THE OXFORD HAN

LATE ANTIQUITY

THE OXFORD HANDBOOK OF

LATE ANTIQUITY

EDITED BY

SCOTT FITZGERALD JOHNSON

UNIVERSITY PRESS

OXFORD
UNIVERSITY PRESS

Oxford University Press is a department of the University of Oxford.
It furthers the University's objective of excellence in research, scholarship,
and education by publishing worldwide.

Oxford New York
Auckland Cape Town Dar es Salaam Hong Kong Karachi
Kuala Lumpur Madrid Melbourne Mexico City Nairobi
New Delhi Shanghai Taipei Toronto

With offices in
Argentina Austria Brazil Chile Czech Republic France Greece
Guatemala Hungary Italy Japan Poland Portugal Singapore
South Korea Switzerland Thailand Turkey Ukraine Vietnam

Published in the United States of America by
Oxford University Press
198 Madison Avenue, New York, NY 10016

First issued as an Oxford University Press paperback, 2016.

Library of Congress Cataloging-in-Publication Data
The Oxford handbook of late antiquity /edited by Scott Fitzgerald Johnson.
p. cm.
Includes bibliographical references and index.
ISBN 978-0-19-533693-1 (hardcover); 978-0-19-027753-6 (paperback)
1. Civilization, Greco-Roman. 2. Civilization, Medieval. 3. Rome—Civilization.
4. Byzantine Empire—Civilization—527–1081.
I. Johnson, Scott Fitzgerald, 1976– II. Title: Oxford Handbook of Late Antiquity.
DE80.O84 2012
937—dc23 2011018578

Frontispiece: The Barberini Ivory, depicting a sixth-century Roman emperor,
possibly Anastasius I or Justinian I (Réunion des Musées Nationaux/Art Resource, NY).

1 3 5 7 9 8 6 4 2

Printed in the United States of America
on acid-free paper

To Averil Cameron and Peter Brown

Contents

Preface: On the Uniqueness of Late Antiquity xi
Scott Fitzgerald Johnson, Georgetown University and Dumbarton Oaks

Acknowledgments xxxi

List of Abbreviations xxxiii

Note on Transliteration xxxvii

Contributors xxxix

Maps xlii

Introduction: Late Antique Conceptions of Late Antiquity 3
Hervé Inglebert, Université Paris Ouest Nanterre—La Défense (Paris X)
(Translation from French prepared by Scott Fitzgerald Johnson)

Part I. Geographies and Peoples

1. The Western Kingdoms 31
Michael Kulikowski, Pennsylvania State University

2. Barbarians: Problems and Approaches 60
Michael Maas, Rice University

3. The Balkans 92
Craig H. Caldwell III, Appalachian State University

4. Armenia 115
Tim Greenwood, St. Andrews University

5. Central Asia and the Silk Road 142
Étienne de la Vaissière, École des Hautes Études en Sciences Sociales, Paris

6. Syriac and the "Syrians" 170
Philip Wood, Sidney Sussex College, Cambridge University

7. Egypt 195
Arietta Papaconstantinou, University of Reading

8. The Coptic Tradition 224
Anne Boud'hors, Centre national de la recherche scientifique (CNRS)
(Translation from French prepared by Arietta Papaconstantinou)

9. Arabia and Ethiopia 247
Christian Julien Robin, Centre national de la recherche scientifique (CNRS), member de l'Institut
(Translation from French prepared by Arietta Papaconstantinou)

PART II. LITERARY AND PHILOSOPHICAL CULTURES

10. Latin Poetry 335
Scott McGill, Rice University

11. Greek Poetry 361
Gianfranco Agosti, University of Rome "La Sapienza"

12. Historiography 405
Brian Croke, Macquarie University and University of Sydney

13. Hellenism and Its Discontents 437
Aaron P. Johnson, Lee University

14. Education: Speaking, Thinking, and Socializing 467
Edward Watts, Indiana University

15. Monasticism and the Philosophical Heritage 487
Samuel Rubenson, Lund University

16. Physics and Metaphysics 513
Gregory Smith, Central Michigan University

17. Travel, Cartography, and Cosmology 562
Scott Fitzgerald Johnson, Georgetown University and Dumbarton Oaks

PART III. LAW, STATE, AND SOCIAL STRUCTURES

18. Economic Trajectories 597
Jairus Banaji, School of Oriental and African Studies (SOAS)

19. Concerning Rural Matters 625
Cam Grey, University of Pennsylvania

20. Marriage and Family 667
Kyle Harper, University of Oklahoma

21. Poverty, Charity, and the Invention of the Hospital 715
Peregrine Horden, Royal Holloway, University of London

22. Concepts of Citizenship 744
Ralph W. Mathisen, University of Illinois at Urbana-Champaign

23. Justice and Equality 764
Kevin Uhalde, Ohio University

24. Roman Law and Legal Culture 789
Jill Harries, St. Andrews University

25. Communication in Late Antiquity: Use and Reuse 815
Andrew Gillett, Macquarie University

Part IV. Religions and Religious Identity

26. Paganism and Christianization 849
Jaclyn Maxwell, Ohio University

27. Episcopal Leadership 876
David M. Gwynn, Royal Holloway, University of London

28. Theological Argumentation: The Case of Forgery 916
Susan Wessel, Catholic University of America

29. Sacred Space and Visual Art 935
Ann Marie Yasin, University of Southern California

30. Object Relations: Theorizing the Late Antique Viewer 970
Glenn Peers, University of Texas at Austin

31. From Nisibis to Xi'an: The Church of the East in Late Antique Eurasia 994
Joel Walker, University of Washington

32. Early Islam as a Late Antique Religion 1053
Robert Hoyland, Oriental Institute and St. Cross College, Oxford University

33. Muḥammad and the Qur'ān 1078
Stephen J. Shoemaker, University of Oregon

PART V. LATE ANTIQUITY IN PERSPECTIVE

34. Comparative State Formation: The Later Roman Empire in the Wider World 1111
John Haldon, Princeton University

35. Late Antiquity in Byzantium 1148
Petre Guran, Institute of South East European Studies, Bucharest

36. Late Antiquity and the Italian Renaissance 1172
Christopher S. Celenza, Johns Hopkins University

Index 1201

Preface: On the Uniqueness of Late Antiquity

SCOTT FITZGERALD JOHNSON
Georgetown University and Dumbarton Oaks

In the year 845 C.E., in a monastery scriptorium in the northwest corner of Ireland, some 3,748 explanations of Latin grammatical points in the language of Old Irish were added by a pair of scribes to a precious manuscript of the *Institutiones grammaticae* (*Elements of Latin Grammar*) by the late antique scholar Priscian (Hofman 1996; Stokes and Strachan 1901). These represent some of the very first instances of an important vernacular tradition in Europe and testify to the vibrant intellectual culture of early medieval Ireland (figure 0.1; Law 1982). The Old Irish scribes were working in a far-flung corner of the former Roman world—really just outside of what was the Roman world at its greatest extent. Their exemplar, Priscianus Caesariensis, had written his influential Latin grammar during the reign of the emperor Anastasius I (see frontispiece) in the Greek milieu of the sixth-century capital of Constantinople, three hundred years prior and half a world away (Averil Cameron 2009; Kaster 1988, no. 126). Constantinople and Ireland are two strange bedfellows, in the ancient world as much as today; yet such boundaries as existed were crisscrossed again and again during Late Antiquity, perhaps even more so at the end than at the beginning, despite the old "Dark Ages" chestnut. Cliché or no, this story is one of intellectual transmission; that is, to quote a recent popular history (Cahill 1995), whether or not the Irish actually "saved" ancient civilization, these scribes were participating in it fully.

Half a century earlier than these Irish scribes, a different sort of real-world *diglossia* was put on display in central China. In 781 C.E., a large stele was set up, inscribed with both Chinese and Syriac inscriptions, to commemorate 150 years of East Syriac (aka "Nestorian") Christian presence in the T'ang capital of Xi'an (figure 0.2). The stele describes on its main face, in elegantly worded (and even more elegantly carved) Chinese, the arrival of the bishop "Aluoben" in 635 C.E.—who may not have even been the first Christian missionary to visit the court (Thompson 2009)—and the emperor's enthusiastic approval of the new religion of *Da Qin*, "from the West" (Malek 2006; Winkler and Tang 2009). Along its sides, the stele evocatively lists, in both Chinese and Syriac, the names of all the Christian bishops of the region for 150 years, from Aluoben to the time of the inscription (figure 0.3; WALKER; Pelliot 1996).[1]

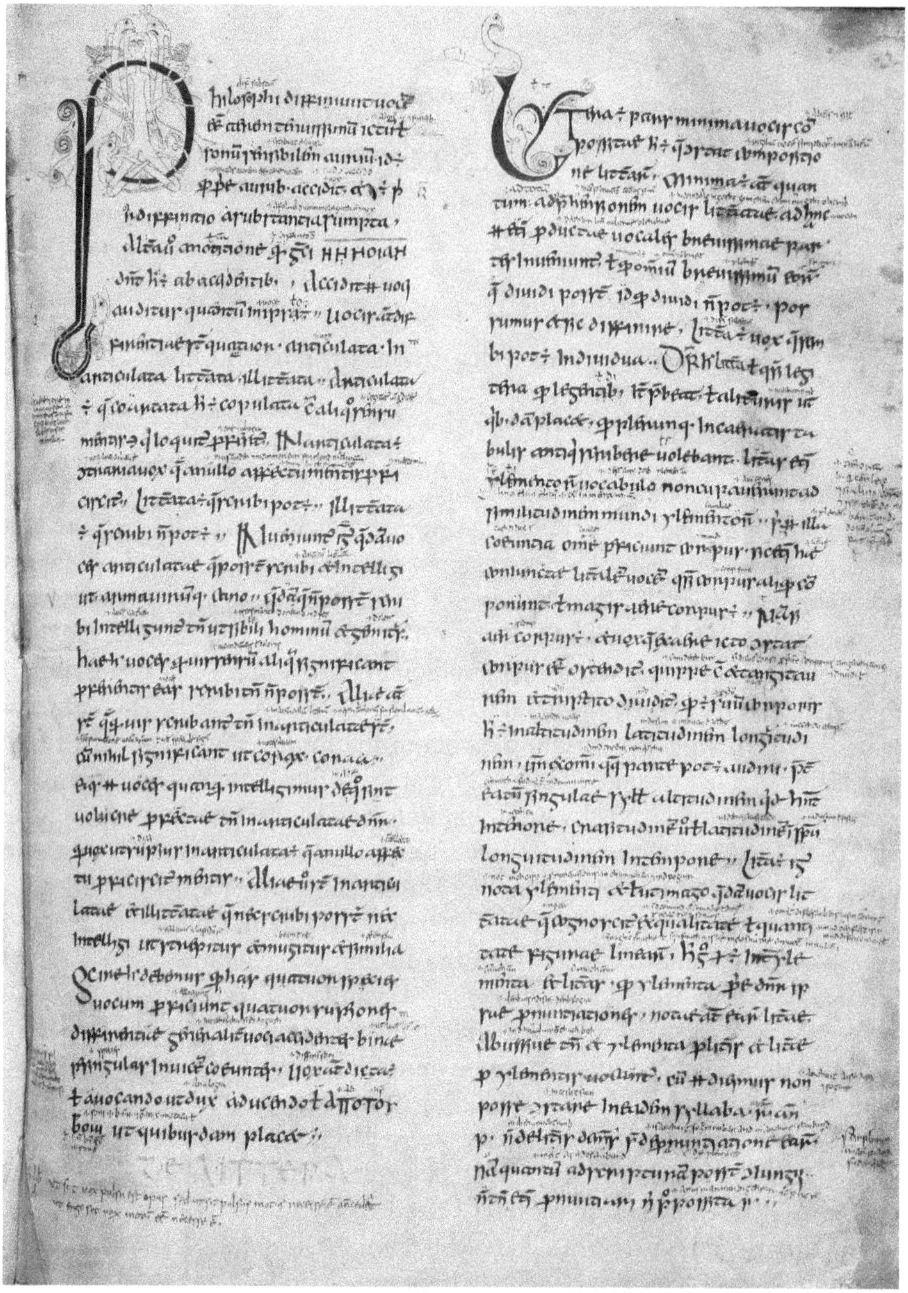

Figure 0.1. Old Irish glosses on Priscian's *Institutiones grammaticae*, 845 C.E. (St. Gallen, Stiftsbibliothek). See also color plate section.

Both the Old Irish Priscian glosses and the Nestorian Monument fall well outside the purview of Edward Gibbon's *Decline and Fall of the Roman Empire* (1776–1788), the standard early-modern touchstone for students of Late Antiquity. Gibbon defined his subject (innovatively, including Byzantium) around the

Figure 0.2. The Nestorian Monument in Xi'an, China, 781 C.E. (Courtesy of Special Collections, Fine Arts Library, Harvard University).

Mediterranean Sea and, specifically, around the portion of that world under the dominion of the Roman state. This state—from the time of the emperor Constantine (307–337) to the fall of Byzantium in 1453—centered on the eastern imperial capital of Constantinople, the institutional successor to Augustus' Rome, in the middle of an ever-shrinking and, in Gibbon's view, ever-degenerating Byzantine empire. For Gibbon, the bulk of six volumes chronicling the long degeneration of the *Rhomaioi*—"the Romans," as the Byzantines called themselves—further

Figure 0.3. Bilingual Chinese-Syriac list of bishops from the Nestorian Monument in Xi'an, China, 781 C.E. (Courtesy of Special Collections, Fine Arts Library, Harvard University).

proved his initial point: ancient civilization never saw a higher point of achievement than at the very beginning of his history, amidst the *pax Romana* of the Antonine emperors in the second century C.E.

Not until the twentieth century was this model substantively problematized, specifically, in the slim book *Mahomet et Charlemagne* by Henri Pirenne (1937), who included the Frankish foundations of Europe and the Islamic caliphate as part of an expansive Mediterranean inquiry. His study focused on the continuity of trade networks and regional identity—subjects hardly touched upon by Gibbon—during the ostensibly cataclysmic events of the sack and ultimate fall of Rome to the "barbarian" Goths in the fifth century (410 and 476) and the capture of much of the eastern Roman empire by the Arabs (630s). For Pirenne, and contrary to Gibbon, the continuity between antiquity and Late Antiquity during these cataclysms was clear in the West: "Romania" remained a unifying force until Charlemagne, around 800. However, the rise of Islam in the East marked a true break with the Greco-Roman world. Spain and North Africa (not to mention Egypt and Syria), long within the orbit of Rome, now looked east for guidance. Thus, despite Pirenne's revision of Gibbon—with new questions and new conclusions for the West—the picture of the East was largely the same disaster that Gibbon had chronicled to death. Islam constituted a different world, a foreign culture and religion, with a separate linguistic identity and disruptive patterns of trade and settlement: ultimately, Islam was responsible for the destruction of the Roman Mediterranean. Moreover, in terms of geography, chronology, and subject matter, strictly cultural events like the Old Irish Priscian glosses and the Nestorian Monument were outside the framework of Pirenne's Mediterranean-centric political and economic argument.

Later in the twentieth century, Peter Brown—soon after a thorough, conservative revision of the late Roman narrative by A. H. M. Jones in *The Later Roman Empire, 284–602: A Social, Economic, and Administrative Survey* (Jones 1964)—abandoned altogether the related concepts of decline, fall, and catastrophe, and focused instead on cultural history, taking his cue from a new interest in anthropological models, versus the political or economic models still dominant at that time. Brown was a pioneer in this approach, especially in his *The World of Late Antiquity: From Marcus Aurelius to Muhammad* (Brown 1971), which expanded even Pirenne's purview by including the lands of the Sasanian Persian empire and by extending the chronology in the East beyond the Islamic conquest. Brown argued for a cultural continuity across the ruptures of the fifth, sixth, and seventh centuries, both West and East, pointing to the similarities of expression among Jews, Christians, and Muslims (as well as Zoroastrians and Manichaeans) in the realms of society, religion, and the arts. These vibrant, hitherto undervalued similarities across time, space, and language continue to offer, for Brown and many others, an argument for the unity and uniqueness of the period. Brown's scholarship thus set a course for the instantiation of Late Antiquity as a category unto its own, and the impact of his approach can be seen throughout the present book.

The examples of the Old Irish Priscian glosses and the Nestorian Monument would therefore slot nicely into Brown's new way of thinking about the period, though neither fit the specific timeline, nor even the much broadened geographical scope, of his narrative in *The World of Late Antiquity*. In fact, in both cases—the glosses and the Monument—the vibrancy of late antique culture is on display at a historical moment when many still today, even those most devoted to sharpening or expanding Brown's model, would consider antiquity to be well and truly over. So, why trot them out at the beginning of a volume on Late Antiquity? To underline the fact that the specific boundaries of our discipline, both chronological and geographical, are still up for debate. While most can agree that these cultural events come near the chronological end of the late antique period—even if early Abbasid Baghdad, around 800, is subsumed under Late Antiquity, for which Brown himself has argued elsewhere (Bowersock, Brown, and Grabar 1999, vii–xiii)—much less often acknowledged is the fact that such extraordinary cultural events as these, drawing directly on the Mediterranean inheritance of antiquity, appear at the extreme West and extreme East of the known world (Ireland and China). Furthermore, in line with Brown's oft-cited (though unpublished) dictum ("Late Antiquity is always later than you think!"), it could be noted that soon after these two examples the picture of far-flung ancient inheritance came to appear more normal, once cultural groups such as these gained a more permanent seat at the table of recorded world history. Not least was the Icelandic world, which would awaken suddenly in the literary consciousness of the West, producing the pagan heroes of the Old Norse sagas while also converting to Christianity along the way (Strömbäck 1975; Cormack 1994). The East Syriac Christians would eventually meet imperial persecution in China from 845 on, just at the time when the Manichaean Uighurs were losing their empire and suffering persecution themselves (Mackerras 1973). By 1000 C.E., the date when Iceland converted to Christianity en masse, more than 500 East Syriac documents had been translated into Chinese, of which a not inconsiderable number came through the unlikely intermediary of the Turkic Uighur language (Baum and Winkler 2003, 49).

The point of offering this vision of the future-past is that these later worlds, although beyond our scope, nevertheless held a claim, direct or indirect, on the legacy of Late Antiquity. It is surely no coincidence that stubborn ancient divisions, such as the previously unbridgeable gulf between the Mediterranean basin and central China, were already being broken down by East Syriac Christians at the very same time as the death of the Prophet Muhammad (d. 632; cf. Shoemaker 2012). In the wake of Brown's attempt to bring early Islam into the conversation, the precise structural or ideational relationship between Islam and the end of Late Antiquity has proven itself to be a persistent and compelling problem, and one that is still primarily conceived of in religious terms (HOYLAND; Shoemaker 2012). In a monumental series of books, Irfan Shahîd has provocatively tried to link the success of Islam with a preceding non-Islamic Arabization of the Roman Near East (Shahîd 1984a, 1984b, 1989, 1995–2009). That may explain (for some) the Islamic Arab conquest of the Levant (cf. ROBIN and Millar 2009), but what about Central Asia, North Africa, or southern Spain? Presumably, these were very different societies without the least hint of prior Arabi(ci)zation (for North Africa, see Kaegi 2010). The solution to this problem largely rests in fields that still need to be tilled: recent research, including groundbreaking chapters in this book, make it clear that, from the sixth to eighth centuries, the interstitial regions between the West, the Middle East, and the Far East became crucially important. Because these regions—namely, Central Asia, the Caucasus, the Danube, Spain, North Africa, and, not least, Asia Minor—all emerge as vibrant microcosms of their own in the medieval period, built directly upon the foundation of Late Antiquity, the transitional period of, roughly, 500 to 800 C.E. now appears more important than previously recognized for defining what Late Antiquity as a whole was really about.

Of course, these regions had all been important before at various times during the preceding millennium, though principally as breadbaskets for their contemporary overlords, be they Greeks, Romans, Persians, or Huns. In Late Antiquity, however, these regions changed into essential spaces for the movement of ideas and the creative interaction of religion, people, and goods. They became places where it was possible, even encouraged, to break down barriers and structures, within the frameworks of the ancient Persian, Greek, and Roman empires (INGLEBERT; HALDON; Fisher 2011). Trading groups such as the Sogdians rose to prominence as cultural enablers for exchange (DE LA VAISSIÈRE), adopting the Syriac Estrangelo script for their prolific east-Iranian lingua franca (Dresden 1983). The detritus of Heraclius' wars with the Sasanians (622–630), on both sides of the fight, as well as the squabbling of the Christian Mediterranean majorities within the empire, were factors that offered in the seventh century a structurally weak resistance to the Arab armies (Howard-Johnston 1999; 2010). However, that same structural weakness was productive of creative possibilities hitherto unknown. It was a fortuitous calamity that could provoke the flourishing of Hellenistic-Umayyad art at Quṣayr 'Amra (Fowden 2004) or the development of an "obsessive taxonomy" of late antique philosophy (SMITH) that proceeded hand in hand with changes to Greco-Roman secular education (WATTS) and (equally so) early Christian education (RUBENSON). On the Central Asian side, the cultural and political situation of Late Antiquity provided fodder for the continued expansion of Manichaeism and Buddhism (Tardieu 1988); on the western European side, Late Antiquity formed the basis of the legal, ecclesiastical, and cultural achievements of the Carolingians (McKitterick 1989).

Recent, magisterial contributions to the question of what happened over time to the infrastructure of Late Antiquity have centered on trade, commerce, and the role of production (McCormick 2001; Wickham 2005; Shaw 2008). The *OHLA* does not eschew debates about economic structures (e.g., BANAJI), but a book such as this is arguably not the best venue to survey archaeological reports or present the results of complicated scientific analyses. Different approaches have been required, such as exploring what the agrarian experience was like in Late Antiquity (GREY), examining the institutional and legal bonds of cohesive families and communities (HARPER; HARRIES), and elucidating the manifold connections between identity formation and legal status (MAAS; MATHISEN; UHALDE). Rather than isolating archaeology or economic theory from the day-to-day lives of late antique individuals by generalizing across the board, the chapters of the *OHLA* show a willingness to experiment with new combinations of evidence and theory in an attempt to understand the smallest moving parts of Late Antiquity.

At the same time, this book is not a "history of late antique private life" or a "people's history of Late Antiquity," even while such a book remains a *desideratum* (cf. Patlagean 1977; Ariès and Duby 1987, vol. 1; Burrus 2005; Krueger 2006). Instead, elite categories have a prominent place—poetry, philosophy, art, architecture, and theology all play their part—though these subjects often appear in different roles from what the word *elite* traditionally suggests (adumbrated by Averil Cameron 1981, §1; Brown 2000). The relationship of the viewer or venerator of a late antique icon to the wealth of associations (social, intellectual, religious) conjured therein, or by the icon's setting, is complex, and this complexity speaks in microcosm to universally relevant engagements between humans and the natural and supernatural worlds (PEERS).

Nevertheless, the uniqueness of the late antique experience is taken up from a number of perspectives: from the designation of certain lands, sites, or buildings as newly holy (YASIN; S. JOHNSON); to the dynamic (i.e., nonepigonal) quality of late antique poetry in its relationship to earlier models (AGOSTI; MCGILL); to the robust tradition of historiography that set a precedent for all subsequent medieval historians, both East and West (CROKE); to the prominence of seminal themes—such as the seemingly antithetical topics of apocalyptic (GURAN) and the late Latin miscellany (CELENZA)—in the reception of Late Antiquity as an identifiable period among premodern societies.

Critical to any formulation of Late Antiquity's uniqueness is its role as the chronological container for the initial process of self-definition within Christianity: during this period, both the Semitic and Hellenistic primal elements of the religion were vying for attention and qualifying their relationship to one another (WOOD; A. JOHNSON). Yet, during Late Antiquity this competition was asymmetrical, since Hellenism was equally the patrimony of late paganism, and thus Hellenophile Christianity had to vie with insiders as well as outsiders (SMITH; Bowersock 1990; Chuvin 2009; Alan Cameron 2011). This cultural and linguistic competition does not seem to have been as strained before Late Antiquity—witness the easy intercourse between Christian bilingual (Syriac and Greek) scholars at Edessa around 200 C.E., such as Bardaisan and his school (Drijvers 1984, §1)—and it does not seem to have been so at the end of Late Antiquity either, when the "assimilation" of Greek linguistic superiority was assured among Syriac philosophers and translators (Brock 1984, §5; Ruzer and Kofsky 2010). Thus the intense competition over (and against) Christian origins—among Latin writers as well (Courcelle 1969; Maas 2003; Humphries and Gwynn 2010)—remains one of the most compelling reasons to view Late Antiquity as a definable period and a unique field of study unto its own.

Several other topics that could be considered definitive of Late Antiquity take center stage in the *OHLA*. There is, for instance, the emergence of the hospital as a locus for the growing societal concern about health, disease, and the duty of the Christian state toward the sick (HORDEN). The religious fluidity of the period seems today to have produced more cultural innovation than it did anxiety, especially once the old-guard "pagan reaction" is balanced by the evidence of a much more gradual process of Christianization in the fourth to sixth centuries (MAXWELL; Alan Cameron 2011; cf. Dodds 1965). Riding the incoming tide of Christianization was the office of the bishop, which, although prominent in the Church from the early second century on, took on an expanded societal role within and above the curial structure of the late Roman city (GWYNN). Of course, aside from all the lasting local change a bishop or patriarch could effect, his contribution to the ecumenical doctrines of the Church was what garnered him special blessings or *damnatio memoriae* among subsequent generations. None of the so-called heresiarchs of Late Antiquity (Origen, Arius, Apollinarius, Priscillian, Pelagius, Nestorius, Eutyches, et al.) could possibly compete with forged documents (WESSEL). Such forgeries were used by all sides throughout Late Antiquity, and this habit set a precedent for later, more infamous forgeries, such as in the *Donation of Constantine* about 800 C.E. (Bowersock 2007). While admittedly a case study of the process of conciliar theology, forgery nonetheless speaks precisely to the unprecedented value that Christian creeds and anathemas held in late antique society as a whole.

Connected to the promulgation of correct belief in Late Antiquity was the conversion of indigenous people groups at the margins of the empire. The western kingdoms that arose in the fourth century, eventually supplanting the Roman empire in the later fifth, often took sides in the doctrinal debates as a means of distinguishing themselves from one another (O'Donnell 2008, chapter 1). Political savvy such as this cannot legitimately be labeled "barbarian" by any standard and especially since the kingdoms found success on exactly the same playing field—that is, the dense network of city, town, and countryside—that their late Roman counterparts had known in the fourth century (KULIKOWSKI). The subjects of violence and rupture in Late Antiquity are perennially important to studies of the western theater and have resonance in the questions of self-definition and collapse that recur throughout the *OHLA* (MAAS; MATHISEN; MAXWELL; UHALDE; Kelly 2009). Even while the debate over violence in Late Antiquity is evolving, scholars have already produced stimulating treatments that attempt to take in the Christian East and Islam as well (Drake 2006; Watts 2010; Sizgorich 2009). A notable area of exciting work is Greco-Coptic Egypt, where the dichotomy between the upper Nile (with its intractable pagans, Jews, and Christians) and a Mediterranean-savvy Alexandria often breaks down upon close inspection (BOUD'HORS; PAPACONSTANTINOU). Egypt was a cohesive yet very complex region in Late Antiquity, and the massive corpus of surviving Coptic literature is only now receiving the devoted care it deserves (e.g., Emmel 2004). Likewise, the cache of late antique papyri from Egypt continues to grow and continues, proportionally, to affect our understanding of the everyday social, pedagogical, and religious practices of eastern Late Antiquity (Bagnall 2009; 2011; Luijendijk 2008; MacCoull 2009).

On the subject of pedagogy, there is, of course, an argument to be made for the applicability of the modern handbook genre to the study of Late Antiquity. While the late antique world in this book offers the reader a remarkable number of diverse topics and locales—stretching widely from Central Asia in the east, to Ethiopia in the south, to Spain and Ireland in the west, and to Scandinavia in the north—the period can, nevertheless, be recognizably depicted as an era of centralization, consolidation, and compilation (Inglebert 2001; Vessey 2003). On the surface, this view may seem to privilege intellectual or political history, but the metaphor of consolidation can speak equally well of ruptures and transitions in society, politics, economy, religion, architecture, and so on. To buttress such an image of consolidation, one might want to add the quick corollary that, despite the geographical expanse of the period, the Mediterranean Sea was an established, even primal, point of centralization around which late antique microcosms participated in a shared ecology, both physical and metaphorical (Horden and Purcell 2000). Is there a way to talk about the smallest moving parts of Late Antiquity without losing track of unifying metaphors that make the period comprehensible to fellow historians within and outside the field?

The *OHLA* attempts to stretch the possibilities of unifying metaphors while also questioning the value of overused systematic frameworks. Thus, it assumes from the beginning the inherited necessity of problematizing chronological norms, no matter whether the "catastrophist" or the "long" Late Antiquity should arrive closer to the truth (Marcone 2008; James 2008; Ando 2008; Ward-Perkins 2005; Averil Cameron 2002). Quite apart from one's answer to the question of when the ancient world ended, the problematization itself is valuable and contributes substantially to the field, particularly when so many authors from differing professional backgrounds tackle the question in the same book. This book does not accept any single chronological span as necessarily authoritative, though I as editor provisionally offered "Constantine to Muhammad" to the authors (cf. INGLEBERT). Of course, in the end, almost none of the authors subscribe to this exact span, extending it earlier and later as their arguments require. It is important that few, if any, authors in the *OHLA* consider this span too long.

On the other hand, what the *OHLA* does not accept as negotiable is the geographic breadth of the subject, as already mentioned. If there is a notional center to this diversity, it is the rigorous insistence on geographical frameworks that do not privilege the borders of the late Roman and early Byzantine empires. The authors in the *OHLA* certainly do, from time to time, accept political borders for the examination of unifying structures, namely, military or bureaucratic (GILLETT; HALDON), but the intra-Roman narrative of Gibbon has largely been abandoned in every quarter of the field, even among those whose focus is the boundaries of these empires themselves (Millar 1993; 2006; Isaac 2000; Dignas and Winter 2007; Stephenson 2000). Of course, boundaries are more than political, and, for the sake of expert analysis, traditions, languages, and regions have been parceled out to specialists in these subjects. This has resulted in *cursus academicae* from across the spectrum: plenty of authors in the *OHLA* may not even self-identify as "late antiquists," a fact that testifies to the broad appeal of the subject and the expert work being done in numerous adjacent fields.

On this basis, the geography covered here could come as something of a surprise to readers from outside the academic practice of Late Antiquity, particularly, readers from neighboring disciplines such as Classics, Medieval/Byzantine Studies, Renaissance Studies, and other fields that have (a traditional) Late Antiquity as part of their patrimony. To be specific, when compared to previous scholarship, the center of Late Antiquity in this book has demonstrably shifted toward the east and the north, to the degree that the loci of the (formerly Mediterranean-shaped) ellipse are now Seleucia-Ctesiphon (WALKER) in the East—or dare we say Sogdiana? (DE LA VAISSIÈRE)—and the Danube Valley (CALDWELL) in the West. Some readers might think that this is Late Antiquity askew, having moved disproportionately along two different axes. While there is still certainly an *oikoumene*, there is no recognizable *mare nostrum*. In recent years, scholars have considered the value of the Mediterranean—so well studied, since Fernand Braudel at least, as a living phenomenon—as a cipher for other "oikoumenical" regions of the world, but this is ultimately an analogical approach to the problem, even if a "Saharan Mediterranean Desert" could perhaps mean something concrete (Abulafia 2005). Intriguingly, the real-world bodies of water central to the *OHLA* are rivers instead of seas: the Euphrates-Tigris and the Danube were, at various times during Late Antiquity, definitive of imperial boundaries, yet, at other times, they were innocuously well inside or well outside the Roman empire. Ultimately, the status of these rivers as boundary markers between peoples and states, for a limited amount of time in any case, was less significant in the *longue durée* than the innumerable transactions (cultural, linguistic, economic, and otherwise) that took place across or around them.

For both its geographical and chronological spans, the *OHLA* is surprisingly synoptic and synchronic, especially given that Late Antiquity, as a field of study, has so often been defined by debates over the breadth and length of the subject. Thus, recent studies such as Deborah Deliyannis's *Ravenna in Late Antiquity* (2010) and Giusto Traina's *428 AD: An Ordinary Year at the End of the Roman Empire* (2009) resonate with the approaches taken in the *OHLA* because each is a circumscribed topic, geographical or temporal, though with universal relevance for Late Antiquity. Both of these examples generally eschew atomism yet will universalize or theorize only on the basis of close reading. In the *OHLA*, diachrony prominently appears in surveys of specific categories (e.g., BOUD'HORS; ROBIN), but the analysis of individual problems and texts often precedes and directs the diachronic surveys.

It has recently been observed in a review essay for the inaugural volume of the *Classical Receptions Journal* that general collected volumes appear now to be the standard scholarly venue to discuss the methodological remit of Reception Studies as a discipline (Güthenke 2009, 104). The essay quotes the following summary from a volume in that field:

> In place of the comforting illusion that even if times change antiquity no longer does, comparison of histories of scholarship or any series of studies around a single object reminds us of just the opposite illusion (or is it a fact?),

> namely that antiquity is changing all the time, from generation to generation and from scholar to scholar. Such vertigo is hard to bear for long. And yet one wants to believe that the more reflexivity that gets built into one's discipline, the greater the chances there will be of arriving at . . . what? A truer picture of antiquity? Or of the discipline itself? There is something uncontroversially valid-feeling about knowing how we know what we know. (Porter 2008, 470)

Taken as a specific subgenre of the general category of "collected volumes," the modern handbook genre regularly struggles to offer that "valid-feeling" something to its audience, largely due to its superhuman calling of presenting a conspective view of an enormous subject to a reader who will naturally want to know more and, particularly, to know the details of how such conclusions were arrived at. For the *OHLA*, this is doubly difficult because the discipline of Late Antiquity is still comparatively young, having been born out of the work of H. I. Marrou, A. H. M. Jones, Arnaldo Momigliano, and Peter Brown only in the 1950s, 1960s, and 1970s (Brown 1988; 2003; Gwynn 2008; Averil Cameron 2003; Straw and Lim 2004). Moreover, the discipline as it exists today is not nearly as institutionalized as Classics is. Instead, scholars from a number of disciplines must intentionally choose to work on Late Antiquity because of their interest in the material, rather than from an institutional imperative, such as teaching a set canon of classical texts. In other words, the model for the discipline is completely different from that of some of its neighbors, and, from an institutional point of view, one might be justified in saying that Late Antiquity does not exist at all as an autonomous unit.

However, as the reader of the *OHLA* will soon discover, there is a passion among practitioners of Late Antiquity for their material that is almost unparalleled. This passion derives, I would suggest, from the vitality of the period itself and from the productive ways in which survivals from Late Antiquity—texts, sites, coins, icons, and more—have been used and reused to form narratives of the period that are often virulently at odds with one another. Of course, much is at stake, not least the early history of the Christian Church, the decline and fall of the Roman empire, and the rise of Islam, Byzantium, and the medieval West. Late Antiquity is certainly one of the most important hinge periods for the history of the civilizations of Europe and the Middle East and even, as this book claims, Central Asia as well.

So, how does the *OHLA* avoid the Scylla and Charybdis of reflexive vertigo, on the one hand, and anodyne synthesis of accepted opinion, on the other? I began the process of organizing the book and commissioning chapters by asking the contributors to be "experimental" and try to incorporate their current research where appropriate. The goal was to try to make this handbook as cutting edge as possible while still following the design of the well-established and authoritative Oxford University Press series. In other words, although I was intentional about not making it a dictionary or a reference work, we still needed to cover the ground of Late Antiquity. As a result, the contents are comprehensive in a somewhat different manner from other handbooks. Some topics are shared between multiple chapters and do not receive a chapter of their own: for example, there is no single chapter in this book on Sasanian Persia; however, it is thoroughly covered by a combination of DE LA VAISSIÈRE, GREENWOOD, and WALKER. (A reader would be advised also to consult recent full-length studies on the Sasanians, such as Dignas and Winter 2007 and Pourshariati 2008.) Likewise, there is no explicit chapter on late antique warfare, though the topic is dealt with as part of larger arguments by GILLETT and HALDON. (One would want to seek out Lee 2007 for a dedicated treatment.) Most gallingly to historians of religion will be the absence of a chapter on the Jews in Late Antiquity, though Judaism in its late antique instantiations is discussed repeatedly throughout the book, for instance by ROBIN and WOOD. (Katz 2006 provides a comprehensive guide to the subject.) Thus, from such examples it should be clear that not every subject that could be isolated and discussed on its own—even subjects as towering and germane as, say, Augustine or the city of Constantinople—will receive the sustained attention they have garnered in other quarters.

However, the intention of presenting a vibrant, up-to-date image of Late Antiquity as a whole—an image that pushes the field forward while also providing a road map for newcomers—has, if I may say so, been admirably fulfilled by the thirty-seven contributors to the *OHLA*. Our goal was to produce a handbook that scholars and students would actually want to purchase, read, digest, and argue with. This was accomplished in certain cases only by leaving old constrictive paradigms in the dust and assuming new models from the start (e.g., BANAJI; HARPER). In other cases, this goal was accomplished through challenging received paradigms directly (e.g., MAAS; SHOEMAKER). And in still other cases, the vision was achieved through case studies that analyze specific questions with universal relevance (e.g., GREY; HORDEN; WESSEL).

Our hope is that this book will be used alongside, and in conversation with, current narrative surveys of the period, such as the comprehensive and perennially useful *Cambridge Ancient History*, volumes 13 and 14 (Averil Cameron and Garnsey 1998; Averil Cameron, Ward-Perkins, and Michael Whitby 2000). This is true also for the burgeoning number of handbooks, companions, and topical introductions to the period: *Late Antiquity: A Guide to the Postclassical World* (Bowersock, Brown, and Grabar 1999); *Approaching Late Antiquity: The Transformation from Early to Late Empire* (Swain and Edwards 2004); *A Companion to Late Antiquity* (Rousseau 2009); *Late Antiquity: A Very Short Introduction* (Clark 2011); *The Cambridge Companion to the Age of Constantine* (Lenski 2006); and *The Cambridge Companion to the Age of Justinian* (Maas 2005). Of course, there are numerous other companionesque books that could be mentioned here that do not have "Late Antiquity" in the title but that border the subject from various points of view: these and the books just mentioned all appear often throughout the chapters that follow.

A final set of *comparanda* that should be noted are the neighboring volumes of the Oxford Handbook series, such as the *Oxford Handbook of Roman Studies* (Barchiesi and Scheidel 2010), the *Oxford Handbook of Early Christian Studies*

(Harvey and Hunter 2008), and the *Oxford Handbook of Byzantine Studies* (Jeffreys, Haldon, and Cormack 2008). All three of these books touch on subjects and themes that are germane to Late Antiquity and should be consulted when they provide focused coverage on a given subject, even as that subject may appear in an ancillary role in the *OHLA* (e.g., the Roman army, early Christian Christology, or Byzantine sigillography). However, a brief glance at these books side by side will immediately demonstrate the perhaps puzzling fact that the word "Studies" is absent from our title. As explained earlier, this book takes a somewhat more experimental approach to the subject and should not be considered a disciplinary manual in the way that these other handbooks are understood. This aberration arises from the specific goals of the present editor and authors, but it also comes from the state of the field of Late Antiquity. There are still vibrant debates, critical to any definition of an Oxford Handbook, over what constitutes precisely the time frame and subject matter of Late Antiquity. These debates are integral to each chapter of the *OHLA* and cannot be said to be settled at this stage in the development of the field. Thus, if this book is to be used as a manual in any way, it should be used as a manual for developing a taste for the fundamental joys and recurrent challenges of studying Late Antiquity as a unique subject in its own right. The *OHLA* can in this way serve as a milestone, or perhaps an Ebenezer, for the (still freshly minted) uniqueness of Late Antiquity. The wide variety of scholarly pursuits on display in this book are a testament to the significance of Late Antiquity to the Humanities in general, though that same variety shows how many opportunities still remain for scholars and students, from every humanistic corner, to consider afresh the defining elements of Late Antiquity for a new generation.

NOTE

1. I use uppercase names in the Preface to point to the authors of chapters in the *Oxford Handbook of Late Antiquity* (hereafter *OHLA*). Other references can be found in the Works Cited.

WORKS CITED

Abulafia, David. 2005. "Mediterraneans." In *Rethinking the Mediterranean*, ed. William V. Harris, 64–93. Oxford: Oxford University Press.

Ando, Clifford. 2008. "Decline, Fall, and Transformation," *Journal of Late Antiquity* 1: 31–60.

Ariès, Philippe, and Georges Duby, eds. 1987. *A History of Private Life*, 5 vols. Cambridge, MA: Harvard University Press.

Bagnall, Roger S. 2009. *Early Christian Books in Egypt*. Princeton, NJ: Princeton University Press.

———. 2011. *Everyday Writing in the Graeco-Roman East*. Berkeley: University of California Press.

Barchiesi, Alessandro, and Walter Scheidel, eds. 2010. *The Oxford Handbook of Roman Studies*. Oxford: Oxford University Press.

Baum, Wilhelm, and Dietmar W. Winkler. 2003. *The Church of the East: A Concise History*. London: Routledge-Curzon.

Bowersock, G. W. 1990. *Hellenism in Late Antiquity*. Ann Arbor: University of Michigan Press.

———, ed. 2007. *Lorenzo Valla: On the Donation of Constantine*. I Tatti Renaissance Library 24. Cambridge, MA: Harvard University Press.

Bowersock, G. W., Peter Brown, and Oleg Grabar, eds. 1999. *Late Antiquity: A Guide to the Postclassical World*. Cambridge, MA: Harvard University Press.

Brock, Sebastian P. 1984. *Syriac Perspectives on Late Antiquity*. London: Variorum.

Brown, Peter. 1971. *The World of Late Antiquity: From Marcus Aurelius to Muhammad*. London: Thames and Hudson.

———. 1988. "Arnaldo Dante Momigliano," *Proceedings of the British Academy* 74: 407–442.

———. 2000. "The Study of Elites in Late Antiquity," *Arethusa* 33: 321–346.

———. 2003. "A Life of Learning: Charles Homer Haskins Lecture for 2003," *ACLS Occasional Papers* 55: 1–19.

Burrus, Virginia, ed. 2005. *Late Ancient Christianity*. A People's History of Christianity 2. Minneapolis, MN: Fortress Press.

Cahill, Thomas. 1995. *How the Irish Saved Civilization: The Untold Story of Ireland's Heroic Role from the Fall of Rome to the Rise of Medieval Europe*. New York: Doubleday.

Cameron, Alan. 2011. *The Last Pagans of Rome*. New York: Oxford University Press.

Cameron, Averil M. 1981. "Images of Authority: Elites and Icons in Late Sixth-Century Byzantium." In *Continuity and Change in Sixth-Century Byzantium*, §1. London: Variorum.

———. 2002. "The 'Long' Late Antiquity: A Late Twentieth-Century Model." In *Classics in Progress: Essays on Ancient Greece and Rome*, ed. T. P. Wiseman, 165–191. Oxford: British Academy and Oxford University Press.

———. 2003. "Ideologies and Agendas in Late Antique Studies." In *Theory and Practice in Late Antique Archaeology*, ed. Luke Lavan and William Bowden, 1–21. Late Antique Archaeology 1. Leiden: Brill.

———. 2009. "Old and New Rome: Roman Studies in Sixth-Century Constantinople." In *Transformations of Late Antiquity: Essays for Peter Brown*, ed. Philip Rousseau and Emmanuel Papoutsakis, 15–36. Farnham: Ashgate.

Cameron, Averil, and Peter Garnsey, eds. 1998. *The Cambridge Ancient History, Vol. 13: Late Empire, A.D. 337–425*. Cambridge: Cambridge University Press.

Cameron, Averil, Bryan Ward-Perkins, and Michael Whitby, eds. 2000. *The Cambridge Ancient History, Vol. 14: Late Antiquity, Empire and Successors, A.D. 425–600*. Cambridge: Cambridge University Press.

Chuvin, Pierre. 2009. *Chronique des derniers païens: La disparition du paganisme dans l'Empire romain, du règne de Constantin à celui de Justinien*, 3rd ed. Paris: Les Belles Lettres–Fayard.

Clark, Gillian. 2011. *Late Antiquity: A Very Short Introduction*. Oxford: Oxford University Press.

Cormack, Margaret. 1994. *The Saints in Iceland: Their Veneration from the Conversion to 1400*. Subsidia hagiographica 78. Brussels: Société des Bollandistes.

Courcelle, Pierre Paul. 1969. *Late Latin Writers and Their Greek Sources*. Trans. Harry E. Wedeck. Cambridge, MA: Harvard University Press.

Deliyannis, Deborah Mauskopf. 2010. *Ravenna in Late Antiquity*. New York: Cambridge University Press.

Dignas, Beate, and Engelbert Winter. 2007. *Rome and Persia in Late Antiquity: Neighbours and Rivals*. Cambridge: Cambridge University Press.

Dodds, E. R. 1965. *Pagan and Christian in an Age of Anxiety: Some Aspects of Religious Experience from Marcus Aurelius to Constantine*. The Wiles Lectures 1963. Cambridge: Cambridge University Press.

Drake, H. A., ed. 2006. *Violence in Late Antiquity: Perceptions and Practices*. Aldershot: Ashgate.

Dresden, Mark. 1983. "Sogdian Language and Literature." In *The Cambridge History of Iran 3.2: The Seleucid, Parthian, and Sasanian Periods*, ed. E. Yarshater, 1216–1229. Cambridge: Cambridge University Press.

Drijvers, H. J. W. 1984. *East of Antioch: Studies in Early Syriac Christianity*. London: Variorum.

Emmel, Stephen. 2004. *Shenoute's Literary Corpus*, 2 vols. Louvain: Peeters.

Fisher, Greg. 2011. *Between Empires: Arabs, Romans, and Sasanians in Late Antiquity*. Oxford: Oxford University Press.

Fowden, Garth. 2004. *Quṣayr 'Amra: Art and the Umayyad Elite in Late Antique Syria*. Berkeley: University of California Press.

Güthenke, Constanze. 2009. "Shop Talk: Reception Studies and Recent Work in the History of Scholarship," *Classical Receptions Journal* 1: 104–115.

Gwynn, David M., ed. 2008. *A. H. M. Jones and the Later Roman Empire*. Brill's Series on the Early Middle Ages 15. Leiden: Brill.

Harris, William V., ed. 2004. *Rethinking the Mediterranean*. Oxford: Oxford University Press.

Harvey, Susan Ashbrook, and David G. Hunter, eds. 2008. *The Oxford Handbook of Early Christian Studies*. Oxford: Oxford University Press.

Hofman, Rijcklof, ed. 1996. *The Sankt Gall Priscian Commentary, Part 1*, 2 vols. Studien und Texte zur Keltologie 1. Münster: Nodus.

Horden, Peregrine, and Nicholas Purcell. 2000. *The Corrupting Sea: A Study of Mediterranean History*. Oxford: Blackwell.

Howard-Johnston, J. 1999. "Heraclius' Persian Campaigns and the Revival of the East Roman Empire, 622–630," *War in History* 6: 1–44.

———. 2010. *Witnesses to a World Crisis: Historians and Histories of the Middle East in the Seventh Century*. Oxford: Oxford University Press.

Humphries, Mark, and David Gwynn. 2010. "The Sacred and the Secular: The Presence or Absence of Christian Religious Thought in Secular Writing in the Late Antique West." In *Religious Diversity in Late Antiquity*, ed. David Gwynn and Susanne Bangert, 493–509. Late Antique Archaeology 6. Leiden: Brill.

Inglebert, Hervé. 2001. *Interpretatio Christiana: Les mutations des savoirs (cosmographie, géographie, ethnographie, histoire) dans l'Antiquité chrétienne (30–630 après J.-C.)*. Paris: Institut d'Etudes Augustiniennes.

Isaac, Benjamin H. 2000. *The Limits of Empire: The Roman Army in the East*, rev. ed. Oxford: Clarendon Press.

James, Edward. 2008. "The Rise and Function of the Concept 'Late Antiquity,'" *Journal of Late Antiquity* 1: 20–30.

Jeffreys, Elizabeth, John F. Haldon, and Robin Cormack, eds. 2008. *The Oxford Handbook of Byzantine Studies*. Oxford: Oxford University Press.

Jones, A. H. M. 1964. *The Later Roman Empire, 284–602: A Social, Economic, and Administrative Survey*, 3 vols. Oxford: Blackwell.

Kaegi, Walter Emil. 2010. *Muslim Expansion and Byzantine Collapse in North Africa*. Cambridge: Cambridge University Press.

Kaster, Robert A. 1988. *Guardians of Language: The Grammarian and Society in Late Antiquity*. The Transformation of the Classical Heritage 11. Berkeley: University of California Press.

Katz, Steven T., ed. 2008. *The Cambridge History of Judaism, Vol. 4: The Late Roman-Rabbinic Period*. Cambridge: Cambridge University Press.

Kelly, Christopher. 2009. *The End of Empire: Attila the Hun and the Fall of Rome*. New York: W. W. Norton.

Krueger, Derek, ed. 2006. *Byzantine Christianity*. A People's History of Christianity 3. Minneapolis, MN: Fortress Press.

Law, Vivien. 1982. *The Insular Latin Grammarians*. Studies in Celtic History 3. Woodbridge: Boydell Press.

Lee, A. D. 2007. *War in Late Antiquity: A Social History*. Malden, MA: Blackwell.

Lenski, Noel, ed. 2006. *The Cambridge Companion to the Age of Constantine*. New York: Cambridge University Press.

Luijendijk, Annemarie. 2008. *Greetings in the Lord: Early Christians and the Oxyrhynchus Papyri*. Harvard Theological Studies 60. Cambridge, MA: Harvard University Press.

Maas, Michael. 2003. *Exegesis and Empire in the Early Byzantine Mediterranean: Junillus Africanus and the Instituta Regularia Divinae Legis*. Tübingen: Mohr Siebeck.

———, ed. 2005. *The Cambridge Companion to the Age of Justinian*. Cambridge: Cambridge University Press.

MacCoull, L.S.B. 2009. *Coptic Legal Documents*. Tempe, AZ: ACMRS.

Mackerras, Colin. 1973. *The Uighur Empire According to the T'ang Dynastic Histories: A Study in Sino-Uighur Relations, 744–840*, 2nd ed. Columbia: University of South Carolina Press.

Malek, Roman, ed. 2006. *Jingjiao: The Church of the East in China and Central Asia*. Collectanea serica. Sankt Augustin: Institut Monumenta Serica.

Marcone, Arnaldo. 2008. "A Long Late Antiquity? Considerations on a Controversial Periodization," *Journal of Late Antiquity* 1: 4–19.

McCormick, Michael. 2001. *Origins of the European Economy: Communications and Commerce, A.D. 300–900*. Cambridge: Cambridge University Press.

McKitterick, Rosamond. 1989. *The Carolingians and the Written Word*. Cambridge: Cambridge University Press.

Millar, Fergus. 1993. *The Roman Near East, 31 B.C.–A.D. 337*. Cambridge, MA: Harvard University Press.

———. 2006. *A Greek Roman Empire: Power and Belief under Theodosius II (408–450)*. Sather Classical Lectures 64. Berkeley: University of California Press.

———. 2009. "Christian Monasticism in Roman Arabia at the Birth of Mahomet." *Semitica et Classica* 2: 97–115.

O'Donnell, James J. 2008. *The Ruin of the Roman Empire*. New York: Ecco.

Patlagean, Evelyne. 1977. *Pauvreté économique et pauvreté sociale à Byzance, 4e–7e siècles*. Civilisations et sociétés 48. Paris: Mouton.

Pelliot, Paul. 1996. *L'inscription nestorienne de Si-Ngan-Fou*. Ed. Antonino Forte. Kyoto: Scuola di studi sull'Asia orientale.

Pirenne, Henri. 1937. *Mahomet et Charlemagne*. Paris: F. Alcan.
Porter, James I. 2008. "Reception Studies: Future Prospects." In *A Companion to Classical Receptions*, ed. Lorna Hardwick and Christopher Stray, 469–481. Blackwell Companions to the Ancient World. Oxford: Blackwell.
Pourshariati, Parvaneh. 2008. *Decline and Fall of the Sasanian Empire: The Sasanian-Parthian Confederacy and the Arab Conquest of Iran*. London: I. B. Tauris.
Rousseau, Philip, ed. 2009. *A Companion to Late Antiquity*. Malden, MA: Wiley-Blackwell.
Ruzer, Serge, and Arieh Kofsky, eds. 2010. *Syriac Idiosyncrasies: Theology and Hermeneutics in Early Syriac Literature*. Leiden: Brill.
Shahîd, Irfan. 1984a. *Rome and the Arabs: A Prolegomenon to the Study of Byzantium and the Arabs*. Washington, DC: Dumbarton Oaks.
———. 1984b. *Byzantium and the Arabs in the Fourth Century*. Washington, DC: Dumbarton Oaks.
———. 1989. *Byzantium and the Arabs in the Fifth Century*. Washington, DC: Dumbarton Oaks.
———. 1995–2009. *Byzantium and the Arabs in the Sixth Century*, 4 vols. Washington, DC: Dumbarton Oaks.
Shaw, Brent D. 2008. "After Rome: Transformations of the Early Mediterranean World," *New Left Review* 51: 89–114.
Shoemaker, Stephen J. 2012. *The Death of a Prophet: The End of Muhammad's Life and the Beginnings of Islam*. Divinations. Philadelphia: University of Pennsylvania Press.
Sizgorich, Thomas. 2009. *Violence and Belief in Late Antiquity: Militant Devotion in Christianity and Islam*. Divinations. Philadelphia: University of Pennsylvania Press.
Stephenson, Paul. 2000. *Byzantium's Balkan Frontier: A Political Study of the Northern Balkans, 900–1204*. Cambridge: Cambridge University Press.
Stokes, Whitley, and John Strachan, eds. 1901. *Thesaurus Palaeohibernicus: A Collection of Old-Irish Glosses, Scolia, Prose, and Verse*, 2 vols. Cambridge: Cambridge University Press.
Straw, Carole Ellen, and Richard Lim, eds. 2004. *The Past before Us: The Challenge of Historiographies of Late Antiquity*. Bibliothèque de l'Antiquité tardive 6. Turnhout: Brepols.
Strömbäck, Dag. 1975. *The Conversion of Iceland: A Survey*. Trans. Peter Godfrey Foote. London: Viking Society for Northern Research.
Swain, Simon, and M. J. Edwards, eds. 2004. *Approaching Late Antiquity: The Transformation from Early to Late Empire*. Oxford: Oxford University Press.
Tardieu, M. 1988. "La diffusion du Bouddhisme dans l'empire kouchan, l'Iran et la Chine, d'après un Kephalion manichéen inédit," *Studia Iranica* 17: 153–182.
Thompson, Glen. 2009. "Was Alopen a 'Missionary'?" In *Hidden Treasures and Intercultural Encounters: Studies on East Syriac Christianity in China and Central Asia*, ed. Dietmar W. Winkler and Li Tang, 267–278. Berlin: LIT.
Traina, Giusto. 2009. *428 AD: An Ordinary Year at the End of the Roman Empire*. Trans. Allan Cameron. Princeton, NJ: Princeton University Press.
Vessey, Mark. 2003. "Introduction." In *Cassiodorus: Institutions of Divine and Secular Learning and On the Soul*, trans. James W. Halporn, 1–101. Translated Texts for Historians 42. Liverpool: Liverpool University Press.

Ward-Perkins, Bryan. 2005. *The Fall of Rome: And the End of Civilization*. Oxford: Oxford University Press.

Watts, Edward Jay. 2010. *Riot in Alexandria: Tradition and Group Dynamics in Late Antique Pagan and Christian Communities*. Berkeley: University of California Press.

Wickham, Chris. 2005. *Framing the Early Middle Ages: Europe and the Mediterranean, 400–800*. Oxford: Oxford University Press.

Winkler, Dietmar W., and Li Tang, eds. 2009. *Hidden Treasures and Intercultural Encounters: Studies on East Syriac Christianity in China and Central Asia*. Berlin: Lit.

Acknowledgments

To begin, I would like to thank Stefan Vranka, Senior Editor for Classics at Oxford University Press USA, who commissioned me to edit the *OHLA* in 2007 and who, from first to last, has encouraged and supported our work in preparing this book. He believes in the inherent value of Late Antiquity and in its fundamental importance for the future of Classics and the Humanities in general. It has been a pleasure to work with him over the past four years. I am appreciative of the favorable comments from two anonymous reviewers of the proposal, who were instrumental in getting the *OHLA* off the ground at the earliest stage. I would also like to thank the staff at OUP USA, not least the Classics editorial assistants Deirdre Brady, Brian Hurley, and Sarah Pirovitz. Sarah, in particular, played a critical role in my visualizing the finish line and crossing it in one piece. The production team of Ryan Sarver and Joellyn Ausanka at OUP and Joy Matkowski and Jay Boggis, our two copy editors, helped achieve the seemingly impossible task of finalizing the text and getting it ready for publication. Kate Mertes prepared a professional index which adds real value to the book. And Leslie MacCoull proofread the entire manuscript and made innumerable corrections and improvements with a charm and grace that enlivened the final stages.

This book was supported by a generous research grant and subvention (2006–2007) from the William F. Milton Fund at Harvard University. For this project, I also received a Glenn Grant (2008) and Lenfest Grant (2009) from Washington and Lee University. The *OHLA* was conceived while I was in my last year as a Junior Fellow in the Harvard Society of Fellows (2006–2007), it gestated during two years of teaching in the Classics Department at Washington and Lee University (2007–2009), it began to take definitive shape as I was a Fellow in Byzantine Studies at Dumbarton Oaks (2009–2010), and it found its final form while I was a Kluge Fellow at the Library of Congress (2010–2011). I am immeasurably grateful to these institutions for sponsoring my research—even when the *OHLA* was not what I was supposed to be working on! I would like to express my appreciation to individuals at all four institutions (and elsewhere) who contributed, through direct advice or general support, to the completion of this long project: Rebecca Benefiel, Monica Blanchard, Carolyn Brown, Sarah Burke, Miriam Carlisle, Chris Chekuri, Ed Cook, Kevin Crotty, Jenny Davis, Jan Willem Drijvers, David Elmer, Jaś Elsner, Maria Evangelatou, Polly Evans, Doug Frame, Sidney Griffith, Sarah Insley, Noel Lenski, Florin Leonte, Ruth Macrides, Meaghan McEvoy, Diana Morse, Lenny Muellner, Margaret Mullett, Greg Nagy, Eric Nelson, Mary Lou Reker, Christina Ricci, Alex Riehle, Philip Rousseau, Toni Stephens, Columba Stewart, Deb Brown Stewart, Alice-Mary Talbot, Shawqi Talia, Elizabeth Teaff, Janet Timbie, Martin Walraff, Jennifer Westerfeld, and Jan Ziolkowski. I would also like to thank my new colleagues at Georgetown University, who have warmly welcomed both myself and Late Antiquity into their thriving Classics department.

In the summers of 2008 and 2009, I was fortunate to have two excellent student assistants: Lain Wilson and Erik Ball, both budding scholars in their own right, without whom this book would have been a much more difficult prospect. I am particularly grateful to Erik Ball for his preliminary translation of a draft French version of Hervé Inglebert's chapter and for his keen proofreading of several other draft chapters. I am grateful also to Arietta Papaconstantinou for her two translations of draft French versions of the chapters by Anne Boud'hors and Christian Julien Robin. Additionally, Aaron Johnson, David Michelson, Dan Schwartz, and Jack Tannous were crucial sounding boards during the initial phases when I was commissioning chapters and formulating the overall vision. Jack was indefatigable in his help with the Syriac and Arabic transliteration. Kyle Harper and Greg Smith were constant dialogue partners throughout the whole process and helped me especially with the organization of the table of contents and the grouping of chapters. Michael Maas provided inspiration for the preface and also helped with the shape of the volume.

I would be remiss as the privileged editor of such a vanguard publication not to thank the contributors for their hard work in producing so many groundbreaking chapters on Late Antiquity. The best reward of an exceedingly long collaborative book comes when you get to read, hot off the press, the cutting-edge research of your colleagues, who have put their trust in your guardianship of their ideas and writing. I am grateful for their faith in my leadership and for strengthening my resolve to complete the project through their inspiring scholarship. I am very proud of our work together.

My parents, Tom and Jan Linder, and my grandparents, Charles and Geneva Mullinax, continue to be unflagging in their (much-treasured) championing of my work. My wife, Carol, and my children—Susanna, Daniel, and Thomas—are the most delightful, loving, and supportive family I could ever imagine. I am indebted to their patience during the editing of this volume, though they would never think of it as a debt or a burden. Carol, in particular, has been unspeakably gracious during this busy, itinerant stage of our lives. It is impossible to acknowledge the full worth of her love and loyalty.

Finally, during the last year of editing this volume (2010–2011), my two mentors in Late Antiquity retired from full-time teaching. Averil Cameron (Oxford) and Peter Brown (Princeton) are two pillars of our field, who continue to push it forward through new research and writing. I feel privileged beyond expression to have been able to study closely with both of them during a formative stage in my life. Since that time, I have been associated with their larger family of students and have seen how, through their scholarly insight and their pastoral instincts, they have together forged a remarkable, enduring legacy for the study of Late Antiquity. Out of gratitude for their support and in celebration of their academic careers, I dedicate this volume to Averil and Peter.

Scott Fitzgerald Johnson
May 2011
Washington, DC

List of Abbreviations

Where possible the abbreviations in this book conform to the standards of *L'Année Philologique* (Paris, 1928–). Papyrological sources not listed below are abbreviated in accordance with:

Oates, J. F., R. S. Bagnall, W. H. Willis, and K. A. Worp. 1992. *Checklist of Editions of Greek and Latin Papyri, Ostraca, and Tablets.* 4th ed. Bulletin of the American Society of Papyrologists, Supplement 7. Atlanta: Scholars Press.

Epigraphical sources not listed below are abbreviated in accordance with:

Bérard, F., D. Feissel, P. Petitmengin, and M. Sère. 2000. *Guide de l'épigraphiste: Bibliographie choisie des épigraphies antiques et médiévales.* 3rd ed. Paris: Éditions Rue d'Ulm / Presses de l'École Normale Supérieure.

AB *Analecta Bollandiana* (Brussels, 1882–)
ACO Schwartz, E. et al., eds. 1914–1992. *Acta Conciliorum Oecumenicorum.* 4 vols. in 27 parts. Berlin: Walter de Gruyter.
AJP *American Journal of Philology* (Baltimore, 1880–)
ANRW Vogt, J., et al., eds. 1972–. *Aufstieg und Niedergang der römischen Welt.* Berlin and New York: W. de Gruyter.
AntAfr *Antiquités africaines* (Paris, 1967–)
AnTard *Antiquité tardive* (Paris, 1993–)
AntJ *The Antiquaries Journal* (Cambridge, 1921–)
ArchMed *Archeologia medievale* (Florence, 1974–)
BASP *Bulletin of the American Society of Papyrologists* (Urbana, IL, etc., 1964–)
BDAG Bauer, W., F. W. Danker, W. F. Arndt, and F. W. Gingrich, eds. 2000. *A Greek-English Lexicon of the New Testament and Other Early Christian Literature.* 3rd ed. Chicago: University of Chicago Press.
BICS *Bulletin of the Institute of Classical Studies of the University of London* (London, 1954–)
ByzF *Byzantinische Forschungen* (Amsterdam, 1966–)
BHG Halkin, F., ed. 1969. *Bibliotheca Hagiographica Graeca.* 3rd ed. Brussels: Société des Bollandistes.
BJ *Bonner Jahrbücher des Rheinischen Landesmuseums in Bonn und des Vereins von Altertumsfreunden im Rheinlande* (Bonn, 1935–)

BMGS *Byzantine and Modern Greek Studies* (Oxford, 1975–)
BSOAS *Bulletin of the School of Oriental and African Studies* (London, 1940–)
Byz *Byzantion* (Brussels, 1924–)
BZ *Byzantinische Zeitschrift* (Stuttgart, etc., 1892–)
C&M *Classica et Mediaevalia* (Copenhagen, 1938–)
CAH XIII Cameron, Averil, and Peter Garnsey, eds. 1998. *The Cambridge Ancient History, Vol. XIII: The Late Empire (A.D. 337–425)*. Cambridge: Cambridge University Press.
CAH XIV Cameron, Averil, Bryan Ward-Perkins, and Michael Whitby, eds. 2000. *The Cambridge Ancient History, Vol. XIV: Late Antiquity: Empire and Successors (A.D. 425–600)*. Cambridge: Cambridge University Press.
CCSL Corpus Christianorum Series Latina (Turnhout, 1965–)
CFHB Corpus Fontium Historiae Byzantinae (Berlin, Paris, Vienna, Washington, DC)
CH *Church History* (Chicago, 1932–)
CIC Kroll, Wilhelm, et al., eds. 1989–1993 [1963–1965]. *Corpus Iuris Civilis*. 3 vols. Hildesheim: Weidmann.
CIL *Corpus Inscriptionum Latinarum* (Berlin, 1893–)
CJ (or *Cod. Just.*) *Codex Justinianus*
Coptic Encyclopedia Atiya, A.S., ed. 1991. *The Coptic Encyclopedia*. 8 vols. New York: Macmillan.
CPG Geerard, M. et al., eds. 1974–2003. *Clavis Patrum Graecorum*. 5 vols. Turnhout: Brepols.
CPh *Classical Philology* (Chicago, 1906–)
CQ *Classical Quarterly* (Oxford, 1907–)
CR *Classical Review* (London, etc., 1887–)
CSCO Corpus Scriptorum Christianorum Orientalium (Louvain, etc.: Peeters, etc., 1903–)
CSEL Corpus Scriptorum Ecclesiasticorum Latinorum (Vienna)
CSL(P) Corpus Scriptorium Latinorum Paravianum (Turin)
CTh (or *Cod. Theod.*) *Codex Theodosianus*
DOP *Dumbarton Oaks Papers* (Washington, DC, 1941–)
EHR *English Historical Review* (London, etc., 1886–)
Ep(p). *Epistula(e)*
G&R *Greece & Rome* (Oxford, 1931–)
GCS Die griechischen christlichen Schriftsteller der ersten Jahrhunderte (Leipzig and Berlin)
GGM Müller, C., ed. 1990 [1855–1861]. *Geographi Graeci Minores*. Hildesheim: Olms.
GRBS *Greek, Roman, and Byzantine Studies* (Cambridge, MA, 1958–)
HE *Historia Ecclesiastica*

HSCP *Harvard Studies in Classical Philology* (Cambridge, MA, 1890–)
HTR *Harvard Theological Review* (Cambridge, MA, 1908–)
JAC *Jahrbuch für Antike und Christentum* (Münster, 1958–)
JAOS *Journal of the American Oriental Society* (New Haven, CT, etc., 1843–)
JECS *Journal of Early Christian Studies* (Baltimore, 1993–)
JEH *Journal of Ecclesiastical History* (London, 1950–)
JHS *Journal of Hellenic Studies* (London, 1880–)
JJP *Journal of Juristic Papyrology* (New York and Warsaw, 1946–)
JJS *Journal of Jewish Studies* (Cambridge, 1948–)
JLA *Journal of Late Antiquity* (Baltimore, 2008–)
JMEMS *Journal of Medieval and Early Modern Studies* (Durham, NC, 1996–)
JÖB *Jahrbuch der Österreichischen Byzantinistik* (Vienna, 1969–)
JÖBG *Jahrbuch der Österreichischen byzantinischen Gesellschaft* (Graz, etc., 1951–)
JRA *Journal of Roman Archaeology* (Ann Arbor, MI, 1988–)
JRS *Journal of Roman Studies* (London, 1911–)
JTS *Journal of Theological Studies* (London, 1899–)
Lampe Lampe, G. W. H., ed. 1961. *A Patristic Greek Lexicon.* Oxford: Oxford University Press.
LCL Loeb Classical Library (London and Cambridge, MA)
LM *Le Muséon* (Leuven, 1882–)
LSJ Liddell, H. G., R. Scott, and H. S. Jones, eds. 1968. *A Greek-English Lexicon.* 9th ed. with supplement. Oxford: Oxford University Press.
MEFRA *Mélanges de l'école française de Rome: Antiquité* (Paris, 1971–)
MGH Monumenta Germaniae Historica (Hannover, etc.)
MGHAA Monumenta Germaniae Historica: Auctores Antiquissimi (Berlin, 1879–1919)
MGHSRM Monumenta Germaniae Historica: Scriptores Rerum Merovingicarum (Hannover, 1884–1897)
NC *Numismatic Chronicle* (London, 1966–)
Nov. Just. (or *Nov.*) *Novellae Constitutiones Justiniani*
NPNF Nicene and Post-Nicene Fathers (Edinburgh)
OCP *Orientalia Christiana Periodica* (Rome, 1935–)
ODB Kazhdan, A., et al., eds. 1991. *Oxford Dictionary of Byzantium.* 3 vols. Oxford: Oxford University Press.
OLD Glare, P. G. W., ed. 1996. *Oxford Latin Dictionary.* Reprinted with corrections. Oxford: Oxford University Press.

Or(r). *Oratio(nes)*
PBA *Proceedings of the British Academy* (London, 1903/1904–)
PBSR *Papers of the British School at Rome* (London, 1902–)
PCPhS *Proceedings of the Cambridge Philological Society* (London, 1882–)
PG Migne, J. P., ed. 1857–1866. *Patrologiae cursus completus: Series Graeca.* 166 vols. Paris.
PL Migne, J. P., ed. 1844–1864. *Patrologiae cursus completus: Series Latina.* 221 vols. Paris.
PLRE Jones, A. H. M. et al., eds. 1971–1992. *Prosopography of the Later Roman Empire.* 3 vols. Cambridge: Cambridge University Press.
PO Patrologia Orientalis (Paris and Turnhout)
PPTS Palestine Pilgrims Text Society (London, 1884–1896)
RAC Klauser, Theodor, ed. 1950–. *Reallexikon für Antike und Christentum: Sachwörterbuch zur Auseinandersetzung des Christentums mit der antiken Welt.* 23 vols. Stuttgart: Hiersemann.
RAL *Rendiconti (Accademia nazionale dei Lincei: Classe di scienze morali, storiche e filologiche)* (Rome, 1946–)
RBPH *Revue belge de philologie et d'histoire* (Brussels, 1922–)
RE von Pauly, A. F. et al., eds. 1894–1980. *Paulys Real-Encyclopädie der klassischen Altertumswissenschaft.* 49 vols. Stuttgart: Metzler.
REB *Revue des études byzantines* (Paris, 1943–)
RHE *Revue d'histoire ecclésiastique* (Louvain, 1900–)
RHPhR *Revue d'histoire et de philosophie religieuses* (Paris, 1921–)
RN *Revue numismatique* (Paris, 1836–)
SC Sources chrétiennes (Paris)
SH Analecta Bollandiana, Subsidia Hagiographica (Brussels)
SO *Symbolae Osloenses* (Oslo, 1924–)
SP *Studia Patristica* (Berlin and Leuven, 1957–)
TAPA *Transactions of the American Philological Association* (Boston, etc., 1869/70–)
TM *Travaux et Mémoires* (Paris, 1965–)
TU Texte und Untersuchungen zur Geschichte der altchristlichen Literatur (Leipzig)
VC *Vigiliae Christianae* (Amsterdam, 1947–)
YClS *Yale Classical Studies* (New Haven, CT, 1928–)
ZPE *Zeitschrift für Papyrologie und Epigraphik* (Bonn, 1967–)
ZSS RA *Zeitschrift der Savigny-Stiftung für Rechtsgeschichte: Romanistische Abtheilung* (Weimar, 1880–)

Note on Transliteration

The standardization of the transliteration of foreign languages in the *OHLA* is a difficult prospect. Numerous ancient and modern languages are represented in this book, and the contributors themselves come from several different national backgrounds and scholarly communities. My primary goal as editor has been the standardization of orthography and transliteration *within each chapter* on its own terms. A secondary goal has been standardization across groups of chapters dealing with related material or languages (see below). A tertiary goal has been standardization across the whole volume, but this is obviously something of a chimera given its size and complexity and, regardless, the thorough index at the back of the book renders complete standardization unnecessary.

For instance, the name of the sixth-century historian Procopius of Caesarea will appear in some chapters of the *OHLA* in its Latinized form, Procopius, and in others in its Hellenized form, Prokopios. When consistent within chapters this variance in usage is perfectly normal for late antique scholarship and should pose few problems. Nevertheless, the reader of the *OHLA* should be aware of the possibility of variance *between different chapters* and should make use of the index where a question arises. The index lists variants in spelling and collects references to single topics or people under one entry, for example, "Yazdgard [Yazdajird, Yazdegerd, Yazkert] I (Sasanian ruler), 296, 994–95, 1002–3, 1004, 1014." The index also cross-references significant transliteration differences. Please see the headnote to the index for more information.

However, my second goal of standardizing orthography and transliteration across groups of chapters has proved to be a bigger challenge. Toward the goal of professionalism among specialists in ancillary fields, I insisted on certain unifying principles: specifically, the need for standardization among the chapters that deal extensively with Arabic words and names. For these chapters—especially 9 (Robin), 31 (Walker), 32 (Hoyland), and 33 (Shoemaker)—I have sought a more literal mode of transliteration that can satisfy the expectations of scholars in Semitics and Islamic studies. Thus, the name of the Prophet Muhammad is rendered in these chapters as Muḥammad, just as *ḥadīth*, *sīra*, and 'Ā'isha are transliterated with the appropriate diacritical marks.

In other chapters that do not deal extensively with Arabic, common Arabic words do not contain diacritical marks. In such chapters the name Muhammad has been rendered in its Anglicized form, without diacritics. An exception to this rule is the word Qur'ān which appears in this form throughout the volume, not just in the group of chapters mentioned above. Likewise, wherever Arabic and Syriac words occur (not to mention Hebrew, Aramaic, and Ethiopic) I have attempted to maintain consistency with regard to distinguishing the letters *'aleph* (') and *'ayin* ('). The Armenian and Coptic transliterations I have left to the authors of those chapters and checked for consistency.

Overall, the transliteration of ancient languages in this book is a compromise system based upon what I perceived to be the most natural expectations of readers. The main goal was consistency within each chapter. To reiterate my recommendation above, the reader should be aware of possible variance between chapters and make use of the index where necessary.

Contributors

Gianfranco Agosti is Lecturer in Classical Philology at the Universitá di Roma "La Sapienza"

Jairus Banaji is Professorial Research Associate with the Department of Development Studies, School of Oriental and African Studies (SOAS), University of London

Anne Boud'hors is Directeur de recherche à l'Institut de recherche et d'histoire des textes, Centre national de la recherche scientifique (CNRS), Paris

Craig H. Caldwell III is Assistant Professor of History, Appalachian State University

Christopher S. Celenza is the Director of the American Academy in Rome and Professor of German and Romance Languages and Literatures, History, and Classical Studies at Johns Hopkins University

Brian Croke is Adjunct Professor of History at Macquarie University and Honorary Associate in Classics and Ancient History, University of Sydney

Andrew Gillett is Associate Professor in Late Antiquity in the Department of Ancient History at Macquarie University

Tim Greenwood is Lecturer in the School of History at St. Andrews University

Cam Grey is Assistant Professor of Classical Studies at the University of Pennsylvania

Petre Guran is Senior Researcher at the Institute of South East European Studies, Bucharest

David M. Gwynn is Lecturer in Ancient and Late Antique History at Royal Holloway, University of London

John Haldon is Professor of History and Hellenic Studies at Princeton University

Kyle Harper is Associate Professor of Classics and Letters at the University of Oklahoma

Jill Harries is Professor of Ancient History at St. Andrews University

Peregrine Horden is Professor of Medieval History at Royal Holloway, University of London

Robert Hoyland is Professor of Early Islamic History at the Oriental Institute and St Cross College, Oxford University

Hervé Inglebert is Professeur d'histoire romaine à l'Université Paris Ouest Nanterre—La Défense (Paris X)

Aaron P. Johnson is Assistant Professor of Humanities at Lee University

Scott Fitzgerald Johnson is Dumbarton Oaks Teaching Fellow in Postclassical Greek at Georgetown University

Michael Kulikowski is Professor of History, Classics, and Ancient Mediterranean Studies and is Head of the Department of History and the Program in Religious Studies at Pennsylvania State University

Étienne de la Vaissière is Directeur d'études at the École des Hautes Études en Sciences Sociales, Paris

Michael Maas is Professor of History and Classical Studies at Rice University

Ralph W. Mathisen is Professor of History, Classics, and Medieval Studies at the University of Illinois at Urbana-Champaign

Jaclyn Maxwell is Associate Professor of History, Classics, and World Religions at Ohio University

Scott McGill is Associate Professor of Classical Studies at Rice University

Arietta Papaconstantinou is Reader in Ancient History, Department of Classics, University of Reading

Glenn Peers is Professor of Early Medieval and Byzantine Art at the University of Texas at Austin

Christian Julien Robin is Directeur de Recherche au Centre national de la recherche scientifique (CNRS), Paris, Laboratoire "Orient et Méditerranée (Monde sémitiques)," et membre de l'Académie des Inscriptions et Belles-Lettres

Samuel Rubenson is Professor of Church History at the Center for Theology and Religious Studies, Lunds Universitet

Stephen J. Shoemaker is Associate Professor of Religious Studies at the University of Oregon

Gregory Smith is Associate Professor of History at Central Michigan University

Kevin Uhalde is Associate Professor of History at Ohio University

Joel Walker is Associate Professor of History at the University of Washington

Edward Watts is Professor of History at Indiana University

Susan Wessel is Associate Professor of Church History and Historical Theology at the Catholic University of America

Philip Wood is College Lecturer in Medieval History at Sidney Sussex College, Cambridge University

Ann Marie Yasin is Associate Professor of Classics and Art History at the University of Southern California

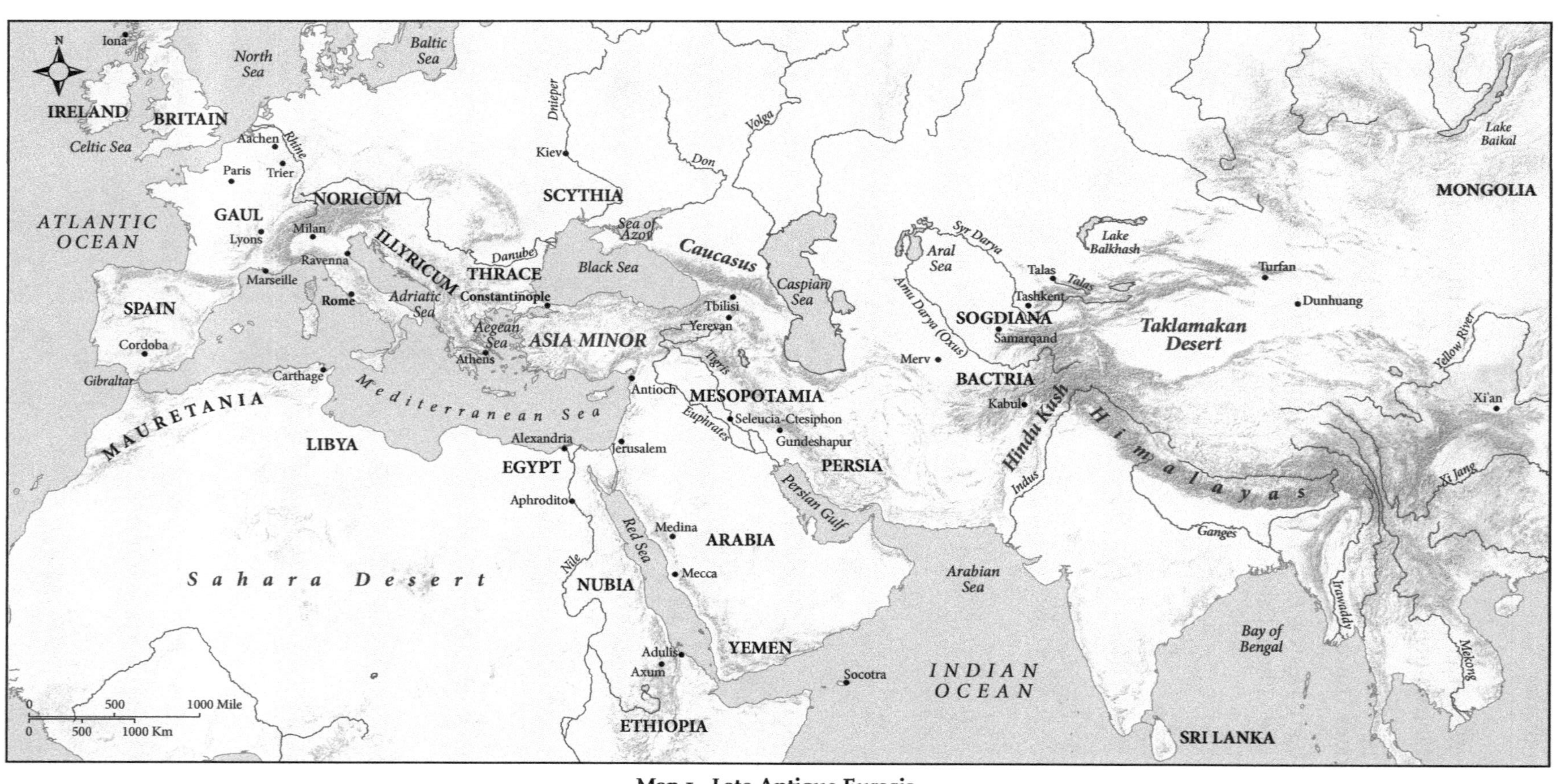

Map 1. Late Antique Eurasia.

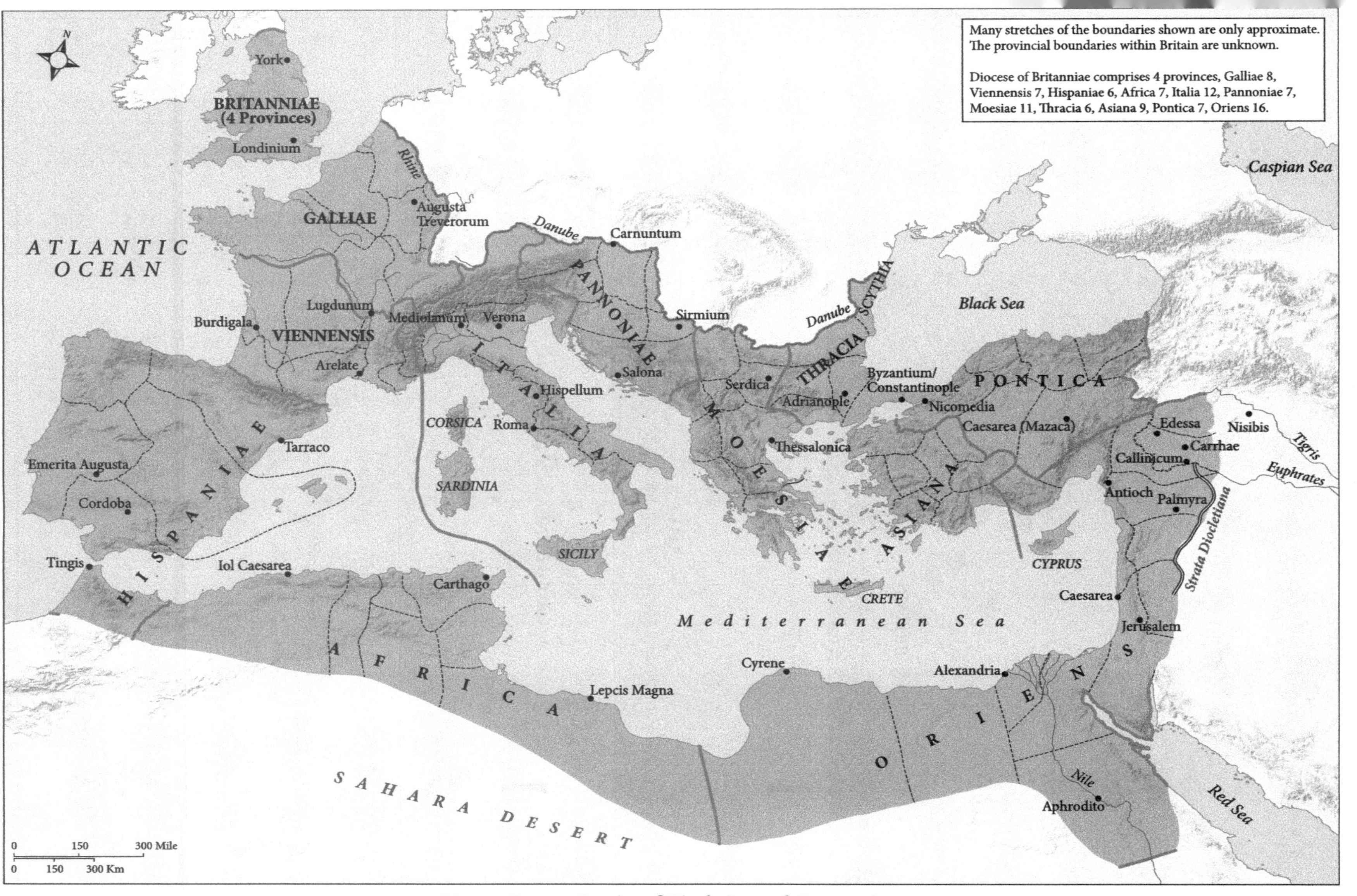

Map 2. Roman Empire of Diocletian and Constantine.

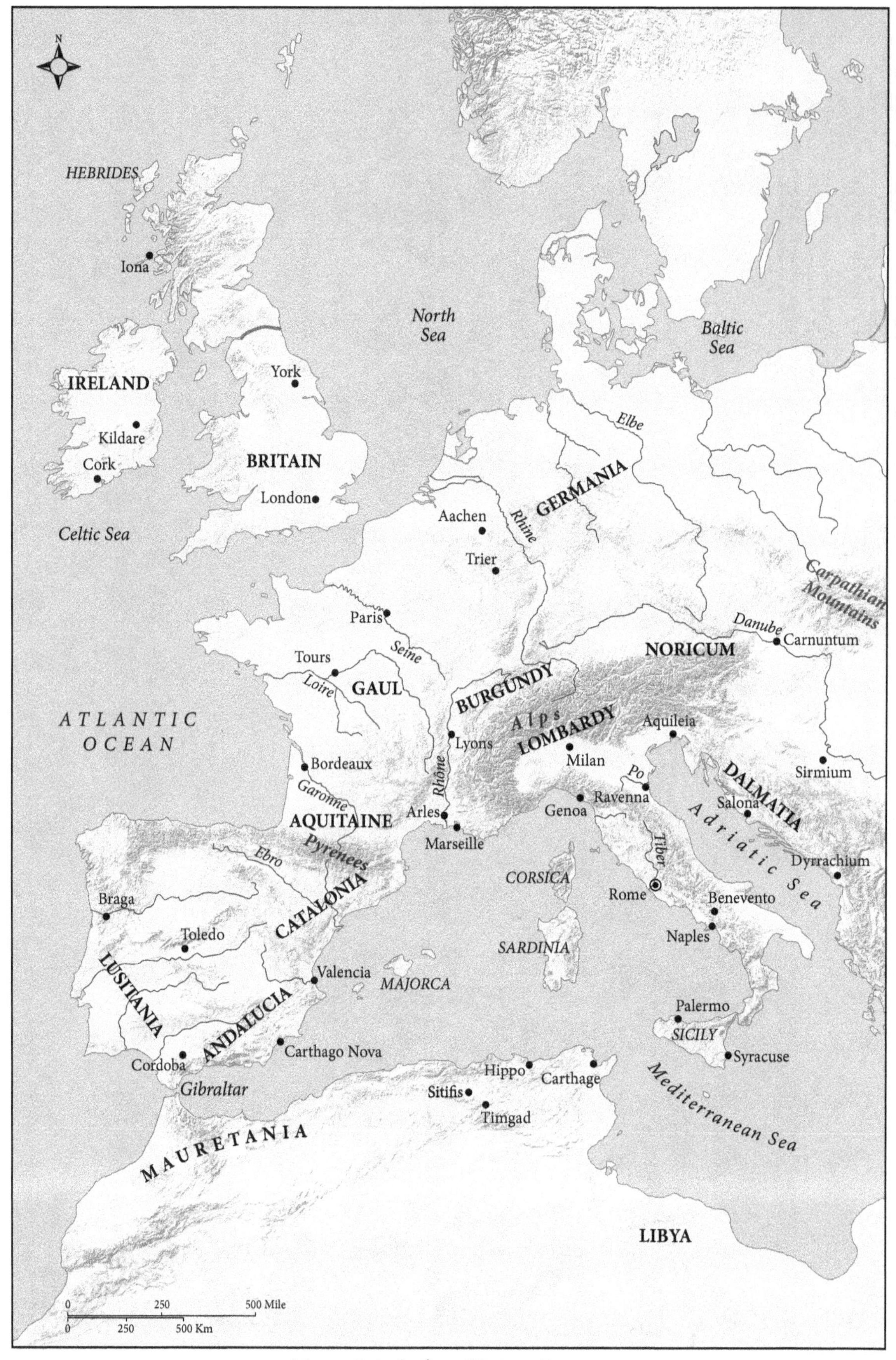

Map 3. Late Antique Western Europe.

Map 4. Late Antique Near East

THE OXFORD HANDBOOK OF

LATE ANTIQUITY

INTRODUCTION: LATE ANTIQUE CONCEPTIONS OF LATE ANTIQUITY

HERVÉ INGLEBERT
Université Paris Ouest
Nanterre—La Défense (Paris X)

For a half century now, a diverse range of historiographical models for the end of antiquity has been increasingly reshuffled (Mazzarino 1959; Demandt 1984; Inglebert 2003; Marcone 2008; James 2008; Ando 2008). "Late Antiquity," a term first attested in German, has, since 1900, been delineated by four main characteristics: (1) a periodization, more or less long in duration; (2) a geographical area, more or less expansive; (3) central themes, either numerous or singular; and, especially, (4) a judgment of overall value. In 1949 (and subsequently), Henri-Irénée Marrou explained why it is preferable to replace the weak adjectives "*bas-empire*," "*spätrömisch*," and "late Roman"—all of which suggest a universal Roman decline that never happened—with the strong nouns "*Antiquité tardive*," "*Spätantike*," and "Late Antiquity" (Marrou 1949; 1977). These latter terms allow for an understanding of the period unto itself, and art historians, under Riegl's influence (Elsner 2002), had already been using such terms for half a century by Marrou's time. But for Marrou, the expression "Late Antiquity" applied above all to the Roman empire and its immediate neighbors, whereas art historians had used it to describe an entire *époque*—applying it even to phenomena attested in Central Asia (Le Coq 1923–1933). What is more, the expression allowed value to be placed on the creative aspects of the period—especially in religious, cultural, and artistic domains—and it took into account all the historical dimensions, understanding these to be linked to the disappearance of the western Roman empire and to the decline of specific regions.

In 1971, a book by Peter Brown, *The World of Late Antiquity*, described Late Antiquity as a long-lasting phenomenon (200–800 C.E.), during which the dissolution of the ancient Mediterranean world led to the creation of three civilizations, all equal heirs of antiquity: western Europe, Byzantium, and Islam. This conception was accompanied by the positive depiction of a period that was altogether creative. Later, in *The Making of Late Antiquity* (1978), Brown proposed defining Late Antiquity by its religious and cultural themes, in their relation to the social evolutions at the heart of the Mediterranean world. Subsequently, Late Antiquity was conceived of as encompassing a vaster area, combining the Roman and Sasanian territories, and later the Umayyad (Fowden 1993)—all the while preserving not only its *longue durée* (250–800) and the central themes defining it (Hellenism, Christianity, Islam) but also the positive judgment it now carried (Hägg 1997; Bowersock, Brown, and Grabar 1999).

However, this new historiographical norm has been sharply criticized in the last ten years or so (Giardina 1999), and some scholars no longer hesitate to take up once more the concept of decline: whether it be in the region-by-region picture of Mazzarino (Liebeschuetz 2001) or even in the universalizing sense of Gibbon (Ward-Perkins 2005). These debates are accompanied by the abandonment of an a priori favorable judgment and by the reassertion of classical themes neglected since 1971. Some favor a new geographical and chronological delimitation of the "Late Roman Empire" (Mitchell 2005); others preserve the broad geographical scope but restrict the time frame (400–800) and keep to economic and social systems (Wickham 2005). This present collective work, *The Oxford Handbook of Late Antiquity*, has chosen to attempt to integrate all the interpretive systems (economic, social, artistic, religious, cultural) while maintaining a broad geographical perspective—from the Atlantic to Central Asia. It offers itself as a thematic complement to the final two volumes of the new *Cambridge Ancient History* (XIII and XIV), which together cover the period 337–600. The *Cambridge Ancient History* volumes emphasize above all classical historiographical themes (political, military, social, and institutional history) and leave out the Sasanian world, which is treated in *The Cambridge History of Iran* (III). By contrast, the *Oxford Handbook of Late Antiquity* tries to extend its reach as far as possible, in terms of both thematic categories and geographical scope.

However, the chronology of this volume is a different matter, since it was announced to the contributors that "from Constantine to Muhammad" was to be the chronological span, and the contributors were asked specifically to problematize this periodization in their chapters. "From Constantine to Muhammad" differs from the periods typically reserved among classicists for the "Late Roman Empire," which begins with the accession of the emperor Diocletian (i.e., 284) and draws to a close—depending on the author—with the death of the emperors Justinian (565), Maurice (602), Phocas (610), or Heraclius (641). To begin with Constantine rather than with Diocletian and to end with the prophet of Islam rather than with a Roman emperor is a choice in favor of religious themes. In the debates over the nature of Late Antiquity, this chronology insists on continuity, as opposed to drastic change. Rupture, by contrast, is what a political periodization usually champions, not least because of the disappearance of the Roman empire in the West.

The fact that this religious periodization favors Christianity (and Islam) in comparison with other religious systems of the *époque* ("paganism," rabbinic Judaism, Manichaeism, Zoroastrianism) is not what some might call "politically scandalous," for Christianity was in fact the major religious movement in the Roman empire, in the Romano-Barbarian kingdoms of the West, among certain neighboring peoples, and even in some regions of the Sasanian Persian empire (Armenia and Mesopotamia). The growing significance of religious sentiment from 250 to 311 is well attested: Christians became more numerous; Manichaeism emerged; general anti-Christian persecutions were perpetrated by the Roman authorities (249–251, 257–260, 303–311), as well as Zoroastrian persecutions ordered by the *Moabadan-Moabad* Kartir (the Zoroastrian "priest of priests" who had Mani executed in 276); and the term "Hellene" began to be used to signify those who were religiously "pagan." However, only the conversion of Constantine, made public at the end of the year 312, crystallized these sentiments by establishing a link between the Roman empire and Christianity, both bearing ambitions of universality. The emperor was able to present himself as a universal protector of Christians, a stance that was immediately understood in Persia by the Christian Aphrahat and by the Zoroastrian "king of kings" Shapur II, persecutor of the Christians after 337.[1] And three centuries later, the expansion of Islam was another example of convergence between a monotheistic religion and a politics of imperial domination. The conversion of Constantine and the Muslim conquest very much had a global impact in allying a religion and a universal power. Even if the rate of conversion to Christianity or Islam diverged region by region, the process persisted into the following centuries.

Nevertheless, this central religious/political/military issue, however important it may be, does not exhaust the significance of the period: one cannot legitimately omit the social dimensions (especially the role of the elites), the economy,[2] or cultural factors. But yet, so long as the evolution of diverse diachronic themes is not rendered in a synchronic manner, it is inevitable that periodizations will vary according to the themes broached. Thus, for Late Antiquity to avoid becoming only a projection of contemporary anachronistic ideas—related to American multiculturalism, to concepts of European Union—or to be only a predictable framework of scholarship,[3] the historian has only two solutions.

The first would be to try to articulate the diverse evolving unsynchronized systems in a unified structure that would describe the appearance, the development, and the disappearance of Late Antiquity and would correspond to the raison d'être of the term itself, as previously described. Such a systematic synthesis, hoped for by Andrea Giardina and necessarily worked out according to the understandings of our time, remains to be written. The second solution would be to describe Late Antiquity from the point of view of the "mentalities" of the *époque* (or of "representations" of its mentalities, though representations are too often understood only as the effects of discourse). This approach would give Late Antiquity what we might call a "psychological" unity.

Such an attempt to re-create the mental world of Late Antiquity—already partially tried (Sambursky 1962)—nevertheless runs into particular difficulties. If one supposes that Late Antiquity existed as a place of shared consciousness—that is to say, as a network of communication—one must admit that it was not a homogeneous space. If one should wish to include the western part of the Roman empire (subsequently the Romano-Germanic kingdoms), the eastern Roman empire (earliest Byzantium), and the Sasanian empire as one geographic unit for the period of 300 to 630, it would be necessary to acknowledge that this unit would not form a "civilization" of Late Antiquity, in the sense that there once existed a Roman civilization.[4] Since this grouping did not know cultural unity (still less political, ideological, or religious unity) before the Muslim conquest—being as it was divided between two large empires and two large official religious systems (leaving aside various others)—the existence of a unity of mentalities seems impossible. However, such a unity might be established in two ways: either according to jointly common ideas (*idées communes*)—which was obviously not the case—or according to shared ideas (*idées partagées*). For example, the idea that the truth was contained in revealed religious texts, even if these texts could be different, was a *shared* idea (*une idée partagée*) among the Jews, Christians, Zoroastrians, Manichaeans, Neoplatonists, and Muslims. On the other hand, the Christian groups (except the Gnostics and the Marcionites) had the *common* idea (*l'idée en commun*) that their revealed text consisted of the Old and the New Testaments, which deterred alternative views of the status of these texts. One could say that a common idea (*une idée commune*) allowed a collective identity to be defined and that a shared idea (*une idée partagée*) led to the definition of a commonwealth. Late Antiquity was not a common civilization (*une civilisation commune*), but a shared commonwealth (*un commonwealth partagé*).

Reconstructing the mental world of Late Antiquity, therefore, returns to describing the representations that peoples had of themselves and of their world (and the connections between these representations). Nevertheless, this world was a real geographical space, which, from the Atlantic to India, had a center of gravity, the imperial Roman power, henceforth Christian. This center, like a very massive star, bent the world of meaning around itself and oriented the mental space-time of people toward its own center. Since it was the most ancient, the most powerful, and the most prestigious empire of Late Antiquity, all other self-definitions referred back to Rome. When the Roman empire disappeared in the West from the fifth century, it was the eastern Roman empire that then assumed the role of reference point. It is for this reason that those who have defined Late Antiquity from the point of view of the Roman East exhibited a correct intuition, but this "East Side Story" was only one facet of the plot. The demographic, economic, military, and cultural importance of the Roman East is alone insufficient to provide us with a definition of Late Antiquity. Rather, the East was only the necessary condition, a central hub around which (and for which) existed a network of traffic in information and meaning—a role that the Muslim world would perform later. In other words, the Roman East was the *material* cause but not the *efficient* cause of Late Antiquity. Late Antiquity arose out of the redefinition, from 312 to 632, of the imperial Roman ideological model of the superiority of the "High Empire," an empire that saw its sovereignty contested in many ways after 230 and that Constantine reformulated from a Christian point of view. Late Antiquity, from Constantine to Muhammad, was both the *époque* of a new Christian assertion of Roman ideology and hegemony and the *époque* of challenges to such an assertion.

Any attempt to describe the "Late Antique Conceptions of Late Antiquity" encounters three methodological problems. The first is the geographical origin of the sources: we have many more documents stemming from the Roman world than from the Sasanian world. Consequently, the reconstruction of a late antique consciousness of the world would be unbalanced in favor of the Roman empire, but at this time, the political and psychological reality always favored Rome. The second difficulty lies in the social origin of the sources: we must lean principally on written sources, and one cannot reconstruct a whole conception of the world from a small selection of works. But in an aristocratic world, there is nothing else that might be used to generalize. The third problem is the criticism that the sources that supply us with information provide more representations than descriptions of reality. However, these are the very representations that structured the shared mentalities (*les mentalités partagées*).

To describe the mental world of the elites of Late Antiquity, it is first necessary to know how they conceived of the late antique geopolitical world. One can then proceed to study the values of late antique societies, the late antique religious world, and ultimately the late antique knowledge of the world, in particular, the history of the *époque* as it was understood by its contemporaries.

To understand the late antique geopolitical world, it is necessary to start from the situation of the High Empire, from Augustus to Gordian III (27 B.C.E. to 244 C.E.). The known world for the Romans (*orbis terrarum*), as it was derived from what was known by Greek geographers from the fourth century B.C.E. (*oikoumene*), had four characteristics: (1) it was assumed that the *oikoumene* was greater in longitude than in latitude by a ratio of 2 to 1; (2) it was divided into three parts: Europe, Asia, Africa; (3) it was composed of a central civilized zone (exemplified by the city), which was surrounded by barbarian peoples living in villages or as nomads, and beyond these lived mythical peoples of the borders (*eschatia*); finally, (4) within the civilized zone, the Roman empire held a dominant position. This image of the world—illustrated by the now lost maps of Eratosthenes and Strabo and also by the surviving itinerary map called the Peutinger Table—remained the common conception until 550, when the first atlas of world and regional maps, derived from the *Geography* of Claudius Ptolemy, was produced in Alexandria (Wolska-Conus 1973). From a Roman point of view, the world could be divided into six political and geographical regions: (1) the Roman empire, (2) European *Barbaricum*, (3) the Iranian world, (4) the Erythrian or Red Sea (Arabia-Ethiopia-India), (5) Scythia (the northeastern steppes), and (6) the country of *Seres* or "silk" (i.e., the Silk Road, including Central Asia and northwestern China). But from a cultural point of view, one might distinguish (within these six regions) four zones of information circulation: (1) the Roman West (Latin), (2) the Roman East (Greek), (3) the Near East (Aramaic), and (4) Persia (Middle-Persian).[5] Each of these cultural zones had its own perception of the world, which did not, however, prevent some exchange of information and knowledge.

From an ideological point of view, Roman power asserted the extension of its own power, or at the least its own influence, into the entirety of the known world, from the Atlantic to the Ganges, ever since the victory at Actium was presented as if it were Rome's victory over the peoples of the East, who had allied themselves with Cleopatra and Marc Antony. The *Imperium Romanum*, which Virgil had defined as *sine fine* (*Aeneid* 1.278), spilled over the provincial frontiers. It is necessary to understand that this pretension, that there was an *urbs* to rule the *orbis terrarum*, was not absurd (Nicolet 1988). On the world maps from the period—such as Strabo's, upon which the coordinates of certain points were fixed according to an astronomical system—the Roman empire extends in longitude over more than half of the known world. In the second century, when Rome controlled the client kingdoms of the Rhine and the Danube, as well as the Red Sea, it was in a position of strength against the Parthians (who were defeated by Trajan, Marcus Aurelius, and Septimius Severus), and it received ambassadors from Central Asia and southern India. The Romans could think without exaggeration that their superiority (*maiestas*) was recognized by all peoples—China was not known—and that the Roman emperor was indeed the master of the world. In the second century, a Roman soldier, to the east of Aqaba (in modern Jordan), inscribed in Greek: "The Romans always prevail. I, Lauricius, wrote this. Greetings Zeno" (IGLJ 4.138 = Sartre 1993); and in Trier, as in Rome, one could write on the stadia, "Parthi occisi, Britto victus, ludite Romani" (*Année Épigraphique* 1949, +00258). The grandeur of Rome was known in China, as claimed by the princes of southern India who used denarii as local money and received a cult of the divine Augustus at the port of Muziris (probably in modern Malabar). Around 200, Bardaisan of Edessa, a Christian aristocrat writing in Syriac, admitted in his *Treatise on the Laws of the Countries* (45 and 48) that the Romans would always be ready to conquer new territories and to extend their laws to others, a concept that harks back to Virgil, *Aeneid* 6.851–853:

> Tu regere imperio populos, Romane, memento
> (hae tibi erunt artes) pacique imponere morem,
> parcere subiectis et debellare superbos.[6]

Only the Parthians, who considered themselves "Philhellenes" (as the successors to Alexander), were able to challenge Roman hegemony. The idea of a division of the universal dominion of the Macedonian empire was affirmed by the Parthians after their victory over Crassus in 53 B.C.E., and at some point accepted by some Romans.[7] But during the Antonine period, Rome was eventually led to consider itself the unique heir of the ancient universal empires, after the Assyrians, the Medes, the Persians, and the Macedonians. What is more, the Roman dominion was conceived of as bigger than its predecessors, because it was tricontinental, as well as perpetual: *Roma aeterna*, which celebrated its millennial anniversary on April 21, 248, was the *telos* of history.

This image of the world was cast aside by the crisis of the third century. From 240 to 275, the Roman empire was attacked on three fronts by adversaries that had become more powerful: the Sasanians in the East, the Goths along the Danube, and the Franks and Alamanni along the Rhine. The defeats, the civil wars, and the fragmentation of the empire into three parts that occurred around 270 created a dramatic situation that stabilized only around 298. But in 300, though Rome had regained a semblance of its former hegemony, this would not last. After 350, the attacks against the Roman empire resumed: troops were withdrawn in the face of the Persian onslaught (Nisibis was lost in 363, Armenia divided in 387); they were defeated by the Goths (Adrianople in 378; the sack of Rome in 410); they were unable to defend the Rhine frontier (407); they suffered losses at the hands of the Vandals (Africa was lost from 429 to 439; Rome was sacked in 455; Roman expeditions were held in check from 460 to 468). All of these events led to the end of the western empire during the years 475 to 480. And even the Justinianic reconquests (533–552) in Africa, Italy, and southern Spain were afterward contested by the *Mauri*/Moors (535–548), the Lombards (after 568), and the Visigoths (until 624). Eventually, the menace of the Slavs in the Balkans (540) and the Sasanians in the East (613–629) was more pressing. But all of these events were henceforth understood in relation to the Christian Roman empire, a mental framework that was the founder of Late Antiquity, ideologically established by Constantine during the years 312 to 337, at the very moment when the notion of Roman superiority was rediscovered. It is now necessary to present the different understandings of this space-time according to the various cultural zones.

In the Latin West, it was still possible in the fourth century to reaffirm the traditional ideology that a Roman hegemony extended all the way to the Ganges (André and Filliozat 1986). This can be seen from the *Panegyrici latini* or in the *Historia Augusta* (*Vita Cari* 9.1–3), which criticizes (even c. 400!) the idea that destiny would prohibit the emperors from going beyond Ctesiphon: for the author of the *Historia Augusta*, Rome rules over a world wherein Persians and barbarians are subordinated. The Peutinger Table offers us a graphic expression of this conception of Roman rule. Even if the surviving copy is medieval, with some early medieval, maybe Carolingian, inclusions (Albu 2005; cf. Talbert 2010), its final conception can be dated to around 360 (Arnaud 1991), and on it the Roman empire represents 80 percent of the depicted space. But the Christian Jerome, who was attuned to the actual state of eastern affairs and wary of an (originally pagan) ideology of Roman domination, wrote around 392, "Persae, Medi, Indi, et Aethiopies regna non modica et Romano regno paria" (*Adversus Jovinianum*, 2.7). For Jerome, Rome was an empire among others in history. The idea of the Roman hegemony became rare after 400. But even after the invasions along the Rhine in 407, it was possible to believe from 417 (Orosius and Rutilius Namatianus) to 470 (Sidonius Apollinaris) that, despite the machinations of the Vandals—in 460 and in 468 it was still possible to hope seriously that they would be destroyed—the Roman empire was surviving (at the least) in the power of the emperor over confederated barbarians henceforth installed within Roman territory. After 470, however, these illusions disappeared. Nevertheless, during the fifth century, men in the West began to think that the "empire of Christ" could take the reins from Rome, perhaps in the form of a Christian commonwealth extending itself beyond the frontier of the empire (Rufinus of Aquileia after 400 in his *Ecclesiastical History*) or perhaps in the form of a spiritual empire of Christ of which Rome would be the citadel in the name of an ideology making the pope the successor of Peter (Leo the Great and Prosper of Aquitaine, around 440–450). The concrete Roman universality could become a Christian universality. This, however, did not prevent barbarians (Odoacer in 476, the Burgundian kings around 520) or the popes—Gregory the Great, who, around 600, was still truly a Roman citizen thanks to the Justinianic conquest—from respecting that the Roman empire was henceforth directed from Constantinople. Throughout the sixth century, however, Visigothic Spain and the Merovingian kingdoms remained outside Justinian's *Romania*.

Seen from the Roman East, the world was rather different because the Roman empire remained in place. Of course, the known world had grown significantly: around 380–390, Ammianus Marcellinus correctly described China, not Central Asia, as the country of the *Seres*. But some still believed in the sovereign superiority of the Roman empire. Recording the Indian voyage of a *scholasticus* from Thebes, Palladius reported the respect that the Roman emperor had inspired in those far-off regions (*Commonitorium* 6.10). And around 550, Cosmas Indicopleustes, a merchant from Alexandria, proudly reported how many eyes of southern Indian princes had been struck by the gold *solidus* after Constantine had gotten the better of the silver money of the Sasanian empire (*Christian Topography* 9.17–19). At that same time, the first atlas of maps based on Ptolemy were created (Wolska-Conus 1973): if the Roman empire appeared smaller, its renown, not only in India, was only appearing greater. However, the fame of Rome was greater than its influence, and the *imperium sine fine* had been replaced with *Romania*, a word that appeared in the fourth century and was prominent thereafter: from now on—that is, after 350, as attested by the *Expositio totius mundi*—the frontier that separated Rome from the barbarians was more insisted upon. And the wars of the fourth century with the Sasanians led Ammianus Marcellinus to reflect on the Persian "other": in his description of the Sasanian territory (23.6), he adopted a model of Persian origins, going from the center to the periphery, thereby recognizing the specificity of an empire that had to be defined for itself. And if the Greek-speaking Romans continued to qualify the Persians as "barbarians," Ammianus—who, though he was a Greek-speaking Syrian-Roman, wrote in Latin—avoids the term, as do other Latin authors. For him, *barbaricum* denotes Germanic areas of Europe, not the powerful and civilized eastern empire.

The Syriac and Armenian Near East, divided between the Roman and Sasanian empires, was without doubt the best place to learn about the late antique geographic world. Already around 200, Bardaisan of Edessa, in his *Laws of the Countries*, describes the world from the *Seres* (probably the Chinese) in the East to the Celts in the West. Around 337, Aphrahat, a Christian from Persian Mesopotamia, was meditating on the Roman and Sasanian empires (*Memra* 5, "On Wars"), and his preferences leaned toward the Roman emperor and the Christian Constantine, who presented himself as the natural protector of Persian Christians. These were Christians who retained lasting suspicion among their Persian rulers and had famously suffered persecutions. Cosmas Indicopleustes, himself a Roman citizen from Alexandria, was in contact with Christians from the Persian empire due to his conversion to "Nestorian" (i.e., East-Syriac) Christianity. For his own theological reasons, he refused to use the maps derived from Ptolemy and instead took up again the very ancient geography of Ephorus (from around 350 B.C.E.), privileging the Celts and the Indians as the peoples at the edges of the world, but he knew China (*Tzinista*), and he gave the number of days for a journey across Eurasia (*Christian Topography* 2.28): 243 days from *Tzinista* to Seleucia on the Euphrates and 150 days from the eastern Mediterranean coast to the columns of Hercules. The Persian empire appears in his work to be comparable in size to the Roman empire. Following Cosmas, it is then possible to continue the investigation after 632, beginning with Ananias of Širak in Armenian, Jacob of Nisibis in Syriac, and the Umayyad frescoes at Quṣayr 'Amra.

Sasanian Persia is the final cultural sphere that concerns us here. Due to their central position in Asia, the Sasanians were a priori very well placed to assemble information (Fr. *information*). But they did not have the Greco-Roman ethnographic and cartographic techniques at their disposal with which to organize their findings into knowledge (*savoir*). They were not in direct contact with the Chinese, except at the end of the Sasanian empire at the time of the Arab invasion, but they knew of their power from Sogdian merchants. They were in contact with northern India, because they fought against the Kushans from 230 to 240. This is shown in a recently discovered bas-relief from Rag-i Bibi, in Afghanistan, which depicts a Sasanian king (no doubt Shapur I) on horseback, attacking a rhinoceros (as a symbol of Kushan India and not of the Afghan mountains!) with a spear. But the Sasanian control over Sogdiana, Bactriana, and Gandhara lasted only until around 360, coming to an end with the arrival of the Ephthalite Huns. The Persians maintained more lasting contact with the Arabs, and they managed to extend their control to Yemen by 575. But in the eyes of the Sasanian "king of kings," only two exterior powers were of any significance: the Romans and the peoples of the Steppe—the Huns and the Turks—the region that the poetic tradition later called Turan. However, Rome was the model, not the nomads. Around 600, Khusro II wrote to the emperor Maurice: "God effected that the whole world should be illuminated from the very beginning by two eyes, namely by the most powerful kingdom of the Romans and by the most prudent sceptre of the Persian state. For by these greatest powers the disobedient and bellicose tribes are winnowed and man's course is continually regulated and guided" (Theophylact Simocatta, *History* 4.11.2–3).[8] This duality and this parity were reiterated shortly afterward by Persian ambassadors: "For it is impossible for a single monarchy to embrace the innumerable cares of the organization of the universe, and with one mind's ruler to direct a creation as great as that over which the sun watches" (4.13.7).[9]

It is known that the Sasanians had asserted their Persian origins, connecting themselves to the Achaemenid Persians; in reality, this pretension was theoretical and aimed less at conquering the Roman East than at justifying their power over the Arsacids, against whom they fought from 224 to 226—though their princes still reigned in Armenia and at Hatra (they had established a rapprochement with Rome by then). Neither in the third century nor in the sixth did the Sasanians endeavor to use their opportune victories over the Romans to annex Syria or part of Anatolia; they did this only at the beginning of the seventh century. But the claim to Achaemenid heritage was real, and it held a strong ideological force.[10] It permitted the rejection of the Parthians as Philhellenes alongside Alexander, an enemy of the Iranians, and it justified animosity toward Rome as Alexander's heir and the eternal enemy of the Iranian people.[11] Indeed, it allowed a claim of, if not sovereign primacy, at least equality with Rome.

After 240, Shapur I proclaimed himself "King of the Iranians and of the non-Iranians" in his inscriptions (e.g., at Naghsh-e-Rostam, near Persepolis), which was a new definition of universality, and around 250, the prophet Mani developed another universality, this one religious, affirming that—after the teaching of Buddha in India, Zoroaster in Iran, and Jesus in the West (the

Roman empire)—he had come to close the cycle of prophets. This Manichaean selection of three great religious spheres was different from the ideological traditions of the Sasanians, which was as much cultural—two civilized empires, Rome and the Sasanians—as it was political: four thrones, China, Central Asia, Persia, and the eastern Roman empire. If the Romans were well acquainted with the Persians after 350 (as the work of Ammianus Marcellinus shows), the Persians were informed about the Romans from the time of Shapur I (as demonstrated by his description of the army of Valerian in 260). The Persians, whether under Shapur I or under Khusro I, were equally receptive to certain Roman models—including political models (ceremonies), military technology (siegecraft), artistic styles (mosaics, the iconographic theme of Victory), philosophical learning (translations of Plato and Aristotle), and scholarship (medicine)—in an effort to be able to claim equality with their great rival, Rome, who was also the great model (Garsoïan 1983).

Thus, beginning after 230, the hegemony of the empire of Rome was called into question, and despite the reestablishment of Roman authority around 300, the question was taken up again after 337 in the East and led to the political and economic disintegration of the Roman West after 400. The Sasanian military power forced the Romans to admit their parity, something they had refused to admit to the Parthians. At the same time, the expansion of Christendom allowed a greater assertion of Christian universality. The world of Late Antiquity was thus organized around four loci: (1) the affirmed primacy of the Christian Roman empire (which became the empire of Constantinople after 476–480), (2) the accepted equality between the Roman and the Sasanian empires, (3) the integration of a number of peripheral regions through the expansion of Christianity (e.g., Ireland, Ethiopia), and (4) the diffusion of culture (e.g., cultural factors of Hellenistic origin in the Arabian peninsula: Bowersock 1990).

In the late antique world, connections among the values of the elites was an important phenomenon; just as under the High Empire, it is easy to simply hold the Roman and Iranian elites in opposition. The former maintained civic, urbane, cultural (*paideia*), and civil values. In effect, the city was the foundation of the municipal Roman civilization, with its double dimension of the local *patria* and the universal city, as found in the dialectic of the "two *patriae*" inherited from Cicero (*De Legibus* 2.2.5). Even still, these civic values expressed themselves best in the towns that (almost without exception) were the civic centers where the aristocrats who governed the cities resided. They levied taxes, maintained the imperial highways, and assured public order. In exchange, the autonomy of the cities and the primacy of the aristocrats were guaranteed by Roman power. Finally, the dominant values were civil values, since the Roman army was composed of professional soldiers who were stationed on the frontier. Classical education in grammar and rhetoric marked membership in the elite class. Public spectacles allowed popular participation in the pleasures of the *pax Romana* and classical culture. Only the senators and a small segment of the *Equites* (those who had entered into the imperial administration) had experience—brief for senators, substantial for *Equites*—of military life as an officer. After Augustus, who had created a professional army to avoid a resumption of civil war, Italian Roman society lost that warlike structural system that had allowed them to conquer the world in only three centuries. After 300, with few exceptions (Isauria, Mauretania), civil values became dominant throughout all of *Romania*. The recruitment of volunteer soldiers, however, became insufficient, and recourse was found through conscriptions beginning during the reign of Diocletian and by the use of Germanic mercenaries.

On the other hand, in the Iranian world, aristocratic values were based in the military; it was necessary to be an excellent horseman and a skilled archer to justify your rank. Furthermore, the Parthian aristocrats lived less in towns and more on their rural estates, where they devoted themselves to hunting, considered to be the best practice for war. The arrival of Sasanian authority did not change this value system, shared by the kings who set their example. Sasanian bas-reliefs and paintings show scenes of hunting because the kings withdrew to their rural palaces surrounded by gardens—the *paradis* inherited from the Achaemenids—which were also hunting reserves. The Sasanian army still remained composed of a substantial rank and file, but it was poorly equipped and poorly trained, consisting of peasants brought by the aristocrats, who, for their part, formed a fearsome cavalry.

The ineffectiveness of the Roman army between 249 and 275 led the emperors to privilege officers who were outside the high ranks for command posts after 262, and the fear of usurpation led them to separate civil administrative careers from military careers after 285. As Rome began to engage many barbarian soldiers after 330, an elite officer corps of barbarian origin arose (Franks, Alamanni, Goths, Alani). They were loyal to the emperor, they adopted some traits of the elite senatorial class (a luxurious life, classical culture), and, sometimes, they married within this class. The "barbarization" of the Roman army in the West, significant after 380, became predominant after 420, whereas in the East after 400, the role of barbarians was limited and controlled. In the West, after 480, the disappearance of the Roman empire led to the devaluation of the civil models of Roman elites (though this was true by 410 in Britain). Euergetism and spectacles had, for the most part, disappeared during the turmoil of the invasions of the fifth century, surviving only in a marginal and dissimilar manner, such as in a royal, imperial, or even an episcopal context (versus a local, elite context).

There was a reduction in the number of administrative posts in the Roman empire's western successor kingdoms because taxation was simplified and some administrative levels—praetorian prefect, dioceses, sometimes even provinces—that were no longer needed after the creation of city counts and court counselors disappeared entirely. This rendered classical culture less attractive, because the effort and investment necessary to master it became less socially profitable. When other careers, especially episcopal ones, opened up to aristocrats in Gaul and Spain, the creation of new cultures was needed: patristic (synthesis of classical and biblical culture) or monastic (primarily biblical). At the same time, the career mode nearest to the kings became, above all, military. Already in 449, at the height of the power of Attila the Hun, Priscus, the ambassador from Constantinople, met with Romans in the service of the Hun king; they were making their careers in an open aristocratic system as administrators or as soldiers (*History* fragment 8). Additionally, in 506, Gallo-Roman aristocrats came from Aquitaine and Auvergne with their peasant militias to support the Visigothic king Alaric II against Clovis; for the first time in many centuries, war became an aristocratic Roman value again (though this was true earlier in Britain and in the time of Sidonius Apollinaris in Gaul). During the same period, aristocrats began to reside less in towns, which were no longer places of spectacles, power, or culture. Thus, urban, cultural, and civil values began to weaken, from 440 in Great Britain, from 500 in Gaul and Spain, and after 530 in Africa and Italy. As for the towns, they became more and more centers of religious power (the bishop), royal power (the count), and military power (the garrison). A similar evolution took place after 550 in the Balkanized regions of the eastern Roman empire. The necessity for pagans to convert to Christianity after 527–529, the increased importance of the law (as opposed to rhetoric) in the formation of civil servants after 540, the progressive clericalization of culture after 550, and the decline of civic life all led to a weakening of classical culture and to the predominance of military and religious values (which supported alms distribution and pious building projects).

This evolution slowly led the aristocrats of the western kingdoms, the Roman East, and the Sasanian empire toward shared dominant values. Everywhere in the sixth century, one can find the elites engaged in military, administrative, and religious pursuits. But these values were shared (*partagées*) differently, and it is because of this that they were not values held in common (*communes*). The bishops of Gaul and Spain often came from the aristocratic senatorial class (Sidonius Apollinaris, Remy of Rheims, Gregory of Tours) and had only a little in common with bishops from Africa, Italy, or the East, who were from a more modest social background, and still less with the hereditary caste of Zoroastrian magi. The social rank of the warrior aristocrats from the West was quite different from that of the Roman officers (and sometimes the barbarian ones) from Constantinople, as well as their Sasanian counterparts. Finally, the administrators of Germanic kingdoms—Roman aristocrats like Cassiodorus or, increasingly as the sixth century advanced, clerics—were not as effective as the huge, meddling bureaucracy of Constantinople: in Africa, reconquered by Justinian, the people felt the difference in tax collection. On the other side, it is possible that after 500, the Sasanian administration had been inspired by Roman models.[12]

Two remarks will suffice for a conclusion to this section. One can observe some convergences between the two states, the Roman one and the Sasanian one: the more centralized placement of power, the organization of an official state church, and increased militarization caused by a greater presence of conflicts (either between the two empires or against barbarians from the north: Germanic tribes, Alani, Huns, Slavs, Turks). This occurred to the detriment of local traditional elites and to the profit of new administrative, military, and religious elites. But these did not all carry the same respective weight, nor the same power relationships, nor the same functions in the different societies (western kingdoms, eastern Roman empire, Sasanian empire). Finally, one can reflect on the evolution of the term *nobilitas*. At the end of the Republic and under the High Empire, this term denoted a small group of aristocrats (around 200 families) whose ancestors had been patricians or consuls. In the fourth century, emperors created a state nobility, which never had the same prestige as the senatorial nobility determined by birth ("*pars melior humani generis*" according to Symmachus, *Ep.* 1.52). On the other hand, one could use the term *nobilis* to denote the quality of individuals (and not of groups) among the local elites of the cities and also among the bishops and the barbarian, German, and Persian nobles—nobles defined in two cases by their status as warriors (i.e., the German ruling class; the Persian aristocratic cavalry class). The Roman senatorial nobility disappeared after 550 in Gaul and after 570 in Italy, but the term "noble" was sufficiently extended to designate the various administrative, military, and religious elites of the late antique world (Badel 2005).

In the late antique world, religious values became the central values, even the supreme values, for conceiving of the world and for justifying discourse and action. However, this was not previously the case, except in a socially marginal manner, before Late Antiquity. Of course, all of ancient life can appear to us as saturated with religion, but this classical religion was not of the same nature as its late antique counterpart. Indeed, in classical communities—cities, *gentes*, and kingdoms—"religion" was comprised of a group of official and family rites maintaining good relations between the community and its gods; religion was thus a part of communal life, side by side with politics and the military, and did not have superior status; in the case of conflicting authority, politics took precedence. Personal religious aspects, beliefs, acts, and sentiments were less glorified (*superstitio*, *δεισιδαιμονία*) and were not to interfere with the communal religion. Marginalized behaviors, scorned but more often tolerated, were not reprimanded unless they questioned or threatened authority: this is the principal reason for the occasional Roman and Sasanian persecutions against Christians or Manichaeans, as well as against the astrologers in Rome.

The principal evolution was that new religious behaviors became the norm. Alongside traditional rituals (above all, sacrifice), others appeared, but explicit beliefs, in particular, took a central place. If the ruling authority continued to privilege some religious aspects with a view toward its own security, it permitted diverse religious systems to coexist, a peace that was occasionally interrupted with phases of persecution. These evolutions took place in a complex way, and through various channels, but it is evident that the most important, in light of the number of people concerned and considering its impact on others, was the development of Christianity from the time of Constantine. The religious mental map was completely transformed. The supreme God, the God of philosophers since Plato, became the principal actor in human history; that which had been evident to Jews, Christians, and Zoroastrians became evident for all (save the Neoplatonists). The supreme God, until then withdrawn from a world that he nevertheless controlled through general Providence—keeping watch over its proper functioning and over the harmonious balance of the cosmos—would henceforth be interfering with collective history,[13] as well as in the details of private life, either directly or through the intermediation of angels or *daimones*. Christianization—and in reaction, the development of a more organized paganism—resulted both in the increased presence of divine providence through its miracles and in man's responsibility for his own salvation, caused by the growing belief in the survival of the whole person because of the Christian faith in resurrection.

In addition to these aspects, linked as they were to the quantitative growth of the number of Christians, the fourth through sixth centuries witnessed the generalization of the model of religious communities, which had all of the characteristics that would be also found later in Islam. These communities were defined by four main principles: (1) a revealed fixed text (the Jewish scriptures of the Hebrew Bible, the Christian Bible including the Old and New Testaments—and some additional apocryphal writings among the East-Syriac and Oriental Orthodox churches—the *Avesta* of the Zoroastrians, the books of Mani, the *Chaldean Oracles* of the Neoplatonists, the works of Homer, Virgil, or Cicero for certain educated pagans); (2) a tradition of interpretive commentaries defining the norms of belief and life, that is, a kind of "orthodoxy" (the Mishna and the Talmud for the Jews, the conciliar decisions and patristic traditions of the Christians, the Neoplatonist philosophical commentaries); (3) the existence of professional religious authorities controlling the others (Christian clerics, pagan philosophical scholarchs, Jewish rabbis, Manichaean clerics, Zoroastrian priests) and holy men who were models for life (Christian ascetics and monks, Neoplatonist ascetics, some rabbis, the Manichaean "elect"); and (4) a sacred geography of pilgrimage to the dead or living saints (the "holy men") but also to certain landscapes, as much for monotheists (Sinai for Egeria), as for pagans, with their landscape relics (Tardieu 1990).

But if the problem of human relations with the divine world and the role of intercessors became more significant for everyone, the proportions of these elements could vary. The Roman polytheists preserved the rituals, such as the sacrifices, even if they were henceforth prohibited in the Roman empire at the end of the fourth century, which led to the birth of new pagan practices: the philosophers added the "Hellenic" practices of Neoplatonic theurgy to their spiritual exercises (those of stoicism and the spiritual asceticism of Plotinus). Christians insisted on the essential intercessory role of Christ—which explains the extreme importance of the theological and Christological debates, but also the centrality of sacramental rituals (from which comes the significance of the Donatist schism in Africa)—and the role of the intercessory rituals of the saints (pilgrimage for the veneration of relics of dead saints or living holy men, a group to whom the Virgin and some angels were later added). Though the Jews privileged rabbinic meditation on the Torah, they also made pilgrimages, and not only to Jerusalem but also to the tombs of the patriarchs.[14] The Manichaeans emphasized instead the salvific asceticism of the "elect," but their discourse was very understandable to Christian monks. The Iranian Zoroastrians were without doubt the most traditional, particularly in their cult of the fire altars, but the fixation on the *Avesta* and the social uses of Iranian religion (such as the Mazdakite movement) were also innovations.

The evolution of mentalities toward a predominance of religion explains the modification of identity categories, principally in the sixth century, since this process was quite slow.[15] Subsequently, in the West, the fact that the homoian Germans (Visigoths, Vandals, Ostrogoths) were considered to be heretics by the Catholics of the vanished Roman empire—who were very much in the majority—limited relations with the new powers, despite the Latin acculturation of the latter (including the adaptation of Roman law in the codes of the new kingdoms). The adoption of religious Catholic orthodoxy by barbarian kings, on the other hand, allowed the growth of post-Roman ethnic identities: around 500 in Britain, formerly Roman people were able to define themselves as Britons, as Goths in Spain around 600, and as Franks north of the Loire at the same time. In the East, in the fifth century, the persistence of the Roman empire was accompanied by the creation of parallel churches: Chalcedonian, "Monophysite" (miaphysite), and "Nestorian" (dyophysite). If this did not contradict loyalty to the empire, it nevertheless allowed men to define themselves religiously, something that became essential after 600 during the Persian and Muslim Arab invasions in the Near East and in Egypt, when communal religious affiliation became more important than imperial affiliation. Thus, the religious factor altered relations within the Roman citizenry, which lost its universal value as an identity.

This recomposition of values explains the construction of a Christian commonwealth, an empire of Christ that spilled over beyond Roman borders. From 300 to 600, a series of regions and peoples converted to Christianity, often with the intention of thereby establishing relations with the Roman empire, sometimes in opposition to the Sasanians: Armenia, Iberia (Georgia), the Ethiopians of Axum, some Himyarites (Arabs from Yemen), some Saracens, some peoples of the Black Sea (Huns and Goths), the Nubian kingdoms—a broad collection of peoples among whom it is necessary to include both the Christians of Persia (especially those in Mesopotamia) and the distant peoples of the far West (Irish Scots, Caledonian Picts, later the Angles and Saxons). This reality does not mean that there was Christian uniformity—since differences in language, doctrine, and monastic regulations were quite real—but it does create a world of common references from the Atlantic to Persia. And above all, this reality redefined what it meant to be civilized: to the Romans, it was henceforth necessary to include the Persians, for political and military reasons, and people formerly scorned as barbarians who had become Christians, for religious reasons. Late Antiquity was not a common civilization (*une civilisation commune*), but a mental space-time with a new, larger definition of civilization that was shared (*partagée*) and accepted (*acceptée*) by Romans who had become Christians.

In this world, more and more modeled on a new definition of religion and on the new role of the elites, culture and learning's place in the world was modified. In classical Greek and Roman culture, poetic and rhetorical composition was central, and erudite learning formed only a complement. Though totalization of learning was the ambition of the Aristotelian school and of the Ptolemaic project of the Museon and the library at Alexandria, erudite learning nevertheless remained outside the *enkyklios paideia*. But the pretension of assembling the totality of knowledge had real ideological significance, and it can be observed in imperial Rome, with its Latin and Greek libraries, and in Sasanian Persia, where the sovereigns supported translation projects of certain Greek and Indian texts. The totalization of late antique knowledge also had an impact on religious hermeneutics: both Christians and Neoplatonist philosophers claimed the ability to exhaust the world's meaning (Inglebert 2008). Another point of connection between the learned Christians and pagan philosophers was their certainty that classical culture (grammar, rhetoric, knowledge) should not be an end in itself, but an instrument in the service of higher religious truths. For Christians, however, the biblical texts held a supreme authority, and because of this, certain literal readings occasionally led to tensions between "Christian (inner) knowledge" and "Greek (outer) knowledge." For instance, there were debates about the shape of the world: the ancient conception (with a flat earth and heavenly dome) or spherical (with a spherical world encompassed by spherical heavens). This debate principally took place from 350 to 550, and above all among the Greek and Syriac Christians. But there were also debates over the existence of a single ocean or closed seas (Cosmas versus Philoponus) and on the comparative efficacies of medicine or prayer for healing; indeed, they even debated the eternity of the world (Philoponus versus the Aristotelians). It is thus possible to propose a typology of the Christian modifications to knowledge about the world (Inglebert 2001).

One must not overlook two sociological factors. The first, already mentioned, is that the elites were now less interested than they had been previously in investing in classical culture to make a career—which brought about a decline in civic schools during the sixth century—whereby it became necessary for bishops to create religious schools to form the clergy. The second is that Christianization of the culture was different, depending on whether one was a member of the *pepaideumenoi*. In regions where there were not any Greco-Roman schools, traditional rhetorical techniques were less important than technical knowledge and ecclesiastical rules, which (in order of priority) were translated from Greek into Syriac and Armenian in the East, or imported in Latin in Ireland. In the sixth century, the school of Nisibis, located in Persian territory since 363 but near Roman Edessa, was the only ancient institution (with the monastery of Qenneshre in the West-Syriac tradition) dedicated to biblical exegesis and Christian theology (Vööbus 1965; Becker 2006); teaching there was done from Greek and Syriac Christian texts. It was a theoretical model for some Christians from Constantinople, Italy, and Africa, but in the Roman world, the Christian cultural shift was actually the founding of monasteries. Thus, for various reasons, linked to the absence (Armenia, Mesopotamia) or to the disappearance (in the Roman empire, first in the West, then in the East) of civic schools, clericalization of the culture became the sociological norm after 550 (the rabbinization of the Jewish tradition had already occurred). In the Mediterranean world at the end of the sixth century, the patristic synthesis, or the coexistence of the profane and Christian between classical and biblical contributions, was replaced by a more strictly theological culture that insisted on criteria of orthodoxy for the selection process of texts, as in the *catenae* (Cameron 1996). But this phenomenon—which selected portions of prior works according to particular rubrics and reorganized knowledge that was formerly distributed in a different mode, that is, according to works by individual authors—was not to be found only in theology. One can find it in other fields where authority had become the criterion for classification: the *Theodosian Code*, the *Code* and *Digest* of Justinian, and the Talmudic tradition.

Another important change was the new status of language and culture that Christianization brought to languages other than Latin and Greek: Syriac, Coptic, Gothic, Armenian, Georgian, and others.[16] This change likewise favored translations of erudite classical knowledge (philosophy, geography, medicine) into Syriac and Armenian. Middle-Persian also served the elaboration of a written corpus of both religious knowledge (*Avesta*) and profane knowledge (translations from Greek or Sanskrit). This cultural evolution thus encouraged the extension of the concept of civilization, via Christianization, to new people groups.

An example of this transformation of knowledge was the manner in which one understood the history of time, which combined political, religious, and intellectual dimensions together. Classical history, beyond its mere description of events, expresses the earthly reflection of a cosmic reality: eternal Rome, the last universal empire, was the *telos* of history and the sign of a unified divine order. With the advent of Christianity, history became another process of realization, in that the expansion of the Church proved the continuity of sacred history. Though the Manichaeans would also use such reasoning, this view was, by contrast, less common among Roman pagans, among Zoroastrians, and among Jews: ecclesiastical history and a universal narrative were Christian specialties. However, contemporary political and military topics, the primary themes of classical history, were central preoccupations of all groups.

For the pagans, Roman military defeats (e.g., Adrianople in 378, the sack of Rome in 410) could be explained by the cessation of divine support, brought about by the coming of the *christiana tempora* (as in Libanius, Eunapius of Sardis, Zosimus). In 417, for instance, Rutilius Namatianus (*De redito suo*, vv. 47–155) could still think that Rome would remain the eternal city, but later pagan hopes—too closely linked to the terrestrial fall of Rome—disappeared. For Latin Christians, the arrival of pagan or heretical barbarians signaled various things: either a sign of the end of the fourth empire of the Book of Daniel, and thus the end of the world (Hydatius, Quodvultdeus); a punishment for the sins of Roman Christians (Salvian); an opportunity for the spread of Christianity (Orosius); or an event to be understood from a philosophico-theological point of view (Augustine, Prosper of Aquitaine). Roman Christians of the East, on the other hand, until the arrival of Arab Muslims, were able to maintain the ideology of Eusebius, Constantine, and Theodosius, that of a Christian Roman empire: God would protect the last empire, Roman and Christian, up to the end of times. As for the Sasanians, they interpreted their victories as victories of Ahura Mazda, and their defeats as resulting from impious leaders, similar in this to the view of pious Romans (pagan or Christian).

The Roman understanding of Persian history was similarly complex. The Sasanian pretension of being the heirs of the Achaemenids was known by the Romans from the third century, but it was not necessarily accepted, and the Persians were considered by some, such as Julian (*On Royalty* 11) and Ammianus Marcellinus (23.6.2) to be merely "Parthians." One Syriac text, the late version of the *Cave of Treasures*, written around 500, presents another history of the Sasanians. The text integrates the Sasanian dynasty with biblical history, making them descended from Sisan the servant of Nimrod, the first king of Babylon (*Cave* 24.25; cf. Genesis 10:8–12)—according to tradition, "Sasan" was the grandfather of Ardashir I, founder of the Sasanian dynasty. Further, with respect to the magi who came to adore the newborn Jesus in Bethlehem, the text specifies that they were certain kings, one of whom was the king of Persia (*Cave* 45.19): this claim once again linked the Persian empire to sacred history. Thus, Syriac Christians proposed a syncretistic history in order to insert Sasanian power into Biblico-Christian history. Cosmas Indicopleustes, a Roman but a "Nestorian," displayed another conception of Sasanian history around 550. According to his *Christian Topography* (2.76), the Sasanians descended neither from the Achaemenids nor from the Parthians. Their empire was actually a kingdom of magi, founded by the descendants of those who came to Bethlehem. This showed that the Sasanian empire, officially Zoroastrian, was in fact willed by God and that it therefore had the same theological foundation as the Roman empire, although with a pagan origin. For Cosmas, the Roman empire since the time of Augustus had been the guardian of the empire of Christ, and it would return it to Christ at the end of time. The association of Christ with the Roman empire of Augustus was ancient (Origen, Eusebius of Caesarea), and the census mentioned in Luke 2:1

was interpreted wrongly during Late Antiquity as Jesus' enrollment as a Roman citizen and was understood as such even by Syriac Christians like Aphrahat (*Memra* 5.24). But the idea that the Sasanian power was linked to the magi of Bethlehem is profoundly original and is not found elsewhere (Panaino 2005), and this idea had, without any doubt, a Persian "Nestorian" origin—perhaps due to the fact that the "king of kings" had given official status to the Church of the East in the fifth century. Such an idea affiliated the two great empires via the same Christian unity and the same chronology focused on the birth of Christ. On one hand, this gave credence to the Sasanian ambitions for parity while, on the other hand, it reserved the first rank for the Roman empire of Justinian.

From the Atlantic to Central Asia, the world of Late Antiquity was neither unitary (*unitaire*) nor common (*commun*), but was fragmented (*fragmenté*) and shared (*partagé*). However, one notices from the fourth to the seventh centuries a convergence of elite values and of conceptions of the world among educated people. And there existed unifying representations of this world, especially religious—those of the Manichaeans, as well as those of Syriac Christians of the sixth century. Situated between the two empires, the Roman and Sasanian, where they formed minority communities and used both Greek and Aramaic, Syriac Christians made simultaneous use of received knowledge from Greco-Roman *paideia* and from data of eastern origin. They were better able than others to affirm the geographical and historical unity of the Mediterranean and Iranian territories based on biblical traditions and the expansion of Christianity.

One can comprehend the late antique world from Constantine to Muhammad from three perspectives. First, there was hardly any upheaval in geographical knowledge: the addition of China, which remained mostly unknown, modified the map of the world only marginally; Christian traits that were inherited from Jewish traditions (e.g., locating the terrestrial paradise in the east, or the central placement of Jerusalem) imposed themselves only slowly as the culture was clericalized; and cartography derived from Ptolemy remained secondary. On the other hand, this world witnessed profound transformations: political (e.g., the disappearance of the western Roman empire and the arrival of the Germanic tribes; the growing power of the Sasanian empire to the east), religious (e.g., the majority victory of Chalcedonian Christianity), social (e.g., the redefinition of the role of elites with respect to military and religious values), and economic (e.g., the decline of economic complexity in the West during the fifth century and in the East after 550).

Finally, representations of this fragmented world were strikingly restructured, and, in this sense, Late Antiquity was above all an *époque* of revolution and of the adaptation of different mentalities. One cannot simply pass from a world dominated by political models to a world dominated by religious models, but, more subtly, we see the transition from a political, classical, uncontested model of Roman hegemony to a religious, Christian, contested model of Roman supremacy. This late antique world was without unity, but nevertheless, there was a structural scheme that created a shared world (*un monde partagé*), a necessary reshuffling that occurred with reference to the model of a Christian Roman empire, inherited from Constantine. The imperial conversion to Christianity was, in effect, the opportunity to reassert, in a new way, the superiority and universality of Roman ideology and values. And it is through this discourse, linking Rome (with its two possible interpretations: the empire and the city) and Christianity, that one can understand the late antique conceptions of Late Antiquity: whether in explaining this new Roman model according to the various categories of time, place, and social and cultural settings; in seeing it transformed according to the whim of emergent circumstances; or, by challenging it, for religious or political reasons.

From Constantine to Muhammad, one can therefore characterize Late Antiquity as an *époque* of "transition," with the condition that the term *transition* is used in a strong sense, distinguishing it from simple transformations that are inherent in every historical period. We pass from a world in the third century wherein identity was primarily political (the principal affiliation being either civic or ethnic), to a world in the seventh century wherein identity became above all religious (the principal affiliation depending on one's religious community). Late Antiquity was a historical period in which the two conceptions coexisted and in which the second overcame the first: this is true whether within the empire of Constantinople, the kingdoms of the West, the Sasanian empire, or in the Qur'ān with "the people of the book." This transition can be explained by the fact that the notion of religion had changed, insisting henceforth less on cosmic and topical aspects and more on soteriology and history (Brown 1978). The main consequence was that the notion of "civilized" was redefined, juxtaposing the ancient political criteria, which permitted the inclusion of the Sasanian empire, and the new Christian religious criteria, which justified the inclusion of converted peoples, even those who were barbarians. The *imperium Romanum*, in theory *sine fine*, became *Romania* in the fourth century, which after 480 denoted the empire ruled from Constantinople. But *Romania* was only one part of the Christian world, which was itself included within a late antique commonwealth. However, this commonwealth did not exist as a unified representation until the sixth century—and only among Sasanian rulers, with the rhetoric of the two "eyes," and among Syriac Christians (or among those, like Cosmas, who were religiously affiliated with them), and only then with reference to Christianity—that is, a common sacred history encompassing the Roman and Sasanian empires, both of which were connected to Christ through Augustus and the magi at Bethlehem. In both cases, this expanded and united "world of Late Antiquity" was that of Rome's (or Constantinople's) political or religious challengers.

But yet, this matrix of discourse, which had been organized by reference to the Christian Roman empire, disappeared with the expansion of Islam. This expansion signaled after 634 the end of any possible Roman and Christian hegemony, a hegemony that had again been reasserted in 629–630 through Heraclius' victory over the Sasanians. In effect, the military victory of the Muslim Arabs—understood as heretical or impious barbarians—was incomprehensible outside of eschatological reasoning,[17] a fact that might explain the end of the Byzantine tradition of ecclesiastical history (which linked Christianity and Roman empire) after 600. The expansion of Islam, by its destruction of the Sasanian empire and the given Roman and Christian certitudes, sealed (in an archaeological sense) a particular conception of the world: Late Antiquity, which lasted from Constantine up to Heraclius, the Roman emperor (610–641) contemporary with both the "king of kings" Khusro II (591–628) and the prophet Muhammad (612–632).

It is therefore possible to say that the analysis of ancient mentalities strengthens the idea of a real Late Antiquity within an expanded geographical framework and is also an argument in favor of a short chronology. Nevertheless, with respect to the chronology, our debate must remain open, if only because the respective roles played by the ancient conceptions of ancient realities and by the contemporary representations of those realities have yet to be delineated clearly.[18]

NOTES

1. Constantine's letter to Shapur, describing himself as protector of the Christians of the world, Eusebius of Caesarea, *Vita Constantini*, 4.9–13; the Sasanian Christians persecuted by Shapur II, Aphrahat, *Memra* 21.

2. That is, the technical decline and general impoverishment of the West, well perceived by Gregory the Great when he described Rome at the end of the sixth century, *Homily on Ezekiel* 1.9.9; 2.10.24; 2.6.22.

3. For this author, at least, the simple juxtaposition in *CAH* XIII and XIV of classical "Late Roman" themes and more innovative "Late Antique" themes is not intellectually satisfying.

4. In the introduction of *Late Antiquity: A Guide to the Postclassical World* (Bowersock, Brown, and Grabar 1999), the editors define Late Antiquity as "a distinctive and quite decisive period that stands on its own" (ix), as "a distinctive civilization" (xi), and "a common civilization, that of Late Antiquity" (xi). However, a period is not a civilization, and such a definition is not, therefore, self-evident—though the confusion of the two terms is already in found in Marrou. For the concept of "Roman civilization," cf. Inglebert 2005.

5. India and China were largely seen through the lens of Persia: see chapter 5, la Vaissière, in this book.

6. "Remember thou, O Roman, to rule the nations with thy sway,
there shall be thine arts, to crown Peace with Law,
to spare the humbled and to tame in war the proud."
Trans. H. Rushton Fairclough (LCL; Cambridge, MA, 1965)

7. Pompey Trogus, who lived during the time of Tiberius, in his *Philippic Histories* 12.13, 12.16, and 41.1, allows the theory that Alexander was the sole ephemeral master of an empire that was actually universal.

8. Theophylact Simocatta 1986, 117.

9. Ibid., 121.

10. It is revealed onomastically through the names Ardashir/Artaxerxes, decoratively through the revival of the Egyptian cornice, used in the buildings of Persepolis, in the palace of Ardashir I at Firuzabad, and through the Zoroastrian religious practice.

11. Around 238, the Roman outposts were located at Hatra, only 300 kilometers from the capital Ctesiphon.

12. Garsoïan 1983, 587–589.

13. Cf. the prayer to the *deus summus* of the army of Licinius in 313 (Lactantius, *De mortibus persecutorum* 46).

14. Maraval 2004, 2–31, 52–53, 194, 275, 276.

15. Cf. the fact that, in 363, the inhabitants of Nisibis wished to remain Romans (Zosimus *Nea historia* 3.33.4), and the same was true for the Arverni around 470; cf. Prévot 1999.

16. The expansion of Manichaeism (which used Aramaic, Coptic, Middle Persian, Parthian, Sogdian, Old Turkish, Chinese), as well as the choice by Jewish rabbis to use Aramaic, had the same effect. Cf. Tardieu 1997.

17. Such as that in the *Apocalypse of Pseudo-Methodius*, a Jacobite Syriac text written around 691/692 in which the future victory of the Roman empire over the Muslims is linked to the end times.

18. In particular, a different presentation is possible: one founded on the ancient *realia*, and not on ancient representations of reality, and one that corresponds to the wishes of Giardina. Such an approach would seek to offer warrant for the different frameworks, both geographical and chronological. I intend to return to these questions in an essay titled "Late Antiquity: A Problem for Historians" (*L'Antiquité tardive: Un problème d'historiens*).

WORKS CITED

Ancient Sources

Aphrahat. 1988–1989. *Les exposés*, 2 vols. Ed. and trans. Marie-Joseph Pierre. Sources chrétiennes 349 and 359. Paris: Éditions du Cerf.

La Caverne des Trésors: Les deux recensions syriaques. 1987. Ed. and trans. Su-Min Ri. 2 vols. CSCO 486–487. Leuven: Peeters.

Cosmas Indicopleustes. 1968–1973. *La topographie chrétienne*, 3 vols. Ed. and trans. Wanda Wolska-Conus. Sources chrétiennes 141, 159, and 197. Paris: Éditions du Cerf.

Eusebius of Caesarea. 1999. *Life of Constantine*. Trans. Averil Cameron and Stuart G. Hall. Oxford: Clarendon.

Gregory the Great. 1986–1990. *Homélies sur Ezéchiel*, 2 vols. Ed. and trans. Charles Morel. Sources chrétiennes 327 and 360. Paris: Éditions du Cerf.

Pseudo-Methodius. 1993. *Die syrische Apokalypse des pseudo-Methodius*, 2 vols. Ed. and trans. G. J. Reinink. CSCO 540–541. Leuven: Peteers.

Rutilius Namatianus. 2007. *Sur son retour.* Ed. and trans. Étienne Wolff. Paris: Les Belles Lettres.

Theophylact Simocatta. 1986. *The History of Theophylact Simocatta.* Trans. Mary Whitby and Michael Whitby. Oxford: Clarendon.

Modern Sources

Albu, Emily. 2005. "Imperial Geography and the Medieval Peutinger Map," *Imago Mundi* 57: 136–148.

Ando, Clifford. 2008. "Decline, Fall, and Transformation," *Journal of Late Antiquity* 1: 31–60.

André, Jacques, and Jean Filliozat. 1986. *L'Inde vue de Rome: Textes latins de l'Antiquité relatifs à l'Inde.* Paris: Les Belles-Lettres.

Arnaud, Pascal. 1991. *La cartographie à Rome.* Ph.D. Thesis, Paris IV.

Badel, Christophe. 2005. *La noblesse de l'empire romain: Les masques et la vertu.* Seyssel: Champ Vallon.

Becker, Adam H. 2006. *Fear of God and the Beginning of Wisdom: The School of Nisibis and Christian Scholastic Culture in Late Antique Mesopotamia.* Philadelphia: University of Pennsylvania Press.

Bowersock, Glen W. 1990. *Hellenism in Late Antiquity.* Ann Arbor: University of Michigan Press.

Bowersock, Glen W., Peter Brown, and Oleg Grabar, eds. 1999. *Late Antiquity: A Guide to the Postclassical World.* Cambridge, MA: Harvard University Press.

Brown, Peter. 1971. *The World of Late Antiquity from Marcus Aurelius to Muhammad.* London: Thames and Hudson.

———. 1978. *The Making of Late Antiquity.* Cambridge, MA: Harvard University Press.

Cameron, Averil. 1996. "Byzantium and the Past in the Seventh Century: The Search for Redefinition." In *Changing Cultures in Early Byzantium*, sec. V. Aldershot: Ashgate.

Cameron, Averil, and Peter Garnsey, eds. 1998. *The Cambridge Ancient History, Vol. XIII: The Late Empire (A.D. 337–425).* Cambridge: Cambridge University Press.

Cameron, Averil, Bryan Ward-Perkins, and Michael Whitby, eds. 2000. *The Cambridge Ancient History, Vol. XIV: Late Antiquity: Empire and Successors (A.D. 425–600).* Cambridge: Cambridge University Press.

Demandt, Alexander. 1984. *Der Fall Roms: Die Auflösung des römischen Reiches im Urteil der Nachwelt.* München: C. H. Beck.

Elsner, Jaś. 2002. "The Birth of Late Antiquity: Riegl and Strzygowski in 1901," *Art History* 25: 358–379.

Fowden, Garth. 1993. *From Empire to Commonwealth: Consequences of Monotheism in Late Antiquity.* Princeton, NJ: Princeton University Press.

Garsoïan, Nina. 1983. "Byzantium and the Sassanians." In *Cambridge History of Iran, Vol. 3.1: The Seleucid, Parthian, and Sasanian Periods*, ed. E. Yarshater, 568–592. Cambridge: Cambridge University Press.

Giardina, Andrea. 1999. "Esplosione di tardoantico," *Studi Storici* 40: 157–180.

Hägg, Tomas, ed. 1997. *The World of Late Antiquity Revisited. Symbolae Osloenses* 72: 5–90.

Inglebert, Hervé. 2001. *Interpretatio Christiana: Les mutations des savoirs (cosmographie, géographie, ethnographie, histoire) dans l'Antiquité chrétienne (30–630 après J.-C.)*. Paris: Études Augustiniennes.

———. 2003. "Peter Brown." In *Les Historiens*, ed. V. Salles, 336–350. Paris: Armand Colin.

———. 2005. *Histoire de la civilisation romaine*. Paris: PUF.

———. 2008. "Les modalités et la finalité de la totalisation du savoir sur le monde dans l'Antiquité gréco-romaine." In *Culture classique et christianisme: Mélanges offerts à Jean Bouffartigue*, ed. Étienne Wolff, 201–214. Paris: Picard.

James, Edward. 2008. "The Rise and Function of the Concept 'Late Antiquity,'" *Journal of Late Antiquity* 1: 20–30.

Le Coq, Albert von. 1923–1933. *Die buddhistische Spätantike im Mittelasien*, 7 vols. Berlin: D. Reimer.

Liebeschuetz, Wolfgang H. W. G. 2001. *The Decline and Fall of the Roman City*. Oxford: Oxford University Press.

Maraval, Pierre. 2004. *Lieux saints et pèlerinages d'Orient: Histoire et géographie des origines à la conquête arabe*, 2nd ed. Paris: Les Éditions du Cerf.

Marcone, Arnaldo. 2008. "A Long Late Antiquity? Considerations on a Controversial Periodization," *Journal of Late Antiquity* 1: 4–19.

Marrou, Henri-Irénée. 1949. "Retractatio." In *Saint Augustin et la fin de la culture antique*, vol. 2. Paris: Boccard.

———. 1977. *Décadence romaine ou Antiquité tardive? IIIe–VIe siècle*. Paris: Seuil.

Mazzarino, Santo. 1959. *La fine del mondo antico*. Milano: A. Garzanti.

Mitchell, Stephen. 2005. *A History of the Later Roman Empire AD 284–641: The Transformation of the Ancient World*. Malden, MA: Blackwell.

Nicolet, Claude. 1988. *L'inventaire du monde: Géographie et politique aux origines de l'empire romain*. Paris: Fayard.

Panaino, A. 2005. "I magi e la stella nei Sermoni di San Pier Crisologo: Qualche riflessione critica a proposito di scienza, fede e metodo storica." In *Ravenna: Da capitale imperiale a capitale esarcale. Atti del XVII convegno internazionale di studio sull'alto medioevo*, 559–592. Spoleto: Centro italiano di studi sull'alto Medioevo.

Prévot, Françoise. 1999. "Sidoine Apollinaire et l'Auvergne." In *L'Auvergne de Sidoine Apollinaire à Grégoire de Tours*, ed. Bernadette Fizellier-Sauget, 63–80. Clermont-Ferrand: Institut d'études du Massif Central.

Rousseau, Philip, ed. 2009. *The Blackwell Companion to Late Antiquity*. Malden, MA: Blackwell.

Sambursky, Samuel. 1962. *The Physical World of Late Antiquity*. London: Routledge and K. Paul.

Sartre, Maurice. 1993. *Inscriptions grecques et latines de la Syrie: Tome XXI, Inscriptions de la Jordanie. Tome IV, Pétra et la Nabatène méridionale du wadi al-Hasa au golfe d'Aqaba*. Paris: P. Geuthner.

Talbert, Richard J. A. 2010. *Rome's World: The Peutinger Map Reconsidered*. Cambridge: Cambridge University Press.

Tardieu, Michel. 1997. *Le manichéisme*. Paris: PUF.

———. 1990. *Les paysages reliques: Routes et haltes syriennes d'Isidore à Simplicius*. Louvain: Peeters.

Vööbus, Arthur. 1965. *History of the School of Nisibis*. CSCO 266, Subsidia 26. Louvain: Peeters.

Ward-Perkins, Bryan. 2005. *The Fall of Rome and the End of Civilization*. Oxford: Oxford University Press.

Wickham, Chris. 2005. *Framing the Early Middle Ages: Europe and the Mediterranean, 400–800*. Oxford: Oxford University Press.

Wolska-Conus, Wanda. 1973. "La Diognôsis ptoléméenne: Date et lieu de composition," *Travaux et Mémoires* 5: 259–273.

PART I

GEOGRAPHIES AND PEOPLES

CHAPTER I

THE WESTERN KINGDOMS

MICHAEL KULIKOWSKI
Pennsylvania State University

I.

THERE are three fundamentally different ways of looking at the kingdoms that were founded on the soil of the western Roman empire in the course of the fifth century. One can view them as a stage in a long history of migrations from northern to central Europe and thence to the Mediterranean, migrations that eventually resulted in the foundation of the early medieval kingdoms, however much the scale of this migration (whole peoples or smaller, tradition-bearing groups) may be open to dispute.[1] Alternatively, the same basic story line can be read not as the laudable prelude to state formation, but rather as a series of barbarian invasions that brought the ancient world to a sudden and violent collapse, perhaps even causing the end of civilization.[2] Finally, the foundation of the western kingdoms can be seen as a relatively peaceful and uneventful process, one that involved regime change at the top but fundamentally preserved the late Roman patterns of political life, albeit on a restricted geographical scale.[3]

None of these approaches is entirely satisfactory. The first and third privilege a false continuity, failing to recognize the scale of economic and political breakdown experienced in the fifth century; seeking the roots of Europe's eighth- and ninth-century landscape, they tend to retroject the concerns of the Carolingian period backward into Late Antiquity. The second approach ignores the diversity of the barbarian kingdoms, in terms of both their inhabitants and the circumstances of their creation, preferring a homogeneous barbarism to any analysis that could make the Roman empire complicit in its own failure. The effects of each of these analyses on the metanarrative of the period are roughly the same: they privilege the perspective of hindsight, which means that the peoples whose fifth-century kingdoms had later progeny—the Visigothic and particularly the Frankish—are treated as more important, or more paradigmatic, than peoples after whom no early medieval kingdom is named. Worse still, all see the fifth-century kingdoms as basically medieval phenomena, no matter how attentive individual scholars might be to the imbrication of the barbarians in Roman political realities. And so, rather than insert the western kingdoms of Late Antiquity into one or another of these longer narratives, it is analytically more useful to consider them within their very specific fifth- and early sixth-century contexts.[4] Doing so allows us to see how fully a part of the late imperial landscape the western kingdoms were and how much their creation was the unintentional consequence of fourth- and fifth-century imperial politics, specifically the accidental importation onto provincial soil of a long-standing model of frontier client kingship. The existence of client kings inside the empire did not in itself make the creation of barbarian kingdoms inevitable, as we shall see. But come into being they did, and when they did so, it was on the basis of existing imperial structures.

That there was a level of continuity between kingdoms and empire is beyond doubt, if not always in the peaceful, transformative sense that some scholars prefer. To take an obvious and sometimes overlooked example, the basic building blocks of empire—towns and their urban territories—remained the basic building blocks of the western kingdoms, the old imperial landscape dissolving very slowly, over generations, and frequently only after several major upheavals in government.[5] Equally, as we shall see, the administrative structures of the imperial period were those on which the first kings came to depend, to the extent that they were able to preserve them. On the other hand, the later fifth century did witness a massive collapse of social and economic complexity, and not simply in the sense that the fifth-century kingdoms were smaller than empire that preceded them.[6] What is more, the period also witnessed a catastrophic decline in living standards, which no appeal to superficial continuities can disguise and which the eastern provinces experienced at a much later date and a much slower rate than did the West.[7] It is wishful thinking, in other words, to see the establishment of the western kingdoms as a fundamentally benign process.[8] Yet it is equally deluded to imagine that fifth-century collapse can be attributed mainly to the impact of external violence: the western kingdoms were undoubtedly born in violence, and the fifth century was undoubtedly catastrophic, but it was a catastrophe that the government of the western empire helped to will on itself.

There are any number of narrative histories of the fifth and sixth centuries on which the reader can safely rely for details.[9] Here, we will chiefly be concerned with the analysis of how kingdoms came into being and functioned in territory that had previously been administered by Roman magistrates. The most important point to make at the outset is that, for much of the fifth century, we are really talking about kings rather than kingdoms. Like the Roman empire, the developed kingdoms of the early Middle Ages could claim to rule over more or less organized territories, as well as over people.[10] But by those standards, there were many more kings than there were kingdoms in the fifth century and even the sixth century. Before that, the western kingdoms were polities made up of the people a king ruled, which was itself something quite nebulous: very few late antique kings specified quite what it was they were king of.[11] This was in large part because their status depended on their shifting relationships to imperial government, and for that reason we are fundamentally mistaken when we treat our late antique *reges* as embryonic versions of early medieval rulers. On the contrary, they have to be understood on the model of the client kings that Roman policy had always encouraged to flourish along the imperial borders, kings who supplied a measure because of the stability that came with continuity of family and status, but who could also be kept weak enough to present very infrequent challenges to the empire.[12] What such client kings actually ruled was always contingent upon what the emperor allowed them to rule at any given time—their royal authority was real, and recognized by their followers, but it was insecurely linked to the land in which that authority happened to be exercised.[13]

The fifth century witnessed the transfer of this model of client kingship from the frontiers into the imperial interior, into something that can be usefully regarded as a frontier diaspora.[14] In other words, the first *regna* of the fifth-century West were simply client kingdoms transposed onto imperial soil, and it was not until the reach of imperial government was irreparably diminished that one or two late antique kings were required to create territorial kingdoms.[15] Note, here, that the territorial kingdom, a polity with which to replace imperial government, was not the goal of any fifth-century king. It is on this point that all the catastrophist readings of the fifth century go so badly wrong. They assume that—because the fifth-century breakdown of the western empire was indeed a catastrophe for much of the population, and because it was barbarian kings who replaced the Roman emperor in providing such government as existed in much of the West from the 450s onward—these kings must therefore have wanted to create barbarian kingdoms in opposition to the empire. But the territorial kingdoms of the late fifth and the sixth centuries were not willed into being by a process of barbarian conquest and royal aggrandizement.[16] They were, rather, the products of failure, the failure of the mechanisms of imperial governance and the failure of various *reges* and *reguli* to find a place within that imperial structure.[17]

Part of the reason the late ancient kingdoms were themselves such transient and fleeting polities was that no one had wanted to create them in the first place, and no one quite knew what to do with them once they were created.

Much as we are conditioned to see a link between the fifth-century kingdoms of the empire and all the early medieval *regna* that were eventually sucked into the Carolingian orbit, that connection is very weak. The strong, successful kingdoms of the early Middle Ages—the Visigoths in Spain from the 570s, the Frankish *Teilreiche* of Clovis' sons, the Lombard state in Italy, even the royal house of Kent—were created with deliberation by rulers who wanted to rule territories as kings and who wanted to do so because that was the only viable model for the exercise of power.[18] The fifth-century kingdoms came into existence *faute de mieux*, and the *mieux* was known to everyone and desired by them: a functional Roman empire in which *reges* had a recognizable place as clients of the empire and participants in its affairs. Only when that prospect became obviously hopeless did they create territorial kingdoms, as a distinctly second-best alternative. Before turning to these themes, it is worth briefly noting the various *reges* of Late Antiquity, both those who founded "kingdoms" and those who did not, for it is only the light of hindsight that distinguishes the trajectory of Goar the Alan from Euric the Goth.

II.

In the fourth century, a large array of kings dotted the edges of the Roman empire. In that respect, if in few others, very little had changed since the first century C.E., when the Augustan empire's developing administrative system relied heavily on client kings to manage frontier regions rather than turn them into provinces.[19] Again as in the early empire, fourth-century *reges* were very closely integrated into the Roman imperial system. They and their families crossed and recrossed notional frontiers; their children were educated in the imperial system both as clients and as hostages, some serving as Roman officers before returning to take up their positions at home. If the paradigmatic example from the early empire is the Herodian dynasty of Judaea, in the fourth century Franks and Alammanni bulk large in the evidence, in part thanks to our reliance on Ammianus and his narrative.[20] Nevertheless, the distribution of this evidence is not entirely the accidental artifact of source survival. The decisive shift of imperial gravity from west to east during the third century had led to the regularization of a fairly stable eastern frontier after the collapse of Parthia and the rise of the Persian Sasanian dynasty.[21] The old client families, earlier buffeted between Roman and Parthian alliances, simply became incorporated into one or the other empire, which now bordered one another directly.[22] The frontier dynamic that had encouraged the maintenance of client kingdoms thus disappeared in the East. Elsewhere, by contrast, the Rhine, Danube, and North African frontiers were still usefully managed in the old way, by a great number of minor *reges* whose authority was enough to dominate their followers but not their neighbors.[23] The regional distribution of client kingship, in other words, had changed between the early and later empires, but the fundamental dynamics of the institution had not.

This is important, because most of the men from beyond the frontiers who rose to power during the disturbances of the fifth century themselves came from the frontier regions or from frontier families.[24] The type of rulership with which they were familiar was one exemplified by two fourth-century figures, Vadomarius, an Alamannic king, and Gildo, a Moorish one.[25] Vadomarius came from a dynasty of kings (his brother Gundomadus was a king, too), and their on-again, off-again friendships with a series of emperors and caesars is fully recounted by Ammianus.[26] As a seemingly loyal client of Constantius, Vadomarius was encouraged to deliberately make life difficult for the caesar Julian, lest the latter become too powerful for the paranoid augustus' liking. When Julian refused to tolerate this, he had Vadomarius seized under false pretenses and exiled to Spain. Vadomarius' son Vithicabius likewise became king, but the last we hear of Vadomarius—now referred to as *ex rege Alamannorum*—he was serving as *dux Phoenices*, an honorable career move for a client king who was no longer to be trusted with his original position.[27] Gildo came from a similar family, one that straddled the line between imperial elites and frontier client kings.[28] Gildo's father, Nubel, was unambiguously a king of sorts (*regulus*: AM 29.5.2), and all his sons (Firmus, Gildo, Mascezel, Sammac, Dius, and Mazuca) could move fluidly between imperial service as officers and hostile commanders, as kings or princes.[29] Gildo himself was *magister militum* in Africa for more than a decade, and it was in this context that his daughter was even married to the nephew of the empress, before the rivalry between Stilicho and the various regents of Arcadius in the East proved fatal.[30] While Gildo and his clan belonged to the central African provinces of Mauretania Caesariensis and Numidia, they were able to exploit the same social dynamic that had existed in the second and third centuries somewhat further west in Tingitania; there, a whole series of inscribed peace treaties document client kings who fell simultaneously inside and outside the empire.[31] In the carefully balanced duality of their roles, men like Vadomarius and Gildo—and one can cite many more such fourth-century examples—represent a very real fact of late imperial politics, which is to say the extent to which lands beyond the putative frontier were functionally a part of the empire, even where they were not administered by imperial officials and therefore failed to benefit from the physical infrastructure that came with imperial administration.[32] It is, in other words, no surprise that the *Laterculus Veronensis* should, in 314, list in its thirteenth chapter the *gentes barbarae quae pullulaverunt sub imperatoribus* as if they were as much a part of the empire as the provinces catalogued in its earlier sections.[33] The *gentes* and their client *reges* were as surely *sub imperatoribus* as was the *diocesis Viennensis* or any other provincial region.

Before the fifth century, that was the context in which one found *reges*: at the frontiers, *sub imperatoribus* but not inside imperial provinces. In the fifth century, by contrast, political disruptions meant that we come to find *reges* everywhere, swept by events into the heart of imperial politics. The old-style frontier kings by no means disappeared. The *Alamannorum rex* Gibuldus, known from the *Vita Severini* and the less reliable *Acta Sancti Lupi*, for instance, is the perfect model of the old-style frontier client.[34] However, that model was no longer tied to the frontiers, spreading out in a type of frontier diaspora that we can trace back to the earliest years of the fifth century. In 402, the Gothic *magister militum* Alaric definitively turned his back on an exhausted East and decided to make his way in western politics.[35] He was viewed as a king retrospectively, but no remotely contemporary source calls him one: instead, he is *phúlarchos, hegoúmenos,* or *dux.* What is more, if he was a king, he was a king without a kingdom and one who spent his career trying to integrate himself into the role of a Roman officer, which had for decades been the route to power and success for ambitious men from subaltern populations. His brother-in-law Athaulf, who married an imperial princess, was clearly regarded as a king and saw himself as potentially the father of emperors: only the swift death of his and Galla Placidia's son Theodosius stopped him from realizing the dream of any successful Roman military man of the period.[36] Athaulf's successors—none of his own blood—are all called kings in sources, both contemporary and retrospective, and the treaty of 439 between the Goth Theoderic and the *magister* Aëtius clearly treats Theoderic as a more or less equal party with a constitutional position to maintain. Yet it is not until the reign of the second Alaric that we find a Gothic ruler unambiguously styling *himself* king in documents emanating from what we might safely call a royal chancery.[37] That there was a Gothic *regnum* in Gaul was accepted by contemporaries by at least the 450s, when Avitus was sent to solicit help from Theoderic (I) against the invading army of Attila.[38] From the vantage point of 455 and the panegyric on his father-in-law, Sidonius Apollinaris could retroject the contemporary de facto independence of the Goths backward by a decade or more.[39] Sigeric, Fl. Wallia, Theoderic, Thorismund, the younger Theoderic, and Euric were all kings, as Frederic may well have been, too, but in that they were not so different from many others in the western provinces of the fifth century.[40]

In 405, for instance, a war leader named Radagaisus invaded Italy through Raetia with a very large army, the composition of which is a matter of controversy, but he was certainly regarded as having been a king very soon after Stilicho had suppressed him.[41] At more or less the same time, and in some not very precise connection with Radagaisus' movements, Alan, Vandal, and Suevic kings led their followers across the Rhine into Gaul.[42] For several decades thereafter, we can document a succession of Vandal, Alan, and Suevic kings without kingdoms in Gaul, Spain, and Africa. The Alan kings are the shadowiest. Among the invaders of 406/407 were leaders named Respendial and Goar, the former called *rex* in the sole source that mentions him.[43] Goar, who went over to the Roman side at the time of the Rhine crossing, was certainly described as a king in the sources of mid-century in which he is most prominent; he and his

Alans soon proceeded to offer military support to the usurper Jovinus in 411.[44] Other Alan kings are nameless, but the campaigns of Wallia that virtually eliminated the Alan *regnum* in Spain during 416–418 imply the existence of more than one *rex* among them: only Addax, killed in 418, is named.[45] Goar's Alans were a long-lasting presence in Gaul, settled for good by Aetius in the mid-440s, after which Alans effectively disappear from western history, save for occasional reminders like Sangibanus, the reluctant ally of Aëtius against Attila, the *rex Alanorum* Beorgor killed by Ricimer in 464, and Sambida, who may or may not have been a king but was likewise active in Gaul at mid-century.[46]

The Vandals are somewhat better documented, their king Godegisel killed at the time of the Rhine crossing, but succeeded by two sons, Gunderic and Gaiseric, each of whom led the Vandals for a time.[47] Gunderic, a source of many raids throughout the western Mediterranean from 421 forward, died in 428, and his brother Gaiseric succeeded.[48] Vandal kings, and Gaiseric perhaps most of all, have a nasty reputation in the modern literature as persecutors and inveterate barbarians, but that is a function of Nicene theological sources that damned the Vandals as Arian heretics.[49] In Gaiseric's case, moreover, his sheer longevity ensures that he looms large in the scholarly imagination. It was he who led his followers into Africa and who, in 439, captured and sacked Carthage, though not so badly that it could not function comfortably as a royal capital for the better part of a century. In 442, Gaiseric was recognized for a time as possessing control of Numidia, Byzacena, and Proconsularis, and later in the 440s, Valentinian's daughter Eudocia was betrothed to Gaiseric's son Huneric.[50] Gaiseric had many sons and grandsons, but his own long life foreshortened the history of the Vandal royal family, since most Vandal kings, thanks to their progenitor's incredible longevity, themselves reached the throne late in life.[51]

The earliest Suevic king known to us (Fredbal) is probably a late invention.[52] In the earlier 420s, a Suevic *rex* named Hermeric contended for control of Gallaecia with his Vandal opposite number Gunderic.[53] The next named Sueve, Heremigarius, is known only from an account of his death that makes his position among his followers quite unclear.[54] Nevertheless, a short-lived but powerful Suevic dynasty established itself in Gallaecia and Lusitania, contending with imperial officials and Gothic armies for control of the diocesan capital at Emerita Augusta: the alliterating Rechila and Rechiar clearly succeeded one another as father and son, while the similarly named Rechimund was presumably a relative who sought to regain something of the familial prominence in the aftermath of the Gothic destruction of Rechiar's kingdom in 456.[55] But Rechimund was a relative nonentity and many others, among them Remismund, Maldras, Framtane, Frumarius, and Aioulfus (supposedly a Varnian, rather than a Sueve), all claimed to be kings of the Sueves.[56] When Hydatius tells us that the Goth Theoderic (II) destroyed the Suevic kingdom in 456, it does not seem like an exaggeration.[57] The rudimentary *regnum* of Rechila, Rechiar, and Rechimund relapsed into a welter of *reges*, who reemerge into the light of history only in the late sixth century, shortly before the assertive Gothic king Leovigild incorporated Suevic Gallaecia into his kingdom.[58]

A similarly rudimentary kingdom was created by Burgundians, straddling what had once been the *limes* in the Jura and Savoy.[59] Earlier, the formal settlement of Jovinus' Burgundian supporters that took place in 413 at Worms must have involved a *rex* or *regulus*, though his name is unrecorded. It was this kingdom—at the time ruled by a king named Gundichar—that Aëtius destroyed in 435–436, possibly with the Hunnic support eventually commemorated in garbled form in the medieval *Nibelungenlied*.[60] The earliest significant *rex* of whom we know is Gundioc, who reigned in the Savoyard kingdom, with his presumed brother Chilperic, and was briefly *magister militum per Gallias*.[61] It was Gundioc's sons Gundobad, Godigisel, Chilperic, and Godomar, however, who succeeded to the kingship in the next generation and divided the kingdom among themselves.[62] Gundobad, much the most ambitious and successful, not only took an active role in Roman politics but also killed off at least one of his brothers, Godigisel, and possibly Chilperic as well. In the next generation, Sigismund and Godomarus saw their kingdom taken over by, and divided among, the Frankish kings.[63]

Frankish kings, for their part, are strangely nameless for most of the fifth century, even though as a collective term for the barbarians opposite the lower German *limes*, Franci are securely attested by the very late third century.[64] Indeed, not long afterward during Constantine's reign, Frankish petty kings could be thrown to the beasts in the arena.[65] Presumably our sketchy sources from the fifth century simply did not know the names of any significant Frankish leaders, not even among the Franks against whom Aetius campaigned in the later 420s, though Sidonius knew the Chlodius who held Cambrai for part of the period.[66] For obvious reasons, we know something of the ancestry of Clovis and the Merovingian dynasty he founded—in particular, Clovis' father, Childeric, whose grave survived into the early modern period—but other rulers come into view solely when they impinge upon that family.[67] Thus the king Chararic, against whom Clovis supposedly harbored an old grudge, was captured treacherously and suppressed shortly before Clovis' death, while the Rhineland kings Sigibert and Chloderic were relieved of their lands in a similarly shady fashion.[68] Clovis' own relatives, the kings Ragnachar, Richarius, and Rignomer, were likewise murdered by their ambitious kinsman.[69] Clovis himself, as known to us in Gregory of Tours, may be more a retrospective construct of the late sixth century than anything resembling the historical founder of the Merovingian kingdoms.[70] Nevertheless, by the time he died in 511, dividing the kingdom among his sons Chlodomer, Theuderic, Childebert, and Chlothar, the family's control of the territory their father had seized from other Franks was secure and remained so for centuries; it was left to the sons to strengthen Merovingian control and extend it into the other territories—particularly Aquitania and Burgundy—either seized or coveted by Clovis.[71]

It is mainly in the Frankish orbit that one begins to find other monarchs behaving very much in the manner of old-fashioned frontier *reguli*, for instance, the Thuringian kings Baderich, Berthacar, and Herminfrid, whose fraternal divisions the Frankish Theuderic exploited early in the sixth century.[72] Before the emergence of this trio, the Thuringi are almost invisible, only their *rex* Bysinus known from the semilegendary history that accumulated around Clovis' ancestors.[73] In a similar sketchy way, the kings of the Rugi are known to us mainly because of a single hagiographic source, Eugippius' *Vita Severini*. In it, the Rugian kings Flaccitheus; his son Feletheus, who was eventually captured by Odoacer; and his son Fredericus all play large enough roles that they are not the mere ciphers that they would be on the basis of the poor chronicle sources that otherwise attest them.[74] The Breton king Riothamus emerges between Gothic and Frankish spheres, suddenly appearing in Gaul in 469 or so, again demonstrating how many more *reges* than *regna* there were in the region well into the later fifth century.[75] Aegidius and Syagrius, both Romans, may well have been kings to the same extent as the barbarians treated elsewhere in this chapter. Aegidius may have been king of the Franks eventually ruled by Clovis, while Syagrius was eventually defeated by that Frankish king, and although the so-called kingdom of Syagrius beloved by an earlier generation of modern scholars is largely invented, there is no reason to believe that Syagrius did not see himself as a *rex* among other competing *reges*.[76] The difficulty of placing either him or Aegidius in a defined "constitutional" position, meanwhile, illustrates the confusion of most of Gaul north of the Loire by the middle of the fifth century.[77]

The situation was more territorially stable in Italy, which went from being the rump of the western empire to a substantial territorial kingdom by way of a perfectly standard military revolt and usurpation: Odoacer declined to continue to serve Orestes, killed him and his allies, and deposed Romulus, departing from the usual script only by declining to nominate a new imperial figurehead. Because Theodoric the Ostrogoth eventually emerged as victor in the campaigns to control Italy, the course of the loser's reign as king is very obscure indeed, but it is interesting that toward the very end of his reign, he promoted his son Thela to the rank of caesar, perhaps thereby intimating a plan to restore some sort of subimperial government system.[78] The eastern Goths—whom we call Ostrogoths in convenient, if ahistorical, defiance of contemporary evidence—have a history that begins for our purposes with the fall of the Hunnic empire in central Europe.[79] The names of many Gothic kings and chieftains from the mid and later fifth century are known in the region.[80] The kingdom founded by Theodoric was painfully short-lived, despite its roots in a Roman infrastructure and the successful efforts of Cassiodorus to make it look like a model of successful *imitatio*.[81] Theodoric was succeeded by his grandson Athalaric, a nonentity, and his daughter Amalasuintha, a ruler on the model of an east Roman princess, who failed to retain the loyalty of her father's following and fell victim to her noble husband, Theodahad.[82] By the time Justinian's army invaded the kingdom in the heady aftermath of the successful Vandal war, the hold of Theodahad on the remnants of the Roman state was tenuous. Though his successors put up a long and bitter fight, and one that basically wrecked Italy for centuries thereafter, they did so increasingly on the model of kings without a kingdom, relying on the loyalty of their followers but increasingly unable to govern a territorial kingdom as Odoacer and Theodoric had done.[83]

In exactly the same way, the defeat of Alaric II at Vouillé forced sixth-century Visigothic kings to revert to the model of kings without a kingdom. Alaric's bastard Gesalic could never secure a reliable following, and the young Amalaric ruled as the ward of his grandfather Theodoric the Ostrogoth.[84] His successors, in turn, controlled only parts—often insignificant parts—of Spain for most of the sixth century, and power in the peninsula devolved almost entirely onto the old Roman civic nobility.[85] Not until the 560s, and even then only slowly and through a process of brutal conquest, was Leovigild able to found an entirely new Visigothic kingdom, one that was consciously postimperial, on Spanish soil. This Visigothic kingdom flourished in the seventh century alongside the contemporary Frankish kingdoms in Gaul, which for their part, with the appropriation of the late Merovingian state by the Carolingian family, provided the model of early medieval kingship that inspired monarchs throughout the early and central Middle Ages.

III.

As the foregoing sketch suggests, the number of kings in the fifth-century West, many of whose *regna* were hardly defined, was huge. Almost nowhere are kings firmly linked to territorial kingdoms until very late in the fifth century or even later. We can usefully explain this by thinking in terms of an analogy between the mid and late Republican transformation in the meaning of the word *provincia* and the fifth-century changes to the significance of *regnum*. In the Republican period, a *provincia* never lacked a territorial component, but for centuries the territorial element was secondary in the term's semantic content, which still primarily signified the sphere of activity in which a magistrate with proconsular or propraetorian *imperium* was active.[86] Similarly, the *regna* of the fifth century, like those of fourth-century client kings, were never without a territorial aspect, but for much of the century, that territorial component was secondary. The territorial component became primary only when the old-fashioned behaviors of a frontier *rex* ceased to be viable in the face of imperial collapse.[87]

When we view the question in these terms, we can distinguish four major stages to the process, all of them implicit in the evidence sketched in the first part of this article. The first stage is the actual movement of *reges* and *reguli* from frontier to imperial interior, that is to say, the movements of population that we normally describe as barbarian invasions. The second stage was the generalized imperial acceptance of the fait accompli, so that, from the 420s and 430s, the existence of *reguli* inside the imperial frontiers came to be tolerated as normal, even if not necessarily desirable. The third stage was the recognition that the western empire could no longer administer areas of its former territory from its own shrinking resources, which meant that it was sensible to cede effective control of imperial lands to the *reges* who were now a permanent part of the landscape, though this de facto cession of control did not necessarily imply that these lands had ceased to be part of the empire conceptually. The fourth and final stage emerged slowly and without most people noticing what had happened until it had done so: left to their own devices for long enough, the western *reges*, as well as the provincial population now living under them, lost the habit of waiting for the empire to again take up its proper function. In those circumstances, the kings started to do what the empire had once done, thus finally turning abstract and ambiguous *regna* into territorial polities on imperial soil.

The starting point of this historical process is, then, the invasions and invitations that brought foreigners onto imperial soil in large numbers. The Roman empire had always been happy to invite large numbers of barbarian neighbors into the imperial provinces, usually with a view to replacing some deficit in the population, military, agricultural, or fiscal. The imperial capacity for *receptio* was almost infinite, but several accidents complicated matters in the late fourth and early fifth century. The mishandled reception of the Goths was, of course, at the heart of the problem, but there is no compelling evidence to suggest that the eventual settlement of the rebellious newcomers in the Balkans by Theodosius was intrinsically doomed to failure.[88] Rather, the usual bane of imperial politics—usurpation and consequent civil war—supervened, with worse than usual consequences.[89] Two civil wars in quick succession, followed by imperial minorities and the cold wars of successive regents, meant that Alaric's Goths (who may have been a very heterogeneous army unit, rather than intimately linked to the Balkan settlers of 382) became an active force in imperial politics; it was also a force that was only tenuously linked to the imperial center, however much Alaric wanted and tried to be a Roman general on the traditional model.[90] When combined with the invasions of Radagaisus and the Alans, Vandals, and Sueves between 405 and 407, the number of uncooperative soldiers with no links to the imperial government, save through the negotiating tactics of their commanders, was very large. We can leave aside the irresolvable question of the numbers involved and the extent to which these barbarian groups represented peoples on the move, with women and children in tow, and how much they were just predatory warrior bands.[91] What mattered was their capacity to challenge the imperial government on the battlefield effectively enough to drive it to concerted military action. The strenuous efforts made by Stilicho and Constantius, as well as lesser commanders, need to be kept in mind, not least by recent commentators who suppose that the empire lacked the good sense to fight back as hard as it ought to have done.

Many of these dangerous, half-foreign forces were led by men who were called or called themselves kings, but their connection, actual and functional, to the barbarian kingdoms of later in the century is much weaker than their connections with the fourth-century frontier *reguli*.[92] This was made clear time and again in the chaotic circumstances of the 410s. The Rhine invaders were kept in check and managed by Constantine III just as frontier client kings had always been; they penetrated the south of Gaul and Spain only after Constantine's regime itself fractured into civil conflict.[93] Similarly, and while Alaric was still alive, one of his chief rivals was a man called Sarus, serving as a loyal Roman officer of Honorius to the same degree that Alaric opposed him.[94] Whatever the initial source of their rivalry, when Sarus' brother briefly made himself king after the assassination of Alaric's brother-in-law and successor Athaulf, we learn that Sarus himself had been "king of part of the Goths."[95] The obscurity of this rivalry cannot disguise its close similarity to the type of conflict that was a regular feature of the fourth-century frontier: rival claimants to a local client kingship (here, Alaric, Athaulf, Sarus, Sigeric, and perhaps others unnamed) both validated their own authority and prosecuted their own feuds through their relationship to the Roman government, which in turn relied upon the mixture of authority and the insecurity caused by local dynastic rivalry to manage the neighbors and to prosecute imperial civil conflict where doing so was useful.[96] The only thing that has changed is the location, transporting the prosecution of these conflicts onto the soil of the empire, so that not just the rivalry but the actual military conflict as well took place there.

One could add further such parallels between the fourth-century frontier kings and the *reges* and *reguli* on western provincial soil in the 400s and 410s, but let us instead note the extent to which these *reges* were managed and handled by the imperial government, and likewise the degree to which Stilicho and thereafter Constantius fought to reduce the power of any such *reges* as declined to knuckle under and behave themselves as good clients should.[97] There was never any intention of allowing these newcomers to operate on their own terms, and all those who tried to were ruthlessly eliminated. Even when the existence of certain *reges* was tolerated—as the Sueves and part of the Vandals were in Gallaecia from 418 to 421 or so—they were tolerated only on imperial terms and at the edge of a not very important province. The Gothic settlement in Aquitania might look like a stark exception to this rule—and the *regnum* of Theoderic I did, indeed, become something very much more significant than its beginnings could ever have suggested—but at its inception, the Gothic settlement was in perfect conformity with the previous norms: Wallia and Theoderic's Goths were treated as the Alamanni of Vadomarius had been seven decades earlier, as provisionally loyal clients of imperial government, available for the chastisement of internal enemies.[98] Aquitania was not ceded to the Goths, no Gothic territorial polity was created, imperial government was envisaged as continuing in the regions where the settlement took place, and the Gallic aristocracy, regardless of whether it actually liked the settlement, was brought into the compact and given its own *concilium* at Arles as a sop to the region's centrifugal tendencies.[99] We can never be sure of just what Constantius had hoped to achieve with the Gothic settlement, but it was clearly the only such expedient that enjoyed official approval and toleration, and we ought to make no assumptions about any permanence it might or might not have been intended to have.[100] What is more, there is every likelihood that Constantius intended to do away with the last of the *reges* in Spain and very well might have, had he not died after holding his arduously acquired throne for a mere nine months. Thereupon, as had happened so frequently since the 380s, the collapse of unity at the highest level meant that dealings with barbarians again became a secondary concern.

That is to say, if the existence of client *reges* on imperial soil was a product of the 400s and 410s, their normalization into the provincial landscape was fundamentally a product of the 420s and 430s and the result of instability at the imperial center. When Constantius died, his policies seem to have been continued—the general Castinus, for instance, was in the midst of prosecuting a war against the barbarian *reges* in Spain.[101] But when Honorius rapidly followed his disliked co-ruler to the grave in 423, the western empire fell apart into one of its periodic bouts of civil war, and barbarian *reges* became useful tools for rival *magistri* more than they seemed threats to imperial power: where Constantius had been able to follow a consistent policy of pushing *reges* and their followers to extinction, or into marginal positions where they could do little harm, for Felix, Boniface, Aëtius, and the other rival soldiers of the 420s and 430s, suppressing the *reges* altogether was undesirable—they were far too useful, which in turn meant the de facto tolerance of semi-independent rulers with their own followers on Roman soil. One says semi-independent, because the 420s and 430s certainly did not witness the creation of actual independent kingdoms on imperial soil, the cession of land to client *reges*, or the recognition of any barbarian *rex* as an equal of the empire. Instead, these two decades saw the acceptance of old-fashioned *reges* as internal players in the politics of controlling the West and the governmental apparatus of its underwhelming emperor Valentinian.[102] The Gothic ruler Theoderic seems to have held himself aloof from politics in the immediate aftermath of Constantius and Honorius' deaths, but by the later 420s, the Gothic *rex* was more or less immovable, and it is at this time that we find the Gothic general Anaolsus investing Arles for reasons of the deepest obscurity.[103] Gothic motives go unrecorded in these years and have to be inferred from Theoderic's behavior, but one should probably envisage an attempt to influence the ongoing rivalries of ambitious *magistri* like Felix, Boniface, Sebastianus, and Aëtius, who set an example the barbarian kings were more than happy to imitate.[104] The Gothic attack on Arles coincided with a period during which Aëtius was intensely active in Gaul, and we should remember that, from the point of view of many contemporaries, Aëtius looked more like a cat's paw of the Huns than the "last of the Romans," however many modern scholars prefer to remember him in that way. Viewed from an alternative perspective, Gothic hostility toward Aëtius might be understood as loyalty to the

Italian regime, with which the Goths had ancestral ties so long as Galla Placidia remained in the ascendant.[105] By choosing sides in Roman political quarrels, barbarian leaders could exercise disproportionate influence. The cack-handed attempts of early Suevic *reguli* to turn themselves into meaningful power players, and the vastly more successful efforts of Gaiseric after his crossing to Africa, need to be read in a similar light.[106]

All told, however, this second stage in the creation of the western kingdoms is the most difficult to assess, because it is far too easy to reify its stages into something inevitable. Here and elsewhere, and bearing in mind the dangers of hindsight, we must force ourselves to concentrate on the contingent, short-term behaviors of all the main political players, rather than trying to discern long-term projects of *Reichsgründung* across decades and innumerable changes of ruler. The initiative still lay with Roman government, however weakened it might have been, because everyone, client kings included, still looked to Roman government as if by a law of nature. Client kings were useful in Roman politics, particularly so long as Aëtius' hold on power remained incomplete, as it did until the very end of the 430s; indeed, not till Galla faded into the political background in the 440s was the patrician's position really safe. But so long as Aëtius had rivals who could contest his position, the Vandal, Gothic, Burgundian, and other *reges*, in a perpetual state of uncertainty as to their own security and always anxious to improve their conditions, were useful to him.

That said, by the time Aëtius' rivals had disappeared, the barbarian kings were a permanent feature of the landscape. Local Roman powers—imperial, ecclesiastical, curial, and aristocratic—had found their own uses for the *reges*, regardless of whether those uses coincided with those of the court. In this respect, one may think of the way the Gothic prince Frederic found his way into papal correspondence on the back of Gallic ecclesiastical disputes, or the way Gallaecian nobles used the Sueves to prosecute their own squabbles.[107] As it happened, these shifting local alliances had the effect of making regional powers less amenable to imperial control, a problem undoubtedly compounded by the fact that the emperors, far away in Italy, could do less and less of what their subjects had once expected them to do. The existence of rival sources of power, though not yet of authority, in the shape of barbarian *reges* meant that local strongmen and aristocrats had greater latitude to ignore the imperial government, and thus by the time Aëtius was in control of the central government, the sway of that government was both narrower and shallower than it had ever been in the past.[108] From the 440s onward, the central government had to engage in really strenuous lobbying to keep its putative subjects in the provinces generally well disposed to it; the fact that Majorian required a full year to bring all the provincial factions into line before actually claiming the imperial purple is still more diagnostic of the shrinking regard for the emperor that beset western politics as the century progressed.[109]

It was in these circumstances that the third stage in the construction of the western kingdoms began, one in which the imperial government recognized the right of *reges* to rule not just in the ambiguous and provisional manner of a client king, but as the territorial governors of parts of imperial territory. The change seems to have been implicit in the treaty between Theoderic and Aëtius of 439. Surrounding circumstances are obscure, and we should not assume, as is too often done, that Aëtius was compelled to make peace against his will after Theoderic had badly beaten Litorius and his Huns.[110] By 439, given his recent successes, Litorius was certainly in a position to threaten Aëtius, something to which Prosper clearly alludes.[111] Though it is perhaps unlikely that Theoderic was acting on the patrician's orders, Aëtius cannot have found the death of Litorius unwelcome. The Gothic treaty may have reflected Aëtius' recognition that the Goths were better "partners for peace" and posed less of a threat than an overmighty subordinate like the dead Roman general. Be that as it may, the same recognition that some territories were more easily left to new masters undoubtedly explains the treaty between Gaiseric and the court in 442. In none of these cases was territory being ceded irrevocably, any more than northern Gaul had been consciously given up just because contemporary authors tended visibly to treat everything north of the Loire (now, tellingly, called Gallia Ulterior) as a foreign land.[112] Cessions were always provisional. But the treaties of the very late 430s and 440s failed to envisage even the pretense of active imperial administration, leaving that task to the local *reges*. That is something new, and it meant that if the government never did get around to reasserting its control over such lands—which it did less and less as the century passed the halfway mark—the foundations for a territorial *regnum* had been laid.

All the same, treaties like those of 439 and 442 did not suddenly create territorial polities for barbarian *reges* to rule; their significance is obvious mainly in retrospect. Until the 460s, the western *reges* generally continued to behave like old-fashioned client kings. We can see this in the way that Aëtius and even his much less competent successors were able to play members of various regal families off one another to maintain the stability that fraternal discord brought with it. While the kings were often successful in intervening in imperial affairs, none more so than Gaiseric in his extracting an imperial betrothal out of Valentinian, the government of Aëtius was equally adept at setting king against king, as had always happened along the frontiers. Nothing, for instance, can explain the Vandal attack on Gallaecia in 445, save Roman determination to use Gaiseric against Rechila.[113] Again, just as in earlier centuries, the empire needed to adjudicate the familial arguments of client rulers, as in the brewing civil war between Theoderic II and Frederic, which Avitus seems to have prevented.[114] Imperial supervision of barbarian marriage connections can also be inferred in many instances.[115] The behavior of the western *reges* at times of imperial regime change is also noteworthy in this context. Theoderic, who had been a loyal client of Avitus, was deeply suspicious of Majorian and had to be brought to heel by him. Yet when Majorian was murdered, he held back, deciding which way to jump—no sign of an independent foreign policy there.

Indeed, most of the *reges* of this third period preferred, when they could, to act in the capacity of Roman *magistri militum*. Thus Gundioc, the Burgundian king and founder of a powerful dynasty, was by preference *magister militum per Gallias*.[116] Gundioc's son Gundobad, the most successful of four brothers and an acolyte of Ricimer, was also primarily interested in his position as *magister militum*. He, like Ricimer, enjoyed the role of kingmaker and preferred it.[117] When the civil war between Anthemius and Ricimer came to an end and both rivals died in quick succession, Gundobad got himself the rank of *patricius* added to his *magisterium* by Olybrius, a man with good connections to both the Vandal court and Ricimer. When Olybrius proved short-lived, Gundobad sponsored Glycerius, after which he seems to have decided that the possibility of sustaining a western emperor capable of holding both Gaul and Italy had ceased to be viable. He chose Burgundian kingship when hopes of a meaningful *magisterium* had collapsed.[118]

The integration of *reges* into imperial politics, which the example of Gundobad illustrates, offered both opportunities and difficult challenges to provincial aristocrats. These aristocrats were used to maneuvering for authority and power in the aftermath of an imperial death, and those in Gaul, in particular, had quite often pursued their own interests in opposition to the Italian center—not least because, with the late-fourth-century retreat of emperors from Gallic to Italian residences, the access of Gallic nobles to the court became attenuated. The centrifugal tendencies of the Gauls were certainly restrained after the crisis of the 400s and 410s, perhaps in part by the Gothic settlement; in the long run, however, all the various settlements created alternative centers of power that became more attractive as successive imperial regimes suffered crises of legitimacy. The assassinations of Aëtius and Valentinian III were undoubtedly traumatic, and Valentinian's death removed the established dynasty from power. However, it was the impossibility of definitively settling on the legitimacy of any given emperor after the death of Majorian that made the possibility of working with alternative, regal sources of power so attractive and simultaneously fraught with danger. Majorian, by dint of careful diplomacy, had won the recognition of every western interest group save the Vandals, but his death meant that every Roman army in the West had the choice of going its own way, and neither armies nor aristocrats had any firm grounds on which to determine where their loyalties should lie, whether or not they actually did lie there.

This utter confusion of legitimacy makes the 450s, and particularly the 460s, very difficult for us to read, but contemporaries were deeply uncertain themselves. Whereas the participation of men like Theoderic and Frederic in local politics had been no more than a normal part of the provincial landscape, the boundaries of legitimate alliance and illegitimate, contemnible behavior became impossible to separate. Part of the reason that the "treason" of the Gallic praetorian prefect Arvandus seemed so appalling, and so embarrassed Sidonius as the urban prefect who should have tried him, was that his alliance with Euric could be portrayed as a betrayal of the emperor and his fellow citizens, where other aristocrats' dealings with the Gothic king could be construed as legitimate.[119] Sidonius' long-term friend, and perhaps cousin, Avitus could negotiate with the Visigoths without any aspersions being cast on his motives; Leo "of Narbonne," who claimed descent from Fronto, the great orator and tutor of Marcus Aurelius, could move from an imperial career in which he had achieved *spectabilis* rank to the court of Euric and then Alaric without anyone holding it against him.[120] Some uses of the barbarian *reges* were understood to be perfectly all right in the game of imperial competition; others were not. The difficulty was telling which was which, when the boundaries were flexible and when they were not. As Arvandus' case shows, correspondence that might be acceptable in a man with a good deal of friendly local support—as had been the case when Avitus bid for imperial office with the backing of Theoderic—was not for a man who had a lot of local enemies.

The tottering late reign of Anthemius and the ephemeral reigns that followed increasingly made such ambiguities an irrelevance, when an emperor like Anthemius, who had won the grudging acknowledgment of most of the regional powers in the West, could achieve next to nothing his aristocratic subjects might desire of him, even in large parts of Italy.[121] Usurpation and the installation of a new regime would have been the old-fashioned way of dealing with an unsatisfying or disliked emperor, but that option looked less and less attractive as the examples of Severus, Glycerius, and Olybrius demonstrated that the imperial title, legitimate or not, guaranteed control of next to nothing. So it was that the West reached the fourth and final stage in the process we are considering here, one that involved barbarian rulers taking on formerly imperial powers of administration and legal authority. More than any of the previous ones, this final stage of regnal formation required the active participation of Roman aristocrats. Some Romans had, of course, hitched their stars to barbarian *reges* from the beginning. We have seen that much of fifth-century Spanish history makes sense only in terms of rival local and regional aristocrats using the presence of barbarian *reges* to prosecute their own quarrels, although that is not quite the same thing as evidence for taking service under a king. Even the latter is visible quite early: the Spaniards Arcadius, Eutychius, Paschasius, and Probus had served Gaiseric for more than a decade before his order to convert to Arianism turned them against him.[122] Nevertheless, it was in this later period, from the 460s and 470s onward, that the service of barbarian kings came to seem not an occasional alternative to, but rather a replacement for, the sort of political and magisterial career that the empire no longer provided. Thus it was the *vir spectabilis* Anianus who edited and authenticated copies of Alaric II's *Breviarium*, and the *comes* Timotheus to whom our manuscript of the code is dedicated.[123] In a similar vein, the Roman Decii and Anicii moved seamlessly from holding prefectures, patriciates, and consulships under the emperors to holding them under Odoacer.[124] Men like Cassiodorus and Boethius are the most prominent examples of this type of service, along with the somewhat younger Liberius, who served Odoacer, Theoderic, and, finally,

Justinian, but many others behaved very similarly to them, in almost every region where the command of territory had shifted definitively out of imperial hands, and where it would have looked to most residents as if the change would be permanent.[125] This sort of service penetrated quite deeply down the social scale, for men from clerical and other minor families needed to work and serve as well, so in every western kingdom, we run into members of the lesser bureaucratic classes serving the kings.[126]

The scale of these regnal administrations differed but was often quite considerable.[127] This need not surprise us. South of the Loire River, the infrastructure of imperial government was all still in place at the end of the fifth century, though the extent to which it survived in northern Gaul and along the Rhine-Danube frontier is much harder to determine. The major difference between the old imperial system and the new royal administrations that did their best to replicate it was their scale: largely because of geographical dislocation—in other words, because there was no longer an imperial court and palatine offices that linked disparate provincial governments together—the administration of the barbarian *regna* was flattened. The size and depth of royal government was tiny compared with the deep pyramid of imperial administration, so that the complexity of governmental functions was reduced. Perhaps the most obvious example of this is the role of the *saiones* in the Ostrogothic kingdom: the ruler's confidential agents have existed under every historical regime, and, at one level, the *saiones* are merely a new version of the old *agentes in rebus*. The salient difference is the way in which *saiones* had to take on a much more diverse portfolio of tasks—enforcement of judgments, adjudication of disputes, investigation of the legal situation on the ground—that would have been handled in the first instance by separate departments of government under the empire. One might suggest that, to some degree, regal government was more responsive to its subjects than imperial, in that there were fewer layers of potentially rebarbative governing apparatus to negotiate. On the other hand, the same attenuation of governing apparatus also meant a restriction of choices and the narrowing of options, if one was unlucky enough to face the hostility or indifference of the few men available, or empowered, to take action in one's case. That is not to say that the kings were unresponsive to the needs of those they governed. Indeed, their responsiveness is one reason that they issued laws, many of which survive to this day.

The exact process by which barbarian kings took on the functions of the emperor as a source of law, its interpretation, and its administration is unclear. At first, the fifth-century kings must have dealt with the legal needs of their own followers alone, presumably according to customary or, dare one say, tribal law and tradition.[128] So long as there was a functioning Roman government or the plausible likelihood of one's being restored, it is difficult to see how provincial Romans would willingly have subjected themselves to a legal system far less sophisticated than, and conceptually alien to, what they had been used to for centuries: for all the ingenuity expended on demonstrating the Romanness of many barbarian law codes, there can be no doubt that a conceptual chasm separates a society based on revenge and compensation from one based on property rights and the civil adjudication of torts.[129] That fifth-century Roman law was not merely a degenerate vulgar law, but rather continued to develop at a sophisticated juridical level into the fifth century, has been demonstrated.[130] Equally, the thriving juristic culture of Italy, Gaul, and Africa into the fifth century and later has received detailed and convincing attention. But to say that the fifth-century kings were unlikely to serve as sources of law for their provincial subjects is not the same thing as to suggest that they took no interest in the administration of justice in their kingdoms; the letters of Sidonius, for instance, contain plenty of evidence for kings being called in on behalf of one injured party or another in places where it was their writ that ran. What will have changed as the prospect of an imperial return faded was thus not the royal exercise of power in the legal lives of their subjects, but rather the need for kings to take on the legislative and responsive function that had belonged to the emperors. This meant providing judgments and decisions, in written form, that could be deployed in courts that would satisfy the majority of their subjects who were not used to being governed by customary law; inevitably, it also meant the need to find a way to work with both groups of subjects. Old disputes about territorial and personal law are now largely dismissed, and the laws issued by the kings of the fifth and sixth centuries are widely accepted as having applied to all their subjects.[131] We must not, however, retroject into the fifth and earlier sixth century the Carolingian habit—perhaps though not certainly following the earlier Merovingian model of the *Lex Salica*—of issuing ethnic or national law codes as an imperialistic propaganda gesture. Unlike Pippin and Charlemagne, the Burgundian, Ostrogothic, and Visigothic kings of Late Antiquity were responding to their subjects' and their own needs in the same way as Theodosius II had done with his code and as Justinian would soon do on an even grander scale.

One last aspect of this final stage in the creation of the barbarian kingdoms as replacements for, rather than components of, the western empire is the development of territorial frontiers, along with the sustained royal management of them. We can see it in the war between Clovis and Gundobad, and in the way Theodoric the Great had to exercise continual diplomacy along his Alpine and Danubian frontiers, intervening in the affairs of the Heruls and seeing to the relocation of Gepids from the Danube to Gaul.[132] Clovis' treatment of the Thuringian brothers was discussed previously, and one might likewise cite the relations between Vandal kings and the Moorish kings on their frontiers.[133] These Moorish kings are themselves another phenomenon of the fourth stage in the creation of western kingdoms: just as the fifth-century client *reges* were compelled to take on the roles that the imperial government could no longer play, so in those areas where neither royal nor imperial writ ran, local options emerged. Thus in Numidia, the *dux* Masties became *imperator* of the Mauri late in the fifth century, and a well-known inscription from the early sixth century honors Masuna, *rex gentium Maurorum et Romanorum.*[134] The *tyranni* of northern Spain are probably to be understood as local usurpers attempting to challenge Gothic control, but the rise of independent local governments in Cantabria, Brittany, and, of course, Britain is part of the same phenomenon, usually taking the form of kingships as limited and undeveloped as those of the earlier client *reges* had once been.[135]

Yet all these late antique kingdoms proved extremely fragile, even the Merovingian *Teilreiche*, which show the greatest superficial level of continuity into the Middle Ages. The fragility of the fifth-century *regna* had many causes, not least the sheer difficulty of forging a stable polity out of a situation that no one had actively tried to create. The Visigothic kingdom collapsed for decades in the sixth century and was re-created almost from scratch in the 570s. The Vandal and Ostrogothic kingdoms were destroyed by Justinian in ways that fundamentally altered the late antique landscape—both physical and political—of their regions.[136] The various smaller kingdoms simply disappear from the evidence, either swallowed up into Francia or lost in the lacunose sources. The new kingdoms that emerge in the later seventh, eighth, and ninth centuries really are new: Umayyad Spain and Africa preserved no more and no less of the late antique heritage than did the Byzantium of the Heraclians; when Lombard Italy emerges from the process of *incastellamento* and the creation of a free peasant economy, little of the Roman infrastructure remains apart from the cities and their names; the Hispano-Christian kingdoms of the ninth century are fundamentally sub-Frankish, as are the Anglo-Saxon kingdoms of the same period. The Frankish kingdom itself, for all that it remembered Roman ideals and aspired to a vague vision of their re-creation, had transformed the late antique mode of governance beyond all recognition. What we saw in embryonic form in the kingdoms of the fifth and earlier sixth century, with the extreme attenuation of government, had developed into a fundamentally personal system of governance, dependent on the powers of, and relationships between, individuals.[137] This new, medieval Europe of the Franks was a world away from the complex, heavily administered, and deeply legalistic world of the late Roman empire, into which the western kingdoms had been born—as fragile, accidental, and short-lived experiments at the very end of antiquity.

NOTES

1. Cf. Musset 1975 and Pohl 2002. See also Maas, chapter 2 in this book.
2. Heather 1996; Heather 2005; Ward-Perkins 2005; to a lesser extent, Kelly 2009.
3. Goffart 2007; Goffart 2008.

4. For *longue-durée* accounts of different barbarian groups and kingdoms, see Courtois 1955; James 1988; García Moreno 1989; Wolfram 1988; Wood 1994; Zöllner 1970.

5. Kulikowski 2004; Brogiolo and Ward-Perkins 1999; Brogiolo et al. 2000; Krause and Witschel 2006.

6. Wickham 2005 is far more convincing on this than is Ward-Perkins 2005.

7. Whittow 1996 illustrates the extent to which the Byzantine empire had changed by 600.

8. Ward-Perkins 2005 is at its most persuasive when criticizing the European Science Foundation's rose-tinted Transformation of the Roman World project on precisely these grounds.

9. Bury 1923; Stein 1949–1959; Jones 1964 are all now dated in their analyses but remain fundamentally sound in their thoroughly documented narrative reconstructions. Halsall 2007 is much the best of many recent narratives but openly polemical against catastrophist approaches like Heather 2005.

10. See McKitterick 1995 for an overview.

11. Gillett 2002.

12. Braund 1984; Sullivan 1990.

13. Barceló 1981.

14. In the postcolonial sense, as argued in Kulikowski (forthcoming).

15. Pohl 1998 recognizes this with its title but not always so much so in its contents.

16. This is the very old model of Stroheker 1937, much in evidence in Wolfram 1988 and Heather 2005. See Gillett 1999 for decisive counterevidence.

17. This analysis implicitly underlies Halsall 2007, 220–319, and the author and I have discussed this analysis at some length since then. I am grateful to Guy Halsall for crystallizing my own thinking on this subject.

18. For the sixth-century and later kingdoms, see n. 4, as well as Ewig 1976, 114–230; Christie 1995.

19. Braund 1984; Elton 1996b; Van Dam 2002.

20. Jones 1938; Matthews 1989 for Ammianus; Drinkwater 2007 for the Alamanni.

21. Dignas and Winter 2007; Potter 2004, 217–241; Johne 2008, 531–571.

22. Johne 2008, 583–816.

23. Whittaker 1994; Johne 2008, 427–582. Wenskus 1961, little read if oft-cited on ethnogenesis, is actually more reliable on this Roman period (esp. pp. 272–428).

24. Throughout the discussions that follow, rather than multiply primary source citations, I provide only *PLRE* references, supplementing them only where absolutely necessary.

25. Vadomarius appears in many parts of Ammianus' narrative, *PLRE* 1.928 (Vadomarius); for Gildo, Amm. Marc. 29.5 is the basic source, *PLRE* 1.395–6 (Gildo).

26. Esp. Amm. Marc. 14.10; 21.3–4.

27. *PLRE* 1.971 (Vithicabius).

28. The best discussion is now Blackhurst 2004; see also Modéran 2003, 417–539.

29. *PLRE* 1.633–4 (Nubel); 1.340 (Firmus); 1.566 (Mascezel); 1.801 (Sammac); 1.262 (Dius); 1.591 (Mazuca). Nubel's daughter, *PLRE* 1.237 (Cyria), was also politically active.

30. In *CTh.* 9.7.9, Gildo is *magister utriusque militiae per Africam*. Flacilla (*PLRE* 1.341–2) was maternal aunt of Nebridius, who married Gildo's daughter Sabina (*PLRE* 1.79); Jerome, *Ep.* 79 is the basic evidence. For the politics of the period, Liebeschuetz 1991; Cameron and Long 1993.

31. Frézouls 1980; Christol 1987.

32. This is an interpretative corollary of treating the frontier as a zone, not a line: Whittaker 1994.

33. *Lat. Veron.* 13.1–47 (ed. Seeck, 251–252). Date: Barnes 1996.

34. Eug., *V. Sev.* 19; *V. Lupi* = AASS July VII, pp. 70, 81, with *PLRE* 2.512 (Gibuldus).

35. *PLRE* 2.43–48 (Alaricus 1). For an interpretation of Alaric's career, Kulikowski 2007, 1–13, 154–177, with which cf. Heather 1996, 146–150.

36. *PLRE* 2.176–8 (Athaulfus); 2.888–9 (Placidia 4), with Oost 1968; *PLRE* 2.1100 (Theodosius 5); Theodosius is only attested in Olymp., frag. 26.

37. *PLRE* 2.49 (Alaricus 3), with Gillett 2002, 92 for the evidence.

38. *PLRE* 2.196–8 (Avitus 5), but with Harries 1994, 52–81; Loyen 1942, 35–58.

39. Sid. Ap., *Ep.* 1.2, *Carm.* 7 are the basic sources; and for Sidonius, see *PLRE* 2.115–8 (Apollinaris 6); Stevens 1933; Harries 1994.

40. *PLRE* 2.987 (Segericus); 2.1147–8 (Vallia); 2.1070–71 (Theodericus 2); 2.1115–6 (Thorismodus); 2.1071–3 (Theodericus 3); 2.427–8 (Euricus); 2.484 (Fredericus 1). Two other brothers are attested only by Jordanes, *Get.* 190, in what may or may not be authentic evidence: *PLRE* 2.565 (Himnerith) and 2.941 (Retemeris). Kulikowski 2008 for Frederic's relationship to Theoderic II.

41. *PLRE* 2.934 (Radagaisus).

42. Kulikowski 2000; Halsall 2007, 200–219; cf. Heather 1996, 98–109.

43. Greg. Tur., *Hist.* 2.9, *PLRE* 2.940 (Respendial); we cannot be sure whether Gregory of Tours drew the royal designation from the contemporary historian Renatus Profuturus Frigeridus or whether he was retrojecting the late-sixth-century model of kingship to the early fifth.

44. See esp. Greg. Tur., *Hist.* 2.9, Constant., *V. Germani* 28; *PLRE* 2.514–5 (Goar).

45. *PLRE* 2.8 (Addac).

46. *PLRE* 2.976 (Sangibanus); 2.224 (Beorgor); 2.975 (Sambida). Neither Bachrach 1973 nor Kouznetsov and Lebedynsky 1997 can be relied on, though the latter is usefully illustrated.

47. Greg. Tur., *Hist.* 2.9, *PLRE* 2.515–6 (Godegisel 1).

48. *PLRE* 2.522 (Gundericus); 2.496–9 (Geisericus).

49. Especially the works of Victor of Vita: Courtois 1954; Moorhead 1992b.

50. Merobaud., *Carm.* 1.17–18; *PLRE* 2.407–8 (Eudocia 1); 2.572–3 (Hunericus).

51. *PLRE* 2.525–6 (Gunthamundus); 2.1116–7 (Thrasamundus 1); 2.564–5 (Hildericus).

52. *PLRE* 2.484 (Fredbalus), but see Burgess 1993, 155; Fredbal appears only in an epitome version of the text and may be the result of invention or confusion.

53. Hyd. 63; *PLRE* 2.546–7 (Hermericus). For a specialist narrative of Spain in this confused period, see Kulikowski 2004.

54. Hyd. 80; *PLRE* 2.546 (Hermenegarius).

55. *PLRE* 2.935–6 (Rechila); 2.935 (Rechiarius); 2.936 (Rechimund).

56. *PLRE* 2.938 (Remismundus); 2.704 (Maldras); 2.483 (Framtane); 2.486–7 (Frumarius); 2.34 (Agiulfus); and 2.39–40 (Aioulfus), with, on this last, Jord., *Get.* 233–234. For a maximalist approach to this evidence, Torres 1977.

57. Hyd. 168: *regnum destructum et finitum est Suevorum.*

58. For later sixth-century Spain, García Moreno 1989.

59. Perrin 1968, 229–369; Favrod 1997, 185–218.

60. Prosper, s.a. 435; *Chron. Gall. a.* 452 118, s.a. 436; *PLRE* 2.523 (Gundicharius).

61. For the *magisterium*, Hilarus, *Ep.* 9 (Thiel), *PLRE* 2.523–4 (Gundioc); Chilperic is only attested in Jord., *Get.* 231, *PLRE* 2.286 (Chilpericus 1).

62. *PLRE* 2.524–5 (Gundobadus 1); 2.516 (Godigisel 2); 2.287–8 (Chilpericus 2); 2.516–17 (Godomarus 1).

63. *PLRE* 2.1009 (Sigismundus); 2.517 (Godomarus 2). For the Frankish conquest, Wood 1994, 51–54.

64. Zöllner 1970, 1–43; James 1988.

65. *Pan. Lat.* 7.10; 10.16.5; Eutr., *Brev.* 10.3.2. See *PLRE* 1.113 (Asacaricus); 1.599 (Merogaisus).

66. For Aëtius: Prosper s.a. 428, Hyd. 88 in 432, thus possibly, though not necessarily, two campaigns; *PLRE* 2.290–91 (Chlogio); another king of this period was named Theudemer, of whom we know next to nothing: *PLRE* 2.1068–9 (Theodemer), citing Greg. Tur, *Hist.* 2.9.

67. *PLRE* 2.288–90 (Chlodovechus); 2.285–6 (Childericus 1).

68. Greg. Tur., *Hist.* 2.37, 40, 41, with *PLRE* 2.283 (Chararicus); 2.287 (Chlodericus).

69. Greg. Tur., *Hist.* 2.42, with *PLRE* 2.934 (Ragnacharius); 2.942 (Richarius); 2.945 (Rignomeris).

70. This is usefully brought out by the arrangement of excerpts in Murray 2000.

71. *PLRE* 2.288 (Chlodomer); 2.1076–7 (Theodericus 6); 2.284–5 (Childebertus); 2.291–2 (Chlothacarius). Wood 1994, 50–54; 88–93; Zöllner 1970, 74–108.

72. *PLRE* 2.208 (Baderichus); 2.225–6 (Berthacarius), who was the father of St. Radegund; 2.549–50 (Herminifridus). Zöllner 1970, 82–84.

73. *PLRE* 2.244 (Bysinus).

74. *PLRE* 2.473 (Flaccitheus); 2.457 (Feletheus), with Eug., *V. Sev.* 44 for his capture; *PLRE* 2.484–5 (Fredericus 2).

75. Sid. Ap., *Ep.* 3.9, Jord., *Get.* 237–238, Greg. Tur., *Hist.* 2.18; *PLRE* 2.945 (Riothamus).

76. Wood 1994, 38–41; Fanning 1992, with *PLRE* 2.11–13 (Aegidius); 2.1041–2 (Syagrius 2) for evidence.

77. Halsall 2001.

78. Most of the events and important figures of this period are attested in the brief entries of the *Chronica minora*, hence the difficulty of reconstructing causation among different pieces of data. *PLRE* 2.791–3 (Odovacer); 2.811–12 (Orestes 2); 2.1064 (Thela), the elevation to the rank of caesar attested only in John of Antioch, frag. 214a.

79. On the Ostrogoths before the Italian conquest, Heather 1996, 166–178.

80. *PLRE* 2.229 (Bigelis).

81. *PLRE* 2.1077–84 (Theodericus 7). In general, Moorhead 1992a; Halsall 2007, 284–293; Wickham 1981, 20–27.

82. *PLRE* 2.175–6 (Athalaricus); Procop., *BG* 1.4 is the basic source of Amalasuntha, and see 2.65 (Amalasuintha); 2.1067–8 (Theodahadus). Halsall 2007, 506–513.

83. The relentless violence of the Gothic wars illustrated in Procopius points this up very well.

84. For Theodoric and Amalaric, see esp. *Cons. Caesaraug.* s.a. 513; *PLRE* 2.509–10 (Gesalicus); 2.64–65 (Amalaricus).

85. Kulikowski 2004, 151–214.

86. Richardson 1986.

87. I deliberately leave aside the question of the mechanisms of settlement. There is no evidence for large-scale expropriation of land from Roman landowners, and the

number of barbarians involved makes it unlikely that very many of them turned to productive labor on the land. On the other hand, the evidence for a complicated restructuring of the system for allocating tax revenue to the newcomers, as argued by Goffart 1980; 2007, 119–186; and Durliat 1990, is extremely tenuous outside of Ostrogothic Italy. The unauthorized settlements, e.g., those of the Sueves in Gallaecia, will have had to rely upon predatory behavior and expropriation to sustain themselves. Elsewhere, if forced to speculate, I would suggest that for the period in which imperial administrators coexisted with the new, tentative *regna*, some portion of a province's revenue simply went to sustaining the settlers, whose kings eventually took over responsibility for revenue gathering, as is visible in the later law codes.

88. Kulikowski 2007, 150–153.

89. Elton 1996a usefully illustrates the ways in which civil wars always took precedence over barbarian problems.

90. Kulikowski 2007, 154–177, and Heather 2005, 211–238 produce very different interpretations of the same evidence for this career.

91. Kulikowski 2002; Halsall 2007, 417–454.

92. No evidence for a king referring to himself as such in an official context occurs before Alaric: see n. 37.

93. Kulikowski 2000.

94. *PLRE* 2.978–9 (Sarus).

95. Marcellinus *comes*, s.a. 406, with Jord., *Rom.* 321.

96. The material basis of these relations is discussed in the articles in Storgaard 2002.

97. Lütkenhaus 1998.

98. Drinkwater 2007, 251–260.

99. Kulikowski 2001.

100. *Pace* Heather 1992, since often repeated.

101. *PLRE* 2.269–70 (Castinus 2).

102. Stickler 2002 is the best account of Aëtius' career and Valentinian's reign.

103. *PLRE* 2.76 (Anaolsus). Wolfram 1988, 172–246 unnecessarily reads all Gothic interaction with the provincial capital at Arles as attempts to renegotiate the Gothic *foedus* with Rome, giving *foedus* a much more precise content than it had at the time.

104. *PLRE* 2.461–2 (Felix 14); 2.237–40 (Bonifatius 3); 2.983–4 (Sebastianus 3); 2.21–30 (Aëtius 7). As in the 470s, the major figures of the later 420s and 430s are mainly attested from laconic and sometimes uninterpretable chronicle entries.

105. See Lawrence (forthcoming).

106. Kulikowski 2004, 176–203.

107. Frederic: Mathisen 1993, 73–74; Kulikowski 2008. Sueves: Kulikowski 2004, 176–188.

108. Stroheker 1948, 43–83 remains the classic account of this process.

109. For Gaul, Harries 1994, 81–102 is the best account.

110. As believed by, e.g., Wolfram 1988, 176.

111. *PLRE* 2.684 (Litorius).

112. Gallia Ulterior: *Chron. Gall. a.* 452, 117, 127.

113. Hyd. 123.

114. Kulikowski 2008.

115. Thus, although some regard the marriage alliance between Theoderic II and Rechiar (Hyd. 132) as part of the Gothic campaign of aggrandizement and the establishment of an independent foreign policy, it is equally legible in terms of an imperial

initiative to encourage the now-loyal Theoderic to rein in the Sueves, whose long quiescence had not been quelled by campaigns in the earlier 440s and who had instead supported Spanish Bacaudae.

116. Hilarus, *Ep.* 9 (Thiel).

117. For Ricimer, *PLRE* 2.942–5 (Ricimer 2). Though we learn from Sid. Ap., *Carm.* 2.363–70, that Ricimer was of royal blood on both sides, there is no reason to think that he ever viewed himself as anything other than a Roman officer.

118. Halsall 2007, 278–280.

119. *PLRE* 2.157–8 (Arvandus). The case of Seronatus (*PLRE* 2.995–6) seems to be a rather more clear-cut example of deliberate slander, the charge of treason used purely to discredit and remove a deeply disliked official. In general, see Harries 1992 and 1994, 41–66; Stevens 1933, 88–107.

120. Sid. Ap., *Ep.* 3.1.5; *PLRE* 2.194–5 (Avitus 1).

121. There is no adequate monograph on Anthemius, but O'Flynn 1983, 104–134 is usable.

122. Prosper, s.a. 437, with *PLRE* 2.130 (Arcadius 2); 2.447 (Eutychius 2); 2.835 (Paschasius 1); 2.910 (Probus 3); 2.662 (Leo 5).

123. *PLRE* 2.90 (Anianus 2); 2.1121 (Timotheus 4).

124. MGH AA 12.445, where Fl. Caecina Decius Maximus Basilius is *agens vice praecellentissimi regis Odovacris*; *PLRE* 2.217 (Basilius 12); his brother was cos. 486, 2.349 (Decius 2); with 2.216–17 (Basilius 11) for their father, cos. 463, and 2.592 (Inportunus) for the next generation, under Theodoric. For the Anicii under the western emperors, *PLRE* 2.452–4 (Faustus 8), under Odoacer, 2.451–2 (Faustus 4) and Theodoric, 2.454–6 (Faustus 9), and note that a descendant of the senatorial usurper Petronius Maximus became consul in 523 under Theodoric: *PLRE* 2.748–9 (Maximus 20). Chastagnol 1966 remains the standard account of the evidence for the senate at this period, but many of the inscriptions on which his conclusions are based may require redating.

125. *PLRE* 2.265–9 (Cassiodorus 4); 2.233–7 (Boethius 5); 2.677–81. See also, e.g., Fl. Rufius Festus, *PLRE* 2.467–9 (Festus 5); 2.652 (Lacanius) = 2.653 (Laconius). Arcadius, grandson of the poet Sidonius who had argued with Euric so forcefully, was a figure of some power in the Auvergne under Clovis' sons, intervening in the struggles between Theuderic and Childebert: *PLRE* 2.131–2 (Arcadius 7).

126. E.g., *PLRE* 2.981 (Saturus), *procurator* under Huneric (Vict. Vit. 1.48–50), or *PLRE* 2.988 (Senarius), *comes patrimonii* under Theodoric (Cass., *Var.* 4.3). That military men, like the *silentiarius* Valentinian had no problem in similar situations is probably less surprising (*PLRE* 2.1137–8 [Valentinianus 3]).

127. A snapshot of the scale of Frankish administration in the sixth and earlier seventh centuries can be grasped, impressively, from the *fasti* in *PLRE* 3.1524–32. A similar exercise might have been attempted for the Visigoths from the 580s onward. For a comprehensive (if not very analytical) survey of this evidence, Barnwell 1997.

128. The nature of the barbarian laws is a wide-ranging and fraught topic of debate. See Halsall 2007, 462–466 and a cautious statement of my own views in Kulikowski 2004, 399–400 n. 37.

129. Wormald 1977.

130. Liebs 1987; 1993; 2002.

131. Wormald 1977; Wood 1994, 102–119.

132. For the Herulian king Rodulf: Cass., *Var.* 4.2, with *PLRE* 2.946 (Rodulfus); for the Gepids, Cass., *Var.* 5.10, to the *saio* Vera, otherwise unattested.

133. For instance, that Cabaon who defeated Thrasamund in the years before Justinian's reconquest: Proc., *BV*. 1.8.15–29, with *PLRE* 2.244 (Cabaon).

134. *PLRE* 2.734 (Masties); 2.734–5 (Masuna), with Modéran 2003, 401–415.

135. For the tyranni, *Cons. Caesaraug.* s.a. 496, 506.

136. Wickham 1981; 2005.

137. Ganshof 1968; McKitterick 2008 for an introduction to the differences in governing style.

WORKS CITED

Bachrach, Bernard S. 1973. *A History of the Alans in the West*. Minneapolis: University of Minnesota Press.

Barceló, Pedro A. 1981. *Roms auswärtige Beziehungen unter den Constantinischen Dynastie (306–363)*. Regensburg: Friedrich Pustet.

Barnes, T. D. 1996. "Emperors, Panegyrics, Prefects, Provinces and Palaces (284–317)," *JRA* 9: 532–552.

Barnwell, P.S. 1997. *Kings, Courtiers and Imperium: The Barbarian West, 565–725*. Chapel Hill: University of North Carolina Press.

Blackhurst, Andy. 2004. "The House of Nubel: Rebels or Players?" In *Vandals, Romans and Berbers: New Perspectives on Late Antique North Africa*, ed. A. H. Merrills, 59–75. Aldershot: Ashgate.

Braund, David C. 1984. *Rome and the Friendly King: The Character of Client Kingship*. London: Croom Helm.

Brogiolo, G. P., N. Gauthier, and N. Christie, eds. 2000. *Towns and Their Territories between Late Antiquity and the Early Middle Ages*. Leiden: Brill.

Brogiolo, G. P., and Bryan Ward-Perkins, eds. 1999. *The Idea and Ideal of the Town between Late Antiquity and the Early Middle Ages*. Leiden: Brill.

Burgess, Richard W. 1993. *The Chronicle of Hydatius and the Consularia Constantinopolitana*. Oxford: Clarendon.

Bury, J. B. 1923. *History of the Later Roman Empire from the Death of Theodosius I to the Death of Justinian*, 2 vols. London: Macmillan.

Cameron, Alan, and Jacqueline Long. 1993. *Barbarians and Politics at the Court of Arcadius*. Berkeley: University of California Press.

Chastagnol, André. 1966. *Le sénat romain sous le règne d'Odoacre*. Bonn: Habelt.

Christie, Neil. 1995. *The Lombards*. Oxford: Blackwell.

Christol, Michel. 1987. "Rome et les tribus indigènes en Maurétanie Tingitane," *L'Africa Romana* 5: 305–337.

Courtois, Christian. 1954. *Victor de Vite et Son Oeuvre*. Algiers: Gouvernement d'Algerie Imprimerie Officielle.

———. 1955. *Les Vandales et l'Afrique*. Paris: Arts et métiers graphiques.

Dignas, Beate, and Engelbert Winter. 2007. *Rome and Persia in Late Antiquity: Neighbours and Rivals*. Cambridge: Cambridge University Press.

Drinkwater, John. 2007. *The Alamanni and Rome, 213–496*. Oxford: Oxford University Press.

Drinkwater, John, and Hugh Elton, eds. 1992. *Fifth-Century Gaul: A Crisis of Identity?* Cambridge: Cambridge University Press.

Durliat, Jean. 1990. *Les finances publiques de Diocletien aux Carolingiens (284–889)*. Beiheft der Francia, 21. Sigmarigen: Thorbecke.
Elton, Hugh. 1996a. *Warfare in Roman Europe, AD 350–425*. Oxford: Clarendon.
———. 1996b. *Frontiers of the Roman Empire*. Bloomington: University of Indiana Press.
Ewig, Eugen. *Spätantikes und fränkisches Gallien: Gesammelte Schriften (1952–1973)*. Munich: Artemis.
Fanning, S. 1992. "Emperors and Empires in Fifth-Century Gaul." In *Fifth-Century Gaul: A Crisis of Identity?* ed. John Drinkwater and Hugh Elton, 288–297. Cambridge: Cambridge University Press.
Favrod, Justin. 1997. *Histoire politique du royaume burgonde (443–534)*. Paris: Bibliothèque Historique.
Frézouls, E. 1980. "Rome et la Maurétanie Tingitane: Un constat d'échec?" *Antiquités Africaines* 16: 65–93.
Ganshof, F. L. 1968. *Frankish Institutions under Charlemagne*. Trans. Bryce and Mary Lyon. Providence: Brown University Press.
García Moreno, Luís. 1989. *Historia de España Visigoda*. Madrid: Catedra.
Gillett, Andrew. 1999. "The Accession of Euric," *Francia* 26.1: 1–40.
———. 2002. "Was Ethnicity Politicized in the Earliest Medieval Kingdoms?" In *On Barbarian Identity: Critical Approaches to Ethnicity in the Early Middle Ages*, ed. Andrew Gillett, 84–121. Turnhout: Brepols.
Goffart, Walter. 1980. *Barbarians and Romans: The Techniques of Accommodation, A.D. 418–584*. Princeton: Princeton University Press.
———. 2007. *Barbarian Tides: The Migration Age and the Later Roman Empire*. Philadelphia: University of Pennsylvania Press.
———. 2008. "Rome's Final Conquest: The Barbarians." *History Compass* 6: DOI 10.1111/j.1478-0542.2008.00523.x. Pp. 1–29.
Halsall, Guy. 2001. "Childeric's Grave, Clovis' Succession and the Origins of the Merovingian Kingdom." In *Society and Culture in Late Roman Gaul: Revisiting the Sources*, ed. Ralph Mathisen and Danuta Shanzer, 116–133. Aldershot: Ashgate.
———. 2007. *Barbarian Migrations and the Roman West, 376–568*. Cambridge: Cambridge University Press.
Harries, Jill. 1992. "Sidonius Apollinaris, Rome and the Barbarians: A Climate of Treason?" In *Fifth-Century Gaul: A Crisis of Identity?* ed. John Drinkwater and Hugh Elton, 298–308. Cambridge: Cambridge University Press.
———. 1994. *Sidonius Apollinaris and the Fall of Rome*. Oxford: Clarendon.
Heather, Peter. 1992. "The Emergence of the Visigothic Kingdom." In *Fifth-Century Gaul: A Crisis of Identity?* ed. John Drinkwater and Hugh Elton, 84–94. Cambridge: Cambridge University Press.
———. 1996. *The Goths*. Oxford: Blackwell.
———. 2005. *The Fall of the Roman Empire: A New History of Rome and the Barbarians*. New York: Oxford University Press.
James, Edward. 1988. *The Franks*. Oxford: Blackwell.
Johne, Klaus-Peter, ed. 2008. *Die Zeit der Soldatenkaiser*, 2 vols. Berlin: Akademie Verlag.
Jones, A. H. M. 1938. *The Herods of Judaea*. Oxford: Clarendon.
———. 1964. *The Later Roman Empire, 284–602*, 3 vols. Oxford: Blackwell.
Kelly, Christopher. 2009. *The End of Empire: Attila the Hun and the Fall of Rome*. New York: Norton. (published in the UK as *Attila the Hun: Barbarian Terror and the Fall of the Roman Empire*, 2008).

Kouznetzov, Vladimir, and Iaroslav Lebedynsky. 1997. *Les Alains: Cavaliers des steppes, seigneurs du Caucase.* Paris: Errance.
Krause, Jens-Uwe, and Christian Witschel, eds. 2006. *Die Stadt in der Spätantike—Niedergang oder Wandel?* Historia Einzelschriften 190. Stuttgart: Franz Steiner.
Kulikowski, Michael. 2000. "Barbarians in Gaul, Usurpers in Britain," *Britannia* 31: 325–345.
———. 2001. "The Visigothic Settlement: The Imperial Perspective." In *Society and Culture in Late Roman Gaul: Revisiting the Sources*, ed. Ralph Mathisen and Danuta Shanzer, 26–38. Aldershot: Ashgate.
———. 2002. "Nation vs. Army: A Necessary Contrast?" In *On Barbarian Identity: Critical Approaches to Ethnicity in the Early Middle Ages*, ed. Andrew Gillett, 84–121. Turnhout: Brepols.
———. 2004. *Late Roman Spain and Its Cities.* Baltimore: Johns Hopkins University Press.
———. 2007. *Rome's Gothic Wars from the Third Century to Alaric.* Cambridge: Cambridge University Press.
———. 2008. "Carmen VII of Sidonius and a Hitherto Unknown Gothic Civil War." *JLA* 1: 335–352.
———. (forthcoming). "Post-Roman, Post-Colonial? Postcolonialism, Diaspora Theory and the Historiography of Late Antiquity and the Early Middle Ages."
Lawrence, Thomas Christopher. (forthcoming). "Spheres of Influence: Romans, Barbarians, and the Hegemony of Aëtius." Diss., University of Tennessee.
Liebeschuetz, J. H. W. G. 1991. *Barbarians and Bishops: Army, Church, and State in the Age of Arcadius and Chrysostom.* Oxford: Clarendon.
Liebs, Detlef. 1987. *Die Jurisprudenz im spätantiken Italien (260–640 n. Chr.).* Berlin: Duncker und Humblot.
———. 1993. *Die römische Jurisprudenz in Afrika: Mit Studien zu den pseudopaulinischen Sentenzen.* Berlin: Akademie Verlag.
———. 2002. *Römische Jurisprudenz in Gallien (2. bis 8. Jahrhundert).* Berlin: Duncker und Humblot.
Loyen, André. 1942. *Recherches historiques sur les panégyriques de Sidoine Apollinaire.* Paris: Honoré Champion.
Lütkenhaus, Werner. 1998. *Constantius III. Studien zu seiner Tätigkeit und Stellung im Westreich 411–421.* Bonn: Habelt.
Mathisen, Ralph Whitney. 1993. *Roman Aristocrats in Barbarian Gaul: Strategies for Survival in an Age of Transition.* Austin: University of Texas Press.
Matthews, John. 1989. *The Roman Empire of Ammianus.* Baltimore: Johns Hopkins University Press.
McKitterick, Rosamund, ed. 1995. *The New Cambridge Medieval History II: c. 700–c. 900.* Cambridge: Cambridge University Press.
———. 2008. *Charlemagne: The Formation of a European Identity.* Cambridge: Cambridge University Press.
Modéran, Yves. 2003. *Les Maures et l'Afrique romaine (IVe–VIIe siècle).* Paris: École Française de Rome.
Moorhead, John. 1992a. *Theoderic in Italy.* Oxford: Clarendon.
———. 1992b. *Victor of Vita: History of the Vandal Persecution.* Translated Texts for Historians. Liverpool: Liverpool University Press.
Murray, Alexander C. 2000. *From Roman to Merovingian Gaul.* Peterborough: Broadview.

Musset, Lucien. 1975. *The Germanic Invasions*. University Park: Pennsylvania State University Press.
O'Flynn, John Michael. 1983. *Generalissimos of the Western Roman Empire*. Calgary: University of Alberta Press.
Oost, S. I. 1968. *Galla Placidia Augusta*. Chicago: University of Chicago Press.
Perrin, Odette. 1968. *Les Burgondes*. Neuchâtel: La Baconnière.
Pohl, Walter, ed. 1998. *Kingdoms of the Empire: The Integration of Barbarians in Late Antiquity*. Leiden: Brill.
———. 2002. *Die Völkerwanderung: Eroberung und Integration*. Stuttgart: Kohlhammer.
Potter, David S. 2004. *The Roman Empire at Bay AD 180–395*. London: Routledge.
Richardson, John. 1986. *Hispaniae: Spain and the Development of Roman Imperialism, 218–282 B.C.* Cambridge: Cambridge University Press.
Stein, Ernst. 1949–1959. *Histoire du Bas-Empire*. Paris: de Brouwer.
Stevens, C. E. 1933. *Sidonius Apollinaris and His Age*. Oxford: Clarendon.
Stickler, Timo. 2002. *Aëtius: Gestaltungsspielräume eines Heermeisters im ausgehenden Weströmischen Reich*. Vestigia 54. Munich: Beck.
Storgaard, Birger, ed. 2002. *Military Aspects of the Aristocracy in Barbaricum in the Roman and Early Migration Periods*. Copenhagen: National Museum of Denmark.
Stroheker, Karl Friedrich. 1937. *Eurich, König der Westgoten*. Stuttgart: Kohlhammer.
———. 1948. *Der senatorische Adel im spätantiken Gallien*. Tübingen: Alma Mater.
Sullivan, Richard. 1990. *Near Eastern Royalty and Rome, 100–130 BC*. Toronto: University of Toronto Press.
Teitler, H. C. 1992. "Un-Roman Activities in Late Antique Gaul: The Cases of Arvandus and Seronatus." In *Fifth-Century Gaul: A Crisis of Identity?* ed. John Drinkwater and Hugh Elton, 309–317. Cambridge: Cambridge University Press.
Torres, Casimiro. 1977. *Galicia Sueva*. La Coruña: Instituto P. Sarmiento.
Van Dam, Raymond. 2002. *Kingdom of Snow: Roman Rule and Greek Culture in Cappadocia*. Philadelphia: University of Pennsylvania Press.
Ward-Perkins, Bryan. 2005. *The Fall of Rome and the End of Civilization*. New York: Oxford University Press.
Wenskus, Reinhard. 1961. *Stammesbildung und Verfassung: Das Werden der frühmittelalterlichen gentes*. Köln–Vienna: Böhlau.
Whittaker, C. R. 1994. *Frontiers of the Roman Empire: A Social and Economic Study*. Baltimore: Johns Hopkins University Press.
Whittow, Mark. 1996. *The Making of Byzantium, 600–1025*. Berkeley: University of California Press.
Wickham, Chris. 1981. *Early Medieval Italy: Central Power and Local Society, 400–1000*. London: Macmillan.
———. 2005. *Framing the Early Middle Ages: Europe and the Mediterranean, 400–800*. Oxford: Oxford University Press.
Wolfram, Herwig. 1988. *History of the Goths*. Berkeley: University of California Press.
Wood, Ian. 1994. *The Merovingian Kingdoms, 450–751*. London: Longmans.
Wormald, Patrick. 1977. "Lex Scripta and Verbum Regis: Legislation and Germanic Kingship from Euric to Cnut." In *Early Medieval Kingship*, ed. P. H. Sawyer and I. N. Wood, 105–138. Leeds: University Press.
Zöllner, Erich. 1970. *Geschichte der Franken*. Munich: Beck.

CHAPTER 2

BARBARIANS: PROBLEMS AND APPROACHES

MICHAEL MAAS
Rice University

AT the beginning of the late antique period, about 250 C.E., the perimeter of the Roman empire looped around its Mediterranean core, enclosing perhaps 50 million Roman citizens in a broad swath of land on three continents.[1] Exceptionally varied populations abutted this enormous frontier, some long familiar to Rome but others strange and with outlandish names. Four hundred years later, the Roman empire, much reduced in scale and might, still confronted a very mixed assortment of peoples and political communities, but perceptions of the outsiders had changed.

The Roman governing elite made sense of this bewildering, unstable array of peoples beyond their borders by labeling them collectively as "barbarians." From the Roman perspective, barbarian lands were hostile, chaotic, and dangerous, while their own empire stood for order and civilization. Yet the opposition of Roman and barbarian was not absolute or final, for despite the sharp contrasts, finding accommodation with the outsiders and even assimilating them within the empire remained necessary. In Late Antiquity Romans drew on diverse traditions to register the differences between themselves and their barbarian neighbors and to consider how those differences might be bridged.

The first section of this chapter considers a number of Roman approaches to the barbarians found in history writing, diplomacy, science, and law, each of which presented the relation of Romans to barbarians in a different fashion. Then it describes how Christianity after Constantine influenced all of these approaches, causing a change in the Roman understanding of their relation to barbarians.

The second part of the chapter sketches a few of the ways that historians from the eighteenth century until today have explained the Roman-barbarian relationship in Late Antiquity. Their interpretations of barbarians, though based to some degree on a reading of ancient evidence, were influenced above all by pressing issues of their own time, such as Gibbon's Enlightenment concern with the social progress of humankind, the pressures of developing nationalism in nineteenth-century Germany, and reactions to both of these approaches in the twentieth century, especially after the Nazi era. Modern views of the Roman relationship with barbarians differ substantially from ancient ones: in antiquity, barbarians often became Romans; in modernity, they have often been turned into Europe's national ancestors.

I.1 Roman Perceptions of Barbarians

Greek science bestowed on Rome a sophisticated body of literature that contrasted civilized people, the Greeks, with all others, whom they called barbarians.[2] Romans adapted the Greek repertoire to suit the needs of their empire. First, they placed Rome at the conceptual center of the world.[3] Their writing about barbarians always registered distance from Rome morally, politically, culturally—or simply geographically. Next, they believed that cultural contact could alter identity and change individuals and communities. The road always lay open between barbarian lands and the Roman empire, offering entry into a cosmopolitan world of stability and peace to all outsiders willing to accept Rome's terms of inclusion. Since foreigners might become Romans, the contrast of Roman and barbarian paradoxically indicated the possibility of change through imperial agency as much as it suggested cultural difference and incompatibility.

I.2 Barbarians in Literature

Romans might write of "the barbarians," and the lands they inhabited as "*barbaria*" or "*barbaricum*,"[4] but no non-Roman group used those terms.[5] Barbarian was a Roman category that revealed Roman values and prejudices. Romans also wrote about individual barbarian groups (*gentes* or *nationes*) whom they named and whose history they often tried to trace.[6] Roman authors and audiences showed interest in exotic lifestyles, clothing and personal habits, political organization, religion, modes of warfare, language, and the places of origin of alien peoples. While references to barbarians are found in all literary genres, extended discussions appeared prominently in historical texts, where they took an ancillary role.[7]

There existed a well-developed repertoire of exemplary Greek and Latin texts, starting with the *Histories* of Herodotus. This classical corpus contained value judgments, names, and descriptions of barbarians that became standard and let current events be described in traditional terms. Scythians, a term used by Herodotus to describe steppe nomads in the fifth century B.C.E., was still used to describe Huns a millennium later.[8]

Roman writers sometimes offered searching critiques of the Roman-barbarian opposition. Priscus of Panium, the fifth-century historian who accompanied an embassy to Attila's court, accepted the dichotomy of Roman and barbarian, but he also believed that cultural identity was something that could be chosen—a remarkable insight that helped him explain the polyethnic empire that Attila controlled. Choice of identity may well have been one of the principal themes of his now-fragmentary narrative.[9] Salvian of Marseilles, a fifth-century Roman cleric in Gaul who was among the first to write after Roman rule had ended, excoriated Roman vice and corruption, finding barbarian vice among the Romans and Roman virtue among the barbarians.[10] He preferred the rule of barbarians, who, though ignorant heretics, he believed offered their subjects a better deal than the Romans. The use of barbarians as a foil for Roman vice was important already in Tacitus' *Germania* at the end of the first century C.E.; Salvian adapted it to suit his immediate circumstances.

Salvian's religious perspective alerts us to the greatest change in literary presentation of barbarians in Late Antiquity, namely, the introduction of Christianity into the descriptive mix. Until the sixth century, history writing and other genres that frequently carried descriptions of barbarians resisted Christian influences, affecting an ever more brittle classical style. In the course of the sixth century, however, a new vision of the world came into focus in Constantinople and the East in which the Roman way of life was understood to be Christian, and the representation of barbarians and the understanding of the Roman-barbarian relationship changed accordingly. For example, Agathias, a Constantinopolitan historian of the late sixth century, described the customs of the Franks in detail. He also praised their orthodox Christianity, indicating that he envisaged them within a larger Christian world dominated by Constantinople.[11] Theophylact Simocatta, whose history of the reign of the emperor Maurice included the last extensive descriptions of barbarians in the classical mode, described how angelic hosts assailed imperial enemies.[12]

I.3 Barbarians and Roman Law

> . . . what is better than that people should wish to live under the rule of justice? . . . [The law] brings . . . people from their wild state into a civilized community.[13]

Romans believed that the rule of law was essential for a community to flourish and that through law's agency, barbarians might be civilized. Roman law was the bridge that barbarians could cross to become members of the imperial community. Yet the legal record does not speak of "barbarians" per se. Instead, we find newcomers within the empire labeled in preexisting categories that revolve around citizenship, the marker of full participation in the Roman state since its earliest days. With the legal condition of citizenship came rights and obligations, as well as the highly desirable protection of civil law. Accordingly, the Roman state awarded citizenship strategically to individuals and non-Roman communities in different degrees.[14]

In 212 C.E., with the *Constitutio Antoniniana*, the emperor Caracalla granted citizenship to all free citizens.[15] Many scholars interpret 212 as the end point of the importance of Roman citizenship because of its universal application, but Ralph Mathisen has recently challenged this opinion, explaining the continued importance of Roman citizenship after that date, especially for the many thousands of barbarians who made arrangements with Rome to settle on Roman territory, subsequently benefiting from citizenship.[16] While no need for formal grants of citizenship remained after 212, free barbarians (*peregrini*) could fully enjoy the benefits of the Roman civil law if they desired.[17] Many of the settlers obtained the status of *laeti*. They enjoyed legal rights, were taxed, and were called upon for military service.[18] Others, called *gentiles*, received land while still in the army,[19] and still others entered the ranks of the *coloni*, farmers with certain obligations to their landlords.[20] Men and women in all of these categories enjoyed the benefits of Roman civil law without having to give up their own cultural identity, however they construed it.

Settlement on Roman soil raises two further problems for historians. First, it is debated whether the newcomers received land or a percentage of tax revenues from the lands on which they were settled.[21] Next, scholars have devoted much attention to the question of how some of these groups (tribes/*gentes*), after spending a generation or so within the empire, threw off the constraints of Roman authority and established independent kingdoms (*regna*) of their own.[22]

Christianity played a role in the settlement and transformation of barbarian communities. Groups such as the Ostrogoths, who came into the empire in the fifth century, assiduously maintained their identity as Arian Christians, partly out of commitment to their beliefs, and partly to maintain a distinctive profile in the midst of the Roman provincial populations that greatly outnumbered them. In sixth-century Italy, barbarian now meant in part having a specific religious allegiance. Only when the leaders of the successor kingdoms converted to Catholicism (Chalcedonian Orthodoxy), as did the Franks in 496[23] and the Visigoths in Spain in 589, could full integration of the newcomers and provincial populations take place.

I.4 Diplomacy: Barbarians between Hostility and Cooperation

In Late Antiquity, diplomacy was as important as open warfare in the Romans' unending efforts to protect their empire and maintain its place among the peoples of the world. Diplomatic efforts accordingly grew in importance and sophistication as a tool of foreign policy in the fourth through seventh centuries, perhaps more in the East then the West.[24] Surrounded by hostile barbarians and often forced to adopt a defensive stance, Romans negotiated agreements of many sorts to protect their interests and seek advantage. The successful transformation of enmity into even the uneasiest of truces entailed careful evaluation of the opponent against the backdrop of Roman resources and strategy. With the spread of Christianity beyond Rome's borders, the empire began to share a common, Christian ground with many of its neighbors, the beginning of a recasting of international relations.[25]

Diplomacy's categories are based on brutal political realities and pressing questions about barbarians: What do we know about those with whom we are negotiating? Are they in any way like us? Can we trust them? How will the agreement ensure their trust or compliance? To obtain answers, Romans needed three things: information about specific groups and previous dealings with them, general principles governing relations with outside communities, and mechanisms through which this knowledge could be put into play.

Information came from soldiers, ambassadors, merchants, travelers, spies, and other sources. Occasionally, "scientific" missions were sent for the purpose of gaining information about geography.[26] Old treaties found a home in archives in Constantinople.[27]

Embedded in Roman ideology of empire lay the general principles of the centrality of Rome in the international community and the subordination of barbarian communities to it. The primacy of the emperor was insisted upon in negotiations, and treaties often spelled out the terms of subordination.[28] The Sasanian empire posed a special challenge to notions of superiority because of its size, stability, long history, and obvious degree of urbanization and rule by law—indicators of civilization to the Roman mind. Roman emperors tolerated being addressed as "brother" by Persian monarchs in treaties and other formal communication, but such concession was exceptional. The international hierarchy did not depend on ideas of complete difference among nations or that differences were unbridgeable. On the contrary, it presumed that the world was not divided into static camps, that accommodations could be found, and that enemies might productively be brought into the Roman orbit.

Treaties and carefully organized ceremonials enacted these relationships. Treaties in which Romans agreed to pay subsidies to foreign barbarians, though roundly criticized by some contemporaries, proved a useful tool in political communication. Sometimes, of course, the Romans were forced to accede to extortion, but when part of a more complex and proactive policy of defensive alliance and war by proxy,[29] the subsidies proved effective. The ceremonial aspects of diplomatic encounters, ranging from the exchange of gifts in foreign places to the elaborate reception of emissaries at the imperial capital, tangibly expressed the international power hierarchy. Because barbarians participated in the ceremonies, giving gifts, and making pledges and demands of their own, an international network dominated by Rome developed, and even the uncompromising Huns acknowledged basic protocols.[30]

Christian emperors struck treaties of the usual sort, but religion played an ever-growing role in the agreements. State-sponsored missions of conversion began in the sixth century.[31] Sometimes the welfare of Christian communities in Persia was a topic of concern.[32] Relics, Bibles, and gifts of religious significance took a place in diplomatic exchange with other Christian monarchs. Thus we witness the slow emergence of what has been called the Byzantine Commonwealth, as the empire at Constantinople forged new connections with the peoples converted to Christianity, perhaps through imperial agency.[33]

I.5 Barbarians and the Forces of Nature

What made barbarians barbaric? It was generally accepted that in addition to the cultural and geographical distance from Rome, the characteristics of individuals, peoples, and their customs were determined either by the physical character of inhabited terrain (geographical determinism) or by the alignment of the stars and planets (astral determinism or fatalism). The latter was the subject matter of astrology.

I.5.i Geographical Determinism

Geographical explanations of cultural difference began in Greece in the fifth century B.C.E., when a body of material developed that explained the dichotomy of Greek and barbarian primarily in terms of geography.[34] The basic assumption was that geographical conditions determine the physical characteristics and even the morality of a people. Many scholars understood the earth to contain seven latitudinal zones (the *klimata*)[35] that influenced their inhabitants differently.

These ideas about the shaping hand of terrain upon human communities spread widely in the Roman empire as an explanation for Roman success. Vitruvius, an architect during the Augustan age, wrote, "By its policy [Rome] curbs the courage of the northern barbarian; by its strength, the imaginative south. Thus the divine mind has allotted to the Roman state an excellent and temperate region in order to rule the world."[36] Strabo (c. 64 B.C.E.—after 21 C.E.), who offered the most thoroughgoing treatment of geographical determinism and civilization, emphasized the importance of climate, terrain, and especially remoteness from Rome as factors shaping human communities.[37] He believed that Romans were to bring the unfortunate barbarians living in remote and harsh landscapes into the civilized space of the empire; Roman civilization could override the imperatives of nature.[38]

Christian writers accepted the influence of environment on individuals and communities.[39] Procopius of Caesarea, the chief historian of Justinian's reign, assumed that remoteness and harsh terrain condemn a people to a barbarous life, but in his scheme it was the emperor's job to bring them into the fold of universal Christian civilization. Only in this way could barbarians attain complete humanity.[40] Other writers accepted environmental determinism without an explicit Christian twist. In Italy, Cassiodorus wrote that climate affected intellect and emotion,[41] while Isidore of Seville (c. 560–636 C.E.), the most important transmitter of these ideas into the Latin West, attributed national characteristic to the environment.[42]

I.5.ii Astral Determinism

Greco-Roman astrological investigation sought to understand the extent of the influence of the unchanging stars on malleable humans and human communities. The second-century polymath Ptolemy applied astronomy to the character of entire races, peoples, and cities in general,[43] though he did not believe that astrology was absolutely causal in shaping an individual's life; non-celestial factors such as an individual's physical strength might play a deciding role.[44] Plotinus and many philosophers took a stance similar to Ptolemy's,[45] while others believed the effects of the stars on human secondary characteristics to be quite variable and not reducible to a few basic "ethnic" types.[46] Many ancient scholars rejected astrology altogether,[47] but among the population at large, astral determinism remained extremely strong, as witnessed by the vigor of Christian efforts against it.

I.6 Alternative Christian Views

> . . . the stars of the nations which have been conquered by the Romans have lost their climates and their portions.[48]

In Late Antiquity, Christian clerics and state officials forcefully condemned astrology in a "power struggle between the stars and God."[49] They rejected the pagan idea that the stars controlled human souls, bodies, minds, and communities.[50] Such a possibility was incompatible with belief in a divine providence that determined individual destiny, even while requiring humans to choose whether to sin.[51] Only God could determine a person's fate and punishment. A Syriac churchman, Bardaisan (Bardesanes, c. 154–222), developed an influential argument against astral determinism. He pointed out that humans live in communities governed by human laws and customs that differ significantly from place to place and that they frequently change despite the fact that they dwell under the same constellations.[52] Human freedom to devise laws is stronger than fate and the power of the stars.[53]

Christian theologians believed that baptism (and other sacraments) freed humans from the bonds of stars and geography, permitting them to enter the Christian community that was not controlled by earthly location or celestial configuration. Gnostic forms of Christianity especially sought to free individuals from astral determinism: "Until baptism, fate is real, but after it the astrologists are no longer right."[54] From this perspective, baptism at the moment of conversion to Christianity meant entry into a new society where it was impossible to be a barbarian. Divine providence always trumped nature, shaping and directing universal Christian community.

I.7 Christianity and the Barbarians

Christianity altered the perception and representation of barbarians in two phases. First, from the earliest days of the faith, many Christians began to develop new ways of looking at the peoples of the world who were neither Jews nor Christians.[55] In addition to barbarians, these gentiles included Romans, who had intermittently persecuted Christians for three centuries after Jesus' death. Christians did not require the Roman community to be the arbiter of civilized values, nor did they mandate that one needed to be Roman to be a Christian. Second, when Christianity began to join with the Roman state after Constantine, it slowly influenced, as we have seen, all of the other approaches to barbarians: literary, legal, diplomatic, scientific. Christianity brought these previously independent approaches together. The sum of this combination amounted to a new perception of the barbarian.[56]

The Bible and the New Testament provided a history of peoples of the world different from that of Greco-Roman civilization. Barbarians, like all of humankind, were understood to be the descendants of Adam and, more specifically, of the three sons of Noah, to whom God apportioned the earth after the Flood.[57] A repertoire of biblical antecedents played a significant role in the late antique view of barbarians by supplying new lineages for ethnic groups and offering biblical names for new groups. Gog, named in various places in the Bible,[58] came to be identified in different sources as the Goths.[59] The Byzantines came to understand themselves as the true recipients of the biblical tradition and successors of the Jews as God's chosen, while they identified the Arabs as the descendents of Ishmael, the son of Abraham and Hagar.[60]

Furthermore, in a Christian environment, barbarians could be seen as participants in a providential history that presumed the eventual salvation of humanity. Conversion to the gospel was understood to be not only desirable for the nations but also necessary to complete a divine plan in which the Roman peace enabled the diffusion of Christianity throughout the world.[61] Thus, outsiders in a history of salvation were no longer "just" barbarians, they were people not yet saved. The apocalyptic tradition found fertile ground within this new time frame. Barbarians and other peoples became actors in the "end times."[62]

Christianity also provided two new broad analytical categories: heretic and pagan. These categories displaced *barbarian* as the most significant appellations of otherness in a Christian worldview. Barbarians could fall into either camp, but being perceived as a member of these categories affected how the Roman empire dealt with them.

When pagan barbarian groups did convert, such as the Goths in the fourth century or the Irish in the fifth, it was due to the efforts of individuals acting alone, often sponsored by the papacy. By the sixth century, however, it had become the emperor's obligation to enable the redemption of barbarians, and missions of conversion within and beyond the empire became a goal of state. An elaborate theory of the emperor's role in God's providential plan for human salvation developed.[63]

Simultaneously, heresiology emerged as a new way of grouping and evaluating the peoples of the world. Charges of heresy rested on perceived deviance from truth claims considered normative by the group that held them. These truth claims, founded on interpretation of Christian scripture, replaced *Romanitas* as the arbiter of correctness. Christian orthodoxy, however construed, became the criterion of full participation in the imperial community.

II.1 New Roles for Barbarians in Modern History

Modern historians remain interested in the relation between Romans and barbarians in Late Antiquity, though their concerns differ markedly from the Romans'. Two broad issues preoccupy scholars. First, to what extent were barbarians implicated in the "fall" of the Roman empire in western Europe in the fifth century? The topic of migration makes a convenient starting point for this discussion because it has been a recurrent and much contested explanatory device for events in Late Antiquity.

The second issue concerns the origins of barbarian groups and the degree of continuity, if any, between prehistoric origin, late antique identity, and modern nations. The concept of ethnogenesis lies at the heart of this issue. A modern version of the ancient "*origines gentium*," ethnogenesis deals with how and where barbarian groups came into being as cultural and political entities.[64] In both of these problems, the barbarians have become the prime movers, displacing Romans from the position of determining events and identity. They acquire a role in shaping events that the Romans did not give them. With the Roman empire far in the past, modern historians have drawn sharper lines between Romans and barbarians than did the Romans themselves. Ethnogenesis theory has largely been directed at western European populations, particularly Germans, but it has broader application to all the peoples on Rome's perimeter.[65]

Understanding migration and ethnogenesis starts with two profoundly influential ancient texts, Tacitus' *Germania* (c. 100 C.E.)[66] and Jordanes' *Getica* (c. 550 C.E.)[67], and one modern one, Edward Gibbon's *History of the Decline and Fall of the Roman Empire* (1776–1788). What did these works contribute to modern discussion?

In his treatise, Tacitus claims that Germania, a vast area roughly equivalent to central Europe beyond the Rhine and Danube, is inhabited by indigenous peoples, "distinct and pure." He says that the names Germania and the *Germani* are "modern," derived from the name of a single tribe. He contrasts the valor, simplicity, and moral rectitude of the *Germani* with the many flaws of the Romans. In particular, he praises their love of independence and freedom so different from Roman servility. Thus Tacitus provides elements that recur in later discussion: a collective identity for a vast population of *Germani* subdivided into different tribal groups, their ethnic "purity" maintained by avoiding intermarriage with foreigners, the possession of political and cultural characteristics over a long time span despite changes in names, and the identification of a geographical area with a particular set of cultural forms. Renaissance scholars who rediscovered the manuscript of the *Germania* in the fifteenth century identified Tacitus' *Germani* with the German language speakers of their own day, and the treatise became fuel for an evolving German national consciousness.[68] German Protestants in turn found ammunition in the *Germania* for their struggle against the papacy. Then, the Romantic Movement beginning in the late eighteenth century injected the idea of an essential, resilient national "spirit" from the earliest days of a nation's existence into the discussion,[69] identifying Tacitus' barbarians as the forebears of the Germans of their own day.

Jordanes, a Goth writing in Constantinople in the mid-sixth century and basing his work on a lost history by Cassiodorus, claimed that the Goths had migrated from "Scandza," or Scandinavia, before the Trojan War, thereby gaining a history older than that of the Romans.[70] Like Tacitus, he drew selectively on a rich set of sources to create a history for the Goths of his day that linked them to a legendary past in the Roman fashion. With his wealth of supposed detail about leaders, places where the Goths stopped in their long migration, connections to stories that were part of the classical tradition, and his understanding that the Goths migrated as a people, with men, women, and children and all their goods, Jordanes created an approach to migration and national history that remains influential today.[71] Widely copied in the Middle Ages,[72] and standard fare since the Renaissance, Jordanes' *History of the Goths* helped European populations explain their origins as a product of migration and heroic adventures in the remote past.

Edward Gibbon's *History of the Decline and Fall of the Roman Empire* (1776–1788) is a benchmark in modern appreciation of late antique barbarians for several reasons. The work's ninth chapter is a riff on Tacitus' *Germania* that brings the Roman treatise directly into the discussion of the late Roman empire. He views Tacitus' *Germani* as the ancestors of the Germans of his own day. Gibbon also uses the savage *Germani* as a foil for Rome's presumed cultural advancement as well as its internal weaknesses. Unlike Romans, the uncivilized *Germani* enjoy political liberty, but this admirable trait prevented them from achieving "national greatness."[73] Thus nation building and national character take a place in his discussion. Gibbon also knew Jordanes' *Gothic History*, and while he does not stress migrations, he speaks of the restlessness of Germanic peoples.[74]

Gibbon famously attributed Rome's decline and fall to "the triumph of barbarism and religion."[75] Religion's contribution to the fall was not simply the emergence of Roman Catholicism. Gibbon drew attention to Rome's inability to control the irrational religious drives that Christianity sparked. Similarly, barbarism referred not only to the violent behavior of non-Roman peoples, but also to their customs and achievements, which were markers of distance from civilized norms. In this regard, Gibbon is quite Roman, as well as a man of the Enlightenment.

Most of all, Gibbon made popular the paradigm of "decline and fall." He turned the slow demise of the Roman empire from the fifth century to the fifteenth into an unfathomable tragedy. In Gibbon's hands, the disappearance of the Roman empire achieved unparalleled dramatic presence in modern historiography.[76]

II.2 Migration

Although migration has been associated with changes in barbarian lands since Roman times, scholars have reached no consensus about what migration means or how it should be evaluated in Late Antiquity.[77] To understand how migration has found a place in discussion of the Roman-barbarian relationship, it is necessary to review how Romans viewed it before considering how German archaeologists of the nineteenth and twentieth centuries brought it into prominence.

II.2.i Romans on Migrations

Though Roman writers often mention migrations, they rarely describe them with precision.[78] There existed no particular Latin or Greek equivalent for our word *migration*,[79] and as a rule, Roman historians did not emphasize migrations in historical analysis. Romans believed the communities of barbarians beyond their borders to be inherently unstable and frequently on the move. From this perspective, barbarian migration was the antithesis of the stability brought by Roman rule. Romans also linked migration to ideas about the origins of peoples. Though some, like the *Germani* as described by Tacitus, were indigenous,[80] other peoples migrated to new homes under some compulsion, a shameful sign of weakness.[81] In Late Antiquity, when imperial conquest stopped and Romans adopted a more defensive military posture, migrations in the form of foreign invasion acquired symbolic value. By the fifth century, contemporaries in the East and the West, pagan and Christian, saw the loss of Roman authority in the western provinces at the hands of barbarian invaders as evidence of divine retribution for Roman sin.[82] Similar explanations of the initial Islamic successes occur in the seventh century.[83] In none of the extant sources is migration singled out as a special cause of Roman collapse.

II.2.ii Archaeology, Migration, and German Nationalism

Archaeological study of migration began in Germany in the nineteenth century in the context of emerging German nationalism. The starting place, however, was not excavation but historical linguistics. With the development of Indo-European philology in the late eighteenth century came new theories of the origin and spread of cultures. Many believed that the Indo-European speakers originated in India, the home of Sanskrit, and then "spread" to Europe, bringing civilization with them.[84] By the mid-nineteenth century, however, scholars motivated by a combination of racism, nationalism, and the discovery that Europe had a deep prehistory of its own, reversed the origin and direction of the spread of Indo-European speakers, whom they called the Aryan race. These fictive Aryans, whom they believed to be the Indo-European-speaking ancestors of the German people, had their beginnings not in India, but in southern Scandinavia and northern Germany.[85] This model seemed to be in accord with various Roman and early medieval origin myths, and archaeological finds were interpreted to corroborate them. Soon, the academic pursuit of Germanic Antiquity (*Germanische Altertumskunde*) developed to study not only linguistic evidence but also material culture and national customs in search of a German origin in remote antiquity. The new science of prehistoric archaeology accompanied this effort. Rudolf Virchow's influential German Society for Anthropology, Ethnology, and Prehistory put forward in 1869 the idea that the tribe was the basic human social unit and that the distribution of ethnically homogeneous tribes could be found in the patterns of prehistoric archaeological evidence.[86] The archaeologist Gustaf Kossinna (1858–1931) took German prehistoric archaeology into the arena of explicitly racial and national discussion.[87] On the assumption that "closed archaeological cultural provinces coincide unconditionally with definite folk and tribal territories,"[88] his examination of archaeological evidence led him to conclude that the Germanic people originated between the Rhine and Vistula Rivers around 1000 B.C.E., with antecedents in the Neolithic period.[89] Kossinna's many works, furthermore, did much to bring into widespread use the idea of a *Völkerwanderung* or Migration Age, during which Germanic tribes spread from a northern homeland.[90] Such ideas became a staple of German scholarship and were widely accepted in other European nations that claimed an Aryan heritage and in the United States as well. During the Nazi period in Germany, archaeology and racial history were used as justification for military expansion and genocide.[91]

For a period of about twenty years, beginning in the 1960s with the appearance of "New Archaeology" in England and the United States—though not in continental Europe, where ideas of ancient national origins on the Kossinna model still held ground—many archaeologists turned away entirely from migrations as an explanatory paradigm.[92] Some continental archaeologists, especially in Germany, avoided discussion of migrations in reaction to the Nazi era.[93] In the last several decades, however, interest in migrations (and the invasions with which they are generally identified) has grown again.[94] Archaeologists understand migration to be an activity as old as humanity[95] and realize that it can be viewed as a human phenomenon without being part of outmoded schemes of the spread of civilization and national origins.[96] They see migration as the consequence of push factors (undesirable conditions or social aspirations at the point of origin) and pull factors (perceived benefits of the target region). Decisions about where to migrate depend on access to information about new destinations, desirable routes, and means and costs of making the trip.[97] Whether the strategic decisions are simple (e.g., get out of the way of the Huns) or far more complex (e.g., obtain lands on which to settle in return for military service through negotiations with Roman officials), they leave no trace in the archaeological record.

Migrations should be considered not just in terms of the point of origin and point of completion of the journey, but rather as a "stream" with internal structures and developments. Only rarely does an entire population migrate; more usually, only a portion of the community makes the decision to leave its home. The migrating group may change by attracting new members in the course of the migration.[98] A simplification of the home culture may occur as well, especially when the final destination is reached and choices are made about what elements of the home culture are appropriate in the new setting.[99] In most migrations, there is a counter-current of people who return to the point of origin or previous stops on the migration route.[100] These perspectives on migration are beginning to enter historical discussion of Late Antiquity's barbarians.[101]

II.2.iii Current Historical Interpretations

Anglophone scholars disagree strongly about late antique migration. At one end of the spectrum, some view migrating barbarians as the cause of Rome's collapse in the West. At the other end lie interpretations that downplay or dismiss the significance of migrations. Regardless of the degree of blame placed on the barbarians' shoulders, the historians are giving different answers to the same questions: why did the western empire fall and what came afterward? Population movements along other parts of the Roman frontier have not received comparable attention.

Bryan Ward-Perkins adopts a "clash of civilizations" interpretation, arguing that migrating barbarian armies knocked down a healthy Roman empire in the fifth century, causing a rapid decline in comfort and prosperity.[102] He challenges ideas of more complex transformation, which he attributes to Peter Brown (see below). Peter Heather adopts a similar approach.[103] He acknowledges the complex interactions of Romans and northern barbarians over many centuries and emphasizes Roman control of barbarian settlement during that time. He argues that the Hunnic onslaught starting in south Russia in the 370s shattered this equilibrium and eventually drove perhaps as many as 200,000 people into the empire. Heather sees the collapse of the western Roman empire as a consequence of uncontrolled barbarian invasion set in motion by the Huns.

At the opposite end of the spectrum, Walter Goffart debunks the idea of a Germanic Migration Age, arguing that the fifth-century newcomers had no collective identity as Germans,[104] no history traceable to an ancestral homeland in the remote past,[105] and no group memory going back more than a century.[106] The northern barbarians had never been in the grip of atavistic urges to hurl themselves against Roman defenses; rather, they were sedentary peoples uprooted by immediate causes.[107] He exposes the long histories devised for the newcomers as unreliable confabulations first produced in the sixth century.[108] Goffart focuses not on barbarian migration but on the terms of barbarian settlement on Roman territory.[109] His dismissal of barbarian migration entails an attack on ethnogenesis theory, as we will see below.

In parallel analysis since 1971, with the publication of his *World of Late Antiquity*, Peter Brown has argued that it is misleading to speak of a Migration Age, for the barbarians did not have the numbers or the force to destroy the Roman empire in the West.[110] Roman power declined due to internal causes, creating a power vacuum filled by barbarian newcomers invited by Roman officials to settle in certain areas in return for military service. These barbarians joined with local Roman elites to control restive peasants and prevent further barbarian incursions. Though small in number in comparison to the Roman provincials, the barbarians caused mayhem but not catastrophe. Brown builds an argument for the gradual transformation of Roman society in the West on this revisionist approach. Barbarians began to settle within the empire, in Gaul, Spain, and eventually Italy. An aristocracy of non-Roman newcomers were supported by armed militias of soldiers, often a very heterogeneous assortment, who swore loyalty to barbarian leaders in return for privileges, and not to the emperor in Constantinople. Brown argues that these new power bases, located in cities, cast themselves as distinct "tribes" or *gentes*, becoming the nuclei of new kingdoms that eventually took control of western Europe and North Africa. Where once settlers had sought to enter the fabric of Roman society, now ethnic diversity was at the fore. Individual groups such as Franks or Goths insisted on their own "tribal identity," for separateness, not integration into the Roman system, had become the shortest route to power. Brown insists that these newly congealed "tribes" were never clearly defined groups, as nineteenth-century scholars once claimed.

Guy Halsall argues that the migrations were not the cause of the fall of the West but the consequence.[111] He follows Brown in describing how local elites turned to barbarians for assistance in the power vacuum caused by the decline of Roman imperial authority, but he emphasizes "the mechanics of migration" drawn from archaeology,[112] pointing to "push and pull" factors, including regular Roman intervention in barbarian affairs, that cumulatively set the stage for large-scale migration.[113] Halsall accepts the complexities of migrations while challenging traditional narratives of barbarian responsibility for Rome's collapse in the West.

II.3 Ethnogenesis

Romans struggled with barbarian peoples throughout Late Antiquity and called them by names that reflect not a classical styling but contemporary usage.[114] Many of these names were in use in the third century C.E. and some even earlier. Many of the new kingdoms that emerged on Roman soil at the end of the late antique period bore these names as well, such as Lombards, Franks, and Ostrogoths. Historians in the nineteenth and most of the twentieth century readily accepted that the peoples with these names had enduring historical ethnic identities.[115] Today, however, most historians no longer accept easy formulas of long-term ethnic tribal identity and state formation. Instead, we are faced with a host of questions. How and when did these peoples come into being? Were they ethnic groups or political constructions? What links, if any, did they have with groups of earlier periods, and how did they understand that continuity, if they did at all? Historians have long struggled to frame these questions of origin and transformation, and their answers are no less varied and contentious than those about migration.[116]

Ethnogenesis theory, which finds mechanisms of ethnic formation *within* a population, perhaps over a very long period time, has become the subject of much debate in early medieval studies, especially regarding the formation of

German cultural identity. Contact with Rome has also been seen as a significant influence on tribal formation.

Ethnogenesis is associated with an approach to origin and identity formulated by Reinhard Wenskus in 1961. His seminal work, *Tribal Formation and Political Organization* (*Stammesbildung und Verfassung*), invigorated debate among historians seeking to explain the emergence of Germanic polities in what had been Rome's western provinces.[117] Determined to break away from the racist gospel of German prehistoric origins favored by the Nazis, Wenskus found threads of continuity among the "Germanic peoples"—tribes that spoke Germanic languages[118]—not in biology but in a political sensibility that he believed had typified their communities for many centuries. Germans shared a political consciousness that he called *Gentilismus* (coining the word from the Latin *gens*), which gave continuity to their communities as they formed and re-formed in very different historical circumstances over time, eventually establishing the tribes that brought down the western Roman empire and created new kingdoms.

With his interest in origins and finding continuity in some elements that were essentially Germanic, Wenskus revealed a connection to the study of German antiquity as it had taken shape in the nineteenth century. He used the word *Stamm* for a Germanic people (usually translated "tribe" or "ethnic group") that understood itself in terms of descent from a common ancestor of the remote past.[119] Wenskus posited a *Traditionskern* or "nucleus of tradition" that carried the consciousness of these tribes through the centuries.[120] It consisted of legends about ancestors and great deeds of the heroic past. Bearers of these traditions were the king, his family, his elite warrior retinue, and any newcomers to the tribe who accepted the figures from the past as their own ancestors. Victorious leaders bound their followers together through ties of personal loyalty and through the ability to reward them with the spoils of battle. Despite the unstable character of Germanic communities, however, or perhaps because of it, hoary legends could instill a sense of continuity and perpetuate group identity.[121] Through conflict with Celts, Slavs, and Romans, the tribes developed their historical forms with distinctly Germanic characteristics.[122]

Herwig Wolfram further developed Wenskus' theories about the political formation of tribes and emphasized the term *ethnogenesis*. Wolfram follows Wenskus in speaking of an elite warrior core around a leader that enabled the formation of a new tribe held together by legends of a heroic past and a common heroic ancestor, and his reading of ancient texts supplies him evidence for reconstructing ancient Germanic legends and beliefs through a method of "historical ethnography." Far more than Wenskus, Wolfram emphasizes Rome's role in the process of ethnogenesis of northern peoples over long centuries of influential contact. Taking Wolfram's lead, Patrick Geary has stated, "The Germanic world was perhaps the greatest and most enduring creation of Roman political and military genius."[123] How contact with an expanding state may lead to the development of "tribal" formations has been an important insight in historical anthropology and deserves further attention in Late Antiquity.[124]

Walter Pohl, Wolfram's successor in Vienna, is influenced by ethnogenesis theory, but he does not accept all of Wenskus's and Wolfram's ideas:[125] questioning ancient and modern preoccupation with origins, he rejects the idea of a German(ic) *Volk* or people, comprised of various tribes, as anything other than a linguistic abstraction. He objects to the elitist notion of a cadre of warriors preserving the nucleus of tradition, and he lifts an eyebrow at the highly subjective definition of ethnicity that lies behind the ideology of *Gentilismus*. The precise distinction that Wenskus made between Roman and Germanic does not adequately explain the complex historical interrelationships of the Roman borderlands. Pohl downplays the agency of a nucleus of tradition as an explanatory model for the remembrance of such traditions,[126] believing that "The barbarians came with neither clear-cut myths nor clear-cut identities."[127] He raises a question that would have shocked Wenskus: "how much did ethnic interpretations matter [in antiquity]?"[128] Pohl provides an understanding of barbarian political formation that does not correspond to any fixed recipe but reflects the confusing realities on the ground. While not ruling out old oral traditions, migration, or lengthy histories of particular ethnic groups, he lets us see the formation of late antique barbarian communities as a kind of societal bricolage, amid which what the Romans called *gentes* and *regna* emerged from many sources and bore the stamp of long interactions with Rome. "They used what they could find, including ancient myths and symbols, Roman ethnography, classical mythology, and biblical history to assert and delineate their difference."[129]

Criticism of *Traditionskern* ethnogenesis, especially as formulated by Wenskus and Wolfram, has been sharp on several grounds.[130] Some historians question the importance of ethnic formation in late antique contexts, and they object to the central role given to ethnic identity formation, rather than to religion, economics, or politics, as an explanation of the transition to the medieval world.[131] They question the applicability of the "historical ethnology" method to developments in prehistory, before even the problematic Greek and Roman source texts were written, and they question how proponents of ethnogenesis theory mine ancient texts for information and use it to narrate the history of complex changes in multiethnic societies. Walter Goffart in particular argues that Roman sources contain no valid, orally transmitted information about barbarians,[132] and they are suspicious of resonances of nineteenth-century concerns with origin and continuity in ethnogenesis theory, especially as presented by Wenskus and Wolfram.

Whether or not identity formation should be given pride of place in understanding the emergence of the Middle Ages, it remains a critical late antique phenomenon.[133] Individuals and groups knew who they were. Their identities might change over time and from circumstance to circumstance, but they did exist and historians must explore them, difficult as that task may be. Certainly, our evidence is woefully fragmentary. We have unreliable texts written long after events, no extant barbarian oral tradition, and an archaeological record that cannot be read, as Kossinna did, as a literal indication of a particular ethnic group's presence on the landscape. We know today that human groups have never been so neatly packaged, and individuals wear many hats. The nineteenth century offered dramatic silhouettes of Late Antiquity's barbarians and their historical role. Ethnogenesis theory points the way to a messier but more realistic picture.

Conclusion

The first part of this chapter sketched Roman registers of seeing, judging, and associating with barbarians and then how they were altered by Christianity. The second reviewed a handful of current interpretations of migration and ethnogenesis that have several things in common. Responding to typical grand theory questions of nineteenth-century historiography, they blame or absolve barbarians from responsibility for Rome's fall in the West, and they are preoccupied with national origins. Migration and ethnogenesis debate grew up in the context of western Europe, especially with the development of German nationalism. Historians today, both Romanists and medievalists, recognize that the time has come to broaden our historical scope when dealing with the Roman-barbarian relationship. This is happening in three areas.

First, population movements and entry into the Roman territory are recognized as empire-wide phenomena. Outsiders had been crossing Rome's borders and settling in Roman territory under different circumstances since the beginning of the Roman state. The scholarly field of frontier studies brings together archaeological and textual evidence and often employs comparative material from beyond the Roman sphere.[134] Roger Batty's meticulous *Rome and the Nomads*, for example, examines economies and movements of peoples in the Danubian provinces, while C. R. Whitaker and many others have trained us to look at the historical implications of the local and the previously uncelebrated.[135]

Second, the interaction of Romans and barbarians can be examined against the much broader map of a late antique Christian world that reached far beyond western Europe to Byzantium and Central Asia. Peter Brown's *The Rise of Western Christendom* (2003; 2nd ed.) exemplifies this approach, letting us appreciate the profound implications of the change to Christian perspectives for understanding and learning to identify with barbarians. In this creation of many Christendoms, the Roman empire lost its leading role.

Finally, many historians approach the transformations of the late antique centuries without focusing on the Roman-barbarian relationship at all, pursuing instead micro-historical investigation of changes in a local economy, food production, and the movements of people on a small scale. Such topics have not previously attracted the attention of grand theory historians interested in the origins of the identities of modern states. Now, however, many economic historians are creating new grand theory interpretations of their own. Ever since

Henri Pirenne's *Mohammed and Charlemagne* (1935) ruled out German responsibility for Rome's fall and substituted the armies of Islam as the culprit for the collapse of Mediterranean unity, economic approaches have grown in importance. We see this in the current interest in microeconomics demonstrated by Chris Wickham's *Framing the Early Middle Ages* and Peregrine Horden and Nicholas Purcell's *The Corrupting Sea*, or by the emphasis on trade and long-distance communications in Michael McCormick's *The Origins of the European Economy*.[136] In these hefty but invaluable works, the barbarians of Late Antiquity do not appear as culture heroes or destroyers of civilization. They are simply actors in a larger story of piecemeal social, political, and economic transformation.

NOTES

1. I wish to thank Scott Johnson, Tolly Boatwright, Noel Lenski, Natalia Lozovsky, Maya Maskarinec, Caroline Quenemoen, Jonathan Shepard, and most of all, Paula Sanders, for assistance of different sorts with this paper.

2. Müller 1980; Thomas 1982, 1–3; E. Hall 1989; J. Hall 1997.

3. Clarke 1999.

4. Tacitus (Rives) 1999, 11–21; see also Müller 1980; Dauge 1981; von See 1981; Thomas 1982; Thollard 1987; Heather 1999; Mitchell and Greatrex 2000; Inglebert 2001.

5. Opelt and Speyer 1967 for usages of *barbar*; Christ 1959; Dauge 1981; *barbaricum*: Eutropius 1979: 7.8, 9.4; Weiler 1965.

6. Tacitus' *Germania* is the best known.

7. Visual representations are not treated in this chapter. See Aillagon 2008, a museum catalogue with fine illustrations and extended historical discussions.

8. Shaw 1982–83.

9. Maas 1995.

10. Maas 1992

11. Maas 2003, 174.

12. Theophylact Simocatta 1972, 7.15.1–3.

13. Cassiodorus 1973, *Variae*, 4.33.

14. Sherwin White 1973.

15. Sasse 1958; Sasse 1962; *Dediticii* were not granted citizenship. Mathisen (chapter 22 in this book and 2006) on their condition as disenfranchised people already within the empire, no longer as defeated barbarians from outside.

16. See Mathisen, chapter 22 in this book.

17. They could make wills and transfer property: Mathisen, chapter 22 in this book.

18. Mathisen, chapter 22 in this book, note 83 for examples.

19. Mathisen, chapter 22 in this book, note 84.

20. Mathisen, chapter 22 in this book, note 85; Jones 1964, 795–812; Sarris 2004, 301; Sarris 2006, 128–129, 150–154.

21. Goffart 1980; Liebeschuetz 2001.

22. Goetz, Jarnut, and Pohl 2003; Gasparri 2001; see Kulikowski, chapter 1 in this book.

23. The date is disputed.

24. Gillett 2002. See also Gillett, chapter 25 in this book.

25. Obolensky 1974; Shepard 2006a. See also Inglebert, Introduction in this book.

26. Lozovsky 2008, 172–173.

27. Lee 1993,33–40; Gillett 2003.

28. Stickler 2007.

29. Blockley 1985.

30. Maas 1995.

31. Ivanov 2008, 307–312.

32. Dignas and Winter 2007, 225–231.

33. Obolensky 1974; Shepard 2006a; Shepard 2006b.

34. Hippocrates (1996), *Airs, Waters, Places* addressed the effects of the environment and climatic variation on human communities and human character; Glacken 1967, 95.

35. Honigmann 1929; Dicks 1955.

36. Vitruvius 6.1.10–11.

37. Maas 2007.

38. E.g., Strabo 3.3.8.

39. Glacken 1967, 254–255.

40. Procopius (1914–1940), *Buildings* 3.6.1–13; Greatrex 2000.

41. Cassiodorus 1973, *Variae* 12.15; Glacken 1967, 257–258.

42. Isidore of Seville 1911, *Etymologies* 9.105; Glacken 1967, 258–259.

43. Ptolemy 1980, *Tetrabiblos* 2.

44. Long 1982, 178–183.

45. Plotinus 1969, *Enneads* 2.3.14.

46. Long 1982, 189.

47. Long 1982, 187–191; Laistner 1941, 255.

48. Ps.-Clement 9.27 (1994: 73–112). Written in the second century, the Ps.-Clementine *Recognitions* were translated from the Greek into Latin by Rufinus of Aquileia (d. 410).

49. Barton 1994a, 62; persecution: *Codex Theodosianus* 9.16; 16.5.62.

50. Trüdinger 1918 reviews astrological ethnography: 81–89; Latin Fathers: Laistner 1941, 254–268; Greek Fathers: Riedinger 1956; Boll 1894, 183; Denzey 2003.

51. Cameron 1993; Boll 1894, 181–238; Barton 1994a, 63–65.

52. Bardesanes/Bardaisan 1965; Drijvers 1966; Peterson 1959; Dihle 1979, 123–135; Cameron 1993, 118–143; Cramer 1993, 102; Honigmann 1929, 92–93, 109.

53. Drijvers 1966, 91 and 1965, 1–3; on the text in later centuries: Adler 2006, 256–258.

54. Theodotus 78.1, in Casey 1934, 88–89; Kelley 2006, 82–134.

55. Scott 1995.

56. Inglebert 2001; Ewig 1976; De Mattei 1939.

57. The *locus classicus* is Genesis 10.

58. Bøe, 2001.

59. Anderson 1932, 6–12.

60. Arabs as children of Hagar: Millar 1993 and 1998, 174–176.

61. Johnson 2006, 153–197.

62. The *locus classicus* is the Book of Daniel, which was fundamental in the development of the Byzantine apocalyptic tradition: Alexander and Abrahamse 1985. See also Inglebert, Introduction in this book.

63. Ivanov 2008, 305–312; Maas 2007, 75–82.

64. Bickerman 1952.

65. For Slavs: Curta 2001, 2005, 2006.

66. Tacitus (Rives) 1999, Introduction, 1–74.

67. Goffart 2006b, 44–48.

68. For history of the manuscript: Tacitus (Rives) 1999, 66–74; Renaissance reception: Borchardt 1971; Krebs 2005

69. Carhart 2007, 4.

70. Jordanes 1991, IV4 and XX20.

71. Goffart 2006b, 45–48; Borchardt 1971.

72. Goffart 2006b, 47.

73. Gibbon 1974, chapter 9.

74. Gibbon 1974, 206.

75. Gibbon 1974, chapter 71:2431; Burke 1976.

76. Bowersock, 1996; Momigliano 1966; Whittow 2003.

77. Goetz, Jarnut, and Pohl 2003, 1–11 on the inherent problems in *gens/regna* discussion, including migrations.

78. Caesar 1972, *Gallic War* 1.2–29; Strabo 1954–61, *Geography* 1.3. 21 viewed migrations as universal phenomena that cause change throughout history.

79. Rosen 2002, 28–37, describes how Latin neologisms for migration were replaced by *Völkerwanderung* in the last three decades of the eighteenth century;

80. Tacitus 1999, *Germania* 2.1; Pohl 2000.

81. Livy 1967–1999, *Ab urbe condita* 5.49.

82. Kaegi 1968, 224–255, summarizing explanations; Croke 1983.

83. Griffith 2007, 25–28.

84. Taylor, 1906, 1–53 summarizes nineteenth-century scholarship.

85. Taylor, 1906, 50–53 on the abandonment of the "Asiatic hypothesis"; Poliakov, 1977; Arvidsson 2006, 124–177.

86. Fetten 2000, 163–170, stressing how he differed from Kossinna on matters of race and national histories; Sklenar 1983.

87. Veit 1996 and 2000.

88. Kossinna 1911, 3.

89. Veit 2002; on scholars with similar ideas: Arvidsson 2006, 141–145; Fehr 2002.

90. Goffart 2006b, chapter 1; Rosen 2002.

91. On Nazi migration theory: Härke et al. 1998, 21–22; Arnold 1990.

92. Chapman 1997, 12–13.

93. Champion 1980, 31–42 for a nonmigrationist perspective.

94. Anthony 2007, 108–120.

95. Chapman and Hamerow, 1997; Chapman 1997, 11–20; Anthony 1997, 21–32.

96. Shennan 1989; Pohl 2009.

97. Anthony 1997, 22.

98. Anthony 2007, 112.

99. Anthony in Härke et al. 1998, 26.

100. Anthony 2007; Tilley 1978.

101. Halsall 2005; for a traditional approach: Musset 1975.

102. Ward-Perkins 2005.

103. Heather 2009 most recently.
104. Goffart 1989a, 132.
105. Goffart 2006b, 12–15, 47.
106. Goffart 2006b, 91–98.
107. Goffart 2006b, 20–22.
108. Goffart 1988, 432–437.
109. Goffart 1980; Liebeschuetz 2006 and 2007.
110. Brown 1971, 122; Brown 1996, 102–105.
111. Halsall 2007, 34 and *passim*.
112. Halsall 2007, 417–422; Halsall 2005.
113. Halsall 2007, 420.
114. For the term, see Goetz, Jarnut, and Pohl 2003, 3–4; Gillett 2006; Innes 2007, 66–71; Geary 1999.
115. Pohl 2002, 226; Heather 1998; Noble 2006, 9–15.
116. Noble 2006 for overview; Pohl 2008; Wood 2008.
117. Wenskus 1961.
118. Wenskus 1961, 152–272.
119. Wenskus 1961, 14–112; Murray 2002, 44–46.
120. Wenskus 1961, 64–76; Murray 2002, 46.
121. Gillett 2002, on Wenskus 1961, 3.
122. Wenskus 1962, parts IV and V.
123. Geary 1988, vi.
124. Fried 1975; Whitehead 1992.
125. Pohl 2002, 224.
126. Pohl 2002, 231.
127. Pohl 2002, 234.
128. Pohl 2002, 237.
129. Pohl 2002, 223.
130. For what follows: Gillett 2002, 1–20; Gillett 2006, 246–253; Murray, 2002; Bowlus 2002; Pohl 2002, 221–239.
131. See Inglebert, Introduction in this book.
132. Goffart 1988.
133. Gillett 2006; Pohl 2002.
134. Whittaker 2004, 199–218; de Ste. Croix 1983, 509–518; Batty 2007; Lenski 2008; Esders 2008.
135. Whittaker 2004; Elton 1996; Poulter 2004.
136. Wickham 2005; Horden and Purcell 2000; McCormick 2001. See also the comparison of these three "grand narratives" made by Shaw 2008.

WORKS CITED

Ancient Sources

Bardesanes/Bardaisan. 1965. *The Book of the Laws of Countries; Dialogue on Fate of Bardaisan of Edessa*. Trans. H. Drijvers. Assen: Van Gorcum.

Basil of Caesarea. 1968. *Basile de Césarée. Homélies sur l'Hexaéméron*. Text, intro., and trans. ed. Stanislas Giet. Paris: Éditions du Cerf.

Caesar. 1972. *C. Iuli Caesaris Commentariorum. Libri VII de Bello Gallico cum A. Hirti Supplemento.* Ed. R. L. A. Du Pontet. Oxford: Clarendon.
Cassiodorus Senator. 1973. *Variarum libri XII.* Ed. Å. J. Fridh. Turnholt: Brepols;
———. 1992. *The Variae of Magnus Aurelius Cassiodorus.* Trans. S. J. B. Barnish. Liverpool: Liverpool University Press. [See also the translation of Thomas Hodgkin. 1886. *The Letters of Cassiodorus, Being a Condensed Translation of the Variae epistolae of Magnus Aurelius Cassiodorus Senator.* London: H. Frowde.]
Eutropius. 1979. *Eutropii breviarium ab urbe condita.* Ed. C. Santini. Leipzig: Teubner.
———. 1993. *The breviarium ab urbe condita of Eutropius.* Trans. H. W. Bird. Liverpool: Liverpool University Press.
Hippocrates. 1983. "Airs, Waters, Places." In *Hippocratic Writings,* ed. G. E. R. Lloyd, trans. J. Chadwick and W. N. Mann, 148–169. New York: Penguin.
———. 1996. *Oeuvres: Tome II, 2e Partie, Airs, Eaux, Lieux.* Ed. and trans. Jacques Jouanna. Paris: Les Belles Lettres.
Isidore of Seville. 1911. *Isidori Hispalensis Episcopi Etymologiarum sive Originum Libri XX.* Ed. W. M. Lindsay. Oxford: Oxford University Press.
———. 2006. *The Etymologies of Isidore of Seville.* Trans. Stephen A. Barney et al. Cambridge: Cambridge University Press.
Jordanes. 1915. *The Gothic History of Jordanes in English Version; Cassiodorus, Senator (Ca. 487–Ca. 580).* Ed. Charles C. Mierow. Princeton, NJ: Princeton University Press. [Repr. New York: Barnes & Noble, 1966.]
———. 1991. *Iordanis De origine actibusque Getarum.* Ed. Francesco Giunta and Antonino Grillone. Rome: Istituto Palazzo Borromini.
Livy. 1967–1999. *Titi Livi Ab urbe condita.* Ed. R. M. Ogilvie. Oxford: Clarendon.
———. 2002. *The Early History of Rome: Books I–V of The History of Rome from Its Foundations.* Trans. Aubrey de Sélincourt. London: Penguin.
Panegyrici Latini. 1964. *XII Panegyrici Latini.* Ed. R. A. B. Mynors. Oxford. Oxford University Press.
———. 1994. *In Praise of Roman Emperors: The Panegyrici Latini.* Trans. C. E. V. Nixon and Barbara Saylor Rodgers. Berkeley: University of California Press.
Plotinus. 1964–1982. *Plotini Opera.* Ed. P. Henry and H.-R. Schwyzer. Oxford: Clarendon.
———. 1969. *The Enneads.* Trans. S. MacKenna and B. S. Page. London: Faber.
Priscus of Panium. 1981. *The Fragmentary Classicising Historians of the Later Roman Empire: Eunapius, Olympiodorus, Priscus, and Malchus.* Ed. and trans. R. C. Blockley, 222–400. Liverpool: F. Cairns.
Procopius of Caesarea. 1914–1940. *Works.* Ed. and trans. H. B. Dewing and G. Downey. Cambridge, MA: Harvard University Press; London: Heinemann.
Ps.-Clement. 1989. In *The Ante-Nicene Fathers. Translations of the Writings of the Fathers down to A.D. 325,* ed. A. Roberts and J. Donaldson; trans. by Thomas Smith, 73–211. Reprint ed. Edinburgh: T&T Clark.
———. 1994. *Die Pseudoklementinen. II, Rekognitionen in Rufins Übersetzung.* Ed. Bernhard Rehm and Georg Strecker. 2nd ed. Berlin: Akademie-Verlag.
Ptolemy. 1980. *Tetrabiblos.* Ed. and trans. Frank E. Robbins. Cambridge, MA: Harvard University Press; London: Heinemann.
Strabo. 1954–1961. *The Geography of Strabo.* Ed. and Trans. H. L. Jones. Cambridge, MA: Harvard University Press; London: Heinemann.
Tacitus, Cornelius. 1999. *Germania.* Ed. and trans. J. B. Rives. Oxford: Clarendon.
Theodosian Code. 1952. *The Theodosian Code and Novels and the Sirmondian Constitutions.* Trans. Clyde Pharr. Princeton, NJ: Princeton University Press.

———. 2000 [1904]. *Codex Theodosianus*. Ed. P. Krueger and Th. Mommsen. Reprint ed. Hildesheim: Wiedmann.

Theophylact Simocatta. 1972. *Theophylacti Simocattae Historiae*. Ed. C. de Boor. Stuttgart: Teubner

———. 1986. *The History of Theophylact Simocatta*. Trans. Michael Whitby and Mary Whitby. Oxford: Clarendon.

Vitruvius Pollio. 1931–1934. *On Architecture*. Trans. Frank Granger. Cambridge, MA: Harvard University Press; London: Heinemann.

Modern Sources

Adler, William. 2006. "Did the Biblical Patriarchs Practice Astrology? Michael Glykas and Manuel Komnenos I on Seth and Abraham." In *The Occult Sciences in Byzantium*, ed. Paul Magdalino and Maria Mavroudi, 245–263. Geneva: La Pomme d'or.

Aillagon, Jean-Jacques. 2008. *Rome and the Barbarians: The Birth of a New World*. Illustrated edition. New York: Skira.

Alexander, Paul Julius, and Dorothy deF. Abrahamse. 1985. *The Byzantine Apocalyptic Tradition*. Berkeley: University of California Press.

Amirav, Hagit, and Bas Ter Haar Romeny, eds. 2007. *From Rome to Constantinople: Studies in Honour of Averil Cameron*. Turnholt: Brepols.

Anderson, Andrew Runni. 1932. *Alexander's Gate, Gog and Magog, and the Inclosed Nations*. Cambridge, MA: Medieval Academy of America.

Anthony, David W. 1990. "Migration in Archeology: The Baby and the Bathwater," *American Anthropologist* n.s. 92.4: 895–914.

———. 1997. "Prehistoric Migration as Social Process." In *Migration and Invasions in Archaeological Explanation*, ed. John Chapman and Helena Hamerow, 21–32. Oxford: British Archaeological Reports.

———. 2007. *The Horse, the Wheel, and Language: How Bronze-Age Riders from the Eurasian Steppes Shaped the Modern World*. Princeton, NJ: Princeton University Press.

Arnold, Bettina. 1990. "The Past as Propaganda: Totalitarian Archaeology in Nazi Germany," *Antiquity* 64: 464–478.

Arvidsson, Stefan. 2006. *Aryan Idols: Indo-European Mythology as Ideology and Science*. Chicago: University of Chicago Press.

Barton, Tamsyn. 1994a. *Power and Knowledge: Astrology, Physiognomics, and Medicine under the Roman Empire*. Ann Arbor: University of Michigan Press.

———. 1994b. *Ancient Astrology*. London: Routledge.

Batty, Roger. 2007. *Rome and the Nomads: The Pontic-Danubian Realm in Antiquity*. New York: Oxford University Press.

Bickerman, Elias J. 1952. "Origines Gentium," *Classical Philology* 47.2: 65–81.

Bintliff, J. L., and Helena Hamerow, eds. 1995. *Europe between Late Antiquity and the Middle Ages: Recent Archaeological and Historical Research in Western and Southern Europe*. Oxford: British Archaeological Reports.

Blockley, R. C. 1985. "Subsidies and Diplomacy: Rome and Persia in Late Antiquity," *Phoenix* 39.1: 62–74.

Bøe, Sverre. 2001. *Gog and Magog: Ezekiel 38–39 as Pre-Text for Revelation 19:17–21 and 20:7–10*. Wissenschaftliche Untersuchungen zum Neuen Testament, 2. Reihe 135. Tübingen: Mohr Siebeck.

Boll, F. 1894. "Studien über Claudius Ptolemaeus: Ein Beitrag zur Geschichte der griechischen Philosophie und Astrologie." *Jahrbuch für klassischen Philologie*, Supplementband 21: 51–243.

Borchardt, Frank K. 1971. *Germanic Antiquity in Renaissance Myth*. Baltimore: Johns Hopkins University Press.

Bowersock, G.W. 1996. "The Vanishing Paradigm of the Fall of Rome." In *Bulletin of the American Academy of Arts and Sciences* 49.8: 29–43. [Repr. in idem, 2000. *Selected Papers in Late Antiquity*, 187–197. Bari: Edipuglia.]

Bowlus, Charles R. 2002. "Ethnogenesis: The Tyranny of a Concept." In *On Barbarian Identity: Critical Approaches to Ethnicity*, ed. Andrew Gillett, 241–256. Turnhout: Brepols.

Brather, Sebastian. 2002. "Ethnic Identities as Constructions of Archaeology: The Case of the Alamanni." In *On Barbarian Identity: Critical Approaches to Ethnicity*, ed. Andrew Gillett, 149–176. Turnhout: Brepols.

Brown, Peter. 1971. *The World of Late Antiquity, AD 150–750*. New York: W. W. Norton.

———. 2003. *The Rise of Western Christendom: Triumph and Diversity, A.D. 200–1000*. 2nd ed. Cambridge, MA: Wiley-Blackwell.

Brown, T. S. 1997. "Gibbon, Hodgkin and the Invaders of Italy." In *Edward Gibbon and Empire*, ed. Rosamond McKitterick and Roland Quinault, 137–161. Cambridge: Cambridge University Press.

Burke, Peter. 1976. "Tradition and Experience: The Idea of Decline from Bruni to Gibbon," *Daedalus* 105.3: 137–152.

Cameron, Averil. 1993. "Divine Providence in Late Antiquity." In *Predicting the Future*, ed. Leo Howe and Alan Wain, 118–143. Cambridge: Cambridge University Press.

Carhart, Michael C. 2007. *The Science of Culture in Enlightenment Germany*. Cambridge, MA: Harvard University Press.

Casey, Robert Pearce. 1934. *The Excerpta ex Theodoto of Clement of Alexandria*. London: Christophers.

Champion, T. C., and J. V. S. Megaw, eds. 1985. *Settlement and Society: Aspects of West European Prehistory in the First Millennium B.C.* Leicester: Palgrave Macmillan.

Champion, T. C. 1980. "Mass Migration in Later Prehistoric Europe." In *Transport, Technology and Social Change*, ed. Per Sörbom, 31–42. Stockholm: Tekniska Museet.

———. 1985. "Written Sources and the Study of the European Iron Age." In *Settlement and Society: Aspects of West European Prehistory in the First Millennium BC*, ed. T. C. Champion and J. V. S. Megaw, 9–22. Leicester: Palgrave Macmillan.

Chapman, John. 1997. "The Impact of Modern Invasions and Migrations on Archaeological Explanation." In *Migration and Invasions in Archaeological Explanation*, ed. John Chapman and Helena Hamerow, 11–20. Oxford: Archaeopress.

Chapman, John, and Helena Hamerow. 1997. "On the Move Again: Migrations and Invasions in Archaeological Explanation." In *Migration and Invasions in Archaeological Explanation*, ed. John Chapman and Helena Hamerow, 1–10. Oxford: Archaeopress.

Chauvot, Alain. 1995a. *Opinions romaines face aux barbares au IVe siècle ap. J.-C.* Paris: De Boccard.

———. 1995b. "Remarques sur l'emploi de Semibarbarus." In *Frontières terrestres, frontières célestes dans l'Antiquité*, ed. Aline Rousselle, 255–271. Paris: De Boccard.

Christ, Karl. 1959. "Römer und Barbaren in der hohen Kaiserzeit," *Saeculum* 10: 273–288.
Christie, Neil. 2004. *Landscapes of Change: Rural Evolutions in Late Antiquity and the Early Middle Ages*. Burlington, VT: Ashgate.
Clarke, Katherine. 1999. *Between Geography and History: Hellenistic Constructions of the Roman World*. New York: Oxford University Press.
Cramer, Peter John. 1993. *Baptism and Change in the Early Middle Ages, c. 200–c. 1150*. Cambridge: Cambridge University Press.
Croke, Brian. 1983. "AD 476: The Manufacture of a Turning Point," *Chiron* 13: 81–119.
Curta, Florin. 2001. *The Making of the Slavs: History and Archaeology of the Lower Danube Region ca. 500–700*. Cambridge: Cambridge University Press.
———. 2005. *Borders, Barriers, and Ethnogenesis: Frontiers in Late Antiquity and the Middle Ages*. Turnhout: Brepols.
———. 2006. *Southeastern Europe in the Middle Ages, 500–1250*. Cambridge: Cambridge University Press.
Dauge, Yves Albert. 1981. *Les Barbares: Recherches sur la conception romaine de la barbarie et de la civilisation*. Bruxelles: Latomus.
De Mattei, Rodolfo. 1939. "Sul concetto di barbaro e barbarie nel medio evo." In *Studi di storia e diritto in onore di Enrico Besta per il xl anno del suo insegnamento* 4: 483–501. Milan: Giuffrè.
Denzey, Nicola. 2003. "A New Star on the Horizon: Astral Christologies and Stellar Debates in Early Christian Discourse." In *Prayer, Magic, and the Stars in the Ancient and Late Antique World*, ed. Scott Noegel et al., 207–222. University Park: Pennsylvania State University Press.
Dicks. D. R. 1955. "The ΚΛΙΜΑΤΑ in Greek Geography," *Classical Quarterly* 3.4: 248–255.
Dignas, Beate, and Engelbert Winter. 2007. *Rome and Persia in Late Antiquity: Neighbours and Rivals*. Cambridge: Cambridge University Press.
Dihle, Albrecht. 1979. "Zur Schicksalslehre des Bardesanes." In *Kerygma und Logos: Beiträge zu den geistesgeschichtlichen Beziehungen zwischen Antike und Christentum; Festschrift für Carl Andresen zum 70. Geburtstag*, ed. Adolf Martin Ritter and Carl Andresen, 123–135. Göttingen: Vandenhoeck and Ruprecht.
Drijvers, H. J. W. 1966. *Bardaisan of Edessa*. Assen: Van Gorcum.
Drinkwater, J. F. 2007. *The Alamanni and Rome 213–496: Caracalla to Clovis*. Oxford: Oxford University Press.
Drinkwater, J. F., and Hugh Elton, eds. 1992. *Fifth-Century Gaul: A Crisis of Identity?* Cambridge: Cambridge University Press.
Elton, Hugh. 1996. *Frontiers of the Roman Empire*. Bloomington: Indiana University Press.
Engelhardt, Isrun. 1974. *Mission und Politik in Byzanz: Ein Beitrag zur Strukturanalyse byzantinischer Mission zur Zeit Justins und Justinians*. Munich: Institut für Byzantinistik und neugriechische Philologie der Universität München.
Esders, Stefan. 2008. "Grenzen und Grenzüberschreitungen: Religion, Ethnizität und politische Integration am Rande des oströmischen imperium, 4.–7. Jh." In *Gestiftete Zukunft im Mittelalterlichen Europa: Festschrift für Michael Borgolte zum 60. Geburtstag*, ed. Wolfgang Huschner and Frank Rexroth, 3–28. Berlin: Akademie Verlag.
Ewig, Eugen. 1976. *Spätantikes und fränkisches Gallien: Gesammelte Schriften 1952–1973*. Ed. Hartmut Atsma. Munich: Artemis Verlag.

Fehr, Hubert. 2002. "Volkstum as Paradigm: Germanic People and Gallo-Romans in Early Medieval Archaeology since the 1930s." In *On Barbarian Identity: Critical Approaches to Ethnicity*, ed. Andrew Gillett, 177–200. SEM 4. Turnhout: Brepols.

Fetten, Frank G. 2000. "Archaeology and Anthropology in Germany before 1945." In *Archaeology, Ideology, and Society: The German Experience*, ed. Heinrich Härke, 140–179. Frankfurt am Main: Peter Lang.

Fried, Morton H. 1975. *The Notion of Tribe*. Menlo Park, CA: Cummings.

Fromentin, Valérie and Sophie Gotteland. 2001. *Origines Gentium: Textes*. Pessac: Ausonius.

Furet, François. 1976. "Civilization and Barbarism in Gibbon's History," *Daedalus* 105.3: 209–216.

Gasparri, Stefano. 2001. *Prima delle nazioni: Popoli, etnie e regni fra antichità e Medioevo*. 3rd ed. Rome: Carocci.

Geary, Patrick. 1988. *Before France and Germany: The Creation and Transformation of the Merovingian World*. New York: Oxford University Press.

———. 1999. "Barbarians and Ethnicity." In *Late Antiquity: A Guide to the Postclassical World*, ed. G. W. Bowersock, Peter Brown, and Oleg Grabar, 107–129. Cambridge, MA: Harvard University Press.

———. 2002. *Myth of Nations: The Medieval Origins of Europe*. Princeton, NJ: Princeton University Press.

Gibbon, Edward. 1974. *The History of the Decline and Fall of the Roman Empire*. Ed. J. B. Bury. London: Methuen.

Gillett, A., ed. 2002. *On Barbarian Identity: Critical Approaches to Ethnicity*. SEM 4. Turnhout: Brepols.

———. 2003. *Envoys and Political Communication in the Late Antique West, 411–533*. Cambridge: Cambridge University Press.

———. 2006. "Ethnogenesis: A Contested Model of Early Medieval Europe," *History Compass* 4.2: 241–260.

Glacken, Clarence J. 1967. *Traces on the Rhodian Shore: Nature and Culture in Western Thought from Ancient Times to the End of the Eighteenth Century*. Berkeley: University of California Press.

Goetz, Hans Werner, Jörg Jarnut, and Walter Pohl. 2003. *Regna and Gentes: The Relationship between Late Antique and Early Medieval Peoples and Kingdoms in the Transformation of the Roman World*. Leiden: Brill.

Goffart, Walter. 1980. *Barbarians and Romans, A.D. 418–584: The Techniques of Accommodation*. Princeton, NJ: Princeton University Press.

———. 1988. *The Narrators of Barbarian History A.D. 550–800: Jordanes, Gregory of Tours, Bede, and Paul the Deacon*. Princeton, NJ: Princeton University Press.

———. 1989a. *Rome's Fall and After*. London: Continuum.

———. 1989b. "The Theme of 'The Barbarian Invasions' in Late Antique and Modern Historiography." In *Das Reich und die Barbaren*, ed. Evangelos Chrysos and Andreas Schwarcz, 87–101. Veröffentlichungen des Instituts für österreichische Geschichtsforschung. Vienna: Böhlau. [= In *Rome's Fall and After*, ed. Walter A. Goffart, 111–132. London: Continuum.]

———. 2006a. "Does the Distant Past Impinge on the Invasion Age Germans?" In *On Barbarian Identity: Critical Approaches to Ethnicity*, ed. Andrew Gillett, 21–37. Turnhout: Brepols. [= 2002. In *From Roman Provinces to Medieval Kingdoms*, ed. Thomas F. X. Noble, 91–109. London: Routledge.]

———. 2006b. *Barbarian Tides: The Migration Age and the Later Roman Empire.* Philadelphia: University of Pennsylvania Press.
Greatrex, Geoffrey. 2000. "Roman Identity in the Sixth Century." In *Ethnicity and Culture in Late Antiquity*, ed. Stephen Mitchell and Geoffrey Greatrex, 267–292. Swansea: Duckworth/The Classical Press of Wales.
Griffith, Sidney H. 2007. *The Church in the Shadow of the Mosque: Christians and Muslims in the World of Islam.* Princeton, NJ: Princeton University Press.
Hall, Edith. 1989. *Inventing the Barbarian: Greek Self-Definition through Tragedy.* Oxford: Clarendon.
Hall, Jonathan. 1997. *Ethnic Identity in Greek Antiquity.* Cambridge: Cambridge University Press.
Halsall, Guy. 2005. "The Barbarian Invasions." In *The New Cambridge Medieval History 1 c. 500–c. 700*, ed. Paul Fouracre, 35–55. Cambridge: Cambridge University Press.
———. 2007. *Barbarian Migrations and the Roman West, 376–568.* Cambridge: Cambridge University Press.
Härke, Heinrich, ed. 2000. *Archaeology, Ideology, and Society: The German Experience.* Frankfurt am Main: P. Lang.
Härke, Heinrich, Stefan Altekamp, David W. Anthony, Bettina Arnold, Stefan Burmeister, Margarita Díaz-Andreu, Pavel M. Dolukhanov, et al. 1998. "Archaeologists and Migrations: A Problem of Attitude? [and Comments and Reply]," *Current Anthropology* 39.1: 19–45.
Heather, Peter. 1991. *Goths and Romans, 332–489.* Oxford: Oxford University Press.
———. 1996. *The Goths.* Cambridge, MA. Harvard University Press.
———. 1998. "Disappearing and Reappearing Tribes." In *Strategies of Distinction: The Construction of Ethnic Communities, 300–800*, ed. W. Pohl and H. Reimitz, 95–111. Leiden: Brill.
———. 1999. "The Barbarian in Late Antiquity: Image, Reality, and Transformation." In *Constructing Identities in Late Antiquity*, ed. Richard Miles, 234–258. London: Routledge.
———. 2006a. *The Fall of the Roman Empire: A New History of Rome and the Barbarians.* Oxford: Oxford University Press.
———. 2006b. "*Foedera* and *foederati* of the Fourth Century." In *From Roman Provinces to Medieval Kingdoms*, ed. Thomas F. X. Noble, 292–308. London: Routledge.
———. 2009. *Empires and Barbarians.* London: Macmillan.
Heather, Peter, and John F. Matthews. 1991. *The Goths in the Fourth Century.* Liverpool: Liverpool University Press.
Honigmann, Ernst. 1929. *Die sieben Klimata und die Poleis Episemoi: Eine Untersuchung zur Geschichte der Geographie und Astrologie im Altertum und Mittelalter.* Heidelberg: Winter.
Horden, Peregrine, and Nicholas Purcell. 2000. *The Corrupting Sea: A Study of Mediterranean History.* Oxford: Wiley Blackwell.
Inglebert, Hervé. 2001. *Interpretatio Christiana: Les mutations des savoirs, cosmographie, géographie, ethnographie, histoire dans l'Antiquité chrétienne (30–360 après J.-C.).* Paris: Institut d'études augustiniennes.
Innes, Matthew. 2007. *An Introduction to Early Medieval Western Europe, 300–900: The Sword, the Plough, and the Book.* London: Routledge.
Ivanov, Sergey. 2008. "Religious Missions." In *The Cambridge History of the Byzantine Empire c. 500–1492*, ed. Jonathan Shepard, 305–332. Cambridge: Cambridge University Press.

Johnson, Aaron P. 2006. *Ethnicity and Argument in Eusebius' Praeparatio Evangelica.* Oxford: Oxford University Press.

Jones, Arnold H. M. 1964. *The Later Roman Empire 284–602. A Social, Economic, and Administrative Survey.* Oxford: Basil Blackwell.

Kaegi, Walter E., Jr. 1968. *Byzantium and the Decline of Rome.* Princeton, NJ: Princeton University Press.

Kelley, Nicole. 2006. *Knowledge and Religious Authority in the Pseudo-Clementines.* Tübingen: Mohr Siebeck.

Kossinna, Gustaf. 1911. *Die Herkunft der Germanen: Zur Methode der Siedlungsarchäologie.* Würzburg: C. Kabitzsch.

———. 1928. *Ursprung und Verbreitung der Germanen in Vor- und Frühgeschichtlicher Zeit.* Leipzig: C. Kabitzsch.

Krebs, Christopher B. 2005. *Negotio Germaniae: Tacitus' Germania und Enea Silvio Piccolomini, Giannantonio Campano, Conrad Celtis und Heinrich Bebel.* Göttingen: Vandenhoeck and Ruprecht.

Laistner, M. L. W. 1941. "The Western Church and Astrology during the Early Middle Ages," *Harvard Theological Review* 34.4: 251–275.

Lee, A. D. 1993. *Information and Frontiers: Roman Foreign Relations in Late Antiquity.* Cambridge: Cambridge University Press.

Lenski, Noel. 2008. "Captivity, Slavery, and Cultural Exchange between Rome and the Germans from the First to the Seventh Century CE." In *Invisible Citizens: Captives and Their Consequences,* ed. Catherine M. Cameron, 80–109. Salt Lake City: University of Utah Press.

Liebeschuetz, J. H. W. G. 2001. *The Decline and Fall of the Roman City.* Oxford: Oxford University Press.

———. 2006. "Cities, Taxes, and the Accommodation of the Barbarians." In *From Roman Provinces to Medieval Kingdoms,* ed. Thomas F. X. Noble, 309–323. London: Routledge.

———. 2007. "Warlords and Landlords." In *A Companion to the Roman Army,* ed. Paul Erdkamp, 479–494. Oxford: Wiley-Blackwell.

Long, A. A. 1982. "Astrology: Arguments Pro and Contra." In *Science and Speculation: Studies in Hellenistic Theory and Practice,* ed. Jonathan Barnes, 165–192. Cambridge: Cambridge University Press.

Lozovsky, Natalia. 2008. "Maps and Panegyrics: Roman Geo-Ethnographical Rhetoric in Late Antiquity and the Middle Ages." In *Cartography in Antiquity and the Middle Ages: Fresh Perspectives, New Methods,* ed. Richard J. A. Talbert and Richard W. Unger. Leiden: Brill.

Maas, Michael. 1992. "Ethnicity, Orthodoxy, and Community in Salvian of Marseilles." In *Fifth-Century Gaul: A Crisis of Identity?* ed. J. Drinkwater and H. Elton, 275–284. Cambridge: Cambridge University Press.

———. 1995. "Fugitives and Ethnography in Priscus of Panium," *Byzantine and Modern Greek Studies* 19: 146–160.

———. 2002. "*Mores et Moenia*: Ethnography and the Decline of Urban Constitutional Autonomy in Late Antiquity." In *Integration und Herrschaft: Ethnische Identitäten und soziale Organisation im Frühmittelalter,* ed. Walter Pohl and Max Diesenberger, 25–35. Vienna: R. Rohe.

———. 2003. "Delivered from Their Ancient Customs: Christianity and the Question of Cultural Change in Early Byzantine Ethnography." In *Conversion in Late Antiquity and the Early Middle Ages,* ed. Kenneth Mills and Anthony Grafton, 152–188. Rochester: University of Rochester Press.

———. 2007. "Strabo and Procopius: Classical Geography for a Christian Empire." In *From Rome to Constantinople: Studies in Honour of Averil Cameron*, ed. Hagit Amirav and Bas ter Haar Romeny, 67–83. Late Antique History and Religion 1. Leuven: Peeters.

Mathisen, Ralph. 2006. "*Peregrini, Barbari*, and *Cives Romani*: Concepts of Citizenship and the Legal Identity of Barbarians in the Later Roman Empire," *American Historical Review* 111.4: 1011–1040.

McCormick, Michael. 2001. *Origins of the European Economy: Communications and Commerce, A.D. 300–900*. Cambridge: Cambridge University Press.

Millar, Fergus. 1993. "Hagar, Ishmael, Josephus, and the Origins of Islam," *Journal of Jewish Studies* 44.1: 23–45.

———. 1998. "Ethnic Identity in the Roman Near East, 325–450: Language, Religion, and Culture," *Mediterranean Archaeology* 11: 158–176.

Mitchell, Stephen, and Geoffrey Greatrex, eds. 2000. *Ethnicity and Culture in Late Antiquity*. London: The Classical Press of Wales.

Momigliano, A. D. 1966. "Gibbon's Contribution to Historical Method." In *Studies in Historiography*, 40–55. New York: Garland.

Müller, Klaus Erich. 1980. *Geschichte der antiken Ethnographie und ethnologischen Theoriebildung: Von den Anfängen bis auf die byzantinischen Historiographen*. Wiesbaden: F. Steiner.

Murray, Alexander Callander. 2002. "Reinhard Wenskus on 'Ethnogenesis,' Ethnicity, and the Origin of the Franks." In *On Barbarian Identity: Critical Approaches to Ethnicity*, ed. Andrew Gillett, 39–68. SEM 4. Turnhout: Brepols.

Musset, Lucien. 1975. *The Germanic Invasions: The Making of Europe, AD 400–600*. University Park: Pennsylvania State University Press.

Noble, Thomas F. X. 2006. *From Roman Provinces to Medieval Kingdoms*. London: Routledge.

Obolensky, Dimitri. 1974. *The Byzantine Commonwealth: Eastern Europe, 500–1453*. History of Civilisation. London: Weidenfeld and Nicolson.

Opelt, I., and W. Speyer. 1967. "Barbar," *Jahrbuch für Antike und Christentum* 10: 251–290.

Peterson, Erik. 1959. "Das Problem des Nationalismus im alten Christentum." In *Frühkirche, Judentum, und Gnosis: Studien und Untersuchungen*, ed. Erik Peterson, 51–63. Freiburg: Herder.

Pohl, Walter. 2000. *Die Germanen*. München: Oldenbourg.

———. 2001. "Conclusion: The Transformation of Frontiers." In *The Transformation of Frontiers: From Late Antiquity to the Carolingians*, ed. Walter Pohl, Ian Wood, and Helmut Reimitz, 247–260. Leiden: Brill.

———. 2002. "Ethnicity, Theory, and Tradition: A Response." In *On Barbarian Identity: Critical Approaches to Ethnicity*, ed. Andrew Gillett, 221–240. SEM 4. Turnhout: Brepols.

———. 2008. "Rome and the Barbarians in the Fifth Century." In *Antiquité Tardive 16: L'Empire des Theodoses*, 93–101. Paris: Brepols.

———. 2009. "Archaeology of Identity: Introduction." In *Archäologie der Identität*, ed. W. Pohl and M. Mehofer. Forschungen zur Geschichte des Mittelalters 16. Vienna: VÖAW.

Pohl, Walter, and Helmut Reimitz, eds. 1998. *Strategies of Distinction: The Construction of Ethnic Communities 300–800*. Leiden: Brill.

Poliakov, Léon. 1977. *The Aryan Myth: A History of Racist and Nationalist Ideas in Europe*. New York: Barnes and Noble.

Poulter, Andrew. 2004. "Cataclysm on the Lower Danube: The Destruction of a Complex Roman Landscape." In *Landscapes of Change: Rural Evolutions in Late Antiquity and the Early Middle Ages*, ed. Neil Christie, 223–254. Burlington, VT: Ashgate.

Riedinger, Utto. 1956. *Die heilige Schrift im Kampf der griechischen Kirche gegen die Astrologie, von Origenes bis Johannes von Damaskos: Studien zur dogmengeschichte und zur Geschichte der Astrologie.* Innsbruck: Universitätsverlag Wagner.

Rosen, Klaus. 2002. *Die Völkerwanderung.* Munich: C. H. Beck Verlag.

Sarris, Peter. 2004. "The Origins of the Manorial Economy: New Insights from Late Antiquity," *English Historical Review* 119: 279–311.

———. 2006. *Economy and Society in the Age of Justinian.* Cambridge: Cambridge University Press.

Sasse, Christoph. 1958. *Die Constitutio Antoniniana.* Wiesbaden: Harrassowitz.

———. 1962. "Literaturübersicht zur Constitutio Antininiana," *Journal of Juristic Papyrology* 14: 329–366.

Scott, James M. 1995. *Paul and the Nations: The Old Testament and Jewish Background of Paul's Mission to the Nations with Special Reference to the Destination of Galatians.* Wissenschaftliche Untersuchungen zum Neuen Testament, 84. Tübingen: Mohr Siebeck.

Shaw, Brent. 1982–83. "'Eaters of Flesh, Drinkers of Milk': The Ancient Mediterranean Ideology of the Pastoral Nomad," *Ancient Society* 13–14: 5–31.

———. 2008. "After Rome: Transformations of the Early Mediterranean World," *New Left Review* 51: 89–114.

Shennan, Stephen. 1989. "Introduction: Archaeological Approaches to Cultural Identity." In *Archaeological Approaches to Cultural Identity*, ed. Stephen Shennan, 1–32. London: Routledge.

Shepard, Jonathan. 2006a. "The Byzantine Commonwealth 1000–1550." In *The Cambridge History of Christianity, Vol. V: Eastern Christianity*, ed. Michael Angold, 3–52. Cambridge: Cambridge University Press.

———. 2006b. "Byzantium's Overlapping Circles." In *Proceedings of the 21st International Congress of Byzantine Studies, London, August 21–26, 2006*, Vol. I: Plenary Papers, 15–56. Aldershot: Ashgate.

Sherwin-White, Adrian Nicholas. 1972. "The Roman Citizenship: A Survey of Its Development into a World Franchise." In *Aufstieg und Niedergang der römischen Welt: Geschichte und Kultur Roms im Spiegel der neueren Forschung*, ed. Joseph Vogt, Hildegard Temporini, and Wolfgang Haase, 1.2:23–58. Berlin: Walter de Gruyter.

———. 1973. *The Roman Citizenship.* 2nd ed. Oxford: Clarendon.

Sklenár, Karel. 1983. *Archaeology in Central Europe: The First 500 Years.* New York: Leicester University Press.

Ste. Croix, G. E. M. de. 1983. *The Class Struggle in the Ancient Greek World from the Archaic Age to the Arab Conquests.* 2nd ed. Ithaca, NY: Cornell University Press.

Stickler, Timo. 2007. "The Foederati." In *A Companion to the Roman Army*, ed. Paul Erdkamp, 495–514. Oxford: Wiley-Blackwell.

Taylor, Isaac. 1906. *The Origin of the Aryans: An Account of the Prehistoric Ethnology and Civilisation of Europe.* 3rd ed. London: Scott.

Thollard, Patrick. 1987. *Barbarie et Civilisation chez Strabon: Étude critique des Livres III et IV de la Géographie.* Paris: Presses Universitaires Franche-Comté.

Thomas, Richard F. 1982. *Lands and Peoples in Roman Poetry: The Ethnographical Tradition.* Cambridge: Cambridge Philological Society.

Tilley, C. 1978. "Migration in Modern European History." In *Human Migration: Patterns and Policies*, ed. William H. McNeill and R. Adams, 48–74. Bloomington: Indiana University Press.

Traina, Giusto. 2001. "Le gentes d'oriente fra identità e integrazione," *Antiquité Tardive* 9: 71–80.

Trüdinger, Karl. 1918. *Studien zur Geschichte der griechisch-römischen Ethnographie.* Basel: Birkhäuser.

Veit, Ulrich. 1989. "Ethnic Concepts in German Prehistory: A Case Study on the Relationship between Cultural Identity and Archaeological Objectivity." In *Archaeological Approaches to Cultural Identity*, ed. Stephen Shennan, 35–56. London: Routledge.

———. 1996. "Kossina, Gustaf." In *The Oxford Companion to Archaeology*, ed. Brian Fagan, 376–377. Oxford: Oxford University Press.

———. 2002. "Gustaf Kossinna and His Concept of a National Archaeology." In *Archaeology, Ideology, and Society: The German Experience*, ed. H. Härke, 40–59. Frankfurt am Main: P. Lang.

von See, Klaus. 1981. "Der Germane als Barbar," *Jahrbuch fur international Germanistik* 13: 42–73.

Ward-Perkins, Bryan. 2005. *The Fall of Rome and the End of Civilization.* Oxford: Oxford University Press.

Weiler, Ingomar. 1965. "Orbis Romanus und Barbaricum," *Carnuntum Jahrbuch* 8: 34–39.

Wenskus, Reinhard. 1961. *Stammesbildung und Verfassung: Das Werden der frühmittelalterlichen Gentes.* Köln: Böhlau.

Whitehead, Neil L. 1992. "Tribes Make States and States Make Tribes: Warfare and the Creation of Colonial Tribes and States in Northeastern South America." In *War in the Tribal Zone: Expanding States and Indigenous Warfare*, ed. R. Brian Ferguson and Neil L. Whitehead, 127–150. Santa Fe, NM: School of American Research Press.

Whittaker, C. R. 2004. *Rome and Its Frontiers: The Dynamics of Empire.* London: Routledge.

———. 2003. "The Use and Abuse of Immigrants in the Later Roman Empire." In *Rome and Its Frontiers: The Dynamics of Empire*, ed. C. R. Whittaker, 199–218. London: Routledge.

Whittow, Mark. 2003. "Decline and Fall? Studying Long-Term Change in the East." In *Theory and Practice in Late Antique Archaeology*, ed. Luke Lavan and William Bowden, 404–423. Leiden: Brill.

Wickham, Chris. 2005. *Framing the Early Middle Ages: Europe and the Mediterranean, 400–800.* Oxford: Oxford University Press.

Wolfram, Herwig. 1997. *The Roman Empire and Its Germanic Peoples.* Berkeley: University of California Press.

———. 2006a. "*Origo et religio*: Ethnic Traditions and Literature in Early Medieval Texts." In *From Roman Provinces to Medieval Kingdoms*, ed. Thomas F. X. Noble, 70–90. London: Routledge.

———. 2006b. "Gothic History as Historical Ethnography." In *From Roman Provinces to Medieval Kingdoms*, ed. Thomas F. X. Noble, 43–69. London: Routledge.

Wood, Ian. 2008. "Barbarians, Historians, and the Construction of National Identities," *Journal of Late Antiquity* 1.1: 61–81.

CHAPTER 3

THE BALKANS

CRAIG H. CALDWELL III
Appalachian State University

"BALKAN" is a word that would be foreign to a learned visitor from Late Antiquity; this archaic Turkish common noun for "mountain" postdates him by many centuries. If you gave him a reference book containing a passage like this one, however, he would certainly grasp where you were talking about: "The Balkans are the ultimate mountain world . . . a tangled network of mountain ranges and valleys . . . the essential character of the region is difficult to define. The common feature is not linguistic. . . . The unity is not political. . . . The region is a kind of minuscule universe."[1] Illyricum, the late antique region that coincides with the modern Balkans, merits much of the same description. Almost 70 percent of its area is elevated, Latin and Greek were used in different subregions, and the landscape is full of niches—some of which might reach down to the underworld, given poetic license.[2] The easy recognition and definition of Illyricum has not been an advantage in the study of Late Antiquity. Amid recent progress in understanding the ancient and medieval worlds in terms of the Mediterranean landscape, most of the Balkan peninsula has escaped consideration because of its perceived isolation. The goal of this chapter is thus to offer a perspective on the late antique Balkans through the interaction of landscape elements (mountains, rivers, plains) and how late-Roman and post-Roman people lived there. "Vika," the prehistoric mammoth, for example, or rather the layers of sediment that contained her bones near Viminacium (Kostolac) are an important part of the history of the lowlands.[3] Following this approach, geological and topographical details overshadow some events of political history, but the result aids in understanding the kinds of events that happened in Illyricum.

To locate Illyricum, the map is both an aid and a bit of a trap, at first simply demarcating the region between Italy and Asia that was administered by a particular late Roman official, the praetorian prefect of Illyricum. Then the going becomes difficult. The government's grand division into three dioceses (Pannonia, Moesia, Thrace; see figure 3.1) rapidly gives way to clusters of provinces with recondite names: Noricum along the River, Inland Noricum, Upper Pannonia (or Pannonia I), Lower Pannonia (or Pannonia II), Savia, Dalmatia, and Valeria; Dacia along the River, Inland Dacia, Upper Moesia, Dardania, Praevalitana, New Epirus, Old Epirus, and Macedonia; Scythia, Lower Moesia, Thrace, Haemus Mountains, Rhodope, and Europe (see figure 3.2).[4] (The modern mapmaker has it no better; Illyricum spans parts of modern Austria, Hungary, Slovenia, Croatia, Bosnia-Herzegovina, Serbia, Montenegro, the Republic of Macedonia, Albania, Greece, Romania, Bulgaria, and Turkey.) Many scholarly pages have described how each of these places came to be, and some of the divisions are still not entirely without controversy.[5]

Theodor Mommsen, the great German assembler of inscriptions (his third volume of the *Corpus Inscriptionum Latinarum* contains Illyricum) and ancient historian, grasped history through multitudes of organized details, but he also

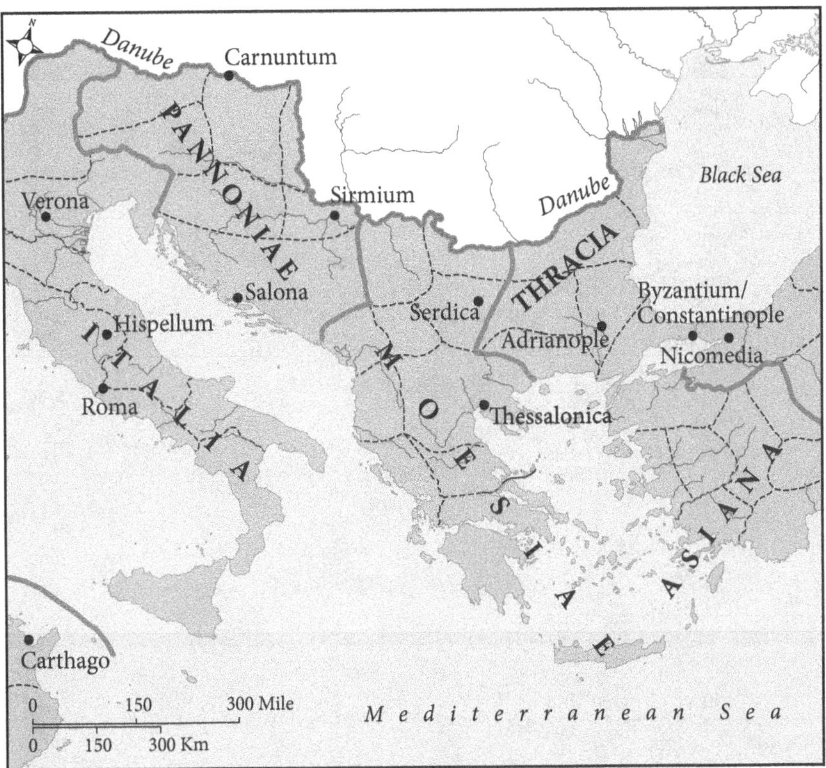

Figure 3.1. Late Roman Balkans, divided into governmental dioceses.

famously used an arboreal simile in his university lectures to imagine the provinces of the Roman empire: "a mighty tree, the main stem of which, in the course of its decay, is surrounded by vigorous offshoots pushing their way upward."[6] This survey of the Illyrian offshoot does not permit the study of every leaf or inch of bark, but it must identify Rome as its parent tree. Roman generals and governors united the Danubian-Balkan lands and peoples into the conceptual region of Illyricum, which embraced a far greater territory than any inhabited by somewhat ambiguous Illyrians.[7] Furthermore, the major late antique institutions of the Balkans, the army and the Christian Church, drew upon a Roman or Greco-Roman root. Exploring three diverse locations (Sirmium, Salona, and Odessos) in different parts of the Balkans provides a local context for the processes that affected the region. Beginning with the physical geography, each section then considers the manmade environment, the contributions of the soldier and churchman, and the evidence for newcomers and change over time.[8]

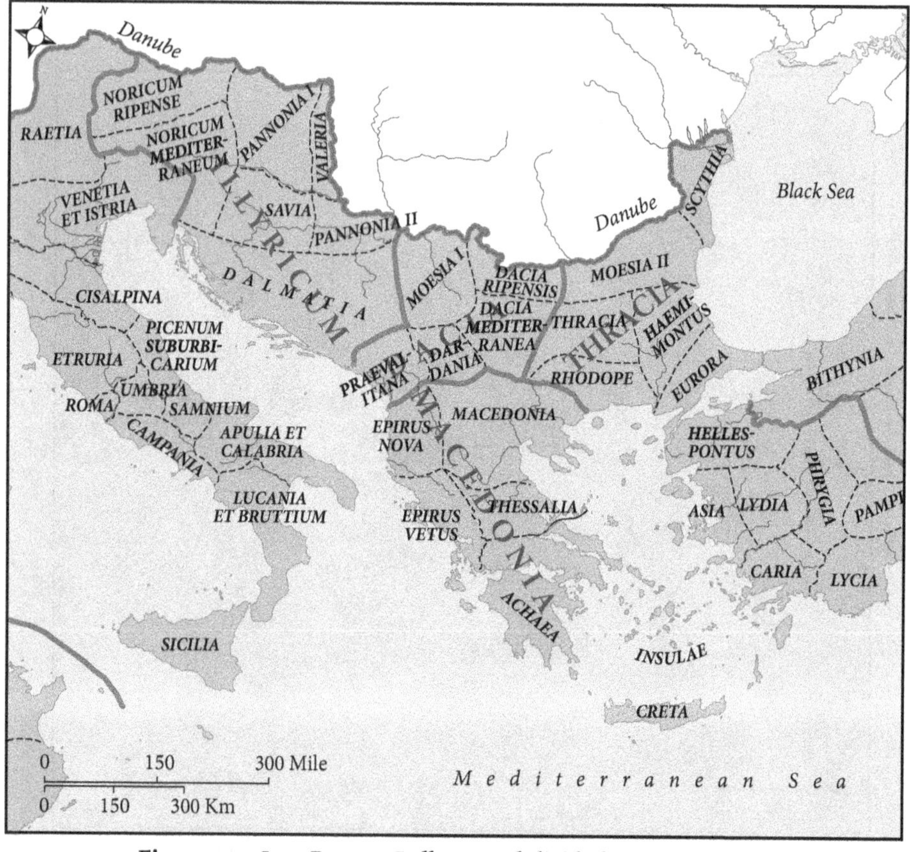

Figure 3.2. Late Roman Balkans, subdivided into provinces.

Pannonia

In the late fourth century, the anonymous author of a rather mercantile geography of the Roman empire (entitled *Expositio totius mundi et gentium*) described what is now the north-central Balkans: "The area of Pannonia is a land rich in everything, in crops and livestock and trade and partly also in slaves. It is also always the residence of the emperors. Sirmium [is among] its very great cities."[9] The landscape can help to explain the late antique thumbnail sketch. Sirmium (Sremska Mitrovica) lies on the southern edge of the Pannonian Plain, which is the legacy of a giant prehistoric sea from the age of the first saber-toothed cats. When that Pannonian Sea drained through the Iron Gates gorge about 600,000 years ago, it left behind miles of sediment crisscrossed by a network of rivers. Sirmium does not adjoin the Danube, the largest of these rivers, but lies along the Savus (Sava) River that parallels it, and therein was its first indispensability to Romans. The Savus valley provided the legions of Augustus with a vital line of east-west communication as they moved north from Dalmatia on the Adriatic, and the Roman generals anchored their control by fortifying Siscia (Sisak) in the west and Sirmium in the east. In this part of northern Illyricum, the plains are fertile, but the rivers determine their use, and the Savus is meandering and wide, frequently flooding and changing course. Caught in the interaction of its tributary rivers and the old seabed, the Savus has wandered over the centuries and left oxbows and marshes across Pannonia. Using and crossing the river was essential, and archaeologists have uncovered a rough port district of Sirmium, as well as bridge piers. The changeable Savus has apparently obliterated the traces of Sirmium's two islands, Casia and Carbonaria, however.[10]

Like Pannonia as a whole, the attributes of Sirmium's location brought it to empirewide prominence only at the beginning of Late Antiquity.[11] During the first and second centuries, Sirmium had receded from its initial importance in favor of legionary forts on the Danube itself, such as strategic Singidunum (Belgrade), fifty miles to the east. No governor or legion was stationed in Sirmium. When renewed warfare against trans-Danubian peoples made defending Illyricum vital to the safety of the Mediterranean core of the empire, however, emperors began to reside in Sirmium. The road network was the determining factor: Sirmium was at the nexus of roads that spanned the vulnerable Pannonian Plain, the vital connection to Italy via the Savus valley and the Alpine passes, southern roads that bore mineral wealth out of the mountains, and the great southeastern route to Macedonia, Thrace, and the Bosphorus. Pannonia was generally a province on the way to other important places, dating back to the incorporation of the Amber Road and Celtic commercial centers (*oppida*) into the Roman north-south highway in western Illyricum. The east-west passages across Pannonia, principally along river valleys like the Savus and the Dravus (Drava) to its north, had been anchored by the monumental urbanization projects of the early second century, which had elevated dozens of towns to the ranks of Roman colonies or *municipia*. Here were the local elites who embraced Roman customs and aided imperial governance; the interior of western Illyricum had assumed Roman form along these arteries. Foreign enemies using these same roads brought about a military crisis that revealed Sirmium as a linchpin. Positioned at a vital crossroads, Sirmium earned mention in the *Antonine Itinerary* as the urban equal of Aquileia, Nicomedia, Antioch, and Alexandria.[12]

Although Sirmium was initially the distant winter base where Marcus Aurelius could have died, it received significant imperial investment in the third and fourth centuries to make it a renowned residence and one of the largest cities in the Balkans. For what the civic aristocracy lost when a palace took over a municipal administrative building, for example, they received increased opportunities for promotion and profit in the emperor's presence. Looking back, late antique authors recalled a profusion of emperors *from* Sirmium and its surrounding towns in this very period, including Decius (249–251), Aurelian (270–275), Probus (276–282), and Maximian (285–305). Just as Illyricum emerged as an essential military theater, Illyrian officers—especially natives of Pannonia—became indispensable in the imperial service. The legions had assumed regional identities and grown Illyrian roots in the preceding decades, and in the third and early fourth centuries, they fought hard to place the purple on their generals' shoulders and defend their corner of the empire. Stories told about the deaths of two emperors at Sirmium illustrate this age of soldier-emperors. Claudius (II) "Gothicus" (268–270) was an Illyrian but not Pannonian, and he won his great victory over the invading Goths in Naissus (Niš) in Moesia, southeast of Sirmium. Yet Sirmium was his final headquarters because it was the hinge between the western menace of the Alamanni and the eastern threat of more raids across the lower Danube.[13]

Probus came to Sirmium and promptly assigned his army to tackle the Savus marshes. He is supposed to have planned a great canal to recover more of the fertile plain and help the citizens of his hometown. This difficult task incensed the soldiers, and a mob of them chased the emperor into another of his projects, a high "ironclad" watchtower that overlooked Sirmium, and killed him. While Claudius died in the strategic center of his theater of operations, the tale of Probus' efforts to improve his native city indicates what could be done and the dangers of alienating the essential constituency of Illyricum and the empire. Along with its higher profile as a frequent imperial residence, Sirmium gained a mint in the third century, which must have assisted construction there. Credit is given to the tetrarchic emperors (Diocletian, Maximian, Constantius, Galerius), all natives of Illyricum, for the greatest period of urban expansion in the city's history.[14] Archaeological finds suggest that the city gained an imperial palace at its center, a hippodrome adjacent to it, large new warehouses, and a bath complex, and its total enclosed area was almost 100 hectares. Significantly, the enormous amount of construction in the city, as in the other new provincial capitals at Savaria, Sopianae, and Siscia, was a product of state expenditure redirected away from the first generation of Roman cities on the Danube itself.[15] Sirmium was the greatest fourth-century beneficiary because it hosted not only its own provincial governor but also one of the praetorian prefects and the master of cavalry for Illyricum at various times. The scale of construction is even more remarkable in light of the poor supply of local stone and the extraordinary (for Pannonia) use of tiles to produce buildings of recognized imperial caliber.

Regardless of whether Probus succeeded in draining any marshes, Sirmium also had numerous suburbs in the nearby Savus valley that were linked to the city by the highway, and sizable vineyards grew outside the city through state support or private initiative. Along with the urban prosperity inaugurated by the Illyrian emperors, farmers and ranchers exploited the wealth of Pannonian land in a parallel boom. Millennia before the Romans arrived, winds had deposited fine-grained loess soil that was well suited to growing grain and raising sheep. Roman control over the Danube and tributaries like the Savus made exports to the East secure and profitable, and large rural estates multiplied across the plains. As one of the great landowners in the region, the imperial fisc benefited from the fourth-century prosperity, but private citizens also built farmsteads and villas. When retired imperial officials and military officers returned home to develop and manage estates in central Pannonia, their efforts were effectively another kind of government investment in a local golden age.[16] The father of the future emperors Valentinian (364–375) and Valens (364–378) acquired property west of Sirmium near the city of Cibalae in just this fashion.[17] Some villas had amenities like baths and fortifications that echoed those of Pannonian cities, and their owners demonstrated independence from the urban markets so long as the boom lasted. In Sirmium and the other new capitals, Diocletian's new governors were keeping better records and placing new obligations upon wealthy citizens who appeared on their radar, and their supervision included both the lowlands and the highlands.

Even this Pannonia of plains and rivers was marked by its mountains. The best hillsides for vineyards were north of Sirmium on the slopes of the Alma Mons (Fruška Gora), where Probus was said to have ordered planting, and Mount Kosmaj to the southwest was rich in another treasure, argentiferous lead ore. Both low mountains had been islands in the Pannonian Sea, and they remained islands of unusual rock on the plain of loamy loess soil. In the case of Kosmaj, these rocks were incredibly productive, with about 1 million metric tons of ancient slag indicating the scale of the lead and silver that Roman miners extracted. By the third century, the Kosmaj mines and the others in the northern Balkans, which included iron mines in Noricum (Austria) and gold mines in Dalmatia (Bosnia), were under direct imperial control. Although the emperors encouraged urbanization, the imperial administration kept mining centers separate from the growing cities and generally "unmunicipalized," restricting the territories of the mines to the enrichment of the fisc. Even so, the Illyrian urban elites had long been the personnel who oversaw the collection of customs duties on the extracted metal, and at least one fourth-century emperor reminded them that service in these procuratorships was necessary if they aspired to greater imperial favor.[18]

The emperors obliged the decurions of Singidunum to tend the Kosmaj mines, but the metalworking industry depended on its larger neighbor Sirmium. To the east and south, Naissus and Viminacium (Kostolac) played similar roles in their local mining economies. When the emperor Licinius (308–324) sought to win and reassure allies in Illyricum during a period of civil war, he bestowed Sirmian silver bowls inscribed with his name. Sirmium was Licinius' favorite residence, and when Constantine (306–337) conquered Pannonia from him, his own long stays in Sirmium may have been efforts to calm a city that remembered his rival's generosity. For Constantine, the mints took precedence over the smiths. The Constantinian coinage from the mint of Sirmium was silver in name only, however, and thus was intended to impress its recipients with its size; its base alloy would not have passed muster in non-Roman markets. Groups of trans-Danubian peoples had been an important audience for pure Roman silver, which they accepted in return for goods and slaves at towns along the Danube. Constantine's unwillingness to mint significant silver coinage at Sirmium or other Illyrian mints may relate to his frequent military expeditions across the Danube and the compensation of his non-Roman allies by reception into Pannonia.[19]

The peoples across the river from Pannonia were usually a threat to Sirmium only insofar as they might raid its hinterland. Periods of peace and trade had advertised Pannonian abundance. War bands of Sarmatians, as the late Romans called them, sought the same things in Pannonian territory as in their neighbors' lands: portable wealth and prisoners. Emperors had an established balancing act to follow, juggling the punishment of raids with decisive military force, along with the cultivation and preservation of client leaders and their followers. As the Romans defined groups into tribes as part of foreign policy, the settlement of some of them in Illyricum after their defeat by Rome or as part of a treaty was possible and sometimes advantageous. Client "kings" who became too strong were dangerous instigators of wars, but exiled tribes were also sources of instability that emperors controlled by permitting immigration. Following a war in the late third century, Galerius (293–311) may have used settled populations of Carpi to make drainage improvements like those attributed to Probus.[20] Constantine fought wars against the Sarmatians and then against the Goths who threatened the security of his Sarmatian allies, and after the emperor settled several groups of Sarmatians in Pannonia, western Illyricum enjoyed two decades without significant external disturbance. With his victory apparently complete, Constantine left Sirmium and Illyricum for the East, and as in the rest of the empire, his promotion of Christianity outlasted all other legacies.

The Christian Church in Sirmium had formed in a pattern familiar to many other Pannonian cities. The important sediment here was the blood of martyrs, of whom St. Irenaeus possesses the most reliable *acta*. According to the preserved narrative, Irenaeus was a young bishop who faced the new administrative apparatus installed in Sirmium by the tetrarchs. In 304, the governor of Pannonia sentenced Irenaeus to be drowned for his disobedience to the imperial command to sacrifice, and the scene of the execution was to be the Pons Basentis over the Savus. Irenaeus is said to have sought beheading as an additional punishment, which was done outside the city near the bridge, and the soldiers then dumped his remains into the river.[21] Excavations have revealed a martyrium within a Christian cemetery on the south bank of the Savus, and this shrine may have catalyzed the urban churches that arose in the later fourth century. Another famous martyr of Sirmium was St. Synerotas, a gardener whose name is frequently found in funerary inscriptions in both Latin and Greek. The cemeteries of Sirmium are the hotspots of Greek inscriptions in Pannonia, which suggests that the Christian population in this large city included significant numbers of easterners. The nearby cities of Cibalae and Singidunum had their own martyrs who were said to have died with Irenaeus in the same persecution from Sirmium. Constantine's victory in civil war just to the west of Sirmium precluded any further anti-Christian measures, and decades passed before the see of Sirmium rose to empire-wide prominence. At the Council of Sirmium in the midst of another civil war, the bishop Photinus of Sirmium was accused of heresy by neighboring churchmen, and the emperor Constantius II's officials were official witnesses to his examination in 351. This theological debate required an imperially guaranteed solution because of its location; Constantine's son Constantius would not permit ecclesiastical disagreement to divide such an important part of the empire. Moreover, Photinus is another example of an eastern immigrant to Sirmium and of Illyrian bilingualism; he came from Galatia and published his "heresy" in both Latin and Greek. The proximity of emperors and their families in Pannonia also influenced the election of Sirmian bishops, as when the empress Justina opposed Ambrose of Milan over the successor to the bishop Germinius. Ambrose's previous career as an imperial official had brought him to Sirmium before, and his victory in confirming his ally Anemius as the new bishop there demonstrated the close connections between ecclesiastical and administrative networks in an important city. But even as Sirmium earned heightened attention in theological disputes, its urban fabric and population faced a crisis of negligence.[22]

When the Pannonian brothers Valentinian and Valens became emperors in the later fourth century, no new golden age of imperial expenditure for Sirmium occurred. They divided the empire just down the road from Sirmium, but neither ruler decided to reside in Pannonia. Sirmium's centrality was a liability when the Roman empire had two other centers of gravity, and ruling the empire in thirds, as Constantine's sons had attempted to do, had proven unstable. So while Valentinian spent significant amounts of money on the Danube fortifications and their garrisons, judging from the enormous issues of Valentinianic coins recovered in the region, the lack of new construction indicates that the administrative centers such as Sirmium did not share in the largesse. Valentinian's building program on the frontier, coupled with unwise appointments to direct the construction, contributed to the beginning of a new war with the Sarmatians, who crossed into Pannonia on their own punitive raid. Their sudden arrival provides a remarkable snapshot of the state of Sirmium and its surroundings. The daughter of Constantius II, who was engaged to Valentinian's son Gratian, was staying at an imperial villa near Sirmium when the Sarmatians came, and she evaded capture only through the intervention of the local governor and his provision of official rapid transportation to Sirmium. Sarmatian invaders disrupted the harvest, and the rural estates could no longer maintain their independence: concessions to unwelcome guests or flight to the cities was necessary.[23]

The situation in the greatest walled city, which had enjoyed a long period of peace, was similarly dire. Petronius Probus, the praetorian prefect, had been an effective collector of Valentinian's taxes, but the revenues he had gathered did not maintain Sirmium's defensive fortifications. Like the emperor's future daughter-in-law at the villa, he had arranged for imperial horses to take him to safety, but Probus heard that the city's population would follow him if he fled. Their refuges would have been in the nearby mountains, where they would wait while the unopposed Sarmatians looted the civic and rural wealth of the Pannonian plains. At this juncture, Probus still had a reserve to draw on: the funds assembled for a theater in Sirmium, which must have been the decurions' project. Deciding to remain in Sirmium, the prefect diverted these resources to repairing the city walls and clearing out its defensive ditches, and he reassigned a unit of archers from a nearby fort to protect the city. With improvisation on this occasion, Sirmium could defend itself as an obstacle to raiders. The emperor Valentinian himself arrived in Pannonia to command a retaliatory campaign, but his presence was said to have been ill omened. The tetrarchic city center of Sirmium was struck by lightning, damaging part of the palace, the decurions' meeting house, and the forum. Valentinian's death while negotiating with allies of the Sarmatians was unfortunate for the security of the frontier, and it also marks the end of the injections of new bronze coinage into northern Illyricum. His reign had not returned the splendor of other Illyrian emperors to Pannonia, however, and his final tour of the region had noted many consequences of decreased imperial investments in the cities.[24]

The imperial decisions that followed confirmed earlier trends, but the local situation became increasingly ambiguous. The closure of the mint of Sirmium by Theodosius I signaled a further pullback from expenditure there, and the settlement of more trans-Danubian peoples in western Illyricum was a nonmonetary way of balancing the imperial checkbook: land and its revenues in exchange for loyal military service. No record exists of the reception of "barbarians" in Sirmium and its environs, but scattered references to Pannonian refugees suggest that the countryside lost its most prominent (and mobile) residents as the empire restricted its attention to the cities. Rural law and order was at best devolved onto local magnates, whether newcomers or villa owners, and at worst nonexistent.[25] On a more modest scale, Jerome writes about the state of his hometown of Stridon, probably on the Dalmatian-Pannonian border, in conflicting ways that reflect the chaos of the period. Jerome alternately describes Stridon as completely destroyed with all the inhabitants dead or, later, as a place where he might sell the dilapidated little farm he had inherited.[26] The general outlook for Pannonia was pessimistic, with Pannonian devastation becoming a catchphrase, but the continual siege there was one of mind-set rather than a universal experience.[27] Outside the cities, a dislocated person's situation and status were fluid and confusing, which the imperial administration recognized in one extant law.[28] Sirmium and some of its population certainly persevered, which indicates that the plains still supplied it with food, and other goods might still flow along the roads, albeit with greater friction due to a lack of Roman maintenance and security. But this economized Pannonia meant the eclipse of urban life in smaller cities such as Savaria, where its martyrs' bones fled to Italy with its prominent citizens.[29] Only in Sirmium did a Pannonian bishop merit mention by name in the fifth century, and the formal cession of large parts of Pannonia to the eastern emperor from his western cousin centered on the control of Sirmium in the midst of the Huns rather than "making the Danube Roman."[30]

Pannonia's strategic position was a liability in the fifth-century empire, and a diminished Sirmium encapsulated what was left of the region's usefulness in the sixth century. As the imperial government retreated from active administration, the northern provinces closest to the Danube served as a corridor for irregular traffic: armed groups called Vandals and Goths marching toward the Alpine passes into Italy. Imperial settlements of Gothic leaders and their followers in Pannonia might have shielded Italy and the western imperial capital at Ravenna for a time, but the provincial situation did not reach a new equilibrium.[31] If the "enemy Pannonians" mentioned by Jerome can be taken at face value, local populations joined in the use of extralegal methods to gain goods and land.[32] The departure of the Goths was followed by the ascent of the Huns, whose influence was first evident not at the court of Attila across the Danube, but in a cemetery west of Sirmium. Hunnic nobles had been interred near Margum (Dubravica), and rumors spread that the local bishop had disturbed their graves in search of treasure.[33] This incident was part of the casus belli for Attila's invasion, but the presence of these important Huns in southern Pannonia indicates the earlier inclusion of the region in the Hunnic world centered on the Pannonian plains. The Huns' familiarity with the Savus valley enabled Attila's success in overcoming the walls of Pannonian cities and even in gaining control of Sirmium itself. But this new order, though regionally rooted, proved fleeting. Whatever anchor Sirmium might have provided for a Hunnic empire evaporated after Attila's death, and Pannonia returned to the nominal control of the eastern Roman empire. Sidonius Apollinaris praised his father-in-law, the western emperor Avitus (455–456), for successful campaigns in the Pannonian provinces, but imperial interests were centered on safeguarding Italy and Gaul, and Sirmium remained too far from civilization. From the perspective of the sixth century, Procopius recalled that after Attila, none but Justinian (527–565) was worthy of mentioning in western Illyricum.[34] Sirmium is conspicuously absent from this imperial secretary's list of Justinianic building projects, with the emperor rebuilding its neighbor Singidunum into a fortress on the Danube instead of Sirmium on the Savus. Procopius and the Byzantine government reduced Pannonia to its still pivotal location; beyond its bastions, the region was said to be barren. After Justinian, Sirmium was still a city of significance under the control of the Gepids, and Justin II (565–578) recovered it as a walled outpost of the empire during a war among the regional powers of the Gepids, Avars, and Lombards. The Avars succeeded the Gepids as the rulers of the Pannonian plains, and their military potential warranted a massive payment of solidi as an annual tribute. While another war occupied the emperor, the Avars isolated Sirmium by turning Roman engineering expertise against it. Roman bridges had joined Sirmium to the imperial road network in preceding centuries, but the Avars hired engineers to bridge the Savus to deny access to Sirmium by water. As a cover story for this stratagem, the Avar khagan claimed that he would use the bridges to bring war to the rebellious Slavs, thus imitating the practices of earlier Roman generals in the region. The local power of the bridges and Avar army ultimately trumped the distant network of the river and the imperial navy. After a three-year blockade, the government in Constantinople yielded Sirmium to the khagan, and the refugees and garrison of the city were ransomed in exchange for three years' tribute. Post-Roman Pannonian insecurity was manifest even as Sirmium disappeared from history. One emperor played upon the plains paranoia of the Avars, using the fear of invasion of their Pannonian homeland by *more* outsiders to turn back an attack.[35]

Dalmatia

Divided from the rest of Illyricum by a shield of mountains, southern Dalmatia was a pocket of Mediterranean urban civilization.[36] The *Expositio* reduces all of Dalmatia to Salona (Solin), "a splendid city flourishing with business," but the topography made its prosperity possible and enduring.[37] The Dinaric Alps rise steeply from the coastal plain around Salona, and carbonate rocks such as limestone are dominant within them. Water easily dissolves this soft rock, creating the landscape of sinkholes, caves, ravines, and disappearing rivers known to modern Europeans as *karst*. Karst can be both cursed and blessed land for its inhabitants, for its undermined surface could be either poor soil with no surface water or agriculturally rich plains called *polje* among the mountains. These naturally irrigated depressions are a consequence of the settling between faults in the mountains, where ongoing tectonic activity folded and split the rock.

Roman land surveyors measured and divided the fertile stretches of agricultural land near cities in Dalmatia, and their centuriated fields stretched outward from Salona to the west and south around the bay. But the forces that fractured this terrain could be terrifying as well as benign: severe earthquakes were a persistent menace in this part of Illyricum. Concentrated urban construction on the narrow coastal plains only amplified the damage. The seismic destruction of Dyrrachium (Durrës) southwest of Salona merited notice in the *Expositio*: "demolished by the gods, it sank and disappeared."[38]

Close proximity to Italy across the Adriatic Sea and the protection of the Dinaric Alps were only two of Salona's assets; it also had islands and access to the inland riches of Dalmatia. Salona's hinterland included nearby islands that contained fine marble and grew olives and grapes, but the islands also protected the ships passing through. Salona received more Adriatic mercantile traffic because Dalmatian harbors were superior to those of eastern Italy. A pass through the mountains (now called Klis) brought timber, minerals, and livestock over a road from Andetrium to Salona for trade. People followed the paths that brought goods to the regional metropolis. The commercial possibilities of Salona attracted waves of immigrants, including significant numbers of families from Italy and Greek-speakers from the East. Importantly, the movement of the legions out of Dalmatia in the early empire meant that few veterans settled in and around Salona. Instead of a military presence gone native, Salona experienced an influx of enfranchised native Dalmatians from the provincial interior at the beginning of Late Antiquity, and its total enclosed area was about ninety-five hectares. Even with its sizable exports, the Dalmatian interior remained relatively isolated until the third century, when the army began recruiting heavily from the rougher areas of Illyricum in place of the veteran colonies to the north. Wealthy landowners seem to have usually lived in the cities and towns, since country villas like those in the Narenta (Neretva) valley to the southwest of Salona are uncommon. Without the imperial investment that transformed Pannonia, Salona welcomed its new residents with civic infrastructure that showed its age.[39]

Salona's amenities indicate the relative peace and prosperity of Dalmatia over several centuries. The walls that distinguished the urban center changed very little. In Late Antiquity, the gates of Salona, which seem to have been designed more for ornamentation than defense, were made still more elaborate. A source of water, however, was not a cosmetic matter, since the surrounding limestone karst meant an irregular groundwater supply for much of the year. Salona had a large enough population and the resources to construct an aqueduct, which brought water from the foot of the nearby mountains down to the city; it passed into Salona at the same northeastern gate where other goods from the interior entered. Within the city, an increasing population led to constant new construction, which submerged the rectangular grid of streets. The erection of fourth-century Christian basilicas over the foundations of a number of large houses added to the complexity and housing pressure in the northern part of the city. The baths across the street continued to operate alongside the new Christian neighbors, and while the building materials of the baths were of high quality, the construction of many components has struck archaeologists as poor workmanship. Salona was evidently a well-used city that was frequently rebuilt in pieces rather than in grand imperial building programs.[40]

The total reconfiguration of part of the Dalmatian landscape awaited the retirement of the most famous native of Salona. After more than twenty years of defending and reorganizing the Roman empire, the emperor Diocletian took the unprecedented step of divesting himself of imperial rule. To house himself in suitable fashion after 305, he ordered the construction of a palace near Salona. Located on a small inlet off the Bay of Salona, it was completely isolated from other structures but only a few miles south of Diocletian's hometown. Expert labor may have come west with the former emperor from Nicomedia, but ample building materials, including two types of limestone, were close at hand in Dalmatia. Whether for purposes of economy or in acknowledgment of their quality, the structure also incorporated roof tiles from the first and second centuries. The slope of ground toward the water compelled the builders to create massive foundations for parts of the complex. Like many Dalmatians in this period, Diocletian had spent much of his adult life in military camps, and his villa resembled a fortress. Its thick walls and four towers made a statement of martial stability, but their everyday use may have favored privacy over the repulse of armed threats. Within his villa, the emperor could not been seen by observers on land. The decoration of the apartments with mosaics was impressive, and Diocletian also brought four sphinxes from Egypt to adorn his mausoleum. The octagonal tomb also included imported crimson stone to honor an emperor who anticipated deification. Diocletian's palace at Spalatum (Split) was ersatz military spending in Dalmatia, and apart from the possible reconstruction of Salona's amphitheater, it was his only known investment in his native area. While the tetrarchic subdivision of Pannonia had profound effects on urban life there, the return of Diocletian to Salona had considerably more muted consequences. In Dalmatia, the former emperor apparently only desired to be the greatest of rural villa owners and the keeper of his own tomb complex, not the founder of a new city or the remodeler of a province. The reversion of the palace to the state upon Diocletian's death made it an occasional residence for members of the imperial family, who stayed safely away from fourth-century disruptions in the rest of Illyricum.[41]

If Diocletian had lived for a century following his retirement, he would have found that few outside events intruded on the peace of Salona. The Dinaric Alps and the Salonitan walls turned aside the raids of Marcomanni and Goths, but the interior of Dalmatia was defenseless, much like that of Pannonia. The flight of refugees to the Adriatic coast was the result, and even an imperial textile factory moved from Pannonia to occupy part of Diocletian's palace. War among the Romans brought a brief armed conflict to Salona in 425. As part of a campaign to remove a usurper in the West, the eastern emperor Theodosius II sent an imperial fleet to Salona from Constantinople, and after the admiral captured the city, he rebuilt the city walls, adding rectangular towers to reinforce the northern defense. Such a conquest was not particularly disruptive. From the age of Diocletian to the mid-fifth century, the Christian Church had wrought more changes in Dalmatia than any external threat. A group of easterners established the Church in Salona, and the first bishop Domnio (probably from Nisibis) was martyred in the early-fourth-century persecution of Diocletian. The recently restored amphitheater of Salona was the site of his death. His nephew and successor Primus survived the persecution and focused the cult of the martyrs around the extramural basilica at Monastirine, just north of the city walls. Inside the walls south of Monastirine, the aforementioned episcopal basilica took the place of a number of houses in the fourth century. In contrast to Sirmium, Salona saw the apex of its episcopal prominence in the fifth century. The bishop Hesychius rebuilt all the major basilicas and shrines of the city on a grander scale, and he constructed a new shrine at Marusinac, farther from Salona. Thereafter, the bishops and the wealthiest Christians were buried at Marusinac while humbler interments continued at the older shrines. Like Odessos in Thrace, the Salonitan Church became a major landowner with powerful friends.[42]

At this juncture, Salona regained a certain significance in imperial politics, and ensuing events detracted from Salona's Christian importance. The general Marcellinus was sent from the western court of Valentinian III (425–455) to defend Dalmatia, and the death of his patron, Aetius, left him as an independent political power on the Adriatic. The security provided by the Salonitan fleet and local troops made Marcellinus a free agent between eastern and western emperors and the various barbarians within the empire.[43] Marcellinus' balancing act came to end with his assassination, but his nephew Julius Nepos (474–480) maintained the separate status of Dalmatia until the late fifth century. Nepos succeeded in deposing the western emperor Glycerius and made him bishop of Salona to keep him out of the way. When Nepos himself was pushed out of Italy, he lived in Diocletian's palace and still merited recognition by the eastern emperor as the lawful ruler of the West. The formal end of the western empire did not occur in Italy, but rather in Dalmatia, with the assassination of Julius Nepos outside Salona in 480. The turmoil around Salona had frayed its connections with Rome such that Glycerius' successor, Honorius, was surprised to receive instructions from the bishop of Rome to combat heresy in his region. The Gothic administration of Dalmatia that followed Nepos' death brought some stability to the situation.

Both the Goths and the bishop of Salona were interested in the Dalmatian countryside in the sixth century. Theodoric, king of the Goths in Italy, sent a special emissary to ask about the functioning of the iron mines of Dalmatia, and Cassiodorus noted the apparent persistence of other imperial infrastructure there.[44] A few decades later, two provincial synods at Salona provide a glimpse of the rest of the Dalmatian churches. With Sirmium imperiled, the bishop of Salona gathered churchmen from Pannonia, as well as the coast, and the synod refers to his entire diocese as Dalmatia. One of the participants from the Illyrian interior understandably complained about how poor his church had become. A subsequent council a few years later dealt with the problems of this expansive diocese of Salona, which several bishops complained was too large. By the end of the sixth century, the Salonitan bishop had a "country bishop" to assist him in administering his see. The accession of Justinian had serious consequences for both the Gothic rule of Dalmatia and the bishop of Salona. Salona traded hands several times during Justinian's reconquest of the West, and its fortifications suffered serious damage. When the Byzantine commander Constantianus finally forced the Goths out of Dalmatia, he ordered the walls of Salona rebuilt, now with triangular towers, and shored up another part of the city wall with a ditch. Justinian subsequently revived the praetorian prefecture of Illyricum and placed a governor for Dalmatia called a proconsul in Salona. Even as his army and navy restored Roman rule in the city, Justinian's religious policies antagonized the Salonitan bishops. The emperor's new bishop at his new city of Justiniana Prima challenged the see of Salona for authority in Illyricum. The Salonitan Church joined with the bishop of Rome in resisting Justinian's efforts to impose a new, more inclusive orthodoxy, and the emperor eventually became so frustrated that he exiled Frontonianus of Salona to Egypt for eight years. The situation of Dalmatia in this period shows the competition of authorities in an important theater. Salona's days as a peaceful backwater had passed.[45]

After Justinian, Salona faced the new threat of the Avars and Slavs with reduced imperial support, and the Salonitan bishops found a new adversary in Gregory the bishop of Rome. Gregory opposed a particularly corrupt bishop of Salona but was unable to secure the election of his own preferred candidate to the see, and he thus refused to recognize the man whom the people and emperor supported. Almost ten years of discord intervened before Rome and Salona were reconciled, and the ensuing cordiality of churchmen was of no help against invasion. After the final fall of Sirmium, Salona was at first untroubled as the Avars shifted their focus to Constantinople. But when Justinian's successors stymied the invasions, the Avars and Slavs turned west toward the Adriatic. Raids swept over the extramural shrines, but the bishop of Salona reported to Gregory that the pass in the surrounding mountains was still guarded. When the invaders breached this defense sometime after 612, Salona fell, and its inhabitants fled. The emperor Heraclius granted Diocletian's palace to the refugees, whose residence there was the beginning of medieval Split. A native Dalmatian who became bishop of Rome was able to retrieve the relics of the Salonitan martyrs and enshrine them in the Lateran. While Pannonia had been erased, the Adriatic connection allowed some bits of the urban and religious life of Dalmatia to endure into the Middle Ages.[46]

Thrace

"Thrace is a province rich in crops, and it has men great and brave in war," says the *Expositio* of southeastern Illyricum.[47] From its history as an independent kingdom and geographic separation by two mountain chains, Thrace remained a distinct subregion even when the later empire administered it as part of a larger Danubian-Balkan region. The historian Ammianus Marcellinus, who had traveled there in the later fourth century, considered Thrace separately from Illyricum:

> Formed in the shape of a crescent moon, [Thrace] presents the appearance of a beautiful theater. At its western summit are the steep mountains through which the narrow pass of Succi opens, separating Thrace from Dacia. The left side, toward the north, is shut in by the lofty heights of the Haemus Mountains and the Danube, which, where it washes Roman soil, borders on many cities, fortresses, and strongholds. On the right, which is the south side, extend the slopes of Rhodope, and where the morning star rises it is bounded by the strait which flows with an abundance of water from the Black Sea, and going on with alternating current to the Aegean, opens a narrow cleft between the lands.[48]

Thrace is composed of the same topographic ingredients as Pannonia, but the result is different. Lacking deep limestone deposits, the Haemus (Balkan) and Rhodope mountains are not as karstic as their counterparts to the west, and they rise more gently from the surrounding plains than the Dinaric Alps do. While their bend forms barriers to movement across the region from east to west, funneling traffic through the Succi Pass and the Iron Gates gorge, they are less of an impediment to passage from north to south. The level terrain in Thrace received layers of sediment from prehistoric flooding, so the Thracian depression and the Black Sea coastal plain (Dobruja) are areas of great agricultural potential, though the mountains deny them the rainfall associated with the Pannonian plain (600–700 mm versus 350–400 mm). Irrigation from the region's rivers and storehouses in the cities were thus vital to supporting a large population. According to Ammianus' late antique ethnography, the mountains also contributed to the martial talents of the inhabitants; pure air, sunshine, and sprinklings with dew enabled the rural population to surpass civilized Mediterranean people in health and strength. The modern historian might add that the close relationship of mountains and plains facilitated the emergence of a people experienced in warfare, as in Macedonia. The well-known characteristics of Thrace thus implicate its geography.[49]

Whereas northern Thrace, with its Danubian riverbank of fortified cities, resembled Pannonia in many respects, including the predominant use of Latin, the south and east of the region was oriented toward the Greek East. The Thracian depression in the farthest southeastern corner of Europe, crisscrossed with Roman roads, was the conduit to the ports of Constantinople and Heraclea (formerly Perinthus, now Marmara Ereğli), which the *Expositio* named as Thrace's greatest cities. Without their own Julian Alps to separate them from an imperial metropolis, Thracian farms were important and familiar assets of Constantine's capital. The Black Sea cities of eastern Thrace lay between these two subregions, and although they shared Greek foundations with the huge commercial hubs on the Aegean and Bosphorus, their northern connections also shaped their history. From its origins as a Greek colony absorbed into the Roman empire, Odessos (Varna), one of these Pontic ports, became a northern bastion of the empire at the close of Late Antiquity.

Odessos lay on a coastal terrace at the northwestern corner of what is now the Bay of Varna, and the nearby river and lake provided connections to its hinterland to the west. The geology here is older than anything around it. Dobruja comprises a zone of rock far more ancient than the dinosaurs, with metamorphic rocks overlain by sedimentary ones and layers of submarine lava, and differences in the hardness of the rock have created complex topography near the sea. The cape and the Franga plateau to the west protect the city from the cold northern winds, which is a substantial advantage: Ammianus refers to the Homeric idea that the north wind itself originates in Thrace. The slopes of the plateau also provide water for the city's aqueduct. When the Romans took over the administration of Thrace, the countryside attached to the city extended north and west to other rivers that separated its lands from those of neighboring Marcianopolis (Devnya) and Dionysopolis (Balchik). The export of crops grown in the countryside was one of Odessos' important roles as an urban center, particularly in the Hellenistic period, but the necropoleis of the city indicate an additional orientation within the Roman empire. The coastal roads north to Dionysopolis and south to Mesembria, the highways to other Greek ports, were where most pre-Roman burials occurred, but the dead gathered along the Marcianopolis road in the second and third centuries. Founded to serve as an administrative center and sometimes called the biggest city in Thrace, Marcianopolis was the inland capital of the late Roman province of Lower Moesia, and Odessos was a node on its newly important road and a nearby harbor. Through immigration and imperial investment, Odessos itself was not small: from its Hellenistic extent of about 16 hectares, early Roman and late antique expansions increased its walled area to 27 and then 35 hectares. Within the city, the greatest monumental buildings were the baths attributed to Septimius Severus in the southeastern quarter, and there was also an impressive theater to the northwest. While grand urban construction with imperial sponsorship ended, along with civic minting of bronze coinage, in the mid-third century, basilicas were erected to serve the Christian community. From the fourth through the sixth centuries, churches rose in all the major areas of the city, including several in existing "religious" locations with Hellenistic or Roman temples. In addition to commerce derived from agriculture and the sea, Odessos also had a neighborhood associated with ceramics production, which had begun alongside a vast array of imports from places as distant as Athens and Egypt.

Like Aquincum, which had diminished in importance due to the rise of new Pannonian provincial capitals such as Sirmium, Odessos remained in the shadow of Marcianopolis until the turmoil of the later fourth century.[50]

A banquet at Marcianopolis and food imports from Odessos have much to do with the return to prominence of the Black Sea coast. Before their infamous encounter with the Roman army at Adrianople (Edirne) in 378, the Goths who sought settlement within the empire were near Marcianopolis, and the Roman supply lines that fed them ran from Odessos and similar Black Sea ports. These supplies were evidently inadequate for the numbers of immigrants, and the Roman general in charge of Thrace hosted a dinner party to assassinate the Gothic leadership. When that failed, the Goths responded by taking what they wanted from the countryside of Marcianopolis and then marching west and south, away from the wealth of the coast. The Goths entered what is now Dobruja only unwillingly, pushed by a Roman army, and Ammianus reports that the newcomers found its landscape barren.[51] Like interior cities such as Marcianopolis, Odessos could withdraw behind its walls. The late antique city possessed a garrison and impressive walls. The old bastion of Odessos had repulsed Philip of Macedon, and the defenses of the Pontic ports remained to provide security against intimidation by the newest entrepreneurs of violence. If Odessos abandoned its hinterland for a time, outlying villages like Galata would no longer have contributed their grain harvests to the city's warehouses. But unlike its neighbor Marcianopolis, whose livelihood depended on the secure network of roads, which themselves now brought seemingly every invader close to the city, supply from the sea could sustain Odessos, and the coastal roads were less frequently used by raiders.[52] Repairs were made to the harbor in the later fourth century to keep trade flowing, and an emissary of Theodosius II traveled by ship to Odessos to negotiate with the Huns. The military commander of Thrace may have resided there while Attila was at large. Increased imperial attention to the city is evident in increasing numbers of coins found from the late fourth and early fifth centuries, and the city achieved even greater notice thereafter.[53]

Such was the strategic importance of Odessos that the city's inhabitants became involved in imperial politics in the sixth century. When the general Vitalian led an uprising against the emperor Anastasius, he captured Odessos with aid of supporters inside the city, and he made use of the city's fleet. Vitalian's promises of decreased taxation may have seemed especially attractive in Odessos, where there was significant wealth but little apparent imperial investment. The rebel faction could have included the immigrant merchants and shipbuilders from Asia who are known from their families' fifth- and sixth-century inscriptions; the possibility of greater profits in Odessos had continued to draw people across the Black Sea.[54] Large finds of Justinianic coins suggest that the emperor did add to the fortifications there, as Procopius describes.[55] One cause of Vitalian's revolt may have been poor provisioning of the army in Thrace, so the emperor Justinian relieved supply problems by creating a new administrative remedy, the *quaestura exercitus*, which was headquartered in Odessos. By linking rich provinces such as Cyprus to those of the Danube frontier, the office of this quaestor formalized and amplified existing trade through the Black Sea ports, and imperial attention must have been a boon to the city at its focal point. This fiscal relationship survived into the later sixth century. As the citizens of Sirmium had grown prosperous during that city's fourth-century golden age, Odessos and its landowners made fortunes in the sixth century. One of Justinian's new laws is evidence of the power of the elites there, as well as the importance of its bishop in imperial eyes:

> We forbade Martinus, holy bishop of Odessos, to sell church property, so that the magnates might not force him to alienate church property according to their pleasure. . . . For now the holy man above mentioned has come to this holy city [Constantinople] and has shown us that many pieces of land, without any definite return, or houses or vineyards have been left for the redemption of captives or the support of the poor, and that the mentioned ends, though pious, are prevented by the prohibited alienation.[56]

The wealthy church of Odessos thus had powerful friends and also formidable local opponents. The law also alludes to problems in the region: the raids of Avars and Slavs elsewhere in Thrace provided many opportunities for ransoming captives. Another part of the law notes that even around Odessos, not all lands were equally fortunate, with some not producing income, or "the house is almost fallen down or the vineyard does not yield the same but various fruits and is perchance subject to the incursions of the barbarians."[57] But as Justinian allowed that these properties could then be sold by the bishop, the landowners around Odessos must have still had venture capital to buy distressed assets. In the later sixth century, while Sirmium was evacuated and Thracian cities north of the Haemus suffered, even disappearing after sacks by Avars and Slavs, Odessos and its coastal neighbors to the south remained. Odessos took its place as a Byzantine border city when the Danube became a notional rather than a practical frontier for eastern Illyricum. Archaeology suggests that it succumbed to destruction sometime in the seventh century, but its vital location attracted rebuilding, and Odessos reemerged several centuries later as medieval Varna.[58]

Through three examples from the diverse corners of the late antique Balkans, some contours of the region are evident. Varying levels of imperial investment overcame geographic impediments to trade and communication, joining niches within Illyricum to each other and to the wider Mediterranean world. Roman involvement in the region also connected it to populations to the north, whose appetite for goods and remunerative employment was the boon and bane of Pannonia in particular. Sirmium was ultimately too strategically convenient to invaders and too far from the protective mountains to remain part of the empire. Dalmatia's interconnection with Italy sustained it for a time when the rest of western Illyricum was neglected, but the absence of the western empire, coupled with its accessibility from the interior, led to the devastation of

Dalmatia. Refugees fled to more defensible ports, and a medieval Dalmatia of coasts and islands replaced its late antique predecessor. The geographic situation of the cities of the Thracian coast was similar to Dalmatia, but here Constantinople invested in and protected what Rome did not.[59] The late Roman city persisted in Dobruja until one of the terminal points of Late Antiquity, when the entire empire had its near-death experience with the armies of Persia and Islam. Within Illyricum, Thrace had the cheapest and least threatened connections to the Mediterranean. When Odessos became the premier city of Thrace, the Roman empire literally retreated out of the fertile valleys and steep passes of the Balkans, leaving late antique Illyricum behind.

NOTES

1. Stillman 1964, 10–11, but see the dangers of "Balkanism" in Todorova 2009.
2. Stat. *Silv.* 4.7.13–16.
3. Gec 2009.
4. Verona List (Barnes 1982, 201–208). The praetorian prefect of Illyricum also had responsibility for Achaea, Thessaly, and Crete.
5. Kulikowski 2000.
6. Mommsen 1906, 4.
7. Plin. *NH* 3.150; App. *Ill.* 1.1.
8. Wilkes 2005 offers a conspectus of recent archaeology; aspects of late antique transformation beyond those mentioned here are discussed in Poulter 2007.
9. *Expositio* 57.
10. For Balkan geologic history, see Reed et al. 2004 and Ager 1980; Sirmium's islands: *Menander Protector* 27.2 (Blockley 1985).
11. Popović 1971–80 for historical overview and prominent archaeological discoveries.
12. *It. Ant.* 124; Póczy 1980, 267–268.
13. Watson 1999, 42–46.
14. Jeremić 1993, 90–96.
15. Poulter 1992.
16. Mulvin 2002.
17. Lenski 2002, 38.
18. *CTh* 1.32.5 (386) = *CJ* 11.7.4; Dušanić 1977.
19. Duncan 1993.
20. Aur. Vict. *Caes.* 40.9.
21. Musurillo 1972, 294–301.
22. Zeiller 1918; McLynn 1994, 92.
23. Amm. Marc. 29.6.6–8; Duncan 1993.
24. Amm. Marc. 29.6.9–10, 30.5.16.
25. Heather 2007, 187–188.
26. Jer. *De vir. ill.* 135; Jer. *Ep.* 66.14; Kelly 1975, 3–6.
27. Claud. *Cons. Hon. Cons. Stil.* 2.191–207.
28. *CTh* 10.10.25 (408).

29. Poulter 2007, 1–50, with particular attention to the decline of the "epigraphic habit," but see Handley 2010.

30. Mócsy 1974, 339–351; Cassiod. *Var.* 11.1.10.

31. Heather 1991.

32. Jer. *Ep.* 123.16.

33. Priscus, Exc. 2.

34. Procop. *Aed.* 4.

35. Mócsy 1974, 352–358.

36. Bratož 1996.

37. *Expositio* 53.

38. *Expositio* 53; Reed et al. 2004.

39. Wilkes 1969, 337–406.

40. Wilkes 1969, 372, 379.

41. Wilkes 1986.

42. Dyggve 1951; Marin 1994.

43. Kulikowski 2002.

44. Cassiod. *Var.* 3.25.

45. Wilkes 1969, 423–433; Procop. *Goth.* 1.7.26–37.

46. Wilkes 1969, 434–437.

47. *Expositio* 50.

48. Amm. Marc. 27.4.5–7, trans. modified from Rolfe (Loeb).

49. Reed et al. 2004; Amm. Marc. 27.4.14.

50. Preshlenov 2002.

51. Amm. Marc. 31.5.4–8, 31.7.3.

52. Liebeschuetz 2007, 101–134, but with caution about the descent of "post-curial government" upon the Balkans.

53. Velkov 1977, 100.

54. Velkov 1977, 271.

55. Procop. *Aed.* 4.11.20.

56. *Nov.* 65 (538), trans. Fred H. Blume.

57. *Nov.* 65, trans. Blume.

58. See Fine 1983 and Curta 2006 for the medieval reconfiguration of the Balkans; Whittow 2007 suggests significant continuities.

59. Dunn 1994.

WORKS CITED

Ager, Derek V. 1980. *The Geology of Europe.* New York: McGraw-Hill.

Barnes, Timothy D. 1982. *The New Empire of Diocletian and Constantine.* Cambridge, MA: Harvard University Press.

Blockley, R. C. 1985. *The History of Menander the Guardsman: Introductory Essay, Text, Translation and Historiographical Notes.* Liverpool: Cairns.

Bratož, Rajko, ed. 1996. *Westillyricum und Nordostitalien in der spätrömischen Zeit.* Ljubljana: Narodni muzej.

Curta, Florin. 2006. *Southeastern Europe in the Middle Ages, 500–1250.* Cambridge: Cambridge University Press.

Duncan, G. L. 1993. *Coin Circulation in the Danubian and Balkan Provinces of the Roman Empire, AD 294–578*. London: Royal Numismatic Society.
Dunn, Archibald. 1994. "The Transition from Polis to Kastron in the Balkans (III–VII cc.): General and Regional Perspectives," *Byzantine and Modern Greek Studies* 18.1: 60–81.
Dušanić, Slobodan. 1977. "Aspects of Roman Mining in Noricum, Pannonia, Dalmatia and Moesia Superior." In *Aufstieg und Niedergang der römischen Welt* 2.6: 52–94. Berlin: De Gruyter.
Dyggve, Ejnar. 1951. *History of Salonitan Christianity*. Cambridge, MA: Harvard University Press.
Fine, John V. A. 1983. *The Early Medieval Balkans: A Critical Survey from the Sixth to the Late Twelfth Century*. Ann Arbor: University of Michigan Press.
Gec, Jovana. 2009. "Mammoth skeleton unearthed in Serbia." Associated Press, 4 June, 2009.
Griffiths, Huw I., Boris Kryštufek, and Jane M. Reed, eds. 2004. *Balkan Biodiversity: Pattern and Process in the European Hotspot*. Dordrecht: Kluwer.
Handley, Mark A. 2010. "Two Hundred and Seventy-Four Addenda and Corrigenda to the *Prosopography of the Later Roman Empire* from the Latin-Speaking Balkans," *Journal of Late Antiquity* 3.1: 113–157.
Heather, Peter J. 1991. *Goths and Romans, 332–489*. Oxford: Oxford University Press.
———. 2007. "Goths in the Roman Balkans c. 350–500." In *The Transition to Late Antiquity: On the Danube and Beyond*, ed. Andrew Poulter, 163–190. Oxford: Oxford University Press.
Ivanov, Rumen Teofilov, ed. 2002. *Римски и ранновизантийски градове в България* [*Roman and Early Byzantine Cities in Bulgaria*]. Sofia: Ivray.
Jeremić, Miroslav. 1993. "Sirmium in the Period of the Tetrarchy." In *Roman Imperial Towns and Palaces in Serbia*, ed. Dragoslav Srejović, 89–114. Belgrade: Serbian Academy of Sciences and Arts.
Kelly, J. N. D. 1975. *Jerome: His Life, Writings, and Controversies*. New York: Harper and Row.
Kulikowski, Michael. 2000. "The *Notitia Dignitatum* as a Historical Source," *Historia* 49: 358–377.
———. 2002. "Marcellinus 'of Dalmatia' and the Fall of the Western Empire," *Byzantion* 72: 177–191.
Lengyel, Alfonz, and George T. Radan, eds. 1980. *The Archaeology of Roman Pannonia*. Budapest: Akadémiai Kiadó.
Lenski, Noel E. 2002. *Failure of Empire: Valens and the Roman State in the Fourth Century A.D.* Berkeley: University of California Press.
Liebeschuetz, J. H. W. G. 2007. "The Lower Danube Region under Pressure: From Valens to Heraclius." In *The Transition to Late Antiquity: On the Danube and Beyond*, ed. Andrew Poulter, 101–134. Oxford: Oxford University Press.
Marin, Emilio, ed. 1994. *Salona Christiana*. Split: Arheološki muzej.
McLynn, Neil B. 1994. *Ambrose of Milan: Church and Court in a Christian Capital*. Berkeley: University of California Press.
Mócsy, András. 1974. *Pannonia and Upper Moesia*. London: Routledge.
Mommsen, Theodor. 1906. *The Provinces of the Roman Empire from Caesar to Diocletian*. New York: Scribner's Sons.
Mulvin, Lynda. 2002. *Late Roman Villas in the Danube-Balkan Region*. Oxford: Archaeopress.

Musurillo, Herbert. 1972. *The Acts of the Christian Martyrs*. Oxford: Clarendon.
Póczy, Klára. 1980. "Pannonian Cities." In *The Archaeology of Roman Pannonia*, ed. A. Lengyel and G. T. Radan, 239–74. Budapest: Akadémiai Kiadó.
Popović, Vladislav, et al., eds. 1971–1980. *Sirmium: Archaeological Investigations in Syrmian Pannonia*, 12 vols. Belgrade: Arheološki Institute.
Poulter, Andrew. 1992. "The Use and Abuse of Urbanism in the Danubian Provinces in the Later Roman Empire." In *The City in Late Antiquity*, ed. J. Rich, 99–135. London: New York: Routledge.
———, ed. 2007. *The Transition to Late Antiquity: On the Danube and Beyond*. Oxford: Oxford University Press.
Preshlenov, Christo. 2002. "Odessos." In *Римски и ранновизантийски градове в България* [*Roman and Early Byzantine Cities in Bulgaria*], ed. R. T. Ivanov, 59–80. Sofia: Ivray.
Reed, Jane M., Boris Kryštufek, and Warren J. Eastwood. 2004. "The Physical Geography of the Balkans and Nomenclature of Place Names." In *Balkan Biodiversity: Pattern and Process in the European Hotspot*, ed. H. I. Griffiths, B. Kryštufek, and J. M. Reed, 9–21. Dordrecht: Kluwer.
Ruseva-Slokoska, Lyudmila, Rumen Ivanov, and Ventsislav Dinchev, eds. 2002. *The Roman and Late Roman City* [*Римският и късноантичният град*]. Sofia: Prof. Marin Drinov Academic Publishing House.
Srejović, Dragoslav, ed. 1993. *Roman Imperial Towns and Palaces in Serbia*. Belgrade: Serbian Academy of Sciences and Arts.
Stillman, Edmund O. 1964. *The Balkans*, Life World Library. New York: Time.
Todorova, Maria. 2009. *Imagining the Balkans*. Oxford: Oxford University Press.
Velkov, Velizar. 1977. *Cities in Thrace and Dacia in Late Antiquity*. 2nd ed. Amsterdam: A. M. Hakkert.
Watson, Alaric. 1999. *Aurelian and the Third Century*. London: Routledge.
Whittow, Mark. 2007. "Nicopolis ad Istrum: Backward and Balkan?" In *The Transition to Late Antiquity: On the Danube and Beyond*, ed. Andrew Poulter, 375–89. Oxford: Oxford University Press.
Wilkes, John J. 1969. *Dalmatia*. Cambridge, MA: Harvard University Press.
———. 1986. *Diocletian's Palace, Split: Residence of a Retired Roman Emperor*. Sheffield: University of Sheffield.
———. 2005. "The Roman Danube: An Archaeological Survey," *Journal of Roman Studies* 95: 124–225.
Zeiller, Jacques. 1918. *Les origines chrétiennes dans les provinces danubiennes de l'Empire romain*. Paris: E. de Boccard.

CHAPTER 4

ARMENIA

TIM GREENWOOD
St. Andrews University

IN 591 C.E., an unexpected visitor came before Gregory of Tours.[1] The stranger introduced himself as bishop Simon and recounted something of his unfortunate life history. Simon claimed that he had been captured in Armenia by the king of the Persians and taken off into Persia, together with his flock. Although numerous churches had been burned down in the course of the Persian campaign, Simon reported that one particular church, dedicated to the Forty-Eight Saints and Martyrs, had been miraculously spared. On learning of Simon's imprisonment, one of his fellow bishops had dispatched a sum of money to the Persian king, and this had secured his release. Simon had then traveled to Gaul seeking unspecified help from the faithful.

This little-known passage from Gregory's *History* presents a number of challenges. Bishop Simon is otherwise unattested; he is a figure who emerges from nowhere and vanishes without trace. His see is not identified beyond being in a region of Armenia that came under Persian attack. Gregory does not tell us when Simon was taken captive, nor why he left Armenia after his ransom, nor the circumstances in which he ended up at Tours. The narrative structure is also problematic. The short description of his travails includes a terse notice referring to the overthrow of Antioch, although whether this refers to a Persian attack or an earthquake is unclear. Moreover, it is followed, again without introduction or explanation, by a self-contained and completely unrelated account of a miracle also associated with devastation in Antioch, this time more obviously by an earthquake.[2] It is hard to see why Simon should wish to frame his own experiences as an Armenian bishop in an Antiochene context, and one is left with the distinct impression that it was Gregory who shaped the report in this way rather than Simon. After all, an earlier passage in Gregory's *History* offers a suspiciously similar combination of elements: the fall of Antioch to a Persian assault, with its inhabitants led away into captivity; the burning of a prominent church in Antioch dedicated to a local martyr; and Armenian visitors, on this occasion attending the emperor in Constantinople rather than Gregory in Tours, who advertise their Christian credentials by recounting how an Armenian bishop had ridiculed the practice of worshipping fire in the presence of Persian envoys and had suffered a severe beating as a result.[3] The structural and thematic correspondences between these two passages are striking.

Yet whilst bishop Simon appears as an isolated figure in the presence of Gregory of Tours and in the pages of his *History*, we should be wary of doubting his very existence. It may well be the case that such a character, and the stories attributed to him—of warfare and burned-out churches and resolute bishops oppressed by impious kings—suited Gregory's wider literary and historical purposes.[4] Nevertheless, the two passages in Gregory's *History* contain sufficient historical detail that is capable of corroboration to suggest that Gregory did, indeed, converse with an Armenian cleric. In other words, although the passages clearly reflect Gregory's role as compiler, they also point to Simon, or someone very like Simon, as the original source.

We know from a range of contemporary sources that in 576 C.E. the Sasanian king of Persia, Khusro I, embarked on an ambitious campaign through Armenia.[5] Unusually, he passed by Theodosiopolis, the capital of a Roman province, Armenia I, and headed further west toward Sebasteia, another provincial capital, this time of Armenia II, which he sacked, before being defeated in a battle west of Melitene, capital of Armenia III, after which he fled back eastward. This is the first instance of a Persian king personally taking charge of a campaign through Armenia since Kavadh's operations against Theodosiopolis and Amida in 502.[6] It therefore seems highly likely that Simon was caught up in Khusro's campaign. No less significant, I would suggest, is Simon's reference to the church of the Forty-Eight Saints and Martyrs.[7] Gregory notes in passing that he had included an account of their martyrdom in his *Books of Miracles*, and indeed this is found in his martyrology, the *Glory of the Martyrs*, under the heading "The Forty-Eight Martyrs who suffered in Armenia."[8] This narrative is without question the well-known passion of the Forty Martyrs of Sebasteia, to which a slight Armenian spin has been applied.[9] Although incapable of being proved, it is tempting to connect the miraculous protection of the church dedicated to these martyrs with Khusro's sack of Sebasteia. After all, Gregory's earlier description of the fall of Antioch to the Persians in 573 and the fate of its inhabitants is followed by a short notice recording the fate of the church of Saint Julian, the martyr of Antioch, and the structural correspondences between the two passages were noted previously.[10] On the other hand, an isolated notice in the *Buildings* of Procopius mentions that a monastery dedicated to the Forty Martyrs was situated near Theodosiopolis.[11] This, too, would fit the route taken by Khusro I in 576. Simon's story can be precisely located in time, in historical context, and in place, that is, Khusro's Armenian campaign of 576.

Another important aspect of the earlier passage lies in its use of "Persarmenians" to describe those who attended upon the emperor Justin II.[12] Again, there are several sources which confirm that the Armenians who rebelled against Khusro I and who subsequently sought refuge in Constantinople were, indeed, from the Persian sector of Armenia. This sector is termed Persarmenia by several sixth-century writers in the east Roman empire, including Malalas and Procopius.[13] Nevertheless, it is most surprising to discover such precision in Gregory's *History* and again points to direct knowledge of the eastern frontier.

These features, when taken collectively, support the proposition that Gregory did indeed meet an Armenian cleric. Simon's particular knowledge about the tradition of the Forty-Eight Saints and Martyrs and the fate of a church "from that region" dedicated to them suggests a personal connection with one of the Roman provinces of Armenia, probably either Armenia I or Armenia II. This is supported by the fine distinction between Armenia, used to describe the territory attacked by Khusro, and Persarmenia, from where the Armenian visitors to Constantinople came. If Simon was a bishop—we do, after all, have only his word for it, although Gregory evidently believed him—and he came from one of these Roman provinces, he therefore held that rank in the imperial Church and so was a Chalcedonian Armenian. Gregory of Tours would then emerge, somewhat improbably, as an important witness for the study of Armenian history in Late Antiquity. Very little material deriving from sixth-century Roman Armenia has been preserved.

The works of Gregory of Tours hardly constitute the most obvious point of departure for a study of Armenia in Late Antiquity. Nevertheless, such an oblique opening does have its advantages. From a historical perspective, it introduces a number of key themes. Armenians emerge from the pages of Gregory's works primarily as fellow Christians under the headship of bishops, with their own churches, martyrs, and traditions. It is as faithful believers that Armenians are forced to defend themselves against an oppressive and impious Persian sovereign. Indeed, the king of the Persians is only portrayed acting in a hostile manner, attacking Armenian districts, setting fire to churches, and leading clerics off into captivity or forcing them into exile. By contrast, the Roman emperor is presented as someone with whom Armenians can negotiate an alliance and whose capital city, Constantinople, can serve as a safe haven. Even Gregory of Tours recognizes the ambiguous status of Armenia in Late Antiquity, partitioned between the two great powers of the Near East, susceptible to both Roman and Persian political and cultural influences. We should not, however, lose sight of the fact that Gregory's account is short and overly simplistic in its analysis. As we shall discover, a plethora of sources offer a far more complex, fluid, and contradictory picture, both of the Armenian Church and of Armenian attitudes toward, and relations with, the great powers of Late Antiquity.

A less obvious historical theme illustrated by Gregory's *History* is that of Armenian dislocation. When the Persarmenians reject the terms offered to them by the envoys of the Persian king, they are forced into exile in Constantinople. Bishop Simon is taken into Persia, ransomed, and eventually arrives in Tours by unknown ways and means. Although the literary aspects of these passages should not be underestimated, we know that Armenians were scattered throughout Roman and Persian territory, both individually and collectively. Some were engaged in military service on a distant frontier. At the end of the sixth century, for example, Armenian contingents could be found stationed on the banks of the Danube in the Balkans and in Vrkan (Wirkān) on the eastern shore of the Caspian.[14] Although the military potential of Armenia had long been appreciated and exploited by the great powers—and I would suggest especially by Persia—this was not the only experience of Armenians outside Armenia. We find Armenians involved in a range of transient activities, traveling to Jerusalem and the holy sites on pilgrimage, pursuing academic study, conducting theological research, and even engaging in commerce, although the evidence for this, examined later, is admittedly slight.[15]

Such a diaspora, whether forced or voluntary, has important consequences for the study of Armenia in Late Antiquity. In the first place, a wide range of literature written originally in Greek or Syriac was translated into Armenian, and the Armenian versions of many of these texts have survived.[16] Some of these represent the only witness to the original text. For example, it is only through its Armenian translation that we have access to the ancillary collection of raw and unreconciled chronological data gathered by Eusebius in the first part of his *Chronicle*, known as the *Chronographia*.[17] By the same token, although original Armenian compositions can provide a different perspective from which to observe the Near East in Late Antiquity, it would be misleading to isolate them from the literary models and cultural influences of their neighbors. Within Armenian historical texts, for example, we find traces of noble epics, blending fact, anecdote, and imaginative reconstruction.[18] These reveal the personalities of the key players in the historical drama through their conversations and sometimes through their confrontations in single combat. Such heroic narratives were strongly influenced by the long-established epic narratives in Sasanian Persia. Without the influence of this Persian literary tradition, it is otherwise hard to account for the similarities across otherwise unrelated Armenian, Arabic, and later Persian versions of Sasanian royal history.[19]

A second feature of this diaspora is that Armenians frequently intrude into non-Armenian sources. Perhaps the most unfortunate was Gilakios, the commander of a small Armenian detachment who served in the Gothic wars in Italy.[20] Procopius records that Gilakios was confronted by enemy soldiers in Lucania in 548 who asked him who he was. Since the hapless Gilakios could not speak Greek, Latin, Gothic, or indeed any language other than Armenian, he kept answering "Gilakios *strategos*" thereby revealing where his loyalties lay. His captors tired of his response and ran him through. Apparently, his lack of linguistic ability cost him his life. Did this really happen, or is this merely included by Procopius to illustrate one Armenian stereotype, the uncomprehending—and incomprehensible—Armenian soldier? It is impossible to tell, but evidently the author had no difficulty in populating his works with Armenians. In another passage, Procopius acknowledges that he had cause to exploit an Armenian historical work.[21] He therefore articulates a very different, almost contradictory perspective, now judging a work of Armenian history to be so significant as to merit open approval.

Approaching Armenia in Late Antiquity is therefore not a straightforward exercise. The preceding paragraphs should be sufficient to demonstrate the pervasive influence of both Rome and Persia on all aspects of Armenian society and culture during these centuries.[22] Arguably, even this is an oversimplification, and we should probably envisage multiple and varied influences, from far-reaching decisions taken at the highest level with immediate implications—redrawing the boundaries between the Roman and Persian sectors of Armenia, for example, or redefining what constituted orthodox belief—to the slow percolation of ideas, traditions, and practices at a regional and a local level. Indeed, it may be more helpful to think of different layers of influence operating across the individual regions and districts of Armenia and engendering different reactions in each of them. The degree to which these influences were themselves conditioned and modified by exposure to existing Armenian traditions and practices should not be underestimated.

The conversion of Armenia at the start of the fourth century illustrates something of this complexity. The significance of both Cappadocian and Syrian missionary impulses in this process has long been recognized.[23] Gregory the Illuminator, the historical founder of the Armenian Church, is recorded as having been raised in Caesarea in Cappadocia. His conversion of the Arsacid (Aršakuni) king of Armenia Trdat took place after the martyrdom of Hrip'simē and her followers, reportedly fleeing eastward from Roman persecution. Subsequently, Gregory was sent back to Caesarea for consecration as bishop by its metropolitan, thereby establishing a connection with, and dependency upon, Caesarea that lasted for several generations. Perhaps unsurprisingly, the Armenian word for bishop, *episkopos*, derives from Greek. On the other hand, an original Armenian composition, the *Buzandaran Patmut'iwnk'* (*Epic Histories*), dating from the last third of the fifth century, tells the story of the famous bishop James of Nisibis (d. 338), who traveled to the mountainous region of Korduk' in southern Armenia in search of Noah's ark.[24] He tried to convert the local lord, Manačihr Rštuni, allegedly without success. Furthermore, although the Armenian script was invented by Maštoc' at the start of the fifth century, even Koriwn's *Life* records an earlier, unsuccessful attempt by a shadowy Syrian bishop named Daniel.[25] The number of Syriac loanwords for fundamental ecclesiastical terminology—*k'ahanay*, for example, meaning priest—strongly hints at the early influence of Syrian Christianity, even if we have little information on the progress or the chronology of

Syrian missionary activity in southern Armenia. Its impact may also be detected in the Armenian tradition that identified Edessa as an Armenian city and Abgar as an Armenian king.

Yet even this does not give a complete picture, for it ignores the early influence of Jerusalem on the Armenian Church. Terian's newly published study on the *Letter to the Armenians* composed by Macarius, archbishop of Jerusalem, proves beyond doubt that a delegation of Armenian clerics visited Jerusalem in 335, requesting guidance on the administration of baptism and the Eucharist (Terian 2008). Macarius and an assembled gathering of bishops responded to their queries, addressing their replies to Vrt'anēs, the "Christ-loving and reverend chief-bishop" (*episkoposapet*) and the whole body of bishops and priests of Armenia. Since all the Armenian sources recording the conversion of Trdat and the spread of Christianity across Armenia are separated from these events by at least a century, the *Letter* emerges as the earliest document to record something of the workings and concerns of the Armenian Church in its formative phase. Not only was Vrt'anēs recognized as holding authority over all the bishops of Armenia; there is even a passing reference in the *Letter* to one Torg, bishop of Basean and Bagrewand, "who for a little time was united with the Arians, then repented through remorse and now again is most insolently minded . . . conferring on himself the honor reserved for an archbishop which he is not worthy to receive" (Terian 2008, 90–91). From its inception, it seems that there were tensions within the Armenian Church over what constituted orthodox belief and practice and the degree of independence enjoyed by individual bishops. Vrt'anēs and his fellow Armenian clerics decided to resolve these issues by seeking the adjudication of Archbishop Macarius of Jerusalem.

Far from being isolated from contemporary doctrinal debates and jurisdictional disputes, the Armenian Church was exposed to, and thoroughly immersed in, such developments from the very beginning. Moreover, the operation of these influences was not limited to the fourth century but persisted throughout Late Antiquity. Several reasons as to why the Armenian Church was so susceptible to such influences may be advanced. As the primary focus of pilgrimage in Late Antiquity, Jerusalem clearly played a prominent role in the transmission of sanctioned teachings back to Armenia. Successive orthodoxies therefore came to be superimposed on top of one another, rather like the layers of sediment at the bottom of a lake, overlaying but not erasing earlier deposits. The transfer of new doctrines and practices was no doubt aided by a permanent Armenian presence in the city, for which an early seventh-century list of monasteries attributed to Anastas *vardapet* provides good evidence; this presence is corroborated by other texts and archaeological finds.[26] The names of the monasteries suggest that they were founded by specific noble families or associated with particular districts; they may also have served as pilgrim hostels. Moreover, a strong case has been made recently by Garsoïan for close ties between Armenian and Palestinian monasticism in Late Antiquity, with Jerusalem as the principal conduit (Garsoïan 2005–2007).

This connection with Jerusalem may go some way toward answering how doctrinal developments or liturgical refinements entered the districts of Armenia, even if the circumstances in which they were received, accepted, and retained remain largely hidden from view. Without doubt, the fragmented and mountainous topography of these districts would have had a major part to play, fostering regional and local traditions and assisting in their unobtrusive preservation. But there may be another means of transmitting ideas and practices. It is striking that the Armenian Church, however one chooses to define it, was surrounded on all sides by neighboring churches—Iberian, East Roman, Syrian Orthodox, Persian, and Albanian—and it seems clear that these also influenced adjacent Armenian sees. By way of illustration, one of the many contentious issues between the Iberian and Armenian Churches at the start of the seventh century concerned the suppression of the Armenian liturgy in the worship of the relics of Saint Šušanik at C'urtaw in Gugark', in what was clearly a bicultural and bilingual diocese. The renegade bishop of C'urtaw Movsēs, who seems to have instigated, and then exacerbated, the dispute between the Churches, is described as knowing both languages and officiating in both as well.[27]

The very fact that there was a separate Armenian Church at all owes much to the collapse of the Roman position in the East after the disastrous campaign of the emperor Julian against the Persians in 363. At some point between 383 and 388—the exact date remains unknown—the emperor Theodosius I and the Sasanian king Šahpur III agreed to a fundamental repartitioning of Armenia, which left approximately four-fifths of Armenian territory under Persian control. It is only in the Persian sector that an autocephalous Armenian Church emerged; those districts that fell under Roman sovereignty were incorporated in the wider imperial Church, and their subsequent ecclesiastical history is largely obscure, hence the value of Gregory of Tours' record.

This is not to say that the Armenian Church did not come under sustained pressure at other times. Although Persian oppression in the middle of the fifth century is stressed by the surviving sources, arguably the threat from Constantinople at the end of the sixth century to impose the doctrines and the authority of the imperial Church was far more serious. One approach to take when tracing the impact of these outside influences on the Armenian Church is to examine the sequence of Catholicoi. After the deposition of Catholicos Sahak in 428, a series of three so-called anti-Catholicoi were imposed on the Armenian Church by the Sasanian king, who seems to have treated it as if it were a counterpart of the Persian Church of the East.[28] The degree of Armenian backing for these pro-Persian leaders is frustratingly obscure, but it would be most surprising if they were without any support. Understandably, the surviving Armenian sources are at pains to stress that an Armenian priest Yovsēp' had been selected and sanctioned by Sahak and that it was, in fact, this figure who was respected as the *de facto* head of the Church.[29] It is hard not to interpret this as a struggle between two evenly matched groups for control of the Armenian

Church, with those who looked eastward to the Persian Church for doctrinal orthodoxy and orthopraxy temporarily ascendant. Full Armenian religious autonomy was conceded by the Sasanian authorities only after the opportunistic and successful Armenian revolt under Vahan Mamikonean in 482 C.E.[30]

A more obvious schism within the Armenian Church occurred a century later, in 591 C.E., with the election of a second rival Catholicos. In that year, Khusro II was forced to concede vast swathes of Armenian territory to the emperor Maurice, all of which had been outside Roman provincial control, and the oversight of the imperial Church, for more than two hundred years.[31] According to a partially preserved letter attributed to Yovhannēs Mayragomec'i, Yovhannēs Bagaranc'i was elected Catholicos by an unidentified group of Armenian bishops in an assembly in Theodosiopolis, convened by T'ēodoros, the local bishop of Karin.[32] Yovhannēs was then established in the newly expanded Roman sector of Armenia at Awan, situated provocatively just across the new frontier opposite the traditional seat of the Catholicos in Dvin, where the existing Catholicos, Movsēs Ełivardec'i, continued to reside.[33]

Yovhannēs Bagaranc'i is usually called an anti-Catholicos and treated as little more than a Chalcedonian cipher of Maurice and the imperial Church, with an ephemeral influence upon Armenia. In fact, it is clear that he enjoyed considerable support, even after Khusro II began his reconquest of Armenia in 603. Following the election of Catholicos Abraham Ałbatanec'i, perhaps in 606 but probably in March 607, we learn that five bishops returned to the miaphysite Armenian Church, confessing faith and condemning Chalcedon: T'ēodoros bishop of Sephakan Gund, Step'anos bishop of Bagrewand, Movsēs bishop of Xorxorunik', K'ristap'or bishop of Apahunik', and Nersēs bishop of Vanand.[34] Four of the five therefore occupied sees in western Armenia, which had come under Roman control in 591. Moreover, on the same occasion, no fewer than nineteen leaders of key religious communities also acknowledged their error, including Abraham, superior of the community of the holy *kat'ułikē* (that is, the cathedral of Vałaršapat/Ējmiacin), Yunanēs of Awan, and Grigoris of Aruč. Evidently, Yovhannēs Bagaranc'i had managed to secure significant backing at and below diocesan level in the years after his election, and his support did not collapse at the first sign of trouble. Their four-year resilience is rarely appreciated.

Further evidence demonstrating the existence of support for Catholicos Yovhannēs has been identified by Cowe in one of the versions of the life and works of Gregory the Illuminator, attributed to Agat'angełos (van Esbroeck 1971; Cowe 1992). The Karshuni variant transposes key events in the original narrative to locations relevant to this period of schism. Thus of the seventy-seven virgins accompanying Hrip'simē, forty are assigned to Dvin and thirty-seven to Avan, establishing and promoting the equal sanctity of both sees. Gregory baptizes in the western district of Ekełeac'; he meets king Trdat in Arcn, ten miles northwest of Theodosiopolis; he dies in Daranałi, again in western Armenia. This radical revision, associating key events in the life and ministry of Gregory with sites in the newly expanded Roman sector of Armenia, represents a very subtle appropriation of Armenian tradition for contemporary confessional and political purposes. It was intended to co-opt none other than Gregory the Illuminator onto the side of the Roman Armenian Church under Yovhannēs Bagaranc'i. Not only does it reflect the environment in which it was composed; it also provides a salutary reminder that other Armenian sources may have been through a similar process of reinterpretation and remodeling.

This general pattern, of short interludes when Roman control extended over much of Armenia followed by longer periods of exclusion, was repeated throughout the seventh century. Its impact on the Armenian Church, however, has not perhaps been fully appreciated. In particular, the reception of the monothelete formulation has not merited much in the way of scholarly consideration, largely because the most familiar contemporary sources are silent on the subject or persist in framing all doctrinal antagonism in Chalcedonian terms. It comes as something of a surprise, therefore, to discover that the repudiation of monotheletism by the Sixth Ecumenical Council in 680–681 is described in both extraordinary detail and reproachful terms by a little recognized but contemporary Armenian source usually known as the *Anonymous Chronicle*.[35] Moreover, monotheletism is referred to approvingly in a late seventh-century Armenian discourse attributed to Catholicos Sahak III.[36] Indeed, chapter 45 opens with the statement "Now that we have demonstrated the single will of Christ after the Incarnation . . . let us show that there is a single will according to one nature and not two."[37] When set alongside the statement by Catholicos Yovhannēs Ōjunec'i in the second decade of the eighth century that no fewer than six successive heads of the Armenian Church in the seventh century (including Sahak III) were heretics, the faint impression of an alternative Armenian ecclesiastical history begins to emerge, in which monotheletism played a much more prominent role than has been credited hitherto.[38]

This spectrum of rival doctrinal currents and conflicting attitudes operating simultaneously across Armenia is very much at odds with the singular quality of the Armenian Church conceived and projected by a number of contemporary authors, as a community of believers, united around a single confession of faith, guided by a single network of bishops and priests, and under the spiritual authority of one leader, the Catholicos. We would do well to remember that this apparent unity within the Armenian Church was carefully constructed by several prominent Armenian writers, notably Ełišē, writing in the third quarter of the sixth century.[39] His narrative of the heroic but doomed uprising of Vardan Mamikonean in 450–451 against the impious Persian king Yazkert II owes much to the books of Maccabees.[40] He devised and was at pains to promote an exclusive Armenian Christian identity, one defined in opposition to an external Persian and Zoroastrian threat. Ełišē studiously avoided any discussion of doctrinal dissonance and portrays only faithful Armenian Christians and renegade apostates. This notion of Armenian identity equating to membership of the Armenian Church proved to be particularly potent in the following centuries.

It is also worth bearing in mind that the overwhelming majority of the surviving sources depict the Armenian Church in two contexts: in terms of its interaction with neighboring churches and clerics, conceived as clearly "other," and through the person and actions of the Catholicos, to the extent that it is often hard to distinguish the history of the Armenian Church from the history of the Armenian Catholicosate.[41] These reinforce the imagined Armenian Church as a united and settled Christian community, staunchly defending its orthodoxy in the face of doctrinal novelty and deviation. It is surely significant that although no fewer than twenty-eight letters over a five-year period (604–608) chart the schism between the Armenian and Iberian Churches, as well as the inevitable breach with the imperial Church that this produced, not a single letter composed by the six Catholicoi between 628 and 705 survives. It cannot be a coincidence that these are the very same six Catholicoi deemed heretical by Yovhannēs Ōjunec'i. The profile of the surviving sources in Armenian may have been more consciously shaped along confessional lines than has generally been appreciated.

Yet we should not forget that the Armenian Church existed outside these confessional and Catholicos-focused contexts. A network of bishops extended across the districts and lordships of historic Armenia, as well as a third tier of village-based priests. The intellectual, spiritual, and financial resources of the Armenian Church needed to be managed and developed. How was the Church administered on a day-to-day basis? What records were kept and where? What was the basis of the Church's wealth, by whom was it controlled, and on what was it expended? What was the nature of the relationship between the bishop and the local lord? What supervisory rights did bishops have over religious communities in their dioceses? Did all bishops enjoy the same rights and have the same responsibilities, or were all the sees slightly different, depending on the circumstances of foundation or contemporary conditions? None of these can be answered with any confidence. But there is no harm in raising them because they provide an important corrective to the content and focus of much of the surviving source material and remind us that there was also a local, mundane quality to the Armenian Church, albeit one that rarely surfaces.

Archbishop Macarius' *Letter to the Armenians* suggests that two particular features of the Armenian Church were present from the outset. The first is implied. The recipient of the *Letter*, Vrt'anēs, is conventionally identified as the elder son of Gregory the Illuminator, who held office between 327 and 342.[42] Several fourth- and fifth-century patriarchs of the Armenian Church came from the family of Gregory the Illuminator, to the extent that they are often called "Gregorid." We cannot be certain how far the hereditary principle was adopted across the Armenian Church, whether bishops of particular sees were related to one another, and if they were also related to the local noble house. We do know, however, that the Quinisext Council *in Trullo*, held in Constantinople in 691–692, repudiated several specifically Armenian practices, including the tradition that "in the country of the Armenians, only persons from priestly families are admitted to the clergy, thus following Jewish customs."[43] It seems that the custom of transmitting ecclesiastical authority within certain Armenian families, evident in the first decades of the fourth century, was still very much alive at the end of the seventh century.

The second feature can be seen in the name of the see occupied by the errant Torg: he is identified as the bishop of Basean and Bagrewand, that is, the bishop of two adjoining regions in northwestern Armenia, situated to the east of Theodosiopolis along the upper Araxes River.[44] From the very beginning, therefore, Armenian bishops were associated with, and defined by reference to, specific regions. More often than not, their titles reflected the individual princely houses to which they were attached. Sometimes this association is obvious. We can be confident that Xabib, bishop of Arcrunik', who attended the First Council of Dvin in 505, was associated with the noble Arcruni house because Arcrunik' was never the name of a region or district.[45] Usually, however, the substantial overlap between the names of princely houses and their territories makes it impossible to tell. Just as occasionally, we find both; so Meršapuh, bishop of Tarōn (district) and Mamikoneayk' (princely family), was closely involved in the letters and documents generated in the context of the Second Council of Dvin in 555.[46] The key point to note is that bishops in the Armenian Church were not generally attached to urban centers—the only exception seems to have been the see of Manazkert.[47] This characteristic distinguishes Armenian bishops from the more familiar city-based bishops found throughout Roman Armenia, including bishop T'ēodoros of Karin/Theodosiopolis.

Quite how this network of bishops developed through Late Antiquity is hard to determine. That it increased numerically can be demonstrated by comparing the lists of signatories to successive sets of canons.[48] The circumstances in which new sees were established remain opaque. Was it in response to political changes within the elite or to spiritual needs for additional bishops? Did the Catholicos attempt to undermine the authority of disobedient or contumacious bishops by splitting their sees in two or by superimposing a new see on top of the existing one? The precise role of the Catholicos in the selection and consecration of bishops remains unclear. One suspects that the Catholicos was the titular head of a confederation of sees whose individual members sometimes acted in concert with him but who could just as easily ignore his strictures or requests and look for recognition from elsewhere. Sadly, we have only a handful of records from outside the archives of the Catholicos that could tell us something about the concerns and attitudes of individual bishops. A single letter, composed in 560 by Gregory, bishop of Arcrunik', while he was staying in Jerusalem, records the contemporary uproar in the city over proposals to change the traditional date of the Feast of the Presentation of the Lord.[49] This illustrates his close ties with Jerusalem. A bare list of twelve bishops of Aršarunik', along with their years of tenure, preserved in a colophon, suggests that episcopal dossiers could have preserved local records stretching back many decades, if not centuries.[50] The fact that the foundation inscription at the seventh-century church of Mastara refers to the years of lord T'eodoros, bishop of Gnunik', implies the use of regional chronologies devised around the local episcopal sequence.[51]

Perhaps the most interesting of these records is a little-heralded document, buried in the bundle of materials from the first decade of the seventh century, charting the breach with the Iberian Church and the confessional repositioning in opposition to the imperial Church. This comprises an acknowledgement of previous dealings with "the disciples of Nestorius," presumably Chalcedonians, by one Sahak, son of Hamazasp from the village of Arac.[52] He admitted this in the presence of two bishops, Manasē of Basean and Yovhannēs of Amatunik'; two lay representatives, Gig of Daštakaran and Sargis Zawrakanean; and one vardapet, K'č'kan. Sahak conceded that he deserved eternal damnation but had now been given the opportunity to repent of his actions. He confirmed that he had taken an oath not to communicate in any manner with "those transgressing and shallow-faithed people," either in prayer, food, or fellowship. Remarkably, they are further defined as including the parents of his wife. From now on, Sahak was to treat them as strangers. Sahak agreed that if he broke his oath in any way, he would be condemned by the Holy Trinity, chastised by those present, and liable to pay the sum of one thousand silver coins to the holy church. Sahak then signed the document, and it was attested and sealed by the five witnesses.

This document is of extraordinary value. It shows how doctrinal differences cut across family loyalties. It indicates the considerable wealth available to Sahak. The fine is calculated in silver coins, revealing a familiarity with Sasanian drams rather than Roman gold and copper and hence Armenian integration into Persian economic systems and structures. It is a document which attests the use of written instruments at a local level and so provides a rare glimpse of episcopal administration in action. But the document also expresses something of the difficulty in enforcing doctrinal uniformity. It is telling that Sahak's acknowledgement of past failings and promise of future orthodoxy is appended to a set of canons that dictated the circumstances under which bishops and priests who had accepted Chalcedon could be readmitted to the Armenian Church.[53] One of the canons contemplates the situation in which a bishop had previously admitted his error, had then returned "to the same vomit," and now wished to return to the Armenian Church once again. It applies therefore to a bishop who had had no fewer than four changes of heart! Not only does this indicate a remarkable degree of confessional fluidity within the ranks of the bishops, much greater than one might have anticipated; it also implies an extraordinary reluctance to exclude heretical bishops, a reluctance that may stem from a weary recognition that it was impossible to do so without condemnation from the princely houses whom the bishops served and from whom they were probably appointed. This could also explain why Sahak's oath was witnessed by both religious and secular figures.

With this timely conflation of the spiritual and the secular, let us move on to consider Armenian society.

The study of Armenian political and social history in Late Antiquity has been dominated for the last century by Adontz's magisterial study of Armenia in the era of Justinian.[54] It has exercised a pervasive influence on subsequent generations of historians, to the extent that no scholar embarks on research without consulting it. Although individual contentions have been modified or rejected, notably by Toumanoff's rightful stress on dynastic principles, the work as a whole continues to command great respect.[55] Without wishing to downplay or reduce Adontz's extraordinary achievement, it is perhaps time to adopt a more critical attitude, especially from a methodological perspective.

Given the relative dearth of contemporary source material for the study of either the Roman or the Persian sectors of Armenia in the sixth century, Adontz adopted two solutions. First, he elected "to have recourse to the genetic method of investigation *i.e.* to illuminate a historical problem through a study of its successive phases of development leading up to the period interesting us."[56] Such an approach either requires that the sources employed are demonstrably free from the twin challenges of retrojection (subsequent features being introduced into an earlier era) and anachronism (historic but outdated features intruding into later periods) or acknowledges where such features are present. Unfortunately Armenian *Quellenforschung* is not yet at a point where either condition has been met. Adontz's approach therefore had the unintended consequence of highlighting continuities and downplaying or glossing over times of change and development. The remarkable stability and permanence of form which Adontz perceived in Armenian society was therefore generated by the methodology he employed; in tracing certain social and political features through time, he lost sight of the potential for evolution and change.

The second approach adopted by Adontz was to filter his study of Armenian social structure in Late Antiquity through the prism of feudalism, as it was defined for the medieval West. Indeed, the concluding chapter of his work is titled "The Feudal Bases of the *Naxarar* System."[57] The development of that chapter is highly revealing, for it confirms that the sociopolitical model was in fact driving Adontz's interpretation of the evidence and not the other way around. Late antique Armenian society looked feudal to Adontz because that is what his theoretical template was prompting him to look for. Adontz surely crossed the line between classification and reification, leading him to stress similarities across Armenian society at the expense of difference and distinction.

Adontz himself admitted some of these shortcomings. He noted the unsatisfactory character of some of the evidence found in Armenian literature. He recognized the incomplete, fragmented nature of the historical record and the likelihood that it had been reworked over time.[58] Despite these perceptive comments, all too often Adontz failed to pay sufficient heed to his own anxieties about Armenian sources, exploiting works separated by several centuries for specific information without first subjecting them to critical scrutiny. He therefore jumbled together elements of pre-modern Armenian society that may never have existed at the same time or in the same place.

This is certainly not the occasion on which to embark upon a comprehensive reevaluation of Armenian social and political history in Late Antiquity. Nevertheless, a number of broad contentions may be advanced which could form the basis of future research. In the first place, it is quite possible that a full reconstruction of Armenian social structure is illusory, that such an ambition is unrealistic. Although the surviving sources reveal something about the most prominent princes, they have much less to say about everyone else. Frustratingly, it is not possible to trace the internal dynamics of a single noble family with any degree of continuity. Nor, incidentally, is it possible to study in any detail the fortunes of an individual district or region in Late Antiquity, how patterns of ownership, settlement, or inheritance across that district changed, if indeed they did, or how they compared with neighboring districts. The non-noble population barely surfaces in the surviving sources, and the urban populations of cities such as Dvin or Naxčavan in Persarmenia or Theodosiopolis in the Roman province of Armenia I fare no better. Who lived in cities, and what did they do there? Garsoïan has argued convincingly that cities were alien elements in the Armenian landscape, the preserve of Persian or Roman governors and their forces.[59] The location of the residence of the Catholicos in Dvin therefore comes as something of a surprise until one appreciates that the transfer from Vałaršapat occurred only at the very end of the fifth century, perhaps under Yovhannēs I Mandakuni (478–490) but more probably in the time of his successor, Babgēn I Ot‘msec‘i (490–515/516), when the city was, unusually, under direct Mamikonean control. Yet it was only in 656 that Catholicos Nersēs III moved back to a new complex near Vałaršapat. Could it be that staying in Dvin, the seat of the Persian governor or *marzpan*, brought the Catholicos certain advantages? It may have enabled the Catholicos to stand outside the political volatility and violence which characterized the Armenian elite, as well as avoiding undue pressure from any one noble house.

Although the final collapse of the Arsacid kingdom in 428 came to be interpreted by later commentators as a key moment of transition in the political fortunes of Armenia, in many ways it was the inevitable outcome of a much longer process, namely, the progressive deterioration in relations between the two great powers during the fourth century. The late-fourth-century partition of Armenia represented an attempt by both sides to draw a line under previous actions and prevent future antagonisms by delineating specific sectors. This encouraged individual noble houses to seek preferment in the service of one or other of the powers, even if this meant breaking ranks with other Armenian princes. Thus Siwnik‘ is repeatedly presented as the domain of perfidious princes whose commitment to the Armenian cause was inherently suspect. The treachery of Andovk, prince of Siwnik‘, in the fourth century was mirrored by the actions of Vasak, prince of Siwnik‘, during the rebellion of 450–451.[60] Yet the degree to which Siwnik‘ perceived itself to be Armenian remains very open.

Zachariah of Mitylene, writing in the sixth century, believed that Siwnik‘ had a separate language, on a par with Armenia, Iberia, and Arran (Ałuank‘ or Caucasian Albania).[61] According to the *History* attributed to Sebēos, Prince Vahan of Siwnik‘ asked the Sasanian king Khusro I to transfer the *diwan* of Siwnik‘ from Dvin to the city of P‘aytakaran "so that the name of Armenian would no longer be applied to them."[62] This distinction is confirmed in one of the final notices of this composition, which records that T‘ēodoros Rštuni was granted authority over Armenia, Iberia, Ałuank‘, and Siwnik‘ by the future caliph Mu‘āwiya; this probably occurred in 654.[63] Since an Armenian geographical text dating from the middle of the seventh century identifies Sisagan as a separate Sasanian province distinct from 'Armn,' there are good grounds for supposing that the very status of Siwnik‘ as Armenian was a matter of contention throughout Late Antiquity.[64]

The extension of direct Roman and Persian control over their designated sectors after the end of the Arsacid line did not bring about an immediate reconfiguration of Armenian society. Persarmenia continued to be dominated by a group of noble houses who maintained a tenacious grip over the patchwork of individual districts and territories which collectively made up historic Armenia. Political power was fragmented, depending upon possession of these lands and their material and human resources. Although largely hidden from view, this was a violent and competitive world, with rival figures jostling for preeminence. Those with energy, ambition, and ability, especially on the battlefield, attracted support both from family members and from others who were not directly related but who judged that their best prospects lay in loyal service to them. Inevitably, we tend to hear about those who were successful in such enterprises; we rarely encounter the failures, those who lost their lands, whose support haemorrhaged away, who chose the wrong side.

It would, however, be mistaken to assume that Sasanian Persia simply left its Armenian subjects to their own devices. We know that a Persian governor, *marzpan*, was appointed immediately after the deposition of the last Arsacid king in 428, and the sequence of appointments to this office extends to 628; other than in times of crisis, this office was reserved for non-Armenians. The issue of military recruitment raised previously is worth revisiting. The third book of the *History* of Łazar P‘arpec‘i offers a detailed description of the rebellion of Vahan Mamikonean against Pērōz (459–484) and the settlement negotiated with his successor Vałarš/Walāxš (484–488). The revolt was instigated in 482 among Armenian troops newly returned from Albania, where they had been operating under the overall command of one Zarmihr *hazarawuxt/hazāruft* to put down unidentified rebels.[65] The agreement reached between Nixor Všnaspdat and Vahan Mamikonean after the revolt included a provision that the native Armenian cavalry should be raised once again to attack a rival claimant to the Sasanian throne, Zareh, son of Pērōz. This was duly dispatched, this time under an Armenian commander, Vrēn Vanandac‘i.[66] In other words, within a year of Vahan's uprising, erstwhile rebel Armenian troops were once more serving Sasanian interests outside Armenia, just as they had been before the uprising. This looks very like a return to the normal state of affairs after a brief hiatus. Moreover, this tradition of Armenian military service in Persian armies persisted to the very end of the Sasanian era. The self-styled *sparapet/spāhbed* of Armenia, Mušeł Mamikonean, and Grigor, lord of Siwnik', were both killed at the battle of Qādisiyya fighting with their contingents of 3,000 and 1,000 men, respectively, under Persian command against the Muslim invaders (January 6, 638).[67]

Currently, the structure, operation, and evolution of Sasanian provincial administration across Armenia can be articulated in only the barest of details. The term currently is used advisedly, for significant recent advances in the field of Sasanian sigillography, combined with a reassessment of contemporary Armenian sources, hold out the prospect of substantial definition in the future.[68] Nevertheless, it seems that Sasanian government was predicated on cooperation rather than confrontation with the local Armenian elite. The noble houses held their ancestral lands in perpetuity and controlled their own armed forces, despite their inclusion within the Sasanian provincial structure. They also retained other rights. Łazar P'arpec'i reports that at some point before his rebellion in 482, Vahan Mamikonean became embroiled in a dispute over the exploitation of gold mines in Armenia that resulted in his having to attend before Pērōz to plead his case. While the details need not concern us, it is very striking that Vahan had an associate called Vriw, "of insignificant family and inexperienced, the son of a Syrian," who acted on behalf of the royal treasury and who had accused Vahan of preventing him from carrying out his duties.[69] Gyselen has recently identified a seal that refers to the office of *zarrbed* of Armin, Ardān, Wirōzān, Sīsagān, and Marz ī [Nēsawan], that is, head of the gold of Armenia, Ałuank', Iberia, Siwnik', and the march of Nesawan.[70] It appears that Vahan and Vriw were jointly responsible for the exploitation of these bullion reserves, Vriw as the duly appointed official and Vahan as the landowner.

A different picture emerges from the Roman sector of Armenia. Admittedly, there is a good deal more information on the structure and development of the Roman provincial administration, although its day-to-day operations across its Armenian territories remain similarly obscure. Much of this evidence dates from the opening years of the reign of Justinian. As Adontz recognized, there were both military and civilian aspects to the reforms of Justinian.[71] A *magister militum per Armeniam et Pontum Polemoniacum et gentes* was created, the office of *comes Armeniae* was abolished, and the military responsibilities of six independent satraps were removed.[72] Moreover, Malalas recorded that the first *magister militum per Armeniam*, Sittas, was granted soldiers from the capital and from the East, that is, from the field armies under the *magister militum praesentalis* and the *magister militum per Orientem*.[73] This introduction of regular troops has not perhaps been sufficiently stressed. Henceforth, Roman defenses would not be dependent on local princes and their contingents. *Novella XXXI*, dated to 18 March 536, established four governors for Armenia, incorporating all the Armenian territories within the regular provincial structure of the empire.[74] At approximately the same time, two other imperial instruments came into operation, the first an edict bearing the title "Concerning the order of inheritance among Armenians" and the second, *Novella XXI*, carrying the heading "That the Armenians should follow Roman laws in all ways."[75] The first prescribed that inheritance should be by testamentary disposition and should treat men and women equally, specifying that women should receive a share in family estates. The second replaced all customary traditions and practices with Roman law. Although specific instances concerning inheritance and dowries are cited, the wider implications of this *Novella* are evident in its heading. Justinian was attempting to undercut the power of the noble families by ensuring that in the future, all family estates would be divided between eligible men and women, that is, between sons and daughters and even the children of daughters who had died intestate, in accordance with Roman law. This was intended to override customary succession, which had been both agnatic (limited to male relatives) and collective. The inalienable family estates were vested in the control of the leading prince, the *tēr*, who granted them to male members of his extended family as he deemed appropriate. In effect, the *tēr* distributed life interests in these estates which terminated at his death, when the estates returned to common ownership, pending reallocation once a new *tēr* had emerged. By sanctioning individual wills, Justinian transferred legal title to the noble estates from the collective to the individual, thereby exciting tensions within the nobility; by recognizing the rights of women to share in those estates, he precipitated the breakup of the family landholdings.

Evidently, this legislation was designed to subvert Armenian customs and traditions, causing the power of the leading families to fragment and thereby dissipate. At the same time, the military reorganization was intended to reduce dependence on forces supplied through the local networks of power and authority, in other words, the noble families once more. Such direct intervention is a considerable distance from the Sasanian approaches to regional government, as explored previously. But the long-term impact of the inheritance legislation is harder to assess. We do not know how widely it was intended to operate or how rigorously it was enforced. Nor do we have much sense of its reception or whether it represented wider Roman attitudes towards, and suspicions of, Armenia. Although there is evidence of unrest within the newly defined provinces of Armenia in the later 530s, the one source that records this describes it as a violent response to increased taxation, not the legislation.[76] Moving forward to the end of the sixth century, while there seems little doubt that Maurice and Khusro II set out to strip their respective sectors of Armenian soldiers for service on distant frontiers in the 590s—to the consternation and bewilderment of some, judging from the two disorganized and desperate revolts undertaken in the middle of that decade—there is no suggestion of radical social engineering along the lines envisaged under Justinian.[77] The hegemony enjoyed by Heraclius in the decade after 630 was too short-lived, and the circumstances too constrained, to contemplate sustained intervention. The most that Heraclius accomplished was to use "new men" from little-heralded noble houses as his principal clients; whether this was through choice or dictated by the long-standing Sasanian sympathies and loyalties of the leading houses cannot be determined.[78]

One of the means by which Heraclius and his successor, Constans II, attempted to secure the loyalties of Armenian princes seems to have been through the distribution of cash subsidies. Seven different issues of silver hexagrams from the reign of Heraclius and four of Constans II have been discovered in hoards or during excavations in Armenia, the latest issue struck between 654 and 665.[79] As noted previously, Armenia had been integrated into the Sasanian silver-based monetary system for centuries, and it is likely that this familiarity with silver influenced the decision to mint silver hexagrams. Unfortunately, the wider commercial context into which these coins were introduced remains obscure. The economic history of Armenia in Late Antiquity has not attracted much recent scholarly attention, and Manandyan's study remains influential.[80] His work is not without its challenges. In addition to adopting a rigid theoretical framework through which to interpret the fragmentary evidence, Manandyan also concentrated on international trade, specifically Armenian participation in the transit trade from Central Asia, from the Achaemenid era to the end of the fifteenth century. Regional commercial networks and local production and consumption were largely ignored. This is not to say that the trade routes through Armenian districts were insignificant in Late Antiquity. Procopius comments very favorably on the numerous *emporoi* busily engaged in commercial transactions around the city of Dvin, bringing unspecified merchandise from India, the neighboring regions of Iberia, Persia, and lands under Roman dominion.[81] Unfortunately, he does not identify them further, and we should be cautious about accepting his testimony uncritically; Procopius may well have decided to stress commercial activities being undertaken just outside Roman territory to contrast with the straitened circumstances he wished to portray within the empire. Gregory of Tours records that the Persarmenians who attended upon Justin II in 572 brought with them "a great quantity of unwoven silk," but whether it was theirs in the first place is decidedly unclear.[82] Manandyan also argued that composite lists of Roman and Persian weights and measures allegedly composed by Anania of Širak supported his thesis of an Armenian dimension to long-distance trade.[83] He did not appreciate that this was an Armenian redaction of the well-known *De Mensuris et Ponderibus* of Epiphanius of Salamis or that its principal concern was establishing the mathematical relationships between the terms.[84] It seems rather doubtful, therefore, whether this text had any practical application. Nevertheless, it contains a significantly higher quotient of Persian terms—"A weight of three grains according to the Persian tongue is called a *p'šit*"—than any of the other surviving redactions.[85] It also incorporates the weights of Roman and Persian coins, including the *nomisma* and the *dram* but not the *follis*. Although it offers little evidence for long-distance trade or commercial practice in late antique Armenia, the text does reflect a society at ease with both Roman and Persian metrology and numismatics.

Another short mathematical text attributed to Anania of Širak, however, provides a fascinating insight into the thought world of late antique Armenia, including aspects of its commercial and economic activities. The text is titled *Questions and Answers* and consists of twenty-four mathematical problems, each of which is given an everyday context.[86] Several are clearly intended to be amusing. Problem 3, for instance, describes thieves stealing three-quarters of the treasure from a room in the Great Palace in Constantinople and having given the amount left (421 *kendinar* and 4,600 *dahekan*), invites the student to work out the original weight of treasure. Problem 4, on the other hand, asks the student to calculate the total salary of all the clergy of Hagia Sophia; the answer given is 3,200 *litra* or pounds of gold, equivalent to 230,400 *nomismata*! Nine of the problems involve coins or transactions in coin, thereby supporting the contention that late antique Armenia was at least partially monetized. Several of the other problems contemplate commercial situations. Problem 2, for example, envisages a relative of the author traveling from Bahl to Širak via Ganjak, Naxčavan, and Dvin, selling fractions of a pearl in each place.[87] Problem 11 considers a merchant traveling through three cities and being subject to a levy on his merchandise in each. Problem 18 considers the melting down of a large silver vessel in order to fashion several smaller vessels, including two drinking vessels and three plates, one of which weighed 210 drams, just over two and a half pounds; the original vessel weighed a rather improbable 4,200 drams, or fifty-two and a half pounds. Of course, it is hardly likely that these problems reflect actual situations: Problem 6, for instance, involves a greedy "Roman" eating vast quantities of lettuce! But collectively I would suggest that they afford invaluable insight into the experiences and prejudices of contemporaries. Even if the specific details have been exaggerated, the varied contexts needed to be comprehensible to a contemporary. Those problems that contemplate fishing in the Axurean or Araxes rivers or hunting for wild boar or buying and selling horses, cattle, and sheep or paying stonecutters in the construction of a church all seem to touch on familiar situations and so deserve our close attention.

One final issue needs to be confronted. What impact did the Arab conquests have on Armenia? As one might expect, the emergence of a new power in the Near East prompted a range of reactions. The first raid, undertaken in autumn 640, was guided by one Armenian noble—Vardik, the prince of Mokk'—and confronted by another—T'ēodoros *tēr* of Rštunik'.[88] Thereafter, the rhythm of campaign and counterattack is bewildering in its complexity, but it is clear that Constans II and his successors mounted a vigorous defense alongside their Armenian clients when in the ascendancy and tried to recover the initiative when excluded. Three general observations may be advanced. First, after the conclusion of the first *fitna* in 660, Byzantine operations in Armenia were limited to periods of internal instability within the caliphate. Second, from the little information afforded by our sources, the principal noble houses recovered or reasserted their authority, acting as clients of the new Islamic polity. From being a vital strategic zone of interaction and rivalry, partitioned between great powers of Rome and Persia, Armenia was suddenly relegated to a relative backwater. Mu'āwiya could afford to soothe local sensibilities, and thereby avoid protracted entanglement, by working through a single client in return for a nominal tribute. This may explain why the second half of the seventh century witnessed the construction of several very large churches; the elite were no longer remitting taxes to the Sasanian state and so could invest in major capital projects instead, of which only the stone churches survive. But third, this benign situation in the central Caucasus changed when the Khazars suddenly attacked in 685. The timing of this campaign, coinciding with prolonged internal strife and the second *fitna*, was not accidental and implies strenuous Byzantine diplomatic activity. Thereafter, the Islamic caliphate could not afford to ignore this northern theater with its independent-minded and militarily significant elite. It is at the start of the eighth century when substantial social, political, and cultural changes began to operate across Armenia, when the Armenian Church made a definitive break with its neighbors and the elite were forced to adjust to the unfamiliar circumstance of a single dominant power.[81]

NOTES

1. Gregory of Tours, *Histories* X.24 (Krusch and Levison [1951] 1965, 515.6–516.5).
2. Gregory of Tours, *Histories* X.24 (Krusch and Levison [1951] 1965, 516.6–517.15).
3. Gregory of Tours, *Histories* IV.40 (Krusch and Levison [1951] 1965, 171.18–173.12).
4. Heinzelmann 2001, 207, proposing that Gregory wanted a society in which bishops were more powerful and exercised their authority in cooperation with royal government and shaped his narrative accordingly.
5. Whitby 1988, 263–268; Greatrex and Lieu 2002, 153–158.
6. Greatrex and Lieu 2002, 62–69.
7. Gregory of Tours, *Histories* X.24 (Krusch and Levison [1951] 1965, 515.14–516.1).
8. Gregory of Tours, *Glory of the Martyrs* 95 (Krusch [1885] 1969, 552.13–553.14).
9. See Basil of Caesarea, *Homily* 19, and Gregory of Nyssa, *In Laudem SS Quadraginta Martyrum*.
10. Gregory of Tours, *Histories* IV.40 (Krusch and Levison [1951] 1965, 172.12–13).
11. Procopius, *Buildings* III.iv.14 (Dewing and Downey 1940, 198).
12. Gregory of Tours, *Histories* IV.40 (Krusch and Levison [1951] 1965, 173.1).
13. See, for example, John Malalas, *Chronicle* XVIII.26 and 66 (Thurn 2000, 368.57 and 392.42); Procopius, *Wars* VIII.ii.26 and VIII.viii.21–23 (Dewing 1928, 70 and 124).
14. Sebēos, *History* 90.12–91.7 and 98.3–17.

15. For pilgrims, see Stone 1986; Ervine, Stone, and Stone 2002; for translation and academic research, see Mahé 1996; Shirinian 2005.

16. For general studies, see Thomson 1982b; Renoux 1993; Mahé 1995; for individual authors, see Thomson 1995; 2007.

17. For a recent reconsideration, see Greenwood 2008a, 198–207.

18. Garsoïan 1989, 22–35; 41–55; Garsoïan 1981.

19. Greenwood 2002, 327–347.

20. Procopius, *Wars* VII.xxvi.25–27 (Dewing 1924, 384–386).

21. Procopius, *Wars* I.v.40 (Dewing 1914, 42).

22. Garsoïan 1976; 1996.

23. Garsoïan 1999, 1–43; Mardirossian 2004, 61–71.

24. *Buzandaran* III.x.

25. Koriwn, *Life of Maštoc'* vi (Abełyan [1941] 1985, 42).

26. Garsoïan 2002. Other texts include a letter of John IV patriarch of Jerusalem (574/5–593 C.E.) to Catholicos Abas of Caucasian Albania (Tēr Mkrtč'ean 1896) and the letter from Grigor bishop of Arcrunik' (Połarean 1964). For archaeological finds, see Stone 1997; 2002.

27. *GT'* 1901, 110–111, 164–165; *GT'* 1994, 244–245, 316–318.

28. Garsoïan 1984, 242–248; 1999, 60–66.

29. Łazar, *History*, I.19, II.23 (Tēr Mkrtč'ean and Malxasean 1904, 38, 44).

30. Łazar, *History*, III.lxv–ic (Tēr Mkrtč'ean and Malxasean 1904, 116–178).

31. Sebeos, *History* 76.8–18, 84.20–32.

32. *History of Ałuank'* II.xlvi (Arak'elyan 1983, 267.16–268.11).

33. Sebēos adds that all the vessels of the church of St. Grigor in Dvin had been taken to Theodosiopolis, boosting Yovhannēs' claims to be the legitimate Catholicos: Sebeos, *History* 91.14–23.

34. *GT'* 1901, 131–132; *GT'* 1994, 298–299.

35. *Anonymous Chronicle* = Sargisean 1904, 77.6–79.26; Abrahamyan 1944, 398.3–399.22. For a recent study of this passage, see Greenwood 2008a, 245–248, 251–254.

36. van Esbroeck 1995.

37. *GT'* 1901, 447.

38. *GT'* 1901, 222; *GT'* 1994, 476.

39. Ełišē, *History* [1957] 1993, 5–14.

40. Thomson 1982a, 11–18.

41. This reflects the Catholicos-centered focus of the *Girk' Tłt'oc'*.

42. Terian 2008, 45–51, 79, 108–109.

43. *Council in Trullo* XXXIII (Nedungatt and Featherstone 1995, 110–111).

44. Terian 2008, 54–55, 91, 137.

45. *GT'* 1901, 41; *GT'* 1994, 148.

46. *GT'* 1901, 70–71, 72–75; *GT'* 1994, 196–198, 199–203.

47. *GT'* 1901, 76–77; *GT'* 1994, 204–205.

48. Hewsen 1997.

49. Połarean 1964.

50. Hovsep'yan 1951, no. 17. The colophon is dated 155 of the Armenian era (June 3, 706—June 2, 707 C.E.). Intriguingly, it records that the see originally comprised Bagrewand and Aršarunik'.

51. Greenwood 2004, 47–48, A.10.1.

52. *GT'* 1901, 108–109; *GT'* 1994, 242–243.

53. *GT'* 1901, 146–148; *GT'* 1994, 292–295.
54. Adontz 1970. The original study was published in Russian in 1908.
55. Toumanoff 1963, 33–144, especially 108–139.
56. Adontz 1970, 6.
57. Adontz 1970, 327–371.
58. Adontz 1970, 4–5.
59. Garsoïan 1984–1985, 74–78.
60. Andovk: see *Buzandaran* IV.xx. Vasak: see Łazar, *History*, II.30–34, 45–46 (Tēr Mkrtč'ean and Malxasean [1904] 1986, 57–64, 82–86).
61. Zachariah of Mitylene xii.7 (Brooks [1919] 1953, 214).
62. Sebēos, *History* 67.32–68.2.
63. Sebēos, *History* 169.14–16.
64. *Ašxarhac'oyc'* V.29 (Soukry 1881, 40).
65. Łazar, *History*, III.66 (Tēr Mkrtč'ean and Malxasean [1904] 1986, 118–120).
66. Łazar, *History*, III.94 (Tēr Mkrtč'ean and Malxasean [1904] 1986, 171–172).
67. Sebēos, *History* 137.4–29.
68. For sigillography, see Gyselen 1989; 2007; for Armenian sources, see Greenwood 2008b; Garsoïan 2009.
69. Łazar *History*, III.65 (Tēr Mkrtč'ean and Malxasean [1904] 1986, 116–118).
70. Gyselen 2002, 31, 91–93, 120–122.
71. Adontz 1970, 103–164.
72. *Codex Iustinianus* I.xxix.5 (Krueger 1898, II, 82).
73. John Malalas, *Chronicle* XVIII.10 (Thurn 2000, 358.7–359.12).
74. *Novella XXXI* (Krueger 1895, III, 235–239).
75. *Edict III* (Krueger 1895, III, 760–761); *Novella XXI* (Krueger 1895, III, 144–146).
76. Procopius, *Wars* II.iii.1–31 (Dewing 1914, 270–278). This account may be colored by the author's own views on Justinian's taxation policies.
77. Sebēos, *History* 86.24–90.7.
78. Greenwood 2008c, 340.
79. Mousheghian et al. 2000a; 2000b.
80. Manandyan 1965, 67–127. The first edition was published in 1930 and the second edition, from which the translation was made, appeared in 1946.
81. Procopius, *Wars* II.xxv.2–3 (Dewing 1914, 480).
82. Gregory of Tours, *Histories* IV.40 (Krusch and Levison 1951, 172.13–173.1).
83. Manandyan 1965, 116–122.
84. Epiphanius, *De Mensuris et ponderibus* VII and VIII (Stone and Ervine 2000, 78–81, 103–108).
85. Epiphanius, *De Mensuris et ponderibus* VIII.2 (Stone and Ervine 2000, 80).
86. Abrahamyan 1944, 227–231. Although Manandyan was aware of this composition, he did not comment on its economic potential (Manandyan 1965, 125). For a full translation and commentary, see Greenwood 2011.
87. This route is partially echoed in another composition associated with Anania of Širak. His *Młonoč'apk'* (*Itinerary*) comprises eight routes, the fourth of which describes the route from Dvin to Naxčavan to Ganjak Šahastan, but it then swings south to Ctesiphon and Basra rather than continuing east to Bahl (Abrahamyan 1944, 355; trans. Hewsen 1992, 321–322).
88. Sebeos *History* 138.8–139.3. For a narrative, see Greenwood 2008c, 341–347.
89. Mardirossian 2004, 268–288.

WORKS CITED

Ancient Sources

Anania of Širak, *Questions and Answers* = Abrahamyan 1944, 227–231. Trans. Greenwood 2011, 158–165.

Anonymous Chronicle = *Ananun Žamanakagrut'iwn* 1904. Ed. Barseł Sargisean, 1–80. Venice: Surb Łazar. See also Abrahamyan 1944, 357–399.

Ašxarhac'oyc' = *Géographie de Moïse de Corène d'après Ptolémée* 1881. Ed. Arsène Soukry. Venice: Surb Łazar. Trans. Robert H. Hewsen. 1992. *The Geography of Ananias of Širak (Ašxarhac'oyc') The Long and Short Recensions.* Tübinger Atlas des vorderen Orients Reihe B (Geisteswissenschaften) Nr 77. Wiesbaden: Dr Ludwig Reichert Verlag.

Basil of Caesarea, *Homily* 19. *Patrologia Graeca* 31:507–526.

Buzandaran = *P'awstosi Buzandac'woy' Patmut'iwn hayoc'* [1883] 1984. Ed. Kerovpe Patkanean. St. Petersburg: Tparan kayserakan čemaranin gitut'eanc'. Reprinted Delmar, NY: Caravan. Trans. Garsoïan 1989.

Codex Iustinianus = *Corpus Iuris Civilis volumen secundum* 1898. Ed. and trans. Paul Krueger. Berlin: Weidmann.

Council in Trullo = *The Council in Trullo Revisited* 1995. Ed. George Nedungatt and Michael Featherstone, 41–186. Kanonika 6. Rome: Pontificio Istituto Orientale.

Ełišē, *History* = *Ełišēi vasn Vardanay ew Hayoc' paterazmin* [1957] 1993. Ed. Ervand Ter Minasyan. Erevan: Haykakan SSR Gitut'yunneri Akademiayi tparan. Reprinted Delmar, NY: Caravan. Trans. Robert W. Thomson 1982a. *Eghishē: History of Vardan and the Armenian War.* Harvard Armenian Texts and Studies 5. Cambridge, MA: Harvard University Press.

Epiphanius, *De mensuris et ponderibus* = *The Armenian Texts of Epiphanius of Salamis De Mensuris et ponderibus.* 2000. Ed. Michael E. Stone and Roberta R. Ervine. Corpus Scriptorum Christianorum Orientalium, vol. 583, Subs. 105. Louvain: Peeters.

Girk' T'łt'oc' (Book of Letters) = *GT'* 1901. Ed. Yovsēp' Izmireanc'. Tiflis: T. Rawtineanc' and M. Sharadze. *GT'* 1994. Ed. Norayr Połarean. Jerusalem: St. James Press. Partial French trans. Garsoïan 1999, 411–583.

Gregory of Nyssa, *In Laudem SS Quadraginta Martyrum. Patrologia Graeca* 46: 749–788.

Gregory of Tours, *Glory of the Martyrs* = *Gregorii episcopi Turonensis Miracula et Opera minora* [1885] 1969. Ed. Bruno Krusch. Scriptores rerum Merovingicarum Pars 2. Hannover: Impensis Bibliopolii Hahniani. Trans. Raymond van Dam 1988. *Gregory of Tours: Glory of the Martyrs.* Translated Texts for Historians 4. Liverpool: Liverpool University Press.

———. *Histories* = *Gregorii episcopi Turonensis libri historiarum X* [1951] 1965. Ed. Bruno Krusch and Wilhelm Levison. Scriptores rerum Merovingicarum Tomi 1 Pars 1. Hannover: Impensis Bibliopolii Hahniani. Trans. Lewis Thorpe 1974. *Gregory of Tours The History of the Franks.* Harmondsworth: Penguin.

History of Ałuank' (variously attributed to Movsēs Dasxuranc'i or Kałankatuac'i) = *Movsēs Kałankatuac'i Patmut'iwn Ałuanic' ašxarhi* 1983. Ed. Varag Arak'elyan. Erevan: HSSH GA Hratarakč'ut'yun. Trans. Charles Dowsett 1961. *The History of the Caucasian Albanians by Moses Dasxuranc'i.* London: Oxford University Press.

John Malalas, *Chronicle* = *Ioannis Malalae Chronographia* 2000. Ed. Ioannes Thurn. Corpus fontium historiae Byzantinae 35. Berolini: W. de Gruyter. Trans. Elizabeth Jeffreys, Michael Jeffreys, and Roger Scott 1986. *The Chronicle of John Malalas.* Byzantina Australiensia 4. Melbourne: Australian Association for Byzantine Studies.

Koriwn, *Vark' Maštoc'i* [1941] 1985. Ed. Manuk Abełyan. Erevan: Haypethrat. Reprinted Delmar, NY: Caravan.

Łazar, *History* = *Łazaray P'arpec'woy Patmut'iwn Hayoc'* [1904] 1986. Ed. Galust Tēr-Mrktč'ean and Stepan Malxasean. Tiflis: Mnacakan Martiroseanc'. Reprinted Delmar, NY: Caravan. Trans. Robert W. Thomson 1991. *The History of Łazar P'arpec'i.* Occasional Papers and Proceedings 4. Atlanta: Scholars.

Novellae constitutiones = *Corpus Iuris Civilis volumen tertium* [1895] 1954. Ed. and trans. Rudolf Schoell and Guilelmus Kroll. Berolini: Apud Weidmannos.

Procopius, *Wars* = *History of the Wars* 1914–1928. 5 vols. Ed. and trans. Henry B. Dewing. Loeb Classical Library 48, 81, 107, 173, 217. Cambridge, MA: Harvard University Press.

———. *Buildings* = *Buildings* 1940. Ed. and trans. Henry B. Dewing and Glanville Downey. Loeb Classical Library 343. Cambridge, MA: Harvard University Press.

Sebeos, *History* = *Patmut'iwn Sebēosi* 1979. Ed. Gevorg V. Abgaryan. Erevan: Haykakan SSH Gitut'yunneri Akademiayi Hratarakč'ut'yun. Trans. Robert W. Thomson, with commentary by James Howard-Johnston 1999. *The Armenian History Attributed to Sebeos,* 2 vols. Translated Texts for Historians 31. Liverpool: Liverpool University Press.

Zachariah of Mitylene, *Historia ecclesiastica Zachariae Rhetori vulgo II adscripta* [1919] 1953. Ed. and trans. Ernest W. Brooks. Corpus Scriptorum Christianorum Orientalium, vol. 84. Scriptores Syri 39. Louvain: L. Dubecq.

Modern Sources

Abrahamyan, Ašot G. 1944. *Anania Širakac'u matenagrut'yunĕ.* Erevan: Matenadarani hratarakč'ut'yun.

Adontz, Nicholas. 1970. *Armenia in the Period of Justinian.* Trans. and partially rev. Nina G. Garsoïan. Lisbon: Calouste Gulbenkian Foundation.

Cowe, S. Peter. 1992. "An Armenian Job Fragment from Sinai and Its Interpretation," *Oriens christianus* 76: 123–157.

Ervine, Roberta, Michael Stone, and Nira Stone, eds. 2002. *Armenians in Jerusalem and the Holy Land.* Hebrew University Armenian Studies 4. Leuven: Peeters.

Garsoïan, Nina G. 1976. "Prolegomena to a Study of the Iranian Elements in Arsacid Armenia," *Handes Amsorya* 90: col. 177–234. Reprinted in Nina G. Garsoïan. 1985. *Armenia between Byzantium and the Sasanians,* no. X. London: Variorum Reprints.

———. 1981. "The Locus of the Death of Kings: Iranian Armenia—the Inverted Image." In *The Armenian Image in History and Literature,* ed. Richard Hovannisian, 27–64. Studies in Near Eastern Culture and Society 3. Malibu, CA: Undena.

———. 1984. "Secular Jurisdiction over the Armenian Church (Fourth–Seventh Centuries)." In *Okeanos: Essays Presented to Ihor Ševčenko on His Sixtieth Birthday,* ed. Cyril A. Mango, Omeljan Pritsak, and Uliana M. Pasiczynk, 220–250. Harvard Ukrainian Studies 7. Cambridge, MA: Harvard University Press. Reprinted in Nina G. Garsoïan. 1985. *Armenia between Byzantium and the Sasanians,* no. IX. London: Variorum Reprints.

———. 1984–1985. "The Early Mediaeval Armenian City—An Alien Element?" *Journal of the Ancient Near Eastern Society* 16–17: 67–83 = *Ancient Studies in Memory of Elias Bickerman.*
———. 1985. *Armenia between Byzantium and the Sasanians.* London: Variorum Reprints.
———. 1989. *The Epic Histories (Buzandaran Patmut'iwnk').* Harvard Armenian Texts and Studies 8. Cambridge, MA: Harvard University Press.
———. 1996. "The Two Voices of Armenian Mediaeval Historiography: The Iranian Index," *Studia Iranica* 25: 7–43.
———. 1999. *L'Église arménienne et le grand schisme d'Orient.* Corpus Scriptorum Christianorum Orientalium vol. 574. Subs. 100. Louvain: Peeters.
———. 2002. "Le témoignage d'Anastas *vardapet* sur les monastères arméniens de Jérusalem à la fin du VIe siècle," *Travaux et Mémoires* 14: 233–245 = *Mélanges Gilbert Dagron.*
———. 2005–2007. "Introduction to the Problem of Early Armenian Monasticism," *Revue des études arméniennes* 30: 177–236.
———. 2009. "Armenian Sources on Sasanian Administration," *Res Orientales* 18: 59–81.
Greatrex, Geoffrey, and Samuel L. C. Lieu. 2002. *The Roman Frontier and the Persian Wars Part II AD 363–630.* London: Routledge.
Greenwood, Timothy W. 2002. "Sasanian Echoes and Apocalyptic Expectations: A Re-Evaluation of the Armenian History Attributed to Sebeos," *Le Muséon* 115.3–4: 323–397.
———. 2004. "A Corpus of Early Medieval Armenian Inscriptions," *Dumbarton Oaks Papers* 58: 27–91.
———. 2008a. "'New Light from the East': Chronography and Ecclesiastical History through a Late Seventh-Century Armenian Source," *Journal of Early Christian Studies* 16.2: 197–254.
———. 2008b. "Sasanian Reflections in Armenian Sources," *E-Sasanika* 5: www.humanities.uci.edu/sasanika/pdf/e-sasanika5-Greenwood.pdf.
———. 2008c. "Armenian Neighbours (600–1045)." In *The Cambridge History of the Byzantine Empire c. 500–1492*, ed. Jonathan Shepard, 333–364. Cambridge: Cambridge University Press.
———. 2011. "A Reassessment of the Life and Mathematical Problems of Anania Širakac'i," *Revue des études arméniennes* 33: 129–184.
Gyselen, Rika. 1989. *La géographie administrative de l'empire sassanide: Les témoignages sigillographiques.* Res orientales 1. Paris: Groupe pour l'étude de la civilisation du Moyen-Orient.
———. 2002. *Nouveaux matériaux pour la géographie historique de l'empire sassanide: Sceaux administratifs de la collection Ahmad Saeedi.* Studia Iranica 24. Paris: Association pour l'avancement des études iraniennes.
———. 2007. *Sasanian Seals and Sealings in the A. Saeedi Collection.* Acta Iranica 44. Leuven: Peeters.
Heinzelmann, Martin. 2001. *Gregory of Tours: History and Society in the Sixth Century.* Trans. Christopher Carroll. Cambridge: Cambridge University Press.
Hewsen, Robert H. 1997. "An Ecclesiastical Analysis of the Naxarar System: A Re-Examination of Adontz's Chapter XII." In *From Byzantium to Iran: Armenian Studies in Honour of Nina G. Garsoïan*, ed. Jean-Pierre Mahé and Robert W. Thomson, 97–149. Columbia University Program in Armenian Studies 8. Atlanta: Scholars.

Hovsep'yan, Garagin. 1951. *Yišatakarank' jeragrac'*. Ant'ilias: Tparan Kat'ołikosut'ean Hayoc' Kilikioy.

Mahé, Jean-Pierre. 1995. "L'Arménie et les Pères de l'Église: Histoire et mode d'emploi." In *La documentation patristique*, ed. Jean-Claude Fredouille and René-Michel Roberge, 167–179. Paris: Presses de l'Université de Paris-Sorbonne.

———. 1996. "Connaître la Sagesse: Le programme des anciens traducteurs arméniens." In *Arménie entre Orient et Occident*, ed. Raymond Kévorkian, 40–61. Paris: Bibliothèque nationale de France.

Manandyan, Hakob A. 1965. *The Trade and Cities of Armenia in Relation to Ancient World Trade*. Trans. Nina G. Garsoïan. Lisbon: Calouste Gulbenkian Foundation.

Mardirossian, Aram. 2004. *Le livre des canons arméniens (Kanonagirk' hayoc') de Yovhannēs Awjnec'i*. Corpus Scriptorum Christianorum Orientalium vol. 606. Subs. 116. Louvain: Peeters.

Mousheghian, Khatchatur, Anahit Mousheghian, and Georges Depeyrot. 2000a. *History and Coin Finds in Armenia: Coins from Duin, Capital of Armenia*. Collection Moneta 18. Wetteren: Moneta.

———. 2000b. *History and Coin Finds in Armenia: Coins from Ani, Capital of Armenia*. Collection Moneta 21. Wetteren: Moneta.

Połarean (Bogharian), Norayr. 1964. "Tułt' yErusałemē i Hays vasn Tearněndarajin," *Sion* 38: 33–36. [Trans. Terian 2008, 155–162]

Renoux, Charles. 1993. "Langue et littérature arméniennes." In *Christianismes orientaux*, ed. Micheline Albert, 109–188. Paris: Éditions du Cerf.

Shirinian, M. Erna. 2005. *K'ristoneakan vardapetut'yan antik ev hellenistakan tarrerě*. Erevan: Maštoc'i anvan hin jeragreri Institut Matenadaran.

Stone, Michael E. 1986. "Holy Land Pilgrimage of Armenians before the Arab Conquest," *Revue Biblique* 93: 93–111.

———. 1997. "The New Armenian Inscriptions from Jerusalem." In *Armenian Perspectives: 10th Anniversary Conference of the Association Internationale des Études Arméniennes*, ed. Nicholas Awde, 263–268. Richmond: Curzon.

———. 2002. "A Reassessment of the Bird and Eustathius Mosaics." In *Armenians in Jerusalem and the Holy Land*, ed. Roberta Ervine, Michael Stone, and Nira Stone, 203–219. Hebrew University Armenian Studies 4. Leuven: Peeters.

Tēr Mrktč'ean, Galust. 1896. "Erusałemi Yovhannēs episkoposi tułt," *Ararat* 252–256. [Trans. Garsoïan 1999, 490–501]

Terian, Abraham. 2008. *Macarius of Jerusalem Letter to the Armenians AD 335*. AVANT Series 4. Crestwood, NY: St. Vladimir's Seminary Press.

Thomson, Robert W., trans. 1982a. *Eghishē: History of Vardan and the Armenian War*. Harvard Armenian Texts and Studies 5. Cambridge, MA: Harvard University Press.

———. 1982b. "The Formation of the Armenian Literary Tradition." In *East of Byzantium: Syria and Armenia in the Formative Period*, ed. Nina Garsoïan, Thomas Mathews, and Robert W. Thomson, 135–150. Washington, DC: Dumbarton Oaks Center for Byzantine Studies.

———. 1995. *A Bibliography of Ancient Armenian Literature to 1500 AD*. Corpus Christianorum. Turnhout: Brepols.

———. 2007. "Supplement to *A Bibliography of Ancient Armenian Literature to 1500 AD*. Publications 1993–2005," *Le Muséon* 120.1–2: 163–223.

Toumanoff, Cyril. 1963. *Studies in Christian Caucasian History*. Washington, DC: Georgetown University Press.

van Esbroeck, Michel. 1971. “Un nouveau témoin du livre d’Agathange,” *Revue des études arméniennes* 8:13–167.

———. 1995. “Le discours du Catholicos Sahak III en 691 et quelques documents arméniens annexes au Quinisexte.” In *The Council in Trullo Revisited*, ed. George Nedungatt and Michael Featherstone, 323–451. Kanonika 6. Rome: Pontificio Istituto Orientale.

Whitby, Michael. 1988. *The Emperor Maurice and His Historian*. Oxford: Clarendon.

CHAPTER 5

CENTRAL ASIA AND THE SILK ROAD

ÉTIENNE DE LA VAISSIÈRE
École des Hautes Études en Sciences Sociales, Paris

Central Asia is known mainly through such images as the "Silk Road," a term invented by a German geographer in 1877 and reinvigorated recently by the development of mass travel. Another image is the path of Buddhism from India to China, exemplified by the art of the Buddhist grottoes, and it is certainly well known for its nomadic world empires, particularly that of the Mongols. But its precise history, especially during Late Antiquity, is mostly unknown to the Western reader.[1] A brief introduction in English is thus sorely needed and complementary to the global spectrum of this book.[2]

Climatic, Geographical, and Cultural Milieux

Central Asia may be described as the region situated north of the Sasanian empire and the Hindu-Kush range, west of the area settled by ethnic Han Chinese (that is, west of the Gansu corridor in China), east of the Caspian Sea, and south of the Altay Mountains. (See figure 5.1.) Four main natural environments dominate this enormous region of Asia: (1) the steppe in the north; (2) the mountains (Tianshan, Pamir, Kunlun), which divide Central Asia into western, eastern, and northern sections; (3) the deserts (Gobi, Taklamakan, Kyzil Kum, Kara Kum); and (4) the oases along the tributaries of the main rivers. The climate is hypercontinental, but the combination of winter rains and high mountains provide water in the rivers from melted snow during the vegetative period. The whole period from the fifth century to the ninth might be a milder episode between two periods of high aridity.[3] Two main economies were created to deal with these formidable climatic and geographical conditions. First, a pastoral economy dominates in the steppe, on the numerous plateaus of the mountains, and on the periphery of deserts. The second, an agricultural system, has always been confined to the alluvial fans of rivers among the foothills and along the smaller rivers. With the exception of the terminal delta of the Amu Darya (i.e., the region of Khorezm),[4] the main rivers—Amu Darya, Syr Darya, and Tarim—are too powerful to be of use for irrigated agriculture.[5] No north-south divide between pastoralism and agriculture can be drawn, since the nomadic and settled populations were interspersed, given that the nomads grazed their flocks on the peripheries of the oases and circulated into the semideserts of western Central Asia.[6]

Two main linguistic groups (Middle-Iranian and Turkish) and several smaller ones can be delineated: in the western part of Central Asia (i.e., the territories of the former USSR) and also on the other side of the Pamir range, as far as the oasis of Khotan (i.e., in the south of the Taklamakan desert of present-day China), Middle-Iranian languages prevailed. There were four main linguistic subgroups in this region: (1) Khorezmian, quite isolated in the delta of the Amu Darya,[7] and (2) Sogdian, between the Amu Darya and the Syr Darya, both written with scripts derived from Aramaic;[8] (3) Bactrian, written with the Greek alphabet (inherited from Alexander's conquests), in Northern Afghanistan and along the upper course of the Amu Darya;[9] and (4) Khotanese, in the Tarim basin, written in an Indian script (Brahmi).[10] In the north, but also in eastern Afghanistan and in the oases to the north of the Taklamakan, the process of "Turkicization" of the nomadic peoples went on throughout our period.[11]

Some groups are not reducible to these two main cultural-linguistic groups, such as the Tokharians of the oases to the north of the Taklamakan (Kucha, Qarashahr, Turfan). These speakers of an Indo-European language that had separated itself from the common Indo-European long before the others wrote in another variant of Brahmi.[12] Additionally, speakers of Tibeto-Birman

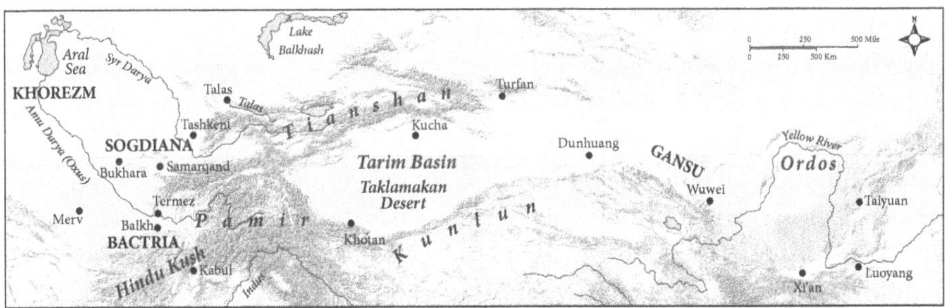

Figure 5.1. Silk Road Regions

languages were found on the vast stretches of the Tibetan plateau. Finally, the Chinese were mostly confined to the three main oases of the far east: Turfan, Hami, and Dunhuang. Each oasis can be described as having its own history and culture, alongside these wide-ranging linguistic provinces. From a religious point of view, the principal belief systems were Buddhism, at home in northern Afghanistan and in the oases of the Tarim basin;[13] a Central Asian polytheistic form of Zoroastrianism, which dominated the settled land of western Central Asia;[14] and the Sky and Earth cult of the Turks, poorly understood from contemporary sources.[15]

The Great Invasion

Western Central Asia opens directly on the steppe belt and its nomadic empires, while eastern Central Asia is protected by the Tianshan mountains and the deserts. Thus the Hunnic invasion that marked the beginning of our period was an important factor only in western Central Asian history. Several independent but corroborating texts show the arrival of a wave of northeastern invaders in western Central Asia in about 350. Some climatic reasons might be adduced to explain this migration: paleoclimatology has proven that the climate of the Altay range changed dramatically in the middle of the fourth century, driving the nomads away from their mountain grazing grounds.[16] In addition to Chinese texts mentioning the death of the king of Samarkand in the face of Xiongnu invaders, Ammianus Marcellinus describes how in 356 Shāpūr II fought against the Chionites in the East and subsequently formed an alliance with them, evidenced by the fact that the king of the Chionites, Grumbates, participated in the siege of Amida (Diyarbakir) at the side of Shāpūr II in 359. The Armenian sources next show that between 368 and 379, the Sasanians were routed in the east on several occasions by a "king of the Kushans" reigning at Balkh.[17] No wars between Sasanians and nomads are known for the following period, from approximately 375 to 425. Several sources attest to significant wars around Merv, or launched from there, during the second part of the reign of Vahrām V (420–438). Many drachms were then struck at Merv, a fact that testifies to the role played by the city in the Sasanian policy of defense.[18] These drachms could have been specifically used to pay the troops. The Arabic and Persian texts on Vahrām Ghor attribute the presence and activity of the king at Merv to a great attack by the "Qagan of the Türks," an anachronistic figure behind whom we must understand a nomadic power from the east or north. A third period of war began with the defeat of the Kidarites by the Sasanian emperor Pērōz in 468 and his subsequent death in 484 in the face of the emerging dynasty of the Ephthalites (first mentioned by Chinese sources in 457).[19] Pērōz's successor, Kawād I (484, 488–497, 499–531) was their protégé. Until the beginning of the reign of Khusrō Anōshervān (531–579), the Sasanians paid a colossal tribute to the Ephthalites.[20] The Ephthalites then controlled the whole of Central Asia, including the Tarim Basin, which had been untouched by the Chionites or Kidarites. This was before the Ephthalites were defeated by the alliance between a new Altaic power, in the form of the Turks, and the Sasanians in 560.[21]

This period is certainly one of the most obscure of Central Asian history, and in this regard, the contrast with the following period, from the middle of the sixth century to the middle of the eighth, is stark. Along with the Byzantine and Chinese texts, numismatic evidence is our other main source. Hundreds of different coins created by these nomadic dynasties have been discovered in Afghanistan.[22] The chronology established by the numismatists is sometimes at odds with that derived from textual sources: for instance, while all the Byzantine and Chinese texts are in agreement, situating the Kidarites during and after the 420s, the numismatists would place them in the 380s because of some rare gold coins discovered near Kabul, with a blurred Bactrian legend that can be read, among other possibilities, as *κιδορο*.[23]

Nevertheless, there have been great recent advances in our understanding of this period. Some 150 new documents from a notarial archive originating in Bactria and dating from the third to the eighth century have been published and offer much new data about the daily life of the small mountainous kingdoms of the Hindu-Kush.[24] It seems that the reign of Ardashir, the creator of the Sasanian empire, serves to date these Bactrian documents—from then up to the Abbasids—because of the conquest of Bactria by the Sasanians under Ardashir's reign. The ebb and flow of the nomadic kingdoms in Bactria is reflected via the titles and the taxes mentioned in these texts. The modern archaeological pillaging of Afghanistan brings to the art market a constant flow of new coins and documents.

There have also been other improvements to our historical understanding of this long period of nomadic turmoil. For instance, the very old question of the ethnic and political identity of the invaders has been solved, after perplexing historians for a quarter of a millennium, that is, since De Guignes in the middle of the eighteenth century proposed identifying the invading Huns with the old foes of Ancient China, the Xiongnu. By a combination of textual and archaeological sources, De Guignes's theory has been confirmed. First, a letter by a Central Asian merchant, sent in 313 to Samarkand and describing the Xiongnu pillages of northern China, calls them "Huns." Next, a Bactrian monk's translation (from Dunhuang) of a Buddhist sutra into Chinese renders the Indic work "Huna" by the Chinese "Xiongnu" at the end of the third century. As for archaeological evidence, the huge Xiongnu cauldrons from Mongolia are virtually identical to the Hunnic ones from Hungary; what is more, they were found in similar locales (i.e., on the banks of rivers), thus proving continuity in ritual as well. Therefore, it is now possible to demonstrate conclusively that the invaders were under Xiongnu/Hunnic leadership and left the Altay mountains in the middle of the fourth century, some of them heading south to western Central

Asia, and some of them heading west and reaching the Volga River. The Huns are beyond doubt the political and ethnic inheritors of the old Xiongnu empire.[25]

It has also been demonstrated that there was a single wave of invasions in Central Asia and not several waves, as previously thought. Formerly, at least three waves were contemplated, due to the multiplicity of nomadic ethnic and dynastic names in Central Asia from about 350 to about 460: a Chionite one in the middle of the fourth century, a Kidarite one from 380 or 420 onward, and then an Ephthalite one in the middle of the fifth century. We now know that all these dynasties and ethnic groups were part of a single episode of massive migration in about 350–360. A well-informed Chinese source mentions the Ephthalites—previously thought to be the latest group—as among the earliest invaders of about 350–360.[26] These invaders were thus the origins of the nobility that would control all of Central Asia during Late Antiquity. Though this is well known for Bactria from coins and seals, the same has also been demonstrated recently for Sogdiana. For instance, a recently published seal gives the title of a fifth-century lord of Samarkand as "king of the Oglar Huns."[27] In Bactria, the name of the king of the Chionites at Amida, Grumbates, is also known as the name of a local noble in 470. Furthermore, the old titles inherited from antiquity, such as "King of the Kushans" in Bactria, were abandoned after the formation of the Kidarite dynasty.

The Postinvasion Economic Shift

This great invasion had a profound impact on the economy.[28] Southern Central Asia—that is, Bactria—was devastated during the wars between the nomads and the Sasanians. Northern Central Asia—that is, Sogdiana—fell easily under the yoke of the invaders and was quickly reconstructed. Archaeology testifies to the divergent fates of these two regions: all of the available data support the idea of a sharp decline in Bactria from the second half of the fourth century to the sixth. In the valley of the Wakhsh River, for example, the irrigation network was partially abandoned. Layers of burning are visible at most of the sites of the region of Kunduz. At Chaqalaq-tepe, a fortified village eleven kilometers south-southeast of Kunduz, three layers of burning can be seen in the middle level (end of the fourth century and first half of the fifth century), despite the simultaneous construction of a double rampart.[29] At Balkh, excavations at Tepe Zargaran show significant barren layers separating two series of Sasanian layers.[30] Farther to the west, at Dil'beržin tepe and Emshi tepe, the sites were abandoned after the middle of the fifth century.[31] At Termez and Dal'verzintepe, necropolises appeared in large numbers over the old urban area in the fourth and fifth centuries, while the Buddhist monasteries around Termez (Karatepe) were pillaged by the troops of Shāpūr II and later abandoned and filled with sepulchres.

A comprehensive study of eastern Bactrian ceramics reveals the desertion of traditionally populated areas in this period (the plain of Taluqan and plain of Kunduz).[32] Up to the sixth century, the low valleys of the tributaries north of the Amu Darya seem to have been sparsely populated. The plain of Bactra, as well as the central Amu Darya, seems to have undergone a decline that was much more significant than that suffered by the regions farther east. Bactra (i.e., Balkh in the Arabic sources), although often claimed as a capital by the various political powers, became once again an important town in the region only much later, during the Muslim period.

The contrast is strong with Sogdiana: for sure, the ancient cohabitation of sedentary peoples and local nomads, established on the immediate frontier of the oases, seems to have been swept away. The nomad kurgans at the peripheries of the oases have disappeared and, with them, an economic osmosis attested by the abundance of sedentary ceramics found in the tombs.[33] The development of ceramic forms is particularly instructive, for parallel to the local forms that continued to be produced, a molded ceramic appears in the archaeological layers of this period, notably in the oases of Bukhara and the Kashka Darya. During the preceding period, this new form of ceramic, molded and not turned, was characteristic of the region of the Syr Darya. It is as if populations arriving from the Syr Darya had to take refuge in Sogdiana due to Hunnic pressure or, bringing their ceramics with them, came to return to cultivation lands that a stricken population had partially abandoned. Conversely, the sites of the Džety-asar culture in the delta of the Syr Daria were widely abandoned, and on the middle course of the Syr Darya, the town of Kanka diminished to a third of its initial surface area. The people arriving from the north added to the local population, which did not disappear. Sogdiana, separated from the steppe by a fragile agricultural zone along the Syr Darya, reaped the benefits of the withdrawal of these populations to the south and the experienced labor these populations had contributed, despite whatever ravages were caused by the invasions in Sogdiana itself. Sogdiana indisputably experienced a great agricultural expansion in the fifth and sixth centuries. The population markedly increased. Detailed archaeological surveys have proven that on the margins of all the Sogdian oases, new lands were reclaimed from desert and irrigated. For instance, to the west of Bukhara, after the advance of the desert in the first centuries C.E., the oasis of Bukhara was extended twenty-two kilometers by irrigation in the sixth century. The Sogdian countryside also benefited from the construction of gigantic walls, intended to fight against nomadic raids as much as against the advance of desert sands. The landscape was dotted with the castles of the settled nomadic aristocracy. The towns of Sogdiana entered a remarkable period of growth as well. The urban network was profoundly modified by the creation of new towns in the Zarafshan Valley, which were often built on older sites. Bukhara, Paykent, and Panjikent developed rapidly on plans of the Hippodamian type (i.e., rectangular walls, an orthogonal network of streets), examples of which are also found in eastern Sasanian Iran.[34]

The economic and demographic dynamism of Sogdiana after the great invasion is thus an established fact. Sogdiana under its nomadic elites became the principal center of agricultural wealth and population in Central Asia.

The Shift of the Trade Routes

Following the decline of Bactria—one of the major points along the Silk Road in antiquity—the principal roads of international trade shifted north. The term "Silk Road" up to the third century could describe a mainly Sino-Indian trade route through the Pamir and Bactria, due to the wealth of the Kushan empire, which controlled northern India and southern Central Asia from the first to the third century C.E.[35] However, the new Silk Road that emerged from the nomadic invasion in the fifth century went through eastern Central Asia and the steppe to Sogdiana, and from there to the Sasanian empire and Byzantium. It linked the main centers of wealth and population, bypassing a half-deserted Bactra. This shift to the north explains the domination of the Sogdian traders on the Silk Road from the fifth century to the eighth. Moreover, with this dynamism in Sogdiana, these traders controlled in their homeland the main market of Central Asia.

But the history of Sogdian international trade has deep roots in antiquity. Even from the very foundations of the Silk Road by Indian and Bactrian traders in the first century B.C.E., Sogdian traders have been mentioned. It seems that during antiquity, they were the apprentices of the wealthier merchants from Bactra or Taxila. The Sogdian vocabulary of trade is a testimony to this phase, as it is replete with Bactrian and Indian loanwords.[36] The Buddhist sources that mention Sogdian traders becoming monks describe them as emigrants, trading and converting in India.[37] However, it seems that already in the third century, before the great invasion, Sogdian trade had progressed enough to be on a par with Bactrian trade: in 227, during the troubled period following the fall of the Han dynasty, the heads of the Bactrian and Sogdian communities of Liangzhou, in the middle of Gansu, were in charge of negotiations with advancing armies.[38] The Hunnic invasion and the Sasanian counteroffensives in Bactria cleared the ground for the Sogdian traders.

This is well demonstrated with the help of a Byzantine text of the middle of the sixth century, the *Christian Topography* of Cosmas Indicopleustes. An Alexandrian spice merchant who had retired to a monastery in the Sinai, Cosmas was accurately informed about the commerce of the Indian Ocean. He mentions silk and states:

> For the country in question deflects considerably to the left, so that the loads of silk passing by land through one nation after another, reach Persia in a comparatively short time; whilst the route by sea to Persia is vastly greater.

> For just as great a distance as the Persian Gulf runs up into Persia, so great a distance and even a greater has one to run, who, being bound for Tzinitza (China), sails eastward from Taprobane (Sri Lanka); while besides, the distances from the mouth of the Persian Gulf to Taprobane; and the parts beyond through the whole width of the Indian sea are very considerable. He then who comes by land from Tzinitza to Persia shortens very considerably the length of the journey. This is why there is always to be found a great quantity of silk in Persia.[39]

Cosmas very precisely distinguishes two routes by which silk was traded: the Central Asian caravan route and the maritime route via Ceylon (Taprobane/Sri Lanka). But above all, he posits a hierarchical relationship between them: for silk, the Central Asian caravan route was primary. The Persians procured silk in two very distinct locations: on the one hand, the peoples of Central Asia brought it to them, and on the other, they went to buy it in Ceylon. The merchants of northwestern India and Bactria were no longer capable of adequately supplying the main Indian ports with silk from distant sources: according to another part of the text, Sind (Pakistan) obtained its silk from Ceylon, not from Bactra.[40] The main road in antiquity—through Bactria, northern India, and then by sea—had become divided into two quite distinct routes, one of which, the most important for silk, was in the hands of the Sogdians in Central Asia.

This text is corroborated by epigraphic evidence from the high passes on the Upper Indus, where caravaneers left graffiti while waiting to cross the river. There are hundreds of Indian and Sogdian graffiti, but only a few Bactrian are known, a fact indicating that even on this mountainous road linking India with Bactria, the Bactrian traders had been superseded by the Sogdian ones.[41]

The Silk Road, the Turks, and the Chinese

This shift to the north of the economic and demographic landscape of Central Asia was reinforced by the close links established between Central Asia and the Turks. The Turkish tribes, under the sacred clan of the Ashinas, took power by revolting against the Rouran in the Altay and the Mongolian steppe in 552 and had established power over all of Central Asia by 560.[42] At its greatest extent, their empire would include the entire steppe belt from the Crimea in the west, where its armies besieged Byzantine towns, to Manchuria in the east. This first Turkish empire, although divided into western and eastern parts after 580, would last until 630 (East) or 659 (West) and later, after a period of disunion and submission to the Chinese, would be reborn from 681 to 744, comprising, however, a reduced Mongolian territory (without most of Central Asia). Central Asian peoples, especially the Sogdians and the Tokharians, played an enormous role in the administration, social life, and economy of the empire: the Turks made use of Sogdian as their diplomatic and administrative language, and their first known inscriptions are in Sogdian.[43] Tokharian Buddhism made inroads in the steppe under their protection.[44] The Ashinas emperors themselves arose out of the ethnically mixed milieu of western China, and the names of the two founding brothers of the empire, Bumın and Istämi, cannot be Turkish.[45] A military-commercial symbiosis was created: the Turkish military integrated itself through marriages and military occupation among the elites of the various oases of Central Asia, whereas the Sogdians were in charge of diplomatic and commercial exchanges in the empire.[46] The Turkish rule was indirect, exacting tribute while keeping the local princes on their thrones.

Sogdiana thrived during this period. Its culture expanded to the north in a movement of agricultural colonization, along the foothills of the Tianshan Mountains.[47]

We have a very good idea of the social life in the various subregions due to the numerous Soviet excavations of towns and villages all over Central Asia. The life of the nobility is especially well known. The transfer of the agricultural wealth to the towns has thus been analyzed precisely. Numerous mural paintings, rich in information, have also been uncovered, notably at Panjikent near Samarkand. An aristocratic culture clearly prevails in the iconography: scenes of legendary combats, the epic of Rostam, armored heroes on horseback, persons carrying long swords (even during banquets). But some depictions of Indian tales (*Pañcatantra*) are also known. Religious iconography pervades western Central Asia: with its characteristic Indian features—gods with numerous arms or heads—it reflects the dominant polytheistic kind of Zoroastrianism. For instance, the image of the goddess Nana, with her four arms holding the sun and the moon and seated on a lion, is known from Khorezm to Bactria, as well as in Panjikent.[48]

Numerous written sources describe the region, including some eyewitness accounts: for example, Xuanzang, the most famous Chinese pilgrim, went to India in search of Buddhist texts and traveled through Central Asia in 629–630.[49] Chinese diplomatic sources are especially valuable.[50] We also have two sets of local archives, one Bactrian, and another Sogdian, the latter of which is political and economic and dated 708–722.[51] It was compiled during the reign of a king of Panjikent who fought against the Arabs. The Turkish *qaghans* described their empire in the Orkhon inscriptions of 720–735.[52] Some Byzantine embassies to the Turks have left reports as well.[53] Moreover, all these data can be checked against the Arabic texts describing the conquests of Islam. Thus, western Central Asia, especially Sogdiana, is certainly better known in the seventh and early eighth centuries than many regions of Europe or the Near East.

The same can be said of eastern Central Asia, except for the more limited documentation of Khotan and Kucha. In Turfan, more than 27,000 fragments of Chinese documents, used to cut hats, shoes, and belts of paper for the dead, were found in the Astana cemetery, dating mainly from the sixth to eighth century. These documents are to be added to the 40,000 manuscripts discovered at the beginning of the twentieth century in a grotto in Dunhuang, dating mainly from the eighth to the tenth century, a discovery that has become the starting point for much of our knowledge of the history and languages of Central Asia. Mostly in Chinese (and in Tibetan at Dunhuang), these documents testify to the "Sinicization" of the eastern end of Central Asia and reflect the Chinese conquest of the region from 640 on. The Tang superseded the Turks as protectors of the small kingdoms of the Silk Road. They organized a western protectorate, theoretically integrating the local nobility into the ranks of the Mandarin hierarchy. Militarily speaking, the Tang occupied most of Central Asia, except for Sogdiana, Bactria, and Khorezm. The recently created Tibetan empire, however, also tried to control the oases of the Tarim basin.[54] This period saw intense movements of population: Turkish mercenaries, Indian and Chinese Buddhist monks, and Sogdian traders. Some are more surprising than others, such as the hundreds of Sogdian peasants mentioned in the sources of Turfan or Dunhuang, more than 2,000 kilometers east of Sogdiana.[55]

The world religions did not miss this opportunity to expand. Buddhism probably had been established in southern Central Asia at least since the first century B.C.E., and during this period, it expanded among the Turks.[56] Two western religions already present in Central Asia expanded to China: Syriac Christianity and Manichaeism.[57] The Church of the East (aka Nestorianism) was at Merv as early as 424 and arrived in Sogdiana in the fifth or sixth century. It arrived in China as early as 635.[58] However, many mistakes have marred our understanding of the Syriac churches in China: the latest interpretations of the famous Nestorian Stele of Xi'an, inscribed in 781, suggest that the Church of the East in China was limited to a small community of foreigners, possibly even without many Chinese converts.[59] It is in northern Central Asia that it took deeper roots, reinforced during the Muslim period, up to its flourishing in the Mongol empire.[60] Sogdian was one of its liturgical languages up to the fourteenth century. Manichaeism, which arrived in China earlier than Christianity, had been chased out of Iran by the persecutions at the end of the third century.[61] It spread to China as early as the second half of the sixth century, as demonstrated by the recent discovery in Xi'an of the funerary bed of a Sogdian immigrant dated to 579, which displays Mani and the Manichaean judgment of the soul (but also Zoroastrian and Buddhist motifs) among its carved reliefs.[62]

Central Asia during this period can certainly be regarded as united by the movements of populations and ideas, and the elites saw themselves at the center of the known world. A fascinating illustration of this idea can be seen on the four painted walls of the reception room of a Sogdian noble's house discovered in Samarkand: here are depicted, on the left, the Iranian world, with the Persian nobility attending a religious ceremony during the Nowruz (Iranian new year festival); on the right, the Chinese civilization, with the emperor shown hunting while the empress and her suite are riding on a dragon-head boat; on the back wall, the Indian world with its astrologers and its dwarfs fighting cranes, reflecting a surprisingly Hellenistic image of India; and on the front wall, painted at the very period during which the balance of power switched from the Turks to the Chinese, embassies from all other Asian territories rendering homage to an unknown figure now destroyed, but who probably was the Turkish *qaghan* because Turkish soldiers are guiding the embassies and surrounding the missing top figure.[63] The old idea of the four empires of the world is here geographical and not chronological. Central Asia was indeed in touch with the entire known world through its trade and its emigration.

The Apogee of the Silk Road: The Chinese Section

Late Antiquity was the heyday of the Silk Road. A single commercial network organized the long-range exchanges along the caravan roads. Proofs of its existence are to be found in all the regions of Asia, but curiously, very few come from Central Asia itself. The *Sogdian Ancient Letters* are the first important documents in this regard: left in 313 amid the ruins of a Han watchtower ninety kilometers west of Dunhuang, they had been sent by some Sogdian traders from Gansu to the West (one of them to Samarkand). They describe the ruin of the Sogdian trading network in these towns:

> The last emperor, so they say, fled from Luoyang because of the famine and fire was set to his palace and to the city, and the palace was burnt and the city [destroyed]. Luoyang is no more, Ye is no more! . . . And, sirs, if I were to write to you about how China has fared, it would be beyond grief: there is no profit for you to gain from it . . . [in] Luoyang . . . the Indians and the Sogdians there had all died of starvation.[64]

However, the Sogdian network was well established in Gansu, and, one century later, it was still there. A Chinese text explains how: "Merchants of that country [Sogdiana] used to come in great number to the district Liang [the present Wuwei in Gansu] to trade. When Guzang [i.e., Wuwei] was conquered [by the Wei in 439] all of them were captured. In the beginning of the reign of Gaozong [452–465] the king [of Sogdiana] sent embassies to ask for their ransom."[65]

We have few other direct testimonies of the existence of long-distance trade in Central Asia. Among the 27,000 fragments of Astana, there is a list of taxes paid on caravan trade in the Gaochang kingdom (Turfan) in the 620s. The text is not complete but gives a fairly good idea of the identity of the main traders in Turfan: out of thirty-five commercial operations in this text, twenty-nine involved a Sogdian trader, and in thirteen instances, both the seller and the buyer were Sogdians.[66] In Astana, more than 800 Sogdian names can be found in the Chinese documents. By contrast, only a handful of Bactrians are named.[67]

Though the documents pertaining directly to the Silk Road are most infrequent in Central Asia itself, it is nevertheless certain that long-distance trade was very much active from the fifth century on. Chinese art is familiar with forms deriving from Mediterranean models. Products, ideas, and images circulated.[68] The Sogdian traders were familiar figures in the main towns all over northern China. In the tombs of the elites, Sogdians, depicted in a stereotyped way with prominent noses and beards—on camels, playing the lute, or presenting horses—are common figures among the various small statues of daily life that were usually placed in the tombs. Poetry, narrative texts, and fables depict these foreigners in the markets of the big towns.[69] Their ubiquitous presence can be socially analyzed, thanks to numerous texts and funerary epitaphs of Sogdian families in China that describe how an ancestor came to China during the Wei period as *Sabao* (i.e., chief caravaneer) before climbing the social ladder. *Sabao* is a transcription of the Sogdian word *sartapao*, itself a Sogdian transcription of the Middle-Indic *sârthavâha*, chief caravaneer, through a Bactrian intermediary.[70] In India, the *sârthavâha* was not only the chief caravaneer but also the head of the traders guild. But *Sabao* was also the title of the head of the Sogdian communities in China. This double meaning demonstrates that the Sogdian communities in China were deeply rooted in the caravan trade. These families established themselves first in Gansu. The next generation entered into the main Chinese towns, and subsequently, some Sogdians even managed to reach the court. The Sogdian community in the main towns of northern China during the sixth and seventh centuries was headed by a *Sabao*, who received a Mandarin rank in the official hierarchy, at least from the Northern Qi dynasty to the Tang.[71]

Some discoveries from Guyuan in the Chinese province of Ningxia (Southern Ordos) provide a very good example of such Sogdian families.[72] Six graves of one Sogdian family were excavated there. They probably originated from the Sogdian town of Kesh (Shahr-i Sabz, in Uzbekistan), and indeed the texts of the funerary epitaphs describe how the family migrated from the western countries. The archaeological content of these tombs confirms these western links, in that some Byzantine and Sasanian coins, a seal stone inscribed in Pahlavi, and a Zoroastrian symbol were found there. While the ancestors were *Sabao*, a member of the fourth generation in China, Shi Shewu, was the great man of the family, and through his work for the Chinese army, the family was integrated into Chinese society. He died in 610, and his grave and funerary epitaph are Chinese. His sons and grandsons were translators or soldiers or in charge of horse-breeding farms for the Chinese dynasties.[73] Some of the names are plain transcriptions of Sogdian names: Shewu is the honorific personal name, but the public name was Pantuo. By reuniting both names, we have Zhimatvande, a well-known Sogdian name meaning "servant of Demeter" and one that was inherited from the period of Alexander the Great in Central Asia. This name was divided in two halves only for the sake of *interpretatio sinica*. The elder branch kept Sogdian names, while the other ones were Sinicized. After five generations in China, some of the members of the families still married within the Sogdian milieu: for example, Shi Hedan, who married one "Kang" (the Chinese surname of the natives of Samarkand), and Shi Suoyan, who married one "An" (from Bukhara). These data are fascinating because we can follow closely how one Sogdian family in China evolved socially and became integrated.[74]

Some other recent archaeological discoveries have uncovered the tombs of the heads of the Sogdian communities in the capital. These nouveaux riches had expensive funerary beds carved for them on which they displayed both their Sogdian culture and their integration into Chinese society—in a sense, this was the iconographical counterpart of the epitaphs of the Shi family. One of the most interesting tombs was discovered a few years ago near Taiyuan by a team of the Shanxi Archaeological Institute. The tomb of Yu Hong, who died in 593 at age fifty-eight, contained a funerary bed in the shape of a Chinese house, adorned with fifty-three carved panels of marble, originally painted and gilded. Yu Hong had traveled extensively, acting as an ambassador for the Ruanruan in Persia, Bactria, and Gandhara (Yuezhi) and among the Tuyuhun tribes near Lake Qinghai. He later served the Northern Qi and Zhou and the Sui. He became *Sabao* in 580, and then nominal governor of a town, as indicated by the funerary epitaphs of Yu Hong and his wife that were discovered in the tomb. The iconography fits very well with the geography of the texts: on the panels, we see Yu Hong hunting with nomads on horses, hunting on an Indian elephant, and banqueting with his wife. Zoroastrian symbols are clearly displayed: two priests, half-bird and half-human, wearing the traditional *padam* (a piece of cloth in front of the mouth), along with Mithra and his sacrificial horse.[75]

The conquest of Central Asia by Chinese armies from 640 on changed the economic conditions within which the Sogdian merchants operated. To finance their expansion and pay their troops, the Tang empire sent more than 10 percent of its fiscal receipts to the West, for the most part in the form of silk and hemp rolls, from which the Sogdians benefited as the main intermediaries of this long-distance trade.[76] Sogdian trade was firmly integrated into the Chinese military expansion in less than one century, even in regions far removed from Central Asia: on its northeastern frontier, the Tang placed Sogdian traders in its garrison towns to ease the economic situation there.[77] The same period saw an evolution in the official position of the Sogdian communities. It seems that the Tang transformed independent and autonomous Sogdian communities—which had been loosely integrated in the Mandarin hierarchy—into villages that were more closely controlled and lacking a Sogdian hierarchy. The *Sabao* disappear from the epigraphical and textual sources after the middle of the seventh century. But this period, up to the middle of the eighth century, was certainly the climax of Iranian influence on Chinese civilization. Although the communities were suppressed, the families and individuals who were formerly inclined to stay within the Sogdian communities now became more thoroughly integrated into Chinese society. We can see people with typical Sogdian surnames getting involved in all the fields of Tang social life.[78]

Many of these Sogdians remained merchants: around the main markets of the capitals, Chang'an and Luoyang, Sogdian temples, Sogdian taverns, and

Sogdian shops flourished. They sold to the Tang elite the western goods that were then à la mode. Many young nobles and drunken poets celebrated the charms of the Sogdian girls. However, other Sogdians were not merchants: soldiers, monks, and high or low officials were also of Sogdian descent. Likewise, not all the foreign traders were Sogdian: some of them were Indian, Bactrian, or Khotanese. These, however, were more specialized traders: for instance, the Khotanese traded in precious stones, since jade came from boulders of the Khotan River.[79] Nevertheless, even these foreigners merged into the dominant immigrant group, the Sogdians: a tomb of an Indian discovered in the capital was modeled on the Sogdian ones. In southern China, by contrast, the sea trade brought numerous Persian traders to the ports in a very different context.

The Apogee of the Silk Road: The Western Section

Information on the links between Central Asia and the West, be it the Sasanian empire or the Byzantine empire, is much more limited. But it is quite certain that the Sogdians moved from their position of merchants and ambassadors in the Turkish empire to a much more long-distance commercial role. The best textual source for this transition is a depiction by a Byzantine author, Menander the Guardsman, of Turkish embassies sent to the two empires in the 570s:

> As the power of the Turks increased, the Sogdians, who were formerly subjects of the Ephthalites and now of the Turks, asked their king to send an embassy to the Persians, to request that the Sogdians be allowed to travel there and sell raw silk to the Medes. Sizabul agreed and dispatched Sogdian envoys, whose leader was Maniakh. . . . When they reached the king of the Persians, they asked that they be given permission to sell the raw silk there without any hindrance. The Persian king, who was not at all pleased by their request, and was reluctant to grant to these men henceforth free access to the territory of Persia [. . . was advised] not to return the silk, but to buy it, paying the fair price for it, and to burn it on a fire before the eyes of the envoys, so that he would not be held to have committed an injustice but that it would be clear that he did not wish to use raw silk from the Turks. So the silk was burned, and the Sogdians returned to their homeland not at all pleased with what had happened. . . . Maniakh, the leader of the Sogdians, took this opportunity and advised Sizabul that it would be better for the Turks to cultivate the friendship of the Romans and send their raw silk for sale to them because they made more use of it than other people.[80]

Several embassies were then exchanged between the Turks and the Byzantine empire, taking a road from the Aral Sea to the north of the Caspian Sea and then through the Caucasus Mountains or via the Crimea. In the Caucasus, tombs have been discovered along the high passes leading to Byzantium that do indeed contain some remains of silk fabrics, and at least one of them has provided archaeologists with Chinese documents.[81] During the great Armenian revolt of 571, Vardam Mamikonian, while on an embassy to Constantinople, brought with him a great quantity of silk thread via the Caucasus. The seventh-century *Geography*, attributed to the Armenian author Ananias of Širak, notes the precious products that could be found in each of the lands he describes and mentions "the Chorasmians [who are] merchants [dwelling] towards the northeast." It states additionally that "the Sogdians are wealthy and industrious merchants who live between the regions of Turkestan and Aria." To the north and northeast of Armenia, these were the only merchants Ananias knew. A commercial town was founded in the Crimea, the other major access point to Byzantine territories, at the end of the seventh century. Seals of the imperial warehouse of Constantinople have been discovered there, as well as eighth-century seals of Byzantine *commerciarii*, officials who dealt with luxury goods. It is by no mere chance that this town was named Sogdaia. Some Sogdian ostraca have been found nearby, near the strait of Kertch, and religious legends seem to recall the existence of a Sogdian population on the northern coast of the Black Sea.

This region, with the rich and proximate Byzantine market, had everything necessary to attract the Sogdian merchants—as the text of Menander the Guardsman already demonstrates. Although a chronological hiatus exists between the attempt mentioned by Menander and the first archaeological traces of Sogdaia, it is nonetheless tempting to postulate the continuity of the Sogdian presence in the region. Sogdaia was a frontier market, like those found in the Ordos at the other end of the steppe, where Sogdo-Turks and Chinese met.[82] The Sogdians thus settled in Turk territory, at that time controlled by the Khazars—the successors of the Turks in the western steppe from the seventh century on—within range of substantial commerce, but without being subject to strict Byzantine control over the silk trade. Some goods that were traded at one stage or another by Central Asian merchants made their way even further west, to the Latin world: the bones and relics of saints were often wrapped in luxury fabrics produced in Central Asia. Some fabrics discovered in the Dunhuang grotto are very similar to those kept in the treasuries of western cathedrals. In both cultures, these were used to wrap their most precious objects, whether the bones of Christian saints or Buddhist sutras. One of the extant textiles still retains a short Sogdian inscription written in ink.[83] No literary text, however, describes this trade. The situation is similar in the north: in the Russian forest belt, dozens of silver plates originating from the Iranian world—be it the Sasanian empire itself or Iranian-speaking Central Asia—have been discovered, without any source describing this trade. But we know for sure that they arrived in the forest zone through Central Asian hands, because their weights are inscribed in Sogdian or Khorezmian. During the eighth century, 75 percent of these plates were traded via Central Asia. Some Central Asian coins have also been discovered in Russia. These northern areas, in the ninth and tenth centuries, are described by the Muslim texts as exporters of furs, honey, amber, and slaves. We can suppose that this was also the case in the preceding periods. Eighth-century Baltic amber has been found in Samarkand and in Panjikent, and even in the Shoshoin repository of Nara, Japan.[84]

On the western roads, Sogdian traders might have been in direct competition with Khorezmian traders. In addition to the text of Ananias quoted previously, a Chinese text states: "Among all of the Central Asian peoples, this people [the Khorezmians] is the only one which [yokes] oxen [to] wagons. The merchants ride [in these vehicles] in order to travel to various kingdoms." But the Chinese knew very little about Khorezm and its commerce. Khorezmian commerce, without doubt important in the western steppe, never possessed the eastern counterpart of the Sogdian commercial network. The silver Khorezmian coins of the middle of the eighth century begin to bear legends in Sogdian, as if they had been included lately in the Sogdian commercial sphere. However, the pre-Islamic long-distance trade network had already ended by this point. Later, when east-west trade resumed in the western steppe in the tenth century—after a gap in the ninth century dominated by north-south trans-Caucasian trade—the Khorezmian traders superseded their Sogdian rivals.[85]

The End of the Network

The end of Central Asian long-distance trade came abruptly in the middle of the eighth century for several reasons. The first is the Arab conquest that took place during two different periods. The fall of the Sasanian empire and the death of its last emperor, Yazdegerd III, near Merv (in present-day Turkmenistan) brought the Arab armies to southern Central Asia as early as 651. For the regions situated to the north of the Amu Darya, however, the conquest begins only in the eighth century. Bukhara was conquered in 705, Khorezm (with a systematic murder of the elites) and Samarkand in 712.[86] Shortly thereafter, a general uprising of the nobility was crushed in 722.[87] But the war went on: all these painful conquests were lost by the Arabs during the 730s in the face of an alliance of the Sogdians with the Türgesh, a Turkish confederation of tribes who occupied the steppe north of western Central Asia. A peace was established under the last Umayyad governor of Central Asia, Naṣr b. Sayyar (from 740 on), but it lasted only a few years.[88] After the Abbasid revolution, which began in Merv in 747, Central Asia beyond the Amu Darya was forced to submit once more to Abū Muslim, who decimated its elites. It is only after this event that the whole of western Central Asia can be regarded as firmly integrated (militarily speaking) into the political commonwealth of Islam.[89] By then, the power and economy of China had been destroyed by a rebellion.

In China, the end of the network came at Sogdian hands. An Lushan was the main military governor of northeastern China, on the frontier of Korea and the Kitans. His father was a Sogdian installed in the Turkish empire, and his mother was Turk. As a young boy, he established himself in northeastern China, acted as a translator in the markets there, became a soldier, and climbed from the rank and file to the top of the army. His rebellion in 755 narrowly destroyed the Tang dynasty and put an end to one of China's golden ages.[90] Many texts describe it as a Sogdian rebellion and state that numerous Sogdian traders supported An Lushan. Some new discoveries demonstrate conclusively that this characterization of the rebellion is not due to a xenophobic bias in the Chinese accounts but is in a way something claimed by the rebels themselves. Shi Seming, himself a Sogdian and the second successor of An Lushan, put the Sogdian royal title of Jamuk ("Jewel," transcribed Zhaowu in Chinese) on a par with Huangdi ("Emperor") on his recently discovered ceremonial jades.[91] The troops of the rebels bore the Sogdian name of Zhejie, a fair transcription of the Sogdian Châkar, "professional soldier."[92] The Sogdian milieu was torn apart by the rebellion, since many Sogdians in China sided with the Tang. The rebellion was quelled only in 763 with the help of the Uighur nomads. To fight against the rebels, the Tang emperors had to call back all their troops from Central Asia. It would take a millennium for the Chinese to return, with the Qing conquest in the eighteenth century. Eastern Central Asia entered into a continuous period of war between the Uighurs, the Tibetan empire in the south, local kingdoms, and a few isolated Chinese garrisons.[93]

The end of the Chinese presence marked the conclusion of the enormous amount of silk spent for the colonial empire, as well as the peace maintained along the trade roads. The international trade was thus completely disrupted in the second half of the eighth century and reconstituted on a very low level (if at all) during the ninth century, and only then with the help of the Uighur empire (though under strong Sogdian influence).[94] But in China, the western communities and religions dwindled. When Manichaeism, Zoroastrianism, and Nestorianism were forbidden in 845—coincident with the persecution of Buddhism—a Chinese official wrote that "the monasteries of these three foreign religions throughout the whole empire are not equal in number to our Buddhist monasteries in one small city."[95] The Nestorian Stele of 781 can be seen, therefore, as a last remnant of this vanishing world, and these religions survived thereafter mainly in Central Asia. Chinese economic centers shifted to the south and the coasts, and no inland Silk Road reemerged before the advent of the Mongol empire.

NOTES

1. The bibliography and notes focus on works in western languages, mainly English, German, and French. However, tools for making use of the bibliography in eastern languages (Chinese and Japanese) and Russian are provided below.

2. There are few global introductions to the history of Central Asia. The UNESCO volumes are of disparate quality, although the third one, devoted to Late Antiquity (Litvinsky 1996), is quite good, if slightly outdated. On economy and trade, see la Vaissière 2005a.

3. Much paleoclimatic research is currently underway. No global synthesis has been published yet, and this qualification of the late antique climate in Central Asia as milder should be regarded as provisional.

4. There is no synthesis on Central Asian irrigation. For an earlier period, see Francfort and Leconte 2002–2003 and the bibliography given there, especially the works of Andrjanov on Khorezm. On Bactria: Gentelle 1989.

5. Example of Ferghana: Gorbunova 1986.

6. On the sedentary-nomadic interaction: Khazanov 1984. During the Turkish period in Central Asia: Stark 2008, parts 3 and 4.

7. Khorezmian is mainly known from texts of the Islamic period: Durkin-Meisterernst 2008.

8. Yoshida forthcoming; Gharib 1995. On material life: Litvinskij 1998.

9. Sims-Williams 1996; 2000b; 2007.

10. Skjærvø 2002 gives a state of the art of Khotanese studies in his introduction. See also Emmerick 1992. Of the numerous philological studies of Bailey, see especially Bailey 1982 for daily life in Khotan.

11. Linguistics: Sims-Williams and Hamilton 1990; Yoshida 2009. Politics and daily life: la Vaissière 2007, 41–44, Stark 2008.

12. Recent bibliography and translated texts in Pinault 2008. See also on Tokharian Buddhism: Pinault 1994. On economic life: Pinault 1998. Translation of the Chinese texts on Kucha in Liu 1969.

13. There are numerous studies on Buddhism in Central Asia. For the results of Soviet archaeology, see Stavisky 1993–1994; in eastern Central Asia: Zürcher 1990; Brough 1965. Art: Rhie 2002.

14. No synthesis but numerous archaeological and art studies: Grenet 1984; 1994; 1995–1996; 2000; Grenet and Marshak 1998; Marshak 2002b; Marshak and Raspopova 1987; 1990b; 1991; 1994; Sims-Williams 1991a; 2000a; Shkoda 1996. Toward China: Zhang Guangda 1994; 2000; Marshak 2002a; Riboud 2005.

15. On the religion of the Turks: Roux 1984; Golden 1992, 149–151, 174–176.

16. Schlütz and Lehmkuhl 2007.

17. Weishu 102.2270; Ammianus Marcellinus 16.3.1, 16.9.3–4, 17.5.1, 19.1.7; Faustus of Byzantium, 5.7 and 5.37.

18. Loginov and Nikitin 1993, 271.

19. Some Chinese texts on the Ephthalites translated in la Vaissière 2007b.

20. Christensen 1944, 293–296.

21. Grignaschi 1984. See also on the Ephthalites: Kuwayama 1989.

22. Göbl 1967 is still the main work on Hunnic numismatics. However, its chronology should be revised according to the new coins and historical analysis. M. Alram is preparing an updated version of this monumental catalogue.

23. Enoki 1969; Grenet 2002, 205–209.

24. Sims-Williams 1996; 2000b; 2007.

25. la Vaissière 2005b.

26. la Vaissière 2007b.

27. ur-Rahman, Grenet, and Sims-Williams 2006.

28. This section is a summary of la Vaissière 2005a, chapter 4, in which more precise references and analysis are provided.

29. Higuchi and Kuwayama 1970, 26.

30. Gardin 1957, 95.

31. See Rtveladze 1989, 54, 63; Grenet 1996, 371.

32. Lyonnet 1997, 268–284.

33. Marshak and Raspopova 1990a, 181.

34. Grenet 1996; Shishkina 1994; la Vaissière 2005a, chapter 4.

35. la Vaissière 2005a, part 1 is devoted to this question of transcontinental Central Asian trade in antiquity.

36. Sims-Williams 1983.

37. la Vaissière 2005a, 77–79.

38. *Sanguo zhi* 4.895. See Rong 2000, 134.

39. *Christian Topography* 2.46, McCrindle's translation 1887, 138.

40. *Christian Topography* 11.15, McCrindle's translation 1887, 366.

41. Sims-Williams 1997.

42. Excellent synthesis on the Turkish empires in Golden 1992. Translation of the Chinese texts in Chavannes 1903; Liu 1958.

43. Kljaštornyj and Livšic 1972.

44. Moriyasu 1990.

45. Golden 1992, 121.

46. la Vaissière 2005a, chapter 7; la Vaissière 2007a, chapter 3; Stark 2008, parts 3 and 4.

47. la Vaissière 2005a, 112–117.

48. Azarpay 1981; Marshak 2002b. In Khotan: Mode 1991–1992. On silverware: Marschak 1986.

49. Texts of Xuanzang and other pilgrims are translated in Beal 1884.

50. See especially Chavannes 1903.

51. Corpus translated only in Russian, but see for the political documents, Grenet and la Vaissière 2002.

52. There is no reliable translation of these inscriptions. See, however, Tekin 1968. Regarding the other Turkish inscriptions, see Moriyasu and Ochir 1999.

53. Menander the Guardsman: trans. Blockley 1984. Theophylact Simocatta: transl. Whitby and Whitby 1986.

54. Beckwith 1987.

55. la Vaissière and Trombert 2004.

56. Laut 1986; Moriyasu 1990; Tremblay 2007.

57. Texts gathered in Leslie 1981–1983.

58. Pelliot 1973; Colless 1986; see also Walker, chapter 31 in this book.

59. Tardieu 2008; Gernet 2008.

60. Klein 2000.

61. Lieu 1985. Tremblay 2001 is a good bibliographical tool but is unreliable with respect to historical analysis.

62. la Vaissière 2005c; Grenet, Riboud, and Yang 2004.

63. Articles on its interpretation gathered in Compareti and la Vaissière 2006. Also Mode 1993.

64. Sims-Williams 2001. Commentary in la Vaissière 2005a, chapter 2. See also Grenet, Sims-Williams, and la Vaissière 1998.

65. *Weishu* 102.2270.

66. Skaff 1998; la Vaissière 2005a, 133–135.
67. Hansen 2005.
68. Laufer 1919; Schafer 1963; Trombert 1996; 2000; Trombert and la Vaissière 2007. On coins: Thierry 1993; Thierry and Morrisson 1994.
69. Schafer 1963 on the Tang exotics.
70. On *sabao*, see Dien 1962; la Vaissière 2005a, 151–152.
71. la Vaissière and Trombert 2004, 944–949.
72. Sogdian colonies in the Ordos: Pulleyblank 1952.
73. Luo Feng 2001.
74. Several other examples in la Vaissière and Trombert 2004.
75. Marshak 2002a; Riboud 2005.
76. Trombert 2000.
77. Pulleyblank 1955, 80, 159 n. 6.
78. la Vaissière and Trombert 2004.
79. Schafer 1963, 223–227.
80. Menander, ed. Blockley 1985, 111–115.
81. Ierusalimskaja 1996.
82. la Vaissière 2006.
83. Shepherd and Henning 1959; Shepherd 1980.
84. la Vaissière 2000.
85. Noonan 1982; 1985; la Vaissière 2005a, 292–299.
86. Gibb 1923. See also Barthold 1968.
87. Grenet and la Vaissière 2002.
88. la Vaissière 2007a, 44–54.
89. Karev 2002; la Vaissière 2007a, 55–58, 115–120.
90. Pulleyblank 1955.
91. Rong 2000, 150.
92. la Vaissière 2007a, 77–82.
93. On the Tibetan empire, see Beckwith 1987; on the Uighurs: Mackerras 1972. On their wars: Moriyasu 1981; Yoshida 2009.
94. la Vaissière 2005a, 306–322.
95. Leslie 1981–1983.

WORKS CITED

Bibliographic Tools for Russian, Japanese, and Chinese

It is beyond the aim of this volume to provide a bibliography in non-Western languages. However, some bibliographic tools are available that might help to find references among the numerous publications in Russian, Japanese, and Chinese, of foremost importance. For Russian, the journal *Abstracta Iranica* annually (from 1977) provides abstracts in French and English of most of the publications in Russian on Central Asia. Abstracts regarding pre-Islamic Central Asia published from 1977 to 1986 have been gathered in Grenet 1988. See also the *Bulletin of the Asia Institute* 8. For Japanese, some Japanese scholars have published annotated bibliographies on Central Asia in English in the journal *Acta Asiatica*: 78 (2000), 94 (2007). For Chinese historiography, see *China Art and Archaeology Digest* 4 (2000).

Ancient Sources

Ammianus Marcellinus: Rolfe, J. C. 1939. *Ammianus Marcellinus, with an English Translation.* Loeb Classical Library. London: Heinemann.

Ananias of Širak: Hewsen, R. H. 1992. *The Geography of Ananias of Širak (Ašxarhac'oyc'): The Long and the Short Recensions.* Beihefte zum Tübinger Atlas des Vorderen Orients, Reihe B (Geisteswissenschaften), 77. Wiesbaden: Reichert.

Cosmas Indicopleustes: McCrindle, J. W. 1897. *The Christian Topography of Cosmas, an Egyptian Monk.* New York: Franklin.

Faustus of Byzantium: Garsoïan, N. 1989. *The Epic Histories Attributed to P'awstos Buzand (Buzandaran Patmut'iwnk).* Cambridge, MA: Harvard University Press.

Menander: Blockley, R. C. 1985. *The History of Menander the Guardsman.* ARCA 17. Liverpool: F. Cairns.

Sanguo zhi: Chen Shou. 1962. *Sanguo zhi.* Beijing.

Theophylact Simocatta: Whitby, Michael, and Mary Whitby. 1986. *The History of Theophylact Simocatta: An English Translation with Introduction and Notes.* Oxford: Clarendon Press.

Weishu: Wei Shou. 1974. *Weishu.* Beijing.

Xuanzang: Beal, S. 1884. *Si-Yu-Ki: Buddhist Records of the Western World. Translated from the Chinese of Hiuen Tsiang, AD 629.* London: Trübner.

Modern Sources

Azarpay, Guitty. 1981. *Sogdian Painting: The Pictorial Epic in Oriental Art.* Berkeley: University of California Press.

Bailey, Harold. 1982. *The Culture of the Sakas of Ancient Iranian Khotan.* Delmar, NY: Caravan.

Barthold, Wilhem. 1968. *Turkestan down to the Mongol Invasion.* Trans. T. Minorsky. London: Luzac.

Beckwith, Christopher. 1987. *The Tibetan Empire in Central Asia: A History of the Struggle for Great Power among Tibetans, Turks, Arabs, and Chinese during the Early Middle Ages.* Princeton, NJ: Princeton University Press.

Brough, John. 1965. "Comments on Third-Century Shan-Shan and the History of Buddhism," *Bulletin of the School of Oriental and African Studies* 28.3: 582–612.

Chavannes, Édouard. 1903. *Documents sur les Toukiue (Turcs) occidentaux.* Saint Petersburg: Commissionnaires de l'Académie impériale des sciences.

Christensen, Arthur. 1944. *L'Iran sous les Sassanides,* 2nd ed. Copenhagen: Annales du Musée Guimet.

Colless, B. E. 1986. "The Nestorian Province of Samarqand," *Abr-Nahrain* 24: 51–57.

Compareti, Matteo, and Étienne de la Vaissière, eds. 2006. *Royal Nawruz in Samarkand: Proceedings of the Conference Held in Venice on the Pre-Islamic Painting at Afrasiab.* Supplemento n°1 alla Rivista degli Studi Orientali 78. Pisa-Rome: Instituto Editoriali e Poligrafici Internazionali.

Dien, Albert. 1962. "The Sa-pao Problem Re-Examined," *Journal of the American Oriental Society* 82–83: 335–346.

Durkin-Meisterernst, Desmond. 2008. "Khwarezmian in the Islamic Period." In *Islamisation de l'Asie centrale: Processus locaux d'acculturation,* ed. Étienne de la Vaissière, 199–213. Cahier de Studia Iranica 39. Paris-Leuven: Peeters.

Emmerick, Ronald. 1992. *A Guide to the Literature of Khotan*. Tokyo: International Institute for Buddhist Studies.
Enoki, Kazuo. 1969. "On the Date of the Kidarites (I)," *Memoirs of the Research Department of the Toyo Bunko* 27: 1–26.
Francfort, Henri-Paul, and Olivier Leconte. 2002–2003. "Irrigation et société en Asie centrale des origines à l'époque achéménide," *Annales: Histoire, Sciences Sociales* 57: 625–663.
Gardin, Jean-Claude. 1957. *Céramiques de Bactres*. Mémoires de la Délégation Archéologique Française en Afghanistan 15. Paris: Klincksieck.
Gentelle, Pierre. 1989. *Prospections archéologiques en Bactriane orientale (1974–1978), 1: Données paléogéographiques et fondements de l'irrigation*. Mémoires de la MAFAC III. Paris: Éditions Recherches sur les civilisations.
Gernet, Jacques. 2008. "Remarques sur le contexte chinois de l'inscription de la stèle nestorienne de Xi'an." In *Controverses des chrétiens dans l'Iran sassanide*, ed. Christelle Jullien, 227–243. Cahier de Studia Iranica 36. Paris-Leuven: Association pour l'avancement des études iraniennes and Peeters.
Gharib, B. 1995. *Sogdian Dictionary: Sogdian-Persian-English*. Tehran: Farhangan.
Gibb, H. A. R. 1923. *The Arab Conquest in Central Asia*. London: Royal Asiatic Society.
Göbl, Robert. 1967. *Dokumente zur Geschichte der iranischen Hunnen in Baktrien und Indien*. Wiesbaden: Harrassowitz.
Golden, Peter. 1992. *An Introduction to the History of the Turkic Peoples*. Turcologica 9. Wiesbaden: Harrassowitz.
Gorbunova, N. G. 1986. *The Culture of Ancient Ferghana, VI Century B.C.–VI Century A.D.* Oxford: B.A.R.
Grenet, Frantz. 1984. *Les pratiques funéraires dans l'Asie centrale sédentaire de la conquête grecque à l'islamisation*. Paris: Éditions du CNRS.
———. 1988. *L'Asie centrale préislamique: Bibliographie critique 1977–1986. Abstracta Iranica*, volume hors-série 3. Tehran-Paris: Institut Français de Recherche en Iran.
———. 1994. "The Second of Three Encounters between Zoroastrianism and Hinduism: Plastic Influences in Bactria and Sogdiana (2nd–8th c. A.D.)." In *James Darmesteter Memorial Lectures*, ed. G. Lazard and D. R. SarDesai, 41–57. Bombay: Asiatic Society of Bombay.
———. 1995–1996. "Vaishravana in Sogdiana: About the Origins of Bishamon-ten," *Silk Road Art and Archaeology* 4: 277–297.
———. 1996. "Crise et sortie de crise en Bactriane-Sogdiane aux ive–ve s. de n. è.: De l'héritage antique à l'adoption de modèles sassanides." In *La Persia e l'Asia Centrale da Alessandro al X secolo*, 367–390. Atti dei Convegni Lincei 127. Rome: Accademia Nazionale dei Lincei.
———. 2000. "Avatars de Vaishravana: Les étapes sogdienne et tibétaine." In *La Sérinde, terre d'échanges*, ed. M. Cohen, J.-P. Drège, and J. Giès, 169–179. Paris: Documentation française.
———. 2002. "Regional Interaction in Central Asia and North-West India in the Kidarite and Hephtalite Period." In *Indo-Iranian Languages and Peoples*, ed. Nicholas Sims-Williams, 203–224. London: British Academy.
Grenet, Frantz, and Zhang Guangda. 1996. "The Last Refuge of the Sogdian Religion: Dunhuang in the Ninth and Tenth Centuries," *Bulletin of the Asia Institute* 10: 175–186.

Grenet, Frantz, and Étienne de la Vaissière. 2002. "The Last Days of Panjikent," *Silk Road Art and Archaeology* 8: 155–196.

Grenet, Frantz, and Boris Marshak. 1998. "Le mythe de Nana dans l'art de la Sogdiane," *Arts Asiatiques* 53: 5–18.

Grenet, Frantz, Pénélope Riboud, and Yang Junkai. 2004. "Zoroastrian Scenes on a Newly Discovered Sogdian Tomb in Xi'an, Northern China," *Studia Iranica* 33: 273–284.

Grenet, Frantz, Nicholas Sims-Williams, and Étienne de la Vaissière. 1998. "The Sogdian Ancient Letter V." In *Alexander's Legacy in the East: Studies in Honor of Paul Bernard, Bulletin of the Asia Institute* 12: 91–104.

Grignaschi, M. 1984. "La chute de l'empire hephthalite dans les sources byzantines et perses et le problème des Avar." In *From Hecataeus to al-Huwārizmī*, ed. Janos Harmatta, 219–248. Collection of the Sources for the History of Pre-Islamic Central Asia, ser. I, 3. Budapest: Akadémiai Kiadó.

Hansen, Valerie. 2005. "The Impact of the Silk Road Trade on a Local Community: The Turfan Oasis, 500–800." In *Les Sogdiens en Chine*, ed. Étienne de la Vaissière and Éric Trombert, 283–310. Études thématiques 13. Paris: EFEO.

Higuchi, T., and Sh. Kuwayama. 1970. *Chaqalaq Tepe: Fortified Village in North Afghanistan Excavated in 1964–1967*. Kyoto: Kyoto University Scientific Mission.

Ierusalimskaja, A. A. 1996. *Die Gräber der Moščevaja Balka: Frühmittelalterliche Funde an der nordkaukasischen Seidenstrasse*. Munich: Editio Maris.

Karev, Yuri. 2002. "La politique d'Abu Muslim dans le Mawaraannahr: Nouvelles données textuelles et archéologiques," *Der Islam* 79.1: 1–46.

Khazanov, Andrei. 1984. *Nomads and the Outside World*. Cambridge: Cambridge University Press.

Klein, Wassilios. 2000. *Das nestorianische Christentum an den Handelswegen durch Kyrgyzstan bis zum 14. Jh*. Turnhout: Brepols.

Kljaštornyj, Sergei, and Vladimir Livšic. 1972. "The Sogdian Inscription of Bugut Revised," *Acta Orientalia Academiae Scientiarum Hungaricae* 26.1: 69–102.

Kuwayama, S. 1989. "The Hephthalites in Tokharestan and Northwest India," *Zinbun* 24: 89–134.

la Vaissière, Étienne de. 2000. "Les marchands d'Asie centrale dans l'empire khazar." In *Les centres proto-urbains russes entre Scandinavie, Byzance et Orient*, ed. Michel Kazansky, Anne Nercessian, and Constantin Zuckerman, 367–378. Paris: Lethielleux.

———. 2005a. *Sogdian Traders: A History*. Leiden: Brill.

———. 2005b. "Huns et Xiongnu," *Central Asiatic Journal* 49.1: 3–26.

———. 2005c. "Mani en Chine au VIe siècle," *Journal Asiatique* 293.1: 357–378.

———. 2006. "Saint André chez les Sogdiens," In *La Crimée entre Byzance et le Khaganat khazar*, ed. C. Zuckerman, 171–180. Paris: Association des amis du Centre d'histoire et civilisation de Byzance.

———. 2007a. *Samarcande et Samarra: É lites d'Asie centrale dans l'empire abbasside*. Paris: Association pour l'avancement des études iraniennes; Leuven: Peeters.

———. 2007b. "Is There Any 'Nationality of the Ephtalites'?" In *Hephtalites = Bulletin of the Asia Institute* 17, ed. Madhuvanti Ghose and Étienne de la Vaissière, 119–137.

———, ed. 2008. *Islamisation de l'Asie centrale: Processus locaux d'acculturation du VIIe au XIe siècle*. Paris: Association pour l'avancement des études iraniennes; Leuven: Peeters.

la Vaissière, Étienne de, and Éric Trombert. 2004. "Des Chinois et des Hu: Migrations et intégration des Iraniens orientaux en milieu chinois durant le Haut Moyen-Âge," *Annales: Histoire, Sciences Sociales* 59.5–6: 931–969.

———, eds. 2005. *Les Sogdiens en Chine.* Études thématiques 13. Paris: EFEO.

Laufer, Berthold. 1919. *Sino-Iranica. Chinese Contributions to the History of Civilization in Ancient Iran.* Chicago: Field Museum of Natural History.

Laut, J. P. 1986. *Der frühe türkische Buddhismus und seine literarischen Denkmäler.* Veröffentlichungen der Societas Uralo-Altaica 21. Wiesbaden: Harrassowitz.

Leslie, D. D. 1981–1983. "Persian Temples in T'ang China," *Monumenta Serica* 35: 275–303.

Lieu, Samuel. 1985. *Manichaeism in the Later Roman Empire and Medieval China: A Historical Survey.* Manchester: Manchester University Press.

Litvinskij, B. A. 1998. *La civilisation de l'Asie centrale antique.* Archäologie in Iran und Turan 3. Rahden: Verlag Marie Leidorf.

Litvinsky, Boris, ed. 1996. *History of Civilizations of Central Asia, Vol. III: The Crossroad of Civilizations, A.D. 250 to 750.* Paris: UNESCO.

Liu, MauTsai. 1958. *Die chinesischen Nachrichten zur Geschichte der OstTürken (T'uKüe).* Göttinger asiatische Forschungen 10. Wiesbaden: Harrassowitz.

———. 1969. *Kutscha und seine Beziehungen zu China, vom 2. Jh. v. bis zum 6. Jh. n. Chr.* Wiesbaden: Harrassowitz.

Loginov, S. D., and A. B. Nikitin. 1993. "Sasanian Coins of the Third Century from Merv"; "Coins of Shapur II from Merv"; "Sasanian Coins of the Late 4th–7th Centuries from Merv"; "Post-Sasanian Coins from Merv," *Mesopotamia* 28: 225–246, 247–270, 271–312, 313–318.

Luo Feng. 2001. "Sogdians in Nothwest China." In *Monks and Merchants: Silk Road Treasures from Northwest China*, ed. Annette Juliano and Judith Lerner, 239–245. New York: Abrams and the Asia Society.

Lyonnet, Bertille. 1997. *Céramique et peuplement du Chalcolithique à la conquête arabe: Prospections archéologiques en Bactriane Orientale (1974–1978)*, vol. 2. Mémoires de la Délégation Archéologique Française en Asie Centrale 8. Paris: Éditions Recherches sur les Civilisations.

Mackerras, C. 1972. *The Uighur Empire (744–840) according to T'ang Dynastic Histories.* Columbia: University of South Carolina Press.

Maršak, Boris. 1986. *Silberschätze des Orients: Metallkunst des 3.–13. Jahrhunderts und ihre Kontinuität.* Leipzig: Seemann Verlag.

———. 2002a. "La thématique sogdienne dans l'art de la Chine de la seconde moitié du vi[e] siècle," *Comptes rendus des séances de l'Académie des Inscriptions et Belles-Lettres* 227–264.

———. 2002b. *Legends, Tales, and Fables in the Art of Sogdiana.* New York: Bibliotheca Persica.

Maršak, Boris, and Valentina Raspopova. 1987. "Une image sogdienne du Dieu-Patriarche de l'agriculture," *Studia Iranica* 16.2: 193–199.

———. 1990a. "Les nomades et la Sogdiane." In *Nomades et sédentaires en Asie centrale: Apports de l'archéologie et de l'ethnologie*, ed. Henri-Paul Francfort, 179–185. Paris: Éditions du CNRS.

———. 1990b. "Wall Paintings from a House with a Granary, Panjikent, 1st Quarter of the Eighth Century A.D.," *Silk Road Art and Archaeology* 1: 122–176.

———. 1991. "Cultes communautaires et cultes privés en Sogdiane." In *Histoire et cultes de l'Asie centrale préislamique*, ed. Paul Bernard and Frantz Grenet, 187–195. Paris: Éditions du CNRS.

———. 1994. "Worshippers from the Northern Shrine of Temple II, Penjikent," *Bulletin of the Asia Institute* 8: 187–207.

Mode, Markus. 1991–1992. "Sogdian Gods in Exile: Some Iconographic Evidence from Khotan in the Light of Recently Excavated Material from Sogdiana," *Silk Road Art and Archaeology* 2: 179–214.

———. 1993. *Sogdien und die Herrscher der Welt: Türken, Sasaniden und Chinesen in Historiengemälden des 7. Jahrhunderts n. Chr. aus Alt-Samarqand.* Europäische Hochschulschriften, Kunstgeschichte 162. Frankfurt: Peter Lang.

Moriyasu, Takao. 1981. "Qui des Ouïghours ou des Tibétains ont gagné en 789–92 à Beš-Balïq?" *Journal Asiatique* 279: 193–205.

———. 1990. "L'origine du bouddhisme chez les Turcs et l'apparition des textes bouddhiques en turc ancien." In *Documents et Archives provenant de l'Asie centrale: Actes du colloque franco-japonais Kyoto 4–8 octobre 1988*, ed. A. Haneda, 147–165. Kyoto: Association franco-japonaise des Études Orientales.

Moriyasu, Takao, and A. Ochir. 1999. *Provisional Report of Researches on Historical Sites and Inscriptions in Mongolia from 1996 to 1998.* Osaka: Society of Central Eurasian Studies.

Noonan, Theodor. 1982. "Russia, the Near-East, and the Steppe in the Early Medieval Period: An Examination of the Sasanian and Byzantine Finds from the Kama-Urals Area," *Archivum Eurasiae Medii Aevi* 2: 269–302.

———. 1985. "Khwārazmian Coins of the Eighth Century from Eastern Europe: The Post-Sasanian Interlude in the Relations between Central Asia and European Russia," *Archivum Eurasiae Medii Aevi* 6: 243–258.

Pelliot, Paul (posth.). 1973. *Recherches sur les Chrétiens d'Asie Centrale et d'Extrême-Orient*, ed. J. Dauvillier. Paris: Imprimerie Nationale.

Pinault, Georges-Jean. 1994. "Aspects du bouddhisme pratiqué au Nord du désert du Taklamakan, d'après les documents tokhariens." In *Bouddhisme et cultures locales: Quelques cas de réciproques adaptations*, ed. Fukui Fumimasa and Gérard Fussman, 85–113. Paris: EFEO.

———. 1998. "Economic and Administrative Documents in Tocharian B from the Berezovsky and Petrovsky Collections," *Manuscripta Orientalia* 4.4: 3–20.

———. 2008. *Chrestomathie tokharienne: Textes et grammaire.* Paris-Leuven: Peeters.

Pulleyblank, Edwin. 1952. "A Sogdian Colony in Inner Mongolia," *T'oung Pao* 41: 317–356.

———. 1955. *The Background of the Rebellion of An Lu-shan.* Oxford: Oxford University Press.

Rhie, Marylin. 2002. *Early Buddhist Art of China and Central Asia*, vol. 2. Leiden: Brill.

Riboud, Pénélope. 2005. "Réflexions sur les pratiques religieuses désignées sous le nom de xian." In *Les Sogdiens en Chine*, ed. Étienne de la Vaissière and Éric Trombert, 73–91. Études thématiques 13. Paris: EFEO.

Rong Xinjiang. 2000. "The Migrations and Settlements of the Sogdians in the Northern Dynasties, Sui and Tang," *China Archaeology and Art Digest* 4.1: 117–163.

Roux, Jean-Paul. 1984. *La religion des Turcs et des Mongols.* Paris: Payot.

Rtveladze, Eduard. 1989. "Pogrebal'nye sooruženija i obrjad v severnom Toxaristane." In *Antičnye i rannesrednevekovye drevnosti Južnogo Uzbekistana*, ed. G.A. Pugačenkova, 53–72. Tashkent: FAN.

Schafer, Edward. 1963. *The Golden Peaches of Samarkand: A Study of T'ang Exotics.* Berkeley: University of California Press.

Schlütz, Frank, and Frank Lehmkuhl. 2007. "Climatic Change in the Russian Altai, Southern Siberia, based on Palynological and Geomorphological Results, with Implications for Climatic Teleconnections and Human History since the Middle Holocene," *Vegetation History and Archaeobotany* 16: 101–118.

Shepherd, D. G. 1980. "Zandanîjî Revisited." In *Documenta Textilia: Festschrift für S. Müller-Christensen*, 105–122. Munich: Bayerisches Nationalmuseum.

Shepherd, D. G., and Walter Henning. 1959. "Zandanîjî Identified." In *Aus der Welt der islamischen Kunst: Festschrift für E. Kühnel*, 15–40. Berlin: Gebr. Mann.

Shishkina, Galina. 1994. "Ancient Samarkand: Capital of Soghd," *Bulletin of the Asia Institute* 8: 81–99.

Shkoda, Valentin. 1996. "The Sogdian Temple: Structure and Rituals," *Bulletin of the Asia Institute* 10: 195–206.

Sims-Williams, Nicholas. 1983. "Indian Elements in Parthian and Sogdian." In *Sprachen des Buddhismus in Zentralasien: Vorträge des Hamburger Symposions vom 2. Juli bis 5. Juli 1981*, ed. K. Röhrborn and W. Veenker, 132–141. Wiesbaden: O. Harrassowitz.

———. 1991a. "Mithra the Baga." In *Histoire et cultes de l'Asie centrale préislamique*, ed. Paul Bernard and Frantz Grenet, 177–186. Paris: Éditions du CNRS.

———. 1991b. "Christianity: iii. In Central Asia and Chinese Turkestan; iv. Christian Literature in Middle Iranian languages." *Encyclopaedia Iranica* 5.5: 530–532.

———. 1996. "Nouveaux documents sur l'histoire et la langue de la Bactriane," *Comptes rendus des séances de l'Académie des Inscriptions et Belles-Lettres* 633–654.

———. 1997. "Zu den iranischen Inschriften." In *Die Felsbildstation Shatial*, ed. Gérard Fussman and D. König, 62–72. Materialen zur Archäologie der Nordgebiete Pakistans 2. Mainz: Ph. von Zabern.

———. 2000a. "Some Reflections on Zoroastrianism in Sogdiana and Bactria." In *Silk Road Studies, IV: Realms of the Silk Roads, Ancient and Modern*, ed. D. Christian and C. Benjamin, 1–12. Turnhout: Brepols.

———. 2000b. *Bactrian Documents from Northern Afghanistan, I: Legal and Economic Documents.* London: Nour Foundation, Azimuth Editions, and Oxford University Press.

———. 2001. "The Sogdian Ancient Letter II." In *Philologica et Linguistica: Historia, Pluralitas, Universitas: Festschrift für Helmut Humbach zum 80. Geburtstag am 4. Dezember 2001*, ed. M. G. Schmidt and W. Bisang, 267–280. Trier: Wissenschaftlicher Verlag Trier.

———. 2007. *Bactrian Documents from Northern Afghanistan, II: Letters and Buddhist Texts.* London: Nour Foundation, Azimuth Editions.

Sims-Williams, Nicholas, and James Hamilton. 1990. *Documents turco-sogdiens du ixe–xe siècle de Touen-houang.* Corpus Inscriptionum Iranicarum II/III. London: SOAS.

Skaff, Jonathan. 1998. "Sasanian and Arab-Sasanian Silver Coins from Turfan: Their Relationship to International Trade and the Local Economy," *Asia Major* 9.2: 67–115.

Skjærvø, Oktor. 2002. *Khotanese Manuscripts from Chinese Turkestan in the British Library: A Complete Catalogue with Texts and Translations.* Corpus inscriptionum

Iranicarum, pt. 2: Inscriptions of the Seleucid and Parthian Periods and of Eastern Iran and Central Asia, vol. 5: Saka, Texts 6. London: British Library.

Stark, Sören. 2008. *Die Alttürkenzeit in Mittel- und Zentralasien: Archäologische und historische Studien*. Nomaden und Sesshafte 6. Wiesbaden: Reichert Verlag.

Stavisky, B. 1993–1994. "The Fate of Buddhism in Middle Asia," *Silk Road Art and Archaeology* 3: 113–142.

Tardieu, Michel. 2008. "Le schème hérésiologique de désignation des adversaires dans l'inscription nestorienne chinoise de Xi'an." In *Controverses des chrétiens dans l'Iran sassanide*, ed. Christelle Jullien, 207–225. Cahier de Studia Iranica 36. Paris: Association pour l'avancement des études iraniennes.

Tekin, Talat. 1968. *A Grammar of Orkhon Turkic*. Bloomington: Indiana University Press.

Thierry, François. 1993. "Sur les monnaies sassanides trouvées en Chine." In *Circulation des monnaies, des marchandises et des biens*, ed. R. Gyselen, 89–139. Res Orientales 5. Bures-sur-Yvette: Groupe pour l'étude de la civilisation du Moyen-orient; Leuven: Peeters.

Thierry, François, and C. Morrisson. 1994. "Sur les monnaies byzantines trouvées en Chine," *Revue Numismatique* 36: 109–145.

Tremblay, Xavier. 2001. *Pour une histoire de Sérinde: Le manichéisme parmi les peuples et religions d'Asie Centrale d'après les sources primaires*. Veröffentlichungen der Kommission für Iranistik 28. Vienna Verlag der Österreichischen Akademie der Wissenschaften.

———. 2007. "The Spread of Buddhism in Serindia: Buddhism among Iranians, Tocharians, and Turks before the 13th Century." In *The Spread of Buddhism*, ed. Ann Heirman and Stephan Peter Bumbacher, 75–130. Handbook of Oriental Studies: Section 8, Uralic & Central Asian Studies 16. Leiden: Brill.

Trombert, Éric. 1996. "Une trajectoire d'ouest en est sur la route de la soie: La diffusion du coton dans l'Asie centrale sinisée (6e–10e siècles)." In *La Persia e L'Asia Centrale da Alessandro al X secolo*, Atti di Convegni Lincei 127, 205–227. Rome: Accademia Nazionale dei Lincei.

———. 2000. "Textiles et tissus sur la Route de la Soie: Éléments pour une géographie de la production et des échanges." In *La Sérinde terre d'échanges*, ed. Monique Cohen, Jean-Pierre Drège, and Jacques Giès, 107–120. Paris: La Documentation Française.

Trombert, Éric, and Étienne de la Vaissière. 2007. "Les prix du marché à Turfan en 742." In *Études de Dunhuang et Turfan*, ed. J.-P. Drège, 1–52. Paris: EPHE-Droz.

ur-Rahman, A., Frantz Grenet, and Nicholas Sims-Williams. 2006. "A Hunnish Kushanshah," *Journal of Inner Asian Art and Archaeology* 1: 125–131.

Yoshida, Yutaka. 2009. "The Karabalgasun Inscription and the Khotanese Documents." In *Literarische Stoffe und ihre Gestaltung in mitteliranischer Zeit: Kolloquium anlässlich des 70. Geburtstages von Werner Sundermann*, ed. Desmond Durkin-Meisterernst, Christiane Reck, and Dieter Weber, 349–362. Wiesbaden: Ludwig Reichert Verlag.

———. 2009. "The Sogdian Language." In *The Iranian Languages*, ed. G. Windfuhr, 279–335. London: Routledge.

Zhang, Guangda. 1994. "Trois exemples d'influences mazdéennes dans la Chine des Tang," *Études chinoises* 13.1–2: 203–219.

———. 2000. "Iranian Religious Evidence in Turfan Chinese Texts," *China Archaeology and Art Digest* 4.1: 193–206.

Zürcher, Erick. 1990. "Han Buddhism and the Western Region." In *Thought and Law in Qin and Han China. Studies Dedicated to Anthony Hulsewé on the Occasion of His Eightieth Birthday*, ed. W. L. Idema and E. Zürcher, 158–182. Sinica Leidensia 24. Leiden: Brill.

CHAPTER 6

SYRIAC AND THE "SYRIANS"

PHILIP WOOD
Sidney Sussex College, Cambridge University

The historiography of writing in Syriac has traditionally focused upon the importance of Syriac during the formation of "the Great Church" in the third and fourth centuries. The existence of the Peshitta Bible text, the writings of the "gnostic" Bardaisan, and the contributions of the great poet-theologians Ephrem and Aphrahat have received the greatest emphases in this assessment.

The early surveys of Wright and Duval recognize the importance of this early period as a source of information for the transmission of the Old Testament from Hebrew and for the historical content of Ephrem's Nisibene hymns (Wright 1894, 3–12 and 27–38). The focus of these surveys is "factual" information: the Syrians are said "to shine neither in war nor science," though we should be grateful for "a plodding diligence that has preserved Greek fathers who might otherwise have been lost" (Wright 1894, 3). That is, interest in Syriac could be justified only insofar as it preserved the literature of a patristic golden age.

The reaction against this early positivism has taken two broad strands. The first, seen originally in the work of Walter Bauer, has been to use Syriac as a window into heterodoxy, presenting Mesopotamia in particular as a world where the "orthodoxy" of men like Ephrem remained a minority into the fourth century (Bauer 1971 5 and 39–45). The work of H. J. W. Drijvers, beginning with his study of the Bardaisanite text *On the Laws of the Countries*, fits into this tradition, with its emphasis on the variety of Christian and pagan practices in

Edessa, where a Middle Platonic intellectual culture was mixed with a Christian scholastic culture and active pagan cults (H. J. W. Drijvers 1966; 1980; 1983). Drijvers argued that "the Great Church" incorporated modified versions of radically ascetic texts of the third century in the Syriac language and that this resulted in several of the distinctive features of the developing Syriac-speaking churches, such as their ascetic reputation and the incorporation of the foundational myths of groups on the fringes of what became "orthodox" Christianity (H. J. W. Drijvers 1970; 1983).

In parallel to this, Sebastian Brock and Robert Murray examined the literature of Syriac Christianity as a body of shared biblical imagery, a collection of assumptions, with a strong Old Testament focus, an intellectual world that Ephrem and Aphrahat imbibed. Like Drijvers, Murray's work in particular emphasizes the importance of the Jewish context for these early theologians, both in terms of shared interests in the exegesis of the Old Testament and their shrill opposition to Jewish populations that were close to Christians both geographically and culturally. Notably, Murray highlights the fact that these early theologians embody a shared religious culture rather than an ecclesiology—their concern is more for proper discipleship by Christians than the institutions of the church (Murray 1975; 2004).

Sebastian Brock's voluminous and sensitive contributions to the same field have characterized the important and distinctive contributions made by Ephrem and his followers, as well as the writings of later mystics in "the Syriac tradition," as "a third lung of the church," who complemented patristic authors who wrote in Latin and Greek (Brock 2005b). Brock's approach has been to link the study of the early history of the Syriac-speaking church with that of its subsequent development after the council of Chalcedon, as well as the practice of its descendants in the contemporary Middle East and its diaspora in Europe and the Americas (Brock 2006).

The contributions of Brock, Murray, and Drijvers have allowed historians and theologians to view Syriac literature as a worthy topic of study in its own right. They have recognized it as the product of a culture with a distinctive position between the Roman and Persian worlds, a Christian literature on the fringes of empire, with a unique relationship to local Judaisms and paganisms that used similar Aramaic dialects but lacked the prestige of Syriac as a Christian language in an increasingly Christian empire.

However, the bulk of Syriac scholarship has remained focused on the earlier formative period. Many of the great contributors to the developing field of Syriac studies have been theologians and biblical scholars, and this has led to an understandable continuation of the emphasis of Wright's generation on the Syriac Bible. Their scholarly endeavors are hugely important for all they tell us about the translation of the Peshitta in Edessa and the subsequent use and re-translation of the Bible in Syriac in later generations (Petersen 1994; Weitzman 1999). But this focus has sometimes come at the cost of removing Syriac-speakers from their Roman context, seeing them instead as embodiments of an unchanging "Syriac spirituality" (e.g., Harvey 1990, 1–21). This tendency is abetted by the absence of many secular texts from Syriac (though Syriac translations of Aristotle are an exception to this rule).

Furthermore, the interest in a patristic golden age has, if anything, increased since Wright wrote. Sources of the fifth century and afterward are all too frequently mined for information about the past they purport to describe rather than seen as interesting inventions of history in their own right. Scholarship on the Edessene *Doctrina Addai* (c. 440s), the vita tradition of Ephrem (fifth and sixth centuries), and the Arabic *Chronicle of Seert* (tenth century) provides examples of this tendency to pillage later sources without sensitivity for their context.

If the late twentieth century saw the admission of the variety of Christian practice in Mesopotamia within the shared discourse and references of the Syriac literature of Ephrem and Aphrahat, one of the problems that awaits Syriac studies is to integrate this into the broader study of the culture and politics of the Roman, Persian, and Islamic worlds in Late Antiquity.

I.1 Syriac, *Suryaye*, and the Syriac tradition

The Christian Suryaye of today's Tur 'Abdin (southeast Turkey) are, like many of the Jewish communities of the early-twentieth-century Middle East, a distinct community, bound by shared religious practices, a shared language, and a shared sense of history. It is with this sense of ethnic difference that some groups of Suryaye claimed a status as a distinct nation, with its own Mesopotamian homeland of Aram, during and after the First World War (Brock and Taylor 2001).

Yet the Syriac speakers in the third century did not display any such sense of their difference. As I hope to show, Christianity contributed to their sense of cultural independence within the Roman world, and it provided the impetus for Christian foundational histories and the identification of great men of a Syriac tradition in the fourth century, of whom Ephrem is the most famous. But to write of Syriac-speakers as "les syriaques," as Duval (1899) does, with its implications of ethnic distinctiveness, is to retroject later ideas of ethno-religious difference and consciousness onto earlier generations.

There were undoubtedly distinctive features of Christianity in Syria, many of which were extremely ascetic, and these attracted both praise and blame from commentators such as Theodoret of Cyrrhus. These existed as *potential* boundaries for identity, which certain authors might appeal to. But the monitoring of religious practice, as opposed to belief, was only emphasized as a guarantee of local orthodoxy well into the debates that followed the

Christological crises. Similarly, any emphasis on Ephrem as a great Suryoyo father of the church was also tempered by the wish of churchmen to participate in debates across a whole universal church and to minimize the identification of Syriac-speakers with the darker heteropractic reputation that was attached to greater Syria. Thus an examination of Syriac literature and its reception should be seen in terms of the tension between the wish to champion the local—in terms of the distinctive history and traditions of Syriac-speakers—and the wish (and ability) to participate in wider debates of theology, culture, and politics.

In an influential article (1984), Sebastian Brock charted the development of the relationship between Syriac and Greek culture from the antagonism of Ephrem's invective against "the poison of the Greeks" to the cultural acceptance of the translation movements that flourished in seventh-century Mesopotamia and ninth-century Baghdad. He identified the sixth century as the hinge point for the acceptance of this Greek culture, pointing in particular to Philoxenus of Mabbug's insistence on the superiority of the Greek Bible and the danger of the use of more imprecise terms in the Syriac Peshitta (1984, 20–22).

Brock's article set out the aim of charting the relationship of Syriac and Greek *cultural production*. It placed in the background of its argument the discussion of attitudes towards the Christian empire and the political contexts for the relationship between Greek and Syriac literary culture and theology. Here, I should like to place the cultural production of the Syriac world more in the forefront and explicitly in its pan-Roman context to investigate aspects of the re-invention of the literary and religious history of Syriac speakers to suit the broader and more Christian political context in which they found themselves in the late fifth and sixth centuries. I will do this by focusing primarily on the foundation history of the city of Edessa, the *Doctrina Addai*, before returning to the examples of Brock's article, to Philoxenus of Mabbug, and to the re-invention of the Syriac heritage in the context of the Christological controversies.

I.2 A Christian Political Context

The gradual adoption of Christianity as a religion of empire meant that Greek, already a language of administration and of civic prestige, also became a language of religious prestige. As the language of the Gospels, it provided the medium for the spread of the new religion and for its distinctive institutional forms. For the local languages of eastern Anatolia, which had resisted Hellenization during the rule of Alexander's successors and the Principate, Christianity provided the nail in the coffin. Frank Trombley has observed how Homeric names, Greek literacy, and Christianity all appear at the same time in the funerary epigraphy of Laodikea in Phrygia (c. 340), and, in the same century, Greek was used to proclaim the religion of villagers of the Aleppine massif or the Hauran (Trombley 2001, 2:102–104; Millar 1998, 165; Mitchell 1993). Similarly, in Roman Palestine, the Latin-speaking pilgrim Egeria recorded that the liturgy would be said in Greek by the priest and then translated into "Syriac" (probably Palestinian Aramaic) for the population at large (*Itinerarium Egeriae* 47).

Yet, further north, Syriac, the Aramaic dialect of Edessa, resisted this trend. In an era in which most local languages were being absorbed by Greek, Syriac seems to have developed into a prestige dialect for speakers of other Aramaic tongues. Edessa had long witnessed the bilingual coexistence of Syriac and Greek, as befitted a buffer state against the Parthians and Sasanians, where Greek had long been a "comprehensible language of power" (Millar 1998, 73). The relatively sudden appearance of Syriac in epigraphy west of the Euphrates—as an epigraphic language and script that could contest Greek's monopoly as a language of religious prestige—must be tied to the prominence of Edessa as a prestige site for Christianity.

Edessa is identified as a missionary center both by the stories in Syriac, such as the *Doctrina Addai*, and by Sozomen (2.8.2). This early role for Edessene missionaries, and the production of texts suited to proselytizing, such as Tatian's *Diatessaron*, might have given Syriac its prestigious role as a Christian language and, potentially, have spread ascetic customs peculiar to the city of Edessa to a wider area. In the same way that Manichaean missionaries devised a distinctive script in the third century to set apart their writings from those of their rivals, so the script and language of the city of Edessa acquired this role for Christian communities in Roman Syria (Brock and Taylor 2001, 2:244–245).

The public culture and law of the Roman empire and of its institutional church was undoubtedly a feature that was shared by all communities within its bounds, to a greater or lesser extent. And the growing importance of Syriac as a language of religious prestige should not be connected with any notions of particularism or a predisposition to doctrinal "heresy" (see Jones 1959). Instead, what I wish to stress in the analysis that follows is that inclusion within Roman cultural and religious norms did not preclude Syriac-speakers from *using their difference to matter*, that is, emphasizing the cultural and religious prestige of their heritage on a broader political canvas than had been possible in a pagan empire.

We should remember, of course, that even Jews and Samaritans, excluded from participation within a Christian empire, were able to use its forms of display to mark out their difference or to practice their religion. Witness, for instance, the depiction of God as a solar deity in synagogue mosaics; the teaching of Homer in the patriarchal schools; and, most striking of all, the use of Roman imperial behavior by the Samaritans in the coronation and chariot races of their emperor-messiah Julian of Neapolis (Goodman 2003, 133–148; Holum 1982, 72–73). In these cases, Jews and Samaritans naturalized the less Christian aspects of imperial display and employed them to reinforce their distinctiveness, in a process that Seth Schwartz has labeled the "Judaization" of the Jews (Schwartz 2003).

Like the Jews, Suryaye could employ Roman discourses of power to magnify their own prestige and to police the boundaries of proper behavior. The difference was, of course, that the Suryaye were Christians within an increasingly Christian empire; indeed, their very importance and cultural independence relied on this. And as such, their expressions of self-identity, such as the foundation history of Christian Edessa, the *Doctrina Addai*, began to participate in and interact with the increasingly Christian Roman empire.

I.3 *Doctrina Addai*

The *Doctrina Addai* is a composite text of the fifth century, attributed to one Labubna, a fictional scribe of first-century Edessa. This dating is based on its emphasis on charitable giving, its use of the *Diatessaron*, the occasional appearance of Cyrilline Christology, and an anti-Jewish bias, contentious factors of the time, which, when taken altogether, connect it with the episcopate of Rabbula (d. 435) (Griffith 2003; H. J. W. Drijvers 1999). The *Doctrina Addai* contains within it various earlier missionary accounts, some of which may be of Manichaean origin, but its constituent parts were gathered together in the fifth century and chiefly reflect concerns of that era (see Wood 2010, chapter 4, for a full version of this argument).

The text's opening narrative (*Doctrina Addai* 1–7), the Abgar correspondence, describes how Abgar, a king of Edessa as Roman client in the first century, corresponded with Christ and received both a letter from him guaranteeing Edessa's invulnerability and a missionary visit from his apostle Addai (Gr. Thaddeus). The same material, with certain variations, had been employed previously by Eusebius in his *Ecclesiastical History* (1.13), a work that had been translated into Syriac probably in the early fifth century and helped to ensure the city's fame as a pilgrimage center.

Yet the *Doctrina* itself is ten times longer than the Abgar legend. A pivotal moment for the invention of Edessene history must be the development of the earlier story into something much grander that could encompass, challenge, and annex the justificatory legends of other places, re-working them and embedding them into the apostolic history of Edessa.

As Griffith has emphasized, rather than focusing on its questionable historicity, the Abgar legend can be seen as a vehicle, a widely acknowledged and popular story to which other tales could be attached. These included the doctrine-laden sermons of the apostle Addai, which have been described as a paradigm for Christian behavior in late antique Edessa, and the re-writing or embedding of apocryphal tales in Greek: for instance, the discovery of the

"True Cross" by Helena, re-worked in Syriac as the *Protonike Legend*, and the correspondence between Pilate and Tiberius, appearing in Syriac as correspondence between Abgar and Tiberius.

In the *Doctrina* (7–10), Addai heals Abgar of his disease and preaches to him a sermon that focuses on the need to spread Christianity to the whole world and to avoid heresy. Addai then tells Abgar the Protonike tale, a re-writing of Helena's discovery of the cross that makes it contemporary with Abgar V in the reign of Tiberius and Claudius.

The narrative continues (*Doctrina* 10–17) with a list of the nobles present, the *bnay hire*, who rejoice at Addai's sermon and ask for it to be proclaimed publicly after one of them has been ordained. His subsequent speech (*Doctrina* 18) to the people is filled with invective against local pagan cults and the Jews, as well as more disguised attacks on Manichaean and Marcionite theology. After this (*Doctrina* 19–31), Abgar and all the citizens convert to Christianity, and the king builds a church for Addai and presents gifts for his mission. Addai then answers the Christological questions of some of the nobility, and the old pagan priests overturn their altars.

Next (*Doctrina* 32–34), Addai trains his successors, emphasizing the ascetic conduct of the priesthood, as well as knowledge of the scriptures, and they also read the *Diatessaron* to the people. Abgar then corresponds with the king of Assyria, sends him a report of happenings in Edessa, and petitions the emperor Tiberius to destroy the Jews in Judaea, which leads to a pogrom of Jewish princes (*Doctrina* 37–39). Finally, Addai, on his deathbed, ordains his successor, Aggai, and tells the nobility that they must preserve the true doctrine that he has laid down (*Doctrina* 39–48).

Addai's sermons and actions function as a model for the correct behavior of the church in the era in which the *Doctrina* was compiled: the apostle's behavior and his instructions to his successors could be modeled on the compiler's view of correct behavior in the present. In particular, he establishes the *bnay qyama*, lay "sons of covenant," who are to be kept "alone and chaste," and instructs the priests in an ascetic ideal, in which they should "keep their bodies pure in order to act as priests of God," sentiments that may reflect ascetic trends in local Christianity deep into Late Antiquity.

Importantly, the religious paradigms set out by the *Doctrina* all have a very local slant. The pagan cults that the text attacks are those of neighboring Aramaic-speaking cities that shared the same pagan cults as Edessa. Paganism could then be identified as a Harranian or Arab practice, alien to a Christian Edessa. Similarly, an ascetic priesthood and the *bnay qyama*, which were a distinguishing feature of Syro-Mesopotamian Christianity, were identified as apostolic injunctions and could be traced back to the missionary success of the Edessene church. A Christian Edessa was made distinct not only from its pagan neighbors and from its own pagan past, but thanks to its ascetic emphasis, from other groups of doctrinally orthodox Christians as well. The *Doctrina* did not solely demarcate proper Christian practice; it gave local Christian practice special significance as apostolic Christian practice and used this to emphasize the city's prestige.

I.4 The Protonike Legend and the Jews

But if the original compilation of the *Doctrina Addai* was concerned with local religious norms and behavior, then the development of this compilation over the century shows us how this distinctive religious culture was brought to bear on the Roman empire as a whole. The critical passages in the compilation are the two sets of embedded vignettes, notable for their anti-Jewish sentiment: the Protonike Legend and the Tiberius correspondence, which clearly interrupt the main flow of the narrative, centered on the sermons of Addai.

There is already an anti-Jewish tone in the original compilation of the *Doctrina*. For instance, Addai counters the kinds of criticisms that might have been made by Jewish interlocutors by stressing the Pentecost and the mission to all the nations and tells the *bnay hire* to preserve the faith from the snares of the Jews (*Doctrina* 19–21 and 29).

Even when Addai goes to visit Tobias the Jew or is mourned by Jews at his death, these are indications of the *potential* of converting the Jews, thereby criticizing those obstinate Jews who, in fifth-century Edessa, had still not converted, and whose culture seems to have been well-known by the compiler (*Doctrina* 5 and 48). These passages, which discuss the Jewish allies of Addai, can be understood in the context of fifth-century attempts to convert Edessene Jews during Rabbula's episcopate, during which a synagogue was appropriated as the cathedral of St. Stephen and when wider debates within the Roman empire about the status of Jews emerge in the law codes (H. J. W. Drijvers 1985).

So the *Doctrina* provides a model of classical arguments against the Jews and a definition of Christianity against a Jewish other. Much of this is not surprising; we would expect Christian authors to delineate their religion against Judaism. Andrew Jacobs (2005, esp. 109–117) has discussed the academic imperialism of Roman Christian writers upon Jews and upon Palestine. Eusebius' *Ecclesiastical History* distinguished the good, proto-Christian traditions and knowledge to be gleaned from the Old Testament as he decried the Jews of his day, while to the Bordeaux pilgrim, the Jews of Palestine only served as memorials to a pre-Christian past, rather than a living alternative to Christianity.

But the absorption of Jewish history and culture by Christian intellectuals that Jacobs reports is, in part, a product of their Palestinian context, where Christians had come to a holy land already inhabited by Jews. The intellectual imperialism he reports is different from the casual, everyday anti-Judaism of Ephrem or the *Doctrina*'s vision of the Jewish past: for pseudo-Labubna, the Jews are not the people of the Old Testament prophets, but the people who rejected the prophets (Hayman 1985). The anti-Judaism of the *Doctrina* reflects a milieu in which Christians and Jews might argue in a shared language over exegesis, and where the long proximity of Judaism and Christianity meant that the former continued to present a real lure to Christians, forcing Christian leaders to assert religious boundaries more starkly (H. Drijvers 1985, 98–100).

The first of these embedded vignettes was already present in the *Doctrina* when the London manuscript was written in the early fifth century, though it breaks the flow of the Edessene narrative, suggesting that the scene was added to the compilation after the writing of Addai's sermons but before our first surviving manuscript was written (J.-W. Drijvers 1992, 153). It describes how Abgar wrote to the emperor Tiberius after hearing Addai's sermon and asks him to punish the Jews and to dismiss Pilate, which Tiberius does, killing the Jewish princes (*Doctrina* 38–39).

The second embedded vignette, the *Protonike Legend*, a variant of the *Helena Legend*, was added later than the Tiberius correspondence. In the *Helena Legend*, the mother of Constantine discovers the Cross in Jerusalem, while in the former the protagonist is the wife of the emperor Claudius, Protonike (J.-W. Drijvers 1992, 79–80 and 147–150). The *Protonike Legend* first appears in the *Doctrina* in the early-sixth-century Leningrad manuscript, but J.-W. Drijvers (1992, 152–162 and 173–174) has argued convincingly that the legend must have been embedded much earlier; dating it to the period 400–440 (the later end of this period seems more likely).

The *Protonike Legend* describes how the wife of the emperor Claudius discovered the True Cross in Jerusalem, anticipating the events of the *Helena Legend*. In it, Protonike abjures paganism after meeting Simon Peter in Rome, before traveling to Jerusalem and being greeted by James, brother of Christ. Here she learns that Golgotha, the True Cross, and Christ's tomb are all in the possession of the Jews, who persecute those who are trying to spread Christianity. Protonike commands their return and tests the three crosses for their miraculous powers by using one of them to resurrect her dead daughter. Next Protonike constructs a church at Gologtha, anticipating Constantine's construction and causing all the Jews and pagans of the city to be thrown into despair, before returning to Rome, where she persuades Claudius to expel all the Jews from Italy (*Doctrina* 10–17).

The anti-Jewish features of the *Protonike Legend* are in keeping with the rest of the *Doctrina*. These features clearly set it apart from the fourth-century *Helena Legend*, which does not mention the Jews at all (Feiertag 2000). Here the *Protonike Legend* has re-worked a popular Greek legend to fit the paradigms of the *Doctrina Addai* and the prejudices and needs of an Edessene audience.

Both the *Protonike Legend* and the Tiberius correspondence feature petitions to the emperor to persecute the Jews. This may reflect the ongoing tensions between imperial authorities and those independent monastic and ecclesiastical authorities that acted against the Jews in the early fifth century. The same issues seem to be at hand in a contemporary saint's life, that of Barsauma of Samosata, who led his bands of monks and "mountain people" across

Palestine, a land of Jews and Samaritans, in the 420s–440s, destroying a luxurious synagogue built by Solomon at Rabbat Moab and ambushing Jews in Jerusalem in spite of opposition from the imperial authorities and Palestinian Christians (Nau 1927). In Jerusalem, he engaged in a public quarrel with the empress Eudocia, who banned him from further destruction, invoking the laws of 423 that prevented Jewish, Samaritan, and pagan places of worship from being attacked (Nau 1927, 191). His response was an attack on her public piety in Jerusalem, highlighting her failure to give alms to the poor. Essentially, the saint groups the empress with the Jews: her building project parallels the luxurious synagogue that Barsauma destroys, while the empress's pagan origins and her defense of the Jews present her as a bad Christian.

A similar scene exists in the fifth-century Syriac *Life of Symeon the Stylite* (121–122), where he attacks the emperor Theodosius II (401–450), the husband of Eudocia, for his defense of the Jews in his legislation. The life reports how a "wicked advisor" caused an edict to be proclaimed returning captured synagogues to the Jews, causing Jews and pagans to dress in white and rejoice, and much distress among the Christians. After certain priests appeal to Symeon, he writes to the emperor saying, "Your heart is exalted and you have disregarded the Lord who gave you diadem and throne and become a friend to the Jews. Behold! The anger of God will overtake you."

The *Doctrina*, and the additional vignettes embedded within it, was compiled in the same era and region as the *Life of Barsauma of Samosata*. The *Doctrina*, like the Syriac *Life of Symeon* and the *Life of Barsauma*, presents attacks on recalcitrant Jews as an approved Christian activity, in contrast to the attitudes of the discovery of the cross in the *Helena Legend*, which does not mention the Jews, or the Theodosian legislation (*CTh* 16.8), which sought to defend them against violence. Thus there were two sides to arguments about the treatment of Jews. The strand that Jacobs observed from his Palestinian texts and the imperial legislation, which sought to absorb and control contemporary Jews as symbols of the past, was accompanied by a more radical strand that advocated a more direct approach. For Barsauma and Symeon, though not for Eudocia and Theodosius, attacking synagogues could be an intrinsic part of orthodox behavior. The stance of this hagiography is borne out by riots in nearby Tella, caused by Jews eating with Christians at Passover, and the massacre of Jews that accompanied the Persian siege of that city in 502 (*Chronicle of Joshua the Stylite* 58).

I.5 A Mesopotamian *Kaiserkritik*

The evidence cited here suggests that anti-Jewish activity was an expected part of Christian identity, at least for some Syrian and Mesopotamian populations, and that, as such, it could form a reasonable focus for *Kaiserkritik*, that is, that discrimination against the Jews was an expected part of good Christian government. An anti-Jewish stance would become increasingly important in the laws and behavior of the emperors: in a gradual process stretching from the banning of Jews from civic honors in the novel of 439, to mob violence against Jews during the reigns of Leo and Zeno, and later to the anti-Jewish legislation of Justinian (Dauphin 1998, 1:297–301). But even then, hagiographers might take emperors to task for failing to discriminate harshly enough against the Jews, a field in which Syrian ascetics and polemicists had a long pedigree of activity.

Like the saints' lives, the *Doctrina* presented a Mesopotamian image of the relationship between Jews and Christians that opposed the intentions of the lawmakers. The *Doctrina* presents Abgar both as a Christian monarch trying to do his duty and persecute the Jews and, in the two embedded texts of the *Protonike Legend* and the Tiberius correspondence, as a Roman magnate petitioning his emperor to deal with the Jewish princes. Simultaneously, the emphasis on Protonike's devotion to Simon Peter portrays Addai's mission as part of the history of an orthodox church that had always acknowledged Roman primacy and continued to do so in the fifth century (*Doctrina* 16). Thus the compilation can be seen as part of a wider movement that opposed the more tolerant agenda regarding the Jews adopted by the Theodosian Code.

However, the embedding of the Tiberius correspondence and the *Protonike Legend* into the *Doctrina Addai* changed the way the text's anti-Jewish agenda was pursued. The compilation that preceded the anti-Jewish vignettes had presented an ideal of Christian rule through the figure of Abgar, who functions as a prototype of Constantine, prefiguring the conversion of the Roman empire in the city of Edessa alone. The text of the *Doctrina Addai*, without the Tiberius correspondence and *Protonike Legend*, is a repository for the independent history of Edessa, in an era when Abgar is said to have converted before any other monarch and in which his aristocratic courtiers served as the repository for a pure faith, in belief and ascetic practice, which was not practiced in most of the empire.

The embedded anti-Jewish vignettes place Abgar into a Roman context. The original text presents Abgar threatening to invade Palestine, supervising the conversion of the people of Edessa, and receiving correspondence from the king of Assyria. But the embedded texts present Edessa not as an independent kingdom but as a client state of the Roman empire. While Abgar's rule is presented as a model for anti-Jewish action by the state in the original text, the embedded vignettes give this role to Roman imperial figures, to Claudius, Tiberius, and Protonike, with whom Abgar is made contemporary.

H. J. W. Drijvers (1998) suggested that the later compilation of the *Doctrina*, with the *Protonike Legend* included, reflects a wish to tie together Edessa and Jerusalem and to create a history of Edessene co-operation with Roman emperors. And Mirkovic proposes that the embedded texts reflect a pro-Roman move on the part of the later compiler, in an era when religious refugees from Persia prompted a closer identification of the Roman empire with the Christian world (Mirkovic 2006, 53–66). But the *Doctrina*'s presence within wider debates about imperial action and attitudes to the Jews does not mean that it seeks to submerge an Edessene identity entirely within a Roman political world, but that Edessene ideas required a Roman history, which presented the city as an actor within the entire empire, in order to be persuasive.

The use of a Roman historical context for the anti-Jewish ideas in the two vignettes embedded into the *Doctrina* reflect the text's position in an empire-wide contest over the emperor's duties, especially those regarding the Jews, in an environment where part of the emperor's authority rested on a church in orthodoxy and at unity. If this meant that provincial religious identity discussed its own past in terms of Roman history as well as in on its own terms, then it was because its opinions could affect the actions of the center: the ideals of orthodox rule provided a framework to criticize an emperor, as well as support for his rule. Just as Barsauma had asserted a specific kind of religious conduct for Eudocia, the embedded vignettes of the *Doctrina Addai* did the same at one remove, using stories about Protonike, Tiberius, and Claudius to make suggestions for the behavior of Theodosius II and Eudocia. The centripetal pull that Mirkovic correctly detected in the *Protonike Legend* also shows us the potential of certain kinds of religious pressure against the Jews in the fifth-century empire: arguments were phrased in terms of the Roman past in protest against contemporary state policy.

Yet these anti-Jewish arguments also emphasized the pious history of the city of Edessa, as opposed to the failure of contemporary emperors to enact proper Christian government: the inclusion of the new vignettes was simultaneously centripetal and centrifugal. The *Protonike Legend* shows us Edessa contesting the special claims of the dynasty of Constantine: by pushing the first discovery of the cross back to the reign of Claudius, its author could emphasize the antiquity of Abgar's conversion and the antiquity of Edessene religious practice compared to other centers. The effectiveness of the re-working of the Protonike and Tiberius legends as models for contemporary anti-Jewish action by emperors relied on their use of a Roman past. Emperors' assertions of universal rule and the equation of the Roman empire with the Christian world provided a framework into which the compiler of the final text of the *Doctrina* could present Edessene history, but they did not exclude other claims to prestige using Christian history.

Within the later compilation, the older parts of the *Doctrina* (such as Addai's sermons) preserved the image of an independent, pre-Roman Edessa alongside that of the Tiberius correspondence and the *Protonike Legend*. The *Doctrina Addai*, after the inclusion of the anti-Jewish vignettes, remains a story about a pre-Roman past, except that now it spells out Abgar's precedence over Constantine and uses Abgar as a model for contemporary Christian government.

II.1 Piety or Danger: The Reinvention of the Christian Past in Syriac

The development of the *Doctrina Addai* in the course of the fifth century suggests that Edessenes, or at least an aristocratic faction within Edessa, sought to use the pious history of the city, first, to cement the Christianization of the city and, second, to contest the claims of Roman emperors to a monopoly on Christian history. By asserting the place of Abgar as "the prelude to Constantine" (in the words of Mirkovic), we can see how the pre-existent symbolic material of the city was brought to bear within the wider empire and overlaid on older local hagiography (such as the Diocletianic martyrs Shmouna, Guria, and Habib).

I should like to set this process alongside the trimming and reinvention of the Syriac ascetic tradition that occurred from the episcopate of Rabbula until the Arab conquests. In this era, Mesopotamian religious leaders sought to use their indigenous ascetic tradition as part of their claim for prestige vis-à-vis other ecclesiastical traditions within the Roman world. Yet at the same time, they also needed to ensure that these indigenous traditions did not go outside the norms of Roman orthopraxy (even if these norms were imported from elsewhere, as in the case of Egyptian cenobitism).

Rabbula's contribution to this process of reformation was decisive. He banned ascetics from living among secular people, from growing their hair long or hanging irons on themselves (except for those who are solitary), from owning heretical books, from taking on lawsuits, from distributing holy oil (especially to women), from giving the Eucharist if they are not ordained, and from practicing self-castration (*Laws of Rabbula, On Monks*, 3, 5, 7, 10, 15, 20 and *On the bnay qyama*, 10, 18, 22, 53). This ecclesiastical legislation makes it clear that he was confronted by a popular religious culture that blurred the boundaries between the priesthood and lay ascetics and practiced the extreme ascetic customs that had been polemically associated with various heretical groups, such as the Messalians (see Caner 2002). He also commands his *bnay qyama* to root out wizards and cut down sacred trees (*Rules for the bnay qyama* 17 and 53–54), both of which suggest an environment that was only semi-Christianized (in spite of the protestations of the *Doctrina Addai*).

At the same time, Rabbula's episcopate was significant for his ban on the Syriac *Diatessaron*, the Gospel harmony that had been attributed to Tatian and upon which Ephrem had composed a commentary. It is hard to judge whether his command that a copy of the independent Gospels be placed in every church was fulfilled, but his hagiographer prominently notes that he was responsible for the translation of the Peshitta Gospels.

Interestingly, similar reforming trends are detectable in the actions and hagiography of Rabbula's opponent, Theodoret of Cyrrhus. Like Rabbula, Theodoret banned the *Diatessaron* in his dioceses. And while his hagiographic collection, the *Historia Religiosa*, celebrates the ascetics of Mesopotamia and Syria—and at times emphasizes the barbarity of his saints—he is also at pains to show them as obedient to their bishop and willing to work within ecclesiastical structures. Theodoret describes himself preventing them from going too far in their asceticism and suppressing the prophetic injunctions that had brought fame to one of his female saints (*Historia Religiosa* 31). Despite the fact that Rabbula and Theodoret were on separate sides of the Christological debates that surrounded the expulsion of Nestorius (431), as well as the second council (the "Robber Synod") of Ephesus (449), they shared a wish to tame and "normalize" the asceticism and popular religion of their own provinces. Christological division and the engagement with empire-wide doctrinal debates—epitomized in Rabbula's sponsorship of the Syriac translations of Cyril of Alexandria (Wright 1894, 48–49)—brought with it a wider concern to bring religious variation into line with a single orthopraxy, lest variations in religious practice provide a hostage to fortune for opponents.

II.2 *Doukrono de Mor Ephrem*: Changing Images in the Hagiography

This normalization of Mesopotamian asceticism was directed through the rewriting of hagiography, as well as through ecclesiastical legislation and church government. Sidney Griffith (1994) has pointed to Theodoret's re-imagining of Julian Saba, the wandering cave-dweller of the pseudo-Ephremic *madrashe*, as the founder of cenobitic monasteries in the style of Egypt, with its more formal relationship with the clergy. Griffith stresses that Julian Saba was no "monk," in the sense that word was understood by the sixth century, but an *ihidaya*, a practitioner of a Mesopotamian proto-monasticism who found a place for celibates in the heart of secular communities (and possibly taking a special role in singing and the liturgy: see Brock 1973 and Griffith 1993). Notably, these Greek rewritings were readily absorbed into the Syriac tradition by the sixth century, as has been demonstrated for Jacob of Nisbis, Julian Saba, and Symeon the Stylite (Peeters 1920; Harvey 1993).

This normalizing process has been most strikingly identified in the reputation of Ephrem "the Syrian." The poet-theologian himself appears in his own compositions as "a bishop's man." He was a deacon who supported a series of bishops in Nisibis and later Edessa: he was active in the midst of his church as a composer of *madrashe* ("teaching-hymns") for men and women, a public celibate in the midst of his congregation, an organizer of famine relief, and a prominent opponent of contemporary heresy (Griffith 1986).

Ephrem himself had proved particularly influential as a heresiologist. We can distinguish two differing approaches in his method. First, while he continued to champion sexual continence within the church, his polemic against the Marcionites in his *Hymns against Heresies* focuses on exposing "their real beliefs," in a text aimed at Palutian ("orthodox") Christians who might have been tempted by a "lifestyle and piety congruent with their own" (Bundy 1988, 31–32; Murray 2004, 343–344). Importantly, this attack offers no criticism of Marcionite spirituality, ethics, or religious canon, all of which featured as points of criticism against ascetic heretics elsewhere, such as the Priscillianists of fourth-century Spain (Chadwick 1976). Instead, Ephrem focuses on orthodoxy, rather than orthopraxy, as the defining feature of membership of the true church: his quarrel with the Marcionites was one waged within the borders of Syriac-speaking religion and culture.

The second strand of Ephrem's heresiology was aimed against the Arians (on this term, see Gwynn 2006). It is in this context specifically that Ephrem made his attack on the "poison of the Greeks" as part of a wider criticism of the attempt to use dialectical theology to categorize God, which Ephrem condemns as an act of pride on the part of the heretics (Russel 1994, 22–27). He praises Paul for entering the capital of the Greeks, for using their language in debate against them, and for "then discarding their equipment once he was finished" (*Hymns of Faith* 161; cf. Acts 17). But Ephrem is referring only to one strand of Greek thought: Greek culture could be tied to Athens and its paganism, but it need not be. Ephrem was content to use Stoic ideas in other contexts (such as his attacks on Bardaisan) and does not label these features as Greek: much of this philosophical terminology seems to have been naturalized into Ephrem's thought world (Possekel 1999, 231–234). And just as Ephrem used Greek philosophical ideas to attack those who used philosophy themselves, he was also drawn into consideration of the imperial church by his opposition to the Arians and his desire for orthodox emperors who would oppose heresy.

Ephrem's literary products won him great fame in the Nicene church he defended. He was widely imitated in the following generations in Edessa, and the associations of orthodoxy that surrounded his name meant that a broad literature of pseudo-Ephremic material appeared in Syriac and Greek, where single lines of Ephrem were combined with new compositions to illustrate points of faith or behavior (Murray 2004, 33–34). Ironically, this popularity would allow Ephrem's image to be repeatedly reformed to fit the new circumstances of the church, in which the idiosyncrasies of Mesopotamian Christianity, with its alternative canon and distinctive ascetic emphasis, were increasingly seen as heteropraxy, especially in the critical atmosphere of the Christological controversies.

Sebastian Brock (1999) has demonstrated how the Syriac *Life of Ephrem* updated the saint's image to accord with sixth-century monastic expectations, making him a hater of women—on the model of some of the Egyptian *Apophthegmata Patrum*—as well as a pilgrim to Egypt and Cappadocia. The *Life* also records how he was given two scrolls by an angel that he was to give to Awgin and Julian Saba (Amar 1992, 135). The *Life* has connected him with the fictitious founder of monasticism in Syria, the Egyptian Awgin (cf. Fiey 1962), and made Ephrem part of this narrative of the origins of cenobitism (just as Theodoret had done earlier for Julian Saba). Similarly, the *Life* enlarges upon the poet's connection with Basil of Caesarea, making him able to miraculously speak Greek as part of his ordination (Amar 1992, 146–148).

In sum, the Syriac *Life* seems to accept the efforts of other traditions to annex the prestige of the great Syrian hymnographer to their own narratives, emphasizing Egypt as the source of monasticism and the cultural prestige of the Greek language. If Theodoret had magnified the importance of Jacob of Nisibis, Julian Saba, and other ascetics in his hagiography (even as he normalized their ascetic practices and made them obedient to their bishops), then the transformation of Ephrem's vita shows that, while his name remained associated with orthodoxy and was appealed to by both sides in the Christological controversies of the sixth century, little of his actual personality remained.

Lucas Van Rompay (2004) has approached the same problem of the changing memory via the works of Philoxenus of Mabbug, the great Miaphysite polemicist of the late fifth and early sixth centuries. Van Rompay notes that Philoxenus' early work, such as his *Memre against Habib* (484), make heavy use of Ephrem, mimicking the titles of his *memre* and appealing to the poet as a touchstone of orthodoxy. Yet his later works, such as his *Letter to the Monks of Senoun* (521), appeals to Ephrem only as the last in chains of authority otherwise entirely composed of Greek writers: the "Syrian teacher" is not quoted directly, but only added to confirm a list of Greek authorities. Just as hagiographers had re-molded his asceticism to fit contemporary expectations, so Philoxenus reduced his emphasis on a figure whose once-huge theological importance had become tarnished because of the requirements of sixth-century debate: Philoxenus criticizes Ephrem for his careless use of clothing language (Christ "put on his flesh"), which could allow Dyophysite interpretations of the Son, and for his archaic use of the feminine when referring to the Holy Spirit (Tanghe 1960). Similarly, Ephrem's commentary on the *Diatessaron* might also have troubled theologians in the era that followed Rabbula's ban: this might account for the very late discovery of Ephrem's commentary in the 1950s and the assertions of the Karshuni *Life of Ephrem* (Amar 1993), where Gregory of Nyssa is said to praise Ephrem's commentaries on *all* the books of the Bible.

Philoxenus' role in the creation of a new Syriac translation of the Bible has long been seen as a red-letter day in the secondary literature. Commentary has focused on his alteration of "Nestorian" terminology, his coinage of new terms based on the Greek, and his fresh translations of Greek Old Testament citations within the New Testament (where the Peshitta New Testament had used its own Old Testament, taken directly from the Hebrew, to furnish these, rather than translating the Greek citations anew). The translation he commissioned might be seen as a mid-point between Rabbula's suppression of the *Diatessaron* and the production of the even more literal Harklean translation in 615 (cf. Brock 2005a).

This drift toward a literal Greek translation, like Rabbula's earlier initiative, was prompted by the ever-widening sphere of the Christological debate: arguments had to depend on a text of undisputed orthodoxy, and this necessitated a series of concessions from the native Syriac tradition. In the same way, we can see Philoxenus' suppression of Ephrem as another attempt to edit out inconvenient aspects of the Syriac ascetic heritage and leave him as a vehicle for orthodoxy, shreds of whose original writings could be used as the core of later, more "relevant," theological compositions.

II.3 Being Syrian and Being Roman: Jacob of Serug and John of Ephesus

The ecclesiastical reforms and writings of Rabbula, Theodoret, and Philoxenus, despite their different theological positions, can be drawn together to show a single narrative in which a Syrian past was molded to emphasize its orthopraxy in an increasingly broad political context, where Syriac-speaking theologians needed to defend their ideas in the terms and language shared by the whole empire.

Yet there is a danger of overstating this case: other texts provide a different perspective on the "compromise" of the Syriac past to fit the context of the Christological debates. Jacob of Serug's *Homily on Ephrem* continues to preserve much of the poet we see from his own *madrashe*: he focuses on the poet's role as an opponent of heretics and as a composer of hymns for choirs of women, going against the image of Ephrem as a cenobitic monk preserved in the *Life* and leaving him as an *ihidaya*, working in the middle of a mixed congregation: "Your teaching signifies a new world, for in the kingdom, men and women are equal / Your labor devised two harps for two groups, treating men and women as one to give praise" (*Homily on Ephrem* 35 and 55).

This archaic vision of the theologian is supplemented by an uncompromising assertion of his origins: he is "the crown of the Syrian nation" and "the master orator of the Syrians," "a divine philosopher who vanquished the Greeks in his speech" (*Homily on Ephrem* 65). Ephrem himself had presented his native Aram as "a holy land," "the treasury from which Zion grew rich in the sons of Jacob" (*Hymns on Julian Saba* 4.8.46). But Ephrem's point here seems to be to contrast his chosen land of Mesopotamia with that of the Jews, to focus on the Mesopotamian origins of the Old Testament patriarchs. The poet certainly has a distinctive sense of territoriality, but it is employed as part of a broader, traditional criticism of the Jews' claim to be the chosen people. While Jacob's means of expression as a symbolic theologian do recall Ephrem while also recalling the poet's own historical behavior, his emphasis on Ephrem *as a Syrian*, as opposed to a Greek, may be a notable innovation (at least within Syriac writing).

A similar emphasis is found in Jacob's recollection of the early Edessene martyrs, Shmouna and Guria, and of the Abgar legend, in his *Homily on Shmouna and Guria*. Here he praises the martyrs as "the salt of our land, by whom it was sweetened" and calls them "two precious pearls, which were /An ornament for the bride of my lord Abgar, the Aramaean's son." The *Homily* seems to deliberately invoke the history of the city and to blend it with different claims for special status, from both the martyr acts and the *Doctrina Addai*. It finishes its account by comparing Edessa favorably with Jerusalem: "her (Zion's) old men were false / and dared to shed innocent blood on the floor, / but behold! The truth is spoken here by these witnesses" (Jacob of Serugh, *Homily on Shmouna and Guria*, 131 and 143).

The context for Jacob's invocation of Edessa's past may be provided by the attempts of other Mesopotamian theologians, such as Philoxenus, to re-write the past of figures such as Ephrem to fit the demands of a sixth-century orthopraxy. At the same time as some thinkers sought to align Mesopotamian practice and the Syriac language to broader currents in the empire, there emerged a stronger appeal to Edessa's own distinctive heritage that refused to surrender the city's pious history or the religious associations of its language. One striking example of this resistance is Elias' *Life of John of Tella* (39–42), the Miaphysite missionary of the 530s, who, as part of his development as an ascetic, rejects the useful education in Greek intended for him by his mother and instead learns the psalms in secret in Syriac. Another is the Syriac *Julian Romance*, a mythical history of the fourth century—probably written in early sixth-century Edessa—that pursues the interests of the *Doctrina Addai* in presenting Edessa as an orthodox stronghold, purged of Jews, and contrasting it to the fallen cities of Harran, Antioch, and Constantinople. Here the author's choice of "pagan cities" corresponds to the centers of sixth-century Chalcedonianism and provides a long-running parallel between the pagan Julian and his Jewish allies and the Chalcedonian Justinian (Wood 2010, chap. 5).

This re-emphasis on "indigenous" pious history and ascetic tradition is perhaps at its most developed in the following generation in the hagiographies of the exiled Miaphysite bishop, John of Ephesus, a native of Amida. His *Lives of the Eastern Saints* are almost entirely set in his native Mesopotamia: their occasional forays into Constantinople serve principally to highlight the difference between them and their heretical persecutor Justinian (e.g., Zu'ra's opposition to the emperor in Life 2). This sense of territorial unity is supplemented by John's praise for ascetic practices peculiar to Syria. Several of his saints give out *hnana*, the dust of saints mixed with earth and water, to heal their petitioners, a custom that had courted controversy in the fifth century but is presented here as a natural element of the saints' aid.

A similar analysis can be applied to John's Nazarite saints, who refuse to cut their hair. This custom had been banned by Rabbula, but, here again, John expressly presents this long-standing but contentious practice as the distinguishing characteristic of two ascetics, John the Nazarite, who withdraws from his monastery at Zuqnin when its leading monks become Chalcedonian, and Sergius, who is "shaved of the hair [that marked his] *naziruta*" when captured by the Chalcedonians (*Lives* 1.39–48 and 1.104). Here, in failing to recognize Sergius' holiness and cutting off his hair, the Chalcedonians deny both the importance of his ascetic activity and the local manner in which it was signified. By oppressing this custom, the Chalcedonians show themselves to be outside this indigenous tradition.

The third of these traditions with specific local resonance is the portrayal of *ihidayuta*, lone asceticism. In the *Historia Religiosa* Theodoret tried to subvert aspects of Syrian *ihidayuta* by making the great lone ascetics of the past the founders of cenobitic monasteries as part of a wider attempt to tame ascetic practice and place it under episcopal control. Most of John's ascetics did exist in a cenobitic environment. Nevertheless, he highlights individual ascetics who practice their religion alone, either within a cenobitic environment or after exile by the Chalcedonians. Thus the two pairs of saints with which John opens the *Lives*, Habib and Zu'ra and Simeon and Sergius, are lone ascetics in preparation for their public ministries in their villages, whether this is as stylites or, like Sergius, walled up in a house (Lives 1, 2, and 5).

These emphases on indigenous ascetic custom are part of a wider critique that presents the Roman empire as a world in disarray, where the characteristics of the emperors, as defenders of the populace and judges of orthodoxy, have been imputed to Mesopotamian holy men (Wood 2010, 198–208). In this world, where the emperor and the Chalcedonians could be presented in parallel with Mesopotamian Jews (e.g., Life 5), the continuity of ascetic practice was an assurance of continued orthodoxy.

For John and his monastic audience, it was more important to maintain distinctive practice as part of a guarantee of the continuing orthodoxy of their chosen land, with its center in Amida and Edessa. Whereas Philoxenus had reduced his reliance on the legacy and example of a figure such as Ephrem—partly because of concerns over the canon he used and partly because of his local appeal—John of Ephesus, by contrast, placed the localism of the ascetic customs of his saints (and their local action against the Jews) at the center of their preservation of orthodoxy in the face of imperial persecution.

Conclusions

The patterns in which Syriac-speakers invented and re-invented their own history could be complex and contradictory. The local history of the city of Edessa was closely tied to the prestige the city had earned in Eusebius' use of the Abgar legend, with its Christian presentation of the city's pre-Roman kings and its focus on the city's role as a missionary base. The *Doctrina Addai* would build on this tradition, first by emphasizing the apostolic authority of local ascetic custom and the Christian heritage of the local notables and, second, by placing this Edessene history into a Roman imperial framework. In so doing, the adapters of the *Doctrina* were not subordinating themselves to the Roman world; instead, they emphasized their own antiquity as a Christian city, with Abgar and the aristocrats who surrounded him as forerunners to Constantine.

Ephrem shares many of the heresiological concerns of the *Doctrina*, especially in his opposition to Jews and Marcionites, a cultural and religious contest that took place within the boundaries of Syriac Christianity and culture. Yet the struggle against Arianism also shows him becoming ever more involved with the imperial Church (which remains on the sidelines in the *Doctrina*).

The debates over Nicaea ensured the fame of Ephrem and his bishop, Jacob of Nisibis, as anti-Arian champions, and it is in these roles that both were always remembered. But their importance also necessitated their transformation: Ephrem in particular was re-imagined as a monk in sixth-century terms, and his *Diatessaron* commentaries may have proved an embarrassment in spite of his reputation for orthodoxy. In the context of the Christological controversies of the fifth and early sixth centuries, when imperial favor swung from one side to the other, protagonists on both sides sought both to use the Syriac ascetic tradition and to trim it to suit their own purposes. The greater involvement in the wider Church that these controversies brought was accompanied by a greater concern over orthopraxy than had existed in fourth-century Edessa, when Ephrem had battled the Marcionites.

But this was not a one-way process. The distance that emerges in Philoxenus' treatment of Ephrem was not universal: for Jacob of Serug, more isolated from demands to normalize his religious discourse, Ephrem was distinctively Syrian (perhaps more obviously so than he had been in his own lifetime). And for John of Ephesus, it was the ascetic customs of Mesopotamia, which might have seemed heteropraxy for Rabbula, that showed the orthodoxy of his holy men.

John's localism in this matter might be seen as a generational shift within Miaphysitism: where John Hephaestu had ordained priests across the Aegean, Rhodes, and Cyprus (*Lives of the Eastern Saints* 2.527 and 2.535–537), and Severus had benefited from an education and career across the eastern Mediterranean (Allen and Hayward 2004, 5–11), the generation after Severus was subject to a rural displacement into its Syriac-speaking hinterland (Frend 1972, 294–295). Thus, while there was no intrinsic connection between the culture of Edessa or Syriac speakers and Miaphysitism, the displacement of Miaphysite leaders into a Syriac-speaking hinterland gradually increased Syriac's prominence within Miaphysitism from the sixth century, into the period of Arab rule. It was in this context that John and others enlarged upon the distinctiveness of Mesopotamian Christian culture and of the Syriac language and of their connection to Miaphysitism as an eternal orthodoxy.

So in one sense, John's hagiography represents a return to focus on older ascetic customs. However, like the *Kaiserkritik* of the later stages of the *Doctrina Addai*, this cultural focus was rendered significant by its broader context. His emphasis on Mesopotamian orthodoxy was important because it was set against the Chalcedonianism of the wider empire, and "the East" he evokes in his hagiography acts a guarantor of orthodoxy for the whole empire. Notably, he includes the "international" missions of his saints, John Hephaestu and John of Tella, both within and beyond the empire, as part of his demonstration that Miaphysitism remained an "orthodoxy in waiting" for the whole empire.

Like the later versions of the *Doctrina Addai*, the significance of John's work was not only the content of its local emphasis and histories, but also the Roman context into which they were placed. In both cases, we see Suryoyo cultural independence functioning as a control on Roman Christian identity as a whole, a process that is tied both to the increasingly Christian nature of Roman imperial politics and to specific disagreements between certain Suryaye and the church of Constantinople. The opposite trend, which we have witnessed here in the "normalizing" legislation of Rabbula or the re-editing of Ephrem's *Life*, belongs, ironically, to those periods when a Miaphysite/Cyrilline party was, or looked to become, an imperial orthodoxy, and when the monastic support network that John appealed to in his hagiographic collection seemed proportionally less important.

The generations that followed the Arab conquests saw these monasteries become ever more important as a focus for Christian society. Important monasteries, especially the academic centers of Qenneshre and Gubo Barrayo, became the nurseries of future patriarchs. The authority given to bishops and holy men in Miaphysite hagiography was confirmed by a century-long incubation, when the Sufyanid Jazira was left ungoverned by states (Robinson 2000, 50–62) and the influence of bishops and monasteries had few rivals when they set out communal boundaries in religious terms (seen most notably in the canons of Jacob of Edessa).

The literary production of major monasteries such as Qenneshre was not exclusively religious: both were centers for the translation of Greek secular works. In this sense, they were better examples of the continuation of late antique academic traditions than Anatolia, Palestine, or Iraq. But this academic prestige, which would later underlie the translation of Greek philosophy into Arabic and send Edessene scholars to Baghdad, was fueled by a Syriac-speaking, Christian educational system that was controlled by the clergy (Watt 1999). By the Abbasid period, the Arab conquests had brought greater political independence, opportunities, and prosperity *within* the Miaphysite monastic culture of Syria and Mesopotamia.

WORKS CITED

Ancient Sources

Acts of Shmouna and Guria. In *Euphemia and the Goth, with the Act of Martyrdom of the Confessors of Edessa,* ed. and tr. F. C. Burkitt, 3–25. Oxford: Williams and Norgate, 1913.

Aphrahat. *Demonstrations,* tr. K. Valavanolickal. Kottayam: Saint Ephrem Ecumenical Research Institute, 2005.

Codex Theodosianus, ed. T. Mommsen and P. Meyer. Berlin: Preußische Akademie der Wissenschaften, 1905; tr. C. Pharr et al. Princeton: Princeton University Press, 1952.

Doctrina Addai, ed. and tr. G. Phillips. In *The Doctrine of Addai.* London: Trübner, 1876; reprinted with new tr., G. Howard. Chico: Scholars' Press, 1981; tr. A. Desreumaux. In *Histoire du roi Abgar et de Jésus.* Turnhout: Brepols, 1993.

Egeria. *Itinerarium,* tr. J. Wilkinson. In *Egeria's Travels to the Holy Land,* 3rd ed. Warminster: Aris and Phillips, 1999.

Elias. *Life of John of Tella.* In *Vitae vivorum apud Monophysitas celeberrimorum. Pars prima,* ed. and tr. E. W. Brooks. Louvain, 1907; CSCO Scriptores Syri 3:5, tr. J. Ghanem. PhD thesis, University of Wisconsin, Madison, 1968.

Ephrem. *Hymns on Faith.* In *Des heiligen Ephraems des Syrers Hymnen De Fide,* ed. and tr. E. Beck. Louvain, 1955: CSCO 154–155 SS 73–74.

———. *Hymns on Julian Saba.* In *Des heiligen Ephraem des Syrers Hymnen auf Abraham Kidunaya und Julianos Sabax,* ed. and tr. E. Beck, Louvain, 1972: CSCO 322–3 SS 140–141.

John of Ephesus, *Lives of the Eastern Saints,* ed. and tr. E. W. Brooks, PO 17–19. Paris, 1923–1925. 1.1–304; 2.513–697; 3.153–227.

Jacob of Serugh. *Homily on Ephrem,* ed. and tr. J. Amar, PO 47. Turnhout, 1995.

———. *Homily on Shmouna and Guria,* ed. P. Bedjan. In *Acta Sanctorum et Martyrorum.* 7 vols. Paris: Harrassowitz, 1890–1897, 1:131–143; tr. W. Cureton. In *Ante-Nicene Fathers.* Edinburgh: T & T Clarke, 1871, 8:94–106.

(Ps.-) Joshua the Stylite. *Chronicle,* ed. and tr. W. Wright. Cambridge: Cambridge University Press, 1882; comm. and tr. F. Trombley and J. Watt. TTH 15. Liverpool, 2000.

Rabbula of Edessa. *Laws for the Monks.* In *Syriac and Arabic Documents Regarding Legislation Relative to Syrian Asceticism,* ed. A. Vööbus, 24–33. Stockholm: Etse, 1960.

———. *Laws for the Bnay Qyama.* In *Canons for the Church of the East.* In *Syriac and Arabic Legislation,* ed. A. Vööbus, 27–33. Stockholm: Etse, 1960.

Sozomen. *Ecclesiastical History.* In *Sozomenus: Kirchengeschichte,* GCS n.f. 4, 2nd ed., ed. J. Bidez and G. Hansen. Berlin: Akademie Verlag, 1995.

Theodoret of Cyrrhus, *Historia Religiosa.* In *L'histoire des moines de Syrie: Histoire Philotheé,* ed. and tr. P. Canivet and A. Leroy-Molinghen. SC 257. Paris: Cerf, 1979.

Modern Sources

Allen, P., and C. Hayward. 2004. *Severus of Antioch.* London and New York: Routledge.

Amar, J. 1992. "Byzantine Monasticism and Greek Bias in the Vita Tradition of Ephrem the Syrian." *OCP* 58: 123–156.

———. 1993. "An Unpublished Karshuni Arabic Life." *LM* 106: 119–144.

Bauer, W. 1971. *Orthodoxy and Heresy in Earliest Christianity*. Trans. Philadelphia Seminar on Christian Origins and ed. R. Kraft and G. Krodel. Philadelphia: Fortress Press.

Beck, E. 1958. "Asketentum und Monchtum bei Ephraem." *OCP* 153: 341–362.

Brock, S. P. 1973. "Early Syrian Asceticism." *Numen* 22: 1–19.

———. 1984. "Antagonism to Assimilation: Syriac Attitudes to Greek Learning." In idem, *Syriac Perspectives on Late Antiquity*, sec. V. London: Variorum.

———. 1999. "St. Ephrem in the Eyes of the Later Syriac Tradition." *Hugoye* 2.

———. 2005a. "Du grec en syriaque: L'art de traduction chez les syriaques." In *Les syriaques: Transmetteurs du civilisations*, ed. M. Attallah, 10–33. Antelias: Centre d'études et de recherches orientales.

———. 2005b. "The Syriac Orient: A Third Lung for the Church." *OCP* 71: 5–20.

———. 2006. "Christology of the Church of the East." In idem, *Fire from Heaven: Studies in Syriac Theology and Liturgy*, sec. III. Aldershot: Variorum.

Brock, S.P. and D. Taylor. 2001. *The Hidden Pearl: The Syrian Orthodox Church and Its Ancient Aramaic Heritage*. 3 vols. Rome: Transworld Film.

Bundy, D. 1978. "Jacob Baradeus: The State of Research, a Review of Sources and a New Approach." *LM* 91: 45–86.

———. 1988. "Marcion and the Marcionites in Early Syriac Apologetics." *LM* 101: 3–32.

Caner, D. 2002. *Wandering, Begging Monks: Spiritual Authority and the Promotion of Monasticism in Late Antiquity*. Berkeley: University of California Press.

Chadwick, H. 1976. *Priscillian of Avila: The Occult and the Charismatic in the Early Church*. Oxford: Clarendon Press.

Dauphin, C. 1998. *La Palestine byzantine: Peuplement et populations*. 3 vols. BAR International Series 726. Oxford: Archaeopress.

Desreumaux, A. 1987. "La naissance du nouvelle écriture aramaique." *Semitica* 37: 95–107.

———. 1996. *L'histoire du roi Abgar et de Jesus*. Turnhout: Brepols.

———. 1998. "Ephraem in Christian Palestinian Aramaic." *Hugoye* 1.

Drijvers, H. J. W. 1966. *Bardaisan of Edessa*. Studia Semitica Neerlandica 6. Assen: Van Gorcum.

———. 1970. "Edessa und das jüdische Christentum." *VC* 22: 4–33.

———. 1980. *Cults and Beliefs at Edessa*. Leiden: Brill.

———. 1983. "Addai und Mani, Christentum und Manichaismus im dritten Jahrhundert." *OCA* 221: 171–185.

———. 1985. "Jews and Christians in Edessa." *JJS* 36: 88–102.

———. 1996. "The Man of God of Edessa, Bishop Rabbula, and the Urban Poor: Church and Society in the Fifth Century." *Journal of Early Christian Studies* 4: 235–248.

———. 1998. "Syriac Culture in Late Antiquity: Hellenism and the Local." *Mediteraneo Antico* 1: 95–113.

Drijvers, J.-W. 1999. "Rabbula, Bishop of Edessa: Spiritual Authority and Secular Power." In *Portraits of Spiritual Authority: Religious Power in Early Christianity, Byzantium, and the Christian Orient*, ed. J.-W. Drijvers and J. Watt, 139–154. Religions in the Greco-Roman World, 137. Leiden: Brill.

———. 1992. *Helena Augusta: The Mother of Constantine the Great and the Legend of Her Finding of the True Cross*. Leiden: Brill.

———. 1997. "The *Protonike Legend*, the *Doctrina Addai* and Bishop Rabbula of Edessa." *VC* 51: 288–315.

Drijvers, J.-W., and H. J. W. Drijvers. 1997. *The Finding of the True Cross: The Judas Kyriakos Legend in Syriac: Introduction, Text and Translation*. Leiden: Brill.

Duval, R. 1899. *La littérature syriaque*. Paris: Lecoffre.

Feiertag, J.-L. 2000. "À propos du rôle des Juifs dans les traditions sous-jacentes aux récits de l'Invention de la Croix." *AB* 118: 241–265.

Fiey, J. 1962. "Aonès, Awun, et *Awgin* (Eugène): Aux origines de monachisme mesopotamien." *AB* 80: 52–81.

Frend, W. H. C. 1972. *The Rise of the Monophysite Movement: Chapters in the History of the Church in the Fifth and Sixth Centuries*. Cambridge: Cambridge University Press.

Goodman, M. 2003. "The Jewish Image of God in Late Antiquity." In *Jewish Culture and Society under the Christian Roman Empire*, ed. R. Kalmin and S. Schwartz, 133–148. Leuven: Peeters.

Griffith, S. 1986. "Ephraem, the Deacon of Edessa and the Church of the Empire." In *Diakonia: Studies in Honour of R. Meyer*, ed. R. Hatton and J. Williman, 22–52. Washington, DC: CUA Press.

———. 1993. "Monks, 'Singles,' and the 'Sons of the Covenant': Reflections on Syriac Ascetic Terminology." In *Eulogema: Studies in Honor of Robert Taft*, 141–160. Studia Anselmiana 110. Rome: S. Anselmo.

———. 1994. "Julian Saba: Father of the Monks of Syria." *JECS* 2: 185–218.

———. 2003. "The *Doctrina Addai* as a Paradigm of Christian Thought in Edessa in the Early Fifth Century." *Hugoye* 6.

———. 2004. "Abraham Qidunaya, St. Ephraem, and Early Monasticism." In *Il monachesimo tra eredita e aperture*, ed. M. Bielawski and D. Hombergen, 239–264. Studia Anselmiana 140. Rome: S. Anselmo.

Gwynn, D. 2006. *The Eusebians: The Polemic of Athanasius of Alexandria and the "Arian" Controversy*. Oxford: Oxford University Press.

Harvey, S. A. 1990. *Asceticism and Society in Crisis: A Study in John of Ephesus' Lives of the Eastern Saints*. Berkeley: University of California Press.

———. 1993. "The Memory and Meaning of a Saint: Two Homilies on Simeon Stylites." *Aram* 5: 222–235.

Hayman, A. 1985. "The Image of the Jew in Syriac Anti-Jewish Polemical Literature." In *To See Ourselves as Others See Us*, ed. J. Neusner and E. Frierichs, 423–431. Chico: Scholars Press.

Holum, K. G. 1982. "Caesarea and the Samaritans." In *City, Town, and Countryside in the Early Byzantine Era*, ed. R. Hohlfelder, 70–85. Byzantine Series, 1. Boulder: East European Monographs.

Jacobs, A. 2005. *Remains of the Jews: The Holy Land and Christian Empire in Late Antiquity*. Stanford: Stanford University Press.

Jones, A. H. M. 1959. "Were Late Roman Heresies National Movements in Disguise?" *JTS* n.s. 10: 280–298.

Millar, F. 1998. "Il ruolo delle lingue semitiche nel vicino oriente tardo-romano, V–VI secolo." *Mediterraneo Antico* 1: 71–94.

———. 2007. "Theodoret of Cyrrhus: A Syrian in Greek Dress." In *From Rome to Constantinople: Studies in Honour of Averil Cameron*, ed. B. Romeny and H. Amirav, 105–126. Oxford: Oxford University Press.

Mirkovic, Alexander. 2006. *Prelude to Constantine: The Abgar Tradition in Early Christianity*. Frankfurt am Main and Oxford: Lang.

Mitchell S. 1993. *Anatolia: Lands, Men and Gods in Asia Minor*. 2 vols. Oxford: Oxford University Press.

Murray, R. 1975. "The Features of the Earliest Christian Asceticism." In *Christian Spirituality: Essays in Honour of E. G. Rupp*, ed. P. Brooks, 65–77. London: SCM Press.

———. 2004. *Symbols of Church and Kingdom*. 2nd ed. London: T. & T. Clark.

Nau, F. 1927. "Deux épisodes de l'histoire juive sous Théodose II (423 et 438), d'après la vie de Barsauma le Syrien." *Revue des études juives* 83: 184–202.

Nedungatt, G. 1973. "The Covenanters of the Early Syriac-Speaking Church." *OCP* 39: 191–215 and 419–444.

Peeters, P. 1920. "Jacob de Nisibe." *AB* 38: 287–373.

Petersen, W. 1994. *Tatian's Diatessaron: Its Creation, Dissemination and Significance in Scholarship*. Supplements to Vigiliae Christianae 25. Leiden: Brill.

Possekel, U. 1999. *Evidence of Greek Philosophical Concepts in the Writings of Ephraem the Syrian*. Leuven: Peeters.

Robinson, C. 2000. *Empires and Elites after the Muslim Conquest: The Transformation of Northern Mesopotamia*. Cambridge: Cambridge University Press.

Russel, P. 1994. *St. Ephraem the Syrian and St. Gregory the Theologian Confront the Arians*. Kottayam: Saint Ephrem Ecumenical Research Institute.

Schwartz, S. 2003. "Jewish-Christian Interaction in Late Antiquity." In *Jewish Culture and Society under the Christian Roman Empire*, ed. R. Kalmin and S. Schwartz, 197–210. Leuven: Peeters.

Tanghe, J. 1960. "Memra de Philoxène de Mabboug sur l'inhabitation du saint-Esprit." *LM* 73: 39–71.

Trombley, F. 2001. *Hellenic Religion and Christianization, 370–529*. 2 vols. Leiden: Brill.

Van Rompay, L. 2004. "Ephrem in the Works of Philoxenus of Mabbug: Respect and Distance." *Hugoye* 7.

Watt, J. 1999. "A Portrait of John bar Aphthonia, Founder of Qenneshre." In *Portraits of Spiritual Authority*, ed. J. Watt and J.-W. Drijvers, 155–169. Leiden: Brill.

Weitzman, M. 1999. *The Syriac Version of the Old Testament: An Introduction*. Cambridge: Cambridge University Press.

Wood, P. 2010. *We Have No King but Christ: Christian Political Thought in Greater Syria on the Eve of the Arab Conquest*. Oxford: Oxford University Press.

Wright, W. 1894. *A Short History of Syriac Literature*. London: A. and C. Black.

CHAPTER 7

EGYPT

ARIETTA PAPACONSTANTINOU
University of Reading

> We depart from the Ionians' opinion, and here is what we personally have to say about the matter: Egypt is all that country which is inhabited by Egyptians, just as Cilicia is inhabited by Cilicians and Assyria by Assyrians, and we know of no border which is properly so called between Asia and Libya except the borders of the Egyptians. But if we follow the belief of the Greeks, we shall consider the whole of Egypt, beginning from the Cataracts and the city of Elephantine, to be divided into two parts, and to have both names; one part of it belonging to Libya, and the other to Asia. For the Nile, beginning from the Cataracts, runs through the middle of Egypt separating it into two parts on its way to the sea.[1]

To counter the belief "of the Ionians" that the Nile marked the separation between the continents of Asia and Africa, Herodotus felt compelled to argue that like any other place, Egypt was a single country on a single continent inhabited by a single people. Today, a quick look at a satellite image leaves no doubt that Herodotus was right. The "Ionians' opinion," however, perceiving the Nile as a sea that could separate two continents, highlights the importance of the river in the country's existence. To a great extent, Egypt *was* the Nile, or rather the Nile Valley and its Delta. This did not escape Herodotus, of course, and he insisted strongly on the ways in which Egypt's life and civilization were based on the Nile and its annual flood.[2] However, it was also what marked, in his eyes, the limits of the country's resemblance to other countries: he famously described at great length how and why the land of the Nile was in every aspect entirely different from the rest of the world. The longevity of his judgment can be measured by the energy still expended by students of late Roman Egypt to convince nonspecialists that it was a province of the empire like any other.[3] In his *Egypt in Late Antiquity*, the only comprehensive treatment of the subject to this day, Roger Bagnall devotes the entire concluding chapter to demonstrating that what his book describes is "a Mediterranean Society."[4]

It is undeniable that by the fourth century Egypt had become totally integrated in the Roman empire, whatever allowance one might make for specific traits arising from local history and culture. The discussion concerning the degree to which Egypt can be seen as representative of the Roman empire as a whole, however, is still alive and well. Understandably so, because even though the case for official, administrative, and socioeconomic integration is strong, it is not entirely by chance that it has been so slow to convince most scholars. If its perception as "different" has persisted with such strength, it is because it rests on two important realities.

The first is objective and has to do with the country's geography. Egypt is made up of a narrow strip of cultivable land slivering through the desert. This valley has been cut through the sandstone by the Nile, whose annual flood brought with it and deposited a layer of silt that boosted the soil's fertility. This aesthetically unique landscape also involved both a high degree of isolation and an equally high ease of penetration and control, as the desert margins formed a very effective border and the navigable river created an easy link with the Mediterranean for a country whose length was more than fifty times its average width. As a result of this, Egypt had proverbial wealth based primarily on its extraordinary fertility and could support a very dense population for the standards of the time.

The second reality determining this view of Egypt's uniqueness within the empire is historiographical and lies with the sources through which we know and write its history. The papyri preserved by its dry climate offer evidence of a kind unknown for the rest of the ancient world. They document different areas of life from literary sources (or shed a different light on them), they are not ideal or normative but the result of practice, and they capture strata of society and forms of activity that might otherwise have remained unknown.[5] Using these sources, historians of Roman Egypt have constructed a narrative that effectively sets the country apart from other areas of the empire, if only because of the research questions asked and the subjects treated, inevitably dictated by the sources at hand.

Yet the gift of the papyri has also had the detrimental effect of sending to sleep the need for other types of evidence, which have proved extremely fruitful in the study of other provinces. The most obvious victim of this has been archaeology. The vast amount of archaeological work carried out in the country since the late nineteenth century has focused to a large extent on the pharaonic and Ptolemaic remains. For later periods, it has concentrated on monumental remains and, more specifically for Late Antiquity, overwhelmingly on monastic art and architecture. Generally, archaeology in Egypt has not been driven by the same questions as in other areas of the empire, namely, society, economy, and institutions, areas for which scholars have predictably turned to the papyri.

Only recently has there been a rising awareness not only of the significance of archaeological data but also of the importance of recording the archaeological context and the artifactual nature of the papyri themselves, important information that had hitherto been overlooked because the text they are inscribed with was considered to be the only bearer of meaning.[6]

Literary evidence from late antique Egypt is mostly of ecclesiastical or monastic origin, and much of it comes from Alexandria and the surrounding region. At the beginning of the period, it is essentially in Greek, but from the sixth century onward there is a rise in the literary production in Coptic in cities of the valley, also mainly within the ecclesiastical realm.[7] The bias toward religious questions that is created by this situation is reinforced by the external literature dealing with Egypt, which tends to focus on monasticism or the Christological controversies in which the country was such an important actor.

To many ancient historians, Egypt justifiably looks like a treasure-house of sources. Yet much remains to be done. Few attempts have been made to combine the various types of evidence in order to gain a fuller picture of late antique Egypt, except for the fourth and early fifth centuries, for which Roger Bagnall has offered a full and thorough account based on all the available sources. The period after 450, although not exactly neglected, has not been covered in the same systematic way. In part, this is because research on late antique Egypt was long fragmented among different disciplines that did not communicate very much: Coptic studies, papyrology, patristics, legal and administrative history, monastic archaeology, and history of monasticism, among others. Integration between the various groups of scholars working on this society has been slow to come, but it is now well under way, and some very interesting work is being carried out. Another area where improvement is not only possible but necessary is the quality, variety, and quantity of the archaeological evidence collected, for instance by shifting part of the weight of late antique archaeology from monastic to other types of settlements and structures. Also, as has been demonstrated by several scholars in recent years, it is possible to enhance our understanding of papyri by taking their materiality and archaeological context into account. Finally, making this extraordinary evidence more widely accessible to nonspecialists is an important task that has only recently begun to be addressed by specialists of late antique Egypt.[8]

Late Antiquity is a period of important political transformations that affected Egypt in various ways. The adoption of Christianity by Constantine and the initiation of an imperial policy of control over religious matters brought about a significant development, namely a much stronger connection between the political and the religious history of the empire, both institutionally and in terms of events; tensions between center and periphery increasingly crystallized around issues of religion and were carried by religious institutions and officials. Because of its economic importance and the cultural dominance of Alexandria in the eastern Mediterranean, Egypt pioneered those developments, followed closely by Syria and partly Palestine.

The move of the imperial capital to Constantinople involved a new destination for the annual grain delivery intended for the annona, which Egypt had previously provided for Rome. The convoy of ships normally left Egypt for the capital from the port of Alexandria, which gave the local authorities there tremendous leverage on important issues played out at the time of its departure. During the Arian crisis, for example, there were allegations that the archbishop of Alexandria, Athanasius, was planning to prevent the grain fleet (σιτοπομπία) from leaving the port.[9] While Dioscorus of Alexandria was in exile and his see occupied by Proterios, the supporters of the former are again said to have threatened to prevent the departure of the grain fleet and were taken seriously to the point that the emperor Marcian had the fleet depart from Pelusium instead of Alexandria to ensure it would reach the capital.[10] Thus Egypt—or rather Alexandria—could use its role as granary of the capital to push forward its position during times of deteriorating relations with the imperial center.

The first such crisis was in the fourth century, when the see of Alexandria with its bishop Athanasius was at the center of the Arian controversy. In the fifth century, it was once again at the forefront of contestation of the imperial line with Dioscorus of Alexandria, in a rift that went much deeper than the first and was ultimately to persist until the end of Roman rule in the country. Even while successive emperors from Constantine to Justinian reinforced the institutional position of the church in the empire, the Egyptian hierarchy was using this newfound power to contest imperial authority. The result was a series of tense episodes between Alexandria and Constantinople, and imperial attempts to bring the country to conformity, first under Justinian and then under Heraclius, had no other result than to reinforce the opposition's determination.

From the sixth century onward, an important part of the Egyptian church, which included the majority of the monastic institutions, was openly in conflict with the imperial line in terms of doctrine, to the point that it created and maintained a parallel hierarchy that mirrored that of the imperial church. There were not only two patriarchs in Alexandria but also two bishops for Valley sees, one Chalcedonian, the other not.[11] Even though this found explicit justification in their disagreement concerning theological questions, it was not a purely religious phenomenon: it was an act of direct defiance toward imperial power, and the energy deployed by successive emperors to bring the Church of Alexandria back into their orbit leaves little doubt that it was understood in that way. Apart from the tension on that front, the sixth century was one of overall political stability, marked by Justinian's series of administrative reforms. On the contrary, the seventh century was from the beginning one of instability, first with the Alexandrian revolts against Maurice, then with Egypt's involvement in the civil unrest under Phocas, and finally with its reluctant alignment with Heraclius and the subsequent vexations it underwent during the Monothelite crisis.

The period of the Persian occupation from 619 to 629 is poorly documented, even though a number of papyri have survived, including a decent number of Pahlavi papyri produced by the Sasanian occupants (around 950 known to this day). The paleographical difficulties they present, however, have prevented their systematic exploitation as sources for the period, while the documents produced by the local population do not bring out any distinctive traits. The Pahlavi papyri deal primarily with military supply, although there are also some private letters indicating that the Persian presence was not exclusively male and military, but that some soldiers at least were in Egypt with their families. On the whole, the evidence we have is remarkable for the absence of any sign of cultural interaction between the Persians and the local population.[12] Neither the texts nor any archaeological data give the impression of a major disruption.

Another blank in our knowledge of the country is the ten-odd years between the departure of the Persians and the arrival of the Arabs. We have fewer than 100 dated texts for a period longer than ten years—even though a large number of undated papyri could potentially date from this period. Several later texts refer to this period, but they are strongly biased by hindsight and partiality. Many are dominated by their hostility to the figure of Kyros, who is claimed to have been appointed both as patriarch and as provincial governor by Heraclius, and by accounts of the persecutions he unleashed against the non-Chalcedonians. Conversely, those sources give a very positive view of Benjamin, who was at the time the anti-Chalcedonian patriarch and who had to spend a number of years in exile because of the persecutions. After the defeat of the Romans, Benjamin is presented in anti-Chalcedonian sources as the main interlocutor of the new Muslim rulers.

In the years 641–642, an Arab force led by ʻAmr ibn al-ʼĀṣ conquered the country with relative ease. Alexandria was briefly recaptured by Roman forces in 645 but definitively lost in 646. The provincial governor and the army settled in the newly built military camp of Fusṭāṭ, next to the ancient city of Babylon at the apex of the Delta, a very strategic position from where both the valley and the Delta could be easily controlled. Like the sixth century, the first period of Arab rule was marked by the combination of administrative reform with a relative political stability that hardly reflected the situation outside Egypt, where the Caliphate was torn by civil wars. The reappointment of ʻAmr as governor by Muʻāwiya in 659 has been understood as an attempt to keep the province under control, and it seems to have been successful.[13] Only from the beginning of the eighth century did the situation gradually begin to change, but that lies beyond the scope of this book.

As already mentioned, the Nile was central in the life of the country, if only because it created a number of preconditions that determined to a large extent the forms of exchange in the country. First of those was, of course, the fertility brought about by the annually renewed silt deposit, which boosted Egypt's agricultural productive capacity. Combined with the ease of transport by river toward the Mediterranean and also within the country itself, it gave Egypt a huge advantage and required a relatively low level of investment in transport and irrigation infrastructures. Even so, as early as the Ptolemaic period and through to Umayyad times, artificial irrigation was extensively used to gain additional land on the valley's margins.

Agriculture was not Egypt's only resource. The deserts on both sides of the valley, despite the impression of void they give on a satellite image, played an important part in the country's economic life. The eastern desert, also known as the Arabian desert, was rich in mineral resources, and throughout the Roman period, its gold mines were exploited, as were various mines for gems such as amethyst, beryl, or jasper. It is especially well known today for the imperial quarries at Mons Porphyrites and Mons Claudianus, which provided, respectively, the red porphyry that became the imperial color in Late Antiquity and the gray granite used in imperial building projects. Other quarries were less heavily exploited and provided a variety of different stones and colored marbles, also often used in imperial contexts.[14] Those two important quarries were protected by the army, and the settlements of soldiers and workers created there are plentifully documented by the ostraka and inscriptions the inhabitants left behind. Their production seems to have been exported for the most part: for their own monuments, the Egyptians used mainly the sandstone and limestone of the valley's cliffs, as well as the red granite quarried at Aswān, even though some important architectural elements were sometimes made of imported stone.[15]

The western desert, known as the Libyan desert, is less rich in minerals, even though it produced alum, and just south of Alexandria, the rich natron deposits of the Wādī al-Natrūn were the empire's main source for this mineral, essential for glassmaking. Several oases from the Fayyūm in the north to Khargha in the south had important settlements with some agricultural production, especially in Dakhla, and they are now being more systematically investigated.[16] As yet, however, very little is known on the period between the fourth century, when they seem to have rapidly declined, and the reoccupation during the Middle Ages.

The annual flood of the Nile had another important effect on social life. It lasted for three months every year, beginning after the harvest period in early June and ending in early September with the new sowing season. This also marked the beginning of the Egyptian year. The result was that Egypt's seasons did not work entirely in tune with those of other provinces, as there was a long period of agricultural inactivity when much of the social life and religious festivals took place. Much traveling and trading was also done in that period, as transport was made easier by the water. Finally, the flood determined in large part the form of the habitat, in that most settlements were perched on small mounds that allowed the houses to be above the water.

Because of its fertility and the barrenness of the surrounding areas, the Nile Valley was very densely populated throughout antiquity. Estimates of Egypt's population in Roman times range from 2.5 to more than 4 million inhabitants, and it is generally accepted that they were supported by local production and were moreover able to produce sufficient surplus to supply the annona.[17] Even though the Antonine plague in the second half of the second century did hit Egypt severely in some areas, there seems to have been almost complete recovery, and Egypt remained one of the most densely populated areas in the ancient world.[18] This density varied in the valley, and it has been suggested that it was higher in the Delta and in the narrower parts of the valley that were easier to exploit.[19]

This population, still ethnically diverse at the arrival of the Romans, had become reasonably homogeneous by the fourth century, and even more so by the time of the Arab conquest. The bilingual, Greek- and Coptic-speaking inhabitants of the valley do not seem to have differentiated between themselves as they had under the Ptolemies and in the early Roman period.[20] On the other hand, they mention with ever greater insistence members of nomadic groups such as Saracens, Nobades, Blemmyes, and Berbers. Saracens are mentioned from the fourth century in various documents and inscriptions, both in the valley and in the Great Oasis, and seem to have been integrated with the local population even though identified ethnically. One Ἰωάννης Σαλαγηνός (for Σαρακηνός) even acts as scribe for a dromedarius of a garrison stationed at Kysis, in the Kharga Oasis, in the fourth century:[21]

> *Παταῦτ δρομεδ(άριος) Λατοπολίτων Ἰσοκράτει ἐπιμελητῇ ιδ ἰνδ(ικτίωνος) οἴνου. ἔσχομεν παρὰ σοῦ οἴνου ξέστας εἴκοσι ὑπὲρ τῆς ἱερᾶς ἀννώνης μό(νον)*
> *Ἰωάνης Σαρακηνὸς ἀξιωθεὶς ἔγραψα ὑπὲρ αὐτοῦ.*
>
> Pataut, dromedarius of (the garrison of) the Latopolites to Isocrates *epimelētēs* of wine for the 14th indiction. We have received from you twenty *xestai* of wine for the sacred annona, 20 only.
> I, John the Saracen, was found worthy to write for him.

In the sixth century, the Saracens, like the Blemmyes, seem to have become more threatening in the valley itself, not only on the margins and the desert regions. In the draft of a long petition to an unidentified official by a group of citizens of Antaiopolis, they are both accused of raiding the city of Antaiopolis and characterised as ἀλιτήριοι (criminals).[22] The theme of heightened insecurity in the sixth century runs through much of the literature and is often invoked to explain some of the changes visible between the beginning and the end of the century. Why it was easier for nomads to raid towns is not entirely clear. Study of the Eastern Desert has shown that from the fourth century the presence of the army there was drastically reduced, and there are hardly any traces of it after the fifth century. The army's main job was to keep away the raiders, and the effects of its withdrawal seem almost mechanical.

In part, the weakening of security and protection may have been connected with the depopulation brought about by the plague of 541–542. Yet it is difficult to assess the effect of the plague on the population of Egypt, as we have no estimates of its size either before or after the spread of the disease.[23] According to John of Ephesus, it spread to Egypt from Ethiopia and Himyar (South Arabia).

"When the majority of the people had perished, to the point that Egypt came to be deprived of its inhabitants, ruined and deserted, it fell upon Alexandria and killed a throng of people."[24] Procopius says the disease spread throughout the Mediterranean from Pelusium,[25] which concords perfectly with John's account because that is precisely where it would have arrived if traveling up the Red Sea from Ethiopia. Considering that the papyri hardly mention it, it is tempting to imagine that, having traveled mainly by sea, the plague did not have as devastating an effect on the valley as in other areas, despite John's assertion that Egypt was left empty.[26] Indeed, even though an eyewitness, John was traveling by land from Alexandria to Constantinople at the moment of the outbreak and thus did not see what was happening in the Valley. It is entirely possible that by "Egypt" he meant essentially the Delta.

It is true, as Peter Sarris has argued, that a number of objective signs indicating a strong fall in population numbers are valid for Egypt, as they are for other areas. One of these, however, is imperial monetary policy, and that would not have varied from province to province. The other is the rise in the security of tenants in land leases, which indicates a readiness of landowners to make concessions resulting from a need for labor.[27] Even if we accept this admittedly tenuous sign, it could conceivably have been prompted by a sharp fall of population in the north of the country and a subsequent fear that lands might be abandoned in the Valley in order to obtain better conditions in the Delta.

The only occurrence of *loimos* in the papyri, precisely a short time after 542, is in a petition of the inhabitants of Aphroditō to the empress Theodora, where they are complaining about the way the officials of Antaiopolis are treating them on tax matters. However, there are two problems with this reference: first, it is partly restored (only the genitive ending]*μου* actually remains), and second, it occurs in a very rhetorical passage where the empress is expected to "bring a healing hand" to the disease (*ὑγιοῦσθαι διὰ χειρὸς τῆς εὐσεβεστάτης ἡμῶν δεσποίνης*)—which thus lends it a moral rather than a medical meaning.[28] One hardly imagines such a metaphor being used if the plague was raging in the country.

This absence of the plague in the papyri is intriguing and cannot be dismissed by saying that the documentation is too haphazard.[29] In contrast to the fifth century, the sixth century yielded large archives, and even though they are not exhaustive, it is implausible that only the nonpreserved documents should have mentioned an event such as the plague if it had hit the valley as fiercely as it had hit other areas. In his study of a fiscal register from Aphroditō, Constantin Zuckerman maintains that the impact in Constantinople was high, despite the continued provision of the annona, which should not be taken as a sign that the population of the capital had not been affected by the disease.[30] He does not use this evidence, however, to discuss the impact of the plague on the population levels of Egypt. It seems clear that for production to continue at the same scale in 542 and 543, there must have been sufficient manpower to carry it out. In 546–547, Aphroditō was still supplying the same amount of wheat as before the outbreak.[31] Later, in the late seventh and early eighth century, requisitions of men for construction work in Fusṭāṭ, but also in Jerusalem and Damascus, were made in Middle and Upper Egypt, which could indicate that the Nile Valley had more manpower to supply than did Syria and Palestine.[32]

That said, there are indeed signs of fragility in the second half of the sixth century. The document that mentions Saracen and Blemmye raids on Aphroditō, a draft of a petition to an unspecified authority, also shows a rise in the arbitrariness of tax collection and complains about the number of irregular taxes.[33] This is not an isolated case and could be the sign of a certain diminution of the tax base.

In terms of settlement, however, the only clearly recognizable trend where more systematic work has been carried out is a certain redistribution of the population and its concentration in larger centers, especially in rural areas. While cities generally diminished in size, some rural sites were abandoned and others became larger, so that the earlier hierarchy of size was slowly undermined, and the frontier between formally recognized cities and larger rural towns became more and more blurred. The strong economic specialization of villages seems to have eroded as time went by, and by the sixth century, a wider variety of economic activities can be observed there than earlier. At the same time, some rural, agricultural functions gradually moved into urban areas, so that the various types of settlement were more integrated within the wider agricultural economy.[34] Only hints of this are archaeologically detectable in Egypt, but the phenomenon of the partial ruralization of cities and the economic expansion of villages is much more clearly observable in neighboring North Africa and Syria, where archaeological evidence has been better exploited.[35]

A parallel phenomenon touched the monastic world from the late sixth century. The multiplicity of small monasteries seems to have gradually given way to larger, richer, and more powerful structures, some of which functioned as independent settlements, owning and exploiting their own land and, at least in the Arab period, having their own dependent tenants.[36] The two documentary archives usually studied for the sixth century, those of Oxyrhynchos and Aphroditō (aka the "Apion" and "Dioskoros" archives), reflect a situation that had not yet reached that point. In the Oxyrhynchite, despite the large Apion estate that dominated agricultural production and relations in the nome,[37] the number of small shrines and monasteries was high. The same can be said of Aphroditō, where we also have the possibility of comparing it with the eighth-century situation. By then, the number of monastic centers had diminished, and their status was enhanced. Such monastic centers kept archives, and several are preserved today, especially from Middle and Upper Egypt. The famous Bawīṭ, for instance, has yielded papyri whose edition has already produced three volumes and a number of articles.[38]

What has generally been seen as the prime sign of "the decline of cities," namely, the slow demonumentalization of city centers in favor of urban models based on very different principles, is not something that strikes only modern scholars. In the previously mentioned petition of 566 from Antaiopolis, the perception of this phenomenon as a form of decline is very explicitly expressed—by a group of what were presumably the city's affluent inhabitants. After describing an "old" Blemmye raid, the text continues:[39]

> After that, while the imperial and public baths had been very large to that day, today all that is left in the city is a private bath functioning for the poor, who can bathe there for a couple of *nummi*.

The demonumentalization, however, was only relative. Large colonnaded streets and classical-looking public buildings and temples were no longer the favorites of the day, and indeed smaller public buildings became more common. Yet building activity did not stop; on the contrary, it went on unremittingly. The multiplication of churches and chapels from the end of the fifth century onward is a very striking phenomenon. Even though some of those were private foundations, they all had a public function: at least once a year, the bishop officiated there.[40] Towns like Aphroditō could have as many as twenty-six churches and chapels, and this is without counting monastic establishments. In 535, Oxyrhynchos had at least twenty-five functioning churches, and most probably more than thirty of them.[41] Neither were those churches all tiny, as a simple glimpse at the plates of Peter Grossmann's compendium of Christian architecture in Egypt can easily show.[42] In Oxyrhynchos itself, the church of St. Philoxenos was expanded in the late sixth or early seventh century, an operation that involved the delivery of 120 new column bases and capitals, which makes for a rather large church for a provincial city.[43]

The foundation of Fusṭāṭ marked a new move toward urban monumentality. The conqueror of Egypt, ʻAmr ibn al-'Āṣ, is said to have built a mosque at the site where his tent stood during the Arab siege of the Roman fort of Babylon. By the mid-eighth century, this mosque had been altered and extended twice, under governors Maslama ibn Mukhallad al-Anṣārī and Qurra ibn Sharīk.[44] It is still standing today and known as the "mosque of ʻAmr." At the beginning of the eighth century, the governor Qurra ibn Sharīk was also building a palace in the city for which men and materials were being requisitioned in the valley, as testified by demand letters preserved in the archive of the pagarch of Aphroditō Basilios.[45]

> Regarding split palm branches and palm-leaves. In the name of God. Qurra ibn Sharīk, the governor, to Basilios, the pagarch of *kome* Aphroditō. We have issued an assessment for provisions on account of the roofing of the buildings of the palace that is being built at the order of the Commander of the Faithful (i.e. the caliph) along the inner harbour at Phossaton . . . under Ata, son of Abderaaman and Yahya, son of Andala, in the present eighth indiction, and we have made an assessment through your pagarchy of provisions in accordance with the attached requisition notice, and after drawing up the orders (*entagia*) for these things we sent them to you. Thus once you receive the present letter, work towards fulfillment of the orders and send the needed provisions to Babylon on account of the said palace, as has been described. This was written on the twenty-third of the month of Thoth in the eighth indiction. . . .

Despite their gradual physical transformation, urban centers remained nodal points in the life of the country, in great part because they retained their administrative functions as intermediaries between the center and the rural areas. The administration—civil, military, and ecclesiastical—is an area that has been abundantly studied and described for Egypt because of the important complement of information brought by the papyri, and I shall not repeat at length what can easily be found elsewhere;[46] rather, I shall highlight some aspects I find important or insufficiently studied to date.

The imperial administration was centered in Alexandria and relayed by several officials to the three provinces created by Diocletian, and below them to the lower levels of local administration. In a similar fashion, the caliphal administration was based in Fusṭāṭ, with a provincial governor whose authority rested ultimately on the network of district governors still called pagarchs. As often in large empires, the local levels of administration were extremely important in defining the form of the relation between state and individuals or local communities. The local elites were initially city magistrates, and increasingly, as the traditional structures of the ancient city became obsolete, members of those groups of local notables can be found in various roles ranging from pagarch in the capital of a pagarchy to *protokometes* in a village, but also bishop or some rank in the clergy. Some were lawyers or had some judicial function such as *defensor civitatis*. It is not easy to follow the evolution of this pattern through time, as the necessary groundwork of collecting and analyzing the sources has not yet been carried out. For the same reason, it is also difficult to tell whether the changes in settlement or the Arab conquest changed the composition of those groups, or whether the same individuals and families adapted to new circumstances and remained in power. There are some examples of notables passing the Arab conquest without casualties, and even a case of one being promoted to a higher rank,[47] but only a systematic long-term study based on a multitude of dispersed sources can analyze and describe Egyptian society as a whole and the transformations it underwent during those crucial centuries.

In many respects, the ecclesiastical administration in Egypt was built on the civil one, based on a network of cities that were the bases of episcopal sees. One important difference, however, was the absence of a regional level centralizing groups of bishoprics under the intermediate hierarchical echelon of the metropolitan. This may have initially been felt as unnecessary because of the peculiar geographical structure of the diocese, but with time, it resulted in a very monarchical ecclesiastical structure, with the patriarch having absolute and direct control over bishops and being surrounded by courtiers whose real influence extended well beyond their nominal ecclesiastical rank.[48] Perhaps unsurprisingly in such a structure, simony was very common.[49] Another feature of Egypt's ecclesiastical administration from the late fifth century onward is the parallel Chalcedonian and non-Chalcedonian hierarchies resulting from the church's division after the Council of Chalcedon. It is clear from the papyrological evidence that this meant not only that there were two competing patriarchs in Alexandria but also that episcopal sees as remote from the capital as Hermonthis in Upper Egypt could have two competing bishops.

Like everywhere, ecclesiastical careers became more and more prestigious with time and most certainly attracted members of the local social elites. However, this is not easy to substantiate from the surviving evidence without a more systematic study. As clerics often dropped their patronyms in favor of the title they bore, it is difficult to determine their family background in the individual sources in which they appear. However, many seem to have had some basic education and fortune or income. Bishop Hierakiōn of Oxyrhynchos, for instance, had founded one of the churches of the city, presumably from his own funds.[50] After the Arab conquest, the church became the main institution that could confer social capital on Christians, who still formed the large majority of the population—although the administration retained its allure, and still in the tenth century, many Christians were working for it.

Throughout Late Antiquity, the higher echelons of the ecclesiastical hierarchy were increasingly chosen from the monastic milieu, and by the eighth century, bishops had almost always previously been monks.[51] On the one hand, this facilitated the control of bishops over the monastic institutions that tended to function with some autonomy; on the other hand, it allowed the monastic world to brand the secular church with a strongly monastic character. This was probably reinforced by the fact that non-Chalcedonian bishops often resided in monasteries to avoid confrontation with their Chalcedonian counterparts in the official episcopal city.[52]

The various administrative structures ensured political, social, and fiscal control; they also allowed the organization and maintenance of infrastructures that would make such control easier and at the same time facilitate economic activity. Evidence for this is less abundant and has been less systematically studied than for the period before Diocletian, but it is clear that efforts were made in a number of areas.

Throughout Late Antiquity, there was much investment in maintaining and even expanding the irrigation infrastructure, which had allowed successive rulers of Egypt since the pharaohs to improve agricultural productivity. As the population of Constantinople rose very quickly after its foundation, the pressure for annona wheat must have been strong. The multiplication of *saqiya*-type waterwheels in the fifth and sixth centuries testifies to further attempts to extend the cultivable area.[53] This drive to encroach onto the desert is strikingly visible today on satellite images of the margins of the Valley—although the expansion is not necessarily located in the same areas as in antiquity. Another way to improve productivity, which also demanded good irrigation, was the rotation of crops, traditionally attributed to the Arabs[54] but already practiced from Roman times.[55] The monitoring of the flood also continued, and it is a tribute to its importance that the famous abbot Shenoute attempted to appropriate its symbolic value by presenting himself as being in control of the flood.[56]

One area of state investment was the protection and maintenance of the communication system. Since the Nile ensured north-south communication, land routes were mainly needed for desert transport to and between the oases and especially to the mines and quarries of the Eastern Desert and to the Red Sea. Access to the Red Sea could also be gained through the canal from the eastern branch of the Nile Delta to the port of Klysma, known as Trajan's canal because of that emperor's re-excavation of it after it had fallen into disuse. The canal is usually considered to have been left unused by "the Byzantines" and put back into use by the Arabs in the later seventh century. New archaeological and survey work in the area by John Cooper, together with a more systematic analysis of the sources, suggest otherwise. There is also documentary evidence for maintenance work on the canal until well into the fifth century. It is not clear if at that time it was open along its entire length, but the parallel increase in activity at Klysma indicates that the canal must have been active at the time. When it was, according to a tradition recounted by the ninth-century historian Ibn 'Abd al-Ḥakam, reopened by the Arabs, its closure was described as recent and temporary. 'Amr, we are told, suggested the reopening to the caliph 'Umar as a solution to a drought in the Ḥijāz, in the following terms:

> You know that before Islam, ships used to come to us carrying traders of the people of Egypt. When we conquered Egypt, that canal was cut, having been blocked off, and the traders had abandoned it.[57]

In his *Historia Francorum*, Gregory of Tours mentions the canal as being in operation—although admittedly his description is somewhat vague.[58] Reopened to facilitate the grain supply to the Ḥijāz, it was, again according to Ibn 'Abd al-Ḥakam, blocked up by al-Manṣūr in the eighth century to cut supplies to the Ḥijāz and the anti-'Abbāsid rebels there.[59]

Coherent though it sounds, Ibn 'Abd al-Ḥakam's explanation is a little intriguing. If the grain for the Ḥijāz was because of a drought, this would suggest that normally the Ḥijāz did not need that grain. Also, if that grain came from Egypt, it did not depend entirely on the availability of the canal—and conversely, closing the canal did not entirely cut off the Ḥijāz from Egypt. Admittedly, the land routes through the desert were less straightforward but not impracticable. Grain was produced in the Delta but also largely in the Valley, which would have involved shipping it north to the canal, through the canal to Klysma, and then from Klysma back south to Medina, a rather laborious voyage. The most important reason for the continued maintenance of the canal in that period probably lies elsewhere. We know from the papyri that from the 660s onward, Klysma had been turned into a shipyard for the construction of the Arab raiding fleet and probably, with time, for the regular fleet.[60] This protected the building site from Byzantine raids, as the Red Sea ports were inaccessible to them, but made the canal necessary if the Arab fleet was to reach the Mediterranean.

The mountainous eastern desert was cut through by valleys that had allowed the construction of a series of routes between sites in the valley and ports on the

Red Sea. One of the most important and best documented was the route from Kainopolis/Qena on the bend of the Nile to the port of Myos Hormos/Quṣayr al-Qadīm.[61] Beyond the access they provided to the mines and quarries exploited in the eastern desert, those routes were important for the eastern trade, especially with India but also South Arabia and Ethiopia, from where such goods as ivory, ebony, incense, pepper, and spices were imported and then traveled up the Nile to the ports on the Mediterranean, Alexandria and Pelusium.

The land route from Myos Hormos to Qena, well documented for the early Roman period, seems to have been abandoned after the third century, and the *praesidia* housing the army units that guarded it fell into disrepair. This followed the abandonment of the port of Myos Hormos at that time, although at the more southern Berenikē, there are signs of occupation until the sixth century. Activity also continued at the more northern port of Abū Shar, where a fort was built in the fourth century for a military unit of about 200, as well as various military installations along the road from the port to Qena on the bend on the Nile via the quarry of Mons Porphyrites.[62] These were active through the fifth century and slowly abandoned. The garrison and outposts protected against desert raiders not only the goods and the people that traveled on that road (a Latin military inscription found on the site mentions *mercatores*)[63] but also probably the nearby monasteries of St. Anthony and St. Paul. In the late fifth and sixth centuries, a Christian settlement including a church, possibly a monastery, developed at the fort.

Even though it was not a big settlement, the port of Abū Shar seems to have participated in the trade with India. A Greek inscription of the fifth or sixth century found in the southwest corner of the fort mentions one of its practitioners:

> † ἐγὼ Ἀνδρέας . . . ἰνδικοπλεύσ[της] ἦλθον ὧδε . . . Παῦν[ι.]
> ἰνδ(ικτίωνος) θ †
>
> I, Andreas, traveler to India, came here . . . Pauni., 9th indiction.

Although there is much skepticism about whether traders really went to India or simply to Ethiopia and Somalia,[64] archaeological evidence from India increasingly vindicates those who gave themselves the epithet.[65] The little-cited account of the Theban *scholastikos* who visited India at the end of the fourth century, preserved in the guise of a letter by Palladios in his *De gentibus Indiae et Bragmanibus*, shows not only that Axum and Adulis were clearly distinguished from "real" India at the time but also that exchange with India was regular and that a Roman could reasonably expect to be able to communicate in Sri Lanka, presumably because of the permanent presence of interpreters.[66] Confusion has probably been introduced by the fact that the actual crossing of the Indian Ocean was undertaken from Axumite or Yemenite ports, where travelers seem to have transboarded after sailing down the Red Sea. The *scholastikos*, for instance, boarded a ship with an Indian crew at an Axumite port.[67] Thus Ethiopia and Yemen were part of "the India voyage" and were even sometimes qualified as "India," but that does not mean that they were mistaken for India in Late Antiquity.[68]

The foundation of ʿAydhab south of Berenikē in the later seventh century allowed the new rulers, who now possessed both coasts of the Red Sea, to establish their control over it. It soon became an important port for the transfer of slaves from the Sudan to work in the mines of the Ḥijāz, and from the ninth century onward, it was established as an important commercial port also used for the exploitation of the Sudanese gold mines, the *ḥajj*, and the India trade. The route to the Nile initially went across the Wādī al-ʾAllāqī to Aswān, and in the eleventh century, as the Fāṭimids tried to gain control of trade with India through ʿAydhab, it was moved northward to arrive at Qūṣ on the bend of the Nile, boosting the city into prominence.[69]

It is very difficult to give a global assessment of the state of the Egyptian economy, whether in agriculture, manufacturing, or trade, from the late sixth century to the end of the period covered by this book, as there has been no systematic exploitation of the full range of documents available. This is in great part because they come in three different languages and are handwritten and difficult to read and understand. Recent work is beginning to reverse this situation. The most important impetus for the study of the later part of late antique Egypt (sixth to eighth centuries) was undoubtedly Jean Gascou's enormously influential and controversial essay on the Apion estate, which sparked a lively debate among papyrologists and specialists of late antique social history, which in turn has led much of the subsequent research on sixth-century Egypt to focus on the issue of landholding patterns, especially the development and function of large estates.[70] A new impulse was given to the study of postconquest Egypt by the creation in 2002 of the International Society for Arabic Papyrology and its regular conferences that bring together those working on documentary material of the Arab period in any language.[71] Unsurprisingly, much of the work to date has focused to a great extent on fiscal questions, as this is the subject of the overwhelming majority of preserved documents. The subject also allows one to study the administration and thus the formation or organization of the state and the army. This has generally resulted in an insistence on the increasing fiscal burden the Arab conquest represented for most Egyptians.

Surprisingly, however, there has been no analysis of the economic effect on the Egyptian agricultural system of the end of the annona. An *embolē* continued to be levied to cater to the soldiers (*μωαγαρίται*) in Fusṭāṭ, but this could hardly have equaled the quantities needed for the population of Constantinople. The assertion that a form of annona continued to cater for the needs of the Holy Cities is not supported by any contemporary evidence,[72] and the fact that Ibn ʿAbd al-Ḥakam mentions an emergency levy under ʿAmr ibn al-ʾĀṣ and the caliph ʿUmār because of a drought touching Medina (discussed earlier) clearly indicates that it was not initially conceived as a regular extractive practice. Besides, contrary to Rome, the Caliphate also controlled Mesopotamia, which meant that Egypt was no longer the one and only fertile province of the empire. Ibn 'Abd al-Ḥakam's account does mention regular imports from Egypt to the Ḥijāz, not only grain but also textiles, lentils, and other goods. In any case, there was certainly a substantially lower demand for Egyptian grain after the Arab conquest, the consequences of which still need to be investigated—whether, for example, it meant the abandonment of cultivable areas and transfer of manpower to different sectors, or whether the same amount of land and effort produced a surplus that allowed the population to deal with the new tax demands of the Arab rulers, and the new Arab rulers to express such demands.

More generally, there is a strong need for systematic exploration of the period between the sixth century and the tenth, when Fāṭimid Egypt emerged as a considerably rich province. The conditions for that wealth were slowly created in its early post-Roman years, even if they could be exploited to their full potential only under the political conditions created by the Fāṭimid Caliphate. This is, of course, a story that takes us much beyond Late Antiquity.

Egypt has been at the center of debates on literacy in the ancient world because of the detailed evidence offered by the papyri. Ewa Wipszycka has argued very convincingly for a relatively high degree of literacy in the country compared with what is generally estimated for the ancient world.[73] Indeed, a simple glimpse at the sort of texts found on papyri makes it clear that this was a society that functioned to a great extent on written documents. Orders of delivery and receipts were written out for transactions that even today might have remained oral. For example, the steward of a given church would write out an order of delivery to a wine merchant to deliver a certain amount of wine to such and such social group. This would be followed by a receipt written out by the recipients and archived at the church. Presumably, the merchant also made a receipt to the steward who paid him for the wine delivered. Such orders and receipts were made even for small sets of nails to repair a stable door or small quantities of tin and lead for the repair of kitchenware.[74] Two monasteries on the Apion estate in the Oxyrhynchite could share a waterwheel located on the premises of one of them, but both would contribute to its maintenance, and records of their contributions were kept.[75]

One could argue that so important a role afforded to the written word in the conclusion of everyday transactions denotes a fundamental lack of trust within society and a high degree of latent conflict. There is also, as Wipszycka points out, the long bureaucratic tradition of temple scribes who noted and archived everything. Whatever the case, some basic literacy was clearly necessary to carry out a great number of activities. That this literacy was often indeed rather basic is also clear from the variety of grammatical and stylistic registers of privately written documents such as letters. The way in which it was acquired has been described in some detail by Raffaella Cribiore, at least for the early period, and new papyri and ostraka containing school exercises are regularly published.

What this documentation makes clear is that there was large-scale bilingual education, which means that, contrary to a common model for bilingual societies, Egyptians did not learn to write only in the dominant language while using the vernacular orally; rather, they were biliterate, and even if most of them must have had a stronger and a weaker language, whether this was Greek or Coptic was not immediately obvious but depended on a number of factors. Collection and analysis of the equivalent documentation in Arabic could shed much light on the gradual linguistic transition from Coptic to Arabic after the Arab conquest: yet another task that remains to be undertaken.

Education was not confined to teaching basic literacy for everyday needs, however. Jean Gascou describes Hermoupolis in the early seventh century as "un centre d'études littéraires et juridiques fort développé."[76] The focus on Alexandria as a center of learning has mostly obscured the fact that several cities in the Nile Valley were important centers of learning in their own right. Not only had they produced famous figures like Nonnos of Panopolis but also they sustained a cultural life of some quality, considering their provincial status and their distance from major centers. Individuals like Dioskoros and the anonymous *scholastikos* from Thebes who traveled to India and described the habits of the Brahmans were not exceptions: they constituted the typical educated elite of the country. This group was still thriving in the second half of the seventh century under Mu'āwiya and controlled the local administration, like Papas, the pagarch of Apollōnos Anō, whose archive from the 660s has been preserved, and his various correspondents, like the notary Helladios or Plato, the pagarch of neighboring Latopolis.[77]

From early on, books in the form of codices replaced rolls, even on papyrus. Although the passage from roll to codex has often been associated with the symbolic role of the book in Christianity, the relation is far from obvious. The capacity of the codex to hold a larger quantity of text and its practicality for reference offer a more plausible explanation;[78] they also made it a popular form in the administration, in particular for tax registers.[79] Literary codices were produced with a basic division of labor, which indicates that a relatively high quantity of them were made. Text, illustration when there was any, and binding were done by different individuals, who seem to have worked individually, taking something akin to postal orders. Orders were sent to them, and the final product was sent back: papyri have preserved a number of such documents. The fascinating dossier of Frange, a bookbinder who in the eighth century had set up shop in an ancient Theban tomb, sheds new light on the entire process. Among the documents are orders sent to him for specific jobs, as well as his own orders and receipts for the materials necessary to his trade.[80]

We preserve today the trace of a variety of book collections about which we usually have very little information. Some of those, like the personal library of Dioskoros of Aphroditō, are connected to otherwise known dossiers and can be understood in their context. Others, however, survive only as fragments of individual works[81] or in the form of fragmentary book lists on papyri,[82] and much less can be said about them—they could be anything from an order to a copyist to part of a library catalogue, from a reading list to a list of borrowed books.

Despite their shortcomings, those lists give us an idea of the most popular works in late antique Egypt. Generally, lists are either "classical" or "Christian," although this is not entirely consistent. Classical book collections, moreover, do not necessarily denote someone with little Christian interest: the most well-known case is Dioskoros, whose father had founded a monastery and who quotes biblical texts regularly in his works.[83] A catalogue in Coptic of the library of Apa Elias in the Theban region contains biblical, patristic, and hagiographical texts and a "book of medicine."[84] Other technical books and treatises are known, and their role in producing the knowledge necessary in various economic activities and in trade was without doubt larger than reflected in current scholarship.

That books circulated and were read is attested by a number of letters from the Theban region that offer a vivid image of book-related practice in the seventh and eighth centuries. For example, a monk of St. Phoibammon wrote to an anchorite in the seventh or eighth century:[85]

> The book that I sent you . . . can it be sent back to me, so that I can read it during the vigil of Saint Apa Phoibammon.

In the sixth century, before the monastery moved to its final location on the ruins of the temple of Hatshepsut, a certain David wrote to a monk who had placed an order with him:[86]

> *Recto*: Before [all things] I greet my [beloved] brother Kouloudje. [When] I left [thee] (thou saidst), "Write the Deuteronomy." Now, I did not write it, but [I] have written the Leviticus and the Numbers in their order. If I am able, I shall write the Deuteronomy.
>
> *Verso*: Give it to the master, Kouloudj, from David, the most humble sinner. Farewell in the Lord. The Holy Trinity.

As has often been pointed out, the copying seems to have been mainly done by monks, but nothing really indicates that provincial or rural monasteries had proper scriptoria like the well-known medieval ones. More plausibly, some establishments hosted one or two monks who worked individually, as the letter shows.

Late Antiquity is often treated as a single, chronologically undifferentiated unit, and this has also been the case for Egypt. In some cases, scholars cover the entire period from the late third to the seventh century;[87] in others, they concentrate on a given period within Late Antiquity, generally the fourth or the sixth century.[88] Implicitly, this reflects the fact that the period covered by the expression is one of very important transformations, for which the fifth century seems to have been pivotal. This is clearly recognized, to the point that Andrea Giardina suggested calling Egypt "late antique" until the mid-fifth century and "Byzantine" after that[89] (a suggestion that has found favor against the old periodization calling "Byzantine" the period from Diocletian to the Arab conquest). There has been as yet no full survey work on Egypt during the so-called "long" Late Antiquity, which includes the Umayyad period, although the sections devoted to Egypt in Chris

Wickham's *Framing the Early Middle Ages* can largely stand as an independent introduction to the country's history over those centuries.[90] Very much like for the rest of the Mediterranean, the divide is clearly visible between the early fourth century, when the country is still recognizably Roman, and the late seventh to early eighth century, when it is unambiguously on the medieval side of the border. Christianity, a key element in definitions of Late Antiquity whether explicitly or implicitly, is in the fourth century a rising force, fighting—very efficiently—for position and power; in the seventh century, it is established and totalizing, especially in Egypt and Syria, where it is beginning to feel the threat of Islam.

The differences between the beginning and the end of the period are not necessarily linked to Christianity, however. Many of those changes happened over the late fifth and early sixth centuries within an empire that was already Christian. The evolution described before of the settlement pattern toward greater concentration and the concomitant developments in administrative structures probably have little to do with religious questions. The rise of large estates and rich landowning aristocracies in the sixth century, a theme that has been very prominent in recent research largely because of the conservation of the Apion archive, also happened independently from the influence of Christianity. Even though the economic importance given to this phenomenon as a specificity of the sixth century seems greatly exaggerated, considering that in the early empire there were also great landowners with large estates producing industrial amounts of agricultural goods and shipping them across the Mediterranean, there were a number of qualitative changes that gave sixth-century *oikoi* a different social function. The fact that they levied some taxes, for example, has been at the center of heated debates as to whether they were acting as agents of the state[91] or usurping the state's attributions and thus undermining its power and authority.[92] To some extent, the two suggestions are not entirely incompatible. As research on late medieval and early modern regional aristocracies has repeatedly shown, such groups were both using their status as representatives of the state locally to acquire authority and wealth, and then used those to undermine and control the sovereign's power. It was not in their interest, however, for the system of the state to collapse, because their own power was based on it. After all, consular families like the Apions can be said to be one of the parts that constitute "the state" in the first place. Even though we are not, as was once argued,[93] witnessing the beginnings of feudalism in sixth-century Egypt, this is a marked departure from the Roman municipal system toward one based on a centralized monarchy both relying on and resisted by powerful aristocracies, a form that appears as distinctly medieval and early modern.

Like everywhere in the empire, the rise of the influence of the church was exponential throughout Late Antiquity. By the sixth century, it was a central institution in the political, economic, social, and cultural life of the country.[94] From the late fifth century, it began marking the cities and the surrounding landscape with a multitude of shrines of various sizes, in parallel with the rise of the cult of saints that gave an impetus for the construction of those new cultic buildings.[95] By the mid-sixth century, the physical aspect of both urban and rural space had been transformed and so had the temporal experience of that space, since the shrines, deliberately different in form from temples, were also visited by communities at given times of the year for the eponymous feasts.[96] Within the church, the monastic element was steadily on the rise, so that what had initially been a movement of contestation and rejection of institutional hierarchy and authority was by the sixth century becoming the moving force behind the institutional church itself, and the higher echelons of church administration were more and more occupied by monks. This was supported by the massive production, in the form of holy biographies and sermons, of a discourse that presented ascetic virtue as the best quality a churchman could exhibit. Monasteries were also landowning institutions with some financial means. By the seventh century, they had also largely appropriated the cult of the saints and used its persuasive power to obtain donations of cattle, consumables, land, and urban property.[97] In the early Arab period, they seem to have served as centers for the levy of taxes and thus acquired a status that allowed them to exert control over the corresponding communities.

The political power of the church was, of course, curbed by the Arab conquest, since the new governmental structures did not take account of ecclesiastical sensitivities. Within the Christian communities themselves, however, its power eventually came to a zenith, as it was the only institution officially representing the Christians within the Caliphate. This was probably much slower than usually thought, however, and did not come about during the period covered by this book.[98] In the seventh century, local officials and tax collectors were lay Christians, and they were the most important individuals in everyday life for most of the population.

I have not given here a full account of late antique Egypt—an impossible task within the allotted space. Instead, I chose to highlight a number of subjects that have received less attention in recent general overviews. By looking from a slightly different angle at a country that is generally associated, for this period, with monasticism, administration, taxes, the Apions, Dioskoros, Alexandria, and Coptic art, and has often been seen as a closed entity, I hope to have shown that it was also a dynamic participant in the life of the empires of which it was part and that its fate was dialectically rather than passively linked to theirs.

NOTES

1. Herodotus 2.17.
2. For a vivid description of the Nile's role in the country, see Bowman 1986, 12–13; for a thorough coverage, see Bonneau 1964; 1993.
3. Wipszycka 1992b; Gascou 2004 among others; see Papaconstantinou 2005a.
4. Bagnall 1993, 310.

5. There have been many surveys of the advantages and caveats of papyrological evidence, and I shall not repeat them here; for a recent overview of the type of texts preserved on papyrus, see Palme 2009, and more generally Bagnall 2009b.

6. This is best exemplified in the importance afforded to archaeology in Bagnall and Rathbone 2004.

7. See Boud'hors, chapter 8 in this book.

8. Bagnall and Cribiore 2006 is an excellent example of such outreach, and its publication as an e-book with links to the original text of the documents and images where available is a model of its kind.

9. Athanasius, *Apology against the Arians* 87.1–3 (PG 25.405); Socrates, *Hist. eccl.* 1.35.2 (Hansen 1995, 85); Theodoret of Cyrus, *Hist. eccl.* 1.31.5 (Hansen-Parmentier 1998, 88); Theodore Anagnostes, *Epitomè* 49 (Hansen 1995, 24).

10. Theodoros Anagnostes, *Epitomè* 362 (Hansen 1995, 102); Theophanes, *Chronographia* (de Boor 1883, 106–107).

11. Wipszycka 2007; more generally on the Near East, Ford (forthcoming).

12. See Fournet 2009, 419–421.

13. Kennedy 1998; Sijpesteijn 2007a, 449.

14. See http://archaeology-easterndesert.com/html/appendix_k.html for a useful list of the Eastern Desert's mineral resources, and the map and localizations in Baines and Málek 1980, 21; for more detailed analyses of its geology, see www.utdallas.edu/~rjstern/egypt/.

15. For instance, *P.Lond.* III 755 (4th c.), an inventory of columns from abandoned buildings for subsequent reuse, clearly distinguishes between local and imported stone.

16. See especially the Dakhleh Oasis Project and the online annual reports: http://arts.monash.edu.au/archaeology/excavations/dakhleh/index.php; http://www.amheida.org/index.php?content=home.

17. Bowman (forthcoming) with further references.

18. See Bagnall and Frier 1994, 173–178 with further references.

19. See the map in Baines and Málek 1980, 16–17.

20. Torallas Tovar 2010.

21. *O.Douch* V 625. Unsurprisingly, Saracens were also present in the Eastern Desert: Power (forthcoming).

22. *P.Cair.Masp.* I 67009, l. r 22 and v 17–18 (566); the term could also be taken in the sense of "vagabonds," i.e., nomads.

23. The plague has been discussed at great length in recent years: see Little 2007; Zuckerman 2004, 207–212; Sarris 2002; Stathakopoulos 2004, all of which cite previous literature.

24. Quoted by Michael the Syrian, *Chronicle* 9.28, Chabot 1901, 235–236.

25. Procopius, *De bello persico* 2.22, Veh 1970, 356. See also Morony 2007, 62–63.

26. In an influential article of 1989, Jean Durliat makes this point, along with a general revision of the effects of the plague on the empire's population. His position is criticized by Peter Sarris (2002), who argues convincingly for a much stronger impact empirewide. Neither, however, seems to seriously consider the possibility that the situation might have been different in Egypt.

27. Sarris 2007, 128–131.

28. *P.Cair.Masp.* III 67283, l. 15 (dated a little before 547). MacCoull 1988, 21 sees it as a joint reference to the Thucydidean plague and that of Exodus and does not even mention the Justinianic epidemic as a possibility. Rea 1997, 191, note to l.7 considers

the restoration *[loi]mou* very improbable, mainly because of the rarity of the term in Egypt (see Casanova 1984).

29. Hickey 2007, 290–291.

30. Zuckerman 2004, 207–212.

31. Zuckerman 2004, 210.

32. Foss 2009a, 18–22.

33. *P.Cair.Masp.* III 67283, l. 32–33.

34. Bagnall 2005; Keenan 2003.

35. Leone 2007 and Decker 2009a, with further references.

36. Boud'hors et al. 2008; Wipszycka 2009.

37. Mazza 2001; Sarris 2006; Ruffini 2008.

38. *P.Mon.Apollo; P.Bawit Clackson; P.Brux.Bawit*, with the previous literature cited therein.

39. P.Cair.Masp. I 67009, 22–24: *ἔκτοτε γὰρ καὶ τὰ βασιλικὰ ἡμῶν καὶ δημόσια λουτρὰ . . μέγιστα ἦσαν μέχρι τῆς δεῦρο, ἔστι δὲ νῦν πριβάτιον λουτρὸν ἐν τῇ πόλει, χρηματίζον τοῖς πένησι λουομένοις τῶν νουμμίων.*

40. See Papaconstantinou 1996.

41. Papaconstantinou 2001a, 286–288; 1996, 152–155.

42. Grossmann 2002, pl. 55 (Antinoe), 59 (Hermoupolis)

43. Papaconstantinou 2005b.

44. Kennedy 1998, 69, 72.

45. *P.Ross.Georg.* IV 7, dated 20 September 709; transl. from APIS (http://www.columbia.edu/cgi-bin/cul/resolve?ATK2059). An overview of the relevant documents is given by Morelli 1998.

46. See Palme 2007; Falivene 2009; Sijpesteijn 2007a; 2007b; Wipszycka 1992a; 2007; Keenan 2000; Gascou 2008; Zuckerman 2004; Kennedy 1998.

47. This was the *defensor* Athanasios, whose documentary dossier has been assembled by Ruey-Lin Chang, and was presented at Roger Bagnall's Inaugural Sather Conference "Papyrology: New Directions in a New Generation," November 11–12, 2005, at the University of California, Berkeley. I am very grateful to the author for providing a copy of his paper prior to publication.

48. Wipszycka 2007.

49. Wipszycka 1992a, 195–212.

50. Papaconstantinou 2005c, 321–322.

51. Wipszycka 2007, 337–338.

52. Wipszycka 2007, 344–345.

53. Bonneau 1993, 221–222, 307; in general on the late antique period, 291–305.

54. Bonneau 1993, 307, based on Watson 1983.

55. See Decker 2009b, 189.

56. Bonneau 1964, 436–437.

57. Cited in Cooper 2009, 198.

58. Gregory of Tours, *Historia Francorum* 1.10 (MGHSRM 1.1, p. 11–12).

59. What precedes draws heavily on Cooper 2009, esp. 197–198.

60. This is clear from the Papas archive from Apollōnos Anō (*P.Apoll.*), dating from the 660s, and later in the early eighth century from the archive of Basilios, pagarch of Aphrodito under Qurra ibn Sharīk (a practical survey of the texts of the archive in Richter 2010). For a historical analysis of the Papas archive, see now Foss 2009a and 2009b.

61. Cuvigny 2006.

62. See Sidebotham, Zitterkopf, and Riley 1991.

63. Bagnall and Sheridan 1994a, 163.

64. Bagnall and Sheridan 1994b, 112; Mayerson 1993, 174; Gascou 2004, 407.

65. Desanges 1969, 632 with further references; Tomber 2007; 2008.

66. Desanges 1969, 634–635.

67. Desanges 1969, 629; see also Munro-Hay 1982.

68. See already Dihle 1964.

69. Power 2008; Garcin 1976; 1978, 308–309; on the localization of 'Aydhab, see Peacock and Peacock 2008.

70. Gascou 1985. Later works entirely or partially focusing on the Apion archive are Hickey 2001; Mazza 2001; Banaji 2001; Sarris 2006.

71. See the Society's Web site at http://www.ori.uzh.ch/isap.html. A new project, "The Formation of Islam: The View from Below," funded by the European Research Council and led by Petra Sijpesteijn in Leiden, aims to identify and edit the most significant papyri of the early Arab period so as to lay the groundwork for the study of that very important period in Egypt's history; see http://eurasianstates.org/foi/.

72. Foss 2009b, 260. Foss cites *CPR* XIV 1 as an example of the continuation of the annona. Indeed, the document mentions the grain for the *aisia embolē* and is dated 651 by the editor—with a question mark, however. The protocol of the document is totally incompatible with an origin in the Arab administration, since it mentions Christ the Saviour and the Theotokos in the manner of Heracleian documents (see Bagnall and Worp 1981).

73. Wipszycka 1984; 1996.

74. *SPP* VIII 948; *P.Oxy.* VI 1001.

75. *P.Oxy.* I 147, of 556.

76. Gascou 1994, 64.

77. The milieu is very well characterized by Foss (2009a, 8–9, with further references).

78. Bagnall 2009a; Johnson 2009, 266–267.

79. Gascou 1989.

80. The dossier is still under study for final publication; a preliminary presentation of the material is in Boud'hors and Heurtel 2002; Heurtel 2003. More generally on book production in this period, see Kotsifou 2007 with further references.

81. See the Leuven Database of Ancient Books (www.trismegistos.org/ldab/).

82. Otranto 2000.

83. Fournet 1999.

84. Coquin 1975, 212, text line 36.

85. *P.Mon.Epiph.* 389, 3–6.

86. *O.Mon.Phoib.* 7; several similar texts are cited in Kotsifou 2007.

87. Gascou 2004, for example.

88. Bagnall 1993; Keenan 2000.

89. Giardina 1989.

90. Wickham 2005, 22–25, 242–255, 411–428, 609–613, 759–769, and *passim.*

91. Gascou 1985 (60, "des institutions de droit public"), followed by Mazza 2001; Hickey 2001.

92. Sarris 2006.

93. See Bachrach 1967.

94. Wipszycka 1972 and the essays in Wipszycka 1996 are the best guide to the church's role in late antique Egypt.

95. Papaconstantinou 2001a; 2007.
96. Papaconstantinou 1996; 2001b.
97. Papaconstantinou (forthcoming).
98. On this issue, see Papaconstantinou 2008.

WORKS CITED

Bachrach, Bernard. 1967. "Was There Feudalism in Byzantine Egypt?" *Journal of the American Research Center in Egypt* 6: 163–166.

Bagnall, Roger S. 1993. *Egypt in Late Antiquity*. Princeton, NJ: Princeton University Press.

———. 2005. "Village and City: Geographies of Power in Byzantine Egypt." In *Les villages dans l'empire byzantin*, ed. Jacques Lefort, Cécile Morrisson, and Jean-Pierre Sodini, 553–565. Realités Byzantines 11. Paris: Lethielleux.

———, ed. 2007. *Egypt in the Byzantine World, 300–700*. Cambridge: Cambridge University Press.

———. 2009a. *Livres chrétiens antiques d'Égypte*. Hautes études du monde gréco-romain 44. Geneva: Droz.

———, ed. 2009b. *The Oxford Handbook of Papyrology*. Oxford: Oxford University Press.

Bagnall, Roger S., and Raffaella Cribiore, 2006. *Women's Letters from Ancient Egypt, 300 BC–AD 800*. Ann Arbor: University of Michigan Press. E-book reference: http://quod.lib.umich.edu/cgi/t/text/text-idx?c=acls;idno=heb90014.

Bagnall, Roger S., and Bruce W. Frier. 1994. *The Demography of Roman Egypt*. Cambridge: Cambridge University Press.

Bagnall, Roger S., and Jennifer A. Sheridan. 1994a. "Greek and Latin Documents from 'Abu Sha'ar, 1990–1991." *Journal of the American Research Center in Egypt* 31: 159–168.

———. 1994b. "Greek and Latin Documents from 'Abu Sha'ar, 1992–1993." *BASP* 31: 109–120 and pl. 24.

Bagnall, Roger S., and K. A. Worp. 1981. "Christian Invocations in the Papyri." *Chronique d'Égypte* 56: 112–133.

Bailey, Donald M. 1998. *Excavations at el-Ashmunein V: Pottery, Lamps and Glass of the Late Roman and Early Arab Periods*. London: British Museum Press.

Baines, John, and Jaromír Málek. 1980. *Atlas of Ancient Egypt*. Oxford: Phaidon Press.

Banaji, Jairus. 2001. *Agrarian Change in Late Antiquity: Gold, Labour, and Aristocratic Dominance*. Oxford: Oxford University Press.

Bonneau, Danielle. 1964. *La crue du Nil: Divinité égyptienne à travers mille ans d'histoire (332 av.–641 ap.J.C.) d'après les auteurs grecs et latins, et les documents de l'époque ptolémaïque, romaine et byzantine*. Études et commentaires 52. Paris: Klincksieck.

———. 1993. *Le régime administratif de l'eau du Nil dans l'Égypte grecque, romaine et byzantine*. Probleme der Ägyptologie 8. Leiden: Brill.

Boud'hors, Anne, James Clackson, Catherine Louis, and Petra Sijpesteijn, eds. 2008. *Monastic Estates in Late Antique and Early Islamic Egypt: Ostraca, Papyri, and Studies in Honour of Sarah Clackson*. American Studies in Papyrology 46. Atlanta: American Society of Papyrologists.

Boud'hors, Anne, and Chantal Heurtel. 2002. "The Coptic Ostraca from the Tomb of Amenemope," *Egyptian Archaeology* 20: 7–9.

Bowman, Alan K. 1986. *Egypt after the Pharaohs: 332 BC–AD 642, from Alexander to the Arab Conquest.* Berkeley: University of California Press.

———. Forthcoming. "Ptolemaic and Roman Egypt: Population and Settlement." In *Settlement, Urbanisation and Population*, ed. A. K. Bowman and A. I. Wilson. Oxford Studies in the Roman Economy 2. Oxford: Oxford University Press.

Bowman, Alan K., Revel A. Coles, Nikolaos Gonis, Dirk Obbink and Peter J. Parsons, eds. 2007. *Oxyrhynchus: A City and Its Texts.* Graeco-Roman Memoirs 93. London: Egypt Exploration Society.

Casanova, Gerardo. 1984. "Epidemie e fame in Egitto," *Aegyptus* 64: 163–201.

Chabot, Jean-Baptiste, ed. and trans. 1901. *Chronique de Michel le Syrien Patriarche Jacobite d'Antioche (1166–1199)*, tome II. Paris: Ernest Leroux.

Cooper, John P. 2009. "Egypt's Nile-Red Sea Canals: Chronology, Location, Seasonality and Function." In *Connected Hinterlands: Proceedings of Red Sea Project IV, Held at the University of Southampton, September 2008*, ed. Lucy Blue, John P. Cooper, Ross Thomas, and Julian Whitewright, 195–209. Society for Arabian Studies Monographs 8, British Archaeological Reports S2052. Oxford: Archaeopress.

Coquin, René-Georges. 1975. "Le catalogue de la bibliothèque du couvent de Saint-Élie 'du rocher' (ostracon IFAO. 13315)." *Bulletin de l'Institut français d'archéologie orientale* 75, 207–39.

Cribiore, Raffaella. 1996. *Writing, Teachers and Students in Graeco-Roman Egypt.* American Studies in Papyrology 36. Atlanta: Scholars Press.

———. 1999. "Greek and Coptic Education in Late Antique Egypt." In *Ägypten und Nubien in spätantiker und christlicher Zeit, 2: Schrifttum, Sprache und Gedankenwelt*, 279–286. Sprachen und Kulturen des Christlichen Orients 6/2. Wiesbaden: Reichert.

———. 2001. *Gymnastics of the Mind: Greek Education in Hellenistic and Roman Egypt.* Princeton, NJ: Princeton University Press.

———. 2009. "Higher Education in Early Byzantine Egypt." In *The Oxford Handbook of Papyrology*, ed. Roger S. Bagnall, 320–337. Oxford: Oxford University Press.

Cuvigny, Hélène, ed. 2006. *La Route de Myos Hormos: L'armée dans le désert Oriental d'Égypte*, 2nd ed. (1st ed. 2003). Fouilles de L'IFAO 48. Cairo: Institut français d'archéologie orientale.

Decker, Michael. 2009a. *Tilling the Hateful Earth: Agricultural Production and Trade in the Late Antique East.* Oxford Studies in Byzantium. Oxford: Oxford University Press.

———. 2009b. "Plants and Progress: Rethinking the Islamic Agricultural Revolution," *Journal of World History* 20: 187–206.

Desanges, Jehan. 1969. "D'Axoum à l'Assam, aux portes de la Chine: Le voyage du 'Scholasticus de Thèbes' (entre 360 et 500 après J.-C.)," *Historia* 18: 627–639.

Dihle, Albrecht. 1964. "The Conception of India in Hellenistic and Roman Literature," *Proceedings of the Cambridge Philological Society* 190: 15–23.

Durliat, Jean. 1989. "La peste du VIe siècle: Pour un nouvel examen des sources byzantines." In *Hommes et richesses dans l'Empire byzantin, I: IVe–VIIe siècle*, 109–110. Réalités byzantines. Paris: Lethielleux.

Falivene, Maria Rosaria. 2009. "Geography and Administration in Egypt (332 BCE–642 CE)." In *The Oxford Handbook of Papyrology*, ed. Roger S. Bagnall, 521–540. Oxford: Oxford University Press.

Ford, Simon. Forthcoming. "Patriarchs." *Encyclopedia of Ancient History*. Oxford and Malden: Wiley-Blackwell.

Foss, Clive. 2009a. "Egypt under Mu'āwiya. Part I: Flavius Papas and Upper Egypt." *BSOAS* 72: 1–24.

———. 2009b. "Egypt under Mu'āwiya. Part II: Middle Egypt, Fusṭāṭ and Alexandria," *BSOAS* 72: 259–278.

Fournet, Jean-Luc. 1999. *Hellénisme dans l'Égypte du VIe siècle: La bibliothèque et l'œuvre de Dioscore d'Aphrodité.* MIFAO 115. Cairo: Institut français d'archéologie orientale.

———. 2009. "The Multilingual Environment of Late Antique Egypt: Greek, Latin, Coptic and Persian Documentation." In *The Oxford Handbook of Papyrology*, ed. Roger S. Bagnall, 418–451. Oxford: Oxford University Press.

Garcin, Jean-Claude. 1976. *Un centre musulman de la Haute-Egypte médiévale: Qūṣ.* Cairo.

———. 1978. "Transport des épices et espace égyptien entre le XIe et le XVe siècle." In *Les transports au moyen age: Actes du VIIe congrès des médiévistes de l'enseignement supérieur, Rennes, juin 1976 = Annales de Bretagne et des pays de l'Ouest* 85: 305–314.

Gascou, Jean. 1985. "Les grands domaines, la cité et l'état en Égypte byzantine (Recherches d'histoire agraire, fiscale et administrative)," *Travaux et Mémoires* 9: 1–90. Reprinted in Gascou 2008: 125–213.

———. 1989. "Les codices documentaires égyptiens." In *Les débuts du codex*, ed. Alain Blanchard, 71–101. Bibliologia 9. Turnhout: Brepols.

———. 1994. *Un codex fiscal hermopolite (P.Sorb. II 69)*. American Studies in Papyrology 32. Atlanta: Scholars Press.

———. 2004. "L'Égypte byzantine (284–641)." In *Le monde byzantin, I: L'Empire romain d'Orient (330–641)*, ed. Cécile Morrisson, 403–436. Nouvelle Clio. Paris: Presses universitaires de France.

———. 2008. *Fiscalité et société en Égypte byzantine.* Bilans de recherche 4. Paris: Association des Amis du Centre d'histoire et civilisation de Byzance.

Giardina, Andrea. 1989. "Egitto bizantino o tardoantico?" In *Egitto e storia antica dall'ellenismo all'età araba: Bilancio di un confronto. Atti del Colloquio Internazionale, Bologna, 31 agosto—2 settembre 1987*, ed. Lucia Criscuolo and Giovanni Geraci, 89–103. Bologna: CLUEB.

Godley, A. D. 1920. *Herodotus, with an English Translation.* Cambridge, MA: Harvard University Press.

Grossmann, Peter. 2002. *Christliche Architektur in Ägypten.* Handbuch der Orientalistik 1. Nahe und Mittlere Osten 62. Leiden: Brill.

Hansen, Günther Christian. 1995. *Sokrates Kirchengeschichte.* Die griechischen christlichen Schriftsteller der ersten drei Jahrhunderte, n.s. 1. Berlin: Akademie Verlag.

Hansen, Günther Christian and Léon Parmentier. 1998. *Theodoret Kirchengeschichte.* Die griechischen christlichen Schriftsteller der ersten Jahrhunderte, n.s. 5. Berlin: Akademie Verlag.

Heurtel, Chantal. 2003. "Que fait Frange dans la cour de la tombe TT 29? Fouilles dans la cour de la tombe TT 29." In *Études coptes VIII: dixième Journée d'études, Lille, juin 2001*, ed. Christian Cannuyer, 177–204. Cahiers de la Bibliothèque copte 13. Lille-Paris: Association francophone de coptologie.

Hickey, Todd M. 2001. *A Public 'House' but Closed: Fiscal Participation and Economic Decision Making on the Oxyrhynchite Estate of the Flavii Apiones.* Ph.D. thesis, University of Chicago.

———. 2007. "Aristocratic Landholding and the Economy of Byzantine Egypt." In Bagnall 2007, 283–308.
Husson, Geneviève. 1990. "Houses in Syene in the Patermouthis Archive," *BASP* 27: 123–137.
Johnson, William A. 2009. "The Ancient Book." In *The Oxford Handbook of Papyrology*, ed. Roger S. Bagnall, 257–281. Oxford: Oxford University Press.
Kaegi, Walter E. 1998. "Egypt on the Eve of the Muslim Conquest." In Petry 1998: 34–61.
Keenan, James. 1985. "Village Shepherds and Social Tension in Byzantine Egypt," *Yale Classical Studies* 28: 245–260.
———. 1989. "Pastoralism in Roman Egypt." *BASP* 26: 175–200.
———. 2000. "Egypt." In *Cambridge Ancient History, XIV. Late Antiquity: Empire and Successors, A.D. 425–600*, ed. Averil Cameron, Bryan Ward-Perkins, and Michael Whitby, 612–637. Cambridge: Cambridge University Press.
———. 2003. "Deserted Villages: From the Ancient to the Medieval Fayyūm," *BASP* 40: 119–139.
Kennedy, Hugh. 1998. "Egypt as a Province of the Islamic Caliphate, 641–868." In Petry 1998, 62–85.
Kotsifou, Chrysi. 2007. "Books and Book Production in the Monastic Communities of Byzantine Egypt." In *The Early Christian Book*, ed. William E. Klingshirn and Linda Safran, 48–66. Washington, DC: Catholic University of America Press.
Leone, Anna. 2007. *Changing Townscapes in North Africa from Late Antiquity to the Arab Conquest*. Munera: Studi storici sulla tarda antichità 28. Bari: Edipuglia.
Little, Lester K., ed. 2007. *Plague and the End of Antiquity: The Pandemic of 541–750*. Cambridge: Cambridge University Press.
MacCoull, Leslie S. B. 1988. *Dioscorus of Aphrodito: His Work and His World*. Transformation of the Classical Heritage 16. Berkeley: University of California Press.
Mazza, Roberta. 2001. *L'archivio degli Apioni: Terra, lavoro et proprietà senatoria nell'Egitto tardoantico*. Munera: Studi storici sulla tarda antichità 17. Bari: Edipuglia.
Mayerson, Philip. 1993. "A Confusion of Indias: Asian India and African India in the Byzantine Sources," *JAOS* 113: 169–174.
Minnen, Peter van. 2007. "The Other Cities in Later Roman Egypt." In *Egypt in the Byzantine World, 300–700*, ed. Roger S. Bagnall, 207–225. Cambridge: Cambridge University Press.
Morelli, Federico. 1998. "Legname, palazzi e moschee: *P. Vindob.* G 31 e il contributo dell'Egitto alla prima architettura islamica," *Tyche* 13: 165–190.
Morony, Michael G. 2007. "'For Whom Does the Writer Write?' The First Bubonic Plague Pandemic According to Syriac Sources." In Little 2007, 59–86.
Munro-Hay, Stuart C. H. 1982. "The Foreign Trade of the Aksumite Port of Adulis," *Azania* 17: 107–125.
Otranto, Rosa. 2000. *Antiche Liste di Libri su Papiro*. Sussidi eruditi 49. Rome: Edizioni di storia e letteratura.
Palme, Bernhard. 2007. "The Imperial Presence: Government and Army." In Bagnall 2007, 244–270.
———. 2009. "The Range of Documentary Texts: Types and Categories." In *The Oxford Handbook of Papyrology*, ed. Roger S. Bagnall, 358–394. Oxford: Oxford University Press.
Papaconstantinou, Arietta. 1996. "La liturgie stationale à Oxyrhynchos dans la première moitié du 6e siècle: Réédition et commentaire de P.Oxy. XI 1357," *Revue des études byzantines* 54: 135–159.

———. 2001a. *Le culte des saints en Égypte des Byzantins aux Abbassides: L'apport des papyrus et des inscriptions grecs et coptes*. Paris: Éditions CNRS.

———. 2001b. "'Là où le péché abondait, la grâce a surabondé': Sur les lieux de culte dédiés aux saints dans l'Égypte des Ve–VIIIe siècles." In *Le sacré et son inscription dans l'espace à Byzance et en Occident: Études comparées*, ed. Michel Kaplan, 235–249. Byzantina Sorbonensia 18. Paris: Publications de la Sorbonne.

———. 2005a. "Aux marges de l'empire ou au centre du monde? De l'Égypte des Byzantins à celle des historiens," *Journal of Juristic Papyrology* 35: 195–236.

———. 2005b. "La reconstruction de Saint-Philoxène à Oxyrhynchos: L'inventaire dressé par Philéas le tailleur de pierres." In *Mélanges Jean-Pierre Sodini = Travaux et Mémoires* 15: 183–192. Paris: Association des Amis du Centre d'histoire et civilisation de Byzance.

———. 2005c. "La Prosopographie chrétienne du Bas-Empire: Le cas du volume égyptien." In *Prosopographie et histoire religieuse: Actes du colloque tenu en l'université Paris XII—Val de Marne les 27 & 28 octobre 2000*, ed. Marie-Françoise Baslez and Françoise Prévot, 315–328. Paris: De Boccard.

———. 2007. "The Cult of Saints: A Haven of Continuity in a Changing World?" In *Egypt in the Byzantine World, 300–700*, ed. Roger Bagnall, 350–367. Cambridge: Cambridge University Press.

———. 2008. "Between *umma* and *dhimma*: The Christians of the Middle East under the Umayyads," *Annales islamologiques* 42: 127–156.

———. 2010. "Administering the Early Islamic Empire: Insights from the Papyri." In *Money, Power, and Politics in Early Islamic Syria*, ed. J. F. Haldon, 57–74. Farnham: Ashgate.

———. Forthcoming. "Donation and Negotiation: Formal Gifts to Religious Institutions in Late Antiquity." In *Donations et donateurs dans la société et l'art byzantins*, ed. Jean-Michel Spieser and Elisabeth Yota. Réalités byzantines. Paris: Desclée.

Peacock, David, and Andrew Peacock. 2008. "The Enigma of 'Aydhab: A Medieval Islamic Port on the Red Sea Coast," *International Journal of Nautical Archaeology* 37: 32–48.

Petry, C.F., ed. 1998. *The Cambridge History of Egypt, I: Islamic Egypt, 640–1517*. Cambridge: Cambridge University Press.

Power, Timothy. 2008. "The Origin and Development of the Sudanese Ports ('Aydhāb, Bāḍi', Sawākin) in the Early Islamic Period," *Chroniques Yéménites* 15: 92–110.

———. Forthcoming. "The Material Culture and Economic Rationale of Saracen Settlement in the Eastern Desert of Egypt." In *Le Proche-Orient de Justinien aux Abbassides*, ed. Dominique Pieri, Jean-Pierre Sodini, Antoine Borrut, Muriel Debié, and Arietta Papaconstantinou, 331–44. Bibliothèque d'Antiquité tardive 19. Turnhout: Brepols.

Rea, John. 1997. "Letter of a Recruit: *P.Lond.* III 982 Revised," *ZPE* 115: 189–193.

Richter, Tonio Sebastian. 2010. "Language Choice in the Qurra Dossier." In *The Multilingual Experience in Egypt from the Ptolemies to the 'Abbāsids*, ed. Arietta Papaconstantinou, 189–220. Farnham: Ashgate.

Ruffini, Giovani R. 2008. *Social Networks in Byzantine Egypt*. Cambridge: Cambridge University Press.

Sarris, Peter. 2002. "The Justinianic Plague: Origins and Effects," *Continuity and Change* 17: 169–182.

———. 2006. *Economy and Society in the Age of Justinian*. Cambridge: Cambridge University Press.

———. 2007. "Bubonic Plague in Byzantium: The Evidence of Non-Literary Sources." In *Plague and the End of Antiquity: The Pandemic of 541–750*, ed. Lester K. Little. Cambridge: Cambridge University Press.
Sidebotham, Steven E., Ronald E. Zitterkopf, and John A. Riley. 1991. "Survey of the 'Abu Sha'ar-Nile Road," *American Journal of Archaeology* 95: 571–622.
Sijpesteijn, Petra M. 2007a. "The Arab Conquest of Egypt and the Beginning of Muslim Rule." In *Egypt in the Byzantine World, 300–700*, ed. Roger Bagnall, 437–459. Cambridge: Cambridge University Press.
———. 2007b. "New Rule over Old Structures: Egypt after the Muslim Conquest." In *Regime Change in the Ancient Near East and Egypt, from Sargon of Agade to Saddam Hussein*, ed. H. Crawford, 183–200. Proceedings of the British Academy 136. Oxford: Oxford University Press for the British Academy.
———. 2009a. "Arabic Papyri and Islamic Egypt." In *The Oxford Handbook of Papyrology*, ed. Roger S. Bagnall, 452–472. Oxford: Oxford University Press.
———. 2009b. "Landholding Patterns in Early Islamic Egypt," *Journal of Agrarian Change* 9: 120–133.
Stathakopoulos, Dionysios. 2004. *Famine and Pestilence in the Late Roman and Early Byzantine Empire: A Systematic Survey of Subsistence Crises and Epidemics*. Birmingham Byzantine and Ottoman Monographs 9. Aldershot: Ashgate.
Tomber, Roberta. 2007. "Rome and Mesopotamia: Importers into India in the First Millennium AD," *Antiquity* 81: 972–988.
———. 2008. *Indo-Roman Trade: From Pots to Pepper*. London: Duckworth.
Torallas Tovar, Sofia. 2010. "Linguistic Identity in Graeco-Roman Egypt." In *The Multilingual Experience in Egypt from the Ptolemies to the 'Abbāsids*, ed. Arietta Papaconstantinou, 17–43. Farnham: Ashgate.
Veh, Otto. 1970. *Prokop Werke, 3: Perserkriege*. Munich: E. Heimeran.
Watson, Andrew. 1983. *Agricultural Innovation in the Early Islamic World*. Cambridge: Cambridge University Press.
Wickham, Chris. 2005. *Framing the Early Middle Ages: Europe and the Mediterranean, 400–800*. Oxford: Oxford University Press.
Wipszycka, Ewa. 1972. *Les ressources et les activités économiques des églises en Égypte du IVe au VIIIe siècle*. Brussels: Fondation Égyptologique Reine Élisabeth.
———. 1984. "Le degré d'alphabétisation en Égypte byzantine," *Revue des études augustiniennes* 30: 279–296. Reprinted in Wipszycka 1996: 107–129.
———. 1992a. "Fonctionnement de l'Église égyptienne aux IVe–VIIIe siècles (sur quelques aspects)." In *Mélanges offerts au père Maurice Martin*, 115–145. Cairo: Institut français d'archéologie orientale. Reprinted in Wipszycka 1996: 195–224.
———. 1992b. "Le nationalisme a-t-il existé dans l'Égypte byzantine?" *Journal of Juristic Papyrology* 22: 83–128. Reprinted in Wipszycka 1996: 9–61.
———. 1996. *Études sur le christianisme dans l'Égypte de l'antiquité tardive*. Studium Ephemeridis Augustinianum 52. Rome: Institutum Patristicum Augustinianum.
———. 2007. "The Institutional Church." In *Egypt in the Byzantine World, 300–700*, ed. Roger Bagnall, 331–349. Cambridge: Cambridge University Press.
———. 2009. *Moines et communautés monastiques en Égypte (IVe–VIIIe siècles*. Journal of Juristic Papyrology Supplement 11. Warsaw: University of Warsaw.
Zuckerman, Constantin. 2004. *Du village à l'Empire: Autour du registre fiscal d'Aphroditô (525/526)*. Paris: Association des Amis du Centre d'histoire et civilisation de Byzance.

CHAPTER 8

THE COPTIC TRADITION

ANNE BOUD'HORS
Centre national de la recherche scientifique (CNRS)

THE pages that follow aim to give an idea of the remit of literature in the Coptic language. One should bear in mind that Coptic, the final transformation of the Egyptian language (the word *Coptic* itself being etymologically a synonym of *Egyptian*), first appeared as a literary language in manuscripts attributable to the end of the third century C.E. and remained alive until around the twelfth century. It is the product of the creative drive of intellectual circles whose composition and activities are unknown to us. Breaking with the previous stages of Egyptian, Coptic is written with the twenty-four letters of the Greek alphabet, to which seven additional letters have been attached to render the specifically Egyptian sounds that do not exist in Greek. The vocabulary of the language also contains a great number of Greek words of all grammatical categories, and its syntax, even though it remains essentially Egyptian, is marked by the influence of Greek. Those characteristics should be related to the fact that the initial function of Coptic was to produce translations of Greek Christian and para-Christian texts, until it became a literary and vernacular language in its own right. Finally, one must keep in mind that during the first centuries of its existence (c. fourth to sixth centuries), Coptic existed in various dialectal forms (at least six main ones) whose witnesses are very erratically preserved. As early as the fourth century, however, the Sahidic dialect established itself as the dominant literary language for the entire Nile Valley and remained in that position until around the tenth century, when Bohairic, the language of the north of Egypt, took over, remaining the liturgical language to this day. From the tenth century onward, also, Arabic began to spread, establishing itself progressively in the following centuries for the transmission of Christian literature.[1] A large part of the literature of the Copts thus exists also—or only—in Arabic, but it shall not be taken into consideration here except in passing.[2]

Compared with related fields of study, like that of later Greek literature, that of Coptic literature is still very young. The language itself is still far from well known, and many texts still remain unedited or have not even been identified; the twentieth century regularly saw the emergence of new manuscripts that contributed in fleshing out such and such section of literature.[3] As a result, despite a number of survey articles published since the beginning of the twentieth century, any synthesis remains difficult and risky, as points of view and approaches are still varying and changeable. The repeated efforts by Tito Orlandi over several decades to put Coptic literature into perspective have resulted in a number of fundamental articles (see among others Orlandi 1978; 1991; 1997), studies that have proved very fruitful both for the hypotheses they contain and for the polemics to which they have given rise. An overview of the established results and an analysis of the different positions on a number of questions are regularly published in a "Literature" report in the Acts of the International Congresses of Coptic Studies (Orlandi 1992, 1993, 1999; Emmel 2006). *The Coptic Encyclopedia* also includes a large number of articles relating to literature.

It is on those reference works that the following presentation is based, so as to give an overview both of the contents of Coptic literature and of the general questions within which it unfolds. I shall also attempt to develop a number of viewpoints that are still too neglected, in my opinion, and some that seem promising as avenues to further progress in our knowledge of the field.

I. Content and Questions

I.1 The Difficulty of a Straightforward Presentation

In 1993, a book was published in French under the title *Christianismes orientaux: Introduction à l'étude des langues et des littératures*. The section devoted to Coptic language and literature was written by René-Georges Coquin (Coquin 1993). After noting the difficulties outlined here, Coquin did not even attempt a synthetic presentation, but limited his survey to describing the texts and indicating the reference works.[4] The result is a separation in two parts, one part containing the texts translated from the Greek, the other containing original works, each part in turn divided into literary genres. Thus, in the first part, one finds biblical texts, apocryphal and intertestamental texts, patristic texts, hagiography (with no detail on the works themselves in the last three categories), law (Apostolic canons, ecclesiastical canons, council acts), history (a category considered very rare and containing a single work),[5] liturgy, and legends and folklore (this category includes certain martyrdom accounts, as well as the two romances of Alexander and Cambyses);

two categories, that of grammatical texts and that concerning medicine and the sciences, belong to slightly marginal areas that one could consider "paraliterary." In the section devoted to original works, one finds almost the same categories: apocryphal or intertestamental texts (in this category one finds in particular those texts for which there is no Coptic version, without consideration of the original language of composition); patristics (for the fourth and fifth centuries, Anthony, Pachomius, Shenoute, and his successor, Besa, namely, the great monastic authors and founders, the last two represented exclusively by the Coptic tradition); for the end of the sixth century, the hagiographical and homiletic works of Constantine of Asyut, Rufus of Shotep, John of Parallos, and John of Shmun; for the seventh century, the period following the Arab conquest, the works of Benjamin of Alexandria, his successor Agathon, John II of Alexandria, and Zacharias bishop of Saha and the *World Chronicle* of John, bishop of Nikiu, known only through an Ethiopic version; the latest works in Coptic, early ninth century, are those of Mark II of Alexandria); in the part concerning hagiography are listed all the lives of saints and accounts of martyrdom, with reference to the three principal studies on the question (Delehaye 1922, O'Leary 1937, and Baumeister 1972), to which should now be added Papaconstantinou 2001; the law category reproduces what has been said for the first section; then comes a very long section on the liturgy, a very particular area that I shall not be treating here;[6] poetry is also a marginal field, late and scarcely represented;[7] and one last category mentions documentary sources (administrative and legal texts, private letters) and calls for their better integration: indeed, even though they are also called "nonliterary," those texts stemming from everyday life are first-rate sources, whose contribution completes and corrects that of the literary sources, most notably for the history of monasticism,[8] the transmission of literature,[9] dating, and toponymy.[10] In many cases, the distinction between literary and documentary can be contested.

On the whole, even though it gave a fairly complete panorama of preserved works, Coquin 1993 treated Coptic literature like one Eastern Christian literature among many, which is justified in the sense that other East Christian literatures were born of a similar necessity, that of evangelization. However, that approach does not sufficiently highlight its specificity and the historical conditions of its creation and development (Orlandi 1999 had already noted the drawbacks of that presentation). But is it possible to put Coptic literature into perspective in this way? Before attempting it, it is important to bring to light a number of questions and difficulties so as to give an idea of the complexity of the situation.

I.2 Various Sides of the Question

I.2.1 *Shreds of Literature*

Although Egypt is justifiably seen as a natural conservatory, Coptic literature has come down to us in pieces. The observation has become a truism, but this reality remains one of the major obstacles to the advancement of knowledge.

The principal witnesses of Coptic literature that we possess are the remains of the library of the White Monastery, also called the monastery of Shenoute, in Upper Egypt. Discovered en masse at the end of the nineteenth century by the Egyptologist Gaston Maspero, those manuscripts, already badly damaged (they had probably been lying abandoned since the thirteenth century), were then dismembered and dispersed throughout the world.[11] Their reconstitution (they are all codices, that is, books made of quires like books are today, and no longer rolls as in antiquity) started at the beginning of the twentieth century, especially for the biblical manuscripts. It took a systematic turn with the database *Corpus dei Manoscritti Copti Letterari* created by Tito Orlandi in the 1970s, but it is far from being finished. The *CMCL* database, which lists the works, authors, and manuscripts, is an essential reference tool for anyone wishing to venture into the labyrinth of Coptic literature.[12]

I.2.2 *Poorly Dated and Often Late Manuscripts*

To the last issue must be added that of the date of the manuscripts.[13] Most of them are attributable to the ninth to eleventh centuries, a period much later than the texts they contain. Most of those manuscripts are collections put together for liturgical purposes, bringing together texts of various origins and dates. Those texts may have been rewritten through the centuries, which considerably blurs historical perspective. The few remains of seemingly older manuscripts that were found at the White Monastery (chance survival or a conscious wish to preserve them?) are all the more precious for the history of the texts.

I.2.3 *Literature and Monastic Libraries*

Although the White Monastery is the principal repository of Coptic literature,[14] there are other, smaller groups of manuscripts, sometimes older or in better condition, predating the reorganization into collections. Thus it is important to know which manuscript preserves each text. Manuscript groups that postdate the sixth century can all be related to monastic institutions: the monasteries of Skete, in Lower Egypt (eighteen composite codices in Bohairic, ninth to twelfth century: see Hebbelynck and van Lantschoot 1937); the monastery of St. Michael of Phantoou in the Fayyūm (about fifty codices, mainly patristic and hagiographical collections, ninth to tenth century: see Depuydt 1993); the monastery of John the Baptist in This, Upper Egypt (remains of seventeen papyrus codices, seventh to eighth century: see Orlandi 1974); monasteries of the Theban region (remains of forty-five codices, seventh to eighth century: see Boud'hors, forthcoming); monasteries or churches of the region of Esna (twenty-one codices, patristic and hagiographical collections, tenth to eleventh century: see Layton 1987). For the preceding period, the milieu of origin is less clear: some manuscripts are isolated; there is no general consensus on the hypothesis that the Nag Hammadi Gnostic manuscripts were a collection compiled or preserved in a monastic milieu (see the discussion by Shelton in the

Introduction of Barns, Browne, and Shelton 1981), nor on the very tempting hypothesis that, in the fourth- and fifth-century Greek and Coptic manuscripts found in Dishna (Upper Egypt) in 1952 and now scattered in various collections (among them that of the Bodmer Foundation in Geneva), the remains of the library of the Pachomian monastery of Pboou can be found (see Robinson 1990).

I.2.4 *Are There Any Original Coptic Works?*

A crucial question that constantly feeds discussions when there is no identified Greek underlying text is that of the original language of the texts. Apart from the biblical, Gnostic, and Manichaean texts, which constitute independent fields of study in their own right, opinion has always been divided. The extreme position is represented by Enzo Lucchesi, an expert in eastern Christian literatures, who has made multiple contributions to the reconstruction of Coptic literature. According to him, "Every Coptic literary text presupposes a Greek original, unless there is proof to the contrary" (Lucchesi 2000, 87).[15] However, most specialists agree that Pachomius, Shenoute, and his successors were indeed Coptic authors.[16] They equally recognize that at least until the seventh century, the patriarchs of Alexandria must have written in Greek, but also consider that the great names of the later sixth century may have written in Coptic. Linguistically, there is no way of being certain that a text was not translated from the Greek, which points in Lucchesi's direction. Syntactical and lexical arguments are too subjective and easily taken apart. A decisive criterion, the presence of biblical quotations translated directly from a Greek text rather than following the existing Coptic version, can only be used to confirm that a text is translated from the Greek.[17] Whatever the case, more attention should be paid to the respective quality of translations. Coptic texts certainly do not all reflect translations made with the same degree of accuracy.[18] As time went by, authors of new works must have taken liberties with the original text. The martyrologies of the eighth century, for instance, rarely conform to the Greek versions we know for the same saints. Homilies composed from various documents required an important effort of redaction and homogenization that led to modification of the translations, pruning or amplifying the texts, thus producing a new sort of work, often placed under the patronage of a famous name.[19]

The question of authenticity is, of course, closely linked to that of the original language. Pseudepigrapha are more common in Coptic than in any other Eastern Christian literature. Works of one author were, voluntarily or not, attributed to another; literary authorities were entirely made up to mask condemned theological positions, flee from persecution, or give greater authenticity to what was being said (motivations could differ at different times). Thus, without losing sight of the original language,[20] it is probably more fruitful to consider Coptic literature as a whole and to study it according to its contents.

I.2.5 *Contents and Literary Genres*

If one leaves aside texts that can be inserted into a precise category (biblical texts, some apocrypha, letters, etc.), the Coptic literary genre par excellence is the homily, which includes a mixture of hagiographical narration, extracts of apocrypha, sections of oratory, and the like. Thus the *History of Joseph the Carpenter*, even though it is usually considered a "Christian apocryphon," is not a homogeneous text that goes back to the beginnings of Christianity, but a homily composed from materials borrowed from various texts and genres (central account of Joseph's death, marked by Gnostic reminiscences and anti-Docetist doctrinal elements, apocrypha of the childhood of Jesus such as the *Protevangelium Jacobi*, Testaments of the Patriarchs). Its composition could go back to the seventh century, and in its finished form, it was used for the celebration of the saint's feast (the date of the feast is given in the preamble).[21]

Indeed, Coptic literature is not "gratuitous"; it is not "a spontaneous phenomenon of varying expression and content" (Orlandi 1997, 46). Nor is it confined to transmitting sacred texts to those who had no Greek.[22] It answers needs that are both ideological and practical, either combined or independent of each other. On the one hand, it is built following political and theological pressure; on the other, being in its majority produced by and used in monastic circles, it is more centered on ascetic preoccupations and moral prescriptions than on theological speculation. Those two aspects are important to understand why some works came into being and the form they have taken. That is why the historical synthesis attempted by Orlandi, even though it can be questioned in many places, offers the advantage of a presentation that takes into account those aspects, as well as all the difficulties mentioned here.

II. Coptic Literature in Its Development

The first literary works are translations of biblical, Gnostic, and Manichaean texts. The last two categories, for which Coptic witnesses are especially precious in the absence of the Greek originals, are of crucial importance for the history of earliest Christianity.[23] Early patristic and apocryphal texts are also preserved in Coptic, some known for a long time[24] and others (re)discovered recently, like the "Gospel of the Saviour,"[25] the "Gospel of Judas," or the unidentified text contained in a papyrus codex in Berlin (Schenke Robinson 2004). Some of these texts reflect Gnostic preoccupations and doctrinal positions that allow us to date them or situate them in relation to each other. In his "Letteratura copta e cristianesimo nazionale egiziano," Orlandi (1997) paints a history of Coptic literature revolving around three great crises that modeled the character of Egyptian Christianity while significantly influencing its literary activity. Those three crises are the Origenist controversy (fourth century), the schism that followed the Council of Chalcedon (451), and the Arab conquest of 641. This does not mean that all literary works attributable to the same period are equally marked by these theological and political events, but taking them into account is of great help in better understanding the existence and contents of certain texts.

II.1 The Importance of the Bible

Questions relating to the identification of a text or to its authenticity often demand quite thorough philological analyses. The different versions of a text, as well as its relation to the Greek original, must be studied closely if we want to progress in our knowledge of Coptic literature, from not only the quantitative but also the qualitative point of view. The first area concerned is that of biblical versions. There is something paradoxical in saying that the translation of biblical texts played a fundamental role in the formation of the Coptic language, since those translations were the first manifestation of that language, and then excluding those texts from a presentation of the literature on the grounds that they constitute a separate area. In fact, it is an area that is much less separate than Gnostic or Manichaean texts, which, despite their interest for their own sake at a given period, did not durably influence Coptic literature. Contrary to those, the Bible is omnipresent in it, as well as in everyday life, as reflected in the documentary texts. An example is afforded by a group of eighth-century documents described as "child donations" to the monastery of St. Phoibammon in the Theban region, whose formulary uses a passage from 1 Samuel 2:1–10 ("Hannah's prayer") as its narrative basis. Two very different studies have shown how this passage can be exploited: Papaconstantinou (2005) notes its importance as a textual witness; Richter (2005) shows how a literary account is built up from the biblical reference. Without claiming to exhaust the subject, I would like to underline some points that, it seems to me, illustrate how the study of biblical texts is indispensable for studying the literature.

Translations of biblical texts have not escaped the general fate of Coptic literature and thus are also, if not in shreds, at least incomplete, especially for the Old Testament, even in Sahidic. Apart from the direct witnesses, which regularly complete the pieces of the puzzle,[26] the abundant quotations in other texts often constitute first-class indirect witnesses. The works of Shenoute, which go back to the fourth and early fifth century, hold pride of place in that respect, because biblical quotations are long and numerous, with a preference for the Prophets, most notably the book of Jeremiah, the Sahidic version of which has important lacunae.[27] Except for some rare exceptions, translations into Sahidic Coptic were quite standardized as early as the fourth century.[28] If one can assess their degree of accuracy (and some criteria make this possible), the quotations of an author like Shenoute can often be considered as reliable witnesses of the biblical text.

Standardization means stability in transmission but not homogeneity of all translations. Even though we know little about the dates, the places, and the circumstances in which they were made, it is clear that those translations were not the work of a single milieu in a single place; rather, they seem to be the result of work carried out on groups of books, in different regions, based on Greek models that were varied and not always easy to identify precisely. This is indicated, on the one hand, by the diversity of dialects[29] and, on the other, by the linguistic differences between texts or groups of texts of the same dialect.[30] Now to various degrees, this could be found in Coptic literature in general, at least that of the beginnings. Similarly, for texts attested in different dialects, one could raise the issue of the dependence of different versions on one another. As Funk (1994: 330–331) notes, the degree of dependence is not necessarily linked to the type of underlying Greek text[31] and should rather be assessed on the basis of lexical and syntactic criteria that are internal to the Coptic. Thus from the very beginnings of Coptic literature, one is faced with what constitutes both its specificity and its difficulty.

II.2 The Role of the Origenist Controversy

Between the third and the fifth centuries, two currents of thought opposed each other: on the one hand, the so-called Alexandrian school, heir of Origen, influenced by neo-Platonism and based on an allegorical interpretation of scripture and a spiritualist conception of sacred history; on the other hand, the so-called Antiochene or Antiochean school, influenced by the Stoics, which promoted a literal interpretation of scripture. The Egyptian church was Origenist until Archbishop Theophilos shifted his loyalty in 401, which provoked a split in monastic circles. According to Orlandi, although the monks of Lower Egypt, as also the Pachomian monks, were Origenist from the start, one also finds early traces of the opposite position in the texts of Upper Egypt.

II.2.1 *Origenist Texts and Pachomian Literature*

Thus, the Origenist milieu is where the *Letters* of Anthony were written. If they are authentic, they could have been composed in Greek or in Coptic.[32] Origenist tendencies, as well as echoes of the difficulties raised by Theophilos's change of heart, can be discerned in a group of theological texts collected in a manuscript that once belonged to a monastic library of the Theban region. Several of those texts are attributed to Agathonikos, bishop of Tarsus, a fictional character; another describes an exchange between Horsiesi, successor of Pachomios, and Theophilos.[33] Those texts, which are quite particular, not only because of their contents but also because of their literary form (several of them are presented as *erotapokriseis*, questions and answers), seem to have originated in a Pachomian milieu. However, the literature attributed to Pachomius and his first successors is far from being entirely marked by the Origenist controversy. As Goehring shows in various studies on monasticism, the early Pachomian ideal was, above all, of an ascetic nature, and theological divisions were not in the foreground.[34] This earliest Pachomian literature, which contains works attributed to Pachomios himself, to Theodore, and to Horsiesi, is made up of monastic rules (or canons), catecheses,[35] and some letters[36]—with the exception of everything that concerns the *Lives* of Pachomios, a large dossier belonging to hagiographical literature of a later date. The examination of the manuscript witnesses of this early group of texts is instructive: some letters do not come from codices but appear to be isolated documents of an early date (fifth century); the rules, together with similar texts about monastic obedience, are preserved in one of the oldest manuscripts of the White Monastery (datable to the sixth or seventh century); other texts are in later manuscripts of the White Monastery that are either collections or florilegia. Thus, the authenticity of that literature seems to be beyond doubt, since it appears to have been the object of a concerted effort of conservation and transmission.

II.2.2 *Texts of the "Asiatic" Strand*

According to Orlandi, this category contains some patristic translations predating the translations of the "classical" period, some apocrypha, and some monastic *vitae*. Among the patristic texts, the *Homily on Easter* by Melito of Sardis (late second century), one of the main representatives of the Asiatic school, is especially significant because its Greek version is rare. The Coptic translation is known from an early manuscript (fourth century?) that contains, in addition to the homily of Melito, a composite collection of biblical texts (2 Maccabees, 1 Peter, Jonah).[37] It seems that another fragment of this homily has been identified in a White Monastery manuscript of a later date,[38] which would be one more sign of the favor that text found within Coptic literature. The relevant apocryphal texts are the *Apocalypse of Elijah*, the *Ascensio Isaiae*, the *Acta Pauli*, the *Epistula Apostolorum*, and the *Acta Petri*. They all have in common that they are known from early manuscripts, which indicates that their translation into Coptic followed their original composition very closely. Another common characteristic is that they are attested in "southern" dialects, especially Akhmimic and "L" dialects, which corroborates Orlandi's hypothesis that those texts were produced in Upper Egypt.[39] As for the monastic texts of this period showing elements of the doctrinal positions of the Asian school, they form a tradition specific to Middle Egypt, in which most noteworthy are the works of Paul of Tamma, an individual who was unknown to the Greco-Latin traditions and whose writings essentially consist of rules and ascetic exhortations,[40] as well as the *Life of Aphou*, a hermit of the fourth–fifth century who later became bishop of Oxyrhynchos, credited with having influenced Theophilos's theological change of heart.[41]

II.3 The Period of Shenoute and the Classical Translations

The abatement of the fourth-century theological controversies marked the beginning of a period of prosperity for Coptic literature, with results that can be observed partly in the works of Shenoute and partly in the massive translation of patristic and hagiographical texts.

II.3.1 *Shenoute*

Most specialists agree that Shenoute, the superior of the White Monastery from about 380 to his death in 465, is the Coptic author par excellence, the one who raised the Coptic language to the rank of a fully autonomous literary language, with a degree of complexity that cannot be found in any other corpus of texts.[42] Even though Shenoute had always been famous and venerated in Egypt, his works were discovered only in the nineteenth century with the publication of the first manuscripts from the White Monastery, and their study was long delayed by the dispersion of those manuscripts described previously. The reconstitution of the corpus of Shenoute's writings was the work of Stephen Emmel, who systematically reconstructed all of the codices, more than a hundred in number.[43] That corpus is made up of nine volumes of monastic canons and eight volumes of "sermons," texts of an edifying and moral nature addressed to a larger audience, to which can be added a collection of letters. A critical edition of the entire corpus is in preparation within the framework of the international project "Editing Shenoute," directed by Emmel. In parallel to this, research on the content and the transmission of the texts is being conducted in various directions. Its aim is to study the socioeconomic aspects of the form of monasticism established by Shenoute[44] to gain a more accurate notion of its position in relation to Pachomian monasticism, from which it derives;[45] to assess the historical value of a number of events mentioned in the *Vita Sinuthii*, a later hagiographical text;[46] and to bring a corrective to the widely held idea that Shenoute's is a corpus with no theological dimension whatsoever.[47] As for the literary and linguistic importance of those texts, it can hardly be overstated. Pioneering studies in this area are those by Ariel Shisha-Halevy, whose *Coptic Grammatical Categories* is entirely devoted to the syntax of Shenoute's works (Shisha-Halevy 1986). The study of Shenoute's rhetoric is currently at the heart of several scholars' interests.[48] Even though he wrote in Coptic, displaying an intimate knowledge of his own tongue and its cultural references,[49] he was also well versed in Greek rhetoric and widely used its procedures, especially those of the second sophistic.

A remarkable point regarding Shenoute's works is the stability of their transmission within the White Monastery. The texts attested by several manuscripts reveal an insignificant number of variants, a situation whose only equivalent is biblical texts; the situation is very different for other homiletical texts or hagiographical narratives, where variations from one version to the other are significant. The fixed, almost sacred character of Shenoute's works contrasts with the almost total absence of copies of his works in other monastic libraries.[50] Whatever the reasons for this lack of circulation (secret nature of the canons, language too difficult for the texts to be understood and used), it leads to two questions of some importance for the history of Coptic monasticism: (1) Did "Shenoutean" monasticism have a real influence on Egyptian monastic life outside the White Monastery? (2) Should one consider that with Shenoute, the language attained a sort of acme that could be neither imitated nor even pursued?[51] Those two questions cannot yet be answered. As for the second one, the large number of preserved writings of Shenoute probably skews the comparison with other works, translated or not, that cannot be considered as a corpus. The successor of Shenoute, Besa, also left significant works behind,[52] and the writings of further successors are still waiting to be edited and analyzed.

Orlandi's hypothesis, according to which Shenoute, in addition to his work as an author, also supervised the large-scale translation of patristic texts, as well as the standardization of biblical translations, does not seem to rest on very solid arguments. As has been said, the numerous biblical quotations in Shenoute's sermons show that he was using texts that were already standardized. It is certain that the White Monastery played an important role in the transmission and preservation of the texts, but the history of its library in that early period is not yet well enough known to allow us to draw further conclusions.

II.3.2 *Patristic and Hagiographical Translations*

As Orlandi underlined, it remains difficult to classify the various periods of translation and to avoid the traps set up by pseudepigrapha. Contrary to what happens in other Eastern Christian literatures, the great patristic corpora do not seem to be systematically translated, the criteria of choice are difficult to apprehend, and the personality of the translators, as well as the principles of their work, remains obscure. On the whole, among the works translated in this period and preserved today (Athanasius of Alexandria, Cyril of Alexandria, John Chrysostom, Basil of Caesarea, Gregory of Nazianzus, Gregory of Nyssa), one observes a relative paucity of great works as opposed to texts centered on pastoral, edifying, or ascetic preoccupations. It remains possible, however, that this impression is largely the effect of the fragmentary character of the manuscripts and of the fact that the texts were reused and grouped together in the surviving witnesses according to principles that no longer corresponded to the original principles of the translators. The existence of monographic manuscripts, such as those of the White Monastery that contain several works of Basil of Caesarea, favors the opposite hypothesis, mainly illustrated by the work of Enzo Lucchesi, namely, the existence of systematic translations of collections of works that were not only ascetic but also theological.[53] A manuscript of the monastery of John the Baptist at This contains three authentic homilies by John Chrysostom, while most of the other Coptic texts under his name are pseudepigrapha, regardless of whether there was a Greek original behind them. One of those homilies, *On David and Saul III*, was the object of a recent study (Barone 2009) that shows the importance of the Coptic version for the history of the text: generally very faithful to the Greek, it contains several readings that are not attested in the Greek tradition directly but are reflected in the indirect tradition and, considering that the Coptic witness is the oldest of the entire manuscript tradition, should be taken into account in the establishment of the text.

Thus the value of this translation literature is not to be neglected. As for the actual quality of the translations, one should keep in mind that certain texts attributed to Shenoute, the greatest authority in literary matters, were later revealed to be translations of Greek patristic texts.[54] It is often instructive to take a close look at the work of the translator or the compiler, for example, the small dossier of texts by Gregory of Nyssa.[55] Among those texts, the *Panegyric of Gregory Thaumaturgus* was translated from Greek into Sahidic, then from Sahidic into Bohairic. The interest in this hagiographical text with a plethora of miraculous episodes can be easily understood. The Sahidic translation is preserved in one of the collections of the White Monastery containing a variety of ascetic and hagiographical texts.[56] It is faithful to the underlying Greek text, but some passages have been cut, clearly the most speculative passages where the narration slows down (and also passages that are linguistically complex). Those cuts look like they are marked in the Bohairic manuscript[57] but not in the Sahidic one. This raises the question of whether they existed in the original translation or whether they were the result of later emendations. Another homily, *De deitate Filii et Spiritus Sancti*, is preserved in Coptic in a Bohairic version, made on a lost Sahidic translation.[58] Also of liturgical use (celebration of the feast of the three patriarchs of the Old Testament), this homily seems to have been much more tampered with than the *Panegyric of Gregory*: omissions, additions, different redactions. Were these reworkings already a part of the Sahidic version? Is the Coptic text transmitted in Bohairic the reflection of a different Greek version that was not preserved? These are questions that cannot be answered as things stand.

It is in this period that one can situate the first translations of hagiographical texts sparked off by the great persecutions (for Egypt, mainly that of Diocletian, at the end of the third century), the narratives of martyrdoms like that of Kollouthos or of Peter of Alexandria. The massive production of epic-style passions, their organization in cycles, where characters and stereotypical episodes are repeated, probably belongs to later periods. However, a number of elements were already in place in Late Antiquity. This is indicated by the fragments of the martyrdom of Cyriacus, transmitted by a manuscript in the Middle Egyptian dialect that is attributable to the fifth century (the translation thus preceding this date), and their comparison with fragments of a Sahidic version attested by later manuscripts.[59]

II.4 The Repercussions of the Council of Chalcedon (451)

Following the Christological controversies of the fifth century concerning the nature of Christ and the various theological positions they engendered, the Egyptian church, behind Bishop Dioscorus of Alexandria, separated itself from the churches that recognized the dogma of the Council of Chalcedon. It is especially after the hardening of Justinian's position (mid-sixth century), once all hope of reconciliation had vanished, that the break began to be felt in the cultural sphere. Many homiletic and hagiographical texts composed from a variety of documents of apologetic or polemical purpose bear evidence to this closure and to a certain rise of national consciousness within the Egyptian church. The *History of the Church of Alexandria*, the only historical work in Coptic literature, is a good example of this. Composed of two parts, the first being the translation of the first seven books of Eusebius's *Ecclesiastical History* and the second an account in five books of the events from the persecution of Diocletian to the troubled period of Timothy II Aelurus (457–477), it could have been compiled and translated soon after Timothy's death. Another important text in that respect is the encomium of Macarius of Tkoou by Dioscorus, a composite text whose central theme is the trip of Bishop Macarius with Dioscorus to Constantinople and his martyrdom in Alexandria in the name of the anti-Chalcedonian faith. That text, which displays a certain savoir faire in the assemblage of literary pieces, seems to have known great popularity, judging by the number of witnesses in Coptic and Arabic.[60] The *Life of Athanasius*; the *Life* and works of Theodosius of Alexandria, a patriarch of the time of Justinian; and those of Severus of Antioch, exiled in Egypt, where his works also knew great popularity, belong to the same circle of influence.

To this literary genre, called *plerophoria* (an account with miraculous elements aiming to prove the orthodoxy of a dogmatic position), can also be attributed a series of *vitae* and panegyrics of monks who founded new communities after having been persecuted for their non-Chalcedonian faith and thrown out of their monasteries. Those narratives are also interesting for the history of the forms of monastic life and its norms. Some concern monks from Upper Egypt: the *Life* of Shenoute attributed to his successor, Besa;[61] the *Life* and *Encomion* of Abraham of Pboou (see Goehring 2006); and the *Life* and *Rule* of Moses of Abydos (see Coquin 1986). Others are linked to places in Middle or Lower Egypt: the *Lives* of Apollo, of Daniel, of Longinus, and of Samuel of Qalamun.[62]

Two homilies attributed, respectively, to Theophilus of Alexandria (end of fourth or beginning of fifth century) and Timothy Aelurus contain elements that allow us to date them in this period. The first one, commonly called the *Visio Theophili* (the events are told by the Virgin to the archbishop in a vision), is attested only in Arabic, Syriac, and Ethiopic,[63] the Arabic having a Coptic substratum; it follows the itinerary of the Holy Family in Egypt and the foundation by Jesus in person of the first church in Qosqām, the southernmost point of the itinerary. The other homily, known only by a fragment in Coptic but preserved entirely in Arabic, deals with the consecration of the church of Pachomius at Pboou and has a strong anti-Chalcedonian flavor.[64] Those two texts form the basis for a third text equally put under the name of Timothy Aelurus, attested in Coptic, Arabic, and Ethiopic.[65] That text of complex construction merges traditions relating to the Holy Family (some being very ancient, others rather borrowed from the *Visio Theophili*), anti-Chalcedonian elements borrowed from various *plerophoriai* (probably secondary elements that mainly reflect the Pachomian milieu where the texts may have been composed), and several accounts concerning the history of the site, which is ultimately the main subject of the homily: the rocky cliff of Gabal al-Tayr in Middle Egypt and its church. Here one reaches the deeper motivation of the text, namely, to demonstrate the legitimacy of the site by making it the equal of the church of Qosqām and by consecrating it to the Virgin. Thus, this homily testifies to the movement, probably subsequent to the Arab conquest, which tended to transfer to the Virgin and to other great national saints several sites of local saints.[66]

II.5 The Period of Damian

Patriarch Damian (578–605) is known as the initiator of a period of spiritual and moral reconstruction. Traces of this can be seen in the long inscriptions datable to the seventh century that are painted on the walls of the establishment known as the monastery of Epiphanius in the Theban region.[67] Among the works and the authors attributed to this period are at least two important figures.

The first is Rufus of Shotep, an author who is unknown both in the Greco-Latin tradition and in other oriental traditions, to whom are attributed a number of Origenist-leaning commentaries on the Gospels attested in several codices from the White Monastery (texts edited in Sheridan 1998). The authenticity of those homilies has been contested by Luisier 1998 and Lucchesi 2000, according to whom they are texts translated from the Greek in the fourth or fifth century and put under a fictional name.[68] One can easily understand that authors so patently in conflict with what was official doctrine from the fifth century onward should have been driven to write anonymously. If this hypothesis is correct, those texts should instead be counted as part of the Origenist controversy.

The other figure is that of Pisenthios, a monk of the Theban region and bishop of Koptos in the first half of the seventh century.[69] A single Coptic work has come down to us, but his life is the object of many accounts, one of which is attested by a manuscript found recently in the Theban region.[70] That manuscript dates to the eighth century at the latest. As Pisenthios died in 632, his *Life* must have been written directly in Coptic in the second half of the seventh century. Also preserved is an important epistolary dossier documenting his administrative activity.[71] The use of Coptic in that correspondence is quite significant in terms of the autonomy that the language had achieved in that period, at least in this area, and there is no reason to think that things were different elsewhere.

II.6 The Consequences of the Arab Conquest (641)

Even if at first the Copts could believe they were liberated from the Byzantine yoke by the new masters of the country, the illusion did not last long. Certainly in cultural terms, the consequences were not immediately felt, and many Coptic works of the late seventh and early eighth centuries have been preserved (described in Coquin 1993 and Orlandi 1991). However, the rapid progress of Arabicization and Islamization irresistibly choked literary creation in a language that was dying. It is probably in this period (seventh to ninth centuries) that literature shifted its focus to liturgical needs: texts were reworked and reorganized in collections designed for feasts and ceremonies, which constituted privileged moments for exhortation and propaganda in an existence that was under pressure. More than ever, those texts were placed under the authority of ancient and prestigious authors announced in long titles that are characteristic of the manuscripts of the ninth to the eleventh century.[72] Those adjustments were especially important in the field of hagiography, with the creation of cycles,[73] even though it remains difficult to establish a finer chronology for the texts of this category, which must very soon have contained typically "Egyptian" characteristics.[74] The final spurt of literary activity in Coptic was the composition of grammars and Coptic-Arabic lexica destined to standardize the structures of a language on its way to extinction, which were to be at the basis of the first modern grammars. From the fourteenth century onward, it was almost exclusively biblical texts and liturgical rituals that were copied and transmitted, in the Bohairic dialect, which were the first witnesses of Coptic literature to arrive in the West in the sixteenth century.

NOTES

1. On all these points, one can consult Layton 2004, 1–4 (Introduction) and the corresponding bibliography.

2. Coptic literature has also been partially transmitted in Ethiopic, through the intermediary of Arabic.

3. The most recent and most striking example is, of course, the *Gospel of Judas*, which has already spawned scores of publications (see the long bibliography in the report presented in 2008 at the last International Congress of Coptic Studies [Dubois forthcoming]).

4. That part of his presentation remains very useful but needs to be updated.

5. Known as *History of the Church of Alexandria, Historia Ecclesiastica* (see later). The historical genre does not seem to have been in great favor among the Copts.

6. Except to mention the constitution of collections with a liturgical purpose: see later.

7. See the article "Poetry" by K. H. Kuhn in *The Coptic Encyclopedia* 6:1985–1986.

8. Their importance is now fully recognized: see Goehring 2007a and, most recently, Wipszycka 2009.

9. See, for instance, Boud'hors 2008; MacCoull 2009.

10. Papaconstantinou 2001 shows the contribution of those texts to hagiography.

11. The story of this scattering is told in various works: see, for instance, the introduction by Henry Hyvernat to Porcher 1933 (105–116).

12. See http://rmcisadu.let.uniroma1.it/~cmcl (accessed by subscription). An excellent description of the resources can be found in Emmel 2006, 176–178. That report (Emmel 2006) is exemplary, in that for every text and work cited, it refers the reader to the reference works of Greek and oriental patrology and hagiography, as well as the identification number of the manuscript in the CMCL database.

13. Coptic manuscripts bear no date before the ninth century, and in later, fragmentary manuscripts, the dates have often disappeared.

14. There are traces of about a thousand codices, according to Orlandi 2002.

15. This position is explicitly described in Emmel 2006, 180–181.

16. The original language of the *Vitae Pachomii* has been at the center of a lively debate, reviewed in Goehring 1986, 3–33. For Shenoute, see later.

17. See later for the role played by this argument in the debate concerning the figure of Rufus of Shotep. The argument cannot be reversed, of course: biblical quotations that conform to the Coptic version could also be found in a translated text.

18. We shall see, for instance, the case of the translations of Gregory of Nyssa.

19. A good example of this work can be seen in the *enkômion* of Makarios of Tkoou or in a homily attributed to Timothy II Ailouros (see later).

20. A question that is closely linked to that of bilingualism in Egypt, which is a larger question than that of literature. See especially Papaconstantinou 2008.

21. On that text, see Boud'hors 2005.

22. Orlandi has raised a voice against this preconception in several of his studies: Greek was part of basic education, and it is difficult to imagine that people with no Greek could have been able to read translated texts in a literary language that is just as complex. However right, such reasoning should not obliterate the fact that the necessities of evangelization played a crucial role in the birth of the Coptic language.

23. As has already been said, they constitute separate fields that are not treated here, even though they are not without influence on some sectors of properly Christian literature. In both fields, there is a large bibliography. See, for instance, Layton 1995 for Gnostic texts and Gardner and Lieu 2004 for Manichaean literature. See also the reports on those disciplines in the Acts of the International Congresses of Coptic Studies.

24. For example, the dossier of the "Apostolic Fathers," published in Lefort 1952.

25. An account of the discussions around this text is in Emmel 2006, 181–184.

26. The list of new editions of Coptic biblical texts is kept up to date in the Acts of the International Congresses of Coptic Studies.

27. See Feder 2002.

28. Perhaps the most striking exception is that of the Gospel of Mark, which clearly shows two different traditions, one being the revision of the other but the two continuing to be transmitted by even late manuscripts (see Boud'hors 1993).

29. See Kasser 1990.

30. On this subject, see Funk 1995, devoted to the Nag Hammadi texts but very useful for the reflection on biblical texts. Shisha-Halevy 2007, a work on Bohairic

syntax, is exclusively based on a manuscript of the Pentateuch dating from the fourteenth century and considered as a homogeneous corpus, distinct from other biblical corpora in the same dialect (see Shisha-Halevy 2007, 20).

31. The study of the place of different Coptic versions in the history of the Greek text of the Bible is a different field, that of textual criticism.

32. The fundamental work, which has overturned the traditional vision of an illiterate and ignorant Anthony, is Rubenson 1990. See also Rubenson, chapter 15 in this book.

33. Edited in Crum 1915. A study of the texts of Agathonikos is in Orlandi 1981a.

34. Especially Goehring 1999. Some of Evagrius Ponticus's ascetic works were certainly transmitted in Coptic, despite their author's Origenism (see Lucchesi 1999 for extracts contained in a codex of works by Ephrem the Syrian), and we know they circulated in Theban monastic circles in the seventh century.

35. Ed. Lefort 1956. According to Orlandi, everything that is catechetical and not merely normative in Pachomian literature should be attributed to a later period (Orlandi 1997, 61).

36. Noticed more recently: see Robinson 1990 (in Goehring 1990), xxxi.

37. Codex Crosby-Schoyen, edited in Goehring 1990.

38. See Lucchesi 1981a, 72. To my knowledge, the fragment he identified (BnF Copte 131(2), f. 134) has not been published.

39. Orlandi 1997, 65–68. However, I do not think one can, as he does, attribute some of those ancient papyrus codices to the White Monastery. There is no certainty on that matter. Besides, what that attribution leads to is clear: the White Monastery, which had produced all those Asiatic texts, did not, on the contrary, preserve any texts of Origenist tendency. Now this last point could be entirely wrong if, for instance, the texts attributed to a certain Rufus of Shotep and copied at the White Monastery are in fact Origenist texts transmitted under a false name (see later on the debate concerning this character).

40. See the entry "Paul of Tamma" in *The Coptic Encyclopedia* 6:1923–1925.

41. Orlandi 1997, 51–52.

42. Lucchesi 1988 put forward the idea that Shenoute wrote in Greek, on the basis of the existence of a bilingual, Graeco-Coptic text. See the response in Depuydt 1990 and the presentation of the two positions in Behlmer 1996, lxx–lxxi.

43. Emmel 2004 is now the major reference work concerning the life and the works of Shenoute. It should be kept in mind that issues of authenticity are not lacking for the author. The corpus, as reconstituted, is made up of collections of texts attributed to Shenoute in the manuscripts themselves.

44. Layton 2002; 2007.

45. See Goehring 2007b.

46. Cf. Lubomierski 2007.

47. Shenoute's anti-Origenist positions in particular have been at the center of renewed interest: see Orlandi 1997, 77.

48. Shisha-Halevy 2010.

49. See especially Aufrère 2006.

50. One should consult Emmel 2004, 379–382, for the rare examples of works preserved outside the White Monastery.

51. This was the opinion expressed in one of the earliest articles on Coptic literature (Leipoldt 1907).

52. See Kuhn 1956.

53. Lucchesi and Devos 1981. The two manuscripts of this Basilian corpus do not seem to predate the ninth century: this could mean that transmission in this form continued in parallel to the previously mentioned "liturgical" reorganization. See also Lucchesi 1981b on the existence of a corpus of Epiphanius, and Lucchesi 1998 on a corpus of Ephrem.

54. See Lucchesi 2004, 281.

55. On that dossier, see Orlandi 1981b and the entry in the *CMCL* database.

56. Edition van Esbroeck 1975–1976 and Lucchesi 2004.

57. Cf. Evelyn White 1926, 144–156.

58. Edition Chaîne 1912–1913; in the manuscript, the homily is attributed to Gregory of Nazianzus.

59. See Schenke 1999. The remains of literature transmitted in dialects other than Sahidic and Bohairic, limited though they are, are of crucial importance because of the early date of the manuscripts. See previously on apocryphal texts transmitted in Akhmimic and "L" dialects; on Fayyumic, see Boud'hors 2005.

60. Cf. Emmel 2006, 184–186; Moawad 2007.

61. Probably wrongly: see Lubomierski 2007. Even though he died several years after the Council of Chalcedon, Shenoute probably never participated directly in the debates, but his person could easily serve as a caution to non-Chalcedonian orthodoxy.

62. Coquin 1993, 204, attributes this text to the period after the Arab conquest.

63. Cf. *CPG* 2628.

64. The text's editor thinks it could have circulated as early as the seventh century (van Lantschoot 1934).

65. Ed. Boud'hors and Boutros 2001 (Coptic and Arabic), Colin 2001 (Ethiopic); analysis of the sources in Boud'hors and Boutros 2000.

66. Another characteristic reaction of grouping around a figure who was more and more venerated in Egypt from the council of Ephesus (431) and the adoption of the dogma of the Theotokos ("mother of God"). The Arabic and Ethiopic witnesses are preserved in collections of texts devoted to the Virgin. The state of the Coptic witnesses, datable to the tenth century, does not offer as much information. There is a large bibliography on the cult of the Virgin. Coptic materials are very usefully collected and classified in Orlandi 2008. See also on shrines Papaconstantinou 2000.

67. See Crum 1926, appendix 1, 331–341. The character and works of Severus of Antioch also seem to have known great favor in the Theban region at that time.

68. Quotations from the New Testament are made from the Greek versions, which seems to me a decisive argument in favor of a translated work; see previously.

69. See Gabra 1984.

70. Cf. Dekker 2008.

71. The reedition of those texts, published only in a rudimentary way in Revillout 1900 and 1902, is in preparation under the direction of Jacques van der Vliet.

72. Cf. Buzi 2005.

73. See the entry "Cycle" by Tito Orlandi in *The Coptic Encyclopedia* 3:666–668.

74. On the question of the "koptischer Konsens," see above all Baumeister 1972. Another example of a synthetic study based on the dossier of Victor can be found in Horn 1988. Behlmer 2007 studies the relations between nationalism and hagiography until the modern period. On the cult of the Virgin, see previously.

WORKS CITED

Alcock, Anthony. 1983. *The Life of Samuel of Kalamun by Isaac the Presbyter.* Warminster: Aris and Phillips.

Aufrère, Sydney. 2006. "Chénouté, hellénisme ou démotisme?" *Lingua Aegyptia* 14: 265–280.

Barns, John Wintour Baldwin, Gerald Michael Browne, and John Shelton. 1981. *Nag Hammadi Codices: Greek and Coptic Papyri from the Cartonnage of the Covers.* Leiden: Brill.

Barone, Francesca Prometea. 2009. "Una versione copta dell'omelia *De Dauide et Saule III* di Giovanni Crisostomo trádita da un papiro del Museo Egizio di Torino (VIII Orlandi)," *Orientalia Christiana Periodica* 75: 463–473.

Baumeister, Theofried. 1972. *Martyr Invictus: Der Martyrer als Sinnbild der Erlösung in der Legende und im Kult der frühen koptischen Kirche, zur Kontinuität des ägyptischen Denkens.* Münster: Regensberg.

Behlmer, Heike. 1996. *Schenute von Atripe: De Judicio.* Catalogo del Museo Egizio di Torino: Serie Prima. Monumenti e Testi 8. Turin: Ministero per i beni culturali e ambientali.

———. 2007. "Patriotische Heilige in Ägypten: Wunsch oder Wirklichkeit?" In *Patriotische Heilige: Beiträge zur Konstruktion religiöser und politischer Identitäten in der Vormoderne,* ed. Dieter R. Bauer, Klaus Herbers, and Gabriela Signori, 157–178. Stuttgart: Franz Steiner.

Boud'hors, Anne. 1993. "L'évangile de Marc en copte sahidique: Essai de clarification." In *Acts of the Fifth International Congress of Coptic Studies,* ed. David W. Johnson, vol. 2.1: 53–65. Rome: Centro Italiano Microfiches.

———. 2005. "Manuscripts and Literature in Fayoumic Coptic." In *Christianity and Monasticism in the Fayoum Oasis,* ed. Gawdat Gabra, 21–31. Cairo: American University in Cairo Press.

———. 2008. "Copie et circulation des livres dans la région thébaine (7e–8e siècles)." In *"Et maintenant ce ne sont plus que des villages . . .": Thèbes et sa région aux époques hellénistique, romaine et byzantine,* ed. Alain Delattre and Paul Heilporn, 149–161. Papyrologica Bruxellensia 34. Bruxelles: Association Égyptologique Reine Élisabeth.

———. Forthcoming. "A la recherche des manuscrits coptes thébains." In *Scripta Coptice (In Honour of Bentley Layton),* ed. David Brakke, Stephen J.Davis, and Stephen Emmel. Leuven: Peeters.

Boud'hors, Anne, and Ramez Boutros. 2000. "La sainte Famille à Gabal al-Tayr et l'homélie du Rocher." In *Études coptes VII,* ed. N. Bosson, 59–76. Cahiers de la Bibliothèque Copte 12. Paris-Louvain: Peeters.

———, eds. 2001. *L'homélie sur l'église du Rocher attribuée à Timothée Ælure: Texte copte et traduction par A. Boud'hors; deux textes arabes et traductions par R. Boutros.* Patrologia Orientalis 49/217. Turnhout: Brepols.

Buzi, Paola. 2005. *Titoli e autori nella tradizione copta: Studio storico e tipologico.* Pisa: Giardini.

Chaîne, Marius. 1912–1913. "Une homélie de saint Grégoire de Nysse traduite en copte, attribuée à saint Grégoire de Nazianze," *Revue de l'Orient chrétien* 17: 395–409 and 18: 36–41.

Colin, Gérard. 2001. *L'homélie sur l'église du Rocher attribuée à Timothée Ælure (texte éthiopien et traduction)*. Patrologia Orientalis 49/218. Turnhout: Brepols.
Coquin, René-Georges. 1986. "Moïse d'Abydos." In *Deuxième journée d'études coptes*, 1–14. Cahiers de la Bibliothèque Copte 3. Louvain-Paris: Peeters.
———. 1993. "Langue et littérature coptes." In *Christianismes orientaux: Introduction à l'étude des langues et des littératures*, 167–217. Paris: Cerf-CNRS.
Crum, Walter Ewing. 1915. *Der Papyruscodex saec. VI–VII der Phillipsbibliothek in Cheltenham*. Strasbourg: Trübner.
———. 1926. *The Monastery of Epiphanius at Thebes, Part II: Coptic Ostraca and Papyri; Greek Ostraca and Papyri*. New York: Metropolitan Museum of Art.
Dekker, Renate. 2008. "The Sahidic Encomium of Pesunthios, Bishop of Keft: Towards a New Understanding, Based on a Recently Discovered Manuscript." M.Phil. Thesis, University of Leiden.
Delehaye, Hippolyte. 1922. "Les Martyrs d'Egypte," *Analecta Bollandiana* 40: 5–154, 299–364.
Depuydt, Leo. 1990. "In Sinuthianum Graecum," *Orientalia* 59: 67–71.
———. 1993. *Catalogue of Coptic Manuscripts in the Pierpont Morgan Library*. 2 vols. Leuven: Peeters.
Dubois, Jean-Daniel. Forthcoming. "Études gnostiques 2004–2008 avec un appendice sur le manichéisme en Égypte." In *Actes du 9e congrès international d'études coptes (Le Caire, septembre 14–20, 2008)*.
Emmel, Stephen. 2004. *Shenoute's Literary Corpus*. 2 vols. CSCO 599 and 600; Subsidia 111 and 112. Leuven: Peeters.
———. 2006. "A Report on Progress in the Study of Coptic Literature, 1996–2004." In *Huitième congrès international d'études coptes (Paris 2004) I: Bilans et perspectives 2000–2004*, ed. Anne Boud'hors and Denyse Vaillancourt, 174–204. Cahiers de la Bibliothèque Copte 15. Paris: De Boccard.
———. 2007. "Coptic Literature in the Byzantine and Early Islamic World." In *Egypt in the Byzantine World, 300–700*, ed. Roger S. Bagnall, 83–102. Cambridge: Cambridge University Press.
Evelyn White, Hugh G. 1926. *The Monasteries of the Wadi'n Natrun, Vol. 1: New Coptic Texts from the Monastery of Saint Macarius*. New York: Metropolitan Museum of Art.
Feder, Frank. 2002. *Biblia Sahidica: Ieremias, Lamentationes (Threni), Epistula Ieremiae et Baruch*. Berlin: De Gruyter.
Funk, Wolf-Peter. 1994. "Zur Frage der achmimischen Versionen der Evangelien." In *Coptology: Past, Present and Future. Studies in Honour of Rodolphe Kasser*, ed. Soren Giversen, Martin Krause, and Peter Nagel, 327–339. Orientalia Lovaniensia Analecta 61. Leuven: Peeters.
———. 1995. "The Linguistic Aspect of Classifying the Nag Hammadi Codices." In *Les textes de Nag Hammadi et le problème de leur classification*, ed. Louis Painchaud and Anne Pasquier, 125–146. Bibliothèque Copte de Nag Hammadi, section "Etudes" 3. Québec: Peeters.
Gabra, Gawdat. 1984. *Untersuchungen zu den Texten über Pesyntheus, Bischof von Koptos (569–632)*. Bonn: Habelt.
Gardner, Iain, and Samuel N. C. Lieu. 2004. *Manichaean Texts from the Roman Empire*. Cambridge: Cambridge University Press.
Goehring, James. 1986. *The Letter of Ammon and Pachomian Monasticism*. Patristische Texte und Studien 27. Berlin: De Gruyter.

———. 1990. *The Crosby-Schøyen Codex MS 193 in the Schøyen Collection*. CSCO 521; Subsidia 85. Leuven: Peeters.

———. 1999. "Monastic Diversity and Ideological Boundaries in Fourth-Century Christian Egypt." In *Ascetics, Society and the Desert: Studies in Early Egyptian Monasticism*, ed. James Goehring, 196–218. Harrisburg, PA: Trinity.

———. 2006. "Remembering Abraham of Farshut: History, Hagiography, and the Fate of the Pachomian Tradition," *Journal of Early Christian Studies* 14: 1–26.

———. 2007a. "Monasticism in Byzantine Egypt: Continuity and Memory." In *Egypt in the Byzantine World, 300–700*, ed. Roger S. Bagnall, 390–407. Cambridge: Cambridge University Press.

———. 2007b. "Pachomius and the White Monastery." In *Christianity and Monasticism in Upper Egypt*, ed. Gawdat Gabra and Hany H. Takla, 47–57. Cairo: American University in Cairo Press.

Hebbelynck, Adolphe, and Arnold van Lantschoot. 1937. *Codices Coptici Vaticani*. Rome: Bibliothèque Vaticane.

Horn, Jürgen. 1988. *Untersuchungen zu Frömmigkeit und Literatur des christlichen Ägypten: Das Martyrium des Viktor, Sohnes des Romanos*. Göttingen: Georg-August Universität.

Kasser, Rodolphe. 1990. "A Standard System of Sigla for Referring to the Dialects of Coptic," *Journal of Coptic Studies* 1: 141–151.

Kuhn, K. H. 1956. *Letters and Sermons of Besa*. CSCO 157–158. Louvain: Peeters.

Layton, Bentley. 1987. *Catalogue of Coptic Manuscripts in the British library Acquired Since the Year 1906*. London: The British Library.

———. 1995. *The Gnostic Scriptures: A New Translation with Annotations and Introductions*, 2nd ed. New York: Yale University Press.

———. 2002. "Social Structure and Food Consumption in an Early Christian Monastery: The Evidence of Shenoute's Canons and the White Monastery Federation A.D. 385–465," *Le Muséon* 115: 25–55.

———. 2004. *A Coptic Grammar: Second Edition, Revised and Expanded*. Wiesbaden: Harrassowitz.

———. 2007. "Rules, Patterns, and the Exercise of Power in Shenoute's Monastery: The Problem of World Replacement and Identity Maintenance," *Journal of Early Christian Studies* 15: 45–73.

Lefort, Louis-Théophile. 1952. *Les Pères Apostoliques en copte*. CSCO 135–136. Louvain: Peeters.

———. 1956. *Œuvres de Pachôme et de ses disciples*. CSCO 159–160. Louvain: Peeters.

Leipoldt, Johannes. 1907. "Geschichte der koptischen Literatur." In *Geschichte der christlichen Literatur des Orients*, ed. Carl Brockelmann, 131–182. Leipzig: Amelang.

Lubomierski, Nina. 2007. "Towards a Better Understanding of the So-Called 'Vita Sinuthii'." In *Actes du huitième congrès international d'études coptes*, ed. Nathalie Bosson and Anne Boud'hors, 2.527–536. Orientalia Lovaniensia Analecta 163. Leuven: Peeters.

Lucchesi, Enzo. 1981a. *Répertoire des manuscrits coptes (sahidiques) publiés de la Bibliothèque nationale de Paris*. Cahiers d'Orientalisme 1. Genève: Cramer.

———. 1981b. "Un corpus épiphanien en copte," *Analecta Bollandiana* 99: 95–100.

———. 1988. "Chénouté a-t-il écrit en grec?" In *Mélanges Antoine Guillaumont: Contributions à l'étude des christianismes orientaux*, ed. René-Georges Coquin, 201–210. Cahiers d'Orientalisme 20. Geneva: Cramer.

———. 1998. "Un corpus éphrémien en copte: *Novum Auctarium* au dossier copte de l'Ephrem grec," *Analecta Bollandiana* 116: 107–114; 117: 80.
———. 1999. "Evagrius Copticus," *Analecta Bollandiana* 117: 285–288.
———. 2000. "La langue originale des commentaires sur les Évangiles de Rufus de Shotep," *Orientalia* 69: 289–301.
———. 2004. "Deux nouveaux fragments sahidiques du Panégyrique de Grégoire le Thaumaturge par Grégoire de Nysse," *Analecta Bollandiana* 122: 277–282.
Lucchesi, Enzo, and Paul Devos. 1981. "Un corpus basilien en copte," *Analecta Bollandiana* 99: 75–94, 100.
Luisier, Philippe. 1998. "Review of Sheridan 1998," *Orientalia Christiana Periodica* 64: 471–473.
MacCoull, Leslie S.B. 2009. *Coptic Legal Documents*. Tempe, AZ: ACMRS.
Moawad, Samuel. 2007. "Zur Datierung des Panegyrikos auf Makarios von Tkoou." In *Actes du huitième congrès international d'études coptes*, ed. Nathalie Bosson and Anne Boud'hors, 2.549–562. Orientalia Lovaniensia Analecta 163. Leuven: Peeters.
O'Leary, De Lacy Evans. [1937] 1974. *The Saints of Egypt: An Alphabetical Compendium of Martyrs, Patriarchs, and Sainted Ascetes in the Coptic Calendar, Commemorated in the Jacobite Synaxarium*. [London: The Church Historical Society]. Reprint, Amsterdam: Philo.
Orlandi, Tito. 1974. "Les papyrus coptes du musée égyptien de Turin," *Le Muséon* 87: 115–127.
———. 1978. "The Future of Studies in Coptic Biblical and Ecclesiastical Literature." In *The Future of Coptic Studies*, ed. R. McL. Wilson, 143–163. Leiden: Brill.
———. 1981a. "Il *Dossier* Copto di Agatonico di Tarso: Studio Letterario e Storico." In *Studies Presented to Hans Jakob Polotsky*, ed. Dwight W. Young, 269–299. Beacon Hill: Pirtle and Polson.
———. 1981b. "Gregorio di Nissa nella letteratura copta," *Vetera Christianorum* 18: 333–339.
———. 1991. "Literature, Coptic." In *Coptic Encyclopedia*, 5:1450–1460.
———. 1992. "The Study of Literature, 1976–1988." In *Actes du IVe congrès copte (Louvain-la-Neuve, septembre 5–10, 1988), II: De la linguistique au gnosticisme*, ed. Marguerite Rassart-Debergh and Julien Ries, 211–223. Louvain-Paris: Peeters.
———. 1993. "The Study of Biblical and Ecclesiastical Literature, 1988–1992." In *Acts of the Fifth International Congress of Coptic Studies*, ed. David W. Johnson, 1.129–149. Rome: Centro Italiano Microfiches.
———. 1997. "Letteratura copta e cristianesimo nazionale egiziano." In *L'Egitto cristiano: Aspetti e problemi in età tardo-antica*, ed. Alberto Camplani, 39–120. Rome: Istituto Patristico Augustinianum.
———. 1999. "Lo studio della letteratura copta, 1992–1996." In *Ägypten und Nubien in spätantiker und christlicher Zeit: Akten des 6. Internationalen Koptologenkongresses, Münster, 20.–26. Juli 1996*, ed. Stephen Emmel, Martin Krause, Siegfried G. Richter, and Sofia Schaten, 2.23–37. Wiesbaden: Reichert.
———. 2002. "The Library of the Monastery of Saint Shenute at Atripe." In *Perspectives on Panopolis: An Egyptian Town from Alexander the Great to the Arab Conquest*, ed. A. Egberts, Brian P. Muhs, and Jacques van der Vliet, 211–231. Leiden: Brill.
———. 2008. *Coptic Texts Relating to the Virgin Mary: An Overview*. Rome: CIM.
Papaconstantinou, Arietta, 2000. "Les sanctuaires de la Vierge dans l'Égypte byzantine et omeyyade: L'apport des textes documentaires." *Journal of Juristic Papyrology* 30: 81–94.

———. 2001. *Le culte des saints en Égypte des byzantins aux abbassides: L'apport des inscriptions et des papyrus grecs et coptes.* Paris: CNRS.

———. 2005. "La prière d'Anne dans la version sahidique du *Premier livre des Règnes*: Quelques témoins méconnus," *Adamantius* 2: 227–231.

———. 2008. "Dioscore et la question du bilinguisme dans l'Égypte du VIe siècle." In *Les archives de Dioscore d'Aphrodité cent ans après leur découverte: Histoire et culture dans l'Égypte byzantine*, ed. Jean-Luc Fournet, 77–88. Paris: De Boccard.

Porcher, Émile. 1933. "Analyse des manuscrits coptes 131[1–8] de la Bibliothèque Nationale, avec indication des textes bibliques," *Revue d'Égyptologie* 1: 105–160.

Revillout, Eugène. 1900 and 1902. "Textes coptes extraits de la correspondance de St. Pésunthius, évêque de Coptos," *Revue égyptologique* 9: 133–177; 10: 34–47.

Richter, Tonio Sebastian. 2005. "What's in a Story? Cultural Narratology and Coptic Child Donation Documents," *Journal of Juristic Papyrology* 35: 237–264.

Robinson, James. 1990. "The Manuscript's History and Codicology." In *The Crosby-Schøyen Codex MS 193 in the Schøyen Collection*, ed. James Goehring, xix–xlvii. CSCO 521; Subsidia 85. Leuven: Peeters.

Rubenson, Samuel. 1990. *The Letters of St. Antony: Origenist Theology, Monastic Tradition and the Making of a Saint.* Lund: Lund University Press.

Schenke, Hans-Martin. 1999. "Mittelägyptische 'Nachlese' III: Neue Fragmente zum Martyrium des Cyri(a)cus und seiner Mutter Julitta im mittelägyptischen Dialekt des Koptischen," *Zeitschrift für ägyptische Sprache* 126: 149–172.

Schenke Robinson, Gesine. 2004. *Das Berliner "Koptische Buch" (P. 20915): Eine wiederhergestellte frühchristlich-theologische Abhandlung.* CSCO 610–611. Leuven: Peeters.

Sheridan, Mark. 1998. *Rufus of Shotep: Homilies on the Gospels of Matthew and Luke.* Rome: CIM.

Shisha-Halevy, Ariel. 1986. *Coptic Grammatical Categories: Structural Studies in the Syntax of Shenoutean Sahidic.* Analecta Orientalia 53. Rome: Pontificium Institutum Biblicum.

———. 2007. *Topics in Coptic Syntax: Structural Studies in the Bohairic Dialect.* Orientalia Lovaniensia Analecta 160. Leuven: Peeters.

———. 2010. "Rhetorical Narratives: Notes on Narrative Poetics in Shenoutean Sahidic Coptic." In *Narratives of Egypt and the Ancient Near East: Literary and Linguistic Approaches*, ed. F. Hagen et al., 451–498. Orientalia Lovaniensia Analecta 189. Leuven: Peeters.

van Esbroeck, Michel. 1975–1976. "Fragments sahidiques du Panégyrique de Grégoire le Thaumaturge par Grégoire de Nysse," *Orientalia Lovaniensia Periodica* 6–7 (Miscellanea in honorem Josephi Vergote): 555–568.

van Lantschoot, Arnold. 1934. "Allocution de Timothée d'Alexandrie prononcée à l'occasion de la dédicace de l'église de Pachôme à Pboou," *Le Muséon* 47: 13–56.

Wipszycka, Ewa. 2009. *Moines et communautés monastiques en Egypte, ive–viiie siècles.* Warsaw: Journal of Juristic Papyrology.

CHAPTER 9

ARABIA AND ETHIOPIA

CHRISTIAN JULIEN ROBIN
Centre national de la recherche scientifique (CNRS), membre de l'Institut

At various moments during antiquity, Arabia and Ethiopia, so different from each other today, were united by strong links that were primarily commercial and cultural but sometimes also political. The Ethiopians borrowed their script from the Arabians, and this was made easier by the fact that the two peoples spoke kindred languages, belonging to the same Semitic family. Arabia and Ethiopia also shared the same off-center position in relation to the great poles of civilization in the Near East, with which, however, they maintained intense relations that went back at least to the beginning of the first millennium B.C.E.

Ethiopia, a large group of mountain massifs and highlands, lies more than 2,000 kilometers from the Mediterranean, far from Egypt and separated from the upper Nile Valley. Immense Arabia, a long peninsula situated between Asia and Africa, probably was in contact with the Mediterranean, but it projected very far, with large zones of steppe and desert.

I. A Long History, Mainly Known through Inscriptions and Archaeology

I.A Arabia

Arabia takes its name from its population: it is the land of the Arabs. The name *Arabs* appears in Akkadian in the eighth century B.C.E. to describe the populations of the steppe and the desert, or some of them; it appears later with the same meaning in Hebrew, Greek, Latin, and Saba'ic (the language of the kingdoms of Saba' and Ḥimyar). Greek and Latin created the word *Arabia* to name the land of the Arabs, and then the entire peninsula, even though it is not inhabited by Arabs alone, as we shall see. The inhabitants of Arabia appropriated the name *Arabs* for themselves at a relatively late date: the first occurrences, found in Yemen, date from around C.E. 200; they are followed by the famous al-Namāra inscription (L 205), discovered in southern Syria, where the Naṣrid Imru' al-Qays gave himself the title "king of all the Arabs" (Eph'al 1982; Macdonald 2001; Robin 2006a).

Arabia, which resembles a rectangle of 2,000 by 1,000 kilometers, is characterized, first of all, by its immensity (figure 9.1). The major part of its territory is arid, with a dry, torrid climate, so that one could describe it as a desert surrounded by seas. The population mainly lived from nomadic stockbreeding, except in the oases where agriculture was the principal activity. Only the highlands of Yemen are an exception: with its mountains rising to 3,700 meters, it has a high rainfall rate that allows its dense population to practice agriculture. Facing Yemen, on the African continent, the Ethiopian highlands have a climate that is also very favorable to agriculture and sedentary stockbreeding, but over a much wider area.

The two seas that separate Arabia from Africa and from Iran place the peninsula at the center of the exchange routes between the Indian Ocean and the Mediterranean. They are very different from each other, however. The Red Sea is a 2,200-kilometer-long corridor, practicable with difficulty because of the irregularity of the winds, the currents, the aridity of the coasts, and the coral reefs. Without doubt, the Arab-Persian Gulf, which is 850 kilometers long, is hardly more favorable to navigation because of the shallow waters, the sandbanks, and the violence of the winds, but it is easier to obtain supplies, especially in sweet waters, and above all, it links together densely populated and complementary regions (Sanlaville 1988).

In Arabia, history begins at the beginning of the first millennium B.C.E. In the northern Ḥijāz, on the Arabian coast of the Arab-Persian Gulf and in southwestern Arabia (Yemen and neighboring regions), numerous ancient cities have left important remains that are especially spectacular since many of those sites were deserted before Islam and have never been reoccupied since. The monuments (surrounding walls, shrines, palaces, and dwellings), the hydraulic works (dams, gates, and canals), the works of prestige (statues, gold and silver work, decorations on bronze plates, and stone slabs), the objects of everyday life, and the many inscriptions reveal a great mastery of technical knowledge of various kinds—architecture, control of streaming water, and the work of stone, metal, and wood, as well as agriculture. The remains form two cultural groupings: western Arabia, along the Red Sea from the Levant to Yemen, on the one hand, and the Arab-Persian Gulf, on the other.

In the north of the Ḥijāz, three sites illustrate the antiquity and brilliance of pre-Islamic Arabia. The oasis of al-'Ulā (ancient Dedān, 300 kilometers to the

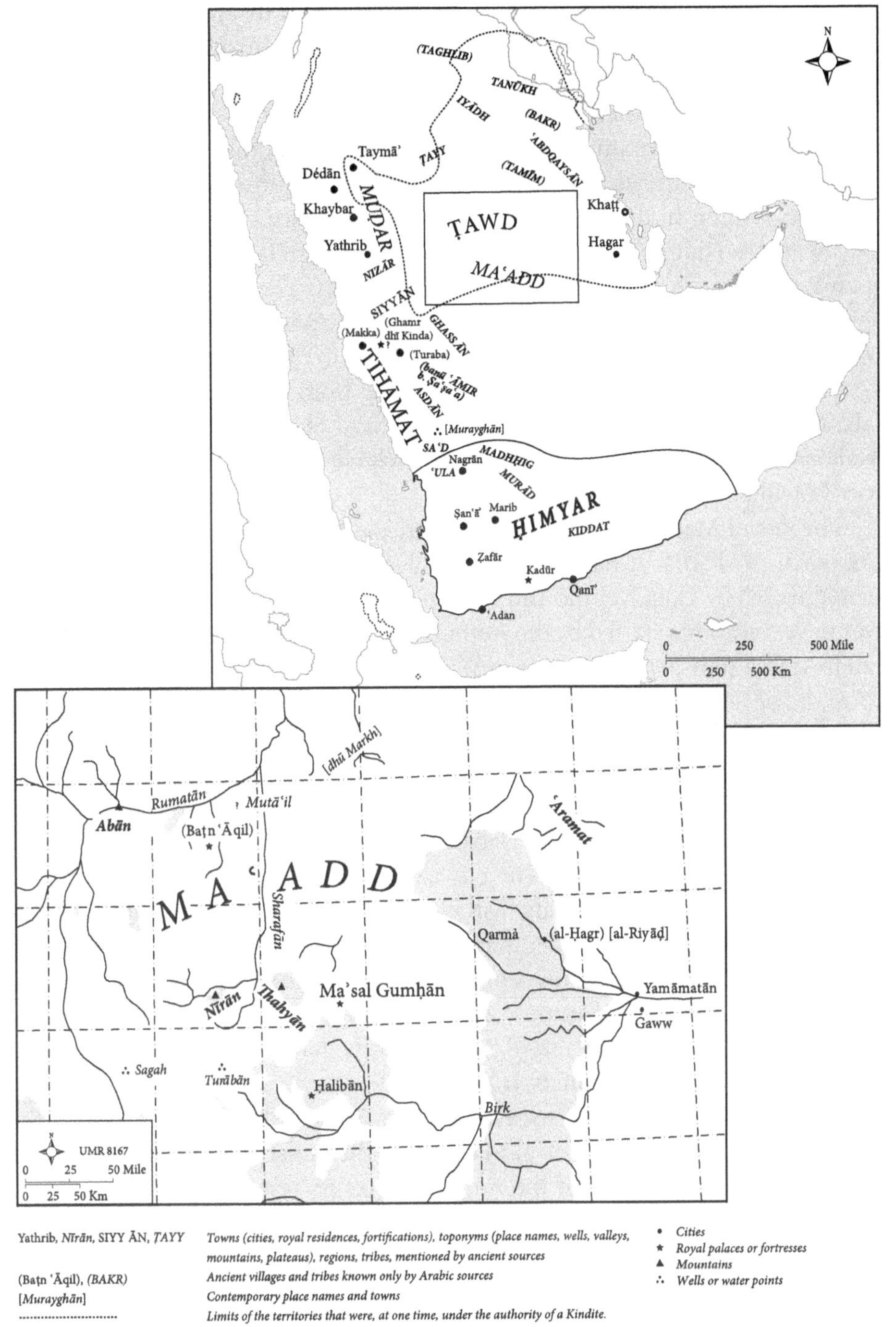

Figure 9.1. The Arabian Peninsula.

north-northeast of al-Madīna, the ancient Yathrib), which has been under excavation since 2004 by King Sa'ūd University of al-Riyāḍ, was the capital of a small kingdom called Dedān, and later Liḥyān, which disappeared toward the beginning of the Christian era. The most spectacular remains are those of two temples in which were found statues (probably representing worshippers of the divinity, since one of these statues is identified as a king) and numerous inscriptions (commemorating the fulfillment of rites and the presentation of offerings). In all, we already know about a thousand monumental texts, composed with care, written in the Dedānite alphabet (a northern variety of the alphabet specific to pre-Islamic Arabia) and in a North-Arabian language (a group comprising the ancestors of Arabic; Macdonald 2004). The Dedān Oasis was for several centuries (c. eighth–third centuries B.C.E.) an important stop on the caravan route linking Yemen to the Levant. Initially (c. eighth–sixth centuries B.C.E.), it catered principally to caravans coming from the Yemenite kingdom of Saba', and then it associated with the kingdom of Ma'īn, also Yemenite, which established a trading post there (Jaussen-Savignac 1909; 1914; Farès-Drappeau 2005; Al-Ghabbān et al. 2010a; 2010b).

The site of Madā'in Ṣāliḥ (ancient Ḥigrā'; al-Ḥijr in Arabic) lies 25 kilometers north of al-'Ulā. It has been under investigation since 2001 by a French team directed by Laïla Nehmé and François Villeneuve; in 2007, the team took over the excavations started by the Authority of the Antiquities and Museums of Saudi Arabia (Jaussen-Savignac 1909; 1914; Nehmé 2004; 2005; Nehmé et al. 2006; 2008; Al-Ghabbān et al. 2010a; 2010b). The city, which appears in the third century B.C.E., takes the place of Dedān as a caravan relay station. It becomes Nabatean toward the beginning of the Christian era: that is when the superb graves were sculpted in the sandstone, their facades rivaling those of Petra. The inscriptions are in the Nabatean language and script (a variety of the Aramaic language and script). The city came under Roman dominion in C.E. 106, together with the entire Nabatean kingdom. An official inscription in Latin dated between 175 and 180, under Marcus Aurelius (161–180), was recently found at the site (al-Talhi and al-Daire 2005). Al-Ḥijr, deserted somewhere between the fourth and the sixth centuries, was a phantom city in the seventh century. According to the Qur'ān (XV, 80–84), it was a city that God annihilated because it did not believe in his prophets.

The Taymā' Oasis (under excavation by a German team since 2004), 380 kilometers north-northwest of al-Madīna, is the most important site of the region because of its size and the importance of its remains (Eichmann et al. 2006; Al-Ghabbān et al. 2010a; 2010b). Its occupation goes back the second millennium B.C.E. at least. It was for ten years the residence of Nabonidus, king of Babylon (556–539), who conquered the oases of the northern Ḥijāz (from north to south Taymā', Dédān, Khaybar, and Yathrib) in 552 (Beaulieu 1989). A stele discovered *in situ*, bearing a much-damaged text in the Akkadian language and script, probably dates from that period. Furthermore, the name of Nabonidus has turned up in several graffiti not far from Taymā' (texts of varying care, usually scratched by travelers along their route) in the Taymānite language and script, a variety of the Arabian alphabet and of the North-Arabian languages (al-Saʿīd 2000; Hayajneh 2001; Müller and Al-Said 2002). However, even though in and around Taymā' graffiti are written in Taymānitic, monumental texts are usually in Aramaic (Lemaire 1995), a language that seems to have been spoken by part of the population until the eve of Islam.

In those oases of the Ḥijāz, monumental inscriptions are found in large numbers before the Christian era and slightly less so in the subsequent centuries (Al-Najem and Macdonald 2009; Macdonald 2009a). The latest dates from the middle of the fourth century (Stiehl 1970). After that date, only rock graffiti are to be found (generally undated but late, judging by the type of script).

The ancient remains—but also the medieval and modern ones—of al-Madīna and Makka have been systematically destroyed over the last decades, so that we know nothing of the archaeology of those cities.

To have an accurate image of the cultural context of where Islam was born, one must also see the southwest of the peninsula, where the archaeological remains are exceptionally dense and spectacular (Robin and Vogt 1997; Robin and Brunner 1997). First, there are the scores of cities (Breton 1994; Fontaine and Arbach 2006; Schiettecatte 2011). The large ones are the capital of the kingdom of Saba' (Maryab/=Marib, mod. Ma'rib; c. 115 hectares) and that of the kingdom of Ḥaḍramawt (Shabwat, mod. Shabwa; c. 15 hectares). Those cities are protected by stone walls that can reach fourteen meters in height. They contained temples and aristocratic dwellings. The most important temple is often outside the walls, protected by its sacrality alone. In the irrigated perimeters of the foothills and the lands of the mountainous zones, the numerous hydraulic and agricultural installations—dams, canals, gates, wells, or terraces—are evidence of a high degree of technical knowledge.

There are thousands of inscriptions between the eighth century B.C.E. and the end of the third century C.E. Subsequently, they become progressively scarcer and completely disappear soon after the middle of the sixth century; over the whole of South Arabia, their number during the period 300 to 560 is around 150 (Robin 2009b). They are all written in the same alphabet, the Sabean one (the southern variety of the Arabian alphabet), but in four different languages. One of them, Saba'ic, is quite close to Arabic; the others diverge from it slightly (Minaic and Qatabānic) or considerably (Ḥaḍramitic).

Most of the inscriptions are commemorative, relating the execution of rites or the completion of works. Their aim is not to write history or describe political, religious, and social institutions, but in fact they commonly do so in passing. The few normative texts sometimes betray the same sort of preoccupations one later finds in Islamic legislation. Thus, a decree dating from before the Christian era and promulgated by the "commune" (or, in other words, the sedentary tribe) Maṭirat (40 kilometers northeast of Ṣanʿā') prohibits the murder of daughters (Robin 1979, 185–190; Beeston 1981, 21–25; Kropp 1998), just like the Qur'ān condemns the *wa'd* (the murder of female newborns) (*EI* 2, s.v.).

Inscriptions allow us to reconstruct chronology with precision (thanks to their dating formulae using various eras) from the middle of the second century C.E. (Robin 1998); for previous centuries, the chronology is less and less certain as we move back in time.

A special category of texts are archival documents, incised on wooden sticks in the cursive Sabaean alphabet. There are several thousand of them, found in recent clandestine excavations. They are difficult to read and interpret, and so their study is still in its infancy (Ryckmans et al. 1994; Robin 2001b, esp. 528–537; P. Stein 2010).

In the zone of contact between Yemen and inner Arabia lies Nagrān (mod. Najrān), which was the capital of a small kingdom before being annexed by Saba' in the second century C.E. It owes its fame, above all, to a tragic event: the massacre of the Christian pro-Byzantine elite by a Jewish king of Ḥimyar (see later) in 523 (Schiettecatte 2010). Qaryat (mod. Qaryat al-Fāw), 300 kilometers to the northeast of Najrān, was also the capital of a small kingdom, controlled first by the tribe of Madhḥig (Arabic Madhḥij) and then by that of Kiddat (Arabic Kinda) during the first centuries C.E. This large city invites us to reconsider our idea of the reputedly "nomadic" tribes: the excavators from King Sa'ūd University uncovered a large building devoted to exchange, numerous temples, a large residential quarter, and a necropolis with monumental tombs. The palaces, whose walls were decorated with figurative frescoes, have yielded rich finds, both produced locally and imported. The inscriptions, written in the Sabean alphabet, are in Minaic, Saba'ic, and Old Arabic (an archaic form of Arabic written in the Sabaean or the Nabatean alphabet: Macdonald 2008) (al-Ansary 1981; Al-Ghabban et al. 2010a).

There are also several important archaeological sites on the coast of the Arab-Persian Gulf. On the continent alone, the most significant are Thāj, al-Dūr, and al-Mulayḥa (Potts 1990), which were all progressively abandoned during the first centuries of the Christian era. As in the north of the Ḥijāz, a large proportion of the surviving documents are written in the Aramaic language and script, or rather in various varieties of the two (Puech 1998). It would seem that Aramaic was the mother tongue of part of the population, especially the elites (Contini 2003). Besides, a large number of Aramaic-speaking churchmen and religious authors in the Nestorian Church came from the Gulf, especially in the seventh century (Brock 1999). The texts in Sabaean script, relatively common before the Christian era, become exceptional in later centuries (Robin 1974).

In the Gulf, as in the north of the Ḥijāz, texts in foreign languages (Akkadian, Imperial Aramaic, Nabatean, Greek, Latin) are common (Beaucamp and Robin 1981; Gatier et al. 2002); they are exceptional in southern Arabia, where five inscriptions have been found in Ge'ez (*gəʿz* or Classical Ethiopic), two in Hebrew, three Saba'ic-Nabatean bilinguals and a Greek-Latin one, one inscription in Greek, one in Nabatean, and finally one in Palmyrenian—to which one can add some graffiti in Greek, Nabatean, Palmyrenian, and especially a fine group of Indian and Ge'ez graffiti in a cave on Suquṭra (*RIÉth* 195 and 263–266;

Degen 1974; Costa 1977; Bowersock 1993; Macdonald 1994; Robin and Gorea 2002; Strauch and Bukharin 2004). Those documents show that the Gulf, northwest Arabia, and Yemen underwent foreign domination but also that, from earliest times, circulation had been intense and varied.

It is today possible to give names to the populations, languages, and places, thanks to inscriptions, which are often very rich in information of all sorts (Macdonald 2000). But one must not forget that these texts throw light on only the higher classes of society and on individuals who are close to power circles, and that they inform us only on events about which such people feel confident.

The lacunae left by inscriptions are not filled by local narrative sources, which are now lost, assuming they ever existed. As for external sources, they are of little help. The oldest ones—Mesopotamian sources or some books of the Hebrew Bible—mention the commercial contacts made with merchants from the South and recount Assyrian and Neo-Babylonian attempts at controlling that trade (Eph'al 1982; Potts 2010a and b). During the Hellenistic and Roman periods, the progress of knowledge incited several scholars to write treatises on Arabia. Those works were based on the reports of the explorers and merchants who crisscrossed its bordering seas from the reign of Alexander onward (336–323 B.C.E.), of which the *Periplus Maris Erythraei* offers a good example (Casson 1989; Robin 1997), and on those of military leaders like Aelius Gallus, whom the emperor Augustus sent to conquer the country of incense around 25 B.C.E. (Marek 1993; Robin 1996, cols. 1131–1133). Unfortunately, their content is known to us only by the brief quotations that later authors inserted into large thematic syntheses, like those of Theophrastus, Strabo, Dioscorides, Pliny, or Ptolemy (Rodinson 1984).

External sources are only really useful for a single episode of Arabian history: the long period of political and religious disorder that shook the kingdom of Ḥimyar in the first decades of the sixth century C.E. and led to its disappearance (c. 500–570). These include historical works in Greek (most notably those of Procopius, Malalas, and Theophanes) and Syriac (such as the *Chronicles* of the monastery of Zuqnin and Michael the Syrian); one of those works, the Greek *Chronicle* composed by the Egyptian John of Nikiu, is known only by a Ge'ez translation. We also possess Photios' summary of a diplomatic report written by the Byzantine ambassador Nonnosos, whom the emperor Justinian (527–565) had sent to Arabia and Ethiopia at an unknown date, probably at the beginning of the 540s (after the notes taken by Photius). The Ḥimyarite crisis is also known thanks to the texts, also in Greek and Syriac, produced within the churches to celebrate the martyrs of South Arabia and to establish their cult. These are accounts in the form of letters (Guidi *Letter*, attributed to Simeon of Beth Arsham, and Shahîd *Letter*), homilies, hymns, and hagiographical texts (*Book of the Ḥimyarites* and *Martyrdom of Arethas*) (Beaucamp et al. 1999).

With the exception of the Ḥimyarite crisis, external late antique sources are not interested in Arabia. At most, Byzantine chroniclers mention the Arabs of the desert when they raid the eastern provinces of the empire (which make up the Diocese of Oriens) or when the empire asks them to engage in an alliance against Sāsānid Persia. As for the ecclesiastical historians who wrote in Greek (Philostorgius, *Ecclesiastical History*) or in Latin (Rufinus, *Ecclesiastical History*), they mention Arabia only in connection with attempts to convert it to Christianity.

One Syriac source sheds light on ecclesiastical institutions: the acts of the synods of the Nestorian Church, known as *Synodicon orientale,* which offer much information on the episcopal sees of the Arab-Persian Gulf up to the year 676 (that is about forty years after the Muslim conquest). Another short document in Ge'ez must be cited here: the *Martyrdom of Azqīr,* probably translated from an Arabic original, which mentions oppression of Christians in Najrān in the 470s, that is, about fifty years before the famous massacre of 523.

To reconstruct the history of pre-Islamic Arabia, we also have at our disposal the information offered by the Islamic tradition, a convenient expression describing the group of texts produced or recorded in the first centuries of Islam (*akhbār,* poetry, genealogies, etc.). That tradition is especially precious for toponymy and tribal geography. It has also preserved many individual accounts of the events experienced by the companions of Muḥammad or by their immediate ancestors. For the periods preceding the sixth century, that collective memory remembers only some personal names (Robin 2005).

I.B Ethiopia

Ethiopia stretches over a territory whose limits have often varied in the north of the Horn of Africa, between the Nile to the west and the Red Sea to the east. The heart of the country is in Aksūm, on the immense central plateau whose altitude varies between 1,800 and 3,000 meters, with mountains whose altitude reaches 4,620 meters (Ras Dashan). The climate is temperate, with very plentiful rains in the summer, so that agriculture and the breeding of cattle are important resources. In antiquity, the Red Sea's coastal regions, around the port of Adulis with its dry and torrid climate, belonged to Ethiopia. The same was true, at some periods, of regions located within the Nile Valley. The name *Ethiopia* comes from the Greek and derives from the adjective *aithiops,* "with a burnt face" (from the sun). For the Greeks and Romans, Ethiopia was Nubia, to the south of Egypt and, more generally, all the areas inhabited by blacks: this is true for Herodotus, the New Testament, and even Philostorgius, who wrote the following at the beginning of the fifth century: "From this great Arabia, [Theophilus the Indian] proceeded to the Ethiopians, who are called Axumites, who dwell along the first coasts of the Erythaean Sea. . . . They are called like that from their metropolis: because they have Axum as their metropolis" (*Ecclesiastical History,* 3.6).

In the inscriptions of Ethiopia, the name *Ethiopia* primarily describes the Nile Valley and perhaps more specifically Nubia. This meaning can be read in a Greek inscription dating from the beginning of the third century C.E.: "The greatest of my gods, Arēs, from whom I am descended and thanks to whom I have brought under my dominion all the peoples bordering my country, in the east to the region of incense, and in the west to the territories of Ethiopia and Sasou" (*RIÉth* 277/36).

A new habit was introduced around the middle of the fourth century C.E., when 'Ēzānā, "king of Aksūm, etc." translated the Ge'ez term *Ḥabashat* (*RIÉth* 185 and 185bis, *Ḥbśt*), which has produced "Abyssinia" in European languages, by the Greek term *Ethiopians* (*RIÉth* 270 and 270bis, *Aithiopōn*). *Ḥabashat* was then one of the many peoples that 'Ēzānā mentions in his titulature and claims to govern. Considering that the term does not appear in all of 'Ēzānā's titulatures, but only in some of the ones that date from the polytheistic period, he was arguably describing a peripheral region that was imperfectly controlled.

The way in which the Sabean and Ḥimyarite inscriptions of southern Arabia describe the sovereign of Aksūm varies considerably. In the third century, the Arabians speak of the "king of the Aksūmites" (*mlk 'ks*^{1}*m*^{n}), of the "king of the Abyssinians" (*mlk Ḥbs*^{2}*t*^{n}), of the "king of Abyssinia" (*mlk Ḥbs*^{2}*t*), or of the "king of Abyssinia and the Aksūmites" (*mlk Ḥbs*^{2}*t w-'ks*^{1}*m*^{n}). Three centuries later, in the sixth century, they mention the "king of Abyssinia," the "kings of the Aksūmites," and the "negus of the Aksūmites," with "negus" in the plural or the singular (Müller 1978; 1998; Beeston 1987; Robin 1988). The same inscriptions call the country "Abyssinia" (*Ḥbs*^{2}*t*), the "country of Abyssinia," and the country of Abyssinia and of the Aksūmites. As for the inhabitants, they are the "Abyssinians" (*'ḥbs*^{2n}) or the "Aksūmites" (*'ks*^{1}*m*^{n}). Apparently, the Arabians describe the kingdom of Aksūm by one of its parts, probably the one that is most familiar to them, which leads us to situate *Ḥabashat* (Saba'ic *Ḥbs*^{2}*t*) on the African coast of the Red Sea.

To sum up, in the local inscriptions, the name *Ethiopians* was applied above all to the black populations of Nubia (early third century) and by extension to those of the Red Sea coast, whose Semitic name is *Ḥabashat* (mid-fourth century).

"Ethiopia" is thus not the name of the ancient kingdom. In the local sources, the sovereign is called "king of Aksūm" and of a series of peoples, among whom the "Ethiopians" only appear during a short period. It seems preferable, insofar as it is possible, to maintain the terminology of the sources and to speak of Aksūm rather than of Ethiopia. We do not really know if, initially, Aksūm was the name of a people or that of a city (Schneider 1996, Müller 1998). Whatever the case, it is without any doubt the name of the capital of the kingdom for the period we are dealing with.

Finally, it must be remembered that in later Greek and Roman authors, our "Ethiopia" is called "India," like the other areas bordering the Indian Ocean (more precisely, "exterior India," *India ulterior*, in Rufinus, *Ecclesiastical History*, which is apparently opposed to the "interior India" of Philostorgius, *Ecclesiastical History*, or Kosmas Indikopleustēs, *Christian Topography* 3.49, describing Arabia).

In Ethiopia, the beginnings of history go back to the seventh century B.C.E., perhaps even to the end of the eighth century. In many sites of the Aksūm region, the oldest remains show special features, especially in the architecture, the decorative repertoire, and the inscriptions (alphabet, writing style, wording, and content), which were borrowed at that time from South Arabia (more precisely, from the kingdom of Saba'). Without doubt, they also contain indigenous characteristics in varying proportions.

At that time, the country is called Da'mat. Royal titulature makes explicit its extension through the formula "its Orient and its West, its Sabeans and its immigrants, its Reds and its Blacks" (*D'mt* *ms²rq-hy w-m'rb-hy S¹b'-hy w-'br-hy 'dm-hy w-ṣlm-hy, RIÉth* 5, 8, 9, 10).

As this titulature and a number of texts explicitly mention the presence of Sabaeans, various explanatory models have been suggested. It has been thought that the Sabaean sovereign had conquered the region of Aksūm, that he had created a network of commercial trading posts, or that he had simply sent artisans for the construction of some prestigious monuments. It is still difficult to chose between those different suggestions, especially as the Da'matites seem to be closely related to the Sabaeans.

The most important site in this period is Yeḥa, where a superb temple of South Arabian style still stands, almost entirely preserved (Robin and Maigret 1998). A few dozen inscriptions going back to this period are written in the Sabaean alphabet and in two varieties of a local language very similar to Sabaic.

A second phase of the history of Ethiopia begins in the first century C.E. The country now has two major centers, the metropolis Aksūm and the port of Adulis, as the *Periplus Maris Erythraei* indicates (4–5):

> From Adulis it is a journey of three days to Koloe, an inland city that is the first trading post for ivory, and from there another five days to the metropolis itself, which is called Axōmitēs. . . . The ruler of these regions, from the Moschophagoi to the rest of Barbaria, is Zōskalēs, a stickler about his possessions and always holding out for getting more, but in other respects a fine person and well versed in reading and writing Greek.

It is in Aksūm that the most impressive remains have been preserved. First, there is a group of very large monolithic stelae, cut in granite and dominating a vast necropolis. The six preserved stelae measure between fifteen and thirty-three meters in height and weigh between 43 and 520 tons. They are decorated with false windows and doors, suggesting a succession of floors: four for the most modest one, up to thirteen for the tallest one (Phillipson 2003, 19ff.). The monumental tombs that have been uncovered in the necropolis were erected for very important individuals, perhaps the sovereigns and their entourage.

The city had large palaces of which only the substructures remain. A South Arabian inscription from the beginning of the third century informs us that the palace of the king was called *Zrr*ⁿ (*CIH* 308/14). Four of them have been excavated. Remains were also found of thrones in stone (with one or two seats) where royal inscriptions were usually engraved. They are called *manbar/mabbar* in Ge'ez (*RIÉth* 187/12; 188/24; 189/39, 44, 49, 51–52; 191/5 and 38; 192/A38; see also 277/43), a term that Arabic borrowed in the form *minbar* (with the meaning of "chair" for the Friday preacher).

The second urban site of the kingdom is Adulis, thirty-five kilometers south-southeast of Masawwa' and six kilometers from the coastline, on the river Haddas, near modern-day Zula (a name that could be derived from Adulis). The excavations that have taken place there were disappointing; they uncovered only a certain number of buildings, which were interpreted as Byzantine-era churches.

In the sixth century, the port was called Gabaza (see the drawing by Kosmas in Wolska-Conus 1968, 1.367, and comm. at 1.366–367), to be perhaps identified with the *Gbzm* of *RIÉth* 186/11.

Adulis, whose name a Greek would automatically relate to the noun *doulos*, "slave" (which explains the myth of the foundation of Adulis by fugitive slaves: *Pliny Nat. Hist.* 6.172), exported among other things ivory, rhinoceros horns, and turtle shells (*Periplus* 4). The Byzantine Kosmas Indikopleustēs (*Christian Topography* 2.54–64) passed through there at the beginning of the reign of Justin I (518–527), as "Ellatzbaas" (Kālēb Ella Aṣbəḥa), king of the Aksūmites, was preparing to invade Yemen. He copied two long Greek inscriptions that are now lost (*RIÉth* 276 and 277).

Two last Aksūmite sites, widely explored, Anza and Matara, also deserve to be mentioned (Bernand et al. 1991, 1.53–57).

The number of inscriptions of the Aksūmite period is slightly above a hundred. Of the thirty that come from Aksūm, the majority are historical texts authored by the king. Two periods are especially well represented: the middle of the fourth century (the reign of 'Ēzānā) and the first half of the sixth century (the reigns of Kālēb and his son Wa'zeb).

The majority of those inscriptions are written in Ge'ez, an extinct Semitic language to which several languages of modern Ethiopia are related (in particular, Tigrigna and Amharic), and all the languages (ancient and modern) of Arabia. The term *Ge'ez* also designates the alphabet and the syllabary with which that language was written.

The first documents in Ge'ez language are the inscriptions of the kingdom of Da'mat (region of Aksūm, seventh to sixth centuries B.C.E.). Ge'ez then witnessed a long period of eclipse and reappeared when it became the language of the kingdom of Aksūm, toward the beginning of the Christian era. It stopped being spoken toward the end of the first millennium of the Christian era, but, because the Ethiopian ("Monophysite") church had chosen it as its liturgical language, it survived as a language of culture in the Christian kingdoms until the nineteenth century, and only since then has it been overtaken by the vernacular languages.

Aksūmite Ge'ez is written in three different scripts. The oldest, "consonantal Ge'ez," is attested from the origins to the third and fourth century, in the reigns of two polytheist sovereigns, Gadara (one text, *RIÉth* 180) and ʿĒzānā (two texts of almost identical content, *RIÉth* 185-II and 185bis-II). It is a consonantal alphabet derived from the Sabean script, with many modifications in the details that are probably due to a cursive intermediary.

The second script is the "Ge'ez syllabary." Its modest modifications to the consonantal alphabet, such as the lengthening of a vertical stroke or the addition of a circle, allow it to note the seven vowels and the absence of a vowel. The sovereigns who used this syllabary were the polytheist king ʿĒzānā (*RIÉth* 188); an apparently polytheist king whose name has disappeared, possibly the same ʿĒzānā (*RIÉth* 187); a monotheist king also called ʿĒzānā (*RIÉth* 189); and a Christian king whose name has disappeared, probably Kālēb (*RIÉth* 195, found in Yemen).

The Ge'ez syllabary is still in use today, not only for Ge'ez but also for several modern languages like Tigrigna and Amharic. It has twenty-six consonants that take seven different forms each to note the various vowels; four consonants can also receive a diphthongal vowel. It has 202 signs in total.

Those two Ge'ez scripts, consonantal and syllabic, are written from left to right, contrary to the Semitic alphabets (Phoenician, Aramaic, Hebrew, Arabic, and Sabean), which are written from right to left. Words are separated by a double dot or a space.

The third script used in Aksūm is more unexpected. It is the Sabaean alphabet in an especially ornate and irregular local form. The language of the inscriptions that use this script presents some interesting characteristics: it is Ge'ez made up as Saba'ic through the addition of an *m* ("*mīm*") at the end of words, in an erratic manner, in order to pastiche Sabaic *mīmation*, and through the use of some characteristic words like the Saba'ic *mlk*, "king" (instead of the Ge'ez *ngśy* [*RIÉth* 180] or *ngś*). All the sovereigns who had inscriptions made in this script—known as "Ge'ez in the Ḥimyarite fashion" (*RIÉth* 185-I, 185bis-I, 186, 190, 191, and 192)—mention the South Arabian kingdom of Ḥimyar in their titulature. Some inscriptions, almost all royal, are written in Greek. Those that can be dated were written before the end of the fourth century. They go back to the reign of ʿĒzānā (polytheist or Christian) or of previous kings. Greek thus stops being used in monumental inscriptions relatively early, while it continues being preferred to Ge'ez on coin legends, especially for gold and silver issues (see later).

To reconstruct the history of the kingdom of Aksūm, we also have at our disposal some external sources in Greek, Latin, and Syriac, which throw light on the conversion of the kingdom to Christianity in the reigns of Constantine I (306–337) and Constantius II (337–361) (the *Ecclesiastical History* of Rufinus and the *Apology to Constantius* by Athanasius of Alexandria) or on its expansion in Arabia in the sixth century (sources mentioned in the section on Ḥimyar). Some observation on the fauna and flora, on the resources and trade, and on the royal palace (the "royal dwelling with the four towers") can be found in accounts written by two Byzantines, a traveler and an ambassador, who both visited Aksūm in the sixth century, Kosmas Indikopleustēs (*Christian Topography* 2.54–64; 6.1; 11.1 and 7) and Nonnosos (Photios, *Bibliotheca* 3). We also possess the description of the very exotic reception that the king of Ethiopia (Kālēb, called "Elesboas") offered for Ioulianos, an ambassador of Justinian, in the months preceding September 531 (John Malalas, 18.56). We learn, among other things, that Kālēb does not speak Greek, since he needs an interpreter. One last source on the kingdom of Aksūm is the Ethiopian learned tradition, which has compiled lists of kings and myths on the foundation of the kingdom (going back to Solomon and the Queen of Saba') and on its conversion to Christianity (*Kəbra nagast*; Conti Rossini 1909). Saints' lives (summarized in the Synaxarium) contain some additional information.

I.C Important Resources Derived from Long-Distance Trade

Aksūm and ancient Arabia had in common the fact that they both benefited greatly from the trade of rare and costly products, sold on the markets of the Near East and the Eastern Mediterranean. However, if we have some indication of the goods exchanged, we know next to nothing about their transport, itineraries, markets, and financial techniques. This is because direct sources are sparse.

During the entire first millennium before the Christian era, caravan trade between Yemen and the Near East saw considerable development, echoes of which can be found among the Assyrians, in the Bible, and in classical literature (Avanzini 1997). The goods transported are the aromatic resins produced in South Arabia (incense and myrrh), tortoise shells and various dyeing and aromatic products of Suquṭra, probably African animals and products (ivory, gold, precious wood, monkeys, etc.), and perhaps others originating from India and the Far East.

As for the markets from which the caravans leave, the only relatively safe hypothesis concerns incense. This market is to be found in Ḥaḍramawt, since the principal production regions (Ẓafār in Oman, eastern Ḥaḍramawt, and the island of Suquṭra) all belong to that kingdom. Pliny (*Nat. Hist.* 12.32) actually locates it at "Sabota," in other words, Shabwat.

We know nothing of the organization of the caravans and the financial arrangements. The itineraries, which have hardly left any archaeological traces, are reconstructed from commonsense arguments (Potts 1988). It is assumed that they took the same routes as the Muslim pilgrimage, that they tried to avoid natural obstacles, and that they took into account the water and fodder resources. They also allowed for security conditions (Maraqten 1996), the tax burden, and political conditions in general—but such parameters almost entirely escape us. As for the destination markets, from which the goods are redistributed, they were probably the Middle Euphrates in the Assyrian period, Gaza in the Persian period, and Petra during Hellenistic times (Liverani 1992).

A unique description of this caravan trade can be found in the *Natural History* (esp. 6.32 and 12.20–48) of Pliny, who died in 79 C.E. during the eruption of Vesuvius. South Arabian inscriptions have only about a dozen allusions to it, while those of Ethiopia, of the great oases of the Ḥijāz, and of Nabatene have none at all.

After the conquest of Egypt by Rome in 30 B.C.E., caravan trade witnessed strong competition from the many Roman ships that, from that time forward, sailed down the Red Sea bound for India. Here we have a direct source that is exceptionally precise: the *Periplus Maris Erythraei* (Casson 1989), a small aide-mémoire written in Greek in Alexandria during the first century C.E. This maritime route seems to have been very active for more than two centuries.

The last centuries of antiquity are the most obscure. References to caravans or ships become rare and allusive. A single source contains relatively precise factual data, the *Christian Topography* of the Alexandrian traveler Kosmas Indikopleustēs, which contains many personal observations. Those concern, among other questions, the maritime trade between the Mediterranean and Ceylon/Sri Lanka and relations between the Sasou and the Aksūmites, who exchange gold for beef, salt, or iron (2.51–53; 11.13–24) (Mango 1996). As far as one can judge, the sea remained the most commonly used commercial route. The trans-Arabian caravan trade saw only a modest revival from the fifth century onward, between Yemen and the Sāsānian lower Euphrates.

To assess the prosperity of ancient Aksūm and Arabia and the importance of their trade, one can also rely on monetary issues. However, it would be a mistake to mechanically link a successful and prosperous trade with coinage. Many trade powers in the ancient Near East only had mediocre coinage (Ḥaḍramawt, Nabatene, and Palmyra) or no coinage at all (Maʿīn). In general, coins are issued not for the needs of trade but to serve financial and political needs: to finance large expenses (most often military), to levy taxes by giving the coinage a higher value than that of the metal it contains, or else to assert one's sovereignty.

Coinage appeared in southern Arabia in the fourth century B.C.E. and in Ethiopia some 600 years later, in the third century C.E. South Arabian coinage is characterized by very lightweight silver coins and small issues, whether in silver or in bronze. It declines in the third century C.E. and disappears toward the end of the century. It is noteworthy that the unified Ḥimyarite state no longer struck significant series. At most, one can attribute to it some issues of minuscule bronze coins (Munro-Hay 2003; Huth 2010; Huth and Alfen 2010).

When looking on the other coast of the Red Sea, at the kingdom of Aksūm, the contrast is striking. Coinage, which began around 270—that is, precisely at the time when it declined in Arabia—continued for more than 300 years. It used bronze, silver, but also gold, in large quantities. The captions of the gold coins and of the large majority of the silver ones are in Greek. The choice of Greek was not designed to facilitate the circulation of Aksūmite coinage in the Mediterranean world, where it remained unknown, but perhaps in the Red Sea and toward India. It also proclaimed that Aksūm was an exemplary ally of the Roman empire.

Monetary captions mention more than twenty kings, among whom five are polytheists and the others Christian. Only three or four of those kings are known from other sources, epigraphic or manuscript, Ethiopian or foreign: numismatics is thus an important documentary source for Aksūmite chronology.

A coin hoard found in the southern Yemen is particularly illuminating (Munro-Hay 1989). It is composed of 1,194 gold coins, 868 of which are Aksūmite and 326 Roman. The latest coins are the four dating from the reign of Kālēb (c. 500–540); the Byzantine ones were all struck before 450. It is probably a hoard that was buried during one of Kālēb's five expeditions to Arabia (Robin 2010d), probably one of the last because the four coins of Kālēb are worn, according to their editor.

The distribution of the Ethiopian coins by reign follows neither the coin quantities otherwise known nor the fame of the corresponding sovereigns. The obscure Ebana is represented by 525 coins. Kings Eōn, Nezeoōl, and Ousas are present with 156, 43, and 24 coins respectively. King ʿĒzānā, who reigned almost two centuries before the hoard was buried, is also present with 26 coins.

It is striking that coins of very different dates circulated together and that the only foreign coins were from Byzantium. Strangely, the hoard contains no Byzantine coins contemporary with Kālēb, which leads one to believe that during the period broadly from 450 to 530, Byzantine money flowed neither into Ethiopia nor into Yemen.

I.D Sedentary Populations and Nomads

Arabia is often considered to be the archetypal area of a very particular way of life, nomadism. It is true that the great majority of its territory is not conducive to agriculture. It is composed of arid mountains, rocky plateaus, and sand seas. In those inhospitable regions, the only mode of subsistence is stockbreeding, a practice of moving the animals from one zone of pasture to another, according to erratic rainfall.

Agriculture is practiced in many zones, however: the well-irrigated mountains of the southwest of the peninsula; the foothills of those mountains when the streaming waters reach them; the oases, especially numerous in the east and northeast of the peninsula; and, to a certain extent, the vast plateaus of central Arabia.

Further, agriculture is the only economic activity that is much mentioned in epigraphic texts. The authors of offerings in temples often express the wish that the divinity grant them a good harvest in fresh products and in cereals. They hope that the rains of the spring and the autumn will be plentiful and that they will be spared by the various natural disasters.

In the past, many scholars thought that the population of Arabia on the eve of Islam was majority nomadic. Historical research in the last decades, based on renewed examination of Arab-Muslim sources and also on the study of archaeological sites and of the thousands of inscriptions discovered in Yemen and the Ḥijāz, have led us to revise that opinion. It is, of course, difficult to give numbers, or even estimates. It seems very plausible, however, that the sedentary population largely exceeded that of pastoralists. This is certainly true for the twentieth century, before the intrusion of modernity. It is even more plausible for antiquity, when the surface of cultivable land was higher than in the twentieth century. At all times, it was not the nomads who dominated, but the peasants and the merchants. The error came mainly from the identification of "nomads" with "tribes." However, while it is true that nomads have a tribal and segmented organization, this is also the case for a considerable portion of the sedentary populations of Yemen and of inner Arabia.

The traditional presentation of the relations between sedentary and nomadic populations also needs revising. The nomad is seen as the natural enemy of the farmer: well versed in war, taking refuge in the desert to escape retaliation, mobile and elusive, he represented a permanent threat that was diverted, thanks to the payment of a heavy tribute. Observation of contemporary societies invites us to change this model. In a given territory, agriculture is not practiced exclusively by one group of inhabitants and stockbreeding by another: all, or almost all, members of the group practice both activities to varying degrees. A complete range going from the pure nomad to the pure farmer can be found, with all possible combinations in between. Pastoralists are not averse to sowing some fields in the arid zones when the rainfall allows it; as for peasants, rare are those who do not breed some animals. Thus, there is not a group of sedentary people opposed to the nomads, but many groups practicing agriculture and stockbreeding in different proportions. Those groups, economically interdependent, can belong to a single tribe or include members of different tribes. These observations cannot be extended to Ethiopia, however; while it also had a considerable sedentary population in the highlands, only a certain portion of the population was organized into tribes.

II. Arabia Dominated by Ḥimyar (Fourth and Fifth Centuries c.e.)

During the major part of its ancient history, Yemen had been divided among several rival kingdoms. That division ended in the first quarter of the third century c.e. The kingdom of Ḥimyar, having driven back an Aksūmite invasion (or "Abyssinian," if we adopt the most common term in local inscriptions), subjected the kingdom of Saba' (around 275) and then conquered Ḥaḍramawt (soon before 300). Those events took place under the reigns of Yāsirum Yuhan'im (c. 265–287) and his son Shammar Yuhar'ish (c. 287–311). They gave Ḥimyar a dominant position in Arabia for close to 250 years.

The unification of southern Arabia was above all political, with sovereigns who were now called "king of Saba', of dhu-Raydān (Ḥimyar), of Ḥaḍramawt and of the South" (*mlk S¹b' w-ḏ-Rydⁿ w-Ḥḍrmwt w-Ymnt*). It was also linguistic, since the only language used in the written documents was now Saba'ic. It soon became institutional, too, with the general adoption of the Ḥimyarite calendar and era, and especially with an important religious reform.

II.A Two Dynasties Favoring Judaism

Following the disappearance of Shammar Yuhar'ish, sometime after 310, the kingdom of Ḥimyar witnessed a period of instability. Three sovereigns without kinship links succeeded each other in less than fifteen years:

—Karib'īl Watār Yuhan'im (c. 311–314) (Ir 28; Ja 666; Ja 667)

The inscriptions of his reign mention a revolt in the capital, an epidemic, and an embassy sent to Aksūm.

—Yāsirum Yuhan'im II (c. 314–321) (Gl 1539; Ir 29; Ja 664; Ja 665; Capuzzi *AION* 1969; Pirenne, *Raydān*, 328 and pl. 6c)

He associated Tha'rān Ayfa' with the throne (Ja 664 and Gl 1539), and then his son Dhra''amar Ayman (Ir 29; Ja 665; Capuzzi *AION* 1969). During his reign, there was renewed war against Ḥaḍramawt: we do not know for sure if it was still incompletely conquered or if it was staging a revolt. The only chronological indication is given by two unpublished inscriptions dating from [31]4–[31]5 and [31]6–[31]7.

—Dhamar'alī Yuhabirr (c. 321–324?) (Ir 31; Ir 32; Schmidt-Ma'rib 28 + Ja 668; Garb Sab. Fragm. 5; Graf 5), finally, is the first sovereign of a new and remarkably stable dynasty.

II.A.a *The Dynasty Founded by Dhamar'alī Yuhabirr*

II.A.a.1 Dhamar'alī Yuhabirr (c. 321–324?): For contemporaries, the memorable event of the reign was probably the definitive submission of the eastern Ḥaḍramawt. For us, it is rather the stabilization of the regime. The confusion of the preceding decade was succeeded by a long period of stability, unique in the history of southern Arabia. From about 320 to 500, there were only two dynasties. Two major developments can be observed: first, the hereditary transmission of the throne became systematic; second, the king surrounded himself with co-regents, whose number tended to rise.

The founder of the dynasty seems to have had a rather short reign. He reigned alone first (Ir 31 and 32) and then with a co-regent, his son and successor

Tha'rān Yuhan'im (Schmidt-Ma'rib 28 + Ja 668). The Islamic tradition has retained only the name of this sovereign, strangely distorted: Yuhbir dhū 'l-Mar'alī b. Yankuf b. 'Abd Shams (al-Hamdānī, *Iklīl* 2.97/3–5; *Mushtabih*, 438 and 462). The poem devoted to great men attributed to As'ad Tubba' gives the name as Yuhbir dhū 'l-Mar'alīn (*Iklīl* 2.390/1–2; see also 97/7, a quotation of the second verse).

II.A.a.2 Tha'rān Yuhan'im (c. 324–375): In 324–325, Tha'rān Yuhan'im, son of Dhamar'alī, was already reigning. The authors of the inscription Maṣna'at Māriya 1 invoke him as if he were the only sovereign, but it is possible that he was only his father's co-regent.

Tha'rān Yuhan'im's reign is known from ten inscriptions (Maṣna'at Māriya 1, just cited; 'Abadān 1; YM 1950; Ja 669, 670 and 671 + 788; DhM 201; DhM 204; MQ-Minkath 1; Khaldūn-Balās 1, still unpublished), of which he is never the author. One should add to this list the texts already mentioned, where Tha'rān is still a king of second rank, next to his father.

One inscription throws particular light on Ḥimyar's military interventions in inner Arabia: 'Abadān 1 (dated 360), which commemorates the military exploits and achievements of an important family of the eastern Yemen over three generations. The king is mentioned twice, without titulature (ll. 5 and 16), just like the kings Tha'rān Ayfa' (possibly identified with Yāsirum Yuhan'im's coregent) and Dhamar'alī Ayfa' (his brother or his son, it would seem).

A second inscription (YM 1950) reveals that certain high-ranking individuals already publicly expressed their adhesion to monotheism. That text can be situated toward the end of the reign, since the king is invoked with one or more sons, whose names have disappeared.

We also know that king Tha'rān Yuhan'im associated several of his sons with the throne:

—Hypothetically, Malkīriyām (if the king Tha'rān of Veerman 2 = BaynM 1 is identical to Tha'rān Yuhan'im)
—Malkīkarib Yuha'min (Ja 669, 670 and 671 + 788; Khaldūn-Balās 1; maybe YM 1950)
—Malkīkarib Yuha'min and Dhamar'alī Yuhabirr (DhM 204; probably MQ-Minkath 1)

The reign of Tha'rān seems to have been exceptionally long, on the order of fifty to fifty-five years, even if the end of the reign is not precisely dated. His son and successor, Malkīkarib Yuha'min, is not yet mentioned in the 'Abadān 1 inscription (composed in 360 C.E.). He came to the throne apparently at an advanced age, since he immediately associated one of his sons (probably Abīkarib As'ad; Ja 856 = Fa 60) and then two of them (Abīkarib As'ad and Dhara''amar Ayman; Garb Bayt al-Ashwal 2 and *RES* 3383, texts dated January 384). Provisionally, then, we can propose about 375 for the end of the reign of Tha'rān Yuhan'im.

For Yemeni traditionist al-Hamdānī, Tha'rān Yuhan'im was the son of the founder of the Ḥimyarite dynasty, the famous al-Rā'ish: "al-Rā'ish son of Ilī-Shadad begat Abraha dhū 'l-Manār and Yun'im Tārān Aklab (with a *fatḥ* on the *alif* and the *lām*; name, title, and qualifier), as if he said Tārān Aklab al-Mun'im—that is Yun'im the Elder—and Shuraḥbīl, three males, sons of al-Ḥārith al-Rā'ish" (al-Hamdānī, *Iklīl* 2.52/5; *Mushtabih*, 181). In the poem devoted to the great men attributed to As'ad Tubba', his name becomes Yun'im Tārān, "the first of the kings" (*ra's al-mulūk: Iklīl* 2.389/12). In a list of fantasy sovereigns, Ibn Ḥabīb also mentions him in the form of Bārān Yuhan'im (*al-Muḥabbar*, 366/4). Al-Hamdānī knows two other Tārān Yun'im, one in the genealogy of Baynūn (Tārān Yun'im b. Nawf Yuhashqir b. Sharāḥīl Nufayl, *Iklīl* 2.99/9) and the other in that of dhū Ru'ayn (dhū Rumāniḥ, who is Ta'rān Yun'im al-Abādh, b. al-Ghawth b. Lahī'a Yun'im b. Ya'fur Yankuf b. Fahd Tārān, *Iklīl* 2.351/14). Note that this Ru'aynid is the father of a Malkīkarib Yuhāmin (Malkīkarib Yuhāmin b. Tārān Yun'im, *Iklīl* 2.351/15), like the historical king.

II.A.a.3 Malkīkarib Yuha'min (c. 375–400): In the reign of Malkīkarib Yuha'min (Gajda 2009, 43–46), a political and diplomatic reorientation was decided: Ḥimyar rejected polytheism and adhered officially to a consensual form of monotheism. The inscriptions written by private individuals reveal, however, that this neutrality was only a facade. In fact, the dynasty offered its support to Judaism. Such a choice necessarily implied distancing themselves to some extent from Byzantium, which forty years earlier had sent an embassy headed by Theophilus the Indian to convert the Ḥimyarites to Christianity, or, as Philostorgius puts it (*Ecclesiastical History* 3.4–6), "to piety" (Rodinson 2001, 228–236).

The new religious orientation probably provoked great upheavals. Three centuries later, the Islamic tradition still remembers the event. However, even though it does mention the introduction of Judaism in Yemen, it does not attribute it to Malkīkarib Yuha'min, but to his son and co-regent Abīkarib As'ad. We can deduce from this that the latter's role was more decisive and more memorable; after all, did Abīkarib As'ad not become the hero of a Yemenite saga (Robin 2004b)?

King Malkīkarib Yuha'min was in power for a relatively long period, around twenty to thirty years. First, he reigned with only one son, whose name has disappeared (Ja 856 = Fa 60), probably Abīkarib As'ad since his name always comes first in the list of his co-regents. That inscription is particularly significant. It commemorates the construction of a *mikrāb* named Barīk in Marib, the ancient capital of the kingdom of Saba'. The name of the *mikrāb*, Barīk, comes from Aramaic, the principal language of Near Eastern Judaism. That *mikrāb* was built in Marib to replace the polytheist temple of the great god Almaqah, which the king and his son had just closed down. As for the term *mikrāb* itself, it appears in this text for the first time and is attested only in Ḥimyarite inscriptions of the Jewish period. Thus it very probably designates a public space intended for the practice of the Jewish religion and teaching, namely, a synagogue.

Later, Malkīkarib Yuha'min associated two of his sons to the throne, Abīkarib As'ad and Dhara''amar Ayman (*RES* 3383 and Garb Bayt al-Ashwal 2, dated January 384). That co-regency is certainly later than the previous one, because these two sons continue to reign together after the disappearance of Malkīkarib.

Of Malkīkarib (Yuha'min), traditionists, including al-Hamdānī, know nothing, except that he is the father of Abīkarib As'ad. According to al-Hamdānī, he reigned thirty-five years (al-Hamdānī, *Qaṣīdat al-Dāmigha*, 534/18–19; mistakenly Kalīkarib instead of Malkīkarib).

II.A.a.4 Abīkarib As'ad (c. 400–445): Like his father, Abīkarib As'ad never reigned alone (Gajda 2009, 47–58). He is always mentioned as co-regent with a brother and several sons:

—Abīkarib As'ad, his brother Dhara''amar Ayman, and his sons Ḥaśśān Yu'min ["Yu'min" is the Arabic pronunciation of Sabaic "Yuha'min"], Ma'dīkarib Yun'im ["Yun'im" is the Arabic pronunciation of Sabaic "Yuhan'im"], and Ḥugr Ayfa' (Garb Minkath 1; see also the fragmentary texts Ja 520 and Garb Framm. 7).

—Abīkarib As'ad and his sons Ḥaśśān Yuha'min, Ma'dīkarib Yuhan'im, Marthad'ilān Yaz'an, and Shuriḥbi'īl Ya'fur. This co-regency is attested by a only single text, Ry 534 + MAFY-Rayda 1, dated August 433.

—Abīkarib As'ad and his son Ḥaśśān Yuha'min (Ry 509, undated royal text, engraved in Ma'sal al-Jumḥ, in the heart of the Najd, in central Arabia, 200 kilometers to the west of modern al-Riyāḍ). This joint reign of Abīkarib and Ḥaśśān comes at the extreme end of Abīkarib's political career. This is based on the fact that the royal titulature appears for the first time presented in its longest form and that the modifications introduced are then found in the following reigns.

Abīkarib and Ḥaśśān added the following to their titulature: "and of the Arabs of the Highlands (Ṭawd, apparently the Ḥimyarite name of the Najd) and of the Coast (Tihāmat, the name of the coastal regions of western Arabia)" (*''rb Ṭwd w-Thmt*), a formula that later became "and of their Arabs in the Highlands and on the Coast" (*w-''rb-hmw Ṭwd*^{m} *w-Thmt*).

It should also be noted that the three other co-regents of Ry 534 + MAFY-Rayda 1 (Ma'dīkarib Yuhan'im, Marthad'ilān Yaz'an, and Shuriḥbi'īl Ya'fur) are not mentioned in this text. This silence cannot be interpreted with certainty. One hypothesis is that Ḥaśśān Yuha'min, having replaced his brothers, was now the only co-regent; this is not very likely because after the death of Abīkarib, Ḥaśśān Yuha'min seems to have reigned for some time in co-regency with his brother Shuriḥbi'īl Ya'fur. According to another hypothesis, the text mentions only those sovereigns who had really ordered its engraving, present at the heart of central Arabia, but this is also quite improbable because, when the expedition commemorated by Ry 509 took place, king Abīkarib As'ad had been on the throne for more than fifty years, and one does not imagine an old man taking part in such an expedition. We must therefore consider that Ry 509 names only the sovereign of the highest rank (probably absent) and the co-regent who had authority on central Arabia.

In the Islamic tradition, Abīkarib As'ad, under the names of Tubba', As'ad Tubba' or Abū Karib As'ad the Perfect (al-Kāmil), is the hero of a legendary cycle whose major elements are fantasy conquests, the recognition of the sanctity of the Meccan shrine, and the introduction of Judaism in Yemen. But he is also a tragic character. Some say he died, having been assassinated by his people (*Akhbār 'Ubayd*, 493–494), and that his son and successor Ḥassān was killed by another of his sons. The difficulty of reconciling those data led the Yemenite traditionist al-Hamdānī to split the character into two and to attribute to the second one the introduction of Judaism to Yemen and the violent death (*Iklīl* 8 ed. Fāris, 72/4–6; Nashwān, *Mulūk Ḥimyar*, 138/1–2). Abū Karib is also called "Tibān," "Tubān," or dhū Tabbān (al-Hamdānī, *Qaṣīda al-Dāmigha*, 531, verse 546). The origin and meaning of this surname are unknown. In the commentary of the *Qaṣīda al-Dāmigha*, al-Hamdānī adds: "Tubba' the intermediate [b.] Kalīkarib, who is As'ad Abū Karib, whose *kunya* is Abū Ḥassān, that is dhū Tabbān, 680 years, while it is said: 326 years. Then reigned his son Ḥassān, who led an expedition against Ṭasm and Jadīs" . . . (534/19–535/1).

II.A.a.5 A reign of Ḥaśśān Yuha'min (c. 445–450?): Ḥaśśān Yuha'min seems to have succeeded his father Abīkarib As'ad and reigned for some time, in co-regency with his brother Shuriḥbi'īl Ya'fur. A fragmentary inscription has as its authors "[X X] and his brother Shuriḥbi'īl Ya'[fur, kings of Saba]', dhu-Raydān etc." (Garb Framm. 3). The most likely restitution for the missing name, based on the length of the lacuna and on the obvious hierarchy of Abīkarib As'ad's co-regents, is Ḥaśśān Yuha'min. Another fragment, with even more lacunae, probably had the same authors: "[Ḥaśśān Yuha'min] and his [brother] Shuriḥbi'īl Ya'f[ur, kings of Saba', dhu-Raydān, Ḥaḍramawt, the South and their Arabs in] the Highland and on the Coast" (*RES* 4105).

During the reign of his father, Abīkarib As'ad, Ḥaśśān Yuha'min had a de facto preeminent position that designated him as the natural successor. He was the coregent of the young generation and was always mentioned first. He was the one who carried out the policy of expansion toward central Arabia. The length of his reign is unknown but was probably quite short: one could suggest a length of about five years, from 445 to 450.

The Arab Muslim traditionists give Ḥaśśān Yuha'min, called Ḥassān, a memorable role. His name is associated with wars in central Arabia, more precisely in the Yamāma, against the tribes of Ṭasm and Jadīs (Ṭabarī, *Ta'rīkh al-rusul*, 1.880–881, 914–915; *The History of al-Ṭabarī*, 5.121–124, 183–184, etc.). He is mentioned as one of the founders of the "kingdom of Kinda" in central Arabia, in competition with Tubba' (a frequent surname of Abīkarib As'ad) or with Tubba' b. Karib (Olinder 1927, 38–39). Finally, it is reported that he was assassinated by his brother 'Amr (see later).

II.A.a.6 Shuriḥbi'īl Ya'fur (c. 450–465): The real successor of Abīkarib As'ad was not his son Ḥaśśān Yuha'min, but another son, already mentioned, Shuriḥbi'īl Ya'fur (Gajda 2009, 58–63).

Four inscriptions date from his reign. Two have the king as their author. The first (*CIH* 540), dated January 456, relates in detail the restoration work on the Marib dam, which lasted for more than a year. The second one (ẒM 1, dated December 462) commemorates the construction of a palace called *Hrgb* in Ẓafār; it refers in passing to the repair of the Marib dam (ll. 10–12), which the king clearly considered as one of his glorious deeds, since the event was already more than six years old. Two other texts, Dostal 1 and the fragment *CIH* 45 + 44, celebrate the construction of palaces by private individuals. The first of these dates from May 456.

Shuriḥbi'īl Ya'fur was the last descendant of Dhamar'alī Yuhabirr to occupy the throne. He was the only sovereign of the dynasty whose name was not remembered by the Islamic traditionists, unless he should be identified with the Ya'fur of some imaginary accounts. Al-Ṭabarī (*Ta'rīkh al-rusul*, 1.889–890; *The History of al-Ṭabarī*, 5.140–143, etc.), for example, relates that the Ḥujrid sovereign al-Ḥārith b. 'Amr, after having obtained the control of the west bank of the Lower Euphrates from the Sāsānid sovereign Qubādh (488–496 and 499–531), wrote to Tubba' to incite him to go to war against Persia. Tubba' sent his nephew Shammar dhū 'l-Janāḥ to make war against Qubādh, who was beaten and killed, while his son Ḥassān was invading Sogdia and another nephew, Ya'fur, was taking Constantinople, before being crushed outside the city. The chronological framework of that story is the beginning of the sixth century (as indicated by the reference to al-Ḥārith and Qubādh), but the mention of Tubba' and his son Ḥassān brings us backward to the time of king Abīkarib. It is thus impossible to know whether the Ya'fur of this fable is Shuriḥbi'īl Ya'fur or Ma'dīkarib Ya'fur (519–522).

Furthermore, it might be possible to identify Shuriḥbi'īl Ya'fur with the fateful 'Amr of tradition. Ḥassān son of Abū Karib had allegedly launched faraway expeditions until the day when, in 'Irāq, the Ḥimyarite army refused to follow him, inciting 'Amr, his brother, to seize power. 'Amr responded positively and killed Ḥassān, but punishment came immediately in the form of permanent insomnia (*Ta'rīkh al-rusul*, 1.914–917; *The History of al-Ṭabarī*, 5.140–143, 183–188).

The framework of this account may have preserved a historical fact, namely, the assassination of Hassān by his brother and successor. In favor of this assumption, one should remember that later traditions are exceptionally well informed on the reign of Abīkarib and on his dynasty in general. Moreover, the extinction of the dynasty after Shuriḥbi'īl Ya'fur signaled a political crisis.

II.A.b *The Dynasty of Shuriḥbi'īl Yakkuf*

II.A.b.1 Shuriḥbi'īl Yakkuf (c. 468–480): The successor of Shuriḥbi'īl Ya'fur, whose name was Shuriḥbi'īl Yakkuf (Gajda 2009, 65–69), never gives his patronymic, which leads us to think that he inaugurated a new dynasty. He is known from seven texts, four of which are dated.

It seems that Shuriḥbi'īl Yakkuf first reigned alone, then with three co-regents, and finally with only two:

—Shuriḥbi'īl Yakkuf alone: Ẓ̣M 2000 (April 470), *RES* 4298 (not dated)
—Shuriḥbi'īl Yakkuf, in co-regency with Abīshimr Nawf, Laḥay'at Yanūf, and Ma'dīkarib Yun'im: *RES* 4919 + *CIH* 537 = L 121 (August 472); *RES* 4969 = Ja 876 (not dated)
—Shuriḥbi'īl Yakkuf, in co-regency with his sons Abīshimr Nawf and Laḥay'at Yanūf: Ma'sal 3 (474–475); perhaps the fragment *CIH* 644 (February [47]5).

King Shuriḥbi'īl Yakkuf is also mentioned as the persecutor king in a Ge'ez hagiographical text, the *Martyrdom of Azqīr* (Conti Rossini 1910; Beeston 1985). His name is slightly distorted: "Sarābhīl/Sarābhēl Dānkəf king of Ḥamēr" (Conti Rossini 1910, 729/6) or "king Sarābḥēl" (Conti Rossini 1910, 731/2).

The opinion according to which this king was Jewish (defended in particular by Jacques Ryckmans 1964, 436, and more recently by Zeev Rubin) seems all the more plausible since the authors of a recently discovered inscription in the capital declare themselves explicitly to be Jews (Ẓ̣M 2000).

Shuriḥbi'īl Yakkuf did not leave a lasting memory in Islamic traditions. Only the Yemenite al-Hamdānī knows a character of that name among the descendants of Baynūn: Sharaḥbīl Yankuf b. Nawf Yuhashqir b. Sharāḥīl Nufayl (*Iklīl* 2.99/9). It is remarkable that this Sharaḥbīl Yankuf had a son called Abū Shimr (*Mushtabih*, 144), just like the king (Abīshimr in Ma'sal 3), and a brother bearing a royal name, Tārān Yun'im (see previously "Tha'rān Yuhan'im").

Al-Hamdānī also knows two "Sharaḥbīl son of Yankuf"—'Abd Shams dhū Yahar b. Shuraḥbīl b. Yankuf b. 'Abd Shams (*Mushtabih*, 35) and Ma'dī Karib b. Shuraḥbīl b. Yankuf (*Mushtabih*, 106)—whose names could be a distortion of Shuriḥbi'īl Yakkuf.

II.A.b.2 Marthad'īlān Yun'im (c. 480–485?): The successor of Shuraḥbīl Yankuf was probably Marthad'īlān Yun'im (Gajda 2009, 69–71). The restitution of two very fragmentary texts (*CIH* 620 et YM 1200) suggests he is the son of Laḥay'at Yanūf and the grandson of Shuriḥbi'īl Yakkuf. Inscription YM 1200 commemorates the construction of a *mikrāb*, that is, a synagogue, by the king. It thus confirms the engagement of this dynasty in favor of Judaism. The dates and the length of this reign are very uncertain. After Marthad'īlān Yun'im, it seems that Ḥimyar witnessed a period of disorder of about fifteen years, as not a single inscription of the period mentions a sovereign.

II.B The Choice of Judaism

After the annexation of Saba' (around 275) and the conquest of Ḥaḍramawt (shortly before 300), the sovereigns of Ḥimyar undertook the unification of their vast kingdom. They imposed the use of Saba'ic—the official language—in Ḥaḍramawt. The Ḥimyarite dating system was generally adopted within a couple of generations. Finally, in the religious domain, the kings innovated radically: instead of favoring one of the existing cults, they made the choice to reject polytheism and give their support to Judaism (Robin 2003; 2004b). This policy became official around 380. Before that date, one guesses that the country was divided: the kings abstained from putting up inscriptions; as for private individuals, some continued to invoke polytheist deities, others refrained from doing so, and some expressed their support for monotheism publicly.

The rejection of polytheism as dictated by the kings was radical and definitive. The last traces of the old religion—one inscription commemorating a construction with a polytheistic invocation (Khaldūn-'Albaj 1) and another one mentioning a temple of the god Ta'lab (MAFY-Banū Zubayr 2)—date from just after 380 (the first from the reign of Dhara''amar Ayman and the second from the year 402–403). In all of Yemen, none of the some 120 other inscriptions postdating 380 (Robin 2009b) is explicitly pagan. Of course, the exclusion of polytheism from the public sphere does not mean it disappeared; it is very probable that the pagan cults survived discreetly, in all sorts of places, except in ruling circles.

The last active temples were abandoned around that time. In the Great Temple of Ma'rib, no inscription is dedicated after about 375. This is especially significant because the number of inscriptions found in that temple, all of which date from the first four centuries of the Christian era, is close to 800. A temple of Ta'lab is probably still mentioned in 402–403, but it must be noted that this is in a clumsy inscription from a small village to the north of Ṣan'ā': the closure of the rural temples was thus spread over several decades. One should also note that the rejection of polytheism is not the result of an internal evolution that progressively transformed a pagan divinity into a supreme and unique god. There was a break, as can be seen by the abandonment of the old terminology and the sudden invasion of terms of Aramaic or Hebrew origin, such as *amen*, *'ālam* (world), *bāraka* (bless), *haymanōt* (guarantee), *kanīsat* (meeting hall), *shalōm*, *ṣalāt* (prayer), *zakāt* (grace), and *Yisra'īl* (Israël). Some Hebrew personal names also appear: Isaac (*Yṣḥq*), Juda (*Yhwd'*), Joseph (*Ywsᶦf*), and possibly Benjamin (*[Bny]mn*) (Beeston 1994; Robin 2000; 2004b).

From 380–400 onward until 525–530, the only religion attested in the inscriptions of Ḥimyar was Judaism. Thirteen documents are very probably Jewish. Among the eleven that are written in the Saba'ic script and language (Robin 2003; 2004b):

—Three invoke the "people of Israel" (Garb Bayt al-Ashwal 1/3, ẒM 2000/8 and Garb Framm. 7).

—Another begins with the prayer: "May the name of Raḥmānān who is in heaven, Israël and their god, the Lord of the Jews, who helped his servant, bless and be blessed" (*CIH* 543 = ẒM 772 A + B).
—The fifth is a decree instituting a cemetery reserved for Jews (Ḥaṣī 1).
—Three name as their author a general of king Joseph (in Saba'ic *Ys^{1}f* [or *Yws^{1}f*] *'s^{1}'r Yṯ'r*); a king who bore a name that was very probably Jewish (Ry 508, Ja 1028, and Ry 507). These inscriptions mention anti-Christian measures, the most explicit being the destruction of churches. One calls God *''lh^{n}* (determined plural of *'lh*, "god"), a calque of the Hebrew Elohim (Ry 508/10); another ends with an invocation to the "Lord of the Jews" (Ja 1028/12).
—One inscription ends with the exclamation "Lord of the Jews" (Ry 515/5).
—A fragment of an inscription has as its author a person whose name, *Yṣḥq*, is certainly Jewish (Robin 2004b).
—A seal with two names depicts a menorah (Robin 2004b).

To those eleven documents in Saba'ic should be added two in Hebrew or Judeo-Aramaic:

—The Hebrew inscription from Bayt Ḥāḍir, which reproduces part of the list of the twenty-four priestly classes given by the book of Chronicles (1 Chronicles 24:7–18) (DJE 23).
—A seal representing a sort of tabernacle on legs in a niche (probably the Ark where the rolls of the Torah are kept), with the Judeo-Aramaic inscription "Isaac son of Ḥanīnah" (*Yṣḥq br Ḥnynh*), was recently discovered by Paul Yule in Ẓafār (Yule 2005, 28 fig. 10).

Finally, ten texts are plausibly considered to be Jewish because they contain the liturgical exclamations *s^{1}lwm* (*shalôm*) and *'mn* (*amen*). *Shalom* appears in Ir 71 (second monogram from the right), Robin-Najr 1/3, Ry 534 + Rayda 1/5 and the epitaph of Leah (in Saba'ic and in Aramaic). The texts containing *amen* are: Garb NIS 4/8, Gl 1194/11, Müller-Tan'im, Ry 403/6, Ry 513/5 et ẒM 5 + 8 + 10 (without repeating Ir 71/6 and the epitaph of Leah, already cited for *shalôm*; Garb Bayt al-Ashwal 1 and ẒM 2000/11 already cited for mentioning the "people of Israël").

All those documents are undated. Those that can be dated predate the fall of king Joseph (between 525 and 530). Conversely, until that date, no epigraphic text conveys any form of support for Christianity or even simple proximity with it. However, if Judaism seems to have enjoyed a privileged position, it did not have the status of an official religion: while the sovereigns were probably Jewish personally, their inscriptions never state this conviction, only a careful monotheism with no particular affiliation, which was probably the model of the *ḥanīf* of Islamic tradition (that is, the pre-Islamic Arabs who had made the choice of monotheism without subscribing to one of the great established faiths; see Rippin 1991; de Blois 2002). External sources confirm that Judaism was the dominant religion in the kingdom of Ḥimyar, at least at the beginning of the sixth century.

II.C The Conquest of Arabia Deserta

The unification of southern Arabia at the end of the third century considerably reinforced the power of the kings of Ḥimyar. It is not impossible that they benefited from the crisis of paganism to confiscate the treasures of great shrines, thus making available extra resources for themselves.

While in the third century the Sabaean armies did not venture beyond Qaryat al-Fāw (300 kilometers north-northeast of Najrān), in the fourth century, the Ḥimyarite armies were operating in the Ḥijāz, the Najd, and the Ḥasā'. In the following century, around 445, large territories of central and western Arabia were annexed, which translated into a new titulature: "king of Saba', of dhu-Raydān, of Ḥaḍramawt, and of the South, and of the Arabs of the Highlands and of the Coast," soon changed into ". . . and of their Arabs in the Highlands and on the Coast," as we have seen. In central Arabia, Ḥimyar imposed its domination over the tribal confederation of Ma'addum, Arabic Ma'add (as is recalled by three royal Ḥimyarite inscriptions engraved at Ma'sal al-Jumḥ, 200 kilometers to the west of al-Riyāḍ), while in western Arabia, it is the tribal confederation of Muḍar (to which Quraysh belonged) that submitted (Robin 2008a).

The consolidation of Ḥimyarite domination over inner Arabia was not contested by the Islamic tradition, but it is presented in such a way that it magnifies certain Arab princes from the tribes of Kinda and Salīḥ, who are raised to the dignity of kings of Ma'add and Muḍar. One can here observe the work of collection and rewriting of the past, probably carried out by the descendants of those kings, who had an obvious interest in celebrating the antiquity and the power of their lineage. The principal Kindite kings reigning over Ma'add were Ḥujr son of 'Amr "the Eater of the Bitter Herbs" (*ākil al-murār*), his son 'Amr, and his grandson al-Ḥārith (killed in 528); only one is known from epigraphy, "Ḥugr son of 'Amrum," who gave himself the title of "king of Kiddat," and not that of "king of Ma'add" (*Ḥgr bn 'mr^m mlk Kdt*, Gajda 1996).

It is not easy to trace the precise limit of the territories controlled by Ḥimyar. There is no doubt, however, that it was almost the totality of inner Arabia up to the vicinity of Lower 'Irāq and perhaps Palestine. Inscriptions mention:

—In central Arabia, the tribal confederation of Ma'addum; the toponyms Ma'sal Gumḥān (Arabic Ma'sal al-Jumḥ, 200 kilometers to the west of al-Riyāḍ), Ḥalibān (90 kilometers to the west-southwest of Ma'sal), and Khargān (Ar. al-Kharj, 280 kilometers to the east of Ma'sal and 80 kilometers to the south of al-Riyāḍ), as well as a whole series of sites in the same region: Gawwān (Ar. al-Jaww), Birkum (Ar. Birk), Sharafān (Ar. al-Sharaf), Nīrān (Ar. al-Nīr), Yamāmatān (Ar. al-Yamāma),

'Aramatum (Ar. al-'Arama), Abānum (Ar. Abān), Rumatān (Ar. al-Ruma) (for the identifications, see Robin 2008a), Turabān (Ar. Turabān).

— In eastern and northeastern Arabia, the tribes of 'Abdqaysān (Ar. 'Abd al-Qays), Iyādhum (Ar. Iyād), and Tanūkh; the toponym Hagarum (Ar. Hajar).

— In western Arabia, the tribal confederation of Muḍar; the tribes Nizārum and Ghassān; the toponyms Sigāh (Ar. Sijā) and Siyyān (Ar. al-Siyy, 100–200 kilometers to the east-northeast of Makka), and finally dhu-Murākh, whose location is uncertain.

These inscriptions clearly indicate that the Ḥimyarites intervened in all areas of inner Arabia, to the exception perhaps of the great oases of the southern Ḥijāz. This expansion of the Ḥimyarites probably happened to the detriment of the Naṣrid kings of al-Ḥīra, clients of the Sāsānids: in 328, in the inscription placed on his tomb, one of them, Imru' al-Qays, son of 'Amr, boasts of having conquered Ma'addū (Arabic Ma'add) and having launched raids all the way to the surroundings of Najrān, the "city of Shammar" (a king whose reign ended c. 312) (inscription of al-Namāra, L 205).

It is rather implausible, however, that the unification of Yemen and the conquest of inner Arabia were accomplished without some form of consent from the Sāsānid sovereigns, who were themselves established on the Arabian coast of the Arab-Persian Gulf (*EI* 2, s.v. Sāsānids). We know of an embassy sent by the king Shammar Yuhar'ish to the Persian sovereign, apparently between 300 and 312. Furthermore, a relief of the Sāsānid Narseh II (293–302) could represent the reception of a Ḥimyarite embassy (Overlaet 2009).

III. 'Ēzānā's Ethiopia Chooses Byzantium

III.A Conversion to Christianity

Early on, Ethiopia made a vote for Hellenism. In the first century C.E., the author of the *Periplus Maris Erythraei* already noted that the sovereign with authority over the port of Adulis was "a cultivated man who knew how to read and write Greek" (par. 5). In the centuries that followed, Greek became the language most commonly employed in coin captions and was one of the languages of royal inscriptions. In the cultural sphere, this vote for Hellenism probably translated into the policy of a narrow alliance with Rome, a fact that in turn explains the rapid conversion of the kingdom of Aksūm to Christianity toward the end of the reign of Constantine (306–337).

The account of that conversion is found in a single source, Rufinus of Aquileia (Tyrannius Rufinus), who shortly after spring 402 wrote an *Ecclesiastical*

History, containing both a translation into Latin of Eusebius of Caesarea's *Ecclesiastical History* and two books he composed dealing with "the time of Constantine after the persecution until the death of Theodosius" (Thélamon 1981). Rufinus' aim is to show that despite the ravages wrought by the invasion of Alaric's Goths in northern Italy, Christians should not despair because the economy of salvation is being fulfilled. It is especially visible outside the empire, where three barbarian peoples, the Indians (the name given to the Aksūmites by Rufinus), the Iberians (the Georgians of the Caucasus), and the Arabs of Queen Māwiya, have just converted.

Rufinus tells the story of a Tyrene philosopher who went to India proper, accompanied by two young children. During the return journey, their ship was attacked by barbarians who killed everyone aboard except the two children, who were offered to the king of the region. The elder, Frumentius, was made responsible for the accounts and archives, while the other one was made cupbearer. At the death of the king, whose son was still very young, the queen liberated the two young men but begged them to stay and administer the kingdom until her son came of age. Frumentius was thus associated with the ruler. He had the Christians among the Roman merchants sought out and ensured everything was done to facilitate their assemblies and prayers according to the Roman religious rite (*romano ritu*).

When the royal child came of age, Frumentius and his companion decide to return "to our world" (*ad orbem nostrum*). Frumentius goes to Alexandria, where he described to the Bishop Athanasius, who "had recently (*nuper*) received the episcopate," the progress of Christianity. He asks him to send a bishop. Athanasius, confident of his qualities, confers the episcopate upon him and sends him back "to the place where he came from." Back in "India," Frumentius worked the same miracles as the apostles, converted a huge number of barbarians, founded communities and churches, and inaugurated the episcopate. Rufinus claims to have this information from a direct account of the companion of Frumentius, who became a priest in Tyre. It is, in fact, possible that the two men did meet: Rufinus was in the Near East from 372–373 to 397; he was in Jerusalem, where he assumed the headship of a male monastery on the Mount of Olives from 380 onward. In his account of the story of Frumentius, Rufinus remains happily vague: he does not give the name of the country, of the port where they are captured, of the sovereigns, or of the capital. He offers a very confused localization of the country where Frumentius founded the episcopate, "India ulterior," which suggests actual India rather than the African coast of the Indian Ocean.

Fortunately, the chronological information he gives is clearer, even if it presents some difficulties. The country received the first seeds of the faith at the time of Constantine (d. 337), although it remains unclear what we are to understand by "first seeds": the first initiatives, the foundation of the first community, or the setting up of a new hierarchy? In fact, one should not place too much historical value on this statement: Rufinus mainly wants to magnify the reign of Constantine and to inscribe the conversion into a period of exceptional religious events.

Frumentius was ordained bishop when Athanasius had not been bishop of Alexandria for long. Athanasius occupied that see three times, from June 8, 328, to July 11, 335; from November 27, 337 (after the death of Constantine on May 22 that year), to April 16, 339; and from October 21, 346, to February 356. The most plausible date would be the period following October 346.

If we had nothing but the account of Rufinus, we could ask ourselves whether it really concerns Aksūm and whether the chronology is reliable. By extraordinary chance, an independent source confirms those two points. It is a letter of the emperor Constantius II (337–362) addressed to the sovereigns of Aksūm, most probably from 357. Athanasius, the bishop of Alexandria who consecrated Frumentius, was deposed from the see of Alexandria by Constantius II, who favored Arianism. He was replaced by George of Cappadocia on February 24, 357. Athanasius, while in flight, wrote his apology to Constantius to justify himself, and in it, he reproduces an imperial letter addressed to the "tyrants" of Aksūm, who are called Aizanas and Sazanas. The letter, which mentions the deposition of Athanasius, could not have been written much later than that deposition. It does not say explicitly that the two "tyrants" of Aksūm were Christian, but it implies it by expressing the concern of the emperor and asking them to attend to their doctrine.

Although there is no doubt that Christianity was solidly implanted at Aksūm around 357 and that it was protected and supported by the monarchs, does that imply that it is already the official religion? This seems plausible since, in any case, Christianity was the official religion of Aksūm before the end of the reign of 'Ēzānā (the Aizanas of the *Apology to Constantius II*), as can be seen from the inscriptions and the coins. The pagan inscriptions of king 'Ēzānā/Aizanas thus certainly predate 357.

The question remains whether this conversion (partial or total) was lasting. We have no precise information on whether an ecclesiastical hierarchy was maintained beyond the beginnings. At best, we have mention of two bishops, one at Adulis, called Moses, in an account of travel to "India" dating from the late fourth or early fifth century, and another one in the "land of the Abyssinians" around 478–486. The fact that the archaeologist Jean Doresse dated the churches in Ethiopia and Eritrea to the fifth century does not necessarily mean that Christianity was the official religion.

The question should be asked because John Malalas (18.15) and the works that copy him relate that a king of Aksūm converted to the Christian faith in the 520s because he had beaten a king of Arabia. In addition, the Ethiopian tradition tends to confuse fourth-century and sixth-century characters (respectively, Frumentius/'Ēzāna and Kālēb/Abraha), all venerated in the Ethiopian church under the names Abrəha and Aṣbəḥa (see later).

To this question, coins bring a sufficiently clear answer: all the coins that postdate 'Ēzāna's reign (seven kings between 'Ēzānā and Kālēb and another seven after Kālēb) bear Christian symbols. If we add to this that no polytheistic document has been discovered that postdates ʿĒzānā, the conversion of Ethiopia appears to have been indeed definitive. Of course, this conversion initially touched only the elites, principally those of the capital. It is quite plausible that polytheism kept many supporters among the population for a long time.

III.B The Reign of ʿĒzānā

King ʿĒzāna/Aizanas, who made Christianity the official religion of Aksūm, is the sovereign about whom we possess the most plentiful epigraphic documentation. He is the author of seven inscriptions in Ge'ez (*RIÉth* 185/I–II, 185 bis/I–II, 188, 189, 190, plus two where the name is reconstructed, *RIÉth* 186 and 187) and of three in Greek (*RIÉth* 270, 270bis, 271, where he is called Aeizanas/Azanas). Those inscriptions allow us to recognize three successive phases in his reign:

1. ʿĒzānā begins his reign while he is still a polytheist. He proclaims himself son of the pagan god Maḥrəm (Greek Arēs); his inscriptions, which are in Greek (*RIÉth* 270 and 270bis), in consonantal Ge'ez (*RIÉth* 185-II and 185bis-II), and in Ge'ez in the Sabaean fashion (*RIÉth* 185-I, 185bis-I), commemorate a campaign against the rebellious Bedja (*Bg*, Greek *Bougaeitai*).
2. ʿEzana, while still a polytheist, then mentions in the titulature of an inscription, using for the first time the Ge'ez syllabary (*RIÉth* 188), not only his divine ascendancy ("son of Maḥrəm") but also the name of his father (Ellē ʿAmīdā) and that of his clan. The titulature, of an intermediate type between the one that preceded it and the one that followed it, and the use of a new script lead us to consider that *RIÉth* 188 postdates *RIÉth* 185, 185bis, and 270.
3. ʿEzana, with the same patronymic and the same clan name, finally adopts monotheism, which is mentioned in neutral terms in an inscription known in two versions, one in syllabic Ge'ez (*RIÉth* 189) and the other in Ge'ez in the Sabaean fashion (*RIÉth* 190). On the same stone as *RIÉth* 190, the Greek version of this text uses explicitly Christian and Trinitarian wording (*RIÉth* 271). Very logically, divine ascendancy disappears from the titles. These inscriptions commemorate a campaign against the Nubians (*Nobā, Nbm, Nb*; Greek *Nōba*).

As king ʿĒzānā, in at least one inscription, presents himself as a Christian, he can be identified with the "tyrant" of Aksūm mentioned in the *Apology to Constantius II*. One more detail confirms it. Constantius addresses two tyrants, Aizanas and Sazanas. In fact, ʿĒzānā's polytheistic inscriptions mention this brother (*Śʿzn, Śʿznh; S²ʿḏnm, S²ʿznh; Saiazana, Sazanan*), who was then a simple army commander.

King ʿĒzānā's titulature and the account of military operations are the only means we have to assess the extent of the kingdom of Aksūm. In Africa, ʿĒzānā reigned over Aksūm, Ḥabashat (*Ḥbśt, Ḥbštm*; Greek *Aithiopōn*), Ṣəyāmō (*Ṣym, Ṣymm*; Greek *Tiamō*), the Bedja (Bəgā, *Bg, Bgm*; Greek *Bougaeitai*), and the Koushites (Kāsū, *Ks, Ksm, Kswm*; Greek *Kasou*). Although we cannot precisely locate any of those peoples, it is certain that the Koushites (Kāsū) lived toward the Upper Nile Valley and that the Bedja (Bəgā) lived between Ethiopia and Egypt.

A lacunar Greek inscription discovered in Meroe (*RIÉth* 286) has as its author a "[king of the Axō]mites and the Homērit[es]." As the text also mentions the god Arēs, many believe that the author of this inscription is 'Ēzānā. If this is the case, we would have one more argument for the identification of the Kāsū (Kūsh) with the people of Meroe.

In his titulature, 'Ēzānā also claims domination over Saba' and Ḥimyar in Arabia. There are sufficient Ḥimyarite inscriptions at our disposal to disprove that Ḥimyar was at the time a tributary of Aksūm. No conflict between Ḥimyar and Aksūm is mentioned. Besides, from about 321, Ḥimyar enjoyed great political stability, so that its sovereigns probably had the political means to resist such domination.

One can thus wonder if the reference to Saba' and Ḥimyar in 'Ēzānā's titulature does not identically reproduce an older model. Such a model is probably not attested, but it must have existed, since we know without question that Aksūm did dominate a large part of western Arabia from about 200 to about 275.

Our witness to this first Aksūmite saga in Arabia is an Aksūmite inscription in Greek, copied by Kosmas Indikopleustēs in Adulis:

> . . . In the same way, after having sent against the Arabitai and the Kinaidokolpitai, who live beyond the Red Sea, a fleet and an army, and after having subjected their kings, I ordered them to pay a tribute for their territory and to leave in peace navigation and land traffic, and from the town of Leukè to the territories of the Sabaeans I led the war. All those peoples, I was the first and only one of the kings that preceded me to have subjected them. . . . (*RIÉth* 277/26–33)

The author of this inscription, whose name has disappeared with the beginning of the text, was a polytheist. He thus presumably predated 'Ēzānā. One can suggest that it was the king of Gadara (Ge'ez *Gdr*; Saba'ic *Gdrt*), under whose reign Aksūm saw a real renaissance. In Ethiopia, a single inscription, engraved on a curious curved object, can be attributed to him with certainty: *Gdr ngśy 'ksm tb'l mzlt l-'rg w-l-Lmq*, "Gadara, negus of Aksūm, has taken possession of the *mzlt* for *'rg* and for *Lmq* [probably the Sabaean god Almaqah]" (*RIÉth* 180). This text, whose translation is very hypothetical, sheds no light on the dates and the activity of Gadara. Note that it renders the word *king* with *ngśy* (which produced the Arabic *najāšī*), while all later texts have *ngś*, which produced our "negus."

Sabaean inscriptions offer more information, particularly King Gadara's military intervention in Yemen while he was the ally of the Sabaean kings

'Alhān Nahfān (c. 195–210) (*CIH* 308/11; see also Nāmī N'J 13 + 14) and Sha'rum Awtar (c. 210–230) (Ja 631/13) (Cuvigny and Robin 1996), who seem to have asked for his assistance. Those alliances allow us to date Gadara around 200 to 220. It is not impossible that the Aksūmite intervention in Arabia was encouraged by the Romans, who, around 200, had probably evacuated the position they occupied fifty years earlier on the Farasān islands, on the present frontier between Saudi Arabia and Yemen (Villeneuve et al. 2004).

Gadara's conquests were consolidated by his successors. Aksūm, alternating alliances with the kingdoms of Saba' and of Ḥimyar, gained possession of the totality of western Yemen, from Nagrān to 'Adan. But this domination was short-lived. It ended in the 270s, when the Ḥimyarite sovereign Yāsirum Yuhan'im (c. 265–287) succeeded in expelling the Aksūmites from Arabia. Sabaean and Ḥimyarite inscriptions recounting these alliances and wars give the name and the order of succession of several otherwise unknown neguses and princes: after Gadara, there are "*'ḏbh* king of the Aksūmites" (Ja 576/11), "*Bygt* son of the negus" (Ja 631/21), "*Grmt* son of the negus (king of the Aksūmites)" (Ja 577/3 and 6, Ja 585/14–15), and finally "*Dtwns*[1] et *Zqrns*[1], the two kings of Abyssinia" (al-Mi'sāl 5/10).

Another explanation for the mention of Saba' and Ḥimyar in 'Ēzānā's titulature could be the presence of Abyssinian tribes that more or less recognized the authority of the negus in western Yemen. Those tribes are mentioned in the Ḥimyarite and Sabaean inscriptions of the third century, sometimes by name. We do not know if they invaded Yemen with Gadara or if their presence goes back to earlier times. The presence of those Abyssinian tribes in Yemen could also explain how Ḥimyar slipped into Aksūmite domination so easily at the beginning of the sixth century.

One last point deserves to be raised: the question has often been asked whether there had been one or several 'Ēzānā. The latest study tends toward the distinction of a first pagan 'Ēzāna ("phase 1" in the preceding list) and a second one who was pagan and then Christian ("phases 2 and 3"): the evidence used is the mention of Ḥabashat, present in the titulature of the first 'Ēzāna but not of the second 'Ēzāna, and palaeography (Drewes 2002). The 'Ēzānā to whom Constantius addressed his letter was the first one (since he had a brother called Sazana).

The hypothesis of two 'Ēzānā creates more problems than it solves. Drewes's reconstruction bizarrely identifies Constantius' correspondent, who seems to be Christian or at least a man devoted to the cause of the true faith, with a polytheist sovereign, while we know a Christian homonym who would fit perfectly. The mention (or not) of Ḥabashat in the titulature is not a decisive argument for distinguishing two different kings: the ethnic term *Ṣrd(m)* can be found (*RIÉth* 185bis) or not found (*RIÉth* 185) in the titulature of the first 'Ēzāna and is not enough of a reason to invent a second one. One can also object that the titulature of the first 'Ēzānā varies considerably from one text to another, especially in the order of the terms, but that there is one that has an almost identical formulation to the titulature of the second one (compare *RIÉth* 185-I and 188).

It seems preferable, for lack of any decisive evidence, to prefer the simplest solution, that of a single ʿĒzānā. It is important, nevertheless, to keep in mind that the attribution of all the inscriptions and coins bearing ʿĒzānā's name to one king is still a matter of debate.

Whatever the case, the conversion of Ethiopia happened under the reign of a sovereign called ʿĒzānā, toward the middle of the fourth century, as has been established since the beginning of the twentieth century through the work of Enno Littmann. This religious reform presents many similarities with the processes observed in Arabia. In Aksūm as in Ḥimyar, the religious reform was not the culmination of a long evolution that progressively transformed one of the pagan gods of the local pantheon into a supreme god. It was a sudden and radical reorientation with the adoption of a foreign religion that permits us to use the term *conversion*. This is particularly clear in Aksūm, where king ʿĒzānā begun his reign as a polytheist and ended it as a Christian.

In Ethiopia as in Arabia, the change was total and definitive. After ʿĒzānā, the coinage systematically bore Christian symbols. As for inscriptions, admittedly not very numerous, they were all Christian. This, of course, does not mean (far from it) that polytheism had disappeared, but that, as in Ḥimyar, it was now excluded from public space.

The date of the official conversion to monotheism, which implies proof of adherence to the new faith and total rejection of polytheism in official documents, is nearly the same in the two kingdoms. In Ḥimyar, it was around 380: the first dated monotheist royal inscription goes back to January 384, but another one, undated, seems to be slightly older, judging by the names of the coregents (Fa 60 = Ja 856). In Aksūm, the official conversion to Christianity predates that of Ḥimyar by fifteen to twenty years (c. 360–365), judging only by documents of the same type, namely, ʿĒzānā's monotheist inscriptions (in which the king is mentioned without a coregent).

We have seen that the apology to Constantius (dated c. 357) is addressed jointly to two sovereigns ("tyrants") of Aksūm, Christian or at least favorable to Christianity, who are called Aizanas and Sazanas. This co-regency of Aizanas and Sazanas, which is not attested epigraphically, presumably predates the sole reign of the Christian Aizanas/ʿĒzānā. Indeed, Sazanas—or rather Shaʿzana (*Śʿzn /Saiazana*)—is mentioned in some of ʿĒzānā's polytheistic inscriptions as the brother of the king at the head of an army. On this basis we can reconstruct a plausible sequence of successive reigns:

1. Pagan ʿĒzānā
2. Pagan or Christian ʿĒzānā, associating his brother Shaʿzana with the throne
3. co-regency of ʿĒzānā and Shaʿzana, probably as Christians: *Apology to Constantius II* (c. 357)
4. Reign of Christian ʿĒzānā alone

The first epigraphic evidence of the conversion of Ethiopia thus dates later than c. 360. It is also remarkable that the Aksūmite (at least in inscriptions in local languages) and Ḥimyarite sovereigns adopt the same careful attitude in their religious policy: they simply display a minimalist monotheism, naming God the "Lord of Heaven," without indicating whether they incline toward Christianity or Judaism. It is only in Greek that the sovereign of Aksūm declares himself explicitly Christian; as for the Ḥimyarite sovereign, his support for Judaism can be detected thanks only to the inscriptions of his subjects.

However, some substantial differences can be observed. I have just mentioned the choice of Christianity in Aksūm and that of Judaism in Ḥimyar. A second one is that the rejection of polytheism brought about several important innovations in Aksūm but not in Ḥimyar. This is, first of all, the creation of a new script that notes vowels. It is plausible that this script was a response to a demand on the part of the Christians. It allowed them to read the liturgy easily, even without knowing the language very well (which was often the case for foreign members of the clergy). It also offered a more reliable instrument for the translation of the Bible, which was probably undertaken at that time. A second innovation is the adoption of the cross as a symbol of identity: the cross appeared in an inscription of 'Ezana and on his last coin issues; it is then to be found on all coins. Finally, it is quite possible that the first efforts to translate the Bible go back to this period (Knibb 1999), as does the creation of the Ethiopian Christian calendar, even if the first evidence for it is later.

On the other hand, in the kingdom of Ḥimyar, the rejection of polytheism did not bring about any big changes: the language, script, calendar, and year were preserved without modification. No symbol was introduced to underline the change, not even in the inscriptions that are explicitly Jewish. If we take the example of the seven-branched candelabra (*menorah*), so common in Byzantine Palestine, we find it in Yemen only once, on a seal of unknown provenance.

The conversion of Aksūm to Christianity is the consequence of a policy favoring Hellenism and Rome that the sovereigns had adopted as early as the first century C.E. It took place very soon after the Christianization of the Roman empire and was a convenient way of reasserting a strategic alliance with a grand gesture. It had important ideological and political consequences. Even if the Byzantine emperor in theory reigned over the entire known world (*oikoumenē*), in practice he had authority only over the empire itself, identified with the civilized world and also called the *oikoumenē*. At first, the limits of the Christian world coincided approximately with those of the empire. But very quickly the conversion of neighboring barbarians such as the Caucasian Iberians and the Arabs of Queen Māwiya, or of barbarians further afield like the Aksūmites, raises the question of the limits of the empire. The Christian hierarchies that were appointed were attached to sees located within the empire, and the emperor himself did not hesitate to intervene in matters of religious policy, as illustrated by the *Apology to Constantius II*.

One should not overestimate Aksūm's degree of dependence on Byzantium. Distance weakened the links. The best proof resides in the quasi-total silence of classical sources on that kingdom. A constitution of the Theodosian

Code might also be mentioned, dated January 15, 356/7, under Constantius II. It orders that envoys on their way to countries bordering on the Red Sea should not spend more than one year in Alexandria at the expense of the state:

> Idem AA. et Iulianus C. Musoniano P(raefecto) P(raetori)o. Nullus ad gentem Axumitarum et Homeritarum ire praeceptus ultra annui temporis spatia debet Alexandriae de cetero demorari nec post annum percipere alimonias annonarias. Dat. XVIII Kal. Feb. Med(iolano) indictione XV Constantio A. VIII et Iuliano C. Conss.
>
> The same Augusti and Julian Caesar to Musonianus, Praetorian Prefect. No person who has been instructed to go to the tribe of the Axumites or the Homerites shall henceforth tarry at Alexandria beyond the space of the time-limit of one year, and after a year, he shall not receive subsistence allowance. Given on the eighteenth day before the kalends of February at Milan in the fifteenth year of the indiction and in the year of the eighth consulship of Constantius Augustus and the consulship of Julian Caesar. (*C.Th.* 12.12.2, trans. Pharr)

This measure suggests that commercial expeditions between Alexandria and Aksūm were not that frequent, since the envoys could wait up to a year before they could find a convoy. Diplomatic contact itself seems to have been rather irregular: when king Kālēb received an ambassador in 531, he was delighted to finally establish "links of friendship" "after many years" (probably close to thirty years) (see later).

From the reign of 'Ēzānā to that of Kālēb, that is, from the 360s to about 500, we know next to nothing of the political history of Aksūm. Coins, our only source, give the names of at least six kings: Ousanas, Ouazebas, Eōn/Nōah, *Mḥdys*, Ebana, Nezana/Nezoōl. Their number is not easy to establish because the Greek captions are clumsy and often corrupted and it is always difficult to distinguish homonyms. There are also many anonymous issues. Numismatic classifications thus still present many uncertainties in their details, even if the general framework is the object of general consensus (Munro-Hay and Juel-Jensen 1995; Hahn 2000).

IV. Ḥimyar as Aksūm's Tributary State (c. 500–570)

Around 500, the kingdom of Ḥimyar, which exerted more or less direct control over a great part of the Arabian Peninsula, seemed powerful. However, it was then that it became a tributary of Aksūm. This reversal, which probably began in the reign of Marthad'īlān Yanūf (around 500–515) (Gajda 2009, 73–76), seems to have been complete by the reign of Ma'dīkarib Ya'fur (519–522), who was placed on the throne by the Aksūmites, was Christian, and launched a military campaign against lower ‘Irāq, with the support of Arab allies of Byzantium (Ry 510) (Gajda 2009, 76–81). Around the same time, the Kindite prince that Ḥimyar had placed at the head of Ma‘add in central Arabia concluded an alliance with the Byzantine emperor Anastasius (491–518) (Robin 2010d).

IV.A The Najrān Massacre and the Defeat of Joseph

At the death of Ma‘dīkarib Ya‘fur, which can be dated between June 521 and June 522, a *coup de force* brought to power a prince named Joseph (Saba’ic Yūsuf As’ar Yath’ar, *Ys^{1}(w)f ’s^{1}’r Yṯ’r*), who had already attempted to take the throne several years earlier (Robin 2008b; 2010d; Gajda 2009, 82–109). That prince bears quite different names depending on the source: in Syriac, he is called Masrūq, probably a personal name; in Greek, Dounaas; and in Arabic, Zur‘a dhū Nuwās. Joseph succeeded in killing the 300 Aksūmites who were in garrison at Ẓafār, the Ḥimyarite capital, and set fire to their church. He then took the head of an army that devastated the coastal regions of the Red Sea that faced Abyssinia. One can assume that Joseph doubted their loyalty. The arson in a church of the port of Mukhawān (Arabic al-Mukhā’) indicates that the population of those regions was at least partly Christianized. The toll of that campaign is impressive: between 12,500 and 14,000 killed, with 11,000 prisoners and 290,000 animals seized.

The king then set up camp at Mukhawān to prevent any possibility of an Aksūmite sea landing. At the same time, he sent an army under the command of a Jewish prince called Sharaḥ’īl Yaqbul dhu-Yaz’an against the oasis of Najrān, which did not recognize his authority (Robin 2008b).

At the time, the population of Najrān included pagans and Jews, but it was dominated by Christians. Those Christians belonged to two different and antagonistic Christological denominations. One group had been converted as a result of their contacts with Christians of the Persian empire, especially those of al-Ḥīra, who insisted on the complete humanity of Christ, introducing a clear distinction between the son of Mary and the son of God. They belonged to a dissident Church, often called "Nestorian," even though the members of that Church did not claim the heritage of Patriarch Nestorius (see Walker, chapter 31 in this book). The Nestorian community of Najrān was founded in the first half of the fifth century, during the reign of a Sāsānid king called Yazdagird, probably Yazdagird II (438–457) (*Chronicle of Seert*, ed. Scher 1910, 330–331). This works well with the chronology of the introduction and growth of Christianity in the Gulf, where the mention of the first bishopric goes back to 410 (*Synodicon orientale*; Beaucamp and Robin 1983).

The other Christians of Najrān were converted during an important missionary effort initiated in Byzantine territory, more precisely in northern Syria, in anti-Chalcedonian circles (rejecting the Christological definitions of the Council of Chalcedon, which convened in 451) (Robin 2006b, 327–329). Asserting the indissoluble unity of God and man in Christ, they were suspected of privileging his divine nature to the detriment of his human nature, which earned them the name of "Monophysites" (see Wood, chapter 6 in this book). They were Christians of Byzantine allegiance, though from 518 imperial support swung toward the compromise decided at Chalcedon and thus against the anti-Chalcedonians. The first conversions in Najrān do not seem to have happened earlier than the middle of the fifth century. One movement of repression against the community is recorded in the 470s. As for the appointment of the first bishop, it was after 485 (*Martyrdom of Azqīr*; Robin 2010d). Syriac and Greek sources underline the wealth and financial power of the Monophysites of Najrān.

In June and July 523, Sharaḥ'īl, who was in command of an army of King Joseph, began the blockade of Najrān, but there he met with strong resistance. He was then joined by King Joseph, who promised to respect the lives of the dissidents if they offered him their submission. The promise was not kept: a great number of Christians, all of Byzantine allegiance it seems, were executed, in particular, their leader called al-Ḥārith son of Ka'b (in Greek, Arethas). Al-Ḥārith and his companions were immediately beatified by the anti-Chalcedonians, soon followed by the Chalcedonians. According to the accounts in Syriac and Greek, this massacre was committed in November 523 (Beaucamp et al. 1999).

According to the *Martyrdom of Arethas*, the Byzantine emperor Justin I (518–527), having heard about it from a diplomatic mission returning from al-Ḥīra, sent a letter to the Aksūmite king Kālēb Ella Aṣbəḥa, inviting him in a very firm and threatening manner to "attack, by land or by sea, the abominable and criminal Hebrew" to take revenge for the martyrs of Najrān. A fleet of sixty ships with "Roman, Persian, and Indian merchants" coming from Aeila (Ayla/Elath, fifteen ships), from Klysma (twenty) and from Berenike (two) in Egypt, from the island of Iotabe in the Gulf of al-'Aqaba (seven), from Pharsan (the Farasān Islands, on the present frontier between Saudi Arabia and Yemen, seven), and India (nine) was put together. It was completed by ten ships that Kālēb had especially built (par. 27–28). This intervention by Justin is probably apocryphal, because it does not agree with another source that insists on the absence of direct relations between Byzantium and Ethiopia; according to Malalas, who probably relied on a report of the ambassador Ioulianos, whom Justinian I had sent to Kālēb shortly before 531, "when [Ioulianos] was introduced to the emperor of the Indians, the latter, filled with great joy, was deeply moved because after many years he finally achieved a link of friendship with the emperor of the Romans" (Malalas 18.56). One might add that Kālēb did not need a demand from Byzantium to avenge the massacre of his troops and reestablish his dominion over Ḥimyar (Beaucamp 2010).

Kālēb's army left Aksūm after Pentecost 525. It boarded the seventy ships at Adulis and crossed the Red Sea. King Joseph was killed while trying to oppose its landing. His death precipitated the crushing defeat of the Ḥimyarite army. The date of the defeat is still under discussion: after Pentecost 525 and before September 531. It could have been around the autumn of 525 or around 528–530, depending on the source to which one chooses to give priority. Joseph's death definitively ended the independence of the kingdom of Ḥimyar, which survived under Aksūmite domination for about fifty years before it disappeared.

The Aksūmites took possession of the capital, Ẓafār, and of Ṣan'ā', Ma'rib, the Jawf (Robin 2004a), and Najrān. It was a remarkable success, which they commemorated at Ma'rib, the cradle of South Arabian civilization, with an inscription in syllabic Ge'ez (*RIÉth* 195). Unfortunately, only two fragments of this document survive, fragments that do not join and do not give the name of its author. The second fragment mentions the conquest of Yemen and the death of the king of Ḥimyar.

The Jews were systematically massacred, churches were founded in great numbers, and an ecclesiastical hierarchy was established. However, Kālēb changed nothing in the political structures of the country: he maintained the Ḥimyarite throne, on which he placed a Christian Ḥimyarite prince, Sumūyafa' Ashwa' ("Esimiphaios" in Procopius, *Wars* 1.20.1), and soon returned to Africa, while leaving part of his army in Arabia to control the country and guarantee payment of an annual tribute. Kālēb remained in Arabia for seven months, according to one source (*Book of the Ḥimyarites*, cxlii and 65a), or three years according to another, which seems less reliable (*Life* of Gregentios 19; and Fiaccadori 2006, 63). A slightly different version, possibly based on the ambassador Ioulianos (mentioned previously), can be found in John Malalas: Kālēb, he says, "made emperor of the Amorite Indians . . . someone of his own family, Anganes."

IV.B The Christian Aksūmite Abraha on the Ḥimyarite Throne

The Byzantine emperor Justinian I (527–565) was persuaded that the conquest of Ḥimyar by an ally opened new economic and military possibilities for him in the war against Persia, which had restarted in 527. He sent an embassy to South Arabia and Aksūm, probably between April and September 531, under the leadership of the aforementioned Ioulianos. He asked the Aksūmites to invest in the trade of Chinese silk: if they could send ships to India, they could divert toward the Red Sea and Roman Egypt a trade route that at the time enriched Persia and offered great wealth. Of the Ḥimyarites and the Arabs (Saracens) who were their dependents, he expected diversionary military operations against Persian territory (Procopius, *Wars* 1.20).

But the Aksūmite Kālēb soon lost his direct control over Arabia. The Christian Ḥimyarite he had installed on the throne, Sumūyafa' Ashwa' (Greek Esimiphaios) (Gajda 2009, 111–115), was overthrown by the leader of his army in Arabia, Abraha. Even though Abraha reigned with the support of this army (mentioned both in inscriptions and in the Islamic tradition), he presented himself as a Ḥimyarite king. He had inscriptions made in Saba'ic and adopted the traditional royal titulature, entirely accepting the political and cultural heritage of Ḥimyar. The only changes were in foreign policy and religion (Gajda 2009, 116–146).

The length of Abraha's reign, probably around thirty years from 535 to 565, is not easy to define with precision. Dated inscriptions give us information only on the period 547 to 558. To help offer an approximate date for his death, we have two indications. First, we know that Aksūmite power collapsed at the very beginning of the 570s according to Byzantine sources, or around 575 according to the Islamic tradition. Furthermore, Abraha had two successors, two sons who did not reign very long. It is thus plausible that Abraha died a few years before 570.

The principal source on Abraha's reign is a series of six inscriptions, of which four were written by the sovereign himself. The most detailed one commemorates a rebellion of the tribe of Kiddat (Arabic Kinda), followed by important works on the Ma'rib dam, which had just broken (547/8). This repair conveys the will to maintain, if not to restore, the brilliance of the cradle of South Arabian civilization and thus to consolidate a contested legitimacy by acting as an indigenous sovereign (*CIH* 541). While he was at Ma'rib, Abraha had a church consecrated. Shortly after that, in the autumn of 547, he organized a diplomatic meeting in which delegations from all the powers of the region participated. Those delegations were classified in three categories: those representing the two suzerain powers (the negus and the "king of the Romans") were called "embassies" (*mḥs²kt*); that of the king of Persia was called a "diplomatic mission" (*tnblt*); those of the Arab princes who were vassals of Persia and Byzantium were described as "envoys" (*rs¹l*). It is noteworthy that no delegation came from Arabia itself, in particular from Ma'addum or from Muḍar: this implies that Abraha considered himself their suzerain. We do not know why these delegations went to Ma'rib. It is possible that it was to talk about the division of the zones of influence between Byzantium, Aksūm, and Persia in Arabia after the conflict between Byzantium and the Persians from 540 to 546.

A second inscription by Abraha, dated 552, recounts military operations in central Arabia, described as "the fourth expedition" (Murayghān 1 = Ry 506). Two auxiliary Arab columns were in charge of raiding Ma'addum, the great tribal confederation of central Arabia. They confronted the Banū *'mr^m* ('Amr or 'Āmir) and were victorious, taking booty and prisoners in battles whose localization is disputed. King Abraha then went to Ḥalibān (300 kilometers southwest of al-Riyāḍ), where the tribe of Ma'addum declared its allegiance and returned its hostages. Abraha's success at Ḥalibān struck contemporaries, since it has left an echo in pre-Islamic Arabic poetry.

The first, generally accepted interpretation of this text was based on the identifications proposed by the Belgian scholar Jacques Ryckmans. He situated the two battles in western Arabia, not far from Makka, and believed that the adversaries of Abraha's two columns were the Banū ʿĀmir (b. Ṣaʿṣaʿa), an important tribe of western Arabia whose territory was south of Makka. From those identifications, the British scholar A. F. L. Beeston inferred that two sets of operations should be distinguished: one in western Arabia, where the king had sent two columns, and another in central Arabia, where the king was himself at the head of his troops (Beeston 1954, 391). In that model, it was not impossible to imagine that a secondary action against Makka had failed.

The Israeli scholar M. J. Kister (1965a) offered another argument that Sabaeologists considered decisive. The inscription Murayghân 1 = Ry 506 is dated 552 C.E. This is one of the dates that the Islamic tradition assigns to the "year of the Elephant." According to the famous traditionist Hishām ibn al-Kalbī (d. 204/819 or 206/821):

> Before the chronology of the Prophet, Quraysh counted time from the time of the Elephant. Between the Elephant and (the battle of) Fijār, they counted 40 years. Between Fijār and the death of Hishām b. al-Mughīra, they counted 6 years. Between the death of Hishām and the construction of the Kaʿba, they counted 9 years. Between the construction of the Kaʿba and the departure of the Prophet for al-Madīna, they counted 15 years. (al-Zubayr b. Bakkār, *Nasab Quraysh*, 668 par. 1649; Kister 1965a, 427)

In this chronological reconstruction, there were seventy years between the Elephant and the hijra (622 C.E.), which puts the Elephant in 552. Abraha's military operations described in Murayghān 1 = Ry 506 thus offered a framework in which Abraha's mythical campaign against Makka, which could be named "the Battle of the Elephant," could find its place. Here is how the Islamic tradition recounts this campaign (Daghfous 1995, 130ff.; de Prémare 2000). Abraha, who had just built a splendid church in Ṣanʿā', wanted to make the city a major center of pilgrimage in Arabia. But Makka, with the Kaʿba, presented an obstacle to that project and had to be made to submit. Abraha took the excuse of a provocation of which we have two divergent versions (Kister 1965a, 431; 1972, 63–65). According to some, Hijāzi Arabs from a tribe allied to Makka had polluted the Ṣanʿā' church with excrement. According to others, Makkans attacked and robbed at Najrān a grandson of Abraha's on their way back from the pilgrimage to Makka, and they also looted a church.

Furious with this provocation, Abraha decided to take revenge on the Makkans and destroy the Kaʿba. He put together an army composed of Abyssinians, Ḥimyarites, and Arabs. In the vanguard, he put an elephant—several, according to some traditions. He arrived in the vicinity of the city of al-Ṭā'if, whose tribe submitted, and progressed toward Makka. It is then that the miracle happened: the elephant placed at the head of the army refused to move. Abraha's army was then threatened by birds that bombarded it with "pellets of hard-baked clay." Some collectors of traditions, probably less prone to believing in miracles, also mention that an unknown disease ravaged the army (Daghfous 1995, 128–129). That victory was one of the foundational myths of the Qurayshite supremacy in western Arabia at the eve of the hijra, echoed in the Qur'ān (105, "The Elephant"):

> Do you not see how the Lord dealt with the army of the Elephant? Did He not utterly confound their plans? He sent ranks of birds against them, pelting them with pellets of hard-baked clay.

It probably has a historical basis since it is also mentioned in pre-Islamic poetry (Rubin n.d., "Abraha"; Robin 2010c; for a different opinion, de Prémare 2000).

Today, however, the hypothesis that the inscription Murayghân 1 = Ry 506 offers a plausible framework for the "Battle of the Elephant" has been abandoned. This is, first of all, because the text has been reinterpreted. There were not two different settings for the operations but a single one, as is indicated by the single mention of booty and prisoners. Ma'addum and the Banū *'mr*^{m} are not two tribes, but a single tribe and its royal dynasty, the Banū 'Amrum (who were descended from Ḥujr, son of 'Amr, the first Kindite king of Ma'add).

This also follows from the discovery in 2009 of a new inscription (Murayghān 3). It contains a declaration of Abraha's victory, undated, which cannot predate the campaign of 552 commemorated in Murayghān 1 = Ry 506. Abraha proclaims that he has reestablished his authority on Ma'addum and that he has extended it over new territories in northeastern, northern, and northwestern Arabia, in particular, Hagar (eastern Arabia), Ṭayyum (north Arabia), and Yathrib (northwest Arabia). He also proclaims that he has chased out 'Amrum, son of Mudhdhirān (Ar. 'Amr son of al-Mundhir III), the son of the Naṣrid king of al-Ḥīra. It is thus the totality of Arabia that now recognized his authority. Islamic tradition confirms this point: it relates anecdotes showing that Abraha intervened directly in the affairs of several tribes of northern Arabia.

Thus it is important to distinguish, on the one hand, the campaign of 552, which allowed Abraha to reestablish his authority over almost all of inner Arabia, and on the other hand, the Battle of the Elephant, which happened later and could be the cause of the collapse of Ḥimyarite domination over inner Arabia. This Battle of the Elephant could be dated between 555 and 565, probably closer to 565, toward the end of Abraha's reign.

Abraha's failure before Makka offers a plausible explanation for the primacy that Quraysh—a poor and not very large tribe, which was established in an inhospitable region—exercised in western Arabia in the last decades of the sixth century. If we believe the Islamic tradition, it is after that failure of Abraha's that Quraysh was called "the people of God" (*ahl Allāh*) (Kister 1972, 75), and it was fifteen years later that the great fair of Quraysh, held at al-'Ukāẓ, was founded. The cult association of the *ḥums*, which tied the members of many tribes of western Arabia to the Makkan shrine, also postdates the Battle of the Elephant. It is of no consequence that the victorious resistance of Quraysh, quite naturally attributed to the local god, was in fact the result of an epidemic that decimated the army of the enemy, as some traditions relate.

After Abraha's death (around 565?), the Islamic tradition relates that his sons Yaksūm/Aksūm and Masrūq succeed each other briefly on the throne of

Ḥimyar (Gajda 2009, 148–156). The first one is mentioned in the inscription *CIH* 541/82–83 while he is still crown prince ("Aksūm dhu-Ma'āhir, son of the king"). But their authority is undermined by dissension. When the Aksūmite kingdom of Arabia collapsed, around 570 or 575, Byzantium lost its main ally in the peninsula. It was the final failure of Justinian's Arab policy and of the older strategy that aimed for control of the Red Sea.

IV.C Kālēb Ella Aṣbəḥa, King of Aksūm

The full name of the Aksūmite king who made Ḥimyar a tributary and then a subject kingdom is "Kālēb Ella Aṣbəḥa, son of *Tzn*, the man of *Lzn*," as indicated by the inscription *RIÉth* 191, of which he is the author (ll. 7–8). His son called him simply Ella Aṣbəḥa (*'l 'ṣbḥ*, *RIÉth* 192/7). External sources use either "Kālēb" (a biblical name) or "Ella Aṣbəḥa." This last name is preferred in the Yemeni inscriptions (Saba'ic Ella A<ṣ>bəḥa, *'l'bḥh*, with omission of the ṣ, in Ist. 7608bis/6) and in the Byzantine sources, in which various orthographic variations can be found: Elesbaas (*Martyrdom of Arethas*, par. 1 and *passim*; Nonnosos, in Photios, *Bibliotheca*, 3); Elesboas (Malalas, 18.56); Ellatzbaas (Kosmas, *Christian Topography*, 2.56); Hellēstheaios (Procopius, 2.20.1ff.; 1.20.9ff., probably with a *bēta* erroneously read as *thēta*).

In Syriac, on the other hand, the king is called Kālēb (Shahîd *Letter*, IX B and 63; *Book of the Ḥimyarites*, index, xci). The same goes for Arabic, where the name is written Kālib (Nashwān, *Mulūk Ḥimyar*, 148). Logically, the Ge'ez translation of the *Martyrdom of Arethas* (Bausi and Gori 2006) replaced Elesbaas with Kālēb.

The Syrian-Byzantine chronicler John Malalas, who gives two versions of the war between Aksūm and Ḥimyar, calls the Aksūmite king "Andas" in the second version (Malalas, 18.9 and 15). For the authors who use this account, the name becomes Adad (Theophanes), Andug (*Chronicle of Zuqnin*), Anzug (*Chronicle of Michael the Syrian*), or Endās (*Chronicle of John of Nikiu*). We do not know the origin of this strange name.

A single source gives King Kālēb's titulature, the Ge'ez inscription *RIÉth* 191/7–8: "Kālēb Ella Aṣbəḥa son of *Tzn*, the man of *Lzn*, king of Aksūm, of Ḥamēr and of za-Raydān, of Saba' and of Salhīn, of the Highlands and of the South, of the Coast and of Ḥaḍramawt and of all the Arabs, the Bedja and the Nubians, the Kūshites and the Ṣəyamo, and the *Drbt*" (*Klb* [8]*l 'ṣbḥ wld Tzn b's Lzn ngš 'ksm w-Ḥ[mr]w-z-Rydn w-*[9]*Sb' w-Slḥn w-Ṭdm w-z-Ymnt w-Thmt w-Ḥḍrmwt w-kl '*[10]*rbm w-z-Bg w-Nb w-z-Ks w-Ṣym w-z-Drbt*). It enumerates in a rather disorderly manner, common in the inscriptions of Ethiopia, his African possessions and the ones in Arabia. In Africa, Kālēb reigned over Aksūm; the Bedja (*Bg*; in 'Ēzāna's titulature, *Bg*, *Bgm*, *Bəgā*, in Greek *Bougaeitai*) between Ethiopia and Egypt; the Nubians (*Nb*) and the Kūshites (*Ks*; in 'Ēzāna's titulature, *Ks*, *Ksm*, *Kswm*, *Kāsū*, in Greek *Kasou*) in the upper Nile Valley; and finally two unidentified peoples, the Ṣəyamo (*Ṣym*; in 'Ēzāna's titulature, *Ṣym*, *Ṣymm*, in Greek

Tiamō) and the *Drbt*. In Arabia, it is the kingdom of Ḥimyar with its various parts: Ḥamēr (*Ḥmr*) and its royal palace, Raydān (*Rydn*); Saba' (*Sb'*) and its royal palace, Salḥīn (*Slḥn*); the South (*Ymnt*); Ḥaḍramawt (*Ḥḍrmwt*); and finally all the Arabs (*kl 'rbm*), those of the Coast (*Thmt*) and those of the Highlands (*Ṭdm*). It is a hardly recognizable copy of Ḥimyarite titulature: "king of Saba', of dhu-Raydān, of Ḥaḍramawt and of the South, and of their Arabs in the Highlands and on the Coast" (*mlk S*[1]*b' w-ḏ-Ryd*^{n} *w-Ḥḍrmwt w-Ymnt w-''rb-hmw Ṭwd*^{m} *w-Thmt*).

In the same inscription, Kālēb commemorates with a wealth of detail a victorious expedition that he conducted against the Agwezāt (*'gzt*) and the *Ḥst*, two peoples that should probably be located to the east of Aksūm (the first had already clashed with 'Ēzānā). He mentions in passing the success of an expedition to Arabia, under the leadership of Ḥayyān *Slbn* za-Samīr (ll. 34–37). The mention of Ḥayyān allows us to date this text to the beginning of Kālēb's reign (see later). At that time, Kālēb did not reign directly over Ḥimyar, but we can assume he controlled the kingdom tightly by stationing a small detachment there, choosing the king, and levying taxes, probably in the form of a tribute. The way the Ethiopian titulature is composed then becomes clear: logically, it mentions the kingdom and then enumerates the territories that are more or less under its control, including those—most probably—that only paid an annual tribute.

A comparison between Kālēb's titulature and that of his son Wa'zeb (*RIÉth* 192/5–7) confirms this. Kālēb's son calls himself: "Wa'zeb king of Aksūm, of Ḥimyar and of dhu-Raydān, of Saba' and Salḥ, of the Bedja, the Kūshites, the Ṣəyamo, the *Wyt(l)*, the man of *Ḥd(f)n*, son of Ella Aṣbəḥa, servant of Christ" (*W'zb n(g)š [']ksm w-ḏ-Ḥmyrm w-*[6]*ḏ-Rdn w-ḏ-Sb' w-ḏ-Sl(ḥ) w-ḏ-Bg w-ḏ-Ks w-ḏ-Ṣy(m) w-ḏ-Wyt*[7]*(l) b's Ḥd(f)n wld 'l 'ṣbḥ g(b)r Krśtś*). In the territory he claims in Africa, the disappearance of the Nubians and the replacement of *Drbt* with *Wyt(l)* is notable. In Arabia, the royal titulature is reduced to Ḥimyar and Saba' (with their respective palaces). As Wa'zeb had no direct authority in Arabia but only received tribute from Ḥimyar (Procopius, *Wars*, 1.20.8, who does not name him but speaks of "the one who succeeded [Hellēstheaios = Kālēb] in the kingdom of the Ethiopians"), it is certain that the titulature of that king enumerates territories under his direct control and those who paid tribute.

The precise date of Kālēb's accession to the throne is not known. The only certainty is that it predates the "beginning of the reign of Justin." The end of his reign is equally unknown, but it is at least several years subsequent to the Byzantine embassy of 531.

A number of separate indications allow us to situate the beginning of Kālēb's reign long before the expedition against Joseph, which postdates Pentecost 525. These are the Aksūmite expeditions to Yemen ordered by Kālēb, which happened before the one that eliminated Joseph; the anti-Jewish persecutions that accompanied those expeditions; and the progressive passage of the kingdom of Ḥimyar into the Byzantine orbit.

Before the great expedition that eliminated Joseph and put an end to Ḥimyar's independence, Kālēb had initiated two other expeditions. The first one, placed under the command of Ḥayyān *(S)lbn* za-Samīr/Ḥyōnā, is known from two independent sources, one Ge'ez inscription from Aksūm, *RIÉth* 191/34–37, and the *Book of the Ḥimyarites* (CI and 3b). The second expedition, led in person by Kālēb (*Martyrdom of Arethas*, pars. 1 and 2), is mentioned by the Byzantine traveler Kosmas, who was present during the preparations, "at the beginning of the reign of Justin [I], emperor of the Romans" (Kosmas, *Christian Topography*, 2.56), namely, 518 or 519 (since Justin I came to the throne in August 518).

Those expeditions resulted in a brutal change of religious policy. The Jews, who had enjoyed the support of the authorities and were present in the entourage of the king (Philostorgius, *Ecclesiastical History*, about the embassy of Theophilus the Indian; *Martyrdom of Azqīr*, ch. 3), were now the object of persecutions and massacres (Shahîd *Letter*, VI C and 56). Those anti-Jewish persecutions began prior to the massacre of the Christians in 523, since one of the victims of that massacre declared: "Ḥayyān is my father, the one who once burnt your synagogues" (*Book of the Ḥimyarites*, CXXIII, 32b).

In the kingdom of Ḥimyar, many small details suggest there was a progressive alignment with Byzantium: the appointment of a bishop for Ḥimyar under Anastasius (before August 518), the Christian faith of the Ḥimyarite King Ma'dīkarib Ya'fur (who died around June 522), the participation of the Arabs of Byzantium in a campaign of the Ḥimyarite king in northeastern Arabia in 521, and finally the peace concluded between Byzantium and the Ḥimyarite viceroy for central Arabia under Anastasius (before August 518). If we add that the succession rules to the throne of Ḥimyar seem to change around 500, with the abandonment of the principle of heredity, we can infer that Aksūm began interfering in Arabian affairs around 500.

Because Aksūm intervened twice (Ḥayyān's expedition and that of Kālēb) and because we know of only two occupants of the Ḥimyarite throne for the period 500–522 (Marthad'ilān Yanūf attested from July 504 to March 509; Shuriḥbi'īl Ya'fur attested in June 521), it can be assumed that each of those expeditions had as its aim to appoint a new king. If all those hypotheses are accepted, it is possible to situate the beginning of Kālēb's reign around 500 (Robin 2010d).

There is also much uncertainty concerning the end of Kālēb's reign. Narrative sources give two contradictory versions. According to the *Martyrdom of Arethas* (par. 39), Kālēb renounced the throne on his return from Arabia. To show his gratitude to God, he left the world, took the monastic habit, and adopted an ascetic way of life. At the same time, he consecrated his diadem to Christ and sent it to Jerusalem.

This version of the *Martyrdom of Arethas* is contradicted by Procopius, *Wars* (1.20.1–8), who mentions two military expeditions ordered by King Kālēb after his return from Arabia. According to Procopius, after having crushed

Joseph and conquered Ḥimyar, King Kālēb ("Hellēstheaios") appointed to the Ḥimyarite throne a local Christian called Esimiphaios, who is to pay an annual tribute. But that Esimiphaios was soon overthrown by the Ethiopians who were left in Arabia and others, who sent to the throne a man from the servant class called Abraha ("Abramos"). Kālēb reacted by sending an army of 3,000 men under the command of one of his kinsmen. But the troops sided with Abraha, and instead of attacking him, they killed their leader and joined the rebels. Kālēb insisted and sent a second army, which had to withdraw after a heavy defeat. Finally, Kālēb gave up trying to recover control of Ḥimyar. It is only after his death that the situation returned to normal. Abraha agreed to pay tribute to his successor and thus consolidated his power. According to that account, a long time passed—certainly more than five years—between the moment when Kālēb left Arabia and the date of his death, with the reign of Esimiphaios, the two expeditions, and finally the period of cold war between Kālēb and Abraha.

Two decisive factors recommend favoring Procopius' version (*pace* Fiaccadori 2007). The first is that the reign of Esimiphaios is mentioned in another narrative source (Photios, *Bibliotheca*, par. 3) and in a Ḥimyarite inscription (Ist. 7608bis + Wellcome A103664). The second factor is that the *Martyrdom of Arethas* is an apologetic work that, although it is based on historical facts, aims to celebrate Kālēb's great deeds and have him recognized as a saint of the Christian Church and a model for the faithful.

It is reasonably certain that Kālēb did not abdicate upon his return from Arabia, but when he did leave the throne remains undetermined. It probably happened long after the reign of Esimiphaios, since, according to Procopius, relations between Abraha and Kālēb's successor were only pacified "at a later date" (*Wars*, 1.20.8). But it was before the autumn of 547, since at that time Abraha received at Marib the diplomatic delegations from Rome, Persia, and Aksūm (*CIH* 541). The presence of an Aksūmite delegation implies a reconciliation between Abraha and Aksūm that could only have been possible after Kālēb's death (Procopius, *Wars*, 1.20.8).

Another argument has used the decline of Aksūmite power over the Nubians, which happened before the conversion of Silko (king of the "Noubadai") to Christianity shortly after 540, to date Kālēb's death to about 535 (Smith 1954, 432). Indeed, it seems that Aksūm did lose its control over Nubia at that point, since it is mentioned in Kālēb's titulature (*RÉth* 191/10) but not in that of his son Wa'zeb (*RÉth* 192). This does not precisely date the moment when the king left the throne.

Based on the political aims of Nonnosos' embassy to the kings of Ḥimyar and Aksūm ("Elesbaas" = Kālēb), it would seem that Kālēb was still on the throne after 540. Nonnosos' mission was to convince an Arab leader from central Arabia, the Ḥujride Qays ("Kaïsos"), to give up power and go to Constantinople (Photios, *Bibliotheca*, par. 3). If such complex procedures were undertaken to replace this Qays, it is probably because the renewed war between Persia and

Byzantium in 540 was compelling Constantinople to replace its allied leaders who had proved inefficient.

One last indication is provided by the chronology of Abraha's inscriptions. The oldest ones date from February and March 548 (DAI GDN 2002/20 and *CIH* 541). One could note that they celebrate the consolidation of Abraha's power. The king recounts, among other things, crushing a revolt led by the Kindite prince Yazīd b. Kabshat in the summer of 547 (ll. 10–11), an operation that was impossible while the relations between Abraha and Aksūm were still conflict-ridden.

Although it is impossible to conclude with certainty, we can situate Kālēb's death before 547 and probably after 540. Thus this sovereign reigned for more than forty years. Such a high number as this is not without parallels in the region (e.g., the Ḥimyarite Abīkarib) or worldwide.

IV.D Kālēb and Abraha in the Legend, Known as "Abrəha and Aṣbəḥa"

The portrait of Abraha ("Abramos") as drawn by Procopius in the *Wars* (1.20) is not flattering. He was a clever individual who betrayed the trust of his lords: by taking the throne of Ḥimyar, he revolted against his king; besides, he did not fulfill his commitments toward Justinian I. Is he not, after all, from the class of servants?

Christian sources present the relations between Kālēb and Abraha very differently. According to the *Martyrdom of Arethas* (par. 38), Kālēb appointed Abraha ("Abraam") as king of Ḥimyar immediately after his victory over Joseph. That Abraha is "sensible, God-fearing, and very Christian." This idyllic version—which probably reflects the terms of the reconciliation between Abraha and Kālēb's successor—served as the basis of legendary developments. The Church of Ethiopia celebrates two brothers named Abrəha and Aṣbəḥa (an abbreviated form of Kālēb Ella Aṣbəḥa), under whose reign Christianity was introduced into Ethiopia (Munro-Hay 2003).

In Arabia, the two enemy kings are also reconciled but in a different way: the Islamic tradition turned Abraha into a descendant of the famous lineage of the dhū Aṣbaḥ (Saba'ic *ḏ-Hṣbḥ*), princes of the commune of Maḏḥām (*Mḏḥy*^{m}) in southern Yemen (Ibn al-Kalbī, Caskel 1966-I, table 278). Dhū Aṣbaḥ is, of course, reminiscent of (Kālēb Ella) Aṣbəḥa. Abraha's genealogy is: Abraha b. al-Ṣabbāḥ b. Lahī'a b. Shaybat al-Ḥamd b. Marthad al-Khayr b. Yankif b. Yanif b. Ma'dīkarib b. 'Abd Allāh [Maḏḥā] b. 'Amr b. al-Ḥārith [dhū Aṣbaḥ]. This Abraha was the sixth-century king: the Yemenite traditionist al-Ḥasan al-Hamdānī calls him Abū Yaksūm, "Father of Yaksūm." And indeed, the historical king did have a son called Aksūm (*CIH* 541/82–83), who is also mentioned by the Islamic tradition as his successor on the throne of Ḥimyar.

IV.E Byzantium and Sāsānid Persia in Arabia

From early on, Roman and Byzantine policy had been to develop narrow links with the powers on the coast of the Red Sea. Success had been striking with Aksūm. Greek culture had taken root: as shown here, from as early as the third century, Greek was the language of inscriptions and coin captions. But the most dazzling success was, in the fourth century, under Constantine (306–337) and Constantius II (337–361), the conversion to Christianity of the Aksūmites, who within two generations had gone through all the phases: foundation of churches, appointment of a religious hierarchy, conversion of the king, establishment of Christianity as the official religion.

With Ḥimyar, on the other hand, the results were disappointing. An embassy sent by Constantius II to its king did not result in a conversion to Christianity as hoped. It is only the establishment of Aksūmite domination over Ḥimyar at the beginning of the sixth century that finally offered the possibility of controlling a great part of the eastern coast of the Red Sea.

To complete the circuit, only the northwestern part of Arabia was missing, between Yathrib/al-Madīna and Ayla/Elath. It was enough to develop alliances with the Arab tribes neighboring Byzantium to take control of this region. At the beginning of the sixth century, a first attempt was supported by the Ghassānite Thaʿlaba and the Kindite al-Ḥārith, respectively, at the head of Muḍar and Maʿadd. But this policy did not truly bear fruit for the empire until 530/1: Justinian I bestowed the "dignity of king" upon the Arab leader al-Ḥārith son of Jabala of the house of Jafna, also from the tribe of Ghassān (Paret 1958). It seems that al-Ḥārith, who normally lived in the Byzantine province of Arabia (between present-day Syria and Jordan), received authority over part of the Arabs of the Byzantine provinces in the diocese of Oriens and that his power also extended to some tribes neighboring Byzantium. To complement this and to obtain territorial continuity from Syria to Yemen, Justinian I accepted the Palm Grove (Greek *Phoinikōn*, a term describing the great oases of the northern Ḥijāz) from an Arab leader named Abocharabos; this Abocharabos can be identified with Abīkarib, son of Jabala, the brother of the Jafnid al-Ḥārith.

The hypothesis that there was a direct link between the conquest of Ḥimyar by Aksūm and the rise of the Jafnid al-Ḥārith to royal status seems very plausible. The collapse of Aksūmite domination over southern Arabia (570–575) did indeed lead to the suppression of the Jafnid monarchy with the deposition and exile of al-Mundhir, the son and successor of al-Ḥārith, son of Jabala (528–569/570), in 582.

Ancient historians assert a parallel between the creation of the Jafnid kingdom by the Byzantines and that of the Naṣrid kingdom by the Persians. For Procopius, al-Ḥārith's elevation can be explained by the desire to counter the power and the prestige of the Naṣrid Arab King al-Mundhir III, a vassal of the Sāsānids. The two kingdoms, however, are not really similar. The Naṣrid kingdom, founded in the third century, lasted more than 300 years and exercised great influence in Arabia at various occasions, in particular at the beginning of the fourth century and in the second half of the sixth century. The Jafnid kingdom, on the other hand, lasted only some fifty years (Nöldeke 1887; Devreesse 1945, 241ff.; Robin 2008a).

More important, the Naṣrid kingdom was a geopolitical reality: even though it was placed under a Sāsānid governor, it had its own territory, a capital, and stable institutions, in particular, a real army composed of mercenaries and Persians (Rothstein 1899; Kister 1968, 165). The Jafnid kingdom, on the other hand, had none of that: the authority of its "king" was limited to the Arabs of one or more Byzantine provinces; it did not have regular troops or a permanent residence.

Some historians call the Jafnid kingdom "Ghassānid." It is a misleading name: it is not the tribe of Ghassān (settled in the center of the Ḥijāz in the fourth century) that one finds in Syria in the sixth century, but only some scattered groups, mainly from the house of Jafna, a princely lineage of that tribe. Moreover, sovereigns are usually described with reference to their lineage, not their nation. The same is true concerning the kings of al-Ḥīra, who were the Banū Naṣr, apparently from the tribe of Lakhm: they should thus be called Naṣrids and not "Lakhmids" (Kister 1968, 165).

The names Jafnids and Naṣrids are based on the Islamic tradition that connects the sovereigns of the two kingdoms to the houses of Jafna and Naṣr. This is probably arbitrary, at least in part. While it is certain that the last sovereigns of the two kingdoms are indeed members of the Banū Jafna and the Banū Naṣr, as the first Muslim historians noted, it is far from certain that this was the case for the earlier kings. Islamic tradition tends to unite all the sovereigns of a given kingdom into a single genealogical tree, even when it is very much removed from historical reality.

We do not know whether these kings had a real titulature. Ḥimyarite inscriptions of the fifth century call the kingdom of al-Ḥīra "Tanūkh," from the main tribe of the region; as for sixth-century Syriac sources, they frequently use the expression "king of Ḥirtâ' (Nu'mān)." For the Jafnids, we have a Syriac text that mentions "the camp of Gebâlâ (Jabala), king of the 'Assanites (Ghassānites)."

From the religious point of view, being part of the Byzantine zone of influence usually meant conversion to Christianity. This is certain for the Arabs who settled on Byzantine territory, especially the Jafnids al-Ḥārith and al-Mundhir. It is probable for Abīkarib, brother of al-Ḥārith, whom we see intervening in Byzantine territory at Petra (Kaimio and Koenen 1997, 461–462, Papyri Scroll 83; Shahîd 2002, 29), but we have no idea whether the *Phoinikōn* over which Abīkarib's authority extended and which he gave to Justinian I as a gift became Christian.

In southern Arabia, the kingdom of Ḥimyar did become officially Christian. From that time on, royal inscriptions start with Christian religious invocations, for example, *CIH* 541, "With the power, help and mercy of Raḥmānān (Arabic al-Raḥmān, a name of God for the Jews and Christians of Arabia), of his

Messiah, and of the Holy Ghost." That text, by Abraha, also mentions the consecration of a church at Ma'rib, "thanks to the presence of a priest, abbot of his monastery." However, it is striking that these inscriptions never quote the Bible (Old or New Testament), while those of the Aksūmite kings of the same period are full of such quotations (Knibb 1999, 46–54). We can infer that no biblical book, not even the Psalms or the Gospels, had been translated into Saba'ic. Ḥimyar became a refuge for those Byzantine bishops who were deemed heretical, most notably those who followed the Julianist doctrine, like a certain Sergius, who remained there the last three years of his life and died there.

Byzantine interventions in western Arabia are echoed in the Islamic tradition. Quṣayy, the ancestor of Quraysh who in the first half of the sixth century is said to have unified the Qurayshite clans and managed to take control of Makka, received help from "Cesar (*Qayṣar*)," according to Ibn Qutayba (*al-Ma'ārif*, 640–641); several decades later, it is a certain 'Uthmān, son of Ḥuwayrith, who obtained Byzantine endorsement as king of Makka ('Athamina 1998, 35).

The same tradition recounts that Abraha received the help of Byzantine artisans for the marble work and the mosaics when he had a superb church built in Ṣan'ā' (which the tradition calls *al-Qalīs*, derived from the Greek *ekklesia*). The construction of that monument, described in detail by al-Azraqī (*Akhbār Makka*), should probably be dated after 548 (Finster and Schmidt 1994).

Even more than Byzantium, Sāsānid Persia was interested in Arabian affairs and intervened in them frequently. Geographically, this is understandable, since the Sāsānid empire, a neighbor of Arabia overland in the Syrian desert, as well as by crossing the Arab-Persian Gulf, had its capital in the heart of Mesopotamia, in close contact with Arabia (Morony n.d., "Sāsānids"). Immediately after seizing power, the first Sāsānid sovereign, Ardashīr I (224–242), moved to occupy the southern coast of the Gulf. His successor Shāpūr I (242–272) actually mentions Arabia (Bēth 'Arbāyē) and Oman (Mazon) in his titulature, as evidenced in the inscription engraved on the eastern wall of the Ka'ba of Zoroaster in Naqsh-i Rustām.

Persian interest in Arabian affairs is also clear from the relief representing King Narseh II (293–302) receiving an Arabian embassy (Overlaet 2009). It is also during Narseh's reign that we have the first mention of the kingdom of al-Ḥīra: in a bilingual inscription in Parthian and Pahlavi found at Paikūlī (Kurdistan) and written soon after 293, Narseh notes that a certain "'Amr king of Lahmāy [= Lakhm]" offered him his support, with many others, although it is unclear whether he was a subject or an ally.

Under Shāpūr II (309–379), huge works were undertaken to build long walls and dig a ditch (*Khandaq Sāpūr*) along the desert frontier in southwest Mesopotamia. Military operations in the Baḥrayn (the Arabic name of the Arabian coast of the Gulf) probably aimed at reestablishing a declining influence. It must be remembered that in Arabia, Sāsānid presence had always been quite loose, since it has left no archaeological traces (Schiettecatte and Robin 2009).

It would seem that Ḥimyar, who intervened in central and western Arabia at this time already, was doing so with the approval of Persia.

The Arabs, who do not appear very much in the internal history of the Sāsānid empire, stop being anonymous around the beginning of the fifth century. After the death of Yazdajird I in 420, his elder son succeeded him but was soon assassinated. His brother Bahram opposed the usurper. Having been raised in al-Ḥīra by a king called al-Mundhir, he found it easy to raise an Arab army with which he reconquered the throne. He reigned as Bahrām V (420–438).

Yazdajird II (438–457), son of Bahrām V, who undertook important religious reforms, is the first Sāsānid king to be qualified as "divine" on his coinage. It is a time when the kings of Ḥimyar were annexing central and western Arabia and taking the title "king of Saba', of dhu-Raydān, of Ḥaḍramawt and of the South, and of the Arabs in the Highlands and on the Coast." The first conversions to Christianity in Najrān also date from his time.

From the end of the fifth century, the recurrent conflicts opposing Persia and Byzantium offered the Arabs of al-Ḥīra the chance to play a major military role. According to the Syriac *Chronicle of Joshua the Stylite* (Wright 1882, par. 57), King al-Nu'mān II participated in the campaigns of Kubādh I (488–496 and 499–531). It was during one of those campaigns that he was wounded near Kirkesion and died shortly afterward (502). The successor of al-Nu'mān II, possibly after a short interlude, was al-Mundhir III, who reigned until 554. This sovereign, whose reign was exceptionally long, was a formidable warrior. He launched many victorious raids into Byzantine territory, described by Procopius in his *Wars*. Procopius calls him "king of the Saracens" (*Wars*, 1.17.30) and the Syriac sources "king of Ḥîrtâ'" or "king of Ḥîrtâ' də-Nu'mān" (Guidi *Letter*, Syriac text, 501, 502, and 507; transl., 481–482 and 486–487; *Book of the Ḥimyarites*, 5a/12). Three of his sons succeeded him on the throne: 'Amr b. al-Mundhir III (554–569), Qābūs b. al-Mundhir III (569-c. 573), and al-Mundhir IV b. al-Mundhir III (c. 575–c. 580).

Until about 560, the Sāsānids controlled without challenge only the eastern fringe of Arabia, either directly or through the mediation of the kings of al-Ḥīra. They did not succeed in extending their domination on inner Arabia, except during short spells, perhaps at the beginning of the fourth century if we follow the epitaph of Imru' al-Qays in al-Namāra (L 205) or around 530–550, after the murders of the Ḥimyarite King Joseph (between 525 and 530) and of the Ḥujrid Prince al-Ḥārith (528), and before Abraha's victorious campaign (552). The diplomatic initiatives and the interventions of Anastasius, followed by those of Justin I and Justinian I, pushed the kings of Ḥimyar, the princes of the Ḥijāz, and those of central Arabia, into an alliance with Byzantium.

The interest shown by Byzantium for Arabian affairs declined with the end of Justinian's reign, possibly because Byzantium had not been supported in its Persian wars by this policy of alliance and possibly also because the relations with the Jafnid kings in Syria had never been easy. Whatever the case, toward the end of the reign of Khusraw I Anūshirwān "with the immortal soul" (531–579), about 570 according to a Byzantine source or about 575 according to the Arabic tradition, the Sāsānids helped a Ḥimyarite prince to overthrow Abraha's successor (see later); it was especially easy as the Ethiopian dynasty of Ḥimyar was very weak, probably as a result of the failure of a campaign launched by Abraha against Makka (c. 560). Finally, some twenty-five or thirty years after the Ethiopian dynasty of Ḥimyar had been overthrown, under Khusraw II (591–628), grandson of Khusraw I, the Sāsānids annexed Yemen and made it a province of their empire.

The Persians, like the Byzantines some decades earlier, finally became weary of their Arab tributaries. In 602, they impoverished and condemned to death the last king of al-Ḥīra, al-Nu'mān III, son of al-Mundhir IV (c. 580–602). A revival of the war against Byzantium allowed them to conquer Syria, Palestine, and Egypt. However, a new Byzantine emperor, Heraclius (610–641), reversed the situation. In 628, Khusraw II, weakened by his defeats, was evicted from the throne. He was followed by a four-year succession crisis that weakened the empire; its Arabian possessions (Yemen, Oman, and Baḥrayn) were then lost to the principality of al-Madīna. The arrival to power of Yazdajird III (632–651), Khusraw II's grandson, did not allow the situation to be reestablished permanently. As early as 633, an Arab army led by Khālid b. al-Walīd attacked and destroyed the Sāsānid fortress that protected the empire from attacks coming from Arabia. In 636, the defeat at Qādisiyya brought about the loss of Mesopotamia and the flight of the emperor to Iran. The loss of the capital and other important sources of revenue proved to be fatal.

V. The Emergence of Makka (560–630)

V.A The End of the Arabian Kingdoms

From the 550s onward, the kingdoms still controlling the major part of Arabia started falling apart, and within less than fifty years, they disappeared, one after another. In the south, Abraha's kingdom was the first to collapse. Around 560–565, it lost control of inner Arabia, and some five or ten years later, it was prey to a succession crisis. While Abraha's two sons (Yaksūm/Aksūm and Masrūq) fought over his heritage and successively imposed their authority with difficulty, a Yemenite Jewish prince called Sayf b. dhī Yazan (a kinsman of Sharaḥ'īl Yaqbul dhu-Yaz'an, the general sent by King Joseph against Najrān) rebelled and easily overthrew the last sovereign of Aksūmite origin with the help of a small Sāsānid troop (around 570 or 575). Ḥimyar then recovered some influence: according to al-Wāqidī, Sayf sent his son to Makka to be its governor (*wālī*) (Kister 1972, 76). But Sayf was soon assassinated, and

Yemen was reduced to the rank of a Sāsānid province with a governor resident in Ṣanʿāʾ (Daghfous 1995, 130–179; Gajda 2009, 157–167). In Ḥaḍramawt as in Najrān, local authorities clearly enjoyed great autonomy, and it is plausible that the same was true in all of Yemen. We know of no monument or inscriptions dating from this period, a fact that illustrates the collapse of South Arabian civilization and its general impoverishment (Finster 1996; Schiettecatte and Robin 2009).

At the center of the peninsula, the authority of the last Ḥujrid princes was virtual. Decline had begun with al-Ḥārith's murder in early 528. Byzantine sources mention only a single successor to al-Ḥārith, his grandson Kaisos (Qays) (c. 530–540), who ended his career in Palestine in the service of Byzantium. In 552, the inscription Murayghān 1 = Ry 506 mentions a revolt of the Banū ʿAmrum (a name that probably designates the Ḥujrids), which suggests that they had kept a certain influence until that date.

According to the Islamic tradition, the Ḥujrid principality was divided between the sons of al-Ḥārith, who were soon fighting against each other. The last representatives of the dynasty wandered from tribe to tribe, like the famous poet Imruʾ al-Qays, a grandson of al-Ḥārith, and finally returned to Ḥaḍramawt. It was then that the Naṣrid princes of al-Ḥīra, agents of the Sāsānids, replaced the Ḥujrids in inner Arabia. It is said, for example, that the Naṣrid ʿAmr son of al-Mundhir III (also grandson of the Ḥujrid al-Ḥārith from his mother Hind) sponsored a peace treaty between Bakr and Taghlib at the market of dhū ʾl-Majāz, thirty-five kilometers to the east of Makka (Lecker 2005c, 39). Such mediation seems possible in the 540s: in 552, if this is the date of the Murayghān 3 inscription, Abraha rejoiced in having chased ʿAmr from inner Arabia; besides, it is improbable that ʿAmr went to a market far from his kingdom after his accession to the throne of al-Ḥīra in 554.

In the Byzantine diocese of Oriens, the second Jafnid sovereign, al-Mundhir, son of al-Ḥārith, was deposed and exiled in 582. There are two easily identifiable causes of the fall of the Jafnid monarchy. First, the support that the Arab tribes in Byzantine territory brought to the religious dissidents of the anti-Chalcedonian (or Monophysite) party required control. Moreover, the collapse of the Christian Aksūmite dynasty in Yemen ten years earlier definitively ruined any hope of leading the Arab tribes of the peninsula into an alliance against Persia. The consequences were nevertheless disastrous according to the *Chronicle of Michael the Syrian* (2.350–351): "The kingdom of the Ṭayyayê (= Arabs) was divided between fifteen princes. Most of them sided with Persia, and at that point the empire of the Christian Ṭayyayê met its end and was over, because of the perfidy of the Romans."

In the Sāsānid empire, at al-Ḥīra, the Naṣrid monarchy, founded at the end of the third century, was eliminated in 602. This elimination was probably a consequence of the Byzantine withdrawal and a reflection of Byzantium's increasing loss of interest for Arabia, which was no longer a threat because of the acute economic and demographic crisis that had hit it.

It was a period of disorder. Communication routes were no longer secure. The Sāsānid kings had to negotiate the security of their messengers and their caravans one by one with tribal chiefs, to whom they offered titles or honorific attributes such as the right to wear the diadem on a turban or headdress (hence the name *dhū 'l-tāj*, "diadem-wearer," given by the Islamic tradition to many of those princes). Sometimes the caravans were looted by the very groups who were escorting them.

The Persians kept a military presence in Yemen and the Gulf, thus maintaining some influence there. All local claims of authority are addressed to them. There are even allusions to taxes levied for them in Yathrib (al-Madīna): a tradition recounts that the Persian governor of the Gulf entrusted the Jews of the tribes of Qurayẓa and al-Naḍīr—and later a member of the tribe of Khazraj, "king" 'Amr, son of al-Iṭnāba—with this responsibility. According to these traditions, the Sāsānids had control over the oasis during the entire second half of the sixth century (Lecker 2002; 2005a).

V.B The Retreat of Aksūm

As we have seen earlier, a son of Kālēb's came to the throne. He is the author of an inscription found at Aksūm in 1959 (*RIÉth* 192). His name, "Wa'zeb . . . man of *Ḥdfn* son of Ella Aṣbəḥa Gabra Krəśtoś (*W'zb . . . b's Ḥdfn wld 'l 'ṣbḥ Gbr Krśtś*)," was not remembered by the Ethiopian tradition, which calls Kālēb's successor "Gabra Maskal" (Munro-Hay 1991, 13–14; Phillipson 2003, 42–46). His titulature reveals that he had no authority left in Arabia or among the Nubians (see previously).

Wa'zeb, apparently the Ge'ez form of the Greek "Ouazebas" (a name borne by a previous king), did not strike coinage either under that name or under that of Gabra Krəśtoś. Moreover, numismatists have noted that a single die was used to strike coins with the names of Kālēb and "Allamidas," which implies that those two sovereigns followed each other very closely (Munro-Hay 1991, 89). It is thus very difficult to reconstruct the sequence of these reigns with any certainty.

From this point, Aksūmite chronology escapes us completely. All we have at our disposal is a list of kings who struck coinage and whose chronological classification has been the object of various hypotheses. They are "Israēl/*Ysr'l*," "Gersem/*Grsm*," "Iōēl/*'y'l*," "Iathaz/*Ḥtz*," "Allagabaz," and "*'rmḥ*," plus other names whose reading—on effaced legends—is doubtful or could be alternative names. The royal series of coins should be filled out with a number of others that do not bear the sovereign's name (Munro-Hay and Juel-Jensen 1995; Hahn 2000). The quality of the issues declined, and the quantities of coins struck were small or symbolic. But the number of different types implies that the coinage dating to a time after Kālēb was produced over a long period. However, as the style always reflects Byzantine models, it is probable that the Aksūmite coinage did not continue beyond the conquest of Yemen, the Near East, and

Egypt by the theocratic principality of al-Madīna, which soon controlled the whole of the Red Sea, disrupting and reorienting the long-distance trade circuits by sea or by land.

The kingdoms of the Nile Valley that were previously dominated by Aksūm (or were their tributaries) were emancipated and definitively passed over into the Byzantine sphere of influence. Around 540 (after 538 and before 545), the Byzantine empress Theodora sent a mission led by a notorious anti-Chalcedonian to convert the king of the Nobades to Christianity (his name was Silkō, unless that was his successor). The emperor Justinian I, who wanted that king to adopt a Chalcedonian form of Christianity, sent a competing mission that arrived too late. The king of the Nobades consented to convert to the faith of Theodora, and, from an ecclesiastical point of view, his kingdom was attached to the Byzantine see of Philae (E. Stein 1949, 301–302; Munro-Hay 1982).

One last echo comes from the Islamic sources. Ethiopia (*al-Ḥabasha*) and its sovereign, the negus (*al-najāshī*), appear several times in Muḥammad's career. Some members of the small community founded by Muḥammad at Makka took refuge in Ethiopia, where they were welcomed. After the creation and consolidation of the theocratic principality of al-Madīna (previously Yathrib), Muḥammad addressed diplomatic correspondence to the negus inviting him to convert. Minor anecdotes show that the negus, who professed a religion that was more Muslim than Christian, sent gifts to Muḥammad and, on the day of his death, was the object of a prayer by Muḥammad (Raven 1988). Finally, in an allegory of the world paying homage to its master, painted in the Umayyad palace of Quṣayr 'Amrā in Jordan, the negus appears with five other sovereigns: the Byzantine emperor, the king of Persia, the Visigothic king of Spain, and two others whose names have disappeared (Van Donzel n.d., "al-Nadjāshī"; Fowden 2004).

From this disparate set of data, one can infer that Ethiopia was still a regional power and that commercial exchange with the Arabian peninsula continued at more or less the same level of intensity. It also seems that the negus was well disposed toward the Muslims he received. Did he see in them potential allies who could allow him to regain some influence in Arabia? Or did his sympathies tend toward Muḥammad's religious reform? Our sources do not permit a clear answer. But they suggest that Muḥammad himself had some familiarity with Ethiopia: according to Ibn Qutayba, his nurse had been Ethiopian, and Ibn Sa'd thinks he even spoke Ethiopic (Van Donzel n.d., "al-Nadjāshī").

Muḥammad's contemporary negus was called al-Aṣḥam b. Abjar, Aṣḥama, Aṣmaḥa, or Saḥama. This is reminiscent of "*'rmḥ*," but this is too uncertain a sign to serve as a basis for identification.

V.C Makka, a Commercial Power

Toward the middle of the sixth century, it is easy to imagine that trans-Arabian trade was disorganized. After its conquest by Aksūm, Abraha's takeover, and finally the Kinda revolt, Ḥimyar found a certain stability again only at the end of the 540s. Abraha then started the reconquest of inner Arabia. An inscription dated 552 and a second one, probably of the same date or shortly later (Murayghān 1 and 3), celebrate the reestablishment of Ḥimyarite control over almost the entire peninsula. But it was a short-lived conquest. At an unknown date between 555 and 565, Abraha was defeated by Makka. That mythical battle, known only by the Islamic tradition, was very striking because Abraha's army was preceded by an elephant (as discussed earlier). It was undertaken after the building of al-Qalīs, the great church of Ṣan'ā'.

It is difficult to understand with precision what Makka was at the time. The town was certainly not a first-rate military or commercial power. First of all, it is not unambiguously mentioned in any source predating Muḥammad. Moreover, according to the Islamic tradition, its trade network developed after Abraha's reign: two of the pillars of that network—the famous fair of al-'Ukāẓ and the guild of the *ḥums*—were founded after the "year of the Elephant." One can also add that Makka was a recently founded town: again, according to the Islamic tradition, it goes back to Quṣayy, the ancestor of the Quraysh, who settled there six generations before Muḥammad (son of 'Abd Allāh, son of 'Abd al-Muṭṭalib [Shayba], son of Hāshim, son of 'Abd Manāf, son of Quṣayy).

Several strategies were employed to counter the disastrous effects of anarchy. The simplest one was to establish or reactivate the sacred months, during which every act of violence was prohibited. During those sacred months, it was possible to participate in pilgrimages or fairs without running into any great danger. An eight-month truce was established by the Banū Murra b. 'Awf (faction of Dhubyān, 250 kilometers to the north of al-Madīna) while the Quraysh defended the principle of two annual truces, one of one month and the second of three months, resulting in a total of four months of truce. For all tribes, respect for the Qurayshite truce implied a recognition of the sacred character of the Makkan Sanctuary (*Ḥaram*); the tribes that accepted this principle were called *muḥrimūn* (as opposed to *muḥillūn*, who refused it).

The Quraysh tribe, which proposed to the Arabian tribes an affiliation among equals, is distinguished by its inventiveness and sense of initiative. This affiliation, which M. J. Kister called the "Commonwealth of Makka" (1965b, 116, 121), could take various forms. The least restrictive was the *ilāf*, a security pact between the Quraysh and a tribe, allowing free movement in the territory of that tribe without having arranged an alliance (*ḥilf*). The cult association of the *ḥums*, which brought together individuals and groups sharing the same demanding rites, was above all religious, but it naturally had important economic consequences: it was the start of a community that went beyond tribal divides and allowed the Qurayshites to develop relations of trust with distant partners. Finally, the Quraysh associated several tribes very closely with its affairs: thus several Tamīmites served as judges at the al-'Ukāẓ fair, Tamīm participated in a sort of intertribal militia, and many Tamīmite women married Qurayshites (Kister 1965b, 146–147, 157–160, 142–143).

The complex trade networks developed by the Makkans after their victory over Abraha led a Belgian scholar of the early twentieth century, Henri Lammens (1911), to qualify Makka as a "merchant republic." That vision has been criticized by Patricia Crone (1987), who demonstrated that on the eve of Islam, Makka was a rather modest town with limited resources, where inhabitants often suffered from hunger (Peters 1988). Compared with the great caravan cities of the Near East like Petra and Palmyra, Makka cut a sorry figure. It was nevertheless one of the most active towns of the peninsula, along with Najrān and 'Adan, and probably one of the most prosperous and secure, since, contrary to many towns of the time (like Najrān), it did not have surrounding walls (Simon 1989).

V.D The End of Arabian Polytheism: The Time of the Prophets

The crisis and disorder of Arabia was made worse by the fact that there were many causes of division. Religion was one of the most important ones. The kingdom of Ḥimyar rejected polytheism as early as 380 and turned toward Judaism, which became the dominant religion in Yemen and the oases of the Ḥijāz. Christianity took root in the Arab-Persian Gulf. Like the rest of the ancient world, Arabia yearned for a more spiritual form of religion and began believing in an afterlife. Moreover, the choice of religion increasingly became an individual rather than a collective issue.

In some circles, conversion to a foreign religion gave rise to hesitancy; however, those religions were, in Muḥammad's time, the principal intellectual and spiritual reference points. Everywhere, including Makka, the old Arabic pagan vocabulary was replaced by terms borrowed from Jewish and Christian Aramaic, terms that were already common in the Yemeni inscriptions from about 400 onward (Jeffery 1938; Robin 2000). The categories and concepts that circulated through those borrowings (angels, devil, paradise, prayer, alms, etc.) naturally made their way into the culture. Above all, the extraordinary familiarity of Muḥammad's audience with biblical stories is most striking. There is no doubt that on the eve of Islam, Makkan polytheism was already dying (Hawting 1999).

The distribution of the polytheistic temples known in Muḥammad's time confirms that Arabian paganism was marginalized. Among the urban centers and oases, the only known temples were at Dūmat al-Jandal, Makka (Rubin 1986 and *EI* 2, s.v. "Ka'ba"), al-Ṭā'if (Kister 1979), and Tabāla (300 kilometers southeast of Makka); none are mentioned in Yemen, in the Gulf, in central Arabia, or in the great oases of the Ḥijāz (Yathrib, Khaybar, al-'Ulā/al-Ḥijr, and Taymā'). Polytheistic cults were no longer practiced except in the steppe and the desert.

If we take the case of Yathrib (studied in detail by the Israeli scholar Michael Lecker, 1995; see also Gil 1984; 2004; Hasson 1989), where two tribes with a polytheistic majority and three Jewish tribes coexisted (without mentioning the many small Jewish factions), there was no polytheistic public cult building. Islamic tradition does note "idols" repeatedly, but they belonged to the various lineages and factions. Yathrib's polytheism was confined to the private sphere (Lecker 2005, iii, whose conclusions are different). If polytheism had been the dominant religion, as in Makka at the beginning of the seventh century, there should be evidence for temples inside the town or in its immediate neighborhood.

The decline of paganism presented people with two options. One was conversion to an already established religion, the main ones being Judaism, Manichaeism (Tardieu 1992; 1994), and the various denominations of Christianity. That was the choice made by a large number of individuals and groups. We have significant evidence concerning Christianity but little concerning Judaism. The clearest one is found in al-Bakrī (*Muʿjam mā ʾstaʿjam*), following Ibn Shabba: before offering refuge to the tribe of Balī, the inhabitants of Taymāʾ demanded they convert to Judaism (Lecker 1995, 66–67).

The second option was to transform the old cults and adapt them to the new demand of a single God and the expectation of an afterlife. This approach did, of course, involve a formal break with the past, but it allowed the faithful to preserve the cultural references to which they were attached, such as traditional rites, rhythmical prose (*sajʿ*), and the enigmatic images of poets and soothsayers.

Muḥammad was not the only one to take that path (Piotrovskij 1984; Halperin 1976; Landau-Tasseron 1997; Hämeen-Anttila 2000). Half a dozen rival prophets are mentioned by the tradition, which puts much effort into demonstrating that they were all mediocre imitators. That is probably true for most of them but not for the principal figure, Musaylima, prophet of the Ḥanīfa in central Arabia. That reformer, much older than Muḥammad, was already active when the latter was still at Makka. He proclaimed a God named al-Raḥmān from whom he received, through the archangel Gabriel, a revelation called a "qur'ān." The theocratic principality founded by Musaylima seems to have been a particularly fierce adversary for the Muslims, who did not succeed in crushing it until AH 12/633 C.E., after a number of failed attempts (Kister 2002).

It must be emphasized that Muḥammad, Musaylima, and others recruited their first partisans in the regions where Judaism and Christianity were well rooted; their reform underlined the defiance those religions inspired. Their monotheism was not the heir of a primitive Arabian religion—an argument developed by Islam—but a reaction against acculturation. There were many who preferred to the established religions a form of monotheism that did not reject their ancestral manifestations of religiosity.

For polytheism, still lively among the Bedouin and in the south of the Ḥijāz, the evidence given by the Islamic tradition mainly concerns Makka and Quraysh. First of all, it is important to distinguish the pantheon of Quraysh and that of the tribes that Quraysh had federated into various cult and commercial associations, especially that of the *ḥums* (Kister 1965b, 131–134; Simon 1970; Fabietti 1988).

The Qurayshite pantheon was composed principally of idols that were in the *Ḥaram* of Makka, that is, Hubal (the most important and oldest deity), Manāf, Isāf, and Nā'ila. The pantheon of the *ḥums* and other associations was superimposed on the Qurayshite one; their principal deities were Allāh (the god who brought victory to Quraysh against Abraha at the Battle of the Elephant) and three goddesses, Allāt, al-'Uzzà, and Manāt. Allāh's shrine was the Ka'ba in Makka, but the three goddesses had neither idols nor a shrine in that city. To find a shrine consecrated to one of them, one must look as far as Buss, about 100 kilometers northeast of Makka, where there was a temple of al-'Uzzà.

The question has been raised whether Hubal (the main god of Quraysh) and Allāh (main god of the entire tribal federation around Quraysh) were not one and the same deity under two successive names: indeed, Allāh (which is probably a contracted form of al-Ilāh, "the God") could be a designation that consecrated Hubal's superiority over the other gods.

In favor of this identification (which goes back to Wellhausen 1887), one should note that the idol of Hubal was "within the Ka'ba," that is, in the shrine of Allāh, according to mainstream opinion (for al-Wāqidī, it was outside, next to the door). Another argument is that Quraysh, whose pantheon was dominated by Hubal, was called the "people of Allāh" (*ahl Allāh*) after their victory over Abraha.

However, evidence supporting the hypothesis of two distinct gods is not lacking. The temple dedicated to Allāh—the Ka'ba—is very different from the rest of the *Ḥaram*. According to some traditions, the Ka'ba contained no statue, but its interior was decorated with images of Mary and Jesus, of prophets, angels, and trees. Another argument is that the two gods clearly had different functions: Hubal was invoked and venerated only by the Qurayshites, while Allāh was the supreme God of a large group of individuals belonging to different tribes (Rubin 1986; Robin 2001a). According to this hypothesis, it should be assumed that the temple of Makka was first consecrated to a supreme god named Allāh and then hosted the pantheon of Quraysh after the conquest of Makka by that tribe, about a hundred years before Muḥammad's time.

A second question concerns the nature of Allāh. Was he the God of the supporters of monotheism or a god of pagan origin? In the oldest revelations of the Qur'ān, the name of Allāh does not appear. When Muḥammad refers to God, he says "the Lord" or, if he want to give him a proper name, it is al-Raḥmān (the name of the one God of the Jews and Christians of Arabia, but also of the followers of Musaylima) (Peters 1991, 300–301).

Allāh is thus a god originating in polytheism. Inscriptions seem to confirm it. At Qaryat al-Fāw, for example, a certain 'Igl entrusts the tomb he has built to "Kahl, Allāh, and 'Aththar the Oriental." The text is dated by the writing style to the beginning of the Christian era (just before or just after).

We know nothing precise about the nature of this god Allāh. He was probably a deity whose name was replaced by a ritual term describing him as "the god" par excellence; in favor of this hypothesis, at Qaryat al-Fāw, al-Lāt ("the goddess") was also venerated.

At the very beginning of Islam, the competition faced by the old polytheistic religions, already rejected by the elites of the major part of Arabia, was twofold: that of the foreign religions and that of the new cults, preached by various religious reformers. It is not surprising that they collapsed so suddenly. The only uncertainty concerned the nature of the monotheistic religion that was going to prevail.

V.E A Time of Crisis

The Arabia of this disorder was also an Arabia experiencing economic crisis (Schiettecatte and Robin 2009). The British scholar Derek Kennet (2005; 2007) was the first to observe that the principal archaeological sites in eastern Arabia show no signs of occupation in the centuries that preceded Islam. Many Christian monuments (churches or monasteries) do seem to have been built on the coast or the islands at that time (Langfeldt 1994; Bin Seray 1996; King 1997), but Robert Carter (2008) has demonstrated that, based on the archaeological material, they should be dated to the seventh and eighth centuries. The most plausible hypothesis is that the Muslim conquests provoked a redistribution of wealth and an economic revival. This benefited all communities, especially the Christians, who at that time built magnificent monuments. This dating concurs with a study by Sebastian Brock (1999) that shows that the peak of Christianity in the Arab-Persian Gulf was in the seventh century.

In the north of the Ḥijāz, in Taymā', the German archaeologists Ricardo Eichmann and Arnulf Hausleiter have not yet found a single zone that was occupied from the fourth to the sixth century, even while the oasis, according to the Islamic narrative sources, was one of the main political and military powers of the region.

There is general consensus on the idea that in the fifty years preceding the *hijra* Arabia was ruined and devastated, but no agreement in determining the reasons for this disaster. The most frequently expressed hypothesis is that Arabia brutally collapsed in the course of the sixth century as a consequence of wars, massacres, and epidemics (such as the famous Justinianic plague).

Other factors also played a role. There was, first of all, an increasing aridity of the climate, a process that had begun several millennia earlier but at this time was beginning to touch the flora of the Yemeni mountains and made agriculture less predictable in many areas of inner Arabia. In the irrigated zones of Yemen, which had already been developed for several centuries, the accumulation of alluvium raised the level of the fields and made it necessary to continuously raise the dams and dig the canals anew, making those facilities increasingly fragile. Such difficulties can be observed particularly at Ma'rib, where the maintenance and repair of the dam became impossible after the collapse of the only central authority capable of mobilizing the necessary resources; the final ruin of the dam, mentioned in the Qur'ān (34.16), certainly occurred before the *hijra*.

A group of Russian scholars led by Andrey Korotayev (1999) has also suggested that the crisis might have been heightened by a natural cataclysm, a major volcanic eruption that provoked great climatic disorders and several years of famine. Indeed, several sources mention that during Justinian's tenth year (536), the sun was veiled to the point of resembling the moon and that that phenomenon lasted between twelve and eighteen months (Hirschfeld 2006, 25).

In short, in the second half of the sixth century, Arabia witnessed a dramatic crisis following brutal and unpredictable events. This cataclysmic approach is in harmony with the Islamic tradition. However, the hypothesis is beginning to attract support that this crisis was severe because of its onset during a long cycle of increasing climatic aridity and an impoverishment that had been perceptible for years.

VI. The Birth of an Arab Identity

From its beginnings to the end of antiquity, Arabia's cultural model was the kingdom of Saba' (and its successor, the kingdom of Ḥimyar), whose script, language, material culture, and iconographic repertoire were imitated in neighboring regions and, to a lesser extent, in the northern Ḥijāz and the Gulf region. Up to around the second century C.E., there was no perceptible manifestation of an Arab identity common to all the populations of inner Arabia. The term *Arab* is indeed attested from the middle of the ninth century B.C.E. but always in external sources and in foreign languages (Akkadian, Hebrew, Greek, Latin, Saba'ic, etc.) and apparently describing the nomadic stockbreeding populations of the steppe and the desert (Eph'al 1982; Macdonald 2001; Retsö 2003).

Not until the end of the second century or the third century C.E.—in two minor inscriptions in Ḥaḍramawt—did locals use the ethnic term *Arab* to describe themselves (Ja 950 and 961; Robin 2006a). And some decades later, in 328, a sovereign of the Syrian desert, the Naṣrid Imru' al-Qays, son of 'Amr, proclaims himself "king of all the Arabs" (L 205, an inscription found at al-Namāra in southern Syria, in Arabic but using the late Nabatean script, i.e., the one that postdated the end of the kingdom of Nabatene). However, at the very time when the populations of inner Arabia began claiming the name Arabs, foreign sources stopped using this term and preferred Saracens in Greek and Tayyites, Ma'addites, or Hagarites in Syriac (Retsö 2003).

Arab identity, once it began asserting itself, was founded mainly, as far as we can tell, on language and culture: thus in the Qur'ān, the term *Arab* describes a language or a document, but not an ethnic group. Very logically, the Arabic language was written in its own alphabet from the beginning of the sixth century. It was a new variety of the Aramean script that borrowed letters from the late Nabatean alphabet (used by the Arabs of the Near East and the northern Ḥijāz) and combined them in the manner of the Syriac script. It appears for the first time in Zabad, some sixty kilometers southeast of Aleppo, in a small text that enumerates some personal names on the lintel of a Christian shrine in honor of Saint Sergius; that document can be dated to 512, like the long bilingual inscription in Greek and Syriac engraved on the same lintel.

The second text, chronologically speaking, is engraved on a rock of Jabal Usays (about 100 kilometers east of Damascus); its author indicates that "al-Ḥārith the king has sent him in garrison to Usays in the year 423 (of the era of the province of Arabia)," namely, 528–529 C.E. That king is surely the Jafnid al-Ḥārith, son of Jabala.

The third text, written by an Arab phylarch in Arabic and Greek, commemorates the construction of a church dedicated to Saint John in 568 at Ḥarrān, in the Lajā' (south of present-day Syria).

Those three inscriptions, to which can be added a fourth, that of the foundation of the convent of Hind at al-Ḥīra, known only by the copy preserved in al-Bakrī and Yāqūt, show that the Arabic script appeared in Syria and in Lower 'Irāq in a Christian milieu. Its development probably aimed to facilitate teaching the Christian religion to the Arabs of the desert. That script was still rudimentary: it noted the long vowels *ī* and *ū*, but it did not note *ā* (which was only transcribed by *alif* at the time of the Medinan Caliphate); the twenty-eight consonants of Arabic were transcribed with the help of only fifteen symbols, some of which could register two, three, or even five different articulations (like *rā'* and *zayn*; *jīm*, *ḥā'*, and *khā'*; or *bā'*, *tā'*, *thā'*, *nūn*, and *yā'*). The diacritics, which indicate how to pronounce the symbols with different phonetic values, do not seem to have been known before the Medinan Caliphate, since their oldest attestation goes back to AH 22/642 C.E. (Robin 2006b; Abbott 1938).

The Islamic tradition does not contradict this reconstruction. It states that the Arabic script was "invented" in the Euphrates Valley and from there reached al-Ḥīra. It gives some chronological reference points. For example, Zayd b. Ḥammād is said to have learned Arabic *first*, and then Persian. Given that he was in charge of Khusraw I's (532–579) postal system and regent of the kingdom of al-Ḥīra around 575, between the reigns of Qābūs (569–c. 573) and al-Mundhir IV (c. 575–c. 580), it is possible to date his acquisition of Arabic to the second quarter of the sixth century. His son 'Adī b. Zayd, the famous Christian poet from al-Ḥīra, was Khusraw I's secretary and remained in that post until the beginning of the reign of Khusraw II (590–628). He was the first to write in Arabic in Khusraw's chancellery; he died around 590, executed by al-Nu'mān III (c. 580–602). His son Zayd b. 'Adī succeeded him as secretary for affairs with the "Arab kings." From al-Ḥīra, the Arabic script reached various centers of northern and western Arabia, mainly Dūmat al-Jandal and Makka (Abbott

1938, 5–7). In the latter city, it is said to have appeared while Muḥammad was still young and was only practiced by a small number of people at the arrival of Islam (al-Balādhurī mentions the names of seventeen men and some women).

The emergence of an Arab identity is also manifested through the development of a poetic language that was common to all tribes, of which the Islamic tradition has preserved significant examples. The origin of that poetic language is not yet clear. The place to look might be Yemen, where three rhymed poems have already been found, ranging between 100 and 330 C.E. (P. Stein 2008). For many scholars, the poetic language of pre-Islamic Arabia was a form of *koinē*. However, that term is not appropriate: a *koinē* is a language understood, but also spoken, by the majority. It is better to reserve the term for middle Arabic, which developed in the first centuries of Islam in the conquered provinces and gave birth to today's dialects.

Arab identity was also founded on a peculiar undertaking, begun at the eve of Islam and followed up over several generations, which seems to have no parallel in human history: collecting all the particular genealogies—above all, those of the leaders and nobles whose legitimacy was based on the antiquity of their lineage—into a single tree that gave a faithful image of the totality of the nation (Kennedy 1997). The most accomplished of those contributions was that of a scholar of the second century A.H. (eighth century C.E.), Hishām, son of Muḥammad al-Kalbī (d. c. A.H. 204/C.E. 819); his *Jamharat al-nasab* (Caskel 1966), which contains some 35,000 names, definitively fixed the contours of the Arab nation, as well as the "kinship" links that united the tribes and aristocratic lineages.

Of course, the genealogical tree of the Arab nation, which divides it into two branches, the descendants of ʿAdnān in the North and those of Qaḥṭān in the South, is an allegory that records only a minute proportion of the people who really existed and defines *kinship* by simply translating geographical proximity and political alliances during the second century A.H./eighth century C.E. The genealogies nevertheless played an important role in the struggle for power during the first Islamic centuries by giving an easily comprehensible form to coalitions, and it is not rare to see them still invoked today in Arabia and the Middle East.

VII. Pre-Islamic Arabia According to the Islamic Tradition

According to the Islamic tradition, the main characteristic of Arabia at the eve of Islam is anarchy (Caussin 1847). The tribes, most of which were resistant to all forms of subjection, were quarrelsome. It is enough to refer to the poems, transmitted generation after generation within tribes and lineages, to celebrate the bravery, generosity, and eloquence of their ancestors: one finds the echo of many a memorable battle (the famous *yawm*, pl. *ayyām*). There was no state authority capable of ensuring a minimum of order and security, especially by punishing raids and pillaging. For that reason, travel—and thus trade—were dangerous except during the sacred months that some tribes had negotiated with their neighbours under the patronage of some deity. Even in the regions that were in theory dominated by the Sāsānids—Yemen, Oman, and the Arabian coast of the Gulf—caravans had to put themselves under the protection of the most powerful tribes to reduce risks (Lecker 2003, 57–58). Although several chiefs in inner Arabia or Yemen claimed the title of "king" or "diadem-bearer" ('Athamina 1998; Lecker 2003), their authority was recognized by only a very small territory of tribal entities.

The opinion common among specialists of early Islam that Arabia was dominated by the nomadic world is certainly erroneous. If we take the example of Makka, we see that the town mainly lived from long-distance trade, which is conceivable only in an urban framework (with warehouses, offices, and financial establishments), involving an urban lifestyle. The Makkans are not dominated by the nomads; rather, they take the nomads in their service and bind them in multiple commercial and religious networks. The overstatement of the role of the nomads comes from the important place they had in pre-Islamic poetry, one of the foundations of Arab identity; it is also because in the Abbasid period, the scholars of Lower 'Irāq considered the nomads as models, especially in questions of language and genealogy. Among modern European scholars, it comes from the inherited fascination of the explorers of colonial times for the desert and the Bedouin.

Again, according to the Islamic tradition, the anarchy of Muḥammad's Arabia went hand in hand with great poverty. Destitution was extreme, even in Makka, where famine was endemic. When the Makkan sanctuary had to be rebuilt (the famous Ka'ba), during Muḥammad's younger years, the beams were made with wood reclaimed from a Byzantine shipwreck. Intellectual poverty was also great, since Quraysh (the tribe of Makka) was not to discover writing until the end of the sixth century. In Muḥammad's generation, there were so few Makkans who knew how to read and write that al-Balādhurī can actually list them.

Many think that Arabia was struck by unprecedented disasters. Many tribes—settled in 'Irāq, in Syria, or in various regions of the peninsula—came from Yemen, which they had left because of the breach of the great dam of Ma'rib (120 kilometers east of Ṣan'ā'), an event that occurred at the end of the sixth century. Of course, the simple breach of a dam that allowed the irrigation of an oasis of only several dozen square kilometers did not provoke an exodus of that extent, but it struck the imagination: it was a symbol of the final fading of the kingdom of Ḥimyar, which had dominated a great part of the peninsula for two centuries (c. 350–550 C.E.), and its consequence, the rise of lawlessness. Many towns, like al-Ḥigr (Arabic al-Ḥijr), once well populated and prosperous, were deserted and ruined, something the religious reformers explained as a divine punishment (Qur'ān, 15, "al-Ḥijr," vv. 80–84). In other towns, the population took the place of older inhabitants who dispersed or disappeared: this was the case of Makka, where the Quraysh tribe settled under the leadership of Quṣayy, six generations before Muḥammad. Whole tribes of which we no longer know anything (e.g., 'Ād, Thamūd, Ṭasm, or Jadīs) were wiped out for various reasons.

The Islamic tradition calls the pre-Islamic period "the state of ignorance" (*jāhiliyya*), ignorance of the Revelation above all. It highlights the contrast between polytheistic Arabia, fallen to the lowest degree of degradation because it had forgotten the one God, and triumphant Islam; only some emblematic individuals, the *ḥanīf* / pl. *ḥunafā'*, escaped the general disrepute because they believed, even before the Revelation, in the one God. According to the tradition, those who opposed Muḥammad's message associated God with other deities. In fact, Muḥammad mainly fought against monotheists, the Jews of the northern Ḥijāz and Musaylima's followers in central Arabia. The Makkan polytheists, from the famous episode of the "satanic verses," had shown that they were ready to accept a compromise if their economic interests were not threatened.

The trace of that compromise can be found in sura 53, "al-Najm," verses 19–21, whose initial form was:

> *Consider al-Lāt and al-'Uzzà*
> *and the third one, Manāt?*
> *[They are the sublime goddesses*
> *and their intercession is hoped for],*
> *Are you to have the male and He the female?*

The two verses between brackets were not included in the Vulgate because they were "repealed." According to the Islamic tradition, they were not dictated by God, but by Satan, who abused the Prophet. Historians think those verses reflect a bargain proposed by Muḥammad to his opponents: against the acceptance of the one God and the recognition of his prophetic authority, Muḥammad made the concession that three polytheistic goddesses were divine messengers who could intercede between God and men. The acceptance of the compromise by the Makkans was so enthusiastic, it seems, that Muḥammad rapidly changed his mind, realizing that his suggestion ruined the force and coherence of his religious reform.

This image of Arabia before the Revelation, elaborated by the Islamic tradition, is not devoid of any historical foundations, even if it is biased by an apologetic reinterpretation of the events and by an oral transmission that selects and often manipulates the facts (Robin 2009a). But the tradition is shortsighted: its visual range does not exceed two generations; of the most ancient periods, only vague reminiscences remain, drowned in legends and folk themes. It is not surprising that the archaeology of the Arab Peninsula, which began developing in the 1970s, has important corrections to bring to it.

WORKS CITED

I. Ancient Sources

A. Epigraphic Sources

1. Sabaic

For a full bibliography of each text, see K. A. Kitchen. 2000. *Bibliographical Catalogue of Texts: Documentation for Ancient Arabia 2*. The World of Ancient Arabia Series. Liverpool: Liverpool University Press.

'Abadān 1: Christian Robin and Iwona Gajda. 1994. "L'inscription du wādī 'Abadān," *Raydān* 6: 113–137, 193–204; Müller 2010: 50–55.

Av Būsān 4 (= BynM 4): Alessandra Avanzini. 1985. "Problemi storici della regione di al-Ḥadā' nel periodo preislamico e nuove iscrizioni." In *Studi Yemeniti* 1, raccolti da Pelio Fronzaroli, = *Quaderni di Semitistica* 14: 53–115; Müller 2010: 39.

BynM = Baynūn Museum.

BynM 1 = Veerman 2: http://csai.humnet.unipi.it.

BynM 4 (= Av Būsān 4): http://csai.humnet.unipi.it.

Capuzzi *AION* 1969: Anna Capuzzi. 1969. "Yasir Yuhan'im in una nuova iscrizione sabea," *Annali dell'Istituto Orientale di Napoli* 29 (N.S. 19): 419–422.

CIH 6, 45 + 44, 46 (= Gl 799), 308, 325, 353 (= Louvre 81), 407, 430 (= Louvre 84), *CIH* 431 + 438 (= Louvre 86) + 948, 448 (*CIH* 448 + Garb Hakir 1), 537 (voir *RES* 4919 + *CIH* 537 = L 121), 540, 541, 543 (= ẒM 772 A + B), 596 + 597 (*CIH* 596 + 597 + *RES* 4157 + 4158), 620, 621, 628, 644, 948 (see 431): *Corpus Inscriptionum Semiticarum ab Academia Inscriptionum et Litterarum Humaniorum conditum atque digestum 4, Inscriptiones Ḥimyariticas et Sabaeas continens*. Paris: Imprimerie nationale. *CIH* 6, 325, 537, 540, 541, 621, 644: see also Müller 2010.

DAI GDN 2002/20: Norbert Nebes. 2004. "A New 'Abraha Inscription from the Great Dam of Mārib," *Proceedings of the Seminar for Arabian Studies* 34: 221–230; Müller 2010: 107–109.

DhM = Dhamār Museum.

DhM 201, 204, 287, 290 (= Khaldūn-Hirrān 1): http://csai.humnet.unipi.it.

DJE = Deutsche Jemen-Expedition.

DJE 23: Rainer Degen. 1974. "Die hebräische Inschrift DJE 23 aus dem Jemen," *Neue Ephemeris für Semitische Epigraphik* 2: 111–116.

DJE 25 see Maṣna'at Māriya 1.

Dostal 1: Walter W. Müller. 1974. "Eine sabäische Inschrift aus dem Jahre 566 der ḥimjarischen Ära," *Neue Ephemeris für Semitische Epigraphik* 2: 139–144; Müller 2010: 74.

Epitaph of Leah: Joseph Naveh. 2003. "A Bilingual Burial Inscription from Saba," *Låšonénu* 65.2: 117–120. (In Hebrew, English Summary: II).

Fa = Fakhrī/Fakhry.

Fa 60 (= Ja 856): Gonzague Ryckmans. 1952. *Epigraphical Texts*. In Ahmed Fakhry, *An Archaeological Journey to Yemen (March–May 1947)*, Part II. Cairo: Government Press.

Fa 74: ibid.; most recently Walter W. Müller. 1976. "Neuinterpretation altsüdarabischen Inschriften *RES* 4698, *CIH* 45+44, Fa 74," *Annali dell'Istituto Orientale di Napoli* 36 (N.S. 26): 55–67; Müller 2010: 89–90.

Garb Ant Yem 9 d: Giovanni Garbini. 1970. "Antichità yemenite," *Annali dell'Istituto Orientale di Napoli* 30 (N.S. 20): 400–404, 537–548; Müller 2010: 92.

Garb Bayt al-Ashwal 1: Giovanni Garbini. 1970. "Una bilingue sabeo-ebraica da Ẓafar," *Annali dell'Istituto Orientale di Napoli* 30 (N.S. 20): 153–165.
Garb Bayt al-Ashwal 2: *ibid.*; Müller 2010: 59.
Garb Framm. 3, 6, 7: Giovanni Garbini. 1971. "Frammenti epigrafici sabei [I] and II," *Annali dell'Istituto Orientale di Napoli* 31 (N.S. 21): 538–542 and 1973. *Annali dell'Istituto Orientale di Napoli* 33 (N.S. 23): 587–593.
Garb Hakir 1 (*CIH* 448 + Garb Hakir 1): Giovanni Garbini. 1971. "Iscrizioni sabee da Hakir," *Annali dell'Istituto Orientale di Napoli* 31 (N.S. 21): 303–311; Müller 2010: 35.
Garb Minkath 1: Giovanni Garbini. 1971. "Una bilingue sabeo-ebraica da Ẓafar," *Annali dell'Istituto Orientale di Napoli* 30 (N.S. 20): 153–165.
Garb NIS 4: Giovanni Garbini. 1973. "Nuove iscrizioni sabee," *Annali dell'Istituto Orientale di Napoli* 33 (N.S. 23): 31–46; Müller 2010: 91.
Garb Sab. Fragm. V: Giovanni Garbini. 1978. "Sabaean fragments," *Raydān* 1: 33–35.
Garb Shuriḥbi'īl Ya'fur (= ẒM 1): Giovanni Garbini. 1969. "Una nuova iscrizione di Šaraḥbi'il Ya'fur," *Annali dell'Istituto Orientale di Napoli* 29 (N.S. 19): 559–566; 1974. "Note di Epigrafia Sabea II," *Annali dell'Istituto Orientale di Napoli* 34 (N.S. 24): 294–298; Müller 2010: 75–76.
Ghul-YU 100: Hani Hayajneh. 2004. "Eine Sammlung von fragmentarischen altsüdarabischen Inschriften aus dem Jemen," *Arabian Archaeology and Epigraphy* 15: 120–148.
Gl = Glaser.
Gl 799 (=*CIH* 46), 1194, 1537, 1539, 1593, 1594, 1596: Brigitte Schaffer. 1972. *Sabäische Inschriften aus verschiedenen Fundorten*. Sammlung Eduard Glaser 7. Österreichische Akademie der Wissenschaften, Philosophisch-historische Klasse, Sitzungsberichte, 282. Band, 1. Abhandlung. Vienna: Hermann Böhlaus Nachf. Gl 799, 1594: see also Müller 2010.
Gl 1541: Helga Tschinkowitz. 1969. *Kleine Fragmente (I. Teil)*. Sammlung Eduard Glaser 6, Österreichische Akademie der Wissenschaften, Philosophisch-historische Klasse, Sitzungsberichte, 261. Band, 4. Abhandlung. Vienna: Hermann Böhlaus Nachf. Gl 1541: see also Müller 2010.
Graf 5: Walter W. Müller. 1972. "Sabäische Inschriften aus dem Museum in Ta'izz," *Neue Ephemeris für semitische Epigraphik* 1: 87–101.
Ḥaṣī 1: Christian Robin (with Serge Frantsouzoff). 2001. "Les inscriptions de Ḥaṣī," *Raydān* 7: 182–191, 207–215, 223.
Ir 14 (= Sharaf 29), 15, 16, 17, 28, 29, 30 (= Ja 657), 31, 32, 37: Muṭahhar 'Alī al-Iryānī. 1973. *Fī ta'rīkh al-Yaman: Sharḥ wa-ta'līq 'alà nuqūsh lam tunshar, 34 naqsh^{an} min majmū'at al-qāḍī 'Alī 'Abd Allāh al-Kuhālī*. Ṣan'ā': Markaz al-dirāsāt al-yamaniyya.
Ir 71: Muṭahhar 'Alī al-Iryānī. 1988. "Naqsh min Nā'iṭ (Iryānī 71)," *Dirāsāt Yamaniyya* 33: 21–46.
Ist 7608 bis + Wellcome A 103664: Jacques Ryckmans. 1976. "L'inscription sabéenne chrétienne Istanbul 7608 bis," *Journal of the Royal Asiatic Society* 96–99; A. F. L. Beeston. 1980. "The South Arabian Collection of the Wellcome Museum in London," *Raydān* 3: 11–16; most recently, Robin 2008b: 96–100.
Ja 516: Albert Jamme. 1955. "Inscriptions sud-arabes de la collection Ettore Rossi," *Rivista degli Studi Orientali* 30: 103–130; see now Christian Robin. 1982. *Les Hautes-Terres du Nord-Yémen avant l'Islam* II. Publications de l'Institut historique et archéologique néerlandais de Stamboul 50: 113–114. Istanbul: Nederlands Historisch-Archaeologisch Instituut in het Nabije Oosten.
Ja 520 (= YM 327): Albert Jamme. 1955. "Inscriptions sud-arabes de la collection Ettore Rossi," *Rivista degli Studi Orientali* 30: 103–130.

Ja 544–547: Albert Jamme. 1955. "Inscriptions des alentours de Mâreb (Yemen)," *Cahiers de Byrsa* 5: 265–281; Müller 2010: 120–121.

Ja 576, 577, 585, 631, 646, 647, 648, 649, 650, 651, 652, 653, 654, 655, 656 (= Sharaf 33), Ja 657 (= Ir 30), 658, 660, 661, 662, 664, 665, 666, 667, 668 (Schmidt-Ma'rib 28 + Ja 668), 669, 670, 671 + 788: Albert Jamme. 1962. *Sabaean Inscriptions from Maḥram Bilqîs (Mârib)*. Publications of the American Foundation for the Study of Man 3. Baltimore: Johns Hopkins University Press.

Ja 856 = Fa 60: Albert Jamme. 1960. "The Late Sabaean Inscription Ja 856," *Bibliotheca Orientalis* 7: 3–5.

Ja 876 (= *RES* 4969): Albert Jamme. 1961. *La dynastie de Šaraḥbi'il Yakûf et la documentation épigraphique sud-arabe*. Publications de l'Institut historique et archéologique néerlandais de Stamboul 9. Istanbul: Nederlands Historisch-Archaeologisch Instituut in het Nabije Oosten.

Ja 950, 961: Albert Jamme. 1963. *The Al-'Uqlah Texts: Documentation Sud-Arabe 3*. Washington, DC: Catholic University of America Press.

Ja 1028: Albert Jamme. 1966. *Sabaean and Ḥasaean Inscriptions from Saudi Arabia*. = *Studi Semitici* 23: 39–55. Rome: Istituto di Studi del Vicino Oriente, Università di Roma; more recently, see Robin 2008b: 87-89, 103; Müller 2010: 100–102.

Ja 2484: Albert Jamme. 1972. *Miscellanées d'ancient* [*sic*] *arabe* 3: 85–86; Müller 2010: 97.

Khaldūn-Aḍra'a 1; Khaldūn-al-Basātīn 1; Khaldūn-'Albaj 1; Khaldūn-Balās 1; Khaldūn Hakir 1: unpublished.

Khaldūn-Hirrān 1: see DhM 290.

Khaldūn-Nūna 1 (al-Khānūq): unpublished.

Kitchen, *PSAS* 25: K. A. Kitchen. 1995. "A Royal Administrator in Nashqum and Najran under the Himyarite King Shammar Yuhar'ish, c. AD 290, and a Squire from Sanaa. With an addendum by A. F. L. Beeston," *Proceedings of the Seminar for Arabian Studies* 25: 75–81.

L = Louvre.

L 11 (=*RES* 4230), 81 (=*CIH* 353), 84 (=*CIH* 430), 86 (*CIH* 431 + 438 [= Louvre 86] + 948), 121 (=*RES* 4919 + *CIH* 537), 205 (al-Namāra): see Calvet and Robin 1997.

Ma'sal 3: unpublished. Discovered by the Mission française de Najrān.

MAFRAY = Mission archéologique française en République arabe du Yémen.

MAFRAY-Abū Thawr 4: Christian Robin. 1986. "Du nouveau sur les Yaz'anides," *Proceedings of the Seminar for Arabian Studies* 16: 181–197; Müller 2010: 85.

MAFRAY-Banū Ṣā' 2: unpublished.

MAFRAY-Quṭubīn 37 and 47: unpublished.

MAFY = Mission Archéologique Française au Yémen.

MAFY-Banū Zubayr 2: unpublished.

MAFY-Bayt Ghufr 1: Christian Robin. 2005. "Les rôles respectifs des rois ḥimyarites Abīkarib et Dhara''amar (vers 380–420 de l'ère chrétienne)." In *Arabia Vitalis, Arabskij Vostok, islam, drevnjaja Aravija*. Sbornik statej, posvjashchennyj 60-letiju V.V. Naumkina: 371–379. Moscow: Rossijskaja Akademija Nauk, Institut vostokovedenija, Moskovskij Gosudarstvennyj Universitet im. M.V. Lomonosova, Fakul'tet mirovoj politiki, Institut stran Azii i Afriki.

MAFY-Rayda 1: voir Ry 534 + MAFY-Rayda 1.

MAFYS = Mission archéologique française au Yémen-Sud.

MAFYS-Ḍura' 3 (unedited) = *RES* 4069.

Maṣna'at Māriya 1 = DJE 25: Walter W. Müller. 1978. "Die Sabäische Felsinschrift von Maṣna'at Māriya," *Neue Ephemeris für Semitische Epigraphik* 3: 137–148;

Christian Julien Robin. 2006. "Muhaqra'um (arabe Muqrā), une tribu ḥimyarite méconnue." In *Le pèlerin des forteresses du savoir* (Hommage au qāḍī Ismā'īl b. 'Alī al-Akwa' à l'occasion de son 85e anniversaire, Recueil d'articles réunis par Christian Julien Robin et Muḥammad 'Abd al-Raḥīm Jāzim), 93–135. Sanaa: Centre français d'Archéologie et de Sciences sociales de Sanaa; Müller 2010: 44–45.

M Bayḥān = M[useum of] Bayḥān

M Bayḥān 5: Christian Robin and Muḥammad Bāfaqīh. 1980. "Inscriptions inédites du Maḥram Bilqīs (Mārib) au musée de Bayḥān," *Raydān* 3: 83–112. (Arabic Summary: 61–62 of the Arabic section).

al-Mi'sāl 5: Christian Robin. 1981. "Les inscriptions d'al-Mi'sāl et la chronologie de l'Arabie méridionale au IIIe siècle de l'ère chrétienne," *Académie des Inscriptions et Belles-Lettres, Comptes rendus 1981*: 315–339; Müller 2010: 28–31.

al-Mi'sāl 18 (unedited): see YMN 13.

MQ = Mission Qatabān.

MQ-Ḥayd Mūsà 1 (=*RES* 4196): Robin 1998.

MQ-Minkath 1: unpublished.

Müller-Tan'im: Walter W. Müller. 1973. "Ergebnisse der Deutschen Jemen-Expedition 1970," *Archiv für Orientforschung* 24: 150–161; G. W. Nebe. 1991. "Eine spät-sabäisch-jüdische Inschrift mit satzeinleitendem doppelten Amen aus dem 4./6. Jahrhundert nach Chr.?" *Journal for the Study of Judaism* 22: 235–253.

Murayghān 1: see Ry 506.

Murayghān 2: see Sayyid *PSAS* 1988.

Murayghān 3: unpublished. Discovered independently by Sālim Ṭayrān and by the Mission française de Najrān.

al-Namāra: see L 205.

Nāmī N'J 13 + 14: Jacques Ryckmans. 1969. "L'inscription sud-arabe Nami NAG 13–14," *Eretz-Israel* 9 (= W. F. Albright Volume): 102–108.

Ph 124 g: H. St. J. B. Philby and A. S. Tritton. 1944. "Najran Inscriptions," *JRAS*: 119–128; Müller 2010: 63.

Pirenne Baynūn 3 = YM 1695: Jacqueline Pirenne. 1987. "Documents inédits de Baynūn." In *Ṣayhadica: Recherches sur les inscriptions de l'Arabie préislamique offertes par ses collègues au Professeur A. F. L. Beeston*, ed. Christian Robin and Muḥammad Bāfaqīh, 99–112. L'Arabie préislamique 1. Paris: Geuthner; Müller 2010: 42–43.

Pirenne. *Raydān* 3: 238. Cf. Jacqueline Pirenne. 1980. "Prospection historique dans la région du royaume de 'Awsān," *Raydān* 3: 213–255.

RES 3383, 3910, 4069 (= MAFYS-Ḍura' 3), 4105, 4157 + 4158 (*CIH* 596 + 597 + *RES* 4157 + 4158), 4196 (= MQ-Ḥayd Mūsà 1), 4230 (= L 11), 4298, 4790, 4919 (*RES* 4919 + *CIH* 537 = L 121), 4938, 4969 (= Ja 876): *Répertoire d'épigraphie sémitique*, publié par la Commission du Corpus Inscriptionum Semiticarum. Académie des Inscriptions et Belles-Lettres. Vols. 1–8: 1900–1967. Paris: Imprimerie nationale.

RES 3383, 4069, 4196, 4919, 5085: see also Müller 2010.

Robin-Najr 1: Christian Robin. 1982. *Les Hautes-Terres du Nord-Yémen avant l'Islam* II. Publications de l'Institut historique et archéologique néerlandais de Stamboul 50: 87–89, pl. 54. Istanbul: Nederlands Historisch-Archaeologisch Instituut in het Nabije Oosten; Müller 2010: 86.

Robin-Viallard 1: Christian Robin. 1981. "Documents de l'Arabie antique II," *Raydān* 4: 43–65. (Arabic Summary: 74–75 of the Arabic section); Müller 2010: 94.

Ry 403: Gonzague Ryckmans. 1949. "Inscriptions sud-arabes. 8e série," *Le Muséon* 62: 55–124; for the reading *mn* at l.6, see Jacques Ryckmans. 1964. "Le christianisme en Arabie du sud préislamique." In *Atti del Convegno internazionale sul tema: L'Oriente cristiano nella storia della Civiltà (Roma 31 marzo–3 aprile 1963; Firenze 4 aprile 1963)*, 413–454, 438 n. 126 (from an unpublished photograph). Rome: Accademia nazionale dei Lincei.
Ry 506 = Muraygħān 1: Gonzague Ryckmans. 1953. "Inscription sud-arabes. Dixième série," *Le Muséon* 66: 267–317; 'Abdel Monem A. H. Sayed. 1988. "Emendations to the Bir Murayghan Inscription Ry 506 and a New Minor Inscription from There," *Proceedings of the Seminar for Arabian Studies* 18: 131–143; Müller 2010: 118–119.
Ry 507 and 508: Gonzague Ryckmans. 1953. "Inscriptions sud-arabes. Dixième série," *Le Muséon* 66: 267–317; most recently, Robin 2008b: 82–85, 91–93, 102–103; Müller 2010: 98–99, 103–104.
Ry 509 and 510: Gonzague Ryckmans. 1953. "Inscriptions sud-arabes. Dixième série," *Le Muséon* 66: 267–317; most recently, Christian Robin. 1996. "Le Royaume Ḥujride, dit 'royaume de Kinda', entre Ḥimyar et Byzance," *Académie des Inscriptions et Belles-Lettres, Comptes rendus* 1996: 665–714. Ry 510, see also Müller 2010: 95-96.
Ry 520: Gonzague Ryckmans. 1954. "Inscriptions sud-arabes. Onzième série," *Le Muséon* 67: 99–119; Müller 2010: 79.
Ry 534 + MAFY-Rayda 1: Christian Robin. 1996. "Le Royaume Ḥujride, dit 'royaume de Kinda," entre Ḥimyar et Byzance," *Académie des Inscriptions et Belles-Lettres, Comptes rendus 1996*: 665–714; Müller 2010: 62.
al-Sayla al-Bayḍā' 1: unpublished. Discovered by Fahmī 'Alī 'l-Aghbarī and Khālid al-Ḥājj.
Sayyid *PSAS* 1988: 136 (= Murayghān 2). 'Abdel Monem A. H. Sayed. 1988. "Emendations to the Bir Murayghan Inscription Ry 506 and a New Minor Inscription from There," *Proceedings of the Seminar for Arabian Studies* 18: 131–143; Müller 2010: 119.
Schmidt-Ma'rib 28 + Ja 668: Norbert Nebes. 1996. "Ein Kriegzug ins wadi Ḥaḏramawt aus der Zeit des Ḏamar'alī Yuhabirr und Tha'rān Yuhan'im," *Le Muséon* 109: 179–297.
Sharaf 29 (= Ir 14), 31, 32, 33 (= Ja 656), 34, 35: Aḥmad Ḥusayn Sharaf al-Dīn. 1387h/1967. *Ta'rīkh al-Yaman al-thaqāfī*, 3 fasc. Cairo: Maṭba'at al-Kaylānī.
Shu'lān-Shibām Kawkabān: unpublished.
Veerman 2 (= BynM 1): Ja[c]ques Veerman. 1998. "Baynun," *Halaqa* 2 (*al-Ḥalqa*, majalla yamaniyya faṣliyya thaqāfiyya fanniyya siyāḥiyya): 20–33.
Yanbuq 47: Muḥammad Bāfaqīh and Christian Robin. 1979. "Inscriptions inédites de Yanbuq (Yémen démocratique)," *Raydān* 2: 15–76. (Summary in Arabic: 25–27 of the Arabic section); Müller 2010: 93.
YM = Yemen Museum.
YM 327: see Ja 520.
YM 1200: Iwona Gajda. 1998. "A New Inscription of an Unknown Ḥimyarite King, Marṯad'ilān Yun'im," *Proceedings of the Seminar for Arabian Studies* 28: 81–88.
YM 1950: Iwona Gajda. 2005. "The Earliest Monotheistic South Arabian Inscription," *Archäologische Berichte aus dem Yemen* 10: 21–29; Müller 2010: 57.
YM 1695: see Pir Baynūn 3.
YMN = Yaman, Mudawwanat al-Nuqūsh.
YMN 13 (= al-Mi'sāl 18): Yūsuf 'Abd Allāh. 1979. "Mudawwanat al-nuqūsh al-yamaniyya al-qadīma," *Dirāsāt yamaniyya (Ṣan'ā')* 3: 29–64; Müller 2010: 40–41.

ẒM = Ẓafār Museum.
ẒM 1: see Garb Shuriḥbiʾīl Yaʿfur.
ẒM 5 + 8 + 10: Walter W. Müller. 2009. "Eine sabäische Inschrift aus Ẓafār aus dem Jahre 542 der himjarischen Ära." In *Philologisches und Historisches zwischen Anatolien und Sokotra: Analecta Semitica, In Memoriam Alexander Sima*, ed. Werner Arnold, Michael Jursa, Walter W. Müller, and Stephan Procházka, 247–255. Wiesbaden: Harrassowitz Verlag; Müller 2010: 61.
ẒM 772 A + B: Yusuf M. Abdallah. 1987. "The Inscription *CIH* 543. A New Reading Based on the Newly-Found Original." In *Ṣayhadica: Recherches sur les inscriptions de l'Arabie préislamique offertes par ses collègues au Professeur A. F. L. Beeston*, ed. Christian Robin and Muḥammad Bāfaqīh, 3–9. L'Arabie préislamique 1. Paris: Geuthner.
ẒM 2000: Iwona Gajda. 2004. "Une nouvelle inscription juive de Ẓafār." In *Scripta Yemenica*, Issledovanija po Yuzhnoj Aravii, Sbornik nauchnykh statej v chest' 60-letija M. B. Piotrovskogo, 197–202. Moscow: Vostochnaja literatura, Rossijskaja Akademija Nauk; Christian Robin. 2004. "Ḥimyar et Israël," *Académie des Inscriptions et Belles-Lettres, Comptes rendus 2004*: 831–906; Müller 2010: 81.

2. *Epigraphic Ge'ez*

RIÉth 5, 8, 9, 10, 180, 185, 185 bis, 186, 187, 188, 189, 190, 191, 192, 195, 263, 264, 265, 266: E. Bernand, A. J. Drewes, and R. Schneider. 1991. *Recueil des inscriptions de l'Éthiopie des périodes pré-axoumite et axoumite*. Académie des Inscriptions et Belles-Lettres. 3 vols. Paris: Diffusion de Boccard.

3. *Epigraphic Greek*

RIÉth 270, 270 bis, 271, 276, 277, 286: ibid.

4. *Old Arabic*

L[ouvre] 205 (funerary monument of Imru' al-Qays at al-Namāra): see now Calvet and Robin 1997, 265–269.

B. *Manuscript Sources*

1. *Syriac*

Book of the Ḥimyarites: Axel Moberg, ed. and trans. 1924. *The Book of the Himyarites: Fragments of a Hitherto Unknown Syriac Work*. Skrifter utgivna av Kungl. Humanistiska Vetenskapssamfundet i Lund 7. Lund: C. W. K. Gleerup.
Chronicle of Joshua the Stylite: W. Wright, ed. and trans. 1882. *The Chronicle of Joshua the Stylite, composed in Syriac A.D. 507*. Cambridge: Cambridge University Press.
Chronicle of Michael the Syrian: Jean-Baptiste Chabot, ed. and trans. 1963. *Chronique de Michel le Syrien, Patriarche Jacobite d'Antioche (1166–1199)*. Paris: Ledoux. First printed 1899.
Chronicle of Zuqnin:
—Amir Harrak, trans. 1999. *The Chronicle of Zuqnīn, Parts III and IV, A.D. 488–775*. Medieval Sources in Translation 36. Toronto: Pontifical Institute of Medieval Studies.

—Witold Witakowski, trans. 1996. *Pseudo-Dionysius of Tel-Mahre, Chronicle (known also as the Chronicle of Zuqnin), Part III*. Translated Texts for Historians 22. Liverpool: Liverpool University Press.

Guidi *Letter*: Ignazio Guidi, ed. and trans. 1880 (1945). "La lettera di Simeone vescovo di Bêth-Arḥam sopra i martiri omerita." In *Atti della Reale Accademia dei Lincei, anno cclxxviii*, 1880–81, Serie terza, Memorie della Classe di Scienze morali, storiche e filologiche 7, 417–515. (Reprint 1945. *Raccolta di scritti, 1. Oriente cristiano 1, Pubblicazioni dell'Istituto per l'Oriente*, 1–60. Rome: Istituto per l'Oriente).

Shahîd *Letter*: Irfan Shahîd. 1971. *The Martyrs of Najrân. New Documents*. Subsidia Hagiographica 49. Brussels: Société des Bollandistes.

Synodicon orientale: J.-B. Chabot, ed. and trans. 1902. *Synodicon orientale*. Notices et extraits des manuscrits de la Bibliothèque nationale et autres bibliothèques, publiés par l'Académie des Inscriptions et Belles-Lettres 37. Paris: Imprimerie nationale.

2. *Greek*

Apology to Constantius II: Athanase d'Alexandrie. Jan-M. Szymusiak, ed. and trans. 1958. *Apologie à l'empereur Constance*. Sources chrétiennes 56. Paris: Cerf.

John Malalas: see Malalas.

Kosmas Indikopleustēs, *Christian Topography*: Cosmas Indicopleustès. Wanda Wolska-Conus, ed. and trans. 1968–1973. *Topographie chrétienne*. Sources chrétiennes 141, 159, 197. 3 vols. Paris: Cerf.

Life of Gregentios: Albrecht Berger, ed. and trans. 2006. *Life and Works of Saint Gregentios, Archbishop of Taphar*. Millennium Studies 7. Berlin: Walter de Gruyter.

Malalas: John:

—L. Dindorf. 1831. *Johannis Malalae Chronographia*. Bonnae: Impensis Ed. Weberi.

—Elizabeth Jeffreys, Michael Jeffreys, and Roger Scott. 1986. *The Chronicle of John Malalas: A Translation*. Byzantina Australiensia 4. Melbourne: Australian Association for Byzantine Studies.

Martyrdom of Arethas (Greek): Marina Detoraki, ed., and Joëlle Beaucamp, trans. 2007. *Le martyre de Saint Aréthas et de ses compagnons* (BHG 166). Collège de France, Centre de Recherche d'histoire et civilisation de Byzance, Monographies 27. Le massacre de Najrān 1. Paris: Association des amis du Centre d'histoire et civilisation de Byzance.

Nonnosos: Photius. René Henry, ed. and trans. 1959. *Bibliothèque, Tome I ("codices" 1–84)*. Collection byzantine. Paris: Les Belles Lettres.

Periplus Maris Erythraei: Lionel Casson, ed. and trans. 1989. *The Periplus Maris Erythraei*. Princeton, NJ: Princeton University Press.

Philostorgius, *Ecclesiastical History*:

—J. Bidez, ed. Second edition F. Winkelmann, ed. 1972. *Kirchengeschichte*. Die griechischen christlichen Schriftsteller der ersten drei Jahrhunderte 3, 4. Berlin: Akademie Verlag.

—Philip R. Amidon, trans. 2007. *Church History*. Writings from the Greco-Roman World 23. Atlanta: Society of Biblical Literature.

Procopius:

—Jacobus Haury. 1905. *Procopii Caesariensis opera omnia*. Leipzig: Teubner.

—H. B. Dewing, trans. 1914 (2006). *Procopius, History of the Wars*. Cambridge, MA: Harvard University Press.

Theophanes the Confessor: Carolus De Boor, ed. 1883. *Theophanis chronographia*. Leipzig: Teubner.

3. Latin

Pliny the Elder, *Natural History*:
—Book VI: H. Rackham, trans. 1969. *Natural History*, vol. 2. Loeb Classical Library. Cambridge, MA: Harvard University Press.
—Book XII: A. Ernout, trans. 1949. *Histoire naturelle, Livre XII*. Paris: Les Belles Lettres.
Rufinus, *Ecclesiastical History*: Françoise Thélamon. 1981. *Païens et chrétiens au IVe siècle: L'apport de l'"Histoire ecclésiastique" de Rufin d'Aquilée*. Paris: Études augustiniennes.

4. Ge'ez (Classical Ethiopic)

John of Nikiu, *Chronicle*:
—Hermann Zotenberg, ed. and trans. 1883. "Chronique de Jean, évêque de Nikiou," *Notices et extraits des manuscrits de la Bibliothèque nationale* 24.1: 125–608.
—Robert Henry Charles, trans. 1916. *The Chronicle of John (c. 690 A.D.), Coptic Bishop of Nikiu*. Text and Translation Society 3. London: Text and Translation Society.
Kəbra Nagast: Robert Beylot. 2008. *La Gloire des rois ou l'Histoire de Salomon et de la Reine de Saba*. Apocryphes, collection de poche de l'AELAC 12. Turnhout: Brepols.
Martyrdom of Arethas (Ge'ez): Alessandro Bausi and Alessandro Gori, ed. and trans. 2006. *Tradizioni orientali del "Martirio di Areta": La prima recenzione araba e la versione etiopica*. Quaderni di Semitistica 27. Firenze: Dipartimento di Linguistica, Università di Firenze.
Martyrdom of Azqīr:
—Carlo Conti Rossini. 1910. "Un documento sul cristianesimo nello Iemen ai tempi del re Šarāḥbīl Yakkuf," *Rendiconti della Reale Accademia dei Lincei, Classe di Scienze morali, storiche e filologiche*, Serie quinta 14: 705–750.
—Hugo Winckler. 1896. "Zur geschichte des Judentums in Jemen," *Altorientalische Forschungen* 4: 329–336.
—Ze'ev Rubin. 2000. "Judaism and Raḥmanite Monotheism in the Ḥimyarite Kingdom in the Fifth Century." In *Israel and Ishmael: Studies in Muslim-Jewish Relations*, ed. Tudor Parfitt, 32–51. London: Curzon.

5. Arabic

Akhbār 'Ubayd: see Wahb b. Munabbih. *Kitāb al-tījān*.
Al-Azraqī, Abū 'l-Walīd Muḥammad b. 'Abd Allāh b. Aḥmad. 1403h/1983. *Akhbār Makka wa-mā jā'a fī-hā min al-āthār*, vol. 1, ed. Rushdī al-Ṣāliḥ Malḥas. Makka al-Mukarrama: Dār al-Thaqāfa.
al-Bakrī, Abū 'Ubayd 'Abd Allāh b. 'Abd al-'Azīz . . . al-Andalusī. 1364h/1945. *Mu'jam mā 'sta'jam min asmā' al-bilād wa-l-mawāḍi'. al-Ma'had al-khalīfī li-l-abḥāth al-maghribiyya, Bayt al-Maghrib*. 4 vols., ed. Muṣṭafā Saqqa. Cairo: Maṭba'at Lajnat al-Ta'līf wa-'l-Tarjama wa-'l-Nashr.
al-Balādhurī, Abū 'l-'Abbās Aḥmad ibn Jābir. 1350h/1932. Arabic Text: *Futūḥ al-buldān li-l-imām Abī 'l-Ḥasan al-Balādhurī*, ed. Riḍwān Muḥammad Riḍwān. Cairo: Al-Azhar.
—English translation: Francis Clark Murgotten. 1924. *The Origins of the Islamic State*. Columbia University Studies in the Social Sciences 163a. (Reprint 1969. New York: AMS.)

Chronicle of Seert: Addaï Scher, ed. and M. l'abbé Pierre Dib, trans. 1910. *Histoire nestorienne (Chronique de Séert)*. Patrologia Orientalis 5.2. Paris: Firmin Didot.
Al-Hamdānī, Abū Muḥammad al-Ḥasan b. Aḥmad b. Ya'qūb.
—*Iklīl* 2: 1386h/1967. *Kitāb al-Iklīl, al-juz' al-thānī, li-Lisān al-Yaman Abī Muḥammad al-Ḥasan b. Aḥmad b. Ya'qūb al-Hamdānī*. ed. Muḥammad b. 'Alī 'l-Akwa' al-Ḥiwālī. al-Maktaba al-yamaniyya 3. Cairo: al-Sunna al-muḥammadiyya.
—*Iklīl* 8: Nabīh Amīn Fāris, ed. 1940. *al-Iklīl (al-juz' al-thāmin)*. Princeton Oriental Texts 7. Princeton, NJ: Princeton University Press.
—*Iklīl* 8: Nabih Amin Faris, trans. 1938. *The Antiquities of South Arabia*. Princeton Oriental Texts 3. Princeton, NJ: Princeton University Press.
—*Mushtabih*: Oscar Löfgren, ed. 1953. *Südarabisches Muštabih: Verzeichnis homonymer und homographer Eigennamen*. Bibliotheca Ekmaniana Universitatis Regiae Upsaliensis 57. Uppsala: Almqvist & Wiksell.
—*Qaṣīdat al-Dāmigha: Kitāb Qaṣīdat al-dāmigha*, ed. Muḥammad b. 'Alī al-Akwa' al-Ḥiwālī, 1978. Min dhakhā'ir al-'Arab. Cairo: al-Sunna al-muḥammadiyya.
Ibn al-Kalbī, Hishām: Wahib Atallah, ed. and trans. 1969. *Le Livre des idoles de Hicham ibn al-Kalbi*. Paris: Klincksieck.
Ibn al-Nadīm.
—Gustav Flügel, ed. 1871. *Kitâb al-Fihrist*. Leipzig: F. C. W. Vogel.
—English Translation: Bayard Dodge, ed. and trans. 1970. *The Fihrist of al-Nadīm*. Records of Civilization: Sources and Studies 83. New York: Columbia University Press.
Ibn Ḥabīb, Abū Ja'far Muḥammad. n.d. *Kitāb al-Muḥabbar li-Abī Ja'far Muḥammad b. Ḥabīb b. Umayya b. 'Amr al-Hāshimī'l-Baghdādī . . ., riwāyat Abī Sa'īd al-Ḥasan b. al-Ḥusayn al-Sukkarī*, ed. Ilse Lichtenstädter. Dhakhā'ir al-turāth al-'arabī. Beirut: Manshūrāt Dār al-ufuq al-jadīda.
Ibn Hishām.
—Muṣṭafà 'l-Saqqā, Ibrāhīm al-Abyārī, and 'Abd al-Ḥāfiẓ Shalabī, ed. n.d. *al-Sīra al-nabawiyya. Turāth al-Islām*. 2 vols. Beirut: Dār al-Ma'rifa.
—English translation: A. Guillaume, trans. 1955. *The Life of Muhammad*. Oxford: Oxford University Press. Abridged French translation: Wahib Atallah, trans. 2004. *Ibn Hishâm, La biographie du prophète Mahomet*. Paris: Fayard.
Ibn Qutayba, Abū Muḥammad 'Abd Allāh b. Muslim. Tharwat 'Ukāsha, ed. 1379h/1960. *al-Ma'ārif*. Cairo: Wizārat al-Thaqāfa wa-'l-Irshād al-qawmī, al-Idāra al-'āmma li-l-thaqāfa.
Ibn Shabba, 'Umar. Fahīm Muḥammad Shaltūt, ed. 1979. *Ta'rīkh al-madīna al-munawwara*. Mecca: H. M. Aḥmad.
Martyrdom of Arethas (Arabic): Alessandro Bausi and Alessandro Gori, ed. and trans. 2006. *Tradizioni orientali del "Martirio di Areta": La prima recenzione araba e la versione etiopica*. Quaderni di Semitistica 27. Firenze: Dipartimento di Linguistica, Università di Firenze.
al-Mas'ūdī, Abū 'l-Ḥasan 'Alī b. al-Ḥusayn.
—Barbier de Meynard and Pavet de Courteille, ed., revised by Charles Pellat. 1965–1979. *Murūj al-dhahab wa-ma'ādin al-jawhar*. Manshūrāt al-Jāmi'a al-lubnāniyya, Qism al-Dirāsāt al-ta'rīkhiyya 11. 7 vols. Beirut: al-Jāmi'a al-lubnāniyya.
—Barbier de Meynard and Pavet de Courteille, trans., revised by Charles Pellat. 1962–1997. *Les prairies d'or*. Société asiatique, Collection d'ouvrages orientaux. 5 vols. Paris: Société asiatique.
Nashwān, b. Sa'īd al-Ḥimyarī. 'Alī b. Ismā'īl al-Mu'ayyad and Ismā'īl b. Aḥmad al-Jarāfī, ed. 1378h/1958–1959. *Mulūk Ḥimyar wa-aqyāl al-Yaman, qaṣīdat Nashwān*

b. *Sa'īd al-Ḥimyarī wa-sharḥu-hā 'l-musammà Khulāṣat al-sīra al-jāmi'a li-'ajā'ib akhbār al-mulūk al-tabābi'a*. Cairo: al-Maṭba'a al-Salafiyya.
Al-Ṭabarī, Abū Ja'far Muḥammad b. Jarīr.
—M. J. De Goeje, ed., revised by J. Barth and Th. Nöldeke. 1964. *Ta'rīkh al-rusul wa-'l-mulūk: Annales quos scripsit Abu Djafar Mohammed Ibn Djarir at-Tabari*. Leiden: Brill.
—English translation: C. E. Bosworth, trans. 1999. *The History of al-Ṭabarī*, vol. V, *The Sāsānids, the Byzantines, the Lak(h)mids, and Yemen*. Bibliotheca persica. Albany: State University of New York Press.
Wahb b. Munabbih. Markaz al-Dirāsāt wa-'l-Abḥāth al-yamaniyya, ed. n.d. *Kitāb al-tījān fī mulūk Ḥimyar*. Ṣan'ā'; *Akhbār 'Ubayd*: 323–501.
Al-Ya'qūbī, Aḥmad b. Abī Ya'qūb b. Ja'far. (known as al-Ya'qūbī). 1379h/1960. *Ta'rīkh al-Ya'qūbī*. Beirut: Dār Ṣādir and Dār Bayrūt.
Yāqūt, Shihāb al-Dīn Abū 'Abd Allāh [Yāqūt] b. 'Abd Allāh al-Ḥamawī 'l-Rūmī 'l-Baġdādī. *Mu'jam al-Buldān*. 1955–1957. Beirut: Dār Ṣādir and Dār Bayrūt.
al-Zubayr b. Bakkār. Maḥmūd Muḥammad Shākir, ed. 1419h/1999. *Jamharat nasab Quraysh wa-akhbāri-hā*. al-Riyāḍ: Dār al-Yamāma.

II. Modern Sources

Abbott, Nabia. 1938. *The Rise of the North Arabic Script and Its Ḳur'ānic Development, with a Full Description of the Ḳur'ān Manuscripts in the Oriental Institute*. University of Chicago Oriental Institute Publications 1. Chicago: University of Chicago Press, Oriental Institute Publications.
al-Ansary, A. R. 1981. *Qaryat al-Fau: A Portrait of Pre-Islamic Civilisation in Saudi Arabia*. Al-Riyāḍ: University of Riyadh Press.
Apology to Constantius II: see Manuscript Sources, Greek.
'Athamina, Khalil. 1998. "The Tribal Kings in Pre-Islamic Arabia: A Study of the Epithet *malik* or *dhū al-tāj* in Early Arabic Traditions," *al-Qanṭara* 19: 19–37.
Avanzini, Alessandra. 1997. *Profumi d'Arabia* (Atti del convegno a cura di Alessandra Avanzini). Saggi di Storia antica 11. Rome: L'Erma di Bretschneider.
Beaucamp, Joëlle. 2010. "Le rôle de Byzance en mer Rouge avant 531, mythe ou réalité?" In *Le massacre de Najrân: Regards croisés sur les sources*, ed. Joëlle Beaucamp, Françoise Briquel Chatonnet, and Christian Robin, 197–218. Paris: Association des amis du Centre d'histoire et civilisation de Byzance.
Beaucamp, Joëlle, Françoise Briquel-Chatonnet, and Christian Robin. 1999. "La persécution des chrétiens de Nagrān et la chronologie ḥimyarite," *Aram* 11: 15–83.
———, eds. 2010. *Le massacre de Najrân: Regards croisés sur les sources* (Actes du colloque organisé par Joëlle Beaucamp, Françoise Briquel-Chatonnet et Christian Robin, mercredi 19 et jeudi 20 novembre 2008). Paris: Association des amis du Centre d'histoire et civilisation de Byzance.
Beaucamp, Joëlle, and Christian Robin. 1981. "Le christianisme dans la péninsule Arabique d'après l'épigraphie et l'archéologie," *Travaux et mémoires* 8 (Hommage à Paul Lemerle): 45–61.
———. 1983. "L'évêché nestorien de Māšmāhīg dans l'archipel d'al-Baḥrayn (v^e^–ixe siècle)." In *Dilmun: New Studies in the Archaeology and Early History of Bahrain*, ed. D. Potts, 171–196. Berliner Beiträge zum Vorderen Orient 2. Berlin: Dietrich Reimer Verlag.

Beaulieu, Paul-Alain. 1989. *The Reign of Nabonidus, King of Babylonia 556–539 B.C.* Yale Near Eastern Researches 10. New Haven, CT: Yale University Press.

Beeston, A. F. L. 1954. "Notes on the Mureighan Inscription," *Bulletin of the School of Oriental and African Studies* 16: 389–392.

———. 1981. "Miscellaneous Epigraphic Notes," *Raydān* 4: 9–28.

———. 1985. "The Martyrdom of Azqir," *Proceedings of the Seminar for Arabian Studies* 15: 5–10.

———. 1987. "Ḥabashat and Aḥābīsh," *Proceedings of the Seminar for Arabian Studies* 17: 5–12.

———. 1994. "Foreign Loanwords in Sabaic." In *Arabia Felix: Beiträge zur Sprache und Kultur des vorislamischen Arabien, Festschrift Walter W. Müller zum 60. Geburtstag,* ed. Norbert Nebes, 39–45. Wiesbaden: Harrassowitz.

Beeston, A. F. L., M. A. Ghul, W. W. Müller, and J. Ryckmans. 1984. *Sabaic Dictionary (English-French-Arabic)—Dictionnaire sabéen (anglais-français-arabe)—al-Muʿjam al-sabaʾī (bi-'l-injilīziyya wa-'l-faransiyya wa-'l-ʿarabiyya).* Publication of the University of Sanaa. Louvain-la-Neuve: Éditions Peeters.

Bin Seray, Hamad M. 1996. "Christianity in the East of the Arabian Peninsula," *Aram* 8.2: 315–332.

Blachère, Régis. 1947. *Le Coran: Traduction selon un essai de reclassement des sourates.* Vol. 1. *Introduction au Coran.* Islam d'hier et d'aujourd'hui 3. Paris: Éditions G.P. Maisonneuve.

Book of the Ḥimyarites: see Manuscript Sources, Syriac.

Bowersock, Glen. 1993. "The New Greek Inscription from South Yemen." In *ΤΟ ΕΛΛΗΝΙΚΟΝ: Studies in Honor of Speros Vryonis, Jr., Vol. 1, Hellenic Antiquity and Byzantium,* ed. John S. Langdon, Stephen W. Reinert, Jelisaveta Stanojevich Allen, and Christos P. Ioannides, 3–8. New Rochelle, NY: Aristide D. Caratzas.

Breton, Jean-François. 1994. "Les fortifications d'Arabie méridionale du 7e au 1er siècle avant notre ère," *Archäologische Berichte aus dem Yemen* 8: 142–345.

Brock, Sebastian. 1999. "Syriac Writers from Beth Qaṭraye," *Aram* 11.1: 85–96.

Calvet, Yves, and Christian Robin. 1997. *Arabie heureuse, Arabie déserte: Les antiquités arabiques du Musée du Louvre.* Notes et documents des Musées de France 31. Paris: Réunion des Musées nationaux.

Carter, R. A. 2008. "Christianity in the Gulf during the First Centuries of Islam," *Arabian Archaeology and Epigraphy* 19: 71–108.

Caskel, Werner. 1966. *Ǧamharat an-nasab: Das genealogische Werk des Hišām ibn Muḥammad al-Kalbī.* 2 vols. Leiden: Brill.

Casson, Lionel. 1989. *The Periplus Maris Erythraei: Text with Introduction, Translation, and Commentary.* Princeton, NJ: Princeton University Press.

Caussin de Perceval, A. P. 1847. *Essai sur l'histoire des Arabes avant l'islamisme, pendant l'époque de Mahomet, et jusqu'à la réduction de toutes les tribus sous la loi musulmane,* vols. 1–3. Paris: Firmin-Didot. (Reprint 1967. Graz: Akademische Druck-u. Verlagsanstalt.)

Chronicle of Joshua the Stylite: see Manuscript Sources, Syriac.

Chronicle of Seert: see Manuscript Sources, Arabic.

Chronicle of Zuqnin: see Manuscript Sources, Syriac.

Conti Rossini, Carlo. 1909. "Les listes des rois d'Aksoum," *Journal asiatique* 14: 263–320.

———. 1910. "Un documento sul cristianesimo nello Iemen ai tempi del re Šarāḥbīl Yakkuf," *Rendiconti della Reale Accademia dei Lincei,* Classe di Scienze morali, storiche e filologiche, 5th ser. 14: 705–750.

Contini, Riccardo. 2003. "La lingua del Bēt Qaṭrāyē." In *Mélanges David Cohen (Études sur le langage, les langues, les dialectes, les littératures, offertes par ses élèves, ses collègues, ses amis, présentés à l'occasion de son quatre-vingtième anniversaire)*, ed. Jérôme Lentin and Antoine Lonnet, 173–181. Paris: Maisonneuve et Larose.

Costa, Paolo. 1977. "A Latin-Greek Inscription from the Jawf of the Yemen," *Proceedings of the Seminar for Arabian Studies* 7: 69–72.

Crone, Patricia. 1987. *Meccan Trade and the Rise of Islam*. Oxford: Blackwell.

Cuvigny, Hélène, and Christian Robin. 1996. "Des Kinaidokolpites dans un ostracon grec du désert Oriental (Égypte)," *Topoi* 6: 697–720.

Daghfous, Radhi. 1995. *Le Yaman islāmique des origines jusqu'à l'avènement des dynasties autonomes (Ier–IIIème S. /VIIème–IXème S.)*. Publications de la Faculté des Sciences humaines et sociales. Série 4: Histoire 25. 2 vols. Tunis: Université de Tunis, Faculté des Sciences humaines et sociales.

de Blois, François. 2002. "*Naṣrānī* (*Nazōraios*) and *ḥanīf* (*ethnikos*): Studies on the Religious Vocabulary of Christianity and Islam," *Bulletin of the School of Oriental and African Studies* 65: 1–30.

de Prémare, Alfred-Louis. 2000. "'Il voulut détruire le Temple.' L'attaque de la Ka'ba par les rois yéménites avant l'islam: Aḫbār et Histoire," *Journal asiatique* 288: 261–367.

Degen, Rainer. 1974. "Die hebräische Inschrift DJE 23 aus dem Jemen," *Neue Ephemeris für Semitische Epigraphik* 2: 111–116.

Devreesse, Robert. 1945. *Le Patriarcat d'Antioche, depuis la paix de l'Église jusqu'à la conquête arabe*. Paris: Gabalda.

Drewes, A. J. 2002. "La question de 'Ezânâ, roi d'Axoum," *Semitica* 52–53: 125–136.

Eichmann, Ricardo, Hanspeter Schaudig, and Arnulf Hausleiter. 2006. "Archaeology and Epigraphy at Tayma (Saudi Arabia)," *Arabian Archaeology and Epigraphy* 17: 163–176.

Eph'al, Israel. 1982. *The Ancient Arabs: Nomads on the Borders of the Fertile Crescent, 9th–5th Centuries B.C.* Leiden: Brill.

Fabietti, Ugo. 1988. "The Role Played by the Organisation of the 'Hums' in the Evolution of Political Ideas in Pre-Islamic Mecca," *Proceedings of the Seminar for Arabian Studies* 21: 25–33. (Reprint in F. E. Peters, ed. 1999. *The Arabs and Arabia on the Eve of Islam*, 348–356. The Formation of the Classical Islamic World 3. Farnham: Ashgate.)

Fahd, T. ed. 1989. *L'Arabie préislamique et son environnement historique et culturel* (Actes du Colloque de Strasbourg, 24–27 juin 1987). Université des sciences humaines de Strasbourg, Travaux du Centre de recherche sur le Proche-Orient et la Grèce antiques 10. Leiden: Brill.

Farès-Drappeau, Saba. 2005. *Dédan et Lihyân: Histoire des Arabes aux confins des pouvoirs perse et hellénistique (IVe–IIe s. avant l'ère chrétienne)*. Travaux de la Maison de l'Orient et de la Méditerranée 42. Lyon: Maison de l'Orient et de la Méditerranée.

Fiaccadori, Gianfranco. 2006. "Gregentios and the Land of the Homerites." In *Life and Works of Saint Gregentios, Archbishop of Taphar*, ed. Albrecht Berger, 48–82. Berlin: Walter de Gruyter.

———. 2007. "Kaleb," In *Encyclopaedia Aethiopica* 3: 329–332.

Finster, Barbara. 1996. "Arabien in der Spätantike: Ein Überblick über die kuturelle Situation der Halbinsel in der Zeit von Muhammad," *Archäologischer Anzeiger*: 287–319.

Finster, Barbara, and Jürgen Schmidt. 1994. "Die Kirche des Abraha in Ṣan'ā'." In *Arabia Felix: Beiträge zur Sprache und Kultur des vorislamischen Arabien, Festschrift Walter W. Müller zum 60. Geburtstag*, ed. Norbert Nebes, 67–86. Wiesbaden: Harrassowitz.
Fontaine, Hughes, and Mounir Arbach. 2006. *Yémen: Cités d'écritures*. Manosque: Éditions Le bec en l'air.
Fowden, Garth. 2004. *Quṣayr 'Amra: Art and the Umayyad Elite in Late Antique Syria*. Berkeley: University of California Press.
Gajda, Iwona. 1996. "Ḥuğr b. 'Amr roi de Kinda et l'établissement de la domination ḥimyarite en Arabie central," *Proceedings of the Seminar for Arabian Studies* 26: 65–73.
———. 2009. *Le royaume de Himyar à l'époque monothéiste: L'histoire de l'Arabie du Sud ancienne de la fin du IVe siècle de l'ère chrétienne jusqu'à l'avènement de l'islam*. Mémoires de l'Académie des Inscriptions et Belles-Lettres 40. Paris: Diffusion de Boccard.
Gatier, Pierre-Louis, Pierre Lombard, and Khalid M. al-Sindi. 2002. "Greek Inscriptions from Bahrain," *Arabian Archaeology and Epigraphy* 13: 223–233.
al-Ghabban, Ali Ibrahim, Béatrice André-Salvini, Françoise Demange, Carine Juvin, and Marianne Cotty. 2010a. *Routes d'Arabie: Archéologie et histoire du royaume d'Arabie séoudite*. Paris: Louvre éditions et Somogy éditions d'art.
———.2010b. *Roads of Arabia: Archaeology and History of the Kingdom of Saudi Arabia*. English translation of Al-Ghabban et al. 2010a. Paris: Louvre éditions et Somogy éditions d'art.
Gil, Moshe. 1984. "The Origin of the Jews of Yathrib," *Jerusalem Studies in Arabic and Islam* 4: 203–224. (Reprint in F. E. Peters, ed. 1999. *The Arabs and Arabia on the Eve of Islam*, 145–166. The Formation of the Classical Islamic World 3. Farnham: Ashgate.)
———. 2004. *Jews in Islamic Countries in the Middle Ages*. Trans. David Strassler. Études sur le judaïsme médiéval 28. Leiden: Brill.
Guidi *Letter*: see Manuscript Sources, Syriac.
Hahn, Wolfgang. 2000. "Aksumite Numismatics: A Critical Survey of Recent Research," *Revue numismatique* 155: 281–311.
Halperin, D. J. 1976. "The Ibn Ṣayyād Traditions and the Legend of al-Dajjāl," *Journal of the American Oriental Society* 96: 213–225.
Hämeen-Anttila, Jaakko. 2000. "Arabian Prophecy." In *Prophecy in Its Ancient Near East Context—Mesopotamian, Biblical, and Arabian Perspectives*, ed. Martti Nissinen, 115–146. Society of Biblical Literature Symposium Series 13. Atlanta: Society of Biblical Literature.
Hasson, Isaac. 1989. "Contributions à l'étude des Aws et des Ḫazrağ," *Arabica* 36: 1–35.
Hawting, G. R. 1999. *The Idea of Idolatry and the Emergence of Islam: From Polemic to History*. Cambridge: Cambridge University Press.
Hayajneh, Hani. 2001. "First Evidence of Nabonidus in the Ancient North Arabian Inscriptions from the Region of Taymā'," *Proceedings of the Seminar for Arabian Studies* 31: 81–95.
Hirschfeld, Yizhar. 2006. "The Crisis of the Sixth Century: Climatic Change, Natural Disasters and the Plague," *Mediterranean Archaeology and Archaeometry* 6: 19–32.
Hoyland, Robert. 2001. *Arabia and the Arabs from the Bronze Age to the Coming of Islam*. London: Routledge.

Huth, Martin. 2010. *Coinage of the Caravan Kingdoms: Ancient Arabian Coins from the Collection of Martin Huth*. Ancient Coins in North American Collections. New York: The American Numismatic Society.

Huth, Martin, and Peter G. van Alfen, eds. 2010. *Coinage of the Caravan Kingdoms*, Studies in Ancient Arabian Monetization (Numismatics Studies 25). New York: The American Numismatic Society.

Jaussen, Antonin and R. Savignac. 1909. *Mission archéologique en Arabie (mars–mai 1907), de Jérusalem au Hedjaz, Médain-Saleh*. Publications de la Société des fouilles archéologiques 2. Paris: Leroux. (Reprint 1982. Lausanne: Roth-Hotz; Reprint 1997. Cairo: Institut français d'Archéologie orientale.)

———. 1914. *Mission archéologique en Arabie II: el-'Ela, d'Hégra à Teima, Harrah de Tebouk*. 2 vols. Publications de la Société des fouilles archéologiques. Paris: Paul Geuthner (Reprint 1997. Cairo: Institut français d'Archéologie orientale.)

Jeffery, Arthur. 1938. *The Foreign Vocabulary of the Qur'ān*. Gaekwad's Oriental Series 79. Baroda: Oriental Institute (Reprint 2007. Leiden: Brill, Texts and Studies on the Qur'ān 3.)

Kaimio, Maarit, and Ludwig Koenen. 1997. "Reports on Decipherment of Petra Papyri (1996/97)," *Annual of the Department of Antiquities of Jordan* 41: 459–462.

Kennedy, Hugh. 1997. "From Oral Tradition to Written Record in Arabic Genealogy," *Arabica* 44: 531–544.

Kennet, Derek. 2005. "On the Eve of Islam: Archaeological Evidence from Eastern Arabia," *Antiquity* 79: 107–118.

———. 2007. "The Decline of Eastern Arabia in the Sasanian Period," *Arabian Archaeology and Epigraphy* 18: 86–122.

King, G. R. D. 1997. "A Nestorian Monastic Settlement on the Island of Ṣīr Banī Yās, Abu Dhabi: A Preliminary Report," *Bulletin of the School of Oriental and African Studies* 60: 221–235.

Kister, M. J. 1965a. "The Campaign of Ḥulubān: A New Light on the Expedition of Abraha," *Le Muséon* 73: 425–436. (Reprint 1980. *Studies in Jāhiliyya and Early Islam*. Farnham: Ashgate.)

———. 1965b. "Mecca and Tamīm (Aspects of Their Relations)," *Journal of Economic and Social History of the Orient* 8: 113–163. (Reprint 1980. *Studies in Jāhiliyya and Early Islam*. Farnham: Ashgate.)

———. 1968. "Al-Ḥīra. Some Notes on Its Relations with Arabia." *Arabica* 15: 143–169. (Reprint 1980. *Studies in Jāhiliyya and Early Islam*. Farnham: Ashgate.)

———. 1972. "Some Reports Concerning Mecca from Jāhiliyya to Islam," *Journal of Economic and Social History of the Orient* 15: 61–93. (Reprint 1980. *Studies in Jāhiliyya and Early Islam*. Farnham: Ashgate.)

———. 1979. "Some Reports Concerning al-Ṭā'if," *Jerusalem Studies in Arabic and Islam* 1: 1–18. (Reprint 1980. *Studies in Jāhiliyya and Early Islam*. Farnham: Ashgate.)

———. 2002. "The Struggle against Musaylima and the Conquest of Yamāma," *Jerusalem Studies in Arabic and Islam* 27: 1–56.

Knibb, Michael A. 1999. *Translating the Bible: The Ethiopic Version of the Old Testament*. Oxford: Oxford University Press.

Korotayev, Andrey, Vladimir Klimenko, and Dimitry Proussakov. 1999. "Origins of Islam: Political-Anthropological and Environmental Context," *Acta Orientalia Academiae Scientiarum Hungaricae* 52: 243–276.

Kropp, Manfred. 1998. "Free and Bound Prepositions: A New Look at the Inscription MAFRAY / Qutra 1," *Proceedings of the Seminar for Arabian Studies* 28: 169–174.
Lammens, Henri. 1911. "La république marchande de La Mecque, en l'an 600 de notre ère," *Bulletin de l'Institut égyptien*. Series 5, 4: 23–54.
Landau-Tasseron, Ella. 1997. "Unearthing a Pre-Islamic Arabian Prophet," *Jerusalem Studies in Arabic and Islam* 21: 42–61.
Langfeldt, J. 1994. "Recently Discovered Early Christian Monuments in North-Eastern Arabia," *Arabian Archaeology and Epigraphy* 5: 32–60.
Lecker, Michael. 1995. *Muslims, Jews and Pagans: Studies on Early Islamic Medina*. Islamic History and Civilization, Studies and Texts 13. Leiden: Brill.
———. 2002. "The Levying of Taxes for the Sassanians in Pre-Islamic Medina (Yathrib)," *Jerusalem Studies in Arabic and Islam* 27: 109–126. (Reprint 2005. *People, Tribes and Society in Arabia around the Time of Muḥammad*. Farnham: Ashgate.)
———. 2003. "King Ibn Ubayy and the *quṣṣāṣ*." In *Methods and Theories in the Study of Islamic Origins*, ed. H. Berg, 29–71. Leiden: Brill. (Reprint 2005. *People, Tribes and Society in Arabia around the Time of Muḥammad*. Farnham: Ashgate.)
———. 2005a. "Were the Jewish Tribes in Arabia Clients of Arab Tribes?" In *Patronate and Patronage in Early and Classical Islam*, ed. M. Bernards and J. Nawas, 50–69. Leiden: Brill.
———. 2005b. "Was Arabian Idol Worship Declining on the Eve of Islam?" In *People, Tribes and Society in Arabia around the Time of Muḥammad*, sec. III, 1–43. Farnham: Ashgate.
———. 2005c. "Tribes in Pre-and Early Islamic Arabia." In *People, Tribes and Society in Arabia Around the Time of Muḥammad*, sec. XI, 1–106. Farnham: Ashgate.
Leemhuis, F. "Wa'd al-Banāt," *Encyclopedia of Islam*, 2nd ed. Leiden: Brill.
Lemaire, André. 1995. "Les inscriptions araméennes anciennes de Teima: Sur les pistes de Teima." In *Présence arabe dans le Croissant fertile avant l'hégire* (Actes de la Table ronde internationale organisée par l'Unité de recherche associée 1062 du CNRS, Etudes sémitiques, au Collège de France, le 13 novembre 1993), ed. Hélène Lozachmeur, 59–72. Paris: Editions Recherches sur les Civilisations.
Life of Gregentios: see Manuscript Sources, Greek.
Liverani, Mario. 1992. "Early Caravan Trade between South-Arabia and Mesopotamia," *Yemen (Studi archeologici, storici e filologici sull'Arabia meridionale)* 1: 111–115.
Macdonald, M. C. A. 1994. "A Dated Nabataean Inscription from Southern Arabia." In *Arabia Felix: Beiträge zur Sprache und Kultur des vorislamischen Arabien, Festschrift Walter W. Müller zum 60. Geburtstag*, ed. Norbert Nebes, 132–141. Wiesbaden: Harrassowitz.
———. 2000. "Reflections on the Linguistic Map of Pre-Islamic Arabia," *Arabian Archaeology and Epigraphy* 11: 28–79. Reprint in Macdonald 2009b.
———. 2001. "Arabi, Arabie e Greci: Forme di contatto e percezione." In *I Greci: Storia Cultura Arte Società 3.1: I Greci oltre la Grecia*, ed. S. Settis, 231–266. Turin: Giulio Einaudi. (English Translation: Macdonald 2009b. "Arabians, Arabias, and the Greeks: Contact and Perceptions.")
———. 2004. "Ancient North Arabian." In *The Cambridge Encyclopedia of the World's Ancient Languages*, ed. R. D. Woodard, 488–533. Cambridge: Cambridge University Press.
———. 2008. "Old Arabic (Epigraphic)." In *Encyclopedia of Arabic Language and Linguistics*, ed. K. Versteeg, 464–477. Leiden: Brill.

———. 2009a. "The Decline of the 'Epigraphic Habit' in Late Antique Arabia: Some Questions." In *L'Arabie à la veille de l'Islam: Bilan clinique*, ed. Jérémie Schiettecatte and Christian Robin, 17–27. Orient et Méditerranée 3. Paris: de Boccard.
———. 2009b. *Literacy and Identity in Pre-Islamic Arabia*, Variorum Collected Studies 906. Farnham: Ashgate.
Mango, Marlia Mundell. 1996. "Byzantine Maritime Trade with the East (4th–7th Centuries)," *Aram* 8: 139–163.
Maraqten, Mohammed. 1996. "Dangerous Trade Routes: On the Plundering of Caravans in the Pre-Islamic Near East," *Aram* 8: 213–236.
Marek, Christian. 1993. "Die Expedition des Aelius Gallus nach Arabien im Jahre 25 v. Chr.," *Chiron* 23: 121–156.
Martyrdom of Arethas (Arabic): see Manuscript Sources, Arabic.
Martyrdom of Arethas (Ge'ez): see Manuscript Sources, Ge'ez.
Martyrdom of Arethas (Greek): see Manuscript Sources, Greek.
Martyrdom of Azqīr: see Manuscript Sources, Ge'ez.
Morony, M. n.d. "Sāsānids." *Encyclopedia of Islam*, 2nd ed. Leiden: Brill.
Müller, Walter W. 1978. "Abessinier und Ihre Namen und Titel in vorislamischen südarabischen Texten," *Neue Ephemeris für semitische Epigraphik* 3: 159–168.
———. 1998. "Südarabisches zum Namen Aksum," *Aethiopica* 1: 217–220.
———. 2009. "Eine sabäische Inschrift aus Ẓafār aus dem Jahre 542 der himjarischen Ära." *In Philologisches und Historisches zwischen Anatolien und Sokotra: Analecta Semitica, In Memoriam Alexander Sima*, ed. Werner Arnold, Michael Jursa, Walter W. Müller, and Stephan Procházka, 247–255. Wiesbaden: Harrassowitz.
———. 2010. *Sabäische Inschriften nach Ären datiert: Bibliographie, Texte und Glossar.* Akademie der Wissenschaften und der Literatur—Mainz, Veröffentlichungen der Orientalischen Kommission 53. Wiesbaden: Harrassowitz.
Müller, Walter W., and Said F. Al-Said. 2002. "Der babylonische König Nabonid in taymanischen Inschriften." In *Neue Beiträge zur Semitistik: Erstes Arbeitstreffen der Arbeitsgemeinschaft Semitistik in der Deutschen Morgenländischen Gesellschaft vom 11. bis 13. September 2000 an der Friedrich-Schiller-Universität Jena*, ed. Norbert Nebes, 105–122. Wiesbaden: Harrassowitz.
Munro-Hay, Stuart C. H. 1982. "Kings and Kingdoms of Ancient Nubia," *Rassegna di Studi Etiopici* 29: 87–137.
———. 1989. "The al-Madhāriba Hoard of Gold Aksumite and Late Roman Coins," *Numismatic Chronicle* 149: 83–100.
———. 1991. *Aksum: An African Civilisation of Late Antiquity*. Edinburgh: Edinburgh University Press.
———. 2003. *Coinage of Arabia Felix: The Pre-Islamic Coinage of the Yemen.* Nomismata 5. Milan: Edizioni ennerre.
Munro-Hay, Stuart, and Bent Juel-Jensen. 1995. *Aksumite Coinage.* London: Spink.
al-Najem, Mohammed, and M. C. A. Macdonald. 2009. "A New Nabataean Inscription from Taymā'," *Arabian Archaeology and Epigraphy* 20: 208–217.
Nehmé, Laila. 2004. "Explorations récentes et nouvelles pistes de recherche dans l'ancienne Hégra des Nabatéens, moderne al-Hijr /Madâ'in Sâlih, Arabie du Nord-Ouest," *Comptes rendus de l'Académie des inscriptions et Belles-Lettres*: 631–682.
———. 2005. "Inscriptions vues et revues à Madâ'in Sâlih," *Arabia* 3: 179–225.
———. 2009. "Quelques éléments de réflexion sur Hégra et sa région à partir du IIe siècle apr. J.-C." In *L'Arabie à la veille de l'Islam: Bilan clinique*, ed. Jérémie Schiettecatte and Christian Robin, 37–58. Orient et Méditerranée 3. Paris: de Boccard.

Nehmé, Laila, Th. Arnoux, J.-Cl. Bessac, J.-P. Braun, J.-M. Dentzer, A. Kermorvant, I. Sachet, L. Tholbecq, and J.-B Rigot. 2006. "Mission archéologique de Madâ'in Sâlih (Arabie Saoudite): Recherches menées de 2001 à 2003 dans l'ancienne Hijrâ des Nabatéens," *Arabian Archaeology and Epigraphy* 17: 41–124.
Nehmé, Laila, D. al-Talhi, and F. Villeneuve. 2008. "Résultats préliminaires de la première campagne de fouille à Madâ'in Sâlih en Arabie Saoudite," *Comptes rendus de l'Académie des Inscriptions et Belles-Lettres:* 651–691.
Nöldeke, Th. 1887. *Die Ghassânischen Fürsten aus dem Hause Gafna's.* Abhandlungen der königl. Akademie der Wissenschaften zu Berlin, Philos.-histor. Abh. II. Berlin: Königl. Akademie der Wissenschaften.
Olinder, Gunnar. 1927. *The Kings of Kinda of the Family of Âkil al-Murār.* Leipzig: Harrassowitz.
Overlaet, Bruno. 2009. "A Himyarite Diplomatic Mission to the Sasanian Court of Bahram II Depicted at Bishapur," *Arabian Epigraphy and Archaeology* 20: 218–221.
Paret, Roger. 1958. "Note sur un passage de Malalas concernant les phylarques arabes," *Arabica* 5: 251–262.
Periplus Maris Erythraei: see Manuscript Sources, Greek.
Peters, F. E. 1988. "The Commerce of Mecca before Islam." In *A Way Prepared: Essays in Islamic Culture in Honor of Richard Bayly Winder*, ed. R. Bayly Winder, Farhad Kazemi, and R. D. McChesney, 3–26. New York: New York University Press.
———. 1991. "The Quest of the Historical Muḥammad," *International Journal of Middle East Studies* 23: 291–313.
Phillipson, David W. 2003. *Aksum: An Archaeological Introduction and Guide.* = *Archaeological Sites of Eastern Africa*, reprint in *Azania* 38. Nairobi: British Institute in Eastern Africa.
Piotrovskij, M. B. 1984. "Prorocheskoe dvizhenie v Aravii VII v." (The Prophetic Movement in Seventh-Century Arabia). In *Islam: Religija, obshchestvo, gosudartsvo*, 19–26. Moscow: Akademija Nauk SSSR, Institut Vostokovedenija.
Pliny the Elder, *Natural History*: see Manuscript Sources, Latin.
Potts, D. T. 1988. "Trans-Arabian Routes of the Pre-Islamic Period." In *L'Arabie et ses mers bordières*, I: *Itinéraires et voisinages*, ed. Jean-François Salles, 127–162. Lyon: Maison de l'Orient.
———. 1990. *The Arabian Gulf in Antiquity.* 2 vols. Oxford: Clarendon Press.
———. 2010a. "L'histoire des origines." In *Routes d'Arabie: Archéologie et histoire du royaume d'Arabie séoudite*, ed. Ali Ibrahim, Al-Ghabban, Béatrice André-Salvini, Françoise Demange, Carine Juvin, and Marianne Cotty, 80–99. Paris: Louvre éditions et Somogy éditions d'art.
———. 2010b. "The Story of the Origins." English translation of 2010a. In *Roads of Arabia: Archaeology and History of the Kingdom of Saudi Arabia*, ed. Ali Ibrahim, Al-Ghabban, Béatrice André-Salvini, Françoise Demange, Carine Juvin, and Marianne Cotty, 70–79. Paris: Louvre éditions et Somogy éditions d'art.
Prémare, Alfred-Louis de: see de Prémare.
Puech, Émile. 1998. "Inscriptions araméennes du Golfe: Failaka, Qala'at al-Baḥreïn et Mulayḥa," *Transeuphratène* 16: 31–55.
Raven, Wim. 1988. "Some Early Islamic Texts on the Negus of Abyssinia," *Journal of Semitic Studies* 33: 197–218.
Retsö, Jan. 2003. *The Arabs in Antiquity: Their History from the Assyrians to the Umayyads.* London: Routledge.

Rippin, Andrew. 1991. "*Rḥmnn* and the *ḥanīfs*." In *Islamic Studies Presented to Charles J. Adams*, ed. Wael B. Hallaq and Donald P. Little, 153–168. Leiden: Brill. (Reprint in Rippin 2001.)

———. 2001. *The Qur'an and Its Interpretative Tradition*. Farnham: Ashgate.

Robin, Christian. 1974. "Monnaies provenant de l'Arabie du Nord-Est," *Semitica* 24: 83–125.

———. 1979. "Mission archéologique et épigraphique française au Yémen du Nord en automne 1978," *Académie des Inscriptions et Belles-Lettres, Comptes rendus des séances de l'année 1979*: 174–202.

———. 1988. "La première intervention abyssine en Arabie méridionale (de 200 à 270 de l'ère chrétienne environ)." In *Proceedings of the Eighth International Conference of Ethiopian Studies*, vol. 2, ed. Taddese Beyene, 147–162. Addis Ababa: University of Addis Ababa Institute of Ethiopian Studies.

———. 1991. "L'Arabie antique de Karib'îl à Mahomet: Nouvelles données sur l'histoire des Arabes grâce aux inscriptions," *Revue du Monde musulman et de la Méditerranée* 61.

———. 1996. "Sheba, II: Dans les inscriptions d'Arabie du Sud." In *Supplément au Dictionnaire de la Bible 70, Sexualité–Sichem*, cols. 1047–1254. Paris: Letouzey et Ané.

———. 1997. "The Date of the *Periplus of the Erythrean Sea* in the Light of South Arabian Evidence." In *Crossings: Early Mediterranean Contacts with India*, ed. F. De Romanis and André Tchernia, 40–65. New Delhi: Manohar.

———. 1998. "Décompte du temps et souveraineté politique en Arabie méridionale." In *Proche-Orient ancien: Temps vécu, Temps pensé: Actes de la Table-Ronde du 15 novembre 1997 organisée par l'URA 1062*, ed. Françoise Briquel-Chatonnet and Hélène Lozachmeur, 121–151. Paris: Jean Maisonneuve.

———. 2000. "À propos de la prière: Emprunts lexicaux à l'hébreu et à l'araméen relevés dans les inscriptions préislamiques de l'Arabie méridionale et dans le Coran." In *Prières méditerranéennes hier et aujourd'hui (Actes du colloque organisé par le Centre Paul-Albert Février à Aix-en-Provence les 2 et 3 avril 1998)*, ed. Gilles Dorival and Didier Pralon, 45–69. Textes et documents de la Méditerranée antique et médiévale 1. Aix-en-Provence: Publications de l'Université de Provence.

———. 2001a. "Les 'Filles de Dieu' de Saba' à La Mecque: réflexions sur l'agencement des panthéons dans l'Arabie ancienne," *Semitica* 50: 113–192.

———. 2001b. "Les inscriptions de l'Arabie antique et les études arabes," *Arabica* 48: 509–577.

———. 2003. "Le judaïsme de Ḥimyar," *Arabia* 1: 97–172.

———. 2004a. "'Les Deux Villes' (*Hagarəynē* /*Hgrnhn*) sont-elles Nashshān et Nashqum?" *Arabia* 2: 119–122.

———. 2004b. "Ḥimyar et Israël," *Académie des Inscriptions et Belles-Lettres, Comptes rendus de l'année 2004*: 831–906.

———. 2005. "Ḥimyar, des inscriptions aux traditions," *Jerusalem Studies in Arabic and Islam* 30: 1–51.

———. 2006a. "Les Arabes vus de Ḥimyar," *Topoi* 14: 121–137.

———. 2006b. "La réforme de l'écriture arabe à l'époque du califat médinois," *Mélanges de l'Université Saint Joseph* 59: 157–202.

———. 2008a. "Les Arabes des 'Romains,' des Perses et de Ḥimyar (IIIe–VIe s. è. chr.)," *Semitica et Classica* 1: 167–202.

———. 2008b. "Joseph, dernier roi de Ḥimyar (de 522 à 525, ou une des années suivantes)," *Jerusalem Studies in Arabic and Islam* 32: 1–124.

———. 2009a. "Faut-il réinventer la Jāhiliyya?" In *L'Arabie à la veille de l'Islam: Bilan clinique*, ed. Jérémie Schiettecatte and Christian Robin, 5–14. Orient et Méditerranée 3. Paris: de Boccard.

———. 2009b. "Inventaire des documents épigraphiques provenant du royaume de Ḥimyar aux IVe–VIe s." In *L'Arabie à la veille de l'Islam: Bilan clinique*, ed. Jérémie Schiettecatte and Christian Robin, 165–216. Orient et Méditerranée 3. Paris: de Boccard.

———. 2010a. "L'Antiquité." In *Routes d'Arabie: Archéologie et histoire du royaume d'Arabie séoudite*, ed. Ali Ibrahim Al-Ghabban, Béatrice André-Salvini, Françoise Demange, Carine Juvin, and Marianne Cotty, 80–99. Paris: Louvre éditions et Somogy éditions d'art. (English translation: "Antiquity." In Al-Ghabban et al. 2010b: 80–99.)

———. 2010b. "Langues et écritures." In *Routes d'Arabie. Archéologie et histoire du royaume d'Arabie séoudite*, ed. Ali Ibrahim Al-Ghabban, Béatrice André-Salvini, Françoise Demange, Carine Juvin, and Marianne Cotty, 118–131. Paris: Louvre éditions et Somogy éditions d'art. (English translation: "Languages and Scripts." In Al-Ghabban et al. 2010b: 118–131.)

———. 2010c. "L'Arabie à la veille de l'islam: La campagne d'Abraha contre La Mecque, ou la guerre des pèlerinages." In *Les sanctuaires et leur rayonnement dans le monde méditerranéen de l'Antiquité à l'époque moderne*, ed. Juliette de La Genière, André Vauchez et Jean Leclant, 213–242. Cahiers de la Villa "Kérylos" 21. Paris: Diffusion de Boccard.

———. 2010d. "Nagrān vers l'époque du massacre: Notes sur l'histoire politique, économique et institutionnelle et sur l'introduction du christianisme (avec un réexamen du *Martyre d'Azqīr*)." In *Le massacre de Najrân: Regards croisés sur les sources* (Actes du colloque organisé par Joëlle Beaucamp, Françoise Briquel-Chatonnet et Christian Robin, mercredi 19 et jeudi 20 novembre 2008), ed. Joëlle Beaucamp, Françoise Briquel-Chatonnet, and Christian Robin. Paris: Association des amis du Centre d'histoire et civilisation de Byzance.

———. Forthcoming. "La péninsule Arabique à la veille de la prédication muḥammadienne." In *Les débuts du Monde musulman (siècle VIIe–Xe): De Muhammad aux dynasties autonomes*, ed. Thierry Bianquis, Pierre Guichard, and Mathieu Tillier. Paris: Presses universitaires de France.

Robin, Christian, and Ueli Brunner. 1997. *Map of Ancient Yemen—Carte du Yémen antique, 1:1,000,000*. Munich: Staatliches Museum für Völkerkunde.

Robin, Christian, and Maria Gorea. 2002. "Les vestiges antiques de la grotte de Ḥôq (Suquṭra, Yémen)," *Académie des Inscriptions et Belles-Lettres, Comptes rendus des séances de l'année 2002*: 409–445.

Robin, Christian, and Alessandro de Maigret. 1998. "Le Grand Temple de Yéha (Tigray, Éthiopie), après la première campagne de fouilles de la Mission française (1998)," *Académie des Inscriptions et Belles-Lettres, Comptes rendus des séances de l'année 1998*: 737–798.

Robin, Christian, and Burkhard Vogt. 1997. *Yémen, au pays de la Reine de Saba'*. Exposition présentée à l'Institut du monde arabe du 25 octobre 1997 au 28 février 1998. Paris: Institut du monde arabe et Flammarion.

Rodinson, Maxime. 1984. "L'Arabie du sud chez les auteurs classiques." In *L'Arabie du Sud, histoire et civilisation*, I: *Le peuple yéménite et ses racines*, ed. Joseph Chelhod,

55–88. Islam d'hier et d'aujourd'hui 21. Paris: Éditions G.-P. Maisonneuve et Larose.
———. 2001. "La conversion de l'Éthiopie," *Raydān* 7: 225–262.
Rothstein, Gustav. 1899 (1968). *Die Dynastie der Lahmiden in al-Ḥîra: Ein Versuch zur arabisch-persischen Geschichte zur Zeit der Sasaniden.* Berlin: Reuther und Reichard.
Rubin, Uri. n.d. "Abraha," *Encyclopaedia of Islam*, 3rd ed., 27–32. Leiden: Brill.
———. n.d. "Ka'ba," *Encyclopedia of Islam*, 2nd ed. Leiden: Brill.
———. 1986. "The Ka'ba: Aspects of Its Ritual Functions and Position in Pre-Islamic and Early Islamic Times," *Jerusalem Studies in Arabic and Islam* 13: 97–131.
Ryckmans, Gonzague. 1953. "Inscriptions sud-arabes. Dixième série," *Le Muséon* 66: 267–317.
Ryckmans, Jacques. 1964. "Le christianisme en Arabie du sud préislamique." In *Atti del Convegno internazionale sul tema: L'Oriente cristiano nella storia della Civiltà* (Roma 31 marzo–3 aprile 1963; Firenze 4 aprile 1963), 413–454. Rome: Accademia nazionale dei Lincei.
Ryckmans, Jacques, Walter W. Müller, and Yusuf M. Abdallah. 1994. *Textes du Yémen antique inscrits sur bois (with an English Summary).* Louvain-la-Neuve: Université catholique de Louvain, Institut orientaliste.
al-Sa'īd, Sa'īd b. Fāyiz Ibrāhīm. 2000. *Ḥamlat al-malik al-bābilī Nabūnīd 'alà shimāl gharb al-Jazīra al-'arabiyya.* Dirāsa fī ta'rīkh al-'Arab al-qadīm. al-Jam'iyya al-ta'rīkhiyya al-sa'ūdiyya, Buḥūth ta'rīkhiyya, Silsilat muḥkama min al-dirāsāt al-ta'rīkhiyya wa-'l-ḥaḍāriyya 8.l. Riyadh: Saudi Historical Society.
Salles, Jean-François, ed. 1988. *L'Arabie et ses mers bordières, I: Itinéraires et voisinages.* Travaux de la Maison de l'Orient 16. Lyon: GS Maison de l'Orient.
Sanlaville, Paul. 1988. "Des mers au milieu du désert, mer Rouge et golfe Arabo-persique." In *L'Arabie et ses mers bordières, I: Itinéraires et voisinages*, ed. Jean-Francois Salles, 9–26. Travaux de la Maison de l'Orient 16. Lyon: GS Maison de l'Orient.
Sayed, 'Abdel Monem A. H. 1988. "Emendations to the Bir Murayghan Inscription Ry 506 and a New Minor Inscription from There," *Proceedings of the Seminar for Arabian Studies* 18: 131–143.
Schiettecatte, Jérémie. 2010. "L'antique Najrān: confrontation des données archéologiques et des sources écrites." In *Le massacre de Najrân: Regards croisés sur les sources* (Actes du colloque organisé par Joëlle Beaucamp, Françoise Briquel-Chatonnet, et Christian Robin, mercredi 19 et jeudi 20 novembre 2008), ed. Joëlle Beaucamp, Françoise Briquel-Chatonnet, and Christian Robin. Paris: Association des amis du Centre d'histoire et civilisation de Byzance.
———. 2011. *D'Aden à Zafar: Villes d'Arabie du Sud préislamique*, Orient et Méditerranée / Archéologie 6. Paris: de Boccard.
Schiettecatte, Jérémie, and Christian Robin, eds. 2009. *L'Arabie à la veille de l'Islam: Bilan clinique.* Orient et Méditerranée 3. Paris: de Boccard.
Schneider, Roger. 1996. "Remarques sur le nom 'Aksum'," *Rassegna di Studi Etiopici* 38: 183–190.
Shahîd *Letter* (= Shahîd 1971): see also Manuscript Sources, Syriac.
Shahîd, 'Irfan. 1971. *The Martyrs of Najrân: New Documents.* Subsidia Hagiographica 49. Brussels: Société des Bollandistes.
———. 1989. *Byzantium and the Arabs in the Fifth Century.* Washington, DC: Dumbarton Oaks Research Library and Collection.
———. 1995. *Byzantium and the Arabs in the Sixth Century.* 2 vols. Washington, DC: Dumbarton Oaks Research Library and Collection.

———. 2002. "Toponymy, Monuments, Historical Geography and Frontier Study." In *Byzantium and the Arabs in the Sixth Century, Part 1*. Washington DC: Dumbarton Oaks Research Library and Collection.

———. 2009. "Economic, Social and Cultural History." In *Byzantium and the Arabs in the Sixth Century, Part 2*. Washington, DC: Dumbarton Oaks Research Library and Collection.

Simon, Róbert. 1970. "Ḥums et Īlāf, ou commerce sans guerre (sur la genèse et le caractère du commerce de La Mecque)," *Acta Orientalia Academiae Scientiarum Hungaricae* 23: 205–232.

———. 1989. *Meccan Trade and Islam: Problems of Origin and Structure*. Bibliotheca Orientalis Hungarica 32. Budapest: Akadémiai Kiadó.

Smith, Sydney. 1954. "Events in Arabia in the 6th century A.D," *Bulletin of the School of Oriental and African Studies* 16: 425–468.

Stein, Ernest. 1949. *Histoire du Bas-Empire*, II: *De la disparition de l'Empire d'Occident à la mort de Justinien (476–565)*. Paris: Desclée de Brouwer.

Stein, Peter. 2008. "The 'Ḥimyaritic' Language in Pre-Islamic Yemen: A Critical Re-Evaluation," *Semitica et Classica* 1: 203–212.

———. 2010. *Die altsüdarabischen Minuskulinschriften auf Holzstäbchen aus der Bayerischen Staatsbibliothek in München*, I: *Die Inschriften der mittel- und spätsabäischen Periode*. Tübingen: Ernst Wasmuth Verlag.

Stiehl, Ruth. 1970. "A New Nabatean Inscription." In *Beiträge zur alten Geschichte und deren Nachleben: Festschrift F. Altheim*, 87–90. Berlin: De Gruyter.

Strauch, Ingo, and Michael D. Bukharin. 2004. "Indian Inscriptions from the Cave Ḥoq on Suquṭrā (Yemen)," *Annali* (Università degli Studi di Napoli "L'Orientale") 64: 121–138.

Synodicon Orientale: see Manuscript Sources, Syriac.

al-Talhi, Dhayfallah, and Mohammed al-Daire. 2005. "Roman Presence in the Desert: A New Inscription from Hegra," *Chiron* 35: 205–217.

Tardieu, Michel. 1992. "L'arrivée des manichéens à al-Ḥīra." In *La Syrie de Byzance à l'Islam, VIIe–VIIIe siècles* (Actes du Colloque international, Lyon [Maison de l'Orient méditerranéen] Paris [Institut du Monde arabe], 11–15 septembre 1990), ed. Pierre Canivet and Jean-Paul Rey-Coquais, 15–24. Damas: Institut français de Damas.

———. 1994. "L'Arabie du nord-est d'après les documents manichéens," *Studia Iranica* 23: 59–75.

TAVO = *Tübinger Atlas des vorderen Orients.*

TAVO B VI 7 Riplinger, Thomas, Herbert Benner, and Margit Sauer. 1988. *Der Vordere Orient zur Zeit des Byzantinisch-Persischen Konflikts (6.–7. Jh. n. Chr.), The Middle East during the Byzantine-Persian Conflict (6th–7th Century A.D.)*. Wiesbaden: Ludwig Reichert.

——— B VI 18 Bloedhorn, Hanswulf, Aharon Oppenheimer, Benjamin Isaac, Michael Lecker, Michael Hartmann, Sabine Körtje, and Gert Lüderitz. 1992. *Die jüdische Diaspora bis zum 7. Jahrhundert n. Chr., The Jewish Diaspora until the 7th Century A.D.* Wiesbaden: Ludwig Reichert.

——— B VII 1 Rebstock, Ulrich. 1987. *Das islamische Arabien bis zum Tode des Propheten (632/11 h), Islamic Arabia until the Death of the Prophet (632/11 h)*. Wiesbaden: Ludwig Reichert.

Thélamon, Françoise. 1981. *Païens et chrétiens au ive siècle: L'apport de l'Histoire ecclésiastique de Rufin d'Aquilée*. Paris: Études augustiniennes.

Christian Topography: see Manuscript Sources, Greek, Kosmas Indikopleustēs.
van Donzel, Emeri. n.d. "al-Nadjāshī." In *Encyclopedia of Islam*, 2nd ed. Leiden: Brill.
Villeneuve, François, C. Phillips, and W. Facey. 2004. "Une inscription latine de l'archipel Farasān (sud de la Mer Rouge) et son contexte archéologique et historique," *Arabia* 2: 143–192.
Wellhausen, Julius. 1887. *Reste arabischen Heidentumes*. Berlin: Georg Reimer.
Yule, Paul. 2005. "Zafar—The Capital of the Ancient Himyarite Empire Rediscovered," *Jemen-Report* 36.1: 22–29.
———. 2007. *Spätantike im Jemen—Late Antique Yemen*. Aichwald: Linden Soft Verlag.

PART II

LITERARY AND PHILOSOPHICAL CULTURES

CHAPTER 10

LATIN POETRY

SCOTT MCGILL
Rice University

WHAT makes the Latin poetry of Late Antiquity late? Negative appraisals in the history of scholarship yield an answer that looks beyond when the poetry was written to how it was written. The criticism ascribes to it attributes commonly used to stigmatize lateness: decadence, a lack of aesthetic harmony, frivolity, and creative exhaustion. The foil to that body of work is the classical Latin verse of the first century B.C.E. and especially the early Augustan era, the tradition's golden noon, whose salient features are order, proportion, moral and political seriousness, and emotional weight. The way late antique poetry deviates from the literature of that ideal age implies debasement and devolution, to the point where it validates talk of Roman decline and fall.[1]

Such blanket characterizations of Late Antiquity have largely gone the way of the discredited label "Silver Age" to describe the Latin poetry of the first century C.E.[2] Along with making the perceived classical past and late antique texts both more uniform than they actually were, the broadsides have an obvious subjective quality that should keep them from seizing the mantle of objective truth. What is more, the classicizing narrative of Latin poetry's degeneration applies external standards of judgment to Late Antiquity. To echo Michael Roberts, the poetry of the later Roman world indeed differs from its classical antecedent. But just as we do not fault Augustan poetry for being unlike late antique verse, so we should not fault late antique poetry for its distinctive character. To get an accurate measure of the later literature, it is instead necessary to view it on its own terms and in its own cultural setting.[3] This methodology, with its sensitivity to historical change and diversity, offers a way of getting around classicizing assumptions about what Late Latin poetry should have been, and of getting at what it in fact was. In recent decades, literary criticism has awakened more and more to the necessity and value of this approach. Just as the period from Ovid through the Flavians now stands as a separate chapter in ancient literary history rather than as a silver pendant to a golden age, so late antique poetry has come to be examined in its own right, not criticized in accordance with hypostatized classical norms.[4]

One area where critics (notably Roberts) have distanced inquiry from prejudicial, classicizing standards of judgment is in analyses of late antique poetic style. Of the period's general stylistic trends and traits, scholars have highlighted the subordination of narrative continuity to the individual episode, the tendency toward visual description, the taste for spectacle, fondness for verbal juxtaposition and paradox, and the frequency of enumeration or catalogues.[5] The predominance of these elements sets the poetry of Late Antiquity apart from classical poetics. Yet instead of stigmatizing this as a lapse or a deficiency, interpreters have sought to bring out what the prevailing "mannerist" style tells us about the literary aesthetics of the era, as well as about individual authors and their poetic techniques. One of the things this has led them to do is to connect late antique Latin poetry to the literature of the first century C.E., rather than viewing it to its disadvantage against first-century B.C.E. classicism.[6] From the "poetic revival" of the fourth century through the sixth century—the chronological boundaries I set for this chapter[7]—poets activate and intensify features of first century C.E. verse as part of developing a second late style in the Latin tradition.[8]

Deviating even more sharply from classical standards and tastes are the multiple pattern poems that survive from Late Antiquity. By pattern poems, I mean not only figurative or shaped poetry (e.g., a description of an egg in the shape of an egg) but also works in which extraordinarily stringent verbal and metrical patterning occurs in accordance with ad hoc rules. These include acrostics, rhopalic lines, reciprocal verses, and anacyclic poems.[9] The most insistent late antique author of such texts is the fourth-century Publilius Optatianus Porfyrius, who in works mainly addressed to Constantine from exile displays a singular ability to manipulate verbal surfaces in varied ways.[10] Another kind of pattern poem, as I am using the term, is the Virgilian cento (lit. "patchwork"), in which an author pieces together discrete lines or segments of lines found in the *Eclogues*, *Georgics*, and *Aeneid* to produce a text with a new narrative. Sixteen of these centos survive from antiquity, twelve on mythological and secular topics and four with Christian content. Most probably date from the fourth century C.E. up to the sixth.[11] The most prominent of the late antique centonists is the fourth-century C.E. Ausonius, whose *Cento Nuptialis*, on the wedding of the emperor Gratian, concludes with a graphic account of the deflowering of the bride (a delicate way of describing a brutally pornographic passage).[12]

Some readers may know Ausonius from Edward Gibbon's caustic comment that "the poetical fame of Ausonius condemns the taste of his age."[13] Similar attacks on the poet target his centos and other pattern pieces, and Optatian has likewise received bad notices for his efforts.[14] Detectable in the criticism is impatience with the way the authors reduce poetry to mere language games and tricks, as well as a feeling that the texts demonstrate how far below the classical ideal their authors had sunk. (With the centos, there is also the imputation that authors directly mar a classic.)[15] One could reconcile these responses with historical analysis by viewing them against the negative remarks on such texts that emerge in antiquity.[16] But fundamentally, the hostile notices seem ahistorical or antihistorical, in that they appear to rest upon modern assumptions about what is and is not authentic literary practice. The literature on pattern poems has increasingly moved beyond such unfavorable value judgments and toward literary criticism, with focuses on formal analysis, on how the texts relate to broader late antique aesthetics and literary practices, and on such topics as the settings in which the poems arose, the purposes for which they were written, and the interpretive choices and challenges that they offer.[17] This scholarship provides perhaps the most striking example of how readers might transcend prejudice and examine the texts of Late Antiquity on their own terms. The works in question are as nonclassical as can be. Yet instead of ghettoizing them as contemptible outliers from "real poetry" and the canon, one can show them the respect of interpretation, to the benefit of our knowledge of the poems and of late antique poetry and literary culture generally.[18]

In the case of the Virgilian cento, one element of late antique Latin poetry finds extreme expression: its productive engagement with preceding literature, especially the classical Latin tradition.[19] This aspect of the period manifests itself not only in the centonic refashioning of Virgil and in the renewal of silver age style but also in generic innovation. Authors take up traditional forms like epic, lyric, and elegy, as well as subgenres like verse panegyric and the epithalamium or wedding poem, but endow them with new qualities and use them to new expressive ends. It is also the case that late poets consistently rework earlier poetry on a smaller scale, through the practice of *imitatio*. As it had for hundreds of years, imitation stood as a fundamental principle of Latin poetic composition throughout Late Antiquity. Poets commonly turned to their predecessors and reused especially their passages and individual lines, with Virgil a predominant source. Often, too, the content of the later poem operates with (or against) that of its precursor to produce an allusion.[20] Critics have given significant attention to imitation and allusion in late antique poetry.[21] Because, moreover, textual parallels are some of the more unstable (and therefore exciting) objects of literary inquiry—that is, because of the ambiguities inherent in determining what is and is not an instance of imitation or allusion, as well as in interpreting an allusion's significance—the area of study has proven to be a vital and sometimes disputatious one.[22]

The consistent pursuit of *imitatio* joins with other facets of late antique poetry to demonstrate how both change and continuity mark the relationship between that poetry and its classical precedents. Certainly, activities and forms emerge in the later age (and particularly in the Christian arena) without parallel in the poetry of the republic and early empire.[23] Yet much more often, authors orient their work to the classical past and update its models. What emerges is a body of work that shows how latecomers can bring fresh life to an enduring inheritance. While Late Antiquity is, of course, when the history of ancient Latin poetry comes to an end, it is also a time when that history continues to unfold and evolve. This it does, moreover, in a great profusion of texts. So much Latin verse survives from the fourth century through the sixth that the age seems more a final flourish than a time of faltering senescence. This is not to deny that the work is of varied quality and, indeed, that some texts can almost be seen to justify Gibbonian pessimism. But it is the case that poetic productivity, a feature not typically associated with decline, is a defining trait of the age.[24] Any student or scholar who stays within the confines of the republic and early empire misses a great amount of the poetry that survives from Latin antiquity and in the process loses opportunities to arrive at a more thorough and richer picture of ancient literary history.

The abundance of late antique Latin poetry reveals itself across a wide geographical range. An author who spanned East and West, traveling from Egypt to Rome and then to the imperial courts of Milan and Ravenna, was Claudius Claudianus. Usually seen as one of the Egyptian "wandering poets," or the professional writers who moved from place to place in search of commissions,[25] Claudian had arrived in Rome by the mid-390s.[26] At that point, he made a name for himself with a hexameter panegyric for Olybrius and Probinus, members of the prominent Roman aristocratic family, the Anicii, and consuls for 395.[27] He then entered the court of Honorius at Milan, probably through the influence of one of his Roman patrons.[28]

Over the better part of the following decade until his presumed death around 404, Claudian consistently wrote for (and on) the emperor and imperial family but worked particularly in the service of Stilicho, the general and regent of Honorius.[29] The poetry he produced includes verse panegyrics, invectives against his patrons' political opponents, and historical epics—categories that at times overlap[30]—as well as occasional pieces. To fault Claudian for flattery or for aping the imperial or Stilichoan party line in these texts is, of course, to miss their point. To understand Claudian's court compositions at all, one must recognize the necessity of their tendentiousness, rather than wishing it away or, in a strong expression of presentism (which amounts to [post-]Romantic biographical criticism), criticizing it as unbecoming a true poet. Certainly Claudian's efforts were viewed well in imperial circles, as his extended stint at court shows. Another mark of Claudian's prominence, achieved through his skill at producing interested poetry for the powerful, is the statue of him placed in the Roman Forum of Trajan, probably in 400. The extant inscription reports that he attained the post of tribune and notary in the imperial service and that he was a senator.[31] Yet the very existence of the statue speaks to how far this "wandering poet" had come in just a few years, so that he was memorialized in the city where so recently he had begun his Latin poetic career.[32]

Claudian's Latin poetry is not limited to the political works just mentioned.[33] Both *carmina minora* (i.e., a miscellany of epigrams and other relatively short works)[34] and a longer mythological epic survive from him. The latter text is the *De raptu Proserpinae* (*DRP*), an unfinished work in three books on the myth of Proserpina. Written with some gap in time between books 1 and 2, and containing a preface to book 2 that announces Florentinus, probably the urban prefect of Rome from 395 to 397, as the dedicatee,[35] the *DRP* has been characterized as an experimental departure from Claudian's court poetry, begun perhaps during his earlier Roman years.[36] The poem stands today as the work for which Claudian is best known. It is mainly on the basis of the *DRP*, moreover, that some modern critics have given Claudian the title of the last classical poet of antiquity.[37] Yet on the level of style, the *DRP* is a late antique text par excellence. An emphasis on the individual scene over narrative continuity; a striving for verbal effect and paradox; a penchant for visual description—all these characteristic features of late antique verse are manifest in the poem, as elsewhere in his corpus.[38] Rather than blurring the facts of literary history and placing Claudian at the end of the line of classical poets,[39] one can thus view him as an exemplar of contemporary stylistic tendencies. This is a step toward recognizing Claudian as a specifically late antique writer, whose output exemplifies some general features of the era's poetry: its recurrently political cast, its variety, and its continued engagement with classical forms and material.

The city where Claudian embarked on his Latin poetic career was, of course, home to other late antique poets as well. Despite losing its political primacy from the Tetrarchy onward, Rome not only continued to have symbolic value as a "city of memories"[40] but also remained a vital cultural center at least into the 400s.[41] The fourth- and fifth-century poets who either lived in the city or visited it reflect that vitality,[42] as does the erection of statues of two late antique poets besides Claudian in the Forum of Trajan: Flavius Merobaudes (in 435) and Sidonius Apollinaris (in 456). The elegist Maximian, meanwhile, who wrote largely on his old age,[43] and the Christian poet Arator, who in 544 recited his two books of hexameters on the Acts of the Apostles in the church of San Pietro in Vincoli,[44] confirm that poetic activity endured in Rome into the sixth century, despite the increasing distress there that came particularly with Constantinople's campaigns against the Goths from the 530s to the 550s.

The struggles that Rome faced in Late Antiquity do not go unnoticed by poets, however. Claudian and other late-fourth- and early-fifth-century writers are relevant here. The threats posed by Alaric and the Goths, the instability caused by political unrest, and the conflict between Christians and polytheists-traditionalists are reflected in several texts.[45] One poem that strikes an emotional chord is Rutilius Namatianus' *De reditu suo*, which recounts in two books of elegiac couplets[46] the author's journey to his native Gaul around 415 after a stint in Rome, where he was master of the offices around 412 and urban prefect in 414. Namatianus comes across in the poem as a passionate Romanophile, so much so that he equates his return to his homeland with going into exile (a message he conveys with echoes of Ovid's poetry from Tomis).[47] Making Namatianus' commitment to Rome, as well as his admiring descriptions of it, especially resonant is the date of the *De reditu suo*.[48] The poet's stance can be seen as a defiant assertion of Rome's unbowed greatness and its ability to recover from the barbarian invasions, even as he balances that optimism by recognizing the wound, more psychological than physical, that the Goths had inflicted on the city.[49] In Namatianus, personal and historical narratives intersect, leaving a forceful picture of how a person devoted to the traditional idea (and ideal) of Rome might respond to the parlous events of the age.

The Gaul to which Namatianus reluctantly returned was itself an active seat of poetic activity and, indeed, appears to have been more a cradle of poetry in Late Antiquity than Rome. In the fourth century, the outstanding representative of Gallic literary culture is Ausonius.[50] Not only does this longtime teacher of high standing from Bordeaux present in his texts a lively roster of grammarians and rhetoricians in the region,[51] thus providing glimpses into the world of education that lay at the heart of Gaul's cultural vitality, but also he stands as a prolific author in his own right. Along with his *Cento Nuptialis*, Ausonius produced other pattern poems, epigrams, verse epistles, and a range of still more works that defy economical categorization. A conspicuous trait is his devotion to a scholarly and arcane Muse, which he demonstrates not only in his language games but also in his treatment of intellectual trivia and esoterica in various texts (particularly the *Eclogae, Technopaegnion, Ludus Septem Sapientum*, and *Griphus Ternarii Numeri*). At the same time, humor and emotional power mark several of Ausonius' poems, especially those dealing with personal subjects.[52] Throughout his work, moreover, he displays a wide knowledge of the classical tradition and an ability to reuse his models to rich formal and thematic effect.[53] These features show him to be a poet in full, whose characteristics include wit, sensitivity, and artistic control, as well as cleverness.

Ausonius also joins with Claudian in pointing up a factor in the geographical spread of Latin poetry in Late Antiquity: texts often emerged in connection with the imperial courts, which lay outside Rome. Thus having been called to Trier to tutor Valentinian's son Gratian in the mid-360s, Ausonius produced several pieces, including the *Cento Nuptialis* and the well-regarded *Moselle*.[54] The impression the poet gives is that a bubble of *otium* existed at court (and on military campaign) in which he trifled away at his poetry. This image of the light, idling author is part and parcel of Ausonius' rhetoric of modesty,[55] however, and anyway it gives only a partial view of his time with Valentinian and Gratian, in which he was not only a teacher and poet but also a politician, becoming quaestor, praetorian prefect, and consul in the 370s and securing important appointments for family members, friends, and associates. Ausonius' career suggests someone with ample worldly ambition and a skilled political hand.

Another Gallo-Roman in Late Antiquity who combined poetic and political activity is Sidonius Apollinaris. Through much of the fifth century, the aristocratic Sidonius found himself close to imperial power and in positions of authority. Married around 452 to Papianilla, the daughter of the emperor Avitus, he retained imperial favor when Majorianus came to power in 457. A decade later, the emperor Anthemius appointed Sidonius urban prefect of Rome. Soon thereafter, Sidonius became bishop of Auvergne, a political more than religious post that he held until 480.[56]

An important element in Sidonius' political success was his poetry, specifically the verse panegyrics he composed on the emperors Avitus, Majorianus, and Anthemius. Indeed, it was as a reward for his encomium that Anthemius gave Sidonius the prefecture of Rome.[57] The panegyrics are only three of the many poems that survive from Sidonius. Twenty-four appear in a volume from 469 that, as Jill Harries has shown, brings together works originally published separately.[58] Apparently a farewell to pagan and secular poetry before Sidonius took up his position as bishop (although as things turned out, the good-bye was not a final one),[59] the *carmina* include his panegyrics and pieces connected to people and events in Gaul. Filled with challenging and arcane vocabulary, and featuring lists, antitheses, and elaborate verbal patterning, Sidonius' work is something of a ne plus ultra of late antique mannerist style. Other poems appear sporadically among Sidonius' letters, which also contain references to requests for his poetry and to his addressees' and others' poetic compositions.[60] Nine books of the letters are preserved, which establish Sidonius as an important figure in the area of Roman epistolography.

In the context of fifth-century Gaul, one can read something deeper into the cultivation of literary interests by Sidonius and by those who appear in his letters. To quote Ralph Mathisen, "Literary pursuits shored up the sagging morale of Gallo-Roman aristocrats who were faced on all sides by the decline of Roman imperial authority and the rise of Germanic power."[61] The act of writing and sharing poetry established oases of *Romanitas* and functioned as a marker of class and cultural solidarity.[62] This line of interpretation offers an example of how the study of poetry can bring counterbalance and shading to the grand narrative of Rome's (Western) late antique decline, as well as detail and nuance to the grand narrative of social, political, and cultural continuity. While still recognizably Roman and vital in its literary culture, Gaul was a different place in the fifth century from what it had been in the fourth, and examining the century's poets and poetry casts light on that fact and on the specific historical and cultural conditions in which authors continued to write and to circulate their works.

The abiding interest in producing and sharing Latin poetry amid barbarian ascendancy also characterizes late antique North Africa. In 429, the Vandals, led by Gaiseric, crossed over into Africa from Spain, an area with its own rich history of late antique poets.[63] Having made their way eastward, the Vandals were first recognized as Roman *foederati*, but subsequently took Carthage and became an independent kingdom in the early 440s. They proceeded to hold power until 534, when the king Gelimer surrendered to Belisarius, the emperor Justinian's general, to end the Vandalic War.[64]

Despite their caricatured reputation for brute destruction and an insensibility to culture, the Vandals proved to be tolerant of and open to the Roman cultural and intellectual traditions they encountered. North Africa, with Carthage at its center, had long been a place where learning, rhetoric, and literature were cultivated, and it remained so—though quite possibly in diminished form—into the early fifth century, as Augustine notably shows.[65] Included in this was an enthusiasm, though often not any particular aptitude, for composing poetry. Under the Vandals, North African literary culture lived on with what appears to have been at least a modestly renewed vigor, with productive poets and new poetic texts as one result.[66]

Two significant North African poets during the period of Vandal domination were Dracontius and Luxurius. The biographies of both men are largely obscure to us, although we do discover from Dracontius' poetry that he suffered imprisonment under Gunthamund between 484 and 496.[67] In an attempt to secure his release, Dracontius wrote the *Satisfactio*, an apology in elegiac couplets, and the *De laudibus Dei*, three books of hexameters on God's benevolence, clearly an apposite topic for someone seeking a king's pardon. The indications are that Dracontius had been a poet before his detention[68] and that he turned to writing while in prison in the belief that poetry could still have practical effects in the corridors of power and could help to bring about his freedom. After gaining his liberty (with what assistance from his poems we cannot know), Dracontius probably continued to produce poetry, though now without a political stamp and function. A collection that seemingly represents his work from different periods of his life is the *Romulea*. The ten poems in the volume include rhetorical exercises, epithalamia, and epyllia on mythological themes.[69] Rounding out his corpus is the *Orestis tragoedia*, a 974-line text that joins with the rest of Dracontius' output to reveal an author of considerable learning, facility, and typically late antique stylistic copiousness.

A single genre, meanwhile, predominates in Luxurius' corpus.[70] Dating to the period of the Vandal kings Thrasamund, Hilderic, and Gelimer (496–534), Luxurius devoted himself to epigram, a form well represented in Late Antiquity.[71] About ninety epigrams survive from him on a range of topics, from his own poetry to various oddities, the circus and amphitheater, works of art and architecture, and occasional subjects.[72] Also linked to a specific occasion is Luxurius' sixty-eight-line Virgilian cento, the *Epithalamium Fridi*.[73] A wedding poem on (and presumably presented to) the groom Fridus and his bride, the cento highlights Luxurius' thorough familiarity with Virgil, as well as his command of other past literature[74]—a command that his epigrams, with their debts to multiple authors (including, unsurprisingly, Martial), also demonstrate.[75]

Luxurius' poems come down to us in the Codex Salmasianus, which contains a collection of poems, originally in twenty-four books, that forms the basis of the Latin anthologies put together by modern editors.[76] The collection appears to represent largely the work of North African poets and to have been put together in the region sometime close to 534.[77] It gathers a multiplicity of works along with Luxurius', many of them of dubious quality. They include several more Virgilian centos, other pattern poems, occasional verses, short pieces on mythological themes, variations on passages and subjects in Virgil, the *Pervigilium Veneris*,[78] and a book of riddles by the poet Symphosius.[79] While its contents are partly organized on the basis of affiliated form or of common authorship,[80] the Salmasianus remains more uneven welter than well-tended anthology. The motley collection points to a lively but rather indiscriminate North African literary scene, still tethered to the classical past but, with its enthusiasm for light pieces and curiosities, floating in its own ether.

After the fall of the Vandals in 534, Africa makes a further contribution to the history of ancient Latin poetry in the person of Flavius Cresconius Corippus. Two poems survive from this author of African origin. One is the *Johannis*, a historical epic in eight books (the last incomplete) on the *magister militum* John Troglita, who overthrew the Moors in 546. The other is a verse panegyric on Justin II, written sometime soon after 565, when the poet had migrated to Constantinople.[81] The *Johannis* in particular exemplifies once more a point of emphasis in this survey: late antique authors continued to work from and to rework classical models.[82] In addition, Corippus provides another example of how Latin poetry in Late Antiquity formed a nexus between culture and power. Like other authors in the period, Corippus wrote on and for those in authority and thus produced poetry that opens a window onto history, however refracted through generic and rhetorical filters.[83] This public poetic voice is one of the many voices that make up the varied chorus of late antique Latin authors. From Rome and Italy to Gaul, North Africa, and beyond, poets worked in a multitude of forms, in a wide range of contexts, and for divergent purposes, and the survival of so much of their material makes it so that this late period comes to be characterized by a robust flow of sources and to bring a renewed energy to the Latin poetic tradition.

So far, I have given only glancing attention to a distinctive feature of late antique Latin poetry that adds much to its variety and interest. This is the emergence of texts on Christian themes but written in traditional forms and quantitative meters and endowed with the devices and linguistic and stylistic details of classical Latin verse.[84] Such works appear in the fourth century and go on to have a firm and significant presence in the late Roman literary world.

The existence of this hybrid poetry illustrates the symbiotic relationship between Christianity and classical culture. As David Scourfield reminds us, Christianity grew within the classical Graeco-Roman world and took much from it, whatever the differences and conflicts between the two spheres.[85] The classico-Christian poetry of Late Antiquity vividly illustrates this interconnection. To build on Alan Cameron's and Peter Brown's observations, a culture based on the classical authors and ancient mythology would have been a given for the Christian writers, simply part of the air they breathed,[86] and to produce Christian poetry on classical models necessarily meant blending that culture with Christianity and Christianity with that culture.[87]

Standing at the vanguard of this development in the Latin tradition is Juvencus, from Spain. Around 330, Juvencus wrote the *Evangeliorum libri IV*, four books of hexameters on the Gospels, and apparently the first substantial Christian Latin poem in classical form and meter.[88] Juvencus' text is classified as a biblical epic, as are several poems written over the next two centuries.[89] This is due not only to the works' length, meter, and voice but also to the way the poets consistently reuse classical epic themes, formal conventions, and specific models. The result is transformation in two directions. On the one hand, Christian topics give new shape and identity to traditional epic material; on the other hand, the traditional material modifies the Christian content. Thus when Christian poets endow Christ with the traits of a classical epic hero, for example, the figure that emerges stands as a new kind of divinely descended, questing leader and at the same time as a new kind of Christ, with features belonging to the classical literary tradition.[90] A parallel to this phenomenon appears in the apse mosaic in the Basilica of Santa Pudenziana in Rome, which presents Christ in imperial guise and the Apostles dressed as Roman senators.[91] In the mosaic, secular markers of authority take on a new appearance and function in their new context, while Christ and the Apostles are simultaneously recast by being Romanized and secularized.

In the *Evangeliorum libri IV*, Juvencus retells the Gospel story, with Matthew as his primary source.[92] The method is largely that of the rhetorical exercise of paraphrase.[93] For Juvencus, the aim is to stay true to the biblical narrative, while taking some paraphrastic license and using the tools of poetic ornamentation to highlight particular passages and ideas and to heighten the emotional power and instructional efficacy of his text.[94] But why did Juvencus choose in the first place to recast the New Testament as he does? Roberts provides a cogent explanation: Juvencus follows the program laid out by Lactantius in the *Divinae Institutiones* that called for writers to put classical eloquence to Christian use.[95] Having thought to heed that directive by writing biblical poetry, Juvencus avails himself of the verbal code, motifs, imagery, and sources of classical epic, logically with an eye to an audience that would appreciate such literary treatment of the Gospels. Virgil stands as Juvencus' most prevalent model.[96] The consistent imitation, especially of the *Aeneid*, puts the Bible narrative and classical poetry in contact on the level of individual passages and lines over the course of the work. One of the challenges (and pleasures) of reading Juvencus, as well as other similarly imitative late antique Christian texts, is to locate and understand these debts. The reader is faced first with determining whether an echo is accidental, generic, or the result of imitating a specific author. If *imitatio* is identified, the choice next becomes whether to consider it ornamental or meaningful on the level of content. Should the reader then conclude that the relationship between the narratives generates an allusive message, he must decide how much to bring that message into his interpretation of the imitating poem.[97]

While the fourth-century Virgilian centonist Proba's 694-line work, in which she recasts both Old Testament and New Testament scenes, can be classified as a sui generis biblical epic,[98] it is not until the fifth century that other such hexameter poems appear with regularity. An author who, like Juvencus, dealt with New Testament material was Sedulius. Probably during the period from 425 to 450, Sedulius composed the *Carmen Paschale*, a hexameter "Easter song" in five books. In a dedicatory letter to Macedonius, Sedulius indicates that he wrote the *Carmen* to instruct his audience and that he used poetry to stoke his readers' enthusiasm and see to it that they committed his message to memory through the frequent repetition of his text.[99] Whether or not these remarks entirely capture Sedulius' purposes, his many explanatory passages, exclamations, apostrophes, and first-person plurals bring an explicit didactic and protreptic quality to the *Carmen*.[100] The concern to instruct is also evident in a third New Testament epic, Arator's aforementioned two-book hexameter poem on the Acts of the Apostles. Perhaps taking his cue from Sedulius, who seems to have achieved renown by the time the *De actibus Apostolorum* was written in the mid-sixth century,[101] Arator asserts that he aims to relate the mystical meaning of the Acts.[102] This he does by interspersing his account with considerable exegesis and spiritual interpretation.

Exegesis and instruction also come to figure prominently as the corpus of Old Testament biblical epics develops in Late Antiquity. Probably the earliest surviving example is the poem conventionally called the *Heptateuch*, which has been attributed to Cyprian the Gaul and placed between 397 and 430. Originally a paraphrase of the historical books of the Old Testament, the work is now incomplete and contains just the seven books from Genesis to Judges.[103] Though not devoid of exegetical features,[104] the *Heptateuch* for the most part stays true to the biblical narrative and seems meant more to entertain its Christian readership than to instruct it. By contrast, Claudius Marius Victorius of Marseilles, the fifth-century author of a poem titled *Alethia* that covers Genesis to the story of Abraham, states that his intention is to teach the young.[105] The three surviving hexameter books (out of an original four) that ensue make up a layered, dense, and sometimes difficult work, whose central theme is the history of salvation. The author is concerned to direct his audience on how to read sections of the Bible in accordance with Christian exegesis, but at the same time he draws on varied non-Christian poetic and philosophical sources.

An animating interest in how to understand the Bible is likewise apparent in the final Old Testament epic, Alcimus Avitus' *De spiritalis historiae gestis*. Written probably in the last decade of the fifth century, the five-book poem treats particular episodes from Genesis and Exodus.[106] Informing Avitus' selective approach (which especially marks books 4 and 5) is an interest in drawing typological connections between the Old and New Testaments, so as to praise Christ. In addition, Avitus uses his material to touch on issues of soteriology and to counter Arianism and Pelagianism.[107] The result is still another striking hybridization of the Christian and the classical, in which hexameter verse and epic verse techniques acquire new narrative, ideological, and didactic functions.

Similarly arresting in their mixture of the Christian and the classical are two examples of Christian bucolic poetry. One is Pomponius' *Versus ad Gratiam Domini*, a Virgilian cento that dates probably to the early fifth century.[108] The author not only draws as directly and dramatically on a classical source as a late antique work can but also Christianizes the characters and situation of Virgil's first *Eclogue*. In this particular (and, given its form, peculiar) case of Christian poetic innovation, Virgil's Tityrus is saved by the Christian *deus* from paganism rather than by the *deus* Octavian from the land confiscations of the 40s B.C.E. and tries to teach his interlocutor Meliboeus about his new religion.[109] The second example of Christian bucolic, known as the *De mortibus boum*, appears not in centonized hexameters, but in a lyric meter (second asclepiads)—an example of generic "mixing," which we also find elsewhere in Christian poetry and Late Antiquity generally.[110] Ascribed to one Endelechius, the poem dates probably to the early fifth century.[111] As in Pomponius' cento, Virgil's *Eclogues* 1 is the essential model. Two herdsmen, Bucolus and Aegon, discuss a cattle plague that is afflicting Bucolus' animals, until Tityrus appears with a healthy herd. Tityrus proceeds to explain that he saved his animals by making the sign of the cross over them, thus ensuring the protection of the God who is worshipped in the big cities. The poem is of interest for how it relates to contemporary Christian efforts to convert the countryside. Yet as another transitional text in the history of bucolic, the *De mortibus* also epitomizes the principle, vividly illustrated in the Christian poems of Late Antiquity, that literary genres are open and adaptable and can evolve when an author combines new formal properties and a new system of ideas with traditional expression and content.[112]

A possible reference to Endelechius leads us to a far more significant and accomplished Christian poet of Late Antiquity. This is Paulinus of Nola, who in a letter (*Ep.* 28.6) refers to the rhetor Endelechius, perhaps the very person who wrote the *De mortibus*.[113] Paulinus was born in Bordeaux in the 350s into a wealthy aristocratic family and had as his teacher Ausonius, whose father had been friendly with Paulinus'. The surviving correspondence between Ausonius and Paulinus shows that the two maintained ties through the period when the adult Paulinus embarked on his senatorial career and after his conversion to ascetic Christianity in 389.[114] The letters capture an affecting human drama: both men seek to come to terms with what Paulinus' ascetic turn means for their relationship, which is so bound up with the pleasures of classical and secular literature.

As Ausonius discovered through the verse epistles that Paulinus sent him after his conversion, the turn to a severe (or, from another perspective, pure) form of Christian life did not cause Paulinus to renounce poetic composition. In fact, he produced a variety of works that demonstrate his command of classical literature and the keen ability he had to reuse that literature to Christian ends. To paraphrase Paulinus, the concern was to dedicate to God his learning and the resources of his mind and tongue, which naturally sprang from the classical tradition.[115] Thus Paulinus adapted such conventional forms as the epithalamium and propemptikon to Christian content and rhetorical purposes[116] and wrote several natalicia for performance on the anniversary of the death of Saint Felix, to whose cult he dedicated himself in Nola after his conversion.[117] In Paulinus' poetics and in his poetry, there is no doubt a break with classical verse, expressed most vigorously in his programmatic resistance to pagan material.[118] Yet he also bridges the divide by continuing to work within the traditional poetic grid and recasting its forms, conventions, and models—in short, by continuing to write classically rooted poetry, which naturally led him to reuse the components of the inherited textual system.

Contemporary with Paulinus is another prolific Christian poet and fierce champion of Christianity, the Spaniard Prudentius.[119] In an autobiographical preface to an edition of his poems, Prudentius describes a life whose elements would translate well to contemporary American politics: a full education, a misspent period of youthful indulgence, a career in law, and subsequent political appointments. Yet Prudentius goes on to reject that life in light of the realization that worldly things will do him no good once he is dead. Faced with that existential truth, Prudentius commits himself to Christianity and, as he writes, to honoring God at least with his voice, if he cannot do so with his deeds.[120] However rhetoric and reality meet in this portrait, it provides the underpinning for a body of poetry given over to Christian material and advocacy.

The boldest of Prudentius' poems is the *Psychomachia*, or "The Battle for the Soul." This over 900-line hexameter work (with a preface in iambic trimeters) depicts the fight that faith wages against idolatry and other vices. The essential approach is allegory, which Prudentius presents in a vivid and often macabre narrative, as well as with a consistently epic, and especially Virgilian, coloring.[121] Very different in subject matter and treatment are two works of lyric poetry, the *Cathemerinon*, or "Daily Round," a collection of twelve lyric hymns for everyday acts and events, Christmas, and the Epiphany, and the *Peristephanon*, or "Crown of the Martyrs," a collection of fourteen lyric hymns on Christian martyrs of Spain and Rome. These works, and especially the *Cathemerinon*, reveal a "Christian Horace" who possesses a strong command of lyric forms, deep classical and Christian learning, and a capacity for arresting thought and aesthetic refinement.[122]

Other poems appear from Prudentius in which Christian argumentation is the guiding concern.[123] In one, the *Contra Symmachum*, Prudentius harks back to the well-known dispute of 382–384 over removing the altar of Victory from the senate house.[124] The poem, in two energetic books of hexameters, offers a teleological view of history, with accompanying efforts to refashion the Roman past along Christian lines, as well as to present the Theodosian city of Rome as the realization of a divine scheme.[125] Classical history stands as a necessary precursor to Christian history, in which Christianity takes hold throughout a world brought together under the Roman empire.[126]

Prudentius and Paulinus of Nola both wrote during the most active period for ancient Christian Latin poetry, which extended later into the fifth century as well.[127] The sixth century, by contrast, yields fewer examples of poets working on Christian themes. One is Ennodius, bishop of Pavia from 513 until his death in

521.[128] Among the extensive literary output that survives from him, which includes some 300 letters, are two books of poems. These combine secular and Christian works, notably hymns and Christian epigrams. Yet it is in Venantius Fortunatus that the fullest flowering of sixth-century Christian Latin verse occurs. Fortunatus was born in northern Italy and educated at Ravenna. In the mid-560s, he migrated to Gaul, earning his living as a writer (and winning the patronage of Gregory of Tours) during his travels. Upon settling at Poitiers, Fortunatus became connected to Radegunda, King Clotaire I's widow, for whom he played many roles while continuing to write poetry, including works on and for her.[129] Eleven books of short poems survive from Fortunatus, as well as a hagiographic epic on St. Martin of Tours and Christian hymns. Again, we see immense productivity from a late antique author, as well as a continued Christian engagement with classical poetic forms and models. But Fortunatus is a *rosa sera*, a flower at the end of the season. After his death in about 600, it would not be until the Carolingian period that Latin poetry in classical forms and quantitative meters again flourished.[130] The gap implies a terminal point and makes it appropriate to consider Fortunatus the last Latin poet of classical antiquity, a Christian conclusion to a history that began deep in the pagan world.

It is rare for students and scholars to follow the Latin poetic tradition to its end point. Even the poetry going back to the fourth century, moreover, remains far less examined and known than that of the late republic and early empire, particularly in the Anglophone world. To take an optimistic view, this means that many readers can look ahead to discovering an unfamiliar library. This chapter has given a summary tour of that library, with stops to briefly examine many of the poets and texts of Late Antiquity. The survey has benefited from the scholarship of those who were intrepid enough to deal with the period from 300 to 600 C.E. when even Ovid, Lucan, and the Flavians were considered sunset figures. These critics laid a path for successors who have continued to make strides in opening up late antique verse and thus in giving it a place in the study of the period alongside such topics as art and architecture, politics, warfare, ethnicity, and Christian community, controversy, and spiritual life.[131] But much still has to be done, many texts, commentaries, translations, and monographs to be produced, to make the Latin poetry of Late Antiquity more accessible, as well as to come to a greater understanding of it. In the study of this material, we still stand closer to the beginning than to the end.

NOTES

1. Roberts 1989, 1–5, shapes my discussion. Examples of such hostile critics whom Roberts cites (p. 1, nn. 2–3) are Rose 1936, 529, and Hadas 1952, 381–382. Relevant comments on how modern scholarship constructs Late Antiquity also appear in Formisano 2007, 277–284. See, too, Shanzer 2009, 917–954.

2. Hinds 1998, 83–98, treats well the problems with the label "Silver Age."

3. So Roberts 1989, 3–4, with an acknowledged debt to Marrou 1958, 689–690.

4. I closely paraphrase Roberts 1989, 3.

5. Along with Roberts 1989, see Charlet 1988, 74–85, and Nugent 1990, 26–50, on late literary aesthetics and literary techniques.

6. See Roberts 1989, 61 and Fontaine 1981, 187–188.

7. Beginning this survey in the fourth century not only stays within the chronological boundaries of this book but also seems justified because of how the poetry of Late Antiquity really began to flourish in the 300s. Starting where I do, however, means that I will overlook poets commonly placed in the third century, like Nemesianus and Vespa. On these authors, see Herzog 1993, 292–293 (Vespa) and 352–360 (Nemesianus). Herzog 1993, 251–388, is a valuable source on many other late antique authors as well.

8. Alan Cameron 1984, 54–58, and 2004, 349–351, discusses the late antique rediscovery of first-century C.E. poets. (Worth noting as well is his critique of the label "Silver Age" [1984, 42].)

9. For examples of some of these forms, see Alan Cameron 1980, 133–135. Other examples from Late Antiquity include Ausonius' *Technopaegnion*; Sidonius, *Ep.* 9.14.4–6; and pieces in the Codex Salmasianus (*AL* 25–69 and 205, Shackleton Bailey). I feel free to broaden the category "pattern poem" as I have because the term captures the concern with extreme verbal patterning in the relevant texts. See, too, Levitan 1985, 246, who similarly expands the reach of the term *technopaegnion*.

10. Levitan 1985, 245–269, is an important source on Optatian.

11. On the Virgilian centos, with an emphasis on the non-Christian texts, see McGill 2005. Italian classicists have long been at the forefront of Latin cento studies; an early example is Ermini 1909. For more recent scholarship, see Salanitro 1997, 2314–2360, and Paolucci 2006. Greek centos were also written in antiquity, principally from Homer. See Agosti, chapter 11 in this book.

12. Green 1991, 132–139 and 518–526, and McGill 2005, 92–98 and 103–114, examine Ausonius' cento. I will discuss Ausonius' other poetry, as well as his life, shortly.

13. Gibbon 1974, chapter 27, n. 1 (vol. 3, p. 134, n. 1 in Bury's edition).

14. For criticism of Ausonius, examples include Evelyn White 1919, 1:xvi–xvii, and Raby 1934, 1:59. For criticism of Optatian, see Raby 1934, 1:45, and Alan Cameron 1980, 134, who refers to the poet as "the unspeakable Publilius Optatianus Porfyrius." Browning 1982, 2:696, is also biting.

15. This is surely an underlying idea in Shackleton Bailey 1982, iii, who asserts that the centos are "an affront to literature" (*opprobria litterarum*).

16. Thus in a dedicatory letter prefacing his cento, Ausonius slights the poem as a worthless, trifling game and laments his treatment of Virgil. This, however, all forms a *captatio benevolentiae*, that is, a rhetorical device in which the author takes a self-effacing stance to win the favor of an audience. (See n. 55.) See, too, Aulus Gellius, *NA* 14.6.4 and Jerome, *Ep.* 53.7 (though this criticism centers upon the use of Virgil to relate Christian subject matter and the interpretation of that activity).

17. Levitan 1985 and the texts cited in nn. 10–11 are relevant here. See, too, Roberts 1989, 58 and 2007, 146–147.

18. My comments here owe much to Scourfield 2007, 2, on the interpretation of late antique poetry generally.

19. I use the term *classical* more broadly now than just to denote the early Augustan golden age and mean by it Latin poetry up to and including the first century C.E., and Juvenal.

20. There is a vast bibliography on imitation theory, particularly as it relates to Latin antiquity, and with it on the nature of allusion. I have found especially useful Conte 1986, 23–95, Pucci 1998, 3–98, and Hinds 1998.

21. Roberts 1989, 57 n. 64, provides a bibliography, and 57–58 offers a discussion of his own. See, too, Charlet 1988, 76–77.

22. Thus disagreements arise, for example, in the interpretation of Prudentius' reuse of Virgil in the *Psychomachia*; see Mastrangelo 2008, 14–40, contra Smith 1976. For examples related to another late antique author, Claudian, see Hall 1969, 108–110, and Alan Cameron 1970, 279–284.

23. I think particularly of Christian hymns not in classical, quantitative meters, including those that rhyme; Raby 1953, 20–41, gives an overview. A notable example is Augustine's *Psalm against the Donatists*. Also worth mentioning as a Christian departure from classical verse is the third-century Commodian's quasi-hexameter poetry.

24. I follow Scourfield 2007, 1–2.

25. On the "wandering poets," see Alan Cameron 1965, 470–509. Mulligan 2007, 285–310, offers a cogent defense of Claudian's eastern origin.

26. Though presumably a native Greek speaker, moreover, Claudian came to Rome endowed with a keen understanding of Latin and its verse techniques, as his poetic career reveals.

27. Wheeler 2007, 97–133, insightfully examines this poem.

28. Alan Cameron 1970, 36, suggests that Probinus specifically used his influence to help Claudian in the matter.

29. Stilicho also married into the imperial family: his wife was Serena, the emperor Theodosius I's adopted daughter.

30. That is, panegyric elements can be found in the invectives and historical epics, and elements of invective in the historical epics. Comments to this effect appear in Dewar 1996, xxi. See, too, Garambois-Vasquez 2007.

31. *CIL* 6.1710. Mulligan 2007, 305, provides the text and a translation of the inscription, which was discovered in 1493. (The statue itself, however, is lost.)

32. It would seem a priori that Claudian had acquired some reputation as a poet before delivering his panegyric on Olybrius and Probinus, for the incoming consuls are very unlikely to have given a commission to just any author. (This does not mean, however, that he had to have won his reputation in Rome, or even necessarily in Latin.) Alan Cameron 1970, 31 makes a similar observation.

33. Fragments of Claudian's Greek poetry also survive, including lines from a *Gigantomachia*. Hall 1985, 429–435, presents the fragments in his edition of Claudian's poetry. For a collection of recent essays on Claudian's work generally, see Ehlers, Felgentreu, and Wheeler 2004.

34. Ricci 2001 is a good source on these poems. Great variety marks the collection, which was gathered and ordered after Claudian's death. To give just a taste, it contains a description of a marble chariot (*CM* 7), a sepulchral epigram on a beautiful woman (11), a scoptic poem on a gout-ridden poet (13), a piece on Gallic mules (18), an epithalamium (25), the *Laus Serenae* (30), a series on a crystal enclosing a drop of water (33–39), and a *Gigantomachia* (53).

35. On Florentinus' identity, see Hall 1969, 95–100;.

36. So Gruzelier 1993, xx. For more on the date of the *DRN* and the circumstances of composition, see Hall 1969, 93–105 and Alan Cameron 1970, 452–466.

37. Examples are Hadas 1952, 388, and Browning 1982, 2:706. Surely the poem's identity as the last multibook Latin epic on a mythological topic to survive from antiquity has much to do with this.

38. For a full treatment of Claudian's style generally, see Alan Cameron 1970, 253–304. Hall 1969, 111–112, and Gruzelier 1993, xxi–xxvii, examine the style of the *DRP*.

39. To echo Roberts 2007, 144, representing Claudian in this way distorts matters by minimizing the Latin poetry that arises after Claudian and by highlighting the features that Claudian shares with the poets of the Augustan Age and early empire while downplaying their differences.

40. I take this phrase from Alan Cameron 1970, 365.

41. See Lancon 2001, 149–154.

42. A good portion of the poets I treat in this survey belong to this group. To them, we can add the Roman Avienus, who in the late fourth century translated both Aratus' *Phaenomena* and Dionysius Perigetes into Latin. Also worth noting are the *Epigrammata Bobiensia*, a collection of epigrams, including those translated from the Greek, gathered in the city sometime in the first decades of the 400s. The instances of translation are in themselves signs of cultural vitality, presuming as they do a familiarity with the Greek language and with Greek literature.

43. Schneider 2003 is an important recent source on Maximian. Also worth noting is Boethius, who combined prose and verse in his Menippean *De consolatione philosophiae*. It would appear, moreover, that Maximian and Boethius knew each other (see Max., *El.* 413–438 [3.47–72]).

44. Hillier 1993, 1–19, examines Arator's biography and historical context. See, too, Rapp 2005, 379.

45. See Alan Cameron 1970, 349–389, and Roberts 2001, 533–565.

46. The opening of the poem is lost, however, and Namatianus' narrative breaks off at only line 68 in the second book, when he has reached Luna on the bay of La Spezia.

47. See *De red.* 1.1–18 and 43–204. Tissol 2002, 435–446, examines Namatianus' reuse of Ovid. Namatianus is also notable for his paganism and his hostility toward Stilicho. For an introduction to Namatianus and the most recent text of his work, see Wolff 2007.

48. While the date of the poem has been disputed, 417 is a good possibility; see Wolff 2007, xxi–xxii. At any rate, it is safe to suppose that Namatianus wrote at least sometime close to that year.

49. So Roberts 2001, 540–541. Maas 2000, 26–29, provides a selection of other contemporary reactions to the so-called sack of Rome in 410. While the physical damage to Rome from the sack (and earlier sieges) was small, the Goths and other barbarians did do significant harm in Gaul and northern Italy, as Namatianus himself relates (1.19–42; relevant as well are 1.325–336 and 2.41–60, where Namatianus also expresses his animus toward Stilicho). See, too, the *De providentia divina* (PL 51, cols. 617–638).

50. A point made by Alan Cameron 1984, 54, who provides an overview of the Gallic cultural revival of the late third and fourth century (54–55).

51. See his *Commemoratio Professorum Burdigalensium*, as well as his *Epistles* 2–7 and 10 (Green). Ausonius was himself a teacher both on the grammatical and rhetorical levels. On his life and career, see Green 1991, xxiv–xxxii. Sivan 1993 is also a worthwhile source on Ausonius' biography and historical context.

52. For humor in Ausonius, see, e.g., the verse letters to Theon (*Ep.* 13–15, Green), as well as the end of the *Cento Nuptialis* (which, however, might not be to everyone's taste). For poems of strong emotion, see some of the *Commemoratio* and the *Parentalia*, with *Parentalia* 9, on Ausonius' deceased wife, a work of particular power. One can also look to the letters that Ausonius wrote to Paulinus of Nola, to which I will return later, for moments of emotional force. Finally, the feeling for Gaul that Ausonius expresses in the *Moselle* is striking in its affection and tinge of nostalgia.

53. See Green 1991, xx—xxii, and O'Daly 2004, 141–154, who focuses on Ausonius' most common classical model, Virgil.

54. O'Daly 2004, 152, offers a representative response when he calls the *Moselle* "the artistic climax of Ausonius' poetry."

55. The rhetoric of modesty is a vital component of Ausonius' *captationes benevolentiae*, which are recurrent in his work. McGill 2005, 166, n. 36, is a starting point for examination.

56. Sidonius suffered imprisonment and exile when the Goths captured Auvergne in the mid-470s. Euric, king of the Goths, however, restored him to his position as bishop (perhaps in 476). Harries 1994, 1–19, provides an overview of Sidonius' life and career.

57. The statue erected to Sidonius in Rome, moreover, appears to have resulted from his encomium on Avitus. A fundamental study of Sidonius is Gualandri 1979.

58. Harries 1994, 5–6.

59. For Sidonius' farewell, see *Ep.* 9.16 *carm.* 57–76. See also *Ep.* 9.12 and 9.13.1–4. Poems of a Christian cast appear among the letters apparently written after 470 (see, e.g., *Ep.* 4.11.6, 4.18.5, and 7.17.2). Yet Sidonius also writes non-Christian verses after becoming bishop (see *Ep.* 8.9.5 and 9.15).

60. See the previous note for examples of Sidonius' poems. For requests for Sidonius' verses, see, e.g., *Ep.* 9.12 and 13. For references to the poetry of his addressees and others, see, e.g., *Ep.* 8.4.2, 9.13.2 *carm.* 20–23, 9.13.4, and 9.15.1 *carm.* 19–49. See, too, *Carm.* 9.302–317.

61. Mathisen 1993, 108.

62. So Mathisen 1993, 110–112.

63. Thus Merobaudes resided in Spain, as did Juvencus and Prudentius, whom I will treat later. Another Spaniard was Damasus, pope from 366 to 384 and author of several epigrams, mainly epigraphic (with the calligrapher Filocalus enlisted to inscribe them).

64. For an overview of the Vandals, see Liebeschuetz 2003, 55–83, and Kay 2006, 7–11.

65. Rosenblum 1961, 25, suggests that African intellectual culture declined in the fourth century, as have scholars since. For more on Roman North Africa, see Shaw 1995a and 1995b (as well as many articles) and Cherry 1998.

66. The idea of fourth-century cultural decline, mentioned in the previous note, obviously sets up the narrative of cultural revival (however modest) under the Vandals.

67. Bright 1987, 15–18, discusses this topic. Bright 1987, 14 and 17, also notes that Dracontius, who was also a lawyer, must have enjoyed some prominence to attract the attention of and incite disapproval from the Vandal king. Certainly his *nomen*, Aemilius (his full name was Blossius Aemilius Dracontius), suggests a Roman line, "generally estimated as senatorial" (Bright 1987, 14).

68. Indeed, it was apparently Dracontius' praise for a foreign king in a poem that got him in trouble in the first place (see *Sat.* 93–96).

69. As Bright 1987, 18, notes, however, the surviving volume almost certainly does not represent the original collection. On Dracontius' epyllia, see Bright 1987, 21–221; on the chronology of his poems, see Bright 1999, 193–206. Kaufmann 2006 provides a thorough study of *Romulea* 10, along with broader remarks on Dracontius and his work. One epyllion often ascribed to Dracontius, though without any firm basis, is the *Aegritudo Perdicae*, which Bright 1999, 222–244, examines.

70. For arguments in favor of this spelling of his name (rather than Luxorius), see Happ 1986, 1:142–58, and Kaster 1988, 415.

71. Other notable sources for late antique Latin epigrams are Claudian, Ausonius, and the *Epigrammata Bobiensia*.

72. The poems, however, do not reveal much personal information. On Luxurius' biography, see Happ 1986, 1:83–91, and Kaster 1988, 415–416.

73. McGill 2005, 98–108, examines this cento.

74. Thus Luxurius strongly appears to refer to Statius, *Silv.* 1.2.107–108—an epithalamium—in line 36 (from *Aen.* 4.150) and to *Silv.* 1.2.189 in line 49 (from *Aen.* 4.103). (Luxurius also composes a wedding poem whose form [minus, of course, the overlaid cento technique] goes back to Statius; see McGill 2005, 99–103.) Ausonius' *Cento Nuptialis* is another model (lines 65-66).

75. See Rosenblum 1961, 52–53, and Happ 1986, 1:105–108 and vol. 2 *passim*.

76. McGill 2005, xix and 158, nn. 36 and 37, and Kay 2006, 13–18, discuss the Codex.

77. Kay 2006, 5–7.

78. *AL* 191, Shackleton Bailey. Currie 1993, 207–224, is a useful source on this much-appreciated poem.

79. On Symphosius, see Herzog 1993, 285–289. Other late antique poets who appear in the Salmasianus are Pentadius (Herzog 1993, 279–280); Reposianus, author of the *Concubitus Martis et Veneris* (Herzog 1993, 283–285); Tiberianus (Herzog 1993, 301–304); and Vespa (see n. 7).

80. So Tarrant 1983, 10.

81. Shea 1998 examines the *Johannis*, and Averil Cameron 1976 the panegyric. See, too, Rapp 2005, 383–384. A difference between Corippus and his classical models, however, is the attention he gives to Christianity. So Shea 1998, 27–38, and Averil Cameron 1976, 8–10.

82. Corippus makes this especially clear in the preface (in elegiac couplets) to the *Johannis*, where he connects his poem to Virgil, as well as to Homer and classical epic generally (*Ioh. Praef.* 7–16).

83. Charlet 1988, 75, discusses the need to take stock of a late antique poem's literary and rhetorical character when using it as a historical source. Shea 1998, 6–25, demonstrates the point, particularly by comparing Corippus' epic narrative with Procopius' *De bello Vandalico*. See, too, Averil Cameron 1976, 12–14.

84. One also certainly finds Christian verse without such roots in the classical past (see n. 24), as well as Christian material in late antique poetry that is not specifically Christian in its overarching plot and subject matter—for instance, in Corippus. But I want to focus upon the classico-Christian poetry just described, which was widespread in Late Antiquity and constitutes a striking and important development not only in Latin literature but also in Western literary history.

85. Scourfield 2007, 4.

86. Alan Cameron 2004, 343, and Brown 1982, 93. Educated Christians would have had this point driven home in the schools, whose curricula continued through Late Antiquity to center on classical texts.

87. We should, of course, not assume unanimity in Christian attitudes toward classical poetry or toward the Christianization of that poetry; see the similar thoughts of Scourfield 2007, 3–4. One area where divergent ways of conceptualizing the Christian relationship to the classical past become apparent is in Christian poets' programmatic statements, on which see Klopsch 1980, 15–17 and White 2000, 6–11.

88. So Roberts 1985, 74.

89. Roberts 1985 is a fundamental source on this corpus of poems. See also Green 2006, on the New Testament poets. Green 2006, xiv–xvii, gives an overview of the question of whether to classify the biblical texts as epics (responding primarily to Herzog 1975); he is in favor of that classification (and see Green 2006, 50–71, 209–226, and 321–350).

90. On Christ as epic hero, see Clark and Hatch 1981a, 31–39, Springer 1988, 79–80, and Green 2006, 66–67.

91. Under this church, moreover, the remains of a house and bath are still visible—a literal manifestation of Christian Rome's classical foundations (as is, e.g., the church of San Clemente, with its underground house-church and Mithraeum).

92. Green 2007, 135–171, treats Juvencus' handling of the Bible.

93. There is some debate over how much to link Juvencus' technique to paraphrase (see Green 2006, 44–50), as well as good reason not to think of other biblical epics as paraphrastic works. But I am comfortable in seeing Juvencus' method at least in such terms. Roberts 1985 is vital on the role of paraphrase in biblical epic.

94. As Roberts 2008, 629, observes.

95. Roberts 2004, 47. Lactantius himself composed poetry, including the *De ave phoenice* in the early fourth century, a text that lies open to a Christian reading.

96. On Juvencus' reuse of Virgil, see Roberts 2004, 47–61 and Green 2006, 50–71.

97. This discussion builds on my previous remarks on imitation. Thraede 1962, 1034–1041, and Herzog 1975, 185–202, are important sources on the subject of Christian *imitatio*.

98. Literature on this cento is quite extensive. A good place to start is Clark and Hatch 1981b. See, too, McGill 2007, esp. 173, 175–176, and the bibliography on 190–193.

99. See *CSEL* 10.4.15–5.10.

100. So Roberts 1985, 168–172 and 179–180, as well as 2008, 635. See, too, Green 2006, 226–250.

101. On Sedulius' late antique renown, see Green 2006, 351–353.

102. Schwind 1990 and 1995 and Hillier 1993 are valuable sources on Arator and his Christian thought.

103. Hence the title *Heptateuch*, used by the nineteenth-century editor Peiper (*CSEL* 23), obviously reflects only the text's current state, not its original one.

104. See Nodes 1993, 25–36 and 83–87.

105. *Precatio*, 104–105: *dum teneros formare animos et corda paramus / ad verum virtutis iter puerilibus annis* (While I prepare to direct the tender minds and hearts of the young to the true path of virtue, *CSEL* 16.362). Nodes 1993, 10–12, discusses Victorius' didactic aims.

106. Avitus also wrote a sixth book addressed to his sister Fuscina, a consolation in praise of chastity.

107. As bishop of Viennes, Avitus likewise worked to combat Arian and Pelagian doctrine. For more on Avitus' Christian thought in his poem, see Nodes 1993, 55–73 and 118–127. For anti-Arian material in New Testament epic, see Green 2006, 117–120, 179 and 312–316.

108. See McGill 2001, 15–26.

109. Note especially *Vers.* 9–10, *o Meliboee, deus haec nobis otia fecit. / namque erit ille mihi semper deus* (O Meliboeus, God granted me this peace. For that one will always be God to me), which comes from *Ecl.* 1.6–7, on Octavian.

110. On such mixing in Prudentius, for example, see Fontaine 1980, 1–23.

111. On this poem, see Schmid 1953, 101–165; Korzeniewski 1976, 4–6 and 58–71; and Barton 2000.

112. I discuss bucolic poetry as a genre with full awareness of the critical debates over ancient conceptions of genre and how to characterize bucolic verse (i.e., whether it is a genre or a mode). To me, it is clear that Latin bucolic texts belong to a recognizable generic category and tradition, defined particularly by "inner form" or content; and I consider it safe to suppose that their authors were conscious of working within that category and tradition.

113. See Trout 1999, 110–111.

114. On their relationship and correspondence, see Trout 1999, esp. 55–59, 68–84, and 86–89; Amherdt 2004; and Ebbeler 2007, 303–315. The thorough and sensitive treatment of Witke 1971, 3–74, also merits attention.

115. See Paulinus, *Ep.* 16.9.

116. For the epithalamium, see *Carm.* 25, and for the propemptikon (i.e., a "send-off" or farewell poem before a journey), *Carm.* 17.

117. On the natalicia, see Trout 1999, 160–197. A good portion of Paulinus' surviving poetic corpus consists of these poems (*Carm.* 12–16, 18–21, 23, and 26–28).

118. A striking example appears in Paulinus' epithalamium (*Carm.* 25.9–10). See, too, *Carm.* 10, notably 19–76.

119. Prudentius was born in 348 and lived probably to after 405, and perhaps to 413. Paulinus' dates are 353–431.

120. *Praef.* 36 ([*peccatrix anima*] *saltem voce Deum concelebret, si meritis nequit* [Let my sinful soul at least honor God with its voice, if it cannot with its deeds]).

121. There is a good amount of secondary literature on this poem. Along with Smith 1976 and Mastrangelo 2008, esp. 14–40 and 82–159, a worthwhile English-language monograph is Nugent 1985. On allegory in Prudentius, see Herzog 1966. For a monumental (more than 1,000 pages) study of Prudentius' poetry, see Gnilka 2000.

122. Modern readers who view Prudentius similarly include Raby 1953, 45 and 57, and Slavitt 1996, ix–xix. The great eighteenth-century British classicist Richard Bentley dubbed Prudentius the Horace and Virgil of the Christians.

123. These include the *Apotheosis*, arguing for the divinity of Christ, and the *Hamartigenia*, which deals with the question of evil and attacks Gnostic dualism. Prudentius also produced a collection of four-line strophes on scenes from the Old and New Testament, the *Dittochaeon*. These might have served as captions for church paintings and mosaics.

124. Croke and Harries 1982, 28–51, collect primary material on this dispute. Testa 2007, 251–262, provides a recent interpretation of events.

125. So Mastrangelo 2008, 10, with 41–81, and Bastiaensen 1993, 126–129.

126. When Prudentius closely echoes Jupiter's prophecy of Rome's imperial dominance in *Aen.* 1.541–542 to describe Theodosius' achievement in Christianizing the city, he offers perhaps the most striking example of how he brings classical and Christian history together. The passage in question is *CS* 1.541–543: *denique nec metas statuit nec tempora ponit: / imperium sine fine docet, ne Romula virtus / iam sit anus, norit*

ne gloria parta senectam ("Finally he sets no spatial limits, no bounds of time; he teaches about empire without end, so that Rome's virtue not grow old, so that its achieved glory know no age"). While one could be tempted to see in this act of imitation an adversative quality, the tone of the passage points more to a teleological scheme. Roberts 2008, 632, influences this discussion.

127. Other Christian Latin poems in the late fourth and fifth century, which I will not treat because of space constraints, include those of Prosper of Aquitaine, Paulinus of Pella, Paulinus of Périgueux, and Orientius, as well as the anonymous *Carmen contra paganos, De ligno Crucis*, and *De providentia divina.*

128. Ennodius was also a rhetorician in Milan before being elevated to his see.

129. Fortunatus was also later made bishop in Poitiers. George 1995, xvii–xxv and 123–132, discusses Fortunatus' life, poetry, and historical context. Among Fortunatus' poems are the well-known hymns *Pange lingua gloriosi proelium certaminis* and *Vexilla regis prodeunt.*

130.Roberts 2007, 163, makes this point similarly. Roberts 2007, 158–160, discusses Fortunatus' use of quantitative meter, as distinguished from rhythmic poetry.

131. I start this list with art and architecture because the notion of the period "Late Antiquity" arose principally in connection with art history; see James 2008, 20–21. The other topics I mention figure in Bowersock, Brown, and Grabar 2001.

WORKS CITED

Amherdt, D., ed., trans., and notes. 2004. *Ausone et Pauline de Nole: Correspondance.* Bern: Peter Lang.

Barton, M. 2000. *Spätantike Bukolik zwischen paganer Tradition und christlicher Verkündigung: Das Carmen De mortibus boum des Endelechius.* Trier: Wissenschaftlicher Verlag.

Bastiaensen, A. A. R. 1993. "Prudentius in Recent Literary Criticism." In *Early Christian Poetry: A Collection of Essays*, ed. J. D. Boeft and A. Hilhorst, 101–34. Leiden: Brill.

Bowersock, G. W., Brown, P., and Grabar, O., eds. 2001. *Interpreting Late Antiquity: Essays on the Postclassical World.* Cambridge, MA: Belknap Press of Harvard University Press.

Bright, D. F. 1987. *The Miniature Epic in Vandal Africa.* Norman: University of Oklahoma Press.

———. 1999. "The Chronology of the Poems of Dracontius," *C&M* 50:193–206.

Brown, P. 1982. *Society and the Holy in Late Antiquity.* Berkeley: University of California Press.

Browning, P. 1982. "Poetry." In *The Cambridge History of Classical Literature*, ed. E. J. Kenney and W. V. Clausen, 2:692–722. 2 vols. Cambridge: Cambridge University Press.

Cameron, Alan. 1965. "Wandering Poets: A Movement in Byzantine Egypt," *Historia* 14: 470–509.

———. 1970. *Claudian: Poetry and Propaganda at the Court of Honorius.* Oxford: Oxford University Press.

———. 1980. "Poetae Novelli," *HSCP* 84: 127–175.

———. 1984. "The Latin Revival of the Fourth Century." In *Renaissances before the Renaissance: Cultural Revivals of Late Antiquity and the Middle Ages*, ed. W. Treadgold, 42–58. Stanford, CA: Stanford University Press.

———. 2004. "Poetry and Literary Culture in Late Antiquity." In *Approaching Late Antiquity: The Transformation from Early to Late Empire*, ed. S. Swain and M. Edwards, 327–354. Oxford: Oxford University Press.

Cameron, Averil, ed., trans., and comm. 1976. *Flavius Cresconius Corippus: In laudem Iustini Augusti minoris*. London: Athlone.

Charlet, J. L. 1988. "Aesthetic Trends in Late Latin Poetry," *Philologus* 132: 74–85.

Cherry, D. R. 1998. *Frontier and Society in Roman North Africa*. Oxford: Oxford University Press.

Clark, E. A., and D. F. Hatch. 1981a. "Jesus as Hero in the Vergilian Cento of Faltonia Betitia Proba," *Vergilius* 27: 31–39.

———, eds. and trans. 1981b. *The Golden Bough, the Oaken Cross: The Virgilian Cento of Faltonia Betitia Proba*. Chico, CA: Scholars Press.

Conte, G. B. 1986. *The Rhetoric of Imitation: Genre and Poetic Memory in Virgil and Other Latin Poets*, ed. C. Segal. Ithaca, NY: Cornell University Press.

Croke, B., and J. Harries. 1982. *Religious Conflict in Fourth-Century Rome: A Documentary Study*. Sydney: Sydney University Press.

Currie, H. M. 1993. "Pervigilium Veneris." In *ANRW* II.34.1, ed. W. Haase, 207–224. Berlin: Walter De Gruyter.

Dewar, M., ed., trans., and comm. 1996. *Claudian: Panegyricus de sexto consulatu Honorii Augusti*. Oxford: Oxford University Press.

Ebbeler, J. 2007. "Mixed Messages: The Play of Epistolary Codes in Two Late Antique Correspondences." In *Ancient Letters: Classical and Late Antique Epistolography*, ed. R. Morello and A. D. Morrison, 301–324. Oxford: Oxford University Press.

Ehlers, W. W., F. Felgentreu and S. M. Wheeler, eds. 2004. *Aetas Claudianea: Eine Tagung an der Freien Universität Berlin vom 28. bis 30. Juni 2002*. Leipzig: Saur.

Ermini, F. 1909. *Il centone di Proba e la poesia centonaria latina*. Rome: Ermanno Loescher.

Evelyn White, H. G., intr. and trans. 1919. *Ausonius*, 2 vols. London: Heinemann.

Fontaine, J. 1980. *Études sur la poésie latine tardive d'Ausone à Prudence: Recueil de travaux*. Paris: Les Belles Lettres.

———. 1981. *Naissance de la poésie dans l'occident chrétien: Esquisse d'une histoire de la poésie latine chrétienne du IIIe au VIe siècle*. Paris: Études augustiniennes.

Formisano, M. 2007. "Toward an Aesthetic Paradigm of Late Antiquity," *AnTard* 15: 277–284.

Garambois-Vasquez, F. 2007. *Les invectives de Claudien: Une poétique de la violence*. Brussels: Latomus.

George, J., trans. and notes. 1995. *Venantius Fortunatus: Personal and Political Poems*. Liverpool: Liverpool University Press.

Gibbon, E. 1974. *The History of the Decline and Fall of the Roman Empire*, ed. J. B. Bury. New York: AMS.

Gnilka, C. 2000. *Prudentiana I–III*. Munich: Saur.

Green, R. P. H., ed. and comm. 1991. *The Works of Ausonius*. Oxford: Oxford University Press.

———. 2006. *Latin Epics of the New Testament: Juvencus, Sedulius, Arator*. Oxford: Oxford University Press.

———. 2007. "Birth and Transfiguration: Some Gospel Episodes in Juvencus and Sedulius." In *Texts and Culture in Late Antiquity: Inheritance, Authority, and Change*, ed. J. H. D. Scourfield, 135–171. Swansea: Classical Press of Wales.

Gruzelier, C., ed., trans., and comm. 1993. *Claudian: De raptu Proserpinae*. Oxford: Oxford University Press.

Gualandri, I. 1979. *Furtiva lectio: Studi su Sidonio Apollinare*. Milan: Cisalpino-Goliardica.

Hadas, M. 1952. *A History of Latin Literature*. New York: Columbia University Press.

Hall, J. B., ed. and comm. 1969. *Claudian: De raptu Proserpinae*. Cambridge: Cambridge University Press.

———, ed. 1985. *Claudii Claudiani Carmina*. Leipzig: Teubner.

Happ, H., ed. and comm. 1986. *Luxurius*, 2 vols. Stuttgart: Teubner.

Harries, J. 1994. *Sidonius Apollinaris and the Fall of Rome AD 407–485*. Oxford: Oxford University Press.

Herzog, R. 1966. *Die allegorische Dichtkunst des Prudentius*. Munich: Beck.

———. 1975. *Die Bibelepik der lateinischen Spätantike: Formgeschichte einer erbaulichen Gattung*. Munich: Fink.

———, ed. 1993. *Restauration et Renouveau: la littérature latine de 284 à 374 après J.-C.* Turnhout: Brepols.

Hillier, R. 1993. *Arator on the Acts of the Apostles: A Baptismal Commentary*. Oxford: Oxford University Press.

Hinds, S. 1998. *Allusion and Intertext: Dynamics of Appropriation in Roman Poetry*. Cambridge: Cambridge University Press.

James, E. 2008. "The Rise and Function of the Concept 'Late Antiquity'," *JLA* 1: 20–30.

Kaster, R. A. 1988. *Guardians of Language: The Grammarian and Society in Late Antiquity*. Berkeley: University of California Press.

Kaufmann, H., ed., trans., and comm. 2006. *Dracontius: Romul. 10 (Medea)*. Heidelberg: Winter.

Kay, N. M. ed., trans., and comm., 2006. *Epigrams from the Anthologia Latina*. London: Duckworth.

Klopsch, P. 1980. *Einführung in die Dichtungslehren des lateinischen Mittelalters*. Darmstadt: Wissenschaftliche Buchgesellschaft.

Korzeniewski, D., ed., trans., and comm. 1976. *Hirtengedichte aus spätrömischer und karolingischer Zeit*. Darmstadt: Wissenschaftliche Buchgesellschaft.

Lancon, B. 2001. *Rome in Late Antiquity: Everyday Life and Urban Change, AD 312–609*. Trans. A. Nevill. New York: Routledge.

Levitan, W. 1985. "Dancing at the End of the Rope: Optatian Porfyry and the Field of Roman Verse," *TAPA* 115: 245–269.

Liebeschuetz, J. H. W. G. 2003. "*Gens* into *Regnum*: The Vandals." In *Regna and Gentes: The Relationship between Late Antique and Early Medieval Peoples and Kingdoms in the Transformation of the Roman World*, ed. H. W. Goetz, J. Jarnut, and W. Pohl, 55–83. Leiden: Brill.

Maas, M. 2000. *Readings in Late Antiquity: A Sourcebook*. London: Routledge.

Marrou, H. I. 1958. *Saint Augustin et la fin de la culture antique*, 4th ed. Paris: E. de Boccard.

Mastrangelo, M. 2008. *The Roman Self in Late Antiquity: Prudentius and the Poetics of the Soul*. Baltimore: Johns Hopkins University Press.

Mathisen, R. W. 1993. *Roman Aristocrats in Barbarian Gaul: Strategies for Survival in an Age of Transition*. Austin: University of Texas Press.

McGill, S. 2001. "*Poeta Arte Christianus*: Pomponius' Cento *Versus ad Gratiam Domini* as an Early Example of Christian Bucolic," *Traditio* 56: 15–26.

———. 2005. *Virgil Recomposed: The Mythological and Secular Centos in Antiquity*. New York: Oxford University Press.

———. 2007. "Virgil, Christianity, and the *Cento Probae*." In *Texts and Culture in Late Antiquity: Inheritance, Authority, and Change*, ed. J. H. D. Scourfield, 173–193. Swansea: Classical Press of Wales.

Mulligan, B. 2007. "The Poet from Egypt? Reconsidering Claudian's Eastern Origin," *Philologus* 151: 285–310.
Nodes, D. J. 1993. *Doctrine and Exegesis in Biblical Latin Poetry*. Leeds: Francis Cairns.
Nugent, S. G. 1985. *Allegory and Poetics: The Structure and Imagery of Prudentius' Psychomachia*. Frankfurt am Main: Peter Lang.
———. 1990. "Ausonius' 'Late-Antique' Poetics and 'Post-Modern' Literary Theory," *Ramus* 19: 26–50.
O'Daly, G. 2004. "*Sunt etiam Musis sua ludicra*: Vergil in Ausonius." In *Romane memento: Vergil in the Fourth Century*, ed. R. Rees, 141–154. London: Duckworth.
Paolucci, P., ed., trans., and comm. 2006. *Il centone Virgiliano Hippodamia dell'Anthologia Latina*. Hildesheim: Georg Olms.
Pucci, J. 1998. *The Full-Knowing Reader: Allusion and the Power of the Reader in the Western Literary Tradition*. New Haven, CT: Yale University Press.
Raby, F. J. E. 1934. *A History of Secular Latin Poetry*, 2 vols. Oxford: Oxford University Press.
———. 1953. *A History of Christian-Latin Poetry from the Beginning to the Close of the Middle Ages*. Oxford: Oxford University Press.
Rapp, C. 2005. "Literary Culture under Justinian." In *The Cambridge Companion to the Age of Justinian*, ed. M. Maas, 376–397. Cambridge: Cambridge University Press.
Ricci, M. L., trans. and comm. 2001. *Claudii Claudiani Carmina Minora*. Bari: Edipuglia.
Roberts, M. 1985. *Biblical Epic and Rhetorical Paraphrase in Late Antiquity*. Liverpool: Francis Cairns.
———. 1989. *The Jeweled Style: Poetry and Poetics in Late Antiquity*. Ithaca, NY: Cornell University Press.
———. 2001. "Rome Personified, Rome Epitomized: Representations of Rome in the Poetry of the Early Fifth Century," *AJP* 122: 533–565.
———. 2004. "Vergil and the Gospels: The *Evangeliorum Libri IV* of Juvencus." In *Romane memento: Vergil in the Fourth Century*, ed. R. Rees, 47–61. London: Duckworth.
———. 2007. "Bringing Up the Rear: Continuity and Change in the Latin Poetry of Late Antiquity." In *Latinitas Perennis, Vol. 1: The Continuity of Latin Literature*, ed. W. Verbaal, Y. Maes, and J. Papy, 141–167. Leiden: Brill.
———. 2008. "Poetry and Hymnography (1): Christian Latin Poetry." In *The Oxford Handbook of Early Christian Studies*, ed. S. A. Harvey and D. G. Hunter, 628–640. Oxford: Oxford University Press.
Rose, H. J. 1936. *A Handbook of Latin Literature from the Earliest Times to the Death of St. Augustine*. London: Methuen.
Rosenblum, M., ed., trans., and comm. 1961. *Luxorius: A Latin Poet among the Vandals*. New York: Columbia University Press.
Salanitro, G. 1997. "Osidio Geta e la poesia centonaria." In *ANRW* II.34.3, ed. W. Haase, 2314–2360. Berlin: Walter de Gruyter.
Schmid, W. 1953. "Tityrus Christianus," *RhM* 96: 101–165.
Schneider, W. C., ed. and trans. 2003. *Die elegischen Verse von Maximian: Eine letze Widerreder gegen die neue christliche Zeit*. Stuttgart: Franz Steiner.
Schwind, J. 1990. *Arator-Studien*. Göttingen: Vanderhoeck and Ruprecht.
———. 1995. *Sprachliche und exegetische Beobachtungen zu Arator*. Stuttgart: Franz Steiner.
Scourfield, J. H. D. 2007. "Textual Inheritances and Textual Relations in Late Antiquity." In *Texts and Culture in Late Antiquity: Inheritance, Authority, and Change*, ed. J. H. D. Scourfield, 1–32. Swansea: Classical Press of Wales.

Shackleton Bailey, D. R, ed. 1982. *Anthologia Latina I.1*. Stuttgart: Teubner.
Shanzer, D. 2009. "Literature, History, Periodization, and the Pleasures of the Latin Literary History of Late Antiquity," *History Compass* 7.3: 917–954.
Shaw, B. D. 1995a. *Environment and Society in Roman North Africa: Studies in History and Archaeology*. Aldershot: Variorum.
———. 1995b. *Rulers, Nomads, and Christians in Roman North Africa*. Aldershot: Variorum.
Shea, G. W., intr. and trans. 1998. *The Iohannis or De Bellis Libycis of Flavius Cresconius Corippus*. Lewiston, ME: E. Mellen.
Sivan, H. 1993. *Ausonius of Bordeaux: Genesis of a Gallic Aristocracy*. London: Routledge.
Slavitt, D. R., trans. 1996. *The Hymns of Prudentius: The Cathemerinon, or The Daily Round*. Baltimore: Johns Hopkins University Press.
Smith, M. 1976. *Prudentius' Psychomachia: A Reexamination*. Princeton, NJ: Princeton University Press.
Springer, C. P. E. 1988. *The Gospel as Epic in Late Antiquity: The Paschale Carmen of Sedulius*. Leiden: Brill.
Tarrant, R. G. 1983. "Anthologia Latina." In *Texts and Transmission: A Survey of the Latin Classics*, ed. L. D. Reynolds, 9–13. Oxford: Oxford University Press.
Testa, R. L. 2007. "Christian Emperor, Vestal Virgins and Priestly Colleges: Reconsidering the End of Roman Paganism," *AnTard* 15: 251–262.
Thraede, K. 1962. "Epos," *RAC* 5: 983–1042.
Tissol, G. 2002. "Ovid and the Exilic Journey of Rutilius Namatianus," *Arethusa* 35: 435–446.
Trout, D. E. 1999. *Paulinus of Nola: Life, Letters, and Poems*. Berkeley: University of California Press.
Wheeler, S. 2007. "More Roman Than the Romans of Rome: Virgilian (Self-) Fashioning in Claudian's *Panegyric for the Consuls Olybrius and Probinus*." In *Texts and Culture in Late Antiquity: Inheritance, Authority, and Change*, ed. J. H. D. Scourfield, 97–133. Swansea: Classical Press of Wales.
White, C. 2000. *Early Christian Latin Poets*. London: Routledge.
Witke, C. 1971. *Numen Litterarum: The Old and the New in Latin Poetry from Constantine to Gregory the Great*. Leiden: Brill.
Wolff, E., ed. 2007. *Rutilius Namatianus: Sur son retour*. Paris: Les Belles Lettres.

CHAPTER 11

GREEK POETRY

GIANFRANCO AGOSTI
University of Rome "La Sapienza"

I. Introduction

For a long time, late Greek poetry was considered an epigonal production, a tiresome continuation of the great classical and Hellenistic poetry. Despite the great critical and philological efforts in the last half of the nineteenth century and the beginning of the twentieth century, which finds expression in the edition of Nonnus of Panopolis' *Dionysiaca* by Rudolf Keydell (Keydell 1959), few were disposed to acknowledge not only the aesthetic qualities but also the reasons for reading the rich production of poetry following the third century C.E.* Since the 1970s, the methodological changes in historiography on Late Antiquity, which brought us to see it not only as a passing and decadent period but also as an age of transformation (Athanassiadi 2006; cf. Giardina 1999), has led consequently to the re-evaluation of the autonomous features and peculiarities of the literary culture of Late Antiquity (Averil Cameron 1998 and 2006; Bowersock 1990). Slowly but surely, the image of bookish and contrived poetry gave way to a growing regard for composition strategies, social functions, and audience response.† The definition of an autonomous profile of Christian literature (compare Vessey 2008) has, moreover, permitted us to consider Christian poetry also as an integral part of the literary production of Late Antiquity. This new critical attitude is summarized in the words of one of its major promoters: "the resurgence of poetry . . . is one the most intriguing features of the literary culture of Late Antiquity" (Alan Cameron 2004a, 328).

Thanks to editorial efforts in the last few years, philological and literary interests have intensified, and the bibliography has grown rapidly (Carvounis and Hunter 2008, 1–3). A general history of Greek poetry of Late Antiquity is nonexistent, and only somewhat detailed outlines are available (Thraede 1962; Garzya 1984; Vian 1986; Gigli Piccardi 2003, 8–13; Hose 2004; Alan Cameron 2004a; Miguélez Cavero 2008; Agosti 2009a), nor are general works on the aesthetics of this poetry comparable to the thought-provoking book by Michael Roberts on Latin poetry (1989; see also McGill, chapter 10 in this book). However, the book on Byzantine aesthetics by Averintsev (1988), which contains innovative views and suggestions on late antique poetry and should be much better known among historians of later Greek literature, deserves to be mentioned. In the following pages, I sketch only some outlines of late antique Greek poetic production, focusing mainly on the issues of relationships between poetry and prose, of rhetorical structures, of social contexts, and of performances.

II. A World of Poetry

First of all, studying late antique poetry means acknowledging a rebalance, evident to contemporaries but underestimated by modern historiography. The enormous amount of artistic and technical writings in prose, as well as the great personalities of orators and philosophers of the fourth and fifth century C.E., encouraged scholars to outline a literary world where poetry was quite marginal. It is significant that among the late antique orators, only Gregory of Nazianzus dedicated himself to poetry, even if placing it secondary to his homiletic and theological works

But the general primacy of prose does not imply the marginalization of poetry. First of all, late antique poets were not afraid of length: Gregory of Nazianzus left about 18,000 verses, Nonnus about 25,000, Quintus Smyrnaeus 10,000, the author of the *Metaphrase of the Psalms* more than 5,000—not to mention what has been lost (as is the case of the sixty books of the *Heroikai Theogamiai* by Peisander of Laranda). Such a "gigantism" resembles the overwhelming production in prose by orators such as Libanius or of theologians, homilists, and Church historians, such as Eusebius, the Cappadocian Fathers, John Chrysostom, or Socrates of Constantinople.

In some geographical areas, there is a notable chronological continuity. In Egypt, above all in the Thebaid and at Alexandria, from at least the beginning of the third century, poetry enjoyed popularity that was to lead to the creation of a new style, brought to a complete codification by Nonnus of Panopolis in the fifth century and used by the "Nonnian" poets up to the age of Justinian (527–565). In an often quoted passage, Eunapius (beginning of the fifth century), regarding the sophist Prohaeresius, observes, "as for rhetoric, suffice it to say that he was Egyptian, for this race is mad for poetry (ἐπὶ ποιητικῇ μὲν σφόδρα μαίνονται), whereas the serious Hermes (ὁ δὲ σπουδαῖος Ἑρμῆς) has departed from them" (*Vitae Sophistarum* 10.7.12, pp. 78.25–27; ed. Giangrande).

One can sense certain irritation and reductive judgment in this phrase regarding the activity and style of poetry, which was evidently considered to be subsidiary and ludicrous, not worthy of a true sophist (Alan Cameron 1965, 491; latest discussion in Miguélez Cavero 2008, 86–88). The haughty Eunapius denounced, however, an undeniable fact: that the public continued to favor poetry, and not only in Egypt. The number of known poets in Asia Minor, in Palestine, and Constantinople; the growing diffusion of verse inscriptions from the fourth to the sixth century; and the testimonies of poetic performances (see §IV.2) reveal evidence that even in the age of prose, poetry had a precise social position (compare Roueché 2006).

Poetry continued to be the base of cultural formation (Cribiore 2001; 2007a) and constituted the principal part of the classical *paideia*, the common language retained as being a fundamental requisite of late antique élites (Brown 1992; Alan Cameron 2004a, 341–346). As a consequence of such, poetry assumed a promotional-political function, as it is easy to see from the honorary inscriptions (Robert 1948; Merkelbach and Stauber 1998–2004) and from the abundant panegyric production in verse—in competition with that of prose—practiced by brilliant intellectuals and able versifiers, often of Egyptian origin, who put their culture and professional qualities at the service of the emperors, important officials of the imperial court, dignitaries, and citizens and who composed praises for single individuals, as well as for celebrative events and city traditions (the so-called *πάτρια*), along with *ἐκφράσεις* of works of art and monuments (Viljamaa 1968; Garzya 1984; Fournet 1999, 673–681; Alan Cameron 2004a, 330; Miguélez Cavero 2008, 343–353). The popularity and success of these professional poets, called after a memorable article by Alan Cameron (1965) "wandering poets," is perhaps the most tangible sign of the prestige of poetry. Along with the epigraphic monuments, quite a few papyrus fragments remain of this official poetry (Page 1942; Heitsch 1963–1964). Many of the poets had brilliant careers, such as Cyrus of Panopolis (Alan Cameron 1982) and Pamprepius of Panopolis (Livrea 1979); important poets such as Claudian, Horapollon, Hermeias, and Christodorus of Coptos wrote patriographic poems, in hexameters and in iambics. All these poems are lost, as well as the Christian *patria* of Alexandria by a certain Theodorus (Fournet 2003a), whose poem is comparable to the Christian ideological images of towns in Near Eastern mosaics (on which see Bowersock 2006); the only notable exception is a fragment of the *patria* of Hermopolis Magna (xxiv, ed. Heitsch; Gigli Piccardi 1990). But we can get a good idea of them by reading the long digressions devoted to Tyre and Beirut in Nonnus' *Dionysiaca* (Chuvin 1991; 1994).

II.1 A Short Prosopography

To assign a *terminus ante quem* to late antique poetry is relatively easy: the last poet still able to manage "classicizing" hexameter was George of Pisidia, who in the thirties of the seventh century wrote the poem *De vanitate vitae* in

Nonnian style (ed. Gonnelli 1991; see also §V). As for the beginning, many scholars point out the continuity of poetry of the first two centuries C.E., especially of the didactic poetry, with the later one (Alan Cameron 2004a, 327–328).[1] It is in any case only from the age of Diocletian (284–305) that some features of late antique aesthetics—or "ancient-Byzantine" according to Averintsev's definition (1998)—such as the restructuring of literary genres, where Christianity played an important role, or the increasing presence of rhetoric become evident.

Some papyrus fragments point to the renaissance of an encomiastic poetry connected to contemporary events at the end of the third century C.E. We know unfortunately only the titles of the poems by Soterichus of Oasis, the most relevant poet of the Tetrarchy: he wrote verse biographies on Alexander and on the pagan holy man Apollonius of Tyana, as well as mythological poems such as *Calydoniaca*, *Bassarica*, and *Ariadne*. The poems on Dionysiac themes probably influenced Nonnus (Bowersock 1994): recently, some fragments preserved by *P.Oxy.* 4352 (c. 298; see Agosti 2002b)—a poem on Antinous and an encomium to Diocletian—along with the already quoted (§I) fragment of the *Patria* of Hermopolis have been attributed to Soterichus (Livrea 2002; but compare Janiszewski 2006, 228–235). The latter poem, preserved in a fourth-century papyrus, is attributed by the last editor to Andronicus of Hermopolis (Gigli Piccardi 1990). To this period belonged also Peisander of Laranda, author of the perhaps longest Greek epic poem, the *Heroikai Theogamiai* in sixty books, a sort of omnicomprehensive mythological handbook in hexameters. There is a general consensus that Quintus of Smyrna should be assigned to the third century; this is the author of the *Posthomerica* in fourteen books, a sequel to the *Iliad* (ed. Vian 1963–1969; for the date, see now Baumbach and Bär 2007, 1–8; Carvounis 2008, 60). About him, we know only that he had a link with Smyrna, where he claims to have received his alleged poetic inspiration (12.308–313, ed. Vian; Campbell 1981; Hopkinson 1994b, 106). His poem was already known and imitated by Triphiodorus of Panopolis (Kaster 1988, no. 157), probably a grammarian, who wrote a short poem (691 hexameters) on *The Fall of Troy* and who composed mythological epics, *Marathoniaca* and *Hippodameia*, a paraphrase of Homeric similes and a lipogrammatic *Odyssey* (all lost). The *Fall of Troy* is the only extant Greek source of the story of the Trojan horse and the fatal night (on the relationships and differences with Virgil's narrative, see Gerlaud 1982, 41–47; Dubielzig 1996, 20–27). This poem is dated to the second half of the third century, thanks to *P.Oxy.* 2946 (Alan Cameron 1970, 478–482); his style and his metrics are very close to that of Nonnus but a little less strict. Before the publication of the papyrus, Triphiodorus was considered a "bad" pupil of Nonnus: it is evident now that he is instead a forerunner. Dating on stylistic grounds can be sometimes seriously misleading.

To the end of the third or the beginning of the fourth century C.E. is dated the choliambic poem on the destruction of Thebes in Ps.-Callisthenes' *Romance of Alexander* (Braccini 2004). A codex from the fourth–fifth century in the Bodmer Library of Geneva has revealed a group of new Christian poems (around 700 lines) that date to the middle of fourth century (ed. Hurst and Reverdin and Rudhardt 1984 and 1999). The codex, usually called the "codex of visions" on account of the majority of its content (the *Visions* of Hermas' Pastor and a visionary poem), contains a collection (cf. Crisci 2004) of eight Christian classicizing poems dealing with sin and salvation. The first three poems (*P.Bodmer* 29–31) are centered on a key figure, Dorotheus, who is also the narrator-protagonist of the first and most important poem, the *Vision of Dorotheus*, where he narrates his experiences in God's palace (described as an imperial palace); there follows a poem on Isaac's sacrifice, reflections on theodicy (the poem *To the Righteous*, the only one in elegiacs; ed. Livrea 2009), dialogue poems on Cain and Abel, *encomia* of Christ, and exhortatory poems. The Bodmer papyri are part of a library that belonged to a religious community of Upper Egypt, not far from Panopolis: these poems may represent the Christian side of the flourishing poetry school of the Thebaid (Agosti 2001c and 2002a and the essays collected in Hurst and Rudhardt 2002). To the second half of the century belongs the poem *On Stones* attributed to Orpheus (*Orphei Lithica*): it is a refined hexametric "didactic" poem on stones' therapeutic virtues, with a mystical prologue in a bucolic setting, whose author was involved in the milieu of Maximus of Ephesus, the teacher of the emperor Julian (Livrea 1992). The same philosopher could also be the Maximus who is author of elegant Callimachean poems on astrological forecasts, *περὶ καταρχῶν* (in hexameters; ed. Ludwich 1877). In this period, there was a renewal of interest in astrology, as some passages in Nonnus' *Dionysiaca* show (for example 6.1–108). Book IV (and maybe V) of the didactic astrological poem that goes under the name of Manetho might also be assigned to this period. Palladas, who lived in Alexandria in the second half of the fourth century (according to the *communis opinio*: for a predating to the age of Constantine, see now Wilkinson 2009; 2010), was a grammarian and a prolific epigrammatist and is well represented in the *Greek Anthology* (about 150 epigrams; for the problems related to the transmission of his *corpus* see Lauxtermann 1997). He is the true successor to Lucilius' satirical tradition, and in his epigrams, iambic themes and personal invective play an important role. He wrote attacks against public individuals, governors, and Christians.

Papyrogical findings have enriched our knowledge of Egyptian verse production (for an updated catalogue, Miguélez Cavero 2008, 33–79). Most of the poems transmitted by papyri are in hexameters, and there are epic panegyrics, often composed for local audiences: among them should be mentioned the fragments of a *Blemyomachia*, a Homeric-style poem on a successful Roman campaign against the Blemyes, a barbarian people living in the south. The papyrus codex (three fragments in different collections) preserving it is dated to around 400, and the poem has been tentatively attributed to the diplomat and historian Olympiodoros of Thebes (Livrea 1978; see

Steinrück 1999; Miguélez Cavero 2008, 59–61). It is noteworthy that, following the tradition of didactic poems in iambics of the first two centuries of the imperial age, a handful of Egyptian poets composed iambic poems. Photius the Patriarch in the ninth century was still able to read an anthology of authors from Middle and Upper Egypt (*Bibl.* cod. 279, 563a.8–20 Henry) containing *patria* of Hermopolis and of Alexandria, works by Hermias of Hermopolis and by Horapollo (Kaster 1988, no. 71 and 77), *dramata* in various meters by Andronicus and Serenus, didactic poems and *patria* by Helladius of Antinoe (Kaster 1988, no. 227), and the encomium of Count Phoibammon by Andronicus of Hermopolis and the praises of Duke Mauricius by Cyrus of Antaiopolis (Kaster 1988, no. 41; on this codex see Hammerstaedt 1997; Agosti 2001a, 222; Alan Cameron 2004a, 336; Miguélez Cavero 2008, 79–83). All these works, unfortunately lost, offer a secular background to the development of another important innovation of the fourth century: Gregory of Nazianzus' cousin, Amphilochius of Iconium, wrote a didactic iambic poem, the *Iambi ad Seleucum* (337 lines), dealing with the education and culture of young Christians.

The greatest poetic personality of the last part of the century is undoubtedly Gregory of Nazianzus (c. 330–390), who practiced all classic meters, hexameters, elegiacs, iambics, and ionics, and a great variety of literary genres: didactic poems, theological poems, personal and autobiographical poems, polemical poems (he was well versed in attacking his adversaries: Agosti 2001a, 231–233), hymns (McGuckin 2008), and epigrams later collected in what is now the eighth book of the *Greek Anthology*. Most of the poems were composed after 380, when Gregory was forced to abandon the episcopal see of Constantinople and came back to Nazianzus. The autobiographical poems, one of his more successful generic innovations for Byzantine literature (*Carm.* 2.1.1–11), allow us to know many aspects of his life and his struggles, and his poetry has been frequently interpreted as a retreat into himself and a "consolation" in old age, following what he says in the programmatic poem *On His Own Verses* (2.1.39, *PG* 37.1329–1336, ll. 54–57). But this is only one side of Gregory's verse production: he also wanted to make of his poetry an instrument of a cultural, didactic, and doctrinal program. A reaction against heretical popular poems and hymns (Simelidis 2009, 25–29) and the project of creating a tradition of Christian classicizing poetry (McGuckin 2006) are also to be taken into account. The only complete edition of Gregory's poems is still Migne's *Patrologia Graeca* volumes 37 and 38, but in recent years some editions and commentaries of single poems have appeared (see Ancient Sources; English translations: White 1996; Moreschini and Sykes 1997; Daley 2006, 162–171; Simelidis 2009).

Between the end of the fourth and the beginning of the fifth century, Synesius of Cyrene (414), orator and bishop, composed nine hymns in ionic meter, poems that combine Neoplatonism and Christian thought (McGuckin 2008; Baldi 2011).

The undisputed protagonist of Greek poetry in fifth century is Nonnus of Panopolis, author of the *Dionysiaca*, telling the life of Dionysus, his triumph in India, and his progress from the Near East to Thebes, in forty-eight books (the longest extant epic poem of antiquity), and of a hexametric *Paraphrase of St John's Gospel* (in general: Golega 1930; Keydell 1936; Vian 1976, ix–lxviii; Livrea 1989; Gigli Piccardi 2003, 27–83; Hernández de la Fuente 2008). Author of a reform of the hexameter (see §IV.1) and of a new poetic style, based on manneristic exuberance, Nonnus is the prime mover of the "late antique renaissance of epic poetry": his style and metrics, usually called "Nonnian style" or "modern style" (in opposition to the "archaic, i.e. Homeric, style" of poets like Quintus of Smyrna or the author of the *Blemyomachia*; Agosti and Gonnelli 1995, 293; Whitby 1994, 128–129), was followed by a group of poets who recognized in him a new model to imitate. The "modern style" will last until the first decades of the seventh century (up to the aforementioned George of Pisidia); the definition "school of Nonnus" became a commonplace in scholarship from the eighteenth century onward, but since the presumed Nonnus' pupils show significant differences each from other, nowadays one prefers to speak of the followers of the "modern style," who accepted the innovative character of Nonnus' metrics and style (Agosti and Gonnelli 1995, 219; Gonnelli 2003, 7–8; Miguélez Cavero 2008, 93–96; Agosti 2009a, 102–107). A couple of hexameters in the *Greek Anthology* (9.198), which Wifstrand interpreted rightly as a *Buchepigramm*, informs us that Nonnus' poems were composed, or at least recited, in Alexandria (Wifstrand 1933, 166–167; Livrea 1989, 32–35). The coexistence of a poem on Dionysus and a Christian poem caused endless discussions about author's faith (§IV.4) until recent research demonstrated beyond all doubt that Nonnus was a Christian and that the *Dionysiaca* and the *Paraphrase* were composed in parallel. Establishing a date is more difficult: the range goes from the early fifth century to about 470 (the date of the first "Nonnian" poets). Vian (1976, xviii) suggests for the major poem the period 457–470; Livrea (1987, 445; 2000, 55–76) offers a date of 445–450 for both poems, but a date around the period 430–450 is nowadays favored by scholars (Agosti 2003, 177, n. 6; Whitby 2007a, 200; compare Miguélez Cavero 2008, 17–18). We do not have any ancient account of Nonnus' biography (for his links with Egypt, see Gigli Piccardi 1998), though Enrico Livrea has suggested identifying the poet with the bishop Nonnus of Edessa (1987; 2000, 55–76; identification rejected by Alan Cameron 2001, but compare Livrea 2003).

The manuscripts assign to Apollinarius of Laodicea a long hexametric *Metaphrase of the Psalms*, which was instead composed by an Egyptian author around 460 and dedicated to a bishop, Marcianus of Constantinople (Golega 1960; Agosti and Gonnelli 1995, 363; De Stefani 2008a). This poem has a long prologue (110 hexameters), which is a real manifesto of Christian poetry (see §IV.3). The style of the paraphrase is rather archaizing, according to the author's aim to translate the Psalms into Homeric language (but in the prologue, where the poet was not obliged to follow the biblical model, language and metrics are closer to the "modern style"). The *Orphic Argonautica*, a strange poem in 1,376 hexameters that deals with the Argonauts' expedition and highlights the role of Orpheus in it, while summarizing and correcting Apollonius Rhodius' poem, is generally assigned to the second half of the fifth century (Vian 1987, 45–47). The language of this poem is an odd mixture of vulgarisms and epic forms. Around the middle of the century, empress Aelia Eudocia (414–460), wife of Theodosius II, composed an epic poem on her husband's war against the Persians, a verse paraphrase of the Octateuch and of Zacharias and Daniel (all lost), and a poetic hagiography on St. Cyprian of Antioch, following a prose model. Only book 1 and the first part of book 2 are preserved (ed. Ludwich 1897; compare Bevegni 2006). This interesting poem deserves to be better known: Cyprian, a pagan wizard who became bishop and martyr, is a precursor of Faust. Eudocia participated in (and possibly initiated) the project of composing a Hellenized Gospel, built entirely with Homeric material: she revised the first version of the *Homeric Centos* written by a certain bishop Patricius, a patchwork composed of hemistichs or entire verses from the *Iliad* or *Odyssey*, known in four different versions in medieval manuscripts (ed. Schembra 2007a; editions of single versions Rey 1998; Usher 1999). We have also an epigraphic poem on the bath complex of Gadara, composed by Eudocia visiting the Holy Land around 440 (Busch 1999, 84–98; *SGO* 21/22/01; Sowers 2008, 26–40).

The "earliest extant reader of Nonnus" (Alan Cameron 1982, 239) was his fellow countryman Cyrus of Panopolis: he had a rapid career under Theodosius II (408–450), being both Prefect of Constantinople and Praetorian Prefect of the East in 439. After his consulate in 441, he fell into disgrace and was sent as bishop to a small town in Phrygia. Only after Theodosius' death could he return to Constantinople. The *Greek Anthology* preserves seven epigrams under his name, but only some of them are authentic (Alan Cameron 1982, 226–227; Tissoni 2008). The hexametric *Hymns* by Proclus, which combine the tradition of Orphic hymns and Chaldaic oracular poetry, share stylistic features and some vocabulary with Nonnus' poetry, but it is difficult to demonstrate direct relationships (Vogt 1957; Gigli Piccardi 1985, 242–244; Van den Berg 2001; Agosti 2003, 105).

After the second half of the fifth century, all the highbrow poets are followers of the "modern style." The first of them was the openly pagan Pamprepius of Panopolis (440–484; Kaster 188, no. 114), a talented and very ambitious man. He frequented Neoplatonic circles in Alexandria and was also a pupil of Proclus in Athens, where he entered the profession of *γραμματικός* enjoying the patronage of Theagenes. In 476, he arrived in Constantinople, where he attached himself to the powerful Illus, general of emperor Zeno, obtaining a public chair of Greek. Thanks to Illus, he became quaestor and then consul in 479, notwithstanding his overt paganism. Pamprepius was later involved in Illus' and Leontius' rebellions against Zeno (484) and was finally executed

(Alan Cameron 2007, 35–36; Chuvin 2009, 100–103). In a papyrus codex of the sixth century (xxxv Heitsch; Miguélez Cavero 2008, 72–74), there are three poems attributed convincingly to Pamprepius (ed. Livrea 1979): an hexametric fragmentary text, an elegant and refined description of a day (of spring or autumn), and an encomium to the patrician Theagenes (a patron of Athenian Neoplatonists; cf. Di Branco 2006, 159–179). At the end of the fifth century, a certain Musaeus the grammarian composed his famous epyllion *Hero and Leander* (Kaster 1988, no. 102; ed. Koster 1971; Livrea 1982), narrating the tragic story of the love of two young people who live on opposite banks of the Hellespont (Leander dies in the sea, and Hero commits suicide after finding his corpse). Musaeus knew Christian poetry: he quotes Gregory of Nazianzus, Nonnus' *Paraphrase*, and the *Metaphrase of the Psalms* (Gelzer 1975, 298–299). Under the reign of Anastasius (491–518) lived Colluthus, Christodorus, and probably John of Gaza (for literary culture under Anastasius, see Nicks 2000). Only the 394 hexameters of the *Rape of Helen* survived among the poems by Colluthus of Lycopolis (Kaster 1988, no. 33), author also of mythological poems and epic panegyrics (*Calydoniaca*; and the *Persika*, perhaps on Anastasius' victory over the Persians in 506). The epyllion tells the story of the abduction, beginning with the wedding of Thetis and Peleus and the judgment of Paris, who goes to Sparta, where he easily seduces Helen (ed. Livrea 1968; Schönberger 1993). Colluthus is possibly the same grammarian to whom "George the Grammarian" dedicated an anacreontic poem (no. 9, Ciccolella 2000, 252–263). Christodorus of Coptos was a prolific poet, having composed historical poems and many *patria*, a poem on the disciples of Proclus, and a description of the statues of the thermae of the Zeuxippos gymnasium in Constantinople (Bassett 2004). This poem has survived in the second book of the *Greek Anthology* (ed. Beckby 1965; commentary by Tissoni 2000; cf. Kaldellis 2007b). John of Gaza (Kaster 1988, no. 83) lived between the second half of the fifth and the first part of the sixth century (Alan Cameron considers 526 C.E. as *terminus ante quem*; for other attempts to specify John's dating: Ciccolella 2000, 119). He composed a description of a cosmic painting (or wall painting) in the winter baths at Gaza or Antioch: a poem of about 700 hexameters, inspired by Neoplatonic doctrine (Gigli Piccardi 2005; 2008; Bargellini 2006; Renaut 2009). Under the name of John, six anacreontic poems are transmitted in the anthology of the codex *Barberinianus gr.* 310 (tenth century), together with the anacreontics attributed to the so-called George the Grammarian, a poet probably of Egyptian origin; to the latter have been recently attributed the ethopoeic epigrams of *AP* 9.449–480 (Lauxtermann 2005).

In the Justinianic age (527–565), there is a renewal of literary epigram, thanks to a group of learned *scholastikoi* (lawyers) in Constantinople (Averil Cameron and Alan Cameron 1966; Rapp 2005, 387–389; a survey of late Greek epigram in Galli Calderini 1987), whose classicizing epigrams have been collected in Agathias' *Cycle*, published probably at the beginning of Justin II's reign, about 567–568 (Alan Cameron 1993, 69–75). Agathias of Myrina

(c. 532–after 580), well known for his *Histories* in five books, also wrote an epic poem in nine books, the *Daphniaca*, and hundreds of epigrams (McCail 1971). A close friend of his was Paul the Silentiary, an officer at the court, one of the best epigrammatists of Greek literature and the author also of the celebrated description of Hagia Sophia (ed. De Stefani 2010). This poem, longer than 1,000 hexameters, was recited after the second restoration of the dome, a few days after Christmas of 562 (Whitby 1985, 215–228; Macrides and Magdalino 1988; for the language, see Fayant 2003); a second description of the ambo (nearly 300 hexameters) was performed some days later. In the sixth century, official Latin poetry was also produced in Constantinople (Priscian composed an epic panegyric of Anastasius, Corippus an encomium of Justin II and other epic poems). The Latin language was obviously known, and Latin books circulated in Constantinople, but a wider knowledge of Latin literature among Greek writers is difficult to prove (recently De Stefani 2006). The last Egyptian poet we know is Dioscorus of Aphrodito (c. 520–585), a contemporary of Agathias and Paul the Silentiary. Dioscorus was a local administrator and notary who was fluent in both Coptic and Greek (cf. MacCoull 2003) and who had the habit of composing poems that followed his prose petitions, as a sort of "dialogue" in the language of the *paideia* between the officer, to whom the request was addressed, and the petitioner. Dioscorus' poems are mostly laudatory poems for dukes and governors, written in a flawed and sometimes obscure language and style: we have the autographs, written on the back of legal documents (ed. Fournet 1999). Considered for a long time the "worst poet" of antiquity, he has recently profited from re-evaluation, in the light of the historical and even literary interest of his "documentary" poetry (Fournet 1999 and 2003b; Agosti 2008c).

III. Rhetoric

III.1 Genres

If the traditional epic genre is somehow furthered by the *Posthomerica* of Quintus of Smyrna (and lately in the epic panegyric, see Viljamaa 1968; Livrea 1978; and Steinrück 1999 for the *Blemyomachia*), the short epic poems by Triphiodorus and the Homeric epyllion of Colluthus combine Callimachus' lesson about short poetry with the mixing of genres (for pastoral tones in Colluthus, see Harries 2006; for his depiction of Paris characterized by irony and humor, see Magnelli 2008c). Musaeus wrote a hexametric elegy, whose meaning is still controversial (simply an erotic poem or a Neoplatonic allegory?; compare Gelzer 1975, 322; Lamberton 1986, 157–161). The *Dionysiaca* is a full-scale attempt at deconstructing the traditional epic poem (Chuvin 2006):

in his forty-eight books, the poet had the ambition to compose a poem that could match the *Iliad* and *Odyssey* together (Shorrock 2001), narrating the story of the world through a "biography" of Dionysus that follows the rhetorical rules of the *encomium* (Stegemann 1930, 116; Vian 1976, xx–xxi; Lasky 1978; Miguélez Cavero 2008, 355–366; Miguélez Cavero 2010). If the overall structure is quite evident (recent analysis in Vian 1976, xxii–xxiv; Gigli Piccardi 2003, 27–30; Chuvin 2006; Miguélez Cavero 2008, 19–21), the plan is programmatically complicated by long and short digressions, *ekphraseis*, praise of cities, and erudite mythological narrations, all according to a predetermined disharmony that corresponds in language and style to the aesthetic of "variety" (ποικιλία; see Riemschneider 1957; String 1966; Fauth 1981), and there is the constant presence of irony, buffoonery, parody, and eroticism. All literary genres are represented in this great literary container, from war epic (books 25–40), to tragedy (Pentheus' story in books 43–45), pastoral poetry, elegy, comedy, and novel (Gigli Piccardi 1985; Tissoni 1998; Harries 2006; Miguélez Cavero 2008, 167–180; 2010): the *Dionysiaca* is a literary macrocosm that embraces all possible microcosms, according to Neoplatonic aesthetics (Gigli Piccardi 2003, 14–26). Dionysus as epic hero goes back to Roman literature, but the living popularity of Dionysiac themes in late antique visual art shows that the story of Dionysus was all but foreign to the contemporary social context (for Dionysus in Egypt, see Bowersock 1990). The same goes for the revival of mythological poetry, as well as of verse encomia and antiquarian poems on the mythical origins of cities (πάτρια: for this genre in Nonnus, see Chuvin 1991). Mythology and classical culture were a cohesive and distinctive social component, as well as an essential requirement for administrative and political careers (see §2). As a consequence, poetry was appreciated among educated élites much more than one might imagine, and there is no reason to identify mythological poetry as a sign of paganism, since mythology was simply a part of the liberal education shared by Christian and pagan élites (Alan Cameron 2004a, 342–343; §IV.4).

Also Christian poetry is innovative in literary genres, even though not as much as contemporary Latin literature is (compare Stella 2005; McGill, chapter 10 in this book). Gregory of Nazianzus deals with a wide range of genres in his poems: autobiographical and didactic poems are particularly innovative, for their formal features and for their metrics, too (Alan Cameron 2004a, 333; Whitby 2008; Simelidis 2009, with further references). He is an extraordinary and unique figure, who nonetheless had a tradition before him: the publication of the Bodmer codex has now shown that there was a continuity between the initial period of Christian poetry, represented by the Christian books in the *Sibylline Oracles*,[2] and Gregory (Agosti 2001c; 2002a). Among the Bodmer poems, there are some paraphrases of Old Testament passages, revealing that also in the East the context favorable to Christianity after Milan's edict (313) gave impulse to literary experiments. The most characteristic Christian genre, biblical verse paraphrases, began actually more or less at the same time in West and East: the poetic Gospel harmony by the Spanish priest Juvencus, the *Evangeliorum libri*, dates to 329–330, and the Bodmer poems were composed in the middle of the fourth century. In the fifth century, biblical paraphrase enjoyed a short but fruitful season with Nonnus' *Paraphrase* of John's Gospel, the *Metaphrase of the Psalms*, the lost metaphrases of the Octateuch and of Zacharias and Daniel by Eudocia, and the *Homeric Centos*. Christian poets transformed the rhetorical exercise into a refined literary genre, based on the principles of abbreviation, amplification, and exegetical explication of the biblical model (compare Roberts 1985; Johnson 2006b, 67–112; on Nonnus' methods, Livrea 1989, 54–57, and the other commentaries on the *Paraphrase* listed in Ancient Sources). In Greek, a tradition of narrative paraphrases did not develop as it did in Latin (with Cyprianus Gallus, Sedulius, Arator, Marius Victorius, Avitus; see McGill, chapter 10 in this book). Greek Christian paraphrases tend rather toward poetic hagiographies, as probably were the life of Apollonius of Tyana by Soterichus or, better, the verse paraphrases of the Neoplatonic school, such as Christodorus' poem on the auditors of Proclus, or the hexametric version of Marinus' *Life of Proclus* (all lost; on Neoplatonic poetry, see Agosti 2005b; 2009c). Also, a difficult poem such as the *Orphic Argonautica* could be defined as a paraphrase of Apollonius Rhodius using procedures of strong abbreviation and selection of episodes, and even "corrections" (Vian 1987, 18–45); the author clearly intended to reestablish the right role of Orpheus in the Argonautic saga, while asserting at the same time a conscious agonistic attitude toward its authoritative model (Hunter 2005).

The epigram is one of the most productive genres in Late Antiquity (surveys in Mattsson 1942; Keydell 1962; Galli Calderini 1987; and see §2.1 on Palladas). Gregory of Nazianzus ennobles the Christian literary epigram (*Greek Anthology* VIII: other Christian epigrams of the fifth and sixth centuries are found in the first book, Baldwin 1996). The poets collected in Agathias' *Cycle* are the protagonists of the last flourish of literary epigram (for Agathias, see McCail 1971, 217–220; for Macedonius, Madden 1995). But it is true that such a production is only a small part compared with the thousands of epigraphic epigrams, whose number and diffusion grows increasingly from the fourth century onward (collections of texts: Robert 1948; Peek 1955; Bernand 1969; Merkelbach and Stauber 1998–2004). Epigraphical poetry is an important part of late antique verse production, which had an immediate and lively impact on its audience. From the perspective of history of literature, the analysis of epigraphic poems could provide a better understanding of some developments and features of highbrow literature (Alan Cameron 2004a, 331; Agosti 2008b). According to a tendency that began to be more popular from the end of the second century onward (Wifstrand 1933, 151–177), many epigraphical epigrams are in stichic hexameters or trimeters. The disregard for short measures, which it is possible to observe in literary epigrams (Agosti 2008a, 674–680; Magnelli 2008b for the proem of Agathias), is even more accentuated: there are *epigrammata longa*, even up to forty hexameters (*SEG* 39.449, from Tanagra, fifth century); unusually long are the ecphrastic epigrams of the Justinianic age, among which a special place is occupied by the highbrow epigram that extols the magnificence of the church of St. Polyeuktos and her patron, Anicia Juliana (Whitby 2006). Close reading of epigraphic epigrams leads to a better understanding of the presence of classical culture in single regions and cities (Robert 1948; Bernand 1969; Feissel 1998; 2006; Sartre-Fauriat 1998; Magnelli 2005; Agosti 1997; 1998; 2005c). While Homer and the Hellenistic poets are the preeminent literary models up to the fourth century, afterward, epigrams following the modern style begin to appear, in a range of literary levels, from highbrow poems that show consistent or occasional presence of modern stylistic features to ordinary poems whose authors were aware of features such as rare adjectives or four-word hexameters. There are also "bad" poems, where imperfect prosodies and metrics coexist with the insertion of poetic *tesserae*. Poetic flavor, the display of noble and recognizable models, and the insertion of poetic syntagmas were essential features of epigraphic poems, and as such, they appear also in texts composed by poets of mediocre education. Epigraphic texts had, first and foremost, a pragmatic function since they were a rich and complex medium for displaying and communicating information. Inscriptions were devised to be seen and to be read aloud (as their arrangement very often suggests: Agosti 2008b, 206–209 on *mise en page* and metrics; 2010); as a consequence, we must always consider the audience's response. For example, in the case of epigrams arranged on a single continuous line, reading them aloud could help to identify the verses' structure; a brilliant example is the long (seventy-six hexameter) inscription in St. Polyeuktos' church, *AP* 1.10, whose arrangement was particularly complex, since lines 1–41 "were written round in a circle inside the church" (according to the lemma in the manuscript) and lines 42–76 were inscribed on six plaques at the entrance of the church.

III.2 From School to Poetry

We have seen that one of the most important innovations in literary genres is verse paraphrase (§3.1). Paraphrase (μετάφρασις) was an exercise normally practiced at school: to a larger extent than before, late poetry was influenced and structured by rhetorical rules taught at school (Viljamaa 1968; Fournet 1999, 258–290, 685–690; Webb 1997, 346–366). With the grammarian (γραμματικός, the profession of many late poets), students learned to compose προγυμνάσματα, "preliminary rhetorical exercises," that looked forward to the μελέται "declamations," putting into practice the rules of literary genres in order to acquire a skillful eloquence. Such rules were codified in rhetorical handbooks (Kennedy 2003), among which the handbook of Menander Rhetor stands out in importance (Heath 2004) as a real key for a proper understanding of all late antique literature. Having learned the rules, authors were supposed to follow them in their works, producing a continuity between school and literary activity that is typical of this period (Cribiore 2001, 239–244; 2007b, 159–165). Rhetorical handbooks give examples only of prose *progymnasmata*, but we know many examples of verse exercise from Egyptian papyri (Fournet 1999, 325–326; Cribiore 2001, 226; Agosti 2005a; Miguélez Cavero 2008, 264–366). Ἐγκώμιον, "praise," ἠθοποιΐα, "impersonation," and ἔκφρασις, "description"—the most important exercises, present in every late antique poem—are the basic grammar of poetry. "Success was assured by following the rules" (Cribiore 2001, 239), a statement even more true in the case of encomiastic poetry (Viljamaa 1968). Poets' skill lay in innovating structures from the inside, to create something new but also recognizable at the same time.

Rhetoric also had consequences for style and language (one of the best analyses is offered by Demoen 1996 in his volume on Gregory's rhetorical use of pagan and biblical *exempla*). Take, for instance, the *ethopoea*, "impersonation," an imitation of a character working in direct style (τίνας ἂν λόγους εἴποι ὁ δεῖνα). In Nonnus' *Dionysiaca*, direct speeches, much more frequent than in Homer, are composed in an emphatic and dramatic style, asyndetic and based on antithesis, oxymoron, sound effects, wordplays, synonyms, participial constructions, and short cola (Wifstrand 1933, 140–150; Vian 1976, 140). Such a style was codified in school practice, going back to the *ethopoea* (Viljamaa 1968, 17). Speeches constructed on the techniques of *ethopoea* are present in every late poem (Agosti 2005a), from mythological poetry to the anacreontics (for example, John of Gaza, *Anacr.* 6, a dialogue between Aphrodite and Zeus), to Christian poetry (*P.Bodmer* 33 and 35 are *ethopoeae* on Cain and Abel; for Gregory of Nazianzus, see Demoen 2009). Rhetorical structures were suited to different subjects and meanings: for instance, a comparison between *P.Bodmer* 33, "Cain's Words," and a passage of Nonnus (*Dion.* 2.115–162, laments of an anonymous nymph) shows clearly that both derive from a common progymnasmatic model, that is to say, that both their authors had the same rhetorical training (Agosti 2005a, 43–44; 2009b, 62–63).

Another preliminary exercise, the ἔκφρασις, "description," of objects, places, situations, people, and works of art, heavily influenced late antique poetry (Tissoni 2000, 49–52; Gigli Piccardi 2003, 24–26; Miguélez Cavero 2008, 283–309), reaching the status of a self-standing poem in Christodorus, in John of Gaza, and in the poems by Paul the Silentiary, the masters of the genre, but almost every late poem has an ἔκφρασις, usually long and elaborate (for example, the description of the Trojan horse in Triphiodorus 57–107, or the description of lamps in Nonnus' *Paraphrase* 18.16–24). The habit of description has important consequences for style and narration: the poets concentrate on details, developing a visual language characterized by the use of rare words, fragmentation, and juxtaposition of scenes. It is possible to compare such a "jeweled style" with the cumulative and miniaturized aesthetics of works of art, such as appear in mosaics or in the reuse of *spolia* in monuments and public buildings (Riemschneider 1957; Roberts 1989, 66–121; Elsner 2004, 306–309; Agosti 2004–2005). In the *Homeric Centos*, for instance, Homeric materials are carefully assembled to give them new meanings, different from the original context. In Nonnus' *Paraphrase*, rare words, compound adjectives, and *hapax legomena* all function to advance the literary embellishment of the prose model, alongside its exegetical purposes (Accorinti 1996, 45–50; Livrea 2000, 92–105; Agosti 2003, 149–174). Composition becomes analytic; scenes are linked by juxtaposition; narrative is based on discontinuity and disharmony (the reason scholars considered many passages unaccomplished or incomplete); in narration, antecedents and preparatives of a story (i.e., its details) are much more important than its accomplishment. On the other hand, *ekphrasis* had the aim to describe with clarity and vividness (*ἐνάργεια*) and to bring before sight what the physical eye is not able to catch, going beyond the sensible world (James and Webb 1991): this anagogic meaning is evident in the *Description* of Paul the Silentiary, in passages such as the one concerning the "landscape" drawn by the marbles of the ambo (*Amb.* 224–240; cf. *S. Soph.* 617–646), the description of church lighting and of the church as a harbor of salvation (ll. 806–820; Agosti 2009a, 118–119). Such a visual aesthetic is heavily indebted to Neoplatonic theories (compare Plotinus 4.3.11 and Grabar 1945). An effective definition of the aesthetics of late antique poetry, which points out both its doctrinal and literary components, is that of a union of Plato and Homer (Gigli Piccardi 2003, 14–26; compare Gigli Piccardi 2005 for John of Gaza's *ekphrasis*).

III.3 Old and New Classics

Homer remained the literary model par excellence. Homeric intertextuality among late antique poetry goes from the simple, evident quotation to the most refined allusions, as carried out by Hellenistic poets. Nonnus has an agonistic attitude toward the father of epic poetry (Vian 1991; Hopkinson 1994a; Shorrock 2001); he also experiments with a complete paraphrase of *Iliad* 23 (the Games) in *Dionysiaca* book 37 (Frangoulis 1995). It is perhaps rather surprising to find a good knowledge of Homeric poetry and of its interpretation in authors less cultivated, as among the poets of the Bodmer codex: a flawless prosody and metrics could coexist with a certain competence in epic poetry (Agosti 2002a). The author of the *Metaphrase of the Psalms* "translates" the Psalter in a perfect Homeric style to give back its "metrical grace" (*μέτρων χάρις*) to biblical poetry (grace lost in the translation from Hebrew into Greek); Eudocia's *Homeric Centos* aim to extract Christian truth from Homer's *ipsissima verba*. Such a radical attempt at Christianizing Homer was possible thanks to the long-standing tradition of allegorical interpretation and the spiritualization of the Homeric poems (Agosti 2005b).[3]

From the second half of the fifth century, Nonnus became a "new classic" (Vian 1976, xx; Miguélez Cavero 2008, 3–105; Agosti 2009a, 102–107): his modern style (§II.1) became widespread in Egypt, Constantinople, Asia Minor, and Palestine. If there was not a "school of Nonnus," properly speaking, there were many followers of the modern style (the poets that Agathias calls νέοι, "moderns"). The definition of "formular *koiné*" has been recently applied to one aspect of this style, namely, the repetitions and slight variations of recurrent expressions (D'Ippolito 2003; materials also in Ludwich 1873, Golega 1930, Hopkinson 1994a, Schmiel 1998). This type of formulation came also from the fact that Nonnus' poems were studied at school, as Dioscorus' poems show (Fournet 1999; Agosti 2008c).

IV. Orality

IV.1 Metrics: Many Rules for a Simple Game

In schools, teachers continued to teach quantitative prosody, knowledge of which was necessary not only to read the ancient poets but also especially to compose verses according to the classical style. But since Greek had changed into an accentual language, distinguishing between long and short syllables, especially in the *dichrona* (α, ι, υ), became a difficult task.[4] For instance, the Bodmer poems and Eudocia's *St. Cyprian* prosodies are full of mis-scansions (Agosti and Gonnelli 1995, 333–348); also, even as learned an author as Gregory could not escape some false quantities (Agosti and Gonnelli 1995, 399–400), though one might consider those iambics as a conscious, innovative choice to follow the pronunciation of the fourth century (Alan Cameron 2004a, 339; Simelidis 2009, 54–56; Whitby 2008, 93).

On the opposite side, in the *Dionysiaca* Nonnus has only one mis-scansion in the quantity of an iota (Alan Cameron 2004a, 339) and a few more in the *Paraphrase*, due to the necessity of retaining expressions of the Gospel (Agosti 2003, 195–205). They are not enough, in any case, to deny Nonnian authorship of the poem (for such an opinion, see Sherry 1996). Despite his perfect knowledge of classical prosody (or, better, thanks to it), Nonnus had the idea of adapting hexameter to the new linguistic conditions (Wifstrand 1933; Whitby 1994; Agosti and Gonnelli 1995, 389–395). In the nineteenth century, scholars patiently discovered and described an endless series of "laws" and restrictions in Nonnian hexameters,[5] but it was left to Albert Wifstrand (1933) to make the decisive step, realizing that Nonnus used regulation of stress accent, together with restrictions of word ends: verses end with a long syllable (90 percent), preferably with a word with an accent on the penultimate syllable (72 percent),[6] and the proparoxytone ending is strictly forbidden; other regulations affect stress accent before main caesurae. As a result, he gave shape to a verse tending to isosyllabism, with a stress accent at the clausula (showing the audience that the verse was about to end) and at the main caesura, and with a loss of synapheia at the caesura. All such features tend to build a paired colon structure (*A / B //*), with the minimum possible rhythm patterns and a regular number of syllables. In Averintsev's words, "Nonnus' metrics is a traditional metrics, refashioned into a partial transformation of its opposite . . . a risky balance between two divergent languages, the school tradition and the living language" (1988, 192): the result is indeed an extremely monotonous verse, according to our sensibility, but an easily recognizable rhythmical structure for the contemporary audience, a structure that was due particularly to the attention given to the opposition between open and closed syllables (Michael Jeffreys 1981, 315–319; Agosti and Gonnelli 1995, 356; Lauxtermann 1999, 71; Steinrück 2008 for open and closed syllables). The followers of the modern style used Nonnian metrics, even if with differences in certain features.[7] The presence of Nonnian metrical rules can help in determining authorship, as in the case of "Claudian," the author of two Christian epigrams (*AP* 1.19, 20; and of 9.139), to be distinguished from Claudian the panegyrist (Alan Cameron 1970, 11–13).

IV.2 Performance

There would have been no reason to take into account the regulation of intensive accent, if poetry were written only to be read. In Late Antiquity, reading aloud and performing were actually the common ways of enjoying literature. For instance, at Alexandria, in the Kom el-Dikka quarter, archaeological excavations have brought to light a structure with lecture halls, which could have served on occasion as classrooms, halls for public lectures, and places for declamations (Majcherek 2007; for the recent publication of another Egyptian schoolroom of the fourth century with epigrams *dipinti*, see Cribiore, Davoli, and Ratzan 2008). Following a practice that had become common from the Hellenistic age onward, publishing a text meant to read it in a public auditorium or in restricted circles of listeners (Agosti 2006, 46; Cavallo 2006; 2007). It has been recently suggested that, in such a circle at Nazianzus, Gregory recited some of his poems (McLynn 2006, 228–233; compare Demoen 2009, 65–66, and Simelidis 2009, 191, 219–220 on word plays suggesting an oral performance). Also declamations (ἐπιδείξεις) of school exercises could occasionally be performed publicly: for example, John of Gaza says in the iambic prologue of his *Cosmic Description* that he faced competition (ἀγών) in elaborating a subject proposed to him by his masters (δεσπόται), either his professors or the notables of Gaza (Renaut 2005; Gigli Piccardi 2005). There is plenty of evidence of poetic competitions: in the prologue of his Greek *Gigantomachy*, Claudian alludes to his performance in front of an Alexandrian audience (I 1–17 Hall; Livrea 2000; Alan Cameron 1970, 26). The iambic prologues of verse panegyrics allude to the occasion of the performance, employing stock expressions to catch audience approval (Viljamaa 1968, 79–81; Alan Cameron 1970;

2004a, 346–347).[8] Even the anacreontics of the school of Gaza were conceived to be performed in public declamations or in festivals (Ciccolella 2006). Paul the Silentiary's *Description* was performed in front of the emperor, the patriarch, and the court élite, and the poet often appeals to the indulgence of his audience (*S. Soph.* 86, 89, 125–129, 177–185, 350–353). It has been reasonably suggested that Christodorus' *ekphrasis*, too, was publicly performed (Tissoni 2000, 50).

We have no direct information about the performance of Nonnus' poems. One can assume that the *Dionysiaca* were performed partially many times, probably according to the progress of the composition. Their structure favored performances of single *epyllia* (for the concept, see D'Ippolito 1964), as books 15–16 (the story of Hymen and Nicaea) or 38 (the myth of Phaethon), of sections on towns (as 40–41 on Tyre), or even of parts that are characterized by a strong narrative coherence (1–2, the Typhonomachy, or 43–45, the Pentheid); single sections of the *Paraphrase* could have been recited on different occasions. This way of "editing" (i.e., publicly reciting) both poems could also well explain similarities between Nonnus and some of his contemporaries, such as Cyrus of Panopolis (Tissoni 2008, 79–80) or Proclus, who seem to have had some knowledge of the Nonnian style but did not adopt it.

One consequence of orality is the fondness for sound effects and word plays: this Hellenistic feature, which increases in the imperial period, especially with Ps.-Oppian (Whitby 2007b), became an essential stylistic feature of late poetry. Gregory is fond of alliteration, assonances, rhymes, and word games, as are Triphiodorus and Nonnus (Gigli Piccardi 1985; Dubielzig 1996, 14; Whitby 2008, 91–92; Simelidis 2009, 219–220); the *Posthomerica*, Triphiodorus' poem, and the *Dionysiaca* all are full of noise and sounds. In the modern style, alliteration, emphatic repetition, anaphorae, polyptota, etymological variations, and synonyms are all systematically employed (Opelt 1958; Newbold 2003; Miguélez Cavero 2008, 127–130). Nonnus defines writing (and literature) as *γράμματα φωνήεντα*, "speaking letters," and employs metaphors and images like the oxymoron "eloquent silence" (Accorinti 2009, 83–89) or the *σάλπιγξ*, "trumpet," which describes both Homer's poetry in *Dion.* 25.269 and the voice of Scripture in *Par.* 5.155–157 (Gigli Piccardi 2003, 354–357; Rotondo 2008; Agosti 2009a, 110).

IV.3 Audience

Were the élites of the local governments or the imperial courts, both of which facilitated the recitations of epic panegyrics, capable of perceiving each aspect of such refined poetry? Such a question probably makes more sense to us than it would have to the contemporaries of that period. The recitation of these poems constituted an integral part of public life: an encomium for a governor, duke, or general was a definite political act, along with being an important test for the poet's career (Alan Cameron 1965). From the professional poets, people expected a good piece following the style of ancient classics and the *paideia*, the common language of the ruling classes (Brown 1992; on Hellenism and Greek mythology as a mandatory mark of culture, see also Alan Cameron 2004b, Kaldellis 2007a). The recognition of the *topoi* of praise, the quotations and allusions to Homer in the description of a battle, and the appreciation of the autonomy of a poet within literary tradition was certainly within reach of the audience (or, at least, of a part of it).

According to the epigram in *Greek Anthology* 9.198, Nonnus performed his poems in Alexandria (§II.2). Alexandrian reading rooms were frequented by a mixed public, both pagans and Christians, both educated in the antique *paideia*, who attended the lectures of philosophers (as attested in the *Life of Severus* by Zacharias Scholasticus: Cribiore 2007a, 51) and who were passionate about poetry performance, according to Claudian's Greek *Gigantomachy* prologue (§IV.2). Such an audience would have been attracted to Nonnus' syncretistic reading of divine polymorphy (see §IV.4), as well as to his rewriting of John's "philosophical" Gospel—the Gospel that Neoplatonic philosophers had already been interested in for a while (Agosti 2001b, 97–99; 2003, 100–101; Whitby 2007a, 197). As is the case for other Christian poems (see later), the *Paraphrase* assumes a double audience: the Christians who were interested in poetic biblical exegesis and in Nonnus' contribution to Christological debate and the pagans who viewed the biography of θεὸς ἀνήρ read against that of Neoplatonic θεῖοι ἄνδρες (Livrea 2000, 54; Agosti 2009c). It has been correctly noted that "in the multicultural world of fifth-century Alexandria these views were not exclusive" (Whitby 2007a, 207). It is also possible that the *Paraphrase* was recited in a church: a century later, in 544, the verse paraphrase of the *Acts of the Apostles* by Arator was publicly performed in Rome, in the church of San Pietro in Vincoli, and it was so appreciated by Pope Vigilius and the clergy that the performance lasted for more than four days, in front of an enthusiastic public. Ancient sources speak of a great public, composed of "all kinds of people"; this reminds us also of the fact "that the appreciation of literature did not necessarily depend on literacy and recondite learning" (Rapp 2005, 379). A wider public could appreciate the sound and visual effects of Nonnian poetry, even without perceiving refined intertextual relationships.

But Alexandria is certainly an exceptional case. A few decades before Nonnus, Synesius, speaking allegorically of his writings, explicitly presents his severe Doric-style hymns to a high-level and selected audience (*De prov.* 1.18). A century later, Paul the Silentiary's *Description* was performed before a small audience, whereas a *kontakion* was recited for the broader public (Macrides and Magdalino 1988).

An entire section of Gregory of Nazianzus' poems (section 2.2, ed. Caillau) is reserved to poems concerning other people (*carmina quae spectant ad alios*). These poems are directed to members of the community of Nazianzus and deal with social, educational, and ethical issues and were therefore pitched to both specific and wider audiences. This is particularly evident in the case of the poem to Hellenius, which contains a lengthy praise of monasticism (2.1.1), or in that to Olympia, an exhortatory poem to a young wife (Whitby 2008). *Poems* 2.17 is a poem seeking to convert Nemesius, who "should be considered as an actual reader of this . . . pamphlet, but certainly not as the only one: the text was probably directed to a public of open-minded pagan intellectuals" (Demoen 1997, 9–10). Some of Gregory's poems were conceived for didactic and dogmatic purposes, as were the *Carmina Arcana* (Moreschini and Sykes 1997, 58–59). Recently, it has been supposed that Gregory continued to remain active in the local educational system of Nazianzus, within which he imagined his own poetry as playing a didactic role (McLynn 2006). The iambic poem *To Seleucus* by Gregory's cousin Amphilochius of Iconium had expressly didactic purposes. Other poems by Gregory are addressed to the clergy, as is the hexametric *On His Life* (*carm.* 2.1.1, ed. Jungck 1974; Tuilier and Bady 2004).

The Bodmer poems were primarily addressed to members of the community who produced them. The library of this community demonstrates that Greek culture was well established and that imitation of the classical models was appreciated (see the essays collected in Hurst and Rudhardt 2002; Miguélez Cavero 2008, 214ff.). As for Nonnus' *Paraphrase*, these poems envisage a double audience: one immediate and one ideal. These texts came from the area of Panopolis; it is difficult to view their mingling of Christian content and epic form as alien from the surrounding context. The ideal audience for this poetry could have come from a still pagan, educated élite or have been represented by the Christian upper classes (it is the same ambivalence we find in works of art with mythological subjects).

The dialogue with pagans characterizes the experiments in the brief season of Greek biblical epic of the fifth century. In the debate on Christian poetry that animated the Christian intellectuals of the milieu of Constantinople and the empress Eudocia (Alan Cameron 1982; Agosti 2001b, 93–97 and Whitby 2007a), the production of paraphrases and of Homeric centos had the purpose of showing the potential of the Christianized *paideia* (Smolak 1979; Agosti 2009b). The anonymous author of the *Metaphrase of the Psalms* expressly states that his metrical rewriting intended to show to the pagans (*Met. Pss.* prologue 32, *ἵνα γνώωσι καὶ ἄλλοι*, lit. "in order that others might know too") the beauty and the authenticity of the Scriptures (Agosti 2001b, 88–91).[9] The *Homeric Centos* were pitched to a public of intellectual Christians, well versed in the Scriptures but also expert in Homer. Nonetheless, cultivated pagan readers are implicitly addressed, particularly with regard to the relationships between classical culture and Christian doctrine and the allegorical interpretation of the Homeric poems that centonary poetry puts forward (Whitby 2007a, 217; Agosti 2009b, 77–79).

IV.4 Religion

Focusing on the audience's response could be a helpful way to reconsider a problem much discussed, that of the religious confession of certain late poets. It has been a tendency to identify poems' subjects and poets' faith: the authors of mythological and of occasional poems, especially the "wandering poets," have been considered pagans, and the Egyptian poetic renaissance has been connected with the last vestiges of paganism (Alan Cameron 1965). The more difficult question arises with Nonnus. From the fifteenth century onward, the coexistence of an epic poem full of paganism and a Christian poem raised doubts: the easy solution of the poet's conversion from pagan to Christian faith (or even in the other direction!) has often been suggested. Since we do not have an ancient biography of Nonnus, every discussion should start from a literary and linguistic analysis of his poems. The *Dionysiaca* does not show expressions that one could define as "sincerely pagan," whereas the *Paraphrase* has some antipagan allusions (already listed by Kuiper 1918; Golega 1930; compare Agosti 2003, 89–94; Caprara 2005, 17–28, 40–44). But the poet's habit of employing the same syntagmas and expressions in both the poems complicates the problem. Not only do we find epithets of Dionysus transferred to Christ and vice versa, but also Nonnus often depicts "parallel" scenes with the same language: for instance, the miracle of water transformed into wine in *Par.* 2 and the Dionysiac miracle of a lake changed into wine in *Dion.* 14, or the miraculous healing of a blind Indian in *Dion.* 25.281–291, which appears to be a linguistic "summary" of the healing of the blind man at Siloam in *Par.* 9, and so on. Already in the 1980s, scholars engaged the task of cross-analyzing the Nonnian poems, revealing in the *Dionysiaca* influences not only of the *Paraphrase* but also of biblical texts (for example, Gigli Piccardi 1984; Livrea 1989). The obvious conclusion was that the poet had always been a Christian, one who knew both Scripture and the exegetical literature (Livrea 2000, 74–92; and all the commentaries on the *Paraphrase*, see Ancient Sources). After Vian's (1997) demonstration that the poems were composed simultaneously—perhaps with the *Paraphrase* begun first—and once archaeology and art history showed that Dionysiac imagery was perfectly integrated in Christian Egypt (Bowersock 1990; Willers 1992), there has been little room for doubts about Nonnus' Christianity (and the same goes for most of the authors of mythological and classicizing poems, now considered Christians: see Alan Cameron 2007, 33–44). Recent historiography tends to look at relationships between pagan and Christian cultures in terms of dialogue and coexistence rather than of conflict (Athanassiadi 2006; Salzman 2008), and it has been demonstrated that Christians did not consider mythology and classical *paideia* as foreign or dangerous (with the exception of some rigoristic statements). As a consequence, the *Dionysiaca* may be read not as a religious poem (Dionysus is not represented as a Savior) but as a learned and secular literary work (Liebeschuetz 2003, 231–239). Analyses of Nonnus' poems tend now to bring to light Christian aspects and thoughts in both of them (for a good example, see Spanoudakis 2007, on Icarius' episode in *Dion.* 47; Frangoulis 2008; Caprara 2008; Greco 2008; Shorrock 2011). Nonnus emphasizes some affinities between Dionysiac religion and Christianity but always from a Christian perspective: in the *Paraphrase*, he draws a parallel between Christ and Hermes (Accorinti 1995); in the prologue of the *Dionysiaca*, he eloquently describes Dionysus' birth in terms of Christian baptism (Gigli Piccardi 2003, 50–51; compare Shorrock 2008, 107); and his aim has been persuasively described as a syncretistic reading of divine polymorphy (Gigli Piccardi 2003, 74–83).

There were also sincerely pagan poets, of course, such as Palladas or Pamprepius (§II.2); the Orphic *Lithica* and the poem on astrology by Maximus come probably from the Neoplatonic milieu close to Emperor Julian; the Orphic *Argonautica* show not only some interest in theurgical rites but also an attention to the Argonauts' ancient relics, an attention that may be evidence of anti-Christian polemic (Agosti 2008d). The hagiographical poetry of Neoplatonic schools, such as the poem by Marinus, as well as Christodorus' poem on Proclus and his auditors, can be read as a reaction against the similar Christian poetry; some passages in Nonnus' *Paraphrase* reveal his polemic against Neoplatonism (Agosti 2003, 102–104, 138–139; 2009c).[10]

V. Reception

In the fifth and sixth centuries, some inscriptional epigrams show quotations, or echoes, of Nonnus' *Dionysiaca* or, at least, of the style represented in his poems. Quite exceptional is the case of an epigraphical epigram from Apameia on the Orontes (ed. Feissel 1998), whose author(s) clearly knew both Nonnus' poems and, more unexpectedly, the *Metaphrase of the Psalms*, Eudocia's *St. Cyprian*, and Gregory Nazianzen's poetry (Agosti 2005c, 14–18; Simelidis 2009, 61–63). Later, in the cultural context of the so-called Macedonian Renaissance of the tenth century, the funerary epigram for Michael, synkellos of the Patriarch Nicholas Mysticus, was composed in the Nonnian style, which presupposes an acquaintance with Nonnus' poetry among the cultivated readers of Hagia Sophia (Ševčenko 1987).

A comprehensive history of the fortune of late antique Greek poetry in Byzantium and in modern times is lacking. The authors who had a real *Fortleben* were mainly Nonnus, Gregory, and Musaeus, who became a best seller in the Western Renaissance. For Nonnus, the spare account by Keydell (1959, 9–10*) has been partially supplemented by recent studies. The first Byzantine classic, George of Pisidia, panegyrist of Emperor Heraclius (610–641), was still able to compose ninety impeccable Nonnian hexameters in his poem *On Human Life*, imitating Nonnus and Paul the Silentiary, and his epic panegyrics (in dodecasyllables) in honor of Heraclius are full of Nonnian words and expressions (Gonnelli 2003, 11–13). Afterward, in the ninth century, Photius considered Eudocia's paraphrases of the Old Testament so effective as to substitute for the reading of the originals (*Bibl.* codd. 183–184, ed. Henry); in the same period, Cometas composed a long epigram on Lazarus' resurrection, *AP* 15.40, showing a knowledge of the *Paraphrase* (Tissoni 2003). Poets such as John Geometres (De Stefani 2002, 29–30; van Opstall 2008, 44–46) and Theodore Prodromus (Magnelli 2003, 181–182) were clearly acquainted with the poetry of Nonnus and Gregory of Nazianzus. Eustathius (twelfth century) quotes some of Nonnus' verses, without giving the author's name, in his commentaries on Homer. Still waiting to be studied systematically is the possible influence of Nonnus' poems (especially the *Dionysiaca*) on figurative art.[11] Late antique epigrams also clearly exercised some influence on Byzantine epigrammatic poetry (Lauxtermann 2003, 19–270; Tissoni 2003; for *AP* 9.363, see De Stefani 2008b).

In accordance with his great reputation, Gregory of Nazianzus' poems were well known in Byzantium and greatly influenced Byzantine poetry. It is, therefore, not so surprising that they were taught in classrooms: the prose paraphrases, the commentaries, and the lexica (in certain manuscripts) do not leave many doubts about the didactic use of Gregory's poems (Simelidis 2009, 57–88).

Nonnus' *Dionysiaca* and Triphiodorus' poem emerged again in the thirteenth century in the collection of epic and didactic poets assembled by Maximus Planudes (*Laur.* 32.16), where the *Dionysiaca* is anonymous. Also, in the oldest manuscript that contains poems of Gregory and Eudocia's *St. Cyprian* (*Laur.* 7.10; tenth century), the *Paraphrase* is anonymous: Maximus Planudes likewise hesitated in the attribution (in the colophon of *Marcianus gr.* Z 481), notwithstanding that the poem is attributed to Nonnus in the index of *Palatinus Heidelbergensis* 23 (see Livrea 1989, 73–74; Alan Cameron 1993, 101). Other poets, such as Colluthus and Quintus (and Triphiodorus, too), were part of a branch of the manuscript transmission in southern Italy (Cavallo 2002, 136–137). The rich manuscript tradition of the Orphic *Argonautica* is due to the fact that they joined the hymnic collection (Vian 1987, 47–51). On the other hand, the Orphic *Lithica*'s manuscripts were quite few; John Tzetzes in the twelfth century was the first to know this poem well (Schamp 1985, 67–71).

From the Renaissance onward, Musaeus was the most appreciated among late antique poets, and translations, paraphrases, and rewritings of his work appeared in France, Spain, Italy, Germany, and England (Kost 1971, 69–85; Gelzer 1975, 323–326; Braden 1978, 55–153). Nonnus had a considerable afterlife, too, though not comparable to Musaeus. The first to have an extensive knowledge of him was Politian, who was also able to identify Nonnus as the author of the *Dionysiaca*, anonymous in the codex *Laur.* 32.16, as noted earlier (Pontani 1983). The *editio princeps* of the *Dionysiaca* came out much later, only in 1569 by G. Falkenburg. Nonnus' major poem began to have a slow but constant circulation, while the *Paraphrase* received a *damnatio memoriae* under the severe condemnation by Daniel Heinsius, who had accused Nonnus of heresy in his book *Aristarchus sacer* (1627: see Livrea 1989, 45). In the sixteenth and seventeenth centuries, Nonnus began to be a well-known author, especially in France and Italy. In France, thanks to the translation of the *Dionysiaca* by Claude Boitet de Frauville (1570–1625), who also translated Homer and Quintus of Smyrna, Nonnus offered many topics to the figurative arts: for example, Nicholas Poussin drew inspiration from him (Bull 1998). But the greatest admirer of Nonnus in France came two centuries later in the Comte de Marcellus (Accorinti 2009, 70–72), whose editions and translations (1856; 1861) are still useful. In Italy, the *Dionysiaca*, together with Claudian's poetry, was explicitly highlighted by Giovanni Battista (Giambattista) Marino (1569–1625) as a model for his new baroque epic. Marino, especially in his poem the *Adone* (1623), imitated Nonnus' styles, metaphors, and figures of sound and created a new style, founded on the aesthetic principles of digression and description (Agosti 1995, 148–150; Tissoni 1998, 56–61; Gonnelli 2003, 26–31).

After some isolated admirers in the eighteenth century, it was in the nineteenth century that interest for late antique poetry was revived from a scholarly and literary point of view (Lind 1978; Gonnelli 2003, 31–37). Thomas Love Peacock, for example, considered the *Dionysiaca* "the finest poem in the world after the *Iliad*" (see Hernández de la Fuente 2007b); Richard Garnett (1835–1906) wrote a short novel, *The Poet of Panopolis* (1888), trying to imagine a solution to the double confession of the poet. Appreciation of late antique writers among the intellectuals of the Decadent movement did not gain much traction in the twentieth century. The great Greek poet Konstantinos Kavafis in his poem *Exuls* (1914) extolled the language and the harmony of Nonnus' verses and was also "an admiring reader" of Gregory of Nazianzus (Gonnelli 2003, 40; Simelidis 2009, 8). Even a lesser-known poem such as the *Homerocentones* has had exceptional modern readers: one scholar suggests it as a model for James Joyce's *Finnegans Wake* (Faj 1968). Finally, the Italian novelist and essayist Roberto Calasso recently drew inspiration from Nonnus' *Dionysiaca* for his novel on Greek mythology and religion, *The Marriage of Cadmus and Harmony* (1988).

NOTES

* For their philological contributions, the innumerable works on metrical and textual problems by German scholars of the nineteenth century and the first half of the twentieth century are still irreplaceable. Every study of later Greek poets should start from the articles and books by scholars such as Arthur Ludwich, Hermann Koechly, Heinrich Tiedke, Augustinus Scheindler, Joseph Golega (for Christian poetry), and especially Rudolf Keydell. A special mention should be given to the great Gottfried Hermann, who, in his *Orphica* (1805), opened the way to the scientific study of late epic.

† The metrical and stylistical analyses by Wifstrand (1933) changed the way of looking at late epic and epigrammatic poetry (some of his conclusions are expanded by Whitby 1994). The collections of essays of Keydell (1981), Alan Cameron (1982), Livrea (1991, 1995), and Vian (2005) are a treasure trove of erudition, philological investigation, and literary observations. The studies by Averil Cameron (1991), Alan Cameron (especially 1970 and 1973), Bowersock (1990), and Chuvin (1991 and 2009) examine

poetry against its social and cultural background: in this field a real masterpiece is Robert 1948, and now the collection of Feissel 2006. Even though not directly concerned with poetry, the books by Peter Brown are essential for a proper understandig of late antique education and culture: see, for example, Brown 1992.

1. Among the particularly important didactic poets of the first two centuries are Dionysius Periegetes (author of a *Periegesis of the World*, under Hadrian), Oppian of Cilicia (author of the *Halieutica*, dedicated to Marcus Aurelius and Commodus), and the so-called Oppian of Apamea (author of the *Cynegetica*, dedicated to Caracalla). For Dionysius and Oppian of Cilicia, see, respectively, Lightfoot 2008 and Kneebone 2008; for Oppian of Apamea, see Whitby 2007b (all with further bibliography). Mythological poetry in the early imperial age is represented by the interesting but scanty fragments of Dionysius, author of *Bassarica* and *Gigantias* (ed. Livrea 1973; for the longest fragment of *Bassarica*, see Agosti 2001d). On Nestor of Laranda, father of Peisander, see now Ma 2007.

2. On this collection, dating from the end of Hellenistic age to the third century (the Christian books), see now Lightfoot 2007, 3–212.

3. Among the other *auctores* of late poets, one should mention at least Hesiod—viewed as a model of didactic poetry, as well as visionary poetry (compare the ethopoea in *P.Oxy*. 3537r)—Pindar, and Aristophanes (Viljamaa 1968; Agosti 2001a). Hellenistic poets were also widely read and imitated: Apollonius of Rhodes (Vian 2001), Euphorion (Magnelli 2002, 115–122), Theocritus (Harries 2006), and especially Callimachus, who was the model for Nonnus' hexameter reform. From Nonnus' imitations and allusions alone, it is possible to uncover new Callimachean fragments (Hollis 1994); the same goes for Gregory of Nazianzus (Hollis 2002, 43–49).

4. Some scholastic papyri show prosodical signs on *dichrona* vowels (ex. TLond. Inv. GR 1906.10–20.2). But cultivated people also had their difficulties: Damascius in his *Life of Isidorus* (fr. 48a, ed. Athanassiadi) records that his master, though well versed in poetry (cf. fr. 106 Ath. on his expertise in poems), did not pay much attention to formal features, asking his pupil to correct metrical defects: *ὕμνους ὅσους ἔγραψεν . . . τοῖς δὲ ἔπεσιν οὐ πάνυ συνηρμοσμένους, ἀλλὰ τούτων ὅσον ἄμετρον ἀπέβαινε καὶ ἄλλως οὐ κατὰ τῶν πρεπώδη ῥυθμὸν ἐμοὶ ἐπανορθοῦσθαι ἐπέτρεπε* ("all the hymns that he wrote . . . (are) not properly arranged to the epic style, but he gave me to amend whatever went against meter and did not follow correct rhythm").

5. Main features: dactylic words are predominant, only nine patterns of hexameter are admitted (32 in Homer, 20 in Callimachus), and the holodactylic represents an average of 38.07 percent, spondaic hexameters are forbidden, two consecutive spondees are quite rare, the main caesura is always present (81 percent is trochaic); there is a series of strict regulations on the placing of word end (see Keydell 1959, 35*–42*; Maas 1979, 83–89; Vian 1976, L–LV; West 1982, 177–180; Agosti 2004, 37–41; Magnelli 2008a).

6. In the second century C.E., Babrius ends his choliambs with a paroxytone. For a brief discussion, see West 1982, 162; Agosti and Gonnelli 1995, 329, n. 151 (with further bibliography). In the hemiambs of Gregory of Nazianzus, the tendency appears to avoid proparoxytone endings, as well as in Synesius' hymns. The Ionic a minore dimeters and trimeters of the Anacreontics of John of Gaza and the so-called George the Grammarian (fifth to sixth century C.E.) tend to close with a paroxytone syllable and avoid strictly proparoxytone endings (West 1982, 167–172; Lauxtermann 1999, 77; Ciccolella 2000, xxvi); recently, it has been plausibly argued that these authors were influenced by the rhythm of Nonnian hexameters (Ciccolella 2009).

Iambic meter also tends gradually to prefer paroxytone endings, as well as to limit the number of resolved feet to one per verse (West 1982, 184–185; Alan Cameron 2004a, 337–338); this is the road to the Byzantine dodecasyllable, which is already evident in George of Pisidia's poems. For the parallel development of accentual poetry of the fifth and sixth centuries up to Romanos, who is likely drawing on the Syriac memra form, see Maas 1910; Brock 1985; Lauxtermann 1999, 79, with further bibliography.

7. Further bibliography in Agosti and Gonnelli 1995; Whitby 2006. All the recent editions and commentaries on single poets usually have a detailed chapter on metrics (see Ancient Sources). For the other meters used in late poetry, see West 1982, 162–185; Lauxtermann 1999.

8. As a consequence, the traditional metaphor of the *ἀγών* with the literary tradition is particularly frequent: for example, Triphiodorus 666–667 (the poem as a race horse); Nonnus, *Dionysiaca* 25.27 (the competition with ancient and modern poets, *νέοισι καὶ ἀρχεγόνοισι ἐρίζων*). Agathias presents his cycle as a "wise contest" (*σοφὸν στήσαντ' ἀγῶνα, AP* 4.4.55) between ancient and contemporary epigrammatistis.

9. Compare Athanasius, *Life of Anthony* 94.2, where he recommends reading the work to the pagans: *ἐὰν δὲ χρεία γένηται, καὶ τοῖς ἐθνικοῖς ἀνάγνωτε*, "if it is of use, read it to the pagans."

10. In religious polemic, the metrical oracles on the "true God and Savior" played an important role: from the fourth to sixth century, Apollinian oracles were adapted by Christians to show that even pagan gods had predicted the embodiment of Christ in human flesh (Busine 2005). The more complete collection of Christianized verse oracles is the so-called *Tübingen Theosophy*, a Byzantine *résumé* of a treatise *On the Right Belief* composed probably in Alexandria around the beginning of the sixth century (see Erbse 1995; Beatrice 2001).

11. An exception is the famous ivory casket from the Cathedral of Veroli, now at the Victoria and Albert Museum, with figural carvings displaying mythological scenes. Nonnus' poem has been proposed as a source for some of them (Simon 1964, but see recently Eastmond 2008).

WORKS CITED

Ancient Sources

AMPHILOCHIUS OF ICONIUM

Oberg, Eberhard. 1969. *Iambi ad Seleucum*. Berlin: De Gruyter (Greek text).

COLLUTHUS

Livrea, Enrico. 1968. *Colluto: Il ratto di Elena*. Bologna: Patron (Greek text, Italian translation and commentary).

Mair, Alexander W. 1928. *Oppian, Colluthus, Tryphiodorus*. London: Heinemann (Greek text with English translation).

Schönberger, Otto. 1993. *Kolluthus: Raub der Helena*. Würzburg: Königshausen und Neumann (Greek text and German translation).

CHRISTODORUS

Tissoni, Francesco. 2000. *Cristodoro: Un'introduzione e un commento.* Alessandria: Edizioni dell'Orso (Greek text and commentary).

DIOSCORUS OF APHRODITO

Fournet, Jean-Luc. 1999. *Hellénisme dans l'Égypte du VIe siècle: La bibliothèque et l'œuvre de Dioscore d'Aphrodité.* Cairo Institut Français d'Archeologie Orientale (Greek text, French translation and commentary).

EUDOCIA

a. Saint Cyprian

Ludwich, Arthur. 1897. *Eudociae Augustae Procli Lyci Claudiani Carminum graecorum reliquiae.* Leipzig: Teubner (Greek text).

b. Homeric centos

Rey, André-Louis. 1998. *Patricius, Eudocie, Côme de Jérusalem: Centons Homériques.* Paris: Du Cerf (Greek text with French translation).

Schembra, Rocco. 2006. *La prima redazione dei centoni omerici: Traduzione e commento.* Alessandria: Edizioni dell'Orso (Italian translation and commentary).

———. 2007a. *Homerocentones.* Turnhout: Brepols (Greek text).

———. 2007b. *La seconda redazione dei centoni omerici: Traduzione e commento.* Alessandria: Edizioni dell'Orso (Italian translation and commentary).

Usher, Mark D. 1999. *Homerocentones Eudociae Augustae.* Stuttgart: Teubner (Greek text).

GEORGE OF PISIDIA

Gonnelli, Fabrizio. 1991. "Il *De vita humana* di Giorgio Pisida." *Bollettino dei Classici* 12: 118–138 (Greek text, Italian translation and commentary).

GREEK ANTHOLOGY

Beckby, Hermann. 1965. *Anthologia Graeca: Griechisch-Deutsch*, 2nd ed. Munich: Heimeran.

Paton, W. R. 1916. *The Greek Anthology.* 5 vols. Cambridge, MA: Heinemann.

GREGORY OF NAZIANZUS

Caillau, A. B. 1840. *Carmina* reprinted in *Patrologia Graeca*, vols. 37 and 38 (Greek text and Latin translation).

Bacci, Lucia. 1996. *Gregorio Nazianzeno: Ad Olimpiade [carm. II.2.6].* Pisa: ETS (Greek text, Italian translation and commentary).

Beckmann, U. 1988. *Gregor von Nazianz: Gegen die Habsucht (Carmen 1, 2, 18).* Paderborn: F. Schöningh (Greek text and commentary).

Crimi, Carmelo, and Manfred Kertsch. 1995. *Gregorio Nazianzeno: Sulla virtù. Carme giambico [I, 2, 10].* Introduzione, testo critico e traduzione di Carmelo Crimi.

Commento di Manfred Kertsch. Appendici a cura di Carmelo Crimi e José Guirau. Pisa: ETS (Greek text, Italian translation and commentary).

Domiter, K. 1999. *Gregor von Nazianz: De humana natura (c. 1, 2, 14)*. Frankfurt am Main: Lang (Greek text, German translation and commentary).

Jungck, C. 1974. *Gregor von Nazianz: De vita sua*. Heidelberg: Winter (Greek text, German translation and commentary).

Knecht, Andreas. 1972. *Gregor von Nazianz: Gegen die Putzsucht der Frauen*. Heidelberg: Winter (Greek text, German translation and commentary).

Meier, Bruno. 1996. *Gregor von Nazianz: Über die Bischöfe (Carmen 2, 1, 12)*. Paderborn: F. Schöningh (Greek text, German translation and commentary).

Moreschini, Claudio, and D. A. Sykes. 1997. *St. Gregory of Nazianzus: Poemata arcana*. Oxford: Oxford University Press (Greek text, English translation and commentary).

Moroni, Maria Grazia. 2006. *Gregorio Nazianzeno: Nicobulo jr. al padre [carm. II,2,4], Nicobulo sen. Al figlio [carm. II,2,5]. Una discussione in famiglia*. Pisa: ETS (Greek text, Italian translation and commentary).

Oberhaus, M. 1991. *Gregor von Nazianz: Gegen den Zorn (Carmen 1, 2, 25)*. Paderborn: F. Schöningh (Greek text, German translation and commentary).

Palla, Roberto, and Manfred Kertsch. 1985. *Gregor von Nazianz: Carmina de virtute Ia/Ib*. Graz: Universität Graz (Greek text, German translation and commentary).

Simelidis, Christos. 2009. *Selected Poems of Gregory of Nazianzus: I.2.17; II.1.10, 19, 32: A Critical Edition with Introduction and Commentary*. Göttingen: Vandenhoeck & Ruprecht (Greek text and commentary).

Sundermann, Karl. 1991. *Gregor von Nazianz: Der Rangstreit zwischen Ehe und Jungfräulichkeit (Carmen 1, 2, 1, 215–732)*. Paderborn: F. Schoningh (Greek text, German translation and commentary).

Tuilier, André, and G. Bady. 2004. *Saint Grégoire de Nazianze: Œuvres poétiques. Tome I, 1re partie. Poèmes personnels: II, 1, 1–11*. Traduit et annoté par Jean Bernardi. Paris: Les Belles Lettres (Greek text, French translation and commentary).

Werhahn, Heinrich M. 1953. *Gregorii Nazianzeni σύγκρισις βίων*. Wiesbaden: Harrassowitz (Greek text and commentary).

White, Carolinne. 1996. *Gregory of Nazianzus: Autobiographical Poems*. Cambridge: Cambridge University Press (Greek text and English translation).

Zehles, F. E., and M. J. Zamora. 1996. *Gregor von Nazianz: "Mahnungen an die Jungfrauen" (Carmen 1, 2, 2)*. Paderborn: F. Schöningh (Greek text, German translation and commentary).

JOHN OF GAZA

a. Ecphrasis

Friedländer, Paul. 1912. *Johannes von Gaza und Paulus Silentiarius*. Leipzig: Teubner. (New forthcoming editions by Daria Gigli Piccardi [Alessandria: Edizioni dell'Orso] and by Delphine Renaut [Paris: Les Belles Lettres]).

b. Anacreontics

Ciccolella, Federica. 2000. *Cinque poeti bizantini*. Alessandria: Edizioni dell'Orso (Greek text, Italian translation and commentary).

MACEDONIUS

Madden, John. 1995. *Macedonius Consul: The Epigrams*. Hildesheim: Olms (Greek text, English translation and commentary).

MAXIMUS

Ludwich, Arthur. 1877. *Maximi et Ammonii carminum de actionum auspiciis reliquiae*. Leipzig: Teubner (Greek text).

MUSAEUS

Gelzer, Thomas, ed. 1975. "Musaeus: *Hero and Leander*." In *Callimachus: Aetia, Iambi, Hecale, and Other Fragments*. Text, translation, and notes by Constantinos A. Trypanis; Musaeus: Hero et Leander. Introduction, text, and notes by Thomas Gelzer; translation by Cedric Whitman, 289–389. Cambridge, MA: Harvard University Press; London: Heinemann (Greek text, English translation).

Hopkinson 1994b, 42–52 and 136–185 (Greek text and notes).

Kost, Karlheinz. 1971. *Mousaios: Hero und Leander*. Bonn: Bouvier (Greek text, German translation and commentary).

Livrea, Enrico, and Paolo Eleuteri. 1982. *Musaeus: Hero et Leander*. Leipzig: Teubner (Greek text).

NONNUS OF PANOPOLIS

a. Dionysiaca

Gigli Piccardi, Daria, Fabrizio Gonnelli, Gianfranco Agosti, and Domenico Accorinti. 2003–2004. *Nonno di Panopoli: Le Dionisiache*, 4 vols. (Greek text, Italian translation and commentary). Milan: Rizzoli.

Keydell, Rudolf. 1959. *Nonni Panopolitani Dionysiaca*. Berlin: Weidmann (Greek text).

Rouse, W. H. D. 1940. *Nonnos: Dionysiaca*. Mythological introduction and notes by Herbert J. Rose and notes on text criticism (1984) by L. Roger Lind, 3 vols. Cambridge, MA: Heinemann (Greek text and English translation).

Vian, Francis, et al. 1976–2006. *Nonnos de Panopolis: Les Dionysiaques*, 19 vols. Paris: Les Belles Lettres (Greek text, French translation and commentary).

b. Paraphrase of St. John's Gospel

Accorinti, Domenico. 1996. *Nonno di Panopoli: Parafrasi del Vangelo di San Giovanni, Canto XX*. Pisa: Scuola Normale Superiore (Greek text, Italian translation and commentary).

Agosti, Gianfranco. 2003. *Nonno di Panopoli: Parafrasi del Vangelo di San Giovanni, Canto V*. Florence: Università degli Studi di Firenze (Greek text, Italian translation and commentary).

Caprara, Mariangela. 2005. *Nonno di Panopoli: Parafrasi del Vangelo di San Giovanni, Canto IV*. Pisa: Scuola Normale Superiore (Greek text, Italian translation and commentary).

De Stefani, Claudio. 2002. *Nonno di Panopoli: Parafrasi del Vangelo di San Giovanni, Canto I*. Bologna: Patron (Greek text, Italian translation and commentary).

Greco, Claudia. 2005. *Nonno di Panopoli: Parafrasi del Vangelo di San Giovanni, Canto XIII*. Alessandria: Edizioni dell'Orso (Greek text, Italian translation and commentary).

Livrea, Enrico. 1989. *Nonno di Panopoli: Parafrasi del Vangelo di San Giovanni, Canto XVIII*. Naples: D'Auria (Greek text, Italian translation and commentary).

———. 2000. *Nonno di Panopoli: Parafrasi del Vangelo di San Giovanni, Canto B*. Bologna: Dehoniane (Greek text, Italian translation and commentary).

Prost, Mark A. 2003. *Nonnos: The Paraphrase of the Gospel of John*. Ventura: Writing Shop Press (English translation).

Scheindler, Augustinus. 1873. *Nonni Panopolitani Paraphrasis S. Evangelii Joannei accedit S. Evangelii textus et index verborum*. Leipzig: Teubner (Greek text).

ORPHIC ARGONAUTICA

Vian, Francis. 1987. *Les Argonautes Orphiques*. Paris: Les Belles Lettres (Greek text, French translation and commentary).

ORPHIC LITHICA

Giannakis, Georgios. 1982. *ΟΡΦΕΩΣ ΛΙΘΙΚΑ*. Ioannina: Ioannina University (Greek text and commentary).

Schamp, Jacques. 1985. *Les Lapidaires grecs*. Texte établi et traduit par Robert Halleux and Jacques Schamp. Paris: Les Belles Lettres (Greek text, French translation and commentary).

PAMPREPIUS OF PANOPOLIS

Livrea, Enrico. 1979. *Pamprepii Panopolitani Carmina (P. Gr. Vindob. 29788 A–C)*. Leipzig: Teubner (Greek text and commentary).

PAPYRI BODMER 29–37

Hurst, André, Olivier Reverdin, and Jean Rudhardt. 1984. *Papyrus Bodmer XXIX: Vision de Dorothéos*. Cologny: Fondation Bodmer (Greek text, French translation and commentary).

Hurst, André, and Jean Rudhardt. 1999. *Papyri Bodmer XXX–XXXVII: "Codex des Visions," Poèmes divers*. Munich: Saur (Greek text, French translation and commentary).

Kessels, A. H. M., and Peter W. Van der Horst. 1987. "The Vision of Dorotheus (Pap. Bodmer 29)." *Vigiliae Christianae* 41: 313–359 (Greek text and English translation).

Livrea, Enrico. 2006–2008. "Dorothei carmen *Ad Justos (= P. Bodmer XXXI)*." *Analecta Papyrologica* 18–20: 27–43.

PAPYRUS FRAGMENTS

Heitsch, Ernst. 1963–1964. *Die griechischen Dichterfragmente der römischen Kaiserzeit*. 2 vols. Göttingen: Vandenhoeck & Ruprecht (Greek text).

Page, Denys L. 1942. *Select Papyri III, Literary Papyri: Poetry*. Cambridge, MA: Heinemann (Greek text and English translation).

PAUL THE SILENTIARY

a. Ekphrasis

De Stefani, Claudio. 2010. *Paulus Silentiarius: Descriptio Sanctae Sophiae; Descriptio Ambonis.* Berlin: De Gruyter (Greek text).

Friedländer, Paul. 1912. *Johannes von Gaza und Paulus Silentiarius.* Leipzig: Teubner (Greek text and commentary).

Fayant, Marie-Christine, and Pierre Chuvin. 1997. *Paul le Silentiaire: Description de Sainte-Sophie de Constantinople.* Die: A Die (Greek text with French translation).

b. Epigrams

Viansino, Giovanni. 1963. *Paolo Silenziario: Epigrammi.* Turin: Loescher (Greek text, Italian translation and commentary).

PROCLUS

Van den Berg, Robert M. 2001. *Proclus' Hymns.* Leiden: Brill (Greek text, English translation and commentary).

Vogt, Ernst. 1957. *Procli Hymni.* Wiesbaden: Harrassowitz. (Greek text and commentary).

PSEUDO-APOLLINARIS, METAPHRASE OF THE PSALMS

Gonnelli, Fabrizio. 1987. "Il Salterio esametrico: I–II," *Koinonia* 13: 51–60, 127–151 (Greek text and commentary of *Ps.* 21).

Ludwich, Arthur. 1912. *Apolinarii Metaphrasis Psalmorum.* Leipzig: Teubner (Greek text).

QUINTUS OF SMYRNA

Bär, Silvio. 2009. *Quintus Smyrnaeus, Posthomerica 1: Die Wiedergeburt des Epos aus dem Geiste der Amazonomachie. Mit einem Kommentar zu den Versen 1–219.* Göttingen: Vandenhoeck & Ruprecht (commentary).

Campbell, Malcolm. 1981. *A Commentary on Quintus Smyrnaeus, Posthomerica XII.* Leiden: Brill (commentary).

James, Alan. 2005. *Quintus of Smyrna: The Trojan Epic; Posthomerica.* Baltimore: Johns Hopkins University Press (English translation).

James, Alan, and Kevin Lee. 2000. *A Commentary on Quintus of Smyrna: Posthomerica V.* Leiden: Brill.

Pompella, Giuseppe. 2002. *Quinti Smyrnaei Posthomerica.* Hildesheim: Olms (Greek text).

Vian, Francis. 1963–1969. *Quintus de Smyrne, La suite d'Homère.* 3 vols. Paris: Les Belles Lettres (Greek text, French translation and commentary).

SYNESIUS

Gruber, Joachim, and Hans Strohm. 1991. *Synesios von Kyrene: Hymnen.* Heidelberg: Carl Winter (Greek text, German translation, and commentary).

Lacombrade, Christian. 1978. *Synésios de Cyrène: Hymnes*. Paris: Les Belles Lettres (Greek text, French translation and commentary).
Terzaghi, Nicola. 1949. *Synesii Cyrenensis Hymni*. Rome: Typis Publicae Officinae Polygraphicae (Greek Text and commentary in Latin).

TRIPHIODORUS

Dubielzig, Uwe. 1996. *Thriphiodor: Die Einnahme Ilions*. Tübingen: Gunter Narr Verlag (Greek text, German translation and commentary).
Gerlaud, Bernard. 1982. *Triphiodore: La Prise d'Ilion*. Paris: Les Belles Lettres (Greek text, French translation and commentary).
Livrea, Enrico. 1982. *Triphiodori Ilii excidium*. Leipzig: Teubner (Greek text).
Mair, Alexander W. 1928. *Oppian, Colluthus, Tryphiodorus*. London: Heinemann (Greek text with English translation). [New forthcoming edition by Laura Miguélez Cavero]

Modern Sources

Accorinti, Domenico. 1995. "Hermes e Cristo in Nonno," *Prometheus* 21: 24–32.
———. 2004. *Nonno di Panopoli: Le Dionisiache, Canti XL–XLVIII*. Milan: Biblioteca Universale Rizzoli.
———. 2009. "Poésie et poétique dans l'œuvre de Nonnos de Panopolis." In *Actes du colloque Doux remède: Poésie et poétique à Byzance (EHESS 24–26 février 2006)*, ed. Paolo Odorico, Panagiotis Agapitos, and Martin Hinterberger, 67–98. Paris: De Boccard.
Accorinti, Domenico, and Pierre Chuvin, eds. 2003. *Des Géants à Dionysos: Mélanges de mythologie et de poésie grecques offerts à Francis Vian*. Alessandria: Edizioni dell'Orso.
Agosti, Gianfranco. 1995. "Poemi digressivi tardoantichi (e moderni)," *Compara(i)son* 1: 131–151.
———. 1997. "The ποικιλία of Paul the Bishop," *Zeitschrift für Papyrologie und Epigraphik* 116: 31–38.
———. 1998. "L'alba notturna (ἔννυχος ἠώς)," *Zeitschrift für Papyrologie und Epigraphik* 121: 53–58.
———. 2001a. "Late Antique Iambics and *iambikè idéa*." In *Iambic Ideas: Essays on a Poetic Tradition from Archaic Greece to the Late Roman Empire*, ed. Antonio Aloni, Alessandro Barchiesi, and Alberto Cavarzere, 217–254. Lanham, MD: Routledge.
———. 2001b. "L'epica biblica nella tarda antichità greca: Autori e lettori nel IV e V secolo." In *La scrittura infinita: Bibbia e poesia in età medioevale e umanistica*, ed. Francesco Stella, 67–104. Florence: SISMEL.
———. 2001c. "Considerazioni preliminari sui generi letterari dei poemi del Codice Bodmer," *Aegyptus* 81: 115–147.
———. 2001d. "Crudeltà dionisiache dall'alto impero," *Analecta Papyrologica* 13: 115–147.
———. 2002a. "I poemetti del codice Bodmer e il loro ruolo nella storia della poesia tardoantica." In *Le Codex des Visions: Recherches et Rencontres*, ed. André Hurst and Jean Rudhardt, 73–114. Geneva: Droz.
———. 2002b. "*POxy* 4352, fr. 5.II.18–39 (Encomio a Diocleziano) e Menandro Retore," *Zeitschrift für Papyrologie und Epigraphik* 140: 51–58.

———. 2004. *Nonno di Panopoli: Le Dionisiache, Canti XXV–XXIX.* Milan: Biblioteca Universale Rizzoli.

———. 2004–2005. "Immagini e poesia nella tarda antichità: Per uno studio dell'estetica visuale della poesia greca fra III e VI sec. d.C." In *Incontri Triestini di Filologia Classica* 4, ed. Lucio Cristante, 351–374. Trieste: Edizioni Università di Trieste.

———. 2005a. "L'etopea nella poesia greca tardoantica." In *ΗΘΟΠΟΙΙΑ: La représentation des caractères entre fiction scolaire et réalité vivante à l'époque imperiale et tardive*, ed. Eugenio Amato and Jacques Schamp, 34–60. Salerno: Helios.

———. 2005b. "Interpretazione omerica e creazione poetica nella tarda antichità." In *Κορυφαίῳ Ἀνδρί: Mélanges offerts à André Hurst*, ed. Antje Kolde, Alessandra Lukinovich, and André-Louis Rey, 19–32. Geneva: Droz.

———. 2005c. "Miscellanea epigrafica I: Note letterarie a carmi epigrafici tardoantichi," *Medioevo Greco* 5: 1–30.

———. 2006. "La voce dei libri: Dimensioni performative dell'epica greca tardoantica." In *Approches de la Troisième Sophistique: Hommages à J. Schamp*, ed. Eugenio Amato, Alexandre Roduit, and Martin Steinrück, 33–60. Brussels: Latomus.

———. 2008a. "L'epigramma lungo nei testi letterari ed epigrafici fra IV e VII sec. d.C." In *Epigramma longum: Da Marziale alla tarda antichità; From Martial to Late Antiquity*, ed. Alfredo Mario Morelli, 663–692. Cassino: University of Cassino Press.

———. 2008b. "Literariness and Levels of Style in Epigraphical Poetry of Late Antiquity." In *Signs of Life? Studies in Later Greek Poetry = Ramus: Critical Studies in Greek and Roman Literature* 37.1–2, ed. Caterina Carvounis and Richard Hunter, 191–213.

———. 2008c. "Il ruolo di Dioscoro nella storia della poesia tardoantica." In *Les Archives de Dioscore d'Aphrodité cent ans après leur découverte: Histoire et culture dans l'Égypte byzantine. Actes du colloque international (Strasbourg 8–10 décembre 2005)*, ed. Jean-Luc Fournet and Caroline Magdelaine, 33–54. Paris: De Boccard.

———. 2008d. "Reliquie argonautiche a Cizico: Un'ipotesi sulle *Argonautiche orfiche*." In *Incontri triestini di filologia classica X*, ed. Lucio Cristante and Ireneo Filip, 17–36. Trieste: Edizioni Università di Trieste.

———. 2009a. "Niveaux de style, littérarité, poétiques: Pour une histoire du système de la poésie classicisante au VIe siècle." In *Actes du colloque Doux remède: poésie et poétique à Byzance (EHESS 24–26 février 2006)*, ed. Paolo Odorico, Panagiotis Agapitos, and Martin Hinterberger, 99–119. Paris: De Boccard.

———. 2009b. "Cristianizzazione della poesia greca e dialogo interculturale," *Cristianesimo nella Storia* 31: 59–81.

———. 2009c. "La *Vita di Proclo* di Marino nella sua redazione in versi: Per un'analisi della biografia poetica tardoantica," *CentoPagine* 3: 30–46 (http://musacamena.units.it/iniziative/SCA2009_Agosti.pdf).

———. 2010. "*Saxa loquuntur?* Epigrammi epigrafici e diffusione della *paideia* nell'Oriente tardoantico," *Antiquité Tardive* 18: 163–180.

Agosti, Gianfranco, and Fabrizio Gonnelli. 1995. "Materiali per la storia dell'esametro nei poeti cristiani greci." In *Struttura e storia dell'esametro greco*, ed. Marco Fantuzzi and Roberto Pretagostini, 289–434. Rome: Giardini.

Ashbrook Harvey, Susan, and David G. Hunter, eds. 2008. *The Oxford Handbook of Early Christian Studies.* Oxford: Oxford University Press.

Athanassiadi, Polymnia. 2006. "Antiquité tardive: Construction et déconstruction d'un modèle historiographique," *Antiquité Tardive* 14: 311–324.

Audano, Sergio. 2008. *Nonno e i suoi lettori*. Alessandria: Edizioni dell'Orso.

Averintsev, S. 1988. *L'anima e lo specchio: L'universo della poetica bizantina*. Italian trans. by Giuseppe Ghini. Bologna: Il Mulino (*Poétika rannevizantiiskoi literatury*. Moscow: Nauka, 1977).

Bagnall, Roger, ed. 2007. *Egypt in the Byzantine World 300–700*. Cambridge: Cambridge University Press.

Baldi, Idalgo. 2011. *Gli Inni di Sinesio: Vicende testuali di un* corpus *tardoantico*. Berlin: De Gruyter.

Baldwin, Barry. 1985. *An Anthology of Byzantine Poetry*. Amsterdam: Hakkert.

———. 1996. "Notes on Christian Epigrams in Book One of the Greek Anthology." In *The Sixth Century: End or Beginning?* ed. Pauline Allen and Elizabeth Jeffreys, 92–104. Brisbane: Australian Association for Byzantine Studies.

Bargellini, Francesco. 2006. "Per un'analisi strutturale dell' *ἔκφρασις τοῦ κοσμικοῦ πίνακος* di Giovanni di Gaza," *Medioevo Greco* 6: 41–68.

Baumbach, Manuel, and Silvio Bär, eds. 2007. *Quintus Smyrnaeus: Transforming Homer in Second Sophistic Epic*. Berlin: de Gruyter.

Beatrice, Pier Franco. 2001. *Anonymi monophysitae Theosophia: An Attempt at Reconstruction*. Leiden: Brill.

Bernand, Étienne. 1969. *Inscriptions métriques de l'Égypte gréco-romaine*. Paris: Les Belles Lettres.

Bevegni, Claudio. 2006. *Eudocia Augusta: Storia di San Cipriano*. Milan: Adelphi.

Boeft, J. den, and A. Hilhorst, eds. 1993. *Early Christian Poetry: A Collection of Essays*. Leiden: Brill.

Børtnes, Jostein, and Thomas Hägg, eds. 2006. *Gregory of Nazianzus: Images and Reflections*. Copenhagen: Museum Tusculanum Press.

Bowersock, G. W. 1990. *Hellenism in Late Antiquity*. Ann Arbor: University of Michigan Press.

———. 2006. *Mosaics as History: The Near East from Late Antiquity to Islam*. Revealing Antiquity 16. Cambridge, MA: Belknap Press of Harvard University Press.

Bowie, Ewen L. 1989. "Greek Sophists and Greek Poetry in the Second Sophistic." In *ANRW II* 33.1: 209–258.

———. 1990. "Greek Poetry in the Antonine Age." In *Antonine Literature*, ed. D. A. Russell, 53–90. Oxford: Oxford University Press.

Braccini, Tommaso. 2004. *Carmen choliambicum quod apud Ps.-Callistheis* Historiam Alexandri *reperitur*. Munich: Saur.

Braden, Gordon. 1978. *The Classics and English Renaissance Poetry*. New Haven, CT: Yale University Press.

Brock, Sebastian P. 1985. "Syriac and Greek Hymnography: Problems of Origin," *Studia Patristica* 16: 77–81.

Brown, Peter Robert Lamont. 1992. *Power and Persuasion in Late Antiquity: Towards a Christian Empire*. The Curti Lectures 1988. Madison: University of Wisconsin Press.

Bull, Malcom. 1998. "Poussin and Nonnos," *Burlington Magazine* 140: 724–738.

Busch, Stephan. 1999. *Versus Balnearum: Die antike Dichtung über Bader und Baden im römischen Reich*. Stuttgart: Teubner.

Busine, Aude. 2005. *Paroles d'Apollon: Pratiques et traditions oraculaires dans l'Antiquité Tardive (IIe-IVe siècles)*. Leiden: Brill.

Cameron, Alan. 1965. "Wandering Poets: A Literary Movement in Byzantine Egypt," *Historia* 14: 470–509.

———. 1970. "*Pap. Ant.* III. 115 and the Iambic Prologue in Late Antiquity." *Classical Quarterly* 20: 119–129.
———. 1973. *Porphyrius the Charioteer.* Oxford: Oxford University Press.
———. 1982. "The Empress and the Poet." *Yale Classical Studies* 27: 217–289.
———. 1985. *Literature and Society in the Early Byzantine World.* London: Ashgate.
———. 1993. *The Greek Anthology from Meleager to Planudes.* Oxford: Oxford University Press.
———. 2001. "The Poet, the Bishop, and the Harlot." *Greek, Roman and Byzantine Studies* 41: 175–188.
———. 2004a. "Poetry and Literary Culture in Late Antiquity." In *Approaching Late Antiquity*, ed. Simon Swain and Mark Edwards, 327–354. Oxford: Oxford University Press.
———. 2004b. *Greek Mythography in the Roman World.* Oxford: Oxford University Press.
———. 2007. "Poets and Pagans in Byzantine Egypt." In *Egypt in the Byzantine World 300–700*, ed. Roger Bagnall, 21–46. Cambridge: Cambridge University Press.
Cameron, Averil. 1991. *Christianity and the Rhetoric of Empire: The Development of Christian Discourse.* Sather Classical Lectures. Berkeley: University of California Press.
———. 1998. "Education and Literary Culture." In *The Cambridge Ancient History, XIII: The Late Roman Empire, A.D. 337–425*, ed. Averil Cameron and Peter Garnsey, 665–707. Cambridge: Cambridge University Press.
———. 2006. "New Themes and Styles in Greek Literature, A Title Revisited." In *Greek Literature in Late Antiquity: Dynamicism, Didacticism, Classicism*, ed. Scott F. Johnson, 11–28. London: Ashgate.
Caprara, Mariangela. 2008. "La 'vite parlante' di *Par.* XV 1–19." In *Nonno e i suoi lettori*, ed. Sergio Audano, 57–66. Alessandria: Edizioni dell'Orso.
Carvounis, Caterina. 2008. "Transforming the Homeric Models: Quintus' Battle among the Gods in the Posthomerica." In *Signs of Life? Studies in Later Greek Poetry = Ramus: Critical Studies in Greek and Roman Literature* 37.1–2, ed. Caterina Carvounis and Richard Hunter, 60–78.
Carvounis, Caterina, and Richard Hunter, eds. 2008. *Signs of Life? Studies in Later Greek Poetry = Ramus: Critical Studies in Greek and Roman Literature* 37.1–2.
Cavallo, Guglielmo. 2002. "Conservazione e perdita dei testi greci: fattori materiali, sociali, culturali." In *Dalla parte del libro*, 49–175. Urbino: QuattroVenti.
———. 2006. *Lire à Byzance.* Paris: Les Belles Lettres.
———. 2007. "Places of Public Reading in Late Antiquity." In *Alexandria: Auditoria of Kom el-Dikka and Late Antique Education*, ed. Tomasz Derda, Tomasz Markiewicz, and Ewa Wipszyska, 151–156. *The Journal of Juristic Papyrology Supplement VII.* Warsaw: University of Warsaw.
Chuvin, Pierre. 1991. *Mythologie et géographie dionysiaques: Recherches sur l'œuvre de Nonnos de Panopolis.* Clermont-Ferrand: ADOSA.
———. 1994. "Local Traditions and Classical Mythology in the *Dionysiaca*." In *Studies in the* Dionysiaca *of Nonnus*, ed. Neil Hopkinson, 167–176. Cambridge: Cambridge Philological Association.
———. 2006. "Nonnos de Panopolis et la 'deconstruction' de l'épopée." In *La poésie épique grecque: Métamorphoses d'un genre littéraire*, ed. Franco Montanari and Antonios Rengakos, 249–268. Vandœuvres-Geneva: Fondation Hardt.
———. 2009. *Chronique des derniers païens: La disparition du paganisme dans l'Empire romain, du règne de Costantin à celui de Justinien.* 3rd ed. Paris: Les Belles Lettres.

Ciccolella, Federica. 2006. "'Swarms of the Wise Bees': Literati and Audience in Sixth-Century Gaza." In *Approches de la Troisième Sophistique: Hommages à J. Schamp*, ed. Eugenio Amato, Alexandre Roduit, and Martin Steinrück, 81–95. Brussels: Latomus.

———. 2009. "Octosyllables, Dodecasyllables, or Hexameters? Reading Anacreontic Poetry in Byzantium." In *Actes du colloque Doux remède: Poésie et poétique à Byzance (EHESS 24–26 février 2006)*, ed. Paolo Odorico, Panagiotis Agapitos, and Martin Hinterberger, 245–265. Paris: De Boccard.

Collart, Paul. 1930. *Nonnos de Panopolis: Études sur la composition des Dionysiaques*. Cairo: IFAO.

Cribiore, Raffaella. 2001. *Gymnastics of the Mind: Greek Education in Hellenistic and Roman Egypt*. Princeton, NJ: Princeton University Press.

———. 2007a. "Higher Education in Early Byzantine Egypt." In *Egypt in the Byzantine World 300–700*, ed. Roger Bagnall, 47–66. Cambridge: Cambridge University Press.

———. 2007b. *The School of Libanius in Late Antique Antioch*. Princeton, NJ: Princeton University Press.

Cribiore, Raffaella, Paola Davoli, and David M. Ratzan. 2008. "A Teacher's Dipinto from Trimithis (Dakhleh Oasis)," *Journal of Roman Archaeology* 21: 171–191.

Crisci, Edoardo. 2004. "I più antichi codici miscellanei greci: Materiali per una riflessione," *Segno&Testo* 2: 109–144.

Daley, Brian. 2006. *Gregory of Nazianzus*. London: Routledge.

Demoen, Kristoffel. 1996. *Pagan and Biblical Exempla in Gregory Nazianzen: A Study in Rhetoric and Hermeneutics*. Turnhout: Brepols.

———. 1997. "'Gifts of Friendship That Will Remain for Ever': Persons, Addressed Characters, and Intended Audiences of Gregory Nazianzen's Epistolary Poems," *Jahrbuch der Österreichischen Byzantinistik* 47: 1–11.

———. 2009. "Poétique et rhétorique dans la poésie de Grégoire de Nazianze." In *Actes du colloque Doux remède: Poésie et poétique à Byzance (EHESS 24–26 février 2006)*, ed. Paolo Odorico, Panagiotis Agapitos, and Martin Hinterberger, 47–66. Paris: De Boccard.

Derda, Tomasz, Tomasz Markiewicz, and Ewa Wipszyska, eds. 2007. *Alexandria: Auditoria of Kom el-Dikka and Late Antique Education*. The Journal of Juristic Papyrology Supplement VII. Warsaw: University of Warsaw.

De Stefani, Claudio. 2006. "Paolo Silenziario leggeva la letteratura latina?" *Jahrbuch der Österreichischen Byzantinistik* 56: 101–112.

———. 2008a. "La *Parafrasi di Giovanni* di Nonno e la *Metafrasi dei Salmi* dello Pseudo-Apollinare: Un problema di cronologia." In *Nonno e i suoi lettori*, ed. Sergio Audano, 1–16. Alessandria: Edizioni dell'Orso.

———. 2008b. "L'*epigramma longum* tardoantico e bizantino e il *topos* dell'arrivo della primavera." In *Epigramma longum: Da Marziale alla tarda antichità; From Martial to Late Antiquity*, ed. Alfredo Mario Morelli, 571–600. Cassino: University of Cassino Press.

Di Branco, Marco. 2006. *La città dei filosofi: Storia di Atene da Marco Aurelio a Giustiniano*. Florence: Olschki.

D'Ippolito, Gennaro. 1964. *Studi nonniani: L'epillio nelle Dionisiache*. Palermo: Università di Palermo.

———. 2003. "Sulle tracce di una koinè formulare nell'epica tardo-greca." In *Des Géants à Dionysos: Mélanges de mythologie et de poésie grecques offerts à Francis Vian*, ed. Domenico Accorinti and Pierre Chuvin, 501–520. Alessandria: Edizioni dell'Orso.

Eastmond, Anthony. 2008. "The Veroli Casket." In *Byzantium 330–1453*, ed. Robin Cormack and Maria Vassilaki. London: Royal Academy of Arts.
Elsner, Jaś. 2004. "Late Antique Art: The Problem of Concept and Cumulative Aesthetic." In *Approaching Late Antiquity*, ed. Simon Swain and Mark Edwards, 271–308. Oxford: Oxford University Press.
Erbse, Hartmut. 1995. *Theosophorum Graecorum Fragmenta*. Stuttgart: Teubner.
Faj, Attila. 1968. "Probable Byzantine and Hungarian Models of *Ulysses and Finnegans Wake*," *Arcadia* 3: 48–72.
Fauth, Wilhelm. 1981. *Eidos Poikilon: Zur Thematik der Metamorphose und zum Prinzip der Wandlung aus dem Gegensatz in den Dionysiaka des Nonnos von Panopolis*. Göttingen: Vandenhoeck & Ruprecht.
Fayant, Marie-Christine. 2003. "Paul le Silentiaire héritier de Nonnos." In *Des Géants à Dionysos: Mélanges de mythologie et de poésie grecques offerts à Francis Vian*, ed. Domenico Accorinti and Pierre Chuvin, 583–592. Alessandria: Edizioni dell'Orso.
Feissel, Denis. 1998. "Deux épigrammes d'Apamène et l'éloge de l'endogamie dans une famille syrienne du VIe siècle." In *AETOS: Studies in Honour of Cyril Mango*, ed. Ihor Ševčenko and Irmgard I. Hutter, 116–136. Stuttgart: Teubner.
———. 2006. *Chroniques d'épigraphie byzantine 1987–2004*. Paris: Association des Amis du Centre d'Histoire et de Civilisation de Byzance.
Fournet, Jean-Luc. 2003a. "Théodore, un poète chrétien alexandrin oublié: L'hexamètre au service de la cause chrétienne." In *Des Géants à Dionysos: Mélanges de mythologie et de poésie grecques offerts à Francis Vian*, ed. Domenico Accorinti and Pierre Chuvin, 521–539. Alessandria: Edizioni dell'Orso.
———. 2003b. "Between Literary Tradition and Cultural Change: The Poetic and Documentary Production of Dioscorus of Aphrodito." In *Learned Antiquity: Scholarship and Society in the Near-East, the Greco-Roman World, and the Early Medieval West*, ed. Alasdair A. MacDonald, Michael W. Twomey, and Gerrit J. Reinink, 101–114. Leuven: Peeters.
———. 2007. "L'enseignement des belles lettres dans l'Alexandrie antique tardive." In *Alexandria: Auditoria of Kom el-Dikka and Late Antique Education*, ed. Tomasz Derda, Tomasz Markiewicz, and Ewa Wipszyska, 97–111. *The Journal of Juristic Papyrology Supplement VII*. Warsaw: University of Warsaw.
Frangoulis, Hélène. 1995. "Nonnos transposant Homère: Étude du chant 37 des Dionysiaques de Nonnos de Panopolis," *Revue de Philologie* 69: 145–168.
———. 2008. "L'eau et le vin dans le mythe d'Ampélos." In *Culture classique et christianisme: Mélanges offerts à Jean Bouffartigue*, ed. Daniel Auger and Étienne Wolff, 285–291. Paris: Picard.
Galli Calderini, Ginevra. 1987. "L'epigramma greco tardoantico: Tradizione e innovazione," *Vichiana* 16: 103–134.
Garzya, Antonio. 1984. "Retorica e realtà nella poesia tardoantica:" In *La poesia tardoantica: Tra retorica, teologia e politica. Atti del V corso della Scuola superiore di archeologia e civiltà medievali presso il Centro di cultura scientifica "E. Majorana,"* 11–49. Messina: Università di Messina.
Giardina, Andrea. 1999. "Esplosione di tardoantico," *Studi Storici* 40: 157–180.
Gigli Piccardi, Daria. 1984. "Dioniso e Gesù Cristo in Nonno *Dionys*. 45, 228–239," *Sileno* 10: 249–256.
———. 1985. *Metafora e poetica in Nonno di Panopoli*. Florence: Università di Firenze.
———. 1990. *La "Cosmogonia di Strasburgo."* Florence: Università di Firenze.
———. 1998. "Nonno e l'Egitto," *Prometheus* 24: 61–82; 161–182.

———. 2003. *Nonno di Panopoli: Le Dionisiache, Canti I–XII*. Milan: Biblioteca Universale Rizzoli.
———. 2005. "AEPOBATEIN: L'ecfrasi come viaggio in Giovanni di Gaza," *Medievo Greco* 5: 181–199.
———. 2008. "Questioni di cronologia nell'opera di Giovanni di Gaza," *Prometheus* 34: 65–86.
Golega, Joseph. 1930. *Studien über die Evangeliendichtung des Nonnos von Panopolis*. Breslau: Müller & Seiffert.
———. 1960. *Der Hexametrische Psalter*. Ettal: Buch-Kunstverlag.
Gonnelli, Fabrizio. 1991. "Il *De Vita Humana* di Giorgio di Pisidia," *Bollettino dei Classici* 12: 118–138.
———. 2003. *Nonno di Panopoli: Le Dionisiache, Canti XIII–XXIV*. Milan: Biblioteca Universale Rizzoli.
Grabar, André. 1945. "Plotin et les origines de l'esthétique médiéval," *Cahiers Archéologiques* 1: 15–34.
Greco, Claudia. 2008. "La cena di Betania e l'Ultima Cena: Esegesi cristiana e motivi dionisiaci in *Par*. M 7–16." In *Nonno e i suoi lettori*, ed. Sergio Audano, 43–55. Alessandria: Edizioni dell'Orso.
Hammerstaedt, Jürgen. 1997. "Photios über einen verlorenen Codex mit Autoren des vierten Jahrhunderts n.Chr. aus Mittel- bzw. Oberägyptens," *Zeitschrift für Papyrologie und Epigraphik* 115: 105–116.
Hardie, Philip. 2005. "Nonnus' Typhon: The Musical Giant." In *Roman and Greek Imperial Epic*, ed. Michael Paschalis, 117–130. Heraklion: Crete University Press.
Harries, Byron. 2006. "The Drama of Pastoral in Nonnus and in Colluthus." In *Brill's Companion to Greek and Latin Pastoral*, ed. Marco Fantuzzi and Theodor Papanghelis, 515–547. Leiden: Brill.
Heath, Malcolm. 2004. *Menander: A Rhetor in Context*. Cambridge: Cambridge University Press.
Hernández de la Fuente, David. 2007a. "Nonnus' Paraphrase of the Gospel of St John: 'Pagan Models and Christian Literature.'" In *Eastern Crossroads: Essays on Medieval Christian Legacy*, ed. Juan Pedro Monferrer-Sala, 169–191. Piscataway, NJ: Gorgias.
———. 2007b. "Nonnus, Peacock, & Shelley: A Note on the First English Translations of the *Dionysiaca*," *Res Publica Litterarum* 30: 188–198.
———. 2008. *Bakkhos Anax: Un estudio sobre Nono de Panópolis*. Madrid: CSIC.
Hollis, Adrian S. 1994, "Nonnus and Hellenistic Poetry." In *Studies in the* Dionysiaca *of Nonnus*, ed. Neil Hopkinson, 43–62. Cambridge: Cambridge Philological Association.
———. 2002. "Callimachus: Light from Later Antiquity." In *Callimaque*, ed. Franco Montanari and Luigi Lehnus, 35–57. Geneva-Vandœuvres: Fondation Hardt.
Hopkinson, Neil. 1994a. "Nonnus and Homer." In *Studies in the* Dionysiaca *of Nonnus*, ed. Neil Hopkinson, 9–42. Cambridge: Cambridge Philological Association.
———. 1994b. *Greek Poetry of the Imperial Period: An Anthology*. Cambridge: Cambridge University Press.
Hose, M. 2004. *Poesie aus der Schule: Überlegunden zur spätgriechischen Dichtung*. Munich: C.H. Beck.
Hunter, Richard. 2005. "Generic Consciousness in the *Orphic Argonautica*?" In *Roman and Greek Imperial Epic*, ed. Michael Paschalis, 149–168. Heraklion: Crete University Press.
Hurst, André, and Jean Rudhardt, eds. 2002. *Le Codex des Visions: Recherches et Rencontres*. Geneva: Droz.

James, Liz, and Ruth Webb. 1991. "'To Understand Ultimate Things and Enter Secret Places': Ekphrasis and Art in Byzantium," *Art History* 14: 1–17.

Janiszewski, Pawel. 2006. *The Missing Link: Greek Pagan Historiography in the Second Half of the Third Century and in the Fourth Century AD*. Warsaw: Warsaw University Press.

Jeffreys, Elizabeth. 2006. "Writers and Audiences in the Early Sixth Century." In *Greek Literature in Late Antiquity: Dynamicism, Didacticism, Classicism*, ed. Scott F. Johnson, 127–139. London: Ashgate.

Jeffreys, Michael J. 1981. "Byzantine Metrics: Non-Literary Strata," *Jahrbuch der Österreichischen Byzantinistik* 31: 313–334.

Johnson, Scott F., ed. 2006a. *Greek Literature in Late Antiquity: Dynamicism, Didacticism, Classicism*. London: Ashgate.

———. 2006b. *The Life and Miracles of Thekla, A Literary Study*. Washington, DC: Harvard University Press.

Kaldellis, Anthony. 2007a. *Hellenism in Byzantium: The Transformation of Greek Identity and the Reception of Classical Tradition*. Cambridge: Cambridge University Press.

———. 2007b. "Christodoros on the Statues of the Zeuxippos Baths: A New Reading of the *Ecphrasis*," *Greek, Roman and Byzantine Studies* 47: 361–383.

Kaster, Robert A. 1988. *Guardians of Language: The Grammarian and Society in Late Antiquity*. Berkeley: University of California Press.

Kennedy, George. 2003. *Progymnasmata: Greek Textbooks of Prose Composition and Rhetoric*. Leiden: Brill.

Keydell, Rudolf. 1936. "Nonnos von Panopolis," *RE* 17.1: 904–920.

———. 1953. "Wortwiederholung bei Nonnos," *Byzantinische Zeitschrift* 53: 1–17.

———. 1962. "Epigramm." In *Reallexicon der Antike und Christentum* 5: 539–577.

———. 1982. *Kleine Schriften zur hellenistischen und spätgriechischen Dichtung (1911–1979)*, ed. Werner Peek. Leipzig: Zentralantiquariat der DDR.

Kneebone, Emily. 2008. "ΤΟΣΣ' ΕΔΑΗΝ: The Poetics of Knowledge in Oppian's Halieutica." In *Signs of Life? Studies in Later Greek Poetry = Ramus: Critical Studies in Greek and Roman Literature* 37.1–2, ed. Caterina Carvounis and Richard Hunter, 32–59.

Kuhn, A. 1906. *Literarhistorische Studien zur Paraphrase des Johannes-Evangeliums von Nonnos aus Panopolis*. Jahresb. d. Gymn. Ges. Jesu in Kalksburg.

Kuiper, Karl. 1918. "De Nonno Evangeli Johannei interprete," *Mnemosyne* 46: 225–270.

Lamberton, Robert. 1986. *Homer the Theologian: Neoplatonist Allegorical Reading and the Growth of the Epic Tradition*. Berkeley: University of California Press.

Lasky, Edward D. 1978. "Encomiastic Elements in the Dionysiaca of Nonnus," *Hermes* 106: 357–376.

Lauxtermann, Marc. 1997. "The Palladas Sylloge," *Mnemosyne* 50: 329–337.

———. 1999. *The Spring of Rhythm: An Essay on Political Verse and Other Byzantine Metres*. Vienna: Verlag der Österreichischen Akademie der Wissenschaften.

———. 2003. *Byzantine Poetry from Pisides to Geometres*. Wien: Verlag der Österreichischen Akademie der Wissenschaften.

———. 2005. "All about George," *Jahrbuch der Österreichischen Byzantinistik* 55: 1–6.

Liebeschuetz, Wolfgang J. H. 2003. *The Decline and Fall of the Roman City*. Oxford: Oxford University Press.

Lightfoot, Jane. 2007. *The Sibylline Oracles, with Introduction, Translation and Commentary on the First and Second Books*. Oxford: Oxford University Press.

———. 2008. "Catalogue Technique in Dionysius Periegetes." In *Signs of Life? Studies in Later Greek Poetry = Ramus: Critical Studies in Greek and Roman Literature* 37.1–2, ed. Caterina Carvounis and Richard Hunter, 11–31.
Lind, L. Roger. 1978. "Nonnos and His Readers," *Res Publica Litterarum* 1: 159–170.
Livrea, Enrico. 1973. *Dionysii Bassaricon et Gigantiadis fragmenta*. Rome: Ateneo.
———. 1978. *Anonymi fortasse Olympiodori Thebani Blemyomachia (P. Berol. 5003)*. Meisenheim am Glan: A. Hain.
———. 1987. "Il poeta e il vescovo: La 'questione nonniana' e la storia," *Prometheus* 13: 97–123.
———. 1991. *Studia Hellenistica*. 2 vols. Florence: Gonnelli.
———. 1992. "I *Lithica* orfici," *Gnomon* 64: 204–211.
———. 1995. *Da Callimaco a Nonno: Dieci studi di poesia ellenistica*. Messina: D'Anna.
———. 1998a. "L'imperatrice Eudocia e Roma: Per una datazione del *De S. Cypr.*," *Byzantinische Zeitschrift* 91: 70–79.
———. 1998b. "La chiusa della *Gigantomachia* greca di Claudiano e la datazione del poemetto," *Studi Italiani di Filologia Classica* 16: 194–201.
———. 2000. "La *Gigantomachia* greca di Claudiano: Tradizione manoscritta e critica testuale," *Maia* 52: 415–451.
———. 2002. "Poema epico-storico attribuito a Soterico di Oasi," *Zeitschrift für Papyrologie und Epigraphik* 138: 17–30.
———. 2003. "The Nonnian Question Revisited." In *Des Géants à Dionysos: Mélanges de mythologie et de poésie grecques offerts à Francis Vian*, ed. Domenico Accorinti and Pierre Chuvin, 447–455. Alessandria: Edizioni dell'Orso.
Ludwich, Arthur. 1873. "Beiträge zur Kritik des Nonnos von Panopolis," *Programm des Königlichen Friedrichs-Collegiums zu Königsberg in Pr. October*: 1–145.
Ma, John. 2007. "The Worlds of Nestor the Poet." In *Severan Culture*, Ed. Simon Swain, Stephen Harrison, and Jaś Elsner, 83–113. Cambridge: Cambridge University Press.
Maas, Paul. 1910. "Das Kontakion," *Byzantinische Zeitschrift* 19: 285–306.
———. 1979. *Metrica greca: Traduzione e aggiornamenti di A. Ghiselli*. Florence: Le Monnier.
MacCoull, Leslie S. B. 1988. *Dioscorus of Aphrodito: His Work and His World*. The Transformation of the Classical Heritage 16. Berkeley: University of California Press.
———. 2003. "Dioscorus (and Nonnus) at the Feast: Late Antiquity and After." In *Des Géants à Dionysos: Mélanges de mythologie et de poésie grecques offerts à Francis Vian*, ed. Domenico Accorinti and Pierre Chuvin, 489–500. Alessandria: Edizioni dell'Orso.
Macrides, Ruth, and Paul Magdalino. 1988. "The Architecture of Ekphrasis: Construction and Context of Paul the Silentiary's Poem on Hagia Sophia," *Byzantine and Modern Greek Studies* 12: 47–82.
Magnelli, Enrico. 2002. *Studi su Euforione*. Rome: Quasar.
———. 2003. "Reminiscenze classiche e cristiane nei tetrastici di Teodoro Prodromo sulle Scritture," *Medioevo Greco* 3: 181–198.
———. 2005. "Su un epigramma greco tardoantico da Scitopoli," *Zeitschrift für Papyrologie und Epigraphik* 152: 57–60.
———. 2008a. "Nuovi dettagli sull'esametro nonniano: Le appositive nel quarto piede." In *Nonno e i suoi lettori*, ed. Sergio Audano, 33–42. Alessandria: Edizioni dell'Orso.
———. 2008b. "I due proemi di Agazia e le due identità dell'epigramma tardoantico." In *Epigramma longum: Da Marziale alla tarda antichità; From Martial to Late Antiquity*, ed. Alfredo Mario Morelli, 559–570. Cassino: University of Cassino Press.

———. 2008c. "Colluthus' 'Homeric' Epyllion." In *Signs of Life? Studies in Later Greek Poetry = Ramus: Critical Studies in Greek and Roman Literature* 37.1–2, ed. Caterina Carvounis and Richard Hunter, 151–172.

Majcherek, Grzegorz. 2007. "The Late Roman Auditoria of Alexandria: An Archaeological Overview." In *Alexandria: Auditoria of Kom el-Dikka and Late Antique Education*, ed. Tomasz Derda, Tomasz Markiewicz, and Ewa Wipszyska, 11–49. *The Journal of Juristic Papyrology Supplement VII*. Warsaw: University of Warsaw.

Mattsson, Axel. 1942. *Untersuchungen zur Epigrammsammlung des Agathias*. Lund: Gleerup.

McCail, Roger C. 1971. "The Erotic and Ascetic Poetry of Agathias Scholasticus," *Byzantion* 41: 205–265.

McGuckin, John A. 1986. *St. Gregory Nazianzen: Selected Poems*. Oxford: SLG.

———. 2006. "Gregory: The Rhetorician as Poet." In *Gregory of Nazianzus: Images and Reflections*, ed. Jostein Børtnes and Thomas Hägg, 193–212. Copenhagen: Museum Tusculanum Press.

———. 2008. "Poetry and Hymnography (2): The Greek World." In *The Oxford Handbook of Early Christian Studies*, ed. Susan Ashbrook Harvey and David G. Hunter, 641–656. Oxford: Oxford University Press.

McLynn, Neil. 2006. "Among the Hellenists: Gregory and the Sophists." In *Gregory of Nazianzus: Images and Reflections*, ed. Jostein Børtnes and Thomas Hägg, 213–238. Copenhagen: Museum Tusculanum Press.

Merkelbach, Reinhold, and A. Stauber. 1998–2004. *Steinepigramme aus dem griechischen Osten*. 5 vols. Stuttgart [I]; Munich [II–V]: Saur.

Miguélez Cavero, Laura. 2008. *Poems in Context: Greek Poetry in the Egyptian Thebaid 200–600 AD*. Berlin: De Gruyter.

———. 2009. "The Appearance of Gods in Nonnus' *Dionysiaca*," *Greek, Roman and Byzantine Studies* 49: 557–583.

———. 2010. "Invective at the Service of Encomium in the *Dionysiaca* of Nonnus of Panopolis," *Mnemosyne* 63: 23–42.

Newbold, Roland F. 2003. "The Power of Sound in Nonnus' *Dionysiaca*." In *Des Géants à Dionysos: Mélanges de mythologie et de poésie grecques offerts à Francis Vian*, ed. Domenico Accorinti and Pierre Chuvin, 457–468. Alessandria: Edizioni dell'Orso.

Nicks, Fiona. 2000. "Literary Culture in the Reign of Anastasius I." In *Ethnicity and Culture in Late Antiquity*, ed. Stephen Mitchell and Geoffrey Greatrex, 183–203. London: Duckworth.

Opelt, Ilona. 1958. "Allitteration im Griechischen? Untersuchungen zur Dichtersprache des Nonnos von Panopolis," *Glotta* 27: 205–232.

Peek, Werner. 1955. *Griechische Versinschriften, I: Grab-Epigramme*. Berlin: Akademie-Verlag.

———. 1968–1975. *Lexikon zu den Dionysiaka des Nonnos*. 4 vols. Berlin: Akademie-Verlag.

Pontani, Filippo Maria. 1983. "Nonniana," *Museum Patavinum* 1: 353–378.

Rapp, Claudia. 2005. "Literary Culture in the Age of Justinian." In *The Cambridge Companion to the Age of Justinian*, ed. Michael Maas, 376–397. Cambridge: Cambridge University Press.

Renaut, Delphine. 2005. "Les déclamations d'ekphraseis: Une réalité vivante à Gaza au VIe siècle." In *Gaza dans l'Antiquité Tardive: Archéologie, rhétorique, histoire*, ed. Catherine Saliou, 197–220. Salerno: Helios.

———. 2009. *La Description du Tableau répresentant le monde par Jean de Gaza. Édition, traduction, commentaire*. Paris: Thèse Paris IV-Sorbonne.

Riemschneider, Margarete. 1957. "Der Stil des Nonnos." In *Aus der byzantinistischen Arbeit der DDR*, ed. J. Irmscher, 46–70. Berlin: Akademie-Verlag.

Robert, Louis. 1948. *Hellenica IV: Épigrammes du Bas-Empire*. Paris: Maisonneuve.

Roberts, Michael. 1985. *Biblical Epic and Rhetorical Paraphrase in Late Antiquity*. Liverpool: Francis Cairns.

———. 1989. *The Jeweled Style: Poetry and Poetics in Late Antiquity*. Ithaca, NY: Cornell University Press.

Rotondo, Arianna. 2008. "La voce divina nella *Parafrasi* di Nonno di Panopoli," *Adamantius* 14: 287–310.

Roueché, Charlotte. 2006. "Written Display in the Late Antique and Byzantine City." In *Proceedings of the 21st International Congress of Byzantine Studies*, ed. Elizabeth Jeffreys, 235–254. London: Ashgate.

Salzman, Michele R. 2008. "Pagans and Christians." In *The Oxford Handbook of Early Christian Studies*, ed. Susan Ashbrook Harvey and David G. Hunter, 186–202. Oxford: Oxford University Press.

Sartre-Fauriat, Annie. 1998. "Culture et société dans les Hauran (Syrie du Sud) d'après les épigrammes funéraires (IIIe–Ve siècles ap. J.-C.)," *Syria* 75: 213–224.

Schmiel, Robert. 1998. "Repetition in Nonnos' *Dionysiaca*," *Philologus* 142: 326–334.

———. 2003. "Composition and Structure: The Battle at the Hydaspes (Nonnos' *Dionysiaca* 21.303–24.178)." In *Des Géants à Dionysos: Mélanges de mythologie et de poésie grecques offerts à Francis Vian*, ed. Domenico Accorinti and Pierre Chuvin, 469–481. Alessandria: Edizioni dell'Orso.

Ševčenko, Ihor. 1987. "An Early Tenth-Century Inscription from Galakrenai with Echoes of Nonnus and the Palatine Anthology," *Dumbarton Oaks Papers* 41: 461–468.

Sherry, Francis Lee. 1996. "The Paraphrase of St. John Attributed to Nonnus," *Byzantion* 66: 409–430.

Shorrock, Robert. 2001. *The Challenge of Epic: Allusive Engagement in the Dionysiaca of Nonnus*. Leiden: Brill.

———. 2008. "The Politics of Poetics: Nonnus' *Dionysiaca* and the World of Late Antiquity." In *Signs of Life? Studies in Later Greek Poetry = Ramus: Critical Studies in Greek and Roman Literature* 37.1–2, ed. Caterina Carvounis and Richard Hunter, 99–113.

———. 2011. *The Myth of Paganism: Nonnus, Dionysus and the World of Late Antiquity*, London: Bristol Classical Press.

Simelidis, Christos. 2009. *Selected Poems of Gregory of Nazianzus. I.2.17; II.1.10, 19, 32: A Critical Edition with Introduction and Commentary*. Göttingen: Vandenhoeck & Ruprecht.

Simon, Erika. 1964. "Nonnos und das Elfenbeinkästchen aus Veroli," *Jahrbuch des Deutschen archäologischen Instituts* 79: 279–336.

Smolak, Kurt. 1979. "Beobachtungen zur Darstellungsweise in den Homerzentonen," *Jahrbuch der Österreichischen Byzantinistik* 28: 29–49.

Sowers, Patrick Brian. 2008. *Eudocia: The Making of a Homeric Christian*. PhD diss., University of Cincinnati.

Spanoudakis, Konstantinos. 2007. "Icarius Jesus Christ? Dionysiac Passion and Biblical Narrative in Nonnus' Icarius Episode (*Dion.* 47, 1–264)," *Wiener Studien* 120: 35–92.

Stegemann, Viktor. 1930. *Astrologie und Universalgeschichte: Studien und Interpretationen zu den* Dionysiaka *des Nonnos von Panopolis*. Leipzig–Berlin: Teubner.

Steinrück, Martin. 1999. "Neues zur Blemyomachie," *Zeitschrift für Papyrologie und Epigraphik* 126: 99–114.

———. 2008. "Comment lire les verses de Nonnos?" *Lexis* 26: 319–324.

Stella, Francesco. 2005. "Epic of the Biblical God: Intercultural Imitation and the Poetics of Alterity." In *Roman and Greek Imperial Epic*, ed. Michael Paschalis, 131–147. Heraklion: Crete University Press.

String, Martin. 1966. *Untersuchungen zum Stil der Dionysiaka des Nonnos von Panopolis*. Dissertation, University of Hamburg.

Thraede, Klaus. 1962. "Epos," *Reallexikon für Antike und Christentum* 5: 983–1042.

Tissoni, Francesco. 1998. *Nonno di Panopoli: I canti di Penteo (Dionisiache 44–46). Commento*. Florence: La Nuova Italia.

———. 2003. "Il Tardoantico a Bisanzio: La ricezione della poesia tardoantica in alcuni epigrammi bizantini del IX–X secolo tràditi nel XV libro dell'*Anthologia Graeca*." In *Des Géants à Dionysos: Mélanges de mythologie et de poésie grecques offerts à Francis Vian*, ed. Domenico Accorinti and Pierre Chuvin, 621–635. Alessandria: Edizioni dell'Orso.

———. 2008. "Ciro di Panopoli riconsiderato (con alcune ipotesi sulla destinazione delle *Dionisiache*)." In *Nonno e i suoi lettori*, ed. Sergio Audano, 67–81. Alessandria: Edizioni dell'Orso.

Van Opstall, Emilie M. 2008. *Jean Géomètre: Poèmes en hexamètres et en distiques élégiaques*. Leiden: Brill.

Vessey, Mark. 2008. "Literature, Patristics, Early Christian Writings." In *The Oxford Handbook of Early Christian Studies*, ed. Susan Ashbrook Harvey and David G. Hunter, 43–65. Oxford: Oxford University Press.

Vian, F. 1976. *Nonnos de Panopolis: Les Dionysiaques I–II*. Paris: Les Belles Lettres.

———. 1986. "L'Épopée grecque de Quintus de Smyrne à Nonnos de Panopolis," *Bulletin Association Guillaume Budé* 1: 333–343.

———. 1991. "Nonno ed Omero," *Koinonia* 15: 5–18.

———. 1994. "Quelques aspects de la technique narrative de Nonnos." In *Studies in the* Dionysiaca *of Nonnus*, ed. Neil Hopkinson, 285–292. Cambridge: Cambridge Philological Association.

———. 1997. "ΜΑΡΤΥΣ chez Nonnos de Panopolis: Étude de sémantique et de chronologie," *Revue des Études Grecs* 110: 143–160.

———. 2001. "Echoes and Imitations of Apollonius Rhodius in Late Greek Epic." In *A Companion to Apollonius Rhodius*, ed. Theodoros D. Papanghelis and Antonios Rengakos, 285–308. Leiden: Brill.

———. 2003. *Nonnos de Panopolis: Les Dionysiaques, Chant XLVIII*. Paris: Les Belles Lettres.

———. 2005. *L'épopée posthomérique: Recueil d'étude*, ed. Domenico Accorinti. Alessandria: Edizioni dell'Orso.

Viljamaa, Toivo. 1968. *Studies in Greek Encomiastic Poetry of the Early Byzantine Period*. Helsinki: Societas Scientiarum Fennica.

Webb, Ruth. 1997. "Poetry and Rhetoric." In *Handbook of Classical Rhetoric in the Hellenistic Period 330 B.C.–A.D. 400*, ed. Stanley E. Porter, 339–369. Leiden: Brill.

West, Martin L. 1982. *Greek Metre*. Oxford: Clarendon Press.

Whitby, Mary. 1985. "The Occasion of Paul the Silentiary's Ekphrasis of S. Sophia," *Classical Quarterly* 35: 215–228.

———. 1994. "From Moschus to Nonnus: The Evolution of the Nonnian Style." In *Studies in the* Dionysiaca *of Nonnus*, ed. Neil Hopkinson, 99–155. Cambridge: Cambridge Philological Association.

———. 2003. "The Vocabulary of Praise in Verse Celebration of 6th-Century Building Achievements: *AP* 2.398–406, *AP* 9.565, *AP* 1.10 and Paul the Silentiary's Description of St. Sophia." In *Des Géants à Dionysos: Mélanges de mythologie et de poésie grecques offerts à Francis Vian*, ed. Domenico Accorinti and Pierre Chuvin, 593–606. Alessandria: Edizioni dell'Orso.

———. 2006. "The St. Polyeuktos Epigram (*AP* 1.10): A Literary Perspective." In *Greek Literature in Late Antiquity: Dynamicism, Didacticism, Classicism*, ed. Scott F. Johnson, 159–187. London: Ashgate.

———. 2007a. "The Bible Hellenized: Nonnus' *Paraphrase* of St John's Gospel and 'Eudocia's' Homeric Centos." In *Texts and Culture in Late Antiquity: Inheritance, Authority, and Change*, ed. J. H. D. Scourfield, 195–231. Swansea: Classical Press of Wales.

———. 2007b. "The *Cynegetica* Attributed to Ps.-Oppian." In *Severan Culture*, ed. Simon Swain, Stephen Harrison, and Jaś Elsner, 125–134. Cambridge: Cambridge University Press.

———. 2008. "'Sugaring the Pill': Gregory of Nazianzus' Advice to Olympias (*Carm.* 2.2.6)." In *Signs of Life? Studies in Later Greek Poetry = Ramus: Critical Studies in Greek and Roman Literature* 37.1–2, ed. Caterina Carvounis and Richard Hunter, 79–98.

Wifstrand, Albert. 1933. *Von Kallimachos zu Nonnos*. Lund: Gleerup.

Wilkinson, Kevin. 2009. "Palladas and the Age of Constantine," *Journal of Roman Studies* 99: 36–60.

———. 2010. "Palladas and the Foundation of Constantinople," *Journal of Roman Studies* 100: 179–194.

Willers, Dietrich. 1992. "Dionysus und Christus: Ein archäologisches Zeugnis zur 'Konfessionsangehörigkeit' des Nonnos," *Museum Helveticum* 42: 141–151.

CHAPTER 12

HISTORIOGRAPHY

BRIAN CROKE

Macquarie University and University of Sydney

If the hallmark of what modern scholarship has come to label "Late Antiquity" is the emergence of a common pan-Mediterranean religious, cultural, and intellectual outlook whose influence has endured to modern times, then the *Chronicle* of Eusebius is its exemplary historiographical text. Written in Greek, in the early fourth century, by a Christian scholar and apologist at the major Roman port capital of Caesarea in Palestine, the chronicle was translated into Latin at Constantinople in 380 and then found its way to Italy, Gaul, Spain, Africa, Britain, and Ireland, where over the ensuing centuries it was simplified, adapted, augmented, and continued by others. Surviving manuscript copies of its Latin translation, from the fifth to the sixteenth centuries, reinforce its central role in medieval European historiography. By the sixth century, the chronicle had also been translated into Syriac and Armenian, thereby becoming the core of subsequent historiography in those languages and cultures. By the seventh century, directly or indirectly, it was also possibly available in Coptic, Ethiopic, and Georgian. For more than a millennium, in its original Greek form, it was recast and reformulated, absorbed and adapted by the Byzantine historiographical tradition and its Slavic offshoots.

The translation and reworking of Eusebius' chronicle, from the fourth century to the seventh century and beyond, reflects the gradual spread of Christianity, with its novel understanding of the nature and importance of history. Conversion entailed a notion of history as the totality of past events meaningfully linked to the present and the future. Believers of all levels of education and culture were exposed to the same history, including the story of the Jewish nation embodied in various books of the Old Testament. The chronicle was a sophisticated document in two parts: the former, a collection of relevant lists of datable rulers extracted from earlier writers; the latter, an annalistic record, making space for each year from Abraham in 2016 B.C.E. to Eusebius' day and progressively interspersed with short narratives of particular events. In historiographical works, the Christian and classical past stood side by side, then merged into each other, and then one fully displaced the other throughout the late antique world. While Eusebius' chronicle originated in a polemical moment, its successors were more concerned to demonstrate the continuity of history under Christian emperors.

For historiographical purposes, "Late Antiquity" is a convenient unifying concept, both chronologically (covering the period from c. 250 to c. 700) and geographically (covering the area from Ireland to Iran), but there are different ways of approaching the story of late antique historiography: by nation or language (Inglebert 2001b), by separate genres (Croke 2007; Woods 2009), by a series of individual writers, especially those whose texts have been wholly or partly preserved to the present (Rohrbacher 2002; Treadgold 2007), by traditions preserved or overturned (Momigliano 1969), or by development over time (Momigliano 1963; Croke and Emmett 1983). Further, recent discussions of late antique historiography (e.g., Rohrbacher 2002; Marasco 2003; Janiszewski 2006) have tended to overvalue categorical differences between "pagan" and Christian, "secular" and "religious," "history" and "chronicle," and Latin and Greek modes of writing about the past (cf. Inglebert 1996, 3–24). At the same time, they have arguably undervalued the prevalent fluidity of historiographical genres in Late Antiquity (cf. Croke 2001b) and the extensive translation of texts (principally Greek to Latin, Latin to Greek, Greek to Syriac and Armenian, Syriac to Greek and Armenian). Translations such as those of Eusebius' chronicle played a key role in spreading the shared religious and intellectual concerns, including historiographical perspectives, that characterize Late Antiquity.

Taking due account of these factors, as well as recognizing that in Late Antiquity responses to the passing of years and centuries are manifest in several new ways—sermons, saints' lives, monuments, and artifacts (Cameron 1999; Bowersock 2001)—the preferred option here is to concentrate on the development of late antique historiography over time, drawing significant connections and continuities between authors of historical works. More detailed introductions to individual authors and genres are readily available elsewhere (Inglebert 2001a; Rohrbacher 2002; Marasco 2003; Croke 2007; Treadgold 2007). A developmental approach exposes the diverse scope of late antique historiography by also considering known works that are now merely fragmentary or completely lost. It also highlights the delimited cultural circles in which old and new forms of history writing were adapted and created from generation to generation as the Graeco-Roman world turned progressively Christian. It also brings into clearer focus how the past was remembered, conceived, presented, explained, and exploited. The recurring themes to be explored are the importance in shaping all historiography of a common rhetorical education across languages (cf. Brown 1992, 35–61, 118–126; Greatrex 2001) and the impact of Christianity on the changing realities of who wrote and read history and how history was composed and communicated (cf. Inglebert 2001a, 533–570). What emerges is the proposition that late antique historiography is more culturally unified and less compartmentalized than has been generally assumed, with Antioch, then Constantinople, providing a central role from the fourth century to the seventh. This applied to historiographical texts not only in Greek but also in Latin, Syriac, and Armenian.

The Emergence of New Historiographical Forms, 250–337

At the turn of the fourth century, reading and writing about the past were minor pursuits for the educated aristocracy of the Roman world, essentially a literary activity with political and moral purposes. It had been that way for centuries. One way of memorializing the recent past was to follow the model established by Herodotus and Thucydides in the fifth century B.C.E., which meant attention to literary style, a focus on speeches, and set-piece narratives. Greeks and Romans also had other ways of recording past events, such as local histories, biographies, and chronicles, but they generally lacked the dating systems required to construct more geographically comprehensive accounts, except for Olympiads, Roman consuls, and Athenian archons. The Athenian sophist Dexippos, writing in the 270s (G. Martin 2006; Janiszewski 2006, 39–54), used Olympiads in his chronological history of Greece and Rome in twelve books, culminating (frag. 12) in his explanation for how, in terms of power and geographical extent, the Roman empire had surpassed the previous realms of the Assyrians, Persians, and Macedonians. In Dexippos' day, Christians had come to the view that the coincidence of Christ's birth and the reign of Augustus as first emperor was providential; that is, the Roman empire would be the vehicle for spreading Christ's message. The empire and the emperor would eventually become Christian. Such reflections formed part of the stimulus for Eusebius, who was writing his *Chronicle* in about 303 (Burgess 1997) against a background of sophisticated critiques of Christianity and imperial persecution of the small but rapidly growing community of Christians.

The *Chronicle* was one of many key polemical works compiled by Eusebius (Kofsky 2000), who drew on an already conventional Christian chronology, stimulated by a quest to establish the date of creation, as in the *Chronography* of Africanus (Mosshammer 1979; Croke 1983a; Burgess 2006; Adler 2006), as well as a quest for precision about the chronology of the successive kingdoms in the biblical book of Daniel. In a single sweep, the chronicle's layout and content defined the Christian understanding of history, in which all known past and present kingdoms, including Dexippos' Assyrians, Persians, and Macedonians, were both embraced and united as part of the divine time span. At Caesarea, Eusebius had access to a large library (Carriker 2003, 139–154, 157–163) and knew the whole repertoire of historical and philosophical texts deployed by his intellectual adversaries, most notably Porphyry and Hierocles (Barnes 1981; Adler 1992; 2008). Eusebius' *Chronicle* appeared around the same time as Christianity became a legitimate public practice and belief system sanctioned by the emperor Constantine (306–337). Questions of Christian history and chronology were familiar and debated at the court of Constantine at Nicomedia and his newly founded capital of Constantinople after 330. Porphyry and Hierocles were countered not only in Greek by Eusebius but also in Latin by both the African rhetor Arnobius (Simmons 1995, 22–31) and his pupil Lactantius (Digeser 2000, 92–107). By regularly quoting memorable examples and incidents, both Arnobius and Lactantius presupposed in their audience a sufficient knowledge of history, wherever they were educated.

The newly legitimized and publicly endowed Christian nation also had its own self-contained story, which was covered by Eusebius in another pioneering historiographical work, the *Church History* (Ferguson 2005, 15–56; Adler 2008, 589–598). The Eusebian form of church history drew inspiration from Josephus' account of the Jewish nation (his *Antiquities*) and the classical tradition of histories of philosophical schools (Momigliano 1990, 140–141). The history, in which suitable attention was paid to use of documents to argue the historical point, was a story of triumph over persecution, the establishment of clear lines of episcopal lineage in key sees, and the production of Christian ideas and texts. As with his other works, Eusebius' history was a sustained apology for his own theological tradition. Like the *Chronicle*, the *Church History* was later translated into Syriac (fourth century), then Latin (early fifth), Coptic (mid-fifth), and Armenian (fifth), thereby providing a model and a unifying impulse for later histories in all those languages and cultures.

Adjusting to the New Forms, East and West, 337–378

Constantine's nephew Julian (emperor 361–363) enjoyed the best available rhetorical and philosophical education. He was therefore familiar with the Greek historians and at Constantinople in 361 even wrote a historical work of his own, the *Caesars*, a panoramic view of the emperors from Julius Caesar to his own day in the form of a satirical dialogue set at a banquet where all the Caesars were gathered together. Since he was educated in a newly Christianized household, he was also familiar with the new forms of history writing pioneered by Eusebius and others. A significant mentor of Julian was George, who became bishop of Alexandria. When George was killed in 362, the now anti-Christian emperor sought to retrieve his library because among the contents of interest to him were "Christian historical works" (Julian, *Ep.* 38). Another influential mentor and friend of Julian was the famous rhetor Libanius, who taught at Constantinople in the 340s and then at Nicomedia and Antioch, where his students shared in the close study of Thucydides, noting the pleasure their teacher took in his personal copy of the historian (Lib., *Or.* 1.148).

Libanius wrote no historical works himself, although in 365 he considered narrating the history of Julian's Persian war but preferred instead to exhort Seleucus (*Ep.* 142) to write an eyewitness account, which resulted in his "Two Books on Persian Affairs" (Janiszewski 2006, 136–144). Other participants in Julian's Persian campaign were also spurred to write up their experiences of the war, notably Magnus of Carrhae (Janiszewski 2006, 123–129), Eutychianus (Janiszewski 2006, 130–132, 270–272), and the Persian convert Chorohbut (Janiszewski 2006, 132–135), but their works have not survived. Even in Gaul, the leading rhetorician Alcimus Alethius at Bordeaux felt inspired to write the story of Julian's reign (Aus., *Prof.* 2.20–4). Also, by this time histories of the reign of the Christian emperor Constantine were being produced by young Praxagoras at Athens (Janiszewski 2006, 352–371) and the sophist Bemarchius from Caesarea (Janiszewski 2006, 371–380), a fierce rival of Libanius.

Julian was educated in Latin as well as Greek. At Sirmium on his way to Constantinople in 361, he met Aurelius Victor, whose recent history he evidently read. Like Lactantius previously, Victor was an African of modest lineage educated at Rome, and his personal efforts advanced his education and then secured him an imperial career. His so-called abbreviated history began with Augustus, was organized by successive imperial reigns, and terminated in his own day (Den Boer 1972, 19–113; Bird 1994; Rohrbacher 2002, 42–48). It was conceived as a continuation of the history of Livy, by which Victor meant one of the epitomes of Livy, such as the one found at Oxyrhynchus in Egypt. Epitomes of multivolume histories like those of Polybius and Livy had always existed but were popular at the time. Since he wrote history in provincial Sirmium, he must have had the few materials he needed close to hand. Although Victor was writing under the aegis of Constantius II (337–361), Julian appointed him as provincial governor at Pannonia and honored him with a bronze statue (Amm. Marc., 20.10.6).

A similar need was filled by the two complementary works of the imperial officials Eutropius and Festus, written at Marcianople for the soldier-emperor Valens (364–378) in 369–370, while he was still in the Balkans fighting the Goths but planning a campaign against the Persians for the following spring. As several scholars have noted previously, Eutropius had been part of Julian's retinue during the ill-fated Persian expedition in 363, then served under Julian's successor Jovian in 363–364, and then served at the court of Jovian's successor Valens, which was based mainly at Antioch (Den Boer 1972,114–172; Bird 1993; Ratti 1996; Rohrbacher 2002, 49–56; Burgess 2001c). His *Roman History* in ten books provides a summary account from the foundation of Rome to the present day, but with a military emphasis and didactic purpose. He left recent history, which required more elaborate narrative, to another day (*Brev.*, 10.18). Festus, older and more experienced than Eutropius, was also invited by Valens to write a short work explaining the background to the expansion of Roman authority in the East, followed by a focus on Roman-Persian relations and the conflicts between them, concluding that Roman success was underpinned by its native manliness. Festus claims to be not writing a narrative so much as merely itemizing events in the manner of an accountant (Den Boer 1972, 173–233; Rohrbacher 2002, 57–63). Research has identified the common source of information behind Victor, Eutropius, and Festus as a lost historian usually known as the "Imperial History" ("Kaisergeschichte," the title bestowed by its original German proponent), although it may have covered all of Roman history (Burgess 2005).

While Valens needed Eutropius and Festus to compensate for the shortcomings in his historical education, his young nephew Gratian (emperor in the West from 367 to 383) had benefited from reading historians under the guidance of his tutor Ausonius, the eminent rhetor summoned from Bordeaux to the court at Trier. He was well versed in the historians, not only in Latin such as Sallust (*Ep.* 3; 22.61, 23.2; *Grat.* 8) but also in Greek, and he praised other local rhetors for their skills in teaching history (*Prof.* 21.26, 26.3), especially Staphylius, who knew the whole of Herodotus and Livy (Aus., *Prof.*, 20.8). Ausonius even owned copies of Herodotus and Thucydides (*Ep.* 10.32) and wrote a consular book designed to culminate in his own consulship in 379, as well as a verse summary of emperors based on Suetonius' *Caesars*. He even provided a copy of Nepos' *Chronica* for the distinguished Christian aristocrat Sextus Petronius Probus while he was holding prefectural authority at Sirmium in the early 370s (Aus., *Ep.* 12.1).

Writing so close together at the eastern imperial court, Eutropius and Festus would have been read by the same educated courtiers and other local officials, Christian and non-Christian. Eutropius was corresponding at the time with both Symmachus at Rome (Symm., *Ep.* 3.46–51) and Gregory of Nazianzus (Greg.Naz., *Ep.* 70–71). Although Antioch, where Valens was then based, included a large Latin community, there was also demand for a historical work such as Eutropius' *breviarium* from the majority Greek population. It was translated in the late 370s by Libanius' pupil, the lawyer Paeanius. Among the local readers of Eutropius and Festus was Jerome, who was in Antioch at the time. Jerome had been educated in Rome in the 350s by its most illustrious teacher, Donatus, from whom he acquired close familiarity with the Latin historians. Yet at the same time, other distinguished Roman rhetors, such as Marius Victorinus, were turning to Christianity and discovering Christian chronology, such as we find in the work of the *Chronographer of 354* (Salzman 1990).

At Antioch, Jerome was also reading the history of Aurelius Victor, having arranged to have a copy sent to him there (Jerome, *Ep.* 10.3). All these new histories by educated officials were serving a clear historiographical function. They were not, as often characterized, minor works reflecting a strictly limited literary ability and outlook. Aurelius Victor, Eutropius, and Festus were not Christians, nor was most of their audience, and the new religion scarcely crosses their path. However, as more and more of the classically educated eastern and western aristocracies turned to Christianity between the 340s and the 390s, Jerome foremost among them, they encountered a new understanding of history and new ways of writing about it. Still, Eutropius in particular came to be used directly by Jerome and almost all subsequent historians over the following decades, Christian and non-Christian alike.

Among the pupils of Libanius at Constantinople were Basil of Caesarea in Cappadocia (330–379), educated by his rhetor father and his fellow Cappadocian Gregory of Nazianzus, while Eustochius, another scholastic friend from Caesarea and later sophist (Janiszewski 2006, 380–382), was to produce a history of the recent reign of Constans (337–350). Both Basil and Gregory later shone out in the competitive educational culture at Athens, where they met the future emperor Julian and where an intellectual tussle was emerging between the traditional Greek and the new Christian understanding of society and history. In Basil's treatise on Greek literature, addressed to young men, he encouraged the enduring value and use of Greek literature by Christians, with the classical historians still worth reading in particular because they provide examples of virtue (*Address to Young Men*, 5). Basil's younger brother Gregory, bishop of Nyssa, shared the education and the friendship with Gregory of Nazianzus and never forgot his Herodotus (*On Infants' Early Deaths*, 395). All three found themselves engaged in theological polemic and caught up in the persecution by the Arian emperor Valens in the 370s.

In 382, Gregory of Nyssa considered writing a history of that period but decided it would have to be too long and detailed. Moreover, the difficult experiences of his contemporaries were already well known, and he would face the uncomfortable fact of including himself in the story, so it would be better left to others (*Against Eunomius* 1.12). Perhaps he had in mind Diodore, bishop of Tarsus, who had also been educated in Athens with Basil and Julian before turning to theology and Christian polemic. At Antioch in 362–363, he had opposed Julian, who accused him of deploying the learning and eloquence of Athens against the immortal gods (Julian, *Ep.* 55), and in 372, he was exiled by Valens. Diodore was the first to lend his learning to improving the *Chronicle* of Eusebius and its chronology, possibly building on a recent Antiochene continuation of Eusebius to the 350s (Burgess and Witakowski 1999). At the same time, his friend Epiphanius of Cyprus was also making good use of Eusebius (*De mensuris et ponderibus*, 56), and Epiphanius' work was to later have considerable influence further east, especially on Armenian writers (Greenwood 2008, 228–229). It was possible that in late 378–379, when Jerome was living in Antioch, he met Diodore, recently returned from exile. At least he mentions him in his list of Christian writers (*De vir. ill.*, 119). Otherwise, Jerome may have encountered

Diodore in Constantinople in 380–381, at the same time he met up with Basil, Gregory of Nyssa, and Gregory of Nazianzus.

More important, it was in Constantinople at precisely this time that Jerome produced his Latin translation and continuation of Eusebius' *Chronicle* (Inglebert, 1996, 203–295; Burgess 2002; Jeanjean and Lançon 2004). Jerome explains to his audience that it is a complex work full of unfamiliar names and its structure is not easy to follow. From Abraham to the fall of Troy, it is "pure translation", thereafter, to fill gaps in Eusebius, adding and editing especially for the Roman period, using Suetonius' *Lives of Famous Men* and other Latin sources, including the "Kaisergeschichte" (Burgess 1995; 1998). Then he adds the period from 325 to 378, reserving the reigns of Gratian and Theodosius I (379–395) for another work in a grander style, but confesses that it is currently impossible because the Gothic invasions have created such uncertainty. Although he dictated the original entries in a hurry, the design and copying of the chronicle was a complex and time-consuming task (Williams 2006, 210–211).

Western Aristocracies Straddling Old and New, 379–410

In Rome, meanwhile, the educated aristocracy of Jerome's generation, only a minority of whom were yet Christian, continued to read and copy the Roman historians and occasionally turn their own hand to historical topics. Naucellius translated an unspecified Greek work on the early Roman republic (Symm., *Ep.* 3.11), another aristocrat wrote his own Roman history (Symm., *Ep.* 9.110), and Symmachus offered to lend Protadius his copies of Julius Caesar's *Gallic War* and the later books of Livy for a history of Gaul he was writing (Symm., *Ep.* 4.18). He also hinted to Eutropius that maybe the time had come for him to take up his earlier promise to write up contemporary history (Symm., *Ep.* 3.46; cf. Eutropius, *Brev.* 10.18). The most significant new history, written in the late 380s, was the lost *Annales* of Nicomachus Flavianus, which was dedicated to the emperor Theodosius. Nothing more is known about it and the period it might have covered, despite much recent speculation (Bleckmann 1992; Baldini 2000, 97–178; Ratti 2003; 2007). Another of the young friends Symmachus recommended to Eutropius was Postumianus (Symm., *Ep.* 3.48), scion of a great noble family and whose uncle presumably knew Eutropius because he, too, had held office in Antioch in the 370s. Postumianus' regular citation of Thucydides and Herodotus reached the ears of the aging Libanius in Antioch (Lib., *Ep.* 181.5).

Also reaching Libanius from Rome was news of the successful reception of a new history by a local Antiochene named Ammianus Marcellinus, a former soldier whose history was written in Rome in installments in the 380s and early

390s. Not long after, the history also reached Jerome in Bethlehem (Rohrbacher 2006), perhaps secured at his request by friends at Rome. Ammianus was certainly sensitive to the demands of his audience (14.6.2, 16.7.8, 28.1.15, 31.5.10), and in modern times, his *Res Gestae* is considered one of the great works of its era. It continued the history of Tacitus from C.E. 96 but is extant only for the period from 353 to 378 and includes several dramatic firsthand descriptions of the author's participation in civil wars, as well as conflicts with the Persians and Goths. Recent research on his history (Matthews 1989; Barnes 1998; Sabbah 2003) has focused on his personal and cultural background, the lost books, sources, his religious views (particularly on Christianity), and how his literary artistry illumines his viewpoint (Kelly 2008). Ammianus' education at least included familiarity with Thucydides, Herodotus, Polybius, and Sallust. He also made good use of Libanius and Julian, Aurelius Victor, Eutropius, and Festus, whom he may have encountered at Antioch. Compared with his literary bulk, their relative brevity had to be defended (15.1.1), and he often draws on the historians in discussing the comparative fortunes of past and present (17.1.4, 23.4.21, 25.9.8–9, 26.6.18, 30.4.6–8, 31.5.9).

Ammianus was particularly critical of the tastes of the Roman aristocrats of his day because of their preference for sensational biography (14.6.18; 28.4.14–15). This was precisely the time when some clever Roman teacher produced the *Historia Augusta*, a series of imperial lives from Hadrian to 285, purporting to have been written by several different people in the late-third to early-fourth century (Birley 2003). The author justified any blemishes by noting that Sallust, Livy, and Tacitus had all made mistakes in their histories (*HA*, Aurel. 2). Otherwise, the inclination to history was diminishing, except for the four books of Sulpicius Alexander, who was possibly a friend of Symmachus (*Ep.* 1.107). Sulpicius' history may have continued that of Ammianus to its terminus in 392. By the turn of the fifth century, Nicomachus Flavianus, the Theodosian historian's son, was still having manuscripts of Livy copied (Hedrick 2000, 177–190), while around the same time an unknown author produced the so-called *Epitome de Caesaribus* (Festy 2002), which began where Livy left off, as Aurelius Victor had done. Its author sprang from a Roman senatorial milieu and continued to 395 with a series of individual imperial profiles, but without ever mentioning Christianity.

Jerome's generation witnessed the conversion of the senatorial elite to Christianity from the 390s, including men like Nummius Aemilianus Dexter, proconsul of Asia under Theodosius in the 380s, the very office held by Eutropius and Festus during the previous reign, and Meropius Pontius Paulinus, governor of Campania in 381. Dexter was a zealous Christian who befriended Jerome and wrote a "multifaceted history" (*de vir. ill.* 132); Paulinus had been another of the pupils of Ausonius at Bordeaux but shocked his teacher and fellow senators by converting to an ascetic Christian life. He had come under the influence of the bishop Ambrose at Milan in the mid-380s, as had many other young aristocrats and aspiring courtiers, including the African friends

Alypius and Augustine. Paulinus (*Ep.* 28.5) tells us he was never keen on history, despite Jerome's repeating to him the recommendation he must already have received from Ausonius: that is, the best examples of histories are Thucydides, Sallust, Herodotus, and Livy (Jerome, *Ep.* 68.2). In fact, Jerome introduced many young students to Sallust and Livy (Rufinus, *Apology* 28) and presumed well-educated adolescents would read works such as Aemilius Asper's commentary on Sallust (Jerome, *In Rufinum* 1.16). Now a Christian, the learned Paulinus could no longer ignore history.

Historical reading and understanding were rapidly changing and expanding for these narrowly educated circles, while new Christian modes of presenting the past were being tried. In 395, Paulinus (*Ep.* 3.3) wrote to Alypius, who had met Jerome in Palestine, saying he had arranged to send him a copy of Jerome's chronicle, while a few years later (403), he was asked by his fellow student of Ausonius, Sulpicius Severus, about points of universal history. Paulinus thought it best to refer Sulpicius' queries instead to Rufinus from the mercantile city of Aquileia. A friend (now adversary) of Jerome and his former fellow student at Rome, Rufinus had recently returned to Italy after several years in Egypt and Palestine, following the monastic life that Jerome had now adopted for himself. Both Rufinus and Sulpicius understood that their Christian commitment involved reinterpreting and explaining the past and its meaning. Accordingly, in 400 Rufinus set about translating Eusebius' *Church History* into Latin but adding two extra books to cover the period from 325 to the death of Theodosius in 395 (Inglebert 1996, 324–350; Amidon, 1997; Rohrbacher 2002, 93–107; Ferguson 2005, 81–124; Humphries 2008). Eusebius' history may have been continued by a later bishop of Caesarea, Gelasius (van Deun 2003, 152–160), but Rufinus' translation took the opportunity to update, correct, and amplify Eusebius as required. His continuation also provided a consolidated account of the development of the Christian community in the West in the fourth century.

Rufinus' history was commissioned by the bishop Chromatius of Aquileia against a background of threatening Gothic raids in the neighborhood. As customary, it was read aloud to the local audience (Ruf., *HE* prol.). Sulpicius' *Sacred History* or *Chronicle* appeared not long after Rufinus' history (c. 403) and provided an innovative and independent attempt to turn the history and chronology of the Old Testament into a coherent summary narrative in the Roman tradition (Inglebert 1996, 365–386; De Senneville-Grave 1999). The author claims to be responding to popular demand for such a work and remains conscious of the need for brevity and accuracy. He carries his story through to recent times (383), with the latter part focused on what was, in effect, church history. However, Sulpicius envisaged his work as merely a supplement to the Scriptures, not a replacement, and as designed for a very wide audience, not just his learned friends. By now, Augustine was bishop of Hippo and beginning to formulate an educational program for Christians to complement their rhetorical training. It involved reading and memorizing the Scriptures and understanding the chronology of the period from Genesis to 2 Chronicles and of the time of Christ (*On Christian Teaching* 2.27). "History," says Augustine, "is of the greatest assistance in interpreting the holy books, even if learnt outside the church as part of primary education" (2.105), because it "relates past events in a faithful and useful way" (2.109), just as Sulpicius Severus was doing.

Making Historiographical Sense of the Barbarian Irruption, 410–500

A couple of decades later, the usefulness of Augustine's own historical knowledge was required to explain the meaning of the disruption to Roman life and government caused by the movement of the Alans, Vandals, and Suevi across the Rhine and into Gaul in 405–406. The Goths who were menacing northern Italy when Rufinus was writing his *Church History* had now reached Rome and in 410 captured the city. Debate sprang up about the association between Rome's recent fate and the adoption of Christianity by the imperial court, with Augustine undertaking a systematic attack on the whole argument in the early books of his monumental *City of God*. History was central to Augustine's elaborate analysis. He drew on Livy and Sallust in particular to contradict the claim that Rome had not suffered such misfortunes when it subscribed to its traditional deities and rituals, and he used the chronicle of Eusebius from time to time.

With the first three books of the *City of God* complete by 414, Augustine encountered a Spanish priest, Orosius, who had come to Africa preoccupied with contemporary concerns about defining the nature of divine grace and human free will, whereupon he set off for Palestine to meet Jerome, armed with a commendation from Augustine. Besides active public engagement with the disputed theological issues, they doubtless spent much time discussing the aftermath of the Goths in Rome, which had immediately astounded Jerome in Bethlehem. On calling in Hippo on his way back to Spain, Orosius was invited by Augustine to deepen the historical case he had developed in the *City of God*. By 416–417, Orosius had completed his *History against the Pagans* (Inglebert 1996, 507–592; Rohrbacher 2002, 135–149). Using the histories familiar to all educated Romans, he provided a clear and continuous account focused on highlighting the disasters inflicted on Rome before "Christian times" and contrasting them with the milder pattern of misfortunes under Christian emperors. Distress and destruction were now less (Orosius, 3.20), civil wars were milder than before Christ (5.22), and the sack of Rome was comparatively restrained (7.39). He wove together the notion of Christianity as marking the advent of a temporal universality, with the "Augustan peace" making way for the birth of Christ, as well as a geographical universality (Merrills 2005, 35–99). Orosius went further than Augustine and others in proposing that, as Christians, the

Goths were the agents for spreading the Christian message beyond the boundaries of the Roman empire. Their historical role, as reflected in subsequent historiography, was not as alien and hostile nations to be excluded from any account of Rome's past. Rather, they were increasingly influential and integral to it. Beside Jerome's translation of the *Chronicle* of Eusebius, Orosius' was to prove the most influential work of Latin historiography in Late Antiquity. In addition to more than 200 manuscripts of the original history, in the ninth century it was still available in Constantinople, as well as in translations as diverse as Anglo-Saxon and Arabic.

At the same time as Augustine and Orosius were setting in perspective the Gothic sack of Rome, Prosper was beginning to deal with the same issue following his expulsion by the Goths from Aquitaine to Marseilles in about 406 (Muhlberger 1990, 48–135; Humphries 1996). Like Ausonius, Sulpicius Severus, and Paulinus of Nola, Prosper had enjoyed the full literary and rhetorical education available at Bordeaux and elsewhere. Like Severus and Paulinus at least, he also acquired solid learning in the Christian Scriptures and histories. He was a correspondent of Augustine, a productive theologian, and later an official of Pope Leo I. Among his literary works was his *Chronicle*, first written in 433 and later updated several times by its author. While the chronicle was a continuation of Jerome, in Prosper's own simplified version, its content reflected a significantly different culture, pressed by the double anxiety over the occupation of Roman territory by alien groups and stubbornly different interpretations of the Christian tradition. It is clear that his chronicle was itself later updated anonymously in many places, but at the same time other such works were being produced in Gaul, such as the so-called *Chronicle of 452*, whose author is unknown but also from Marseilles (Muhlberger 1990, 136–192; Burgess 2001a).

Another of the continuators of Jerome was Hydatius from northwest Spain, who, like Orosius, had traveled as a young boy with his mother to meet Jerome in Palestine and may also have known Prosper. His *Chronicle* from 379 to 468 was focused on the impact of successive nations and armies on Spain and Gaul; attention devoted to a range of portents and natural disasters gives the work an apocalyptic flavor (Muhlberger 1990, 193–266; Burgess 1993). An educated aristocrat with literary ability such as Sidonius, son-in-law of the emperor Avitus, prefect of Rome in 468, and later bishop of Clermont, always possessed the potential to produce a substantial history. Indeed, he once commenced writing a history of the war with Attila in Gaul in the early 450s but was overwhelmed by the magnitude of the subject and terminated his efforts. He never even managed to read a first installment to a willing audience (Sid., *Ep.* 8.15.1–2). Around the same time, there appeared the history of Renatus Profuturus Frigeridus, which may have continued that of Sulpicius Alexander. It was in at least twelve books and terminated about 455. Thereafter, the only extant historiographical text is the so-called *Gallic Chronicle of 511* (Burgess 2001b), which continued Jerome and made use of Orosius, Hydatius, and the *Gallic Chronicle of 452*. Into the late fifth century, the Roman schools of Gaul continued to provide the conventional grammatical and rhetorical education that underpinned the reading and writing of history, but the production of narrative histories had virtually ended in the West, except for Italy. This was not the case in the East, especially at Constantinople.

Continuity and Christian History in the East, 395–500

The emperor Valens' successor Theodosius I had a special interest in finding out about the deeds of his ancestors (*Epit.* 48.11), which gave rise to Nicomachus Flavianus' *Annales* and Theodosius' advice to his son Honorius to study and learn from Greek and Roman history (Claudian, *IV cons.Hon.* 395–418). It was from the reign of Theodosius that Constantinople became the focus of higher education, literary activity, and public careers for what was now a Christian majority. As provincials flocked to imperial service, the increasingly Greek senatorial aristocracy and imperial bureaucracy expanded. Their education was secured by the establishment of sufficient teachers of Greek and Latin grammar and rhetoric in the city. Works of history were listened to, read, exchanged, and shared. In addition, capital and court bestowed patronage of power and belief. The city grew rich and secure. It also developed into a vibrant center of theological discussion and urban monasticism. The now foremost imperial capital gave shape and centrality to a well-established Christian imperial identity, which was quickly reflected in historical narrative. Almost every known historian writing in Greek from the beginning of the fifth century to the mid-seventh was a highly educated lawyer or rhetorician who, if not educated in Constantinople, at least wrote his history and found his first audience there (cf. Treadgold 2007, 380–381). Such was the cultural and historiographical dominance of the city.

In the reign of Theodosius' son Arcadius (395–408), a Christian sophist, Helikonios, produced a (now lost) history from Adam to Theodosius I (Janiszewski 2006, 411–415; Treadgold 2007, 48–49), and a pagan sophist, Eunapius from Sardis (Blockley 1981, 1–26; 1983, 1–150; Baldini 1984; Liebeschuetz 2003, 177–201; Treadgold 2007, 81–89), wrote a work (now fragmentary) continuing that of Dexippus, although berating him for indulging in the Christian preoccupation with chronology by asking, "For what do dates contribute to the wisdom of Socrates or the acuity of Themistocles?" (Frag. 1). The history appeared in two separate versions covering events to 404, the latter recast as less anti-Christian than the former, but their dates are disputed. Eunapius saw the point of a history like his as demonstrating how to "gain experience of old age while still young so that we know what is to be avoided and what sought after" (Frag.1). What was to be avoided was Christianity, hence his hostility to Constantine and

Theodosius I, and what was to be sought after was a restoration of the ideals of the emperor Julian. Although his history was first read to his close cultural circle, he was conscious that a much wider audience enjoyed the stories, even if they failed to appreciate the high style (frag. 66).

Like Eunapius, Olympiodorus also studied philosophy at Athens before arriving at the court of the young Theodosius II (408–450) via his native Egypt (Blockley 1981, 27–47; 1983, 152–220; Liebeschuetz 2003, 201–206; Baldini 2004; Treadgold 2007, 89–96). He worked in close liaison with western courtiers and even helped the father of Theodosius' future bride Eudocia obtain a chair of philosophy at Athens. As an envoy, Olympiodorus journeyed to the Huns in 412 and to the Blemmyes in 419, as well as to Italy in 424 to help install the emperor Valentinian III. His detailed history covering eighteen years in twenty-two books would have been designed for a familiar audience of courtiers and imperial officials at Constantinople. Christianity seems to have found no place in it, although Christian ritual was now fully integrated into court and civic life in the imperial capital, while the imperial church was increasingly focused on affirming right belief and stamping out unapproved variations, such as that promoted by the local patriarch Nestorius in 428.

These theological contests were soon manifested historiographically, as successive historians sought to retell the story of the church from Eusebius' day to their own, using all the historical materials available. Olympiodorus' history was first exploited by Philostorgius (Marasco 2003, 257–284; Ferguson 2005, 125–164; Treadgold 2007, 126–134; Amidon 2007), and they were probably known to each other in that Philostorgius had been in Constantinople since the reign of Theodosius I, following a rhetorical, philosophical, and medical education, all of which are evident in his history. In the 430s, he wrote a partially preserved *Church History* that continued Eusebius but from the Arian and Eunomian viewpoint. Consequently, he attributed the disasters of the early fifth century not to pagans or to Goths and Huns but to the anti-Arian policies of the imperial court. Another large and amorphous (but lost) history written at the same time was the *Christian History* of Philip of Side (Heyden 2006).

Not long after, a local scholar named Socrates produced his *Church History* in continuation of Eusebius to 439, which has been the object of substantial recent research (Leppin 1996; 2003; Wallraff 1997; Urbainczyk 1997; Bäbler and Nesselrath 2001; Rohrbacher 2002; Van Nuffelen 2004; Treadgold 2007, 134–145). Socrates used Rufinus' *Church History*, which helped reinforce the theological tradition in which he was writing, even though he subsequently had to correct some of the information he took from Rufinus. While Eusebius was writing before and during the reign of the first Christian emperor, by the 440s in Constantinople, the Christian story inevitably required adaptation to a community in which imperial, conciliar, and local episcopal authority loomed large. Based on what he had seen or heard (*HE* 6, praef), Socrates sought to explain the connection between the fortunes of both church and state under the watchful eye of divine providence. Accordingly, he emphasized the importance of studying classical literature (3.16) and wrote for a wide audience. His history was evidently read out at Constantinople, as were other histories (Urbainczyk 1997, 64–67). Before long, and covering almost the same scope, appeared the *Church History* of Sozomen, a much younger person from Palestine but a longtime resident in Constantinople (Leppin 1996; 2003; Rohrbacher 2002; Van Nuffelen 2004; Treadgold 2007, 145–155). The history is replete with documents, and he is more overtly polemical than Socrates. Sozomen dedicated his history to the emperor Theodosius II.

Finally, Theodoret's *Church History* in five books was designed to fill gaps left by Socrates and Sozomen (Theod., *HE*, praef.) and to argue the case for the see of Antioch and the theology of its local community, now under threat from Alexandria and Constantinople (Leppin 1996; 2003; A. Martin 2006–2009). He received the traditional education in Greek, complemented by Christian instruction from his mother and neighboring Syrian monks. Although Theodoret was neither a lawyer nor Constantinopolitan but a bishop of provincial Cyrrhus, he was drawn into the intense theological politics of the court. His history makes extensive use of documents at key points to support his case, but he is careful about overburdening his audience (*HE*, 1.2, 4.18, 5.21). In sum, the church historians of the 420s to 440s suggest that the same circles were listening to and reading both Eunapius and Socrates (Croke 2010), except that the new church historians were also of interest to the educated clergy.

The argument of the Theodosian church historians, where the emperor is portrayed as deriving power from God reinforced by miracles (cf. Brown 1992; 134–135), was countered by a treasury lawyer at Constantinople, Zosimus, either now or possibly closer to 500. In his incomplete *New History*, meaning new interpretation of history, Zosimus sought to trace the decline of Rome over a fifty-three-year period, just as Polybius had traced its rise (Paschoud 1971–1989; 2006; Liebeschuetz 2003, 206–215; Treadgold 2007, 107–114). Harnessing Eunapius and Olympiodorus to his cause, he was particularly hostile to Constantine and Theodosius I, the two heroes of the church historians. Monarchy was not the fertile soil that enabled Rome to grow and flourish, as the Christian tradition had come to believe. Instead, it was the source of maladministration leading to the political incoherence and barbarian incursions that diminished Roman authority and hegemony (Zos., *NH* 1.5.2–3, 2.38.1, 3.1.1, 4.29.1, 4.33.3, 4.59.2).

Through the following reigns of Marcian (451–457) and Leo I (457–474), no known histories appeared until that of Priscus from Panion in 474–475 (Blockley 1981, 48–70; 1983, 222–400; 2003, 293–312; Rohrbacher 2002, 82–92; Treadgold 2007, 96–102). Priscus wrote up the period from the 430s to the 460s in eight books in which, like Olympiodorus, he played a periodic role himself in embassies to the Huns in 448–489 and to Isauria (450),

Rome (450), Egypt (453), and Georgia (c. 471). Like Eunapius and Olympiodorus, as well as the church historians Philostorgius, Socrates, and Sozomen, Priscus was probably a lawyer and even wrote rhetorical exercises. Only extracts of his history remain, but they are sufficient to show his close knowledge of Thucydides and his capacity to rival any ancient historian by his firsthand account of an embassy to the court of the Hun king Attila (frag. 11). Priscus was perhaps continued by Malchus (Blockley 1981, 71–83; 1983, 402–462; 2003, 293–312; Treadgold 2007, 103–107), a rhetor from Philadelphia whose detailed *Byzantine History* appeared in the 490s, covering the period from the city's foundation in 330 until the reign of Zeno (474–491). Next was Candidus (Blockley 1983, 464–473; 2003, 312–313; Roberto 2000; Treadgold 2007, 103–104), an Isaurian whose history may have been a corrective to that of Malchus by casting the Isaurian emperor Zeno in a positive light. Then otherwise unknown histories entitled *Isaurika* were written by the philosopher Pamprepius in the 470s and by Capito early in the sixth century. Capito also translated Eutropius' *Breviarium* into Greek, although the impetus for another translation of such a straightforward work is hard to explain.

Conflict within the Christian communities intensified in the reigns of Zeno and Anastasius (491–518) before it was partly resolved by Justin I (518–527). The need to explicate the orthodoxy of belief and action through the events and personalities of these years gave rise to different ecclesiastical histories (Whitby 2003, 459–472; Treadgold 2007, 167–175). At an early age, Gelasius of Cyzicus sought to clinch an argument with Monophysites by writing a history in Constantinople of the Council of Nicaea in three books using a copy of the acts of the council he read at his father's house (Marasco 2003, 284–287). He was followed by two Monophysites close to the court of Anastasius—Zachariah from Gaza and John Diacrinomenos. The former, a lawyer in the imperial capital but later bishop at Mitylene, wrote his history at the request of the imperial chamberlain Eupraxius (Whitby 2003, 459–466; Blaudeau 2006, 589–618); the latter covered the period from the first council of Ephesus in 431 to about 515. Neither history has survived, except that an abridged version of Zachariah was incorporated into a Syriac church history written in the late 560s that consciously revised Socrates and Theodoret before continuing from where they terminated (Greatrex 2006).

Not long after, perhaps in response, Theodore Lector at Hagia Sophia in Constantinople compiled a condensed summary account (partly extant) of Socrates, Sozomen, and Theodoret in four books (Whitby 2003, 467–472; Blaudeau 2006, 619–654; Treadgold 2007, 169–174). He had been prompted to it while exiled in Gangra with the former patriarch Macedonius. After 518, he wrote his own history from the 440s to the reign of Justin. Another Chalcedonian, Basil the Cilician, wrote from 450 to about 540 in three books (lost) at Antioch, replete with episcopal letters. Each of these church histories reflected the theology and religious identity of the writer's church community.

The Spreading of Christian Historiography: Syriac and Armenian

The Persian siege of Amida in 502 was the subject of the first known history in Syriac, which goes under the name of Joshua and is titled *A Historical Narrative of the Distress which occurred in Edessa, Amida, and All Mesopotamia* (Trombley and Watt 2000). It is basically a history of the period 502 to 506, focused on the war with Persia and its consequences for Edessa "so that when they read and see what happened to us they may guard against our sins and escape our punishments." The influence of Herodotus and Thucydides is discernible in Joshua's account (Watt 1999). Indeed, by the later fifth century, a fine Greek education could also be obtained at bilingual Edessa in Mesopotamia, where Syriac was the medium for many Christian texts. They learned their history from Eusebius, whose *Church History* had been translated into Syriac by the mid-fourth century, with the *Chronicle* translated not long after. Joshua's history was probably written by a leading official in Edessa at the request of a local abbot, Sergius. A more systematic program of instruction in Christian Scripture and tradition had emerged at Edessa but now mainly at Nisibis. Educated speakers of Syriac were spread throughout Roman Mesopotamia and Persia. Their historiographical productions included the *Chronicle of Edessa* in the 540s and the controversial "Chronicle of Arbela," essentially a series of short biographies of successive bishops of the city to 544, many of whom had spent time at the Nisibis school.

A similar experience was felt by the Armenian community when they converted to Christianity in the early to mid-fourth century. Conversion eventually brought them an alphabet and a literate language for the first time, created by a demand for Armenian versions of Christian texts in Greek and Syriac. Armenian students were educated in Antioch and Constantinople, where they were exposed to classical grammar and rhetoric, including the Greek historians, as well as at Edessa and Nisibis. The Armenian civilian and military aristocracy functioned in Greek and Syriac, which were also key languages of the Persian court, where so many Armenians were located or conducted business. The late antique Armenian historians succeeded in translating both the Greek and emerging Christian historiographical traditions into a very different cultural idiom.

The first Armenian historian was a man of classical culture named Agathangelos, whose work survives in a fifth-century redaction (Thomson 1974). It provided a model for Armenian history writing and was dedicated to the Armenian king Tiridates III, who "has ordered me to narrate not a false account of his brave deeds, but what really happened in the battles, the plundering of provinces, the capture of towns, the struggles of men for renown or revenge." The history also covered "how the teaching of the Gospel came to be honored in

Armenia, by the king and then by all his subjects." Agathangelos sees his history as "a chronicle in the literary style of the Greeks," so that it is based on "what we ourselves saw and heard," echoing a classical motif. The history of Agathangelos was continued from Tiridates to 387, when Armenia was divided into separate Roman and Persian spheres of influence, by the so-called *Epic Histories* attributed to Faustus and written in the 470s (Garsoïan 1989). They combined a narrative of the increasingly Christian Armenian court and nobility with the heroic deeds of bishops and holy men.

Renewed Persian insistence on Zoroastrian fire worship in Armenia gave rise to a major revolt in 450, which forms the core of the historical accounts of Lazar of Parpec'i (c. 500) and Elishe. Lazar, a contemporary of Malchus of Philadelphia, had studied literature and philosophy at Constantinople, where he was doubtless exposed to classical historians and the new church historians. His history was commissioned by Vahan, leader of the Mamikonian family; is organized by the successive reigns of Persian monarchs; and was read to his audience (Thomson 1991). Lazar consciously indicates the amount of reading that underpins his narrative, especially the care required in dealing with oral sources. Documents and speeches abound in his clear and vivid account. Elishe, by contrast, writing in the early mid-sixth century, focuses on similar events but employs a more overt biblical tone and language (Thomson 1982). He dedicated his work to David Mamikonian, who commissioned it, and it was written to be read aloud to its audience (Thomson 1982, 105, 191).

Reading and Writing History at Constantinople, 500–600

By the turn of the sixth century, there was no longer an emperor in the West, although the Gothic king Theodoric at Ravenna had established a royal court and culture. Historians were still read and copied by those with the means and leisure. Caesar's *Gallic War*, for instance, was being studied by Flavius Licerius Firminus Lupicinus, a nephew of bishop Ennodius of Pavia. Among Theodoric's chief courtiers was Cassiodorus, who in 519 wrote a *Chronicle* occasioned by the consulship of the king's son-in-law Eutharic. The chronicle largely copies and condenses entries from the *Chronicle* of Prosper and an anonymous continuation but carefully excludes those of hagiographical or ecclesiastical content. Sometimes he rewrites Prosper to reslant the story in favor of the Goths (s. a. 382, 402, 410, 427, 451). Theodoric later persuaded Cassiodorus to produce a history of the Goths in which he would make "Roman history of the origins of the Goths" (Cass., *Var.* 9.25), an obscure phrase ensuring its character and content remain contested (Momigliano 1966; Goffart 1988, 21–42; Croke 2003, 361–367). Another lost work from around the same time was the seven-book

Roman History of Symmachus, consul in 485 and great-grandson of the famous orator. Symmachus enjoyed the same literary and rhetorical education as his forebears and was a renowned philosopher and orator in his own day. His history has been the subject of protracted but unproductive speculation (Croke 1983b; Zecchini 1993; Festy 2003).

Both Ennodius and Symmachus had spent time at Constantinople on royal service. Cassiodorus, too, lived there in the 540s. There they would have been exposed to a wide range of historical works and encountered a large Latin-speaking community, not only Italians but also Africans and Illyrians. Constantinople was where Jerome had composed his chronicle, and in 518–519 it was continued from 379 to 518 by an Illyrian named Marcellinus who was close to the court of the new Illyrian emperor Justin and his nephew Justinian. It was then updated for the emperor Justinian (527–565) in 534 (Croke 1995; 2001a; Treadgold 2007, 227–234). Marcellinus' chronicle, which was known to Cassiodorus, concentrated on events at Constantinople and the East, as well as the successive invasions of Goths, Huns, and Bulgars into the Balkans and how Roman armies dealt with them. His outlook is decidedly Illyrian and orthodox and suggests that he was writing for an immediate audience of local Illyrians in Constantinople. Within a generation or two, the chronicle was being used in Italy and Ireland, then Britain. Meanwhile, other summary histories based on Christian chronology were being written elsewhere. Eustathius of Epiphaneia produced two books, the first reaching from Adam to the fall of Troy and the second from there to the Persian siege of Amida in 502–503, where death interrupted him (Brodka 2006; Treadgold 2007, 114–120, with reservations). It was possibly something similar in scale and structure to the chronicle of Sulpicius Severus. It was first used by John Malalas, a local imperial official in nearby Antioch in the late 520s to early 530s (Jeffreys 1986; 1990 et al.; 2003 et al.; Beaucamp et al. 2004; Agusta-Boularot et al. 2006; and, with reservations, Treadgold 2007, 235–255). His eighteen-book world chronicle began with creation and continued to his own day, both reflecting local Antiochene traditions and perspectives and incorporating his own distinctive blend of classical and Christian history. Indeed, it provides a valuable insight into how classical and Near Eastern history was viewed in Justinian's reign.

At Antioch, Malalas may have met Procopius, secretary of the Roman general Belisarius as he set out on his campaigns against the Persians in 528 and remained in the East until 531. Procopius will already have been compiling notes with a view to writing a history of the Persian war. In 533, he found himself accompanying Belisarius to Africa to wrest authority from the Vandals and from 535 to 540 was by the general's side fighting the Gothic regime in Italy. Around 550, Procopius produced his substantial history of all three campaigns, marking himself as one of the greatest of classical historians. He devoted two books each to the Persian and Vandal wars and three to the Gothic war, with another book covering all three fronts published around 553 or 554. Recent research has focused on whether the historian's own political and religious views can be discerned in the text of the history, and whether Procopius is to be characterized as an orthodox Christian or a Platonist (Cameron 1985; Kaldellis 2004; Brodka 2004, 14–151; Whitby 2007). Also relevant to his perspective is determining when and how he wrote his histories and how they relate to his two other works, the *Secret History* and the *Buildings* (Cataudella 2003, 391–415; Greatrex 2003; Croke 2005b; Kaldellis 2009). Procopius was educated in his native Caesarea and possibly also at the flourishing sixth-century schools in Gaza. His history displays classical literary dimensions, such as speeches and digressions, but also reflects the contemporary Christian culture in which its writer lived and worked.

Well known to Procopius was Peter the Patrician, a distinguished lawyer and diplomat, who wrote a Roman history covering the period from Julius Caesar to the emperor Julian, plus a detailed account of his embassies to and from the Persian court in the 550s and 560s (Cataudella 2003, 431–441; Treadgold 2007, 264–269). His contemporary, Hesychius, another Constantinopolitan lawyer from an eminent family in Miletus, wrote both a summary world history and another detailed one from 518 into the reign of Justinian (Kaldellis 2005; Treadgold 2007, 270–278). Only fragments of these works still survive. Their ready audience consisted of men like John the Lydian and other literary-minded imperial officials in the capital whose identity embraced Christian and classical culture. To judge by John, they were familiar with a wide range of historians, including Thucydides, Diodorus, Arrian, and Cassius Dio, in addition to Julius Caesar and Sallust, and Aemilius Asper's commentary, which Jerome had recommended (*de mag.* 3.8.4). The only late antique historians cited by John are Eusebius, Aurelius Victor, and Eutropius, but he would have been well equipped to prosecute Justinian's unfulfilled invitation to write up the Persian war in 530 (*de mag.* 3.28.5).

Also at Constantinople, at precisely the time Procopius' first books appeared in 550–551, two other Latin works were commissioned and produced by Jordanes, former secretary to a Roman general of Gothic background (Goffart 1988, 20–111; 2006, 56–72; Christensen 2002; Croke 2003, 367–375; 2005a; Merrills 2005, 100–169). He was working on his *Romana* when interrupted by a certain Castalius to produce his *Getica*, making major use of the lost *Gothic History* of Cassiodorus. The extent of his use of Cassiodorus and the accuracy of his geography and Gothic genealogy are much debated. The *Romana* covered world history, derived from Jerome, and that of Rome from its foundation to 550. For this overview, Jordanes had to hand the few required texts, namely, Florus, Eutropius, Orosius, and Marcellinus. As with Marcellinus, a local audience could be found at Constantinople for the Latin chronicle of Victor of Tunnuna, an exiled African bishop (Placanica 1997; Cardelle de Hartmann 2002). Victor continued the chronicle of Prosper to 563, concentrating on ecclesiastical politics of the major patriarchates and, for more recent events, drawing on the *Church History* of Theodore Lector and his own experience. He probably knew the Spanish cleric John of Biclaro, who spent seventeen years in Constantinople and wrote a chronicle in 590 after he had returned to Spain (Wolf 1990, 61–80; Cardelle de Hartmann 2000, 121; 2001). Apparently continuing Victor's work, his chronicle balances East and West. John knew Greek, as well as his native Latin, and utilized memory and local informants.

The emperor Maurice (582–602) delighted in passing the evening hours in the palace with his history books and was prepared to offer financial inducement to potential historians (Menander, frag.1). One of them may have been a local official named Theophanes who, in the 580s, wrote a history in ten books from 567 to 577, but it had little impact, probably because it was superseded by two more substantial histories that covered the same ground, namely, those of Agathias and Menander, both locally educated lawyers. Agathias' five-book history was written in the early 580s and continued Procopius from 553–554 to 557–558, before being interrupted, probably by the historian's death (Cameron 1970; Kaldellis 1999; Brodka 2004, 152–192; Treadgold 2007, 279–290). The centerpiece of Menander's history, preserved only in extracts, was the negotiations and protocols for establishing peace with the Persian king (Blockley 1985; Whitby 1992, 39–45; Brodka 2007). Procopius, Agathias, and Menander encountered many educated Persians and learned about their history. Although Procopius took details of Persian history from envoys and others, he frequently distorted his sources in recounting them (Börm 2007). Agathias, however, claimed superior accuracy on the basis of information from his Syrian friend Sergius, who provided the historian with translated excerpts from the Persian royal annals (Cameron, 1969–1970, 112–113). These annals came to form part of the seventh-century Book of Lords ("Khwadaynamag") but are now accessible only through the opaque layers of later Arabic and Persian texts (Howard-Johnston 2010). Otherwise, late antique Sasanian historiography remains mainly a blank.

In the 590s, the Thucydidean tradition was continued by John of Epiphaneia, who, like most recent historians, studied law at Constantinople but settled in Antioch as an adviser to its archbishop Gregory. Later he met the Persian king Chosroes and took part in an embassy to Persia in 594, but his history of the Persian wars of the 570s and 580s is largely lost (Whitby 1992; Cataudella 2003, 439–441; Treadgold 2007, 308–310). John's cousin Evagrius, also from Epiphania and likewise an adviser to Gregory at Antioch (Allen 1981; Whitby 2000; 2003, 480–492; Blaudeau 2006, 655–696), and John of Ephesus, originally from Amida, took up writing ecclesiastical histories. The former continued Socrates with an orthodox perspective, but the latter retold the whole history of Christianity from his well-established Monophysite position. Both Evagrius and John of Ephesus used the chronicle of John Malalas, with the former also utilizing Zosimus, Priscus, Procopius, and other local historians, especially justifying to his audience the relevance of attacking the claims of Zosimus in a church history (Evagrius, *HE* 3.41).

Reading and Writing History under Christian Kings, 500–600

At Rome under Gothic rule in the 530s, Cassiodorus had unsuccessfully sought to raise funds to establish a Christian school of higher learning, like the one he had heard about in faraway Nisibis. By the 560s, with imperial authority restored in Italy, Cassiodorus had returned from Constantinople with a fuller knowledge of the Nisibis school. He was now settled in a monastery at coastal Vivarium, where he supported the education of his monks by compiling a guide to Christian literature in Latin, including history. It consisted of Josephus' *Antiquities of the Jews*, which he had translated, and his *Jewish War*, which formed a prelude to the church history of Eusebius. Both works had been translated by Rufinus, and the latter was continued by him. Reading these books, so Cassiodorus assured his monks, illustrates that the pagans were wrong. History is guided by the will of the Creator. Cassiodorus then goes on to recommend the church histories of Socrates, Sozomen, and Theodoret, which he had arranged to be combined and translated by Epiphanius as the so-called *Historia Tripartita*, along with Orosius, who brought together Christian and pagan times. In addition, there were the chronicles of Eusebius translated and continued by Jerome, followed by those of Marcellinus and Prosper and their unspecified continuators (*Inst.* 1. 17.1–2). Cassiodorus would have known Maximian, bishop of Ravenna, but he does not cite Maximian's lost chronicle (Agnellus, *Lib.Pont.*, 78) which may be partly preserved in the *Excerpta Valesiana*.

By the sixth century, imperial authority no longer extended to Gaul and Britain, Spain and Ireland, but the Cassiodoran historiographical model could now be found there. Reading and writing history was still the preserve of the best educated, but the best educated were now mainly bishops and monks, so classical rhetoric was de-emphasized (Brown 2003, 235). In Gaul, Gregory the bishop of Tours wrote a history in ten books covering the period from Adam to 594, focused on the period after the death of the king Sigibert in 575 and linked into a Christian chronology (Goffart 1988, 112–234; Heinzelmann 2001; Halsall 2007). Regularly resorting to oral sources, his history of kings and bishops was written for officials of the court of the Frankish king, as well as local clergy at Clermont and Tours, and was influenced by Gregory's need to deal with local apocalyptic concerns. Gregory was placing himself in the same tradition as Rufinus and Orosius, whom he used extensively. Meanwhile, the equally educated Marius, bishop of Avenches, chose the chronicle format to tell the story from 455 (end of Prosper) to the 580s (Favrod 1993). In Britain, the monk Gildas, although probably educated in Gaul, was able to acquire sufficient grammatical and rhetorical education to become familiar with not only Vergil but also Jerome, Sulpicius Severus, Rufinus, and Orosius, as displayed in his *de excidio*, in which he set out to persuade his educated audience of the shortcomings of their rulers (Croke 2003, 375–381).

In the newly Catholic kingdom of Visigothic Spain, Isidore, the bishop of Seville, educated in a monastery but to a high level, became a prolific writer. His chronicle (615), which ran from creation to the time of the emperor Heraclius and the Gothic king Sisebut, was built up from the established chronicles of Jerome, Prosper, Victor, and John of Biclaro (Wolf 1990, 81–110; J. C. Martin 2003; Merrills 2005, 170–228). It became a popular chronicle in subsequent centuries. Isidore also wrote histories of all the nations that had been settled in Spain for two centuries, namely, the Suevi, the Goths, and the Vandals. Finally, he produced an encyclopedic *Etymologiae* (c. 630) that expressed the unity of culture across an increasingly divergent set of "regional Christianities" (Brown 2003, 350). In explaining "history," Isidore used traditional Roman categories (borrowed from the grammarian Servius) to sum up the state of historiography as it had evolved in Late Antiquity: history is what is seen in the past and written down (*Etym.* 41); the first historian was Moses (42), as he was for Evagrius (*HE* 5.24); and the past can be described in three ways: diaries, annals (earlier years), and history (years in the author's lifetime). Chronicles were a separate matter (28).

Connections between Spain and Ireland were close and frequent, so Isidore's works quickly appeared there, as did literary texts from Constantinople, including Marcellinus' chronicle. This was facilitated by the trade routes linking the capital with the west country of England and southern Ireland (Hillgarth 1985), not to mention by occasional visitors to Constantinople, such as Isidore's brother Leander in the 580s. In England and Ireland, monastic culture was already flourishing by 565, when Columba set out to establish a new monastery on the isolated and bleak island of Iona, just off the coast of modern Scotland. At Iona, he had a copy of the chronicles of Jerome and Marcellinus, which formed the basis of a new *Irish Chronicle*, first compiled at Iona and later spread across many of the monasteries of Ireland, where it was expanded and updated, as chronicle manuscripts always were (Charles-Edwards 2006). So between the *Institutes* of Cassiodorus and the *Etymologiae* of Isidore, the basic shape of history reading and writing in the Latin West was set for a millennium (cf. McKitterick 2007, 15–16).

Consolidating Late Antique Historiography, 600–700

Imperial territory in the eastern provinces was being overrun in the early seventh century by the Persians in Mesopotamia and Asia Minor, as well as by the Avars and Slavs in the Balkans. The education and literary culture that had supported the classical tradition of historiography and its audience was contracting and in some places disappearing (cf. Meier 2004). However, at Constantinople, where the public provision for education in grammar and rhetoric continued, there was still an audience for a history like that of Theophylact Simocatta, written in the 630s and continuing that of Menander, nearly half a century later, until the death of Maurice in 602 (Whitby and Whitby 1986; Whitby 1988; Brodka 2004, 193–227; Treadgold 2007, 329–339). Theophylact had been educated to the highest level in literature, law, and philosophy at Alexandria, where such opportunity was still available. His history covered events in the Balkans and on the Persian frontier, but with its elaborate rhetorical style, it turned out to be the last of its genre. Theophylact's history was dedicated to the local patriarch Sergius, as was the so-called *Chronicon Paschale*, which ran from Adam to 630 (Whitby and Whitby 1989; Treadgold 2007, 340–348). Shortly before (or a century sooner, as argued by Mariev 2008), there appeared in Constantinople the history from Adam to 610 of John of Antioch (Roberto 2005; Treadgold 2007, 311–329). John knew the Latin historians and gave unusual space to the Roman republic, whose political freedom he saw as politically exemplary.

The swiftly spreading conquests of the Islamic armies from the 630s eventually raised the question of the Roman empire's place in the interpretation of Daniel and in Christian chronography, while on the shrinking imperial frontiers, the historiographical response was more active and creative. Young Armenians like Ananias of Shirak were still being educated in Constantinople, and even in Trebizond in the 640s, he could find a library full of histories and chronicles. Writing around the same time, the Armenian historian known as Sebeos (Thomson and Howard-Johnston 1999; Greenwood 2002) considered the Persian invasion, followed by that of the Arabs, as a divine punishment for sin (Ps-Sebeos, *Hist.* 47). Moreover, he revised Daniel's providential prophecy interpreting the "fourth beast" as signifying the Arab invasion (44), thereby accommodating Byzantine chronology to contemporary purposes. In producing a record of recent events, he saw himself as the successor of Lazar and Elishe but built on his Armenian predecessors by using classical elements such as speeches, dialogue, and documents, including an exchange of letters between the emperor Heraclius and the Persian king Chosroes (11, 38) and by highlighting eyewitness accounts (42).

There were many other Armenian historical works produced in the seventh century, such as the anonymous history from 572 to 655. Some can be traced in other texts, such as Moses Daskhurantsi's *History of Albania* (Howard-Johnston 2002), but most are lost. Of particular interest is the anonymous chronicle sometimes attributed to Ananias of Shirak. It appears to have been written in the late 680s and was based on an earlier Armenian translation of the chronicle of Annianos of Alexandria, who in 411–412 reworked the chronology of Eusebius' chronicle (Greenwood 2008). Similarly, Syriac chronicles, extant in anonymous and fragmentary form and linked to Syriac versions of Eusebius, began to proliferate (Palmer 1993): the so-called Melkite Chronicle from Adam to 641, the Chronicle of Thomas to 640, and the "Maronite Chronicle" after 664. Most important was Jacob of Edessa, a learned and prolific author whose *Chronicle* continued Eusebius from 325 to 692, including the addition of an extra column to the original Eusebian layout. This addition enabled the reader to connect within each Olympiad the years of Roman emperors, Persian monarchs, and, from 632, Muhammad and the successive "emperors" of Islam to his time of writing in 692 (Palmer 1993, 36–38).

As eastern centers of Hellenic and Christian culture were progressively captured and occupied by Persians and then Arabs, many naturally retreated to safety elsewhere. When Tarsus, for instance, was overtaken by the Persians in 614, a young local student, Theodore, was of an age to be introduced to Thucydides and Herodotus by a teacher of grammar. A few years later, he studied at Antioch and may also have been in Edessa. Certainly, he was well versed in Syriac literature and culture. Theodore's career was well established by 637, when Tarsus was captured by the Arabs, whereupon he fled to Constantinople, where he remained until the 660s, deepening his knowledge of historical and theological texts. Next he is found in Rome, living in a community of Greek and Syriac monastic refugees. To a scholarly knowledge of texts in Greek and Syriac, Theodore added Latin. In 669, despite his advanced years, he arrived in Canterbury as its new bishop, complete with his working library in Greek and Latin and presumably Syriac (Lapidge 1995).

The so-called *Laterculus Malalianus*, composed by Theodore at Canterbury, demonstrates his direct use of the *Chronographia* of John Malalas, which he probably had copied in Constantinople originally and brought to Britain (Stevenson 1995). Through Theodore's writing and teaching at Canterbury, in Greek as well as Latin and for both Anglo-Saxon and Irish students, it is evident that he had absorbed the established set of late antique historiographical texts available to scholars from Canterbury to Nisibis: Josephus' *Jewish War* translated by Rufinus and his *Antiquities* in the translation organized by Cassiodorus, Eusebius' *Chronicle* translated and continued by Jerome, his *Church History* translated and continued by Rufinus, Eutropius' *Breviarium* (which was available in the East in multiple Greek translations), and the *Historia Tripartita* of Theodore Lector, translated by Epiphanius, and Orosius.

This collection of texts, which covered all the required biblical and Roman history for any learned seventh-century Christian, Greek or Latin speaking, constituted Late Antiquity's narrow historiographical legacy to the medieval West and much of the East. It came to represent the history section of Bede's library at Jarrow, for example, and all Anglo-Saxon libraries (Lapidge 2006); it was also the pattern discernible through much of western Europe (McKitterick 2004, 39–50). At Constantinople, most classical and late antique histories written in Greek and probably known to Theodore were still readily available to Photius in the ninth century (Croke 2006) and well beyond. In a single lifetime, Theodore had traversed the entire late antique world, both geographically and culturally, from Mesopotamia to England. His life and work neatly encapsulate the cross-cultural coherence that defines late antique historiography as it developed from a source of rhetorical exempla, in a society where Christianity was marginal, into a more central literary activity that explained the story of human existence, in a society permeated by Christianity.

WORKS CITED

Adler, W. 1992. "Eusebius' Chronicle and Its Legacy." In *Eusebius, Christianity and Judaism*, ed. H. Attridge and G. Hata, 467–491. Leiden: Brill.

———. 2006. "Eusebius' Critique of Africanus." In *Julius Africanus und die christliche Weltchronik*, ed. M. Wallraff, 147–160. Berlin: Walter de Gruyter.

———. 2008. "Early Christian Historians and Historiography." In *The Oxford Handbook of Early Christian Studies*, ed. S. Ashbrook Harvey and D. G. Hunter, 584–602. Oxford: Oxford University Press.

Agusta-Boularot, S., J. Beaucamp, A.-M. Bernardi, and E. Caire. 2006. *Recherches sur la chronique de Jean Malalas*. Vol. 2. Paris: Association des Amis du Centre d'Histoire et Civilisation de Byzance.

Allen, P. 1981. *Evagrius Scholasticus: The Church Historian*. Louvain: Spicilegium Sacrum Lovaniense.

Amidon, P. 1997. *The Church History of Rufinus of Aquileia, Books 10 and 11*. Oxford: Oxford University Press.

———. 2007. *Philostorgius: Church History*. Atlanta: Society for Biblical Literature.

Bäbler, B., and H.-G. Nesselrath, eds. 2001. *Die Welt des Sokrates von Konstantinopel*. Munich: Saur.

Baldini, A. 1984. *Ricerche sulla Storia di Eunapio di Sardi*. Bologna: CLUEB.

———. 2000. *Storie perdute (III secolo d.C.)*. Bologna: Pàtron.

———. 2004. *Ricerche di tarda storiografia (da Olimpiodoro di Tebe)*. Bologna: Pàtron.

Barnes, T. D. 1981. *Constantine and Eusebius*. Cambridge, MA: Harvard University Press.

———. 1998. *Ammianus Marcellinus and the Representation of Historical Reality*. Ithaca, NY: Cornell University Press.

Beaucamp, J., S. Agusta-Boularot, A.-M. Bernardi, B. Cabouret, and E. Caire. 2004. *Recherches sur la chronique de Jean Malalas*. Vol. 1. Paris: Association des Amis du Centre d'Histoire et Civilisation de Byzance.

Bird, H. W. 1993. *Eutropius: Breviarium*. Liverpool: Liverpool University Press.

———. 1994. *Aurelius Victor: De Caesaribus*. Liverpool: Liverpool University Press.

Birley, A. 2003. "The Historia Augusta and Pagan Historiography." In *Greek and Roman Historiography in Late Antiquity*, ed. G. Marasco, 127–150. Leiden: Brill.

Blaudeau, P. 2006. *Alexandrie et Constantinople (451–491): De l'histoire à la gloire de l'église*. Rome: École française de Rome.

Bleckmann, B. 1992. *Die Reichskrise des III. Jahrhunderts in der spätantiken und byzantinischen Geschichtsschreibung*. Munich: Tuduv.

Blockley, R. 1981. *The Fragmentary Classicising Historians of the Later Roman Empire*. Vol. 1. Leeds: Francis Cairns.

———. 1983. *The Fragmentary Classicising Historians of the Later Roman Empire*. Vol. 2. Leeds: Francis Cairns.
———. 1985. *The History of Menander the Guardsman*. Leeds: Francis Cairns.
———. 2003. "The Development of Greek Historiography: Priscus, Malchus, Candidus." In *Greek and Roman Historiography in Late Antiquity*, ed. G. Marasco, 289–316. Leiden: Brill.
Börm, H. 2007. *Prokop und die Perser: Untersuchungen zu den römisch-sasanidischen Kontakten in der ausgehenden Spätantike*. Stuttgart: Steiner.
Bowersock, G. 2001. "Recapturing the Past in Late Antiquity," *Mediterraneo Antico* 4: 1–15.
Brodka, D. 2004. *Die Geschichtsphilosopie in der spätantiken Historiographie: Studien zu Prokop von Kaisareia, Agathias von Myrina und Theophylaktos Simokattes*. Bern: Peter Lang.
———. 2006. "Eustathios von Epiphaneia und das Ende des Weströmischen Reiches," *JÖB* 56: 59–78.
———. 2007. "Zum Geschichtsverständnis der Menander Protektor." In *Continuity and Change: Studies in Late Antique Historiography*, ed. D. Brodka and M. Stachura, 95–104. Crakow: Jagiellonian University Press.
Brown, P. 1992. *Power and Persuasion in Late Antiquity: Towards a Christian Empire*. Madison: University of Wisconsin Press.
———. 2003. *The Rise of Western Christendom*, 2nd ed. Oxford: Blackwell.
Burgess, R. W. 1993. *The Chronicle of Hydatius and the Consularia Constantinopolitana: Two Contemporary Accounts of the Final Years of the Roman Empire*. Oxford: Oxford University Press.
———. 1995. "Jerome and the Kaisergeschichte," *Historia* 44: 349–369.
———. 1997. "The Dates and Editions of Eusebius' *Chronici canones* and *Historia Ecclesiastica*," *Journal of Theological Studies* 48: 471–504.
———. 1998. "Jerome's *Chronici canones*, Quellenforschung, and Fourth-Century Historiography." In *Historiae Augustae Colloquium Argentoratense: Atti dei Convegni sulla Historia Augusta VI*, ed. G. Bonamente, F. Heim, and J.-P. Callu, 83–104. Bari: Edipuglia.
———. 2001a. "The Gallic Chronicle of 452: A New Critical Edition with a Brief Introduction." In *Society and Culture in Late Antique Gaul: Revisiting the Sources*, ed. R. W. Mathisen and D. Shanzer, 52–84. London: Ashgate.
———. 2001b. "The Gallic Chronicle of 511: A New Critical Edition with a Brief Introduction." In *Society and Culture in Late Antique Gaul: Revisiting the Sources*, ed. R. W. Mathisen and D. Shanzer, 85–100. London: Ashgate.
———. 2001c. "Eutropius *v.c. Magister memoriae?*" *CPh* 96: 76–81.
———. 2002. "Jerome Explained: An Introduction to His Chronicle and Guide to Its Use," *Ancient History Bulletin* 16: 1–32.
———. 2005. "A Common Source for Jerome, Eutropius, Festus, Ammianus, and the *Epitome de Caesaribus* between 358 and 378, along with Further Thoughts on the Date and Nature of the *Kaisergeschichte*," *CPh* 100: 166–192.
———. 2006. "Apologetic and Chronography: The Antecedents of Julius Africanus." In *Julius Africanus und die christliche Weltchronik*, ed. M. Wallraff, 17–44. Berlin: Walter de Gruyter.
Burgess, R. W., and W. Witakowski. 1999. *Studies in Eusebian and Post-Eusebian Chronology*. Stuttgart: Steiner.
Cameron, Averil. 1969–1970. "Agathias on the Sasanians," *DOP* 23–24: 69–183.

———. 1970. *Agathias*. Oxford: Oxford University Press.
———. 1985. *Procopius*. London: Duckworth.
———. 1999. "Remaking the Past." In *Late Antiquity: A Guide to the Postclassical World*, ed. G. Bowersock, P. Brown, and O. Grabar, 1–20. Cambridge, MA: Belknap.
Cardelle de Hartmann, C. 2000. "Historie und Chronographie: Entstehung und Frühzeit Lateinischer Chronistik," *Minerva* 14: 107–127.
———. 2001. *Victoris Tunnunensis Chronicum cum reliquiis ex Consularibus Caesaraugustanis et Iohannis Biclarensis Chronicon*. Turnhout: Brepols.
Carriker, A. 2003. *The Library of Eusebius of Caesarea*. Leiden: Brill.
Cataudella, M. R. 2003. "Historiography in the East." In *Greek and Roman Historiography in Late Antiquity: Fourth to Sixth Century A.D.*, ed. G. Marasco, 391–448. Leiden: Brill.
Charles-Edwards, T. M. 2006. *The Chronicle of Ireland*. Translated Texts for Historians 44. Liverpool: Liverpool University Press.
Christensen, A. 2002. *Cassiodorus, Jordanes and the History of the Goths: Studies in a Migration Myth*. Copenhagen: Museum Tusculanum Press.
Croke, B. 1983a. "The Origins of the Christian World Chronicle." In *History and Historians in Late Antiquity*, ed. B. Croke and A. M. Emmett, 116–131. Oxford: Pergamon. (Reprinted in B. Croke. 1992. *Christian Chronicles and Byzantine History*. London: Ashgate)
———. 1983b. "AD 476: The Manufacture of a Turning Point," *Chiron* 13: 81–119. (Reprinted in B. Croke. 1992. *Christian Chronicles and Byzantine History*. London: Ashgate)
———. 1992. *Christian Chronicles and Byzantine History*. London: Ashgate.
———. 1995. *The Chronicle of Marcellinus*. Sydney: Australian Association for Byzantine Studies.
———. 2001a. *Count Marcellinus and His Chronicle*. Oxford: Oxford University Press.
———. 2001b. "Chronicles, Annals and 'Consular Annals' in Late Antiquity," *Chiron* 31: 291–331.
———. 2003. "Latin Historiography in the Barbarian Kingdoms." In *Greek and Roman Historiography in Late Antiquity: Fourth to Sixth Century A.D.*, ed. G. Marasco, 349–389. Leiden: Brill.
———. 2005a. "Jordanes and the Immediate Past," *Historia* 53: 473–494.
———. 2005b. "Procopius' *Secret History*: Rethinking the Date," *GRBS* 45: 405–432.
———. 2006. "Tradition and Originality in Photius' Historical Reading." In *Byzantine Narrative*, ed. J. Burke et al., 59–70. Melbourne: Australian Association for Byzantine Studies.
———. 2007. "Late Antique Historiography, 250–650 CE." In *A Companion to Greek and Roman Historiography*, ed. J. Marincola, 567–581. Oxford: Blackwell.
———. 2010. "Uncovering Byzantium's Historiographical Audience." In *Byzantine History as Literature*, ed. R. Macrides, 25–53. London: Ashgate.
Croke, B., and A. M. Emmett. 1983. "Historiography in Late Antiquity." In *History and Historians in Late Antiquity*, ed. B. Croke and A. M. Emmett, 1–12. Oxford: Pergamon.
De Senneville-Grave, G. 1999. *Sulpice Sévère: Chroniques*. Paris: Éditions du Cerf.
Den Boer, W. 1972. *Some Minor Roman Historians*. Leiden: Brill.
Digeser, E. D. 2000. *The Making of a Christian Empire: Lactantius and Rome*. Ithaca, NY: Cornell University Press.

Favrod, J. 1993. *La Chronique de Marius d'Avenches*. Lausanne: Université de Lausanne.
Ferguson, T. C. 2005. *The Past Is Prologue: The Revolution of Nicene Historiography*. Leiden: Brill.
Festy, M. 2002. *Pseudo-Aurélius Victor, Abrégé des Césars*. Paris: Les Belles Lettres.
———. 2003. "De l'*Epitome de Caesaribus* à la *Chronique* de Marcellin: l'*Historia Romana* de Symmaque le Jeune," *Historia* 52: 251–254.
Garsoïan, N. 1989. *The Epic Histories*. Harvard Armenian Texts and Studies 8. Cambridge, MA: Harvard University Press.
Goffart, W. 1988. *The Narrators of Barbarian History*. Princeton, NJ: Princeton University Press.
———. 2006. *Barbarian Tides: The Migration Age and the Later Roman Empire*. Philadelphia: University of Pennsylvania Press.
Grafton, A., and M. Williams. 2006. *Christianity and the Transformation of the Book*. Cambridge, MA: Harvard University Press.
Greatrex, G. 2001. "Lawyers and Historians in Late Antiquity." In *Law, Society and Authority in Late Antiquity*, ed. R. W. Mathisen, 148–161. Oxford: Oxford University Press.
———. 2003. "Recent Work on Procopius and the Composition of *Wars* VIII," *Byzantine and Modern Greek Studies* 27: 45–67.
———. 2006. "Pseudo-Zachariah of Mitylene: The Context and Nature of His Work," *Journal of the Canadian Society for Syriac Studies* 6: 39–52.
Greenwood, T. 2002. "Sasanian Echoes and Apocalyptic Expectations: A Re-Evaluation of the Armenian History Attributed to Sebeos," *Le Muséon* 115: 323–397.
———. 2008. "'New Light from the East': Chronography and Ecclesiastical History through a Late Seventh-Century Armenian Source," *JECS* 16: 197–254.
Halsall, G. 2007. "The Preface to Book V of Gregory of Tours' *Histories*: Its Form, Context and Significance," *EHR* 122: 297–317.
Hedrick Jr., C. W. 2000. *History and Silence: Purge and Rehabilitation of Memory in Late Antiquity*. Austin: University of Texas Press.
Heinzelmann, M. 2001. *Gregory of Tours: History and Society in the Sixth Century*. Cambridge: Cambridge University Press.
Heyden, K. 2006. "Die Christliche Geschichte des Philippos von Side mit einem kommentierten Katalog der Fragmente." In *Julius Africanus und die christliche Weltchronistik*, ed. M. Wallraff, 209–243. Berlin: Walter de Gruyter.
Hillgarth, J. 1985. *Visigothic Spain, Byzantium and the Irish*. London: Ashgate.
Howard-Johnston, J. D. 2002. "Armenian Historians of Heraclius: An Examination of the Aims, Sources and Working Methods of Sebeos and Mouses Daskhurantsi." In *The Reign of Heraclius (610–641): Crisis and Confrontation*, ed. G. Reinink and B. Stolte, 41–62. Louvain: Peeters.
———. 2010. *Witnesses to a World Crisis: Historians and Histories of the Middle East in the Seventh Century*. Oxford: Oxford University Press.
Humphries, M. 1996. "Chronicle and Chronology: Prosper of Aquitaine, His Methods and the Development of Early Medieval Chronography," *Early Medieval Europe* 5: 155–175.
———. 2008. "Rufinus' Eusebius: Translation, Continuation, and Edition in the Latin *Ecclesiastical History*," *JECS* 16: 143–164.
Inglebert, H. 1996. *Les Romains chrétiens face à l'histoire de Rome*. Paris: Institut d'Etudes Augustiniennes.
———. 2001a. *Interpretatio Christiana: Les mutations des savoirs (cosmographie, géographie, ethnographie, histoire) dans l'Antiquité chrétienne (30–630 après J.-C.)*. Paris: Institut d'Etudes Augustiniennes.

———. 2001b. "Le développement de l'historiographie chrétienne dans le monde méditerranéen (IIe–VIIe siècles de notre ère)," *Mediterraneo Antico* 4: 559–584.
Janiszewski, P. 2006. *The Missing Link: Greek Pagan Historiography in the Second Half of the Third Century and in the Fourth Century AD*. The Journal of Juristic Papyrology Supplement 6. Warsaw: University of Warsaw.
Jeanjean, B., and B. Lançon. 2004. *Saint Jérôme Chronique*. Rennes: Presses Universitaires de Rennes.
Jeffreys, E. 2003. "The Beginning of Byzantine Chronography: John Malalas." In *Greek and Roman Historiography in Late Antiquity*, ed. G. Marasco, 497–527. Leiden: Brill.
Jeffreys, E., B. Croke, and R. Scott, eds. 1990. *Studies in John Malalas*. Sydney: Australian Association for Byzantine Studies.
Jeffreys, E., M. Jeffreys, and R. Scott. 1986. *The Chronicle of John Malalas*. Melbourne: Australian Association for Byzantine Studies.
Kaldellis, A. 1999. "The Historical and Religious Views of Agathias: A Reinterpretation," *Byzantion* 69: 206–252.
———. 2004. *Procopius of Caesarea: Tyranny, History and Philosophy at the End of Antiquity*. Philadelphia: University of Pennsylvania Press.
———. 2005. "Hesychios the Illoustrios of Miletos," *GRBS* 45: 381–403.
———. 2009. "The Date and Structure of Prokopios' *Secret History* and His Projected Work on Church History," *GRBS* 49: 585–616.
Kelly, G. 2008. *Ammianus Marcellinus: The Allusive Historian*. Cambridge: Cambridge University Press.
Kofsky, A. 2000. *Eusebius of Caesarea against Paganism*. Leiden: Brill.
Lapidge, M. 2006. *The Anglo-Saxon Library*. Oxford: Oxford University Press.
———, ed. 1995. *Archbishop Theodore: Commemorative Studies on His Life and Influence*. Cambridge: Cambridge University Press.
Leppin, H. 1996. *Von Constantin dem Großen zu Theodosius II: Das christliche Kaisertum bei den Kirchenhistorikern Socrates, Sozomenus und Theodoret*. Göttingen: Vandenhoeck & Ruprecht.
———. 2003. "The Church Historians (I): Socrates, Sozomenus and Theodoretus." In *Greek and Roman Historiography in Late Antiquity*, ed. G. Marasco, 219–254. Leiden: Brill.
Liebeschuetz, W. 2003. "Pagan Historiography and the Decline of the Empire." In *Greek and Roman Historiography in Late Antiquity*, ed. G. Marasco, 177–218. Leiden: Brill.
Marasco, G. 2003. "The Church Historians (II): Philostorgius and Gelasius of Cyzicus." In *Greek and Roman Historiography in Late Antiquity*, ed. G. Marasco, 257–288. Leiden: Brill.
———, ed. 2003. *Greek and Roman Historiography in Late Antiquity*. Leiden: Brill.
Maraval, P. 2004–2007. *Socrate de Constantinople: Histoire Ecclésiastique*. 4 vols. Paris: Éditions du Cerf.
Mariev, S. 2008. *Ioannis Antiocheni fragmenta quae supersunt*. Corpus Fontium Historiae Byzantinae 47. Berlin: Walter de Gruyter.
Martin, A. 2006–2009. *Théodoret de Cyr: Histoire Ecclésiastique*. 2 vols. Paris: Éditions du Cerf.
Martin, G. 2006. *Dexipp von Athen: Edition, Übersetzung und begleitende Studien*. Classica Monacensia 32. Tübingen: G. Narr.
Martin, J. C. 2003. *Isidori Hispalensis Chronica*. Turnhout: Brepols.

Matthews, J. 1989. *The Roman Empire of Ammianus*. London: Duckworth.
McKitterick, R. 2004. *History and Memory in the Carolingian World*. Cambridge: Cambridge University Press.
———. 2007. "The Migration of Ideas in the Early Middle Ages." In *Foundations of Learning: The Transfer of Encyclopaedic Knowledge in the Early Middle Ages*, ed. R. H. Bremmer and K. Dekker, 1–18. Leuven: Peeters.
Meier, M. 2004. "Prokop, Agathias, die Pest und das 'Ende' der antiken Historiographie: Naturkatastrophen und Geschichtsschreibung in der ausgehenden Spätantike," *Historische Zeitschrift* 278: 281–310.
Merrills, A. H. 2005. *History and Geography in Late Antiquity*. Cambridge: Cambridge University Press.
Momigliano, A. 1963. "Pagan and Christian Historiography in the Fourth Century A.D." In *The Conflict between Paganism and Christianity in the Fourth Century*, ed. A. Momigliano, 79–99. Oxford: Clarendon.
———. 1966. "Cassiodorus and Italian Culture of His Time." In *Studies in Historiography*, 181–210. London: Harper and Row.
———. 1969. "L'età del trapasso fra storiografia antica e storiografia medievale (320–550 d.C.)," *Rivista Storica Italiana* 81: 286–303.
———. 1990. *The Classical Foundations of Modern Historiography*. Berkeley: University of California Press.
Mosshammer, A. 1979. *The Chronicle of Eusebius and Greek Chronographic Tradition*. Lewisburg, PA: Bucknell University Press.
Muhlberger, S. 1990. *The Fifth Century Chroniclers*. Leeds: Francis Cairns.
Palmer, A. 1993. *The Seventh Century in the West Syrian Chronicles*. Translated Texts for Historians 15. Liverpool: Liverpool University Press.
Paschoud, F. 1971–1989. *Zosime: Histoire Nouvelle*. 3 vols. Paris: Les Belles Lettres.
———. 2006. *Eunape, Olympiodore, Zosime: Scripta Minora*. Bari: Edipuglia.
Placanica, A. 1997. *Vittore da Tunnuna, Chronica: Chiesa e impero nell'età di Giustiniano*. Florence: Edizioni di Galluzzo.
Ratti, S. 1996. *Les Empereurs romains d'Auguste à Dioclétien dans le "Bréviaire" d'Eutrope: Les livres 7 à 9 du "Bréviaire" d'Eutrope*. Paris: Les Belles Lettres.
———. 2003. "L'historiographie latine tardive, IIIe–IVe siècle: État des recherches 1987–2002," *Pallas* 63: 209–232.
———. 2007. "Nicomaque Flavien senior auteur de l'Histoire Auguste." In *Historiae Augustae Colloquium Bambergense*, ed. G. Bonamente and H. Brandt, 305–317. Bari: Edipuglia.
Roberto, U. 2000. "Sulla tradizione storiografica di Candido Isaurico," *Mediterraneo Antico* 3: 685–727.
———. 2005. *Ioannis Antiocheni Fragmenta ex Historia chronica*. Berlin: Walter de Gruyter.
Rohrbacher, D. 2002. *The Historians of Late Antiquity*. London: Routledge.
———. 2006. "Jerome, an Early Reader of Ammianus Marcellinus," *Latomus* 65: 422–424.
Sabbah, G. 1983–2008. *Sozomène: Histoire Ecclésiastique*. 4 vols. Paris: Éditions du Cerf.
———. 2003. "Ammianus Marcellinus." In *Greek and Roman Historiography in Late Antiquity*, ed. G. Marasco, 43–84. Leiden: Brill.
Salzman, M. 1990. *On Roman Time: The Chronographer of 354*. Berkeley: University of California Press.

Simmons, M. 1995. *Arnobius of Sicca: Religious Conflict and Competition in the Age of Diocletian*. Oxford: Oxford University Press.
Stevenson, J. 1995. *The* Laterculus Malalianus *and the School of Archbishop Theodore*. Cambridge: Cambridge University Press.
Thomson, R. W. 1974. *Agathangelos: History of the Armenians*. Albany: State University of New York Press.
———. 1982. *Elishe: History of Vardan and the Armenian War*. Cambridge, MA: Harvard University Press.
———. 1991. *The History of Lazar P'arpec'i*. Atlanta: Scholars Press.
Thomson, R. W., and J. Howard-Johnston. 1999. *The Armenian History Attributed to Sebeos*. Liverpool: Liverpool University Press.
Thurn, H. 2000. *Ioannis Malalae Chronographia*. Berlin: Walter de Gruyter.
Treadgold, W. 2007. *The Early Byzantine Historians*. London: Palgrave.
Trombley, F. R., and J. W. Watt. 2000. *The Chronicle of Pseudo-Joshua the Stylite*. Liverpool: Liverpool University Press.
Urbainczyk, T. 1997. *Socrates of Constantinople: Historian of Church and State*. Ann Arbor: University of Michigan Press.
Van Deun, P. 2003. "The Church Historians after Eusebius." In *Greek and Roman Historiography in Late Antiquity*, ed. G. Marasco, 151–176. Leiden: Brill.
Van Nuffelen, P. 2004. *Un héritage de paix et de piété: Étude sur les histoires ecclésiastiques de Socrate et de Sozomène*. Leuven: Peeters.
Wallraff, M. 1997. *Der Kirchenhistoriker Sokrates: Untersuchungen zu Geschichtsdarstellung, Methode und Person*. Göttingen: Vandenhoeck and Ruprecht.
Watt, J. 1999. "Greek Historiography and the 'Chronicle' of Joshua the Stylite." In *After Bardaisan*, ed. G. J. Reinink and J. A. Klugkist, 317–327. Louvain: Peeters.
Whitby, Michael. 1988. *The Emperor Maurice and His Historian*. Oxford: Oxford University Press.
———. 1992. "Greek Historical Writing after Procopius: Variety and Vitality." In *The Byzantine and Early Islamic Near East, I: Problems in the Literary Source Material*, ed. Averil Cameron and L. Conrad, 25–80. Princeton, NJ: Princeton University Press.
———. 2000. *The Ecclesiastical History of Evagrius Scholasticus*. Liverpool: Liverpool University Press.
———. 2003. "The Church Historians and Chalcedon." In *Greek and Roman Historiography in Late Antiquity*, ed. G. Marasco, 449–495. Leiden: Brill.
———. 2007. "Religious Views of Procopius and Agathias." In *Continuity and Change: Studies in Late Antique Historiography*, ed. D. Brodka and M. Stachura, 73–94. Crakow: Jagiellonian University Press.
Whitby, Michael, and Mary Whitby. 1986. *The History of Theophylact Simocatta*. Oxford: Oxford University Press.
———. 1989. *Chronicon Paschale 284–628 AD*. Liverpool: Liverpool University Press.
Williams, M. H. 2006. *The Monk and the Book: Jerome and the Making of Christian Scholarship*. Chicago: Chicago University Press.
Wolf, K. 1990. *Conquerors and Chroniclers of Early Medieval Spain*. Liverpool: Liverpool University Press.
Woods, D. 2009. "Late Antique Historiography: A Brief History of Time." In *A Companion to Late Antiquity*, ed. P. Rousseau, 357–371. London: Wiley-Blackwell.
Zecchini, G. 1993. *Ricerche di storiografia latina tardoantica*. Rome: L'Erma di Bretschneider.

CHAPTER 13

HELLENISM AND ITS DISCONTENTS

AARON P. JOHNSON
Lee University

In the earlier years of Late Antiquity, a second-century orator from Smyrna speaking at Athens heralded the force and vibrancy with which Greek (in particular Atticizing) culture had come to conquer his world.[1] The early Greeks "so divided the land [of the Mediterranean world] among them and settled upon it, extending the measure of Hellas to some other mark, as it were, until they had filled the whole basin. Even now, at both ends of our world there dwell children of your [Attica's] children, for some have moved all the way to Gades from Massalia, while others have taken possession of allotments along the Tanais and the lake [Maeotis]" (Aristides, *Or.* 1, *Panath.*, 65–66 Behr).[2] The claims of Aelius Aristides (117–181 C.E.) here echo those made nearly five hundred years before by Isocrates (436–338 B.C.E.; Said 2001; Hall 2002, 172–228).[3] The classical orator had similarly exuberant claims for Greekness and had set about looking for a powerful leader to incise politically and militarily his Hellenocentric vision of cultural superiority onto the broader landscape of the known world. The ideal leader would be one who could transform peoples who had sunk into the slough of barbarism to become philhellenes adopting civic structures, martial virtues, and *paideia*.[4] In Philip of Macedon, and then Alexander, he seems to have found his man. Indeed, Isocrates (had he lived long enough) might well have agreed with Droysen's celebrated claim that the name of Alexander spelled the end of one period of world history and the beginning of another.[5] Alexander was romantically remembered as having slept with a copy of the *Iliad* underneath his pillow as he led Greek culture into exotic and barbarian lands at the head of a

Greco-Macedonian army, following the footsteps of Dionysus and Heracles as far as India (Plutarch, *V.Alex.* 26; Arrian, *Anabasis* 6.28; Julian, *Ad Themist.* 253c).[6] For his part, Aristides was less certain about the importance of Alexander: under the Athenian flagship, the Greeks had been civilizing the world with their *logos* and *paideia* long before the Macedonian kings with their questionably Greek pedigree came on the larger Mediterranean scene (Aristides, *Or.* 1, *Panath.*, 314–316, 331–335 Behr).[7]

Even in the face of such blue-blooded detractors of Macedonian rule, Alexander seems to carry off the prize as the greatest contributor to the process known by modern historians as Hellenism (Jüthner 1923; cf. Julian, *Symp.* 25.323d). Most important, however, is the enduring, if misleading, picture of this process that such ancient rhetoric leaves us: a unified force of Greek cultural superiority was the active vanquisher of weak eastern cultures who passively yielded to the advance of Greek rationality, piety, and beauty. Behind the oratorical fanfare, one can also hear the murmur of historians and philosophers who carefully codified native traditions, histories, and ancestral wisdom within a hegemonic Greek conceptual framework. Withering under the panoptic gaze of a Hellenocentric vision, barbarian knowledge survived in the reformulations of Greek historians, geographers, and philosophers, from the Hellenistic successor dynasties through the period of Roman domination of the eastern Mediterranean.[8] What historians often name an *interpretatio Graeca* thus seems to have embalmed the decrepit remains of barbarian peoples within a Greek cultural museum.[9]

Yet there are other, potentially more fruitful ways of telling the story, especially since problems with the uncritical adoption of the picture sketched here have been recognized with greater clarity in recent decades. Most fundamentally, the historiographic model of a clash of monolithic cultures fails to do justice to the complexity of the ancient sources, as well as being inadequate in general for any analysis of cultural conflict—and indeed, a conflict model itself may be insufficient (Bowersock 1987; Frankfurter 2000). Hellenism as either a colossal cultural force obliterating native cultures or a flimsy veneer overlaying older and deeper cultures (Baynes 1946, 24–25), to be worn away at varying speeds over time, lacks the analytical nuance requisite for a more robust account of the diverse tendencies and tensions expressed variously in the ways of thinking and living in the eastern Mediterranean between the times of the eastward conquest of Alexander (fourth century B.C.E.) and the westward conquest of the Arabs (seventh century C.E.; Gruen 1998; 1984, 1.250–272; Levine 1998, 3–32). Furthermore, the description of cultures as active or passive occludes the complexities of ancient cultural engagements, where multiple nodes of contestation were fraught with varying levels of significance at various times and with varying degrees of intensity by a host of often quite different cultural actors (Frankfurter 2000). This situation even complicates notions of cultural fusion (Millar 1983; Woolf 1994) and the recently popular notion of cultural hybridity (Bhabha 1994; Schott 2008). A more productive framework requires an assessment of how ancient authors conceptualized their world and the identities of the peoples inhabiting that world over the *longue durée* of Hellenism, from the times of the Greco-Macedonian dynasties to the Byzantine period (Kaldellis 2007, 7).

We might start by seeing Hellenism as forming a sort of rhetorical and conceptual toolbox (to use a metaphor at once Themistean and Wittgensteinian) from which the educated could draw in building their own visions of who they and others were.[10] Together with Aristides, the literati (*pepaideumenoi*) of Late Antiquity could employ a wide range of tools from the collections of Greek texts at their disposal to construct philosophical arguments, deliver speeches, write histories or biographies, compose novels, draft chronologies, appreciate visual representations, and (among Christian sophists) craft apologetic treatises or heresiological compendia. The tools that these thinkers might wield at any point in their activity of building (or repair) included at the most basic level the use of the Greek language (Lechner 1954, 11–12; Casevitz 1991). More interesting is the range of other tools, however, which were used with more or less artistry depending on any builder's previous apprenticeship (to continue our metaphor) and the constraints of the particular situation. Such tools included the citation of or allusion to classical authors (Aerts 2003); mythological exempla; genealogies; ethnographic topoi; the literary or rhetorical structuring of an oratorical or other piece; the varied elements of religious cult, doctrine, or iconography; the invocation of historical figures or events; personal dress or grooming (Dio Chrys., *Borysth.*, Or. 36.16–17; Julian, *Misopogon* 338bc, passim; Vout 2006); and, at the most basic level, generic conceptual categories for classifying the world (*genos*, *ethnos*, and so on; A. P. Johnson 2006b, 25–54). No one tool was essential for this toolbox; rather, Hellenism was an aggregate of potentially useful tools for negotiating identity, proving a point, or ostentatious display. What unites them is that they are all (though this point could be debated) attributable to a Greek identity, or Hellenicity, by the ancient authors who used them.

This last point is crucial since an individual in an eastern province of the later Roman empire might speak Greek, employ an erudite classicizing (even Atticizing) style when writing, incorporate anthropomorphic imagery adopted from classical Greek artistic models within one's religious practices, consider one's Syrian or Egyptian neighbor with the disdain built upon "barbarian" stereotypes introduced in earlier Greek literature, and have a mosaic of Dionysus or Heracles installed in a main room of one's house—all this, and yet one need not identify oneself or one's behavior as Greek. As with any toolbox, we must be wary of too readily limiting the possible edifices or monuments for which variously trained builders might use its tools. Indeed, we should even be prepared to find some builders renaming the tools or claiming that many of those in Hellenism's box did not belong there at all. In the second century, for instance, the biographer of Hadrian, Philo of Byblos in Phoenicia (64–141 C.E.), had scathingly criticized the Greeks for theft of what he claimed were native Phoenician goods.

> But the Greeks, surpassing all in genius, appropriated most of the earliest stories, and then variously decked them out with ornaments of tragic phrase and adorned them in every way, with the purpose of charming by the pleasant fables. Hence Hesiod and the celebrated Cyclic poets framed their own Theogonies, Gigantomachies, Titanomachies, and castrations; and making adaptations to them, they conquered and drove out the truth. (Philo ap. Eus., *PE* 1.10.40)[11]

The accusation that the Greeks had stolen their tools from the toolboxes of other, older nations was not uncommon in the period following the conquests of Alexander and later Pompey, though it occurs already in Herodotus (e.g., Herod. 2.43–45, 143–146). If we do likewise and attempt to determine what isolable elements were originally Greek and what were originally Phoenician, Egyptian, and so on, and then proceed to trace the ways in which those Greek elements influenced other cultures in a process of Hellenization that followed close upon military advancement, we will no doubt make interesting and politically important claims (see Most 2008). But it will remain unclear how such an approach will help us appreciate the variety of uses to which the ancient claims themselves could be put.

It is, therefore, more helpful to locate the ways in which ancient sources sought to describe Greeks, their practices, and their past in sometimes carefully crafted and rhetorically powerful constructions of Greek identity. These acts of identity construction and manipulation were at once rooted *both* in discourses of great durability and sluggish conservatism *and* within the shifting constraints of social, economic, and political situations. We must attend, therefore, to the rhetorical contours of the identities under construction and the scope and valences of the textually articulated visions of Hellenism and Hellenicity produced in the pages of Late Antiquity's philosophers, orators, poets, and preachers (Hall 1997, 17–66; A. P. Johnson 2006b, 25–33; Kaldellis 2007, 6–8). Ours cannot be a history of culture in any grand or monolithic sense, but a history of perception, of identification (Bowie 1991, 182; J. Bouffartigue, 1991, 252). How did late antique thinkers use the term *Hellēnismos*? Who was perceived as being a Greek (*Hellēn*)? What processes were presumed under the label *hellēnizein*?[12]

Hellenism and Hellenicity between Porphyry and the Christians

When we read a narrative from the later end of Late Antiquity, the *Record of the Miracles of Saints Cyrus and John* by Sophronius (c. 560–638), the bishop of Jerusalem who lived to see the Arab invasion of Palestine, we see the tools in Hellenism's toolbox being put to rather different uses than those of Aristides and his peers. We might at first be tempted to see Sophronius' Hellenism in his adoption of the Greek language—and indeed the verb *hellēnizein* originally carried this sense (Casevitz 1991)—or we might see his composition of poems in anacreontic meter as exhibiting Hellenism, in the sense of the performance of Greek literary *paideia*. Yet, his own explicit identifications in the *Narratio* of what he saw as Greekness hardly involved language or literary form; instead, they emphasized traditional "pagan" cult activity.[13] Agapius the Greek, we are told, not only dealt in silver but "openly Hellenized, even reverencing statues, and 'worshiping the creation instead of the Creator' (Rom. 1:25)" (*Narratio* 32.2–4 Fernández Marcos). He attempted to pass himself off as a Christian to obtain healing from Cyrus and John, who had been martyred in Alexandria during the Great Persecution (c. 304). The two saints were unimpressed by his covert hypocrisy and duly allowed a daemon to lacerate him severely and eventually choke him to death after leaving their shrine. For Sophronius, dire consequences were thus attendant on Agapius' Hellenizing tendencies. Hellenism and Christianity are here discursively construed as mutually exclusive categories. For Sophronius and other late antique Christians, like his friend John Moschos, the identities were simple and directly religious postures: "Are you a Christian or a Greek?" (*Pratum spirituale* 136 [PG 87.3.3000B]; Jüthner 1923, 99; Ševčenko 1980, 63). While we may congratulate ourselves on knowing better than these late antique Christians, having long recognized and developed grand narratives for ourselves of the Hellenization of Christianity (Jüthner 1923; Jaeger 1969), such accounts ought not muffle the voices from Late Antiquity whose identifications of themselves and others might differ from ours.

Sophronius reports another miracle involving "Theodore," who was also labeled a Greek: snorting derisively after Holy Communion, the impious Theodore was struck with a blindness that was only cured by divine grace after three days. Those who saw or heard his outrageous bellow were naturally horrified, for the deed was "of a rank with Hellenic impiety" (*Narratio* 31.18–19 Fernández Marcos). As the saints declared in a dream, "everyone must keep their lives from all this sort of thing [snorting at church], since it is Hellenic and dear to the daemons" (*Narratio*, 31.43–44 Fernández Marcos). Sophronius' explanatory remark regarding the problematic nature of snorting at church is noteworthy:

> Porphyry says that the Greeks, when they are bringing their accursed sacrifices to the idols, snort violently with their noses, evincing such a noise by a violent inhalation and a force of wind (*pneuma*), they deem it a sacred hymn, so that the sacrificers have great fearlessness for this reason, and they compete in a great contest, [in order to see] who will beat the other in snorting; in order that the best might be named first, and become most pleasing to daemons. The very making of such noises has been established for the worship of daemons, compelling those emitting it to hymn inadvertently unclean daemons. (*Narratio*, 31.19–28 Fernández Marcos)

Both sacrifices and snorting, polytheism and impiety, were marks of Sophronius' literary portrayal of Hellenism. It is surely impressive that the seventh-century bishop invokes Porphyry of Tyre (c. 233–c. 305 C.E.), the great anti-Christian polemicist of the third century, since the latter is sometimes deemed one of the greatest defenders of Hellenism in antiquity.[14] Two points are, however, readily apparent: first, the relevant passage from Porphyry's *Philosophy from Oracles* (as we have it today) does not specifically mention snorting with one's nose, but rather burping and flatulence after eating meat (fr. 326 Smith; cf. Greg. Naz. *Or.* 5.41); second, he does not designate such behavior as Greek, as Sophronius would have it, though he does refer to Egyptian and Phoenician cultic practices, which serve to drive away the daemons—and this, without any report of ritualized snorting contests. The religion of various national groups had been renamed as Hellenic by the later bishop, not the pagan theologian. The invocation of Porphyry remains appropriate, however, since the exhalation of wind (or a spirit, *pneuma*) from any bodily orifice could, according to the philosopher, mark the presence of a daemon.

The connection of Porphyry to the Greeks and hence to Hellenism deserves further reflection.[15] Contrary to the prevailing opinion, which relies on the hostile testimony of later Christians, there is no solid basis for naming the Phoenician philosopher residing in Rome and Sicily during his literarily productive years a champion of Hellenism (whatever that might mean) or a claimant to Hellenicity;[16] on the contrary, there are clear expressions of a critical attitude toward the Greeks in some puzzlingly overlooked fragments. Though the Greeks were "most familiar" to Porphyry and his peers (*Abst.* 4.2.1), they based their ideas on conjectures (*Ep.Aneb.* 1 Sodano, p. 2.12–14), were constantly discordant toward each other (*Ep.Aneb.* 2 Sodano, p. 29.19–20), and had neglected true piety and wisdom (*Abst.* 4.18.4; *Phil.Orac.* fr. 324 Smith). The philosophical vision that Porphyry developed in his wide-ranging oeuvre marked itself off from Greek identity, even while being steeped in the Greek heritage. An author does not necessarily foster an Hellenocentric position merely because he exhibits scarcely any knowledge of a language other than Greek (Millar 1997), composed texts on the sources of the Nile (a quintessentially Greek ethnographic concern) and the prologue of Thucydides, commented on the poems of Homer and the dialogues of Plato, or carefully collected Apolline oracles (Smith 1993, L–LIII.). A recurrent phrase like "Greeks and barbarians" could vaguely carry the meaning "everyone" and scarcely conveyed the ethnocentric biases of earlier authors (cf. Jüthner 1923, 97; Lechner 1954, 12; Bouffartigue 1991, 256).

On the contrary, the elements, concerns, and emphases in Porphyry's corpus could be, and were, put to rather un-Hellenic uses. For instance, in speaking of the "road to the gods," which was neither smooth nor easily trod, he deftly manipulated what were presumably Greek elements in a manner deliberately dismissive of the Greek traditions (*Phil.Orac.*, fr. 324 Smith). While we may recognize the metaphor of the path to the gods as rooted in the Greek poetic tradition (particularly, Hesiod)[17] and note its occurrence in Porphyry's own corpus within an oracle given in solid hexameters (*Phil.Orac.*, fr. 323 Smith), the philosopher pried the metaphor loose from its Greek underpinnings and claimed that the road to the gods had been discovered by the ancient

Egyptians, Phoenicians, and Hebrews. Then comes a crucial claim: the path discovered by barbarians had only been muddled by the Greeks. Though we do not possess enough of the fragment to know the precise nature of his complaint, it seems clear that his vision of the world and its nations displaced the Greeks from the center of wisdom and dignity so boldly asserted by authors of the so-called Second Sophistic, among whom Aelius Aristides had held foremost place.

Porphyry, of course, did not reject the Greeks altogether, yet he passed over some potential features of Greek identity (e.g., Atticism), renamed others, and construed many in ways that were at once disruptive to the Hellenocentric visions articulated by earlier authors and constructive of visions that saw the centers of wisdom, piety, and theological astuteness to be scattered across the ethnic landscape of the East (among Egyptians, Jews, and especially the Indians; see *On the Styx*, fr. 376 Smith; cf. Numenius, *On the Good*, fr. 1a DesPlaces). "By Late Antiquity most of the leading exponents of Hellenism were orientals. Inheriting a tradition which once had professed respect for the wisdom of the Orient from a safe distance, they tipped the whole centre of gravity eastwards. . . . Hellenism, then, was held captive by those it had conquered" (Fowden 1983, 73, albeit not referencing Porphyry).[18] Discomfort with the ideologically loaded term *oriental* (Traina 2002) is not sufficient to detract from the perceptiveness of such a description. The ethnic modifier of the *interpretatio Graeca* was thrust aside as Phoenician, Egyptian, and other national knowledges were given consideration, if not priority, by philosophers of Late Antiquity. In the case of Porphyry, it seems more appropriate to name his interpretive program an *interpretatio philosophica* (rejecting any one ethnic modifier; Clark 1999). In his openness to eastern barbarian wisdom, Porphyry is startlingly similar to Christian apologists, like Origen, to whom he polemically assigned the sole instance of *hellēnizein* in his surviving corpus (*c.Christ.* fr. 39 Harnack), and even (or rather, especially) the two prolific defenders of the faith who are recognized as his foremost critics, Eusebius of Caesarea (c. 263–339) and Theodoret of Cyrrhus (c. 393–c. 457).

The two bishops had learned from Clement of Alexandria (c. 150–211), rather than from Porphyry, the effectiveness of locating the origins of various inventions and cultural advances among the forefathers of different barbarian nations in order to detract from Greek claims to cultural superiority (Clem., *Stromateis* 1.14, 16; Thraede 1962; Droge 1989; Ridings 1995). Yet, like their unwitting Phoenician ally, they expressed a vision of the world that severely decentered Greek cultural hegemony and forcefully curtailed the claims for an ancient Greek wisdom by showing the Greeks as younger than the more ancient nations, more fragmented by discord than the harmonious picture of other peoples, and less a source of civilizing advancement than the others.[19] Criticism of Porphyry was certainly part of both bishops' apologetic programs,[20] but a shared ethnographic vision and suspicion of Hellenocentrism exhibit the unexpectedly mutual ways in which the great anti-Christian and his detractors were reassessing and relabeling the discursive tools of the Greek tradition. Or to draw Theodoret's unkind parallel, Porphyry was like Balaam's ass inadvertently supporting the claims of truth (*Curatio* 3.65).[21]

The early apologetic tradition carried the marked distinction from Porphyry, however, in insisting on a simplified, yet powerful, threefold schema that contained, while not fully resisting, the diversification of the sort of ethnic and cultural vision he had articulated. "Christianity," the bishop of Caesarea claimed, "is neither Hellenism nor Judaism, but bears a certain character of worship of its own, and this is nothing new or strange but of the greatest antiquity" (*DE* 1.2.1; see A. P. Johnson 2006b, 218–232).[22] Hardly suspicious of metanarratives as such, Eusebius developed a world-historical vision that drew on more tools from the various Greek discourses than any apologist before (and possibly even after) him. His often densely periodic Greek prose played host to a polyphony of voices from the Greek camp in constructing a Greek identity that could be easily assailed by his truth-loving students. Within Eusebius' fifteen-book *Praeparatio Evangelica*, Homer could be criticized by a Greek philosopher (*PE* 2.7.4–7, citing Plato, *Rep.* 2.377e–378d), Orpheus could be shown as an Egyptianizing interloper by a Greek historian (*PE* 2.1.22–26, citing Diod. Sic. 1.23), the disharmony and *logomachia* of the Greeks could be expressed in the voices of later "Greek" philosophers (including Porphyry himself; *PE* 14–15, citing Numenius, Plutarch, Aristocles, and others), the Greek language could be seen as derivative of earlier barbarian languages (*PE* 10.5), ancient inhabitants of Greece could be depicted as travelers in search of a wisdom that could not be found at home, and so on (A. P. Johnson 2006b, 55–93, 126–152).[23]

A century after Eusebius, Theodoret of Cyrrhus created his own apologetic system that dismantled the narrative structure of his Caesarean predecessor while nonetheless heavily drawing on it (see his explicit claim to be abbreviating Eusebius' *Praeparatio* at *Curatio* 2.97). Eusebius' grand narrative of the place of the Greeks among the nations of ancient history was reformulated incisively in short, yet powerful, assaults against Greek claims to cultural superiority in Theodoret's *Cure for Greek Diseases* (or the *Curatio*).[24] Heavy concentration was placed on not only the place of the Greeks in the history of nations but also the relatively low place of Greek eloquence in the pursuit of truth (e.g., *Curatio* 1.26–31; Lechner 1954, 27–28). But all of this was reorganized within topical categories, from philosophical anthropology and psychology, to Providence and oracles (Books 5, 6 and 10, respectively). Throughout his work, Theodoret deftly reformulated Greek identity for polemical purposes and artfully placed a vast amount of historical, poetic, and philosophical material at critical points in his argument. In a passage reminiscent of the better-known claims in Basil's *Letter to Young Men*, Theodoret represents his activity as a doctor for the Greek disease and apologist for the Christian faith: just as those picking roses keep the flower and reject the thorns, and "bees go to both sweet and bitter flowers, yet get rid of the bitter qualities and produce from different qualities . . . the sweetest honey, we imitate them when we produce sweet honey for your benefit from your own bitter meadows" (*Curatio* 1.125–127).[25]

The single occurrence of *hellēnizein* in the *Curatio* is in the context of a critique of Greek idol worship.[26] "I am amazed at the shamelessness of those who now Hellenize; for, being ashamed that the world is [now] sensible and has turned from its former error, they say that the things said about the gods by the poets are false myths and are, when accused, not embarrassed by what the gods do. For they worship idols constructed in accordance with the myths; for the image of Aphrodite is more shameful than any courtesan standing on a roof" (*Curatio* 3.79–84). It was Plato's fear of the Greeks that kept him from clearly proclaiming the irrationality of their idolatry (*Curatio* 3.74–76). The importance of his connection of "Hellenizing" to Greek religion, and in particular to the cult of images within Greek religion, should not be missed. Hellenism as an analytic approach to late antique iconography is not an entirely modern art historical concern (e.g., Baynes 1946, 33–34; Bowersock 1996, 15–28; Fowden 2004, 25–145); at least some ancient authors were linking iconographic elements (especially anthropomorphism of divine figures) to what they articulated as a Greek identity (see also Procopius, *Bell.* 5.15.13). The fact that these connections were being made for others, rather than for their own identities, should not detract from the significance of these perceptions within the envisioned worlds of their authors. Religious iconography could be, and was, an efficient tool in constructing a Christian edifice of truth, or (to maintain Theodoret's metaphor) the art of the Greeks was a symptom of the Greek disease, as well as a formal element in crafting his own vision of Greek identity.

Hellenism, History, and Julian

Theodoret's fifth-century peers, who sought to continue the work of Eusebius within the genre of ecclesiastical history, exhibit different emphases within the history of the constructions and perceptions of Hellenism in Late Antiquity. Yet, in concert with the apologetic texts of Eusebius and Theodoret, the historical writings of Socrates (fl. 439 C.E.) and Sozomen (c. 400–c. 450 C.E.) (as well as their continuator Evagrius Scholasticus and other sixth-century historians) provide a caveat against our adopting a more singularly religious set of associations for Greek identity and its processes. But first we should appreciate the force of those religious associations. Certainly, the Church historians of the Theodosian age (401–450) evince a repeated emphasis on the religious tenor of Greek identity in their portrayals of Hellenism. If we consider their narratives of the reign of Julian (360–363) or their accounts of religious violence in Alexandria and Gaza, our modern proclivity to read late antique Hellenism as "paganism" might at first seem justified. For instance, when the bishop Theophilus attempted to dismantle key centers of polytheism in Alexandria, his opponents are invariably named Hellenes or Hellenizers, while the supporters of Theophilus are named "Christianizers" (Socrates, *HE* 5.16).

The violence at Gaza under Julian marks a fascinating and equally violent precursor to the Alexandrian conflict. Unruly crowds apprehended three Christian brothers who had committed "insult and injury to Hellenism" under earlier Christian emperors. The violence was extreme: their bodies were dragged, lashed, poked with spinning needles (by women) or roasting spits (by cooks); their skulls were crushed; and the remains were burned in ignominy and mingled with the bones of camels and donkeys (Sozomen, *HE* 5.9; cf. Greg. Naz. *Or.* 4.61, 86–93). The literary battles against the Greeks seen in the pages of the apologists might thus be portrayed by the historians as erupting with brute force and physicality in the streets of late antique cities.

The apostate emperor Julian was, according to the Church historians, a central catalyst in this crescendo of religious violence. During Julian's reign, it would be "Hellenizers" at Antioch who brought a certain Theodore before the praetorian prefect, himself "a Hellene by religion," to be tortured for his adamantine faith (Socrates, *HE* 3.19). Julian is depicted as openly Hellenizing after his rise to sole rule, and many are described as Hellenizing along with the emperor. Some may have been merely religious chameleons. For instance, Ecebolius the sophist "pretended to Christianize (*Christianizein*) ardently [under Constantius], then he appeared a vehement Greek under Julian, and again he wanted to Christianize after him" (Socrates, *HE* 3.13).[27] Not all were so inconstant, however; the Church historians represent an anonymous collectivity who were Hellenizing (in the sense of performing sacrifice and frequenting temples) before, during, and after the Apostate's brief reign (e.g., Socrates, *HE* 3.1; Sozomen, *HE* 5.3).

Christianizers and Hellenizers often seem to form starkly polar oppositions within the historians' identity constructions. The temples of the Greeks stood opposite the martyria and churches of the Christians; the many gods of Hellenism contrasted strongly with the one true God of Christianity. Yet the historians' vision was not so simplistic. Boundary crossing was represented and its dangers eschewed. The father-and-son intellectual team, both bearing the name Apollinarius and both seeking to maintain their faith and their intellectual integrity during the disconcerting reversals of Julian's reign, diligently composed metrical renditions of the Pentateuch, as well as a poetic paraphrase of the entire Old Testament, and transformed the Gospels into Platonic-styled dialogues (Socrates, *HE* 3.16; Sozomen, *HE* 5.18).[28] Not only was their education solidly ensconced within the Greek tradition but also their network of friends and associates placed them within circles of Greek literati. Such a background and set of relationships threatened the purity of Christian truth, however, and both Socrates himself and the pastoral supervisors whom he records as directly concerned with the Apollinarii cautioned against their collusion with Hellenicity.

When Socrates later offered his own disquisition on the promises and pitfalls of their Hellenizing activity, he carefully outlined a middle course between outright rejection of what was good in Greek literature and what he characterized as the excesses of the Apollinarii. Like Theodoret and Basil, Socrates saw the proper engagement with the Greek traditions as a cautious selection of the good and rejection of the bad; like Eusebius and Theodoret, he saw primarily an oppositional usefulness in reading the literature of the Greeks—that is, the aim must be the acquisition of ammunition from Greek arsenals in fighting Hellenism (Socrates, *HE* 3.16; see Allen 1987, 372–373). The *paideia* of the Apollinarii, however, had fostered friendship with the Greeks rather than making them more effective combatants in the assault on Greek thought.

Already before the reign of Julian, two successive bishops of Laodicea had sought to dissuade the father and son from fellowship with the non-Christian sophist Epiphanius, "fearing lest they would incline towards Hellenism by their continual association with the man" (Socrates, *HE* 2.46). The warning (and eventual excommunication) went unheeded, and the consequences were dire: they became innovators of their own brand of heresy. The connection of Hellenism to heresy had already become an important feature in theological polemic of Late Antiquity (see esp. Epiphanius, *Panarion* 1.3, pp. 176–179 Holl; Averil Cameron 2003; Lyman 2003). Socrates' representation of the dalliance with Greek *paideia* by the Apollinarii is reminiscent of what he had rendered as an earlier act of Christian Hellenization in his *Church History*. Like tares among wheat, Socrates had averred, "a Hellenizing Christianism arose along with the true Christianism" before the times of Constantine (Socrates, *HE* 1.22). Altering the classical distinction between word and deed, he described the writings of the third-century Mani as "Christianizing in word, but Hellenizing in doctrine," since they recommended the veneration of many gods (Socrates, *HE* 1.22; Lechner 1954, 28–29).

The evidence so far noted lends itself to a particularly religious reading of Hellenism in the fifth-century Church historians. Hellenes, Hellenizers, and Hellenism are labels generously applied to those who venerate images, participate in non-Christian cult activity, and believe in and worship many gods. In their histories, Julian was the harbinger of Hellenism par excellence; but their hostile representation and vocabulary of Hellenicity in describing Julian and his co-religionists was not an entirely Christian invention. Julian's own writings, some of which were quoted verbatim by Socrates and Sozomen, ostentatiously donned the dress of Greek identity. The identification is, at least in part, both emic and etic (to adopt anthropological terminology). And in Julian's writings, too, a specifically religious reading of Hellenism might be readily apparent (Koch 1928, 539; Alan Cameron 1993); Hellenism might even be deemed "an article of faith" for the Apostate (Jaeger 1969, 72). After all, the emperor had bluntly declared: "Show us a man purely Greek, for I see that some do not want to sacrifice, while a few others want to but do not know how" (*Epistle* 78 Bidez-Cumont, 375c). Or again, in a letter quoted by Sozomen: "Hellenism is not yet going according to our plan because of those who pursue it; for the things of the gods are to be bright, great and better than every prayer and hope. . . ." The letter goes on to describe Hellenism's other, Christianity, or rather the Galileans (*HE* 5.16 [= Julian, *Ep.* 84 Bidez-Cumont, 429c]). Resonant with this letter, the polemical *Against the Galileans* is often taken as a manifesto of Hellenism as paganism, since Hellenes are strictly marked off from Christians and Jews in that treatise (e.g., *c.Galil.* 42e–43a; 238b; 305d).

Yet, for all the "paganism" we see looming behind the usage of Hellenism and similar labels in Julian and his historians, we are struck by the inclusiveness of their use of the verb *hellēnizein* and the label "Hellene" as denoting an ethnic and cultural as well as religious identity. Hellas maintained its status as a topographical marker, and "Hellenes" identified its inhabitants (e.g., Julian, *Or.*1.13b, 14b). Importantly, "Hellenize" continued to carry its early sense of speaking Greek. For instance, the emperor Constantine "Hellenized" to a room full of bishops at Nicaea and so was "rather sweet and pleasant" to hear (Socrates, *HE* 1.8; see Van Dam 2007, 184–216). While it is doubtful that the emperor identified himself as a Greek, the historian's representation of his speech could remain part of the larger cluster of ideas associated with his concept of Hellenization. Recent studies have indeed shown the importance of the continued usage of the Greek language in the eastern provinces throughout Late Antiquity (Dagron 1969; Charanis 1972b; Averil Cameron 1996; Millar 2007). Resonant with this linguistic phenomenon, the historians construed Hellenizing processes as including the possibilities of immersion in a literary tradition (*paideia*) and assumption of religious doctrines and practices.

If the historians' concept of Hellenizing could embrace both speech acts and cult acts, both knowledge of a language and belief in the gods, and if, furthermore, Greek identity could contain a number of possible markers of distinction from other identities (including ethnic, historical, geographical, literary, or religious associations), a fruitful reading of the studied ambiguity of the historians toward Hellenism must appreciate more fully the particular contexts and characterizations being crafted by their authors, rather than attempting to discover the cultural realia *behind* the text (Allen 1987). This is true even for the flamboyantly pagan Julian. It may, in fact, be due more to the enchanting distinctions carefully drawn by his posthumous opponents than to the emperor himself that we suppose he adopted the Christianizing definition of Hellenism as paganism. On the contrary, his Christian antagonists, most notably Gregory Nazianzen, assiduously raised a rhetorical smokescreen following Julian's death in Mesopotamia, separating the originally more unified cluster of ideas that were joined under the emperor's conceptualization of Greek identity (Greg. Naz. *Or.* 4.103–104). The severance of religious from cultural elements in Gregory's polemic against Julian refused to work within the contours of Julian's own conception of Hellenicity (Dostálová 1983, 8–9). Since Hellenism was one of the central sites of contention in Late Antiquity's culture wars, we should not be surprised by the rhetorical precision with which Gregory sought to make religion separable from literature. We fail to appreciate both the holistic Hellenicity of Julian and the elegance and force of Gregory's anti-Julianic orations when we readily adopt the latter's characterization of the former's thought.[29]

In spite of the "Constantinian revolution," Julian maintained a full-bodied expression of Hellenicity, in contrast to the characterizations of Gregory Nazianzen or the formulations produced by the other pagans of the period (Themistius, Synesius who later converted, or, differently, Libanius; Dostálová 1983, 10–11).[30] Only in its contextually limited heightening of emphasis on religious elements, driven by anti-Christian antagonism, does Julian's Hellenicity differ from what we find in earlier Greeks such as Plutarch, Aristides, or Philostratus. Both before and after his assumption of sole rule and, hence, both before and after his public acknowledgment of his religious position, Julian attaches a broad sense to Greek identity, which incorporates religion and geographical, historical, racial, and literary features within its embrace (see Bouffartigue 1991, who nonetheless attempts to keep these senses distinct in the various occurrences in Julian). For instance, in an encomium honoring Eusebia, the wife of Constantius II, the young Caesar praised the empress for her good birth. Her mother was "very Greek in her birth, and from very Greek [ancestors]" (*Or.* 3.110b). She came from Thessalonike, the metropolis of Macedonia, which had long before been settled by the Heracleidae, who "had left behind memorials of the Greek character" (*Or.* 3.106d). Geographic and quasi-historical marks of Greek identity are invoked here. The empress also aided his attempt to spend time in Athens: "When I longed to behold my true fatherland the empress and emperor made it possible; for we who dwell in Thrace and Ionia are the sons of Greece, and whoever of us is not excessively mindless desires to greet our fathers and to welcome the land itself" (*Or.* 3.118d; contrast Greg. Naz. *Or.* 4.109).

A slightly different representation of the connection between Thracian and Greek occurs in Julian's later work, *The Beard-Hater*. Part of his difficulty in building an amicable relationship with the Antiochenes, against whom the satiric piece was directed, was that he presumed that they shared a Greek identity. They were "children of the Greeks," and he, even if a Thracian by race, was a Greek by training (*Misopogon* 367c). The self-identification recalls that of the eunuch sophist Favorinus in the second century, who had played his multiple identities as a Gaul, a Roman, and a Greek against one another. In spite of his racial origins in Gaul, Favorinus boldly claimed "not only to seem, but to be" a Greek (*Corinthian Oration* [= Ps.-Dio, *Or.* 37], 25). Julian's tense relationship with the Antiochenes had not been helped by a common Greekness. Their mutual identity should have entailed a mutual love for each other, but this had not been realized. Of course, the Antiochenes had inherited the corrupt morals of their eponymous founder (*Misop.* 348d–349a; Kaegi 1964, 30). In response, the emperor determined, like Favorinus, to play with his own hybrid identity as well. Turning from his previous claim that Thracians were Greeks, he touted the boorish rusticity of his Thracian character (*Misop.* 348b–d) and reminded his audience that his tutor had been a Scythian eunuch (*Misop.*, 352a). His native simplicity had failed to meet the fastidious pleasure-seeking of the Antiochenes.

A final passage from another late work, the *Hymn to Helios the King*, is again resonant of the sort of identity constructions typical in earlier Greek authors, whether a Favorinus or an Aristides. Roman and Greek were frequently identified with each other in crucial rhetorical manipulations. Apollo had civilized the greater part of the world by means of Greek colonies, Julian averred, and so had prepared it to submit easily to the Romans, "for they not only are Greek by race, but have also established and guarded as Greek from first to last the sacred ordinances and belief in the gods, and besides these things they have established the order of their city in a manner no worse than the best governed cities, if not better than all others. . . . The city was Greek in respect to both race and constitution" (*Or.* 4.152d–153a). The identification of Rome as a Greek city was traditional and long-lived; there is little original in Julian's perception of Greek and Roman identity here (see esp. Dion. Hal. 1.41–44, 89; Gruen 1992, 6–51; Erskine 2005).[31] What is most important for the scope of our current concerns is the unmistakable inclusion of much more than merely religious features in his conception of Hellenicity. While the boundaries between identities could be breached or made to overlap, race, religion, region, history, and national character were all elements of Julian's vision of the Greeks, Romans, and others.

One can conclude from all this that Hellenism certainly included pagan religious activity and theology but that it was not simply to be equated with paganism in Julian's conceptual universe. The evidence noted previously, which is hardly exhaustive, certainly supports this conclusion. Yet the reader of Julian's oeuvre may still balk at such an interpretation. The term *Hellēnismos* occurs, after all, only once in Julian's extant corpus: in the well-known letter to Arsacius, quoted by Sozomen (and cited previously), the emperor had spoken of Hellenism within the context of the worship of the gods in contrast to Christianity (Sozomen, *HE* 5.16 (= Julian, *Ep.* 84 [Bidez-Cumont]).* A minimalist reading of the letter finds only a religious sense of *Hellēnismos* (Bouffartigue 1991, 252–253). The letter seems, furthermore, to show the unmistakable signs of working within a Christian frame of thinking: the identities contrasted with the Greeks are the Galileans (or Christians) and the Jews. Especially given the dominant reading of Julian's Hellenism as one that had been formed within the crucible of Christian religious conceptions of Hellenism, his adoption of the threefold schema in this letter (as well as in the *Against the Galileans*) might seem to further support this interpretation.

As argued here, however, even the Christian conception of Hellenism and Greek identity went beyond the simply religious valences of that identity and its labels. Furthermore, if Hellenism was the art of using tools from the Greek heritage in rhetorically contingent and socially particular contexts, then the letter must be located within his policy of religious revitalization, as well as his economic policy in the civic revitalization of Asia Minor (Huart 1978; Athanassiadi 1981, 98–114, 184–189).[32] The Greeks referred to in this letter had allowed the traditional cult practices to fall into abeyance, and the priests were using their office to pursue worldly advancement. Julian's letter marks an attempt to put pressure on priestly and civic religious standards at once. His economic aid depended on religious commitment and hieratic seriousness. The letter focuses on religion but not to the exclusion of other elements of Greek identity (even if these elements remain indistinct because of his particular emphasis and aims). The fact that the "Greek villages" were not religious enough by Julian's standards amply indicates this. Religion, then, was a necessary, but not sufficient, part of Greek identity. This conclusion remains true even of the religiously vituperative *Against the Galileans*, where broader ethnic senses are conveyed in his usage of the labels Greeks, Jews (or Hebrews), and Galileans (never Christians; see esp. *c.Galil.* 138ab, 176bc; Bouffartigue 1991, 259–260; Dostálová 1983, 4).

Philosophy and Hellenism

We have so far recognized a breadth in the conception of Hellenism and Greek identity in Late Antiquity that is often limited in modern discussion to a simply religious, iconographic, or literary set of phenomena. Greek identity and the processes of adopting one or more elements of that identity were constructed by literary craftsmen wielding the tools variously provided by the visions and re-visions of the Greek past and its ideas, literary forms, doctrines, stories, and ethnic and geographical boundaries. We may ask, did any late antique authors themselves seek to limit Hellenicity to a single identity category, or is such a narrowing the result of modern preoccupations and assumptions alone?

The philosophers of the fifth and sixth centuries may come closest to constructing Greek identity as a distinctly philosophical or, more precisely, theological (and hence, we might say, religious) identity. As one of the greatest systematizers of pagan theology in a Neoplatonic framework, Proclus of Lycia (412–485 C.E.), the head of the Academy at Athens, sought to engage fully with the theological implications of the wisdom of Plato (Watts 2006, 100–110 for context). His *Platonic Theology* may justly be seen as the high point of Neoplatonic theological reflection. As a Lycian born at Constantinople, he avoided the other cultural and religious options available to him and chose the difficult road of defending his pagan religious commitments as distinctly Greek in character (Marinus, *V.Procli* 6, 10).[33] In a number of instances, he makes it explicit that the theology found in the dialogues of Plato is a Greek theology. For instance, after discussing what he labels the "indefinite and common teaching" about the gods, he proceeds, "Let us bring into our midst the Greek report about them passed down to us by Plato and let us show that he follows the theology of the Greeks even as far as [using their] names. . . . [For] Plato had not departed from the Greek interpretation" (*Plat. Theol.* 5.35 [5.127 Saffrey-Westerink]). Anyone, Proclus averred, who knew anything at all about Greek *theosophia* (an allusion to Orphic thought) would know that "in their ineffable mysteries and in their other activity about the gods the order of the Kouretes [that is, the guardian gods, who served as a sort of buffer between the demiurgic and created levels] is especially hymned by them" (*Plat. Theol.* 5.35 [5.127 Saffrey-Westerink]; cf. 5.3 [5.17 Saffrey-Westerink]). Later he would reiterate: "It seems to me that Plato was looking to all the Greek theology, and especially the Orphic mystagogy, when he said that God possesses the beginning, middle and end of all things" (*Plat. Theol.* 6.8 [6.40 Saffrey-Westerink]).[34] Orpheus was, in what by Proclus' time had become the standard appellation, "the theologian of the Greeks," and Plato was consistently exhibited as being in harmony with him. The context of references to the Greeks in the *Platonic Theology* is almost invariably religious, whether elements of mythology, the mystery rites, or "Greek theology" generally. In a treatise on the subject of theology, however, this is not necessarily surprising. If we turn to a work of a different nature, namely, his *Commentary on the Timaeus*, we find a broader range of associations for Greek identity.

Proclus' explication of a passage from Plato's *Timaeus*, which had provided ammunition for those who would attack Hellenicity in previous generations, is instructive (see Staab 2006, 63–67). The Egyptian priest's response to the Greek sage in that dialogue, "Solon, Solon, you Greeks are always children and there is no elderly Greek" (*Tim.* 22b), offered exegetes a rich opportunity for their own articulations of ethnic and cultural commitments, since the longer historical memory of the Egyptians recalled a greater antiquity for the Greeks that they had forgotten. Proclus' extensive discussion of the individual features of the Platonic passage formulates an equivocal stance. On the one hand, the priest's native city of Sais is claimed to be a colony of Athens (though Proclus cites dissenting voices that reverse their relationship; *Comm.Tim.* 1.98),[35] which repeatedly receives a position of superiority to that of the Egyptians; yet, on the other hand, Proclus shifts to assertions for the greater antiquity of the Egyptians (even defending the Egyptians against detractors who accuse them of exaggerating; *Comm.Tim.* 1.100, 102) and allegorizes the *Timaeus'* Egyptians and Greeks as figures of, respectively, higher and lower divine levels of reality (*Comm.Tim.* 1.95, 101, 103, 108, 127). There is, then, a degree of ambivalence in the Hellenocentric cultural moves of Proclus that distinguishes his commentary from those of the *Timaeus* itself (contrast Hermeias, *Comm.Phdr.* 254 Couvreur).[36]

In spite of his repeated allegorizing of the details of the Platonic dialogue, Proclus also takes seriously the ethnic nature of the identities raised therein. In fact, it was due to certain markers of ethnic identity, for instance, the invoking of antiquity and well-known ancestors, that the reader of Plato was to recognize the necessity of a deeper understanding of the text. The environmental differences between various regions, the divergence in the relative antiquity of Greeks and other nations, and the diversity in the chronologies of different Greek groups (particularly, the Athenians, the Argives, and the Thessalians) indicated that Plato's "narrative must be dealing, not with minor matters, but with the universal and the whole" (*Comm.Tim.* 1.100–101). The closeness between Sais and Athens, for instance, was not absolute, according to the commentator:

> For one should realize this, that variations occur in various races according to the different areas in which each lives, according to the make-up of the air, to the position in relation to the heavens, and still more specific, if you like, in accordance with the seminal formal principles. You might say that they differed most of all in relation to the herd-tending management of the gods and the differences among their overseers, thanks to which you will detect variations in coloring, stature, language and movements in different places. The result is that even colonists often undergo change in the coloring and the dialect of the settlers when they come to different places, just as plants change together with the quality of the soil if they are transplanted. . . . (*Comm.Tim.* 1.99, trans. Tarrant)

The notion of regional divine guardians reminiscent of earlier Christian and pagan thought was thus combined with the notion of environmental determinism reminiscent of Herodotus and Hippocrates.[37] Language was also an important feature of Greek identity for the Neoplatonist commentator. The verb *hellēnizein*, in fact, occurs only in the linguistic sense (and then, only in a commentary on a dialogue that itself contained the verb; *Comm.Alcib.* 258–9 [2.303 Segonds]). The linguistic differences of various peoples were raised only to relativize their particular claims to express more fully the truth; all languages were equally capable of signifying reality (*Comm.Tim.* 1.98; 2.305).

Proclus confronts us, then, with a more inclusive conception of Hellenicity similar to what we have found in other authors of Late Antiquity, while nonetheless putting this broader range of elements to work within an emphatically religious and spiritual program (see Dillon 2007). The Neoplatonist had more limited, if more sublime, aims than Julian in the previous century. The emperor's scope for Hellenism was on a much grander scale and predicated upon concerns at all levels: imperial, civic, cultural, literary, spiritual, and religious. Had they been contemporaries, their visions of Greek identity might well have aligned nicely. Furthermore, if Proclus had composed public speeches, panegyrics, or satires, he might have more frequently evinced a range of valences of Hellenicity in a manner similar to that of Julian. We must constantly be mindful of the rhetorically specific nature of articulations of Hellenicity and Hellenism. In a corpus dominated by theological reflection and philosophical commentary, Proclus evinces a religious focus for what it meant to be Greek.

Proclus was followed in highlighting the religious nature of Greek identity by Damascius, his later successor at the Athenian school (c. 458–538; for context, Watts 2006, 125–128). The latter's vivid account of the pagan intellectual circles of his time in the *Life of Isidore*, or rather *Philosophical History*,[38] clearly articulates the identities of the various figures that cross its fragmentary pages by their religious commitments (Fowden 1982; Athanassiadi 1993; 1999, 19–57; Dillon 2007). Severian was "excessively pious and a Greek," Marcellinus was "a Greek in his doctrine," and Maximinus was "a Greek with respect to reverence."[39] The concern with Greek language crops up occasionally,[40] but it does little to offset the religious intensity of Hellenicity in the fragments of this pagan hagiographical text. Those who worship the old gods are invariably Greek.

Given the religious agenda of Proclus and Damascius, a final question remains: what became of Hellenism in the bleak years of Christian imperial persecution of religious dissidents in the sixth century? Had the pagan Hellenists at Athens provoked (or accelerated) their own demise? In the onset of what might be seen as cultural decrepitude beginning with the reign of Justinian in the sixth century, whither Hellenism? Whatever conclusions we may draw from the meager evidence of Malalas and Agathias, some sort of blow fell against the already dwindling school of Platonic philosophers in Athens.[41] Furthermore, in the same era that Justinian was prohibiting the practices of the "unholy Greeks" (Lemerle 1971, 68–69), his praetorian prefect, John Lydus (490–c. 565), was lamenting the decline of Latin in the eastern empire and clinging to a strongly Roman identity (and all this, ironically, in Greek; *Magist.* 3.42).[42] Indeed, it is precisely during this period that Roman self-identification was most clearly established in the East (even if the trend had commenced centuries earlier; Jüthner 1923, 104–111; Charanis 1972b; Ando 2000; Kaldellis 2007, 42–74).

Though our conclusions must be tentative, there is something striking in the fact that, aside from Proclus and Damascius, the other pagan philosophers of the fifth and sixth centuries, especially those of the Alexandrian school, were not as concerned to construct a well-developed Greek identity.[43] While modern readers may find them Hellenizing at every turn—speaking Greek, educating themselves in classic Greek texts, being possessed of pagan religious commitments—there is little indication that they wanted others to perceive them as doing something distinctively Greek. This fact cannot simply be explained, however, by the increasingly hostile imperial pressure against the purveyors of pagan religious and philosophical commitments. Non-philosophical texts of the same period exhibit the durability of a broad conception of Hellenicity as a linguistic, ethnic, or broadly cultural identity into the sixth century and beyond. Procopius, for instance, moved unproblematically (even somewhat playfully) between the different associations of those he labeled "Greeks." Those who received this appellation in his historical oeuvre could in different contexts be Christian speakers of the language, cultured literati, inhabitants of Hellas, or even non-Hellenophone pagans.[44] The evidence of Procopius shows that what it meant to be Greek was still not limited to religious identity in the sixth century.

It could be that philosophers like Ammonius, Olympiodorus, and Simplicius refused this range of Greek identity and instead, following Proclus, considered it a religious identity; thus, out of fear, they avoided it in a hostile Christian environment. Yet, while they did allude to Christian domination and continued to embrace pagan philosophical doctrines (for instance, the eternity of the world), there is simply insufficient evidence of a concern with Greek identity as such, whether of a religious or broader type.[45] They were certainly preservers of what we might label the Greek heritage and perpetuated a pagan theology (Tarrant 1997), but they generally avoided self-ascription as Greek.

The reasons for the silence in articulating a Greek identity among these late antique pagan philosophers must be due to other reasons. It could very well be that we merely lack sufficient extant works from them. Or their commentaries on Aristotle's works, many of which do survive, may have been deemed unsuitable texts for formulating Hellenicity (Sheppard 2000, 843). It may be that they sought to transcend the particularity of such an ethnic-specific identity. This possibility is less likely, however, since a rhetoric of transcendence need not involve a silence about ethnicity: other late antique philosophers who eschewed ethnic allegiances for transcendent philosophical aims, like Porphyry or Proclus himself, were frequently at pains to describe the blessings and curses of such bodily identities. Ammonius, Olympiodorus, and Simplicius were at no such pains.[46] They continued to use many of the tools ascribed to the Greeks by many of their predecessors, but they were untroubled by the precise label affixed to these elements. Greek identity, for pagan philosophers in Alexandria, may have merely lost its luster as an identity to ascribe either to themselves or to others. One wonders if Hellenicity died among them for sheer lack of interest rather than from reserved taciturnity.[47]

Christian philosophers of the sixth century, on the contrary, would continue to lavish attention on Hellenicity and construct a polemically charged vision of the Greeks in their works. Their philosophical ruminations achieved a fresh vigor from the stimulus of their pagan peers, especially Proclus, and, related to this, a renewed focus on cosmological matters. For Aeneas of Gaza (c. 465–c. 534), who continued traditional apologetic configurations of Greek identity, the Greeks were polytheists (*Theophrastus* 33–34) or those who believed in the preexistence of souls (*Theophrastus* 18). The doctrine of the eternity of the world was a mark of Greek identity for Zacharias of Mytilene (c. 465–c. 540; see *Ammonius* 1.2ff) and John Philoponus (c. 490–c. 570; see *De aeternitate mundi* 86, 245, 287); both the eternity and the sphericity of the world were assigned to the Greek way of thinking by Cosmas Indicopleustes (admittedly a philosopher in only a loose sense; fl. c. 550; see e.g., *Topogr. Christ.* 5.178; 6.25, 30, passim). For these Christian thinkers, Hellenicity comprised cosmological and philosophical traits, but these were frequently seen as part of broader ethnic and historical significations (see esp. Cosmas Indic., *Topogr. Christ.* 5.54; 12.7ff.). For these men and many of their contemporaries, Greek identity remained a potent cluster of ideas, Greek language and literature were preserved, and the construction of Greek identities (though rarely self-ascribed) persisted as an important task for thinkers, as we saw earlier with Sophronius, inhabiting a rather different world than that of Aristides in the second century.

The sketch offered here is necessarily cursory and tells only part of a more complicated story that would include the representations of other cultural, ethnic, and religious identities, which formed the discursive field in which Hellenicity was articulated.[48] The present discussion has touched on only a small and by no means representative selection of late antique authors and texts. What if we were to continue our inquiry to consider the eloquent speeches of Late Antiquity's highly trained orators, the popular sermons steeped in biblical allusions of classically educated bishops, the seemingly tedious ruminations on scriptural details in the vast wealth of early Byzantine biblical commentaries, the compendious and erudite (if sometimes inaccurate) chronographical works from Africanus to Malalas, the often vitriolic preciseness of theological treatises, the exciting austerity of saints' lives, or the encyclopedic collections of anthologies? The task of analyzing the carefully constructed, as well as the glibly presumed, acts of Greek identity construction is nearly endless. Inquiry into Hellenism and Greek identity in Late Antiquity is far from moribund (see, e.g., Fowden 2004, 25–145; Kaldellis 2007; Sandwell 2007; Elm forthcoming), and it is salutary to remember, "Hellenism never ends" (Grant 1959, 209; quoted in Bichler 1983, 2). The present discussion has sought only to indicate continuity of certain trends and habits in the late antique use of the labels of Greek identity: *Hellēn* continued to identify an individual by perceived markers of religious, ethnic, cultural, or regional differences; *Hellēnismos* remained exceptionally rare in pagan authors but nonetheless bore more than a merely religious resonance; *Hellēnizein* maintained its sense of speaking Greek but widened its range to incorporate notions of thinking like a Greek and performing polytheist ritual. All of these were persistently dynamic features of the fashioning and refashioning of one's self and one's world throughout Late Antiquity.

NOTES

* Van Nuffelen 2002 provides a strong argument against the authenticity of this letter. For defense of authenticity, see Bouffartigue 2005.

1. The author is grateful to Susanna Elm and Isabella Sandwell for discussion and prepublication drafts of their work, and especially to Erich Gruen for criticisms of an earlier version of this article.

2. Trans. Oliver 53; compare *Or.* 27 (*Paneg. Cyzic.*), 32 Behr, for similar rhetoric. Translations throughout are my own, unless otherwise noted (as here).

3. The distinctly Roman context for Aristides has been emphasized, however, by Said 2006.

4. See, e.g., *Evagoras* 47–50, 66–67.

5. For the theological and philosophical contexts of Droysen's historical vision, see Momigliano 1955, 181–185; Bichler 1983, 33–109; Vogt 1988, 2–4.

6. See also Aristides, *Or.* 41.8; 40.4–5, 16–17 Behr. For a possible late antique manifestation, see Socrates, *HE* 3.21, with Kaegi 1964, 37; Huart 1978, 106–107, 120.

7. Aristides and other orators of the period favored the history of classical Greece before the rise of Alexander (see Swain 1996, 65–100); for the differing valences of the Greek past for Romans and Greeks, see Woolf 1994. For the question of Macedonian genealogy, see Herodotus 5.22.

8. For an ancient expression of the Greek philosopher's panoptic gaze, see, e.g., Maximus Tyrius, *Diss.* 16.6; 22.5; 38.3; Ps.-Julian, *Ep.* 187 (Bidez-Cumont), 405d–406a.

9. For the term, see Pliny, *NH* 16.249; a striking expression of the phenomenon occurs at Josephus, *Ant.Jud.* 1.121. For the difficulties of clarifying what processes exactly are meant by an *interpretatio Graeca*, see Dillery 1998; Fowden 1983, 45; see also, *mutatis mutandis*, the critical remarks about *interpretatio Romana* by Ando 2005.

10. See Themistius, *Or.* 4.59d–60c: The books and letters of wise men are like their tombstones, and "like the edifices in the treasure-house of memory they risk being entirely annihilated"; but Constantius has ordered to restore them to life. "These works [of restoration] are performed for you not by bronzesmiths, carpenters and stonemasons, but by the craftsmen of the art of Kadmos and Palamedes [i.e., letters and rhetoric], who are able to build a new home for the mind from its old languishing tent to a freshly-fixed and new-made one. . . . Plato is restored to life; Aristotle is restored to life. . . ." L. Wittgenstein 1968, §11: "Think of the tools in a tool-box: there is a hammer, pliers, a saw, a screw-driver, a rule, a glue-pot, glue, nails and screws. The functions of words are as diverse as the functions of these objects. . . . Of course, what confuses us is the uniform appearance of words when we hear them spoken or meet them in script and print. For their *application* is not presented to us so clearly." For "words," we might read "elements of the Hellenic tradition (ideas, language, literature, artistic representations, historical events and figures) variously construed."

11. Trans. E. H. Gifford; see A. P. Johnson 2006b, 64–73.

12. I have intentionally left the Latin side out of discussion here for reasons of space, but it should be noted that a fruitful and varied discourse representing the *Graeci* and *Graecitas* had been carried on in Latin literature for centuries and remained significant in Late Antiquity (unfortunately, the important study of Alan Cameron 2011, 14–32, was published too late to receive a response in the present discussion, which is in any case dedicated to the Hellenophone articulation of Hellenicity). For one of the more complicated instances, see Ammianius' self-ascription as *miles quondam et Graecus* in the last sentence of his *History* (31.16.9); the scholarly discussion remains diverse, but see especially Matthews 1994; Barnes 1998, 54–78, 79–80.

13. Following Chuvin, 1990, 7–9, I continue to use the terms *paganism* and *pagan* (in the sense of "people of the place," i.e., adherents of the established ancestral religion, as opposed to *alieni*, "people from elsewhere"), in spite of the criticism of such language for its dependence upon a particularly Latin Christian derogation of the religious other (see Fowden 2005, 521–522; also now, but differently, Alan Cameron 2011, 14–25). It has been suggested that we use *Hellenism* to refer to paganism in the eastern Mediterranean (Bowersock 1996), but this continues to employ the derogatory language of Greek Christian authors and can hardly help us in determining the self-identification of, e.g., a Syriac-speaking devotee of a non-Christian and non-Jewish cult dwelling in Mesopotamia. Another suggestion has been to adopt the term *polytheists* to describe adequately all those who previously went under the label "pagan" on both sides of the Mediterranean (see Fowden 2005, 521–523). Even if "pagan monotheism" is a misnomer (as this author believes), "polytheist" is somewhat

misleading as a label for intellectuals who, while believing in the existence of many gods, nonetheless considered them as comprising only one level within a theological hierarchy and not at all as the summit of that hierarchy. The establishment of adequate modern terminology for ancient religious self-identification in terms of generic categories that appropriately encompass their subject is a nearly insoluble problem. As with the label "Hellene" treated in this discussion, religious self-identification must be examined in terms of the particular social, theological, philosophical, and rhetorical contingencies of the ancient evidence (for further, albeit quite brief, considerations, see A. P. Johnson 2009, note 4, and the discussion of Jacqueline Maxwell, chapter 26 in this book; see now also Alan Cameron 2011, 14-32).

14. Bidez 1913, 6, 118, 128–129, 131 (Porphyry became "the soul of Hellenism").

15. A more thorough reassessment of Greek identity in Porphyry's fragments will soon be offered in A. P. Johnson 2011 and in *Religion and Identity in Porphyry of Tyre: The Limits of Hellenism in Late Antiquity*, forthcoming.

16. There are insufficient grounds for attributing to Porphyry the claims of an anonymous Greek at Eusebius, *PE* 1.2.1ff (= *c.Christ.* fr. 1 Harnack); see A. P. Johnson, forthcoming. Likewise, the criticism of Origen's Hellenizing exegetical method (*c.Christ.* fr. 39 Harnack [= Eus., *HE* 6.19.2ff.]) is hardly a defense of Hellenism.

17. See Hesiod, *Works* 287–291; Porph. *ad Marc.* 6.277–7.278; the metaphor of the road is widespread in poetry and prose, especially of a philosophical nature; see Callimachus, *Aetia* fr. 1; Lucr., *de Rerum Nat.*, 1.921–930; for discussion and extensive comparanda, see Knox 1999.

18. In a different context, the opposite claim has been made by Ševčenko 1980; see also Jüthner 1923, 95.

19. On this apologetic project in early Christian apologists before Eusebius, see Pilhofer 1990; Boys-Stones 2001; the best treatment remains Droge 1989.

20. Eusebius, after all, wrote a *Contra Porphyrium*. The point must be emphasized, however, that Eusebius' and Theodoret's extant criticisms of Porphyry almost entirely excluded his great *Against the Christians*; only frr. 1 (dubium), 38 (which is actually favorable toward Porphyry), and 39 in Harnack's collection of the *c.Christ.* can be found in the *PE*, *DE*, or *Curatio*. See Morlet 2009; A. P. Johnson 2010.

21. For the biblical story of Balaam, see Numbers 22–24; for a Christian interpretation of Balaam's oracle, see Eusebius, *Ecl.Proph.* 1.13–14 (PG 22.1069A–1072C). Elsewhere, Theodoret demeans Porphyry for being like an ape in imitating the truth without understanding it: *Curatio* 7.36–37 (which may be adapting Greg. Naz. *Or.* 4.112).

22. For the identification of Christians as a (third) race or nation, see A. P. Johnson 2006b, 9, n.39; for the traditional, nonracial, interpretation, see, e.g., Jüthner 1923, 91–95.

23. A more favorable invocation of Homer can be found elsewhere in Eusebius' corpus; see A. P. Johnson 2006a.

24. For an overly critical assessment of Theodoret's apologetic approach, see Siniossoglou 2008 (with A. P. Johnson 2009).

25. See also Themistius, *Or.* 4.54b. On Basil's letter and its context, see Ševčenko 1980, 61.

26. The only other occurrence of this verb in Theodoret's corpus seems to be at *Comm.Dan.* 11.30 (PG 81.1520D), where it is contrasted with *Ioudaizein*.

27. See Athanassiadi 1981, 28–29; cf. Greg. Naz. *Or.* 4.11; Julian *Ep.* 194 (Bidez-Cumont), with discussion at Wright 2003, xlvii–xlviii.

28. The *Paraphrase of the Psalms* is printed at PG 33.1313–1538; for defense of authorship, see Scheidweiler 1956; the best treatment of Christian paraphrase in Late Antiquity is now S. F. Johnson 2006, 67–112.

29. See Elm 2003, 507: "Hellenism was not, at least then, the same as paganism. Indeed, Hellenism only could have become a synonym for paganism because Gregory made Greekness essential to Christianity." On Gregory's Hellenism, see also Ševčenko 1980, 53–73. For general discussion of Julian's holistic view, see Huart 1978; Athanassiadi 1981, 20, 123. For further analysis of Gregory's conception of Hellenism, see Elm forthcoming. For reasons of space, I have omitted discussion of other late antique evaluations of Julian, especially those of Ammianus, Eunapius, Libanius, and Zosimus.

30. On Themistius, see Cracco Ruggini 1972; Dagron 1968; Downey 1957; on Synesius, see Bregman 1982; Alan Cameron 1993, 27–29; on Libanius, see Sandwell 2007.

31. This is not to deny that he makes important moves in relating Romans to Greeks, sometimes to the disfavor of the latter; see Bouffartigue 1991, 261–264; also Weiss 1978.

32. In spite of the well-founded criticisms of the historical value of Athanassiadi's study (the most incisive being that of Bowersock 1983, but see also Kaegi 1984), it remains invaluable for the particular texts of Julian's corpus that are important for delineating his Hellenism. Bouffartigue 1991 now offers the best brief treatment of Julian's Hellenism.

33. A Lycian would not have had difficulty claiming a Greek identity, since purportedly the eponymous Lycus had been an exile from Athens; see Herodotus 1.173. This need not entail a positive evaluation, however; see Aristotle ap. Porphyry *Quaest. homer. ad Iliadem* 4.88 Schrader.

34. The reference is to a line of an Orphic poem, which has just been cited: "Zeus is the beginning, Zeus is the middle, all things come from Zeus" (= *Orph.* fr. 168 Kern; also quoted by Porphyry, *de Simulac.* fr. 354 Smith).

35. See also *Comm.Tim.* 1.134, where Athens is asserted to be more ancient than Sais (with Festugière 1966, 182, n. 4); 1.144–145, 150, 160.

36. For discussion of the *Timaeus'* use of Egypt and early responses to it, see Vasunia 2001, 216–247.

37. National guardians: Porphyry, *in Tim.*, fr. 17 Sodano; Julian, *c.Galil.* 143a–148c; Origen, *c.Cels.* 1.24; 3.35; 5.26–32, 46; 7.68, 70; Eusebius, *DE* 4.6, 155d; Philoponus, *De op. mundi* 21; environmental determinism: see Isaac 2004, 56–74.

38. See Athanassiadi 1999, 58–69, for the reconstruction of the text.

39. Severian: *Hist.Phil.*, fr. 108 Athanassiadi (= 304 Zintzen); Marcellinus: fr. 69D Athanassiadi (= E91 Zintzen); Maximinus: fr. 139 Athanassiadi (= E204 Zintzen).

40. See *Hist.Phil.*, fr. 47 Athanassiadi (=E60 + 111 Zintzen); cf. fr. 60 Athanassiadi (= E81–2, 138 Zintzen).

41. The bibliography is extensive; see variously Lemerle 1971, 68–73; Alan Cameron 1969; Blumenthal 1978; Maas 1991, 166, n. 18; Watts 2004; 2006, 111–142.

42. Cf. Phlegon of Tralles, *FGrH* 257 F 36 Jacoby; on Lydus generally, see Maas 1991. For the limits of Romanness in this period, see Browning 1989a, 114–117.

43. It must be remembered that there was much exchange between the Athenian and Alexandrian Neoplatonist schools (both Proclus and Damascius studied there before moving to Athens, and many of their own students later moved to Alexandria). There were, however, differences of context, orientation, and attitude. Alexandria had a noted history of pagan-Christian tension and violence, which Athens did not share.

The Alexandrian pagan philosophers learned to develop a greater tolerance of Christians and were less devoted to expressions of theurgy, at least after Ammonius. See Sheppard 2000, 843–852; Watts 2006, 204–256.

44. On religious uses of the label "Hellene," see Procopius *Bell.* 1.19.35; 1.20.1; 1.25.10; *Hist. Arcan.* 11.31; on geographic uses, see *Bell.* 2.4.11; 5.15.24 (with Charanis 1972a; Trombley 2006); on linguistic uses, see *Bell.* 2.25.4; 5.18.6; 8.14.48; *Hist. Arcan.* 2.17 (the verb *hellēnizein* seems to have an exclusively linguistic sense in Procopius).

45. The exception would be Olympiodorus' *Comm.Alcib.* 95–96 Creuzer (63–64 Westerink), but here the attention is only due to the use of *hellēnizein* in Plato's dialogue.

46. Hermeias, the father of Ammonius and head of the school at Alexandria for a brief period, might be something of an exception; see *Comm.Phdr.* 77–78 Couvreur, where the Greeks signify the intelligible realm while the Trojans represent the material. Less flattering to the Greeks, though, is *Comm.Phdr.* 254. As his sole surviving work, the *Comm.Phdr.* does not offer sufficient material to make a firm judgment on the importance of the Greeks for Hermeias.

47. For a different account of this decline in self-ascribed Hellenicity, see Kaldellis 2007, 173–187, where he dates the decline to c. 400.

48. The author has attempted such an analysis of a single late antique text in A. P. Johnson 2006b. See also Jones 2004; briefly Browning 1989b, 1–2.

WORKS CITED

Ancient Sources

Aelius Aristides:

Behr, C. A. 1976. *P. Aelii Aristidis Opera Quae Exstant Omnia.* Leiden: Brill. Translated by J. H. Oliver. 1968. *The Civilizing Power.* Philadelphia: American Philosophical Society.

Damascius:

Athanassiadi, P. 1999. *Damascius: The Philosophical History.* Athens: Apamea Cultural Association.

Epiphanius:

Holl, K. 1915. *Epiphanius.* GCS 25. Leipzig: Hinrichs.

Eusebius:

Mras, K. 1954, 1956. *Eusebius Werke VIII: Die Praeparatio Evangelica.* Berlin: Akademie-Verlag. Transated by E. H. Gifford. 1981. *Preparation for the Gospel.* 2 vols. Grand Rapids, MI: Baker Book House.

Heikel, I. A. 1913. *Eusebius Werke VI: Die Demonstratio Evangelica.* Berlin: Akademie-Verlag.

Hermeias:

Couvreur, P. 1971. *Hermeias von Alexandrien: In Platonis Phaedrum scholia.* Hildesheim: Olms.

Julian:

Bidez, J., and F. Cumont. 1922. *Imp. Caesaris Flavii Claudii Iuliani Epistulae Leges Poematia Fragmenta Varia.* Paris: Les Belles Lettres.

Olympiodorus:

Westerink, L. G. 1956. *Olympiodorus: Commentary on the First Alcibiades of Plato.* Amsterdam: North-Holland.

Porphyry:

Smith, A. 1993. *Porphyrius: Fragmenta.* Leipzig: Teubner.

Proclus:

Diehl, E. 1965. *Procli Diadochi in Platonis Timaeum Commentaria.* 3 vols. Amsterdam: Adolf M. Hakkert. Translated by H. Tarrant. 2007. *Proclus: Commentary on Plato's* Timaeus, vol. 1. Cambridge: Cambridge University Press.

Saffrey, H. D., and L. G. Westerink. 1968–1997. *Proclus: Théologie platonicienne.* 6 vols. Paris: Les Belles Lettres.

Segonds, A. Ph. 1985–1986. *Proclus: Sur le premier Alcibiade de Platon.* 2 vols. Paris: Les Belles Lettres.

Socrates:

Hansen, G. C., text; Pierre Périchon and Pierre Maraval, trans. 2004–2007. *Socrate de Constantinople: Histoire Ecclésiastique,* SC 477, 493, 505, 506. Paris: Les Éditions du Cerf.

Sophronius:

Fernández Marcos, N. 1975. *Los Thaumata de Sofronio: Contribución al studio de la incubaión cristiana.* Emerita suppl. 31. Madrid: Instituto Antonio de Nebrija.

Sozomen:

Bidez, J., text; André-Jean Festugière, trans. 1983–2008. *Sozomène: Histoire Ecclésiastique,* SC 306, 481, 495, 516. Paris: Les Éditions du Cerf.

Theodoret:

Canivet, Pierre. 1958. *Théodoret de Cyr: Thérapeutique des Maladies Helléniques,* SC 57.1–2. Paris: Les Éditions du Cerf.

Modern Sources

Aerts, Willem J. 2003. "*Imitatio* and *Aemulatio* in Byzantium with Classical Literature, Especially in Historical Writing." In *Constructions of Greek Past: Identity and Historical Consciousness from Antiquity to the Present*, ed. Hero Hokwerda, 89–99. Groningen: Egbert Forsten.

Allen, Pauline. 1987. "Some Aspects of Hellenism in the Early Greek Church Historians," *Traditio* 43: 368–381.

Ando, Clifford. 2000. *Imperial Ideology and Provincial Loyalty in the Roman Empire*. Berkeley: University of California Press.

———. 2005. "Interpretatio Romana," *CPh* 100: 41–51.

Athanassiadi, Polymnia. 1981. *Julian and Hellenism*. Oxford: Clarendon.

———. 1993. "Persecution and Response in Late Paganism: The Evidence of Damascius," *JHS* 113: 1–29.

Barnes, Timothy D. 1998. *Ammianus Marcellinus and the Representation of Historical Reality*. Ithaca, NY: Cornell University Press.

Baynes, Norman H. 1946. *The Hellenistic Civilization and East Rome*. London: Geoffrey Cumberlege, Oxford University Press.

Bhabha, Homi K. 1994. *The Location of Culture*. London: Routledge.

Bichler, Reinhold. 1983. *Hellenismus: Geschichte und Problematik eines Epochenbegriffs*. Darmstadt: Wissenschaftliche Buchgesellschaft.

Bidez, Joseph. 1913. *Vie de Porphyre*. Leipzig: Teubner.

Blumenthal, H. J. 1978. "529 and Its Sequel: What Happened to the Academy?" *Byzantion* 48: 369–385.

Bouffartigue, J. 1991. "Julien ou l'Hellénisme décomposé." In *ΕΛΛΗΝΙΣΜΟΣ: Quelques jalons pour une histoire de l'identité Grecque*, ed. S. Said, 251–266. Leiden: Brill.

———. 2005. "L'authenticité de la Lettre 84 de l'empereur Julien," *Revue de philologie, de la littérature et d'histoire anciennes* 79: 231–242.

Bowersock, G. W. 1983. Review of P. Athanassiadi 1981, *CR* 33: 81–83.

———. 1987. "The Hellenism of Zenobia." In *Greek Connections*, ed. J. T. A. Koumoulides, 19–27. Notre Dame, IN: University of Notre Dame Press.

———. 1996. *Hellenism in Late Antiquity*. Ann Arbor: University of Michigan Press.

Bowie, E. L. 1991. "Hellenes and Hellenism in Writers of the Early Second Sophistic." In *ΕΛΛΗΝΙΣΜΟΣ: Quelques jalons pour une histoire de l'identité Grecque*, ed. S. Said, 182–204. Leiden: Brill.

Boys-Stones, G. R. 2001. *Post-Hellenistic Philosophy*. Oxford: Oxford University Press.

Bregman, Jay. 1982. *Synesius of Cyrene, Philosopher-Bishop*. Berkeley: University of California Press.

Browning, Robert. 1989a. "The Continuity of Hellenism in the Byzantine World: Appearance or Reality?" In *History, Language and Literacy in the Byzantine World*, sec. I. Northampton: Variorum.

———. 1989b. "Greeks and Others: From Antiquity to the Renaissance." In *History, Language and Literacy in the Byzantine World*, sec. II. Northampton: Variorum.

Cameron, Alan. 1969. "The Last Days of the Academy at Athens," *PCPhS* 145: 7–29.

———. 1993. "Julian and Hellenism," *Ancient World* 24: 25–29.

Cameron, Averil. 1996. "The Eastern Provinces in the 7th Century A.D.: Hellenism and the Emergence of Islam." In *Changing Cultures in Early Byzantium*, sec. IV. Aldershot: Variorum.

———. 2003. "How to Read Heresiology," *JMEMS* 33: 471–492.
Casevitz, M. 1991. "*Hellenismos*: Formation et fonction des verbes en-ΙΖΩ et de leurs dérivés." In *ΕΛΛΗΝΙΣΜΟΣ: Quelques jalons pour une histoire de l'identité grecque*, ed. S. Said, 9–16. Leiden: Brill.
Charanis, Peter. 1972a. "Hellas in the Greek Sources of the Sixth, Seventh, and Eighth Centuries." In *Studies in the Demography of the Byzantine Empire: Collected Studies*, sec. XVIII. London: Variorum.
———. 1972b. "How Greek Was the Byzantine Empire?" In *Studies in the Demography of the Byzantine Empire: Collected Studies*: London: Variorum, XXII.
Chuvin, Pierre. 1990. *A Chronicle of the Last Pagans*. Trans. B.A. Archer. Cambridge, MA: Harvard University Press.
Clark, Gillian. 1999. "Translate into Greek: Porphyry of Tyre on the New Barbarians." In *Constructing Identities in Late Antiquity*, ed. R. Miles, 112–132. London: Routledge.
Cracco Ruggini, Lellia. 1972. *Simboli di battaglia ideologica nel tardo ellenismo (Roma, Atene, Constantinopoli; Numa, Empedocle, Cristo)*. Pisa: Pacini.
Dagron, Gilbert. 1968. *L'Empire Romain d'Orient au IVe siècle et les traditions politiques de l'Hellénisme*, T&MByz. Paris: Éditions E. de Boccard.
———. 1969. "Aux origines de la civilisation byzantine: Langue de culture et langue d'État," *Revue Historique* 241: 23–56.
Dillery, John. 1998. "Hecataeus of Abdera: Hyperboreans, Egypt, and the *Interpretatio Graeca*," *Historia* 47: 255–275.
Dillon, John. 2007. "The Religion of the Last Hellenes." In *Rites et croyances dans les religions du monde romain*, ed. J. Scheid, 117–138. Entretiens 53. Genève: Fondation Hardt.
Dostálová, Růžena. 1983. "Christentum und Hellenismus," *Byzantinoslavica* 44: 1–12.
Downey, Glanville. 1957. "Themistius and the Defense of Hellenism in the Fourth Century," *HTR* 50: 259–274.
Droge, Arthur. 1989. *Homer or Moses? Early Christian Interpretations of the History of Culture*. Hermeneutische Untersuchungen zur Theologie 26. Tübingen: Mohr Siebeck.
Elm, Susanna. 2003. "Hellenism and Historiography: Gregory of Nazianzus and Julian in Dialogue," *JMEMS* 33: 493–515.
———. forthcoming. *Sons of Hellenism, Fathers of the Church: The Emperor Julian and Gregory of Nazianzus*. Berkeley: University of California Press.
Erskine, Andrew. 2005. "Unity and Identity: Shaping the Past in the Greek Mediterranean." In *Cultural Borrowings and Ethnic Appropriations in Antiquity*, ed. E. Gruen, 121–136. Münich: Franz Steiner Verlag.
Festugière, A.-J. 1966. *Proclus: Commentaire sur le Timée*, Vol. 1. Paris: Vrin.
Fowden, Garth. 1982. "The Pagan Holy Man in Late Antique Society," *JHS* 102: 33–59.
———. 1983. *The Egyptian Hermes*. Princeton, NJ: Princeton University Press.
———. 2004. *Studies in Hellenism, Christianity and the Umayyads*. Athens: Center of Hellenic and Roman Antiquity.
———. 2005. "Late Polytheism: The World-View." In *The Cambridge Ancient History*, Vol. 12, ed. A. K. Bowman, P. Garnsey, and Averil Cameron, 521–537. Cambridge: Cambridge University Press.
Frankfurter, David. 2000. "The Consequences of Hellenism in Late Antique Egypt: Religious Worlds and Actors," *Archiv für Religionsgeschichte* 2: 162–194.
Grant, F. C. 1959. "Hellenismus." In *Die Religion in Geschichte und Gegenwart*, Bd. 3, ed. K. Galling et al. Tübingen: Mohr Siebeck.

Gruen, Erich. 1984. *The Hellenistic World and the Coming of Rome*. Berkeley: University of California Press.

———. 1992. *Culture and National Identity in Republican Rome*. Ithaca, NY: Cornell University Press.

———. 1998. *Heritage and Hellenism*. Berkeley: University of California Press.

Hall, Jonathan. 1997. *Ethnic Identity in Greek Antiquity*. Cambridge: Cambridge University Press.

———. 2002. *Hellenicity: Between Ethnicity and Culture*. Chicago: University of Chicago Press.

Huart, Pierre. 1978. "Julien et l'Hellénisme: Idées morales et politiques." In *L'Empereur Julien: De l'histoire à la légende (331–1715)*, ed. R. Braun and J. Richer, 99–123. Paris: Les Belles Lettres.

Isaac, Benjamin. 2004. *The Invention of Racism in Classical Antiquity*. Princeton, NJ: Princeton University Press.

Jaeger, Werner. 1969. *Early Christianity and Greek Paideia*. Oxford: Oxford University Press.

Johnson, Aaron P. 2006a. "The Blackness of Ethiopians: Classical Ethnography and the Commentaries of Eusebius," *HTR* 99: 179–200.

———. 2006b. *Ethnicity and Argument in Eusebius' Praeparatio Evanglica*. Oxford: Oxford University Press.

———. 2009. Review of N. Siniossoglou 2008, *BMCR*, 5 May.

———. 2010. "Rethinking the Authenticity of Porphyry, *contra Christianos*, fr. 1," *Studia Patristica* 46: 53–58.

———. 2011. "Porphyry's Hellenism." In *Le traité de Porphyre contre les chrétiens*, ed. Sebastien Morlet, 165-181. Paris: Études Augustiniennes.

———. forthcoming. *Religion and Identity in Porphyry of Tyre: The Limits of Hellenism in Late Antiquity*.

Johnson, Scott F. 2006. *The Life and Miracles of Thekla, A Literary Study*. Washington, DC: Center for Hellenic Studies.

Jones, Christopher P. 2004. "Multiple Identities in the Age of the Second Sophistic." In *Paideia: The World of the Second Sophistic*, ed. B. Borg, 13–21. Berlin: Walter de Gruyter.

Jüthner, Julius. 1923. *Hellenen und Barbaren*. Leipzig: Dieterichische Verlagsbuchhandlung.

Kaegi, Walter E. 1964. "The Emperor Julian's Assessment of History," *PAPhS* 108: 29–38.

———. 1984. Review of P. Athanassiadi 1981, *CPh* 79: 349–351.

Kaldellis, Anthony. 2007. *Hellenism in Byzantium*. Cambridge: Cambridge University Press.

Knox, Peter E. 1999. "Lucretius on the Narrow Road," *HSCP* 99: 275–287.

Koch, W. 1928. "Comment l'Empereur Julien tacha de fonder une église païenne," *Rev. belge de phil. et d'hist.* 7: 511–550.

Lechner, Kilian. 1954. *Hellenen und Barbaren im Weltbild der Byzantiner: Inaugural-Dissertation*. Münich: Ludwig-Maximilians-Universität.

Lemerle, Paul. 1971. *Le premier humanisme byzantin*. Paris: Presses Universitaires de France.

Levine, Lee. 1998. *Judaism and Hellenism in Antiquity: Conflict or Confluence?* Seattle: University of Washington Press.

Lyman, Rebecca. 2003. "Hellenism and Heresy," *JECS* 11: 209–222.

Maas, Michael. 1991. *John Lydus and the Roman Past.* London: Routledge.
Matthews, J. F. 1994. "The Origin of Ammianus," *CQ* 44: 252–269.
Millar, Fergus. 1983. "The Phoenician Cities: A Case-Study of Hellenization," *PCPhS* 29: 55–71.
———. 1987. "Empire, Community, and Culture in the Roman Near East: Greeks, Syrians, Jews and Arabs," *JJS* 38: 143–164.
———. 1997. "Porphyry: Ethnicity, Language, and Alien Wisdom." In *Philosophia Togata II: Plato and Aristotle at Rome,* ed. J. Barnes and M. Griffin, 241–262. Oxford: Clarendon Press.
———. 2007. *A Greek Roman Empire.* Berkeley: University of California Press.
Momigliano, Arnaldo. 1955. "Genesi e funzione del concetto di Ellenismo." In *Contributo alla Storia degli Studi Classici,* Vol. 1, 165–193. Rome: Edizioni di Storia e Letteratura.
———. 1975. *Alien Wisdom.* Cambridge: Cambridge University Press.
Morlet, Sebastien. 2009. *La Démonstration évangélique d'Eusèbe de Césarée: Étude sur l'apologétique chrétienne à l'époque de Constantin.* Paris: Institut d'Études Augustiniennes.
Most, Glenn. 2008. "Philhellenism, Cosmopolitanism, Nationalism." In *Hellenisms: Culture, Identity, and Ethnicity from Antiquity to Modernity,* ed. Katerina Zacharia, 151–167. Aldershot: Ashgate.
Pilhofer, Peter. 1990. *Presbyteron Kreitton: Der Altersbeweis der jüdischen und christlichen Apologeten und seine Vorgeschichte.* Tübingen: Mohr Siebeck.
Ridings, Daniel. 1995. *The Attic Moses: The Dependency Theme in Some Early Christian Writers.* Goteborg: Acta Universitatis Gothoburgensis.
Said, Suzanne. 2001. "The Discourse of Identity in Greek Rhetoric from Isocrates to Aristides." In *Ancient Perceptions of Greek Ethnicity,* ed. I. Malkin, 275–299. Washington, DC: Center for Hellenic Studies.
———. 2006. "The Rewriting of the Athenian Past: From Isocrates to Aelius Aristides." In *Greeks on Greekness: Viewing the Greek Past under the Roman Empire,* ed. D. Konstan and S. Said, 47–60. Proceedings of the Cambridge Philological Society Suppl. 29. Cambridge: Cambridge Philological Society.
Sandwell, Isabella. 2007. *Religious Identity in Late Antiquity: Greeks, Jews, and Christians in Antioch.* Cambridge: Cambridge University Press.
Scheidweiler, F. 1956. "Zur Protheoria der unter dem Namen des Apollinarios überlieferten Psalmenparaphrase," *BZ* 49: 336–344.
Schott, Jeremy. 2008. *Christianity, Empire, and the Making of Religion in Late Antiquity.* Philadelphia: University of Pennsylvania Press.
Ševčenko, Ihor. 1980. "A Shadow Outline of Virtue." In *Age of Spirituality,* ed. K. Weitzmann, 53–73. New York: Metropolitan Museum of Art.
Sheppard, Anne. 2000. "Philosophy and Philosophical schools." In *Cambridge Ancient History Vol. 14,* ed. Averil Cameron, B. Ward-Perkins, and Michael Whitby, 835–854. Cambridge: Cambridge University Press.
Siniossoglou, Niketas. 2008. *Plato and Theodoret.* Cambridge: Cambridge University Press.
Staab, Gregor. 2006. "Chronographie als Philosophie: Die Urwahrheit der mosaischen Überlieferung nach dem Begründungsmodell des Mittelplatonismus bei Julius Africanus." In *Julius Africanus und die christliche Weltchronik,* ed. M. Wallraff, 61–82. Berlin: Walter de Gruyter.
Swain, Simon. 1996. *Hellenism and Empire.* Oxford: Clarendon.

Tarrant, Harold. 1997. "Olympiodorus and the Surrender of Paganism," *ByzF* 24: 181–192.
Thraede, K. 1962. "Erfinder II," *RAC* 5: 1191–1278.
Traina, G. 2002. "Hellenism in the East: Some Historiographical Remarks," *Electrum* 6: 15–24.
Trombley, Frank. 2006. "Autochthons and Barbarians in Early Medieval Greece: Identity and Symbiosis," *Ancient World* 37: 157–178.
Van Dam, Raymond. 2007. *The Roman Revolution of Constantine*. Cambridge: Cambridge University Press.
Van Nuffelen, Peter. 2002. "Deux fausses lettres de Julien l'apostat (La lettre aux Juifs, Ep. 51 [Wright], et la lettre à Arsacius, Ep. 84 [Bidez])," *VC* 55: 131–50.
Vasunia, Phiroze. 2001. *The Gift of the Nile: Hellenizing Egypt from Aeschylus to Alexander*. Berkeley: University of California Press.
Vogt, E. 1988. "Hellenismus II." In *Kleines Wörterbuch des Hellenismus*, ed. H. H. Schmitt and E. Vogt, 2–4. Wiesbaden: Otto Harrassowitz.
Vout, C. 2006. "What's in a Beard? Rethinking Hadrian's Hellenism." *In Rethinking Revolutions through Greece*, ed. S. Goldhill and R. Osborne, 96–123. Cambridge: Cambridge University Press.
Watts, Edward. 2004. "Justinian, Malalas, and the End of the Athenian Philosophical Teaching in A.D. 529," *JRS* 94: 168–182.
———. 2006. *City and School in Late Antique Athens and Alexandria*. Berkeley: University of California Press.
Weiss, Jean-Pierre. 1978. "Julien, Rome et les Romains." In *L'Empereur Julien: De l'histoire à la légende (331–1715)*, ed. R. Braun and J. Richer, 125–140. Paris: Les Belles Lettres.
Wirth, G. 1988. "Geschichtsschreibung." In *Kleines Wörterbuch des Hellenismus*, ed. H. H. Schmitt and E. Vogt, 205–230. Wiesbaden: Otto Harrassowitz.
Wittgenstein, Ludwig. 1968. *Philosophical Investigations*. Oxford: Blackwell.
Woolf, Greg. 1994. "Becoming Roman, Staying Greek," *PCPhS* 40: 116–143.
Wright, Wilmer C. 2003. *Julian*, Vol. 3. Loeb Classical Library. Cambridge, MA: Harvard University Press.

CHAPTER 14

EDUCATION: SPEAKING, THINKING, AND SOCIALIZING

EDWARD WATTS
Indiana University

> Libanius to Symmachus (Ep. 1004 F=177 N)
>
> The day proceeded up to the third hour when, as I was in the midst of my work, Quadratus, the most excellent and noble . . . came to me and placed in my hand a letter, saying that it had come from you. And immediately all my troubles fled . . . When I found a translator, I thought it would be terrible if I did not fill the city with the gift of Fortune, and so I handed the letter to three of my friends and told them to go through the whole city and show it . . . [the city] counted me blessed for the honor received and you for that bestowed, for you had obliged the gods of eloquence by rousing the students.

The Antiochene rhetorician Libanius and Symmachus, a prefect of the city of Rome, authored two of the largest surviving collections of late antique Greek and Latin letters. This letter, the only surviving exchange between them, represents a natural point from which to begin a discussion of late antique education. Libanius and Symmachus had never met and, evidently, could not even comfortably communicate in the same language. Nevertheless, Symmachus' letter so excited Libanius that he immediately commissioned and circulated a translation among his friends. Libanius' excitement arose not from the senator's political achievements or the (likely quite mundane) contents of his message but from Symmachus' mastery of the arcane rules of rhetorical composition. Libanius, Symmachus, and the Antiochenes who subjected themselves to the public reading of their correspondence all were initiates into the common culture of the educated man (*paideia*). In Late Antiquity, *paideia* represented a universal cultural currency that distinguished the cultivated from the average man[1] through an expensive and time-consuming education that drilled students to follow linguistic rules and taught them to master a code of socially acceptable behavior.[2] Men like Libanius and Symmachus could exchange pleasantries over thousands of miles because the Roman educational system had implanted a deep appreciation of the value of *paideia* among the urban elites of the Mediterranean world. Throughout the empire, men had come to assume that the educated man was better than his uneducated contemporaries. His learning guided his soul "towards excellence and the condition proper to humanity" while his uneducated contemporaries languished in a less refined and more primitive state.[3] Many devotees of *paideia* saw their cultivation as so much of a defining feature of their elite identities that they highlighted it explicitly in epitaphs,[4] public inscriptions,[5] and the letters that they circulated and published.[6]

This sentiment rested on a solid foundation. Although fundamentally literary in character, later Roman education did as much to socialize students as it did to familiarize them with the works of a classical canon. Students learned about, commented on, and practiced the behaviors that marked one as a member of polite society.[7] Their teachers went to great pains to outline for young gentlemen how they should treat other men and what role they ought to play in their home cities.[8] They also learned to maintain their composure at all times and to extend to other educated men the respect that they expected to receive.[9] *Paideia* then created and sustained the reciprocal relationships and codes of conduct essential to the functioning of an elite social system that had spread across the Roman world.

This chapter explores both the literary and social aspects of late antique education. It begins by discussing, in general terms, the nature of teaching. Although some attention is paid to basic reading and writing instruction, most of the discussion focuses on elite literary education, the best documented and most influential teaching in the late antique world. It describes the nature of the curriculum and the places in which teaching occurred. It then examines the ways in which teachers and their students crafted a distinctive scholastic social world with its own particular hierarchy and rules. Finally, it concludes by considering Christian responses to an educational system that retained strong pagan influences even as it shaped the ways that students conceived of their world.

The Levels of Late Antique Education

Later Roman education, at its most accessible level, was not geared toward the literary training of *paideia*.[10] The vast majority of people in the Roman world were effectively illiterate, and most young people probably received little formal education at all.[11] Most of those who did attend class received only a functional education, undertaken at a school of letters,[12] in which they acquired basic literacy. If they completed their training (which, undoubtedly, most did not), these students could presumably read and/or write, but they would not possess any detailed familiarity with classical literature or the literary style of famous authors. Additionally, many of the people who once possessed these skills were likely to forget some of them as their lives went on. Literacy is a skill that must be developed, but it is also one that must be practiced constantly if it is not to be lost. Many average Romans who once possessed some degree of literacy would have seen these skills gradually atrophy through disuse.

This rarely happened to those fortunate few who undertook the expensive and time-consuming training of the elite. Those men received a specialized education that emphasized grammatical rules, eloquent composition, and mastery of a canon of authors. Late antique students followed a variety of paths to develop these skills, but the most conventional one began at the school of the grammarian.[13] Students generally spent their preteen and early teenage years with grammarians and got from them a flexible education that responded to their individual needs.[14] Grammarians taught everything from basic reading and writing skills to the rudiments of rhetorical composition.[15] Their teaching imparted to students a sense of the correct pronunciation of words and the behavior of each part of a sentence. During the initial phase of training, their classes often consisted of the detailed reading of a text that explained its grammatical constructions as well as its moral and historical significance.[16] When students were sufficiently advanced, the grammarian began a series of exercises called the *progymnasmata* that taught students how to elaborate upon stories or themes using the grammatical skills they had developed earlier.[17]

Probably around the age of thirteen or fourteen, these students began moving on to schools of rhetoric.[18] Sometimes this represented an abrupt jump from one teacher to another, but it seems to have been common for a student to take a bit of time to adjust to the new environment. Libanius, for example, spent his fourteenth year taking classes in both grammar and rhetoric.[19] Even when a student enrolled exclusively under a rhetorician, he often continued with the *progymnasmata* under the tutelage of one of the rhetorician's assistants.[20] Rhetorical schools ultimately geared their training toward the production of complete student orations, but this was done in a systematic fashion. The second-century sophist Lucian, for example, used the apt metaphor of climbing a mountain to describe this progression. He marks the rhetorician as a guide (though, in reality, rhetoricians usually lacked the "hard muscles, manly stride, and sun-tanned body" Lucian details) who leads his students in the footsteps of Demosthenes and Plato toward "a lawful marriage with Rhetoric."[21] The path began with relatively simple exercises designed to teach students to interpret short memorable sayings. As they progressed through their training, students developed this modest base into a detailed knowledge of the texts and tendencies of a range of esteemed authors. They read and commented on the work of orators and historians, they composed rhetorical exercises based on literary and mythological situations, and they developed anthologies by copying favorite passages.[22] Eventually, students progressed to the point where they were ready to write, memorize, and deliver their own rhetorical compositions. These products and the eloquence that they displayed grew out of their scrutiny and dissection of the finest works of Greek and Latin literature.

A typical course in rhetoric took about three years. Although some students remained attached to their teachers for much longer,[23] most probably moved on by the age of twenty.[24] In Late Antiquity, those who wished to continue their education could pursue legal, medical, or philosophical training. Each of these paths led to different outcomes, but, at their early stages, they were not completely parallel. Indeed, philosophy represented something of a common point of contact. Perhaps because of its importance to Galen, philosophy (in particular, the first half of Aristotle's *Organon*) eventually came to occupy an important place in the medical curriculum passed down from the late antique to the medieval world.[25] Law schools never incorporated philosophical study into their curricula, but individual students seem often to have come to law schools with some background in philosophy.[26] Indeed, in the 480s, the future lawyer Zacharias Scholasticus and the physician Gessius both attended lectures in Aristotelian philosophy in the same Alexandrian classroom.[27]

Because of its intimate association with paganism, philosophy is often seen by modern scholars as the most contentious subject treated by conventional late antique teachers. Late antique philosophers did occasionally find themselves faced with serious political problems, but the actual teaching of philosophy was usually a rather banal and uncontroversial affair. In the classroom of a philosopher, students would listen to and participate in what amounted to line-by-line discussions of philosophical texts and their meaning.[28] While focused on well-known works, these discussions could contain a surprising amount of originality and critical examination.[29] Lecture notes taken down by students of the Neoplatonist Damascius, for example, show that his seminars used detailed critiques of the commentaries of Proclus to interpret Platonic texts.[30] In a routine session, Damascius introduced a Platonic passage, provided Proclus' interpretation of it, and then offered his own analysis of both the Platonic text and Proclus' explanation.[31] Sessions like these both presented the particular ideas contained within a text and, in the aggregate, helped to demonstrate the principles of a larger doctrinal system.[32]

Philosophers also tried to shape the behavior of their students in even more profound ways than grammarians and rhetoricians. Their discussions often laid out ideals of philosophical conduct and used examples to illustrate their practical applications.[33] The *Prolegomena to Platonic Philosophy*, the best known introduction to a late antique philosophical curriculum, groups a set of ideal behaviors under the headings of moral and political virtue and indicates that the first part of philosophical training was devoted to their explanation.[34] Indeed, these virtues were so important to teachers of philosophy that some turned away students whose moral failings seemed without remedy.[35]

Places of Study in Late Antiquity

Teaching occurred in a variety of locations in Late Antiquity. Some classes were held in dedicated classrooms, but the vast majority of late antique professors gave their lessons in less formal spaces, like temples, tombs, and the open air.[36] In a career that spanned more than five decades, Libanius taught classes in his home, beside a pool in a bath house, alongside a temple, and in a lecture room within Antioch's *bouleuterion*.[37] This last space included a "covered lecture room and four colonnades with a courtyard that had been turned into a garden with vines, figs, and other trees."[38] No remains of Libanius' various teaching spaces have been found, but a number of "classrooms" have been uncovered in other cities throughout the Eastern Mediterranean. In Athens, for example, it was customary for professors to teach in their own houses. Eunapius provides a detailed description of one such house, which belonged to the sophist Julianus at the turn of the fourth century. It contained a small theater of marble and was decorated with statues of his pupils.[39] The remains of a number of late antique Athenian houses contain apsidal rooms like those described by Eunapius and, in one case, a cache of statuary.[40] One of these houses even sits in a spot that corresponds to the place where Marinus, the biographer of Proclus, locates his master's school.[41]

Even more interesting are the remains of a late antique university quarter unearthed at Kom el-Dikka in Alexandria. In the late fifth and early sixth centuries, perhaps as many as twenty-five lecture halls were constructed in the center of the city abutting a late Roman bath.[42] These seem to have been part of a larger scholastic quarter that included a public theater, a colonnaded portico, and a large open space in which people could congregate. Intriguingly, all of the lecture halls were entered from the portico, all contained two or three rows of stone benches built to line three walls, and all had a raised central seat from which (presumably) the professor conducted class.[43] Their capacity varied, but, aside from the much larger theater in the south of the complex, twenty to thirty people could sit in each room.[44] Literary references suggest that similar complexes existed in Berytus[45] and Constantinople, too.[46] From all indications, use of these dedicated classroom spaces was reserved for only the most accomplished professors. The Neoplatonist Ammonius, who held a publicly funded professorship in Alexandria, probably taught in the Kom el-Dikka auditoria, as did Horapollon, a *vir clarissimus* who similarly held a public chair.[47]

Although very different spaces, the elementary teacher's modest accommodations, Libanius' space in the Antiochene city hall, Proclus' Athenian house, and the Alexandrian scholastic complex all played the same functional roles. Whatever its physical layout, a late antique classroom helped to separate a teacher and his students from the rest of the world by defining the space in which teaching occurred. This could be done by adorning the walls with thematically appropriate artwork like the statues of Julianus' students or the *tondos* of Greek philosophers that decorated an apsidal room in the Atrium house of Aphrodisias, but the simple act of sitting in a group around a teacher helped students to focus their attention on his words.[48] In addition, teachers used these spaces to communicate the undeniable hierarchy of a school. Although most apparent in the raised seats for professors at the center of the Alexandrian classrooms, ancient depictions of teachers usually show them seated in an imposing chair before a student or a class of students.[49] Even the unfortunate elementary teachers described as *chamaididaskaloi* ("teachers sitting on the ground") seem to have sat upon rocks as humble signs of their modest authority.[50]

The Scholastic Worldview

The existence of communal intellectual spaces and the emphasis placed on scholastic hierarchy within them enhanced pedagogy while simultaneously contributing to the informal social formation of students. We have already discussed how elements of the late antique grammatical, rhetorical, and philosophical curricula taught students to behave in specific ways. The physical and social environment both within and beyond a school influenced the behavior of students as much as or more than this teaching. When a student enrolled at a school, he entered into a new social world. The majority of late antique students probably continued to live at home and attend the classes of a local teacher, but many young men also traveled to teachers based in Athens, Alexandria, Rome, Antioch, and any number of less famous centers of teaching. Regardless of the distance traveled, teachers made great efforts to make enrollment in an intellectual circle seem like the beginning of a new life. Teachers and students alike commonly described the members of their school as a second family. Students called their teachers "father" or "mother" and their peers "brothers." Teachers saw the boys they taught as their children.[51] This was not empty rhetoric; late antique sources offer many examples of students depending on their professors for protection and assistance.[52] Students reciprocated by cheering if their professors gave a public performance,[53] avoiding the lectures of other professors,[54] and even fighting the students of rival schools.[55] In the years that they remained at school, students were expected to function as a part of this scholastic family.

Most students arrived fully prepared to participate in this new world. Libanius, for example, grew up hearing "from older men about Athens and the doings there."[56] Sometimes these highlighted great rhetorical triumphs, but many of the stories involved "tales of the fighting between the schools . . . and all of the deeds of daring that students perform to raise the prestige of their teachers."[57] Later in his life, Libanius even speaks fondly about the fathers who used to take pride when they saw "on their sons' bodies the evidence of the battles they fight on their teacher's behalf, the scars on the head, face, hands, and on every limb."[58]

Among the other activities Libanius had heard about and longed to take part in were "the kidnapping of arriving students, being taken to Corinth for trial on kidnapping charges, giving many feasts, blowing all (his) money, and looking for someone to give a loan."[59]

Libanius' words show that students, teachers, and even magistrates understood that schools operated under a different set of rules than the rest of late Roman society. Students were encouraged to develop new loyalties to their scholastic families and permitted to demonstrate those loyalties through actions (like brawling or kidnapping) that would normally be considered criminal. Indeed, in a justly famous passage, Augustine comments that students "often commit outrages that ought to be punished by law, were it not that custom protects them."[60] One's student status legitimized normally unacceptable behaviors and, in some cases, even marked these as positive contributions to the fabric of an intellectual community.

Rituals of inclusion particular to intellectual communities helped to reinforce the sense that students lived in a social world with its own particular set of rules. The best attested of such rituals come from the Athenian rhetorical schools of the mid- to late fourth century. When students arrived at an Athenian school, they swore an oath to study under a specific teacher.[61] They were then led in procession through the Agora (which was filled with their fellow students) until they reached the baths.[62] This procession was intended to be a frightening thing, and it included screamed threats and some physical violence.[63] Once the initiates reached the bathhouse, they were "washed, dressed, and received the right to wear the scholarly robe."[64] When this was completed, Gregory Nazianzus says, the students received the newcomer "as an equal."[65]

The initiation ceremony represented a liminal phase in a student's academic life. He had now become a part of the school, and, if a student of rhetoric, he also now wore a robe to distinguish himself from the wider public.[66] He was now a scholar, not a civilian, but he occupied the lowest rung of a scholastic hierarchy that defined his interaction with other students and professors. Professors, the heads of these intellectual families, rested atop a steep pyramid. Below them were the assistant teachers and senior students who, in larger circles, served as intermediaries between the professor and his youngest and least advanced charges.[67] The average students represented the broad base of this pyramid. Their ranks, too, were organized according to a well-defined hierarchy. They were led by a designated student leader and ranked based on their time in the school.[68] Not surprisingly, hazing of the youngest and newest students occurred, evidently with some regularity.[69]

The experience of studying under the same teacher helped many students forge strong friendships. Gregory Nazianzus' description of the bond he developed with Basil of Caesarea in Athens is perhaps the best-known portrait of a scholastic friendship, but others offer equally interesting (and often more reliable) snapshots. Eunapius, for example, tells how Prohaeresius and Hephaestion both arrived in Athens so impoverished that they shared not only a room but even a scholarly robe.[70] Synesius, whose wealth never forced him into such a situation, still could reminisce about the intimacy that he enjoyed with fellow students.[71] Indeed, late antique graduates looked back on their student days with the same fondness as their modern counterparts. Many of them maintained the social networks that they first built while studying. In some cases, they even organized ancient versions of the thoroughly modern institution of the class reunion.[72]

Education's Influence

Unfortunately, the reality of late antique education was often much messier than these idealistic portraits suggest. The interactions that joined students and their professors in a shared intellectual enterprise enhanced the bonds of companionship that the curriculum urged them to develop, but the cost of schooling and the uncertainties of late antique life meant that a significant portion of those attending classes did not develop a particularly strong identification with their scholastic families. Additionally, some students tried to sample the offerings of a range of teachers and may have enjoyed only a casual association with any one particular school and its students. Others were forced by their financial or personal circumstances to drop out before they could develop these strong bonds. Late antique evidence suggests that only a minority of those attending classes in rhetoric at any one time would complete even a three-year course of study.[73] In addition, some of the students who stayed for the full course would sullenly separate themselves from the activities of their fellows. Libanius, who proudly counted himself among that group, found himself ostracized by his classmates.[74] In the 480s, the Alexandrian student Paralius even received a beating because of his negative attitude toward his teachers and peers.[75] Despite these circumstances, both men remained friends with some of their classmates for the rest of their lives.[76]

Even after noting these exceptions, the influence of late antique education on elite behaviors and the social relationships they supported cannot be denied. Letters, the lifeblood of elite social networks, show how the literary knowledge and mutual expectations of behavior that *paideia* engendered combined to fashion a powerful yet extremely idiosyncratic code of conduct. A typical example of this dynamic can be found in a letter sent by Procopius of Gaza to the physician Gessius around the turn of the sixth century. This letter, which aims to comfort Gessius following the death of his wife and some of his children, offers sincere condolences for the "terrible tragedy" inflicted on Gessius by the "whims of fortune."[77] The death of Gessius' wife, which Procopius chose to attribute to her grief at the loss of her children, came about because she was a "Phrygian and a barbarian, and she did not prepare her soul with the medicines of philosophy for the drink of fortune."[78] While this was perhaps understandable, Procopius reminded Gessius of an anecdote in which the philosopher Anaxagoras shrugged off news of an untimely death because he understood his own mortality.[79] He then urged Gessius to respond to this situation philosophically by showing the appropriate restraint and emotional detachment. Intriguingly, when Gessius failed to rouse himself after reading Procopius' inspiring Anaxagoran allusion, Procopius wrote a second letter in which he offered an extended anecdote featuring Pythagoras as a way to again urge the doctor to "wisely guide our affairs towards greater things."[80] Procopius' letters, and myriad others like them, combine the florid language and literary allusions emphasized in the late antique classroom to exhort their recipient to behave with the rationality and restraint expected of a man of *paideia*. Prompts like these reminded elites of the ancient culture that they all shared, the basic values it upheld, and the actions it required them to take.

The tendency to look back in time for exemplary figures, illustrative anecdotes, and powerful turns of phrase made the system of *paideia* an inexact fit for the needs of an increasingly Christian Roman empire. *Paideia* was a system born in a different world, and its contents reflected the ideas and values of its creators. Its teaching focused extensively on classical mythology and pagan theology[81] and, in its classical incarnation, even offered direct instruction in "how a man must bear himself in his relationships with the gods."[82] Although some teachers continued to offer religious instruction like this to select students into the sixth century,[83] most had wisely begun to downplay this curricular element by the beginning of the Theodosian era.[84] Nevertheless, classical mythology and pagan theology remained present in classrooms throughout Late Antiquity.[85]

The hierarchy and personal dynamics of late antique schools meant that social factors could enhance the appeal and importance of these pagan elements of the curriculum. On occasion, these factors could encourage students to engage in religious behaviors that they would not otherwise have considered. A number of Christian sources speak about this danger. In the fourth century, Gregory Nazianzus characterizes the Athens of his student days as "harmful to the soul and this is of no small consequence to the pious. For the city is richer in those evil riches—idols—than the rest of Greece and it is hard not to be carried along and led away with their devotees."[86] Two late-fifth-century sources speak in greater detail about the ways in which peers could encourage the sort of spiritual drift to which Gregory alludes. Zacharias Scholasticus' *Life of Severus* offers an extremely rich portrait of the religious dimensions of late antique student life. A section of the text describing the schools of Alexandria details the conversion to Christianity of a young pagan student of grammar named Paralius, a conversion brought about in part through his friendships with a group of devout Christian peers.[87] Another section of the text describes how John, a young Christian student of law, grew close to a group of colleagues who experimented with pagan and magical rituals in Berytus in the 490s.[88] After a failed love affair, John turned to these friends and participated in their rites until he was discovered, chastised by some Christian students, and brought back into the Church. While studying in Berytus, no less a Christian figure than Severus, the future bishop of Antioch, followed young men whose minds were "polluted by Hellenic myths" and participated in decidedly non-Christian rituals.[89]

At times, true conversions did occur among students. Pagan sources occasionally speak about men from Christian backgrounds who adopted pagan religious practices because of their educational experiences. The emperor Julian, of course, offers the most famous example, but a range of others—from the third-century Platonist Ammonius Saccas[90] to the fifth-century Alexandrian intellectuals Epiphanius and Euprepius—also fit into this category.[91] The occasional Christian source also speaks about pagan students converted by Christian teachers or students.[92] These conversions are notable precisely because they were extraordinary; there is no evidence of overwhelming numbers of student religious conversions in the period. Leaving aside the rare conversion, student religious experimentation seems to have had few long-term consequences. For most students, this sort of religious experimentation seemed a type of adolescent misbehavior that differed little from punching a stranger in the nose for studying under the wrong teacher. It was something that could be done while a student because of the special rules of the scholastic environment.

This helps to explain the general comfort that most Christians seem to have had with an educational system that remained dominated by pagan teachers and included significant pagan content. To be sure, some Christians offered rather extreme rejections of classical learning. Caesarius of Arles, for example, once fell asleep over a book and dreamed that it changed into a threatening serpent.[93] Such comments are memorable, but they are the isolated (and often hypocritical) complaints of a minority. In truth, the growth of Christianity and the development of Christian culture did little to change the influence of *paideia* over late antique literary habits and social relationships. Many of Late Antiquity's Christian leaders were themselves highly educated men who expressed their ideas and managed their friendships through the exchange of rhetorically polished compositions and letters. These Christians adopted the spirit, and often even the language, of Basil of Caesarea's suggestion that Christians "apply themselves especially to literature" to take the "deeds of good men to heart" and from this "trace out a kind of rough sketch of what virtue is."[94] They saw the utility of the personal and social skills taught in schools and were willing to cull from this curriculum whatever was useful "while smiling at the myths."[95]

Emperors and imperial officials tended to share their subjects' relaxed view of the religious connotations of late antique education. Two emperors, however, proved memorable exceptions to this trend. In the 360s, the pagan emperor Julian issued a series of laws designed to use the educational system as a protreptic tool.[96] His efforts began in June 362 with a rather innocuous law requiring that both local officials and the imperial court certify the good personal character of every teacher in the empire.[97] Julian followed this law with another issued later that summer. This second law explained that teachers were of good character only if they taught what they believed to be true,[98] and, for this reason, Christian teachers were left with a choice: "either do not teach the things which (you) do not think honorable or, if (you) wish to teach, first persuade (your) students that neither Homer nor Hesiod nor any one of these, the authors about whom (you) lecture and explain, is guilty of any impiety."[99] Teachers then could neither criticize pagan content nor even disregard it. They were instead required to "persuade" students to accept pagan piety.[100] Under Julian's heavy hand, education had become a tool for religious as well as cultural instruction. Perhaps not surprisingly, his restrictive second law was quickly reversed by his successor.[101]

Justinian intervened in Roman scholastic life in less dramatic but no less memorable fashion in the late 520s and early 530s. In 529, a law ordering that "no one should teach philosophy nor interpret astronomy" was issued in Justinian's name and sent to the city of Athens.[102] This law has often been interpreted as a blanket restriction placed on the teaching of philosophy throughout the empire, but our sources do not support so broad an interpretation. Instead, it is better to see Justinian's intervention as a specific response to local conditions in Athens at the time.[103] In 531, however, the emperor issued a series of two laws that, while not specifically concerned with regulating education, deeply influenced the legal standing and opportunities available to pagan teachers.[104] These two edicts attacked paganism by undermining both the political standing of individual pagans and the viability of institutions that supported the private practice of paganism. Included among the restrictions of the second law was a prohibition against pagans teaching and receiving a municipal salary.[105] Imperial agents enforced these laws in a rather desultory fashion. Excavations in the important pagan intellectual centers of Athens and Aphrodisias show the hasty abandonment in the early sixth century of buildings that may once have housed pagan teachers.[106] Elsewhere, however, pagan teaching survived. The pagan Neoplatonist Olympiodorus of Alexandria, for example, continued teaching without interruption into the 560s.[107]

Conclusion

Pagans and Christians alike responded negatively to the educational interventions of both Julian and Justinian. From the Christian side, Gregory Nazianzus attacks Julian at length for absurdly claiming Hellenic ownership of learning and language while debarring Christians from teaching.[108] Other Christian observers went so far as to call his law an act of persecution.[109] Intriguingly, even Julian's pagan defenders offer little support for his policy.

Eunapius and Libanius both remain conspicuously silent, while Ammianus Marcellinus classifies Julian's "harsh decree forbidding Christians from teaching rhetoric and grammar" as an exception to the emperor's tendency to enact laws that "were not oppressive."[110] Oblique but no less firm criticism of Justinian's actions appears in sources authored by both pagans and Christians. In a commentary on the Epictetan *Handbook*, the Neoplatonist Simplicius adds a long section detailing the appropriate political behavior for a philosopher.[111] In proper Platonic fashion, it marks the philosopher as "a father and teacher for all in common, their corrector, counselor, and guardian."[112] Simplicius argues that, in a corrupt polity, the philosopher "ought to ask to be an exile from these incurable affairs, and, if indeed it is possible, he will go to another, better state."[113] This discussion seems innocuous unless one understands that Simplicius and six of his colleagues anticipated these ideas when they fled from the Roman empire following Justinian's laws of 529 and 531. Indeed, even the Christian historian Agathias shows himself sympathetic to Simplicius' rationale when he says that these seven men, "the flower of those who philosophized at that time," fled to Persia "because it was impossible for them to live without fear of the laws."[114]

The unease expressed by pagan and Christian authors about imperial restrictions placed on teachers shows that many Romans thought it essential to segregate traditional education from the larger politics of religious identity. Despite the dramatic religious, political, and social changes that rocked the Roman world in Late Antiquity, traditional culture remained prized. Indeed, Late Antiquity saw the influence of traditional educational curricula and methods spread from the Greek and Latin classrooms of Roman cities to a surprisingly diverse range of settings. For example, across the Persian frontier, the School of Nisibis offered Syriac-language instruction in elements of the Neoplatonic curriculum.[115] In the later sixth century, its scholastic culture even resembled that of a late antique Greek or Latin rhetorical or philosophical circle. The School of Nisibis emphasized the same strict loyalty to one's master and established a scholarly *habitus* that distinguished scholarly appearance, dress, and behavior from others.[116] A similar scholastic culture also developed at Qenneshre, a center of Syriac scholarship that produced a succession of seventh- and eighth-century Syriac commentators on Aristotle.[117] The influence that Roman philosophical and (especially) medical schools had on late antique Syriac thinkers like those based in Nisibis and Qenneshre also helped set the stage for the important role their ideas would play in the cultural life of the late antique and medieval Arab world.[118]

Late antique schools mattered because they offered access to the ideas, language, and experiences that transformed well-born youths into the respected gentlemen of a large empire. The education they provided centered ostensibly on learning grammar, mastering rhetorical approaches, and developing a facility with a literary canon. But it occurred in an environment with its own rules and its own hierarchy that offered students the freedom to engage in otherwise impermissible social and religious experimentation. Loosened from the bonds that restricted normal behavior, young men were free to interact, develop friendships, and show personal loyalty in an exciting range of ways. This process of socialization allowed young men to create the relationships that their polished words and literary allusions then sustained. It also enabled classical education to endure as a cultural institution throughout and beyond the late antique Roman world.

NOTES

1. For this idea, see most notably Matthews 1989, 78, and Brown 1992, 35.

2. For education as a process of socialization, see Bloomer 1997, 57–78.

3. *IPriene* 112.73; see also Marrou 1938, 209, and Kaster 1988, 15–16.

4. See the example of Didius Taxiarches, *CIL* VI.16843.

5. For example, the Epicurean inscription erected by Diogenes in his hometown of Oinoanda, published in English by Smith 1996.

6. One of the best expressions of this idea is Libanius, *Ep.* 1036.

7. For this line of thought, see Brown 1992, 122. Bloomer (1997, 59–63) has described the particular role that *fictio personae* played in developing a student's conception of gentlemanly behaviors.

8. Plutarch, *Moralia*, 7 E.

9. Plutarch, *Moralia*, 10 C, f; 37 C; and Philostratus, *Vit. Soph.* 561. For the evolving view of anger in antiquity, see Harris 2001, 112–127, and Brown 1992, 48–52.

10. For broader treatments of ancient education, see Marrou 1956; Morgan 1998; and Cribiore 2001.

11. Arguing largely from empirical evidence, the most compelling estimates of literacy rates in the high imperial period suggest that between one-tenth and one-third of the population was literate to the degree that they could write and read simple documents. For the lower figure, see Harris 1989, 256–283. Note, however, the more optimistic figures of Hopkins 1991, 133–158, and Hanson 1991, 159–198. In addition to the materials noted previously, see the important work of Youtie 1971a, 161–176, and 1971b, 239–261.

12. The *grammatodidaskaleia*.

13. What follows is a description of the ideal path a student followed. The realities of late antique education were often more complicated, however. Grammar schools, for example, that taught elementary letters as well as rhetoric are attested as well. See Dionisotti 1982, 98–101.

14. Instruction in grammar could begin as early as age seven or eight (cf. Kaster 1988, 11), but a later age may be more typical. Libanius, for example, finished his grammatical training at thirteen (Cribiore 2007a, 31).

15. See, for example, Cribiore 1996, no. 160 and no. 379.

16. For the function of the grammarian, see Kaster 1988, 12–14; Bonner 1977; and Marrou 1956, 243.

17. For an especially thorough discussion of the *progymnasmata*, see Cribiore 2001, 221–230. For the exercises as a sort of primer for the lifestyle of the cultivated, see Webb 2001, 289–316.

18. One student, Euphemius, enrolled under Libanius at age eleven (Libanius, *Ep.* 634=Cribiore 16; for the age of eleven, see Cribiore 2007a, 240). Eunapius famously joined a school of rhetoric at age sixteen (*VS* 485), perhaps a bit later than usual.

19. Cribiore 2007a, 31, based on the arguments of Booth 1983, 157–163.

20. This seems to be the role played by Eusebius and Thalassius in Libanius' school. For a description of their role, see *Ep.* 905–909 and 922–926, as well as *Oration* 31. For a discussion, see Norman 1990, 454–461, as well as the comprehensive discussion of Cribiore (2007a, 33–37).

21. Lucian, *Rhetorum praeceptor* 9.

22. Cribiore 2001, 226–230.

23. E.g., the particular case of Prohaeresius, discussed in Watts 2006, 49–54.

24. *CTh* 14.9.1; a law of 370 seems to have limited rhetorical training in the city of Rome to those twenty and under. This may then be taken as a rough baseline.

25. Roueché 1999, 153–169.

26. This much is suggested by the *proemium* of Zacharias Scholasticus' dialogue, the *Ammonius*.

27. Zacharias, *Ammonius* ln. 360–368.

28. This was the basic pattern. For the probable variations of approach from school to school, see Lamberton 2001, 442–445, esp. 455.

29. On the nature of late antique commentaries, see Baltussen 2007, 247–281.

30. Westerink 1977, 10–14.

31. Westerink 1977, 11. For a typical example of this structure, see *In Phaedonem*, 1.100.

32. The various prolegomena to philosophy that were written in Late Antiquity played a crucial part in making this possible. They introduced each philosopher's system of thought before a student studied the texts. By starting with a complete picture of the system, it was easier for students to understand where each individual text fit. For these discussions, see Mansfeld 1994 and 1998.

33. Even the initial introduction to philosophy that students received emphasized things like "the care of morals, the administration of a household, and the state and its preservation" (Alcinous, *Didaskalikos*, 3).

34. *Prolégomènes à la philosophie de Platon* (ed. and trans. Westerink 1990) 26.30–33. Aristotle's *Ethics* was used for moral virtues, and his *Politics* (along with Plato's *Laws* and the *Republic*) was used to teach political virtues.

35. As Proclus did with the Antiochene Hilarius: Damascius, *Vit. Is.* fr. 91B.

36. Cribiore 2001, 21–34.

37. For discussion of Libanius' various locations, see Cribiore 2007b, 145–146; cf. Cribiore 2007a, 30. Libanius mentions the bathhouse at *Or* 1.55 and describes the space in the city hall at some length in *Or.* 22.31 and *Or.* 5.45–52. For the temple and his use of his own house in Antioch, see *Or.* 1.101–4.

38. *Or.* 22.31 (trans. Norman).

39. *Vit. Soph.* 483.

40. See Frantz 1988, 88–89, and, for a more detailed discussion, Shear 1973, 156–164. It has been suggested that these houses were connected with the philosophical school of Damascius, a link initially proposed by Frantz 1975, 36, and reiterated later (Frantz 1988, 44–47). More recently, Athanassiadi (1999, 343–347) has suggested linking House C, the largest of the Areopagus houses, with Damascius. As she admits, this is a "necessarily speculative theory."

41. *Vit. Proc.* 29. Karivieri 1994, 115–139.

42. The remains are described and analyzed in detail by Majcherek 2007, 11–50, and placed in their urban context by McKenzie 2007, 53–83. Cf. MacCoull 2007.

43. Majcherek 2007, 23–25. These remains seem to correspond to the space in which Zacharias Scholasticus describes an Alexandrian class (*Amm.* 92–99).

44. Majcherek 2007, 25.

45. *Expositio Totius Mundi et Gentium* 25; cf. Jones Hall 2004, 66–67.

46. *CTh* 14.9.3; cf. *CTh* 6.21.1. For discussion of how these laws regulating scholastic organization relate to spatial arrangements in the city, see Cribiore 2007b, 148–149.

47. For Ammonius' position, see Watts 2006, 209–210. For Horapollon, see Maspero 1914, 166 ln. 15.

48. For Aphrodisias, note R. Smith 1990, 151–153. For the possible identification of the Atrium House as a school, see Welch 2007, 130.

49. This evidence, much of which predates Late Antiquity, is masterfully discussed by Cribiore 2001, 29–32.

50. These are, admittedly, a rather elusive group. In the fourth century B.C.E., however, one teacher was mocked for "sitting on stones teaching the children of Gargara their alphabet" (*Anth. Pal.* 11.437). Note the discussion of Cribiore 2001, 27.

51. E.g., Libanius, *Ep.* 931, 1009, 1070, 1257; Synesius, *Ep.* 16. For a discussion of these terms, see Petit 1957, 35–36, and Cribiore 2007a, 138–143.

52. Students called upon their teachers for support if they were arrested (e.g., Eunapius, *Vit. Soph.* 483), they asked that influence be used to help their families (Libanius, *Ep.* 359), and they even used them to suggest a raise in their allowances (Libanius, *Ep.* 428).

53. Among many other references, see Eunapius, *Vit. Soph.* 483.

54. Libanius, *Or.* 18.13–14 indicates that such a restriction was placed upon Julian.

55. Libanius watched this happen to a classmate while he was a student (*Or.* 1.21).

56. Libanius, *Or.* 1.11.

57. Libanius, *Or.* 1.19.

58. *Or.* 3.22. Other scholastic riots in the fourth century may have been motivated by a similar desire to win prestige for teachers. See, for example, Eunapius, *Vit. Soph.* 483; Himerius, *Or.* 67; and Libanius, *Or.* 1.21 on the great riot.

59. Libanius, *Or.* 1.19.

60. Augustine, *Conf.* 5.8.

61. This oath was either "coerced" (as in the case of Libanius) or given willfully (as Eunapius experienced). Libanius, in *Or.* 1.16, describes being abducted and held against his will. Himerius, *Or.* 48.37, describes something similar. For the more agreeable experience of Eunapius, see *Vit. Soph.* 485–487.

62. Gregory Nazianzus, *Or.* 43.16. This ritual is known as well from Eunapius, *Vit. Soph.* 486, and Olympiodorus of Thebes, fr. 28=Photius, *Bib. Cod.* 80.177f.

63. Gregory describes the performance as "seeming very fearful and brutal to those who do not know it, (but) it is to those who have experienced it quite pleasant and humane, for its threats are for show rather than real" (*Or.* 43.16). Eunapius, who was quite ill when he arrived in Athens, suggests that it was nonetheless a physically draining experience (*Vit. Soph.* 486).

64. Olympiodorus, fr. 28.

65. Gregory, *Or.* 43.16.

66. The necessity of wearing a student cloak while engaged in basic rhetorical study is suggested by Eunapius, *Vit. Soph.* 487. This was not only an Athenian convention. Heraclas in Alexandria was forced by his teacher to wear a *tribōn*, and, once he

began, it seems he continued to wear the garment whenever he engaged in intellectual pursuits (Eusebius, *HE* 6.19.12–14).

67. For assistant teachers, see Watts 2006, 49–53; Cribiore 2001, 28.

68. The student leaders have different names in ancient sources. Their role in the school is not particularly clear, nor is it evident that they were distinct from the upper level students. Olympiodorus (fr. 28), for example, mentions that newly initiated students had to pay them a fee upon the commencement of their studies. On this hierarchy in conventional schools, as well as the privileges attached to the head of a teacher's *choros*, see Cribiore 2007a, 201, and Libanius, *Ep.* 886.

69. In fourth-century Athens, for example, it was common for first-year students to be ganged up on whenever they argued a point (Gregory Nazianzus, *Or.* 43.17). Zacharias Scholasticus (*Life of Severus* 47) records a similar situation in the law schools of Berytus in the later 480s.

70. Eunapius, *Vit. Soph.* 487.

71. E.g., Synesius, *Ep.* 139 to Herculianus.

72. Libanius, *Or.* 58.33; cf. Cribiore 2007a, 104.

73. Kaster 1988, 26–27; based on Petit 1957, 62–65. See Libanius, *Ep.* 379, for a case of a student who left his care before completing his course. Note, however, the cautions of Cribiore 2007a, 177.

74. Libanius describes his attitude and the reaction to it in *Or.* 1.17.

75. For this incident, see Zacharias Scholasticus, *Life of Severus*, 20–24.

76. For Libanius, see Cribiore 2007a, 48, and *Ep.* 147. For Paralius, see Zacharias, *Life of Severus*, 40–43.

77. *Ep.* 125.1–2.

78. *Ep.* 125.8–9.

79. *Ep.* 125.9–13.

80. *Ep.* 164.29–30.

81. This was especially true of the philosophy classrooms of the time. For mythology and its role in teaching, see Hermogenes, *Progymnasmata.*

82. Plutarch, *Moralia*, 7 E.

83. E.g., the Athenian scholarch Hegias, as suggested by Damascius (*Vit. Is.* 145B).

84. The philosopher Antoninus, who taught at the Serapeum in Canopus in the later fourth century, is a good example of this. For Antoninus, see Eunapius, *Vit. Soph.* 472, as well as Frankfurter 2000, 184–189.

85. For theology, it is worth noting the defense of basic pagan ideas that Olympiodorus offered before his students in the late 520s (e.g., *In Gorgiam* 47.2).

86. Gregory Nazianzus, *Or.* 43.21. For the nature of fourth-century Athenian life, see Watts 2006, 48–78.

87. This process is laid out in Zacharias, *Life of Severus*, 14–40.

88. Zacharias, *Life of Severus*, 57–63.

89. Garitte 1966, 335–386.

90. Note Porphyry's comments that "Ammonius (Saccas) was a Christian who was brought up in Christianity by his parents. However, when he began to think and study philosophy, he immediately changed (*metebaleto*) to a way of life that conformed with the laws" (Porphyry quoted in Eusebius, *HE* 6.19.6–7).

91. Damascius, *Vit. Is.*, fr. 41.

92. A situation described, for example, by Gregory Thaumaturge in his *Address to Origen*. On this text, see Trigg 2001, 27–52.

93. *Vit. Caes*, 1.8–9.

94. Basil, *Letter to Young Men on How to Derive Benefit from Pagan Literature*, 5.1; 4.1; 10.1.

95. Choricius, *Laud. Marc.* 1.4 (see also Kaster 1988, 80–81). This is actually taken from a description of the bishop of Gaza.

96. For a more detailed discussion of this process, see Watts 2006, 67–71; Matthews 2000, 274–277; and Banchich 1993, 5–14.

97. *CTh*, 13.3.5 (trans. Pharr, with slight revisions).

98. On this idea, see Averil Cameron 1991, 138.

99. Julian, *Ep.* 61 (ed. Bidez-Cumont).

100. The emperor's goal in this, he explained in a letter, was to allow "any youth who wishes to attend school . . . for we ought, I think, to teach but not punish the demented" (*Ep.* 61).

101. Jovian's law is *CTh* 13.3.6. Though the law states that it was issued under Valens and Valentinian, the date places it in the reign of Jovian.

102. John Malalas, *Chronicle*, 18.47 (ed. Thurn).

103. Watts 2004, 168–182.

104. *CJ* 1.11.9 and 10.

105. This is the probable meaning of *dēmosia sitēsis*.

106. For Athens, see Frantz 1988, 88–89, and Shear 1973, 156–164. For Aphrodisias, see Welch 2007, 130.

107. Olympiodorus' lectures on Aristotle's *Meteorology* took place in March and April of 565. For this date, see Neugebauer 1975, 1043–1045.

108. Gregory Nazianzus, *First Oration against Julian*, 4–5; 104–112.

109. For this as a persecution, see Socrates, *HE* 3.12. Note as well Sozomen, *HE* 5.18; Rufinus, *HE* 1.32; and Theodoret, *HE* 3.8.

110. Ammianus, 25.4.20.

111. For a detailed discussion of this section of the text, see O'Meara 2004, 89–98.

112. *In Ench.* 65.3.

113. *In Ench.* 65.35.

114. Agathias, 2.30.3–4. Agathias' account of the philosophers' flight and return may well have been influenced by one of their own accounts (cf. Averil Cameron 1970, 101–102).

115. For the School of Nisibis, see Becker 2006.

116. The specific structures of the sixth-century school were laid out in the *Cause of the Foundation of the Schools*. On this, see now the useful translation of Becker 2008. The scholastic culture described in the *Cause* permitted less student freedom than a conventional school of letters because its students were expected to go into the service of the Church.

117. On Qenneshre, note Watt 1999 and Brock 1993.

118. For discussion of this process and its representation in the literature, see Gutas 1999.

WORKS CITED

Athanassiadi, P., ed. and trans. 1999. *Damascius: The Philosophical History*. Athens: Apamea Cultural Association.

Baltussen, H. 2007. "From Polemic to Exegesis: The Ancient Philosophical Commentary," *Poetics Today* 28: 247–281.

Banchich, T. 1993. "Julian's School Laws: *Cod. Theod.* 13.3.5 and *Ep.* 42," *The Ancient World* 24: 5–14.

Becker, A. 2006. *Fear of God and the Beginning of Wisdom: The School of Nisibis and the Development of Scholastic Culture in Late Antique Mesopotamia.* Philadelphia: University of Pennsylvania Press.

———, trans. 2008. *Sources for the Study of the School of Nisibis.* Liverpool: Liverpool University Press.

Bloomer, M. 1997. "Schooling in Persona: Imagination and Subordination in Roman Education," *Classical Antiquity* 16.1: 57–78.

Bonner, S. F. 1977. *Education in Ancient Rome.* Berkeley: University of California Press.

Booth, A. 1983. "À quel age Libanius est-il entré à l'école du rhéteur?" *Byzantion* 53: 157–163.

Brock, S. 1993. "The Syriac Commentary Tradition." In *Glosses and Commentaries on Aristotelian Logical Texts: The Syriac, Arabic and Medieval Latin Traditions,* ed. C. Burnett, 3–18. London: Warburg Institute, University of London.

Brown, P. 1992. *Power and Persuasion in Late Antiquity: Towards a Christian Empire.* Madison: University of Wisconsin Press.

Cameron, Averil. 1970. *Agathias.* Oxford: Oxford University Press.

———. 1991. *Christianity and the Rhetoric of Empire.* Berkeley: University of California Press.

Cribiore, R. 1996. *Writing, Teachers, and Students in Graeco-Roman Antiquity.* Atlanta: Scholars Press.

———. 2001. *Gymnastics of the Mind: Greek Education in Hellenistic and Roman Egypt.* Princeton, NJ: Princeton University Press.

———. 2007a. *The School of Libanius in Late Antique Antioch.* Princeton, NJ: Princeton University Press.

———. 2007b. "Spaces for Teaching in Late Antiquity." In *Alexandria: Auditoria of Kom el-Dikka and Late Antique Education,* ed. T. Derda, T. Markiewicz, and E. Wipszycka, 143–150. Warsaw: University of Warsaw.

Dionisotti, A. C. 1982. "From Ausonius' Schooldays? A Schoolbook and Its Relatives," *JRS* 72: 83–125.

Frankfurter, D. 2000. "The Consequences of Hellenism in Late Antique Egypt: Religious Worlds and Actors," *Archiv für Religionsgeschichte* 2: 162–194.

Frantz, A. 1975. "Pagan Philosophers in Christian Athens," *Proceedings of the American Philosophical Society* 119: 29–38.

———. 1988. *The Athenian Agora XXIV: Late Antiquity: A.D. 267–700.* Princeton, NJ: Princeton University Press.

Garitte, G. 1966. "Textes hagiographiques orientaux relatifs à S. Leonce de Tripoli: II. L' homélie copte de Sevère d'Antioche," *Le Muséon* 79: 335–386.

Gutas, D. 1999. "The 'Alexandria to Baghdad' Complex of Narratives: A Contribution to the Study of Philosophical and Medical Historiography among the Arabs," *Documenti e Studi sulla Tradizione Filosofica Medievale* 10: 155–194.

Hanson, A. 1991. "Ancient Illiteracy." In *Literacy in the Roman World,* ed. J. L. Humphrey, 159–198. Ann Arbor: University of Michigan Press.

Harris, W. V. 1989. *Ancient Literacy.* Cambridge, MA: Harvard University Press.

———. 2001. *Restraining Rage: The Ideology of Anger Control in Classical Antiquity.* Cambridge, MA: Harvard University Press.

Hopkins, K. 1991. "Conquest by Book." In *Literacy in the Roman World,* ed. J. L. Humphrey, 133–158. Ann Arbor: University of Michigan Press.

Jones Hall, L. 2004. *Roman Berytus: Beirut in Late Antiquity*. London: Routledge.
Karivieri, A. 1994. "The House of Proclus on the Southern Slope of the Acropolis: A Contribution." In *Post-Herulian Athens: Papers and Monographs of the Finnish Institute at Athens*, ed. P. Castrén, 115–139. Helsinki: Suomen Ateenan-instituutin säätiö.
Kaster, R. 1988. *Guardians of Language: The Grammarian and Society in Late Antiquity*. Berkeley: University of California Press.
Lamberton, R. 2001. "The Schools of Platonic Philosophy of the Roman Empire: The Evidence of the Biographies." In *Education in Greek and Roman Antiquity*, ed. Y. L. Too, 433–458. Leiden: Brill.
MacCoull, Leslie S.B. 2007. "Philosophy in its Social Context." In *Egypt in the Byzantine World, 300–700*, ed. R. S. Bagnall, 67–82. Cambridge: Cambridge University Press.
Majcherek, G. 2007. "The Late Roman Auditoria." In *Alexandria: Auditoria of Kom el-Dikka and Late Antique Education*, ed. T. Derda, T. Markiewicz, and E. Wipszycka, 11–150. Warsaw: Warsaw University.
Mansfeld, J. 1994. *Prolegomena: Questions to be Settled Before the Study of an Author or Text*. Leiden: Brill.
———. 1998. *Prolegomena Mathematica: From Apollonius of Perge to Late Neoplatonism*. Leiden: Brill.
Marrou, H. I. 1938. *ΜΟΥΣΙΚΟΣ ΑΝΗΡ: Étude sur les scenes de la vie intellectuelle figurant sur les monuments funéraires romains*. Grenoble: Didier & Richard.
———. 1956. *Histoire de l'éducation dans l'Antiquité*. Paris: Éditions du Seuil.
Maspero, J. 1914. "Horapollon et la fin du paganisme égyptien," *BIFAO* 11:163–195.
Matthews, J. 1989. *The Roman Empire of Ammianus*. London: Duckworth.
———. 2000. *Laying Down the Law*. New Haven, CT: Yale University Press.
McKenzie, J. S. 2007. "The Place in Late Antique Alexandria 'Where the Alchemists and Scholars Sit . . . Was Like Stairs.'" In *Alexandria: Auditoria of Kom el-Dikka and Late Antique Education*, ed. T. Derda, T. Markiewicz, and E. Wipszycka, 53–83. Warsaw: University of Warsaw.
Morgan, T. 1998. *Literate Education in the Hellenistic and Roman Worlds*. Cambridge: Cambridge University Press.
Neugebauer, O. 1975. *A History of Ancient Mathematical Astronomy*. New York: Springer-Verlag.
Norman, A. F. 1990. *Libanius: Autobiography and Selected Letters*, Vol. 2. Cambridge, MA: Harvard University Press.
O'Meara, D. 2004. "Simplicius on the Place of the Philosopher in the City (*In Epictetum* Chap. 32)," *Mélanges de l'Université Saint-Joseph* 57: 89–98.
Petit, P. 1957. *Les étudiants de Libanius*. Paris: Université de Paris.
Roueché, M. 1999. "Did Medical Students Study Philosophy in Alexandria?" *BICS* 43: 153–169.
Shear, T. L. 1973. "The Athenian Agora: Excavations of 1971," *Hesperia* 42: 156–164.
Smith, M. 1996. *The Philosophical Inscription of Diogenes of Oinoanda*. Vienna: Verlag der österreichischen Akademie der Wissenschaften.
Smith, R. R. R. 1990. "Late Roman Philosopher Portraits from Aphrodisias," *JRS* 80: 127–155.
Trigg, J. W. 2001. "God's Marvelous *Oikonomia*: Reflections of Origen's Understanding of Divine and Human Pedagogy in the *Address* Ascribed to Gregory Thaumaturgus," *JECS* 9: 27–52.
Watt, J. W. 1999. "A Portrait of John bar Aphtonia, Founder of the Monastery of Qenneshre." In *Portraits of Spiritual Authority*, ed. J. W. Drijvers and J. W. Watt, 155–169. Leiden: Brill.

Watts, E. 2004. "Justinian, Malalas, and the End of the Athenian Philosophical Teaching in A.D. 529," *JRS* 94: 168–182.

———. 2006 *City and School in Late Antique Athens and Alexandria.* Berkeley: University of California Press.

Webb, R. 2001. "The Progymnasmata as Practice." In *Education in Greek and Roman Antiquity*, ed. Y. L. Too, 289–316. Leiden: Brill.

Welch, K. 2007. "Some Architectural Prototypes for the Auditoria at Kom el-Dikka and Three Late Antique (Fifth Century AD) Comparanda from Aphrodisias in Caria." In *Alexandria: Auditoria of Kom el-Dikka and Late Antique Education*, ed. T. Derda, T. Markiewicz, and E. Wipszycka, 115–134. Warsaw: University of Warsaw.

Westerink, L. G., ed. and trans. 1977. *The Greek Commentaries on Plato's Phaedo.* Vol. 2. New York: North-Holland.

———, ed. and trans. 1990. *Prolégomènes à la philosophie de Platon.* Paris: Les Belles Lettres.

Youtie, H. C. 1971a. "*Agrammatos*: An Aspect of Greek Society in Egypt," *HSCP* 75: 161–176.

———. 1971b. "*Bradeos graphon*: Between Literacy and Illiteracy," *GRBS* 12: 239–261.

CHAPTER 15

MONASTICISM AND THE PHILOSOPHICAL HERITAGE

SAMUEL RUBENSON
Lund University

The famous quotation from the third-century theologian Tertullian, "*Quid ergo Athenis et Hierosolymis, quid academiae et ecclesiae* . . . (what has Jerusalem to do with Athens, the Academy with the Church . . .)?"[1] could well be applied also to the relation between the Greek philosophical heritage and early monasticism: "What has the desert monk to do with the learned philosopher?" In the search for the roots of the sudden rise of monasticism in the fourth century, a rich variety of sources have been suggested, but almost no attention has been given to the schools of philosophy.[2] The monks of emergent monasticism in the fourth, fifth, and sixth centuries, Eastern as well as Western, have generally been seen as the stark opposites of the classical philosophers, as anti-intellectual representatives of a new community and society replacing Greek culture and *paideia*.[3] Numerous sayings of the desert fathers, seen as the epitomes of early monasticism, as well as early hagiographic descriptions of monks, can be found to support such a view. Antony the Great, regarded as the father of the monastic tradition, has been depicted as not only illiterate but also antiphilosophical, based on significant passages in the *Vita Antonii*, probably the most influential text for the rapid spread of monastic ideals and practices. In it, he is said to have refused to learn letters,[4] to have been taught by God, and, in a series of chapters recounting his encounters with philosophers, to be the exact opposite of what they are. His is the uninhabitable desert landscape, not the schools of the cities of learning.

Such an understanding of the relation between the early Christian monks and the representatives of classical philosophy in Late Antiquity has been, however, increasingly undermined by recent scholarship. Early monasticism can no longer be identified with the sudden establishment of a pristine counterculture outside the confines of civilization by individuals leaving society behind, Heussi's "Sonderwelt." The study of early Christian asceticism has shown that monasticism developed out of a variety of forms of ascetic life, such as ascetic households tied to Christian communities in the cities and groups of itinerant ascetic preachers and disciples in the countryside. When defining monasticism as the socially and ecclesiastically recognized institution of a communal ascetic life separated from family (as well as congregation) that emerged in the fourth century, we need to realize that the emergence was not sui generis, but a gradual process in which a variety of traditions made an impact.[5] This is evident in the results of the archaeological excavations of early monastic sites, as well as in what the study of Egyptian papyri related to monastic settlements have revealed. Both provide an image of these settlements as much less isolated, less simple, and less uncivilized than previously imagined.[6] More detailed studies of the literary character and rhetoric of the texts describing early monastic life have furthermore revealed that many of these are to be read as idealizations in which the depictions of the monks are loaded with strongly symbolical connotations.[7] When these texts are read more carefully, we find that the monks are depicted not only as simple and rustic but also as philosophers and most civilized.[8] The large quantity of letters, written by and to monks, as well as monastic educational texts that have been largely neglected, also reveal close contacts with the educational traditions of their own days. Without denying differences in interpretation and social status, there is a growing awareness that the role of the ascetic in society and the ascetic practice had very much in common, whether Christian or pagan.[9]

This tension between the traditional image, based on ideals and symbols transmitted by what have been seen as the main sources, and the growing evidence for a quite different historical setting forces us to revise our interpretation of the rise of monasticism in Late Antiquity. It also opens up perspectives that might contribute to new solutions to some of the still puzzling issues related to early monasticism, such as its sudden and rapid spread and the models for its institutionalization.

On the basis of recent studies of the historical evidence related to the social setting and early history of monasticism and on the literary character of the early monastic texts, in this chapter I suggest a closer link between traditional Greek society and culture and the rise of monasticism than is usually assumed. Not denying the innovative character of much of early monastic life, the rich variety of forms of monasticism, and the strong anti-Hellenic polemic of monastic texts in general, I think we are obliged to situate the innovations, variations, and polemic in much closer relation to the society in which it all happened.

I. The Social Setting

Already the excavations of Kellia, regarded as probably the earliest monastic settlement, revealed (to the surprise of the archaeologists) that the monks in the fifth and sixth centuries lived in what was a much more settled, prosperous, and organized society than expected. Here, not far from Alexandria, on the western arm of the Nile, archaeologists have found a landscape dotted with late antique monastic cells, almost like a suburban housing area.[10] The cells were well built, communications seem to have been excellent, and there was a division of labor and signs of clear societal organization. Detailed studies of monastic cells show a regular pattern in which a master lived with one or several disciples in a complex that was more or less self-sufficient. The similarities between some of the settlements and larger villas excavated closer to Lake Mareotis are striking. The social background of the people establishing the settlements is much more likely urban middle or upper class than rural peasantry.

Other excavations at Naqlun, at the edge of the Fayoum Oasis, have revealed a similar conglomerate of ancient cells, although carved out of natural caves and cliffs, and also here we find clear evidence for close relations to the society at large.[11] Again, the most important architectural features are the communal character of self-sufficient complexes with rooms for a master and one or several disciples and the good communications between the independent monastic complexes and between these and the society. Also significant is the fact that both in Kellia—and in the adjacent settlements of Nitria and Scetis—and in Naqlun, there is ample evidence of writing, inscriptions on the walls and on ostraka, as well as texts on papyri, including probably production of manuscripts.[12]

Even though most of the archaeological finds date to a later period, there is no reason to think that the origins in the fourth and fifth centuries were much different, albeit on a smaller scale. The fact that the early monastic settlements rapidly attracted the attention of the literate elite in Alexandria and beyond makes it unlikely that the origins were unconnected to these circles. It is thus no longer possible to think of the centers of early Egyptian desert monasticism in Lower Egypt as isolated, simple, and countercultural. The monks who inhabited these cells in the fifth and sixth centuries, and probably already in the fourth, were, no doubt, persons with social standing, with resources of various kinds, and to a large extent, persons capable of reading, writing, and organizing their own society and its relations to the towns and cities of the late Roman empire.

The evidence from other places regarded as important centers of early monasticism, such as the monastic centers of Upper Egypt, yield similar results.[13] As has been demonstrated in detail, the creation of the network of large monasteries headed by Pachomius of Tabennesi in the 320s and 330s cannot have been accomplished without significant intellectual and social resources or without the support of the local society into which the monasteries were well integrated.[14] The emergence of several series of rules manifests both the need for and the ability to establish a strict organization, and thus regular teaching and written communication; that is, an educational system within the monasteries. The texts related to Pachomius himself, primarily the various *Lives* of Pachomius but also his sermons, actually depict Pachomius primarily as a teacher, and in addition to the rules, the texts emphasize the educational aspect of monastic life.[15] In addition, Pachomius is depicted as an intellectual equal to pagan philosophers and Christian opponents alike.[16] The information given about the disciples and their backgrounds and about other monasteries also contributes to the impression that the monastic tradition had the support of people who were both educated and of a higher social standing and was hardly confined to or even dominated by the poor and uneducated rural population. The architectural remains of the large cathedral at Pbow indicate the same. The ongoing work on the texts by Shenoute of Atripe, the dominant monastic leader of the early fifth century, and the archaeological work at his main monastery, the White Monastery, give further evidence for the early Egyptian monastic tradition as part of a literate and socially integrated enterprise.[17]

The large amounts of papyri of the fourth and fifth centuries preserved in Egypt testify further to the social status of the monks and the monasteries. Monks are visible in papyri already from the year 324 as a recognizable social category.[18] In fact, several archives with monastic correspondence of the fourth century are known.[19] These attest not only to the existence of literate monks but also to the rather intense relations between the monasteries and the surrounding society, economically and socially. Most (if not all) of the larger collections of early Christian papyri found in Egypt are remains of monastic archives and libraries, and they testify to the importance of education and books in the early monasteries.[20] It is likely that the Nag Hammadi codices also have their origins in a monastic setting, and the intensive debate about this shows how difficult it has been for scholars to think of monasteries as places for the study and transmission of philosophical texts.[21]

Unfortunately, papyrological and archaeological sources for early monasticism outside Egypt are more meager. However, the archaeological evidence from Palestine shows that already beginning in the early fifth century, large churches and monastic complexes were built with skilled labor (figure 15.1).[22] Particularly in Palestine, we have ample evidence for large donations to monastic settlements by the aristocracy in the fourth century, as well as for the role of well-educated upper-class men and women, like Melania the Elder and Jerome, in establishing and running monasteries at the end of the century. The literary activity of the Latin settlements in and around Jerusalem, as well as the Greek around Gaza, is well attested.[23] Not only the number of letters exchanged but also the emphasis on spiritual therapy and the fact that the monks often became involved in conflicts about doctrines and literature give the impression that intellectual training by reading, teaching, and reflection was important. A similar intellectual background is, moreover, presupposed in the description of the monks of the Judean desert by the sixth-century author Cyril of Scythopolis.

For Syria and Asia Minor, the archaeological and documentary evidence is even less. The remains of the large monastic complexes in northern Syria have yet to be studied in detail. Literature on early Syrian monasticism has tended to focus on the radical and anticultural character of the monastic movement, mainly based on the description of the early monks of Syria by the fifth-century bishop Theodoret of Cyrrhus.[24] The literary character of the work and its rhetoric should, however, make us cautious about its historical veracity.[25] For all its harshness, monastic life was for Theodoret the life of the true philosophers, for those who through Christian faith fulfilled what ancient philosophy aimed at but could not achieve. References to the early monastic settlements of Syria by other writers like Jerome and John Chrysostom manifest both the intellectual character and a strong link not only to the society but also even to the educated upper class. The role of the monks in Syria in the bitter conflict over the Council of Chalcedon (451) in the late fifth and early sixth centuries also testifies to a movement with strong social and intellectual resources.[26]

Figure 15.1. Mar Saba Monastery in the Kidron Valley, Palestine (Photo: Inga-Lill Rubenson). See also color plate section.

Recent studies have emphasized the role of wandering monks in Syrian and Cappadocian monastic tradition.[27] The fact that they were begging monks without property of their own does not, however, mean that they necessarily had a background among the poor or that they had no education. Their lifestyle, with a strong emphasis on freedom from worldly concern as well as teaching, is related not only to first-century apostolic preachers but most probably also to Cynic philosophers. The harsh denunciation of the wandering monks by bishops like Nilus of Ancyra in the mid-fifth century actually echoes the satirist Lucian's caricature of the house philosophers of the aristocrats.[28]

At the end of the fifth century, the major cities in the East—such as Alexandria, Gaza, Jerusalem, Antioch, Cappadocian Caesarea, Ancyra, and Constantinople—all had large monasteries either inside the city or just outside. The monks of these monasteries were, moreover, actively engaged in ecclesiastical and doctrinal affairs, both locally and at the level of the imperial administration and the ecumenical councils. Monks were, moreover, essential to the establishment of new social institutions, in particular the poorhouses and hospitals that were established in the cities beginning in the first half of the fourth century, the most famous established in Caesarea by Basil in the 360s.[29] Also in the rural areas, evidence points to the rich landowning classes. In Annisa, Macrina the Younger, herself a philosopher according to her brother Gregory of Nyssa, turned the family estate into a monastic community in about 340.[30] All the ancient Church historians writing in the fifth and sixth centuries mention the significant role the monks played in the major dogmatic conflicts in the East at that time. They were not only at the center of the first and second Origenist controversies in the 390s and 540s but also prominent in the deposition of John Chrysostom in 403 and of Nestorius in 431, as well as the councils of Ephesus in 449 and Chalcedon in 451. The strongest opposition to the Council of Chalcedon and the most virulent attacks on the proponents, as well as the subtlest argumentation for a non-Chalcedonian position, came from monastic centers.[31]

Turning to the West, there is no doubt that monasticism started among the Christian elite through their contacts with developments in the East. The first centers were Rome and other important cities, and the earliest establishment of monasteries was in general closely connected with the episcopate and its clerics.[32] With the exception of figures like Martin of Tours, the early propagators of the fourth century, like Eusebius of Vericelli, Chromatius of Aquileia, Ambrose, Augustine, Jerome, and Rufinus, were all well educated and wealthy, and they attracted people with the same background. An important role was, moreover, played by some of the most affluent ladies in the Roman aristocracy in the late fourth and early fifth centuries: Marcellina, the sister of Ambrose, Marcella, Paula, Melania the Elder, and Melania the Younger, as well as Olympias in Constantinople, all of whom were well read.

At the monastery of Lérins, established in the early fifth century, the emphasis was clearly on intellectual activity, and the monastery soon became a famous school for future bishops. Of great importance were the spread and translation of seminal Greek texts, such as the *Vita Antonii*, the ascetic writings of Basil of Caesarea, and the Pachomian rules. Equally important were the compilation of Latin texts inspired by these or by direct contact with the East, the most important being the works by John Cassian, written around 420. Cassian wrote on the basis of his experiences of monasticism, material he collected during his period as a monastic disciple in Egypt. The early monastic rules in the West, the rules of Augustine and the early-sixth-century bishop Caesarius of Arles, reflect the problem of how to deal with monks from the upper classes—classes not used to physical labor—and how to avoid conflicts between them and monks of humbler origin.

This social setting of early Western monasticism begins to change in the sixth century, when we find a number of rural monastic establishments not connected to any bishopric or affluent landlord. Nevertheless, even in these, education was seen as important. Models and rules were mostly imported from the classical centers of learning, often via the transmission of Eastern Christian literature in Latin translation. This is, for example, evident in the early development of the monastic center in the Jura Mountains in the mid-sixth century. Although it might seem strange, the stories about rustic, uneducated desert monks were primarily read and transmitted by educated urban teachers and clerics, like Augustine and his friends.[33] The texts prompted them to abandon civil service and political ambitions, but not necessarily to turn against the ideals of a classical education. On the contrary, as in the East, the monastic life was considered to be a philosophical life, the natural choice for a Christian philosopher.

II. Monastic Literature

In view of this broader historical background and social setting of early monasticism, it has become increasingly important to reinterpret the literary sources, both those produced by and those read by the early monks. We also need to look more carefully at the descriptions of the monks made by non-monastic authors in relation to the purpose of the texts. It is evident that a traditional literal reading of the lives of the early monks and the sayings in the *Apophthegmata patrum* as reliable historical accounts can no longer be upheld. We can no longer take for granted that the *Life of Antony* is an accurate historical description of what happened to Antony or that the sayings of the desert fathers are faithful reproductions of their own words. But neither can we be satisfied with a blank rejection of the texts as products of pious fiction without any value for historical research. Here the cultural turn in late antique studies, and especially recent developments in literary studies, are of great value.[34]

To interpret the sources, we have to ask how the monks are presented (and present themselves) and for what purposes. We have to look not only at what the texts say about their background, education, and activities but also at why we get this information and what is revealed by other aspects of the texts. The early monastic tradition is represented by a rich literary legacy, so we have to reflect on how this literature was produced, what models were used, for whom the texts were intended, and what kind of knowledge they presupposed. It is only in relation to such questions that we can say anything about the educational patterns of early monastic life and its relation to the general cultural and educational background.[35]

II.a Hagiography

Traditionally, scholarship on early monasticism has had its focus on the descriptions of the early monastic generation produced by others, especially the various *Lives* of the early monks. The most famous of these is, no doubt, the *Life of Antony*, written by Athanasius of Alexandria, most probably in the early 360s. Its rapid translation and dissemination, its authoritative character, and its popularity made it a widely used model and standard for monastic biographies. Although Antony is said to have learned from ascetics in the neighborhood, the *Vita* depicts him as the founder of monasticism by being the first to settle in the desert and by attracting disciples, thereby making the desert into a city.[36] The conscious polarization between desert and city is as manifest as between divine inspiration and Greek learning, both interpreted as expressions of a deeper opposition between divine and human, between solitude and strife. Through *askesis*, the monk defeats the disturbances, becomes open for divine intervention, and is thus both saved and made capable of saving the world around him.

As mentioned, a main feature is the reference to Antony's lack of literary education, his repudiation of Greek learning, and his mockery of the Greeks who travel in vain to gain wisdom.[37] It is, however, evident that these references cannot be taken at face value. Even the *Vita* itself admits that Antony received and sent letters,[38] that he exhorted his disciples to write down their thoughts,[39] and that he appeared as a shrewd philosopher when he was questioned.[40] The reason for this tension in the text is the apologetic setting. As I have demonstrated elsewhere, the *Vita* is actually construed to match a description of a philosopher, namely, the *Life of Pythagoras*.[41] Antony is in every aspect similar or superior to Pythagoras, but unlike him, he has no need to travel anywhere or obtain worldly learning. Wisdom and virtue are given by God and thus inherent in the ideal monk.[42] What Athanasius makes clear is that Antony was the true philosopher, the philosopher of a divine wisdom in contrast to the merely human teachings of the neo-Pythagoreans, one of the most active opposition groups to Christianity in the fourth century. The *Vita* must thus be seen as a weapon in what has been termed a war of biographies and through which Christians and pagans competed over whose saint was the most divine philosopher.[43] The emphasis on Antony being unlettered has quite a specific purpose and cannot be taken literally. On the contrary, the *Vita* actually supports an interpretation of the early monks as in many ways similar to pagan philosophers, sharing many of the same ideals, methods, and ways of life.

A rereading of other monastic biographical texts reveals a similar close connection to the philosophical heritage, although interpreted differently. It is striking that in Jerome's lives of early monastic saints, both the desert heroes Paul and Hilarion, the pioneer of Palestinian monastic life, are said to have been well educated and, moreover, that when they left the world they did not reject their learning, but rather transcended its limits.[44] In contrast to Antony, Hilarion studies, and when he is disturbed by too many visitors and decides to retreat into the desert to find Antony, only to learn that he has died, he does not settle down but embarks on travels that actually remind us of Apollonius or Pythagoras. In *Historia Philotheos*, the first description of Syrian monastics, written about 345 by Theodoret, bishop of Cyrrhus, the monastic saints are often extremely rustic but are nonetheless depicted as philosophers searching out the truth, integrating it into themselves, and then often teaching their philosophy (figure 15.2). In spite of their rusticity, they are described as philosophers, their monasteries as schools, and their pursuit as a life of virtue. Echoes from the classical *paideia* actually permeate the entire text.[45] It is tempting to see this simply as the result of Theodoret's own training and ambition to impress the educated elite of the city, but there are good reasons to think that what Theodoret aims at is an interpretation of the Church as a school with the monks as its great philosophers.

If we read these and other biographical texts, such as the *Historia Monachorum in Aegypto*, dated to the 390s, and Palladius' *Historia Lausiaca* from the 420s, not as quarries for historical information but as depictions of ideals propagated both by monks and by those interested in supporting certain forms of monastic life, it is evident that the most important model used is that of philosophy and the life of the philosophers. It is within this framework that the biblical models and the quotations from the Bible are interpreted.

II.b The *Apophthegmata patrum*

The most important and by far the most influential texts emerging from early monasticism are the *Apophthegmata patrum*, the various collections of sayings and anecdotes about the desert fathers. A collection of sayings of monastic fathers is first attested in an appendix to one of Evagrius' texts, the *Praktikos*, written probably in the 390s, and seems to lie behind the works of John Cassian some twenty-five years later.[46] For the large collections preserved and transmitted in many languages, scholars usually assume an origin in fifth-century Palestine.[47] The sayings emphasize a radical rejection of society, harsh ascetic practices, extreme humility, and a fierce struggle for solitude and silence. The images are, however, by no means uniform. The monks are penitent, escaping

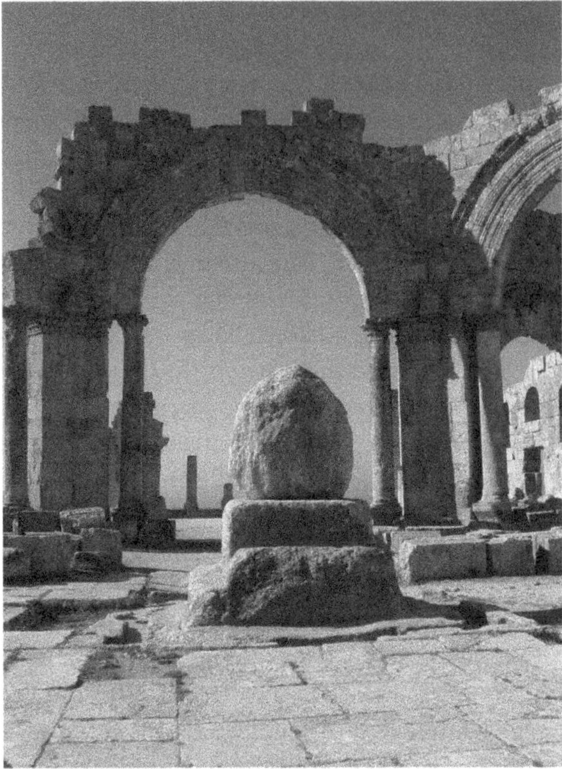

Figure 15.2. St. Simeon Pillar and Cathedral, Qal'at Sim'ān, Syria (Photo: Inga-Lill Rubenson). See also color plate section.

from sin as well as fiery angels, merciful brothers as well as sharp critics, examples of fanatic excess as well as teachers of moderation. Any attempt to discern one specific image and way of life, or to distill the most authentic sayings, runs into great problems in both method and content.

In spite of these difficulties, the sayings have generally been seen as the most reliable and authentic source for the ideals, as well as everyday life, of the early monastic tradition of Egypt. Thus they have often been used to support an understanding of the early monastic tradition as rustic, illiterate, anti-intellectual, and extremely hostile to society at large. The early monastic tradition has traditionally been seen as especially hostile to the Greek cultural tradition and civilization and as having established a world of its own, a counterculture in the desert. But this picture has been asserted in disregard of the fact that even in the *Apophthegmata patrum*, books, readers, copyists, and teachers are well represented, as are merchants, peasants, prostitutes, and bishops, as well as communal gatherings, building activities, and visits to the cities. In spite of the strong emphasis on solitude and distance, the actual descriptions reveal a life that is to a large extent communal and closely related to the world (figure 15.3). The virtues and practices taught are in reality related to the needs of monastic communities in the world.[48]

Recent studies have increasingly come to realize that the sayings can no longer be taken at face value as historical recollections and need to be seen as a

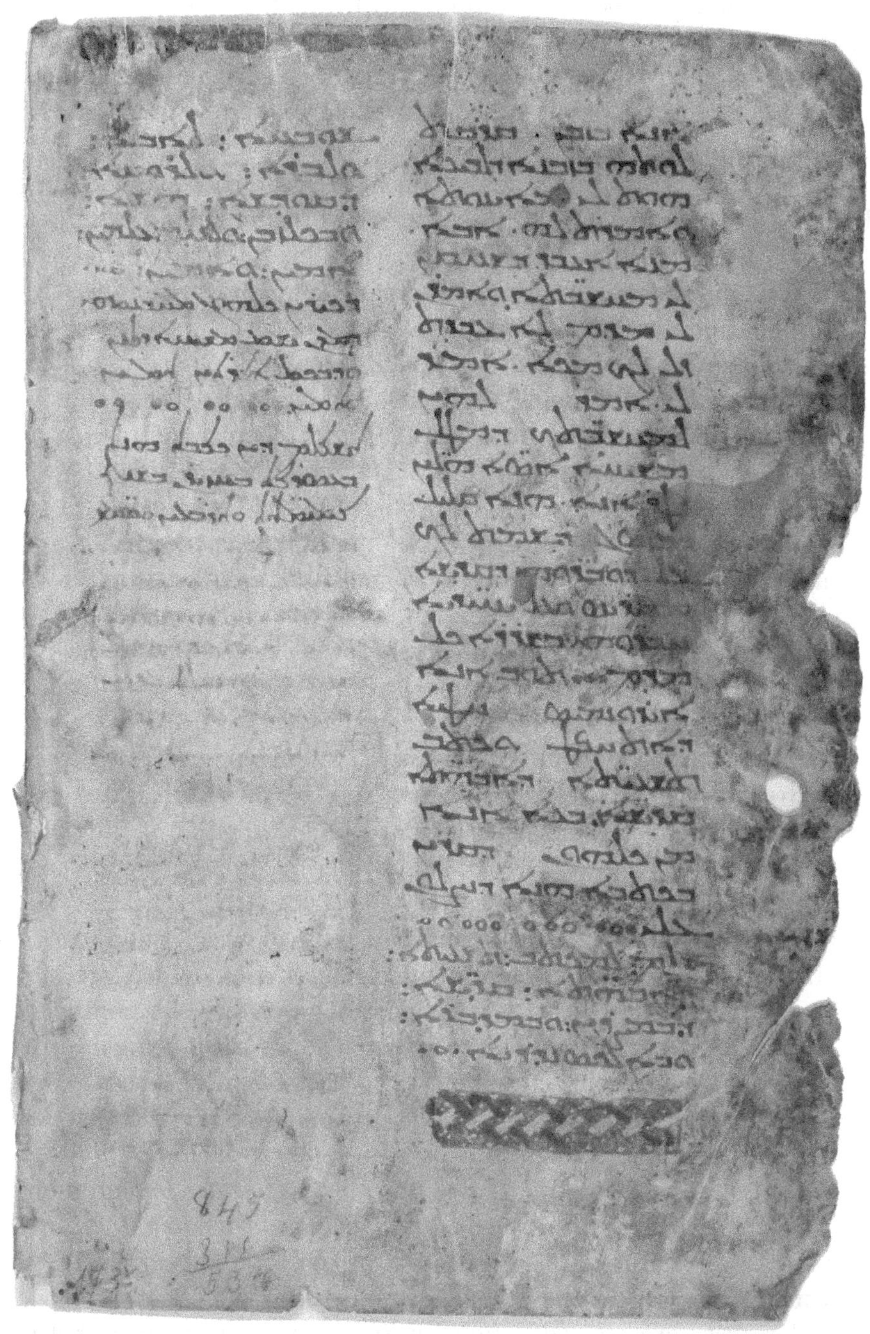

Figure 15.3. *Apophthegmata patrum* (in Syriac), Folio 173v. (Courtesy of the Biblioteca Ambrosiana, Milano © Veneranda Biblioteca Ambrosiana).

literature produced with certain aims. As James Goehring has shown, the desert in the sayings is not to be understood as a factual description of the geographical setting and social environment of the early monks, but rather as a strong symbol for basic ideals taught by the sayings.[49] In the same manner, the portraits of the monastic figures are icons highlighting virtues and embodying maxims to be reflected upon, rather than photographs revealing daily life or true recordings of actual expressions.

There is thus good reason to suspect that the rejection of books and learning, when it occurs in the sayings, is to be interpreted, as in the *Vita Antonii*, not as a historical fact. A close reading of these sayings instead reveals that the point is to remind monks, who were actually reading and studying, of the ultimate goal of their endeavors and to warn them against intellectual pride.[50] There are also good reasons to think that these sayings also reflect a concern to avoid the temptation to become strongly involved in theological debates and heresy hunting. The devastating experience of the first Origenist controversy in the 390s for the monastic centers in Lower Egypt and the expulsion in 399 of a large number of the leading monks of Nitria, Kellia, and Scetis happened during the lives of many of the monks quoted in the *Apophthegmata patrum*, and the first attempts to produce collections of sayings were done by people who had been part of the controversy.[51] When the larger collections were made in the latter part of the fifth century, the controversy over Chalcedon was at its height, and in the mid-sixth century, the second Origenist controversy broke out. In all of these, monks were very prominent participants.

On a more structural and functional level, recent studies of the *Apophthegmata patrum* have, moreover, revealed that there are clear similarities between them and pagan late antique collections of sayings.[52] From a literary point of view, the *Apophthegmata patrum* are akin to other maxims, sentences, and poignant stories used for educational purposes, and although this has not yet been studied in greater detail, it appears to be the case that the collections were later used in the formation of the monks in the monasteries, as they are in present-day monasteries in the East. A clear indication that the collections had educational aims is the early ambition to systematize the sayings under different topics. Although the alphabetical collection has become the best known in recent scholarship, it is the thematic organization of the material that we find best represented in the early transmission of the texts, as, for example, in the very early Latin and Syriac translations. In their system of organization, the collections of sayings are similar to educational texts such as the *Praktikos* of Evagrius of Pontus or the *Ladder of Heavenly Ascent* by John Climacus.[53]

If indeed the larger collections are products of cenobitic monasteries in which they were used for educational purposes, it is no surprise that many sayings are extracts from other writings, be they hagiographical texts such as the *Vita Antonii*, monastic letters, or writings by known monastic authors like Evagrius. Instead of using the *Apophthegmata patrum* to gain information about the actual historical life of the first generations of Egyptian monks in an uninhabited desert, we need to see how they constitute a link between educational material and patterns of the late antique schools and the emergence of forms for monastic formation. In later monastic authors like Barsanuphius of Gaza in the mid-sixth century. the sayings are cited as the words of the fathers of the monastic life, the founders of their way of philosophy. It is quite likely that it was for such a use that not only the collections but also many of the individual sayings were produced. This, however, does not rule out that many of the sayings actually may reflect the teachings of the fathers and mothers mentioned, teachings that were preserved and edited by their disciples. The attribution of almost a fifth of the entire alphabetical collection to a certain Abba Poimen, not known from any other source, might indicate exactly such a process of forming a monastic philosophical school by creating a collection of the teachings of the school.[54]

II.c The Letters

In contrast to the biographical texts and the collections of sayings, letters by the early monks have received little attention, and that only recently. A major reason is that their textual transmission tends to be much more complicated, since the letters were by far not as popular as the biographies or the sayings. A large number of the letters, in some cases entire collections, are not preserved in their original Greek, and often only partly in translations into other languages, such as Latin, Coptic, Syriac, Armenian, Georgian, and Ethiopic. Many letters are quite enigmatic, and others have been regarded as too repetitive to be of much interest. But probably just as important is the fact that the letters do not fit the general image of early monasticism that has been created on the basis of a particular reading of the main sources. For a better understanding of the development of early monasticism, a closer study of the letters is, however, of major importance, especially for the relation of late antique monasticism to the philosophical heritage. In the letters, we have a much better opportunity to hear the voice of the early monks than in either biography or sayings.

The most important early collections are the letters of Pachomius, the letters of Antony, the letters of Ammonas, his disciple, and the letters of Evagrius. To these can be added singular letters by the successors of Pachomius and probably also some of the letters attributed to Macarius and to Arsenius, both prominent figures in the *Apophthegmata Patrum*.[55] Later collections include the large number of letters attributed to the fifth-century monk Isidore of Pelusium, as well as the letters by Barsanuphius and John, and occasional letters by others, including some of the early Western monastic authors.

Among the earliest letters, those of Antony are the only letters that have yet received a major analysis, which in its turn has created an intense debate among scholars.[56] The letters clearly reveal that the author sees himself as a teacher of spiritual knowledge and the recipients as students or disciples. He is furthermore not only acquainted with some form of popular philosophy reflecting both Stoic and Platonic views but also seems to know some of the basic teachings of Origen of Alexandria. If accepted as genuine, as most scholars do, the letters force us to revise a more traditional view of the early monks and draw them closer to the intellectual environment of Alexandria. Related to this collection of seven letters is another collection of letters attributed to a certain Ammonas, most likely the Ammonas who is mentioned in other sources as a disciple of Antony. The letters, preserved in varying numbers, orders, and in several languages—the largest collection being the Syriac—reveal a teacher writing to his disciples in a manner similar to Antony's.[57] The main contents are, however, quite different and center on how to gain and preserve a mystical knowledge based on sensory experiences that transform the monk into a heavenly being while still on earth. The similarities with esoteric Jewish schools are manifest in the quotations of Jewish apocryphal texts and the descriptions of visions of the heavenly realm.[58]

Except for most of the letters of Evagrius, which are clearly written to individuals in special circumstances and are thus more similar to letters preserved among the papyri or to the letters by the Cappadocian fathers, to whom Evagrius was related, the other collections are all letters by teachers aimed at a larger audience of disciples. Of the Macarian letters—the least studied of these collections—the first two, in particular, are quite similar in style and content to the letters of Antony, and the first letter undoubtedly belongs to the same tradition of monastic philosophical formation.[59] Due to the use of enigmatic alphabetical symbols, the letters of Pachomius have been hard to interpret.[60] It is, however, evident that Pachomius in these is primarily transmitting interpretations of biblical texts seen as keys to spiritual knowledge and a spiritual life and also that this interpretation requires both initiation into secret teachings and a searching mind.

For the question of the relation between emergent monastic tradition and the philosophical heritage, both the vast collection of letters by Isidore of Pelusium and the collection of letters by Barsanuphius and John are very important. Unfortunately, we still lack detailed studies of their literary character and the philosophical and rhetorical background of the authors.[61] In both cases, it seems clear that the authors were well educated and in touch with intellectual centers of their own time, which is particularly striking in the case of Barsanuphius, who seems to have been an Egyptian monk retiring into solitude outside Gaza. The concern in many of the letters of Barsanuphius and John is to guide the recipient, often a person from the higher levels of society, in his life, and the themes are reminiscent of themes treated in the non-Christian moral philosophy of the first centuries C.E.

The most important conclusion to be drawn from the (still preparatory) studies of the monastic letters is that the early monks not only were capable of writing letters, a fact well known from papyrological studies, but also used letters to teach their disciples. Several letters mention that the author longs for the disciples and hopes to meet them, creating the impression that the letters were sent to disciples far away. But from collections of letters found at monastic sites, as well as from descriptions of monks who refused to speak to visitors, like Barsanuphius, we do know that letters were in the early monastic tradition used also in cases where there was little or no geographical distance. The writing of letters seems to have become an important aspect of teaching and especially of spiritual guidance.

II.d Other Writings

Turning from these texts to the literature produced by the early monks themselves, we see a surprising amount of philosophical writing. Authors like Evagrius of Pontus, John Cassian, Diadochus of Photike in the mid-fifth century, Dorotheus of Gaza a century later, and John Climacus in the seventh century all produced instructive texts based on their own philosophical and rhetorical education and their own practice of philosophy as it was understood in antiquity. The setting of texts such as these is amply illustrated by some of the ascetic texts collected under the name of the fourth-century monk Isaiah of Gaza, in which we hear about monks traveling widely, visiting each other, sharing knowledge, borrowing books, and caring for the quality of the copies.[62] The letters of Nilus of Ankyra, a monastic fifth-century bishop, furthermore reveal an emphasis on the necessity of monks being educated and an anger toward rich, and probably educated, Christians who turned to a monastic, that is, philosophical, lifestyle only to be lazy.[63] For some monks, like Dorotheus of Gaza, we know about their education at a proper center of learning; he was a student from the famous school of rhetoric and Christian Neo-Platonism in early-fifth-century Gaza.[64] His texts are undoubtedly worth a deeper analysis as to their rhetorical and philosophical content. Except for Evagrius, John Cassian, and (recently) John Climacus,[65] this literature has unfortunately not received much scholarly attention, some of it not even proper scholarly editions.

By far the most prominent early Christian monastic author was Evagrius of Pontus.[66] After receiving a good education in Cappadocia and Constantinople, he settled in Nitria, on the outskirts of the desert not far from Alexandria. According to the ancient sources, he worked as a scribe, but on account of his writings, as well as the image given by Palladius, one of his disciples, he was primarily a teacher. Because of his later condemnation, Evagrius has often been regarded primarily as a speculative theologian deeply influenced by Origen and a foreigner to the early monastic tradition. But recent studies have made it clear that Evagrius belonged to a wider monastic setting in Egypt and that his background was as much Stoic as Platonic, with a focus on moral philosophy and psychology, not metaphysics. Except for the letters and a few other texts, Evagrius' writings are organized in series of short, seemingly independent sayings, *sententiae*, called *kephalaia* or *centuriae*. There is no doubt that the purpose is educational and that the reader or listener is intended to reflect on and practice the sayings. In this, they remind us of the spiritual exercises of the late antique schools of philosophy.[67]

John Cassian was a student of Evagrius and lived for more than a decade in the monastic community of Nitria. Although nothing is known about his background, he evidently had a good education and was fluent in both Greek and Latin.[68] After leaving Egypt as a result of the first Origenist crisis, he was involved in ecclesiastical diplomacy to defend first the so-called Origenist monks and later John Chrysostom, but finally he settled near Marseille, where he established his own community. His writings are presented as accounts of the organization and teachings of the Egyptian monks, reflecting the tradition represented by Evagrius but adapting its language and tenor to the circumstances of the West. Although less philosophical than much of Evagrius' writings, Cassian also writes for an educated audience, an audience that was prepared and free to implement the teachings and practice the spiritual exercises prescribed.

A further development of early monastic teaching is to be found in the very influential text known as the *Ladder*, written by John of Sinai, nicknamed *Klimax* or Climacus.[69] Of John we know very little, only that he probably was a *scholastikos*, that is, a learned man, most often a teacher of law, from Constantinople. In the late sixth century, he became the abbot of the monastery of St. Catherine in Sinai, a monastery that was enriched and supported by the emperors. The *Ladder* is a step-by-step practical guide to a life in solitude and is organized in a series of chapters based on earlier monastic traditions, primarily Evagrius and the systematic collection of *apophthegmata*. As has been demonstrated in a recent study, Climacus is strongly dependent upon a classical rhetorical formation and writes in the tradition of late antique moral philosophy, with clear parallels to Plutarch, among others.[70]

Not all texts coming out of the early monastic environment are, however, as clearly connected to a Greek educational background and to the school traditions of moral philosophy. The most prominent examples of a quite different style are the writings attributed to Macarius the Great, a series of homilies that probably originated in late-fourth-century Syria. On account of their rich use of metaphors, as well as their use of biblical stories and imagery, they have been seen as representing a tradition quite opposite to that of Evagrius: more biblical, less intellectual, and more emotional mysticism, similar to that found in the letters of Ammonas.[71] The sharp distinction between an Evagrian and a Macarian, or a philosophical and emotional, monastic spirituality has, however, recently been questioned.[72] Although we know almost nothing about the historical and social setting of the Macarian homilies, not even the identity of the author, it is significant that the homilies presuppose a certain tension between the Church as an institution and the community to which the homilies are addressed. The impression given by the homilies is that they were delivered to a group adhering to a teacher who directs them in how to live. Their function is in a sense similar both to treatises of moral philosophy and to Egyptian monastic exhortation. Differences in imagery, language, and style should not make us blind to similarities in function.

III. Monastic Life as a School of Philosophy

These recent developments in the study of the social setting and literary character of emergent monasticism make it necessary to question the traditional image of an anti-intellectual and anti-social movement cutting all ties with traditional Greek *paideia*. Instead of a dichotomy between monastery and school, we need to search for the models used for training and formation within monastic life and for developments within the traditions of philosophical formation that can bridge the gap between the city and the desert. This is not to suggest a new one-sided interpretation of the rise of monasticism or to deny the great variety of forms of early monasticism, nor the combination of different factors in promoting the tradition, but only to suggest one important and often missing link.

Estimates of the level of literacy and the percentage of the population attending school in late Roman society vary greatly. Against a more negative view that allows for only a small percentage of literate people, the papyri documentation from Egypt shows that schools were found even in small towns in fairly remote areas.[73] But even the more optimistic estimates agree that only a small minority of adult men were literate and that illiteracy was not uncommon even among people with good social standing and positions of responsibility.[74] The strong emphasis on teaching in early monastic texts, the early monastic rules demanding literacy of all monks, and the evidence for regular correspondence between monks and persons in society, as well as between the monks themselves, are thus worth noting. Even if some of this emphasis on education and literacy is directly related to the strongly scriptural orientation of early monasticism, the models for learning, both on an elementary level of reading and writing and on higher levels of composition, rhetoric, and philosophy, must necessarily have been taken from contemporary society and its school tradition.

Recent studies of the schools of Late Antiquity show that the traditions remained largely unchanged throughout the late Roman period. On all levels, the school was in essence the teacher surrounded by his students, not a specific building constructed for educational purposes. Teaching was largely a matter of presenting models that the students were to imitate. Letters and syllables were to be copied, subsequently sentences and short anecdotes, and, later, arguments and ideas. The models were taken from established collections of classical texts. On a more basic level, these were taken from texts such as Homer and the *Sentences* of Menander. When the student had mastered a saying, the task was to elaborate on it and thus to learn composition by a development from set texts into a personal text that was strongly reminiscent of the models and into which these were integrated. Since texts were supposed to be read aloud and usually to an audience, a text was basically a speech, whether a short saying or a long oration. For each kind of writing or speech, specific characteristics were to be learned on the basis of models. Even in the philosophical school, the basic pattern was the same: models had to be studied and emulated but also commented on, elaborated, and applied to the questions raised or issues dealt with.

If we look at early monastic texts such as the letters of Antony or Pachomius, the *Apophthegmata patrum*, the writings attributed to Isaiah of Gaza, or even the *Life of Pachomius*, we can easily recognize such an educational formation, although the formative texts are here taken from the Bible. The authors knew and used the Bible as a collection of sayings that they combined and elaborated upon freely, and they also imitated it when composing sentences and passages. An intriguing issue is whether the collections of monastic *apophthegmata* can be regarded as part of such a process of monastic formation, as the shaping of an alternative to the *Sentences* of Menander to be used for monastic education. For many of the early monastic authors, we know that they had received a thorough classical education, and there are good reasons to think that the study of their works can gain much from a closer attention to the educational formation underlying the texts. But is it also possible to establish a link between the traditions of elementary education, as well as higher rhetorical and philosophical education, and see the rise of monasticism as a direct Christian adaptation of the schools of antiquity? Were the monks schoolteachers, albeit teachers of a different alphabet, as a saying attributed to Arsenius puts it?[75]

The tangible evidence we have for elementary teaching in a monastic setting, for the monastery as school, has up to now been centered on Upper Egypt and emerges from the archaeological excavations of monasteries of a somewhat later period (sixth to eighth centuries), where numerous papyri and ostraka used for school exercises, as well as copies of Homer and the *Sentences* of Menander, have been found in situ.[76] But no thorough investigation of all material indicating school activity in early monastic sites has yet been done. A possible reason for the fact that the evidence for elementary education comes from monasteries in Upper Egypt may well be that it was mainly here that monastic communities were receiving monks who had not received any or much elementary education. As suggested elsewhere, it is reasonable to think that the creation of an elementary education on a Christian basis first happened in the periphery of traditional Greek culture.[77]

On a more general level, there are, however, obvious parallels between what we know of the lives of the early monks and of the teachers of antiquity, especially teachers of rhetoric and philosophy. Both the archaeological evidence from Kellia and Naqlun and the texts describing the lives of the early monks indicate the central role of the Abba, the teacher, and the disciples or students who were closely attached to him and whose task was both to provide for and to learn from him. The similarities between some monastic biographical texts and, for example, the descriptions of the lives of neo-Pythagorean and neo-Platonic teachers are obvious.[78] Also in these we find teachers who established themselves outside the city and disciples who settle down in the neighborhood, forming a new community, which in the *Life of Pythagoras* by Porphyry is actually called a *koinobion*.

Although noted in previous scholarship, it is somewhat startling that the fact that the monastic texts regularly describe the monastic life as the philosophical life has not received more attention. *The Life of Antony*, as well as the *Life of Pachomius*, makes it clear that the monks were seen as rivals to the Greek philosophers; less developed texts, such as the Coptic *Life of Abba Aphou of Pemdje*, indicate that the desert ascetic was a more secure source for theological insight and wisdom than the archbishop. When the synod of Gangra denounces monks disliked for their radicalism, one issue is that the monks dressed in the garb of philosophers, a description probably not to be taken literally but, rather, to indicate that monks should not pretend to be philosophers.[79] The criticisms of bishop Nilus of Ancyra directed toward wandering and begging monks who pretended to be great teachers echo a similar critique of philosophers who spend their time on nothing useful, divesting themselves of their responsibilities in society.

Although much more work has to be done on the details of the formative structures within early monasticism and the relations between various forms of early monasticism and the varieties of educational traditions in Late Antiquity, it seems evident that the traditional forms of elementary and higher education need to be taken into account in studying the emergence of monasticism. In view of the literature produced by the monks of the first generations, Eastern as well as Western, a special emphasis has to be put on the role of traditional philosophical schools in shaping monastic ideals and teachings. It is no longer possible to regard the monastic authors manifesting a strong philosophical background—for example, Evagrius of Pontus, Dorotheus of Gaza, or Augustine—as foreigners to the emergent monastic tradition. What is exceptional is their influence but probably not their ideals or the models of life they followed and made use of.

NOTES

1. Tertullian, *De praescriptione haereticorum* 7.9.

2. For the variety of traditional explanations, see the influential study by Karl Heussi (1936), in particular, 108–115 and 280–304 with its emphasis on rural simplicity, echoing themes from Gibbon. Recently, more emphasis has been put on a variety of social and political factors, as well as internal developments in Christian spirituality. See, for example, Griggs 1990, 100–106; Goehring 1999, 13–35; Dunn 2000, 1–24; and Caner 2002, 12–18.

3. The dichotomy between "the philosophically influenced Christian circle" of Alexandria and "a new type of Christian wisdom" being the opposite of the "pagan philosophical schools" is highlighted in Watts 2006, 169–170. For a survey and critique of earlier scholarship concerning the "anti-intellectualism" of early Egyptian monasticism, see Casiday 2007, 131–160.

4. *Vita Antonii*, 1.

5. See Rubenson 2007a.

6. See Wipszycka 1995 for the importance of archaeology in reinterpreting early monasticism and Wipszycka (the articles in Wipszycka 1996b, 281–392) for discussions on the papyrological evidence. For early monastic architecture, see Grossman 2002, 40–63 and 245–315. For a recent survey of the archaeological evidence, see Brooks Hedstrom 2007, 368–389.

7. See Goehring 1993 and 2007.

8. As in the encounter between Antony and the philosophers in *Vita Antonii*, 72–73.

9. The rather sharp distinction between Christian and pagan ascetic ideals made by Peter Brown tends to overlook this common ground by focusing on idealizations. See, for example, Brown 1998, 601–631, echoing the sharp distinction between pagan and Christian views on the body in Brown 1988, 160–177 and 213–240.

10. For Kellia, see Grossman 2002. For an interpretation of the social and economic conditions, see Wipszycka 1986. For a summary and recent bibliography, see Brooks Hedstrom 2007, 378–380.

11. For the excavations at Naqlun see Brooks Hedstrom 2007, 375–377, and Derda 2008, 3–11, with references.

12. For the production of biblical manuscripts at Naqlun, see Derda 1995a; for the Naqlun texts, see Derda 1995b and 2008.

13. See Goehring 2007 for an excellent survey of the early development as evidenced by material culture.

14. See Rousseau 1985, 149–173, and Goehring 2007.

15. Education and teaching are strongly represented in the rules; see *Regula Pachomii, Praecepta* 3, 13, 15, 17, 19–21, 25, 31, and in the *Vita Pachomii* 31, 41, 56–57. For a detailed discussion, see Scholten 1988, 144–157.

16. Rousseau 1985, 163–169.

17. On the monasteries of Shenoute, see Krawiec 2002 and Schroeder 2007.

18. See Judge 1981, 613–620.

19. For a general discussion, see Rubenson 1995, 120–122.

20. On early monastic libraries, see Gamble 1995, 170–174, and, more recently, Kotsifou 2007, with references to detailed studies (51, n. 7).

21. For the debate, see Goehring 2001, 234–256. For a new perspective, see Rousseau 2007, 140–157.

22. The archaeological evidence is almost exclusively confined to the Judean desert monasteries. See Hirschfeld 1992 and Patrich 1995. For the Gaza region, see Hirschfeld 2004, 71–88.

23. The classical survey of early Palestinian monasticism is Chitty 1966. More recent studies include Binns 1994, Hevelone-Harper 2005, and Bitton-Ashkelony and Kofsky 2006.

24. The classic study is Vööbus 1958–1988.

25. For recent discussions on Theodoret, see Pásztori-Kupán 2006.

26. See Harvey 1990.

27. Caner 2002.

28. For a discussion of the parallels and references to the texts, see Caner 2002, 183–184.

29. Although Basil's *xenodocheion* is central in Brown 2002, the monks are strangely absent. For another view with an emphasis on the role of the monks, see Crislip 2005, 103–120 and 138–142.

30. For Macrina and the importance of rich women for the establishment of monastic households, see Elm 1994, 39–47 and 78–105.

31. For the monks and the anti-Chalcedonian propaganda, see Steppa 2002.

32. For the early developments in the West and the aristocratic background of Western monasticism, see Dunn 2000, 59–75 and 82–84.

33. A vivid example is the description of the impact the *Life of Antony* made on Augustine. See Augustine, *Confessiones* VIII.14–19.

34. See, for example, Cameron 1991 and Clark 1999 and the discussions in Martin and Miller 2005, esp. 1–21.

35. Questions on the issue of monastic education, its models, character, and practice have rarely been asked. But for a recent contribution, see Larsen 2006.

36. Athanasius, *Vita Antonii* 14.

37. Athanasius, *Vita Antonii* 1, 14, 90.

38. Athanasius, *Vita Antonii* 81.

39. Athanasius, *Vita Antonii* 55.

40. Athanasius, *Vita Antonii* 72–80.

41. Rubenson 2006, 191–208.

42. Athanasius, *Vita Antonii* 20.

43. This is excellently worked out in Urbano 2008.

44. See Rubenson 2000, 119–124.

45. See Gaspar 2008.

46. Evagrius Ponticus, *Praktikos* 91–100. For John Cassian, see Stewart 1998, 133–140.

47. Regnault 1987, 65–83; Gould 1993, 9–17.

48. For the strong emphasis on community in the *Apophthegmata Patrum*, see Gould 1993. There is as yet no major study of the interactions between the monks and society, but see important comments in Caner 2002, 19–49.

49. Goehring 1993, 2005, and 2007.

50. See, for example, the sayings attributed to Arsenius and Evagrius in *Apophthegmata patrum*.

51. For the sources on and the debate about the controversy, see Rubenson 1999.

52. See Larsen 2006, 74–115, and Rönnegård 2007, 206–218.

53. See Rydell Johnsén 2007, 196–277.

54. See Harmless 2000.

55. For a survey of some of the early collections, see Rubenson 2007b, 75–87.

56. See Rubenson 1995 and for the debates, Bumazhnov 2009, 1–9.

57. Rubenson 2009.

58. For discussions on this connection, see Bumazhnov 2009, 11, with its references.

59. For editions and discussion, see Rubenson 2007b.

60. For the problems and solutions, see Joest 2002a and 2002b.

61. For the letters of Isidore of Pelusion, see Evieux 1997, and for the letters of Barsanuphius and John, Hevelone-Harper 2005.

62. There is unfortunately no critical edition of the corpus and consequently no detailed scholarly study. For a translation with introduction, notes, and an extensive bibliography, see Chryssavgis and Penkett 2002.

63. Also here a critical edition is wanting. For references and Nilus' views, see Caner 2002, 177–190.

64. For Dorotheus of Gaza, see Hevelone-Harper 2005.

65. See Rydell Johnsén 2007.

66. An excellent introduction with all references is Casiday 2006. More emphasis is given to the philosophical background in Guillaumont 1966, 1104–1107.

67. For this connection, see Hadot 1995, 126–144.

68. For John Cassian, see Casiday 2007.

69. *Klimax* in Greek means "ladder."

70. Rydell Johnsén 2007, 160–162.

71. For the Macarian corpus, see Stewart 1991 and Plested 2004.

72. Plested 2004.

73. On education in Egypt in Late Antiquity, see Cribiore 2001.

74. See Wipszycka 1984, 279–296, and 1996a, 127–135.

75. *Apophthegmata patrum*, the alphabetical collection, Arsenius 6.

76. See the reference to the material found at the monastery of Epiphanius at Thebes in Cribiore 2001, 24–25, and Larsen 2006, 67–76 and 147–151. Unfortunately no similar material emerging from the Pachomian monasteries has yet been found.

77. Rubenson 2000, 136.

78. See Rubenson 2006 and Urbano 2008.

79. Canon 12 of the synod of Gangra: "If any man, from supposed asceticism, uses the philosopher's mantle and, as if by this he were maintaining righteousness, despises those who with piety wear ordinary cloaks and make use other common clothing as is customary, let him be anathema." See Silvas 2005, 486–494.

WORKS CITED

Ancient Sources

Apophthegmata patrum, the alphabetical collection. Ed. Migne, J. P. *Patrologia Graeca* 65.71–440.

Athanasius, *Vita Antonii*. Ed. J. Bartelink 2004. *Athanase d'Alexandrie: Vie d'Antoine*. Paris: Cerf.

Augustine, *Confessiones*. Ed. L. Verheijen 1981. *Sancti Augustini Opera: Confessionum libri XIII*. Turnhout: Brepols.

Evagrius Ponticus, *Praktikos*. Ed. A. and C. Guillaumont. 1971. *Évagre le Pontique, Traité pratique ou le moine*. Sources chrétiennes 170–171. Paris: Cerf.

Regula Pachomii. Ed. A. Boon. 1932. *Pachomiana Latina: Règle et épîtres de s. Pachôme, épître de s. Théodose et 'Liber' de s. Orsiesius. Texte latine de s. Jérome*. Louvain: Bibliothèque de la Revue d'histoire ecclésiastique 7.

Tertullian, *De praescriptione haereticorum*. Ed. R. Refoulé. 1957. *Traité de la prescription contre les hérétiques*. Sources chrétiennes 46. Paris: Cerf.

Vita Pachomii. Ed. F. Halkin. 1932. *Sancti Pachomii Vitae Graecae*. Brussels: Société des Bollandistes.

Modern Sources

Binns, John. 1994. *Ascetics and Ambassadors of Christ: The Monasteries of Palestine, 314–631*. Oxford: Clarendon Press.

Bitton-Ashkelony, Brouria, and Aryeh Kofsky. 2006. "Monasticism in the Holy Land." In *Christians and Christianity in the Holy Land: From the Origins to the Latin Kingdom*, ed. Ora Limor and Guy Stroumsa, 257–291. Turnhout: Brepols.

Brooks Hedstrom, Darlene L. 2007. "Divine Architects: Designing the Monastic Dwelling Place." In *Egypt in the Byzantine World, 300–700*, ed. Roger S. Bagnall, 368–389. Cambridge: Cambridge University Press.

Brown, Peter. 1988. *The Body and Society: Men, Women and Sexual Renunciation in Early Christianity*. London: Faber and Faber.

———. 1998. "Asceticism: Pagan and Christian." In *The Cambridge Ancient History, Vol. 13: The Late Roman Empire, A.D. 337–425*, ed. Averil Cameron and Peter Garnsey, 601–631. Cambridge: Cambridge University Press.

———. 2002. *Poverty and Leadership in the Later Roman Empire*. Hanover, NH: University Press of New England.

Bumazhnov, Dimitrij. 2009. *Visio Mystica im Spannungsfeld frühchristlicher Überlieferungen*. Tübingen: Mohr Siebeck.

Cameron, Averil. 1991. *Christianity and the Rhetoric of Empire: The Development of Christian Discourse*. Berkeley: University of California Press.

Caner, Daniel. 2002. *Wandering, Begging Monks: Spiritual Authority and the Promotion of Monasticism in Late Antiquity*. Berkeley: University of California Press.

Casiday, Augustine. 2006. *Evagrius Ponticus*. London: Routledge.

———. 2007. *Tradition and Theology in St. John Cassian*. Oxford: Oxford University Press.

Chitty, Derwas. 1966. *The Desert a City*. Oxford: Blackwell.

Chryssavgis, John, and Pachomios Penkett. 2002. *Abba Isaiah of Scetis: Ascetic Discourses*. Kalamazoo, MI: Cistercian Publications.

Clark, Elizabeth. 1999. *Reading Renunciation: Asceticism and Scripture in Early Christianity*. Princeton, NJ: Princeton University Press.

Cribiore, Raffaela. 2001. *Gymnastics of the Mind: Greek Education in Hellenistic and Roman Egypt*. Princeton, NJ: Princeton University Press.

Crislip, Andrew. 2005. *From Monastery to Hospital: Christian Monasticism and the Transformation of Health Care in Late Antiquity*. Ann Arbor: University of Michigan Press.

Derda, Thomas. 1995a. "The Naqlun Papyri and the Codex Alexandrinus." In *The Spirituality of Ancient Monasticism: Acts of the International Colloquium Held in Cracow-Tyniec, November 16–19th, 1994*, ed. Marek Starowieyski, 13–34. Cracow: Tyniec.

———. 1995b. *Deir el-Naqlun: The Greek Papyri (P.Naqlun I)*. Warsaw: Wydawnictwa Uniwersytetu Warszawskiego.

———. 2008. *Deir el-Naqlun: The Greek Papyri, Volume II (P.Naqlun II)*. Journal of Juristic Papyrology Supplement 9. Warsaw: University of Warsaw.

Dunn, Marilyn. 2000. *The Emergence of Monasticism: From the Desert Fathers to the Early Middle Ages*. Oxford: Blackwell.

Elm, Susanna. 1994. *"Virgins of God": The Making of Asceticism in Late Antiquity*. Oxford: Oxford University Press.

Evieux, Pierre. 1997. *Isidore de Peluse: Lettres*. Sources chrétiennes 422. Paris: Cerf.

Gamble, Harry Y. 1995. *Books and Readers in the Early Church: A History of Early Christian Texts.* New Haven, CT: Yale University Press.
Gaspar, Christian. 2008. "An Oriental in Greek Dress: The Making of a Perfect Christian Philosopher in the *Philotheos Historia* of Theodoret of Cyrrhus," *Annual of Medieval Studies at CEU* 14: 193–229.
Goehring, James. 1993. "The Encroaching Desert: Literary Production and Ascetic Space in Early Christian Egypt," *JECS* 1: 281–296.
———. 1999. *Ascetics, Society, and the Desert: Studies in Early Egyptian Monasticism.* Harrisburg: Trinity Press.
———. 2001. "The Provenance of the Nag Hammadi Codices Once More," *Studia Patristica* 35: 234–256.
———. 2005. "The Dark Side of the Landscape: Ideology and Power in the Christian Myth of the Desert." In *The Cultural Turn in Late Ancient Studies: Gender, Asceticism and Historiography*, ed. Dale Martin and Patricia Cox Miller, 136–149. Durham, NC: Duke University Press.
———. 2007. "Monasticism in Byzantine Egypt: Continuity and Memory." In *Egypt in the Byzantine World 300–700*, ed. Roger Bagnall, 390–407. Cambridge: Cambridge University Press.
Gould, Graham. 1993. *The Desert Fathers on Monastic Community.* Oxford: Oxford University Press.
Griggs, C. Wilfred. 1990. *Early Egyptian Christianity: From Its Origins to 451 C.E.* Leiden: Brill.
Grossman, Peter. 2002. *Christliche Architektur in Ägypten.* Handbuch der Orientalistik 1. Der Nahe und Mittlere Osten. Leiden: Brill.
Guillaumont, Antoine. 1966. "Evagrius Ponticus," *Reallexikon für Antike und Christentum* 6: 1088–1107.
Hadot, Pierre. 1995. *Philosophy as a Way of Life.* Oxford: Blackwell.
Harmless, William. 2000. "Remembering Poemen Remembering: The Desert Fathers and the Spirituality of Memory," *Church History* 69: 483–518.
Harvey, Susan Ashbrook. 1990. *Asceticism and Society in Crisis: John of Ephesus and the Lives of the Eastern Saints.* Berkeley: University of California Press.
Heussi, Karl. 1936. *Der Ursprung des Mönchtums.* Tübingen: Mohr Siebeck.
Hevelone-Harper, Jennifer. 2005. *Disciples of the Desert: Monks, Laity, and Spiritual Authority in Sixth-Century Gaza.* Baltimore: Johns Hopkins University Press.
Hirschfeld, Yitzhar. 1992. *The Judean Desert Monasteries in the Byzantine Period.* New Haven, CT: Yale University Press.
———. 2004. "The Monasteries of Gaza: An Archaeological Review." In *Christian Gaza in Late Antiquity*, ed. Brouria Bitton-Ashkelony and Aryeh Kofsky, 71–88. Leiden: Brill.
Joest, Christoph. 2002a. "Die Pachom-Briefe 1 und 2: Auflösung der Geheimbuchstaben und Entdeckungen zu den Briefüberschriften," *Journal of Coptic Studies* 4: 25–98.
———. 2002b. "Das Buchstabenquadrat im pachomianischen Briefcorpus," *Le Muséon* 115: 241–260.
Judge, E. A. 1981. "Fourth-Century Monasticism in the Papyri." In *Proceedings of the Sixteenth International Congress of Papyrology*, 613–620. Chico, CA: Scholars Press.
Kotsifou, Chrysi. 2007. "Books and Book Production in the Monastic Communities of Byzantine Egypt." In *The Early Christian Book*, ed. William E. Klingshirn and Linda Safran, 48–66. Washington, DC: Catholic University of America Press.
Krawiec, Rebecca. 2002. *Shenoute and the Women of the White Monastery: Egyptian Monasticism in Late Antiquity.* Oxford: Oxford University Press.

Larsen, Lillian. 2006. *Pedagogical Parallels: Re-Reading the Apophthegmata Patrum*. PhD Thesis, Columbia University.

Martin, Dale, and Patricia Cox Miller, eds. 2005. *The Cultural Turn in Late Ancient Studies: Gender, Asceticism and Historiography*. Durham, NC: Duke University Press.

Pásztori-Kupán, István. 2006. *Theodoret of Cyrus*. London: Routledge.

Patrich, Joseph. 1995. *Sabas, Leader of Palestinian Monasticism: A Comparative Study in Eastern Monasticism, Fourth to Seventh Centuries*. Washington, DC: Dumbarton Oaks Research Library.

Plested, Marcus. 2004. *The Macarian Legacy: The Place of Macarius-Symeon in the Eastern Christian Tradition*. Oxford: Oxford University Press.

Regnault, Lucien. 1987. *Les Pères du désert à travers leurs Apophthegmes*. Sablé-sur-Sarthe: Solesmes.

Rönnegård, Per. 2007. *Threads and Images: The Use of Scripture in the Apophthegmata Patrum*. Lund: Centre for Theology and Religious Studies.

Rousseau, Philip. 1985. *Pachomius: The Making of a Community in Fourth-Century Egypt*. Berkeley: University of California Press.

———. 2007. "The Successors of Pachomius and the Nag Hammadi Codices: Exegetical Themes and Literary Structures." In *The World of Early Egyptian Christianity: Language, Literature and Social Context. Essays in Honor of David W. Johnson*, ed. James E. Goehring and Janet A. Timbie, 140–157. Washington, DC: Catholic University of America Press.

Rubenson, Samuel. 1995. *The Letters of St. Anthony, Monasticism and the Making of a Saint*. Minneapolis: Fortress.

———. 1999. "Origen in the Egyptian Monastic Tradition of the Fourth Century." In *Origeniana Septima: Origenes in den Auseinandersetzungen des 4. Jahrhunderts*, ed. Wolfgang Bienert, 319–337. Leuven: Peeters.

———. 2000. "Philosophy and Simplicity: The Problem of Classical Education in Early Christian Biography." In *Greek Biography and Panegyric in Late Antiquity*, ed. T. Hägg and P. Rousseau, 110–139. Berkeley: California University Press.

———. 2006. "Anthony and Pythagoras: A Reappraisal of the Appropriation of Classical Biography in Athanasius' *Vita Antonii*." In *Beyond Reception—: Mutual Influences between Antique Religion, Judaism, and Early Christianity*, ed. D. Brakke, A.-C. Jacobsen, and J. Ulrich, 191–208. Frankfurt: Peter Lang.

———. 2007a. "Asceticism and Monasticism I: Eastern." In *The Cambridge History of Christianity*, vol. 2, ed. A. Casiday and W. Löhr, 637–668. Cambridge: Cambridge University Press.

———. 2007b. "Argument and Authority in Early Monastic Correspondence." In *Foundations of Power and Conflicts of Authority in Late-Antique Monasticism*, ed. A. Camplani and G. Filoramo, 75–87. Orientalia Lovaniensia Analecta 157. Leuven: Peeters.

———. 2009. "'As Already Translated to the Kingdom While Still in the Body': The Transformation of the Ascetic in Early Egyptian Monasticism." In *Metamorphoses: Resurrection, Body and Transformative Practices in Early Christianity*, ed. Turid Karlsen Seim and Jorunn Økland, 271–289. Berlin: Walter de Gruyter.

Rydell Johnsén, Henrik. 2007. *Reading John Climacus: Rhetorical Argumentation, Literary Convention and the Tradition of Monastic Formation*. Lund: Lund University.

Scholten, Clemens. 1988. "Die Nag-Hammadi-Texte als Buchbesitz der Pachomianer," *JAC* 31: 144–157.

Schroeder, Caroline. 2007. *Monastic Bodies: Discipline and Salvation in Shenoute of Atripe.* Philadelphia: University of Pennsylvania Press.
Silvas, Anna. 2005. *The Asketikon of Basil of Caesarea.* Oxford: Oxford University Press.
Steppa, Jan-Eric. 2002. *John Rufus and the World Vision of Anti-Chalcedonian Culture.* Piscataway, NJ: Gorgias Press.
Stewart, Columba. 1991. *"Working the Earth of the Heart": The Messalian Controversy in History, Texts, and Language to AD 431.* Oxford: Clarendon.
———. 1998. *Cassian the Monk.* Oxford: Oxford University Press.
Urbano, Arthur. 2008. "'Read It Also to the Gentiles': The Displacement and Recasting of the Philosopher in the *Vita Antonii*," *Church History* 77: 877–914.
Vööbus, Arthur. 1958–1988. *History of Asceticism in the Syrian Orient: A Contribution to the History of Culture in the Near East.* 3 vols. Corpus Scriptorum Christianorum Orientalium Subsidia 14, 17, 81. Louvain: Peeters.
Watts, Edward. 2006. *City and School in Late Antique Athens and Alexandria.* Berkeley: University of California Press.
Wipszycka, Ewa. 1984. "Le degré d'alphabétisation en Égypte byzantine," *Revue des Études Augustiniennes* 30: 279–296. (Reprinted in Wipszycka 1996b, 107–126)
———. 1986. "Les aspects économiques de la vie de la communauté des Kellia." In *Le site monastique des Kellia: Sources historiques et explorations archéologiques*, ed. Philippe Bridel, 117–144. Geneva: Mission Suisse d'archéologie Copte. (Reprinted in Wipszycka 1996b, 337–362.)
———. 1994. "Le monachisme égyptien et les villes," *Travaux et mémoires* 12: 1–44. (Reprinted in Wipszycka 1996b, 281–336)
———. 1995. "Apports de l'archéologie à l'histoire du monachisme égyptien." In *The Spirituality of Ancient Monasticism: Acts of the International Colloquium Held in Cracow-Tyniec, November 16–19th, 1994*, ed. Marek Starowieyski, 63–78. Cracow: Tyniec.
———. 1996a. "Encore sur la question de la 'Literacy' après l'étude de W. V. Harris." In *Études sur le christianisme dans l'Égypte de l'antiquité tardive*, 127–135. Studia Ephemeridis Augustinianum 52. Rome: Institutum Patristicum Augustinianum.
———. 1996b. *Études sur le christianisme dans l'Égypte de l'antiquité tardive.* Studia Ephemeridis Augustinianum 52. Rome: Institutum Patristicum Augustinianum.

CHAPTER 16

PHYSICS AND METAPHYSICS

GREGORY SMITH
Central Michigan University

> The finest-particled kind of matter is air, the finest air is soul, the finest soul is mind, the finest mind is God.
>
> —Stobaean Hermetica 12.14

THERE is a well-known passage in Porphyry's *Life of Plotinus* that invokes some of the most important issues in the history of late ancient thought. That these are all more or less directly connected to problems we might label physical or metaphysical (or both) is not quite a coincidence, given the theme of the present contribution. But the wide-ranging importance of physical and metaphysical ideas in the history of Late Antiquity as a whole, not just the history of philosophy or science, is something that many readers may be reluctant to accept without the further demonstration that is one of this article's primary goals. And since, as Plotinus discovered, some demonstrations can take a long time, it is best to reflect on Porphyry's words without further delay.

> When Plotinus spoke his mind was manifest even in his countenance, which radiated light; lovely as he was to see, he was then especially beautiful to the sight. Fine sweat suffused [his skin], and his kindness shone forth, and his gentleness displayed itself in answering questions, along with his vigor. Even when I, Porphyry, spent three days asking him how the soul is present to the body, he kept on explaining.[1]

The last sentence of this passage is probably the most quoted because it usefully underscores an important point: Plotinus and the philosophers who followed him were very interested in the relationship between body and soul. Since these men and women, the Neoplatonists, are widely recognized as the most important philosophers of Late Antiquity, exerting profound influence on premodern Christian thought in particular, their preoccupation with the question of body and soul was momentous not just for the period but for the history of philosophy.

This, then, is the first observation of central if basic importance. If, for the moment, we let the more specific categories of body and soul stand in for physics and metaphysics, as only the most important among a number of philosophical questions on related themes, we may reasonably (and, as it turns out, accurately) conclude that at least some people in Late Antiquity spent a lot of time thinking and talking about both physical and metaphysical things—and particularly about how these things were related to each other. That virtually all extant discussions addressed at least the possibility of a literal, physical connection between bodily and nonbodily things offers a salutary reminder that late ancient people did not think in the categories most of us assume more or less instinctively. True, many of the best-known discussions from Late Antiquity raise the possibility only to deny it: even if we cannot be sure exactly what Plotinus said on the occasion in question, it is safe to assume that he did not come down in favor of a physical link between body and soul.[2] But it also took him three days to explain how an alternative might work. It is hard to avoid the suspicion that Porphyry, at least, was still not quite sure about the answer.

And so to a second point, easier to miss than the first. Three days makes for a long discussion, especially when the question at issue is both familiar and precise. The primary point of the anecdote, to be sure, is to illustrate Plotinus' exemplary character, his graceful and tireless dedication to the philosophical life. But even if we make allowance for the treatment of earlier theories and other reasonable digressions, this extended question-and-answer session would be remarkable for its length in the context of ancient philosophy—at least before the period under consideration in this book. What I want to suggest here is that the extent and persistence of Plotinus' response to Porphyry might be used as a kind of rough index to the novelty of his answers and, more precisely, to the newly uncompromising rigor of his commitment to an immaterial (not just an incorporeal) soul.

Now it may well be that Porphyry's reluctance was the principal bottleneck, but this comes to the same thing.[3] For some reason, the Plotinian kind of distinction between body and soul seems to have been a hard sell, at least around the middle of the third century. This raises two further questions, both of which lurk behind the pages that follow. First, why should this be so? Was not "dualism" the order of the day in the later centuries of the Roman empire, especially for Platonists? Second, was the connection between corporeal and incorporeal things just as hard to explain at the end of our period as it was at the beginning? In other words, did Late Antiquity make a difference?

Before addressing these and related questions, however, I would like to draw attention to a third feature of Porphyry's story, the part where Plotinus' mind makes light shine out of his face. This was because of the luminous splendor of his intellect, Porphyry tells us, but we should not let our hackneyed image of a "brilliant mind" mislead us into thinking it merely a metaphor. There is, on the contrary, little reason to think that Porphyry meant the light (φῶς) coming from Plotinus' face any less literally than the fine sheen of sweat (ἱδρώς) that covered it. We can be confident about this for two different kinds of reasons. First, comparable accounts in late ancient biography offer more examples, as well as more details, about luminescent sages, including philosophers, in ways that leave no doubt about their conviction that literal, visible light could be produced by a great man's soul. Setting aside, for the moment, accounts of glowing Christian saints,[4] the fifth-century life of the philosopher Proclus is decidedly more explicit than Porphyry on Plotinus.

> He was lovely indeed to behold, for not only did he fully possess that symmetry [of body], but also the force of his soul, blooming in his body like a living light, produced an astonishing radiance which it is scarcely possible to convey in words.[5]

Second, we also have detailed attempts to explain with more or less scientific precision the mechanisms behind the glow. A preliminary summary of the late ancient explanation is that an important class of late ancient things, occupying a pivotal place on the scale of being, was often equated or closely associated with light in one form or another. The fact that the human soul could be directly or indirectly included in this class, together with the related principle that higher and better things tend to be both clearer and brighter (not to mention more real), helps make a bit more sense of a visibly shining mind.

This, then, is one of the places where late ancient physics and metaphysics merge, sometimes insensibly but always remarkably. Before we turn to fundamental principles, however, some further observations will help to clarify this chapter's scope and approach.

First, the range and diversity of the available sources. Whose ideas are these, anyway? For several reasons, Plotinus himself dominates much of the discussion to follow.[6] It is conventional, correct, and probably sufficient to observe at this point his abiding influence on both pagan and Christian thought from the third century clear through the Middle Ages and beyond.[7] But it seems equally important to recall that Plotinus and what we call Neoplatonism (for Plotinus and his followers, it was merely Platonism, of course) represent less the ascendancy of a single school of thought, narrowly defined and scrupulous in its boundaries, than the culmination of a long process of consolidation. Frans A. J. de Haas has characterized the two or three centuries leading up to Plotinus as a time when "the vexed issue of the criterion of truth was surpassed by the growing belief in a universal truth from which all human wisdom had drawn from times immemorial."[8] Along with the retreat of skepticism, this entailed a considerable amount of latitude and even the combination of doctrines from previously disparate traditions.[9] The intellectual debts of Neoplatonism itself extend well beyond Plato, to Aristotle above all, but also to Stoics and Pythagoreans.[10]

While I have tried to indicate a few places where later authors diverged from the acknowledged founder of Neoplatonism, it has also seemed important to read Plotinus (along with other sources) as a potential index of certain deep-seated assumptions that rarely made it to the surface of explicit discussion. More particularly, the centuries leading up to and including Late Antiquity have long been recognized as a period when a range of evidently related ideas, often labeled "Platonic," spread well beyond the circles of professional philosophy. The varied texts of the *Corpus hermeticum*, the tantalizing fragments of the *Chaldean Oracles*, and the esoteric doctrines of gnostic masters like Valentinus, for example, have memorably been described in the aggregate by John Dillon as "the underworld of Platonism."[11] If we extend the shadow of this rather catholic Platonism only slightly to include its celebrated or notorious influence on Christian thought in the same period, it is easier still to justify an emphasis on Plato's most important exponents after Aristotle. In any case, the methodological point should be clear: without wishing to elide crucial differences between any number of theorists and a still greater number of diverse sources from Roman and later antiquity, I would suggest that there are several common if not quite universal metaphysical and physical assumptions worth considering together, for their practical no less than their theoretical implications.

Another reason for lingering over deep-seated instincts is the fact that most of them are no longer with us. To modern people who have not spent their lives immersed in the ancient world, this distance can make a wide range of late ancient thought and practice seem alien or absurd. More dangerous still are those ideas that seem familiar but, in fact, depend on quite different assumptions about the world or the human person. In these cases, it is not always possible to argue for definitive and permanent change in Late Antiquity itself, nor has it always been easy to determine whether the most influential figures—Plotinus and Augustine above all—serve as normative representatives or extraordinary exceptions.

In fact, the rather old-fashioned problem of Plotinus as representative example or exceptional "man of genius" has turned out to be a good deal more central than expected.[12] For all his influence, for all the (sometimes) sophisticated adoption and modification of his central ideas in his own and succeeding centuries, and for all his dominance of much of the discussion here, writing this chapter has strengthened a long-growing suspicion that certain crucial ideas or suggestions in Plotinus' thought were rarely, if ever, taken as far as he meant them and that sometimes it is more helpful to understand him as a negative example, even as the exception that proves the rule. Similar things, I will suggest, might be said about Augustine. In both cases, I restrict myself to highly qualified conclusions about how both men approached the subject of material and immaterial things, especially the relationship of body and soul. I feel confident, in any case, that I am not the first to envy Porphyry his three days of questions.

Finally, to talk about a "scale of being" as I have already done is to talk about metaphysics, and it is hard to think of a period in intellectual history where scales of being were more important than in Late Antiquity. For better or worse, these sometimes elaborate rankings rank among the best-known features of late ancient thought. Not quite so well known, perhaps, is the fact that the hierarchies very often involved physical things as well—and not just as an undifferentiated mass on the bottom rung of the ladder. Familiar modern categories apply but poorly here or break down altogether. Moral, metaphysical, and material distinctions march together or entail one another in ways that can be hard to understand, at first. For this, with only slightly exaggerated specificity, we can thank Descartes.

Dualism and Descartes

Among Descartes' many contributions to modern thought is a way of thinking about the world that is still very much with us, despite the fact that few specialists nowadays defend its original assumptions. Usually known as Cartesian or substance dualism, this view holds that there are two kinds of things in the world: things that think (minds) and things that have spatial dimensions (bodies). For Descartes, these were mutually exclusive categories, and this categorization has proven tenacious indeed.[13] Upon being asked about the physical attributes of the human mind or soul, for example, an ordinary educated modern person will think this a mischievous or nonsensical question. Everyone knows that to describe minds as sharp or slow or brilliant or dull, or hearts as stony or heavy or light, is to speak figuratively, without any danger that people will think you are talking literally about squishy pulsing organs or physical qualities describing objects that can be located, seen, or otherwise measured in three-dimensional space.

In pursuit of late ancient mentalities, there are several reasons for pausing over what may seem obvious observations about how we ordinarily conceive of mind and body. In the first place, it is only a little misleading to suggest that Descartes got some of his most famous ideas from Late Antiquity.[14] More important, it is essential to be clear about certain similarities and differences between the Cartesian sort of dualism and the several dualisms that have been ascribed to ancient thought. More often than not, the similarities are misleading. Differences, on the other hand, are everywhere to be found and are very often illuminating. In classical and later antiquity, for example, the question about the soul's constitution would not have been nonsensical to many (and probably most) people. In fact, theorists like Plotinus and Augustine had to spend a good deal of effort trying to persuade educated and intelligent people that it was.

Thinking with Shadows

In Plato or Plotinus, one often encounters a basic contrast between intelligible and sensible reality, between the immaterial world of thought (more or less) and the tangible world of ordinary experience. At first, this seems very nearly the same as Descartes' contrast between mind and body, but the similarity can be misleading. In what remains one of the best single introductions to Plotinus in English, Dominic O'Meara neatly summarizes the problem in historical terms:

> For almost 2,000 years many philosophers took for granted the Platonic belief that the visible world is the shadow of a higher, more substantial, immaterial world. Even Aristotelians, inasmuch as they believed in the existence of a superior, immaterial divine substance, came near to this view, although they did not follow the Platonists in condemning the material world to a sort of semi-existence. A decisive change and a new beginning came only in the seventeenth century, with René Descartes. In his effort to break away from ancient and medieval philosophy and found a new, resolutely modern philosophy Descartes took as the fundamental metaphysical distinction that between mind and body. The question whether "mind" (however defined) is "different" (and in what sense) from body (whatever that may be) remains unresolved and crucial in modern philosophy.[15]

While the ancient part of this sketch demands further attention, we cannot afford much more space for the Cartesian kind of substance dualism to which most of us instinctively revert unless we are trying very hard to avoid it. It must be enough to underscore, instead, the consequential fact that Cartesian dualism makes mind and body categorically distinct by definition. By definition, Descartes' mental things cannot be described in terms of physics or biology or anything else that involves extension. No matter how kind or keen, a Cartesian mind cannot shine through a philosopher's face. For all the same reasons, it follows that the Cartesian world can hardly be much like its ancient counterparts. Defined by extension and wholly real, its bodies cannot serve as the "shadow" of its thinking things, as the imperfect reflection of a purely mental world that is somehow more real or substantial than the bodily one. This is where modern differences with ancient and especially late ancient thought become especially important. In Late Antiquity, the distinction between true reality and its several shadows was as crucial as it was complicated.

Being and Reality

"Semiexistence" seems particularly difficult nowadays, perhaps. How can a material world whose bare existence is not really in question be "less real," by degrees, than the higher world or worlds of which it is said to be a shadow?

After all, for most of us who are not professional metaphysicians, the question of being is roughly the same as the question of existence. Like the standard dualism of body and mind, the issue is a binary one. A thing either exists or it doesn't. Either there is or there is not such a thing as a unicorn. In English at least, a common way of talking about this involves the words *real* or *reality*, often again with the assumption of two possible answers. Is a unicorn real?

Even in ordinary conversation, however, this kind of question can involve considerably more complexity than the yes-or-no matter of existence. Asking whether a man's Christian faith or his Shaker table is "real" might conceivably expect a yes-or-no answer about the existence of his faith or the table, but it is considerably more likely to preface a discussion about the degree to which his faith or the table corresponds to some understanding of the essential nature or qualities of Christianity or Shaker furniture—qualities without which a thing is not really what it appears or is claimed to be. This kind of question is concerned with the distinction between reality and appearance rather than that between what does and does not exist. Unlike the question of existence, it is also the kind of question to which an answer somewhere between yes and no is conceivable, even likely. One might in ordinary conversation describe a man's table or his faith as more or less real, or more or less genuine, without fear of absurdity or hopeless ambiguity.

Familiar enough from everyday habits of speech, these two approaches to the question of being and reality correspond broadly to two major ontologies or approaches to metaphysics, described with helpful clarity by Julius Moravcsik in one of the most important and challenging books on Platonism to appear in the 1990s.[16] While many modern ontologies have focused on the contrast between real and unreal, aiming at an exhaustive inventory of existing things, Platonic metaphysics is not primarily interested in the question of unpredicated existence.[17] It seeks instead to identify "the most fundamental elements of reality and then shows in terms of these how one can account for much that is less fundamental or merely surface appearance." This in turn has important implications for the motivation behind doing metaphysics in the first place. For one thing, the Platonic approach is productive by design. Its conceptual structure is "explanatory rather than that of an inventory. It explains the less fundamental in terms of the more fundamental." Among other things, this also means that Plato and his diverse successors (including late ancient ones) were less concerned with exhaustiveness, with making everything fit into its own "metaphysical cage," than with the ability to get beyond appearances, to identify the essence of a thing in order to discover its fundamental relation to other things.

That these relationships are usually expressed in terms of priority or dependence will come as no surprise to anyone possessed of even a passing acquaintance with Plato, Plotinus, or especially the elaborate metaphysical hierarchies of later Neoplatonism. In the midst of Late Antiquity's reputation for levels of being at untouchably distant levels of abstraction, however, it is easy to lose sight of the fact that what may seem at first to be obsessive taxonomy for its own sake has certain practical implications. The essentially explanatory framework of this sort of metaphysics has already been suggested—although a frustrated nonspecialist hunting for practical applications might well counter that the "explanations" in question seem quite technical or abstract, and usually both. The precise way in which or indeed the reason why the Neoplatonic One generates Divine Intellect, for example, has few immediately obvious implications for how even a thoughtful person should try to think, much less live as an embodied person in the material world. Although I address some objections of this kind in more detail later, here I want to draw attention to another implication of the Platonic way of doing metaphysics.

This depends on the commonsense observation that when we talk about things that are more fundamental or essential than others, we are usually also making a statement about importance. "Priority," even before its conversion into a barbarous verb, has always had a practical side. Knowing what is fundamental or essential or substantial, in contrast to what is accidental or secondary or indeed the merest deceptive appearance, helps in any number of contexts to produce useful recommendations about where one's energy is best directed—which is to say, about what a person ought to do. In other words, this kind of essentializing metaphysics can lead by easy, sometimes insensible steps, to ethics.[18] When, as in Late Antiquity, this approach to reality is combined with a set of scientific ideas that assume that the physical world embodies, reflects, or otherwise reveals analogous principles of priority, the results can be more practical still.

But how can you tell if one thing is more fundamental than another? Much has been implied already, but it is time for a more systematic summary.

First Principles

These are exciting times for the study of late ancient intellectual history, especially for scholars whose formal training lies outside philosophy itself. While the twentieth century as a whole witnessed a remarkable surge of professional interest in Neoplatonism and its precedents,[19] the last four decades in particular have produced an especially useful array of authoritative introductions and syntheses.[20] Monographs have multiplied apace, but some of the most promising and already fruitful developments have come in the form of collaborative translations, commentaries, and source collections whose utility extends well beyond the classroom.[21] All of this makes it easy to justify the summary nature of this overview, and easier still to combine some potentially disparate strands of late ancient thought and practice in a relatively brief compass.

Unity, Simplicity, and Priority

It is hard to think of a philosophical axiom older or more enduring than what O'Meara has justifiably capitalized as "the Principle of Prior Simplicity." The conviction that "everything made up of parts, every composite thing, depends and derives in some way from what is not composite, what is simple" is evident from the earliest phases of Greek philosophy through some of the most influential projects in modern science: in evolutionary biology or the "theory of everything," for example, no less than in Presocratic attempts to explain the complexity of the cosmos by means of a single fundamental substance and the smallest possible set of basic processes.[22] But it is also hard to think of a time when the principle of prior simplicity was applied with more consequential force than in Late Antiquity. Indeed, the simplicity of a thing (always a matter of degree) determined its place in the scale of being: the more complex, the less real.

Consider Plotinus' insistence on the need for unity or oneness if a thing is to exist at all.

> It is by the one [or "oneness"[23]] that all beings are beings, both those which are primarily beings and those which are in any sense said to be among beings. For what could be anything if it was not one? For if things are deprived of the one which is predicated of them they are not those things. For an army does not exist if it is not one, nor a chorus or a flock if they are not one. But neither can a house or a ship exist if they do not have their one, since the house is one and so is the ship, and if they lose it the house is no longer a house nor the ship a ship.[24]

This is a distinctive way of describing and explaining unity. Decidedly more than a description or mathematical attribute, the unity of composite things comes from and depends on something else altogether, "oneness" or "the one," an independent and prior thing that houses or flocks can have or lose. Of course, if they do lose their oneness—or, in Plotinus' suggestive words, "flee" or "escape" it—they cease to exist altogether. "They are no longer what they were but have become other things, and are those other things in so far as each of them is one."[25] In other words, whereas most of us would probably say that there has to be a house before you can talk about its unity, Plotinus puts it the other way round. Oneness or "the one" comes before the house (and everything else that exists), in a very strong sense.

In this case, Plotinus borrowed his examples, along with the basic argument, from the Stoics,[26] but the use of houses, armies, ships, and choruses helps to illustrate some further important points. In a way more immediately obvious, perhaps, than in the case of a rock, an organizing intelligence is responsible for the unity and order of these human creations. This intelligence is clearly prior and superior to the things that depend on it for their existence, structure, and so on. As the term is most characteristically used by Plotinus, however, *priority* suggests both less and more than we might suspect. "Priority by nature"—a concept used by Aristotle (with a nod to Plato) to indicate a thing's capacity for existence independent of those posterior things that depend on it for their own being[27]—further entails for Plotinus "priority by power and dignity."[28] What may seem less obvious is the claim that prior things are necessarily simpler and more unified than the things that depend on them—but then for Neoplatonists, this amounts to something like a tautology.

> There must be something simple before all things, and this must be other than all the things which come after it, existing by itself, not mixed with the things which derive from it, and all the same able to be present in a different way to these other things, being really one, and not a different being and then one. . . . For if it is not to be simple, outside all coincidence and composition, it could not be a first principle; and it is the most self-sufficient, because it is simple and the first of all: for that which is not the first needs that which is before it, and what is not simple is in need of its simple components so that it can come into existence from them.[29]

It should now be clear that late ancient applications of the principle of prior simplicity leads to results quite different from those to which we have been accustomed by, say, atomic theory. As I understand it, when scientists hunt for the simplest particles of which compound things are composed, they generally expect the particles to outnumber the compounds. The entities multiply with the descent toward simplicity. Plotinus, again, has it the other way round. His path to simplicity (always described as an ascent, when a spatial metaphor is necessary) leads back from multiplicity through increasing unity to a single thing "existing by itself."

Part of the problem comes from the inevitably material metaphors that emerge in ordinary talk about parts and wholes. Plotinus knew this, of course; few ancient philosophers used metaphorical language more deliberately, critically, and fruitfully.[30] In this case, however, the discussion of simplicity quoted in the previous paragraph avoids the material examples (houses and ships) used in the discussion of unity in *Enneads* 6.9.1. Even Armstrong's authoritative translation might just lead us astray by rendering τῶν ἐν αὐτῷ ἁπλῶν as "simple components" rather than the more literal "simple things in it."[31] For "in" also has a special meaning in Plotinus, and these simpler, prior things must not be confused with material parts, analogous to the timbers, say, in a house or ship. For Neoplatonists, "simple" and "prior" point in exactly the opposite direction, to things that cause and unify rather than merely comprise what is complex and posterior.

Lloyd Gerson has aptly described this aspect of Platonism as "top-down," by contrast to ancient and modern systems that find the world's elemental building blocks in material particles and then move up the chain of complexity and sophistication. This top-down approach is, moreover, one of the most pervasive and distinctive features of Platonism in any period. Although it proceeds in the opposite direction, Platonic top-downism is quite as reductivist as materialism (paradigmatically "bottom-up"). But its ultimate irreducible principle is intelligible rather than material. Its simple or prior things impose unity from above, beginning with an ultimate and unqualifiedly simple explanatory principle on which all else depends. At the heart of Platonism, then, lies a consequential axiom inherited from the Presocratics, namely, that the universe itself, the *kosmos*, is an intelligible unity.[32] And since it is evident that this intelligible unity could not emerge on its own, or as some emergent property of the parts it unifies, cosmic unity itself requires a cause outside itself or its parts, a prior principle of unity.[33]

Plotinus described the relationship between prior and posterior in terms that appear paradoxical in other ways, too. In one obvious way, the prior or higher levels of his metaphysical hierarchy can be said to "contain" everything below them, inasmuch as the prior is a sufficient cause of the unity and therefore the existence of what is posterior.[34] In this sense, the posterior is "in" the prior.[35] On the other hand, as evident from passages already examined, Plotinus is perfectly willing to describe a prior thing as "in" the things that come from it.[36] Obviously, this second use of "in" is not to be construed spatially any more than the first one, nor does it imply containment or constraint. On the contrary, Plotinus insists in the strongest possible terms on the independent existence and superior power of prior things. But perhaps this is not so far from the way we habitually talk about people and their creations, after all. However much we might say that we see a man (his intelligence, his character, his skill, and so on) "in" the book he writes or the boat he builds, it is only in very special circumstances that we would claim that his actual existence depends on the book or the boat. The man was there, had to be there, first. Equally special circumstances would be required for us to say that his intelligence or character or skill has been diminished because of its evident "presence" in the book or the boat or, indeed, as a result of the process of making it. The parallel does not get us very far, perhaps, especially if the rather weak and figurative way in which we talk about this kind of presence obscures the remarkably pervasive if nonspatial sense in which Plotinus thinks prior things really are "in" posterior ones.[37] By way of further illustration, then, let us turn briefly instead to the problem with which this article began.

"How is the soul present to the body?" Behind this question lies a good deal more than the status of body and soul in ordinary human life, including the problems of how the prior, superior soul comes to be embodied and why there are multiple individual souls at all.[38] But setting the how-did-this-happen questions aside for the moment, Plotinus' famously counterintuitive remarks on how things are remain instructive. First,

> We must say in general that neither any of the parts of the soul nor the whole soul are in body as in a place. For place is something encompassing, and encompassing body, and where each divided part is, there it is, so that the whole is not [as a whole] in any place; but soul is not a body, and is no more encompassed than encompassing. It is certainly not in the body as in a receptacle either.[39]

So much for any spatial sense in which soul is "in" body. But "how then is it that the soul is said by everyone to be in the body?" Ordinarily, Plotinus does not spend much time considering "what everyone says," but evidently this was a more than usually important problem. Plotinus' immediate answer, however, is quite simple: people say that the soul is in the body because they can see the body but not the soul.

> But if the soul was visible and perceptible, in every way surrounded by life and extending equally to all the [body's] extremities, we should not have said that the soul was in the body, but that the unimportant was in the more important, and what is held together in what holds it together, and that which flows away in that which does not.[40]

This is a consistent application of the principle of prior things described previously. Drawing on the analogy between the soul of the universe—for the universe, possessing both life and order, necessarily has a soul—and referring to the considerable authority of the *Timaeus* (together with the *Parmenides*, the most important Platonic dialogue in the late ancient curriculum),[41] Plotinus then put the conclusion more strongly still. "Plato rightly does not put the soul in the body when he is speaking of the universe, but the body in the soul."[42] So also, necessarily, with human beings. Except in a qualified way,[43] the soul is not in the body; better to say that the body is in the soul. Earlier in the same treatise, he famously illustrated the relationship by comparing the body to a net in the sea. "It is as if a net immersed in the waters was alive, but unable to make its own that in which it is. The sea is already spread out and the net spreads with it, as far as it can."[44]

Once the essential features of the top-down version of Prior Simplicity have been granted, the explanation works without a hitch—so long, that is, as one heads in the right direction, ascending from complexity and multiplicity to necessary levels or principles of increasing unity and simplicity. But if that were the only way to the view the problem, it seems likely that Plotinus could have explained it to a willing disciple in less than three days. To cite only one rather obvious question, why should there be a net in the sea in the first place?

Three Hypostases

Plotinus identified three levels of reality in the intelligible universe, usually known as the three "hypostases" or principles (*archai*).[45] These are, in descending order of simplicity and priority, the One, Intellect, and Soul. Since the basic features of the *archai*, including their relation to one another and to the material world, have been particularly well served by both introductions and surveys in the last few decades,[46] and since several key principles have already been introduced, what follows is a very brief sketch.

For all his attempts to demonstrate its consistency with and even its recognition by prior philosophers, especially Plato,[47] Plotinus' doctrine of the One that is above being itself has long been seen as his most important innovation. Indeed, together with its manifold implications, it is traditionally the doctrine par excellence by which Neoplatonism is distinguished from its precedents.[48] The One is, as we have seen, the unqualifiedly simple first principle. It is "other than all the things which come after it, existing by itself, not mixed with the things which derive from it, and all the same able to be present in a different way to these other things, being really one, and not a different being and then one."[49] We have also seen that such a thing must exist. Unity and order, evident in the cosmos, the human person, and so on, demand an explanation that necessarily culminates in an ultimate simple.[50] In the *Republic*'s Form of the Good, Plotinus found Platonic precedent for his assertion that the One is even "beyond being,"[51] a claim that should not be taken to imply nonexistence but in relation to the One's status as the ineffable cause of being itself, beyond any of the characteristics ordinarily predicated of beings. The One is literally unspeakable—even calling it "the One" is misleading if taken as a positive affirmation of its essence—and all language used to describe it is figurative and incomplete. Plotinus would prefer not to give it a name at all.[52] Apart from necessarily ineffable direct apprehension, what we would call mystical experience,[53] the One is therefore unknowable in any ordinary sense. When we do talk about it, we are really talking about things that depend on it and, above all, about ourselves.[54]

Being, in the sense that we can talk about it, as well as about the particular essence that makes various beings what they are, belongs instead to the second hypostasis or principle, Intellect (*νοῦς*). Intellect, to borrow from Gerson's summary, is "the principle of essence or whatness or intelligibility in the world as the One is the principle of being."[55] In other words, Intellect unifies being and knowledge, or ontology and epistemology.[56] This is the level of Plato's famous Forms or Ideas, eternal paradigms that serve as the proper objects of knowledge. In one of his most important moves—characteristically both the culmination and an innovative synthesis of a complex tradition—in his second hypostasis, Plotinus linked the Forms with Aristotle's God, a divine intellect that thinks itself and is wholly united with the objects of its thought.[57] The Forms or intelligibles are Intellect's thoughts. In the immediate intuitive apprehension of its objects, the "intellection" (*νόησις*) of Intellect is to be distinguished from ordinary reason, argumentation, or discursive thought. This suggests a more practical reason for positing Intellect as a higher principle. Most of the time, after all, we go about thinking or perceiving the sensible world in a limited and fragmented way. The processes of reasoning (*διάνοια*) itself, its "propositions and syllogisms," work sequentially toward their conclusion rather than by a single act of apprehension and contemplation.[58] Defined by the latter kind of thinking, Intellect is thus a higher, simpler, more unified principle prior to ordinary reason; it is also something whose existence and nature Plotinus knew by experience.[59] In any case, whereas Aristotle and other predecessors had identified divine intellect with the first principle, for Plotinus the necessary multiplicity of the things Intellect thinks, as well as the inherent duality of subject and object, means it cannot be the ultimate principle of unity and simplicity.[60] Its unity borrowed from the One, it remains the locus of both real being and perfect knowledge.

Apart from its dependence on the One, the principle of Intellect therefore remains as austere and simple and self-contained as it is possible for a self-thinking thinker to be. Its thoughts, moreover, are the paradigmatic structures of being, eternal and unchanging. What, then, about the world of growth and change we know from ordinary experience? To help explain this, a third principle is required, the hypostasis of "Soul." In a fundamental sense, Soul is a principle of life itself: it "makes alive all the other things which do not live of themselves."[61] The inherent connection between soul and life is a basic axiom that Platonists share with virtually everyone else in classical or later antiquity. For Platonism, moreover, "the psychological constitutes an irreducible explanatory category."[62] Just as the unity of a thing or the cosmos cannot be an emergent property but demands explanation by a prior principle of unity, so the life of living things comes from Soul. As we might expect from the necessarily greater complexity of the third hypostasis, however, Soul is a good deal more complicated than this. Indeed, for most ancient thinkers, it accounts for or is closely involved in a wide variety of functions that few people nowadays are inclined to ascribe to a single thing: reason, sensation, passions, appetite, and so on, but also life and growth, the "vegetative" functions people share with plants and the living, growing earth.[63]

But there are distinctive Neoplatonic features. While Plotinus insists repeatedly on the unity of Soul (and all souls), he describes at least three distinct kinds: the transcendent intelligible hypostasis, whose activities are difficult to distinguish from those of Intellect; the world soul that animates the cosmos; and individual human souls.[64] To this list might be added "nature," a kind of embedded principle of growth and basic order in living things.[65] In these forms, soul serves as the principle immediately prior to living bodies (of plants, people, earth, cosmos), unifying and organizing what it animates. To each living body, soul "gives it what is better in it." A piece cut off from a living (ensouled) plant is merely a stick.[66] Above all, perhaps, soul provides the crucial link between intelligible reality and the sensible world.

> For it is the rational principle of all things, and the nature of soul is the last and lowest rational principle of the intelligibles and the beings in the intelligible world, but first of those in the whole world perceived by the senses.[67]

The way in which this link might work remained as problematic for Plotinus and his successors as it had been for Plato. Indeed, the problem could only be sharpened by the Neoplatonic insistence—much stronger than Plato's, using terminology and concepts that emerged only after (and sometimes well after) Plato's death—that soul is not just part of the intelligible world but wholly immaterial in all its manifestations and activities.[68] Plotinus further maintained, in a position he knew to be suspiciously original (it would be rejected by later Neoplatonists), that the rational part of the human soul never entirely "descends" from the realm of Intellect, that is, from the unified ceaseless contemplation of the eternal Forms.[69] Among other consequences, this meant that the path to union with Intellect and the One lay not just upward but within or, as Plotinus put it, "into the inside."[70] Turning in the other direction, to what is outside oneself, is pretty nearly the cause of everything that is wrong with or misunderstood by ensouled bodies in the sensible world. On the other hand, this outward turn or "desire for externals" is as much an inherent characteristic of soul as its all too often unnoticed or "forgotten" participation in eternal Intellect.[71] Recognizing the danger, then, but also the fact that as an embodied soul even a philosopher has to think about externals every now and then, let us examine a few of them in more detail.

A Hierarchy of Bodies

Naturally enough, top-down Platonism—and the Plotinian kind of Platonism is about as top-down as it gets—emphasizes the exposition of things at the top of the scale of being. The three hypostases are all aspects of the intelligible rather than the sensible world. The principles we have discussed so far are thus metaphysical both in the strict sense, with their inherent relation to the nature of being and reality, and in the more general way the word is often used, to indicate something like the opposite of ordinary, visible, tangible life. To be sure, as the third hypostasis, Soul provides the crucial link between Intellect and the physical world of bodies—as we have seen, its nature is "twofold, partly intelligible and partly perceptible," at once the lowest principle in the intelligible and the highest of the sensible worlds—but Plotinus repeatedly insists that Soul's relation to material things is necessarily immaterial: as a primary hypostasis, world soul, or the individual human soul,[72] its "presence" to body is in no way spatial, nor are its connections physical. While this entailed certain problems, related if not quite identical to those famously generated by Cartesian minds and bodies, for Plotinus, the absolute immateriality of soul was also the solution to other dilemmas.[73]

This kind of thoroughgoing attention to the intelligible rather than the sensible world suggests that we should not expect from Neoplatonists a detailed exposition of bodies. Equally forbidding are the famous opening words of Porphyry's biography: "Plotinus, the philosopher of our times, seemed ashamed of being in a body." But this does not mean that Plotinus, and still less his successors, thought human and other bodies unworthy of analysis. While the sometimes scattered remarks this occasioned are generally less known than the main principles of Neoplatonic metaphysics, they have much to tell us, especially when set in a broader context. But to make more sense of what are often technical explanations, it is more than usually important to understand how and why people came to think and talk about bodily and nonbodily things in the first place.

Body and Its Opposites

Late ancient discussions about the corporeality of things relied on a tradition that was long and complex but not sempiternal. Immaterial existence is, after all, deeply counterintuitive. In antiquity, the concept of the incorporeal first appears in Plato, who seems to have invented the word *asōmatos*, "not-bodily."[74] Robert Renehan may be correct in linking its emergence to the "reflection on the relationship between Body and Soul" characteristic of late Presocratic and Academic philosophy rather than to cosmological or theological speculations on the possibility of immaterial existence, but the word was never restricted to the human body as a whole.[75] Instead, Plato and subsequent authors more often used it to negate or qualify specific bodily characteristics like visibility and tangibility.[76]

According to Aristotle, incorporeality could be conceived as a matter of degree; Democritus and the atomists considered the soul to be the "finest and most incorporeal" of bodies.[77] This is an essential point. For materialists as well as the many people who reserved absolutely immaterial existence for God or a first principle, a thing that could not be seen or touched in the usual ways might nonetheless be described as "incorporeal"—not like an ordinary body but not strictly immaterial, either. According to Origen in the third century C.E., this usage reflected "general custom."[78] Origen knew better, but he also used "incorporeal" freely in reference to souls, angels, and other "rational natures," despite his repeated insistence that absolute immateriality belongs only to God.[79] The same equivocation was recognized as a problem in Late Antiquity, as Jerome observed in the course of a letter detailing his mature views on the followers of Origen.

> "We believe," they say, "in the future resurrection of bodies." If this be rightly said, it is an innocent confession. But since there are both celestial and terrestrial bodies and since the air as well as subtle breath are called bodies according to their proper nature, they say "body" (*corpus*), not "flesh" (*caro*), so that the orthodox when hearing "body" will think "flesh," while the heretic will understand it as "spirit" (*spiritus*).

According to Jerome, people who believe in the resurrection of "body" but not "flesh" will go along with orthodox doctrine only until the questions of visibility and tangibility arise. After this point, the heretics, unable to contain themselves, dissolve in laughter at the gross materialism of a literal belief in the resurrection of noses and toes. And thus their equivocal use of "body" is exposed, along with their heretical lack of faith in the letter of Scripture.[80]

The ambiguity of calling something "unbodily" thus generated questions and problems throughout classical and later antiquity; sometimes these are easy to miss. But the emergence of a rather different and stronger word adds to the complexity. Aristotle appears to have invented the concept of matter when he borrowed the word ὕλη ("forest" or "wood") to indicate "the substratum to which change happens, including coming into existence and passing away."[81] To claim that something was "immaterial" was thus a good deal more precise and extreme than calling it incorporeal, although the terms were obviously related. Εἰ δὲ ἄϋλον, οὐ σῶμα, the Christian bishop Nemesius of Emesa could write against materialists near the turn of the fifth century. "If something is immaterial it is not a body."[82] But this was a formula whose strict logic worked in only one direction. Extremely fine or invisible bodies like air might just be called ἀσώματος, "incorporeal," but not ἄϋλος (or ἄνυλος), "immaterial." They may lack the usual bodily characteristics accessible to human sensation but still be made of physical stuff. In neither Greek nor Latin, however, did words for "immaterial" enjoy early or widespread popularity. The more familiar, accessible, and flexible "incorporeal" was much preferred.[83]

Characteristically, Plotinus anticipated and steered later trends by means of rigorous and sometimes radical application of principles inherited from predecessors. In the first place, his clear distinction between matter and body allowed him to refer to both without fear of equivocation. Matter's utter formlessness led him to speak of it as "nonbeing," as "privation," and as "evil itself."[84] While matter's nonbeing does not quite entail nonexistence,[85] the important point for present purposes is that matter never really exists apart from some kind of qualification.[86] In practice, then, the lowest level of being is that of bodies, organized masses with the characteristic property of magnitude or extension (μέγεθος).[87] This conception of body means that anything that has any kind of magnitude, be it ever so small or fine or evasive to ordinary sensation, is necessarily corporeal. Plotinus therefore never uses "incorporeal" in the weaker sense described previously. An additional consequence of his rigorous definition, however, is that "incorporeal" and "immaterial" can be used interchangeably (unlike "body" and "matter"). Apart from the special case of matter itself,[88] each negation implies the other. Not surprisingly, in Late Antiquity the two negations begin to used as synonyms, at least by those who talked about immateriality at all.[89] A final consequence worth noticing here is that matter and body are conceived hierarchically, at the bottom end of the spectrum of being. If matter's absolute deprivation of form, limit, and unity amounts to "nonbeing," body's possession of a minimal degree of structure, of "magnitude," puts it higher on the scale—but only just. It is a "shadow" of being.[90]

The coalescence of "incorporeal" and "immaterial" appears to get us quite close to familiar modern ideas about matter and its opposite, body and mind, matter and spirit, and so on. Nowadays the terms are synonymous, and we are not inclined to think of them in relative terms. But then Plotinus says something that pulls us up short. Or at least it should.

> Fire itself is more beautiful than all other bodies, because it has the rank of form in relation to all the other elements; it is above them in place and is the finest and subtlest (λεπτότατον) of all bodies, being close to the incorporeal (ἐγγὺς ὂν τοῦ ἀσωμάτου).[91]

This is not quite the same as saying that incorporeality admits of degree, but it certainly suggests that corporeality can be conceived on a sliding or graduated scale.[92] More explicit still is the claim in *Enneads* 3.6.6 that fire is "already at the point of escaping bodily nature." This is because it is lighter, less "earthy" (γεωδέστερος) than other bodies. In short, some things are "more body" than others, and this has important metaphysical consequences.[93]

I do not know enough about Descartes to assert with perfect certainty that he would never, after the *Meditations*, say such a thing, but it seems safe to assume that most of us would find it unscientific or illogical, a category mistake, perhaps, to talk about a material body "approaching" the incorporeal, especially when body itself has been defined and maintained with Plotinian rigor. But alleging absurdity does not get us much closer to a world where such a statement appears to have rarely been challenged. When, moreover, we find no less clear-headed and influential a champion of Neoplatonic immateriality than Augustine making just the same kind of claims for light and fire, above all, but also air and ether—based on the evidently axiomatic principle that "the finer the nature of a corporeal thing, the closer it is to the nature of spirit"[94]—it seems clear that modern categories will not get us very far.[95] In search of an explanation, let us turn instead to some ancient precedents.

Air, Fire, and the Heavens

For the production of philosophical speculation, as well as less technical observations about the way the world is and how it works, it is hard to find a more fruitful topic than the heavens. When people went outside and looked up or around in classical or later antiquity, they arrived at a number of conclusions that are as remarkable for certain consistent patterns as for some unexpected metaphysical implications. It is important in the first place to recognize the importance of the moon, which according to a ubiquitous scheme marked the crucial division between the labile diversity of earth and its atmosphere, on the one hand, and the eternal permanence of the heavens, on the other. Aristotle's postulation of a fifth element is only the most famous among many ancient theories advanced to explain the circular movement of the heavens.[96] It was also a theory that inspired a notable flurry of sophisticated rebuttals in Late Antiquity, culminating in the consequential rejection of ether (among other major features of Aristotelian physics) by the Christian author John Philoponus in the sixth century.[97] Classical and later ideas about the atmosphere of the sublunar world are less familiar, perhaps, but equally important for several of the issues just discussed.

If the moon marked the most important distinction between the terrestrial atmosphere and the heavens, layers of air could also be identified between earth and moon. The general model was quite simple: the air was known to get thinner the higher you went. Some of the most detailed descriptions appear in one of the classic sites of the Roman "underworld of Platonism," the Hermetica, especially as providentially (or, for classicists of an older generation, diabolically) preserved in the excerpts made by Johannes Stobaeus, probably in the fifth century C.E.[98] As we might expect, Hermetic accounts of the air have little to do with idle meteorological speculation. "Air is the instrument or mechanism of all the gods," as one treatise puts it, "through which all things are made."[99] The text that follows this intriguing claim seems to be corrupt, but it can hardly be accidental that it is concerned with the interconnectedness of everything *ab imo ad summum*, "from bottom to top."

Sorting out the hierarchy, however, could be complicated. Another Hermetic text describes four divisions organizing no fewer than sixty distinct layers of air above the earth. As evident from the ordinary experience of valleys and mountains, the air got thinner and better as one ascended, culminating in the finest, purest, clearest air of all.[100] The telling technical term in these and related passages is λεπτός, "light, thin, delicate," which, together with its usual Latin equivalent *tenuis*, is the most common word used for exceptionally fine material things that pass beyond the limits of ordinary human sensation but are bodies all the same. More telling still are comparative or superlative forms of the adjective—like Plotinus writing about fire, the Hermetist here uses λεπτότατος, "finest, thinnest"—indicating degrees of solidity and materiality.

These cosmological conceptions so far present only loose parallels with the metaphysical principles we have examined before: common features include an ascending hierarchy (literally ascending, in the case of the atmosphere), an evident conviction about the general superiority of higher entities, and an emphasis on simplicity—on being "unmixed," to use a word favored by ancient cosmologists and metaphysicians alike. But three further observations suggest the need for deeper scrutiny. First, for the Hermetists at least, the metaphysical implications of a materially graduated world were patent, and they went all the way to the top.

> The finest-particled (λεπτομερέστατον) kind of matter is air, the finest air is soul, the finest soul is mind, the finest mind is God.[101]

Second, ideas about the ascending material hierarchy or continuum of the visible cosmos were hardly restricted to Platonic or other underworlds. They are, on the contrary, ubiquitous in the classical or late Roman world, a fact that doubtless owes much to the influence of Stoic cosmology, perhaps especially as mediated or transformed by authors like Posidonius in the final centuries of the Roman republic.[102] Cicero, for example, has much to tell us about contemporary understandings of Stoic and other ideas about the importance of air, its density and rarefaction, and so on.[103] Augustine reports that Varro divided the regions above the earth into two parts, consisting of ether and air, with two further terrestrial regions of water and land. Plotinus, too, envisions a hierarchical cosmos in which the fires of heaven are materially distinct from their analogous element beneath the moon. The quantity and quality of the air is essential to his explanation.

> We must not suppose that the flame down here mingles with the fires of heaven; it reaches a certain way and then is extinguished when it encounters a greater quantity of air, and as it takes earth with it on its ascent it falls back and is not able to get up to the upper fire but comes to a standstill below the moon, so as to make the air finer (λεπτότερον) there.[104]

But there is more to the story, for Cicero, Varro, and a broad range of authors in classical and later antiquity also populated this graduated world with souls whose natures (mortal or immortal) corresponded precisely to where they live: gods above the moon, invisible "aerial souls" (heroes, lares, and *genii*, in Augustine's summary of Varro) between clouds and the moon, and mortal ones on the earth.[105]

This brings us to a third feature of the hierarchical cosmos. Owing above all to their constitutional likeness to air or ether, the intermediate regions between heaven and earth were very often seen as the natural home of souls and kindred spirits like demons and angels. Indeed, the idea that souls ascend after death to the airy or ethereal level of the cosmos best suited to their ambiguously material nature is attested on tombstones as early as the fifth century B.C.E.[106] While Cicero again offers an evocative description of the human soul winging up through the atmosphere before coming to rest "among the rarefied air and the modified glow of the sun" in regions that most closely resemble its fine-material constitution,[107] few ancient sources can rival Plutarch for details about how the process works. Among much else, he reminds us that a soul's ascent is sharply conditioned by how one has lived while body and soul were still together. Souls that have become too enmeshed with bodily pursuits (including material substances, alcohol being a particular culprit)[108] remain heavy and sluggish, unable to ascend to the superlunary zones reserved for purer souls or, indeed, intellect itself.[109] By the middle of the fourth century C.E., this model of ascent was conventional enough that the emperor Julian could take it for granted by way of setting the celestial scene for a dinner party in his satire on the emperors. While the gods were placed at the highest part of heaven, Romulus, the symposiarch, decided to entertain his imperial guests in the upper air just below the moon. The lightness of the bodies with which they had been invested (after death, of course) held them quite naturally in place.[110]

For the idea that souls could be weighed down by immoderate living, later authors could rely in part on the authority of Plato, who had advanced the theory that some people allow their souls to become so "permeated with the corporeal" by overindulgence in food and sex that the soul itself becomes "heavy," "dragged back to the visible region." Evidence for this was as close as a graveyard, where the shadowy apparitions people sometimes see lurking around the tombs are just these wretchedly ponderous and visible souls.[111] This account, from the mouth of Socrates in no less "dualistic" a dialogue than the *Phaedo*, remained current if not precisely popular throughout later antiquity. Origen, Porphyry, Iamblichus, Gregory of Nyssa, Proclus, and John Philoponus cite or allude to it with approval.[112]

It is hardly surprising, perhaps, that Plotinus' closest allusion to the theory of visible souls is purely metaphorical.[113] Nor should we expect his relentlessly nonspatial conception of soul to generate much discussion on the possibility of souls finding a "natural home" in the physical space of the heavens, once separated from the body.[114] Once again, however, expectations may be misleading.

> The souls when they have peeped out of the intelligible world go first to heaven, and when they have put on a body there go on by its means to earthier bodies (γεωδέστερα σώματα), to the limit to which they extend themselves in length. And some souls [only] come from heaven to lower bodies; others pass from one body into another, those whose power is not sufficient to lift them from this region because they are weighed down and forgetful, dragging with them much that weighs upon them.[115]

About "earthier bodies," we already know a little: these are the tangible bodies of everyday experience. Their degree of earthiness or solidity corresponds to the literal proportion of earth, a physical element like water, air, and fire. But what about those souls that put on a manifestly different body in heaven before descending all the way to earthy bodies and terrestrial life? We are still a long way from Cicero or Plutarch, perhaps, and we can be certain that Plotinus will have rejected the Hermetic treatise that neatly assigned sixty ranks of fine-material souls to the progressively material regions of heaven we have already encountered, but once again it seems there must be something not quite Cartesian going on.

Between Soul and Body?

In *Enneads* 2.2, Plotinus takes up the problem of the movement of the heavens. Because of the world soul, he naturally has a good deal to say about the parallel between the cosmos and the human body, moved by their respective souls. For reasons that need not detain us, Plotinus concludes that the soul's motion is circular, movement around a center.[116] Because of their own tendency to move in a straight line, ordinary earthly bodies arrest this circular movement.[117] In the case of heaven, however, things are substantially—and materially—different.

> There the body of heaven follows along with soul, being light and easy to move (λεπτὸν καὶ εὐκίνητον); why ever should it stop when it goes on moving, whatever its motion? And in us, too, it seems that the *pneuma* which is around the soul moves in a circle.[118]

So much for the circular movement of the stars, but the passage has more to tell us. First, there is the telling word λεπτός again. "Easily moved" (εὐκίνητος) is another clue: bodies thus described are not only light in weight but also preternaturally agile. They are lithe and speedy in all the ways that a boulder is not.

More suggestive still, however, is the passing reference to the *pneuma* that surrounds the soul. This is (almost certainly) one of Plotinus' rare references to something known to Neoplatonic scholars as the "vehicle of the soul."[119] Its precise origins are obscure, but the second-century doctor Galen may preserve one of the first unambiguous references to the theory, in a discussion of the "luminous and ethereal body" that is either the substance of the soul itself or else its "vehicle" (ὄχημα). Even if the soul itself is incorporeal rather than tenuously material (Galen was consistently agnostic on the subject), it still requires a material substance by means of which it can interact with the corporeal world. But a doctor need not be concerned about the metaphysical question, Galen continued, so long as he realizes that the soul's role in vision and other sensory processes is to be explained by the luminous ethereal substance that pervades the human brain, identical or closely related to the *pneuma* or "spirit" that was essential to a host of biological and psychological processes in the human body.[120] As we might expect, later Neoplatonic proponents of the vehicle of the soul found authoritative precedents in Plato,[121] supplemented by Aristotle's influential remarks linking *pneuma* both to "the element of the stars" and to the human soul.[122]

In its developed form, then, the vehicle of the soul is a semi- or quasi-material body that performs a number of functions. It surrounds or carries the soul on its descent from the intelligible to the sensible world, and then again, when properly purified or lightened, on the way back up. A second major set of benefits has to do with ordinary life on earth, for the vehicle is naturally intermediate between the incorporeal soul and the visible, tangible body.[123] It can receive the literal stamps or impressions of bodily sensation and transmit them to the soul; it can also endow a soul with the shape and (limited) visibility associated with the apparitions flickering around a tomb, as Origen observed in one of his several allusions to the vehicle.[124] The fine-material stuff of which it is composed was identified with *pneuma* or with the ethereal bodies of the stars, whence its frequent designation as the soul's "astral body." As we might expect from something made of ether or *pneuma* (generally conceived as a mixture of fire and air), the vehicle is frequently described as glowing or luminous.

It is hard to know whether to make more of the fact that Plotinus obliquely refers to the vehicle of the soul at several points or of the fact that it seems to play such a small role in his philosophy as a whole.[125] The special body is evidently acquired, as we have seen, in that part of the heavens whose constitution corresponds to its own. Plotinus elsewhere alludes to how the process might work in reverse as the soul ascends, leaving its fine-material body behind. He begins, however, with what seems an unambiguously noetic account of ascent.

> The purification of the part [of the soul] subject to affections is the waking up from inappropriate images and not seeing them, and its separation is effected by not inclining much downwards and not having a mental picture of the things below.

So far so good. And then this:

> But separating it could also mean taking away the things from which it is separated when it is not [carried] on *pneuma* that is turbid from gluttony and

> full of impure meats, but that in which it resides is so attenuated that it can ride on it in peace.[126]

This presentation of two alternative (or are they complementary?) methods for promoting the soul's ascent—easily obscured by confusion about what Plotinus could possibly mean by the second sentence—seems momentous, in retrospect. The first kind of purification relies altogether on the rigorously intellectual turn for which Plotinus is justly famous, but the second underscores the importance of a different kind of rigor, an ascetic discipline. Keeping your *pneuma* pure, fine, and buoyant demands sober appreciation of the bluntly physical effects of everyday life. For later Neoplatonists, at least, this also left the door open for alternative means of purification.

In any case, where Plotinus was content with cautious allusions, later Neoplatonism found the vehicle of the soul a useful theory indeed. Its attractions were strong and quickly felt. Porphyry appears to have linked the pneumatic *ὄχημα* so closely to the soul's lowest part that the two were virtually equated. The crucial role of *pneuma*—according to Augustine, Porphyry distinguished the "pneumatic soul" (*anima spiritalis*) from the soul's intellectual part—in the processes of perception suggests surprising affinities with Stoic psychology.[127] Moreover, while Porphyry denied that theurgical rites could assist the higher intellectual soul in its separation from the physical body, he evidently accepted their efficacy for purifying the soul's vehicle, together with the lower part of the soul itself.[128] But it was Iamblichus who gave the vehicle of the soul its definitive form and central place in later Neoplatonism.[129] He cited Plato's *Timaeus* for his assertion that it was made of ether; elsewhere, he uses the traditional terminology of "luminous *pneuma*."[130] Immortal and permanently attached to the soul, the ethereal vehicle acquires additional bodies and powers in its descent, including bodies corresponding to various regions of the heavens.[131] It can thus be weighed down with the pollutions of material life; these must be purged if the soul is to ascend from the terrestrial through the celestial to the intelligible realm.[132] Iamblichus argued further that the vehicle transferred sensory impressions and other "images" to the soul, enabling not only sensation but also memory and imagination.[133] A crucial doctrine undergirding his theory at many points is the principle (ubiquitous in Roman and later antiquity) that "like approaches like," that constitutional and other similarities between entities enable communication, "sympathetic" interaction, and so on.[134]

Apart from certain minor changes to Iamblichus' seminal conceptions, later Neoplatonists added little to the model, which they endorsed with enthusiasm. Proclus, to take only the most influential example, identified not one but two vehicles of the soul: a luminous astral body acquired in the upper heavens, as well as a thicker one made of *pneuma* for the soul's lower part, the latter being the perishable material vehicle responsible for psychic functions.[135] This is the basic theory adopted by Philoponus in the sixth century, who further elaborated on what several predecessors had suggested, namely, that the soul's pneumatic vehicle could help explain how demons and other "spirits" (*pneumata*) interacted with the immaterial soul.[136] But then demons had pneumatic vehicles, too.[137]

With the introduction of demons, we have moved into decidedly practical territory. I mention them only in passing as perhaps the single most important evidence of the practical importance of knowing what you were about, and what was about you. Knowing where you, and especially your soul, fit on the scales of both physics and metaphysics could make all the difference. Demons enjoyed all the advantages of a fine-material constitution: physical speed and astonishing mental agility, for example, combined with the possibility of direct interaction with the stuff of the human soul.[138]

But let us reflect instead on the further implications of the vehicle of the soul. It seems at first blush a paradigmatic example of Neoplatonic excess, a desperate theoretical construction that does little to solve the fundamental problem brought into such clear relief by the Plotinian conception of body and soul. Most modern readers will find it hard to disagree with the trenchant analysis offered by Joseph Priestley in 1777.

> The vehicle of the soul is altogether a creature of imagination and hypothesis, and in reality without explaining any one phenomenon, or removing one real difficulty. For so long as the matter of which this vehicle consists, has what are supposed to be the essential properties of all matter, viz., solid extent, its union with a truly immaterial substance must be just as difficult to conceive, as if it had been the subject of all our corporeal senses. To the vulgar, indeed, the attenuation of matter may make it seem to approach to the nature of spirit; but the philosopher knows that, in fact, no attenuation of matter brings it at all nearer to the nature of a substance that has no common property with matter.[139]

To this criticism, there is, it seems, no obvious response. Unless, that is, we are dealing with a different definition of matter or, less precisely (from a philosophical perspective) but more significantly (from a historical one), with different instinctive assumptions about just what it is that makes a bodily thing bodily. Plotinus, as so often, helps to put a finer point on it. As we have seen, his most consistent and technical accounts follow Aristotle in identifying magnitude or extension as the essential attribute of bodies.[140] Bodies can be bigger or smaller, but according to this approach, corporeality itself cannot be a matter of degree. Reflections of this kind doubtless have something do with the fact that Plotinus nowhere relies on the vehicle of the soul as a kind of quasi-material hack in order to bridge (or disguise) the gap between bodies and immaterial things, in the way deplored by Priestley.[141]

But Plotinus evidently found the vehicle congenial all the same. Setting aside the mind-body problem he addressed in other ways, the vehicle's astral or pneumatic composition seems to have suggested advantages in quite a different direction. It should be remembered that Plotinus did not only talk about magnitude in relation to body. On the contrary, when the subject at hand approaches the possibility of relative corporeality—of things that have "more completely become body" than others, as he put it—the crucial attribute is "solidity" or "earthiness" rather than magnitude or extension. Let us stipulate at once that this does not form part of Plotinus' formal definitions of body. It does, however, allow one to conceive more readily of material things, like fire, that ascend by degrees toward incorporeality. It is easier to imagine the subtraction of the last bit of "earth" or solidity from a substance, the incremental removal of all the stuff that makes for resistance and pressure, than the graduated diminishing of spatial extension until one arrives by degrees at a thing with no extension at all.[142] In a tradition of enormously fruitful and broad-ranging speculation, Greek doctors and scientists had long made much of just such special bodies, of things like air and fire that seemed to lack either solidity or visibility or both. We have already encountered the special status of fire in Plotinus and the remarkable role of air in Hermetic physics and metaphysics. Air, of course, had a much older history in Greek science, as one of the several Presocratic substances that explained everything else. In the fifth or early fourth century B.C.E., the Hippocratic author of *On the Sacred Disease* identified air as the source of intelligence and reason in the human body; from it, the brain drew all its remarkable powers of intellection.[143]

But it was above all the development of the concept of *pneuma*—air in motion, in the first place, but also, for Aristotle and the doctors, the special airy substance that enabled a wide range of biological and psychological functions in the human body—that bore abundant fruit in Hellenistic and later antiquity.[144] The Stoics are traditionally held to have defined *pneuma* as a mixture of fire and air;[145] more certain is the Stoic identification of *pneuma* as the crucial fine-material element that causes the universe, as well as the human person, to cohere, to live and breathe, to move. The human soul was made of it. *Pneuma*'s constitutional similarities to air, ether, and fire help to explain the cogency of the belief in buoyant souls ascending to their natural place in the cosmos. Its malleability and other special properties account for changes of shape (in demons and souls, for example), as well as the ability of a *pneuma*-wrapped soul or *pneuma*-filled brain to generate, receive, and retain sensory and other data in the form of literal impressions. Its tendency to become "thickened" with corporeal accretions had all sorts of consequences, from the visible souls around tombs to the intermittent visibility of demons, angels, and other "spirits." According to Origen and Porphyry, the pneumatic bodies of demons required sustenance in the form of sacrificial smoke and vapors; they could get fat and sink down toward the earth or be starved back into the heavens like an unballasted balloon.[146] More prosaically, Galen observed that the respiration of ordinary air nourishes a person's own *pneuma* in the same way air feeds fire.[147]

Appreciation for the importance of *pneuma* in Roman and Late Antiquity has been checked by at least four stubborn complications. First, readers familiar with the New Testament, early Christian literature, and especially with gnosticism will be surprised to find the moral and material implications of soul and "spirit" apparently reversed. The theological importance of the "Spirit of God" and the consequential language of 1 Corinthians 15 made "spirit" and "spiritual" higher, better, and (perhaps) finer than "soul" and its cognates. Second, when Augustine drew on the same traditions and defined "spirit"—for the first time in Latin Christendom—as an unqualifiedly immaterial substance, the confusion with traditional, fine-material, instrumental understandings of *pneuma* was institutionalized.[148] Third, a rarely challenged stream of modern scholarship, doubtless influenced by the genius of Augustine himself, has presented the history of *pneuma* as one of progressive refinement and rarefaction: from a primitive material understanding involving air and breath and vapors to the sophisticated fine-materiality of the Stoics to its immaterial apotheosis in the bishop of Hippo and his numberless heirs.[149] Fourth, is there not something vaguely disreputable in all this talk of not-quite-bodily bodies, with their intangible sympathies, their spherical shape-shifting, the suspiciously convenient breadth of their explanatory power?[150] With some reason, it smacks of the heady days of the early twentieth century, when the deep erudition of the most serious scholars of ancient ideas detected "Iranian" influence around virtually every corner.[151] In another, not unrelated vein, it was a learned member of the Theosophical Society, indeed Madame Blavatsky's private secretary, who published *The Doctrine of the Subtle Body in Western Tradition* in 1919.[152]

There is, in fact, little hope of rescuing the pneumatic vehicle of the soul from the murky waters of late ancient theurgy (as it used to be seen). It is more productive, I suggest, to follow the lead of E. R. Dodds in paying more attention to the theory's deep roots in classical philosophy and science.[153] As we have seen, it is not much of a stretch to label empirical or experiential at least some of the evidence mustered in its support. Nor does it seem that the role of the vehicle as a convenient if logically dubious mediator between material and immaterial things was ever a primary reason for its development by later Neoplatonists. While Plotinus himself certainly did not rely on it to bridge an ontological gap, it is equally certain that he saw no reason to reject certain traditional notions of *pneuma*, together with some of its remarkable properties.[154] Thus, while it must be admitted that Plotinus' newly rigorous conceptions of an immaterial soul may have provided an impetus to later speculation about its vehicle as a kind of *tertium quid*—a substance that did not suffer from all of the disadvantages of the solid "earthy" body but enjoyed instead the special properties of fire, air, or ether, right on the border of corporeal existence—more interesting observations emerge from recognizing the degree to which the soul's vehicle could promote the integration of a venerable and sophisticated tradition of thinking with *pneuma* while remaining within or very close to the intellectual austerities of Neoplatonic metaphysics.[155] In the context of late ancient cosmology and physics—much of which we are only now beginning to understand and appreciate, thanks in no small part to the efforts of Richard Sorabji and his collaborators—the pneumatic vehicle of the soul is hardly an oddity at all.

Conclusion: Augustine and Cassiodorus

The second most famous conversion in Christian history was a conversion to the Neoplatonic version of strict immateriality. Or at least it began that way, in the story told by the convert himself. Augustine tells us that when he was a Manichaean, he was unable to conceive of mind except as "a subtle body."[156] Still worse,

> When I wished to think of my God, I was unable to think of him except as a bodily substance, for it seemed to me that no other kind of thing could exist. This was the most important and almost the only cause of my insurmountable error.[157]

The story of Augustine's momentous encounter with "the Platonists" has been told many times, but it was François Masai in 1961 who built on the pioneering work of Pierre Courcelle to demonstrate more decisively than anyone else that the conversion of 386 was partly the result and partly a cause of nothing less than "les débuts du spiritualisme en Occident."[158] It need hardly be said that the *spiritualisme* of Masai's title has nothing to do with séances or "spirituality." It relies instead on the immaterial sense of "spirit" that was invented in Late Antiquity. But for all the importance of the word's abrupt liberation from matter, this was no mere change of terminology. The ascendancy of the concept of immaterial spirit—or immaterial anything, in the strong Plotinian sense—was a revolution in Latin Christendom.[159] Nor is there any need to hypothesize long impersonal changes in currents of thought or the spirit of an anxious (or ambitious) age. At the heart of the revolution were particular people known by name—Marius Victorinus, Simplicianus, Ambrose—people who had read Plotinus. Moreover, these Neoplatonic readings bore their firstfruits quite precisely in the Milan where Augustine encountered Ambrose.[160]

There is much more to the story of Augustine's conversion, but from the perspective of the ideas examined here, it hardly seems a stretch to propose it as a candidate for the single most important consequence of the kind of metaphysics developed by Plotinus and his successors. Of course, there was much in this metaphysics that had to be modified or rejected. The Neoplatonic One is decidedly not a God who might "relent" and pity Augustine after an indulgent laugh at his creature's expense.[161] Nor could Plotinus agree (without careful qualification)[162] that the human soul "is the one thing in the universe nearest to God"—which Augustine tells us is something he first learned from Ambrose, together with the all-important principle that "when one thinks about God, one should not think about a body in any way whatsoever, and the same is true of the soul."[163]

But the more important point for present purposes has less to do with the details of the Augustinian appropriation of Neoplatonic metaphysics than with the very long shadow cast by his conversion to immateriality. As with Plotinus, the chronological length of this shadow is easily mistaken for contemporary breadth, especially when its size is magnified through a Cartesian prism. But what Plotinus and Augustine bequeathed to Descartes and the modern world was less a set of convictions about body and the physical world than a relentlessly inward turn, an unprecedentedly rigorous conception of mind or soul occasioned not by the rejection of hierarchical or fine-material physics but by the consequences of introspection.[164] The full implications of this introspection, especially as Augustine formulated them in his invention of the *cogito* argument from systematic doubt, would not be taken up or pressed to their logical end until the seventeenth century. Indeed, it is difficult to find any ancient thinkers apart from Plotinus and Augustine who explicitly took this path or directly confronted the problems we generally take for granted as the necessary result of making an uncompromising ontological distinction between body and mind.[165]

In Late Antiquity, it was a hard case to make. As I have suggested we might conclude from Plotinus' three days with Porphyry, the enormous efforts Augustine expended in explaining and proving his new position might serve as a rough but useful indicator of what he was up against. It requires only a glance through book 7 of his treatise *On the Literal Interpretation of Genesis* to appreciate the depth of his commitment to the principle of an immaterial soul. In his view, potentially ambiguous allusions to an "incorporeal" soul do not suffice. Instead, Augustine demands explicit rejection of all the principal theories concerning material and fine-material substrates of the soul's constitution: earth, air, ether, the substance of the stars, Aristotle's quintessence. Here and elsewhere, he proposed a number of formal philosophical reasons for his position, some of them quite sophisticated.[166] But the vehemence of his opposition, the voluble consistency with which he maintained its immateriality even in the face of unsolved difficulties and expunged persistent habits of thought hinting at psychic materialism from his writing, ought to give us pause.[167]

Augustine clearly found the flexible features of fine-material constitution appealing from a number of perspectives, along with the fundamental notion of a hierarchy of material existence from visible and thick to very thin.[168] In fact, he very nearly tried to have it both ways, to locate the soul in a hierarchy like this (at the top of the thin list, naturally) while maintaining its difference in kind from all bodies. Light, for example, he recognized as a corporeal substance, *subtilissimum in corpore*, "the finest element in bodies and by virtue of this more closely related (*vicinius*) to the soul than the others."[169] Similar characterizations obtain for fire, air, and ether.[170] Indeed, for Augustine, "light and air" constitute in their marvelous subtlety the crucial fine-material interface between body and soul.[171] It need not be surprising, therefore, to find Augustine warning that demons, with their "airy" bodies, can enter human bodies unawares, "by means of the subtlety of their own bodies," literally "mixing themselves with the person's thoughts."[172] We have already encountered the physical principle underlying a process like this. "The finer the nature of a corporeal thing, the closer it is to the nature of *spiritus*"—"although there is a great distance in kind,"

Augustine added, "since the one is a body and the other is not."[173] But *quamvis* marks a substantial leap indeed, from the flexible physics of daily experience to what seems here a metaphysical axiom rather anxiously maintained.

So did Late Antiquity make a difference? Of course, it did, but it is important to be clear about the nature and extent of innovation and tradition. Discussions of Christian Neoplatonism toward the end of our period, for example, seem necessarily to culminate in the late-fifth- or early-sixth-century achievement of Pseudo-Dionysius, whose famous hierarchies of heavenly and other beings are populated with thoroughly incorporeal beings, the physical or quasi-physical language used about them always symbolic. The influence of Neoplatonic metaphysics, especially as mediated through Proclus, is profound and everywhere apparent.[174] Nor is there much sign of anxiety about creeping corporealism. But this is only part of the story, despite the fact that standard conceptions of late ancient and especially Christian Neoplatonism are deeply colored by the surpassingly top-down, apophatic, and intellectual hierarchies of Pseudo-Dionysius. To be sure, he engaged later Neoplatonic discussions of soul throughout his work, but the kind of practical or experiential speculation about the relation between material and immaterial things evident in earlier pioneers or indeed in near-contemporaries like John Philoponus is conspicuous in its absence. If you want to know how to deal with demons, how to recognize their materially subtle and mentally pervasive impact on the human person, Pseudo-Dionysius is not your man.[175]

By way of contrast and conclusion, then, let us turn to a different milieu, a bit later and further west. Setting aside a persistent if rarely noticed tradition of more or less overt materialism in the Latin West,[176] there is much to be learned from one of those remarkable men who (as we might have put it before the discovery of Late Antiquity) seems to have had one foot each in antiquity and the Middle Ages.

Cassiodorus wrote his little treatise *On the Soul* in 538, a bit more than a century after Augustine's death. Its theological and philosophical debts have been discussed from a number of modern perspectives and need not long detain us.[177] "With few exceptions, the views he reports were the stock-in-trade of late ancient Platonism, readily assimilable and already assimilated to a platonizing Christian anthropology," according to the recent summary of Mark Vessey.[178] Augustine is in fact the only source Cassiodorus names explicitly, and the influence of the bishop's early treatise *Magnitude of the Soul* in particular is clear throughout.[179] In any case, few have wished to defend the philosophical rigor of this late Roman *De anima*.

But the "mistakes" Cassiodorus made, as a self-conscious heir of Augustine on the incorporeal soul, are suggestive indeed. He stoutly maintained the principle of the soul's immateriality—including an Augustinian denial of spatial extension in three dimensions—throughout the treatise.[180] Nonetheless, he used words that Augustine could not have countenanced. The soul is *subtilis*, for example, "thin" and thus comparable to the "angels and other aerial powers" who also retain powers of intellection apart from an ordinary visible body. By God's will, it is "blocked" from escaping through the body's numerous portals. Like fire, whose refined constitution makes it tend upward, the soul inhabits the highest part of the human body, the head. But the clearest clues to the persistence of fine-material instincts in the face of strong protestations emerge when Cassiodorus addresses the substance of the soul directly. Like Augustine, he proceeded apophatically, listing bodies and things that should not be equated with the soul's constitution.

It is not part of the angels, since it is associated with flesh, nor of air, nor of earth, nor of things joined together in mutual combination; rather, it is a simple and unique nature and a substance distinct from other spirits.

Not quite content with this, however, Cassiodorus wanted to make the point perfectly plain.

> We should take note of the fact that the soul is much thinner and more translucent (*lucidior*) than the air, since we commonly behold the latter but cannot see the former because of the condition of the flesh.

While the first part of this passage depends quite directly on Augustine, the language of comparative subtlety and visibility represents Cassiodorus' telling improvement on his model. One searches Augustine in vain for *subtilior* or even *subtilissimus* as a description of the soul's constitution—except in reference to the exceptionally "fine-grained" arguments necessary to counter material or fine-material beliefs.[181] He saw (correctly, we might think) that such comparative language fatally compromises the definition of immateriality itself—however "close" very thin but corporeal things like air, fire, and light came to its wholly spiritual composition.

Things were easier for Cassiodorus. In the next chapter of his treatise, he went on to entertain (without rejecting) the identification of soul with a "fiery substance" before settling with more confidence on "substantial light." While *substantialis* can mean a number of things in Latin, we need not rely on Augustine's assertions that light is a body to draw conclusions about the luminous soul in Cassiodorus. It is something you can see and feel, if only just.

> When deep in thought, we sense within ourselves something tenuous, agile, bright, something that gazes without the sun and sees without external light.[182]

Nescio quid tenue, volubile, clarum: the glittering, tenuous "something" is the soul itself—almost but not quite an Augustinian one. It has more in common with Tertullian, perhaps, or the luminous vehicle of the soul from Galen to Philoponus.[183] Is it so different, after all, from the kind of mind that could kindle the face of a Neoplatonic sage?

One thinks finally of Descartes' description of the soul as an "attenuated something" (*exiguum nescio quid*), that "spontaneous" product of inherited assumptions described and finally rejected with momentous clarity 1,103 years after Cassiodorus published his little book about the soul.[184] The spontaneous description of the soul—"something tenuous, like wind or fire or ether," "a kind of subtle air diffused throughout these limbs"—was a setup for one of the most famous punch lines in philosophical history. "I now admit nothing except what is necessarily true: I am therefore, precisely speaking, only a thing that thinks, mind or rational soul or intellect or reason, words of whose meaning I have been ignorant until now." It is one of the many paradoxical achievements of the period to which this book is devoted that the most important precedents for both *res cogitans* and *exiguum nescio quid* were to be found in Late Antiquity.

NOTES

1. Porphyry, *Life of Plotinus* 13; translation adapted from Edwards 2000, 23.

2. For the problem of identifying the three-day body-soul discussion in Plotinus' *Enneads*, see Blumenthal 1971a, 16, n. 20.

3. For Porphyry's abiding interest in the relationship between body and soul, and a case for the substantial agreement of his psychology with Plotinus, see Smith 1974, 1–19; see also 150, with nn. 2–3, for Porphyry's reputation for hesitance and indecision; cf. Dodds 1951, 286–287.

4. In addition to the examples and explanations discussed, see Golitzin 2002, 17–18, with n. 13; for Syriac literature, see Wagner 1999, 137.

5. Marinus, *Proclus* 3; trans. Edwards 2000, 62. Cf. chapter 23 in the same work for an expanded description.

6. Precedents need not be enumerated, but A. Smith 2004, for example, a useful and important introduction titled *Philosophy in Late Antiquity*, is devoted entirely to Plotinus and his successors, with some seventy pages for Plotinus himself and the rest (fifty-five pages) for "the diffusion of Neoplatonism"; see esp. the book's preface (ix–xi) for defensible reasons for the book's emphases. A similar ratio obtains, on a rather more focused topic but as part of a collection similar to the present volume, in Chadwick 1999. For a more balanced article-length survey of late ancient philosophy, see de Haas 2003; for themes treated in the present article, see especially the sections on physics (261–264), psychology (264–267), and metaphysics (267–270).

7. A. Smith 2004, ix–x; Edwards 2000, lv–lix; Rist 1996, 409.

8. De Haas 2003, 251. After Plotinus, de Haas suggests, late ancient philosophers turned from establishing the essential principles of this "universal truth" (which Plotinus had synthesized so brilliantly and suggestively) to exploring its details and implications (242–251).

9. Once derided as confused and derivative "eclecticism," this shift in emphasis has been recast in much more positive terms in recent decades. For the problem, and a set of important essays instrumental in turning the tide, see Dillon and Long 1988.

10. Porphyry, *V. Plot.* 14.4–7. See Gatti 1996 for a useful summary, equally rich in modern and ancient bibliography, as well as further details on how Plotinus "gathered the legacy of nearly eight centuries of Greek into a magnificently unified synthesis" (10). See also, for Aristotle, the articles collected in Sorabji 1990; Schrenk 1994; Blumenthal 1996; Karamanolis 2006; and especially the provocative case made for the

Neoplatonic harmony of Plato and Aristotle in Gerson 2005a. For Stoicism, see Theiler 1960; Armstrong 1967, 129–131; Graeser 1972; Sorabji 2000; Gill 2003.

11. Dillon 1996, 384–396. Less cautious but equally memorable is Arthur Darby Nock on gnosticism: "Platonism run wild" (1964, xvi). Cf. Willy Theiler's "Proletarierplatonismus" (1955, 78). Since it was the successors of Plotinus, especially Iamblichus and Proclus, who were responsible for the preservation (and celebration) of the *Chaldean Oracles* in the next few centuries, at least part of this underworld continued to flourish. For the *Oracles* and imperial Platonism, see Lewy 1978; Majercik 1989; Saffrey 1990; Dillon 1992; Athanassiadi 1999; Brisson 2003.

12. For a memorable statement of Plotinian exceptionalism, see Dodds 1928, 142: "If anyone doubts that Plotinus was a man of genius, let him study the efforts of Plotinus' nearest predecessors and followers. Let him soak for a while in the theosophical maunderings of Philo and the Hermetists, in the venomous fanaticism of Tertullian, in the tea-table transcendentalism of Plutarch, in the cultured commonplaces of Maximus, in the amiable pieties of Porphyry, in the really unspeakable spiritualistic drivellings of the *de Mysteriis*—let him do that, and if ever he gets his head above water again, he will see Plotinus in his true historical perspective as the one man who still knew how to think clearly in an age which was beginning to forget what thinking meant." Cf. Dodds 1951, 286: "Plotinus is a man who, as Wilhelm Kroll put it, 'raised himself by a strong intellectual and moral effort above the fog-ridden atmosphere which surrounded him.' While he lived, he lifted his pupils with him. But with his death the fog began to close in again, and later Neoplatonism is in many respects a retrogression to the spineless syncretism from which he had tried to escape."

13. It is worth noting that some recent interpreters have argued that Descartes' dualism was not so sharp as once thought. For discussion of these, together with a convincing case for the radical distinction between mind and body sketched here, see Rozemond 1998, 172–213.

14. The several important connections between Descartes and Augustine in particular—including, most famously, Augustine's invention and use of the *cogito* argument (esp. Aug. *Trin.* 10.10)—cannot detain us here. The classic study is Gilson 1930; cf. Taylor 1989, chapter 7; brief remarks in Sorabji 2005, 1:12 (see 1:167–168 for the relevant passages in Augustine); Menn 1998 (a strong view of Descartes' dependence on Augustine for both method and content); and Janowski 2004.

15. O'Meara 1993, 14.

16. See Moravcsik 1992, 55–56, for the remainder of this paragraph; both O'Meara (1996, 67–68) and Remes (2008, 35) invoke Moravcsik's ontology in the context of Neoplatonism.

17. I have benefited from Charles Kahn's stimulating investigations of the semantic and philosophical history of Greek words for "being"; relevant articles are now collected in Kahn 2009. Note that many of the basic points made in this paragraph apply with equal force to Aristotelian metaphysics; cf. Politis 2004, 3.

18. The possibility of discerning not only personal and otherworldly but also practical ethics in Plotinus has in fact received a good deal of attention in the last decade or so. See, e.g., A. Smith 1999; Schniewind 2000; 2003; Remes 2006; 2008, chapter 5.

19. Twentieth-century milestones include translations of Plotinus: two in English, Mackenna 1917–1930 (4th ed. 1969) and Armstrong 1966–1988; for other European languages, see Harder 1930–1937 (2nd ed. 1956–1967); Cilento 1947–1949; Hadot 1988– (an ongoing series by multiple authors). Influential studies and collections

include Inge 1918 (3rd ed. 1929); Arnou 1921 (2nd ed. 1967); Dodds 1928; Bréhier 1928 (2nd ed. 1961); Kristeller 1929; Dodds 1933 (2nd ed. 1963); Armstrong 1940; Fondation Hardt 1960 (*Entretiens* 5); Hadot 1963 (Eng. tr. 1993); Theiler 1966 (reprinting several pioneering articles); Armstrong 1967; Rist 1967.

20. Some notable examples in English include Blumenthal 1971a; Wallis 1972 (2nd ed. 1995, with an updated, annotated bibliography by Lloyd Gerson); Dillon 1977 (2nd ed. 1996); Steel 1978; Lloyd 1990; O'Meara 1993; Gerson 1994, 1996, 2003; de Haas 2003; Smith 2004; Corrigan 2005; Remes 2008.

21. At last count, the *Ancient Commentators on Aristotle* series overseen by Richard Sorabji numbered seventy-eight volumes of translation and commentary on some of the most important philosophy produced in any form in Late Antiquity. Up-to-date lists with much helpful information and supplementary material on the project can be consulted at www.kcl.ac.uk/schools/humanities/depts/philosophy/research/commentators.html. Developed from the same rich and underexploited material, Sorabji 2005 is a three-volume sourcebook whose wide learning and unexpected juxtapositions make it doubly useful, as reference and stimulus. Nor is Neoplatonic commentary on Plato being neglected: to cite only the most recent and substantial example, Dirk Baltzly, Harold Tarrant, and their colleagues have begun to publish a most welcome series of annotated translations of Proclus' monumental commentary on Plato's *Timaeus*. For a brief overview of the importance of philosophical commentaries in Late Antiquity, with a useful table of authors and commentaries, as well as a systematic list of factors involved in make the commentaries so popular, see de Haas 2003, 246–254. The "introductory readings" in Neoplatonism in Dillon and Gerson 2004 were collected and annotated expressly to complement a classic introduction to Neoplatonism (Wallis 1972).

22. O'Meara 1993, 44.

23. For the ambiguity of *τὸ ἕν* in *Enneads* 6.9.1–2, see Meijer 1992, 94–95; Gerson 1994, 228, n. 12.

24. Plotinus, *Enneads* 6.9.1. Translations from Plotinus here and later are taken and sometimes slightly modified from Armstrong 1966–1988.

25. *Enneads* 6.9.1; trans. Armstrong 1966–1988, 7:303.

26. For Stoic versions of the argument, see *SVF* 2.366–368 (von Arnim 1903–1924, 2:124), with important qualifications about the degree of "Stoicizing" by Graeser 1972, 74–75; cf. Wallis 1972, 48. The fragments from Plutarch (*SVF* 2.366–367) contain all of the examples used by Plotinus here.

27. Aristotle, *Metaphysics* 5.11 (1019a1–4); trans. W. D. Ross in Barnes 1984, 1609. Beyond the reference to Aristotle, the discussion of priority in the paragraph owes a great deal to O'Meara 1996.

28. O'Meara 1996, 79.

29. Plotinus, *Enneads* 5.4.1; trans. Armstrong 1966–1988, 5:141.

30. Rappe 1995, 2000; Miller 2001, 3–4; Emilsson 2007, 191–198. For more traditional views of metaphors and imagery in Plotinus, see Ferwerda 1965; Cilento 1967.

31. The phrase, in full: *τό τε μὴ ἁπλοῦν τῶν ἐν αὐτῷ ἁπλῶν δεόμενον, ἵν' ᾗ ἐξ ἐκείνων*. For an explanation of *τῶν ἐν αὐτῷ ἁπλῶν* as "simple components" in the ordinary sense, see Gerson 1994, 4–5; cf. O'Meara 1993, 46, on *Enneads* 5.6.3.10–15.

32. Gerson 1994, 43: "an orderly arrangement of parts perspicuous to an intellect"; cf. Gerson 2005b, 259–261; 2005a, 31–33; Runia 1999.

33. Cf. *Enneads* 4.3.9: "there never was a time when this universe did not have a soul, or when body existed in the absence of soul, or when matter was not set in order." To this might be added Plotinus' view that "the cause is not the same as what is caused" (*Enneads* 6.9.6); cf. Tornau 2005.

34. For a rather different (but important) sense of "contain," see *Enneads* 2.2.1.17–18: *ὥστε εἶναι μικτὴν ἐκ σωματικῆς καὶ ψυχικῆς, τοῦ μὲν σώματος εὐθὺ φερομένου φύσει, τῆς δὲ ψυχῆς κατεχούσης, ἐκ δ' ἀμφοῖν γενομένου φερομένου τε καὶ μένοντος.*

35. The posterior's degree of unity and thus its perfection is necessarily inferior to the prior; it can only be an imperfect reflection or shadow of the higher thing on which it depends. It is to this extent less real, less perfect, although as we have seen, this imperfect being or reality should not be taken to imply nonexistence.

36. Naturally, the paradox appears sharpest when the thing in question is the first principle of all; see, e.g., *Enneads* 5.2.1.

37. For Plotinus' remarks on the utility and inadequacies of a similar analogy (the skill of a pilot "in" a rudder), see *Enneads* 4.3.21. Cf. Blumenthal 1971a, 17–18. For a related analogy (a builder and his "beautiful and richly various house"), see *Enneads* 4.3.9.29–37.

38. See esp. *Enneads* 4.3–5 for detailed treatment of these and related questions. Blumenthal 1971a, esp. 8–19, remains very useful; cf. Emilsson 1988, chapters 2 and 5; 1991; Gerson 1994, 127–139; Clark 1996, 277–281; and, for a recent collection with several helpful and detailed articles, Chiaradonna 2005.

39. *Enneads* 4.3.20.10–16. For the Aristotelian origins of this argument, mediated through Alexander of Aphrodisias, see Armstrong 1966–1988 ad loc.; Blumenthal 1968.

40. *Enneads* 4.3.20.42–51.

41. See the *Anonymous Prolegomena to Platonic Philosophy* 10, ed. and trans. Westerink 1962, 46–49.

42. *Enneads* 4.3.22; Plato, *Timaeus* 36D-E.

43. Partial and qualified, that is, not because there is a part of body outside soul but because, while soul as a prior thing is pervasively present in (or to) the body, this does mean that all of soul is in the body. See, e.g., *Enneads* 1.1.2, 4.2–3.

44. *Enneads* 4.3.9.35–44.

45. For ἀρχή as the more precise term, see Gerson 1994, 3

46. See, e.g., Wallis 1972, 47–72; O'Meara 1993, chapters 3–7; Gerson 1994, chapters 2–3, 6; 2003, esp. 308–312; Emilsson 2007, 1–2; Remes 2008, 47–59.

47. Useful overviews addressing of all or parts of the established or probable pedigree of Plotinus' doctrine of the One include O'Meara 1993, 46–49; and Gatti 1996, with detailed bibliographical analysis. Dodds 1928 is the classic study identifying Plato's *Parmenides* as a fundamental inspiration.

48. See, e.g., Armstrong 1967, 236–237.

49. *Enneads* 5.4.1.

50. For a discussion of reasons why there should be such a thing and why it must be unique, see Gerson 1994, 4–14. For Plotinus' originality in posing the question of the reason for the One's existence, see Gatti 1996, 28–29.

51. Plato, *Rep.* 509b. Other key proof texts include Plato, *Parmenides* 142C and reports of Plato's esoteric oral teaching, which Plotinus appears to have accepted; see O'Meara 1993, 47–48, 54.

52. *Enneads* 5.5.6.23–35.

53. See esp. *Enneads* 5.3.14.8–20.

54. See, e.g., *Enneads* 6.9.3; cf. O'Meara 1993, 56–57.

55. Gerson 2003, 311.

56. Emilsson 2007, 2.

57. Aristotle, *Metaphysics* 12(Λ).7 (1072b19–21); cf. *Enneads* 5.4 and esp. 5.5.1–2. For the history of how the Platonic forms came to be identified with the objects of a divine intellect, see Armstrong 1960; Szlezák 1979; Emilsson 1988, 17–18.

58. *Enneads* 1.3.4.

59. *Enneads* 4.8.1.

60. *Enneads* 5.3.10. This is only one of several ways in which Plotinus finds multiplicity in Intellect.

61. *Enneads* 4.3.10. Entirely independent of their posterior principles, the higher "life" of Intellect and the One are, of course, excluded from this category; cf. *Enneads* 3.6.6; 5.1.4, 5.3.16, 5.5.1.

62. Gerson 2005b, 261.

63. *Enneads* 4.4.27: "But what does the soul give to the body of the earth itself? One should not consider an earthy body the same when it is cut off from the earth and when it remains connected with it, as stones show, which grow as long as they are attached to the earth but remain the size they were cut when they are taken away from it."

64. See, among many possibilities, Wallis 1972, 69–70; Blumenthal 1971b; Kalligas 2000. For the unity of the soul, see *Enneads* 4.3–4, 4.9.

65. Emilsson 1988, 24.

66. *Enneads* 4.4.27.

67. *Enneads* 4.6.3.

68. See esp. *Enneads* 4.7.2–8.

69. *Enneads* 4.8.8.

70. For Plotinus' very frequent use of this phrase (εἰς τὸ εἴσω), see Cary 2000, with n. 67.

71. Cf. Gerson 2003, 211: "The principle of Soul is what accounts for the desire of anything that can have desires for objects or goals that require those things to 'go outside' themselves."

72. For the three (and possibly four) kinds of soul in Plotinus, see Blumenthal 1971a; Emilsson 1988, 23–24.

73. Notably, it helps solve the problem of the unity of Soul in light of the existence of the world soul, individual human souls, and so on. See esp. *Enneads* 4.9, with the conclusion in 4.9.4.

74. The word is used five times in Plato's uncontested works and once in the *Epinomis*.

75. Renehan 1980, 130–131.

76. E.g., Plato, *Phaedo* 85e–86a; *Timaeus* 28b; 31b. Cf. Origen, *Against Celsus* 3.47.

77. Aristotle, *On the Soul* 1.5, 409b: οἱ [sc., Democritus and the atomists] δὲ σῶμα τὸ λεπτομερέστατον ἢ τὸ ἀσωματώτατον τῶν ἄλλων.

78. Origen, *On First Principles*, pref. 8; cf. G. Smith 2008, 488–489.

79. Origen, *On First Principles* 1.1.6, 1.6.4, 1.7.1, 2.3.3, etc.; *Against Celsus* 6.71; *Exhortation to Martyrdom* 47.

80. Jerome, *Letters* 84.5.

81. Aristotle, *On generation and corruption* 1.5 (320a).

82. Nemesius, *On the nature of man* 2 (M 71), ed. Morani 1987, 18.

83. Greek: ἄϋλος for "immaterial" is not attested before Plutarch; the alternative form ἄνυλος is later still; see Renehan 1980, 126. Latin: apart from a single instance in Ambrose of Milan and possibly one in Jerome, *immaterialis* is not attested in classical or Late Antiquity (*TLL*, q.v.), although it became popular in medieval Latin.

84. E.g., *Enneads* 1.8.3, 1.8.8, 1.8.13–14, 2.4.16, 2.5.4, 3.6.6–7. Gerson 1996 contains a particularly useful series of articles offering summaries of and different approaches to Plotinus' views of matter, evil, physical substance, and related topics. See esp. the contributions by Corrigan, Wagner, and O'Brien.

85. See O'Brien 1996, 172–174, for a useful explanation based on Plotinus' reliance on Plato's *Sophist*.

86. Cf. Remes 2008, 83.

87. *Enneads* 2.4.12, 3.6.12, etc. See Emilsson 1988, 102, for further discussion and references.

88. That is, matter's complete lack of form and being makes it incorporeal but not, of course, immaterial.

89. This is especially true where both words are used together for emphasis (as in Gregory of Nyssa, for example); Renehan 1980, 126.

90. See *Enneads* 6.2.7, 6.3.8; cf. 1.8.4, where body is "an evil" but not quite the "primal evil" of the matter on which it is based. Cf. Corrigan 1996, 107–108.

91. *Enneads* 1.6.3.

92. Plotinus elsewhere speaks more precisely of "solidity" (στερεότης) as the particular aspect of corporeality with which he is concerned in discussions like this one; see esp. *Enneads* 2.1.6.

93. "The thing which has most completely become body, since it has approached most nearly to non-being, is too weak to collect itself again into a unity," *Enneads* 3.6.6.

94. Augustine, *On the Literal Interpretation of Genesis* 3.4.7. As discussed further later, for Augustine, *spiritus* is unqualifiedly immaterial.

95. Cf. Dillon 1998, in a suggestive article on "nuances of incorporeality in Philo." Noting that Philo appears to describe stars as both "incorporeal" and as composed of fine-material *pneuma* or pure fire, he concludes: "This can be seen as a piece of muddle-headedness, and as a compromise with Stoic materialism, but it can also—more profitably in my view—be seen as an indication that the boundary between the corporeal and the incorporeal was not drawn by many ancient thinkers where we might think it should be drawn" (110).

96. The key text for Aristotle is *On the Heavens* (*De caelo*). For an illuminating summary of ancient alternatives, see Furley 1981, esp. 580–585.

97. Philoponus receives nothing like the attention he deserves in this article. Not surprisingly, he is the single most dominant figure in Sambursky's pioneering survey of late ancient physics (1962). See also Wildberg 1988; the important collection of articles in Sorabji 1987; de Haas 1997; and recent translations of Philoponus in the *Ancient Commentators on Aristotle* series directed by Richard Sorabji. For another major attack on the fifth element, see Proclus, *On the Timaeus*, especially 2.9ff.; cf. Baltzly 2002.

98. For Stobaeus and the Hermetica, see Fowden 1993; Ebeling 2007, esp. 7–36. Nock and Festugière 1938–1954 (3rd ed. 1972) is the indispensable edition, with French translation; Copenhaver 1992 is a partial English translation of the Hermetica but does not include the Stobaean excerpts; see Salaman et al. 1999 for additional translations, including the Armenian *Definitions*.

99. *Asclepius* 19; ed. Nock and Festugière 1972, 2:319–320.

100. *Stobaean Hermetica* 25.11–14; ed. Nock and Festugière 1972, 4:71–72.

101. *Stobaean Hermetica* 12.14: *ἔστιν οὖν τῆς μὲν ὕλης τὸ λεπτομερέστατον ἀήρ, ἀέρος δὲ ψυχή, ψυχῆς δὲ νοῦς, νοῦ δὲ θεός*. For nearly the same formulation, see what appears to be the misplaced final sentence appended to *Stobaean Hermetica* 5: *ὕλης μὲν γὰρ τὸ λεπτομερέστερον ἀήρ, ἀέρος δὲ ψυχή, ψυχῆς δὲ νοῦς, νοῦ δὲ ὁ θεός*.

102. Although the study of Posidonius has been transformed by a sensible retreat from the speculative reconstructions of the first half of the twentieth century (see esp. Reinhardt 1926, more than usually relevant for topics considered here), the older literature is always suggestive and still useful if treated with caution; see, e.g., Cumont 1922, 98–100, for the importance of cosmological ideas in the context of Roman beliefs about the soul, its ascent, and its "natural home" at various levels of the heavens.

103. See, e.g., Cicero, *On the Nature of the Gods* 1.103; 2.65, 84, 101, 117.

104. *Enneads* 2.1.7.

105. Augustine, *City of God* 7.6.

106. For brief discussion of this, the broader context, and further references, see Corrigan 1986, 367. Diogenes of Apollonia (fr. 4) had observed that people and animals require air to live and breathe; air "is for them both soul and intelligence (*nous*)"; Kirk, Raven, and Schofield 1983, 442.

107. Cicero, *Tusculan Disputations* 1.43; cf. Sextus Empiricus, *Against the Professors* 9.71–74.

108. For the material and detrimental effect of alcohol on the soul (not just the body), see Hippocrates, *On Breaths* 14; Aristotle, *On Sleep and Waking* 3 (456B-457A); Lucretius 4.476–483; Soranus, *Gynecology* 1.39, 2.19; Galen, *The Soul's Dependence on the Body* 3 (Kühn 1821–1833, 4:777–779); Philostratus, *Life of Apollonius* 1.8, 2.36, 2.37; Clement of Alexandria, *Paedagogus* 2.1.11, 2.2.29, 2.5.48.

109. Plutarch, *On the Face in the Moon* 24 (943A-D).

110. Julian, *Symposium* or *Kronia (Caesars)* 2 (307C).

111. Plato, *Phaedo* 81B-D.

112. Origen, *Against Celsus* 2.60; Porphyry, *On the Cave of the Nymphs* 11 (a faint echo), *Sentences* 29; Iamblichus, *On the Mysteries* 4.13; Proclus, *On Plato's Republic* 2.156–157 (also faint); Gregory of Nyssa, *On the Soul and the Resurrection* 6 (an extended and important discussion); John Philoponus, *On Aristotle's On the Soul* 19.18–22 (also explicit and illuminating). See van der Eijk 2005, 125, n. 203, for further discussion and bibliography.

113. *Enneads* 5.9.1; cf. the index fontium in Henry and Schwyzer 1964–1982, 3:352. The allusion has little to do with the visibility of soul, being concerned rather with the effect of how one lives one's life.

114. Plotinus explicitly rejects the idea that souls naturally inhabit the air at *Enneads* 1.8.14.30–31

115. *Enneads* 4.3.15.

116. The "center" is to be understood spatially only if body is involved; free of spatial constraints, souls "move" around God as their center.

117. *Enneads* 4.2.1–2.

118. *Enneads* 4.2.2.19–23.

119. Beginning with Dodds's classic account in an appendix to his edition of Proclus' *Elements of Theology* (1963, 313–321), the theory has received a good deal of

fruitful attention in recent decades. See Kissling 1922 and Bidez 1913, 88–97, for important precedents to Dodds. More recent scholarship includes A. Smith 1974, 152–158; Finamore 1985; Di Pasquale Barbanti 1998; Bos 2003, 258–303; Zambon 2005; and Congourdeau 2007, 49–54. Sorabji 2005, 1:221–241, should be singled out for special recommendation as providing useful summaries and bibliography and also a broad array of sources suggestively juxtaposed under coherent headings.

120. The context is a discussion of the *pneuma* found in the eyes, whose constitutional similarity to light is a key part of the explanation of vision; optical *pneuma* is bright or luminous (φωτοειδές, αὐγοειδές), analogous and responsive to the sun's rays (αὐγαί). Galen, *On the Doctrines of Hippocrates and Plato* 7.7.25–26; ed. De Lacy 1978–1984, 474. For *pneuma* in Galen, see Temkin 1951; von Staden 2000; Rocca 2003, 59–66.

121. Plato, *Phaedo* 113D; *Phaedrus* 247B; *Timaeus* 41E, 44E, 69C; and especially *Laws* 898E-899A. As Dodds observes (1963, 315), none of these passages develops a full-blown theory of the vehicle as a pneumatic or astral body, but taken together, most of the important terms and concepts were available.

122. Aristotle, *On the Generation of Animals* 2.3, 736b.27–38. Cf. Proclus, *On the Timaeus* 3.238.20. For *pneuma* in Aristotle, see Solmsen 1957; Freudenthal 1995; Bos 2002.

123. For details and further references for this summary, see the works listed in n. 119.

124. Origen, *Against Celsus* 2.60. For Origin on the vehicle of the soul, and especially its importance as the body received at the resurrection, see Festugière 1959; Crouzel 1977; Dechow 1988; Hennessy 1992; Schibli 1992. Alternatively, the explanation could also work the other way (ghostly souls prove the existence of the vehicle), as in Philoponus, *On Aristotle's On the Soul* 19.18–22.

125. For the minimal impact of the theory in Plotinus, see Dodds 1963, 318; Zambon 2005.

126. *Enneads* 3.6.5. Armstrong (1966–1988, 3:231) has "when it is not standing over a vital breath" for ὅταν μὴ ἐπὶ πνεύματος, but given the evident reference to a pneumatic vehicle and the use of ὀχεῖσθαι later in the sentence, "carried on" seems more appropriate.

127. Augustine, *City of God* 10.9. The problem of an evident confusion between psychic *pneuma* (or pneumatic *psychē*) and the soul's own faculties is thoroughly explored by A. Smith 1974, 155–158, who notes important parallels between Porphyry and Synesius of Cyrene, among others.

128. Augustine, *City of God* 10.9, 10.27; cf. A. Smith 1974, 157; Finamore 1985, 4.

129. Finamore 1985, 168–169.

130. Iamblichus, *On the Timaeus* fr. 84 (Dillon 1973, 196); *On the Mysteries* 3.11 (125); cf. Finamore 1985, 11.

131. Simplicius, *On Aristotle's Categories* (ed. Kalbfleisch 1907, 374).

132. For basic cosmology, as well as theurgical rites involved in this process, Iamblichus drew freely from the *Chaldaean Oracles* and the Hermetica; for a useful overview with additional bibliography, see Clarke et al. 2003, introduction.

133. See Finamore 1985, 145.

134. Shaw 1995, 52. This was naturally a central principle for explaining of the efficacy of magic, as Plotinus had observed (*Enneads* 4.4.40), citing "sympathy and the fact that there is a natural concord of things that are alike."

135. Proclus, *On Plato's Timaeus* 3.237; see van der Eijk 2005, 123–124, n. 183, for an overview, references, and further bibliography.

136. See, e.g., Proclus, *On Plato's Republic* 2.167, *On Plato's Timaeus* 3.237; Philoponus, *On Aristotle's On the Soul* 20; cf. van der Eijk 2005, 124; Sorabji 2005, 1:226–227.

137. See the examples and discussion in Sorabji 2005, 1:75–76.

138. See G. Smith 2008 for further details and an argument for the persistent (fine-)materiality of demons in Roman and later antiquity.

139. Priestley 1777, 74–75.

140. For Aristotle on matter, see the summary (with a view toward Neoplatonism) in Sorabji 1988, 5–22. It should be noted that magnitude (μέγεθος) is not quite the same as extension (διάστημα). As Sorabji summarizes it in his discussion of Simplicius (1988, 9–10), the former is definite while the latter is not; it is extension considered in itself without reference to particular measurements in length, width, or depth.

141. Indeed, Plotinus had little use for "mediation" as an explanatory device in itself, especially by contrast to his successors. See Emilsson 1988 for a convincing case that even Plotinus' complex theory of sensation attempts to dispense with the "images," impressions, or mental representations on which so many other ancient theorists relied; *Enneads* 4.5.4 is particularly suggestive in this regard.

142. Syrianus and Proclus in the fifth century seem to have taken something like the first route when they suggested that vehicles of the soul were "immaterial bodies" (ἄϋλα σώματα) endowed with the special (unique?) ability to interpenetrate other bodies. Cf. Porphyry, as cited by Proclus, *On Plato's Timaeus*, 2.11.10–13, who suggests that some visible corporeal demons offer no resistance to touch; Sorabji 1988, 107.

143. *On the Sacred Disease* 16–17.

144. The classic study, still essential but now long overdue for an update, is Verbeke 1945. See Rocca 2003, 59–63, for an excellent overview and more recent bibliography on the medical context in particular.

145. Sorabji 1988, 85–87, suggests that this is not quite right: that the early Stoics, at least, used *pneuma* for air and fire and other very thin things, rather than positing a mixture of air and fire.

146. G. Smith 2008, 483–489.

147. See von Staden 2000, 114, for references and discussion.

148. Joseph Priestley's use of "spirit" in the passage quoted reflects the Augustinian definition, of course, sharpened still further by the Cartesian notion of mind.

149. See, e.g., Rüsche 1933, titled *Das Seelenpneuma: Seine Entwicklung von der Hauchseele zur Geistseele*. Verbeke 1945 is a more reliable source for the traditional model, although his conclusions are a good deal more nuanced than the summary presented here. For some necessary modifications, see Masai 1961, 15–31.

150. For the spherical shape of the vehicle of the soul, see Iamblichus, *On the Timaeus*, fr. 49 (Dillon 1973); cf. Shaw 1995, 51–53.

151. This is not meant as a characterization of Franz Cumont, but it is significant that his *After Life in Roman Paganism* (1922) remains one of the most important books to treat themes addressed in the second half of this chapter in broad and comparative detail.

152. Mead 1919.

153. Dodds 1963 (orig. 1933), 313–321, is the classic demonstration that unknown "oriental" sources need not be invoked for a theory with sturdy roots in classical philosophy.

154. In addition to the pneumatic soul vehicle references discussed, see *Enneads* 4.4.26.23–31 for *pneuma*'s role in vision, its special translucence, and the power of life or vegetative principle (φυτικός). Plotinus, of course, does not accept the full Stoic doctrine of *pneuma*; see *Enneads* 4.7.4, 7–8c, etc.

155. Consider, for example, Tertullian's much-scorned materialist account of how the human soul gets its shape (recognizable after death as the individual person it animates). Starting as the breath of God, blown in through the nostrils (of Adam, in this case), it spreads throughout the body, "condensed by the divine exhalation and squeezed into every internal channel which the condensed [breath] had filled, and thus it congealed into shape" (*On the Soul* 9.7–8). This is precisely the process described by Philoponus (*On Aristotle's On the Soul* 20)—including solidification of *pneuma*, compression into the body's cavities, and the comparison with ice freezing into shape—to explain why certain souls appear in human form after death. The only difference is a reliance of the soul's pneumatic vehicle rather than the soul itself, as in the Stoicizing Tertullian.

156. Augustine, *Confessions* 5.10.20.

157. Augustine, *Confessions* 5.10.19; cf. 3.7.12, 5.14.25, 7.1, etc.

158. Masai 1961; Courcelle 1950 (2nd ed. 1968). Masai's account, in turn, received what would become its most influential endorsement in Brown 1967, 75–76.

159. This applies even to conceptions of God, as demonstrated by Griffin and Paulsen 2002; cf. Paulsen 1990 for "Origen and Augustine as reluctant witnesses" to widespread belief in a corporeal deity.

160. Masai 1961, 13–29.

161. Augustine, *Confessions* 1.6.7.

162. To be sure, for Plotinus the soul in its pure essential state could be seen as part of the realm of Intellect. Cf. Steel 1978, 155–156: "Plotinus considered the soul as the great 'traveler' in the ontological scheme which, according to the faculty it actualized, could become anything at all." If, moreover, we take "universe" to refer to the sensible cosmos, then Ambrose/Augustine's remark presents few Plotinian problems.

163. Augustine, *On the Happy Life* 1.4.

164. See Emilsson 1991 for soul-body dualism in Plotinus, Augustine, and Descartes; see Matthews 2000 for similar conclusions about Augustine and Descartes. See also Emilsson 1988, 146: "What then does it take to have a Cartesian type of mind (soul)-body problem? I think that someone who uses introspection to make claims about the nature of the soul (or mind) and contrasts his findings with the nature of the body considered from an external and hence public point of view, is about to produce such a problem for himself—and for others too if others find his reasoning persuasive or challenging." For Augustine's "invention of the inner self" and its debts to Plotinus, see Cary 2000.

165. This is not to deny that closely related problems continued to stimulate productive discussion in later Neoplatonism, as demonstrated, e.g., by Steel 1978. Cf. Emilsson 1988, 147: "Plotinus himself was quite aware of the difficulties his position involved. And his claims against Stoic (and Stratonic) materialism could for instance easily and directly generate discussion of the relation between what goes on physically in the body and what goes on in the soul as viewed from inside or a discussion of the possibility of explaining the apparently non-physical features of the soul in terms of the physical. But these seeds did not sprout, no doubt because there were no materialists around who would respond to Plotinus and carry the dialogue further."

166. These are clearly summarized in O'Daly 1986, 325–327.

167. See esp. *On the Literal Interpretation of Genesis* book 7; cf. 3.4.7, 10.25–26, 12.10.21, 12.16–17; and O'Daly 1986 for further references and summary.

168. Along with others mentioned here, agility and susceptibility to impression rank high on the list of fine-material advantages; by means of "subtle bodies," for example, demons move very quickly indeed; *On the Literal Interpretation of Genesis* 12.16.33; 12.17.34–35. For sensation, see esp. 5.7.

169. *On the Literal Interpretation of Genesis* 12.16.32.

170. Fire: *City of God* 21.10 (how else can demons feel the pain of punishment?); Augustine glosses fire as "light and air" and calls it the chief instrument by which the soul governs the body at *On the Literal Interpretation of Genesis* 7.15.21. According to the early (unfinished) *Literal Interpretation of Genesis*, air and ether barely qualify as matter at all: "et aer quidem mobilior est quam aqua; aether autem ipso aere mobilior non absurde creditur aut sentitur; sed aeris uel aetheris nomine minus conuenienter appellaretur materies."

171. *On the Literal Interpretation of Genesis* 7.15.21.

172. Augustine, *Divination of Demons* 5.9; quoted and discussed in more detail in G. Smith 2008, 506–507.

173. *On the Literal Interpretation of Genesis* 3.4.7.

174. Wear and Dillon 2007.

175. Not that Ps-Dionysius has nothing materially interesting to say about angels and demons. While their constitution is never described in detail, demons are both without body (*Divine Names* 4.27) and "conjoined with matter" (*πρόσυλος*; *Divine Names* 4.18); the latter is an adjective commonly used of people not properly turned toward the divine and the good. For their part, angels are immaterial, of course, but Ps-Dionysius also links the symbolic name of "winds" to their surpassing speed (a classic property of fine-material things) just before observing that "wind" can also refer to "aerial *pneuma*" (*Celestial Hierarchy* 15.6).

176. Perhaps the most influential example, contemporary with Augustine, is John Cassian; see esp. *Conferences* 7.13.1–2: "For although we declare that some natures are spiritual—as are the angels, the archangels and the other powers, our soul itself and of course the subtle air—yet these are by no means to be considered incorporeal. They have a body appropriate to themselves by which they subsist, although it is far more refined than our own bodies. . . . From this it is clear that nothing is incorporeal but God alone." To this could be added the dispute over the soul's material composition in late-fifth-century Gaul, involving Faustus of Riez and Claudianus Mamertus, for which see, in English, Mathisen 1989, 235–244; and Brittain 2001 (with discussion of previous scholarship).

177. See, e.g., O'Donnell 1979, 121–130; Di Marco 1985, 93–117; D'Elia 1987.

178. Vessey 2004, 20.

179. Vessey 2004, 20–21.

180. *On the Soul* 4; cf. Augustine, *On the Literal Interpretation of Genesis* 7.21.27. Unless otherwise noted, all citations in the following paragraphs come from chapter 4 of Cassiodorus' *On the Soul.*

181. See, e.g., *Magnitude of the Soul* 31.63, 32, 68. *On the Literal Interpretation of Genesis* 3.5.7 comes close to using *subtilius* of the soul, but actually refers to the *subtilius corpus* by which the soul achieves sensation.

182. Cassiodorus, *On the Soul* 5.

183. Tertullian, *On the Soul* 9.4 and esp. 9.5: "Si enim corpus anima, sine dubio inter illa quae supra sumus professi, proinde et coloris proprietas omni corpori aderit. Quem igitur alium animae aestimabis colorem quam aerium ac lucidum?"

184. All quotations in this paragraph come from Descartes' second Meditation.

WORKS CITED

Armstrong, A. H. 1940. *The Architecture of the Intelligible Universe in the Philosophy of Plotinus: An Analytical and Historical Study*. Cambridge Classical Studies. Cambridge: Cambridge University Press.

———. 1960. "The Background of the Doctrine 'That the Intelligibles are Not Outside the Intellect.'" In *Les sources de Plotin*, 391–413. Geneva: Fondation Hardt.

———, trans. 1966–1988. *Plotinus*. 6 vols. Loeb Classical Library. Cambridge, MA: Harvard University Press.

———, ed. 1967. *The Cambridge History of Later Greek and Early Medieval Philosophy*. Cambridge: Cambridge University Press.

Arnou, R. 1921. *Le désir de Dieu dans la philosophie de Plotin*. Paris: F. Alcan.

Athanassiadi, Polymnia. 1999. "The Chaldaean Oracles: Theology and Theurgy." In *Pagan Monotheism in Late Antiquity*, ed. Polymnia Athanassiadi and Michael Frede, 149–183. Oxford: Clarendon Press.

Baltzly, Dirk. 2002. "What Goes Up: Proclus against Aristotle on the Fifth Element," *Australasian Journal of Philosophy* 80: 261–287.

Barnes, Jonathan, ed. 1984. *The Complete Works of Aristotle: The Revised Oxford Translation*. 2 vols. Bollingen series 71.2. Princeton, NJ: Princeton University Press.

Bidez, J. 1913. *Vie de Porphyre, le philosophe néo-platonicien: avec les fragments des traités Perì agalmátōn et De regressu animae*. Leipzig: Teubner.

Blumenthal, Henry J. 1968. "Plotinus *Ennead* IV.3.20–1 and its Sources: Alexander, Aristotle, and Others," *Archiv für Geschichte der Philosophie* 50: 254–261.

———. 1971a. *Plotinus' Psychology: His Doctrines of the Embodied Soul*. The Hague: Martinus Nijhoff.

———. 1971b. "Soul, World-Soul and Individual Soul in Plotinus." In *Le néoplatonisme*, 55–63. Paris: Editions du Centre national de la recherche scientifique.

———. 1996. *Aristotle and Neoplatonism in Late Antiquity: Interpretations of the De anima*. Ithaca, NY: Cornell University Press.

Bos, Abraham P. 2002. "*Pneuma* and Aether in Aristotle's Philosophy of Living Nature," *Modern Schoolman* 79: 255–276.

———. 2003. *The Soul and Its Instrumental Body: A Reinterpretation of Aristotle's Philosophy of Living Nature*. Brill's Studies in Intellectual History 112. Leiden: Brill.

Bréhier, Emile. 1928. *La philosophie de Plotin*. Bibliothèque de la *Revue des cours et conférences*. Paris: Boivin & Cie.

Brisson, Luc. 2003. "Plato's Timaeus and the Chaldaean Oracles." In *Plato's Timaeus as Cultural Icon*, ed. Gretchen J. Reydams-Schils, 111–132. Notre Dame, IN: University of Notre Dame Press.

Brittain, Charles. 2001. "No Place for a Platonist Soul in Fifth-Century Gaul? The Case of Mamertus Claudianus." In *Society and Culture in Late Antique Gaul: Revisiting the Sources*, ed. Ralph W. Mathisen and Danuta Shanzer, 239–262. Aldershot: Ashgate.

Brown, Peter. 1967. *Augustine of Hippo: A Biography*. Berkeley: University of California Press.

Cary, Phillip. 2000. *Augustine's Invention of the Inner Self: The Legacy of a Christian Platonist*. Oxford: Oxford University Press.

Chadwick, Henry. 1999. "Philosophical Tradition and the Self." In *Late Antiquity: A Guide to the Postclassical World*, ed. G. W. Bowersock, Peter Brown, and Oleg Grabar, 60–81. Cambridge, MA: Harvard University Press.

Chiaradonna, Riccardo, ed. 2005. *Studi sull'anima in Plotino*. Elenchos 42. Naples: Bibliopolis.

Cilento, Vincenzo, trans. 1947–1949. *Enneadi*. 3 vols. Filosofi antichi e medievali: Collana de testi e di traduzioni. Bari: Laterza.

———. 1967. "Stile e linguaggio nella filosofia di Plotino," *Vichiana* 4: 29–41.

Clark, Stephen R. L. 1996. "Plotinus: Body and Soul." In *The Cambridge Companion to Plotinus*, ed. Lloyd P. Gerson, 275–291. Cambridge: Cambridge University Press.

Clarke, Emma C., John M. Dillon, and Jackson P. Hershbell, trans. 2003. *Iamblichus: De Mysteriis*. Writings from the Greco-Roman World 4. Atlanta: Society of Biblical Literature.

Congourdeau, Marie-Hélène. 2007. *L'embryon et son âme dans les sources grecques (VIe siècle av. J.-C.–Ve siècle apr. J.-C.)*. Monographies 26. Paris: Centre d'histoire et civilisation de Byzance.

Cooper, John W., and D. S. Hutchinson, eds. 1997. *Plato: Complete Works*. Indianapolis, IN: Hackett.

Copenhaver, Brian P. 1992. *Hermetica: The Greek Corpus Hermeticum and the Latin Asclepius in a New English Translation*. Cambridge: Cambridge University Press.

Corrigan, Kevin. 1986. "Body and Soul in Ancient Religious Experience." In *Classical Mediterranean Spirituality: Egyptian, Greek, Roman*, ed. A. H. Armstrong, 360–383. New York: Crossroad.

———. 1996. "Essence and Existence in the Enneads." In *The Cambridge Companion to Plotinus*, ed. Lloyd P. Gerson, 105–129. Cambridge: Cambridge University Press.

———. 2005. *Reading Plotinus: A Practical Introduction to Neoplatonism*. Purdue University Press Series in the History of Philosophy. West Lafayette, IN: Purdue University Press.

Courcelle, Pierre. 1968. *Recherches sur les Confessions de Saint Augustin*, 2nd ed. Paris: E. de Boccard.

Crouzel, Henri. 1977. "Le thème platonicien du véhicule de l'âme chez Origène," *Didaskalia* 7: 225–237.

Cumont, Franz. 1922. *After Life in Roman Paganism: Lectures Delivered at Yale University on the Silliman Foundation*. New Haven, CT: Yale University Press.

de Haas, Frans A. J. 1997. *John Philoponus' New Definition of Prime Matter: Aspects of Its Background in Neoplatonism and the Ancient Commentary Tradition*. Philosophia antiqua 69. Leiden: Brill.

———. 2003. "Late Ancient Philosophy." In *The Cambridge Companion to Greek and Roman Philosophy*, ed. David N. Sedley, 242–270. Cambridge: Cambridge University Press.

De Lacy, Phillip, ed. 1978–1984. *Galen: On the Doctrines of Hippocrates and Plato.* 3 vols. 2nd ed. Corpus Medicorum Graecorum 5.4.1.2. Berlin: Akademie Verlag.

Dechow, Jon Frederick. 1988. "Origen and Early Christian Pluralism: The Context of His Eschatology." In *Origen of Alexandria: His World and His Legacy*, ed. Charles Kannengiesser and William L. Petersen, 337–356. Notre Dame, IN: University of Notre Dame Press.

D'Elia, Francesco. 1987. *L'antropologia di Cassiodoro: Tra ispirazione agostiniana e suggestioni del mondo classico; note teoretiche e filologiche sul "De anima."* Rome: Gesualdi.

Di Marco, Michele. 1985. "Scelta e utilizzazione delle fonti nel *De anima* di Cassiodoro," *Studi e materiali di storia delle religioni* 51: 93–117.

Di Pasquale Barbanti, Maria. 1998. *Ochema-pneuma e phantasia nel neoplatonismo: Aspetti psicologici e prospettive religiose.* Symbolon 19. Catania: CUECM.

Dillon, John M. 1973. "The Concept of Two Intellects: A Footnote to the History of Platonism," *Phronesis* 18: 176–185.

———. 1977. *The Middle Platonists: A Study of Platonism, 80 B.C. to A.D. 220.* London: Duckworth.

———. 1992. "Plotinus and the Chaldaean Oracles." In *Platonism in Late Antiquity*, ed. Stephen Gersh and Charles Kannengiesser, 131–140. Notre Dame, IN: University of Notre Dame Press.

———. 1996. *The Middle Platonists, 80 B.C. to A.D. 220.* Rev. ed. Ithaca, NY: Cornell University Press.

———. 1998. "*Asômatos*: Nuances of Incorporeality in Philo." In *Philon d'Alexandrie et le langage de la philosophie*, ed. Carlos Lévy, 99–110. Turnhout: Brepols.

Dillon, John M., and Lloyd P. Gerson, eds. 2004. *Neoplatonic Philosophy: Introductory Readings.* Indianapolis, IN: Hackett.

Dillon, John M., and A. A. Long, eds. 1988. *The Question of "Eclecticism": Studies in Later Greek Philosophy.* Berkeley: University of California Press.

Dodds, E. R. 1928. "The *Parmenides* of Plato and the Origins of the Neoplatonic 'One'," *Classical Quarterly* 22: 129–142.

———. 1951. *The Greeks and the Irrational.* Sather Classical Lectures 25. Berkeley: University of California Press.

———, ed. 1963 [1933]. *Proclus: The Elements of Theology.* 2nd ed. Oxford: Clarendon Press.

Ebeling, Florian. 2007. *The Secret History of Hermes Trismegistus: Hermeticism from Ancient to Modern Times.* Trans. David Lorton. Ithaca, NY: Cornell University Press.

Edwards, Mark Julian. 2000. "Birth, Death, and Divinity in Porphyry's Life of Plotinus." In *Greek Biography and Panegyric in Late Antiquity*, ed. Tomas Hägg and Philip Rousseau, 52–71. Berkeley: University of California Press.

Emilsson, Eyjólfur K. 1988. *Plotinus on Sense-Perception: A Philosophical Study.* Cambridge: Cambridge University Press.

———. 1991. "Plotinus and Soul-Body Dualism." In *Psychology*, ed. Stephen Everson, 148–165. Cambridge: Cambridge University Press.

———. 2007. *Plotinus on Intellect.* Oxford: Clarendon Press.

Ferwerda, R. 1965. *La signification des images et des métaphores dans la pensée de Plotin.* Groningen: J. B. Wolters.

Festugière, A.-J. 1959. *Antioche païenne et chrétienne: Libanius, Chrysostome et les moines de Syrie.* Bibliothèque des écoles françaises d'Athènes et de Rome 194. Paris: E. de Boccard.

Finamore, John F. 1985. *Iamblichus and the Theory of the Vehicle of the Soul*. American Classical Studies 14. Chico, CA: Scholars Press.
Fondation Hardt. 1960. *Les sources de Plotin*. Entretiens sur l'antiquité classique 5. Geneva: Fondation Hardt.
Fowden, Garth. 1993. *The Egyptian Hermes: A Historical Approach to the Late Egyptian Mind*. 2nd ed. Princeton, NJ: Princeton University Press.
Freudenthal, Gad. 1995. *Aristotle's Theory of Material Substance: Heat and Pneuma, Form and Soul*. Oxford: Clarendon Press.
Furley, David J. 1981. "The Greek Theory of the Infinite Universe," *Journal of the History of Ideas* 42: 571–585.
Gatti, Maria Luisa. 1996. "Plotinus: The Platonic Tradition and the Foundation of Neoplatonism." In *The Cambridge Companion to Plotinus*, ed. Lloyd P. Gerson, 10–37. Cambridge: Cambridge University Press.
Gerson, Lloyd P. 1994. *Plotinus*. Arguments of the Philosophers. London: Routledge.
———, ed. 1996. *The Cambridge Companion to Plotinus*. Cambridge: Cambridge University Press.
———. 2003. "Neoplatonism." In *The Blackwell Guide to Ancient Philosophy*, ed. Christopher Shields, 303–323. Malden, MA: Blackwell.
———. 2005a. *Aristotle and Other Platonists*. Ithaca, NY: Cornell University Press.
———. 2005b. "What Is Platonism?" *Journal of the History of Philosophy* 43: 253–276.
Gill, Christopher. 2003. "The School in the Roman Imperial Period." In *The Cambridge Companion to the Stoics*, ed. Brad Inwood, 33–58. Cambridge: Cambridge University Press.
Gilson, Etienne. 1930. *Études sur le rôle de la pensée médiévale dans la formation du système cartésien*. Études de philosophie médiévale. Paris: J. Vrin.
Golitzin, Alexander. 2002. "'The Demons Suggest an Illusion of God's Glory in a Form': Controversy over the Divine Body in Some Late Fourth, Early Fifth Century Monastic Literature," *Studia monastica* 44: 13–43.
Graeser, Andreas. 1972. *Plotinus and the Stoics: A Preliminary Study*. Philosophia antiqua 22. Leiden: Brill.
Griffin, Carl W., and David L. Paulsen. 2002. "Augustine and the Corporeality of God," *Harvard Theological Review* 95: 97–118.
Hadot, Pierre. 1963. *Plotin ou la simplicité du regard*. La Recherche de l'absolu 10. Paris: Plon.
———, ed. 1988–. *Les écrits de Plotin*. Paris: Editions du Cerf.
Harder, Richard. 1930–1937. *Plotins Schriften*. 5 vols. Leipzig: F. Meiner.
Hennessy, Lawrence R. 1992. "A Philosophical Issue in Origen's Eschatology: The Three Senses of Incorporeality." In *Origeniana Quinta: Papers of the Fifth International Origen Congress*, ed. Robert J. Daly, 373–380. Louvain: Peeters.
Henry, Paul, and Hans-Rudolf Schwyzer, eds. 1964–1982. *Plotini Opera*. 3 vols. Scriptorum classicorum bibliotheca Oxoniensis. Oxford: Clarendon Press.
Inge, William Ralph. 1918. *The Philosophy of Plotinus: The Gifford Lectures at St. Andrews, 1917–1918*. 2 vols. London: Longmans, Green.
Janowski, Zbigniew. 2004. *Augustinian-Cartesian Index: Texts and Commentary*. South Bend, IN: St. Augustine's.
Kahn, Charles H. 2009. *Essays on Being*. Oxford: Oxford University Press.
Kalbfleisch, Karl, ed. 1907. *Simplicii In Aristotelis Categorias commentarium*. Commentaria in Aristotelem graeca 8. Berlin: Reimer.

Kalligas, Paul. 2000. "Living Body, Soul, and Virtue in the Philosophy of Plotinus," *Dionysius* 18: 25–38.

Karamanolis, George E. 2006. *Plato and Aristotle in Agreement? Platonists on Aristotle from Antiochus to Porphyry*. Oxford Philosophical Monographs. Oxford: Clarendon Press.

Kirk, G. S., J. E. Raven, and M. Schofield. 1983. *The Presocratic Philosophers: A Critical History with a Selection of Texts*. 2nd ed. Cambridge: Cambridge University Press.

Kissling, R. C. 1922. "The ὄχημα-πνεῦμα of the Neoplatonists and the *De insomniis* of Synesius of Cyrene," *American Journal of Philology* 43: 318–331.

Kristeller, Paul Oskar. 1929. *Der Begriff der Seele in der Ethik des Plotin*. Heidelberger Abhandlungen zur Philosophie und ihrer Geschichte 19. Tübingen: J. C. B. Mohr.

Kühn, Karl Gottlob, ed. 1821–1833. *Claudii Galeni Opera Omnia*. 20 vols. Medicorum Graecorum opera quae exstant. Leipzig: Knobloch.

Lewy, Hans. 1978. *The Chaldaean Oracles and Theurgy: Mysticism, Magic and Platonism in the Later Roman Empire*. 2nd ed. Ed. Michel Tardieu. Paris: Etudes augustiniennes.

Lloyd, A. C. 1990. *The Anatomy of Neoplatonism*. Oxford: Clarendon Press.

MacKenna, Stephen, trans. 1917–1930. *Plotinus*. 5 vols. London: Medici Society.

Majercik, Ruth. 1989. *The Chaldean Oracles: Text, Translation, and Commentary*. Studies in Greek and Roman Religion 5. Leiden: Brill.

Masai, François. 1961. "Les conversions de Saint Augustin et les débuts du spiritualisme en Occident," *Le Moyen Âge* 67: 1–40.

Mathisen, Ralph W. 1989. *Ecclesiastical Factionalism and Religious Controversy in Fifth-Century Gaul*. Washington, DC: Catholic University of America Press.

Matthews, Gareth. 2000. "Internalist Reasoning in Augustine for Mind-Body Dualism." In *Psyche and Soma: Physicians and Metaphysicians on the Mind-Body Problem from Antiquity to the Enlightenment*, ed. John P. Wright and Paul Potter, 133–145. Oxford: Oxford University Press.

Mead, G. R. S. 1919. *The Doctrine of the Subtle Body in Western Tradition: An Outline of What the Philosophers Thought and Christians Taught on the Subject*. London: J. M. Watkins.

Meijer, P. A. 1992. *Plotinus on the Good or the One (Enneads VI, 9): An Analytical Commentary*. Amsterdam Classical Monographs 1. Amsterdam: J. C. Gieben.

Menn, Stephen. 1998. *Descartes and Augustine*. Cambridge: Cambridge University Press.

Miller, Patricia Cox. 2001. *The Poetry of Thought in Late Antiquity: Essays in Imagination and Religion*. Aldershot: Ashgate.

Morani, Moreno, ed. 1987. *Nemesii Emeseni De natura hominis*. Leipzig: Teubner.

Moravcsik, Julius. 1992. *Plato and Platonism: Plato's Conception of Appearance and Reality in Ontology, Epistemology, and Ethics, and Its Modern Echoes*. Issues in Ancient Philosophy 1. Oxford: Blackwell.

Nock, Arthur Darby. 1964. *Early Gentile Christianity and its Hellenistic Background*. New York: Harper & Row.

———, ed. 1972. *Corpus Hermeticum*. Trans. A. -J. Festugière. 3rd ed. 4 vols. Collection des universités de France. Paris: Les Belles Lettres.

Nock, Arthur Darby, and A. -J. Festugière, eds. 1938–1954 [3rd ed. 1972]. *Corpus Hermeticum*. 4 vols. Collection des universités de France. Paris: Les Belles Lettres.

O'Brien, Denis. 1996. "Plotinus on Matter and Evil." In *The Cambridge Companion to Plotinus*, ed. Lloyd P. Gerson, 171–195. Cambridge: Cambridge University Press.

O'Daly, Gerard J. P. 1986. "Anima, Animus." In *Augustinus-Lexikon*, ed. Cornelius Mayer, Erich Feldmann, and Karl Heinz Chelius, 315–340. Basel: Schwabe.
O'Donnell, James J. 1979. *Cassiodorus*. Berkeley: University of California Press.
O'Meara, Dominic J. 1993. *Plotinus: An Introduction to the Enneads*. Oxford: Clarendon Press.
———. 1996. "The Hierarchical Ordering of Reality in Plotinus." In *The Cambridge Companion to Plotinus*, ed. Lloyd P. Gerson, 66–81. Cambridge: Cambridge University Press.
Paulsen, David L. 1990. "Early Christian Belief in a Corporeal Deity: Origen and Augustine as Reluctant Witnesses. *Harvard Theological Review* 83: 105–116.
Politis, Vasilis, ed. 2004. *Routledge Philosophy Guidebook to Aristotle and the Metaphysics*. Routledge Philosophy Guidebooks. London: Routledge.
Priestley, Joseph. 1777. *Disquisitions Relating to Matter and Spirit*. London: J. Johnson.
Rappe, Sara. 1995. "Metaphor in Plotinus' Enneads V 8.9," *Ancient Philosophy* 15: 155–172.
———. 2000. *Reading Neoplatonism: Non-Discursive Thinking in the Texts of Plotinus, Proclus, and Damascius*. Cambridge: Cambridge University Press.
Reinhardt, Karl. 1926. *Kosmos und Sympathie: Neue Untersuchungen über Poseidonios*. München: C. H. Beck.
Remes, Pauliina. 2006. "Plotinus' Ethics of Disinterested Interest," *Journal of the History of Philosophy* 44: 1–23.
———. 2008. *Neoplatonism*. Ancient Philosophies 4. Berkeley: University of California Press.
Renehan, Robert. 1980. "On the Greek Origins of the Concepts of Incorporeality and Immateriality," *Greek, Roman and Byzantine Studies* 21: 105–138.
Rist, John M. 1967. *Plotinus: The Road to Reality*. Cambridge: Cambridge University Press.
———. 1996. "Plotinus and Christian Philosophy." In *The Cambridge Companion to Plotinus*, ed. Lloyd P. Gerson, 386–414. Cambridge: Cambridge University Press.
Rocca, Julius. 2003. *Galen on the Brain: Anatomical Knowledge and Physiological Speculation in the Second Century AD*. Studies in Ancient Medicine 26. Leiden: Brill.
Rozemond, Marleen. 1998. *Descartes's Dualism*. Cambridge, MA: Harvard University Press.
Runia, David T. 1999. "A Brief History of the Term 'Kosmos Noētos' from Plato to Plotinus." In *Traditions of Platonism: Essays in Honour of John Dillon*, ed. John J. Cleary, 151–171. Aldershot: Ashgate.
Rüsche, Franz. 1933. *Das Seelenpneuma: Seine Entwicklung von der Hauchseele zur Geistseele: ein Beitrag zur Geschichte der antiken Pneumalehre*. Studien zur Geschichte und Kultur des Altertums: Ergänzungsband 18.3. Paderborn: Schöningh.
Saffrey, H. D. 1990. *Recherches sur le néoplatonisme après Plotin*. Histoire des doctrines de l'antiquité classique 14. Paris: J. Vrin.
Salaman, Clement, Dorine van Oyen, William Wharton, and Jean-Pierre Mahé, trans. 1999. *The Way of Hermes: New Translations of the Corpus Hermeticum and the Definitions of Hermes Trismegistus to Asclepius*. London: Duckworth.
Sambursky, S. 1962. *The Physical World of Late Antiquity*. New York: Basic Books.
Schibli, H. S. 1992. "Origen, Didymus, and the Vehicle of the Soul." In *Origeniana Quinta: Papers of the Fifth International Origen Congress*, ed. Robert J. Daly, 381–391. Louvain: Peeters.

Schniewind, Alexandrine. 2000. "Quelles conditions pour une éthique plotinienne? Prescription et description dans les *Ennéades*." In *Études sur Plotin*, ed. Michel Fattal, 47–73. Paris: L'Harmattan.

———. 2003. *L'éthique du sage chez Plotin: Le paradigme du spoudaios*. Histoire des doctrines de l'antiquité classique 31. Paris: J. Vrin.

Schrenk, Lawrence P., ed. 1994. *Aristotle in Late Antiquity*. Studies in Philosophy and the History of Philosophy 27. Washington, DC: Catholic University of America Press.

Shaw, Gregory. 1995. *Theurgy and the Soul: The Neoplatonism of Iamblichus*. Hermeneutics: Studies in the History of Religions. University Park: Pennsylvania State University Press.

Smith, Andrew. 1974. *Porphyry's Place in the Neoplatonic Tradition: A Study in Post-Plotinian Neoplatonism*. The Hague: M. Nijhoff.

———. 1999. "The Significance of Practical Ethics for Plotinus." In *Traditions of Platonism: Essays in Honour of John Dillon*, ed. John J. Cleary, 227–236. Aldershot: Ashgate.

———. 2004. *Philosophy in Late Antiquity*. Routledge: London.

Smith, Gregory A. 2008. "How Thin Is a Demon?" *Journal of Early Christian Studies* 16: 479–512.

Solmsen, Friedrich. 1957. "The Vital Heat, the Inborn Pneuma and the Aether," *Journal of Hellenic Studies* 77: 119–123.

Sorabji, Richard, ed. 1987. *Philoponus and the Rejection of Aristotelian Science*. London: Duckworth.

———. 1988. *Matter, Space, and Motion: Theories in Antiquity and Their Sequel*. Ithaca, NY: Cornell University Press.

———, ed. 1990. *Aristotle Transformed: The Ancient Commentators and Their Influence*. Ithaca, NY: Cornell University Press.

———. 2000. *Emotion and Peace of Mind: From Stoic Agitation to Christian Temptation*. The Gifford Lectures. Oxford: Oxford University Press.

———. 2005. *The Philosophy of the Commentators, 200–600 AD: A Sourcebook*. 3 vols. London: Duckworth.

Steel, Carlos G. 1978. *The Changing Self: A Study on the Soul in Later Neoplatonism: Iamblichus, Damascius and Priscianus*. Brussels: Paleis der Academien.

Szlezák, Thomas Alexander. 1979. *Platon und Aristoteles in der Nouslehre Plotins*. Basel: Schwabe.

Taylor, Charles. 1989. *Sources of the Self: The Making of the Modern Identity*. Cambridge, MA: Harvard University Press.

Temkin, Owsei. 1951. "On Galen's Pneumatology," *Gesnerus* 8: 180–189.

Theiler, Willy. 1955. "Gott und Seele in kaiserzeitlichen Denken." In *Recherches sur la tradition platonicienne*, ed. W. K. C. Guthrie, 66–80. Geneva: Fondation Hardt.

———. 1960. "Plotin zwischen Platon und Stoa." In *Les sources de Plotin*, 63–103. Geneva: Fondation Hardt.

———. 1966. *Forschungen zum Neuplatonismus*. Quellen und Studien zur Geschichte der Philosophie 10. Berlin: De Gruyter.

Tornau, Christian. 2005. "Plotinus' Criticism of Aristotelian Entelechism in *Enn.* IV 7(2),8.25–50." In *Studi sull'anima in Plotino*, ed. Riccardo Chiaradonna, 149–178. Naples: Bibliopolis.

van der Eijk, Philip J. 2005. "The Matter of Mind: Aristotle on the Biology of 'Psychic' Processes and the Bodily Aspects of Thinking." In *Medicine and Philosophy in*

Classical Antiquity: Doctors and Philosophers on Nature, Soul, Health and Disease, ed. Philip J. van der Eijk, 206–237. Cambridge: Cambridge University Press.

Verbeke, G. 1945. *L'évolution de la doctrine du pneuma du stoïcisme à s. Augustin: étude philosophique*. Bibliothèque de l'Institut supérieur de philosophie, Université de Louvain. Paris: Desclée de Brouwer.

Vessey, Mark. 2004. "Introduction." In *Cassiodorus: Institutions of Divine and Secular Learning and On the Soul*, ed. James W. Halporn, 1–102. Liverpool: Liverpool University Press.

von Arnim, Hans Friedrich August, ed. 1903–1924. *Stoicorum veterum fragmenta*. 4 vols. Leipzig: Teubner.

von Staden, Heinrich. 2000. "Body, Soul, and Nerves: Epicurus, Herophilus, Erasistratus, the Stoics, and Galen." In *Psyche and Soma: Physicians and Metaphysicians on the Mind-Body Problem from Antiquity to the Enlightenment*, ed. John P. Wright and Paul Potter, 79–116. Oxford: Oxford University Press.

Wagner, Mary Anthony. 1999. "A Reflection on the Use of 'Heart' in Select Prayer Texts in Early Christianity." In *Purity of Heart in Early Ascetic and Monastic Literature: Essays in Honor of Juana Raasch, O.S.B.*, ed. Harriet A. Luckman and Linda Kulzer, 131–139. Collegeville, MN: Liturgical Press.

Wagner, Michael F. 1996. "Plotinus on the Nature of Physical Reality." In *The Cambridge Companion to Plotinus*, ed. Lloyd P. Gerson, 130–170. Cambridge: Cambridge University Press.

Wallis, R. T. 1972. *Neoplatonism*. Classical Life and Letters. London: Duckworth.

Wear, Sarah Klitenic, and John Dillon. 2007. *Dionysius the Areopagite and the Neoplatonist Tradition: Despoiling the Hellenes*. Ashgate Studies in Philosophy and Theology in Late Antiquity. Aldershot: Ashgate.

Westerink, L. G., ed. and trans. 1962. *Anonymous Prolegomena to Platonic Philosophy*. Amsterdam: North-Holland.

Wildberg, Christian. 1988. *John Philoponus' Criticism of Aristotle's Theory of Aether*. Peripatoi 16. Berlin: de Gruyter.

Zambon, Marco. 2005. "Il significato filosofico della dottrina dell' ὄχημα dell' anima." In *Studi sull'anima in Plotino*, ed. Riccardo Chiaradonna, 305–335. Naples: Bibliopolis.

CHAPTER 17

TRAVEL, CARTOGRAPHY, AND COSMOLOGY

SCOTT FITZGERALD JOHNSON
Georgetown University and Dumbarton Oaks

> The map and the library are two aspects of the same project: organizing and codifying knowledge. Both of them rely on accumulation, on tradition, on authority. Some maps could be considered condensed and portable visual libraries, while libraries' catalogs are sometimes organized as a map—a map of culture, of scholarly disciplines, of literary genres. The map and the library are icons of knowledge.
>
> Christian Jacob, *The Sovereign Map*, xix

Travel

The oldest western travel account to have survived from the ancient world (besides Homer's *Odyssey*) is Hanno the Carthaginian's *Periplous* (lit. "sailing around"). It purports to be a translation from Phoenician into Greek and dates (probably) to the fifth century B.C.E.[1] The text consists of a series of episodes along the western coast of Africa. It organizes the ports, the peoples, and the curiosities it contains all within the structure of the voyage itself. This paradigm was a technical genre in the ancient world and provided the framework for sea captains, explorers, and other travelers to publish, at the least, a basic record of the ports along sea or river routes or, at the most, an encyclopedic work containing many disparate types of information. Prominent examples of this mainly Greek genre from the ancient world include Ps.-Scylax,[2] Nearchus the Cretan (as received via Arrian's *Indica*),[3] Pytheas of Marseille (320 B.C.E., fragmentary),[4] the anonymous *Periplous of the Red Sea* (first century C.E.),[5] Arrian's *Periplous of the Black Sea* (second century C.E.),[6] the fragmentary *Stadiasmus Magni Maris* (third century C.E.),[7] Avienus' Latin *Ora Maritima* (fourth century C.E.),[8] and Marcian of Heraclea Pontica's *Periplous of the "Outer" Sea* (c. 400 C.E.).[9] The *periplous* genre often mixed with popular literary forms, such as paradoxography—a typically Hellenistic (i.e., post-Aristotelian) genre that collected natural wonders and portents[10]—and the ancient novels (both Greek and Latin), almost all of which contain at the center an episodic journey. The Greek tradition finds its most popular geographical text in the *Periegesis* ("leading around") of Dionysius Periegetes (fl. 117–138 C.E.).[11] Less technical in tone than the *periplous*, the *periegesis* was also a revered genre in Greek. In form, it is a literary description of the known world, often in verse. The genre was originally associated with the fifth-century B.C.E. writer Hecataeus of Miletus and was known to Herodotus, but Dionysius was its most famous exponent for later readers: his work was translated into Latin numerous times, not least by Avienus in the fourth century and by the grammarian Priscian in sixth-century Constantinople, both in verse.[12] Dionysius' contemporary, Pausanias of Magnesia, wrote an archaizing, compilatory *Description of Greece* that most closely resembles the *periegesis* genre, though the *Description* is in prose and is a much more audacious work in many ways, partly due to its prominent religious content, as well as its association with the Greek *theoria* tradition of corporate pilgrimage.[13] Pausanias is also largely (though not exclusively) anachronistic in his attempt to recapture the classical Greek landscape, in defiance of his Roman imperial context.

Dionysius, Pausanias, and others wrote Greek *periploi* and *periegeseis* under Roman rule, but Roman writers in Latin, generally speaking, preferred the overland genre, the *itinerarium*. This is perhaps due to their mature tradition of land surveying (known from a sixth-century C.E. collection called the *Agrimensores*), as well as to their demonstrable commitment to infrastructure (namely, roads, forts, and way stations).[14] The *Antonine Itinerary* of about 300 C.E. offers an example of an imperial *itinerarium* with a clear dependence on the Roman road network and its overlying provincial system, both of which serve as conceptual frameworks that enable its literary expression.[15] Within these frameworks, an individual could chart his or her own travel experiences, making use of customary habits of writing. The data collected along the way, which could be as bare as merely the number of Roman miles between staging posts, were easily slotted into the genre as a linear narrative, serving imperial or other interests. In an *itinerarium*, both writer and reader make the journey out, to a destination, and the journey back, to the starting point.[16] Additionally, with the broad adoption of the codex in the Mediterranean in the later third and fourth centuries C.E., a reader could access the narrative at multiple random points, without having to read through the linear progression in toto, as with a scroll.[17] For this reason, the *Antonine Itinerary*—originally an early Roman imperial or even republican document—was recopied into an enlarged, late antique form and made more useful via the codex.[18] This tradition depended on the Roman *cursus publicus* and involves, at a basic level, the compilation and repackaging of information from Roman milestones set up all along this imperial road system.[19] The *cursus publicus* dominates the pictorial landscape of the famous Peutinger Table—remarkably, the only surviving world map of Greco-Roman antiquity. This aesthetic choice is discussed later.

The Christian adoption of the *itinerarium* genre began in 333 C.E. with the anonymous Bordeaux pilgrim.[20] Following the unitary Mediterranean rule of the emperor Constantine I (from 324) and the subsequent travels of his mother, Helena, in the eastern empire (326–327), the Holy Land became a livelier destination for well-off travelers.[21] This advent of Christian travel to the East coincided with the monumentalization of the region, with imperially sponsored churches and other buildings.[22] However, the relationship between these two phenomena is a complex one, and I would hesitate to argue that either one was the cause of the other. For instance, it is not clear whether Helena's visit was a pilgrimage based on her Christian faith or was made for some other political or personal reason (e.g., the executions of Crispus and Fausta in 326).[23]

Since the *Bordeaux Pilgrim* is written in the *itinerarium* genre, it mostly reads like a list of cities, miles, and way stations. However, the author manipulates the genre, first, to include various points of interest (mainly pagan/traditional) along the route—not unlike the *periplous* tradition. Second, when it comes to Jerusalem, the narrative blossoms out quite substantially and becomes a topography of the city, based on biblical sites (mainly Jewish) and implementing the cognitive tool of stacking holy sites across the centuries, a hallmark of all subsequent pilgrimage texts. The *Bordeaux Pilgrim* does mention four Constantinian churches—Golgotha, Bethlehem, Mount of Olives, and Mamre—but this number is dwarfed by the huge number of Jewish sites, perhaps signaling an established Jewish pilgrimage network that is unknown from other contemporary sources.[24] Narratively speaking, the *Bordeaux Pilgrim* becomes quite a different type of text in the Jerusalem section, with both space and time being conceived in a more detailed or granular fashion.

Another Constantinian-era text, not a pilgrimage account but a text that bears on the biblical character of early Christian pilgrimage narrative, is Eusebius of Caesarea's *Onomasticon* (c. 300), or "name-book."[25] This alphabetized work proceeds book by book in the Bible (within a given letter of the Greek alphabet) and provides contemporary names and information on sites mentioned therein. Its main purpose was to correlate lost Hebrew toponyms with their Greco-Roman equivalents. This is the kind of book that would have been much less useful without the codex technology, and scholars have recently drawn attention to the glut of technical or informational literature, mainly biblical in orientation, that emerged from the library of Caesarea.[26] This literature includes Origen's famous *Hexapla*, which compared Greek versions of the Hebrew Bible with the Septuagint and the Hebrew text (6 to 9 columns a spread, depending on the edition), and Eusebius' *Chronici Canones*, which became a standard tool in the Middle Ages (as did the *Onomasticon*) through Jerome's Latin translations and extensions.[27] A key difference between the *Onomasticon* and the *Bordeaux Pilgrim*, of course, is that the *Onomasticon* is not organized as a narrative, or linear, text. However, they both use their literary forms as means of accumulation and organization, and both texts presage later developments within their genres and among late antique writers generally. Jerome's scholarly interest in biblical geography, derived from Eusebius, was combined with a keen appreciation for the spiritual value of Christian pilgrimage, a practice that Eusebius does not comment on.[28] Thus, the fourth-century crystallization of these parallel traditions—biblical scholarship and pilgrimage—finds their meeting point in the work of Jerome: this is a conclusion one could make merely from the titles of individual works, but only recently has geography been recognized as a constituent component of Jerome's entire corpus.[29]

Shortly before Jerome's installation in Bethlehem, the western pilgrim Egeria spent the years 381–384 traveling to numerous sites in the Holy Land, in and around Jerusalem, as well as far to the south (Sinai) and north (Edessa).[30] While Egeria makes use of the *itinerarium* form, she also includes many details of the sites she visits and, like the *Bordeaux Pilgrim*, quotes Scripture. However, Egeria's bibliophilia is much more prominent: she notes that she carries around codices of the Bible, which she pulls out whenever an apt passage needs to be read on site (e.g., 10.41, ed. Bieler), but she also has copies (or obtains them on the way) of apocryphal narratives, such as the *Acts of Thomas* and the Abgar correspondence at Edessa in northern Mesopotamia (19) and the *Acts of Thekla* at Seleucia in southern Asia Minor (23). This aspect of her text is very important in that it shows how hagiography, the Bible, and travel literature were all coming together during the late fourth century and how hybrid literary forms were being forged at the same time as the Christian imagination was extending the received history of the Hebrew and apostolic worlds.[31] Another important aspect of Egeria's narrative is the time she takes to describe living holy men in situ in the Holy Land. This is important, of course, for the light it sheds on the emergence of asceticism and monasticism during the fourth century, but for my purposes, it shows how Egeria can connect the holy deeds of the Christian past with the holy people she meets in the flesh.[32] The line between pilgrimage narrative and saint's Life blurs even more in these sections. Finally, and to return to the theme of accumulation, Egeria organizes this diversity of information and observation through two modes: (1) her itinerary itself, which provides a narrative framework, as with the *Bordeaux Pilgrim* (though Egeria makes major detours off the beaten path), and (2) a now truncated account of the Jerusalem Holy Week liturgy, which makes up the second half of the text. I have chosen here not to discuss the latter, but it is an evocative, microcosmical (or cross-sectional) counterpart to the grand tour narrative in the first half. That dual perspective, and the different modes of accumulation and organization within a single text, is deserving of further exploration at length elsewhere.

A secular analogue to the *Bordeaux Pilgrim* and Egeria is the *Expositio totius mundi* (c. 350–360), which has long been prized as a source for the vitality of trade and commerce in the late Roman economy.[33] Alongside this evidentiary value, the text proves to follow the established literary pattern, moving around the empire, province by province, in a linear and episodic fashion. However, this is not an *itinerarium*: the episodes describe the chief cities and exports in each province, and many ancillary details enliven the narrative.[34] Not unlike Egeria in this way, the *Expositio* creatively fills the received literary framework with disparate types of information, so that the reader gets the sense that its synoptic view of the empire is simultaneously encyclopedic in scope.[35] The opening section, a portion of which survives in a later Greek recension, eschews imperial boundaries—as one sees later with Cosmas Indicopleustes—and discusses far eastern people groups, some legendary, in an ethnographical manner (3–21).[36] By contrast, the western extremities of the known world, such as Britannia, are given much less attention in the closing sections (67–68). This compendious quality of the *Expositio*, particularly in its purported knowledge of the East, has often been overlooked because of the text's value for history within the empire, but the *Expositio* nevertheless contributes an important voice to the overarching trend toward literary experimentation within received forms among geographical writers of the fourth century.

To return to Christian pilgrimage, other texts build on Egeria's use of the *itinerarium* model, not least the anonymous *Piacenza Pilgrim* from the mid-sixth century, which demonstrates an even more expressive devotional quality.[37] The New Testament is much more prominent in the *Piacenza Pilgrim*, and established patterns of movement and veneration are readily apparent. At the end of the seventh century, the abbot of the Iona monastery, Adomnán—most famous for his *Life of St. Columba*—produced a work called *On the Holy Places* (*De locis sanctis*).[38] Ostensibly a pilgrimage account dictated by the Frankish bishop Arculf, who had shipwrecked on the western shore of Scotland during his return from Jerusalem (a nearly impossible trajectory), the *De locis sanctis* has been shown to be, in certain sections, a patchwork of scholarly observations taken from earlier authors, particularly Jerome.[39] Significant as it is that the *De locis sanctis* is (1) the first post–Arab Conquest pilgrimage narrative to have survived (thus necessarily including some original material at least, particularly for Alexandria) and (2) the basis for the Venerable Bede's own *De locis sanctis* a generation later, one of its most important qualities has been somewhat overlooked: namely, that it amasses and organizes information about the Holy Land that previously appeared in separate books, synthesizing this material through the (potentially artificial) device of a contemporary pilgrim's own words. This is not the last time a Christian travel narrative makes use of such a device: as late as the fourteenth century, an Anglo-Norman travelogue in the name of Sir John Mandeville is likewise considered largely invention on the basis of previous texts.[40] In the preceding twelfth and thirteenth centuries, the *Imago Mundi* of Honorius Augustodunensis was followed by the gargantuan *Otia Imperialia* by Gervasius of Tilbury and the even more massive *Speculum Maius* of Vincent of Beauvais. These were geographical compendia, with roots in both the *itinerarium* and encyclopedic traditions, that exploded the boundaries of this scholarly invention beyond all recognition.[41]

Cartography

Sometime in the late fourth or early fifth century C.E., a map was produced covering the whole of the known world.[42] This famous map, called the Peutinger Table (*Tabula Peutingeriana*) after its early modern owner Konrad Peutinger (1465–1547), has long been the subject of scholarly investigation and debate.[43] The copy that has come down to us dates to around 1200 but is thought to reproduce its predecessor more or less accurately. In conception, the Peutinger Table is schematic, not resembling anything modern viewers might recognize as a map. It is severely elongated, and its horizontal length—as much as 8.6 meters at one estimate—is the determining visual characteristic.[44] At thirty-three centimeters high, the map squeezes the ancient world into an extraordinarily narrow frame: Italy is completely horizontal, and the Mediterranean Sea occupies a narrow strip of water at its center (figure 17.1). Its visual depiction of the *oikoumene* is thus quite striking and even disorienting for modern viewers who are used to looking at scale maps.[45] The Peutinger Table has been read in recent scholarship as a prime exemplar of Roman imperial mapping techniques and, more generally, as a cipher of the perception of space by late Roman travelers.

As such, the Peutinger Table's second most salient feature is the huge quantity of cities and smaller towns listed on the map, all connected by a vast network of highways and roads. Icons of varying sizes represent cities, hostels, waypoints, baths, and imperial capitals: basic information for a user of the map on the ground but comprehensive in its scope. Not unlike the comparable *Notitia Dignitatum* (figure 17.2), also from the fourth or fifth century, the Peutinger Table appears to be an attempt to take account of the entire material and topographical infrastructure of the late Roman world.[46] Significantly, both documents express this infrastructure through a geographical depiction of the world, however schematic or stylized it may be.

The title *tabula* is a modern moniker and not the standard word for "map" (*forma*) in the Roman world.[47] Nevertheless, the title can perhaps be helpful as an interpretative tool. The modern English adjective *tabular* has connotations of the Latin *tabula*, both in its meaning "table" and in its metaphorical meaning "accounts table" or "register." Here, both connotations deriving from *tabula* are

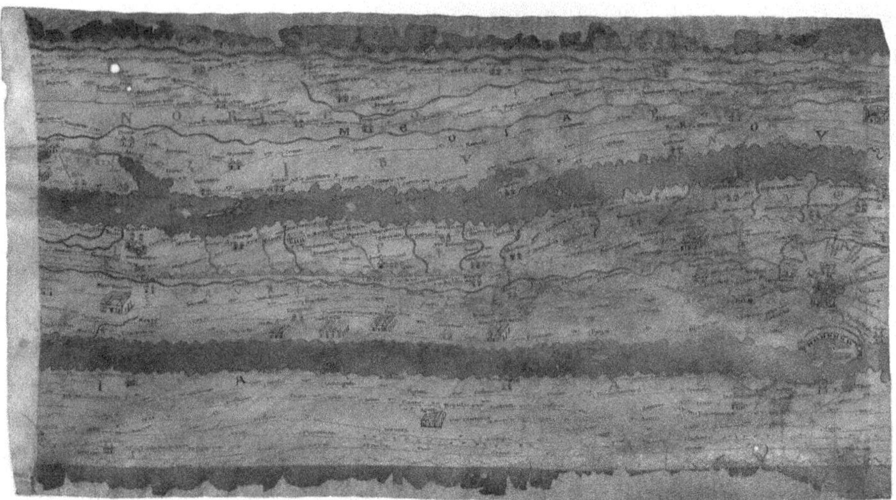

Figure 17.1. Peutinger Table. Section 4, selection of Rome and central Italy (Reproduced with permission of the Austrian National Library). See also color plate section.

appropriate: certainly, the Peutinger Table is able to be spread out and viewed on a table—in fact, that is one of the few ways to view it as a whole—and, moreover, it retains a workmanlike aesthetic in its accumulation of topographical ephemera of the empire. In addition, the word *tabula* also has the meaning "picture" or "painting" (*tabula picta*), which perhaps carries a connotation of the viewer's appreciation of the flat surface of the work. One might adduce here Ptolemy's comments on globes versus planar (i.e., flat) maps in *Geography* 1.20–21: "[Making the map on a globe] does not conveniently allow for a size [of map] capable of most of the things that have to be inscribed on it, nor can it permit the sight to fix on [the map] in a way that grasps the whole shape all at once."[48] So perhaps the Latin word *tabula* is helpful after all. Thus interpreted, it calls to mind three provisional qualities identifiable in the Peutinger Table and, indeed, in geographical literature from Late Antiquity in general, some of which has already been discussed:

1. The accumulation and organization of complete knowledge, "encyclopedism," especially as an aesthetic choice or argument[49]
2. Two-dimensionality, often on a grand scale but with attendant distortion
3. A precarious balance between the apparent intentions of the work and the requirements of the viewer or reader (i.e., with or without practical benefits)

These three fundamental qualities appear in different guises, depending on the work in question, be it visual or literary, but they show up repeatedly, a fact suggesting that the Peutinger Table can be viewed as a product of geographical thought in Late Antiquity as much or more than as a product of its Roman sources.

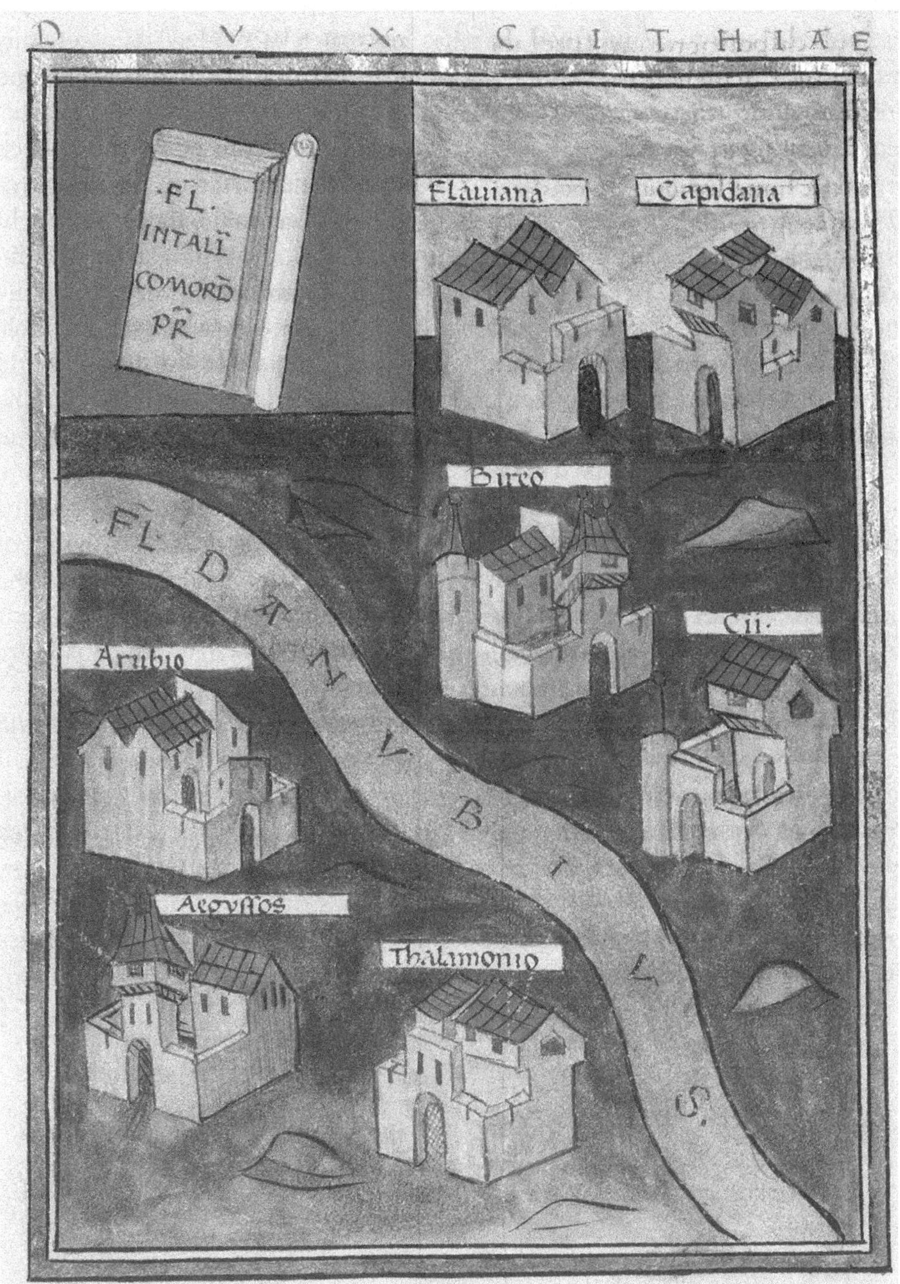

Figure 17.2. *Notitia Dignitatum*. "Dux Cithiae." Fol. 101 verso. Basel, c. 1436. MS Latin 9661 in the Bibliothèque Nationale de France, Paris (Reproduced with permission of the Bibliothèque Nationale de France, Paris). See also color plate section.

A comparable map, in scope if not in content, comes from the earliest stage of our period: namely, the Severan marble plan of the city of Rome, known as the Forma Urbis Romae. Set up by Septimius Severus in the restored Templum Pacis, this gargantuan inscribed map has long been recognized as essentially impractical for the urban traveler in the city.[50] For one, its height, scale, and detail would have made a quick consultation of the map impossible. In particular, a ladder was required to make use of the minute details of the plan, which seems to have prohibited a functional viewing of the map at a distance (figures 17.3 and 17.4). Further, if viewers trusted the information on the map, they might not arrive at their destination, since the map (what survives of it, at least) is inaccurate in a number of places.[51] The question of inaccuracy, however, is not the most pertinent theme. Rather, the Forma Urbis Romae, like the Peutinger Table after it, makes a visual statement about the conception of the (local) world through its accumulation and organization of knowledge. Jennifer Trimble argues that the Forma Urbis Romae should be interpreted in light of "the grand Roman tradition of imperial visual monuments," such as the Column of Trajan. Both of these monuments, according to Trimble, "overwhelm the viewer with a mass of veristic detail."[52] The word *veristic* is helpful in that the huge amount of detail on an overwhelming canvas is what produces the aesthetic effect on the viewer. As Richard Talbert has noted in a comparison of the two maps, "Their design makes a feature of incorporating quantities of items that individually are dull, even trivial, but cumulatively make a powerful impression."[53]

The interplay between the collection of information, practicable or not, and the aesthetic rendering of that information is crucial also to the emergence of pilgrimage literature in the Christian Roman empire. There is thus an important connection between the Peutinger Table and the pilgrimage texts discussed previously. The scholarly debate over the Peutinger Table centers on just how fundamental the *itinerarium* genre is to the composition of the map. Talbert has argued for a "holistic" approach, reading the route network alongside the more decorative elements of the map. In Talbert's words,

> I see it as a project of a single designer, who was already an experienced cartographer, but who was sufficiently creative and ambitious to experiment here both with the map's shape and with featuring land routes. He aimed above all to convey how civilized, peaceful, and united an appearance the entire *orbis terrarum* presented under Roman sway, with the city of Rome at its center and focal point.[54]

This statement stands in contrast to the approach of Kai Brodersen, particularly in his preference to understand the Peutinger Table as merely a visual key to a list of destinations, a true *itinerarium pictum*. In Brodersen's view, the Peutinger Table behaves most like the London Tube map, which connects stations without direct reference to overland geography.[55] Like the Table's Mediterranean strip of water, the only real-world geographical feature on a Tube map is the River Thames (one crucial datum, however, being which side of the river you are

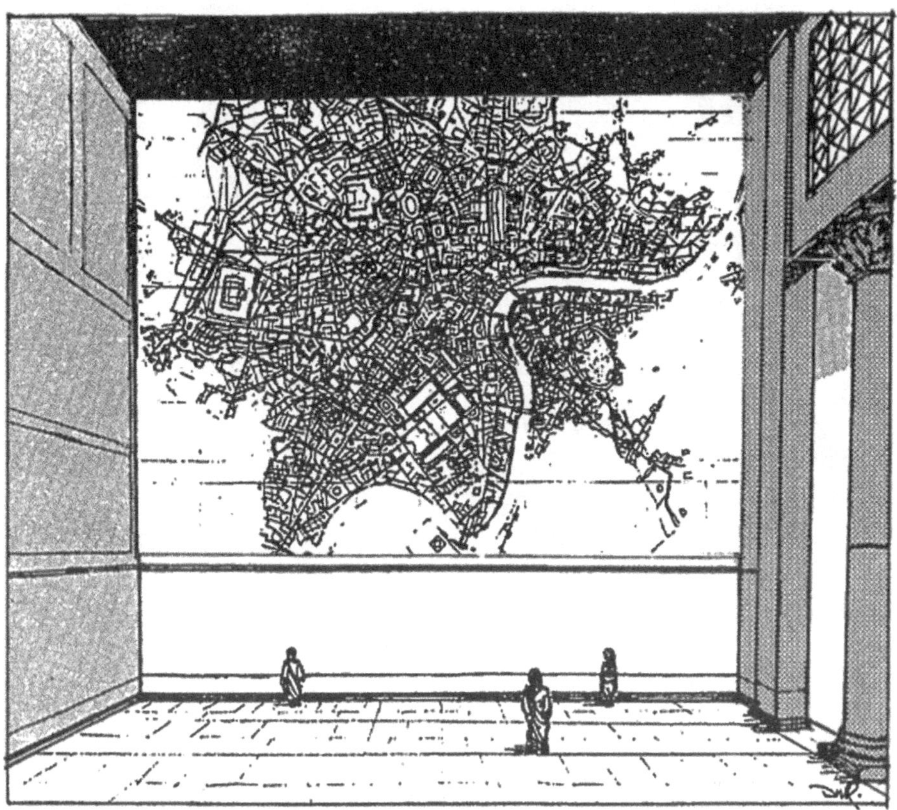

Figure 17.3. Forma Urbis Romae. Reconstruction from D. W. Reynolds, "Forma Urbis Romae: The Severan Marble Plan and the Urban Form of Ancient Rome." Ph.D. Thesis, University of Michigan, 1996 (© David West Reynolds, courtesy Phaeton Group).

on).[56] Talbert, by contrast, underscores the fact that numerous labels of gulfs, inlets, and islands seem to reveal a cartographer very concerned about the physical geography of the seas.[57] However, the Bosporus and Golden Horn are uncharacteristically exaggerated on the Peutinger Table, and Sardinia's route network (known from the *Antonine Itinerary*, c. 300) is completely absent. Thus, the accuracy of the physical geography, even with regard to maritime details, is uneven. Nevertheless, emphasizing the detail of its physical features rather than its hodological qualities, Talbert states, "No one was ever meant to consult it seriously as a guide to land routes"; referring to both the Peutinger Table and the Forma Urbis Romae, he claims, "Neither was ever seriously intended for use."[58]

While these two views of the Peutinger Table—the hodological and the physical/aesthetic—have each been helpful in teaching us how to read this complex map, a central vexing question still remains: why did the author of the Peutinger Table care so much about cartographic detail? If it is merely a route map, or primarily meant to adorn, what is the virtue of minutely rendered (and

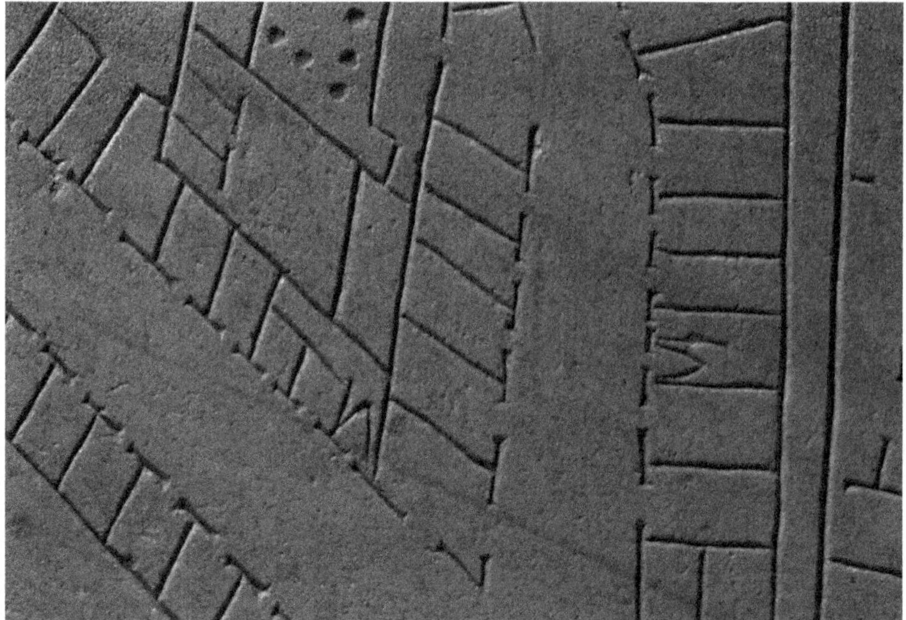

Figure 17.4. Forma Urbis Romae. Detail from Stanford Digital Forma Urbis Romae Project. http://formaurbis.stanford.edu (Reproduced with permission of the Stanford Digital Forma Urbis Romae Project).

often accurate) Mediterranean coastlines? Perhaps here Trimble's felicitous phrase "vertiginous cartography," in reference to the Forma Urbis Romae, is especially helpful as an aesthetic cipher: "The map's totality impinged on the eye."[59] The stockpiling of data is its own artistic argument. Once this principle is accepted, moreover, there are other avenues of inquiry that may yield an even more precise appreciation of the compilatory aesthetic: first, the relation of the Peutinger Table and the *itinerarium* tradition to ancient science (geography, astrology, cosmography) and second, the larger movement of literary history in Late Antiquity, namely, the trend toward encyclopedism across many disparate genres.

Cosmology

The question remains open as to how late antique maps and *itineraria* relate to ancient geographical models, scientific and non-. Talbert states the following in his assessment of the physical features of the Peutinger Table: "Generally speaking, it would seem probable that the map's base reflects the unrivaled geographic and cartographic learning that was developed in third-century [B.C.E.] Alexandria by Eratosthenes and his successors."[60] This view is far from incontrovertible. For one, we know that the scientific trajectory from Eudoxus of Cnidus (c. 408–347 B.C.E.) and Eratosthenes (c. 275–194 B.C.E.) to Ptolemy (c. 90–168 C.E.) was to some degree lost in the high empire and Late Antiquity, only to be recovered by medieval scholars in Muslim Spain.[61] Further, it cannot be overemphasized that the geographical conclusions of Ptolemy and subsequent writers were influenced by their cosmologies and astronomical conclusions. The very influential *Natural History* of Pliny the Elder demonstrated this view in the first century: "The organization of the revolutions of heaven is more appropriately discussed in the section on geography, since it pertains wholly to that subject."[62] This understanding persisted among geographical writers, and late antique depictions of the *oikoumene* should thus be read in concert with contemporary views of the planets and celestial heavens. This is true for fourth-century pilgrimage literature as much as it is for a unique cosmological schema like that of Cosmas Indicopleustes in his *Christian Topography* (c. 550). Before these Christian texts can be brought into focus, however, Ptolemy's reception in subsequent centuries requires further investigation.

Many aspects of Ptolemy's thought were in use in Late Antiquity, but others, such as Ptolemy's relentless commitment to empirical research, were not. In particular, the accurate representation of the longitude and latitude of any given locale is ultimately based on repeated observations of astronomical phenomena, ideally at disparate points on the earth. Hipparchus (fl. c.150–125 B.C.E.) made use of extensive Assyrian and Persian records of celestial observation, particularly observations of eclipses going back 600 years.[63] In turn, Ptolemy, in the second century C.E., made use of Hipparchus' evidence and models but extended and improved on them mathematically, attempting to start afresh with only the observable phenomena as given.[64] His conclusions, famously, drove him to break with the cosmology of Aristotle and to assert the independence of the motion of the planets—philosophically, this is an explicit move back to Platonic conclusions, though derived by different means.[65] Simultaneously, these observations allowed him to produce, it would seem, accurate maps of the *oikoumene* that accompanied his *Geography*. However, it is not at all certain that Ptolemy's maps even survived into Late Antiquity and Byzantium. Certainly, we have medieval copies of maps under the name of Ptolemy, but how these copies relate to maps Ptolemy may have drawn himself is unclear.[66] Some scholars have even denied Ptolemy drew maps at all.[67] Most important, however, is the fact that, among surviving late antique authors, there was no dedicated attempt to replicate Ptolemy's assiduously observational or "positivistic" (to use an anachronistic term) approach to natural phenomena. Stated most bluntly,

> Ptolemy had no successor. No Greek astronomer who followed him managed to advance the enterprise. Pappus and Theon of Alexandria (fourth century CE) wrote commentaries on the *Almagest*, but these had little to add to Ptolemy. After Ptolemy, astronomy marked time for six hundred years, until the Islamic revival of astronomy that began around 800 CE.[68]

Setting aside for the moment the teleological tone of this statement—we will return to the contribution of the commentary tradition later—it nevertheless highlights the following basic point: that any assumption of a Ptolemaic underpinning to the Peutinger Table is perilous, since the Table comes at least three to four hundred years after Ptolemy and, even if it represents earlier traditions, almost certainly does not emerge from a late antique Alexandrian-Ptolemaic school of astronomy.[69] Ptolemy's reception in Late Antiquity was vibrant in two areas of study, and here, at least, he is well represented in the literary history: (1) cosmology and (2) predictions of the movements of the stars and planets.[70] The first area appears primarily in a theological and metaphysical framework, and the second is associated with astrology and divination. Both areas have implications for geographical writing in the period, and both find the encyclopedic mode of writing germane to their subject.

The first area of study, cosmology, focused on Ptolemy's preference, as already noted, for the Platonic view of autonomous or "independent" motion in the planets, over and against the systematic or "unitary" Aristotelian system of eccentrics and epicycles.[71] The Neoplatonist Proclus Diadochus (412–485 C.E.) agreed strongly with Ptolemy on this point. Nevertheless, the received dictum of Plato to "save the appearances" (Simplicius *De Caelo* 488.23)—that is, to strive to account for celestial motion by as simple an explanation as possible—was understood by Neoplatonic writers in a very different way than Ptolemy had interpreted it. Proclus was critical that Ptolemy never sought out the "real" (i.e., theological) cause of planetary motion, which, as Plotinus (c. 204–270 C.E.) had explained, was the perpetual emanation of the ineffable Monad down through the divine "Mind" and "Soul" into the celestial and natural world. Stars were made of divine power, and celestial motion was directly connected to the ongoing emanation of the One.[72] Further, though he was a Neoplatonist, Proclus can even be seen to occasionally lament the loss of a complete, aesthetically simple system like the one Aristotle had devised.[73] Thus, Proclus' central argument, as found in his *Elements of Astronomy* (ed. Manitius 1974 [1909]) and his *Commentary on the Timaeus* (ed. Lang et al. 2001), is that mathematics and philosophical simplicity are of greater explanatory value than observation. Later, Simplicius (c. 490–560 C.E.), in his *Commentary on Aristotle's De Caelo* (ed. Heiberg 1894), would argue along identical lines to Proclus, claiming that nothing in the celestial heaven was changeable since it possessed the divine power.[74] The practice of observation was the domain of mere "astronomers."[75] Ptolemy had valued simplicity, too, but when the mathematics did not fit the data, he had preferred to change the mathematics, rather than ignore the data. We might laud this commitment of Ptolemy's as "scientific" and as contributing to the teleology of modern science, but the point is often overlooked that, for many late antique authors, the theological and metaphysical implications of Ptolemy's approach were more important than the verifiability of his data.

In the sixth century, the Christian philosopher John Philoponus cited Ptolemy in his *Against Proclus on the Eternity of the World* (529 C.E.), arguing that the mutability of the stars and planets was observable in their motions, as proven by observations.[76] Philoponus continued such arguments in his *Against Aristotle on the Eternity of the World* (530–534 C.E.): the only immutable thing, he argued, was God alone, who had created the world *ex nihilo*. Creation *ex nihilo* was, as is well known, anathema to the Neoplatonists, and Simplicius responded directly to this claim of Philoponus in his book *On the Eternity of the World against Philoponus* (after 534 C.E.).[77] Thus, Neoplatonists and Christians alike were unwilling to cede Ptolemy's (accepted) authority to the other camp, and, although each ultimately was more interested in the system than the content, Ptolemy's writings were certainly in circulation and held a gravitas that is unavailable to the historian of science interested only in constructing a teleology of the modern disciplines.

Broader histories of science in the period have highlighted the enormous interest in Ptolemy's *Handy Tables* (Κανόνες πρόχειροι), a summary of astronomical predictions based on the Almagest (i.e., the Μαθηματικὴ σύνταξις), on which, in turn, numerous commentaries were written from the fourth century. Not the least of these were the "Great" and "Little" commentaries on the *Handy Tables* by Theon of Alexandria, the mathematician and father of Hypatia.[78] The *Handy Tables* was translated into Latin, under the title *Preceptum Canonis Ptolomei*, sometime before 550 (probably c. 535), when it was used by Cassiodorus in his survey of basic astronomical terminology in book 2 of the *Institutes* (153–157, ed. Mynors).[79] One might point also to Boethius' (lost) Latin translation of "Ptolemy the astronomer," which Theodoric praised through an official commendation drafted by Cassiodorus (*Variae*, 1.45, 506 C.E., ed. Mommsen). Boethius' desire to construct an encyclopedia of world knowledge, alongside his projected translations of the complete works of Plato and Aristotle, coincides with the late antique goal of systematizing within the framework of the *auctores*, while simultaneously making the works more accessible (through translation and abbreviation) and more coherent within a Christian worldview. Thus, the late antique technical disciplines of commentary, compilation, translation, and systematization—precisely what late authors were very good at—are demonstrably in full swing with geographical and astronomical thought.

On this basis, one might reasonably claim—in contrast to Talbert's previous argument—that the most significant connection between the Peutinger Table and Ptolemy in Late Antiquity was not, primarily at least, a shared scientific view of physical geography but, rather, a shared attraction to the collection and repackaging of preexistent knowledge (from various sources) in a systematic, digestible form. The systematic element is both aesthetic and functional; the mode can be the message. As an additional example of this convergence, one might cite the fact that the ancient disciplines of astronomy and astrology equally made use of mathematics, produced tables of celestial phenomena, and wrote epitomes and commentaries on earlier works. Their shared modus operandi included the observation and collection of celestial phenomena.

Observation was perhaps even more important to the astrologer, since most astronomers, Ptolemy excepted, made the observations fit the schema (rather than vice versa), whereas accurate observation (ἀκρίβεια) was crucial to the trade and profit of an astrologer, as was emphasized by astrologers from Manilius (fl. c. 10–20 C.E.) through Hephaistion (c. 415 C.E.).[80] Of course, astrology and astronomy were socially and professionally overlapping disciplines in the ancient world (unlike today), and Ptolemy himself produced (like Brahe and Kepler after him) a work of astrology, the ἀποτελεσματικά or τετράβιβλος.[81] However, the salient connection between these disciplines in Late Antiquity was not the obvious mutual interest in the stars or movements of the planets but, again, their mode of literary and cartographic production, and in the amassing and streamlining of evidence as an argument unto itself.

To cast the net somewhat wider, the collection of functional data as a literary mode can be found in diverse late antique Latin texts, from Macrobius' *Commentary on the Dream of Scipio* (c. 430),[82] to Martianus Capella's *Marriage of Philology and Mercury* (late fifth century),[83] to Gregory of Tours' *On the Course of the Stars* (after 573),[84] to Aethicus Ister (c. 700),[85] and to the *Ravenna Cosmography* (c. 700).[86] While not a complete list by any means, all of these examples could reasonably be labeled encyclopedic, and all have what might be called an "archival aesthetic."[87] Additionally, all of them mix geographical and cosmological theories within the encyclopedic schema. Far less technical than a Ptolemy or a Philoponus, Macrobius' *Commentary* is best read as a layman's handbook or miscellany on natural science, in the vein of the more philologically oriented *Attic Nights* of Aulus Gellius (b. 125–128 C.E.).[88] However, the work is structured around a classical text, the *Somnium Scipionis*, the last book of Cicero's (now mostly lost) *De republica* (before 50 B.C.E.).[89] Macrobius draws liberally on predecessors in the Neoplatonic mold, notably Porphyry (234–c. 305 C.E.), whose lost *Commentary on the Timaeus* probably provided most of the material for Macrobius' discussion of astronomy.[90] From a medieval Western point of view, we can set Macrobius alongside the fourth-century Chalcidius, a Christian who also knew Porphyry's *Commentary* and produced his own (very popular) translation and commentary on Plato's *Timaeus*.[91]

Martianus Capella, in the late fifth century, holds as high or higher a distinction among medieval writers, though his *Marriage of Philology and Mercury* is structured in a unique manner: not as a commentary but as a pedagogical argument for a system of *trivium* and *quadrivium*, the seven liberal arts, which is addressed to his son and predicated on the mythical apotheosis of the goddess Philologia.[92] While not organized in a dictionary or headword fashion like the later, equally influential *Etymologiae* of Isidore of Seville (c. 600–636), the work is often called an encyclopedia because of its universal scope and also, perhaps, because of how it was later used as a school textbook.[93] In any case, Martianus' text, as unusual as the setting may be, is mainly a culling and compilation of classical authorities on his seven chosen subjects. The astronomical section reproduces the familiar ancient system of standard works, such as Aratus' *Phaenomena* (third century B.C.E.) and Geminus' *Introduction to Astronomy* (c. 50 C.E.), though Capella does cite Ptolemy as an authority on both geographical (Geometria) and astronomical (Astronomica) subjects (once each).[94]

A very different combination of archive and cosmography comes from the bishop Gregory of Tours at the end of the sixth century in his treatise *On the Course of the Stars* (*De cursu stellarum*).[95] This work was intended as a handbook for monks who were in charge of regulating the times of prayer at their monasteries.[96] The requirement that the hours of prayer be governed by watching the stars is first mentioned by John Cassian, but he does not describe the method to be used for such calculations.[97] Gregory provides the earliest surviving technical manual for this,[98] but the book reveals a debt to classical astronomy that extends beyond his immediate practical purposes. In the second half of the book, he provides a comprehensive, if brief, survey of celestial phenomena (mainly specific constellations but also comets). He disputes pagan astrological interpretations while admitting that some phenomena are true supernatural signs.[99] The first half of the book is taken up with a discussion of natural wonders (*miracula*), a subject that aligns well with the persistent late antique view of astronomy that allied it with geography and the work of creation in Genesis.[100]

The literary forgery (*Schwindelliteratur*) preserved under the title *Aethicus Ister*—attributed to Jerome, though almost certainly late seventh century in composition (c. 655–725)—combines the cosmographical and encyclopedic approach with the classical philosophical journey (*Philosophenroman*), a form made famous by Philostratus' *Life of Apollonius of Tyana* (c. 200 C.E.).[101] *Aethicus Ister* includes at the beginning a general narrative of cosmogony, purportedly written by the pagan philosopher and "chosmografus" Aethicus (88.2, ed. Prinz), and next proceeds to recount the journeys of Aethicus around Europe (including Ireland) and the Mediterranean (esp. Greece). Within the playful genre of the literary parody—or even hoax, given that the pseudonymous author pretends to discover a lost work—the two forms of geographical literature are melded into a single literary experiment. This experiment assumes an encyclopedic framework from the outset, based on the creation *ex nihilo* (89.3–5, ed. Prinz) of the cosmos—also not unlike the *Hexaemeron* tradition in this way (see later). Within such a cosmographical structure and, in series, within the structure of the philosophical quest, a plentiful storehouse of information and detail about the (early medieval) inhabited world is built up. As one might expect, such detail is liberally appropriated (often without attribution) from earlier geographical writers: Jerome, Avitus, Orosius, Isidore, and others.[102]

The work known as the *Ravenna Cosmography* (c. 700) is very similar to *Aethicus Ister* in its literary playfulness, authorial misdirection, and citation of authorities.[103] Further, like both the *Expositio totius mundi et gentium* and *Aethicus Ister*, it begins with and concentrates on the East, naming numerous legendary people groups beyond the eastern rim of the Mediterranean basin and describing the details of their habitat. If the felt need for comprehensiveness is both kindled and imposed by the chosen form of the encyclopedic work—for example, imagine a lexicographer reaching the letter *Z*—then the *Ravenna Cosmography* amply demonstrates this process. The anonymous author's chosen metaphor for describing the world is the clock or, more precisely, the hours of the sun's transit across the sky. He thus offers twelve "hours" of space to the countries and peoples north of the Mediterranean and twelve to those below. A difficulty arises when he spends an inordinate amount of this metaphorical time-space on eastern peoples, which is a problematic decision not least because he has strikingly authentic historical sources for the peoples of Europe, especially northern Europe. Thus, certain western areas get short shrift, and his world, which resembles a circle, compresses the geography he is describing. In contrast to the *Expositio totius mundi et gentium*, the geographical world (in a physical sense) of the *Ravenna Cosmography* is not the direct object of description—if it were, then it would comprise its own boundaries, obviously—rather, the schema of the sun's celestial transit, in a temporal framework, creates boundaries that are, ultimately, literary and impose a unique and creative order on the knowledge the text contains.

The Ends of the Late Antique *Oikoumene*

In the early 1150s C.E., a Christian pilgrim from Iceland, the abbot Nikulás Bergsson, made his way to the Holy Land, via Rome, and left a written account of his journey.[104] He came from what was then nearly the western edge of the known world, from the Benedictine Mukathverá monastery on the northern coast of the island, and he wrote in his native tongue of Old Icelandic, or Old Norse.[105] Given such an exotic backdrop, Bergsson's account is all the more striking because he wrote it in the standard Christian pilgrimage genre known from the Latin tradition as far back as the fourth century. Perhaps he had been inspired by Latin writers closer to his own time: Anglo-Latin pilgrim narratives by figures such as Willibald of Eichstätt (723–729) and Saewulf (1102) had demonstrated the relative ease with which an Atlantic pilgrim could reach the Holy Land in the Middle Ages.[106] Bergsson was also writing in a robust tradition of Anglo-Latin pilgrimage to Rome—for instance, Archbishop Sigeric of Canterbury in 990–994.[107] Just as the *itinerarium* tradition finds its cartographical equivalent in the Peutinger Table, the medieval pilgrimage to Rome has its analogue in Giraldus Cambrensis' (c. 1200) map of Europe.[108]

The similarity of a high-medieval, vernacular account of a single pilgrimage to the much earlier pilgrimage narratives of Late Antiquity is striking and very important for intellectual history. At a basic level, it attests to the fundamental assumptions about the world that arose in Late Antiquity—a time frame one medievalist has called the "seminal period" and another "the Venerable Model"

0.1. Old Irish glosses on Priscian's *Institutiones grammaticae*, 845 C.E. (St. Gallen, Stiftsbibliotek).

15.1. Mar Saba Monastery in the Kidron Valley, Palestine (Photo: Inga-Lill Rubenson).

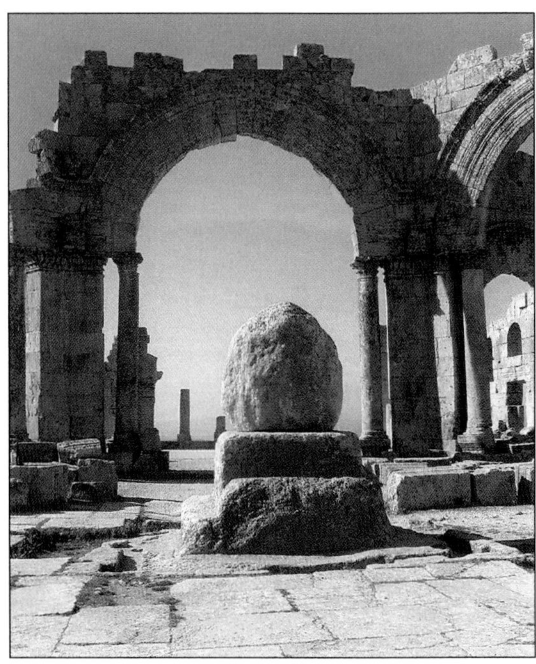

15.2. St. Simeon Pillar and Cathedral, Qalʿat Simʿān, Syria (Photo: Inga-Lill Rubenson).

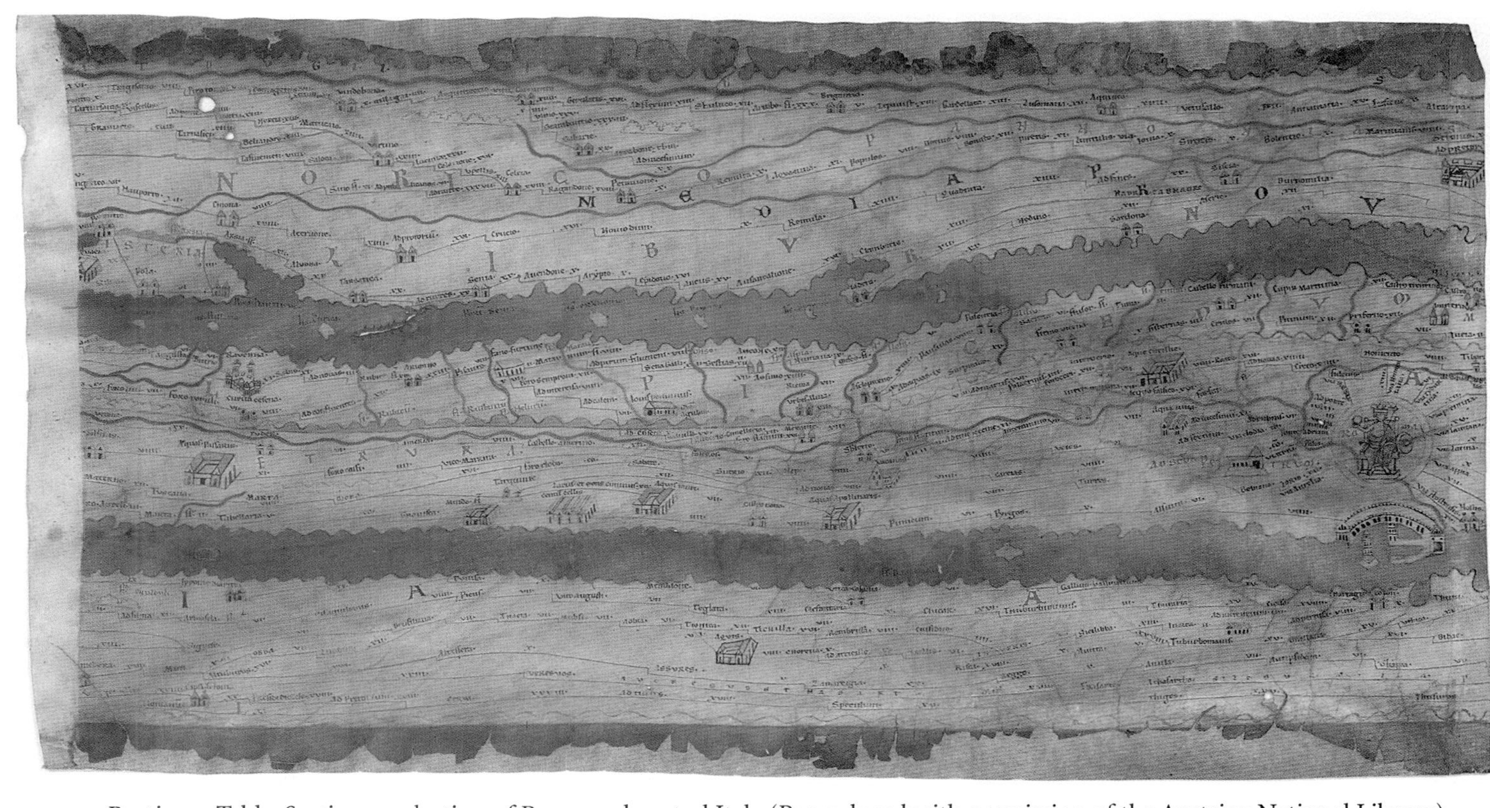

17.1. Peutinger Table. Section 4, selection of Rome and central Italy (Reproduced with permission of the Austrian National Library).

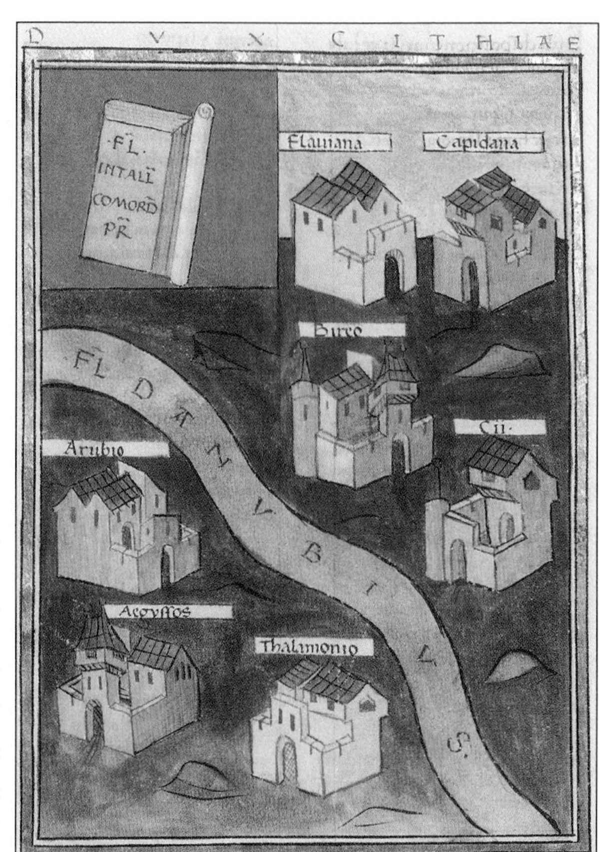

17.2. Notitia Dignitatum. “Dux Cithiae.” Fol. 101 verso. Basel, c. 1436. MS Latin 9661 in the Bibliothèque Nationale de France, Paris (Reproduced with permission of the Bibliothèque Nationale de France, Paris).

29.10. Mosaic pavement of the Chapel of Priest John in the Church of Amos and Kasiseus, Khirbet el-Mukhayyat, Jordan, 565 C.E. (Mount Nebo Museum; photo: A. M. Yasin).

29.11. Sanctuary vault and apse, S. Vitale, Ravenna, sixth century (Photo: Vanni/Art Resource, NY).

29.12. S. Pudenziana apse mosaic, Rome, c. 400 (Photo: Vanni/Art Resource, NY).

29.13. Eufrasius Basilica apse mosaic, Poreč, sixth century (Photo: A. M. Yasin).

30.3. Icon of Saint Peter, Monastery of Saint Catherine, Mount Sinai, sixth–seventh century (By permission of Saint Catherine's Monastery, Sinai, Egypt).

30.1. Icon of Saints Sergius and Bacchus, National Art Museum, Kiev, sixth century (Reproduced with permission © The Bohdan and Varvara Khanenko National Museum of Arts, Kiev, Ukraine).

32.1. Wall Painting, Qaryat al-Faw, possibly third century C.E. or earlier (Riyadh National Museum. © Saudi Commission for Tourism & Antiquities).

for this reason[109]—and to the longevity and dispersal of those assumptions in the wider medieval world. Equally important, I suggest, is the continuity that appears in the very manner of telling or writing: at almost every point (aside from references to the immediate historical circumstances), Nikulás Bergsson's account can be directly compared with disparate texts dealing with travel, geography, and cosmology from Late Antiquity, Byzantium, and the Middle Ages.[110]

This literary continuity arises from three factors: first, the conservative approach to genre that is the legacy of the classical world in that where innovation occurs, it always does so with reference to the *auctores*, "the authorities" of previous centuries; second, the value and success of the literary form of the Roman itinerary, which was in its own way quite innovative, particularly in its Christian adaptations; and third, and most important, authors from Late Antiquity on were drawn to an aesthetic of accumulation and encyclopedism. The organization of knowledge was one of the principles of their literary art. Technical and more general genres mixed and mingled, and the hybridity of form and genre—all within the framework of the Greco-Roman, Jewish, and Christian inheritance—became one of the focal points for authors from the fourth century on.[111] When this aesthetic of accumulation is recognized as a creative force in late antique, Byzantine, and medieval literature, the old juggernauts of "decline" and literary epigonality lose much of their power. As Bergsson's narrative demonstrates—in a language and context admittedly alien to late antique writers, some six to seven centuries prior—the seminal period of late antique literature had long-lasting effects, not least in the arena of geographical thought.

The library of the Archbishop of Canterbury in the seventh century—in the era of Theodore of Tarsus (602–690) and Hadrian (c. 637–709/10)—very likely possessed a copy of Cosmas Indicopleustes' *Christian Topography* (c. 550).[112] This probability is demonstrated by the appearance of precise details from Cosmas' work in Latin biblical commentaries and excerpts produced in Anglo-Saxon England and, specifically, at the Canterbury school.[113] We learn from Bede (*Hist. Abb.* 15, ed. Plummer) that Benedict Biscop, who later accompanied Theodore from Rome to Canterbury, purchased in Rome an expensive *codex cosmographiorum* that he subsequently sold to King Aldfrith of Northumbria (r. 685–705) for a hefty sum. There is good reason to assume this was a text of Cosmas, of the lavishly illustrated variety that existed as early as the reign of Justinian (i.e., very shortly after the work's composition).[114] As one of the most clearly sui generis works from all of Late Antiquity, it is a shame that the *Christian Topography* has been saddled by scholars with such a conventional title. *Topography* does not adequately convey the metaphysical aspirations of the work; likewise, *Christian* ignores the fact that Cosmas was an East Syriac (aka Nestorian) Christian in the middle of Miaphysite (aka Monophysite) Alexandria and that he had as one of his principal opponents the same John Philoponus, also an Alexandrian, who argued so vehemently against the Neoplatonists over creation *ex nihilo*.[115] Despite Philoponus' Christian convictions, Cosmas considered him a heretic because of his commitment to Ptolemaic geography, particularly to the generally acknowledged principle of a spherical universe.

> If, as a Christian, he wanted to refute the pagan [lit. Greek] view, he ought first to have refuted their fundamental principles about the [celestial] sphere and its circular motion, which very thing I, by the will of God, was asked to produce and have done so in a separate treatise.[116]

This passage should be read with the prologue to the *Christian Topography*, in which Cosmas claims to have written two other books: a geography dedicated to "Constantine" and an astronomy dedicated to "the deacon Homologos" (Pr. 1–2). Philoponus responded to Cosmas by writing the work known today as the *De opificio mundi*, a philosophical meditation on the Genesis creation story, not terribly distinct in form from the *Hexaemeron* commentary tradition.[117] Cosmas' own views on cosmology were biblicist in character: the universe was a box with a canopy stretching over the top (like the Mosaic tabernacle) and with the sun rotating around a mountain in the center to produce night and day (again, evocative of the Exodus landscape). The exegetical details of this system have been discussed elsewhere.[118] What is most significant for our purposes is Cosmas' inventiveness and prolific output. The volume of literature and thought on the topic of cosmology in the sixth century is astounding, and more so in that it took place across denominational, religious, philosophical, and linguistic lines and often with a radical repurposing of the intellectual tools at hand.

The categories of travel, cartography, and cosmology are not easily separated in late antique literature: the bulk of Cosmas' narrative is actually a classical *periplous* along the Red Sea coast of Africa. Indeed, it may be doing an injustice to the vitality of the late antique authors discussed here to categorize them too narrowly. An encyclopedic or archival trend ties many of them together in Late Antiquity, as does the (perhaps more adventurous) idea that their archives of knowledge represent an artistic or aesthetic choice that can be shown to define the output of the period to a significant degree. It is clear that most of the texts discussed in this chapter simultaneously assume and challenge the assumptions of their chosen genre. But on this basis, the most difficult texts to understand may be those, like the *Christian Topography* or the Peutinger Table, that have no surviving ancestor from Greco-Roman antiquity.

NOTES

1. Ed. Schoff 1912. See also Malkin 1998.
2. Ed. *GGM* 1.15–96.
3. Ed. Chantraine 2002; *GGM* 1.306–369. Nearchus was chosen by Alexander the Great to command his naval expedition in the East.
4. Ed. Roseman 1994; Cunliffe 2001.

5. Ed. Casson 1989; *GGM* 1.257–305.
6. Ed. Silberman 1995; *GGM* 1.370–423.
7. Ed. Bauer and Cuntz 1905; *GGM* 1.427–514.
8. Ed. Murphy 1977; *PLRE* Festus 12.
9. Ed. *GGM* 1.515–576.
10. Giannini 1963; 1964; 1966.
11. Ed. *GGM* 2.xv–xl, 103–176; Jacob 1990.
12. Avienus: ed. Woestijne 1961. Priscian: ed. Woestijne 1953. Avienus also produced a translation of Aratus' *Phaenomena*: ed. Soubiran 1981.
13. Ed. Pereira and da Rocha 1989; ed. Casevitz et al. 1992; trans. Levi 1979; Alcock et al. 2001; Hutton 2005; Pretzler 2007.
14. Ed. Thulin 1913; ed. Clavel-Lévêque 1993–1996; trans. Campbell 2000; Dilke 1971.
15. Ed. Cuntz and Schnetz 1929–1940, 1–94.
16. Elsner 2000, 183.
17. For emergent book technology during this period, see Gamble 1995; McCormick 1985; O'Donnell 1998.
18. For the redaction and transmission of this text, see Salway 2001.
19. Chevallier 1976, 39–47.
20. Bieler 1965, 1.1–26; trans. Stewart 1887.
21. Elsner 2000.
22. Hunt 1982.
23. Hunt 1982, 30–36; Holum 1990.
24. Wilkinson 1990; Hunt 1999; Taylor 1993, 318–332.
25. Ed. and trans. Timm 2005. Also, trans. Freeman-Grenville et al. 2003. On the date, see Barnes 1975.
26. See Grafton and Williams 2006, with Johnson 2007.
27. See Jeanjean et al. 2004; Notley and Safrai 2005; and Williams 2006.
28. Cain 2010.
29. Weingarten 2005.
30. Ed. Maraval 2002; trans. Wilkinson 1999. For the (formerly contested) date of this text, see Maraval 2002, 27–39.
31. Johnson 2008; 2010.
32. Prudentius' *Peristephanon* could be cited as a near-contemporary comparandum in verse: see McGill, chapter 10 in this book.
33. Ed. Rougé 1966; trans. Vasiliev 1936.
34. The older idea of the mutual dependence of the *Expositio* and Ammianus Marcellinus on a shared geographical source has not found many recent proponents: see Vasiliev 1936, 28–39.
35. The Syrian section is the fullest, leading scholars to suggest this region as home to the author (Rougé 1966, 31): e.g., §33, ed. Rougé, "This is only part [of what could be described] of Syria: we have passed over many things, so that we might not seem to extend the discourse beyond propriety and so that we might be able to describe other regions and cities."
36. See the Greek text in Rougé 1966, appendix 2, entitled in two separate sections, "An Exposition of Stories Concerning the Blessed Ones" (Ἔκθεσις λόγων περὶ Μακαριῶν) and "Land-Routes from the Paradise of Eden to the [lands] of the Romans" (Ὁδοιπορίαι ἀπὸ Ἐδὲμ τοῦ παραδείσου ἄχρι τῶν Ῥωμαίων). The term ὁδοιπορία is the later Greek equivalent of *itinerarium*, though originally it meant

exclusively "walking" (LSJ s.v.). It is worth noting that the second Greek section follows the *itinerarium* structure much more closely than the Latin. This Greek version has been placed within an East Syriac diaspora, similar to that of Cosmas (Wolska-Conus 1962, 255–257; cf. Rougé 1966, 56–69).

37. Ed. Bieler 1965, 1.127–74.

38. Ed. and trans. Meehan 1958; ed. Bieler 1965, 1.175–234. See also O'Loughlin 2007.

39. Meehan 1958, 5–6, 13–14.

40. Ed. Kohanski and Benson 2007.

41. See refs. at Banks and Binns 2002, xlii. Honorius: ed. Flint 1982. Gervasius: ed. and trans. Banks and Binns 2002. On the modes of high-medieval geographical writing, see Ziolkowski 2005. On the organization of disparate information among high-medieval and early-modern Latin writers, see Blair 2011.

42. Emily Albu's argument for a Carolingian date for the Peutinger Table has not won wide support: see Albu 2005; 2008; and, in defense of the c. 400 date, Salway 2005; Talbert 2008, 21–22.

43. For the general background of the map, see Talbert 2004; 2007a; 2008. Talbert 2010 (not available at the time of writing) is a complete reassessment of the Peutinger Table based upon these earlier studies.

44. The map as it has survived is only 670 centimeters, split into eleven parchments of roughly equal size. The discussion is over how far to extend the (lost) western portion: see Talbert 2007b, 222; Talbert 2007a.

45. On the intended scope of the Peutinger Table, see Talbert 2007b, 224: "The sense is thus 'the (part of the) world claimed by Rome,' 'Rome's dominion,' or 'Rome's sway,' rather than "territory under direct Roman control" as can be meant in statements, say, by jurists." Compare to this the traditional interpretation of Vipsanius Agrippa's map in Rome, that it was set up for propaganda purposes to show the dominion of the Romans: Dilke 1998 [1985], 39–54; Nicolet 1991, 95–122.

46. *Notitia Dignitatum* ed. Seeck 1876. See also Berger 1981; Mann 1991; Woods 1996; and the papers in Mann et al. 1976.

47. Dilke 1998 [1985], 196–197, noting that *tabula* is occasionally used to mean "map" (Cicero *Att.* 6.2.3; Propertius 4.3.37) and, in this, mirrors the use of *πίναξ* in Greek.

48. Trans. Berggren and Jones 2000, 82. See also Berggren 1991, which describes Ptolemy's *Geography* and *Planispherium* as two similar attempts to "unfold the sphere" (of the earth and the heavens, respectively): "In the Geography [Ptolemy] presents planar images of the inhabited earth which satisfy the two requirements of presenting some of the major features of the appearance of the terrestrial globe as well as preserving some of the proportions of that globe. In the *Planispherium* he presents a disk that represents the heavens . . . so faithfully that one could even use it, for example, to compute rising times" (143).

49. *Oxford English Dictionary* s.v. "encyclopedism": "the possession of the whole range of knowledge." This is not precisely the definition of *enkuklios paideia* from the Greek world, as mediated through the Roman empire and Late Antiquity: see Odorico 1990; Bovey 2003.

50. Reynolds 1996, 115–127. For the discovery and publication of this monument, see Bloch 1961.

51. Reynolds 1996, 92–106. Cf. Trimble 2007, 368: "Largely accurate, with the exception of a few glaring orientation errors and skewing problems. . . ."

52. Trimble 2007, 374.

53. Talbert 2005, 628.

54. Talbert 2008, 17. See also Talbert 2007b, 221–222.

55. Brodersen 1995, 59–68. Brodersen goes even further than most by claiming Agrippa's map in Rome was not even an image at all but simply a list of places (268–285). See also Brodersen's review of the *Barrington Atlas of the Greek and Roman World*, ed. Talbert (Brodersen 2004).

56. Compare the important observation of Talbert's that the River Tiber on the Forma Urbis Romae received no paint and no special outlining of any kind, appearing only as a blank band in the midst of urban structures (Talbert 2005, 630). Note also that the present London Underground map, first published by Harry Beck in 1933, was preceded by a map (1908) that attempted to include both overland geography and the Tube system.

57. Talbert 2007b, 225–226.

58. Talbert 2008, 18; 2005, 627. A remarkable sentence by Nicholas Horsfall is apropos here: "In the absence of a precise and universally accepted system of orientation, of the means to measure height, distance, or angles with exactitude, of any serious cartography, and, lastly, of the vocabulary which would have enabled [ancient] historians of the Roman world to describe places at all coherently, even had they the science and technology to comprehend their outlines exactly—for it is to be suspected that there exists a conceptual and causal link between the abilities to measure accurately and to describe coherently—then we should perhaps rather marvel that Roman authors preserved *any* exact topographical indications which we can today relate to our precisely arithmeticized world-view" (1985, 205; emphasis original).

59. Trimble 2007, 378, 380.

60. Talbert 2007b, 224.

61. See Evans 1998, 25–26.

62. 2.6.30: "circulorum quoque caeli ratio in terrae mentione aptius dicetur, quando ad eam tota pertinet."

63. See Evans 1998, 22–23. See also Goldstein and Bowen 1991; Berggren 2002 for how empirical data were used in Greek astronomy and cartography.

64. The geocentricity of the universe is, of course, an a priori assumption made by Ptolemy and all ancient astronomers save Aristarchus of Samos (c. 280 B.C.E.), who advocated for a heliocentric model. This proposition was not taken seriously because it implied that there was an enormous distance between earth and the stars, given that their positions were relatively stable throughout the earth's orbit.

65. On Ptolemy's view of Aristotle, see Sambursky 1962, 133–145.

66. Maps based on Ptolemy's *Geography* were known to some Arab geographers and, in the Byzantine world, were famously "discovered" by Maximus Planudes during the Palaiologan period (c. 1300): Diller 1940 and Berggren and Jones 2000, 48–49, agree that Planudes' reference to *geographia* is to his own reconstruction of the maps on the basis of Ptolemy's text rather than to maps in the manuscript of Ptolemy's *Geographia* that he unearthed. Cf. Stückelberger 1996, a critical edition of Planudes' hexameter poem on the *Geography*.

67. This seems unlikely, given the substantial cartographic sections of the *Geography*: for the debate, see Berggren and Jones 2000, 45–50.

68. Evans 1998, 25.

69. Talbert argues Rome was at the center of the Peutinger Table (2007a). Also, Italy was uniquely well suited to being the center of the map because it was easily elongated (2007b, 226); mainland Greece is the most foreshortened (227).

70. James Evans points out that the so-called instrumentalist interpretation of ancient astronomy—that is, that the Greeks were primarily concerned with accurate predictions and not the validity of their physical or philosophical models—does not acknowledge that the earlier Greek astronomers, up to Hipparchus, were solely concerned with modeling the movements of the planets and not with astrological prediction (1998, 216–219). However, that seems to suggest that, after Hipparchus, predictive astronomy dominated, which is certainly not the case if one includes philosophical literature: cosmology and predictive astrology are equally well represented in Late Antiquity.

71. The terminology here is taken from Sambursky 1962, 133–145. See also Evans 1998, 19–20, 247, 310–311.

72. Wilberding 2006. For background, see chapter 16 by Smith in this book.

73. Sambursky 1962, 147–149.

74. Sambursky 1962, 161–162.

75. Sambursky 1962, 148–150.

76. Sambursky 1962, 158–166. On the dating of Philoponus' career, see MacCoull 1995.

77. This tract forms part of his commentary on Aristotle's Physics and includes quotations of a lost work by Philoponus (perhaps the *De contingentia mundi*) that postdates Philoponus' *Against Aristotle*. It has been argued that Simplicius deliberately misrepresents Philoponus' arguments in this work: R. Sorabji in Furley and Wildberg 1991, 97–100. It is worth noting that the name of Simplicius does not appear in any of Philoponus' extant writings (Sambursky 1962, 156).

78. Ed. Mogenet and Tihon 1985; ed. Tihon 1978; and see Tihon 1999 for context. See also Pappus' and Theon's commentaries on the *Almagest* itself: ed. Rome 1931–1943 [only books 1–4]; ed. Halma. 1993 [1822–1825; entire text]. Two different commentaries on the same work suggest, as Theon himself attests, that there were different levels of mathematical knowledge among the educated readership (Cuomo 2001, 243). On Pappus, see Cuomo 2000; Jones 1986; Hultsch 1965.

79. Pingree 1990.

80. Cuomo 2000, 13, citing Firmicus Maternus *Math.* 13.29–15.6. See also Cuomo 2000, 13, n.14 for occurrences of *ἀκρίβεια* in late antique astrological texts. For a balanced approach to Manilius (in particular) and to the overlap between astronomy and astrology (in general), see Volk 2009, 1–13.

81. Ed. Heiberg et al. 1898–1961, 3.1–2; trans. Robbins 1940.

82. Ed. Armisen-Marchetti 2001; trans. Stahl 1990 [1952]. On his dates and intellectual circle, see Alan Cameron 1966 and 1967.

83. Ed. Willis 1983; trans. Stahl 1971–1977.

84. Ed. Arndt et al.1884–1885, 1.2:854–872.

85. Ed. Prinz 1993. See now Herren 2011.

86. Ed. Cuntz and Schnetz 1929–1940, vol. 2.

87. For further thoughts on the archival aesthetic in Late Antiquity, see Johnson 2010.

88. The antiquarian handbook tradition is perhaps even more prominent in his Virgilian *Saturnalia*: Stahl 1990 [1952], 3, 55.

89. The *De republica*, like Macrobius' *Saturnalia* after it and Plato's *Republic* before it, is framed as a dialogue. The encyclopedic qualities of the literary dialogue form, in numerous ancient languages, are still somewhat underappreciated in the scholarship, though there is good recent work on the related late antique dispute and *erotapokriseis*

("question-answer") genres (Averil Cameron 1991; Volgers and Zamagni 2004; Papadoyannakis 2006). The *Somnium Scipionis* is preserved only through the process of being severed from its original and attached to manuscripts of Macrobius' *Commentary*. The rest of the extant *De republica* was discovered in the nineteenth century under a palimpsestic copy of Augustine's *Commentaries on the Psalms* (Stahl 1990 [1952], 9–11).

90. See Stahl 1942; 1990 [1952], 32; Courcelle 1969, 27–28.

91. Ed. Waszink 1977. See McCluskey 1998, 119–120.

92. Lewis 1936, 78: "this universe, which has produced the bee-orchid and the giraffe, has produced nothing stranger than Martianus Capella."

93. See Bovey 2003. On this reception as a fundamentally continental, rather than insular, development, see Teeuwen 2007.

94. Stahl 1977, 227, 318. For Martianus' language of "streams" (*amnes*) in reference to the planetary spheres—probably taken from Porphyry's lost *Commentary on Plato's Republic*—see Shanzer 1986, appendix 1, 187–201.

95. Ed. Arndt, Krusch, and Bonnet 1884, 2.854–872.

96. Isidore assigns this role to the sacristan: *Regula monachorum* 20.1 (ed. *PL* 83.889–90). On Isidore and astronomy, see McCluskey 1998, 123–127.

97. McCluskey 1990, 9–10. Cassian, *De institutis coenobiorum* 2.1–2.6, 2.17 (ed. Guy).

98. The task of determining the proper hours of daily prayer is normally distinguished from the task of organizing the calendar of the Christian year. The latter was typically called *computus* among later medieval writers, and the first manual was prepared by Bede (*De temporum ratione*; c. 725): see Wallis 1999, esp. appendix 4 on the term *computus*.

99. McCluskey 1990, 13.

100. McCluskey 1990, 14. On Gregory's pervading interest in the natural world, see de Nie 1985.

101. Herren 2011; 2004; 2001; 1994. Herren disputes the older attribution of this work to Virgil of Salzburg (cf. Löwe 1952). *The Life of Apollonius* appears in Latin through the translation of Sidonius Apollinaris (c. 430–490), though the original Greek text was known in the Latin West well before then: see Jones 2006. On "literarische Fälschung" and "Schwindelliteratur," see Herren 1989; Speyer 1971, esp. 77–78 on Aethicus Ister.

102. For the reception of late antique Latin astronomy and geography among Carolingian writers, see Eastwood 2007; McCluskey 1998; Lozovsky 2000.

103. On this work generally, see Dillemann 1997. On its date and provenance, see Staab 1976.

104. Ed. Kålund 1908; trans. Magoun 1940; 1944 (Iceland to Rome, Rome to Iceland); Hill 1983 (Holy Land).

105. Far from a "barbaric" vernacular, by this point Old Icelandic had developed a substantial corpus of poetry and prose, and Nikulás was writing on the cusp of the Golden Age of medieval Icelandic literature: see Turville-Petre 1953, 160–162.

106. Willibald of Eichstätt: ed. Holder-Egger 1887, 86–106; trans. Talbot 1954, 153–180; see also Aist 2009. Saewulf: ed. Huygens 1994, 59–77; trans. Brownlow 1892 On medieval Anglo-Latin pilgrimage in general, see Moore 1937.

107. See Magoun 1940.

108. O'Loughlin 1999.

109. Lewis 1964; Crosby 1997, 21–47.

110. See Merrills 2004, 310: "In the absence of any formally defined geographical discipline, the descriptions of the world were fitted into the literary moulds provided by a host of different genres."

111. Not insignificantly, Bergsson's text is preserved within a larger miscellany of encyclopedic knowledge compiled in a fourteenth-century manuscript (now in Copenhagen, AM 194): Hill 1983, 177.

112. Ed. and trans. Wolska-Conus 1968.

113. These details are attributed to an anonymous "Christian historian" (*Christianus historicus*) in the excerpts (found in Anglo-Saxon mss. throughout Europe), as well as in the Canterbury commentaries: see Bischoff and Lapidge 1994, 208–211; Herren 2004, 97–98. On the Antiochene and Syriac background of Theodore of Tarsus, see Brock 1995.

114. Kominko 2006; 2005.

115. On Cosmas' theological allegiances, see Becker 2006. There is, of course, a strong astronomical tradition in later Syriac thought, notably in the work of Severus of Sebokht and Theophilus of Edessa, both writing in the late seventh century under Muslim rule; see Pingree 1973, 34–35. See now Takahashi 2011.

116. *Christian Topography* 7.1.11–15, ed. Wolska-Conus: *Εἰ γὰρ ὡς χριστιανὸς ἀνατρέπειν ἠβούλετο τὴν δόξαν τὴν ἑλληνικήν, τάς γε περὶ τούτου πρῶτον ἀρχὰς ἐχρῆν ἐκ βάθρων ἀνελεῖν, τὴν σφαῖραν καὶ τὴν ταύτης περιφοράν, ὅπερ ἡμεῖς βουλήσει Θεοῦ ἐν ἑτέρῳ συγγράμματι αἰτηθέντες πεποιήκαμεν.*

117. Ed. Reichardt 1897; trans. Scholten 1997; see MacCoull 2006. On the *Hexaemeron* ("six-day") creation literature, see the introduction to Thomson 1995.

118. Wolska-Conus 1962; Pearson 1999.

WORKS CITED

Aist, Rodney. 2009. *The Christian Topography of Early Islamic Jerusalem: The Evidence of Willibald of Eichstätt, 700–787 CE.* Turnhout: Brepols.

Albu, Emily. 2005. "Imperial Geography and the Medieval Peutinger Map," *Imago Mundi* 57: 136–148.

———. 2008. "Rethinking the Peutinger Map." In *Cartography in Antiquity and the Middle Ages: Fresh Perspectives, New Methods*, ed. Richard Talbert and Richard W. Unger, 111–119. Leiden: Brill.

Alcock, Susan, John Cherry, and Jaś Elsner, eds. 2001. *Pausanias: Travel and Memory in Roman Greece.* Oxford: Oxford University Press.

Armisen-Marchetti, Mireille, ed. 2001. *Commentaire au Songe de Scipion.* Paris: Belles Lettres.

Arndt, Wilhelm, Bruno Krusch, and Max Bonnet, eds. 1884–1885. *Gregorii Turonensis Opera.* 2 vols. MGHSRM 1. Hannover: Hahn.

Banks, S. E., and J. W. Binns, eds. 2002. *Otia Imperialia: Recreation for an Emperor.* Oxford Medieval Texts. Oxford: Clarendon Press.

Barnes, T. D. 1975. "The Composition of Eusebius' *Onomasticon*," *Journal of Theological Studies* 26: 412–415.

Bauer, Adolf, and Otto Cuntz, eds. 1905. *Die Chronik des Hippolytos im Matritensis Graecus 121; nebst einer Abhandlung über den Stadiasmus maris magni.* Leipzig: J. C. Hinrichs.

Becker, Adam H. 2006. "The Dynamic Reception of Theodore of Mopsuestia in the Sixth Century: Greek, Syriac, and Latin." In *Greek Literature in Late Antiquity: Dynamism, Didacticism, Classicism*, ed. S. F. Johnson, 29–47. Aldershot: Ashgate.

Berger, Pamela C. 1981. *The Insignia of the Notitia Dignitatum*. New York: Garland.

Berggren, J. L. 1991. "Ptolemy's Maps of Earth and the Heavens: A New Interpretation," *Archive for History of Exact Sciences* 43.2: 133–144.

———. 2002. "Ptolemy's Maps as an Introduction to Ancient Science." In *Science and Mathematics in Ancient Greek Culture*, ed. C. J. Tuplin and T. E. Rihll, 36–55. Oxford: Oxford University Press.

Berggren, J. L., and Alexander Jones. 2000. *Ptolemy's Geography: An Annotated Translation of the Theoretical Chapters*. Princeton, NJ: Princeton University Press.

Bieler, Ludwig, ed. 1965. *Itineraria et Alia Geographica*. 2 vols. CCSL 175–176. Turnhout: Brepols.

Bischoff, Bernhard, and Michael Lapidge. 1994. *Biblical Commentaries from the Canterbury School of Theodore and Hadrian*. Cambridge Studies in Anglo-Saxon England 10. Cambridge: Cambridge University Press.

Blair, Ann. 2011. *Too Much to Know: Managing Scholarly Information before the Modern Age*. New Haven, CT: Yale University Press.

Bloch, Herbert. 1961. "A New Edition of the Marble Plan of Ancient Rome," *Journal of Roman Studies* 51: 143–152.

Bovey, Muriel. 2003. *Disciplinae Cyclicae: L'organisation du savoir dans l'oeuvre de Martianus Capella*. Polymnia 3. Trieste: Edizioni Università di Trieste.

Bremmer, Rolf H., and Cornelis Dekker, eds. 2007. *Foundations of Learning: The Transfer of Encyclopaedic Knowledge in the Early Middle Ages*. Paris: Peeters.

Brock, Sebastian P. 1995. "The Syriac Background." In *Archbishop Theodore: Commemorative Studies on His Life and Influence*, ed. Michael Lapidge, 30–53. Cambridge: Cambridge University Press.

Brodersen, Kai. 1995. *Terra Cognita: Studien zur römischen Raumerfassung*. Spudasmata. Hildesheim: Georg Olms.

———. 2004. "Review Article: Mapping (In) the Ancient World," *Journal of Roman Studies* 94: 183–190.

Brownlow, W.-R. 1892. *Saewulf, 1102–03 A.D.* PPTS 4.2. London: Palestine Pilgrims' Text Society.

Cain, A. 2010. "Jerome's *Epitaphium Paulae*: Hagiography, Pilgrimage, and the Cult of Saint Paula," *Journal of Early Christian Studies* 18: 105–139.

Cameron, Alan. 1966. "The Date and Identity of Macrobius," *Journal of Roman Studies* 56: 25–38.

———. 1967. "Macrobius, Avienus, and Avianus," *Classical Quarterly* N.S. 17: 385–399.

Cameron, Averil. 1991. "Disputations, Polemical Literature, and the Formation of Opinion in the Early Byzantine Period." In *Dispute Poems and Dialogues in the Ancient and Mediaeval Near East: Forms and Types of Literary Debates in Semitic and Related Literatures*, ed. G. J. Reinink and H. L. J. Vanstiphout, 91–108. Orientalia Lovaniensia Analecta 42. Leuven: Peeters.

Campbell, J. B. 2000. *The Writings of the Roman Land Surveyors: Introduction, Text, Translation and Commentary*. London: Society for the Promotion of Roman Studies. [text = Thulin 1913]

Casevitz, M., J. Pouilloux, and F. Chamoux, eds. 1992. *Pausanias: Description de la Grèce*. 8 vols. Paris: Belles Lettres.

Casson, Lionel, ed. 1989. *The Periplus Maris Erythraei: Text with Introduction, Translation, and Commentary*. Princeton, NJ: Princeton University Press.

Chantraine, Pierre, ed. 2002. *Arrien: L'Inde*. 4th ed. Paris: Belles Lettres.

Chevallier, Raymond. 1976. *Roman Roads*. Trans. N. H. Field. Berkeley: University of California Press.

Clavel-Lévêque, Monique, ed. 1993–1996. *Corpus Agrimensorum Romanorum*. 3 vols. Naples: Jovene.

Courcelle, Pierre Paul. 1969. *Late Latin Writers and Their Greek Sources*. Trans. Harry E. Wedeck. Cambridge, MA: Harvard University Press.

Crosby, Alfred W. 1997. *The Measure of Reality: Quantification and Western Society, 1250–1600*. Cambridge: Cambridge University Press.

Cunliffe, Barry. 2001. *The Extraordinary Voyage of Pytheas the Greek*. London: Allen Lane.

Cuntz, Otto, and Joseph Schnetz, eds. 1929–1940. *Itineraria Romana*. 2 vols. Leipzig: Teubner.

Cuomo, S. 2000. *Pappus of Alexandria and the Mathematics of Late Antiquity*. Cambridge: Cambridge University Press.

———. 2001. *Ancient Mathematics*. Sciences of Antiquity. London: Routledge.

de Nie, Giselle. 1985. "The Spring, the Seed, and the Tree: Gregory of Tours on the Wonders of Nature," *Journal of Medieval History* 11: 89–135.

Dilke, O. A. W. 1971. *The Roman Land Surveyors: An Introduction to the Agrimensores*. Newton Abbot: David and Charles.

———. 1998 [1985]. *Greek and Roman Maps*. Baltimore: Johns Hopkins University Press.

Dillemann, Louis. 1997. *La cosmographie du Ravennate*. Ed. Yves Janvier. Collection Latomus 235. Brussels: Latomus.

Diller, Aubrey. 1940. "The Oldest Manuscripts of Ptolemaic Maps," *Transactions and Proceedings of the American Philological Association* 71: 62–67.

Eastwood, Bruce. 2007. *Ordering the Heavens: Roman Astronomy and Cosmology in the Carolingian Renaissance*. History of Science and Medicine Library 4. Leiden: Brill.

Elsner, Jaś. 2000. "The *Itinerarium Burdigalense*: Politics and Salvation in the Geography of Constantine's Empire," *Journal of Roman Studies* 90: 181–195.

Evans, James. 1998. *The History and Practice of Ancient Astronomy*. New York: Oxford University Press.

Flint, V. 1982. "Honorius Augustodunensis: *Imago Mundi*," *Archives d'histoire doctrinale et litteraire du moyen âge* 49: 7–153.

Freeman-Grenville, G. S. P., Rupert L. Chapman, and Joan E. Taylor. 2003. *The Onomasticon: Palestine in the Fourth Century A.D.* Jerusalem: Carta.

Furley, D., and C. Wildberg. 1991. *Philoponus: Corollaries on Place and Void; with Simplicius: Against Philoponus on the Eternity of the World*. London: Duckworth.

Gamble, Harry Y. 1995. *Books and Readers in the Early Church: A History of Early Christian Texts*. New Haven, CT: Yale University Press.

Giannini, Alessandro. 1963. "Studi sulla paradossografia greca," *Accademia dei Lincei, Rendiconti: Classe di lettere e scienze morali e storichi* 97: 247–266.

———. 1964. "Studi sulla paradossografia greca," *Acme* 17: 99–140.

Giannini, Alessandro, ed. 1966. *Paradoxographorum Graecorum Reliquiae*. Milan: Istituto editoriale italiano.

Goldstein, Bernard R., and Alan C. Bowen. 1991. "The Introduction of Dated Observations and Precise Measurement in Greek Astronomy," *Archive for History of Exact Sciences* 43.2: 93–132.

Grafton, Anthony, and Megan Hale Williams. 2006. *Christianity and the Transformation of the Book: Origen, Eusebius, and the Library of Caesarea*. Cambridge, MA: Harvard University Press.

Halma, N.-B., ed. 1993 [1822–1825]. *Commentaire de Théon d'Alexandrie, sur le premier livre de la composition mathématique de Ptolémée*. 2 vols. Bordeaux: Editions Bergeret.

Hamesse, Jacqueline, and Marta Fattori, eds. 1990. *Rencontres de cultures dans la philosophie médiévale: Traductions et traducteurs de l'antiquité tardive au XIVe siècle (Actes du colloque internationale de Cassino, 15–17 Juin 1989)*. Rencontres de Philosophie Médiévale 1. Louvain-la-Neuve: Université catholique de Louvain.

Heiberg, J. L., F. Boll, A. Boer, and F. Lammert, eds. 1898–1961. *Claudii Ptolemaei Opera Quae Exstant Omnia*. 3 vols. Leipzig: Teubner.

Herren, Michael W. 1989. "Wozu diente die Fälschung der Kosmographie des Aethicus." In *Lateinische Kultur im VIII. Jahrhundert*, ed. Albert Lehner and Walter Berschin, 145–159. St. Ottilien: EOS.

———. 1994. "Aethicus Ister and Virgil the Grammarian." In *Mélanges François Kerlouégan*, ed. Danièle Conso, Nicole Fick, and Bruno Poulle, 283–288. Paris: Les Belles Lettres.

———. 2001. "The 'Greek Element' in the *Cosmographia* of Aethicus Ister," *Journal of Medieval Latin* 11: 185–200.

———. 2004. "The Cosmography of Aethicus Ister: Speculations about Its Date, Provenance, and Audience." In *Nova de veteribus: Mittel- und neulateinische Studien für Paul Gerhard Schmidt*, ed. Andreas Bihrer, 79–102. Munich: K. G. Saur.

———, ed. 2011. *The Cosmography of Aethicus Ister: Edition, Translation, and Commentary*. Publications of the Journal of Medieval Latin 8. Turnhout: Brepols.

Hill, Joyce. 1983. "From Rome to Jerusalem: An Icelandic Itinerary of the Mid-Twelfth Century," *Harvard Theological Review* 76: 175–203.

Holder-Egger, Oswald, ed. 1887. *Die Monumenta Germaniae und ihr neuester Kritiker: Eine Entgegnung*. MGHSRM 15.1. Hannover: Hahn.

Holum, Kenneth G. 1990. "Hadrian and St. Helena: Imperial Travel and the Origins of Christian Holy Land Pilgrimage." In *The Blessings of Pilgrimage*, ed. Robert G. Ousterhout, 66–81. Urbana: University of Illinois Press.

Horsfall, N. 1985. "Illusion and Reality in Latin Topographical Writing," *Greece and Rome* 32: 197–208.

Hultsch, Fridericus, ed. 1965. *Pappi Alexandrini Collectionis Quae Supersunt*. 3 vols. Amsterdam: A. M. Hakkert.

Hunt, E. D. 1982. *Holy Land Pilgrimage in the Later Roman Empire, AD 312–460*. Oxford: Clarendon Press.

———. 1999. "Were There Christian Pilgrims before Constantine?" In *Pilgrimage Explored*, ed. J. Stopford, 25–40. York: York Medieval Press.

Hutton, William. 2005. *Describing Greece: Landscape and Literature in the Periegesis of Pausanias*. Cambridge: Cambridge University Press.

Huygens, R. B. C., ed. 1994. *Peregrinationes Tres: Saewulf, John of Würzburg, Theodoricus*. CCSL 139. Turnhout: Brepols.

Jacob, Christian. 1990. *La description de la terre habitée de Denys d'Alexandrie, ou, La leçon de géographie*. Paris: Albin Michel.

———. 2006. *The Sovereign Map: Theoretical Approaches in Cartography throughout History*. Ed. Edward H. Dahl. Trans. Tom Conley. Chicago: University of Chicago Press.

Jeanjean, Benoît, et al. 2004. *Chronique: Continuation de la Chronique d'Eusèbe, années 326–378*. Rennes: Presses Universitaires de Rennes.
Johnson, Scott Fitzgerald. 2007. Review of Grafton and Williams 2006. *Bryn Mawr Classical Review*; http://ccat.sas.upenn.edu/bmcr/2007/2007-06-41.html.
———. 2008. "Reviving the Memory of the Apostles: Apocryphal Tradition and Travel Literature in Late Antiquity." In *Revival and Resurgence in Christian History*, ed. Kate Cooper and Jeremy Gregory, 1–26. Studies in Church History 44. Woodbridge: Ecclesiastical History Society and Boydell Press.
———. 2010. "Apostolic Geography: The Origins and Continuity of a Hagiographic Habit," *Dumbarton Oaks Papers* 64: 5–25.
Jones, Alexander, ed. 1986. *Pappus of Alexandria: Book 7 of the Collection*. New York: Springer-Verlag.
Jones, C. P. 2006. "Apollonius of Tyana in Late Antiquity." In *Greek Literature in Late Antiquity: Dynamism, Didacticism, Classicism*, ed. S. F. Johnson, 49–64. Aldershot: Ashgate.
Kålund, K. ed. 1908. *Alfræði Íslenzk: Islandsk Encyklopædisk Litteratur*. Copenhagen: S. L. Møllers.
Kohanski, Tamarah, and C. David Benson, eds. 2007. *The Book of John Mandeville*. Kalamazoo, MI: Medieval Institute.
Kominko, Maja. 2005. "The Map of Cosmas, the Albi Map, and the Tradition of Ancient Geography," *Mediterranean Historical Review* 20: 163–186.
———. 2006. *The World of Cosmas: The Universe Described and Depicted in Byzantine Manuscripts of the Christian Topography*. 2 vols. D.Phil. thesis, University of Oxford.
Levi, P. 1979. *Pausanias, Guide to Greece*. Rev. ed. 2 vols. London: Penguin.
Lewis, C. S. 1936. *The Allegory of Love: A Study in Medieval Tradition*. Oxford: Clarendon.
———. 1964. *The Discarded Image: An Introduction to Medieval and Renaissance Literature*. Cambridge: Cambridge University Press.
Löwe, Heinz. 1952. "Ein literarischer Widersacher des Bonifatius: Virgil von Salzburg und die Kosmographie des Aethicus Ister," *Akademie der Wissenschaften und der Literatur: Abhandlungen der Geistes- und Sozialwissenschaftlichen Klasse 1951* 2: 903–988.
Lozovsky, Natalia. 2000. *The Earth Is Our Book: Geographical Knowledge in the Latin West c. 400–1000*. Ann Arbor: University of Michigan Press.
MacCoull, L. S. B. 1995. "A New Look at the Career of John Philoponus," *Journal of Early Christian Studies* 3: 47–60. Repr. in 2011. *Documenting Christianity in Egypt*, sec. IX. Farnham: Ashgate.
———. 2006. "The Historical Context of John Philoponus' *De Opificio Mundi* in the Culture of Byzantine-Coptic Egypt," *Zeitschrift für Antikes Christentum* 9: 397–423. Repr. in 2011. *Documenting Christianity in Egypt*, sec. XIII. Farnham: Ashgate.
Magoun, Francis P. 1940. "The Rome of Two Northern Pilgrims: Archbishop Sigeric of Canterbury and Abbot Nikolas of Munkathvera," *Harvard Theological Review* 33: 267–289.
———. 1944. "The Iceland Voyage in the 'Nibelungenlied'," *Modern Language Review* 39: 38–42.
Malkin, Irad. 1998. *The Returns of Odysseus: Colonization and Ethnicity*. Berkeley: University of California Press.
Mann, J. C. 1991. "The *Notitia Dignitatum*: Dating and Survival," *Britannia* 22: 215–219.
Mann, J. C., Roger Goodburn, and Philip Bartholomew, eds. 1976. *Aspects of the Notitia Dignitatum*. BAR Supplementary Series 15. Oxford: British Archaeological Reports.
Maraval, P. ed. 2002. *Egérie, Journal de Voyage: Itinéraire*. Rev. and corr. ed. Paris: Éditions du Cerf.

McCluskey, Stephen C. 1990. "Gregory of Tours, Monastic Timekeeping, and Early Christian Attitudes to Astronomy," *Isis* 81: 8–22.

———. 1998. *Astronomies and Cultures in Early Medieval Europe*. Cambridge: Cambridge University Press.

McCormick, Michael. 1985. "The Birth of the Codex and the Apostolic Life-Style," *Scriptorium* 39: 150–158.

Meehan, Denis, ed. 1958. *Adamnan's De Locis Sanctis*. Dublin: Dublin Institute for Advanced Studies.

Merrills, A. H. 2005. *History and Geography in Late Antiquity*. Cambridge Studies in Medieval Life and Thought 4. Cambridge: Cambridge University Press.

Mogenet, Joseph, and Anne Tihon, eds. 1985. *Le "Grand Commentaire" de Théon d'Alexandrie aux tables faciles de Ptolémée*. Vatican City: Biblioteca Apostolica Vaticana.

Moore, W. J. 1937. *The Saxon Pilgrims to Rome and the Schola Saxonum*. Fribourg: Society of St. Paul.

Müller, Karl Otfried, ed. 1990 [1855–1861]. *Geographi Graeci Minores*. 2 vols. Hildesheim: Georg Olms.

Murphy, J. P., ed. 1977. *Ora Maritima: A Description of the Seacoast from Brittany to Marseilles [Massilia]*. Chicago: Ares.

Nicolet, Claude. 1991. *Space, Geography, and Politics in the Early Roman Empire*. Ann Arbor: University of Michigan Press.

Notley, R. Steven, and Zeev Safrai. 2005. *Onomasticon, the Place Names of Divine Scripture: Including the Latin Edition of Jerome*. Boston: Brill.

O'Donnell, James. 1998. *Avatars of the Word: From Papyrus to Cyberspace*. Cambridge, MA: Harvard University Press.

Odorico, Paolo. 1990. "La cultura della Συλλογή: 1) Il cosiddetto enciclopedismo bizantino; 2) Le tavole del sapere di Giovanni Damasceno," *Byzantinische Zeitschrift* 83: 1–21.

O'Loughlin, Thomas. 1999. "An Early Thirteenth-Century Map in Dublin: A Window into the World of Giraldus Cambrensis," *Imago Mundi* 51: 24–39.

———. 2007. *Adomnán and the Holy Places: The Perceptions of an Insular Monk on the Locations of the Biblical Drama*. London: T&T Clark.

Papadoyannakis, Yannis. 2006. "Instruction by Question and Answer: The Case of Late Antique and Byzantine Erotapokriseis." In *Greek Literature in Late Antiquity: Dynamism, Didacticism, Classicism*, ed. S. F. Johnson, 91–105. Aldershot: Ashgate.

Pearson, Carl. 1999. *Scripture as Cosmology: Natural Philosophical Debate in John Philoponus' Alexandria*. Ph.D. Thesis, Harvard University.

Pelliot, Paul. 1996. *L'inscription nestorienne de Si-Nang-Fou*. Ed. Antonio Forte. Paris: Italian School of East Asian Studies.

Pereira, M. H. da Rocha, ed. 1989. *Pausaniae Graeciae Descriptio*. 2nd ed. 2 vols. Leipzig: Teubner.

Pingree, David. 1973. "The Greek Influence on Early Islamic Mathematical Astronomy," *Journal of the American Oriental Society* 93: 32–43.

———. 1990. "The Preceptum Canonis Ptolomei." In *Rencontres de cultures dans la philosophie médiévale: Traductions et traducteurs de l'antiquité tardive au XIVe siècle (Actes du colloque internationale de Cassino, 15–17 Juin 1989)*, ed. Jacqueline Hamesse and Marta Fattori, 355–375. Rencontres de Philosophie Médiévale 1. Louvain-la-Neuve: Université catholique de Louvain.

Pretzler, Maria. 2007. *Pausanias: Travel Writing in Ancient Greece*. London: Duckworth.

Prinz, O., ed. 1993. *Die Kosmographie des Aethicus.* Munich: Monumenta Germaniae Historica.

Reichardt, Walther, ed. 1897. *Joannis Philoponi De Opificio Mundi Libri VII.* Leipzig: Teubner.

Reynolds, David West. 1996. *Forma Urbis Romae: The Severan Marble Plan and the Urban Form of Ancient Rome.* Ph.D. Thesis, University of Michigan.

Robbins, Frank Egleston. 1940. *Ptolemy: Tetrabiblos.* Loeb Classical Library. Cambridge, MA: Harvard University Press.

Rome, A., ed. 1931–1943. *Commentaires de Pappus et de Théon d'Alexandrie sur l'Almageste.* 3 vols. Rome: Biblioteca Apostolica Vaticana.

Roseman, Christina Horst, ed. 1994. *Pytheas of Massalia: On the Ocean.* Chicago: Ares.

Rougé, Jean, ed. 1966. *Expositio Totius Mundi et Gentium.* SC 124. Paris: Éditions du Cerf.

Salway, Benet. 2001. "Travel, *Itineraria*, and *Tabellaria*." In *Travel and Geography in the Roman Empire*, ed. Colin Adams and Ray Laurence, 22–66. London: Routledge.

———. 2005. "The Nature and Genesis of the Peutinger Map," *Imago Mundi* 57: 119–135.

Sambursky, Samuel. 1962. *The Physical World of Late Antiquity.* London: Routledge and K. Paul.

Schoff, Wilfred H. 1912. *The Periplus of Hanno: A Voyage of Discovery down the West African Coast, by a Carthaginian Admiral of the Fifth Century B.C.* Philadelphia: Commercial Museum.

Scholten, Clemens. 1997. *De Opificio Mundi = Über die Erschaffung der Welt.* 3 vols. Fontes Christiani 23–25. Freiburg: Herder.

Seeck, Otto, ed. 1876. *Notitia Dignitatum: Accedunt Notitia Urbis Constantinopolitanae et Laterculi Prouinciarum.* Berlin: Weidmann.

Shanzer, Danuta. 1986. *A Philosophical and Literary Commentary on Martianus Capella's De Nuptiis Philologiae et Mercurii, Book 1.* Classical Studies 32. Berkeley: University of California Press.

Silberman, A., ed. 1995. *Arrien: Périple du Pont-Euxin.* Paris: Belles Lettres.

Soubiran, J., ed. 1981. *Les Phénomènes d'Aratus.* Paris: Belles Lettres.

Speyer, Wolfgang. 1971. *Die literarische Fälschung im heidnischen und christlichen Altertum: Ein Versuch ihrer Deutung.* Handbuch der Altertumswissenschaft 1.2. Munich: Beck.

Staab, Franz. 1976. "Ostrogothic Geographers at the Court of Theodoric the Great: A Study of Some Sources of the Anonymous Cosmographer of Ravenna," *Viator* 7: 27–64.

Stahl, William Harris. 1942. "Astronomy and Geography in Macrobius," *TAPA* 73: 232–258.

———. 1977. *The Marriage of Philology and Mercury.* New York: Columbia University Press.

———. 1990 [1952]. *Commentary on the Dream of Scipio.* New York: Columbia University Press.

Stewart, Aubrey. 1887. *Itinerary from Bordeaux to Jerusalem.* Palestine Pilgrims' Text Society 1.2. London: Committee of the Palestine Exploration Fund.

Stückelberger, Alfred. 1996. "Planudes und die Geographia des Ptolemaios," *Museum Helveticum* 53: 197–205.

Takahashi, Hidemi. 2011. "The Mathematical Sciences in Syriac: From Sergius of Resh-'Aina and Severus Sebokht to Barhebraeus and Patriarch Ni'matallah," *Annals of Science* 68: 477–491.
Talbert, Richard. 2004. "Cartography and Taste in Peutinger's Roman Map." In *Space in the Roman World: Its Perception and Presentation*, ed. Richard Talbert and Kai Brodersen, 113–141. Münster: LIT.
———. 2005. "Rome's Marble Plan and Peutinger's Map: Continuity in Cartographic Design," *Althistorisch-Epigraphische Studien (Österreichischen Gesellschaft für Archäologie)* 5: 627–634.
———. 2007a. "Konrad Miller, Roman Cartography, and the Lost Western End of the Peutinger Map." In *Historische Geographie der alten Welt: Grundlagen, Erträge, Perspektiven; Festgabe für Eckart Olshausen aus Anlass seiner Emeritierung*, ed. Ulrich Fellmeth, Peter Guyot, and Holger Sonnabend, 353–366. Hildesheim: G. Olms.
———. 2007b. "Peutinger's Roman Map: The Physical Landscape Framework." In *Wahrnehmung und Erfassung geographischer Räume in der Antike*, ed. Michael Rathmann, 220–230. Mainz am Rhein: Verlag Philipp von Zabern.
———. 2008. "Greek and Roman Mapping: Twenty-First Century Perspectives." In *Cartography in Antiquity and the Middle Ages: Fresh Perspectives, New Methods*, ed. Richard Talbert and Richard W. Unger, 9–27. Technology and Change in History 10. Leiden: Brill.
———. 2010. *Rome's World: The Peutinger Map Reconsidered.* Cambridge: Cambridge University Press.
Talbot, C. H. 1954. *The Anglo-Saxon Missionaries in Germany: Being the Lives of SS. Willibrord, Boniface, Sturm, Leoba, and Lebuin, Together with the Hodoeporicon of St. Willibald and a Selection from the Correspondence of St. Boniface.* London: Sheed and Ward.
Taylor, Joan E. 1993. *Christians and the Holy Places: The Myth of Jewish-Christian Origins.* Oxford: Clarendon.
Teeuwen, M. 2007. "Martianus Capella's *De nuptiis*: A Pagan 'Storehouse' First Discovered by the Irish?" In Bremmer and Dekker 2007, 51–62.
Thomson, Robert W., ed. 1995. *The Syriac Version of the Hexaemeron by Basil of Caesarea.* 2 vols. Louvain: Peeters.
Thulin, Carl, ed. 1913. *Corpus Agrimensorum Romanorum.* Leipzig: Teubner.
Tihon, Anne, ed. 1978. *Le petit commentaire de Théon d'Alexandrie aux tables faciles de Ptolémée.* Vatican City: Biblioteca Apostolica Vaticana.
———. 1999. "Theon of Alexandria and Ptolemy's *Handy Tables.*" In *Ancient Astronomy and Celestial Divination*, ed. N. M. Swerdlow, 357–369. Cambridge, MA: MIT Press.
Timm, Stefan, ed. 2005. *Das Onomastikon der biblischen Ortsnamen: Edition der syrischen Fassung mit griechischem Text, englischer und deutscher Übersetzung.* Texte und Untersuchungen zur Geschichte der altchristlichen Literatur 152. Berlin: Walter de Gruyter.
Trimble, Jennifer. 2007. "Visibility and Viewing on the Severan Marble Plan." In *Severan Culture*, ed. Simon Swain, Stephen Harrison, and Jaś Elsner, 368–384. Cambridge: Cambridge University Press.
Turville-Petre, Gabriel. 1953. *Origins of Icelandic Literature.* Oxford: Clarendon.
Vasiliev, A. A. 1936. "*Expositio Totius Mundi*: An Anonymous Geographic Treatise of the Fourth Century A.D.," *Seminarium Kondakovianum* 8: 1–39.

Volgers, Annelie, and Claudio Zamagni, eds. 2004. *Erotapokriseis: Early Christian Question-and-Answer Literature in Context*. Leuven: Peeters.

Volk, Katharina. 2009. *Manilius and His Intellectual Background*. Oxford: Oxford University Press.

Wallis, Faith. 1999. *Bede, The Reckoning of Time*. Translated Texts for Historians 29. Liverpool: Liverpool University Press.

Waszink, J. H., ed. 1977. *Timaeus, a Calcidio translatus commentarioque instructus*. 2nd ed. Plato Latinus 4. London: Warburg Institute and Brill.

Weingarten, Susan. 2005. *The Saint's Saints: Hagiography and Geography in Jerome*. Leiden: Brill.

Wilberding, James. 2006. *Plotinus' Cosmology: A Study of Ennead II.1(40)*. Oxford: Oxford University Press.

Wilkinson, John. 1990. "Jewish Holy Places and the Origins of Christian Pilgrimage." In *The Blessings of Pilgrimage*, ed. Robert G. Ousterhout, 41–53. Urbana: University of Illinois Press.

———. 1999. *Egeria's Travels*. 3rd ed. Warminster: Aris & Phillips.

Williams, Megan Hale. 2006. *The Monk and the Book: Jerome and the Making of Christian Scholarship*. Chicago: University of Chicago Press.

Willis, James, ed. 1983. *Martianus Capella*. Leipzig: Teubner.

Woestijne, Paul van de, ed. 1953. *La Périégèse de Priscien*. Bruges: De Tempel.

———. 1961. *La Descriptio Orbis Terrae d'Avienus*. Bruges: De Tempel.

Wolska-Conus, Wanda. 1962. *La topographie chrétienne de Cosmas Indicopleustès: Théologie et sciences au VIe siècle*. Bibliothèque byzantine 3. Paris: Presses Universitaires de France.

———, ed. 1968–1973. *Cosmas Indicopleustès: Topographie Chrétienne*. 3 vols. Sources chrétiennes 141, 159, 197. Paris: Éditions du Cerf.

Woods, D. 1996. "The Scholae Palatinae and the *Notitia Dignitatum*," *Journal of Roman Military Equipment Studies* 7: 37–50.

Ziolkowski, Jan M. 2005. "La Grèce antique sous le regard de Gervais de Tilbury." In *La Grèce antique sous le regard du moyen âge occidental*, ed. Jean Leclant and Michael Zink, 51–67. Paris: De Boccard.

PART III

LAW, STATE, AND SOCIAL STRUCTURES

CHAPTER 18

ECONOMIC TRAJECTORIES

JAIRUS BANAJI
School of Oriental and African Studies (SOAS)

Introduction

Michael Rostovtzeff concluded his great history of the early Roman empire by suggesting: "The catastrophe of the third century dealt a severe blow to the prosperity of the Empire and weakened the creative energies of the better part of the population."[1] In part, this was a throwback to Weber's thesis about the late empire as a period of expanding natural economy. Yet the distinctiveness of the late empire lies precisely in the fact that *money*, not land, emerged as the general form of wealth. Constantine's restructuring of the monetary system was a major economic watershed in the history of antiquity, inaugurating a period that would see unprecedented levels of monetary circulation. However, for the scholars who made money central to the dynamics of the fourth century, these changes in the monetary system were underpinned by major social transformations. For Mazzarino, the anonymous author of *De rebus bellicis*, a reform tract drafted (probably) in the 350s, had already made the crucial connection by linking the expanding circulation of gold to the consolidation of a new aristocracy, the *clarissimi* of the reigns of Constantine and his sons.[2] Anonymous saw the economic basis of this aristocracy in the rapid accumulation of large masses of gold, and the mechanism of accumulation in Constantine's expansion of the governing class.[3] These are crucial insights into the dramatic transformations of the fourth century, and they offer *one* frame for constructing a more general economic history of Late Antiquity, based, of course, on a much wider range of sources than either Mickwitz (numismatic, legal, papyrological) or Mazzarino (legal, textual) used. In particular, the archaeological revolution of the last, roughly, three decades throws up a huge challenge for historians of Late Antiquity, since they are now confronted, in an acute way, by the problem of how sources that are so diverse in character can be coherently blended into totalizing narratives. Chris Wickham's recent book is probably the most spectacular attempt in this direction, and in the conclusion to this chapter, I shall discuss one or two of its major theses.

Staying with the point about sources for the moment: Anonymous alludes to a process of class formation that was largely true of the western aristocracy. The prosopography of third-century provincial elites (the work of scholars like Pflaum, Alföldy, and Jacques) has shown that that process had much deeper roots. The core of the Constantinian elite comprised powerful aristocrats whose roots go back to the huge economic expansion of the western Mediterranean in the second and third centuries and to the ability of some families to survive the savage conflicts that ended in the victory of Septimius Severus. Generalizing a model first used by Mario Torelli in prosopographical work on Lepcis Magna, it is possible to see that the booming provincial centers of the western Mediterranean, Africa above all, threw up families who used their wealth to establish a wider network of connections, both matrimonial and political, that could help consolidate their business interests and political ambitions.[4] Clodius Albinus himself is said to have come from Hadrumetum in the heart of the Sahel.[5] The backbone of his support among the provincial upper classes was broken in the fierce reprisals that led to large-scale executions in 197.[6] The Anicii are one family that emerged as strong supporters of Septimius. In 196–197, Q. Anicius Faustus from Uzappa near Mactaris was Septimius' chief military commander in Numidia.[7] His descendants can be traced through the whole of the third century[8] and became, of course, one of the wealthiest families of Late Antiquity. Thus in this case, prosopography provides one context for the deeper understanding of an isolated textual source. Archaeology provides another. The explosion of survey archaeology since the late seventies has shown just how densely settled the eastern countrysides were in Late Antiquity. The expansive energies of the fourth century, of Constantine's empire, found their most durable expression in the *east* Mediterranean of the fifth, sixth, and seventh centuries. It was here that gold continued to circulate on a spectacular scale, that the urban traditions of antiquity were at their most resilient, and that the economic base existed, clearly, for the survival of a powerful imperial state. Now a major part of this dramatic transformation was the emergence of a new aristocracy in the east, quite different in nature from the kind of aristocracy that Anonymous saw stuffing its "houses" with gold. Constantius II created a *noblesse de fonction* ("différent de l'aristocratie traditionnelle"), so that the nascent aristocracy of the east was more firmly rooted in the traditions of a bureaucratic state.[9] This remained true of the fifth century, when the Byzantine new aristocracy that emerged in regions like Egypt could reliably be described as "of bureaucratic origin."[10]

Thus Late Antiquity threw up multiple trajectories, and no single formula can do justice to all of them. Even the dissolution of the western aristocracy, when it came, took such different forms and moved in such different ways that the "fall" of the western empire is a mere abstraction unless each context is constructed in its own terms. In particular, the slow erosion of the Gallic aristocracy that proceeded apace with the consolidation of Gothic power in the fifth century stands in sharp contrast to the dramatic and altogether more sudden collapse of the Italian aristocracy in the sixth. And again, the way in which the Merovingian rulers handled the remnants of that class—substantial in southern Gaul—contrasts sharply with the treatment meted out to their north Italian counterparts by the Lombards. There was no unified bloc of "Barbarians," any more than there was a homogeneous or unified class of late Roman aristocrats, and these differences are what late antique history is largely about.

The Late Empire

Whatever one thinks of the "crisis" of the third century, the key consequence of its recurrent monetary instability was the de facto disintegration of bimetallism. The chief expression of this was that *gold came to circulate at a floating rate.* As Lo Cascio says, "With the dissolution of the Roman monetary system in the third century, gold coinage came to occupy a peculiar position within the Roman monetary economy. It was no longer linked through a fixed value relationship to the other denominations and to the unit of account. . . ."[11] Diocletian's attempt to restore a viable bimetallic system ended in failure, and it is no small measure of Constantine's achievement that he was no longer mesmerized by the monetary illusions of the third century and could break so decisively from them. Mazzarino's assessment of Constantine as a "revolutionary" is thus fully justified. The fourth century began, more or less, with a radically different monetary system based on gold as the measure of value and on a calculated decision not to introduce fixed value relations between the metals. But this monometallism of gold had far-reaching economic and social consequences. The division between gold (the *solidus*) and the base-metal coinages was in some sense a metaphor for and replicated in a more rampant stratification of society, where the "abject" strata (*humiliores*) were defined as much by their powerlessness as by economic deprivation or poverty. Thus one way of classifying or dividing up late Roman society was in terms of the contrast, drawn by Ambrose, for example, between the *inopes* and the *potentes.*[12] In one of their several meanings at least, the late antique poor were those who lacked any form of protection and who were thus vulnerable to oppression or more tragic eventualities. They were, in a favorite category of the legal sources, *tenues*, that is, groups vulnerable to domination. The pervasive imagery of power and powerlessness that runs through the discursive worlds of Late Antiquity reflects the peculiar nature of the Constantinian order, where "at the highest levels there was no longer any distinction between senators and bureaucracy" (Mazzarino).[13] A purely civilian aristocracy ceased to exist, in the sense that the clans who dominated the City of Rome in the early fourth century could continue to prosper only as part of a much bigger governing class, a class that would in the future, and in the east for centuries, comprise "the higher officials of the army, the bureaucracy and the church."[14] It was this expanded governing class of the fourth century that formed the powerful social base of a monetary economy based on gold.

The return to a stable, high-value coinage, a single currency that spanned the entire breadth of the empire, had vast economic implications. First, it would mean a sustained increase in the level of monetary activity, which would mean an expansion of the monetized economy. The widespread use of cash payments on rural estates in Egypt (already by the third quarter of the fourth century) is one illustration of this. Second, a growing money supply could match a "long-term increase in the demand for money" to service a larger volume of transactions in the "private" sector (among merchants, landowners, monasteries, and so on).[15] Third, the *solidus* was, as Maurice Lombard noted, the sole means of exchange accepted *par le grand commerce méditerranéen*, so that the return of a stable currency was bound to stimulate an expansion of trade as well.[16] Fourth, it would give government flexibility in terms of how much of its own revenue was exacted in money (gold). The 380s were a watershed in this respect, as Theodosius I decided that a larger share of the land tax should be assessed directly in money. Cerati sifted through the constitutions to show that the fiscal system inherited from Constantine was thus "radically transformed," that is, increasingly monetized.[17] Moreover, late antique taxation was also characterized by widespread commutation of taxes, a movement driven in the first instance by the pressure of the military officers (*militares*) for substantial monetary payments. For example, Valentinian I is said to have made sweeping concessions in this respect.[18] So the result was growing monetization of the economy, increased liquidity, and a tax system based (more and more) on money.

These tendencies reached a sort of climax in the sixth and early seventh centuries. "The extremely plentiful *solidi* of Justinian I through to Heraclius would prove, were anyone heroic enough to undertake the formidable task of checking their dies, to be the survivors of a once vast coinage."[19] Michael Metcalf estimated that Thessalonica alone would have turned out between five and six million *solidi* a year under Justinian.[20] Assuming, for the sake of argument, that the mint of Thessalonica accounted for a tenth of the total number of *solidi* struck in his reign, some 50 to 60 million *solidi* were struck at Constantinople in the main part of the sixth century. This gives us a rough impression of the *size* of the sixth-century money supply, which, of course, was substantially greater than that, since the size of a currency (the amount of money in circulation) includes the coins that have stayed in circulation from previous reigns, the average velocity of circulation (the amount of business transacted by the average *solidus*), *and* the use of credit instruments other than coin. That we are dealing with a *credible* order of magnitude is shown by Procopius' report that Anastasius built up a treasury reserve of 23 million *solidi* in the course of his reign.[21] The sheer scale of monetary circulation is what is so striking about Late Antiquity.

"To ensure that terror was universal, provinces too were cut into fragments; many governors and even more provincials were imposed on individual regions . . . and to these were added numerous accountants, controllers, and prefects' deputies."[22] So wrote Lactantius on Diocletian and the major reforms that overhauled the administration of the empire in the 290s. The proliferation of provinces and the tighter political control and bureaucratic expansion that went with them were, for an unabashedly hostile source, linked to Diocletian's *avaritia*, that is, the drive to tax the expanding wealth of the provinces more effectively. Indeed, the same passage tells us that Africa and Spain were among the wealthiest provinces in the later third century.[23] Spanish olive oil had dominated the Rome market between 140 and 250, and although the massive export drive was now past its peak, the late third century in Spain still absorbed the afterglow of much of that prosperity. The olive oil of North Africa, on the other hand, saw *very* rapid expansion on the Italian market in the middle decades of the third century. So here the ceramic evidence is an even better match for Lactantius' testimony. By the third century, North African producers were bringing vast new areas of the interior into production to sustain this phenomenal drive. Industrial-scale production of the kind exemplified by the villa of Saint-Michel in the commune of La Garde in southern France, still prosperous in the early third century,[24] would have had hundreds of counterparts in the African countryside. Olive oil on this scale was clearly an economic sector dominated by the aristocracy, because it required "massive capital investment" among producers. For Tripolitania alone, Mattingly has surmised a "potential annual export to Rome in excess of one million litres of oil per year" and suggested, plausibly, that this degree of domination of the countryside was only possible through "large-scale organisation of the rural economy."[25] What it implies is a powerful aristocracy backed by the resources of the state, a pattern demonstrated throughout the imperial history of Africa (down to Justin II's laws on the colonate!), and certainly for Tripolitania at least, the amphora stamps are decisive proof (if this were needed) that the senatorial aristocracy of the third century controlled the key enterprises in the region. The same, surely, was true of the areas further west, in Tunisia, where **NUM TUS/CI·ET·ALBin/I·CC Vv** on the body of an amphora found at Carthage takes us to the heart of the third-century aristocracy and to a family that had survived the brutal repression of the 190s.[26] Presumably, these were the sons of M. Nummius Senecio Albinus (cos. 227), the first, M. Nummius Tuscus, consul in 258, the second, Nummius Ceionius Albinus, consul in 263, and descended from the brother or half-brother of Didius Julianus, who was executed (most likely) in 193.[27] At any rate, *AE* (1926, 28) pulls together a number of strands in the overlapping histories that led into the late empire. Like the Nummii, the Aradii, the Anicii, the Anullini, the Memmii, and so on were all ultimately from provincial backgrounds, wealthy landed families that would form the core of the city's aristocracy under Constantine. They were now among the leading elements of the Italian aristocracy, and under Constantine, the new provinces were carefully ordered in a hierarchy that reflected major concessions to them.[28] His creation of "consular" provinces affected mainly regions where families like the Caeonii and the Aradii held a substantial part of their assets. Thus Campania, Sicily, and Numidia all received consular rank in the 320s, and Byzacena about 330.[29] If, as Jones supposed, "Diocletian had very little use for senators," in a Constantinian perspective, the proliferation of provinces also allowed tighter control *by aristocratic families* of regions where their assets were concentrated—by the Caeonii in Numidia, the Aradii in Byzacena, the Anicii in Campania, and so on. No rule barred the aristocracy from governing their home provinces, in other words,[30] and this is surely an important clue to understanding how late Romans themselves understood the distinction between "public" and "private."

Indeed, Rome itself, avoided by the emperors, was almost left to colonization by the aristocracy! Guidobaldi draws attention to its illicit control of real estate within the city and the expansion of aristocratic *domus* in areas of the city formerly occupied by *insulae* or by commercial buildings.[31] Olympiodorus in the fifth century would describe those *domus* as miniature cities.[32] The "private" monumentality of the fourth century reflected a major shift in the culture of urban investment, away from the *evergetismo* of the early empire to a more brutal display of power poised ambiguously on a boundary between public and private that was symptomatic of the kind of social order ushered in by Constantine. The great senatorial clans (*gentes*) had multiple residences in the city. The fourth century saw a "boom in senatorial dwellings of a high standard," with an explosion of new architectural styles and decorative elements.[33] The urban prefecture, controlled by the aristocracy, must have been a key mechanism in the deals that structured the market in real estate. Rufius Volusianus Lampadius, prefect in 366 and notorious for his passion for building, was the owner of a marble workshop (*officina*) in Ostia.[34] Building materials (marble, stone, bricks) were a favorite sphere for the investment of aristocratic capital. The urban aristocracy that effectively ran the city in the 330s was also actively engaged in a range of businesses that included banks (*mensae*) and commercial enterprises (*negotiationes*).[35] One reason there is so little explicit evidence of this side of their economic activities is simply that "the pose of senatorial disregard for trade"[36] endured and meant that the complex or, better still, mediated patterns of business governance discussed by Serrao and Di Porto for a much earlier period were almost certainly still deployed. (The best indication of this is the passage from Firmicus Maternus, with its reference to *praepositi* or agents, who were more properly known as *institores.*) In short, we should be wary of the cliché that sees the late Roman aristocracy as a purely agrarian group, even if in this sector as well there was often rampant speculation (*avara venditio*) and a drive to dominate grain markets. But Ruggini's characterization of the western aristocracy as *latifondisti speculatori* ignores other dimensions of aristocratic economic behavior that were inseparable from their wholesaling of food grains and wine.[37]

The fourth century in particular saw a massive wave of investments in rural estates, in the expansion and reorganization of "villas" in the archaeological sense. This is probably best documented for the Spanish (or "Iberian") countryside, where Gorges could count at least 140 villas whose apogee he could date to the fourth century, and where the villas of the Constantinian period were described, nicely if dramatically, as expressions of a "brutal change in the architectural, artistic, economic and social norms that had governed the countryside till then."[38] In more recent work, Chavarría has proposed a rudimentary taxonomy dividing the middle-size estates along the Mediterranean coast of Spain from the monumental villas of the interior, which were mostly abandoned only gradually from the later fifth century.[39] These different sorts of establishments evolved differently in the fourth century: while the smaller establishments in the coastal areas of eastern and southern Spain converted their residential spaces to productive or industrial use—for example, "mosaics or baths were destroyed and replaced by the installation of agricultural or industrial structures"—the large estates of the interior gained in monumentality and style.[40] Chavarría argues that both movements reflected a common process of rationalization, as the absorption of the lesser properties by the biggest landowners "prompted the abandonment of the residential buildings of these 'bought out' sites and allowed their reuse for new economic activities."[41] This is a rare example of the attempt to explain the archaeology in terms of a coherent economic movement that is, in any case, reasonably well supported by all the other evidence we have for the aristocratic consolidation of the fourth century. But if true, it would suggest an astonishing degree of concentration of landed assets, which is something we can be much less sure about.

At any rate, there is now a substantial though still largely dispersed bibliography of individual sites, and attention to their specific, individual trajectories demonstrates continuing or renewed vitality in the late fourth century. At the villa of Torre de Palma in Lusitania, the 350s saw a "burst of building activity [that] created an array of new structures unmatched in number, novelty, and importance since the building campaigns of the late first century." This included the construction of a new olive press complex with its massive press and a substantial barn in one corner of the old *villa rustica*.[42] A whole clutch of villas in the southern parts of Gaul and Italy show major reconstruction and embellishment toward the end of the fourth century or even late into the fifth. Sometimes an existing villa was demolished and a new, larger one constructed in its place, as at S. Giovanni di Ruoti, where an early-first-century villa abandoned in the third, reoccupied in the mid-fourth, was demolished and rebuilt on a "much more impressive scale and to a coherent plan" in about 400. The large apsidal hall that emerged at this time was emblematic of the new power architecture that characterized the vast majority of the more substantial fourth-century establishments.[43] Elsewhere, and more commonly, major changes were made to existing sites, as villas were redeveloped to underline a new sense of scale and ostentation. This happened at S. Giovanni as well, when the apsidal hall collapsed around 460 and the villa was rebuilt on an even bigger scale till it disappeared in the devastation of the Gothic wars. Many of these "late" structures, villas built or reconstructed in the late fourth and early fifth centuries, continued in production till well into the main part of the sixth century, showing that large parts of the countryside retained their vitality despite the dissolution of the empire in the West. The huge tuna factory built at Ciudadela de Roses (ancient Rhode) in Catalunya in the late fourth century was abandoned only in the late sixth, probably in the last years of the reign of Leovigild, and then deliberately so.[44] The sumptuous establishment at Faragola in Puglia, which saw the construction of a luxurious dining room in the fifth century that used colored marbles and glass paste in its floors, survived in style into the main decades of the sixth, when it fell into ruin and was eventually abandoned.[45] In Italy, the Gothic wars had a devastating impact on the landscape and the resilience of the countryside, but short of the havoc created by prolonged warfare, there is no compelling reason to see the countrysides of the West enduring a dramatic loss of dynamism in the fifth and sixth centuries. The villas themselves were abandoned only gradually as the aristocracy regrouped or was driven back. Thus Chavarría refers to the "continued vitality" of Spanish villas in the fifth century,[46] and Balmelle has made a similar point for Aquitania.[47] In Spain, it is the late fifth century that marks a break in terms of the archaeological evidence for the continued presence of an aristocracy.[48] This was a major transformation that I shall come back to shortly.

What *was* the villa? If the archaeological villa just discussed refers to the physical remains of building complexes connected with rural estates where owners may or may not have resided for at least part of the year, in a more purely historical sense, the term *villa* referred to the estates themselves and to some size of estate *with clear boundaries*. In short, the villa was a physically coherent entity. This is a crucial point, as it has an obvious bearing on how we construe the organization of such estates in terms of their use of labor and the nature of the labor force. The widespread dogma that relations of production in these enterprises were structured as rent tenancies—that is, that the land was broken up into myriad smaller holdings that were simply leased out to peasants who paid some form of rent for them, usually in kind—is simply a cliché transferred to late Roman history from the popular idea of the large landowner (everywhere!) as a landlord. It is quite clear that the *villa* in the Roman sense was a discrete block of land, not a collection of land parcels randomly dispersed through the landscape. Thus in the Llandaff charters, which reflect Roman traditions of landholding and record grants of land of estate size, "There are boundaries which ran from one villa to another." Here the areas enclosed "varied between 125 and 1000 acres, and were, exceptionally, greater." As Wendy Davies notes, terms like *villa*, *ager*, and *terra* referred to "a coherent unit or estate," an integrated unit.[49] Aristocratic patrimonies may well have been characterized by fragmentation, but not the individual estates of which they were made up. Thus one of the estates (*villae*) owned by the Anicii was the *Casas villa Aniciorum* some twenty-eight miles west of Sabratha on the Libyan coast. This turns up in the Antonine Itinerary in a sequence that lists a series of *villae* along the coastal route between the oasis of Gabes and Lepcis Magna.[50] These must have been *very* substantial estates straddling much of the countryside between the stations listed. The *casas* were almost certainly *mapalia*, settlements typical of the nomadic and transhumant communities throughout the Maghreb from whom the estates drew much of their labor. Procopius described them as καλύβαι ("huts") and called them "stuffy."[51] In regions of olive monoculture, landowners would have needed large infusions of labor during the harvest season but practically no permanent workforce otherwise. And since harvests fluctuated, the demand for labor was never constant. Elsewhere, in areas of arable cultivation, estates created more permanent labor settlements, frequently named after the owner, since they lay within or close to the boundaries of the estate. The "vicus Juliani" in Augustine, *Ep.*23A* (from 419) is a good example. As late as the sixth century, estates in Byzantine-controlled Africa contained settlements (*vici*) with labor forces permanently attached to them.[52] Thus, in this crucial respect, there was no substantive difference between the way the biggest estates were organized in the Western provinces and in the East, where the documentation is much better. But having said this, it is important to note how little attention scholars have paid to the sheer variety of estates in the western Mediterranean and the empire more generally. The seeming normality of the *villa* is something of an illusion, and this for two reasons. First, there was simply no counterpart to the ubiquitous western villa in the eastern countryside, except for the very rich rural establishments called *proasteia*, which were largely found in suburban countryside, close to urban centers, and nowhere else. More or less consolidated rural estates in the open countryside, such as that of the Apions in the Oxyrhynchite, were run from the nearest urban center, in this case Oxyrhynchus itself; at least no papyrologist familiar with the Apion material has ever suggested otherwise. This stands in obvious contrast to the substantial managerial role that devolved on the archaeological villa as a complex of buildings from which the surrounding estate was administered. Second, estates differed according to topography. *Saltus* and *castra* are prime examples of this. The *saltus* were vast tracts of woodlands and half-mountainous regions, marshes, lagoons, and so on, or any combination of these. In Africa, local communities within these estates had petitioned the authorities for permission to convert wasteland to productive uses.[53] A powerful Antonine family, the Antistii, owned a *saltus* in the region between Thibilis and Bordj

Sabath near Cirta.[54] Ammianus' remarkable references to a whole series of *fundi* that were mountain strongholds controlled by a family of tribal chieftains in the Grande Kabylie and the areas to its west are a startling reminder of the same diversity. The most famous of these was, he says, "built in the style of a city,"[55] hence my description of estates of this sort as "*agadir*-type." None of these estates were remotely like the *villae* controlled by the Anicii on the coast of Libya. One imagines that the *Petra Geminiani* in the Aurès was precisely of this form: the Berber chief Iaudas stored a massive amount of money there, which helped the Byzantines finance much of their fortification program when it was captured.[56] It is thus fascinating to know that many of the *castra* in Visigothic Spain bore names that suggest they were privately owned strongholds from which a purely local aristocracy dominated the surrounding countryside: *Castrum Liviae, Castrum Leonis, Castrum Rufiana*, and so on.[57] These were the closest counterparts, in the late antique West, to the "strong, stone-built castles" in which the Armenian aristocracy resided,[58] influenced in part by a Sasanian model, where estates had a very different structure.

The late antique sense of scale triumphed here as well, in the emergence of a form of property that conglomerated individual estates (*fundi*) into massive holdings called *massae*. These are, usually, most widely attested in central-southern Italy and the islands, and not just because these parts of the Mediterranean remained under imperial control. There is a consensus among scholars that the *fundi* that made up the *massa* tended to be more or less contiguous, which would mean that the *massa* itself was a very substantial bloc of land.[59] From the distribution of its brick stamps, Adamesteanu suggested that the *massa Calvisiana*, owned by an early-fourth-century (Tetrarchic) governor of Sicily, subsumed much of the countryside east of the Gela, along the southern coast.[60] One of the famous Ravenna papyri (*P. Ital.* 1.58ff.) from the papers of a palatine official at the court of Ravenna shows the amounts of revenue (in *solidi*) that Sicilian *massae* could yield (445, 500, and 756 *solidi* in the three instances listed) and suggests also that *massae* were frequently leased to *conductores*, that is, entrepreneurs who, like the more recent Apulian *massari*, "assumed the management of the estate" for "short-term financial speculation."[61] Like the physical monumentality of the villa, the economic dimensions of the *massa* reflected the sheer scale on which the aristocracy accumulated wealth in the late antique West.

What I have tried to do in the preceding pages is convey some sense of the economic power and resilience of the late empire and the scale on which private wealth was accumulated. Catastrophist images of the fall of antiquity use biological metaphors like decay and decline, but the crisis of the Western empire and its aristocracy was *not* a reflection of deep-seated economic instabilities or of a loss of dynamism. Italy was the worst-case scenario; the sixth century was traumatic for its aristocracy, which effectively disappeared by the beginning of the seventh. But the dramatic changes that reconfigured Italian history in the sixth century had everything to do with the impact of the Gothic war—a major blow for the aristocracy—and the severity of the Lombard settlement that followed. By contrast, the Ostrogoths chose to rule with the collaboration of the aristocracy, and the senatorial houses were still intact and powerful under them. Aristocrats like Caecina Mavortius Basilius Decius were willing to make substantial investment in the reclamation of marshland if they could have the profits.[62] And certainly, southern Italy was still prosperous in the early sixth century. In southern Gaul, where much the best archaeology has been done, the sixth century emerges as a watershed in the history of the landscape, but the transitions are more complex, subtler than any simple "end of the villas" model, as Laurent Schneider has shown. Although a new rural geography began to emerge, the key fact is that there was no demographic contraction in southern France in Late Antiquity.[63] In Spain, the late Roman aristocracy was pushed back more decisively and is much harder to track through the main decades of Visigothic rule. Perhaps the bulk of it migrated to the church. But Chavarría has rejected the idea, argued for Italy, of a desertion of the countryside,[64] which takes us back to the need for more complex transition models than simple catastrophism. There is no doubt that by and large the aristocracy was the chief casualty of the fall of the Western empire, as Wickham now argues, but also that aristocratic forms of property survived on a much bigger scale throughout the West, as argued by medievalists like Rouche for Gaul and Modzelewski for Italy.[65] The "large estate" was one of Rome's chief legacies to the early Middle Ages, certainly in the West, where it had always been a major feature of the landscape.

The Eastern Mediterranean

The eastern Mediterranean threw up a rather different formation, much less comprehensively dominated by its aristocracy, with a more complex pattern of stratification and an almost infinite series of gradations between the imperial top and the wage-laboring bottom. To reflect this, the economy was also more complex and ramified, with a stronger urban legacy, a large urban middle class, and a substantial layer of commercial capital. Indeed, relations between business and the state, and between the aristocracy and business, were altogether more involved here, completely at odds with conventional dichotomies between "public" and "private" or between "aristocrats" and "entrepreneurs." There are several ways of conveying these nuances, but we could just as well start at the bottom. John Chrysostom felt that self-employed artisans were better off than craftsmen in wage employment, since employers often cut a substantial part of the wages of these workers on the pretext that they were fed by the employer.[66] In Egypt, there were rural households who at one extreme could accumulate substantial sums of gold (360 *solidi* in one will!),[67] and of course, many more who simply had no land and relied on work as sharecroppers or rural laborers. The Fayyūm sharecroppers of the sixth to seventh centuries are a good example of the latter, since they were easily evictable.[68] For the salaried middle class, Late Antiquity was an age of comparative affluence. When John the Lydian was taken on as a *chartularius*, he received an annual salary of twenty-four *solidi*.[69] Senior estate managers were sometimes even better paid,[70] and the local garrisons were remarkably well fed.[71] Where the demand for labor was strong, workers could earn six or seven *solidi* a year, as in contracts for irrigation work.[72] In a contract dated 588, a goldsmiths' helper was paid three *solidi*,[73] barely sufficient for a family, but he was lucky to have a regular job at all, since a large proportion of urban wage earners were in casual employment and not even paid in gold but in the copper currency that Anastasius had finally restored to viability. In 553, when Justinian tried to devalue the *follis*, these groups, called πτωχοί (lit., "the poor"), rioted, and Justinian retreated.[74] The exchange between gold and copper was critical to their ability to defend living standards. Justin II had fewer qualms, and from his reign, the undervaluation of the copper coinage effectively condemned it to extinction. A superb analogy for the Byzantine monetary system and its implications for wage earners is Raymond de Roover's description of the way Florence's monetary system affected similar groups in the fourteenth and fifteenth centuries, which is worth citing in full. The Florentines used two currencies,

> the gold florin, which remained more or less stable in weight and fineness, and a silver currency, the *moneta di piccioli*, which was steadily deteriorating . . . *There was no fixed ratio* as in the bimetallic standard of the classical type; instead the ratio of the florin to the *moneta di piccioli* varied from day to day . . . bankers and merchants belonging to the major guilds transacted their business . . . in gold florins, but the retail trade was conducted in *piccioli*. While the *lanaioli* bought wool and sold cloth in gold florins, they paid their workers in *piccioli*. As the chronicler Giovanni Villani relates, the *lanaioli*, whenever there was a shortage of money, induced the government to debase the silver currency without disturbing the gold florin. . . . In other words, they had found the way to reduce real wages without changing nominal wages . . . by simply putting less silver into new coins.[75]

Of course, this could work both ways. The strict correlation between the onset of plague in Justinian's empire and his sharp revaluation of the *follis* is surely not accidental and shows how monetary relations could influence the supply of labor.

If the expansion of wage labor was a striking feature of the late antique eastern Mediterranean, the sheer commercial vitality of its urban centers was even more remarkable. Study of the ceramic assemblages at Marseille, Carthage, and elsewhere in the western Mediterranean has clearly established that the fifth century was an absolute watershed in terms of the breakthrough and partial dominance of exports of wine and olive oil from the eastern Mediterranean.[76] The commercial vitality of the eastern Mediterranean urban centers was a vitality backed by a "widespread late antique boom in the rural economy,"[77] with densely populated countrysides. What is not so obvious in the ceramic evidence are the kinds of *networks* that these massive Mediterranean flows presupposed. The penetration of Western markets that was especially rapid from the second quarter of the fifth century was bound up, almost certainly, with a diaspora of merchant groups from the Levant. The affluence and business acumen of those groups are repeatedly noted by the author of the mid-fourth-century survey called *Expositio totius mundi*; for example, Tyre, densely populated, was well known for its "wealthy businessmen," Ashkelon and Gaza "seethed with business activity," and the Levant in general was characterized by its strong culture of business.[78] These are exceptionally valuable references, as they fill in some of the background to the extraordinary commercial thrust that developed in the fifth century by suggesting that eastern merchants were well placed in terms of capital resources to build networks abroad. At Carthage, they may have dominated the commercial and domestic quarter north of the circular harbor[79] and were a major pressure group behind Justinian's decision to invade Africa.[80] And when Guntram entered Orleans in 585, he was "greeted by acclamations in Hebrew and Syriac as well as Latin."[81] The dispersion of merchant colonies throughout the Mediterranean *may* imply a transformation of commerce such as that involved in the expansion of Venetian trade from the twelfth century. The famous (Alexandrian) financier in the Muziris contract was bound to have had late antique counterparts, but we know almost nothing about them.[82] John of Ephesus describes the "great ship-owners" of Alexandria as the "most powerful class in that wealthy city." That was about 560.[83] Justinian (*Nov.* 106, 540) shows that there were capitalists who specialized in financing shippers and merchants for an expected return of not less than 10 percent. Justinian's attempt to instigate an attack on Sasanian commercial interests and the Sasanian occupation of the Yemen in the last years of Khusro I's reign are striking indications of the money to be made by control of or even just access to the Indian Ocean.[84] This was a trading network ruthlessly controlled by the Sasanians, whose merchants would "buy up whole cargoes [of silk]" by preemptive positioning in the harbors where it first arrived.[85] On the other hand, a whole swath of territory in the Fertile Crescent, from Edessa (indeed even further north, from Dvin) down to Bostra on the edge of the desert, prospered on trade with the (non-Roman) east,[86] which may well be one reason that the urban economies of the Levant held up so much better in the crisis that swept through the Byzantine heartland in the seventh century. Edessa was so prosperous that Khusro I thought he could try to levy 50,000 pounds of gold from its residents,[87] and as late as 622, his grandson could strip 112,000 pounds of silver from its churches![88] And Maurice Sartre explains the wealth of the Hawran in the later sixth century through its contacts with the Ḥijāz, along trade routes whose success depended very largely on a "network of agreements with local tribes."[89]

The Hawran was a countryside dominated by *villages*, more typical in this respect of the east than areas with a dense concentration of estates. Indeed, there was no sector of the countryside in the eastern provinces that did not have villages and usually very substantial ones, like the large Negev villages south of Elusa (and this in a purely marginal zone!) or Aphrodito in Egypt. Even the Fayyūm, which had an exceptional concentration of aristocratic properties by the seventh century, could boast large villages like Psenyris (still described in the seventeenth century as "great and very beautiful") or Sele (Saīla), which Nabulsī (d. 1261) claimed had up to forty churches in the past![90] Both the sheer density of settlements in the rural areas of the east and the astonishing prosperity of so many of them reinforce the sense of a world where "the extraordinary tide of Mediterranean life," which, in Peter Brown's unforgettable image, "had washed further inland than ever previously" by the second century, had, quite simply, still not receded. The richer villages of the Hawran saw the construction of substantial rural houses in the Byzantine period, *maisons de village* that were linked to rich agricultural holdings and owned essentially by a rich peasantry with a strong sense of its own property.[91] The hill country was dominated by wine growing, and the absence of any trace of the olive suggests considerable regional specialization. This was *one* countryside, dominated by villages and within them by a substantial peasantry engaged in cash cropping. Villeneuve's inferences are carefully controlled and a model of how far one should go with purely archaeological evidence. Others have been less restrained and characterize the village populations of the Massif Calcaire farther north in terms like "une petite paysannerie" and "a middle class of peasants."[92] These are meaningless characterizations, since they beg the question of who or what "peasants" were in the late antique world. None of the numerous terms used (in Greek, for example) to describe people who owned or worked the land maps onto our own (sometimes confused) notions of the peasantry with quite the neatness or symmetry we would like. *Geōrgos* comes closest, but with the caveat that in late antique sources it refers often to a purely landless stratum that worked on large estates on a permanent basis. They certainly were not peasants and had little control of the land they worked. The villagers of Aphrodito described themselves as λεπτοκτήτορες (lit., "small landowners") when appealing to the authorities, a term that has no obvious connotation of a peasantry.[93] On the other hand, the ownership of villages was a possible form of landholding in the east, not attested in any of the papyri I am familiar with, but certainly referred to by Libanius and John Chrysostom in the later fourth century. Indeed, even very substantial villages could be bought, as a story in Procopius shows.[94] This tradition appears to have been strongest in Armenia. In the pages of the anonymous late fifth-century compilation called *The Epic Histories*, the aristocracy there is depicted as residing in "inaccessible fortresses protected by the rugged terrain of the country,"[95] and it is possible that their "estates" comprised the villages dominated from these fortresses.

Egypt is the only region where we can track the emergence and evolution of the aristocracy of the eastern Mediterranean with some consistency. The point of saying this is simply that it existed everywhere, from Constantinople to Armenia, and must broadly have reflected the same trends. If the consolidated western aristocracy of the fourth century suffered sustained erosion in the fifth and sixth, in the east by contrast a *new*, "Byzantine" aristocracy would emerge in the middle decades of the fifth century. This was a *Dienstadel*, quite different in formation from the senatorial clans who dominated the western empire in the fourth and fifth centuries, purely urban in character and with a strong sense of the need to preserve their estates against subdivision and structure those estates as corporate entities that could survive the vagaries of individual fortune. For example, Flavius Apion I, described by Procopius as a man of extraordinary energy,[96] and *praefectus praetorio Orientis* (PPO) in 518, had in fact suffered a major setback in the latter part of Anastasius' reign when he was exiled, ostensibly on religious grounds.[97] Yet there is no evidence that the estate in the Oxyrhynchite suffered unduly. Indeed, when the last known Apion, Flavius Apion III, died in about 619 against the background of the Sasanian invasion of Egypt, the estate (οἶκος) continued to function as an integrated organization for some years after that.[98] The corporatism of the Byzantine *oikoi* is a remarkable feature of the new aristocracy and reflected in the repeated occurrence of the expression "the heirs of so-and-so" in the papyri. (When this expression was used, it meant that the estate had remained undivided.)[99] The Apions themselves expanded their holdings through matrimonial alliances, as Azzarello has shown.[100] Indeed, women played a major role in the affairs of the eastern Mediterranean aristocracy. The later papyri are replete with the names of women who presided over major aristocratic households. And at the elite level (the "patricians"), this was a cosmopolitan aristocracy: Praejecta, the mother of Flavius Apion III, was herself the granddaughter of Justinian's niece of the same name,[101] while Apion III married the daughter of Rusticiana, one of a group of Italian aristocrats who had relocated to Constantinople following the Lombard invasion.

Rentiers? Risk-averse? How do we construe the economic characteristics of the new aristocracy? The French papyrologist Jean Gascou argued that they were content with a "relative stagnation of revenues," expressed in fixed, long-term, money rents.[102] There are at least two reasons he espoused this odd view. In the first place, he thought that the substantial long-term leases based on what was called *emphyteusis* were a major source of revenue for the Apions. This implies a whole theory of the way estates were organized economically and in terms of their use of labor. At another level, Gascou believed that the Byzantine *oikoi* were semipublic agencies, regulated by government and its drive to enforce a stable exaction of revenue. Neither of these views is plausible. There are very few leases in the Apion archive,[103] and the estate accounts and water-wheel receipts both show that the *ousia* was structured in terms of labor settlements (*epoikia*) rather than dispersed cash tenancies, let alone the very substantial leases that *emphyteusis* involved.[104] This should not be surprising, as

Dominic Rathbone's work on the third century likewise shows an aristocratic property managed in terms of the use of a regular, permanent labor force, supplemented in this case by casual laborers.[105] The rural workers, usually called *geōrgoi*, were paid in a combination of usufruct plots, estate accommodation, and cash wages (paid in gold), and sometimes also allowances in kind. The bureaucratized methods of estate management also suggest a substantial investment in overhead that is hard to reconcile with a model of dispersed tenancies, where the whole point is to minimize the burden of management. As for the view that aristocrats like the Apions had ceased to have an independent economic existence but that, like the church, the aristocracy was effectively a public agency, Roger Rémondon expressed this idea in a more nuanced way than Gascou when he referred to the Byzantine evolution as one based essentially on a "transfer of public functions to private institutions."[106] In Egypt, the pagarchy was perhaps the most striking expression of this peculiar fusion of public and private power, because pagarchs were, by and large, leading aristocrats, and the "office" was an expression of the control they had established over rural taxation. It is not often noticed that in Edict XIII, ostensibly designed to rein in recalcitrant magnates, Justinian in fact removed the authority of the Augustalis over the pagarchs![107]

Behind the fiscal solidarity of aristocracy and state in the eastern Mediterranean lay a more profound evolution, the fact that the state had come to rely on the church and the aristocracy in a fundamental way in the financial management of the empire. If Byzantine Italy, with its rapid dispersion of the former aristocracy, saw a "clerical take-over of senatorial traditions" and a new, decisively enhanced role for the church (this was true even in the Lombard areas),[108] in the Byzantine East Justinian redrew the map of public and private interests by integrating wealthy individuals, as well as institutions like the church, in the conduct of public business. This was a distinctively Byzantine development, quite different from the way the western senatorial aristocracy had *shared* power with the military and bureaucratic establishment by its own unilateral domination of the civil administration. (Valentinian I hated Petronius Probus but gave him a free hand all the same!) For example, Flavius Anastasius, banker in a famous contract dated 541, was described as *καστρησιανὸς τῆς θείας τραπέζης καὶ ἀργυροπράτης* [*sic*]. That *τραπέζη* should refer to anything other than a bank in this context is unlikely, and the description suggests that Anastasius ran his own banking business and was simultaneously connected with the imperial bank at Constantinople, where he lived.[109] So, too, with the racier and more ambitious Peter Barsymes, who began as a hugely successful banker before Justinian appointed him *comes sacrarum largitionum* (head of the treasury) in 542 and PPO soon afterward. That Peter did not relinquish his own business interests when appointed to those financial posts is clear from Procopius' accusation that "he established a state monopoly on trade in silk and made for himself a great personal profit thereby."[110] In fact, it is the Byzantine silk industry that offers the best example of the subtle forms of integration of state and private capital that had evolved by the sixth century, which expressions like "state monopoly" and "personal profit" describe in a misleading way. The fact that a whole swath of exceedingly high-ranking aristocrats were actively involved in the industry as so-called *kommerkiarioi*[111] certainly suggests that at least down to the main part of the seventh century, they were not simply officials in some purely administrative sense, but, as argued by Oikonomidès, "wealthy businessmen" who bid for monopolistic control of the trade in silk within wide-ranging regional markets. In Oikonomidès's words, "We have here a very small number of very wealthy people, who do business with the state and in the name of the state." Such individuals could form partnerships or business associations when bidding for contracts, and Oikonomidès even describes them as "wealthy individuals at the head of powerful economic organizations."[112]

Scarcely risk-averse, then. The regulation of private commerce by the state can hardly be construed as a sign of "autocratic centralization."[113] Those images were popular at a time when the academic imagination was shaped by the imposing conflict between western-style capitalism with supposedly free markets and Soviet bureaucracy. The vibrant economies of the late antique eastern Mediterranean would have had thousands of commercial establishments, well-organized money markets, and numerous middle-size cities like Scythopolis, where a decline in the architectural quality of the town was in part a reflection of the rampant growth of private businesses and a more densely built-up urban environment.[114] Both church and aristocracy owned *ergastēria*—commercial and industrial establishments of various kinds—the cathedral or Great Church of Constantinople owning no fewer than 1,100 of them.[115] Justinian (*Nov.* 159, 555), in a document reproducing the will of the aristocrat Hierios and describing a *proasteion* he owned in the suburbs of Constantinople he wanted left to his grandson, shows that these rich suburban estates could include *ergastēria* as well.[116] Čekalova suggested that the aristocracy of Constantinople was not mainly a landed group and held the bulk of its assets in liquid form.[117] Whatever one thinks of this, it certainly suggests a more diversified asset base for the late antique aristocracy than the cliché of a purely landed class. However we characterize the aristocracy of Constantinople itself, it is clear that a vast amount of gold was in circulation in the eastern empire, and the urban economies of the east were sufficiently vibrant to allow for the existence of a wide range of monied groups, such as jewel traders, bankers, silversmiths, and silk merchants. Money changers and bankers were among the most prosperous groups in Ephesus,[118] and the eastern Mediterranean money market functioned with considerable autonomy from government control. In Edict XI, Justinian attacked the coin weighers and dealers (*chrysōnes*) of Alexandria for charging the public an exorbitant commission of 12.5 percent on transactions involving loose *solidi* that had lost weight in circulation. This was in 559 during the second prefecture of Peter Barsymes, and Justinian instructed Peter to make sure that the dealers reverted to a rate that would facilitate transactions involving loose coins. As it happens, the papyri show that this particular intervention did bring the commission down to half its former level, 6.25 percent. In *P.Oxy.*I 144, dated 580, a payment of 720 *solidi* described as "in loose coin from the interior districts" attracts a supplement of 45 *solidi* "for deficiencies in purity and weight" (*hyper obryzēs kai apokatastatikōn*); in other words, 1.5 carats per *solidus* or 6.25 percent. Here is an excellent example of the nature of Byzantine regulation, namely, not quite the dramatic model of "autocratic centralization" that Ostrogorsky had in mind but a more pragmatic and flexible attempt to encourage the flow of business by eliminating excesses from the market.

The fiscal system of the sixth century was very largely monetized. A detailed tax register from an Egyptian district, Antaeopolis, is one indication of this.[119] Using this document, A. H. M. Jones was able to calculate that 10,322 *solidi* was the "normal gold assessment of Antaeopolis" in the reign of Justinian.[120] This works out to a cash ratio of almost 63 percent; in other words, close to two-thirds of the total revenue from this district (one of the lesser ones) was paid in gold.[121] The very high levels of money taxation that the Umayyads could extract from Egypt was thus a development of trends established in the sixth and seventh centuries. Michael Metcalf has shown that the truncated Byzantine state of the later seventh century ran into a severe monetary recession, as the treasury was depleted of fresh inflows following the Arab conquests.[122] But this fiscal crisis and the general deflation bound up with it are *not* a reflection of the state of monetary economy in the eastern Mediterranean in these decades. The Mediterranean remained integrated for much of the sixth and seventh centuries, with Byzantine control of Africa playing a pivotal role in preserving the link between its opposite shores. There was an abundance of gold in Africa, Sicily, and the Aegean,[123] and much of the continued circulation of *solidi* and tremisses was undoubtedly due to trade. The very substantial late-seventh-century deposit from the Crypta Balbi in Rome[124] is a microcosm of the continued economic vitality of the Mediterranean in this period, despite the huge changes that swept through it politically. The conquests themselves involved no dramatic economic disruption,[125] and the huge sums that cities like Emesa agreed to settle for shows just how prosperous the urban Levant remained.[126]

Aftermaths

The transition to the early Middle Ages thus certainly requires the complex and differentiated model that Wickham has developed, minus its minimalism and the obsessive focus on taxation. Catastrophist images of Late Antiquity were built on the political dissolution of the Western empire, coupled with the intensity of the dislocations in sixth-century peninsular Italy. Francovich and Hodges build their model of the Italian transformation on the large-scale desertion of the countryside by the aristocracy and a dramatic shift in the settlement pattern over the later sixth and seventh centuries.[127] For his part, Paolo Delogu refers in Italy's case to the "great crisis of the sixth and seventh century."[128] But in Francia, which saw a fairly rapid integration of the surviving aristocracy and the Frankish ruling class, the seventh century was a period of agrarian and demographic expansion, spearheaded by the powerful new nobilities that emerged in the Merovingian *Teilreiche* by the end of the sixth century.[129] The Merovingians inherited the late Roman system of unified estates (*villae*) with their mixed servile labor forces. Slavery was a substantial part of the late antique legacy, but the great movement of manumission that swept through post-Roman societies in the sixth and seventh centuries threw up a less segregated labor force described generically as *mancipia*—not slaves in the rigorous Roman sense but servile all the same, a conglomerate of all the various forms of labor oppression that had survived as part of the debris of the Western empire. Manumission entailed the creation of service holdings and the first assaults on the physical integrity of the unified *villa*.[130] By the *late* seventh century, the Merovingian aristocracy had forged the elements of a new organization of labor, a further break from antiquity, a further move into the pure Middle Ages. Chris Wickham's rejection of the "slavery to serfdom" model is unexceptionable and welcome, except that much of that rejection is based on views about late and post-Roman labor organization that flow more from abstractions than from a closer consideration of the terminology used in sources such as the Merovingian charters. For example, "Most *servi/mancipia* in our period . . . were tenants who *controlled their own holding* and could keep its fruits after rents were paid."[131] But *mancipia* included former *coloni*, bound tenants, and *servi* were still slaves in Francia, Visigothic Spain, and elsewhere, and it is doubtful that these groups in particular were ever thought to "control their own holdings," whatever other groups may actually have done so. Wickham's thesis of the conversion of slaves into self-managing peasants is really equivalent to the thesis that Roman landowners abandoned direct management, a view I have suggested is implausible.[132]

Farther east, Islam emerged as the dominant economic power in the eighth to eleventh centuries,[133] but much of the prosperity of that period flowed from the legacy of vibrant urban economies inherited from Late Antiquity by the Umayyads. A key part of that legacy was the monetary economy of the late Roman and Sasanian worlds. The existing coinages (*solidi* and *drahms*) continued to circulate for some five decades after the conquests, a fact that is usually little emphasized. The general implication is a strong degree of cultural and economic continuity across the political watersheds of the seventh century, an indication surely of the astonishing resilience of the eastern Mediterranean in this period and the vitality of its urban sectors. In Egypt, the province of Arcadia could still be assessed for the substantial sum of 200,000 *solidi* in the early seventh century.[134] Alexandria's population was 300,000 taxable adults at the time of the conquest,[135] which yields a total population of well over a million and puts this great eastern metropolis in the same orbit, demographically, as ninth-century Baghdād, medieval Cordoba, and Tang cities like Xi'an and Luoyang. Baṣra, founded in the late 630s, had a population of roughly half a million by the 680s.[136] None of this suggests a demographic fragility any more extreme than the biological precariousness of all ancien régime populations.[137] Of course, the loss of the affluent eastern provinces was a severe financial blow to the Byzantine state and led directly to the prolonged monetary recession I referred to. But the image of imperial crisis that this suggests can scarcely be extended either to the Merovingians, ruling over what was now the richest region of Europe, or to the Muslim Near East, both of which inherited the mantle of Late Antiquity to become the cutting edge of major new developments.

NOTES

1. Rostovtzeff 1971, 530.
2. Mazzarino 2002; 1980, vol. 3, p. 666ff.
3. Anon., *De rebus bellicis*, 2.1–4 (Giardina, *Le cose della guerra*, p. 12). Cf. Bagnall 1985.
4. Torelli 1973.
5. SHA, *Clod. Alb.*, 4.1–2; Alföldy 1968a.
6. SHA, *Sev.*, 12.1, 13.1–7; Alföldy 1977.
7. Birley 1988, 195.
8. Beschaouch 1969; Christol 1986.
9. Vogler 1979, 232ff., 239.
10. Rémondon 1966, 145 ("la noblesse égyptienne, d'origine bureaucratique"); so, too, Fikhman 1973, 18 ("La nouvelle noblesse issue essentiellement des milieux militaires et burocratiques").
11. Lo Cascio 2008, 172–173. Fluctuations: *P.Oxy.* 3401.7ff. ("everyone is looking for *solidi* and the price is going up every day"), *P. Oxy.* 1223.31ff., cf. Symmachus, *Rel.*, 29.1 (Barrow, p. 162).
12. Ambrose, *De fide*, 4.81, etc., cited Freu 2007, 65.
13. Mazzarino 1980, vol. 3, p. 679: "Ma nei gradi supremi, non c'è più distinzione tra senatori e burocrazia."
14. Morris 1976, 119.
15. See Lo Cascio 1981, 82ff. on the provision of liquidity.
16. Lombard 1971, 138.
17. Cerati 1975, 71–85.
18. Ammianus 27.9.4 (Rolfe, vol. 3, p. 58).
19. Metcalf 2001, 119.
20. Metcalf 1984, 119.
21. Procopius, *Anecd.* 19.7 (Dewing, *Secret History*, p. 228).
22. Lactantius, *De mortibus persecutorum*, 7.4 (Creed, p. 12).
23. Lactantius, *De mort. persec.*, 8.3 (Creed, p. 14).
24. Brun 1989.

25. Mattingly 1988.
26. *AE* (1926), #28, "Sur la panse d'une amphore trouvée à Carthage."
27. Cf. *PLRE* 1, p. 1142 (stemma); Alföldy 1968b, 138 (ancestor).
28. Chastagnol 1966.
29. Kuhoff 1983, 63–64.
30. Kuhoff 1983, 77.
31. Guidobaldi 1999, 58–60.
32. Olympiodorus, fr. 41.1 (Blockley, *The Fragmentary Classicising Historians of the Later Roman Empire*, vol. 2, pp. 204–205).
33. Hillner 2003, 135f., 141f. (more than one house), 144f. (boom); Guidobaldi 1999, 62ff. (architecture).
34. Becatti 1948, 31.
35. Firmicus Maternus, *Mathesis*, 3.10.1 (Monat, t.2, p. 101): *magnorum aut potentium virorum . . . scribas, rationibus, mensis, apothecis negotiationibusque praepositos*, written c. 334. Cf. *CTh* xiii.5.14 (371) for senatorial involvement in commercial shipping.
36. Cooper 2007, 93.
37. Ruggini 1961, 230.
38. Gorges 1979, 48 (apogee), 52 (brutal change).
39. Chavarría 2004, 68–75.
40. Chavarría 2004, 75–80.
41. Chavarría 2004, 87; 2007, 137–138.
42. Maloney and Hale 1996, 290ff.
43. Small and Buck 1994.
44. Nolla-Brufau 1984.
45. Volpe, De Felice, and Turchiano 2005.
46. Chavarría 2004, 75; 2007, 114.
47. Balmelle 2001, 119.
48. Chavarría 2006, 25.
49. Davies 1978, 32–34, 40.
50. *Itin. Ant.*, 61.2 (Cuntz, p. 9).
51. Procopius, *Bell.* 4.6.10 (Dewing, *History of the Wars*, vol. 2, p. 257).
52. Justin II, *Nov.* 6.1 (570) (*Jus Graecoromanum*, t.1, p. 10). So, too, in Sicily, cf. Gregory, *Ep.*, 9.129 (599).
53. Flach 1978.
54. Pflaum 1969–1971.
55. Ammianus 29.5.13, about the fundus Petrensis.
56. Procopius, *Bell.* 4.20.23; 29 (Dewing, *History of the Wars*, vol. 2, p. 390).
57. Martínez Melón 2006, 124–125, esp. nn.152–155.
58. Thomas Artsruni, *History of the House of Artsrunik'*, p. 143 (tr. Thomson).
59. Cf. Brown 1984, 198 ("large blocs"); Ruggini 1980, 12 ("aggregati di fondi contigui"); Castagnetti 1991, 62; De Francesco 2004, 286.
60. Adamesteanu 1955, cf. *Itin. Ant.*, 89.6; 95.7 (Cuntz, p. 12ff.).
61. Snowden 1986, 14.
62. Giardina 2001.
63. Schneider 2007.
64. Chavarría 2006, 34; 2007, 139.
65. Rouche 1979, 220, 328–329; Modzelewski 1978, 41ff.
66. John Chrysostom, *In Ep. I ad Cor., Hom.* xliii, 3 (PG 61.372).
67. *P.Oxy.* I 132, with *BL* 7.127; legacy of a former village headman.

68. E.g., Jördens 1986.
69. John Lydus, *De mag.*, 3.27 (Bandy, p. 174).
70. *P. Oxy.* XVI 1913.40, thirty *solidi* and substantial amounts of wheat and barley for an Apion manager.
71. Gascou 1989, 290ff.
72. E.g., *P.Flor.* I 70 (627).
73. *P. Oxy.* LVIII 3933.
74. John Malalas, *Chron.*, 18.117 (Thurn, p. 415; Jeffreys, p. 293).
75. de Roover 1968, 305.
76. Pieri 2005.
77. Loseby 2005, 631.
78. *Expositio totius mundi*, 24; 29; 33 (Rougé, pp. 158, 162, 166).
79. Procopius, *Bell.* 3.20.3ff., 16 (Dewing, *History of the Wars*, vol. 2, pp. 170, 174). Cf. Clover 1982, 8.
80. Procopius, *Bell.* 3.20.5–6 (Dewing, *History of the Wars*, vol. 2, p. 170).
81. Jones 1964, 865.
82. Rathbone 2000.
83. John of Ephesus, *Third Part of the Ecclesiastical History*, p. 69 (tr. Payne Smith).
84. John Malalas, *Chron.*, 18.56 (Thurn, p. 384–385; Jeffrey, p. 269); Procopius, *Bell.* 1.20.9 (Dewing, *History of the Wars*, vol. 1, p. 192); Theophanes of Byzantium *ap.* Photius, *Bibl.*, t. 1, p. 78 (Henry) (explaining Khusro's decision as a *response* to the Byzantine drive to access the Central Asian silk routes via the Türks!).
85. Procopius, *Bell.*, 1.20.12 (Dewing, *History of the Wars*, vol. 1, p. 192), cf. Whitehouse and Williamson 1973; Whitehouse 1991.
86. *Expositio totius mundi*, 38 (Rougé, p. 176) (Bostra); 22 (p. 156) (Edessa); extrapolating to the sixth century.
87. Procopius, *Bell.*, 2.26.39 (Dewing, *History of the Wars*, vol. 1, p. 498).
88. *Chronicle of AD 1234*, § 31 (Palmer, *The Seventh Century in the West-Syrian Chronicles*, p. 133–134).
89. Sartre 1985, 132ff.; 1985–1986, 197–198; Kennedy 2004, 21. The geographer al-Iṣṭakhrī notes that ʿUmar b. al-Khaṭṭāb (the future caliph) had made his fortune trading with Gaza.
90. al-Nabulsī, *Ta'rīkh al-Fayyūm*, 114 (Moritz).
91. Villeneuve 1985–1986.
92. Sodini 2003, 46.
93. *P.Lond.* V 1674. 95–96; *P.Cairo Masp.* 67002.
94. Procopius, *Anecd.* 30.18–19 (Dewing, *Secret History*, pp. 352ff.)
95. Garsoïan 1989, 52.
96. Procopius, *Bell.*, 1.8.5 (Dewing, *History of the Wars*, vol. 1, p. 63).
97. Sarris 2006, 16–17.
98. E.g., *P.Oxy.* LXVIII 4703 dated 22.5.622.
99. Gonis 2002, 92.
100. Azzarello 2006, 210ff., n. 8.
101. Beaucamp 2001.
102. Gascou 1985, 10.
103. As Gascou himself notes! Cf. Gonis, *P.Oxy.* LXVII 4615 intr. (p. 235).
104. *P.Lond.* II 483 (615 or 616) is a perfectly preserved specimen of an emphyteutic lease. Typically, it involves a monastery, not one of the *oikoi*.
105. Rathbone 1991.

106. Rémondon 1966, 142.

107. Just., *Ed.* xiii, 12; 25. Most likely date: 539.

108. Brown 1984, 35; Pohl 1997, 125.

109. *P.Cairo Masp.* II 67126.

110. *PLRE* IIIb, p. 1001, citing Procopius, *Anecd.* 25.20–6 (Dewing, *Secret History*, p. 298ff.), which claims that management of the industry was centralized under the *comes sacrarum largitionum*, namely, Peter, who siphoned the bulk of its profits. But in *Anecd.* 20.5 (Dewing, *Secret History*, p. 234) Procopius himself makes it clear that the "monopolies" were based on competitive bidding.

111. Morrisson and Seibt 1982, 226f., 228, 231; Cheynet, Morrisson, and Seibt 1991, 103 (#140), 105 (#143), 105f. (#144); with titles like *paneuphemos* and *endoxotatos*.

112. Oikonomidès 1986, esp. 39–40, 43.

113. Ostrogorsky 1968, 253. Marlia Mango (2000, 190) refers, with more preciseness, to "private commerce regulated by the state."

114. Tsafrir 1996, esp. 276. "Numerous middle-sized cities" from Laiou and Morrisson 2007, 26.

115. Just., *Nov.* 43 (536) (*CIC* vol. 3, pp. 269ff.); *Vita S. Olympiadis*, 6 (*Anal. Boll.* 1896, p. 414).

116. Just., *Nov.* 159 pr. (*CIC* vol. 3, pp. 736ff., at 738).

117. Čekalova 1998.

118. Foss 1979, 8.

119. *P.Cairo Masp.* I 67057.

120. Jones 1951, 271.

121. Contrast Wickham's view: "It was in general unlikely that most taxation was moved between regions in the form of money in our period" (2005, 768).

122. Metcalf 2001.

123. Guéry, Morrisson, and Slim 1982; Banaji 2007, 63–64, 83–84.

124. Saguì 2002.

125. Villeneuve 1985–1986, 64, 128; Magness 2003, 215; Loseby 2005, 633; Walmsley 2000, 291–293.

126. al-Balādhurī, *Futūḥ al-buldān*, p. 136 (ed. Ridwan).

127. Francovich and Hodges 2003, 109.

128. Delogu 1994, 23.

129. Sprandel 1957.

130. Banaji 2009, 70ff.

131. Wickham 2005, 560; italics mine.

132. See my discussion of Wickham in Banaji 2009.

133. Lombard 1947, the classic statement.

134. An estimate based on *P.Oxy.* XVI 1909.

135. Al-Maqrīzī, *Kitāb al-mawāʿiẓ wa-al-iʿtibār bi-dhikr al-khiṭaṭ wa-al-āthār*, tr. Bouriant, p. 226, citing Ibn Lahīʿa. A tradition attributed to the renowned and more reliable Egyptian authority ʿUthmān b. Ṣāliḥ claimed that Egypt had a total taxable population (meaning a population of adult males) of "over six million" (Ibn ʿAbd al-Ḥakam, *Futūḥ Miṣr*, ed. Torrey, p. 70, lines 10–12), but this would yield an impossibly high figure for the overall demography. Yāqūt cites "over six million" as the size of the total native population of the country: *Muʿjam al-buldān*, ed. Wüstenfeld, vol. 3, p. 895.

136. Rotter 1982, 69; half a million c. 683.

137. Braudel 1975, vol. 1, p. 413.

WORKS CITED

Adamesteanu, Dinu. 1955. "Due problemi topografici del retroterra gelese," *RAL*, ser. viii, 10: 199–210.

Alföldy, Géza. 1968a. "Herkunft und Laufbahn des Clodius Albinus in der Historia Augusta." In *Bonner Historia-Augusta-Colloquium 1966/1967*, 19–38. Bonn: Habelt.

———. 1968b. "Septimius Severus und der Senat," *BJ* 168: 112–160.

———. 1977. "Eine Proskriptionsliste in der Historia Augusta." In *Bonner Historia-Augusta-Colloquium 1968/1969*, 1–11. Bonn: Habelt.

Azzarello, Giuseppina. 2006. "*P.Oxy.* XVI 2039 e la nascita della *domus gloriosa* degli Apioni," *ZPE* 155: 207–228.

Bagnall, Roger S. 1985. *Currency and Inflation in the Fourth Century Egypt.* Atlanta: Scholars Press.

Balmelle, Catherine. 2001. *Les demeures aristocratiques d'Aquitaine.* Paris: De Boccard.

Banaji, Jairus. 2007. *Agrarian Change in Late Antiquity.* 2nd rev. ed. Oxford: Oxford University Press.

———. 2009. "Aristocracies, Peasantries and the Framing of the Early Middle Ages," *Journal of Agrarian Change* 9.1: 59–91.

Beaucamp, Joëlle. 2001. "Apion et Praejecta: Hypothèses anciennes et nouvelles données," *REB* 59: 165–178.

Becatti, Giovanni. 1948. *Case ostiense del tardo impero.* Rome: Libreria dello Stato.

Beschaouch, A. 1969. "*Uzappa* et le proconsul d'Afrique Sex. Cocceius Anicius Faustus Paulinus," *MEFRA* 81: 195–218.

Birley, Anthony R. 1988. *The African Emperor: Septimius Severus.* Rev. ed. London: Batsford.

Braudel, Fernand. 1975. *The Mediterranean and the Mediterranean World in the Age of Philip II*, tr. Siân Reynolds, 2 vols. London: Fontana/Collins.

Brown, Peter. 1971. *The World of Late Antiquity: From Marcus Aurelius to Muhammad.* London: Thames and Hudson.

Brown, T. S. 1984. *Gentlemen and Officers: Imperial Administration and Aristocratic Power in Byzantine Italy, AD 554–800.* London: British School at Rome.

Brun, Jean-Pierre. 1989. "La villa gallo-romaine de Saint-Michel à La Garde (Var)," *Gallia* 46: 103–162.

Camps, Gabriel. 1984. "*Rex Gentium Maurorum et Romanorum*: Recherches sur les royaumes de Maurétanie des VIe et VIIe siècles," *AntAfr* 20: 183–218.

Castagnetti, A. 1991. "Le strutture fondiarie ed agrarie." In *Storia di Ravenna, 2/1: Dall'età bizantina all'età Ottoniana*, ed. A. Carile, 55–72. Venice: Marsilio.

Čekalova, Alexandra. 1998. "Fortune des sénateurs de Constantinople du IVe au début du VIIe siècle." In ΕΥΨΥΧΙΑ: *Mélanges offerts à Hélène Ahrweiler*, 119–130. Paris: Publications de la Sorbonne.

Cerati, André. 1975. *Caractère annonaire et assiette de l'impôt foncier au Bas-Empire.* Paris: Librairie Générale de Droit et de Jurisprudence.

Chastagnol, A. 1966. "Les consulaires de Numidie." In *Mélanges d'archéologie, d'épigraphie et d'histoire offerts à Jérôme Carcopino*, 215–228. Paris: Hachette.

———. 1970. "Les modes de recrutement du Sénat au IVe siècle." In *Recherches sur les structures sociales dans l'Antiquité classique*, ed. C. Nicolet, 187–211. Paris: CNRS.

Chavarría Arnau, Alexandra. 2004. "Interpreting the Transformation of Late Roman Villas: The Case of Hispania." In *Landscapes of Change*, ed. N. Christie, 67–102. Aldershot: Ashgate.

———. 2006. "Villas en *Hispania* durante la antigüedad tardía." In *Villas tardoantiguas en el Mediterraneo occidental*, ed. A. Chavarría, *Anejos de AEspA* 39: 17–35.

———. 2007. *El final de las villae en Hispania (siglos IV–VII d.C.)*. Turnhout: Brepols.

Cheynet, Jean-Claude, C. Morrisson, and W. Seibt. 1991. *Les sceaux byzantins de la Collection Henri Seyrig*. Paris: Bibliothèque Nationale.

Christol, M. 1986. "À propos des Anicii: le IIIe siècle," *MEFRA* 98.1: 141–164.

Clover, Frank M. 1982. "Carthage and the Vandals." In *Excavations at Carthage 1978, Conducted by the University of Michigan*, vol. 7, ed. J. H. Humphrey, 1–22. Ann Arbor, MI: Kelsey Museum.

Cooper, Kate. 2007. *The Fall of the Roman Household*. Cambridge: Cambridge University Press.

Davies, Wendy. 1978. *An Early Welsh Microcosm: Studies in the Llandaff Charters*. London: Royal Historical Society.

De Francesco, Daniela. 2004. *La proprietà fondiaria nel Lazio secoli IV–VIII: Storia e topografia*. Rome: Quasar.

Delogu, Paolo. 1994. "La fine del mondo antico e l'inizio del medioevo." In *La storia dell'Alto Medioevo italiano (VI–X secolo) alla luce dell'archeologia*, ed. R. Francovich and G. Noyé, 7–29. Florence: All'insegna del giglio.

Fikhman, I. F. 1973. "Quelques considérations sur les données sociales et économiques des papyrus d'Oxyrhynchus d'époque byzantine," *JÖBG* 22: 16–21.

Flach, D. 1978. "Inschriftenuntersuchungen zum römischen Kolonat in Nordafrika," *Chiron* 8: 441–492.

Foss, Clive. 1979. *Ephesus after Antiquity: A Late Antique, Byzantine and Turkish City*. Cambridge: Cambridge University Press.

Francovich, Riccardo, and Richard Hodges. 2003. *Villa to Village: The Transformation of the Roman Countryside in Italy c. 400–800*. London: Duckworth.

Freu, Christel. 2007. *Les figures du pauvre dans les sources italiennes de l'Antiquité tardive*. Paris: De Boccard.

Garsoïan, Nina G. 1989. *The Epic Histories (Buzandaran Patmut'iwnk')*. Cambridge, MA: Harvard University Press.

Gascou, Jean. 1985. "Les grandes domaines, la cité et l'état en Égypte byzantine," *Travaux et Mémoires* 9: 1–90.

———. 1989. "La table budgétaire d'Antaeopolis (*P.Freer* 08.45 c–d)." In *Hommes et richesses dans l'Empire byzantin, t. 1 IV–VII siècle*, 279–313. Paris: P. Lethielleux.

Giardina, Andrea. 2001. "Pubblico e privato nella bonifica Teodericiana delle paludi pontine." In *Zones côtières littorales dans le monde Méditerranéen au Moyen Âge*, ed. J.-M. Martin, 35–50. Rome: École Française de Rome; Madrid: Casa de Velázquez.

Gonis, Nikolaos. 2002. "Studies on the Aristocracy of Late Antique Oxyrhynchus," *Tyche* 17: 85–97.

Gorges, Jean-Gerard. 1979. *Les villas hispano-romaines: Inventaire et problématique archéologiques*. Paris: De Boccard.

Guéry, Roger, C. Morrisson, and H. Slim. 1982. *Le trésor de monnaies d'or byzantines*. Recherches archéologiques franco-tunisiennes à Rougga 3. Rome: École Française de Rome.

Guidobaldi, Federico. 1999. "Le *domus* tardoantiche di Roma come 'sensori' delle trasformazioni culturali e sociali." In *The Transformations of Urbs Roma in Late Antiquity*, ed. W. V. Harris, 53–68. Portsmouth, RI: JRA.

Hillner, Julia. 2003. "Domus, Family, and Inheritance: The Senatorial Family House in Late Antique Rome," *JRS* 93: 129–145.
Jones, A. H. M. 1951. "Review of Johnson and West, *Byzantine Egypt: Economic Studies*," *JHS* 71: 271–272.
———. 1964. *The Later Roman Empire 284–602*. 2 vols. Oxford: Blackwell.
Jördens, Andrea. 1986. "Teilpachtverträge aus dem Arsinoites," *ZPE* 65: 107–122.
Kennedy, Hugh. 2004. *The Prophet and the Age of the Caliphates*. 2nd ed. Harlow: Longman.
Kuhoff, Wolfgang. 1983. *Studien zur zivilen senatorischen Laufbahn im 4.Jhr. n.Chr.* Frankfurt: P. Lang.
Laiou, Angeliki E., and Cécile Morrisson. 2007. *The Byzantine Economy*. Cambridge: Cambridge University Press.
Lebecq, Stéphane. 1990. *Les origines franques, Ve–IXe siècle*. Paris: Éditions de Seuil.
Lombard, Maurice. 1947. "Les bases monétaires d'une suprématie économique: L'or musulman du VIIe au XIe siècle," *Annales* 2: 143–160.
———. 1971. *Études d'économie médiévale I: Monnaie et histoire d'Alexandre à Mahomet*. Paris: Mouton.
Loseby, S. T. 2005. "The Mediterranean Economy." In *The New Cambridge Mediaeval History, Vol. 1: c. 500–c.700*, ed. P. Fouracre, 605–638. Cambridge: Cambridge University Press.
Lo Cascio, Elio. 1981. "State and Coinage in the Late Republic and Early Empire," *JRS* 71: 76–86.
———. 2008. "The Function of Gold Coinage in the Monetary Economy of the Roman Empire." In *The Monetary Systems of the Greeks and Romans*, ed. W. V. Harris, 160–173. Oxford: Oxford University Press.
Magness, Jodi. 2003. *The Archaeology of the Early Islamic Settlement in Palestine*. Winona Lake, IN: Eisenbrauns.
Maloney, Stephanie J., and John R. Hale. 1996. "The Villa of Torre de Palma (Alto Alentejo)," *JRA* 9: 275–294.
Mango, Marlia Mundell. 2000. "The Commercial Map of Constantinople," *DOP* 54: 189–207.
Martínez Melón, José Ignacio. 2006. "El vocabulario de los asentamientos rurales (siglos I–IX d.C.): evolución de la terminología." In *Villas tardoantiguas en el Mediterraneo occidental*, ed. A. Chavarría, *Anejos de AEspA* 39: 113–131.
Mattingly, D. J. 1988. "The Olive Boom: Oil Surpluses, Wealth and Power in Roman Tripolitania," *Libyan Studies* 19: 21–42.
Mazzarino, Santo. 1980. *L'Impero romano*. 3 vols. 3rd ed. Bari: Laterza.
———. 2002. *Aspetti sociali del IV secolo*, ed. Elio Lo Cascio. Milan: Rizzoli.
Metcalf, D. M. 1984. "The Mint of Thessalonica in the Early Byzantine Period." In *Villes et peuplement dans l'Illyricum protobyzantin*, 111–128. Rome: École Française de Rome.
Metcalf, D. M. 2001. "Monetary Recession in the Middle Byzantine Period: The Numismatic Evidence," *NC* 161: 111–155.
Mickwitz, Gunnar. 1965 [1932]. *Geld und Wirtschaft im römischen Reich des vierten Jahrhunderts n. Chr.* Amsterdam: Adolf M. Hakkert.
Modzelewski, Karol. 1978. "La transizione dall'antichità al feudalesimo." In *Dal feudalesimo al capitalismo: Storia d'Italia, Annali* 1, ed. R. Romano and C. Vivanti, 3–109. Turin: Einaudi.
Morris, Rosemary. 1976. "The Powerful and the Poor in Tenth-Century Byzantium: Law and Reality," *Past and Present* 73: 3–27.

Morrisson, Cécile, and Werner Seibt. 1982. "Sceaux de commerciaires byzantins du VIIe siècle trouvés à Carthage," *RN* 24: 222–241.
Nolla-Brufau, J. M. 1984. "Excavaciones recientes en la ciudadela de Roses: El edificio bajo-imperial." In *Papers in Iberian Archaeology*, ed. T. F. C. Blagg, R. F. J. Jones, and S. J. Keay, 430–459. BAR Int. Series 193/2. Oxford: B.A.R.
Oikonomidès, Nicolas. 1986. "Silk Trade and Production: The Seals of *Kommerkiarioi*," *DOP* 40: 33–53.
Ostrogorsky, George. 1968. *History of the Byzantine State*. 2nd ed., tr. Joan Hussey. Oxford: Blackwell.
Pflaum, H. G. 1969–1971. "Glanes épigraphiques dans la région de Constantine," *Recueil de la Société archéologique de Constantine* 71: 59–75.
Pieri, Dominique. 2005. *Le commerce du vin oriental à l'époque byzantine*. Beirut: Institut Français du Proche-Orient.
Pohl, Walter. 1997. "The Empire and the Lombards: Treatises and Negotiations in the Sixth Century." In *Kingdoms of the Empire: The Integration of Barbarians in Late Antiquity*, ed. W. Pohl, 75–134. Leiden: Brill.
Rathbone, Dominic. 1991. *Economic Rationalism and Rural Society in Third-Century A.D. Egypt: The Heroninos Archive and the Appianus Estate*. Cambridge: Cambridge University Press.
———. 2000. "The 'Muziris' Papyrus (*SB* XVIII 13167): Financing Roman Trade with India." In *Alexandrian Studies II in Honour of Mostafa el Abbadi*, ed. Mohammed Abd-el-Ghani et al., 39–50. Alexandria: Société Archéologique d'Alexandrie.
Rémondon, Roger. 1966. "L'Égypte au 5e siècle de notre ère." In *Atti del XI Congresso Internazionale di Papirologia, Milano, 2–8 settembre 1965*, 135–148. Milan: Istituto Lombardo di Scienze e Lettere.
Roover, Raymond de. 1968. "Labour Conditions in Florence around 1400: Theory, Policy and Reality." In *Florentine Studies: Politics and Society in Renaissance Florence*, ed. Nicolai Rubinstein, 277–313. London: Faber.
Rostovtzeff, M. 1971. *The Social and Economic History of the Roman Empire*. 2 vols. 2nd ed., rev. P. M.Fraser. Oxford: Clarendon Press.
Rotter, G. 1982. *Die Umayyaden und der Zweite Bürgerkrieg (680–692)*. Wiesbaden: Kommissionsverlag Franz Steiner GmbH.
Rouche, Michel. 1979. *L'Aquitaine des Wisigoths aux Arabes 418–781*. Paris: Éditions Touzot.
Ruggini, Lellia. 1961. *Economia e società nell' "Italia annonaria": rapporti fra agricoltura e commercio dal IV al VI secolo d. C.* Milan: Giuffrè.
———. 1980. "La Sicilia fra Roma e Bisanzio." In *Storia della Sicilia*, vol. 3, ed. R. Romeo, 3–37. Naples: Società editrice Storia di Napoli e della Sicilia.
Saguì, Lucia. 2002. "Roma, i centri privilegiati e la lunga durata della tarda antichità: Dati archeologici dal deposito di VII secolo nell'esedra della Crypta Balbi," *ArchMed* 29: 7–42.
Sarris, Peter. 2006. *Economy and Society in the Age of Justinian*. Cambridge: Cambridge University Press.
Sartre, Maurice. 1985. *Bostra: des origines à l'Islam*. Paris: P. Geuthner.
———. 1985–1986. "Le peuplement et le développement du Ḥawrān antique à la lumière des inscriptions grecques et latines." In *Hauran I: Recherches archéologiques sur la Syrie du Sud à l'époque hellénistique et romaine*, ed. J.-M. Dentzer, 189–202. Paris: P. Geuthner.

Schneider, Laurent. 2007. "Structures du peuplement et formes de l'habitat dans les campagnes du sud-est de la France de l'Antiquité au Moyen Âge," *Gallia* 64: 11–56.
Small, A. M., and R. J. Buck. 1994. *The Excavations at San Giovanni di Ruoti, Vol. 1: The Villas and Their Environment*. Toronto: University of Toronto Press.
Snowden, Frank M. 1986. *Violence and the Great Estates in the South of Italy: Apulia, 1900–1922*. Cambridge: Cambridge University Press.
Sodini, Jean-Pierre. 2003. "Archaeology and Late Antique Social Structures." In *Theory and Practice in Late Antique Archaeology*, ed. L. Lavan and W. Bowden, 29–56. Leiden: Brill.
Sprandel, Rolf. 1957. *Der merovingische Adel und die Gebiete östlich des Rheins*. Freiburg im Breisgau: E. Albert.
Spufford, Peter. 1988. *Money and Its Use in Medieval Europe*. Cambridge: Cambridge University Press.
Torelli, Mario. 1973. "Per una storia della classe dirigente di Leptis Magna," *RAL* 28: 377–410.
Tsafrir, Y. 1996. "Some Notes on the Settlement and Demography of Palestine in the Byzantine Period." In *Retrieving the Past*, ed. J. D. Seger, 269–283. Winona Lake, IN: Eisenbrauns.
Villeneuve, F. 1985–1986. "L'économie rurale et la vie des campagnes dans le Hauran antique." In *Hauran I*, ed. J.-M. Dentzer, 63–136. Paris: P. Geuthner.
Vogler, Chantal. 1979. *Constance II et l'administration impériale*. Strasbourg: AECR.
Volpe, Giuliano, Giuliano De Felice, and Maria Turchiano. 2005. "Faragola (Ascoli Satriano): Una residenza aristocratica tardoantica e un 'villaggio' altomedievale nella Valle del Carapelle." In *Paesaggi e insediamenti rurali in Italia meridionale fra Tardoantico e Altomedioevo*, ed., G. Volpe and M. Turchiano, 265–297. Bari: Edipuglia.
Walmsley, Alan. 2000. "Production, Exchange and Regional Trade in the Islamic East Mediterranean." In *The Long Eighth Century*, ed., I. L. Hansen and C. Wickham, 265–343. Leiden: Brill.
Whitehouse, David. 1991. "Epilogue: Roman Trade in Perspective." In *Rome and India: The Ancient Sea Trade*, ed. V. Begley and R. D. De Puma, 216–218. Madison: University of Wisconsin Press.
Whitehouse, David, and Andrew Williamson. 1973. "Sasanian Maritime Trade," *Iran* 11: 29–49.
Wickham, Chris. 2005. *Framing the Early Middle Ages: Europe and the Mediterranean 400–800*. Oxford: Oxford University Press.

CHAPTER 19

CONCERNING RURAL MATTERS[1]

CAM GREY
University of Pennsylvania

THE fifth-century agronomist Rutilius Taurus Aemilianus Palladius was long regarded as merely a poor and slavish imitator of his illustrious agronomic forebears, but in recent scholarship his reputation as a reporter and commentator on agricultural matters in Late Antiquity has enjoyed something of a renaissance. Scholars note in particular his sensitivity to the immense diversity in the geography of the Mediterranean world and the corresponding variation in agricultural techniques. Further, while it is clear that his handbook is aimed at his wealthy, leisured peers rather than the *rustici* whom he claims as his audience, we may nevertheless take his reportage as a relatively accurate reflection of the options available to both small and large landowners for managing their agricultural resources in the period.[2]

Concerning the Four Things of Which Agriculture Consists[3]

In the opening chapters of his *Opus Agriculturae,* a text notable among other things for its organization as a month-by-month calendar of the work undertaken over the course of an agricultural year, he writes that the four crucial elements of agriculture are *aere, aqua, terra,* and *industria.*[3] While we might quibble with the precise details of Palladius' catalogue, it provides a useful framework for structuring an account of agriculture and rural life in Late Antiquity. For our current purposes, we might, for example, take *aere* and *aqua* together to mean environmental conditions, climate, and natural resources; *terra* to encompass settlement, exploitation, ownership, and tenure of land; and *industria* to refer to the peasant family and the peasant community more generally.

In what follows, I embrace Palladius' broad geographical scope but adapt his schema and adopt a tripartite division, exploring in turn environmental, practical, and socioeconomic aspects of rural life in the period between the accession of Diocletian in the late third century and the establishment of the Rashidun Caliphate on the eastern fringes of the Roman world in the first half of the seventh century. Palladius and other sources from the period provide a certain amount of information about the first element, and we may in addition draw on a burgeoning body of material detailing the physical and environmental conditions of Late Antiquity.[5] There exists also a relatively rich collection of legal, documentary, and material sources for patterns of land settlement and use in the period, along with a vibrant set of historiographical debates in the secondary literature.[6] By contrast, rural social structures and relations between peasants and other inhabitants of their world receive relatively short shrift from the aristocratic authors of our written sources, who are little interested in the unknown, unknowable masses who dwelt on the margins of their world.[7] However, comparative evidence suggests that rural communities are characterized by highly complex, interwoven systems of socioeconomic interaction, and in pursuit of those systems of interaction in Late Antiquity, we are forced to cast our net widely, read for what our texts do not tell us as much as for what they do, and adopt an explicitly cross-cultural perspective.

Geographically, our inquiry encompasses a vast area, from the windswept and damp confines of northwestern Europe through the irrigated deserts of North Africa and Egypt to the fertile river valleys of the Tigris and Euphrates in Syria and the Middle East.[8] Throughout, I emphasize interregional variation, for, as Palladius himself observes, "The system of working cannot maintain a single method within such a great diversity of lands."[9] Equally, however, I acknowledge broad and recognizable patterns in the strategies employed by rural inhabitants in responding to and managing their physical and socioeconomic environments. We must begin, that is, from two seemingly contradictory assumptions. On the one hand, the rural landscapes of the late Roman world were almost infinitely diverse in terms of physical topography, economic structures, and social systems. On the other hand, peasant communities exhibit certain behaviors that are broadly congruent and comparable across time and space.[10] It is crucial that we entertain both propositions to avoid both the Scylla of a string of overschematic, broad-brush generalizations about rural life in Late Antiquity, which erases differences in pursuit of an ideal and idealized grand narrative, and the Charybdis of a collection of discrete, balkanized microregional studies of individual communities that eschews larger analytical categories and questions.[11]

Concerning the Determination of Climate[12]

The natural environment looms large in the conceptual world of all who live on, and off, the land, but particularly the peasant. The most fundamental aim of the peasant household is, of course, to ensure its subsistence survival by combining the cultivation of food-producing plants with animal husbandry. In the process, peasants must be able to respond to the demands and limitations of their environment if they are to survive. The particular form that those responses take will be specific to context, for different microenvironments pose different challenges, and a host of socioeconomic, familial, political, and cultural factors are also likely to intrude on the peasant household's decision-making ability. The potential for localized climatic conditions to affect agricultural practices is not lost on Palladius, who suggests alternative sets of criteria for determining where to situate fields, according to whether one is in a cold or warm province; offers contrasting advice over ideal sowing times, depending on the prevailing weather of the region; and lards his text liberally with casual observations about the massive variation possible in plowing, sowing, and harvesting techniques.[13]

We should not be surprised to observe this flexibility in ancient agricultural techniques, for year-to-year and interregional variations in climatic conditions and natural resources are a fact of life for agriculturalists. It is more difficult to determine whether there were longer term, more far-reaching climatic changes in the period and, if there were, whether such changes had an impact on agriculture. Although it was once fashionable to attribute the fall of the late Roman empire to a disastrous climatic shift that crippled agricultural production, desiccated the land, and led to the eventual collapse of the entire political superstructure of the state, scholars have long been suspicious of such arguments.[14] The ancient sources speak of plagues, blights, and natural disasters and complain about the exhaustion of the soil, but we should be wary of generalizing from isolated accounts of unusual or extreme weather conditions and cautious about the ulterior motives that lie beyond petitions for relief from taxation or grants of tax concessions on the grounds of agricultural crisis.[15] Nevertheless, in recent research, the issue of climate change and its impact on societal, political, and economic change in the period has once again begun to receive some attention.[16] It is therefore worth briefly exploring what is known or can be surmised of the climate in Late Antiquity.

The study of the climates of antiquity rests largely on a congeries of proxy data, including information on changes to sea levels, palynological assemblies, the distribution of environmentally stable isotopes in ice cores, tree rings, and cave stalagmites. In recent decades, an increasingly clear picture of the climate of Europe and the Mediterranean region has emerged from this combination of evidence. In broad terms, it seems that the climate of the first three centuries of the Common Era was slightly cooler than the present, but around 300 C.E., a slight increase in temperature occurred. This was followed around 400 C.E. by a return to cooler conditions for a period of 100 years or so; then a period of warming again ensued, which culminated in the Little Optimum or Medieval Warm, around 1000 C.E. As a result of the combination of mountains, low-lying countries, and a circuitous shoreline dominated by a sizable body of water, this fluctuation in temperature was accompanied by variable changes in rainfall and humidity in the region. In continental Europe, for example, it seems that warmer weather brought with it some degree of desiccation and a reduction in rainfall, and cooler temperatures were accompanied by increased rainfall. By contrast, in areas closer to the Mediterranean Sea, the opposite held true: increased rainfall accompanied increases in temperature, and colder conditions tended to be dryer.[17]

This interregional variation should warn us against adopting convenient universal schemata in pursuit of the impact of climate change on agriculture, but it is possible that, more generally, the period witnessed an increase in climatic variability.[18] Archaeological evidence suggests, in addition, a process of gradual alluvial aggradation in the streambeds of various parts of the Mediterranean Basin in the middle of the first millennium, although debate currently rages over the relationship between human and natural factors in this process.[19] At any rate, it is conceivable that, in combination, these phenomena necessitated abandonment or movement of some settlements, particularly those in or close to alluvial streambeds.[20] It is possible also that, combined with some falling off in large-scale, long-distance trade networks, increased climatic fluctuation may have led to the abandonment of marginally productive fields, which were no longer worth the investment of labor and resources.[21] Similar combinations of environmental and human factors are likely to be behind evidence for the reforestation of areas formerly given over to agriculture in regions as diverse as northern Britain, Gaul, and Mesopotamia.[22] Although it is certainly possible that these reductions in the proportion of cultivated land were accompanied by some shrinking in the size of both urban and rural populations, clear chains of cause and effect are difficult to establish, and the evidence points to immense interregional variation.[23]

Concerning Opinions on the Labor and Essentials of Agriculture[24]

Palladius offers his readers detailed advice about the physical characteristics they should look for when choosing estates, together with an exhaustive checklist of the buildings, fixtures, livestock, and *instrumenta* that they should expect to find.[25] He also advises them to retain blacksmiths, carpenters, potters, and coopers on their estates, "lest a need for wandering into town distract peasants from their important labor."[26] While this observation once again prompts legitimate questions about Palladius' audience and his firsthand knowledge of small-scale agriculture, it does at least reveal an assumption that urban and rural contexts coexisted symbiotically and an expectation that there were few obstacles to travel between city and country in the period. Palladius' expectations here are not unfounded, for the evidence suggests that the population of the ancient Mediterranean world was highly mobile. Skilled artisans could travel long distances to ply their craft, and merchants and traders moved around the countryside with relative ease.[27] Clergymen and pilgrims, soldiers, brigands, and nomads wandered the landscape.[28] These habitual travelers might be joined by occasional travelers—a young woman, a peasant or tenant farmer with a grievance, a slave traveling on his master's business.[29]

Movement between town and country also appears to have been a relatively regular feature of rural life. The city was a recognized refuge for peasants in the event of subsistence crisis or other perturbations, although it is likely that they would also have been among the first to be banished from cities in times of food shortage.[30] But economic straits were not the only circumstance in which peasants might find themselves living or working in towns. Legislation of the early fifth century suggests that men registered in the tax rolls as tenants on rural estates could be found serving in municipal *curiae* or urban guilds in Gaul.[31] A woman registered in the tax rolls as a *colona* might marry a man and move to live with him in the city.[32] The sixth-century bureaucrat and *littérateur* Cassiodorus remarks on peasant children being sold at a market in Lucania and observes that such sale might provide the opportunity for a better life in the city.[33] Movement from town to country is also evident. A law of Honorius censures town dwellers giving their children over to shepherds for rearing but concedes that they may be given to other *rusticani*, "as is customarily done."[34] Members of municipal councils, urban craftsmen, and members of urban guilds could be found working or living in the countryside. In legislation of the period, this is interpreted as withdrawal from towns, but in the context of continuous movement between the two, this may be overly dramatic.[35] In Noricum, for example, farmers issued daily from towns to cultivate the surrounding fields. It seems reasonable to conclude, therefore, that "most people breathed in a steady dose of both town and country air."[36]

Consequently, any account of agriculture and rural life in Late Antiquity must also take note of the experience of cities in the period.[37] A brief survey of the archaeological evidence reveals infinite variety here, too. It appears that in some circumstances, cities and their hinterlands experienced quite different fates.[38] Where the two remained connected, it is probable that some regional or provincial economic systems fragmented in the period, and the economic horizons of these towns and their hinterlands were consequently reduced.[39] In marginal or transitional economic zones, existing populations may have responded to these circumstances by embracing or reverting to nomadic pastoralism in preference to sedentary agriculture.[40] In some parts of the empire, populations of barbarians were installed in dispersed or nucleated settlements in the early fifth century, which is likely to have caused upheaval for local populations.[41] Natural disasters might also cause disruption, including food shortages for the affected population, and this in turn could lead populations to adopt strategies for dealing with subsistence crisis, including temporary or permanent movement.[42] In each case, the balance or distribution of settlement in a region may have been affected.

The archaeological evidence reveals longer term trends in settlement patterns, and here we may, broadly speaking, draw a contrast between eastern and western provinces. In the west, the period witnessed a gradual process of transformation in the distribution of settlement over the course of the fourth to seventh centuries.[43] Broadly speaking, urban agglomerations continued, with a few notable exceptions such as the Balkans and the Danube region.[44] Some urban sites in northern Europe reveal the construction of town walls, and it is possible that in these regions, some rural dwellings may have been abandoned in favor of the security of those walls. Caution is necessary, however, for changes in settlement distribution need not entail abandonment of fields, and the construction of walls may in some circumstances have more to do with a town's prestige and self-identity than with fear or uncertainty. Further, the area enclosed by fortifications tends to be smaller than the extent of the settlement in earlier periods.[45]

Small, dispersed hamlets, villas, and farmsteads also continued, although, generally speaking, they appear to have gradually reduced in number and increased in relative size.[46] Roman villas continued to be the most recognizable sites, although they appear to have experienced a variety of fates in the period. Some acquired the appearance, at least, of fortification, and a number continued to be inhabited into the sixth century and beyond. The reasons for such fortification are difficult to determine. It is possible that here, too, we witness a response to security concerns in the period, but it is also possible that spectacular building in the countryside amounted to an exercise in social prestige for local aristocrats.[47] Other villa sites continued to be occupied or exploited, but in a different form or for a different purpose. A villa might be reused as the site of a church or monastery, an artisanal installation, or a pottery kiln.[48] It might be reconstituted as the focal point for a small settlement or become a periodic or temporary habitation.[49] In addition, the period witnessed the beginnings of villages in western Europe, as some small sites agglomerated and grew, while others were abandoned in favor of nearby protovillages. But clarity is hampered by the suspicion that most of the archaeological evidence comes from villages that failed, for those that prospered appear in many cases to have continued into modern times and therefore present almost insurmountable challenges to scholars seeking to gather information about their earliest history.[50]

In the eastern provinces, by contrast, preexisting patterns of settlement appear to have continued into the sixth century, at least, and perhaps later. In some regions, the number of sites appears to have increased, although this may be attributed to a new type of territorial organization or, indeed, to sampling techniques used in a survey.[51] At any rate, in these regions the characteristic rural settlement remained the village, occupying a series of landscapes that were geographically and geologically diverse. The general pattern is of continuity, at the very least, and often of increased prosperity in rural contexts in the eastern Mediterranean. Survey evidence from the Methana Peninsula in Greece suggests that the number of rural settlements increased over the course of the fourth and following centuries, and the Mareotis region around the city of Alexandria also experienced a period of prosperity. In Boeotia, the fourth century witnessed reoccupation of sites that had been abandoned during the preceding centuries, combined with new settlements. In northern Syria and the Hauran, the boom was slightly later, beginning sometime in the fifth century and enduring until a falling off in the late sixth or seventh century.[52]

It is difficult to incorporate this variety of changes into a single pattern or even a series of patterns, and in any case, generalizations are of only limited value. A case in point is North Africa, where extensive survey work reveals immense diversity in the distribution, density, size, and location of settlements over the course of the third to seventh centuries. It seems that some regions experienced a loss of sites during this period, while in others settlement appears to have increased. It is possible that this amounts to a redistribution of the population across the landscape, rather than either depopulation or expansion. Equally, however, the evidence strongly suggests that the large-scale agricultural exploitation of the Roman period came to an end, and this is likely to have affected some small-scale agriculturalists as well.[53] At any rate, the archaeological evidence reveals landscapes of change throughout the late and post-Roman world, and a brief survey such as this cannot hope to do justice to the immense diversity in the fates of countrysides, their towns, and their populations. It suffices to observe that scholars no longer expect to find decline in all regions, but they are increasingly wary of swinging to the opposite extreme and positing a booming rural sector throughout the Mediterranean world.

Concerning the Cultivation of Fields[54]

The seventh-century Spanish encyclopedist Isidore of Seville defines the cultivation of fields as involving "ashes, plowing, lying fallow, burning of stubble, dunging, hoeing, and weeding."[55] Isidore here highlights the various techniques for preparing the terrain for sowing. An individual agriculturalist's choice of preparation technique is likely to vary from place to place, for it will be constrained by a number of factors—the availability of oxen for plowing, the type of crop and the density with which it is being sown, the method that best suits the terrain itself, and so on.[56] Peasants did on occasion sell goods in the market, but their production was geared primarily toward subsistence and the satisfaction of the demands of the landlord and the tax man, so it will have only distantly resembled larger productive enterprises devoted to the cultivation of a single crop explicitly for sale.[57] But it is still unhelpfully broad and schematic to speak of a single peasant economy or agricultural regime in Late Antiquity. The annual flooding of the Nile, for example, created an agricultural regime that was unique and had little in common with the practices necessary for the swampy environs of Ravenna or the techniques practiced in the arid environment of North Africa. Nevertheless, a typical agricultural enterprise is likely to have involved some kind of mixed-farming regime involving cereals, legumes, and livestock. We can surmise in addition that peasants characteristically aimed to ensure the long-term productivity of their fields by recourse to a collection of crop-rotation and field management strategies. It is also probable that a number of crops were cultivated concurrently to minimize risks of crop diseases and derive the maximum benefit from the different properties of each plant.[58]

Palladius' evidence suggests that a wide diversity of crops were grown as a matter of course—among them wheat, spelt, barley, millet, chickpeas, and lentils.[59] It seems from both ancient and comparative evidence that these crops were typically planted in combinations and sown in three sowing seasons: an autumn sowing of wheat and barley, a late winter or early spring sowing of pulses, and a summer sowing of various other crops.[60] These could be supplemented by sowing special additional crops as and when necessary, as a response either to crop failure or to particularly propitious conditions.[61] It is likely that different crops were often planted together in the same field as a strategy for maintaining soil fertility, increasing overall yields, and lessening the risk of subsistence crisis. Given the small size of peasant holdings, it is also probable that relay cropping was a regular part of agrarian regimes, and Palladius provides some evidence for this when he recommends second and even third plowing of some fields.[62]

These methods of soil preparation and management were part of broader strategies for maintaining the productivity of fields. The ancient agronomic evidence suggests that agriculturalists characteristically employed a multitude of short-, medium-, and long-term strategies for creating and managing pasturage and for alternating that land with arable cultivation. At any one time, an individual agricultural enterprise is therefore likely to have included a multiplicity of fields under a diversity of crops, including some converted into pasture within an established arable rotation, some transformed into artificial meadows for a period of years, and some designated as permanent or semipermanent pastures for grazing animals.[63] This last phenomenon is a reminder that animal husbandry was also an essential component of these agrarian regimes. Palladius envisages an estate to include horses, asses, cattle, sheep, goats, and pigs, and other sources speak of peasants tending small flocks of sheep or possessing a team of oxen.[64] In addition to their manure, these animals might provide wool, meat, and milk. While oxen and a plow represented a significant investment, they might provide the peasant with income from renting out his team or his labor.

Concerning the Possession of Property[65]

A considerable amount of legislation from the late Roman world is devoted to defining the liturgies and fiscal obligations pendant upon various different types of land, for an individual's liability for taxation in the period rested on the amount and type of land that he or she possessed or cultivated. Landowners were expected to submit a declaration of their assets, called a *professio* or *iugatio*, to the municipal census rolls, and on the basis of these, a community's liability for taxation, or *capitatio*, was determined.[66] There is precious little evidence for the form that these declarations might take, but what does survive indicates that a single landed estate, even a very small one, consisted of a number of different fields, dispersed across the landscape.[67] The economic benefits of such a strategy are clear. Comparative evidence suggests that dispersal of landholdings is a deeply entrenched technique among peasant populations around the world, a conscious strategy to ensure that a natural disaster will not completely destroy all a household's crops. The critical point of equilibrium in this strategy is between the distance of the land from the peasant's home and the return it will give, but even here the rationality of the practice revolves more around risk management and the specific needs of the household than around motivations of profitability or reduction of labor output.[68]

Our best evidence for fragmented landholdings in Late Antiquity concerns the properties of wealthy aristocrats. Paulinus of Pella owned land in several different provinces of the empire and claimed that, in his later years, he was forced to rent land elsewhere, as well as cultivating his own meager plot. Symmachus held land both throughout Italy and in Africa. Legislation detailing senators' liability for taxes in many different regions reveals that, at least among the aristocracy, widely dispersed landholdings remained an accepted norm in the late Roman empire. The sixth-century will of the bishop Remigius of Rheims also reveals widespread personal landholdings, spread over a reasonably wide area, including fields in Portensum, Cesurnicum, and Vindonissa.[69] While we should not uncritically infer the condition of peasants from the behavior of elites, it seems reasonable to suggest that they were simply an extreme (and extremely visible) manifestation of a widespread phenomenon.

Fragmented landholdings had as their corollary an active market in land, participated in by both aristocrats and peasants.[70] Peasants sold to elites.[71] They bought from elites.[72] They also sold to each other.[73] Additionally, it seems that land sales were often made to buyers known or connected to the vendor.[74] Purchase of land was not exclusively for cultivation—papyrological evidence from Egypt reveals that some villagers possessed capital to speculate in land on a small scale for profit.[75] The fluidity of the market in land reflected the life cycle needs of individual peasant households. A pair of land registers from the Hermopolite nome in Egypt, dated around 350, reveal changes in the distribution and amount of land held by both village and metropolitan owners over perhaps a decade.[76] Bowman's analysis of these texts suggests that in that period, more than a third of the land of the nome changed hands. He observes that there is no way of determining what constitutes a normal circulation of land but concludes that the fourth-century Hermopolis land market "was far from ossified."[77] From these registers and other evidence from the late antique world, it seems reasonable to conclude that land was usually transferred as a series of small parcels rather than as an agglomerated holding, and an individual land sale often added only a relatively small amount to the buyer's total holdings.[78]

Concerning Farmers on the Census Lists and Tenants[79]

Alongside dynamic field management strategies and an active market in land, we might expect tenancy and labor arrangements in the period to have been relatively flexible in response to the changing needs of both large landowners and small-scale agriculturalists. However, such an expectation runs counter to a long-held assumption that the period witnessed a fundamental transformation in the condition of formerly free peasant proprietors, who were reduced over the course of the fourth, fifth, and sixth centuries to a position of dependence that so closely resembled slavery that the latter legal status ceased to exist as a separate category. This interpretation was based principally on the evidence of the legal sources, which betray a preoccupation with identifying the individuals responsible for the tax burden assessed on a particular field and ensuring that they continued to fulfill their fiscal responsibilities.[80] It is difficult to imagine that the idealized world of the legislation was matched in reality, and in recent scholarship, the focus has shifted increasingly to the *realia* of rural labor relations.[81] The following brief survey of the diversity of complementary arrangements visible in the late antique sources builds on this literature.

It is clear from the ancient sources that large landowners customarily employed complex, complementary systems of labor for exploiting their rural properties.[82] Registered and unregistered tenants, slaves, and casual or permanent laborers could coexist on the same estate. The farm itself was overseen by a farm manager, who could be a slave, freedman, or freeborn.[83] These complementary systems of exploitation satisfied the needs of peasant households as well, which customarily employed strategies for periodically modifying the productive capacity or personnel of the household. A household might rent additional plots of land to employ its labor force fully or ensure more produce.[84] Adolescent or adult members of the household might become specialist rural laborers, such as reapers.[85] Peasants also labored for their landlords and other large landowners at crucial times in the agricultural year, including harvest time and when the vintage was due.[86] For peasant households, wage labor was a complement to tenancy and ownership of land.[87]

When we turn to the nature of tenancy arrangements in the period, it seems that the *locatio-conductio* arrangement of the legislation is of only limited use for an analysis of tenancy on the scale undertaken by peasants. A variety of tenancy agreements existed, their character determined more by local customs and conditions than by legal directives.[88] There was, in addition, great variety in the wealth and social standing of individuals who undertook small-scale tenancies.[89] Some were wealthy enough to own slaves or a team of plow oxen.[90] Others brought to a tenancy arrangement little more than their own labor and that of their families.[91] Still other tenants might be debtors of their landlord, working off a debt incurred.[92] Contracts were either short- or long-term, although what little evidence we have suggests a preference for long-term tenants.[93] Just as a landlord might expect to rent to more than one tenant, it was possible for an individual to rent from more than one landlord.[94] The benefits of this strategy for the peasant household were twofold. In the first place, it facilitated the fragmentation of landholdings and therefore served to minimize the risk that a natural disaster would completely destroy all of a household's crops.[95] In the second place, it widened the pool of individuals who could be approached at need to act as a patron or intercessor and with whom members of the peasant household could expect to pick up additional wage labor at certain times of the year.

Rent might be paid in cash, in kind, or in a combination of the two.[96] It might include the farmer's tax burden, which the landlord was then expected to pass on to the fisc. The landlord could take responsibility for taxes, expecting his tenant to pay only rents.[97] Or the two might be entirely separate and collected independently.[98] The rent might be a fixed annual sum, in an arrangement of "tenancy proper" (*fermage*),[99] or it might be a negotiated proportion of the harvest as part of a sharecropping arrangement (*métayage*).[100] The economic arrangements between landlord and farmer that underlie these two systems are fundamentally different. In addition to differences in the form of remuneration, the two parties carry different burdens of risk and responsibility.[101] For the peasant, tenancy potentially offered more rewards for high productivity but threatened ruin in the event of a bad harvest. The investment of the landowner in the venture was minimal, although the *instrumenta* with which a tenancy was leased could be fairly comprehensive.[102] Sharecropping, on the other hand, involved sharing risk. The peasant was required to make only a minimal investment of capital. But his freedom in exploiting the plot might be limited. In cases where the landlord provided seed, tools, and/or a team of oxen for plowing, for example, he or his farm manager might be involved in decisions regarding crop rotation and sowing strategies. Thus, while the tenant nominally stood on his own, the sharecropper made his economic decisions in consultation with his landlord.

Some scholars have equated close economic links between landlord and sharecropper with the sharecropper's status and assumed that his apparent lack of economic independence is a product of his low economic and social standing.[103] It has been further suggested that the late Roman period witnessed a move toward sharecropping as a more effective means of exploiting and binding the peasantry.[104] However, this interpretation is overly pessimistic. It is possible that rents in kind became more prevalent in the late Roman period, but this does not amount to the eclipse of fixed-rent tenancy by sharecropping.[105] It seems also that landlords continued to agonize over the debts of their tenants, but there is no reason to assume that debt became more widespread among the peasantry or that peasants in debt became sharecroppers.[106] It is, perhaps, more judicious to conclude that flexibility, not rigidity, was the norm of late Roman tenancy arrangements.

Concerning Laborers and Lands[107]

Casual labor was fundamental to the economies of wealthy landowners and peasants in the late Roman period, and was characteristically enmeshed with both tenancy and patronage alliances.[108] For landlords and patrons, it satisfied the periodic, seasonal needs of the estate more effectively than employment of a permanent, underutilized labor force. For peasant proprietors and tenants, it supplemented the income and resources of the household.[109] A discussion of the landowner's economy in precapitalist societies has argued that Roman estates relied in all periods and in all regions on the availability of free laborers, who could be employed on a casual or periodic basis.[110] The peasant household, too, regularly entered the rural labor market, and in doing so, peasants came into regular contact with aristocratic landowners. Labor could be undertaken for wages.[111] It might also be a negotiated component of a tenancy contract.[112] Some contracts of labor, at least, were part of ongoing relationships between peasant and landowner, patron, or patrons. Comparative literature suggests that landowners hired seasonal labor on a preferential basis, choosing clients over nonclients, and papyrological evidence from the Appianus estate in third-century Egypt reveals that some casual laborers, at least, were related to permanent employees or tenants of that estate.[113]

Palladius' advice about retaining certain specialists permanently on one's estate functions as something of an ideal, however, for not every estate would have merited full-time employment of specialists, and most would have needed extra laborers at harvest time.[114] Skill levels and terms of employment are likely to have varied.[115] The value of skilled casual laborers to the landowner's economy at certain crucial times of the year was not lost on Palladius, who observes that "five *modii* can be gathered from a full field in one day's labor by an experienced reaper, by a mediocre one only three, by a poor one even less," and we can assume that these individuals found themselves employed in gangs at specified times of the year.[116] Skilled woodchoppers, too, could find themselves in high demand at certain points in the agricultural cycle.[117]

In other instances, laborers were neither enmeshed in ongoing relations with a landowner nor regular participants in sedentary agriculture. They could occupy the margins of that society, taking advantage of its occasional needs. In a letter to Augustine, a certain Publicola reveals that nomadic tribesmen might be employed to guard the crops.[118] Publicola's principal concern is that these *barbari*, through their oaths to pagan deities, will pollute the Christian crops they have undertaken to protect. In passing, however, he reveals that these crop guardians were hired on the strength of a letter written by a military officer.[119] This type of letter vouched for the trustworthiness of the laborer and was one way of creating a link between laborer and landowner through the intercession of another. Elsewhere in North Africa, Optatus of Milevus describes gangs of men looking for work who congregated in rural markets, on estates, and around the shrines of the saints to seek work.[120] In Arzuges, however, the rural labor market was partially regulated by members of the military stationed there. In an anonymous, seasonal labor market, such as that described by Optatus, such a letter might provide a link to a potential employer that could be crucial in that employer's choice of one laborer over another.

Concerning Family Relationships and Their Degrees[121]

Palladius observes that the *industria* of agriculture "comprises both supply (*facultas*) and purpose (*voluntas*)."[122] The concept acquires a more theoretically sophisticated form in Chayanov's proposition that the extent to which a peasant household can exploit its own labor is conditioned by the makeup of the family labor unit, on the one hand (Palladius' *facultas*), and its requirements as a consumer, on the other (Palladius' *voluntas*). The link between household composition and household economy is an organic one: the economic requirements of the household necessarily have an impact on the composition of the family, and the makeup of the family influences the economic behavior of the household.[123] Our sources for the period are somewhat obdurate, but a few tentative observations are possible. The sixth-century will of the bishop Remigius of Rheims provides some tantalizing hints of relations between economic behavior and family composition. The will contains evidence for a range of economic activities, including viniculture, pig rearing, and agricultural cultivation, and suggests that variability in family structures could be intra-regional, as well as inter-regional. In some instances, particular economic activities can be ascribed to individuals and their families. The will mentions a certain Enias, a *vinitor* who seems to have been head of a household comprising himself; his wife, Muta; their daughter, Nifastes; and at least one son, Monulfus. Comparative literature suggests that viniculture can be linked to the employment of day laborers, partible inheritance strategies, and perhaps even nuclear family form, and this may be evidence of just such a nuclear family.[124]

The peasant household was not hermetically sealed from other professions, and we might expect soldiers and shepherds, as well as other specialists, to have originally been peasants themselves or counted peasants among their kin.[125] Some division of labor within peasant households is also probable, and we find traces of this in Palladius, who suggests that women and children are particularly suited to the collection and storage of acorns and notes the skills of women in the raising of hens, "insofar as it seems work."[126] It is likely that a corollary of cooperation between households was a keen awareness of the advantages and possibilities of marriage alliances, kinship relations, and friendship as strategies for managing economic risk or mitigating a subsistence crisis. A small amount of evidence exists for peasant marriage strategies in the period, revolving principally around attempts by aristocratic landlords and the state to control or respond to movement of registered *coloni* from one location to another.[127] Likewise, we catch glimpses of collaboration between individual peasants that we may, with caution, label friendships. Characteristically, these relationships entail both conflict and cooperation, as each party negotiates the tension between an impulse toward self-interest, on the one hand, and an acknowledgment of the obligations as well as the benefits of cooperative behavior, on the other.[128]

On Charity Toward One's Neighbor and Love of One's Enemies[129]

When we turn to the internal organization of rural communities, both ancient and comparative evidence reveals that they are characterized by a series of fundamental tensions. A consciously espoused ideology of reciprocity sits uneasily with a reality of factionalism, competition, and petty jealousies. The impression of group solidarity offered to outsiders conflicts with marked divisions in status, power, and access to resources within the community. These tensions hold a community together, for it is thereby forced to create dynamic strategies for managing the resultant pressure. The ideal of reciprocity is a key element in the cohesiveness of rural communities, since it enables craft specialization within the community, and underlies strategies for risk management.[130] By choosing to live in a community, individual households lessen the risk of subsistence crises and increase potential strategies for coping with such crises. If a household in need calls on its neighbors for assistance, they will help—if they can—to safeguard their own survival when their own subsistence crisis arises. At the same time, rural communities are heterogeneous collections of alliances and loyalties, groups of households aware that they may at any moment find themselves in conflict with their neighbors for resources.[131] The village is a stage for internecine disputes, disagreements between sedentary and pastoral populations, and petty crime. The ideology the community espouses and the reality of community behavior can, and frequently do, conflict.[132]

In practice, the tension between an expressed ideal of reciprocity and the perpetual potential for conflict manifested itself in various ways in rural communities. In the eastern Mediterranean, where the characteristic pattern of settlement was the village, tinkers, coopers, and blacksmiths might be found, supplementing their own agricultural activities or trading their labor and goods for agricultural produce.[133] Markets could take place in the village, drawing traders from the surrounding region and serving also as an opportunity for the celebration of communal religious festivals.[134] Woodcutters and shepherds, faith healers and magicians, lived in or on the margins of these communities, often the object of suspicion and distrust but nevertheless essential to the life of the village.[135] In their interactions with these marginal figures, peasants might choose to act together to minimize their risk. For example, we observe villagers collectively entrusting the care of their sheep, cows, or oxen to a few individuals. A crucial component of such a decision was trust: an unscrupulous shepherd might, for example, milk the sheep without their owners' knowledge and consent and sell the milk for his own profit.[136]

The inhabitants of smaller settlements, such as the *vici* of western Europe or the scattered hamlets and farmsteads of North Africa, are likely to have relied on traveling specialists or to have traveled themselves to a larger habitation to meet their need for medical or spiritual aid and the acquisition or repair of household items or small luxuries.[137] In these cases, too, they are likely to have run the risk of exploitation or worse. Consequently, it is probable that such communities tended to embrace collective action as an effective tool for insulating individual members against violence or loss. Such collective action is only occasionally visible in our sources, but we may gain a sense of its potential effectiveness from a letter of Augustine, bishop of Hippo. Augustine remarks on a threat by the inhabitants of the *fundus Thogonoetis* to decamp from their tenancies en masse if an unpopular bishop is imposed on them. In this case, it seems that the threat was heeded and the bishop removed in response to the community's collective resistance.[138]

Concerning the Bringing of Disputes[139]

The foregoing examples illustrate a fundamental element in the behavior of rural communities. The success of communal economic strategies requires individuals to balance the interests of their own households against the interests of the collectivity. Individual households must weigh advantages of communal living against the disadvantages of communal obligations and the potential for dispute and disagreement. Inclusion in a community involves interactions and activities that are theoretically voluntary but effectively compulsory. These activities include communal harvesting; processing and storing grain; constructing agricultural buildings, such as wells and cisterns, threshing floors, olive presses, and granaries; and maintaining irrigation systems.[140]

The advantages of such behavior are clear. Constructing or maintaining large installations or owning a team of oxen represents investment that might be too great for one household to bear alone.[141] But each undertaking is fraught with tension, and the potential for conflict is high. Who determines the order of plowing, harvesting, and threshing each household's grain? Who is responsible for recording the amount of grain each household stores in communal granaries? Who controls the release of that grain and ensures that each individual takes only his share? Who regulates the irrigation system so that each plot of land receives its fair share of water? The answers to these questions are elusive, since internal systems of regulation are visible only when they fail.[142]

Communal living also entailed negotiation. As a result of the flexibility and precariousness of peasant economic strategies, an individual household might acquire or lose wealth and status quite quickly. Consequently, an individual community will display marked divisions in the wealth, status, and power of its inhabitants.[143] The villages of the eastern Mediterranean are likely to have been dominated by an oligarchy of wealthier peasants. These individuals might seek to exclude other members of the community from their ranks and emphasize that exclusion in subtle and not-so-subtle ways.[144] While it is more difficult to determine the internal organization of the smaller communities of the western Mediterranean, it is likely that there, too, a certain degree of competition and inequality was present. We may, for example, interpret commemorations of building activities by named individuals as a means for simultaneously publicizing their actions on behalf of the community and emphasizing the exclusion of their fellows.[145]

Communities characteristically develop strategies for affirming their ideological unity and balancing these antagonisms, while subtly emphasizing difference and inequality. Activities such as the celebration of religious festivals and communal building projects function as an affirmation of the ideology of reciprocity and equality within the community. They benefit the entire community and may also release tensions that rest on social and economic differentiations within the community. Equally, they provide members of the "exclusive" community with an opportunity for displaying their status and wealth, thereby perpetuating and affirming their position of power and privilege.

Concerning Systems of Patronage[146]

In our analysis of the nature and structure of rural communities, we must place alongside their internal organization the relations they enjoyed with wealthy, powerful outsiders. Like all complex societies, the late antique world was structured around inequalities in wealth, social status, and power. A massive gulf separated a man such as the late-fourth-century Italian senator Symmachus, who owned estates distributed across Italy and elsewhere in the Mediterranean world and held both a consulship and prefecture of the city of Rome, from the tenant farmer who cultivated a small field attached to one of his rural estates. But the two were connected by their mutual interest in the productivity of the field in question, and a letter written by the former on behalf of the latter suggests that they might in addition be tied to each other through further bonds of mutual obligation and reciprocity.[147] Relationships such as this are part of broader systems of interaction between rich and poor, the powerful and the relatively powerless. These systems of interaction are often grouped under the analytical rubric of patronage, an enduring, reciprocal relationship of exchange between individuals of unequal status that contains more than one point of common interest and is entered into voluntarily by both parties.[148] But to concentrate solely on relationships that fit all of these criteria is to miss the rich and varied contexts in which the language of patronage might be employed by both "patrons" and "clients" and to ignore the fundamentally dialectical nature of patronage as both a set of ideals and a collection of practices.

The written sources from the late Roman period attest the use of the vocabulary of patronage to describe relationships as diverse as the tenancy agreement between Symmachus and his *colonus*, the intercession offered by a martyred saint to his community or a bishop to his flock, the resort to illegal influence in securing election to a coveted post in the city of Rome, and protection of rural cultivators from the exactions of the tax collector.[149] The broad semantic field covered by the language of patronage in these examples speaks to its continuing importance as an ideological tool for structuring relationships between unequals.[150] But it creates problems for the analysis of those relationships: when is a relationship described as patronage *actually* a patronage relationship? And how do we account for interactions between the powerful and the powerless that are clearly not patronage relationships but are described by one or both participants as if they are?

The line between legitimate patron and illegitimate oppressor was indistinct. Individual relationships were under constant negotiation and renegotiation. The members of a peasant community might find themselves subjected to an aggressive interloper who imposed his authority by force and gave them no choice but to accept it, as in the case of Simeon the Mountaineer, who kidnapped and tonsured the children of the village of M'rbn' in the Euphrates region, before cowing the inhabitants into submission with various threats and acts of violence.[151] Equally, peasants might threaten to reject or resist an individual who overstepped the bounds of acceptable behavior or whose claims to exercise authority were not matched by an acceptance of the obligations that accompanied those claims. Resistance might at times entail physical violence, as in the case of the treatment meted out to a local *eirenarch* in the village of Karanis, or it could involve subtler tools of dissent, as in the carefully worded letter from the inhabitants of the village of Euhemeria to the local *praepositus pagi*.[152] A patron's legitimacy rested on his ability—and the ability of his client or client community—to maintain and negotiate the tension between an ideology of reciprocity and mutuality and the reality of massive inequality in power, resources, and wealth.[153] It also rested on a patron's success in mediating or interceding—a patron who failed was unlikely to receive commemoration and unlikely to retain his clientele. As such, patronage of rural communities was a performance-based, competitive undertaking.[154]

Concerning the Patronage of Villages[155]

The late Roman sources attest a multiplicity of individuals claiming the role of patron or fulfilling portions of that role in rural contexts. The novelty of competition between patrons or would-be patrons in the period should not be overemphasized, but it seems reasonable to suggest that peasants did experience some expansion in the number of individuals claiming a position of authority in the countrysides of Late Antiquity and a corresponding increase in the options available to them for managing subsistence risk and obtaining intercession on their behalf. These individuals might extend their protection to a community, shielding them from the unreasonable demands—and, no doubt, the reasonable demands as well in some circumstances—of other powerful figures. They might be expected to endow public buildings; hold or fund feasts, markets, or festivals; and mediate disputes within the community when internal mechanisms failed. In return, they could expect or demand services and, perhaps, produce or gifts from their clients.

Landlords, of course, were natural patrons. In the western provinces, it is likely that the close proximity of hamlets to some villa sites was matched by close relations between the inhabitants of those hamlets and the owner of the villa. In the east, Libanius describes some villages in the hinterland of Antioch as belonging to a single landowner, and legislation aimed at Egypt appears to attest a comparable phenomenon.[156] Alternatively or additionally, a village community might invite a powerful individual to become their patron or benefit from the euergetism of a rich or influential local.[157] Such a man could be of local birth, a veteran or member of another profession who had become wealthy.[158] He could be a local magistrate or a soldier stationed nearby.[159] In particular, he might be involved in local tax assessment and collection hierarchies—and we may imagine that there were certain advantages attached to having such a patron.[160] The claims to power, legitimacy, and authority of other figures rested on different foundations. In the eastern provinces, some ascetic holy men, at least, provided an alternative and may be observed mediating the internal squabbles of village communities and interceding on their behalf with other figures of power.[161] In both the western and the eastern provinces, bishops gradually came to assume the role of patrons, at least over their urban communities, and it is likely that the influence of some of these individuals extended to the inhabitants of the hinterlands that surrounded those towns.[162]

Imperial or ex-imperial officials, too, may be observed offering their patronage or protection to rural communities in certain contexts. In the legal sources, the circumstances of these relationships are generally presented as involving the evasion of taxes, and we should expect that such behavior did indeed occur. But it is also possible that the individuals involved did not have the evasion of taxation in the forefront of their minds when they chose to enter into the relationships described in the legal sources.[163] That is, we must be wary of uncritically adopting the rhetorical vocabulary employed by the state in our investigation of the realities of these relationships in rural contexts.[164] Arrangements of this type offered other gains to both patron and client community: for the clients, they transformed a disinterested outsider into a stakeholder in the community, while a patron garnered prestige from a grateful community's public commemoration in stone.[165]

In some circumstances, these new elites are likely to have aggressively and consciously conformed to existing patronage ideologies to build their own local power base.[166] This created competition with existing patrons, and the famous oration of Libanius, *Peri Ton Protostasion*, provides a case in point.[167] However, adopting existing patronage frameworks worked only if one possessed the necessary collateral—a government post, for example, or the wealth necessary to purchase land. In the absence of such collateral, a would-be patron might choose to exploit a different armory of power, seeking to impose his authority in an unfamiliar way. The example of Simeon the Mountaineer is a case in point.[168] In normal circumstances, however, it seems that asymmetrical relations continued to be negotiated and renegotiated in the familiar vocabulary of patronage. A would-be patron who rejected that vocabulary in favor of a new and unfamiliar armory of power ran the risk of jeopardizing the legitimacy of his relationship with an individual or community. It is clear also that not every new patron figure benefited rural communities, and not every figure of power was welcomed.[169] The presence of new figures wielding new weapons in rural communities could disrupt preexisting harmonious relations just as often as it could remedy instances of abuse and exploitation.[170] In communities that were fissile at the best of times, competition between patrons or the aggressive intervention of a new figure of power could fragment the fragile harmony of the community or increase and exacerbate existing factionalism.

The sources reveal that rural communities were involved in multiple complementary alliances with powerful figures in the late Roman period. Peasants were prepared to take advantage of an environment of competition between elites and to exploit rivalries between different patrons.[171] They were also capable of manipulating the ideology of reciprocity in negotiating relations with powerful figures.[172] It seems, moreover, that in response to exploitation by rural communities themselves, the role of patron could be shared or fragmented. Some individuals chose to concentrate on one particular aspect of a patronage relationship. Physical protection might best be provided by a strong military presence.[173] The attentions of the tax collector, whether reasonable or unreasonable, might most effectively be resisted by recourse to an imperial official.[174] Divine intervention could be effected through an ascetic holy man or woman.[175] The local monastery or church offered a safety net in the event of subsistence crisis.[176] These alliances were all described using the language and rhetoric of patronage. For both benefactor and recipients, this vocabulary provided a framework within which interactions could be conceptualized and demands made. Rooted as it was in the ideology of reciprocity, the rhetoric of patronage provided a tool for both defusing and accentuating tensions within and between individual relationships in the broader system of vertical interactions.

Subscript[177]

In Late Antiquity, as in all periods, agriculture and rural life revolved around the village, hamlet, or farmstead a peasant lived in or near. Travel to a nearby town or city was an occasional, if not particularly unusual event, motivated by the need for staples the household could not produce, the pursuit of a luxury item, or the desire to sell produce or handiwork at market. This was a world of predominantly first-person relationships, of dispute settlement at a local level. It was characterized by local social alliances, with both fellow villagers and kin, and a variety of more powerful individuals with whom they came into contact. The particular character and form that a community's web of socioeconomic interactions took will have varied from region to region, community to community, according to a multitude of factors: the size, complexity, and cohesion of the community in question; the proximity of a powerful figure or figures, with both the desire to make claims to authority and the capacity to render those claims legitimate; the type of crops under cultivation and the extent to which that production is aimed at subsistence or at the market; and so on.

While our written sources only reluctantly reveal the world of the peasant in Late Antiquity, the cumulative impression that we gain from these snippets of information is of rural communities characterized by the impulse to balance consensus and conflict in their internal interactions and aware also of the possibilities for negotiating the terms of their relations with more powerful outsiders. These communities, both as groups and as collections of individuals, emerge not merely as audiences or victims but rather as actors and agents. The steadily growing body of archaeological evidence also reveals long-term continuities in the fact of rural settlement and cultivation, even where the pattern and distribution of that settlement underwent fundamental changes in the period.

On the other hand, we should be careful not to overplay the impression of dynamic rural collectivities, self-consciously asserting themselves in the face of the tax man, the soldier, the local potentate. There can be no doubt that some communities did suffer, did collapse, and did decline in the period. The fissile tendencies of these collectivities should not be underestimated and must be placed alongside evidence for the capacity of other communities for flexibility and adaptation to their circumstances. It suffices, perhaps, to observe that political transformation, the disintegration of administrative and fiscal bureaucracies, and the fragmentation of the world (and worldview) of the aristocracies of the late Roman world were not inevitably accompanied by a universal crisis of agriculture.

NOTES

1. Isidore *Etym.* 17. tit.: *De rebus rusticis.*

2. Frézouls 1980; Vera 1999; Grey 2007b.

3. Palladius *Op. Ag.* 1.2.tit.: *De quattuor rebus quibus agricultura consistit.*

4. Palladius *Op. Ag.* I.2.

5. For recent surveys, Horden and Purcell 2000; Issar 2003; Wickham 2005b; Haldon 2007; chapter 34 in this book; Cheyette 2008.

6. See, for example, the collection of essays in Lefort, Morrisson, and Sodini 2005. Also Whittaker and Garnsey 1998; Brogiolo, Gauthier, and Christie 2000; Ward-Perkins 2000; Banaji 2001; McCormick 2001; Barceló and Sigaut 2004; Bowden, Lavan, and Machado 2004; Christie 2004; Sarris 2004; 2006.

7. Cf. now Ruffini's stimulating and suggestive account of social networks in sixth-century Oxyrhynchus and Aphrodito: Ruffini 2008. Also, for social mobility among non-elites in late-fifth- and sixth-century Gaul, Jones 2009.

8. Note the surveys of Chavarría and Lewit 2004; Wickham 2005b, 16–55. A huge number of regional accounts now exist, of which I offer a brief selection. Africa: Barker et al. 1996. Europe: van Ossel 1992; Guyon 1996–1997; van Ossel and Ouzoulias 2000; 2001; Faure-Boucharlat 2001; Schneider 2007. The East: Kaplan 1992; Tate 1992; 1997; 1998; Lapin 2001; Casana 2004; Casana and Wilkinson 2005; Decker 2009. Egypt: Bowman and Rogan 1999; Bagnall 2007.

9. Palladius *Op. Ag.* 1.6.3: *Operarum ratio unum modum tenere non potest in tanta diversitate terrarum.* Note also Isidore's discussion of the various different types of rural dwellings: Isidore *Etym.* 15.12.

10. Cf. the survey of Bernstein and Byres 2001. Also, for fuller exposition of the principles advanced here, see Grey 2011.

11. Cf. Wickham 2005b, 3–6, 386–387.

12. Palladius *Op. Ag.* 1.3.tit.: *De aeris probatione.*

13. Palladius *Op. Ag.* I.7. Cf. also *Op. Ag.* II.3; IV.2; IV.10.16; 24.

14. The *locus classicus* is Huntington 1917. Note, however, that the second edition of a collection of papers concerning the fall of Rome replaced Huntington's article with one on dysgenic lead poisoning: Chambers, ed., 1st ed. 1963, 2nd ed. 1970.

15. E.g., an earthquake and tsunami in Constantinople: Ammianus Marcellinus *Res Gestae* XXVI.10.15–9, with Jacques and Bousquet 1984, 456–460; Lepelley 1984; Barceló 1998. A famine in Italy: Symmachus, *Rel.* III.16–7. An earthquake at Constantinople: Augustine, *Sermo de excidio urbis Romae* VI.7, with Woods 1992, 336. A plague of locusts: *Chronicle of Ps.–Joshua the Stylite* c. 38. Further literature is collected and discussed in Gunn 2000; Stathakopoulos 2004; Little 2007.

16. The most comprehensive recent survey of the evidence is Issar 2003. Wickham 2005b, 13–14, 547–550 dismisses the impact of these phenomena, but cf. the more cautious and nuanced comments of Haldon 2007, 227; Cheyette 2008, 157–64. Note also Shaw's critique of climatic determinism in the study of North Africa: Shaw 1981a.

17. Issar 2003, 105.

18. Randsborg 1991, 24, 28–29; Ingram, Farmer, and Wigley 1981, 12–13; Issar 2003, 59.

19. Vita-Finzi 1969; Potter 1976, 209–212; Judson 1963, 898; Neboit 1988, 402; Squatriti 1992, 3–4; Bintliff 1975, 80–81. Debate and dissent: Wagstaff 1981; Barker 1989, 62–73; Randsborg 1991, 29; Mørch, 1994, 107–113; Horden and Purcell 2000, 316–320; Grove 2001.

20. See, for example, Cambi and Fentress 1989, 84–85; Potter 1976, 212–213; Hodges et al. 1984, 158–165; Neboit 1988, 404.

21. Whittaker 1976. Note, however, additional and alternative hypotheses in Grey 2007b.

22. Dark 2000; Issar 2003, 59; Haldon 2007, 220; Cheyette 2008, 150–153.

23. Cf. Chavarría and Lewit 2004, 3 with n. 2.

24. Palladius *Op. Ag.* I.6. tit.: *De industria et necessariis ad rura sententiis.*

25. Palladius *Op. Ag.* I, *passim.*

26. Palladius *Op. Ag.* I.6.2: *ne a labore sollemni rusticos causa desiderandae urbis avertat.* Cf. Paulinus of Pella's expectations of what he wants of his own estate: *Eucharisticus* 204–215.

27. Long-distance movement: Constantius *V. Germani* 31, with Mathisen 1981, 153–154; *V. Genovefae* 26; Gregory of Nyssa *Ep.* 25.1; *SEG* 20, 372 (342 C.E., Kefr Haya). Short-distance movement: Theodoret *Historia Religiosa* VII.2; *Nov. Val.* XXIV.1.1 (447 C.E.); *Ed. Diocl.* 17. More generally, Horden and Purcell 2000, 377–383; McCormick 2001, 237–267. Also Garnsey and Whittaker 1998, 325; Constable 2003, 2–3.

28. Theodoret *Historia Religiosa* XVII.2; Paulinus of Nola *Ep.* 12.12; 17.1; 22.1; Augustine *Ep.* XXII.6; Gregory of Tours *Virt. Jul.* 9; *Virt. Mart.* I.31; *V. Sim. Styl. (S)* 35; Jerome *V. Malchi* 4.

29. *V. Sim. Styl. (S)* 35; 39; Symmachus *Ep.* V.48; VII.56; Sidonius *Ep.* II.10; VI.3; VI.12; Paulinus of Nola *Ep.* 23; Sulpicius Severus *Ep.* 3, with Lepelley 1989, 236–238.

30. Peasants flee to cities: Herodian VIII.2; *Chronicle of Pseudo-Joshua the Stylite* 38, with Garnsey 1988, 3. *Peregrini* banished from cities: Ambrose *De Officiis* III.45–52; Ammianus Marcellinus *Res Gestae* XIV.6.19.

31. *CTh* XII.19.2 (400 C.E., Gaul), with Grey 2007a, 163.

32. *CTh* V.18.1.4 = *CJ* XI.48.16 *mut.* (419 C.E., Italy).

33. Cassiodorus *Var.* VIII.33.4.

34. *CTh* IX.31.1 (409 C.E., Italy): *ut fieri solet.*

35. *CTh* XII.18.1 (367 C.E., Egypt); XII.18.2 = *CJ* X.38.1 (396 C.E., Illyricum); dating following *PLRE* I, 320; *CTh* XII.19.1 (400 C.E., Gaul), with Grey 2007a, 163. Also *Apa Mena: Further Miracles*, 75, 151.

36. Eugippius *V. Severini* X.1; Riggs 2001, 288, with reference to North Africa. Libanius *Or.* L.23 notes regular movement by peasants between country and town. Also Lepelley 1979, 47–48; de Ligt 1993, 129; Horden and Purcell 2000, 385–386; Grey 2011, 47–49. Cf. Garnsey 1979, 4.

37. Whittaker 1995; Guyon 1996–1997; Brandes and Haldon 2000; Gauthiez, Zadora-Rio, and Galinié, 2003; Heijmans 2006. Cf. Ward-Perkins et al. 1986, 83; Whitehead 1994, 188; Hill 1988, 8.

38. E.g., the Biferno Valley: Lloyd, in Barker 1995, 239–240. Tarraco: Keay 1991, 84–85. Note also the case of North Africa, where rural market sites emerged as alternative foci to urban centers: Optatus *Contra Don.* 3.4; Shaw 1981b, 69; Potter 1995, 66–73, 79. Gaul: Loseby 2000, 89–90. Also Brown 1981, 43, discussing the shrine of St. Felix at Cimitile in Italy; Haas 2001, 54–55, describing Apa Mena in the Mareotis region of Egypt.

39. E.g., Petra and its hinterland: Fiema 2001, 121–122. Also the marginalization of Italian towns in the Albegna, Gubbio, and Biferno Valleys: Ward-Perkins 1988, 16–18; Potter 1995, 90; Cambi and Fentress 1989, 81–82; Whitehead 1994, 191; Lloyd, in Barker 1995, 238; Patterson 1987, 136. More general comments in Christie 2000, 55; Bender 2001, 188–189.

40. Rosen and Avni 1993, 197–198.

41. See Maas, chapter 2, and Mathisen, chapter 22, in this book for the means by which these populations were settled. Note that accounts of the ravages of the barbarians tend to come from an urban perspective: a useful catalogue is in Lewit 1991, 69–70 = Lewit 2004, 40–41.

42. Natural disasters as one among a variety of causes of food shortages or famines: Garnsey 1988, 20; Mathisen 1993, 91. Response strategies: *Nov. Val.* XXXIII.1 (451 C.E., Italy); cf. Gallant 1991, 137–139.

43. Ripoll and Arce 2000; Chavarría and Lewit 2004; Cheyette 2008; Grey 2011, 49–51.

44. Gaul: Fixot 2000; Heijmans 2006. Hispania: Díaz 2000. Danube: Poulter 2004. Balkans: Dunn 1994; Brandes and Haldon 2000.

45. Construction of city walls as a possible response to uncertainty: Brühl 1988, 43; Bender 2001, 191. Town walls as an identifying feature of a late Roman town: Christie 2000, 57–58.

46. Hamlets, villas, and farmsteads in Europe: van Ossel 1983, 165; 1992, 87, 171; van Ossel and Ouzoulias 2000, 139. In Africa: Ørsted with Ladjimi Sebaï et al. 1992, 95; Mattingly and Hayes 1992, 414–415; Jones et al. 1982, 258.

47. See the general discussion of Scott 2004. Cf., e.g., Sidonius *Carm.* XXII. 121–125.

48. Paulinus of Nola *Ep.* 31–32; Sidonius *Ep.* IV.24.3–4, with Percival 1997, 1–2; Stern 1992, 490; see also the catalogue of van Ossel and Ouzoulias 2000, 147.

49. van Ossel 1983, 162, 164, 167–168; 1992, 87; Whittaker 1994, 237; Percival 1992, 159; 1997, 3, 5–6. For a recent, cogent survey of the fate of villas in the western provinces, see Lewit 2003, with the important response and critique of Bowes and Gutteridge 2005. Also Wickham 2005b, 465–481.

50. Périn 2004; Arthur 2004; Durand and Leveau 2004; Wickham 2005a; Cheyette 2008.

51. Territorial reorganization: Sanders 2004. Problems with survey sampling: Pettegrew 2007.

52. Greece: Mee et al. 1991, 227. Cf. Alcock 1993, 56–58. Alexandria and the Mareotis region: Haas 2001, 50–53. Boeotia: Bintliff 1991, 124–127. Hauran: Villeneuve 1985, 63; Tate 1992, 243. Also Sapin 1998, 129, with n. 44 for the central basin of the Wādī Sahbān in Arabia. More general comments in Laiou 2005; Wickham 2005b, 442–465; Haldon 2007; Grey 2011, 51–52.

53. Mattingly with Flower in Barker et al. 1996.

54. Isidore *Etym.* 17.2.tit.: *De cultura agrorum.*

55. Isidore *Etym.* 17.2.1: *cinis, aratio, intermissio, incensio stipularum, stercoratio, occatio, runcatio.*

56. Palladius *Op. Ag.* I.42; III.17.8; XII.15.3; IV.10.16, 24. Horden and Purcell 2000, 175–230.

57. Peasants in the market place: *CTh* XIII.1.10 (374 C.E., Italy); *SEG* 20, 372 (342 C.E., Kefr Haya); Cassiodorus *Var.* VIII.33. For larger productive enterprises, cf. now Sarris 2006, 81–95, 115–130.

58. Egypt: Bagnall 2007; Bowman and Rogan 1999. Ravenna: Squatriti 1992. Africa: Barker et al. 1996. The nature of peasant economies in the period: Grey 2007b, 363–367, with further references.

59. Palladius *Op. Ag.* VIII.1; X.2; XII.1; IV.3–4; II.5; III.4.

60. Palladius *Op. Ag.* II.4–6; IV.3; X.2. Cf. Gallant 1991, 37–38. Note also that tax payments were expected three times a year: *CTh* V.15.20 (366 C.E., West); XI.25.1 (393 C.E., East).

61. Gallant 1991, 37–38 offers a survey of the comparative evidence.

62. Palladius *Op. Ag.* X.1. Cf. Gallant 1991, 39, 82–86; Kron 2004.

63. Kron 2000; 2004; 2005; Grey 2007b.

64. Horses: *Op. Ag.* IV.13. Asses: *Op. Ag.* IV.14. Cattle and oxen: *Op. Ag.* IV.11. Also Paulinus of Nola *Carm.* 18; *Farmer's Law* 23–27. Sheep and goats: *Op. Ag.* VI.8; IX.4; XII.13; also *V. Sim. Styl. (S)* 6; 7. Pigs: *Op. Ag.* III.26.

65. Justinian *Inst.* 3.9.tit.: *De bonorum possessionibus.*

66. Fuller discussion of the process in Grey 2007b, 368–369.

67. See the cogent discussion of the evidence by Harper 2008.

68. Fragmentation: Gallant 1991, 41–44, with further references. Also Richardson 2003, providing an important review of the literature for medieval Europe. Equilibrium: Delano Smith 1979, 172.

69. Paulinus of Pella, *Eucharisticus* 273; 480–492; 530–536; Symmachus, *Epp.* I.8; VII.66; *CJ* III.24.2 (390 C.E., *ad Senatum*); *Testamentum S. Remigii*, 20; 26–27; 59–60; 100; 105.

70. Rowlandson 1996, 178–179. Bowman 1985, 143, 162–163, and table VIII B, discusses the Hermopolite nome in fourth-century Egypt.

71. E.g., *CPR* XVIIA.17 = *SPP* XX.80 (321? C.E., Hermopolis); cf. *P. Ital.* 32 (540 C.E.); 35 (572 C.E.).

72. E.g., *BGU* IV.1049 (342 C.E., Arsinoe); *SPP* XX.86 = *CPR* I.19 (330 C.E., Hermopolis); *P. Oxf.* 6 (350 C.E., Heracleopolis); *SB* III.6612 (365 C.E.). Bagnall 1993, 72, n. 169 observes that of the sale documents involving villagers that do survive, the majority record sales from metropolitans to villagers, rather than vice versa.

73. *P. Oxy.* 1470 (336 C.E., Oxyrhynchus); *P. Ness.* III.32 (c. sixth century C.E.).

74. Rowlandson 1996, 184–185, 196. Cf. *TA* 8; *P. Ness* III.15 (512 C.E.), which both provide analogous evidence for a high turnover of small parcels of land in a fluid market in fifth-century Africa and sixth-century Nessana.

75. *P. Vindob.* G 25871 (373 C.E., Arsinoite/Heracleopolite Nome); published by Hoogendijk 1995. Cf. Bowman 1985, 138; Rowlandson 1996, 176.

76. *P. Flor.* 71 and *P. Giss.* 117, republished in *P. Landlisten.* For dating, Bowman 1985, 143–144. He argues that it is impossible to determine the interval between these two lists, but it is certainly short. Bagnall 1993, 72, suggests that the time period between the two registers is perhaps five to ten years.

77. Bowman 1985, 154–155, with table VIII B, 162–163; cf. Bagnall 1993, 73.

78. Bowman 1985, table VIII B; *CTh* III.1.4 (383 C.E.); *P. Oxy.* 1470 (336 C.E., Oxyrhynchus); *TA* V, lines 5–18 (c. 493–494 C.E.); *P. Ital.* 35.10–14 (572 C.E.); *SB* III.6612 (365 C.E.); *CTh* III.1.4 (383 C.E.). Cf. Rowlandson 1996, 184–185, for Egypt in the pre-Diocletianic period.

79. *CJ* 11.48.tit.: *De agricolis censitis vel colonis.*

80. Fuller discussion, with additional references, in Grey 2007a, 165–166.

81. Vera 1997; 1998. Cf. Scheidel 2000. For an account of rural power relations in the period that is not focused solely upon labor, see Grey 2011, 148–177.

82. *CTh* XI.7.2 (319 C.E., Britain); *CTh* II.31.1 = *CJ* IV.26.1 *mut.* (422 C.E., West); *CTh* IX.42.7 = *CJ* IX.49.7 (369 C.E., Illyricum, Italy, Africa). See, in particular, the detailed accounts of Egyptian large estates by Rathbone 1991; Sarris 2006. Also Jones 1964, 788; Finley 1976, 103; Garnsey 1980, 34; Foxhall 1990, 97–98; Banaji 1992, 380; Carlsen 1995, 57.

83. *CTh* IV.12.5 (362 C.E., East); *CTh* XII.1.92 = *CJ* X.32.34 *mut.* (382 C.E., East); *CTh* XVI.5.65.3 (428 C.E., East); *Nov. Theod.* IX.1.1 (439 C.E.); *Nov. Maj.* VII.1.4 (458 C.E., Italy). See the discussions of Scheidel 1990; Teitler 1993. Also Jones 1964, 788–792; Lepelley 1983, 337–339; Carlsen 1995, 68.

84. *P. Cairo Isid.* 98–100 (c. 296 C.E.); Palladius *Op. Ag.* I.6.6; *CTh* XI.1.14 = *CJ* XI.48.4 (371S C.E., East); cf. Gallant 1991, 82, 87–89.

85. *CIL* VIII.11824 (fifth century C.E., Mactar); *CTh* XVI.5.52 (412 C.E., Africa).

86. Percival 1969, 610, with nn. 1–2; MacMullen 1974, 42, with nn. 43–48; Hamel 1990, 153; Rathbone 1991, 174.

87. Cf. Garnsey 1979, 1, with n. 3; Banaji 1992; Erdkamp 1999; Bernstein and Byres 2001, 25–26. *Contra* Wickham 2005b, 272–279.

88. Vera 1997, 185, 196–199, 201, 210–211, 213; also Hamel 1990, 152; Lo Cascio 1993, 297–302; Safrai 1994, 335, 337. A law issued to Ruricius, *praeses* of Tripolitania, concedes that in the matter of tenancy, local custom should be observed above all (*CJ* XI.48.5 (365 C.E.)).

89. De Neeve, rightly, observes that tenants "did and do not comprise a uniform status group": de Neeve 1984b, 15; also Foxhall 1990, 97. For diversity among peasant tenants, Vera 1993, 136–137, 143–149; 1997, 199.

90. *Testamentum S. Remigii* 87–89; Sidonius *Ep.* III.9; Paulinus of Nola *Carm.* 18.

91. *CJ* XI.52.1 directs that the family members of a fugitive *colonus* must be restored to his landlord as well.

92. The most detailed treatment remains Finley 1965; also de Ste. Croix 1981, 136–137, 162–170; Giliberti 1981, 5–6; Lintott 1999; Sirks 2001, 258–259.

93. E.g., Libanius *Or.* XLVII.13; *Testamentum S. Remigii* 19–25; Wickham 2005b, 269–270.

94. In the two land registers of *P. Landlisten*, Olympiodorus is named as a tenant of two separate owners: Bowman 1985, 141, n. 24.

95. Gallant 1991, 43.

96. *CTh* XI.19.3 (364 C.E.); *CTh* V.15.20 = *CJ* XI.65.4 (366 C.E.); Vera 1997, 221.

97. *P. Cairo Isid.* 99; 100 (296 C.E.).

98. *CTh* XI.16.13 (383 C.E.).

99. The term is de Neeve's: de Neeve 1984b, 15.

100. Eitrem 1937, 29–30. See also, with specific reference to Palestine, Safrai 1994, 333.

101. De Neeve 1984b, 16–17.

102. E.g., *Dig.* XIX.2.19.2 (Ulpian) with Frier 1979 but cf. Buck 1982, 256, who observes that there are a number of lists of *instrumenta* in the Digest, no two of which are alike, "and often they take on, in their desire to overlook nothing, something of the dream-like inconsequence of a rummage sale."

103. de Neeve 1984a, 130; 1984b, 17; Hamel 1990, 156–158. See the discussion of Robertson 1980, 412–415. Also Caballero 1983, 107; Foxhall 1990, 107–108.

104. For Palestine, Hamel 1990, 159–160; Safrai 1994, 329.

105. Thus Vera 1997, 213–215, 221, with n. 142.

106. Symmachus *Ep.* VI.81; IX.6. Cf. Pliny *Ep.* III.19; IX.37; X.8; de Ste. Croix 1981, 257.

107. *Leges Burgundionum* 54.tit.: *De mancipiis et terris.*

108. White 1970, 366; Garnsey 1980, *passim*; de Ste. Croix 1981, 187; Foxhall 1990, 97–98.

109. MacMullen 1974, 42, with nn. 43–48; Hamel 1990, 153.

110. Banaji 1992, 379–381.

111. E.g., *P. Oxy.* 3804 (566 C.E.). For waged labor on the Appianus and related estates, see Rathbone 1991, 155–173, 390–393.

112. *CIL* VIII.10570.II.11–13 (second century C.E., Africa); *P. Ital.* 3 (sixth century C.E., Italy).

113. Cf. Banaji, chapter 18 in this book. Comparative evidence: Gallant 1991, 164. Appianus estate: Rathbone 1991, 390–393, summarizing arguments developed in chapters 3, 4, and 5.

114. Although cf. Aubert 1994, 176, arguing that specialists could be employed in other tasks throughout the agricultural year.

115. White 1970, 349–350; de Ste. Croix 1981, 187; Finley 1985, 73; Rathbone 1991, 390–393.

116. Palladius *Op. Ag.* VII.2.1: *quinque modios recidere potest pleni agri opera una messoris experti, mediocris vero tres, ultimi etiam minus.* Cf. *CIL* VIII.11824 (fifth century C.E., Mactar).

117. Palladius *Op. Ag.* VI.4.1. Cf., however, *Farmer's Law* 17, 20, 39, where the woodcutting appears to be carried out by nonspecialists.

118. Augustine *Ep.* XLVI.1. Cf. the fruit guardians of *Farmer's Law* 33.

119. Cf. Goodchild 1950, 31.

120. Optatus *Contra Don.* 3.4, with Shaw 1981b, 70–71. Augustine *Contra Gaudentium* I.32; *Enarr. in Psalm.* 132.3. Cf. the parable of the laborers in the vineyard: Matthew 20:1–16.

121. Isid. *Etym.* 9.5.tit.: *De adfinitatibus et gradibus.*

122. Palladius *Op. Ag.* 1.2.

123. Chayanov 1966/1986, 76, 218; discussed by Thorner 1966/1986, xv–xviii. Also Erdkamp 1999.

124. *Testamentum S. Remigii*, 55–57. The family of Mellaricus, who worked a vineyard in Lugdunum, his wife, Placidia, and their son Medaridus may be similar: *Testamentum S. Remigii*, 80–82. Fuller discussion in Grey 2011, 43–44. Comparative literature: Mitterauer 1992, 150.

125. Shepherds: *CTh* IX.31.1 (409 C.E., Italy); Theodoret *Historia Religiosa* XXVI.2; XXX.3; *V. Sim. Styl. (S)* 1. Cf. Le Roy Ladurie (1978), 69; 72–73. Members of the military: Vegetius *De Re Militari* I.7; *CJ* XI.48.18 (426 C.E., Italy); Eugippius *V. Severini* 20; *CJ* XII.33.3 (Diocletian and Maximian). Cf. also the practice of *oblatio* of children to monasteries: Boswell 1988/1991; de Jong 1996. For a more general treatment of the fluid and permeable boundaries between peasant economies and other economic activities, see now Erdkamp 1999. Also Grey 2011, 26–28.

126. Acorns: Palladius *Op. Ag.* XII.14. Chickens: *Op. Ag.* I.27.1: *quae modo videtur industria.* It is likely that the status of women varied according to the economic role that they fulfilled in agricultural contexts: Scheidel 1995, 204. See also the more general comments of Wickham 2005b, 551–558.

127. E.g., *CTh* V.18.1.3–4 (419 C.E., Ravenna). Sidonius *Ep.* V.19 with Grey 2008. *Testamentum S. Remigii* 66–67. Marriage contracts: *P. Sak.* 48 (343 C.E., Theadelphia); *P. Ness.* III.18 (537 C.E.), 20 (558 C.E.). For fuller discussion, Grey 2011, 64–69.

128. E.g., *Querolus* 27, 30, 65–66, 73, 92–100; *P. Col.* VIII.242 (fifth century C.E., Karanis); *P. Sak.* 38 (312 C.E., Theadelphia). Fuller treatment in Grey 2011, 69-71. Cf. the discussions in Bailey 1971; Aguilar 1984; Chong 1992; Sommier 1996.

129. Caesarius *Serm* 29: *De caritate proximi et de amore inimicorum.*

130. Craft specialization: Theodoret *Historia Religiosa* V.4; de Ligt 1991, 38; 1993, 132–133; cf. Patlagean 1977, 261–277. Risk management: Gallant 1991, 146–147, 156–158. Interconnections among risk, reciprocity, and reputation: Grey 2011, 58–90.

131. Gallant 1991, 143–146. Cf. Keenan 1985; Drinkwater 1983, 175.

132. E.g., Ennodius *V. Epiphanii* 21–26; *P. Cair. Isid.* 68 (309/310 C.E.); *P. Princeton* III.119 (early fourth century C.E., Karanis); *P. Cair. Isid.* 79 (early fourth century C.E., Karanis); *P. Cair. Masp.* I.67087 (sixth century C.E., Aphrodito); *P. Sak.* 46–47 = *P. Thead.* 22–23 = *P. Abinn.* 44 (342 C.E., Theadelphia). General discussion in Wickham 2005b, 434–438. Disputes and disagreements are treated in detail in the collection of legal opinions conventionally known as the *Farmer's Law*. For a recent, balanced account of the debate surrounding this corpus, see Köpstein 1990. Note also the

prominent place accorded disputes pertaining to agricultural contexts in the *Pactis Legis Salicae.*

133. *Hist. Mon. in Aegypt.* XIII.1. *V. Theod. Syc.* 26–27. Not every village would have boasted its full complement of specialists: Kaplan 1992, 277–278.

134. *CIL* III.12336 = *IGBulg* IV.2236 (238 C.E., Thrace); Theodoret, *Historia Religiosa* VII.2–3; Kaplan 1992, 197–198.

135. Woodcutters, foresters, reapers: Palladius *Op. Ag.* VI.4.1; VII.2.1; *CJ* XII.33.3 (Arcadius and Honorius to Pulcher, *mag. mil.*); cf., for Gaul, *V. Genovefae* 49. Faith healers, magicians, holy figures: Theodoret, *Historia Religiosa* VII.2–3, with Grey 2011, 88-89; Horden 1993. Cf. Mathisen 1996.

136. Relations with shepherds: Keenan 1985; Kaplan 1992, 195, 483–488. Owners carry risk: *Farmer's Law* 23–29. Shepherd selling milk: *Farmer's Law* 34. For distrust of shepherds, cf., e.g., *CTh* IX.30.2 (364 C.E., Campania); *CTh* IX.31.1 (409 C.E., Italy).

137. Cf. also the transformation of the villa at Mola di Monte Gelato into a site containing smithing and other facilities: Potter and King 1997.

138. Augustine *Ep.*20* 10, with Grey 2011, 145–146.

139. *Lex Romana Burgundionum* XI.tit.: *De commotione litium.*

140. Reynolds 1997, lii–iii; Kaplan 1992, 195–197; Grey 2011, 112–119. For physical and documentary testimony: Tchalenko 1953, 30, 41, 44; *ILAfr* 7 (219 C.E.); *P. Ness.* III.32 (sixth century C.E.); *PSI* VI.711 (311 C.E., Oxyrhynchus); van Ossel 1992, 143, nn. 55, 56; Kehoe 1988, 230–234; *V. Sim. Styl. (S)* 64, 85; Shaw 1981b, 75–79; Stone 2000, 721–722.

141. MacMullen 1974, 20, with n. 61.

142. Eugippius *V. Severini* 3; *CIL* VIII.18587 = *ILS* 5793, with Shaw 1982, who also provides further references.

143. MacMullen 1974, 16; de Ligt 1990, 50–51, with nn. 82–88; Giliberti 1992, 177. *Contra* Tate 1997, 65, 67; 1998, 923–924. See also the comments of Foss 2000, 796–800; Horden and Purcell 2000, 274–275; Wickham 2005b 443–447.

144. E.g., *IGR* 3.1187 = Wadd. 2546 (282 C.E., Syria); *V. Sim. Styl. (S)* 29, 105; *P. Cair. Masp.* I 67002 (567 C.E., Aphrodito). MacMullen 1974, 23, with nn. 73–77, collects further references; also Keenan 1985, 253; Grey 2011, 95.

145. *CIL* XIII.3475 (n.d.), for the *vicus Ratumagus*; *ILTG* 126 (n.d.), involving the *vicini Spariani.* Fuller discussion in Grey 2011, 92–94.

146. Libanius *Or.* XLVII.tit: *Peri Ton Protostasion.*

147. Symmachus *Ep.* VII.56, with Grey 2004, 29–30.

148. Saller 1982, 1, 194; Garnsey and Woolf 1989, 153–154; Wickham 2005b, 438–441. Also Wolf 1966, 86–87; Scott 1977.

149. Symmachus *Ep.* VII.56; Prudentius *Peristephanon* X.835; Gregory of Tours *Gloria Martyrorum* LXXXII; Gregory the Great *Dial.* II.38.2; Ennodius *Ep.* VIII.8; Sidonius Apollinaris *Ep.* VII.4.4; *CTh* XIII.3.8 (368 or 370 C.E., Rome); *CTh* XI.24.4 (399 C.E., East).

150. Krause 1987 emphasizes the essential continuity of patronage relationships: 75–76, 85, 330. Cf. also Grey 2011, 148–177.

151. John of Ephesus *Lives of the Eastern Saints* 16: *PO* 17.242–247, with Grey 2011, 144–145. Cf. the behavior of the bishop Antoninus toward the residents of Fussala in North Africa: Augustine, *Ep.* 20*.4–6.

152. *P. Col.* VIII.242 (fifth century C.E., Karanis); *P. Ross. Georg.* III.8 (fourth century C.E., Euhemeria), with the reading of Rathbone 2008, although note the contrasting analysis of van Minnen 1997. Cf. St. Martin's experiences when attempting

to eradicate paganism in the countryside of Gaul: Sulpicius Severus *V. Mart.* 13–15. Note also the reception accorded Theodore of Sykeon in the villages of Buzaea and Eukraae: *V. Theod. Syc.* 43, 116.

153. For theoretical approaches to the legitimacy of patronage relationships, see now Silverman 1977, 8, 11; Scott 1977, 22; Gallant 1991, 159.

154. Carrié 1976, 173–174; Garnsey and Woolf 1989, 164; Grey 2011, 121–147.

155. *CTh* XI.24.tit.: *De patrociniis vicorum.*

156. West: e.g., Constantius *V. Germani* XXXIV; *Ep. ad Salvium* 2.9. East: Libanius *Or.* XLVII.11; *CTh* XI.24.3 (395 C.E., Egypt). Also MacMullen 1974, 38–39, with references collected at n. 34.

157. Harmand 1957, 9.

158. *CIL* III.6998 = *ILS* 7196 (second century C.E., Nacolea); MacAdam 1983, 113–114; MacMullen 1967, 113.

159. *CIL* III.14191 (244/247 C.E., Phrygia); *CIL* III.12336 = *IGBulg* IV.2236 (238 C.E., Thrace). Libanius *Or.* XLVII.4. Cf. the example of a village reportedly under the protection of a bandit chief: *Historia Monachorum in Aegypto* VIII.31.

160. *CTh* XIII.10.8 (383 C.E., *ad populum*).

161. Brown 1971 remains seminal, but note now his reassessments in Brown 1997, Brown 1998, and the collection of articles in *JECS* 6.3 (1998). Not all ascetic figures enthusiastically participated in power relationships with local communities: Whitby 1987.

162. Salvian *De Gubernatione Dei* IV.15.74–75 provides an arresting vignette. More generally, see Brown 1981, 38–39; Klingshirn 1985, 185–190; Lepelley 1998; Mayer 2001; Grey 2011, 130–133. Also Corbo 2006.

163. *CTh* XI.24.3 (395 C.E.); 4 (399 C.E.).

164. Grey 2011, 169–170. *Contra* Wickham 2005b, 527–529.

165. Harmand 1957, 332–344, gives a catalogue of inscriptional commemorations of patrons.

166. It is possible that an ex-imperial official by the name of Mixidemus is a case in point: Libanius *Or.* XXXIX.6, 10. Cf. Silverman 1977, 17.

167. Libanius *Or.* XLVII, with the discussions of Carrié 1976; Bagnall 1992. Cf. Theodoret *Historia Religiosa* XIV.4.

168. John of Ephesus *Lives of the Eastern Saints* 16: *PO* 17.242–247.

169. Resistance to a figure of power: *V. Theod. Syc.* 43, 116.

170. Libanius *Or.* XLVII.4; John of Ephesus *Lives of the Eastern Saints* 5: *PO* 17.91–93; cf. conflict between pagans and Christians in the *Passio S. Sabae* III.2. Fuller discussion in Grey 2011, 78–79; 124; 144–145.

171. Peasants exploiting patrons: *CTh* XI.11.1 (368 C.E., Illyricum). Waterbury 1977, 332; Garnsey and Woolf 1989, 164–165, with specific reference to competition between imperial and curial elites.

172. *P. Ross. Georg.* III.8 (fourth century C.E., Euhemeria).

173. Libanius *Or.* XLVII.

174. *CTh* XI.24, *passim.*

175. Theodoret *Historia Religiosa* VIII.14.

176. *Historia Monachorum in Aegypto* VIII.44; Sidonius *Ep.* VI.12; Mathisen 1993 discusses the mobilization of Christian clergy and laymen in response to the Gallic famine of c. 470.

177. I wish to express my gratitude to the colleagues and friends who discussed and read earlier versions of this chapter. In particular, I thank John Haldon and Kim

Bowes for their generosity in offering comments, bibliographic references, and advice. Naturally, they should not be held responsible for infelicities in content or argumentation.

WORKS CITED

Ancient Sources

Ambrose, *De Officiis*. Ed. M. Testard, CCSL 15 (Turnhout, 2000).

Ammianus Marcellinus, *Res Gestae*. Ed. W. Seyfarth, 2 vols., Teubner (Leipzig, 1999).

Apa Mena = *Apa Mena: A Selection of Coptic Texts Relating to St. Menas*. Ed., trans. and comm. J. Drescher. Publications de la Société d'Archéologie Copte: Textes et Documents 3 (Cairo, 1946). References to these texts will be by title, then Coptic text, then English text page numbers.

Augustine, *Contra Gaudentium*. Ed. M. Petschenig, *Scripta Contra Donatistas*, vol. 3, CSEL 53 (Vienna, 1910).

———, *Enarrationes in Psalmos CI–CL*. Ed. D. E. Dekkers and I. Fraipont, CCSL 40 (Turnhout, 1961).

———, *Epistulae*. Ed. A. Goldbacher, CSEL 34, 57 (Vienna, 1898, 1911).

———, *Epistolae ex duobus codicibus nuper in lucem prolatae*. Ed. J. Divjak, CSEL 88 (Vienna, 1981).

———, *Sermo de excidio urbis Romae*. Ed. M. V. O'Reilly, *Opera* XIII.2, CCSL 46 (Turnhout, 1969).

Caesarius of Arles, *Sermones*, vol. 2. Ed. D. G. Morin, CCSL 114 (Vienna, 1953).

Cassiodorus, *Variae*. Ed. T. Mommsen, MGHAA 12 (Berlin, 1894).

Constantius *V. Germani* = Constance de Lyon, *Vie de saint Germain d'Auxerre*. Ed., introd. and trans. R. Borius, SC 112 (Paris, 1965).

Codex Justinianus. Ed. P. Krueger, *Corpus Iuris Civilis* vol. 2 (Berlin, 1954).

Codex Theodosianus. Ed. T. Mommsen (Berlin, 1905).

Digesta Justiniani, 4 vols. Ed. T. Mommsen, P. Krueger, and A. Watson (Philadelphia, 1985).

Ed. Diocl. = *Diokletians Preisedikt*. Ed. S. Lauffer (Berlin, 1971).

Ennodius, *Opera Omnia*. Ed. and comm. G. Hartel, CSEL 6 (Vienna, 1882).

Ep. ad Salvium. Ed. C. Halm, Sulpicius Severus, *Libri Quae Supersunt*, CSEL 1 (Vienna, 1896), 254–6.

Eugippius, *Vita Severini*. Ed. H. Sauppe, MGHAA 1 *pars posterior* (Berlin, 1877).

Farmer's Law = W. Ashburner, 1910/1912. *The Farmer's Law*, *JHS* 30, 85–108; *JHS* 32, 68–95.

Gregory of Nyssa, *Epistulae* = *Lettres*. Ed. and trans. P. Maraval, SC 363 (Paris, 1990).

Gregory of Tours, *Gloria Martyrorum*. Ed. W. Arndt and B. Krusch, MGHSRM I (Berlin, 1885), 484–561.

———, *Liber de virtutibus S. Juliani*. Ed. W. Arndt and B. Krusch, MGHSRM I, (Berlin, 1885), 562–584.

———, *Libri IV de virtutibus S. Martini*. Ed. W. Arndt and B. Krusch, MGHSRM I (Berlin, 1885), 584–661.

Gregory the Great, *Vita S. Benedicti, ex libro II Dialogorum*. Ed. PL 66 (1847).
Herodian, *History*, 2 vols. Ed. C. R. Whittaker, LCL (Cambridge, MA, 1969–1970).
Historia Monachorum in Aegypto. Ed., trans., and comm. A. J. Festugière, Société des Bollandistes, Subsidia Hagiographica 53 (Bruxelles, 1971).
Isidore *Etymologiae sive Origines* = *Isidori Hispalensis Episcopi Etymologiarum sive Originarum Libri XX*. Ed. W. M. Lindsay (Oxford, 1911).
Jerome *Vita Malchi*. PL 23: 53–60.
John of Ephesus, *Lives of the Eastern Saints*. Ed. and trans. E. W. Brooks, Patrologia Orientalis 17 (Paris, 1923), 1–307. References to this text will be by author, text, then page number.
Justinian *Inst*. = *Justinian's Institutes, Translated with an Introduction by Peter Birks and Grant McLeod, with the Latin text of Paul Krueger* (Ithaca, NY, 1987).
Leges Burgundionum. Ed. L. R. de Salis, MGH (Leges) Sectio I, 2 parts 1 and 2 (Berlin, 1892).
Libanius, *Opera*. Ed. R. Foerster, 12 vols., Teubner (Leipzig, 1903–1922).
Nov. Maj. = *Novellae Majoriani*. Ed. P. M. Meyer, *Leges Novellae ad Theodosianum Pertinentes* (Berlin, 1905).
Nov. Theod. = *Novellae Theodosiani*. Ed. P. M. Meyer, *Leges Novellae ad Theodosianum Pertinentes* (Berlin, 1905).
Nov. Val. = *Novellae Valentiniani*. Ed. P. M. Meyer, *Leges Novellae ad Theodosianum Pertinentes* (Berlin, 1905).
Optatus *Contra Don*. = *Sancti Optati Milevitani Libri VII*. Ed. and comm. C. Ziwsa, CSEL 26 (Vienna, 1893).
Pactis Legis Salicae. Ed. K. A. Eckhardt, MGH Legum Sectio I, Leges Nationum Germanicorum 4 part 1 (Berlin, 1962).
Palladius *Op. Ag*. = Palladius, *Opus Agriculturae*. Ed. R. H. Rodgers, Teubner (Leipzig, 1975).
Passio Sancti Sabae. Ed. G. Krüger and G. Ruhbach, *Ausgewählte Märtyrerakten*, 4th ed. (Tübingen, 1965), 119–124.
Paulinus of Nola, *Carmina*. Ed. G. de Hartel, CSEL 29 (Vienna, 1999).
———, *Epistulae*. Ed. G. de Hartel, CSEL 30 (Vienna, 1999).
Paulinus of Pella, *Eucharisticus*. Ed. and trans. H. G. Evelyn White, *Ausonius*, vol. 2. LCL (Cambridge, MA, 1961).
Pliny, *Letters and Panegyrics*. Ed. and trans. B. Radice, 2 vols. LCL (Cambridge, MA, 1969).
Prudentius, *Carmina*. Ed. M. P. Cunningham, CCSL 126 (Turnhout, 1966).
The Chronicle of Pseudo-Joshua the Stylite. Trans and comm. F. R. Trombley and J. W. Watt, Translated Texts for Historians 32 (Liverpool, 2001).
Querolus sive Aulularia. Ed. and trans. C. Jacquemard-Le Saos, Belles Lettres (Paris, 1994).
Salvian, *De Gubernatione Dei*. Ed. C. Halm, MGHAA 1 (Berlin, 1877).
Sidonius Apollinaris, *Poems and Letters*. Ed. and trans. W. B. Anderson, 2 vols., LCL (Cambridge, MA, 1936; 1965).
Sulpicius Severus, *Libri Quae Supersunt*. Ed. C. Halm, CSEL 1 (Vienna, 1896).
Symmachus, *Opera Quae Supersunt*. Ed. O. Seeck, MGHAA 6 part 1 (Berlin, 1883).
TA = *Tablettes Albertini: actes privés de l'époque Vandale*. Ed. C. Courtois, L. Leschi, C. Perrat, and C. Saumagne (Paris, 1952).
Testamentum S. Remigii, in *Defensoris Liber Scintillarum*. Ed. D. H. Rochais. CCSL 117 (Turnhout, 1957), 474–487.

Theodoret of Cyrrhus, *Historia Religiosa* = *Histoire des moines de Syrie*, 2 vols. Ed. and trans. P. Canivet and A. Leroy-Molinghen, SC 234 and 257 (Paris, 1977 and 1979).
Vegetius, *Epitoma Rei Militari*. Ed. C. Lang, Teubner (Leipzig, 1885).
V. Genovefae, in *Acta Sanctorum* 1, January 3, 137–153.
V. Sim. Styl. (S) = *The Lives of Simeon Stylites*. Introd. and trans. R. Doran, Cistercian Studies 112 (Kalamazoo, 1992), 101–198.
V. Theod. Syc. = *Vie de Théodore de Sykéôn (Écrite par Géorgiôs prêtre et higoumène du même monastère*. Ed. and trans. A.-J. Festugière, Subsidia hagiographica 48 (Brussels, 1970).

Modern Sources

Aguilar, J. L. 1984. "Trust and Exchange: Expressive and Instrumental Dimensions of Reciprocity in a Peasant Community," *Ethos* 12.1: 3–29.
Alcock, S. E. 1993. *Graecia Capta: The Landscapes of Roman Greece*. Cambridge: Cambridge University Press.
Arthur, P. 2004. "From *Vicus* to Village: Italian Landscapes, AD 400–1000." In *Landscapes of Change: Rural Evolutions in Late Antiquity and the Early Middle Ages*, ed. N. Christie, 103–133. Aldershot: Ashgate.
Aubert, J.-J. 1994. *Business Managers in Ancient Rome: A Social and Economic Study of Institores, 200 B.C.–A.D. 250*. Leiden: Brill.
Bagnall, R. S. 1992. "Military Officers as Landowners in Fourth Century Egypt," *Chiron* 22: 47–54.
———. 1993. *Egypt in Late Antiquity*, Princeton, NJ: Princeton University Press.
———, ed. 2007. *Egypt in the Byzantine World, 300–700*. Cambridge: Cambridge University Press.
Bailey, F. G., ed. 1971. *Gifts and Poison: The Politics of Reputation*. New York: Schocken.
Banaji, J. 1992. "Historical Arguments for a 'Logic of Deployment' in 'Precapitalist' Agriculture," *Journal of Historical Sociology* 5: 379–391.
———. 2001. *Agrarian Change in Late Antiquity: Gold, Labour, and Aristocratic Dominance*. Oxford: Oxford University Press.
Barceló, P. 1998. "Die Darstellung von Naturkatastrophen in der spätantiken Literatur." In *Naturkatastrophen in der antiken Welt: Stuttgarter Kolloquium zur historischen Geographie des Altertums 6, 1996*, ed. E. Olshausen and H. Sonnabend, 99–104. Geographica Historica 10. Stuttgart: F. Steiner.
Barceló, M., and F. Sigaut, eds. 2004. *The Making of Feudal Agricultures?* Leiden: Brill.
Barker, G. 1989. "The Italian Landscape in the First Millennium A.D.: Some Archaeological Approaches." In *The Birth of Europe: Archaeology and Social Development in the First Millennium A.D.*, ed. K. Randsborg, 62–73. Analecta Romana Instituti Danici suppl. 16. Rome: L'Erma di Bretschneider.
———. 1995. *A Mediterranean Valley: Landscape Archaeology and Annales History in the Biferno Valley*. London: Leicester University Press.
———, et al. 1996. *Farming the Desert: The UNESCO Libyan Valleys Archaeological Survey: Volume One: Synthesis*. Paris: UNESCO.
Bender, H. 2001. "Archaeological Perspectives on Rural Settlement in Late Antiquity in the Rhine and Danube Area." In *Urban Centers and Rural Contexts in Late Antiquity*, ed. T. S. Burns and J. W. Eadie, 185–198. East Lansing: Michigan State University Press.
Bernstein, H., and T. J. Byres. 2001. "From Peasant Studies to Agrarian Change," *Journal of Agrarian Change* 1.1: 1–56.

Bintliff, J. L. 1975. "Mediterranean Alluviation: New Evidence from Archaeology," *Proceedings of the Prehistoric Society* 41: 78–84.

———. 1991. "The Roman Countryside in Central Greece: Observations and Theories from the Boeotia Survey (1978–1987)." In *Roman Landscapes: Archaeological survey in the Mediterranean Region*, ed. G. Barker and J. Lloyd, 122–132. Archaeological Monographs of the British School at Rome 2. London: British School at Rome.

Boswell 1988/1991 = Boswell, J. E. 1988. *The Kindness of Strangers: The Abandonment of Children in Western Europe from Late Antiquity to the Renaissance.* New York: Pantheon. [Republished 1991]

Bowden, W., L. Lavan, and C. Machado, eds. 2004. *Recent Research on the Late Antique Countryside.* Late Antique Archaeology 2. Leiden: Brill.

Bowes, K., and A. Gutteridge. 2005. "Rethinking the Later Roman Landscape," *JRA* 18: 405–418.

Bowman, A. K. 1985. "Landholding in the Hermopolite Nome in the Fourth Century A.D.," *JRS* 75: 137–163.

Bowman, A. K., and E. Rogan, eds. 1999. *Agriculture in Egypt from Pharaonic to Modern Times.* Oxford: Oxford University Press.

Brandes, W., and J. Haldon. 2000. "Tax and Transformation: State, Cities and their Hinterlands in the East Roman World, *c.* 500–800." In *Towns and Their Territories between Late Antiquity and the Early Middle Ages*, ed. G. P. Brogiolo, N. Gauthier, and N. Christie, 141–172. Leiden: Brill.

Brogiolo, G. P., N. Gauthier, and N. Christie, eds. 2000. *Towns and Their Territories between Late Antiquity and the Early Middle Ages.* Leiden: Brill.

Brown, P. R. L. 1971. "The Rise and Function of the Holy Man in Late Antiquity," *JRS* 61: 80–101.

———. 1981. *The Cult of the Saints: Its Rise and Function in Latin Christianity.* Chicago: University of Chicago Press.

———. 1997. "The World of Late Antiquity Revisited." With comments by G.W. Bowersock, Averil Cameron, E. A. Clark, A. Dihle, G. Fowden, P. Heather, P. Rousseau, A. Rousselle, H. Torp, and I. Wood. *Symbolae Osloenses* 72: 5–90.

———. 1998. "The Rise and Function of the Holy Man in Late Antiquity, 1971–1997," *JECS* 6.3: 353–376.

Brühl, C. 1988. "Problems of the Continuity of Roman *Civitates* in Gaul, as Illustrated by the Interrelation of Cathedral and *Palatium*." In *The Rebirth of Towns in the West AD 700–1050*, ed. R. Hodges and B. Hobley, 43–46. CBA Research Report 68. London: Council for British Archaeology.

Buck, R. J. 1982. "Roman Law and Agriculture: The Evidence from San Giovanni," *EMC* 26: 243–258.

Burns, T. S., and J. W. Eadie, eds. 2001. *Urban Centers and Rural Contexts in Late Antiquity.* East Lansing: Michigan State University Press.

Caballero, J.-M. 1983. "Sharecropping as an Efficient System: Further Answers to an Old Puzzle," *Journal of Peasant Studies* 10: 107–118.

Cambi, F., and E. Fentress. 1989. "Villas to Castles: First Millennium A.D. Demography in the Albegna Valley." In *The Birth of Europe: Archaeology and Social Development in the First Millennium A.D.*, ed. K. Randsborg, 74–86. Analecta Romana Instituti Danici suppl. 16. Rome: L'Erma di Bretschneider.

Carlsen, J. 1995. *Vilici and Roman Estate Managers until AD 284.* Analecta Romana Instituti Danici suppl. 24. Rome: L'Erma di Bretschneider.

Carrié, J.-M. 1976. "Patronage et propriété militaires au IVe s.: Objet rhétorique et objet reel du discours Sur les patronages de Libanius," *BCH* 100: 159–176.

Casana, J. 2004. "The Archaeological Landscape of Late Roman Antioch." In *Culture and Society in Later Roman Antioch*, ed. J. A. R. Huskinson and B. Sandwell, 102–125. Oxford: Oxbow.

Casana, J., and A. Wilkinson. 2005. "Settlement and Landscapes in the Amuq Region." In *The Amuq Valley Regional Projects, Volume 1, Surveys in the Plain of Antioch and Orontes Delta, Turkey, 1995–2002*, ed. K. A. Yener, 25–65. Oriental Institute Publication 131. Chicago: Oriental Institute of the University of Chicago.

Chambers, M., ed. 1963/1970. *The Fall of Rome: Can It Be Explained?* New York: Holt, Rinehart and Winston.

Chavarría, A., and T. Lewit. 2004. "Archaeological Research on the Late Antique Countryside: A Bibliographical Essay." In *Recent Research on the Late Antique Countryside, Vol. 2: Late Antique Archaeology*, ed. W. Bowden, L. Lavan, and C. Machado, 3–51. Leiden: Brill.

Chayanov, A. V. 1966/1986. *The Theory of Peasant Economy*. Ed. D. Thorner, B. Kerblay, and R. E. F. Smith, trans. C. Lane and R. E. F. Smith. Madison, WI: R. D. Irwin.

Cheyette, F. L. 2008. "The Disappearance of the Ancient Landscape and the Climatic Anomaly of the Early Middle Ages: A Question to Be Pursued," *Early Medieval Europe* 16.2: 127–165.

Chong, D. 1992. "Reputation and Cooperative Behavior," *Social Science Information* 31.4: 683–709.

Christie, N. 2000. "Construction and Deconstruction: Reconstructing the Late-Roman Townscape." In *Towns in Decline AD 100–1600*, ed. T.R. Slater, 51–71. Aldershot: Ashgate.

———, ed. 2004. *Landscapes of Change: Rural Evolutions in Late Antiquity and the Early Middle Ages*. Aldershot: Ashgate.

Constable, O. R. 2003. *Housing the Stranger in the Mediterranean World: Lodging, Trade, and Travel in Late Antiquity and the Middle Ages*. Cambridge: Cambridge University Press.

Corbo, C. 2006. *Paupertas: La legislazione tardoantica (IV–V sec. d.c.)*. Napoli: Satura.

Dark, P. 2000. *The Environment of Britain in the First Millennium AD*. London: Duckworth.

Decker, M. 2009. *Tilling the Hateful Earth: Agricultural Production and Exchange in the Late Antique East*. Oxford: Oxford University Press.

de Jong, M. 1996. *In Samuel's Image: Child Oblation in the Early Medieval West*. Leiden: Brill.

Delano Smith, C. 1979. *Western Mediterranean Europe: A Historical Geography of Italy, Spain, and Southern France since the Neolithic*. New York: Academic Press.

de Ligt, L. 1990. "Demand, Supply, Distribution: The Roman Peasantry between Town and Countryside; Rural Monetization and Peasant Demand," *MBAH* 9: 24–56.

———. 1991. "The Roman Peasantry: Demand, Supply, Distribution between Town and Countryside II: Supply, Distribution, and a Comparative Perspective," *MBAH* 10: 37–77.

———. 1993. *Fairs and Markets in the Roman Empire: Economic and Social Aspects of Periodic Trade in a Pre-Industrial Society*. Amsterdam: J. C. Gieben.

de Neeve, P. W. 1984a. "Colon et colon partiaire," *Mnemosyne* 37: 125–142.

———. 1984b. Colonus: *Private Farm-Tenancy in Roman Italy during the Republic and the Early Principate.* Amsterdam: J. C. Gieben.

de Ste. Croix, G. E. M. 1981. *The Class Struggle in the Ancient Greek World: From the Archaic Age to the Arab Conquest.* London: Duckworth.

Díaz, P. C. 2000. "City and Territory in Hispania in Late Antiquity." In *Towns and Their Territories between Late Antiquity and the Early Middle Ages*, ed. G. P. Brogiolo, N. Gauthier, and N. Christie, 3–35. Leiden: Brill.

Drinkwater, J. 1983. *Roman Gaul: The Three Provinces, 58 BC–AD 260.* London: Croom Helm.

Dunn, A. 1994. "The Transition from *Polis* to *Kastron* in the Balkans (III–IV cc.): General and Regional Perspectives," *Byzantine and Modern Greek Studies* 18: 60–80.

Durand, A., and P. Leveau. 2004. "Farming in Mediterranean France and Rural Settlement in the Late Roman and Early Medieval Periods: The Contribution from Archaeology and Environmental Sciences in the Last Twenty Years (1980–2000)." In *The Making of Feudal Agricultures?* ed. M. Barceló and F. Sigaut, 177–253. Leiden: Brill.

Eitrem, S. 1937. "A Few Remarks on σπονδή, θαλλός and Other Extra Payments in Papyri," *SO* 17: 26–48.

Erdkamp, P. 1999. "Agriculture, Underemployment, and the Cost of Rural Labour in the Roman World," *CQ* 49.2: 556–572.

Faure-Boucharlat, É., ed. 2001. *Vivre à la campagne au Moyen Âge: L'habitat rural du Ve au XIIe s. (Bresse, Lyonnais, Dauphiné) d'après les données archéologiques.* Lyon: Association Lyonnaise pour la Promotion de l'Archéologie en Rhône-Alpes.

Fiema, Z. T. 2001. "Byzantine Petra—A Reassessment." In *Urban Centers and Rural Contexts in Late Antiquity*, ed. T. S. Burns and J. W. Eadie, 111–131. East Lansing: Michigan State University Press.

Finley, M. I. 1965. "La servitude pour dettes," *RD* 4e série 43: 159–184.

———. 1976. "Private Farm Tenancy in Italy before Diocletian." In *Studies in Roman Property*, ed. M. I. Finley, 103–123. Cambridge: Cambridge University Press.

———, ed. 1976. *Studies in Roman Property.* Cambridge: Cambridge University Press.

———. 1985. *The Ancient Economy.* 2nd ed. Berkeley: University of California Press.

Fixot, M. 2000. "La cité et son territoire: L'exemple du Sud-Est de la Gaule." In *Towns and Their Territories between Late Antiquity and the Early Middle Ages*, ed. G. P. Brogiolo, N. Gauthier, and N. Christie, 37–61. Leiden: Brill.

Foss, C. 2000. "Urban and Rural Housing in Syria: Review Article," *JRA* 13: 796–800.

Foxhall, L. 1990. "The Dependent Tenant: Land Leasing and Labour in Italy and Greece," *JRS* 80: 97–114.

Frézouls, E. 1980. "La vie rurale au Bas-Empire d'après l'oeuvre de Palladius," *Ktèma* 5: 193–210.

Frier, B. W. 1979. "Law, Technology and Social Change: The Equipping of Italian Farm Tenancies," *ZRG* 96: 204–228.

Gallant, T. W. 1991. *Risk and Survival in Ancient Greece: Reconstructing the Rural Domestic Economy.* Stanford, CA: Stanford University Press.

Garnsey, P. D. A. 1979. "Where Did Italian Peasants Live?" *PCPhS* n.s. 25: 1–25.

———. 1980. "Non-Slave Labour in the Roman World." In *Non-Slave Labour in the Greco-Roman World*, ed. P. D. A. Garnsey, 34–47. Cambridge: Cambridge University Press.

———, ed. 1980. *Non-Slave Labour in the Greco-Roman World.* Cambridge: Cambridge University Press.

———. 1988. *Famine and Food Supply in the Graeco-Roman World: Responses to Risk and Crisis.* Cambridge: Cambridge University Press.

Garnsey, P. D. A., and C. R. Whittaker. 1998. "Trade, Industry and the Urban Economy." *CAH* XIII: 312–37.

Garnsey, P. D. A., and G. Woolf. 1989. "Patronage of the Rural Poor in the Roman World." In *Patronage in Ancient Society*, ed. A. Wallace-Hadrill, 153–170. London.

Gauthiez, B., E. Zadora-Rio, and H. Galinié, eds. 2003. *Village et ville au Moyen Age: Les dynamiques morphologiques.* 2 vols., Collection Perspectives "Villes et Territoires" 5. Tours: Presses universitaires François-Rabelais.

Gellner, E., and J. Waterbury, eds. 1977. *Patrons and Clients in Mediterranean Societies.* London: Duckworth.

Giliberti, G. 1981. *Servus quasi colonus: Forme non tradizionali di organizzazione del lavoro nella società romana.* Naples: E. Jovene.

———. 1992. "Consortium vicanorum," *Ostraka* 1: 177–214.

Goodchild, R. G. 1950. "The *Limes Tripolitanus* II," *JRS* 40: 30–38.

Grey, C. 2004. "Letters of Recommendation and the Circulation of Rural Laborers in the Late Roman West." In *Travel, Communication and Geography in Late Antiquity*, ed. L. Ellis and F. L. Kidner, 25–40. Aldershot: Ashgate.

———. 2007a "Contextualizing *colonatus*: The *origo* of the Late Roman Empire," *JRS* 97: 155–175.

———. 2007b. "Revisiting the 'Problem' of *agri deserti* in the Late Roman Empire," *JRA* 20: 362–376.

———. 2008. "Two Young Lovers: An Abduction Marriage and Its Consequences in Fifth-century Gaul," *CQ* 58.1: 286–302.

———. 2011. *Constructing Communities in the Late Roman Countryside.* Cambridge: Cambridge University Press.

Grove, A. T. 2001. "The 'Little Ice Age' and Its Geomorphological Consequences in Mediterranean Europe," *Climatic Change* 48.1: 121–136.

Gunn, J. D. ed. 2000. *The Years without Summer: Tracing A.D. 536 and Its Aftermath.* BAR International Series 872, Oxford: Hadrian.

Guyon, J. 1996–1997. "La Gaule Méridionale pendant l'Antiquité Tardive et le Haut Moyen Âge," *Annals de l'Institut d'Estudis Gironins* 36: 117–150.

Haas, C. 2001. "Alexandria and the Mareotis Region." In *Urban Centers and Rural Contexts in Late Antiquity*, ed. T. S. Burns and J. W. Eadie, 47–62. East Lansing: Michigan State University Press.

Haldon, J. F. 2007. "'Cappadocia Will Be Given Over to Ruin and Become a Desert': Environmental Evidence for Historically-Attested Events in the 7th–10th Centuries." In *Byzantina Mediterranea: Festschrift für Johannes Koder zum 65. Geburtstag*, ed. K. Belke, E. Kislinger, A. Külzer, and M. Stassinopoulou, 215–230. Vienna: Böhlau.

Hamel, G. 1990. *Poverty and Charity in Roman Palestine: First Three Centuries C.E.* University of California Publications, Near Eastern Studies 23. Berkeley, CA: University of California Press.

Harmand, L. 1957. *Le Patronat sur les Collectivités.* Paris: Presses universitaires de France.

Harper, J. K. 2008. "The Greek Census Inscriptions of Late Antiquity," *JRS* 98: 83–119.

Heijmans, M. 2006. "Les habitations urbaines en Gaule Meridionale durant l'Antiquité tardive," *Gallia* 63: 47–57.

Hill, D. 1988. "Unity and Diversity—A Framework for the Study of European Towns." In *The Rebirth of Towns in the West AD 700–1050*, ed. R. Hodges and B. Hobley, 8–15. CBA Research Report 68. London: Council for British Archaeology.

Hodges, R., et al. 1984. "Excavations at Vacchereccia (Rocchetta Nuova): A Later Roman and Early Medieval Settlement in the Volturno Valley, Molise," *PBSR* 52: 148–194.

Hodges, R., and B. Hobley, eds. 1988. *The Rebirth of Towns in the West AD 700–1050*. CBA Research Report 68. London: Council for British Archaeology.

Hoogendijk, F. A. J. 1995. "Zwei byzantinische Landkäufe," *Tyche* 10: 13–26.

Horden, P. 1993. "Responses to Possession and Insanity in the Earlier Byzantine World," *Social History of Medicine* 6.2: 177–194.

Horden, P., and N. Purcell. 2000. *The Corrupting Sea: A Study of Mediterranean History*. Oxford: Blackwell.

Huntington, E. 1917. "Climatic Change and Agricultural Exhaustion as Elements in the Fall of Rome," *Quarterly Journal of Economics* 31: 173–208.

Ingram, M. J., G. Farmer, and T. M. L. Wigley 1981. "Past Climates and Their Impact on Man: A Review." In *Climate and History: Studies in Past Climates and Their Impact on Man*, ed. T. M. L. Wigley, M. J. Ingram, and G. Farmer, 3–50. Cambridge: Cambridge University Press.

Issar, A. S. 2003. *Climate Changes during the Holocene and Their Impact on Hydrological Systems*. Cambridge: Cambridge University Press.

Jacques, F., and B. Bousquet. 1984. "Le raz de marée du 21 Juillet 365: Du cataclysme local à la catastrophe cosmique," *MEFRA* 96: 423–461.

Jones, A. E. 2009. *Social Mobility in Late Antique Gaul: Strategies and Opportunities for the Non-Elite*. Cambridge: Cambridge University Press.

Jones, A. H. M. 1964. *The Later Roman Empire*. Oxford: Blackwell.

Jones, R. F. J., S. J. Keay, J. M. Nolla, and J. Tarrús 1982. "The Late Roman Villa of Vilauba and Its Context: A First Report on Field-work and Excavation in Catalunya, North-east Spain, 1978–81," *AntJ* 62: 245–282.

Judson, S. 1963. "Erosion and Deposition of Italian Stream Valleys during Historical Time," *Science* 140: 898–899.

Kaplan, M. 1992. *Les hommes et la terre à Byzance du VIe au XIe siècle: Propriété et exploitation du sol*. Paris: Publications de la Sorbonne, Université de Paris I-Panthéon-Sorbonne.

Keay, S. 1991. "The *Ager Tarraconensis* in the Late Empire: A Model for the Economic Relationship of Town and Country in Eastern Spain?" In *Roman Landscapes: Archaeological Survey in the Mediterranean Region*, ed. G. Barker and J. Lloyd, 79–87. Archaeological Monographs of the British School at Rome 2. London: British School at Rome.

Keenan, J. G. 1985. "Village Shepherds and Social Tension in Byzantine Egypt," *YClS* 27: 245–259.

Kehoe, D. P. 1988. *The Economics of Agriculture on Roman Imperial Estates in North Africa*. Hypomnemata 89. Gottingen: Vandenhoeck & Ruprecht.

Klingshirn, W. E. 1985. "Charity and Power: Caesarius of Arles and the Ransoming of Captives in Sub-Roman Gaul," *JRS* 75: 183–203.

Köpstein, H. 1990. "Profane Gesetzgebung und Rechtssetzung." In *Quellen zur Geschichte des frühen Byzanz (4.–9. Jahrhundert)*, ed. F. Winkelmann and W. Brandes, 134–148. Berlin: Akademie-Verlag.

Krause, J.-U. 1987. *Spätantike Patronatsformen im Westen des Römischen Reiches.* Munich: C.H. Beck.

Kron, G. 2000. "Roman Ley-Farming," *JRA* 13: 277–287.

———. 2004. "A Deposit of Carbonized Hay at Oplontis and Roman Forage Quality," *Mouseion* 48: 275–330.

———. 2005. "Sustainable Roman Intensive Mixed Farming Methods: Water Conservation and Erosion Control," *Caesarodunum* 39: 285–308.

Laiou, A. E. 2005. "The Byzantine Village (5th–14th Century)." In *Les Villages dans l'Empire byzantin (IVe–XVe siècle)*, ed. J. Lefort, C. Morrisson, and J.-P. Sodini, 31–54. Réalités Byzantines 11. Paris: Lethielleux.

Lapin, H. 2001. *Economy, Geography, and Provincial History in Later Roman Palestine.* Tübingen: Mohr Siebeck.

Lefort, J., C. Morrisson, and J.-P. Sodini, eds. 2005. *Les Villages dans l'Empire byzantin (IVe–XVe siècle).* Réalités Byzantines 11, Paris: Lethielleux.

Lepelley, C. 1979 and 1981. *Les cités de l'Afrique romaine au Bas-Empire*, 2 vols. Paris: Études augustiniennes.

———. 1983. "Liberté, colonat et esclavage d'après la Lettre 24*: La jurisdiction épiscopale 'de liberali causa'." In *Les lettres de Saint Augustin découvertes par Johannes Divjak: Communications présentées au colloque des 20 et 21 Septembre 1982*, 329–342. Paris: Études augustiniennes.

———. 1984. "L'Afrique du Nord et le prétendu séisme universel du 21 Juillet 365," *MEFRA* 96: 463–491.

———. 1989. "Trois documents méconnus sur l'histoire sociale et religieuse de l'Afrique Romaine tardive, retrouvés parmi les *spuria* de Sulpice Sévére," *AntAfr* 25: 235–262.

———. 1998. "Le patronat épiscopal aux IVe et Ve siècles: Continuités et ruptures avec le patronat classique." In *L'Éveque dans la cité du IVe au Ve siècle: Image et autorité*, ed. E. Rebillard and C. Sotinel, 17–31. Collection de l'École Française de Rome 248, Rome: École Française de Rome.

Le Roy Ladurie, E. 1978. *Montaillou: Cathars and Catholics in a French Village.* Trans. B. Bray. Harmondsworth: Penguin.

Lewit, T. 1991/2004. *Agricultural Production in the Roman Economy A.D. 200–400.* BAR Int. Ser. 568, London: Tempus Reparatum [republished, with a new introductory chapter and updated bibliography, as *Villas, Farms and the Late Roman Rural Economy (Third to Fifth Centuries AD)*, London: Hadrian]

———. 2003. "'Vanishing villas': What Happened to Élite Rural Habitations In the West in the 5th–6th C?" *JRA* 16: 260–274.

Lintott, A. 1999. "La servitude pour dettes à Rome." In *Carcer: Prison et privation de liberté dans l'Antiquité classique. Actes du colloque de Strasbourg (5 et 6 décembre 1997)*, ed. C. Bertrand-Dagenbach, A. Chauvot, M. Matter, and J.-M. Salamito, 19–25. Paris: De Boccard.

Little, L., ed. 2007. *Plague and the End of Antiquity: The Pandemic of 541–750.* Cambridge: Cambridge University Press.

Lo Cascio, E. 1993. "Considerazioni sulla struttura e sulla dinamica dell'affitto agrario in età imperiale." In *De Agricultura: In memoriam Pieter Willem De Neeve 1945–1990*, ed. H. Sancisi-Weerdenburg, R. J. van der Spek, H. C. Teitler, and H. T. Wallinga, 296–316. Dutch Monographs in Ancient History and Archaeology 10. Amsterdam: J. C. Gieben.

Loseby, S. T. 2000. "Urban Failures in Late-Antique Gaul." In *Towns in Decline AD 100–1600*, ed. T. R. Slater, 72–95. Aldershot: Ashgate.

MacAdam, H. I. 1983. "Epigraphy and Village Life in Southern Syria during the Roman and Early Byzantine Periods," *Berytus* 31: 103–115.

MacMullen, R. 1967. *Soldier and Civilian in the Later Roman Empire.* Cambridge, MA: Harvard University Press.

———. 1974. *Roman Social Relations: 50 B.C. to A.D. 284.* New Haven, CT: Yale University Press.

Mathisen, R. W. 1981. "The Last Year of Saint Germanus of Auxerre," *AB* 99: 151–159.

———. 1993. "'Nature or Nurture?': Some Perspectives on the Gallic Famine of ca. A. D. 470," *Ancient World* 24.2: 91–105.

———. 1996. "Crossing the Supernatural Frontier in Western Late Antiquity." In *Shifting Frontiers in Late Antiquity*, ed. R. Mathisen and H. Sivan, 309–320. Brookfield, VT: Ashgate.

Mattingly, D. J., and J. W. Hayes. 1992. "Nador and Fortified Farms in North Africa," *JRA* 5: 408–418.

Mayer, W. 2001. "Patronage, Pastoral Care, and the Role of the Bishop at Antioch," *Vigiliae Christianae* 55.1: 58–70.

McCormick, M. 2001. *Origins of the European Economy: Communications and Commerce, A.D. 300–900.* Cambridge: Cambridge University Press.

Mee, C., D. Gill, H. Forbes, and L. Foxhall. 1991. "Rural Settlement Changes in the Methana Peninsula, Greece." In *Roman Landscapes: Archaeological Survey in the Mediterranean Region*, ed. G. Barker and J. Lloyd, 223–232. Archaeological Monographs of the British School at Rome 2. London: British School at Rome.

Mitterauer, M. 1992. "Peasant and Non-Peasant Family Forms in Relation to the Physical Environment and the Local Economy," *Journal of Family History* 17.2: 139–159.

Mørch, H. F. 1994. "Agricultural Landscape: A Geographer's Considerations on the Past." In *Landuse in the Roman Empire*, ed. J. Carlsen, P. Ørsted, and J. E. Skydsgaard, 107–113. Analecta Romana Instituti Danici suppl. 22. Rome: L'Erma di Bretschneider.

Neboit, R. 1988. "Les basses terrasses alluviales, témoins de l'occupation des sols. Italie méridionale, Sicile." In *Structures de l'habitat et occupation du sol dans les pays méditerranéens: Les méthodes et l'apport de l'archéologie extensive*, ed. G. Noyé, 401–405. Rome: Ecole française de Rome; Madrid: Casa de Velázquez.

Ørsted, P. with Ladjimi Sebaï et al. 1992. "Town and Countryside in Roman Tunisia: A Preliminary Report on the Tunisio-Danish Survey Project in the Oued R'mel Basin in and around Ancient Segermes," *JRA* 5: 69–96.

Patlagean, E. 1977. *Pauvreté économique et pauvreté sociale à Byzance 4e–7e siècles.* Paris: Mouton.

Patterson, J. 1987. "Crisis, What Crisis? Rural Change and Urban Development in Imperial Apennine Italy," *PBSR* 55: 115–146.

Percival, J. 1969. "P. Ital. 3 and Roman Estate Management." In *Hommages à Marcel Renard*, ed. J. Bibauw, 607–615. Brussels: Latomus.

———. 1992. "The Fifth-Century Villa: New Life or Death Postponed?" In *Fifth-Century Gaul: A Crisis of Identity?* ed. J. Drinkwater and H. Elton, 156–164. Cambridge: Cambridge University Press.

———. 1997. "Villas and Monasteries in Late Roman Gaul," *JEH* 48.1: 1–21.

Périn, P. 2004. "The Origin of the Village in Early Medieval Gaul." In *Landscapes of Change: Rural Evolutions in Late Antiquity and the Early Middle Ages*, ed. N. Christie, 255–278. Aldershot: Ashgate.

Pettegrew, D. 2007. "The Busy Countryside of Late Roman Corinth: Interpreting Ceramic Data Produced by Regional Archaeological Surveys," *Hesperia* 76: 743–784.

Potter, T. W. 1976. "Valleys and Settlement: Some New Evidence," *World Archaeology* 8.2: 207–219.

———. 1995. *Towns in Late Antiquity: Iol Caesarea and Its Context*. Oxford: Oxbow.

Potter, T. W., and A. C. King, 1997. *Excavations at the Mola di Monte Gelato*. Archaeological Monographs of the British School at Rome 11. London: British School at Rome.

Poulter, A. 2004. "Cataclysm on the Lower Danube: The Destruction of a Complex Roman Landscape." In *Landscapes of Change: Rural Evolutions in Late Antiquity and the Early Middle Ages*, ed. N. Christie, 223–253. Aldershot: Ashgate.

Randsborg, K., ed. 1989. *The Birth of Europe: Archaeology and Social Development in the First Millennium A.D.* Analecta Romana Instituti Danici suppl. 16. Rome: L'Erma di Bretschneider.

———. 1991. *The First Millennium AD in Europe and the Mediterranean: An Archaeological Essay*. Cambridge: Cambridge University Press.

Rathbone, D. W. 1991. *Economic Rationalism and Rural Society in Third-Century A.D. Egypt: The Heroninos Archive and the Appianus Estate*. Cambridge: Cambridge University Press.

———. 2008. "Villages and Patronage in Fourth-Century Egypt: *P. Ross. Georg.* 3.8," *BASP* 45: 189–207.

Reynolds, S. 1997. *Kingdoms and Communities in Western Europe: 900–1300*, 2nd ed. Oxford: Clarendon Press.

Richardson, G. 2003. "What Protected Peasants Best? Markets, Risk, Efficiency and Medieval English Agriculture," *Research in Economic History* 21: 299–356.

Riggs, D. 2001. "The Continuity of Paganism between the Cities and Countryside of Late Roman Africa." In *Urban Centers and Rural Contexts in Late Antiquity*, ed. T. S. Burns and J. W. Eadie, 285–300. East Lansing: Michigan State University Press.

Ripoll, G., and J. Arce. 2000. "The Transformation and End of Roman *Villae* in the West (Fourth–Seventh Centuries): Problems and Perspectives." In *Towns and Their Territories between Late Antiquity and the Early Middle Ages*, ed. G. P. Brogiolo, N. Gauthier, and N. Christie, 63–114. Leiden: Brill.

Robertson, A. F. 1980. "On Sharecropping," *Man* 15: 411–429.

Rosen, S. S., and G. Avni, 1993. "The Edge of Empire: The Archaeology of Pastoral Nomads in the Southern Negev Highlands in Late Antiquity." In *Production and the Exploitation of Resources*, ed. M. G. Morony, 81–91. The Formation of the Classical Islamic World 11. Aldershot: Ashgate.

Rowlandson, J. 1996. *Landlords and Tenants in Roman Egypt: The Social Relations of Agriculture in the Oxyrhynchite Nome*. Oxford: Oxford University Press.

Ruffini, G. 2008. *Social Networks in Byzantine Egypt*. Cambridge: Cambridge University Press.

Safrai, Z. 1994. *The Economy of Roman Palestine.* London: Routledge.

Saller, R. P. 1982. *Personal Patronage under the Early Empire.* Cambridge: Cambridge University Press.

Sancisi-Weerdenburg, H., R. J. van der Spek, H. C. Teitler, and H. T. Wallinga, eds. 1993. *De Agricultura: In Memoriam Pieter Willem De Neeve 1945–1990.* Dutch Monographs in Ancient History and Archaeology 10. Amsterdam: J.C. Gieben.

Sanders, G. D. R. 2004. "Problems in Interpreting Rural and Urban Settlement in Southern Greece, AD 365–700." In *Landscapes of Change: Rural Evolutions in Late Antiquity and the Early Middle Ages,* ed. N. Christie, 163–193. Aldershot: Ashgate.

Sapin, J. 1998. "À l'est de Gerasa: Aménagement rural et reseau de communications," *Syria* 75: 107–136.

Sarris, P. 2004. "The Origins of the Manorial Economy: New Insights from Late Antiquity," *English Historical Review* 119: 279–311.

———. 2006. *Economy and Society in the Age of Justinian.* Cambridge: Cambridge University Press.

Scheidel, W. 1990. "Free-born and Manumitted Bailiffs in the Graeco-Roman World," *CQ* 40: 591–593.

———. 1995. "The Most Silent Women of Greece and Rome: Rural Labour and Women's Life in the Ancient World (I)," *G&R* 42: 202–217.

———. 2000. "Slaves of the Soil: Review Article," *JRA* 13: 727–732.

Schneider, L. 2007. "Structures du peuplement et formes de l'habitat dans les campagnes du sud-est de la France de l'Antiquité au Moyen Âge (IVe–VIIIe S.)," *Gallia* 64: 11–56.

Scott, J. C. 1977. "Patronage or Exploitation?" In *Patrons and Clients in Mediterranean Societies,* ed. E. Gellner and J. Waterbury, 21–39. London: Duckworth.

Scott, S. 2004. "Elites, Exhibitionism and the Society of the Late Roman Villa." In *Landscapes of Change: Rural Evolutions in Late Antiquity and the Early Middle Ages,* ed. N. Christie, 39–65. Aldershot: Ashgate.

Shaw, B. D. 1981a. "Climate, Environment, and History: The Case of Roman North Africa." In *Climate and History: Studies in Past Climates and Their Impact on Man,* ed. T. M. L. Wigley, M. J. Ingram, and G. Farmer, 379–403. Cambridge: Cambridge University Press.

———. 1981b. "Rural Markets in North Africa and the Political Economy of the Roman Empire," *AntAfr* 17: 37–83.

———. 1982. "Lamasba: An Ancient Irrigation Community," *AntAfr* 18: 61–103.

Silverman, S. 1977. "Patronage as Myth." In *Patrons and Clients in Mediterranean Societies,* ed. E. Gellner and J. Waterbury, 7–19. London: Duckworth.

Sirks, A. J. B. 2001. "The Farmer, the Landlord and the Law in the Fifth Century." In *Law, Society, and Authority in Late Antiquity,* ed. R. Mathisen, 256–271. Oxford: Oxford University Press.

Sommier, B. 1996. "Les amitiés dans un village d'Andalousie orientale: Morale, identités et evolution sociale," *Ethnologie française* 36.3: 477–489.

Squatriti, P. 1992. "Marshes and Mentalities in Early Medieval Ravenna," *Viator* 23: 1–16.

Stathakopoulos, D. C. 2004. *Famine and Pestilence in the Late Roman and Early Byzantine Empire: A Systematic Survey of Subsistence Crises and Epidemics.* Aldershot: Ashgate.

Stern, E. M. 1992. "A Fourth-Century Factory for Gathering and Blowing Chunks of Glass?" *JRA* 5: 490–494.

Stone, D. L. 2000. "Society and Economy in North Africa: Review Article," *JRA* 13: 721–724.

Tate, G. 1992. *Les campagnes de la Syrie du Nord du IIe au VIIe siècle*, vol. 1. Institut Français d'Archéologie du Proche-Orient, Bibliothèque Archéologique et Historique 133. Paris: Librarie orientaliste Paul Geuthner.

———. 1997. "The Syrian Countryside during the Roman Era." In *The Early Roman Empire in the East*, ed. S. E. Alcock, 55–71. Oxford: Oxbow.

———. 1998. "Expansion d'une société riche et égalitaire: les paysans de Syrie du Nord du IIe au VIIe siècle," *Comptes Rendus des séances de l'Académie des Inscriptions & Belles-Lettres 1997*, 913–941. Paris: Diffusion de Boccard.

Tchalenko, G. 1953. *Villages Antiques de la Syrie du Nord: Le Massif du Bélus à l'époque romaine*. 3 vols. Paris: P. Geuthner.

Teitler, H. C. 1993. "Free-born Estate Managers in the Graeco-Roman World." In *De Agricultura: In Memoriam Pieter Willem De Neeve 1945–1990*, ed. H. Sancisi-Weerdenburg, R. J. van der Spek, H. C. Teitler, and H. T. Wallinga, 206–213. Dutch Monographs in Ancient History and Archaeology 10. Amsterdam: J. C. Gieben.

Thorner, D. 1966/1986. "Chayanov's Concept of the Peasant Economy." In A. V. Chayanov, *The Theory of Peasant Economy*, ed. D. Thorner, B. Kerblay, and R. E. F. Smith, trans. C. Lane and R. E. F. Smith, xi–xxiii. Madison, WI: R. D. Irwin.

van Minnen, P. 1997. "Patronage in Fourth-Century Egypt: A Note on *P. Ross. Georg.* III.8," *JJP* 27: 67–73.

van Ossel, P. 1983. "L'Établissement Romain de Loën à Lixhe et l'occupation rurale au Bas-Empire dans la Hesbaye Liègeoise," *Helinium* 23: 143–69.

———. 1992. *Établissements ruraux de l'Antiquité tardive dans le Nord de la Gaule*. 51e supplément à Gallia. Paris: Editions du Centre National de la Recherche Scientifique.

van Ossel, P., and P. Ouzoulias. 2000. "Rural settlement economy in Northern Gaul in the Late Empire: An Overview and Assessment," *JRA* 13: 133–60.

———. 2001. "La mutation des campagnes de la Gaule du Nord entre le milieu du IIIe siècle et le milieu du Ve siècle: Où en est-on?" In *Belgian Archaeology in a European Setting II*, ed. M. Lodewijckx, 231–245. Acta Archaeologica Lovanensia Monographiae 13. Leuven: Leuven University Press.

Vera, D. 1993. "Proprietà terriera e società rurale nell'Italia gotica." In *Teoderico il Grande e i Goti d'Italia: Atti del XIII Congresso internazionale di studi sull'Alto Medioevo, Milano, 2–6 novembre 1992*, 133–166. Spoleto: Centro italiano di studi sull'alto Medioevo.

———. 1997. "Padroni, contadini, contratti: *Realia* del colonato tardoantico." In *Terre, proprietari e contadini dell'Impero romano: Dall'affitto agrario al colonato tardoantico (Incontro studio di Capri, 16–18 ottobre 1995)*, ed. E. Lo Cascio, 185–224. Rome: Nuova Italia Scientifica.

———. 1998. "Le forme del lavoro rurale: Aspetti della trasformazione dell'Europa romana fra tarda antichità e alto medioevo." In *Morfologie sociali e culturali in Europa fra Tarda Antichità e Alto Medioevo*, 293–342. Settimane di studio del Centro italiano di studi sull'alto medioevo 45. Spoleto: Centro italiano di studi sull'alto Medioevo.

———. 1999. "I silenzi di Palladio e l'Italia: Osservazioni sull'ultimo agronomo Romano," *AntTard* 7: 283–97.

Villeneuve, F. 1985. "L'économie rurale et la vie des campagnes dans le Hauran antique (Ier siècle avant J.-C.–VIIe siècle ap. J.-C.), une approche." In *Hauran I: Recherches archéologiques sur la Syrie du Sud a l'époque Hellénistique et Romaine*, ed. J.-M. Dentzer, 63–136. Institut Français d'Archéologie du Proche-Orient, Bibliothèque Archéologique et Historique 124. Paris: P. Geuthner.

Vita-Finzi, C. 1969. *The Mediterranean Valleys: Geological Changes in Historical Times.* Cambridge: Cambridge University Press.

Wagstaff, J. M. 1981. "Buried Assumptions: Some Problems in the Interpretation of the Younger Fill Raised by Recent Data from Greece," *Journal of Archaeological Science* 8.3: 247–64.

Ward-Perkins, B. 1988. "The Towns of Northern Italy: Rebirth or Renewal?" In *The Rebirth of Towns in the West AD 700–1050*, ed. R. Hodges and B. Hobley, 16–27. CBA Research Report 68. London: Council for British Archaeology.

———. 2000, "Land, Labour and Settlement." In *CAH* XIV: 315–345.

Ward-Perkins, B., N. Mills, D. Gadd, and C. Delano Smith. 1986. "Luni and the *Ager Lunensis*: The Rise and Fall of a Roman Town and Its Territory," *PBSR* 54: 81–146.

Waterbury, J. 1977. "An Attempt to Put Patrons and Clients in Their Place." In *Patrons and Clients in Mediterranean Societies*, ed. E. Gellner and J. Waterbury, 329–342. London: Duckworth.

Whitby, Michael. 1987. "Maro the Dendrite: An Anti-Social Holy Man?" In *Homo Viator: Classical Essays for John Bramble*, ed. Mary Whitby, P. Hardie and Michael Whitby, 309–17. Bristol: Bristol Classical Press.

White, K. D. 1970. *Roman Farming*. London: Thames and Hudson.

Whitehead, N. 1994. "The Roman Countryside." In *Territory, Time and State: The Archaeological Development of the Gubbio Basin*, ed. C. Malone and S. Stoddart, 188–203. Cambridge: Cambridge University Press.

Whittaker, C. R. 1976. "*Agri Deserti*." In *Studies in Roman Property*, ed. M. I. Finley, 137–165. Cambridge: Cambridge University Press.

———. 1994. *Frontiers of the Roman Empire: A Social and Economic Study*. Baltimore: Johns Hopkins University Press.

———. 1995. "Do Theories of the Ancient City Matter?" In *Urban Society in Roman Italy*, ed. T. J. Cornell and K. Lomas, 9–26. London: UCL.

Whittaker, C. R., and P. D. A. Garnsey, 1998. "Rural Life in the Later Roman empire." in *CAH* XIII: 277–311.

Wickham, C. 2005a. "The Development of Villages in the West, 300–900." In *Les Villages dans l'Empire byzantin (IVe–XVe siècle)*, ed. J. Lefort, C. Morrisson, and J.-P. Sodini, 55–69. Réalités Byzantines 11. Paris: Lethielleux.

———. 2005b. *Framing the Early Middle Ages: Europe and the Mediterranean 400–800*. Oxford and New York: Oxford University Press.

Wigley, T. M. L., M. J. Ingram, and G. Farmer, eds. 1981. *Climate and History: Studies in Past Climates and Their Impact on Man*. Cambridge: Cambridge University Press.

Wolf, E. 1966. *Peasants*. Englewood Cliffs, NJ: Prentice-Hall.

Woods, D. 1992. "An Earthquake at Constantinople: Augustine's *De excidio urbis* VI.7," *Augustiniana* 42: 331–337.

CHAPTER 20

MARRIAGE AND FAMILY

KYLE HARPER
University of Oklahoma

Introduction

In a series of homilies delivered around 400 C.E., John Chrysostom lectured his flock on the foundations of Christian marriage.[1] These sermons represent a *tour de force* of pastoral activism, offering us remarkable insights into late Roman social practices and into the attitudes of the Christian intelligentsia at a moment of brisk religious change. In Chrysostom's vision, Christian matrimony was to be characterized by two distinguishing norms: firm opposition to divorce or remarriage and a single standard of sexual behavior for men and women.[2] At the same time, the preacher was eager to appropriate the highest ideals of Greco-Roman marriage for his own cause. He claimed, shrewdly, that virtue rather than social prestige was the path to concord and companionship. Chrysostom argued that Greco-Roman values of companionship were subverted by the very dynamics of betrothal, since social considerations outweighed moral or personal factors in the selection of partners. Marriage should be a "sharing of life," rather than a business transaction, he asserted in resonant words.[3] He focused relentlessly on the intense strategy behind the making of a match, rehearsing in merciless detail the betrothal process. He exploited anxieties about unequal marriages and parodied the man who sought a rich wife by gambling his entire wealth on a nuptial gift, like a merchant overloading his ship and putting his whole fortune at risk.[4] For Chrysostom, the betrothal process—the jostling of the lawyers and the maneuvering of the matchmakers—was ultimate proof that contemporary marriage was a material rather than spiritual affair.

Like many Christian authors of Late Antiquity, John Chrysostom conjured a deliberately negative image of marriage when it suited his rhetorical purposes. It is worth noting, though, the earnest sense within these sermons of the distance between Christian norms and the realities of marriage in the late empire. Chrysostom stressed the divide between his teaching and the "outside" world, repeatedly counterposing his vision of Christian marriage and Roman law.[5] There was no hint in these lectures that the Roman state might be an instrument for Christianizing social practices.[6] Indeed, modern scholarship on the late ancient family has shown that Christian influence did not deeply affect Roman family law, particularly on the issues closest to Chrysostom's heart: indissolubility and sexual exclusivity. In the larger picture, although from the perspective of a late antique bishop it may not have seemed so, Christianity was more influenced by Greco-Roman structures than vice versa, and the Church ultimately became the principal carrier of the Greco-Roman tradition of the family.[7] Taking its cue from Chrysostom's sermons, this chapter considers both the role of the family in the making of Late Antiquity and the place of Late Antiquity in the history of the family. After briefly surveying the rise of family history in ancient studies, the analysis turns to the influence of law, religion, and social structure on the late Roman family.[8] Throughout, the focus is on marriage as the central strand in the ancient family, indeed, as "a sort of seedbed of human society."[9]

The late Roman family inherited its basic form from the high empire. Affective monogamy was a strong cultural force, but family life was inevitably structured by the needs of a high-mortality, high-fertility society. Late Roman law, following social practice, tended to recognize the nuclear family unit in the rules governing marriage, guardianship, and succession. Christianity reinforced these tendencies and introduced two distinctive norms, articulated precisely by Chrysostom: the doctrine of indissolubility and the ideal of sexually exclusive marriage. These very sermons of Chrysostom have been key documents in the history of the family in Late Antiquity, regularly cited as witnesses to the legal and religious developments of the period. Yet they hold another, neglected clue to the dynamics of family life in Late Antiquity. Chrysostom's warnings about the ambitious groom and the wealthy bride have been dismissed as mere tropes, even though the detailed criticism of matchmaking was the warp and woof of these speeches. Ironically, the rise of the *donatio ante nuptias*, a nuptial gift from the groom to the bride, is recognized as perhaps the principal structural change in the late Roman family, although it remains unexplained.[10] This chapter argues that the social context of the late antique family, in particular the interplay among property transfers, marital strategy, and the reconstitution of the Roman aristocracy, has been underemphasized. The effort to situate Late Antiquity in an overarching narrative of family history has drawn attention toward Roman law and Christianity and away from the ordinary struggles for survival and social success that defined the horizons of the men and women who heard Chrysostom preach.

The Historiographical Tradition

Finding a universal definition of the family is not simple.[11] An inclusive working definition might describe the family as the social form through which the two deeply related processes of biological reproduction and the transmission of property are pursued. The language of family life in Roman antiquity is revealing. *Familia* connoted the legal, proprietary group under the power of a *pater familias*, including biological descendants and slaves; more broadly it referred to the whole agnatic descent group. Yet *domus*, "household," was the more common, idiomatic word.[12] *Domus* made reference to the focal point of matrimonial, biological, and proprietary bonds, including the slaves; slaves were an elemental part of the Greco-Roman family, in Late Antiquity, too.[13] In Greek, *oikos* and *oikia* were the normal expressions for the family.[14] It is immediately significant that, in both languages, the basic word for the family was a term derived from the practical realm (residence) and used as a shorthand for the outcome of complex kinship and inheritance systems. In other words, the family in the Roman empire was not imagined in terms of abstract lineage structures or legal forms, but as the day-to-day experience of links within the household. The ubiquity of slavery, the ravages of death, and the residence of extended relatives made the Roman family a complex organism, but undoubtedly the conjugal bond and the parent-child relationship were at its core.[15]

This insight is the hard-won product of a long historiographical tradition. It is imperative to consider the way in which the modern study of the family emerged and developed, for this background has shaped the questions that have been asked and the sources that have been used to reconstruct the family.[16] Family history came into its own as a distinct subfield during the 1970s, at the convergence of three disciplines: anthropology, social history, and demography. Anthropology could claim the longest pedigree, descending from a nineteenth-century discourse on the problem of kinship.[17] In the 1960s, the family became an object of study among historians who took a broader view of what constituted the proper domain of historical investigation. Ariès's work on childhood was a major impetus, providing an overarching narrative of the modern family that correlated nuclear structure and sentimentality with industrialization, and the rise of women's history provided sustaining momentum.[18] Finally, the study of demography brought into focus the stark differences among past and present families: the ancient family was forced to answer the heavy demands of a high-mortality, high-fertility society.[19]

The late 1970s and 1980s saw two concurrent if somewhat contradictory trends in the field of family history. On the one hand, the results of the previous decade were consolidated in the form of large-scale narratives tracing the history of the family in Europe. The work of Flandrin, Macfarlane, Stone, Goody, Brundage, Herlihy, and *A History of Private Life* not only signaled that the discipline had arrived but also often took the ancient family, or more specifically a legalistic reading of the Roman family, as a foil or a point of departure from which the modern, nuclear, sentimental family would develop.[20] At the same time, ongoing research was undermining the foundations of these narratives. More detailed investigation revealed the extreme temporal and geographic diversity of family life, and it was during this second wave of family history that the modern study of the Roman family emerged. The 1980s and 1990s were the heyday of Roman family history, with a particular emphasis on the early empire, as historians diligently whittled away at stereotypes of the ancient family as a legalistic, agnatic, and emotionally vacuous medium for reproduction.[21]

The model of the Roman family that emerged over the 1980s recognized the cultural value placed on private life under the empire and thus challenged the narratives correlating sentimentality with modernity. The breakthrough studies of Saller and Shaw demonstrated that large, agnatic clans were not the basic form of the Roman family.[22] Nuclear structures, neolocal residence, and conjugal affection were common in the Roman empire. Demographic modeling revealed that the severer features of Roman law, such as *patria potestas*, were tempered by the mortality structures of ancient Mediterranean societies.[23] Epigraphy and papyrology were called into service and have yielded plausible models of nuptuality, fertility, and mortality in antiquity.[24] These studies demonstrated that Roman society was powerfully mobilized for fertility, with a low age at marriage for females (mid to high teens, a decade later for men) and universal marriage.[25] Newer research has explored the role of class, provincial diversity, and socially marginal elements in the construction of mainstream society.[26] Only recently has sufficient attention been given to the basic fact that the Greeks and Romans were unusual for practicing socially-imposed monogamy: this was the essential precondition for the nuclear structures and sentiments that are such striking features of the Roman family.[27] Absorbed by Christianity, monogamy must be reckoned one of the most profound legacies of Greece and Rome to the modern European family.

In sheer volume, study of the late Roman family has lagged behind this rapidly progressing body of work on the Roman family in the high empire. It has also been framed by its own questions, often derived from prior traditions of scholarship and from the particular nature of the evidence. The late Roman family has been framed by the interaction of three disciplinary interests: post-classical law, patristics, and, more recently, the history of gender and sexuality. The search for Christian influence on the development of late Roman law has been a major paradigm of study, not least because the two richest sources of information are the corpus of patristic literature and the late Roman legal codifications.[28] This focus has acted to suppress dialogue between late antique social history and the historiography of the family in early periods of Roman history. The study of gender and sexuality, however, has found fertile ground in the ascetic literature of Late Antiquity.[29] The ascetic impulses of Late Antiquity, in fact, threaten to overshadow the stronger forces of continuity in a society that went on reproducing itself with a great deal of success.

Within the venerable debate over Christian influence, a revisionist consensus of the late Roman family began to emerge in the 1980s among scholars who argued strongly *against* Christian influence.[30] Shaw demonstrated that the patristic sources could be read against the grain for what they reveal about the realities of the late Roman family.[31] Evans Grubbs, in a meticulous case study of Constantine's family law, showed that the social legislation of the first Christian emperor was conservative and status-conscious, rather than inspired by religious conviction.[32] Arjava demonstrated that late Roman family law is more convincingly explained as a ratification of long-standing trends rather than a radical Christian departure.[33] Above all, the monumental work of Beaucamp on women in Late Antiquity, rooted in legal and papyrological evidence, dismantled any easy, linear narrative of Christianization and highlighted the overriding influence of a continued, and perhaps even more strongly inflected, patriarchy.[34]

The study of the late Roman family in the last decades has thus emphasized continuity over change.[35] The Church's ability to alter behavior was ultimately limited. The legal record exhibits no overarching direction, no teleological drive toward Christian, medieval, or modern structures of family life. The legal and literary sources obscure the deep patterns of continuity, and the imperatives of a high-fertility, high-mortality demographic regime, in the context of a monogamous society, continued to shape the form of the family far more strongly than the Church or state could. The pastoral wing of the late antique Church presented a new institutional voice against divorce, remarriage, and the sexual double standard, even as it intensified the earlier Roman valorization of harmonious, affective marriage as "the principal affair in human life."[36] In short, the family in Late Antiquity saw slow and modest cultural change driven by the expanding scope of ecclesiastical institutions, yet deep structural continuity.

The remainder of this chapter is divided into three parts, considering in turn the influence of state, Church, and social structure on the late Roman family.[37] The first section offers a brief survey of the most important developments in postclassical family law. The second section discusses the problem of Christianization, focusing on the new religion's impact on the values and habits of family life. The third section is devoted to social structure, trying to assess the degrees of continuity and change in terms of demography, urbanism, and, in particular, status hierarchies. It has recently been argued that the late antique family was influenced by changing patterns of aristocratic dominance.[38] This is a promising approach. This chapter argues that Late Antiquity saw a new tendency for upwardly mobile men to cement their rising status through socially favorable marriages. John Chrysostom's ferocious attack on the social climber's marital ambition was something more than generic rhetoric; it was an unnerving commentary on the use of marriage in a society where aristocratic status was in flux. Marital strategy is a dimension of late Roman family life that has been unduly neglected and, as the following discussion demonstrates, an avenue for further research.

Roman Family Law from Constantine to Justinian

The constitutions preserved in the *Theodosian* and *Justinianic Codes* are an invaluable source for the history of the family in the postclassical period of Roman law (after c. 235 C.E.). Roman family law sat at the intersection of two complex legal structures—reproduction and the transmission of property. The rules of betrothal, marriage, divorce, succession, and guardianship formed an interrelated system. In the classical period, the Roman family was legally defined by *patria potestas*, the power held by the eldest male ascendant over all of his slaves and direct descendants.[39] The *pater familias* enjoyed extensive control over those in his power and complete rights over their property. This power continued even after the children reached adulthood, and it could be severed only by emancipation or death. Yet the mortality regime of the ancient Mediterranean meant that relatively few adults had a living father.[40] In fact, one of the most important consequences of *patria potestas* was the relative independence it ultimately afforded adult women. In the imperial age, the Romans married *sine manu*, meaning that a married woman remained in the legal power of her father rather than her husband.[41] Women married at a significantly younger age than men, so it was common for a girl's first marriage to be arranged by her parents. But after her emancipation or her father's death, an adult woman was legally independent, a status that many wives in the Roman empire must have enjoyed.[42]

The position of women was also strengthened by the Roman practice of partible inheritance; daughters played a major role in the devolution of property. Moreover, the Romans practiced dotal marriage (with a dowry), so that the woman brought at least part of her share with her into marriage.[43] Yet the dowry remained the property of the wife or, if she was still in his power, her father. The husband had the right to use the dowry during the marriage, but legally it remained a distinct fund. Roman law strictly prohibited the transmission of property between living spouses.[44] All of a woman's property remained technically separate from her husband's goods, so that on divorce or death, it was returned to her or her family. Yet the Romans enjoyed considerable testamentary powers, which allowed individuals to dispose of their property as they wished.[45] Testamentary customs gave nuclear structures additional salience in Roman society; agnatic principles intervened particularly when there was a dispute over property or no will to determine its ownership.[46]

The marriage bond in classical Roman law was only lightly regulated by the state.[47] Marriage was a relationship formed *causa procreandorum liberorum*; it required no formal ceremony or property exchanges. It required only marital intent from the parties to the marriage, consent from all those who were a party to the marriage (including the *patres familias*), and legal capacity to marry (age, degrees of separation, status, and citizenship).[48] Because mutual intent defined marriage in classical law, a marriage could be dissolved by one of the spouses. This system of free and unilateral divorce meant that marriages could be ended, with or without cause, by either the husband or the wife, although judges could award the husband part of the dowry if the wife was culpable for the divorce or if there were children.[49] Yet this liberal legal regime of divorce belies the fact that Romans of the imperial age placed a high value on marriage.[50] Tracts, letters, and tombstones abundantly attest the importance of the marriage bond in imperial society. Monogamy was the bedrock of Roman society, marital concord was a core social value, and private life was a domain of extreme importance.[51]

Roman family law would undergo fundamental transformation in Late Antiquity. The reign of Constantine marked the major departure, in both style and substance. Family law was a central concern for Constantine: in one tally, at least eighty of the nearly four hundred surviving extracts of Constantinian legislation concerned the family.[52] Constantine's legislation often yielded to pragmatism over formalism, yet Constantine's laws fit into no coherent pattern, not even one organized around "Christian" principles. In many cases, especially regulations protecting female sexual honor, the first Christian emperor intensified the state's role but wholly accepted traditional boundaries, with their firm basis in social status.[53]

Among the "most famous and misunderstood" legal enactments of Constantine was his *Ad Populum* edict of 320.[54] This broad and multipart reform repealed the Augustan penalties for celibacy and childlessness.[55] Augustus had limited the ability of unmarried adults to receive inheritances or legacies from outside their close kin and restricted the ability of childless spouses to inherit from one another. Constantine removed the penalties for celibacy and childlessness, although he left in place the limits on inheritance between childless spouses: Roman law continued to protect a family's property against diffusion through daughters who had no children.[56] This edict has been seen as a concession to Christianity, but the enactment itself claimed to be acting against the "lurking terrors of the laws," and the other parts of the *Ad Populum* law demonstrate an effort to simplify and streamline several onerous aspects of the classical law.[57] No less important were the measures that simplified the requirements of formal language and procedure in testation.[58]

Constantine also initiated a series of reforms that gave increasing legitimacy to the succession of property through the nuclear family. The Romans had long believed that children should inherit their parents' property, and they wrote their wills to that effect. But in Late Antiquity, this pattern was increasingly reinforced by public law, even where it intruded on the intricate logic of classical jurisprudence. For instance, Constantine enacted legislation protecting the ability of children to inherit from their mother by limiting the father's ownership over *bona materna*.[59] If a mother died, she could not technically leave her property to her children while they were still in the *potestas* of the father. But women did effectively leave their children property, on the condition of the children's emancipation or through *fideicommissa*. In a law of 315, Constantine declared that fathers could enjoy the *usufruct* of such property but not alienate it.[60] In a later law, fathers who remarried peremptorily lost even the control over the *bona materna* of their children from the first marriage—a solution that "did not fit very elegantly into the Roman legal system" but ensured the transmission of property to children.[61]

On the rules of succession, these reforms of Constantine were a bellwether of change. Later emperors consistently protected the customs of nuclear succession, but these reforms had precedent in the high empire. A law passed under Hadrian helped mothers with the *ius liberorum* inherit from their deceased children, and Marcus Aurelius permitted children to inherit from their mothers on intestacy.[62] Constantine allowed mothers to succeed from their children on intestacy, regardless of their possession of the *ius liberorum*, and allowed mothers to make claims against an ungrateful will.[63] Later laws extended the Constantinian protections of *bona materna* by ruling that a widow with children could not give more than three-quarters of her estate in a dowry to her new husband.[64] Children also gained residual inheritance rights from their maternal grandfather, even if their mother was dead.[65] These reforms reached their natural conclusion in the reign of Justinian, who established equality between the male and female lines in the rules of succession.[66] The late antique reforms of succession exhibit a pattern of slow and piecemeal development, already begun under the high empire, away from agnatic structures (typically residual and overridden by testation) and toward nuclear property structures.[67]

Constantine also initiated dramatic changes to the laws governing exchanges between betrothed couples. In Late Antiquity betrothals became increasingly formalized and enforced by public law; moreover, men began making a contribution similar to the dowry, allotting part of their property as a donation to a conjugal fund.[68] Already in the imperial period, men might make engagement gifts for the sake of contracting a marriage.[69] Third-century rescripts reveal that these gifts could be reclaimed if the engagement was broken, unless the man was responsible for its dissolution.[70] Grooms' gifts were apparently more common in the eastern empire. Disputes over these arrangements increasingly found their way into Roman courts in the aftermath of the Antonine Constitution, so "there was a need for a general imperial ruling" on the fate of betrothal gifts in broken engagements.[71] In 319, Constantine ruled that whichever party broke off the engagement lost all rights to gifts made during the betrothal.[72] He ruled that this would hold *regardless* of cause, since any claims against the character of the fiancé(e) should have prevented the engagement in the first place. He also specified that if the engagement was ended by death, the gifts were returned. Constantine provided a rule covering an area of social life for which there was not a general principle of law, and he thus made betrothal a legally consequential act.

Later laws of Constantine fine-tuned his initial reforms of betrothal, but the system underwent a major overhaul later in the fourth century.[73] At some point before 380, Roman legislators instituted a system in which betrothals were insured by the exchange of earnest payments, called *arrhae*.[74] Breaking the engagement entailed repayment of the *arrhae* times four. The elaboration of this rule encouraged a distinction between the *arrhae* and the husband's contribution to the conjugal fund, which became known as the *donatio ante nuptias*. Such gifts were not an unusual element of local customs throughout the empire, especially in the east, but from the fourth century they rapidly took on increasing significance in Roman law.[75] Ultimately, the *donatio* came to be seen and treated as a counterpart to the dowry. Legal rules governing the management and fate of the dowry were applied to the *donatio*.[76] For instance, both were forfeited by the guilty party in case of divorce.[77] Thus, during Late Antiquity, Roman law moved from a purely dotal system to one based on dual gifts into a conjugal fund. In fact, although dowry would survive in the east, it was eclipsed in the west by a nuptial exchange system dominated by the groom's gifts.[78]

In step with these other reforms, the rules governing guardianship over minors were modified in the fourth century. The Roman family was surrounded by death, and it would be hard to overestimate the significance of the guardianship of minors in ancient society.[79] In the classical period, a minor who lost his or her father received a legal guardian, a *tutor*.[80] The tutor could be appointed by the father in his will.[81] If none was appointed, then the nearest paternal male relative automatically occupied the role, and if no such relative existed, a trustworthy substitute was to be appointed by a magistrate.[82] The widow could not legally act as tutor for her own children, although men evaded this technicality by bequeathing their property to the mother under a trust or usufruct.[83] They also evaded it practically by ordering the widow to monitor the tutor's actions. Already in the early empire, women were often "virtual guardians" of their children, a reality that became increasingly recognized in Roman law.[84] In the fourth century, the guardianship of widows over their children was legally recognized but only if no agnatic relatives existed; later enactments specified that she had to remain unmarried to enjoy the role.[85]

Likewise, the tutelage of women was the object of significant reform, although it is notoriously difficult to follow the path of change in the laws that survive. Women without a living father were *sui iuris*, but even after the age of majority, women were subject to legal incapacities if they acted without a guardian.[86] Augustus allowed women who gave birth to three children—not unusual given the fertility patterns of the Roman population—the *ius liberorum*, enabling them to act without a tutor.[87] During the imperial period, there are signs that guardianship over adult females was becoming obsolete.[88] Little mention of it is made in postclassical law. Yet, in the papyri, women continued to cite the *ius trium liberorum* until 389 C.E.[89] Moreover, they would continue for centuries to specify when they acted without a tutor. In a detailed analysis, Beaucamp demonstrated that women acting without a tutor were widows, while only husbands acted as tutors.[90] The logical conclusion is that a woman could act independently if her husband had died, but living husbands were expected to be present at property transactions, especially ones involving the patrimony.

These developments reflect "the reinforcement of the nuclear family cell, privileging the common patrimony of the couple."[91]

Divorce marks the ultimate test of late Roman legislation on the family, for it sits at the crossroads of the moral, social, and economic aspects of marriage.[92] Yet the complex history of divorce legislation in the late empire demonstrates that no clear pattern of social or ideological change can explain the development of late Roman law. In 331, Constantine overturned the system of unilateral divorce.[93] He issued a law restricting the grounds for divorce to the most heinous crimes.[94] If a woman repudiated her husband for any other cause, she not only lost her dowry but was also deported. If a man repudiated his wife without just cause (limited to a restricted class of offenses but including adultery), he had to return the dowry and remain unmarried. If he took a second wife, his first wife could make a claim against the dowry of the second wife. Constantine abolished a woman's ability to divorce her husband, while making it inconvenient for a man who wished to remarry to seek a divorce.[95] This was an extraordinary reversal of classical principles, but Constantine's reforms were not to endure. His nephew Julian repealed the measure. We are informed about this development only by the comments of the author known as Ambrosiaster, who complained that Julian's law had allowed women to divorce their husbands "freely" and "constantly."[96] Perhaps this was just traditional misogyny, or perhaps men were still able to divorce their wives after the reform of Constantine. Conceivably, it was easier for a husband to coerce his wife into a mutual divorce than the reverse. Nevertheless, during the reign of Julian, the classical regime of free, unilateral divorce was reestablished.[97]

In the fifth century, the law of divorce was the object of a back-and-forth exchange between the western and eastern halves of the empire, in which the east generally supported a more liberal regime. In 421, a law was issued in the western empire that reestablished limits on unilateral divorce.[98] This law promulgated a completely new system of rules. It maintained a double standard between men and women, but now there were three categories of justification: without cause, minor cause, and grave offenses. If a woman repudiated her husband without cause, she lost the dowry and donation and was exiled; for the same offense, a man lost the property and could not remarry. Divorce on the grounds of minor cause entailed loss of the property and inability to remarry for the woman and the loss of property and a two-year inability to remarry for the man. For grave offenses, a man could unilaterally divorce his wife without penalty, and a woman could do the same to her husband but with a five-year inability to remarry. The law thus established penalties for unilateral divorce, albeit much lighter ones than Constantine had decreed. The concern with both dowry *and* nuptial donation is evident, and revealing. Mutual divorce remained entirely permissible.

When the *Theodosian Code* became effective in the east on January 1, 439, the restrictive western standard became generally valid in the eastern empire, but within a year, Theodosius II repealed the law in his provinces and restored the classical system of free divorce.[99] In 448, with the adoption of Theodosius

II's Novels, this more liberal standard temporarily became law in the west, but in 452, Valentinian III returned again to the restrictive law of 421, which would remain the last word of Roman law on divorce in the west.[100] In the east, an attempt at compromise was issued in 449, with a broader list of justifications for unilateral divorce and substantially reduced penalties.[101] The liberal attitude would prevail in the east to the reign of Justinian. Justinian first maintained the outlines of the Theodosian compromise, although he showed opposition to the double standard.[102] But in 542, amid the ravages of the plague, he instituted a rule harsher than anything imagined by Constantine or the other western rulers: he outlawed consensual divorce.[103] This radical innovation was undone by Justin II in 566, who was pressured by unhappy couples to reverse the policy of his uncle.[104]

Even this abbreviated presentation of major legal developments prompts a series of difficult questions about the late antique family. First, what were the driving forces behind the changes to the law in Late Antiquity? The two principal suspects are Christianity, of course, and also provincial custom, whether eastern or western. Second, how are laws to be interpreted as evidence for social practice? Were the laws effective in shaping social habits, or do they represent a conversation that reveals little more than the perception and desires of the state? These are classic problems in the study of late Roman law, and in recent years, new approaches to socio-legal history have brought greater clarity to these issues.

The question of Christian influence on late Roman law has been a dominant theme in the study of the late Roman family. Influence can be construed in different ways. At times, scholars have looked for the Christian—Hosius or Ambrose—whispering into the emperor's ear.[105] More generally, Christian ideology, in favor of a strong or indissoluble conjugal bond, is detected behind trends in lawmaking.[106] But the thesis of Christian influence has been profoundly undermined. Often, the differences between "pre-Christian" habits and Christian ideology have been overstated.[107] The patterns of legal development disprove any neat, linear theory of change; in many cases, Christian doctrine was too formless to be suspected of having influence, or the correspondence between law and doctrine was so weak that influence is doubtful.[108] Divorce is a prime example. Divorce was discouraged in pre-Christian society, the pattern of legislation throws into doubt the suspicion that Christianity was the driving force of change, only around 400 was a consensus Christian view of divorce consolidated, and none of the legal enactments, before Justinian's law of 542, closely reflects Christian teaching.[109]

Provincial custom was a more important influence on late Roman law, but it, too, risks being overstated. Western (under the rubric of "vulgarization") and eastern ("orientalizing") influences have been detected behind the development of late Roman law, but there was no coherent pattern of borrowing.[110] It is often the case that the imperial chancery chose to adapt, rather than adopt, provincial norms, and the impetus behind such change was pragmatic reform, rather than ideological activism or simply a breakdown of classical jurisprudence. The rules governing premarital exchanges are a revealing example. In the fourth century, the Roman state adapted a form of earnest payment drawn from the realm of commerce (the *arrhae*) and applied it to betrothal contracts.[111] At the same time, the government began to regulate premarital gifts from the groom (*donationes ante nuptias*) in slightly different form in the east and the west, recognizing local differences of practice. While such gifts from the groom were not entirely new, they were apparently increasing in importance, so the state responded by regulating an area of social practice for which it lacked an adequate set of rules.

The changes in family law during Late Antiquity are best explained by institutional, rather than social or ideological, change. In the deep background of all late antique lawmaking lies the Antonine Constitution. While the reign of Diocletian saw a massive effort to enforce the rules of classical Roman law across the empire, the reign of Constantine initiated a new period, one more willing to accept regional practices, more open to pragmatism.[112] Constantine was ready to provide public enforcement in areas where the classical law had remained silent and relied on the self-regulating behavior of the upper classes.[113] The Mediterranean scope of Roman jurisdiction in Late Antiquity provided the background for a slow, dialectical accommodation between public law and social praxis.[114] As Menander Rhetor observed late in the third century, "In matters of state an orator considers whether the city fastidiously observes the customs and affairs of law, such as inheritances and female succession to property. But this aspect of praise is also obsolete, since the laws of the Romans are used by all."[115] Roman civil law in Late Antiquity answered to a wider citizen base than ever before.[116]

Not only was Roman law in the late empire universally valid, but it is now broadly recognized that the late Roman administration was more effective and responsible than once believed.[117] A revisionist view emphasizes the quality of legal training, the judicial competence of Roman officials, and the strong interaction between law and society in the late empire. A sharp awareness of Roman law and its significance runs through the literary sources of the period. "When we take wives, make a will, buy slaves, houses, fields, and such, we do it not according to private form, but as the imperial laws command."[118] Yet this passage equally betrays the limits of Roman law as an influence on social habits. With Roman law, the concern with property was always in the fore. The principal function of the state's law was to regulate, to provide publicly enforceable rules for transactions between parties that might result in dispute. And in family law, private contracts were fundamental, as the documentary record shows.[119]

The example of divorce is revealing. The system of free divorce, characteristic of the classical law, was inextricable from an agnatic property regime in which the marriage bond involved few property transfers. In the late empire, the law increasingly recognized the realities of conjugal property, and, in tandem, unilateral divorce became more difficult.[120] The keyword is *unilateral*. The state penalized parties who left a marriage without coming to an agreement. The new rules would have changed the dynamics of negotiating a divorce settlement, but they did not prevent divorce.[121] The papyri of the late empire show that men and women "knew and used imperial law," without strictly following its prescriptions.[122] The conclusion to be drawn is not that the state's law was socially irrelevant, but that its effect (and perhaps purpose) was to discourage couples from separating, in an ever more conjugal property system, without coming to terms. Justinian's ban on mutual divorce was the exception, for his was a piece of moral activism. But it is dangerous to read the pattern of development as though the tendencies of earlier enactments were fulfilled in the reign of the idiosyncratic Justinian, whose reputation as a Christian emperor and a *legislator uxorius* still holds.[123]

If there is an overarching pattern of change in the legal record, it is neither Christianization nor provincialization, but a broad shift toward the recognition and regulation of nuclear principles of property ownership and transmission.[124] This was not driven by social change, for many of the underlying patterns were evident in the practices of the high empire.[125] The institutional setting of Roman law in an empire of universal citizenship and the pragmatic streak in imperial lawmaking reconfigured the relationship between social custom and public rules. Nuclear property structures gained ground in family law; however, this very focus on regulating property marks the essential limit on the law as evidence for the late Roman family. Roman civil law provided a script for the transmission of property through the family across time. To access the cultural and social dimensions of the Roman family, we must broaden the inquiry to include an array of literary and documentary sources.

Christian Triumph and the Family

The conversion of Constantine and the proscription of paganism under Theodosius I catalyzed a process through which Christianity became the dominant religion in the empire.[126] From Gibbon to Gaudemet to Goody, the history of the family in Late Antiquity has been inseparable from the story of Christian expansion. The written record of Late Antiquity is dominated by Christian literature, and one of the principal achievements of late antique scholarship has been simply untangling the theology and cultural logic of the vast textual corpus.[127] The problems, however, become even more daunting when historians try to move outside the texts. In other words, the hardest question is the one that MacMullen so directly posed: What difference did Christianity make?[128] To answer such a question, it is necessary to identify the distinctly Christian norms of marriage and then to evaluate the mechanisms through which Christian ideology could have effected change.

An immediate challenge is that the surviving literature overstates the importance of asceticism in late Roman society.[129] Moreover, Christian authors writing in favor of marriage were often writing *against* ascetic extremism, so that even the tracts written "on the good of marriage" offer a rather stilted perspective.[130] It is thus imperative to seek out the ideals of the family that prevailed among that "silent majority" who continued to reproduce ancient society, generation after generation.[131] For this purpose, conciliar canons, tracts in defense of marriage, and pastoral instruction provide the essential sources. In these texts, one notices immediately the striking similarities between the ideals of pagan marriage and the norms of Christian matrimony. Christianity absorbed the structural elements of Greco-Roman marriage, based on monogamous (which, in its strict, socially-imposed form, was distinctly Greco-Roman rather than Jewish) unions for the purpose of legitimate procreation.[132] The Church accepted the patriarchal arrangements inherent in secular marriage, down to the rules of status required for *connubium*.[133] More profoundly, Christianity embraced the Greco-Roman valorization of marital concord; the ideal of a "partnership of mutual trust based on honorable love" was easily received into Christian ideology.[134] But there were also important divergences between pre-Christian and Christian marriage, of which two deserve special attention: a belief in the indissolubility of marriage and the ideal of sexually exclusive marriage.[135]

The doctrine of indissolubility that prevailed in late Roman Christianity held that a marriage was the joining of two into one flesh.[136] This view entailed strong opposition to both divorce and remarriage, even in the case of a spouse's death.[137] Yet it is dangerous to speak of "Christian" thought as a uniform phenomenon. The late antique Church did not present a united front, and one of the most important developments of the fourth century was the effort, in the context of mass-scale conversion to Christianity, to flesh out a model of Christian marriage.[138] Into the fifth century, there remained disagreement about Christian justifications for divorce (the "Matthean Exceptions") and the capacity of men and women to remarry after a divorce.[139] In parts of the empire, even a man who legitimately divorced his wife on the grounds of fornication was punished with excommunication if he remarried while his spouse was alive.[140] Remarriage after the death of a spouse was strongly discouraged and in some cases punished, and on the question of widowhood, Christian leaders struggled to wrest a coherent position out of a contradictory set of Scriptures.[141] Basil envisaged a short period of penance for a second marriage but regarded a third as a sort of fornication rather than a legitimate union.[142] More abstractly, to discourage remarriage, bishops could evoke the belief in an afterlife and an eternal family that continued to exist after death.[143]

The most distinctive element of Christian marriage was its insistence on sexual exclusivity from both spouses. The Greeks and Romans were monogamous—men married and created children through one legitimate wife.[144] They valued marriage and marital harmony, but the striking fact is that only one surviving author of the Roman empire, Musonius Rufus, made an unambiguously strong case for sexually exclusive marriage.[145] Plutarch, in his *Advice to the Bride and Groom*, ultimately urged women to bear a husband's escapades lightly.[146] The Roman model of marriage simply did not demand sexual exclusivity from men. To call it a double standard is to trivialize the problem. The Greeks and Romans operated with a dual standard, two patently different sets of expectations in sexual behavior. This pattern was rooted in social structure. Female chastity was enforced in the name of ensuring patrimonial legitimacy.[147] While men were viciously punished for violating free women, they were permitted to use dishonored women—prostitutes, concubines, and slaves—as sexual partners. Public law reinforced the system by protecting the sexual honor of respectable women and exposing dishonored women to the remainder of male desire.[148] Salvian complained that Roman policy amounted to "forbidding adulteries, building brothels."[149] The average age at marriage strengthened the dual standard, with men entering marriage nearly a decade after sexual maturity. Young men were simply assumed to enter marriage with sexual experience. Married men also enjoyed sexual freedom with slaves and prostitutes, since adultery was determined by the status of the woman involved.[150] Flagrant excess was poor form, but hardly damnable.[151]

Prostitution, concubinage, and slavery played distinct, complementary roles in this sexual economy.[152] Prostitution was an accepted institution in the ancient city, regulated and taxed by the Roman authorities.[153] The prostitute was defined, legally, as a sexually available woman.[154] While many prostitutes were in fact slaves, what distinguished prostitution from sexual relations with concubines or household slaves was its public nature. The prostitute was the public woman. The sexual use of slaves, on the other hand, was an act of private power; masters enjoyed complete access to the bodies of their slaves, and sexual exploitation was simply a presumptive aspect of the master-slave relationship.[155] Augustine imagined that prostitution existed, in effect, as an alternative for those who could not afford private sexual objects.[156] Concubinage was a more complex institution, in its broadest form any semi-permanent relationship that could not qualify as marriage.[157] But in the late empire, its most common form was a stable sexual relationship between a man and a socially inferior woman, often his own freedwoman.[158] It played a demographically important role, allowing men to enjoy temporary sexual partnerships in the years before marriage or after the death of a wife, especially if an heir existed. Concubinage was thus more open, less casual than mere sex with household slaves, but the distinction was slippery. The lines between prostitution, concubinage, and slavery could be vague because they played such similar roles in the social landscape of ancient sexuality.[159]

This sexual culture was criticized by Paul in the crucial seventh chapter of his first letter to the Corinthians. He specifically allowed marriage as an alternative to fornication. The word *porneia* in this context should not be translated narrowly as prostitution, nor blandly as "extramarital sex."[160] In the Greek cities where Paul moved and preached, the word referred to a culture of sexuality in which men were freely allowed sexual access to dishonored women. In fact, the deeply gendered basis of the term explains Paul's relative silence on the sexual rules regarding women—the sexual limits on women were beyond obvious. It was the sexual laxity afforded to men that he intended to correct. Here he was followed by his late antique successors. The Christian leadership of the late empire found little trouble explaining the need for women to enter marriage as virgins and then to remain faithful to their husbands, but the notion that men were not allowed sexual access to dishonored women was radically unfamiliar.[161] "I am not unaware that most think it is adultery only to violate a married woman. But I say that it is a wicked and licentious adultery for a man with a wife to have an affair even with a public whore, a slave girl, or any other woman without a husband."[162] "What I am saying is paradoxical, but it is true."[163]

Pre-Christian sexual standards urged men to exhibit moderation or self-control in their sexual behavior, but such ideals were compatible with the exploitation of dishonored women before and even during marriage.[164] The Christian model of marriage consistently demanded that men abstain from premarital sex and then remain faithful to their wives. "Among them [the Romans], the bridles of sexual restraint are unloosed for men. The Romans condemn only *stuprum* and *adulterium*, letting lust run wild through whore-houses and slave girls, as though social status makes an offense, and not sexual desire."[165] This was a perceptive description, rightly aware that the dual standard of sexual behavior was immanent in social structure and reinforced by Roman law. Among the most significant legacies of Late Antiquity must be reckoned the Christian adoption of Greco-Roman monogamy, overlaid with a distinctly new sense of sexual exclusivity.[166]

To what extent was the Church in Late Antiquity capable of imposing its view of marriage on society? It is clear that, even after the headlong progress of conversion in the fourth and fifth centuries, the Church as an institution was not able to dominate social mores until much later, perhaps not until the middle Byzantine period in the east, perhaps not until the Gregorian Reform in the west, when it did finally possess the authority to bind and loose on earth.[167] This long delay leaves the serious challenge of characterizing lay spirituality in the centuries of Late Antiquity and the early Middle Ages.[168] The power of the Church in this period rested on the twin foundations of pastoral care and penitential discipline. Moral persuasion and spiritual punishment provided the Church with the ability to influence, but not dictate, the dynamics of marriage in society. These mechanisms allowed the Christian ideology of marriage to become culturally central, if not publicly enforced, in Late Antiquity.

The homilies of Late Antiquity provide invaluable insight into the relation between ideology and social practices. The Christian leadership of the late empire preached, constantly, on the Church's opposition to divorce and remarriage and the requirements of sexual exclusivity. In the sermons of John Chrysostom, Ambrose, Augustine, or Caesarius of Arles, we can watch the effort to convince an audience that Christian marriage required sexual fidelity from men. The campaign against the dual standard of sexual behavior was a common refrain through the preaching of the period. Ambrose despaired that his men felt themselves morally secure for using prostitutes, "like a law of nature."[169] Notably, the bishops found Roman law to be a powerful rival to their vision of Christian marriage. Augustine implored his parishioners to follow the law of heaven, not the law of the forum, on sexual manners, and, in a sermon intended to correct the *cottidiana peccata*, thundered against the sexual exploitation of household slaves.[170] Chrysostom sternly told his audience not to show him "the laws of the outside world."[171] The bishops also struggled, sometimes comically, to rationalize the behavior of the Old Testament patriarchs like Abraham when laymen began to proffer such venerable precedents for their habits.[172]

On the one hand, the pastoral campaign was unprecedented, but on the other, its ability to influence behavior was limited. These limits are detectable in a range of documents. Ausonius the Christian courtier could compose a hymn on his favorite slave girl that left little doubt about the nature of his interest: "My precious, my charmer, my toy, my love, my lust! A barbarian, but even you, ingénue, trump the Latin dames! Bissula, a rough name for a soft girl, a little rude to those who don't know you, but delicious in your master's ears."[173] Paulinus of Pella admitted without remorse—in a poem of thanksgiving to God—that he had restricted his adolescent sexual forays to the slave quarters and had never even known his illegitimate offspring.[174] Agathias could outline the social landscape of sexuality in terms lightly brushed by Christianity; sex with prostitutes and slaves was inconvenient rather than immoral.[175] Nevertheless, the pastoral campaign for sexually exclusive marriage was entirely without historical precedent. It marked a departure from the almost universal acceptance of separate sexual standards for men and women that had prevailed since time immemorial. There is no comparison between the feeble and isolated injunctions of a Musonius or Plutarch and the emergence of a universal institution committed to disseminating to the public a new ideology of sexually exclusive marriage.

The Church did possess a stronger reserve of power in its nascent penitential discipline.[176] The Church's power was ultimately dependent on the need or desire of its congregants to participate in the liturgy, for its only sanction was excommunication. But the Church encouraged adherence to its norms of sexuality and marriage through an elaborate set of rules providing penalties for various violations.[177] Of course, even here a dual standard survived that punished male sexual sins more lightly than female errors.[178] Moreover, we might doubt the ability of the Church to enforce many of its standards, especially sexual ones, which could be difficult to detect or prove. Indeed, in the early fifth century, the bishop of Rome admitted that it was practically impossible to punish wayward husbands for their concealed acts, and Caesarius of Arles lamented that if he were to apply the Church's discipline on sexual mores, his basilica would be empty.[179] On the matter of divorce, even, where detection and enforcement were theoretically easier, there is little concrete evidence that the Church was able to assert its authority.[180] But as the Church grew in social importance throughout the early Middle Ages, it is conceivable that its norms gained institutional grounding through the mechanism of penitential discipline.[181]

The late antique Church was able to wield soft influence over social behavior but not to reshape the dynamics of marriage or family life. It relied on the compliance of individual actors, and thus social agency has become an important dimension in the study of the late Roman family. One of the fundamental achievements of the study of gender in Late Antiquity has been to expose the way that Christianization played off the intricate, internal dynamics of the family.[182] The family was a place of conflict between husbands and wives, parents and children. The family was never a static entity, but a set of processes that involved decisions about property, reproduction, and marriage as family members coursed through the life cycle. The Church was sensitive to this fact, even opportunistic. The call of asceticism resonated with young men languishing under *patria potestas*.[183] More significantly, the Church was responsive to the problem of widowhood. Widows were in a vulnerable position, socially and economically, but they also enjoyed an unusual degree of autonomy for women in ancient society.[184] The Church was able to provide a social niche that simultaneously protected widows and made use of their independence. Thus, the Christianization of society was shaped by the distribution of power within the ancient family and the inherent tensions of private life.

One final way to assess the authority of the Church in the centuries between Theodosius and the Gregorian reforms is to consider the development of ritual.[185] A Christian ritual of marriage developed slowly and unevenly, and throughout antiquity some form of the household-based *deductio in domum* remained the dominant marriage ceremony. In the east, priests slowly became part of the traditional marriage ritual, blessing the couple and even participating in parts of the ceremony such as veiling, crowning, or the joining of hands.[186] Chrysostom acidly noted, however, that episcopal blessings occurred before the *deductio*, which fully retained its vulgar elements.[187] By the fifth century, clerical blessings became routine, although the wedding maintained its profane form and never became truly liturgical in the late antique east. In the west, clerical blessings, in which the couple was veiled, are attested in late fourth-century Italy.[188] The rite of blessing gave the Church a chance to promote its view of marriage: only first marriages were blessed, and Caesarius reports that only virgins received the honor.[189] But Christian *rituals* developed late. Augustine, significantly, never mentioned a Christian ritual of marriage.[190] Paulinus of Nola was the first to mention a marriage inside a church, specifically at the altar.[191] The Verona Sacramentary, reflecting sixth-century practices, finally presents a full-fledged Christian liturgy of marriage, including a nuptial mass.[192] The physical movement of the wedding and the development of a Christian ritual are signs of the Church's growing authority, but not until deep into the Middle Ages was the Church the ultimate arbiter of a marriage's social legitimacy.[193]

The Material Context of Family Life

The ancient family was formed at the intersection of two processes: biological reproduction and the transmission of property. Consequently, the family was shaped by its material context. Family formation was deeply influenced by the demographic, economic, and social structures in which the processes of reproduction and succession took place. In Late Antiquity, the material context of social life in the Roman empire was transformed. The extent, pace, and regional variations of this change may be debated, but in broad terms, the outlines are clear.[194] In the middle of the fourth century, the Mediterranean was home to an exceptionally wealthy and urbanized society, ruled by a single state, and integrated economically and socially. By the end of the sixth century, urbanism had declined, the level of prosperity, particularly in the west, had plummeted, and the imperial state had fragmented.[195] Inevitably, these changes had an effect on the dynamics of marriage and family life in the late empire. The shifting material framework of private life deserves to be considered alongside the legal and religious factors for a complete picture of the family in Late Antiquity.

In a high-fertility, high-mortality society dominated by the basic needs of subsistence and reproduction, deep continuities were inexorable. The ancient family was dominated by its demographic structure, and those structures changed very little in the late empire. That point is too little emphasized in accounts of the late Roman family based on the legal or literary sources, even though texts such as the *Life of Melania* vividly illustrate the human toll of early marriage and infant mortality.[196] The study of late antique demography is less advanced than the study of Roman imperial demography, in part because hundreds of thousands of burial inscriptions and census papyri offer a unique, quantitative perspective on private life in the high empire. The demography of the early empire must act as a starting point for discussion of the late empire.

The two dominant parameters of a population's structure are mortality and fertility.[197] In ancient societies, mortality and fertility were high and relatively stable, although mortality could vary.[198] The Roman empire was characterized by a severe mortality regime. Infant mortality rates were grievously high, in the range of 25 to 35 percent.[199] The commemoration of deceased infants was rare outside of Christian milieux; public documents did not bother to record those of age one year or less, even in the late empire.[200] Life expectancy at birth for women probably fell between twenty and twenty-five years, and life expectancy at age ten between 34.5 and 37.5 years.[201] Death stalked the ancient family. The mortality schedule tempered the structures of *patria potestas*, and marriage itself was mortally precarious. The average marriage lasted twelve years.[202] "Perhaps as many as one in every six marriages would be ended by death within two years of marriage, and approximately one in every four marriages was ended by death after only five years of matrimony."[203] When Christian bishops warned young women that as brides they might soon exchange their white wedding gowns for the black mourner's robes, it was a morbidly real possibility.[204]

If mortality in ancient societies was beyond control, fertility was shaped by a number of contingent factors. Fertility is a function of female age at marriage, rates of marriage and remarriage, child spacing, and mechanisms of fertility control. Greco-Roman society was forcefully mobilized for high fertility. Women married young. Age at first marriage varied, particularly by class, but most women married by their late teens, and marriage was effectively universal.[205] The woman who survived to fifty would have given birth to nearly six children.[206] There was a very low incidence of fertility control in the Roman empire, although moderate rates of remarriage depressed the fertility of older women.[207] Child exposure was not uncommon and provided a means of family limitation; the practice would have raised infant mortality rates but also represented an important passage into slavery.[208] It is doubtful that Christianity deeply affected family limitation practices such as child exposure, although ecclesiastical criticism of the practice is certainly audible.[209] Valentinian is often wrongly credited with banning child exposure, but there were no restrictive measures before the age of Justinian.[210]

The demographic structure of ancient Mediterranean society was practically immovable. It is not likely that Christianity radically affected the basic patterns of life and death. In a fascinating study, Shaw demonstrated that Lenten prohibitions reshaped seasonal birthing patterns in Italian towns, a remarkable example of Christianization, but also one that underscores the absence of basic structural change.[211] In fact, it may ultimately be more profitable to consider how demography shaped religion rather than vice versa. Part of asceticism's appeal was that its practitioners had suspended the absolutely dominant rhythms of ordinary life. Demographic realities even co-opted religious ideals. For example, the dedication of female children as lifelong virgins became a pious alternative to child exposure and a new tactic for the problem of having too many girls in a family.[212] There is little reason to believe that the new religion had any effect on age at first marriage.[213] Perhaps the Church was able to reduce the incidence of remarriage, with its strong and calculated appeal to widows, although there is little reason to believe so.[214] But the decline in the number of inscriptions in Late Antiquity and the lack of census papyri make it difficult to answer questions about the demography of the late Roman population in quantitative terms.

If demography provided the framework for deep continuities in the late antique family, there were nevertheless changes in the material context of private life, of which two deserve mention: the recession of urbanism and the reconfiguration of vertical hierarchies, at the top and bottom of society. The urban lifestyle of the ancient Mediterranean reached its apex in the high Roman empire, but it is clear that throughout the fourth century, even longer in the east, a flourishing urban culture survived. Urbanism influenced family formation in numerous ways. It raised mortality rates.[215] It pulled young men out of the countryside, creating an excess mass of shiftless, unplaceable men.[216] Urbanism seems to have encouraged neolocal marriage and smaller households, a pattern with significant effects on the structure and sentimental texture of family life.[217] In the West, the reassertion of rural life over the fifth and sixth centuries would have encouraged larger residential units and a new focus on the family farm as the centerpiece of patrimonial strategy.

A largely silent development in the background of the late antique family was the decline of slavery. In the fourth century, slavery remained a vital institution. Augustine could claim, in a calm, expository sermon delivered to the middling urban classes of Hippo, that "nearly all households" included slaves, and the corroborating evidence for extensive household slavery is vast.[218] Even in the "poor" household, "the man rules his wife, the wife rules the slaves, the slaves rule their own wives, and again the men and women rule the children."[219] The papyri of the high empire show that slavery may have touched up to one-sixth of urban households in a region not at the forefront of the slave system.[220] In this regard, the Roman empire resembles the protobourgeois societies of the early modern period, in which non-kin residents were an important part of family life, although in the Roman period, non-kin residents were predominantly servile.[221] The ubiquity of slaves had tremendous consequences for the organization of domestic labor, the habits of household violence, the construction of male and female honor, and the practice of wet-nursing and child rearing, not to mention the emotional entanglements caused by slavery.[222] Into the early fifth century, the very foundation of private life, the substance of the *domus felix*, was made of a harmonious marriage, reverent children, and slaves who quaked utterly in fear of their master.[223] Yet, by the sixth century, household slavery appears increasingly restricted to the very wealthiest strata of society.[224]

Rural slavery, too, was far from moribund in the fourth century.[225] An important new inscription from Thera, dating to the fourth century, documents a large group of slaves belonging to a single landowner.[226] The slaves seem to have experienced a relatively normal demographic regime. An imbalance toward females in the older age cohorts may reflect male manumission, and on the whole, the inscription suggests strong patterns of familial life among the slave population.[227] This should be no surprise, since the most convincing models of Roman slavery suggest the need for extensive natural reproduction, but it is necessary to recall that slaves had no legal control over their own relationships.[228] Despite an often misinterpreted law of Constantine, it remained permissible to separate slave families, if the practice was probably rare, until the late fifth or sixth century, and the Church seems not to have objected in the least.[229] The survival of slavery through the fourth century is a reminder that Roman society was complex, structured by legal and economic relationships. The decline of rural slavery over the fifth and sixth centuries was part of a deeper cycle of economic recession that encouraged simpler social hierarchies.

The composition of the upper classes was also transformed in Late Antiquity. In fact, the reorganization of the Roman status system, with the growth of an imperial service aristocracy and new paths of social mobility, was one of the most transformative changes in late antique society and one of the least analyzed in terms of its impact on the family. Starting already in the high empire, the senate began to draw from the provinces, but over the fourth century, the senatorial order expanded precipitously, from some 600 to about 3,000 members, slowly displacing the equestrian ranks and requiring, from the late fourth century, ever finer gradations of status within the order.[230] This expansion was fueled both by the ascendance of local elites, principally decurions, and by the admission of new men, principally through imperial service. In short, the fourth-century aristocracy was transformed by the reorientation of local elites toward the imperial center and by an influx of social risers, a process that manifestly destabilized the normal markers of high status. The effects of this transformation should be sought in the patterns and experience of private life, in particular, marital strategy.[231] It is significant that John Chrysostom's sermons on marriage saw the strategic aspects of matchmaking as a primary obstacle to the spiritualization of marriage that he envisioned.[232] The transformation of the late Roman aristocracy, a process with such momentum in the late fourth century, looms in the background of his preaching, but his plea for Christians to ignore social criteria when contracting a marriage was no less fantastic than his call for them to cease reproducing because the earth was full. His critique, in fact, demonstrates the centrality of social striving in the marriage market of Late Antiquity.

The study of late Roman marriage in terms of social strategy was pioneered by Herlihy, who argued that the growth of property transfers from grooms to brides was driven by a shortage of marriageable women: an inadequate supply of women drove up the price of marriage for men seeking a mate.[233] This was a provocative argument, and he was right to bring property transfers into the equation. But it is hard to credit a sudden lack of eligible females in the fourth and fifth centuries.[234] Instead of looking at the raw force of supply and demand in the marriage market, we should look for imbalances in the social capital men and women brought to marriage in the late empire. Marriages, in antiquity, were supposed to create a suitable match between bride and groom. But families drew on a broad menu of criteria—wealth, status, and reputation—to balance the scales of social parity.[235] In the high empire, men in the Roman aristocracy tended to marry women of moderately lower status.[236] It was acceptable for senatorial men to marry the daughters of equestrians, for equestrians to marry the daughters of decurions, and so on. In such cases, the women were of sufficiently high status to constitute a suitable match, while the slightly unequal marriage conformed to the patriarchal expectation that husbands would be superior to their wives. Men were discouraged, in some cases legally prohibited, from reaching too far down the social scale, while the possibility of marrying a socially superior woman raised the specter of the husband being in submission to his wife. It is exceedingly rare to find, in the high empire, senatorial women married to non-senatorial men.[237]

In an important recent study, Cooper has argued that ambitious men of the late empire increasingly married lower-status women whose families could not deter them from seeking their fortunes on the imperial scene; in her account, the restrictive divorce legislation of the late empire was enacted to consolidate the power of such husbands against their inferior wives.[238] The main evidence for this pattern lies in the fact that late antique laws pay ample attention to the problem of concubines and illegitimate children.[239] This evidence is complex. Concubinage was an important complement to family strategy; it was a stable partnership that allowed men without a wife to enjoy intimate companionship (whatever that means in such grossly asymmetrical relationships). For young men, it was a way of building their social capital for a proper marriage; for older men, it was used as a way to avoid creating additional heirs.[240] But concubinage often *did* produce children. Augustine learned "the difference between the sort of marital unions contracted for the sake of procreation [marriage] and those pacts made for sexual love [concubinage], in which children are born against our wishes, although once they are born they compel our affection."[241] This practice was hardly new in the late empire, but the fragile conspiracy of silence among early imperial elites about their illegitimate offspring gradually broke down.[242] The turning point came in the reign of Constantine. He extended the Augustan marriage restrictions down into the upper ranks of the town councils; as an enforcement mechanism, he prohibited testamentary bequests to concubines and their children.[243] This rule grated against a deep tendency to love or at least pity illegitimate children. The case of Libanius is instructive, for he fully intended to hand down his estate to his only son, born of his slave concubine, either by special permission or by funneling the money through friends.[244]

The use of concubinage in the late empire in fact demonstrates that men were often trying to marry *up*. When concubinage worked as intended, it was a temporary, not permanent, alternative to marriage. Often, young men were trying to acquire the money or status that would allow them to secure a favorable match. We hear about the legitimation of children when men tried to substitute concubinage for marriage, *precisely because* they had failed to complete the transition to a favorable match.[245] The transformation of the late Roman aristocracy created new modes of social ascendance, especially through the imperial service. The social mobility of the late empire meant that the social currency of men was relatively variable; they could change their status through the acquisition of wealth or rank, while the avenues for female mobility were far more limited.[246] This is perhaps the distinctly late antique dynamic that lies in the background of fourth- and fifth-century developments: socially ascendant men seeking to deploy their newfound wealth and status to contract an advantageous match, especially with girls from more established, respectable families. Sometimes they succeeded; sometimes they did not. If this reconstruction is correct, then the idea of men marrying "up" or "down" does not account for the complexity of the marriage market, and it is important to recognize that, with the substance of elite status in flux, men and women were forced to navigate their family strategies through the turbulent waters of a society with an unsettling element of male social mobility.

The broad acceptance of concubinage as a holding pattern for young men, in a society where ambitious marital strategy was common, made for an unstable combination. This tension can help us explain a well-known development in late Roman law: an increased emphasis on the objective modes of proving a marriage's existence. Roman marriage was legally formless, defined by the intent of both partners.[247] Although this remained the case throughout Late Antiquity, the legislation of the fifth and sixth centuries gave more attention to contracts, dowry, ceremonies, and witnesses as objective signs of marital intent.[248] This was hardly a result of Christianity's new focus on the moment of initial intent, nor do we need to imagine mass-scale status confusion in the background of these laws. The legal doctrine of formless marriage was inherently delicate.[249] In Late Antiquity, it was challenged by the realities of universal citizenship, in which any conflict or confusion could end up in Roman jurisdiction.[250] Moreover, the imperial aristocracy in Late Antiquity was broader, socially and geographically more diverse, than during the high empire. Above all, the line between concubinage and marriage would have been blurred by the efforts of men, surely not always successful, to delay proper marriage in the hopes of social ascendance. Augustine's concubine was of sufficiently low social status that she was disposable, but what would have become of her and Adeodatus if he had not been appointed to Milan and engaged to a young girl of high status?[251]

The use of marriage to mediate the process of social ascendance, especially for men with money or rank but little family reputation, illuminates other key developments in late Roman law. Whatever its origins, the rapid expansion of the *donatio ante nuptias*, the gift from groom to bride, over the fourth and fifth centuries was perhaps the most important structural change in the family during this period—and remains an unexplained development.[252] The *arrha* and *donatio* swiftly entered the common parlance of the fourth century.[253] Needless to say, a new tendency for men to marry down hardly explains why they increasingly offered "all the riches of the earth" to lure their brides.[254] These gifts, which joined the dowry as part of the conjugal fund in the wife's ownership, should be considered a form of insurance that was especially useful in situations where *the man's* social position or social intentions were less than fully determinate. The *donatio* functioned more like a safety deposit than a true exchange, since the property went to the wife rather than her natal family—remaining in the husband's control unless he ended the marriage. Roman law, by regulating premarital gifts, was responding to a social development with its own momentum rather than catalyzing change. The divorce laws, in turn, should be seen as part of the state's response to the more conjugal character of property.[255]

There is explicit evidence that the *donatio* was used by men as a bargaining chip to secure a socially favorable marriage. John Chrysostom is again a prime witness. He imagined that a young man would try to find a wife as rich and noble as possible. This would require intense negotiation and the help of attorneys to draft the nuptial agreements. Such an upwardly mobile man would wager his property on the match by placing it legally in the conjugal fund. Here Chrysostom used the analogy of the greedy merchant overloading his ship and thereby risking his entire fortune.[256] Throughout his sermons, Chrysostom talked extensively about the dangers of the "rich wife."[257] These complaints have been read as mere tropes, whereas they might also be put into context as highly acute social observation.[258] A law of 371 explicitly tried to put a stop to men who were trying to "buy noble marriages" by marrying young widows of higher social status.[259] The roughly contemporary letters of Libanius are a rich trove of documents that reveal the inner workings of social life among the urban gentry in the eastern Mediterranean. In one letter, Libanius referred to a recent marriage in which the groom, a young student with upward potential but apparently the social inferior of the bride, was surprisingly *not* made to render his best estate as a nuptial gift because of his father-in-law's generosity.[260] Financial ties made it more difficult for men to leave their wives, as contemporary observers noticed in a society where men might use divorce to shed old wives, "like clothes," as they rose through society.[261] It is widely recognized that the dowry was used as a bargaining chip to secure a favorable match for a girl, but the reverse function of the *donatio*, as a social ploy, has not received sufficient notice.

What is distinctive about the upper classes of Late Antiquity, as the *PLRE* readily reveals, is that upward and downward marriages alike were common (a comprehensive study would be welcome).[262] The grammarians and rhetors of Late Antiquity, avatars of upward mobility, succeeded in attracting wives of superior wealth and reputation.[263] Individual microhistories, when they are available, can also be used to appreciate the complexity of marital strategies. Besides Augustine, the case of Ausonius is familiar and revealing.[264] Both men embodied the upward social mobility that was available to those with talent and education—and savvy family strategy. Ausonius' father was the beneficiary of a favorable match. He was probably the son of a freedman who became a doctor at Bordeaux and obtained curial rank. At the age of only twenty, he was able to marry the daughter of a "relatively impoverished but noble house" who belonged to the old Gallic aristocracy.[265] Ausonius was manifestly proud of his mother's ancestry and reticent about his father's. Ausonius was trained in rhetoric, and already during the early stages of his promising career, he married a girl from an ancient family of senatorial rank.[266] It helped that Ausonius' maternal uncle had connections at the imperial court, but the match was nevertheless a social coup for the young professor. Over three generations, the members of this family—one of the paradigmatic cases of fourth-century social mobility—parlayed their political and cultural capital into "marriages which were socially and financially advantageous to themselves and to the *gens Ausonia*."[267]

The epistolary corpus of Symmachus provides us another glimpse, from the very highest echelons of imperial society, of the marriage market in the west.[268] Symmachus regularly acted, through his social connections, as patron to younger men seeking brides of high status. We can only wonder how well the western senatorial aristocracy—the wealthiest social bloc in the empire—resisted the influx of social risers. Regardless, the letters of Symmachus amply illustrate the complex material considerations that underwrote the strategic game of matchmaking.[269] The potential grooms were advertised as *honestus, clarissimus,* and even, rather indelicately, *re uberior.*[270] Several examples document possible upward social mobility, and in two cases the men—one a philosopher and the other an advocate—had secured favorable engagements that subsequently proved fragile.[271] In another case, the engagement did fall apart, but another bride, of even higher status, was found for the client; the way this sequence of events is described leaves no doubt that "a brilliant match offered the same advantages of career advancement."[272] A sensitive analysis concludes that, in comparison with the idealized representation of matchmaking in the corpus of Pliny, the letters of Symmachus are more transparently "practical" and "utilitarian."[273]

Finally, gender roles must inform the study of marital strategy. There is comparative evidence that, in periods of social dynamism, not only does marriage absorb the shocks of structural change but also women in particular become the arbiters and symbols of social prestige.[274] Because their status is relatively immobile, and because the domestic sphere is a stage for the display of social manners, women occupy a medial role between conservative social values and actual social change. Unsurprisingly, our most acute observer of female society, Jerome, has left us extraordinary portraits of elite women in the salons of Rome acting as the regulators of social prestige.[275] Likewise, Chrysostom was outraged by the habits of conspicuous consumption among women who married upwardly mobile husbands.[276] These critics saw nothing more than vanity in such social circles, but the carefully calibrated display of manners provided a measure of stability in uncertain times. It is surely not mere coincidence that the women of the Theodosian court were more prominent as symbols of legitimacy and as agents of dynastic power than almost any previous empresses: the gender dynamics at the top of the social pyramid are the visible surface of a deeper phenomenon.[277] The late Roman family was not simply a private sphere; it reflected the workings of social prestige in a fiercely competitive world where wealth, status, and reputation were in flux.

From the top of society to the bottom, the processes of family formation were shaped by circumstance, and marital strategy would have differed significantly across the social spectrum. The foregoing discussion can hardly do justice to the diversity and complexity of family life in the late empire. By putting marital strategies in the fore, however, we not only expose an important undercurrent of private life in this period but also are reminded more generally that the patterns of continuity and change cannot be explained by legal and religious factors alone. The late Roman family was shaped, profoundly, by its material context—the imperatives of fertility, the influence of habitat, and the structure of society.

Conclusion

What is the broader significance of the late antique family, both for our understanding of Late Antiquity as a period and for the history of private life in the *longue durée*? Study of the late Roman family must build off the insights earned in the investigation of the Roman imperial family. This body of work has consistently shown that marriage and family life in the high empire were shaped by conjugal structures and nuclear sentimentality, even if pervasive slavery, high mortality, and lingering notions of the agnatic group made the Roman family something different from the modern family. This revisionist model of private life not only challenges the traditional stereotypes of the Roman *familia* but also prompts us to reconsider, fundamentally, the difference that Christianity made. The developments in late Roman law reflect the gradual triumph of conjugal structures rather than Christian change. One of the most important effects of Christianity, in the long term, was its absorption of Greco-Roman norms. John Chrysostom was eager to counterpose Roman and Christian marriage, but in the larger picture, Christianity became an institutionalized carrier of Roman marital ideology.[278] The essential differences in Christian ideology lay in a spiritualized view of marriage that, quite radically, demanded sexual exclusivity from both partners and treated marriage as a unique and indissoluble bond.

Roman law and Christian institutions were the legacy of Late Antiquity to the history of the family in succeeding ages. If we wish to recover the *experience* of the family in the centuries of Late Antiquity, the dynamics of private life must be set within the social and economic structures of the late Roman world. It was a world defined by the interplay of primitive reproductive demands and sophisticated social hierarchies, and it was a world that was changing. The fourth and fifth centuries saw the imperialization of the elite, even as the fifth and sixth centuries were marked by a decline in material conditions that resulted in a less urbanized habitat and simpler social hierarchies. Christian triumph, the Christian absorption and transformation of Roman marital ideology, took place amid these changes. We could measure the distance traveled in Late Antiquity by listening to a Christian observer of marriage writing two centuries after Chrysostom's well-wrought invectives against contemporary social practices. Isidore of Seville, at the opposite end of the old empire, claimed that marriage was instituted for procreation, partnership, and preventing fornication.[279] Here, the mix of Roman and Christian elements was far more settled and more practical than in Chrysostom's world. The loose energy of asceticism had been safely compartmentalized in the monastery, a society apart, while Christian marriage was reconciled to the structures of ordinary life—no contrast here between the Christian way and the "outside" world. In one regard, though, Isidore would have found himself in perfect accord with Chrysostom. "These days wives are sought whom wealth or physical beauty commend, rather than probity of morals."[280] The complaint is familiar, but the material differences between fifth-century

Constantinople and seventh-century Seville measure the gulf that separated these two spokesmen for the complex and adaptable heritage of Christian marriage.

NOTES

1. John Chrysostom, *Propter fornicationes, De libello repudii*, and *Quales ducendae sint uxores*. PG 51: 207–242. On Chrysostom's preaching, see Allen and Mayer 1993 and now Maxwell 2006, esp. 157–161.

2. Frequently asserted by other Christians of the period, too: see Gaudemet 1980, 122.

3. John Chrysostom, *Quales ducendae sint uxores*, 3. PG 51: 230: Οὐ γὰρ καπηλείαν, ἀλλὰ βίου κοινωνίαν εἶναι τὸν γάμον δεῖ νομίζειν. Cf. *Dig.* 23.2.1: *Nuptiae sunt coniunctio maris et feminae et consortium omnis vitae, divini et humani iuris communicatio*. See Sargenti 1985, 371.

4. John Chrysostom, *Quales ducendae sint uxores*, 4. PG 51: 232. See Anné 1941, 271–272.

5. John Chrysostom, *Quales ducendae sint uxores*, 1. PG 51: 226: *μὴ τοὺς ἔξωθεν ἀναγίνωσκε νόμους μόνον*. *Propter fornicationes*, 4. PG 51: 213: *Μὴ γάρ μοι τοὺς ἔξωθεν νόμους εἴπῃς νῦν*.

6. It is worth noting, too, that these sermons were quite possibly delivered to the power set in Constantinople: see Mayer 2005, 256, for the traditional attribution to the eastern capital, though cf. 470 for a more cautious assessment.

7. A thesis inseparable from the work of Gaudemet 1980.

8. Here "late Roman" is c. 300–550 C.E. It is important to admit that while recent studies (esp. George 2005) rightly emphasize the geographic and social diversity of the Roman family, this chapter has a pan-Mediterranean focus that tries to draw general characterizations in the space allotted without eliding important differences. We should note, however, that perhaps never before or since were marriage practices in the Mediterranean so integrated.

9. Augustine, *De civitate Dei*, 15.16. Ed. B. Dombart and A. Kalb, CC 47 (Turnhout, 1955) 478: *quoddam seminarium est ciuitatis*.

10. See Reynolds 2007, 32.

11. Saller and Kertzer 1991, 1–19.

12. Saller 1984, 336–355; Shaw 1987, 10–19; Saller 1994, 74–101; McGinn 1999, 627; Hillner 2003.

13. Emphasized by Bradley 1991; Wallace-Hadrill 1991. On late antique slavery, see Harper forthcoming.

14. Patterson 1998, 1–2; Pomeroy 1994, 214; Alston 2005, 130.

15. Shaw 1987, 50.

16. For general reviews of family history, see Stone 1981; Hareven 1991.

17. Saller 1997, 10–18.

18. Ariès 1960.

19. Laslett and Wall 1972 was seminal. Frier 2006 is an elegant statement of this fundamental difference.

20. Flandrin 1976; Macfarlane 1986; Stone 1977; Goody 1983; Brundage 1987; Herlihy 1985; and Ariès and Duby 1985–1987. See Saller 1991.

21. Selectively, Hallett 1984; Saller and Shaw 1984; Rawson 1986; Bradley 1991; Rawson 1991; Treggiari 1991a; Dixon 1992; Saller 1994; Rawson and Weaver 1997.

22. Saller and Shaw 1984. See also Martin 1996, whose criticisms do not undermine the importance of Saller and Shaw's intervention. Cf. Edmondson 2005, 216–217.

23. Saller 1994.

24. Going back to Hopkins 1966. Shaw 1984; 1987; Bagnall and Frier 1994; Scheidel 2001a.

25. See Scheidel 2001b.

26. Neri 1998; McGinn 1998; 2004; George 2005.

27. MacDonald 1990; Betzig 1992a; 1992b; Herlihy 1995; Scheidel 2009.

28. Gaudemet 1987; Evans Grubbs 1994.

29. Clark 1986; Brown 1988; Clark 1993; Elm 1994; Cooper 1996.

30. Goody 1983 argued for a rather different sort of Christian influence, contending that the Church widened incest prohibitions and constricted the strategies of heirship available to a testator. But see Shaw and Saller 1984. Sargenti 1938 and Gaudemet 1980 were important predecessors to the later work that questioned Christian influence.

31. Shaw 1987.

32. Evans Grubbs 1995.

33. Arjava 1996.

34. Beaucamp 1990–1992.

35. Nathan 2000.

36. Asterius of Amasea, *Homiliae*, 5.2.3. Ed. C. Datema (Leiden, 1970) 46: *γάμος . . . πρᾶγμα τοῦ ἀνθρωπικοῦ βίου κεφάλαιον.*

37. A major subtext throughout will be to consider how the nature of the surviving evidence—legal, ecclesiastical, and documentary—influences the effort to study the family. See Beaucamp 1990, 1–9.

38. Cooper 2007a, 152–160.

39. Arjava 1998.

40. Saller 1986, 7–22; 1987, 21–34. Emancipation was not rare, especially in Late Antiquity: Arjava 2001, 42.

41. Treggiari 1991b, 32–36. Cooper 2009, 195–196, notes that this gave women a better position in Roman law than in the succeeding barbarian law codes of the West.

42. Arjava 1996, 41–42. On the guardianship of adult females, see below.

43. Gardner 1986, 97–116; Treggiari 1991a, 323–364.

44. Gade 2001.

45. Champlin 1991.

46. Treggiari 1991a, 365–396, emphasizes the influence of conjugal property structures already in the classical period.

47. Corbett 1930; Gaudemet 1980, 46–103; Treggiari 1991a. For the late empire, see *CTh* 3.7.3 (428) on the informality of marriage, with Sargenti 1981.

48. Treggiari 1991a, 37–80.

49. Treggiari 1991a, 350–356.

50. Treggiari 1991a.

51. Veyne 1987, 33–50.

52. Evans Grubbs 1995, 2.

53. Beaucamp 1990–1992, 109, 203–204. See, e.g., *CTh* 9.7.1 (326), where the rules of adultery do not apply to women *quas vilitas vitae dignas legum observatione non credidit.*

54. Evans Grubbs 1995, 118–119.

55. Gaudemet 1992. The law originally included *CTh* 8.16.1, 3.2.1, 11.7.3, 4.12.3; *CJ* 6.9.9, 6.23.15, and 6.37.21. Evans Grubbs 1995, 119. See Mommsen, *Codex Theodosianus*, 1.1, ccxiv–ccxv. Seeck 1919, 59–61.

56. Although special exemptions were apparently granted "lavishly." See Arjava 2001, 39.

57. *CTh* 8.16.1: *imminentibus legum terroribus.*

58. *CJ* 6.9.9, 6.23.15, 6.37.21.

59. Arjava 1996, 100–105.

60. *CTh* 8.18.1 (315).

61. Arjava 1996, 102 on *CTh* 8.18.3 (334). Justinian, *Nov.* 117.1 (542), allowed mothers to leave property directly to their children, even if the children remained *in potestate.*

62. Hadrian: *Dig.* 38.17.2. Marcus: *Dig.* 38.17.1. Gardner 1986, 196–200.

63. *CTh* 5.1.1 (318). *CTh* 2.19.2 (321).

64. *CTh* 2.21.1–2 (358 and 357).

65. *CTh* 5.1.4 (389) and *CTh* 5.1.5 (402).

66. *CJ* 6.55.12 (528). *Inst.* 3.1.16. *Nov.* 118 (543).

67. See, too, *Nov. Val.* 21.1 (446).

68. Anné 1941 is fundamental. Evans Grubbs 1995, 156–183; Arjava 1996, 52–62.

69. *Dig.* 39.5.1.1; Arjava 1996, 55.

70. *Epitome Codicum Gregoriani et Hermogeniani Wisigothica,* 2.1 (CE 259) and *CJ* 5.3.1–14.

71. Evans Grubbs 1995, 158.

72. *CTh* 3.5.2 (319).

73. *CTh* 3.5.3–6 (330–335).

74. *CTh* 3.5.10–11 (380). Anné 1941, 87–135.

75. Anné 1941, 239–471; Arjava 1996, 56.

76. Anné 1941, 341–342, 369–372.

77. *CTh* 3.16.2 (421).

78. Bougard et al. 2002; Arjava 1996, 60–62; Hughes 1978. See Falchi 1995 for the long survival of dual gifts in the east.

79. See the demographic simulations of Saller 1997, 28–33; 1991, 37.

80. Crook 1967, 113–118. *Dig.* 26 covers tutelage.

81. *Dig.* 26.2.1.

82. *Dig.* 26.4.1 and 26.5. For the role of the widow in requesting a tutor, Beaucamp 1990, 315–320.

83. Saller 1991, 40–41.

84. Arjava 1996, 90–91.

85. *CTh* 3.17.4 (390), which assumes that female guardianship already exists. Beaucamp 1990, 46–47, 325–330.

86. Gardner 1986, 5–29.

87. Gaius, *Inst.*, 1.145.

88. Gaius, *Inst.*, 1.190.

89. *BGU* 3.943 (389).

90. Beaucamp 1992, 193–267.

91. Bagnall 1995, 77.

92. Bagnall 1987; Arjava 1988; and Memmer 2000.

93. *CTh* 3.16.1 (331).

94. Namely, murder, concocting poisons, and violating tombs.

95. Evans Grubbs 1995, 228–232, for a detailed analysis.

96. Ambrosiaster, *Quaestiones veteris et novi testamenti*, 115.12. Ed. A. Souter, CSEL 50 (Vienne, 1908) 322: *coeperunt enim cottidie licenter viros suos dimittere.* See Arjava 1988, 9–13.

97. For the endurance of Julian's law until 421, see Arjava 1988, 9–12.

98. *CTh* 3.16.2 (421).

99. *Nov. Theod.* 12 (439), with the requirement of a formal *repudium*. See Memmer 2000, 500–501. Sirks 2007, 189, argues that the laws retained the original geographic limitations on their validity, but Honoré 1998, 130–132, is convincing.

100. *Nov. Val.* 35.11 (452).

101. *CJ* 5.17.8 (449). The law also included the requirement of a formal *repudium*.

102. *CJ* 5.17.10–11 (528).

103. *Nov. Just.* 117.8–10 (542).

104. *Nov. Just.* 140 (566). See McCail 1968.

105. Gaudemet 1980, 119–120 (cautiously); Sargenti 1975 suggests that Ablabius was behind the social legislation of Constantine during the later part of his reign; Evans Grubbs 1995, 134 (with further citations for Hosius' influence) and 253–260 (where she allows some Christian influence on the divorce law of Constantine and the abolition of the penalties for celibacy). For Ambrose, e.g., Watson 1995.

106. E.g., Anné 1941, 127–135, 456–460; Wolff 1950. Gaudemet 1962; Reynolds 1994, 64.

107. Evans Grubbs 1995, 54–102.

108. Gaudemet 1980, 123: "c'est l'époque où le dogme s'affirme et se precise." Krause 1994–1995, vol. 1, 171–181.

109. Bagnall 1987, 41–61. For the development of a Christian doctrine of divorce, see esp. Reynolds 1994, 173–226. For pre-Christian attitudes, see Arjava 1988, 6–7.

110. The classic statements are Mitteis 1891; Levy 1951. Cf. Sargenti 1938 and see now esp. Liebs 2008.

111. Anné 1941, 103, 124–125.

112. For Diocletian, see Corcoran 2006, 31–62. Constantine was not alone. Cf. the rescript of Licinius: *CJ* 3.1.8 (314): *placuit in omnibus rebus praecipuam esse iustitiae aequitatisque quam stricti iuris rationem.*

113. Harper forthcoming.

114. See, e.g., Arjava 1998, 158–159, for the diffusion of *patria potestas* in the provinces.

115. Menander, *Division of Epideictic Speeches*, 1.364.10. Ed. Russell and Wilson, 68: *ἐν μὲν τοῖς κοινοῖς εἰ τὰ νόμιμα καὶ περὶ ὧν οἱ νόμοι τίθεται ἀκριβῶς ἡ πόλις, κλῆρον ἐπικλήρων, καὶ ὅσα ἄλλα μέρη νόμων· ἀλλὰ καὶ τοῦτο τὸ μέρος διὰ τὸ τοῖς κοινοῖς χρῆσθαι τῶν Ῥωμαίων νόμοις ἄχρηστον.* See Garnsey 2004, 148–149.

116. Garnsey 2004, 133–155.

117. See esp. Harries 1999 and chapter 24 in this book. Honoré 1994; 1998.

118. John Chrysostom, *Ad populum Antiochenum*, 16.2. PG 49: 164: *κἂν γυναῖκας ἀγώμεθα, κἂν διαθήκας ποιῶμεν, κἂν οἰκέτας ὠνεῖσθαι μέλλωμεν, κἂν οἰκίας, κἂν ἀγρούς, κἂν ὁτιοῦν ἕτερον ποιεῖν, οὐκ οἰκείᾳ γνώμῃ ταῦτα πράττομεν, ἀλλ' ὅπως ἂν ἐκεῖνοι* (sc. *βασιλικοί νόμοι*) *διατάξωσι.*

119. Arnaoutoglou 1995. Bagnall 1995, 73. See also Memmer 2000, 495.

120. Bagnall 1987 is worth quoting in full: "The liberality of the classical Roman law of marriage and divorce is inseparable from a legal structure that largely insulated the transmission of patrimonial property to male heirs from the vicissitudes of

marriage. As property came to be conceived of as the goods of the couple, as *de facto* happened already under the earlier empire, this link became unstable."

121. See Mnookin and Kornhauser 1979, for the classic discussion of how divorces are settled "in the shadow of the law."

122. Beaucamp 1992, 102.

123. Arjava 1996, 260–261; Beaucamp 1990, 23–24.

124. Beaucamp 1989.

125. See Saller 1991, 46–47.

126. MacMullen 1984.

127. E.g., Reynolds 1994.

128. MacMullen 1986.

129. Jacobs and Krawiec 2003, 257–263.

130. Hunter 1989; Clark 1986.

131. Cooper 2007a, esp. 38, is an effort to do just this. Jacobs 2003; Harrison 1996.

132. On the continued existence of polygamy in Roman-era Judaism, see Scheidel 2009; Williams 2005; Satlow 2001, 188–192; Ilan 1996, 85–288. Augustine, for instance, recognized that monogamy was a distinctly Roman custom. Augustine, *De bono conjugali*, 7.7. Ed. J. Zycha, CSEL 41 (Vienna, 1900) 197: *et tamen non licet, et nostris temporibus ac more Romano nec superducere, ut amplius habeat quam unam vivam. CJ* 1.9.7 (393): *Nemo iudaeorum morem suum in coniunctionibus retinebit nec iuxta legem suam nuptias sortiatur nec in diversa sub uno tempore coniugia conveniat.*

133. Basil of Caesarea, *Epistulae*, 199.40. Ed. Y. Courtonne, *Lettres*, 3 vols. (Paris, 1957–1966), 2: 162: Ἡ παρὰ γνώμην τοῦ δεσπότου ἀνδρὶ ἑαυτὴν ἐκδιδοῦσα ἐπόρνευσεν, ἡ δὲ μετὰ ταῦτα πεπαρρησιασμένῳ γάμῳ χρησαμένη ἐγήματο. Ὥστε ἐκεῖνο μὲν πορνεία, τοῦτο δὲ γάμος. Αἱ γὰρ συνθῆκαι τῶν ὑπεξουσίων οὐδὲν ἔχουσι βέβαιον.

134. Augustine, *De civitate Dei*, 14.26. Ed. Dombart and Kalb, CC 48, 449: *inter se coniugum fida ex honesto amore societas.* See Dixon 1996, for the Roman sentimental ideal. Treggiari 1991a, 205–261. Saller 1997 criticizes the practice of using legalistic kinship structures as a paradigm for the Roman family. This is a crucial point as we consider the question of Christian influence, since there is a lingering tendency to contrast the wife's position outside the husband's *familia* in Roman law with the "Christian" view of the family centered on the conjugal bond.

135. Sargenti 1985, 367–391, offers a perceptive discussion.

136. Gaudemet 1980, 230–289.

137. Humbert 1972, 301–345.

138. Crouzel 1971.

139. Reynolds 1994, 173–226.

140. Reynolds 1994, 213–226. See Augustine, *De adulterinis coniugiis*, 2.16.16. Ed. J. Zycha, CSEL 41 (Vienna, 1900) 401–402.

141. E.g., John Chrysostom, *De non iterando conjugio*, 3. Ed. B. Grillet and G. Ettlinger, SC 138, 172–174.

142. Basil of Caesarea, *Epistulae*, 188.4. Ed. Courtonne, 2: 125. See Dauvillier and De Clercq 1936, 195–200.

143. John Chrysostom, *Ad viduam juniorem*, 3. Ed. B. Grillet and G. Ettlinger, SC 138, 126–132. Cooper 2007a, ix. See Shaw 1984 for Christian mortuary practices.

144. Betzig 1992a; 1992b.

145. Treggiari 1991a, 220–222. Musonius Rufus, *Discourses*, 12. Ed. C. Lutz, 84–86.

146. Plutarch, *Conjugalia praecepta*, 140B. Ed. F. C. Babbitt, 2: 308.

147. E.g., Asterius of Amasea, *Sermones*, 5.11.2. Ed. Datema, 51: *Γάμος γὰρ τούτων χάριν τῶν δύο συνίσταται, διαθέσεως καὶ παιδοποιΐας, ὧν οὐδέτερον μετὰ μοιχείας σώζεται . . . Οἱ μὲν γὰρ ἄνδρες, φασί, κἂν πάνυ πολλαῖς γυναιξὶ πλησιάσωσιν, οὐδὲν τῇ ἑστίᾳ λυμαίνονται· αἱ δὲ γυναῖκες, ἐξ ὧν ἁμαρτάνουσι, κληρονόμους ἀλλοτρίους ταῖς οἰκίαις καὶ τοῖς γένεσιν ἐπεισάγουσιν.*

148. Cohen 1991. McGinn 1998, *passim.*

149. Salvian, *De gubernatione Dei*, 7.22. Ed. Halm, 101–102: *adulteria uetantes, lupanaria aedificantes.*

150. Treggiari 1991a, 279–280.

151. The perfect example is preserved in the anecdotes about Cato the Elder, who approved of visits to the brothel, but not too often: Horace, *Sermones*, 1.2. Ed. O. Keller and A. Holder, 1: 14–15. *Pseudacronis scholia in Horatium vetustiora*, 1.2. Ed. O Keller, 2: 20: *postea cum frequentius eum exeuntem de eodem lupanari vidisset, dixisse fertur, adulescens ego te laudavi, tamquam huc intervenires, non tamquam hic habitares.*

152. What follows is developed in greater detail in Harper forthcoming, chapter 7.

153. Until C.E. 498. Procopius of Gaza, *In imperatorem Anastasium panegyricus*, 13. PG 87c:2812–2813. See McGinn 1998, 273.

154. *Dig.* 23.2.43.1–3.

155. Finley 1998, 163.

156. See, for instance, Augustine, *De civitate Dei*, 2.20. Ed. Dombart and Kalb, CC 47, 52: *abundent publica scorta uel propter omnes, quibus frui placuerit, uel propter eos maxime, qui habere priuata non possunt.*

157. Stressed by Friedl 1996.

158. Beaucamp 1990, 297.

159. Jerome, *Epistulae*, 69.5. Ed. I. Hilberg, CSEL 54, 688. Gregory of Nyssa, *In canticum canticorum*, 15.6.8. Ed. H. Langerbeck, 6: 462–463. Asterius of Antioch, *Commentarii in Psalmos*, 11.9. Ed. M. Richard (Oslo, 1956) 80. Augustine, *Epistulae*, 259.3. Ed. A. Goldbacher, CSEL 57, 612–613. Augustine *Sermones*, 224.3. PL 38: 1095. Salvian of Marseilles, *De gubernatione Dei*, 4.5. Ed. C. Halm, MGHAA 1, 40.

160. Jensen 1978; Glancy 1998; Gaca 2003; Osiek 2003. Gaca has shown Paul's dependence on the Septuagint. Moreover, *porneia* is used very sparingly in non-Jewish, pre-Christian authors. This topic is the object of a future study.

161. Clark 1991. See Beaucamp 1990, 17–21, on continuity in the idiom of female sexual morality.

162. John Chrysostom, *Propter fornicationes*, 1.4. PG 51: 213: *Οὐκ ἀγνοοῦμεν γὰρ ὅτι πολλοὶ μοιχείαν νομίζουσιν, ὅταν τις ὕπανδρον φθείρῃ γυναῖκα μόνον· ἐγὼ δὲ κἂν δημοσίᾳ πόρνῃ, κἂν θεραπαινίδι, κἂν ἄλλῃ τινὶ γυναικὶ ἄνδρα οὐκ ἐχούσῃ πρόσχῃ κακῶς καὶ ἀκολάστως, ἔχων γυναῖκα, μοιχείαν τὸ τοιοῦτον εἶναί φημι.*

163. John Chrysostom, *Propter fornicationes*, 1.4, PG 51:213: *Εἰ γὰρ καὶ παράδοξόν ἐστι τὸ εἰρημένον, ἀλλ' ἀληθές.*

164. Brown 1988, 5–32. Foucault 1986. Gaca 2003 is right to stress how different the moral grounding of Christian sexuality was from these earlier modes of self-restraint.

165. Jerome, *Epistulae*, 77.3. Ed. Hilberg, CSEL 55, 39: *Apud illos viris impudicitiae frena laxantur et solo stupro atque adulterio condemnato passim per lupanaria et ancillulas libido permittitur, quasi culpam dignitas faciat, non voluptas.*

166. Herlihy 1995 (though with caution at 581–582). See Beaucamp 1992, 82–104, for the increasing "moralization" of marriage visible in the papyri, especially with reference to male sexuality. Cf. Satlow 2003 for Jewish parallels.

167. For Byzantium, Laiou 1985, esp. 195–196. For the Syriac world, see Selb 2002. For the west, see Daudet 1941; Duby 1978, though see Reynolds 2007, 15–16; 1994, 153; Toubert 1998, 534–535, for the strong legal position of Christian marriage norms in the Carolingian realm.

168. Cooper 2007a, xi.

169. Ambrose, *De Abraham*, 2.11.78. Ed. C. Schenkl, CSEL 32.1, 631: *quia uiri licito se errare credunt, si solo se abstineant adulterio, meretricios autem usus tamquam naturae legi suppetere putant.*

170. Augustine, *Sermones*, 153.6. PL 38: 828. Augustine, *Sermones*, 9.12. Ed. C. Lambot, CC 41, 131.

171. John Chrysostom, *Propter fornicationes*, 4. PG 51: 213.

172. Ambrose, *De paradiso*, 13.65. Ed. C. Schenkl, CSEL 32.1, 324; *De Abraham*, 1.4.23. Ed. Schenkl, CSEL 32.1, 518. Augustine, *Contra Faustum*, 22.25. Ed. J. Zycha, CSEL 25.1, 620.

173. Ausonius, *Bissula*. Ed. C. Schenkl, MGHAA 5.2, 125–127: *Delicium, blanditiae, ludus, amor, voluptas / barbara, sed quae Latias vincis alumna pupas, / Bissula, nomen tenerae rusticulum puellae, / horridulum non solitis, sed domino venustum.*

174. Paulinus of Pella, *Eucharisticos*, lines 159–172. Ed. C. Moussy, SC 209, 68–70.

175. Agathias, in *Anthologia graeca*, 5.302. Ed. H. Beckby, 1: 414.

176. Reynolds 1994, 144–151.

177. Bagnall 1987, 48–50, on the canons pertaining to divorce.

178. Basil of Caesarea, *Epistulae*, 199.21. Ed. Courtonne, 2: 157–158.

179. Innocentius I, *Epistulae*, 6.4. PL 20: 499–500. Caesarius of Arles, *Sermones*, 43.5. Ed. G. Morin, CC 103, 192: *ut in quibus propter infinitam multitudinem non possunt severitatem vel disciplinam ecclesiasticam exercere, monendo vel orando pro eis possint eos vel aliquando ad paenitentiam provocare.*

180. Bagnall 1987, esp. 59–61.

181. See the cautious remarks of Toubert 1998, 527.

182. Clark 1984; Cloke 1995; Cooper 1992; 1996; Vuolanto 2008.

183. See Cooper 2007a. Parental opposition became a principal trope of ascetic literature: e.g., Jerome, *Vita Malchi*, 3. Ed. C. C. Mierow, 37.

184. See Shaw 2002, 216, for epigraphic evidence of the Christian emphasis on widowhood.

185. Ritzer 1970; Hunter 2007, 590–592.

186. Ritzer 1970, 134–141.

187. Anné 1941, 156. John Chrysostom, *Propter fornicationes*, 2. PG 51: 211: Τίνος δὲ *ἕνεκεν καὶ ἱερέας εἰσάγεις, μέλλων τῇ ὑστεραίᾳ τοιαῦτα τελεῖν.* . . . Lack of marriage ritual: Metzger 1992, 218–219.

188. Ambrosiaster, *Comm. in ep. ad Timotheum pr.*, 3.13. Ed. H. Vogels, CSEL 81.3, 268. Siricius, *Epistulae*, 1.4.5. PL 13:1136: *illa benedictio, quam nupturae sacerdos imponit.* Ambrose, *Epistulae*, 19.7. See Ritzer 1970, 223–225; Reynolds 1994, 321–322.

189. Ambrosiaster, *Comm. in ep. ad Corin. pr.*, 7.40. Ed. H. Vogels, CSEL 81.2, 90. Caesarius of Arles, *Sermones*, 42.5. Ed. Morin, CC 103, 188.

190. Hunter 2003, 64.

191. Paulinus of Nola, *Carmina*, 25, lines 199–232. Ed. G. von Hartel, CSEL 30, 244–245. See Crouzel 1983, 622–625.

192. Ritzer 1970, 238–246. The mid-fifth-century *Praedestinatus* may refer to a nuptial mass (see Ritzer 1970, 225), although the allusion (at 3.37. Ed. F. Gori, CC 25B, 123) is indeterminate: *sacerdotes nuptiarum initia benedicentes, consecrantes et in dei mysteriis sociantes.*

193. Daudet 1941; Duby 1978; Reynolds 1994, 153; Toubert 1998, 534–535.

194. Cf., for instance, Wickham 2005, 759–794; McCormick 2001, 115–119, on the timing of eastern economic decline.

195. See, e.g., Alston 2001, 161–204.

196. Melania, forced into marriage at thirteen by her father, lost her first two children in quick succession (a daughter around the age of five and a newborn infant). Gerontius, *Vita Melaniae*, 1–6. Ed. D. Gorce, SC 90, 130–136. For the chronology, see Laurence 2002, 29–76.

197. Scheidel 2001b, 13. Migration is another fundamental factor but less significant for the history of the family (though see below on urbanism and sex ratios).

198. Scheidel 2001a.

199. Bagnall and Frier 1994, 32–36; Scheidel 2001b, 22–23, emphasizes the empirical challenge of estimating infant mortality in antiquity.

200. Shaw 1984, on Christian commemoration. Harper 2008, 108–109, on the lack of infants in the new Thera inscription.

201. Bagnall and Frier 1994, 84–90.

202. Shaw 2002, 29; Bagnall and Frier 1994, 123.

203. Shaw 2002, 231.

204. E.g., Gregory of Nyssa, *De virginitate*, 3.7. Ed. M. Aubineau, SC 119, 290–292.

205. Shaw 1987, 30–46; Saller 1991, 25–41. The Egyptian papyri, perhaps surprisingly, do not show high rates of remarriage for women past thirty: Bagnall and Frier 1994, 153–155.

206. Bagnall and Frier 1994, 138–139.

207. Bagnall and Frier 1994; Frier 2006, 18.

208. Harris 1994; Bagnall 1997.

209. See Harper forthcoming, chapter 10. Evans Grubbs 2009b emphasizes the Church's impact. For the Christian authors, the concern with sex was prominent: Basil, *Epistulae*, 217.52. Ed. Courtonne, 2: 210: *εἰ μὲν οὖν δυναμένη περισώσασθαι κατεφρόνησεν ἢ συγκαλύψειν τὴν ἁμαρτίαν ἐντεῦθεν νομίζουσα ἢ ὅλως θηριώδει καὶ ἀπανθρώπῳ λογισμῷ χρησαμένη, ὡς ἐπὶ φόνῳ κρινέσθω. Εἰ δὲ οὐκ ἠδυνήθη περιστεῖλαι καὶ δι' ἐρημίαν καὶ ἀπορίαν τῶν ἀναγκαίων διεφθάρη τὸ γεννηθέν, συγγνωστὴ ἡ μήτηρ.*

210. *CJ* 8.51.2 (374) mentions a "penalty" for child exposure, but this refers to a measure of Constantine, *CTh* 5.9.1 (331), which denied parents the right to redeem their exposed children from slavery—*that* was the penalty, now applied to masters and patrons whose dependents were exposed and enslaved. See Harper forthcoming, chapter 10; Corbier 2001, 60.

211. Shaw 2001.

212. Arjava 1996, 164–165; Evans Grubbs 2009a, 209.

213. See esp. Shaw 1987, 41–42; Aubin 2000.

214. Beaucamp 1992, 349–350. See esp. Krause 1994–1995, 1: 181–191.

215. Scheidel 2001b, 28.

216. Bagnall and Frier 1994, 121.

217. Alston 2005; Bagnall and Frier 1994, 66–74, on the higher incidence of complex households in the countryside. Complex households were not rare in the cities, of course (see esp. Wallace-Hadrill 1991 for Pompeii and Herculaneum).

218. Augustine, *Enarrationes in psalmos*, 124.7. Ed. E. Dekkers and J. Fraipont, CC 40, 1840–1841: *prima et quotidiana potestas hominis in hominem domini est in seruum. prope omnes domus habent huiusmodi potestatem.* See, in general, Harper forthcoming, chapter 1. Also Bagnall 1993.

219. John Chrysostom, *In epistulam ad Ephesios*, 22.2. PG 62: 158: ἐγὼ δὲ καὶ τὴν τῶν πενήτων οἰκίαν φημὶ πόλιν εἶναι. Καὶ γὰρ καὶ ἐνταῦθά εἰσιν ἀρχαί· οἷον, κρατεῖ τῆς γυναικὸς ὁ ἀνὴρ, ἡ γυνὴ τῶν οἰκετῶν, οἱ οἰκέται τῶν ἰδίων γυναικῶν· πάλιν αἱ γυναῖκες καὶ οἱ ἄνδρες τῶν παίδων.

220. Bagnall and Frier 1994, 70.

221. E.g., Romano 1996.

222. Bradley 1991 for the high empire; Harper forthcoming for the late empire. See also Cooper 2007b.

223. Augustine, *Enarrationes in Psalmos*, 136.5. Ed. Dekkers and Fraipont, CC 40, 1967: *filii obsequuntur, serui contremiscunt, coniux concors, felix dicitur domus.*

224. See Fikhman 1973; 1974; 1997 (unconvincing on the fourth century—see Bagnall 1993—but compelling for the fifth and sixth). Beaucamp 1992, 58.

225. Finley 1998, Whittaker 1987.

226. Geroussi-Bendermacher 2005.

227. Harper 2008.

228. Esp. Scheidel 1997.

229. *CTh* 2.25.1 (325). Basil of Caesarea, *Epistulae*, 199.40. Ed. Courtonne, 2: 162. Cf. Reynolds 1994, 162–172, on the lack of response in the late antique Church (though at 169–170 misinterpreting the law of Constantine).

230. Heather 1998; Arjava 1991.

231. Bourdieu 1972 was the seminal study of "marital strategies." McGinn 2002, 46–93; Raepsaet-Charlier 1993, 147–163, demonstrates that already in the third century, men below senatorial rank began to marry *clarissimae feminae.*

232. Esp. John Chrysostom, *Quales ducendae sint uxores*. PG 51: 225–242.

233. Herlihy 1985, 14–23.

234. See Arjava 1996, 57; Krause 1994–1995, 2: 73.

235. E.g., Himerius, *Orationes*, 9.12. Ed. A. Colonna, 80: φύντες ἴσως καὶ ἐκτραφέντες ὁμοίως, ἐπ' ἴσων ἁπάντων τῆς κοινωνίας ἠράσθησαν. See Treggiari 1991a, 83–124, for the earlier period.

236. McGinn 2002.

237. McGinn 2002, 59.

238. Cooper 2007a, 152–160.

239. The legislative record is extensive indeed. See esp. the laws in *CTh* 4.6; Beaucamp 1990, 195–201; Tate 2008.

240. Caesarius of Arles, *Sermones*, 43.4. Ed. Morin, CC 103, 191–192: *tractant enim apud se, ut prius de multis calumniis et rapinis iniustas divitias et iniqua lucra conquirant, et postea contra rationem plus nobiles quam ipsi sunt vel divitiores uxores accipiant.* Augustine, *De bono conjugali*, 5.5. Ed. Zycha, CSEL 41, 193–194.

241. Augustine, *Confessiones*, 4.2. Ed. L. Verheijen, CC 27, 41. *in qua sane experirer exemplo meo, quid distaret inter coniugalis placiti modum, quod foederatum esset generandi gratia, et pactum libidinosi amoris, ubi proles etiam contra votum nascitur, quamvis iam nata cogat se diligi.*

242. Syme 1960 on the silence in the earlier period. Cooper 2007a, 157–158. Evans Grubbs 1995, 261–316, on mixed-status unions. See also Harper forthcoming, chapter 11; Garnsey 2004 for the argument that these unions were not *more common* in Late Antiquity. Mixed-status liaisons were always common in Roman society but increasingly likely to come into view in Late Antiquity, not only because of universal citizenship and hence universal Roman jurisdiction but also because fourth-century social mobility brought men of lower-class origin onto the historical stage (e.g., Ablabius, on whom see Evans Grubbs 1995, 286–287).

243. *CT* 4.6.3 (336); McGinn 1999, 57–73; Evans Grubbs 1995, 283–294; Beaucamp 1990, 284–288.

244. Libanius, *Orationes*, 1.195. Ed. R. Foerster, vol. 1: 171.

245. Likely the situation imagined by Jerome, *Epistulae*, 69.5. Ed. Hilberg, CSEL 54, 688. See Arjava 1996, 214–215.

246. Hopkins 1961; MacMullen 1964.

247. See Gaudemet 1980, 126, 155.

248. *CTh* 4.6.7 (426) and *CJ* 5.4.21 (426) hint that, for a time, ceremonies may have been formally required, but if so, this did not last long, especially in the east. See esp. *CTh* 3.7.3 (428); Wolff 1950, 293; Beaucamp 1990, 262–264; Arjava 1996, 206; Toubert 1998, 518–519; Evans Grubbs 2007, 86–87. Leo I, *Epistulae*, 167.4. PL 54: 1204, famously used the dowry as a criterion to distinguish marriage from concubinage. *Nov. Maj.* 6.9–10 (458–459) required the dowry and nuptial gift to be of equal value, explicitly because *men* were being forced to pay too much.

249. Arjava 1996, 205. On the ambiguities of concubinage in the classical law, see esp. McGinn 1991.

250. Garnsey 2004.

251. See Shanzer 2002.

252. Anné 1941, 455–460, attributes the growth of nuptial gifts vaguely to an elevated ideal of marriage promoted by Christianity.

253. For the frequent references to *arrhae* and *donationes ante nuptias* in Augustine, see Shaw 1987, 37.

254. Augustine, *In Iohannis ev. tract.*, 2.4. Ed. R. Willems, CC 36, 84: *offerant homines quaelibet ornamenta terrarum; aurum, argentum, lapides pretiosos, equos, mancipia, fundos, praedia.*

255. Arjava 1988, 17–18, also raises the possibility that restrictions on divorce reflected the attitudes of the lower-class men who filtered into the ranks of the imperial government in Late Antiquity.

256. John Chrysostom, *Quales ducendae sint uxores*, 4. PG 51: 232: Καὶ *καθάπερ οἱ τῶν ἐμπόρων ἄπληστοι, μυρίων τὴν ναῦν πλήσαντες φορτίων, καὶ πλέον τῆς δυνάμεως τὸν ὄγκον ἐπιθέντες, κατέδυσαν τὸ σκάφος, καὶ πάντα ἀπώλεσαν.*

257. John Chrysostom, *Quales ducendae sint uxores*, 4. PG 51: 231: Ὁ *μὲν γὰρ εὔπορον λαβὼν γυναῖκα, δέσποιναν μᾶλλον ἔλαβεν ἢ γυναῖκα.* John Chrysostom, *In Matthaeum*, 73.4. PG 58:678: Ἀλλ' *ὁ δεῖνα, φησὶν, ἀπὸ γυναικὸς εὔπορος γέγονεν . . . τί δὲ αἰσχρότερον τοῦ ἐπίσημον εἶναι ἐντεῦθεν, καὶ λέγεσθαι παρὰ πάντων,* Ὁ *δεῖνα ἀπὸ γυναικὸς εὔπορος γέγονε;* John Chrysostom, *De virginitate*, 53–55. Ed. B. Grillet, SC 125, 298–304. John Chrysostom, *In acta apostolorum*, 49.4. PG 60:344: Ὥ*στε οὐκ εὔπορον δεῖ ζητεῖν, ἀλλ' ὥστε κοινωνὸν βίου λάβωμεν εἰς κατάστασιν παιδοποιίας.* John Chrysostom, *Ad Theodorum lapsum*, 1.5. Ed. J. Dumortier, SC 117, 70, warns against rich and poor wives. Also Jerome, *Adv. Iovinianum*, 1.28. PL 23: 261.

258. E.g., O'Roark 1996, 405–406.

259. *CTh* 3.7.1 (371): *nuptias nobiles nemo redimat . . . si pares sunt genere ac moribus petitores, is potior aestimetur, quem sibi consulens mulier approbaverit.* See Reynolds 2007, 58–59; Krause 1994–1995, vol. 1: 138–143.

260. Libanius, *Epistulae*, 371.3. Ed. Foerster, vol. 10, 358: *ἔλεγον τῷ νυμφίῳ μὲν δεδόσθαι παρὰ τῆς μητρὸς γῆν ἀτεχνῶς τὸ μέσον* Κορίνθου *καὶ* Σικυῶνος, *τῆς νύμφης δὲ ταύτην οὐ γενέσθαι μεγαλοψυχίᾳ σῇ.* See Festugière 1959, 164–168.

261. Asterius of Amasea, *Homiliae*, 5.4.1–4. Ed. Datema, 46–47: *ἀκούσατε δὲ νῦν, οἱ τούτων κάπηλοι καὶ τὰς γυναῖκας ὡς ἱμάτια εὐκόλως μετενδυόμενοι . . . οἱ τὰς εὐπορίας γαμοῦντες καὶ τὰς γυναῖκας ἐμπορευόμενοι . . .* Πῶς *δὲ ἀθετήσεις τὰς*

ὁμολογίας ἃς ἐπὶ τῷ γάμῳ κατέθου; Καὶ ποίας με οἴει λέγειν; Ἆρα τῆς προικὸς τῆς συγγραφείσης ἐνταῦθα, ὅτε τῇ σαυτοῦ χειρὶ ἐπεσημήνω τῷ βιβλίῳ ἐπισφραγιζόμενος τὰ τελούμενα;

262. For instance, between women of the senatorial order (*clarissimae feminae*) and men of lower status. See, e.g., *PLRE* I Claudius Amazonicus *v.e.* See Chastagnol 1979, 22–23, for more examples. Another possibility would be to study the intermarriage of Flavii and Aurelii. See Keenan 1974, 295–296, for mixed marriages. *CJ* 10.40.9 (392) imagines women marrying up and down (see Beaucamp 1990, 273).

263. Kaster 1997, 104–105, 129.

264. For Ausonius, see Hopkins 1961; Aivan 1993, 49–66; Evans Grubbs 2009a, 202–206. As Sivan notes (50), "No other Gallic family in Late Antiquity is as well documented as Ausonius'." For Augustine, Shaw 1987; Shanzer 2002.

265. Hopkins 1961, 242.

266. Sivan 1993, 58–59.

267. Hopkins 1961, 243.

268. See now Sogno 2010, 57–70.

269. Especially Symmachus, *Epistulae*, 6.3, 7.120, 9.7, 9.43 and 9.49. Ed. Seeck: 153, 210–2211, 237, 248–249, 250.

270. Symmachus, *Epistulae*, 9.7 and 9.49 (*honestus*), 6.44 and 9.43 (*clarissimus*), and 6.3 (*re fortassis uberior*). Ed. Seeck: 237, 250, 165–166, 248–249, and 153.

271. Symmachus, *Epistulae*, 9.39 (philosopher), 6.44 and 9.43 (advocate). Ed. Seeck: 247, 165–166, 248–249.

272. Sogno 2010, 70. Symmachus, *Epistulae*, 7.125. Ed. Seeck: 212.

273. Sogno 2010, 71.

274. E.g., Davidoff 1973. For Late Antiquity, Cooper 2009.

275. Jerome, *Epist.* 22.16. Ed. Hilberg, CSEL 54, 163–164. On Jerome and women in general, see Arjava 1989 and Laurence 1997. The remarkable passage in the *Scriptores Historiae Augustae: Heliogabalus*, 4.3 (ed. H. Hohl, 1: 225) can also be read as an oblique commentary on late-fourth-century manners. See Chastagnol 1979, 24–25 (whose interpretation may overstress religion).

276. John Chrysostom, *In epist. ad Eph.*, 20.7. PG 62:144.

277. Holum 1982.

278. Gaudemet 1980, 116–139; Toubert 1998, 508–509.

279. Isidore of Seville, *Etymologiae*, 9.7.27, ed. W.M. Lindsay: *causa prolis . . . causa adiutorii . . . causa incontinentiae.*

280. Isidore of Seville, *Etymologiae*, 9.7.29: *Nunc autem illae quaeruntur, quas aut divitiae aut forma, non quas probitas morum commendat.*

WORKS CITED

Ancient Sources

Ambrose, *De Abraham*. Ed. C. Schenkl, CSEL 32.1 (Vienna, 1897) 501–638.
———, *De paradiso*. Ed. C. Schenkl, CSEL 32.1 (Vienna, 1897) 265–336.
———, *Epistulae*. Ed. O. Faller, CSEL 82 (Vienna, 1968).
Ambrosiaster, *Commentarius in epistulam ad Corinthios primam*. Ed. H. Vogels, CSEL 81.2 (Vienna, 1968) 3–194.

———, *Commentarius in epistulam ad Timotheum primam.* Ed. H. Vogels, CSEL 81.3 (Vienna, 1969) 251–294.
———, *Quaestiones veteris et novi testamenti.* Ed. A. Souter, CSEL 50 (Vienne, 1908).
Anthologia Graeca. Ed. H. Beckby, 4 vols. (Munich, 1957–1958).
Asterius of Amasea, *Homiliae.* Ed. C. Datema (Leiden, 1970).
Asterius of Antioch, *Commentarii in Psalmos.* Ed. M. Richard, *Asterii sophistae commentariorum in Psalmos quae supersunt* (Oslo, 1956).
Augustine, *Confessiones.* Ed. L. Verheijen, CCSL 27 (Turnhout, 1981).
———, *Contra Faustum.* Ed. J. Zycha, CSEL 25.1 (Vienna, 1891) 251–797.
———, *De adulterinis coniugiis.* Ed. J. Zycha, CSEL 41 (Vienna, 1900).
———, *De bono conjugali.* Ed. J. Zycha, CSEL 41 (Vienna, 1900) 187–231.
———, *De civitate Dei.* Ed. B. Dombart and A. Kalb, CCSL 47–48 (Turnhout, 1955).
———, *Enarrationes in Psalmos.* Ed. E. Dekkers and J. Fraipont, CCSL 38–40 (Turnhout, 1956).
———, *Epistulae.* Ed. A. Goldbacher, CSEL 34.1–2, 44, 57, 58 (Vienna, 1895–1923).
———, *In Iohannis evangelium tractatus.* Ed. R. Willems, CCSL 36 (Turnhout, 1954).
———, *Sermones.* PL 38–39.
———, *Sermones de vetere testamento* (1–50). Ed. C. Lambot, CCSL 41 (Turnhout, 1961).
Ausonius, *Bissula.* Ed. C. Schenkl, *Opuscula,* MGHAA 5.2 (Berlin, 1883) 125–127.
Basil of Caesarea, *Epistulae.* Ed. Y. Courtonne, *Lettres,* 3 vols. (Paris, 1957–1966).
Caesarius of Arles, *Sermones.* Ed. G. Morin, CCSL 103–104 (Turnhout, 1953).
Epitome Codicum Gregoriani et Hermogeniani Wisigothica. Ed. P. Krueger, *Collectio librorum iuris anteiustiniani,* vol. 3 (Berlin, 1890) 221–35.
Gerontius, *Vita Melaniae.* Ed. D. Gorce, SC 90 (Paris, 1962).
Gregory of Nyssa, *De virginitate.* Ed. M. Aubineau, SC 119 (Paris, 1966).
———, *In canticum canticorum.* Ed. H. Langerbeck, *Opera,* vol. 6 (Leiden, 1960).
Himerius, *Orationes.* Ed. A. Colonna (Rome, 1951).
Horace, *Sermones.* Ed. O. Keller and A. Holder, *Opera,* 2 vols. (Leipzig, 1899–1925).
Innocentius I, *Epistulae.* PL 20: 457–638.
Isidore of Seville, *Etymologiae.* Ed. W.M. Lindsay (Oxford, 1911).
Jerome, *Adversus Iovinianum.* PL 23: 221–352.
———, *Epistulae.* Ed. I. Hilberg, CSEL 54–56 (Vienna, 1996).
———, *Vita Malchi.* Ed. C. C. Mierow, in *Classical Essays Presented to J. A. Kleist* (Saint Louis, 1946) 33–60.
John Chrysostom, *Ad populum Antiochenum.* PG 49: 15–222.
———, *Ad Theodorum lapsum.* Ed. J. Dumortier, SC 117 (Paris, 1966).
———, *Ad viduam juniorem.* Ed. B. Grillet and G. Ettlinger, *A une jeune veuve. Sur le marriage unique.* SC 138 (Paris, 1968) 112–159.
———, *De libello repudii.* PG 51: 217–226.
———, *De non iterando conjugio.* Ed. B. Grillet and G. Ettlinger, *A une jeune veuve. Sur le marriage unique.* SC 138 (Paris, 1968) 160–201.
———, *De virginitate.* Ed. B. Grillet, *La virginité,* SC 125 (Paris, 1966).
———, *In acta apostolorum.* PG 60: 13–384.
———, *In epistulam ad Ephesios.* PG 62: 9–176.
———, *In illud: Propter fornicationes autem unusquisque suam uxorem habeat.* PG 51: 207–218.
———, *In Matthaeum.* PG 57: 13–472. PG 58: 471–794.
———, *Quales ducendae sint uxores.* PG 51: 241–252.
Leo I, *Epistulae.* PL 54: 551–1218.
Libanius, *Epistulae.* Ed. R. Foerster, *Opera,* vols. 10–11 (Leipzig, 1921–2).
———, *Orationes.* Ed. R. Foerster, *Opera,* vols. 1–4 (Leipzig, 1903–8).

Menander, *Division of Epideictic Speeches*. Ed. D. Russell and N. Wilson, Menander Rhetor (Oxford, 1981).
Paulinus of Nola, *Carmina*. Ed. G. von Hartel, CSEL 30 (Vienna, 1999).
Paulinus of Pella, *Eucharisticos*. Ed. C. Moussy, SC 209 (Paris, 1974).
Plutarch, *Conjugalia praecepta*. Ed. F. C. Babbitt, *Plutarch's Moralia*, vol. 2 (Cambridge, MA, 1928).
Praedestinatus. Ed. F. Gori, CCSL 25B (Turnhout, 2000).
Procopius of Gaza, *In imperatorem Anastasium panegyricus*. PG 87c: 2793–2824.
Pseudacronis scholia in Horatium vetustiora. Ed. O. Keller, vol. 2 (Leipzig, 1904).
Salvian of Marseilles, *De gubernatione Dei*. Ed. C. Halm, *Libri qui supersunt*, MGHAA 1 (Berlin, 1877) 1–108.
Scriptores Historiae Augustae. Ed. H. Hohl, 2nd ed., 2 vols. (Leipzig, 1965).
Siricius, *Epistulae*. PL 13: 1131–1196.
Symmachus, *Epistulae*. Ed. O. Seeck, MGHAA 6.1 (Berlin, 1883) 1–278.

Modern Sources

Allen, Pauline, and Wendy Mayer. 1993. "Computer and Homily: Accessing the Everyday Life of Early Christians," *Vigiliae Christianae* 47: 260–280.
Alston, Richard. 2001. "Urban Population in Late Roman Egypt and the End of the Ancient World." In *Debating Roman Demography*, ed. W. Scheidel, 161–204. Leiden: Brill.
———. 2005. "Searching for the Romano-Egyptian Family." In *The Roman Family in the Empire: Rome, Italy, and Beyond*, ed. M. George, 129–157. Oxford: Oxford University Press.
Anné, Lucien. 1941. *Les rites des fiançailles et la donation pour cause de mariage sous le Bas-Empire*. Louvain: Desclée de Brouwer.
Ariès, Philippe. 1960. *L'enfant et la vie familiale sous l'ancien régime*. Paris: Plon.
Ariès, Philippe, and Georges Duby. 1985–1987. *Histoire de la vie privée*. 5 vols. Paris: Seuil.
Arjava, Antti. 1988. "Divorce in Later Roman Law," *Arctos* 22: 5–21.
———. 1989. "Jerome and Women," *Arctos* 23: 5–18.
———. 1991. "Zum Gebrauch der griechischen Rangprädikate des Senatorenstandes in den Papyri und Inschriften," *Tyche: Beiträge zur Alten Geschichte, Papyrologie und Epigraphik* 6: 17–35.
———. 1996. *Women and Law in Late Antiquity*. Oxford: Clarendon.
———. 1998. "Paternal Power in Late Antiquity," *Journal of Roman Studies* 88: 147–165.
———. 2001. "The Survival of Roman Family Law after the Barbarian Settlements." In *Law, Society, and Authority in Late Antiquity*, ed. Ralph Mathisen, 33–51. Oxford: Oxford University Press.
Arnaoutoglou, Ilias. 1995. "Marital Disputes in Greco-Roman Egypt," *Journal of Juristic Papyrology* 25: 11–28.
Aubin, Melissa. 2000. "More Apparent Than Real? Questioning the Difference in Marital Age between Christian and Non-Christian Women of Rome during the Third and Fourth Centuries," *Ancient History Bulletin* 14: 1–13.
Bagnall, Roger. 1987. "Church, State, and Divorce in Late Roman Egypt." In *Florilegium Columbianum: Essays in Honor of Paul Oskar Kristeller*, ed. K.-L. Selig and R. Somerville, 41–61. New York: Italica.
———. 1991. "The Prostitute Tax in Roman Egypt," *Bulletin of the American Society of Papyrology* 28: 5–12.

———. 1993. "Slavery and Society in Late Roman Egypt." In *Law, Politics, and Society in the Ancient Mediterranean World*, ed. B. Halperin and D. Hobson, 220–240. Sheffield: Sheffield Academic Press.

———. 1995. "Women, Law and Social Realities in Late Antiquity: A Review Article," *Bulletin of the American Society of Papyrologists* 32: 65–86.

———. 1997. "Missing Females in Roman Egypt," *Scripta Classica Israelica* 16: 121–138.

Bagnall, Roger, and Bruce Frier. 1994. *The Demography of Roman Egypt*. Cambridge: Cambridge University Press.

Beaucamp, Joëlle. 1989. "L'Égypte byzantine: Biens des parents, biens du couple?" In *Eherecht und Familiengut in Antike und Mittelalter*, ed. D. Simon, 61–76. Munich: R. Oldenbourg.

———. 1990–1992. *Le statut de la femme à Byzance, 4e–7e siècle*. 2 vols. Paris: De Boccard.

Betzig, Laura. 1992a. "Roman Monogamy," *Ethology and Sociobiology* 13: 351–383.

———. 1992b. "Roman Polygyny," *Ethology and Sociobiology* 13: 309–349.

Bougard, François, Laurent Feller, and Régine Le Jan, eds. 2002. *Dots et douaires dans le haut moyen âge*. Rome: Ecole française de Rome.

Bourdieu, Pierre. 1972. "Les stratégies matrimoniales dans le système de reproduction," *Annales: économies sociétés civilisations* 27: 1105–1127.

Bradley, Keith. 1991. *Discovering the Roman Family: Studies in Roman Social History*. Oxford: Oxford University Press.

Brown, Peter. 1988. *The Body and Society: Men, Women, and Sexual Renunciation in Early Christianity*. New York: Columbia University Press.

Brundage, James. 1987. *Law, Sex, and Christian Society in Medieval Europe*. Chicago: University of Chicago Press.

Champlin, Edward. 1991. *Final Judgments: Duty and Emotion in Roman Wills, 200 B.C.–A.D. 250*. Berkeley: University of California Press.

Chastagnol, André. 1979. "Les femmes dans l'ordre sénatorial: Titulature et rang social à Rome," *Revue historique* 262: 3–28.

Clark, Elizabeth. 1984, *The Life of Melania the Younger: Introduction, Translation, Commentary*. New York: E. Mellen.

———. 1986. *Ascetic Piety and Women's Faith: Essays on Late Ancient Christianity*. Lewiston, NY: E. Mellen.

———. 1986. "'Adam's Only Companion': Augustine and the Early Christian Debate on Marriage," *Recherches augustiniennes* 21: 139–162.

———. 1991. "Sex, Shame, and Rhetoric: En-Gendering Early Christian Ethics," *Journal of the American Academy of Religion* 59: 221–245.

Clark, Gillian. 1993. *Women in Late Antiquity: Pagan and Christian Life-Styles*. Oxford: Clarendon.

Cloke, Gillian. 1995. *This Female Man of God: Women and Spiritual Power in the Patristic Age, AD 350–450*. London: Routledge.

Cohen, David. 1991. "The Augustan Law on Adultery: The Social and Cultural Context." In *The Family in Italy from Antiquity to the Present*, ed. David Kertzer and Richard Saller, 109–126. New Haven, CT: Yale University Press.

Cooper, Kate. 1992. "Insinuations of Womanly Influence: An Aspect of the Christianization of the Roman Aristocracy," *Journal of Roman Studies* 82: 150–164.

———. 1996. *The Virgin and the Bride: Idealized Womanhood in Late Antiquity*. Cambridge, MA: Harvard University Press.

———. 2007a. *The Fall of the Roman Household*. Cambridge: Cambridge University Press.

———. 2007b. "Closely Watched Households: Visibility, Exposure and Private Power in the Roman *domus*," *Past and Present* 197: 3–33.
———. 2009. "Gender and the Fall of Rome." In *A Companion to Late Antiquity*, ed. P. Rousseau, 187–200. Malden, MA: Wiley-Blackwell.
Corbett, Percy. 1930. *The Roman Law of Marriage*. Oxford: Clarendon.
Corbier, Mireille. 2001. "Child Exposure and Abandonment." In *Childhood, Class and Kin in the Roman World*, ed. S. Dixon, 52–73. New York: Routledge.
Corcoran, Simon. 2006. "The Tetrarchy: Policy and Image as Reflected in Imperial Announcements." In *Die Tetrarchie: Ein neues Regierungssystem und seine mediale Präsentation*, ed. D. Boschung and W. Eck, 31–62. Wiesbaden: Reichert.
Crook, John. 1967. *Law and Life of Rome*. London: Thames & Hudson.
Crouzel, Henri. 1971. *L'Église primitive face au divorce, du premier au cinquième siècle*. Paris: Beauchesne.
Daudet, Pierre. 1941. *L'établissement de la compétence de l'Église en matière de divorce & de consanguinité, France, Xème–XIIème siècle*. Paris: Recueil Sirey.
Dauvillier, Jean, and Carlo De Clercq. 1936. *Le marriage en droit canonique oriental*. Paris: Recueil Sirey.
Davidoff, Leonore. 1973. *The Best Circles: Women and Society in Victorian England*. Totowa, NJ: Rowman and Littlefield.
Dixon, Suzanne. 1992. *The Roman Family*. Baltimore: Johns Hopkins University Press.
———. 1996. "The Sentimental Ideal of the Roman Family." In *Marriage, Divorce, and Children in Ancient Rome*, ed. Beryl Rawson, 99–113. Oxford: Oxford University Press.
Duby, Georges. 1978. *Medieval Marriage: Two Models from Twelfth-Century France*. Baltimore: Johns Hopkins University Press.
Edmondson, Jonathan. 2005. "Family Relations in Roman Lusitania: Social Change in a Roman Province?" In *The Roman Family in the Empire: Rome, Italy, and Beyond*, ed. M. George, 183–229. Oxford: Oxford University Press.
Elm, Susanna. 1994. *Virgins of God: The Making of Asceticism in Late Antiquity*. Oxford: Oxford University Press.
Evans Grubbs, Judith. 1994. "Pagan and Christian Marriage: The State of the Question," *Journal of Early Christian Studies* 2: 361–412.
———. 1995. *Law and Family in Late Antiquity: The Emperor Constantine's Marriage Legislation*. Oxford: Clarendon.
———. 2007. "Marrying and Its Documentation in Later Roman Law." In *To Have and to Hold: Marrying and Its Documentation in Western Christendom, 400–1600*, ed. Philip Reynolds and John Witte, 43–94. Cambridge: Cambridge University Press.
———. 2009a. "Marriage and Family Relationships in the Late Roman West." In *A Companion to Late Antiquity*, ed. P. Rousseau, 201–219. Malden, MA: Wiley-Blackwell.
———. 2009b. "Church, State, and Children: Christian and Imperial Attitudes toward Infant Exposure in Late Antiquity." In *The Power of Religion in Late Antiquity*, ed. A. Cain and N. Lenski, 119–131. Burlington, VT: Ashgate.
Falchi, Gian Luigi. 1995. "Matrimonio 'cum scriptis' e 'sine scriptis' nel Libro Siro-Romano di diritto," *Studia et Documenta Historiae et Iuris* 61: 875–887.
Fikhman, Itzhak. 1973. "Sklaven und Sklavenarbeit im spätrömischen Oxyrhynchus," *Jahrbuch für Wirtschaftsgeschichte* 2: 149–206.
———. 1974. "Slaves in Byzantine Oxyrhynchus." In *Akten des* XII *internationalen Papyrologenkongresses*, 117–124. Munich: Beck.
———. 1997. "Review of R. Bagnall, *Reading Papyri, Writing Ancient History*," *Scripta Classica Israelica* 16: 279–285.

Finley, Moses. 1998. *Ancient Slavery and Modern Ideology*. Princeton, NJ: Markus Wiener. [originally published 1980]

Flandrin, Jean Louis. 1976. *Familles: Parenté, maison, sexualité dans l'ancienne société*. Paris: Hachette.

Foucault, Michel. 1986. *The Care of the Self*. Trans. R. Hurley. New York: Pantheon.

Friedl, Raimund. 1996. *Der Konkubinat im kaiserzeitlichen Rom: Von Augustus bis Septimius Severus*. Stuttgart: F. Steiner.

Frier, Bruce. 2006. "Marriage and Motherhood in Roman Egypt." In *Ten Years of the Agnes Kirsopp Lake Michels Lectures at Bryn Mawr College*, ed. Suzanne Faris and Lesley Lundeen, 1–31. Bryn Mawr, PA: Bryn Mawr College.

Gaca, Kathy. 2003. *The Making of Fornication: Eros, Ethics, and Political Reform in Greek Philosophy and Early Christianity*. Berkeley: University of California Press.

Gade, Gunther. 2001. *Donationes inter virum et uxorem*. Berlin: Duncker & Humblot.

Gardner, Jane. 1986. *Women in Roman Law and Society*. Bloomington: Indiana University Press.

Garnsey, Peter. 2004. "Roman Citizenship and Roman Law in the Late Empire." In *Approaching Late Antiquity: The Transformation from Early to Late Empire*, ed. Simon Swain and Mark Edwards, 133–155. Oxford: Oxford University Press.

Gaudemet, Jean. 1962. "Les transformations de la vie familiale au Bas Empire et l'influence du Christianisme," *Romanitas: Revista de cultura romana* 5: 58–85.

———. 1980. *Sociétés et mariage*. Strasbourg: Cerdic.

———. 1987. *Le mariage en Occident: Les mœurs et le droit*. Paris: Cerf.

———. 1992. "La constitution 'ad populum' du Janvier 31, 320." In *Droit et société aux derniers siècles de l'empire romain*, 3–22. Naples: Jovene.

George, Michele, ed. 2005. *The Roman Family in the Empire: Rome, Italy, and Beyond*. Oxford: Oxford University Press.

Geroussi-Bendermacher, Eugenia. 2005. "Propriété foncière et inventaire d'esclaves: un texte inédit de Perissa (Thera) tardo-antique." In *Esclavage antique et discriminations socio-culturelles*, ed. V. Anastasiadis and P. Doukellis, 335–358. New York: Peter Lang.

Glancy, Jennifer. 1998 "Obstacles to Slaves' Participation in the Corinthian Church," *Journal of Biblical Literature* 117: 481–501.

Goody, Jack. 1983. *The Development of the Family and Marriage in Europe*. Cambridge: Cambridge University Press.

Hallett, Judith. 1984. *Fathers and Daughters in Roman Society: Women and the Elite Family*. Princeton, NJ: Princeton University Press.

Hareven, Tamara. 1991. "The History of the Family and the Complexity of Social Change," *American Historical Review* 96: 95–124.

Harper, Kyle. 2008. "The Greek Census Inscriptions of Late Antiquity," *Journal of Roman Studies* 98: 83–119.

———. forthcoming. *Slavery in the Late Roman World, AD 275–425*. Cambridge: Cambridge University Press.

Harries, Jill. 1999. *Law and Empire in Late Antiquity*. Cambridge: Cambridge University Press.

Harris, William. 1994. "Child-Exposure in the Roman Empire," *Journal of Roman Studies* 84: 1–22.

Harrison, Carol. 1996. "The Silent Majority: The Family in Patristic Thought." In *The Family in Theological Perspective*, ed. Stephen Barton, 87–105. Edinburgh: T. & T. Clark.

Heather, Peter. 1998. "Senators and Senates." In *Cambridge Ancient History, Vol. 13: The Late Empire, A.D. 337–425*, ed. Averil Cameron and Peter Garnsey, 184–210. Cambridge: Cambridge University Press.

Herlihy, David. 1985. *Medieval Households*. Cambridge, MA: Harvard University Press.

———. 1995. "Biology and History: The Triumph of Monogamy," *Journal of Interdisciplinary History* 25: 571–583.

Hillner, Julia. 2003. "*Domus*, Family, and Inheritance: The Senatorial Family House in Late Antique Rome," *Journal of Roman Studies* 93: 129–145.

Holum, Kenneth. 1982. *Theodosian Empresses: Women and Imperial Dominion in Late Antiquity*. Berkeley: University of California Press.

Honoré, Tony. 1994. *Emperors and Lawyers*. Oxford: Clarendon Press.

———. 1998. *Law in the Crisis of Empire, 379–455 AD: The Theodosian Dynasty and its Quaestors with a Palingenesia of Laws of the Dynasty*. Oxford: Clarendon.

Hopkins, Keith. 1961. "Social Mobility in the Later Roman Empire: The Evidence of Ausonius," *Classical Quarterly* 11: 239–249.

———. 1966. "On the Probable Age Structure of the Roman Population," *Population Studies* 20: 245–264.

Hughes, Diane Owen. 1978. "From Brideprice to Dowry in Mediterranean Europe," *Journal of Family History* 3: 262–296.

Humbert, Michel. 1972. *Le remariage à Rome: etude d'histoire juridique et sociale*. Milan: A. Giuffrè.

Hunter, David G. 1989. "'On the Sin of Adam and Eve': A Little-Known Defense of Marriage and Childbearing by Ambrosiaster," *Harvard Theological Review* 82: 283–299.

———. 2003. "Augustine and the Making of Marriage in Roman North Africa," *Journal of Early Christian Studies* 11: 63–85.

———. 2007. "Sexuality, Marriage, and the Family." In *Cambridge History of Christianity, Vol. 2: Constantine to c. 600*, ed. Augustine Casiday and Frederick Norris, 585–600. Cambridge: Cambridge University Press.

Ilan, Tal. 1996. *Jewish Women in Greco-Roman Palestine*. Tübingen: J. C. B. Mohr.

Jacobs, Andrew. 2003. "'Let Him Guard *Pietas*': Early Christian Exegesis and the Ascetic Family," *Journal of Early Christian Studies* 11: 257–263.

Jacobs, Andrew, and Rebecca Krawiec. 2003. "Fathers Know Best? Christian Families in the Age of Asceticism," *Journal of Early Christian Studies* 11: 257–263.

Jensen, Joseph. 1978. "Does *Porneia* Mean Fornication? A Critique of Bruce Malina," *Novum Testamentum* 20: 161–184.

Kaster, Robert. 1997. "The Shame of the Romans," *Transactions of the American Philological Association* 127: 1–19.

Keenan, James. 1973. "The Names Flavius and Aurelius as Status Designations in Later Roman Egypt 1," *ZPE* 11: 36–63.

———. 1974. "The Names Flavius and Aurelius as Status Designations in Later Roman Egypt 2," *ZPE* 13: 283–304.

Krause, Jens-Uwe. 1994–1995. *Witwen und Waisen in römischen Reich*. 4 vols. Stuttgart: F. Steiner.

Laiou, Angeliki. 1985. "*Consensus facit nuptias—et non:* Pope Nicholas I's *responsa* to the Bulgarians as a Source for Byzantine Marriage Customs," *Rechtshistorisches Journal* 4: 189–201.

Laslett, Peter, and Richard Wall. 1972. *Household and Family in Past Time: Comparative Studies in the Size and Structure of the Domestic Group over the Last Three*

Centuries in England, France, Serbia, Japan and Colonial North America, with Further Materials from Western Europe. Cambridge: Cambridge University Press.

Laurence, Patrick. 1997. "Les représentations de la *domina* chez Jérôme," *Recherches de science religieuse* 85: 41–55.

———. 2002. *La vie latine de sainte Mélanie*. Jerusalem: Franciscan Printing Press.

Levy, Ernst. 1951. *West Roman Vulgar Law: The Law of Property*. Philadelphia: American Philosophical Society.

Liebs, Detlef. 2008. "Roman Vulgar Law in Late Antiquity." In *Aspects of Law in Late Antiquity: Dedicated to A.M. Honoré on the Occasion of the Sixtieth Year of his Teaching in Oxford*, ed. A. J. B. Sirks, 35–53. Oxford: All Souls College.

MacDonald, Kevin. 1990. "Mechanisms of Sexual Egalitarianism in Western Europe," *Ethology and Sociobiology* 11: 195–238.

Macfarlane, Alan. 1986. *Marriage and Love in England: Modes of Reproduction, 1300–1840*. Oxford: B. Blackwell.

MacMullen, Ramsay. 1964. "Social Mobility and the Theodosian Code," *Journal of Roman Studies* 54: 49–53.

———. 1984. *Christianizing the Roman Empire (A.D. 100–400)*. New Haven, CT: Yale University Press.

———. 1986. "What Difference Did Christianity Make?" *Historia* 35: 322–343.

Malina, B. 1972. "Does *Porneia* Mean Fornication?" *Novum Testamentum* 14: 10–17.

Martin, Dale. 1996. "The Construction of the Ancient Family: Methodological Considerations," *Journal of Roman Studies* 86: 40–60.

Maxwell, Jaclyn. 2006. *Christianization and Communication in Late Antiquity: John Chrysostom and His Congregation in Antioch*. Cambridge: Cambridge University Press.

Mayer, Wendy. 2005. *The Homilies of St. John Chrysostom, Provenance: Reshaping the Foundations*. Rome: Pontificio Istituto orientale.

McCail, Ronald. 1968. "Three Byzantine Epigrams on Marital Incompatibility," *Mnemosyne* 21: 76–78.

McCormick, Michael. 2001. *Origins of the European Economy*. Cambridge: Cambridge University Press.

McGinn, Thomas. 1991. "Concubinage and the Lex Iulia on Adultery," *Transactions of the American Philological Association* 121: 335–375.

———. 1998. *Prostitution, Sexuality, and the Law in Ancient Rome*. New York: Oxford University Press.

———. 1999. "Widows, Orphans, and Social History," *Journal of Roman Archaeology* 12: 617–632.

———. 2002. "The Augustan Marriage Legislation and Social Practice: Elite Endogamy versus Male Marrying Down." In *Speculum Iuris: Roman Law as a Reflection of Social and Economic Life in Antiquity*, ed. J.-J. Aubert and B. Sirks, 46–93. Ann Arbor: University of Michigan Press.

———. 2004. *The Economy of Prostitution in the Roman World: A Study of Social History and the Brothel*. Ann Arbor: University of Michigan Press.

Memmer, Michael. 2000. "Die Ehescheidung im 4. und 5. Jahrhundert n. Chr." In *Iurisprudentia universalis: Festschrift für Theo Mayer-Maly zum 70.* Geburtstag, ed. M. Schermaier et al., 489–510. Cologne: Böhlau.

Metzger, Marcel. 1992. "Apports de l'histoire de la liturgie à la théologie du mariage," *Revue de droit canonique* 42: 215–236.

Mitteis, Ludwig. 1891. *Reichsrecht und Volksrecht in den östlichen Provinzen des römischen Kaiserreichs: Mit Beiträgen zur Kenntniss des griechischen Rechts und der spätrömischen Rechtsentwicklung.* Leipzig: B.G. Teubner.

Mnookin, R. H., and L. Kornhauser. 1979. "Bargaining in the Shadow of the Law: The Case of Divorce," *Yale Law Journal* 88: 950–997.

Nathan, Geoffrey. 2000. *The Family in Late Antiquity: The Rise of Christianity and the Endurance of Tradition.* London: Routledge.

Neri, Valerio. 1998. *I marginali nell'Occidente tardoantico: Poveri, "infames" e criminali nella nascente società cristiana.* Bari: Edipuglia.

O'Roark, Douglas. 1996. "Close-Kin Marriage in Late Antiquity: The Evidence of Chrysostom," *Greek, Roman and Byzantine Studies* 37: 399–411.

Osiek, Carolyn. 2003. "Female Slaves, *Porneia*, and the Limits of Obedience." In *Early Christian Families in Context*, ed. David Balch and Carolyn Osiek, 255–274. Grand Rapids, MI: William B. Eerdmans.

Patterson, Cynthia. 1998. *The Family in Greek History*. Cambridge, MA: Harvard University Press.

Pomeroy, Sarah. 1994. *Xenophon, Oeconomicus: A Social and Historical Commentary, with a New English Translation.* Oxford: Clarendon Press.

Raepsaet-Charlier, Marie-Thérèse. 1993. "Les femmes sénatoriales du IIIe siècle: Étude préliminaire." In *Prosopographie und Sozialgeschichte: Studien zur Methodik und Erkenntnismöglichkeit der kaiserzeitlichen Prosopographie. Kolloquium, Köln, 24.–26. November 1991*, ed. W. Eck, 147–163. Vienna: Böhlau Verlag.

Rawson, Beryl, ed. 1986. *The Family in Ancient Rome: New Perspectives.* London: Croom Helm.

———, ed. 1991. *Marriage, Divorce, and Children in Ancient Rome.* Oxford: Clarendon Press.

Rawson, Beryl, and Paul Weaver. 1997. *The Roman Family in Italy: Status, Sentiment, Space.* Oxford: Oxford University Press.

Reynolds, Philip. 1994. *Marriage in the Western Church: The Christianization of Marriage during the Patristic and Early Medieval Periods.* Leiden: E. J. Brill.

———. 2007. "Marrying and Its Documentation in Pre-Modern Europe: Consent, Celebration, and Property." In *To Have and to Hold: Marrying and Its Documentation in Western Christendom, 400–1600*, ed. Philip Reynolds and John Witte, 1–42. Cambridge: Cambridge University Press.

Ritzer, Korbinian. 1970. *Le mariage dans les Églises chrétiennes du Ier au XIe siècle.* Paris: Éditions du Cerf.

Romano, Dennis. 1996. *Housecraft and Statecraft: Domestic Service in Renaissance Venice, 1400–1600.* Baltimore: Johns Hopkins University Press.

Saller, Richard. 1984. "Familia, *domus*, and the Roman Conception of the Family," *Phoenix* 38: 336–355.

———. 1986. "*Patria potestas* and the Stereotype of the Roman Family," *Continuity and Change* 1: 7–22.

———. 1987. "Men's Age at Marriage and Its Consequences in the Roman Family," *Classical Philology* 82: 21–34.

———. 1991. "European Family History and Roman Law," *Continuity and Change* 6: 335–346.

———. 1994. *Patriarchy, Property and Death in the Roman Family.* Cambridge: Cambridge University Press.

———. 1997. "Roman Kinship: Structure and Sentiment." In *The Roman Family in Italy: Status, Sentiment, Space*, ed. Beryl Rawson and Paul Weaver, 7–34. Oxford: Oxford University Press.

Saller, Richard, and David Kertzer. 1991. "Historical and Anthropological Perspectives on Italian Family Life." In *The Family in Italy from Antiquity to the Present*, ed. David Kertzer and Richard Saller, 1–19. New Haven, CT: Yale University Press.
Saller, Richard, and Brent Shaw. 1984. "Tombstones and Roman Family Relations in the Principate: Civilians, Soldiers and Slaves," *Journal of Roman Studies* 74: 124–156.
Sargenti, Manlio. 1938. *Il diritto privato nella legislazione di Costantino: Persone e famiglia*. Milan: A. Giuffrè.
———. 1975. "Il diritto privato nella legislazione di Costantino." In *Accademia romanistica costantiniana: Convegno internazionale* 1, 1–109. Perugia: Libreria universitaria.
———. 1981. "Il matrimonio nella legislazione di Valentiniano e Teodosio." In *Accademia romanistica costantiniana: Convegno internazionale* 4, 239–257. Perugia: Libreria universitaria.
———. 1985. "Matrimonio cristiano e società pagana: Spunti per una ricerca," *Studia et documenta historiae et iuris* 51: 367–691.
Satlow, Michael. 2001. *Jewish Marriage in Antiquity*. Princeton, NJ: Princeton University Press.
———. 2003. "Slipping towards Sacrament: Jews, Christians, and Marriage." In *Jewish Culture and Society under the Christian Roman Empire*, ed. R. Kalmin and S. Schwartz, 65–89. Louvain: Peeters.
Scheidel, Walter. 1997. "Quantifying the Sources of Slaves in the Early Roman Empire," *Journal of Roman Studies* 87: 156–169.
———. 2001a. "Progress and Problems in Roman Demography." In *Debating Roman Demography*, ed. Walter Scheidel, 1–81. Leiden: Brill.
———. 2001b. "Roman Age Structure: Evidence and Models," *Journal of Roman Studies* 91: 1–26.
———. 2009. "A Peculiar Institution? Greco-Roman Monogamy in Global Context," *History of the Family* 14: 280–291.
Seeck, Otto. 1919. *Regesten der Kaiser und Päpste für die Jahre 311 bis 476 n. Chr.: Vorarbeit zu einer Prosopographie der christlichen Kaiserzeit*. Stuttgart: J. B. Metzler.
Selb, Walter. 2002. *Das syrisch-römische Rechtsbuch*. Vienna: Verlag der österreichischen Akademie der Wissenschaften.
Shanzer, Danuta. 2002. "*Avulsa a latere meo*: Augustine's Spare Rib: *Confessions* 6.15.25," *Journal of Roman Studies* 92: 157–176.
Shaw, Brent. 1984. "Latin Funerary Epigraphy and Family Life in the Later Roman Empire," *Historia: Zeitschrift für alte Geschichte* 33: 457–497.
———. 1987. "The Family in Late Antiquity: The Experience of Augustine," *Past and Present* 115: 3–51.
———. 2001. "The Seasonal Birthing Cycle of Roman Women." In *Debating Roman Demography*, ed. Walter Scheidel, 83–110. Leiden: Brill.
———. 2002. "'With Whom I Lived': Measuring Roman Marriage," *Ancient Society* Man n.s. 19: 432–444.
Shaw, Brent, and Richard Saller. 1984. "Close-Kin Marriage in Roman Society?" *Man* n.s. 19: 432–444.
Sirks, A. J. B. 2007. *The Theodosian Code: A Study*. Friedrichsdorf: Éditions Tortuga.
Sivan, Hagith. 1993. *Ausonius of Bordeaux: Genesis of a Gallic Aristocracy*. London: Routledge.
Sogno, Cristiana. 2010. "Roman Matchmaking." In *From the Tetrarchs to the Theodosians: Later Roman History and Culture, 284–450 CE*, ed. S. McGill, C. Sogno, and E. Watts, 55–71. Cambridge: Cambridge University Press.

Stone, Lawrence. 1977. *The Family, Sex and Marriage in England 1500–1800*. London: Weidenfeld & Nicolson.
———. 1981. "Past Achievements and Future Trends," *Journal of Interdisciplinary History* 12: 51–87.
Syme, Ronald. 1960. "Bastards in the Roman Aristocracy," *Proceedings of the American Philosophical Society* 104: 323–327.
Tate, Joshua. 2008. "Inheritance Rights of Nonmarital Children in Late Roman Law," *Roman Legal Tradition* 4: 1–36.
Toubert, Pierre. 1998. "L'institution du mariage chrétien, de l'antiquité tardive à l'an mil." In *Morfologie sociali e culturali in Europa fra tarda antichità e alto Medioevo: Aprile 3–9, 1997*, 503–553. Spoleto: Presso La sede del Centro.
Treggiari, Susan. 1982. "Consent to Roman Marriage: Some Aspects of Law and Reality," *Classical Views* 26: 34–44.
———. 1991a. *Roman Marriage:* Iusti Coniuges *from the Time of Cicero to the Time of Ulpian*. Oxford: Clarendon.
———. 1991b. "Divorce Roman Style: How Easy and How Frequent Was It?" In *Marriage, Divorce, and Children in Ancient Rome*, ed. B. Rawson, 31–46. Oxford: Clarendon Press.
Verdon, Michel. 1988. "Virgins and Widows: European Kinship and Early Christianity," *Man* 23: 488–505.
Veyne, Paul. 1978. "La famille et l'amour sous le Haut-Empire romain," *Annales: economies sociétés civilisations* 33: 36–63.
———. 1987. "The Roman Empire." In *A History of Private Life, Vol. 1, From Pagan Rome to Byzantium*, ed. Philippe Ariès and Georges Duby, 5–234. Cambridge, MA: Harvard University Press.
Vuolanto, Ville. 2008. *Family and Asceticism: Continuity Strategies in the Late Roman World*. Doctoral dissertation, University of Tampere, Finland.
Wallace-Hadrill, Andrew. 1991. "Houses and Households: Sampling Pompeii and Herculaneum." In *Marriage, Divorce, and Children in Ancient Rome*, ed. B. Rawson, 191–227: Oxford: Clarendon Press.
Ward-Perkins, Bryan. 2006. *The Fall of Rome and the End of Civilization*. Oxford: Oxford University Press.
Watson, Alan. 1995. "Religious and Gender Discrimination: St. Ambrose and the Valentiniani," *Studia et documenta historiae et iuris* 61: 313–326.
Whittaker, C. R. 1987. "Circe's Pigs: From Slavery to Serfdom in the Later Roman World." In *Classical Slavery*, ed. M. Finley, 88–122. Totowa, NJ: F. Cass.
Whittaker, C. R., and Peter Garnsey. 1999. "Rural Life in the Later Roman Empire." In *Cambridge Ancient History, Vol. 13, The Late Empire, A.D. 337–425*, ed. Averil Cameron and Peter Garnsey, 277–311. Cambridge: Cambridge University Press.
Wickham, Chris. 2005. *Framing the Early Middle Ages: Europe and the Mediterranean World, 400–800*. Oxford: Oxford University Press.
Williams, Margaret. 2005. "The Jewish Family in Judaea from Pompey to Hadrian—the Limits of Romanization." In *The Roman Family in the Empire: Rome, Italy, and Beyond*, ed. M. George, 159–182. Oxford: Oxford University Press.
Wolff, Hans Julius. 1950. "Doctrinal Trends in Postclassical Roman Marriage Law," *Zeitschrift der Savigny-Stiftung für Rechtsgeschichte, romanistische Abteilung* 67: 261–319.

CHAPTER 21

POVERTY, CHARITY, AND THE INVENTION OF THE HOSPITAL

PEREGRINE HORDEN
Royal Holloway, University of London

> Are we harming anyone in building lodgings [*katagogia*] for strangers, for those who visit us while on a journey and for those who require some care [*therapeias*] because of sickness, and when we extend to them the necessary comforts, such as [male] nurses [*nosokomountas*], those who give medical assistance [*iatrouontas*], beasts of burden, and escorts? All these must apply the skills needed for life and those that have been devised for living decently; they must also have buildings suitable for their work, all of which are an honor to the place, and, as their reputation is credited to our governor, confer glory on him.[1]

I.

THE year is 371 or 372.[2] Basil, the new bishop of Caesarea (modern Kayseri, Turkey), writes to the provincial governor Elias. From the letter's opening, we can infer that Elias has wanted to see the bishop and hear his answers to accusations made against him. Relations between Basil and Elias have, in any case, been strained. Basil's management of the local church and its endowment has now come under scrutiny, and claims have evidently been made that Roman government is being damaged. In writing to Elias, Basil concedes, with heavy irony, that his accusers may have a point. He has erected a magnificent church in a suburb of Caesarea with suitable accommodation for bishop and clergy and a guest suite for the governor. Admittedly, that may have been going too far. But who could possibly object to this charitable "multiplex," with its appropriate personnel and infrastructure, all of which redounds to the governor's glory?

The background to this exchange is not altogether easy to reconstruct. We have to rely on carefully redacted letter collections (in which we have only half the correspondence); on sermons that are hard to date because they mix timeless verities with topicality and were selected for copying with a view to their future pastoral usefulness, not the needs of social historians; and on naturally laudatory accounts by Basil's brother, Gregory of Nyssa, and his friend, Gregory Nazianzen. The latter's funeral oration was reworked for publication after being delivered on the third anniversary of Basil's death in 379.[3] None of these writings displayed much duty to exact chronology or circumstantial detail. It seems, however, that Basil had served as chief advisor to his predecessor as bishop, Eusebius. With him, too, relations had become fraught, although Basil had recently assumed de facto leadership of the local church because Eusebius was elderly and ill.[4] This phase of Basil's career coincided with a period of food stress and epidemic disease that lasted several years into the 370s and so into Basil's early years as bishop. It would be remembered as very severe.[5]

Through sermons deploying all the rhetorical skills that he owed to his Athenian education, Basil induced the local wealthy elites to release onto the market their local grain hoards (from caves that are still such a feature of the area) rather than wait for the price to reach the stratosphere. He may have drawn on his own patrimony to purchase some of it. "Open to the world the dark cave of mammon . . . the hungry are wasting away before your face."[6] He also established a soup kitchen, or at least some organized distributions of soup and meat, working in it himself along with fellow clergy, perhaps supporting "even" Jewish children (a striking detail in Gregory of Nyssa).[7] In this, Basil was following the precocious example of his grandparents' philanthropy in exile in the mountains of Pontus during a time of persecution and, indeed, more recently the philanthropy of his siblings.[8]

Despite the sharply expressed theological differences between them, his activities attracted the attention of the aging emperor Valens (whose name Basil drops artfully in the letter quoted here). For Valens, Caesarea was important as a staging post en route to and from his capital in Antioch and as a source of munitions and horses. At some point, perhaps even before Basil became bishop in 370, the emperor donated land that provided space or revenue for his philanthropic initiatives.[9] Yet Basil still had to struggle for local control of the church with Valens and his "vicar." Perhaps he had not consulted the emperor about the specific use to which his donation would be put. Moreover, Basil's conversion of ad hoc famine relief measures into permanent structures for the overnight shelter of the needy remained controversial for some while. Witness the squabble that erupted between a later director of his hospital, Sacerdos, and the man who would succeed Basil as bishop.[10]

Basil's plans for this philanthropic complex were nothing if not ambitious. After his death, it could be lauded by Gregory Nazianzen as a "new city" and came to bear its founder's own name, being known as the Basileias or some variant on that.[11] With its adjacent monastery and all the workshops, outbuildings, and accommodation, it may indeed have looked like a new city, a secondary conurbation outside the old city center of Caesarea. It may even underlie the nucleus of modern Kayseri, although it is not clear from any other evidence, documentary or archaeological, when that was established.[12]

In this "new city," and in seeming abundance, lay "the common treasury for those with possessions . . . even what people need to live on [implying that, for poorer donors too, their accumulated gifts are earning them a heavenly reward]; a place where disease is studied philosophically [*philosopheitai*: both Christian and medical wisdom?] . . . where compassion is held in genuine esteem." It was "the easiest way up to heaven," for donors as much as for terminally ill inmates.[13] Yet it is hard to tell what exactly the suburban complex comprised. Basil himself described the central charity as a *katagogion* (hostel or lodging house) and a *ptochotropheion* (literally, place where the indigent are looked after). He also refers in his shorter rule for monks to a *xenodocheion*, hospice for strangers, which is likely to be identical with, or at least very similar to, the main "public" hospital, since Basil evinces concern for the sins of its inmates. This hospital seems to have had a chapel. There was also, less ambiguously, a separate establishment for lepers, some of them disfigured beyond recognition. And we can add to the list the orphans looked after in the monastery's school.[14]

On the other hand, we must not add any special medical facility. Basil knew some Galenic medicine.[15] Often in ill health himself, he may have consulted a variety of healers. He was too interested in, and impressed by, learned medicine to ignore its therapeutic potential. This is not a hospital in a modern sense, yet nor is it simply a hospice for the terminally ill, "a stairway to heaven." In his hospital, Basil offered inmates "doctoring" as well as nursing: "doctoring" rather than "doctors." In many ways that was, admittedly, a distinction without a difference. Basil's world lacked any form of professional medical accreditation, and the title "doctor" could be earned only through clinical success. Still, the language suggests attendants in the hospital with a variety of skills rather than specialists.

Who were the beneficiaries of this care, this therapy? In the first place, they were the victims of prolonged "food stress"—not famine in the sense of absolute shortage but as a failure of "entitlement," since the rich had grain stored in their barns that they were reluctant to release until Basil's preaching.[16] An account of a later famine in Edessa (modern Urfa) may evoke some of the demographic circumstances: "the infirm in the villages, along with the elderly and the young, women and children, and those racked by hunger . . . went into the cities to live by begging."[17] At least some of their equivalents in Caesarea would have been sustained by hospital life in the Basileias.

Even when swollen by refugees, Caesarea was not a very large city. In 1500, the earliest date for which any statistics are available, it could boast only 2,287 tax-paying adults. In normal times, it may well not have generated many poor and needy people. Yet it lay in the middle of the horse-rearing countryside for which Cappadocia was famed, with no network of subordinate towns that could help absorb migrants in periods of crisis.[18] It was a major crossroads in Cappadocia's highways linking the capital and Syria and would have seen a considerable number of transients, some of the "strangers" to which Basil's hospital may well explicitly have catered.[19]

Little else can be said. The poor are amply present in the sermons and orations of these years: present in harrowing but stereotypical vignettes.[20] As individuals with life histories—or, indeed, with any personality—they are beneath notice. In the immediate aftermath of the food crisis, all sorts of people might have sought temporary relief at Basil's soup kitchen. But soon, what was becoming an exemplary institution may have accepted only exemplary patients: suitable paupers whose names were already on the bishop's approved list.[21] Basil called his hospital a *ptochotropheion*. *Ptochos* was a commonly used term for the absolutely indigent, dependent for survival on handouts or begging; the *ptochos* was to be contrasted with the *penes*, the "laboring pauper" who had just about adequate resources in good times but not enough to survive a crisis unaided.[22] That might suggest the very poorest as the group targeted for admission. But Basil, like so many others, was inconsistent in his terminology. He stressed the importance of distinguishing the genuinely needy from avaricious scroungers. He generally advocated selectivity in his advice to monastic almoners.[23] In his sermons, he refers to *penetes* more often than to *ptochoi*, and in his shorter rule for monks, echoing Origen, he defines the *ptochos* as he who has fallen from wealth into need (the "shame-faced" pauper of later ages) and is therefore less worthy than the *penes*, who has always been needy.[24]

We can therefore not be sure who was favored in his hospital: Christians, primarily, rather than Jews or pagans; free men and women rather than slaves;[25] perhaps those in "shallow" (or "conjonctural") poverty needing temporary assistance (*penetes*). Overall, it is far from clear that the openhandedness of his famine relief measures was carried over into the governance of his hospital. It is in keeping with his austere, even grim program that the town's lepers, at the extremity of need and sickness, are not mentioned in his surviving writings and that, in his funeral oration, Gregory Nazianzen praises the Basileias for removing the appalling sight of them from the city's streets.[26] Basil emerges as perhaps having more in common than we might expect with a later, more conventional bishop of Caesarea, Firmus (d. 439). In one of his surviving letters, Firmus shows that he does not want the Basileias to be a haven for footloose peasants who have abandoned their landlords and their tax obligations.[27]

II.

"Are we harming anyone?" Basil had asked. What indeed could be more innocent or straightforward than a hospital or hostel for the poor and sick erected in the suburbs? Centuries of Christian teaching, going back to Christ's injunction to the rich man who would be perfect (Matthew 19:21) and encapsulated in the widely read "sentence" of Sextus—"God does not listen to the plea of one who does not himself listen to the plea of those in need"[28]—made it clear that assistance to those most affected by disaster or indigence benefited recipient and donor alike. It might now, in the "hungry '70s," seem natural to give such assistance architectural expression.

A hospital in its basic and, in world-historical terms, most widespread form is a place, an area, designated for the overnight care of the needy.[29] Its ethos is nearly always charitable, and it is to be distinguished from "outdoor" relief centers from which food or goods are distributed. The recipients of the hospital's services are therefore in some sense poor—but they are not necessarily sick. The definition of the modern hospital (from around 1850 onward) as essentially medical—as constituting a vanguard of medical expenditure and research—should not be applied to earlier periods, despite the obsession of many hospital historians with separating out from the rest the "true" hospitals, those with attendant doctors, regardless of the period being studied.[30]

Still, the history of hospitals is far from straightforward, as the outline of Basil's activity on becoming the new bishop of Caesarea should have begun to show. It was less than a decade since the death of a pagan emperor, Julian—and who could be confident that he was the last of his type? There may have been a Christian majority in the population of Caesarea, but, if so, it was probably not an overwhelming one. Christian charity, especially in its most assertive, architectural form, had to earn approbation from several constituencies. These included the imperial court; the governor's office; the local notables, many of them pagan; admirers of the previous bishop, who does not seem to have done much for the poor; the "middling sort" in city and suburbs, whose contributions were in aggregate very important to Church finances (in particular to the stipends of the clergy);[31] and even the various categories of the poor themselves, not all of whom will have been entitled to benefit from Basil's foundation.

The politics of institutional charity in Caesarea in about 370 were shifting and complicated to a degree that we can never hope to recover from the surviving texts. We can, though, sense something of the risk that Basil was taking. The hospital would soon become part of the Christian Church's "reformatting" of the ancient city, replacing a representation of society in terms of citizen and noncitizen with one resting on the polarity of rich and poor (in both city and countryside). Basil's philanthropic project was uncomfortably ambiguous. He was acting in some respects like a wealthy civic benefactor, using his personal means to establish an amenity that was above all a memorial to his wealth and generosity. He was an old-style euergetist, a "nourisher" of his city.[32] The pagan tradition of civic public building and distributions had begun to atrophy in Asia Minor, as in other parts of the empire, during the third century.[33] Even so, enough of it presumably remained, in ideal if not in practice, to provide a template against which Basil's activities sat very awkwardly. His objective was radically new: a foundation that explicitly benefited the pauper, not the citizen. He was advertising his claims to civic leadership, as a "lover of the poor" rather than a lover of his city.[34] It is no coincidence that the Basileias was soon echoed by smaller hospitals dotted across the Cappadocian countryside and overseen by another fourth-century innovation, "country bishops."[35] Neither the old city nor its new suburb, but rather the poor wherever they were, defined the bishop's sphere of action.

III.

This is looking ahead, to some wider ramifications of Basil's initiative. And looking ahead, though tempting, makes it hard to recapture (so familiar does the hospital seem) the sheer novelty of Basil's conception. Let us therefore go back and start at the very beginning of the story—or at least attempt to do so, since the evidence is fragmentary, mostly written some time after the actions described, and often sharply partisan.[36] It has been claimed that we should start in the 320s, with the infirmary (and perhaps the guest house) of what is usually taken as the first monastery, that of Pachomius at Tabennesi (north of Thebes in Egypt). Thus, it is argued, the "place where the sick brothers lie" referred to in, for instance, the Bohairic Coptic *Life* of Pachomius should count as the first Christian hospital.[37] Those who redacted, or even framed, the various rules ("precepts") for Pachomian monks also hint at a designated place for the sick. But the evidence of the infirmary, like so much else in the Pachomian dossier, is uncertain. The biographers and redactors may on some points speak to us of developments after the founder's death in 346. And in any case, still more to the point, Pachomius was not establishing a "public" hospital for the poor. Some paupers might have taken temporary refuge in the guest house, alongside those of greater means. But that is again not a facility with any broad ambition for the relief of the needy. Basil had visited Egypt in the mid-350s after his conversion to the ascetic life as a pilgrim collecting monastic experiences, but he would not have traveled as far south as the Pachomian monasteries; and like so many others in the later fourth century, he seems to have been largely ignorant of what Pachomius had achieved.[38]

For the first instance of a foundation that really seems to anticipate Basil's, we have to look a little later. We are now in the middle of the fourth century.

> The blessed Leontius, the bishop of Antioch in Syria, a man who was in all respects faithful . . . for the true faith [which others dubbed Arianism], who also had responsibility for the hospices [*xenodocheia*] for the care of strangers, appointed men who were devout in their concern for these, among whom were three men exceedingly zealous in piety.

So, under the year 350, writes the author of the *Chronicon Paschale*, perhaps a clerical bureaucrat in the Great Church in Constantinople in the early seventh century, but dependent on local official chronologies as well as on the somewhat unreliable historian Philostorgius.[39] Leontius is mentioned to introduce the three men who help run the hospitals in Antioch; and they in turn appear in the narrative only because they miraculously convert a scornful Jew, who comes to work alongside them in one of those hospitals. We should not put too much emphasis on the date 350. Leontius was patriarch of Antioch from 344 to 358. The hospitals are not represented as his personal creation. But then, to the author of the *Chronicon Paschale*, writing over two and a half centuries later, they are a mere incidental detail, by his time a thoroughly familiar part of the ecclesiastical landscape. He is not interested in their specific origins. On the other hand, there was no reason for him to invent this rather slight incidental detail in the short narration of a miracle, which takes us (we may guess) back into the 340s. It is thus one of the very earliest creditable references that we have to Christian hospitals for the local poor or strangers.[40]

At about the same time in Constantinople, one Macedonius was, after a bloody and protracted struggle and the intervention of the emperor Constantius II, installed as bishop.[41] Some of the support that facilitated his installation apparently came from monasteries that he had already founded in the city. These monasteries were administered by a deacon called Marathonius, "a zealous superintendent [*epitropos*] of the hospitals for the poor [*ptocheia*] and the monastic houses of men and women," according to the mid-fifth-century ecclesiastical historian Sozomen.[42] It is not clear that Macedonius the bishop himself founded hospitals; nor is it clear when those under the deacon Marathonius were established. But we do know that Marathonius, formerly a bureaucrat from the office of the praetorian prefect, was converted to the life of asceticism, monasteries, and charity by Eustathius of Sebaste, some time before 356, and presumably around the time that Macedonius was struggling to become bishop of Constantinople.[43]

Eustathius (c. 300–c. 380) was a powerful and controversial figure, but to us he is wrapped in some obscurity.[44] His father had been bishop of Sebaste (modern Sivas in Turkey) in Byzantine Armenia Minor. He was linked, by his many detractors, to the "Arian" movement in Alexandria. In his middle years, he shuttled among Constantinople, Cappadocia, Armenia, and Pontus. In 339, and then again in 343, his following was condemned by provincial Church councils for, in the words of Sozomen, founding "a society of monks" and propounding "a monastic philosophy."[45] His supporters, at least as characterized by those who condemned them, were extremely ascetic, and also radical in their treatment of slaves and women. It was some refraction of their ideas that underlay the monasteries of Constantinople, the first monasteries in the city. Despite being anathematized by the Council of Gangra, Eustathius was chosen as bishop of Sebaste (his father's see) around 356. There, he founded a *ptochotropheion*. This could have been a soup kitchen, but is more likely, given the term's subsequent usage, not least by Basil, to have been a hospice for the poor, or hospital.[46] The connection between Basil and Eustathius is controversial. Basil had been influenced by him in the early stages of his ascetic career, but perhaps not since, and probably not as a philanthropist.

Next in chronological sequence, under the year 360 the *Chronicon Paschale* reports that Constantius was making provision for the hospitals of Constantinople, and this, too, seems to look forward to Basil and the imperial patronage that he would enjoy from Valens.[47]

A final piece of evidence to add to the dossier takes us outside the empire, to the other side of the Euphrates frontier and into the Christian kingdom of Armenia. Here, some time between 353 and 358, the Patriarch Nerses reportedly used grants of royal land to create a network of rural hospitals for the shelter and, indeed, the confinement of the poor, the sick, lepers, and paralytics, who might otherwise turn into troublesome beggars. The report dates from the later-fifth-century anonymous Armenian *Epic Histories* that have traditionally been attributed to P'austus Buzand (sometimes mistransliterated as Faustus of Byzantium).[48] By itself, neither the information nor its chronology would be very reliable. But the retrospective placing of the patriarch's initiative in the 350s fits well with the phase of hospital foundations to the west that we have just reviewed and is not wholly implausible. Basil visited some part of Armenia in 373. There is also some indirect evidence that the Armenian hospitals reflected the example of hospitals both in Constantinople and also in Eustathius' much nearer episcopal see of Sebaste. The probability that radical ascetic ideas associated with Eustathius achieved some currency in the Armenian kingdom is signaled by the fact that the canons of the Council of Gangra anathematizing his adherents were translated into Armenian and incorporated into the Armenian Church's body of canon law.[49]

IV.

Basil's is the early charitable development documented in contemporary or near-contemporary writing. (There is seemingly no archaeology of Caesarea to help us.) If we allow some later but credible evidence into the dossier—from up to the fifth century—then the background to his initiative is to be found only in immediately preceding decades. It does not come from much earlier than the

340s or 350s. That is, the short-term background is the only background. The hospital—a designated charitable arena for the overnight relief of the needy explicitly designated as such—turns out to be a quite recent invention in Basil's time. Emperors and monks and bishops seem to be the leading players. Especially if we here discount the Pachomian infirmary, many of them can be linked to the circle of Basil's erstwhile mentor, Eustathius, and thus to a particular period of no more than thirty years and a particular set of places: Constantinople and a few cities in Asia Minor.

To make explicit the underlying point: the first hospitals were Christian; and they were mid-fourth century. That entails several negatives. First, we are in the reign of Constantius II (337–361) and then, for Basil's enterprise in welfare, of Valens (364–378). We are not in the reign of Constantine, whose largesse to the Christian Church he "established" was unprecedented in scale and included much charity, but no hospitals—or at least so it appears if we reject what, in this context, is late evidence, projecting onto the founding figure an image actually elaborated by his successors.[50]

A fortiori, we are not in pre-Constantinian times. In its first two centuries at least, early Christian charity was limited, discriminating in its reach, introverted. This is no place to defend that assertion fully.[51] We should simply note its important corollary: hospitals ("indoor" or overnight relief on an institutional scale) seem to have had no place in it. This charity is focused for the most part on distributions—outdoor relief—of money, food, and clothing. The infrastructure of house churches, characteristic of the first two Christian centuries and, to a considerable extent, of the third as well, probably could not support a room or building designated for overnight support. There is no sign of any such accommodation in the tiny early Christian complex at Dura Europos, and nor should we expect there to be.[52] The culture of early Christian charity was, indeed, in some respects the converse of the hospital: a culture of mobility, which comes down to us in letters of "peace" or "recommendation" carried by travelers who are of the faith.[53]

The accommodation required by such people was, or was meant to be, of limited duration, and to be offered mainly by the bishop. But a guest room is not, ideologically speaking, in terms of its public expression, a hospital—although it might have resembled one in a material sense. And when, in early Christian writings, we can catch sight of charity in action, the emphasis is always on the great outdoors of need dispersed across the city. Tertullian outlines the varieties of aid to which the common charitable pot was dedicated in the Carthaginian church of his day (toward 200):[54] no "indoor" relief, no overnight shelter, but support and burial for the poor and help for orphans and the elderly, the shipwrecked, and those condemned to the mines, exile, or imprisonment. Cyprian of Carthage is the best documented charitable bishop from the pre-Constantinian centuries, and even in the extreme circumstances of an epidemic, he does not seem to have provided a roof over the heads of any of the needy.[55] In the middle years of the third century, he was using poor relief—presumably any form of it at his ready disposal—to demonstrate and consolidate the Christian population under his bishopric. But there is no mention of a hospital in his surviving correspondence. From the middle of the third century again (251, to be exact) we have the well-known letter from the bishop of Rome, Cornelius, listing all those maintained by his church, from priests down to doorkeepers and "more than 1500 widows and indigent people."[56] But as well as noting the scale of his operation, in what was probably the largest Christian community in the empire at that time, we should also register what the list seemingly does not contain: no administrators, attendants, or inmates of a hospital, at least not as such. Roman indigents were more likely to have benefited from "outdoor" relief. Distributions were the thing, such as that presumably intended to be made from the store of aristocratic cast-offs itemized in the early-fourth-century inventory of the church at Cirta, North Africa.[57] The Egyptian papyri in many respects take us as close we can get anywhere in the later Roman world to the everyday life of the Church. It is significant that in the surviving fragments there is no mention of hospitals from much earlier than the sixth century.[58]

In all this, the only place of overnight relief was the bishop's house. General episcopal hospitality was urged in Pauline epistles,[59] and shelter of the destitute was attributed to bishops in a parable of *The Shepherd of Hermas*.[60] How was it manifested in practice?

> Coming home late one night, he found a poor woman lying in the street, so much exhausted that she could not walk: he took her upon his back, and carried her to his house, where he discovered that she was one of those wretched females who had fallen into the lowest state of vice, poverty and disease. Instead of harshly upbraiding her he had her taken care of with all tenderness for a long time, at a considerable expense, till she was restored to health.

This was no bishop, but Dr. Johnson as reported by Boswell.[61] It is quite hard to find late antique evidence of such hospitality in action. A letter preserved by Eusebius from the bishop of Corinth to Soter, the bishop of Rome, written in about 170, praises his paternal care for all visitors (not especially the poor).[62] Cyprian, from his exile, urges his priests to support strangers from his personal funds.[63]

V.

So far, all the examples have been Christian and, indeed, the evidence, such as it is, in general suggests that the hospital of this period is a Christian invention of the fourth century. For support, we can look briefly at three other religio-cultural traditions: Zoroastrianism, paganism, and Judaism.

The first can be disposed of briefly. The relevance of Zoroastrianism is to those hospitals of Nerses in the kingdom of Armenia. In Nerses' time, the kingdom lay firmly within the orbit of Sasanid Iran, and part of it would soon be ruled directly by the Iranian shahs. Nerses was a "protector of the poor" in a Christian, but also in an Iranian-Zoroastrian, tradition.[64] Yet, while Zoroastrian charity took many documented forms, several of which resemble Christian charity, the endowment of hospitals was apparently not among them. There are no known Iranian precedents for Nerses' charitable initiative. For inspiration, he might well therefore, as already surmised, have looked westward, into Roman Asia Minor.[65]

As for paganism, now is the moment to introduce one of the greatest tributes paid to Christian charity by one of Christianity's most resolute imperial opponents. In 362, having arrived at Ancyra (modern Ankara) en route to the Persian frontier, the Emperor Julian famously wrote to Arsacius, the high priest of Galatia:[66]

> In every city establish frequent hospitals [*xenodocheia*] in order that strangers [migrant poor?] may benefit from our benevolence [*philanthropia*] . . . whoever is in need. . . . For it is disgraceful that, when no Jew ever has to beg and the impious Galilaeans [i.e., Christians] support not only their own poor but ours as well, our own people should seem destitute of support from us.

That passage is well known to specialists and frequently cited. Less often noticed is the striking range of institutions that the emperor is said (polemically, by Gregory Nazianzen) to want to found. They include not only hospitals for the needy, but inns, houses of virgins, "sacred places" (*hagneuteria*), and academies—a strange refraction of the Judaeo-Christian exemplar.[67] Also less often noticed is the emperor's admiration (reported, it must again be conceded, only by Christians) for the Christian network of contacts and especially of episcopal hospitality represented by the practice of equipping the traveler with letters of recommendation. This, according to Sozomen, was the aspect of Church organization that he chiefly admired.[68] But his own letter attests that what has brought him up short is the recent proliferation of hospitals in certain cities of the empire, especially in Syria and Armenia.

There was no pagan tradition on which Julian could draw. Temples may have offered shelter or distributions to pilgrims (who might be poor on arrival, if not on departure from home). But they did not do this as an explicit contribution to poor relief. Accommodation at healing shrines was there to facilitate prolonged attendance at the shrine. It was not part of the healing, and presumably it had to be paid for, if only in kind.[69]

For a relatively brief period, the Romans had occasionally built hospitals (*valetudinaria*) for slaves and soldiers: buildings within which the two categories of laborers who mattered most to the functioning of the empire might be repaired when broken down and then sent back to work.[70] Slave hospitals were favored by some of the richest owners from the first century B.C.E. to the end of the first century C.E. That is, they came to be built when the supply of slaves through conquest had diminished, prices had risen, and it was worth maintaining those who could work and breed. When the empire's crucial labor force became *coloni*, tied to the land and living in quasi-peasant households, slave hospitals were no longer economical or indeed necessary.

The chronology of the rise and fall of military hospitals is later, but can be explained in similar structural-cum-economic terms. These hospitals date from the time of Augustus until around the middle of the third century C.E. They correspond to the period when the army was often operating well beyond the frontier in areas largely bereft of friendly settlements where sick and wounded soldiers could be helpfully accommodated. When, in the third century, the army was reorganized and a local militia, supported where needed by a mobile field army, defended the frontier, the construction of fortress hospitals ceased. Sick soldiers were thereafter cared for by their families or in their tents—just as sick *coloni* were tended by their wives or relatives. The age of Roman hospitals was over. Even at its height, moreover, neither kind of hospital was at all widespread. The Roman writer known as Hyginus implied that a hospital was to be found in every fortress. Yet the archaeological evidence is slight—slighter than used to be thought because the identification of a number of proposed sites of *valetudinaria* has been questioned.[71] About the number and distribution of slave hospitals even less is known. These hospitals—to repeat—belong to a highly specific niche in Roman history. They reflect a calculation of the economies of scale to be made by the directed reconstitution of the workforce. Such a calculation is quite removed from late antique thinking about the poor, and will not be repeated until the later Middle Ages in Italy, when hospitals will once again attempt a rapid turnover of sick laborers.

Finally, the Jews. Were not Jewish hospitals the model for Christian ones?

> Theodotos, son of Vettenos the priest and *archisynagogos* . . . built the synagogue . . . and as a hostel with chambers and water installations for the accommodation of those who, coming from abroad, have need of it.

So runs a well-known inscription from first-century Jerusalem.[72] It has been claimed as marking the first Jewish medical hospital. But there is no reason to think that doctors attended those staying in it. Three aspects of the establishment should, rather, be stressed. First, as a "hostel with chambers," it resembles the already-mentioned hostels that could be found near any major shrine in the ancient world. The Temple in Jerusalem was perhaps the largest temple of its time, and virtually the sole focus of Jewish pilgrimage. It undoubtedly attracted far more visitors than did most pagan shrines, which would come fully to life only once or twice a year for a great festival. Its facilities were presumably offered in a more charitable spirit than the pagan ones were. Still, it is no surprise that the Jerusalem synagogue of the first century C.E., whether before or after the destruction of the Second Temple in the year 70, should cater to needy visitors. The second, more surprising feature is that there seems to have been no wider system of organized charity in Jerusalem at the time; individual initiatives such as that of Theodotos were crucial.[73] Third, there is little or no specific evidence of other such hospices attached to synagogues in the first three or four centuries C.E.—despite a number of rabbinic texts showing that travelers might be lodged within a synagogue precinct.[74] Clear archaeological, epigraphic, and documentary evidence is simply lacking. If lodging was to be had at synagogues, it was perhaps offered informally, ad hoc—as in the bishop's house. There was, apparently, no distinct, and distinctively named, hospital. The paradox of the Jerusalem hostel is, therefore, that it blends far better into a pagan than a Jewish context. And it looks forward to Christian hospitals of almost three centuries later rather than standing in a demonstrable tradition of its own. Perhaps not coincidentally, the one Jewish charitable institution of Late Antiquity that can be documented, albeit tentatively, is a soup kitchen rather than a hospital.[75]

With the exception, then, of the Roman *valetudinaria*—specialized in function, immensely different in character from later Christian hospitals, and long defunct by the time of the first Christian hospitals—there were probably no hospitals at all in the Mediterranean world or the Middle East before the reign of Constantius II. To that extent, the Christian hospitals of the fourth century really do mark a break with the past.

VI.

How can we measure the success of this novel development? Julian is probably the first and most significant, if hostile, witness to its rapid impact. Granted, he was reacting to Jewish as well as to Christian charity. But it was perhaps only Christian hospitals that he could imitate. A sermon once attributed to John Chrysostom, and presumably of his time, refers to Christian *xenodocheia* as being evident throughout the inhabited world.[76] That was claiming too much. But it is arresting to find the learned Nilus of Ancyra (d. c. 430) redeploying in his correspondence the older metaphor of Christ the physician as active in the "hospital" of the world.[77] The idea had caught on, and it changed the way bishops responded to crisis. If we can trust the detail of Palladius on this, Ephrem the Syrian improvised a hospital in Edessa in a time of food shortage, arranging some 300 beds and covering for them in the city's porticoes. It is unlikely that a bishop would have responded in such a way a few decades earlier.[78] Ephrem's initiative would have been in 372–373, when Basil's hospital complex might not have been finished. By 398, there was at least one hospital in Constantinople besides the monastic foundations outlined earlier. On arrival as bishop, Chrysostom studied the church's accounts (a revealing detail in Palladius' *Life*—would they had survived), transferred to the hospital (*nosokomeion*) the surplus he found in those accounts, and later established other hospitals, installing in them monastic doctors, cooks, and attendants.[79] It was not, however, only in such major centers that the need was felt. Fifth-century Syrian canons decree that *xenodocheia* should be established in each town, and *plebia* (poor houses) are legislated about at the Council of Chalcedon.[80] Occasional inscriptions also reveal to us hospitals in quite minor or remote towns—well below the radar of chronicler or hagiographer.[81]

Most such hospitals will have been small. True, we read from time to time of multistory structures and hospitals of seventy or even two hundred beds.[82] To estimate the numbers of patients, we should also probably double the number of beds, as almost all but the most lavish medieval founders would do. Nor should we take the enumeration of beds for granted, when the more flexible (and space-saving?) provision of straw or pallets was always a possibility.[83] Yet the large places were exceptional. So was the hospital in Constantinople, glimpsed in the prism of seventh-century hagiography, that was big enough to have more than one ward and to offer surgery and specialist help for eye diseases.[84] Other foundations were big enough to segregate the patients by gender.

To conclude that most hospitals were small is not to reduce them to a single model. Although they were all supposed to come under episcopal supervision, hospitals were variously planned, founded, endowed and supported by members of the imperial family, aristocrats, clerics, monks, and private lay families or individuals. We have already seen a variety of labels in the written evidence: *nosokomeia* explicitly for the sick, *xenodocheia* or *xenones* ostensibly for poor transients, *ptocheia* or *ptochotropheia* for the indigent, and leper houses. We can add lying-in hospitals, orphanages, old people's homes, and (mostly after our period) a few houses for the blind and for repentant prostitutes. What we do not find, though it might have been expected, is any sign of a hospital explicitly for plague victims, although foundations of the later sixth century may indirectly reflect the pandemic's ravages: the "plague of Justinian" is a non-event in the world of hospitals, as it is in the medical world.[85]

This variety may tell us more about the ambitions of founders to distinguish their creations than about the specific needs of beneficiaries. The links between poverty, rootlessness, and ill health in premodern or modern developing societies are obvious enough. They blurred most of the boundaries that founders tried to maintain in the functions they set for their establishments. Perhaps less obvious are the equally resilient links between "high" medicine and basic nursing and between secular and religious therapies—links that confound any attempt to separate medical establishments from the rest. In late ancient medical thinking, attention to the patient's psychology and environment—the provision of spiritual comfort, clean water, and wholesome food—*was* part of medicine. Christ, the physician of souls, stood behind, or rather above, the secular physician of bodies, and the two kinds of therapy complemented each other. Granted, a self-styled doctor might cost more than a lay attendant, and hospital benefactors will have taken this into account. But those founders who added *iatroi* to the personnel of their institutions were not necessarily raising them into a superior category of therapeutic excellence. The hospital, as a supposed "revolution in the organization of medical care," in fact had no discernible impact upon—indeed, is not mentioned in—the surviving medical writing of Late Antiquity.[86]

That is also why it is implausible to suggest that Justinian so highly esteemed the medicine available in hospitals that he somehow transferred (in an edict for which there is no direct evidence) the "public physicians" (*archiatroi*) to the hospitals, ensuring the place of hospital medicine in the front line of medical teaching and practice for centuries to come. It was not like that. The medicine of the hospitals we are looking at blends into the wider scene, not only of basic medication and nursing but also of the charitable provision of rest and protection from the elements, vital for sick poor and healthy poor alike. Of course, hospital medicine was not everywhere the same. Those in the capital with doctors on call will have been the more sophisticated in their resources—pharmacopoeias, *instrumentaria*—culminating (perhaps) well after the end of our period in the hospital of the twelfth-century Pantocrator monastery. For the majority, I suggest, it is unhelpful to ask whether medicine was available to the inmates and who dispensed it.[87]

How many hospitals were there? Counting such places in Byzantium has a venerable history. It began in 1680 with Du Cange's *Constantinopolis Christiana*, which listed some thirty-five charitable foundations in the capital. Janin's more recent, but not wholly reliable, tabulation for Constantinople finds thirty-one hospitals (*xenones* and others) and twenty-seven old people's homes.[88] The most recent gathering of material from the provinces, reaching forward to the ninth century, supplies a total of more than 160 charitable facilities, of which the most numerous are *xenodocheia* and *xenones* (71), *nosokomeia* (44), and *ptocheia* (21).[89] All such aggregates are to be greeted with caution. Some small hospitals will have eluded those who produced the extant documents; others—such, anyway, is the lesson of later hospital history—will rapidly have gone out of business. Still, these totals are likely to represent a considerable underestimate. The study of inscriptions and sealings will surely bring further instances to light. And already the Egyptian papyri are presenting a much more densely populated picture than other kinds of evidence could supply.

Overall, we seem to have some seventy-five references to hospitals in Egypt from about 550 to about 700, including those of Alexandria.[90] Most of these derive from papyri related to middle Egypt. A few village hospitals are evident, but the majority cluster in the capitals of three districts (nomes). One of these, Hermopolis, seems, in the first half of the seventh century, to have had as many as seven *nosokomeia* in operation at the same time.[91] Although such foundations all eventually fell to some degree under episcopal supervision, many of the hospitals attested in the papyri will have been small private affairs, and the papyri offer an incomparable (if inevitably very partial and fragmentary) ground-level view of their endowment and staffing. We learn of one hospital run, exceptionally, by a family of *archiatroi*, and another with a female administrator. We may at least entertain the possibility that other relatively small towns and villages across the empire (not to mention the metropolis) were as well supplied with charitable accommodation.

VII.

If that were so, it would complicate the question of why hospitals were founded. The private Egyptian ones, which originally had little to do with bishops or monks, seem, with a few exceptions, to date from the sixth century onward and may therefore represent a second wave of foundations, in which the philanthropic projects of emperors, bishops, and monks of the fourth to fifth centuries were widely required and imitated.

Why were those earlier ones founded? We should at once admit a genuine role for compassion, the "care of the poor" that is such a feature of the "discourse" and practice of the period under review.[92] Of course, there was a degree of self-interest involved, too. The imitation *of* Christ in charitable acts was a form of giving *to* Christ and as such (the Gospels had demonstrated) was a considerable down payment on the "purchase of paradise": Luke 11:41: "give alms and all things will be clean unto you." Both founders of charities and donors to them would hope to have earned the gratitude and prayers of the recipients of their generosity, and the prayers of the poor would benefit their souls in the afterlife more than those of almost anyone else. Founders could also enjoy wider secular renown among their contemporaries, especially if their association with a charity was publicized in its name.[93]

Explanation in this form is too general for hospitals, however. It could apply to a wider range of charitable practices and an extensive variety of charitable foundations, such as the soup kitchen or the distribution of clothing. We need greater precision, an explanation that captures the chronology, types, and distribution of the hospitals we have been looking at. These hospitals cannot—or cannot only—be seen as a normal expression of the charitable imperative; otherwise, we might have found them in pre-Constantinian times. To take an example from outside the Byzantine world that was probably not at all extreme: Augustine's episcopal complex at Hippo (Bone, in modern Algeria) in the early fifth century had 120 or so rooms. There was surely space there for the accommodation of some of the deserving needy (à la Dr. Johnson), and doubtless space was found. Yet it took the energy of a priest, Leporius, whom Augustine had ordained, to bring into being Hippo's first *xenodochium* (the Latinized Greek is telling). Of course, there will have been organizational tasks inherent in that process that now escape us—the assignment of rents and donations, the provision (perhaps) of beds and bedding on a greater scale than ad hoc hospitality demanded, the recruiting of attendants (perhaps even some with medical skills) and of an administrator. Still, the impression given is that to found a hospital is an ideological statement, rather than just the construction or designation of some rooms.[94]

The significance of ideology in the making of hospitals is one reason why an explanation of their proliferation in simple terms of demography will not quite work. The *xenodocheion* is a place for *xenoi*, strangers, migrants, the rootless. Leporius himself had been a refugee. One (probably) fifth-century story from Syria of an anonymous "man of God" has him, as the scion of a senatorial family in Rome, taking ship and ending up in Edessa. There he lived a life of unremitting prayer and austerity among the indigent begging outside the church, an *aksnoyo*, a stranger, who, when ill, was placed in the "place for strangers," the hospital.[95] Having read such narratives, we may be tempted to see the proliferation of hospitals as a reflex response to demographic change, especially migration. Certainly, particular crises could be a stimulus to action, as in Basil's case. Yet it is not clear that, in the fourth or fifth centuries, the countryside of the eastern Mediterranean was on the verge of Malthusian crisis, of a kind that might promote more than the usual influx of migrants to the bigger cities. There is no sign of general overpopulation. We find strong demographic growth and agricultural expansion, undeniably, but they express themselves in prosperous villages and farmsteads that were unlikely to have been generating enough casualties of the system to account, by themselves, for the development of new kinds of poor relief.[96]

The strangers of the "place for strangers," the *xenodocheion*, must be differently conceived. Man is a wanderer, Basil had asserted in a heated exchange with the Prefect Modestus, "confined to no place."[97] All Christians are strangers (*xenoi*) and sojourners, in need of hospitality and accommodation, but not in a commercial, seedy inn or *pandocheion*—to which the hospital is perhaps a deliberate antithesis.[98] We thus need to turn from potential economic or social causes to explanations that have more to do with the Church and theology.

One such associates many of the very earliest hospitals, in fourth-century Constantinople and some cities of Asia Minor, with Arianism—that is, with a Christologically distinct "party" of monks and bishops and a related type of asceticism that could have emphasized poor relief. The difficulty with this approach is that, outside the crude polemics of the self-appointed orthodox, Arianism did not yet exist as a particular affiliation in the middle of the fourth century. There was only a wide spectrum of views on the Christology at issue, and the only evidence of an association between their various proponents and a style of charity is the charity itself, so the argument is circular as well as reductive.[99]

More pertinent, and transcending all such supposed divisions among fourth-century clerics, is the way poor relief generally and hospitals in particular displayed the breadth of the Church's social concerns, its "bracketing" of the whole free population (not slaves), its promotion of a new "aesthetic of society" in which "rich and poor" had replaced "citizen and noncitizen" as the defining polarity.[100] The fourth-century Church benefited from valuable tax immunities. It needed a highly visible symbol of its deployment of the wealth generated not only by these immunities but also by massive imperial and aristocratic largesse, as well as by the small donations of ordinary believers. It needed some form of "conspicuous expenditure." The hospital highlighted the needy as the defining group in the new Christian representation of society. It legitimated the Church's wealth by showing that it was being channeled into purposes that no one could reasonably question.

This explanation applies best in cities, where episcopal leadership had to be asserted and maintained and where wealth was concentrated. But monasteries situated away from major episcopal centers could, however subliminally, deploy a related justification to their benefactors for their poor relief and care for guests. These, too, were a visible return for blessings received.[101] Of course, there were always balances to be struck. How much wealth should be put into charity as against other forms of generally approved expenditure? Should monks cripple their domestic economy through charity to passing vagrants, who might not even be Christian? Should bishops build churches rather than hospitals? Both churches and hospitals came, in law, to fall into the same category of "divine" (*theioi*) or "sacred houses" (*euageis oikoi*),[102] and we should not be swayed by the decoration of churches or the likely austerity of hospitals into separating them too starkly as expressions of piety. Nonetheless, hard choices often presented themselves. Finding a surplus in the accounts, Chrysostom opted for more hospitals. In the Syriac story of the "man of God" in Edessa the great monk-bishop Rabbula is presented as converting from "other business" to charity after finding the empty grave of the anonymous holy man, who had died in hospital. "He desisted from constructing many buildings."[103] Admittedly, his purported reasoning had nothing to do with the involuntary poor. It was of greater concern that any indigent in the hospital might be a saint incognito: "who knows whether there are many like this saint who delight in abasement, but are nobles to God in their souls, not recognized by the people." Rabbula was indeed reputed, by his own biographer, to have shunned great building projects, to have transformed what was a hospital in name only into a well-endowed establishment with clean linen and soft beds, and to have created a hospital for women.[104] A hospital was thus, as we might put it, a step up from outdoor distribution, an architectural expression of the welfare promotion of churches and monasteries. But it was also a step down, or perhaps sideways, from extravagant church building.[105]

Decisions about the direction to take could be controversial. We have seen that in Basil's case. There must have been many other such disputes. When Chrysostom built a suburban leper hospital, the local landowners were reportedly angered because property values declined, as well as fearful of contagion.[106] Wherever they emerged, but especially in the civic context, hospitals reconfigured spaces, much more so than other forms of institutional charity, precisely because of their forcible combination of architecture and ideology. Part of the ideological context within which hospitals have to be understood is thus the Christian "production of space." That did not only involve churches and hospitals as spaces for poverty and its relief. It is no coincidence that the first stages of the history of Christian cemeteries for the poor matches, so far as we can tell from the limited evidence, the chronology of early hospitals. The poor gained their own space in death as they, or some of them, gained their own space in life.[107]

Rehearsing various possible explanations for the first hospitals, sight of the poor patients themselves has been somewhat lost. Apart from a handful of laudatory vignettes (e.g., Rabbula's bed linen), we can say little about the regular inmates or patients of hospitals. Who were they, economically, socially? How long did they stay? In what circumstances, death apart, did they leave? Gregory Nazianzen's advocacy of the hospital as a "sweet stairway to heaven" was hardly a demographic analysis of patient outcomes. How were these hospitals staffed, managed, and endowed? Again, stray glimpses of hospital directors apart, we cannot tell.[108] This is no accident. The church accounts that Chrysostom read, like the lists of paupers in receipt of alms that we know to have been compiled in this period, were of no interest to biographers or chroniclers. Holy ones masquerading as beggars were more to their taste. Not even the rubbish tips of Egypt give us much information about the daily running of a hospital, and what they do tell us is financial rather than personal or therapeutic. Nor does archaeology have much to add. Probably the biggest Byzantine hospital to have been excavated is that of St. Sampson in Constantinople. All that the portion dug reveals is a cluster of rooms around a courtyard—if the site has been correctly identified. Separate wards and a substantial numbers of patients? Doubtless, but that is hardly new or surprising information. It has already come to us from the texts.[109]

VIII.

Of such evidence, we want to ask the major question: what difference did hospitals make? By way of immediate answer, it is easy to advance some negative propositions and, in effect, cut hospitals down to size.

Did hospitals, for example, change the overall pattern of the transfer of alms between donors and recipients?[110] An earlier generation of hospital historians thought that hospitals and related types of institutionalized charity undermined the flow of spontaneous and ad hoc almsgiving from haves to have-nots. But support for both the poor and the clergy had, despite the contrary efforts of some aristocratic families, to a considerable extent been channeled through the bishop since the third century, if not the second. Church orders emphasize that the bishop is in a better position than the laity to identify recipients and organize collections and distributions. Not that begging on the streets or in church porticoes disappeared; far from it. The "man of God" begged in church before sickness consigned him to the hospital. But whereas in the third century the bishops and deacons had to cajole to maintain collections of various forms, in the fourth century we find Chrysostom vehemently preaching that individual lay almsgiving has not been made redundant by such initiatives, and is still required. "What I have to say about alms, I am not saying so that you bring them to me, but so that you yourself distribute with your own hands."[111] The world of almsgiving remained a mixed economy, as it had been in pre-Constantinian times, a public-private partnership. The balance of ingredients varied in ways that will always elude us because of how little we know about the history of church finances. But it is at least reasonable to envisage hospitals as not, by themselves, having dramatically altered the overall blend.

On this somewhat negative side of the balance sheet, three further points of a comparative nature can tentatively be made.[112] First, there will have been many blanks on the map: areas where no hospitals or anything like them were to be found. Second, not only do the figures for size support the view that early medieval hospitals were small in comparison with, say, early modern ones; the figures for total numbers are small even by comparison with later periods within the Middle Ages. We know, for instance, of more than 300 hospitals for lepers alone founded in England between 1100 and 1250. That comfortably exceeds current estimates for the whole Byzantine empire, and over a much longer period.[113] Third, whether measured by average size or total numbers, the scale of hospital provision was easily dwarfed by other sources of social welfare. In Late Antiquity, the *annona* (dole) of grain and other foodstuffs in Rome, Constantinople, and even small towns such as Oxyrhynchus reached a far larger number of poorer people than any estimate we can hazard of the total hospital population. Hospital capacity was not only dwarfed by such state-run measures. It was also probably, in aggregate, surpassed even by the church's own "outdoor" distributions to its local poor—those whose names were inscribed, sometimes in their thousands, on registers of the deserving (3,000 in Antioch, for instance).[114]

What can be said in a more positive vein? First, as argued before, we may entertain the possibility that, thanks to imperial patronage, the new establishments of the fourth century onward represented a massive increase in the scope of formal ecclesiastical charity by comparison with that of the pre-Constantinian centuries.

Second, hospitals could, as we have also seen, achieve in certain areas a considerable density. The patient turnover might also have been considerable. In Alexandria, John the Almsgiver established seven forty-bed hospitals for parturient women. The measure originated in a period of famine, but John's biographer writes as if the hospitals were intended to be permanent. So if the women each stayed for a week (as prescribed), the bishop could have facilitated more than 14,000 births a year.[115]

Third, we should envisage the economic and social difference that hospitals could make as not confined to the effects on inmates. Hospitals were sources of employment for priests, doctors (sometimes), nurses, attendants, gravediggers (if less often than has been imagined), builders, and maintenance staff of all kinds—many of whom will have been almost as poor as the designated inmates. A collectivity of quite small hospitals could, in aggregate, markedly have increased local opportunities in a world characterized by chronic underemployment.[116]

Fourth, hospitals reached beyond their walls in their services to the needy. Their functions sometimes (perhaps often) elided with those of "outdoor" relief centers—soup kitchens, bathing facilities for the poor, charitable grain stores, and so forth. We should not think only in terms of inmates when assessing the impression they made.[117]

Fifth, we should register contemporary perceptions that hospitals had a significant effect on the poor. In the Christian kingdom of Armenia in the 350s, the decade in which the Christian hospital emerged in Byzantium, the patriarch Nerses, having very quickly appreciated the "hospital idea," established a network of hospitals to help keep beggars off the streets. When the patriarch's enemy, King Pap, jealously destroyed these hospitals, the effect was, reportedly, to return the poor to beggary throughout the kingdom. The patriarch's hospitals are represented (admittedly more than a century after they were built) as having been all-embracing.[118]

What would have been the effect of a similar mass closure in Byzantium around 450 or 550? The answer must at least partly depend on our assessment of the effective demand for hospital places. This is not by any means necessarily coincident with the demand perceived by registrars of the poor, who tended to ignore or despise the "laboring poor" (with large families) in favor of the biblically sanctioned categories of the needy, such as widows, orphans, and the sick. This effective demand must have varied markedly from area to area and, of course, cannot now be known with any precision.

Demand for hospital beds has often been measured by reference to estimates of the total population or of the likely number of poor and sick in the society in question—on which measure hospitals often fare poorly, because they could seldom have accommodated the 10 percent or so in absolute penury, let alone the extra 20 to 30 percent who might, at some point in the life cycle, need relief. But the massed ranks of the poor are, of course, only the potential demand. The effective demand—the actualization of that potential at any one time—will have been significantly less, because of self-help among the poor, on the one hand, and sources of charity other than hospitals, on the other.

These two sectors of help for the poor are easily mentioned and impossible to describe in detail.[119] Let us look first at what we can call the sources of "vertical" relief—those from above, in social terms: from the state, the Church, individual benefactors. The respective proportions of these contributions can scarcely be estimated for any part of the period that concerns us. Moreover, it is not enough just to consider explicit sources of charity. The history of poor relief is much wider than the history of charity. We have to look for it in unlikely places and periods—for instance, in the minimal care of sick slaves provided by owners (outside the few *valetudinaria*), in the whole grim history of debt bondage, in rural patronage, in distributions and benefactions that reached impoverished members of the citizen body and were provided by local pagan aristocrats who had no concept of charity, in distributions organized by temples. So in this context to ask what difference hospitals made is hardly worthwhile. We cannot separate out the hospital contribution to the vertical component of poor relief. We cannot even say confidently that the establishment of Christianity and the proliferation of charitable institutions from the fourth century onward marked a decisive change in the relative strength of the vertical component, distinguishing later antiquity from classical antiquity, or the medieval from the ancient world. Charity may not have been a virtue in ancient pagan society, but poor relief could, whether directly or indirectly, have been practiced—to an extent that is now wholly obscure.[120]

As for the "horizontal" component in that relief—self-help and mutual aid among social equals—it has been argued on the basis of a wide comparative survey that we should not overestimate its strength or capacity. The large supportive households to which historians have unthinkingly attributed the overwhelming bulk of premodern support for the poor are hardly ever to be found. Pauper households were small and thus vulnerable. Networks of support operated between more than within them. And those networks were fragile and limited. They needed "vertical" buttressing if their beneficiaries were to avoid sinking into criminality or terminal destitution.[121]

IX.

The hospital is an idea, an invention, and not a reflex response to growing poverty in a Christianizing empire. That much is clear from the way the invention was diffused. It spread first, quite rapidly, around the Mediterranean from its Byzantine homeland in Asia Minor: westward to North Africa and Italy, and from Italy to Spain and parts of the Merovingian kingdoms. And it spread eastward, more slowly, into the "land of Islam" and, with Islam, across Asia. These hospitals are the distant but direct forebears of the modern biomedical hospital, the hospice, the night shelter, and a variety of other, related institutions. Their future does not belong here.[122] The history of hospitals has a beginning, which this chapter has attempted to trace, but, as yet, no end. Basil's ironic question, "are we harming anyone?" continues to resonate—as pertinent to the age of the so-called worried well as it was in the fourth century.

NOTES

1. Basil, *Letter* 94, ed. Deferrari or Courtonne.
2. The best biography remains Rousseau 1994.
3. *Oration* 43, ed. Bernardi.
4. The literature on Basil's career and his philanthropy in this period, late 360s to early 370s, is copious, yet many aspects, not least chronology, remain controversial. The most helpful recent discussions are Finn 2006, 222–236; Holman 2001, 68–76; Brown 2002, 35–42, but see also on philanthropy Giet 1941.
5. Garnsey 1988, 22–23; Stathakopoulos 2004, 200–202 (numbers 22–23); Finn 2006, 222.
6. *Homily* 6.6, ed. Courtonne, with Holman 1999, 342.
7. Finn 2006, 224; Holman 2001, 4.
8. Mitchell 1993, 82; Holman 2001, 76.
9. Theodoret, *HE* 4.16, ed. Parmentier and Hansen; Daley 1999, 440–441; for the imperial arms factory in Caesarea itself, see Mitchell 1993, 76.
10. Gregory Nazianzen, *Letter* 216, ed. Gallay.
11. *Oration* 43.63, ed. Bernardi; Sozomen, *HE* 6.34, ed. Bidez and Hansen.
12. Faroqhi 1987, 41; Daly 1999, 459; Finn 2006, 230–231.
13. Gregory Nazianzen, *Oration* 43.63.
14. Basil, *Letters* 94, 150, 176 (chapel), and cf. 143; Crislip 2005, 117; Holman 2001, 153–158. Orphans: Miller 2003, 115–116; Crislip 2005, 112–113.
15. Temkin 1991, 163, for Basil's own medical know-how.
16. Garnsey 1988, 23; Sen 1981.
17. *Chronicle of Pseudo-Joshua the Stylite*, 38, trans. Watt.
18. Faroqhi 1987, 43, 208.
19. Holman 2001, 70.
20. Neri 1998.
21. Brown 2002, 60, 65.
22. Patlagean 1977, chapter 1.
23. Finn, 2006, 69–70; Caner 2008, 228.
24. Holman 2001, 4–5.
25. Brown 2002, 61–2.
26. Holman 2001, 146–147; *Oration* 43.63.
27. *Letter* 43, ed. Calvet-Sebasti and Gabier.
28. Finn 2006, 3; *Sentences of Sextus* line 217, ed. Chadwick.
29. Henderson et al. 2007.
30. E.g., Miller 1997; van Minnen 1995.
31. Brown 2002, 26, 54–55. For the finances of the Cappadocian clergy, Hübner 2005.
32. Subtle discussion in Finn 2006, 224–226.
33. Zuiderhoek 2009, esp. 18, 156–159, 170.
34. Brown 2002; Rapp 2005, 219–228; Gwynn, chapter 27 in this book.
35. Basil, *Letters* 53, 142, 143; Hübner 2005, 62–63.
36. I shall not here look at early south Asian hospital history, on which see references in Henderson et al. 2007, 29–30; Horden 2005, 371.
37. Crislip 2005, 11, 20, with the Bohairic biography and the Greek *Vita prima* of Pachomius (sections 26, 28, respectively), trans. Veilleux. See also Chitty 1966, 22,

with n. 22. On the Pachomian dossier, see Rousseau 1999, chapter 2. I am indebted also to forthcoming work by J. Grossmann.

38. Basil, *Letter* 223; Rousseau 1994, 54–55.

39. *Chronicon Paschale* s. a. 350, ed. Dindorf; trans. Whitby and Whitby.

40. Agreed by Brown 2002, 123, n. 121, *pace* Miller 1997, 21; note also 77 with 234, n. 62, for the possible mosaic evidence of another hospital "of Leontius" in Daphne, a suburb of Antioch.

41. Elm 1994, 111; see also Dagron 1970, 238–239.

42. Sozomen, *HE* 4.20.2, ed. Bidez and Hansen.

43. Elm 1994, 112; Dagron 1970, 246–253.

44. Elm 1994, 106–110; Brown 2002, 36–39; Rousseau 1994, 233ff.

45. *HE* 3.14.31.

46. Epiphanius, *Panarion* 75.3.7, ed. Holl and Dummer, with the skeptical comments on this evidence of Brown 2002, 37–38.

47. Miller 1997, 76, 93, attributes a "network" of hospitals to the Arian George of Cappadocia after his consecration in 357 but is not supported by the passage from Epiphanius cited: 76.1.6. This reads *ton xenon* (of strangers), not *ton xenonon* (of hospitals).

48. Trans. Garsoïan 1989, 115, 211, with Brown 2002, 42–44.

49. Garsoïan 1983, 166; Rousseau 1994, 64.

50. Miller 1997, 21, relies on an early-ninth-century, and on this topic unreliably late, text, for hospitals supposedly founded or supported by Constantine: the *Chronicle* of Theophanes, sub A. M. 5824, ed. de Boor. Constantelos 1991, 89, uses a late biography of Constantine for that emperor's hospitals—again, I believe, unwisely. Constantelos also cites (47) a canon (number 70) of the Council of Nicaea (325) that "hospitals should be established in every city." But this is a reference to the probably inauthentic Arabic text of over 80 canons, dependent on a Syriac original; hospitals do not appear in the original 20 canons. Compare Brown 2002, 123, n. 121; and see also Gwynn, chapter 27 in this book.

51. The historiography is surveyed in Finn 2006, 26–31; Harnack 1908 remains classic. See also Grant 1977, chapter 6; Garnsey and Humfress 2001, 123–127.

52. Bowes 2008, 49–51; Doig 2008, 1–6.

53. Luijendijk 2008, 102–112.

54. *Apologeticum* 39.5–6, ed. Dekkers.

55. *Letters* ed. Clarke, with Brown 2002, 24–25; Finn 2006, 258–259.

56. Eusebius, *HE* 6.43.11.

57. Finn 2006, 81.

58. van Minnen 1995; Luijendijk 2008; Serfass 2008.

59. 1 Timothy 3:2; Titus 1:8.

60. *Similitude* 9.27.2, ed. Lake.

61. *Life of Johnson*, for 1784.

62. *HE* 4.23.10.

63. *Letter* 7.2, trans. Clarke, with Luijendijk 2008, 103–104.

64. Garsoïan 1981, 21–32.

65. Yarshater 1991, s.v. "Charitable Foundations." The first known Sasanian foundation of a hospital is that of the sixth century C.E. reported by (pseudo-) Zacharias Rhetor: *HE* 12.7, ed. Brooks.

66. *Letter* 22, ed. Wright; 84, ed. Bidez. For context, Kislinger 1984, and for a persuasive re-assertion of this letter's authenticity in the face of some scholarly doubt, Bouffartigue 2005.

67. Gregory Nazianzen, *Oration* 4.111, ed. Bernardi, with Finn 2006, 87.
68. *HE* 5.16.3; Luijendijk 2008, 111.
69. Hands 1968, 132.
70. For references to support what follows, see Horden 2005, 372–373.
71. Baker 2004.
72. Reinach 1920, 46–56; trans. from Fine 1996, 9.
73. Seccombe 1978, 140–143. For other synagogue hostels, see Kraeling 1979, 10ff.; Loewenberg 2001, 141ff., 153.
74. Safrai and Stern 1976, 943; Levine 2000, 381ff.
75. Reynolds and Tannenbaum 1987; Finn 2006, 267. On later Jewish hospitals, see Horden 2005, 374–375.
76. *On Matthew* 6.13; PG 59.571.
77. *Letter* 3.33; PG 79.397; though see also Cameron 1976 on the textual problems presented by these letters.
78. *Lausiac History* 40, ed. Bartelink; Stathakopoulos 2004, 202–203 (number 23).
79. *Dialogue on the Life of St John Chrysostom* 5.128–139, ed. Malingrey and Leclercq.
80. Vööbus 1970, 129, 159; *Acts of the Council of Chalcedon*, canon 8, trans. Price and Gaddis.
81. *CIG* 9256 (Asia Minor).
82. Surveys and further references: Nutton 2004, 308; Constantelos 1991; Miller 1997.
83. *Life of the Man of God*, expanded Syriac version: Doran 2006, 38.
84. *Miracles of St Artemius* 21, trans. Crisafulli and Nesbit.
85. Horden 2005.
86. van Minnen 1995, 154; Temkin 1991, chapter 18.
87. Horden 2006, *contra* Miller 1997.
88. Du Cange 1680, 163–166; Janin 1969, 552–567.
89. Mentzou-Meimare 1982.
90. van Minnen 1995.
91. van Minnen 1995, 161, corrected from 8 to 7 by Serfass 2008, 101.
92. Brown 2002.
93. Horden 2007.
94. Brown 2003, 78; Augustine *Sermon* 356.10, PL 39.1578.
95. *Life of the Man of God*, original Syriac version: Doran 2006, 20–23.
96. Lewit 2009; Laiou and Morrisson 2007, chapter 2; Decker 2009.
97. Gregory of Nazianzen, *Oration* 43.49.
98. Arterbury 2005; Hiltbrunner 2005, pt. 4; Dunning 2009; Constable 2003, 18–36.
99. Miller 1997, 76–85, largely and erroneously accepted in Horden 2004. See now Gwynn 2007.
100. For what follows, see Brown 1992, 94; 2002, 29–33; 2005.
101. Caner 2006; 2008.
102. Justinian, *Novel* 120; *Oxford Dictionary of Byzantium*, s.v. "Euageis oikoi."
103. *Life of the Man of God*, original Syriac version: Doran 2006, 24 (see also xv).
104. *The Heroic Deeds of Mar Rabbula*, Doran 2006, 100–101.
105. For context, see Janes 1998.
106. van Ommeslaeghe 1979, 151.
107. Rebillard 1999a; 1999b.

108. Hübner 2005, 32, 59.
109. Miller 1990; Lavan et al. 2007, 194–197.
110. For what follows, see Finn 2006, 27, 39, 40, 44, 107; Brown 1992, 95.
111. *Hom. on I Cor.* 26.6, PG 61.179, with Finn 2006, 107.
112. For fuller references in support of what follows, see Horden 2004.
113. Rawcliffe 2006, 106–107.
114. Brown 2002, 27–28, 65; Herrin 1986, 153–154; Garnsey and Humfress 2001, 126–127; Finn 2006, 63.
115. *Life of John the Almsgiver* 7, ed. Festugière, trans. Dawes and Baynes.
116. Compare Patlagean 1977, 196–203.
117. For a hospital's distributions, see *P. Amh.* 154, *P. Bingen* 136, the latter discussed by Serfass 2008, 99–100.
118. Garsoïan 1989, 115, 211–212; Brown 2002, 42–43.
119. For what follows, see Horden 1998.
120. Brown 1992, 92–93; Atkins and Osborne 2006.
121. Horden 1998; Hübner 2012; see also for comparison Ben-Amos 2008.
122. But is sketched in Horden 2005; Henderson et al. 2007.

WORKS CITED

Arterbury, A. E. 2005. *Entertaining Angels: Early Christian Hospitality in Its Mediterranean Setting.* Sheffield: Sheffield Phoenix.

Atkins, M., and R. Osborne, eds. 2006. *Poverty in the Roman World.* Cambridge: Cambridge University Press.

Baker, P. A. 2004. *Medical Care for the Roman Army on the Rhine, Danube, and British Frontiers.* Oxford: J. and E. Hedges.

Ben-Amos, I. K. 2008. *The Culture of Giving: Informal Support and Gift Exchange in Early Modern England.* Cambridge: Cambridge University Press.

Bouffartigue, J. 2005. "L'authenticité de la Lettre 84 de l'empereur Julien," *Revue de philologie* 79: 231–242.

Bowes, K. 2008. *Private Worship, Public Values, and Religious Change in Late Antiquity.* Cambridge: Cambridge University Press.

Brown, P. R. L. 1992. *Power and Persuasion in Late Antiquity: Towards a Christian Empire.* Madison: University of Wisconsin Press.

———. 2002. *Poverty and Leadership in the Later Roman Empire.* Hanover and London: Brandeis University Press; Historical Society of Israel.

———. 2003. *The Rise of Western Christendom,* 2nd ed. Malden, MA: Blackwell.

———. 2005. "Remembering the Poor and the Aesthetic of Society," *Journal of Interdisciplinary History* 35: 513–522.

Cameron, Alan. 1976. "The Authenticity of the Letters of St. Nilus of Ancyra," *Greek, Roman and Byzantine Studies* 17: 181–196.

Caner, D. 2006. "Towards a Miraculous Economy: Christian Gifts and Material 'Blessings' in Late Antiquity," *Journal of Early Christian Studies* 14: 329–377.

———. 2008. "Wealth, Stewardship, and Charitable 'Blessings' in Early Byzantine Monasticism." In *Wealth and Poverty in Early Church and Society,* ed. S. R. Holman, 221–242. Grand Rapids, MI: Baker Academic.

Chitty, D. 1966. *The Desert a City*. Crestwood, NY: St. Vladimir's Seminary Press.
Constable, O. R. 2003. *Housing the Stranger in the Mediterranean World*. Cambridge: Cambridge University Press.
Constantelos, D. J. 1991. *Byzantine Philanthropy and Social Welfare*, 2nd ed. New Rochelle, NY: Caratzas.
Crislip, A. 2005. *From Monastery to Hospital: Christian Monasticism and the Transformation of Health Care in Late Antiquity*. Ann Arbor: University of Michigan Press.
Dagron, G. 1970. "Les moines et la ville: Le monachisme à Constantinople jusqu'au concile de Chalcédoine (451)," *Travaux et Mémoires* 4: 229–276.
Daley, B. E. 1999. "Building a New City: The Cappadocian Fathers and the Rhetoric of Philanthropy," *Journal of Early Christian Studies* 7: 431–461.
Decker, M. 2009. *Tilling the Hateful Earth: Agricultural Production and Trade in the Late Antique East*. New York: Oxford University Press.
Doig, A. 2008. *Liturgy and Architecture: From the Early Church to the Middle Ages*. Aldershot: Ashgate.
Doran, R., trans. 2006. *Stewards of the Poor: The Man of God, Rabbula, and Hiba in Fifth-Century Edessa*. Kalamazoo, MI: Cistercian Publications.
Du Cange, C. du F. 1680. *Historia Byzantina, II: Constantinopolis Christiana*. Paris: L. Billaine.
Dunning, B. H. 2009. *Aliens and Sojourners: Self as Other in Early Christianity*. Philadelphia: University of Pennsylvania Press.
Elm, S. 1994. *Virgins of God: The Making of Asceticism in Late Antiquity*. Oxford: Clarendon Press.
Faroqhi, S. 1987. *Men of Modest Substance: House Owners and House Property in Seventeenth-Century Ankara and Kayseri*. Cambridge: Cambridge University Press.
Fine, S. ed. 1996. *Sacred Realm: The Emergence of the Synagogue in the Ancient World*. New York and Oxford: Oxford University Press, Yeshiva University Museum.
Finn, R. 2006. *Almsgiving in the Later Roman Empire: Christian Promotion and Practice (313–450)*. Oxford: Oxford University Press.
Garnsey, P. 1988. *Famine and Food Supply in the Graeco-Roman World*. Cambridge: Cambridge University Press.
Garnsey, P., and C. Humfress. 2001. *The Evolution of the Late Antique World*. Cambridge: Orchard Academic.
Garsoïan, N. 1981. "Sur le titre de *Protecteur des pauvres*," *Revue des études arméniennes* n.s. 15: 21–31.
———. 1983. "Nersês le Grand, Basile de Césarée et Eustathe de Sébaste," *Revue des études arméniennes* n.s. 17: 145–169.
———, trans. 1989. *The Epic Histories Attributed to P'awstos Buzand*. Cambridge, MA: Harvard University Press.
Giet, S. 1941. *Les idées et l'action sociale de Saint Basile*. Paris: J. Gabalda.
Grant, R. M. 1977. *Early Christianity and Society*. New York: Harper and Row.
Gwynn, D. 2007. *The Eusebians*. Oxford: Oxford University Press.
Hands, A. R. 1968. *Charities and Social Aids in Greece and Rome*. London: Thames and Hudson.
Harnack, A. 1908. *Mission and Expansion of Christianity in the First Three Centuries*, 2nd ed. London: Williams and Norgate.
Henderson, J., P. Horden, and A. Pastore, eds. 2007. *The Impact of Hospitals 300–2000*. Oxford: Peter Lang.

Herrin, J. 1986. "Ideals of Charity: Realities of Welfare." In *Church and People in Byzantium*, ed. R. Morris, 151–164. Birmingham: Centre for Byzantine, Ottoman and Modern Greek Studies.

Hiltbrunner, O. 2005. *Gastfreundschaft in der Antike und im frühen Christentum*. Darmstadt: Wissenschaftliche Buchgesellschaft.

Holman, S. R. 1999. "The Hungry Body: Famine, Poverty, and Identity in Basil's *Hom.* 8," *Journal of Early Christian Studies* 7: 337–363.

———. 2001. *The Hungry Are Dying: Beggars and Bishops in Roman Cappadocia*. New York: Oxford University Press.

Horden, P. 1998. "Household Care and Informal Networks: Comparisons and Continuities from Antiquity to the Present." In *The Locus of Care*, ed. P. Horden and R. M. Smith, 21–67. London: Routledge.

———. 2004. "The Christian Hospital in Late Antiquity: Break or Bridge?" In *Gesundheit-Krankheit: Kulturtransfer medizinischen Wissens von der Spätantike bis in die Frühe Neuzeit*, ed. F. Steger and K. P. Jankrift, 76–99. Cologne: Böhlau.

———. 2005. "The Earliest Hospitals in Byzantium, Western Europe, and Islam," *Journal of Interdisciplinary History* 35: 361–389.

———. 2006. "How Medicalised were Byzantine Hospitals?" *Medicina e Storia* 10: 45–74.

———. 2007. "Alms and the Man: Hospital Founders in Byzantium." In *The Impact of Hospitals 300–2000*, ed. J. Henderson, P. Horden, and A. Pastore, 59–76. Oxford: Peter Lang.

Hübner, S. R. 2005. *Der Klerus in der Gesellschaft des spätantiken Kleinasiens*. Stuttgart: Steiner.

———. 2012. *The Family in Roman Egypt: A Comparative Approach to Solidarity and Conflict*. Cambridge: Cambridge University Press.

Janes, D. 1998. *God and Gold in Late Antiquity*. Cambridge: Cambridge University Press.

Janin, R. 1969. *La géographie ecclésiastique de l'empire byzantin, première partie, III: Les églises et les monastères*, 2nd ed. Paris: Institut français d'études byzantines.

Kislinger, E. 1984. "Kaiser Julian und die (Christlichen) Xenodocheia." In *ΒΥΖΑΝΤΙΟΣ: Festschrift für Herbert Hunger*, ed. W. Hörandner et al., 171–184. Vienna: Ernst Becvar.

Kraeling, C. H. 1979. *The Synagogue: The Excavations at Dura-Europos, Final Report VIII, Part I*. Aug. ed. New Haven, CT: Yale University Press.

Laiou, A., and C. Morrisson. 2007. *The Byzantine Economy*. Cambridge: Cambridge University Press.

Lavan, L., E. Swift, and T. Putzeys, eds. 2007. *Objects in Context, Objects in Use: Material Spatiality in Late Antiquity*. Leiden: Brill.

Levine, L. I., ed. 2000. *The Jewish Synagogue: The First Thousand Years*. New Haven, CT: Yale University Press.

Lewit, T. 2009. "Pigs, Presses and Pastoralism: Farming in the Fifth to Sixth Centuries AD," *Early Medieval Europe* 17: 77–91.

Loewenberg, F. M. 2001. *From Charity to Social Justice: The Emergence of Communal Institutions for the Support of the Poor in Ancient Judaism*. New Brunswick, NJ: Transaction.

Luijendijk, A. 2008. *Greetings in the Lord: Early Christians and the Oxyrhynchus Papyri*. Cambridge, MA: Harvard University Divinity School.

Mentzou-Meimare, K. 1982. "Eparchiaka evage idrymata mechri tou telous tes eikonomachias," *Byzantina* 11: 243–308.

Miller, T. S. 1990. "The Sampson Hospital of Constantinople," *Byzantinische Forschungen* 15: 101–135.

———. 1997. *The Birth of the Hospital in the Byzantine Empire*, 2nd ed. Baltimore: Johns Hopkins University Press.

———. 2003. *The Orphans of Byzantium: Child Welfare in the Christian Empire*. Washington, DC: Catholic University of America Press.

Mitchell, S. 1993. *Anatolia: Land, Men, and Gods in Asia Minor*, Vol. 2. Oxford: Oxford University Press.

Neri, V. 1998. *I marginali nell'occidente tardoantico*. Bari: Edipuglia.

Nutton, V. 2004. *Ancient Medicine*. Abingdon: Routledge.

Patlagean, E. 1977. *Pauvreté économique et pauvreté sociale à Byzance 4e–7e siècle*. Paris: Mouton.

Rapp, C. 2005. *Holy Bishops in Late Antiquity*. Berkeley: University of California Press.

Rawcliffe, C. 2006. *Leprosy in Medieval England*. Woodbridge: Boydell.

Rebillard, E. 1999a. "Église et sépulture dans l'antiquité tardive (occident latin, 3e–6e siècles)," *Annales ESC*: 1027–1046.

———. 1999b. "Les formes de l'assistance funéraire dans l'empire romain et leur évolution dans l'antiquité tardive," *Antiquité tardive* 7: 269–282.

Reinach, T. 1920. "L'inscription de Théodotos," *Revue des études juives* 71: 46–56.

Reynolds, J., and R. Tannenbaum. 1987. *Jews and God-Fearers at Aphrodisias*. Cambridge: Cambridge Philological Society.

Rousseau, P. 1994. *Basil of Caesarea*. Berkeley: University of California Press.

———. 1999. *Pachomius*, rev. ed. Berkeley: University of California Press.

Safrai, S., and M. Stern, eds. 1976. *The Jewish People in the First Century*, Vol. 2. Assen: Van Gorcum.

Seccombe, D. 1978. "Was There Organized Charity in Jerusalem before the Christians?" *Journal of Theological Studies*, n.s. 29: 140–143.

Sen, A. 1981. *Poverty and Famines*. Oxford: Oxford University Press.

Serfass, A. 2008. "Wine for Widows: Papyrological Evidence for Christian Charity in Late Antique Egypt." In *Wealth and Poverty in Early Church and Society*, ed. S. R. Holman, 88–102. Grand Rapids, MI: Baker Academic.

Stathakopoulos, D. C. 2004. *Famine and Pestilence in the Late Roman and Early Byzantine Empire*. Aldershot: Ashgate.

Temkin, O. 1991. *Hippocrates in a World of Pagans and Christians*. Baltimore: Johns Hopkins University Press.

van Minnen, P. 1995. "Medical Care in Late Antiquity." In *Ancient Medicine in Its Socio-Cultural Context*, ed. P. van der Eijk, H. F. J. Horstmanshoff, and P. H. Schrijvers, vol. 1: 153–169. Amsterdam: Rodopi.

van Ommeslaeghe, F. 1979. "Jean Chrysostome en conflit avec l'impératrice Eudoxie," *Analecta Bollandiana* 97: 131–159.

Vööbus, A. 1970. *Syrische Kanonessammlungen*, Vol. 1. Louvain: Secrétariat du CSCO.

Yarshater, E., ed. 1991. *Encyclopaedia Iranica*, Vol. 5. London: Routledge and Kegan Paul.

Zuiderhoek, A. 2009. *The Politics of Munificence in the Roman Empire*. Cambridge: Cambridge University Press.

CHAPTER 22

CONCEPTS OF CITIZENSHIP

RALPH W. MATHISEN
University of Illinois at Urbana-Champaign

At the beginning of the Roman empire, Roman citizenship was an elite legal status to which certain rights, privileges, and obligations accrued under civil and criminal law.[1] In private life, *cives romani* ("Roman citizens") could marry, make wills, and carry on business under the protection of Roman law. And under the criminal code, citizens could not be questioned under torture, had the right of appeal, and, if sentenced to death, were given a simple execution rather than crucifixion or death in the arena. But not everyone living in the Roman empire at this time was a citizen. Far from it. The majority of the free population in the empire lived in the provinces and were known as *provinciales* ("provincials") or *peregrini* ("foreigners"). They remained liable to whatever legal system was in effect in their communities at the time of their annexation by Rome. The usual ways for *provinciales* to become citizens were by becoming members of city councils or by serving in the *auxilia*, the provincial branch of the Roman army. Even *servi*, or slaves, had the opportunity to become citizens. A freed slave of a provincial gained citizenship opportunities that were available to provincials. But a freed slave of a Roman gained the legal status of *libertus* (freedman) with partial citizenship rights; his or her children gained full citizenship rights.

The Antonine Constitution

As time progressed, there was a constant filtering up of individuals from less privileged legal status to more privileged legal status, and the Roman citizen body increased as a result not only of grants of citizenship but also by the passing on of citizenship rights by inheritance. Thus, citizenship, along with access to Roman *ius civile* (civil law), became less and less a special status and more a lowest common denominator. This process culminated with the issuance in 212 C.E. of the *Constitutio Antoniniana* (Antonine Constitution), in which the emperor Caracalla (211–217) granted citizenship to nearly all of the inhabitants of the Roman empire who did not already possess it.[2] The only surviving copy, a Greek translation, is fragmentary,[3] but the crucial words are clear: "*δίδωμι τοίνυν ἅπασι τοῖς κατὰ τὴν Ῥωμαικὴν οἰκουμένην πολιτείαν Ῥωμαίων*," that is, "I grant to all those in the Roman world the citizenship of the Romans." Many restorations have been proposed for the gaps in the text, but all that can be said for certain is that a class of persons called the *dediticii* were excluded from the grant.[4]

Caracalla's own justification for the grant was as a thanksgiving for having been saved from a conspiracy supposedly organized by his murdered younger brother. The contemporary historian Dio Cassius cynically opined (78.9.5), "He made all the people in his empire Roman citizens; nominally he was honoring them, but his real purpose was to increase his revenues" (because only citizens were liable to a 5 percent tax on inheritances).[5] But the real reason might be more mundane: the spread of citizenship not only meant that citizenship no longer was an indication of social status but also standardized private legal transactions such as lawsuits, inheritances, property transfers, and contracts, which previously had to negotiate a welter of different legal systems and navigate the differentiations between citizens and provincial noncitizens and were an absolute nightmare.[6] Caracalla's grant of citizenship simply made the administration of Roman private law a great deal easier.

One might suppose that additional information regarding what, from a modern perspective, would seem to have been a ruling of tremendous impact would be forthcoming from other ancient sources. But this is not the case. In addition to Dio, only a few scattered references survive. The contemporary jurist Ulpian referred to "those in the Roman world who were made Roman citizens by the constitution of the emperor Antoninus."[7] And two later sources also mention the law. The *Augustan History* noted that the family of the emperor Septimius Severus had been knights "before citizenship was given to all."[8] And Augustine in the *City of God* referred to the time when "all those associated with the Roman empire received the association of citizenship and became Roman citizens, and thus that which previously had belonged to a few now belonged to many."[9]

On the face of it, the scant attention paid to Caracalla's grant seems surprising. One of the reasons probably is that the statute did not create any significant changes either in social status or legal procedures. Yes, the number of citizens was increased, perhaps by quite a bit,[10] but by 212, being a *civis Romanus* no longer was an inordinately privileged status. In criminal law, legal distinctions now were based on the distinction between *honestiores* (more distinguished people) and *humiliores* (more humble people).[11] And in civil law, the real beneficiaries would have been lawyers, for Roman citizenship was changed to a default status whereby civil law now applied to everyone in the *orbis Romanus* (Roman world). Even legally disadvantaged persons lacking full citizen rights had a place in the legal system,[12] for along with *cives Romani* (full citizens), Roman law also recognized *servi* (slaves) and three classes of *liberti* (freedmen): full citizens, Junian Latins, and *dediticii*.[13]

The last of these must be identified as the *dediticii* who in the Antonine Constitution had been so emphatically excluded from the benefits extended by Caracalla,[14] contrary to assumptions that Caracalla's *dediticii* are to be identified as the *peregrini dediticii* ("surrendered foreigners") who in the Roman Republic were defeated foreign peoples.[15] But by the third century, the definition of *dediticii* had changed. According to the Augustan *Lex Aelia Sentia* (Aelian-Sentian Law), *peregrini dediticii* were legally classified as stigmatized freedmen—who had been branded, or submitted to torture, or had fought in the arena—who were ineligible to become full Roman citizens.[16] This ineligibility was simply maintained in the Antonine Constitution.

Given the grant's lack of immediate, high-profile consequences, it is not surprising that it did not make a bigger splash in the contemporary sources. Nevertheless, the lack of impact in the contemporary sources has led most modern writers to downplay the significance of Caracalla's grant and to suggest that henceforth Roman citizenship had little value.[17] Indeed, most modern discussions of Roman citizenship simply stop at this point,[18] on the assumption that citizen status now ceased to be a meaningful component of personal or legal identity in the Roman world. But there are several reasons not to accept such a simplistic model. For one thing, it took a while for Caracalla's edict to be implemented fully, and, perhaps as a consequence of sheer bureaucratic inertia, formal grants of citizenship, such as those to auxiliary soldiers, continued to be made, at least for a while.[19] There are continued occasional third-century references to groups of Roman citizens, such as the "Roman citizens of Mainz,"[20] as if the distinction still meant something. There also are occasional references to *peregrini* resident in the empire who do not yet seem to be recognized as citizens.[21] But these cases of inertia did not outlast the third century, and soon enough Roman civil law, to a greater or lesser degree, applied to everyone living in the empire.

In broader terms, several other considerations also might cause one to question (1) whether the Antonine Constitution marked the end of citizenship grants and (2) whether Roman citizenship no longer counted for much. Slaves certainly continued to be freed and became *liberti*, and *liberti* became full Roman citizens. A law of 349, for example, decreed that manumitted mothers, "for whom, of course, the rights of Roman citizenship had been obtained," could have their cases heard in court, as could any freed sons and daughters who had become "Roman citizens in a similar manner."[22] And a law of 447 spoke of the testamentary rights of "a *libertus*, who will have obtained the privilege of Roman citizenship."[23] In exceptional cases, slaves could become citizens directly.[24] So, for some people, the process of becoming a citizen still counted. Indeed, nearly all, if not all, of the acquisitions of citizenship attested after 212 resulted from promotions from servile to free status.

Proliferating Definitions of Citizenship

In addition, far from becoming an obsolete concept of little value, citizenship acquired multiple definitions that existed alongside the status of "Roman" citizen, and dual citizenship of various forms existed.[25] For example, there continued to be a parallel concept of municipal citizenship.[26] The territory of the Roman empire was subdivided into a multitude of municipalities under the jurisdiction of *civitates* (cities), which were responsible for overseeing much of Roman administration at the local level. Nominally, every Roman citizen also was a citizen of a city.[27] A large section of Justinian's *Digest* (50.1) was devoted to establishing "origo" and "domicilium" in a *civitas* (city) for all the inhabitants of the empire and hence liability to municipal duties and taxes.

After Roman citizenship became essentially universal, people generally no longer were identified as *cives Romani* but often as *cives* of a city.[28] In the late fourth century, for example, the Gallic poet Ausonius could write, "I love Bordeaux, I esteem Rome: I am a citizen of the one, a consul in both."[29] Even Rhine frontier villagers in 230 C.E. could call themselves "Roman citizens and inhabitants of Taunus by paternal descent."[30] In a similar manner, mid-third-century Thracians could identify themselves ethnically as "Roman citizens and Bessi."[31] Indeed, to be a *civis* of a *civitas* probably was the fundamental status that had made persons eligible for Roman citizenship via the Antonine Constitution in the first place.

In addition, there was regional identity and even regional citizenship, and people increasingly identified themselves as inhabitants of provinces.[32] For example, Justinian's sixth-century *Digest* cites earlier examples of Campanian and Pontic legal identity.[33] The legal term *provinciales* ("provincials") usually referred generically to all nonservile inhabitants of one or more provinces.[34] The law even refers to "citizens" of a province,[35] a status that also is found in popular parlance, with references to citizens of Africa, Gaul, or Spain.[36] A ruling of 385 specified that no one was to serve in any office "within that province in which he was considered to be a provincial and a citizen."[37]

The adoption of Christianity as a state religion during the fourth century brought additional ways of defining citizen status. As Christian clerics, administrators, and emperors became more and more intolerant of anyone who was not an orthodox Christian, the possession of full citizenship rights came to be based on Christian confessional status. Pagans, Jews, and heretics suffered a diminution of their citizenship rights and their ability to avail themselves of Roman civil law: they could "pursue the decisions of no judge in private business."[38] And in a metaphorical sense, the Christian concept of being a citizen of some supernal community, such as heaven or the "City of God," was similar to, and even replaced, the classical philosophical sense of being a citizen of the cosmopolis: Christians were "citizens of the heavenly Jerusalem."[39]

Finally, in popular usage even barbarians were acknowledged to have a form of ethnic citizenship. In 423, a Roman of Florence, for example, described his deceased wife as a "civis Alamanna" ("Alamannic citizen").[40] In the 470s, the Arian Modaharius was depicted as a "civis Gothus" ("Gothic citizen").[41] And a soldier buried near Budapest said on his epitaph, "I am a *civis Francus* ['Frankish citizen'] and a Roman soldier in arms."[42] But this usage never appears in any extant Roman legal sources, and it is unclear what being a barbarian "civis" meant. It may have been the functional or metaphorical equivalent of the civic or provincial citizenship that Romans had.

As a consequence of these varied forms of citizenship, one's personal identification with a city, a province, a religion, or a barbarian people now could be expressed in terms of "citizenship" that in no way conflicted with holding Roman citizenship and may or may not have had anything to do with legal rights. There thus existed multiple legal identities whereby persons who were Roman citizens also could be designated by their municipal, provincial, religious, or ethnic status.

Another element of legal identity relates to the legal jurisdiction under which these different kinds of citizens fell. Even though civil law could be used by all Roman citizens, not all of them did so. Parallel legal systems, variously referred to as provincial, vulgar, civic, or common law, continued to be valid alongside Roman civil law.[43] Even in the sixth century, the *Digest* acknowledged, "Those practices that have been approved by long practice and observed for many years are preserved as law, as if by a tacit agreement of the citizens, no less than those laws that are written."[44] The Roman government even extended official recognition to the dual citizenship created by different forms of religious law. For example, even though Jews could be restricted in their ability to make use of Roman civil law because of their non-Christian beliefs, they nonetheless were extended special privileges regarding the use of their own laws. A ruling of 398 allowed Jews a choice of legal identity: they could use their own laws within their own religious communities or when both parties agreed, but if they identified themselves as "Romans," they then were expected to abide by Roman civil law.[45] In addition, the official recognition of the Christian Church brought with it an acknowledgment of Christian legal jurisdiction in cases involving the maintenance of proper Christian belief and behavior. The result was a growing body of canon law that sometimes competed with or contradicted Roman civil and criminal law.[46]

WHITHER THE *PEREGRINI*?

One of the great hitherto unanswered questions of Roman law relates to the status of *peregrini*—foreign "barbarians"—who settled in the empire after Caracalla's grant. Just how were they treated under Roman law?[47] Did they then (1) constitute a new class of noncitizens, (2) "become" citizens by some as yet undefined process, (3) gain access to Roman civil law by some other means, or (4) likewise become covered by the Antonine Constitution? These are issues that have been rarely discussed in the scholarship[48] and never answered.

During the Principate, there certainly had been established procedures by which newly arrived *peregrini* could become Roman citizens;[49] indeed, there was a long tradition of integration of many barbarians into the Roman world.[50] Ever since the early Principate, barbarians had been resettled en masse on Roman territory.[51] Augustus (27 B.C.E.–14 C.E.) placed 50,000 Getae on the Danube.[52] Tiberius (14–37) reportedly settled 40,000 German captives on the banks of the Rhine in Gaul.[53] During the reign of Nero (54–68), land in Moesia was granted to more than a hundred thousand Transdanubians.[54] Trajan (98–117) settled multitudes of Dacians on Roman territory, and Marcus Aurelius (161–180) settled Quadi, Vandals, Iazyges, Naristae, and Marcomanni.[55] Merely by residing within Roman provinces, these barbarian settlers would have gained the status of *provincialis,* which would have made them eligible for service in the *auxilia* and hence for enrollment as *cives Romani* within a very short time.[56] Thus, by a relatively rapid process, thousands of barbarians would have been quickly cycled into the citizen ranks. In 212, all of these barbarian settlers and their descendants who were not yet citizens would have acquired full Roman citizenship just as automatically as anyone else. But what about subsequent barbarian settlers?

In part, the lack of discussion of the legal status of *peregrini* after 212 is no surprise, for there is no clear exposition of their status in the thousands of surviving laws or in any other source. This can mean only two things: either they remained in some kind of legal limbo, or we have simply been mistaken regarding what kinds of legislation we would expect to find dealing with them. Given the Roman penchant for legal precision, the former seems unlikely. So just what was the legal status of barbarian immigrants? Did they have access to Roman civil law? Were they able to cross the great divide from *peregrinus* to *civis Romanus*?

Now, contrary to some recent assertions, the sense of *peregrinus* as "non-Roman" in a legal sense was alive and well in the late empire.[57] A simple insight into the identity of late Roman *peregrini* comes from Sidonius Apollinaris, who in the late fifth century said about Rome, "In this state (*civitas*) alone of the entire world only barbarians and slaves are *peregrini*."[58] This suggests a reverse definition of citizenship: to be considered a full citizen, one merely needed to be identified as neither a slave nor a barbarian. And given that *servi* (not to mention *liberti*) were "foreign" to Roman citizenship only in the sense that they were not fully covered by *ius civile*, that leaves barbarians as the true *peregrini* who, after 212, were not part of the Roman polity. Indeed, elsewhere Sidonius distinguished citizens from barbarians, as when he lampooned the collaborator Seronatus for pursuing "fighting among citizens and literature among barbarians."[59] But given that, as already seen, barbarians are not to be identified as the *dediticii* excluded from Caracalla's citizenship, there would have been no legal impediment to barbarian immigrants becoming citizens. So the question is how, if at all, did they do so?

The greatest attention to the legal condition of barbarians living in the empire has been given to barbarians in the Roman army. As of the fourth century, barbarians served in all elements of the Roman military.[60] Many barbarian soldiers remained inside the empire after their military service.[61] There also are many examples of barbarians holding high Roman offices, including not only military ones but even the consulate.[62] Just what was the legal status of these barbarians?

It sometimes has been assumed that by some unknown process some barbarians, and in particular soldiers, were made Roman citizens.[63] Demougeot assumed that barbarians who became members of the *comitatenses* (field army), held Roman military or civilian office, or married a Roman must have become citizens.[64] Others suggest that only barbarian officers became citizens.[65] Demougeot also argued that the honorific "Flavius," used by many barbarians, indicated a grant of Roman citizenship, a suggestion recently seconded by Garnsey, even though in the interim Mocsy had shown that Flavius was an inherited title given to soldiers and officials and thus had nothing to do with barbarian ethnicity.[66] Garnsey asserts that "a few individual Goths were honoured with Roman citizenship," a claim repeated by Heather.[67] And Demougeot also suggested that barbarians did not hold full citizenship but some kind of special barbarian citizenship that limited them to only military careers.[68] But this kind of halfway house is both unprecedented and undocumented in Roman law. The problem with these assumptions, however, is that none of those who argue that barbarians were formally granted Roman citizenship can show how the procedure worked or provide a single example,[69] and this in spite of a wealth of legal and prosopographical material. We still have no examples of barbarians actually being "made" citizens, nor are we told what these general statements about barbarians being considered to be "Romans" or "citizens" meant in the real world of Roman law.

A diligent search of the sources does turn up a handful of references to barbarians described as Romans or Roman citizens. In his panegyric to the

Master of Soldiers Stilicho in 400, the poet Claudian observed of Rome, "Those whom she has conquered she calls citizens."[70] Even if Claudian is speaking historically, there is nothing to suggest that this policy did not continue in his own day. This view continued in the mid-sixth century, when the panegyrist Corippus could say, in a North African context, "Whatever *gentes* the Roman empire sees being faithful and subject, it considers them to be Latin citizens."[71] In the late fourth century, the rhetor Synesius even stated that Theodosius I "considered the Goths worthy of citizenship"[72] but did not claim that Theodosius actually "made" Goths citizens. In addition, in 383, the orator Themistius opined that Goths were "no longer called barbarians but Romans," a sentiment seconded by Pacatus, who stated in 389 that Theodosius I (379–395) ordered defeated barbarian soldiers to "become Roman."[73] It is difficult to see how "becoming Roman" would not entail having some degree of Roman citizenship. But the only person of barbarian ancestry specifically to be called a Roman citizen is the Master of Soldiers Stilicho, the son of a Roman mother and a Vandal father, of whom Claudian said, "Rome rejoiced that she deserved to have you as a citizen."[74] But how Stilicho gained this status—whether through his mother, through some action of his own, or just by default—we are not told.

Barbarian Use of Roman Civil Law

Lacking direct evidence for barbarians being formally made citizens, we might take a different approach and investigate whether barbarian *peregrini* who resided or settled in the Roman empire were able to make use of Roman civil law. If so, to what extent could they do so, and did they need to be Roman citizens?

A very widespread way in which barbarians participated in Roman legal procedures was related to landholding and the tax liabilities on their property. Barbarians most commonly gained title to Roman land through their military service. The law codes record many instances of land grants and tax breaks awarded to army veterans.[75] Many of them would have been barbarians, although ethnicity is mentioned in only a few cases.[76] There also are specific examples, the most spectacular being the Master of Soldiers Fl. Valila *qui et* Theodobius, who in 471 established a church at Tivoli and later bequeathed to the church a house on the Esquiline Hill in Rome.[77] Other barbarians also disposed of their property using Roman testamentary law, as when the eastern general Aspar named another barbarian, the Ostrogoth Theoderic Strabo, as one of his heirs.[78] The ability of these barbarians to make property transfers and testamentary bequests certainly attests to their use of Roman civil law.

Multitudes of extraterritorial barbarians gained property in the Roman empire, often in exchange for military service, by means of continuing en masse settlements of barbarians.[79] In 297/298, an anonymous panegyrist reported that "captive processions of barbarians" were "conducted to the cultivation of deserted lands assigned to them" in exchange for military service.[80] Constantine (306–337), it was said, settled more than 300,000 Sarmatians in Thrace, Scythia, Macedonia, and Italy.[81] Ammianus reports settlements of Alamanni in Gaul in the 360s and in the Po River valley in 370, as well as settlements of defeated Goths and Taifals in Italy in 377.[82] Some settlers had the status of *laeti*, who were allowed to settle on Roman land in exchange for military service.[83] Other settlers, known as *gentiles*, received land at the same time they remained enrolled in Roman army units.[84] And still other settlers, such as Scirians settled on the Danube in 409, had the status of full-fledged Roman *coloni* (tenant farmers).[85] The legal or citizenship status of these barbarian settlers has never been elucidated in the scholarship.[86] But the repeated references to the regularization of the status of these barbarian *coloni*, *gentiles*, or *laeti* indicates that they had been assimilated into the Roman legal system and had access to Roman civil law, at least as regards both land tenure and taxpaying.[87]

Roman-Barbarian Marriages

It also has been assumed that the legal distinction between barbarians and provincials meant something in the case of marriages, as seems to be indicated in a law of Valentinian I and Valens, addressed to the Master of Soldiers Theodosius,[88] that decreed, "For none of the provincials may there be a marriage with a barbarian wife, nor may any provincial woman marry any of the gentiles." Such marriages were to be punished by death "because something suspect or culpable is revealed in them."[89] But this ruling would seem to be related more to the legal statuses of "gentilis" (a type of barbarian soldier) and "provincialis," as discussed previously, than to ethnicity,[90] and, irrespective of this, it certainly did not inhibit marriages between Romans and barbarians, a great number of which are attested.[91] And for these marriages to be recognized under Roman law, the barbarian spouse must have had *ius conubii* (right of marriage) of a Roman citizen, a concept also embodied in other spheres of contemporary Roman thought. The late-fourth-century Spanish poet Prudentius, for example, stated: "A common law makes us equal . . . the native city embraces in its unifying walls fellow citizens. . . . Foreign peoples now congregate with the right of marriage (*ius conubii*): for with mixed blood, one family is created from different peoples."[92] Even though Prudentius was speaking metaphorically about the kingdom of God, his words seem uncannily applicable to the world of late Roman marriage and Roman citizenship.

Legal Accommodations

Other evidence also indicates that barbarians were covered by Roman law. One ruling stated that legal cases involving soldiers and civilians were to be tried before a military tribunal as opposed to a civil court, and a law of 405 addressed to the proconsul of Africa stated that appeals were to be heard according to "ancient custom," except that appeals by *gentiles* or their prefects were to be heard by the proconsul.[93] The aforementioned panegyric of 297/298 also reported, "The *laetus*, having been restored by *postliminium*, and the Frank, received into the laws ["receptus in leges"], cultivate the fields of Armorica and Trier."[94] Now, the right of *postliminium* allowed Roman citizens who had been forced into exile to recover lost property, and to say that Frankish settlers had been "received into the laws" also must mean that they were covered by Roman law. These statements also are consistent with Zosimus' report about barbarian soldiers who robbed the Egyptian provincials: "This was not the behavior of men who were ready to live according to the laws of the Romans."[95] Large numbers of barbarians, it would seem, were being assimilated under the umbrella of Roman law.

A particular example is provided by a law of 468, which stated, "But if a testator of a barbarian nation leaves a bequest or trust without a person having been designated, and if some ambiguity appears regarding his homeland (*patria*), the bishop of his city, in which the testator died, likewise shall have the petition of the bequest or trust, in order to fulfill the resolution of the deceased."[96] Here, Roman civil law covered even a deceased barbarian, for the issue was not whether the barbarian had the right to designate an heir or trustee under Roman law—that was taken for granted—but what to do if he or she failed to do so. In addition, the question of the barbarian's *patria* suggests one way in which barbarians might have been legally integrated into the Roman world. In Roman legal terminology, *patria* usually referred to one's native city, but never to a foreign land.[97] A law of 364 addressed "To all the provincials" stated: "We grant to all well-deserving veterans the *patria* that they wish."[98] The opportunity to do so would have been most applicable to those who did not already have a Roman *patria*, a criterion that would have fit barbarian veterans. And given that citizens of cities were ipso facto Roman citizens, the act of choosing a *patria*, or even—as in this case—having the potential right to do so, would have allowed one to exercise the legal rights of a Roman citizen.

Barbarians who lived under the Roman legal umbrella, moreover, did not necessarily give up their barbarian identity. Yes, multitudes of barbarian settlers no doubt were absorbed into Roman society and retained, at most, sentimental attachments to the old country. But others had dual residences, living part-time in the Roman empire and also returning home,[99] and were able to maintain dual citizenship, so to speak.[100] Indeed, this accommodation dated back at least to the 160s, when Roman citizenship was granted to

North African *gentiles* "salvo iure gentis," that is, "with the law of their people preserved."[101] These barbarians retained whatever legal obligations or benefits that accrued from their belonging to a barbarian *gens* (people) at the same time that Roman civil law became available to them. They, like the aforementioned Jews, had the ability to use their own law, when they identified themselves as *gentiles*, or Roman law, when they identified themselves as *cives Romani*.

Universal Citizenship in the Late Roman Empire

In Late Antiquity, Roman citizenship clearly no longer was being "granted" in the same manner as during the Principate. The only formal grants of Roman citizenship were to freedmen and slaves, who thus experienced not so much a change from noncitizen to citizen as a transfer to a greater measure of legal freedom. But the lack of any evidence at all for formal grants of citizenship to barbarians means that if they gained access to citizenship—as the preceding examples demonstrate that they surely did—it must have happened in some other manner. Barbarians held office, owned and transferred property, made wills, went to Roman courts, and generally made use of *ius civile* all without formally "receiving" citizenship. The most reasonable explanation for how this happened, it seems, is that the Antonine Constitution was not a one-time grant but was meant to be self-perpetuating. All free foreign *peregrini* were potential citizens, assuming they settled in the Roman empire and took up the same obligations and identity as had the provincial *peregrini* of 212 C.E. Doing so would make someone both *de facto* and *de iure* a citizen.

Indeed, one never hears about any difference in the degree of access by Romans and barbarians to *ius civile*. The primary distinction in late Roman law was not between citizen and noncitizen, but between free and degrees of legal disability, as denoted by being a slave, freedman, *colonus*, *laetus*, and so on. Free status conveyed full access to Roman civil law, whereas nonfree or impaired status necessarily entailed legal disability. It therefore was a contradiction to suggest that a free person, including a person of barbarian origin, could be a noncitizen. This would explain why there are no cases during the late empire of anyone being denied access to *ius civile* on the basis of ethnic, or any other nonservile, status, a stark contrast to the Principate, when accusations of noncitizens passing themselves off as citizens were rampant.[102]

But this does not mean that all barbarians automatically were considered citizens. It was making use of Roman law—as seen in the case of the barbarian testator—that made someone a citizen. Citizenship was a matter of participation and self-identification:[103] one could just as easily identify oneself as a *civis Alamanna* as a *civis Romanus*. Indeed, given the concept of dual identity, one could do both. There was no process by which a foreigner became a Roman citizen except by functioning as one. Caracalla's edict truly intended that Roman law would apply to everyone, including new immigrants. As expressed by the third-century jurist Modestinus, "Roma communis nostra patria est" ("Rome is our shared homeland").[104] The same ideology also lay behind the *Augustan History*'s proud observation, in the late fourth century, about the emperor Probus: "Did he not defeat all of the barbarian nations and make almost the entire world Roman?"[105] By making their law available to all, the Romans manifested their claim to rule all that mattered of the whole world and established the closest thing ever known to a "citizenship of the world."[106]

NOTES

1. See Sherwin-White 1972; 1979; Gauthier 1986; Giacomini and Poma 1996; Nicolet 1980; 1989; Giacomini 1996; Gardner 1993; Noy 2000a; Ste-Croix 1981; Ratti 2002; Kaser 1971.

2. For the Antonine Constitution, see Condurachi 1958; Sasse 1958; Lukaszewicz 1990; Bell 1947; Hagedorn 1996; Giacomini and Poma 1996, 165; Garnsey 2004.

3. For the text, see Riccobono 1968, no. 88, 445–449; Heichelheim 1940.

4. "χωρὶς τῶν δεδειτικῶν."

5. Followed by Jones 1964, 16: "the main motive was fiscal."

6. See Honoré 2002, 85, for the legal "simplification that common citizenship would bring"; also Millar 1977, 481.

7. *Digest* 1.5.17, "Ulpianus. . . . In orbe Romano qui sunt ex constitutione imperatoris Antonini cives Romani effecti sunt."

8. *Augustan History, Septimius Severus* 9.5: "ante civitatem omnibus datam."

9. Augustine, *City of God* 5.17, "Omnes ad romanum imperium pertinentes societatem acciperent civitatis et romani cives essent, ac sic esset omnium quod erat ante paucorum. . . ."

10. Millar 1977, 477–483; Honoré 2002, 24; Garnsey 2004, 135. New citizens can be identified by their *nomen* (family name) "Aurelius" (from Caracalla's full name of "Aurelius Antoninus"): Sherwin-White 1972, 56; Millar 1977, 481; Garnsey 2004, 143.

11. See Jones 1964, 17; Rilinger 1988; Santalucia 1998; Garnsey 1970, 118.

12. Seen throughout Justinian's *Digest*.

13. See Ulpian, *Regulae* 1.5; for the Junian Latins, see Fear 1990, 149–166; Weaver 1990.

14. Jones 1968; Benario 1954; Sherwin-White 1979, 380–398.

15. See Sasse 1958, 70–104, 111–112; Heichelheim 1940, 16; Kaser 1971: 1.282; Jones 1968, 135: after 212, "no distinction between *peregrini* and *dediticii* would be expected and none was to the best of our knowledge made." Also Sherwin-White 1979, 380–398; Noy 2000b, 15–30.

16. Gaius, *Institutes* 1.13–14: "cuius condicionis sunt peregrini dediticii" ("the *peregrini dediticii* are of this status"); see Sasse 1958, 104–110.

17. Sherwin-White 1979, 444: it "introduced no material alteration"; Garnsey 2004, "an accident of history" (133), a "whim" (135) that "came out of the blue" (137), and "For some modern observers, it was all over for Roman citizenship . . . citizenship had lost whatever residual value it formerly possessed" (140); Williams 1979, 69–72: an "impulsive measure"; Brown 1992, 154: "The brittle privileges and self-respect once associated with the notion of citizenship slipped away"; also Kunkel 1973, 79ff.; Sollner 1980, 97; Giacomini and Poma 1996, 165; Gardner 1993, 187.

18. E.g., Giacomini and Poma 1996, 165.

19. Herodian, *Roman History*, 8.4.2, notes that in 238 the inhabitants of Aquileia received "a sharing of Roman citizenship" ("*παρὰ 'Ρωμαίοις πολιτείας κοινονία*"). For continued military grants as a "combination of utility and legal archaism," see Sherwin-White 1979, 388.

20. For example, Riese 1914, 4.2125, 236 = *CIL* 13.6733: "c(ivium) R(omanorum) Mog(untiaco)" (276 C.E.); also 4.2126, 236–237 = *CIL* 13.6769, (222–235 C.E.). See Sherwin-White 1979, 387.

21. Note Riese 1914, *Germanien* 1.237, 31 = *CIL* 13.4679, "Genio pagi Dervet(ensis) peregrini qui posuer(unt)" (232 C.E.); and see Garnsey 2004, 143, for "geographically, ethnically, and culturally marginal people allowed to slip through the net."

22. *CTh* 8.13.1 (349).

23. *Novel of Valentinian* 25 (447).

24. E.g., *CTh* 9.21.2.1 (321); *CTh* 4.7.1 (321).

25. See Bergh 1992; also Fourgous 1993, for the "double citizenship of Cecrops, Greek and barbarian," cited in Diodorus Siculus 1.28.

26. Garnsey 2004, 137: "local citizenships were tolerated." See also El-Abbadi 1962.

27. See Jones 1968, 136: "all Roman citizens are *municipes* of some *municipium*."

28. E.g., *CTh* 1.10.4 (391), 11.16.6 (346), 12.1.17 (329), 12.1.53 (362), 15.5.3 (409), 15.5.4 (424); Ammianus Marcellinus 19.2.14, 27.3.2.

29. Ausonius, *Poems* 11.20.40–41: "Civis in hac sum / consul in ambabus."

30. Riese 1914, *Germanien* 3.1176 132; see Sherwin-White 1979, 388.

31. *CIL* 3.3505, 7533, 14214; *Année epigraphique* (1924) nos. 142–148 (237–246); see Sherwin-White 1979, 56, 210, 269, 387.

32. See Charlotte Roueché, *CAH* XIV, 572: "Many people chose to describe themselves as inhabitants of their province . . . rather than as citizens of particular towns."

33. *Digest* 50.1.1.2: "Campanus est . . . Ponticus esset."

34. For example, *CTh* 1.5.1, 1.16.6–7, 2.26.3, 2.30.1, 7.4.26, 7.9.1, 7.13.7–8, 7.13.16, 7.20.8, and throughout; also 8.10.2, 11.8.3.1.

35. *CTh* 1.34.1 (400): "cives . . . provinciae"; *CTh* 9.38.9 (398): "civem Lycium."

36. E.g., Gregory of Tours, *Glory of the Confessors* 69.1; Hydatius, *Chronicle* 217, s.a. 462: *Life of Eugendus* 2.

37. *CJ* 9.29.3 (385): "Intra eam provinciam, in qua provincialis et civis habetur."

38. E.g., *Novel of Theodosius* 3.7 (438); see Lo Nero 2001; King 1961, 95.

39. Ephesians 2:19: "estis cives sanctorum" ("you are citizens of sainthood"); and Augustine, *City of God* 22.17: "civis supernae Hierusalem" ("the citizen of the heavenly Jerusalem"). See Garnsey 2004, 150–155; Clévenot 1988, 107–115.

40. *CIL* 11.1731.

41. Sidonius Apollinaris, *Letters* 7.6.2–3.

42. *CIL* 11.3576: "Francus ego cives, Romanus miles in armis." For a different reading of this inscription, see Rigsby 1999.

43. See Levy 1943; Stühff 1966; Sirks 1996, 150 ("Roman and indigenous law still coexisted"); Kunkel 1973, 79; Garnsey 2004, 138–141, 146. For a dissenting opinion, see Honoré 2002, 212, "the contrast between the civil law and common custom was now of purely historical interest."

44. *Digest* 1.3.35.

45. *CTh* 2.1.10.

46. See, e.g., Gaudemet 1985.

47. For this issue, see Mathisen 2006.

48. Note in particular Garnsey 2001; 2004; Demougeot 1981; 1984; also Liebeschuetz 1998.

49. Gaius, *Institutes* 1.93: "Si peregrinus . . . civitatem Romanam petierit. . . ." ("If a foreigner seeks Roman citizenship"); see Visscher 1958.

50. See, e.g., Metzler et al. 1995; Woolf 1998; Whittaker 1997.

51. See, e.g., Chrysos 1989; Claude 1988; MacMullen 1963; Okamura 1997; Ste-Croix 1981, 245–249, 509–518.

52. Strabo 7.303.

53. Eutropius, *Abridgement* 7.9.

54. Dessau 1954–1955, no. 986.

55. Dio Cassius, *Roman History* 71.11.4–5, 71.12.1–3, 71.16.2, 71.31; *Augustan History, Marcus Aurelius* 22.2, 24.3.

56. E.g., Sherwin-White 1979, 310, "barbarian peasantry secured [citizenship] by long service in the provincial militia."

57. E.g., Gaudemet 1958, 211, maintains that the term *peregrinus* "perdre toute signification juridique precise"; followed by Blockley 1982.

58. Sidonius Apollinaris, *Letters* 1.6.3: "in qua unica totius mundi civitate soli barbari et servi peregrinantur"; Sherwin-White 1979, 387, notes, "Sidonius was certainly right when he asserted the continued existence of barbarian *peregrini* within the Roman world."

59. "inter cives pugnas, inter barbaros litteras" (*Letters* 2.1.2).

60. Julian, *Oration* 5.11, recalls how an officer "had exhorted his troops, both peregrines and citizens, to stand by the emperor." Garnsey 2004, 144, suggests that in the army, "peregrines must have heavily outweighed citizens."

61. E.g., Hoffmann 1963.

62. See Bang 1906; Waas 1971; Johne 1988.

63. E.g., Blockley 1982, "a generation or two of residence and service would have been usually necessary"; Liebeschuetz 1998, 138, calls it "a mere formality." But on the other hand, Sirks 1996, 149, states simply, "They did not become Roman citizens."

64. Demougeot 1981: Masters of Soldiers "reçurent la citoyenneté parce qu'ils commandaient aussi les soldats romains" (384); "les généraux barbares de l'armée *comitatensis* devenus citoyens" (384); common barbarian soldiers received citizenship "mais tacitement" (385); "sans doute seuls vivaient en citoyens ceux qui avaient reçu la citoyenneté avant l'*honesta missio*," that is, five years of service (387).

65. Soraci 1968; Sherwin-White 1979, 380ff.

66. Demougeot 1981, 383: "le gentilice de Flavius . . . désigna les nouveaux citoyens"; also Garnsey 2004, 144: "We know of around seventy officers of citizen rank and barbarian origin, almost all of them named Flavius," without citing any examples; Mocsy 1964, 258; also Millar 1977, 481; Keenan 1973–1974.

67. Demougeot 1981, 388; Garnsey 2004, 144; Heather 1991, 164–165: "citizenship [was] limited only to the most important Goths."

68. Demougeot 1981, 384: "un barbare devenu citoyen romain ne pouvait ambitionner qu'une carrière militaire."

69. Observed long ago by Mommsen 1889, 240.

70. Claudian, *On the Consulate of Stilicho* 3.152–153: "civesque vocavit /quos domuit."

71. Corippus, *Praise of John* 8.461–462: "cives putat esse latinos."

72. "*πολιτείας ἄξιον*": *On Kingship* 21/25C = Terzaghi 1944, 50, ll.13–14. Liebeschuetz 1998, 135, suggests that "politeia" (citizenship) here "has acquired a new meaning," being applied to "non-naturalized barbarians who had acquired the right to live within the empire." The old meaning of "citizenship," however, seems to fit perfectly well.

73. Themistius, *Oration* 167.211–212; Pacatus, *Latin Panegyrics* 2/12.36.4, "iussisti esse Romanam."

74. Claudian, *On the Consulate of Stilicho* 3.180–181: "Roma . . . gaudebat . . . quod te . . . meruisset . . . civem." His ancestry: ibid. 1.35–39; Orosius, *History against the Pagans* 7.38.1; John of Antioch, fragment 187; Jerome, *Letters* 123.16; *PLRE* 1.853.

75. E.g., *CTh* 7.20.3 (320), 7.20.4 (325), 7.20.8 (364), 7.20.11 (373).

76. *CTh* 7.20.12 (400), 5.11.7 (365).

77. Tivoli: Duchesne 1886–1892, 1.lcxlvii; Rome: *Book of the Popes* 49: ibid. 250. See *PLRE* 2.1147; Castritius 1972.

78. Malchus, fragment 2.

79. See, e.g., Chrysos 1989; Claude 1988; MacMullen 1963; Okamura 1997; Demougeot 1974.

80. "Ad destinatos sibi cultus solitudinum ducerentur": *Latin Panegyrics* 8[5].9.3.

81. *Anonymus Valesianus* 32; for additional settlements, see MacMullen 1963, 553–554.

82. Ammianus Marcellinus 20.4.1, 28.5.15, 31.9.4.

83. Ammianus Marcellinus 20.4.1, 20.8.13, 1.13.16, 24.1.15; also *CTh* 7.20.10, 7.20.12, 13.11.10, 13.11.10. *Novel of Severus* 2.1; *Latin Panegyrics* 7(6).6. Also, for *laeti*, see Demougeot 1970; Simpson 1977a; 1977b; 1988.

84. *CTh* 7.15.1 (409). Note units of "laeti gentiles" and "Sarmatae gentiles" in the *Notitia dignitatum occidentalis* ("Western Catalogue of Offices") 42.

85. *CTh* 5.6.3 (409).

86. E.g., Garnsey 2004, 134, wrongly supposing that the *dediticii* were defeated barbarians, suggests that they were ineligible for citizenship; Heather 1991, 113, likewise suggests that barbarians submitted "not as full citizens but as dependent subjects."

87. For barbarian settlers as taxpayers, see also Themistius, *Oration* 167.211–212.

88. See Sivan 1996.

89. *CTh* 3.14.1 (365/373): "Nulli provincialium, cuiuscumque ordinis aut loci fuerit, cum barbara sit uxore coniugium, nec ulli gentilium provincialis femina copuletur . . . quod in iis suspectum vel noxium detegitur, capitaliter expietur."

90. See R. W. Mathisen, "*Provinciales, Gentiles,* and Marriages between Romans and Barbarians in the Late Roman Empire," forthcoming, *Journal of Roman Studies.*

91. For marriages between barbarians and Romans, see Demandt 1989; Soraci 1965; Bianchini 1988; Blockley 1982.

92. *Against Symmachus* 2.598–614: "Ius fecit commune pares . . . Cives congenitos concludat moenibus unis / Urbs patria . . . conveniunt nunc . . . / Externi ad ius connubii: nam sanguine mixto / Texitur alternis ex gentibus una propago."

93. *CJ* 3.13.6 (413), *CTh* 11.30.62 (405); also *CTh* 2.1.2 (355); *Nov.Theo.* 4 (438). Contrary to Sirks 1996, 149, "Barbarians were not subjected to Roman courts."

94. *Latin Panegyrics* 8(5).21.1.

95. *New History* 3.30.4.

96. *CJ* 1.3.28.3 (468): "Quod si testato, qui huiusmodi legatum vel fideicommissum non designata persona reliquit, barbarae sit nationis et de eius patria aliqua emerserit ambiguitas, vir reverentissimus episcopus civitatis eius, in qua idem testator defunctus est, itidem habeat legati seu fideicommissi petitionem defuncti propositum modis omnibus impleturus."

97. Municipality: *CTh* 6.4.21.4, 8.12.3, 12.1.98, 12.1.119, 12.1.146, 12.18.2, 14.9.1, 15.1.42; Empire: *CTh* 9.37.2, 10.10.25.

98. *CTh* 7.20.8: "quam volunt patriam damus."

99. E.g., Ammianus Marcellinus 21.4.3, 29.6.5, 18.2.17; see Lee 1993.

100. E.g., Braund 1984, 39: "Gothic leaders easily could have held dual citizenship."

101. *Table of Banasitana* (ca. 161/169), in Labory 1982, 76–91, n. 94; also Sherwin-White 1973. For dual citizenship: Honoré 2002, 24.

102. Reinhold 1971.

103. See Ando 2000, 352, for the pre-212 period.

104. *Digest* 50.1.33; see Thomas 1996.

105. *Augustan History, Probus* 18.4.

106. For Roman rule of the "orbis terrarum" ("circle of the lands"), see Ando 2000, 278–280.

WORKS CITED

Ando, Clifford. 2000. *Imperial Ideology and Provincial Loyalty in the Roman Empire.* Berkeley: University of California Press.

Bang, Martin. 1906. *Die Germanen im römischen Dienst bis zum Regierungsantritt Constantins I.* Berlin: Weidmann.

Bell, H. Idris. 1947. "The *Constitutio Antoniniana* and the Egyptian Poll-Tax," *Journal of Roman Studies* 37: 17–23.

Benario, Herbert W. 1954. "The Dediticii of the Constitutio Antoniniana," *Transactions of the American Philological Association* 85: 188–196.

Bergh, G. C. J. J. van den. 1992. "Legal Pluralism in Roman Law." In *Comparative Legal Cultures*, ed. C. Verga, 338–350. New York: New York University Press.

Bianchini, Mariagrazia. 1988. "Ancora in tema di unioni fra barbari e Romani," *Atti dell' Accademia romanistica constantiana* 7: 225–249.

Blockley, Roger C. 1982. "Roman-Barbarian Marriages in the Late Empire," *Florilegium* 4: 63–79.

Braund, David. 1984. *Rome and the Friendly King: The Character of Client Kingship.* London: Croom Helm.

Brown, Peter. 1992. *Power and Persuasion in Late Antiquity: Towards a Christian Empire.* Madison: University of Wisconsin Press.

Castritius, Helmut. 1972. "Zur Sozialgeschichte der Heermeister des Westreichs nach der Mitte des 5. Jh.: Flavius Valila qui et Theodovius," *Ancient Society* 3: 233–243.

Chrysos, Evangelos. 1989. "Legal Concepts and Patterns for the Barbarian's Settlement on Roman Soil." In *Das Reich und die Barbaren*, ed. E. Chrysos and A. Schwarcz, 13–23. Vienna: Böhlau.

Claude, Dietrich. 1988. "Zur Ansiedlung barbarischer Föderaten in der ersten Hälfte des 5. Jahrhunderts." In *Anerkennung und Integration: Zu den wirtschaftlichen Grundlagen der Völkenwanderungszeit 400–600*, ed. Herwig Wolfram and Andreas Schwarcz, 13–16. Vienna: Verlag der Osterreichischen Akademie der Wissenschaften.

Clévenot, Michel. 1988. "La double citoyenneté: Situation des chrétiens dans l'empire romain." In *Mélanges Pierre Lévêque, I: Religion*, ed. Marie-Madeleine Mactoux and Geny Évelyne, 107–115. Paris: Belles Lettres.

Condurachi, Emil. 1958. "La costituzione Antoniniana e la sua applicazione nell'impero romano," *Dacia* 2: 281–311.

Demandt, Alexander. 1989. "The Osmosis of Late Roman and Germanic Aristocracies." In *Das Reich und die Barbaren*, ed. E. Chrysos and A. Schwarcz, 75–86. Vienna: Böhlau.

Demougeot, Emilienne. 1970. "A propos des lètes gaulois du IVe siècle." In *Festschrift für Franz Altheim*, 101–113. Berlin: de Gruyter.

———. 1974. "Modalités d'établissement des fédérés barbares de Gratien et de Théodose." In *Mélanges d'histoire ancienne offerts à William Seston*, 143–160, Paris: Sorbonne.

———. 1981. "Restrictions à l'expansion du droit de cité dans la seconde moitié du IVe siècle," *Ktèma*: 6: 381–393.

———. 1984. "Le 'conubium' et la citoyenneté conféré aux soldats barbares du Bas-Empire." In *Sodalitas: Scritti A. Guarino*, 1633–1643. Naples: Scientia Verlag.

Dessau, Hermann, ed. 1954–1955. *Inscriptiones Latinae Selectae*, 2nd ed. 5 vols. Berlin: Weidmann.

Duchesne, Louis, ed. 1886–1892. *Liber pontificalis*. Paris: de Boccard.

El-Abbadi, M. A. H. 1962. "The Alexandrian Citizenship," *Journal of Egyptian Archaeology* 49: 106–123.

Fear, A. T. 1990. "*Cives latini, servi publici* and the *lex Irnitana*," *Revue internationale des droits de l'antiquité* 37: 149–166.

Fourgous, Denise. 1993. "L'hybride et le mixte," *Métis* 8.1–2: 231–246.

Gardner, Jane F. 1993. *Being a Roman Citizen*. London: Routledge.

Garnsey, Peter. 1970. *Social Status and Legal Privilege in the Roman Empire*. Oxford: Clarendon Press.

———. 2001. "Citizens and Aliens." In *The Evolution of the Late Antique World*, ed. Peter Garnsey and Caroline Humfress, 88–91. Cambridge: Cambridge University Press.

———. 2004. "Roman Citizenship and Roman Law in the Late Empire." In *Approaching Late Antiquity: The Transformation from Early to Late Empire*, ed. Simon Swain and Mark Edwards, 133–155. Oxford: Oxford University Press.

Gaudemet, Jean. 1958. "L'étranger au bas-empire." *Recueils de la Société Jean Bodin* 9: 209–235.

———. 1985. *Les sources du droit de l'église en occident du IIe au VIe siècle*. Paris: PUF.

Gauthier, Ph. 1986. "La citoyenneté en Grèce et à Rome," *Ktèma* 11: 167–179.

Giacomini, Paulo Donati, and Gabrielle Poma, eds. 1996. *Cittadini e non cittadini nel Mondo Romano: Guida ai testi e ai documenti*. Bologna: CLUEB.

Hagedorn, D. 1996. "Noch einmal zum Volljährigkeitsalter in Ägypten nach der *Constitutio Antoniniana*," *Zeitschrift für Papyrologie und Epigraphik* 116: 224–226.
Heather, Peter. 1991. *Goths and Romans 332–489*. Oxford: Oxford University Press.
Heichelheim, F. M. 1940. "The Text of the Constitutio Antoniniana," *Journal of Egyptian Archaeology* 26: 10–22.
Hoffmann, D. 1963. "Die spätrömischen Soldatengrabschriften von Concordia," *Museum Helveticum* 20: 22–57.
Honoré, Tony. 2002. *Ulpian: Pioneer of Human Rights*, 2nd ed. Oxford: Oxford University Press.
Johne, K. P. 1988. "Germanen im römischen Dienst," *Das Altertum* 34: 5–13.
Jones, A. H. M. 1964. *The Later Roman Empire, 284–602: A Social, Economic and Administrative Survey*. Oxford: Oxford University Press.
———. 1968. "The *dediticii* and the Constitutio Antoniniana." In *Studies in Roman Government and Law*, ed. A. H. M. Jones, 129–140. Oxford: Oxford University Press.
Kaser, Max. 1971. "Das römische Privatrecht." In *Das altrömische, das vorklassische, und das klassische Recht* 1. 2nd ed. Munich: Beck.
Keenan, J. G. 1973–1974. "The Names Flavius and Aurelius as Status Designations in Later Roman Egypt," *Zeitschrift für Papyrologie und Epigraphik* 11: 33–63; 12: 283–304.
King, N. Q. 1961. *The Emperor Theodosius and the Establishment of Christianity*. London: SCM.
Kunkel, W. 1973. *An Introduction to Roman Legal and Constitutional History*, 2nd ed. Trans. J. M. Kelley. Oxford: Oxford University Press.
Labory, Nadine, ed. 1982. *Inscriptions antiques du Maroc II: Inscriptions latines*. Paris: Éditions du CNRS.
Larsen, Jakob A. O. 1934. "The Position of Provincial Assemblies in the Government and Society of the Late Roman Empire," *Classical Philology* 29: 209–220.
Lee, A. D. 1993. *Information and Frontiers: Roman Foreign Relations in Late Antiquity*. Cambridge: Cambridge University Press.
Levy, E. 1943. "The Vulgarization of Roman Law in the Early Middle Ages," *Mediaevalia et Humanistica* 1: 14–40.
Liebeschuetz, Wolf. 1998. "Citizen Status and Law in the Roman Empire and the Visigothic Kingdom." In *Strategies of Distinction: The Construction of Ethnic Communities, 300–800*, ed. Walter Pohl and Helmut Reimitz, 131–152. Leiden: Brill.
Lo Nero, Carolina. 2001. "*Christiana dignitas*: New Christian Criteria for Citizenship in the Later Roman Empire," *Medieval Encounters* 7: 146–164.
Lukaszewicz, Adam. 1990. "Zum Papyrus Gissensis 40 I 9 ("Constitutio Antoniniana")," *Journal of Juristic Papyrology* 20: 93–101.
MacMullen, Ramsay. 1963. "Barbarian Enclaves in the Northern Roman Empire," *Antiquité classique* 32: 552–561.
Mathisen, Ralph W. 2006. "*Peregrini, Barbari*, and *Cives Romani*: Concepts of Citizenship and the Legal Identity of Barbarians in the Later Roman Empire," *American Historical Review* 111: 1011–1040.
Metzler, J., M. Millett, N. Roymans, and J. Slofstra, eds. 1995. *Integration in the Early Roman West*. Luxembourg: Musée Nationale d' Histoire et d'Art de Luxembourg.
Millar, Fergus. 1977. *The Emperor in the Roman World (31 BC–AD 337)*. Ithaca, NY: Cornell University Press.
Mocsy, A. 1964. "Der Name Flavius als Rangbezeichnung in der Spätantike." In *Akten des IV. internationalen Kongresses für griechisches und lateinisches Epigraphie*, 257–263. Vienna: Bohlau.

Mommsen, Theodor. 1889. "Das römische Militarwesen seit Diocletian," *Hermes* 24: 195–279.

Nicolet, C. 1980. *The World of the Citizen in Republican Rome*, trans. P. S. Falla. London: Batsford.

———. 1989. *Le métier de citoyen dans la Rome républicaine*, 2nd ed. Paris: Gallimard.

Noy, David. 2000a. *Foreigners at Rome: Citizens and Strangers*. London: Duckworth.

———. 2000b. "Foreigners in Late Imperial Rome." In *Ethnicity and Culture in Late Antiquity*, ed. S. Mitchell and G. Greatrex, 15–30. London: Duckworth.

Okamura, Larry. 1997. "Roman Withdrawals from Three Transfluvial Frontiers." In *Shifting Frontiers in Late Antiquity*, ed. R. Mathisen and H. Sivan, 11–19. Aldershot: Variorum.

Ratti, Stéphane, ed. 2002. *Antiquité et citoyenneté*. Besançon: Presses Universitaires Franc-Comtoises.

Reinhold, Meyer. 1971. "Usurpation of Status and Status Symbols in the Roman Empire," *Historia* 20: 275–302.

Riccobono, S., ed. 1968. *Fontes Iuris Romani anteiustiniani, I: Leges*. Florence: Barbara.

Riese, A. 1914. *Rheinische Germanien in den antiken Inschriften*. Leipzig: Teubner.

Rigsby, K. J. 1999. "Two Danubian Epitaphs," *Zeitschrift für Papyrologie und Epigraphik* 126: 175–176.

Rilinger, R. 1988. *Humiliores-Honestiores: Zu einer sozialen Dichotomie im Strafrecht der romischen Kaiserzeit*. Munich: Oldenbourg.

Santalucia, B. 1998. *Diritto e processo penale nell'antica Roma*. Milan: Giuffré.

Sasse, Christoph. 1958. "Die constitutio Antoniniana." In *Eine Untersuchung über den Umfang der Bürgerrechtsverleihung auf Grund von Papyrus Gissensis 40 I*. Wiesbaden: Harrassowitz.

Sherwin-White, A. N. 1972. "The Roman Citizenship: A Survey of its Development into a World Franchise." In *Aufstieg und Niedergang der römischen Welt* I.2, 23–58. Berlin: de Gruyter.

———. 1973. "The *Tabula* of Banasa and the Constitutio Antoniniana," *Journal of Roman Studies* 63: 86–98.

———. 1979. *The Roman Citizenship*, 2nd ed. Oxford: Oxford University Press.

Simpson, C. J. 1977a. "*Laeti* in Northern Gaul: A Note on *Pan. Lat.* VIII, 21," *Latomus* 36: 169–170.

———. 1977b. "Julian and the *Laeti*: A Note on Ammianus Marcellinus XX, 8, 13," *Latomus* 36: 519–521.

———. 1988. "*Laeti* in the *Notitia Dignitatum*: Regular Soldiers vs. Soldier Farmers," *Revue belge de philologie* 66: 80–85.

Sirks, A. J. B. 1996. "Shifting Frontiers in the Law: Romans, Provincials, and Barbarians." In *Shifting Frontiers in Late Antiquity*, ed. R. Mathisen and H. Sivan, 146–157. Aldershot: Variorum.

Sivan, Hagith S. 1996. "Why Not Marry a Barbarian? Marital Frontiers in Late Antiquity (The Example of *CTh* 3.14.1)." In *Shifting Frontiers in Late Antiquity*, ed. R. Mathisen and H. Sivan, 136–145. Aldershot: Variorum.

Sollner, A. 1980. *Einführung in die römische Rechtsgeschichte*. Munich: Beck.

Soraci, Rosario. 1968. *Richerche sui conubia tra Romani e Germani nei secoli IV–VI*. Catania: Giannotta. [Rev. 1974]

Ste-Croix, G. E. M. de. 1981. *Class Struggle in the Ancient Greek World*. Ithaca, NY: Cornell University Press.

Stühff, Gudrun. 1966. *Vulgarrecht im Kaiserrecht.* Weimar: Bohlau.

Thomas, Yan. 1996. *L'origine de la commune patrie: Étude de droit public romain (89 av. J.-C.—212 ap. J.-C.).* Rome: École Française de Rome.

Visscher, F. de. 1958. "La condition des pérégrins à Rome jusqu'à la Constitution Antonine de l'an 212." *Recueils de la Société Jean Bodin* 9: 195–208.

Waas, M. 1971. *Germanen im römischen Dienst in 4. Jahrhundert nach Christus.* Bonn: Habelt.

Weaver, P. 1990. "Where Have All the Junian Latins Gone? Nomenclature and Status in the Roman Empire," *Chiron* 20: 275–305.

Whittaker, C. R. 1997. "Imperialism and Culture: The Roman Initiative." In *Dialogues in Roman Imperialism: Power, Discourse, and Discrepant Experience in the Roman Empire,* ed. D. J. Mattingly, 143–164. Journal of Roman Archaeology Supplementary Series 23. Portsmouth: JRA.

Williams, W. 1979. "Caracalla and the Authorship of Imperial Edicts," *Latomus* 38: 67–89.

Woolf, Greg. 1998. *Becoming Roman: The Origins of Provincial Civilization in Gaul.* Cambridge: Cambridge University Press.

Zeller, Joseph. 1905. "Das Concilium der Septem Provinciae in Arelate," *Westdeutsche Zeitschrift für Geschichte und Kunst* 24: 1–19.

CHAPTER 23

JUSTICE AND EQUALITY

KEVIN UHALDE
Ohio University

Philosophical ideas about equality and justice were influential in late Roman imperial and ecclesiastical law. They also stood in conflict with reality, for the law often favored status and influence, and its execution relied upon imperfect judges and procedures. In the *Consolation*, his famous dialogue with the personification of Philosophy, Boethius (c. 480–525) pondered the gap between ideal and reality, justice and law:

> For the proper functioning of wisdom is carried out with greater renown and to better acclaim . . . when prison, death, and all the other tortures that belong to the punishments of the legal process are reserved for the destructive citizens instead, for whom they have in fact been established. Therefore I am utterly amazed that these things are changed and reversed, that punishments for crimes oppress good people, and that evil people snatch away the rewards owed to virtues. And in fact I would be less amazed at this were I to believe that all things are confused together by chance occurrences happening at random. But as it is now, the God who is the helmsman makes my incomprehension that much greater.[1]

Although he had publicly served the Ostrogothic court, Boethius crafted these reflections from an unhappy seclusion, awaiting his own execution around 525. While justice and equality rarely if ever measure up to any society's aspirations, two factors are particular to the later Roman empire. First, the practice of unequal justice—or better justice for better people—was an old and celebrated tradition. Second, the makers of secular law became converts and eventually forceful proponents of Christianity, to whose doctrine the promise of both justice and equality was central. Boethius' complaint, that injustice born of chance was easier to understand than the design of an omnipotent being, would aggravate anyone obliged to deal with the failure of justice and equality. Whether their fullest faith resided in Roman emperors or the Christian God, some worried over the difference between ideal and reality and even tried to bridge the gap, which sometimes meant bending the rules.

Rules to Protect the Innocent

Not long after Carthage fell to the Vandals, the bishop of Rome discovered that Manichaean refugees had taken shelter in his city. Leo I (bishop 440–461) preached in 443 for his congregation "to make known to your priests the Manichaeans, wherever they be hiding."[2] He repeated the summons in an Advent sermon that year. This time he offered evidence that the initial information he had received had led to revelations more disturbing than anyone had anticipated: two women were found to have raised a girl "of at most ten years" for the purpose of having sexual intercourse with an adolescent male, all under the supervision of the Manichaean bishop. The details, Leo said, were in the official record, and one has the sense that his audience knew them already. Leo was not trying to scandalize but instead to convince his audience that the crimes under investigation were horribly real. More specifically, he sought to justify the general call for accusations by Christians against each other. Clearly, some were reluctant to step forward. Leo assured them that his investigation had pursued good information, not "dubious reports and uncertain opinions."[3] The recent revelations came from public testimony given by the accused themselves in open court. (Leo does not mention whether torture was used but it seems likely.) Those who still "believe[d] not that such people must be betrayed" to Leo's investigation must themselves worry, according to the bishop, that they would "be found guilty of silence in the judgment of Christ."[4]

Romans, however, had good reason to refrain from accusing one another. Generation after generation of late Roman emperors decried the "iniquities of calumniators," who accused others falsely or on insufficient grounds, thus polluting "the conduits of law" and making "innocence subject to harm."[5] A 305 edict on accusations, wrongly attributed in the Theodosian Code to Constantine I (r. 306/312–337), warned those who accused others of treason that they were liable to suffer the same penalties as the accused, including torture to corroborate insufficient evidence, regardless of their rank. The same edict prescribed crucifixion for slaves or freedmen who brought accusations against their masters or patrons.[6] The law also provided a variety of procedural restraints against weak or malicious charges. Constantine broke with tradition by forbidding oral accusations and requiring written accusations (*inscriptiones*) in criminal cases.[7] The procedural effect was to mark the path through the increasingly complex system of courts and procedures with a paper trail that higher judges could follow backward if necessary. The reason Constantine gave, however, was "that the license and rashness of such declarations shall be abolished and a charge of crime shall be brought according to the customary form and order of inscription [so] that when anger has been soothed and tranquility of mind restored by these lapses of time, they shall come to the final action with reason and counsel."[8] Procedural restraint was desirable not only in secular contexts. Augustine of Hippo, for example, preached for due process: "If you are a judge, if you take on the power of judging according to the ecclesiastical rules, if there is an accusation before you, if there is a conviction with valid documents and witnesses, then use force, go to trial, excommunicate, degrade."[9]

Leo nonetheless had succeeded at both uncovering Manichaeans and justifying his means of inquiry. Emperor Valentinian III (r. 425–455) wrote admiringly to the praetorian prefect of the West in June 445, recalling how "things that are obscene to tell and to hear have been revealed by their very manifest confession in the court of the most blessed Pope Leo, in the presence of the most august Senate!"[10] Valentinian may have been mindful of how two decades earlier, as a very young ruler, he had ordered Manichaeans "banished from the very sight of the City of Rome."[11] Now he ordered the praetorian prefect to give public notice that "every person who wishes shall have the right to accuse such persons without the risk attendant upon an accusation" (*sine accusationis periculo*).[12] The fear of reprisal for failed accusations was not to deter accusers from making charges. This was not the first time emperors suspended ordinary rules of law to pursue religious criminals. In 382, for example, in Constantinople, Emperor Theodosius I (r. 379–395) instructed the praetorian prefect of the East to hunt down, prosecute, and execute heretics, making use of "informers and denouncers, without the odium attached to informants" (*sine invidia delationis*). The edict also denied the accused the ability to file for a delay or change of venue: accusations should be easy and prosecutions swift.[13] Constantine once decreed in relation to soothsayers "that an accuser of this crime is not an informer, but rather is worthy of a reward."[14] Emperors showed themselves willing to suspend the normal rule of law in the name of piety and justice, though this could leave their officials in an uncomfortable position. Four years after he required written inscriptions for all criminal charges, Constantine invited accusations from every quarter of the Roman populace against his own judges and officials.

> If there is any person of any position, rank, or dignity whatever who believes that he is able to prove anything truthfully and clearly against any judge, count, or any of My retainers or palatines, in that any of these persons has committed some act which appears to have been done without integrity and justice, let him approach Me and appeal to Me unafraid and secure. I Myself will hear everything; I Myself will conduct an investigation; and if the charge should be proved, I Myself will avenge Myself. Let him speak with safety, and let him speak with a clear conscience. If he should prove the case, as I have

> said, I Myself will avenge Myself on that person who has deceived Me up to this time with feigned integrity. The person, moreover, who has revealed and proved the offense I will enrich with honors as well as with material rewards. Thus may the Highest Divinity always be propitious to Me and keep Me unharmed, as I hope, with the State most happy and flourishing.[15]

Rather than reading its exuberance as a sign of Constantine's emotional insanity, as did Edward Gibbon, we can situate this edict into the "culture of criticism" that marks so much late Roman imperial rhetoric: Constantine drew critical attention to the shortcomings of the law, leaving officials of "feigned integrity" to blame, and extolled his own commitment to justice and equality.[16]

Leo's encounter with the Manichaeans has impressed some historians as the "first moment in the history of the Inquisition."[17] But we should not exaggerate either the bishop's ambition or his success.[18] Within a few years, a "most fetid sewage" resurfaced in the Spanish provinces. Its familiar stench was that of Priscillianism, a heresy whose namesake had been tried and executed sixty years earlier. Now there were rumors of magic and astrology, tracts filled with doctrinal errors, and suspicion that the clergy itself was contaminated again. Turibius, bishop of Astorga, one of Spain's oldest episcopal seats, alerted the bishop in Rome. Leo replied in July 447, offering Turibius practical and doctrinal guidance based on his experience with Manichaeans. Their behavior and beliefs were all too similar to those of the Spanish heretics, who mixed their "compound sediment" (*multiplex faeculentia*) "from all the mud of worldly opinions."[19] For instance, their claim that the inequality and injustice of this world derived from some cosmic cause: "So what have the courses of stars to do with this; what the figments of fate; what the changing state and the restless diversity of worldly things?" Leo was contemptuous. "Behold how many unequal people the grace of God makes equal; if they remain faithful throughout all the labors of this life, they cannot be unhappy." What applied to the faithful applied to the Church as a whole: "Therefore the Church, which is the body of Christ, has nothing to fear from the inequalities of the world."[20]

Why Not Equality

When Leo professed equality within the church, he was not suggesting that he presided over a congregation of social peers. True justice and equality, Leo would have said, existed only in another time and place: the eternity of Heaven, which humans awaited until the Final Judgment. Leo was an attentive reader of Augustine of Hippo (bishop 396–430), who distinguished clearly between the imperfections of human society, regardless of its aspirations, and the Christian divine order.[21] Even criminals who stood trial managed to escape justice, but Leo would have agreed with his contemporary, Valerian of Cimiez (bishop c. 439–c. 462), when he preached: "Dead men have their sins still clinging to them. . . . Hell, armed with due punishments, awaits its prisoner."[22] Leo's concept of the Church, however, was not entirely eschatological. In his letter to Turibius, Leo explained how the current "hostile eruption" of heresy no less than "the storms of wars have prevented the execution of the laws." History revealed how to properly execute law, as when Magnus Maximus had Priscillian executed in 385, or Bahram I sentenced Mani to death in 276/277. Then, according to Leo, "the sword of public laws" and their "severity" had served as the appropriate, desirable, and necessary counterpart to "ecclesiastical leniency."[23] Without this balance, should heresy spread unchecked, "all decrees, not only of human laws but even of divine constitutions, will be dissipated."[24] The only recourse at such moments was for the Church to take direct action, as Leo had done in Rome. Thus he sent Turibius the written proceedings of the "most careful inquisitions" (*sollicitissimis inquisitionibus*) that had exposed the Manichaeans to justice.[25]

The correspondence between Leo and the Spanish bishop, however, suggests that problems other than reluctant informants sustained the Priscillianists. According to Turibius, the Church bore much of the blame: priests were reluctant to correct their followers and bishops to excommunicate known heretics. "What kind of disciples will there be where masters such as this are teaching?" Leo fumed, with outrage similar to what Constantine once had unleashed on secular officials "of feigned integrity."[26] Neither Leo nor Turibius was sure that Spanish bishops could even summon a general council among themselves, much less launch a general investigation. Turibius hesitated to try the "force of an official decree" among his own colleagues and instead roused them with "a suggested course of action" for pursuing heretics and enforcing Christian justice.[27] Leo was willing to settle for a regional council, if Turibius could manage that. Neither stars nor fate was thwarting the Church's pursuit of its enemies so much as its own institutional and administrative limitations.

The tension between justice and equality was not new to Late Antiquity. "Equality," wrote Cicero, "is unequal when it does not recognize grades of dignity."[28] The most dignified citizens were the senators, whose dignity consisted in the public offices they held, the responsibilities they shouldered, and the fortunes they spent to maintain public order. Thus they earned the advantages they enjoyed, not least preferential treatment under the law. Ordinary citizens, for their part, were alert, if also submissive, to the "conflict between certain moral aspirations (justice, for instance) and the social institutions (like the law) which attempt to enshrine them."[29] In his landmark study of how social status affected judicial practice, Peter Garnsey observed two distinct ideologies at work in the Roman empire: one, the imperial promise of justice and equality; the other, the judicial privileges for the deserving elite. Emperors often expressed contempt for inequality and injustice and extolled the true justice only they could offer.[30] The turning of late Roman emperors to Christianity did nothing to diminish this ideology. Indeed, Constantine, the first Christian emperor, joined imperial justice with Christian ideas about justice, styling himself as an agent of both. Ecclesiastical writers, especially Lactantius in Constantine's day and later Augustine of Hippo, argued that Christianity revealed to the human race true, perfect justice that the empire had never known.[31] Images from the earliest church mosaics of an imperial Christ, seated with his senatorial apostles or presiding over the Final Judgment, or of his empty throne epitomized the ambition for fusing together these ideals in a "new representation" of justice.[32]

Cicero's criticism of undifferentiated equality reflects the other ancient ideology, which provided for the judicial privileges enjoyed by the Roman elite for centuries. Membership in that group changed with time and situation, extending outward through the provinces, for example, to include the members of city councils, but in Late Antiquity still deriving from family pedigree and public office.[33] Most of its judicial privileges, and most of our evidence for how the ideology of status affected justice, "were grounded not in legislative enactment, but in administrative rules, customary practices, and ultimately the social attitudes of the ruling elite."[34] Some of those privileges had expanded in the later empire, especially with regard to the control wealthy Romans had over the property and people in their power: private bonds of tenancy and dependency became the legal basis for maintaining public order and delivering public revenue.[35] Other privileges, such as immunity from torture or from degrading forms of punishment, were still cherished but far from guaranteed. Changes in judicial procedure, especially the steady rise of the hearing (*cognitio*) over both civil and criminal cases by appointed judges and officials, had accompanied a creeping upward of penalties, including corporal punishment, once fit only for the lowest orders.[36] The response to treason (*majestas*), above all, could level all privilege, as an imperial edict announced in 369: "in [cases of treason] there is only one and the same status for all" (*sola omnibus aequa condicio*).[37] Equality, then, from the mouths of emperors or, as in the case of Boethius, their Germanic successors, had a menacing sound for the privileged elite.

Quintus Aurelius Symmachus (c. 340–402), like Cicero, believed that social status deserved judicial recognition. As a private citizen, he had the requisite prominence, connections, and technical skill to command attention. His orations and letters show him using his eloquence to solicit favors on behalf of friends and clients, favors he suggested they were owed.[38] Symmachus expressed this view succinctly when he appealed for tax relief on behalf of a dear friend, a "noble sister," named Italica. This woman may be the same Italica known from other sources: a Christian widow who corresponded with two of the most famous bishops of the time, John Chrysostom and Augustine of Hippo.[39] "Of course, justice always must be taken into account," wrote Symmachus to his unidentified recipient, someone with the power (*judiciaria auctoritas*) to provide Italica relief. "But when it comes to noble and distinguished persons, moderation is more appropriate, so that the judgment reflects the use of discrimination."[40] Justice was something more to revere and contemplate than to exercise or expect. It stood in the way of the deference due to social distinction. Justice and equality required calibration to reflect the worthy inequality of the Roman social order. Judges, therefore, needed leeway to recognize other estimable qualities—noble birth, social status, and dignity of office, above all. This, for Symmachus, was not merely special pleading for Italica and her particular situation; it should stand as a general principle (*interventum meum generaliter commendum*).

Symmachus, of course, also was powerful. His sympathies and friendships were with other powerful senators whose interests, as he believed, a prefect was obliged to protect.[41] But there were times when great men like Symmachus were obliged to serve the letter of the law and represent the ideal of justice. Symmachus served for brief periods in public office, once a decade over thirty years; his tenure as urban prefect of Rome lasted not much more than half a year (June 384–February 385).[42] Nevertheless, no doubt like most of his fellow aristocrats, when his time came, Symmachus took his work seriously.[43] Urban prefects in the later empire had broader jurisdiction than their earliest predecessors. They heard appeals and also served as the court of first instance in a range of cases, including most civil matters involving members of the senatorial order, who could ask that their cases be transferred to Rome, even when they originated in the provinces.[44] The bulk of business that entered the prefect's court would have been settled there, but the most difficult or controversial cases might be referred to the emperor, in which case the prefect would attach his own report (*relatio*) to whatever documents had been generated up to that point. For this reason, Symmachus' official reports speak of the exceptional: cases that were unusually difficult or terribly sensitive or involved extremely powerful people.[45] Nonetheless, although some the details of the reports are extraordinary, the circumstances and procedures that produced them were the mundane stuff of late Roman law.

Judicial Advantage

During his months as urban prefect, Symmachus encountered every sort of advantage the judicial system allowed the elite. Not justice, as Symmachus had claimed on behalf of Italica, but the law—its rules and procedures and the law itself, in the form of edicts, rescripts, and precedents—constrained his discretion as a judge. There was the case of Musa, a young woman who had come into her inheritance when she turned twenty-five, only to find she shared it with a fictitious brother named Faustinus, who in fact was her guardian's son. Such a transparent swindle should have been easy to undo, yet Musa was "held up by many appeals and various judicial proceedings," as well as the succession of the original judge by another, and so she had missed two filing deadlines. Moreover, each party had cited different imperial edicts as to whether her case could receive another extension. The introduction of conflicting edicts, a common occurrence even in the small sample of cases Symmachus reported, supplied the prefect with his best reason for deferring the case to an imperial decision. Indeed, even when compelling evidence was on the table, by introducing an imperial decree or recommendation, however old or even of dubious authenticity, a litigant could stop a case cold.[46]

Whereas Symmachus sided with dignity over justice in the case of Italica, with Musa he argued from Justice, writ large and represented by *aequitas*:[47] "There may be a reason for it, or it may be chance incidental to lawsuits, that often one party to the controversy bases himself on equity, the other on law. When that happens, merely human counsel wavers and the examining judge, as he considers the question, resorts to a pronouncement by your Clemencies."[48] The law (*jus*) in this case was the array of procedures that a party with the requisite knowledge and resources could work to its advantage. The "chance of lawsuits" (*fortuna causarum*) could wend in unexpected directions, to the greater detriment of those without the time, finances, and legal expertise necessary to survive each new twist and turn. This sort of fortune, unlike the random chance that suggested some comfort to the speaker in Boethius' dialogue, favored the powerful.

The "chance of lawsuits" included time itself—the sheer duration of litigation that could outrun emotional and financial resources and, no less important, outlast the terms of judges, officials, even emperors; even when the law had seemed to provide a remedy, the rules for appeal and change of venue remained complex and open to dispute, which meant still more time before Musa could control her estate in full. All lawsuits, Symmachus suggested on another occasion, were concluded either "by time or by final judgment" (*in negotiis tempore ac judicatione finitis cessare*), after which their discussion became a nuisance. Symmachus wrote this even as he was nettling his emperor with a case whose time, strictly speaking, was up, its period for renewal having passed.[49] Indeed, Symmachus sent on a number of cases that the law should not have admitted, either because some deadline had passed or else the proper moment for filing an appeal had not yet arrived. Even gestures made in the name of justice could forestall its execution. It often is suggested that Symmachus showed excessive caution or even timidity as urban prefect, particularly when he allowed appeals contrary to the law.[50] But emperors were known to change the rules in response to such cases, as indeed happened after at least one of Symmachus' own referrals in the matter of a preemptive appeal.[51]

For those who could bear the costs, an appeal to the emperors might bend the rules in their favor, the same way Symmachus, as private citizen, had sought to bend the rules in favor of Italica. "It is difficult for long-standing disputes to find an ending," he admitted in connection to a particularly vexing suit. "A matter treated in many courts gets into a tangle; the legal processes change, judges move, and the persons implicated are different, My Lords Emperors. I have practical experience of this at the moment. . . ."[52] Symmachus was referring to an inheritance dispute involving three generations of family members, among them two women both named Marciana, one deceased and both represented by agents with their lawyers. Years had passed since the case first opened, with objections and countersuits filed at every stage. "Where there is so much doubt there is only one way of salvation," Symmachus wrote, "to consult an authority which is divine or indeed next to god." So he delivered up the thick packet of documents and waited for the time "when your Majesties' sense of justice (*justitia*) has weighed them all up."[53] When law failed, Symmachus turned to justice. At least a sort of parity, if not equality, existed in this lawsuit. All parties enjoyed social prominence and wealth enough to retain diligent and resourceful representation. The skillful jurisprudence working on both sides is evident from the numerous challenges and new tacks each party made, more often than not, in response to procedural errors or faulty documentation by the other. Where neither party was able to work the process with enough advantage to outmaneuver its opponent, they could make common cause to overwhelm the judge and force the issue to a referral. At this point, both parties appear to have wanted Symmachus simply to get out of the way and send their case to the ultimate decider.

The well-to-do, however, were not always so happy to draw imperial notice. Symmachus also draws criticism from modern historians for not standing up to the violent use of force, another elite privilege, deployed both to resist justice and to afflict the less powerful. Senator Valerianus, for example, who made his home in Epirus, was charged with civil and criminal offenses: he had ignored summonses from a praetorian prefect and a proconsul in turn and remained "influenced neither by respect for rescripts, nor by the severity of laws, nor by loyalty to agreements, nor by regard for the law courts."[54] Now that Symmachus was involved, Valerianus displayed "a discourtesy unbecoming to a citizen" (*inciviliter repugnavit*): he was reported to have beaten the official sent to detain him and bring him to Rome.[55] Not relishing the prospect of the mockery the man might make of his court (*rursus inludi judiciis*), Symmachus suggested that only an emperor had "the right to punish misdemeanors committed by men of the most powerful rank."[56] Even that was easier said than done. Emperor Valentinian II (r. 375–392) once instructed Symmachus to oversee the trial of two enemies of the state. One of them, Macedonius, had only a year earlier, under Emperor Gratian, served as a high officer in the imperial court at Milan. There he had offended the bishop, Ambrose, an aristocrat and former governor himself, by interceding with Gratian on behalf of Priscillian, a convicted heretic. Some ancient and modern commentators see this as the reason for Macedonius' downfall under Valentinian II.[57] Yet, although he seemed to have been taken into custody by the time Symmachus wrote, Macedonius was yet to be delivered up to his court. The prefect was "worried day and night by anxiety to obey [the emperor] quickly" but could do little except wonder at the "various rumors . . . flying around" as to where his tardy defendant was.[58]

Valerianus and Macedonius had gone beyond even the expansive boundaries of elite privilege—*evagari ulterius*, as Symmachus put it in Valerianus' case.[59] Another urban prefect, Quintus Clodius Hermogenianus Olybrius, had been told explicitly in 369 that where the imperial majesty was threatened, "there is only one and the same status for all."[60] More often, force favored the powerful, more so in the later empire than ever before. If the legislation is any guide, for example, land grabbing (*invasio*) was widespread in the fourth century: the "invader" might take over physical possession of an estate in its owner's absence or simply evict the occupant by force. Once in physical possession, the case for ownership would be much easier to make, should it be contested. The law offered some protection to less powerful owners by allowing an order of temporary possession (*possessio momentaria*) to be executed, without the possibility of appeal and without waiting for a hearing on legal ownership.[61] But the law mostly favored the powerful, especially when they took possession against their own tenants or clients.[62] They also had the illicit option of taking violent action first, trusting in their superior status and legal advantage to deal later with the fallout.

Social Advantage

Former prefect Olybrius had precisely those resources and that confidence, as Symmachus discovered in another of the cases to fall under his purview.[63] Other sources describe Olybrius as an honorable and philanthropic man, who served as urban prefect from October 368 to August 370 and later as consul in 379 with the famed rhetorician Ausonius. A less admirable person lurks in the shadows of Symmachus' report. The varying impressions we have of Olybrius may reflect a real difference, not unique to this senator, between the public official and the private citizen. Olybrius' family is known, from Ammianus, to have grown dramatically wealthier around this time.[64] Olybrius himself never appeared in Symmachus' courtroom in connection with this case—another benefit of wealth and power[65]—but even his representatives were slow to show their faces, although their actions were causing the commotion from the outset. The property dispute Symmachus heard very well might have been related to a larger family project that would succeed in making a rich and powerful family richer and more powerful. Depending on how we interpret the record for this difficult case, the law may not have helped this project along, but it almost certainly did little to hinder it.

It appears that Fariana, a woman of senatorial rank, had left instructions for a man named Scirtius to give half her estate to a man named Theseus upon her death. Scirtius, who had imperial rank (*perfectissimus*), may have been the manager of the estate, which lay in the vicinity of Praeneste (modern Palestrina), a city under the jurisdiction of the urban prefect of Rome.[66] Scirtius announced the bequest in a personal letter to Theseus, who requested a document specifying himself and after him also his heirs as recipients. When Theseus died, his heirs claimed their half of the estate, while representatives of Senator Olybrius claimed the half Fariana had asked to be given to Theseus, though on what basis we are never informed. Scirtius claimed that those two halves were one and the same—the half Fariana gave to Theseus had passed to his sons—and that he, Scirtius, owned the other half: if Olybrius had a claim on anything, it would be the half now owned by the heirs. Two or three months before Symmachus entered the dispute, however, agents of Olybrius had forcibly evicted Scirtius from the estate. Now, within the time allowed for a complaint of unlawful dispossession, Scirtius was bringing suit against the heirs and Olybrius. Symmachus agreed to restore temporary possession to Scirtius until the issue of ownership could be settled. The heirs filed an objection to the order, but grudgingly (*reluctarentur*), according to Symmachus, who suspected, at least in hindsight, Olybrius' heavy hand at work again. One of Olybrius' men, by his own admission, refused to let the official sent to carry out the prefect's command onto the estate. When Symmachus called for inhabitants of the estate to be brought to him under escort so that they might clear up the question of possession, they were forcibly abducted en route. Somehow, a freedman of the deceased Theseus was produced in court; he testified that Scirtius' slaves were being kept in a villa owned by Olybrius.[67] Now the prefect summoned members of Praeneste's council to provide evidence for possession from the fiscal records. Finally, no doubt in anticipation of what those records would reveal, a man named Tarpeius came to Symmachus' court. He was Olybrius' estate manager, and this marked Olybrius' first formal involvement in the dispute.

Earlier we saw how much the expert wrangling of lawyers marked the dispute between the two Marcianas. This hearing, by contrast, "was conducted amid much conflict of different kinds waged by the parties," until Symmachus turned to the councilors from Praeneste. They agreed, not only that Scirtius had been in possession of the estate until two or three months earlier but also that Olybrius' men had evicted him. Now that the issue of possession seemed clear, Tarpeius shifted the focus of the hearing to ownership. He recalled the informal and improper means by which Scirtius had executed the instructions of the deceased Fariana, which Scirtius tried to explain but could not entirely defend. Clearly, the matter of ownership would not be settled easily. Nevertheless, Symmachus was certain that Scirtius had a right to temporary possession and so repeated his earlier order. Tarpeius had expected this. He asked that Symmachus deliver him a written copy of the decision and then the very next day filed a joint appeal with the heirs, which fell within the narrow window of two days allowed for an appeal after a ruling was published.[68] There is no mention of legal counsel for Scirtius, but he showed more acumen at this stage than he had with his sloppy handling of the original bequest: he cited "certain enactments" that prohibited appeals of temporary possession orders. As in the case of Italica, conflicting imperial precedents now complicated the proceedings, which Symmachus sent on to Milan, knowing that by doing so he was guilty of allowing an improper appeal. We hear no more of this case. Whether Olybrius prevailed we do not know. But only two years later, Valentinian II issued an edict allowing appeals in the case of orders for temporary possession.[69] Powerful people like Olybrius won another advantage.

If we expand our scope beyond the inner procedural workings of this trial, however, and imagine how Symmachus' report was received in Milan, we find other reasons to think Olybrius carried the day. On the one hand, Olybrius appears to have had the weakest case of all the parties because no documents or other evidence supporting his claims are mentioned in the report and the strong evidence for forcible dispossession undercuts any claim based on possession. On the other hand, the senator knew well how to exercise the privileges the law allowed men of his status and resources. From the beginning, both Scirtius and Symmachus did little more than react to the various tactics Olybrius and his agents employed: "first a game of evasion, then a game of confusion; and when this did not succeed, a stubborn play of superiority by denying responsibility."[70] To evasion and confusion, Symmachus responded well within the limits of his jurisdiction and procedure, which, in the case of abduction, was to do far too little. As for the "stubborn play of superiority," when Tarpeius demanded that the appeal be sent to the imperial court, Symmachus simply "folded."[71] Scirtius would not be moving back onto the estate any time soon. Given the poor state of his own records, losing possession would make his case for ownership still more difficult if and when the case should be heard, by which time it well could be Olybrius who would have paid levies to the Praeneste council and been recorded in its rolls as possessor. Moreover, by including the freedman's testimony about the abduction of Scirtius' slaves, which he claimed would leave no doubt who was behind this "uncivil deed" (*factum incivile*), Symmachus effectively embedded a criminal case in his report: serious charges of violent dispossession, obstruction of justice, and kidnapping, all directly implicating Olybrius. The prefect had upped the ante that Scirtius would have to pay, should he want to see his claim through to completion. If a criminal accusation failed, the accuser suffered the penalty of the crime. Thanks to Symmachus' report, Scirtius' property claim was now entangled in criminal allegations against an extremely powerful man.[72]

Imperial Influence

Finally, as the complexity and gravity of the dispute increased, so did the length of time it might take to reach a final resolution, and much could change in the interval. Symmachus would resign from office and return to the life of dignified leisure he preferred no later than February 385. Because we cannot date this report precisely, we cannot be certain that Symmachus left Scirtius to resume his case under a different judge. But we do know that Symmachus had inherited just such cases himself. The turnover in administrative offices presented problems not only for litigants but also for officials. Two cases bore directly on Symmachus during his prefecture. One involved a "departmental dispute" left unresolved from the prefect who preceded Symmachus' own predecessor, which was complicated by the maneuverings of one of the prefect's own barristers.[73] The other involved the latest of a long series of investigations into the prefecture of his own father-in-law, Memmius Vitrasius Orfitus (urban prefect in 353–356 and 357–359), which threatened the personal fortune of Symmachus' wife. In his own defense, Symmachus hopefully reminded Valentinian of "what course of action best befits the equity [*aequitas*] characteristic of your times."[74] Just as the less powerful turned for help to patrons or officials such as Symmachus, so Symmachus turned to his emperor when he found himself ensnared in the law. As for Scirtius, he well may have been caught in a personal rivalry between Symmachus and Olybrius (although Symmachus insisted that "private hatreds" should not interfere with the law).[75] Unfortunately for Scirtius, Olybrius' influence at the imperial court was on the rise at the same time that Symmachus' waned.

Some of the evidence for this shift in favor from Symmachus to Olybrius is to be found in the circumstances surrounding the most famous report Symmachus sent to Milan: the request in the summer or fall of 384 that the Altar of Victory be restored to the Senate House, from which Gratian had ordered it removed two years earlier. Symmachus in his elegant plea claimed to represent the desire of the Senate's majority. He also would have hoped that influential friends, above all men such as Vettius Agorius Praetextatus, praetorian prefect of Italy, would provide compelling vocal support to his recommendation. Bishop Ambrose of Milan, however, was already campaigning against this request even before he had read Symmachus' report.[76] In the end, Ambrose prevailed in what is often signaled as one of the turning points in Christianity's triumph over paganism.[77] Meanwhile, Praetextatus, Symmachus' strongest ally in the imperial court, died in December 384. In a series of reports, Symmachus conveyed the grief of the Roman people, who wept in the streets; he himself asked to be relieved of office.[78]

The prefect did not need to express what was obvious: as distinguished and well connected as he was, his authority and success, not only as a patron for his friends and clients but also as an official whose duties butted against the privileges of his peers, were contingent on having the emperor's ear. Such influence depended on access to the center of power, where ordinary reassignment, "meteoric rises" and "sudden falls" (as in the case of Macedonius), and natural death (as in the case of Praetextatus) could change the dynamics overnight.[79] In Late Antiquity, the imperial court, including the consistory where edicts and responses to reports like Symmachus' were written, was in many ways a closed orbit. Emperors were increasingly insulated from the appeals not only of ordinary citizens but also even of their high officials.[80] This affected the way late Roman government worked generally and how accessible emperors really were to citizens who suffered injustice. Not only were the resources of a person such as Scirtius, facing a more powerful opponent, outmatched in terms of wealth, influence, legal expertise, and violent force, but also even the highest civil judges could effectively be bypassed. With trial expenses up to the point of deferral or appeal weighing disproportionately on the weaker party, we can easily imagine the impact to have been crushing. Thus the experiences of Symmachus and Scirtius both were subject to larger processes that affected the relationship between late Roman law and justice.

Before concluding, let us consider another of the larger processes that may have affected Symmachus and Scirtius in this case: the Christianization of the empire. With Praetextatus' death, the most powerful official at court became Sextus Petronius Probus, son-in-law of Olybrius and head of one of Rome's most famous Christian senatorial families, later to be buried in St. Peter's with a suitably distinguished tombstone.[81] Unlike Probus and Olybrius, Symmachus was not a Christian. Historians often locate him within a group of senators who resisted the decline of traditional religion in public life, even styling him as a leader of the "last pagan revival" and "paganism's last battle."[82] There is little revivalist or apologetic in Symmachus' writings, not even in the report on the Altar of Victory. We also know that Symmachus counted Christians among his clients, friends, and even relatives—including Ambrose, long after the affair of the altar was settled. Business, patronage, and family interests could still trump religious differences.[83] Yet one commentator on the *Relationes* suggests that Symmachus' judicial behavior, including the opposition he drew between justice (*aequitas*) and the law (*jus*), reflected the working of a "Christian ethical influence," traceable back to Constantine the Great more than a half century earlier.[84]

How religion affected the first Christian Roman imperial laws has never been clear-cut. Constantine banned death by crucifixion, for example, but he also ordered that parricides be sewn in a sack with deadly serpents, a punishment his son extended to adulterers.[85] He may have had a genuine regard for the humanity of slaves, but when he considered their freedom (*libertas*), it was in traditional Roman fashion: as property to be released or not.[86] Constantine's innovations with regard to judicial procedure were part of a familiar endeavor by emperors to reconcile the ideal of justice with judicial reality, at least in their rhetoric. In this respect, he was a "typical Roman emperor," and recent scholarship tends to emphasize Constantine's place in long-term developments, rather than arguing for a sudden "revolution" or a wholesale transformation of "Roman Law" into "Christian Roman Law."[87] This is important for understanding the role he allowed Christian bishops in the Roman judicial system—the so-called episcopal hearing (*audientia episcopalis*). Two pertinent edicts survive from Constantine's reign. The circumstances of their creation reflect the other, inner side of the orbit enclosing the imperial consistory, which sometimes allowed but also repelled contact with citizens and even high officials such as Symmachus.[88] The first responded narrowly to queries from officials, no doubt men like Symmachus, seeking a quick, pertinent response. The emperor showed no generic concern over Christian bishops acting as arbiters or judges but addressed only cases that had changed venue from a public court to an episcopal hearing and how a public judge should treat their outcome. The second surviving decree, from 333, considered Christian episcopal arbitration more broadly and deeply. It allowed bishops actual judicial powers: they might take cases even when only one party desired an episcopal hearing; their decisions were independently binding, without a public judge's endorsement. They also were immune from appeal, "considered as forever holy and revered." A bishop's uncorroborated testimony was incontestable because it was "established with the authority of truth, that is incorruptible, which the consciousness of an undefiled mind has produced from a sacrosanct man." At that time, within the confines of the imperial court, bishops, by virtue of being bishops, were thought to be extraordinary, even infallible, judges: "The authority of sacrosanct religion searches out and reveals many things which the captious restrictions of legal technicality do not allow to be produced in court."[89]

The main purpose of Constantine's edict was to open another channel to justice, boring through the sediment of legal restrictions, lengthy appeals, and social inequalities. Later evidence shows bishops hearing a range of disputes, including some that involved less privileged members of society. We are not surprised that bishops never emerged as the perfect judges Constantine promised. Yet some bishops drew on their secular forensic training to solve religious disputes, actively—even "jealously"—attracted casework to their courts, requested gynecological exams as evidence and inflicted corporal punishment against clergy and laity (including the poor), and sought out legal advice when they found themselves lost in law's "captious restrictions."[90] Indeed, bishops fit well enough into the legal system to become a potential source of confusion and advantage in their own right. More than a decade after Ambrose prevailed in the matter of the Altar of Victory and Symmachus retired from office, we find the former prefect writing to the bishop about a financial dispute (*pecuniaria actio*) between two men: on the one side, Symmachus' client, a young and rapidly rising public official named Classicianus; on the other side, a man of indeterminate status, referred to only as "the Pirate." The Pirate wanted a hearing in Ambrose's court, while Classicianus—"absent as well as caught up in public affairs"—hoped Symmachus could persuade the bishop it was not worth his bother. "There are laws, there are tribunals, there are judges for a litigant to employ," Symmachus wrote, "without violating your conscience."[91] These were people using their connections to find the most advantageous forum, while being careful not to cause needless offense in the process—at least in Classicianus' case; the Pirate's tact, we do not know.

CONCLUSION

Such tactics continued to harry lesser-skilled litigants as well as officials, who throughout the fourth and fifth centuries wrote their emperors with questions about episcopal hearings. The single imperial response to survive wholly intact comes from Valentian III, given at Rome in 452. Although still allowing privileges to clerics and especially bishops, the scope of their judicial authority was restricted much more than Constantine had allowed in 333. Seven years earlier, Valentinian had given extraordinary judicial support to Leo the Great's heresy investigation, even lifting the ordinary restraints on accusations. But as a rule, bishops were part of the legal system. They could be accused in public court of civil and criminal offenses, and, if they should refuse to comply, "the order of the law shall be observed and a sentence shall hold them liable as contumacious."[92]

Both Symmachus and Leo, prefect and pope—one representative of the old elite, the other of a new religious order—grappled with the conflict between the theory and practice of justice. Both were willing to bend the rule of the law, which was imperfect, to serve the cause of justice. Neither man, however, believed that this was an ideal or sustainable solution. After half a year as urban prefect, Symmachus returned to private life, where his many letters show him fully enjoying the pleasures of his privileged social position. Leo was willing to combat heresy in his city the same way emperors destroyed traitors, with extreme severity and disregarding ordinary judicial restraint. But the Church was in no position, practically or theologically, to bring human society into accord with what the philosopher and public official Boethius called "the proper functioning of wisdom." Justice and equality were both served and constrained by the practice of the law. Which way the balance tipped was in the eye of the beholder, who was never without a vested interest.

NOTES

1. *Consolation of Philosophy* 4, Prose 5, Boethius 2001, 110–111 (I changed the translator's "overwhelm" to "oppress").

2. Leo, *Serm.* 9.4, Schipper and van Oort 2000, 25. All translations of Leo's writings are by Schipper and van Oort. The best study of this and related texts remains Lepelley 1961; see also Maier 1996; Neil 2009. More generally on Leo, along with Neil, see recently Armitage 2005; Green 2008; Henne 2008; Wessel 2008.

3. Leo, *Serm.* 16.4, Schipper and van Oort 2000, 27; also see the translation and introduction to this homily in Neil 2009.

4. Leo, *Serm.* 16.5, Schipper and van Oort 2000, 29.

5. Justinian, *Institutiones*, Preface; *C.Th.* 9.1.19 preface; Uhalde 2007, 20–21.

6. *C.Th.* 9.5 (*Ad legem Iuliam maiestatis*), with most recently Corcoran 2002 for the 305 date.

7. Mossakowski 1996. If this seems an obvious improvement, consider Herodotus' critical description of Deioces, the tyrant of Media, who refused to be seen by litigants lest they remember he was their peer and so only dealt with lawsuits through written form (Hdt. 1.100).

8. *C.Th.* 9.1.5 (320), Pharr 1952, 224–225. See generally *C.Th.* 9.1, 10.10.

9. Augustine, *Serm.* 164.11, PL 38: 900; Uhalde 2007, 32–43.

10. *N.Val.* 18 preface, Pharr 1952, 531.

11. *C.Th.* 16.5.62; Enßlin 1937, 369.

12. *N.Val.* 18.2, Pharr 1952, 531.

13. *C.Th.* 16.5.9.1, Pharr 1952, 452. In *C.Th.* 9.19.4, Gratian allowed a litigant to accuse his opponent of forgery for introducing a false document during a trial *without* filing an inscription: Harries 1988, 166–169; 1999, 127. But Gratian also required an inscription from an accuser before even slaves were submitted to torture in connection to a homicide case (*C.Th.* 9.1.14).

14. *C.Th.* 9.16.1 (320), Pharr 1952, 237.

15. *C.Th.* 9.1.4, Pharr 1952, 224.

16. Harries 1999 for "culture of criticism."

17. Batiffol, 1924, 437: "Les *gesta* du procès des manichéens romains, si nous les possédions, seraient le premier monument de l'histoire de l'inquisition"; Caspar 1930, 434–435: "Die Hinrichtung Priscillians hat man wohl als den ersten blutigen Ketzerprozeß, Leos d. Gr. Manichäerverfahren als den ersten 'Inquisitions'prozeß bezeichnet"; Wessel 2008, 38: "he orchestrated what could be considered the first inquisition at Rome." See Maier 1996, 441.

18. Maier 1996, 460: "Of course it is impossible to determine the degree to which Leo's exhortations were followed. Again, his commandments to be vigilant for the enemy within and without may reveal more the absence of real power to survey, discipline and punish than its presence." Also Lieu 1992, 147.

19. Leo, *Ep.* 15 preface, Schipper and van Oort 2000, 53; also see the translation and introduction to this letter in Neil 2009. For Priscillianism generally, see Chadwick 1976; Burrus 1995. With specific regard to this correspondence, see Vollmann 1965; Van Dam 1984, 87–114; Wessel 2008, 106–114.

20. Leo, *Ep.* 15.10, Schipper and van Oort 2000, 65–67.

21. Dodaro 2004; Wessel 2008, 137–178. For an example of how ordinary clergy shared these ideas with their congregations, see Bailey 2008.

22. Valerian of Cimiez, *Hom.* 1, PL 52, col. 694: "defunctis corporibus salua sunt crimina . . . expectat enim reum suum gehenna debitis armata suppliciis"; Humfress 2007, 156.

23. For Priscillian's trial, see note 2 and Girardet 1974. For a summary and bibliography for the date of Mani's death, see Schipper and van Oort 2000, 90–91.

24. Leo, *Ep.* 15 preface, Schipper and van Oort 2000, 53.

25. Leo, *Ep.* 15.16, Schipper and van Oort 2000, 72.

26. *Ep.* 15.16–17, Schipper and van Oort 2000, 75–77.

27. Schipper and van Oort 2000, 80–81.

28. Cicero, *De republica* 1.43: ". . . tamen ipsa aequabilitas est iniqua, cum habet nullos gradus dignitatis"; Garnsey 1970, 3.

29. Morgan 2007, 22, also 40: "Though very keen on justice in principle . . . proverbs (like popular morality in general) are rather sceptical of judicial systems, and nearly all proverbs dealing with actual institutions are rather negative."

30. Voss 1982; Millar 1977, 228–259; Konstan 2001, 114–115.

31. E.g., Konstan 2001, 121–124; Digeser 2000; Bowen and Garnsey 2003, 29–35; Dodaro 2004; Humfress 2007, 149–150.

32. Hellemo 1989; Brenk 1975, 14–19; "new representation": Cameron 1991, chapter 6.

33. E.g., Brown 1992, 3–34; Salzman and Rapp 2000; Salzman 2001; Lizzi Testa 2006.

34. Garnsey 1970, 10.

35. Sirks 2001; Grey and Parkin 2003; Grey 2007.

36. Garnsey 1970, chapters 1–2, 4–5; MacMullen 1986; Harries 1999, 118–152.

37. *C.Th.* 9.35.1, Pharr 1952, 250, with Matthews 1989, 212–213. But also see, e.g., *C.Th.* 9.1.1: "Omnem enim honorem reatus excludit, cum criminalis causa et non civilis res vel pecuniaria moveatur."

38. Matthews 1974, 69, n. 53; Brown 1995, 38–40. See generally Sogno 2006; Brown 1992, 35–47.

39. *PLRE* 1:465–466; Roda 1981, 164–167. She may have married one of the sons of Petronius Probus 5 (see *PLRE* 1:736–740), the praetorian prefect overlapping with Symmachus' urban prefecture.

40. Symmachus, *Ep.* 9.40, Callu 2002, 27 (my translation): "Ratio quidem semper habenda iustitiae est, sed circa nobiles probabilesque personas plus debet esse moderaminis, ut perspiciatur in discretione iudicium." Matthews 1974, 68, n. 54; Roda 1981, 164–165; MacMullen 1988, 61, n. 3.

41. Matthews 1974, 68, n. 51.

42. Matthews 1974, 74–75, observes that terms rarely lasted more than a year.

43. Matthews 1975, 7–12.

44. Chastagnol 1960.

45. Harries 1999, 114–117; 2006, 99; Sogno 2006, 31–57; Hecht 2006; Vera 1981.

46. So Symmachus exclaimed in a case between three women and the imperial treasury, over alleged outstanding payments due on their inheritance (*Rel.* 30.4, Barrow 1973, 165): "This complication made me hold my hand, for I saw that a statement made by an Emperor carried more force than all the receipts in the world." Hecht 2006, 392–406. All translations of the *Relationes* are from Barrow 1973.

47. Cf., e.g., *C.Th.* 1.1.15, to Praetorian Prefect Synegius: "iustitia et aequitate, qua notus es." For *aequitas* see further later.

48. Symmachus, *Rel.* 39.1, Barrow 1973, 201; Hecht 2006, 456–459; Vera 1981, 293, who compares with Symmachus, *Rel.* 33.1: "ius potestatis . . . iniquae iudicationis."

49. Symmachus, *Rel.* 38.1 and 3, Barrow 1973, 197–199.

50. Liebs 1997; Hecht 2006, 522–523, *passim.*

51. Symmachus, *Rel.* 16, Barrow 1971, 93–95; *C.Th.* 11.30.44 and 4.17.4, dated November 29, 384; Vera 1981, 128–131; Hecht 2006, 312–316.

52. Symmachus, *Rel.* 19.1, Barrow 1973, 103; Harries 1999, 105–106, 114–115; Hecht 2006, 326–360.

53. Symmachus, *Rel.* 19.10, Barrow 1973, 107.

54. On fitting this case with the rules of accusation against *clarissimi viri*, see *C.Th.* 9.1.13 (February 11, 376) with Chastagnol 1960, 125–126; Hecht 2006, 522–540.

55. At 31.2, Symmachus writes of this attack: "unus . . . adfectum se a Valeriano gravibus iniuriis indicavit," while at 3.3 the same official (*apparitor*) is identified as the one who "contumaciam senatoris et serviles impetus nuntiavit." Barrow translates the

latter as "attacks made by his slaves," but *serviles* better describes the humiliating nature of the beatings Valerianus had dealt the official.

56. Symmachus, *Rel.* 31, Barrow 1973, 169–171.

57. Vera 1981, 277–280; McLynn 1994, 150–153, 158–159; Sogno 2006, 48. Vera 1981, 278, corrects Chastagnol 1960, 130, n. 4, who mistakenly identifies the two men, Macedonius and Ammianus, as *protectores*, who in fact were those charged with transporting the prisoners and Symmachus' source of information.

58. Symmachus, *Rel.* 36, Barrow 1973, 193.

59. Symmachus, *Rel.* 31.3, Barrow 1973, 171.

60. *C.Th.* 9.35.1, with n. 37 here.

61. Vera 1981, 204; Liebs 1997, 108 with nn. 50–51, observe, *pace* Barrow (who was following Seeks), that *CTh* 11.30.44 on appeals *praeiudicium* does not apply in the case to be considered here (*Rel.* 28).

62. For *invasiones*, see *C.Th.* 2.26.1–2, 4.22, 9.10; Symmachus, *Rel.* 38, Barrow 1973, 196–199; Vera 1981, 206–207; Jaillette 1995; Delmaire 1995; Hecht 2006, 383–389 ("Landraub (invasio) als weitverbretetes Übel"), 564–567.

63. Symmachus, *Rel.* 28, Barrow 1973, 153–161. See Vera 2001, 202–220; Liebs 1997; Harries 1999, 116–117; 2006, 99–101; Hecht 2006, 360–392.

64. Especially Liebs 1997, 111–112, with Matthews 1975, 2; 1989, 278, n. 52.

65. A privilege we find curtailed by an edict of Valentinian II and Theodosius I in 390, regarding criminal accusations against *potentiores*: *C.Th.* 9.1.17.

66. The estate (*massa Caesariana*) has been tentatively identified with a cluster of buildings at a place called Casarina, between Poli and Gallicano: see Vera 1981, 209.

67. It is understandable that Theseus' heirs would have complied to make the freedman available to the court. At that point, only they had made a formal objection to Scirtius' possession and so had reason to distance themselves from the violent, criminal turn the dispute took with the abduction of the slaves.

68. Vera 1981, 218.

69. *C.Th.* 11.37.1 (November 18, 386).

70. Liebs 1997, 113. Harries 2006 is more optimistic about how much Symmachus helped Scirtius.

71. Liebs 1997, 113.

72. On the risk of civil actions becoming criminal actions and its unequal bearing against less powerful parties, see Gratian's 378 edict, *C.Th.* 9.20.1, with Harries 1988, 166–169; 2006, 96–97.

73. Symmachus, *Rel.* 23, Barrow 1973, 122–135; Matthews 1975, 210, n. 4; Vera 1981, 163–180.

74. Orfitus: Symmachus, *Rel.* 34, Barrow 1973, 178–189; Chastagnol 1960, 341–345; Chastagnol 1962, 143–147; Vera 1981, 254–272. The scandal is particularly interesting because Symmachus also wrote about it in a personal letter, *Ep.* 9.150, Callu 2002, 86–87, 137–138.

75. Symmachus, *Rel.* 34.9, Barrow 1973, 187: "privata odia aduersum leges exercenda non esse." For Olybrius and Symmachus, see Vera 1981, 204–208; Liebs 1997.

76. Symmachus, *Rel.* 3, Barrow 1973, 32–47. See Matthews 1975, 183–211, with references.

77. See Maxwell, chapter 26 in this book.

78. Symmachus, *Rel.* 10–12, Barrow 1973, 72–81.

79. Kelly 2004, 194.

80. Kelly 2004, esp. chapter 5; also MacMullen 1988. On the consistory, see Coriat 1997; Harries, chapter 24 in this book, nn. 10 and 84.

81. Matthews 1975, 195–197; Salzman 2001, 364–365.

82. Bloch 1945; Sheridan 1966; Wytzes 1977.

83. Matthews 1986; Barnes 1992; McLynn 1994, 151–152, 263–275; Salzmann 2006; Sogno 2006; Sogno and Ebbeler 2007.

84. Vera 1981, 293, referring to the passage from Symmachus, *Rel.* 39.1 quoted previously: "È evidente, infatti, la derivazione dei suoi concetti dalla legislazione di Costantino nella quale, secondo un'evoluzione in cui è sensibile l'influsso dell'etica cristiana, è molto frequente l'esaltazione della superiorità della *aequitas* sullo *ius* [citations follow]." Musumeci 1977, 433, similarly describes how Valentinian III "fa dell'etica cristiana e dell'umanità il motivo ispiratore di gran parte della sua legislazione." By contrast, Matthews 1974, 69–70, observes Symmachus' chilling insensitivity to the suffering of ordinary people. On *aequitas* in this context, see Pringsheim 1935; Caron 1971, chapter 1.

85. *C.Th.* 15.1, 11.36.4.

86. Lenski 2011; see also Harper, chapter 20 in this book.

87. Van Dam 2007. For "Christian Roman Law," Biondi 1952–1954, especially chapters 1, 4, and 12. Among recent critics, see Crifò 1988; Evans Grubbs 1995; Humfress 2006; 2007, 147–152; Huck 2008b, 11–16, 38–44, *passim* with further citations. See further Harries, chapter 24 in this book, section 6.

88. See especially the work of Olivier Huck cited in the bibliography; his doctoral thesis (Huck 2008b) eventually will appear in the Collection de l'École française. Also see Vismara 1995; Harries 1999, 191–211; Humfress 2007, 156–173.

89. *C.Sirm.* 1, Pharr 1952, 477. On the consistory's "perception" of bishops with relation to this clause, see Huck 2008b, 346, n. 458; Humfress 2007, 161 at n. 31. For the Sirmondian Constitutions, see Landau 1992; Vessey 1993; Huck 2008b: "Étude annexe II: les *Constitutions Sirmondiennes.*"

90. Humfress 2007; Huck 2008b, 509–530 (including "évêques jaloux de leurs prérogatives"); Uhalde 2007, 67–76; Dossey, 2001; Lenski 2001; Humbert 1983; Lepelley 1983.

91. Symmachus, *Ep.* 3.36, Callu 2003, 44–45 (my translation): "Sunt leges, sunt tribunalia, sunt magistratus, quibus litigator utatur salua conscientia tua." See Vismara 1995, 76–82; Huck 2008b, 412–416, 519–522, 524–526.

92. *N.Val.* 35.1, Pharr 1952, 545–546; Humfress 2007, 164–166.

WORKS CITED

Ancient Sources

Barrow, R. H., trans. 1973. *Prefect and Emperor: The Relationes of Symmachus A.D. 384.* Oxford: Oxford University Press.

Bowen, Anthony, and Peter Garnsey, trans. 2003. *Lactantius: Divine Institutions.* Translated Texts for Historians 40. Liverpool: Liverpool University Press.

Boethius. 2001. *Consolation of Philosophy.* Trans. Joel C. Relihan. Indianapolis, IN: Hackett.

Callu, Jean-Pierre, ed. and trans. 2002. *Symmaque: Lettres Tome IV, livres IX–X.* Collection des Universités de France. Paris: Belles Lettres.

———. 2003. *Symmaque: Correspondance, Tome II, livres III–V.* Collection des Universités de France. Paris: Belles Lettres.

C.Th. and *C.Sirm.* = Theodor Mommsen and Paul M. Meyer, eds. 1905. *Theodosiani libri XVI cum Constitutionibus Sirmondianis et Leges novellae ad Theodosianum pertinentes.* Berlin: Weidmann.

Justinian, *Institutiones.* Paul Krueger, ed. *Corpus iuris civilis, vol. 1: Institutiones, Digesta,* 16th ed. Berlin: Weidmann, 1928.

Pharr, Clyde, trans. 1952. *The Theodosian Code and Novels and the Sirmondian Constitutions.* Princeton, NJ: Princeton University Press.

Schipper, Hendrik Gerhard, and Johannes Van Oort, trans. 2000. *St. Leo the Great: Sermons and Letters against the Manichaeans, Selected Fragments.* Corpus Fontium Manicaeorum Series Latina 1. Turnhout: Brepols.

Symmachus, *Rel.* and *Ep.* = Otto Seeck, ed. *Q. Aurelii Symmachi quae supersunt.* Monumenta Germaniae Historica, Auctores Antiquissimi 6:2. Berlin: Weidmann. 1883.

Valerian of Cimiez, *Homiliae* = PL 52: 691–756.

Modern Sources

Armitage, Mark. 2005. *Twofold Solidarity: Leo the Great's Theology of Redemption.* Strathfield, Australia: St. Paul's Publications in association with the Centre for Early Christian Studies, Australian Catholic University.

Bailey, Lisa. 2008. "'No Use Crying over Spilt Milk': The Challenge of Preaching God's Justice in Fifth and Sixth-Century Gaul," *Journal of the Australian Early Medieval Association* 4: 19–31.

Barnes, T. D. 1992. "Augustine, Symmachus and Ambrose." In *Augustine: From Rhetor to Theologian,* ed. Joanne McWilliam, 7–13. Waterloo, ON: Wilfrid Laurier University Press.

Batiffol, Pierre. 1924. *Le siège apostolique (359–451).* Paris: Libraire Victor Lecoffre.

Biondi, Biondo. 1952–1954. *Il diritto romano cristiano.* 3 vols. Milan: Giuffrè.

Bloch, Herbert. 1945. "A New Document of the *Last Pagan* Revival in the West," *Harvard Theological Review* 38: 199–244.

Brenk, Beat. 1975. *Die frühchristlichen Mosaiken in S. Maria Maggiore zu Rom.* Wiesbaden: Steiner.

Brown, Peter. 1992. *Power and Persuasion in Late Antiquity: Toward a Christian Empire.* Madison: University of Wisconsin Press.

———. 1995. *Authority and the Sacred: Aspects of the Christianisation of the Roman World.* Cambridge: Cambridge University Press.

Burrus, Virginia. 1995. *The Making of a Heretic: Gender, Authority, and the Priscillianist Controversy.* Berkeley: University of California Press.

Cameron, Averil. 1991. *Christianity and the Rhetoric of Empire: The Development of Christian Discourse.* Berkeley: University of California Press.

Caron, Giovanni. 1971. *"Aequitas" romana, "misericordia" patristica ed "epicheia" aristotelica nella dottrina dell' "aequitas" canonica (dalle origini al Rinascimento).* Milan: Giuffrè.

Caspar, Erich. 1930. *Geschichte des Papsttums von den Anfängen bis zur Höhe der Weltherrschaft. 1er Band: Römische Kirche und Imperium Romanum.* Tübingen: J. C. B. Mohr.

Chadwick, Henry. 1976. *Priscillian of Avila: The Occult and the Charismatic in the Early Church.* Oxford: Clarendon Press.

Chastagnol, André. 1960. *La préfecture urbaine à Rome sous le Bas-Empire.* Paris: Presses universitaires.

———. 1962. *Les fastes de la préfecture de Rome au Bas-Empire.* Paris: Nouvelles Éditions Latines.

Corcoran, Simon. 2002. "A Tetrarchic Inscription from Corcyra and the *Edictum de Accusationibus,*" *Zeitschrift für Papyrologie und Epigraphik* 141: 221–230.

Coriat, Jean-Pierre. 1997. *Le prince législateur: La technique législative des Sévères et les méthodes de création du droit impérial à la fin du principat.* Bibliothèque des écoles françaises d'Athènes et de Rome 294. Rome: Ecole française de Rome.

Crifò, Giuliano. 1988. "Romanizzazione e cristianizzazione, certezze e dubbi in tema di rapporto tra cristiani e istituzioni." In *I cristiani e l'impero nel IV secolo: Colloquio sul cristianesimo nel mondo antico,* ed. Giorgio Bonamente and Aldo Nestori, 75–106. Macerata: Università degli studi di Macerata.

Delmaire, Roland. 1995. "*Invasor, invasio*: Réflexions sur quelques textes de l'antiquité tardive." In *Aux sources de la gestion publique, Tome II: L'Invasio des villae ou la villa comme enjeu de pouvoir,* ed. Elisabeth Magnou-Nortier, 77–88. Villeneuve d'Ascq: Presses universitaires de Lille.

Digeser, Elizabeth DePalma. 2000. *The Making of a Christian Empire: Lactantius and Rome.* Ithaca, NY: Cornell University Press.

Dodaro, Robert. 2004. *Christ and the Just Society in the Thought of Augustine.* Cambridge: Cambridge University Press.

Dossey, Leslie. 2001. "Judicial Violence and the Ecclesiastical Courts in Late Antique North Africa." In *Law, Society, and Authority in Late Antiquity,* ed. Ralph W. Mathisen, 98–114. Oxford: Oxford University Press.

Enßlin, Wilhelm. 1937. "Valentians III. Novellen XVII und VIII von 445," *Zeitschrift der Savigny-Stiftung für Rechtsgeschichte, Römanistische Abteilung* 57: 367–378.

Evans Grubbs, Judith. 1995. *Law and Family in Late Antiquity: The Emperor Constantine's Marriage Legislation.* Oxford: Oxford University Press, 1995.

Garnsey, Peter. 1970. *Social Status and Legal Privilege in the Roman Empire.* Oxford: Clarendon.

Girardet, Klaus M. 1974. "Der Prozess gegen die Priszillianer," *Chiron* 4: 577–608.

Green, Bernard. 2008. *The Soteriology of Leo the Great.* Oxford: Oxford University Press.

Grey, Cam. 2007. "Contextualizing *Colonatus*: The *Origo* of the Late Roman Empire," *Journal of Roman Studies* 97: 155–175.

Grey, Cam, and Anneliese Parkin. 2003. "Controlling the Urban Mob: The *colonatus perpetuus* of *CTh* 14.18.1," *Phoenix* 57: 284–299.

Harries, Jill. 1988. "The Roman Imperial Quaestor from Constantine to Theodosius II," *Journal of Roman Studies* 78: 148–172.

———. 1999. *Law and Empire in Late Antiquity.* Cambridge: Cambridge University Press.

———. 2006. "Violence, Victims, and the Legal Tradition in Late Antiquity." In *Violence in Late Antiquity: Perceptions and Practices,* ed. H. A. Drake, 85–102. Aldershot: Ashgate.

Hecht, Bettina. 2006. *Störungen der Rechtslage in den Relationen des Symmachus: Verwaltung und Rechtsprechung in Rom, 384/385 n. Chr.* Freiburger Rechtsgeschichtliche Abhandlungen, n.f. 50. Berlin: Duncker & Humblot.

Hellemo, Geir. 1989. *Adventus Domini: Eschatological Thought in 4th-Century Apses and Catecheses*. Trans. Elinor Ruth Waaler. Supplements to Vigiliae Christianae, 5. Leiden: Brill.

Henne, Philippe. 2008. *Léon le Grand*. Paris: Éditions du Cerf.

Huck, Olivier. 2003a. "À propos de *CTh* 1, 27, 1 et *CSirm* 1: Sur deux textes controversés relatifs à l'*episcopalis audientia* constantinienne," *Zeitschrift der Savigny-Stiftung für Rechtsgeschichte, Romanistische Abteilung* 120: 78–105.

———. 2003b. "Encore à propos des *Sirmondiennes*: Arguments présentés à l'appui de la thèse de l'authenticité en réponse à une mise en cause récente," *Antiquité tardive* 11: 181–196.

———. 2008a. "La 'création' de *l'audientia episcopalis* par Constantin." In *Empire chrétien et Eglise aux IV*[e] *et V*[e] *siècles: Intégration ou "concordat"? Le témoignage du Code Théodosien*, ed. Jean-Noël Guinot and François Richard, 295–315. Paris: Cerf.

———. 2008b. *Ad episcopale iudicium provocare: Fondements spirituels, cadre institutionnel et implications sociales des recours laïcs à la justice épiscopale (I*[er]*–V*[e] *siècle)*. Ph.D. thesis., Strasbourg, Université Marc Bloch—Strasbourg II.

Humbert, Michel. 1983. "Enfants à louer ou à vendre: Augustin et l'autorité parentale (*Epist.* 10* et 24*)." In *Les Lettres de saint Augustin découvertes par Johannes Divjak*, 189–204. Paris: Etudes augustiniennes.

Humfress, Caroline. 2006. "Civil Law and Social Life." In *The Cambridge Companion to the Age of Constantine*, ed. Noel Lenski, 205–225. Cambridge: Cambridge University Press.

———. 2007. *Orthodoxy and the Courts in Late Antiquity*. Oxford: Oxford University Press.

Jaillette, Pierre. 1995. "Les atteintes aux biens fonciers: Analyse des termes *invasio* et *invasor* dans le code théodosien et les novelles postthéodosiennes." In *Aux sources de la gestion publique, Tome II: L'Invasio des villae ou la villa comme enjeu de pouvoir*, ed. Elisabeth Magnou-Nortier, 16–76. Villeneuve d'Ascq: Presses universitaires de Lille.

Kelly, Christopher. 2004. *Ruling the Later Roman Empire*. Revealing Antiquity 15. Cambridge, MA: Harvard University Press.

Konstan, David. 2001. *Pity Transformed*. London: Duckworth.

Landau, Peter. 1992. "Findelkinder und Kaiserkonstitutionen: Zur Enstehung der *Constitutiones Sirmondianae*," *Rivista internazionale di diritto comune* 3: 37–45.

Lenski, Noel. 2001. "Evidence for the *Audientia episcopalis* in the New Letters of Augustine." In *Law, Society, and Authority in Late Antiquity*, ed. Ralph W. Mathisen, 16–76. Oxford: Oxford University Press.

———. 2011. "Constantine and Slavery: *Libertas* and the Fusion of Roman and Christian Values." In *Atti dell'Accademia Romanistica Costantiniana* 18, 235–60. Naples: Edizioni scientifiche italiane.

Lepelley, Claude. 1961. "Saint Léon le grand et la cité romaine," *Revue des sciences religieuses* 35: 130–150.

———. 1983. "Liberté, colonat et esclavage d'après la lettre 24*: La juridiction épiscopale *de liberali causa*." In *Les Lettres de saint Augustin découvertes par Johannes Divjak*, 329–342. Paris: Etudes augustiniennes.

Liebs, Detlef. 1997. "Landraub eines Großgrundbesitzers 384 n. Chr. (Symmachus, *Relatio* 28)." In *Aspects of the Fourth Century A.D.*, ed. H. W. Pleket and A. M. F. W. Verhoogt, 97–114. Leiden: Agape.

Lieu, Samuel N. C. 1992. *Manichaeism in the Later Roman Empire and Medieval China.* 2nd ed. Tübingen: J. C. B. Mohr.

Lizzi Testa, Rita, ed. 2006. *Le trasformazioni delle élites in età tardoantica.* Roma: 'L'Erma' di Bretschneider.

MacMullen, Ramsay. 1986. "Judicial Savagery in the Roman Empire," *Chiron* 16: 43–62.

———. 1988. *Corruption and the Decline of Rome.* New Haven, CT: Yale University Press.

Maier, H. O. 1996. "'Manichee!': Leo the Great and the Orthodox Panopticon," *JECS* 4.4: 441–460.

Matthews, John F. 1974. "The Letters of Symmachus." In *Latin Literature of the Fourth Century,* ed. J. W. Binns, 58–99. London: Routledge & Kegan Paul.

———. 1975. *Western Aristocracies and Imperial Court (AD 364–425).* Oxford: Oxford University Press.

———. 1986. "Symmachus and his Enemies." In *Colloque Genevois sur Symmaque,* ed. F. Paschoud, 163–176. Paris: Belles Lettres.

———. 1989. *The Roman Empire of Ammianus.* London: Duckworth.

McLynn, Neil B. 1994. *Ambrose of Milan: Church and Court in a Christian Capital.* Berkeley: University of California Press.

Millar, Fergus. 1977. *The Emperor in the Roman World, 31 BC–AD 337.* London: Duckworth.

Morgan, Teresa. 2007. *Popular Morality in the Early Roman Empire.* Cambridge and New York: Cambridge University Press.

Mossakowski, Wieslaw. 1996. "The Introduction of an Interdiction of Oral Accusation in the Roman Empire," *Revue internationale des droits de l'antiquité,* 3rd ser., 43: 269–281.

Musumeci, Anna Maria. 1977. "La politica ecclesiastica di Valentiniano III," *Siculorum Gymnasium,* n.s. 30: 431–481.

Neil, Bronwen. 2009. *Leo the Great.* Early Christian Fathers. London: Routledge.

Pringsheim, Fritz. 1935. "Römische *aequitas* der christlichen Kaiser." In *Acta congressus iuridici internationalis: VII saeculo a decretalibus Gregorii IX et XIV a codice Iustiniano promulgatis,* 1: 119–152. Rome: Pontificium Institutum Utriusque Iuris.

Roda, Sergio. 1981. *Commento storico al libro IX dell'epistolario di Q. Aurelio Simmaco.* Pisa: Giardini.

Salzman, Michele R. 2006. "Symmachus and the 'Barbarian' Generals," *Historia* 55: 352–367.

———. 2001. "Competing Claims to '*Nobilitas*' in the Western Empire of the Fourth and Fifth Centuries," *Journal of Early Christian Studies* 9.3: 359–385.

Salzman, Michele R., and Claudia Rapp, eds. 2000. *Elites in Late Antiquity = Arethusa* 33(3).

Sheridan, James J. 1966. "The Altar of Victory: Paganism's Last Battle," *L'Antiquité Classique* 35: 186–206.

Sirks, Boudewijn. 2001. "The Farmer, the Landlord, and the Law in the Fifth Century." In *Law, Society, and Authority in Late Antiquity,* ed. R. W. Mathisen, 256–271. Oxford: Oxford University Press.

Sogno, Cristiana. 2006. *Q. Aurelius Symmachus: A Political Biography.* Ann Arbor: University of Michigan Press.

Sogno, Cristiana, and Jennifer V. Ebbeler. 2007. "Religious Identity and the Politics of Patronage: Symmachus and Augustine," *Historia* 56: 230–242.

Uhalde, Kevin. 2007. *Expectations of Justice in the Age of Augustine*. Philadelphia: University of Pennsylvania Press.

Van Dam, Raymond. 1984. *Leadership and Community in Late Antique Gaul*. Berkeley: University of California Press.

———. 2007. *The Roman Revolution of Constantine*. Cambridge: Cambridge University Press.

Vera, Domenico. 1981. *Commento Storico alle* Relationes *di Quinto Aurelio Simmaco*. Biblioteca di Studi Antichi 29. Pisa: Giardini.

Vessey, Mark. 1993. "The Origins of the *Collectio Sirmondiana*: A New Look at the Evidence." In *The Theodosian Code*, ed. Jill Harries and Ian Wood, 1–16. Ithaca, NY: Cornell University Press.

Vismara, Giulio. 1995. *La giurisdizione civile dei vescovi: Secoli I–IX*. Milan: Giuffrè.

Vollmann, Benedikt. 1965. *Studien zum Priszillianismus: Die Forschung, die Quellen, der fünfzehnte Brief Papst Leos des Grossen*. Kirchengeschichtliche Quellen und Studien 7. St. Ottilien: Eos Verlag.

Voss, Wulf Eckart. 1982. *Recht und Rhetorik in den Kaisergesetzen der Spätantike: Eine Untersuchung zum nachklassischen Kaur- und Uberreignungsrecht*. Forschungen zur byzantinischen Rechtsgeschichte 9. Frankfurt-am-Main: Löwenklau.

Wessel, Susan. 2008. *Leo the Great and the Spiritual Rebuilding of a Universal Rome*. Supplements to Vigiliae Christianae 93. Leiden: Brill.

Wytzes, Jelle. 1977. *Der letzte Kampf des Heidentums in Rom*. Études préliminaires aux religions orientales dans l'Empire romain 56. Leiden: Brill.

CHAPTER 24

ROMAN LAW AND LEGAL CULTURE

JILL HARRIES
St. Andrews University

In Late Antiquity, the emperor was the supreme lawgiver. However, his supremacy was both expressed and constrained by the past and the ancient legal tradition within which he and his administration operated. Although the Roman Republic and its constitutional framework were no more, the emperor's authority could be expressed and thereby legitimated in Republican terms as late as Justinian in the sixth century: "what the emperor decides has the force of statute, the people having conferred on him all their authority and power through the *lex regia* [royal law] which was passed concerning his office and authority."[1] Although earlier jurisprudence conceded that the emperor was not bound by the restraints of some laws,[2] in practice the rhetoric of imperial legitimacy paid due deference to a legal tradition, which was itself embedded in the Roman past.

Republican precedent and practice also shaped the forms taken by "law": edicts (formerly issued by magistrates), judicial decisions, and decisions by rescript were all classified as "constitutions."[3] By the fifth century, most "laws" were contained in imperial letters sent to officials and explicitly destined for publication; the imperial law codes, the contents of which are so central to the study of any aspect of Late Antiquity, consist almost entirely of extracts from these official letters and from imperial edicts "to the people" or "to the provincials." But Justinian's *Institutes*, published as part of his *Corpus Iuris Civilis* in 533 C.E., contained a significant innovation. Unlike the jurist

Gaius, writing in the second century C.E., Justinian acknowledged indirectly a problem that had become endemic in the system: the tension between the emerging, rule-based culture of the Byzantine bureaucracy, on the one hand,[4] and the traditional role of the emperor as patron, with the right to exercise judicial discretion, on the other. Some imperial verdicts, Justinian wrote, being "personal," such as conferring a favor or imposing a special penalty, were case-specific and did not count as general precedents; others were "general" and universally applicable. In practice, it was not easy for the emperor's interested subjects to tell the difference—hence the emperors' often reiterated complaints about rescripts, which were *contra ius*, not in accordance with law.

The tension between rules and discretion is also one (though not the only) reason for ancient, and some modern, concern with corruption in late Roman law and government.[5] As Chris Kelly has argued,[6] what we may perceive as "corrupt" practices, such as the purchase of offices, was part of the way the system worked. The structural and cultural tension within the system between the discretion of the autocrat and the legal rules favored by the bureaucracy was, paradoxically, essential to its functioning in practice. Imperial clemency, extended to such fortunate convicts as the *agens in rebus* (spy) brought before Symmachus' court in 384,[7] mitigated the rigors of the law and showed the emperor in a favorable light. But the autocrat could not be seen to be arbitrary. Instead, his deference to "law" was advertised, and much rhetorical emphasis was laid on his concern with corruption and incompetence on the part of his officials.[8] Concern with establishing what precisely the rules were was one motive for the great legal codification projects of Theodosius II and Justinian in the early fifth and sixth centuries. Thus, three years before the inception of the Theodosian Code, a "general law" was formally defined in a long communication to the Roman Senate as being either an *oratio* (imperial address) to the Senate, an edict, or a constitution, which explicitly stipulated that it should apply to other "similar" cases.[9]

The imperial legislators did not act alone. Major legal decisions would have been taken in consultation with the advisory council (consistory) and would have been responses to communications or proposals from officials and from pressure groups, such as bishops or larger city councils with the political clout to gain access to a consistory hearing.[10] The court was also the hub of a wide range of legal advisory activity, as the huge citizen population of the empire made the most of its access to the privileged workings of Roman justice, through questions on points of law prior to verdicts and appeals or referrals after sentence; in December 398, Arcadius ruled that replies to *consultationes*, questions from judges prior to sentence, were to be case-specific and were not to count as "general."[11] How the lawmaking activity at the "center" was shaped by the requirements of the wider empire, the role of rhetoric in imperial constitutions,[12] and the impact in practice of imperial law on the peoples of the Roman empire are much debated and still controversial questions.

Res Publica: Rhetoric and Legitimation

The presence of the Roman People, at least rhetorically, as the legitimator of the emperor as legislator is symptomatic of the continuing importance of the Roman Republic for the ideology of Roman law—and indeed for Late Antiquity in general. For Lactantius, who offered the basics of a divinely ordered legal system in his *Divine Institutes* (before 310), as for Augustine in his *City of God*, Cicero's works on state, law, and citizen were indispensable. At Rome itself, while senators edited Livy, the learned guests at Macrobius' (fictitious) *Saturnalia* (c. 431) delved into the minutiae of the Eternal City's ancient past, while a visitor from Antioch celebrated Rome's gift of laws for her conquered peoples as the "foundation of liberty."[13]

But perhaps the most significant characteristic of Roman law inherited by the empire from the republic was that it revolved round the citizen. The Romans' *ius civile* was the law under which Roman citizens lived, and after Caracalla's grant of universal citizenship in 212, the so-called *Constitutio Antoniniana*, this comprised almost all the inhabitants of the Roman empire. In that sense, the *ius civile* became universal, the law not of a city-state but of a world state. However, as law, it was still distinct from the *ius gentium*, the "law of nations," which applied to all peoples and could not be affected by changes in the *ius civile*.[14] Roman citizen law applied to the status of the citizen, property (including household [*familia*] and succession), obligations, and rights of redress of wrongs through legal actions. Although the interests of the community as a collective were protected under Roman public law (*ius publicum*), which traditionally took in guardianship and other *familia*-law (such as funerals), as well as criminal sanctions, the *ius civile*, the civil—or, more accurately, citizen—law was built round the individual, as a member of the *civitas*.[15] For this reason, legal discourse had an obligation to be consistent with Roman ideals of a citizen community, however oppressive and unjust the legal system might be in practice.

From the time of Virgil[16] onward, Roman law was celebrated as a distinctively Roman achievement. The innate conservatism of the legal tradition was thus enhanced by national pride. In Late Antiquity, legal history mattered—hence the inclusion by Justinian's compilers in the Digest (1.2) of long extracts from two versions of the second-century jurist Pomponius' *Enchiridion* (*Handbook*) of Roman legal history. Pomponius' dubious genealogies of famous jurists extended back to the early kings; the author of the *Historia Augusta*, who was probably based at Rome, had a similar passion for constructing "dynasties" of famous lawyers.[17] The Republic had generated law in many forms and through the medium of multiple legislators: the People (statutes, plebiscites), the Senate (resolutions, or *consulta*), and the edicts of the magistrates, especially the Praetor, whose Edict, along with the Edict of the Aediles, formed the *ius honorarium*, or law of the magistrates (holders of *honos*); after its codification by Salvius Julianus in the reign of Hadrian, the Praetor's Edict became known also as the *Edictum Perpetuum*, the Perpetual Edict. In addition, there was the authority of the jurists, along with unwritten law and custom, based on consent.[18] Of these, a select group of republican statutes and senatorial resolutions formed a framework for legal discourse and appear in the chapter headings of the late Roman law codes; however, it is unlikely that complete texts of republican statutes survived into Late Antiquity. Not mentioned by either Gaius or Justinian (although present in similar lists in Cicero) is the role played by court decisions (*res iudicatae*), although these, as we shall see, had significant implications for the evolution of Christianity.

The long legal past was a mixed blessing. As Justinian commented in the constitution, which set up the Digest commission to codify Roman jurisprudence,[19] the problem with laws that "had come down from the foundation of the city of Rome and the days of Romulus" was that they were confused and unmanageable. For lawyers—and for imperial codifiers—there was simply too much to read. However, with divine assistance, as their merely human efforts would not have availed, Justinian's commission would plough through 3 million lines of text to create the 50 books that comprised the Digest. Rigorous excerpting, avoidance of repetition and contradiction, and, where necessary, stylistic revision and updating, with possible implications for content, would be required, because the jurists had held conflicting opinions—and had infected imperial constitutions with inconsistency as well.[20]

In stating that the classical jurists had been "given authority to compose and interpret the laws" by past "revered" emperors, Justinian showed his ambition to assert imperial control over all law—including, as it would emerge, juristic commentary. In fact, down to the time of Hadrian, although many of the classical jurists were incorporated into the imperial administration or *consilium*, the authority of the early imperial jurists, who were often public figures in their own right, depended largely on their personal contributions as writers, legal advisors, and teachers. By the time of Diocletian, however, jurists and their discipline had been incorporated into the imperial administration. Among the few named writers on law to survive from Late Antiquity (through his inclusion in Justinian's Digest) was Arcadius Charisius, master of petitions in 290–291, who wrote monographs on witnesses, public services, and the remit of the praetorian prefecture.[21] Contemporary with him was an anonymous writer of Opinions (*Sententiae*), probably from Africa, who took the name (and identity) of Paulus, the Severan jurist; his work, as David Johnston put it, was "simple and clear, with no concern for subtleties or controversies."[22]

It is easy to forget when reading Justinian on Romulus that his *Corpus Iuris Civilis*, with its emphasis on an apparently unbroken Latin legal tradition, was in fact issued in Greek-speaking Constantinople, a city imbued with Hellenic culture. From the mid-530s, following the completion of the *Corpus Iuris Civilis*, Justinian increasingly used Greek for his *Novellae*,[23] a development noted and deplored by the bureaucrat and writer John the Lydian.[24] In fact, the symbolic value of Latin in law in the eastern empire must long have outweighed its practical usefulness.[25] Under the early empire, it was accepted by the second century C.E. that *fideicommissa* (trusts) could be drafted in Greek,[26] a privilege that Ulpian under the Severans maintained should be extended to Punic and Syriac.[27] In Late Antiquity, it had been formally accepted that wills, too, were valid in their local languages.[28] Yet Latin continued to be used on legal inscriptions in out-of-the-way Greek-speaking places, where, if no parallel Greek text were supplied, it was expected that the locals would, somehow, have access to a translator.[29] That Latin survived so long as the language of power in an alien cultural environment is tribute to the tenacity of Roman legal and administrative tradition.

Rescripts

A rescript was a response to a query, usually but not always from an official, in any form. In its narrower, more technical sense, a rescript was a reply, framed in simple language, to a specific question on a matter of law, addressed either to an official or to an individual petitioner. In routine cases, where there was no dispute as to the law, rescripts were issued by the office of the *magister libellorum*, the master of petitions, in the emperor's name. While queries on matters of law were often forwarded by governors acting as judges in their provinces,[30] they could also emanate from individuals, not all of high social status. As most rescripts issued by the administrators would have reiterated or reaffirmed existing law, it is unlikely that the emperor was directly involved. However, consultation of the emperor was necessary if any innovation was in prospect, and his signature was to be found on some rescripts, perhaps where the issue or the addressee were especially significant.[31] In theory, rescripts applied only to the cases to which they referred[32] and adjudicated on the legal point at issue, not on the facts of the cases, which, where disputed or where the documentation was incomplete, were for the judges to determine.[33] It should also be remembered that the rescripts that survive do so because those who preserved them believed they were of legal interest; numerous now lost rescripts would have been routine, even boring,[34] although they, too, would have been of practical interest, even benefit, to their recipients.

The opportune citation of a rescript could decide a case: for example, a case of disputed land ownership in Roman Egypt brought before the prefect in 339 was settled by citation of a rescript of Constantine asserting that land owned for forty years without challenge belonged to its possessor, who also became liable for the taxes on it.[35] However, in practice, any legal decision, which emanated from "the emperor," could be argued to be applicable in similar cases. For this reason, two collections of second- and third-century rescripts, beginning with those of Hadrian, who had codified the Praetorian Edict, were assembled by two of Diocletian's legal officers in the 290s and acquired considerable authority.[36] The *Codex Gregorianus* (*CG*), completed in 292, and the *Codex Hermogenianus* (*CH*), which revised and updated the *CG* in 294–295, were used as a general guide to law throughout the fourth century and beyond. Finally the *CG* and *CH* were incorporated in Justinian's *Codex* in 529 (reedited in 534); thenceforward, the rescripts included officially had "general" validity.[37] However, while the *CG* and *CH* are the earliest late antique demonstration of the concern with rules, which would inspire the later codification projects, there remained considerable scope for interpretation by advocates in the courtrooms of the empire. The extending of imperial decisions—which were often themselves interpretations or elucidations of existing law—to analogous cases by advocates by the creative use of arguments from precedents supplied by arguably similar cases could itself affect the content of law. As Caroline Humfress has shown (2007), this is of particular relevance to the Christianization of Roman law and legal custom after Constantine.

Legal Anthologies and Epitomes

Imperial constitutions and important rescripts were customarily read out and posted for all to see, along with decrees from the praetorian prefects or other relevant officials charged with publication and (where necessary) enforcement.[38] Some took the trouble to make copies, and a number of "private collections" of imperial constitutions survive, combining extracts from Gregorius and Hermogenian with imperial constitutions and citations of the classical jurists. The *Fragmenta Vaticana*, from the early fourth century,[39] draws on the *CG*, the *CH*, the jurists, and some Constantinian rulings on gifts.[40] Two centuries later, the so-called *Consultatio veteris cuiusdam iurisconsulti* ("legal consultation of a famous ancient jurist") was put together, probably in Gaul in the early sixth century, after the promulgation of the *Breviary* of Alaric II in 506: it combines rescripts from the *CG* and an "updated" version of *CH* containing seven rescripts from 364–365[41] with citations from the Theodosian Code and the jurists. Collections of constitutions could also be made for more eccentric reasons. The so-called *Collatio of Mosaic and Roman Law*, or *Lex Dei*,[42] for example, features citations of the Roman jurists and imperial constitutions set out in parallel with biblical passages, with the aim of proving that the content of Jewish and Roman law were virtually identical; for historians, it is the sole source for Diocletian's rescript letter to the governor of Africa against the Manichaeans.[43] The citations are arranged in line with the Ten Commandments, with a few supplementary additions at the end.

Private collections were more useful in court cases in the fourth century than might appear. Mastery of the legal literature was impossible for all but a favored few. One exception, Justinian's codifier Tribonian, was commended for his extensive legal library, which contained works of such rarity that even their titles had (allegedly) escaped the notice of his learned colleagues.[44] In fact, while lawyers were satirized, as they had been since at least the time of Cicero, for their obsession with obscure precedents and their deliberate attempts at obfuscation,[45] in practice, as Tribonian and the compilers of Justinian's Digest complained, the legal literature consulted and cited by advocates and judges in court cases was limited to a few accessible brief guides. Paulus' *Opinions* (*Sententiae*), the Book of *Rules* ascribed to Ulpian, and Hermogenian's *Epitome* of law were all found useful in the fourth century. In 426, the long *oratio* issued to the Senate on November 7, following the restoration of Valentinian III by the forces of his cousin Theodosius II, clarified many aspects of law and court practice (as well as providing guidance on the law of succession), stipulating that the writings of only five jurists, Gaius, Papinian, Paulus, Ulpian, and Modestinus, and those earlier jurists cited by them were to be valid in court and that, where the five differed, the majority view should prevail, with Papinian acting as a tie-breaker.[46] Once deplored as the nadir of Roman jurisprudence, the so-called Law of Citations is now recognized as a practical measure to assist judges, who had always faced the problem of whom to believe when confronted with conflicting authorities.[47]

Codification and Control

Complaints about the complexity of law were commonplace in the fourth century; even the eccentric author of the *De Rebus Bellicis* petitioned the emperors Valentinian and Valens to "throw light on the confused and contradictory rulings of the laws."[48] In the early fifth and sixth centuries, the emperors Theodosius II (402–450) and Justinian (527–565) launched ambitious projects to codify and clarify the law. In March 429, Theodosius II issued a constitution (*Cod. Theod.* 1.1.5), which set up a committee that would collect imperial legislation from the time of Constantine and form it into a code of law "in the likeness" (*ad similitudinem*) of the *CG* and the *CH*, although it would contain "general laws" only. The intention was that, subsequently, a second code would be compiled, containing the writings of the jurists, followed by a third, which would synthesize law in perpetuity. In fact, only the first part of the scheme was completed, with the formal issue of the Theodosian Code on February 15, 438,[49] to mark the marriage of Valentinian III with Theodosius' daughter Eudoxia the previous year.[50] Its appearance was preceded by what must have been a frenetic period of activity on the part of a second commission, charged in December 435[51] with the process of arranging extracts of constitutions chronologically under the relevant headings (*tituli*), abbreviating to remove superfluous verbiage, and tidying up the style.[52]

It was left to Justinian a century later to issue the Justinianic Code (*Cod. Just.*) in two editions.[53] This brought together the *CG*, the *CH*, and the *Cod. Theod.*, plus the *novellae* (new laws) of emperors since 438, and made further revisions to the texts; in addition, the sixteen books of constitutions set out in the Theodosian Code were reduced to twelve, and laws on Christianity, which in traditional legal terms might be classified as regulation of right religion, were transferred from the last book to the first. Justinian then went on to complete the project left unfinished by Theodosius, with the issuing of the Digest or *Pandectae* (*Encyclopaedia*),[54] which was to be the set text in law schools and the sole source for citations of jurists in court cases. His quaestor, Tribonian,[55] who had supervised the compilation of the first edition of the *Cod. Just.*, was charged with assembling a group of suitably qualified lawyers and teachers of law who would work under his supervision. Their delegated responsibility was considerable: in cases where learned opinions differed, the compilers were empowered to select their favored version, regardless of the authority of their sources, and were permitted to modify texts at will, where updating appeared necessary. How far these radical instructions affected the texts as we have them can probably never be known; the study of alleged interpolations by later scholars has produced little agreement on the extent of Tribonian's revisions. Finally, as noted before, Justinian's *Institutes*,[56] which drew heavily on Gaius' *Institutes*, written in the mid-second century, set out the guiding principles and structures of Roman law. Both of the latter had an abiding influence on Roman law as adopted in Europe and beyond.

The emperors' professed aim was to be useful. Theodosius and Justinian celebrated the benefits of clarity and their abolition of the obscurities beloved by lawyers.[57] Both also believed that their compilations would assist judicial proceedings, as lawyers would no longer be obliged to compete with rivals to unearth supportive imperial or juristic rulings from diverse—and possibly unreliable—sources. But Justinian's primary aim in the issuance of the Digest, as set out in his *Constitutio Tanta*, was educational. Thirty-six of the fifty books of extracts from juristic commentary were established as set texts for the three "authorized" law schools at Rome (still in theory part of the Roman empire), Constantinople, and Beirut. Departures from Justinian's new "national curriculum" for law were outlawed, although law teachers would not be punished for their possession of now redundant law books. And first-year students were now to be known, not by their previous title, but as "New Justinians."

The imperial codes excluded and invalidated material "outside themselves,"[58] although Theodosius II, characteristically, incorporated an element of confusion by conceding that some constitutions would be included, even though they were no longer valid, because of their interest for historians of the legal tradition.[59] The chronological arrangement of legal extracts under headings (*tituli*) would establish that the later of conflicting rulings had validity. For example, the first law included in the Code as we have it, *Cod. Theod.* 1.1.1 (322) on undated constitutions, was superseded by *Cod. Theod.* 1.1.5, establishing the principles of the Theodosian Code and the validity of laws within it; *Cod. Theod.*

15.6.1 (396) permits the holding of a festival in Gaza, which is banned in the next constitution.[60] But in general, later laws repealed earlier constitutions only insofar as they were inconsistent with them.

The emperors also went to great lengths to protect their texts from interpolations, establishing locations where the texts would be held, rights of access, and proper formatting, which, in copies of the Digest, excluded idiosyncratic scribal abbreviations.[61] The Theodosian Code was formally received at Rome by the Senate there on December 20, 438. The Senate minutes[62] of that occasion featured formal speeches by the praetorian prefect of Italy, Anicius Acilius Glabrio Faustus, and others; the reading out of *Cod. Theod.* 1.1.5; and frequent outbursts of probably prearranged acclamations.[63] The ceremony concluded with a text agreed upon by the Senate, which would regulate the copying and transmission of the *Cod. Theod.*[64] Faustus' text would generate two further copies, one of which would be held by the prefect of the city at Rome, while the second would be given to the *constitutionarii*, Anastasius and Martinus, who alone were permitted to issue and circulate further copies. However, despite attempts to agree that new laws issued by one emperor should be automatically communicated to the other,[65] Theodosius and Valentinian III, and their successors, failed to establish a coherent system for further updating and revision, with the result that the Codes could be used as living law only in conjunction with the *Novellae* (new laws) of subsequent emperors.

The Codes were also exercises in power. By extracting from and revising the texts of previous legislators and legal interpreters, who had acquired authority over the centuries, the emperors claimed ownership of all past law.[66] The point was reinforced by the emperors' concession that the referencing systems used would allow previous lawmakers to take credit for their achievement.[67] But while Theodosius' constitution promulgating his code confined itself to celebrations of the new "light of brevity" shed on the law by his and his (named) officials' efforts, for Justinian the issuing of the *Corpus Iuris Civilis* was a demonstration of a new world order presided over by an emperor favored by the Christians' God, the dawning of an era of "Eternal Peace" following victory over Persia, in which law would come into its own.[68] The two great guardians of the Roman *res publica* had been "arms and the laws,"[69] and Justinian's *Corpus Iuris Civilis* would establish the law, past and present, allowing emperors alone the power to change law in the future.

Reading the Codes

Controversy on the imperial law codes, their contents, and their contexts abounds.[70] Recent studies of the Theodosian Code have differed on the important question of the sourcing of the texts: did the compilers travel round the empire between 429 and 435 before embarking on the perhaps hurried work of collation and revision? Or did they draw most of their material from the archives at Constantinople, supplemented perhaps with the contents of a few private collections?[71] Did the compilers of the Theodosian Code, with their professed interest in legal history, incorporate all the constitutions they could find, regardless of their current validity, or were more excluded than we can ever know? The question matters, because of its impact on the amount of "general" legislation issued by emperors, and remains unresolved.

Numerous further questions of detail surround the rubrics of the individual texts. The extracts were headed by the names of not only the legislator but also all the other emperors in the imperial college responsible for the law, followed by the name of the recipient. At the foot of the text was added the date or dates that the law was issued (*data*), received (*accepta*), and/or posted in a public place for all to read (*proposita*). The rubrics and even the texts of many constitutions, especially the earlier laws of Constantine and his successors, are corrupt, and in several cases, the identity of the emperor responsible, the dating, and the identities of the recipients are uncertain. As the work of editing and compilation took less than two years, from December 435[72] to the marriage of Valentinian III in October 437, mistakes were perhaps inevitable. The research of Simon Corcoran (1993) has uncovered several laws ascribed to Constantine that are in fact the work of Licinius and Maximim Daia; there is also at least one rescript.[73] On Justinian's *Corpus Iuris Civilis*, there has been extensive discussion in legal circles, but no agreement, on the extent and nature of interpolations included by Tribonian and his colleagues in the texts with a view to updating the content, although the focus has shifted away from this in recent years.

An issue of broader interest to historians is the extent to which imperial laws accurately reflected or addressed realities on the ground. How well was the emperor informed of situations far from his capitals? Notorious cases, such as the campaigns of disinformation described by Ammianus on the part of officials with reference to the situation in Africa in the early 370s,[74] suggest that laws issued in ignorance of the problems to be addressed were unlikely to be effective. Other evidence supports a view of imperial impotence, inadequately compensated for by inflated rhetoric; the failure of Diocletian's Maximum Prices edict, issued with much hyperbole in 301 and expensively set up in a limited number of eastern provinces, is a case in point. In particular, it has been assumed that repetition of laws is evidence that imperial lawmaking was ineffectual and that emperors re-enacted laws because previous constitutions had been ignored, a concession occasionally made by frustrated emperors themselves. Certainly some laws, such as that of Julian forbidding Christians to teach the pagan classics, failed in their purpose,[75] although the Theodosian Code acknowledged the validity of some of his views on education.[76]

Repetition, however, is not a reliable indicator of failure. The reissuing of laws was built into the system of petition and response. In a continuation of the practice under the early empire,[77] emperors legislated in response to reports, proposals, and requests for legal rulings advanced by interested parties often far from the imperial court, and it was in the interest of the latter to see the law upheld. If there was doubt as to imperial policy on any matter for any reason—for example, following the accession of a new emperor—cautious judges, administrators, and litigants would play it safe and ask for a ruling confirming or modifying the stance of a predecessor; reaffirmations of existing policy were thus often evidence of the strength of imperial control and the willingness of litigious subjects to defer to the imperial will.[78] This did not mean, however, that the imperial will could not be manipulated; as we shall see, the implications of the responsive nature of law for our interpretation of law as imperial policy are profound. Moreover, although laws on, for example, criminality or taxation required enforcement, much of Roman civil law concerns the resolution of legal disputes between individuals over property and other private matters. In the civil courts, therefore, the emperors operated as a form of legal consultancy and were deferred to as the ultimate source of law (on the courts, see also Kevin Uhalde, chapter 23 in this book). More significant for the effectiveness of imperial and gubernatorial jurisdiction may have been the extent to which litigants preferred alternative forms of dispute resolution, such as the episcopal courts (*episcopalis audientia*), to those administered by the government.[79]

The late Roman law codes are both statements of law and expressions of the ideology of the autocracy that produced them. In theory, the rhetorical justifications, which routinely accompanied imperial legislation, were to be edited out of the extracts included in the Codes, leaving only their legal content; in practice, this was often not the case. Moreover, the extracts in the Codes can be amplified by other texts, both epigraphic, such as the Edict on Maximum Prices,[80] and literary, such as the laws of Constantine preserved in Eusebius, albeit in Greek translation. These preserve in full the rhetoric of imperial lawmaking. Most subjects of the empire would never see the emperor in person, and laws, often in the flexible form of letters (which could have no legal content at all), were an essential form of communication both of the emperors' policies and of their characters. The techniques of persuasion employed by the legal draftsmen in the emperor's name express governmental priorities and assumptions, project the emperor's virtues, and systematically denigrate all who would subvert or ignore his will.[81] Imperial constitutions were thus as much—if not, on occasion, more—about image building and moral exhortation as about law in a strictly juristic sense.

Some constitutions in the Codes do not appear, at first sight, to be law at all, yet their inclusion was appropriate because they advised on appropriate conduct in a specific situation and, by extension, all similar situations. One may question what legal principle, for example, is served by an emperor's ruling that it was unlawful for wild animals destined for export to be held up for months at a city, or that lions could be killed if they endangered livestock but were otherwise to be left unharmed;[82] or the instruction issued to the army that horses were to be washed by their naked grooms downriver and away from the camp, for both hygienic and aesthetic reasons.[83] And inhabitants of the city of Rome were warned that wearing oriental or Germanic trousers was forbidden within the city.[84] Such examples of "generality" serve also as a reminder that "laws" were what the emperor decided, whatever the subject on which he chose to pronounce.

Since the mid-1980s,[85] there has been an increased focus on the men believed to be behind the drafting of the texts of the laws, the imperial quaestors. Originally the emperor's spokesmen, they retained that role but increasingly took on responsibility for drafting the texts of general laws decided by the emperor and his advisory council, or consistory. They also gave legal advice; the first known intervention on a legal matter from a quaestor was Eupraxius' attempt in 370 to correct Valentinian I on the law of treason.[86] In the fifth century, the quaestor Antiochus Chuzon was the guiding hand in the formation of the Theodosian Code (despite other distractions, such as the Council of Ephesus in 431). Under Justinian, his quaestor, Tribonian,[87] took charge, in various capacities, of the great *Corpus Iuris Civilis* project; the imperial constitutions of which he was the author from 527 show a zest for the "ambiguities" of juristic discourse perhaps not entirely appreciated by his imperial master. It is not, however, certain that quaestors drafted every constitution: some may be the work of the *magister memoriae*, and others may reflect revisions inserted by lesser draftsmen in the secretariat for the benefit of specific recipients.[88]

It has become increasingly clear over recent years that the late Roman law codes contain a number of problems for the historian, and much study still remains to be done if imperial constitutions are to be properly understood, both as law and as sources for the general history of the period. Every extant constitution in the Codes requires careful reading; its nominal author (the emperor), the input of the quaestor and perhaps other legal draftsmen, the proposer, and the circumstances that brought the constitution into being may all be relevant to its interpretation. Imperial laws are part of a conversation of which usually only the one voice is audible. Even that one voice may be heard only in part. The power of the Codes' editors to extract "legal content" and exclude "extraneous verbiage" could result in distortion. For example, a law on gladiators issued by Constantine in 325 stated that criminals condemned to fight in the arena should instead be sent to the mines;[89] the *Cod. Just.*, however, deleted the reference to the mines, allowing the first Christian emperor to be credited, erroneously, with a universal ban on gladiators.[90] The editors, therefore, could become, in effect, retrospective legislators.

As we have seen, the process by which the texts came into being involved a number of people other than the emperor. Some constitutions may in fact reflect the agenda of the proposer of the constitution, whose proposal (*suggestio*) had presumably been vetted and passed without revision.[91] Although it is never possible to be sure that the named recipient of a law was also the proposer, further study may identify distinctive features in clusters of laws addressed to individuals. This has important implications for how texts are read. What appears to be a reforming general law may often be a response to a question of detail concerning a situation that already existed; Constantine's famous (and textually corrupt) law on *episcopalis audientia* did not inaugurate a new system of jurisdiction by bishops, but merely ruled on the specific question of what should happen when both episcopal and civil courts were resorted to by a pair of litigants.[92] In fact, imperial policy toward episcopal jurisdiction was benign, in the sense that emperors were willing to enforce episcopal judgments in civil cases with state power if necessary,[93] but in other respects *episcopalis audientia* was treated as another form of binding private arbitration involving a *compromissum*, or arbitration agreement between the parties, an institution long established in Roman legal thought and practice.[94]

An imperial constitution was thus often the product of a negotiation among several interested parties, both at and beyond the court. The process was intensely political and competitive, and turf wars between various sections of the bureaucracy were constant.[95] In 440, for example, the praetorian prefect in the West, Petronius Maximus, succeeded in taking over responsibility for tax collection from the Counts of the Treasury;[96] two years later (after Maximus had been replaced), the reform was reversed.[97] Emperors could also be dragged into local feuds, not least those involving Christians; a series of letters from Augustine in 408 show how Honorius, far away in Italy, was persuaded to send in the troops because of anti-Christian riots in African Calama.[98] Ad hoc legal decisions therefore were as good (or bad) as the information available at the center, and wise emperors made a point of checking their facts first. Despite their best efforts, however, the system could not ensure consistency over time, especially as precedents might be of dubious relevance or inconsistent. Legislation even on so important a matter as the status of *coloni* is found to lack coherence when analyzed over a period of centuries.[99]

Law and Social Change: Family, Crime, Christianity

Emperors took legal advice from members of their consistories and from the now largely nameless jurists in their employ. Despite the distractions of the rhetoric, much civil legislation appears to perpetuate rules established in the "classical" juristic tradition.[100] The implications of this go beyond legal niceties. Constantine I's legislation is often categorized as pro-Christian, thanks largely to Eusebius' representation in his *Life of Constantine*. Yet analysis of his laws, for example, relaxing—or appearing to relax—requirements for legal formalities to be observed in wills[101] shows that his lawmaking was in fact in line with traditional practice, going back, in the case of wills, to the republic and early empire.[102] Even his famous repeal of the Augustan legal penalties for celibates can be seen as part of a wider acceptance of the social usefulness of the unmarried pagan, as well as Christian, philosopher and was a measure designed to benefit Roman aristocrats in general, not Christians as such.[103]

However, the responsive nature of imperial lawmaking to external promptings and the power of emperors to reject legal precedents, if appropriate, permitted emperors to make changes, which reflected shifts in social attitudes, though these did not necessarily result from direct Christian influence.[104] Since the first century C.E., women had gradually acquired more rights to take legal responsibility for themselves and others, and their rights as inheritors of their children's property and vice versa had been recognized in the second century. At the same time, the absolute rights of the *paterfamilias* over his descendants continued to be gradually eroded, as women became empowered to act as independent agents.[105] Widows even took on the responsibility of acting as guardians for their children.[106] Their existing right, if legally independent (*sui iuris*), to inherit, own, and bequeath property made them attractive patrons, not only to traditional beneficiaries but also to the Christian Church and clergy; Valentinian wryly reminded the kinsmen of susceptible women that it was their responsibility to keep grasping and manipulative clerics at bay.[107] It can be argued that, despite the powerful rhetoric to the contrary indulged in by such Christian clients of rich females as Jerome, the claims of family continued to matter, even to the most devout.[108]

The distinction between immorality and criminality was easily blurred. In 331, Constantine diverged from the classical practice concerning divorce, which had allowed either party to end the marriage, although the financial consequences were determined in part by culpability, as well as the requirement to provide financial provision for the children.[109] Constantine decreed that, in cases of contested divorce, grounds for divorce were limited to homicide, sorcery, or destruction of tombs by the husband, or adultery, sorcery, or procuring on the part of the wife.[110] Under classical law, an unjustified unilateral divorce led to loss of the dowry by the offending party, but to this Constantine added exile for the wife, normally a criminal penalty, and restrictions on the rights of both to remarry. The law was repealed by Julian[111] but revived by later emperors, with varying degrees of severity.[112] The interests and honor of the family, headed by the *paterfamilias*, remained dominant; abduction (*raptus*), even when it resulted in honourable marriage, could not be condoned,[113] and the mouth of the nurse who corrupted her charge was "to be stopped with molten lead." On adultery, Constantine changed one provision of the Augustan *Lex Iulia* on adulteries by removing the right of third parties to bring accusations, because of the risks to marriage posed by malicious prosecutions,[114] and updated another, by explaining that owners of taverns could be liable to accusations of adultery but that the waitresses were "cheap" and therefore exempt.[115]

Imperial and court practice in the punishment of adultery seems to have varied, with the death penalty being deemed appropriate in some cases (Jerome, *Letter* 1, on an innocent victim of a false accusation miraculously resurrected), while ecclesiastical rules on penance suggest that some adulteries were admitted but either not prosecuted (although the Julian law made prosecution obligatory) or dealt with more leniently by the courts.

By the early fifth century, charges of heresy were also deemed to be public and therefore "criminal":[116] "that which is committed against divine religion works to the injury of all."[117] Despite the resort to public procedure, which carried moral as well as serious legal implications, convicted heretics did not expect the death penalty. Instead, civil disabilities were imposed concerning the right to make and benefit from wills, and meetings of those labeled as heretics were outlawed (as those of the Christians had been in time of persecution). The civil penalties could be suspended if the "heretic" returned to the fold; the execution by the emperor Maximus of Prisicillian and two of his followers in 386 was a scandalous exception.[118] The identification and labeling of heretics was itself a vigorously contested process, by means of which the Church resolved questions of doctrine and identity; the power of rhetoric is demonstrated in the successful completion of the labeling process, which enabled the rhetorical—then actual—creation of a separatist persona who had diverged from the one right path and was now the follower of a man (Mani, Arius, et al.), not of Christ. While resort by ecclesiastics and officials to the public courts may have criminalized those convicted as heretics, it also serves as a reminder to the modern observer than "public" jurisdiction was not primarily "criminal" in our modern sense (i.e., denoting extreme wickedness) but concerned anything that affected the interests of the community. The Latin *crimen*, from which our word *crime* derives, refers to the public accusatory process, which required a named individual, acting on behalf of the community, to lodge a prosecution and confront the defendant face-to-face. The extension and adaptation of the public process to encompass heresy therefore exemplifies the flexibility of late Roman law and legal process, as it adjusted to changing times.

On traditional criminal law in general, the "judicial savagery" of the courts is well known.[119] There was little substantive change in the laws on "public crimes," such as homicide, treason, adultery, and forgery; imperial clemency, as evidenced in Easter amnesties, did not extend to them.[120] However, many offences were assimilated to crimes, with serious consequences for the accused. Treason, for example, came to encompass *inter alia* the unauthorized use of purple dye and the counterfeiting of the imperial coinage; this had important procedural implications for defendants, as safeguards on the use of torture did not apply when the empire's or the emperor's safety was at stake. One distinctive development was the emergence of a system of fines for derelictions of duty on the part of not only governors but also their office staffs.[121] Officials were expected to prevent their boss from flouting the law and could face fines if they had failed to exert themselves sufficiently.[122] The liveliness of some court proceedings is evoked in sanctions against officials who fail to prevent their convicts from being spirited away by clerics on their way to execution;[123] the emperors conceded that they could be referred to if the governor found himself "at war" with monks and clerics.

More significant than imperial harshness was the role of the judges themselves in eroding legal safeguards. Some lucky third-century appellants were able to overturn unlawful decisions, such as condemnation to the mines in absentia[124] or a verdict reached on the basis of the testimony of a single witness and the improper use of torture.[125] Despite the clear guidance in the juristic tradition that neither prison nor torture was to be used as a punishment, the Roman courts made a practice of both, as accounts of persecutions of Christians make clear.[126]

Reforms benefiting Christianity may also have been driven—and resisted—from below. Theodosius I was the first Christian emperor to target enforcement of a ban on the governors of provinces and their administrators, who were made liable for violations of the law.[127] Without their cooperation, sacrifices would continue and, in fact, did so, even after the laws came into force. The key to making controversial laws efficacious was to ensure their enforcement, where applicable, by local groups with an interest in seeing the law enforced.[128] Thus although various laws were passed about temples, which remained in use for social but not (in theory) cultic purposes,[129] and about statues,[130] which merited preservation because of their artistic value, these were only one element in the vigorous conflicts over religious space pursued by pagans and Christians on the ground. The attacks on temples in the 380s of Theodosius I's Praetorian Prefect Maternus Cynegius and monks backed by him, so deplored in Libanius' speech *Pro Templis*, had a more drastic impact on pagan rites and festival celebrations than any single imperial law.

"Canon law," as it came to be known, is the most striking example of law driven from below and accepted over time as universal.[131] In 407, for example, the African churches agreed on a recommendation concerning remarriage after divorce and that the promulgation of an imperial law should be requested, which would, in effect, activate their decision as a law in the full secular sense.[132] In general, clerics faced with legal problems in their church communities extrapolated principles of Roman law by analogy, but agreement with their findings depended on the informal authority of the ecclesiastical interpreter, not on formal law. In Roman legal culture, this was not problematic; the authority of the jurists, all-important in the secular courts, also had no formal backing. Characteristically, Justinian declared that the canons of four ecumenical church councils (Nicaea, Constantinople, Ephesus I, and Chalcedon) had the "force of law,"[133] almost certainly the formal recognition of an accepted situation. While due deference was to be paid to biblical law, the formulation of ecclesiastical law in the early centuries was dependent on the principles of Roman law and the interpretative use of it made by the clergy, often themselves advocates and trained in the principles of rhetoric.

Laws, Rhetoric, and Advocacy

The rhetorical language of late imperial constitutions is a prominent and often deplored feature of the texts. It can be read as the inevitable expression of the culture of the emperor and his legal draftsmen, all trained in the arts of rhetoric as schoolboys, and many having experience as advocates, perhaps before one of the prefects' courts. But the culture of advocates was also confrontational; their training was based on the handling of controversy and the besting of opponents. The extreme language of late Roman imperial law is partly a reflection of the colorful fashions of the time and the emperor's need to project moral concern, but it was also conditioned by the advocate's determination to win.

Studies by Crook (1995), Heath (2004), and Humfress (2007) have established that the profession of advocate flourished in Late Antiquity, despite the relatively low-key nature of the *cognitio* process, and that there was wide scope for his argumentative and persuasive talents in both the imperial administration and the courts. Before 460, there was no requirement that an advocate listed as eligible to plead in the prefects' courts should have certified legal knowledge. However, the practical advice given by the participants in Cicero's *De Oratore*—that an advocate should have command of the basics at least, and preferably more—was observed by those aspiring careerists who combined a rhetorical education with a more specialist legal education at the schools of Rome, Beirut, and, later, Constantinople. As pleaders, they required access to the relevant legal material and understanding of the issues, including the theory of how those issues should be identified and communicated to greatest effect (Heath 2004). Cases involving advocates, which survive in the papyri, show that two skills were required of the advocate: knowledge of the law and imperial constitutions and the ability to deploy his texts to maximum strategic advantage before the judge.

Once placed in a forensic context, an imperial constitution, though overtly revered, became a part of the evidence to be dissected and interpreted—although never explicitly contradicted. The rhetoric of imperial law was addressed not only to officials and members of the public who read constitutions on notice boards but also to judges and advocates in courtrooms. In the imperial constitutions, *lex* refers to the written enactment. In the wider world, *lex* (and the approximate Greek equivalent, *nomos*) also denoted a "right way of life"; thus the *lex Christiana* denoted the principles by which a Christian should live, and the Theodosian Code itself was designed as a *magisterium vitae*,[134] an education in (right) living. Acting as his own advocate, the emperor as legislator proclaimed that his enactments and decisions were in accord with law in its widest, moral sense; conversely, those who would oppose the imperial order were, by definition, greedy, wicked, and corrupt. The rhetoric of imperial law was thus not merely an exercise in persuasion; it was also an affirmation of the legitimacy of the emperor as lawgiver.

It followed also that the emperor, as guardian of the law, must be above the deficiencies of his own administration. Judges were held to account by both emperors and their assertive subjects. Constantine denounced judges who gave wrong verdicts "having been corrupted" (*depravatus*) by bribery or favor (*gratia*);[135] similar opinions were expressed by Valentinian and Valens[136] and Arcadius.[137] However, while perversions of the system did exist, their scale cannot be measured by the extent of the rhetoric about them. The culture of criticism expressed in the emperors' constitutions is to be explained by the need to justify autocracy by casting the blame of its failings onto others, while preserving for the supreme ruler the credit of remaining accountable to the Roman people.

Nor was he alone. Expectations generated by the language of imperial constitutions were echoed by the emperor's subjects. In Antioch in the 380s, Libanius (*Oratio* 33) turned his talent for invective against the governor of Syria, Tisamenos, accusing him of cruelty (the indiscriminate flogging of defendants), incompetence (delays in the hearing of cases), and frivolity (hearings suspended due to his daughter's wedding). Provincial governors were especially vulnerable to attack from powerful local provincials because of their relatively lowly position in the official hierarchy. Moreover, accusations of *gratia* coexisted with widespread interventions in the judicial system by interested parties on behalf of their clients;[138] the exercise of patronage, like other forms of discretion, was incompatible with a culture of legal rules. It is this clash of cultures, when combined with the self-justifying rhetoric of imperial constitutions, which generated omnipresent accusations of corruption—but as Ulpian cynically remarked, no winner was likely to complain of corruption on the part of a judge.[139]

Conclusions

The law of Late Antiquity has often been viewed as a symptom of wider decline. The very label "postclassical"[140] implies that late Roman legal culture was somehow inferior to that of the "classical" golden age of the Antonines and the Severi. The thesis of E. Levy (1951)—that late Roman law was "vulgarized," and such crucial distinctions as the difference between absolute ownership (*dominium*) and possession (*possessio*) ignored—is reinforced for the casual modern reader by the nature of the surviving texts. Imperial constitutions are often guilty of oversimplification and extreme or eccentric rhetoric (not all quaestors were legal experts). Indeed, rhetoric itself could be viewed as a corrupting influence, far removed from the traditional clarity, conceptual sophistication, and care for accurate use of terminology characteristic of Roman "classical" jurisprudence.

It is now accepted, however, that the law and legal culture of Late Antiquity had a vitality of their own. Behind the rhetoric of imperial constitutions can be detected an often scrupulous adherence to the legal juristic tradition, even while emperors were also willing to implement and justify changes and reform. The responsive nature of imperial lawmaking, combined with the persuasive function of the epistolary form, permitted the emperors' lawmaking activity to serve as a means of two-way communication between subjects and emperor. Laws thus also kept pace with social change; the new and more austere moral climate of the fourth century was reflected in important developments in family and religious law. Despite complaints of corruption and failure to observe the emperors' diktats, the efficacy of much imperial legislation could be guaranteed by the self-interest of those who may originally have prompted it and had an interest in its implementation. The presence of the imperial legal codifications, collections of legal material that have no equivalent under the early empire, allow us to see, in part, the process of negotiation and legislation, which drove legal change and both defined and limited the potential arbitrariness of autocratic rule. And perhaps most significantly, it is becoming increasingly clear that legal change was driven, not only by emperors but also from below by the courts, by judges, by litigants, and by Christian religious reformers.

NOTES

1. Justinian, *Institutes* 2.6 (Birks and MacLeod 1987); cf. Gaius, *Institutes* 1.5 (mid-second century; Gordon and Robinson 1988) and Justinian, *Constitutio "Deo Auctore"* 7 (Krueger 1915, 69–70).

2. Digest 1.3.31, "the emperor is released from the laws" (*princeps legibus solutus est*) refers specifically to the provisions of the Augustan *Lex Iulia et Papia* but is often read as a general rule.

3. For the list of constituent elements of the *ius civile* as it functioned under the republic, see Cicero, *On Invention* 2.67; *Topica* 28.

4. See Stein 1966; Kelly 2004, 11–63.

5. See the connection between corruption and imperial decline argued by MacMullen 1988.

6. Kelly 2004, 138–185, 203–207. Also see his article on corruption in the *Oxford Classical Dictionary*, 3rd ed. rev., ed. Simon Hornblower and Tony Spawforth (2003), 402–403.

7. Symmachus, *Relatio* 49, which refers one Africanus, who had falsely accused two eminent citizens, to the emperor for (expected) clemency. Vera 1981, 388.

8. E.g., at *Codex Justinianus* (*Cod. Just.*) 1.14.4, of 429 (Krueger 1915), stating the emperor's subjection to law as a general principle. As its context in the original constitution is not extant, its full significance cannot be assessed.

9. *Cod. Just.* 1.14.3, November 426. There is some debate as to whether this represents early stirrings of the Theodosian Code project. Although the law shares the culture of the Theodosian compilers, based in the eastern empire, it is, at least on the face of it, a western initiative. On this, see Matthews 2000, 26.

10. Honoré 1986, 136–137, and Millar 2006, 201–204, discussing *Cod. Just.* 1.14.8, which formally included the Senate at Constantinople in legal deliberations; see also Harries 1999, 41. On the proposal process (*suggestio*), see Harries 1999, 47–53; Millar 2006, 207–214.

11. *Cod. Theod.* 1.2.11 (Mommsen 1905; English trans. Pharr 1969); see also Harries 1999, 30.

12. On rhetoric and law in general, see Voss 1982.

13. Ammianus Marcellinus 14.6.5.

14. Gaius, *Institutes* 1.3 and 158. On the *ius gentium* and natural law, see Johnston 2000, 618–622. On the evolution from universalism to autocracy, see Honoré 2004.

15. See Gaius, *Institutes* 1.1 = Justinian *Institutes* 2.1: "quod quisque populus ipse sibi ius constituit, id ipsius proprium civitatis est vocaturque ius civile, quasi ius proprium ipsius civitatis. Justinian, following Ulpian's *Institutes*, also defines private versus public law."

16. *Aeneid* 6.851–853.

17. See Honoré 1987; 1999, 190–211.

18. On custom and consent, Digest 1.3.32 (Julianus); 35 (Hermogenian); 36 (Paulus).

19. *C. Deo Auctore* = *Cod. Just.* 1.17.1, December, 15, 530.

20. *C. Tanta*, preface, Krueger 1915, 70–74.

21. Honoré 1994, 156–162.

22. Johnston 2005, 207.

23. Honoré 1978, 124–133.

24. John the Lydian, *On Magistracies* 2.12; 3.42 (Bandy 1983).

25. For use of Greek for practical purposes by emperors and even eminent subjects such as bishops in the fifth century, see Millar 2006, 20–34, 84–97.

26. Gaius, *Institutes* 2.281.

27. Digest 32.11.pr. and 45.1.1.

28. *Cod. Just.* 7.45.12; *Nov. Theod.* 16.8, Mommsen 1905.

29. Mitchell 1988 on Latin copies of a rescript of Maximinus against the Christians, in the original Latin, found at Colbasa in Pisidia and Arycanda in Lycia.

30. Corcoran 2000, 43ff.; Matthews 2000, 13, 16.

31. See *Cod. Just.* 1.23.3 on rescripts "nostra manu subscripta," with Turpin 1988.

32. *Cod. Just.* 1.19.22, 23.

33. Ulpian, at Digest 49.1.1.1.

34. Turpin 1991.

35. *P. Col.* VII, 175. Crook 1995, 104–107; Heath 2004, 317; Humfress 2007, 127–129.

36. Corcoran 2000, 25–42.

37. *Constitutio Haec* 2.

38. Matthews 2000, 196–199.

39. Text at *FIRA* 2: 463–540.

40. *Fragmenta Vaticana* 248–249, 273–274, 287.

41. *Consultatio* IX.1.1–7.

42. *FIRA* 2: 543–589, edited with commentary by Hyamson 1913; Frakes 2011.

43. *Coll.* 15.3; the collection also contains an alternative version of a law outlawing homosexual practices and several extracts from the jurists not preserved in the Digest.

44. *C. Tanta* 17. Ironically, the contents of Tribonian's library excluded from the Digest would no longer be valid for court citation purposes.

45. Ammianus 30.4.11–12.

46. *Cod. Theod.* 1.4.3, cf. Gaius, *Institutes* 1.7, followed by Just. *Institutes* 1.2.8 for the binding legal force of juristic unanimity. Citation of jurists included by the five depended on careful checking of the manuscripts.

47. Matthews 2000, 24–26.

48. *De Rebus Bellicis* 21; the date (here assumed to be c. 369) for this document is disputed.

49. *Nov. Theod.* 1.1.

50. *Gesta Senatus* 2 and 3, Mommsen 1905, 1–4; Matthews 2000, 1–9.

51. *Cod. Theod.* 1.1.6.

52. Matthews 2000, 62–83.

53. The relevant constitutions are conventionally indicated by their opening word or phrase, and their location can be obscure to the nonspecialist. For convenience, I list the constitutions relevant to the *Cod. Just.* here: *C. Haec*, February 15, 528 (exactly ninety years after the *Cod. Theod.*), Krueger 1915, 1; *C. Summa*, April 529, Krueger 1915, 2–3; *C. Cordi*, Nov. 534, Krueger 1915, 4. For an accessible discussion on law and legal culture in the time of Justinian, see Humfress 2005.

54. Digests had been compiled by second-century jurists, such as Julianus and Cervidius Scaevola; they were commentaries on the Praetor's Edict and a selection of statutes. *Pandectae* (the title is Greek) were less common and occur later. The *Pandectae* of Modestinus, Ulpian's pupil, seem to have been a general guide to law, presumably for educational purposes.

55. Honoré 1978 is the standard account on Tribonian and his context and is also important for the processes by which the *Corpus Iuris Civilis* was created.

56. Birks and MacLeod 1987.

57. *Nov. Theod.* 1.1.1: "discussis tenebris conpendio brevitatis lumen legibus dedimus"; *C. Tanta* 20, on confusion imported into the Praetorian Edict by juristic commentaries.

58. For the Digest, *C. Tanta* 19.

59. *Cod. Theod.* 1.1.5 allows inclusion of laws that "consigned to silence have fallen into disuse;" (*quae mandata silentio in desuetudinem abierunt*) because of their interest to legal scholars.

60. *Cod. Theod.* 15.6.2 (399). See also *Cod. Theod.* 11.22.2 (385), reversed by *Cod. Theod.* 11.22.3 (387); and *Cod.Theod.* 16.5.25 (390), reversed five years later by *Cod. Theod.* 16.5.27.

61. *C. Tanta* 22.

62. *Gesta Senatus*, Mommsen 1905, 1–4. The Senate was also the recipient of the constitutions relevant to the setting up of Theodosius' codification projects and later those of Justinian.

63. Harries 1999, 65–66; Matthews 2000, 31–54.

64. *Gesta Senatus* 7.

65. *Nov. Theod.* 2.1, October 447.

66. For the Digest, *C. Tanta* 10. For the Theodosian Code, *Nov. Theod.* 1.1.

67. *Nov. Theod.* 1.1.4; *C. Tanta* 20 and 20a on lawyers as builders of the "temple of Roman justice."

68. Laiou and Simon, 1994, chapter 1.

69. *C. Summa* preface. Contrast Honoré 1978, 35: "Rome gave civilisation the law—that is to say a certain professional conception of laws as the cement of society—and the arch."

70. For the state of the question, see Lee 2002.

71. Contrast the devolved view taken by Matthews 1993 with the argument of Sirks 1993, that the compilers could resort to the archives at Constantinople for the bulk of their texts.

72. *Cod. Theod.* 1.1.6.

73. *Cod. Theod.* 8.15.1.

74. Ammianus, 28.6.1–29; cf. Ammianus' criticism of Valens (30.4.1–2) for being misled by officials into neglecting his judicial duties, "thus opening the doors for robberies."

75. Cf. Ammianus 22.10.7; 25.4.20.

76. *Cod. Theod.* 13.3.5; Matthews 2000, 274.

77. Millar 1977 passim.

78. Harries 1999, 82–88.

79. Gagos and van Minnen 1994; Harries 1999, 172–211; Humfress 2007, 155–171.

80. Corcoran 2000, 205–233.

81. On rhetoric in law, see Voss 1982. On the quaestor as the emperor's spokesman, as well as legal advisor, see Honoré 1986; Harries 1988; also Honoré 1999 on the late-fourth- and fifth-century quaestors of the Theodosian dynasty.

82. *Cod. Theod.* 15.11.1, 2.

83. *Cod. Theod.* 7.1.13.

84. *Cod. Theod.* 14.10.2.

85. Honoré 1986; Harries 1988.

86. Ammianus 28.1.25; Matthews 1989, 212–213.

87. Honoré 1978, chapters 1 and 2, provide an overview of Tribonian's career in the context of Justinian's early years.

88. Harries 1988, 160–162; Matthews 2000, 179. If authorship of some of the extant texts by officials other than quaestors is conceded, this will affect reading of Honoré's lists of quaestors (1999).

89. *Cod. Theod.* 15.12.1.

90. Matthews 2000, 291, n. 32.

91. Cf. *Cod. Theod.* 6.30.8; 7.8.8.

92. *Cod. Theod.* 1.27.1; Humfress 2007: 156–159.

93. *Cod. Theod.* 1.27.2 = *Cod. Just.* 1.4.7, of 397; Harries 1999, 172–211, on arbitration and dispute settlement.

94. For juristic commentary on the praetor's involvement with arbitrations, see Digest 4.8.

95. Harries 1999, 48–49.

96. *Nov. Val.* 7.1

97. *Nov. Val.* 7.2, of September 442.

98. Harries 1999, 88–91.

99. Grey 2007; but see also Sirks 2008.

100. On Constantine, Humfress 2006, esp. 205–208, 217–218.

101. E.g. at *Cod.Theod.* 2.24.1; *Cod. Just.* 6.23.15; but on witnesses, still, *Cod. Theod.* 4.4.1.

102. Meyer 2004, 265–276; Champlin 1991, 70–75. A relaxed attitude toward mistakes in the wording of wills was taken by, for example, P. Alfenus Varus (consul 39 B.C.E.), at Digest 35.1.27.

103. For references, Cameron and Hall 1999, 321–323.

104. Evans Grubbs 1995.

105. Arjava 1996, 41–52, showing also that vestiges of father power survived under the post-Roman western kingdoms.

106. Arjava 1996, 89–94 (mothers as guardians), 112–123 (guardianship of women).

107. *Cod. Theod.* 16.2.20.

108. Harries 1984 argues that pious Roman women observed the claims of family, provided there were family members available to inherit.

109. Gardner 1986, 81–96.

110. *Cod. Theod.* 3.16.1. See also Harper, Chapter 20 in this book.

111. Ambrosiaster, *Quaestiones Veteris et Novi Testamenti* 115.12.

112. *Cod. Theod.* 3.16.2 (421) reversed by *Nov. Theod.* 12.14.4, of 439.

113. *Cod. Theod.* 9.24.1; Evans Grubbs 1989.

114. *Cod. Theod.* 9.7.2.

115. *Cod. Theod.* 9.7.1 = *Cod. Just.* 9.9.28.

116. For prosecutions, Humfress 2007, 242–255.

117. *Cod. Theod.* 16.5.40, of 407.

118. Chadwick 1978 for Priscillian's career as a whole in Spain and Gaul.

119. MacMullen 1986 is the classic account of the expansion in the number of "criminal" charges in Late Antiquity and the extension of the use of torture up the social scale.

120. *Cod. Theod.* 9.38.3–4, 6–8.

121. Honoré 1999, 26–28.

122. *Cod. Theod.* 14.3.21 and *Nov. Theod.* 17.1.4.

123. *Cod. Theod.* 9.40, 15 and 16.

124. *Cod. Just.* 9.2.6, of 243.

125. Digest 48.18.20.

126. On judicial incompetence see, briefly, Harries 2007, 38–41.

127. *Cod. Theod.* 16.10.10 and 12 of 391 and 392.

128. Laws on, for example, taxation, where the imperial interest was directly involved, were, of course, supported by an enforcement apparatus based locally but answerable to the center. Many laws, as stated previously, were not intended to be "enforced" in the first place.

129. *Cod. Theod.* 16.10.3; 4; 16.

130. *Cod. Theod.* 16.10.8; 15.

131. In general, Humfress 2007, 196–213.

132. *Council of Carthage 407* = CCSL 149: 218, lines 1230–1234.

133. *Nov. Just.* 131.1.

134. *Cod. Theod.* 1.1.5.

135. *Cod. Theod.* 1.16.3.

136. *Cod. Theod.* 9.42.7; 12.1.77.

137. *Cod. Theod.* 11.30.57; Harries 1999, 164, n. 63.

138. Harries 1999, 153–171.

139. Digest 4.6.26.5. In his widely read guide to the *Duties of the Proconsul*, Ulpian advised that where governors delegated a case to another judge, he should give guidance on law but not fact, to avoid accusations of *gratia* (Digest 5.1.79.1). On the "corrupt judge," see Harries 1999, 153–171.

140. Or "epi-classical," as at Johnston 2005, as opposed to "High classical law" (Ibbetson 2005).

WORKS CITED

Ancient Sources

Ambrosiaster. *Quaestiones Veteris et Novi Testamenti*, ed. A. Souter. 1908. CSEL 50. Vienna: Tempsky.

Ammianus. *Res Gestae.* Trans. J. C. Rolfe. 1935–1939. 3 vols. London: Heinemann.

Bandy, A. C., ed. 1983. *John Lydus, On Powers, or The Magistracies of the Roman State*. Philadelphia: American Philosophical Society.
Birks, P., and G. MacLeod. 1987. *Justinian's Institutes: A Parallel Text and Translation*. London: Duckworth.
FIRA = S. Riccobono, ed. 1968. *Fontes Iuris Romani Anteiustiniani*. 3 vols. Florence: Barbèra.
Frakes, R. M. 2011. *Compiling the* Collatio Legum Mosaicarum et Romanarum *in Late Antiquity*. Oxford: Oxford University Press.
Gordon, W. M., and O. F. Robinson. 1988. *The Institutes of Gaius, Translated with an Introduction, with the Latin Text of Seckel and Kuebler*. London: Duckworth.
Hyamson, M., ed. 1913. *Mosaicarum et Romanarum Legum Collatio*. London: Oxford University Press.
Krueger, P., ed. 1915. *Corpus Iuris Civilis II: Codex Justinianus*. Berlin: Weidmann.
Mommsen, Th., ed. 1905. *Codex Theodosianus and Novellae* (also includes the *Gesta Senatus*). Berlin: Weidmann.
P. Col. VII = *Columbia Papyri VII: Fourth Century Documents from Karanis*. Ed. and trans. R. S. Bagnall and Naphtali Lewis. 1979. Missoula: Scholars Press.
Pharr, C. 1969. *The Theodosian Code and Novels and the Sirmondian Constitutions, Translated with Commentary, Glossary, and Bibliography by Clyde Pharr in Collaboration with Theresa Sherrer Davidson and Mary Brown Pharr*. New York: Greenwood Press.
Reinhardt, T., ed. 2003. *Cicero's Topica*. Oxford: Oxford University Press.
Watson, A., ed. 1985. *The Digest of Justinian: Latin Text Edited by Th. Mommsen with the Assistance of P. Krueger; English Translation Edited by Alan Watson*. Philadelphia: University of Pennsylvania Press.

Modern Sources

Arjava, A. 1996. *Women and Law in Late Antiquity*. Oxford: Oxford University Press.
Cameron, A., and S. Hall, eds. 1999. *Eusebius: Life of Constantine*. Oxford: Clarendon Press.
Chadwick, H. 1978. *Priscillian of Avila*. Oxford: Oxford University Press.
Champlin, E. 1991. *Final Judgments: Duty and Emotion in Roman Wills*. Berkeley: University of California Press.
Corcoran, S. 1993. "Hidden from History: The Legislation of Licinius." In *The Theodosian Code: Studies in the Imperial Law of Late Antiquity*, ed. Jill Harries and Ian Wood, 97–119. London: Duckworth.
———. 2000. *The Empire of the Tetrarchs*, 2nd ed. Oxford: Oxford University Press.
Crook, J. 1995. *Legal Advocacy in the Roman World*. London: Duckworth.
Evans Grubbs, J. 1989. "Abduction Marriage in Antiquity: A Law of Constantine (*CTh* 9.24.1) and Its Social Context," *Journal of Roman Studies* 79: 59–83.
———. 1995. *Law and Family in Late Antiquity: The Emperor Constantine's Marriage Legislation*. Oxford: Oxford University Press.
Gagos, T., and P. van Minnen. 1994. *Settling a Dispute: Towards a Legal Anthropology of Late Roman Egypt*. Ann Arbor: University of Michigan Press.
Gardner, Jane. 1986. *Women in Roman Law and Society*. London: Croom Helm.
Grey, Cam. 2007. "Contextualising *Colonatus*: The *Origo* of the Late Roman Empire," *Journal of Roman Studies* 97: 155–175.
Harries, Jill. 1984. "Treasure in Heaven: Property and Inheritance among Senators of Late Rome." In *Marriage and Property*, ed. E. Craik, 54–70. Aberdeen: Aberdeen University Press.

———. 1988. "The Roman Imperial Quaestor from Constantine to Theodosius II," *Journal of Roman Studies* 78: 148–172.
———. 1999. *Law and Empire in Late Antiquity*. Cambridge: Cambridge University Press.
———. 2007. *Law and Crime in the Roman World*. Cambridge: Cambridge University Press.
Harries, Jill, and Ian Wood, eds. 1993. *The Theodosian Code: Studies in the Imperial Law of Late Antiquity*. London: Duckworth.
Heath, M. 2004. *Menander: A Rhetor in Context*. Oxford: Oxford University Press.
Honoré, Tony. 1978. *Tribonian*. London: Duckworth.
———. 1986. "The Making of the Theodosian Code," *ZSS RA* 103: 133–222.
———. 1987. "Scriptor Historiae Augustae," *Journal of Roman Studies* 77: 156–176.
———. 1994. *Emperors and Lawyers: With a Palingenesia of Third-Century Imperial Rescripts, 193–305 AD*, 2nd ed. Oxford: Oxford University Press.
———. 1999. *Law in the Crisis of Empire: The Theodosian Dynasty and Its Quaestors, AD 379–455*. Oxford: Oxford University Press.
———. 2004. "From Cosmopolis to Rechtsstaat: Roman Law AD 200–400." In *Approaching Late Antiquity*, ed. S. Swain and M. Edwards, 109–132. Oxford: Oxford University Press.
Humfress, Caroline. 2005. "Law and Legal Practice in the Age of Justinian." In *The Cambridge Companion to Justinian*, ed. M. Maas, 161–184. Cambridge: Cambridge University Press.
———. 2006. "Civil Law and Social Life." In *The Cambridge Companion to Constantine*, ed. N. Lenski, 205–225. Cambridge: Cambridge University Press.
———. 2007. *Orthodoxy and the Courts in Late Antiquity*. Oxford: Oxford University Press.
Ibbetson, D. 2005. "High Classical Law." In *The Cambridge Ancient History, Vol. 12: The Crisis of Empire, AD 193–337*, ed. A. K. Bowman, A. Cameron, and P. Garnsey, 184–199. Cambridge: Cambridge University Press.
Johnston, D. 2000. "The Jurists." In *The Cambridge History of Greek and Roman Political Thought*, ed. C. Rowe and M. Schofield, 616–634. Cambridge: Cambridge University Press.
———. 2005. "Epiclassical Law." In *The Cambridge Ancient History, Vol. 12: The Crisis of Empire, AD 193–337*, ed. A. K. Bowman, A. Cameron, and P. Garnsey, 200–207. Cambridge: Cambridge University Press.
Kelly, Christopher M. 2004. *Ruling the Later Roman Empire*. Cambridge, MA: Harvard University Press.
Laiou, A., and D. Simon, eds. 1994. *Law and Society in Byzantium, Ninth–Twelfth Centuries*. Cambridge, MA: Dumbarton Oaks.
Lee, A. D. 2002. "Decoding Late Roman Law," *Journal of Roman Studies* 92: 185–193.
Levy, Ernst. 1951. *West Roman Vulgar Law: The Law of Property*. Philadelphia: American Philosophical Society.
MacMullen, Ramsay. 1986. "Judicial Savagery in the Roman Empire," *Chiron* 16: 147–166.
———. 1988. *Corruption and the Decline of Rome*. New Haven, CT: Yale University Press.
Matthews, John. 1989. *The Roman Empire of Ammianus*. London: Duckworth.
———. 1993. "The Making of the Text." In *The Theodosian Code: Studies in the Imperial Law of Late Antiquity*, ed. Jill Harries and Ian Wood, 19–44. London: Duckworth.
———. 2000. *Laying Down the Law: A Study of the Theodosian Code*. New Haven, CT: Yale University Press.

Meyer, Elizabeth. 2004. *Law and Legitimacy in the Roman Empire: Tabulae in Belief and Practice*. Cambridge: Cambridge University Press.

Millar, Fergus. 1977. *The Emperor in the Roman World*. London: Duckworth.

———. 2006. *A Greek Roman Empire: Power and Belief under Theodosius II*. Sather Classical Lectures 64. Berkeley: University of California Press.

Mitchell, S. 1988. "Maximinus and the Christians in AD 312: A New Latin Inscription," *Journal of Roman Studies* 78: 105–124.

Sirks, Boudewijn. 1993. "The Sources of the Code." In *The Theodosian Code: Studies in the Imperial Law of Late Antiquity*, ed. Jill Harries and Ian Wood, 45–67. London: Duckworth.

———. 2008. "The Colonate in Justinian's Reign," *Journal of Roman Studies* 98: 120–143.

Stein, Peter. 1966. *Regulae Iuris: From Juristic Rules to Legal Maxims*. Edinburgh: Edinburgh University Press.

Turpin, W. 1988. "*Adnotatio* and Imperial Rescript in Roman Legal Procedure," *Revue Internationale des Droits de l'Antiquité*, 3rd series, 35: 285–307.

———. 1991. "Imperial Subscriptions and the Administration of Justice," *Journal of Roman Studies* 81: 101–118.

Vera, D. 1981. *Commento Storico alle* Relationes *di Quinto Aurelio Simmaco*. Pisa: Giardini.

Voss, W. E. 1982. *Recht und Rhetorik in den Kaisergesetzen der Spätantike: Eine Untersuchung zum nachklassischen Kauf- und Uberreignungsrecht*. Forschungen zur byzantinischen Rechtsgeschichte 9. Frankfurt am Main: Löwenklau.

CHAPTER 25

COMMUNICATION IN LATE ANTIQUITY: USE AND REUSE

ANDREW GILLETT
Macquarie University

We perceive Late Antiquity, as other periods of the past, largely through the remnants of intentional acts of communication, be they pragmatic or ideological in nature, intended for solitary meditation or for monumental display. What appears new and characteristic of the period, differentiating it from earlier periods, stems from developments in the contents or form of communicative acts: novel messages, of imperial autocracy or monotheistic belief, or changed modes of expression, in newly emerged ecclesiastical literary genres or ceremonial court ritual. The late antique period developed no new communicative media or substantial technological developments (cf. O'Donnell 2010), but the major political and cultural changes of the period prompted new practices of communication: not only new or modified textual genres, such as ecclesiastical history or hagiographic biography, but also new routes of communication, linking different permutations of society; correspondence between emperors, bishops, and "barbarian" kings, or between Roman aristocrats and monks, are obvious examples of such new routes. The fundamental means of direct communication in this period, as in earlier antiquity, was the combination of letter and embassy, a partnership of written text and human accompaniment that undergirded public and private life both in the late Roman empire and in its successor states.

One striking feature of Late Antiquity is an apparent explosion of epistolary practice: there seems to have been an upsurge in the writing of letters among social elites and, particularly, in the publication of their letters in edited collections. This phenomenon is not restricted to the collection of "private" letters of civilian elites. The great Latin and Greek letter-collections of aristocrats and bishops from the fourth to sixth centuries preserve for us evidence of the functioning of elite *amicitia* and interchanges of theological thought; these same centuries, however, also present the great collections of governmental correspondence: imperial and papal dispositive letters, gathered privately or officially to serve as administrative guides or as sources of authority. Collections of "private" letters of *amicitia* and "official" dispositive letters shade into each other: the act of selection emphasizes patronage and friendship in some collections and administrative decisions in another, but aristocrats, bishops, senior officials, and emperors all participated in "social" as well as administrative correspondence; some letter-collections explicitly combine features of both. The chronology of the upsurge of published collections, escalating in the early fifth century with collections of aristocratic, episcopal, imperial, and papal correspondences, is striking and suggestive. The act of collecting and circulating letters, turning the product of a specific occasion into a text for permanent wide consultation, is perhaps more problematic than is usually recognized. On the one hand, the great letter-collections, private and official, provide petrified but skewed evidence of the vast, intersecting mesh of one-to-one correspondences that facilitated public life, social strategies, and cultural and religious developments throughout the later Roman empire and its successor states. On the other hand, the reuse of these communiqués is a different act, sometimes obscured for us by the convenience of letter-collections as reservoirs of evidence. Collections are necessarily removed from the aims of the original correspondence. They are a second-order vehicle of communication with functions that are neither obvious nor consistent, which may have included "targeted" communication through dedication or prescribed official use, as well as "broadcast" communication through publication. As letter-collections are an important lens through which we see many of the specific communicative acts of Late Antiquity, it is necessary to elucidate the compulsion to reuse transient correspondences and turn "leaves" into "books," *chartae* into *libri*, and to contextualize the genre of collected letters through both the documentary evidence of papyrology and the normative accounts of narrative descriptions of communicative acts.

A Communicative Démarche Gone Wrong

When the emperor Theodosius was waging war against the usurper Maximus, Theophilus [bishop of Alexandria] sent gifts to the emperor through [his priest] Isidore and gave him two copies of a letter, [one for the emperor

> and one the usurper[Soz]], and instructed him to present to whoever emerged as victor both the gifts and the appropriate letter. Following his instructions, Isidore arrived at Rome and awaited the outcome of the war. But word of this did not stay quiet for long, for a lector who accompanied Isidore secretly took the letters [and showed them to the emperor[Cass]]. Terrified by this, Isidore straightaway fled to Alexandria, [wishing to hide what he had been ordered to do[Cass]].[1]

Isidore's discomfiture illustrates and arose from many of the fundamental factors of communication in Late Antiquity. We do not know the aim of the embassy commissioned by Theophilus in 388 or the contents of the letters to be presented to the winning emperor;[2] as is not uncommon for narrative descriptions of embassies, it is the embassy itself and its significance for the social credit (or public humiliation) of the envoy or principal that is dramatically important in this anecdote (Mullett 1990, 172; Gillett 2003, 169–171, 276). Effaced of its individual purposes, this embassy stands as a representative example of a traffic in embassies and letters that bulks large in sources for the post-Constantinian period and usefully illustrates several key aspects of how communication functioned in Late Antiquity more broadly.

Framed by premodern technology and Hellenistic culture, active communication—the transfer of information and persuasion in the expectation of effecting a reciprocal response—was determined by the available media, by the physical nature of their infrastructure, and by the geographic and social patterns that marked lines of contact. Three forms of media are combined in this anecdote in the forms of Theophilus' letters, his envoy Isidore, and the gifts he bore: text, person, token. Though it was the letters that got Isidore into hot water and best fulfill our expectations of textual communication, they were not necessarily the most important component of this foiled démarche. Of the three media used, two were intended to function verbally: the letters (with textual language) and the envoy (with oral language); and two to function semiotically: the gifts (creating an expectation of reciprocality) and, again, the envoy (who, in representing his principal, conventionally "performed" requisite acts of greeting and supplication). In the event, Isidore's misfortune prevents us from seeing this semiotic function of the envoy other than by its absence, but the role is apparent in even the most cursory accounts of communication through embassies. "The envoy Felix, after making his greetings and displaying his letters, spoke . . ." (*Felix legatus, salutatione praemissa, ostensis litteris, ait . . .*; Greg. Tur. *Hist.* 9.13): in this passing reference, the gesture of performance and friendship precedes first the presentation of a letter of credence and then the substantive, oral message. The invention of the modern telegraph system was the first form of communication removed from the speed of human transport (Sotinel 2009, 125), but the telegraph and the governmental postal systems that arose in early-nineteenth-century cities were also the first forms of verbal communication that were not, at least potentially, accompanied by human speech or gesture. In the ancient and medieval worlds, the written, oral, performative, and semiotic modes of expression were interdependent.

The physicality of the means of communication impressed itself on the function of these interconnected media. While parts of the (intended) communication of the embassy were ephemeral, namely, Isidore's oral message and his "performance" in presenting the gifts and letter, the items to be presented were inescapably material, to Isidore's chagrin. The physical object of the letter itself had to be produced in Alexandria before Isidore's departure for it to be authenticated with Theophilus' signature (*subscriptio*); otherwise, Isidore could simply have taken notes of Theophilus' intended message and had an appropriately addressed full copy produced in Italy once the civil war had been resolved. This "materiality" of the letter was an essential part of the communication; in addition to authenticating the letter as a genuine message from the bishop of Alexandria and thereby certifying Isidore as Theophilus' representative, it made the object of the letter itself akin to a gift, so assimilating it to the other tokens being presented (Bowman 1994, 123, citing Demetrius, *On Style* 223–224; Constable 1976, 16; Mullett 1990, 182–183). It was the evidential potential of the fixed, physical form of Theophilus' two versions of the letters that caused Isidore grief on this occasion (and at least one other; Russell 2007, 16–17); likewise, it was the fixed evidence of letters that gave them dispositive force in imperial and other administration (as is underscored by a number of incidents in narrative texts that turn on the vexed issue of forgeries or disputed attribution, e.g., Amm. Marc. 15.5, cf. Kelly 1994, 169; Greg. Tur. *Hist.* 6.22, 10.19). Beyond the letter as object, physicality shaped the framework of communication even more fundamentally, in terms of space and time. The remoteness of Alexandria from the emperors' presence in Italy required Theophilus to be represented by his envoy and his letters; they also necessitated the expense and, crucially, the time-delay of travel. Events would progress while the embassy was in train; Theophilus could not know which imperial claimant would have succeeded by the time his envoy sought audience and so attempted to circumvent this time lag by hedging his bets. His idea backfired, but it was not an unreasonable response to the consequences of distance. Not only time but also opportunity were limited by distance: if Isidore's (unspecified) mission failed, further attempts to negotiate Theophilus' request could be made only with difficulty; any such long-range supplication must effectively have been regarded as a one-off opportunity, with limited scope for remedial negotiation should the envoy receive a negative response. To the extent that they could be foreseen, contingencies likely to affect the outcome of an audience—here, the uncertain outcome of a civil war, an extraordinary if not altogether rare event—had to be accommodated. Communication, though frequent and ubiquitous, was not necessarily a continual and reciprocal reverberation; it could be staccato and terminal, and it could readily fail to reach its target or be made redundant by its physical limitations (e.g., Ebbeler 2009, 279).

Isidore's mission presented him with a particular problem in the fundamental element of all communication: route and direction. As the vehicle of an approach from Theophilus to the emperor, he could not be sure which of two possible emperors, two end termini of the communication, he should approach. But what is, in historical terms, more significant in this episode is the starting terminus of the communication, a Christian bishop in a key province of the Roman empire. A century earlier it would, of course, have been improbable, if not dangerous, for a bishop to initiate communication with an emperor, let alone with reasonable expectations of receiving patronage as a result. By contrast, Theophilus, notwithstanding the faux pas of 388, maintained correspondence with Theodosius, parts of which are extant, including a fragment of a report written by the bishop to the emperor on one of the major incidents in the Christian defeat of traditional civic cults, the destruction of the Serapeum in Alexandria (Haas 1997, 159–169; Russell 2007, 7–10, 81–84). The rapprochement wrought by Constantine between imperial authority and the Church, considered in terms of its impact on patterns of elite communication throughout the Mediterranean world, had generated an immense quantity of communiqués between holders of ecclesiastical office and their newfound aristocratic peers and imperial patrons; it inserted a whole new register of correspondents into societal interactions (Sotinel 2009, 128). In modern terms, an equivalent upsurge in the volume of communicative traffic caused by the sudden entry of a new class of participants—such as the large-scale spread of mobile telephone use by children in many countries over the last decade—may well temporarily overload the relevant infrastructure, and Ammianus Marcellinus' oft-cited complaint of bishops' use of the *cursus publicus* is a sign of exactly that in the generation after Constantine (Amm. Marc. 21.16.18). Episcopal correspondence, however, not only piggybacked on governmental and other pre-existing infrastructure but also developed a critical mass sufficient to generate its own routes and carriers and its own *mores* in written and performed expression (Conybeare 2000; Sotinel 2004; Ebbeler 2009). In terms of its human components, one effect of this new traffic was, as in other parts of society, the emergence of individuals noted and deployed for their particular experience gained from repeatedly undertaking embassies. Isidore was such an individual: the first figure described in Palladius' *Lausiac History*, he owes his prominence to his frequent travels on behalf of his see to Rome (even after the events of 388), where he was well acquainted not only with the church establishment but also with the city's senators and their families. The value of his contacts made while in Italy was no doubt complemented by his position as guest master of the Alexandrian church, receiving ecclesiastical visitors to the great city (Palladius, *Laus. Hist.* 1.4; *Dial. de vita Joannis Chrys.* 6; Sozomen, *HE* 8.12). The rapid rise in social status of bishops in the fourth century generated new routes of communication not in geographical but in social and institutional terms. The Christianization of the Roman empire was one of several social and political changes—along inter alia with the movement to new cities of the emperors' courts, the imperial appointment of municipal governors, the development of large-scale monasticism, and the establishment of royal courts in former western provinces—that produced extensive redirections of the social, governmental, and political patterns of communication (Matthews 1989, 254; Slootjes 2006, 106–177; McGuire 1988, 1–90; Gillett 2003).

Communication Practices as Cultural Index

The customary use of such practices as part of societal and institutional infrastructure may be regarded as an index of a society's participation in the fundamentally Hellenistic cultural bloc of Late Antiquity, even if outside the political boundaries of the late Roman or Byzantine empire. The "barbarian kingdoms" of Gaul, Italy, and Spain occupy an ambiguous place in current historical scholarship with regard to the idea of Late Antiquity, vacillating on the one hand between essentially Eurocentric, exceptionalist interpretations of their "post-Roman" society, and on the other acknowledgment of their derivation from the monotheistic, monarchical culture of the late antique empires. This ambiguity pertains to literacy and communication. The government of Merovingian Gaul produced extensive written documentation (Ganz and Goffart 1990, 907–923; Murray 2005, 250–261), yet even when a high degree of elite literacy is recognized, specific practices of communication or literacy may still be subject to "decline" models of interpretation (Wood 1990; Heather 1994, 192–193). These understandings need not, however, offer the only possible readings of the evidence. The production of formularies, books of model or pro forma documents including many types of dispositive and social letters, has been seen as symptomatic of a lack of composition skills; formularies can, however, also be seen as evidence for busy and professionalized chanceries (Rio 2009, 20–21). The evolution of nonclassical, baroque styles of Latinity can be interpreted as the result of failure to grasp the importance of classicizing style as a badge of cultural membership, but changes in Latinity do not apply only to western composition but also to the use of Latin at Constantinople (e.g., *Ep. Austr.* 40–42, letters of the Byzantine exarch in Italy and the emperor Maurice; cf. Malaspina 2001, 287–296; Avitus, *Ep.* 49); common changes in style may signal evolving, rather than fracturing, membership of an increasingly abstruse genre of elite communication (cf. Mullett 1990, 178–179). The publication of letter-collections in Gaul, well attested for the fifth and sixth centuries, drops off thereafter until the Carolingian period; both the rise and decline of Gallic epistolary collections, however, may reflect changes in cultural styles rather than real increases or decreases in activity (Constable 1976, 30; on changes in Gallic literary styles: Wood 1992; 1994). Gregory of Tours certainly knew and used earlier and perhaps contemporary Gallic letter-collections, but he did not collect letters of his own, despite the desire he displays in the valedictory chapter of his *Histories* to preserve his literary writings as a whole, and despite the dedication to him of published books of verse epistles (and other works) by his client Venantius Fortunatus.[3]

Gregory's lengthy historical narrative, while largely if unintentionally responsible for the modern image of his times as chaotic (Goffart 2005, 112–119), in fact regularly demonstrates the centrality of accepted, formal conventions of communication to public life within the kingdom at the end of the sixth century. Two anecdotes may serve as illustrations from his many casual references to written and human instruments of communication and documentation.[4] In 580, Leudast, *comes* of Tours, was accused of spreading calumnies against Chilperic's queen, Fredegund, and against bishop Gregory himself, and was deposed from his position by king Chilperic, driven from the city, and excommunicated by an assembly of bishops. Three years later, he returned to Tours and presented Gregory with an order (*praeceptum*) from Chilperic allowing him to return to the city and a letter (*epistola*) from a group of bishops urging his readmittance to communion, but Gregory hesitated to obey the instructions of these royal and episcopal correspondences because he had received no message (*litterae*) from Fredegund herself advising whether she acquiesced in Leudast's reinstatement; after himself sending to the queen, Gregory received a response (*scripta*), however unreassuring (Greg. Tur. *Hist.* 5.49, 6.32). The correspondences of Chilperic and the bishops had the dispositive force of royal authority and the consensual force of episcopal synodical counsel but needed to be balanced against private communication from the queen. In this politically awkward situation, Gregory had to be alert to multiple channels of communication and to exchange messages, presumably quite quickly, before acting.

In 590, Gregory witnessed another unpleasant political situation when bishop Egidius of Rheims fell foul of king Childebert II. Egidius was accused of conspiring in a recent assassination plot and of having earlier betrayed Childebert's interests in favor of his fellow king Chilperic, now deceased (Greg. Tur. *Hist.* 10.19). The betrayal struck hard, because Egidius had played a major role throughout the previous decade in managing relations between Childebert's court and those of the other Merovingian dynasts; inter alia, Egidius had undertaken several high-profile embassies to the royal courts of Childebert's two fellow Merovingian kings and had led negotiations there.[5] Chilperic arranged for Egidius to be tried canonically by fellow bishops, sending letters to all the bishops in his part of the kingdom (some thirty-odd in all), simultaneously en masse to order them to attend the hearing. The bishops, however, objected to the request on a technicality; Gregory omits the mechanics of the bishops' reply but suggests some sort of consultation to coordinate a response and delay the proceedings. Childebert was forced to reschedule the trial for six weeks later and to dispatch a second round of letters advising the bishops of the deferred date. At the trial, the evidence rested largely on written documentation. Accused of accepting property from Chilperic as a bribe, Egidius produced diplomas (*chartae*) showing that the lands in question had in fact been granted to him by Childebert. But the court official responsible for authenticating documentation on behalf of Childebert, the *referendarius*, testified that the signature (*subscriptio*) on the document was not his own but a forgery. Next, an exchange of incriminating letters (*epistolae*) between Egidius and Chilperic was produced. Egidius denied that the letters had been produced in his name (presumably indicating that they were anonymous, rather than that they were pseudoepigraphic) or that Chilperic's letters were replies (*rescripta*) to any of his own, but a personal servant of the bishop (*puer familiaris*) produced note-form versions of Egidius' letters that had been preserved in his records of correspondence ([*epistolae*] *notarum titulis per tomos chartarum conprehensae*; perhaps Tironian notes; cf. Ganz 1983). The third set of damning written evidence was a set of treaty documents (*pactiones*) in the names of Childebert and Chilperic, confirming negotiations conducted by Egidius seven years earlier and signed at the time by the bishop and his fellow envoys; Childebert claimed that this agreement was a distortion of the mission that had been entrusted to Egidius.[6] The bishop could not impute the legitimacy of these documents as they were Chilperic's own copy of the agreement that had been preserved as a set in the archives of one of his writing offices (*in regestum Chilperici regis in unum scriniorum pariter*), housed in the treasury of one of Chilperic's royal villas, which Childebert later inherited. The final evidence was oral. Other former envoys, leading members of Childebert's court and an abbot, who had accompanied Egidius on his embassies to Chilperic years earlier, testified that Egidius had held private discussions with Chilperic without his fellow envoys, contrary to the usual practice of embassies; these meetings had been the opportunity for conducting his false negotiations and accepting bribery. Convinced by this evidence, the episcopal judges removed Egidius from his bishopric in line with Church canons but convinced the king to reduce his punishment for treason from death to exile.

This episode pays considerable attention to the infrastructure of late antique communication practices that facilitated the exchanges of letters and embassies involved.[7] Archives enabled documentation to be located and authenticated, and they included both brief records of private correspondence and official depositories of original, signed documentation that could be passed on between administrations, aiding institutional continuity. Staff of royal and episcopal *domus* were maintained to produce and authenticate documents, including multiple, simultaneous letters, a kind of pre-electronic "distribution list" that must have required considerable human resources to first produce the documents and then deliver them within a limited time frame. The standing practice of regular episcopal correspondence allowed the bishops to consult with each other, across a geographically scattered area, and reply to the king with a unified response. Experienced envoys were used repeatedly to capitalize on their local knowledge and relationship with correspondents; the convention of dispatching several envoys to attend group audiences was intended to preclude the sort of misuse of opportunity of which Egidius was accused. Such evidence as these two episodes offer is qualitative, not quantitative. It does, however, suggest not only the continuing ubiquity of Hellenistic modes of communication in this post-imperial polity but also confidence in their effectiveness, a significant degree of investment in their maintenance by elites, and a critical mass of regular interchange sufficient to sustain their efficacy. Gregory's narrative indicates that formal practices of communication and their infrastructure remained fundamental to public affairs in Gaul; they were not residual or lapidary affectations.

Communication as an Approach to Sources and Historical Contexts

It is self-evident that much of the material we study for Late Antiquity, as of other periods of history, constitutes vestiges of acts of communication. This is true not only for what is called "direct communication" (including "political communication"), here Theophilus' embassy to Theodosius, but also for less restrictively targeted forms of "display communication," including messages broadcast in public space to assert ideological claims (for example, the monumental architecture of late Roman civic and ecclesiastical building programs or Sasanian rock reliefs) and for private and intimate communications (such as curse tablets or texts for solitary meditation). Most extant cultural artifacts, whether textual or material, represent intercepted messages—sent not, of course, to us but to contemporaries of whoever commissioned the artifact. Certain aspects of "communication" were systematized, analyzed, even to an extent theorized in antiquity, in particular rhetoric in the forms of oratory and letters (Stowers 1986; Malherbe 1988; Mullett 1997, 135; Trapp 2003, 42–46; Rosenmeyer 2006, 1–10; Morello and Morriso 2007; Sullivan 2007; Poster 2007). "Communication" in the broadest sense, however, is a modern abstraction, studied in the technological sciences, social sciences, and humanities (e.g., McQuail 2005; O'Sullivan et al. 1983; Rogers and Kincaid 1981; Windahl, Signitzer, and Olson 2009). With caveats about the nature of historical evidence (cf. Buc 2001; 2007), these studies can provide useful frameworks or analogues for conceptualizing ancient behavior. It has been only relatively recently that studies of ancient and medieval societies have adopted approaches that forefront the act of communication by studying the ways in which cultural practices functioned to communicate messages and to effect purposes, not only at the level of readership (the encoding and decoding of a message within specific conventions) but also within social and political contexts (the elements of society or culture with which a text interacted in order to "work") (Mostert 1999; Lewis 1996; Sotinel 2009).

There are at least two main benefits of an approach to our sources that abstracts the patterns and functions of communication of our sources, parallel to but separate from study of their contents, form, and specific aims (the anecdote about Theophilus' embassy to Theodosius lacks all three of these individualizing features and yet is usefully informative about communicative practices). First, attempting to reconstruct how a text or material artifact may have been intended to operate as an act of communication alerts us to its lost context, the total process of communication of which extant textual sources originally formed only a part. To use letters as an example: the thousands of letters extant in manuscript collections can be studied for their literary form and argumentative content but generally lack the contextual information available in the narrative of Isidore's embassy to Italy, where we learn incidentally that the letter was to accompany gifts and that it was to be presented (we can assume, with an oral message) at a specific, dramatic occasion (the aftermath of a civil war) by an experienced episcopal envoy with strong local contacts. Surviving papyri letters, especially if preserved as part of an archive, sometimes tell us more about their context and function, but in general extant texts preserved in medieval manuscript collections represent a limited fragment of the act of communication of which any one individual letter formed part. We miss the complement to the written letter, the nontextual components, be they verbal or semiotic: "half the letter, the living half, is automatically missing . . . [a letter] was written, oral, material, visual, and it had its own ceremony, lost for us [almost] totally . . ." (Mullett 1990, 182, 183; 1997, 37; Papaioannou 2010, 189). Asking what were the accompanying actions or objects intended to facilitate a particular message cannot supply what is unrecoverable, but it can help build up an outline of what is missing, increasing our awareness of how letters—and other cultural artifacts—operated to fulfill their functions.

Second, analyzing our sources in terms of their communicative functions highlights ways in which social, cultural, and political developments in Late Antiquity changed the way people used the media available, how shifts in power and culture led to "media revolutions" and in part depended on them (Mendels 1999; Ellis and Kidner 2004, xiii–xiv; Cooper and Hillman 2007, 3–4). Late Antiquity developed no new communicative technologies beyond those used in earlier Mediterranean and Near Eastern societies: oral and written verbal expression, bodily gesture, visual representation in two- and three-dimensional media, personal dress and ornamentation, and architectural and urban design and decoration. Because of the general training of students of the period in textual or material artifact-based disciplinary skills, we are (rightly) alert to changes in genre and form of sources produced in the period—for example, the emergence of ecclesiastical history as a new mix of literary and documentary forms, the development of hagiographic biography, the appearance of a specifically Christian genre of chronicle, the explosion of sermon literature as a quotidian vehicle for Christianity (Barnes 1981, 126–147; Grafton and Williams 2006; Haag and Rousseau 2000; Maxwell 2006). Alongside these changes in content and form, however, it is also possible to consider how a new or newly altered genre of expression might have effected its purpose, not only through argumentation and rhetorical strategy but also through factors of its contemporary "transmission" as a communicative medium: its display, declamation, publication, or circulation. Such factors include the direction of communication and the cultural implication of the medium involved. Some late antique changes in these factors are literally obvious, especially in "display" communication: the move of mosaic programs from the floors of villas to the walls and ceilings of churches is in part a shift from a private to a public venue, but other messages are likely to have been encoded in this striking relocation of a long-familiar visual medium from a horizontal and inferior position to a vertical and superior one (Mathews 1999, 95). The adoption by bishops of outward signs of public and aristocratic status, including basilica architecture, Roman senatorial clothing styles, and silver goods, is an unambiguous appropriation of "display" media by the "new men" of late Roman society (Krautheimer 1983, 7–40; Leader-Newby 2004; Janes 1998; Harlow 2004), while the shift from scroll to codex as the format of elite literary production seems to be a Christian adaptation of a hitherto humble medium. There are examples of reoriented "direct" communication also. The sudden appearance of panegyric in epic poetic form in the 390s and 400s in the works of Claudian was an innovation of genre that won immediate and long-lasting appreciation, and the study of both the form and content of his corpus are essential components of our understanding of the cultural and political life of the western empire (Cameron 1970). But Claudian and his patron Stilicho also represent an equally significant redirection of communication through panegyric, away from addresses by representatives of provincial cities to emperors (or their senior magistrates), seeking direct or indirect benefits, toward a continuous "stream" of messages emanating from the imperial authority (in the form of Stilicho) to the senatorial aristocracy of the city of Rome. Stilicho can be seen to "reroute" an existing medium, the public performance of panegyric, to accommodate the needs of an imperial court now located regularly in Italy (Gillett 2001, 137–141; forthcoming). Other examples of new developments of genre also involve redirection of communications (new "senders" and "receivers") or redeployment of media from one social context to another, with eloquent semiotic meaning.

Communication, in its simplest terms, involves a sender, a message, a channel of transmission, and a receiver. Often, as is the way of historical studies, we do not have information on all of these basic elements: we may possess a redaction of the medium or even the object itself (a text, an ivory diptych) but not know the identity of the sender (being careful not to conflate the roles of the artisan-creator and the person who commissioned the artifact and in whose name it was dispatched or displayed). Far more often, however, we have no indication of the identity of the intended or actual receiver (or "audience"), a significant stumbling block to any attempt to analyze extant cultural artifacts in these terms of communication. Whereas early martyrological texts can be more or less contextualized—as part of an annual liturgy of an urban congregation celebrating the martyr's death—the addressees of the vast wealth of later ancient and medieval hagiographic literature remain elusive (Van Egmond 1999). The "audience" remains the holy grail of much ancient and medieval textual scholarship. The implications of this are that we remain uncertain exactly what function hagiographic and other texts served, because in not knowing who their target was, we thereby do not know how they were intended to operate.

The Medium *Epistula*

The most basic means of direct communication in antiquity, however, does by and large preserve for us all four fundamental elements of sender, message, channel, and receiver: the letter (though, as we have seen, the written text is only a part of the channel of communication and, often, of the message). A constant interchange of communication through letters undergirds almost all activities we know of in the late antique Mediterranean world: government, church, aristocratic lifestyle, agricultural management, trade. Although we often use the terms *letter* and *epistle* to refer to personal communiqués between private individuals, such as the letters of Libanios to other nobles in Antioch and beyond or Augustine's letters to fellow bishops, our sources use the term *epistula* and its synonyms far more liberally, ranging from short familial greetings and business transactions to imperial and royal administrative documents and theological and literary tractates; at one extreme of scale, Photius' *Bibliotheca* is cast as a letter to his brother Tarasios (Photius, *Bibl. praef.*, 280 *post.*). This terminology should not automatically be dismissed as loose usage or, in the case of tractates, necessarily be seen as a literary ploy, for it recognizes the basic elements of what constituted a letter: a written substitution for the author's presence, compensating for the "epistolary situation," the inability of the author to be in the presence of the recipient to deliver an oral message. In terms of formal features, an *epistula* is defined only by the presence of a greeting and conclusion demonstrating the intent to transmit from sender to recipient (Constable 1976, 13–14, 24–25). The letter substituted for the author by acting as a representation not only of the sender's message but also of the relationship between the sender and recipient: so, letters were an instrument of *amicitia* between peers (in the letters of aristocratic and episcopal collections), of command between members of a hierarchy (in imperial and papal letters), and of a range of other societal relations, such as this example of submission: "Since I cannot in person cast myself at your feet, I bow to you in this letter, as my proxy" (*epistolae vicarietate prosternor*; Radegund, *Ep. ad episcopos, apud* Greg. Tur. *Hist.* IX 42). The letter, moreover, was not only a means of communication in itself but also a primary means of circulation of other texts. Dedicatory letters prefacing any type of work became a literary subgenre from the late Roman republic onward (Constable 1976, 27); though a convention, this was also a function of the fact that, in a world without mass marketing as a vehicle for publication, the primary means of "publishing" a text aimed at wide circulation was its initial dispatch by the author to one recipient under cover of a letter, an act that could be repeated multiple times. Theophilus sought to establish the primacy of the Alexandrian calculation of the date of Easter through his own table of paschal dates, which he put into circulation by sending as a letter to Theodosius (both the cover letter and the preface to the treatise itself addresses the emperor; Russell 2007, 81–84). Under cover of a letter, Augustine sent a copy of his *Confessions*, decades after it was written, to a senior imperial official (Aug. *Epp.* 230–231; Brown 2000, 431). Published letter-collections themselves were often prefaced by dedicatory letters. "Publication" was not independent from social and political correspondence. The ancient understanding of Greek and Latin *epistula* was much broader than modern "letter" or *Brief*; rather than recognizing a restricted range of written genres as letters, the term (in Greek, literally "what is sent to accompany a journey") evoked the basic means of communication. Like modern postal letters and emails, the ancient *epistula* and its necessary complement the envoy or letter bearer could "cover" and circulate other documents as "attachments."

Categories of Evidence

Our evidence for the use of this ubiquitous medium in Late Antiquity is divided by issues of preservation into a number of categories that tend, because of legitimate distinctions in technical knowledge or content, to obscure commonalities in the processes of epistolary communication. Most fundamentally, extant letters divide into original papyrological documents (including actual papyri, ostraka, and other writing materials)[8] preserving their contents, form, and physical material and letters transmitted to us only through manuscript copies, always edited at least to the extent of the loss of their original layout and often with heavily revised contents. The overlap between letters preserved on papyri and in manuscript is negligible; no papyri archival version of a letter-collection transmitted in manuscript has been found, although papyri copies of texts preserved or known from manuscript have been identified (e.g., the contentious *P. Giss.* 40 I, possibly a fragment of the *Constitutio Antoniniana*).

On the one hand, we have very large numbers of letters on papyrus, realia we can hold in our gloved hands as material artifacts, preserved primarily in Egypt (and regularly being found, in quantity) as the tail end of the vast quantities of documentation generated by Ptolemaic- and Roman-era administration of the ancient kingdom, though smaller quantities have been preserved from other sites, including Ravenna and Dura Europos. These original letters in Greek, Coptic, Latin, or Arabic represent either receivers' copies or senders' files (copybook versions or returned originals), found largely as individual documents packed in cartonnage or as waste but sometimes preserved intentionally and systematically as an archive (e.g., the archives of Abinnaeus: Bell 1962; and Theophanes of Hermopolis: Matthews 2006). They and other preserved papyri documents witness a level of quotidian life and subaltern activity largely absent from the literary sources generated by elites. Some individual documents throw light on the practical impact on urban populations of high-level imperial policy or cultural shifts, as in the case of the *libelli* produced for Decius' persecution of Christianity or evidence for the spread of Christianity (Horsley and Llewelyn 1981–2002; Bagnall 1993, 278–289; Choat 2006).

On the other hand are the thousands of letters preserved or described in manuscript sources. The two most substantial categories of letters preserved in manuscript are the largely literary or theological letter-collections of individual aristocrats and bishops (which are what is usually meant by the term *letter-collections*) and the volumes of dispositive letters of the Roman emperors (the Codes of Theodosius II and Justinian and other collections of imperial *constitutiones*) and of the bishops of Rome (the decretals). There are also a not insignificant number of letters reported in other types of document: purportedly full texts of letters embedded for their evidentiary value in Church council *acta* (Millar 2006, 236, 243–247; e.g., *Conc. Gall.* 1:44–45, 140–141, 197–199; 2:66–69, 195–199, 283–285) and in apologetic ecclesiastical narratives (Eusebius, *HE passim*, e.g., 10.5–7; Athanasius, *Apol. contra Ar.*, *Hist. Ar.*; Aug. *Ep.* 88.2, 4; cf. Greg. Tur. *Hist.* 9.39, 41, 42; 10.16); versions of letters by rulers and others included in historical narratives in classical historiographical style as "speech acts" akin to pre-battle orations, which, though of doubtful authenticity, may preserve some genuine formulas (e.g., possibly the celestial terms of address between Roman emperors and Iranian *shahanshahs* in Amm. Marc. 17.5.3, 10; Dignas and Winter 2007, 232–233; Canepa 2009, 124–125); and descriptions in narrative works of the dispatch of envoys and letters, such as Isidore's mission to Italy for Theophilus, scenes that may lack details of the content of the letters (and even of the embassy's aim) but often provide a fuller account of the whole process of communication and its social context than the contents of individual letters reveal.

The great letter-collections of aristocratic authors such as Symmachus, Ausonius, Julian, and Libanios and of bishops like Ambrose, Augustine, Sidonius, Synesios, John Chrysostom, Gregory of Nazianzus, and Theodoret of Cyrrhus, and the abbot Shenoute include large numbers of letters by the same author, gathered, selected, edited, at least to some extent systematized, copied into manuscripts, "published" through circulation, and preserved by the medieval manuscript tradition as *opuscula* of the authors, who were often the creators of other works to which the letter-collections were seen as *subsidia*. For the Latin tradition, the late Roman republic and early empire produced the great models of both letter writing and letter-collections—Cicero, Pliny, and Horace—that would provide templates in Late Antiquity and again in the "renaissances" of the Carolingian era, twelfth century, and *Quattrocento*; the Greek epistolary tradition looked back further, to Athenian and Hellenistic models that the Apostolic and Pauline letters reinforced (Stowers 1986). Yet late antique letter-collections survive in far greater numbers and bulk than do those of republican or early imperial authors (Dinneen 1929, vi–viii; O'Brien 1930, vii–ix; Constable 1976, 27–30; Leclercq 1929; Mullett 1997, 11; Bradbury 2004, 73; Ebbeler 2009, 271–272). This may not merely be the result of chance survival, though the collected letters of bishops clearly had privileged chances of transmission by medieval monasteries (one of the few extant letter-collections from the high empire, that of Fronto, survived only as a palimpsest beneath a Latin version of the acts of the Council of Chalcedon; Reynolds 1983, 173). Both the writing of letters in large numbers and their collection and publication may have been an aristocratic and episcopal practice, akin to the "epigraphic habit," to a greater extent in the fourth to seventh centuries than in earlier periods. Some provincial areas are particularly well represented in letter-collections: Cappadocia, by Basil of Caesarea and Gregory of Nazianzus (Van Dam 2002; 2003a; 2003b); Antioch, by Libanios and John Chrysostom; Gaul, by Ausonius, Sidonius Apollinaris, Caesarius of Arles, Avitus of Vienne, and Ruricius of Limoges (Wood 1993). Specific social and cultural forces seem to explain certain cases of the high incidence of letter *writing* (as opposed to letter *collecting*): the increasing social prominence of bishops and the drive for homogeneity of belief and practice put in motion by the great councils of the fourth century (MacMullen 2006) and the need of aristocratic elites to adjust social networks when centers of political power shifted, either through the relocation of the imperial court to new residences in the provinces and in Constantinople in the fourth century or because of the dislocation of imperial hierarchy and intermittently turbulent changes in royal authority in the post-imperial West (Matthews 1975; Salzman 2004; Bradbury 2004). The collection and publication of letters may have been a secondary function of these same forces but should not automatically be equated with the initial act of correspondence itself.

These two fundamental categories, papyrological realia and manuscript collections and other attestations, are rarely discussed together and are often implicitly assumed to represent differing genres, "low" and "high" respectively (a noteworthy exception: Trapp 2003). There is of course a substantial difference in the metadata available from the circumstances of survival of each of these categories, but as regards content and genre, the most important difference is one of range versus selectivity. Papyri materials feature both aristocratic and subaltern correspondents, ornate and simple writing styles, and business as well as less quotidian subjects. The manuscript letter-collections are not a different medium but a narrow selection from these types of correspondents, styles, and subjects. The authors of letter-collections exclusively represent social elites, such as large landowners, teachers, and bishops; the more broadly preserved papyri materials include such senders but also other subaltern persons, largely invisible in manuscript sources. If there is a single, overarching function of the individual letters in the great collections, it is not practical matters for which the papyri offer such valuable direct witness but the creation and maintenance of *amicitia*, a term perhaps better translated as *alliance* rather than *friendship* to capture its mix, alongside personal and spiritual friendship, of influence, patronage, and, in the letters of bishops and religious, theological conformity. The letters in these collections are therefore a valuable index into the social interactions that buttressed the positions of late antique aristocratic elites (Matthews 1975; Mullett 1997; Mathisen 2003, 1.11–41; Ebbeler 2009, 274).

One category of manuscript attestation of epistolary communication is even more selectively preserved than "literary" letter-collections: the dispositive letters of the large-scale administrative organizations of Late Antiquity, the Roman imperial government and the Christian Church. Just as Late Antiquity is the period of the great "private" letter-collections of aristocratic and episcopal authors, so, too, is it the period of the great collections and codifications of governmental correspondence. As Fergus Millar has recently brought out vividly, the texts we conventionally think of as sources of Roman law—the *Codes* of Theodosius II and Justinian, the official collections of imperial *Novellae*, and private collections of imperial *constitutiones*, including the codes of Gregorius and Hermogenianus and the *Constitutiones Sirmondiani*—all represent not "statutory law" in the modern sense of acts centrally proclaimed throughout the state by government, but collections of thousands of specific imperial letters to individual officials or other recipients. In the case of the two official *Codes*, the constituent letters have been heavily excerpted and systematized (Millar 2006, 7–13, 34–38, 207–214). Rather than ex cathedra initiatives of central government, most original imperial missives were responses written in reply to incoming petitions, requests for administrative guidance and policy, or appeals for judicial decisions (Kelly 1994, 164). The imperial *constitutiones* themselves represent neither the beginning nor the end of a cycle of communication but a point of relay: each initial appeal generated a series of communiqués from individuals or imperial officials that eventually reached the imperial consistory; the emperor's response, directed to the imperial official with responsibility for the issue, obligated the official in turn to take actions that may have included the communication of the decision to further officials in the prefecture or diocese, to individuals involved, or to post for the public generally (as demonstrated by individual *constitutiones* that record, as well as the date and place at which the emperor issued the letter, the dates on which the official concerned received and posted it for public awareness; e.g., *Const. Sirm.* 4, 12, cf. 16 *ad fin.*; Matthews 2000, 185–190). Like any other letter, the original imperial correspondences were dispatched from one sender, the emperor, to an identified recipient (whether individual or, occasionally, group); this single act of communication could be replicated through multiple copies sent simultaneously to several recipients. The same is true for the components of the other major source of late

Roman (albeit post-imperial) law and administration, Cassiodorus' *Variae*. Like the *Theodosian Code*, the *Variae* contains documents that in modern government would be separately classified as judicial decisions, administrative orders, statutory law, diplomatic correspondence, and letters of appointment to offices. All were prepared originally as letters between the Gothic monarchs of Italy and their senior officials, beneficiaries, and other correspondents (though in principle none of the royal documents had the status of imperial legislation, *lex*, in recognition of the viceregal position of the Gothic kings; Proc. *Wars* 5.1.27, 6.6.17). Unlike all the imperial legal collections, the *Variae* also contain a substantial number of dispositive letters written by a senior magistrate (the praetorian prefect of Italy, Cassiodorus himself), which are attested but barely preserved elsewhere (Cass. *Variae* 11–12; Millar 2006, 137–139; an example in post-imperial Gaul: Greg. Tur. *Hist.* 9.19), providing a glimpse into the sprawling substrata of imperial administrative correspondence otherwise overshadowed by the extant texts of emperors.

Papal collections of *decreta* similarly were gatherings of dispositive letters by the bishops of Rome, selected because of their administrative and canonical value (Jasper 2001; Noble 1990). Just as most imperial *constitutiones* (from which papal *decreta* draw terminology) were drafted in the form of replies to submissions and petitions (*suggestiones* and *preces*) and often incorporated the wording of the original *suggestio*, so the papal epistles that came to be regarded as *decreta* were composed as answers (*responsa*) to incoming reports or queries from bishops (*relationes*). The decision embodied in the papal *responsum* was to be enacted by the recipient bishop and, if necessary, disseminated throughout his province, in much the same way that imperial officials receiving letters were to implement the emperor's wishes and, where appropriate, advertise his pronouncement throughout their jurisdiction (Jasper 2001, 17; Matthews 2000, 181–182; Classen 1977, 99–101). Like the collections of imperial *constitutiones*, too, papal decretal collections are only a selection from a much wider range of episcopal correspondence, including the letters of friendship and theological tractates evidenced in more "literary" episcopal letter-collections; this can be seen in the fuller representations of papal and (sub-)imperial correspondence preserved in Gregory the Great's *Registrum* and Cassiodorus' *Variae*, both of which preserve a wide range of non-dispositive correspondence, though nevertheless representing only a part of their respective original archival registers. Besides deriving administrative terminology from imperial letters, papal *decreta* collections also resemble imperial *constitutiones* collections in chronology. Official moves to collect and systematize imperial *constitutiones* arose in the 420s–430s (*CTh* 1.1.5–6). The earliest attested collections of papal *decreta* were also compiled in the second quarter of the fifth century, in Gaul and Italy; so, too, apparently was the earliest version of the collection known as the *Constitutiones Sirmondiani*, a gathering of imperial dispositive letters on church matters (Jasper 2001, 23–26; cf. Vessey 1993). Like the Gregorian and Hermogenian collections of imperial *constitutiones* (and unlike the *Theodosian Code*), these ecclesiastical collections were private compilations, not official codifications ordered by the bishops of Rome. Pope Leo I (440–461), however, may have either initiated an official collection of papal *decreta* or granted official status to one of the already existing Gallic or Italian collections; if the latter, this would again have been analogous to the quasi-official status that had been granted to the codes of Gregorius and Hermogenianus and to the works of certain jurisprudents prior to publication of the *Theodosian Code* (Jasper 2001, 26; *CTh* 1.4.3). Like the *Theodosian Code,* though in a less rigorous format, the decretal collections generalized from the precedents of individual decisions made in specific earlier letters to provide legislation on a more or less comprehensive coverage of ecclesiastical administrative issues (Jasper 2001, 59–60). The terminology of papal *decreta* reflects imperial chancery usage; the timing of the compilation of the papal *decreta* may reflect stimulus from the development of imperial legal codification.

These categories of letter-collection—literary, episcopal, dispositive—are conveniences only and far from exclusive. Perhaps the clearest example of the range of permutations possible, both in the original texts included and in the nature of the collection, is Cassiodorus' *Variae*: a single-author collection, edited by the author, in which ten of the thirteen books present letters written in the name of other figures, the Gothic monarchs of Italy (this includes eight books of actual letters and two of generic *formulae* provided for the use of future senior officials, *quaestores*); a further two books, as mentioned before, of letters written in Cassiodorus' own name as praetorian prefect; and one book not of letters at all but a treatise on the nature of the soul (Gillett 1998, 40; Halporn and Vessey 2004, 19–22; Bjornlie 2009, 155–161). The collection includes the types of administrative letters found in the collections of imperial *constitutiones,* but Cassiodorus' collection (according to the extensive preface by the author) had no secondary dispositive purpose like the *Theodosian Code,* nor were the texts gathered as a dossier to be reused as a source of authority or evidence, like the *Constitutiones Sirmondiani.* The professed purposes of the collection are those of "private" aristocratic letter-collections: *amicitia* (bowing to demands of friends to publish, and commemorating them through publication of their letters of appointment to high office) and literary style as a monument to Cassiodorus himself and as a model for those employing literary skills in governmental service. It is a private, literary collection of public, administrative letters. An analogous example of a single-author collection of letters written not in the author-editor's own name but in the *persona* of a high office holder is the (unfortunately lost) collection of letters and other documents by the Church historian Evagrius, written for Gregory, patriarch of Antioch. Several small collections of letters by multiple authors, such as the late-sixth-century *Epistulae Austrasicae,* which mixes episcopal and governmental letters of literary, dispositive, and diplomatic natures, may represent stylistic models for these different epistolary situations, analogous in intent to Cassiodorus' collection and a complement to the collection of generic *formulae* (Malaspina 2001, 9–11).

Chartae and *Libri*: Use and Reuse of Letters

Letter-collections, as cultural artifacts and as historical sources, present a phenomenon discrete from original individual letters on papyrus. The contents of collections provide evidence for the act of letter writing by their authors, for the contents of at least a proportion of their correspondence, and especially for the networks of friendship, patronage, or hierarchal administration in which the authors participated. But manuscript collections present documents that may be edited (without indication of how extensively), that lack the visual forms of originals, and that characteristically are "deconcretized" through removal of dating, localization formulas, and other indicators of context (Mullett 1990, 184). Consequently, manuscript letter-collections cannot be regarded as lucid windows onto ancient letter-writing and communication processes, any more than narrative histories and biographies can be treated as transparent windows onto "events." Because of this distance between letters and collections, and because manuscript collections nevertheless constitute a large proportion of our evidence for the behavior of elites, especially outside of Egypt, in communication practices (and many other topics), it is necessary to distinguish firmly between letters and letter-collections in modern discussions and to consider why collections were produced and published and why they were copied and preserved. The distinction between letters and letter-collections is not a modern categorization but one made clearly in contemporary sources: Latin works generally refer to individual letters as *chartae* and to collections as *libri*. *Charta* refers to the form of the document, a single papyrus "page," *liber* to a different form, in scroll or (in this period) codex, and to a different nature, setting collections among literary, technical, administrative, or other "books." So the nine books of letters of Sidonius Apollinaris are his *libri*, as are Cassiodorus' *Variae*; likewise, the topically arranged books of imperial letters we know as the *Theodosian Code* were in fact named the *Libri Theodosiani* (by imperial command: *Gesta senatus* 2), the modern name giving a somewhat misleadingly technical turn to the more generic original title.

The copying of a letter into a manuscript collection changed its form and nature. The layout of the text on a single sheet, the *charta*, was compressed into more-or-less continual block text with letter following letter, punctuated by changes in script or spacing to indicate the beginning of a new letter, to fit as much text per folio as was visually practical, like any other substantial work. Consequently, most formatting of the original letter was lost, as was its metadata, information conveyed outside the actual body of the letter itself in layout, annotations, or the circumstances of composition and delivery. Metadata conventionally though not universally omitted from manuscript collections include the full opening address to the recipient (commonly replaced with a brief heading noting the names and positions of sender and receiver without full titles and greetings), concluding dating formula, and, for imperial and royal letters, localizing formulae. These deletions made the texts of letters into timeless literary, theological, or legal pronouncements (however frustrating for future historians). Other information lost by change in format includes the sender's *subscriptio*, a salutation at the end of the letter but set apart from the main text, conventionally in the sender's autograph and therefore visually distinct in calligraphy from the script of the rest of the letter, which, usually, was prepared by a scribe. Most manuscript copies of letters either incorporate these salutations as part of the main text, without indication of their original visual distinction, or leave them out altogether. Some letter-collections, however, record these visual additions by marking them as *alia manu*, "in another hand," indicating that when the letter was first copied for compilation in manuscript form, the scribe had access to either the actual received copy of the letter displaying the original *subscriptio* or an archival copybook of dispatched letters that included annotations of the sender's *subscriptiones*. This record was made particularly where the *subscriptio* was an autograph with probative value, as in the case of western collections of imperial *novellae* marking the salutations of the emperors (signed *manu divina*; Seeck 1919, 3–4; Classen 1977, 61–64; Matthews 2000, 189; Millar 2006, 23; similarly, Church conciliar *acta* recording the signatures of bishops *alia manu*). But manuscripts of the collected letters of Augustine of Hippo include a large number of annotations, in different formulae, of his *subscriptiones*, indicating a concern to record this personal addition by some individual editors of collections also (Leclercq 1929, 2838–2839). Another attempt to preserve metadata is seen in the brief annotations in a few letter-collections of the names and offices of the individuals who delivered the letters, in most cases presumably the envoys who would present the sender's message or supplication orally in audience with the recipient. Again these details seem to have been recorded in archival file copies of governmental and ecclesiastical *officia* and sometimes copied into manuscript letter-collections (e.g., imperial and papal envoys in *Coll. Avell.* 51, 52 [*ad fin.*], 105 [in dating formula], 110–114–118, 120–127, 149, 167, 191–192 [in headings]; *Ep. Austr.* 43 [in heading]). Rarer still is the preservation, again presumably from archival annotations, of the name of an official or subordinate who drafted a letter in the name of the office bearer (most obviously Cass. *Variae* 1–5, 8–10, and see previously regarding Evagrius; also *Ep. Austr.* 43 [confused in transmission], 48). These limited attempts to record aspects of the production and dispatch of the original letters were motivated by legal concerns, institutional needs, or thoughts of publication.

Letter-collections served a fundamentally different function from an original epistle. Though letter-collections are very familiar to us as a type of source, the functions of collections are not necessarily obvious; they seem misleadingly like other literary or theological works in their authors' *opera*. A letter, reproduced years after its original dispatch without its identifying metadata and, perhaps more important, with no substitute for the oral and "living" role of the bearer or envoy, is no longer any part of an exchange of correspondence. This is underscored by the fact that most letter-collections contain only letters of the one author, some occasionally including a limited number of received letters or other documents (such as the inclusion of Symmachus' third *relatio* alongside Ambrose's letters to Honorius on the Altar of Victory). Generally, the other side of a correspondence is absent altogether, evoked only by references to received letters to which the author is now replying—that is, an interlocutor's letter is mentioned as a stimulus to composition but is not seen as necessary to include. Only rarely can two sides of an exchange be reconstructed, and usually uncertainly (as in the case of sewing together the correspondence of Ausonius and Paulinus of Nola). Even when it is possible to reconstruct a bilateral exchange, it is an outline of only two points of communication from a far more complex web of contact (cf. the diagrammatic representations of the epistolary network of Theophylact of Ochrid in Mullett 1997, 180–181, 192). Moreover, many aristocratic and episcopal *libri* of letters are clearly far from reflecting the full contents of the authorial archive from which they may have been generated, not only truncated in time but also regularly omitting whole categories of workaday correspondence. It is a topos for epistolary authors to complain of their *curae*, but readers are usually spared cares of the more mundane kind (in favor of the burdens of prestige and authority), further reducing the potential of overlap between original papyri letters and manuscript collections. Though we understand aristocratic and episcopal letters and collections as the products of *amicitia* behavior, collections are not true portrayals of the exchanges involved in Roman social practices because they lack interchange and complexity; by and large, we see only one figure, without multiple correspondents and letter bearers supplementing the message of the letter. It is reasonable to assume that in many cases, where a collection has been produced using the author's files, it would have been possible to produce collections including both incoming and outgoing letters, reflecting the apparently common filing practices of individuals and *officia* in Late Antiquity of keeping separate in and out records (Noble 1990, 87). Some epistolary exemplars used in Late Antiquity, particularly Cicero's *Ad familiares*, included many letters of his correspondents (Reynolds et al. 1983, 138). Nevertheless, the editors of collections, whether the authors themselves or later enthusiasts, rarely chose to present multiple sides of correspondence.[9]

Functions of Letter-Collections

The most common interpretations of the function of the publication and copying of personal letter-collections are social and literary, that they served as monuments to the social status of their authors and as literary models for later imitation. It should be underscored that these interpretations refer to two distinct events, the first-generation initial editing and circulation of a *liber* and its second- and subsequent-generation preservation and distribution. A letter-collection displayed the author's literary prowess by the style of its contents, and its addressees demonstrated his (or rarely her) social standing in the patterns of *amicitia* and patronage among aristocratic peers (best exemplified by Symmachus' letters). A number of epistolary *libri* are in fact collections of several different types of documents, revealing the author's prowess in more than one social or literary field. Where a collection echoed the device of Pliny's editor by gathering "official" letters written while in imperial service into a separate tenth book, the author's "professional" status in governmental hierarchy was displayed (most obviously the *Relationes* of Symmachus, but both Ambrose of Milan and Cassiodorus present variations on this device). Some collections include philosophical, religious, or other types of work alongside letters, indicating both the range of their author's talents and the looseness of generic categorization (e.g., the collections of Ennodius, Avitus of Vienne, Cassiodorus, Venantius Fortunatus, and the lost collection of Evagrius). The beneficiaries of these displays of social and literary status could be the author himself or his immediate descendants, whether the collection was made in the author's lifetime or posthumously (Salzman 2004, 83; in many cases, we have no clear indication of who complied a collection or when). The value of such a collection as an indication of the status and influence of a family, however, would inherently have been limited to one or two generations (Bradbury 2004, 73–74). Collections copied beyond that, or initially compiled after the author's death, were valued for literary worth as models of epistolary style, just as Pliny's collection was (Mullett 1990, 173; Bradbury 2004, 73; Ebbeler 2009, 272). For official correspondence, the production of formularies of letters and other documents explicitly addresses this function, anticipating to some extent the *ars dictaminis* genre of the high Middle Ages (Rio 2008; Witt 2005).

Other functions are conceivable. A letter was a vehicle for direct communication from one speaker to one identified recipient; was a collection, by contrast, necessarily a form of display communication, broadcast to peers and posterity rather than directed to targeted recipients? In some cases at least, *libri epistularum* were themselves direct communication, recycling letters as a means to further *amicitia* activities. Sidonius Apollinaris published his books of letters sequentially, providing each group with dedicatory and concluding letters to the friends who had urged him to collect his writings (Sid., *Epp.* 1.1 and 7.18; 8.1 and 16; 9.1 and 16; Harries 1994, 7–10). The *libri* circulated more widely, but the initial publication and subsequent circulation followed the same paths of *amicitia* as had Sidonius' individual original letters; collection reinforced the cultivation of ties among the author's peers, a sort of second-order *amicitia*. The dedicatory letters, direct communications to their addressees albeit intended for wider public recognition, are clearly signposted as compositions made at the time of editing the collection, not as earlier letters now reproduced. But direct communication could also be made by the inclusion of earlier letters, acknowledging before a public audience the ties between the author and the individual addressee for the benefit of that recipient. The addressee of the penultimate letter in Sidonius' final book of letters, one Gelasius, had complained that Sidonius had not hitherto included a letter to him in his works (*necdum nomine tuo ullas operi meo litteras iunxerim*, Sid. *Ep.* 9.15.1); he did not complain that he had not *received* a letter from Sidonius, but that his name had not appeared as an addressee in one of the collected and circulated *libri*. Sidonius obliged. Similarly, the inclusion in Cassiodorus' *Variae* of many pairs of letters of appointment of Italian aristocrats to high office (one to the appointee, one to the Senate announcing the appointment) may be seen as a form of publicly monumentalizing Cassiodorus' peers and friends (Gillett 1998).

It has been suggested that some letter-collections possess an intrinsic narrative, albeit obscured by the conventional omission of dating formulae; sometimes a letter-collection is assumed to have been compiled as a form of historical account, a kind of memoir (Mullett 1997, 20; cf. Harries 1994, 11–19). Some collections do preserve strict chronological order (the *Registrum* of Gregory I marks years and months, which is rare) or collocate letters on similar themes, making possible a reconstruction of the authors' activities on a chronological or topical basis for the period covered by the letters. In several cases, late antique and medieval biographers availed themselves of this possibility when writing *vitae* of the authors: Paulinus for Ambrose of Milan, John the Deacon for Gregory I, and the author of the *Life* of Desiderius of Cahors. Ambrose's assemblage of his letters to emperors in a tenth book, evoking Pliny's correspondence with Trajan, may not have been intended as materials for a biography, but it was certainly a means to represent his public life in a politicized and loosely sequential manner. It is clear that many aristocratic and episcopal authors had an eye to possible future publication of a letter-collection when writing individual epistles; if records of correspondence had to be maintained as a necessary component of maintaining correspondence, they could be exploited for literary publication also. But there seems to be no explicit record of authors regarding their letters, their archives, or a published letter-collection as basic materials for future historical or biographical narrative, in the way that some records were identified as materials, *commentaria* or *hula*, for classicizing historiography (cf. Olymp. *Test.*, Blockley 1981, 32; Fornara 1983, 181). The apparent narrative of a letter-collection, where one is discernible, may be incidental rather than intentional.

The functions of the imperial and papal dispositive letter-collections seem more immediately obvious but warrant consideration. Some collections were *ad causam* dossiers of materials to be used as evidence, for example, in ecclesiastical disputes, as is the case for the subcollections gathered together in the sixth-century collection of papal, episcopal, and imperial letters known as the

Collectio Avellana (Blair-Dixon 2007). Other collections of imperial or papal correspondence served as sources of authority to buttress the position of specific ecclesiastical dioceses, evident in the collection of papal letters on the church of Thessaloniki and possibly the case for the imperial correspondence of the *Constitutiones Sirmondiana* (Jasper 2001, 81–82). Overshadowing these local collections, however, are the vast editorial projects embodied in the *Codes* of Theodosius II and Justinian, in which several thousand individual imperial letters of various natures were gathered and key passages excerpted and arranged under the headings of the sixteen books (derived from the format of the extant Praetor's Edict; Matthews 2000, 106–108), an epistolary florilegium on a grand scale. Both codes are, of course, monuments of legal history: from a modern perspective, they are the models for Napoleonic legal codifications, and from the standpoint of antiquity, the *Libri Theodosiani* of the fifth century C.E. are the first attempt to systematize Roman law since the Twelve Tablets of the fifth century B.C.E. and therefore the first legal codification of the Roman imperial period (Matthews 2000, 19). But as a project, the *Libri Theodosiani* was left incomplete: the projected resolution of each series of excerpts under a subheading into a single authoritative statement was not undertaken, leaving the full series of relevant texts arranged in chronological order, even where individual imperial decisions are superseded by later *constitutiones*. Justinian's commission a century later did complete this final stage, producing a more practical, less historical legal resource.

As an attempt to produce a definitive text that would serve as a unifying and definitive source of law, a collection of imperial correspondence was not the only option and perhaps not the most obvious one. Some imperial letters constituted edicts, intended for public dissemination; others were essentially internal administrative directions for imperial bureaucrats; others again were rescripts, judicial decisions in specific cases and in theory applicable only to the legal case that generated the determination. Alongside specific imperial decisions embodied in individual letters, however, was another source of law: the writings of the "classical" Roman jurisconsultants Papian, Paulus, Gaius, Ulpian, and others, deriving legal principles from the individual enactments of emperors, the Senate, and other republican and early imperial sources of law. Written in the first centuries of the empire, these texts were studied, added to, and reworked through to the fifth century. The official validity of the works of selected jurisconsultants was recognized by imperial law in the early fifth century and incorporated into the *Libri Theodosiani* (*CTh* 1.4.3); when the project of ordering Roman law was revisited by Justinian's commissions a century later, the juristic writings were systematized as the *Digesta* and stood alongside the new *Code*, together with the textbook *Institutes*, also derived from juristic writings. Even before Justinian's project, however, the heavily abridged version of the *Libri Theodosiani* issued in 506 in southern Gaul by the Gothic king Alaric II, conventionally known as the *Breviarium Alarici*,[10] dealt with the shortcomings of the original codification. The *Breviarium* omitted many *constitutiones* that addressed aspects of imperial administration irrelevant to provincial needs and complemented the imperial texts with extracts from the juristic writings of Gaius and Paulus and with *interpretationes* (brief explanations of the intent of selected imperial *constitutiones*; Haenel 1848). Although juristic principles were from time to time modified by new laws of imperial edicts, they formed the basis for most of the work of judges because of their systematic coverage of legal situations; by contrast, the codification of imperial decisions from individual letters could never be comprehensive but was rendered incomplete as soon as new imperial dispositive letters were issued, resulting in the subsequent collections of *Novellae*, selected but unsystematized new imperial statements (the *Novellae* of Theodosius II and the western emperors from Valentinian III to Majorian were complied into a legal collection in the 460s, and those of Theodosius II and Valentinian III were later incorporated into Justinian's *Code*, but Justinian's own far more extensive and complete collection of novels remained unsystematized). Given that both Alaric's and Justinian's commissioners thought it necessary to update the *Libri Theodosiani* project by complementing imperial letters with jurisconsultants' writings, the original decision by Theodosius II and his advisors to publish imperial texts without accompanying juristic writings is not self-explanatory. Imperial dispositive letters did provide orders for civilian and military administration, governmental situations not covered by the civil and criminal law of the jurists. But the sources and functioning of law were not limited to the dispositive letters of the emperors, and it is possible that the vast proportions of the *Libri Theodosiani*, lacking the systematic guidance of jurisconsults, limited the practical value of the work (Kelly 1994, 171–173; Humfress 2009).

For *libri* of both private and official letters, where the collection of letters was undertaken by their authors rather than by later editors, the establishment of a corpus of letters may have served as a means of reclaiming authority and establishing a definite version of the texts. Private letters, because of their aspect as a gift, were sometimes seen as the property of the recipient; this is expressed by the frequent topos of the author asking the recipient to correct and improve the letter (and any attached literary work). The publication of an author-edited collection brought the individual letters back under the control of their composer and enabled him to produce a final, definitive form, albeit perhaps significantly changed from the document as originally dispatched (Constable 1976, 16, 49). The recipients of imperial letters never had the right to own the text, but reclaiming control of dispositive letters, and therefore their legal force, was central to the project of imperial codification. The *Libri Theodosiani* established both a final, highly edited form for individual *constitutiones* and a delineated corpus of legal texts, omitting individual rulings (*rescripta*) that could be employed illegally as precedents. The provisions for authenticating the reproduction of the *Libri Theodosiani* (and also of the Gallic provincial version ordered by Alaric II) were attempts to enforce the fixed forms of these collections (*Gesta senatus* 3, 7, 8; *Const. de const.* [*apud CTh* I.2: 1–4]; *Brev. Alarici*: *Praesc.*, *Auct.*, *Subscr. Aniani* [*apud CTh* I.1: xxxi–xxxv]).

Like private letter-collections, the imperial codes reused and reformatted transient documents and redirected them for a different audience. Analogy between aristocratic and episcopal letter-collections on the one hand and imperial codifications on the other is not intended to suggest that the imperial collections are solely cultural or ideological artifacts. To be sure, both original imperial letters and the official collections of edited *constitutiones* and *novellae* did serve ideological functions—not least, in the case of the *Libri Theodosiani*, an implied assertion of the unity of the two halves of the Roman empire and assertion of imperial authority (Gillett 1993, 18–26; Matthews 1993, 43–44; Humfress 2009, 380)—while the works of Cassiodorus and John Lydus, together with the lawyerly professionalism of imperial *quaestores*, suggest that senior palatine bureaucrats involved in the tasks of epistolary and legal drafting constituted a type of textual community that was itself one audience for the ideological elements of their own writings (Honoré 1978; 1993; 1998; Maas 1992; Gillett 1998; Kelly 2004, 11–17; Sotinel 2009, 135). Clearly, however, the *Libri Theodosiani* were nevertheless intended as a functional administrative tool to address a major problem in public life, the sheer size and complexity of Roman laws. The imperial codifications share three key features with private or literary letter-collections: first, the process of collection of transient texts and their deployment for new purposes and recipients; second, the desire to control both the definition of the corpus and the texts of its constituent documents; and third, timing: the compilation of the *Libri Theodosiani* was undertaken not only in a context of significant legal study (Matthews 2000, 20–23) but also against a background of growing cultural activity in the reuse of private, official, and episcopal letters and the appearance of collections of both imperial and papal letters as administrative and apologetic dossiers in the service of the Church.

Both private and dispositive letter-collections are very slanted windows onto the communicative practices of the times of their authors. The evidence of papyrological documents and narrative dramatizations of embassies and audiences sketch in some of the framework of communicative processes, within which letters played a significant but not necessarily central role; these other evidences should provide a constant check on the representation of communication implied by epistolary *libri*. At the same time, letter-collections are not only problematic sources for reconstruction of primary correspondences but also acts of communication themselves, secondary in the sense that they reuse materials originally prepared for specific situations and reroute them into a new situation. The purposes of this secondary communicative practice could be as multifarious as that of original epistolary correspondence. This reuse of communication is a phenomenon distinct in itself, requiring analysis alongside investigation of the individual components of letter-collections to elucidate those practices of communication that facilitated the developments of late antique societies.[11]

NOTES

1. Socrates, *HE* 6.2, with additions as indicated from Sozomen, *HE* 8.2 and Cassiodorus-Epiphanius, *Hist. Tripart.* 10.2.

2. Context: most likely the disputes at Alexandria between the Church and supporters of traditional civic cults, leading up to (and continuing after) the destruction of the Serapeum; cf. Haas 1997, 159–169; Russell 2007, 7–13, 81–84. Russell doubts the veracity of the story, but even if it were a hostile fabrication (which is not firm), the anecdote illustrates contemporary understanding of processes and problems of communication.

3. Gregory's use of letter-collections: Greg. Tur. *Hist.* 224, 25 (= Sid. Ap. *Ep.* 7.6), 2.31 (Remigius of Rheims = *Ep. Austr.* 2; cf. Sid. Ap. *Ep.* 9.7.1: a published collection of Remigius' *declamationes*, presumably his sermons), 6.7 (letter-collection of bishop Ferreolus of Uzès in imitation of Sidonius). Valediction: 10.31, his own letters: 5.5, 5.14, 10.19; Roberts 2009, 278–280 (four letters and two poems to Venantius Fortunatus). Fortunatus' verse epistles: Roberts 2009, 244–319.

4. For a full tabulation of royal, episcopal, and other documents and of embassies in the *Histories*: Weidermann 1982, 1.1–9, 1.103–106.

5. Greg. Tur. *Hist.* 6.3, 31; 7.14; possibly 7.6.

6. Greg. Tur. *Hist.* 6.31, 7.6; cf. 9.20, the full text of another agreement, the Treaty of Andelot of 587.

7. Cf. Greg. Tur. *Hist.* 6.22: another episcopal trial, also turning on the evidence of letter and the question of authenticity. Greg. Tur. *Hist.* 5.18 and 5.49 are longer accounts of two episcopal trials, but with no reference to written evidence; likewise, the briefer accounts of trials in 5.20, 27; 6.37.

8. Among other materials used for letters in Mediterranean antiquity, including parchment, wax tablets, wooden sheets, and slates, the most extravagant must be the late antique ivory diptychs, preserved in medieval treasuries as items of value and emulated for the art of their exteriors, not for the messages, which are now mostly lost from their interiors.

9. One example: the Carolingian collection of the letters of the seventh-century bishop Desiderius of Cahors, reproducing sent letters in the first *liber* and received ones in the second; Desiderius, *Epp.* A proportionately smaller but still significant number of received letters is included in the collection of Ruricius of Limoges; Mathisen 1999, 52.

10. The heading of the text, probably its actual title, reflects awareness of the multiple sources of law: *Leges atque species iuris de Theodosio vel de diversis libris electae*; *CTh.* I xxxi, xxxvi.

11. The research for this chapter forms part of a project funded by the Australian Research Council.

WORKS CITED

Bagnall, Roger S. 1993. *Egypt in Late Antiquity.* Princeton, NJ: Princeton University Press.

Barnes, Timothy D. 1981. *Constantine and Eusebius.* Cambridge, MA: Harvard University Press.

Barnwell, P. S. 1997. *King, Courtiers, and Imperium: The Barbarian West, 565–725.* London: Duckworth.

Bell, H. I. 1962. *The Abinnaeus Archive: Papers of a Roman Officer in the Reign of Constantius II.* Oxford: Clarendon Press.

Bjornlie, Shane. 2009. "What Have Elephants to Do with Sixth-Century Politics? A Reappraisal of the 'Official' Governmental Dossier of Cassiodorus," *Journal of Late Antiquity* 2: 143–171.

Blair-Dixon, Kate. 2007. "Memory and Authority in Sixth-Century Rome: The *Liber Pontificalis* and the *Collectio Avellana.*" In *Religion, Dynasty, and Patronage in Early Christian Rome, 300–900*, ed. Kate Cooper and Julia Hillman, 59–76. Cambridge: Cambridge University Press.

Blockley, R. C. 1981. *The Fragmentary Classicising Historians of the Later Roman Empire.* Vol. 1. Liverpool: Francis Cairns.

Bowman, Alan K. 1994. "The Roman Imperial Army: Letters and Literacy on the Northern Frontier." In *Literacy and Power in the Ancient World*, ed. Alan K. Bowman and Greg Woolf, 109–125. Cambridge: Cambridge University Press.

Bowman, Alan K., and Greg Woolf, eds. 1994. *Literacy and Power in the Ancient World.* Cambridge: Cambridge University Press.

Bradbury, Scott. 2004. "Libanius' Letters as Evidence for Travel and Epistolary Networks among Greek Elites in the Fourth Century." In *Travel, Communication, and Geography in Late Antiquity*, ed. Linda Ellis and Frank L. Kidner, 73–80. Aldershot: Ashgate.

Brown, Peter. 2000. *Augustine of Hippo: A Biography*, 2nd ed. Berkeley: University of California Press.

Buc, Philippe. 2001. *The Dangers of Ritual: Between Early Medieval Texts and Social Scientific Theory.* Princeton, NJ: Princeton University Press.

———. 2007. "The Monster and the Critics: A Ritual Reply," *Early Medieval Europe* 15: 441–452.

Cameron, Alan. 1970. *Claudian: Poetry and Propaganda at the Court of Honorius.* Oxford: Clarendon.

Canepa, Matthew. 2009. *The Two Eyes of the Earth: Art and Ritual of Kingship between Rome and Sasanian Iran.* Berkeley: University of California.

Choat, Malcolm. 2006. *Belief and Cult in Fourth-Century Papyri.* Turnhout: Brepols.

Classen, Peter. 1977. *Kaiserreskript und Königsurkunde: Diplomatische Studien zum Problem der Kontinuität zwischen Altertum und Mittelalter.* Thessaloniki: Byzantina.

Constable, Giles. 1976. *Letters and Letter-Collections.* Typologie des sources du Moyen Âge occidental 17. Turnhout: Brepols.

Conybeare, Catherine. 2000. *Paulinus Noster: Self and Symbols in the Letters of Paulinus of Nola.* Oxford: Oxford University Press.

Cooper, Kate, and Julia Hillman, eds. 2007. *Religion, Dynasty, and Patronage in Early Christian Rome, 300–900.* Cambridge: Cambridge University Press.

Dignas, Beate, and Engelbert Winter. 2007. *Rome and Persia in Late Antiquity: Neighbours and Rivals.* Cambridge: Cambridge University Press.

Dinneen, Lucilla. 1929. *Titles of Address in Christian Greek Epistolography to 527 A.D.* Washington, DC: Catholic University of America Press.

Ebbeler, Jennifer. 2009. "Tradition, Innovation, and Epistolary Mores." In *A Companion to Late Antiquity*, ed. Philip Rousseau, 270–284. Malden, MA: Wiley-Blackwell.

———. 2010. "Letters." In *The Oxford Handbook of Roman Studies*, ed. Alessandro Barchiesi and Walter Scheidel, 464–476. Oxford: Oxford University Press.

Ellis, Linda, and Frank L. Kidner, eds. 2004. *Travel, Communication, and Geography in Late Antiquity*. Aldershot: Ashgate.

Fornara, Charles W. 1983. *The Nature of History in Ancient Greece and Rome*. Berkeley: University of California Press.

Ganz, David. 1983. "Bureaucratic Shorthand and Merovingian Learning." In *Ideal and Reality in Frankish and Anglo-Saxon Society*, ed. Patrick Wormald, Donald Bullough, and Roger Collins, 58–75. Oxford: Blackwell.

Ganz, David, and Walter Goffart. 1990. "Charters Earlier Than 800 from French Collections," *Speculum* 65: 906–932.

Gillett, Andrew. 1993. "The Date and Circumstances of Olympiodorus of Thebes," *Traditio* 48: 1–29.

———. 1998. "The Purposes of Cassiodorus's *Variae*." In *After Rome's Fall: Narrators and Sources of Early Medieval History*, ed. Alexander C. Murray, 37–50. Toronto: University of Toronto Press.

———. 2001. "Rome, Ravenna, and the Last Western Emperors," *Papers of the British School in Rome* 69: 131–167.

———. 2003. *Envoys and Political Communication in the Late Antique West, 411–533*. Cambridge Studies in Medieval Life and Thought 4th ser. 55. Cambridge: Cambridge University Press.

———. Forthcoming. "Epic Panegyric and Political Communication in the Fifth-Century West."

Goffart, Walter. 2005. *The Narrators of Barbarian History (A.D. 550–800): Jordanes, Gregory of Tours, Bede, and Paul the Deacon*. Notre Dame, IN: University of Notre Dame Press.

Grafton, Anthony, and Megan Williams. 2006. *Christianity and the Transformation of the Book: Origen, Eusebius, and the Library of Caesarea*. Cambridge, MA: Belknap Press.

Häag, Tomas, and Philip Rousseau, eds. 2000. *Greek Biography and Panegyric in Late Antiquity*. Berkeley: University of California Press.

Haas, Christopher. 1997. *Alexandria in Late Antiquity: Topography and Social Conflict*. Baltimore: Johns Hopkins University Press.

Haenel, Gustav. 1848. *Lex Romana Visigothorum*. Leipzig: Teubner.

Halporn, James W., and Mark Vessey, trans. 2004. *Cassiodorus: Institutions of Divine and Secular Learning*. Translated Texts for Historians 42. Liverpool: Liverpool University Press.

Harlow, Mary. 2004. "Clothes Maketh the Man: Power Dressing and Elite Masculinity in the Later Roman World." In *Gender in the Early Medieval World: East and West, 300–900*, ed. Leslie Brubaker and Julia M. H. Smith, 44–69. Cambridge: Cambridge University Press.

Harries, Jill. 1994. *Sidonius Apollinaris and the Fall of Rome*. Oxford: Clarendon Press.

Harries, Jill, and Ian Wood, eds. 1993. *The Theodosian Code*. Ithaca, NY: Cornell University Press.

Heather, Peter. 1994. "Literacy and Power in the Migration Period." In *Literacy and Power in the Ancient World*, ed. Alan K. Bowman and Greg Woolf, 177–197. Cambridge: Cambridge University Press.

Honoré, Tony. 1978. *Tribonian*. London: Duckworth.

———. 1993. "Some Quaestors of the Reign of Theodosius II." In *The Theodosian Code*, ed. Jill Harries and Ian Wood, 68–94. Ithaca, NY: Cornell University Press.

———. 1998. *Law in the Crisis of Empire, 379–455 AD: The Theodosian Dynasty and Its Quaestors with a Palingenesia of Laws of the Dynasty*. Oxford: Clarendon Press.

Horsley, G. H. R., and S. R. Llewelyn, eds. 1981–2002. *New Documents Illustrating Early Christianity: A Review of the Greek Inscriptions and Papyri*. Sydney and Grand Rapids, MI: Eerdmans.

Humfress, Caroline. 2009. "Law in Practice." In *A Companion to Late Antiquity*, ed. Philip Rousseau, 377–391. Malden, MA: Wiley-Blackwell.

Janes, Dominic. 1998. *God and Gold in Late Antiquity*. Cambridge: Cambridge University Press.

Jasper, Detlev. 2001. "The Beginning of the Decretal Tradition." In *Papal Letters in the Early Middle Ages*, ed. Detlev Jasper and Horst Fuhrmann, 3–133. Washington, DC: Catholic University of America Press.

Kelly, Christopher M. 1994. "Later Roman Bureaucracy: Going through the Files." In *Literacy and Power in the Ancient World*, ed. Alan K. Bowman and Greg Woolf, 161–176. Cambridge: Cambridge University Press.

———. 2004. *Ruling the Later Roman Empire*. Cambridge, MA: Belknap Press.

Krautheimer, Richard. 1983. *Three Christian Capitals: Topography and Politics*. Berkeley: University of California Press.

Leader-Newby, Ruth E. 2004. *Silver and Society in Late Antiquity: Functions and Meanings of Silver Plate in the Fourth to Seventh Centuries*. Aldershot: Ashgate.

Leclercq, Henri. 1929. "Lettres chrétiennes." In *Dictionnaire d'archéologie chrétienne et de liturgie*, 8.2: 2683–2885. Paris: Libraire Letouzey et Ané.

Lewis, Sian. 1996. *News and Society in the Greek Polis*. London: Duckworth.

Maas, Michael. 1992. *John Lydus and the Roman Past: Antiquarianism and Politics in the Age of Justinian*. London: Routledge.

MacMullen, Ramsay. 2006. *Voting about God in Early Church Councils*. New Haven, CT: Yale University Press.

Malaspina, Elena, ed. 2001. *Il Liber epistolarum della cancelleria austrasica (sec. V–VI)*. Rome: Herder.

Malherbe, Abraham. 1988. *Ancient Epistolary Theorists*. Atlanta: Scholars Press.

Mathews, Thomas F. 1999. *The Clash of Gods: A Reinterpretation of Early Christian Art*, 2nd ed. Princeton, NJ: Princeton University Press.

Mathisen, Ralph W. 1999. *Ruricius of Limoges and Friends: A Collection of Letters from Visigothic Gaul*. Liverpool: Liverpool University Press.

———. 2003. *People, Personal Expression, and Social Relations in Late Antiquity*. Ann Arbor: University of Michigan Press.

Matthews, John F. 1975. *Western Aristocracies and Imperial Court, A.D. 364–425*. Oxford: Clarendon.

———. 1989. *The Roman Empire of Ammianus*. London: Duckworth.

———. 1993. "The Making of the Text." In *The Theodosian Code*, ed. Jill Harries and Ian Wood, 19–44. Ithaca, NY: Cornell University Press.

———. 2000. *Laying Down the Law*. New Haven, CT: Yale University Press.

———. 2006. *The Journey of Theophanes: Travel, Costs, and Diet in the Later Roman East*. New Haven, CT: Yale University Press.

Maxwell, Jaclyn L. 2006. *Christianization and Communication in Late Antiquity: John Chrysostom and His Congregation in Antioch*. Cambridge: Cambridge University Press.

McGuire, Brian Patrick. 1988. *Friendship and Community: The Monastic Experience 350–1250*. Kalamazoo, MI: Cistercian Press.

McKitterick, Rosamund, ed. 1990. *The Uses of Literacy in Early Mediaeval Europe*. Cambridge: Cambridge University Press.

McQuail, D. 2005. *McQuail's Mass Communication Theory*, 5th ed. London: Sage.
Mendels, Doron. 1999. *The Media Revolution of Early Christianity: An Essay on Eusebius's Ecclesiastical History*. Grand Rapids, MI: Eerdmans.
Millar, Fergus. 2006. *A Greek Roman Empire: Power and Belief under Theodosius II, 408–450*. Berkeley: University of California Press.
Morello, Ruth, and A. D. Morriso. 2007. *Ancient Letters: Classical and Late Antique Epistolography*. Oxford: Oxford University Press.
Mostert, Marco, ed. 1999. *New Approaches to Medieval Communication*. Turnhout: Brepols.
Mullett, Margaret. 1990. "Writing in Early Mediaeval Europe." In *The Uses of Literacy in Early Mediaeval Europe*, ed. Rosamund McKitterick, 156–185. Cambridge: Cambridge University Press.
———. 1997. *Theophylact of Ochrid: Reading the Letters of a Byzantine Bishop*. Birmingham Byzantine and Ottoman Monographs 2. Aldershot: Ashgate.
Murray, Alexander C. 2005. "Review Article: The New MGH Edition of the Charters of the Merovingian Kings," *Journal of Medieval Latin* 15: 246–278.
Noble, Thomas F. X. 1990. "Literacy and the Papal Government in Late Antiquity and the Early Middle Ages." In *The Uses of Literacy in Early Mediaeval Europe*, ed. Rosamund McKitterick, 82–108. Cambridge: Cambridge University Press.
O'Brien, Mary Bridget. 1930. *Title of Address in Christian Latin Epistolography to 543 A.D.* Washington, DC: Catholic University of America Press.
O'Donnell, James J. 2010. "New Media (and Old)." In *The Oxford Handbook of Roman Studies*, ed. Alessandro Barchiesi and Walter Scheidel, 7–29. Oxford: Oxford University Press.
O'Sullivan, T., et al. 1983. *Key Concepts in Communication*. London: Methuen.
Poster, Carol. 2007. "A Conversation Halved: Epistolary Theory in Greco-Roman Antiquity." In *Letter-Writing Manuals and Instruction from Antiquity to the Present*, ed. Carol Poster and Linda C. Mitchell, 21–51. Columbia: University of South Carolina Press.
Papaioannou, Stratis. 2010. "Letter-writing." In *The Byzantine World*, ed. Paul Stephenson, 188–199. Abingdon: Routledge.
Reynolds, L. D., et al., eds. 1983. *Texts and Transmission: A Survey of the Latin Classics*. Oxford: Clarendon Press.
Rio, Alice. 2008. *The Formularies of Angers and Marculf: Two Merovingian Legal Handbooks*. Translated Texts for Historians 46. Liverpool: Liverpool University Press.
———. 2009. *Legal Practice and the Written Word in the Early Middle Ages: Frankish Formulae, c. 500–1000*. Cambridge: Cambridge University Press.
Roberts, Michael. 2009. *The Humblest Sparrow: The Poetry of Venantius Fortunatus*. Ann Arbor: University of Michigan Press.
Rogers, E. M., and D. L. Kincaid. 1981. *Communication Networks: Toward a Paradigm for Research*. New York: Free Press.
Rosenmeyer, Patricia A. 2006. *Ancient Greek Literary Letters: Selections in Translation*. London: Routledge.
Rousseau, Philip, ed. 2009. *A Companion to Late Antiquity*. Malden, MA: Wiley-Blackwell.
Russell, Norman. 2007. *Theophilus of Alexandria*. London: Routledge.
Salzman, Michele R. 2004. "Travel and Communication in the *Letters* of Symmachus." In *Travel, Communication, and Geography in Late Antiquity*, ed. Linda Ellis and Frank L. Kidner, 81–94. Aldershot: Ashgate.

Seeck, Otto. 1919. *Regesten der Kaiser und Päpste für die Jahre 311 bis 476 n. Chr.: Vorarbeit zu einer Prosopographie der christlichen Kaiserzeit*. Stuttgart: Metzler.

Slootjes, Daniëlle. 2006. *The Governor and His Subjects in the Later Roman Empire*. Leiden: Brill.

Sotinel, Claire. 2004. "How Were Bishops Informed? Information Transmission across the Adriatic Sea in Late Antiquity." In *Travel, Communication, and Geography in Late Antiquity*, ed. Linda Ellis and Frank L. Kidner, 63–72. Aldershot: Ashgate.

———. 2009. "Information and Political Power." In *A Companion to Late Antiquity*, ed. Philip Rousseau, 125–138. Malden, MA: Wiley-Blackwell.

Stowers, Stanley K. 1986. *Letter Writing in Greco-Roman Antiquity*. Philadelphia: Westminster.

Sullivan, Robert G. 2007. "Classical Epistolary Theory and the Letters of Isocrates." In *Letter-Writing Manuals and Instruction from Antiquity to the Present*, ed. Carol Poster and Linda C. Mitchell, 7–20. Columbia: University of South Carolina Press.

Trapp, Michael. 2003. *Greek and Latin Letters: An Anthology, with Translation*. Cambridge: Cambridge University Press.

Van Dam, Raymond. 2002. *Kingdom of Snow: Roman Rule and Greek Culture in Cappadocia*. Philadelphia: University of Pennsylvania Press.

———. 2003a. *Becoming Christian: The Conversion of Roman Cappadocia*. Philadelphia: University of Pennsylvania Press.

———. 2003b. *Families and Friends in Late Roman Cappadocia*. Philadelphia: University of Pennsylvania Press.

Van Egmond, Wolfert S. 1999. "The Audience of Early Medieval Hagiographical Texts." In *New Approaches to Medieval Communication*, ed. Marco Mostert, 41–67. Turnhout: Brepols.

Vessey, Mark. 1993. "The Origins of the *Collectio Sirmondiana*: A New Look at the Evidence." In *The Theodosian Code*, ed. Jill Harries and Ian Wood, 178–199. Ithaca, NY: Cornell University Press.

Weidermann, Margarete. 1982. *Kulturgeschichte der Merowingerzeit nach den Werken Gregors von Tours*. 2 vols. Mainz: Römisch-Germanisches Zentralmuseum.

Windahl, Sven, Benno Signitzer, and Jean T. Olson. 2009. *Using Communication Theory*. London: Sage.

Witt, Ronald G. 2005. "The Arts of Letter-Writing." In *The Cambridge History of Literary Criticism, Vol. 2: The Middle Ages*, 68–83. Cambridge: Cambridge University Press.

Wood, Ian. 1990. "Administration, Law, and Culture in Merovingian Gaul." In *The Uses of Literacy in Early Mediaeval Europe*, ed. Rosamund McKitterick, 63–81. Cambridge: Cambridge University Press.

———. 1992. "Continuity or Calamity? The Constraints of Literary Models." In *Fifth-Century Gaul: A Crisis of Identity?* ed. John Drinkwater and Hugh Elton, 9–18. Cambridge: Cambridge University Press.

———. 1993. "Letters and Letter-Collections from Antiquity to the Early Middle Ages: The Prose Works of Avitus of Vienne." In *The Culture of Christendom: Essays in Medieval History in Commemoration of Denis L. T. Bethell*, ed. Marc Meyer, 29–43. London: Hambledon.

———. 1994. *The Merovingian Kingdoms, 450–751*. London: Longman.

PART IV

RELIGIONS AND RELIGIOUS IDENTITY

CHAPTER 26

PAGANISM AND CHRISTIANIZATION

JACLYN MAXWELL
Ohio University

Introduction

THE history of religion in Late Antiquity can be presented as a compelling narrative with an inevitable outcome: after Constantine's Edict of Toleration in 313, the Christian emperors became increasingly intolerant toward the traditional religions of their empire and legislated accordingly, outlawing by the end of the century not only animal sacrifice but also everything from burning incense in household shrines to tying ribbons on trees. Justified by imperial edicts and urged on by bishops, Christian monks destroyed cult images and ancient temples. Pagan mobs and philosophers sometimes attempted to defend their traditions, but they ultimately failed to change the course of history that had begun with Constantine. Meanwhile, Christian holy men began to receive acclaim for feats of ascetic endurance and miraculous healings, and a wave of not especially pious converts joined the Church. In the middle of the fourth century, the emperor Julian's failed attempt to revive paganism served only to underline the doomed nature of his cause and to prove that the old religions were lacking the same appeal that was the key to Christianity's success. The linked processes of declining paganism and rising Christianity continued through the fifth century, with the destruction of more temples and the building of more churches until the final blow came under Justinian and his successors: the forced baptism of pagans. This is the familiar story of Christianity's rise to dominance in Late

Antiquity. The Christian emperors and their laws mandating the end of paganism, along with aggressive or even violent clergy and monks, are often presented as the chief driving forces in this transformation.[1]

Although these factors were certainly important, they do not explain why people decided to become Christians or their conception of what this religious identity entailed. Accounts of the Christianization of the Roman empire can easily rest too heavily on the story constructed and promoted by Church Fathers (almost always referred to now in quotation marks as the "triumphal narrative"), which presents the decline of the old religions and the rise of Christianity as inevitable and glorious.[2] Moreover, the imperial law codes seem to back this up, providing evidence of growing Christian power and the gradual disappearance of official support for traditional cult. At the same time, though, we know that some of the Christian emperors made concessions to tradition. Constantius and Constans decreed that temples related to spectacles should be preserved; the title of Pontifex Maximus was still used by emperors until Gratian's refusal in 383; even Theodosius, known for his harsh policies against pagan worship, associated with leading pagans.[3] Also, the laws compiled in the Theodosian Code show us that, overall, the Christian emperors paid much more attention to other matters of imperial rule—stamping out paganism does not appear to have been at the forefront of their agenda. For example, many more entries were dedicated to regulating the public post service than to limiting pagan worship.[4] Indeed, even in the realm of religious policy, intra-Christian conflicts were perceived as more urgent than the persistence of pagan practices: more legislation was passed, more sermons preached, and more blood spilt in response to rival Christian sects. By scratching the surface of the religious changes in Late Antiquity, it is easy to see how complicated this transformation was.

The chronology of the decline of paganism and the Christianization of Roman society is similar in some ways to the "Fall of the Roman Empire." Both of these processes elude our attempts to pin them down and to say *when* exactly they happened. Historians (especially when teaching undergraduates) tend to seek, if not a definitive date, then at least a key turning point. There are many candidates for the decisive moment in the decline of paganism and the acceleration (or completion) of Christianization: the conversion of Constantine in 312; the removal of the Altar of Victory from the Roman Senate House in 382; 391 saw Theodosius' law prohibiting pagan sacrifice, as well as the destruction of the Serapeum in Alexandria; perhaps the condemnation of the Lupercalia by Pope Gelasius in 494 spelled the end of the old religions; or the persecutions of pagans and the closure of the Academy in Athens during the reign of Justinian. All of these events are revealing, but there is always an argument to be made that the real turning point was a bit earlier or later.[5] No specific moment or event can explain such gradual processes that took place across so many diverse regions.[6] Instead of searching for specific key events, we should focus our sights on changes and continuities in religious behaviors and attitudes, which are, arguably, what matter the most when discussing religious patterns in Roman society as a whole.

Although the decline of traditional Mediterranean religious systems and the rise in prominence, and then dominance, of orthodox Christianity have long been a focus of both scholarly and popular interest, there are still many unanswered questions about the manner of and reasons for this transformation. What, precisely, was changing and what was remaining the same, who was leading and who was following? Scholars continue to debate the nature of the old religions, the importance of the conversion of Constantine, the role of violence and coercion in Christianization, the specific appeals of Christianity that attracted converts, and the significance of religious practices that persisted, regardless of religious affiliation. In current scholarship, the traditional categories that have shaped much of the debate are being reconfigured. These categories—not only pagan and Christian but also monotheism and polytheism, elite and popular, magic and religion—reflect the polarized view of our sources, not the religious syncretism and fluid identities that appear to have been the norm for ordinary people. More and more scholars are turning away from the idea of an epic "conflict between pagans and Christians" to discuss the period in terms of religious diversity and overlapping beliefs and practices.[7] This chapter, then, provides an overview of the problem of religious conflict and coercion but also focuses on the transformation of religious identity and religious practices in connection with the experience of the general population, rather than remaining focused on the views and actions of emperors, bishops, and philosophers.

Sources

The study of religious change in Late Antiquity is usually based on evidence from prolific theologians, bishops, hagiographers, and Church historians. The quantity of texts that survive from these Christian writers surpasses anything that exists from previous eras. Despite their obvious biases, these are invaluable sources that allow us to examine a broad expanse of the religious landscape. The bishops addressed their lay audiences in sermons, the saints' lives reflect popular interests, and theology attracted widespread interest in this period.[8] These texts should not be written off as belonging only to the small circle of Christian intellectuals cut off from the rest of society. That said, it is also important to avoid identifying Christianity with the most rigorously orthodox Church figures. Despite their prominence and eloquence, the Church Fathers did not necessarily represent the mainstream religious ideas of the time. The bishops' and preachers' unrelenting promotion of their brands of Christianity, together with the rise in prestige and influence of ascetic Christians, has led studies of this period to focus perhaps too much attention on the "overachievers" who made lay devotion look feeble by comparison.[9] By reflexively agreeing with our sources in identifying "real" Christianity with rigorous or even ascetic Christianity, we tend to see the laity, if we think of them at all, as the weak link in the Christianization of society. In this way, their reluctance to conform—their persistence in practicing old traditions, their failure to realize that Christianization meant a complete transformation of *everything*—meant that the triumphal narrative of Christianity had to include "pagan survivals," bits of the past smuggled into, and leaving a stain on, the developing Christian society. But if we think in terms of the ordinary layperson and move rigorous, ascetic Christianity away from the spotlight, then the issues of religious identity and the process of change look quite different.[10] Before discussing the matter of Christianization, however, we must examine the state of traditional religions in Late Antiquity, which is often distorted by the claims of Christian writers.

"Paganism" and Christian Categories

The most common term for ancient Mediterranean religions, *paganism*, is problematic, yet difficult to replace. Originally, there was no overarching name for the various forms of traditional religion in the ancient Mediterranean.[11] The concept of paganism was a creation of Christians who aimed to define their religious rivals as a coherent group. Such a label made traditional beliefs and practices an easier target for the attacks of Christian polemicists. As a result, the Christian conception of paganism centered on what differed most dramatically from Christianity: polytheism, the use of idols, and animal sacrifice.[12] Not only did this category allow Christians to condemn their opponents in sweeping terms but also they were able to emphasize the lines between the two religions and avoid acknowledging any middle ground between paganism and Christianity. This tendency has influenced our perception of this period to the extent that it is easy to overlook shared attitudes and practices.[13] In the process of defining traditional religion in negative terms, Christian writers associated almost anything they deemed undesirable with paganism, a measure that also led to long-lasting assumptions about decadent pagan morality. The focus on difference and accusations of demon worship set the stage for aggressive actions against traditional religions.[14]

In addition to these negative connotations, the term *paganism* implies a coherence and self-consciousness that, for the most part, did not exist. Other terms, however, present their own problems: "Greek" or "Greco-Roman" religion leaves out Egyptian, Syrian, and other local traditions. "Polytheism" excludes monotheistic and henotheistic views.[15] Even "traditional" religion raises questions, since it implies that these beliefs and practices were incapable of innovation. Pierre

Chuvin has offered a particularly appealing solution to the problem, embracing the term *pagan* as meaning "the people of a place": the pagans were people rooted in local customs of an ancient religious landscape.[16] Ultimately, however, any sort of generalization tends to impose a false consistency on the wide range of local traditions. Of course, the term *Christianity* poses similar problems. David Frankfurter warns against accepting that "a monolithic Christianity and 'paganism' might be faced off in a uniform struggle across the Roman Empire. . . . To buy into such a category is thus to render oneself immediately imprecise, subject far more than is commonly thought to the worldview of ancient polemicists."[17] Still, surveys and syntheses of Late Antiquity, such as this one, require an attempt to make reasonable generalizations. Despite the clear problems with the terms, this chapter uses the terms *paganism* and *pagan* because the alternatives ("non-Christian/non-Jew"?) are so awkward; just as using "Christianity" in a general sense is imprecise but practical.[18]

Traditional Religion and Change in Late Antiquity

For generations of scholars, it seemed obvious that for paganism to be wholly displaced by another religion, like one empire falling to another, it must have had a crucial weakness that led to its demise. Why else would its adherents have offered so little resistance to the new religion? Resistance is what we expect from a persecuted religion: historians have relished the stories of pagan senators and philosophers who defied the Christian emperors with their stubborn refusal to end traditional worship of the gods. These noble examples are presented as braver and more dedicated than the average pagan and therefore able to withstand the pressure to convert to Christianity.[19] This is certainly part of the story, but too much emphasis on the heroes runs the risk of identifying them with paganism in general, making the more ordinary adherents appear lackluster (semi-pagan?) by comparison. We should be wary of judging the majority by the standards of the fervent minority.

Awareness of its ultimate fate inevitably affects the study of late paganism. Consequently, the vitality of these beliefs and practices is often underestimated. Some scholars have reckoned that the traditional cults declined in the mid-third century C.E. and never recovered, giving Christianity the chance to fill the void. Others have found evidence for continuing vigor of paganism well into the fifth and sixth centuries. Still others point to this evidence as exceptions proving the rule, mere pockets of resistance for a lost cause. There is a middle ground between these two interpretations that comes across best in studies that concentrate on particular regions.[20] Traditional cults flourished in some areas for years after imperial laws were passed against them: Heliopolis and Carrhae (Harran) are the best-known examples. Likewise, in certain regions of Asia Minor and Egypt, a strong Christian presence is already evident by the early fourth century.[21] Given the length of time and the number of regions involved, there can be no conclusive date or even decade marking "when paganism ended." Just as all politics are local, so are all conversions. Nevertheless, some patterns do emerge.

Many of the changes in religious practice in the late empire can be tied to the vicissitudes of the Roman economy. During the upheavals of the third century, the lack of public money and changes in attitudes toward private benefaction weakened many public ceremonies.[22] Under Diocletian, resources were again available to repair temples and reinvigorate festivals (and to renew the persecution of Christians). But Constantine would soon shift imperial favor to Christianity, while many of the old cults had not fully recovered from the neglect brought on by the financial collapse.[23] Later Christian emperors intensified restrictions, targeting blood sacrifice in particular because of its association with illicit divination. Imperial attention to this issue demonstrated through repeated laws and warnings can be interpreted as evidence for the intimidation of the adherents to traditional cults or as evidence for the continuation of old ceremonies in the face of the laws, which led to the need for repeated laws. Or of course, both of these scenarios could be true simultaneously.[24]

The decline in public ceremonies should not be confused with a general decline in religious life. For instance, pagan monotheism has attracted attention as a window onto the vitality of paganism in Late Antiquity. The tendency to worship one god or goddess developed in several contexts: the philosophical schools (Neoplatonism), the pagan-Jewish "god-fearers" and the worshippers of Zeus Hypsistos (Zeus "The Highest"), and in the consolidation of deities into one overarching figure, as happened with the cult of Isis.[25] This development has been seen as a precursor to the acceptance of Christianity: a monotheistic (or even henotheistic) outlook would make the transition to Christianity easier.[26] But putting aside the issue of future conversions to Christianity, pagan monotheism should be seen as an example of the diversity within ancient Mediterranean religions and philosophies, and as a reminder that it was not a coherent system. Pagan monotheism did not necessarily lead to a yearning for Jewish or Christian monotheism. The main connection between pagan monotheism and Christian success is rhetorical: Christian polemicists were able to adopt philosophers' arguments in favor of one deity.[27]

Sacrifice

The primary target of imperial antipagan legislation (and much Christian rhetoric) was animal sacrifice. But this does not necessarily mean that the forbidden practice was essential to ordinary pagans. According to the early

Christian imagination, paganism centered on the killing of animals, the burning of their entrails for demons mistakenly believed to be gods residing in idols (cult statues), and the consumption of polluted meat at banquets. (Of course, these images of paganism still persist.) Christian writers contrasted the messy business of killing animals with the pure sacrifice of the Christians, who offered prayers and good deeds rather than livestock to God.[28] But not surprisingly, the Christians' characterization of paganism is distorted. Rather, it was quite possible, and certainly acceptable, to worship the gods without killing animals.

Blood sacrifice was a central ritual in pre-Christian Mediterranean religions, attested in the earliest historical evidence. When Christian emperors began restricting sacrifice, though, they were not doing something entirely new. Certain types of sacrifice related to divination had been condemned in earlier centuries as *superstitio*, as bad for society, and, especially, as threatening to emperors. Private divination was feared by sitting emperors as a method of predicting future emperors. Therefore, the fourth-century condemnations of nocturnal sacrifices and various types of *superstitio* were consistent with previous imperial policies.[29] But some Christian emperors went further than this, singling out sacrifices and the veneration of statues in temples to criminalize the worship of old gods.

Putting Christian expectations and condemnations aside, how important were these rituals to the ordinary pagan? Epigraphical and literary evidence, on the one hand, demonstrates that some pagans continued to conduct sacrifices into the sixth century. On the other hand, epigraphical evidence also suggests a steep decline in cult practices starting in the third century.[30] The persistence of traditional worship in places like Stratonicea, Apamea, and Carrhae (Harran) can be seen as a glimpse of a larger, undocumented picture of pagan religious life of the time or, alternatively, as exceptions to the rule.[31] In either case, though, the decline in evidence for sacrifice should not be identified with the decline of paganism. Traditional religious identity and practice was not necessarily tied to the practice of animal sacrifice: not all pagans believed it was a good or necessary way to worship the gods. Instead, there are signs that, starting in the third century, divination and prayer were more prominent than public rituals.[32] If we think about religion practiced on a small scale by individuals, including practices typically categorized as magic, it is clear that the same religious worldview and assumptions continued to address the same basic human needs, regardless of what happened to the public temples. David Frankfurter demonstrates that Egyptian religion remained alive and well in this period, despite the decline or even destruction of monumental temples. The success of Christianity, he argues, did not result from a "spiritual vacuum" or the decline of the temple-centered cult.[33]

The attempted revival of sacrifice by the emperor Julian provides additional perspectives on late Roman paganism. Julian's religious agenda emphasized the reinvigoration of public sacrificial rituals. His actions were certainly in tune with Christian characterizations of paganism, but the emperor was shocked at how unenthusiastic pagans were about the revival of these ceremonies.[34] Ammianus Marcellinus comments on the excess of the sacrifices and refers to Julian as superstitious.[35] Libanius, otherwise an avid supporter of the emperor, was lukewarm about the massive blood sacrifices.[36] Broad estimates suggest that more than half of the population still identified with the traditional religions, but, according to our sources, they did not openly embrace the return of public money and social prestige to the worship of the gods. Julian's revival appears to have failed because ritual sacrifice had never recovered from its decline in the third century. Comments from Julian's contemporaries confirm the impression that animal sacrifice was by then uncommon and, therefore, nonessential to pagan identity. Although some people still performed traditional sacrifices, most people saw it as too risky: not only because they could be punished under Christian emperors but also because they did not wish to alienate the Christians in their communities and families.[37]

Although Julian's massive public sacrifices did not make the impression he had hoped for, sacrificial rituals continued in various guises and in unexpected ways. People continued to hold banquets and butcher animals. The line between these events and pagan animal sacrifice was not always clear. In Libanius' oration "For the Temples," the orator rails against monks who attacked rural temples, harassing the already overburdened peasants. The monks claimed that the peasants were breaking laws against sacrifice, but Libanius argued that slaughtering animals for a feast was no longer a religious act. Whereas "it used to be the custom for country folk to assemble in large numbers at the homes of the village notables at holiday time, to make a sacrifice and then hold a feast," a very similar feast would still be legal (*Or.* 30.19). The ambiguous nature of meat-centered feasts caught the attention of bishops, who expressed concern about the similarities between Christian banquets and traditional sacrificial banquets.[38] Surprisingly enough, some Christian leaders adopted variations on the ritual. In addition to the incorporation of sacrifice into Armenian Christian liturgy, we have evidence of at least two well-known Christian bishops who encouraged a version of animal sacrifice as part of Christian worship: Paulinus of Nola's sacrifices honoring St. Felix, and Nicholas, bishop of Myra in Lycia, who allowed sacrifices patterned after ancient Jewish practices.[39]

Pragmatic Religion and Popular Religion

My undergraduate students have tended to see a sharp contrast between the practicality of pagan worship and the loftier nature of Christian devotion based on spirituality, selflessness, and morality. They easily lose sight of the practicality of Christianity. If pressed, the students acknowledge that many Christians did (and still do) pray for personal benefits and turn to religion for help in difficult times such as illness, political upheaval, or natural disaster. Nevertheless, worldly concerns remain marginal for "good" Christians. It is certainly not surprising that they would expect Christianity to be completely different from paganism and reflexively categorize any common ground with the old religions as "superstitions" or "pagan survivals." As we have seen, this view is based on the Church Fathers' characterization of the old religions as completely alien to Christianity. But the common ground was quite extensive because much of life remained the same regardless of religious affiliation. Pagan and Christian responses to critical needs such as safety and subsistence were based on shared assumptions about the human and divine realms. By taking these pragmatic concerns seriously, we can move away from the stark dichotomies that often distort our understanding of religion in this period.[40]

The role of pragmatic concerns in religious life is often discussed in terms of "popular religion" or magic. This, in turn, tends to be identified with the more exotic aspects of religious life and contrasted with the official religious norms promoted by Church leaders. The juxtaposition of popular and official religion usually takes on class connotations, setting the poor and uneducated majority in contrast to the elite. This is another instance in which these categories and associations have been profoundly influenced by the worldviews of our main sources, the Church Fathers. In the process of defining orthodoxy, they aimed to stigmatize unacceptable beliefs and activities as vulgar, ignorant, pagan, and demonic. What they categorized as magic or as pagan survivals, though, should now be seen in terms of local religious systems and pragmatic concerns. Most of the condemned practices were not confined to the uneducated peasants; religious practices and attitudes did not, in fact, vary greatly according to social and economic class.[41] Numerous examples reveal educated people who held beliefs typically classified as "popular." For instance, pagan and Christian elites shared the masses' concern over the dangers of the evil eye.[42] Magicians were depicted as educated men: St. Cyprian had been a scholar and magician before his conversion to Christianity, and both Libanius and Apuleius were accused of performing magic. Libanius was also a victim of magic: he recognized a curse placed on him when he spotted a dead chameleon in his classroom. The famous orator did not laugh it off: the dead reptile was, for him, a real threat.[43] Curses and the need for protective amulets were facts of life for everyone, regardless of religious affiliation, class, status, or education. Archaeologists have discovered numerous amulets, from cheap metal bells to beautifully carved gems, but regardless of monetary value, the hopes for their protection were the same.[44]

"Pagan Survivals"

One approach to the study of Christianization is to look at its rough edges: the various beliefs and behaviors that most troubled the clergy. Church leaders' efforts to uproot certain traditions and activities, which are preserved in the vast number of surviving sermons, letters, and treatises, tell us a great deal about the process of Christianization. Their complaints and advice regarding the laity's misbehavior have often been taken as evidence of the wave of insincere Christians who joined the Church once it became legal and fashionable after the conversion of Constantine. These were the Christians who, against their bishops' wishes, insisted on celebrating the Kalends of January with drinking parties, decorations, and gift exchange. These people could not have been genuine Christians, or so the Church Fathers claimed.[45] But we should be careful not to adopt our sources' perspectives as our own. A number of practices they condemned as magic, pagan, and/or demonic were actually based in Christian beliefs.

In southern Egypt, the abbot Shenoute referred, unfavorably, to a fox-claw amulet that had been made for a layperson by a monk. The monk and his client, though, did not see themselves as operating outside the bounds of their religion. Shenoute also condemned the independent use of oil or water for religious purposes, whether people obtained these materials from enchanters or from monks.[46] In Antioch, John Chrysostom was suspicious of people who washed too carefully before church. For him (but clearly not for everyone), the unsupervised use of water for purification was a holdover from pagan or Jewish traditions and inconsistent with Christian faith.[47] Augustine complained about the uneducated who irrationally kissed the columns of the church.[48] Fervent worship at saints' shrines and too much enthusiasm for the cult of angels were singled out for censure. Leo the Great worried about Christians in Rome who greeted the rising sun before they entered their church. Maximus of Turin was surprised by "seemingly devout Christians" who attempted to help the moon through an eclipse by shouting. Further west, Martin of Braga condemned many behaviors that would later be broadly acceptable, such as the use of pagan names for the days of the week.[49] In these cases, the practices denounced as pagan or magical were broadly accepted and often based on Christian beliefs and performed in the context of Christian worship.

Even for many Church leaders, the dividing line between magic and orthodox Christianity was not absolute when it came to practical concerns. In some cases, the only difference between old magic and Christian miracles was whether the power originated with demons or with God. The similarities are clear in confrontations between pagan magicians and Christian holy men such as Martin of Tours and Theodore of Sykeon.[50] Jerome unabashedly describes how St. Hilarion of Thavatha helped a Christian charioteer defeat a pagan charioteer by applying holy water and pronouncing the name of Jesus over him.[51] Some of the Christian "magical" ritual manuals from this period were written by monks.[52] Christians, including clergy and ascetics, used Scriptures and relics from holy sites and people for divine protection, creating new types of amulets based on Christian beliefs but serving old purposes.[53] These examples reveal the continuity between pagan and Christian worldviews, demonstrating that the pragmatic use of religion for problem-solving was not confined to the uneducated lower classes or to a semi-Christian, semi-pagan fringe. Most Christians had no qualms about practices that were strikingly similar to pagan ones: for them, the protection came from God rather than demons, which was the crucial difference. Likewise, pagans had also defined magic in terms of motive rather than types of rituals or the problems that were addressed.[54]

Conflict, Coercion, and . . . Coexistence?

What role did coercion play when people converted to Christianity and renounced traditional religions? Laws banned pagan worship with increasingly harsh punishments, Christian enthusiasts destroyed ancient temples, and, in the sixth century, the emperor Justinian mandated the forced baptism of pagans. These factors, plus the aggressive antipagan rhetoric of a number of Christian writers, demonstrate that coercion certainly figured into both the suppression of old religions and the spread of Christianity. The transition of the Christians from persecuted to persecutors can seem jarring, and their treatment of non-Christians appears to conflict with precepts such as "Turn the other cheek" and "Love thy enemies." The use of intimidation and force by Christians, though, should not surprise us; equally, our fascination with this topic should not lead to an exaggeration of its magnitude. It would be mistaken to expect open-minded tolerance from the Christians: aggressive elements existed in Christianity from the beginning, side by side with, and in contradiction to, peacefulness and tolerance.[55] At the same time, the use of force was not as widespread or as fierce as some accounts claim. That said, it is still necessary to examine (and question) the significance of the sporadic instances of violence that broke out between pagans and Christians and the extent to which intimidation by both Church and state encouraged the abandonment of one religion and the adoption of another. Outbursts of violence on both sides occurred, as did attempts at compromise and reconciliation; it is up for debate which should be given greater emphasis.

Our sources tell a distorted story, embellishing certain events to glorify their heroes and, especially, to demonize their opponents. Moreover, the study of the "struggle" between pagans and Christians has focused a great deal of attention on certain bloody events, taken out of their largely nonviolent contexts. Recent studies, though, have turned the emphasis away from conflict, arguing that disproportionate attention has been paid to conflict at the expense of other types of interaction among religious groups. For example, in a recent overview of religious violence in late antique Italy, North Africa, and Gaul, Michele Salzman demonstrates that the violent episodes reported in our sources were isolated events that had as much to do with social concerns as religious fervor. The

Christians simply were not very combative, even in the case of Martin of Tours, the "militant converter of Gaul," who was involved in only nine confrontations with pagans over the course of a long career.[56] Even his few confrontations were more often than not directed against buildings, statues, or trees, rather than people.[57]

Violent Anecdotes

While it is important not to overemphasize the worst instances of violence or present them as typical of the relationship among religious groups, it is worth retelling a few of the most disturbing anecdotes here to gauge their relevance to the processes of Christianization and the decline of paganism. The Church historian Theodoret reports atrocities committed against Christians during the reign of Julian by going through the empire, region by region, describing tortures inflicted out of religious hatred: in Palestine, men and women were mutilated and fed to pigs; in Phoenicia, a deacon was mutilated and even subjected to cannibalism; in Thrace, a Christian was burned alive by a pagan governor; in Syria, a bishop's tortures included being stabbed by the styluses of schoolboys.[58] If true, these were terrible deeds, but it would be misleading to take them at face value or to see them as representative of how pagans and Christians interacted in this period. At the same time, though, we should not be *too* skeptical, because such things were possible in a society that accepted the use of torture.[59]

We have multiple accounts for two cases of mutilation and murder by angry mobs in Alexandria, one Christian and the other pagan. Both incidents were reported by pagan and Christian writers, all of whom indicate that religious hatred played a role in the events. The first victim was George, the Arian bishop of Alexandria, who was an unpopular man due to his work as an informer and his attacks on pagan worship.[60] In the events leading up to his murder and mutilation by an angry crowd, he publicly insulted the Genius (guiding spirit) of the city, wondering aloud how long this temple would stand. Previously, he had offended many Alexandrians after he discovered what he claimed were "implements" for initiation rites and, according to one account, evidence of human sacrifice to Mithras. The Christians exhibited these discoveries to the public, mocking the pagans' "mysteries" in a parade. This provoked an attack by a pagan mob that killed some of the Christians and stopped the building project. In the course of this fighting, the enraged crowd killed, mutilated, and burned the unpopular Arian bishop. Both Socrates and Sozomen mention (and deny) the rumor that orthodox Christians also played a role in the violence. Instead, they point to the bishop's overly abrasive attitude toward the city's pagans as the inspiration for the attack, which is supported by a pagan account. Ammianus tells us that, in addition to the bishop, the crowd also singled out and killed two other Christians: the superintendent of the mint who had destroyed an altar in his workplace and another prominent man who was overseeing the construction of a new church.[61] These attacks were clearly newsworthy at the time, but unusual. Both pagan and Christian writers, though, presented the violence as an unsurprising result of rising tensions over religious difference, insults, and the growing vulnerability of traditional places and ways of worship.

A similar attack occurred in 415, when a Christian mob in Alexandria attacked and killed the pagan philosopher Hypatia. The clash stemmed from a disagreement between Orestes, the prefect of Egypt, and Cyril, the city's bishop, over the latter's plan to seize Alexandria's synagogues. Hypatia, a respected public figure and a supporter of Orestes, became Cyril's enemy by association and was publicly attacked, mutilated, and killed by a crowd of the bishop's supporters. There are variations in the reports of this murder—different emphases and different conclusions regarding the justification of the deed emerge from the pagan and Christian sources. Socrates does not sympathize with his coreligionists here: he presents the pagan Hypatia as a respected philosopher and public figure, and the Christians as guilty of an atrocity, whereas a separate Egyptian tradition lauded the killing as a triumph over the female philosopher's demonic power.[62]

The study of religious conflict invariably draws our attention to the most striking actions of the extremists. Rather than illuminating a deep current of intolerance within pagan and Christian communities, these events primarily reveal the intolerance of fanatics: just as most early Christians did not suffer martyrdom during the persecutions, the majority of Christians in Late Antiquity did not participate in the destruction of ancient temples or other aggressive measures.[63] Torture and murder were not the inevitable result of the rise of Christianity; at certain times in the "wavering" fourth century, coexistence and cooperation took precedence over conflict.[64]

To put this issue into proper perspective, we should note that conflicts among Christian sects resulted in more bloodshed than those between Christians and pagans. Likewise, Christian emperors devoted more effort to outlawing heresies than they did to paganism.[65] It is safe to assume that not all pagans and Christians were locked in perpetual combat. At the same time, however, violent confrontations could be indicative of simmering tensions that were more widely experienced. Extraordinary episodes of violence would surely have affected the worldview of those not directly involved. Furthermore, while religious rivalry was never the sole reason for the conflicts, religious motives were still significant; in cases like George of Alexandria, religious insults appear to have provoked people who already hated him for other, more practical reasons. Although scholars may wish to avoid constructing a lachrymose history of religion in Late Antiquity, it is also important to acknowledge the pressure resulting from sporadic violence. Dramatic events, such as the demolition of an ancient temple or the murder of a public leader, would have been the catalyst for greater awareness of and adherence to religious loyalties on both sides.[66]

Legislation and Coercion

Imperial legislation against pagan practices is an important part of the narrative of the decline of paganism and the Christianization of the Roman world. These laws can be used to gauge the level of oppression or tolerance experienced by pagans under each emperor. The Theodosian Code demonstrates that the emperors' efforts to limit pagan practice were not consistent in the fourth century. In 340, Constantine II prohibited divination through entrails as superstition but did not condemn pagan ceremonies per se. Constans and Constantius banned pagan sacrifice in 341 but the next year issued a decree protecting pagan temples from plunderers.[67] In the first half of the fourth century, this legislation focused on activities that were already marginalized: illicit divination and other forms of *superstitio* were the targets rather than pagan religion in general. The Christian emperors followed the example of their pagan predecessors, who condemned the same practices and arrested people suspected of using amulets, hiring dream interpreters, or performing animal sacrifice. In 341, Constantius was the first emperor to condemn sacrifice and pagan worship in general; Theodosius later reaffirmed and elaborated on this ban.[68] It is unclear whether the initial distinction between condemned practices and paganism resulted from efforts to promote coexistence or whether the idea of pagans as a distinct group simply had not yet developed. In this context, some scholars have argued that clear anti-pagan intentions existed as early as Constantine, while others have seen indications of religious pluralism until the reign of Theodosius.[69]

It is difficult to judge whether the legislation against pagan practices reflects widespread attitudes or just the intentions of the emperors. It is also unclear whether the reiteration of the laws is evidence that the laws were important or that they were largely ignored. Libanius describes how people still worshipped the gods and visited temples but considered sacrifice and the public worship of cult images to be dangerous offenses.[70] Some people continued to perform sacrifices, but the nearby presence of the imperial court presumably increased the general level of compliance.[71] One particular law also reveals the ambiguity of the emperors' intentions for the laws: a law from the year 423 protected from Christian attacks Jews and pagans who lived "quietly." This reflects imperial concern for the safety of non-Christians, the threat of Christian aggression, and also the legitimacy of this aggression if its objects were not "quiet." Here, the goal appears to have been the suppression of non-Christians but not their extinction or even their conversion.[72]

Conversion, Christianization, and Orthodoxy

In his oration "For the Temples," Libanius defended peasants accused of illicit sacrificial rituals and rebuked monks who were destroying ancient temples. In this context, he observed that forcing people to abandon traditional practices would not cause them to convert to a new religion.[73] Indeed, hostile imperial laws, powerful bishops, and Christian mobs working toward the suppression of paganism do not fully explain why people decided to become Christians. A number of theories have been proposed. Ramsay MacMullen's explanation focuses on the practical appeal of Christianity: Christian holy people and objects became famous for their effectiveness in healing and, especially, exorcism.[74] For A. H. M. Jones, the new elite that emerged after the upheavals of the third century provided the key to religious transformation. The upwardly mobile were less attached to old traditions and more open to influence from the imperial family.[75] During the fourth century, if not earlier, Christianity became more and more associated with the middle and upper classes. Michele Salzman has tracked the conversion of the highest level of the Roman aristocracy, demonstrating that the effect of elite values on Christianity were as significant as the mark Christianity left on the aristocracy. The consequences of upper-class conversions would be magnified when their dependents followed, whether out of compulsion or general self-interest.[76] Garth Fowden has observed that the increase in mobility in Late Antiquity meant that having a consistent community and a sense of belonging in Churches spread across vast regions contributed to Christianity's appeal and success.[77] David Frankfurter argues that conversion depended on the charisma of particular bishops or abbots and that the change in religious affiliation did not necessarily require an end to all previously held beliefs and traditions.[78] In this perspective, the reasons for conversion were not necessarily great or pressing; the converts themselves did not always perceive this shift in allegiance as a drastic change. And of course, the conversions took place across an extended period of time. Averil Cameron has observed that disagreements about the pace of Christianization are due to varying definitions of what counted as conversion or Christianization and proposes that more attention should be paid to ways in which this happened.[79] Peter Brown concludes that by 425 C.E., the Roman empire was not yet Christianized; instead, "pockets of intensely self-confident Christianity had merely declared the Christian religion to have been victorious."[80] The adding of Christian beliefs and practices, the rooting out of pagan beliefs and practices, and the combination of the two were always negotiations between ordinary Christians and local Church leaders. No single explanation or turning point can provide the key to the conversion of pagans to Christianity.

Fluid Religious Identities

For a variety of reasons, more and more people began to identify themselves as Christians during this period. Most likely, the motivations are difficult to discern because the conversions themselves were not necessarily clear-cut, permanent changes. Idealized conversions to "genuine" Christianity are depicted in numerous saints' lives: an ordinary pagan, perhaps even a magician or a prostitute, suddenly accepts Christianity, renounces his or her old way of life, undergoes catechism and baptism, and thereafter leads a completely transformed (and usually ascetic) life.[81] In these accounts, conversion changed lives from one extreme to another. But not everyone experienced such a dramatic transformation. Indeed, recent studies point more and more toward the fluid nature of religious identity: many people may have seen themselves as Christian without necessarily denouncing all aspects of pagan religions; they may have attended Christian festivals or visited holy sites without a firm recognition of this religion to the exclusion of all others; they may have been condemned as pagans by Church leaders while considering themselves to be good Christians.

Material evidence indicates that many people respected the power of a mix of religions: curse tablets and amulets show a combination of Christian, Jewish, and pagan influences. One amulet aimed to protect a Christian child by calling on pagan powers; a ring was made with an image of Venus and a Christian inscription; curse tablets often called on any and all divine powers, without concern for theological consistency.[82] Christian texts provide glimpses of Christians who either knew little about the official requirements of their religion or combined traditions without regard to the Church Fathers' strict lines between religions.[83] Perhaps the most extreme example of unofficial Christianity appears in the sixth century, when, according to John of Ephesus, a holy man named Simeon the Mountaineer discovered a village in Syria where the people called themselves Christians and had a Church but did not know anything about the liturgy, doctrine, or Scriptures. After learning that they were not concerned about the lack of priests, he wondered, "How are you Christians, when you do not follow the custom of Christians?" Astonished, Simeon declared them to be apostates of both pagan and Christian religion and endeavored to set them straight.[84]

In other cases, the mere fact that Christians had to be reminded not to observe pagan festivals is illuminating: these warnings can be read as evidence for the ambiguity of religious affiliation, rather than merely documenting the prevalence of "bad" Christians. Various terms have been used to describe this lack of religious consistency, but it is impossible to distinguish "sincere" Christians from "semi-Christians," "paganized-Christians," and "crypto-pagans" without implicitly accepting the biases of the Church Fathers' standards.[85] Instead, we should acknowledge that there were different levels of commitment to Christianity and that the accepted norms varied in different communities.

The conception of a coherent, standardized religious belief and practice was new for most people; aside from Jews and Christians, this concept was familiar only within certain philosophical circles.[86] Libanius serves as an example of a pagan who was actually quite flexible in his conception of religious affiliation and opposed to rigid extremism of any sort. Isabella Sandwell argues convincingly that this attitude is more representative of trends and mentality in broader society than the more extreme religious identities adhered to by Church Fathers and certain pagans, such as the emperor Julian.[87] Indeed, it seems that except for these religious leaders, there was not necessarily a hard-and-fast boundary between Christianity and other religions.[88]

Although they may have attempted to do so, Church leaders could not force or convince everyone to adopt their interpretations of Christianity and paganism. In one anecdote, the Church historian Socrates gives an account of a father and son who were both teachers of grammar and rhetoric, members of the clergy, and friends of a certain pagan sophist. Worried that this association would lead them astray, their bishop forbade the friendship. The two men ignored their bishop, who, in turn, excommunicated them. The bishop did not have the final word; the younger man began his own sect, the "Apollinarians."[89] This instance is an example of the different currents of the time: friendly coexistence of committed Christians with pagans, Christian hostility to paganism, the use of coercion, and the limits of a bishop's authority.

While the conversion of the pagans to Christianity is of great interest to us, the Church Fathers of the fourth and fifth centuries were much more interested in the Christianization of people already in the Church and the creation of a uniform system of belief and practice. A great deal of Christian writing—theological texts, hagiography, sermons—is focused on the development of an ideal system of Christian life and belief and a striving for uniformity among the most devoted followers. This project aimed far beyond mere conversion or even Christianization and is perhaps better described as "hyper-Christianization."[90] But it is clear that the majority of Christians did not view the increasingly ascetic vision of their religion as the norm. Recent studies of Late Antiquity point to the lack of control Church Fathers had over the Christianization of the general population and culture.[91]

What Difference Did Christianity Make?

For the groups that were, indeed, Christianized during this period, it is unclear the degree to which religious affiliation affected the rest of their lives. Again, it is necessary to point out the difference between the ideals of Church leaders and the way of life of ordinary Christians, regardless of social status. Ramsay MacMullen has argued that most social relationships—including slavery—remained the same.[92] Recent studies have examined the connection between Christian and pagan moral thought: most of the ideas—even those underlying the Christian ascetic movement—were not new, but the "democratization" of these philosophical values in Christian culture was a new element.[93] MacMullen concluded that, along with changes in sexual mores, the most striking innovation was the Christian care for the poor, and recent work on wealth, poverty, and almsgiving bears this out. The "love of the poor" became a new, fundamental virtue in Christian society, even as Christian leadership and culture became increasingly aristocratic. Wealthy Christian patrons built hostels and hospitals, and their beneficiaries were now thought of in terms of "the poor" rather than "the people." Of course, while the ideas about the poor were transformed, there is no clear indication that the experience of being poor and the disparity in wealth changed significantly.[94]

If social relationships and moral ideals were largely unaffected by the conversion to Christianity, it is safe to say that in the context of Christian worship, people were engaging in new activities. As emphasized earlier, the religious practices of pagans and Christians were not *opposites*; many aspects overlapped. Yet, new practices emerged with the spread of Christianity. The most obvious practice that would have distinguished Christians from pagans was church attendance. Just *showing up* was a sign of affiliation, however incomplete in the eyes of the Church Fathers. Preachers complained about the decline in attendance on certain days or the laziness of the absent portion of the congregation and praised those who were present for the sermons. In his sermon "Against the Pagans," Augustine at one point addresses his listeners as the "real Christians," in contrast to the so-called Christians who had opted for the chariot races. Later, he further acknowledges their presence in church: "Thank heaven that you have come here together at all."[95] In addition to church attendance, identification with particular theological doctrines was new.[96] Meanwhile, as we have seen, some fundamental things remained the same: belief in invisible beings (demons, gods, angels) and attempts to ask them for help.[97] The cultural life of the cities, to the Church Fathers' annoyance, changed slowly. In this case, bishops could rely on less imperial help than with the closure of temples. The spectacles that Church leaders found so deeply threatening to the life and belief of a "true" Christian were still embraced by the Christian public of all socioeconomic backgrounds.[98]

Conclusions

The gray area is often missing from studies of religion in Late Antiquity: most people were neither strict Christians nor devoted pagans; the worldviews of the elite certainly overlapped with popular religion; many people surely vacillated between "heresy" and "orthodoxy." The way we use these categories is based too much on the testimony of the devotees who wrote the bulk of our texts. Most people, it seems, would have tended toward different practices or religious affiliations, moving one way or another depending on the situation, the time of year, or the particular occasion. This flexibility helps to explain the apparent contradiction between the growing dominance of Christianity, on the one hand, and the continued importance of traditional religions, on the other. The religious transformation that took place in Late Antiquity used to be attributed to the "spiritual vacuum" left by old, inadequate religions, which gave way to the superiority of Christianity.[99] But when the vitality of late paganism is brought to the forefront, then it appears that violence and coercion must be the explanation for its ultimate decline. As we have seen, this is part of the answer, but flexible identities and the possibility of incomplete conversions should be addressed as important aspects of these changes. While many Christian values, institutions, and behaviors were based at least in part on previously existing models, religious norms were changing and Christian communities were developing, just not as consistently, dramatically, or completely as the "triumph of Christianity" would make it seem.

NOTES

1. E.g., Chuvin 1990; Fowden 1978.
2. On "triumphal narrative," see Brown 1995, 1–26; Clark 2004, 14–15.
3. On protecting temples, *C.Th.* 16.10.3. On the title Pontifex Maximus, see Alan Cameron 1968. On Theodosius' pagan officials, see Chuvin 1990, 59–64.
4. On the post service, see *C.Th.* 8.5.1–66. On Constantine as an emperor rather than a "Christian emperor," see Van Dam 2007, 11.
5. For the third and early fourth century as decisive time for decline of paganism and growth of Christianity, see Geffcken 1978, 25–32; Jones 1963; Barnes 1981, 191; For the fourth century as decisive, see Lane Fox 1987; Veyne 2007. For emphasis on the long survival of paganism into the fifth and sixth centuries, see Harl 1990; Frankfurter 1998. Averil Cameron addresses this wide range of decisive turning points, suggesting, "Perhaps we are not all talking about the same thing:" Averil Cameron 1997, 25.
6. Geographical variation illustrated in Harl 1990; Mitchell 1993; Hahn 2004; Trombley 2007; Salzman 2007.
7. For example, Frankfurter 1998, 7; Lim 2003, 8; Clark 2004, 14; Bowes 2008, 10–11.
8. Gregory 1979; Perrin 2001; Garnsey and Humfress 2001, 134–136; Maxwell 2006.
9. On lay devotion, see Frank 2007.
10. Sandwell 2007.
11. On the unselfconsciousness of traditional religions, see Fowden 1999, 83–87.
12. For examples of Christian anti-pagan polemic, see Firmicus Maternus; Arnobius of Sicca; Augustine, *Serm.* 198.
13. Frankfurter 1998; 2007; Fowden 1988; 1999; Sandwell 2007.
14. Pagels 1995, 112–148; Flint 1999.
15. See essays in Athanassiadi and Frede 1999.

16. Chuvin 1990, 8–9. For recent discussions and solutions: Clark 2004, 35; North 2005, 127–128, 134–137; Sandwell 2007, 10–11; Frankfurter 2007, 174; Salzman 2008, 187–189.

17. Frankfurter 1998, 33.

18. Cf. the lack of clear boundaries between Judaism and Christianity: Fonrobert 2005; between Judaism and paganism: Mitchell 1999.

19. For emphasis on elite pagans as the fighters: Bloch 1963; Geffcken 1978; Chuvin 1990; Harl 1990. Other scholars downplay or reject the notion of an organized pagan "resistance movement": Alan Cameron 1984; Salzman 2008, 191–194.

20. For regional studies: see note 6.

21. On Heliopolis and Carrhae, see Harl 1990, 14; for Asia Minor, see Mitchell 1993; Egypt, Bagnall 1993, 278–283.

22. Bradbury 1995.

23. On Constantine's intentions, see Barnes 1994. Cf. Lane Fox 1987, 671–672; Van Dam 2007.

24. On the difficulties of gauging the religious changes resulting from the Theodosian Code, see Hunt 1993. For laws as prescriptive rather than descriptive, see Salzman 1993, 362.

25. On pagan monotheism, see essays in Athanassiadi and Frede 1999.

26. Geffcken 1978, 30.

27. North 2005, 142.

28. For Christian descriptions of sacrifice and idolatry, see note 12.

29. Sandwell 2005. See note 66.

30. Bradbury 1995, 351.

31. Harl 1990, 10, 14; cf. Bradbury 1995, 345.

32. Sandwell 2007, 74–80, 251–252; Frankfurter 1998, 24–25.

33. Frankfurter 1998, 20; See also MacMullen 1984, 104; 1997, 32–73.

34. Julian, *Misop*. 361d–62b.

35. Amm. Marc. 22.12.6–7, 25.4.17.

36. Bradbury 1995, 342; Sandwell 2007, 96–86, 216–225.

37. Bradbury 1995, 345.

38. Council of Laodicea, canon 28.

39. On sacrifice in Armenian Christianity, see Conybeare 1903. Paulinus of Nola, *Carm*. 20. See Trout 1995. On Nicholas, see Trombley 2007, 202–203. On the changing notions about sacrifice during this time, especially in Judaism, see Stroumsa 2005.

40. Emphasis on common ground: see Frankfurter 1998; 2005, 267–268; Graf 1997, 15–19; Flint, 1999.

41. On "popular religion," see Frankfurter 2005, 255–271; Brown 1981; MacMullen 1997, 80.

42. See examples of Christian clergy involved in magic in Wortley, 2001. On evil eye, see Dickie 1995; Limberis 1991.

43. Libanius, *Or*. 1.245–249. Sandwell 2005, 111–113; Luck 2006, 461–462.

44. On the continuity of images on amulets in addition to Christian themes, see Luck 2006, 467. On Christian use of texts as amulets, see van der Horst 1998. For translations of Christian magical texts, see Meyer et al. 1999.

45. On the Kalends festivities, see Meslin 1970. Augustine singles out the "real Christians" in contrast to those who attended the spectacles: *Serm*. 198.3.

46. Shenoute, *Acephalous Works* A14, quoted and discussed by Frankfurter 2005, 261–262. For similar issues in Asia Minor, see Trombley 2007, 191–194.

47. Maxwell 2006, 118–119, 165–167.

48. Aug. *Serm.* 198.10, 16; Brown 1998a.

49. Saints' shrines: Brown 1981. Angels: Council of Laodicea, canon 35. Leo the Great, *Serm.* 27.4. Maximus of Turin, *Serm.* 30.2; cf. Caesarius of Arles, *Serm.* 13.5, 52.3. Martin of Braga, *De Correctione rusticorum*, 8.

50. *Life of Theodore of Sykeon* 37–38; *Life of St. Martin* 1, 26–27. Frankfurter 2005, 276–277. See also examples in Wortley 2001, 295–307.

51. Jerome, *Vita S. Hilarionis* 20; Flint 1999, 341–342. On the centrality of such supernatural events to late antique Christianity, see MacMullen 1997, 92–96.

52. Meyer et al. 1999, esp. 259–262.

53. Luck 2006, 464–468; Flint 1999, 324–348.

54. Graf 1997, 46.

55. Drake 1996.

56. On Martin, see Salzman 2006, 278–282; against focus on religious conflict, see Clark 2004, 115–116; Hahn 2004; Salzman 2008.

57. On the destruction of temples as both events and as part of Christian discourse, see the essays in Hahn et al. 2008.

58. Theodoret *H.E.* 3.7.1; cf. Socrates *H.E.* 3.15; Sozomen *H.E.* 5.8–11.

59. For graphic examples of judicial torture, see Harries 1999, 122–134; Shaw 2003, esp. 538–540.

60. Accounts of the murder of George: Amm. Marc. 22.11.3ff.; Socrates *H.E.* 3.2; Sozomen *H.E.* 5.7.

61. Amm. Marc. 22.11.1–11.

62. On an additional account from a seventh-century Monophysite source that demonized the philosopher and championed her killers, see Watts 2006, 338–340.

63. See Gaddis 2005, who emphasizes the role of "extremists" or "zealots" in violent conflicts. For example, Theophilus and Shenoute are placed squarely out of the mainstream as a "tyrant bishop" and a zealot: 251–254.

64. According to Drake, conflicts arising from competing Christian sects and Julian's pagan revival encouraged the development of a combative approach toward rivals from Christian emperors and bishops: Drake 1996, 27–35. Against this view of Constantine as tolerant, see Barnes 1994, 322–325. On Constantine's restrictions of pagan worship, see also Chuvin 1990, 28–35.

65. Salzman 1993, 375. The full context of violence and coercion includes the conflicts among Christian sects, as well as Christian aggression against Jewish communities, which are both beyond the scope of this chapter.

66. Frankfurter 2007, 186.

67. Ban on sacrifice: *C.Th.* 16.10.2; protection of temples: *C.Th.* 16.10.3.

68. Constantius: *C.Th.* 16.10.2–6; Theodosius: *C.Th.* 16.10.104–111. On second- and third-century laws against certain pagan religious practices, see Sandwell 2005, 94–95.

69. On the influence of Constantine's religion on his laws, see Biondi 1952–1954; Barnes 1981, 210–212, 246–248, 254–255; 1994, 322–325. Cf. Sandwell 2005, 119–123; Salzman 1987, 177–180. See also Uhalde, chapter 23 in this book.

70. Libanius, *Or.* 1.201; *Or.* 14; *Or.* 30. On the limited role of imperial laws in the destruction of temples, see Fowden 1978.

71. Sandwell 2005, 121.

72. *C.Th.* 16.10.24. See Watts 2006, 335, esp. note 12 on "acceptable violence."

73. Libanius, *Or.* 30.26–27.

74. MacMullen 1984, 27–28, 59–62. More recently, see Clark 2004, 24.

75. Jones 1963.

76. Salzman 2002, esp. 66, 202. See Maximus of Turin's call for landowners to end pagan practices among the peasants working their land, *Serm.* 107.

77. Fowden 1988.

78. Frankfurter 1998, 19–20, 31–32.

79. Averil Cameron 1997, 23–25.

80. Brown 1998b, 664.

81. For the conversion of a prostitute, see the *Life of Saint Mary of Egypt.* For the conversion of a magician, see Gregory of Nazianzus' account of St. Cyprian in *Or.* 24.

82. Ogden 2002, 213–214, 220, 268. For examples of Christian magic, see Meyer et al. 1999; Kotansky 2001. On the continuity of themes and usage across religions, see Engemann 1975.

83. Lim 2003; Piepenbrink 2005, 47–48, 283–291; Klingshirn 1994.

84. John of Ephesus, *Lives of the Eastern Saints,* PO 17.1, 236–237.

85. For "semi-Christians" and "paganized Christians" as people outside the mainstream, see Bonner 1984, 350–351. On good, bad, and semi-Christians, see Piepenbrink 2005, 132–161.

86. Fowden 1999, 84–85.

87. Sandwell 2007.

88. Beard, North, and Price 1998, 387–388.

89. Socrates, *H. E.* 2.46.

90. On "hyper-Christianization," see Brown 1998b, 655.

91. Garnsey and Humfress 2001, 165; Klingshirn 1994; Lim 2003; McLynn 2003; Elm 2003; Uhalde 2007; Bowes 2008.

92. MacMullen 1986. Cf. Clark 2004, 106. See also Harper, chapter 20 in this book.

93. Carrié 2001; Salamito 2001; Garnsey and Humfress 2001, 151; Maxwell 2006, 171–175.

94. On the poor as "the people": Brown 2002, 33–35; little change in living conditions: 92–94.

95. Augustine, *Serm.* 198.3,7. On the originality of Church gatherings, Brown 1998b, 653.

96. On violence and religious factions, see Gregory 1979; Gaddis 2005.

97. Frankfurter 1998; Brown 1995, 8–13.

98. Curran 2000, 218–259.

99. Dodds 1990. Frankfurter 1998, 19–20.

WORKS CITED

Ancient Sources

Ammianus Marcellinus. *Ammiani Marcellini rerum gestarum libri qui supersunt.* Ed. W. Seyfarth. Leipzig, 1999.

Arnobius of Sicca. *Adversus nationes.* Ed. C. Marchesi, CSL Paravianum 62. Turin, 1934.

Augustine. *Sermon 198 (Mayence 62).* Ed. François Dolbeau, *Augustin d'Hippone: Vingt-Six sermons au people d'Afrique.* Paris, 1996.

Besa. *Life of Shenoute*. Ed. J. Leipoldt and W. E. Crum, *Sinuthii Archimandritae Vita et Opera Omnia*. CSCO 41, Scriptores Coptici 1. Paris, 1906.
Caesarius of Arles. *Sermones*. Ed. G. Morin, CCSL 103–104. Turnhout, 1953.
Codex Theodosianus. Ed. T. Mommsen and P. Meyer, *Theodosiani libri XVI cum constitutionibus Sirmondianis: et leges novellae ad Theodosianum pertinentes*, 2 vols. in 3. Berlin, 1954. For *C. Th.* 16, see SC 497. Paris, 2005.
Council of Laodicea. Ed. J. Mansi, *Sacrorum conciliorum collectio* 2. Paris, 1758–1798.
Firmicus Maternus. *De errore profanarum religionum*. Ed. Robert Turcan. Paris, 1982.
Georgios Hegoumenos. *Vita Theodori Syceotai* (Theodore of Sykeon). Ed. A. J. Festugière, *Vie de Théodore de Sykéôn*, SH 48. Brussels, 1970.
Gregory of Nazianzus. *Oratio* 24. Ed. J. Mossay and G. Lafontaine, *Discours 24–26*, SC 284. Paris, 1981.
Jerome. *Vita S. Hilarionis*. Ed. E. Morales, in *Trois Vies de Moines: Paul, Malchus, Hilarion*, SC 508. Paris, 2007.
John of Ephesus. *Lives of the Eastern Saints*. Ed. E. W. Brooks, PO 17–19. Turnhout, 1923.
Julian. *Opera*. Ed. J. Bidez, *Oeuvres complètes*. Paris, 1924–1932.
Leo the Great. *Sermones*. Ed. A. Chavasse, *Tractatus*, CCSL 138–138A. Turnhout, 1973.
Libanius. *Orationes*. Ed. R. Foerster, *Opera*, vols. 1–4. Leipzig, 1903–1908.
Martin of Braga. *De Correctione rusticorum*. Ed. Mario Naldini. Florence, 1991.
Maximus of Turin. *Collectio sermonum*. Ed. Almut Mutzenbecher, CCSL 23. Turnhout, 1962.
Paulinus of Nola. *Carmina*. Ed. G. von Hartel, CSEL 30^2. Vienna, 1999.
Shenoute. *Acephalous Works*. Ed. Tito Orlandi, *Contra Origenistas*. Rome, 1985.
Socrates. *Historia ecclesiastica*. Ed. G. C. Hansen, GCS N. F. 1. Berlin, 1995.
Sozomen. *Historia ecclesiastica*. Ed. J. Bidez, GCS 50. Berlin, 1960.
Sulpicius Severus. *Vita S. Martini*. Ed. Jacques Fontaine, SC 133–135. Paris, 1967–1969.
Theodoret. *Historia Ecclesiastica*. Ed. Léon Parmentier, GCS N. F. 5. Berlin, 1998.
Vita S. Mariae Aegyptiacae, Meretricis. PG 87(3): 3693–3726. PL 73: 671–690.

Modern Sources

Athanassiadi, Polymnia, and Michael Frede, eds. 1999. *Pagan Monotheism in Late Antiquity*. Oxford: Clarendon Press.
Bagnall, Roger. 1993. *Egypt in Late Antiquity*. Princeton, NJ: Princeton University Press.
Barnes, Timothy D. 1981. *Constantine and Eusebius*. Cambridge, MA: Harvard University Press.
———. 1994. "Christians and Pagans in the Reign of Constantius." In *From Eusebius to Augustine*, 322–337. Aldershot: Ashgate.
Beard, Mary, John North, and Simon Price. 1998. *Religions of Rome*, 2 vols. Cambridge: Cambridge University Press.
Biondi, Biondo. 1952–1954. *Il Diritto Romano Cristiano*, 3 vols. Milan: Dott. A. Giuffrè Editore.
Bloch, Herbert. 1963. "The Pagan Revival in the West at the End of the Fourth Century." In *The Conflict between Paganism and Christianity in the Fourth Century*, ed. Arnaldo D. Momigliano, 193–218. Oxford: Clarendon Press.
Bonner, Gerald. 1984. "The Extinction of Paganism and the Church Historian," *Journal of Ecclesiastical History* 35.3: 339–357.

Bowes, Kim. 2008. *Private Worship, Public Values, and Religious Change in Late Antiquity*. Cambridge: Cambridge University Press.

Bradbury, Scott. 1995. "Julian's Pagan Revival and the Decline of Blood Sacrifice," *Phoenix* 49: 331–356.

Brown, Peter. 1981. *The Cult of the Saints: Its Rise and Function in Latin Christianity*. Chicago: University of Chicago Press.

———. 1995. *Authority and the Sacred: Aspects of the Christianisation of the Roman World*. Cambridge: Cambridge University Press.

———. 1998a. "Augustine and a Practice of the Imperiti." In *Augustin Prédicateur (395–411): Actes du Colloque International de Chantilly*, ed. Goulven Madec, 367–375. Paris: Institut d'Études Augustiniennes.

———. 1998b. "Christianization and Religious Conflict." In *Cambridge Ancient History, Vol. 13: The Late Empire, A.D. 337–425*, ed. Averil Cameron and Peter Garnsey, 632–664. Cambridge: Cambridge University Press.

———. 2002. *Poverty and Leadership in the Later Roman Empire*. Hanover, NH: University Press of New England.

Cameron, Alan. 1968. "Gratian's Repudiation of the Pontifical Robe," *Journal of Roman Studies* 58: 96–102.

———. 1984. "The Latin Revival of the Fourth Century." In *Renaissances before the Renaissance: Cultural Revivals of Late Antiquity and the Middle Ages*, ed. Warren Treadgold, 42–58. Stanford, CA: Stanford University Press.

Cameron, Averil. 1997. "Christianity and Communication in the Fourth Century: The Problem of Diffusion." In *Aspects of the Fourth Century A.D., Proceedings of the Symposium Power & Possession: State, Society, and Church in the Fourth Century A.D.*, ed. H. W. Pleket and A. M. F. W. Verhoogt, 3–42. Leiden: Agape.

Carrié, Jean-Michel. 2001. "Antiquité Tardive et 'Démocratisation de la Culture': Un paradigme à géométrie variable," *Antiquité Tardive* 9: 27–46.

Chuvin, Pierre. 1990. *A Chronicle of the Last Pagans*. Trans. B. A. Archer. Cambridge, MA: Harvard University Press.

Clark, Gillian. 2004. *Christianity and Roman Society*. Cambridge: Cambridge University Press.

Conybeare, Fred. 1903. "The Survival of Animal Sacrifices inside the Christian Church," *American Journal of Theology* 7.1: 62–90.

Curran, John. 2000. *Pagan City and Christian Capital: Rome in the Fourth Century*. Oxford: Clarendon.

Dickie, M. W. 1995. "The Fathers of the Church and the Evil Eye." In *Byzantine Magic*, ed. Henry Maguire, 9–34. Washington, DC: Dumbarton Oaks Research Library and Collection.

Dodds, E. R. [1965] 1990. *Pagan and Christian in an Age of Anxiety: Some Aspects of Religious Experience from Marcus Aurelius to Constantine*. Cambridge: Cambridge University Press.

Drake, H. A. 1996. "Lambs into Lions: Explaining Early Christian Intolerance," *Past &Present* 153: 3–36.

Elm, Susanna. 2003. "Inscriptions and Conversions: Gregory of Nazianzus on Baptism (*Or.* 38–40)." In *Conversion in Late Antiquity and the Early Middle Ages: Seeing and Believing*, ed. Kenneth Mills and Anthony Grafton, 1–35. Rochester, NY: University of Rochester Press.

Engemann, Josef. 1975. "Zur Verbreitung magischer Übelabwehr in der nichtchristlichen und christlichen Spätantike," *Jahrbuch für Antike und Christentum* 18: 22–48.

Flint, Valerie. 1999. "The Demonisation of Magic and Sorcery in Late Antiquity: Christian Redefinitions of Pagan Religions." In *Witchcraft and Magic in Europe: Ancient Greece and Rome*, ed. Bengt Ankarloo and Stuart Clark, 279–348. Philadelphia: University of Pennsylvania Press.

Fonrobert, Charlotte Elisheva. 2005. "Jewish Christians, Judaizers, and Christian Anti-Judaism." In *Late Ancient Christianity*, ed. Virginia Burrus, 234–254. A People's History of Christianity 2. Minneapolis, MN: Fortress Press.

Fowden, Garth. 1978. "Bishops and Temples in the Eastern Roman Empire," *Journal of Theological Studies* 29.1: 53–78.

———. 1988. "Between Pagans and Christians," *Journal of Roman Studies* 78: 173–182.

———. 1999. "Religious Communities." In *Late Antiquity: A Guide to the Postclassical World*, ed. G. W. Bowersock, Peter Brown, and Oleg Grabar, 82–106. Cambridge, MA: Belknap Press of Harvard University Press.

Frank, Georgia. 2007. "From Antioch to Arles: Lay Devotion in Context." In *Cambridge History of Christianity, Vol. 2: Constantine to c. 600*, ed. Augustine Casiday and Frederick W. Norris, 531–547. Cambridge: Cambridge University Press.

Frankfurter, David. 1998. *Religion in Roman Egypt: Assimilation and Resistance*. Princeton, NJ: Princeton University Press.

———. 2005. "Beyond Magic and Superstition." In *Late Ancient Christianity*, ed. Virginia Burrus, 255–284. A People's History of Christianity 2. Minneapolis, MN: Fortress Press.

———. 2007. "Christianity and Paganism I: Egypt." In *Cambridge History of Christianity, Vol. 2: Constantine to c. 600*, ed. Augustine Casiday and Frederick W. Norris, 173–188. Cambridge: Cambridge University Press.

Gaddis, Michael. 2005. *There Is No Crime for Those Who Have Christ: Religious Violence in the Christian Roman Empire*. Berkeley: University of California Press.

Garnsey, Peter, and Caroline Humfress. 2001. *The Evolution of the Late Antique World*. Cambridge: Orchard Academic.

Geffcken, Johannes. [1929] 1978. *The Last Days of Greco-Roman Paganism*. Trans. Sabine MacCormack. New York: North-Holland.

Graf, Fritz. [1994] 1997. *Magic in the Ancient World*. Trans. Franklin Philip. Cambridge, MA: Harvard University Press.

Gregory, Timothy. 1979. *Vox Populi: Popular Opinion and Violence in the Religious Controversies of the Fifth Century A.D.* Columbus: Ohio State University Press.

Hahn, Johannes. 2004. *Gewalt und religiöser Konflikt: Studien zu den Auseinandersetzungen zwischen Christen, Heiden und Juden im Osten des Römischen Reiches [von Konstantin bis Theodosius II]*. Berlin: Akademie Verlag.

Hahn, Johannes, Stephen Emmel, and Ulrich Gotter, eds. 2008. *From Temple to Church: Destruction and Renewal of Local Cultic Topography in Late Antiquity*. Leiden: Brill.

Harl, Kenneth. 1990. "Sacrifice and Pagan Belief in Fifth- and Sixth-Century Byzantium," *Past & Present* 128: 7–27.

Harries, Jill. 1999. *Law and Empire in Late Antiquity*. Cambridge: Cambridge University Press.

Horst, Pieter van der. 1998. "*Sortes*: Sacred Books as Instant Oracles in Late Antiquity." In *The Use of Sacred Books in the Ancient World*, ed. L. V. Rutgers, 143–173. Leuven: Peeters.

Hunt, David. 1993. "Christianising the Roman Empire: The Evidence of the Code." In *The Theodosian Code*, ed. Jill Harries and Ian Wood, 143–158. Ithaca, NY: Cornell University Press.

Jones, A. H. M. 1963. "The Social Background of the Struggle between Paganism and Christianity." In *The Conflict between Paganism and Christianity in the Fourth Century*, ed. Arnaldo Momigliano, 17–37. Oxford: Clarendon Press.

Klingshirn, William. 1994. *Caesarius of Arles: The Making of a Christian Community in Late Antique Gaul.* Cambridge: Cambridge University Press.

Kotansky, Roy. 2001. "An Early Christian Gold Lamella for Headache." In *Magic and Ritual in the Ancient World*, ed. Paul Mirecki and Marvin Meyer, 3–24. Leiden: Brill.

Lane Fox, Robin. 1987. *Pagans and Christians.* New York: Knopf.

Lim, Richard. 2003. "Converting the Un-Christianizable: The Baptism of Stage Performers in Late Antiquity." In *Conversion in Late Antiquity and the Early Middle Ages: Seeing and Believing*, ed. Kenneth Mills and Anthony Grafton, 84–126. Rochester, NY: University of Rochester Press.

Limberis, Vasiliki. 1991. "The Eyes Infected by Evil: Basil of Caesarea's Homily, 'On Envy'," *Harvard Theological Review* 84.2: 163–184.

Luck, Georg, ed. [1985] 2006. *Arcana Mundi: Magic and the Occult in the Greek and Roman Worlds: A Collection of Ancient Texts.* Baltimore: Johns Hopkins University Press.

MacMullen, Ramsay. 1984. *Christianizing the Roman Empire, A.D. 100–400.* New Haven, CT: Yale University Press.

———. 1986. "What Difference Did Christianity Make?" *Historia* 35: 322–343.

———. 1997. *Christianity and Paganism in the Fourth to Eighth Centuries.* New Haven, CT: Yale University Press, 1997.

Matthews, John F. 2000. *Laying Down the Law: A Study of the Theodosian Code.* New Haven, CT: Yale University Press.

Maxwell, Jaclyn. 2006. *Christianization and Communication in Late Antiquity: John Chrysostom and His Congregation in Antioch.* Cambridge: Cambridge University Press.

McLynn, Neil. 2003. "Seeing and Believing: Aspects of Conversion from Antoninus Pius to Louis the Pious." In *Conversion in Late Antiquity and the Early Middle Ages: Seeing and Believing*, ed. Kenneth Mills and Anthony Grafton, 224–270. Rochester, NY: University of Rochester Press.

Meslin, Michel. 1970. *La Fête des Kalendes de Janvier dans l'Empire Romain: Étude d'un rituel de nouvel an.* Bruxelles: Latomus.

Meyer, Marvin, Richard Smith, and Neal Kelsey, eds. [1994] 1999. *Ancient Christian Magic: Coptic Texts of Ritual Power.* Princeton, NJ: Princeton University Press.

Mitchell, Stephen. 1993. *Anatolia: Land, Men, and Gods in Asia Minor.* Oxford: Clarendon Press.

———. 1999. "The Cult of Theos Hypsistos between Pagans, Jews and Christians." In *Pagan Monotheism in Late Antiquity*, ed. Polymnia Athanassiadi and Michael Frede, 81–148. Oxford: Clarendon Press.

North, J. A. 2005. "Pagans, Polytheists and the Pendulum." In *The Spread of Christianity in the First Four Centuries: Essays in Explanation*, ed. W. V. Harris, 125–143. Leiden: Brill.

Ogden, Daniel. 2002. *Magic, Witchcraft, and Ghosts in the Greek and Roman Worlds: A Sourcebook.* Oxford: Oxford University Press.

Pagels, Elaine. 1995. *The Origin of Satan.* New York: Random House.

Perrin, Michel-Yves. 2001. "À propos de la participation des fidèles aux controverses doctrinales dans l'Antiquité Tardive: Considérations introductives," *Antiquité Tardive* 9: 179–199.

Piepenbrink, Karen. 2005. *Christliche Identität und Assimilation in der Spätantike: Probleme des Christseins in der Reflexion der Zeitgenossen*. Frankfurt: Verlag Antike.

Salamito, Jean-Marie. 2001. "Christianisation et démocratisation de la culture: Aspects aristocratiques et aspects populaires de l'être-chrétien aux IIIe et IVe siècles," *Antiquité Tardive* 9: 165–178.

Salzman, Michele. 1987. "'Superstitio' in the Codex Theodosianus and the Persecution of Pagans," *Vigiliae Christianae* 41: 172–188.

———. 1993. "The Evidence for the Conversion of the Roman Empire to Christianity in Book 16 of the *Theodosian Code*," *Historia* 42: 362–378.

———. 2002. *The Making of a Christian Aristocracy: Social and Religious Change in the Western Roman Empire*. Cambridge, MA: Harvard University Press.

———. 2006. "Rethinking Pagan-Christian Violence." In *Violence in Late Antiquity*, ed. H. A. Drake, 263–284. Aldershot: Ashgate.

———. 2007. "Christianity and Paganism III: Italy." In *Cambridge History of Christianity, Vol. 2: Constantine to c. 600*, ed. Augustine Casiday and Frederick W. Norris, 210–230. Cambridge: Cambridge University Press.

———. 2008. "Pagans and Christians." In *The Oxford Handbook of Early Christian Studies*, ed. Susan Ashbrook Harvey and David Hunter, 186–202. Oxford: Oxford University Press.

Sandwell, Isabella. 2005. "Outlawing 'Magic' or Outlawing 'Religion'? Libanius and the Theodosian Code as Evidence for Legislation against 'Pagan' Practices." In *The Spread of Christianity in the First Four Centuries*, ed. W. V. Harris, 87–123. Leiden: Brill.

———. 2007. *Religious Identity in Late Antiquity: Greeks, Jews and Christians in Antioch*. Cambridge: Cambridge University Press.

Shaw, Brent. 2003. "Judicial Nightmares and Christian Memory," *Journal of Early Christian Studies* 11: 533–563.

Stroumsa, Guy. 2005. *La fin du sacrifice: Les mutations religieuses de l'antiquité tardive*. Paris: Odile Jacob.

Trombley, Frank. [1993–1994] 2001. *Hellenic Religion and Christianization, c. 370–529 CE*. 2 vols. Religions in the Graeco-Roman World 115. Boston: Brill Academic.

———. 2007. "Christianity and Paganism II: Asia Minor." In *Cambridge History of Christianity, Vol. 2: Constantine to c. 600*, ed. Augustine Casiday and Frederick W. Norris, 189–209. Cambridge: Cambridge University Press.

Trout, Dennis. 1995. *Paulinus of Nola: Life, Letters, and Poems*. Berkeley: University of California Press.

Uhalde, Kevin. 2007. *Expectations of Justice in the Age of Augustine*. Philadelphia: University of Pennsylvania Press.

Van Dam, Raymond. 2007. *The Roman Revolution of Constantine*. Cambridge: Cambridge University Press.

Veyne, Paul. 2007. *Quand notre monde est devenu chrétien (312–394)*. Paris: Albin Michel.

Watts, Edward. 2006. "The Murder of Hypatia: Acceptable or Unacceptable Violence?" In *Violence in Late Antiquity: Perceptions and Practices*, ed. H. A. Drake, 333–342. Aldershot: Ashgate.

Wortley, John. 2001. "Some Light on Magic and Magicians in Late Antiquity," *Greek, Roman, and Byzantine Studies* 43: 289–307.

CHAPTER 27

EPISCOPAL LEADERSHIP

DAVID M. GWYNN

Royal Holloway, University of London

Introduction

The emergence of the Christian bishop as a figure of fundamental religious, social, and political importance is one of the defining characteristics of Late Antiquity. The spread of Christianity across the Mediterranean world, before and particularly after the conversion of Constantine, the first Christian Roman emperor, placed enormous strains on the fabric of the Church. In this changing environment, episcopal leadership became ever more crucial, both within the Christian community and in the wider empire. Bishops acquired new responsibilities in their cities and provinces, at the imperial court, and beyond the frontiers. This chapter explores the widely varying roles that bishops came to play in Late Antiquity and the debates over the nature and functions of episcopal leadership inspired by the rising status of bishops and of the Christian Church.

The roles open to the late antique bishop took many forms, and so of course did the bishops themselves. Much of our evidence derives from the great fathers of the Church: Athanasius of Alexandria, Basil of Caesarea, Gregory of Nazianzus, Ambrose of Milan, John Chrysostom, Augustine of Hippo, Gregory the Great. Their careers and writings were to exert vast influence on later centuries. But the models of episcopal leadership that they offer at times conceal the sheer diversity of the backgrounds, motivations, and actions of those who held the office of bishop during Late Antiquity. It is important to look as broadly as possible at bishops in different social, geographical, and chronological contexts and to seek to identify the essential elements that remain constant in defining the nature and functions of episcopal leadership. We therefore need to begin with the origins of the office of the bishop and to assess the impact of the reign of Constantine on that office and on the opportunities now open to those who attained episcopal status. The changing place of the bishop within the Christian Roman empire must then be traced through the collapse of imperial power in the West and the roles played by bishops in the early Germanic kingdoms and in the eastern empire down to the rise of Islam.

The Office of the Bishop before Constantine

> Whoever aspires to the office of bishop (*episkopos*) desires a noble task. Now a bishop must be above reproach, married only once, temperate, sensible, respectable, hospitable, an apt teacher, not a drunkard, not violent but gentle, not quarrelsome, and not a lover of money. He must manage his own household well, keeping his children submissive and respectful in every way—for if someone does not know how to manage his own household, how can he take care of God's church? He must not be a recent convert, or he may be puffed up with conceit and fall into the condemnation of the devil. Moreover, he must be well thought of by outsiders, so that he may not fall into disgrace and the snare of the devil.[1]

The origins of the office of the bishop, like so much of the early history of Christianity, is controversial.[2] The clerical hierarchy that had emerged by the end of the late antique period did not evolve along a single consistent path, and the early Church saw considerable debate over the position and role of the *episkopos* ("overseer"). If we are to assess the place of the episcopate in Late Antiquity, it is essential to look briefly at these debates across the first three Christian centuries. Those years witnessed the gradual rise of the monarchical bishop as the leading representative of his see and laid the foundations for the further development of episcopal leadership following the conversion of Constantine in the early fourth century.

In New Testament texts, the term *episkopos* is often used synonymously with presbyter (elder) to identify the local leaders of the first Christian communities.[3] Thus Paul addressed his Epistle to the Philippians to "the bishops and deacons,"[4] who were responsible for overseeing church property and who performed the earliest version of the liturgy. There could evidently be multiple *episkopoi* within a given community in this early period, and these local clergy were seen to possess less authority than inspired traveling apostolic teachers such as Paul himself who instructed them.[5] The same context is visible in the *Didache*, the oldest extant church order, probably composed in early-second-century Syria or Palestine.[6] The *Didache* urges that good men should be chosen for clerical office and saw the need to defend their authority as not to be despised in comparison with the itinerant charismatic teachers.[7] The only New Testament text to discuss the episcopate in any detail, the pseudo-Pauline First Letter to Timothy quoted above,[8] similarly emphasizes that a bishop should be moral and respected.[9] But it is not apparent that the author of 1 Timothy wished to set the episcopate apart as superior to all other clerical offices, and the bishop's role is primarily that of a moral exemplar rather than a spiritual leader.

The earliest explicit defense of what would become known as the monarchical episcopate, a single bishop at the head of each individual Christian community, is approximately contemporary to the First Letter to Timothy. Ignatius of Antioch, martyred in Rome under the emperor Trajan in about 115, composed a series of letters as he traveled to meet his fate.[10] In those letters, he repeatedly upholds the bishop as the representative of God on earth and the sole guarantee of unity within his see. Only the bishop could administer the sacraments, with no role for the wandering charismatic teacher and the presbyters and deacons now clearly defined as subordinate clergy. The bishop must still provide an exemplar of Christian conduct, as in the First Letter to Timothy. But for Ignatius, the bishop is also responsible for spiritual, pastoral, and liturgical leadership, for only through him can the community share in the wider Church of Christ.

> Follow, all of you, the bishop, as Jesus Christ followed the Father; and follow the presbytery as the apostles. Moreover, reverence the deacons as the commandment of God. Let no man do aught pertaining to the Church apart from the bishop. Let that Eucharist be considered valid which is under the bishop or him to whom he commits it. Wheresoever the bishop appears, there let the people be, even as wheresoever Christ Jesus is, there is the Catholic Church. It is not lawful apart from the bishop either to baptize, or to hold a love-feast. But whatsoever he approves, that also is well-pleasing to God, that everything which you do may be secure and valid.[11]

The views of Ignatius were by no means necessarily representative of the Church of his time. The early Christian communities varied widely in structure as in much else,[12] and the transition from the more diverse hierarchy of the first Christian generations to the later principle of "one community, one bishop" was not a simple or uniform process. Nevertheless, in the course of the second and third centuries, the monarchical bishop gradually became the dominant institution of the early Church. By the time of Ignatius in the early second century, the original apostles were dead, and with their passing and the fading of immediate eschatological expectations, the Church faced a crisis of authority. Organization and unity became ever more important to maintain a common faith and a common moral life, reaffirmed by the shared rituals of baptism and the Eucharist. In this period of Christian redefinition, episcopal leadership was to prove the most effective guarantee to uphold and strengthen the bonds within and between communities. It was thus the bishops who emerged as the heirs of the apostles, ensuring the continuity of Christian teaching and morality through the rule of apostolic succession, which received its classic evocation in the *Adversus Haereses* of Irenaeus of Lyons (c. 130–c. 200).[13]

The rise of the monarchical bishop did not go unchallenged. There were those who regretted the decline of the charismatic wandering teachers and who decried the autocratic insistence on a single episcopal leader. The question of authority and who had the right to guide the Christian community was a recurring theme of the Montanist controversy,[14] and of the debates over what is now known as "Gnosticism", within which context Irenaeus wrote his *Adversus Haereses.*[15] These conflicts of the second and third centuries failed to halt the growing importance of episcopal leadership in the early Church, but they highlighted the permanent tension that underlay the monarchical episcopate. The office of the bishop united charismatic and administrative authority in a single figure.[16] Yet the concept of apostolic succession in particular placed increasing emphasis on the office rather than the person of the bishop, whose status rested on his hierarchical relationship to the apostles rather than on his own virtue. This left bishops vulnerable to challenge from others who could lay claim to charismatic inspiration. Origen in early third-century Alexandria recognized the authority of the bishop but also believed that a teacher might challenge an unworthy cleric.[17] As we shall see, the same tensions would revive in the fourth century with the appearance of the ascetic holy man.

By the middle of the third century, the authority and roles of the bishop had become far more clearly defined.[18] Yet debates over the scope and nature of episcopal authority continued. This changing environment is perhaps best encapsulated in the career of Cyprian, bishop of Carthage 248/9–258.[19] Born into a well-off family and converted as an adult, Cyprian as bishop played important roles both within his community and in wider society. He led his congregation through preaching and the liturgy and oversaw the wealth he used to support the poor and the sick, in one instance sending money to Numidian bishops to aid them in ransoming Christian captives taken by marauding nomads.[20] He also represented the Carthaginian church before the local imperial officials and in correspondence with other churches,[21] roles that had become increasingly important as Christianity expanded in the third century.

After Cyprian fled his see during the persecution of Decius in 251, however, he faced potential opposition from the confessors whose witness to the faith gave them their own spiritual authority. The confessors and the bishop particularly came into conflict over penitential discipline, over who had the authority to judge those who had lapsed and to alleviate their sins.[22] In two great works, *On the Lapsed* and *On the Unity of the Catholic Church*, Cyprian insisted upon the bishop as the focus of Christian unity on earth, although the bishop could heed the confessors' advice. Thus he upheld the status of the bishop's office, but in defending his position, he confronted a question that would continue to trouble later generations, whether a bishop who failed to maintain the standards required by his office could claim the authority of that office. This question was to divide the North African church for centuries through the Donatist Schism, which began in the early fourth century.[23] Cyprian further insisted on the equality of all bishops, particularly during the controversy over the rebaptism of schismatics that brought him into conflict with Stephen of Rome (254–257), the first bishop of Rome to begin to claim a degree of supremacy through his Petrine authority.[24]

When Eusebius of Caesarea began to compose his *Ecclesiastical History* in the late third century, the Christian Church had spread widely across the Mediterranean world.[25] Bishops were now public figures. The deposition of Paul of Samosata as bishop of Antioch in 268 was followed in 272 by an appeal to the emperor Aurelian to expel Paul from the church property he occupied.[26] Bishops were targeted for special persecution under Valerian in 257–260, when Cyprian died, and particularly during the Great Persecution of Diocletian, 303–313.[27] By the accession of Constantine in 306, the traditional pattern of episcopal leadership was thus already firmly in place. The rise of the monarchical bishop had played a crucial part in securing the unity of the Church through the difficult years of the second and third centuries, and the spiritual, moral, and administrative roles of the episcopate were well established. This model would exert vast influence upon the bishops of Late Antiquity, although much would inevitably change in the fourth century with the emergence of a Christian emperor.

The Impact of Constantine

> The event was beyond all description. Guards and soldiers ringed the entrance to the palace, guarding it with drawn swords, and between these the men of God passed fearlessly, and others relaxed nearby on couches on either side. It might have been supposed that it was an imaginary representation of the kingdom of Christ.[28]

Eusebius of Caesarea's famous account of the bishops at the Council of Nicaea in 325 entering the imperial palace to celebrate Constantine's *vicennalia* dramatically evokes the new world opened for the bishops by the conversion of the first Christian emperor. Following his victory over Maxentius at the Battle of the Milvian Bridge in 312, Constantine in the West had already begun to pour resources and privileges into the Church, which he extended to the eastern regions of the empire after his conquest of Licinius in 324. From this time onward, with only the very short interlude of Constantine's pagan nephew

Julian "the Apostate" (361–363), the Christian hierarchy would be intimately tied to the state and would exert an ever-increasing influence on all areas of late Roman society.

The reign of Constantine marks a watershed in Roman and Christian history, yet we must not exaggerate his impact on the nature and functions of episcopal leadership.[29] Many of the privileges he granted to bishops were not new but developed and extended existing roles, and recent scholarship has rightly emphasized that the interaction between Constantine and the bishops was very much a two-way relationship rather than a simple story of imperial domination.[30] The opportunities raised by Christian imperial rule were in any case not fully realized under Constantine and continued to develop under his successors, particularly the Theodosian emperors (379–450). With these cautions in mind, this is not the place for a lengthy assessment of Constantine's policies toward Christianity, which have been well covered in numerous books.[31] But a short survey of his major measures is required if we are to assess the consequences, both positive and negative, of imperial recognition and support for the Church and its bishops.

At a very practical level, Constantine's reign had a profound impact on episcopal wealth. The Church had already acquired considerable resources in the third century, and charity and building works had become central to a bishop's duties, as Cyprian attests for Carthage. This only increased as Constantine gave money directly to individual clergy[32] and in 321 formally legalized the Church to receive bequests.[33] His restoration of property lost in the Great Persecution[34] was in turn followed by new construction in Rome and in the Holy Land, which received rich endowments.[35] Later emperors and wealthy elites added further benefactions, inspiring the pagan Ammianus Marcellinus' satirical description of bishops in Rome who, "enriched by the gifts of matrons, ride in carriages, dress splendidly, and outdo kings in the lavishness of their table."[36] Several well-known bishops expressed concern that resource management was occupying too much of their time,[37] and the misuse of wealth became a topos of accusations against unpopular church leaders.[38] But there was little explicit clerical opposition to deter further bequests,[39] and the rising wealth at their command made bishops valuable urban patrons.

Constantine's support for the Church was also expressed through legal privileges that gave the bishops official recognition and new or enhanced powers.[40] Episcopal immunity from taxation and curial duties reflected their favored status and left them free to devote themselves to charity and the piety that ensured the well-being of the state.[41] Bishops gained the right to grant asylum,[42] could preside over the manumission of slaves,[43] and could hear legal cases through the *audientia episcopalis* (bishop's court of arbitration).[44] There is limited evidence for how these powers functioned in practice,[45] but both care for the unfortunate and the settling of disputes were traditional episcopal roles, and the episcopal courts offered an attractive alternative to the secular courts, quicker and cheaper and upheld by the emperor's decree.[46]

The bishops of the early fourth century thus gained further avenues for power and patronage, status that from Constantine onward was in turn increasingly reflected in their social background. In the third century, bishops like Cyprian of Carthage had begun to be recruited from the upper levels of urban society, the curial class.[47] In the course of the fourth century, this became the norm, particularly after Constantine's law giving bishops exemption from curial duties.[48] Members of the curial class varied widely in wealth and status, from the relatively poor family of Augustine to the richer Cappadocians, Basil, and the two Gregories. But the Church now offered to such men a serious alternative to local or imperial service, which still allowed the exercise of social authority.

There were certain exceptions. A few fourth-century bishops are reported to have had lower-class origins, although this may on occasion derive from the polemic of their opponents.[49] At least two soldiers also reached the episcopate, although this was rare.[50] Perhaps most significantly, the fourth century for the first time saw bishops beginning to appear from the very highest social class, the senatorial order. Eusebius of Nicomedia, bishop of the eastern imperial capital at the time of Constantine's defeat of Licinius in 324, was a relative of Licinius' praetorian prefect Julius Julianus and so of the later emperor Julian "the Apostate", for whom Eusebius would briefly act as guardian.[51] However, Eusebius was most probably of high curial birth, and the only certain senatorial bishops known in the fourth century are Ambrose of Milan and his contemporary, Nectarius of Constantinople.[52] Both were highly exceptional appointments who had followed political rather than clerical careers. Nevertheless, the very appearance of senatorial bishops reflected the new prestige of the episcopal office, and the senatorial aristocratic bishop would become a more widespread figure in the fifth century.

The rising status that bishops now held in the Constantinian empire was further confirmed by the increasing correlation between the episcopal hierarchy and the structure of Roman provincial government.[53] This development again had begun well before the conversion of Constantine and received explicit confirmation in the canons of the Council of Nicaea in 325. Every city was expected to have a bishop,[54] and the leading bishop in each province was the metropolitan, the bishop of the provincial capital. The metropolitan had a right of veto over episcopal appointments within his province[55] and was expected to preside over provincial synods twice per year to resolve local disputes.[56] Above the metropolitans, the bishops of Rome, Alexandria, and Antioch held special authority by "ancient custom."[57] This neat organization left certain unresolved difficulties. The bishops at Nicaea acknowledged the status of the bishop of Jerusalem while maintaining the dignity of his metropolitan the bishop of Palestinian Caesarea (in 325, of course, this was Eusebius),[58] a tension that remained for over a century until the Council of Chalcedon in 451 recognized the primacy of Jerusalem over Caesarea. More significantly, the foundation of Constantinople five years after the Council of Nicaea posed a new challenge. The Council of Constantinople in 381 affirmed the status of the bishop of the imperial capital as "next after the bishop of Rome, because Constantinople is new Rome."[59] This claim was to lead to conflict both with Rome and with Alexandria, but over the next century, the bishops of these three cities, together with Antioch and Jerusalem, were to exert great authority as the five patriarchs of the late antique Church, later termed the Pentarchy.

The holders of these great sees were ideally placed to benefit from the closer relationship that Constantine encouraged between the Church and the imperial court. Recent scholarship has challenged older assumptions that there emerged around early Christian emperors "court bishops" who influenced their political and religious policies.[60] Yet certain episcopal figures do appear to have played prominent roles under Constantine,[61] notably the Spanish bishop Ossius of Cordova in the years before 326[62] and later Eusebius of Nicomedia,[63] who baptized Constantine in 337 and who, under Constantine's son Constantius II, became the first imperial nominee to be appointed as bishop of Constantinople.[64] In 360, another ambitious bishop, Eudoxius of Antioch, was translated to the see of Constantinople,[65] while in 379, Ambrose became bishop of Milan and exerted a powerful influence on successive emperors Gratian, Valentinian II, and Theodosius I.[66] Such power, however, came at a cost. The career of John Chrysostom reflected the new pressures that a bishop of an imperial residence might face.[67] Despite his popularity and spellbinding preaching, John's asceticism and lack of diplomacy alienated the wealthy citizens of Constantinople and the empress Eudoxia, whose opposition helped to bring about his fall.

Bishops lower down the episcopal hierarchy could also gain the emperor's ear.[68] Eusebius of Caesarea's account of the bishops at Nicaea dining with Constantine was quoted earlier, and successive fourth-century councils passed canons seeking to prevent excessive episcopal appeals to the imperial court.[69] It is true that already during Constantine's reign there were voices calling for the separation of the Church from secular interference.[70] Yet in this period, the voices were those of the minority and came from bishops who themselves allied with imperial power when the emperors acted in their favor. In reality, Constantine's support for Christianity reaffirmed the bond between the Church and the empire that already had begun to emerge under the pagan emperors. The privileges that Constantine gave to the bishops did not fundamentally alter the nature of the episcopal office but did dramatically expand the power and influence that a bishop could wield. And the emperor himself, no less than the bishop, could now claim both institutional and spiritual authority as God's representative and act (in the words of Constantine) as "a bishop perhaps appointed by God over those outside."[71]

The Bishop in the Later Roman Empire: Image and Reality

> The duties of his office he discharged in the same spirit as that in which he had been preferred to it. . . . He was sublime in action, lowly in mind; inaccessible in virtue, most accessible in intercourse; gentle, free from anger, sympathetic, sweet in words, sweeter in disposition; angelic in appearance, more angelic in mind; calm in rebuke, persuasive in praise, without spoiling the good effect of either by excess, but rebuking with the tenderness of a father, praising with the dignity of a ruler, his tenderness was not dissipated, nor his severity sour; for the one was reasonable, the other prudent, and both truly wise; his disposition sufficed for the training of his spiritual children, with very little need of words; his words with very little need of the rod, and his moderate use of the rod with still less for the knife.[72]

The bishop in the later Roman empire had many parts to play. Within his church, he was a preacher and teacher, responsible for the celebration of the liturgy, the imposition of penance, and the charitable care of his congregation. As a prominent social leader within his city, the bishop was also now a central figure in civic administration and an important source of wealth and patronage. He represented the local community in the great church councils, before imperial officials, and potentially even before the emperor or foreign powers. These duties were not unprecedented, for they had their origins in the evolution of the episcopal office in the first three centuries of the Christian era. But with imperial support from Constantine onward, the range and scale of the duties expected of the bishop had expanded dramatically. This in turn inspired new debates over the nature of episcopal leadership and how it should be held and exercised, debates that were themselves part of a wider dialogue over the nature of authority in the changing late antique world.[73]

The existence of these debates is an important caution that we cannot impose upon the fourth and fifth centuries later preconceptions of how a bishop should live and act. The office of the bishop in this period was the subject of an ongoing process of definition, and the men who filled the episcopate came from diverse social backgrounds and understood their position in different ways. A number of contemporary church fathers composed their own models of the ideal bishop, including Gregory of Nazianzus, Ambrose of Milan, John Chrysostom, and Augustine of Hippo.[74] However, while these models exerted a powerful influence, there is always an inherent tension between an image and reality. No one model ever became definitive, and nor can we assume that these great fathers were necessarily representative of their own times. All our patristic sources emphasize the struggles that bishops faced to reconcile their spiritual and worldly duties and the need for virtue and morality to overcome the temptations of ambition and vice. But every bishop must be set as far as possible in his own individual context to understand how he faced the obligations and challenges of his office.

The one quintessential role that every bishop played was as the leader of his own Church community. The increased numbers and greater social prominence that imperial patronage brought to the Church accelerated the ongoing formalization of Christian liturgy and ceremonial that had already begun before the conversion of Constantine.[75] The rituals of baptism and the Eucharist became more standardized, although regional variations still remained,[76] and increasing use was made of wider urban spaces with processions and festivals.[77] These developments both shaped and were shaped by the leadership of local bishops, expressed above all through the central liturgical rites of the life of the Christian community.

Only those who received baptism at the hands of their bishop could become full members of the church, membership that was confirmed by the celebration of the Eucharist over which the bishop presided. The fourth century saw an influx of new converts, and while adult baptism had previously been the norm, the practice of infant baptism now began to emerge.[78] The adult candidate for baptism was expected to undergo a lengthy period of instruction as a catechumen,[79] exemplified by the *Catechetical Lectures* of the mid-fourth-century bishop Cyril of Jerusalem.[80] Through this pre-baptismal instruction, the bishop played a crucial role in the ethical and doctrinal formation of the future members of his congregation. Through his penitential authority and the threat of excommunication, the bishop could also determine who possessed the right to receive the Eucharist and so remain within the body of the Church.

The bishop was also expected to be the leading preacher of his church.[81] The hundreds of homilies that survive preserve only a fraction of the words that poured forth to inspire the expanding congregations of the fourth and fifth centuries. Of course, not all bishops were as successful as preachers as the men who dominate our evidence, men like John Chrysostom[82] and Augustine of Hippo.[83] These men had received an extensive education and drew upon the models of classical oratory, skills they now turned to biblical exegesis and spiritual exhortation. Nor can we assume that those who heard these sermons actually heeded the lessons they were taught.[84] Nevertheless, sermons were the primary vehicle through which bishops could fulfill their role as moral and doctrinal guardians and teachers. Preaching was thus itself a statement of episcopal leadership, asserting the authority of the bishop to provide guidance to his congregation.

Outside of the liturgical context, the late Roman bishop continued to perform other roles that likewise derived from earlier episcopal practices but expanded in scale and significance under the Christian emperors. As has long been recognized, perhaps the most important of these roles was charity. Christian charity differed from Greco-Roman elite euergetism in its concern for the very poor and its explicitly religious motivation.[85] Offering care for widows and orphans and for the sick and injured, providing food in times of shortage, and ransoming prisoners all fell within the oversight of the bishop, as we have previously seen with Cyprian in the third century. The increase in church wealth from Constantine onward expanded these activities,[86] as, too, did the imperial legislation that formally recognized concern for welfare as part of a bishop's public duty. Already in the mid-third century, the church in Rome cared for "over 1500 widows along with others in distress."[87] According to John Chrysostom late in the fourth century, the Antiochene church provided for 3,000 widows and virgins each day, as well as for the male poor, the sick, and those in jail.[88] Not every bishop possessed the wealth of the sees of Rome and Antioch, but the measure of what could now be achieved is well demonstrated by the "new city" of hospitals and hostels that Basil of Caesarea is said to have created in his region of Cappadocia.[89]

The expanding charitable role of the bishop in the fourth and fifth centuries reflected the new prestige of the episcopal office within its wider urban context. The place of the bishop in the late antique city has been the subject of several major studies in recent years.[90] Many of the activities now expected of bishops were those also expected of provincial governors and local notables. Thus bishops now had the resources to promote major public works. The majority of these were naturally churches, such as the basilicas that Ambrose built in Milan (and sanctified with relics) and the churches that the bishops of Rome added to the great foundations of Constantine.[91] But by the early fifth century, bishops could also patronize more secular structures, including baths and bridges, as Theodoret claimed to have done for his see of Cyrrhus.[92] The episcopal residence (*domus episcopi*) also began to attain a new prominence, reflecting the bishop's status and concern for self-presentation.[93] Such residences varied widely in form, but the few so far identified mirror the designs of gubernatorial residences and elite villas, and like the episcopal churches, they moved from the periphery to the center of the civic landscape in the century following Constantine's conversion.

As a community leader with wealth and authority equal to or greater than that of other local notables, the bishop was an important patron not only for his congregation but also for the entire urban population. Bishops could intervene in disputes, another role further reinforced by Constantine through his legislation on episcopal courts. As they were now increasingly drawn from the upper levels of civic society, bishops moved easily within the elite social networks that dominated late Roman society. Numerous letters from the collections of Basil of Caesarea, Theodoret of Cyrrhus, and Augustine of Hippo, like those of their pagan contemporaries Libanius and Symmachus, were written to governors and officials, including petitions for benefactions (frequently tax exemptions)[94] and letters of recommendation for friends and clients. Bishops could also intervene on behalf of their cities at the imperial court. In 387, Bishop Flavian of Antioch played a crucial role in placating the emperor Theodosius' anger after the destruction of imperial images in the Riot of the Statues, a role he shared with Libanius, the pagan civic orator.[95] If the situation demanded, bishops could likewise represent their cities before external foes. Ammianus Marcellinus describes the bishop of Bezabde negotiating with the Persian shah Shapur in 360,[96] and Leo of Rome famously came out from his city to face the dread Attila the Hun.[97]

The late Roman bishop thus performed a number of essential civic functions, and the status of the bishop as a leader of the urban community was recognized at both local and imperial levels. Episcopal elections acquired a new significance, and whereas early bishops were traditionally selected by their congregations, from the fourth century onward, other bishops and civic leaders played a central role.[98] In the great sees, conflict over rival candidates could easily turn to violence, as occurred in the riots in Constantinople in 342 between Paul and Macedonius[99] and the deaths of 137 in a Roman church in 366 when Damasus defeated Ursinus.[100] Despite their notoriety, however, such episodes were very much the exception rather than the norm. Unlike civic officials, a bishop, once elected, served for life, and in the increasingly Christian late Roman world, bishops were now inseparable from the smooth operation of city government. By the early fifth century, this had been confirmed by imperial legislation. The earliest law that formally placed the bishop among the highest civic officials was passed in 409, ordering the bishop together with the *honorati*, *possessores*, and *curiales* to appoint the *defensor civitatis*.[101] By the late fifth century under Anastasius, the bishop was also required to aid the chief magistrate in distributing supplies to soldiers and to oversee the *sitōnes* responsible for the grain supply.[102]

In older scholarship, as has already been observed, the rising prominence of the bishop in civic government was cited as proof that imperial patronage had transformed the episcopate into simply another secular office. The bishop was also regarded as a beneficiary of the so-called "decline of the *curiales*", moving into the vacuum believed to have been created by the gradual disappearance of the old civic elite.[103] It is true that curial numbers did decrease in the fourth and fifth centuries, with a corresponding concentration of civic wealth and power in fewer hands, including those of the bishop. Yet the bishops were themselves largely drawn from the curial order and did not replace the leading citizens but cooperated with them.[104] Moreover, even though the late Roman bishops did share a number of the roles they played with secular officials, the position of the bishop and the nature of episcopal leadership remained separate. The values and virtues expected of a bishop were rooted in the early Christian past, and the religious character of their office gave them additional authority but also additional burdens. The unique pressures of the episcopal office are perhaps best reflected in the involvement of the bishops in the dramatic religious changes and controversies that helped to shape the late Roman world in the centuries following Constantine's conversion.

The "Christianization" of the Roman empire is too wide-ranging and complex a subject to discuss in any depth here.[105] Nor should we exaggerate the role of the bishop, for many factors were at work in the expansion of

Christianity. Nevertheless, episcopal leadership played its part. As the head of the urban Christian community, the bishop could set the tone for local Christian-pagan relations. In some famous instances, this led directly to violence.[106] The city of Alexandria provides several vivid glimpses of religious conflict with episcopal figures at their heart.[107] One bishop, George, was lynched by pagans in 361 in reaction against his attacks on pagan temples.[108] In 391, it was Bishop Theophilus of Alexandria who oversaw the destruction of the great Serapeum,[109] while Theophilus' nephew Cyril has long been suspected of involvement in the murder of the pagan philosopher Hypatia in 415.[110] As always, however, it is difficult to generalize from isolated examples. Other bishops preferred to promote Christianity without direct conflict, as Paulinus did in Nola,[111] although not all were as broad-minded as Pegasius, the bishop of Troy, who according to Julian honored Achilles and Hector just as he did the Christian martyrs.[112] Much the same could be said of episcopal attitudes toward Judaism. A few examples of organized violence are known, most notably the actions of Bishop Severus of Minorca,[113] and Ambrose of Milan convinced Theodosius I not to enforce the rebuilding of a synagogue destroyed by Christians in Callinicium in Mesopotamia in 386.[114] But other bishops could condemn overly close Christian-Jewish relations without resorting to persecution, as we see from John Chrysostom.[115] Here again individual bishops could follow their own judgments on the roles they should play.

The doctrinal and schismatic controversies that divided the late Roman church raise further questions regarding the nature of episcopal leadership and how that leadership was exercised. These controversies dominate much of our evidence, particularly the "Arian" Controversy in the fourth century and the Christological debates of the fifth century.[116] They also exerted a profound influence on the careers of a number of leading bishops, many of whom, such as Athanasius of Alexandria and Ambrose of Milan, faced a struggle to maintain their authority against rivals for their sees.[117] It is more difficult to determine how influential the controversies were on the daily lives of less prominent bishops and their congregations. Sermons and catechetical texts from this period usually contain little reference to contemporary theological debates, although this may reflect their genre and purpose rather than lack of interest. It might equally be asked to what extent many bishops actually understood the complex doctrinal issues debated at the Councils of Nicaea in 325 or Chalcedon in 451.[118]

As the representatives of their communities, however, every bishop was responsible for the orthodox faith taught to his flock. No bishop could ignore the theological debates of their times, and hundreds of bishops attended the numerous councils of the fourth and fifth centuries, aided by the emperor's patronage, which placed the imperial communication system at their disposal.[119] The *Acts of Chalcedon*, the most detailed extant record from one of the great early councils, preserve the acclamations of those present during the council's sessions.[120] Those acclamations confirm that individual bishops even from relatively minor sees could and did express their own opinions on controversial questions, at times in opposition to the direction of the leading bishops or the imperial commissioners.[121] We cannot accurately judge the widely varying levels of doctrinal knowledge and engagement of the highly diverse body of late Roman bishops, but nor should we underestimate the importance of the issues at stake to those present at the first ecumenical councils.

Two last themes highlight the scale of episcopal responsibilities within and beyond the later Roman empire. In the first three centuries of the Church, bishops do not appear to have played a particularly significant role in spreading the Christian message outside their communities. In the fourth century, we encounter bishops directly involved in missionary movements beyond the Roman frontiers. Athanasius of Alexandria supported the two merchants who inspired the conversion of Ethiopia, and he consecrated Frumentius, one of those merchants, as the first bishop of Ethiopia.[122] But perhaps more important was the action of Athanasius' great rival, Eusebius of Nicomedia, who consecrated Ulfila, the "Apostle to the Goths."[123] Ulfila was responsible for inventing the Gothic alphabet and for the translation of the Gothic Bible. Although his own episcopal career was not entirely successful, he thus played a crucial part in the conversion of the Goths and of other Germanic tribes. The fact that Ulfila's theology, like that of Eusebius, was one that men like Athanasius regarded as "Arian" would have serious repercussions for the subsequent history of the Goths and of the western Roman empire.

Finally, we must consider what is arguably the greatest potential challenge to episcopal leadership within late Roman Christianity: the ascetic movement.[124] The rising prominence of ascetic holy men and women in the fourth and fifth centuries brought into renewed focus the uneasy tension between spiritual and institutional authority that the position of the bishop had embodied from its beginnings. Antony the hermit, Symeon Stylites, and other great ascetics derived their influence from their personal holiness and charisma, not from the possession of clerical office. There had always been those in the early Church who had questioned whether the worldly concerns of the episcopate were truly compatible with the bishop's moral and spiritual duties, and those debates had gained new impetus with the social prominence and privileges that came with imperial patronage. The ascetic renunciation of society to follow the life in Christ now threatened to create an alternative Christian elite, one that might undermine or even supersede the bishop in offering leadership and guidance to the Christian community.

Yet asceticism was never necessarily incompatible with ecclesiastical office. John Cassian famously wrote that "monks should flee bishops,"[125] but several leading bishops made great efforts to maintain close relations with the ascetic populations of their regions, and a number of monks took clerical office.[126] Athanasius of Alexandria in his *Life of Antony* expresses his respect for Antony while insisting on Antony's obedience to episcopal authority.[127] His relationship with Antony reinforced Athanasius' own spiritual position, and it was Athanasius who began the ordination of monks in Egypt that was continued by his successors.[128] In the West, the hermit Martin became the bishop and later saint of Tours,[129] and ascetically minded bishops like Augustine founded monastic communities from whom they could recruit their clergy.[130] Tensions continued to arise, but across the Church the ascetic movement strengthened rather than weakened episcopal leadership and provided a counterbalance to the worldly obligations of the late Roman bishop.

West and East: The Bishop in a Changing World

By the end of the fourth century, the bishop was an established figure within the elite of an increasingly Christian Roman empire. The foundations of episcopal leadership remained rooted in the office's origins in the first three Christian centuries, but the scale and diversity of the roles that bishops played had expanded dramatically in the decades that followed the conversion of Constantine. This complex dynamic of continuity and change continued to characterize the evolution of the episcopate in the later fifth and sixth centuries, years that saw an increasing separation between the churches of the eastern and western regions of the empire. The collapse of imperial power in the West and the emergence of the Germanic kingdoms raised new dangers but opened new opportunities for many western bishops, particularly for the see of Rome. The bishops of the East were forced to confront the deep theological debates dividing their church and witnessed in the reign of the emperor Justinian a further stage in the ongoing relationship between episcopal and imperial power.

This is not the place for an in-depth analysis of the much-debated "Decline and Fall" of the western Roman empire.[131] As has long been recognized, the gradual disappearance of imperial structures in the West was accompanied by significant continuity and transformation. The Christian Church, while suffering from the negative consequences of the Roman decline, was itself a primary example of continuity and in turn helped to preserve and reshape elements of Roman culture. It is against this background that we must place the evolution of episcopal leadership in the post-Roman West. The older models of how a bishop should act and the roles that a bishop should play still exerted a powerful influence. But now those models had to be adapted once more, maintaining the connection to the past while meeting the challenges of the present.

The breakdown of centralized imperial authority weakened the bishops of the western provinces, who had become closely bound to that authority during the fourth and early fifth centuries. In the chaos of the barbarian invasions, bishops also offered a tempting target, traditionally nonviolent and commanding substantial wealth. Yet the bishops were now prominent community figures in a predominantly Christian world, to whom their congregations and their cities looked for guidance. In regions where secular officials were increasingly unable to provide local leadership, bishops frequently took on that role. Churches became the focus for urban life, and educated bishops preserved the classical literary heritage. The Christianity of the majority of the Germanic tribes, even if they were regarded by many Romans as heretical "Arians", made it easier for bishops to act as mediators between the existing populations and the newcomers. The dangers of a changing world were thus offset by new opportunities. In the emerging Germanic kingdoms, the place of episcopal authority could be reestablished and redefined, while in the void left by the fall of the last western emperor in 476, the see of Rome began to assert its status as the spiritual heir of the empire.

An early example of one possible path now open to an ambitious western bishop is provided by the career of Sidonius Apollinarius (c. 430–489) in southern Gaul.[132] A member of the Gallo-Roman aristocracy, he was the son-in-law of the emperor Avitus and urban prefect of Rome before becoming bishop of Clermont-Ferrand in Auvergne in 470 or 472. In addition to the liturgical duties of his clerical office, Sidonius continued to act as he had as an aristocrat, as a patron and writer. There was a particular need for charity in times of crisis,[133] while Sidonius also acted as a mediator in resolving disputes[134] and played a central role in the defense of Auvergne against the Visigothic king Euric.[135] After his city fell to Euric, Sidonius was temporarily imprisoned but able to retain his office,[136] while still providing the spiritual and practical leadership that his community looked for in their bishop.[137]

It is inevitably difficult to determine how far one may generalize from a career like that of Sidonius. Through his letters and other sources, we are informed of several other aristocratic southern Gallic bishops who enjoyed prominent secular careers before entering the episcopate.[138] A slightly different career path is reflected in the next generation by another well-known figure, Caesarius of Arles (bishop 502–542).[139] Although born into a wealthy family, Caesarius was initially a monk on the monastic island of Lerins, and as a bishop he drew on his ascetic life to reinforce his episcopal authority. He was renowned for his charity to those who suffered loss or captivity under Gothic rule,[140] and he was a great preacher, whose sermons were copied and circulated for use by bishops in Gaul, Italy, Spain, and beyond.[141] A very different personality from Sidonius, Caesarius played the same essential roles of local patron and leader in the uncertain period in which southern Gaul passed from Visigothic to Frankish rule, and he was later held as a model for episcopal behavior in the Carolingian world.

Sidonius and Caesarius reflect the capacity of Gallo-Roman bishops to retain their social status and cooperate successfully with Germanic kings, both "Arian" Goths and Catholic Franks. Similarly, Avitus of Vienne (bishop c. 494–c. 518)[142] held a prominent place at the court of the "Arian" Burgundian king

Gundobad and wrote to Clovis congratulating the Frankish king on his adoption of Catholicism.[143] Avitus, himself a relative of Sidonius and a correspondent of Caesarius, offers a further insight into the roles that bishops could play in the post-Roman kingdoms, once again adapting traditional models of behavior to the new context. A leading theologian of his time, he took part in contemporary doctrinal debates[144] and maintained correspondence with other leading bishops in Italy and Gaul.[145] Avitus also wrote letters to the eastern emperor Anastasius on behalf of Gundobad's son Sigismund (who had converted to Catholicism before his father's death in 516)[146] and so paralleled the better-known work of his younger contemporary Cassiodorus on behalf of Theoderic the Ostrogoth in Italy.

Not every bishop enjoyed the relatively smooth relationships that Avitus established with his Germanic rulers. The reign of Theoderic in Italy was initially well received by Italians and Ostrogoths alike.[147] But tensions grew in the closing years of his life.[148] John, bishop of Rome, was one of those to suffer, and he died in prison upon his return from an embassy to Constantinople in 526.[149] The persecution of Catholic bishops in Vandal North Africa, although possibly exaggerated by our sources, notably Victor of Vita, further suggests the dangers as well as the privileges that episcopal status could bring.[150] Accounts of bishops who faced similar dangers may likewise be found in Visigothic Spain.[151] The "Arianism" of the Vandal and Gothic rulers may have provided one motive for persecution, but it was above all as the leaders of their local communities that bishops posed a potential threat. It was through the courage and conviction, as well as the ambition, of the men who held episcopal office in these years that bishops would continue to exert social and political as well as religious influence on western Europe for centuries to come.

Two generations after Avitus, we may examine the nature of episcopal leadership in a Francia now firmly under Merovingian rule through the life of our major source for this period: Gregory of Tours (bishop 573–594).[152] The final book of the so-called *History of the Franks*, Gregory's most widely read work, sheds valuable light on Gregory himself and his career as bishop of Tours. Like Sidonius, Gregory was the scion of a highly aristocratic family, and he counted a number of bishops in his ancestry.[153] As Gregory proudly records, he in turn contributed significantly to support building and charitable works in the city, particularly for the greater veneration of the patron saint of Tours, the ascetic bishop St. Martin.[154] During his episcopate, Gregory fought to protect the shrine of St. Martin and his see from the threat of strife between rival Merovingian kings.[155] He offered asylum to those in need,[156] mediated in local disputes,[157] and was forced to defend himself from charges of misbehavior brought by malicious rivals.[158] Seen in this light, it is not difficult to view Gregory as a traditional aristocrat now pursuing an elite career through the Church. Yet Gregory was also a theologian, proclaiming his orthodox doctrine proudly in his *History*[159] and famously misrepresenting the life of Clovis, the first Catholic Merovingian ruler, as an anti-"Arian" crusade.[160] His praise of Clovis was not misplaced, for the conversion of the Franks to Catholicism aided the status and influence of Catholic bishops like Gregory, and episcopal leadership was to remain an essential feature of social and political life throughout Merovingian and later Carolingian Francia.[161]

This short survey of episcopal leadership in the post-Roman West must conclude with some consideration of the greatest of all western bishoprics, the see of Rome.[162] In the opening Christian centuries, the Roman church derived great prestige from the status of Rome as the center of the empire and from its association with Peter and Paul, for Rome alone of the western churches could claim apostolic foundation. Yet despite later claims, the monarchical episcopate developed only gradually in Rome, as it did elsewhere. The *Shepherd of Hermas* describes a divided Roman hierarchy in the late first or early second century,[163] and the first bishop of Rome to exert a major influence outside his city was Victor (bishop 189–199), through his intervention in the eastern debates over the date of Easter.[164] Even so, tensions over legitimate authority still remained in Rome, reflected in the career and writings of Hippolytus (c. 170–c. 236).[165] As we have already seen, the Petrine doctrine was first cited by Stephen (bishop 254–257) in the mid-third century in his clash with Cyprian of Carthage,[166] and the special status of the bishop of Rome was recognized at the Council of Nicaea.[167]

Constantine's patronage then brought further prestige and wealth to the Roman church,[168] however legendary may be the later stories of the emperor's baptism in Rome and the so-called "Donation of Constantine."[169] Miltiades of Rome (bishop 310–314) was asked by Constantine to hold a Roman synod in a failed attempt to resolve the Donatist schism.[170] During the fourth century, a number of eastern bishops appealed to Rome for aid, notably Athanasius of Alexandria,[171] and the right of the bishop of Rome to hear appeals was affirmed by the western Council of Serdica in 343.[172] By the episcopate of Damasus (bishop 366–384), the Roman bishop was a leading figure in both the imperial church and elite society.[173] In the ironic words of the great pagan senator Praetextatus, "Make me bishop of Rome, and I will become a Christian at once."[174]

The expansion of Roman episcopal authority in the fifth and sixth centuries was neither consistent nor inevitable and depended heavily on the personality of the occupant of the see at a given time. Two bishops in particular illustrate the potential power of the Roman church, and both were to receive the title "the great" from later generations: Leo (bishop 440–461) and Gregory (bishop 590–604).[175] Leo I was one of the few late antique bishops of Rome to play a central role in the eastern doctrinal controversies, and his *Tome* was upheld as a statement of orthodoxy at the Council of Chalcedon.[176] He was also a great preacher, who placed renewed emphasis on his status as the heir of Peter and Paul and further secured the place of the bishop at the heart of Roman civic life.[177] The decline of western imperial power by the mid-fifth century had created a vacuum of authority in Italy as elsewhere, and Leo led the defense of the city against the threat of Attila in 452 and during the sack of Rome by the Vandals in 455.[178]

The disappearance of the last western emperor in 476 further strengthened the position of the Roman bishop, despite internal schisms and periodic tensions with the "Arian" Ostrogoths. Justinian's "reconquest" in the mid-sixth century temporarily restored a degree of imperial control, as Vigilius (bishop of Rome 537–555) learned to his cost,[179] but the twenty-year war to destroy the Ostrogothic regime also crippled the Italian elite and was followed almost immediately by the arrival of the Lombards into Italy.[180] By the turn of the seventh century, Gregory I not only led the Roman church but also had taken over many of the roles once played by the Roman emperors. He was responsible for the grain supply that fed Rome[181] and represented the city to both the imperial exarch in Ravenna and the various Lombard rulers, Catholic and "Arian" alike.[182] Gregory also exerted significant influence throughout the western church, most famously through the mission that led to the Catholic conversion of Britain.[183]

The career of Gregory the Great witnessed a high-water mark in the early history of the Roman see and laid the foundations for future developments. But in the world of Late Antiquity, the Roman church possessed only a shadow of the power and prestige of the medieval "papal monarchy". Moreover, despite their emerging claims to superior authority, the bishops of Rome were expected to fulfill the same roles as other members of the episcopate, and it was upon the execution of those roles that their leadership rested. Gregory placed great emphasis on his responsibilities as the moral and spiritual guide of his community. His involvement with the grain supply and in diplomatic negotiations was on a greater scale than previously known but continued the traditional obligations of the bishop to provide charitable support and community representation. He encapsulated his vision of the episcopate in the most influential of his numerous writings, the *Regula pastoralis* (*Pastoral Rule*):

> Necessity demands that one should carefully examine who it is that comes to the position of spiritual authority; and coming solemnly to this point, how he should live; and living well, how he should teach; and teaching rightly, with what kind of self-examination he should learn of his own weakness. Necessity also demands that humility does not flee when the office is assumed, nor the way of life contradict the assumption of the office, nor teaching abandon the way of life, nor presumption outshine teaching. Ideally, therefore, trepidation will restrain desire. But when authority is received by one who was not seeking it, may his life commend him because afterwards it will be necessary that the goodness that is displayed by the shepherd's actions be multiplied by his words. Finally, it should be added that a consideration of one's weakness should subdue his every achievement so that the swell of pride not abolish his good works before the eyes of the secret Judge.[184]

For Gregory, as for his predecessors, the bishop was to be an example to others, dignified but humble, contemplative but social, able to deal well with people from all walks of life. It was a vision that was to inspire the courts and clergy of Charlemagne and Alfred the Great.[185]

The evolution of episcopal leadership in the eastern Roman empire in the fifth and sixth centuries followed a slightly different path from that in the West. The relative military and political stability of the East ensured that the bishop remained an essential feature of imperial and urban society, and a number of developments that had begun under Constantine and his successors were further extended under the greatest of the sixth-century emperors, Justinian (527–565).[186] The great legislative project of Justinian's reign included a series of laws that confirmed and advanced the official status of the bishop within the empire. In 530, the bishop, together with three respectable citizens, was made responsible for the annual audit of city funds and building work.[187] Later, bishops were allowed to report protests against provincial governors to the emperor[188] and to sit alongside the judge in cases in which the judge might prove guilty of bias.[189] Such laws tied bishops closely to the apparatus of imperial government. Yet still the episcopate remained distinct from secular office, and the relationship of the eastern bishops with their emperor did not differ significantly in nature from that of men like Gregory of Tours with their Merovingian kings. The duties that Justinian required of the bishops reflected their underlying role as moral overseers, separate from the secular administration. In Justinian's own words:

> The priesthood and the empire are the two greatest gifts which God, in His infinite clemency, has bestowed upon mortals. The former has reference to divine matters, the latter presides over and directs human affairs, and both, proceeding from the same principle, adorn the life of mankind. Hence nothing should be such a source of care to the emperors as the honour of the priests who constantly pray to God for their salvation.[190]

The close involvement of the eastern bishops in the life of the empire, like that of their counterparts in the western kingdoms, came at a cost. Older arguments that viewed Justinian as the archetypal "Caesaropapist", dictating imperial decisions to a passive church, have long been discredited.[191] As the language of his law here suggests, however, Justinian took to heart the need for Christian morality and orthodoxy in his realm. In his efforts to reunite the ongoing divisions within the eastern church that had existed since the Council of Chalcedon in 451, Justinian's policies fluctuated from persuasion and conciliar debate to outright persecution.[192] Few of the bishops who attended the fifth ecumenical council that Justinian summoned to Constantinople in 553 were prepared to openly defy the emperor's wishes. Nevertheless, Justinian was unable to secure the unity he sought, and it was during his reign that the Syrian monk Jacob Baradeus began the formation of those who rejected Chalcedon into what would become the "Monophysite" or "Miaphysite" Syrian Orthodox Church.[193] What differentiated Jacob from earlier opponents of Chalcedon was his widespread ordination of anti-Chalcedonian bishops, who formed their own separate hierarchy. Episcopal leadership was the essential requirement that confirmed the existence of a distinct Miaphysite Church and created a division within eastern Christianity that has endured to the present day.

In the closing decades of the sixth century and the early years of the seventh century, eastern bishops increasingly faced challenges not dissimilar from those western bishops like Sidonius had faced in the fifth century. In the conflicts between the eastern Roman and Persian empires, bishops once again were expected to play a leading role within their communities.[194] Bishop Zacharias of Jerusalem sought to negotiate the surrender of the city to the Persians in 614, although he was unable to avert the sack in which the relics of the True Cross were seized, and he led the survivors into captivity.[195] More successful was Sergius, bishop of Constantinople (610–638). One of the leading men left in command of the besieged capital by the emperor Heraclius on the latter's invasion of Persia, Sergius furnished a practical and spiritual example that helped to preserve Constantinople from the Persians and Avars. The procession carrying the image of Christ that Sergius led around the Land Walls of the city in its hour of need would be immortalized in Byzantine tradition.[196] The bishop as the savior of the great Christian imperial capital provides a final compelling vision of the fundamental importance of episcopal leadership in the life and survival of the eastern Roman empire.

> Our Moses [the patriarch Sergius] having raised in his pure hands the image of the only-begotten God at which the demons tremble (which, they say is not made by human hands) . . . showing it just like an invincible weapon with tears to the aerial powers of darkness and the troops of the West [the Avars], he walked along the entire walls of the city. In a suppressed voice just as the first Moses cried towards God when he made the tabernacle to proceed before the people: "Arise, O Lord, let your enemies be scattered abroad, and all the ones who hate you run away" [Numbers 10:35; Psalm 68(67):1].[197]

NOTES

1. 1 Timothy 3:1–7.

2. For an overview of the debates, see Hatch 1881; Kirk 1946; Telfer 1962; Faivre 1977; Hanson 1985; Bobertz 1992; Nasrallah 2003; and now Torjesen 2008.

3. Acts 20:17, Titus 1:5 (the term *episkopos* is never used in the Gospels). See further Schweizer 1961; Ysebaert 1994.

4. Philippians 1:1.

5. According to Paul, apostles, prophets, and teachers stood at the head of the Christian hierarchy of gifts, followed by miracle workers and healers, and only then by helpers and administrators (1 Corinthians 12:28).

6. Niederwimmer 1989.

7. "Elect therefore for yourselves bishops and deacons worthy of the Lord, men meek and not covetous, and true and approved, for they also minister unto you the ministry of the prophets and teachers. Therefore despise them not, for these are they which are honoured of you with the prophets and teachers" (*Didache* XV.1–2).

8. The three Pastoral Epistles (1 and 2 Timothy and Titus) date to at least several decades after Paul's death, probably to the early or mid-second century. The injunction

to appoint an appropriate person as bishop in 1 Timothy 3:1–7 is repeated in very similar language in Titus 1:5–9.

9. For the central role that this passage would play in later debates over episcopal leadership, see Rapp 2005, 32–41.

10. For an introduction to Ignatius, see Trevett 1992; Brent 2007.

11. Ignatius, *Letter to the Smyrnaeans* VIII.1–2; cf. *Letter to the Trallians* III.1.

12. The classic if controversial account of diversity in early Christianity is Bauer 1934.

13. Irenaeus, *Adversus Haereses* III.2.2–4.3, IV.40.2–42.1. Clement of Rome in the late first century had warned the church of Corinth against deposing those who led them in succession from the apostles (1 Clement 42–44), and the first succession lists tracing lines of episcopal descent from the apostles appeared in the mid- to late second century. See Molland 1954; von Campenhausen 1969, esp. 156–177.

14. Trevett 1996; Tabbernee 2007.

15. See Pagels 1978 and, on the "Gnostic" controversy more broadly, Logan 1996; King 2003.

16. Here one might still cite Weber's famous classification of the three pure types of legitimate authority: legal, traditional, and charismatic (Weber 1978, 212–254, esp. 246–254: "The Routinization of Charisma").

17. Origen urged all bishops to follow the virtues laid down in 1 Timothy 3:1–7 (*Com. Rom.* 8.10; *Com. Matt.* 15.21–28), but also maintained that those who possessed such virtues were as bishops before God, even if they did not hold that office among men (*Com. Matt.* 16.19). See further Völker 1931.

18. A comparison between the early-second-century *Didache* and the later *Didaskalia*, from northern Syria in the early third century, reveals a far greater degree of organization in the latter work, including clerical salaries and a structured episcopal role in charity and the liturgy. See Schöllgen 1988.

19. On the career and context of Cyprian, see Sage 1975; Rives 1995, 285–307; Burns 2002.

20. Cyprian, *Letter* 62. He also wrote a treatise *On Almsgiving*.

21. Letters to bishops in Spain (*Letter* 67), Gaul (68), Cappadocia (75), and repeatedly to Rome (e.g., 9, 20, 27).

22. On the importance of penance and penitential authority in the early Church, see Watkins 1920; Dassmann 1973.

23. The standard work, although increasingly dated, is still Frend 1971. See also Shaw 1992; Tilley 1997.

24. On the rebaptism controversy, see Sage 1975, 295–335. The evolution of Roman episcopal authority is discussed further later in this chapter.

25. "How great, how unique were the honour, and liberty too, which before the persecution of my time were granted by all men, Greeks and non-Greeks alike, to the message given through Christ to the world, of true reverence for the God of the universe. . . . How could one describe those mass meetings, the enormous gatherings in every city, and the remarkable congregations in places of worship?" (Eusebius, *HE* VIII.1).

26. Eusebius, *HE* VII.30.19. See further Millar 1971.

27. For the respective imperial decrees, see Cyprian, *Letter* 80.1 (Valerian); Eusebius, *HE* X.2 (Diocletian).

28. Eusebius of Caesarea, *Life of Constantine* III.15.

29. For the older argument, now rightly rejected, that regarded Constantine as absorbing the bishops into the secular power structure, see Klauser 1953, with the criticisms of Jerg 1970.

30. Particularly emphasized by Drake 2000.

31. Among many others, see Barnes 1981; Drake 2000; Odahl 2004; and now Van Dam 2007.

32. Constantine, *Letter to Caecilian of Carthage* (313), quoted in Eusebius, *HE* X.6.

33. *CTh* XVI.2.4. The law presupposes that such bequests were already being made, but they now became far more common.

34. Constantine, *Letter to Anulinus, Proconsul of Africa* (313), quoted in Eusebius, *HE* X.5.

35. See most famously the long list of treasures given to the Roman church by Constantine, recorded in *Liber Pontificalis* 34, and his letter to the bishop of Jerusalem regarding construction of the Holy Sepulchre (quoted in Eusebius, *Life of Constantine* III.30–32).

36. Ammianus Marcellinus, *Res Gestae* XXVII.3.14.

37. John Chrysostom, *Hom. Matt.* 85.3–4; Augustine according to Possidius (*Life of Augustine* 23–24).

38. E.g., Cyril of Jerusalem (Sozomen, *HE* IV.25.3–4; Theodoret, *HE* II.27.1–2); John of Jerusalem (Jerome, *Against John of Jerusalem* 14); John Chrysostom (Photius, *Bibliotheca* 59.19–22, 39–40).

39. In one rare exception, Martin of Tours is said to have refused gifts offered by Valentinian I (Sulpicius Severus, *Dialogue* II.5.10).

40. See further Rapp 2005, 236–260, who emphasizes that these laws drew on privileges previously granted to pagan priests and *collegia*, and largely reaffirmed and extended existing episcopal roles.

41. "This [clerical exemption from civic duties] will ensure that by no error or sacrilegious fall from grace will they be drawn away from the worship owed to the Godhead; rather will they be completely free to serve their own law at all times. In thus rendering wholehearted service to the Deity, it is evident that they will be making an immense contribution to the welfare of the community" (Constantine, *Letter to Anulinus, Proconsul of Africa*, quoted in Eusebius, *HE* X.7). Similarly *CTh* XVI.2.1–2, XVI.2.6.

42. *CTh* XVI.2.4, *CJ* I.12.2. See Herman 1935; Ducloux 1994.

43. *CJ* I.13.1; *CTh* IV.7.1.

44. Initially, both parties had to agree to accept the bishop's jurisdiction (*CTh* I.27.1), but this was then altered to allow either party to appeal for episcopal judgment (*Sirmondian Constitution* 1 (333)). Later, the requirement of agreement from both parties was restated (*CJ* I.4.7 (398)), and the bishop's involvement was limited to religious not criminal cases (*CTh* XVI.2.23 (376); *CTh* XVI.11.1 (399)). See further Cimma 1989; Lamoreaux 1995.

45. Augustine complained of the amount of legal work his episcopal duties involved (Augustine, *Letter* 24* (Divjak); Possidius, *Life of Augustine* 19). On the evidence for the *audientia episcopalis* provided by the newly discovered Divjak letters of Augustine, see Lenski 2001.

46. Constantine himself in a law of 333 referred to episcopal courts as a means to escape the "long and almost endless toils of litigation" (*Sirmondian Constitution* 1).

47. On the social origins of clergy in the third century, see Schöllgen 1988. For the fourth century, see in general Jones 1964, 920–929; Gilliard 1984; Rapp 2005, 172–207.

48. This exemption proved so popular that Constantine was forced to issue further laws denouncing those "who in evasion of public duties have taken refuge in the number of the clergy" (*CTh* XVI.2.3; cf. *CTh* XVI.2.6).

49. Spyridon of Cyprian Trimithis was a sheep farmer (Socrates, *HE* I.12; Sozomen, *HE* I.11), Zeno of Maiuma a linen weaver (Sozomen, *HE* VII.28). Accusations of low origins were also brought against a number of men condemned as heretics, notably the so-called "Neo-Arian" Aetius (Gregory of Nyssa, *Contra Eunomium* I.37–46).

50. Martin of Tours (Sulpicius Severus, *Life of Martin* 2–4); Victricius of Rouen (Paulinus of Nola, *Letter* 18.7). As the *Life of Martin* attests, the army and the clergy were not easy careers to reconcile.

51. Ammianus Marcellinus, *Res Gestae* XXII.9.4. Eusebius is most likely to have been a relative of Julianus' unnamed Christian wife, possibly her brother (see Vanderspoel 1999, 410–411).

52. For the career of Ambrose, see McLynn 1994; on the election of Nectarius, see Socrates (*HE* V.8); Sozomen (*HE* VII.8). Approximately ten other possible senatorial bishops from Italy, Gaul, and North Africa have been tentatively identified in the late fourth and early fifth century, but the evidence is weak: see Gilliard 1984; Rapp 2005, 188–195.

53. The evidence is well summarized in Jones 1964, 873–894.

54. Bishops outside of municipal centers were rare. Rural bishops (*chorepiscopi*) still existed in some eastern regions in the fourth century but, in theory at least, were subordinate to the nearest civic bishop (Ancyra (314) canon 13; Laodicea (date uncertain) canon 57).

55. Nicaea (325) canon 4. For further discussion of this and the following canons, see L'Huillier 1996.

56. Nicaea (325) canon 5. Cf. Antioch (327) canons 9 and 20.

57. Nicaea (325) canon 6. I will return to the status of the see of Rome later. The authority of the see of Antioch does not appear to have been clearly defined in the early church (Wallace-Hadrill 1982), but the see of Alexandria exerted considerable influence throughout Egypt and its surrounding regions. For the evolution of Alexandrian episcopal leadership in Late Antiquity, see Davis 2004.

58. Nicaea (325) canon 7.

59. Constantinople (381) canon 3.

60. Warmington 1989; Hunt 1989.

61. Such a role was once widely attributed to Constantine's biographer Eusebius of Caesarea. For a strong critique of that view, see Barnes 1981, 265–267.

62. The standard work on Ossius' career remains de Clercq 1954. For a far more minimalist assessment of Ossius' influence on Constantine's reign, see Warmington 1989, 119–122.

63. Gwynn 1999.

64. The problems caused by the role played by the "Arian" Eusebius in the baptism of Constantine contributed significantly to the legends that later placed Constantine's baptism in Rome: see Fowden 1994; Lieu 1998.

65. McLynn 1999. Eudoxius had previously moved from the see of Germanicia to that of Antioch. Such translations had previously been condemned at Nicaea (canon 15), but this ruling was never easy to enforce, as Eusebius of Nicomedia's translation to Constantinople similarly attests.

66. McLynn 1994; Williams 1995.

67. Liebeschuetz 1990, 166–227; Kelly 1995.

68. For the relationship between bishops and the emperor, set within the wider context of the workings of imperial government, see Millar 1977, 551–607.

69. Antioch (327) canons 11, 12; Western Serdica (343) canon 8.

70. Donatus of Carthage, "What has the Church to do with the emperor?" (quoted in Optatus of Milevis, *Against the Donatists* III.3); Ossius of Cordova, "Intrude not yourself into ecclesiastical matters, neither give commands to us concerning them. . . . God has put into your hands the kingdom; to us He has entrusted the affairs of His Church" (Letter to Constantius, quoted in Athanasius, *Historia Arianorum* 44).

71. Quoted in Eusebius, *Life of Constantine* IV.24. See further Rapp 1998.

72. Gregory of Nazianzus, *Oration* XXI (On the Great Athanasius, Bishop of Alexandria) 9.

73. For further general reading on the material discussed here, see Chadwick 1980; Liebeschuetz 1997; Rapp 2005; Lizzi Testa 2009.

74. Gregory of Nazianzus, *Oration* XXI (On the Great Athanasius, Bishop of Alexandria), *Oration* XLIII (Funeral Oration on the Great St. Basil, Bishop of Caesarea in Cappadocia); Ambrose of Milan, *On the Duties of the Clergy*; John Chrysostom, *Homily on 1 Timothy, On the Priesthood*; Augustine of Hippo, *De Doctrina Christiana* IV. Also the *Life of Ambrose* (by Paulinus of Milan), *Dialogue on the Life of Chrysostom* (by Palladius), and the *Life of Augustine* (by Possidius). See further Lochbrunner 1993; Sterk 1998; Rapp 2005, 41–55; and the articles collected in *Vescovi e pastori in epoca teodosiana* 1997.

75. On the history of the liturgy, see the older classics of Dix 1945 and Jungmann 1960, although Dix in particular exaggerates the impact of Constantine on Christian liturgical practice, and more recently, Jones et al. 1992; Bradshaw 1996.

76. Eucharist: Laverdiere 1996; Smith 2003. Baptism: McDonnell and Montague 1994; Saxer 1998.

77. Baldovin 1987; Bauer 1996.

78. On the much-debated evolution of infant baptism, see Jeremias 1960, 1963; Aland 1963; Wright 2005, 2007.

79. For the history of the catechumenate, see Dujarier 1979.

80. In addition to Cyril, contemporary catechetical works are preserved from Ambrose of Milan and Augustine of Hippo in the West and from John Chrysostom (composed while a presbyter in Antioch rather than as a bishop) and Theodore of Mopsuestia in the East. For an introduction to these works, see the collection of Whitaker and Johnson 2003.

81. On the importance of preaching in Late Antiquity, see in general Brown 1992; Dunn-Wilson 2005; and the edited volumes of Hunter 1989 and Cunningham and Allen 1998.

82. The sermons and preaching of Chrysostom have received renewed attention in recent years: see Allen and Mayer 1997; Mayer 2000; 2005; Maxwell 2006.

83. For the significance of Augustine's sermons both for his role as a bishop and for our knowledge of his life and thought, see the classic work of Brown 2000, esp. 443–462 on the newly discovered sermons identified by Dolbeau; Lancel 2002.

84. In the provocative view of A. H. M. Jones, the high standards demanded by clerical preaching in fact encouraged moral decline, leading many Christians to conclude that as they could not avoid sin, "they might as well be hanged for a sheep

as a lamb" (Jones 1964, 985). See further MacMullen 1989; more optimistically, Rousseau 1998.

85. See in general Patlagean 1977; Brown 2002.

86. For an overview of the evidence for Church wealth and its use in this period, see Jones 1960; 1964, 894–910; Rapp 2005, 208–234.

87. Letter of Cornelius of Rome (251–253), quoted in Eusebius, *HE* VI.43.11.

88. John Chrysostom, *Hom. Matt.* 66.3.

89. Gregory of Nazianzus, *Oration* XLIII.63. See further Daley 1999 and Horden, chapter 21 in this book.

90. See Lizzi Testa 1989; Rebillard and Sotinel 1998; Liebeschuetz 2001, 137–168; Brown 2002; Rapp 2005, 208–234.

91. For a convenient introduction to the evidence from Milan and Rome, see Krautheimer 1983.

92. Theodoret of Cyrrhus, *Letters* 79, 81. On Theodoret, see further Urbainczyk 2002.

93. For the evolution of the *domus episcopi*, primarily in the West, see Müller-Wiener 1989; Loseby 1992; Miller 2000.

94. See, for example, Theodoret, *Letters* 42–47.

95. John Chrysostom, *Homilies on the Statues*; Libanius, *Orations* XIX–XXIII. See French 1998.

96. Ammianus Marcellinus, *Res Gestae* XX.7.7–9.

97. Prosper, *Chronica Minora* I, 482; Jordanes, *Getica* 223; *Liber Pontificalis* 47.7.

98. Gryson 1979 and now Norton 2007.

99. Socrates, *HE* II.12–13; Sozomen, *HE* III.7.

100. Ammianus Marcellinus, *Res Gestae* XXVII.3.11–13.

101. *CJ* I.55.8 (a western law, repeated in the East by Anastasius in 505: *CJ* I.55.11).

102. Respectively *CJ* I.4.18 and *CJ* X.27.3.

103. On the "decline" or "flight" of the *curiales*, see Rostovtzeff 1926, 502–541; Jones 1964, 724–763; more recently, Liebeschuetz 2001.

104. Rapp 2005, esp. 280–289.

105. For initial reading, see Trombley 1993–1994; MacMullen 1997; Brown 1993; 1998a; and Maxwell, chapter 26 in this book.

106. On religious violence in Late Antiquity, and the role of bishops in that violence, see Gaddis 2005.

107. The religious topography of Alexandria was greatly contested in Late Antiquity: see Haas 1997.

108. Ammianus Marcellinus, *Res Gestae* XXII.11.8–11; Socrates, *HE* III.2–3; Sozomen, *HE* V.7. Julian, the emperor, rebuked the people of Alexandria (*Letter* 21) but appears to have been equally concerned to acquire the dead bishop's impressive library (*Letter* 23).

109. Rufinus, *HE* XI.22–30; Socrates, *HE* V.16–17; Sozomen, *HE* VII.15.

110. Socrates, *HE* VII.15.

111. For the career of Paulinus, see Trout 1999.

112. Julian, *Letter* 19.

113. Bradbury 1996.

114. Ambrose, *Letters* 40–41.

115. See Wilken 1983.

116. The literature on the theological controversies is vast. For an introduction, see on the "Arian" Controversy, Hanson 1988; Ayres 2004 and on the Christological

controversies, Frend 1972; Grillmeier 1975; 1987; Grillmeier with Hainthaler 1995; 1996.

117. On the ecclesiastical career of Athanasius, see Barnes 1993 and Gwynn 2012. For the involvement of Ambrose in the controversies, see in particular Williams 1995.

118. For one interesting approach to answering this difficult question, see MacMullen 2006.

119. Hence the famous complaint of Ammianus Marcellinus, that the repeated Church councils of the reign of Constantius "only succeeded in hamstringing the post service" (*Res Gestae* XXI.16.18).

120. The *Acts* are translated by Price and Gaddis 2005. On the role of acclamations at the council, see Roueché 2009.

121. Thus a number of the bishops at Chalcedon opposed the request of the imperial commissioners that they recognize the authority of the Constantinopolitan creed of 381: see Gwynn 2009, 16–18.

122. Socrates, *HE* I.19; Sozomen, *HE* II.24. For the significance of this episode, see Munro-Hay 1997; and Robin, chapter 9 in this book.

123. Philostorgius, *HE* II.5. For the texts and debates surrounding Ulfila's life, see Heather and Matthews 1991.

124. On the much-debated relationship between ascetic and episcopal authority in Late Antiquity, see among many others Rousseau 1978; Chadwick 1993; Leyser 2000; Rapp 2005, 137–152. On the closely related question of the rise of the late antique holy man, see in particular Brown 1971; 1995; 1998b; Cox Miller 1983.

125. John Cassian, *Institutes* XI.18. Monastic reluctance to face ordination became a hagiographical topos, although it must on occasion have had a basis in truth.

126. See the works cited in n. 124 and also Sterk 2004; Demacopoulos 2007.

127. On his deathbed, Antony left for Athanasius "the garment whereon I am laid, which he himself gave me new, but which with me has grown old" (*Life of Antony* 91). For Athanasius' relationship with Antony and Egyptian asceticism, see further Brakke 1995.

128. Brakke 1995, 99–110.

129. On the career and legacy of Martin, see Stancliffe 1983.

130. Augustine, *Sermon* 355.

131. For a few recent contributions to the debate, see Heather 2005; Ward-Perkins 2005; O'Donnell 2009.

132. Harries 1994. On the survival of the Roman church and aristocracy in southern Gaul and their interaction with their new rulers, see in general Heinzelmann 1976; Van Dam 1985; Mathisen 1993.

133. See Sidonius, *Letter* VI.12.5–7, celebrating the charity of Bishop Patiens of Lyons, whose distribution of grain "throughout all the ruined land of Gaul" surpassed even the achievements of Triptolemus, to whom the goddess Demeter first taught the art of agriculture.

134. Sidonius, *Letters* IV.24, VI.2.

135. Sidonius, *Letters* II.1, III.3, III.7, VII.7 (the last mourning the treaty of 474/5 by which his city and people fell under Gothic rule).

136. He secured his position in part through a letter, written to a friend who had Euric's favor, which contained a short poem celebrating the fame of the Gothic court (Sidonius, *Letter* VIII.9).

137. Sidonius lays down at length his vision of the ideal bishop in *Letter* VII.9, in which he records the address he delivered in the church at Bourges to justify his choice of Simplicius as the bishop of that city.

138. For the evidence, see Mathisen 1993, 89–104. Two other major figures who merit attention are Ruricius, bishop of Limoges (c. 485–510), and Ennodius, a Gallic aristocrat who became bishop of Pavia (514–521). See, respectively, Mathisen 1999; Kennell 2000.

139. Klingshirn 1994.

140. *Life of Caesarius* I.20, I.32, I.38, II.8.

141. *Life of Caesarius* I.55.

142. On the life and works of Avitus, see Shanzer and Wood 2002.

143. Avitus, *Letter* 46.

144. Avitus indeed debated scriptural theological questions with his "Arian" king (*Letters* 21, 22), who also requested the two rather inaccurate works that Avitus wrote concerning the eastern theological debates under the emperor Anastasius (*Contra Eutychianam haeresim* 1–2).

145. The relevant letters are collected with commentaries in Shanzer and Wood 2002, esp. 285–314.

146. Avitus, *Letters* 78, 93, 94.

147. According to Ennodius' *Life of Epiphanius of Pavia*, Epiphanius (bishop 466–496) interceded with Theoderic on behalf of the followers of Theoderic's defeated rival Odovacer (*Life* 122–147) and later was able to obtain from Theoderic one year's tax relief for the province of Liguria (*Life* 182–189).

148. Moorhead 1992a, esp. 212–252.

149. *Anonymous Valesianus* 93; *Liber Pontificalis* 55.1–6.

150. For a rather overcritical analysis of Victor, see Courtois 1954 and now Moorhead 1992b; Howe 2007. According to Victor's *History of the Vandal Persecution*, the Vandal king Huneric sent into exile 4,966 bishops, priests, deacons, and other Catholics (II.26). In a subtler form of persecution, Victor also reports that the Vandals "forbade the ordination of bishops for Zeugitana and the proconsular province. There used to be 164 of them, but little by little this number has diminished, and now they seem to number just three" (I.29).

151. See the sufferings of Bishop Masona of Merida, who endured repeated persecution under the Visigothic king Leovigild (*Lives of the Fathers of Merida* V.4–8).

152. The literature on Gregory is extensive. For the close relationship between his episcopal and literary activities, see in particular Breukelaar 1994; Heinzelmann 2001; and the articles collected in Mitchell and Wood 2002.

153. Gregory's predecessor as bishop of Tours was Eufronius (555–573), his first cousin once removed (Gregory, *History of the Franks* X.31).

154. "When I took over Tours cathedral, in which Saint Martin and all these other priests of the Lord had been consecrated to the episcopal office, it had been destroyed by fire and was in a sorry state of ruin. I rebuilt it, bigger and higher than before" (Gregory, *History of the Franks* X.31). Gregory proceeds to report that he also located a number of relics, restored the walls of St. Martin's church, and added an adjacent baptistery.

155. The greatest threat came when Chilperic's fugitive son Merovech sought asylum in Tours in 577. When Gregory refused Chilperic's demand that he expel Merovech, Chilperic sent an army against Tours, which was turned aside only by

Merovech's decision to leave to prevent the church and lands of St. Martin being defiled on his account (*History of the Franks* V.14). On a less violent note, Gregory also resisted the efforts of Childebert II to tax the city of Tours (IX.30).

156. In addition to Merovech (see preceding note), Gregory gave asylum to duke Guntram Boso, who had served Chilperic's brother and rival Sigibert (*History of the Franks* IV.50). Chilperic's official Roccolen attempted to violate the asylum and threatened to destroy Tours if Gregory did not give way, but he was struck down by the wrath of God and Saint Martin (V.4).

157. E.g., Gregory, *History of the Franks* VII.47.

158. Gregory was put on trial for treason during the reign of Chilperic, on false charges that he had spread rumors regarding a liaison between Bishop Bertram of Bordeaux and Chilperic's Queen Fredegund (*History of the Franks* V.49).

159. The Preface to *History of the Franks* III, following the death of Clovis at the end of Book II, proclaims "the happy outcome of the Christians who have believed in the Holy Trinity and the disasters which have befallen those who have sought to destroy it" and asserts Gregory's belief in a coequal Trinity. Gregory also describes debates in which he refuted the "Arians" Agilan (V.43) and Oppila (VI.40). On the importance of Gregory's conception of orthodoxy and heresy in his *History*, see further Heinzelmann 1998.

160. Gregory, *History of the Franks* II.27–43; Wood 1985.

161. For further discussion of Merovingian episcopal leadership, see Prinz 1973; Wood 1994, 71–87. On the wider religious world of Merovingian Gaul, see also Hen 1995.

162. On the church of Rome in Late Antiquity, see for a general overview Pietri 1976; Richards 1979; more broadly, Schatz 1996; Duffy 2002. Our major source, the *Liber Pontificalis*, is translated with notes in Davis 2000. The term *pope* did not carry the meaning in the late antique period that it would later acquire and has therefore been avoided here.

163. "You will write two little books and send one to Clement and one to Grapte. Clement will send his to the other cities, for he is charged with this responsibility. Grapte will admonish the widows and orphans. But you will read it in this city with the presbyters who preside in the church" (Hermas, *Vision* II.4.3). The date and context of the text remain controversial, and it is uncertain if the Clement named here is the author of the Roman letter to the church of Corinth known as 1 Clement. See further Osiek 1999; more generally, Jeffers 1991.

164. Eusebius, *HE* V.23–24.

165. See Brent 1995.

166. "You are Peter, and on this rock I will build my church, and the gates of Hades will not prevail against it. I will give you the keys of the kingdom of heaven, and whatever you bind on earth will be bound in heaven, and whatever you loose on earth will be loosed in heaven" (Matthew 16:18–19). Stephen's claim to authority in succession to Peter was denounced by Firmilian, bishop of Cappadocian Caesarea, who in a letter to Cyprian (preserved as Cyprian, *Letter* LXXV) sarcastically parodied Stephen's use of this verse (LXXV.17).

167. Nicaea (325) canon 6.

168. The buildings, estates, and other gifts that Constantine is reported to have given to the church of Rome are recorded in great detail in *Liber Pontificalis* 34.9–33.

169. For the text of the "Donation" with commentary, see Edwards 2003; for a recent reassessment, see Fried 2007.

170. Constantine's letter to Miltiades is quoted in Eusebius, *HE* X.5.18–20.

171. For the assertion of Roman authority to hear such appeals, see the letter of Julius (bishop of Rome 337–352) on behalf of Athanasius and of Marcellus of Ancyra, quoted in Athanasius, *Apologia Contra Arianos* 20–35.

172. Western Serdica (343) canons 3c, 4, 7, and 10a (following the numbering of the Latin canons in Hess 2002, 212–225). The Western Serdica canons were later claimed to be Nicene by Zosimus (bishop of Rome 417–418), an error denounced to Zosimus' successor Boniface (bishop 418–422) by the bishops of North Africa (Letter of the Council of Carthage 419, preserved as Boniface, *Letter* 11). See Merdinger 1997, 111–135.

173. See further Lizzi Testa 2004; for the concept of Roman primacy in the time of Damasus, see Piepkorn 1974.

174. Quoted in Jerome, *Against John of Jerusalem* 8. Needless to say, Jerome was not amused.

175. For Leo, see Jalland 1941; McShane 1979; and now Wessel 2008. For Gregory, see Richards 1980; Markus 1997.

176. Older scholarship (e.g., Grillmeier 1975, 543–544) rather exaggerated Leo's influence upon the decisions of Chalcedon, where the dominant voice was that of the deceased Cyril of Alexandria. There is a recent reexamination of the role of Leo at Chalcedon in Uthemann 2005; see also chapter 28 by Susan Wessel in this book.

177. "[June 29, the Feast of Peter and Paul] is to be honoured with special and peculiar exultation in our city, that there may be a predominance of gladness on the day of their martyrdom in the place where the chief of the Apostles met their glorious end. . . . These are they who promoted thee to such glory, that being made a holy nation, a chosen people, a priestly and royal state, and the head of the world through the blessed Peter's holy See thou didst attain a wider sway by the worship of God than by earthly government" (Leo the Great, *Sermon* LXXXII.1). See further Wessel 2008, 285–321, on Leo and Roman primacy.

178. For Leo and Attila, see n. 97; for his role in limiting the excesses of the Vandals, Victor of Tonnena, *sub anno* 455.

179. Vigilius was summoned to Constantinople by the emperor and compelled to accept Justinian's condemnation of the "Three Chapters." For the evidence and further discussion of papal-imperial relations in the sixth century, see Sotinel 2005.

180. For the significance of this crucial period of transition, see Markus 1990, esp. 216–228.

181. The evidence is collected in Markus 1997, 112–124.

182. Gregory clashed repeatedly with the exarch Romanus, who hindered his efforts to negotiate a truce with the Lombards (*Letters* II.38, V.36, VI.33), and he appealed to the Catholic Lombard queen Theodelinda to influence her "Arian" husband Agilulf to maintain the peace (*Letter* IX.43). See further Markus 1997, 97–107.

183. On the organization of the mission, see in particular Gregory, *Letters* VI.51–59, and on its success *Letter* VIII.30. The classic study is still Mayr-Harting 1991.

184. Gregory the Great, *Pastoral Rule*, Prologue.

185. Study of the *Pastoral Rule* was encouraged for all Carolingian bishops by the councils of Rheims (canon 10) and Tours (canon 3) summoned by Charlemagne in 813, while Alfred ordered translations of the *Pastoral Rule* to be circulated throughout his kingdom as one of the books "which are most needful for all men to know" (Alfred, *Translation of Gregory's Pastoral Care*, Preface).

186. For a general introduction, see Evans 1996 and the articles collected in Maas 2005.

187. *CJ* I.4.26. In 545, the bishop and other members of the local elite were also required to oversee those responsible for the tax collection in their region (Justinian, *Novel* CXXVIII.16).

188. Justinian, *Novel* VIII.8 (535).

189. Justinian, *Novel* LXXXVI (539).

190. Justinian, *Novel* VI, Preface. *Novel* VI.1 lays down the moral life required of someone who sought to become a bishop, reflecting in imperial law the ideal vision of the episcopate laid down by earlier Christian writers.

191. Geanakoplos 1965; Dagron 1996.

192. For the debates that continued after Chalcedon and an overview of Justinian's religious policies, see Gray 1979; Grillmeier 1987; Grillmeier with Hainthaler 1995; 1996; Gray 2005; Van Rompay 2005.

193. Frend 1972; Bundy 1978; Menze 2008.

194. This was already true during the Persian wars of Justinian: for the evidence, see Claude 1969, 125–129.

195. The role of Zacharias is celebrated in Antiochus Strategos' *The Capture of Jerusalem by the Persians*, an eyewitness account that is preserved only in a tenth-century Georgian manuscript. There is a partial English translation in Conybeare 1910.

196. For the primary sources, see Pentcheva 2002, 4–12.

197. Theodore Synkellos, *Sermon on the Siege of the City* (Makk 1975, 80–81); cf. George of Pisidia, *The Avar War* 366–373.

WORKS CITED

Aland, K. 1963. *Did the Early Church Baptize Infants?* London: SCM.

Allen, P., and W. Mayer. 1997. "Traditions of Constantinopolitan Preaching: Towards a New Assessment of Where Chrysostom Preached What," *BZ* 24: 94–114.

Ayres, L. 2004. *Nicaea and Its Legacy: An Approach to Fourth-Century Trinitarian Theology*. Oxford: Oxford University Press.

Baldovin, J. 1987. *The Urban Character of Christian Worship: The Origins, Development, and Meaning of Stational Liturgy*. Rome: Pontificium Institutum Studiorum Orientalium.

Barnes, T. D. 1981. *Constantine and Eusebius*. Cambridge, MA: Harvard University Press.

———. 1993. *Athanasius and Constantius: Theology and Politics in the Constantinian Empire*. Cambridge, MA: Harvard University Press.

Bauer, F. A. 1996. *Stadt, Platz und Denkmal in der Spätantike: Untersuchungen zur Ausstattung des öffentlichen Raumes in den spätantiken Städten Rom, Konstantinopel und Ephesos*. Mainz: P. von Zabern.

Bauer, W. 1934. *Rechtgläubigkeit und Ketzerei im ältesten Christentum*. Tübingen: Mohr.

Bobertz, C. A. 1992. "The Development of Episcopal Order." In *Eusebius, Christianity and Judaism*, ed. H. W. Attridge and G. Hata, 183–211. Leiden: Brill.

Bowersock, G. W. 1986. "From Emperor to Bishop: The Self-Conscious Transformation of Political Power in the Fourth Century A.D.," *CPh* 81: 298–307.

Bradbury, S. 1996. *Severus of Minorca: Letter on the Conversion of the Jews*. Oxford: Clarendon Press.
Bradshaw, P. F. 1983. *Liturgical Presidency in the Early Church*. Bramcote: Grove.
———. 1996. *Early Christian Worship: A Basic Introduction to Ideas and Practice*. London: SPCK.
Brakke, D. 1995. *Athanasius and the Politics of Asceticism*. Oxford: Clarendon.
Brent, A. 1995. *Hippolytus and the Roman Church in the Third Century: Communities in Tension before the Emergence of a Monarch-Bishop*. Leiden: Brill.
———. 2007. *Ignatius of Antioch: A Martyr Bishop and the Origin of Episcopacy*. London: Continuum.
Breukelaar, A. H. B. 1994. *Historiography and Episcopal Authority in Sixth-Century Gaul: The Histories of Gregory of Tours Interpreted in Their Historical Context*. Göttingen: Vandenhoeck & Ruprecht.
Brown, P. 1971. "The Rise and Function of the Holy Man in Late Antiquity," *JRS* 61: 80–101. Reprinted and revised in P. Brown, *Society and the Holy in Late Antiquity*, 1982, 103–152. London: Faber and Faber.
———. 1992. *Power and Persuasion in Late Antiquity: Towards a Christian Empire*. Madison: University of Wisconsin Press.
———. 1993. "The Problem of Christianization," *PBA* 82: 89–106.
———. 1995. *Authority and the Sacred: Aspects of the Christianisation of the Roman World*. Cambridge: Cambridge University Press.
———. 1998a. "Christianization and Religious Conflict." In *Cambridge Ancient History Vol. 13: The Late Empire, A.D. 337–425*, ed. Averil Cameron and P. Garnsey, 632–664. Cambridge: Cambridge University Press.
———. 1998b. "The Rise and Function of the Holy Man in Late Antiquity, 1971–1997," *JECS* 6: 353–376.
———. 2000. *Augustine of Hippo: A Biography*. Rev. ed. London: Faber and Faber.
———. 2002. *Poverty and Leadership in the Later Roman Empire*. Hanover, NH: University Press of New England.
Bundy, D. D. 1978, "Jacob Baradeus: The State of Research, a Review of Sources, and a New Approach," *Le Muséon* 91: 45–86.
Burns, J. P. 2002. *Cyprian the Bishop*. London: Routledge.
Carroll, T. K. 1984. *Preaching the Word*. Wilmington, DE: M. Glazier.
Chadwick, H. 1980. *The Role of the Christian Bishop in Ancient Society*. Berkeley: Center for Hermeneutical Studies in Hellenistic and Modern Culture.
———. 1993. "Bishops and Monks," *Studia Patristica* 24: 45–61.
Cimma, M. R. 1989. *L'episcopalis audientia nelle costituzioni imperiali da Costantino à Giustiniano*. Turin: Giappichelli.
Claude, D. 1969. *Die byzantinische Stadt im 6. Jahrhundert*. München: Beck.
Conybeare, F. C. 1910. "Antiochus Strategos' Account of the Sack of Jerusalem in A.D. 614," *EHR* 25: 502–517.
Courtois, C. 1954. *Victor de Vita et son oeuvre: Étude critique*. Algiers: Imprimerie officielle.
Cox Miller, P. 1983. *Biography in Late Antiquity: A Quest for the Holy Man*. Berkeley: University of California Press.
Cunningham, M. B., and P. Allen, eds. 1998. *Preacher and Audience: Studies in Early Christian and Byzantine Homiletics*. Leiden: Brill.
Dagron, G. 1996. *Empereur et prêtre: Étude sur le 'cesaropapisme' byzantine*. Paris: Gallimard.

Daley, B. E. 1999. "Building a New City: The Cappadocian Fathers and the Rhetoric of Philanthropy," *JECS* 7: 431–461.

Dassmann, E. 1973. *Sündenvergebung durch Taufe, Busse und Martyrerfürbitte in den Zeugnissen frühchristlicher Frömmigkeit und Kunst.* Münster: Aschendorffsche Verlagsbuchhandlung.

Davis, R. 2000. *The Book of Pontiffs (Liber Pontificalis): The Ancient Biographies of the First Ninety Roman Bishops to AD 715*, rev. ed. Liverpool: Liverpool University Press.

Davis, S. J. 2004. *The Early Coptic Papacy: The Egyptian Church and Its Leadership in Late Antiquity.* Cairo: American University in Cairo Press.

de Clercq, V. C. 1954. *Ossius of Cordova: A Contribution to the History of the Constantinian Period.* Washington, DC: Catholic University of America Press.

Demacopoulos, G. E. 2007. *Five Models of Spiritual Direction in the Early Church.* Notre Dame, IN: University of Notre Dame Press.

Dix, G. 1945. *The Shape of the Liturgy.* London: Dacre.

Drake, H. A. 2000. *Constantine and the Bishops: The Politics of Intolerance.* Baltimore: Johns Hopkins University Press.

Ducloux, A. 1994. *Ad ecclesiam confugere: Naissance du d'asile dans les églises (IVe-milieu du Ve s.).* Paris: De Boccard.

Duffy, E. 2002. *Saints and Sinners: A History of the Popes*, 2nd ed. New Haven, CT: Yale University Press.

Dujarier, M. 1979. *A History of the Catechumenate: The First Six Centuries.* New York: William H. Sadlier.

Dunn-Wilson, D. 2005. *A Mirror for the Church: Preaching in the First Five Centuries.* Grand Rapids, MI: Eerdmans.

Edwards, M. 2003. *Constantine and Christendom.* Liverpool: Liverpool University Press.

Evans, J. A. S. 1996. *The Age of Justinian: The Circumstances of Imperial Power.* London: Routledge.

Faivre, A. 1977. *Naissance d'une hierarchie.* Paris: Editions Beauchesne.

Ferguson, E. 2001. "Catechesis and Initiation." In *The Origins of Christendom in the West*, ed. A. Kreider, 229–268. New York: T. & T. Clark.

Fowden, G. 1994. "The Last Days of Constantine: Oppositional Views and Their Influence," *JRS* 84: 146–170.

French, D. R. 1998. "Rhetoric and the Rebellion of A.D. 387 in Antioch," *Historia* 47: 468–484.

Frend, W. H. C. 1971. *The Donatist Church: A Movement of Protest in Roman North Africa*, 2nd ed. Oxford: Clarendon.

———. 1972. *The Rise of the Monophysite Movement: Chapters in the History of the Church in the Fifth and Sixth Centuries.* Cambridge: Cambridge University Press.

Fried, J. 2007. *Donation of Constantine and Constitutum Constantini: The Misinterpretation of a Fiction and Its Original Meaning.* Berlin: Walter de Gruyter.

Gaddis, M. 2005. *There Is No Crime for Those Who Have Christ: Religious Violence in the Christian Roman Empire.* Berkeley: University of California Press.

Geanakoplos, D. J. 1965. "Church and State in the Byzantine Empire: A Reconsideration of the Problem of Caesaropapism," *CH* 34: 381–403.

Gilliard, F. D. 1984. "Senatorial Bishops in the Fourth Century," *HTR* 77: 153–175.

Gray, P. T. R. 1979. *The Defense of Chalcedon in the East (451–553).* Leiden: Brill.

———. 2005. "The Legacy of Chalcedon: Christological Problems and Their Significance." In *The Cambridge Companion to the Age of Justinian*, ed. M. Maas, 215–238. Cambridge: Cambridge University Press.

Grillmeier, A. 1975. *Christ in Christian Tradition, Vol. 1: From the Apostolic Age to Chalcedon (451)*, 2nd rev. ed. Trans. J. Bowden. London: Mowbray.

———. 1987. *Christ in Christian Tradition, Vol. 2: From the Council of Chalcedon (451) to Gregory the Great (590–604), Pt. 1, Reception and Contradiction: The Development of the Discussion about Chalcedon from 451 to the Beginning of the Reign of Justinian.* Trans. P. Allen and J. Cawte. London: Westminster/John Knox.

Grillmeier, A., with T. Hainthaler. 1995. *Christ in Christian Tradition, Vol. 2.2: The Church of Constantinople in the Sixth Century*. Trans. J. Cawte and P. Allen. Louisville, KY: Westminster/John Knox.

———. 1996. *Christ in Christian Tradition, Vol. 2.4: The Church of Alexandria with Nubia and Ethiopia after 451*. Trans. O. C. Dean Jr. Louisville, KY: Westminster/John Knox.

Gryson, R. 1979. "Les élections épiscopales en orient au IVe siècle," *RHE* 74: 301–345.

Gwynn, D. M. 1999. "Constantine and the Other Eusebius," *Prudentia* 21: 94–124.

———. 2009. "The Council of Chalcedon and the Definition of Christian Tradition." In *Chalcedon in Context: Church Councils 400–700*, ed. R. Price and M. Whitby, 7–26. Liverpool: Liverpool University Press.

———. 2012. *Athanasius of Alexandria: Bishop, Theologian, Ascetic, Father*. Oxford: Oxford University Press.

Haas, C. 1997. *Alexandria in Late Antiquity: Topography and Conflict*. Baltimore: Johns Hopkins University Press.

Hanson, R. P. C. 1985. "Office and Concept of Office in the Early Church." In R. P. C. Hanson, *Studies in Christian Antiquity*, 117–143. Edinburgh: T. & T. Clark.

———. 1988. *The Search for the Christian Doctrine of God: The Arian Controversy 318–381*. Edinburgh: T. & T. Clark.

Harries, J. 1994. *Sidonius Apollinaris and the Fall of Rome, A.D. 407–485*. Oxford: Clarendon Press.

Hartney, A. M. 2004. *John Chrysostom and the Transformation of the City*. London: Duckworth.

Hatch, E. 1881. *The Organization of the Early Christian Churches*. London: Clarendon Press.

Heather, P. 2005. *The Fall of the Roman Empire: A New History*. London: Macmillan.

Heather, P., and J. Matthews. 1991. *The Goths in the Fourth Century*. Liverpool: Liverpool University Press.

Heinzelmann, M. 1976. *Bischofsherrschaft in Gallien: Zur Kontinuität römischer Führungsschichten vom 4. bis 7. Jahrhundert: Soziale, prosopographische und bildungsgeschichtliche Aspekte*. Munich: Artemis.

———. 1998. "Heresy in Books I and II of Gregory of Tours' *Historiae*." In *After Rome's Fall: Narrators and Sources of Early Medieval History*, ed. A. C. Murray, 67–82. Toronto: University of Toronto Press.

———. 2001. *Gregory of Tours: History and Society in the Sixth Century*. Trans. C. Carroll. Cambridge: Cambridge University Press.

Hen, Y. 1995. *Culture and Religion in Merovingian Gaul, AD 481–751*. Leiden: Brill.

Herman, E. 1935. "Zum Asylrecht im byzantinischen Reich," *OCP* 1: 204–238.

Hess, H. 2002. *The Early Development of Canon Law and the Council of Serdica*. Oxford: Oxford University Press.

Howe, T. 2007. *Vandalen, Barbaren und Arianer bei Victor von Vita*. Frankfurt: Verlag Antike.

Hunt, E. D. 1989. "Did Constantius II Have 'Court Bishops'?" *Studia Patristica* 19: 86–90.

Hunter, D. G., ed. 1989. *Preaching in the Patristic Age*. New York: Paulist Press.

Jalland, T. 1941. *Life and Times of St. Leo the Great.* New York: Society for Promoting Christian Knowledge.

Jeffers, J. S. 1991. *Conflict at Rome: Social Order and Hierarchy in Early Christianity.* Minneapolis, MN: Fortress Press.

Jeremias, J. 1960. *Infant Baptism in the First Four Centuries.* Trans. D. Cairns. London: SCM.

———. 1963. *The Origins of Infant Baptism: A Further Study in Reply to Kurt Aland.* Trans. D. M. Barton. London: SCM.

Jerg, E. 1970. *Vir venerabilis: Untersuchungen zur Titulatur der Bischöfe in den ausserkirchlichen Texten der Spätantike als Beitrag zur Deutung ihrer öffentlichen Stellung.* Vienna: Herder.

Jones, A. H. M. 1960. "Church Finance in the Fifth and Sixth Centuries," *JTS* n.s. 11: 84–94.

———. 1964. *The Later Roman Empire 284–602: A Social, Economic, and Administrative Survey*, 3 vols. Oxford: Blackwell.

Jones, C., G. Wainwright, E. Yarnold, and P. F. Bradshaw, eds. 1992. *The Study of Liturgy*, rev. ed. London: SPCK.

Jungmann, J. 1960. *The Early Liturgy to the Time of Gregory the Great.* Trans. F. A. Brunner. London: Darton, Longman & Todd.

Kelly, J. N. D. 1995. *Golden Mouth: The Story of John Chrysostom—Ascetic, Preacher, Bishop.* London: Duckworth.

Kennell, S. A. H. 2000. *Magnus Felix Ennodius: A Gentleman of the Church.* Ann Arbor: University of Michigan Press.

King, K. L. 2003. *What Is Gnosticism?* Cambridge, MA: Belknap Press of Harvard University Press.

Kirk, K. E., ed. 1946. *The Apostolic Ministry: Essays on the History and the Doctrine of Episcopacy.* London: Hodder & Stoughton.

Klauser, T. 1953. *Der Ursprung der bischöflichen Insignien und Ehrenrechte*, 2nd ed. Krefeld: Scherpe-Verlag.

Klingshirn, W. 1994. *Caesarius of Arles: The Making of a Christian Community in Late Antique Gaul.* Cambridge: Cambridge University Press.

Krautheimer, R. 1983. *Three Christian Capitals: Topography and Politics.* Berkeley: University of California Press.

Lamoreaux, J. C. 1995. "Episcopal Courts in Late Antiquity," *JECS* 3: 143–167.

Lancel, S. 2002. *St Augustine.* Trans. A. Nevill. London: SCM.

Laverdiere, E. 1996. *The Eucharist in the New Testament and the Early Church.* Collegeville, MN: Liturgical Press.

Lenski, N. 2001. "Evidence for the *Audientia episcopalis* in the New Letters of Augustine." In *Law, Society and Authority in Late Antiquity*, ed. R. Mathisen, 93–97. Oxford: Oxford University Press.

Leyser, C. 2000. *Authority and Asceticism from Augustine to Gregory the Great.* Oxford: Clarendon Press.

L'Huillier, P. 1996. *The Church of the Ancient Councils: The Disciplinary Work of the First Four Ecumenical Councils.* Crestwood, NY: St. Vladimir's Seminary Press.

Liebeschuetz, J. H. W. G. 1990. *Barbarians and Bishops: Army, Church, and State in the Age of Arcadius and Chrysostom.* Oxford: Clarendon.

———. 1997. "The Rise of the Bishop in the Christian Roman Empire and the Successor Kingdoms," *Electrum* 1: 113–125.

———. 2001. *The Decline and Fall of the Roman City.* Oxford: Oxford University Press.

Lieu, S. N. C. 1998. "From History to Legend and Legend to History: The Medieval and Byzantine Transformation of Constantine's *Vita*." In *Constantine: History, Historiography and Legend*, ed. S. N. C. Lieu and D. Montserrat, 136–176. London: Routledge.
Lizzi Testa, R. 1989. *Vescovi e strutture ecclesiastiche nella città tardoantica ("L'Italia Annonaria" nel IV–V secolo d. C.)*. Como: Edizioni New Press.
———. 2004. *Senatori, popolo, papi: Il governo di Roma al tempo dei Valentiniani*. Bari: Edipuglia.
———. 2009. "The Late Antique Bishop: Image and Reality." In *A Companion to Late Antiquity*, ed. P. Rousseau, 525–538. Chichester: Wiley-Blackwell.
Lochbrunner, M. 1993. *Über das Priestertum: Historische und systematische Untersuchung zum Priesterbild des Johannes Chrysostomus*. Bonn: Borengässer.
Logan, A. 1996. *Gnostic Truth and Christian Heresy: A Study in the History of Gnosticism*. Edinburgh: T. & T. Clark.
Loseby, S. 1992. "Bishops and Cathedrals: Order and Diversity in the Fifth-Century Urban Landscape of Southern Gaul." In *Fifth-Century Gaul: A Crisis of Identity?* ed. J. Drinkwater and H. Elton, 144–155. Cambridge: Cambridge University Press.
Maas, M., ed. 2005. *The Cambridge Companion to the Age of Justinian*. Cambridge: Cambridge University Press.
MacMullen, R. 1989. "The Preacher's Audience (AD 350–400)," *JTS* n.s. 40: 503–511.
———. 1997. *Christianity and Paganism in the Fourth to Eighth Centuries*. New Haven, CT: Yale University Press.
———. 2006. *Voting about God in Early Church Councils*. New Haven, CT: Yale University Press.
Makk, F. 1975. *Traduction et commentaire de l'homélie écrite probablement par Théodore le Syncelle sur le siège de Constantinople en 626*. Szeged: JATE.
Markus, R. A. 1990. *The End of Ancient Christianity*. Cambridge: Cambridge University Press.
———. 1997. *Gregory the Great and His World*. Cambridge: Cambridge University Press.
Mathisen, R. W. 1989. *Ecclesiastical Factionalism and Religious Controversy in Fifth-Century Gaul*. Washington, DC: Catholic University of America Press.
———. 1993. *Roman Aristocrats in Barbarian Gaul: Strategies for Survival in an Age of Transition*. Austin: University of Texas Press.
———. 1999. *Ruricius of Limoges and Friends: A Collection of Letters from Visigothic Gaul*. Liverpool: Liverpool University Press.
Maxwell, J. L. 2006. *Christianization and Communication in Late Antiquity: John Chrysostom and His Congregation in Antioch*. Cambridge: Cambridge University Press.
Mayer, W. 2000. "Who Came to Hear John Chrysostom Preach? Recovering a Late Fourth-Century Preacher's Audience," *Ephemerides Theologicae Lovanienses* 76: 73–87.
———. 2005. *The Homilies of St John Chrysostom, Provenance: Reshaping the Foundations*. Rome: Pontificium Institutum Studiorum Orientalium.
Mayr-Harting, H. 1991. *The Coming of Christianity to Anglo-Saxon England*, 3rd ed. London: Batsford.
McDonnell, K., and G. T. Montague. 1994. *Christian Initiation and Baptism in the Holy Spirit: Evidence from the First Eight Centuries*, 2nd ed. Collegeville, MN: Liturgical Press.

McLynn, N. 1994. *Ambrose of Milan: Church and Court in a Christian Capital.* Berkeley: University of California Press.
———. 1999. "The Use and Abuse of Eudoxius of Germanicia," *Kyoyo-ronso* 110: 69–99.
McShane, P. A. 1979. *La Romanitas et le Pape Léon le Grand: L'apport culturel des institutions impériales à la formation des structures ecclésiastiques.* Tournai: Desclée and Bellarmin.
Menze, V.-L. 2008. *Justinian and the Making of the Syrian Orthodox Church.* Oxford: Oxford University Press.
Merdinger, J. 1997. *Rome and the African Church in the Time of Augustine.* New Haven, CT: Yale University Press.
Millar, F. 1971. "Paul of Samosata, Zenobia, and Aurelian: The Church, Local Culture, and Political Allegiance in Third Century Syria," *JRS* 61: 1–17.
———. 1977. *The Emperor in the Roman World (31 BC–AD 337).* London: Duckworth.
Miller, M. C. 2000. *The Bishop's Palace: Architecture and Authority in Medieval Italy.* Ithaca, NY: Cornell University Press.
Mitchell, K., and I. Wood, eds. 2002. *The World of Gregory of Tours.* Leiden: Brill.
Molland, E. 1954. "La développement de l'idée de succession apostolique," *RHPhR* 34: 1–29.
Moorhead, J. 1992a. *Theoderic in Italy.* Oxford: Clarendon Press.
———. 1992b. *Victor of Vita: History of the Vandal Persecution.* Liverpool: Liverpool University Press.
Mühlenberg, E., and J. van Oort, eds. 1994. *Predigt in der Alten Kirche.* Kampen: Kok Pharos.
Müller-Wiener, W. 1989. "Bischofsresidenzen des 4.–7. Jhs. im östlichen Mittelmeer-Raum." In *Actes du XIe Congrès International d'Archéologie Chrétienne,* 1: 651–709. Vatican City: Pontificio Istituto di Archeologia Cristiana; Rome: École Française de Rome.
Munro-Hay, S. 1997. *Ethiopia and Alexandria: The Metropolitan Episcopacy of Ethiopia.* Warsaw: ZAS PAN.
Nasrallah, L. S. 2003. *"An Ecstasy of Folly": Prophecy and Authority in Early Christianity.* Cambridge, MA: Harvard Divinity School.
Niederwimmer, K. 1989. *Die Didache.* Göttingen: Vandenhoeck & Ruprecht.
Norton, P. 2007. *Episcopal Elections 250–600: Hierarchy and Popular Will in Late Antiquity.* Oxford: Oxford University Press.
Odahl, C. M. 2004. *Constantine and the Christian Empire.* London: Routledge.
O'Donnell, J. J. 2009. *The Ruin of the Roman Empire.* London: Profile.
Osiek, C. 1999. *Shepherd of Hermas: A Commentary.* Ed. H. Koester. Minneapolis, MN: Fortress Press.
Pagels, E. 1978. "Visions, Appearances and Apostolic Authority: Gnostic and Orthodox Traditions." In *Gnosis: Festschrift für Hans Jonas,* ed. B. Aland, 415–430. Göttingen: Vandenhoeck & Ruprecht.
Patlagean, E. 1977. *Pauvreté économique et pauvreté sociale à Byzance, 4e–7e siècles.* Paris: Mouton.
Pentcheva, B. V. 2002. "The Supernatural Protector of Constantinople: The Virgin and Her Icons in the Tradition of the Avar Siege," *BMGS* 26: 2–41.
Piepkorn, A. C. 1974. "From Nicaea to Leo the Great." In *Papal Primacy and the Universal Church,* ed. P. C. Empie and T. A. Murphy, 73–97. Minneapolis, MN: Augsburg.

Pietri, C. 1976. *Roma Christiana: Recherches sur l'Eglise de Rome, son organisation, sa politique, son idéologie de Miltiade à Sixte III (311–440)*, 2 vols. Rome: École Française de Rome.

———. 1981. "Aristocratie et société clericale dans l'Italie chrétienne au temps d'Odoacre et de Théoderic," *Mélanges d'archéologie et d'histoire de l'école française de Rome: Antiquité* 93: 417–467.

Price, R., and M. Gaddis. 2005. *The Acts of the Council of Chalcedon, Translated with an Introduction and Notes*. Liverpool: Liverpool University Press.

Prinz, F. 1973. "Die bischöfliche Stadtherrschaft im Frankenreich," *Historische Zeitschrift* 217: 1–35.

Rapp, C. 1998. "Imperial Ideology in the Making: Eusebius of Caesarea on Constantine as 'Bishop,'" *JTS* n.s. 49: 685–695.

———. 2005. *Holy Bishops in Late Antiquity: The Nature of Christian Leadership in an Age of Transition*. Berkeley: University of California Press.

Rebillard, É., and C. Sotinel, eds. 1998. *L'évêque dans la cité du IVe au Ve siècle: Image et autorité*. Rome: École Française de Rome.

Richards, J. 1979. *The Popes and the Papacy in the Early Middle Ages, 476–752*. London: Routledge & Kegan Paul.

———. 1980. *Consul of God: The Life and Times of Gregory the Great*. London: Routledge & Kegan Paul.

Rives, J. B. 1995. *Religion and Authority in Roman Carthage from Augustus to Constantine*. Oxford: Clarendon Press.

Rostovtzeff, M. I. 1926. *The Social and Economic History of the Roman Empire*, 2 vols. Oxford: Clarendon Press.

Roueché, C. 2009. "Acclamations at the Council of Chalcedon." In *Chalcedon in Context: Church Councils 400–700*, ed. R. Price and M. Whitby, 169–177. Liverpool: Liverpool University Press.

Rousseau, P. 1978. *Ascetics, Authority, and the Church in the Age of Jerome and Cassian*. Oxford: Oxford University Press.

———. 1998. "'The Preacher's Audience': A More Optimistic View." In *Ancient History in a Modern University*, vol. 2: *Early Christianity, Late Antiquity and Beyond*, ed. T. W. Hillard, R. A. Kearsley, C. E. V Nixon, and A. M. Nobbs, 391–400. Grand Rapids, MI: Ancient History Documentary Research Centre, Macquarie University, and William B. Eerdmans.

Sage, M. M. 1975. *Cyprian*. Cambridge, MA: Philadelphia Patristic Foundation.

Saxer, V. 1998. *Les rites de l'initiation chrétienne du IIe au VIe siècle: Esquisse historique et signification d'après leurs principaux témoins*. Spoleto: Centro Italiano di Studi sull'Alto Medioevo.

Schatz, K. 1996. *Papal Primacy: From Its Origins to the Present*. Collegeville, MN: Liturgical.

Schöllgen, G. 1988. *Die Anfänge der Professionalisierung des Klerus und das kirchliche Amt in der syrischen Didaskalie*. Münster: Aschendorffsche Verlagsbuchhandlung.

Schweizer, E. 1961. *Church Order in the New Testament*. London: SCM.

Shanzer, D., and I. Wood. 2002. *Avitus of Vienne: Letters and Selected Prose*. Liverpool: Liverpool University Press.

Shaw, B. D. 1992. "African Christianity: Disputes, Definitions, and 'Donatists'," In *Orthodoxy and Heresy in Religious Movements: Discipline and Dissent*, ed. M. R. Greenshields and T. A. Robinson, 5–34. Lewiston, ME: Edwin Mellen.

Smith, D. E. 2003. *From Symposium to Eucharist: The Banquet in the Early Christian World*. Minneapolis, MN: Fortress.

Sotinel, C. 2005. "Emperors and Popes in the Sixth Century: The Western View." In *The Cambridge Companion to the Age of Justinian*, ed. M. Maas, 267–290. Cambridge: Cambridge University Press.

Stancliffe, C. 1983. *St. Martin and His Hagiographer*. Oxford: Clarendon Press.

Sterk, A. 1998. "On Basil, Moses, and the Model Bishop: The Cappadocian Legacy of Leadership," *CH* 67: 225–253.

———. 2004. *Renouncing the World Yet Leading the Church: The Monk-Bishop in Late Antiquity*. Cambridge, MA: Harvard University Press.

Tabbernee, W. 2007. *Fake Prophecy and Polluted Sacraments: Ecclesiastical and Imperial Reactions to Montanism*. Leiden: Brill.

Telfer, W. 1962. *The Office of a Bishop*. London: Darton, Longman and Todd.

Tilley, M. A. 1997. *The Bible in Christian North Africa: The Donatist World*. Minneapolis, MN: Fortress Press.

Torjesen, K. J. 2008. "Clergy and Laity." In *The Oxford Handbook of Early Christian Studies*, ed. S. A. Harvey and D. G. Hunter, 389–405. Oxford: Oxford University Press.

Trevett, C. 1992. *A Study of Ignatius of Antioch in Syria and Asia*. Lewiston, ME: Edwin Mellen.

———. 1996. *Montanism: Gender, Authority and the New Prophecy*. Cambridge: Cambridge University Press.

Trombley, F. R. 1993–1994. *Hellenic Religion and Christianization, c. 370–529*, 2 vols. Leiden: Brill.

Trout, D. E. 1999. *Paulinus of Nola: Life, Letters, and Poems*. Berkeley: University of California Press.

Urbainczyk, T. 2002. *Theodoret of Cyrrhus: The Bishop and the Holy Man*. Ann Arbor: University of Michigan Press.

Uthemann, K. H. 2005. "Zur Rezeption des Tomus Leonis in und nach Chalkedon." In *Christus, Kosmos, Diatribe: Themen der frühen Kirche als Beiträge zu einer historischen Theologie*, ed. K. H. Uthemann, 1–36. Berlin: Walter de Gruyter.

Van Dam, R. 1985. *Leadership and Community in Late Antique Gaul*. Berkeley: University of California Press.

———. 2007. *The Roman Revolution of Constantine*. Cambridge: Cambridge University Press.

Vanderspoel, J. 1999. "Correspondence and Correspondents of Julius Julianus," *Byzantion* 69: 396–478.

Van Rompay, L. 2005. "Society and Community in the Christian East." In *The Cambridge Companion to the Age of Justinian*, ed. M. Maas, 239–266. Cambridge: Cambridge University Press.

Vescovi e pastori in epoca teodosiana: XXV Incontro di studiosi dell'antichità cristiana, Roma, 8–11 maggio 1996. 1997. 2 vols. Rome: Institutum Patristicum Augustinianum.

Völker, W. 1931. *Das Vollkommenheitsideal des Origenes: Eine Untersuchung zur Geschichte der Frömmigkeit und zu den Anfängen christlicher Mystik*. Tübingen: J. C. B. Mohr.

von Campenhausen, H. 1969. *Ecclesiastical Authority and Spiritual Power in the Church of the First Three Centuries*. Trans. J. A. Baker. London: Adam and Charles Black.

Wallace-Hadrill, D. S. 1982. *Christian Antioch: A Study of Early Christian Thought in the East*. Cambridge: Cambridge University Press.

Ward-Perkins, B. 2005. *The Fall of Rome and the End of Civilization*. Oxford: Oxford University Press.

Warmington, B. H. 1989. "Did Constantine Have 'Religious Advisers'?" *Studia Patristica* 19: 117–129.
Watkins, O. D. 1920. *A History of Penance*, 2 vols. London: Longmans, Green.
Weber, M. 1978. *Economy and Society: An Outline of Interpretative Sociology*. Ed. G. Roth and C. Wittich, 2 vols. Berkeley: University of California Press.
Wessel, S. 2008. *Leo the Great and the Spiritual Rebuilding of a Universal Rome*. Leiden: Brill.
Whitaker, E. C., and M. Johnson. 2003. *Documents of the Baptismal Liturgy*, 3rd ed. London: SPCK.
Wilken, R. L. 1983. *John Chrysostom and the Jews: Rhetoric and Reality in the Late Fourth Century*. Berkeley: University of California Press.
Williams, D. H. 1995. *Ambrose of Milan and the End of the Nicene-Arian Conflicts*. Oxford: Clarendon Press.
Wood, I. 1985. "Gregory of Tours and Clovis," *RBPH* 63: 249–272.
———. 1994. *The Merovingian Kingdoms 450–571*. London: Longman.
Wright, D. F. 2005. *What Has Infant Baptism Done to Baptism? An Enquiry at the End of Christendom*. Milton Keynes: Paternoster.
———. 2007. *Infant Baptism in Historical Perspective: Collected Studies*. Milton Keynes: Paternoster.
Ysebaert, J. 1994. *Die Amtsterminologie im Neuen Testament und in der Alten Kirche: Eine lexikographische Untersuchung*. Breda: Eureia.

CHAPTER 28

THEOLOGICAL ARGUMENTATION: THE CASE OF FORGERY

SUSAN WESSEL
Catholic University of America

Introduction

Theological argumentation can be viewed as a rhetorical process by which certain doctrinal beliefs, institutional practices, and norms of behavior are determined to be legitimate and authoritative. It has long been recognized that this was especially complicated, multidimensional, and even problematic for the period being considered here, that of the Ecumenical Councils from Nicaea I (325) to Constantinople III (680/1).[1]

Even before Nicaea I, this rhetorical process was evident in the evolving beliefs, practices, and norms of the letters of Paul and deutero-Paul, the letters of Ignatius of Antioch and Clement of Rome; the early church orders, and the pre-Nicene conciliar decrees, to name only a few. The deutero-Pauline corpus, which was incorrectly attributed to the apostle Paul, and the early church order, the *Didache*, which purported to be an apostolic document, illustrate one way in which this process occurred. By suggesting that their beliefs, practices, and norms of behavior were connected to the authority of the apostolic past, the anonymous authors of such documents argued for their legitimacy and eased the transition from charismatic to institutional authority.

The creation of the pseudo-Dionysian corpus, a stunning integration of neo-Platonist and Christian thought penned under the name of an associate of the apostles, Dionysius, attests to the continuing relevance of this line of argument for the theological discourse of the sixth century. No matter how improbable the authorial claim in this case was, the fact remained that to link the pseudo-Dionysian corpus to the apostolic past was the most direct way to assert its legitimacy. That the anonymous author dared to make such an argument approximately 500 years after the apostolic period separates his pretension to apostolic authority from that of the pre-Nicene Christians just mentioned, who, in many instances, advanced their apostolic connection plausibly, if not always accurately.

The discrepancy between the rhetoric, on the one hand, and the historical reality, on the other, requires some discussion. To make such an erroneous claim in the sixth century was not simply to continue, but to alter subtly in the light of new circumstances, the method of theological argumentation that the early Christians had used. Patrick Gray has argued persuasively: "The success of this forger [i.e., pseudo-Dionysius] is at once an admission of the inescapability of the need in the period to validate the truth by ascribing it to the past, and a magnificent revolution against the closing of the patristic canon by his contemporaries" (1989, 36). The false attribution to apostolic authority that in the pre-Nicene period had been the reasonable means by which the transition from charismatic to institutional authority was made legitimate became, in the theological discourse of the sixth century, the ethically ambiguous method of argumentation that might be characterized as forgery.

Pseudo-Dionysius was not, of course, the first author whose false attribution rendered him, according to the broadest definition of the term, a forger. Beginning with the New Testament, the *Historia Augusta*, and other works too numerous to mention, attributing one's work to another, perhaps to a respected teacher or to an orthodox school of thought with which one hoped to be associated, was such a common practice that it generally went unchallenged.[2] Because these attributions were not controversial, they might well be placed among the literary corpus known as the apocrypha and pseudepigrapha, texts whose authorship was assigned to someone other than the person who wrote them.[3] In the case of forgery, however, there is the sense that a deeper level of deception has occurred. What separates the most extreme cases of forgery from the apocrypha and pseudepigrapha is, I suggest, the polemical context for which the forged literary work has been either purposefully written, or later appropriated, to advance arguments unforeseen by the author.

Because these categories are far from stable, there are significant cases in which they overlap, that of Cyril of Alexandria and the Apollinarian forgeries being one of them. Prior to the Nestorian controversy, the start of which can be traced to Nestorius' unwillingness to ascribe the title *Theotokos* to the Virgin Mary, Cyril had built his Christology partly around several texts he believed to have been written by the orthodox father, Athanasius. His critics were only too happy to point out that the texts had actually been written by heretics who followed Apollinarius and who had taken the name of Athanasius merely to lend their corpus legitimacy.[4] While even the original deception was conniving enough to render the Apollinarian texts a forgery, when Cyril relied on them to construct his orthodox Christology, a new level of duplicity was achieved. Due to his miscalculation, the forgeries were absorbed into the orthodox tradition, though they were a source of contention over the next 250 years as his supporters and critics alike struggled to make sense of the continuing implications of the original deception. What had begun as a false attribution to Athanasius was dramatically transformed into a full-fledged forgery, including the polemics and controversy that this implied, only to recede again as the forged passages that Cyril had used were reinterpreted by such neo-Chalcedonians as the emperor Justinian and Leontius of Jerusalem to make them consistent with orthodoxy.

Unlike the pseudepigraphical authors, who generally ascribed their texts to like-minded authors, the Apollinarians had committed a duplicitous forgery.[5] Condemned by the Council of Constantinople in 381, they as heretics believed that there was one composite nature in the divine and human natures in Christ and that in Christ the human soul was replaced by the Logos. To make their texts legitimate, they attributed them to the orthodox author, Athanasius, who never would have uttered such words. By securing what they perceived to be their rightful place in the lineage of orthodoxy, the Apollinarians carried out a deception that resulted not only in constructing themselves as deceivers but also in an unwitting object of their deception—someone who had been deceived.

The consequences for the formation of orthodoxy were dramatic. It is not an exaggeration to say that Cyril's naive reception of the Apollinarian forgeries contributed to the schism of the eastern churches, which never came to terms with the proliferation of meanings and contexts that were the unforeseen result of the original deception.

In tracing the unwieldy consequences of literary deception, Gray has uncovered what he calls "the double movement" in the quest to imagine a particular, monolithic vision of the religious past during the age of Justinian, an ideological construct that simultaneously "chang[ed] the past while denying and repressing knowledge of the change." At issue here was "the age's repressed, subconscious or semi-conscious tension about its reconstruction of the religious past in its struggle to achieve conformity" (1997, 195).[6] After the Council of Chalcedon (451), the challenge for its supporters was to prove that Cyril's teaching, including the thorny problem of his unwitting use of Apollinarian and decidedly un-Chalcedonian forgeries, was consistent with orthodoxy. The predicament for the neo-Chalcedonians was to interpret his use of the Apollinarian phrase "one incarnate nature of the Word of God" in the light of the Chalcedonian formula "two natures in one *prosopon* or *hypostasis*." The double movement that Gray has identified came about when Leontius of Jerusalem in his *Contra Monophysitas* argued that Cyril intended "one *hypostasis*" and "two natures" when he said "one incarnate nature," "the existence of the second, human nature being implied . . . by the addition in Cyril's own formula of the word 'incarnate.'" (1997, 198). Leontius changed the past by making Cyril's use of the "one-nature formula" consistent with the two natures that Chalcedon championed more than twenty years later. And he repressed that change by arguing that Cyril had intended to make such a theological statement all along.

In this chapter, I plan to further explore the tension that Gray has identified in the religious ideology of the age of Justinian, a tension that, I suggest, is rooted in the earliest period of the Church and that extends at least until the Council of Constantinople III (680/1). The tension is between the ideology of continuity and the inevitability of change. Forgery, the act of both committing the deception and alleging it against one's opponents, was, as I shall argue here, the rhetorical tool par excellence by which this tension between continuity and change was superficially resolved. I say "superficially" because new ideas flourished in the sixth and seventh centuries in spite of the conscious attempts to suppress them. It might be more accurate to say that the tension was navigated by means of this rhetorical tool but never fully resolved. The example of Leontius of Jerusalem just mentioned attests, in fact, to the originality of the period, even while those like him who adhered to the ideology of conformity attempted to define themselves and their theological productions solely in relation to a past that they imagined as unchanging.

The Work and Self-Understanding of the Forgers

In modern times, forgery is punished in both civil and criminal courts.[7] A term in prison might result for someone who has made fraudulent alterations to a legal instrument, such as a will or a contract, by signing someone else's name, by making unauthorized changes, or by wholly fabricating it. Before someone can be found guilty of having committed such a crime, the court must conclude that the forger altered or fabricated the document with the intent to deceive.[8] Not only the act itself but also the mind of the forger must be scrutinized to evaluate the ethical quality of the action. If a person has received permission to sign the name of another, or has done so in jest, then he is not guilty of forgery. Those whose interest is to profit monetarily, as when someone forges a letter, a work of art, a piece of literature, or coins or bills, are tried and punished by either the criminal or civil courts, which can exact monetary fines. In the medieval West, the most striking legislation against forged documents was promulgated by Pope Innocent III in the year 1198. His law made it a crime not only to fabricate a document but also to alter an otherwise authentic document by changing the names, dates, signature, or seal or by tampering with the content. Those who were found guilty of having committed such a crime were imprisoned.

While such laws suggest that the moral and ethical dimensions of the problem have been addressed unambiguously in the medieval and modern context, that was not the case in Late Antiquity, where the act of forgery, in and of itself, was not considered a crime. The later concern with forgery as a crime, therefore, contrasts sharply with the late antique world's seeming non-interest in considering forgery a crime at all. The only legislation I know of that condemned it, canon 63 of the Council in Trullo (692), punished the audience who continued to listen to the forged work (in this case, the forged Acts of the martyrs), rather than the person who was responsible for the deception.[9] Only the audience was punished because forgery was generally considered problematic according to the extent to which the forged text undermined the prevailing conception of orthodoxy. After the experience of the Council of Constantinople III (680/1) (which I consider later), it was understood that both the charge and the act of forgery were part of the polemical arsenal by which certain texts were construed as orthodox and others dismissed as heretical. The lack of moral clarity had nothing to do, as Gray has remarked (1988, 284), with insufficient philological tools to ferret out the deception. In fact, the opposite was true. By the seventh century, the philological methods for unearthing forgery were not only available but also in widespread use, as the Acts of Constantinople III attest. To make something as complex and multidimensional as forgery a crime would have undermined the fluid process by which theological ideas were transmitted.

Given this fluidity, it was not always possible to distinguish the deceiver from the deceived, the same party being, at various times, a victim of forgery, a forger himself, and an accuser of, or a defender against, the charge. The underlying coherence lay merely in the fact that each argument was made in the name of orthodoxy. Eutyches, the archimandrite of a large monastery in Constantinople, is a case in point.[10] In constructing his Christology, he had relied on Cyril of Alexandria's use of the documents forged by the Apollinarians to conclude that Christ was composed of two natures before the union, but of only one nature after the union. Duped by this Apollinarian formula, he accused the orthodox bishop of Constantinople, Flavian, of Nestorianism for having taught that Christ consisted in two natures after the Incarnation. Nestorius had been sanctioned by the Council of Ephesus in 431 for articulating a Christology that failed to integrate the two natures in a single *prosopon*. In mistakenly equating Flavian's orthodox formula with Nestorius' heresy, Eutyches was himself a victim of the deception that had been committed by the Apollinarians.

In a new context, he became an accuser of forgery when he decided to defend himself against the charge of heresy. To address Eutyches' erroneous charges of Nestorianism against those who continued to subscribe to orthodoxy, Flavian of Constantinople held a synod at Constantinople in 448. Having determined that Eutyches' reliance on the Apollinarian formula was heretical, the synod deposed and excommunicated him. There was no indication in its decision that Eutyches was merely an innocent victim of the continuing effects of the Apollinarian forgery. Not even Eutyches himself raised this possibility. Rather he defended himself before the emperor Theodosius II, with whom he filed a petition in 449 to reexamine the Acts of the synod, by alleging that the Acts had been falsified by the notaries and clerics who had prepared them.[11] Although there is not space here to consider in depth all of Eutyches' allegations, suffice it to say that he claimed to have uncovered several discrepancies in the Acts. First, the Acts apparently failed to record his refusal to anathematize everyone who did not confess two natures after the Incarnation, citing as the reason for his refusal that he would never anathematize the holy fathers. Second, that Eutyches had allegedly appealed to Rome, Alexandria, Jerusalem, and Thessaloniki to judge his orthodoxy had also been omitted from the Acts, as had his supposed willingness to submit to specific orders issued by Rome and Alexandria. Persuaded by these arguments, a new synod overturned the judgment against Eutyches on the grounds that the Acts that condemned him had been falsified.

Although the Acts did not examine the theological content of his beliefs, his allegation that they omitted his refusal to anathematize those he considered to be holy fathers unwittingly confirmed that his views were unorthodox. (His definition of "holy fathers" included those who subscribed to his heretical views.) His additional allegations, that the Acts failed to record evidence of his readiness to submit to patriarchal authority, suggested at most that, despite his views, he wished to be reckoned among the orthodox. Nor was there evidence that the Acts had been falsified in the ways that Eutyches indicated. To the contrary, the notary in charge of the transcripts testified that he had no knowledge that the conciliar record had been distorted.[12] The record provides no compelling evidence, in other words, that the Acts condemning Eutyches had reached their decision unjustly. Yet the mere allegation that the conciliar record had been forged sufficed, without convincing evidence to support it, to overturn his conviction temporarily. This incident marked a turning point in which theological discourse and debate gradually receded from the work of the councils in favor of technical examinations into the transmission and authenticity of texts.

This same trajectory was apparent at the Council of Constantinople II (553), where the charge of forgery was used strategically to prevent a document from being absorbed into the orthodox tradition. They feared that recognizing the document as orthodox might enlarge the boundaries of orthodoxy in ways that the dominant party, the neo-Chalcedonians, found threatening. At issue was the letter that the fifth-century Church Father Ibas of Edessa had written in which he criticized the Apollinarian formula that Cyril had used (the same formula that had deceived Eutyches). Because Cyril had emerged by the middle of the fifth century as one of the orthodox fathers, to criticize him was considered by many to be the equivalent of heresy. The opposition party in this case was the Dyophysites, strict Chalcedonians who were critical of Cyril's use of the Apollinarian formula. They argued that the letter by Ibas was an orthodox expression of the faith that the Council of Chalcedon (451) had accepted. To settle these competing claims, the Council of Constantinople II (553) examined not only the theological content of the letter, which it determined to be heretical, but also its authenticity.

Several tests were used to evaluate whether the letter was genuine. First, the council examined whether the letter was consistent with the statements that Ibas had made at the Council of Chalcedon (451), where he acknowledged the orthodoxy of the Council of Ephesus (431) and anathematized the teaching of Nestorius as heretical. Because the letter subscribed to a two-nature view of Christ that the Council of Constantinople II (553) decided was consistent with Nestorianism, the council (553) concluded that it could not have been written by Ibas. Second, the council (553) examined a more complete body of evidence, which the earlier council had omitted, including testimony by the papal legates that Ibas was orthodox. Finally, the council (553) considered Ibas' own assurances in the record that he had not blasphemed against Cyril.[13] It might be argued that the last test presumed the existence of the very letter that it was determined to remove from the record as a forgery: without the letter, there would have been little evidence that Ibas had questioned Cyril's orthodoxy. From the preceding tests, logical though they may have been, the council (553) reached the incorrect conclusion that the letter was a forgery. But in making this erroneous claim, the council accomplished its greater task of preserving orthodoxy as exclusively Cyrillian. They strategically used the charge of forgery as a ploy by which to remove from the conciliar record a document that undermined the vision of orthodoxy that the Council (553) championed.

Forgery was also committed, and charged, in the exceedingly polemical context of the Monothelete controversy of the seventh century. The question being debated was whether Christ had a natural will that was a property of each of his two natures, as the Dyothelites maintained, or whether he had a personal will that was a property of his person, as the Monotheletes contended. The answer was significant for understanding the characteristics of Christ's human nature and the quality of its actions. The solution of the Dyothelites envisioned a real human nature that suffered indecision and contemplated despair, while that of the Monotheletes saw that nature as guided by a divine-human person. Such questions were addressed by the Council of Constantinople III (680/1) mainly through the lens of the philological issues raised by the charge of forgery. In the highly self-conscious, philological discourse of this council (680/1), the tendency to suppress theological debate, which had begun with the councils of the fifth century, culminated.

The emperor, Constantine IV, who convened the council (680/1), as well as the conciliar members who administered it, were confident that the solution to their theological problems resided in books. Among the patristic collections and conciliar books that were retrieved from the patriarchal library was a letter purportedly written by the orthodox patriarch Menas of Constantinople to pope Vigilius, around the time of the Council of Constantinople II (553), in which the disputed phrase "one will" appeared. If the letter were proven genuine, then the Monotheletes would have adduced significant proof of the antiquity and orthodoxy of their doctrinal position. The technical way in which this letter was examined by the council reveals its determination to channel the discussion of the deeper Christological issues away from fluid theological debate and into the stable purview of the authenticated text.

Philological analysis of the letter, which was preserved as part of a two-volume collection of the Acts of Constantinople II (553), revealed two important discrepancies: the three unpaginated *quaterniones* in which the letter of Menas to Vigilius was found had been inserted at the beginning of the book, while the pages that followed began with the number 1; the handwriting of the letter differed from that of the rest of the book.[14] Alerted to the forgery, the emperor asked the conciliar secretary to examine the second book of the Acts of Constantinople II (553) for documents that had been similarly forged. This new examination revealed two letters by Pope Vigilius that contained the Monenergist confession that Christ consisted in one operation. Protesting that the letters were forgeries, the papal legates present at the council (680/1) insisted that the Acts of Constantinople II (553) be examined for any indication that they taught either one will or one operation. When a close reading of the Acts (553) confirmed that they taught neither, these additional letters by Vigilius were determined to have been forged.

I find it particularly striking that the inquiry did not end there. The council (680/1) proceeded to examine the history of textual transmission by which the forged letters of Vigilius had been inserted into the Acts (553).[15] Macrobius of Seleuceia testified that the copy of the Acts of Constantinople II (553) that he had received from Philip, the *magister militum*, contained documents that had been forged in the handwriting of George, a scholar employed by Makarios of Antioch. George had inserted the falsified letters at the request of Makarios and Theodore, the patriarch of Constantinople, both of whom were Monotheletes. Additional copies of the Acts of Constantinople II (553) were similarly altered by George to include the falsified letters. The ethical extent of his involvement in the matter was clear: by copying and then inserting the falsified letters, George merely carried out the orders of Makarios and Theodore, Monotheletes who had probably altered the documents to support their theological views. Yet they themselves probably would not have considered their actions unethical. As one candid forger admitted to the council (680/1) when confronted with evidence of his having misinterpreted passages from the orthodox fathers to endorse his Monotheletism: "I selected only those passages that supported my point of view."[16] There was no sense on the part of the forger of his having done anything ethically wrong. Makarios and Theodore may have similarly altered the letters of Vigilius, rationalizing that they had simply made the pope say what he would have said had he been confronted with the opportunity to address the theological problem. Forgers in such cases justified their actions as being a reasonable attempt to make the past speak to the shifting theological demands imposed on them in the present.

The reason the ethical dimensions of forgery were never fully explored by either the victims or perpetrators of forgery during the period of Late Antiquity was that forgery was an essential tool not only for reconstructing the past, as Gray has shown (1988), but also for negotiating the inherent tension of the theological enterprise. They could not risk acknowledging that forgery was an ethical problem, because maintaining continuity with the traditions of the fathers in the light of new theological questions required the rhetorical ploys and self-deception that forgery provided. Philological examination of texts whose authenticity had been questioned enabled those engaged in intractable theological controversy to conduct those debates on what they hoped would be stable ground. But in making that presumption, they were mistaken, as the following sections show. They deceived themselves in thinking that theological discourse might be contained and limited by shifting that discourse into the sphere of philological examination.

The Limits of Context

I and others have argued that forgery—both accusing one's opponent of forgery and committing it oneself—was an attempt to control the corpus of patristic authors and texts that were becoming canonized as the tradition of the fathers.[17] It can also be viewed more broadly as an attempt to control context. By "context," I mean every conceivable circumstance in which a theological work might appear.[18] The best example of the unruly proliferation of context was Cyril's use of the Apollinarian formula "one incarnate nature of the Word of God" and then the rhetorical complexity of his subsequent elevation, in spite of his error, as an orthodox father in both the Chalcedonian and non-Chalcedonian traditions. Cyrillians in Egypt interpreted this phrase not as the unfortunate consequence of the original deception, but as an orthodox expression of Cyril's Monophysite views. The charge of forgery was irrelevant to such devotees of Cyril because everything that Cyril said—no matter the reason he had said it—was thought to be sufficient to promote orthodoxy. Dyophysites, however, who interpreted this phrase as evidence of Cyril's Apollinarian views, were not interested in absorbing his error into the orthodox tradition. That task was left, rather, to the neo-Chalcedonians, those who not only accepted Chalcedon as legitimate but also viewed that council as an expression of Cyrillianism. Because of their commitment to a Cyrillian Chalcedonianism, they needed to account for his use of the Apollinarian forgery, it being simply unacceptable for such supporters of Cyril to leave unchallenged the charges that the Dyophysites had raised against his orthodoxy. Cyril's use of the Apollinarian formula—language he had mistakenly attributed to Athanasius—was, therefore, reinterpreted as an expression of his abiding Chalcedonian intent.[19] Each party to the neo-Chalcedonian debate—the Monophysites, Dyophysites, and neo-Chalcedonians—argued that Cyril should be interpreted in the theological context that supported their point of view.

What is unusual is the fact that Cyril was being recognized as the archetypal orthodox father by nearly everyone engaged in the post-Chalcedonian debates. I have already suggested elsewhere the reasons for his striking success in this regard, but suffice it to say that Cyril had constructed an image of himself as orthodox that went far beyond not only the boundaries of Egypt but also the theological circumstances that he could have reasonably envisioned.[20] That a canon of the fathers was being established is clear, therefore, from the case of Cyril. The Church's success in establishing such a canon through its methods of theological argumentation, including the arguments of forgery being considered here, resulted in a limited number of Church Fathers being celebrated as orthodox. Because there was an evolving consensus about which fathers should be included in the orthodox canon, all parties to the neo-Chalcedonian debates argued from the same limited number of Church Fathers, Cyril being the most eminent among them. That the canon was increasingly limited meant, however, that each side of the controversy not only alluded to and competed for the same authors but also read them in vastly different contexts.

The quest to control the boundaries of orthodoxy by limiting the canon of the fathers led to the paradox that each of these canonized fathers was being increasingly reinterpreted. Meaning, in other words, was far from stable and was instead proliferating far beyond what might be called the original intent of the author. Forgery emerged as the rhetorical tool that concealed the impossibility of controlling the proliferation of meaning that resulted from this limited body of canonized authors being read in unforeseen circumstances. The examples considered in the previous section also apply here. Ibas of Edessa became the object of controversy some 200 years after his death because he, an orthodox father, had criticized Cyril, who had since been recognized as the paragon of orthodoxy. To eliminate his letter from the corpus and to preserve the memory of Cyril, the charge of forgery was used. In making such an argument, it did not seem to matter much that the letter was, in fact, genuine. Nor did it matter that those involved in the episode probably knew that the letter was genuine. The charge, and not the reality, of forgery, which was supported by several philological arguments, sufficed to remove the offending letter from the orthodox corpus.

The altered letters of Pope Vigilius provide an example of forgery from the opposite perspective, that of the work of the forger. Contained in the Acts was an examination of evidence detailing how the altered letters came to be inserted, as well as the forger's method of doing so. By exploring this evidence, the council intended to show that philological examination yielded demonstrable results: texts whose authenticity was questioned might be examined in a conciliar text, judged to be inauthentic, and then removed from the conciliar record. That the text was, in this case, a "genuine forgery" meant that the charge might be used ethically and successfully to remove an altered document from the orthodox corpus. While it is reasonable to conclude that the letters had, in fact, been altered, it is also plausible to assume that the legates themselves, as Gray has suggested, knew about the deception all along. In being thus informed, the legates permitted the investigation into the letters to continue as if the philological discussion, in and of itself, put on display the magnitude of the deception.

There were certainly other ways to conduct a theological debate, engaging in earnest intellectual inquiry being the most obvious. Philological investigation had the merit, however, of shifting the locus of the debate toward a method of argumentation that appeared to be objective. And those who conducted such investigations were also assured that orthodoxy was being built on a genuine body of canonized texts and authors. That is not to suggest that theological debate never took place, only that it receded into the background as the implications of this discourse unfolded at the councils. Once the texts that were written by Church Fathers whose orthodoxy had been established were proven genuine, then orthodoxy developed along tracks that had been authenticated by the authority of a continuous tradition.

The philological method of inquiry, which was limited mainly to demonstrating the authenticity of texts, was related to the deeper problem of tradition mentioned before. In the attempt to control the boundaries of orthodoxy, we have already seen that a canon of fathers emerged, which all the parties to the theological debates appealed to in making their case for orthodoxy. The proliferation of meaning that resulted from this limited canon's being mined for widely different purposes generated the further incentive to control these meanings, either by alleging forgery or by committing it. Making orthodox popes and fathers speak the words one wanted to hear by altering the very texts in which those words appeared was the logical consequence of this way of thinking. Another possibility was simply to allege forgery when the text being questioned no longer served the purposes of orthodoxy, as in the case of the letter by Ibas of Edessa. Forgery emerged, therefore, as the rhetorical tool by which each party attempted to limit—but, significantly, did not succeed in limiting—the context of orthodoxy in the ways in which they envisioned. Given these concerns, it is no accident that the councils gradually came to see their work as involved not exclusively in theological argumentation, which one might say they attempted to suppress, but in sorting out philological issues.

The Undermining of Writing

The act of writing presumes that a text can exude authority even when the author is absent.[21] It presumes that words that are written have a life of their own in contexts unimagined by the author. The rhetoric of forgery, however, undermines this presupposition by insisting that texts are unreliable unless the presence of the author can be demonstrated. This is apparent in many of the tests that the councils of the fifth through seventh centuries conducted to determine whether a text had been forged. Whenever a council examined the intent of the author, for instance, it was attempting to limit the meaning, and validity, of the text to an original context that was defined by the presence of the author. Such a test was used, but with strikingly different results, to determine whether the letters by Ibas and Vigilius were forgeries, that is, in the case of Ibas to remove a genuine letter from the orthodox corpus and in that of Vigilius to restore an altered document to its original orthodox intent. Far from being objective, therefore, the test alone did not ensure that the authenticity of a document had been evaluated correctly.

The practice of forgery was only one of the rhetorical tools and methods of argumentation that were being used to form an orthodox consensus. By the time of the Council of Ephesus (431), a canon of patristic authors was gradually emerging under the theological designation "the traditions of the fathers."[22] The phrase was significant for implying that a new authoritative category had emerged—alongside the settled categories of Scripture, oral tradition, church practice, and canon law—to describe the growing corpus of patristic literature. The word *tradition* translates something close to the Greek word *paradosis*, which refers to doctrines or teachings that have been transmitted over time. While the phrase "the traditions of the fathers" appeared as early as the fifth century, the word *tradition* was not used frequently in the Acts of the Council of Constantinople III in the seventh century. The idea that it conveyed, however, was expressed in such phrases as "the teachings of the fathers," "patristic testimony," or simply "the holy fathers said." The few times the word did appear, it was introduced by Pope Agatho, who spoke of a "living tradition" of the apostles whose authority was embraced by the councils and by the orthodox fathers.[23] Whether expressed directly or indirectly, the idea of the "traditions of the fathers" gradually became established as a valid source of authority from the fifth to the seventh centuries. To maintain that a theological concept was consistent with the traditions of the fathers was to argue for its place in the orthodox lexicon.

As the traditions of the fathers were being recognized as a legitimate source of theological authority, a new genre of writing emerged, that of the *florilegium*. While the genre had antecedents in the secular literature and could be traced perhaps to the early Christian period, the *florilegium* was embraced in the fifth century as particularly well suited to make the argument from tradition. The *florilegium* consisted of excerpts from patristic authors, whose writings the compiler of the *florilegium* considered to be orthodox.[24] Because the excerpts were collected to advance a theological argument, these were not, in any sense, impartial documents.

Two such documents compiled for the Council of Ephesus (431) illustrate the point: the first was a collection of patristic authors that the council, under the direction of Cyril of Alexandria, considered to be orthodox, including such authors as Athanasius, Theophilus of Alexandria, Cyprian, Ambrose, Gregory of Nazianzus, Basil of Caesarea, and Gregory of Nyssa, as well as several bishops of Rome. In compiling this collection, the Cyrillian party intended to demonstrate that orthodoxy consisted in a limited number of authors whose teachings were consistent with each other. The second collection of texts compiled by the Cyrillian party consisted of excerpts of writings by their opponent, Nestorius. Both *florilegia* were composed, in other words, to show that Nestorius was a heretic. After the Nestorian *florilegium* was read into the conciliar record, for instance, one of the bishops exclaimed that the words of Nestorius were terrible and blasphemous and that all of them should be inserted into the Acts to secure his condemnation. The *florilegia* served the additional purpose of making the conciliar process appear to be objective and, therefore, legitimate. Cyril defended the methods of his council, for example, by arguing that they had compared Nestorius' letters, writings, and several of his public homilies to both the Nicene Symbol of Faith and to the patristic *florilegium*, which his party had compiled. What is striking about such compilations is that the authority of the Church Father, rather than the persuasiveness of his reasoning, was adduced as proof of the orthodoxy of a particular theological claim.

The introduction of patristic and heretical *florilegia* into the conciliar discourse of the fifth through eighth centuries (the Councils of Constantinople III (680/1) and Nicaea II (787) were especially rich with *florilegia*[25]) suggests that patristic proof-texts were gradually being accepted as legitimate sources of theological argumentation. That such compilations of excerpts were proof-texts implied that they were considered legitimate merely because a particular author had written them. The *florilegium*, in other words, was an example of a text whose legitimacy depended on the presence of the author.

It is worth mentioning that the logic of the *florilegium* could be subverted when it served the interests of the dominant orthodox party. During the Council of Constantinople III (680/1), the heretic Makarios defended his Monenergism by introducing a *florilegium* of patristic texts that the council then criticized for being selectively truncated.[26] Surrounding passages that were inconsistent with the opposing theological view had been, the council implied, strategically omitted. Makarios, however, argued that he was justified in collecting and systematizing texts that supported his theology and did not view his method as deceptive.[27] The difference in perception lay not only in the council's subjective theological concerns but also in its way of understanding literary context. As Athanasius had articulated in his fight against Arianism, the intent of the fathers must be preserved to interpret passages and phrases correctly. The council argued that Makarios had violated that intent by removing passages from the larger theological context that might have imbued them with orthodox meaning.[28] To promote the interests of orthodoxy, therefore, a *florilegium* might be dismantled by restoring one of its patristic excerpts to the broader context. The absolute authority of the Church Father no longer sufficed in such instances to advance orthodoxy.

While the *florilegium* was generally rooted in the assumption that the traditions of the fathers were authoritative statements of orthodoxy simply because an orthodox father had said them, an inherent tension in the discourse occasionally surfaced. The concept of absolute authority, which was embodied in the traditions of the fathers, was simply at odds with the act of writing, the very existence of which presumed that the text lived beyond the absence of the author in circumstances unforeseen by him. Writing, in other words, presupposed the absence of the author, yet his presence was repeatedly asserted by the councils to demonstrate that their theological positions were consistent with the tradition that the author embodied.[29] An interesting result ensued. Because of this tension, the theological discourse of the fifth through eighth centuries never moved entirely into the realm of proof-texting, and original theological production continued, including the work of Maximus the Confessor and John of Damascus. Because of this tension, the uneasy sense remained that the legitimacy of the text could not be accounted for merely by associating it with the author, as the following section suggests.

Copies, Originals, and an Act of Theodicy

It has long been recognized that for a work to be authentic it must be either the original or an exact duplicate.[30] Any number of alterations to a work might compromise its authenticity and, if serious enough, leave open the possibility that it has been intentionally and duplicitously forged. (Note that a work that has been altered over time due to deterioration and neglect might be rendered "inauthentic" but not necessarily a forgery.) In ferreting out authentic texts from those that have been forged, the councils addressed the very real problems of textual authenticity that might—and often did—arise in the process of copying, referred to here (to borrow a phrase from Walter Benjamin) as "manual reproduction." Texts were, indeed, altered by those who copied them in ways that surely undermined their content and integrity. Yet establishing a succession of authentic, orthodox texts—a "tradition of the fathers"—depended on the possibility that texts could be reproduced manually without undermining their authenticity and legitimacy. In the period of Late Antiquity, this movement from the copy to the original often required a leap of faith insofar as copyists, by altering the texts they copied, acted more like authors than neutral transmitters of texts.

In considering the legitimacy of texts that had been manually reproduced, the councils pondered a number of issues.[31] Suspicious that the copy might not embody the authenticity and legitimacy of the original text, the councils asked implicitly: what happens when a text is reproduced and severed from the authority of the Church Father who wrote it? How might that authority continue to reside in the copy? In proposing that the councils implicitly pondered such questions, I mean to elicit the deeper sense of anxiety that, in my view, resulted from the temporal distance they perceived between the copy and the original. Insofar as the original was presumed to embody the greatness of its author, the copy was judged as inferior and as having lost something of its original legitimacy. One need only consider the minute attention that the Council of Constantinople III (680/1) gave to uncovering the provenance of texts to realize that they saw their work as establishing an unbroken line of connection to an original. An unspoken tension remained, nonetheless, between the councils' desire to confirm the presence of the author in the copy—through whatever philological tools were available to them—and the intuition that the very idea of the copy itself, no matter what tools they used, implied that the author was just beyond their grasp. Manual reproduction continued to evoke a kind of metaphorical journey away from the author, even while the "tradition of the fathers" required that the original connection be kept alive.

These contradictory impulses are brought into focus by a particularly strange event that the Acts of the Council of Constantinople III recorded in its fifteenth session.[32] The episode is an example of how one man's confidence in the power of the text was brought to light, examined, and eventually deflated, as his claims to doctrinal and textual authenticity were publicly undermined.

A Monothelete monk and priest named Polychronios was apparently inspired by a vision he had while traveling from Herakleia to Chrysopolis. In it, he claimed to have seen a man dressed in white standing before him, saying, "He who does not confess one will and theandric operation (i.e., Monotheletism) is not a Christian." He offered to demonstrate his conviction that Monotheletism was synonymous with orthodoxy by laying a written copy of his confession, sealed with a bull bearing the monogram, "Polychronios, the Confessor," upon a dead man. If the man were to rise from the dead, then the council was to accept his Monothelete confession as a legitimate statement of orthodoxy. The conciliar judges agreed to carry out the experiment in the court of the public baths, so that not only they and the council members might witness it but also anyone who happened to be present. Standing over the dead man, he placed his written confession upon the body, whispering over it for hours. When nothing happened and his test had failed, he stubbornly refused to renounce his Monothelete views.

This unusual act of theodicy unwittingly illustrates Polychronios' belief that words were legitimate only when they conveyed special powers. Benjamin's observations about the origins of writing are appropriate here: the words that were used in rituals were eventually written down in manuals and codified, their authenticity being validated *only* when the event happened again.[33] When Polychronios attempted to prove the validity of his confession by bringing such ancient principles to bear on his current problem, the crowd erupted in laughter. I suggest that they were laughing not only at the implausibility of resuscitating a dead man but also at Polychronios' awkward attempt to limit the legitimacy of the written text to the truth claims of theodicy. His test was a failure on all counts: not only did he fail to revivify the dead man and prove the validity of his confession but also he failed implicitly to limit the authority of texts to particular acts of theodicy. The crowd did not merely reject the Monothelete confession; they also rejected the test that Polychronios had so foolishly performed.

Because this test was embedded in the circumstances of the Council of Constantinople III (680/1), where Monotheletism was being examined through the philological methods discussed previously, the implications of his failure can be interpreted more broadly. Polychronios' misunderstanding of how words functioned in the context of his Monothelete confession demonstrated to the laughing crowd that original texts were not necessarily imbued with special powers. Having witnessed that reciting the words of his text could not revive a dead man, it is striking that the crowd did not respond by reciting a Dyothelite confession. They were no more likely to perform such a ridiculous test than they were to be persuaded by his Monotheletism. The crowd had perhaps learned not only that Polychronios' confession was unorthodox but also that the legitimacy of a text depended on the theological content that its words conveyed. In the light of that revelation, the copies of Dyothelite texts that the council had carefully authenticated might exude as much authority as or—in comparison to Polychronios' text—more authority than an original. After witnessing the episode, the crowd was poised to consider the possibility of taking the metaphorical journey away from the author and of accepting the legitimacy of texts that had been manually reproduced.

Conclusion

Forgery, and the conceptual problems with respect to writing that it generated, was the rhetorical tool by which theological ideas were either accepted or rejected by the ecumenical councils. One might even go so far as to say that the councils used the argument of forgery rhetorically to support the theological position that they had initially championed. Because a text that was judged to be forged did not bear the stamp of the original, it was no longer considered to be an authentic conveyer of the orthodox tradition. The charge of forgery was, therefore, closely bound to such concepts as continuity and tradition. To argue that a text had been forged was to sever its link to the continuous chain of orthodoxy.

Although theological argumentation was generally made legitimate by emphasizing the continuity with the past, theological discourse flourished, and new ideas were formed. A tension existed, in other words, between the ideology of continuity and the inevitability of change. The councils negotiated that tension, as I have suggested here, by conducting philological investigations into texts whose authenticity had been questioned. But the tension was never fully resolved through philological examination; the limits that the councils attempted to place on theological discourse and texts could not be contained in the ways that they had intended. The logical momentum of writing, by which texts were severed from their connection to the author and placed in unforeseen contexts, prevailed over every attempt to contain it.

This is not to suggest that forgery, as it was practiced, alleged, and imagined during the period of Late Antiquity, was an evil that should have been eliminated. Maintaining continuity with tradition in the light of new theological problems actually benefited from the rhetorical arguments, and even self-deception, that forgery provided. I say "benefited" because such arguments enabled the councils to maintain the discourse of a continuous orthodox tradition, and "self-deception" because the richness of theological ideas throughout the period of the ecumenical councils attests not only to the expanding corpus of orthodox texts but also to the continuing relevance of theological discourse.

NOTES

1. For a recent critical edition of the decisions and canons of the Council in Trullo and the Council of Nicaea II, see Alberigo 2006. The volume lists the critical editions and describes the history of the manuscript tradition.
2. Metzger 1980.
3. Charlesworth 1988, 3919–3968.
4. Gray 1989, 24.
5. Tuilier 1987, 581–590.
6. Gray 1997, 198.
7. For the modern law of forgery in Western nations, see Black 2001.
8. Speyer 1971, 13; according to Metzger 1980, 2, "A literary forgery is essentially a piece of work created or modified with the intention to deceive." Constable generally agrees: "Forgers attribute their own work to some one else and plagiarists pass off some one else's work as their own, but both intend to deceive. Neither term is commonly used for unintentional deceptions" (1996, 3). See also Grafton 1990; Bardy 1936.
9. Joannou 1962, 200.
10. Wessel 2001, 205–207.
11. *Acta Conciliorum Oecumenicorum* = *ACO* II.1.1, 152–153.
12. *ACO* II.1.1, 178–179.
13. *ACO* IV.1, 144–146.
14. *ACO* Ser. 2.II.1, 40, 42.
15. *ACO* Ser. 2.II.2, 650.
16. *ACO* Ser. 2.II.1, 238.
17. Gray 2000.
18. Culler 1982, 123–125.

19. See Gray 2006, 11–15.
20. Wessel 2004.
21. Culler 1982, 92–96, 103, 106, 200–201.
22. Graumann 2002, 410–419.
23. Wessel 2006, 36.
24. In the latter half of the seventh century, the Byzantines developed a genre they called "collection of exegetical fragments," which was known by the fifteenth century as "*catena*": *ODB* 1991, 391. On the Syriac *catenae*, see Romeny 2007a; 2007b.
25. On *florilegia* and the councils, see Alexakis 1996, 1–42.
26. *ACO* Ser. II.2.1, 240.
27. *ACO* Ser. II.2.1, 238, 242.
28. *ACO* Ser. II.2.1, 272.
29. Derrida 1971, 316, 328.
30. Benjamin 1968, 220.
31. As Benjamin has remarked, "Confronted with its manual reproduction, which was usually branded as a forgery, the original preserved all its authority" (1968, 220).
32. *ACO* Ser. II.2.2, 674–682.
33. Benjamin 1968, 223–224.

WORKS CITED

Acta Conciliorum Oecumenicorum. 1914–1940, 1971, 1984–1992. 4 vols. in 27 parts, ed. Eduard Schwartz, Johannes Straub, and Rudolf Riedinger. Berlin: Walter de Gruyter.

Alberigo, Giuseppe, ed. 2006. *Conciliorum Oecumenicorum Generaliumque Decreta, Editio Critica, I: The Oecumenical Councils from Nicaea I to Nicaea II (325–787)*. Corpus Christianorum. Turnhout: Brepols.

Alexakis, Alexander. 1996. *Codex Parisinus Graecus 1115 and Its Archetype*. Washington, DC: Dumbarton Oaks.

Bardy, Gustave. 1936. "Faux et fraudes littéraires dans l'Antiquité chrétienne," *Revue d'histoire ecclésiastique* 32: 5–23, 275–302.

Benjamin, Walter. 1968. *Illuminations*. Trans. Harry Zohn. Repr. New York: Schocken.

Black, Henry Campbell, ed. 2001. *Black's Law Dictionary*. Repr. St. Paul, MN: West Group.

Charlesworth, James H. 1988. "Research on the New Testament Apocrypha and Pseudepigrapha." In *Aufstieg und Niedergang der Römischen Welt*, II.25, ed. Wolfgang Haase, 3919–3968. Berlin: Walter de Gruyter.

Constable, Giles. 1996. *Culture and Spirituality in Medieval Europe*. Aldershot: Variorum.

Culler, Jonathan. 1982. *On Deconstruction: Theory and Criticism after Structuralism*. Ithaca, NY: Cornell University Press.

Derrida, Jacques. 1971. "Signature, Event, Context: A Communication to the Congrès internationale des Sociétés de philosophie de langue française." In *Margins of Philosophy*, trans. Alan Bass, 307–330. Repr. Chicago: University of Chicago Press, 1985.

Grafton, Anthony. 1990. *Forgers and Critics: Creativity and Duplicity in Western Scholarship*. Princeton, NJ: Princeton University Press.

Graumann, Thomas. 2002. *Vätertheologie und Väterbeweis in den Kirchen des Ostens bis zum Konzil von Ephesus (431)*. Tübingen: Mohr Siebeck.

Gray, Patrick. 1988. "Forgery as an Instrument of Progress: Reconstructing the Theological Tradition in the Sixth Century," *Byzantinische Zeitschrift* 81: 284–289.

———. 1989. "The Select Fathers: Canonizing the Patristic Past," *Studia Patristica* 23: 21–36.

———. 1997. "Covering the Nakedness of Noah: Reconstruction and Denial in the Age of Justinian." In *Conformity and Non-Conformity in Byzantium*, ed. L. Garland, = *Byzantinische Forschungen* 24: 193–206.

———. 2000. "Theological Discourse in the Seventh Century: The Heritage from the Sixth Century," *Byzantinische Forschungen* 26: 219–228.

———. 2006. *Leontius of Jerusalem, Against the Monophysites: Testimonies of the Saints and Apostles*. Oxford Early Christian Texts. Oxford: Oxford University Press.

Joannou, Périclès-Pierre. 1962. *Discipline générale antique: Les canons des conciles oecuméniques*. Rome: Italo-Orientale.

Metzger, Bruce Manning. 1980. "Literary Forgeries and Canonical Pseudepigrapha." In *New Testament Studies: Philological, Versional, and Patristic*, ed. Bruce Manning Metzger, 1–22. Leiden: Brill.

Romeny, R. B. ter Haar. 2007a. "Les Pères grecs dans les florilèges exégétiques syriaques." In *Les Pères grecs dans la tradition syriaque*, ed. Andea B. Schmidt and Dominique Gonnet, 4.63–76. Paris: Geuthner.

———. 2007b. "Procopius of Gaza and His Library." In *From Rome to Constantinople: Studies in Honor of Averil Cameron*, ed. Hagit Amirav and R. B. ter Haar Romeny, 173–190. Leuven: Peeters.

Speyer, Wolfgang. 1971. *Die literarische Fälschung im heidnischen und christlichen Altertum: Ein Versuch ihrer Deutung*. Munich: Beck.

Syme, Ronald. 1983. *Historia Augusta Papers*, 1–11, 12–29, 98–108. Oxford: Clarendon Press.

Tuilier, André. 1987. "Remarques sur les fraudes des Apollinaristes et des Monophysites." In *Texte und Textkritik: Eine Aufsatzsammlung* Berlin: Akademie-Verlag.

Wessel, Susan 2001. "Forgery and the Monothelete Controversy: Some Scrupulous Uses of Deception," *Greek, Roman, and Byzantine Studies* 42: 201–220.

———. 2004. *Cyril of Alexandria and the Nestorian Controversy: The Making of a Saint and of a Heretic*. Oxford Early Christian Studies. Oxford: Oxford University Press.

———. 2006. "The Politics of Text and Tradition in the Council of Constantinople III (AD 680/1)," *Annuarium Historiae Conciliorum* 38: 35–54.

CHAPTER 29

SACRED SPACE AND VISUAL ART

ANN MARIE YASIN
University of Southern California

Sacred Sites and Landscapes

As early as the year 333 C.E., when a Christian traveler from Bordeaux arrived via Constantinople to the area of Roman Palestine, the landscape was punctuated by biblical landmarks. This anonymous author, known to us as the Bordeaux Pilgrim, wrote an itinerary of his eastern journey; much of his account is a relatively bare-bones list of staging posts along the route, but in places his text swells to draw associations between the geographical cities through which he passed and the scriptural events that had been staged there. He wrote, for example, of a place called Sychar near the city of Neapolis, "where the Samaritan woman went down to draw water, at the very place where Jacob dug the well, and our Lord Jesus Christ spoke with her. Some plane trees are there, planted by Jacob, and there is a bath which takes its water from this well" (*Itinerarium Burdigalense* 588).[1] The Bordeaux Pilgrim testified, in other words, to a landscape that offered witness to the events of the Scriptures: the visitor could observe trees planted by Jacob himself and touch water supplied by the well he dug. The physical landscape provided the traveler with direct connection to sacred figures and events. Visiting the ruins of Solomon's Temple in Jerusalem, for example, our author described the still-palpable traces of Zechariah's death: "there is marble in front of the altar which has on it the blood of Zechariah—you would think it had only been shed today. All around you can see the marks of the hobnails of the soldiers who killed him, as plainly as if they had been pressed into wax" (*Itinerarium Burdigalense* 591).[2] The Bordeaux Pilgrim's account does not simply attest to the past events that occurred at the site, but stresses that material evidence of those events is to be witnessed in the present tense.[3] The marble before the altar was not simply the site of Zechariah's murder, but *still* appeared to have fresh blood on it; the pavement was scarred not by the indistinct traces of wear and weathering, but bore the crisp evidence of a recent scuffle. Rather than merely signposting the location of centuries-old events, the stones at the site gave the visitor the sensation of coming upon a fresh crime scene. The impressions made on the visitor's senses by such places could thus create a sense of immediacy that defied any rational sense of historical distance.

Fifty years or so later, when the intrepid Christian woman Egeria traveled across the eastern Mediterranean, she, too, wrote of sites identified as holy due to their association with biblical events or holy figures. Her itinerary even expanded beyond the strictly biblical to incorporate living holy men, as well as burial places of martyrs, among the sacred sites mapped on her journey.[4] Much as for the pilgrim from Bordeaux, the physical landscape made the sacred past immediately perceptible to the senses: the water, for example, from the spring Moses struck from a rock near Mount Nebo was, she says, "beautifully clear and with an excellent taste" (*Itinerarium Egeriae* 11.2).[5] Indeed, at one point in her text, Egeria even indicated that this sensory immediacy was a central concern driving not only her own journey but also the very penning of the account of her travels for her readers back home: "I know it has been a rather long business writing down all these places one after the other. . . . But it may help you, loving sisters, the better to picture what happened in these places when you read the holy Books of Moses" (*Itinerarium Egeriae* 5.8).[6] For Egeria and the pilgrim from Bordeaux, the landscape of the eastern Mediterranean was unique. It offered direct and perceptible access to the material traces of scriptural events and thus allowed the visitor to partake in, and to pass on to their readers, a profoundly sensory encounter with sacred history.

At the same time, Egeria's late-fourth-century text also opens a telling window onto the social mechanics behind this invention of the concept of a Christian Holy Land.[7] As far as we can tell, along much of her journey, the sacredness of the landscape was not immediately apparent. Rather, Egeria repeatedly testified to her dependence on local religious experts—monks or clergymen—who identified for her the location of a particular scriptural event and then led her in prayers, appropriate biblical readings, and offerings. Much of the rough desert landscape of the valley before Mount Sinai, for example, had not been marked with man-made monuments or religious structures. Rather, Egeria wrote, "all the way along the valley the holy men were showing us the different places. . . . They pointed out the place where the children of Israel had their camp. . . . They showed us where the calf had been made . . . and the bed of the stream from which, as you read in Exodus, holy Moses made the children of Israel drink" (*Itinerarium Egeriae* 5.1–6).[8] This was, in other words, a Christian sacred topography in the process of becoming, and it was being directly shaped by the authority vested in religious experts: members of the clergy and ascetic holy men. The performance of place-based ritual—the formalized structures of prayer, readings, and instruction by the religious experts—was beginning to codify certain sites recognized as sacred through repeated symbolic actions, at the same time as built structures and commemorative markers also began to alter the physical appearance of the wilderness of Egypt and Palestine.[9] The late antique Christian sacred landscape of the Holy Land was thus woven from multiple threads: the perception of direct connection to sacred history through personal sensory experience of the physical terrain, the validation of the places' special status through repeated performance of ritual actions and prayers, and the investment in the sacred authority of a class of individuals set apart from the normal population.[10]

Special Structures

Yet, even before the "special" status of certain places came to be widely recognized and acted upon, generations of Christians in cities and villages throughout the Mediterranean had been gathering together in private houses for prayer and celebration of the Eucharist. These were spaces that accommodated local groups' communication with God; they served as venues for the collective and increasingly formalized ritual actions and speech of the liturgical prayer and offerings. Though we have numerous literary sources testifying to Christian meetings held in private houses, only one securely attested example of a pre-Constantinian so-called house-church survives in the archaeological record.[11] In a third-century house at the remote site of Dura Europos in eastern Syria, renovations carried out in about 241 included the expansion of a dining room and adjacent storage room into a single larger chamber with a raised platform at one end. The house's refurbishments also included the conversion of another room into a baptismal chamber with the installation of a permanent masonry font surmounted by a columnar canopy and the decoration of the room's walls with Christian frescoes, including imagery of the Women at the Tomb, David and Goliath, the Woman at the Well, and the Healing of the Paralytic, among other subjects (fig. 29.1).[12] The survival of the Dura Europos church is a precious anomaly, but the fact that we have such thin archaeological testimony of first- to third-century Christian meeting places undoubtedly has more to do with our difficulty in identifying them from preserved traces than with their actual distribution and degree of frequency.

Moreover, private houses continued to serve as venues for Christian church services well into Late Antiquity. Indeed, it has been argued that for many Christians in the city of Rome, the day-to-day practice of prayer and worship would have remained relatively consistent from the third through fourth centuries.[13] Ample literary evidence testifies to the home as a site of Christian prayer and devotion and even to the existence of clergymen to officiate at rituals

Figure 29.1. Dura Europos Baptistery, excavation photo of west end of north wall (Yale University Art Gallery, Dura-Europos Collection).

in the patrons' private domiciles.[14] Nevertheless, archaeological identification of such sites remains frustratingly elusive, though it has been suggested that many of the apsidal *aulae* halls found in elite Roman houses could have served as Christian worship spaces.[15] Saints could also be venerated at the household level, and we may find material evidence for this in, for example, the scenes of martyrdom painted on the walls of a small shrine added in the late fourth century to a house on Rome's Caelian Hill under the later church of SS. Giovanni e Paolo.[16]

By the early fourth century, we also see in some places the construction of free-standing buildings built explicitly to accommodate Christian religious meetings. With this new development, the scale and architectural language of the purpose-built ecclesiastical structures began to mark, and often radically transformed, the preexisting urban landscape. For example, two early monumental church buildings constructed in Rome, the Lateran basilica, originally dubbed the Basilica Constantiniana or Basilica Salvatoris, and St. Peter's basilica at the Vatican, utterly transformed the appearance and function of their respective quarters of the city.

The Lateran, the first monumental church built by the emperor Constantine in the city of Rome, was constructed directly atop military barracks of his rival Maxentius' imperial horse guards, the *equites singulares*.[17] Sometime shortly after defeating Maxentius and routing his army at the Battle of the Milvian Bridge in 312, Constantine converted the powerful symbol of his opponent's military presence, the camp of his *equites* located on the Caelian Hill, just inside the monumental Aurelian walls in the southeast corner of the city, into a church building measuring some 75 by 55 meters (250 by 180 feet).[18] The barracks themselves were razed and filled in to serve as the base for the new church and official residence of the bishop of Rome. Constantine's first monumental church construction in the city was thus coupled with an act of urban demolition aimed directly at the eradication of a site immediately associated with the emperor's political rival. As such, the Lateran needs to be seen as part of a larger image-shaping campaign, which, like the renovation of the enormous secular Basilica Nova (also called the Basilica Maxentii/Constantini) originally built by Maxentius at the east end of the Roman Forum, manipulated urban topography, large-scale architecture, and public monuments to underscore Constantine's victory and legitimacy of rule.[19]

At the Vatican, the construction of the enormous basilica of St. Peter dramatically transformed the extramural landscape west of the Tiber River. The walls of the new basilica rose directly on top of what had been an actively used cemetery, heavily built up with houselike family tomb structures, in an area that was also home to a large chariot-racing arena (the *Circus Gai et Neronis*) and the Phrygianum, a sanctuary of the divinities Attis and Cybele.[20] Shaving off the roofs of the mausolea and filling the tombs with rubble to serve as a level support ground, the builders of the new structure converted the necropolis's streets of family graves into a lavish, monumental memorial for Rome's celebrated apostle, which, with an interior length of 119 meters (391 feet), could have accommodated the gathering of thousands of pilgrims and other devout Christians.[21] As became apparent, thanks to excavations carried out in the 1940s under the pavement of the nave, imposing the monumental basilica atop the extramural cemetery transformed the landscape both physically and socially, for the tombs of numerous distinct households were supplanted by a collective monument directed toward a larger community of Christians.[22] At the same time, both the Lateran and St. Peter's, together with other Constantinian basilicas on the outskirts of the city, declared a dramatically new monumental prominence for Christian buildings in Rome. By the second quarter of the fourth century, anyone traveling along any number of the major arteries leading into and out of the city would have encountered the massive brick structures of a major Christian sanctuary.[23]

In their architectural forms, these early Roman churches and others that arose in urban and extra-urban areas across the Mediterranean demonstrate a significant degree of variety within certain typological norms. The original Lateran structure is illustrative of a longitudinal basilica plan in which a wide central nave stretches from the principal entrance to the altar (fig. 29.2). The altar itself stood at the opposite end, framed and aggrandized by the monumental apse and its capping semidome. (At the Lateran, the altar was also grandly

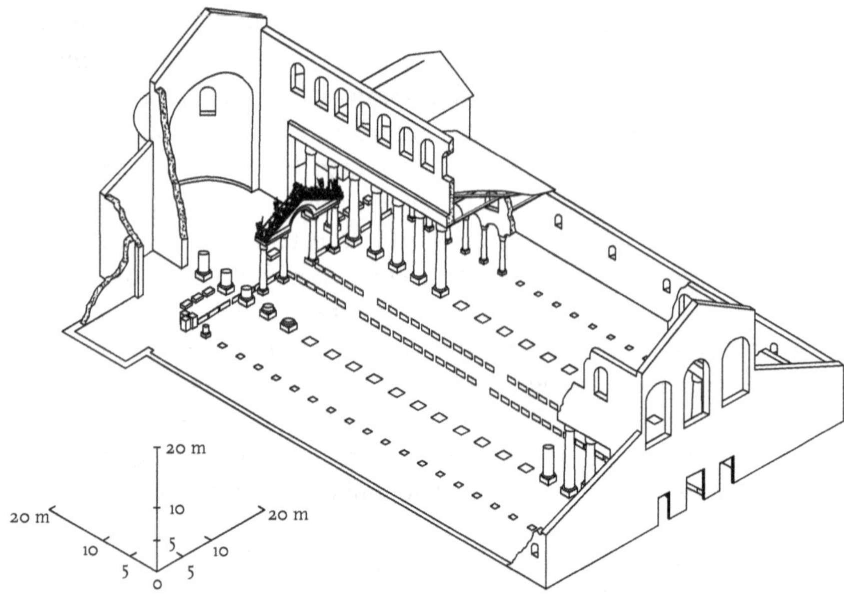

Figure 29.2. Isometric reconstruction of the Lateran Basilica in the Constantinian period with *fastigium* before the sanctuary (from S. de Blaauw 1994, vol. 2, fig. 2).

framed by a free-standing silver screen, or *fastigium*, which bore aloft statues of Jesus and the apostles, all donated by the emperor Constantine, as the *Liber Pontificalis* (1.172) reports.)[24] Further contributing to the longitudinal pull of the basilica are the regular rows of monumental columns lining either side of the nave which support the wall of the clerestory windows above and visually separate it from the darker and lower-ceilinged aisles to either side. St. Peter's presents a variation on the basilica theme by the addition of a transept that created a transverse space at right angles to the length of the nave, an arrangement that was to become immensely influential later in the Middle Ages.[25] Over time, the plan of St. Peter's was also modified by the addition of funerary mausolea appended to the church's sides.[26]

The basilica at the Vatican shared this funerary function in common with the large U-shaped structures built near martyrs' tombs in subterranean catacombs, such as the Basilica Maior structure at S. Lorenzo fuori le mura, S. Sebastiano fuori le mura, S. Agnese fuori le mura (fig. 29.3), and SS. Peter and Marcellinus (also called the "inter (or 'ad') duas lauros" cemetery), each of which accommodated the burials of numerous individuals beneath the pavement, as well as in semi-independent mausoleum structures attached to their walls.[27] Unlike the basilica types of the Lateran and St. Peter's, however, the shape of these structures, with their unusual round-ended plans, was not regularly adopted after the early fourth century or outside of Rome.

Other early churches combine basilica-shaped halls with centrally planned architectural elements that monumentalized special holy sites. The Church of the Nativity in Bethlehem and the site of the Holy Sepulcher in Jerusalem, both

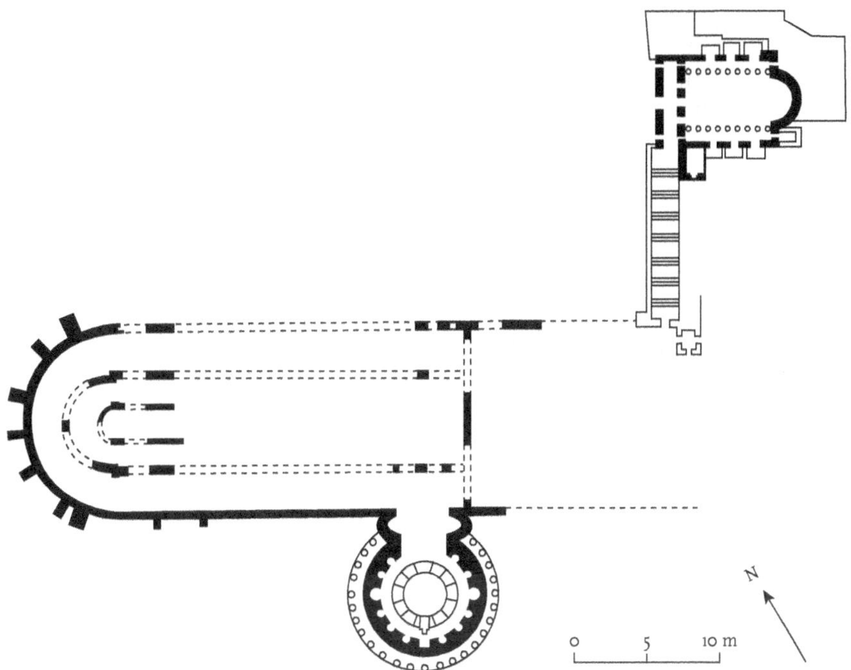

Figure 29.3. Plan of S. Agnese, Rome, with the mausoleum dubbed "S. Costanza" added to the south and the seventh-century basilica to the north (J. Marston, after Deichmann and Tschira 1957, fig. 27).

Constantinian foundations of the second quarter of the fourth century, deployed architecturally complex forms that simultaneously accommodated a congregation gathered before the liturgical altar and underscored the special status of the sacred sites they housed. At Bethlehem, the basilica hall terminated not in the usual apse, but in an octagonal chamber elevated several steps above the pavement of the nave and side aisles, from which visitors could gaze down on the grotto associated with the site of Jesus' birth.[28] The basilica at the Holy Sepulcher incorporated a number of ritual focal points into a single architectural complex (fig. 29.4). Approaching from the north-south street on the east side of the complex, a visitor would have passed through a monumental propylaeum and an airy, marble-bedecked atrium courtyard before reaching the basilica.[29] This structure was focused, as we might expect, on the altar situated before the apse, but beyond the west wall of the basilica and its apse lay a second colonnaded courtyard that embraced two hallowed biblical sites: the place of the crucifixion (Rock of Calvary) in the southeast corner and, to the west, Jesus' rock-cut tomb, which was converted to a freestanding *aedicula*, the so-called Anastasis Rotunda, and later enveloped by a C-shaped ambulatory crowned by a domed or conical roof.[30]

Though churches of the fifth and sixth centuries are frequently categorized as either basilican halls or centralized buildings (e.g., circular, cross-shaped, or octagonal), these stripped-down typological labels mask a wide range of

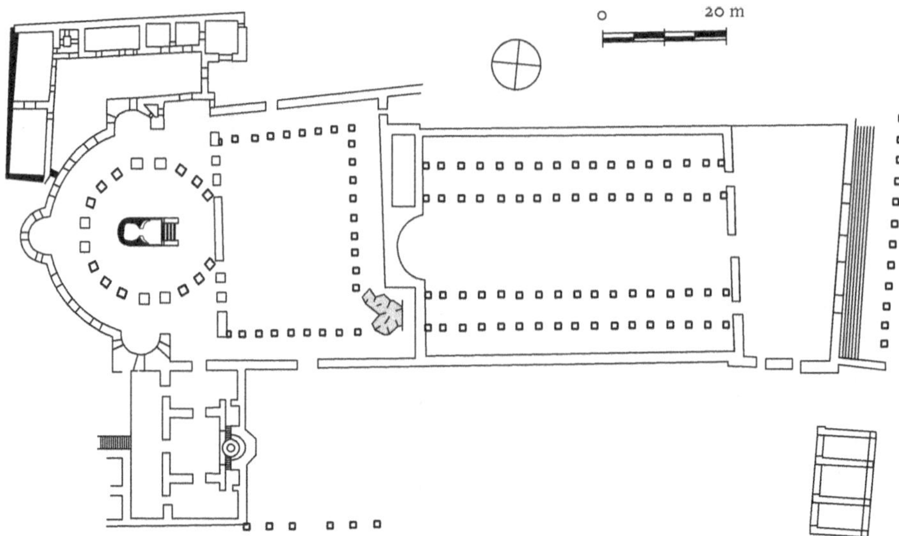

Figure 29.4. Reconstruction of the plan of the Holy Sepulcher, Jerusalem, mid-fourth century (Wharton 1995, 89; after Ousterhout 1990 and Corbo 1981).

regional and local architectural diversity, as well as functional variation.[31] Most centralized church buildings served as martyria; that is, they housed the remains of a venerated saint or marked a holy site (the word *martyrium* derives from a Greek word meaning "witness").[32] This is the case at Jerusalem and Bethlehem, as seen in the cases of the Anastasis Rotunda and the chamber over the hallowed site of the Nativity. It also applies to sites such as Constantine's Church of the Holy Apostles, which, though no longer extant, had a centralized plan and was designed to house memorials of the twelve followers of Christ, as well as the emperor's own tomb.[33] Likewise, the centralized shapes of an octagonal church at Philippi in northern Greece and the famous cross-shaped structure outside of Antioch have been associated with St. Paul's visit and the relics of St. Babylas, respectively.[34]

Basilica structures also demonstrate considerable variation in their formal architectural arrangements. In North Africa, for example, a number of basilicas survive with apses on both ends of the nave, occasionally even preserving evidence for the existence of multiple altars.[35] Early Christian basilicas in Greece and other areas of the eastern Mediterranean often included low screens or parapet walls between the columns, which drew a sharp spatial division between the nave and side aisles.[36] In the area of northern Syria, where numerous small-scale village churches are well preserved, basilicas typically featured monumental entrances along their long, south side instead of or in addition to on the short wall opposite the altar and apse (fig. 29.5).[37] It was, moreover, common in this region for a basilica's apse to be flanked on either side by distinct chambers at the terminus of each of the side aisles in an arrangement dubbed a "tripartite" sanctuary.[38] Though the functions of these rooms were not necessarily consistent, in a number of cases it is clear that one of them, often the south room,

Figure 29.5. Basilica of Mshabbak (Syria), c. 460, exterior view of south side (Photo: A. M. Yasin).

accessible from the side aisle through a wide archway, held the relics of a saint or saints displayed in large stone reliquaries from which holy oil could be obtained.[39]

Each of these typological variations would have substantively altered the experience of the visitors of the space, though frequently we can only speculate on the particulars. Someone entering from the south side of a basilica in northern Syria, for example, would not have had a direct view down the long space of the nave to the altar before the apse. Unlike the experience of one entering St. Peter's or the Lateran, he or she would instead have faced the row of columns lining the side aisle and had only an oblique view through them toward the choir and altar area off to the side. Likewise, the lay congregation standing in the side aisles of a church such as the Acheiropoietos in Thessaloniki or Basilica A at Amphipolis in northern Greece, where the spaces between the nave columns were closed off with a parapet, would have had a view of the nave and sanctuary partially impeded by the nave colonnade.[40]

It is also important to recognize that church buildings rarely stood alone. Rather, they were frequently surrounded by other structures and urban features that would have powerfully affected the visual, spatial, and even symbolic impact of the church. Episcopal complexes, for example, declared their status as seats of the local bishop through architectural and decorative programs that distinguished them from other church buildings and provided a venue for

Figure 29.6. Baptistery of Archbishop Neon ("Orthodox Baptistery"), Ravenna, mid-fifth century (Photo: SEF/Art Resource, NY).

competitive display between cities. For one thing, they included baptisteries, which in the late antique period were usually either monumental free-standing structures in their own right or specialized annexed chambers whose centralized ground plan focused on the small pool (*piscina*) at the center in which the catechumen would stand.[41] The monumental baptistery built adjacent to the Lateran by Constantine (and later rebuilt by Sixtus III in the fifth century), for example, declared the basilica's status as the seat of the bishop of Rome.[42] In the northern Italian city of Ravenna, two surviving, magnificently decorated monumental baptisteries pronounced architectonic claims of legitimacy for the independent Orthodox and Arian bishoprics to whose basilicas they were originally associated (fig. 29.6).[43]

Similarly, surrounding structures associated with a bishop's residence or designed for the accommodation of large numbers of monastics or pilgrims set some church buildings proper within a wider architectural and ideological frame. The well-preserved sixth-century ecclesiastical complex at Poreč (ancient Parentium) in Istria, for example, uses a central courtyard space to connect a lavishly decorated basilica dedicated to the Virgin to a monumental baptistery, which is in turn linked to an impressive episcopal palace (fig. 29.7).[44] Here the axiality of the baptistery and basilica and the monumental constructions of the

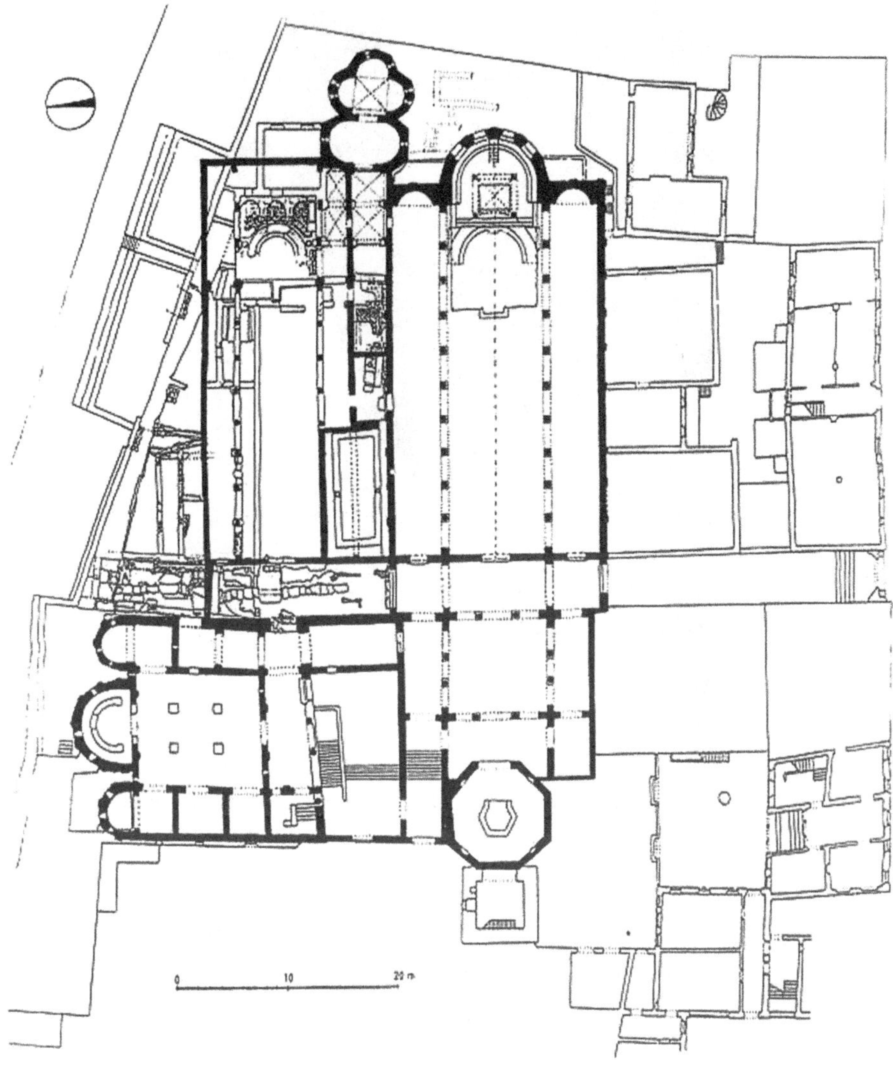

Figure 29.7. Plan of ecclesiastical complex at Poreč (Croatia), mid-sixth century (Courtesy of Ivan Matejčić).

episcopal apartments created a complex that underscored the office of the bishop to all who gazed toward or visited the church. At the late-fifth-century shrine built up around St. Simeon's column at Qal'at Sem'ān (fig. 15.2) in northern Syria and the fortified Justinianic complex at the site of the Burning Bush on the Sinai peninsula, the accumulation of large masses of monastic buildings and those that accommodated the feeding and housing of religious pilgrims fundamentally structured the visitors' experience of the site. Monumental architectural features such as gates and passageways and other transitional spaces marked and mediated one's progress toward the holy relics and the liturgical altar. The precinct of the pilgrimage church and martyrium at Tebessa in North Africa, for example, was accessed by a monumental triumphal arch–inspired

Figure 29.8. In situ wooden lintel over central western doorway of the Basilica of the Monastery of St. Catherine, Sinai, sixth century (Photo: A. M. Yasin).

gateway.[45] Visitors to the site of the Burning Bush at Sinai had to pass through the fortification wall and basilica portal, both of which called attention to the spatial transition with a monumentally inscribed text taken from Psalm 118:20: "This is the gate of the Lord: the righteous shall enter by it" (fig. 29.8).[46]

While the variety in ecclesiastical structures, whether from regional differences in architectural types or from the exigencies of particular sites, meant that the experience of visiting different late antique churches could vary widely, in general, church buildings deployed formal and decorative elements toward closely related ends. For one thing, from their initial appearance in the early fourth century and continuing into the fifth and sixth, purpose-built churches distinguished themselves from other kinds of buildings in the urban and suburban landscape. With forms originally drawn from a classical architectural vocabulary—including civic basilicas, private apsidal audience halls, and centralized tomb buildings—the combination of scale and increasingly distinctive formal elements nevertheless made late antique ecclesiastical structures readily recognizable as churches and distinct from domestic houses, governmental structures, and meeting places of other religious groups. As such, early church buildings throughout the Mediterranean functioned as material markers of Christian identity. As social spaces in which the religious group assembled, church buildings could define the boundaries of that community, communicate its divisions, and define its relationships to others past and present.[47] Moreover, as spaces of Christian gathering and liturgical ritual, they were directly charged with focusing and articulating the community's collective encounter with the divine.

Encountering the Holy, Engaging the Senses

Church buildings framed and structured this encounter both through the forms of their physical spaces and through the shapes of the rituals and actions they housed. Walking into an early Christian church and participating in the liturgy was a dynamic, sensory-filled experience. Many complexes began to prime the visitor's senses even before he or she entered the church building proper. Fountains of running water, for example, were frequently incorporated into the design of entrance courtyards.[48] The refreshing sound and sparkling light from the water bouncing off reflective marble surfaces would delight the senses, much as Roman fountains and nymphaea did, but would also, and critically in its ecclesiastical context, provide both a means of ritual purification and a constant sensory reminder of the symbolic waters of baptism that defined membership in the Christian community and signaled the promise of eternal life. As early as Eusebius' panegyric of the bishop of Tyre, probably composed on the occasion of his cathedral's dedication in about 317 C.E., water seems to have been an integral element of the courtyard's infrastructure and symbolism.[49] Paulinus of Nola, writing in 396, provides an early literary description of the bright atrium courtyard stretching out before St. Peter's, where a *baldacchino* supported by four columns covered a *cantharus* from which streams of water flowed to serve, he says, "our hands and faces" (*Ep.* 13.13).[50] Undoubtedly inspired by his visit to St. Peter's, Paulinus' descriptions of his own renovations of the complex built up around the site of St. Felix's tomb in Cimitile/Nola reveal the strong emphasis he placed on the sensory effects and symbolism of water and other precious materials in the courtyard that joined the two basilicas on the site (e.g., *Carm.* 27.365–384, 480–504; 28.28–52).[51] Paulinus' fountains, like that in the atrium at St. Peter's, are long gone, but evidence for the incorporation of monumental water features before church entrances survives, for example, at Basilica A in Nea Anchialos (Greece) and the Fountain Court between the cathedral and the Basilica of St. Timothy at Gerasa (modern Jerash, Jordan).[52]

The water, sound, colorful materials, and refreshing breezes could call to mind (and body) the sensory experiences of earthly gardens and heavenly paradise. Such paradisiacal references were carried out on an even more dramatic scale in the interior decorations of many early churches. The surfaces of the

Figure 29.9. Monastery of St. Catherine at Mount Sinai, apse mosaic (Courtesy of the Michigan-Princeton-Alexandria Expedition to Mount Sinai).

floors, walls, and vaults of the wealthiest churches, covered with marble revetment and glass mosaic, were praised not only for the colorful variety of their materials but also especially for their radiant ability to transmit light from their reflective or highly polished surfaces.[53] Well-preserved churches, such as the mid-fourth-century basilica at Mshabbak in northern Syria, reveal how integral a multitude of windows was to the original architectural design and help us imagine the brilliance of daytime illumination that would have flooded the nave from rows of clerestory windows above the colonnade and from openings in the façade and apse walls (see fig. 29.5).[54] The supernatural significance of the natural light could be magnified by its echoes in a church's figural imagery. At the Sinai basilica, for example, the central apse imagery of Christ's theophany (fig. 29.9), as well as the Moses scenes laid out in glass mosaic to either side of the window on the triumphal arch above, use the imagery of light to underscore the message of God's divine intervention.[55]

The heavenly symbolism of light and brilliance that contributed to the aesthetic of golden vaults and polished reflective surfaces was pushed to extremes in the extraordinary architecture of Justinian's Hagia Sophia.[56] Here, the highest level of imperial commission resulted in a building whose interior was coated with costly marble cladding and gold and silver mosaic and whose dome appeared to hover above a ring of light. The row of windows that pierced the springing of the enormous dome, one opening between each of the forty ribs, admitted celestial rays of light at all times of the day, which, reflecting off the dome's original golden mosaic surface, inspired late antique descriptions that likened the building to the vaults of heaven itself.[57] The overhead illumination was redoubled by the dozens of additional windows piercing the clerestory, conch vaults, and apse wall.[58] In addition, lamps of precious metal hung between the columns, and candelabra stood atop the chancel screen; at least 140 additional lamps were suspended on long chains from the dome and hung in a ring around the cornice overhead.[59] Their flames, like the rays of sunlight in the daytime, reflected off the silver-covered columns of the screen and bishop's throne against the apse wall and the highly polished gray, green, yellow, white, red, and other colored marbles used for the church's pavement, columns, and wall revetment.[60]

In addition to the array of diverse colored and reflective materials, the subject matter of church decoration often explicitly evoked the abundance of the terrestrial or celestial paradise.[61] In this respect, as with architectural typologies discussed in the previous section, regional differences defy any obvious sense of uniformity of style, but the functional aims share much in common across the Mediterranean. The surfaces of many churches practically overflowed with imagery of the abundance of the natural world—both vegetal and animal—and the richness of the heavenly kingdom. The composition of the pavement mosaic of the mid-sixth-century Chapel of Priest John, attached to a church near Mount Nebo in Jordan, presents a lush example, with a personification of Earth itself (labeled "ΓΗ") surrounded by evidence of its bounty (fig. 29.10).[62] The mosaic bands that articulate the ribs of the sanctuary vault at the sixth-century church of S. Vitale in Ravenna, for example, are cast as fictive polychrome garlands, and the triangular spaces between them are covered in a pattern of lush bird- and animal-filled vegetation of stylized acanthus leaves (fig. 29.11).[63] Even the soffits under the arches of basilica colonnades and of the round-topped windows were exploited to fill the space with floral and vegetal plenty as, for example, in the stucco relief decoration still in situ at the Eufrasius Basilica in Poreč.[64] Large numbers of surviving mosaic pavements from late antique churches in North Africa and the Levant presented either so-called inhabited scrolls of vines "peopled" with birds and animals or schematic fields of rosebuds, across which a wide variety of terrestrial beasts give chase or are pursued.[65] The broad compositions of which they form a part represent terrestrial bounty while recalling the virtues on display in aristocratic hunt scenes and infusing them with symbolism of the abundance of God's creation.[66]

If lush fields of multicolored flowers and golden, gem-studded walls were envisioned as attributes of paradise, the evocation of such features on the floors and walls of churches turned these spaces into approximations or simulacra of the next world.[67] In the iconography depicted in the apses of churches, the connection could be drawn even more literally.[68] At the small, early-fifth-century church of S. Pudenziana in Rome, which preserves our earliest extant monumental church apse mosaic, Jesus appears on a jewel-studded golden throne surrounded by his twelve apostles, who sit before the sparkling golden rooftops of a luxurious city, understood as a representation of the heavenly Jerusalem apparently

Figure 29.10. Mosaic pavement of the Chapel of Priest John in the Church of Amos and Kasiseus, Khirbet el-Mukhayyat, Jordan, 565 C.E. (Mount Nebo Museum; photo: A. M. Yasin). See also color plate section.

modeled on the earthly city (fig. 29.12).[69] Above, a magnificent, bejeweled golden cross dominates the composition and, together with the four winged creatures of the apocalypse arrayed around it who come to symbolize the Evangelists, draws unmistakable attention to eschatological themes of Christ's triumphant second coming.[70] Surviving sixth-century apse compositions frequently depict Christ in majesty. Whether he stands draped in golden robes as at SS. Cosmas and Damian in Rome, sits upon an orb as at S. Vitale in Ravenna, or as an infant sits on his mother's lap as at the Eufrasian basilica at Poreč (fig. 29.13), his paradisiacal surroundings are signaled by the lily- and rose-sprouted landscape and golden or cloud-bedecked heavens. When, in addition, Jesus is positioned atop a hillock from which four flowing streams sprout, as at S. Vitale and SS. Cosmas and Damian, the reference to the four fabled rivers of Paradise is made graphically explicit (see fig. 29.11).[71]

Imagery like this, precious testimony of the vibrant brilliance of the original late antique church interior, transports the viewer standing in the church into another temporal and spatial realm (e.g., figs. 29.9, 29.11–29.13). It also presents him or her with a powerful theophanic vision. The monumental figure of Christ, either alone or together with his mother, Mary, is at the center and the

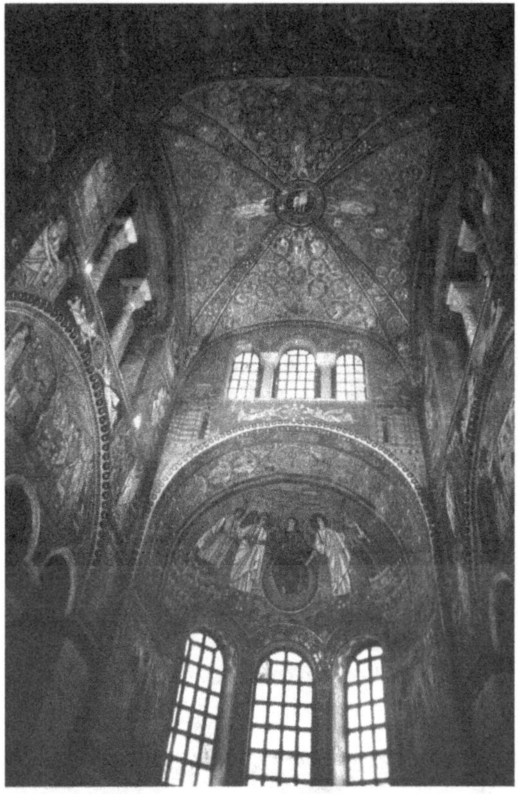

Figure 29.11. Sanctuary vault and apse, S. Vitale, Ravenna, sixth century (Photo: Vanni/Art Resource, NY). See also color plate section.

one to whom the gestures and movement of the surrounding figures—angels, martyrs, and ecclesiastical donors or, in the case of Sinai, prophets and apostles—are directed. The hierarchical arrangement of the compositions thus powerfully direct the viewer's attention toward the divine Christ.

At this point, it is also critical to note the larger pattern of decorative and architectural organization of the church space. Not only the figures immediately flanking Jesus but also the vertical and horizontal arrangement of other elements duplicate the figure of Christ, sometimes depicted in allegorical (lamb) or symbolic (cross or chi-rho) form, and stress the centrality of the monumental apse figure. Ravenna's S. Vitale provides a particularly lavish and well-preserved assembly of mosaic decorations (see fig. 29.11). Here, beginning at the boundary of the sanctuary and nave, the soffit beneath the arch that delineates the space of the choir is ringed with medallion portraits of the apostles and two local saints and presents at its center a frontal image of the bearded Christ.[72] Guiding the eye back along the axis of the choir, a second medallion image appears at the apex of the vault over the altar: a haloed lamb in a garland frame held aloft by four angels. These two images of Christ lead directly to the figure of Jesus enthroned above the rivers of paradise in the apse. Similarly, at the Eufrasian basilica in Poreč (see fig. 29.13), the strict organization of the

Figure 29.12. S. Pudenziana apse mosaic, Rome, c. 400 (Photo: Vanni/Art Resource, NY). See also color plate section.

Figure 29.13. Eufrasius Basilica apse mosaic, Poreč, sixth century (Photo: A. M. Yasin). See also color plate section.

composition stresses the centrality of Christ by figuring three versions of his image along the sanctuary's vertical axis: enthroned on an orb flanked by gift-bearing apostles on the triumphal arch, as haloed lamb in the medallion at the center of the soffit, and upon the Virgin's lap in the curve of the apse. Each representation of Christ confronts the viewer directly with frontal gaze, allowing for a face-to-face encounter with the divine.

The organization also, however, underscores the degree to which the decorative program mediates the viewer's own approach to the divinity. Christ is at the center, but to either side of him, and below, closer to the viewer's own realm, are the figures who guide and direct one's attention to God. The angels, apostles, saints, and clerical donors model proper reverential deportment and literally point the way to the Godly vision. What is more, the axiality also extends all the way to the ground, for directly beneath the string of images of Christ is a final, symbolic image of the Savior: the eucharistic bread and wine prepared at the actual altar below. The architectural and decorative elements of the church interior work in concert with the performance of liturgical ritual to present a message about the path to salvation, eternal paradise, and the company of Christ: they are to be found through following the examples of the angels and saints and through the sacrament of the Eucharist made possible by the institution of the church.

Ritual and Authority

While the layout and decoration of the church stressed both the visitor's direct experiences of heavenly sensations—the brilliance, color, variety, and imagery calling to mind a heavenly paradise—they also created a privileged space in the sanctuary around the altar where the richest decoration and most spiritually elevated iconography were to be found. The church building as a whole and the sanctuary in particular were stages for liturgical performance, elaborate theaters for ceremonial and processional performance.[73] Study of fifth- to sixth-century Constantinople, where we have substantial textual and architectural sources for early Byzantine liturgical ritual, reveals the emphasis on movement and the orchestrated shifting of attention to different ecclesiastical spaces.

The early Byzantine liturgy of Constantinople began with the First Entrance, the ceremonial procession of clergy and congregation into the church.[74] An atrium and narthex are key features of many urban early Christian churches and are especially prevalent in the early churches of Constantinople, where, as liturgical evidence testifies, great stress was placed on spectacular entrance processions.[75] A Prayer of Entry (Introit Prayer) performed at the architectural juncture between the sacred space of the church and the everyday world outside further ritually charged the site of the church doors and thresholds in a way analogous to the monumental decoration adorning entrances, such as the psalm inscribed on the lintel of the church at Sinai (see fig. 29.8).[76] Processing through the nave of the church and bearing aloft the gospel book, the clergy ended arrayed as a collective group on raised tiers of benches (the *synthronon*), which were built against the apse, and with the principal celebrant seated on the central throne (*cathedra*).[77]

The rest of the ritual enlivened the space of the sanctuary and the area immediately preceding it. In the Liturgy of the Word, which was the first part of the liturgical ritual following the processional entrance, all attention was focused on the deacon as he moved ceremonially from the sanctuary, though the chancel barriers, and into the space of the nave along a special, cordoned-off path (*solea*). His goal was an elevated platform, or ambo, from which he performed the scriptural readings of the service. The famous description of the liturgical furnishings at Hagia Sophia written by Paul the Silentiary in the sixth century offers an extended metaphor of the ambo that likened its connection with the sanctuary to a sort of surf-buffeted island that is tethered to the mainland, a "wave-washed land, extended through the white-capped billows by an isthmus into the middle of the sea."[78] This passage, together with accounts of various clergymen who expressed frustration at instances of distracting or unruly behavior by their congregations, has been taken as evidence that arrangements of liturgical furnishings also responded to a need for a certain degree of crowd control during the liturgy.[79] The gospel book from which the deacon read the culminating text of this portion of the liturgy would have been carried with him from the altar to the ambo along the *solea* and then back again into the sanctuary. The liturgical performance, as well as the ornate decoration of the exterior binding of the codex, would therefore have ceremonially dramatized the gospel book itself as a precious sacred object.[80] Its theatrical but temporary movement from the clerical space of the sanctuary into the congregational space allowed churchgoers to see and hear the word of God, while it also underscored the clergy's role in providing access to and safekeeping of the holy book. After the sermon (if there was one), all those who had not yet been baptized (the catechumens) were dismissed, and the main entrance doors were closed, for the remainder of the liturgy was reserved for full, baptized members of the Christian community only.[81]

The celebration of the liturgy then moved into its most solemn chapter. During the Entrance of the Mysteries, deacons carried rich chalices and patens filled with bread and wine, together with candles, incense, and ritual fans (*flabella*), into and through the church to the altar.[82] The assembled then exchanged the Kiss of Peace and recited the Nicene Creed, elements of the ritual that reaffirmed the tight bonds of community through gestures performed by each member. The ritual focus during the subsequent Anaphora, the series of Eucharistic prayers that accompanied the preparation of the bread and wine, was on the celebrant and the altar. Unlike later Byzantine churches in which the altar itself was both visually and spatially inaccessible behind a high, image-bearing

Figure 29.14. Reconstructed silver altar revetment from the Sion Treasure, sixth century (Dumbarton Oaks; photo: A. M. Yasin).

screen or *iconostasis*, in the early Byzantine churches of Constantinople, altars and the ritual actions performed at them during the liturgy appear to have been largely visible to the congregation beyond the chancel barriers.[83] Many late antique altars were highly ornate furnishings in their own right, richly adorned with carving or precious metal revetment, like the sixth-century silver-clad altar from the Sion Treasure found in southern Turkey, now partially reconstructed in the Dumbarton Oaks Museum in Washington, D.C. (fig. 29.14), and/or covered with the kind of expensive decorated altar cloths attested by literary sources.[84] After the Communion, in which the Eucharistic bread and wine were distributed to the clergy and congregation, presumably at the entrance of the chancel, the ritual concluded as it began, with the clergy's processional exit from the sanctuary through the space of the church.

Throughout the Eucharistic ceremony, therefore, the key ritual focal points of the liturgy were anchored by furnishings whose prominence was framed and monumentalized by the architectural forms and decoration of the surrounding church structure. The *solea* and ambo delineated and dramatized the movement of the deacon and the gospel book between the sanctuary and congregational space. The chancels materially underscored the spatial division between lay and clerical space, and the altar provided the symbolic and visual focus of the liturgy at the culmination of the eucharistic ritual.

This sense of the sanctuary's distinction, its spatial separateness and elevation, also can be seen to underscore a fundamental social division between clergy and lay members of the community. The sixth-century Basilica of Eufrasius in Poreč again offers the opportunity to study a relatively well-preserved late antique sanctuary's decorative ensemble (see fig. 29.13). If we think away

Figure 29.15. Eufrasius Basilica cathedra, Poreč (Photo: A. M. Yasin).

the square ciborium erected above the altar in the thirteenth century, the organization of the sanctuary space becomes apparent. Strict symmetry and axiality reign. The clerical zone of the sanctuary is clearly set off from and elevated above the congregational space by the steps and decorated marble slabs of the chancel barrier.[85] The decoration of the nave walls of the congregational space is now lost to us, but the walls were probably painted with frescoes and undoubtedly would have contrasted greatly with the rich marble and shell inlay work (*opus sectile*) of the lower portions of the apse wall and the luminous gold of the semi-dome and vertical triumphal arch wall marking the sanctuary. In the upper reaches of the mosaic decoration, as we have seen, a compositional line vertically links the enthroned Christ on the triumphal arch, the haloed lamb on the soffit, the enthroned Virgin and Child in the apse conch, and the altar below. In addition, these aligned representations of Christ also point directly to the seat of the presiding bishop built against the center of the apse wall (fig. 29.15). This *cathedra* was constructed of marble, flanked by fictive, ever-burning candles on tall, iridescent stands depicted in *opus sectile*, and topped by a representation of a golden triumphal cross set on a porphyry hillock. The extravagant, polychrome decoration not only visually and symbolically elevated the bishop who occupied this seat above the congregation in the nave and even the other clergymen within the sanctuary but also put him literally in direct line with the figure of Jesus represented in the numerous depictions above him.

What is more, the presiding bishop would be understood as the successor to the office held by the clerical benefactor of the church, Bishop Eufrasius, who figures in the mosaic program directly (see fig. 29.13). The beautifully lettered, monumental inscription, which runs the width of the apse above the windows, explicitly praises the bishop's pious generosity.[86] Moreover, Eufrasius is among the figures depicted bearing gifts to the Virgin and Child in the semidome of the apse. The first figure on the left of Mary and the angel attendants is haloed and carries the crown symbolizing his martyr's victory; the inscription set next to his head identifies him as "St. Maurus," who was one of the city's first bishops. Behind him, in deep purple ecclesiastical robes and accompanied by a deacon and child carrying a jeweled book and candles, is a figure identified by inscription as "Bishop Eufrasius," the same benefactor credited with this church's renovation and decoration in the monumental inscription below. In the apse composition, Eufrasius approaches the holy figures holding a representation of a church building in his reverently veiled arms. Through this balanced composition, the mosaic graphically equates the bishop's pious act of church benefaction to the sacrifice offered by the accompanying martyrs. His deeds have earned him company with the angels and saints beyond this world before the Lord. The clergy's distinctive access to the holy and the authority of the local bishop as Christ's representative on earth was, in other words, engrained into the very fabric of the church building. At the same time, this exceptional figure is held up before the congregation as a subject to be both remembered and emulated.

Here as well as in less wealthy churches, permanent structural features and surface decoration inscribed the hierarchical ordering of the Christian community within the space of the church. Ecclesiastical buildings could, in other words, also serve as a means of public communication by the church as an institution. Church officials could regulate access to the holy and teach lessons of faith and behavior through the location, form, and decoration of churches, as well as the shape of the activities permitted inside. While the church building as a whole was a space made sacred through the performance of ritual, it in turn also shaped and elevated the ritual actions performed there and legitimated the social positions of the various members of the Christian community.

Whether an unadorned site of a scriptural event, a rich, monumental urban cathedral, or a relatively modest provincial basilica, early Christian sacred spaces conditioned believers' approach to the divine in immediate, personal, and palpably sensory ways. Like the water from Jacob's well described by the Bordeaux Pilgrim or the landscape of the Sinai peninsula that Egeria visited, through their form, decoration, and the activity they housed, late antique churches reinforced the veracity of scriptural accounts, provided evidence of

God's glory and intervention on earth, and created venues for offering pious responses through ritual and prayer. It is not that all early Christian churches looked alike. On the contrary, different communities, patrons, and craftsmen offered architectural and artistic responses that differed in scale, shape, materials, and style in response to local political, social, economic, and liturgical situations. Yet, by various means—such as windows admitting golden rays of light, attention-focusing arrangements of columns and liturgical furniture, heightened adornment of sanctuary zones, and decorative programs that underscored the promise of eternal life and other articles of faith—churches across the early Christian world offered physical spaces in which God's presence could be sensed and appropriate responses could be made.

NOTES

1. Trans. after Wilkinson 1999, 27.
2. Trans. after Wilkinson 1999, 30. Note that three different Zechariahs, who could be variously conflated by different Christian authors, were associated with the site of the Temple Mount. The Bordeaux Pilgrim's text seems to follow Matthew 23:35, in which the prophet Zechariah, author of the biblical book of Zechariah, is taken to be one and the same as the Zechariah who prophesied against Joash and was martyred in the Temple courtyard (Wilkinson 1999, 30, n. 3; Johnson 2010, 14). See also Johnson, chapter 17 in this book.
3. E.g., *etiam parent vestigia clavorum militum* (*Itinerarium Burdigalense* 591; Geyer and Cuntz 1965, 15–16).
4. On the itineraries of late antique pilgrims to the Holy Land, see Maraval 1995; 2002; 2004, as well as Talbot 2002 on female pilgrimage in particular.
5. Trans. Wilkinson 1999, 120.
6. Trans. Wilkinson 1999, 113.
7. On the concept of the Holy Land, see especially Wilken 1992; Taylor 1993; Eliav 2005.
8. Trans. Wilkinson 1999, 112–113.
9. Cf. Renfrew's discussion of archaeological indicators of religious sites (1994, esp. 52).
10. On the creation and definition of early Christian sacred landscapes more broadly, see Smith 1987; Wilken 1992; MacCormack 1990; Markus 1994; Taylor 1993; Yasin 2009.
11. Literary sources on early Christian as well as Jewish and pagan gatherings in private houses are very usefully assembled in White 1997.
12. On the Dura house-church, which was destroyed along with the rest of the town in the Persian attacks of 256 C.E., see White 1997, 123–134; Kraeling 1967.
13. Bowes 2008, 71–73.
14. Sessa 2006; Bowes 2005; Bowes 2008, esp. 76–84.
15. Bowes 2008, 74.
16. Bowes 2008, 88–92; Brenk 1995; 2003, 82–113; Krautheimer 1937b.
17. On the *castra nova* built to accommodate the corps of *equites singulares* at the site of the earlier *castra priora*, see Buzzetti 1993.

18. On the transfer of imperial property and the foundation date of the Lateran basilica, see Curran 2000, 93–96. More detailed discussion of the measurements, plan, and materials of the Constantinian structure can be found in Krautheimer 1986, 47–48; Krautheimer and Corbett 1977.

19. Constantine's conversion of the Maxentian basilica included opening a second major entrance on the long southwest side facing the Sacred Way leading into the forum, adding a monumental apse directly across from this entranceway, and installing a colossal seated statue of himself, many fragments of which survive. On the Constantinian reorganization of this building and the surrounding monuments, see Curran 2000, 57–61, 80–83; Marlowe 2006.

20. On the preexisting topography of the Vatican area, see Castagnoli 1992; Guarducci 1960; Krautheimer and Frazer 1977, 177–183.

21. Krautheimer 1986, 54–56, and the more detailed presentation of Krautheimer and Frazer 1977; MacMullen 2009, 79.

22. On the preexisting cemetery, see Toynbee and Ward-Perkins 1956; Mielsch and von Hesberg 1996.

23. Krautheimer 2000, 24–31.

24. de Blaauw 1994, 1.117–127; Davis 1989, 16.

25. E.g., McClendon 2005, 90; Krautheimer 1969.

26. The mausoleum of Sextus Petronius Probus was added against the apse between 390 and 410, and the rotunda mausoleum of the Honorian dynasty was appended to the south transept arm in c. 400 (Krautheimer and Frazer 1977, 173).

27. On this class of buildings in general, see Tolotti 1982; La Rocca 2000; Torelli 1990. On the Basilica Maior, see Krautheimer and Frankl 1959; on S. Sebastiano, see Krautheimer and Corbett 1970. On S. Agnese: Krautheimer 1937a; Cianetti and Pavolini 2004. For SS. Marcellino e Pietro, see Krautheimer 1962; Deichmann and Tschira 1957.

28. The church standing on the site today, which dates to the sixth century, replaced the Constantinian structure, the outlines of which are known thanks to excavations carried out in the 1930s (Bagatti 1952, 9–54; Ovadiah, 1970, 33–37; Krautheimer 1986, 60).

29. Corbo 1981, 1.115–117, 227.

30. See Ousterhout 1990; Krautheimer 1986; Biddle 1999; Corbo 1981, 1.39–137, English summary: 223–228. The complex is described by Eusebius in *Vita Constantini* 3.33–40 (Cameron and Hall 1999, 135–137).

31. For an overview of the diversity of architecture and liturgical arrangements of late antique churches, see Duval 1999.

32. The classic study of martyria is Grabar 1946. More recent analyses include Yasin 2009; Deichmann 1970; the essays in Lamberigts and van Deun 1995.

33. Mango 1990a; 1990b; Krautheimer 1986, 69–70; Eusebius, *Vita Constantini* 4.58–60 (trans. Cameron and Hall 1999, 176–177).

34. Saradi 2006, 393–394; Bakirtzis and Koester 1998; Lassus 1938; Downey 1938.

35. Duval 1973. For a catalogue of North African early Christian church architecture, see Gui et al. 1992.

36. Peschlow 2006.

37. Sodini 1989, 349–351.

38. On the range of functions of these north Syrian side rooms, see Descoeudres 1983, esp. 13–25. On the early ecclesiastical architecture of Syria in general, see Sodini 1989; Butler 1929; Lassus 1947; Tchalenko 1953–1958; Krautheimer 1986, 137–156.

39. Yasin 2009, 164–170; Descoeudres 1983; Lassus 1947, 161–183; Donceel-Voûte, 1995. On the oil-producing reliquaries, see Gessel 1988.

40. Peschlow 2006.

41. For a typological overview and catalogue of early Christian baptisteries plus older bibliography, see Ristow 1998. Falla Castelfranchi investigates a number of eastern examples associated with important martyria (1980).

42. Krautheimer 1986, 90–92, 176–177; Pelliccioni 1973.

43. See Wharton 1995, 105–136; Wharton 1987; Deichmann 1969, 1.130–157, 209–212; 2.17–47, 251–255.

44. For an overview of the complex, see Terry and Maguire 2007, 2–6; Molajoli 1943. There is some debate about whether the episcopal palace dates to Bishop Eufrasius or was added slightly later in the sixth century (Matejčić and Chevalier 1998; Chevalier and Matejčić 2004).

45. Yasin 2009, 164; Christern 1976.

46. Coleman and Elsner 1994, 78–79.

47. See Yasin 2009.

48. Picard 1989, 536–538.

49. *Historia Ecclesiastica* 10.4.39–40: "But he did not permit the one passing inside the gates to come immediately with unholy and unwashed feet upon the holy places within . . . and he left an atrium in the middle for beholding the sky, providing it with an airy brightness, open to the rays of light. Herein he placed the symbols of holy purification; he erected opposite the front (façade) of the temple fountains whose plenteous streams of flowing water provide cleansing for those who will proceed into the interior of the sacred enclosure" (text and translation in White 1997, 2.94–99).

50. van den Hoek and Herrmann 2000, 174–175. On the evidence for the plan of Old St. Peter's atrium, see Krautheimer and Frazer 1977, 261–271; Picard 1974.

51. Goldschmidt 1940; Kiely 2004.

52. On Basilica A at Nea Anchialos with its unusual, richly decorated hemicycle atrium and fountain, see Krautheimer 1986, 122–123; Soteriou 1931, 33–39. At Gerasa, the fountain was in the middle of the atrium on the west side of the cathedral (Crowfoot 1938, 210–212).

53. James 2003; Janes 1998, 94–152. See also Saradi 2010, 92–105.

54. Butler 1929, 62–64.

55. Nelson 2006.

56. Krautheimer 1986, 205–219; Mainstone 1988.

57. The dome we see today was the second one, completed in 563 after the collapse in 558 of the first, shallower shell of the structure dedicated in 537 (for a report of structural changes made since the church's construction, see Mainstone 1988, 85–114). The original dome was apparently decorated with a solid gold mosaic (Procopius, *De aedificiis* 1.1.56; translated in Mango 1986, 76), while the second bore the image of a large cross, neither of which survives (Mango 1962, 87–91). The mosaic cross of the rebuilt dome is described and likened to the heavens in Paul the Silentiary's *Description of Hagia Sophia* (489, 506; translated in Mango 1986, 83). See also Mainstone 1988, 126.

58. Krautheimer 1986, 214; Mainstone 1988, 124–126.

59. Bouras and Parani 2008, 31–36.

60. See the contemporary description by Paul the Silentiary (translated in Mango 1986, 87–91); cf. Procopius, *De aedificiis*, 1.1.23ff. (translated in Mango 1986, 72–75).

For a summary of the marbles used in the church's decoration, see Kleinbauer 1999, 39–42, and see Barry 2007 on the perception and symbolism of the marble pavement.

61. Maguire 1987, Kessler 2007.

62. Piccirillo 1993, 174–175.

63. Maguire 1987, 76–80.

64. Cantino Wataghin 2006; Matejčić 2006.

65. Maguire 1987; Hachlili 2009, 111–147; Donceel-Voûte 1988, esp. 476–479.

66. Maguire 1987.

67. On paradisiacal and other apocalyptic imagery in early Christian churches, see Engemann 1976, as well as Kinney 1992; Maguire 1987; Kessler 2007; Herrmann and van den Hoek 2009.

68. Ihm's catalogue of early Christian apse programs remains essential (1960).

69. Ihm 1960, 130–132, cat. no. 2; Christe 1972; Dassmann 1970. Further discussion of the identification of the architecture represented can be found in Pullan 1997–1998; Schlatter 1995. For a controversial interpretation of the figure of Christ in this church, see Mathews 1999, 92–114. On the architecture and chronology of the structure, see Krautheimer and Corbett 1967.

70. In addition to the sources in the previous note, on the interpretation of eschatological themes in the mosaic, see Schlatter 1992; Steen 1999; Kinney 1992, 208–210. More generally on the history of the literary and iconographical connection between the prophet Ezekiel's famous apocalyptic vision (Ezekiel 1:4–28), the winged creatures described in Revelation 4:6–8, and the four Evangelists, see Minasi 2000.

71. Maguire 1987. On the significance of the donors and local saints often included in such compositions, see Yasin 2010.

72. On this and other sequences of medallion portraits at the edge of the sanctuary space, see Yasin 2009, 260–271.

73. Not only during the regular liturgical services examined later but also on special feast days and nighttime vigils were churches the settings for multisensory celebrations (e.g., Frank 2006).

74. The most accessible overview to early Byzantine liturgy is Taft 1992; see also Dix 1945. Translations of many of the earliest liturgical texts appear in Brightman 1896.

75. Mathews 1971, 145; Taft 1992, 33–35.

76. Mathews 1971, 141; Taft 2006, 52–56.

77. Mathews 1971, 107–109, 138–144.

78. *Description of Hagia Sophia* 244 (translated in Mango 1986, 95). On the ambo, *solea*, and chancels of Hagia Sophia, see Xydis 1947.

79. Taft 2006, 76–79.

80. Mathews 1971, esp. 110, 148–149. On the appearance and symbolism of the early Christian gospel book as a sacred object, see Lowden 2007; Rapp 2007.

81. Mathews 1971, 149–152.

82. This procession of liturgical items probably entered through one of the church's side doors (Mathews 1971, 155–162).

83. In some areas of the Mediterranean, however, there is evidence that curtains were sometimes hung between the colonnettes of the *templon* barrier, which supported a narrow architrave above the chancel blocks (Mathews 1971, 168–171, 178; Chatzidakis 1978, esp. cols. 326–330).

84. Mathews 1971, 166–177; Boyd and Mango 1992, 32–33.

85. The chancel barrier we see today is not, however, the original (which was dismantled in the thirteenth century) but a reconstruction of 1937 that reused numerous slabs from the chancel of the sixth-century church (Molajoli 1943, 50).

86. For the text of the inscription, as well as discussion of the figures, see Yasin 2009, 271–275; Yasin 2010; Terry and Maguire 2007; Maguire 2007.

WORKS CITED

Bagatti, Bellarmino. 1952.*Gli antichi edifice sacri di Betlemme*. Jerusalem: Tip. dei PP. Francescani.

Bakirtzis, Charalambos, and Helmut Koester, eds. 1998. *Philippi at the Time of Paul and after His Death*. Harrisburg, PA: Trinity.

Barry, Fabio. 2007. "Walking on Water: Cosmic Floors in Antiquity and the Middle Ages," *Art Bulletin* 89.4: 627–656.

Biddle, Martin. 1999. *The Tomb of Christ*. Stroud: Sutton.

Bouras, Laskarina, and Maria G. Parani. 2008. *Lighting in Early Byzantium*. Washington, DC: Dumbarton Oaks.

Bowes, Kim. 2005. "Personal Devotions and Private Chapels." In *A People's History of Christianity, Vol. 2: Late Ancient Christianity*, ed. V. Burrus, 188–210. Minneapolis, MN: Fortress Press.

———. 2008. *Private Worship, Public Values, and Religious Change in Late Antiquity*. Cambridge: Cambridge University Press.

Boyd, Susan A., and Marlia Mundell Mango, eds. 1992. *Ecclesiastical Silver Plate in Sixth-Century Byzantium: Papers of the Symposium Held May 16–18, 1986, at the Walters Art Gallery, Baltimore and Dumbarton Oaks, Washington, D.C.* Washington, DC: Dumbarton Oaks.

Brenk, Beat. 1995. "Microstoria sotto la Chiesa dei SS. Giovanni e Paolo: La cristianizzazione di una casa privata," *Rivista dell'Istituto nazionale d'archeologia e storia dell'arte*, ser. 3, 18: 169–206.

———. 2003. *Die Christianisierung der spätrömischen Welt: Stadt, Land, Haus, Kirche und Kloster in frühchristlicher Zeit*. Wiesbaden: Reichert.

Brightman, F. E. 1896. *Liturgies, Eastern and Western: Being the Texts, Original or Translated, of the Principal Liturgies of the Church*. Oxford: Clarendon Press.

Butler, Howard Crosby. 1929. *Early Churches in Syria, Fourth to Seventh Century*. Princeton, NJ: Department of Art and Archaeology of Princeton University.

Buzzetti, C. 1993. s.v. "Castra Equitum Singularium, Singulariorum." In *Lexicon Topographicum Urbis Romae*, ed. Eva Margareta Steinby, 1.246–248. Rome: Quasar.

Cameron, Averil, and Stuart G. Hall, eds. and trans. 1999. *Eusebius: Life of Constantine*. Oxford: Clarendon Press.

Cantino Wataghin, Gisella. 2006. "Lo stucco nei sistemi decorative della tarda antichità." In *Stucs et décors de la fin de l'antiquité au moyen âge (v^{e}–xiie siècle): Actes du colloque international tenu à Poitiers du 16 au 19 septembre 2004*, ed. Christian Sapin, 115–124. Bibliothèque de l'antiquité tardive 10. Turnhout: Brepols.

Castagnoli, Ferdinando. 1992. *Il Vaticano nell'antichità classica*. Vatican City: Biblioteca Apostolica Vaticana.

Chatzidakis, Manolis. 1978. s.v. "Ikonostas." In *Reallexikon zur byzantinischen Kunst*, ed. Klaus Wessel and Marcell Restle, 3: 326–354. Stuttgart: Anton Hiersemann.
Chevalier, Pascale, and Ivan Matejčić. 2004. "Du *cardo* au 'narthex' de la cathédrale: contribution à l'étude du développement du groupe episcopal de Poreč." In *Mélanges d'antiquité tardive: Studiola in honorem Noël Duval*, 149–164. Bibliothèque de l'antiquité tardive 5. Turnhout: Brepols.
Christe, Y. 1972. "Gegenwärtige und endzeitliche Eschatologie in der frühchristlichen Kunst: Die Apsis von Sancta Pudenziana in Rom," *Orbis scientiarum* 2: 47–60.
Christern, Jürgen. 1976. *Das frühchristliche Pilgerheiligtum von Tebessa: Architektur und Ornamentik einer spätantiken Bauhütte in Nordafrika*. Wiesbaden: Franz Steiner.
Cianetti, Marina Magnani, and Carlo Pavolini, eds. 2004. *La basilica costantiniana di Sant'Agnese: Lavori archeologici e di restauro*. Milan: Electa.
Coleman, Simon, and John Elsner. 1994. "The Pilgrim's Progress: Art, Architecture and Ritual Movement at Sinai," *World Archaeology* 26.1: 73–89.
Corbo, Virgilio C. 1981. *Il Santo Sepolcro di Gerusalemme: Aspetti archeologici dalle origini al period crociato*, 3 vols. Studium Biblicum Franciscanum, Collectio Maior 29). Jerusalem: Franciscan Printing Press.
Crowfoot, J. W. 1938. "The Christian Churches." In *Gerasa: City of the Decapolis*, ed. Carl H. Kraeling, 171–294. New Haven, CT: American Schools of Oriental Research.
Curran, John. 2000. *Pagan City and Christian Capital: Rome in the Fourth Century*. Oxford: Clarendon.
Dassmann, Ernst. 1970. "Das Apsismosaik von S. Pudenziana in Rom: Philosophische, imperiale und theologische Aspekte in einem Christusbild am Beginn des 5. Jahrhunderts," *Römische Quartalschrift für christliche Altertumskunde und Kirchengeschichte* 65: 67–81.
Davis, Raymond, trans. 1989. *The Book of Pontiffs (Liber Pontificalis): The Ancient Biographies of the First Ninety Roman Bishops to AD 715*. Liverpool: Liverpool University Press.
de Blaauw, Sible. 1994. *Cultus et Decor: Liturgia e architettura nella Roma tardoantica e medievale*, 2 vols. Vatican City: Biblioteca apostolica vaticana.
Deichmann, Friedrich Wilhelm. 1969. *Ravenna: Hauptstadt des spätantiken Abendlandes*. 3 vols. Wiesbaden: Franz Steiner.
———. 1970. "Märtyrerbasilika, Martyrion, Memoria und Altargrab," *Mitteilungen des Deutschen Archäologischen Instituts, Römische Abteilung* 77: 144–169.
Deichmann, Friedrich Wilhelm, and Arnold Tschira. 1957. "Das Mausoleum der Kaiserin Helena und die Basilika der Heiligen Marcellinus und Petrus an der Via Labicana vor Rom," *Jahrbuch des Deutschen Archäologischen Instituts* 72: 44–110.
Descoeudres, Georges. 1983. *Die Pastophorien im syro-bysantinischen Osten: Eine Untersuchung zu architecktur- und liturgiegeschichtlichen Problemen*. Wiesbaden: Otto Harrassowitz.
Deliyannis, Deborah Mauskopf. 2010. *Ravenna in Late Antiquity*. Cambridge: Cambridge University Press.
Dix, Gregory. 1945. *The Shape of the Liturgy*. Westminster: Dacre.
Donceel-Voûte, Pauline. 1988. *Les pavements des églises byzantines de Syrie et du Liban: Décor, archéologie et liturgie*. Publications d'histoire de l'art et d'archéologie de l'Université catholique de Louvain 69. Louvain-la-Neuve: Départment d'archéologie et d'histoire de l'art, Collège Érasme.

———. 1995. "L'inévitable chapelle des martyrs: identification." In *Martyrium in Multidisciplinary Perspective*, ed. M. Lamberigts and P. van Deun, 179–195. Leuven: Leuven University Press.

Downey, Glanville. 1938. "The Shrine of St. Babylas at Antioch and Daphne." In *Antioch-on-the-Orontes, Vol. 2: The Excavations of 1933–1936*, ed. Richard Sidwell, 45–48. Princeton, NJ: Princeton University Press.

Duval, Noël. 1973. *Les églises africaines a deux absides: Recherches archéologiques sur la liturgie chrétienne en Afrique du Nord, vol. 2: Inventaire des monuments–interpretation.* BEFAR 218, pt. 2. Paris: de Boccard.

———. 1999. "Les installations liturgiques dans les églises paléochrétiennes," *Hortus Artium Medievalium* 5: 7–30.

Eliav, Yaron Z. 2005. *God's Mountain: The Temple Mount in Time, Place and Memory.* Baltimore: Johns Hopkins University Press.

Engemann, J. 1976. "Auf die Parusie Christi hinweisende Darstellungen in der frühchristlichen Kunst," *Jahrbuch für Antike und Christentum* 19: 139–156.

Falla Castelfranchi, Marina. 1980. *Βαπτιστήρια: Intorno ai più noti battisteri dell'oriente.* Roma: Libreria Editrice Viella.

Frank, Georgia. 2006. "Romanos and the Night Vigil in the Sixth Century," in *A People's History of Christianity Vol. 3: Byzantine Christianity*, ed. Derek Krueger, 59–78. Minneapolis, MN: Fortress.

Gessel, Wilhelm. 1988. "Das Öl der Märtyrer: Zur Funktion und Interpretation der Ölsarkophage von Apamea in Syrien," *Oriens Christianus* 92: 183–202.

Geyer, P., and O. Cuntz, eds. 1965. "Itinerarium Burdigalense." In *Itineraria et Alia Geographica*, 1–26. CCSL 175. Turnhout: Brepols.

Goldschmidt, R. C. 1940. *Paulinus' Churches at Nola: Texts, Translations and Commentary.* Amsterdam: Noord-Hollandsche Uitgevers Maatschappij.

Grabar, André. 1946. *Martyrium: Recherches sur le culte des reliques et l'art chrétien antique*, 2 vols. Paris: Collège de France.

Guarducci, Margherita. 1960. *The Tomb of St. Peter.* New York: Hawthorn.

Gui, Isabelle, Noël Duval, and Jean-Pierre Caillet. 1992. *Basiliques chrétiennes d'Afrique du Nord (inventaire et typologie)*, 2 vols. Collection des Études Augustiniennes, Série Antiquité, 130. Paris: Institut d'Études Augustiniennes.

Hachlili, Rachel. 2009. *Ancient Mosaic Pavements: Themes, Issues, and Trends.* Leiden: Brill.

Herrmann, John, and Annewies van den Hoek. 2009. "Apocalyptic Themes in the Monumental and Minor Art of Early Christianity." In *Apocalyptic Thought in Early Christianity*, ed. Robert J. Daly, 33–80. Grand Rapids, MI: Baker Academic.

Ihm, C. 1960. *Die Programme der christlichen Apsismalerei vom vierten Jahrhundert bis zur Mitte des achten Jahrhunderts.* Wiesbaden: Steiner.

James, Liz. 2003. "Color and Meaning in Byzantium," *Journal of Early Christian Studies* 11.2: 223–233.

Janes, Dominic. 1998. *God and Gold in Late Antiquity.* Cambridge: Cambridge University Press.

Johnson, Scott Fitzgerald. 2010. "Apostolic Geography: The Origins and Continuity of a Hagiographic Habit," *Dumbarton Oaks Papers* 64: 5–25.

Kessler, H. L. 2007. "Bright Gardens of Paradise." In *Picturing the Bible: The Earliest Christian Art*, ed. J. Spier, 111–139. New Haven, CT: Yale University Press.

Kiely, Maria M. 2004. "The Interior Courtyard: The Heart of Cimitile/Nola," *Journal of Early Christian Studies* 12.4: 443–479.

Kinney, Dale. 1992. "The Apocalypse in Early Christian Monumental Decoration." In *The Apocalypse in the Middle Ages*, ed. Richard K. Emmerson and Bernard McGinn, 200–216. Ithaca, NY: Cornell University Press.

Kleinbauer, W. Eugene. 1999. *Saint Sophia at Constantinople: Singulariter in Mundo.* Dublin, NH: William L. Bauhan.

Kraeling, Carl H. 1967. *The Christian Building.* The Excavations at Dura-Europos Conducted by Yale University and the French Academy of Inscriptions and Letters, Final Report 8, pt. 2. New Haven, CT: Dura-Europos.

Krautheimer, Richard. 1937a. "S. Agnese f.l.m." In *Corpus basilicarum christianarum Romae: The Early Christian Basilicas of Rome (IV–IX cent.)*, 1: 14–39. Vatican City: Pontificio Istituto di Archeologia Cristiana.

———. 1937b. "SS. Giovanni e Paolo." In *Corpus basilicarum christianarum Romae: The Early Christian Basilicas of Rome (IV–IX cent.)*, 1: 265–300. Vatican City: Pontificio Istituto di Archeologia Cristiana.

———. 1962. "SS. Marcellino e Pietro on the Via Labicana." In *Corpus basilicarum christianarum Romae: The Early Christian Basilicas of Rome (IV–IX cent.)*, ed. Richard Krautheimer, Wolfgang Frankl, and Spencer Corbett., 2.2: 191–204. Vatican City: Pontificio Istituto di Archeologia Cristiana.

———. 1969. "The Carolingian Revival of Early Christian Architecture." In *Studies in Early Christian, Medieval and Renaissance Art*, 203–256. New York: New York University Press.

———. 1986. *Early Christian and Byzantine Architecture*, 4th rev. ed., with Slobodan Ćurčić. New Haven, CT: Yale University Press.

———. 2000. *Rome: Profile of a City, 312–1308, with a New Foreword by Marvin Trachtenberg.* Princeton, NJ: Princeton University Press.

Krautheimer, Richard, and S. Corbett. 1967. "S. Pudenziana." In *Corpus basilicarum christianarum Romae: The Early Christian Basilicas of Rome (IV–IX cent.)*, ed. Richard Krautheimer, Spencer Corbett, and Wolfgang Frankl, 3: 277–302. Vatican City: Pontificio Istituto di Archeologia Cristiana.

———. 1970. "S. Sebastiano." In *Corpus basilicarum christianarum Romae: The Early Christian Basilicas of Rome (IV–IX cent.)*, ed. Richard Krautheimer, Spencer Corbett, and Wolfgang Frankl, 4: 99–147. Vatican City: Pontificio Istituto di Archeologia Cristiana.

———. 1977. "S. Giovanni in Laterano." In *Corpus basilicarum christianarum Romae: The Early Christian Basilicas of Rome (IV–IX cent.)*, ed. Richard Krautheimer, Spencer Corbett, and Alfred K. Frazer, 5: 1–92. Vatican City: Pontificio Istituto di Archeologia Cristiana.

Krautheimer, Richard, and Wolfgang Frankl. 1959. "S. Lorenzo fuori le mura." In *Corpus basilicarum christianarum Romae: The Early Christian Basilicas of Rome (IV–IX cent.)*, ed. Richard Krautheimer, Wolfgang Frankl, and Spencer Corbett, 2.1: 1–144. Vatican City: Pontificio Istituto di Archeologia Cristiana.

Krautheimer, Richard, and A. Frazer. 1977. "S. Pietro." In *Corpus basilicarum christianarum Romae: The Early Christian Basilicas of Rome (IV–IX cent.)*, ed. Richard Krautheimer, Spencer Corbett, and Alfred K. Frazer, 5: 165–279. Vatican City: Pontificio Istituto di Archeologia Cristiana.

Lamberigts, M., and P. van Deun, eds. 1995. *Martyrium in Multidisciplinary Perspective.* Leuven: Leuven University Press.

La Rocca, Eugenio. 2000. "Le basiliche cristiane 'a deambulatorio' e la sopravvivenza del culto eroico." In *Aurea Roma: Dalla città pagana alla città Cristiana*, ed. Serena Ensoli and Eugenio La Rocca, 204–220. Rome: 'L'Erma' di Bretschneider.

Lassus, Jean. 1938. "L'Église cruciforme Antioch-Kaoussié 12-F." In *Antioch-on-the-Orontes, Vol. 2: The Excavations of 1933–1936*, ed. Richard Sidwell, 5–44. Princeton, NJ: Princeton University Press.

———. 1947. *Sanctuaires chrétiens de Syrie: Essai sur la genèse, la forme et l'usage liturgique des edifices du culte chrétien en Syrie, du IIIe siècle à l conquête musulmane.* Paris: Librairie orientaliste Paul Geuthner.

Lowden, John. 2007. "The Word Made Visible: The Exterior of the Early Christian Book as Visual Argument." In *The Early Christian Book*, ed. William E. Klingshirn and Linda Safran, 13–47. Washington, DC: Catholic University of America Press.

MacCormack, Sabine. 1990. "Loca Sancta: The Organization of Sacred Topography in Late Antiquity." In *The Blessings of Pilgrimage*, ed. Robert Ousterhout, 7–40. Urbana: University of Illinois Press.

MacMullen, Ramsay. 2009. *The Second Church: Popular Christianity* A.D. *200–400.* Atlanta: Society of Biblical Literature.

Maguire, Henry. 1987. *Earth and Ocean: The Terrestrial World in Early Byzantine Art.* University Park: Pennsylvania State University Press.

———. 2007. "Eufrasius and Friends: On Names and Their Absence in Byzantine Art." In *Art and Text in Byzantine Culture*, ed. Liz James, 137–160. Cambridge: Cambridge University Press.

Mainstone, Rowland J. 1988. *Hagia Sophia: Architecture, Structure and Liturgy of Justinian's Great Church.* New York: Thames and Hudson.

Mango, Cyril. 1962. *Materials for the Study of the Mosaics of St. Sophia at Istanbul.* Washington, DC: Dumbarton Oaks.

———. 1986. *Art of the Byzantine Empire, 312–1453, Sources and Documents.* Medieval Academy Reprints for Teaching 16. Toronto: University of Toronto Press.

———. 1990a. "Constantine's Mausoleum and the Translation of Relics," *Byzantinische Zeitschrift* 83: 54–61.

———. 1990b. "Constantine's Mausoleum: Addendum," *Byzantinische Zeitschrift* 83: 434.

Maraval, Pierre. 1995. "Les itinéraires de pèlerinage en Orient (entre le 4e et le 7e s.)." In *Akten des XII. internationalen Kongresses für christliche Archäologie. Bonn 22.–28. September 1991*, 1: 291–300. Münster: Aschendorff.

———. 2002. "The Earliest Phase of Christian Pilgrimage in the Near East before the 7th Century," *Dumbarton Oaks Papers* 56: 63–74.

———. 2004. *Lieux saints et pèlerinages d'Orient: Histoire et géographie des origines à la conquête arabe*, 2nd ed. Paris: Éd. du Cerf.

Markus, R. A. 1994. "How on Earth Could Places Become Holy? Origins of the Christian Idea of Holy Places," *Journal of Early Christian Studies* 2.3: 257–271.

Marlowe, Elizabeth. 2006. "Framing the Sun: The Arch of Constantine and the Roman Cityscape," *Art Bulletin* 88.2: 223–243.

Matejčić, Ivan. 2006. "Breve nota e novità sulle decorazioni a stucco del periodo paleocristiano in Istria." In *Stucs et décors de la fin de l'antiquité au moyen âge (v[e] –xiie siècle): Actes du colloque international tenu à Poitiers du 16 au 19 septembre 2004*, ed. Christian Sapin, 125–132. Bibliothèque de l'antiquité tardive 10. Turnhout: Brepols.

Matejčić, Ivan, and Pascale Chevalier. 1998. "Nouvelle interpretation du complex épiscopal 'pré-euphrasien' de Poreč," *Antiquité Tardive* 6: 355–365.

Mathews, Thomas F. 1971. *The Early Churches of Constantinople: Architecture and Liturgy.* University Park: Pennsylvania State University Press.

———. 1999. *The Clash of Gods: A Reinterpretation of Early Christian Art*, rev. ed. Princeton, NJ: Princeton University Press.

McClendon, Charles B. 2005. *The Origins of Medieval Architecture: Building in Europe, A.D. 600–900*. New Haven, CT: Yale University Press.

Mielsch, Harald, and Henner von Hesberg. 1996. "Die heidische Nekropole unter St. Peter in Rom: Mausoleen E-I, Z, PSI," *Atti della Pontificia Accademia romana di archeologia, Memoria*, 3rd ser. 16.2: 143–208.

Miller, Maureen Catherine. 2000. *The Bishop's Palace: Architecture and Authority in Medieval Italy*. Ithaca, NY: Cornell University Press.

Minasi, Mara. 2000. s.v. "Evangelisti." In *Temi di iconografia palocristiana*, ed. Fabrizio Bisconti, 174–177. Vatican City: Pontificio Istituto di Archeologia Cristiana.

Molajoli, Bruno. 1943. *La basilica eufrasiana di Parenzo*. Padova: Le tre Venezie.

Nelson, Robert S. 2006. "Where God Walked and Monks Pray." In *Holy Image, Hallowed Ground: Icons from Sinai*, ed. Robert S. Nelson and Kirsten M. Collins, 1–33. Los Angeles: J. Paul Getty Museum.

Ousterhout, R. 1990. "The Temple, the Sepulchre and the *Martyrion* of the Savior," *Gesta* 29.1: 44–53.

Ovadiah, Asher. 1970. *Corpus of the Byzantine Churches in the Holy Land*. Bonn: Peter Hanstein.

Pelliccioni, Giovanni. 1973. *Le nuove scoperte sulle origini del battistero Lateranense*. Vatican: Tipografia Poliglotta.

Peschlow, Urs. 2006. "Dividing Interior Space in Early Byzantine Churches: The Barriers between the Nave and Aisles." In *Thresholds of the Sacred: Architectural, Art Historical, Liturgical, and Theological Perspectives on Religious Screens, East and West*, ed. Sharon E. J. Gerstel, 53–71. Washington, DC: Dumbarton Oaks.

Picard, Jean-Charles. 1974. "Le quadriporticus de Saint-Pierre du Vatican," *Mélanges d'archéologie et d'histoire publiés par l'École Française de Rome. Antiquité* 86.2: 851–890.

———. 1989. "L'atrium dans les églises paléochrétiennes d'occident." In *Actes du XIe Congres International d'Archéologie Chrétien, 21–28 septembre 1986*, 1: 535–542. Vatican City: Pontificio Istituto di Archeologia Cristiana.

Piccirillo, Michele. 1993. *The Mosaics of Jordan*. Amman: American Center of Oriental Research.

Pullan, Wendy. 1997–1998. "Jerusalem from Alpha to Omega in the Santa Pudenziana Mosaic," *Jewish Art* 23–24: 405–417.

Rapp, Claudia. 2007. "Holy Text, Holy Men, and Holy Scribes: Aspects of Scriptural Holiness in Late Antiquity." In *The Early Christian Book*, ed. William E. Klingshirn and Linda Safran, 194–222. Washington, DC: Catholic University of America Press.

Renfrew, Colin. 1994. "The Archaeology of Religion." In *The Ancient Mind: Elements of Cognitive Archaeology*, ed. Colin Renfrew and Ezra B. W. Zubrow, 47–54. Cambridge: Cambridge University Press.

Ristow, Sebastian. 1998. *Frühchristliche Baptisterien*. Münster: Aschendorff.

Saradi, Helen G. 2006. *The Byzantine City in the Sixth Century: Literary Images and Historical Reality*. Athens: S.M.A.S.

———. 2010. "Space in Byzantine Thought." In *Architecture as Icon: Perception and Representation of Architecture in Byzantine* Art, ed. Slobodan Ćurčić and Evangelina Hadjitryponos, 73–111. New Haven, CT: Yale University Press.

Schlatter, Fredric W. 1992. "Interpreting the Mosaic of Santa Pudenziana," *Vigiliae Christianae* 46: 276–295.

———. 1995. "A Mosaic Interpretation of Jerome, *In hiezechielem*," *Vigiliae Christianae* 49: 64–81.

Sessa, Kristina. 2006. "Christianity and the *Cubiculum*: Spiritual Politics and Domestic Space in Late Antique Rome," *Journal of Early Christian Studies* 15.2: 171–204.

Smith, Jonathan Z. 1987. *To Take Place: Toward Theory in Ritual*. Chicago: University of Chicago Press.

Sodini, Jean-Pierre. 1989. "Les églises de Syrie du Nord." In *Archéologie et histoire de la Syrie, vol. 2: La Syrie de l'époque achéménide à l'avènement de l'Islam*, ed. Jean-Marie Dentzer and Winfried Orthmann, 347–372. Saarbrücken: Saarbrücker Druckerei und Verlag.

Soteriou, G. A. 1931. *Αἱ χριστιανικαὶ Θῆβαι τῆς Θεσσαλίας καὶ αἱ παλαιοχριστιανικαὶ βασιλικαὶ τῆς Ἑλλάδος* [= *Christian Thebes in Thessalia and Christian Basilicas in Greece*]. Athens: Typographeion 'Estia' Maesner and Kargadouri.

Steen, Olaf. 1999. "The Proclamation of the Word: A Study of the Apse Mosaic in S. Pudenziana, Rome," *Acta ad archaeologiam et artium historiam pertinentia*, ser. altera in 8, 11: 85–113.

Taft, Robert F. 1992. *The Byzantine Rite: A Short History*. Collegeville, MN: Liturgical Press.

———. 2006. *Through Their Own Eyes: Liturgy as the Byzantines Saw It*. Berkeley, CA: InterOrthodox Press.

Talbot, Alice-Mary. 2002. "Female Pilgrimage in Late Antiquity and the Byzantine Era," *Acta Byzantina Fennica* n.s. 1: 73–88.

Taylor, Joan E. 1993. *Christians and the Holy Places: The Myth of Jewish-Christian Origins*. Oxford: Clarendon Press.

Tchalenko, Georges. 1953–1958. *Villages antiques de la Syrie du Nord: Le massif Bélus à l'époque romaine*, 3 vols. Paris: P. Geuthner.

Terry, Ann, and Henry Maguire. 2007. *Dynamic Splendor: The Wall Mosaics in the Cathedral of Eufrasius at Poreč*, 2 vols. University Park: Pennsylvania State University Press.

Tolotti, Francesco. 1982. "Le basiliche cimiteriali con deambulatorio del suburbio romano: Questione ancora aperta," *Mitteilungen des Deutschen Archäologischen Instituts, Römische Abteilung* 89: 153–211.

Torelli, Mario. 1990. "Le basiliche circiformi di Roma: Iconografia, funzione, simbolo." In *Milano capitale dell' Impero romano 286–402 d.c.*, 203–217. Milan: Silvana.

Toynbee, J. M. C., and J. Ward-Perkins. 1956. *The Shrine of St. Peter and the Vatican Excavations*. London: Longmans, Green.

van den Hoek, Annewies, and John J. Herrmann. 2000. "Paulinus of Nola, Courtyards, and Canthari," *Harvard Theological Review* 93.3: 173–219.

Wharton, Annabel Jane. 1987. "Ritual and Reconstructed Meaning: The Neonian Baptistery in Ravenna," *Art Bulletin* 69.3: 358–375.

———. 1995. *Refiguring the Post-Classical City: Dura Europos, Jerash, Jerusalem and Ravenna*. Cambridge: Cambridge University Press.

White, L. Michael. 1997. *The Social Origins of Christian Architecture, Vol. 2: Texts and Monuments for the Christian Domus Ecclesiae in Its Environment*. Valley Forge, PA: Trinity.

Wilken, Robert L. 1992. *The Land Called Holy: Palestine in Christian History and Thought*. New Haven, CT: Yale University Press.

Wilkinson, John, trans. 1999. *Egeria's Travels to the Holy Land*, 3rd ed. Oxford: Aris and Phillips.

Xydis, Stephen G. 1947. "The Chancel Barrier, Solea, and Ambo of Hagia Sophia," *Art Bulletin* 29.1: 1–24.

Yasin, Ann Marie. 2009. *Saints and Church Spaces in the Late Antique Mediterranean: Architecture, Cult, and Community*. Cambridge: Cambridge University Press.

———. 2010. "Making Use of Paradise: Church Benefactors, Heavenly Visions, and the Late Antique Commemorative Imagination." In *Looking Beyond: Visions, Dreams and Insights in Medieval Art and History*, ed. Colum P. Hourihane, 39–57. Princeton, NJ: Index of Christian Art.

CHAPTER 30

OBJECT RELATIONS: THEORIZING THE LATE ANTIQUE VIEWER[1]

GLENN PEERS
University of Texas at Austin

A STUDY of late antique relations with objects needs to begin at a point where those relations were fluid and contingent, where a powerful surfeit of matter was revealed. In a hagiography from the sixth or seventh century, paint was divinely saturated medicine:

> [The woman] depicted them on all the walls of her house, being as she was insatiable in her desire of seeing [Saints Cosmas and Damian], for which reason she had been struck by this excessive desire. Perceiving herself to be in danger, she crawled out of bed and, upon reaching the place where these most wise Saints were depicted on the wall, she stood up leaning on her faith as upon a stick and scraped off with her fingernails some plaster. This she put into water and, after drinking the mixture, she was immediately cured of her pains by the visitation of the Saints. (Deubner 1907, 137–138 [15]; Mango 1986, 139; see now Cox Miller 2009, 131–133, 144)

How late antique people understood this episode is a crucial aspect of their attitude to matter, and how historians have understood this story says a great deal about our own attitudes. Moreover, those attitudes have colored our historical explanations of late antique images and materiality, for that episode reveals the essential traits of the connection between divinity and matter as relational, in short, a worldview without objects—all are subjects. The fact that the hagiography survives in this form demonstrates fault lines in the positions of theologians, because that episode was also adduced as a proof for proper worship of icons at the Second Council of Nicaea in 787 (Mansi 1901–1927, 12:68). Despite the clear evidence of the healing presence of God in the paint, theologians espoused an apparently self-contradictory position from which idolatry was rid but a species of animism admitted.

This chapter examines a small number of objects made in the late antique period (here c. 200–c. 750) in conjunction with texts to make a case for a deeply relational sympathy between late antique Christians and their objects. It offers an understanding of the extension of that relation into the material world around those people, and in doing so, it argues that distinctions among humanity, objects, and world were sometimes blurred or masked. The natural world, then, provided insight into God's immanence, renewed after the Incarnation of Christ, and even physical apprehension of it. Divinity infused matter, and when properly activated and perceived, that matter mediated and transformed, as the woman so devoted to Cosmas and Damian knew.

This icon of the saints Sergius and Bacchus (now in Kiev; fig. 30.1) probably dates to the sixth century, roughly contemporary to the hagiography already mentioned, and it shows the two saints as young men with martyrs' crosses (Nelson and Collins 2006, 126–127). Sergius and Bacchus were military saints, but they are dressed in court costume, with red and gold tunics partly covered by white cloaks. The panel is small (approximately 28 by 42 cm), and it was probably once a lid, likely for a reliquary.

In this period, relics and images were equivalent, and the images of the saints had that same physical reality and presence as did bodily remains. As the woman here knew, figuration was relation. Another episode from the late-sixth-century *Miracles of Symeon the Younger* vividly showed the ellipsis between saint and matter. When a priest asked the saint to heal his son, Symeon sent the anxious pair home: "So take this eulogia made of my dust, depart and when you look at the imprint of our image, it is us that you will see" (Van den Ven 1962–1970, 1:205–206 [231]). The dust is the matter collecting at the base of his column, that material that had soaked up the sanctity channeling through the saint from God. It is not just the dust that works miraculously, but its reshaping into the image of the saint, like this eulogia, or token, from the Menil Collection in Houston (fig. 30.2). Here a line between image and saint, representation and relic, loses meaning; agency extends from saint to relic to image, and the network of relations among them is a constant operation of power (Bennett 2004; *pace* Cox Miller 2009, 128–129, 145–147).

Likewise, the small medallion of Christ between the two saints on the painted panel is a relic. Without bodily relics, Christ left traces in his representation, and this image is also his relic: his likeness is his trace. In this same period, the miraculous icon of Christ, the Mandylion and its relatives, came into being (Belting 1994, 59–63; also Dagron 2007, 181–201; Frommel and Wolf 2006; Wolf, Dufour Bozzo, and Calderoni Masetti 2007). From the fourth

Figure 30.1. Icon of Saints Sergius and Bacchus, National Art Museum, Kiev, sixth century (Reproduced with permission © The Bohdan and Varvara Khanenko National Museum of Arts, Kiev, Ukraine). See also color plate section.

Figure 30.2. Clay token of Saint Symeon the Stylite, Menil Collection, Houston, sixth–seventh century (Courtesy Menil Collection, Houston).

century, Christ's letter to the king of Edessa, Abgar, had circulated, and so his voice also circulated, but the image (*acheiropoieta*, "not made by [human] hands") that he produced by miraculous means (either by blood or sweat or some other medium) came to assume a cultural priority by the sixth century. In the course of this period, then, Christ and his saints, like Cosmas and Damian,

Figure 30.3. Icon of Saint Peter, Monastery of Saint Catherine, Mount Sinai, sixth–seventh century (By permission of Saint Catherine's Monastery, Sinai, Egypt). See also color plate section.

assumed an essential relation with their images. Images' object relations with viewer and models freighted divinity in that world.

Such freighting occurred because these painted panels could be mistaken visually for the real thing, even though they do not possess verisimilitude in our terms of visual correspondences. Indeed, the Sergius and Bacchus icon is strongly abstract and two-dimensional to our eyes and therefore lacks natural likeness with its models on our terms. An extraordinarily skilled painting like the icon of St. Peter, probably from the sixth century also and now at the Monastery of St. Catherine on Mount Sinai (fig. 30.3), reveals the volumetric mass of the saint, and the decorated niche indicates a depth of space around the saint. And yet the figure is clearly two-dimensionalized, and the awkward passages in the painting, like the left ear, help ensure a viewer's recognition of its artifice. Flatness is a defining feature of these paintings, in other words, and those visual qualities may have ensured the survival, even the success, of this format, because of their divergence from the three-dimensional statues that Romans had included in worship. Eastern Christians and Jews alike appear to have gravitated toward this pronounced two-dimensionality because it allowed figural art without taint of idolatry (Kogman-Appel 2009; Bland 2004). But this more pronounced two-dimensionality does not imply that these icons were mere incidentals in that environment. Great power resided in the face, most markedly the Mandylion and its cognates, and from the earliest period, this concentration on face distinguished Christian art and theology from Judaism and Islam (Epstein 2006, 173–203). Apparently free from untoward idolatry—at least from the point of view of the large silent majority—icons were objects with strong relation and power, as the rise in private and public devotion to them in this period reveals (Kitzinger 1954; Cameron 1992; Belting 1994).

Eighth-century iconoclasm marked a terminating point in late antique culture in which highly stressful discussion over idolatry came to a head and in which each side accused the other of serious misdeeds and heretical thinking (Barber 2002). The stress arose from the apparently overweening authority that made-things—that is, *art*—were assuming (Cameron 1992). As Hans Belting points out, images had power, and theologians limited means to counter it (Belting 1994). That stress was then largely restricted to theologians, at least with regard to the sources available to us, and it arose out of an irresolvable conflict: trying to suppress an irrepressible desire in that culture to render the divine material (Küper 2008).

Perhaps new interpretations can break the impasse and reveal more relational realities than we have admitted. As Clifford Ando has recently argued, for example, Platonic metaphysics of representation profoundly affected powerful late antique and modern understandings of idols and icons (Ando 2008; also Johnston 2008; Frankfurter 2008). The value of copies in relation to a model is low, on the one hand, because a Platonic reading asserts that copies are different from and lesser than the model. On the other hand, representation cannot contain divinity because God exists on a higher, absolute plane. "Recognizing further hypostases beyond or between the divine and corporeal, people in the ancient world might well have understood that Cybele somehow was, and yet was not coextensive with, their black stone; and in that way, she might have been, but not been identical with, other black stones" (Ando 2008, 42). The relation between representation and stone is explored later, too, because stone in the late antique world was also in relation to God and his saints. Those hypostases operated in this world but need to be explained for us in ways unnecessary for those late antique Christians. Likewise, idols do not enter in those Christians' self-conceptions. Despite theological worries, those Christians knew they did not have idols, simply because their images "worked," as Richard Trexler pointed out in another context (Trexler 1991, 72). Such understandings chase binaries like God and matter, icon and idol, and representation and nature, and they smooth apparent tensions into a collaborative, relational materiality.

Capgras: A General Condition

Ernst Kitzinger (1912–2003) once asserted that this culture arrived at the fever stage of idolatry by the end of the period (Kitzinger 1954, 85). However, late antique attitudes to its objects are in clear need of a new diagnosis that recognizes problems with real things. Let me propose another pathology to help explain late antique Christians' apparent difficulties with object relations. Capgras syndrome is known after its first discussant, Joseph Capgras (1873–1950), and it is a relatively rare affliction with unclear causes, but it has strong attestation and is consistent in its features (Capgras and Reboul-Lachaux 1923; Luauté 2009). It is a problem of cognition that affects a subject's ability to recognize the true identity of persons or objects. The subject looks at a familiar face, for example, and sees an impostor, whom he or she may love and trust yet hate and fear at the same time. Vivid narratives of the dislocation this syndrome brings can be found in works of fiction, for instance, in Richard Price's *The Echo Maker* (2006), but psychological literature also presents powerful cases where a subject has lost moorings in social life that undermine one's very grip on self. One such case described the affliction of a young man who began to suspect, and then believe, that his parents were no longer who they claimed to be (Ramachandran and Blakeslee 1998, 158–173). The young man saw the physical and psychological resemblances these new strangers had to his parents, but he could not accept that those resemblances were true. He came to believe that they were impostors, whose role-playing must have been arranged by his real parents for reasons he could not understand or explain. His parents tried to reason around this mistrust by telling their son that the impostor-father had been sent to China and his real one was now in place, but he could accept this only intellectually, and his emotional distrust led him to revert within a week to seeing his father as an actor with unclear motives. This unsettling miscognition finally led him to doubt his own previously secure sense of self, and he came to admit that he was also possibly an impostor. The real one had left him in place, now untethered from his formerly inviolable selfhood that had somehow gone elsewhere. That paradigmatic I, which we all take as a truth of existence, had split and become a truly disorienting position within a formerly safe world of people and things.

Capgras syndrome focuses its miscognition most forcefully on persons or objects nearest and most familiar to the subject. The subject retains the ability to recall and identify persons and objects but makes an essential error by not accepting the truth of that ability; in other words, the subject knows the person or object, recognizes individual features, but cannot accept that what is before him or her is the true person or object.

Late antique (and also Byzantine) theologians reveal the most extreme symptoms of a general condition of Capgras syndrome. They argued that Christians were free of idolatry because images were not real, and others argued against images altogether because images were so unreal as to be pointless. They were responsible for infecting the rest of their culture with this syndrome, but they were not entirely successful in spreading it fully and deeply—natural antibodies existed. Many Christians, the silent majority again, simply accepted the world to be deeply divinized after the Incarnation and matter newly charged with God, and they were able to counteract the Capgras in the theological elite with their own practice of relational Christianity. The issue for historians is that we have taken the symptoms expressed by theologians at face value; we have misunderstood them because we share many of them and have read their hysteria without asking about our investments in it and without searching deeply enough for the condition's root causes.

In proposing that late antique culture suffered from Capgras, and theologians more than any others, this chapter uses a metaphor, and perhaps a highly simplifying one, to offer a way of expressing a blind spot that existed then and exists still. We have believed that Late Antiquity falls into our Western tradition, as we understand it, and that tradition offered humans secure definitions of the discrete self and safe relations of that self to the world outside it. This chapter tries to argue for a diagnosis of late antique cognition and relation to the world that reads the patients' description of the condition in a critical fashion. In short, some late antique Christians—notably theologians in their theoretical texts—insisted that their miscognition of things around them was correct. They naturally followed their Capgras in theory as the right way to interpret persons and objects in their world (on this natural fallacy, see Berlinerblau 2005), but this chapter contends that we should interpret the theology of images as symptoms of the Capgras disorder. While insisting on safe relations between images and models, image theory disguised the fact that the "normal condition" for the late antique world was the following: in the first place, that persons and objects, which were said to be not essentially related to a "real model," were essentially related after all; and in the second, that that understanding of the world, so fundamental as almost never to be addressed as such, made the world fully open, relational, and contingent.

Touching Sight

This argument describes important differences in late antique intuition and sense in the culture and reclaims them for that distant world (Gumbrecht 2008; Vance 2008). Naturally, living and thinking with senses in the late antique world were different in many ways from our own, but the implications of that difference need to be applied to understandings of things and persons in that world. We ourselves very often experience the world and its effects in strangely immaterial ways; our intuitive point of reference is our discretion that we exist as separate Cartesian beings (Latour 1993; also Davis 2008; Smith 2008, 489). Many effects arise from that intuitive stance, namely, a basic alienation from the world. Our bodies are strikingly disembodied as we experience the world, since our senses follow a mechanistic model of cause and effect, or at least as "common sense" tells us. And it is only when our body fails or betrays us, with pain or malfunction, that we want that other body back, and we fall out with ourselves (Leder 1990).

That alienation, its recognition and grudging support, is a necessary condition, in these views, and animism—its opposite—was widely discredited as an explanatory model, let alone as a belief. Animism has had a long history as an explanatory model for religions of so-called primitive cultures in various academic fields of the modern period. It fit easily into a developmental framework of human cultural and religious evolution, but scholars understood animism, for the most part, as a phase closer to the origins of religion than to its evolved state in the modern, developed world. Animists were children to our adults, in this view, voiced most influentially by the pioneering anthropologist Edward Burnett Tylor (1832–1917) (Stringer 1999; Barnhart 1999; Sharpe 1986, 51–58). Sigmund Freud (1856–1939) worked hard at extirpating that root evil from our psyche, and he did so through art—a kind of homeopathic remedy, in a way, to rid us of the residue of animism that we all have (Nixon 2006). But this chapter attempts to recover some of the productive aspects of discussing animism seriously, along the lines followed by contemporary anthropologists like Tim Ingold and Nurit Bird-David. It makes an argument that the condition disguised by late antique image theory was a kind of animism—a relational, dialogical, contingent view of the world and its things. Like Capgras patients, those people in Late Antiquity claimed that they did not see the real thing, but like them, they really did. Image theory sometimes lets it slip, practice almost always does (if we read it with this worldview in mind), and the way matter is understood and made reveals its sensual existence and extensions.

As Eugene Vance has recently written, we need to overturn our own senses, our own understanding of cause and effect, to come close to comprehending the senses of Late Antiquity (Vance 2008; Gumbrecht 2008). Perhaps the most difficult aspect to understand with full implications is the haptic quality of seeing. The physical contact that arises from looking is a natural outcome of the way that world understood vision to function. Vision either worked through extramission (the eye sends out atoms that return to the eye with sensory information) or intramission (things send out atoms), but in either case, the eye participated physically in the act of looking, not at all like the disembodied light-ray model that we use as the basis for understanding how we see. The outcomes of that looking are radically different from our own.

In the first place, inner seeing—that is, with the inner eye so valued by late antique theologians—was not solely in the mind but also participating in the material world. All seeing had moral content; no innocent gaze or imagining was truly possible. In the ancient world, where these ideas originated, pleasures and dangers of sight were fully recognized (for example, Webb 2008, 182–183). In the second century, Achilles Tatius wrote,

> You do not know what a thing it is when a lover is looked at. It has a greater pleasure than the Business. For the eyes receive each other's reflections and impress from little images as in mirrors. Such an emanation of beauty, flowing down through them into the soul, is a kind of copulation at a distance. This is not far from the intercourse of bodies. For it is a novel kind of embrace of bodies. (*Leucippe and Cleitophon*, 1.9.4)

That moral ambiguity inherent in seeing was deeply troubling for theologians, and Tertullian (c. 160–c. 220) and Clement of Alexandria (c. 150–211/16), for example, may have seen too vividly the moral danger posed by statues, even inadvertently seen, and statues therefore were not worth the risk to the Christian soul. Their attitudes to art, as normally presented by scholars, were probably more complex and accommodating than we credit them (Murray 1981), but Simon Goldhill's observation, "How you look is part of your relation to God," is fully in keeping with the moral imperatives behind seeing in the late antique world (Goldhill 2001; Frank 2000).

In the second place, outer, or physical, seeing was also a means of making actual contact with the seen. What Paula really saw when she approached the place of the Crucifixion in Jerusalem can never be known, but in 404, Jerome (c. 340–420) wrote that "she fell down and worshipped before the cross as if she could see the Lord hanging on it" (*Epistola ad Eustochium*, 9.2; Wilkinson 1977, 49; also Frank 2000; Wharton 2006, 42). The crux in such statements is always the "as if." We take it normally to implicate metaphorical force behind the observation, so that it was a quasi reality and took place only in her mind. But perhaps that kind of seeing was real enough in that world, after all, and so when that vision is extroverted, put into the world, we encounter real presence of the reality seen and participants both. The survival of pilgrims' tokens from the Holy Land is extraordinary in itself; a number went to Italy and were kept in church treasuries, and the small, fragile objects would otherwise have been lost. But they also reveal a miraculous outcome of seeing places where divinity lived and died: before the kneeling pilgrims at the foot of the cross is the crucified Lord (fig. 30.4). The relative "as if" is forceful indeed in this context and does not hedge or fence off (see also Smith 2008, 482–483).

Such seeing characterized the world of Late Antiquity, and at the end of that period, a particularly vivid example is provided by a monk living on the edge of the Mediterranean world and outside the Christian empire. Dadīšōʿ lived in a monastery in the Qatar region of the Persian Gulf (Carter 2007), and he wrote in Syriac several works that became influential, one of

Figure 30.4. Pilgrimage ampulla, Monza, sixth–seventh century (©Monza, Museo e Tesoro del Duomo di Monza, foto di Piero Pozzi).

which was the *Treatise on Solitude and Prayer*. In that work, Dadīšōʿ instructed his disciples in the proper ways to find relation with God:

> After this rise from both your knees, embrace and kiss our Lord on His Cross, and then immediately perform ten prostrations, and believe and trust what I am about to tell you: As your sight perceives the light of the Crucifix and your lips feel also its heat when the sun shines on it and you pray to it and kiss it, although the sun itself is in the sky and the Crucifix is on the wall, so also, and in a greater measure, although the man of our Lord Christ in the flesh sits in heaven on the throne of majesty, according to the preaching of the blessed Paul, yet His power, His glory, His working and His dominion are in the cross; and you kiss our Lord Himself and embrace Him with love, as it is written: "Who is like unto our Lord Jesus Christ, who dwelleth on high and beholdeth the depth" (paraphrasing Psalm 113:4)—in Heaven and in the Cross. (Mingana 1934, 136; Brock 1999–2000)

That sense of pressing immanence of the holy in matter was strongly communicated in Dadīšōʿ's prescriptive exercises here for his disciples, and vision was the multifaceted means by which that immanence was triggered. Touch and sight were tightly interwoven, of course, but God was in—*on*—that cross, like the energy of the sun is in the wood and yet the sun itself remains in the sky; he is coextensive like Cybele was with her stones (Ando 2008). Lips, hands, and eyes made his living presence there in that wood.

Can one call such late antique object relations animistic? Animism is not simply a way of imputing life or spirit to things that are actually inert. As Tim Ingold writes, this view of life is not *about* the world but provides a way of being *in* it, and it provides the potential for dynamic transformations, in which "beings of all kinds, more or less person-like or thing-like, continually and reciprocally bring one another into existence" (Ingold 2006). Dadīšō' advised his students to make themselves closer to God through making their images more subject and thereby transforming all those beings present into divinized things in the world (for comparison, Jung 2000, 632). In that reciprocal fashion, a purified, realized Christian came into being through his contact with wood, which is Christ.

Nature and Relation

In the third place, materials in relics and icons were not dead, inert matter, nor were places inactive, and none was more animate than the wood of the cross in the Holy Sepulcher. That wood had ceaseless capability for regeneration, and its active power never diminished. As Paulinus of Nola (c. 354–431) wrote after receiving and distributing some of that wood:

> Indeed this cross of inanimate wood has living power, and ever since its discovery it has lent its wood to the countless, almost daily, prayers of men. Yet it suffers no diminution; though daily divided, it seems to remain whole to those who lift it, and always entire to those who venerate it. Assuredly, it draws this power of incorruptibility, this undiminishing integrity, from the Blood of that Flesh that endured death yet did not see corruption. (*Epistulae*, 36–125–33; Wharton 2006, 20)

Gregory of Tours (538–594) later lauded the power of the ground on which Christ had lain after death and, from that soil, of the tokens fashioned and dispersed throughout Christendom (*In gloria martyrum*, Krusch 1885/1969, 42.21–26). Wood and soil store up power from those contacts, they gain unique powers of expansion and growth, and they retain that relational energy when sent away and made into other things.

How one sees the regenerative potential in the world around oneself implicates all manner of thinking. The wood of the cross was a special case, unique in the world, of course, but it shared that quality of potential regeneration and inexhaustibility with other materials that we think of as being finite and inert, for instance, metals. In the ancient world, natural philosophers held that metals grew beneath the earth like plants; they were lower forms than plants, but they reproduced themselves in a similar manner, through seeds, and their root systems, which we would call veins—rather suggestively, actually—were like

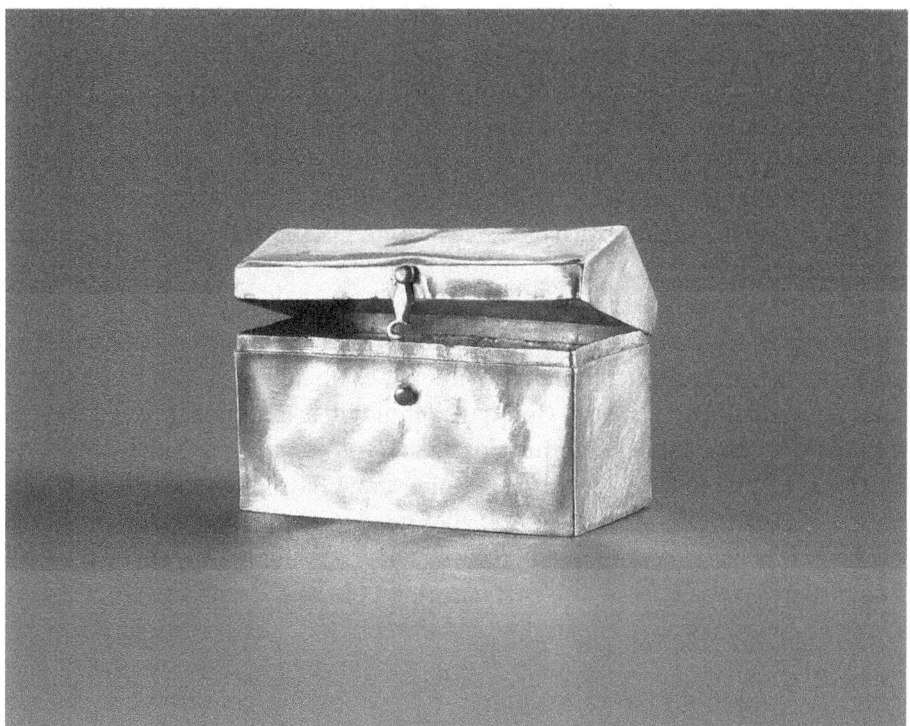

Figure 30.5. Gold reliquary box, Menil Collection, Houston, sixth–seventh century (Courtesy Menil Collection, Houston).

another of the earth's vascular systems. This idea of the earth's minerals being renewable resources was not seriously questioned or even explored really, and it remained viable into the modern period (Bachelard 2002, 159–162; Merchant 1980, 29–30; Healy 1978, 15–19; Vogel 1967, 287; also Janes 1998). Such views had an impact on how metals like gold and silver were perceived, that is, as potentially or formerly living parts of matter. This small gold box from the Menil Collection in Houston was likely a reliquary container, but its history is largely obscure (fig. 30.5). The lack of decoration, however, intensifies the impact of the material properties of sheen and light, and those properties have a history, which is part of that matter's origins and life. They also generate experiential meaning, for the contents of the box, now lost, were triggers for radiations of sacred energy. Such objects react to light (sunshine, candles, lamps) and create this sense of radiation, so that as they demonstrate their materiality, they also dematerialize, withdraw into their halations. In that sense, as they mediate between the divine and the human, they themselves enrich, enliven that very mediation in their material histories and properties.

The connection between nature and nature made into object, which I am arguing for here, of course seeks to suppress once again binarisms, in this case, a nature-culture split. Nature was not a neutral screen on which late antique Christians could project human activities, nor was it simply a symbolic, analogical domain. It was a sphere in which humans and God, and all other actors in the terrestrial economy, were engaged in establishing self-transforming processes turned toward divinity. Stories like Gregory's and Paulinus' revealed how the world could be opened and remain open to God. The cross is divine wood made into a cross, and the soil under Christ's body was made into tokens. Nature and artifact are different, of course, but in that world, essential relations remain, wherever we ourselves would put them along the spectrum of culture and nature.

If earth and the wood of the cross continued to multiply from their singular contact with the body of God, then nature was clearly no less responsive to God's presence and touch. Such attempts at establishing relations among the natural world, humanity, and God have often fallen to the field of folklore and ethnography and not been admissible to serious considerations of deep structures of the late antique world (see, however, Wharton 2006). But stories of nature and its contingency with God abounded, and the places where that contingency was present were highly prized. They proved not only that such flashpoints were accessible but also that nature was widely, deeply open to God. For example, Sozomen, writing sometime between 439 and 450, described a tree, located at Hermopolis in Egypt, that was transformed by the presence of Jesus into a healing thing (Davis 2008, 132–133). More dramatically even, the tree, named Persis, had a sufficient amount of sentience that it could recognize the Messiah—an ability remarkable indeed during the lifetime of Jesus.

> At Hermopolis, in the Thebaid, is a tree called Persis, of which the branches, the leaves, and the least portion of the bark, are said to heal diseases, when touched by the sick; for it is related by the Egyptians that when Joseph fled with Christ and Mary, the holy mother of God, from the wrath of Herod, they went to Hermopolis; when entering at the gate, this largest tree, as if not enduring the advent of Christ, inclined to the ground and worshipped Him. I relate precisely what I have heard from many sources concerning this tree. I think that this phenomenon was a sign of the presence of God in the city; or perhaps, as seems most probable, the tree, which had been worshipped by the inhabitants, after the pagan custom, was shaken, because the demon, who had been an object of worship, started up at sight of Him who was manifested for purification from such agencies. It was moved of its own accord. (5.21.8–10, Hartranft 1890/1952, 2.343)

Sozomen stated that the worshipping tree was due to the presence either of God or, more probably in his opinion, of a demon shaken by his presence in the vicinity. The inclination of the tree and its worship imply an energy and will, however, directed toward the acknowledgment of Christ, and the two (not necessarily exclusive) explanations of Sozomen are means to show God's immanence in nature then and now.

Other trees flourished in these conditions of relationality of God and nature. The well-known complex at Mamre, which was built under Constantine, was a monument built specifically for the sacred oak tree, the Terebinth, believed to have been the tree under which Abraham entertained the three angels (Bar 2008, 284–285; Fleischer 2004, 151; Taylor 1993, 86–95). The shrine was widely popular among Christians, Jews, and pagans alike. Trees have deep connections to shrines throughout the late antique world, and they can be benign like these examples and protective. They can attack, if they or the shrine is threatened, and they can be appeased with offerings like rags tied to their branches. These attitudes—often dismissed as superstition—are deeply embedded in late antique and Eastern Christian attitudes toward the world around them. Not only in elite literature do they survive (for example, see *Aeneid* 3.19–48 among others) but also in stories relegated to folklore, texts, and oral histories difficult to date but ubiquitous. (Alexiou 2002 is exemplary in taking this richness of the Hellenic tradition as seriously as it deserves.)

Late Antique Animism

The episode discussed earlier from the hagiography of Saints Cosmas and Damian in which paint became an antidote was less a symptom of irrational behavior, from this point of view, than a natural interpretation of the lively ingredients of matter. That woman's yearning for the saints found expression in her eyes and mouth, and she satisfied part of her desire by having the saints painted in her home, but her desire was greater than the touch of the eyes could satisfy. The woman wanted to have them inside more thoroughly than sight alone allowed, and so she flaked off pigments with her own hand and drank pigmented water. The word *epiphoitêsis* was translated by Cyril Mango, whose version was cited, as "visitation," but that word choice also marks our own interpretative position on the process of presence and healing. *Epiphoitêsis* is actually a stronger term than *visitation* would suggest in English. *Visitation* is relatively weak, where the word is translatable as *manifestation, intervention*, or even *haunting*, which in the context of this passage indicates a more direct, dramatic attendance by the saints. The unfolding story retells elements of romance after all, where the lover desires the absent beloved, makes him-her-them present by portrayal, and finds the portrait nearly real enough to satisfy. The sequence recalls stories like Pygmalion, for example, where the icon comes to supersede the referent (Stoichita 2008; Bettini 1999). In that legend, Pygmalion entreated the gods to make Galatea real, but in the hagiography, the woman's act—faith supporting her like a cane, as the texts stated—and matter's cooperation silently make the paint healing. And the passage in the hagiography leaves serious doubt as to the manner of the manifestation or intervention: the saints are not said to appear to her directly but must have acted through the matter, we are left to infer, that the woman shaped in their likenesses on her walls and then ingested.

That apparent ambiguity is serious, if the passage is read carefully, but seen in another light, the ambiguity is just a natural implication of potent, multiple effects of art that relates, that mediates holy and mortal bodies. Perhaps an unusual parallel might make this familiar late antique tale less ordinary, even easy. For example, Algonquin tribes made great efforts to acquire beads, and they admired them for their material beauty and radiance. But they also understood power to reside in them. Part of the power derived to the tribes from their visual qualities, but another standard means of gaining full benefit from powerful substances was respiration, and so Algonquins also ground up the beads and smoked them (von Gernet 1996, 170–176). Icons in the late antique world did not, likewise, exist on a safe, purely mental plane, but belonged to a similar world where "every artifact embodies a particular sensory mix" (Howes 2006, 166). Everything is therefore touchable and ingestible, with eye, nose, mouth, and body, and everything potentially reverses the inside and outside through that sensory mix. The icon that is on a wall can become internalized, and the outside of that viewer is transformed into a purer human form. When the woman is healed by ingesting the saints, her body is returned to a state less alienated to God than was her ill, desiring self. That powerful substance changes her from the inside out, and the sensory mix of that process goes some way to revealing the relational, tactile continuum between God and humanity. Furthermore, incense's odors intensify another aspect of sensory contact with the divine (S. A. Harvey 2006, 186–188). The interaction between humanity and divinity was mediated by smell, and the interiorization of the smell altered the communicant. Just as God smelled the offering of Noah as a "sweet savor" (Genesis 8:20–21), all the participating entities took in that smell and came into sensory contact.

Stone Objects

Doing fieldwork in Manitoba before the Second World War, the anthropologist Alfred Hallowell (1892–1981) asked an Ojibwa elder if all the stones that they could see were alive (Hallowell 1960; G. Harvey 2006; Bird-David 1999). The elder thought for a moment and answered, "No, but some are." Hallowell collected views on the liveliness of stones, and he heard that stones move, open their mouths, and appear unexpectedly from the ground. He cautioned that these stories revealed only that certain classes of objects have the potential for animation under certain circumstances, but the potential is real, as stone is a grammatically active word in Ojibwa, and flint, for instance, is a living person in their mythology.

That potential exists in the Judeo-Christian tradition, if passages like Deuteronomy 32:13 ("He made him draw honey from the rock, and oil from the flinty rock") and 1 Peter 2:4 ("Coming to Him *as to* a living stone, rejected indeed by men, but chosen by God *and* precious") are read with this same sympathy. And episodes from pilgrimage sites also revealed this empathy and life of stones. For example, the Piacenza Pilgrim, who traveled to the Holy Land in about 570, spoke of living stones, too, such as the "ugly stone" that murmured to anyone listening to it. In the same passage, he described the column at Sion that softened itself to the degree that it had been able to accept the impression of the suffering body of Christ: "his chest clove to the stone" (*Antoni Placentini Itinerarium*, 22; Wilkinson 1977, 84). Likewise, Arculf (in Adomnan's recounting), himself traveling between 679 and 688, spoke of the portrait-bearing column at the church of St. George at Diospolis that swallowed the offending hand of a "witless fellow," as well as his lance. After killing the man's horse, the column released his hand only when the man had admitted the truth of Christianity. The finger holes were still visible in Adomnan's time, and the stone floor had still not allowed the horse's blood to be released (*De locis sanctis*, 3.4.1–13; Wilkinson 1977, 114–115). At Jabal al-Tayrin in Egypt, Christ had left the impression of his hand in the living rock, and moreover, an opening in the rock oozed a black substance called collyrium or kohl:

> The church is hewn out of the mountainside, and in the rock is the mark of the palm of the hand of the Lord Christ—to whom be glory!—which was made when he touched the mountain, when it bowed in adoration before him, after he had gone down thither from Syria. He grasped the mountain, when it worshipped before him, and restored it to its place with his hand; so that the mark of his palm remains impressed upon that mountain to the present day. In the impression of the hand there is a fine perforation, large enough to admit a collyrium-needle, into which the needle is inserted, and, when it is pulled out, brings up a black collyrium which makes an indelible mark. (Evetts 1895/1969, 218)

This emanation could be used to mark pilgrims' bodies, to leave indelible markings on their bodies with real contact to the body of Christ himself. As Stephen Davis recently wrote, "Received from the palm of Jesus' own hand, as it were, this sanctified substance marked the bodies of pilgrims and functioned as a physical sign of their identification with Christ" (Davis 2008, 140).

Ojibwa traditions are perhaps not as remote from the late antique views of the potentials of stone as one might think. Evidently, stone was able to speak, to transform, to accommodate itself to contact with the holy, and to possess sufficient sentience to realize it was under attack and react. The episode related by Adomnan makes no mention at all of George working through the stone, nor did the Piacenza Pilgrim state that Christ made the stone move to provide a cavity for his chest. In both accounts, the stone was the active character, and it self-made its representation, made itself reflective of divine presence, and made itself combative if divinity was doubted. One can say that not all late antique stones were alive, in other words, but special ones were and could be so again.

Figure 30.6. View of interior, Hagia Sophia, Istanbul, constructed 532–537 (© Dumbarton Oaks, Image Collections and Fieldwork Archives, Washington, DC).

Stones in special clusters could say things in ways nothing else could, and the famous marble slabs in Hagia Sophia were splendid showing stones (figs. 30.6 and 30.7). Not made by human hands, those split marble panels clad much of the vast interior of the church, and they were also miraculous abstract images. Their figuration cannot be identified by our de-educated eyes; to late antique eyes, it was limpid (Markham 1859, 38; Trilling 1998). Evidently, late antique viewers of all aspects of a church like Hagia Sophia found content and connection in areas that our eyes skim. They recognized that nature revealed divine truths: that divinity worked through nature and was in constant relation

Figure 30.7. View of the North Gallery, northwest pier, Hagia Sophia, Istanbul, constructed 532–537 (© Dumbarton Oaks, Image Collections and Fieldwork Archives, Washington, DC).

to it. This mode of understanding geology is related to perceiving nature as in constant, contingent states of divinization: God works himself out in the world, he is immanent in all of it, and he reveals that presence in answering stone.

Hagia Sophia on the whole was replete with nature, too; its stones spoke of inherent forms of holy figures, and they recapitulated the world outside it. Paul Silentiarius, for example, wrote a fulsome description of the church, which appears to have been delivered in 563. In his ekphrasis, Paul made the church a cosmos in which stars, hills, flowing streams with flowery banks, wheat fields and wood, along with sheep and olives and vines can be seen, as well as the "limpid calm upon the blue-grey sea, whipped to foam by the sailor's oar" (*Ekphrasis tou naou tes Agias Sophias*, ll. 286–293; Fobelli 2005, 114–116; Trilling 1998, 125). Such seeing was encouraged on many levels, as Paul reveals, and in liturgy also, in the sense that veins of laid marble in the floor of Hagia Sophia were markers of rivers of paradise and of stagings for episcopal consecrations (Majeska 1978). Germanus, patriarch of Constantinople from 715 to 730, wrote a highly influential liturgical treatise in which he provided a strongly literalist approach to church space, in which the altar, for example, was identified with sites like Bethlehem, Golgotha, and the Sepulcher (Meyendorff 1984). Late antique subjects were evidently open to reading and relating to the world around themselves with full attention to labile meanings and responding objects—including stones, buildings, altars, and paint. Everything could act, exchange, and transform.

Looking at Objects with Animism

Icons, and by extension all things that were made and were inhabiting the late antique world, were constantly alert sites. In fact, this argument is a view into the abyss, as Ernst Kitzinger memorably put it (Kitzinger 1954, 147, but see Freedberg 1989, 29), the abyss that rationalists like Kitzinger feared to impute to a civilized, Western society, that depth where things were capable of life. Naturally, that fear of the abyss says more about us than it does about the culture we study. The modernist position normally draws a dividing line between the world of objects and the world of meaning, but that separation is an illusion, and a reading of late antique animism would view all objects as potentially communicative subjects. This animism is a relational position; that is, all human and material things relate in transformative and productive ways, and they do so in conversation as equal participants.

The question always arises of how we know what is alive and what is not, and the answer is usually determined through experience. As the Ojibwa elder implied, we know when it shows us. Of course, late antique culture had a whole set of complex strategies in play that established ways of understanding what was living and what was not. These strategies were always politically inscribed, and they permit the "spread of agency" throughout the world. For example, the attacking portrait-column of George was serving the purpose, on one level, of enforcing respect for institutional objects. One always needs to recognize the stakes when we read their texts with their elaborate, compelling, and *nearly* persuasive explanations of their "art." However, texts and things demonstrate how to evaluate that liveliness in the world, even if that evaluation is always tentative and provisional. For as Aristotle (384–322 B.C.E.) wrote, "Nature proceeds little by little from the inanimate to living creatures in such a way that we are unable, in the continuous sequence, to determine the boundary line" (*Historia Animalium*, 588b.4–589a.10; and Thomson 1995). That contingency of animation, its mysteriously omnipresent possibilities, demands a critical reading of the world. Western culture believes this reading is straightforward for the most part, but it relies on the objectification of the world to make it so. In an animist-friendly world, everything is potentially subjectified, and that world therefore demands a more creative, open, and fluid understanding of matter (Rooney 2000). In that sense, overcoming Capgras syndrome happens when we recognize that we are in front of the real thing and that our miscognition has led us to interpret the meanings of objects wrongly. Likewise, admitting the contingency of the world into late antique understandings of matter is the cure for that Capgras. Now we know we are experiencing the actual thing, as subject with real relation, and we can know that those people did, too. The objects we experience are really themselves and not impostors.

So where are the dividing lines for objects, and what are the triggers that make them sometimes alive? These icons, boxes, and crosses, these *things*, were surely active participants in their ritual and devotional performances, and they are not then "*objects* of devotion" at all because that wording implies that they receive only, that they are passive receptacles. Not wholly discrete, their materiality gave means to act in the world—they are in the world like us—and through their images and their words, they look and speak. The point, then, is that not only did objects alter subjectivities but also they actively participated themselves, as entities in a process of exchange among desiring bodies. This animism is a kind of perceptual strategy, after all, to make the world as full of God as they could wish it (Guthrie 1993).

Even our own safest category, the apparently disembodied word, was alive and corporeal. Christian words were also animating presences in that world. Erik Thunø has examined living writing in late antique culture from this point of view: "The special significance given by Christians to the written word changed its status from a transparent to an opaque self-referential signifier, where the subject signified (Christ) was himself also the signifier" (Thunø 2007; also Krueger 2004, 13–57; Nelson 2005). In such a world, the words in a manuscript are not empty, but full of participation by the writer, calligrapher, reader, and God, and the dividing line across objects disappears in a Christian fusion.

So every animism has its own project, its own shifting horizons, and Ojibwa stones and Algonquin beads are not the same as late antique objects—though they have *things* in common. Late antique animism is fraught with its own special histories. We can see forcefully other ways in which late antique objects worked so energetically on their viewers and why they broke down apparent differences in identity of viewer and thing. Late antique objects were part of an ecology of social, ideological, and material relations: live and let live.

Suggested Reading

Recent exhibition catalogues provide good grounding in the material and bibliography: *Byzantium 330–1453*, ed. R. Cormack and M. Vassilaki, London: Royal Academy, 2008; *Picturing the Bible: The Earliest Christian Art*, ed. J. Spier, New Haven, CT: Yale University Press, 2007; and *In the Beginning: Bibles before the Year 1000*, ed. M. Brown, Washington, DC: Freer Gallery of Art and Arthur M. Sackler Gallery, Smithsonian Institution, 2006. Recommended on specific media: *La sculpture byzantine VIIe–XIIe siècles: Actes du colloque international organisé par la 2e Éphorie des antiquités byzantines et l'École française d'Athènes (6–8 septembre 2000)*, ed. C. Pennas and C. Vanderheyde, Athens: École française d'Athènes, 2008; B. Pitarakis, *Les croix-reliquaires pectorales byzantines en bronze*, Paris: Picard, 2006; A. Cutler, *Late Antique and Byzantine Ivory Carving*, Aldershot: Ashgate, 1998; G. Noga-Banai, *The Trophies of the*

Martyrs: An Art Historical Study of Early Christian Silver Reliquaries, Oxford: Oxford University Press, 2008; and E. D. Maguire and H. Maguire, *Other Icons: Art and Power in Byzantine Secular Culture*, Princeton, NJ: Princeton University Press, 2007.

NOTE

1. Georgia Frank, Ann Marie Yasin, and Caitlin Haskill read versions of this essay and offered encouragement and excellent criticisms; I thank them warmly for that engagement. In spring 2009, the graduate students in my seminar "Byzantine Things" were stimulating discussants over these questions, as was my collaborator, Kristina Van Dyke, and I am grateful to them all for a memorable experience. This essay is part of a project directed toward an exhibition, Byzantine Things in the World, which will take place at the Menil Collection, Houston, in 2013.

WORKS CITED

Alexiou, M. 2002. *After Antiquity: Greek Language, Myth, and Metaphor*. Ithaca, NY: Cornell University Press.

Ando, C. 2008. *The Matter of the Gods: Religion and the Roman Empire*. Berkeley: University of California Press.

Bachelard, G. 2002. *The Formation of the Scientific Mind: A Contribution to a Psychoanalysis of Objective Knowledge*. Trans. M. McAllester Jones. Manchester: Clinamen.

Bar, D. 2008. "Continuity and Change in the Cultic Topography of Late Antique Palestine." In *From Temple to Church: Destruction and Renewal of Local Cultic Topography in Late Antiquity*, ed. J. Hahn, S. Emmel, and U. Gotter, 275–298. Leiden: Brill.

Barber, C. 2002. *Figure and Likeness: On the Limits of Representation in Byzantine Iconoclasm*. Princeton, NJ: Princeton University Press.

Barnhart, J. E. 1999. "Anthropomorphism." In *Modern Spiritualities: An Inquiry*, ed. L. Brown, B. C. Farr, and R. J. Hoffman, 171–178. Amherst, NY: Prometheus.

Belting, H. 1994. *Likeness and Presence: A History of the Image before the Era of Art*. Trans. E. Jephcott. Chicago: University of Chicago Press.

Bennett, J. 2004. "The Force of Things: Steps toward an Ecology of Matter," *Political Theory* 32.3: 347–372.

Berlinerblau, J. 2005. "Durkheim's Theory of Miscognition: In Praise of Arrogant Social Theory." In *Teaching Durkheim*, ed. T. F. Godlove Jr., 213–333. Oxford: Oxford University Press.

Bettini, M. 1999. *The Portrait of the Lover*. Trans. L. Gibbs. Berkeley: University of California Press.

Bird-David, N. 1999. "'Animism' Revisited: Personhood, Environment, and Relational Epistemology," *Current Anthropology, Supplement* 40:S67–79.

Bland, K. 2004. "Icon vs. Sculpture in Christian Practice and Jewish Law," *Jewish Studies Quarterly* 11:201–214.
Brock, S. 1999–2000. "Syriac Writers from Beth Qatraye," *Aram* 11–12: 85–96.
Cameron, Averil. 1992. "The Language of Images: The Rise of Icons and Christian Representation." In *The Church and the Arts*, ed. D. Wood, 1–42. Studies in Church History 25. Oxford: Oxford University Press.
Capgras, J., and J. Reboul-Lachaux. 1923. "L'illusion des 'Sosies' dans un délire systématisé chronique," *Bulletin de la Société Clinique de Médecine Mentale* 11: 6–16.
Carter, R. A. 2007. "Christianity in the Gulf during the First Centuries of Islam," *Arabian Archaeology and Epigraphy* 19: 71–108.
Cox Miller, P. 2009. *The Corporeal Imagination: Signifying the Holy in Late Ancient Christianity*. Philadelphia: University of Pennsylvania Press.
Dagron, G. 2007. *Décrire et peindre: Essai sur le portrait iconique*. Paris: Gallimard.
Davis, S. J. 2008. *Coptic Christology in Practice: Incarnation and Divine Participation in Late Antique and Medieval Egypt*. Oxford: Oxford University Press.
Deubner, L., ed. 1907. *Kosmas und Damian: Texte und Einleitung*. Leipzig: Teubner.
Epstein, S. A. 2006. *Purity Lost: Transgressing Boundaries in the Eastern Mediterranean, 1000–1400*. Baltimore: Johns Hopkins University Press.
Evetts, B. T. A., trans. 1895/1969. *History of the Churches and Monasteries: The Churches and Monasteries of Egypt and Some Neighbouring Countries Attributed to Abu Sâlih, the Armenian*. Oxford: Clarendon Press; repr. London: Frome, Butler & Tanner.
Fleischer, J. 2004. "Living Rocks and *locus amoenus*: Architectural Representations of Paradise in Early Christianity." In *The Appearances of Medieval Rituals: The Play of Construction and Modification*, ed. N. H. Petersen, M. Birkedal Bruun, J. Llewellyn, and E. Ostrem, 149–171. Turnhout: Petersen.
Fobelli, M. L. 2005. *Un tempio per Giustiniano: Santa Sofia di Constantinopoli e la Descrizione di Paolo Silenzario*. Rome: Viella.
Frank, G. 2000. "The Pilgrim's Gaze in the Age before Iconoclasm." In *Visuality before and beyond the Renaissance: Seeing as Others Saw*, ed. R. S. Nelson, 98–115. Cambridge: Cambridge University Press.
Frankfurter, D. 2008. "The Vitality of Egyptian Images in Late Antique Egypt: Christian Memory and Response." In *The Sculptural Environment of the Roman Near East*, ed. Y. Z. Eliav, E. A. Friedland, and S. Herbert, 659–678. Leuven: Peeters.
Freedberg, D. 1989. *The Power of Images: Studies in the History and Theory of Response*. Chicago: University of Chicago Press.
Frommel, C. L., and G. Wolf, eds. 2006. *L'immagine di Cristo dall'acheropite alla mano d'artista: Dal tardo medievo all'età barocca. Studi e testi* 432. Vatican City: Biblioteca Apostolica Vaticana.
Goldhill, S. 2001. "The Erotic Eye: Visual Stimulation and Cultural Conflict." In *Being Greek under Rome: Cultural Identity, the Second Sophistic and the Development of Empire*, ed. S. Goldhill, 154–194. Cambridge: Cambridge University Press.
Gumbrecht, H. U. 2008. "Erudite Fascination and Cultural Energies: How Much Can We Know about the Medieval Senses?" In *Rethinking the Medieval Senses: Heritage, Fascination, Frames*, ed. S. G. Nichols, A. Kablitz, and A. Calhoun, 1–10. Baltimore: Johns Hopkins University Press.
Guthrie, S. 1993. *Faces in the Clouds: A New Theory of Religion*. New York: Oxford University Press.
Hallowell, A. I. 1960. "Ojibwa Ontology, Behavior and World View." In *Culture in History: Essays in Honor of Paul Radin*, ed. S. Diamond, 19–52. New York: Columbia University Press.

Hartranft, C., trans. 1890/1952. *Nicene and Post-Nicene Fathers, Vol. 2: Socrates, Sozomenus: Church Histories.* 2nd ser. New York: Christian Literature Company; repr. Grand Rapids, MI: Eerdmans.
Harvey, G. 2006. *Animism: Respecting the Living World.* New York: Hurst.
Harvey, S. A. 2006. *Scenting Salvation: Ancient Christianity and the Olfactory Imagination.* Berkeley: University of California Press.
Healy, J. F. 1978. *Mining and Metallurgy in the Greek and Roman World.* London: Thames & Hudson.
Howes, D. 2006. "Scent, Sound and Synaesthesia: Intersensoriality and Material Culture Theory." In *Handbook of Material Culture,* ed. C. Tilley et al., 161–172. London: Sage.
Ingold, T. 1993. "The Temporality of the Landscape," *World Archaeology* 25: 152–174.
———. 2006. "Rethinking the Animate, Re-Animating Thought," *Ethnos* 71: 9–20.
Janes, D. 1998. *God and Gold in Late Antiquity.* Cambridge: Cambridge University Press.
Johnston, S. I. 2008. "Animating Statues: A Case Study in Ritual," *Arethusa* 41: 445–477.
Jung, J. E. 2000. "Beyond the Barrier: The Unifying Role of the Choir Screen in Gothic Churches," *Art Bulletin* 82: 622–657.
Kitzinger, E. 1954. "The Cult of Images in the Age before Iconoclasm," *Dumbarton Oaks Papers* 8: 83–150 [= Kitzinger, E. 1976. *The Art of Byzantium and the Medieval West: Selected Studies,* ed. W. E. Kleinbauer, 90–156. Bloomington: Indiana University Press].
Kogman-Appel, K. 2009. "Christianity, Idolatry, and the Question of Jewish Figural Painting in the Middle Ages," *Speculum* 84: 73–107.
Krueger, D. 2004. *Writing and Holiness: The Practice of Authorship in the Early Christian East.* Philadelphia: University of Pennsylvania Press.
Krusch, B., ed. 1885/1969. *Gregori Episcopi Turonensis Miracula et Opera Minora.* MGHSRM 1.2. Hannover: Hahnsche Buchhandlung.
Küper, J. 2008. "Perception, Cognition and Volition in the Arcipreste de Talavera." In *Rethinking the Medieval Senses: Heritage, Fascination, Frames,* ed. S. G. Nichols, A. Kablitz, and A. Calhoun, 119–153. Baltimore: Johns Hopkins University Press.
Latour, B. 1993. *We Have Never Been Modern.* Trans. C. Porter. Cambridge, MA: Harvard University Press.
Leder, S. 1990. *The Absent Body.* Chicago: University of Chicago Press.
Luauté, J.-P. 2009. "Neuropsychiatrie cognitive des délires d'identification des personnes: Une revue historico-critique," *L'Évolution Psychiatrique* 74.1: 93–121.
Majeska, G. 1978. "Notes on the Archeology of St. Sophia at Constantinople: The Green Marble Bands on the Floor," *Dumbarton Oaks Papers* 31: 229–308.
Mango, C. 1986. *The Art of the Byzantine Empire 312–1453.* Toronto: University of Toronto Press.
Mansi, G. D. 1901–1927. *Sacrorum conciliorum nova et amplissima collection.* 53 vols. in 58 pts. Paris: Welter.
Markham, C. R., trans. 1859. *Narrative of the Embassy of Ruy Gonzalez de Clavijo to the Court of Timour at Samarcand.* London: Hakluyt Society.
Merchant, C. 1980. *The Death of Nature: Women, Ecology and the Scientific Revolution.* San Francisco: Harper & Row.
Meyendorff, J., ed. 1984. *St. Germanus of Constantinople: On the Divine Liturgy.* Crestwood, NY: St. Vladimir's Seminary Press.
Mingana, A. 1934. "Dadisho: Treatise on Solitude and Prayer." In *Woodbrooke Studies,* 7: 70–143. Cambridge: Heffer.

Murray, C., Sr. 1981. *Rebirth and Afterlife: A Study of the Transmutation of Some Pagan Imagery in Early Christian Funerary Art*. Oxford: B.A.R.
Nelson, R. S. 2005. "Byzantine Art vs. Western Medieval Art." In *Byzance et le monde extérieur: Contacts, relations, échanges*, ed. M. Balard, É. Malamut, and J.-M. Spieser, 255–270. Paris: Publications de la Sorbonne.
Nelson, R. S., and K. M. Collins, eds. 2006. *Holy Space, Hallowed Ground: Icons of Sinai*. Los Angeles: J. Paul Getty Museum.
Nixon, M. 2006. "Dream Dust," *October* 116: 63–86.
Ramachandran, V. S., and S. Blakeslee. 1998. *Phantoms in the Brain: Probing the Mysteries of the Human Mind*. New York: William Morrow.
Rooney, C. 2000. *African Literature, Animism and Politics*. London: Routledge.
Sharpe, E. J. 1986. *Comparative Religion: A History*, 2nd ed. La Salle, IL: Open Court.
Smith, G. A. 2008. "How Thin Is a Demon?" *Journal of Early Christian Studies* 16: 479–512.
Stoichita, V. I. 2008. *The Pygmalion Effect: From Ovid to Hitchcock*. Trans. A. Anderson. Chicago: University of Chicago Press.
Stringer, M. D. 1999. "Rethinking Animism: Thoughts from the Infancy of Our Discipline," *Journal of the Royal Anthropological Institute* 5.4: 541–555.
Taylor, J. E. 1993. *Christians and the Holy Places: The Myth of Jewish-Christian Origins*. Oxford: Oxford University Press.
Thomson, M. 1995. "The Representation of Life." In *Virtues and Reasons: Philippa Foot and Moral Theory: Essays in Honor of Philippa Foot*, ed. R. Hursthouse, G. Lawrence, and W. Quinn, 252–268. Oxford: Oxford University Press.
Thunø, E. 2007. "Looking at Letters: 'Living Writing' in S. Sabina in Rome," *Marburger Jahrbuch für Kunstwissenschaft* 34: 19–41.
Trexler, R. C. 1991. *Public Life in Renaissance Florence*. Ithaca, NY: Cornell University Press.
Trilling, J. 1998. "The Image Not Made by Hands and the Byzantine Way of Seeing." In *The Holy Face and the Paradox of Representation*, ed. H. L. Kessler and G. Wolf, 109–127. Bologna: Nuova Alfa Editoriale.
Vance, E. 2008. "Seeing God: Augustine, Sensation and the Mind's Eye." In *Rethinking the Medieval Senses: Heritage, Fascination, Frames*, ed. S. G. Nichols, A. Kablitz, and A. Calhoun, 13–29. Baltimore: Johns Hopkins University Press.
Van den Ven, P. 1962–1970. *La vie ancienne de S. Syméon le Jeune*, 2 vols. Brussels: Société des Bollandistes.
Vogel, K. 1967. "Byzantine Science." In *The Cambridge Medieval History, Vol. 4: The Byzantine Empire, Part 2: Government, Church and Civilisation*, ed. J. M. Hussey, 264–305. Cambridge: Cambridge University Press.
von Gernet, A. 1996. "Reactions to the Familiar and the Novel in Seventeenth-Century French-Amerindian Contact." In *Cultural Transfer: America and Europe*, ed. L. Turgeon, D. Delâge, and R. Ouellet, 170–176. Québec: Presses de l'Université Laval.
Webb, R. 2008. *Demons and Dancers: Performance in Late Antiquity*. Cambridge, MA: Harvard University Press.
Wharton, A. J. 2006. *Selling Jerusalem: Relics, Replicas, Theme Parks*. Chicago: University of Chicago Press.
Wilkinson, J. 1977. *Jerusalem Pilgrims before the Crusades*. Warminster: Aris and Phillips.
Wolf, G., C. Dufour Bozzo, and A. R. Calderoni Masetti, eds. 2007. *Intorno al Sacro Volto: Genova, Bisanzio e il Mediterraneo (XI–XIV secolo)*. Venice: Marsilio.

CHAPTER 31

FROM NISIBIS TO XI'AN: THE CHURCH OF THE EAST IN LATE ANTIQUE EURASIA*

JOEL WALKER
University of Washington

IN 410 C.E., forty bishops of the Church of the East gathered in Seleucia-Ctesiphon, twenty-nine kilometers south of modern Baghdad. They had traveled from as far away as the Roman frontier and the shores of the Persian Gulf to reach the Sasanian capital, a sprawling urban complex nearly twice the area of ancient Rome. The cathedral where they met lay somewhere within the imposing walled district of Vēh-Ardashīr, on the western bank of the Tigris across from the Sasanian royal palace at Ctesiphon.[1] Upon arrival, the bishops paid their respects to Mār Isaac, the "grand metropolitan" bishop of Seleucia-Ctesiphon, who had convened the synod under the aegis of the Persian king himself, Yazdgard I (r. 399–421). There must have been considerable excitement, and perhaps also trepidation, at the meeting, since royal support for the church was unprecedented. Old men and women could still vividly recall the terrible abuses inflicted on the clergy and other Christian ascetics during the reign of Yazdgard's grandfather, Shapur II (r. 309–379). But the climate at the Sasanian court had shifted dramatically since Yazdgard's accession, reducing the influence of the *magi*, hereditary priests of Zoroastrianism.[2] According to the synod's official transcript, preserved in the eighth-century compilation known as the *Synodicon Orientale*, the Persian king ordered that:

> In his entire kingdom, the temples (i.e., churches) that had been overturned by his ancestors be grandly rebuilt during his days and that the altars that had been demolished be carefully restored to service, and that those who had been tried and tested for the sake of God by imprisonments and beatings be freed, and (that) the priests and leaders (of the church) together with the entire holy covenant (*qyāmā*) circulate freely in public without fear.[3]

Yazdgard's repeal of the persecution against the Christians of his empire marks a decisive innovation in royal policy, which paved the way for the gradual integration of Christians into the political and social fabric of the Sasanian empire.[4] Although converts from Zoroastrianism and other prominent Christians remained vulnerable to harassment, and even execution, during periods of crisis—for instance, early in the reign of Bahram V Gor (r. 421–439) and under Yazdgard II (r. 439–447)[5]—Yazdgard's endorsement of the synod established a precedent that would continue to guide Christian relations with their non-Christian rulers even after the fall of the Sasanian empire. In exchange for their taxes, political loyalty, and technical expertise, Christians gained a recognized position in the imperial order of the Sasanian world.

Names and Historiography of the Church of the East

Modern writers have adopted a variety of names to describe the Christian community represented by the bishops at Seleucia in 410. Until the 1980s, most scholars outside the Middle East identified them as "Nestorians," a rather ironic misnomer, since Nestorius, the Greek theologian and archbishop of Constantinople (428–433), seems never to have set foot east of the Euphrates.[6] The modern Christian communities descended from the Church of the East often object to the label "Nestorian" because of its heretical associations, which authorized Catholic missionaries in the sixteenth and seventeenth centuries to destroy precious Syriac manuscripts in India and the Middle East. The modern branches of the Church of the East thus prefer the names "Assyrian" (popularized in the nineteenth century) or "Chaldean" (the name for the Uniate branch of the church, established in the seventeenth century).[7] For historians, the choice of names remains difficult, since none of the options is fully satisfactory. In this chapter, I use the names "East-Syrian" and "Nestorian" interchangeably, since, as we shall see, some leaders of the Church of the East eventually embraced the name "Nestorian" as an acceptable label for their community.

The history of East-Syrian Christianity has always been confined to the margins of the dominant narratives of church history. Philip Jenkins is not entirely wrong to call the story of the East-Syrian Church the central thread of the "lost history" of Christianity.[8] Textbooks and handbooks on the history of Christianity in Late Antiquity still routinely allot scant attention to Christianity outside the Greco-Roman world.[9] The roots of this historical amnesia run deep. As Sebastian Brock has observed, Eusebius' *Church History* is essentially a history of Christianity inside the Roman empire.[10] The father of church history never acknowledges the existence of a Christian community in the Persian empire, a region he discusses only as the source for the "deadly poison" of the prophet Mani (c. 216–276).[11] Church historians of the later Roman empire and Byzantium perpetuated this bias. While they honored the memory of the "Persian martyrs" executed in Mesopotamia, their presentation of Christianity east of the Euphrates generally remained brief, ill informed, and polemical. Even the most learned scholars of medieval Europe had no idea that there were myriads of fellow Christians living in Mesopotamia, Iran, India, Central Asia, and China.[12] European awareness of the Christians of Asia received a major boost in the twelfth century, as rumors emerged of the existence of "Prester John," a powerful Christian king ruling somewhere in Asia. Though much distorted in transmission, these reports echoed the genuine presence of Nestorians in Mongolia and Inner Asia.[13] As the Mongols extended their power into the Middle East, sacking Baghdad in 1258, they regularly employed Nestorian Christians as ambassadors in their diplomatic negotiations with Europe.[14] In the thirteenth century, Nestorian prelates appeared at the courts of Constantinople and Rome, where they had rarely been seen since the age of Justinian. Latin envoys to the Mongol courts at Tabriz, Sarai on the Volga, and Qaraqorum reported the prominence of Nestorian queens (*khatuns*) and courtiers in the Mongol aristocracy.[15] This flurry of thirteenth-century contacts could not, however, overcome the limitations of medieval Europe's horizons. After the conversion of the Ilkhanids and the Golden Horde to Islam during the fourteenth century, contacts between Europe and the Church of the East withered. With the cessation of embassies, so, too, faded Europeans' memory of Asian Christianity.

Two separate but complementary currents helped launch the modern historiography of the Church of the East. In 1625, Jesuit missionaries in China announced the discovery of a magnificent Christian stele, found near Chang'an (modern Xi'an), capital of the Chinese empire under the Tang dynasty (618–907). The Xi'an stele, erected in 781, quickly became the linchpin of a protracted and heated debate over the origins of Christianity in China, pitting the Jesuits against their numerous critics, such as Voltaire, who denounced the stele as a fake.[16] Efforts to translate and contextualize the stele's bilingual Chinese-Syriac inscription (on which, see further below) contributed to the gradual emergence of systematic studies of the Nestorian heritage in China and Central Asia, culminating in the posthumous publications of the eminent Sinologist Paul Pelliot (1878–1945).[17] As Pelliot reconstructed one portion of Nestorian church history, scholars of the Christian Middle East began to assemble other pieces of the puzzle. Between 1870 and the outbreak of the First World War, a cluster of learned bishops published major histories of the "Chaldean" church in Arabic.[18] During the same period, European Orientalists published first editions of many of the fundamental textual sources for East-Syrian church history, including the *Synodicon Orientale*, the *Acts of the Persian Martyrs*, and the letters of the patriarch Timothy I (r. 780–823). This flood of new Syriac and Arabic texts laid the foundation for Jerome Labourt's pioneering synthesis, *Le christianisme dans l'empire perse sous la dynastie sassanide (224–632)*, which was published as a thesis at the University of Paris in 1904.[19] With its rigorous historical methodology, Labourt's monograph overturned a number of pious myths about the Church of the East and long served as the standard scholarly account (although less reliable surveys surpassed its popularity in the English-speaking world).[20] No work of comparable scope and rigor appeared until 1970, when Jean-Maurice Fiey, a Dominican priest resident in Mosul, published his *Jalons pour une histoire de l'église en Iraq*. In a publication career that spanned more than five decades (1943–1995), Fiey applied his unparalleled command of the primary sources to contribute to nearly every subfield of East-Syrian studies. His most enduring achievement came in the field of ecclesiastical geography, where his publications reconstructed, province by province, the history of nearly two hundred East-Syrian dioceses.[21]

Study of the Church of the East today has grown and evolved in ways that Fiey could hardly imagine. Since his death in 1995, the field has burgeoned with research conducted under a variety of overlapping disciplinary rubrics, including Syriac studies, Sasanian history, Middle Eastern archaeology, Islamic and Central Asian studies, the history of medicine and philosophy, and, increasingly, Late Antiquity.[22] This chapter can convey the insights of only some of these many advances. Recent Middle Eastern history has made such research all the more urgent, as two decades of political upheaval beginning with the Iran-Iraq War (1980–1988) have threatened to extinguish the Church of the East from some of its most ancient dioceses. This turmoil has accelerated the demographic shift toward the diaspora that was already well under way by the early twentieth century. It would be disingenuous to ignore the unsettling contrast between the rising tide of scholarship on the East-Syrian tradition on which this chapter is based and the steady diminution of the church's modern descendants in the contemporary Middle East.

Christian Origins in Mesopotamia and Iran

The origins of the Church of the East lie shrouded in a tangle of fragmentary reports and legends first attested in the late Sasanian and Islamic periods. According to these traditions, Christianity was first brought to the Parthian empire by the apostle Thomas (en route to India), Addai (after his mission to Edessa), or one of Addai's disciples, Mārī or Aggai.[23] While the historicity of these apostolic claims is dubious, Christianity does appear to have taken root in the Parthian empire by the end of the second century. Bardaisan, a Christian philosopher at the Edessan court, notes the presence of Christians in several regions of the Parthian world in the *Book of the Laws of the Countries*, completed in about 196 by one of his disciples.[24] Several later Syriac accounts emphasize the role of merchants in this process of evangelization. The *Acts of Mār Mārī*, for instance, claims that traders from Fars and Khuzistan in southwestern Iran traveled to the "West," where they were "led to the religion of God by the blessed apostle Addai" before returning to their home districts.[25] The "West" refers here not to Rome or Italy, but to Roman Syria and, in particular, to the holy city of Edessa. Greco-Roman writers were equally aware of Edessa's pivotal role in Christian expansion into the Persian world. Writing in Constantinople in the mid-fifth century, the church historian Sozomen attributed the origins of Christianity in Persia to the dual influence of the churches of Osrhoene (the region of Edessa) and Armenia.[26]

Sasanian military expansion inadvertently facilitated the church's growth in both Mesopotamia and western Iran. Reviving a practice of earlier Near Eastern empires, King Ardashir (r. 224–239) and his son Shapur I (r. 239–270) forcibly resettled thousands of captives from Roman Syria in the most fertile agricultural zones of their empire.[27] Among these deportees were an unknown, but clearly significant, number of Christians.[28] The trauma of the deportations was long remembered; according to the *Chronicle of Siirt*, the captive patriarch of Antioch, Demetrios, "became ill and died of grief."[29] But stronger and more adaptable deportees survived, and many learned to accept their new land as home. They and their descendants, such as the royal craftsman Mār Poṣi, often intermarried with the local population. In the 320s or 330s, Mār Poṣi, his Persian wife, and their children were resettled in Karkā d-Lēdān, a new royal capital near Susa, where Poṣi was later arrested and died a martyr under Shapur II.[30] In cases like this, the Sasanian policy of deportations had the unintended consequence of implanting small but resilient Christian communities in the heartlands of the empire.

Under early Sasanian rule, Mesopotamia and Iran had a highly variegated religious landscape, with Zoroastrians, Jews, Christians, and a variety of polytheist and Judeo-Christian sects.[31] Zoroastrians generally enjoyed the highest status with the Sasanian court, an advantage that the *magi* exploited to harass and dominate other religious communities. Under the reign of Bahram II (r. 276–293), the chief priest Kirdīr erected a set of impressive cliff reliefs in Fars, inscribed in Middle Persian, to celebrate his repression of sects promoting the "false doctrines of Ahriman and the demons (*dēv*)." Ironically, Kirdīr's enumeration of opposing sects is itself valuable evidence for the religious pluralism of the early Sasanian empire: he boasts of destroying the cult sites of "the Jews (*yahūd*), Buddhists (*šaman*), Hindus (*bramān*), Nazarenes (*nāčarāy*), Christians (*kristiyān*), Baptists (*makdag*), and Manichaeans (*zandīk*)."[32] The relative size and distribution of these religious communities within the third-century empire cannot be reconstructed with much precision. Despite much learned debate it remains frustratingly unclear whether the "Nazarenes" were separated from the "Christians" by language, ethnicity, or doctrine. Brock's suggestion that the "Nazarenes" were indigenous Syriac-speaking Christians while the "Christians" were descendants of the deportees from Roman Syria offers one plausible solution.[33]

The career of the prophet Mani (c. 216–276) further attests to the multiplicity of Christian sects active in third-century Mesopotamia. The *Cologne Mani Codex*, a miniature Manichaean book produced in late Roman Egypt, has confirmed Islamic reports that Mani was raised among the "Baptists" of southern Iraq, a Judeo-Christian sect founded by a teacher named "Alchasios."[34] After leaving the Baptists, Mani began to circulate letters and treatises in which he presented himself as "the apostle of Jesus Christ." The foundational texts of his syncretistic doctrine drew extensively on a wide range of early Christian literature.[35] Both the cosmology of Bardaisan and the Marcionites' rejection of the Old Testament made an acute impression on the young Babylonian prophet. In debates with other religious groups, Mani and his disciples often presented themselves, as did the Marcionites, as the true Christians.[36] With its strong emphasis on both literacy and mission, the religion of Mani presented, in turn, a threatening but stimulating adversary for the dispersed churches of the Sasanian empire, which were only loosely woven together prior to the end of the third century. Later East-Syrian sources preserve multiple stories of Christian clashes with Mani and his disciples. At Karkā d-Bēt Selōk (Kirkuk), local Christian memory accurately preserved the names of two Manichaean missionaries, "Addai and Abzakiya, the offspring of evil," who preached in the city in the twentieth year of Shapur I's reign (260/261).[37] Early Manichaean teaching and ritual retained a heavily Christian flavor. According to a vignette in the *Chronicle of Siirt*, the Persian king Bahram II initially persecuted both groups since he had difficulty distinguishing between them.[38] Modern liturgical scholars have also emphasized this similarity, noting, for instance, how closely the Manichaean bema festival, at which Mani's followers commemorated the "passion" of their prophet, paralleled the Easter liturgy of the East-Syrian church.[39] The sibling religions would continue to compete and influence each other throughout the Sasanian period and beyond.

Christian-Jewish relations were similarly close and yet fraught with tensions. In cities such as Nisibis, Arbela (Erbil), and Karkā d-Bēt Slōk, Christians often lived in the midst of much older and larger Jewish communities.[40] Jews and Christians shared a spoken language (proximate dialects of Aramaic), a common sacred text (closely related versions of the Aramaic or Syriac Bible), and key ritual traditions. Some Christians may have continued to attend synagogue services and festivals even after the church developed its own calendar.[41] Areas of divergence and potential conflict included the definition and interpretation of Scripture, the Sabbath, circumcision, and sexual renunciation. Gradually, over the course of the third century, the church grew by attracting both Jewish and non-Jewish converts, although the stages of this expansion remain obscure due to the dearth of reliable literary sources.[42] This documentary lacuna extends into the early fourth century, when under the pressure of renewed and more severe persecution, Sasanian Christians found new literary forms to articulate their identity and history.

From the "Great Slaughter" to the Synod of 410

In the early 340s, Shapur II unleashed a ferocious persecution against the Christians of his empire.[43] Several factors account for this turn in Sasanian policy. The Christianization of the Roman imperial court under Constantine (r. in the East, 324–337) and his successor Constantius II (r. 337–361) created a setting in which the Christians of Persia could be perceived as unreliable subjects—a potential fifth column—particularly in areas of Mesopotamia that were contested between the empires of Rome and Iran.[44] Constantine may have unwittingly endangered the Christians of the Sasanian empire when he informed his "brother" Shapur how pleased he was "to hear that the most important parts of Persia are also richly adorned (with Christians)!"[45] The safety of Sasanian Christians became more precarious after Shapur's abortive siege of the Roman city of Nisibis in 337/338. As the war between Shapur and Constantius intensified, the Persian king ordered the arrest of Simeon bar Ṣabbāʿē, metropolitan bishop of Seleucia-Ctesiphon, and sought to impose "a double head tax and double tribute on all the Nazarene people in the land of our Divinity."[46] According to fifth-century accounts of the persecution, Jews incited Shapur and the *magi* with accusations that the Christians "although dwelling in our land are co-religionists (*bnay tarʿīteh*) with our enemy Caesar."[47] While the Jewish community probably had allies at Shapur's court (the king's mother, 'Ifra Hormizd, was rumored to admire the powers of the rabbis), the historicity of this particular accusation remains uncertain.[48] Talmudic denunciations of apostasy may obscure a relatively fluid situation, in which many Christians remained enmeshed in Jewish social and cultural contexts.[49]

The homilies of Aphrahat, a Christian ascetic living in northern Iraq during the mid-fourth century, illustrate this ambiguity. In the first ten of his twenty-three surviving Syriac homilies or *Demonstrations*, circulated in 337, Aphrahat explicates proper Christian conduct, rooted in faith, humility, and prayer. His exegetical methods and style reveal close parallels with contemporary Jewish traditions and hardly a trace of the virulent anti-Judaic polemics common in later Byzantine and West-Syrian writers.[50] His remaining homilies, dated to 344 and thus composed within the context of Shapur's persecution, address more directly the question of Christianity's relationship to Judaism. In these homilies, Aphrahat explains how and why Christians had become the rightful heirs to the divine covenant, which God had originally formed with the Jews.[51] This chronology strongly suggests that the experience of persecution forced Aphrahat and his fellow Christians in Mesopotamia—many, it seems, of Jewish descent—to define more sharply their relationship to their Jewish neighbors and interlocutors. To explain why God allowed the Christians to be persecuted, Aphrahat invoked the full spectrum of slain or exiled biblical heroes, from Abel and Moses to Judas Maccabee, Stephen of Jerusalem, and Christ: "I have written to you these memorials, my beloved, about Jesus who was persecuted and the righteous who were persecuted, so that those who are persecuted today may be comforted."[52]

The "Great Slaughter" (c. 344–379), as it came to be known in Syriac sources, generated a vast and diverse martyr literature.[53] This literature brings into focus for the first time the strength of Christian communities in regions such as Adiabene (northern Iraq), Bēt Arāmāyē (central Iraq), and Khuzistan (southwestern Iran). In each of these territories, Zoroastrian authorities targeted clergy and ascetics, hoping to cripple the Christian community by removing its leaders. In the capital, royal officials executed three bishops of Seleucia-Ctesiphon during the first six years of the persecution.[54] After the death of the third bishop (c. 350), the Church of the East was left without a chief pastor for more than two decades. In other regions, the martyrs included numerous bishops, priests, deacons, and ascetics (women as well as men). Some Christians cracked under pressure and renounced their faith, although it is difficult to extract any credible portraits of apostasy from the martyr literature, in which turncoats appear as stock Judas-like characters.[55] Apostasy may have been rare, since East-Syrian literature preserves little sign of debates about readmission to the church, analogous to the schisms that erupted in Egypt and North Africa after the Great Persecution in the Roman empire.[56] The Sasanian martyr literature emphasizes rather the solidarity of Christian families and communities.[57] In the fifth year of the persecution, a large group of clergy and ascetics (111 men and 9 women) were rounded up from across the capital and imprisoned for the entire winter. During their six-month incarceration, a devout woman of Arbela named Yazdāndukt paid for every aspect of their care, bolstering their resolve through her monetary and spiritual support. As the confessors exited the prison, Yazdāndukt greeted each of them, kissing their hands and feet as they were led in chains to the executioner.[58] After their death, she provided linen burial garments for each martyr and hired pairs of "believing men" from the marketplace to place them in graves (dug "in haste" out of fear of the *magi*).[59] This account, both credible and moving in its details, is exceptional for its attention to the deeds of a laywoman; most accounts of the Great Slaughter focus on the heroism of clergy and "children of the covenant."

The prominence of clergy in the martyr literature reflects not only Sasanian tactics of persecution in the mid-fourth century but also the maturation of clerical authority during the preceding century.

The conflicting depictions of Pāpā bar Aggai, the first definitively historical bishop of the Sasanian capital (285/91–327), provide further insight into the growing authority of the East-Syrian bishops.[60] Hostile sources depict Pāpā as a haughty power-monger, who ran roughshod over the traditional privileges of other bishoprics. His opponents represented sees in Khuzistan, Mayshān, and Bēt Arāmāyē (southwestern Iran, southern and central Iraq) that could legitimately claim to be as old as or older than the see of Seleucia-Ctesiphon. Led by the bishop of Susa, Pāpā's detractors successfully campaigned for his deposition.[61] Sources sympathetic to Pāpā present the same events in a very different light, describing the conflict as a schism provoked by "insolent and unruly bishops who were severely rebuked for their disgraceful behavior by the holy and triumphant chief priest, the faithful Mār Pāpā, the *catholicos*."[62] In the wake of the controversy, defenders of the primacy of Seleucia-Ctesiphon developed two crucial lines of argument. First, they claimed that the stalwart support of the "Western fathers" had confirmed Pāpā's authority over the other bishoprics of the Sasanian empire; they even generated apocryphal correspondence between Pāpā and "the Greeks" as evidence of this alliance.[63] Second, they asserted the apostolic origin of the see of Seleucia-Ctesiphon (also known as Kokhe) by elaborating stories about the travels of the apostle Mār Mārī in Mesopotamia.[64] Neither line of argument—the appeal to "Roman" authority or the invocation of apostolic origins—was fully articulated before the fifth or sixth century, yet they both served to justify centralizing ambitions that were already emerging in the mid-fourth century. In a homily written in about 345, Aphrahat launches a scathing attack on the arrogance of an unnamed chief pastor of the church, possibly to be identified as Simeon bar Ṣabbā'ē.[65] Rather than weakening the clergy, Shapur's persecution appears to have enhanced the bishops' authority.

As the Church of the East coalesced under the authority of the bishop of Seleucia-Ctesiphon, it borrowed extensively (but selectively) from the ecclesiastical standards of the late Roman empire. The unusually amicable relationship between the two empires during the reign of Yazdgard I (r. 399–420) facilitated this ecclesiastical dialogue.[66] The Roman ambassador Marutha of Maiferqaṭ, guest of honor at the synod of 410, brought with him an official letter from the bishops of Syria, "fully demonstrating the charity of their love towards us."[67] With the help of Isaac, bishop of Seleucia-Ctesiphon, the letter was translated from Greek into Persian and read before the "victorious and triumphant king of kings."[68] The forty or so bishops in attendance, rejoicing in the protection of a sympathetic monarch, then approved all the contents of the letter—a complete paradigm for church organization based on the Council of Nicaea.[69] Henceforth, throughout the Persian empire, each city was to have just one bishop, the festivals of the church were all be observed at the proper time, and the rules for the selection and comportment of the clergy should be strictly enforced.

Anyone who refused to ratify "these glorious laws and orthodox canons" was expelled from the church.[70] Roman ecclesiastical models remained conspicuous down to the end of Yazdgard's reign. At the synod of 420, the Roman ambassador Acacius, bishop of Amida, played a role similar to that of his predecessor Marutha in 410. In the synod's signature list, Acacius' name appears second, immediately after that of the *catholicos* Yabhalāhā (Syriac for "Gift of God"), followed by ten Sasanian bishops, who ratified the validity of the Western canons for the Church of the East, including the canons from the Councils of Ancyra (314), Neocaesarea in Cappodocia (314/319), Antioch (324), Gangra (c. 340), and Pisidian Laodicea (347/395). To avoid confusion over the new rules, each signatory received a copy of the canons.[71]

In the case of the Council of Nicaea, the temptation to rewrite history proved too powerful to resist. Only one Sasanian bishop attended Nicaea, a certain "John the Persian" attested in the earliest Greek participant lists.[72] East-Syrian tradition placed an assortment of other Persian churchmen there, including, in one version, the future metropolitan bishops of the Sasanian capital, Simeon bar Ṣabbā'ē and Šahdōst.[73] Such invented traditions attached the patriarchal see of Seleucia-Ctesiphon to the undisputed authority of Nicaea. Canons approved by the East-Syrian bishops at subsequent synods reveal growing confidence in the autonomy of the East. At the synod of 424, the bishops readily acknowledged the invaluable intervention of the "Western fathers" and Roman ambassadors at previous synods but insisted that henceforth "easterners will not be allowed to make an appeal about our patriarch before the western patriarchs."[74] Acceptance of Western models at the synods of the early fifth century enabled the Sasanian bishops to forge a remarkably strong and enduring ecclesiastical structure. Canons 18 through 21 of the synod of 410 established the hierarchy and privileges of the core metropolitan provinces of the Church of the East. These six provinces or eparchies—Khuzistan, Mayshān, Bēt Arāmāye Bēt Garmai, Adiabene, and Bēt 'Arbāyē—would remain the demographic heartland of the Church of the East for the next half millennium.[75]

Christian Expansion and Diversity: Fifth and Sixth Centuries

The steps taken to unify the Christians of the Sasanian empire were, on the whole, highly effective. Although ambitious provincial bishops continued to challenge the primacy of Seleucia-Ctesiphon (leading to periodic schisms), the *catholicos'* proximity to the Sasanian court ensured that the new hierarchy prevailed. During the course of the fifth century, the East-Syrian bishops convened at least five more times in or near the Sasanian capital, with as many as thirty-nine bishops in attendance.[76] Discipline was required to enforce the new hierarchy. The bishops assembled by the *catholicos* Dadīšōʿ in 424 excoriated eleven dissident clergy who refused to acknowledge the *catholicos'* position as "the father and chief and director of all Christianity in the East."[77] Proximity to the court also produced a situation in which powerful courtiers increasingly controlled the selection of the *catholicos*. Candidates who could speak Persian were favored; bribes ensured that the right names were placed before the king.[78] Increased access to the court also brought new forms of danger. During periods of warfare between Rome and Persia, when Christians were viewed with heightened suspicion, the *catholicos* had to answer for his flock—a situation that could lead to banishment or worse. The end of Yazdgard's reign was marked by a flurry of executions aimed at Christian converts from Zoroastrianism and extremists who had courted confrontation by attacking regional fire temples.[79] The Sasanian court was particularly intolerant of any sign of pro-Roman sentiment. In 484, King Pērōz (r. 459–484) had Dadīšōʿ's successor, Babowai, hung by his finger until death, after learning of a secret letter that the *catholicos* had sent the Roman emperor Zeno.[80] Such incidents, though rare, underscored the fragility of the détente between church and state in the Sasanian empire.

One factor that constantly threatened to undermine the détente was the church's success in attracting ethnic Persian converts. How early this trend began remains unclear. Christians bearing typical Persian Zoroastrian names appear, occasionally, in the earliest East-Syrian sources, but names alone are an unreliable indicator of ethnicity. The proportion of Christians bearing traditional Persian names rose steadily as the church expanded its presence in the highland provinces of the Iranian plateau. Bishops participating in the early-fifth-century synods represented churches in the regions of Fars (Rev-Ardashīr and Istakhr), Media (Ḥulwān and Ray), Khurasān (Merv and Herat), and Segestān (southeastern Iran).[81] Formed through a combination of deportation and conversion, these communities were probably polyglot and multiethnic rather than exclusively Persian.[82] By the early sixth century, though, there were enough Persian Christians in Fars and other regions to inspire the creation of Pahlavi translations of Syriac Christian literature. According to a well-known passage in the *Chronicle of Siirt*, Maʿnā, metropolitan bishop of Fars in the mid-sixth century, produced Persian "hymns, homilies, and responses to be sung in church" and distributed them to "the maritime lands (*Bēt Qaṭrāyē*) and India."[83] The near total loss of Persian Christian literature has made it difficult to recapture the history of this Iranian (or, more precisely, Persophone) branch of the Church of the East. The lone, fragmentary Pahlavi Psalter, preserved in the Turfan Oasis of northwestern China, is virtually all that survives as direct evidence for what was once a widespread effort to provide Persian-speaking Christians with sacred texts in their own language.[84]

The influx of Persian Christians during the fifth and sixth centuries coincided with a broader pattern of acculturation in which many Christians adopted (or maintained) Sasanian social traditions. Foremost among these issues was the practice of consanguineous marriage, a custom vigorously promoted by the *magi* and apparently common among Sasanian elites.[85] The bishops assembled at Gundēshāpūr in 486 were appalled to learn that "many of the faithful, in various places, imitate the *magi*, by the impure marriage in which they are united, and transgress the steadfast law of the Church of Christ."[86] Sixty years later, the synod convened by the patriarch Mār Abā (540–552) specified thirty-four degrees of kinship within which marriage was prohibited.[87] In districts with powerful Persian laity, the pressure to tolerate such unions could be intense. Mār Abā, who was himself a convert from Zoroastrianism, faced down demands that he respect the legitimacy of consanguineous marriages formed prior to his patriarchate.[88] The bishops' battle against incestuous unions was part of a larger campaign to promote legitimate monogamous unions untainted by "pagan" customs. The synod of 486 forbade not only consanguineous marriage but also bigamy, concubinage, abductions, and forced marriages.[89] The drive to reform Christian marriage paralleled and sometimes conflicted with the anti-ascetic legislation of the same period, which made marriage compulsory for all clergy beneath the rank of bishop.[90] Critics of this policy attacked it as a concession to royal pressure and Zoroastrian custom. At the synod of 497, the Persian king Zamasp (r. 496–498) explicitly instructed the East-Syrian bishops to encourage "orderly marriage and the begetting of children among all the clergy (*bnay qyāmā*) everywhere."[91] This dramatic innovation in canon law generated its own complications. The bishops assembled in Ctesiphon in 554 felt compelled to address the issue of clergy who had taken "pagan" wives but were unable to shield them and their children from the danger of apostasy.[92] Offenders were removed from the priesthood but not excommunicated, a more lenient punishment than that imposed in 486 on clergy who tolerated incestuous unions in the congregations. Collectively, this legislation highlights the array of thorny challenges raised by the growing number and influence of Persian Christians in the late fifth and sixth centuries.

Other ethnic and linguistic groups, though less prominent in the hierarchy, also joined the ranks of the Church of the East. Since doctrine rather than ethnicity determined membership, new bishoprics were established wherever East-Syrian missionaries won converts. The city of Ḥīra (seven kilometers southeast of modern Najaf), capital of the Arab dynasty of the Lakhmids, possessed a mixed population of Arameans and Arabs with strong elements of Persian culture.[93] By the early fifth century, Ḥīra had a significant Christian community and soon thereafter a special relationship with the bishops of Seleucia-Ctesiphon.[94] Bishop Dadīšō' (r. 421–456) became the first of six East-Syrian *catholicoi* or patriarchs buried in the city's churches and monasteries.[95] Christianity was not the only religion to flourish at Ḥīra; pre-Islamic Arab poets indicate that polytheists, Zoroastrians, and Jews were also present. But it was Christianity that ultimately gained the support of the ruling Lakhmid clan, first among its women, and eventually its king.[96] The strength of the church at Ḥīra encouraged the spread of Christianity among the various Arab tribes connected to the Lakhmid capital through commerce, tribute, or warfare. As M. J. Kister has shown, the rulers of Ḥīra used their status as Sasanian allies to extend their influence across much of the Arabian Peninsula during the two centuries preceding the emergence of Islam.[97] Christianity spread along the same networks. According to an early-eighth-century source, the oasis town of Najrān (in southwestern Saudi Arabia, near the Yemeni border) gained its first converts through a merchant who had been baptized at Ḥīra.[98] A second line of expansion introduced Christianity to eastern Arabia and the Persian Gulf. By the 420s, there were at least three bishoprics clustered around the shores of the Gulf of Bahrain (modern Bahrain, Qatar, and northeastern Saudi Arabia).[99] With remarkable speed, the Church of the East was becoming an institution that mirrored the enormous geographic breadth and diversity of its host empire.

Monks, Schools, and Scholars

As in other parts of the late antique world, ascetics played a prominent role in the Church of the East's expansion and literary production. Much of the earliest East-Syrian literature, such as the homilies of Aphrahat, appears to have been written by and for Christians committed to the "holy war" of renunciation.[100] Early Syrian ascetics were known under a variety of names: they were the "single ones" (*iḥīdāyē*), the "virgins" (*btūlē*/*btūlātā*), the "holy ones" (*qaddīšē*), and the "sons and daughters of the covenant" (*bnay* or *bnāt qyāmā*).[101] As indicated previously, both male and female ascetics were among those imprisoned and executed during the Great Slaughter under Shapur II. While many ascetics—especially, it seems, "the children of the covenant"—lived in domestic settings under the protection of their parents or other guardians, others settled (or roamed) outside the cities and villages of Mesopotamia. The rugged hills of Mount Sinjār, in northern Iraq, and Mount Izla, the eastern extension of the Tur 'Abdin on the Persian side of the frontier, were already populated with Christian ascetics by the late fourth or early fifth century.[102] The boundary between these ascetics and the laity remained permeable. The *Book of Steps*, a manual of ascetical exhortation composed in Persian Mesopotamia (possibly Adiabene) during the mid- to late fourth century, assumes a mixed audience of "upright" men and women striving to join the ranks of the "mature" or "perfect" (*gmīrē*): "the Upright," the author counsels, "do not curse anyone, nor call a person a fool or stupid or contemptible and do not lie against anyone; but the Perfect honor and bless everyone, teaching everyone not to lie against his neighbor."[103]

The origins of formal monasticism in Mesopotamia are similarly difficult to pin down. The *Chronicle of Siirt* preserves a cluster of intriguing stories about the abbot Mār 'Abdā and his disciples active in regions of central and southern

Iraq between the mid-fourth and mid-fifth centuries. These stories, full of obscure place-names, emphasize the role of monasteries in Christian mission to remote areas. One such story describes how a certain 'Abdīšō' of Arphelouna (a village in Mayshān, in southern Iraq) left the monastery of Mār 'Abdā after being rebuked for helping women fill their water jugs on the banks of the Tigris near Ctesiphon. 'Abdīšō' returned first to Mayshān, where he founded a monastery and "converted Rimoun and its environs."[104] He later founded two further monasteries, one in the desert "three miles from Ḥīra" and a second on the island of Ramath in the Persian Gulf, "sixty-eight parasangs from Uballah [a port at the head of the Persian Gulf, near modern Basra]."[105] Another disciple of Mār 'Abdā, Yabhalāhā, established a "great monastery" near a newly converted village in Bēt Arāmāyē ("near the monastery of Mār Ezekiel the Prophet") and a second "on the banks of the Tigris," where the monks were organized into three shifts, "so that their prayer would never be interrupted, thus imitating the angels."[106] Further study is needed to determine how much basis these reports have in actual events of the late fourth and fifth centuries.[107]

From the early sixth century, the landscape of East-Syrian asceticism was transformed by two interlocking trends: the rise of the school movement centered at Nisibis and the monastic revival spearheaded by Abraham of Kashkar (d. c. 588) and his disciples. At the famous East-Syrian School of Nisibis, founded with the assistance of the bishop Barsauma in the late fifth century, students (boys and men only) combined fastidious training in Scripture, liturgy, theology, and disputation with a quasi-monastic existence guided by explicit sets of rules that suggest, among other things, the difficulty of keeping the "brothers" focused on their studies.[108] By the end of the sixth century, residence at the school was mandatory, and room and board were provided.[109] The success of this model of intensive education quickly became apparent as graduates of the School of Nisibis fanned out across Sasanian Mesopotamia, founding satellite schools that taught basic literacy (including the copying of manuscripts) and, in some cases, more advanced skills of exegesis, theology, and Aristotelian logic. The reputation of the School of Nisibis and its graduates soon reached beyond the Sasanian empire. At Vivarium in southern Italy, the retired Italian aristocrat Cassiodorus (c. 485–c. 585) expressed his great admiration for Paul of Nisibis, the East-Syrian contributor to a treatise on biblical interpretation written at the court of Justinian.[110]

The impact of this East-Syrian school tradition was greatly intensified by its confluence with the rising tide of cenobitic monasticism inspired by the reforms of Abraham of Kashkar (d. c. 588). In the words of one modern scholar, Abraham's reforms were "destined to set monastic life in Persia on an entirely new footing."[111] A native of Bēt Arāmāyē in central Iraq, Abraham traveled to "Egypt, Scetis, and Mount Sinai" after education in his village school and a period of missionary work among the "pagans" of Ḥīra.[112] When he returned to the Sasanian empire and the School of Nisibis, he carried with him zeal to reinvigorate East-Syrian monastic tradition, which had grown lax over the course of the fifth century. At the Great Monastery, which he founded on Mount Izla, the "brothers" lived according to the austere regimen of their founder's *Rule* issued around 571. Canon 8, which concerns the monks' Sunday services, illustrates the *Rule*'s "back to basics" approach inspired by Egyptian models:

> On Sunday, when the brothers come together, let the first brother who arrives in Church take the Holy Book and seat himself in his assigned place and meditate [on the Scripture] until all the brothers have arrived. Just so, as each one arrives, his spirit will be seized by the hearing of Scripture, and they will not engage in empty talk.[113]

The assumptions implicit in this canon are revealing. It assumes, first, that every monk will be able to read; second, that his reading will be audible to his peers; and third, that the hearing of Scripture is inherently beneficial and can even inspire ecstatic experiences. Following Abraham's death in about 588, his successor, the abbot Dadīšō', issued twenty-eight further canons, affirming the core principles of the original rule but insisting on more specific guidance for the monks' daily lives.[114] Dadīšō' reinforced, for instance, the centrality of literacy for the monastic life and clarified the boundaries of blameless behavior.[115] With its rigorous standards and charismatic leadership, the Great Monastery attracted monks from across Mesopotamia and beyond. The "reformed" monasticism at Mount Izla developed in parallel with the School of Nisibis, and the two movements, though initially separate, soon became deeply intertwined and mutually reinforcing.[116] Abraham's numerous disciples—listed at length in both the *Chronicle of Siirt* and the eighth-century *Book of Chastity*—dispersed like a starburst across the western Sasanian provinces, founding scores of monasteries in a diverse range of cultural and physical landscapes, from the Arab desert of Ḥīra to the Kurdish-speaking villages along the base of Jabal Jūdī on the modern Turkish-Iraqi border.[117] Crucially, this geographic breadth was matched by openness to ethnic (and, to a lesser extent, linguistic) diversity: the monastic founders listed in the *Book of Chastity* include "Ishmaelites" (i.e., Arabs), Persians, and Romans. Reformed Nestorian monasticism was also characterized by a significant degree of geographic mobility, with many monks traveling beyond their home districts for the sake of education or mission. The long-standing tension in Christian asceticism between the ideals of wandering and stability played out in Nestorian lands, as elsewhere, with the bishops coming down firmly against unsupervised movement.[118]

The patriarchate of Mār Abā marks a key transition in the status of asceticism in the Church of the East. His decision to reinstate the church's policy of clerical celibacy, which had been in abeyance since the synod of 484, effectively curtailed the type of episcopal succession through familial lines that was widely practiced in other areas of Sasanian society. Following his conversion from Zoroastrianism, Mār Abā had cut himself off from his own family roots, recognizing that converts who remained close to their home districts were more likely to be arrested for apostasy. Freed from the constraints of family life, Mār

Abā immersed himself in Christian monastic culture while studying in Nisibis, Edessa, and Antioch. A prolific scholar, he deployed his fluency in both Syriac and Greek to prepare new Syriac translations of the Old Testament (from the Septuagint) and to write commentaries on the Pentateuch, the Psalms, the Wisdom of Solomon, and the Pauline epistles.[119] Later, less bookish patriarchs emphasized other aspects of the monastic tradition. The future patriarch Sabrīšō' studied in the School of Nisibis as a young man, then spent nine years as an ascetic in the mountains of Iraqi Kurdistan (Syriac *Qardū*), then further years living in a cave at Mount Ša'rān (the Jabal Qandīl) in eastern Iraq.[120] Elected patriarch in 596, Sabrīšō' I brought into the patriarchal palace an ascetic lifestyle that shocked and offended some visitors. According to one story, a Roman ambassador dispatched by the emperor Maurice failed to recognize the patriarch, whom he found "seated on a piece of rough cloth in the corner of his cell, dressed in dirty clothes with a cap on his head."[121] The story may be pure fiction, but it exemplifies the patriarch's enduring reputation as a pious ascetic.

Orthodoxy and Dissent

Modern audiences, misled by the label "Nestorian," sometimes assume that the Church of the East simply adopted the theology of Nestorius, the "heretical" patriarch of Constantinople (428–433).[122] In fact, the East-Syrians possessed a distinctive theological tradition, which they developed in dialogue with the patristic heritage of Antioch, Cappadocia, and Edessa.[123] While they honored Nestorius as an inspired teacher in the Antiochene tradition, they lavished far greater attention and praise on another Antiochene theologian, Theodore of Mopsuestia (c. 350–428).[124] Within a decade of Theodore's death, Persian students at Edessa were already immersed in Syriac translations of his major works. By the end of the fifth century, Theodore's exegetical and theological treatises held a central place in the curriculum of the School of Nisibis, ensuring their enduring status as touchstones for East-Syrian orthodoxy.[125] Thus rooted in the Antiochene tradition, the clergy of the Church of the East firmly rejected any Christology that blurred the distinction between Christ's dual nature as fully human and fully divine. Responding to the *Henoticon* issued by the emperor Zeno in 482, the East-Syrian Synod of 486 declared in its first canon: "Regarding Christ, our faith consists in the confession of the two natures of divinity and humanity, and let none of us dare to introduce into the distinction between these two natures a blending, mixing, or confusion."[126] As refined by Babai the Great (c. 551–628) and other East-Syrian theologians, the official position of the Church of the East was that the incarnate Christ possessed two natures and two *qnōmē* (a Syriac concept similar to, but not identical with, the Greek *hypostasis*), but only one *prosōpon*.[127] This formulation placed the Church of the East at odds not only with Chalcedon but also with the opponents of Chalcedon, the West-Syrian or Miaphysite ("One Nature") Church, which formed in the final decades of the fifth century.

The spread of this West-Syrian or Jacobite Church into Mesopotamia during the early sixth century forced East-Syrian bishops to sharpen their skills of theological argumentation. Barsauma of Nisibis (d. 484) was among those East-Syrian bishops who greeted this intra-Christian rivalry with gusto. To this day, churches in the Miaphysite tradition remember Barsauma as a fearsome persecutor of the West-Syrian clergy in northern Iraq.[128] Led by a generation of remarkable teachers, the West-Syrian Church steadily gained ground over the course of the sixth century. Writing in Constantinople in the late sixth century, John of Ephesus joyfully reported on the career of the West-Syrian missionary Simeon of Bēt Arsham, who was nicknamed the "Persian Debater" for his habit of openly challenging the Nestorians to public disputations throughout Mesopotamia.[129] While John of Ephesus may exaggerate the success of itinerant Jacobite teachers like Simeon, the growth of the West-Syrian community in Sasanian lands unquestionably presented the Church of the East with a serious challenge. West-Syrian advances were particularly noticeable in the lowlands of northern Iraq and, more ominously, at the royal court, where the powerful royal physician Gabriel of Sinjār defected to the their side.[130] Gabriel's penchant for seizing East-Syrian monasteries and handing them over to the Jacobites culminated in his effort to control the monastery of St. Sergius, which Khusro II had built in the mountains northeast of Ctesiphon.[131] The metropolitan bishop of Bēt Garmai was able to block the confiscation, but Gabriel avenged the defeat by exposing the East-Syrian monk George of Izla as a convert from Zoroastrianism. In 618, George, formerly known as Mihrmagushnasp, was executed for his apostasy in the hay market of Vēh-Ardashīr; he would not be the last casualty in the struggle between the Church of the East and its West-Syrian rivals.

East-Syrian synodical records of the late Sasanian period admit no anxiety over these divisions. If anything, the bishops advanced more forcefully than ever their vision of the Church of the East as untainted by heresy. In their eyes, there was a manifest divergence between the purity of faith, which they had maintained in the Persian empire, and the corrupted Christian traditions of the Roman empire. In the words of the East-Syrian synod of 612:

> In the land of the Persians, from the days of the apostles and up to the present, no heresy has ever showed itself against this faith or stirred up schisms and factions. In the land of the Romans, by contrast, from the time of the apostles to the present, there have been numerous and diverse heresies. They have infected many of the people; (and) when they were chased from there, in the course of their flight, their shadows have extended up to here.[132]

This bold formulation conveniently ignored the Church of the East's long history of clashes with Manichaeans and Marcionites—both groups still active in some corners of the late Sasanian empire.[133] It also inveighed against the Nestorians' chief rivals, the West-Syrians, without ever naming them, dismissing them instead as one more example of the "numerous and diverse heresies" that had plagued the Roman empire and, having been expelled from there, arrived in the East.

The Laity and Varieties of Christian Practice

How far these theological debates penetrated lay society remains unclear. Partisans attempted to mobilize the laity through public debates or organized violence (against, for instance, "heretical" monasteries), but hagiographic sources probably exaggerate the frequency and ferocity of these clashes.[134] The prevalence of ascetics and the clergy in surviving literary sources should not blind us to the fact that the vast majority of the adult Christian population were married men and women whose contact with monks and bishops might be limited to the periodic festival. Bishops were fully aware of this problem and tried to instill habits of appropriate Christian behavior from the cradle to the grave. Infant baptism, rare at first, became routine by the sixth or seventh century, and babies were welcomed into the church amid the sweet odor of incense.[135] The consequences of ignoring or delaying this sacrament were made clear at the graveside. Baptized infants or children received proper Christian burial, while the unbaptized were allowed a funeral procession led by a priest, but without prayers in Christ's name.[136] Analogous provisions highlighted the punishment of laity who formed consanguineous marriages yet still expected Christian burial. The synod of 544 insisted that neither clergy nor laity should accompany the casket of these lapsed Christians, "whether secretly or in public," so that those who had "separated themselves by their actions from the lofty conduct of Christianity and soiled themselves by unlawful marriage, like beasts without reason, should likewise on their deaths be separated and removed from any communion with the faithful."[137] Such rules, asserting clerical authority at the crucial junctures of life and death, challenged deeply ingrained and highly visible customs among the laity. The bishops assembled by the patriarch Ezekiel in 576, for instance, rebuked Christians who "imitate the pagans (*ḥanpē*) by their actions," marking funerals "with ululations, lamentations, the beating of drums, songs and the cutting of trees."[138] The bishops proposed, instead, solemn, silent commemoration "in churches, monasteries, or their houses" consistent with local Christian custom. No punishment is specified for offenders, probably because the bishops recognized how difficult it would be to enforce such measures.

The distinctive features of East-Syrian architecture and liturgy framed the laity's experience in church.[139] Men and women typically entered the consecrated space of the church through separate portals along the southern or northern exterior wall of the basilica. Once inside, men gathered in the east end of the nave facing the apse or sanctuary, while the women (and presumably the children) clustered behind them.[140] The ten or so East-Syrian churches that have been adequately published suggest that a typical church—such as one of the two churches excavated by the British at Ḥīra in 1931—could hold, when full, between 300 and 400 people.[141] In non-monastic churches, the laity usually shared the space of the nave with a raised platform for the reading the Scripture known as the bema. Derived from similar structures in synagogues, the bema was part of the liturgical package that the Church of the East inherited from Antioch but modified to suit its own needs.[142] The synod of 410 specified: "On Sunday, in the presence of the bishop, the archdeacon will preach upon the bema of the deacons' proclamation and read the Gospel."[143] In practice, the bema's position in the nave accentuated the congregation's participation in the liturgy. Standing around the base of the bema, the laity chanted their responses and pressed close to hear the reading of Scripture from its pulpits. Those standing near the *šqāqonā* (a walled floor-level pathway connecting the bema to the altar area) could sometimes touch or kiss the sacred books as they were carried from the deacons' chamber to the bema and from the bema to the altar.[144] After the consecration of the wine and bread in the sanctuary, baptized Christians came forward to receive the Eucharist.[145] The expectations of bishops and laity sometimes diverged even in this final stage of the liturgy, as, for instance, when unruly parishioners refused to exchange the pre-Eucharistic peace with their neighbors.[146] Others erred (in the eyes of their bishops) by excessive displays of piety, reaching out to touch the chalice or paten with their unsanctified hands or lips.[147]

The behavior of clergy and laity outside of church also diverged, in various ways and degrees, from the high standards articulated by the bishops. Despite episcopal admonitions, many Christians retained commercial, political, and familial bonds with their non-Christian neighbors. As the historian of Zoroastrianism Albert de Jong observes, we should not be fooled by the "rhetoric of insularity" that depicts each Sasanian religious community as autonomous and self-contained.[148] We have already noted the synod of 544's defrocking of clergy who had taken "pagan" wives. The synod of 585 issued several canons to deal with the larger problem of social relations with non-Christians and heretics. Canon 15 is particularly revealing:

> We have learned that some Christians, either through ignorance or through imprudence, are going to see people of other religions (*deḥlātā*) and taking part in their festivals (*'īdayhōn*), that is to say, going to celebrate festivals with Jews, heretics, or pagans, or accepting something sent to them from the festivals of other religions. We thus order, by heavenly authority, that no Christian is allowed to go to the festivals of those who are not Christians, nor accept anything sent to the Christians from their festivals, for it [the gift] is part of the oblation made in their sacrifice.[149]

Apparently, members of different religious communities were willing—perhaps even expected—to share portions of banquet meats as a sign of social solidarity. The patriarch Īšōʿyabh I and his fellow bishops were equally troubled by the close ties that some Sasanian Christians had forged with "heretics" through marriage, the exchange of blessings, and even the sharing of altars.[150] Such prohibitions hint at the codes of respectful coexistence that developed in some cities and villages with mixed religious populations. More elemental attractions also encouraged social mixing. At the synod of 676, the bishops assembled in Bēt Qaṭrāyē (modern Bahrain and its environs) irately complained of parishioners who flocked to Jewish taverns after the Eucharistic liturgy, when they could at least have gone to Christian taverns![151]

In sum, the range of Christian values and behavior in the Church of the East was probably considerably broader than the sources composed by clergy and monks imply. Many laity and some clergy had their own interpretations of the acceptable parameters of Christian piety. The boundaries between religious communities, which were lowered in certain social settings (such as festivals, feasts, and taverns), are even less visible in the diverse assortment of unsanctioned techniques of healing, divination, and prayer, which modern scholars usually lump under the category "magic." Here, the documentary evidence is vast, at least for Mesopotamia, where excavations (mostly illegal) have produced a corpus of more than 1,100 incantation bowls with drawings of demons and inscriptions in a mixture of Aramaic dialects and scripts.[152] The bowls' inscriptions alternately ban or invoke a bewildering array of demons, angels, and other nonhuman spirits, a rich mélange drawn from Jewish, Babylonian, Hellenistic, Mandean, Iranian, and Christian traditions. A small fraction of these incantations—roughly a third of the ones written in Syriac—employ crosses or Christian prayer formulae, leading some scholars to identify them as written by Christians.[153] Far more often, the affiliation of both the magician and his (or her) client remains ambiguous, pointing to the existence of a shared pool of "popular religion" in Mesopotamia that linked Christians to their non-Christian neighbors. The bishops were adamant in their opposition to these "demonic" practices, repeatedly enumerating and denouncing them. At the synod of 576, for instance, the patriarch Ezekiel and the bishops ruled that clergy caught wearing amulets, ligatures, or charms (*qmīʿē w-qeṭrē w-lūḥšātā*) should be removed from office; offending members of the laity were banned from church until completion of penance.[154] The variety of surviving incantation bowls and amulets with Christian associations suggests that the clerical fulminations had limited effect. Magical objects preserve the names and prayers of Christian men and women otherwise unknown to history, such as Pērōzduxt, the owner of a fifth-century seal-amulet with a Middle Persian inscription invoking Jesus, and Xvarr-veh-zād, the owner of a trio of Syriac leather amulets of the sixth or seventh century that feature prominent Trinitarian invocations.[155] A stern seventh-century monk of northern Iraq devoted an entire treatise to denouncing such popular practices, forbidding even semi-Christian variations such as the wearing of cross amulets by children. Sadly for historians, the treatise has not survived.[156]

Warfare, Diplomacy, and Court Politics

In contrast to the general reticence of the sources on the nature of lay piety, East-Syrian writers are often voluble and highly informative on Christian relations with the late Sasanian court. Everyone understood that shifts in royal favor could bring tremendous opportunity or danger. The court's regular intervention in patriarchal elections, beginning with the reign of Yazdgard, drew the upper echelons of the church hierarchy tightly into the orbit of Sasanian politics, as bishops and their allies jockeyed for access to the royal family. Court doctors and astrologers appear to have been particularly influential. According to the *Chronicle of Siirt*, the patriarch Babai (497–502) was elected through his family ties to Mūsā, "a Christian astrologer," who had the king's ear.[157] Babai's successor and former secretary, the patriarch Silas, gained the favor of King Kavad, after one of his allies, the bishop of Susa, healed the king and his daughter of some unspecified malady.[158] Silas' death in 523 threw the church into turmoil, as two viable candidates emerged, each with determined supporters. One of them, Elisha, was a physician, Silas' own nephew whom he had groomed for the position after noticing how Elisha's medical skills had earned him "the friendship of the king and his ministers."[159] Similarly, Mār Abā's fluency in Persian (his native language) and professional experience as a secretary for the *marzbān* of Bēt Arāmāyē probably facilitated his relations with the court. After Mār Abā's death, Kavad's successor, Khusro I (r. 531–579), nominated his personal physician, Joseph, to the patriarchal throne. Duly consecrated by the bishops, the former royal doctor held the office of patriarch for the next fifteen years.

The East-Syrian clergy's close relationship with the Sasanian court was complicated by the repeated efforts of Roman rulers, beginning with Constantine, to assert themselves as protectors of Persia's Christian community. This Roman policy occasionally provided concrete legal protections for the Christians of Iran, most conspicuously as part of the treaty of 561, which stipulated that Sasanian Christians should be free to build churches, bury their dead, and not be coerced into participating in "Magian worship."[160] The policy's inadvertant effect, however, was to goad the Sasanian court into placing intense pressure on Persia's Christians to demonstrate their loyalty. Bishops who demonstrated their complete fealty to the Persian king were promoted. In the patriarchal election of 582, Īšōʿyabh I, bishop of Arzon on the upper Tigris, received the decisive royal nod from King Hormizd IV (r. 579–590), who "knew him and cherished him, since he . . . had reported on the movements of the

Greek army."[161] As the head of the church, the East-Syrian patriarch had the weighty responsibility of ensuring his flock's loyalty to the throne. King Khusro was duly impressed when Mār Abā exercised the church's most serious weapon, excommunication, against the Christians of Gundēshāpūr, where Khusro's eldest son, Anošazad, was leading a rebellion.[162] Bishops or patriarchs caught wavering in their support fell precipitously from royal favor. The case of the *catholicos* Babowai, hung by his offending seal-finger from the gate of the royal palace, illustrates the danger of any hint of pro-Roman sentiment.

Christian influence at the Sasanian court reached its apex in the reign of Khusro I's grandson, Khusro II Aparvez ("The Victorious") (r. 590–628). Khusro regained the Persian throne with the support of a Roman army, after the short-lived usurpation of the Sasanian general Bahram Chubin in 589/90.[163] Following his restoration, Khusro not only married a local Christian, an Aramean named Shirin, but also built in her honor, in the highlands above Ctesiphon, a well-appointed monastery dedicated to the martyr St. Sergius.[164] Meanwhile, in Ctesiphon, Khusro surrounded himself with a coterie of powerful Christian advisors, including Sabrīšō', the new patriarch he handpicked for consecration in 596.[165] This close alliance between church and state served both sides well when Khusro's relations with his former Roman patrons soured. In 591, four East-Syrian bishops supported the Persian viceroy (*nekhurgān*) sent to repress a major rebellion in the frontier city of Nisibis.[166] A decade later, in 603/4, the patriarch Sabrīšō' accompanied the royal army when Khusro and his troops besieged the Roman fortress at Dara. Following the Sasanian capture of Jerusalem in 614, Khusro rewarded his Christian allies by entrusting them with the greatest relic in all of Christendom. Sasanian soldiers had recovered the True Cross from its hiding place in a vegetable garden by torturing the clerical guardians who knew its location. To celebrate the relic's arrival in Persia, the wealthy Christian courtier Yazdin of Kirkuk arranged a "great festival," shaving off a sliver of the precious relic to be placed "with (other) sacred vessels in the new treasure house that he (Khusro) had built in Ctesiphon."[167] Yazdin mounted another fragment inside a bejeweled golden cross and presented it to Babai the Great, the Church of the East's leading theologian.[168] Byzantine sources maintain a stony silence about this reverential reception of the True Cross by Khusro and his East-Syrian subjects.

The Church of the East under Early Islamic Rule

The Islamic conquest of the Sasanian empire (637–651) brought dramatic new dangers and opportunities for the Church of the East.[169] Although some of the invading Arab tribes were Christian, this did not prevent bloodshed of fellow

Christians in cities that resisted the conquerors. After a two-year siege, the city of Shushtar in Khuzistan fell in about 640, betrayed by a resident from Bēt Qaṭrāyē, and "blood flowed like water"; in the massacre, the Arab army "killed the exegete (*mpašqānā*) of the city and the bishop of Hormizd-Ardashīr, along with the rest of the city's students, priests, and deacons."[170] After the turmoil of the initial conquest ended, however, a rather different picture emerged, as Christians recognized the relative lenience of their new rulers. John of Phenek (John bar Penkāyē), an East-Syrian monk writing in about 687 in northwestern Mesopotamia, believed that God had prepared the Arabs beforehand "to hold Christians in honor," monks in particular.[171] The East-Syrian patriarchs assiduously cultivated good relations with the new Arab elites, an effort reported to have begun even before the fall of the Sasanian monarchy. According to the *Chronicle of Siirt*, Īšō'yabh II (628–646) dispatched Gabriel, bishop of Mayshān, to Medina with a "gift" of 1,000 silver staters. Confronted by the Persian king Yazdgard III, the patriarch claimed the money was simply an effort to assist the Christians of Najrān.[172] Gabriel's embassy led, in turn, to a treaty with the caliph Umar (r. 634–644), which guaranteed the safety of the Christians of Seleucia and their buildings. It is likely that both this treaty and the initial embassy are apocryphal—later inventions to confirm the same type of protections that the Christians had enjoyed under the late Sasanian monarchy.[173] But the stories illustrate the expectation for respectful relations between Christian subjects and their Muslim rulers. By the mid-seventh century, another patriarch bearing the same name, Īšō'yabh III (649–660), could speak of the Arab rulers in almost glowing terms: "As for the Arabs, to whom God has given rule over the world at this time, you know well how they act towards us. Not only do they not oppose Christianity, but they praise our faith, honor our priests and saints of our Lord, and give aid to the churches and monasteries."[174] Even if, as Robert Hoyland recommends, we interpret such statements with a pinch of salt, recognizing them as part of an ongoing struggle for political favor between the Nestorians and their West-Syrian rivals, they highlight the speed with which the East-Syrian episcopal hierarchy adapted to life under Islamic rule.[175]

The advent of Islamic rule reconfigured the playing field for competition between the two major churches of Mesopotamia (East- and West-Syrians). In principle, both groups were subject to discriminatory legislation that limited the public manifestations of their faith.[176] In practice, both East- and West-Syrian churches were able to expand their reach into districts that were formerly dominated by the other.[177] The Nestorians made the larger gains, especially in the former Roman provinces of Syria and Palestine, where new bishoprics were established at Damascus, Jerusalem, and other cities between the mid-eighth and mid-ninth centuries.[178] Literary sources for this western branch of the Nestorian church are fairly sparse, but archaeology has provided evidence for the diverse origins of the Nestorian immigrants. For example, a cluster of thirty-three Syriac inscriptions (alongside one each in Pahlavi and Greek), found at a quarry in the Bekaa Valley in northern Lebanon and dated to about 715, record the names and professions of a group of mostly East-Syrian stonecutters from northern Iraq. The inscriptions do not reveal whether these migrants came voluntarily or (perhaps more likely) were forcibly resettled by the caliph al-Walīd (r. 705–715) as part of a professional building crew.[179] Further south, near Jericho, a road repair team working in 1933 struck a mosaic floor that proved to be part of a ninth-century Nestorian monastery. Its founders, honored in the mosaic's Syriac inscription, are identified as "Daniel of Khuzistan, John of Fars, Īšō'dad of Qaṭar, and Ba'ya of Šahrzūr," striking evidence that geographic mobility and ethnic mixing continued to characterize East-Syrian monasticism in the West, as it did in Mesopotamia.[180] In the early 1970s, German archaeologists excavated a smaller, but earlier, Nestorian monastery in the Negev, where it probably served as a stop for pilgrims traveling from Jerusalem to Sinai.[181]

Islamic rule also brought new opportunities in the East, where increased trade through the Persian Gulf encouraged the construction of new Nestorian settlements. In a cagey move designed to outflank the schismatic bishop of Fars, the patriarch Īšō'yabh III (649–660) raised the provinces of Bēt Qaṭrāyē and India to metropolitan status. Recent archaeological research suggests that this strategy of promoting the Persian Gulf churches—further advanced after Īšō'yabh's death by the convocation of a major synod held in Bēt Qaṭrāyē in 676—anticipated a flurry of new church and monastery construction beginning in the late seventh century and extending into the ninth century.[182] French excavations on the island of Khārg, in the northern Persian Gulf fifty-five kilometers north of the modern Iranian port of Bushīr, uncovered, for instance, the remains of a monastery built on the rocky and previously uninhabited southwestern side of the island between the mid-seventh and ninth centuries.[183] This island monastery is part of a growing corpus of archaeological evidence for the southern wing of the Church of the East. Excavations in at least four modern countries in the Persian Gulf region have produced evidence for churches, monasteries, or other Christian settlement between the sixth and ninth centuries.[184] This accumulation of evidence is all the more striking when one notes how many of these sites were recorded by rushed or incomplete excavations. On the small island of Failaka, off the coast of Kuwait, a team of French archaeologists excavated a triple-aisled church with a central nave (19 by 5.6 meters) and a rectangular apse flanked by side chambers for relics and deacons. As in the monastic church on the island of Khārg, which it resembles, the surviving decor of the Failaka church consists entirely of stucco panels, featuring jeweled crosses framed by thick bands of intricate and stylized foliage that parallel Umayyad decorative patterns.[185] Here, too, however, no inscriptions were found, and the name of the church—possibly part of another monastic complex—remains unknown. In fact, literary sources preserve no reference to Christianity on any of the three islands in the northern gulf that have yielded Christian remains.[186] A comparable silence surrounds the remains of the late Sasanian church at al-Jubail and three further sites near the coast of northeastern Saudi Arabia, where the Australian and American archaeologists recorded crosses made of bronze and mother-of-pearl and several crudely marked Christian graves.[187] Further south, on the island of Ṣīr Banī Yās, about 250 kilometers west of Abu Dhabi, British archaeologists have excavated a centrally planned monastic complex similar in layout and decor to the one found on the island of Khārg, but equally anonymous. It, too, has now been tentatively redated to the period between the late seventh and mid-eighth centuries, making it roughly contemporary with the East-Syrian monastery in the Negev and the stonecutter inscriptions at Kamid el-Loz in northern Lebanon.[188]

Despite this steady accumulation of evidence for Christian expansion in the Persian Gulf under Islamic rule, scholars have not been able to identify any of the archaeological sites with the Christian settlements named in the literary sources. As Yves Calvet has observed, the episcopal sees of the gulf region, attested in the *Synodicon* and other East-Syrian texts, have so far remained archaeologically mute.[189] This disjuncture underscores how much we still have to learn about the late Sasanian and early Islamic archaeology of the Persian Gulf. Other regions of the Arabian Peninsula, such as Ḥimyar and Ḥaḍramawt in Yemen and the oasis of Najrān in Saudi Arabia, where Syriac and Islamic literary sources indicate the existence of East-Syrian clergy and major churches, have been even less explored.[190] Even at Ḥīra, where the Lakhmid king al-Nuʿmān had sheltered one fleeing patriarch (Īšōʿyabh I in 596) and received baptism from a second (Sabrīšōʿ I c. 602, leading to the Arab king's deposition and execution by Khusro II), the correspondence between history and archaeology remains elusive. British and Japanese excavators have recorded the remains of three churches at Ḥīra and the nearby site of ʿAyn Shāʾia, dated between the sixth and ninth centuries; yet, not one of these structures can be identified with the renowned churches and monasteries of Ḥīra named in the relatively abundant Syriac and Arabic sources.[191] The archaeological data thus complement the literary sources without matching them. The archaeological data also provide new insight into the regional subcultures within the Church of the East. As Stefan Hauser has argued, most of the Christian artifacts from northern Iraq—the ground plans of the churches at Qaṣr Serīj (in the Jabal Sinjār) and Tell Museifnah (near Eski Mosul), the oil lamps from Nineveh, and the mosaic from Tell Khwāris (south of Erbil in the flood plain of the Lower Zab River)—suggest intensive artistic interchange with Byzantium.[192] The Christian churches from southern Mesopotamia and the Persian Gulf, by contrast, possess their own distinctive architectural style, with domed rectangular apses that echo Babylonian temple architecture.[193]

Christian Expansion into India and Central Asia

Long before the Arab conquests of the Sasanian empire, the Church of the East had begun to extend its reach beyond the Middle East. Its earliest and ultimately most successful expansion focused on the coasts of southern India, which were connected to Mesopotamia and southern Iran by maritime trade routes that had flourished since the Hellenistic and Parthian periods. Even if, as archaeologists now contend, activity along these trade routes declined during the Sasanian period, some Christian merchants and missionaries continued to use them to reach India.[194] The *Chronicle of Siirt* reports that David, the bishop of Basra (ancient Perat d-Mayšān), left his see to preach in India in the early fourth century—a story that could well be true, given the fact that the prophet Mani traveled along the same route in the early 240s.[195] The earliest indisputable evidence for Nestorians in India, however, belongs to the mid-sixth century, when an Alexandrian spice merchant known from the manuscript tradition as Cosmas Indicopleustes ("the one who sailed to India") became a pupil of the future East-Syrian patriarch Mār Abā.[196] In his magnum opus on Christian topography, Cosmas preserves unique information about the East-Syrian bishoprics of the Indian Ocean. As part of his account of the spread of the gospel through the East, Cosmas observes, "Even in Taprobane [Sri Lanka] . . . there is a Christian church with clergy and laity (*pistoi*)." Elsewhere, he specifies that the island's priest was "appointed by Persia," as were also the clergy on the island of Socotra (at the mouth of the Gulf of Aden) and the bishop at "Calliana" (modern Quilon) in "Malé, where pepper grows" (i.e., the Malabar Coast of southwestern India, modern Kerala).[197] Cosmas' dutiful observation of the distribution of Nestorian churches briefly opens a window onto the entire southern wing of the Church of the East, where Syriac and Persian coexisted as languages of business and Christian instruction. A collection of stone crosses (80–100 centimeters high) with Middle Persian inscriptions, erected at five ports along the Malabar and Coromandel coasts, attest to the piety of one particularly rich Nestorian merchant, possibly from an Iranian family of Fars.[198] Although East-Syrian chroniclers add a few scraps of information about these Nestorian outposts in southern India, the evidence remains far too scanty to construct a coherent history. When and how these outposts grew into the sizable population of Christians encountered by Vasco da Gama in 1498 remains a mystery.[199]

The diffusion of Christianity across late antique Central Asia (c. 400–800) is significantly better documented than for the parallel period in India. East-Syrian chronicles and synodical documents make it clear, for instance, that the oasis city of Merv (Turkmenistan), principal garrison city of the northeastern Sasanian frontier, had an established Christian community by the fifth century.[200] Legend credited the city's evangelization to the bishop Bar Shabbā, who arrived in Merv in the entourage of an exiled Sasanian princess.[201] A bishop of the same name participated in the East-Syrian synod of 424—a duty performed by subsequent bishops at the synods of 486 and 497 and thereafter by proxy in 554 and 585.[202] Merv's position on the frontier made it an important base for Christian mission among the nomadic peoples of the desert and steppe surrounding the Aral Sea. A colorful story in the *Khuzistan Chronicle* recounts the missionary success of Elias, bishop of Merv in the 650s, among "the Turks and other nations."[203] Challenged by a local chief *(malkūnā)* to prove the power of the Christians' God, Elias silenced the storms raised by the tribe's shamans and then led them "to a certain river and baptized them all and appointed for them priests and deacons and returned to his land."[204] East-Syrian writers treasured such stories since they explained, with appropriate attention to clerical authority, how bellicose tribes living beyond the Sasanian frontier could be brought into the church. Anecdotal evidence from both Syriac and Byzantine sources suggests that this process was already well under way by the mid- to late sixth century. During his patriarchate, Mār Abā the Great responded favorably to the Hephthalites' request to consecrate a bishop for their people.[205] Forty years later, in 591, a group of "eastern Scythians"—captured soldiers from the army of the Sasanian usurper Bahram Chubin—were paraded through Constantinople, where the Romans marveled at the crosses tattooed on their foreheads.[206]

The archaeology of Central Asia complements these literary anecdotes with a variety of physical evidence. Although some finds are ambiguous and many are difficult to date, recent syntheses have documented the overall size and richness of the corpus.[207] For instance, the Merv oasis, under nearly continuous investigation since 1946, has yielded an assortment of Christian artifacts—a mold for making crosses, Christian burials, ceramics with crosses and other stamped motifs—and one possible example of a large church.[208] The bishopric of Herat in northern Afghanistan (c. 350 kilometers due south of Merv), which was raised to metropolitan status at some stage between 497 and 585, has never been properly investigated, but an inscribed processional cross dated to the mid-eighth century confirms the use of Middle Persian as one of the city's Christian languages.[209] By the eighth century and possibly as early as the sixth, there were substantial Christian communities in the cities and towns of Sogdia (southern Uzbekistan and western Tajikistan), where archaeologists have found traces of their presence in the form of graves, metal crosses, and even local bronze coinage with crosses.[210] Ossuaries painted with crosses found at Afrasiyab (Samarkand) and Mizdaxkan (a tell in ancient Khoresmia, in western Uzbekistan) appear to illustrate the processes of syncretism that facilitated Christian expansion.[211] The earliest churches discovered so far in the region date to the eighth century and later, by which time Samarkand was recognized as a metropolitan bishopric, a promotion that probably occurred in around 720 (rather than the early sixth century, as some later East-Syrian writers claimed). No trace of the episcopal cathedral of Samarkand has survived, but at nearby Urgut (c. thirty kilometers southeast of Samarkand), a team led by the Ukrainian archaeologist Alexei Savchenko has found the remains of a mud-brick monastic complex near a site already known for its collection of East-Syrian pilgrim graffiti. During his visit to this monastery in the mid-tenth century, the Islamic geographer Ibn Hawqal encountered "many Iraqi Christians."[212]

The strength of the Church of the East in Sogdia had important ramifications for the spread and evolution of Christianity across the entire Silk Road. Sogdian merchants, writing their East-Iranian language in a modified Syriac script, created a network of communication and family-based commercial ties that spread across Asia like a giant spiderweb.[213] In the Chu Valley in modern Kyrgyzstan (medieval Semirečʹe), Sogdian emigrants introduced not only urbanization but also Christianity. In the city of Suyab (modern Ak-Beshim), Russian archaeologists excavated in 1954 a church with *ad sanctos* burials and a ground plan that closely recalls the East-Syrian churches at Ḥīra. This eighth-century church, located in the merchant or *rabad* quarter, was replaced, sometime after the Chinese sack of Suyab in 748, by an unusual triple-aisled church built in the most prominent part of the city (the *shahristan*)—a shift that seems indicative of the growing prestige of Christianity in the region.[214] Of course, there is a danger in seeing such buildings in isolation. At Suyab, as at Merv and numerous other oases between eastern Iran and China, local Christian communities lived in close proximity to other religious groups, particularly Buddhists, Zoroastrians, and Manichaeans.[215] The habits of literacy that underpinned East-Syrian spiritual life provided a versatile tool for competing with these other religious communities. Archaeologists have found traces of this tradition of Christian literacy at multiple sites across Central Asia, though typically only small fragments, such as the Syriac ostrakon from the Sogdian town of Panjikent (Tajikistan). Found in a building dating to the first half of the eighth century, the ostrakon bears excerpts of the first two Psalms ("Blessed is the man who does not follow the example of the impious . . ."), studiously copied by a Sogdian Christian seeking to learn the sacred language of the Peshitta.[216] More advanced monks put their linguistic skills to good use, creating entire libraries of Sogdian Christian literature based on translations from the Syriac. In 1905, German archaeologists excavated the remnants of one such library at Bulayïq, on the northern edge of the great Turfan oasis in northwestern China (Xinjiang Province). Thousands of paper fragments found at the site and now housed in Berlin provided the key for the modern decipherment of the Sogdian language. Collectively, these fragments, dated by their paleography to the ninth and tenth centuries, show how intensely the Christianity of Central Asia was steeped in the literary traditions of East-Syrian monasticism. The Bulayïq library included a variety of liturgical texts, multiple copies of Scripture, apocrypha on the life of Jesus and the prophets, and many volumes of hagiography and spiritual instruction drawn from the monastic traditions of Egypt, Syria, and Mesopotamia.[217] The excavations at Bulayïq also yielded numerous fragments of Christian texts in Syriac, Middle Persian, and medieval Uighur, the textual residue of a vigorous tradition of translation for the purposes of teaching and mission.[218]

The Uighur translations of Sogdian Christian texts are especially intriguing, since they represent one important route by which Nestorian Christian teaching penetrated the cultures of the steppe, reaching, by the eleventh century, the principal tribal confederations of Mongolia.

Coda: The Church of the East in the Era of Timothy I (780–823)

Two nearly contemporary events in the early 780s illustrate many of the fundamental features of the Church of the East at the end of Late Antiquity. The first was the erection, in 781, of the so-called Nestorian Monument in Chang'an (modern Xi'an), the grand and teeming capital of China under the Tang dynasty. The second event, in Baghdad in 782/783, was a philosophical defense of Christianity presented by invitation before the caliph al-Mahdī by the newly consecrated East-Syrian patriarch, Timothy, later dubbed "The Great."

Standing over nine feet (2.77 meters) high, the black monolith known as the Nestorian monument or Xi'an stele belongs to a long tradition of stone stelae erected in the courtyards of Chinese temples and monasteries (see figs. 0.2 and 0.3). Its purpose, like that of many similar stelae, was to articulate the privileges and honors of the religious community that it represented. By the time of its erection in 781, Christianity already had a 150-year history in China. The stele's inscription, in beautiful engraved Chinese, describes how the "Luminous Religion of the Daqin" (*Daqin jingjiao*)—a phrase indicating the religion's origin in the Roman empire (Daqin)[219]—was first brought to China in 635 by a teacher named Aluoben bearing "sacred books."[220] It recounts with pride how the emperor Taizong (r. 626–649) ordered Chinese translations of the new teaching and, three years later, in 638, showed his approval by ordering the construction of a Nestorian church (*Daqinsi*, "The Temple of the Daqin") within the walls of the imperial capital.[221] The stele's inscription also details the support of subsequent emperors. Taizong's successor, the emperor Gaozong (r. 656–684), for instance, "caused monasteries of the Luminous Religion to be founded in every prefecture," and as a result, the new teaching "spread throughout the ten provinces."[222] Near the bottom of the stele, beneath the Chinese text of 1,756 characters, stands a brief Syriac text (fifteen vertical lines) naming the inscription's author, a priest named Adam (Chinese: Jing-Jing), and its chief donor, Yazdbozid (Ch. Yissi), followed by the names and titles of seventy further Christians, most identified in both Syriac and Chinese.[223] Modern scholars, impressed by the inscription's elegant Chinese style, have argued that Adam, whose name also appears prominently in the prologue to the main Chinese text on the stele, must have worked closely with a learned Chinese collaborator to whom he "related" or "explained" (Ch. *shu*) the beliefs of his community.[224]

The stele presents a fascinating fusion of Chinese and Nestorian Christian culture. Its summary of Christian doctrine, although framed in Chinese and especially Daoist terminology, echoes the language and themes of the East-Syrian literary tradition.[225] For example, Adam (Jing-Jing) highlights Persia's positive response to the birth of the Messiah: "An angel promulgated the good news, and a Virgin gave birth to the holy one in Syria (*Daqin*); a bright star announced the felicitous event, and Persia (*Bose*), observing the splendor, came to present tribute."[226] Other East-Syrian writers, including Timothy the Great, similarly present the gift-bearing *magi* ("Persia") as forerunners of the Church of the East. Other echoes are more muted. If the recent argument by Michel Tardieu is correct, the unnamed false religions alluded to in the stele's inscription refer not to Daoists, Buddhists, and Confucians—as has been widely assumed since the mid-seventeenth century—but to the followers of Mani, Marcion, and the Messalians, the traditional bêtes noires of East-Syrian heresiology.[227] Part of the challenge of interpreting the stele is the distance between the context of its erection in 781 and the history of Christianity in China that it presents, which extends back to the 630s. As Antonino Forte has suggested, the positive reception that Aluoben received from the emperor Taizong may well reflect the general rapprochement in Chinese-Persian diplomatic contacts during the mid-seventh century, as increasingly imperiled Sasanian monarchs sought aid and later refuge from the Tang court.[228] The original Chinese name for Christianity underscored the importance of this Sasanian connection: before it became the "Luminous Religion of the Daqin," Christianity was known simply as the "Religion of Persia" (*Bose-jiao*).[229]

At a more general level, the history of Christianity in Tang China fits logically within the larger trajectories of the Church of the East. Its chronology, from its origin in the 630s to its aggressive suppression in 845, closely corresponds to the period of East-Syrian monasticism's most explosive growth in other regions (for instance, in the Persian Gulf). A space of less than fifty years separates the death of Abraham of Kashkar at Mount Izla in 588 from Aluoben's arrival in Chang'an in 635. Between Nisibis and Xi'an lay several stages of adaptation and translation, as Christian doctrines passed from Syriac into Middle Persian and Sogdian, and then from Sogdian into Turkish and Chinese. The last step in this chain involved the greatest disjuncture. Whereas Sogdian, Middle Persian, and even Turkish Christian texts consist primarily of translation literature, the earliest Chinese Christian texts to survive—a series of at least six scrolls composed between about 635 and the second half of the eighth century, which were preserved in the Buddhist cave library at Dunhuang (Gansu Province in northern China)—are original compositions.[230] Suffused with Daoist and Buddhist concepts, these Nestorian Chinese texts reveal the "Chinese face of Jesus Christ."[231] The role of Adam (Jing-Jing) and his fellow monks at Chang'an in the creation of these Chinese compositions remains unclear. Their ethnicity is disputed, since their Syriac names, presumably given at baptism, do not reveal whether they were ethnic Chinese or, more likely, mostly foreigners, a mixture of speakers of Syriac, Sogdian, and Uighur.[232] Whatever its precise ethnic composition, the monastery at Xi'an recognized its place within the Church of the East. Ecclesiastical titles are carefully recorded: the community included one bishop, one sacristan (*qankāyā*), and thirty-one "priests" (*qaššīšē*), four of whom were also recognized as "solitaries" (*iḥīdāyē*) and one as an elder (*sābā*).[233] The monastery's patron, a powerful Chinese official named Yazdbozid (Ch. *Yissi*), is identified in the Syriac text as the son of an East-Syrian priest of Balkh (Afghanistan).[234] Most decisively, the stele's Syriac text is dated by the patriarchate of the "father of fathers, Mār Ḥnānīšō', the *catholicos*-patriarch"—that is, Ḥnānīšō' II (r. 775–778/79), a native of Bēt Garmai in central Iraq and the immediate predecessor of Timothy the Great.[235]

Meanwhile, in Baghdad, Timothy, a native of the Erbil district in northern Iraq and former bishop of Bēt Bgash (the hill country north of Arbela), was settling into his new duties as the patriarch of a church that spanned Asia. In some respects, Timothy's forty-three-year patriarchate (780–823) marks a new and rather different phase of East-Syrian history, one shaped by the political, cultural, and economic currents of the Abbasid caliphate, which moved its capital to Baghdad in 762. In other respects, though, Timothy still lived in a Christian culture deeply attached to its Sasanian roots. His philosophical defense of Christianity presented before the caliph al-Mahdī in 782 or 783 built upon a dual East-Syrian tradition: first, the expositions of the faith prepared for Sasanian monarchs, such as Yazdgard I, Kavad, and Khusro II; and second, the techniques of religious disputation honed by centuries of East-Syrian rivalry with Manichaeans, Jacobites, and Chalcedonians.[236] Timothy's themes were specific to his era: the defense of Trinitarian doctrine, the contrast between Muḥammad's humanity and the divinity of Christ, and the place of Islam in world history.[237] But his intellectual toolkit, with its combination of scriptural proofs and Aristotelian logic, owes an obvious debt to the pedagogical traditions of the School of Nisibis. As is well known, the Abbasid court recognized and valued the Syrians' mastery of the Greek intellectual heritage. Under the caliphs al-Manṣūr (r. 774–775), al-Mahdī (r. 775–785), and Harūn al-Rashīd (r. 786–809), the Abbasid court, like the late Sasanian court that it emulated, bustled with Christian doctors, astrologers, and other technical experts.[238] Summoned from Gundēshāpūr to treat the caliph al-Manṣūr, George Boktīšō' (a Middle Persian name meaning "Jesus saves") became the first of six generations of Nestorian court doctors. Similarly, when the caliph al-Manṣūr requested an Arabic translation of the *Topics* of Aristotle, the patriarch Timothy promptly supplied it. Christian scholars became instrumental in the Abbasid translation movement, drawing on their long tradition of philosophical studies to produce, often for Muslim patrons, many of the earliest Arabic translations of Aristotle, Galen, and other influential Greek writers. Such high-level scholarship sometimes required collaboration with West-Syrians (as was also the case at the late Sasanian court). For his translation of Aristotle's *Topics* and parts of the *Organon*, Timothy acquired manuscripts from the Monastery of Mār Mattai near Mosul, a four-hundred-year-old institution controlled by the Jacobites.[239]

East-Syrian tradition also shaped Timothy's approach to political relations with the court, ecclesiastical administration, and mission. At least in his public statements, the patriarch was quick to emphasize the benefits of living under a non-Christian monarchy. In this perspective, Muslim rule was no worse than what had come before and even had certain advantages. As he wrote to one monastic community:

> We never had a Christian king. First it was the Magians for about four hundred years; then the Muslims. Neither the first nor the second ever attempted to add or subtract anything from our Christian faith, but took care not to suppress our faith, especially the blessed kings of the Muslims who never imposed anything in religious matters.[240]

Timothy may have been more critical of Muslims in safe company, but he knew how to get what he needed in the public sphere. After the caliph al-Mahdī destroyed churches as retribution for the military victories of the Byzantine emperor Leo IV (775–780), Timothy successfully petitioned for permission to rebuild them. Although his election was tainted by accusations of simony, he proved to be an exceptionally meticulous administrator of the church's sprawling and often contentious hierarchy. The surviving portion of his patriarchal correspondence (59 of about 200 letters) reveals his skilled efforts to manage the affairs of a church that had ballooned, under his leadership, to include some nineteen metropolitan provinces.[241] Like his predecessor Īšōʻyabh III (650–660), Timothy expanded the traditional structure of the Church of the East to encourage and nourish the growth of Christian communities in regions beyond the church's core provinces in the Middle East. The breadth of his geographic vision is staggering. As he joyfully proclaimed in one letter, "I have just consecrated a new metropolitan for the Turks, and will soon consecrate one for Tibet."[242] He also created new provinces based in Samarkand, Kashgar, the land of the Tangut (in northern China), and Chang'an (Xi'an). Timothy's foot soldiers in this campaign were the monks, many of them drawn from Bēt ʻĀbe and other monasteries in northern Iraq. Thomas of Marga describes, for instance, how one such monk, Mār Elijah, marched off with nothing but a staff and a gospel book to assume his new post as the new metropolitan bishop of Gilān in the wild highlands along the southern coast of the Caspian Sea.[243] Forbidden to proselytize among Muslims, the Church of the East shifted its missionary efforts to marginal and distant regions, expanding from bases established in the sixth and seventh centuries.

Most fundamental of all, Timothy sought to preserve unsullied the "pearl of faith" transmitted to him from his ancestors. He closes his *Apology* with an elaborate parable about this "precious pearl" of Christian teaching, whose luster is reflected in the miracles of the saints.[244] Like the bishops who signed the creed of 612, Timothy had utter confidence in the orthodoxy of his community. He knew that some objected to the term "Nestorian" but saw no reason to reject it since Nestorius was indeed a revered authority.[245] As he wrote in a public letter to the bishop of Nineveh: "We, however, have received the pure gold and splendid pearl of faith, while rejecting, purging, washing away and distancing (ourselves) from the stain and filth of blasphemies."[246] As proof, Timothy cites the suppression of the Manichaean and Marcionite heresies and the status of Seleucia-Ctesiphon as the fifth patriarchal see. In a burst of almost lyrical prose (and rather curious logic), Timothy explains how the Church of the East was, in fact, the earliest and more pristine branch of Christianity, since "We Easterners . . . publicly gave a demonstration of our faith through the twelve messengers who were guided by the star."[247] Seleucia's position in the East was thus no political accident, but a providential fulfillment of Scripture: Eden was in the East, and the Fountain of Life placed in Eden supplied the water for the four rivers flowing from it. Nimrod, the first king of earth, ruled in the East, and Abraham, the forefather of Jesus through the line of David, came from the East. For all of these reasons, Timothy announces, the honor of primacy belongs to the East, "queen of all regions."[248] Modern readers do not have to agree with Timothy to recognize the historical significance of his position. From its humble origins among resettled captives and other converts in the early Sasanian empire, the Church of the East had grown into a vast and variegated Christian community confident of its mission to preserve the faith in a non-Christian empire and to carry that faith to the ends of the earth.

NOTES

*The author wishes to thank Scott McDonough, Étienne de la Vaissière, Scott Johnson, Naomi Koltun-Fromm, Kira Druyan, and the History Research Group at the University of Washington for valuable comments and corrections on drafts of this article.

1. On the complex topography of the Sasanian capital, see Hauser 2007a. In the Sasanian period, Seleucia became another name for Vēh-Ardashīr, which was joined by a bridge to Ctesiphon on the eastern bank of the Tigris.

2. Royal toleration of the church may have begun already under Shapur III (r. 383–388). See McDonough 2008a, 90, n. 9.

3. *Synodicon Orientale*, ed. Chabot, 18, lines 5–9; trans. 254. The Syriac term *qyāmā* seems to refer here to the entire clergy, including the ascetics, the "sons and daughters of the covenant (*bnay qyāmā*)."

4. For the parallel with the Edict of Milan and the description of Yazdgard as a "Second Constantine" in modern scholarship, see McDonough 2008b.

5. Fiey 1970a, 91–94, including discussion of the scanty evidence for an alleged persecution under King Peroz (r. 459–484); Brock 2008, 82–83 (nos. 44–56) for a guide to the martyr literature.

6. For objections to the name "Nestorian," see Brock 1996; Baumer 2006, 7–8.

7. Joseph 2000, 1–32, charts the development of each of these names. On "Assyrian" identity, see also Heinrichs 1993 and, convincingly, Becker 2008.

8. Jenkins 2008, a popularizing survey with vague and inconsistent documentation.

9. See, for instance, Esler 2000; also Harvey and Hunter 2008. French scholarship has generally been more cognizant of the importance of eastern Christian communities, a legacy of France's colonial history in Syria and Lebanon.

10. Brock 1992, 212; 1982, 2, on the deleterious consequences of Eusebius' geographic parameters for subsequent church history.

11. Eusebius, *Church History*, 7.31.2, ed. Winkelmann, 2:716; trans. Williamson, 249; Eusebius mentions the allotment of "Parthia" to the apostle Thomas in *Church History*, 3.1.1 (Winkelmann, 1:188; trans. 65).

12. Population estimates for Christianity in premodern Asia vary widely. Baumer 2006, 5, proposes a population of 7 to 8 million Christians spread across the church's twenty-seven metropolitan dioceses by the beginning of the fourteenth century.

13. On the origins of the Prester John legend, see de Rachewiltz 1972; Jackson 1997; 2005, 20–21, 97. The original figure behind the legend was apparently the warlord Yelü Dashi, founder of the Qara Khitai dynasty in 1131; he was probably a Buddhist.

14. See, for instance, Jackson 2005, 173, and the amazing story of the Öngüt Turkish monk and Mongol ambassador Rabban Sawma, translated with valuable annotations in Borbone 2000.

15. On Nestorians at the Mongol courts, see, in general, Ryan 1998; Jackson 2005, 97–102; Baumer 2006, 197–233; Halbertsma 2008, 48–57.

16. For the controversy over the stele's authenticity that continued into the 1850s, see *Xi'an stele*, 147–166; Keevak 2008; Billings 2004, with a well-organized précis of the vast secondary literature on the stele (32–33).

17. For full references, see Gilmann and Klimkeit 1999, 374.

18. For a brief, rather ungenerous description of these ecclesiastical authors, see Fiey 1970a, 1–5. New in-depth studies would be welcome.

19. Labourt 1904, dedicated to his teachers, Ignazio Guidi and Rubens Duval. Only two of the thirty primary sources in his bibliography were published before 1874; most were published in the 1890s.

20. Especially the books by the English clergyman William W. Wigram published in London in 1910 and 1929.

21. His pivotal contributions include Fiey 1965–1968; idem 1970a; and idem 1993a, 42–145. For further bibliography, see Walker 2006, 91, 311–312.

22. On the merits of making the Sasanian world an integral part of late antique studies, see Morony 2008; Gnoli 1998; Walker 1998.

23. For a meticulous sifting of these traditions, see Jullien and Jullien 2002a, 68–82.

24. *Book of the Laws of the Countries*, ed. and trans. Drijvers, 60–61. The reference, part of Bardaisan's proof that Christian morality trumped regional customs, is too rhetorical to inspire confidence in its details. A nearly identical list of regions appears in the description of the Pentecostal miracle at Acts 2:9.

25. *Acts of Mār Mārī*, 31, ed. Jullien and Jullien, 43–44; trans. Harrak 2005, 71–75. Written in the sixth or seventh century, this narrative of the apostle of Persia preserves elements of earlier traditions, as the editors demonstrate in their commentary and in 2002a, 215–224.

26. Sozomen, *Church History* II.8.1, ed. Bidez, 1:264; trans. 265.

27. See esp. Kettenhofen 1998. Many of the deportees were settled in new urban foundations (or annexes to existing settlements), which were given triumphant names, such as Vēh-Andiyok-Šāpūr, "the better Antioch (built by) Shapur," later abbreviated as Gundēshāpūr.

28. Jullien and Jullien 2002a, 153–187, is characteristically thorough in their analysis, although the evidence is often undatable (for example, rock-cut crosses near Susa), ambiguous (East-Syrian bishops with Greek names), or preserved only in literary sources of the sixth century and later.

29. *Chronicle of Siirt*, ed. Scher, I/I (PO 4), 221 (chap. 2). Preserved in an Arabic version from the early eleventh century, this East-Syrian chronicle remains a fundamental source for the Church of the East, since it frequently paraphrases earlier sources, such as the (otherwise lost) seventh-century *Ecclesiastical History* of Daniel bar Miriam, cited here as the chronicler's source for his account of Demetrios.

30. *Acts of Mār Poṣi*, 2, ed. Bedjan, 208–209; German trans. Braun, 58.

31. On the empire's religious diversity, see Wiesehöfer 1996, 199–216; Morony 1984, 280–430.

32. *Kirdīr's Inscription*, 11, ed. MacKenzie, 42; trans. 58; Wiesehöfer 1996, 199. For the image of Kirdīr on the so-called Ka'ba of Zoroaster (an Achaemenid tomb) at Naqsh-ī-Rustam, see MacKenzie, fig. 2 and plates 1 and 15.

33. Brock 1975, 91–95; also Chaumont 1988, 111–117, refined by Jullien and Jullien 2002b, 324–329. For objections to this political interpretation, cf. de Blois 2002, 7–10.

34. On the codex's decipherment and significance, Henrichs 1979; Lieu 1994, 78–87. See also Lieu 2008, 224, for the identification of the sect's founder as the early-second-century teacher Elchasai condemned by early Christian heresiographers. Lieu 1985, 28–32; de Blois 1995, 46–47, document the sect's longevity into the Abbasid period.

35. See Lieu 2008, 228, on Mani's appropriation of the *Diatesseron*, the Pauline letters, and the *Acts of Thomas*. On his Christology, see Franzmann 2003.

36. Drijvers 1974; Lieu 1985, 37–44; de Blois 2004, 37–38; on the disputations, Hutter 1991, 129. On the difficulty of identifying Mani's earliest rivals, see Lieu 1994, 1–21.

37. *History of Karkā d-Bēt Selōk*, ed. Bedjan, 512, ll. 10–15; Lieu 1985, 81–82. On the identity of Mani's disciples, known also from Manichaean sources, see Chaumont 1988, 97–99.

38. *Chronicle of Siirt*, ed. Scher, I/I (PO 4), 237–238 (chap. 9), where the Persian king observes that "the Manichaeans call themselves Christians, dress like them, and renounce marriage and the procreation of children." On this remarkable passage, see Decret 1979, 126–128.

39. Rouwhorst 1981.

40. The Jewish communities of Mesopotamia were founded by deportations under the Neo-Assyrian and Neo-Babylonian empires. Gafni 2002 provides a lucid overview.

41. Rouwhorst 1997; Emlek 2000, 330–334, both emphasize the profound debt of the East-Syrian liturgy to its Jewish antecedents; see also Brock 2006, 141–146. Stern 2004 demonstrates the use of different calendars, contra Burgess and Mercier 1999.

42. Though often cited as a source for this period, the *Chronicle of Arbela* is a highly problematic text and may even be a modern forgery. For doubts about its authenticity, see Fiey 1967a; 1981; Walker 2006, 287–290. For a vigorous defense of its value, see Jullien and Jullien 2001; 2002a, 133–136.

43. The date of the persecution's onset is disputed. See Burgess and Mercier 1999, revised by Stern 2004, but both accepting the date of 344 for the beginning of executions in the capital (Stern 2004, 454, n. 23).

44. For a clear articulation of this view, see Brock 1982, 7–8. I am not persuaded by the revisionist arguments of Mosig-Walburg 2007, though she is right to emphasize the paucity of evidence for pro-Roman sentiments among Sasanian Christians.

45. Eusebius, *Life of Constantine*, IV.13, ed. Winkelmann, 125; trans. Cameron and Hall, 158. On the political context, see Fowden 1993, 93–97. For doubts about the letter's authenticity (misplaced in my view), cf. Mosig-Walburg 2007, 171–172, n. 4; Cameron and Hall, 311–315.

46. *History of Simeon bar Ṣabbā'ē*, 4, ed. Kmosko, 791–792, lines 9–11. The hagiography probably dates to the early fifth century. On this phase of the Roman-Persian wars, see the documents collected in Dodgeon and Lieu 1991, 164–210.

47. *History of Simeon bar Ṣabbā'ē*, 4, ed., Kmosko, 791–792, lines 14–16. Byzantine sources likewise foreground the role of the Jews in inciting the persecution. See Sozomen, *Church History* II.9.1, ed. Bidez, 1:266; trans. 267. Neusner 1972 provides long extracts from all the major sources.

48. For Jewish relations with the Sasanian court, see Neusner 1972, 98; 1969, 35–39, 55–57; Brody 1990; Gafni 2002, 235–236.

49. Becker 2003, 376–377. See also Becker 2002 for the hypothesis, based on Aphrahat's *Demonstration* 20, that some Christians were flocking to the synagogues for alms.

50. Aphrahat's relationship to Judaism has generated an extensive bibliography. See Pierre 2008; Becker 2002, 307, n. 4. At one end of the spectrum, Neusner 1971, 5, finds an "utter absence of anti-Semitism in Aphrahat's thought."

51. Aphrahat, *Demonstration* 16 ("On the Peoples [*'ammē*] who replaced the People [*'ammā*]"), ed. Parisot, 759–784. Neusner 1971 includes annotated translations of Aphrahat's *Demonstrations* against the Jews.

52. Aphrahat, *Demonstration* 21 ("On Persecution"), 21.21, ed. Parisot, 982, 16–20; trans. Neusner 1971, 110.

53. Rist 1996 provides a well-annotated synopsis of the sources and modern scholarship. See also Bettiolo 2006, 446–449; Walker 2006, 113–115; Brock 2008.

54. Simeon bar Ṣabbā'ē (d. 344), Šahdōst (d. 345), and Barb'ašmīn (d. 350). The names of all three martyrs appear in a Syriac martyrology copied in Edessa in 411. For details, see Fiey 2004, nos. 72, 327, and 421; Burgess and Mercier 1999, 43.

55. See, for instance, the image of the apostate priest, who executed five "daughters of the covenant" in the fifteenth year of the persecution in the *Martyrdom of Thecla and Her Companions*. Fiey 2004, 186–187 (no. 438); Brock 2008, 80 (no. 25).

56. For this key insight, Neusner 1969, 25. As Koltun-Fromm 1996 suggests, some Christians may have returned to Judaism to escape persecution.

57. See, for instance, Walker 2006, 222–223, on the affirmation of Christian family bonds in the earliest Sasanian martyr literature.

58. *Martyrdom of the Hundred-and-One Men and Nine Women*, 5, ed. Bedjan, 294, lines 8–11; trans. Braun, 99. On the Sasanian state's use of temporary imprisonment and torture prior to execution, see Jany 2007, 379–381. Prisoners were often loaded with heavy chains: C. Jullien 2004, 251–252.

59. *Martyrdom of the Hundred-and-One Men and Nine Women*, 6, ed. Bedjan, 295, lines 10–14; trans. Braun, 99. For the Greek and Sogdian versions of the *Acta*, see Brock 2008, 79 (no. 17); also 194 (no. 459) on Yazdāndukt.

60. For his shadowy predecessors, beginning with the apostle Mārī, see Jullien and Jullien 2002a, 231–235.

61. See the list of Pāpā's principal opponents and their sees in the *Chronicle of Siirt*, ed. Scher, I/I (PO 4), 236 (chap. 8).

62. *Acts of the Synod of Dadīšō'* (424 CE), in *Synodicon Orientale*, ed. Chabot, 46, lines 15–17; trans. 289; Chaumont 1988, 142; Jullien and Jullien 2002a, 238. On the origins of the title *catholicos* (from the Gr. *katholikos*), see Fiey 1967b.

63. Published in 1894, the apocryphal correspondence includes letters from the bishops of Rome, Jerusalem, and Nisibis, and the empress Helena. For orientation and bibliography, see Macomber 1968, 179–180; Chaumont 1988, 143–145; Jullien and Jullien 2002a, 238–239.

64. Jullien and Jullien 2002a, 240.

65. Pierre 1995, acknowledging that the chronology is problematic. As she also notes (257), it may be significant that we know virtually nothing about Simeon's episcopacy except for the events of his martyrdom.

66. On Yazdgard's alliance with the Roman court, see Blockley 1992, 46–59; Dignas and Winter 2007, 94–96. I agree, however, with Börm 2007, 308–311, that one should view with skepticism Procopius' report that Yazdgard was made the legal guardian of the child-emperor Theodosius II.

67. *Synodicon Orientale*, ed. Chabot, 18, lines 27–28; trans. 256. The letter's principal authors—the bishops Porphyrius of Antioch, Acacius of Aleppo, Paqida of Edessa, Eusebius of Tella, and Acacius of Amida—are all reliably attested in other Greek and Syriac sources.

68. *Synodicon Orientale*, ed. Chabot, 19, lines 3–4; trans. 256. On Isaac and Marutha's positive relations with the Persian king, see Schwaigert 1995, 180–182; Fowden 1999, 52–56.

69. The exact number and identity of the bishops at the synod remains uncertain due to corruption of the signature list during the process of transmission. On this vexing issue, see Chabot's note at *Synodicon*, 616–618.

70. *Synodicon Orientale*, ed. Chabot, 21, lines 9–12; trans. 260.

71. *Synodicon Orientale*, ed. Chabot, 42, lines 8–9; trans. 283. For useful summaries of the councils and their canons, see Erhart 2001; McCullough 1982, 121–124; Dauvillier 1938.

72. Chaumont 1988, 147–151, outlines the evidence. Eusebius, *Life of Constantine*, 3.7, ed. Winkelmann, 84; trans. Cameron and Hall, 124, mentions, but does not name, the Persian bishop (*Persês episkopos*) present at the council.

73. *Chronicle of Siirt*, ed. Scher, I/I (PO 4), 277 (chap. 18), where the chronicler also lists several alternate traditions.

74. *Synodicon Orientale*, ed. Chabot, 51, lines 16–17; trans. 296.

75. *Synodicon Orientale*, ed. Chabot, 31–35, line 15; trans. 270–273. For an introduction to the ecclesiastical geography of these eparchies, see Walker 2006, 94–102.

76. For a convenient summary, see McCullough 1982, 124–126, 131–134. Smaller synods were sometimes held in other cities, such as the dissident synod convened in 484 by Barsauma of Nisibis at Gundēshāpūr (Syriac Bēt Lapaṭ), the Sasanian summer capital.

77. *Synodicon Orientale*, ed. Chabot, 44, lines 10–11; trans. 286.

78. See, for instance, the description of the election of Dadīšō''s predecessor, Ma'nā of Rev-Ardashīr, in the *Chronicle of Siirt*, ed. Scher, I/II (PO 5), 328–330 (chap. 72).

79. For the sources and sensible analysis, see Van Rompay 1995.

80. *Chronicle of Siirt*, ed. Scher, II/I (PO 7), 99–102 (chap. 1); Gero 1981, 107.

81. *Synodicon Orientale*, ed. Chabot, 35–36, 43; trans. 274–275, 285; Fiey 1993a, 89, 92, 97, 110, 124, 129. On the Persian population in Mesopotamia, see Morony 1984, 181–190, 594–595, focusing on the late Sasanian and early Islamic evidence.

82. According to the *Chronicle of Siirt*, ed. Scher, I/I (PO 4), 222 (chap. 2), the liturgy in third-century Fars was conducted in Syriac and Greek. For communities of deportees in other parts of Iran, see, for instance, Fiey 1993a, 92.

83. *Chronicle of Siirt*, ed. Scher, II/I (PO 7), 117 (chap. 9).

84. Brock 1982, 18; Sims-Williams 1992; Buck 1996, 81–84.

85. For the Zoroastrian ideology underpinning *xwēdōdah*-unions (i.e., consanguineous marriages), see de Jong 1997, 424–432; Macuch 2003.

86. *Synodicon Orientale*, ed. Chabot, 623, lines 9–10; trans. Gero 1981, 79. For polemic against incestuous unions in Syriac, Armenian, and Georgian hagiography, see Panaino 2008. Elman 2007 documents analogous debates about "Iranization" among Sasanian Jews.

87. *Synodicon Orientale*, ed. Chabot, 82–85; trans. 335–338. On Mār Abā's legislation, see Dauvillier 1938, 313–317; Erhart 2001, 127.

88. *History of Mār Abā*, 17, ed. Bedjan, 234–236; trans. 200–202. See also Hutter 2003, 168, though one can be skeptical of the hagiographer's claim that it was the chief Zoroastrian *mobād* who made these demands.

89. Gero 1981, 80, with full references.

90. *Synodicon Orientale*, ed. Chabot, 56–57; trans. 303–306. Gero 1981, 81.

91. *Synodicon Orientale*, ed. Chabot, 63, lines 12–13; trans. 312.

92. *Synodicon Orientale*, ed. Chabot, 102, lines 12–17; trans. 359–360. Only "some" of the wives were converted to Christianity (*w-menheyn mettalmadān*).

93. On the varieties of Arab settlement in Sasanian Iraq, see Morony 1984, 214–223; for Ḥīra's intimate relations with the Sasanians, see Morony 1984, 150–153, Bosworth 2004.

94. For the signature of its bishop Hosea at the Synod of 410, see *Synodicon Orientale*, ed. Chabot, 36, line 26; trans. 275. Fiey 1965–1968, 3:203–243, reviews the city's long and complex ecclesiastical history.

95. Hunter 2008, 43; Fiey 1965–1968, 3:210.

96. On the conversion in 593 of the last king of Ḥīra, al-Nu'mān ibn al-Mundhīr, see the discussion of the patriarchate of Sabrīšō' I (596–604) in Tamcke 1988, 22–23.

97. Kister 1968. Dependent tribes paid the Lakhmids tribute in livestock; even an "independent" tribe sent a few of its members to Ḥīra "as merchants, relatives, and visitors": Kister 1968, 154, paraphrasing Abū al-Baqā'.

98. *Chronicle of Siirt*, ed. Scher, I/II (PO 5), 330–331 (chap. 73), based on the (lost) *Ecclesiastical History* of Barṣahdē of Kirkuk. For the various accounts of Najrān's initial conversion, see Tardy 1999, 97–109, here 102, dating the event to the reign of Yazdgard II (r. 439–457).

99. Beaucamp and Robin 1983, 180–181; Carter 2008; the first coastal bishoprics in eastern Arabia (as opposed to island-based bishoprics) are not securely attested until the synod of 576.

100. See, for instance, Corbett 2003, on "holy war" imagery in Aphrahat and the *Book of Steps*.

101. The secondary literature is very extensive. See esp. Griffith 1993, a probing study of the ascetical terminology in Aphrahat's *Demonstration* 6. There is, however, a need for further work on the *bnay qyāmā* in later East-Syrian contexts.

102. Sozomen, *Church History* VI.33.1–2, ed. Bidez, 3: 422–425, describes the "grazers" (Gr. *boskoi*) of Mount Sinjār, a distinctive form of asceticism "among the people of Nisibis" (*para men Nisibēnois*). For the varieties of early Syrian asceticism, see Escolan 1999, 11–69; Caner 2002, 52–82; Brock 2005, chap. 5.

103. *Book of Steps*, 14.3, ed. Kmosko, 329, lines 20–25; trans. Kitchen and Parmentier, 137. The text's East-Syrian provenance is implied by a single reference to swimming across the Little Zab River in northern Iraq. See p. l in the translators' introduction (xiii–lxiii).

104. *Chronicle of Siirt*, ed. Scher, I/II (PO 5), 310–312 (chap. 62). For the bishops of Rimoun (Syriac Rīmā), first attested in the early fourth century, see Fiey 1993a, 125–126.

105. Carter 2008, 102; Potts 1994 place this island somewhere in northern Persian Gulf, possibly near al-Jubayl (Saudi Arabia), where archaeologists have found evidence of several Christian graves and portable crosses.

106. *Chronicle of Siirt*, ed. Scher, I/II (PO 5), 321–322 (chap. 68). The chronicler's identification of this abbot with the *catholicos* Yabhalāhā (415–420) may be a later conflation.

107. For a preliminary account, see F. Jullien 2008, 93–96. The story of 'Abdīšō', for instance, while rich in topographic detail, is also marked by chronological inconsistencies. Cf. Baumer 2006, 291, n. 43; Bin Seray 1997, 223, n. 20.

108. See, in general, Becker 2006, 77–97, an adroit reconstruction of the sociology of learning at the school. For distractions, see, for instance, canon 5 (from the school's first set of canons, dated to 496; Becker 2006, 82–83), prohibiting students from engaging in business or crafts for longer than three months.

109. Becker 2006, 80, 326, n. 22, noting the contrast with the earlier provisions, which allowed students to rent rooms in the city of Nisibis.

110. Walker 2006, 173, with full references to recent scholarship on this treatise, the *Institutes* of Junillus Africanus, Justinian's chief legal officer

111. Jullien 2008, 2, quoting Arthur Vööbus. See F. Jullien 2008, 57–92, for an attempt to clarify the murky chronology of Abraham's career.

112. Īšō'dnaḥ of Basra, *Book of Chastity*, ed. Chabot, 7–9 (quotation at p. 7, line 18); trans. 232–234 (no. 14). This mid-ninth-century collection of short biographies is an indispensable source for the history of East-Syrian monasticism. For Abraham's journey to Egypt (probably, but not certainly, historical), see F. Jullien 2008, 71–78.

113. *Rule of Abraham of Kashkar*, canon 8, in F. Jullien 2008, 137; trans. 133.

114. See F. Jullien 2008, 106, on the "codification progressive du quotidien" in the rules of the Great Monastery.

115. *Rule of Dadīšō'*, canon 7, in F. Jullien 2008, 145; trans. 140, stipulating the ability "to read Scripture" as a prerequisite to joining the monastery. On blameless behavior, see, for instance, canons 8 (no lingering in a brother's cell) and 17 (no youths [*ṭlayē*] to be admitted to the monastery).

116. Becker 2006, 169–203.

117. For the Jabal Jūdī region as the "land of the Kurds," see, for instance, Walker 2006, 26, on this language in the early seventh-century *History of Mar Qardagh*, where the mountain is also identified (as customary in Syriac tradition) as the landing spot for Noah's Ark after the Flood. According to the *Chronicle of Siirt*, ed. Scher, II/II (PO 13), 446–447 (chap. 45), Rabban Bar 'Īdta "went to the region of Marga, where he converted many Kurds and built a monastery."

118. *Synodicon Orientale*, ed. Chabot, 145; trans. 406 (Synod of 585, canon 7), the first explicit statement on the topic, part of a broader program to discredit "Messalian" monks.

119. *Chronicle of Siirt*, ed. Scher, II/I (PO 7), 157–158 (chap. 27). None of these treatises has survived.

120. See the summary of the patriarch's Syriac *Vita* in Fiey 2004, 168–169 (no. 392).

121. *Chronicle of Siirt*, ed. Scher, II/II (PO 13), 494 (chap. 67).

122. Nestorius and his teaching were condemned as heretical at the East-Roman Councils of Ephesus in 431, Chalcedon in 451, and Constantinople in 553.

123. For an overview of the stages of this development reflected in the *Synodicon Orientale*, see Brock 1985.

124. The name Nestorius never appears in the *Synodicon*'s account of the eight East-Syrian councils held between 486 and 612, while Theodore's name is repeatedly cited as an authority on doctrinal matters: Brock 1996, 29.

125. Becker 2006, 117.

126. *Synodicon Orientale*, ed. Chabot, 55, lines 1–3; trans. 302; Brock 1995, 133. Baumer 2006, 83, interprets the language as a direct rebuttal to the *Henoticon*, which is not, however, explicitly mentioned.

127. Brock 1996, 25, for the East-Syrian objections to the dual hypostases of Chalcedon.

128. Gero 1981 qualifies the historicity of this image of Barsauma as an arch-persecutor.

129. Walker 2006, 174–177, with full references. The story of West-Syrian expansion in the Sasanian empire deserves greater attention than it can receive here.

130. For the alliance between Gabriel and Khusro's Christian wife, Shirin, see Hutter 1998, 378.

131. On Khusro's dedications to St. Sergius, see n. 164.

132. *Synodicon Orientale*, ed. Chabot, 567, lines 18–22; trans. 585. For the elaboration of this claim by the ninth-century East-Syrian chronicler of heresies Theodore bar Kōni, see Fiey 1970a, 49.

133. On references to the Marcionites in sixth-century East-Syrian sources, see Fiey 1970b.

134. See, for instance, the enthusiastic account of the destruction of West-Syrian monasteries in the *History of Rabban Hormizd*, ed. Budge, 1: 76–78; trans. 2: 112–116 (chaps. 14–15), esp. 78, lines 4–6, on the villagers who plundered the Jacobite monastery at Bezkin near Alqosh after an initial assault by East-Syrian monks.

135. For East-Syrian baptismal tradition, see Schmitz 2007 (282 on child baptism becoming standard by the sixth or seventh century "at the latest"; 291 on incense).

136. Macomber 1977, 331, citing a provision found in "many of the older manuscripts" of the Chaldean funeral liturgy for laymen. Emlek 2000, 348, suggests a seventh-century date for the revised version of the larger ritual.

137. *Synodicon Orientale*, ed. Chabot, 85, lines 1–3; trans. 338.

138. *Synodicon Orientale*, ed. Chabot, 117, lines 3–6 (canon 4). Braun's translation of the passage (p. 174) is more accurate than Chabot's (p. 376), but the meaning of the "tree-cutting" (*wa-ba-psāqā d-'ilānē*) remains opaque.

139. For overviews of Sasanian church archaeology, see Okada 1991; Lerner 1992; Hauser 2007b. For the East-Syrian liturgy, see Emlak 2000; Varghese 2007, with references.

140. Taft 1968, 332, on the sequestering of women at the west end of the nave according to the anonymous ninth-century *Expositio* of the East-Syrian liturgy attributed to George of Arbela.

141. This is a very rough estimate (excluding small children) based on the sizes of the churches illustrated by Hauser 2007b, 122–125. The church known as Ḥīra V, for instance, measures 25 by 16.5 meters, making it the same size as the church at Vēh-Ardashīr (27 by 15 meters) excavated by the Germans in the 1930s. Monastic churches were generally smaller.

142. On the functions and symbolism of the bema in the East-Syrian liturgy, see Taft 1968 (esp. 336); 1970, with additional comments in Taft 1995, 3–6. On the "Antiochization" of the East-Syrian liturgy, beginning in 410, see Varghese 2007, 272.

143. *Synodicon Orientale*, ed. Chabot, 27, line 27–28, line 1; trans. 267 (canon 15, on the qualifications and duties of archdeacons). Emlek 2000, 342–346, surveys the liturgical rules in the *Synodicon*.

144. The church at Museifneh (Eski Mosul) in northern Iraq preserves archaeological evidence of this feature (Taft 1995, 3, but cf. Hauser 2007b, 97, on the dating). On the geographical distribution of churches with bemas, see Cassis 2002, 10.

145. East-Syrian liturgical commentaries suggest that the tradition of the catechumenate (an intermediate stage before baptism) was abandoned during the sixth century. References in Varghese 2007, 276.

146. The patriarch Īšō'yabh I (582–596) describes the problem of the irreconcilable parishioners—and even priests!—in his response to the bishop of the island of Dayrīn (modern Tarut, Saudia Arabia). *Synodicon Orientale*, ed. Chabot, 171–174; trans. 431–433, where the patriarch exhorts the bishop to deny the sacrament to such unforgiving men.

147. *Nestorian Questions on the Administration of the Eucharist by Isho'yabh* [*sic*] *IV*, ed. Van Unnik, nos. 21–22 (M. 10b—11a); trans. 165, an early-eleventh-century source but possibly applicable to much earlier periods.

148. de Jong 2004, 58–60, an important article.

149. *Synodicon Orientale*, ed. Chabot, 157, lines 31–158, line 8; trans. 417–418. I adopt here the translation of Williams 1996, 42, with minor changes based on the Syriac. On animal sacrifice in Zoroastrianism, see de Jong 2002, esp. 141, on priestly opposition to the sharing of meat with non-Zoroastrians.

150. *Synodicon Orientale*, ed. Chabot, 158, 20–159, line 2; trans. 418 (canon 27): "nor shall they hand over (*nšalmūn*) the holy altars of Christ for the service of heresy."

151. *Synodicon Orientale*, ed. Chabot, 225, lines 1–10; trans. 489 (canon 17): "and [they do] this, even though they do not lack Christian taverns (*ḥānwātā*) in which they could satisfy their desire for wine drinking as is their custom."

152. Shaked 1997; Morony 2003 offer excellent introductions to the corpus, the latter with illustrations and preliminary statistical tables. For the iconography of the demons, see Hunter 1998.

153. Shaked 2000, 63, n. 23, though Callieri 2001, 24, plausibly argues that the language and script may reflect the demands of the client, rather than the magician. For recent additions to the corpus of bowls in Syriac (c. 13 percent of the total corpus), see Müller-Kessler 2006. Gorea 2004 stresses the difficulty of distinguishing between Christian and Manichaean inscriptions.

154. *Synodicon Orientale*, ed. Chabot, 116, lines 15–34; trans. 375–376 (canon 3). Earlier councils had issued similar legislation. See the *Synodicon*, 24, trans. 264 (synod of 410, canon 5); 548–549, trans. 559 (synod of 544, canon 22); 106; trans. 363 (synod of 554, canon 19).

155. For the seal-amulet depicting a wild-haired demon, see Harper et al. 1992; Jesus is the only divine name in the amulet's nearly 100-word inscription. For the leather amulets, see Gignoux 1987: the second amulet opens its prayer "in the name of the Father, Son, and Holy Spirit" (p. 29) and closes it "by the seal (*ḥatmā*) of the Father, Son, and Spirit" (p. 35, line 55).

156. The monk was Rabban Hormizd, the same man who reputedly led the assault on the West-Syrian monastery at Bezkin near Alqosh in northern Iraq. For a brief description of his book "containing the precepts obligatory for Christians," see the *Chronicle of Siirt*, ed. Scher, II/II (PO 13), 596 (chap. 99).

157. *Chronicle of Siirt*, ed. Scher, II/I (PO 7), 128–130 (chap. 15). Babai had a second line of influence through his service as the secretary to the *marzbān* of Bēt Arāmāyē.

158. *Chronicle of Siirt*, ed. Scher, II/I (PO 7), 135–136 (chap. 19). Silas also excommunicated one of his rivals, a physician, "who had reproached him for his conduct," which allegedly included giving richly adorned altar cloths to his daughter.

159. *Chronicle of Siirt*, ed. Scher, II/I (PO 7), 148 (chap. 25), specifying that these men were "Magians," that is, Zoroastrians. The grooming process for Elisha included marriage to Silas' daughter, his first cousin.

160. Menander the Guardsman, *History*, ed. Blockley, 74–76; trans. 75–77 (frag. 6.1); Greatrex and Lieu 2002, 133–134.

161. *Chronicle of Siirt*, ed. Scher, II/II (PO 13), 438 (chap. 42).

162. *Chronicle of Siirt*, ed. Scher, II/I (PO 7), 163 (chap. 27). On the revolt, c. 551, see Greatrex and Lieu 2002, 275, n. 4.

163. Faced with an unenviable choice, the patriarch Īšō'yabh refused to accompany Khusro on his flight into Roman territory; he could hardly expect a warm reception in Constantinople, since as bishop of Nisibis he had provided damaging military intelligence on Roman troop movements.

164. On this monastery, as well as Khusro's votive dedications to the principal shrine of St. Sergius at Rusafa in northern Syria, see Greatrex and Lieu 2002, 173, 176; Fowden 1999, 137–141.

165. *Khuzistan Chronicle*, ed. Guidi, 17; trans. 16; Nöldeke, 10 (on this invaluable East-Syrian chronicle composed in the 660s, see Hoyland 1997, 182–183). Later tradition claimed that Sabrīšō' first appeared to Khusro in a vision. *Chronicle of Siirt*, ed. Scher, II/II (PO 13), 481–482 (chap. 65).

166. Greatrex and Lieu 2002, 184–186. Here again, later tradition elaborated the story to remove any blame from the venerable patriarch. *Chronicle of Siirt*, ed. Scher, II/II (PO 13), 513–514, where the Persian general tricks Sabrīšō' to help him gain access to the rebellious city, where his soldiers then massacre its inhabitants.

167. *Khuzistan Chronicle*, ed. Guidi, 25, lines 17–21; trans. 22; Nöldeke, 25.

168. *Khuzistan Chronicle*, ed. Guidi, 24; trans. 21; Nöldeke, 23.

169. The topic deserves a much longer treatment than can be given here. For orientation, see Fiey 1993b; Baumer 2006, 137–168.

170. *Khuzistan Chronicle*, ed. Guidi, 37, lines 10–12; trans. 30–31; Nöldeke, 44. See also Hoyland 1997, 184. As Nöldeke observes (n. 2), the chronicler also blames a student from "Qatar" for the fall of Alexandria to the Persian army in the summer of 619.

171. John of Phenek (John bar Penkāyē), *Rīš Mellē*, ed. Mingana, 141, lines 16–20; Hoyland 1997, 196 (with bibliography and partial translations).

172. *Chronicle of Siirt*, ed. Scher, II/II (PO 13), 618–620 (chap. 104).

173. Cf. Erhart 1996, 66–68, who defends the historical plausibility of both the embassy and the treaty. If so, the ambassador Gabriel of Mayshān would have been a

very old man by about 633 (the date of his embassy), assuming that he is the same Gabriel, bishop of Karkā d-Mayshān, who participated in the East-Syrian synods of 585 and 605.

174. Hoyland 1997, 181, with full reference (Išō'yabh III, Letter 14C). The patriarch's letter was sent to Simeon of Rev-Ardashīr, the schismatic metropolitan bishop of Fars.

175. Even after his long days of correspondence and crisis management, Īšō'yabh found the time for his other ecclesiastical duties. For his pivotal contribution to the reform of the East-Syrian liturgy, see Emlek 2000, 348–349.

176. For a summary of this legislation, see Baumer 2006, 150–151.

177. See, for instance, Allard 1962, 377, on the construction of an East-Syrian church at Takrit in 762, while the East-Syrian bishop of Nisibis was obliged to hand over one of his congregation's churches to the Jacobites.

178. This process of Nestorian expansion may have had roots in the pre-Islamic period, in the wake of the Sasanian conquest of Syria, Palestine, and Egypt in 611 to 619, but the sources credit Timothy with the creation of the metropolitan province based in Damascus.

179. Kassis, Yon, and Badwi 2004, 32–35, present a reliable summary. The inscriptions are mostly very brief but include precise (and rarely attested) terms for the building trade and several typical East-Syrian names See Mouterde 1939, 88–89 (no. 16), for the site's intriguing collection of clergy.

180. Stephan 1937. Desreumaux 2004, 46, misinterprets the final two toponyms. For Šahrzūr, a mountainous district in the eastern Bēt Garmai (central Iraq), see Walker 2006, 99.

181. Fritz and Kempinski 1983, 138–185, esp. 183–185, for the approximate dates of occupation between the monastery's foundation in the second half of the seventh century and its destruction in the first half of the eighth century. On East-Syrian pilgrimage to Jerusalem and the Holy Land, see Fiey 1969; Teule 1994.

182. For this revised chronology, see Carter 2008 (esp. 72); Kennet 2007 (esp. 89). For the Synod of 676, which finally resolved the long-standing schism between Seleucia-Ctesiphon and the Persian Gulf bishoprics, see *Synodicon Orientale*, ed. Chabot, 215–226; trans. 480–490; Bin Seray 1997, 209; Beaucamp and Robin 1983, 182–184.

183. The whole complex, enclosed by an exterior wall, measures approximately 123 by 88 meters.

184. The countries are Iran (Khārg Island only), Kuwait, Saudi Arabia, and the United Arab Emirates (Abu Dhabi). The most complete survey is now Carter 2008, but see also Calvet 1998; Bin Seray 1996, 325–332; Finster 1996, 303–306.

185. Calvet 1998, figs. 5–8. Fieldwork on Failaka was interrupted after the 1989 season by the Iraqi invasion of Kuwait in August 1990. For the similar stucco decor in the monastic church at Khārg, see Steve 2003, 114–130—all to be redated to the eighth or ninth century, according to Carter 2008, 97–98 (citing a forthcoming study by St. John Simpson).

186. For the badly damaged church and stucco cross recorded during salvage excavations on the island of Akkaz, in Kuwait Bay, see Calvet 1998, 674.

187. Potts 1994; Langfeldt 1994, esp. 52, on the neglect and further damage to the church at al-Jubayl following its accidental discovery. See also Calvet 1998, 675–678; Hauser 2007b, 103–104.

188. King 1997, a valuable preliminary report; Carter 2008, *passim*.

189. Calvet 1998, 678. For the literary sources, see also Jullien and Jullien 2003.

190. For the late antique churches at Najrān, Ẓafār, Ṣan'ā', and other sites described in the literary sources, see Finster 1996, 295–297. The chronology and extent of East-Syrian activity in Yemen (esp. after the Sasanian conquest of 572) remain disputed. Fiaccadori 1985 offers a bold assessment drawing upon very late sources. But cf. Bowersock 2004, 271, n. 27.

191. On the numerous churches and monasteries of Ḥīra, see Fiey 1965–1968, 3: 205–225; Hunter 2008, 45–51. See also Hauser 2007b, 99, on three further churches recorded by a German survey in the desert northwest of Ḥīra.

192. Hauser 2007b, 98–99. For the Tell Khwāris mosaic, now in the Iraqi National Museum, see Costa 1971. The mosaic of uncertain date and architectural setting depicts an ornamental band of peacocks and a stag eating from a tree. For additional Christian finds from Nineveh, long buried in the storerooms of the British Museum, see Simpson 2005.

193. Okada 1991; Hauser 1997b, 99–103, with careful parsing of variants. For the astonishing architectural parallels with the prehistoric temples from Uruk (Uruk IVb–V), see Potts 1996 200–207.

194. Kennet 2007 presses the revisionist case for decline, citing "a very dramatic decline in burials, rural settlement, coin deposition, and urbanisation" throughout the Persian Gulf between the first century B.C. and the Sasanian periods.

195. *Chronicle of Siirt*, ed. Scher, I/I (PO 4), 292 (chap. 25). For Mani's journey to India, see Lieu 1985, 55–57; also Tardieu 1993, on Mani's letters to his followers in the ancient Persian Gulf port of Ḥaṭṭā (Ar. *ḥṭ'*; Middle-Persian *ht'*), which Beaucamp and Robin 1983, 171, identify as the oasis of al-Qaṭīf on the northeastern coast of Saudi Arabia.

196. *Christian Topography*, II.2, ed. Wolska-Conus, 1: 306–307, where Cosmas proudly describes his association with Mār Abā ("Patrikios" in Greek). On Cosmas' worldview, see Wolska-Conus 1962, esp. 3–9, on his presentation of India, and 65–85, on his intellectual ties to the School of Nisibis.

197. Cosmas Indicopleustes, *Christian Topography*, II.65, ed. Wolska-Conus, 1: 502–505 and XI.14, ed., 3:342–345. In the latter passage, Cosmas specifies that the Persian Christian community was resident (*epidēmountōn*) in Sri Lanka and not simply transient.

198. The six crosses, which could be as late as the ninth century, bear variants of the same inscription: "May our lord Messiah show mercy over Gabriel, son of Čahār-buxt. May there be long life for him who made (this cross)." For the distribution, paleography, and hypothesis about the merchant's family background, see Gropp 1991; Baumer 2006, 27–28, has excellent photos of the cross in Kottayam and another, much larger stone cross with a Middle Persian inscription (seventh to ninth century) at Kuravalangad, also in Kerala. See also Baum and Winkler 2003 51–58.

199. Gillman and Klimkeit 1999, 154–175, attempt a survey but have precious little reliable data for the early period beyond a set of inscribed copper tablets from late-ninth-century Quilon. For instance, not one of the sixty-two Syriac inscriptions recorded by recent fieldwork in Kerala (Briquel Chatonnet et al. 2004, 155–167) securely predates the sixteenth century.

200. Here again, Manichaean missionaries preceded them. For the Manichaean community at Merv, important in the late fourth century but thereafter absent from the sources, see Lieu 1985, 183; Gillman and Klimkeit 1999, 210, on Mani's Parthian-speaking disciple Mār Ammō.

201. *Chronicle of Siirt*, ed. Scher I/II (PO 5), 253–258 (chap. 40). Brock 1995 clarifies the relationship among the several versions of the legend in Syriac, Arabic, and Sogdian.

202. Fiey 1993a, 110: the sources are contradictory on when the city was raised to metropolitan status, possibly in the early fifth, but certainly by the early sixth century.

203. *Khuzistan Chronicle*, ed. Guidi, 34, line 13; trans. 28; Nöldeke, 39. The chronicler is vague on the geography of the "Turkic" lands, in striking contrast to his relatively well-informed description of the Merv oasis.

204. *Khuzistan Chronicle*, ed. Guidi, 35, lines 8–10; trans. 29; Nöldeke, 40.

205. *History of Mār Abā*, 37, ed. Bedjan, 266–269; trans. 217–218.

206. Theophylact Simocatta, *History*, 5.10.13–15, ed. Bekker, 225; trans. Whitby and Whitby, 146–147; also cited by Brown 2003, 267.

207. See esp. Comneno 1997; Baumer 2006, 169–193. Gillman and Klimkeit 1999, 212–226, is also valuable, though less consistently rigorous in its choice of secondary literature.

208. The rectangular (51 by 13 meters) fifth- to sixth-century building was found at Charoba-Koshuk, 15 kilometers north of Merv on the northern periphery of the oasis. Comneno 1997, 28–32, with figs. 3–7, carefully reviews the debate over its identification as a church.

209. Gignoux 2001; Fiey 1993a, 89. Bishops representing the city participated in the East-Syrian synods of 424 and 497 and, by proxy, the synod of 585.

210. Comneno 1997, 34–40, provides a good overview, duly noting instances where the evidence is ambiguous. For the coins, see Gillman and Klimkeit 1999, 213; esp. Baumer 2006, 170–171, on the series of coins with a lion on the obverse and a cross on the reverse issued by Khudak, ruler of Varaksha (ancient Bukhara) in the late seventh and early eighth centuries.

211. Comneno 1997, 32–33 (fig. 12); Baumer 2006, 171–172, with illustrations.

212. Savchenko 1996. See also Baumer 2006, 170, and the cautious summary by Comneno 1997, 34–36.

213. De la Vaissière 2004, a landmark study; see, for instance, p. 151 on the importance of family-based networks among the Sogdian traders. See also de la Vaissière, chapter 5 in this book.

214. Klein 2004 describes both the eighth-century church (now destroyed) and the triple church complex (60 by 46 meters) discovered in 1999 in the *shahristan* or walled inner city of medieval Suyab. Ceramic and other finds in the *shahristan* church suggest occupation extending into the early eleventh century. On the earlier church in the *rabad* quarter, see also Comneno 1997, 41–45, esp. 45, on the *ad sanctos* burials, including Muslim graves in the church's courtyard.

215. Archaeologists have found at Suyab, for instance, a Zoroastrian burial ground of the seventh to eighth century, a sixth-century Buddhist temple (38 by 38 meters), and a massive second Buddhist temple (76 by 22 meters) built beneath the southwestern corner of the *shahristan* in the eighth century.

216. The identification of the scribe as Sogdian is based on spelling errors that might be expected in the pedagogical context of dictation. Syriac would not have been an easy language for native speakers of Sogdian, an East-Iranian language closely related to Parthian and Bactrian.

217. For well-documented introductions to the Bulayïq library, see Baumer 2006, 176–178; Gillman and Klimkeit 1999, 251–256. Texts attested in the fragments include histories of the Persian martyrs, the legend of Bar Shabbā of Merv, and the *Antirrheticus* of Evagrius of Pontos. On Evagrius in Sogdian, see also the comments of Brown 2003, 285.

218. It is disappointing that the Syriac fragments have yet to be published, a full century after their discovery. For a description of the Uighur texts, which were apparently translations from Sogdian, see Gillman and Klimkeit 1999, 254–256.

219. On the ambiguity of the geographical term Daqin (the "Great Qin"), which could signify various parts of the Greco-Roman world or Syria, see Barrett 2002, 556.

220. *Xi'an stele*, trans. Pelliot, 175 (x–xii). On this mysterious figure, named three times in the inscription, see Barat 2002, who persuasively identifies the name as a title (*a-rabān*, from the Syriac *rabbān*, "our teacher," an honorific sometimes applied to East-Syrian holy men).

221. For the location of this church and monastery complex in the northwestern quarter of Chang'an, the district for Western merchants, see Gernet 2008, 234. On Taizong's edict of 638, see Forte's essay in *Xi'an stele*, 349–373.

222. *Xi'an stele*, trans. Pelliot, 176 (xv); English from Eskildsen 2002, 182.

223. Barat 2002 provides a useful list of the Syriac names (a mixture of biblical, Syriac, and Persian names, which are consistent with those found throughout East-Syrian monastic literature) and the Chinese translations (based on Buddhist onomastics).

224. *Xi'an stele*, trans. Pelliot, 173 (ii). For the hypothesis about collaborative translation, see Gernet 2008, 233, building on the observations of Pelliot.

225. In addition to its Syriac postscript, the stele also employs a few key loan-words. Its first term for God, for instance, is a calque based on the Syriac (Ch. *A-lo-ho*, from Syriac *Alāhā*).

226. *Xi'an stele*, trans. Pelliot, 174 (vi); English based on Pelliot's French translation.

227. Tardieu 2008. The ambiguity could also be deliberate: heresy, by its nature, was multiform but repetitive.

228. Forte in *Xi'an stele*, 362–367, 375–418, although his identification of Aluoben as "Vahrām . . . a distinguished member of the Persian aristocracy" (413) should be viewed with caution. On Sasanian-Chinese relations, see also Lieu 2000, 54–56.

229. For this change in terminology, see Baumer 2006, 184, emphasizing the role of the Umayyad ambassador—a Christian astronomer and bishop (!) named George (Syr. *Giwargis*; Ch. *Jihuo*)—who arrived in China via the sea route in 713. Cf. also Barrett 2002, for a different (but less plausible) explanation.

230. For orientation, see Baumer 2006, 187–193, supplemented by Mikkelsen 2007.

231. Eskildsen 2002 argues that Christian doctrines became increasingly distorted or muted in the eighth-century texts, a pattern that may suggest the influence of Chinese Manichaean teaching.

232. For the debate, which impinges on the larger question of the apparent disappearance of Christianity from China after the persecution of 845, see Tardieu 2008, 209, n. 6. The Dunhuang texts certainly imply the existence of ethnic Chinese converts, but the size and age structure of that community are impossible to gauge.

233. The high number of priests would become a regular feature of Nestorian Christianity in Asia, noted, for instance, by European visitors to the Mongol court. For a very different interpretation of these titles, cf. Ammassari 2003, 35–44; his approach, however, like that of Yves Raguin, emphasizes parallels with New Testament terminology at the expense of more immediately relevant East-Syrian models.

234. The Chinese text details Yazdbozid's lofty titles and foreign origins. See *Xi'an stele*, trans. Pelliot, 178 (xxiii), with Pelliot's commentary at 277, n. 199, and 280, n. 205.

235. News of the former patriarch's death in 778 or 779 had not yet reached Xi'an. The patriarchal dating is followed by the date in the Seleucid calendar (the year 1082 = 781 C.E.), which remained the preferred dating system in the Syrian churches into the modern period.

236. For expositions, see, for instance, earlier on the East-Syrian creed of 612. For disputations in the Sasanian period, see Walker 2006, 172–180.

237. Timothy the Great, *Apology before the Caliph al-Mahdī*, trans. Mingana, with a facsimile of the Syriac text from a late-nineteenth-century manuscript. Heimgartner 2007 outlines its themes and explains the limitations of Mingana's text and translation. See also Griffith 2008, 104–105.

238. For Christians' vital contributions to the intellectual life of Abbasid Baghdad, see Watt 2004; Griffith 2007; 2008, 106–128, with an important critique of Dimitri Gutas's work on the Abbasid translation movement.

239. Griffith 2008, 113. For this monastery, an important center for West-Syrian scholarship, see Fiey 2004, 137–138.

240. Becker 2003, 375, with full references to text and translation.

241. See the chart at Gillman and Klimkeit 1999, 137, which cites, for the year 820, nineteen eparchies and eighty-five bishoprics. For a guide to Timothy's letters, see Heimgartner 2007, 41.

242. Gillman and Klimkeit 1999, 218; Borbone 2000, 43–44. Baumer 2006, 175, includes a photograph of the Sogdian Christian inscription near Tanktse, in eastern Ladakh (India), carved in 825/826, recording the passage of a merchant from Samarkand "with the monk Nosfarn, as ambassadors to the Tibetan king."

243. Thomas of Marga, *Book of Governors*, V.8, ed. Budge, 1:506; trans. 2:227.

244. *Apology before the Caliph al-Mahdī*, Mingana, 160–62; trans. 88–90; Heimgartner 2007, 54–56. A pearl, guarded by two dragons, also appears in a prominent position on the top of the Xi'an stele.

245. Tardieu 2008, 208, n. 1.

246. Timothy the Great, *Letter 23*, ed. Braun, 147, lines 10–12; trans. 99; French trans. Briquel Chatonnet et al., 9.

247. Timothy the Great, *Letter 23*, ed. Braun, 149, lines 13–15; trans. 101; French trans. Briquel Chatonnet et al., 10, n. 24, on the tradition of the twelve *magi*, which was extensively developed in Syriac literature. Fiey 1970a, 84, on his tone.

248. Timothy the Great, *Letter 23*, ed. Braun, 149, line 21; trans. 101; French trans. Briquel Chatonnet et al., 11.

WORKS CITED

Ancient Sources

Acts of Mār Mārī. Ed. Christelle and Florence Jullien. CSCO Scriptores Syri 234. Louvain: Peeters, 2003; also Amir Harrak, ed. and trans. *The Acts of Mār Mārī the Apostle*. Leiden: Brill, 2005.

Aphrahat, *Demonstrations*. Ed. with Latin trans. J. Parisot. In *Patrologia Syriaca* 1: 893–930. Paris: Firmin-Didot, 1894 and 1907.

Book of the Laws of the Countries: Dialogue on Fate of Bardaisan of Edessa. Ed. and trans. Han Drijvers. Assen: Van Gorcum, 1967. [Repr. Piscataway, NJ: Gorgias Press, 2007]

Book of Steps. Ed. with Latin trans. Michael Kmosko, *Liber Graduum*, in *Patrologia Syriaca* 3: cols. 1–1168. Trans. Robert A. Kitchen and Martien F. G. Parmentier. Kalamazoo, MI: Cistercian Publications, 2005.
Cosmas Indicopleustes, *Christian Topography*. Ed. with French trans. Wanda Wolska-Conus. 3 vols. Paris: Les Éditions du Cerf, 1968–1973.
Chronicle of Siirt. Ed. with French trans. Addaï Scher et al. *Histoire Nestorienne (Chronique de Séert)*. In *Patrologia Orientalis* 4(1): 215–313; 5(2): 219–344; 7(2): 99–203; 13(4): 437–639. Paris: Firmin-Didot, 1908–1950.
Eusebius, *Church History*. Ed. Friedhelm Winkelmann. *Eusebius Werke: Band 2: Kirchengeschichte*. Berlin: Akademie Verlag, 1999. 3 vols. Trans. G. A. Williamson, rev. by Andrew Louth. London: Penguin, 1989.
———. *Life of Constantine*. Ed. Friedhelm Winkelmann, *Eusebius Werke: Band 1: Über das Leben des Kaisers Konstantin*. Berlin: Akademie Verlag, 1975. Trans. Averil Cameron and Stuart Hall. Oxford: Clarendon Press; New York: Oxford University Press, 1999.
History of Karkā d-Bēt Selōk. Ed. P. Bedjan 1891, 2: 507–535; Partial German trans. O. Braun 1915, 179–187.
History of Mār Abā. Ed. P. Bedjan 1895, 206–274; German trans. O. Braun 1915, 188–229.
History of Rabban Hormizd. Ed. with English trans. E. A. Wallis Budge. 2 vols. London: Luzac, 1902. [Repr. Piscataway, NJ: Gorgias Press, 2003]
History of Simeon bar Ṣabbā'ē. Ed. with Latin trans. Michael Kmosko, *Narratio de beato Simeone bar Sabba'e*, in *Patrologia Syriaca* 2, pt. 1, 778–960. Paris: Firmin-Didot, 1907.
Īšō'dnaḥ of Basra, *Book of Chastity*. Ed. Jean-Baptiste Chabot, *Le livre de la chasteté composé par Jésusdenah, évêque de Baçrah*. Rome: École française de Rome, 1896.
John of Phenek (John bar Penkāyē), *Rīš Mellē*. Ed. Alphonse Mingana. *Sources Syriaques, Vol. I*, 1*–202*. Leipzig: Otto Harrassowitz, 1907.
Khuzistan Chronicle. Ed. Ignazio Guidi, *Chronica Minora* 15–39; Latin trans. 15–32. Louvain: L. Durbecq, 1903. German trans. Theodor Nöldeke, "Die von Guidi herausgegebene syrische Chronik übersetzt und commentiert," *Sitzungsberichte der kaiserlichen Akademie der Wissenschaften in Wien, Philosophisch-historische Klasse* 128 (1893): 1–48.
Kirdīr's Inscription. Ed. D. N. Mackenzie. In *Iranische Denkmäler: Iranische Felsreliefs I: The Sasanian Rock Reliefs at Naqsh-i Rustam*, 35–72. Berlin: D. Reimer, 1989.
Martyrdom of the Hundred-and-One Men and Nine Women. Ed. P. Bedjan 1891, 2: 291–295. German trans. O. Braun 1923, 97–104.
Martyrdom of Mār Poṣi. Ed. P. Bedjan 1891, 2: 208–232. German trans. O. Braun 1923, 58–75.
Menander the Guardsman, *History*. Ed. and trans. R. C. Blockley. Liverpool: Francis Cairns, 1985.
Nestorian Questions on the Administration of the Eucharist by Isho'yabh IV. Facsimile edition of Syriac MS trans. by Willem Cornelis Van Unnik. Haarlem: Enschedé, 1937. [Repr. Piscataway, NJ: Gorgias Press, 2006.]
Sozomen, *Church History*. Ed. J. Bidez. French trans. André-Jean Festugière. Paris: Les Éditions du Cerf. 4 vols. 1983–2005.
Synodicon Orientale (ou Recuil de synodes nestoriens). Ed. with French trans. J.-B. Chabot. Paris: Librairie C. Klincksieck, 1902. See also Oscar Braun, *Das Buch der Synhados oder Synodicon Orientale*. Stuttgart and Vienna, 1900; repr. Amsterdam: Philo Press, 1975.
Theophylact Simocatta, *History*. Ed. with Latin trans. Immanuel Bekker, *Theophylacti Simocattae Historiarum libri 8*. Bonn: Weber, 1924. Trans. Michael and Mary Whitby. Oxford: Clarendon Press, 1986.

Thomas of Marga, *Book of Governors*. Ed. and trans. E. A. Wallis Budge. London: Kegan Paul, Trench, Trübner, 1893. [Repr. Piscataway, NJ: Gorgias Press, 2003]

Timothy the Great, *Apology before the Caliph al-Mahdī*. Facsimile of Syriac MS with English trans. by Alphonse Mingana in *Woodbrooke Studies: Christian Documents in Arabic, Syriac, and Garshūni*, vol. 2: 1–162. Cambridge: Heffer, 1928.

———. *Letters*. Ed. Oscar Braun with Latin trans. *Timothei patriarchae I epistulae*. 2 vols. CSCO 74–75. Louvain: Imprimerie Orientaliste, 1914. Reprint: Paris: Durbecq, 1953. French trans. of letter 26 in Françoise Briquel Chatonnet, Christelle Jullien, Florence Jullien, Christine Moulin Palliard, and Marwan Rashed, "Lettre du patriarche Timothée à Maranzekhā, évêque de Nineve," *Journal Asiatique* 288.1 (2000): 1–13.

Xi'an stele. Trans. Paul Pelliot. 1996. *L'inscription nestorienne de Si-ngan-fou*. Edited with supplements by Antonio Forte. Kyoto: Scuola di studi sull'Asia orientale; Paris: Collège de France, Institut des hautes études chinoises.

Modern Sources (including editions listed by editor or translator)

Allard, Michel. 1962. "Les chrétiens à Bagdâd," *Arabica* 9: 375–388.

Ammassari, Antonio. 2003. "La struttura carismatica della Comunità Siro-Cinese a Xian-fu (635–845) e il suo Tempio di Daqin: Tradizioni proto-evangeliche del "Sutra di Gesù Messia," *Orientalia Christiana Periodica* 69: 29–71.

Barat, Kahar. 2002. "Aluoben, a Nestorian Missionary in 7th Century China," *Journal of Asian History* 36.2: 184–197.

Barrett, T. H. 2002. "Buddhism, Taoism, and the Eighth-Century Chinese Term for Christianity: A Response to Recent Work by A. Forte and Others," *Bulletin of the School of Oriental and African Studies* 65.3: 555–560.

Baum, Wilhelm, and Dietmar Winkler. 2003. *The Church of the East: A Concise History*. London: RoutledgeCurzon. German original: Klagenfurt, 2000.

Baumer, Christoph. 2006. *The Church of the East: An Illustrated History of Assyrian Christianity*. London: I. B. Tauris.

Beaucamp, Joëlle, and Christian Robin. 1983. "L'évêché nestorien de Māšmāhīg dans l'archipel d'al-Baḥrayn (Ve-IXe siècle)." In *Dilmun: New Studies in the Archaeology and Early History of Bahrain*, ed. Daniel T. Potts, 171–203. Berlin: Dietrich Reimer Verlag.

Becker, Adam H. 2002. "Anti-Judaism and Care for the Poor in Aphrahat's *Demonstration* 20," *Journal of Early Christian Studies* 10.3: 305–327.

———. 2003. "Beyond the Spatial and Temporal *Limes*: Questioning the 'Parting of the Ways' Outside the Roman Empire." In *The Ways That Never Parted: Jews and Christians in Late Antiquity and the Early Middle Ages*, ed. Adam H. Becker and Annette Yoshiko Reed, 373–392. Tübingen: Mohr Siebeck.

———. 2006. *Fear of God and the Beginning of Wisdom: The School of Nisibis and the Development of Scholastic Culture in Late Antique Mesopotamia*. Philadelphia: University of Pennsylvania Press.

———. 2008. "The Ancient Near East in the Late Antique Near East: Syriac Christian Appropriation of the Biblical East." In *Antiquity in Antiquity: Jewish and Christian Pasts in the Greco-Roman World*, ed. Gregg Gardner and Kevin L. Osterloh, 394–415. Tübingen: Mohr Siebeck.

Bedjan, Paul, ed. 1890–1897. *Acta Martyrum et Sanctorum*. Paris: Otto Harrassowitz. Repr. Hildesheim: Georg Olms, 1968.

———, ed. 1895. *Histoire de Mar-Jabalaha, de trois autres patriarches d'un prêtre et de deux laïques nestoriens*. Paris: Otto Harrassowitz.

Bettiolo, Paolo. 2006. "Syriac Literature." In *Patrology: The Eastern Fathers from the Council of Chalcedon (451) to John of Damascus*, ed. Angelo di Berardino; trans. Adrian Walford, 407–490. Cambridge: James Clarke. Italian original: Turin: Marietti, 2000.

Billings, Timothy. 2004. "Jesuit Fish in Chinese Nets: Athanasius Kircher and the Translation of the Nestorian Tablet," *Representations* 87: 1–42.

Bin Seray, Hamid M. 1996. "Christianity in East Arabia," *ARAM: Journal of Syro-Mesopotamian Studies* 8: 315–332.

———. 1997. "The Arabian Gulf in Syriac Sources." In *New Arabian Studies 4*, ed. G. Rex Smith, J. R. Smart, and B. R. Pridham, 205–232. Exeter: Exeter University Press.

Blockley, R. C. 1992. *East Roman Foreign Policy: Formation and Conduct from Diocletian to Anastasius*. Leeds: Francis Cairns.

Borbone, Pier Giorgio, ed. and trans. 2000. *Storia di Mar Yahballaha e di Rabban Sauma: Un Orientale in Occidente ai tempi di Marco Polo*. Turin: Silvio Zamorani.

Börm, Henning. 2007. *Prokop und die Perser: Untersuchungen zu den römisch-sasanidischen Kontakten in der ausgehenden Spätantike*. Stuttgart: Franz Steiner Verlag.

Bosworth, C. Edmund. 2004. "Ḥira." In *Encyclopaedia Iranica 12*.

Bowersock, Glen W. 2004. "The Ḥaḍramawt between Persia and Byzantium." In *La Persia e Bisanzio (Roma, 14–18 ottobre, 2002)*, 263–273. Rome: Accademia Nazionale dei Lincei.

Braun, Oscar. 1915. *Ausgewählte akten Persischer Märtyrer, mit einem Anhang: Ostsyrisches Mönchsleben*. Kempten: Verlag der Jos-Köselschen Buchhandlung.

Briquel Chatonnet, Françoise, Muriel Debié, and Alain Desreumaux, eds. 2004. *Les inscriptions syriaques*. Paris: Librarie Orientaliste Paul Geuthner.

Brock, Sebastian P. 1973. "Early Syrian Asceticism," *Numen* 20.1: 1–19. Repr. in 1984, *Syriac Perspectives on Late Antiquity*, sec. 1. London: Variorum.

———. 1975. "Some Aspects of Greek Words in Syriac." In *Synkretismus im syrisch-persischen Kulturgebiet*, ed. A. Dietrich, 80–108. Göttingen: Vandenhoeck & Ruprecht. Reprinted in 1984, *Syriac Perspectives on Late Antiquity*, sec. 4. London: Variorum.

———. 1980–1981. "Notes on Some Monasteries of Mount Izla," *Abr-Nahrain* 19: 1–19. Repr. in 1984, *Syriac Perspectives on Late Antiquity*, sec. 15. London: Variorum.

———. 1982. "Christians in the Sasanian Empire: A Case of Divided Loyalties." In *Religion and National Identity: Papers Read at the Nineteenth Summer Meeting and the Twentieth Winter Meeting of the Ecclesiastical History Society*, ed. Stuart Mews, 1–19. Oxford: Basil Blackwell. Repr. in 1984, *Syriac Perspectives on Late Antiquity*, sec. 6. London: Variorum.

———. 1984. *Syriac Perspectives on Late Antiquity*. London: Variorum Reprints.

———. 1985. "The Christology of the Church of the East in the Synods of the Fifth to Early Seventh Centuries: Preliminary Considerations and Materials." In *Aksum-Thyateira: A Festschrift for Archbishop Methodios of Thyateira and Great Britain*, ed. George Dion Dragras, 125–142. London: Thyateira House.

———. 1992. "Eusebius and Syriac Christianity." In *Eusebius, Christianity and Judaism*, ed. Harold W. Attridge and Gohei Hata, 212–234. Leiden: E. J. Brill.

———. 1995. "Bar Shabba/Mar Shabbay, First Bishop of Merv." In *Syrisches Christentum weltweit: Studien zur syrischen Kirchengeschichte: Festschrift Prof. Wolfgang Hage*, ed. Martin Tamcke, Wolfgang Schwaigert, and Egbert Schlarb, 190–201. Münster: LIT.

———. 1996. "The 'Nestorian' Church: A Lamentable Misnomer," *Bulletin of the John Rylands Library* 78: 23–35.

———. 2004. "Changing Fashions in Syriac Translation Technique: The Background to Syriac Translations under the Abbasids," *Journal of the Canadian Society for Syriac Studies* 4: 3–14.

———. 2005. *Spirituality in Syriac Tradition*, 2nd rev. ed. Kottayam, India: St. Ephrem Ecumenical Research Institute (SEERI).

———. 2006. "Some Distinctive Features in Syriac Liturgical Texts." In *Worship Traditions in Armenia and the Neighboring Christian East: An International Symposium in Honor of the 40th Anniversary of St. Nerses Armenian Seminary*, ed. Robert R. Ervine, 141–160. Crestwood, NY: St. Vladimir's Seminary Press.

———. 2008. "A Guide to the Persian Martyr Acts." In *The History of the Holy Martyr Mar Ma'in*, ed. Sebastian P. Brock, 77–125. Piscataway, NJ: Gorgias Press.

Brody, Robert. 1990. "Judaism in the Sasanian Empire: A Case Study in Religious Co-Existence." In *Irano-Judaica II: Studies Relating to Jewish Contacts with Persian Culture throughout the Ages*, ed. Shaul Shaked and Amnon Netzer, 52–62. Jerusalem: Ben-Zvi Institute.

Brown, Peter. 2003. *The Rise of Western Christendom: Triumph and Diversity, A.D. 200–1000*, 2nd rev. ed. Malden, MA: Blackwell.

Buck, Christopher. 1996. "The Universality of the Church of the East: How Persian Was Persian Christianity?" *Journal of the Assyrian Academic Society* 10.1: 54–89.

Burgess, Richard, and Raymond Mercier. 1999. "The Dates of the Martyrdom of Simeon bar Sabba'e and the 'Great Massacre'," *Analecta Bollandiana* 117: 9–66.

Callieri, Pierfrancesco. 2001. "In the Land of the Magi: Demons and Magic in the Everyday Life of Pre-Islamic Iran." In *Démons et merveilles d'Orient*, ed. Rika Gyselen, 9–35. Bures-sur-Yvette, France: Groupe pour l'Étude de la Civilisation du Moyen-Orient.

Calvet, Yves. 1998. "Monuments paléo-chrétiens à Koweit et dans la région du Golfe." In *Symposium Syriacum VII: Uppsala University, Department of Asian and African Languages, 11–14 August 1996*, ed. René Lavenant, 655–685. Rome: Pontificio Istituto Orientale.

Caner, Daniel. 2002. *Wandering, Begging Monks: Spiritual Authority and the Promotion of Monasticism*. Berkeley: University of California Press.

Carter, R. A. 2008. "Christianity in the Gulf during the First Centuries of Islam," *Arabian Archaeology and Epigraphy* 19: 71–108.

Cassis, Marica. 2002. "The Bema in the East Syriac Church in Light of New Archaeological Evidence," *Hugoye* 5. http://syrcom.cua.edu/Hugoye/Vol5No2/HV5N2Cassis.html

Cereti, Carlo G., Mauro Maggi, and Elio Provasi, eds. 2003. *Religious Themes and Texts of Pre-Islamic Iran and Central Asia: Studies in Honour of Professor Gherardo Gnoli on the Occasion of His 65th Birthday on 6th December 2002*. Wiesbaden: Dr. Ludwig Reichert Verlag.

Chaumont, M.-L. 1988. *La christianisation de l'empire iranien des origines aux grandes persécutions du IVe siècle*. Louvain: Peeters.

Comneno, Maria Adelaide Lala. 1997. "Nestorianism in Central Asia during the First Millennium: Archaeological Evidence," *Journal of the Assyrian Academic Society* 11.1: 20–67. [Italian original in *Orientalia Christiana Periodica* 61 (1995): 495–535]

Corbett, John H. 2003. "They Do Not Take Wives, or Build, or Work the Ground: Ascetic Life in the Early Syriac Church," *Journal of the Canadian Society for Syriac Studies* 3: 3–20.

Costa, P. M. 1971. "The Mosaic from Tell Khwāris in the Iraq Museum," *Iraq* 33.2: 119–124.

Curtis, John. 1997. "The Church at Khirbet Deir Situn," *Al-Rāfidān* 18: 369–379 (with plates 1–6).
Dauvillier, J. 1938. "Chaldéen (droit)." In *Dictionnaire de Droit canonique* 13–14: 292–388. Paris: Letouzey Ané.
De Blois, François. 1995. "The 'Sabians' (*Ṣābi'ūn*) in Pre-Islamic Arabia," *Acta Orientalia* 56: 39–61.
———. 2002. "*Narṣrānī (Ναζωραῖος)* and *ḥanīf ((ἐθνικός)*: Studies on the Religious Vocabulary of Christianity and of Islam," *Bulletin of the School for Oriental and African Studies* 65.1: 1–30.
———. 2004. "Elchasai—Manes—Muḥammad: Manichäismus und Islam in religionhistorischem Vergleich," *Der Islam* 81: 31–48.
De Jong, Albert F. 1997. *Traditions of the Magi: Zoroastrianism in Greek and Latin Literature.* Leiden: Brill.
———. 2002. "Animal Sacrifice in Ancient Zoroastrianism: A Ritual and Its Interpretations." In *Sacrifice in Religious Experience*, ed. Albert I. Baumgarten, 127–148. Leiden: Brill.
———. 2004. "Zoroastrian Religious Polemics and Their Contexts: Interconfessional Relations in the Sasanian Empire." In *Religious Polemics in Context: Papers Presented to the Second International Conference of the Leiden Institute for the Study of Religions (Lisor) Held at Leiden, 28 April 2000*, ed. Theo Leonardus Hettema, Arie van der Kooij, and Joannes A. M. Snoek, 48–63. Assen: Royal Van Gorcum.
De la Vaissière, Étienne. 2004. *Histoire des Marchands Sogdiens.* Paris: Collège de France, Institut des Hautes Études Chinoises.
De Rachewiltz, Igor. 1972. *Prester John and Europe's Discovery of East Asia.* Canberra: Australian National University Press.
Decret, François. 1979. "Les conséquences sur le christianisme en Perse de l'affrontement des empires romain et sassanide de Shâpur Ier à Yazdrard Ier," *Recherches Augustiniennes* 14: 91–152.
Desreumaux, Alain. 2004. "Des inscriptions syriaques de voyageurs et d'émigrés." In *Les inscriptions syriaques*, ed. Françoise Briquel Chatonnet, Muriel Debié, and Alain Desreumaux, 45–53. Paris: Librarie Orientaliste Paul Geuthner.
Dignas, Beate, and Engelbert Winter. 2007. *Rome and Persia in Late Antiquity: Neighbors and Rivals.* Cambridge: Cambridge University Press [German original: 2001].
Dodgeon, Michael H., and Samuel N. C. Lieu, eds. 1991. *The Roman Eastern Frontier and the Persian Wars, A.D. 226–363: A Documentary History.* London: Routledge.
Drijvers, H. J. W. 1974. "Mani und Bardaisan: Ein Beitrag zur Vorgeschichte des Manichäismus." In *Mélanges d'histoire des religions offerts à Henri-Charles Puech*, 459–469. Paris: Presses Universitaires de France.
Elman, Yaakov. 2007. "Middle Persian Culture and Babylonian Sages: Accommodation and Resistance in the Shaping of Rabbinic Legal Tradition." In *The Cambridge Companion to the Talmud and Rabbinic Literature*, ed. Charlotte Elisheva Fonrobert and Martin S. Jaffee, 164–197. Cambridge: Cambridge University Press.
Emlek, Idris. 2000. "Vielfalt und Einheit der ostsyrischen Liturgie: Grundzüge einer liturgiehistorischen Untersuchung." In *Zu Geschichte, Theologie, Liturgie und Gegenswartslage der syrischen Kirchen: Ausgewählte Vorträge des deutschen Syrologen-Symposiums von 2.–4. Oktober 1998 in Hermannsburg*, ed. Martin Tamcke and Andreas Heinz, 329–350. Münster: LIT.
Erhart, Victoria. 1996. "The Church of the East during the Period of the Four Rightly-Guided Caliphs," *Bulletin of the John Rylands Library* 78: 55–71.

———. 2001. "The Development of Syriac Christian Canon Law in the Sasanian Empire." In *Law, Society, and Authority in Late Antiquity*, ed. Ralph W. Mathisen, 115–129. Oxford: Oxford University Press.
Escolan, Philippe. 1999. *Monachisme et église: Le monachisme syrien du IVe au VIIe siècle: un ministère charismatique*. Paris: Beauchesne.
Eskildsen, Steve. 2002. "Christology and Soteriology in the Chinese Nestorian Texts." In *The Chinese Face of Jesus Christ*, vol. 1, ed. Roman Malek, 180–218. Sankt Augustin: Institut Monumenta Serica and China-Zentrum.
Esler, Philip Francis, ed. 2000. *The Early Christian World*. London: Routledge.
Fiaccadori, Gianfranco. 1985. "Yemen Nestoriano." In *Studi in onore di Edda Bresciani*, ed. S. F. Bondi, S. Pernigotti, F. Serra, and A. Vivian, 195–212. Pisa: Giardini.
Fiey, Jean-Maurice. 1964. "Les laïcs dans l'histoire de l'Eglise syrienne orientale," *Proche-Orient* 14: 169–183.
———. 1965–1968. *Assyrie chrétienne: Contribution á l'étude de l'histoire et de la géographie ecclésiastiques et monastiques du nord de l'Iraq*, 3 vols. Beirut: Imprimerie catholique.
———. 1967a. "Auteur et date de la *Chronique d'Arbèles*," *L'Orient Syrien* 12: 267–302.
———. 1967b. "Les étapes de la prise de conscience de son identité patriarchale par l'église syrienne orientale," *L'Orient Syrien* 12: 3–22.
———. 1969. "Le pèlerinage des Nestoriens et Jacobites à Jérusalem," *Cahiers de civilisation médiévale* 12: 113–126.
———. 1970a. *Jalons pour une histoire de l'église en Iraq*. Louvain: Sécretariat du CorpusSCO.
———. 1970b. "Les Marcionites dans les textes historiques de l'église de Perse," *Le Muséon* 83: 183–188.
———. 1981. "Review of *Die Chronik von Arbela*," *Revue d'histoire ecclésiastique* 181: 544–548.
———. 1993a. *Pour un Oriens Christianus novus: Répertoire des diocèses syriaques orientaux et occidentaux*. Beirut: Franz Steiner Verlag.
———. 1993b. "Naṣārā." In *Encyclopedia of Islam*, new ed. 7: 970–973. Leiden: Brill.
———. 2004. *Saints syriaques*, ed. Lawrence I. Conrad. Princeton, NJ: Darwin Press.
Finster, Barbara. 1996. "Arabien in der Spätantike: Ein Überblick über die kulturelle Situation der Halbinsel in der Zeit von Muhammad," *Archäologischer Anzeiger* n.s. 2: 287–319.
Fowden, Elizabeth Key. 1999. *The Barbarian Plain: Saint Sergius between Rome and Iran*. Berkeley: University of California Press.
Fowden, Garth. 1993. *Empire to Commonwealth: Consequences of Monotheism in Late Antiquity*. Princeton, NJ: Princeton University Press.
Franzmann, Majella. 2003. *Jesus in the Manichaean Writings*. London: T. & T. Clark.
Fritz, Volkmar, and Aharaon Kempinski. 1983. *Ergebnisse der Ausgrabungen auf der Hirbet el-Mšāš (Tēl Māśōś): 1972–1975*. Wiesbaden: Otto Harrassowitz.
Gafni, Isaiah. 2002. "Babylonian Rabbinic Culture." In *Cultures of the Jews: A New History*, ed. David Biale, 222–265. New York: Schocken.
Gernet, Jacques. 2008. "Remarques sur le contexte chinois de l'inscription de la stèle nestorienne de Xi'an." In *Controverse des chrétiens dans l'Iran sassanide*, ed. Christelle Jullien, 227–243. Paris: Association pour l'avancement des études iraniennes.
Gero, Stephen. 1981. *Barṣauma of Nisibis and Persian Christianity in the Fifth Century*. CSCO 426. Louvain: E. Peeters.
Gignoux, Philippe. 1987. *Incantations magiques syriaques*. Louvain: E. Peeters.

———. 2001. "Une croix de procession de Hérat inscrite en pehlevi," *Le Muséon* 114: 291–301.

Gillman, Ian, and Hans-Joachim Klimkeit. 1999. *Christians in Asia before 1500*. Ann Arbor: University of Michigan Press.

Gnoli, Gherardo. 1998. "L'Iran tardoantico e la regalità sassanide," *Mediterraneo antico: economie, società, culture* 1.1: 115–139.

Gorea, Maria. 2004. "Coupes magiques syriaques et manichéennes en provenance de Mésopotamie." In *Les inscriptions syriaques*, ed. Françoise Briquel Chatonnet, Muriel Debié, and Alain Desreumaux, 107–116. Paris: Librarie Orientaliste Paul Geuthner.

Greatrex, Geoffrey B. 2003. "Khusro II and the Christians of His Empire," *Journal of the Canadian Society for Syriac Studies* 3: 78–87.

Greatrex, Geoffrey, and Samuel N. C. Lieu, eds. 2002. *The Roman Eastern Frontier and the Persian Wars, Part II: AD 363–630: A Narrative Sourcebook*. London: Routledge.

Greenwood, Tim. 2008. "Sasanian Reflections in Armenian Sources," *e-Sasanika* 5, www.humanities.uci.edu/sasanika/pdf/e-sasanika5-Greenwood.pdf.

Griffith, Sidney H. 1993. "Monks, 'Singles,' and the 'Sons of the Covenant': Reflections on Syriac Ascetic Terminology." In *Eulogema: Studies in Honor of Robert Taft, S. J.*, ed. Ephrem Carr, Stefano Parenti, and Abraham Thiermeyer, 141–160. Rome: Pontificio Ateneo S. Anselmo.

———. 2007. "From Patriarch Timothy I to Ḥunayn ibn Isḥāq: Philosophy and Christian Apology in Abbasid Times: Reason, Ethics, and Public Policy." In *Christians and Muslims in Dialogue in the Islamic Orient of the Middle Ages/ Christlich-muslimische Gespräche im Mittelalter*, ed. Martin Tamcke, 75–98. Beirut: Orient-Institut der DMG Beirut.

———. 2008. *The Church in the Shadow of the Mosque: Christians and Muslims in the World of Islam*. Princeton, NJ: Princeton University Press.

Gropp, Gerd. 1991. "Christian Maritime Trade of Sasanian Age in the Persian Gulf." In *Golf-Archäologie: Mesopotamien, Iran, Kuwait, Bahrain, Vereinigte Arabische Emirate und Oman*, ed. Klaus Schippmann, Anja Herling, and Jean-François Salles, 83–88. Buch am Erlbach: Verlag Marie L. Leidorf.

Halbertsma, Tjalling H. F. 2008. *Early Christian Remains of Inner Mongolia: Discovery, Reconstruction and Appropriation*. Leiden: Brill.

Harper, P. O., O. Skjaervø, L. Gorelick, and A. J. Gwinnet. 1992. "A Seal-Amulet of the Sasanian Era: Imagery and Typology, the Inscription, and Technical Comments," *Bulletin of the Asian Institute* n.s. 6: 43–58.

Harvey, Susan Ashbrook, and David G. Hunter, eds. 2008. *The Oxford Handbook of Early Christian Studies*. Oxford: Oxford University Press.

Hauser, Stefan R. 2007a. "Vēh Ardashīr and the Identification of the Ruins at al-Madā'in." In *Facts and Artefacts: Art in the Islamic World: Festschrift for Jens Kröger on His 65th Birthday*, ed. Jens Kröger, Annette Hagedorn, and Avinoam Shalem, 461–488. Leiden: Brill.

———. 2007b. "Christliche Archäologie im Sasanidenreich: Grundlagen der Interpretation und Bestandsaufnahme der Evidenz." In *Inkulturation des Christentums im Sasanidenreich*, ed. Arafa Mustafa and Jürgen Tubach, with G. Sophia Vashalomidze, 93–136. Wiesbaden: Reichert Verlag.

Heimgartner, Martin. 2007. "Die Disputatio des ostsyrischen Patriarchen Timotheos (780–823) mit dem Kalifen al-Mahdī." In *Christians and Muslims in Dialogue in the Islamic Orient of the Middle Ages/Christlich-muslimische Gespräche im Mittelalter*, ed. Martin Tamcke, 41–56. Beirut: Orient-Institut der DMG Beirut.

Heinrichs, W. 1993. "The Modern Assyrians—Name and Nation." In *Semitica: Serta Philologica Constantino Tsereteli Dicata*, ed. Richard Contini, Fabrizio A. Pennachietti, and Mauro Tusco, 99–114. Turin: Zamorani.

Henrichs, Albert. 1979. "The Cologne Mani Codex Reconsidered," *Harvard Studies in Classical Philology* 83: 339–367.

Hoyland, Robert. 1997. *Seeing Islam as Others Saw It: A Survey and Evaluation of Christian, Jewish and Zoroastrian Writings on Early Islam*. Princeton, NJ: Darwin Press.

Hunter, Erica C. D. 1998. "Who Are the Demons? The Iconography of Incantation Bowls," *Studi epigraphici e linguistici sul Vicino Oriente antico* 15: 95–115.

———. 2008. "The Christian Matrix of al-Hira." In *Controverse des chrétiens dans l'Iran sassanide*, ed. Christelle Jullien, 41–56. Paris: Association pour l'avancement des études iraniennes.

Hutter, Manfred. 1991. "Mani und das Persische Christentum." In *Manichaica Selecta: Studies Presented to Professor Julien Ries on the Occasion of His Seventieth Birthday*, ed. Alos van Tongerloo and Søren Giversen, 125–135. Louvain: International Association of Manichaean Studies.

———. 1998. "Shirin, Nestorianer, und Monophysiten: Königliche Kirchenpolitik im späten Sasanidenreich." In *Symposium Syriacum VII: Uppsala University, Department of Asian and African Languages, 11–14 August 1996*, ed. René Lavenant, 373–386. Rome: Pontificio Istituto Orientale.

———. 2003. "Mār Abā and the Impact of Zoroastrianism on Christianity in the 6th Century." In *Religious Themes and Texts of Pre-Islamic Iran and Central Asia: Studies in Honour of Professor Gherardo Gnoli on the Occasion of His 65th Birthday on 6th December 2002*, ed. Carlo G. Cereti, Mauro Maggi, and Elio Provasi, 167–173. Wiesbaden: Dr. Ludwig Reichert Verlag.

Jackson, Peter. 1997. "Prester John Redivivus: A Review Article," *JRAS*, series 3, 7: 425–432.

———. 2005. *Mongols and the West, 1221–1410*. Harlow: Pearson.

Jany, János. 2007. "Criminal Justice in Sasanian Persia," *Iranica Antiqua* 42: 347–386.

Jenkins, Philip. 2008. *The Lost History of Christianity: The Thousand-Year Golden Age of the Church in the Middle East, Africa, and Asia—and How It Died*. New York: HarperOne.

Joseph, John. 2000. *The Modern Assyrians of the Middle East: Encounters with Western Christian Missions, Archaeologists, and Colonial Powers*. Leiden: Brill.

Jullien, Christelle. 2004. "Peines et supplices dans les Actes des martyrs persans et droit sassanide: Nouvelles prospections," *Studia Iranica* 33: 243–269.

———, ed. 2008. *Controverse des chrétiens dans l'Iran sassanide*. Paris: Association pour l'avancement des études iraniennes.

Jullien, Christelle, and Florence Jullien. 2001. "La *chronique d'Arbèles*: Propositions pour la fin d'une controverse," *Oriens Christianus* 85: 41–83.

———. 2002a. *Apôtres des confins: Processus missionnaires chrétiens dans l'empire iranien*. Paris: Groupe pour l'étude de la civilisation du Moyen-Orient.

———. 2002b. "Aux frontières de l'iranité: '*naṣrāyē*' et '*krīstyonē*' des inscriptions du *mobad* Kirdīr. Enquête littéraire et historique," *Numen* 49: 282–385.

———. 2003. "Le monachisme dans le Golfe Persique: Six siècles d'histoire." In *L'île de Khārg: Une page de l'histoire du Golfe Persique et du monachisme oriental*, ed. Marie-Joseph Steve, 155–184. Neuchâtel: Recherches et publications.

Jullien, Florence. 2008. *Le monachisme en Perse: La réforme d'Abraham le Grand, père des moines de l'Orient*. CSCO 622. Louvain: Peeters.

Kassis, Antoine, Jean-Baptiste Yon, and Abdo Badwi. 2004. "Les inscriptions syriaques du Liban: Bilan archéologique et historique." In *Les inscriptions syriaques*, ed. Françoise Briquel Chatonnet, Muriel Debié, and Alain Desreumaux, 29–43. Paris: Librarie Orientaliste Paul Geuthner.

Keevak, Michael. 2008. *The Story of a Stele: China's Nestorian Monument and Its Reception in the West, 1625–1916*. Hong Kong: University of Hong Kong Press.

Kennet, Derek. 2007. "The Decline of Eastern Arabia in the Sasanian Period," *Arabian Archaeology and Epigraphy* 18: 26–122.

Kettenhofen, Erich. 1998. "Deportations (ii): In the Parthian and Sasanian Periods," *Encyclopaedia Iranica* 8: 297–308.

King, G. R. D. 1997. "A Nestorian Monastic Settlement on the Island of Ṣīr Banī Yās, Abu Dhabi: A Preliminary Report," *Bulletin of the School of Oriental and African Studies* 60: 221–235.

Kister, M. J. 1968. "Al-Ḥīra: Some Notes on Its Relation with Arabia," *Arabica* 15: 143–169.

Klein, Wassilios. 2004. "A Newly Excavated Church of Syriac Christianity along the Silk Road in Kyrghyzstan," *Journal of Eastern Christian Studies* 56.1: 25–47.

Koltun-Fromm, Naomi. 1996. "A Jewish-Christian Conversation in Fourth-Century Persian Mesopotamia," *Journal of Jewish Studies* 46: 45–63.

Langfeldt, John A. 1994. "Recently Discovered Early Christian Monuments in North-eastern Arabia," *Arabian Archaeology and Epigraphy* 5: 32–60.

Lavenant, René, ed. 1998. *Symposium Syriacum VII: Uppsala University, Department of Asian and African Languages, 11–14 August 1996*. Rome: Pontificio Istituto Orientale.

Lerner, Judith. 1992. "Christianity II: In Pre-Islamic Persia: Material Remains," *Encyclopaedia Iranica* 5: 529–531.

Lieu, Samuel N. C. 1985. *Manichaeism in the Later Roman Empire and Medieval China: A Historical Survey*. Manchester: Manchester University Press.

———. 1994. *Manichaeism in Mesopotamia and the Roman East*. Leiden: E. J. Brill.

———. 2000. "Byzantium, Persia, and China: Interstate Relations on the Eve of the Islamic Conquest." In *Silk Road Studies IV: Realms of the Silk Road, Ancient and Modern*, ed. David Christian and Craig Benjamin, 47–65. Turnhout: Brepols.

———. 2008. "Manichaeism." In *The Oxford Handbook of Early Christian Studies*, ed. Susan Ashbrook Harvey and David G. Hunter, 221–236. Oxford: Oxford University Press.

Macomber, William F. 1968. "The Authority of the Catholicos Patriarch of Seleucia-Ctesiphon." In *I Patriarchi Orientali nel Primo Millennio: Relazione del Congresso tenutosi al Pontificio Istituto Orientale nei giorni 27–30 Dicembre 1967*, 179–200. Rome: Pontificium Institutum Studiorum Orientalium.

———. 1977. "Two Unusual Liturgical Ceremonies of the Chaldean Rite." In *A Tribute to Arthur Vööbus: Studies in Early Christian Literature and Its Environment, Primarily in the Christian East*, ed. Robert H. Fischer, 329–336. Chicago: Lutheran School of Theology at Chicago.

Macuch, Maria. 2003. "Zoroastrian Principles and the Structure of Kinship in Sasanian Iran." In *Religious Themes and Texts of Pre-Islamic Iran and Central Asia: Studies in Honour of Professor Gherardo Gnoli on the Occasion of His 65th Birthday on 6th December 2002*, ed. Carlo G. Cereti, Mauro Maggi, and Elio Provasi, 231–245. Wiesbaden: Dr. Ludwig Reichert Verlag.

McCullough, W. Stewart. 1982. *A Short History of Syriac Christianity to the Rise of Islam*. Chico, CA: Scholars Press.

McDonough, Scott. 2008a. "Bishops or Bureaucrats? Christian Clergy and the State in the Middle Sasanian Period." In *Current Research in Sasanian Archaeology, Art, and History: Proceedings of a Conference Held at Durham University, November 3rd and 4th, 2001*, ed. Derek Kenner and Paul Luft, 87–92: Oxford: Archaeopress.

———. 2008b. "A Second Constantine? The Sasanian King Yazdgard in Christian History and Historiography," *Journal of Late Antiquity* 1: 127–141.

Mikkelsen, Gunnar. 2007. "Review of Li Tang's *A Study of the History of Nestorian Christianity in China and Its Literature in Chinese* (2004)," *China Review International* 14.1: 232–235.

Morony, Michael G. 1984. *Iraq after the Muslim Conquest*. Princeton, NJ: Princeton University Press.

———. 2003. "Magic and Society in Late Sasanian Iraq." In *Prayer, Magic, and the Stars in the Ancient and Late Antique World*, ed. Scott Noegel, Joel Walker, and Brannon Wheeler, 83–107. University Park: Pennsylvania State University Press.

———. 2008. "Should Sasanian Iran Be Included in Late Antiquity?" *e-Sasanika* 6, www.humanities.uci.edu/sasanika/pdf/e-sasanika6-Morony.pdf.

Mosig-Walburg, Karin. 2007. "Die Christenverfolgung Shâpurs II. vor dem Hintergrund des persisch-römischen Krieges." In *Inkulturation des Christentums im Sasanidenreich*, ed. Arafa Mustafa and Jürgen Tubach, with G. Sophia Vashalomidze, 171–186. Wiesbaden: Reichart Verlag.

Mouterde, Paul. 1939. *Inscriptions en syriaque dialectal a Kāmed (Beq'a)*. Beirut: Imprimerie Catholique.

Müller-Kessler, Christa. 2006. "Syrische Zauberschalen—Korrekturen und Nachträge," *Die Welt des Orients* 36: 116–130.

Mustafa, Arafa, and Jürgen Tubach, with G. Sophia Vashalomidze, eds. 2007. *Inkulturation des Christentums im Sasanidenreich*. Wiesbaden: Reichert Verlag.

Neusner, Jacob. 1969. *A History of the Jews in Babylon, IV: The Age of Shapur II*. Leiden: E. J. Brill.

———. 1971. *Aphrahat and Judaism: The Christian-Jewish Argument in Fourth-Century Iran*. Leiden: E. J. Brill.

———. 1972. "Babylonian Jewry and Shapur II's Persecution of Christianity from 339 to 379 A.D.," *Hebrew Union College Annual* 43: 77–102.

Okada, Yasuyoshi. 1991. "Early Christian Architecture in the Iraqi South-Western Desert," *Al-Rāfidān* 12: 71–83.

Panaino, Antonio. 2008. "The Zoroastrian Incestuous Unions in Christian Sources and Canonical Laws: Their (Distorted) Aetiology and Some Other Problems." In *Controverse des chrétiens dans l'Iran sassanide*, ed. Christelle Jullien, 69–87. Paris: Association pour l'avancement des études iraniennes.

Paykova, A.V. 1979. "The Syrian Ostracon from Panjikant," *Le Muséon* 92: 159–169.

Pierre, Marie-Joseph. 1995. "Un synode contestataire à l'époque d'Aphraate le sage persan." In *La controverse religieuse et ses formes*, ed. Alain Le Boulluec, 243–279. Paris: Cerf and Centre d'études des religions du livre.

———. 2008. "Thèmes de la controverse d'Aphraate avec les tendances judaïsantes de son église." In *Controverse des chrétiens dans l'Iran sassanide*, ed. Christelle Jullien, 115–128. Paris: Association pour l'avancement des études iraniennes.

Potts, Daniel T. 1994. "Nestorian Crosses from Jabal Berri," *Arabian Archaeology and Epigraphy* 6: 61–65.

———. 1996. *Mesopotamian Civilization: The Material Foundations*. Ithaca, NY: Cornell University Press.

Rist, Josef. 1996. "Die Verfolgung der Christen im spätantiken Sasanidenreich: Ursachen, Verlauf und Folgen," *Oriens Christianus* 80: 17–42.

Rouwhorst, G. 1981. "Das manichaeische Bemafest und das Passafest der syrischen Christen," *Vigiliae Christianae* 35.4: 397–411.

———. 1997. "Jewish Liturgical Traditions in Early Syriac Christianity," *Vigiliae Christianae* 51: 72–93.

Ryan, James. 1998. "Christian Wives of Mongol Khans: Tartar Queens and Missionary Expectations in Asia," *Journal of the Royal Asiatic Society* n.s. 8: 411–421.

Savchenko, Alexei. 1996. "Urgut Revisited," *ARAM: Journal of Syro-Mesopotamian Studies* 8: 333–354.

Schmitz, Bertram. 2007. "Die Tauftradition der nestorianischen Kirche und die Frage der Inkulturation." In *Inkulturation des Christentums im Sasanidenreich*, ed. Arafa Mustafa and Jürgen Tubach, with G. Sophia Vashalomidze, 281–293. Wiesbaden: Reichert Verlag.

Schwaigert, Wolfgang. 1995. "Katholikos Isaak (399–410 n. Chr.) und seine Zeit: Ein Beitrag zur nestorianischen Patriarchengeschichte." In *Syrisches Christentum weltweit: Studien zur syrischen Kirchengeschichte: Festschrift Prof. Wolfgang Hage*, ed. Martin Tamcke, Wolfgang Schwaigert, and Egbert Schlarb, 180–189. Münster: LIT.

Shaked, Shaul. 1997. "Popular Religion in Sasanian Babylonia," *Jerusalem Studies in Arabic and Islam* 21: 103–117.

———. 2000. " Manichaean Incantation Bowls in Syriac," *Jerusalem Studies in Arabic and Islam* 24: 58–92.

Simpson, St. J. 2005. "Christians at Nineveh in Late Antiquity," *Iraq* 67.1: 285–294.

Sims-Williams, Nicholas. 1992. "Christianity iv: Christian Literature in Middle Iranian Languages," *Encyclopaedia Iranica* 5: 534–535.

Stephan, St. H. 1934. "A Nestorian Hermitage between Jericho and the Jordan," *Quarterly of the Department of Antiquities in Palestine* 4: 81–86.

Stern, Sacha. 2004. "Near Eastern Lunar Calendars in the Syriac Martyr Acts," *Le Muséon* 117: 447–472.

Steve, Marie-Joseph. 2003. *L'île de Khārg: Une page de l'histoire du Golfe Persique et du monachisme oriental.* Neuchâtel: Recherches et publications.

Taft, Robert. 1968. "Some Notes on the Bema in the East and West Syrian Traditions," *Orientalia Christiana Periodica* 34: 326–359. [Reprinted in Taft, 1995, *Liturgy in Byzantium and Beyond*, sec. 7. Aldershot: Variorum.]

———. 1970. "On the Use of the Bema in the East-Syrian Liturgy," *Eastern Churches Review* 3: 30–39. [Reprinted in Taft, 1995, *Liturgy in Byzantium and Beyond*, sec. 8. Aldershot: Variorum.]

———. 1995. *Liturgy in Byzantium and Beyond.* Aldershot: Variorum.

Tamcke, Martin. 1988. *Der Katholikos-Patriarch Sabrišo' I. (596–604) und das Mönchtum.* Frankfurt am Main: Peter Lang.

———, ed. 2007. *Christians and Muslims in Dialogue in the Islamic Orient of the Middle Ages/Christlich-muslimische Gespräche im Mittelalter.* Beirut: Orient-Institut der DMG Beirut.

Tamcke, Martin, Wolfgang Schwaigert, and Egbert Schlarb, eds. 1995. *Syrisches Christentum weltweit: Studien zur syrischen Kirchengeschichte: Festschrift Prof. Wolfgang Hage.* Münster: LIT.

Tardieu, Michel. 1993. "Le golfe Arabo-persique dans la littérature manichéene," *Annuaire du Collège de France* 93: 449–554.

———. 2008. "Le schème hérésiologique de désignation des adversaires dans l'inscription nestorienne chinoise de Xi'an." In *Controverse des chrétiens dans l'Iran sassanide*, ed. Christelle Jullien, 207–226. Paris: Association pour l'avancement des études iraniennes.

Tardy, René. 1999. *Najrân: Chrétiens d'Arabie avant l'islam*. Beirut: Dar el-Machreq Éditeurs.

Teule, Herman G. B. 1994. "The Perception of the Jerusalem Pilgrimage in Syriac Monastic Circles." In *VI Symposium Syriacum 1992: University of Cambridge, Faculty of Divinity, 30 August–2 September 1992*, ed. René Lavenant, 311–321. Rome: Pontificio Istituto Orientale.

———. 2002. "Middle Eastern Christians and Migration: Some Reflections," *Journal of Eastern Christian Studies* 54: 1–23.

Varghese, Baby. 2007. "East Syrian Liturgy during the Sasanian Period." In *Inkulturation des Christentums im Sasanidenreich*, ed. Arafa Mustafa and Jürgen Tubach, with G. Sophia Vashalomidze, 269–280. Wiesbaden: Reichert Verlag.

Van Rompay, Lucas. 1995. "Impetuous Martyrs? The Situation of the Persian Christians in the Last Years of Yazdgard I (419–420)." In *Martyrium in Multidisciplinary Perspective: Memorial Louis Reekmans*, ed. M. Lamberigts and P. van Deun, 363–375. Louvain: Louvain University Press.

Walker, Joel Thomas. 1998. "The Limits of Late Antiquity: Philosophy between Rome and Iran," *Ancient World* 33: 45–69.

———. 2006. *The Legend of Mar Qardagh: Narrative and Christian Heroism in Late Antique Iraq*. Berkeley: University of California Press.

Watt, John. 2004. "Syriac Translators and Greek Philosophy in Early Abbasid Iraq," *Journal of the Canadian Society for Syriac Studies* 4: 15–26.

Wiesehöfer, Josef. 1996. *Ancient Persia: From 550 BC to 650 AD*. Trans. Azizeh Azodi. London: I. B. Tauris.

Wigram, William W. 1910. *An Introduction to the History of the Assyrian Church or the Church of the Sasanid Persian Empire: 100–640 A.D.* London: Society for Promoting Christian Knowledge.

———. 1929. *The Assyrians and Their Neighbors*. London: G. Bell and Sons. [Repr. Piscataway, NJ: Gorgias Press, 2002].

Williams, A. V. 1996. "Zoroastrians and Christians in Sasanian Iran," *Bulletin of the John Rylands Library of Manchester* 78.3: 37–57.

Wolska-Conus, Wanda. 1962. *La Topographie chrétienne de Cosmas Indicopleustès: Théologie et science au VIe siècle*. Paris: Presses Universitaires de France.

CHAPTER 32

EARLY ISLAM AS A LATE ANTIQUE RELIGION

ROBERT HOYLAND

Oriental Institute and St. Cross College, Oxford University

Introduction

> His [Henri Pirenne's] thesis that the advent of Islam in the Mediterranean sealed the end of Late Antiquity remains valid.
>
> —(Herrin 1987, 134)

> We have expended a good deal of energy, both scholastic and intellectual, on taking seriously the obvious fact that the formation of Islamic civilisation took place in the world of Late Antiquity.
>
> —(Crone and Cook 1977, vii)

At first sight, the developments in the seventh-century Middle East seem very new. They do not seem to fit into the world of Late Antiquity as we know it. A man named Muḥammad, described by seventh-century Christian sources as a military leader, a legislator, and a monotheist preacher (Hoyland 2000), persuaded a number of his own people in west Arabia to form a community (*umma*) united in "belief in God and the Last Day," to dissociate themselves from those who would not follow them by making an exodus (*hijra*), and finally to make war (*jihād*) on their opponents to bring them over to their cause or to make them submit (Cook 1983). The movement snowballed until it

Figure 32.1. Wall Painting, Qaryat al-Faw, possibly third century C.E. or earlier (Riyadh National Museum. © Saudi Commission for Tourism & Antiquities). See also color plate section.

engulfed Arabia, and eventually the Arab armies of Muḥammad and his successors (called caliphs), in a series of lightning campaigns, swept away the old empire of Iran and wrested the southern and eastern provinces of the Byzantine empire from its grasp (Kennedy 2007). The kinsmen of the third caliph ʿUthmān, the Umayyads, governed the ever-expanding Muslim Arab world until 132 A.H./750 C.E. (Hawting 2000), and under their rule, new cities sprang up to house the new troops, new sacred buildings (mosques) were erected for their worship, the teachings of Muḥammad were proclaimed in inscriptions written in a new language and new script (Arabic), and so on. And this sense of discordance with Late Antiquity's rhythms is reinforced by the Muslim sources for this early period, which speak principally of internal quarrels among the Muslims, names of holders of high office, and battles against amorphous external foes; the colorful characters of Late Antiquity are no more than faceless taxpayers and occasional rebels. So in what sense can we consider early Islam a late antique religion, or should we call it such at all (Robinson 2003)?

It is helpful when considering this question to look a little at the history of the idea of Late Antiquity. One might start with Henri Pirenne (1937), who, though negative about the effects of the Muslim conquest, is actually a positive influence in that he extended the life of Roman civilization. Gibbon was wrong; not all was lost with the Germanic invasions; rather, urban life and the culture that went with it continued until the Muslim invasions. This extension of Rome's dominion was given very concrete realization with the publication of A. H. M. Jones's *The Later Roman Empire* (1964), which offered a very thorough and detailed account of the history and institutions of the Roman realm up until 602. The focus and interest of both scholars were firmly rooted in the Roman sphere of things, and other cultures and peoples only got a look when they affected Rome—so Iran features only when it launches incursions into Roman territory. Nevertheless, the door had been pushed ajar, and this laid the ground for it to be thrown open a few years later by Peter Brown, with his *The World of Late Antiquity* (1971a), an incredibly rich and influential work that gave birth to the discipline of Late Antiquity by virtue of its evocative and sensitive portrayal of this, in his view, vibrant and exotic period. Late Antiquity as an explanatory model was thus devised in reaction to the Gibbonesque model of decline and fall and wariness toward the barbarians at the gates, so it stresses inclusivity, welcomes diversity and difference, and irons out change and rupture by appealing to the *longue durée*. Under this model, it is relatively easy to slip in Islam as another facet of the kaleidoscope world of Late Antiquity, as indeed Peter Brown does very nicely. And in Patricia Crone and Michael Cook's *Hagarism* (1977), Islam becomes a mêlée of Jewish, Christian, and Manichaean ingredients, the ultimate late antique concoction.

This approach has been applied to a whole variety of phenomena across the fourth- to eighth-century Middle East, constituting a veritable "Late Antiquity to early Islam" industry, spawning numerous conferences, workshops, seminars, and collaborative volumes. All are responding to the fact that the Middle East in the fourth century looks very different in the eighth century. A particularly graphic example is provided by changes in cities: straight streets to winding alleys, temples to churches and mosques, wide open public spaces to tightly packed industrial and commercial complexes, and so on (Kennedy 1985; Whittow 1990; Liebeschuetz 2001). The question is what it all means, and here is where the difference of views is evident, ranging from decadent decline to exciting evolution. The emergence of Islam is omnipresent in this debate, representing for the advocates of a long Late Antiquity the consummation of changes already under way long before. However, the traditional Muslim model would argue that Muḥammad and the Qur'ān usher in a new age, one that erases all before it, one that generates its own concepts and principles, one that neither needed nor heeded foreign elements and alien wisdoms. And the clash of civilizations model of Samuel Huntington and others has impelled a number of late antique historians to emphasize that the Muslim world was very different from its predecessors, to be less shy of speaking of confrontation and conquest, and to cut off Late Antiquity before the emergence of Islam, seeing it as the straw that broke Late Antiquity's back and pushed the Middle East into the medieval age.[1]

In what follows, I shall first adduce a few examples of ways in which early Islam might be seen as conforming to the late antique model and then return at the end to the question of whether it makes sense to see early Islam as a late antique religion.

The Problem of the Sources

> The creation of the past which was achieved through this creation of [an Arabic historical] tradition tacitly excluded all outsiders to Arabia. Jews and Christians, Persians and East Romans were allotted "walk-on parts," but little more. The immensely rich but inward-looking Arabic historical tradition virtually ignored the intimacy and the complexity of the relations between the Arabs and the other cultures of the Near East.
>
> —(Brown 2003, 301)

Before proceeding, however, I should add a cautionary note, namely, that tracing the development of the early Islamic religion is a very difficult task. The source material tends to give the impression that Muḥammad and his companions brought forth Islam complete and that later scholars merely codified and interpreted it. Moreover, many Western scholars would argue that the numerous accounts we have of the life of Muḥammad and his companions are a late distillation of an oral history that has been much transformed and distorted in the course of its transmission and, more important, that alternative versions have been edited out (Humphreys 1991, 25–68; see also Shoemaker, chapter 33 in this book). This means, as one critic has put it, that "one can take the picture presented or one can leave it, but one cannot work with it" (Crone 1980, 4). Such a situation has had the effect of polarizing the study of early Islam into two camps: traditionalists who accept the picture and revisionists who reject it (Nevo and Koren 1991). In the hope of breaking the deadlock, attempts have been made to rely solely on non-Muslim sources (Crone and Cook 1977) and archaeological evidence (Nevo and Koren 2003), both of which, though yielding important insights, are too scanty to provide a credible alternative vision (Hoyland 1997; 2006). This situation has been made worse by recent political events such as September 11, 2001, and the invasion of Iraq, which have tended to engender and heighten tensions between the civilizations of the West and the Middle East and to push scholars into either being apologists for Islam (supporting the traditional account) or polemicists against Islam (opposing the traditional account). Yet though a detailed depiction of the evolution of early Islam over its first two centuries is not yet possible, its general outlines are clear enough (and confirmed by non-Muslim and archaeological evidence) to be able to permit some assessment of the question of Islam's place in Late Antiquity.

Rapprochement between Religion and Politics and Universalist Vision

The Islamic empire was implicit in Late Antiquity.
—(Fowden 1993, 138)

Although one of the most important features of the late antique model is to stress continuity, the period before the advent of Islam was nevertheless one of great upheaval and transformation. In the first place, the loose territorial empires of the Romans and Parthians had given way to the integrated ecumenical empires of the Byzantines and Sasanians (Garsoïan 1983; Howard-Johnston 1995). Their close proximity, the result of Rome's shift to the east in the second century, and the assertiveness of the Sasanian dynasty of Iran, in comparison with their complacent predecessors, led to confrontation (Greatrex and Lieu 2000). Inevitably, such emulation between states of similar standing engendered large-scale political, social, and cultural change. Both moved toward greater administrative centralization and absolutist government, to the detriment of civic autonomy in Byzantium and of the provincial nobility in Sasanian Iran. In the second place, the ruling elites no longer remained indifferent to the beliefs of the masses. Indeed, the emperors of both realms, now sharing their creed with the majority of their subjects, evinced an interest in the promotion of religious uniformity within their lands, intervening in matters of religious dispute among their subjects.

Thus the religions of Late Antiquity tend to be intricately linked with power. Christianity provides the most visible illustration, the conversion of Constantine the Great ensuring an intimate connection that became ever closer. But Judaism, too, won over ruling elites in various times and places, most famously the Himyarite dynasty of south Arabia (Robin 2003; 2004), which in the sixth century instigated a persecution of the Christians in their land. The reason for this was that the latter were loyal to the Byzantines, who supported the Ethiopians, who had territorial ambitions in south Arabia, another example of the enmeshing of religion and politics at that time (Shahîd 1979; Munro-Hay 1991, esp. 85–92). Zoroastrian clergy were keen to court the overlords of Iran and to emphasize how much religion and politics were twins, each reinforcing the other (Huyse 1998). And Manichaeism, though ultimately unsuccessful, tried hard to enlist the support of states: the prophet Mani himself visited the courts of three successive Persian emperors.

Seen in this light, early Islam looks very much like a child of Late Antiquity. Muḥammad was not just a preacher, but leader of the Muslim community of Medina: its legislator, military director, and arbiter in all matters of religion. His successors, who led the young Muslim community to capture and rule the Middle East, were termed "commander of the believers" and "deputy of God" (Crone and Hinds 1986). Disagreement over the powers and conduct of such leaders led to a number of civil wars, the upshot of which was a split in the Muslim community between those who believed that the leaders should combine political and religious power (eventually crystallizing into the Shīʿī sect) and those who preferred a separation of powers (eventually crystallizing into the Sunnī sect), handing matters of religion over to scholars and government to secular rulers (sultans). But this was still in the future, and in early Islamic times a majority felt that the community was best served by a leader who combined both powers, the only source of dispute being the election and identity of such a person.

The eyes of the rulers of Byzantium and Iran were not only on their own lands but also on those beyond, for indeed one of the appeals of Christianity to Constantine and his successors was its universalism. This made the emperor the representative of God over all mankind, in whose name the message could be carried via military campaigns to the whole world. Zoroastrianism was closer to Judaism than Christianity in that it was chiefly the religion of a nation and evinced little sensitivity to the problem of the clash between orthodoxy and heresy that so affected Christianity, and it was therefore more tolerant than the latter in the face of religious difference. Yet the Sasanian emperors did urge some conformity (enacting calendrical and liturgical reforms, outlawing images in favor of sacred fires), suppressed overt dissent (e.g., Mazdakism), were usually hostile to missionary efforts by Christians, and occasionally struck a more universalist note (e.g., Shapur II asks a Christian martyr: "What god is better than Ahuramazda? Which one is stronger than Ahreman? What sensible human being does not worship the sun?"—cited by Shaked 1994, 91).

Again, viewed against this background, it becomes evident that Islam did not, initially at least, "seal the end of Late Antiquity," but rather continued one of its most salient features. The expansionist aims of Justinian, Khusrau II, and other late antique emperors were pursued with alacrity by the youthful Muslim state. And via the bold and dramatic visual statement of the structure and location (on the Temple Mount in Jerusalem) of the Dome of the Rock, as well as via the inscriptions upon it, the caliph ʿAbd al-Malik proclaimed that "the true religion with God is Islam" and felt justified in remonstrating the Jews and the Christians for their lax monotheist views. Evidently, the Dome of the Rock was meant for them as well and was not just a Muslim monument (Raby and Johns 1979; 2000). This echoes the Qur'ān's appeal to Jews and Christians to return to the original message of God given to Abraham, Moses, and Jesus, subsequently corrupted by later generations, but brought again pure by Muḥammad. This is what lies behind the quotation from Fowden cited previously, a sense that Islam is the fulfillment of Late Antiquity's dynamic, by virtue of its achievement of politico-religious universalism.

Autonomous Religious Communities

> Large Christian groups, Chalcedonians quite as much as Monophysites, were prepared to forget ancient loyalties to their cities. Religion provided them with a more certain, more deeply felt basis of communal identity. Even when they lived in villages and cities where their own church predominated, they had come to see themselves first and foremost, as members of a religious community. They were fellow-believers. They were no longer fellow citizens.
>
> —(Brown 2003, 189)

> The arrival of the Arabs merely cut the last threads that had bound the provincials of the Near East to the Roman Empire.
>
> —(Brown 1971a, 187)

> Wansbrough considers the Qur'ān . . . to be a product of what he has aptly called the "sectarian milieu" of interconfessional and political polemics. In this arena . . . Christians, Jews, Zoroastrians, and Believers, or proto-Muslims, bounced ideas and claims off one another until . . . all groups had clearly defined their theological, ritual, and sociological boundaries.
>
> —(Donner 1998, 69)

The drive toward greater integration and conformity on the part of the state, which intensified during the sixth century as a result of an escalation of the conflict between the two superpowers, provoked those sectarian groups jealous of their own independence to establish a certain distance between themselves and imperial culture. Gradually, and especially in pluralist Iraq, they transformed themselves into communal organizations with their own schools, law courts, places of worship, religious hierarchy, and so on. They were effectively socio-legal corporations ordered along religious lines, and this is one of the most salient features of Late Antiquity (Morony 1974; Fowden 2001). It was within this environment that Islam grew up, and it willingly continued and even extended these trends. It divided up the world primarily along religious lines, seeing only believers (*ahl al-islām*) and infidels (*ahl al-kufr*). The latter were generally left—indeed, expected—to manage their own affairs and to conduct themselves according to their own laws and beliefs (Edelby 1950–1951;

Fattal 1951; Goitein 1970). The only major demand made of them was that they pay a special tax (*jizya*) to demonstrate their twin shame of having been conquered and having rejected the true religion and its prophet Muḥammad. This laissez-faire attitude was noted of the Muslim conquerors by a north-Mesopotamian resident, John bar Penkāyē, writing in the 680s: "Their robber bands went annually to distant parts and to the islands, bringing back captives from all the peoples under the heavens. Of each person they required only tribute, allowing them to remain in whatever faith they wished. . . . There was no distinction between pagan and Christian, the faithful was not known from a Jew" (Mingana 1907, 147/175, 151/179). For their part, the early Muslims preferred to distance themselves from the conquered population, living in separate garrison towns and eschewing the customs and practices of others (Kister 1989). But their possession of wealth and power meant that the conquered peoples would inevitably seek them out, whether to win their support in internal conflicts, earn a share in their privileges and riches, or simply to seek a living in their employ. So the garrison towns became cosmopolitan cities in which Muslims and non-Muslims interacted in a variety of different ways.

In return for paying their taxes, the non-Muslims received a guarantee of protection (*dhimma*) with regard to their lives and property and the right to practice their faith without hindrance (Ayoub 1983). Since certain Qur'ānic verses (e.g., 22:17, 98:1) distinguish between possessors of a Scripture sent by the one God (*ahl al-kitāb*) and polytheists (*ahl al-shirk*), some Muslims argued that only the former qualified for protection, whereas the latter should be fought to the death. But as the Muslims pushed further east, vanquishing such peoples as the Zoroastrians and the Hindus, any initial objections were soon brushed aside, and the category of people qualifying for protected status (*ahl al-dhimma*) expanded to comprise pretty much all non-Muslims. Thus Muḥammad ibn al-Qāsim (d. 96/715), the first Muslim general to conquer an Indian town and to face the problem of what to do with its population, ruled that their holy places were "akin to the churches of the Christians and the synagogues of the Jews and the fire-temples of the Zoroastrians" (Baladhuri 1866, *Futūḥ* 439). And this judgment formed the theoretical basis for subsequent Muslim tolerance of Hindus and their worship. The only major exception to this principle involved non-Muslim Arabs, who, whether the pagan Arabs of Muḥammad's Arabia or the Christian Arabs of the Fertile Crescent, were sometimes the target of Muslim missionary efforts.

Besides the requirement to pay taxes and abide by their own laws, there were a number of rules for social conduct that non-Muslims were expected to observe. These most famously appear listed in the so-called Pact of 'Umar, which purports to be a letter sent at the time of the Muslim conquests from the Christians of Syria to the caliph 'Umar I, requesting protection and promising observance of certain obligations. The document has provoked much discussion regarding both its authenticity and its significance. Earlier scholars tended to consider it a late invention and as an indication of the discrimination and isolation endured by non-Muslims of later times. More recently, it has been argued that the list does reflect the conditions of the earliest period of the conquests and that its contents were intended for the benefit of the Muslims rather than for the detriment of the non-Muslims (Noth 1987). Faced with a massive majority population of non-Muslims, the conquerors instituted measures to erect boundaries between themselves and the conquered peoples to prevent their assimilation after the fashion of the Germanic conquerors of Rome and so many Central Asian conquerors of China. For example, one item on the list concerns the belt known as the *zunnār* (*cf. Gr. zōnē*). Since Christians wore such a thing before Islam, it is evident that the initial aim of the prescription to wear it was not to humiliate Christians, but rather to make it possible to distinguish them from Muslims. By this and many other measures, the Muslims thus made themselves into a distinct religious community.

Wansbrough's term *sectarian milieu* (1978) could be applied to the late antique and early Islamic Middle East in general, for groups of numerous different persuasions devoted a considerable amount of time to defining their own doctrinal stance and refuting that of others. This is reflected in the very high number of disputation texts produced in this period (Cameron 1991; 1994; 2003). These would be disseminated by religious leaders of confessional communities whose task it was to reinforce allegiance to their respective communities. Islam was born into this sectarian milieu and, from its very beginnings, would seem to have embraced it. A large proportion of the Qur'ān is devoted to discussions with and polemic against Jews, Christians, those who ascribe partners to God (*mushrikūn*), and hypocrites. The inscriptions on the aforementioned Dome of the Rock are much preoccupied with admonishments to the Jews and Christians, in particular urging the latter "not to say three; refrain, it is better for you; God is only one god." And Muslim scholars argued heatedly among themselves about such issues as determinism versus free will, the relationship between revelation and reason, the ingredients of right belief, the relative weight to be given to faith and good works, the nature of the caliphate, and membership of the Muslim community (in particular, whether evil deeds voided your membership, so making you an infidel and your life forfeit). Over time, this resulted in the emergence of a mainstream position, who came to be called Sunnīs, and those who refused to accept this mainstream position, most famously Shī'īs and Khārijīs, were labeled heretics by the Sunnīs. The Sunnī position was then strenuously asserted by an array of creeds and heresiographies that aimed to show Sunnīs as the one saved sect and all other groups as damned (Wensinck 1932; Van Ess 2002, 17–44; 2006).

The disputes between the different monotheisms also gave rise to a very substantial literary production. The roots of these controversies between the Muslims and their subject peoples went back to the late seventh and early eighth centuries, when Islam first began to present itself on coins and other media as "the true religion," so challenging other faiths. But the literary manifestation of the debate only gathered momentum once Arabic, established as the administrative language of the empire by late Umayyad times, had become accepted as the international medium of scholarship. The presence of a lingua franca enabled the debate to cross sectarian lines, as did the universal deployment of dialectical reasoning based on categorical definitions, and also the proliferation of converts and apostates, which meant that there were many with a genuine knowledge of two religions and with a real will to champion one over the other. But also, quite simply, there were matters that needed debating. Islam prompted questions that had not previously arisen, such as what were the attributes of a true prophet (a question scarcely considered by pre-Islamic Christian and Jewish authorities) and how could one recognize an authentic Scripture, and one can observe these and other questions being broached in an original way (Griffith 1979).

The Qur'ān and Late Antique Piety

> The Qur'ānic emphasis on piety and morality thus informs and dominates each of the . . . different forms of Qur'ānic material. . . . Qur'ānic piety continued these late antique traditions of piety.
>
> —(Donner 1998, 72)

In this quotation, Donner argues that we should view the Qur'ān as a late antique text on account of its firm emphasis on piety, a piety that had its roots in deep-seated trends and currents in Late Antiquity. By this, he means the way in which the Qur'ān, whether it is imparting a story, law, or admonition, always couches it in the language of obedience and disobedience to God, of carrying out his will and doing good works or rejecting his message and acting wickedly in the world. Donner sees this as being fully in tune with Late Antiquity's preoccupation with religion and piety. He extends this "concern for piety" to the early Islamic community at large, and it is indeed striking how much early Islamic inscriptions are focused on demonstrations of piety and how much their content is related to Qur'ānic and wider monotheistic ideas of piety. The religious devotional vocabulary of these early inscriptions is inspired by and suffused with the lexicon of the Qur'ān. For example, the three most common wishes of these texts, particularly the graffiti, are to ask for forgiveness (*gh-f-r*), seek compassion (*r-ḥ-m*), and make a declaration of/bear witness to the faith (*'-m-n/sh-h-d*), each of these a prominent theme and root in the Qur'ān: *gh-f-r* 234 times, *r-ḥ-m* 339 times, *'-m-n* 767 times (i.e., *āmana*/believe 537 times and *mu'min*/believer 230 times), and *sh-h-d* 199 times (including *shahīd*/witness 56 times).

Commonly, especially in the case of graffiti, an inscription consists of a collage of phrases assembled from different verses of the Qur'ān, it presumably being considered that creative citation and handling of the Qur'ān was acceptable. For example, the text from Medina, "my Lord, Lord of the heavens and earth and what is between them, there is no God but He, and so I adopt him as a protector" (al-Rāshid 1993, no. 21), is put together from Q 26.24 (or 37.5, 38.66, 44.7, 38) and 73:9, with a small amendment to personalize the quotation ("I adopt him" rather than "you adopt him!"). And the text "I believe that there is no god except Him in whom the children of Israel believed, (believing as) a Muslim *ḥanīf* nor am I among the associators" quotes verbatim part of Q 10.90 and then adapts a statement about Abraham (3.67) to suit the inscriber (Donner 1984, W1).

There are two other ways the Qur'ān plays a role in early inscriptions that are worth mention. One is brief allusion to a Qur'ānic topic, and this has the effect of clearly indicating one's allegiance to and membership of the community of those who understand the reference. A nice example is a short graffito found in the Ḥijāz on the Syrian pilgrimage route, dated 83/702 (Hamed 1988, III.238), that states simply: "I believe in what the residents of al-Ḥijr denied" (*āmantu bi-mā kadhdhaba bi-hi aṣḥāb al-Ḥijr*). This refers to Q 15.80: "The residents of al-Ḥijr denied the messengers," that is, the ones sent by God to exhort the people of al-Ḥijr to heed God's message. This graffito is clearly a profession of faith but decipherable as such only to those familiar with the Qur'ān.

A second way of using the Qur'ān is to engrave on one's chosen, usually highly visible, rock face a single unadapted verse of the Qur'ān, with no additional verbiage, bar one's name and a date. Onto a basalt rock face south of Mecca, for example, there have been etched, in a fine imperial Umayyad hand,[2] two verses of the Qur'ān, 4.87 and 38.26, both by a certain 'Uthmān and dated 80 A.H./699 (Fahmī 1987). What are we to make of this practice? Donner focuses on the religious content of these texts, observing that "the Believers at first seem to have had little interest in leaving for posterity any reference to tribal ties, politics, confessionalism, or systematic theology, all of which paled into insignificance in comparison with their need to prepare for the impending Judgment through proper piety" (Donner 1998, 88). This, however, does not take into account that inscriptions are not mere statements of fact, but are public declarations intended to portray a particular image of their commissioners, thereby to obtain respect, status, prestige, and the like via a display of virtue (however that might be construed in the pertinent culture) and, if well engraved, a display of wealth, for to hire a good stonemason was expensive.[3] However, Donner is right inasmuch as the very etching of a Qur'ānic verse was evidently perceived as symbolic of pious action and perhaps as a reminder or call to others of the word of God, without any need for further comment or elaboration. It was presumably also a declaration of religious allegiance in a world where one's Scripture was a badge of identity.

Holy Persons and Holy Places

> Under Islam, monasteries and their holy men continued to fill a niche in the landscape and society of the late antique Middle East. Only now, the visitors who passed through the monastic complexes included Muslims. . . . For many early Muslims it seems that Christian practices and beliefs acted as stimuli along the way to the formation of a distinctively Islamic way of holiness and asceticism.
>
> —(Fowden and Fowden 2004, 162)

Probably the single most popular topic of late antique studies has been the tendency of Christianity and Judaism to locate spiritual power in particular persons, who then serve as objects of veneration, models for imitation, or intercessors with God, holy men in the terms of Peter Brown (1971b). Though the Qur'ān is strongly monotheist, insisting on a concentration of the sacred in the godhead, early Islam nevertheless allowed a certain degree of seepage, which in later times became a flood. In particular, visiting tombs and shrines of holy people (*ziyāra*) and seeking out those exceptional, blessed people who are close to God (*walī*) were intrinsic features of medieval Islam (Meri 2002).

Assuming one can believe the general tenor of what one reads in the later sources, then there are a number of different contenders for the role of holy man in early Islam (Robinson 1999). First, there are the fiery rebels against the centralizing and nepotistic use of power by the Umayyad dynasty, whom we know as Khārijīs. They are portrayed as Zorro-style bandits living a life of asceticism, raiding, and revolution on behalf of their version of Islam and Islamic rule. A good example is Saliḥ ibn Musarriḥ, who was a thorn in the Umayyads' side in Mesopotamia and fought on a platform of, so we read, "fear of God, abstinence in this world, desire for the next, frequent remembrance of death, separation from the sinners, and love for the believers" and preparedness "to fight against . . . the oppressive errant leaders" (Morony 1984, 475–476). Sālih was perhaps a holy man after the fashion of the Prophet Muḥammad, marrying piety and military activism in God's way, but it was inevitably one that the authorities tried to suppress, especially when they were its targets, and they might well be responsible for the promulgation of the idea that jihad is, in postconquest times, of the heart and mind.

Second, there are the various 'Alid leaders, that is, those who were of the family of 'Alī ibn Abī Ṭālib (perceived by many to be owed loyalty because of his marriage to Muḥammad's daughter Fāṭima) or those who led movements on behalf of this family. Examples of the former include Muḥammad ibn al-Ḥanifiyya and ʿAbd Allāh ibn Muʿāwiya, and of the latter, Bayān ibn Samʿān, Abū Manṣūr al-ʿIjli, and al-Mughīra ibn Saʿid. Such figures not only combined piety and activism but also were alleged to have possessed prophetic powers, tapping into a different aspect of Muḥammad's holy-man qualities. The teachings attributed to them often seem to draw on Zoroastrian and/or Gnostic ideas, such as the transmigration of souls (*tanāsukh*), indwelling of God's spirit (*ḥulūl*), dualism of light and darkness, the existence of a chosen elite, and elaborate cosmologies and creation myths (Tucker 2008). Such teachings seemed, however, highly suspect in the eyes of the religious mainstream, who labeled those who held them to be *ghulāt*, "extremists," and the possession of supernatural powers among ʿAlids became restricted to a defined series of imams in the direct line of Fāṭima and ʿAlī.

These two types of holy man seem rather distant from the classic type so beloved by fans of late antique religious history. However, there is a third type in early Islam who seems much closer to the late antique spiritual hero, namely, the more pluralist, end-of-the-world-fearing kind, who believes, as allegedly did the most famous exponent of this type, Ḥasan al-Baṣrī, that one should make this world a bridge over which one crosses but on which one does not build (Mourad 2005). Mālik ibn Dīnār al-Sāmī, a preacher and ascetic in late-seventh-to early-eighth-century Basra, would frequent monasteries and is reported to have conversed about ascetic practices with a monk and to have replied to the monk's query about whether he was a follower of the Qur'ān that indeed he was, but that that would not deter him from sitting at the feet of the Christian master. Khālid ibn Maʿdān, another late-first-century A. H. ascetic, advocated going hungry and rebuking the soul so that one might perchance see God. And indeed he himself died fasting, and from his habit of doing 10,000 rosaries per day, his fingers still kept moving after his death, so reported the washer of his corpse. Numerous such figures are encountered in the annals of the early Islamic world (Mourad 2004; Avdinli 2007), and it is with them that we are closest to the heroic holy men of Late Antiquity who spent decades perched on columns or lodged up trees, engaged in constant prayer and devotion and dispensing wisdom and miracles to their throngs of admirers and petitioners. Not surprisingly, it is this sort of holy man that proponents of the long Late Antiquity highlight, and, indeed, examples of this type continued to be found in the Muslim Middle East, but officially there was a toning down of their sacred powers. The official version, the *walī Allāh*, "friend of God," performed miracles privately rather than in public (*karāmāt* versus *muʿjizāt*), received inspiration and insight rather than revelation (*ilhām* and *firāsa* versus *waḥy*), and their asceticism is moderate and measured. Or perhaps we should see them as different types: other-worldly ascetics, who reject this earthly existence and minimize their interaction with it, and inner-worldly ascetics, who work to remedy the injustice of this world while minimizing what they take from it for themselves (Cooperson 1997).

Apocalypticism

> His (Muḥammad's) fundamental doctrine . . . is that the times announced by Daniel and Jesus having now come, Muḥammad was the last prophet, chosen by God to preside, together with Christ, returned to earth for that purpose, at the end of time, over the universal resurrection and the Last Judgement.
>
> —(Casanova 1911, 8)

Judaism, Zoroastrianism, and Christianity all shared a teleological view of history, and consequently, all produced their fair share of visionaries to interpret the significance of events and to depict the end of times. At the approach of some significant date or on the occasion of some momentous disaster, eschatological speculation could become apocalyptic. Thus when it was the 500th anniversary of the Incarnation, supposedly marking the 6,000th year since Creation, "the end of the world was awaited as never before"; and when in 557, Constantinople was shaken by a series of tremors, "immediately fantastic and fallacious pronouncements began to circulate, to the effect that the whole world was on the point of perishing. For certain deceivers, behaving like self-inspired oracles, prophesied whatever came into their heads and terrified all the more the populace who were already thoroughly disposed to be terrified" (Magdalino 1993, 5–6, citing the sixth-century writers Simplicius and Agathias). The great war between Byzantium and Iran in the years 603 to 628 spawned much apocalyptic agonizing, for it seemed to reflect the final battles spoken of in the book of Daniel and in the New Testament, and Heraclius was portrayed as a redeemer-like figure, come to save Christianity and to hand it over to the Messiah himself (Reinink 2002).

Early Islam would seem to have caught this spirit, and indeed the very earliest teaching of Muḥammad was suffused with such a mood, if we can judge from the Qur'ān, which devotes much space to a depiction of the events preceding the Day of Judgment and of the day itself. It seems worthwhile giving an example to demonstrate the vividness and drama of the description: "When heaven is split open, when the stars are scattered, when the seas swarm over, when the tombs are overthrown, then a soul shall know its own works" (82.1–5). This mood continued for several decades, and numerous apocalyptic predictions survive that infer from the trials and triumphs of the early Muslim community the date of time's end. Their greatest worry was whether they would manage to hold on to their acquisitions from their conquests. And at certain key times—such as during their various civil wars, when it looked as if they might lose all, and during their siege of Constantinople in 717, when it looked as if they might gain all—these fears and hopes found their voice in a veritable explosion of apocalyptic sentiment. The battles with their enemies, chiefly the Byzantines, were identified with the *malāḥim*, the final wars at the end of the world that would eventually, after many setbacks, conclude with the Muslim capture of Constantinople and the appearance of the Antichrist. This construction aided the Muslim warriors in weathering any reverses, for they could see that they would ultimately triumph, and it gave added meaning to their efforts, since it was no ordinary war they were fighting, but Armageddon itself (Cook 2003).

In their turn, the Muslims and, in particular, their stunning military victories stimulated apocalyptic fervor among the conquered peoples as they grappled to understand the swift pace of change. Christians viewed Arab rule as the time of testing before the final peace, when the churches would be renewed, the cities rebuilt, and the priests set free from tax. To the Zoroastrians, it was the age of adversity that closed the millennium of Zoroaster and preceded the millennium of Ushedar, in which the Good Religion would flourish. In both cases, the ousting of the Muslims and regeneration of the religion was to be achieved by a savior figure, whether an idealized Christian emperor in the image of Alexander the Great, Constantine, and Jovian or the warrior Bahram coming from India with an army and a thousand elephants to destroy Iran's enemies. Apocalypses thus offered an interpretation for historical change, thereby rendering it more meaningful, and hope for redemption in the near future, thereby encouraging steadfastness (Hoyland 1997, 26–31, 257–335).

Greek Thought

> Islam . . . builds upon and preserves Christian-Antique Hellenism. . . . A time will come when one will learn to understand late Hellenism by looking back from the Islamic tradition.
>
> —(Becker 1924–1932, 1.201)

> Those scholars of Late Antiquity and of medieval Europe who ponder about when the late-antique era ended and the medieval began, can infer from my book that at least as far as the history of metaphysics is concerned, the decisive moment occurred around 1001, in the Samanid library in the city of Bukhara in the Central Asian province of Transoxania, far outside their traditional area of focus.
>
> —(Wisnovsky 2003, 266)

These two quotations point to the feature that most induces Classicists and Byzantinists to see in early Islam a continuation of Late Antiquity, namely, the continued study of the Greek language and Greek scientific texts. Indeed, thousands of texts were translated from Greek into Arabic in the course of the eighth through tenth centuries C.E. So extensive was this activity that modern

Western scholars have labeled it "the translation movement."[4] The appellation is well deserved in that the activity was not sporadic or haphazard, but, to a substantial degree, thorough and systematic. Thus almost all nonliterary and nonhistorical secular Greek works that were available throughout the Byzantine empire and the Middle East were translated into Arabic. A variety of factors lent impetus to this movement. The Arab conquests created a single empire from Morocco to India, which promoted greater movement of goods, people, and ideas across this vast region. Not much more than a century later, the language of the conquerors, Arabic, had established itself as the official language of this empire, further accelerating the flow of ideas. A military encounter between Arab and Chinese forces at Talas in Central Asia in 136/754 resulted in the knowledge and spread in Islamic lands of paper, which was much cheaper and easier to make than papyrus and so lowered the price and raised the availability of the written word. These and other factors were crucial for creating an environment conducive to the translation movement, but perhaps the most direct stimulus was the transfer of the Muslim seat of government from Syria to Iraq in 132/750 and the building of the new capital of Baghdad in 145/762. This placed the 'Abbasids, the dynasty that had carried out the transfer, in the heartlands of the former Sasanian Persian empire. Whereas in Damascus, only a provincial and in any case semi-Arabized city of the Byzantine empire, the Muslim Arabs had been able to withstand pressure to assimilate, in Baghdad they felt very strongly the pull of Persian ideas and style of government (Ahsan 1979; Kennedy 2004). One feature of this was an interest in alien wisdom. So just as the Persian emperors Ardashir, Shapur, and Khusrau I sent to India, China, and Byzantium for books and had them translated into Persian, "such as those of Hermes the Babylonian who ruled over Egypt, Dorotheus the Syrian, Phaedrus the Greek from the city of Athens, famed for its science, and Ptolemy the Alexandrian," so 'Abbasid caliphs did the same, "modelling their conduct on that of the past Sasanian emperors" (Ibn al-Nadīm 1872, *Fihrist* 239; Mas'ūdī 1866–1874, *Murūj* 8.300–301). The caliph Manṣūr (r. 136–158/754–775), for example, had translated for him "books by Aristotle on logic and other subjects, the Almagest by Ptolemy, the Arithmetic (by Nichomachus of Gerasa), the book by Euclid (on geometry), and other ancient books" (Mas'ūdī 1866–1874, *Murūj* 8.291).

One might say that this has nothing to do with religion. However, given the sectarian milieu into which Islam was born and its parvenu status, its practitioners spent an enormous amount of time right from the beginning in defining and delimiting their faith vis-à-vis other faiths. For this purpose, Greek logic was extremely important:

> Mahdī (r. 158–69/775–85) devoted all his efforts to examining heretics and apostates. These people appeared in his days and publicly proclaimed their beliefs during his caliphate on account of the wide dissemination of books by Mani, Bardesanes, and Marcion, which were translated from Old and New Persian into Arabic. . . . In this way Manichaeans increased in number

> and their opinions came out into the open among people. Mahdi was the first caliph to command the theologians who used dialectic disputation in their research to compose books against the heretics and other infidels we have just mentioned. The theologians then produced demonstrative proofs against the disputers, eliminated the problems posed by the heretics, and expounded the truth in clear terms to the doubters. (Mas'ūdī 1866–1874, *Murūj* 8.292–93)

This translation movement was not, however, merely imitative. Once the Greek corpus had been absorbed and digested, Muslim scholars felt competent to challenge and respond critically and creatively to the Greek tradition. Thus Ibn Zakariyyā' al-Rāzī (d. 313/925) penned *Doubts about Galen*, Ibn al-Haytham (d. 430/1039) *Doubts about Ptolemy*, and Ibn Sīnā (d. 428/1037) his *Eastern Philosophy*, which is an exposition of his doubts about Aristotle. It is with this in mind that Wisnovsky makes his slightly tongue-in-cheek remark, cited earlier, about the end of Late Antiquity, for Muslim scholars spent a good three centuries working through the Greek scientific patrimony, translating it, and commenting on it, before moving beyond it. If this process of absorption of the Greek scientific heritage by Islamic civilization is still part of Late Antiquity, then it is true that only by the late tenth or early eleventh century C.E. did Late Antiquity finally come to an end.

A Solution: Late Antique Arabia?

> The relevance of the geographical region of central Arabia to that emergent definition of what we have come to know as the religion of Islam is highly questionable; Islam (in its clearly defined and developed form) had its formative developing period outside the Arabian context and, while the initial impetus for the religion is clearly tied to the Ḥijāz in Arabia, the character the religion adopted was molded by more widespread Near Eastern precedents than would appear historically possible within the narrow isolation of Arabia.
>
> —(Rippin 2005, 10)

In recent decades, there have been two approaches to conceptualizing the rise and formation of the religion of Islam: either as a child of Late Antiquity, conceived and nourished wholly by the late antique world, or as a force that was formed outside the late antique world (in Arabia) from outside (Arabian) ingredients and only entered that world once it was fairly well developed and so was only marginally influenced by it. The latter view, the "out of Arabia" approach, is the traditional Muslim one, and it is accepted by a good many Western scholars as well. However, the former view, the "born of Late Antiquity" approach, is gaining ground at present. Not surprisingly, it has been very popular with late antique historians, since it widens the scope of their field to include a new geographical region, a new religious phenomenon, and a greater span of time (Cameron 2002). Indeed, it was adopted already by the architect of late antique studies, Peter Brown (1971a, 189): "The preaching of Muḥammad and the consequent rise of a new religious grouping of the Arab world—the religion of Islam—was the last, most rapid crisis in the religious history of the late antique period. . . . We know just enough about the Ḥijāz in the early seventh century to see how this sudden detonation fitted into the culture of the Near East. . . . The caravans of the Meccan merchant-adventurers had come to permeate Byzantium and Persia: Muḥammad himself had once made the trek to Syria. . . ."

An increasing number of Islamic historians are also now backing this perspective, putting forward the argument that the emergence of Islam has to be set in a wider Middle Eastern context and to be seen as the result of a long process (Kennedy 1999; Conrad 2000). Of course, most, including many Muslim thinkers past and present, would accept that the early Muslim conception of their prophet and their faith evolved over time, resulting in a different conception from that of later Muslims, but these revisionist scholars would go much further. To allow Islam to be properly integrated into the late antique world, they deem it necessary to break totally with the Arabian past. For example, they have postulated that Mecca was not Muḥammad's birthplace or the Ḥijāz Islam's home (Crone and Cook 1977, esp. 21–23; Crone 2005), that there was no Arabian paganism for Muḥammad to fight and fulminate against (Hawting 1999), that the Qur'ān was not compiled in the seventh century (Wansbrough 1977) or written in Arabic (Luxenberg 2000), and even that Muḥammad himself and the conquests he initiated were a later invention (Nevo and Koren 2003; Popp 2007).

Most of the impetus for such radical theories stems from a belief, already articulated by Russian Islamologists in the 1930s (Ibn Warraq 2000, 44–49), that a major world religion could not have been born in such a remote corner of the Middle East, but rather must have been nourished more fully within the heartlands of the late antique Middle East. Its practitioners worry about the fact that "in its equation of the origins of Islam with the career of Muḥammad and its detailed depiction of Muḥammad's life in Mecca and Medina, Muslim tradition effectively disassociates Islam from the historical development of the monotheist stream of religion as a whole. Islam is shown to be the result of an act of divine revelation made to an Arab prophet who was born and lived most of his life in a town (Mecca) beyond the borders of the then monotheistic world" (Hawting 1997, 24). The solution, they say, is to relocate the origins of Islam to the Fertile Crescent: "We need to rethink more drastically our ideas about when and where Islam emerged," for "it is easier to envisage such an evolution occurring in those regions of the Middle East where the tradition of monotheism was firmly established."[5]

But does Arabia play no part at all in all this? Did it not contribute any ingredients to the formation of Islam? For Julius Wellhausen, one of the most famous of all Islamic historians, it is in the "rough-hewn pieces of paganism" that we can most clearly see Arabia's contribution to Islam, such as "the processing around the Ka'ba and the kissing of the black stone, the running between Ṣafā and Marwa, and the rituals at 'Arafa" (Wellhausen 1897, 68–69). South Arabianists have long pointed to the numerous common traits to be found in Islamic and pre-Islamic south Arabian rituals. The south Arabian expiation texts from the first to third centuries C.E., for example, seemed to Ryckmans (1975, 457) to "prove that the Islamic laws of ritual purity were already in use in pagan Arabia and that it is there, rather than in Judaism, that their origin must be sought." And this approach has been pursued by other scholars, notably Serjeant (1962), who cast Muḥammad as a holy man in charge of a sacred enclave, such as were commonly found in south Arabia, and de Blois, who has tried to elucidate various passages in the Qur'ān by reference to attested Arabian parallels. Certainly, the references in the Qur'ān to the irrigated lands of Saba' (Sheba) destroyed by a flood (34.15–17), the raiders on Mecca coming from Yemen with elephants in their ranks (105), "the people in ditches" burned in the fields of Najran (85.4–7), and the subjects of the dynastic rulers of Himyar known as the *tubba'* (44.37, 50.14) suggest that the Ḥijāz was influenced by its southern neighbor. Indeed, new finds of inscriptions in Yemen are making it clear that a substantial body of religious vocabulary is common to the Qur'ān and the epigraphic record of south Arabia, most famously the three "daughters of God" (cf. 53.19–20) and the name Muḥammad, but also a variety of religious practices and regulations (Ryckmans 1975; Robin 2001; see also Robin, chapter 9 in this book).[6]

If we endorse the validity of these Arabian contributions to Islam's formation, would this mean that the "out of Arabia" theory trumps the "born of Late Antiquity" theory? It seems to me that there is a way out of this dichotomy, namely, to accept that Arabia by the time of Muḥammad was already a part of the late antique world. To some degree, of course, Arabia had been exposed to the attention of empires ever since the domestication of the camel made its vastnesses crossable and made those of its inhabitants who could ride camels useful as either merchants or soldiers. Not only do we have the records of great emperors—such as the Assyrian king Esarhaddon and the Persian rulers Cambyses and Artaxerxes, who all crossed north Arabia to march on Egypt; the Babylonian monarch Nabonidus, who made the north Arabian oasis of Taymā' his base for ten years; and Caesar Augustus, who sent his general Aelius Gallus to march down the west coast of Arabia to conquer its southern corner (Hoyland 2001, chapter 2)—but also we have a few documents from locals. For example, from the reign of the emperor Marcus Aurelius (161–180 C.E.), two inscriptions in north Arabia reveal to us that the Roman empire already influenced communities even in this region: the first, in Greek and Nabataean Aramaic, commemorates the construction of a temple in honor of the emperor by a military detachment from the tribe of Thamud at Rawwafa (between Hegra and Tabuk in northwest Arabia); the second, in Latin, relates how the community of the people of Hegra (300 kilometers north of Medina) restored the Nabataean covered market under the supervision of 'Amr son of Ḥayyān, the headman of the community (*primus civitatis*). This influence increased as the cold war between Byzantium and Iran warmed up in the fourth to sixth centuries, and the two powers fought to bring peripheral regions into their orbit. Religion was an important factor in this struggle, and we see missionaries peddling their messages and rulers instigating persecutions in Arabia as well as elsewhere.

Probably our best witness to these influences in sixth- to seventh-century Arabia is the Qur'ān. It has long been known that it bears the imprint of numerous late antique texts. However, it has usually been discussed in terms of borrowing and originality, what Muḥammad took from the Jews and the Christians (Geiger 1902; Bell 1926; Torrey 1933; Luxenberg 2000).[7] This is, however, unhelpful, in part because it strikes a polemical note, which muddies the issue, and in part because it misses the point. By the time of Muḥammad, stories like the sleepers of Ephesus; the lives of figures like Adam, Abraham, Alexander the Great, and Jesus; and issues like the extent of God's oneness and justice were all part of late antique common knowledge. The Qur'ān is not borrowing, but creatively using this common knowledge for its own ends and giving its own take on current religious problems. The vast majority of the religious texts that have survived from this period were written by official religious authorities and so give us the party line, the strict version of their creed. The Qur'ān, however, gives us an insight into the unofficial world, which was much more flexible and pluralist. Scholars tend to assume that where the Qur'ān offers a version of a story or a doctrine that does not conform to the official version, then either the Qur'ān and/or Muḥammad has got it wrong or it reflects the views of some heretical sect that has survived in Arabia. More likely, it is just that it gives us a hint of the broad array of narratives and beliefs that existed below the level of canonized and codified texts. The Qur'ān is in many ways the ultimate late antique document and provides us with a means to link Arabia, the origins of Islam, and Late Antiquity. This has been illustrated by a number of interesting recent studies that have put the Qur'ān in dialogue with late antique texts (Reynolds 2006; Griffith 2007; van Bladel 2007; Mourad 2007). This has yielded useful insights, which is in the end the only real reason for us to consider the question at all of whether early Islam fits within Late Antiquity.

NOTES

1. Good examples of this clash-of-civilizations approach in the field of Late Antiquity are Heather 2005 and Ward-Perkins 2005.

2. It is the same script as is used for the coinage (with long upright strokes for the letters alif and lām) but differs from the so-called Ḥijāzī or *mā'il* (slanting) style. Some consider the latter older (e.g., Déroche 2003, 258), but they could be contemporary.

3. And possibly also to demonstrate political allegiance; in general, individuals' inscriptions tend to adhere quite closely to the phraseology of imperial inscriptions, and it is possible that the verse about the caliphate of David was chosen to demonstrate support for 'Abd al-Malik's decision to publicize his caliphate on coins.

4. Most recently by Gutas 1998 in his very informative monograph, though in calling it "the Graeco-Arabic translation movement," he undermines its universalism. For a recent and excellent study of the translations and translators, see Endress 1997. A representative and readable selection of the material translated from Greek is given in Rosenthal 1975.

5. Hawting 1999, 13; cf. Wansbrough 1978, 99: "The elaboration of Islam was not contemporary with but posterior to the Arab occupation of the Fertile Crescent," and Bashear 1997, 113: "The proposition that Arabia could have constituted the source of the vast material power required to effect such changes in world affairs within so short a span of time is, to say the least, a thesis calling for proof and substantiation."

6. A nice example is the practice of intercalation (*al-nasī'*), which is forbidden by the Qur'ān (9.37) and which has turned up in a South Arabian expiation text with the same significance as in the Qur'ān, namely, moving sacred festivals from their prescribed time (de Blois 2004).

7. In particular, one finds this approach adopted in Web sites, which tend to have apologetic or polemical aims; see, for example, www.islamic-awareness.org and www.answering-islam.org, which are nevertheless very informative.

WORKS CITED

Ahsan, M. M. 1979. *Social Life under the Abbasids.* London: Longman.

Avdinli, Osman. 2007. "Ascetic and Devotional Elements in the Mu'tazilite Tradition: The Sufi Mu'tazilites," *Muslim World* 97: 174–189.

Ayoub, Mahmoud. 1983. "Dhimmah in Qur'ān and Hadith," *Arab Studies Quarterly* 5: 172–182.

Baladhuri, Ahmad ibn Yahya al-. 1866. *Futūḥ al-buldān*, ed. M. J. de Goeje. Leiden: Brill.

Bashear, Suliman. 1997. *Arabs and Others in Early Islam.* Princeton, NJ: Darwin Press.

Becker, C. H. 1924–1932. *Islamstudien: Vom Werden und Wesen der islamischen Welt.* Leipzig: Quelle und Meyer.

Bell, Richard. 1926. *The Origin of Islam in Its Christian Environment.* London: Macmillan.

Brown, Peter. 1971a. *The World of Late Antiquity, from Marcus Aurelius to Muḥammad.* London: Thames and Hudson.

———. 1971b. "The Rise and Function of the Holy Man in Late Antiquity," *Journal of Roman Studies* 61: 80–101.

———. 2003. *The Rise of Western Christendom: Triumph and Diversity AD 200–1000*, rev. ed. Oxford: Blackwell.

Cameron, Averil. 1991. "Disputations, Polemical Literature, and the Formation of Opinion in the Early Byzantine Period." In *Dispute Poems and Dialogues in the Ancient and Medieval Near East*, ed. G. J. Reinink and H. L. J. Vanstiphout, 91–108. Leuven: Peeters.

———. 1994. "Texts as Weapons: Polemic in the Byzantine Dark Ages." In *Literacy and Power in the Ancient World*, ed. A. K. Bowman and G. Woolf, 198–215. Cambridge: Cambridge University Press.

———. 2002. "The Long Late Antiquity: A Late Twentieth-Century Model?" In *Classics in Progress: Essays on Ancient Greece and Rome*, ed. T. P. Wiseman, 165–191. Oxford: Oxford University Press.

———. 2003. "How to Read Heresiology," *Journal of Medieval and Early Modern Studies* 33: 471–492.

Casanova, Paul. 1911. *Mohammed et la fin du monde*. Paris: Paul Geuthner.

Conrad, Lawrence. 2000. "The Arabs." In *The Cambridge Ancient History, Vol. 14: Late Antiquity: Empire and Successors AD 425–600*, ed. Averil Cameron, B. Ward-Perkins, and Michael Whitby, 678–700. Cambridge: Cambridge University Press.

Cook, David. 2003. *Studies in Muslim Apocalyptic*. Princeton, NJ: Darwin Press.

Cook, Michael. 1983. *Muḥammad*. Oxford: Oxford University Press.

Cooperson, Michael. 1997. "Ibn Hanbal and Bishr al-Hafi: A Case Study in Biographical Traditions," *Studia Islamica* 86: 71–101.

Crone, Patricia. 1980. *Slaves on Horses: The Evolution of the Islamic Polity*. Cambridge: Cambridge University Press.

———. 2005. "How Did the Quranic Pagans Make a Living?" *Bulletin of the School of Oriental and African Studies* 68: 387–399.

Crone, Patricia, and Michael Cook. 1977. *Hagarism: The Making of the Islamic World*. Cambridge: Cambridge University Press.

Crone, Patricia, and Martin Hinds. 1986. *Religious Authority in the First Centuries of Islam*. Cambridge: Cambridge University Press.

de Blois, Francois. 2004. "Qur'ān 9:37 and CIH547," *Proceedings of the Seminar for Arabian Studies* 34: 101–104.

Déroche, Francois. 2003. "Manuscripts of the Qur'ān." In *Encyclopaedia of the Qur'ān*, ed. J. D. McAuliffe, 3:254–275. Leiden: Brill.

Donner, Fred. 1984. "Some Early Arabic Inscriptions from al-Hanakiyya, Saudi Arabia," *Journal of Near Eastern Studies* 43: 181–203.

———. 1998. *Narratives of Islamic Origins*. Princeton, NJ: Darwin Press.

Edelby, Néophyte. 1950–1951. "L'autonomie législative des chrétiens en terre d'islam," *Archives d'histoire du droit oriental* 5: 307–351.

Endress, G. 1997. "The Circle of al-Kindi: Early Arabic Translations from the Greek and the Rise of Islamic Philosophy." In *The Ancient Tradition in Christian and Islamic Hellenism*, ed. G. Endress and R. Kruk, 43–76. Leiden: Brill.

Fahmī, S. 'A. 1987. "Naqshan jadidan min Makka al-mukarrama mu'arrakhan li-sanat thamanīn hijriyya," *al-Manhal* 48: 346–361.

Fattal, Antoine. 1951. "Comment les Dhimmis étaient jugés en terre d'Islam," *Cahiers d'histoire égyptienne* 3: 321–341.

Fowden, Garth. 1993. *Empire to Commonwealth: Consequences of Monotheism in Late Antiquity*. Princeton, NJ: Princeton University Press.

———. 2001. "Varieties of Religious Community." In *Interpreting Late Antiquity: Essays on the Postclassical World*, ed. G. W. Bowersock, P. Brown, and O. Grabar, 82–106. Cambridge, MA: Belknap Press of Harvard University Press.

Fowden, E.K., and G. Fowden. 2004. *Studies on Hellenism, Christianity, and the Umayyads*. Athens: Kentron Hellēnikēs kai Rōmaïkēs Archaiotētos, Ethnikon Hidryma Ereunōn.

Garsoïan, Nina. 1983. "Byzantium and the Sasanians." In *Cambridge History of Iran, Vol. 3.1: The Seleucid, Parthian and Sasanian Period*, ed. Ehsan Yarshater, 568–592. Cambridge: Cambridge University Press.

Geiger, A. 1902. *Was hat Muḥammad aus dem Judenthume ausgenommen?* Leipzig: M. W. Kaufmann.

Goitein, S. D. 1970. "Minority Self-Rule and Government Control in Islam," *Studia Islamica* 31: 101–116.

Greatrex, Geoffrey, and Samuel N. C. Lieu. 2000. *The Roman Eastern Frontier and the Persian Wars, Part II: AD 363–630*. London: Routledge.

Griffith, Sidney H. 1979. "Comparative Religion in the Apologetics of the First Christian Arabic Theologians." In *Proceedings of the Patristic, Medieval, and Renaissance Conference (University of Villanova, Pennsylvania)*, 4: 63–86. Villanova, PA: Augustinian Historical Institute.

———. 2007. "Christian Lore and the Arabic Qur'ān: The 'Companions of the Cave' in *Surat al-Kahf* and in Syriac Christian Tradition." In *The Qur'ān in its Historical Context*, ed. Gabriel Reynolds, 109–138. London: Routledge.

Gutas, Dimitri. 1988. *Greek Thought, Arabic Culture: The Graeco-Arabic Translation Movement in Baghdad and Early Abbasid Society*. London: Routledge.

Hamed, 'Ali Ibrahim. 1988. *Introduction à l'étude archéologique des routes syriennes et égyptiennes de pélérinage au nord-ouest de l'Arabie Saoudite*. Ph.D. diss., University of Aix-en-Provence.

Hawting, Gerald. 1997. "John Wansbrough, Islam and Monotheism," *Method and Theory in the Study of Religion* 9: 23–38.

———. 1999. *The Idea of Idolatry and the Emergence of Islam*. Cambridge: Cambridge University Press.

———. 2000. *The First Dynasty of Islam: The Umayyads, AD 661–750*. London: Routledge.

Heather, Peter. 2005. *The Fall of the Roman Empire*. London: Macmillan.

Herrin, Judith. 1987. *The Formation of Christendom*. Princeton, NJ: Princeton University Press.

Howard-Johnston, James. 1995. "The Two Great Powers in Late Antiquity: A Comparison." In *The Byzantine and Early Islamic Near East, III, States, Resources, and Armies*, ed. Averil Cameron, 157–226. Princeton, NJ: Darwin Press.

Hoyland, Robert G. 1997. *Seeing Islam as Others Saw It*. Princeton, NJ: Darwin Press.

———. 2000. "The Earliest Christian Writings on Muḥammad: An Appraisal." In *Muḥammad: The Issue of the Sources*, ed. Harald Motzki, 276–297. Leiden: Brill.

———. 2001. *Arabia and the Arabs from the Bronze Age to the Coming of Islam*. London: Routledge.

———. 2006. "New Documentary Texts and the Early Islamic State," *Bulletin of the School of Oriental and African Studies* 69.3: 395–416.

Humphreys, R. Stephen. 1991. *Islamic History: A Framework for Enquiry*. Princeton, NJ: Princeton University Press.

Huyse, Philip. 1998. "Kerdir and the First Sasanians." In *Proceedings of the Third European Conference of Iranian Studies*, ed. Nicholas Sims-Williams, 1: 109–120. Wiesbaden: Reichert.

Ibn al-Nadīm, Muḥammad ibn Isḥāq. 1872. *Fihrist*. ed. G. Fluegel. Leipzig: F. C. W. Vogel.

Ibn Warraq. 2000. "Studies on Muḥammad and the Rise of Islam." In *The Quest for the Historical Muḥammad*, ed. Ibn Warraq, 15–88. Amherst, NY: Prometheus.

Jones, A. H. M. 1964. *The Later Roman Empire, 284–602*. Oxford: Blackwell.

Kennedy, Hugh. 1985. "From Polis to Madina: Urban Change in Late Antique and Early Islamic Syria," *Past and Present* 106: 3–27.

———. 1999. "Islam." In *Late Antiquity: A Guide to the Postclassical World*, ed. G. W. Bowersock, P. Brown, and O. Grabar, 219–237. Cambridge, MA: Belknap Press of Harvard University Press.

———. 2004. *The Court of the Caliphs*. London: Weidenfeld and Nicolson.

———. 2007. *The Great Arab Conquests.* Philadelphia: Da Capo.
Kister, M. J. 1989. "'Do Not Assimilate Yourselves . . . (*Lā tashabbahū . . .*),'" *Jerusalem Studies in Arabic and Islam* 12: 321–353.
Liebeschuetz, J. H. W. G. 2001. *The Decline and Fall of the Late Roman City.* Oxford: Oxford University Press.
Luxenberg, Christoph. 2000. *Die syro-aramäische Lesart des Koran.* Berlin: Das Arabische Buch.
Magdalino, Paul. 1993. "The History of the Future and Its Uses: Prophecy, Policy, and Propaganda." In *The Making of Byzantine History: Studies Dedicated to Donald M. Nicol,* ed. Roderick Beaton and Charlotte Roueché, 3–34. Aldershot: Ashgate Variorum.
Mas'ūdī, 'Ali ibn al-Husayn al-. 1866–1874. *Murūj al-dhahab.* Ed. and trans. C. Barbier de Meynard and Pavet de Courteille. Paris: Imprimerie impériale.
Meri, Josef. 2002. *The Cult of Saints among Muslims and Jews in Medieval Syria.* Oxford: Oxford University Press.
Mingana, Alphonse. 1907. *Sources syriaques.* Part 2, 1–171/172–197 (edition and translation of John bar Penkāyē's *Ktābā d-rīsh mellē*). Leipzig: Harrassowitz.
Morony, Michael G. 1974. "Religious Communities in Late Sasanian and Early Muslim Iraq," *Journal of the Economic and Social History of the Orient* 17: 113–135.
———. 1984. *Iraq after the Muslim Conquest.* Princeton, NJ: Princeton University Press.
Mourad, S. A. 2004. "Christian Monks in Islamic Literature: A Preliminary Report on Some Arabic *Apophthegmata Patrum,*" *Bulletin of the Royal Institute for Interfaith Studies* 6: 81–98.
———. 2005. *Early Islam between Myth and History: Al-Hasan al-Basri and the Formation of His Legacy in Classical Islamic Scholarship.* Leiden: Brill.
———. 2007. "Mary in the Qur'ān: A Reexamination of Her Presentation." In *The Qur'ān in Its Historical Context,* ed. Gabriel Reynolds, 163–174. London: Routledge.
Munro-Hay, Stuart. 1991. *Aksum: An African Civilization in Late Antiquity.* Edinburgh: Edinburgh University Press.
Nevo, Yehuda D., and Judith Koren. 1991. "Methodological Approaches to Islamic Studies," *Der Islam* 68: 87–107.
———. 2003. *Crossroads to Islam: The Origins of the Arab Religion and the Arab State.* Amherst, NY: Prometheus.
Noth, Albrecht. 1987. "Abgrenzungsprobleme zwischen Muslimen und Nicht-Muslimen: Die Bedingungen 'Umars' unter einem anderen Aspekt gelesen," *Jerusalem Studies in Arabic and Islam* 9: 290–315.
Pirenne, Henri. 1937. *Mahomet et Charlemagne.* Paris: F. Alcan.
Popp, Volker. 2007. "Von Ugarit nach Samarra." In *Der frühe Islam: Eine historisch-kritische Rekonstruktion anhand zeitgenössischer Quellen,* ed. Karl-Heinz Ohlig, 13–222. Berlin: Hans Schiler.
Raby, Julian, and Jeremy Johns, eds. 1979 and 2000. *Bayt al-Maqdis: 'Abd al-Malik's Jerusalem, 2 parts.* Oxford: Oxford University Press.
Rashed, R. 1989. "Problems of the Transmission of Greek Scientific Thought into Arabic: Examples from Mathematics and Optics," *History of Science* 27: 199–209.
Rāshid, Sa'd ibn 'Abd al-'Aziz. 1993. *Kitābāt islāmīya ghayr manshūra min 'Ruwāwa' al-Medina al-munawwara.* Riyad.
Reinink, Gerrit. 2002. "Heraclius the New Alexander: Apocalyptic Prophecies during the Reign of Heraclius." In *The Reign of Heraclius (610–641): Crisis and Confrontation,* ed. Gerrit Reinink and Bernard Stolte, 81–94. Leuven: Peeters.

Reynolds, Gabriel. 2006. "Redeeming the Adam of the Qur'ān." In *Arabische Christen—Christen in Arabien*, ed. D. Kreikenbom, F.-Ch. Muth, and J. Thielmann, 71–83. Frankfurt: Lang.

Rippin, Andrew. 2005. *Muslims and Their Beliefs*. London: Routledge.

Robin, Christian. 2001. "Les 'Filles de Dieu' de Saba' à la Mecque," *Semitica* 50: 113–192.

———. 2003. "Le judaïsme de Himyar," *Arabia: revue de Sabéologie* 1: 97–172.

———. 2004. "Himyar et Israël," *Comptes rendues de l'Académie des Inscriptions et Belles-Lettres*: 831–908.

Robinson, Chase. 1999. "Prophecy and Holy Men in Early Islam." In *The Cult of Saints in Late Antiquity and the Middle Ages*, ed. James Howard-Johnston and P. A. Hayward, 241–262. Oxford: Oxford University Press.

———. 2003. "Reconstructing Early Islam: Truth and Consequences." In *Method and Theory in the Study of Islamic Origins*, ed. Herbert Berg, 101–134. Leiden: Brill.

Rosenthal, Franz. 1975. *The Classical Heritage in Islam*. London: Routledge and Kegan Paul.

Ryckmans, Jacques. 1975. "Les inscriptions sud-arabes anciennes et les études arabes," *Annali dell'Istituto Orientale di Napoli* 35: 443–463.

Serjeant, R. B. 1962. "Haram and Hawtah, the Sacred Enclave in Arabia." In *Mélanges Taha Husain*, ed. A. R. Badawi, 41–58. Cairo: Dar al-Ma'arif.

Shahîd, Irfan. 1979. "Byzantium in South Arabia," *Dumbarton Oaks Papers* 33: 27–94.

Shaked, Shaul. 1994. *Dualism in Transformation: Varieties of Religion in Sasanian Iran*. London: Routledge Curzon.

Torrey, Charles. 1933. *The Jewish Foundation of Islam*. New York: Jewish Institute of Religious Press.

Tucker, William F. 2008. *Mahdis and Millenarians: Shi'ite Extremists in Early Muslim Iraq*. Cambridge: Cambridge University Press.

Van Bladel, Kevin. 2007. "The Legend of Alexander the Great in the Qur'ān 18:83–102." In *The Qur'ān in Its Historical Context*, ed. Gabriel Reynolds, 175–203. London: Routledge.

Van Ess, Josef. 2002. *Prémices de la théologie musulmane*. Paris: Albin Michel.

———. 2006. *The Flowering of Muslim Theology*. Cambridge, MA: Harvard University Press.

Wansbrough, John. 1977. *Qur'ānic Studies: Sources and Methods of Scriptural Interpretation*. Oxford: Oxford University Press.

———. 1978. *The Sectarian Milieu: Content and Composition of Islamic Salvation History*. Oxford: Oxford University Press.

Ward-Perkins, Brian. 2005. *The Fall of Rome and the End of Civilization*. Oxford: Oxford University Press.

Wellhausen, Julius. 1897. *Reste arabischen Heidentums gesammelt und erläutert*. Berlin: Georg Reimer.

Wensinck, A. J. 1932. *The Muslim Creed: Its Genesis and Development*. Cambridge: Cambridge University Press.

Whittow, Mark, 1990. "Ruling the Late Roman and Early Byzantine City: A Continuous History," *Past and Present* 129: 13–20.

Wisnovsky, Robert. 2003. *Avicenna's Metaphysics in Context*. London: Duckworth.

CHAPTER 33

MUḤAMMAD AND THE QUR'ĀN

STEPHEN J. SHOEMAKER
University of Oregon

At the midpoint of the nineteenth century, Ernest Renan famously wrote of Islam's founding prophet that it was possible to know "year by year the fluctuations of his thoughts, his contradictions, his weaknesses," further exclaiming that Islam, unlike so many of the world's other religions, had been born "in the full light of history" (Renan 1851, 1025; trans. Renan 2000, 129). Such remarks are particularly noteworthy for their source: Renan was one of the pioneers of historical Jesus research, whose *Life of Jesus* remains one of the most important and influential biographies of Jesus (Renan 1863; cf. Baird 1992, 375–384). Given Renan's critical rejection of much that the Christian Gospels sought to pass for history, his full-throated endorsement of the Islamic historical tradition and its memory of Muḥammad's life is remarkable. If a critic of Renan's stature would vouch so forcefully for the authenticity of Muḥammad's traditional biographies, one might expect that they would, in fact, be historical sources of the highest quality. Unfortunately, however, Renan's initial enthusiasm now appears to be altogether unwarranted, and with the turning of a new century, fresh doubts concerning the traditions of earliest Islam and their accuracy began to emerge. Ignác Goldziher's groundbreaking studies of Islam's prophetic traditions, the *ḥadīth*, called attention to the highly tendentious, contradictory, and artificial qualities of early Islamic literature (Goldziher 1889–1890; trans. Goldziher 1967–1971). Goldziher's studies were shortly followed by the important work of Henri Lammens (Lammens 1910; 1911; 1912; trans. Lammens 2000c; 2000a; 2000b) and Leone Caetani (Caetani 1905–1926) on the biographical and historical traditions, which dimmed considerably the "full light" imagined by Renan and found the origins of Islam instead shrouded beneath a cloak of pious memories.

By consequence, it is now widely recognized in Western scholarship on Islamic origins that almost nothing conveyed by the early Islamic sources can be taken at face value, and indeed, most of what these narratives relate concerning Muḥammad and his earliest followers must be regarded with deep suspicion.[1] As no less of an authority than Marshall Hodgson concludes, "On the face of it, the documentation transmitted among Muslims about his life is rich and detailed; but we have learned to mistrust most of it; indeed, the most respected early Muslim scholars themselves pointed out its untrustworthiness" (Hodgson 1974, 160). Yet despite this widely held recognition, it is peculiar that so many modern scholars have continued to write as if nothing has changed. Any number of introductory works on Islam or biographies of Muḥammad present only a very lightly edited, more or less uncritical version of the traditional Islamic narratives of Muḥammad's life, the *sīra* traditions.[2] Perhaps the most famous example of this phenomenon is the work of Montgomery Watt, whose biographies of Muḥammad often seem to have attained a near canonical status in the modern study of Islam (esp. Watt 1953; 1956; 1961). In his defense of the traditional sources, Watt appeals to the existence of "a solid core of fact" underlying the traditional accounts, particularly for Muḥammad's Medinan period. This "historical kernel" guarantees the accuracy of their "basic framework" and provides a reliable chronological foundation (Watt 1958; 1983; cf. Andræ 1935, 31): such reasoning allows Watt to reproduce essentially unaltered the traditional Islamic accounts of Muḥammad's activities at Mecca and Medina. Nevertheless, despite his frequent invocation of this "authentic core," Watt merely asserts rather than demonstrates its existence, amounting to little more than a *petitio principii* that fails to confront significant problems with the source material (cf. Schacht 1949, 146–147).

Early Islamic Biographies of Muḥammad: The *Sīra* Traditions

The earliest biographies of Muḥammad are arrestingly late: the first *sīra*, or "life," of Islam's prophet was compiled only in the middle of the eighth century, some 120 years after Muḥammad's death, by Ibn Isḥāq (d. 767).[3] Even more troublesome, however, is the fact that Ibn Isḥāq's biography itself does not survive; rather, its contents are known only through later recensions of his foundational work, the most important of which are the ninth-century *Sīra* of Ibn Hishām (d. 833) and al-Ṭabarī's *History* from the early tenth century. When these and other related sources converge in assigning a particular tradition to Ibn Isḥāq, the probability is high that his biography was indeed their common source. Nevertheless, many details of Muḥammad's life survive only in Ibn Hishām's more recent adaptation, and insofar as Ibn Hishām does not always reproduce Ibn Isḥāq's biography faithfully but has "abridged and vigorously edited" his source, the authorship of such material is often questionable.[4] By way comparison with Christian origins, it is as if, as Patricia Crone observes, the earliest Gospel had been compiled by Justin Martyr and yet was known only in a recension by Origen (Crone 1980, 202, n. 10). One can only imagine what such a Gospel might have looked like, but presumably Jesus would have appeared much more like a Hellenistic philosopher and somewhat less like a Jewish eschatological prophet.

Of course, it is clear that Ibn Isḥāq did not simply create his biography of Muḥammad from whole cloth, and occasionally he identifies his sources, frequently attributing material to Ibn Shihāb al-Zuhrī (d. 742), a renowned early authority on the life of Muḥammad. According to the Islamic tradition, al-Zuhrī was Ibn Isḥāq's teacher, and while it is doubtful that al-Zuhrī himself actually composed a life of Muḥammad (Goldziher 1889–1990, 2:210–211; M. Cook 1997, 459–466; Robinson 2002, 25), it certainly seems plausible that much of Ibn Isḥāq's biography derives from al-Zuhrī's teaching at the beginning of the second Islamic century. Nevertheless, despite occasional attributions to earlier authorities, it is much less certain that Ibn Isḥāq actually transmits material authored by these more legendary figures, such as 'Urwa ibn al-Zubayr (d. 712) (Robinson 2002, 24). To be sure, al-Zuhrī's teachings were almost certainly rooted, at least in part, in a tradition of oral lore that he inherited, but the nature of his own personal contribution to these collective memories is unclear: how he shaped or added to what he received is largely unknown.

Recently, a handful of scholars have sought to escape the apparent limitations of the early Islamic sources through a method known as "*isnād* criticism," which seeks to date individual traditions on the basis of their alleged patterns of transmission. In general, each of the biographical traditions, like Islam's other prophetic traditions (the *ḥadīth*), is prefaced by an "*isnād*," a pedigree that purports to record the chain(s) of transmitters by which a given tradition eventually reached a particular collector. Unfortunately, however, these testimonies of transmission are notoriously unreliable, and rather than conveying accurate records of a tradition's provenance, *isnād*s were easily manipulated and became a favorite forger's device. New traditions could be introduced with the appearance of antiquity by simply adorning them with impeccable ancestry, tracing their origins to Muḥammad himself through his closest and most trusted companions. Likewise, existing *isnād*s were often edited to fill out gaps in their early transmission history, and individual transmitters could be added or deleted according to their changing reputations.

That such widespread manipulation of *isnād*s occurred is not in dispute: the Islamic tradition itself has long acknowledged that forgery occurred on a massive scale in the Middle Ages. Al-Bukhārī (d. 870), for instance, the most authoritative early collector of *ḥadīth*, is said to have considered some 600,000 traditions attributed to Muḥammad by their *isnāds*, rejecting more than 593,000 as later forgeries (Crone 1987b, 33). In its suspicion of *isnāds*, modern scholarship has merely intensified the healthy skepticism already introduced by traditional Islamic scholars. Goldziher and, more recently, Joseph Schacht have persuasively argued that the earliest tradents of most *isnāds* are, in fact, almost always false (Goldziher 1967–1971, vol. 2; Schacht 1949; 1950). As Schacht in particular has observed, *isnāds* exhibit a tendency to grow backward, as later generations sought to validate individual traditions by assigning them directly to Muḥammad through his companions and their successors (Schacht 1950, 3, 163–175; cf. Goldziher 1967–1971, 2:148). The earliest *isnāds* generally do not include such venerable transmitters, which more than likely is a consequence of the *isnād*'s relatively late implementation only around the turn of the second Islamic century. Consequently, any record of transmission during the first Islamic century is almost certainly artificial and mythologized, making it nearly impossible to date any Islamic traditions other than the Qur'ān to before the mid-seventh century.

Nevertheless, with most *isnāds*, there comes a point at which the list of transmitters passes from the legendary figures of Islamic origins and begins to reflect an often accurate record of actual historical transmission. As Schacht recognized, it is often possible to identify this moment of transition with some probability by comparing a large number of *isnāds* that are assigned to the same tradition by different sources. When all of these *isnāds* trace their divergent paths back to a single transmitter, the "common link," one can reasonably conclude, as Schacht suggests, that either this figure was the first to circulate that tradition or, alternatively, that perhaps a student or someone else initially circulated the tradition in that person's name. Otherwise, it is difficult to explain how so many different *isnāds* could independently converge on this single individual. Nevertheless, a number of scholars, including Schacht himself, have pointed to potential problems with this method, raising in particular the issue of the manipulation of *isnāds* during the process of transmission: such alterations could lead to the identification of false common links and, by consequence, false datings of traditions (Schacht 1950, 166–175; M. Cook 1981, 107–116; Crone 1987b, 27–34; Calder 1993, 236–241). These concerns are certainly real, as Michael Cook has demonstrated (M. Cook 1992), and such potential deficiencies in the chains of transmission can be offset, it would appear, only by a network of transmission that is sufficiently dense to rule out the possibility of distortion by manipulation of *isnāds*. Consequently, this method not only is laborious but also can be used to date only traditions that are preserved in a large number of collections and display a complex pattern of transmission involving several "partial common links" who can confirm the original transmission from the common link (Juynboll 1983, 206–217; 1989; 1993). Although such traditions are rare, when these conditions are satisfied the results are quite persuasive.

G. H. A. Juynboll and Harald Motzki have recently applied this method to certain *ḥadīth* from the Islamic legal tradition with some success, convincingly dating a number of traditions to the beginnings of the second Islamic century.[5] Motzki, however, often argues aggressively for an even earlier dating, to the first Islamic century, yet in doing so he generally must ignore the safeguards established by partial common links and engage in special pleading on behalf of early tradents (e.g., Motzki 1991a, 3–4, 6–7, 9, etc.; 1996a; 1996b). As several critics have noted, these efforts to push certain traditions back into the seventh century are methodologically problematic and not very convincing.[6] Nevertheless, Motzki and others, particularly Gregor Schoeler and Andreas Görke, have used this same method of common-link analysis in an effort to date material from the *sīra* traditions, albeit with somewhat limited success. The primary difficulty is that the data of the biographical traditions generally cannot meet the demanding requirements of this methodology: their networks of transmission usually are not dense enough to establish sufficiently meaningful patterns. Consequently, one often cannot exclude the possibility that an apparent common link is in fact the result of a corrupt *isnād*, a "dive" as Juynboll names it, which aims to create the illusion of greater antiquity by ascribing a tradition to an early authority (Juynboll 1993). Absent the reassurances of a complex pattern of transmission by a number of sources through several partial common links, the method is much less persuasive.

Despite such shortcomings, Motzki has applied this approach to a tradition in which Muḥammad orders the assassination of a Jewish opponent, Ibn Abī al-Ḥuqayq, and while he persuasively assigns the tale to al-Zuhrī, his efforts to find an earlier source are not convincing (Motzki 2000). To do so, he must conflate two traditions that appear to be independent (Mattock 1986; Newby 1986) and ignore the deeply problematic nature of one of his tradents, Abū Isḥāq (Juynboll 1982, 170–171; 1983, 141–142). Schoeler has made a similar analysis of the traditions of the beginnings of Muḥammad's revelations (the *iqra'* episode) and the rumors that 'Ā'isha had committed adultery (*ḥadīth al-ifk*) (Schoeler 1996), and Görke has studied accounts of Muḥammad's treaty at al-Ḥudaybiya (Görke 2000). Together, Görke and Schoeler have published a very brief article on a complex of traditions purportedly linked with the events of Muḥammad's *hijra* (Görke and Schoeler 2005). In each instance, they attempt to link these traditions with 'Urwa ibn al-Zubayr, whose "biography" of Muḥammad they aim to reconstruct using the methods of common-link analysis (Schoeler 2003; Görke and Schoeler 2005). While all of these traditions are convincingly assigned to al-Zuhrī and occasionally other authorities of his generation, the reach back to 'Urwa is generally not very persuasive. Their arguments often require a great deal of optimism regarding the accuracy of certain *isnāds* and an occasional willingness to accept hypothetically reconstructed lines of transmission. In the case of the tradition complex associated with the *hijra*, for instance, a large body of material transmitted by only a single source is received as genuine, while *isnāds* belonging to only specific parts of the alleged tradition complex are represented as authenticating the entire block of material.

Görke and Schoeler are most successful in arguing that the traditions of Muḥammad's experience of visions and voices at the onset of his revelations and a basic narrative of his flight to Medina in the face of opposition had already begun to circulate during the second half of the first Islamic century. Likewise, the story of 'Ā'isha's suspected adultery and her acquittal is persuasively assigned to this period through the study of its *isnāds*. Yet one should recognize just how meager these results are, particularly given the amount of effort involved. Even if all the methodological questions regarding such an *isnād*-critical approach to the *sīra* traditions are placed to the side, the resultant biography of Muḥammad is disappointingly minimal. Motzki himself expresses some doubt whether "the outcome will justify the time and energy needed for such an enterprise," and he forecasts that "the historical biography which will be the outcome of all these source-critical efforts will be only a very small one" (Motzki 2000, 234–235).

Perhaps even more important is the failure so far of this arduous method to reveal anything particularly "new" about the historical Muḥammad that could not already be determined using simpler approaches. For instance, there can be little doubt that the early Muslims believed that Muḥammad had been the recipient of divine revelation, and its representation as a vision of light and auditions merely reflects a well-established biblical pattern (Rubin 1995, 103–112). Moreover, dating according to the *hijra* is attested by early documentary sources, signaling the importance of a tradition of Muḥammad's flight for the earliest Muslims (Crone and Cook 1977, 7, 157, n. 39; Humphreys 1991, 19). The accusations against 'Ā'isha are also credibly early, inasmuch as they reflect negatively on a figure who later came to be revered as the "mother of the faithful," and one would thus imagine that the story had begun to circulate before 'Ā'isha had attained this status in Sunni piety (Schoeler 2002, 362; 1996, 164). Even if one were to accept the more problematic arguments presented on behalf of the traditions of al-Ḥudaybiya and Ibn Abī al-Ḥuqayq's murder, very little is added to our portrait of Muḥammad. It is certainly credible that Muḥammad may have concluded an unfavorable treaty regarding fugitives at al-Ḥudaybiya or ordered the assassination of an opponent. But these traditions reveal almost nothing about the nature of Muḥammad's religious movement and its early history. In these areas, the *sīra* traditions remain not only unproven but also highly suspect, presenting modern scholars with an undesirable choice: as Patricia Crone concludes, "one can take the picture presented [by the *sīra* traditions] or one can leave it, but one cannot *work* with it" (Crone 1980, 4). Either one must accept the basic narrative of Muḥammad's traditional biography, placing faith in the existence of a reliable historical kernel embedded therein, as Watt suggests, or, abandoning the *sīra* traditions as hopelessly tendentious and artificial, one is left to reconstruct the beginnings of Islam solely on the basis of the Qur'ān, whose traditions are generally regarded as having a direct connection with the historical Muḥammad.[7]

The Historical Muḥammad and the Qur'ān

Régis Blachère first undertook to write such a biography of Muḥammad based solely on the Qur'ān, and the limited results of this endeavor attest to the inherent difficulties of any attempt to reconstruct the origins of Islam using the Qur'ān only (Blachère 1952; see also Blachère 1959). The Qur'ān is, as Fred Donner observes, a "profoundly ahistorical" text (Donner 1998, 75–85, esp. 80). In contrast to the Gospels of the Christian New Testament, for instance, its contents do not concern the events of Muḥammad's life or the early history of the religious community that he founded (Peters 1991). Rather, the Qur'ān serves primarily to "bring strands of earlier biblical and Arabian traditions together through the person of Muḥammad" (Wansbrough and Rippin 2004, xvii), excluding from its purview the "incidentals of time and space" (Halevi 2007, 207). As Michael Cook effectively summarizes, based on the Qur'ān alone, "we could probably infer that the protagonist of the Koran was Muḥammad, that the scene of his life was in western Arabia, and that he bitterly resented the frequent dismissal of his claims to prophecy by his contemporaries. But we could not tell that the sanctuary was in Mecca, nor that Muḥammad himself came from there, and we could only guess that he established himself in Yathrib" (M. Cook 1983, 70).

Everything else that we "know" about Muḥammad comes from these later biographical collections, which in their nature are much more comparable to the apocryphal writings of early Christianity than they are to the Gospels and letters of the Christian New Testament. Peters is thus quite correct when he likens the efforts of modern scholars to recover the historical figure of Muḥammad with the notion of producing a historical-critical biography of the Virgin Mary (Peters 1991, 292). Although Peters's primary intent is to note the impact of religious piety on how such endeavors might be received by the respective religious communities, the comparison is apt with regard to the source materials as well. Mary, like Muḥammad, was merely the vessel by which the divine Word came into the world, and like the historical Muḥammad, the historical figure of Mary is similarly obscured from view. While minuscule information can be gleaned from the writings of the New Testament, the details of her life and her involvement in the beginnings of Christianity remain largely a mystery. Various early Christian documents, however, relate certain episodes of her life with great detail. The *Protevangelium of James*, for instance, composed just over a century after the death of Christ (and Mary), purports to give an account of Mary's childhood, and likewise the early Dormition apocrypha of the third century describe the events of Mary's departure from this world. Although these texts compile older traditions that had previously circulated in either oral or written form (Zervos 1997; 2002), no scholar of early Christianity would use these narratives to reconstruct actual events from the life of Mary and her son. They are highly tendentious and mythological texts whose purpose is to memorialize the time of origins and to inscribe the beliefs and practices of second- and third-century Christianity onto its beginnings. The apocryphal acts of the various apostles are similarly comparable. For example, no historian would take the second-century *Acts of Peter* as a more or less accurate record of Peter's actual preaching and martyrdom in Rome. Yet when Watt and others invoke the existence of a reliable historical kernel at the core of Muḥammad's traditional biography, it is hard to see how this assumption is very different (cf. Robinson 2003, 123).

Consequently, when faced with such problematic and limited sources for knowledge of Muḥammad's life, one may rightly wonder if it is in fact possible to know anything of Islam's founder and its early history separately from the mythological narrative of origins composed by the Muslim scholars of Medina during the mid-eighth century. Is the historical Muḥammad at all identifiable, or has he been obscured almost to the point of invisibility, like the mother of Jesus? Can one hope to achieve a kind of historical-critical reconstruction of Islamic origins comparable in nature to the accomplishments of Early Christian Studies, or are we faced instead with the prospect of writing, as Jacqueline Chabbi has recently suggested, "la biographie impossible de Mahomet" (Chabbi 1996)? If the Qur'ān is ahistorical and the traditions of the *sīra* and the *ḥadīth* are so determined and overlaid by the concerns of later generations, is there any possibility of excavating earlier traditions from these sources that reveal the changing nature of Islam over the course of its first century? Or must we simply be resigned to complete silence and skepticism with regard to the beginnings of Islam, as John Wansbrough has proposed (Wansbrough 1978b, 116–119; cf. Wansbrough 1978a)?

Fortunately, as Blachère was perhaps the first to recognize, the Qur'ān provides a unique window into the first century of Islam, and although the Qur'ān reveals frustratingly little about the events of Muḥammad's life and the early history of the religious community that he founded, it nevertheless is alleged to preserve a record of Muḥammad's teaching. As the oldest surviving piece of Islamic literature and the only document from Islam's first century, the Qur'ān presents a precious witness to Muḥammad's religious beliefs as interpreted by his earliest followers. Thus, the Qur'ān offers the most promising chance of peering behind the veil of the Islamic myth of origins. By attempting to read the Qur'ān against, rather than with, the traditional narratives of Islamic origins, it may be possible to excavate an older stratum in the development of the Islamic faith. This endeavor, of course, is not simply a matter of interpreting the Qur'ān at every instance in a manner opposite to the received tradition simply for the sake of doing so. Rather, the aim is to locate, following methods from biblical studies, places where the text of the Qur'ān appears to be in tension with the traditional accounts of Islamic origins, while searching for parallel anomalies in the early tradition that similarly resist interpretive closure. By finding such hermeneutic gaps between the sacred text and tradition, we discover a space that invites the potential discovery of a different sort of Islam at these earliest stages, a religious movement perhaps not completely discontinuous from what would follow but that has a distinctive character nonetheless.

The methods and perspectives developed in the study of Christian origins are particularly well suited for such an endeavor, yet unfortunately, as Wansbrough rightly observes, the Qur'ān "as a document susceptible of analysis by the instruments and techniques of Biblical criticism . . . is virtually unknown" (Wansbrough 1977, ix).[8] Resistance to the use of methods from biblical studies in the investigation of the Qur'ān and Islamic origins established itself quite early and has remained remarkably persistent. Any historical-critical study of the Qur'ān analogous to New Testament criticism of the nineteenth and twentieth centuries has been long forestalled by the influential views of Theodor Nöldeke, who from the very beginning pronounced that "the development of the Islamic canon is utterly unique—one could say that it took place in the opposite fashion" from the biblical texts (Nöldeke and Schwally 1909–1919, 2:120; cf. Wansbrough 1977, 43–44). Likewise, Nöldeke's insistence that "the Qur'ān contains only authentic material" left little opportunity for investigating the history of the Qur'ānic text or for raising questions about any potential influence that the early community may have had on its contents (Nöldeke 1892, 56; cf. Gilliot 2008, 100). For well more than a century now, such views have continued to hold sway over the study of the Qur'ān in the West. For example, F. E. Peters, in his article on the "quest for the historical Muḥammad," rejects outright the methods of biblical studies as having no pertinence to study of the Qur'ān. Inasmuch as "our copy of the Qur'ān is, in fact, what Muḥammad taught, and is expressed in his own words," there is little need or even possibility for historical-critical study of the Qur'ānic text (Peters 1991, esp. 293–295). The fact that Angelika Neuwirth, one of the most respected Western scholars of the Qur'ān, would recently describe Nöldeke's work as "the rock of our church" reveals the degree to which his views continue to determine the modern study of the Qur'ān (see Higgins 2008).

Nöldeke's apparent resistance to the application of methodological perspectives from biblical studies may owe something to his training under Heinrich Ewald, a notoriously martinet *Doktorvater* whose fierce resistance to the emergent critical methods of Early Christian Studies and to the groundbreaking work of F. C. Baur in particular is legendary.[9] More generally, however, the relative quarantine of these methods from study of the Qur'ān may also reflect the early marriage of the study of Islamic origins with philology (Semitics) and study of the Hebrew Bible, rather than New Testament and Early Christian Studies, during the nineteenth century (Fähndrich 1976; Irwin 1999, esp. 91–101, 104–107). Accordingly, such comparisons as Qur'ānic scholars have drawn to the study of the Bible tend to compare the Islamic sacred text with the Christian Old Testament. Insofar as the historical process by which these two corpora formed differs considerably, Nöldeke and others could rightly insist that the history of the Qur'ān and its canonization were radically different, thus obviating the need to subject Islam's sacred writing to the same level of scrutiny given to the Hebrew Bible. Such thinking is readily apparent, for example, when Fred Donner more recently explains that methods from biblical studies are not "applicable to the study of the Islamic materials, which crystallized much more rapidly than the Old Testament tradition" (Donner 1998, 29). Indeed, Julius Wellhausen, another of Ewald's students, achieved radical breakthroughs in the study of both the Hebrew Bible and the early Islamic historical tradition (Wellhausen 1883; 1902). Nevertheless, Wellhausen failed to apply his insights into the Bible's formation to a similar study of the Qur'ān, no doubt because the traditional accounts of the Qur'ān's rapid collection could not allow for the sort of slow evolution that Wellhausen discovered within the Hebrew Bible. And neither he nor any of his contemporaries brought to bear on the early Islamic tradition the sort of radical critique that Baur and others had begun to apply to the origins of Christianity with increasing intensity.

The Collection of the Qur'ān

The Qur'ān's virtual segregation from the critical perspectives applied to the Jewish and Christian Scriptures depends largely on certain assumptions about the Qur'ān's formation, which many modern scholars have adopted almost unaltered from the traditional Islamic accounts of the Qur'ān's collection. According to the most widely accepted narrative of the Qur'ān's formation, Muḥammad's teachings circulated orally for only a brief period before they were gathered together and written down at the direction of the caliph 'Uthmān (r. 644–656), during the second half of his reign. For the most part, modern scholarship has followed the early precedent established by Nöldeke in accepting the claims of the Islamic tradition that the *ne varietur* text of the Qur'ān was collected both early and under official supervision by some of Muḥammad's closest followers, thereby ensuring the complete authenticity of the Qur'ān as a witness to Muḥammad's teachings. In this regard and many others, as Andrew Rippin has recently observed, "when modern scholars approach the Qur'ān, the core assumptions of the Muslim tradition about the text are not challenged."[10] Indeed, such an early collection would leave very little time for the early Islamic community to have effected significant changes in the text of the Qur'ān, potentially securing a strong connection between the Qur'ānic *textus receptus* and Muḥammad's religious teaching.

Nevertheless, the Islamic tradition itself preserves several divergent accounts of the Qur'ān's collection, including one ascribing the task to the first caliph Abū Bakr (d. 634). In his article on the Qur'ān in the second edition of the *Encyclopaedia of Islam*, Alfred Welch considers this alternative tradition, concluding that "there are serious problems with this account" and dismissing it because "most of the key points in this story are contradicted by alternative accounts in the canonical *ḥadīth* collections and other early Muslim sources." Yet Welch further remarks that the story of the Qur'ān's 'Uthmānic collection "stands up to critical analysis no better than the first [i.e., Abū Bakr's collection]," and he estimates it to be "another story whose particulars cannot be accepted." Despite this negative judgment, Welch nonetheless resolves that "the unanimity with which an official text is attributed to 'Uthmān, in the face of a lack of convincing evidence to the contrary," ensures that the consonantal text of the Qur'ān can be assigned to the reign of 'Uthmān (Welch 1960–2005, 405). Motzki has published an *isnād*-critical study of the tradition of an 'Uthmānic collection in an effort to demonstrate its veracity (Motzki 2001). Although Motzki identifies a probability that this tradition may be associated with al-Zuhrī, this finding certainly does not decide the question of the Qur'ān's origins; rather, it merely reveals that this story had begun to circulate by the middle of the eighth century, presumably alongside other rival accounts. Indeed, despite the widespread acceptance of this account of the Qur'ān's 'Uthmānic origins, there seems to be little reason for investing this tradition with any more veracity than scholars of early Christianity have allowed Papias' account of the Gospels' formation, particularly in light of the significant problems that Welch identifies with the 'Uthmānic tradition.[11]

There is in fact considerable evidence suggesting that the text of the Qur'ān remained in flux beyond the reign of 'Uthmān, as Wansbrough has argued rather persuasively on the basis of the Qur'ānic text itself and early Islamic literature concerning the Qur'ān.[12] Likewise, Gerald Hawting and Crone have demonstrated that certain aspects of the Islamic legal tradition seem to suggest the Qur'ān's later redaction (Hawting 1989; Crone 1994), and Claude Gilliot has argued for an understanding of the Qur'ān as a product of collective work, calling attention to the traditions of Muḥammad's "informants" (Gilliot 1998; 2004; 2005; 2008). Perhaps the most intriguing alternative to the 'Uthmānic collection is the recent revival of Paul Casanova's earlier hypothesis that the Qur'ān was redacted under 'Abd al-Malik (685–705), a position championed in particular by Alfred-Louis de Prémare, whose works have been unfortunately overlooked by much recent scholarship on the Qur'ān and Islamic origins.[13] De Prémare points to compelling evidence for the instability of the Qur'ānic text still at the end of the seventh century (see also M. Cook 2000, 118–122; Welch 1960–2005, 404b), while also noting the existence of traditions reporting that 'Abd al-Malik worked in concert with his governor of Iraq, al-Ḥajjāj, to standardize the text of the Qur'ān. 'Abd al-Malik's strategy was, de Prémare proposes, to displace various divergent codices that were being used in different cities, with the goal of establishing a religious unity that would foster cohesion of the Islamic polity around his central authority. As for the legend of a collection under 'Uthmān, de Prémare regards this as a piece of Umayyad propaganda, designed to bolster their dynastic claims by ascribing to the first caliph from their family this pious act of collecting the Islamic Scripture. The legend ultimately attained its canonical status through inclusion in al-Bukhārī's highly influential collection of *ḥadīth*.

Chase Robinson has recently endorsed the idea of the Qur'ān's collection under 'Abd al-Malik, noting that even if 'Uthmān may have made an effort to standardize the text, he lacked the means by which to enforce his new version: "in a polity that lacked many rudimentary instruments of coercion and made no systematic attempt to project images of its own transcendent authority—no coins, little public building or inscriptions—the very idea of 'official' is problematic." 'Abd al-Malik, however, not only "had the resources to attempt such a redaction and to impose the resulting text," but his reign also witnessed a concerted effort to Islamicize political authority "by broadcasting ideas of order and obedience in a distinctly Islamic idiom" (Robinson 2005, 102–104). Even Angelika Neuwirth seems to have more or less conceded the possibility that the text of the Qur'ān remained in flux and was not standardized before the reign of 'Abd al-Malik. Although she clearly remains loyal to the traditional position of the Qur'ān's collection under 'Uthmān, Neuwirth allows, in addressing de Prémare's work, that the *ne varietur textus receptus* of the Qur'ān was perhaps not established until 'Abd al-Malik's rule. Nevertheless, she insists that even if the text was fixed only at this later date, this would allow a period of at most only sixty years between "the completion of the text" (apparently the end of Muḥammad's life) and its publication in an authoritative edition. "Contrary to de Prémare's conclusions," she maintains, such a brief interval "is too short to allow sufficient room for significant, that is, deliberate, theologically relevant modifications of the text" (Neuwirth 2007, 18*–22*, esp. 19*).

The comparanda of the Christian Gospels, however, show such claims to be unfounded. If once again writings of the Hebrew Bible are the model, then the time frame is indeed comparatively short. But the Christian Gospels, by contrast, took literary form fairly quickly: the Q collection was compiled perhaps as early as twenty to thirty years after the death of Jesus, while the first Gospels appeared within forty to fifty years. It is a fundamental principle of New Testament criticism that during this short interval, the so-called tunnel period, the early Christian community shaped and reshaped—even "invented"—traditions about Jesus' life and teachings.[14] If we follow Robinson's prescription that the study of early Islam should be "committed to the idea that the history made by Muslims is comparable to that made by non-Muslims" (Robinson 2005, 103), then one must allow the possibility that similar changes occurred during the early oral transmission of the Qur'ānic traditions. One certainly cannot, as Neuwirth resolves, simply exclude this possibility as a matter of principle. Indeed, future study of the Qur'ān will need to confront more seriously the potential impact of oral transmission on the shape of the Qur'ān. It will no longer suffice, in a methodologically comparative context, to insist on its complete authenticity and integrity with hollow appeals to the brevity of its transmission.

Muḥammad's Message: Eschatological Herald or Social Reformer?

At the most general level, the Qur'ān reveals a monotheist religious movement grounded in the biblical and extrabiblical traditions of Judaism and Christianity, to which certain uniquely "Arab" traditions have been added. These traditions, however, are often related in an allusive style, which seems to presuppose knowledge of the larger narrative on the part of the audience. There is clear emphasis on articulating the boundaries of this religious community, particularly in relation to other Arab "polytheists," but also with regard to Jews and Christians. The Qur'ān also regulates social practices and boundaries within the community, proclaiming God's divine law in a fashion reminiscent of the Jewish Scriptures. Likewise, there is pressing concern with the impending arrival of "the Hour," or "God's command (*amr*)," terms that designate the final judgment: Muḥammad and his earliest followers seem to have believed that this eschatological event was about to take place or indeed had already begun. Muḥammad thus appears as a monotheist prophet within the Abrahamic tradition who called his followers to renounce paganism, to submit to the divine laws, and to prepare themselves for the impending doom: altogether, it is a portrait rather familiar from the Jewish and Christian Scriptures.

Nevertheless, recent scholarship on Islamic origins, particularly in English, has often failed to give the eschatological aspect of Muḥammad's message the proper emphasis that it deserves. From the beginnings of Western study of Islam, scholars have recognized the importance of "the Hour" in Muḥammad's preaching: the coming judgment is in fact the second most common theme of the Qur'ān, preceded only by the call to monotheism (Bell and Watt 1970, 158). Yet despite the Qur'ān's frequent focus on the impending eschaton, many modern experts have sought to minimize the significance of this belief within the early community. In presenting Muḥammad and his message to a modern audience, these scholars generally portray him as a great social reformer and preacher of ethical monotheism. While neither of these traits is inherently contradictory with belief in the world's imminent destruction, these biographers of Muḥammad would have him appear, as Richard Bell explains, not as "a crack-brained enthusiast" ranting about impending doom, but rather as a great leader whose religious message was "from the very start quite a rational and practical one" (Bell 1926, 71–72, 80, 83). Yet in diminishing Muḥammad's eschatological fervor, these studies efface what is perhaps one of the most clearly identifiable features of both the historical figure of Muḥammad and the religious community that he founded.

Snouck Hurgronje seems to have been the first to locate imminent eschatology at the heart of Muḥammad's message. Muḥammad's appearance was itself reckoned to be a sign of the world's impending destruction, and Hurgronje further suggests that his followers did not expect him to die before the

Hour's arrival (Hurgronje 1886, 26). The coming end of the world was the primary inspiration for Muḥammad's preaching, and from beginning to end, he was "haunted" by the notion of divine judgment and its immediate proximity. Other elements of his message were "more or less accessories" to the fundamental theme of the world's imminent judgment and destruction, which always remained "the essential element of Muḥammad's preaching" (Hurgronje 1894, 149–151, 161–162). Frants Buhl also shared this view, arguing that Muḥammad's overpowering concern with the looming eschaton and dread of the horrifying punishments "ruled all of his thoughts" and stood at the core of his message (Buhl 1930, 126–127, 132–133, 144–145, 157; 1936, 645–646). It was Paul Casanova, however, who developed this hypothesis most forcefully. Much like Hurgronje, Casanova proposed that Muḥammad and his followers believed that the end of the world was imminent and could be expected before Muḥammad's death. Casanova went a bit further, however, in offering an explanation for those parts of the Qur'ān that could seem to soften the Hour's immediacy: according to him, these passages reflect the work of Abū Bakr, 'Uthmān, and others, who either "falsified" or carefully "concealed" the true nature of Muḥammad's original eschatological teachings (Casanova 1911–1924, 4). In their day, Casanova's ideas were widely rejected, in particular because they challenged the Qur'ān's integrity as a transparent record of Muḥammad's religious teaching (e.g., Hurgronje 1916, 15–18; Bergsträsser and Pretzl 1938, 6–8; Bell and Watt 1970, 53–54). The reaction is somewhat surprising, in light of the contemporary "discovery" of the importance of apocalyptic and eschatology in early Judaism and Christianity (e.g., Weiss 1892; Schweitzer 1910).

Nevertheless, Bell's 1925 Gunning Lectures, published as *The Origin of Islam in Its Christian Environment*, mark the beginnings of a shift in English-language scholarship away from an eschatological understanding of primitive Islam. Since Bell, Muḥammad has often been portrayed as primarily a prophet of ethical monotheism, who aimed above all else to reform the social order rather than warning of its impending divine dissolution. According to Bell, the heart of Muḥammad's preaching was not the imminence of the Hour but instead a call "to recognize and worship the one true God and show thankfulness for His bounties." Only when his fellow Meccans refused to heed this admonition did Muḥammad eventually turn to themes of eschatology and divine judgment, hoping to frighten his audience into changing their ways. For a time, Muḥammad himself came to believe that such eschatological warnings were indeed the message of revelation that he had been charged to deliver, but once he attained authority over Medina, the last judgment passed "into the realm of assured dogma in Muḥammad's mind" (Bell 1926, 72, 102–107). Thus, Muḥammad's fervent warnings of impending doom were merely a passing phase, a "practical-minded" effort to accommodate his message to his audience.

This reconstruction of Muḥammad's evolving message, however, depends primarily on Bell's idiosyncratic attempt to date individual traditions within the Qur'ān (Bell 1958, 72–138), which even Watt, Bell's most sympathetic disciple, found somewhat questionable (Watt 1957). Only by assigning a very specific order to various elements of the Qur'ān can Bell marginalize its considerable eschatological content in this fashion. Bell's hypothesis demands that a handful of non-eschatological traditions focused on the revelation of "signs" should be identified with Muḥammad's earliest preaching. Nevertheless, Bell's views concerning the order of the Qur'ān have not found much acceptance, and there seems to be a broad consensus that it is not possible to define the precise chronology of the earliest Qur'ānic *sūras*. Even among those scholars who have adopted Nöldeke's influential fourfold chronological schema of the Qur'ān (Nöldeke and Schwally 1909–1919, 1:174–164), there is general agreement that the precise order of the earliest *sūras* cannot be known, but they must instead be "understood as a group rather than as standing in the exact chronological order of their revelation" (Böwering 2001–2006, 322–326). Yet Nöldeke's system, despite its widespread acceptance, is no more reliable than Bell's: as Welch rightly notes, this prevailing hypothesis is "little more than a European variation of the traditional dating," and those scholars embracing this approach to the Qur'ān "have not demonstrated the validity of the historical framework or the development of ideas and key terms assumed by their system" (Welch 1960–2005, 417; see also Reynolds 2008, 9; Donner 2008, 29).

Harris Birkeland advanced a hypothesis similar to Bell's, arguing that Muḥammad's fundamental religious message was rooted not in eschatological urgency but "the recognition of God's merciful guidance in the life of himself [i.e., Muḥammad] and his people" (Birkeland 1956, 5). Yet Birkeland reaches this conclusion only through a rather arbitrary selection of five *sūras* to represent Muḥammad's earliest preaching. Likewise, Watt, despite his criticism of Bell's system, follows his mentor's decisions regarding both the earliest traditions of the Qur'ān and the relatively marginal role of eschatology in Muḥammad's religious system. Eschatology is not a major factor in the small group of passages that Watt identifies as the earliest, and when Muḥammad later turns to themes of divine judgment, he has in mind either temporal chastisement or a distant final judgment that will come "at some unspecified future time" (Watt 1953, 62–66). This displacement of Muḥammad's eschatological urgency enables Watt to portray Muḥammad as the social and moral reformer for which his work is so famous (Watt 1953, 1–25, 72–85; cf. Crone 1987a). Instead of a "crack-brained" eschatological enthusiast who mistakenly forecast the world's destruction, Watt imagines Islam's founder to have been a much more "practical" and "rational" prophet striving for economic justice and an increase in personal piety.

Rudi Paret has rightly criticized these efforts to exclude eschatological themes from Muḥammad's earliest preaching, calling attention in part to their basis in an arbitrary selection of a primitive core of Qur'ānic passages. Paret observes that in the *sūras* assigned by Nöldeke to the earliest Meccan period, eschatology is simply too prominent to be so lightly cast aside. Perhaps more important, Paret suggests that it is misguided to insist that Muḥammad's initial preaching must have focused on either monotheism or eschatology exclusively. The two ideas are complementary, and one would expect that as Muḥammad began to preach, he offered a message of impending judgment grounded in ethical monotheism (Paret 2005, 69–79). Nevertheless, and most important, Paret resists any notion that Muḥammad believed the final judgment to be imminent. Rather, Paret views the Qur'ān's warnings of impending judgment as Muḥammad's threats against his opponents that they would suffer temporal chastisement, while the final judgment was an event belonging to the distant future. In this regard, Paret ultimately does not depart very far from Bell and Watt's uneschatological prophet: Muḥammad may have preached eschatological ideas from the very start, but according to Paret, these were lacking any sense of urgency (Paret 2005, 96–98).

On the whole, Watt's views in particular continue to hold sway in most English-language scholarship. A prime example can be found in Welch's revision of Buhl's article on Muḥammad for the *Encyclopaedia of Islam*: Welch transforms the eschatological prophet of Buhl's original article into Watt's social and economic reformer (Buhl and Welch 1960–2005, 363–364). Peters seems to favor Birkeland's hypothesis (Peters 1994, 152–156), but most other scholars have embraced the non-eschatological reformer imagined by Watt.[15] Presumably, such apparent consensus inspired Karen Armstrong to misleadingly claim that "the Last Judgment was only mentioned briefly in the earliest suras, or chapters, of the Qur'an but the early message was essentially joyful." According to Armstrong, Muḥammad preached the benevolence of God as manifest in the creation and struggled tirelessly on behalf of the poor and oppressed against the rich and powerful. Any apparent Qur'ānic references to "the approaching Last Judgment are essentially symbolic representations of divine truths and should not be understood as literal facts" (Armstrong 1993, 91–107, esp. 91, 99). While a handful of scholars have recently proposed resurrecting the eschatological prophet revealed by the Qur'ān (Donner 1998, 30, n. 78, 46; 2002, 10–13; Ayoub 2003, 145–146; D. Cook 2002, 30), Asma Afsaruddin perpetuates the status quo in dismissing their arguments as "hardly convincing." Instead, she identifies "the Qur'an's clear and powerful message" not as a warning before the impending judgment of the Hour, but as a call to "egalitarianism and social justice" aimed especially at "those who were on the periphery of society" (Afsaruddin 2008, 3, 26).

It is hard not to hear in these descriptions of Muḥammad as a non-eschatological prophet of ethical monotheism and social justice an echo of the various nineteenth-century "liberal" biographies of Jesus. One would likewise suspect that a similar tendency is at work in shaping this image of Muḥammad: sympathy for their subject has inspired these scholars to find a timeless great teacher whose message can speak to modern men and women, rather than an eschatological preacher who, together with his followers, mistakenly expected the world to end in their day (cf. Schweitzer 1910, 402–403; Sanders 1985, 154; Ehrman 1999, 127). Yet if we approach the issue of eschatology in the Qur'ān in the same manner as it has been pursued in the New Testament, it is difficult to escape the conclusion that Muḥammad and his earliest followers, like Jesus and the first Christians, believed themselves to be living in the last days.

"It Is Knowledge of the Hour": Muḥammad, the Qur'ān, and Eschatology

The Qur'ān is rife with eschatological warnings of the impending judgment and destruction of the Hour: the Qur'ān itself defines the very subject of its revelation as "knowledge of the hour—do not doubt concerning it" (43.61).[16] "Nigh unto men has drawn their reckoning," warns another passage (21.1), while one verse declares that "God's command [*amr*] comes" or, even more literally, "God's command has arrived" (16.1). Such pronouncements recall the declaration with which Jesus allegedly began his ministry: "the Kingdom of God is at hand" (Mark 1:15 and parallels). Likewise, the Qur'ānic "parable of the two men" (18.31–44) resembles Jesus' parable of the rich fool (Luke 12:13–21), particularly in its emphasis on the short eschatological window that remains. "The matter of the Hour is as a twinkling of the eye, or nearer" (16.79), warns the Qur'ān. The coming judgment is "imminent" (40.18), or, with even greater force, "the Imminent is imminent" (54.57).[17] The "Lord's chastisement"—or "judgment" or "the terror"—"is about to fall" upon the world; "none denies its descending," and "there is none to avert it" (52.7–8; 51.6; 56.1–2). The chastisement is indeed near (78.40; cf. 27.72; 36.49), and the Qur'ān promises that the punishments of Hell and the bliss of paradise will be known soon "with the knowledge of certainty" (102.3–5). The Qur'ān threatens that all who disregard its warning will soon behold the Hour and its punishments with their own eyes (19.75).

Other passages refer to certain astronomical events that will signal the Hour's arrival: "surely that which you are promised is about to fall! When the stars shall be extinguished, when heaven shall be split, when the mountains shall be scattered and when the Messenger's time is set, to what day shall they be delayed? To the Day of Decision" (77.7–13; see also 45.17; 52.9; 75.7–9; 81.1–2; 82.1–2). Many such signs had already occurred "in the heavens and on the earth" and yet had gone unheeded (12.105): "The Hour has drawn nigh: the moon is split. Yet if they see a sign they turn away" (54.1–2; cf. 69.16). Presumably, as David Cook suggests, these and other passages refer to some remarkable astronomical event that Muḥammad and other inhabitants of the Ḥijāz had recently witnessed (D. Cook 2001a). The Qur'ān often refers to such signs to refute the doubts of skeptics regarding the Hour's immediacy: "Are they looking for aught but the Hour, that it shall come upon them suddenly? Already its tokens have come" (47.20).

Other passages similarly respond to disbelief in the Hour and its imminent arrival: "soon they shall know!" warns the Qur'ān. "Already Our Word has preceded to Our servants. . . . So turn thou from them for a while, and see them; soon they shall see! What, do they seek to hasten Our chastisement?" (37.170–179). In the face of such doubts, the Qur'ān counsels the faithful, "be thou patient with a sweet patience; behold they see it as far off; but We see it is nigh" (70.5–7); similar sentiments are echoed in a number of other passages (e.g., 15.3; 36.49; 75.34–35; 78.4–5; 79.46). When the unbelievers ask to know precisely when the Hour will arrive, the Qur'ān declares that knowledge of the Hour lies with God alone (7.187; 31.34; 41.47; 43.85). Nevertheless, this acknowledgment of the limits to human knowledge does not necessarily indicate weakening of belief in the Hour's immediacy. Although "the knowledge is with God," the Qur'ān rebuffs its audience, "assuredly you will soon know who is in manifest error" (67.26–29; cf. 33.63; 79.44–46). Yet perhaps such uncertainties are also an early sign of efforts to accommodate the Hour's unanticipated delay: while the Hour is still believed to be nigh, it has not arrived with the haste that was initially anticipated.

Other passages betray this redactional tendency more clearly. For instance, the Qur'ān explains that although the Hour is imminent, one should recall that for God a day is a thousand years (22.47; cf. 32.5) or even 50,000 years (70.4). Yet despite the difference between divine and mortal calendars, belief in the Hour's impending arrival remains constant in these passages: "they see it as if far off, but We see it is nigh" (70.6–7; cf. 22.55). In a few places, the Qur'ān proclaims the Hour's imminence with slightly more hesitancy. "It is possible [*'asa an*] that it may be nigh," but when it comes, "you will think you have tarried but a little" (17.51–52). Indeed, "it may be [*'asa an*] that riding behind you already is some part of that which you seek to hasten on" (27.72). Although God alone knows when the Hour will descend, "Haply [*la'lla*] the Hour is nigh" (33.63; cf. 42.17). Various other passages urge persistence in light of the Hour's unexpected delay (e.g., 11.8; 40.77), but only once does the Qur'ān allow even the possibility that the eschaton may in fact not be imminent. Despite its pervasive and fervent warnings of the Hour's threatening immediacy, a single passage equivocates, conceding, "I do not know whether that which you are promised is nigh, or whether my Lord will appoint it for a space" (72.25).

Bell, Watt, Blachère, and others adduce these passages as evidence of Muḥammad's evolving eschatological timetable, using them to relegate any concern with the Hour's fearful imminence to a mere passing phase in Muḥammad's religious development (e.g., Bell 1926, 86–90, 102–107; Bell and Watt 1970, 54; Blachère 1952, 43–51; 1959, 22–24; Rodinson 1971, 120–123). Although Muḥammad for a time experimented with ideas that he borrowed from Jewish and Christian apocalyptic, primarily in an effort to win converts, once he achieved power over Medina, this perspective was abandoned as no longer useful. At this point, the Hour was increasingly pushed into the distant future, and this new orientation can be detected in the Qur'ān's occasionally more guarded forecast of the Hour's impending arrival. Such passages are understood as Muḥammad's direct cancellation of his earlier focus on eschatological immediacy. In this way, the Qur'ān's ethical teaching and its program for the early Islamic community are made to emerge as the true core of Muḥammad's message. Admittedly, this hypothesis effectively resolves an apparent tension within the Qur'ān: its frequent warnings of impending eschatological doom can seem difficult to reconcile with the parallel concern to define the nature and structure of the early community. Such attention to details of social and political order would appear to be contradicted by the belief that the world itself would soon pass away, a dissonance that Bell, Watt, and others have chosen to resolve by determining the priority of the former. Yet a comparison with formative Christianity suggests that any such conflict may be more imagined than real: the writings of the New Testament often show concern for defining and maintaining a well-ordered community, even in the face of the world's impending judgment and destruction.[18] One would assume such ideas could similarly coexist in earliest Islam.

Perspectives from New Testament studies are also helpful for understanding the different shades of urgency with which certain passages from the Qur'ān proclaim the Hour's impending arrival. The sayings of Jesus occasionally exhibit similar ambivalence regarding the Kingdom's immediacy: although most statements about the Kingdom proclaim its immediacy, a minority tradition suggests that its coming should be expected further into the future. Innumerable studies have examined this eschatological tension in the Gospels, with the clear majority concluding that the historical Jesus preached the world's imminent judgment, heralding the eschaton's arrival within the lifespan of his earliest followers.[19] By applying the same principles to analysis of the Qur'ān, one finds that Muḥammad and his earliest followers seem to have similarly believed that their generation would live to see the end of the world.[20] Although the Qur'ān reflects some diversity of opinion regarding the timing of the Hour's arrival, as with the Jesus traditions, one eschatological position clearly predominates, namely, the Hour's pressing imminence (cf. Sanders 1985, 152–153; 1993, 176–177). Likewise, the response of the unbelievers as depicted by the Qur'ān suggests that Muḥammad's preaching had led them to believe that they would soon behold the Hour's arrival for themselves (e.g., 19.75; 37.170–179; 102.3–5). More important, however, it seems highly unlikely that this prevailing voice, warning of the Hour's immediate approach, is the invention of the later Islamic community, inasmuch as such promises were soon falsified by the passing of Muḥammad and his early followers. The criteria of embarrassment and dissimilarity (i.e., dissimilarity with the experience of the early community) strongly suggest that the historical Muḥammad and the religious community that he founded professed that the world would soon end in divine judgment and destruction. To be sure, a strong eschatological perspective would persist in later Islam (as it did in Christianity), but it seems highly improbable that later Muslims would insert traditions into the Qur'ān wrongly predicting the Hour's appearance in the immediate future (cf. Schweitzer 1910, 360–363; Sanders 1993, 180).

Qur'ānic traditions that may seem to suggest a less narrow eschatological horizon are, like similar elements in the New Testament, the result of efforts to accommodate the primitive kerygma of the impending Hour to the passage of time. For instance, as noted earlier, the Qur'ān occasionally maintains, particularly in responding to its critics, that knowledge of when the Hour will arrive belongs to God alone. While some Western scholars have appealed to such statements as evidence that the early Muslims did not in fact expect the Hour's arrival within their lifetimes (e.g., Rüling 1895, 11; Smith 2002, 46), comparison with the Jesus traditions suggests otherwise. Jesus seems to have similarly preached that the timing of the Kingdom's arrival was known by the Father alone, while insisting that its appearance was imminent (e.g., Matthew 24:32–25:12; cf. Schweitzer 1910, 239). Far from contradicting the Hour's immediacy, these passages instead complement the Qur'ān's emphasis on its sudden and unexpected appearance. Yet it is certainly not out of the question that such sentiments first arose shortly after Muḥammad's lifetime, as the early community struggled to make sense of the Hour's protracted delay.

As the writings of the New Testament evidence, the early Christians adopted a variety of hermeneutic strategies to "correct" Jesus' inaccurate forecast of impending doom (e.g., Sanders 1993, 179–182), and one should expect to find similar tendencies at work in the early Islamic tradition. The gulf between divine and human perceptions of time, for instance, explained the parousia's delay for many early Christians (cf. 2 Peter 3:8, referring to Psalm 90:4), and the Qur'ān likewise invokes this contrast on occasion. While the Qur'ān situates such reflections within the context of the Hour's immediacy, these passages seem designed to soften the blow of the Hour's delay, and as even Bell observes, they have the appearance of interpolations, added by the early Islamic community "to obviate the difficulty of the delay in the coming event" (Bell 1937–1939, 2:604). Likewise, those verses introducing a note of hesitancy regarding the Hour's imminence probably reflect the perspective of the early community rather than Muḥammad's preaching: often by adding only a single word or two, statements heralding the Hour's imminent arrival could easily be qualified to meet the inconsistencies of its continued delay. One should note, however, that such alterations of the text need not be crudely judged as acts of "forgery" somehow inconsistent with the Qur'ān's status as divine revelation. To the contrary, insofar as the primitive Islamic community treasured the Qur'ān as God's infallible revelation through Muḥammad, it would be absolutely essential that its contents should comport with the reality of continued existence. If, as appears to be the case, Muḥammad warned his initial followers that the Hour would arrive very soon, a more conditional tone would have to be discovered to make sense of this eschatological promise for future generations. As in the New Testament, but to a more limited extent, the Qur'ān shows traces of the early community's efforts to adjust Muḥammad's eschatological warnings to the persistence of human history.

It is particularly important that the Qur'ān's imminent eschatology finds significant confirmation in a number of early *ḥadīth*. For instance, at the end of Ibn Isḥāq's biography, when Muḥammad dies, 'Umar, the future caliph, refuses to accept Muḥammad's death, swearing, "By God he is not dead: he has gone to his Lord as Moses b. 'Imrān went and was hidden from his people for forty days, returning to them after it was said that he had died. By God, the apostle will return as Moses returned and will cut off the hands and feet of men who allege that the apostle is dead" (Ibn Hishām 1858–1860, 1:1012; trans. Guillaume 1955, 682–683). When 'Umar is later asked to clarify his behavior, he explains that he truly believed that Muḥammad would remain with the people until the Hour to serve as a witness for them regarding their final deeds, citing Qur'ān 2.143 (Ibn Hishām 1858–1860, 1:1017–1018), while in another account, he justifies himself "because he [Muḥammad] said that he thought that he would be the last of us [alive]" (Ibn Sa'd 1904–1928, 2.2:56; cf. al-Ṭabarī 1990, 200, n. 1328).

Other early traditions describe Muḥammad as having been "sent on the breath of the Hour," noting that his appearance and that of the Hour were concomitant to the extent that the Hour had almost outstripped his own arrival (Bashear 1993, 76–80). According to another tradition, Muḥammad offered his followers a promise (reminiscent of Matthew 16:28, 24:34) that the Hour would arrive before some of his initial followers died (D. Cook 2002, 4; Livne-Kafri 1999, 76, n. 22). In another tradition, Muḥammad responds to questions about the Hour's timing by pointing to the youngest man in the crowd and declaring that "if this young man lives, the Hour will arrive before he reaches old age" (e.g., Muslim b. al-Ḥajjāj 1995, 4:1795–1796). One senses here the beginnings of a process of chronological extension, the growth of which can be seen in a promise that "at the end of one-hundred years there will be no one alive on the earth" (Bashear 1993, 87–92; D. Cook 2001b). Yet as this deadline and still others passed, new predictions continued to arise, refreshing the Hour's immediacy for each generation (Bashear 1993, 92–98). As with the eschatological predictions assigned to Jesus, it is difficult to imagine the fabrication of such eschatological urgency by the later Muslim community, let alone its attribution to Muḥammad. The same can be said of certain traditions concerning the first mosque at Medina: as Meir Kister observes, Muḥammad's instruction not to build a roof for the structure "because the affair [*al-amr*] will happen sooner than that" (Kister 1962, 150) seems to suggest a primitive belief in the Hour's imminence. The dissonance of such material with the Hour's manifest delay speaks very strongly in favor of its antiquity if not even authenticity. When joined with the Qur'ān's unmistakable warning that the end of the world had come upon its audience, it is difficult to avoid the conclusion that Muḥammad and his earliest followers ardently believed themselves to be living in the shadow of the eschaton, in the waning moments of human history.

Consequently, the present "quest for the historical Muḥammad," finds itself confronted by a dilemma rather similar to the one identified by Albert Schweitzer in his seminal study of the "historical Jesus": one must choose to follow either a "thoroughgoing skepticism" or a "thoroughgoing eschatology" (Schweitzer 1910, 330–403). Like the Christian Gospels, the earliest narratives of Islamic origins are heavily determined by the theological interests of the later community (i.e., "salvation history"), inviting the conclusion, with Wansbrough, that all "historical" knowledge of Muḥammad and the origins of Islam has been lost, obscured by the imagination of medieval Islam. Alternatively, however, one may adopt the position of "thoroughgoing eschatology," which reveals a historically probable Muḥammad, who, like Jesus, was an eschatological prophet of the end times. The imminent eschatology of the Qur'ān and many early *ḥadīth* invites recovery of this apocalyptic preacher who, with his followers, expected to see the end of the world very soon, seemingly even in his own lifetime. The preservation of such material against the interests of the later tradition suggests that it preserves a credible approximation of the *ipsissima vox Machometi*. While such an image of Muḥammad will perhaps be of little relevance for modern believers, much like Schweitzer's Jesus, it nevertheless presents a plausible reconstruction worthy of standing alongside the historical Jesus, having been recovered using comparable methods and assumptions.

NOTES

1. E.g., the article on "sīra" in the second edition of the *Encyclopaedia of Islam* evaluates these biographical traditions as essentially useless for knowledge of either the historical figure of Muḥammad or the rise of Islam: Raven 1960–2005, 662. See also Buhl 1930, 372–377; Rodinson 1971, xi; Wansbrough 1978b; Crone 1980, 3–17; 1987a, 214–230; Peters 1991, 301–306; Hawting 1997; 1999; Robinson 2002, 8–25; 2003, 121–124.

2. For specific examples, see Donner 1998, 7–9; Hoyland 2007, 597, n. 6. Hodgson, for his part, despite his critical assessments of the sources, nevertheless gives a rehash of the traditional account. Even F. E. Peters, who in one place writes, "Goldziher, Lammens and Schacht were all doubtless correct" with regard to historical knowledge of Muḥammad's life (Peters 1991, 303), later composed his own biography of Muḥammad largely according to the accounts of the traditional sources (Peters 1994).

3. On the date of Ibn Isḥāq's biography, see Sellheim 1967, 33. For general discussions of the early *sīra* traditions, see Rubin 1998, xiii–xxxvi; 1995, 5–17; Jones 1983, 343–346; Humphreys 1991, 77–80; and esp. Hinds 1983.

4. Robinson 2002, 25; see also al-Samuk 1978, 160–161; Conrad 1993, 260–261; Motzki 2003, 174.

5. Juynboll 1989; 1991; 1992; 1993; 1996; Motzki 1991a; 1991b; 1998; 2002; 2003; 2005.

6. Calder 1993, 194–195; Hawting 1996; Berg 2000, 36–38, 112–114; Melchert 2003, 301–304; Hoyland 2007, 587.

7. The main exception to this consensus would be John Wansbrough, who argued that the Qur'ān was much later in forming. While many of the particulars of

his hypothesis, such as the final redaction of the Qur'ān only around 800, are admittedly somewhat questionable, Wansbrough's broader argument that the Qur'ān was in fact redacted later than the Islamic tradition remembers and under different circumstances is well made. Moreover, allowance for a historical connection between Muḥammad and the traditions of the Qur'ān need not entail an acceptance of the "authenticity" of all the traditions collected in the Qur'ān. Despite Western scholarship's long-standing acceptance of the Islamic tradition's views on the Qur'ān's identification with Muḥammad, the possibility of both additions and alterations to the text needs to be more widely considered, as discussed later.

8. For similar, more recent assessments, see Donner 2008, 29–30; Gilliot 2008, 88.

9. On Ewald's fierce opposition to the new approaches that had emerged within early Christian studies, as well as his nature as a mentor, see Davies 1903, 23, 36–40, 63–64, 68–71; Fück 1955, 167, 217; Harris 1975, 43–48; Baird 1992, 287–293; Hurgronje 1931, 245. For remarks on Ewald's methodological conservatism and resistance to the emergent historical-critical approaches within early Christian studies from perhaps the two greatest innovators of the field, see Baur 1860, 122–171; Schweitzer 1910, 116 (esp. n. 4), 135.

10. Rippin 2006, 240–247, esp. 242. See also, e.g., Rippin 1985, 153, 158–159; 1992, 641–642; Arkoun 1982.

11. Alfred-Louis de Prémare draws a similar comparison with Papias' testimony: de Prémare 2004b, 176, 183. The fragments of Papias are most readily accessible in Ehrman 2003, 91–119. The most important fragments, regarding the Gospels of Mark and Matthew, are preserved in Eusebius, *Ecclesiastical History* III.39. Regarding the accuracy of Papias' account, see Kümmel 1975, 53–56, 94–97, 241–244; Schoedel 1993; Ehrman 1999, 42–45.

12. Wansbrough 1977, esp. 43–51. See also Rippin 1985; 1997; Wansbrough and Rippin 2004, xiv–xviii; Berg 1997; Hawting 1997; Mojaddedi 2000; Reynolds 2008, 12.

13. Casanova 1911–1924, 103–142; de Prémare 2001; 2002, 278–306; 2004a, esp. 57–136; 2004b; 2005. Cf. Mingana 1916; Crone and Cook 1977, 17–18; Hoyland 1997, 500–501.

14. See, e.g., Sanders 1993, 57–63; Ehrman 1999, 21–53; Dunn and McKnight 2005; Koester 1995, 2:59–64.

15. E.g., Rodinson 1971, 81–98; Rahman 1980, 37–64, 106–120; Muranyi 1986; Bennett 1998, 19, 128–132; Afzaal 2003; Zeitlin 2007.

16. Unless otherwise indicated, translations of the Qur'ān are from Arberry 1955. Nevertheless, I have followed the Egyptian system of numbering the verses for easier reference to the Arabic text.

17. Alternatively, one might translate the passage as: "the hastening [Hour] is at hand."

18. As much is reflected in the very title of John Gager's influential *Kingdom and Community*: Gager 1975. See also, e.g., Martin 1995; Theissen 1982; Overman 1990; Saldarini 1994; Balch 1991; Neyrey 1991.

19. While a small minority of New Testament scholars continue to argue that Jesus' message was non-eschatological, Ehrman dispenses with such hypotheses both swiftly and judiciously: Ehrman 1999, 132–134.

20. For comparison, see, e.g., Sanders 1985, 123–156, although one could still explore Weiss 1892 or Schweitzer 1910, 330–397, on this topic with profit, even at such a chronological distance. For more popular presentations of the same ideas, see Sanders 1993, 169–188; Ehrman 1999, 125–139.

WORKS CITED

Afsaruddin, Asma. 2008. *The First Muslims: History and Memory*. Oxford: Oneworld.
Afzaal, Ahmed. 2003. "The Origin of Islam as a Social Movement," *Islamic Studies* 42: 203–243.
Andræ, Tor. 1935. *Mohammed: The Man and His Faith*. Trans. Theophil William Menzel. New York: Barnes and Noble.
Arberry, A. J. 1955. *The Koran Interpreted*. London: Allen & Unwin.
Arkoun, Mohammed. 1982. "Bilan et perspectives des études coraniques." In *Lectures du Coran, v–xxxiii*. Paris: G. P. Maisonneuve et Larose.
Armstrong, Karen. 1993. *Muhammad: A Biography of the Prophet*. New York: Harper San Francisco.
Ayoub, Mahmoud. 2003. *The Crisis of Muslim History: Religion and Politics in Early Islam*. Oxford: Oneworld.
Baird, William. 1992. *History of New Testament Research, Vol. 1: From Deism to Tübingen*. 2 vols. Minneapolis, MN: Fortress Press.
Balch, David L., ed. 1991. *Social History of the Matthean Community: Cross-Disciplinary Approaches*. Minneapolis, MN: Fortress Press.
Bashear, Suliman. 1993. "Muslim Apocalypses and the Hour: A Case-Study in Traditional Reinterpretation," *Israel Oriental Studies* 13: 75–100.
Baur, Ferdinand Christian. 1860. *Die Tübinger Schule und ihre Stellung zur Gegenwart*, 2nd ed. Tübingen: L. Fr. Fues.
Bell, Richard. 1926. *The Origin of Islam in Its Christian Environment*. London: Macmillan.
———. 1937–1939. *The Qur'ān*. 2 vols. Edinburgh: T.&T. Clark.
———. 1958. *Introduction to the Qur'ān*. Edinburgh: At the University Press.
Bell, Richard, and W. Montgomery Watt. 1970. *Bell's Introduction to the Qur'ān*. Edinburgh: Edinburgh University Press.
Bennett, Clinton. 1998. *In Search of Muhammad*. London: Cassell.
Berg, Herbert. 1997. "The Implications of, and Opposition to, the Methods and Theories of John Wansbrough," *Method and Theory in the Study of Religion* 9: 3–22.
———. 2000. *The Development of Exegesis in Early Islam: The Authenticity of Muslim Literature from the Formative Period*. Richmond, Surrey: Curzon.
Bergsträsser, Gotthelf, and Otto Pretzl. 1938. *Geschichte des Qorāns III: Geschichte des Qorāntexts*, 2nd ed. Leipzig: Dieterich'sche Verlagsbuchhandlung.
Birkeland, Harris. 1956. *The Lord Guideth: Studies on Primitive Islam*. Skrifter utg. av det Norske videnskaps-akademi i Oslo, II: Hist.-filos., klasse, 1956, no. 2. Oslo: I kommisjon hos H. Aschehoug (W. Nygaard).
Blachère, Régis. 1952. *Le problème de Mahomet: Essai de biographie critique du fondateur de l'Islam*. Paris: Presses universitaires de France.
———. 1959. *Introduction au Coran*, 2nd ed. Paris: Besson and Chantemerle.
Böwering, Gerhard. 2001–2006. "Chronology and the Qur'ān." In *Encyclopaedia of the Qur'ān*, ed. Jane Dammen McAuliffe, 1:316–335. Leiden: Brill.
Buhl, Frants. 1930. *Das Leben Muhammeds*. Trans. Hans Heinrich Schaeder. Leipzig: Quelle & Meyer.
———. 1936. "Muḥammad." In *The Encyclopaedia of Islām*, ed. M. Th. Houtsma et al., 3:641–657. Leiden: E. J. Brill.
Buhl, Frants [and A. T. Welch]. 1960–2005. "Muḥammad." In *The Encyclopaedia of Islam*, ed. P. J. Bearman et al., 7:360–376. New ed. Leiden: E. J. Brill.

Caetani, Leone. 1905–1926. *Annali dell'Islām*. 10 vols. Milano: U. Hoepli.
Calder, Norman. 1993. *Studies in Early Muslim Jurisprudence*. Oxford: Clarendon.
Casanova, Paul. 1911–1924. *Mohammed et la fin du monde: Étude critique sur l'Islam primitif*. Paris: P. Gauthier.
Chabbi, Jacqueline. 1996. "Histoire et tradition sacrée: La biographie impossible de Mahomet," *Arabica* 43: 189–205.
Conrad, Lawrence I. 1993. "Recovering Lost Texts: Some Methodological Issues," *Journal of the American Oriental Society* 113: 258–263.
Cook, David. 2001a. "Messianism and Astronomical Events during the First Four Centuries of Islam." In *Mahdisme et millénarisme en Islam*, ed. Mercedes García-Arenal, 29–52. Revue des mondes musulmans et de la Méditerranée, Série Histoire. Aix-en-Provence: Édisud.
———. 2001b. "The Beginnings of Islam as an Apocalyptic Movement," *Journal of Millennial Studies* 1.1, www.bu.edu/mille/publications/winter2001/cook.html.
———. 2002. *Studies in Muslim Apocalyptic*. Studies in Late Antiquity and Early Islam 21. Princeton, NJ: Darwin Press.
Cook, Michael. 1981. *Early Muslim Dogma: A Source-Critical Study*. Cambridge: Cambridge University Press.
———. 1983. *Muhammad*. Oxford: Oxford University Press.
———. 1992. "Eschatology and the Dating of Traditions," *Princeton Papers in Near Eastern Studies* 1: 25–47.
———. 1997. "The Opponents of the Writing of Tradition in Early Islam," *Arabica* 44: 437–530.
———. 2000. *The Koran: A Very Short Introduction*. Oxford: Oxford University Press.
Crone, Patricia. 1980. *Slaves on Horses: The Evolution of the Islamic Polity*. Cambridge: Cambridge University Press.
———. 1987a. *Meccan Trade and the Rise of Islam*. Princeton, NJ: Princeton University Press.
———. 1987b. *Roman, Provincial and Islamic Law*. Cambridge Studies in Islamic Civilization. Cambridge: Cambridge University Press.
———. 1994. "Two Legal Problems Bearing on the Early History of the Qur'ān," *Jerusalem Studies in Arabic and Islam* 18: 1–37.
Crone, Patricia, and M. A. Cook. 1977. *Hagarism: The Making of the Islamic World*. Cambridge: Cambridge University Press.
Davies, T. Witton. 1903. *Heinrich Ewald, Orientalist and Theologian 1803–1903: A Centenary Appreciation*. London: T. Fisher Unwin.
de Prémare, Alfred-Louis. 2001. "Coran et Hadîth." In *Des Alexandries*, ed. Luce Giard and Christian Jacob, vol. 1, *Du livre au texte*, 179–195. 2 vols. Paris: Bibliothèque nationale de France.
———. 2002. *Les fondations de l'islam: Entre écriture et histoire*. L'Univers historique. Paris: Éditions du Seuil.
———. 2004a. *Aux origines du Coran: Questions d'hier, approches d'aujourd'hui*. L'Islam en débats. Paris: Téraèdre.
———. 2004b. "La constitution des écritures islamiques dans l'histoire." In *Al-Kitāb: La sacralité du texte dans le monde de l'Islam. Actes du Symposium International tenu à Leuven et Louvain-la-Neuve du 29 mai au 1 juin 2002*, ed. D. de Smet, G. de Callatay, and J. M. F. van Reeth, 175–184. Acta Orientalia Belgica, Subsidia 3. Brussels: Belgian Society of Oriental Studies.
———. 2005. "Abd al-Malik b. Marwān et le Processus de Constitution du Coran." In *Die dunklen Anfänge: Neue Forschungen zur Entstehung und frühen Geschichte des*

Islam, ed. Karl-Heinz Ohlig and Gerd-R. Puin, 179–210. Berlin: Verlag Hans Schiler.

Donner, Fred McGraw. 1998. *Narratives of Islamic Origins: The Beginnings of Islamic Historical Writing*. Studies in Late Antiquity and Early Islam 14. Princeton, NJ: Darwin Press.

———. 2002. "From Believers to Muslims: Confessional Self-Identity in the Early Islamic Community," *al-Abḥāth* 50.1: 9–53.

———. 2008. "The Qur'ān in Recent Scholarship: Challenges and Desiderata." In *The Qur'ān in Its Historical Context*, ed. Gabriel Said Reynolds, 29–50. Routledge Studies in the Qur'ān. London: Routledge.

Dunn, James D. G., and Scot McKnight. 2005. *The Historical Jesus in Recent Research*. Sources for Biblical and Theological Study 10. Winona Lake, IN: Eisenbrauns.

Ehrman, Bart D. 1999. *Jesus: Apocalyptic Prophet of the New Millennium*. New York: Oxford University Press.

———. 2003. *The Apostolic Fathers*. 2 vols. Loeb Classical Library 24–25. Cambridge, MA: Harvard University Press.

Fähndrich, Hartmut. 1976. "Invariable Factors Underlying the Historical Perspective in Theodor Nöldeke's *Orientalische Skizzen* (1892)." In *Akten des VII. Kongressesfür Arabistik und Islamwissenschaft*, ed. Albert Dietrich, 146–154. Göttingen: Vandenhoeck & Ruprecht.

Fück, Johann. 1955. *Die arabischen Studien in Europa bis in den Anfang des 20. Jahrhunderts*. Leipzig: Harrassowitz.

Gager, John G. 1975. *Kingdom and Community: The Social World of Early Christianity*. Englewood Cliffs, NJ: Prentice-Hall.

Gilliot, Claude. 1998. "Les 'informateurs' juifs et chrétiens de Muhammad: Reprise d'un problème traité par Aloys Sprenger et Theodor Nöldeke," *Jerusalem Studies in Arabic and Islam* 22: 84–126.

———. 2004. "Le Coran, fruit d'un travail collectif?" In *Al-Kitāb: La sacralité du texte dans le monde de l'Islam. Actes du Symposium International tenu à Leuven et Louvain-la-Neuve du 29 mai au 1 juin 2002*, ed. D. de Smet, G. de Callatay, and J. M. F. van Reeth, 185–223. Acta Orientalia Belgica, Subsidia 3. Brussels: Belgian Society of Oriental Studies.

———. 2005. "Les traditions sur la composition ou coordination du Coran (*ta'līf al-qur'ān*)." In *Das Prophetenḥadīṯ: Dimensionen einer islamischen Literaturgattung*, ed. C. Gilliot and T. Nagel, 14–39. Göttingen: Vandenhoeck & Ruprecht.

———. 2008. "Reconsidering the Authorship of the Qur'ān: Is the Qur'ān Partly the Fruit of a Progressive and Collective Work?" In *The Qur'ān in Its Historical Context*, ed. Gabriel Said Reynolds, 88–108. Routledge Studies in the Qur'ān. London: Routledge.

Goldziher, Ignác. 1889–1890. *Muhammedanische Studien*. 2 vols. Halle: M. Niemeyer.

———. 1967–1971. *Muslim Studies*. Ed. S. M. Stern. Trans. C. R. Barber and S. M. Stern. 2 vols. London: Allen & Unwin.

Görke, Andreas. 2000. "The Historical Tradition about al-Hudaybiya: A Study of 'Urwa b. al-Zubayr's Account." In *The Biography of Muhammad: The Issue of the Sources*, ed. Harald Motzki, 240–275. Leiden: E. J. Brill.

Görke, Andreas, and Gregor Schoeler. 2005. "Reconstructing the Earliest *Sīra* Texts: The Hiǧra in the Corpus of 'Urwa b. al-Zubayr," *Der Islam* 82: 209–220.

Guillaume, Alfred. 1955. *The Life of Muhammad*. London: Oxford University Press.

Halevi, Leor. 2007. *Muhammad's Grave: Death Rites and the Making of Islamic Society*. New York: Columbia University Press.

Harris, Horton. 1975. *The Tübingen School.* Oxford: Clarendon Press.
Hawting, Gerald R. 1989. "The Role of the Qur'ān and *ḥadīth* in the Legal Controversy about the Rights of a Divorced Woman during Her 'Waiting Period' (*'idda*)," *Bulletin of the Jewish Palestine Exploration Society* 52: 430–445.
———. 1996. "Review of Harald Motzki, *The Origins of Islamic Jurisprudence: Meccan Fiqh before the Classical Schools*," *Bulletin of the School of Oriental and African Studies* 59: 141–143.
———. 1997. "John Wansbrough, Islam, and Monotheism," *Method and Theory in the Study of Religion* 9: 23–38.
———. 1999. *The Idea of Idolatry and the Emergence of Islam: From Polemic to History.* Cambridge Studies in Islamic Civilization. Cambridge: Cambridge University Press.
Higgins, Andrew. 2008. "The Lost Archive." *Wall Street Journal*, 12 January.
Hinds, Martin. 1983. "'Maghāzī' and 'Sīra' in Early Islamic Scholarship." In *La vie du Prophète Mahomet: Colloque de Strasbourg, Octobre 1980*, ed. Toufic Fahd, 57–66. Paris: Presses universitaires de France.
Hodgson, Marshall G. S. 1974. *The Venture of Islam: Conscience and History in a World Civilization*, Vol. 1: *The Classical Age of Islam.* 3 vols. Chicago: University of Chicago Press.
Hoyland, Robert G. 1997. *Seeing Islam as Others Saw It: A Survey and Evaluation of Christian, Jewish and Zoroastrian Writings on Early Islam.* Studies in Late Antiquity and Early Islam 13. Princeton, NJ: Darwin Press.
———. 2007. "Writing the Biography of the Prophet Muhammad: Problems and Solutions," *History Compass* 5.2: 581–602.
Humphreys, R. Stephen. 1991. *Islamic History: A Framework for Inquiry.* Princeton, NJ: Princeton University Press.
Hurgronje, C. Snouck. 1886. "Der Mahdi," *Revue coloniale internationale* 1: 25–59.
———. 1894. "Une nouvelle biographie de Moḥammed," *Revue de l'histoire des religions* 30: 48–70, 149–178.
———. 1916. *Mohammedanism; Lectures on Its Origin, Its Religious and Political Growth, and Its Present State.* New York: G. P. Putnam's Sons.
———. 1931. "Theodor Nöldeke: 2. März 1836–25. Dezember 1930," *Zeitschrift der deutschen morgenländischen Gesellschaft* 85: 238–281.
Ibn Hishām, 'Abd al-Malik. 1858–1860. *Kitāb sīrat Rasūl Allāh [Das leben Muhammed's nach Muhammed ibn Ishâk bearbeitet von Abd el-Malik ibn Hischâm].* Ed. Ferdinand Wüstenfeld. 2 vols. Göttingen: Dieterichsche Universitäts-Buchhandlung.
Ibn Sa'd, Muḥammad. 1904–1928. *Ṭabaqāt [Biographien Muhammeds, seiner Gefährten und der späteren Träger des Islams, bis zum Jahre 230 der Flucht].* Ed. E. Sachau. 9 vols. Leiden: E. J. Brill.
Irwin, Robert. 1999. "Oriental Discourses in Orientalism," *Middle Eastern Lectures* 3: 87–110.
Jones, J. M. B. 1983. "The Maghāzī Literature." In *Arabic Literature to the End of the Umayyad Period*, ed. A. F. L. Beeston et al., 344–351. The Cambridge History of Arabic Literature. Cambridge: Cambridge University Press.
Juynboll, G. H. A. 1982. "On the Origins of Arabic Prose: Reflections on Authenticity." In *Studies on the First Century of Islamic Society*, ed. G. H. A. Juynboll, 161–175. Papers on Islamic History 5. Carbondale: Southern Illinois University Press.

———. 1983. *Muslim Tradition: Studies in Chronology, Provenance, and Authorship of Early Ḥadīth.* Cambridge Studies in Islamic Civilization. Cambridge: Cambridge University Press.

———. 1989. "Some *Isnād*-Analytical Methods Illustrated on the Basis of Several Woman-Demeaning Sayings from *Ḥadīth* Literature," *Qantara* 10: 343–383.

———. 1991. "The Role of *Mu'ammarūn* in the Early Development of the *Isnād*," *Wiener Zeitschrift für die Kunde des Morgenlandes* 81: 155–175.

———. 1992. "Some Notes on Islam's First *Fuqahā'* Distilled from Early *Ḥadīth* Literature," *Arabica* 39: 287–314.

———. 1993. "Nāfi', the *Mawlā* of Ibn 'Umar, and His Position in Muslim *Ḥadīth* Literature," *Der Islam* 70: 279–300.

———. 1996. *Studies on the Origins and Uses of Islamic Ḥadīth.* Brookfield, VT: Variorum.

Kister, M. J. 1962. "'A Booth Like the Booth of Moses . . .': A Study of an Early *Ḥadīth*," *Bulletin of the School of Oriental and African Studies* 25: 150–155.

Koester, Helmut. 1995. *Introduction to the New Testament*, Vol. 2: *History and Literature of Early Christianity.* 2 vols. 2nd ed. New York: Walter de Gruyter.

Kümmel, Werner Georg. 1975. *Introduction to the New Testament*, rev. ed. Trans. Howard Clark Kee. Nashville, TN: Abingdon.

Lammens, Henri. 1910. "Qoran et tradition: Comment fut composée la vie de Mohamet?" *Recherches de Science Religieuse* 1: 25–61.

———. 1911. "L'âge de Mahomet et la chronologie de la Sîra," *Journal Asiatique* ser. x, 17: 209–250.

———. 1912. *Fatima et les filles de Mahomet.* Rome: Pontificium Institutum Biblicum.

———. 2000a. "Fatima and the Daughters of Muḥammad." In *The Quest for the Historical Muḥammad*, ed. Ibn Warraq, 218–329. Amherst, NY: Prometheus.

———. 2000b. "The Age of Muḥammad and the Chronology of the Sira." In *The Quest for the Historical Muḥammad*, ed. Ibn Warraq, 188–217. Amherst, NY: Prometheus.

———. 2000c. "The Koran and Tradition: How the Life of Muḥammad Was Composed." In *The Quest for the Historical Muḥammad*, ed. Ibn Warraq, 169–187. Amherst, NY: Prometheus.

Livne-Kafri, Ofer. 1999. "Some Notes on the Muslim Apocalyptic Tradition," *Quaderni di Studi Arabi* 17: 71–94.

Martin, Dale B. 1995. *The Corinthian Body.* New Haven, CT: Yale University Press.

Mattock, J. N. 1986. "History and Fiction," *Occasional Papers of the School of Abbasid Studies* 1: 80–97.

Melchert, Christopher. 2003. "The Early History of Islamic Law." In *Method and Theory in the Study of Islamic Origins*, ed. Herbert Berg, 293–324. Leiden: Brill.

Mingana, Alphonse. 1916. "The Transmission of the Kur'ān," *Journal of the Manchester Egyptian and Oriental Society* 5: 25–47.

Mojaddedi, Jawid A. 2000. "Taking Islam Seriously: The Legacy of John Wansbrough," *Journal of Semitic Studies* 45: 103–114.

Motzki, Harald. 1991a. "The *Muṣannaf* of 'Abd al-Razzāq al-Ṣan'ānī as a Source of Authentic *ḥādīth* of the First Century A.H.," *Journal of Near Eastern Studies* 50: 1–21.

———. 1991b. "Der Fiqh des al-Zuhrī: Die Quellenproblematik," *Der Islam* 68: 1–44.

———. 1996a. "*Quo vadis, Ḥadiṯ* Forschung? Eine kritische Untersuchung von G. H. A. Juynboll: 'Nāfi', the *Mawlā* of Ibn 'Umar, and His Position in Muslim *Ḥadiṯ* Literature'," *Der Islam* 73: 40–80.

———. 1996b. "*Quo vadis, Ḥadīṯ*-Forschung?: Eine kritische Untersuchung von G.H.A. Juynboll: 'Nāfi', the *Mawlā* of Ibn 'Umar, and His Position in Muslim *Ḥadīṯ* Literature,' Teil 2," *Der Islam* 73: 193–231.

———. 1998. "The Prophet and the Cat: On Dating Mālik's *Muwaṭṭa'* and Legal Traditions," *Jerusalem Studies in Arabic and Islam* 22: 18–83.

———. 2000. "The Murder of Ibn Abī l-Ḥuqayq: On the Origin and Reliability of Some Maghāzī Reports." In *The Biography of Muḥammad: The Issue of the Sources*, ed. Harald Motzki, 170–239. Leiden: E. J. Brill.

———. 2001. "The Collection of the Qur'an: A Reconsideration of Western Views in Light of Recent Methodological Developments," *Der Islam* 78: 1–34.

———. 2002. *The Origins of Islamic Jurisprudence: Meccan Fiqh before the Classical Schools*. Islamic History and Civilization, Studies and Texts 41. Leiden: Brill.

———. 2003. "The Author and His Work in the Islamic Literature of the First Centuries: The Case of 'Abd al-Razzāq's *Muṣannaf*," *Jerusalem Studies in Arabic and Islam* 28: 171–201.

———. 2005. "Dating Muslim Traditions: A Survey," *Arabica* 52: 204–253.

Muranyi, Miklos. 1986. "Die ersten Muslime von Mekka—soziale Basis einer neuen Religion?" *Jerusalem Studies in Arabic and Islam* 8: 25–35.

Muslim b. al-Ḥajjāj. 1995. *Ṣaḥīḥ Muslim*. 5 vols. Beirut: Dār Ibn Ḥazm.

Neuwirth, Angelika. 2007. *Studien zur Komposition der mekkanischen Suren: Die literarische Form des Koran—ein Zeugnis seiner Historizität?* 2nd ed. Berlin: de Gruyter.

Newby, Gordon D. 1986. "The Sirah as a Source for Arabian Jewish History: Problems and Perspectives," *Jerusalem Studies in Arabic and Islam* 7: 121–138.

Neyrey, Jerome H., ed. 1991. *The Social World of Luke-Acts: Models for Interpretation*, Peabody, MA: Hendrickson.

Nöldeke, Theodor. 1892. *Orientalische Skizzen*. Berlin: Paetel.

Nöldeke, Theodor, and Friedrich Schwally. 1909–1919. *Geschichte des Qorāns*, 2nd ed. 2 vols. Leipzig: Dieterich.

Overman, J. Andrew. 1990. *Matthew's Gospel and Formative Judaism: The Social World of the Matthean Community*. Minneapolis, MN: Fortress Press.

Paret, Rudi. 2005. *Mohammed und der Koran: Geschichte und Verkündigung des arabischen Propheten*, 9th ed. Stuttgart: W. Kohlhammer.

Peters, F. E. 1991. "The Quest of the Historical Muhammad," *International Journal of Middle East Studies* 23: 291–315.

———. 1994. *Muhammad and the Origins of Islam*. Albany: State University of New York Press.

Rahman, Fazlur. 1980. *Major Themes of the Qur'an*. Minneapolis, MN: Bibliotheca Islamica.

Raven, W. 1960–2005. "Sīra." In *The Encyclopaedia of Islam*, new ed., ed. P. J. Bearman et al., 9:660–663. Leiden: E. J. Brill.

Renan, Ernest. 1851. "Mahomet et les origines de l'Islamisme," *Revue des deux mondes* 12: 1023–1060.

———. 1863. *Vie de Jésus*. Paris: M. Lévy frères.

———. 2000. "Muhammad and the Origins of Islam." In *The Quest for the Historical Muḥammad*, ed. Ibn Warraq, 127–166. Amherst, NY: Prometheus.

Reynolds, Gabriel Said. 2008. "Introduction: Qur'ānic Studies and Its Controversies." In *The Qur'ān in Its Historical Context*, ed. Gabriel Said Reynolds, 1–25. Routledge Studies in the Qur'ān. London: Routledge.

Rippin, Andrew. 1985. "Literary Analysis of Qur'ān, Tafsīr, and Sīra: The Methodologies of John Wansbrough." In *Approaches to Islam in Religious Studies*, ed. Richard C. Martin, 151–163, 227–232. Tucson: University of Arizona Press.

———. 1992. "Reading the Qur'ān with Richard Bell," *Journal of the American Oriental Society* 112: 639–647.

———. 1997. "Qur'anic Studies, Part IV: Some Methodological Notes," *Method and Theory in the Study of Religion* 9: 39–46.

———. 2006. "Western Scholarship and the Qur'ān." In *The Cambridge Companion to the Qur'ān*, ed. Jane Dammen McAuliffe, 235–251. Cambridge: Cambridge University Press.

Robinson, Chase F. 2002. *Islamic Historiography*. New York: Cambridge University Press.

———. 2003. "Reconstructing Early Islam: Truth and Consequences." In *Method and Theory in the Study of Islamic Origins*, ed. Herbert Berg, 101–134. Leiden: Brill.

———. 2005. *'Abd al-Malik*. Makers of the Muslim World. Oxford: Oneworld.

Rodinson, Maxime. 1971. *Mohammed*. Trans. Anne Carter. New York: Pantheon.

Rubin, Uri. 1995. *The Eye of the Beholder: The Life of Muhammad as Viewed by the Early Muslims: A Textual Analysis*. Studies in Late Antiquity and Early Islam 5. Princeton, NJ: Darwin Press.

———, ed. 1998. *The Life of Muhammad*. The Formation of the Classical Islamic World 4. Aldershot: Ashgate.

Rüling, Josef Bernhard. 1895. *Beiträge zur Eschatologie des Islam*. Leipzig: G. Kreysing.

Saldarini, Anthony J. 1994. *Matthew's Christian-Jewish Community*. Chicago Studies in the History of Judaism. Chicago: University of Chicago Press.

Samuk, Sadun Mahmud al-. 1978. "Die historischen Überlieferungen nach Ibn Ishaq: Eine synoptische Überlieferung." Ph.D. diss., Johann Wolfgang Goethe Universität, Frankfurt.

Sanders, E. P. 1985. *Jesus and Judaism*. Philadelphia: Fortress Press.

———. 1993. *The Historical Figure of Jesus*. London: Allen Lane.

Schacht, Joseph. 1949. "A Revaluation of Islamic Traditions," *Journal of the Royal Asiatic Society* 49: 143–154.

———. 1950. *The Origins of Muhammadan Jurisprudence*. Oxford: Clarendon Press.

Schoedel, William R. 1993. "Papias," *Aufsteig und Niedergang der römischen Welt*. II.27.1: 235–270.

Schoeler, Gregor. 1996. *Charakter und Authentie der muslimischen Überlieferung über das Leben Mohammeds*. Studien zur Sprache, Geschichte und Kultur des islamischen Orients 14. Berlin: Walter de Gruyter.

———. 2002. "Character and Authenticity of the Muslim Tradition on the Life of Muhammad," *Arabica* 48: 360–366.

———. 2003. "Foundations for a New Biography of Muḥammad: The Production and Evaluation of the Corpus of Traditions from 'Urwa b. al-Zubayr." In *Method and Theory in the Study of Islamic Origins*, ed. Herbert Berg, 19–28. Leiden: Brill.

Schweitzer, Albert. 1910. *The Quest of the Historical Jesus: A Critical Study of Its Progress from Reimarus to Wrede*. Trans. W. Montgomery. London: Adam and Charles Black.

Sellheim, Rudolf. 1967. "Prophet, Chalif und Geschichte: Die Muhammed-Biographie des Ibn Isḥāq," *Oriens* 18–19: 32–91.

Smith, Jane I. 2002. "Eschatology." In *Encyclopaedia of the Qur'ān*, ed. Jane Dammen McAuliffe, 2:44–54. Leiden: Brill.

Ṭabarī, Muhammad ibn Jarīr al-. 1990. *The History of al-Tabarī, Vol. 9: The Last Years of the Prophet*. Trans. Ismail K. Poonawala. SUNY Series in Near Eastern Studies. Albany: State University of New York Press.

Theissen, Gerd. 1982. *The Social Setting of Pauline Christianity: Essays on Corinth*. Trans. John H. Schütz. Philadelphia: Fortress Press.

Wansbrough, John E. 1977. *Quranic Studies: Sources and Methods of Scriptural Interpretation*. London Oriental Series 31. Oxford: Oxford University Press.

———. 1978a. "Review of Patricia Crone and Michael Cook, *Hagarism: The Making of the Islamic World*," *Bulletin of the School of Oriental and African Studies* 41: 155–156.

———. 1978b. *The Sectarian Milieu: Content and Composition of Islamic Salvation History*. London Oriental Series 34. Oxford: Oxford University Press.

Wansbrough, John E., and Andrew Rippin. 2004. *Quranic Studies: Sources and Methods of Scriptural Interpretation*. Amherst, NY: Prometheus.

Watt, W. Montgomery. 1953. *Muhammad at Mecca*. Oxford: Clarendon Press.

———. 1956. *Muhammad at Medina*. Oxford: Clarendon Press.

———. 1957. "The Dating of the Qur'ān: A Review of Richard Bell's Theories," *Journal of the Royal Asiatic Society of Great Britain and Ireland* 1957: 46–56.

———. 1958. "The Materials Used by Ibn Isḥāq." In *Historians of the Middle East*, ed. Bernard Lewis and P. M. Holt, 23–34. Historical Writings of the Peoples of Asia 4. London: Oxford University Press.

———. 1961. *Muhammad: Prophet and Statesman*. London: Oxford University Press.

———. 1983. "The Reliability of Ibn Isḥāq's Sources." In *La vie du Prophète Mahomet: Colloque de Strasbourg, Octobre 1980*, ed. Toufic Fahd, 31–43. Paris: Presses universitaires de France.

Weiss, Johannes. 1892. *Die Predigt Jesu vom Reiche Gottes*. Göttingen: Vandenhoeck & Ruprecht.

Welch, A.T. 1960–2005. "al-Ḳur'ān." In *The Encyclopaedia of Islam*, new ed., ed. P. J. Bearman et al., 5:400–429. Leiden: E. J. Brill.

Wellhausen, Julius. 1883. *Prolegomena zur Geschichte Israels*. 2nd ed. Berlin: G. Reimer.

———. 1902. *Das arabische Reich und sein Sturz*. Berlin: G. Reimer.

Zeitlin, Irving M. 2007. *The Historical Muhammad*. Cambridge: Polity.

Zervos, George T. 1997. "An Early Non-Canonical Annunciation Story," *SBL Seminar Papers* 36: 664–691.

———. 2002. "Seeking the Source of the Marian Myth: Have We Found the Missing Link??" In *Which Mary? The Marys of Early Christian Tradition*, ed. F. Stanley Jones, 107–120. Society of Biblical Literature Symposium Series 19. Atlanta: Society of Biblical Literature.

PART V

LATE ANTIQUITY IN PERSPECTIVE

CHAPTER 34

COMPARATIVE STATE FORMATION: THE LATER ROMAN EMPIRE IN THE WIDER WORLD

JOHN HALDON
Princeton University

WHEN in the year 589 C.E. Wen-Ti, the founder of the short-lived Sui dynasty, invaded and defeated the armies of the southern Ch'en, he brought China under unified rule again for the first time since the breakdown of Han rule in the late second century. In the course of his rule, he dealt effectively with the threat posed by the nomadic peoples to the north, most particularly the great T'u-chüeh (Turk) empire, partly by promoting factional strife among the eastern T'u-chüeh, partly by encouraging the ruler of the western Turks, Ta T'eou (Turkish *Tarduš*; *Tardou* [*Τάρδου*] in the Greek sources), in his efforts to secure his own rule.[1] In so doing, of course, Chinese diplomacy met eastern Roman diplomacy (although commercial and cultural contacts were much older, and the arrival of Nestorian churchmen at the T'ang court during the 630s would be the first direct cultural contacts we know of since the reign of Leo I),[2] for it was only twenty years earlier that Byzantium had begun regular contact with the Turkish court over the question of the Avars and over the role of the Sasanian court in central Asian affairs, a contact that seems to have been maintained regularly thereafter. Two great empires, one of which, the Roman, had suffered the permanent loss of its western lands over a century earlier (even if under

Justinian some of these territories were recovered), the other of which was to remain united, under the T'ang dynasty, from 618 until the early tenth century, thus touched, as it were, in Central Asia. Yet the contact took place at a time when China was on the road to a dramatic recovery of its political and military fortunes, whereas for the hard-pressed eastern Roman state, the problems posed by various "barbarians" in the Balkans, the threat from Sasanian Iran, and, in the 630s, the Arab Islamic invasions, were to end once and for all any idea of a united Roman world stretching from the Atlantic to the Syrian desert and from the North Sea to the High Atlas.

We have long grown accustomed to understanding the late ancient world, and in particular the world of the later Roman empire, as only one element of a more complex and varied cultural and geographical setting. More often than not, though, we look at this broader context as just that, the "setting," and pay lip service to its existence and the connections between people in the Roman world and these other regions, and the emphasis is generally on either the immediate geographical neighbors of Rome—barbarians in the north and west, the peoples of the Caucasus region, the Parthian or Sasanian realm to the east, the steppes to the north, stretching away across to China, or the Arabian peninsula and the Red Sea and Gulf territories, with their mercantile and sometimes political associations with east Africa or with the Indian Ocean and beyond. We rarely place the Roman state as such—as a political, cultural, and economic system—in such a context, however, which means that while comparisons with its nearer neighbors are not unusual, its place in a wider world of political systems is neglected. Yet looking at the Roman state from such a comparative perspective can be enlightening, not only from the point of view of the dynamics of Roman state power but also in respect of how best to think about states and other political-cultural forms in a premodern world.[3] We shall return to this theme later.

Context and Environment

The question of the nature, constitution, and dynamics of states and empires has been at the forefront of much comparativist and specialist discussion. In a recent contribution, empires have been described very straightforwardly as the effects of the imposition of political sovereignty by one polity over others, however achieved, and the key marker of an "imperial" state was thus the degree of "foreignness" perceived to exist between rulers and ruled, conquerors and conquered.[4] In the simplest terms, then, the study of empires becomes the study of the subordination of one "state" or social formation by another and of the extent to which the conquerors are successful in converting these peripheral zones into a part of their original state, both ideologically and in terms of fiscal, military, and administrative structures. In some respects, this overlaps with the issue of the nature of the "segmentary" state, intended to suggest a multi-centered, confederated political structure in which ideological elements and consensus play as great a role as centrally exercised coercive power.[5] Although many early states functioned on the basis of a series of concentric zones of power distribution, focused around a political core, we might reasonably describe empires on the same lines, in which case the issue of their success and longevity will revolve around the same key questions: to what extent are empires of conquest able to impose upon the conquered lands and cultures their own ideological/cultural values, patterns of administration, and elite formation and thereby create out of a range of different sociocultural formations a more or less homogeneous set of political values and ideological identities? Of all the ancient empires that arose in the western Eurasian world, the Roman state, and its medieval Byzantine successor in the east Mediterranean basin, was perhaps the most successful in this respect. In the East, the various ancient and early medieval Chinese states, in particular the earlier and later Han states and the T'ang empire, achieved similar rates of successful integration.

While some empires about which historians are informed evolved through strategic alliances based on kinship or inheritance through gift or marriage, the majority of those political formations we conventionally label as empires were the direct result of military conquest. Four key questions attract our interest: how did they come into being? How did they survive? What was the structure of power relations that facilitated this (or not)? What was their economic basis in respect of both the production, distribution, and consumption of wealth, on the one hand, and in respect of the expansion of the basis upon which wealth could be generated—whether quantitative (territorial expansion, for example) or qualitative (changing technologies of production, expanding trade, or shifting the structures of capital investment)?

The later Roman empire was, in many respects, already an ancient and very mature political system, the result of a continuous process of evolution from the first century B.C.E., as the political system and the economic structures of the circum-Mediterranean world adjusted to shifts and changes in its conditions of existence. The last two or three generations of historians have been, on the whole, less concerned with the question why it "fell" than with that of how it worked. In recent years, however, the issues of change and transformation have been brought back into the limelight, partly a reflection of an accumulation of more accessible archaeological data, partly on account of a revival of metatheoretical interest in comparative world systems and long-term social evolution.[6] In particular, setting the Roman state against other comparable state systems in the late ancient or early medieval worlds has forced historians to consider a range of issues outside the immediate confines of local social, political, economic, and cultural history.

Demography and related issues play an important role here. It has been argued, for example, on the basis of admittedly problematic statistical evidence, that western Eurasia was more heavily affected by epidemics (and invasions) than China in the late ancient and early medieval period.[7] But while attempts to relate the collapse of late Roman state forms in the West to population decline and concurrent dislocations caused by epidemic disease or other environmental crises are currently experiencing a revival,[8] they remain at the least ambiguous in their implications.[9] Archaeological survey work makes it clear that (with the exception of southwest Asia) population in western Eurasia was considerably lower in the seventh century C.E. than it had been in the second century C.E. In contrast, conditions in China differed significantly from those in the West. There does appear to have been some fairly marked decline across the period from the middle of the third century C.E. into the early sixth century. But its extent cannot be measured, partly because dramatic fluctuations in Chinese census results seem to reflect the ability of the states in question to control and tax their populations (rather than the size of the population itself). On the other hand, the Sui state counted roughly the same number of people and households in 609 C.E. as the Han government had registered in the mid-second century C.E., indicating that by the later sixth century overall population densities were back at the levels of the later Han period.[10] But that population loss in the West should be understood as a principal factor in the weakening of state institutions and the failure of the state seems dubious—to take but one example, the Achaemenid empire covered an area almost as large as that of the Roman empire but controlled a far smaller population—and demographic conditions in themselves seem to be a poor indicator of the feasibility of an extensive state system.

In this respect, our view of and approach to the issue of catastrophic events such as outbreaks of plague become important. For example, we still do not know enough about the effects of the sixth-century pandemic and its regional incidence to understand just how significant it was for the demographic or economic and social impact on the western Eurasian world. Definitive evidence from DNA analysis has shown, for example, that it was caused by an exceptionally virulent and lethal biovar of *Yersinia pestis*, the bubonic plague. It was significantly different from that which caused the plague narrated by Thucydides; it was indeed an entirely new pathogen for the populations of the empire in 541, a fact that would have rendered it particularly virulent. It is possible that the sixth-century plague had a more dramatic impact on populations than is generally thought, even if several scholars have been right to emphasize that the archaeological data suggest a highly regionalized pattern.[11]

The interpretation of this sort of environmental evidence is clearly fraught with difficulties and pitfalls, and much of it can be made only with difficulty to match cycles of political or economic growth and decline. This does not mean there is no connection, only that the connections are likely to be complex, multistranded, and indirect. While the plague fits in with some aspects of change in the sixth century, there has as yet been no clear evidence of an obvious causal association between environment and socioeconomic change. Climate has remained, within certain margins, relatively constant across the late ancient and medieval periods. Minor fluctuations, when combined with natural events such as earthquakes, man-made phenomena such as warfare, and catastrophes such as pandemic disease, could have dramatic short- to medium-term results for populations, settlement patterns, land use, resource extraction and consumption, and political systems.[12] From the second century B.C.E. into the second century C.E., the climate was relatively warmer and milder than in the preceding period and constituted a "climatic optimum" that favored the expansion of agriculture. This expansion is reflected in the so-called Beyşehir Occupation Phase in the southern Balkans and southwestern Turkey, for example.[13] By about 500 C.E., the climatic situation was changing, with colder and wetter conditions persisting up to the mid-ninth century. But within this broad pattern, there were also microclimatic shifts: stable isotope analysis from lake beds in the Levant and Asia Minor suggest that from about 300 C.E. until about 450, conditions were slightly dryer and warmer than in the preceding centuries (tree-ring analysis also suggests that drought was frequent between the 420s and 480s in several regions of the Levant).[14] In the course of the later fifth century, the climate became cooler and wetter, until a period of very gradual warming and desiccation began in the seventh century. Precipitation levels declined, affecting, in particular, highland zones. At the same time, the evidence suggests that during the fifth century the level of the Mediterranean began to rise, although the impact of this, which reflects a global phenomenon, remains unclear.[15]

Such microclimatic fluctuations are important because climate change does not affect all areas in the same way. The textual evidence assembled for the late antique period, as well as the paleoclimatological evidence, suggests marked regional variations across quite short periods of fifty or a hundred years, with droughts alternating with extremely cold and wet conditions, bringing serious difficulties for irrigated lands on the one hand and for marginal dry-farming zones on the other. In regions such as the Mediterranean coastal plains, where the prevailing winds are westerly, a warmer climate brings less rainfall and desertification of arid marginal regions, whereas in more continental zones, such as the Iranian plateau and the drainage areas of the Caspian, rainfall increases. A colder climate brings more rainfall in the former regions—thus exerting pressure on hydrological systems in general—whereas in the continental zones, such as the Anatolian or Iranian plateaux, it brings less precipitation and thus desiccation. Evidence from the Susiana plain suggests that the period of about 500 to 650 C.E. was relatively dry, for example.[16] Intermediate zones—such as the Mesopotamian lowlands—are affected according to their position in relation to prevailing winds, rain- and highland-shadow, and distance from the sea. Climate change tends to show up first in marginal zones and in temperate or humid regions later.

We are not yet in a position to judge the impact of these shifts on either land use or the social and economic history of the regions concerned.[17] But it is clear that they have played a role and cannot be written out of the causal relationships that determined the pattern of historical change in the late ancient world. It is also likely that they have rendered the human environment of the later fifth to seventh centuries more challenging in many areas, and the economy of existence more fragile. For the eastern provinces of the later Roman empire, it would seem that after a period of demographic expansion and intensification of agriculture lasting into the sixth century, a slow decline and retrenchment seems to set in from sometime around about 540 to 550 in some areas, from the early or middle years of the seventh century in others. In certain Anatolian provinces, some marginal lands were abandoned, soil erosion increased where agriculture receded, the colder climate generated increasing water volume in rivers and watercourses, and this contributed to alluviation and flooding in more exposed areas. Yet, while there is some support for an overall reduction in agrarian activity around the early 540s, as reflected in the carbon dioxide content of polar ice cores, the sources of this change cannot be geographically fixed, and the pattern does not seem to be repeated in Syria and Palestine—the settlement at Nessana in the Negev, for example, flourished well into the later seventh century on the basis of its irrigation agriculture.[18] In other regions, an overall reduction in population and thus in the rate of exploitation of natural resources such as forests is shown by an increased variation in woodland flora over the same period. It is important to bear in mind the very different effects such shifts had on different regions, and we must not assume that similar outcomes were exhibited in Anatolia, the Balkans, the Iranian plateau, Mesopotamia, or the north Syrian uplands, each subject to its own particular microclimatic system.[19] How far all this affected the state's fiscal base in the East and the degree to which it affected western European politics and society remains both unclear and debated.

Economies

Similar considerations apply to a range of other phenomena that had different effects on society, economy, and therefore politics. The trajectory of Mediterranean economic development from well before the Principate onward demonstrates how the Roman sphere of economic activity was but one part of a much wider set of relationships stretching across into Asia, connections that also had a causal role, even if that is as yet only dimly understood. Sea-borne commerce and trade massively expanded from the later third century B.C.E. and began to fall off during the later second and into the third century C.E.—a pattern that bears only a very indirect relation either to the political configuration or the fiscal demands of the developing Roman state. Late republican and early imperial levels of pollution generated by metal extraction and working (as evidenced in Greenland ice cores) reached a peak not to be attained until the modern period, falling off rapidly after the second century. Patterns of building activity based on accurately dated wood remains from parts of Germany show a peak in the first and early second centuries C.E., a dramatic decline thereafter, and a limited recovery in the fourth century.[20] Evidence for diet—and, in particular, the wider access to meat that skeletal and other material seems to suggest for the western provinces during the period of the early Principate in western and northwestern Europe—suggests again very dramatic improvements in standards of living and diet, followed by an equally dramatic reduction in the later second century, with a minor recovery in the fourth century. Whether the Antonine plague can be made responsible for some or all of these changes at this time is not an issue that can be pursued here, although comparative work on the effects of the pandemics of the second and sixth centuries remains to be done. It is significant that comparable demographic collapse is not evident from the Chinese records of the later Han, whereas some aspects of climate change that, it has been argued, had adverse effects in western Eurasia had positive results in China. In either case, we are faced here with issues of global or near-global significance, where the fate of the western Eurasian late ancient world is but one part of a bigger picture that historians need to bear in mind when drawing conclusions about their own particular area.[21]

The erosion of central state power in terms of control of surplus and surplus extraction must always have multiple causes. The collapse of fiscal control and the ability of a central regime to extract revenues sufficient to maintain it independent of provincial elites, indeed, to disempower such elites, is a key element in such a process. While the reasons underlying this erosive process remain debated, recent work has done much to establish a model for the late Roman world, although at the same time, more sharply defined concepts of "decline" have reappeared in some of the literature, partly reflecting a response to the notions of gradual cultural and social transformation that have become typical of much of the literature of the late antique period. A persuasive case has been made that the strong and (relatively) centralized late Roman state (which could register and tax a civilian population in order to support a substantial standing army) suffered especially from the perceived vested interests of provincial elites, who in effect by the later fourth century were beginning to starve the state of the resources it needed to survive, at least in the West.[22] This process generated in its turn the relatively weak successor states that sprang up on western Roman territory, polities whose rulers gradually lost the ability to tax or where, as in some regions such as Britain, the institutions of the state disappeared altogether. The rulers of states that maintained registration, taxation, and centrally controlled military forces (in this case, the eastern Roman empire or the early caliphate) continued to enjoy greater autonomy from elite interests, while the elites themselves depended to a significant extent on the state for positions, income, and status.[23] In contrast, the elites of weak states relied on the resources they themselves controlled and concomitantly enjoyed greater independence of the ruler, while the power and authority of the latter depended largely on cooperation or forms of collaboration that depended heavily on ideological structures, since they lacked centralized resource control and coercive capacities. Local elites rather than state rulers dominated and at the same time, since there was only limited transregional economic integration (which had been characteristic of the strong Roman state), could be less wealthy, and these conditions further contributed to the erosion of interregional exchange. Fiscal decline, together with the high degree of regionalization of political and military power, made it more difficult to maintain state capabilities (especially in the military sphere) and, combined with the curtailment of economic activity, meant that the potential for the reestablishment of any sort of stable empirewide core was very limited.

The apparent paradox in this is that it seems to have been the reestablishment of a stable monetary system and of an effective and more centralized fiscal apparatus under Constantine I that encouraged closer ties of regional elites to the imperial system at all levels. Political stability coupled with state demands led to the recovery of trans-Mediterranean commerce after the relative breakdown of the later third century. Henceforward, as has been argued by Wickham, it was the state and its fiscal apparatus that acted to facilitate and stimulate this recovery, clearly demonstrated in the archaeological and written record. While it may not have been the Roman state alone that generated the vast commercialized market system of Late Antiquity, it did act as an agent for stability and market expansion. As the system became progressively independent of the conditions that created it, these fiscal mechanisms remained key inflecting factors with specific consequences. When they eventually broke down or were weakened or suborned by local elites, fragmentation of the empirewide economy and its elite was a necessary consequence for several sectors, even if not all, of the economy.

On this model, regardless of whether fiscal centralization was a key element in the establishment of empire,[24] it was certainly a key factor in the breakdown of the late Roman imperial system. And although it is difficult to generate a model that is universally applicable in all its details from this specific historical instance (for example, in late ancient and medieval India, local elites generally continued to derive substantial incomes from commercial exchange, usually managed and dominated by merchant lineages—the existence of a strong centralizing political authority seems to have added only marginal advantages), the case of the conquest of the southern Ch'en state by the Sui ruler in the 580s C.E. does appear to reinforce the idea that central fiscal control and a centrally managed military and administrative apparatus confer decided advantages in most circumstances. Recent work on the history of the main northern "successor states" in fifth- and sixth-century C.E. China brings out the gradual reestablishment of centrally managed taxation and military organization and the ability of rulers to limit elite autonomy, permitting an increase in the mobilization of resources for military purposes that eventually resulted in imperial reunification.[25] While the evidence from state censuses is problematic, it is nevertheless clear that the breakdown of Han power and ideological authority led to a radical reduction in the state's ability to raise taxes. By the later sixth century C.E., the successor states of Northern Ch'i and Northern Zhou appear to have massively increased their ability to count and control households and thus resources, and within twenty years of the Sui conquest of the Ch'en state in the south, this had risen even more dramatically.[26] In stark contrast, the extant census figures for the southern successor states are consistently low, and it seems that the southern successor state was unable to tax more than a small proportion of the actual households and potential taxpayers. Distribution maps showing the geographical spread of the census population in 140 and 609 C.E. indicate that even by the Sui period the government had not been able to restore Han standards of registration in the southern provinces.[27] The relatively small size of the military forces reportedly marshaled by southern regimes, compared with some of the centralizing northern states, reinforces this impression. The main problem in the south lay in the fact that more or less autonomous elites dominated rural populations and resources,[28] elites who could successfully compete with central authorities for surplus and control of other forms of resource in labor power and skills, so that southern states came to rely on tolls and commercial taxes generated by the dynamic economies of coastal provinces in particular—an economic dynamism that foreshadowed later growth in the T'ang and Song periods.[29] Such income was further supplemented by fees and "gifts" extorted by provincial officials and shared with the central government, so that in the southern state of Ch'en, a combination of elite resistance to census and registration and its commercial dynamism promoted a dependency on the latter, which was in the short term easier and cheaper to exploit than regular taxation. The whole encouraged an equilibrium between elite demands, which dominated the agrarian surplus, and state demands, which targeted indirect taxes on commercial activity and the extraction of tribute through fees and the activities of tax and contract farmers outside the political center. This was a balance that could sustain the state and ensure equilibrium between central and elite power, but it proved inadequate in direct competition with the more centralized Sui state, with its greater potential for resource concentration and management.

Geography

The period we now by common agreement all refer to as Late Antiquity stretches from the third or fourth/fifth centuries to the seventh or eighth, depending on who is writing about what. As we have seen, Late Antiquity is not just the Roman world, and as the essays in this book make clear, it was an immensely complex period, with enormously significant changes and transformations proceeding at every level of social and political life. While inevitably the Roman world receives most attention from those whose prime focus is on the West, even the most Romanocentric accounts need to be set in their broader context. This is especially the case for the history and evolution of the Roman state and its successors.

One of the more obvious issues arising from any such comparison is the question of the degree to which states repeatedly arise within a particular territory and the reasons for the maintenance, or regular reassertion, of empire or at least of political unity across such wider territories. China, in spite of its frequent periods of disunity—in territorial blocs that in the south certainly and in the north frequently reflected geographical and environmental conditions—has tended from the first Ch'in emperor in the later third century B.C.E. toward political unification, even if it was regularly contested and often difficult to achieve. This tendency reflects a number of factors, but geography is certainly a key element, a geography that from the beginning favored the evolution of cultural phenotypes bound to and contributing to the reproduction of specific cultural, economic, and social forms, which in turn tended to make the promotion of political unity a norm to be achieved. The same points can be made for other regions in which stable cultural forms have evolved, especially those with a favorable ratio between the length of frontiers and surface area, where the core territory is relatively well shielded by geographical features such as mountains, desert, or seas. Such features all confer certain key advantages or at least promote certain types of social-cultural-political development and identity. "China" as a geographical zone is demarcated by the Tibetan plateau to the west, by the Tarim basin and the Tian Shan and Altai Mountains to the northwest, and by the Mongolian steppe and related mountains to the north and northeast (see fig. 5.1). In spite of the vast differences in climate and geography within this macroregion, these major features separate it very clearly from the regions beyond. By the same token, Iran is demarcated in the east by the Makran desert and mountains and the mountains of Afghanistan, in the north by the Caspian Sea and the steppe and desert of the Karakum, and in the west by the fertile lands of Iraq, although Iraq and Iran have historically generally formed a unity, since beyond Iraq the great Syrian desert has always marked another clear geopolitical divide. In the same way, Syria and Egypt, with the outlying lands westward along the North African coast, have generally been associated politically; both the struggle over Syria between Egypt and the Hittite kingdom in the second and first millennium B.C.E., as well as the tendency for Egypt-based Islamic dynasties to move north and east—the Tulunids in the ninth century, the Fatimids in the tenth, the Mamluks in the thirteenth—testify to this. Asia Minor, similarly clearly marked off by the Taurus, Anti-Taurus, and Caucasus ranges, likewise forms a geographical entity that has often reflected political separateness. This is not to suggest that such divisions cannot be overcome or are the sole determinants—the example of the Achaemenid empire is a case in point. But each of these areas has generated distinctive cultural and political types, and they have repeatedly fallen together in particular political formations. They represent, so to speak, relative geopolitical constants.

The Roman empire contrasts very clearly with this pattern, so much so, indeed, that it ought to be seen as an exception, a historical aberration, and analyzed from that perspective. Perhaps its geographical openness played a much greater role than is often assumed, for more than anywhere in the extended western Eurasian world, the absence of any major obstacle in its northern regions—in the form of mountain ranges or deserts—rendered it more vulnerable and exposed to population movements. Its origins lie in very particular Mediterranean circumstances, and its fragmentation is in many respects far easier to explain. Certainly its eastern successor, the medieval Byzantine state, constitutes (more or less) a natural geopolitical entity, since in terms of the regions around them, both Asia Minor and the southern Balkans form a geographical continuum.[30] In thinking about states and how they evolve and develop, we need to pay attention to these admittedly crude geophysical aspects. Geographical features alone are unlikely to account for divergent trends in the strength of state systems, as opposed to their size or the tendency for specific zones to favor their formation. Yet without our sliding into a geographical determinism, it does seem clear that some, at least, of the political fate of state systems should be anchored in their physical context and the cultural phenotypes these contexts have generated.[31]

States and the Later Roman State: Current Debates and Approaches

So far, then, we have considered the Roman state in a broad context, but we have taken several concepts for granted, and it is important to think a little about the technical or theoretical implications of the vocabulary we use in discussion. For example, the term *state* is often seen as problematic, because it reflects too much of the modern understanding of the concept. Yet it seems otherwise rather difficult to describe the set of institutions, system of government and administration, and ideology of political systems such as the Roman empire without recourse to it. Historians and sociologists have produced a wide range of definitions, each reflecting the particular intellectual and political backgrounds of those who have worked on the problem. As a descriptive starting point, we may begin with the general definition that has been evolved by recent commentators, notably Skalnik and Claessen, Krader, and, most recently, Mann.[32] This posits that "the state" represents a set of institutions and personnel, concentrated spatially at a single point, and exerting authority over a territorially distinct area. As Mann notes,[33] this description combines both institutional and functional elements, pertaining to the appearance of the state's apparatuses, as well as to their functions and effects. But in addition, we may qualify the definition by adding that the central point at which state power is nominally located may be mobile; that authority is in principle normative and binding and usually enshrined in legal and juridical prescription and practice, yet relies ultimately on coercion; and that the effectiveness of such authority depends upon a series of contextual factors: geographical extent, institutional forms through which power is actually exercised (for example, through a centralized and supervised central bureaucracy or through a dispersed provincial ruling elite). And while, with Radcliffe-Brown, we can agree that the state is the product of social and economic relations and must, therefore, not be reified or personified in the process of analysis, it is important to stress that the state possesses an identity as a field of action, as a role-constituting site of power and practices that can be independent, under certain preconditions, of the economic and political interests of whose who dominate it. As a general point, this consideration has been expressed frequently in historical and sociological literature in recent years, although it has not always been put into practice in the actual examination and interpretation of ancient and medieval state formations.[34]

At one extreme of social-political organization, the term *state* can refer to a relatively short-lived grouping of tribal or clan communities united under a warlord or chieftain who is endowed with both symbolic and military authority—in anthropological terms, a "Big-man" confederacy. Such "states" rarely survive for long, however, and are sometimes referred to as *protostates*, since they have not yet attained a degree of institutional permanence. Examples would include the majority of the "nomad empires" that arose on the Eurasian steppe zone from the beginning of the first millennium B.C.E. and periodically reappeared until the seventeenth century C.E., with the possible exception—although the point is certainly debatable—of the postconquest Mongol "empire" in the early thirteenth and fourteenth centuries.[35] Their problematic nature as states will become evident in the following discussion, so it seems on the whole simpler and less misleading to refer to them as chieftaincies, confederacies, or some such term more expressive of their ephemeral nature and absence of infrastructural continuity or permanence. At the other extreme, we find more or less territorially unified political entities, with a "center" (which may be peripatetic) from which a ruler or ruling group exercises political authority and that maintains its existence successfully over several generations; a key element in the formation and degree of permanence of such formations is that the authority of the ruler or ruling group is recognized as both legitimate and exclusive. In this respect, the ideological aspect is absolutely fundamental to state building, again as we will see later. One approach to these issues[36] (rooted in both Weberian and Marxian approaches) distinguishes a number of evolutionary tracks that may or may not lead from one to another but in which the degree of social stratification, social division of labor, and development of contradictory relations of production play a fundamental role. These are articulated together to form modes of the distribution of power, in which the forms of economic, ideological, and coercive power, distributed among differently located roles, give each social structure its particular form and content.[37] In their turn, the combining and recombining of such different elements can generate various forms of political structure, ultimately leading to the creation of states. In the earliest stages of social-political evolution, there are social formations with either "dissipated power" or "shared power"—in social-anthropological terms, small societies characterized by segmentary lineage organization (that is, where "stratification" exists as a vertical line between kin groups and attributed functions within the society, rather than horizontally between groups with different economic power), such as hunter-gatherer groups. Second, there are semistates, usually temporary extensions of the power of a single chieftain as a result of warfare or internal conflict. Third, involving a greater elaboration of both coercion and more explicitly political ideology, there are protostates that develop "from the existence of specialised political roles which fall short of an effective monopoly of the means of coercion to the existence of potentially permanent institutions of government properly so-called." A final track is represented by full-fledged states with the sort of political and institutional potential described already.[38]

More permanent state formations of this type were generally territorially demarcated (even if lands and frontiers were ill defined or fluctuating, reflecting the process of formation through amalgamation, conquest, inheritance, and so forth) and controlled—at least in their early phases of development—by centralized governing or ruling establishments of some sort, which usually possessed the coercive power to assert their authority over the territories they claim, even if only on an occasional "punitive" basis. How exactly such central authorities achieved these ends varied enormously from state to state and society to society. In all premodern states, there have been gaps in the extent of state authority—border or mountainous regions, for example, difficult to access and untouched by state supervision; or "tribal" groups nominally owing allegiance and occupying territory claimed by the state, but not always easily brought under the state's authority or control (such as the Isaurians at times in Anatolia or the Daylamites of the Elburz region in Iran).[39] In areas where geography favors a tribal pastoral and/or nomadic economy, the latter frequently formed important elements in the armies of conquest states, certainly in the initial stages of their evolution. Because of the mobility of such people, their internal social cohesion and self-sufficiency, and the fact that their wealth is generally easily moved away from the reach of state officials, they are both able and sometimes inclined to resist any central authority that does not directly favor their own interests. Local elites may likewise have presented difficulties, even if ideologically committed to the existence of a particular state. By the same token, the relative patchiness of central control may represent a point on the line from local to supralocal state to empire (and back again), as with Assyrian control over neighboring territories in the early period of expansion (ninth century B.C.E.). Ideological power can overcome this at certain times but by itself generally remains a short-term means of cementing such power relationships.[40] The very different configuration of power relationships within three late ancient/early medieval states, for example—late Rome/early Byzantium, Sasanian Iran, and the early Umayyad caliphate—provides striking examples of the ways in which these features combined.

States, Legitimation, and Politics

Another central aspect of state formation is the generation of fairly complex ideological and legitimating systems, on the one hand, and at the same time more impersonalized and institutionalized modes of surplus extraction, on the other, than protostates or clan or tribal groupings are capable of developing. Administration based on kinship and lineage relationships and the exploitation of kin-based modes of subordination tend in the more successful and enduring states to be replaced by non-kinship-based bureaucratic or administrative systems (although kin and lineage are rarely entirely absent—again the Assyrian example, on the one hand, with provincial governors appointed from among the ruling families, and that of the later Byzantine empire, with its close familial networks, provide useful but very different illustrations). In most examples, a bureaucratic-administrative structure of some sort confers a clear advantage and appears to be a necessity if the political system is to retain its nontribal existence and cohesion. This point was made already by the Muslim philosopher and political analyst Ibn Khaldun, for example, who saw this process as generally following the initial formation of a supratribal political entity from tribal elements under a chieftain of some sort, in which a crucial role was played by religion as a unifying element providing a new, suprakinship set of relationships, identities, and loyalties. While Ibn Khaldun was clearly working on the basis of his knowledge of the evolution of Islamic states, his main point remains valid for any state-formative process.[41]

An obvious reason for preferring a relatively open-ended account of state formation and characteristics is that the formation of a state is never a single event and only rarely a set of closely compressed events, but rather a longer term evolutionary process in which social praxis and economic relationships respond to changing conditions through what has been referred to as "competitive selection" of practices; where social and cultural praxis fail to respond adequately to shifts in their conditions of existence, the state fails to develop further and succumbs. There are many different shades of "stateness," both in respect of the degree of actual physical control and in the degree of ideological integration of the varying and often antagonistic elements occupying the territory claimed by a given central authority. Some historical states have been represented by claims to legitimacy based on a consensus agreed among various powerful elements, but where the actual ruler has little or no power of coercion, and have survived generally for only a relatively short time. Those state elites who have military coercion at their disposal, at least in the early stages of their development, may remain relatively isolated from the social structures they live off, surviving only as long as they can coerce or persuade support and resources. Others may move toward establishing a permanent and self-regenerating body of administrators that draws its recruits from either specific groups within the state (tribal groups, for example), from particular family dynasties, or from those of a particular social or cultural background (which includes the establishment of slave bureaucracies and armies, deracinated from their original social and cultural context and dependent entirely on the system to which they owe their position). They tend thus to evolve institutional structures—fiscal systems, military organizations, and so forth—that establish their own sets of roles and discourses, divorced from the daily practices of ordinary society. The state becomes a specialist and dominant set of institutions that may even undertake the creation *ab initio* of its own administrative personnel and that can survive only by maintaining control over the appropriation and distribution of surplus wealth these specialized personnel administer.[42] This certainly became the case in Rome and Byzantium and—to a different degree—in the Umayyad and Abbasid caliphates, for example. And it seems also that this deracination or distancing of administrative apparatus from a social base, as well as from the kinship ties of the royal household, represents a developmental shift, a process of maturation, as we follow the evolution of state formation through time. Whereas the Assyrian and Achaemenid empires recruited their administrative infrastructure from the elite families of the center and provinces, bound together through kinship ties or vested interests shared with the ruling dynasty and its kin, developed bureaucratic systems, such as came to typify Rome and the Chinese Han state, recruited their personnel from a wider social range and depended upon more broadly available literary and educational possibilities. Of course, the picture is in all cases uneven and patchy, and this simplification does a certain amount of injustice to the historical cases we know about.

A particularly important aspect is represented by the potential for state formations to reproduce themselves, in contrast to the potential of a particular dynasty with its retinues based upon personal loyalties and notions of honor, obligation, and reciprocity, to maintain itself in power over a number of generations. The evolution of a bureaucratic elite with a sense of its own function within the state/society (even if this elite remains closely tied to a particular social stratum, such as the slave administrators of the imperial household in first-century imperial Rome or the royal household in Sasanian Iran), which identifies with a particular set of ideological and symbolic narratives, and which can recruit and train its personnel into the institutional roles and behavioral patterns relevant to the maintenance and even expansion of these structures, is a crucial factor. The relative success of the first Islamic caliphates, the Roman and Byzantine empires, or the Chinese and Ottoman states, in their different forms over time in this regard, to name just a few examples, provides good illustrations of the ways in which some political formations evolved stable yet flexible structures sufficient to permit their survival over a long period regardless of often major shifts in dynastic arrangements and the nature of the central authority itself. The failures of the early Frankish kingdoms illustrate the fate of political formations that failed to generate such structures.

The case of ancient Athens may be used as an illustration. In spite of its success in mobilizing a vast resource catchment area, in the form of allies and dependent cities and territories, Athens remained remarkably jealous of its rights of citizenship, although this by no means reflected an impermeable system. But the failure to expand citizenship, on the one hand, and to create identities between center and periphery, on the other (with notable exceptions—Samos, for example, toward the end of the Peloponnesian war), reflected the failure to evolve a broader tax base within the core territories. Athens was thus always parasitical in respect of its allied and subordinate territories, and this deprived it of the sort of structural flexibility that would have permitted it to survive the crisis of 405–404 and the defeat at Aegospotami.[43] Just as, in some states, problems of both regional and lineage identities (however spurious or artificial the latter may usually in fact have been) dramatically vitiated attempts by a central authority, even when supported by elements of a permanent civil or military bureaucracy, to maintain itself as an effective power with real coercive potential over more than a few generations, so the failure to generate common identities within Athenian tributary territories vitiated Athenian strength at precisely the point at which it was most severely challenged. The maintenance of ideological legitimacy and hegemony must accompany the maintenance of appropriate coercive potential in situations during which external pressures build up, and the combination must be seen as a central element in considering the reasons for the long-term survival of a particular state system. The relatively short life span of the Athenian empire must owe something to these systemic weaknesses. In contrast, the neo-Assyrian state of the tenth to eighth centuries B.C.E. does appear to have been able to maintain an administrative apparatus, which, although dependent upon a social and ethnic identity with the palace, was founded upon a combination of taxation and tribute raising (and associated bureaucratic skills). This was in turn integrated into a system of vassalage and dependency upon both the royal dynasty and the cult of Assur, which was quite deliberately introduced into the pantheon of conquered peoples.[44]

The Sasanian state offers a good example of a remarkably successful dynasty in which ideological legitimacy and a bureaucratic administrative structure were successfully combined to hold powerful centrifugal tendencies and the competition of several equally powerful clans in check for some four centuries. The power of the Sasanian royal house depended very largely on two interlinked factors: an ideological commitment by a powerful group of regional clan or dynastic chiefs (the Sasanian "aristocracy," from whom the royal house was itself drawn) to the legitimacy of the dominant dynasty (which claimed also a certain politico-religious authority sanctioned both by a claim to ancient lineage and military leadership) and the maintenance of a degree of equilibrium between the interests of the ruling house and those of the aristocracy, which supported the claims to legitimate power and accepted royal authority only as long as Sasanian rule did not challenge their own interests, whether ideological, political, or economic.[45] Dynastic rivalries, and questions of honor, shame, and competition were inevitably also integral elements in this picture. The Abbasid Caliphate itself (750–1258) can be understood from this perspective, for already by the later ninth century the central power was heavily compromised by the growing autonomy of provincial governors and by generals commanding armies in the central lands. It could be argued that only the need to attain ideological legitimacy within Islam held the wider polity together, and successful religious-ideological opposition in Africa, Egypt, and the Arabian peninsula threatened even this.

Medieval Indian states exemplify some elements of the relationship between the success or failure of a state center to survive over a longer or shorter period, the networks of power between other actual or potential centers of social power (spatially or socially) and the rulers and their dependent elite, and control over the appropriation and distribution of resources, whether economic or ideological. It is clear from a cursory comparison of a number of ancient and medieval state formations that a central authority can survive for substantial periods simply through the manipulation of key ideological and symbolic elements in the cultural system of the social formation as a whole. South Indian temple culture and the attendant state structures, particularly as exemplified in the Chola empire, offer good illustrations. The Chola empire also illustrates the central importance of legitimation within symbolic terms of reference—within the symbolic universe of a given cultural formation—and of the social/cultural groups that are generally responsible for their maintenance, whether priestly groups, official churches, cult organizations, or aristocratic elites endowed with particular symbolic authority.[46] This is especially relevant when we consider that states may have an ideological life that is not necessarily tied to their actual political and institutional efficacy or power. Political ideologies and belief systems, once in existence, are sometimes quite able to adapt and survive in conditions that have evolved well away from those within which they were originally engendered, provided the contradictions between the two are not too extreme or insurmountable in terms of social praxis and psychology.

Those that respond to long-term functional needs in human society provide the best examples and include religious systems in particular, such as Hinduism, Islam, or Christianity—systems that do, to a greater or lesser degree, free themselves in certain respects from both the political and the social and economic conditions that produced them (although they may at the same time constrain the direction of socioeconomic evolution within those societies). But "political" ideologies, too, can be extremely flexible. They may provide a rationale for conflict where no visible or obvious reason in terms of competition for material resources exists, for example. And they can also be extremely powerful. Many states were, in effect, little more than territories under the nominal authority of a ruler, but in which actual power was exercised by a tribe-, clan-, or family-based socioeconomic elite. The position of such an elite might originally have depended upon the central ruler and/or the conditions in which the state came into being (by conquest, for example), but, because of their actual control over resources and other historical conditions, they became in practice independent of the center. Yet in such cases, we find that the very idea of a centralized kingdom or state and the residual power of concepts such as honor or loyalty to a particular dynastic succession or set of constitutional arrangements were enough to maintain at least a fictional unity of identity. The later history of the Byzantine state from the thirteenth century to its final extinction in 1453 exemplifies this particular type of development. The Assyrian empire in the later ninth and first half of the eighth centuries B.C.E. survived partly at least, it appears, because of the strength of these symbolic and ideological relationships, in spite of political strife at the center and the loss of certain more distant western territories.

Ideological Integration and Ritual Penetration

These points suggest that a crucial element in the longer term success of a state formation is that of the degree of consensus and reciprocity (between its own demands and structures, those of social elites, and those of the populations from which it draws its resources) upon which the state is built or upon which it comes to depend. This is not to revive a "consensus" theory of state formation, but rather to stress the significance in the structuring of political relations of power and resource distribution of rules, "law," and forms of normative behavioral patterns. This differed enormously between different historical cases. Some survived only by virtue of their ability to coerce submission and the extraction of surplus wealth on a more or less continuous basis. But over the longer term, this has not been a particularly effective way of evolving or maintaining state power. A good example is provided by the development from republic to empire in the case of Rome, in which a conquest state was able to evolve an ideological hegemony, which in turn generated a consensual identity with the conceptual world delivered by the Roman conquerors, stimulated by the deliberate erasure of preexisting political structures in many—although by no means all—the conquered territories.[47] Although most states first evolved in the context of an imbalance between military coercion and cooperative participation, those that have been most successful have usually generated increasingly complex relationships of reciprocity, consensus, and interdependence with other elements of the social formations upon which they draw (but which, it must not be forgotten, they also influence), in particular with leading elements of conquered groups or previous political formations, whether these are tribal and clan leaders, merchant elites, or aristocracies. Many states, established after a relatively brief period of military expansion and conquest, came to rest very heavily on such structures, and the Indian examples mentioned already provide a good illustration of such systems. Equally, the Merovingian kingdom during the sixth and seventh centuries depended very heavily on the support and goodwill of the pre-existing Gallo-Roman elite and the episcopal establishment (the two were anyway very closely integrated), especially in its southern regions,[48] while the caliphate during the later seventh and well into the ninth century relied on the complicity of non-Muslim (or only slowly Islamizing) local elites in both the former Roman provinces, as well as in Iran and Iraq, for the management of their fiscal affairs at grassroots level.[49]

Ideological integration has been a major feature of most major recent state formations. In the western tradition, this has generally been seen as a secondary aspect of state formation, a reflection, perhaps, of the dominance of military institutions and coercion in the political history of the western Eurasian world. In fact, comparison with different types of states suggests that this prioritization may be misplaced.[50] In the pre-Islamic Indian subcontinent, political power rested on the exploitation of a core region, the source of immediate royal income, while the areas farthest away from the center of military and political coercion were attached primarily through occasional military expeditions and by connections of a ritual nature. Royal rituals were centered on key religious centers and temples, through whose religious-ideological authority the rulers reinforced their legitimacy and claims to overlordship, and in return for which they undertook to support such institutions through a variety of endowments, regular gifts in cash and in kind, grants of labor services, and so on. It was through their involvement in such rituals that members of dominant social groups could be incorporated within what was in practice a network of royal and spiritual patronage. At the same time, the rituals legitimated more localized authority and power, so that the system as a whole provided a rationale for the prevailing political institutions and social-economic relations.[51]

The political relationships that are represented by those of ancient and early medieval Indian polities, such as the Mauryan empire from the late fourth to early second century B.C.E., or the empire of the Guptas (c. 320–540 C.E.), in which religious/priestly elites and temple economies play such an important role, have been described by the concept "ritual polity"[52] or as the "intense ritual penetration of everyday life" in cultural systems that broadly share the same basic tenets (in cases where markedly different belief systems exist within the framework established by a state and not shared by the political elite, of course, such relationships may only operate to a limited degree, or not at all). One of the most prominent features of the ideological underpinnings of such systems, in particular from the time of the Gupta state, was the emphasis placed on social order (*dharma*), which it was the king's or ruler's duty to protect; while it cannot be said that this was the main reason for the lack of emphasis on large state building in India, it played a significant role. There is also a danger in modern conceptualization of this notion of turning a specifically structured system of social praxis, which reflects and maintains also a given symbolic universe, into an idealist notion of theocratic, "Asiatic" stability, in which the rise and fall of states and power elites is determined by "religion" and in which economic relationships are created by the demands of religious observance and beliefs or perceptions. In fact, it is clear that rulers were generally quite aware of the process of religious-political manipulation necessary to the maintenance of their power, especially of the need to maintain control over resources in order to invest in this ritual system on a grand scale in order to continually legitimate their position. More significantly, it is clear that when we examine a number of ancient state formations more closely, this ritual incorporative facet and the ways in which cultic systems function at both the political and economic levels to bind a wider territory together were widespread and represented in practice one of the commonest means of empire building—whether we are concerned with the Babylonian, Assyrian, or later states and empires. In the case of both ancient Assyrian and Achaemenid Persian kingdoms, for example, the rulers of both empires became actively involved in the dominant cults of conquered territories, which were then assimilated into a broader network of divine relationships, participation in which guaranteed both continuing divine support and therefore political and institutional stability. The same might be said, in a different degree according to region, for pre-Christian Rome.

Such "ritual" consists not simply in ideas or attitudes. Ritual practice was itself constitutive of, and reproduced by, social praxis and represented in consequence an aspect of the social relations of production, that is, the sets of socioeconomic relations that enabled the social formation to reproduce itself. It is less the fact that such interactional networks existed that is important, than the role they played, for they functioned as networks of distribution and redistribution of surplus wealth—through a priestly caste or ruling elite, for example—organized in favor of a particular religious center (such as a temple or similar locus of the divine) at a given moment. The fact that many rulers derived their original status from an ancestral role as chief priest or similar, on the one hand, and that much of the political expansion of ancient states was legitimated by appealing to the claims to overlordship of a particular divinity, on the other hand, is indicative of how usual this actually was.

Indeed, the "ritual penetration" of a society as represented by specific sets of social practices, which are themselves the expression of the structure of social relations of production (expressed through a given religious and symbolic vocabulary), is common to all premodern (or precapitalist) social formations, but in different degrees. In some societies, they have come to be the dominant expression of relations of production, since as Godelier has pointed out, each social-cultural formation represents and practices economic relations in different forms, the location and origins of which must be the subject of specific empirical analysis.[53] In each case, the combination of a specific political universe, ecological context, kinship structure, and religious configuration promoted the varying role and position of such ritual, transactional networks. Their importance was enhanced or diminished by the structure of political demands of state centers and rulers in respect of control over surplus distribution. In pre-Islamic central India, the incorporation of social praxis into a temple-oriented system of redistribution of surplus wealth and political legitimacy, combined with the particular, highly fragmented character of the political geography of the region, meant that the process of state formation was always inscribed within such relationships and the structures they generated, producing a highly inflected set of political-religious relationships in which legitimacy depended to a very great extent on consensual acceptance. The situation was not so different in ancient Assyria and Babylon.

But in the case of Indian states, there is an additional factor to be taken into account. The ideological structures of Hinduism, and its contingent social practices, which came to mark every aspect of social and political life across the whole subcontinent, tended under certain conditions to render the functions normally assumed and required of any state structure, especially those of maintaining order and internal cohesion, dangerously redundant. If we assume that states provide both centralized authority and, more important, normative rules for legal, social, and economic relationships, then it becomes clear that in the Hindu context, these characteristics of state organization are already present in the internal order of religious and social life—the lineage structures and caste attributions alone provide for much of this.[54] A similar case could, in fact, be made for certain forms of Islam, given the permeative strength of Sharīʿa as a guide to day-to-day patterns of behavior down to the humblest levels of household existence; in a few cases within Christianity—more especially, in certain post-Reformation movements—one could draw similar conclusions about the interface among state structures (and their functions), law, and normative social behavior. It would be interesting to examine some of the ancient state formations about which we have evidence in an attempt to see whether similar relationships did, or could, prevail or whether, as argued by Mann, it is only the most recent salvationist or soteriological systems that can achieve these results.[55] In the case of China, for example, the longevity of Confucian prominence and its penetration into society seems to be due to the fact that the Confucian-Legalist system that was characteristic of the state from the early Han period welded political and ideological power together, so that even in a situation of fragmented state authority, as long as no competing ideology could better legitimize the state and as long as Confucian scholars survived as a social-cultural group, new rulers inevitably came to rely on imperial Confucianism for legitimization and on Confucian scholars—who were at once both priests and bureaucrats—to manage the fiscal and institutional structures through which the country was governed, which in turn reinforced notions of imperial unity and promoted the reproduction of key administrative-cultural practices.[56]

Of course, the power-relations in any culture are legitimated through systems of belief, ideologies in which the "necessary" duty of individuals, states, communities to defend their beliefs, values, and identities and to promote the variety of associated activities are represented through culturally-specific ideas and concepts. Similar forms of ritual penetration can be seen in the Islamic world or in Christendom as in India or China. In the case of both Christianity and Islam, one aspect of ritual incorporation—that is to say, conversion—served as a fundamental tool of political integration and domination, while the religious systems established both the framework for social praxis as well as the thought-world within which it was conceived and apprehended. The observance of specific modes of behavior in social intercourse determined the degree to which an individual was identified as a member of a community or group (or not), while medieval Christian and Muslim rulers had to be seen to reinforce and re-affirm their particular symbolic universe through ritualized expressions of faith and the redistribution of considerable amounts of surplus wealth through certain ideologically legitimating ritual actions, such as through endowing or supporting religious foundations. In the late Roman world, the complex ceremonial of the imperial palace, the detailed hierarchy of ranks and offices, and the daily acting-out of rituals designed expressly to recall and to imitate the harmony and peace of the heavenly order were all fundamental expressions of the symbolic order. The close relationship between the emperor and the Church, and the supervision by the Church of popular beliefs and, increasingly, of kinship arrangements, for example, embodied an impressive ideological and symbolic system of legitimation. But it did not itself express also, or serve as, a key institution of surplus distribution necessary to the economic survival of the state institution. Yet religious ideology *as social praxis* directly affected relations between individuals and the Church, as well as between the latter and rulers. A key strand in late Roman imperial ideology was that of imperial universalism, embodied in its Christian form from the later fourth century C.E. and marked by both exclusivism and an increasing intolerance towards competing belief-systems. By the middle and later years of the sixth century this imperialism identified the *imperium Romanum* with "orthodox" Christianity, equated with the civilized, God-protected empire of the Christian Romans. In the following period, especially from the ninth century onwards, imperialism through territorial expansion was accompanied by a growing emphasis on imperialism as the spiritual conquest of the world through mission, conversion, and the establishment of an orthodox Christian *oikoumene* under imperial leadership, although this motif was present in Justinian's time also.[57] The Church represented one of the most powerful ideological and economic institutions of the late Roman and Byzantine world. Through its formal teaching and theology it came to be presented by the clergy and the literate and learned minority as the single correct form of belief—orthodoxy—even though its first centuries were marked by a series of intellectual and political clashes over the definitions at issue.[58]

An important characteristic of the late Roman Church was the close political-ideological relationship it held with the secular power, embodied by the emperor. The development in the course of the fourth century of an imperial Christian ideological system rooted in both Romano-Hellenistic political concepts and Christian theology established an unbreakable association, which was thereafter to set limits to, yet also to legitimate, the actions of emperor and patriarch. In its most abstract form it was understood as a relationship of mutual dependence, but the duty of the secular ruler was both to defend "correct belief" (*orthodoxia*) as well as to protect the interests of the Church—in the form of the honor and respect accorded the priestly office—which catered for the spiritual needs of the Christian flock. Accordingly it was understood that the health of the state was assured only when the traditions of orthodox belief (as derived from the Apostles and the Fathers of the Church) were faithfully practiced and handed down. This utopian expression of harmony and order—which the earthly kingdom was meant to strive to achieve, in imitation of Heaven—was reflected in imperial religious and secular politics, and in the ways in which the emperors understood their practical role in respect of the Church, especially with regard to the convening of ecclesiastical councils and the incorporation of the principles embodied in these ideas in imperial legislation.[59]

Now patterns of investment of wealth directly reflected what people believed about their world—whether they invested in civic infrastructure and amenities, as in the Hellenistic and Roman world up to the third century; whether they invested in church- or temple-building or the endowment of religious foundations, artwork and decoration, or charity; or whether they invested in court offices, tax-farms or commercial ventures, or a combination of all of these, all reflect prevailing values and assumptions about what was important in their world. Religious belief can be seen directly to affect patterns of wealth investment and, in consequence, the ways in which elites, for example, appropriate and consume wealth, as well as the ways in which political regimes are able to maintain themselves, or not. If we want to understand, causally, changes in such phenomena, we need to take beliefs and the framework they set seriously into consideration as one key element in the notion of change, otherwise we end up merely describing them and seeing them as epiphenomena with no causal value. Indeed, since beliefs certainly had an impact at times on political action and thus, indirectly, on economic relationships, it seems obvious that if we want to understand the processes of change, we need to build beliefs and their contingent social effects into our model of causal relationships.

Power and the Politics of Resource Distribution

State centers that are unable to maintain control and participation in the process of primary surplus distribution (through direct taxation, for example, or the ability always to coerce militarily) must attempt to survive by promoting their interests through alternative, *secondary* means of surplus *re*distribution. Such means include both the "devolution" of military and other authority, for example, to the level of the fief or an equivalent institution, as in western Europe during the period from the sixth to the eleventh century. They include also networks of redistribution reinforced and operated through primarily religious structures.

Of course, both Islamic and Christian rulers in East and West legitimated the extraction and distribution of surplus—which is to say, in effect, the continued existence of their respective states—through political theologies, ideological narratives that highlighted the necessary duty of the state and its rulers to defend the faith and to promote the variety of associated activities this entailed. At the same time, they had to be seen to reinforce and reaffirm their particular symbolic universe through ritualized expressions of faith and the redistribution of considerable amounts of surplus wealth to religious foundations of various types or through certain ideologically legitimating ritual actions. In the Byzantine world, for example, the complex ceremonial of the imperial palace, the close relationship between the emperor (with the state) and the church, and the supervision by the church of popular beliefs and kinship structures created an impressive ideological and symbolic system of legitimation, a system whose origins can be followed from the reign of Constantine I through that of Justinian and beyond. Yet, in this particular case, in contrast with the south Indian examples, it did not itself express also, or serve as, a key institution of surplus distribution necessary to the economic survival of the state institution. Similar networks can be seen in the Islamic world, in western Christendom, and in the Chinese empire. And in the case of both Christianity and Islam, ritual incorporation (that is to say, conversion) served as a fundamental tool of political integration and domination. The "segmentary" states of South and Central America provide closer parallels to the south Indian case, for here temple-centered redistribution of surplus and tribute was a crucial means through which surplus appropriation and political authority were maintained.[60]

The structure of the power relations that dominate within state apparatuses and between them and the broader social formation are another important facet of the ways in which states function and how they evolve. How independent of society were state functionaries, individually or as a group? How limited were state apparatuses by the social and economic relationships that dominated a given society? Was the state, as a set of institutions, dependent upon a social and economic elite or "ruling class," upon an alliance of tribal lineages and identities (which may or may not have had any historical substance), or upon some combination of these?[61] To what extent did emergent states incorporate existing elites? The relationships between these considerations and the origins of a given state system, on the one hand, and the appropriation, allocation, and distribution or redistribution of resources, on the other, constitute a series of focal issues.

These considerations are important because the state, while it provides a framework for, or sets limits to, the development of certain social and economic relationships, through its need to establish and then maintain a regular and predictable structure of surplus extraction, also enables or facilitates the evolution of new practices and relationships. This is as true of relations of dependence between groups and between individuals as it is of relationships between sets of institutions and the practices through which they are lived out and reproduced. A clear example of this can be seen in the way in which the east Roman/Byzantine state transferred the focus of its attention in fiscal matters away from urban centers to village communities during the course of the seventh and eighth centuries, thereby radically altering the ways in which social relationships between landlords and tenants, on the one hand, and among peasant producers, the state, and towns, on the other, functioned.[62] Similar examples exist in the cases of the Ottoman and Mughal states. In the Ottoman case, the growth during the seventeenth century of a local nobility, together with the garrisoning of imperial salaried troops and Janissaries in the provinces on a permanent basis, radically altered the relationship between central government and regions (generally seen as to the disadvantage of the former), yet such changes were made possible precisely because of the state's perceived fiscal and military requirements.[63]

The state thus established or generated spaces in which new developments could take place. The role of tax farmers provides an interesting case, since their activities both involved the extraction of surplus and acted as a stimulus to changed patterns of investment or consumption of wealth, to changed structures of money use on the part of both producers and state administrations, and so on. In some cases, the existence of a central fiscal administration may have given hitherto unimportant local leaders—village headmen, small-scale local landlords—a more significant role in the process of surplus appropriation and accumulation, leading to shifts in the political order of power at the local level and ultimately reacting back on the state itself. This might lead to a consideration of how the role of village elites or rural social rank attributions could have an influence on the ways a state or its regional predecessors and successors could organize, just as the existence of centralized state apparatuses and their demands for surplus in turn affected the ways in which these local relationships worked, opening up new social space within which they could evolve.[64] And this leads in turn to a consideration of how such elements form part of a social totality, especially in the context of both local and international pools of influence—the concentric, overlapping, and reciprocally (but unevenly) influencing relationships that cross the boundaries of social formations.[65]

As was implied in the first part of this chapter, one important aspect of any discussion on states and their histories must be the differential processes of evolution reflected in their age or maturity. "Mature" states confront very different problems from "young" states. The degree to which their various institutional and ideological systems become well established, entrenched, and embedded into the basic fabric of the social formations that support them must play an important role. In newly formed conquest states, the conquerors are rarely integrated into the wider structure of social and economic relationships: they remain, often for some considerable time, in effect, parasitic consumers of wealth extracted by force, or the threat of force, alone. In other cases, while this may once have been the case, centuries of "state embedding" have occurred, so that the state elite, its apparatuses, and its ideology are inextricably interwoven into the social fabric of society at large. The later Roman state and the Sasanian empire would seem to represent such formations. Looking at traits such as the way in which the economic relationship between center and elites evolved across the medium and longer term is just one way of expanding the basis for comparative discussion about states, because it enables us to construct models of state formations or social-economic systems that can then help in asking questions about other cultural and social systems and states. It encourages us to look behind the institutional and political forms that each society presents through its particular symbolic universe and to locate explanations of change that incorporate both the general (or systemic) and the particular (or culture-specific).

Finally, broader issues of power must play a role in any discussion of the ways state systems function, whether as political or sociocultural entities or both. Conflict is an unavoidable aspect of human history, perhaps given more emphasis than we always appreciate in many of our literary sources because conflict is frequently what interested the contemporary historians, chroniclers, and other commentators. Conflict at court, disagreements and tensions or conflict between emperors and patriarchs, conflict between elite families and clans, conflict between individuals before a court, conflict between provincial commanders and their armies, all conflict revolved around a struggle for power and influence, whether at court and over policy, over economic resources in the provinces, or over imperial religious policy and the perceptions ordinary people had about it. Power must therefore occupy an important role in much of the discussion, and definitions of power, or how the notion might best be conceptualized, are therefore of central importance. Power has two aspects—the ways in which it could be wielded and the ways in which it was represented and portrayed by those who wielded it or wished to give that impression. In much contemporary social history debate, power is generally understood as social power, as a generalized means to specific ends. Power is thus control over various types of resources (wealth, people, knowledge) and can thus be exercised at a variety of levels—from the most personal (of the individual over other individuals) to the most public (of political-military power over armies, food supplies, and so on).

In one sense, therefore, power is the political and psychological expression of economic dominance (since resources are, in the end, an essentially economic category). Yet this is an element that may not always be obvious to the modern commentator or be clearly conceptualized as such by those who wield it: social relationships are generally represented in an ideological form that has no obvious single economic point of reference. Power is a product of the combination and articulation of human psychology, cultural forms, and economic context. And while it may be exercised in relative autonomy from other structures in respect of its immediate *effects*, it does not spring out of nothing. Power, coercion, and ideology are forms or expressions of *praxis*, that is to say, of the socially determined way people in different contexts in a culture do things. They are modes through which particular sets of relationships can be maintained and reproduced. Power is central to social theory, but the struggle for, attainment, and exercise of power are about resources, and while it must by definition be understood as a reflection of the economics of society, it must also be seen as something that can be realized or implemented at the level of cultural and psychological resources.[66] In this context, we may bear in mind the extension of postcolonial theory to the premodern empires and to the study of subaltern and subordinated cultures, which have largely remained invisible in the historiographical record, even if efforts are being made to address the issue through a range of new approaches that recenter cultural or sociocultural elements that have been marginalized in the debate, ranging from ethnic and linguistic identities to gender or to belief systems written out of the picture as "heresies."[67] Postprocessual archaeology is but one bundle of such approaches, but they have an impact also on literature, the study of buildings, and the use of private and public space in ancient and medieval urban environments, as well as on studies of visual and representational culture.[68] By the same token, the application of complexity theory in the study of state systems will certainly open up significant new avenues of approach and generate new questions, even if this has barely begun to occur, and especially since the issue of the appropriateness of some uses of complexity theory remains at issue, since this is a highly contested and much-debated issue in current discussions within the humanities.[69] Subordination and oppression are as much a key element in state formation and evolution as political and fiscal administration, military organization, or the structure of social and religious elites, and all are about power and how it is achieved, maintained, reproduced, or denied. Since much of the history of the late antique world revolves around issues of access to and exercise of social power, in one form or another,[70] this must be understood as a central feature of any effort to describe and to understand the period as a whole.

NOTES

1. See Wright 1978; Moravcsik 1958, 2, 299.

2. Leslie and Gardiner 1996; Lieu 1992; Pelliot 1996.

3. This chapter draws to some extent on my sections of Haldon and Goldstone 2009.

4. Doyle 1986, 45.

5. For the "segmentary" state, see Southall 1956; 1965; also Stein 1977. For criticisms of the way this concept has been used, however, see Champalakshmi 1981; Kulke 1982.

6. See, for example, Sanderson 1995; 1999; Mann 1986a; Runciman 1989. Most recently on Rome and China see the essays in Scheidel 2009; and the short comparative survey in Burbank and Cooper 2010, 23–59.

7. Adshead 2000, 58–63.

8. Little 2007; Rosen 2007; Stathakopoulos 2004; Keys 1999.

9. Wickham 2005, 548–549.

10. Bielenstein 1987, 12, 19.

11. Wiechmann and Grupe 2005.

12. For some of the literature on climate change and its impact, especially in respect of societal collapse, see Diamond 2005; Nüzhet Dalfes, Kukla, and Weiss 1997; Rosen 2001; 1997.

13. Bottema, Woldring, and Aytug 1986; Eastwood, Roberts, and Lamb 1998.

14. Lev-Yadun, Lipschitz, and Waisel 1987.

15. Jones, Roberts, Leng, and Türkeş 2006; see also Haldon 2007; England, Eastwood, Roberts, Turner, and Haldon 2008.

16. Wenke 1975–1976, see 82; Cullen and de Menocal 2000; Jones, Roberts, Leng, and Türkeş 2006.

17. See the careful discussion in Decker 2009, 7–11.

18. See Hirschfeld 1997, 50ff.; in general, Shereshevski 1991; for the ice cores: Ruddiman 2003.

19. See Morony 2004a, 172–175; Wickham 2005, 17–31, 609ff.

20. See de Calataÿ 2005; Hopkins 1980; Parker 1992; Jongman 2003; Schmidt and Gruhle 2003.

21. Kron 2002; Bakels and Jacomet 2003. For Chinese population and climate, see Adshead 2000, 58–60.

22. Wickham 2005; more narrowly but with very different emphases, see also Ward-Perkins 2005; Heather 2006.

23. Haldon 1997; 2005.

24. As maintained in part by Wickham 2005. But there are some difficulties with this part of his construct: see Haldon 2008; Sarris 2006.

25. Pearce 1987; Graff 2002.

26. Graff 2002, 127, 136, n.19, for example.

27. Bielenstein 1987, 194, 199. For later Han census figures and taxable households, see Graff 2002, 93, n. 1; de Crespigny 2004, table 2; 1990, 7–58.

28. Graff 2002, 127.

29. Liu 2001.

30. On one fundamental element, see Horden and Purcell 2000; Belke, Hild, Koder, and Soustal 2000; or the much older work of Phillipson 1939 for the Byzantine successor state.

31. For some discussion of these issues, see Diamond 1997, 411–417.

32. Mann 1986b; Claessen and Skalník 1978b; Cohen 1978, together with the papers in section 3 of the same volume.

33. Mann 1986b, 112.

34. For some older literature, see Cipolla 1970; Cohen and Service 1978; Claessen and Skalnik 1978a; Claessen and Skalnik 1981; Eisenstadt 1967; Kautsky 1982.

35. See Runciman 1989, 152f., for example.

36. Runciman 1989, 150ff.

37. See Runciman 1989, 12ff., 148ff.

38. Runciman 1989, 153.

39. See Hild and Hellenkemper 1990, 30–43 for Isauria.

40. This is not only a premodern phenomenon: see, for example, Fabietti 1982.

41. See Ibn Khaldun 1958, 1.247ff.

42. For the extent of recent discussion on the nature and form of state power in premodern state formations: Mann 1986a; Runciman 1989.

43. See Finley 1985, 61ff.; Strauss 1986; Raaflaub 1979; 1989.

44. See Pećirková 1977; 1987; Postgate 1974; also Liverani 1984.

45. For Sasanid Persia (third–seventh century C.E.), see Howard-Johnston 1995, esp. 211–226; Rubin 1995; in general, Christensen 1944; Rubin 2000.

46. See, for example, Appadurai and Breckenridge 1976.

47. See Woolf 1998.

48. See especially the valuable discussion of Wood 1979; and Heinzelmann 1975; Lewis 1976. Bishops represented a very important focus of spiritual power and authority, backed by sometimes quite extensive ecclesiastical revenues, quite independent of the royal and lay establishment. By the middle of the seventh century, the blending of Frankish and Gallo-Roman elites meant that the episcopate was more closely connected, through kinship, to the secular elites of the Merovingian kingdom.

49. E.g., Morony 2004b.

50. See the discussion in Acien Almansa 1998.

51. See Stein 1980, esp. 264ff.

52. See Heitzman 1991; Preston 1980; Spencer 1969.

53. Godelier 1978; 1984.

54. See in particular Stein 1985, esp. 74ff.; in general Saraswati 1977. For a detailed discussion of these points, with further literature, see Haldon 1993, 242ff.

55. Mann 1986a, 301–340 and esp. 341–372.

56. Zhao 2006.

57. Dagron 1993; Ivanov 2008.

58. Christianity and the evolution of Orthodoxy: Winkelmann 1980; Dagron 1993, 9–371; Hussey 1986; Dvornik 1966, 2: 614–615, 652–653.

59. Imperial ideology and the role of the emperor: Dvornik 1966, vol. 2; Hussey 1986, 297–310.

60. For "ritual penetration," see Mann 1986a, 361; but against his argument that *only* the major world-salvationist-religious systems offered such possibilities, see Wickham 1988, esp. 68–72. For the function of "ritual enclosure" in pre-Columbian South American cultures, see Marcus 1976; 1984.

61. See for discussion Haldon 1993, 140ff.

62. See Haldon 1997, 132ff.

63. See, for example, Goffman 1990, 26ff.

64. See on these issues in a somewhat later historical context the excellent discussion of Perlin 1993, esp. 36ff., 51–74.

65. For the "overlapping" character of socioeconomic and cultural structures, and the ways in which such reciprocal influences are hierarchized according to the relative strengths of the state, social, or cultural forms, see Rowlands 1987, 1–11; Hedeager 1987. On relations of dependence and their structural significance in the dynamic of a social formation, see also Manzano Moreno 1998 esp. 906–913.

66. See Mann 1986a, 6; Foucault 1979, 81ff.

67. Pohl and Reimitz 1998; Mitchell and Greatrex 2000.

68. The issue has polarized but also focused discussion: see Kabir and Williams 2005, for example; for a critical perspective, Parry 2004 or Bartolovitch and Lazarus 2002; and for the burgeoning literature, Riemenschneider et al. 2004. On "postprocessual archaeology," see Shanks and Tilley 1987; Hodder 1992; Tilley 1993.

69. Some social theorists and social historians, following recent work in literary theory, have begun to exploit the potential of approaches drawn from "complexity theory"—the science of "nonlinear dynamics"—drawn in their turn from mathematics (for example, chaos theory), computer science, and the physical sciences. Complexity theory challenges the principles of linear explanation and causation. It places emphasis instead on the randomness of causation, in which the interplay of multiple human actors with one another, within behavior-determining social and institutional contexts, and with the physical environment, generates "emergent" social praxis. Societies—and state systems, therefore—may thus be seen as complex adaptive systems, and emphasis is placed on the unpredictability of possible outcomes (or, in historical terms, of knowing all the causal elements leading to a particular outcome). While there has been some misuse or misconstrual of the original mathematical and computer science notions, this nevertheless does serve to emphasize the causal pluralism of social interaction and warns against simplistic linearity in historical explanation. For some perspectives on aspects of the appropriation of complexity theory by literary and social theorists, see Bricmont and Sokal 1998 (a strongly critical appraisal); Plotnisky 2002 (critical of Bricmont and Sokal). For general introductions, see Lewin 1999; Byrne 1998.

70. As is abundantly clear from Brown 1992, for example.

WORKS CITED

Acien Almansa, M. 1998. "Sobre el papel de la ideología en la caracterización de las formaciones sociales: La formación social islamica," *Hispania* 58.3: 915–968.

Adshead, S. A. M. 2000. *China in World History*. New York: St. Martin's Press.

Appadurai, A., and C. Breckenridge. 1976. "The South Indian Temple: Authority, Honour, and Redistribution," *Contributions to Indian Sociology* 10.2: 187–211.

Bakels, C., and S. Jacomet. 2003. "Access to Luxury Foods in Central Europe during the Roman Period," *World Archaeology* 34: 542–557.

Bartolovitch, C., and N. Lazarus. 2002. *Marxism, Modernity, and Postcolonial Studies*. Cambridge: Cambridge University Press.

Belke, K., F. Hild, J. Koder, and P. Soustal, eds. 2000. *Byzanz als Raum: Zu Methoden und Inhalten der historischen Geographie des östlichen Mittelmeerraumes*. Vienna: Verlag der österreichischen Akademie der Wissenschaften.

Berktay, H. 1991. "Three Empires and the Societies They Governed: Iran, India and the Ottoman Empire," *Journal of Peasant Studies* 18: 242–263.

Bielenstein, H. 1980. *The Bureaucracy of Han Times*. Cambridge: Cambridge University Press.

———. 1987. "Chinese Historical Demography A.D. 2–1982," *Bulletin of the Museum of Far Eastern Antiquities* 59: 1–288.

Blockmans, W. 1989. "Voracious States and Obstructing Cities: An Aspect of State Formation in Preindustrial Europe," *Theory and Society* 18: 733–755.

Bonney, R., ed. 1995. *Economic Systems and State Finance*. Oxford: Clarendon.

Bottema, S., H. Woldring, and B. Aytug. 1986. "Palynological Investigations on the Relations between Prehistoric Man and Vegetation in Turkey: The Beyşehir Occupation Phase." In H. Demirez and N. Özhatay, eds., *Proceedings of the 5th Optima Congress, September 1986*, 315–328. Istanbul.

Brown, P. R. L. 1992. *Power and Persuasion in Late Antiquity: Towards a Christian Empire*. Madison: University of Wisconsin Press.

Burbank, J., and F. Cooper. 2010. *Empires in World History: Power and the Politics of Difference*. Princeton, NJ: Princeton University Press.

Byrne, D. 1998. *Complexity Theory and the Social Sciences: An Introduction*. London: Routledge.

Cameron, Averil, ed. 1995. *The Byzantine and Early Islamic Near East, III: States, Resources and Armies: Papers of the Third Workshop on Late Antiquity and Early Islam*. Princeton, NJ: Darwin Press.

Cameron, Averil, B. Ward-Perkins, and Michael Whitby, eds. 2000. *The Cambridge Ancient History, XIV: Late Antiquity, Empire and Successors, A.D. 425–600*. Cambridge: Cambridge University Press.

Champalakshmi, R. 1981. "Peasant State and Society in Medieval South India: A Review Article," *Indian Economic and Social History Review* 18.3–4: 411–426.

Chang, C. 2007. *The Rise of the Chinese Empire, Vol. 1: Nation, State, and Imperialism in Early China, ca. 1600 B.C.–A.D. 8*. Ann Arbor: University of Michigan Press.

Christensen, A. 1944. *L'Iran sous les Sassanides*. Copenhagen: Levin & Munksgaard.

Cipolla, C. M., ed. 1970. *The Economic Decline of Empires*. London: Methuen.

Claessen, H. J. M., and P. Skalník, eds. 1978a. *The Early State*. The Hague: Mouton.

———. 1978b. "The Early State: Theories and Hypotheses." In *The Early State*, ed. H. J. M. Claessen and P. Skalník, 3–29. The Hague: Mouton.

———, eds. 1981. *The Study of the State*. The Hague: Mouton.

Cohen, R. 1978. "State Origins: A Reappraisal." In *The Early State*, ed. H. J. M. Claessen and P. Skalník, 31–75. The Hague: Mouton.

Cohen, R., and E. R. Service. 1978. *Origins of the State: The Anthropology of Political Evolution*. Philadelphia: Institute for the Study of Human Issues.

Cullen, H. M., and P. B. de Menocal. 2000. "North Atlantic Influence on Tigris-Euphrates Stream-Flow," *International Journal of Climatology* 20: 853–863.

Dagron, G. 1993. "Le Christianisme byzantin du VIIe au milieu du XIe siècle." In *Histoire du Christianisme, IV: Évêques, moines et empereurs (610–1054)*, ed. G. Dagron, P. Riché, and A. Vauchez, 216–240. Paris: Desclée-Fayard.

de Calataÿ, F. 2005. "The Greco-Roman Economy in the Super Long Run: Lead, Copper and Shipwrecks," *Journal of Roman Archaeology* 18: 361–372.

De Crespigny, R. 1990. *Generals of the South: The Foundation and Early History of the Three Kingdoms State of Wu*. Canberra: Faculty of Asian Studies, Australian National University.

———. 2004. "South China in the Han Period," www.anu.edu.au/asianstudies/decrespigny/southchina_han.html.

Decker, M. 2009. *Tilling the Hateful Earth: Agricultural Production and Trade in the Late Antique East*. Oxford: Oxford University Press.

Diamond, J. 1997. *Guns, Germs, and Steel: The Fates of Human Societies.* New York: Norton.

———. 2005. *Collapse: How Societies Choose to Fail or Succeed.* New York: Viking.

Dien, A., ed. 1990. *State and Society in Early Medieval China.* Stanford: Stanford University Press.

———. 2001. "Civil Service Examinations: Evidence from the Northwest." In *Culture and Power in the Reconstitution of the Chinese Realm, 200–600*, ed. S. Pearce, A. Spiro, and P. Ebrey, 99–121. Cambridge, MA, and London: Harvard University Asia Center.

———. 2007. *Six Dynasties Civilization.* New Haven, CT, and London: Yale University Press.

Doyle, M. 1986. *Empires.* Ithaca, NY: Cornell University Press.

Dvornik, F. 1966. *Early Christian and Byzantine Political Philosophy*, 2 vols. Washington, DC: Dumbarton Oaks

Eastwood, W. J., C. N. Roberts, and H. F. Lamb. 1998. "Palaeoecological and Archaeological Evidence for Human Occupance in Southwest Turkey: The Beyşehir Occupation Phase," *Anatolian Studies* 48: 69–86.

Eisenstadt, S. N., ed. 1967. *The Decline of Empires.* Englewood Cliffs, NJ: Prentice-Hall

England, A., W. J. Eastwood, C. N. Roberts, R. Turner, and J. F. Haldon. 2008. "Historical Landscape Change in Cappadocia (Central Turkey): A Paleoecological Investigation of Annually-Laminated Sediments from Nar Lake," *Holocene* 18.9: 1229–1245.

Fabietti, U. 1982. "Sedentarization as a Means of Detribalization: Some Policies of the Saudi Government Towards the Nomads." In *State, Society, and Economy in Saudi Arabia*, ed. T. Niblock, 186–197. London: Croom Helm.

Finley, M. 1985. *Democracy Ancient and Modern.* London: Hogarth Press.

Foucault, M. 1979. *The History of Sexuality.* New York: Vintage Books.

Frantz-Murphy, G. 2006. "The Economics of State Formation in Early Islamic Egypt." In *From al-Andalus to Khurasan: Documents from the Medieval Muslim World*, ed. P. M. Sijpesteijn, L. Sundelin, S. Torallas Tovar, and A. Zomeño, 101–114. Islamic History and Civilization 66. Leiden: Brill.

Godelier, M. 1978. "Infrastructures, Societies, and History," *Current Anthropology* 19.4: 763–771.

———. 1984. "Modes of Production, Kinship, and Demographic Structures." In *Marxist Analyses and Social Anthropology*, ed. M. Bloch, 3–27. London: Malaby Press.

Goffman, D. 1990. *Izmir and the Levantine World, 1550–1650.* Seattle: University of Washington Press.

Graff, D. A. 2002. *Medieval Chinese Warfare, 300–900.* London and New York: Routledge.

Haldon, J. F. 1993. *The State and the Tributary Mode of Production.* London: Verso.

———. 1997. *Byzantium in the Seventh Century: The Transformation of a Culture.* Cambridge: Cambridge University Press.

———. 2005. "The Fate of the Late Roman Elite: Extinction or Assimilation?" In *Elites Old and New in the Byzantine and Early Islamic Near East (Papers of the VIth Workshop in Late Antiquity and Early Islam)*, ed. J. F. Haldon, 178–232. Princeton, NJ: Darwin Press.

———. 2007. "'Cappadocia Will Be Given Over to Ruin and Become a Desert': Environmental Evidence for Historically-Attested Events in the 7th–10th Centuries." In *Byzantina Mediterranea: Festschrift für Johannes Koder zum 65. Geburtstag*, ed.

K. Belke, E. Kislinger, A. Külzer, and M. Stassinopoulou, 215–230. Vienna: Verlag der österreichischen Akademie der Wissenschaften.

———. 2008. Review of Wickham 2005, *Millennium* 5:27–351.

Haldon, J. F., and J. Goldstone. 2009. "Ancient States, Empires, and Exploitation: Problems and Perspectives." In *The Dynamics of Ancient Empires*, ed. I. Morris and W. Scheidel, 3–29. Oxford: Oxford University Press.

Halsall, G. 2003. *Warfare and Society in the Barbarian West, 450–900*. London and New York: Routledge.

Heather, P. 2006. *The Fall of the Roman Empire: A New History of Rome and the Barbarians*. London: Macmillan.

Hedeager, L. 1987. "Empire, Frontier, and the Barbarian Hinterland: Rome and Northern Europe from A.D. 1–400." In *Centre and Periphery in the Ancient World*, ed. M. Rowlands, K. Larsen, and K. Kristiansen, 125–140. Cambridge: Cambridge University Press.

Heinzelmann, M. 1975. "L'Aristocratie et les évêchés entre Loire et Rhin jusqu'à la fin du VIIe siècle," *Revue d'Histoire de l'église de France* 62: 75–90.

Heitzman, J. 1991. "Ritual Polity and Economy: The Transactional Network of an Imperial Temple in Medieval South India," *Journal of the Economic and Social History of the Orient* 34.1: 23–54.

Hild, Friedrich, and Hansgerd Hellenkemper. 1990. *Kilikien und Isaurien*. 2 vols. Tabula Imperii Byzantini 5. Vienna: Verlag der österreichischen Akademie der Wissenschaften.

Hirschfeld, Y. 1997. "Farms and Villages in Byzantine Palestine," *DOP* 51: 33–71.

Hodder, Ian. 1992. *Theory and Practice in Archaeology*. London: Routledge.

Hopkins, K. 1980. "Taxes and Trade in the Roman Empire (200 B.C.–A.D. 400)," *Journal of Roman Studies* 70: 101–125.

Horden, P., and N. Purcell. 2000. *The Corrupting Sea: A Study of Mediterranean History*. Oxford: Blackwell.

Howard-Johnston, J. D. 1995. "The Two Great Powers in Late Antiquity: A Comparison." In *The Byzantine and Early Islamic Near East, III: States, Resources and Armies: Papers of the Third Workshop on Late Antiquity and Early Islam*, ed. Averil Cameron, 157–226. Princeton, NJ: Darwin Press.

Hussey, J.M. 1986. *The Orthodox Church in the Byzantine Empire*. Oxford: Oxford University Press.

Ibn Khaldun. 1958. *The Muqaddimah*. 3 vols. Trans. F. Rosenthal. Princeton, NJ: Princeton University Press.

Ivanov, S. 2008. "Religious Missions." In *The Cambridge History of the Byzantine Empire, c. 500–1492*, ed. J. Shepard, 305–332. Cambridge: Cambridge University Press.

Jones, M. D., C. N. Roberts, M. J. Leng, and M. Türkeş. 2006. "A High-Resolution Late Holocene Lake Isotope Record from Turkey and Links to North Atlantic and Monsoon Climate," *Geology* 34: 361–364.

Jongman, W. M. 2003. "A Golden Age: Death, Money Supply and Social Succession in the Roman Empire." In *Credito e moneta nel mondo romano*, ed. E. Lo Cascio, 181–196. Bari: Edipuglia.

Kabir, A. J., and D. Williams, eds. 2005. *Postcolonial Approaches to the European Middle Ages: Translating Cultures*. Cambridge: Cambridge University Press.

Kautsky, J. 1982. *The Politics of Aristocratic Empires*. Chapel Hill: University of North Carolina Press.

Keys, D. 1999. *Catastrophe: An Investigation into the Origins of the Modern World.* London: Century.

Khalidi, T., ed. 1984. *Land Tenure and Social Transformation in the Middle East.* Beirut: American University of Beirut.

Kron, G. 2002. "Archaeozoology and the Productivity of Roman Livestock Farming," *Münstersche Beiträge zur antiken Handelsgeschichte* 21: 53–73.

Kulke, H. 1982. "Fragmentation and Segmentation versus Integration? Reflections on the Concept of Indian Feudalism and the Segmentary State in Indian History," *Studies in History* 4.2: 237–263.

Leslie, D. D., and K. H. J. Gardiner. 1996. *The Roman Empire in Chinese Sources.* Rome: Bardi.

Lev-Yadun, S., N. Lipschitz, and Y. Waisel. 1987. "Annual Rings in Trees as an Index to Climate Changes Intensity in Our Region in the Past," *Rotem* 22:6–17, 113.

Lewin, R. 1999. *Complexity: Life at the Edge of Chaos.* New York: Macmillan.

Lewis, A. R. 1976. "The Dukes in the 'Regnum Francorum' A.D. 550–751," *Speculum* 51: 381–410.

Lieu, S. N. C. 1992. *Manichaeism in the Later Roman Empire and Medieval China.* Tübingen: J.C.B. Mohr.

Little, L. K., ed. 2007. *Plague and the End of Antiquity: The Pandemic of 541–750.* Cambridge: Cambridge University Press.

Liu. X. 2001. "Jiankang and the Commercial Empire of the Southern Dynasties: Change and Continuity in Medieval Chinese Economic History." In *Culture and Power in the Reconstitution of the Chinese Realm, 200–600*, ed. S. Pearce, A. Spiro, and P. Ebrey, 35–52. Cambridge, MA, and London: Harvard University Asia Center.

Liverani, M. 1984. "Land Tenure and Inheritance in the Ancient Near East: The Interaction between 'Palace' and 'Family' Sectors." In *Land Tenure and Social Transformation in the Middle East*, ed. T. Khalidi, 33–44. Beirut: American University of Beirut.

Mann, M. 1986a. *The Sources of Social Power, I: A History of Power from the Beginnings to A.D. 1760.* Cambridge: Cambridge University Press.

———. 1986b. "The Autonomous Power of the State: Its Origins, Mechanisms, and Results." In *States in History*, ed. J.A. Hall. 109–136. Oxford: Blackwell.

Manzano Moreno, E. 1998. "Relaciones sociales en sociedades precapitalistas: Una critica al concepto de 'modo de producción tributario'," *Hispania* 58.3: 881–913.

Marcus, J. 1976. *Emblem and State in the Classic Maya Lowlands.* Washington, DC: Dumbarton Oaks.

———. 1984. "Lowland Maya Archaeology at the Crossroads," *American Antiquity* 48: 454–488.

Mitchell, S., and G. Greatrex, eds. 2000. *Ethnicity and Culture in Late Antiquity.* London: Duckworth.

Moravcsik, Gy. 1958. *Byzantinoturcica, I: Die byzantinischen Quellen der Geschichte der Türkvölker; II: Sprachreste der Türkvölker in den byzantinischen Quellen.* BBA 10, 11. Berlin: Akademie-Verlag.

Morony, M. G. 2004a. "Economic Boundaries? Late Antiquity and Early Islam," *Journal of the Economic and Social History of the Orient* 47: 166–194.

———. 2004b. "Social Élites in Iraq and Iran: After the Conquest." In *Élites Old and New in the Byzantine and Early Islamic Near East (Papers of the VIth Workshop in Late Antiquity and Early Islam)*, ed. J. Haldon and L. Conrad, 275–284. Princeton, NJ: Darwin Press.

Nüzhet Dalfes, H., G. Kukla, and H. Weiss, eds. 1997. *Third Millennium BC Climate Change and Old World Collapse.* New York: Springer.

Parker, P. 1992. *Ancient Shipwrecks of the Mediterranean and the Roman Provinces.* Oxford: Tempus Reparatum.

Parry, B. 2004. *Postcolonial Studies: A Materialist Critique.* London and New York: Routledge.

Pearce, S. A. 1987. "The Yü-Wen Regime in Sixth Century China." Ph.D. diss., Princeton University.

———. 2001. "Form and Matter: Archaizing Reform in Sixth-Century China." In *Culture and Power in the Reconstitution of the Chinese Realm, 200–600,* ed. S. Pearce, A. Spiro, and P. Ebrey, 149–178. Cambridge, MA, and London: Harvard University Asia Center.

Pearce, S., A. Spiro, and P. Ebrey, eds. 2001. *Culture and Power in the Reconstitution of the Chinese Realm, 200–600.* Cambridge, MA, and London: Harvard University Asia Center.

Pećirková, J. 1977. "The Administrative Organization of the Neo-Assyrian Empire," *Archiv orientální* 45: 211–228.

———. 1987. "The Administrative Methods of Assyrian Imperialism," *Archiv orientalni* 55: 162–175.

Pelliot, P. 1996. *L'inscription nestorienne de Si-Ngan-Fou.* Ed. A. Forte. Kyoto: Scuola di studi sull'Asia orientale; Paris: Collège de France, Institut des Hautes Études Chinoises.

Perlin, F. 1993. *"The Invisible City": Monetary, Administrative, and Popular Infrastructures in Asia and Europe, 1500–1900.* London: Ashgate.

Phillipson, A. 1939. *Das byzantinische Reich als geographische Erscheinung.* Leiden: Brill.

Plotnisky, A. 2002. *The Knowable and the Unknowable.* Ann Arbor: University of Michigan Press.

Pohl, W., and H. Reimitz, eds. 1998. *Strategies of Distinction: The Construction of Ethnic Communities.* Leiden: Brill.

Postgate, J. N. 1974. *Taxation and Conscription in the Assyrian Empire.* Rome: R. Denicola.

Preston, J. J. 1980. "Sacred Centers and Symbolic Networks in South Asia," *Mankind Quarterly* 20.3–4: 259–293.

Raaflaub, K. 1979. "Beute, Vergeltung, Freiheit? Zur Zielsetzung des delisch-attischen Seebundes," *Chiron* 19: 1–22.

———. 1989. "Contemporary Perceptions of Democracy in Fifth-Century Athens," *Classica et Mediaevalia* 40: 33–70.

Reinhard, W., ed. 1996. *Power Elites and State Building.* Oxford: Clarendon Press.

Riemenschneider, D., et al. 2004. *Postcolonial Theory: The Emergence of a Critical Discourse.* Tübingen: Stauffenburg Verlag.

Rosen, A. 1997. "Environmental Change and Human Adaptational Failure at the End of the Early Bronze Age in the Southern Levant." In *Third Millennium BC Climate Change and Old World Collapse,* ed. H. Nüzhet Dalfes, G. Kukla, and H. Weiss, 25–38. New York: Springer.

———. 2001. "Determinist or Not Determinist? Climate, Environment, and Archaeological Explanation in the Levant." In *Studies in the Archaeology of Israel and Neighboring Lands in Memory of Douglas L. Esse,* ed. S. Wolff, 535–554. Chicago: Oriental Institute of the University of Chicago.

Rosen, W. 2007. *Justinian's Flea: Plague, Empire, and the Birth of Europe.* London: Jonathan Cape.

Rowlands, M. 1987. "Centre and Periphery: A Review of a Concept." In *Centre and Periphery in the Ancient World*, ed. M. Rowlands, K. Larsen, and K. Kristiansen, 1–11. Cambridge: Cambridge University Press.

Rowlands, M., K. Larsen, and K. Kristiansen, eds. 1987. *Centre and Periphery in the Ancient World*. Cambridge: Cambridge University Press.

Rubin, Z. 1995. "The Reforms of Khusro Anushirwan." In *The Byzantine and Early Islamic Near East, III: States, Resources and Armies: Papers of the Third Workshop on Late Antiquity and Early Islam*, ed. Averil Cameron, 227–297. Princeton, NJ: Darwin Press.

———. 2000. "The Sasanid Monarchy." In *The Cambridge Ancient History, XIV: Late Antiquity, Empire and Successors, A.D. 425–600*, ed. Averil Cameron, B. Ward-Perkins, and Michael Whitby, 638–661. Cambridge: Cambridge University Press.

Ruddiman, W. F. 2003. "The Anthropogenic Greenhouse Era Began Thousands of Years Ago," *Climatic Change* 61: 261–293.

Runciman, W. G. 1989. *A Treatise on Social Theory, II: Substantive Social Theory*. Cambridge: Cambridge University Press.

Sanderson, S. K., ed. 1995. *Civilizations and World Systems: Studying World Historical Change*. Walnut Creek, CA, London, and Delhi: Altamira Press.

———. 1999. *Social Transformations: A General Theory of Historical Development*. Oxford: Rowman & Littlefield Publishers.

Saraswati, B. 1977. *Brahmanic Ritual Traditions in the Crucible of Time*. Simla: Indian Institute of Advanced Study.

Sarris, P. 2006. "Review of Wickham 2005," *Journal of Agrarian Change* 6: 400–413.

Scheidel, W., ed. 2009. *Rome and China: Comparative Perspectives on Ancient World Empires*. Oxford: Oxford University Press.

Schmidt, B., and W. Gruhle. 2003. "Klimaextreme in römischer Zeit—eine Strukturanalyse dendrochronologischer Daten," *Archäologisches Korrespondenzblatt* 33: 421–427.

Shanks, Michael, and Christopher Y. Tilley. 1987. *Re-Constructing Archaeology: Theory and Practice*. Cambridge: Cambridge University Press.

Shereshevski, J. 1991. *Byzantine Urban Settlements in the Negev Desert*. Beer-Sheva: Ben-Gurion University of the Negev Press.

Sokal, Alan D., and J. Bricmont. 1998. *Fashionable Nonsense: Postmodern Intellectuals' Abuse of Science*. New York: Picador.

Southall, A. 1956. *Alur Society*. Cambridge: Cambridge University Press.

———. 1965. "A Critique of the Typology of States and Political Systems." In *Political Systems and the Distribution of Power*, ed. M. Barton, 113–140. New York: Tavistock.

Spencer, G. 1969. "Religious Networks and Royal Influence in Eleventh Century South India," *Journal of the Social and Economic History of the Orient* 12.1: 42–56.

Stathakopoulos, D. C. 2004. *Famine and Pestilence in the Late Roman and Early Byzantine Empire: A Systematic Survey of Subsistence Crises and Epidemics*. Aldershot: Ashgate.

Stein, B. 1977. "The Segmentary State in South Indian History." In *Realm and Religion in Traditional India*, ed. R. G. Fox, 3–51. Durham: University of North Carolina Press.

———. 1980. *Peasant State and Society in Medieval South India*. Delhi and New York: Oxford University Press.

———. 1985. "Politics, Peasants, and the Deconstruction of Feudalism in Medieval India," *Journal of Peasant Studies* 12: 54–86.

Strauss, B. 1986. *Athens after the Peloponnesian War.* London: Croom Helm.
Tang, C. 1990. "Clients and Bound Retainers in the Six Dynasties Period." In *State and Society in Early Medieval China*, ed. A. Dien, 111–138. Stanford, CA: Stanford University Press.
Tilley, Christopher Y. ed. 1993. *Interpretative Archaeology.* Providence: Berg.
Trigger, B. G. 2003. *Understanding Early Civilizations.* Cambridge: Cambridge University Press.
Ward-Perkins, B. 2005. *The Fall of Rome and the End of Civilization.* Oxford: Oxford University Press.
Wenke, R. J. 1975–1976. "Imperial Investments and Agricultural Development in Parthian and Sasanian Khuzistan: 150 B.C. to A.D. 640," *Mesopotamia* 10–11: 31–221.
Wickham, C. J. 1988. "Historical Materialism, Historical Sociology," *New Left Review* 171: 63–78.
———. 2005. *Framing the Early Middle Ages: Europe and the Mediterranean, 400–800.* Oxford: Oxford University Press.
Wiechmann, I., and G. Grupe. 2005. "Detection of *Yersinia Pestis* in Two Early Medieval Skeletal Finds from Aschheim (Upper Bavaria, 6th Century A.D.)," *American Journal of Physical Anthropology* 126: 48–55.
Winkelmann, F., 1980. *Die östlichen Kirchen in der Epoche der christologischen Auseinandersetzung (5.-7. Jahrhundert).* Kirchengeschichte in Einzeldarstellungen I/6. Berlin: Akademie-Verlag.
Wood, I. 1979. "Kings, Kingdoms, and Consent." In *Early Medieval Kingship*, ed. P. H. Sawyer and I. N. Wood, 6–29. Leeds: University of Leeds.
Woolf, G. 1998. *Becoming Roman.* Cambridge and New York: Cambridge University Press.
Wright, A. F. 1978. *The Sui Dynasty.* New York: Knopf.
Zhao, D. 2006. *Eastern Zhou Warfare and the Formation of the Confucian-Legalist State.* Shanghai.

CHAPTER 35

LATE ANTIQUITY IN BYZANTIUM

PETRE GURAN

Institute of South East European Studies, Bucharest

Introduction

To write a chapter on Late Antiquity in Byzantium supposes knowing when Late Antiquity ends and Byzantium begins. If for Peter Brown in his *World of Late Antiquity* (1971) the closing date was about the mid-eighth century,[1] for Henri-Irénée Marrou[2] the year 600 was a more meaningful moment to put an end to the ancient world. In fact, if we look into social structure, economy, or political organization, we may find arguments for several dates in this large period from Justinian to the iconoclastic emperors to describe a significant change.[3] Nevertheless, in his *Rise of Western Christendom* Peter Brown extends his period[4] to the year 1000. In more recent historiography of Western Europe, the "Middle Ages" subtly vanishes as an object of study, squeezed between modernity's eagerness to push its roots further into the "medieval" world and our expanding Late Antiquity.[5] Why would a Byzantinist then stick to "Byzantium"? As much as the Middle Ages, Byzantium is a historiographic construct. Historians from the Renaissance to the twentieth century favored such constructs, only to oppose them to the beautiful world of classical antiquity. At the same time, for Western confessional history, Eastern Christianity was the wrong type of Christianity. Ironically, to oppose bourgeois historiography, Marxist historiography continued to build up Byzantium as a competitor of Western

European civilization. Byzantium was for all these Western European intellectual endeavors a word of contempt or dismissal.

Today, Late Antiquity appropriates half of Byzantium's millennial history. Byzantinists are left with what Evelyne Patlagean called *Le Moyen Age grec* (ninth/tenth century to the fifteenth century). Part of this Greek Middle Age is either a history without Constantinople (1204–1261) or a history of Constantinople alone (most of the fourteenth and fifteenth centuries until the fall of the city in 1453). The first question then I will have to answer in this chapter is: was this Greek Middle Age conscious of a Late Antiquity? How does Late Antiquity relate to Byzantium, but also to a more discrete continuation of Greek or antique or late antique culture under the Ottomans, called by Iorga *Byzance après Byzance*?[6]

There are three ways to tackle this issue. First, we can speak of continuity of the Roman empire (with the capital in Constantinople and Greek as the language of state and culture)[7] down to 1453 and argue that the Greeks in Constantinople were in the right to think that they were Romans. This acknowledged continuity was the reason for a thorough condemnation and disdain for a thousand years of Roman history, as in Edward Gibbon's *Decline and Fall of the Roman Empire*, or with a more lenient judgment and sometimes a pinch of sympathy, but not less convinced that it was distant, dead, and not related to their own world, by French scholars like Charles Diehl in *Byzance: grandeur et décadence*, or Louis Bréhier's *Vie et mort de Byzance*.

The second solution is to consider Byzantium in the way of Arnold Toynbee, as one of the twenty-three world civilizations he identifies in his *Study of History*, which means to offer a chronology and to describe the distinctive features of this civilization: for example, in Toynbee's vision, to consider Orthodoxy as a separate religion and to take the Greek language as a national identification. This view was partially embraced by Hélène Ahrweiler in her *L'idéologie politique de l'Empire byzantin*.

The third way is to describe Byzantium as part, or even the core, of this separate span of the ancient world, called Late Antiquity, which has emerged today as a more powerful instrument of research than the Middle Ages. Without claiming it, this view was already advocated by Herbert Hunger in his book *Das Reich der neuen Mitte*.[8] The problem arises in this case when it comes to describe the appendix of Byzantine history after 1204.[9] But here we are in the special case of Eastern Europe (particularly for the Black Sea region—Asia Minor included—the Balkans, and Russia), where the historical chronology of the West hardly applies.

It is obvious that Late Antiquity and Byzantium have a common opponent and *comparandum*: antiquity. In the tradition of classical scholarship, whatever followed on the territory of the Roman empire after its fall was the opposite of civilization, as in Bryan Ward-Perkins's *The Fall of Rome and the End of Civilization*. And this view is now more than a clash of historians; it is a public debate, if we include the recent movie *Agora*, in which the death of Hypatia precipitates the death of ancient science and civilization, whereupon the long night of the

Christian Middle Ages sets in.[10] Thus, in parallel to the comparison with antiquity, some historians' distaste for Late Antiquity and Byzantium shares another common factor: Christianity. The paradigm for this view is still Gibbon's *Decline and Fall*: the famous chapters 15 and 16.

If we had to characterize an entire period and geographical space, as we often do for the ancient world, through a religious system, then Late Antiquity, together with its less "antique" continuations toward and after the year 1000, could simply be called a Christian civilization. From the point of view of a post-Christian civilization, historians enjoy the freedom to say this. The essence of this period, which extends to the beginnings of early modernity, lies in its Christian character, with all its good and bad features. It is only from this point of view that we can understand the elements of continuity. Peter Brown's *Rise of Western Christendom* has its parallels in Herbert Hunger's *Reich der neuen Mitte* and in Marrou's *Décadence romaine ou antiquité tardive?* where Marrou tried to distinguish the religious fervor of Late Antiquity, Judeo-Christian in its essence, from the sacral conceptions of the Hellenistic and Classical stages of antiquity. Successful or not—this question requires a subjective evaluation—what is still conventionally called Byzantium was a world built upon and around the religion founded by Jesus of Nazareth. The Greek and Roman ingredients underwent a systematic effort of Christianization.

Historians who chose to defend this continuity, either in the form of the Roman empire or in the form of an emergent Byzantine civilization, found a good excuse in the fact that these Byzantines, defined as Greek-speaking Christians who called themselves Romans, had their capital uninterruptedly to 1204 in the same city. From this point of view, the disruption happens with the conquest of Constantinople by the Latins in 1204. At the same time, the Byzantine state, as it shrank to the smaller dimensions of an eastern Mediterranean state, found itself surrounded by its "copies," Christian kingdoms that grew out of the lost territories of the empire, labeled by Dimitri Obolensky (1971) as a "Byzantine Commonwealth." It is a world that shares much of the Christian civilization produced by Byzantium, allots to Constantinople a central role in world history, but progressively resigns any political allegiance to it. The paradox is that this Byzantine Commonwealth integrates in its history predominantly that part of Byzantium that was produced in Late Antiquity, as emphasized by the huge, impressive product of cultural transfer called "Elinskij Letopis," which contains the early Slavonic translation of the *Chronicle* of John Malalas, together with the *Chronicle* of George Hamartolos, the *Romance of Alexander*, Flavius Josephus, and various hagiographies.[11]

If one could walk around the Constantinople of the year 600 and then again in the year 1200, one would recognize almost nothing. People of the two historical times would be dressing differently, fighting differently, building or rebuilding their city differently, and organizing their society differently. What would be common to the two periods, however, is the fact that they are praying to the same God, almost in the same way. The memory and inheritance of Late Antiquity lies precisely in this area.

Christianity

Such an introduction was necessary to avoid the error of considering the "classical heritage" as being of a piece with the late antique one. What Byzantines inherited from classical antiquity is a language and its written production, a portion of the ancient content and method of education, the pleasure and necessity of philosophical speculation (with an emphasis on Plato and Platonism), a general interest in things past (which is secular historiography), and the organization of society by written law. Late Antiquity in turn bequeathed to Byzantium something completely different, which classical antiquity did not pass on: its new religion—Christianity—and the cultural universe produced by the practice of this religion for several centuries. For example, many of the Byzantine philosophers and teachers at some point in their lives took on the black cloak of monasticism (Michael Psellos, Nikephoros Blemmydes, Maximos Planoudes, Thomas Magistros, Nikephoros Gregoras, Georgios Gennadios Scholarios). With very few exceptions, the exercise of scholarship was linked to and depended upon the ascetical practice of the Christian religion. Who would recognize the elegance of an antique or late antique philosopher[12]—such elegance emphasizes the continuity of antiquity with Late Antiquity—in the years of Laskarid Nicaea, or in the Thessaloniki of the Angeloi, during the black plague in Constantinople, or in the schools and libraries of Mount Athos? Clothing fashions changed for the bearers of knowledge. Nevertheless, the Christianized content of the knowledge produced in Late Antiquity was passed on throughout the Byzantine centuries. The garment eventually expressed an emphasis, a nuance that marked more the sense of a development than the content of a change. To visualize the new dress code, we should compare the depiction of the second ecumenical council in the imperial manuscript of the *Homilies* of Gregory of Nazianzus (Parisinus graecus 510, ninth century) with the depiction of the council of 1351 held in Constantinople in the manuscript of the works of John Kantakuzenos (Parisinus graecus 1342, 1369–1370).[13] The first image displays a number of bishops, dressed in blue, brown, green, or golden chitons like high officials, distinguished only by their pallium or omophorion; the second depicts a large mass of black-clad monks and four bishops clad in their liturgical *polystavria* but affirming their monastic status by the black cowl. Theodore Metochites, a lover of antique culture and science and thus a contributor to the Byzantine classical Renaissance, chose to end his life in a cell inside the complex liturgical building of the Chora monastery, situated between the *naos*/sanctuary and the funerary chapel, a symbolic form of living burial. The grand logothete in the donor's portrait exchanged the worldly glory for the new dress of the Wisdom he eventually chose.

But the evaluation of any late antique heritage in Byzantium is blurred by what Steven Runciman labeled as *The Last Byzantine Renaissance* (1970), a book in which he discussed the notable works of scholars who took a particular interest in classical Greek literature: John Tzetzes (especially his *Verse Chronicle*),[14] Eustathius (metropolitan of Thessalonica), Michael Acominatos (metropolitan of Athens), Maximos Planoudes, Manuel Moschopoulos, Theodore Metochites,[15] Thomas Magistros, Manuel Chrysoloras,[16] with the peak of this revival arriving in the person of Georgios Gemistos Plethon.[17] Paul Lemerle also blurred the evaluation of the late antique heritage in his book *Premier Humanisme Byzantin* (1971), in which the flourishing of Byzantine culture in the ninth and tenth centuries was presented merely as a revival and transmission of classical Greek learning.

To avoid this trap, I try here to identify those elements from the late antique centuries that are clearly distinguishable from elements of classical culture.

Hagiography: The New Literary Fashion

Christian hagiography is certainly one late antique creation that continued to be read, admired, and emulated throughout the Byzantine world, both as a literary genre and in its social guise, the holy man. It became thus the main vehicle to propagate an icon of Late Antiquity. Not only had the collection of these texts grown in cultural and social relevance as hagiography gradually entered the cult but also it legitimately joined the realm of literary fiction. In the tenth century, the corpus of saints' lives was standardized by Symeon Metaphrastes. The reasons for this interest in writing and rewriting saints' lives are much debated by scholars. It was not only a matter of adapting the popular level of some of the ancient texts to a higher stylistic expectation or a narrative pattern that better fitted the tenth-century religious feeling but also a rise of hagiography at the level of a state affair. The Metaphrastic attempt to "modernize" hagiography did not achieve an elimination of earlier hagiography and perhaps did not aim at it. It was rather that the emperors and their court theologians recognized in hagiography an important tool for strengthening their role within Christian society.[18] The complex and colorful late antique world passed from its own time to the Byzantine Renaissance in the form of literary fiction. Examples of the taste for late antique environments can be found in a long list of hagiographic fictional narratives: *Life of Saint Mary of Egypt, Life of Alexios the Man of God, Life of Symeon of Emesa, Life of Leo of Catania, Life of Gregorios Bishop of Agrigentum, Revelation of the Nun Anastasia, Life of Niphon of Constantianae* (BHG 1371),[19] *Life of Irene of Chrysobalanton*, the second *Vita of Kosmas and John* (BHG 394, written in the eleventh or twelfth century), *Life of Theodore of Edessa* (BHG 1744–1744e), *Life of Gregentios* (mid-tenth century).[20] The category of fictional writing comprises also lives of saints whose historicity may be attested by other sources, but the hagiographical text has a fictional character. In this sense, even the Metaphrastic rewriting of hagiographies sometimes had a fictional character, which shows that these Byzantine authors were eager and able to display an ancient world that they considered to be meaningful for their own religious experience. Among these literary productions, two hagiographic texts, the *Life of Barlaam and Josaphat* and the *Life of Saint Andrew the Fool* (BHG 264b), were so successful in re-creating a world of knowledge and sensibility specific to Late Antiquity that even modern scholars have argued over whether to ascribe them to the late antique (seventh or early eighth century) environment or to the high point of Byzantine medieval culture (tenth to eleventh century).[21] Through their encyclopedic interest in a wide range of religious phenomena, these two hagiographies are related to the genuine late antique *Alexander Romance*, which displays a similar taste for the extravagant experience of the past. All three literary pieces are marginal to Greek culture and to Christianity: geographically the first, socially and psychologically the second, chronologically the third. The *Life of Barlaam and Josaphat* unfolds in spaces far removed from usual Byzantine geopolitical notions. The *Life of Saint Andrew the Fool* goes up against the notion of order (*taxis*) and hierarchy so important in the Byzantine social construction. The *Alexander Romance* lies outside the mainstream of antique material relevant to Christians. Yet these texts express the effort to Christianize a whole range of historical, anthropological, and social experiences and to make them relevant to the future of mankind.

The *Legend of Alexander*, circulated under the name of Callisthenes of Olynthos (the pseudonymous publication, as in eschatological literature, gives authority to the text), started as a literary production in the third century but underwent a significant revision in the seventh century, when a strong sense of relationship between Alexander's empire and the Christian empire was developed. The Syriac *Legend of Alexander* offers the most coherent version within the historical context of the seventh century: Heraclius' war with Persia.[22] The empire created by Alexander is understood as a foreshadowing and announcement of the Christian empire. At the same time, the same thought process was applied in Theodore Synkellos' *Homily on the Siege of Constantinople of 626*, where the contemporary event is seen as the accomplishment of the Old Testament prophecy contained in the description of the siege of Jerusalem through the Assyrian king Sennacherib, when an angel of God miraculously destroyed the besieging army (2 Kings 19; Isaiah 37).[23] The sense of the mythical reconstruction of Alexander's endeavor was to show the connection of Greek past to the Christian present.

The *Life of Barlaam and Josaphat* is a much more puzzling composition. Based on a Near Eastern variant of the legend of Buddha but derived directly from the Georgian *Balavariani*, the text includes pieces of late antique scholarship such as excerpts from the *Apology* of Aristeides, the *Chapters* of Deacon Agapetus, fragments from the *Ekloga* of the homilies of John Chrysostom compiled by Theodoros Daphnopates (died 961/963), material from the *Life of Mary of Egypt* (BHG 1042), and the *Narrationes* by Pseudo-Nilus of Ancyra (BHG 1301–1307/CPG 6044).[24] The creation of the text shows a particularly good knowledge of early Christian literature.[25] Regarding the political culture of Byzantium, the *Life of Barlaam and Josaphat* shows an astonishing aspect in the fact that Christian perfection justifies abandoning the exercise of power. It nevertheless recalls a genuine late antique hagiography destined to achieve literary success in Byzantium, the *Martyrdom of Saint Arethas and of His Companions*, a narrative of Christian martyrdom in pre-Islamic Arabia, where the Ethiopian king Elesbaa, after a victorious campaign against the Jewish kingdom of Himyar, abandons power, retires into monastic confinement, and dispatches his crown to the Anastasis in Jerusalem.[26]

All three texts enjoyed enormous success in Byzantine, post-Byzantine, and Slavonic Orthodox cultures.

Theology: The New Philosophy

We can hardly imagine Byzantium and its world of intellectual references without the corpus of late antique Church Fathers, and here we should mention only some of the most famous in Byzantine theology: Ignatius of Antioch, Irenaeus of Lyons, Justin Martyr,[27] Origen, Athanasius of Alexandria, Cyril of Jerusalem, Cyril of Alexandria, Basil of Caesarea, Gregory of Nazianzus ("Gregory the Theologian"), Gregory of Nyssa, John Chrysostom,[28] Macarius the Great,[29] Dionysius the Areopagite, Gregory *ho Dialogos* (pope of Rome), Maximus Confessor, John Climax, John Damascene, Theodore the Stoudite. Most of the writings of the Church Fathers were produced in response to important religious challenges. These come from competitors in the large religious bazaar of Late Antiquity, particularly different types of Dualisms and Gnosticisms, or from a more fine-tuned religious differentiation born out of the encounter between the effort to define the indefinable and very particular political and human circumstances. Their writings were not meant to be theology, but they were turned into orthodox theology by subsequent generations of clergy. As Christianity grew more into the Byzantine era, from the available amount of religious thought, a selection was used that best expressed, in the view of each later generation, orthodoxy. A tragic case of selection was the postmortem condemnation of writings and authors by Justinian's religious policy. Later, the treasury of patristic thought was gathered in collections of writings and fragments of an author or of several authors. Such are the collections of John Chrysostom's writings (e.g., *Margaritai, etoi Logoi diaphoroi, tou en agiois patros hemon Ioannou, archiepiskopou Kostantinoupoleos tou Chrysostomou, kai heteron hagion Pateron*).[30] or different collections, organized in the form of response to predefined heresies, the dogmatic Panoplies.[31] The first and only attempt to give a systematic and comprehensive overview of Christian belief was John Damascene's *Fountain of Knowledge* (*Pege gnoseos*). The patristic era ends with the early defenders of the cult of holy images, when a selection of religious literature of the earlier centuries was acknowledged as the ultimate form of Christian thought. Dogmatic debates of the importance of patristic literature never came up again in Byzantium. Among the later authors of theological writings, only Gregory Palamas attained such a reputation as to be compared to the Church Fathers. Modern scholars and theologians still dispute whether Palamas should be considered such an authority in matters of dogma. It is a fact, nonetheless, that Gregory Palamas and his followers never pretended to produce anything other than a defense and a reiteration of patristic positions.

Despite this official affirmation, the theology of Gregory Palamas resumes an important theological debate with Neoplatonism, which, as part of the philosophical heritage of Late Antiquity, had seemed to have merged in a perfect way with Judaic thought to produce a Christian theology. Gregory Palamas, however, opposed Pseudo-Dionysius' hierarchical model of the communication of God and thus broke with the tradition of Platonic and Neoplatonic thought and vocabulary in Byzantine mystical theology.[32] The intensity of this debate, which assumes the importance of the Neoplatonic tradition and the prestige of the works of Pseudo-Dionysius, demonstrates the fourteenth-century vividness of a thought world produced almost a thousand years earlier.

Soon after the establishment of the imperial church in the fourth century, in parallel and in competition with public theological debates emerged the spiritual writings of the desert fathers. Their interest lay in describing the direct and personal experience of God: this was mystical theology. Byzantium made its true theology out of the wisdom of this spiritual guidance. In the memory of later ages, only a handful of Greek Christian writers received the nickname "the Theologian": first was the apostle John, second was Gregory of Nazianzus, third was the eleventh-century mystical author Symeon (called the "New Theologian"), and last was Gregory Palamas.

The first collections of sayings of the desert fathers are late antique creations: the *Apophthegmata patrum* (fifth to sixth centuries),[33] Palladius' *Lausiac History* (419), and John Moschos' *Spiritual Meadow* (d. 619/634). They were highly valued in Byzantine monasteries and were among the most successful cultural exports of Byzantium to the Slavic world. The importance of ascetic writings grew within the monastic world and reached a peak of historical relevance with the spiritual movement of Symeon the New Theologian in the eleventh century and again with the Hesychast movement in the fourteenth century. Publishing this literature produced a new type of *florilegia* of ascetic and mystical authors (published in the seventeenth century with the title *Philokalia*).[34] The aim of this selection of ascetic and mystical authors was to guide the monk on his path toward *theosis* (deification). Among these ascetic authors we find also a Latin father, John Cassian, whose works were translated into Greek probably by the end of the fifth century and were well known to readers of monastic spirituality. The cult of John Cassian was promoted on the basis of his writings and inscribed in the Constantinopolitan *Synaxarion* on February 28/29.[35]

Liturgy: The New Religious Lyricism

As patristic theology declined in Late Antiquity, a new literary genre began its storied career: Christian liturgical poetry. It is certainly the most widespread Christian literature after the Holy Scriptures and can be found in complete collections in every Orthodox monastery, as it is the basis for the daily prayer. The prototype of Christian poetry is the Old Testament Book of Psalms, with its complex character of prophecy, prayer, personal and collective address to God, and finally the mystical experience of God's answers. The structure of Christian prayers is thus given by the Psalms.

The evolution of the Eucharistic celebration in connection with the morning and evening prayers borrowed from Judaism reaches its first stable formula in the fourth century. The names given to the basic Orthodox liturgies, Saint Basil and Saint John Chrysostom, attest to this initial period of completion. Thus liturgy faithfully preserves a form achieved in early Late Antiquity. The oldest manuscript to preserve the liturgical structure in use in the Orthodox Church (up to today) is an eighth-century manuscript from Italy, the Barberini graecus 336. But the process of liturgical creation continued uninterrupted throughout the Byzantine millennium until Nikephoros Kallistos Xanthopoulos' *Triodion Synaxaries* (exegetical text about the significance of the celebration of the day to be read during office) in the fourteenth century.

The Eucharistic liturgy was expanded in the fifth and sixth centuries by several adjustments and prayers, like the Cherubic hymn in the time of Justinian I or Justin II, but the main new creation consists in the liturgical use of the poems (*kontakia*) of Romanos the Melode, which were originally composed as homilies in verse.[36]

Andrew of Crete (also known as the Jerusalemite, b. Damascus 660–d. Lesbos 740) is the author of the *Great Kanon* (a prayer of repentance, which impresses with its length). Together with the *Life* and the *Kanon* of Mary of Egypt, the *Great Kanon* was probably the hymnographic and hagiographic core of the *Triodion* book of seventh-century Palestine (according to the notice of Xanthopoulos). It was meant as a spiritual exercise for the Lenten period, a preparation for the paschal celebration. This time of preparation has its origin in the late antique practice of initiating those who were to be baptized during the Resurrection celebration, as attested by the baptismal catecheses of Cyril of Jerusalem in the fourth century. This period was marked by two traditional fasting times, the Holy Week of Passiontide (the week that precedes the Resurrection and begins with Palm Sunday) and the forty days of fasting observed in memory of Christ's sojourn in the desert following his baptism. The liturgical celebration was continually enriched by other texts (*kanones*) written in the eighth century by John Damascene and Kosmas of Maïouma (particularly for Holy Week and the week after Resurrection) and in the ninth century by Theodore the Stoudite, Joseph the Hymnographer (i.e., Joseph of Thessalonica or Joseph the Stoudite, brother of Theodore the Stoudite), Theophanes Graptos (the brother of Theodore Graptos), and another Theophanes of Sicily. Although a monastic Palestinian *Triodion* may have existed in the seventh to eighth centuries, the first manuscripts that preserve the actual structure of the liturgy are from the tenth century. This structure includes also the three weeks that precede Lent.[37] Some of the hymns for the celebration of Lazarus (the Saturday before Palm Sunday) are ascribed to Leo the Wise and to a certain Andrew Typhlos.

This literary development of the liturgical cult was systematized in the ninth and tenth centuries in the form of three prayer books added to the *Horologion* and *Euchologion*, the daily prayer structure of Late Antiquity: the *Octoechos*, which covers most of the year, contains *kanones* in honor of the saints and movable feasts; the *Triodion* initially covered the Lenten period and the fifty days from the Resurrection to Pentecost, but this last period was detached in the fourteenth century into a separate book, the *Pentecostarion*.

Nikephoros Kallistos Xanthopoulos' *Triodion Synaxaries* (short explanatory notices to be read in church during the office) are a recapitulation of the whole theological, hagiographical, and liturgical creation of Late Antiquity. The author carefully notes various traditions linked to the celebrations of each feast of the *Triodion* and their spiritual sense. Nikephoros notes, for example, for the first Sunday of the *Triodion* that the image of the Prodigal Son could apply both to the Jews and to the Christians. On one hand, the Jews, the former Chosen People, are expected to return to Christ through an act of repentance at the end of time. On the other hand, the Christians, the new Chosen People, have by their sins forsaken God's love and thus need to return to God in an equally dramatic act of repentance. As a proof of this interpretation, Nikephoros invokes the present ruin of the Christian empire. By recalling the two possible exegeses of the passage, the author delineates a historical evolution in which the late antique self-confidence of the Christians faces a medieval sense of collective repentance. Xanthopoulos uses a wide variety of sources, including the Pseudo-Macarian homily collections and the *Dialogues* of Gregory the Great. The amount of erudition displayed in his writings and his care to collect various opinions on a subject place Xanthopoulos in the context of the Palaiologan Renaissance, with the particularity that his sources are imbued with the cultural essence of Late Antiquity.

Eschatology: The New Sense of Life

One of the great religious contributions of Late Antiquity seems to consist in the creation of a strong and socially functional link between earthly life and eternal life. Peter Brown's studies have shown that the belief in a direct connection between the two realms succeeded in supplementing and replacing the antique social system and power structure.[38] The fourth- to sixth-century religious phenomenon, of which the "holy man" is a key figure, bequeathed to Byzantium the importance of the relation between the society of the living and the society of the departed.[39] The issue consisted in defining the religious status of the soul between the individual's death and the Last Judgment.[40] It is what theologians call the "little eschatology."[41]

Passing through several metamorphoses, due to a tense relation with imperial power, as attested by the imperial attempt to confine monasticism inside specialized and controlled institutions (the canons of the Council *in Trullo*), the mediator of the holy (holy man/holy image) continued to be a key figure in Byzantine society as an iconodule contestant of the iconoclastic imperial power in the eighth and ninth centuries (mostly monastic figures), as a founder of monasteries and reformer of monastic life in the tenth to twelfth centuries, and ultimately as a Hesychast or Palamite (supporter of Gregory Palamas' mystical theology) in the fourteenth century. Alongside this monastic development, we should view as part of the same tradition the holy fool, whose presence (in more or less discrete forms) never vanished from Byzantium's religious environment. Even the post-Byzantine Slavonic Orthodox tradition retained this mediating role in the form of the *starets*. Their function was to assure the believers that the earthly present had an immediate and just continuation in the afterlife. This concern finds a strong literary expression in the visionary literature of the tenth and eleventh centuries: the *Life of Mary the Younger*, the *Life of Basil the Younger*, the *Apocalypse of Anastasia*, the *Apocalypse of the Theotokos*.[42]

Eschatology meets liturgy in a most wonderful manner in the *Life of Saint Mary of Egypt*. Written by Sophronios, patriarch of Jerusalem in the mid-seventh century, this piece of hagiography played a special role liturgically, as noted previously. It became a symbol of the encounter between moral and spiritual endeavor and the Eucharistic celebration. The dramatic force of this late antique story continued to astonish generations of ascetics. Not only did it enter the *Triodion* and occupy the place of the fifth Sunday of the Lenten period but also the whole text in Sophronios' version was appended as a reading to the *Triodion*.

As Eucharistic symbolism grew stronger in the decoration of churches, the final scene of the *Life of Saint Mary of Egypt*, in which she receives communion from Abba Zosima in the desert, was depicted on the walls around the entrance in the nave of the church. It became thus the sign of the new ascetic understanding and practice of the Eucharist. What seemed so specific in the text of Sophronios for the monastic environment of sixth-century Palestine entered the liturgical theology of Byzantine monasticism. The relevant passage is worth quoting in full:

> And when again the monks returned and the day of the Last Supper dawned, he [Zosima] did as he had been ordered and, placing some of the most pure Body and Blood into a small chalice and putting some figs and dates and

> lentils soaked in water into a small basket, he departed for the desert and reached the banks of the Jordan and sat down to wait for the saint. He waited for a long while and then began to doubt. Then raising his eyes to heaven, he began to pray: "Grant me, O Lord, to behold that which Thou hast allowed me to behold once. Do not let me depart in vain, being the burden of my sins." And then another thought struck him: "And what if she does come? There is no boat; how will she cross the Jordan to come to me who am so unworthy?" And as he was pondering thus he saw the holy woman appear and stand on the other side of the river. Zosima got up rejoicing and glorifying and thanking God. And again the thought came to him that she could not cross the Jordan. Then he saw that she made the sign of the Cross over the waters of the Jordan (and the night was a moonlit one, as he related afterwards) and then she at once stepped on to the waters and began walking across the surface towards him. And when he wanted to prostrate himself, she cried to him while still walking on the water: "What are you doing, Abba, you are a priest and carrying the divine Gifts!" He obeyed her and on reaching the shore she said to the elder: "Bless, father, bless me!" He answered her trembling, for a state of confusion had overcome him at the sight of the miracle: "Truly God did not lie when He promised that when we purify ourselves we shall be like Him. Glory to Thee, Christ our God, Who has shown me through this thy slave how far away I stand from perfection." Here the woman asked him to say the Creed and the Our Father. He began, she finished the prayer and according to the custom of that time gave him the kiss of peace on the lips. Having partaken of the Holy Mysteries, she raised her hands to heaven and sighed with tears in her eyes, exclaiming: "Now lettest Thou Thy servant depart in peace, O Lord, according to Thy word; for my eyes have seen Thy salvation."
>
> Then she said to the elder: "Forgive me, Abba, for asking you, but fulfill another wish of mine. Go now to the monastery and let God's grace guard you and next year come again to the same place where I first met you. Come for God's sake, for you shall again see me, for such is the will of God." He said to her: "From this day on I would like to follow you and always see your holy face, but now fulfill the one and only wish of an old man and take a little of the food I have brought for you." And he showed her the basket, while she just touched the lentils with the tips of her fingers, and taking three grains said that the Holy Spirit guards the substance of the soul unpolluted. Then she said: "Pray, for God's sake pray for me and remember a miserable wretch." Touching the saint's feet and asking for her prayers for the Church, the empire and himself, he let her depart with tears, while he went off sighing and sorrowful, for he could not hope to vanquish the invincible. Meanwhile she again made the sign of the Cross over the Jordan, and stepped on to the waters and crossed over as before. And the elder returned filled with joy and terror, accusing himself of not having asked the saint her name. But he decided to do so next year.

The encounter between Mary and Zosima is a dramatic enactment of the meaning of communion that prevailed throughout Byzantium, the moral and ascetic. The liturgical-ceremonial and hierarchical aspects of communion apparently succumb in front of the free hierophany of the man or woman of

God. The priest holding the holy elements wants to bow at the sight of the saint, but at the last moment the saint reestablishes the *taxis* and stops Zosima from performing his *proskynesis*. The topography described by the text also emphasizes the liturgical meeting between priest and communicant at the liturgical frontier between nave and sanctuary. The Jordan River plays this liturgical role, but as the priest is not capable of coming out of the sanctuary (i.e. crossing the river), the saint, although a half-naked woman, miraculously abolishes the frontier and approaches communion. The scene reconciles the wilderness of holy man/woman with liturgical communal practice. It is in this sense that the scene became a symbol of communion depicted on the entrance walls to the nave in late Byzantine Orthodox monastic churches. The narrow entrance and the small nave of late Byzantine monastic communities are a reenactment of the Jordan encounter.

From Christianity to Orthodoxy

The period between the dusk of Late Antiquity and the dawn of Byzantium (seventh to ninth centuries) witnessed a moment when Christianity crystallized into a civil religion. The term for this momentous but fragile synthesis might be called Orthodoxy, which was subsequently the political and religious bequest of Late Antiquity to Byzantium.

The transformation of the coronation ritual in the seventh century accompanies the process of full identification of the Roman power with Christianity.[43] It is in this context and in advance of the Council *in Trullo* that imperial propaganda began to use the idea of the emperor as guardian of Orthodoxy. A letter of Justinian II to Pope Konon (dated February 17, 687), regarding the acts of the sixth ecumenical council (Constantinople III, 553), describes Justinian himself as representative of God and guardian of Orthodoxy. The emperor tells the pope that he assembled patriarchs, papal legates, archbishops, bishops, functionaries, bodyguards, the demes, the excubitors, and representatives of the army; ordered the acts to be read out; and then asked the assembly to sign them. Afterward, he ordered the acts to be kept in the imperial archive and not in the patriarchal archive as a sign of his role of "guardian of Orthodoxy."[44]

The canons of the Council *in Trullo* offer a definition, sanctioned by an assembly of bishops, of imperial power. Kingship is described as follows in the preamble of the Trullan canons:

> As we conduct our lives in great sloth and slumber in the idleness of our thoughts, so that the enemy can come upon us unawares, Christ our Lord, who steers this greatest of ships, the entire world, has now set you over us, the wise governor, the pious emperor . . . you who dispense your words in

> discernment. . . . *Wisdom bore you in her womb* and nurtured you with her virtues; she brought you up and educated you and filled you with the Spirit of God; she has made you the *eye of the universe*, you who brightly illumine your subjects with the pureness and splendor of your mind. To you she has entrusted her Church and has taught you to meditate on her law day and night [Psalm 1:2], for the correction and edification of the people subject to you . . . [like Phinehas in Numbers 25:7–11, the emperor transfixes sin by piety and understanding] . . . and you have chosen to lead your flock away from iniquity and corruption.[45]

The emperor steers the ship through the swells of turbulence and transgression. Because the last two ecumenical councils have not established canons, therefore,

> it follows that the holy nation, the royal priesthood [1 Peter 2:9], on whose behalf Christ died, is torn asunder and led astray through the many passions resulting from indiscipline, and is detached little by little and cut off from the divine fold, . . . through ignorance and neglect [quoting Hebrews 10:29].
>
> It was your [the emperor's] great desire, therefore, after the example of Christ, the good shepherd [John 10:1–14], searching for the sheep lost in the mountains, to bring together this holy nation, as a special people [1 Peter 2:9], and to return it to the fold and convince it to keep the divine commandments and statutes . . . [The council's mission is to purify the Church of the remnants of Judaizing and pagan practices].[46]

The preamble alludes to the fact that assaults of devilish legions at the gates of the church coincide in a meaningful way with the assaults of huge Arab armies from the east and equally threatening pagan invasions from the north. The defeat of the former opens the possibility of victory over the latter. To formulate this political interpretation, the text appeals to an eschatological framework, which develops new forms of expression at the end of the seventh century and describes, as we shall see, the empire as near to the Heavenly Kingdom as the available vocabulary could express it.

In the description of the emperor, a series of topoi are borrowed from earlier rhetorical texts: the imperial *Christomimesis* already appears in Eusebius' *Life of Constantine*; the steering of the cosmic ship by Christ and of the earthly empire by the emperor appears in both Eusebius and Agapetus' *Mirror of Princes*. Some parallels with the *Life of Constantine* are more striking, such as the description of the image that represented Constantine and his sons trampling or stabbing a serpent or dragon, which was cast into the depths of the sea, while the cross was depicted above their head. It is possible that the labarum itself was that weapon.[47] Eusebius explains the image by citing Isaiah 27:1 and Psalms 90:13, references that are more often applied to Christ, such as in the chapel of the archbishop's palace in Ravenna. If, for Eusebius, the dragon is the devil in this context, in a different context it is Licinius who is called "that dragon."[48] The eternal enemy of mankind thus finds specific, historical expressions in threats to the Christian empire; this is what the preamble conveys through the juxtaposition of "dragon" and "Assyrian." Thus, in his description of the opening of the Council of Nicaea in 325, Eusebius presents the emperor walking into the hall "like some heavenly angel of God," and, at the Vicennalia celebrations, the palace "might have been supposed . . . an imaginary representation of the Kingdom of Christ."[49] In the Trullan preamble, it is not a palace or a church, or the presence of the emperor, that alludes to the Kingdom of God, but the Christian community, as a holy people and a political body of the empire, which has already exchanged servitude for the Kingdom of Heaven. The vocabulary is both Pauline, stressing the moral and individual aspects of the struggle with evil, and political, in its use of words like *servitude, kingdom, rebellion,* and *tyranny.*

Certain passages in the *Life of Constantine,* particularly Constantine's letter to the provincials of the East,[50] as well as passages in the treatise *In Praise of Constantine,* where Eusebius draws the analogy between the cosmos ruled by God and the empire ruled by Constantine,[51] display numerous themes resonant in the Trullan preamble: the new sacrifice, as opposed to the pagan sacrifice; Christ's war on the demons, and the emperor's war against its terrestrial enemies; the friendship between Christ and the emperor, who is thus acting as an interpreter of the Word of God. Even though there is no textual borrowing from Eusebius in the preamble, the thematic proximity cannot be denied.

Unlike Eusebius' more restricted term-by-term comparison of God's monarchy over the universe with the empire, built on the idea of imitation or reflection, in the preamble the empire is already an actor in the dramatic development of the Last Things. The objective of the council itself is to establish canons, as rules of righteousness. If in the first and second parts the preamble emphasizes the religious and political unity, the empire as actor, in its third part the emperor Justinian II assumes the preeminent role. Divine Wisdom "has entrusted her Church [to the emperor] and has taught [the emperor] to meditate on her law day and night, for the correction and edification of the peoples [once again in the plural]."[52] More than a divine attribute, the Wisdom of God in this text seems to be a kind of political manifestation of God. "Wisdom bore you in her womb," referring to the emperor, could be visualized as the description of a quite obvious ceremonial image: the emperor crossing Saint Sophia with the holy gifts, penetrating in the sanctuary, rising at the ambo to address the people and to receive the crown under the cosmic dome/womb of Wisdom.

The name *ho Assyrios* given to the devil, as historical enemy of the holy city, inspired by Cyril of Alexandria's *Commentary on Micah* but possibly also related to the corresponding rhetorical themes of the *Homily* of Theodore Synkellos, presents the church of the living God typologically as Zion, and mystically as icon of the heavenly Jerusalem. By these references, Constantinople itself becomes a besieged Jerusalem, in which church and empire merge into an undifferentiated unity. If in Cyril's commentary, following Clement of Alexandria,[53] the church is the icon of the heavenly Jerusalem, the preamble extends this function to the empire. The same confusion/identification is employed by Pseudo-Methodius when he applies the reference in Matthew 16:18 ("the gates of Hades shall never prevail over the Church") to the kingdom of the Christians (i.e., that of the Greeks; i.e., that of the Romans), whose power is justified by the Holy Cross.[54]

Canons 36, 38, and 69 correspond to the political scope of the preamble. First, the apparently unnecessary repetition of the canons 3 and 28 from the second and fourth ecumenical councils, which equate Constantinople and Rome ecclesiastically, reiterates, very appropriately in the context of the Council *in Trullo*, the role of Constantinople as both political and religious capital.[55] Canon 38 reinforces this intention through invocation of the principle of geographic accommodation of ecclesiastical authority on civil authority, going even further in this logic by replacing the dignity of ecclesiastical centers based on the antiquity of the see with the hierarchical order of cities created by imperial authority.[56] Canon 36 is thus in fact the very logical consequence of canon 38. Ultimately, canon 69 addresses, albeit in an ambiguous form, the question of the sacred status of the emperor.[57] Although this canon is part of the segment of the canonic collection that deals with laity, it creates an exception for imperial power.

To close our demonstration with the case of Justinian II, we have to add the numismatic evidence: the gold coins (*nomismata*) of his reign represent on the recto the image of Christ *rex regnantium* and on the verso the image of the emperor with the inscription *servus Christi*, thus pointing to the joint government of the emperor with Christ.[58] The homology of Heavenly Kingdom with Earthly Kingdom was placed in a vertical orientation on the Barberini Ivory (first half of the sixth century, probably Justinian; see Frontispiece)[59] and on the apse of the domed hall of the Chrysotriklinos in the imperial palace: Christ above, the emperor below.[60] However, Justinian II chose to depict the relationship through a double-sided image, the coin. The intimacy of the two grew that much stronger.

Conclusion

Why does Byzantium look so Christian to us? If we interpret Christianity as a means to achieve social cohesion in the empire, and if we are willing to define Christianity as a strictly recognizable and controlled form of worship (as the Trullan canons might suggest), in the context of multiple political and religious challenges, then we have to return to the theme of civil religion, rather than to political theology. Neither did the empire force Christianity to approve of a political doctrine dedicated to the empire, nor did Christianity shape the political doctrine of the empire, because empire and Christianity were not coherent, willful historical actors. Nevertheless, the impetus producing Orthodoxy—viewed at the moment of the late seventh century as orthopraxy—lies within the imperial palace. In this place it seemed that, if God granted the empire to go on, this survival was in exchange for its members' commitment to the one true faith in God. Such a belief found a stronger expression with emperors like Justinian, Heraclius, and Justinian II, but it was shared by all the others.

The claims of imperial guardianship of Orthodoxy[61] and the harsh treatment of peripheral groups were not new, in fact, but the novelty consisted in their official written form. The canons of the Council *in Trullo* compelled monks to remain in their monastic establishments (canons 34, 41, 42), but already an imperial constitution of Theodosius II ordered recalcitrant and noisy monks to be kept out of the councils' gatherings. This attitude shows an early awareness of the subversive power of monasticism. If the palace of the emperor is a dwelling of Orthodoxy, as long as the non-Chalcedonians sought refuge in Theodora's palace in Constantinople they were not yet labeled as heretics. A heresy was not a heresy until it was expelled from the center. If the marginal groups were to claim their righteousness or to proclaim their challenge, they had to do it in the center.

From the second half of the seventh and into the eighth century, the system started functioning the other way round. A severe trial in Constantinople could assure a religious dissenter of his posthumous success. In the seventh century, the trial of Maximus Confessor took place in Constantinople, and, in the eighth century, the trial of Saint Stephen the Younger by the iconoclast emperor Constantine V was even held in the Hippodrome. The initial defeat of the dissenter was eventually turned into triumph when a change of policy occurred in Constantinople. The narrator of the saint's life transforms the castigatory examination in Constantinople into an opportunity to proclaim the truth to the whole world. The official history of Orthodoxy records the later triumphant point of view and expels the discordant view from the sources.[62] If political will seems primordial in establishing Orthodoxy, later narrative strategies about orthodox heroes insert coherence into what looks, from a political point of view, like a change of actors and contexts. Creators of Orthodoxy are thus both those who act directly on the battlefield of political action and those who tell the story of the religious conflict.

The conflict around Orthodoxy, or the succession of orthodoxies throughout these centuries, accentuates the fact that the emperor held his own version of Christianity. Historians, in their attempts to retrace the rise and function of the imperial Church, are privileged in the amount of sources produced by and near political power. What the historian should avoid, however, is simply to take the latter for Christianity.[63] We have to group the evidence carefully into small temporal units. What makes sense in the fourth century does not in the sixth. What one believes in Palestine is still unknown in Constantinople at the same time.

Nevertheless, the ninth and tenth centuries know of one political and religious center, Constantinople. Thus the tremendous effort to recall a large world of Christianity, including West and East, was designed to strengthen the claim that Constantinople represented the *oikoumene*. The large world of Late Antiquity found its way in the synaxaries, menologia, universal chronicles, and various hagiographical narratives as a testimony of Christianity's universal character, and the Byzantine imperial power was able to keep up the pretense of being essentially universal for another few centuries. Late Antiquity was thus important for the definition of both power and faith. As long as Byzantium stood firm in this tradition, Late Antiquity survived surprisingly well as part of the cultural memory of a world that continued to change regardless.

NOTES

1. At the same time, the eighth century witnessed a form of religious change analyzed in Brown 1973, although he notes divergent evolutions also on a geographic basis in Brown 1976.
2. Marrou 1977.
3. Cameron 1993 or Cameron, Ward-Perkins, and Whitby 2000; discussion of the issue in Cameron 2006.
4. Brown 1996.
5. Boureau 2007, 179–202.
6. Iorga 1935.
7. Dagron 1969, 23–56.
8. Hunger 1965.
9. Guran 2006a, 41–52.
10. Turcan 1979 brought up the same "Hypatia" argument against Marrou 1977.
11. Sorlin 1973, 385–408.
12. Justin Martyr, *Dialogue with Trypho*, Introduction:

> "Hail, O philosopher!" And immediately after saying this, he turned round and walked along with me; his friends likewise followed him. And I in turn having addressed him, said, "What is there important?" And he replied, "I was instructed," says he, "by Corinthus the Socratic in Argos, that I ought not to despise or treat with indifference those who array themselves in this dress, but to show them all kindness, and to associate with them, as perhaps some advantage would spring from the intercourse either to some such man or to myself. It is good, moreover, for both, if either the one or the other be benefited. On this account, therefore, whenever I see any one in such costume, I gladly approach him, and now, for the same reason, have I willingly accosted you; and these accompany me, in the expectation of hearing for themselves something profitable from you."

13. Guran 2001, 73–121.
14. Hunger 1955, 13–49.
15. Müller and Kiessling 1966 [1821].
16. Dagron 1987, 281–288.
17. Woodhouse 1986.
18. Flusin 2001, 29–54.

19. Ivanov 2006, 168–172; Rydén 1990; Rystenko and Potapow 1928, 17–186; Noret 1977.

20. Berger 2006, 43–45.

21. Dölger 1953 versus Aerts 1993, 357–364; Volk 1993–1994, 442–462; finally Volk 2009, 1–95, see conclusion 92–95, established the authorship of Euthymios Hagioreites (died 1028). Mango 1982, 297–313, versus Rydén 1978, 129–155.

22. Reinink 1985, 263–281; 2002, 81–94.

23. Guran 2009, 35–55.

24. Caner 2010, 73–135; 2004, 135–147.

25. Volk 2009 (ed.), 118–120.

26. Detoraki and Beaucamp 2007, 285 (text), 55 (commentary).

27. Transmitted by a wonderful late Byzantine manuscript edition of the complete work in Parisinus graecus 450 (A) dated September 11, 1364, which shows the fourteenth-century interest in early patristic authors.

28. In the tenth century, to avoid a competition among the three Cappadocians, Basil of Caesarea, Gregory of Nazianzus, and Gregory of Nyssa, and John Chrysostom, the clergy of the Great Church established a common liturgical celebration on January 30.

29. The Macarian literature is contained in PG 34. For Pseudo-Macarius, *The Fifty Spiritual Homilies and the Great Letter* see Maloney 1992.

30. Bady 2010, 149–164.

31. The best product of this type is Euthimios Zygabenos, *Panoplía dogmatike tes orthodóxou písteos*, PG 128–131, edited by the fourteenth-century scholar Gregoras and first published in the post-Byzantine atmosphere of eighteenth-century Wallachia by Târgovişte in 1711.

32. von Ivánka 1964; Guran 2006c, 291–320.

33. Ward 1980; 1975.

34. Pseudo-Anthony the Great, Evagrios Pontikos, John Cassian, Isaiah the Solitary, Mark the Ascetic, Hesychios the Priest (of Jerusalem), Neilos the Ascetic (of Ankyra), whose name was used to cover the transmission of the works of Evagrios, Diadochos bishop of Photike, John of Karpathos (*Consolations to the Monks of India*), Theodoros the Great Ascetic, Maximos Confessor, Thalassios the Lybian, John of Damascus, Abba Philemon, Theognostos, and the rest are later Byzantine authors.

35. Guran 2003, 239–255.

36. Maas and Trypanis 1963; Grosdidier de Matons 1964–1981; English translation: Carpenter 1970–1973; selected English translation: Lash 1996.

37. Taft 1982, 358–370.

38. Brown 1971, 80–101; 1981; 1982; 1983, 1–25.

39. Patlagean 1981, 201–221.

40. Dagron 1980, 84–92; 1984, 419–430.

41. Beck 1979, 5–71.

42. Baun 2000, 241–268.

43. Guran 2006b, 292–296.

44. Dölger 1924, 31, nr. 254.

45. Nedungatt and Featherstone 1995, 49–50.

46. Nedungatt and Featherstone 1995, 52–53.

47. Eusebius, *Life of Constantine* III.3; trans. Cameron and Hall 1999, 122, 255–256 (commentary).

48. The same kind of identification of the Avar khagan with the dragon in Theodoros Synkellos' *Homily on the Siege of Constantinople 626*, ed. L. Sternbach, *Analecta avarica*, 302–303 (Greek text), 16–17 (trans.).

49. Eusebius, *Life of Constantine* III.10 and 15; trans. Cameron and Hall 1999, 125–127, 264–267 (commentary).

50. Eusebius, *Life of Constantine* II.48–60; trans. Cameron and Hall 1999, 111–114.

51. Eusebius, *Tricennalia* II; ed. Heikel 1902, 199–200.

52. Nedungatt and Featherstone 1995, 50.

53. Clement of Alexandria, *Stromateis* 4.8, 18, *PG* 8, col. 1277B.

54. Pseudo-Methodius, *Apocalypse*; trans. Alexander 1985, 42; ed. Aerts and Kortekaas 1998; German translation: Reinink 1993.

55. Canon 36: "Renewing the enactments by the 150 Fathers assembled at the God-protected and imperial city, and those of the 630 who met at Chalcedon; we decree that the see of Constantinople shall have equal privileges with the see of Old Rome, and shall be as highly regarded in ecclesiastical matters as that is, and shall be second after it. After Constantinople shall be ranked the See of Alexandria, then that of Antioch, and afterwards the See of Jerusalem."

56. Canon 38: "the canon which was made by the Fathers we also observe, which thus decreed: If any city be renewed by imperial authority, or shall have been renewed, let the order of things ecclesiastical follow the civil and public models."

57. Canon 69: "it is not permitted to a layman to enter the sanctuary [Gk., holy altar], though, in accordance with a certain ancient tradition, the imperial power and authority is by no means prohibited from this when he wishes to offer his gifts to the Creator."

58. Grabar 1957, 37–45; Morrisson 1970, 1: 396–398, pl. LXI, LXIII, LXIV.

59. Gaborit-Chopin 1993, nr. 20, 63–65.

60. Cameron 1980, 62–84.

61. Dölger 1924, 31, nr. 254 in a letter of Justinian II to Pope Konon, February 17, 687.

62. Auzépy 1981, 415–436; 1990, 445–492; 2004, 127–169 (all reprinted in Auzépy 2007).

63. Rebillard 1994, 232, draws attention to the significant changes that allow him to speak of several "christianismes dans l'histoire." To his view, we may add our distinction between simultaneous zones of Christianities, of which one is that which appears in proximity to political power.

WORKS CITED

Aerts, W. J. 1993. "Einige Überlegungen zur Sprache und Zeit der Abfassung des griechischen Romans 'Barlaam und Joasaph'." In *Die Begegnung des Westens mit dem Osten: Kongressakten des 4. Symposiums des Mediävistenverbandes in Köln 1991 aus Anlass des 1000. Todesjahres der Kaiserin Theophanu*, ed. O. Engels and P. Schreiner, 357–364. Sigmaringen: Jan Thorbecke Verlag.

Aerts, W. J., and G. A. A. Kortekaas, eds. 1998. *Die Apokalypse des Pseudo-Methodius: Die ältesten griechischen und lateinischen Ubersetzungen.* 2 vols. CSCO 569–570. Louvain: Peeters.

Alexander, P. J., trans. 1985. *The Byzantine Apocalyptic Tradition.* Berkeley: University of California Press.

Auzépy, M.-F. 1981. "Une lecture 'iconoclaste' de la Vie d'Etienne le Jeune," *Travaux et Memoires* 8: 415–436. [Repr. Auzépy 2007.]

———. 1990. "La destruction de l'icône du Christ de la Chalcé par Léon III: Propagande ou réalité?" *Byzantion* 60: 445–492. [Reprint: Auzépy. 2007. *L'histoire des iconoclastes.* Paris]

———. 2004. "Les enjeux de l'iconoclasme." *Cristianità d'Occidente et Cristianità d'Oriente: Settimane di Studio* 51: 127–169. Spoleto. [Repr. Auzépy 2007]

———. 2007. *L'histoire des iconoclastes.* Paris: Association des Amis du CHCB.

Bady, G. 2010. "La tradition des œuvres de Jean Chrysostome, entre transmission et transformation," *REB* 68: 149–164.

Baun, J. 2000. "The Moral Apocalypse in Byzantium." In *Apocalyptic Time,* ed. Albert I. Baumgarten, 241–268. Leiden: Brill.

Beck, H.-G. 1979. *Die Byzantiner und ihr Jenseits: Zur Entstehungsgeschichte einer Mentalität (Sitzungsberichte der Bayerischen Akademie der Wissenschaften, philosophisch-historische Klasse, Jahrgang 1979 Heft 6)*, 5–71. Munich: Verlag der Bayerischen Akademie der Wissenschaften.

Berger, A., ed. 2006. *Life and Works of Saint Gregentios, Archbishop of Taphar.* Berlin: Walter de Gruyter.

Boureau, Alain. 2006. *La religion de l'état: La construction de la république étatique dans le discours théologique de l'occident médiéval, 1250–1350.* Paris: Belles Lettres.

Brown, P. 1971. "The Rise and Function of the Holy Man in Late Antiquity," *Journal of Roman Studies* 61: 80–101.

———. 1973. "A Dark Age Crisis: Aspects of the Iconoclastic Controversy," *English Historical Review* 88: 1–34.

———. 1976. "Eastern and Western Christendom in Late Antiquity: A Parting of the Ways." In *The Orthodox Churches and the West: Papers Read at the Fourteenth Summer Meeting and the Fifteenth Winter Meeting of the Ecclesiastical History Society,* ed. Derek Baker, 1–24. Oxford: Blackwell.

———. 1981. *The Cult of the Saints: Its Rise and Function in Latin Christianity.* Chicago: University of Chicago Press.

———. 1982. *Society and the Holy in Late Antiquity.* Berkeley: University of California Press.

———. 1983. "The Saint as Exemplar in Late Antiquity," *Representations* 2: 1–25.

———. 1996. *The Rise of Western Christendom, Triumph and Diversity, A.D. 200–1000.* Oxford: Blackwell.

Cameron, Averil. 1980. "The Artistic Patronage of Justin II," *Byzantion* 50: 62–84.

———. 1993. *The Mediterranean World in Late Antiquity, AD 395–600.* London: Routledge.

———. 2006. *The Byzantines.* Oxford: Blackwell.

Cameron, Averil, and Stuart G. Hall, eds. and trans. 1999. *Eusebius: Life of Constantine.* Oxford: Clarendon.

Cameron, Averil, Bryan Ward-Perkins, and Michael Whitby, eds. 2000. *The Cambridge Ancient History, 14: Late Antiquity, Empire and Successors, A.D. 425–600.* The Cambridge Ancient History 14. Cambridge: Cambridge University Press.

Caner, Daniel. 2004. "Sinai Pilgrimage and Ascetic Romance: Pseudo-Nilus's *Narrationes* in Context." In *Travel, Communication and Geography in Late Antiquity: Sacred and Profane,* ed. L. Ellis and F. L. Kidner, 135–147. London: Ashgate.

———. 2010. *History and Hagiography from the Late Antique Sinai.* Translated Texts for Historians 53. Liverpool: Liverpool University Press.

Carpenter, M., trans. 1970–1973. *Kontakia of Romanos, Byzantine Melodist.* 2 vols. Columbia, MO.

Clement of Alexandria. *Stromatum liber 4.* PG 8.

Dagron, G. 1969. "Aux origines de la civilisation byzantine: Langue de culture et langue d'état," *Revue historique* 489: 23–56.

———. 1980. "La perception d'une différence: Les débuts de la *querelle du Purgatoire.*" In *Actes du XVe Congrès International d'Études Byzantines, Athènes, Septembre 1976, 4: Histoire, Communications,* 84–92. Athens: Association internationale des études byzantines.

———. 1984. "Troisième, neuvième et quarantième jour dans la tradition byzantine: temps chrétien et anthropologie." In *Le temps chrétien de la fin de l'Antiquité au Moyen Âge, IIIe–XIIIe siècles (Colloques internationaux du CNRS 604, Paris 9–12 mars 1981),* 419–430. Paris: Éditions du CNRS.

———. 1987. "Manuel Chrysoloras: Constantinople ou Rome," *Byzantinische Forschungen 12 = Mélanges F. Thiriet:* 281–288.

Detoraki, Marina, ed., and Joëlle Beaucamp, trans. 2007. *Le martyre de saint Arethas et de ses compagnons (BHG 166).* Paris: ACHByz.

Dölger, F. 1924. *Regesten der Kaiserurkunden des Oströmischen Reiches, 1: Regesten von 565–1025.* Munich and Berlin: Oldenbourg.

———. 1953. *Der griechische Barlaam-Roman, ein Werk des Johannes von Damaskos.* Studia Patristica et Byzantina 1. Ettal: Buch-Kuntsverlag.

Eusebius. 1902. *Werke.* Ed. Ivar Heikel. Leipzig: Hinrichs.

Euthymios Zygabenos. *Panoplía dogmatike tes orthodóxou písteos.* PG 128–131.

Flusin, B. 2001. "L'empereur hagiographe: Remarques sur le rôle des premiers empereurs macédoniens dans le culte de saints." In *L'empereur hagiographe: Culte des saints et monarchie byzantine et post-byzantine,* ed. P. Guran and B. Flusin, 29–54. Bucharest: New Europe College.

Gaborit-Chopin, D. 1993. "Catalogue description of the Barberini Ivory, nr. 20." In *Byzance, l'art byzantin dans les collections publiques françaises (catalogue de l'exposition au musée du Louvre, 3 novembre 1992–1 er février 1993),* 63–65. Paris: Réunion des musées nationaux.

Grabar, A. 1957. *L'iconoclasme byzantin: Dossier archéologique.* Paris: Collège de France.

Grosdidier de Matons, J., ed. 1964–1981. *Romanos le Mélode: Hymnes.* 5 vols. SC 99, 110, 114, 128, 283. Paris: Cerf.

Guran, P. 2001. "Jean VI Cantacuzène, l'hésychasme et l'empire: Les miniatures du codex Parisinus graecus 1242." In *L'empereur hagiographe: Culte des saints et monarchie byzantine et post-byzantine,* ed. P. Guran and B. Flusin, 73–121. Bucharest: New Europe College.

———. 2003. "Le culte de Jean Cassien dans l'Église d'Orient." In *Jean Cassien entre l'Orient et l'Occident,* ed. C. Badilita and Atilla Jakab, 239–255. Paris: Beauchesne.

———. 2006a. "From Empire to Church and Back: In the Aftermath of 1204," *Revue des études sud-est européennes* 44: 41–52.

———. 2006b. "Genesis and Function of the Last Emperor Myth in Byzantine Eschatology," *Bizantinistica* 8: 292–296.

———. 2006c. "L'eschatologie de Palamas entre théologie et politique," *Études byzantines et post-byzantines* 5: 291–320.

———. 2009. "The Constantinople-New Jerusalem at the Crossing of Sacred Space and Political Theology." In *New Jerusalems: Hierotopy and Iconography of Sacred Spaces*, ed. Alexei Lidov, 35–55. Moscow: Indrik.

Hunger, Herbert, ed. 1955. "Die Allegorien aus der Verschronik," *JÖBG* 4: 13–49.

———. 1965. *Reich der neuen Mitte: Der christliche Geist der byzantinischen Kultur*. Graz: Verlag Styria.

Iorga, N. 1935. *Byzance après Byzance: Continuation de l'histoire de la vie byzantine*. Bucharest: Institut des Études Byzantines.

Ivanov, S. A. 2006. *Holy Fools in Byzantium and Beyond*. Oxford: Oxford University Press.

Lash, E., trans. 1996. *St. Romanos the Melodist: Kontakia on the Life of Christ*. San Francisco: HarperCollins.

Maas, P., and C. A. Trypanis, eds. 1963. *Sancti Romani melodi cantica: Cantica genuina*. Oxford: Clarendon Press.

Makk, F. 1975. *Traduction et commentaire de l'Homélie écrite probablement par Théodore le Syncelle sur le siège de Constantinople en 626*. Szeged: JATE.

Maloney, George A., ed. and trans. 1992. *Pseudo-Macarius: The Fifty Spiritual Homilies and the Great Letter*. New York: Paulist Press.

Mango, C. 1982. "The Life of St. Andrew the Fool Reconsidered," *Rivista di studi bizantini e slavi* 2 = *Miscellanea A. Pertusi* 2: 297–313.

Marrou, H.-I. 1977. *Décadence romaine ou antiquité tardive? (IIIe–VIe siècle)*. Paris: Éditions du Seuil.

Morrisson, C. 1970. *Catalogue des monnaies byzantines de la Bibliothèque nationale* 1. Paris: Bibliothèque nationale.

Müller, G., and T. Kiessling, eds. 1966. *Theodore Metochites: Miscellanea philosophica et historica*. Amsterdam: Hakkert. [Originally published 1821]

Nedungatt, George, and Michael Featherstone, eds. 1995. *The Council in Trullo Revisited*. Rome: Pontificio Istituto Orientale.

Noret, J. 1977. "Une recension fantôme de récits sur saint Niphon de Constantiana," *Analecta Bollandiana* 95: 118.

Patlagean, E. 1981. "Byzance et son autre monde: Observations sur quelques récits." In *Faire croire: Modalités de la diffusion et de la réception des messages religieux du XIIe au XVe siècle*, 201–221. Rome: École Française de Rome.

Rebillard, Eric. 1994. *In hora mortis: Evolution de la pastorale chrétienne de la mort au IVe et Ve siècles*. Rome: École Française de Rome.

Reinink, G. J. 1985. "Die Entstehung der syrischen Alexanderlegende als politisch-religiöse Propagandaschrift für Herakleios' Kirchenpolitik." In *After Chalcedon: Studies in Theology and Church History Offered to Professor Albert van Roey for His Seventieth Birthday*, ed. C. Laga, J. A. Munitiz, and L. van Rompay, 263–281. Orientalia Lovanensia Analecta 18. Leuven: Peeters.

———. 1993. *Die syrische Apokalypse des Pseudo-Methodius*. CSCO 540–541. 2 vols. Louvain: Peeters.

———. 2002. "Heraclius, the New Alexander: Apocalyptic Prophecies during the Reign of Heraclius." In *The Reign of Heraclius (610–641): Crisis and Confrontation*, ed. G. J. Reinink and B. H. Stolte, 81–84. Leuven: Peeters.

Rydén, L. 1978. "The Date of the Life of Andreas Salos," *DOP* 32: 129–155.

———. 1990. "The Date of the Life of St. Niphon, BHG 1371z." In *Greek and Latin Studies in Memory of C. Fabricius*, ed. S.-T. Teodorsson, 33–40. Göteborg: University of Göteborg.

Rystenko, A. V., and P. O. Potapow, eds. 1928. *Materialien zur Geschichte der byzantinisch-slavischen Literatur und Sprache*. Odessa: n.p.

Sorlin, I. 1973. "La transmission et la diffusion de la littérature chronographique byzantine en Russie prémongole du XIe au XIIIe siècle," *Travaux et Mémoires* 5: 385–408.

Taft, R. F. 1982. "The Byzantine Office in the Prayerbook of New Skete," *OCP* 48: 358–370.

Turcan, R. 1979. "Review of H.-I. Marrou, *Décadence romaine ou antiquite tardive?*" *Revue d'Histoire religieuse* 196.2: 216–218.

Volk, R. 1993–1994. "Urtext und Modifikationen des griechischen Barlaam-Romans: Prolegomena zur Neuausgabe," *Byzantinische Zeitschrift* 86–87: 442–462.

———, ed. 2009. *Die Schriften des Johannes von Damaskos, herausgegeben vom Byzantinischen Institut der Abtei Scheyern, VI/I: Historia animae utilis de Barlaam et Ioasaph (spuria)*. Berlin: Walter de Gruyter.

von Ivánka, Endre. 1964. *Plato Christianus: Übernahme und Umgestaltung des Platonismus durch die Väter*. Einsiedeln: Johannes Verlag.

Ward, B. 1975. *The Wisdom of the Desert Fathers: Apophthegmata Patrum from the Anonymous Series*. Oxford: SLG.

———. 1980. *The Desert Christian: Sayings of the Desert Fathers: The Alphabetical Collection*. New York: Macmillan.

Woodhouse, C. M. 1986. *George Gemistos Plethon: The Last of the Hellenes*. Oxford: Clarendon Press.

CHAPTER 36

LATE ANTIQUITY AND THE ITALIAN RENAISSANCE

CHRISTOPHER S. CELENZA
Johns Hopkins University

RENAISSANCE thinkers did not possess a concept analogous to today's "Late Antiquity," diversely as its modern scholars might understand the term. Yet at least one of the polarities inherent in current debates about the designation can be detected: that of evolution and change, on the one hand, versus continuity and plurality on the other. The first set of historical discourses, tied to stories of "decline," belonged to a foundational, older era in modern historiography, stretching from Edward Gibbon to the twentieth century, whereas the second is most often identified with Henri Marrou and, especially, Peter Brown.[1] If we take the period denominated Late Antiquity as broadly as current historiography seems to permit, from (roughly) 250 C.E. to 800 C.E., Renaissance thinkers have a lot to say, often in ways that, though unfamiliar to much modern historiography, form part of the intellectual genealogy of both sides.

On the one hand, when it comes to evolution and change, one fact that cannot be disputed is that, at some point in the centuries that led to the early Middle Ages, Latin ceased to become a native language. Or at the very least, Latin changed radically, moving from a multi-registered form of oral and written discourse to the primary language of early medieval graphic culture; there is a difference between, say, Cicero and Gregory the Great, or Tacitus and Isidore of Seville.[2] Fifteenth-century humanists reflected on the problem of ancient Latin's evolution in ways that grew increasingly pointed as that century wore on, even as these debates revealed much about how these thinkers saw themselves in relation to classical antiquity. Steeped in a culture whose members routinely used the basic biological metaphor of birth, growth, flourishing, and decline, Renaissance thinkers had no hesitation in linking the changes in the Latin language with the "decline" of ancient Roman greatness. Certain thinkers, too, in their history writing recognized unabashedly that the invasions had changed the shape of Europe irrevocably, but the directions in which they saw things moving thereafter can seem surprising to modern readers.

Moreover, throughout the fifteenth century, there were thinkers on the vanguard of scholarly accomplishment who were interested not only in later Latin but also in miscellany-oriented scholarship, well represented in the second century of the common era by the work of Aulus Gellius, early though he may be in the traditional chronologies of Late Antiquity. This type of scholarly endeavor, in which the particular is favored over the general, flourishes once a moment arrives when leading cultural actors believe that a phase of "classicism" has been reached. Again, evolution, change, and finality are implied, as canons solidify and as certain works take pride of place as acknowledged classics among literate elites.

On the other hand and on the "continuity and plurality" side of the ledger, one focal point within recent scholarship on Late Antiquity has been an emphasis on religion and philosophy (themselves now disciplinary phenomena that have been retrospectively separated but that, in late ancient practice, were often intimately linked).[3] For Renaissance thinkers, the recovery of an at times bewildering variety of ancient texts hinted at this late ancient plurality of religious and philosophical visions, even as some Renaissance thinkers, for a short time, attempted to recover the plurality suggested by those texts. What can it mean when one is a devoted fifteenth-century Christian who discovers texts and practices from the late ancient world, promulgated by notorious anti-Christians, that nevertheless are similar in kind to texts and practices that were part of the fabric of Christianity? How does one integrate these texts into a coherent vision of one's place in the world and one's own relation to the divine?

These three tendencies—the realization on the part of Renaissance thinkers that ancient Latin had been a "living" ancient language and the links to history writing, the miscellany-oriented style of scholarship, and the diversity of late ancient religiosity—serve to frame the fifteenth-century Italian Renaissance's relation to Late Antiquity.

The Latin Language

Renaissance "humanism" can be defined in many ways, but any definition would have to include respect for the ancient Greco-Roman world; a desire to excavate its texts, monuments, and eventually material culture; and, importantly, an attempt to integrate that passion for the ancient world with a renewed attention to the Latin language.[4] Humanism in this respect represented a broad intellectual movement that contained within it different strands, one of the most distinctive of which was the decision to write classicizing Latin. If this project began in northern Italy in the late thirteenth century, certainly one of its most prominent milestones was reached during the life and career of Francesco Petrarca, or Petrarch (1304–1374), the first humanist who achieved a Europe-wide fame.[5] It was with Petrarch that humanism acquired a historical self-consciousness, an important part of which was tied to the Latin language.

For Petrarch, Latin was the "root of our arts and the foundation of every branch of knowledge."[6] It was in Latin, rather than in his vernacular works, he told Boccaccio in a letter, that he wished to make his mark, given that Latin seemed the more serious and durable language. And while all medieval and Renaissance students of Latin learned by imitation, Petrarch's commitment to his beloved ancient Latin authors goes further than stylistics, as one observes, again, in a letter to Boccaccio, when Petrarch explains that there are certain authors that have, quite simply, become a part of him:

> I have read Virgil, Flaccus [i.e., Horace], Severinus [i.e., Boethius], Tullius [i.e., Cicero] not once but countless times, nor was my reading rushed but leisurely, pondering them as I went with all the powers of my intellect; I ate in the morning what I would digest in the evening, I swallowed as a boy what I would ruminate upon as an older man. I have thoroughly absorbed these writings, implanting them not only in my memory but in my marrow, and they have so become one with my mind that were I never to read them for the remainder of my life, they would cling to me, having taken root in the innermost recesses of my mind.[7]

This intimate commitment to certain Latin authors led Petrarch to scrutinize ancient texts, to do fundamental work reconstructing the text of Livy, and to recognize that there was something about the Latin then in use in schools and in the church that simply did not match the ancient Latin he loved so well. This sense in Petrarch was inchoate. He at times recognized the notion that custom changes speech, citing or alluding to traditional ancient sources that propound this position; elsewhere, for polemical purposes, Petrarch argues that certain varieties of Latin are immutable, as he does when he writes in his *Invectives against a Physician*, that "in the case of the Latin poets there is no change."[8] He was responding there to his adversary's charge that the truths of medical science were immutable whereas language was mutable, so that Petrarch had a polemical purpose in mind. Yet he does not consider this question in great depth, and if there is something to be sought in Petrarch on this question, it is the previously mentioned intimate connection to Latinity, something that he passed on to later generations, even if he never theorized it in an extended manner.[9]

Petrarch's successor in the generational scheme of Italian humanism, Coluccio Salutati (the figure with whom humanism became rooted for a time in Florence), did take a position regarding the progress of ancient Latin, though in his case one that was not worked out in a very schematic fashion.[10] Still, two letters from among his large epistolary production are worthy of note, given that each possesses the elements that contributed to the growing sense among humanists that Latin was a language that needed to be studied as a historical phenomenon. The first letter allows Salutati to explain his growing conviction that there was something inorganic about the use of the plural *vos* as an honorific singular, a phenomenon that had grown in medieval Latin alongside evolving Romance languages.[11] Elsewhere, he wrote that the singular *tu* was used faithfully until recent times, though he does not specify exactly when the change took place.[12]

The second letter, from August 1395 and written to a Paduan cardinal, presents an evolutionary scheme.[13] Salutati is responding to the cardinal's earlier praise, to the effect that Salutati was such a good and prodigious letter writer that he surpassed even a respected ancient like Cassiodorus. Salutati avers that this cannot be the case, since antiquity supersedes modernity by an almost unimaginable extent. Salutati continues: "if you don't believe me, I'll place the writers themselves before your eyes."[14] If one considers that the height of ancient eloquence is to be placed in Cicero and in Cicero's era (Salutati asserts this judgment as a self-evident truth), then it becomes clear by what extent modernity falls short. Salutati then presents a short portrait of those writers found in Cicero's day, including a number whom he knows (and whom we know) primarily from Cicero's correspondence.[15] Salutati moves on to the next era, to those who "succeeded these times": Seneca (3 B.C.E.–65 C.E.), Valerius Maximus (20 B.C.E.–50 C.E.), and Livy (59 B.C.E.–17 C.E.). Tacitus (56–117) does not find himself in the same rank as these earlier writers. Then come Suetonius (71–135), Pliny the Younger (63–113), Martianus Capella (fl. fifth century), Apuleius (123/5–80), Macrobius (fl. 395–423), and others (the ordering is Salutati's), "in whose writings it can be seen . . . to what extent that majesty of ancient speech which reached its apex in Cicero had diminished."[16] Church fathers come next (and Salutati again places in one group figures whose dates span a number of centuries): Cassiodorus (490–585), Ambrose, Symmachus (ob. 514), Jerome, Augustine, Ennodius (474–521), Sidonius (430–485), and others. All lived in a time of an eloquence that had revived "in a certain way" (*quodammodo*), though Salutati emphasizes that they all form part of one age in which only a few were still able to raise their style to an appropriate level.[17]

Then there occurs a momentous change, and we find ourselves in the time of what we might term the "plural" medieval writers—that is, writers who had fallen off into such decadence of style that they could only be referred to in the plural: "Ivos, Bernards, Hildeberts, Peters of Blois, Peters of Abelard, Richards de Pofi, Johns of Salisbury and many others who never worried themselves too much about eloquence."[18] These authors cannot even be compared to any of those ancient writers, from whom they differ as much in style as they do in temporal distance.

Commenting on his own time, Salutati writes: "The study of literature has risen somewhat in our day; and the first cultivator of eloquence was your own Paduan, [Albertino da] Mussato, as well as Geri d'Arezzo, the greatest imitator . . . of the orator Pliny the Younger."[19] Salutati ends his historical survey: "Those Florentine lights have also risen: I will pass over Dante Alighieri, the highest glory of vernacular eloquence, who can be compared to no one who has flourished in our day or even to any of the ancients in his knowledge or intelligence. Petrarch and Boccaccio have also come forth, all of whose works, if I am not mistaken, posterity will celebrate. Still, I think no one capable of judging rightly is unaware how much they differ in capacity of speaking from those ancients."[20] How then could Salutati ever imagine that he might come out ahead of Cassiodorus, when he cannot be preferred not only to any of the ancients but also to any of the moderns?

Salutati's view, then, is that the Latin language went through phases of evolution that one could roughly chart, with its apogee in the time of Cicero (when no one would have dreamed of using the plural honorific). Latin eloquence was then kept alive by a number of writers up to about the sixth century; it declined thereafter, arriving at its nadir in the era of the scholastics, and then, beginning with Mussato, the study of Latin literature began its slow upward progress, even if it was obvious how great was the distance between even the best modern writers and the giants of antiquity.

Members of the next intellectual generation both felt and, to an extent, questioned this sense of living in a time of revival. The circle of intellectuals who gathered around Salutati proved energetic and able both in their continuing investigation of the ancient world and in their perfection in writing an appropriately classicizing Latin. There emerged from that group one thinker, Leonardo Bruni (1370–1444), who embodied a number of that generation's most prominent tendencies.[21] He had learned Greek quite well at the feet of Manuel Chrysoloras, the visiting Greek diplomat whom Salutati and his circle persuaded to stay in Florence for three years in the late 1390s.[22] Bruni translated any number of Greek works, even as he wrote some of the early fifteenth century's most lasting Latin literature: a *Panegyric of Florence* modeled on Aelius Aristides' panegyric of Athens; a short dialogue in two books that showed Bruni's generation's thoughts on the question of where they stood in relation both to their beloved ancients and to Florence's most famous fourteenth-century thinkers, Dante, Petrarch, and Boccaccio; and a host of other works, from a famous *History of Florence* to a series of biographies, all of which had wide circulation.[23]

Bruni was also for a time a prominent member of the papal court as an apostolic secretary. Bruni's association with the papal court was long and occasionally interrupted, until 1427, when he returned definitively to Florence to assume the post of chancellor (the same position held by his beloved mentor,

Salutati). Toward the end of that period, a debate emerged among the court's humanist members, regarding the question, as one of them put it, "whether the language spoken in Rome was its own particular idiom"; in other words, did the revered ancients possess a formalized language with its own set of seemingly permanent rules and also have a day-to-day vernacular? Or did the ancients actually speak Latin, in more or less the way its written remains would indicate?[24]

Among those intellectuals serving at the papal court was Biondo Flavio (1392–1463), and it was he who initiated this fifteenth-century debate with Bruni.[25] Biondo begins his lengthy epistolary treatise by reminding Bruni of the recent discussion that took place at the papal court. Bruni, along with a few others, had argued that in antiquity there were indeed two very distinct registers, not dissimilar from the modern era. Biondo, on the other hand, argued, as he wrote to Bruni, "that the words, as they were spoken, were Latin of the sort that we now call 'literate.'"[26] Biondo, in short, believed that the ancients wrote more or less as they spoke, and in making his case, he used many of the arguments that continued to be part of the debate for the next fifty years: examples in Cicero (specifically his *Brutus*, Cicero's account of the great orators of his day) show that it was possible to become an eloquent, admired speaker in Rome without a formal education; in the Roman General Assembly, the *contio*, the audience would not have understood what the orator was saying had there been a totally separate vernacular; people also would not have understood the comedies and tragedies that were performed as plays in front of a live audience if the written language was not formally similar to the spoken; and even the ancients themselves show a consciousness of change in the Latin language. For this last point Biondo draws only on Cicero's *Brutus*, again, but the next decades would see humanists expand upon this argument. Finally, almost as an afterthought, Biondo addresses the question of change: how did things get to be the way they are? How did our vernacular emerge from this pristine ancient tongue? His answer is worth noting: "But after the City of Rome was taken by Goths and Vandals and began to be inhabited by them, it was not only one or two men who were tarnished, but rather everyone who was polluted and indeed made deeply impure [*penitus sordidati*] by foreign speech. So it gradually happened that, in place of Roman Latinity, we have this common vernacular that has been mixed together with foreign Latinity [*barbarica* sc. *latinitate*], that has the character of something inauthentic."[27]

Biondo Flavio can justly be described as the first historian of medieval Europe. He wrote a "History" in the familiar Livian "decade" model from "the decline of the Empire of the Romans," beginning essentially with Alaric's 410 Sack of Rome and moving to his own era.[28] Biondo's comments to Bruni reveal that there was a language-based foundation for his interest in "decline." Bruni, in his laconic response, maintains the traditional position that the ancients, like the moderns, had two distinct languages, a vernacular and a polished language. Tellingly, Bruni does not address the question, raised at the end of Biondo's letter, regarding the changes in the Latin language in the wake of the barbarian invasions.

As this debate progressed in the fifteenth century, other thinkers did address those changes, seeing the barbarian invasions as a key factor in the transformation of ancient Latin. Here is the famed polymath Leon Battista Alberti (1404–1472), in the preface to book three of his Tuscan classic, *Della famiglia*, as he tries to answer the question why the Latin language fell into disuse. He writes: "Italy was occupied and possessed more than once by various peoples: Gauls, Goths, Vandals, Lombards, and other similarly barbarous ones who were extremely harsh."[29] To facilitate communication among different language communities, Latin speakers learned other languages, and the newly arrived peoples learned Latin, though the foreigners learned Latin, "I believe, with many barbarisms and corruption in the pronunciation. Because of this mixture our language, which once was quite cultivated and refined, gradually became rough and spoiled."[30]

The educator Guarino of Verona (1370–1460) adopted and adapted a distinction from the medieval tradition to describe Latin's evolution in a fourfold fashion. After the perfection of the third age (the time of Cicero), the fourth age followed, characterized by a mixing together of different forms and the subsequent corruption of the language.[31] The "undeleted footsteps [*indeleta vestigia*]" of the barbarians "stained the splendid brilliance of Roman eloquence."[32] Others could be cited who reflected what became, by the end of the fifteenth century, a common position: since on the one hand Latin was a "dead" language, but on the other was still necessary for education, politics, and the Roman Catholic religion, one needed to educate Europe's elites in a form of the language that was authentically ancient but that also encompassed the fact that Latin ceased to be a native language in what we would term the early Middle Ages.[33]

As leading humanist thinkers reflected over time on the progress of ancient Latin and came to the realization that it had, indeed, been a natural language, the understanding was also implicit that historicity as such was a force with which one always needed to reckon. The sense that there were provable changes in Latin, a language that at least in theory had seemed the one form of human expression that was permanent and unchanging, went hand in hand with a more sophisticated historical sense, or at least one that included more sources than had been previously available. A number of the Renaissance's leading thinkers carried this new historical sense forward in ways that impinge directly on their understanding of what is now called Late Antiquity. Biondo Flavio, as mentioned, chose to begin his history precisely at the moment of "decline." There were many literary and historical monuments to Rome's period of flourishing, Biondo wrote in his preface, "but," he continued, "the greatest darkness obscures and covers over that same City's [i.e., Rome's] defeats and the end of its fame. It therefore seemed to me to be worth the effort to unmask and bring to light for all posterity the remarkable misdeeds of those 1030 years since the City was captured by the Goths up to the present day."[34] Biondo covers in his history the fate of the former Roman provinces (including ultramontane ones) up to about the year 600 but then restricts himself to the evolution of Rome and Italy, with a focus on Christianization, the positive result, as it happened, of the calamitous invasions.

Another monument of fifteenth-century historiography was Leonardo Bruni's *History of the Florentine People*. There, Bruni's focus is precisely on the great deeds and overall character of the "Florentine people" over time. His uses of Late Antiquity are revealing in the way that they contribute to his pro-Florentine goals, even as they manifest clearly the basic perception that the "late antique" was a time of decline. Yet if the typology of "decline" seems an indivisible element of a common historiographical scheme, Bruni does put that scheme to interesting use. He writes: "Before the Romans took over, many cities and peoples flourished magnificently in Italy, and under the Roman empire all of them declined. After the fall of Rome, on the other hand, the other cities began immediately to raise their heads and flourish. What her growth had taken away, her decline restored."[35] As he explores the prehistory of Florence, he idealizes the pre-Roman Etruscans, since "before the Roman empire [he means here, as previously, simply Roman power] the greatest wealth and power in Italy and the greatest fame in war and peace belonged to the Etruscans."[36]

For Bruni, it is the destruction of the Republic that represented the real decline of Rome. A series of emperors took away the people's liberty, and from the time of Nero on, "the emperors were all of the same mind, fearing anyone in whom they could detect some excellence, hating whomever they feared, and killing with the sword whomever they hated. At last hatred would overcome fear, and they themselves would also be cut down."[37] Bruni goes on: "So many murders and assassinations, and the revolutions that in the end followed them, could not but lead to the weakening and decline of the Empire. Roman power began little by little to drain away and her grandeur to decline, eventually falling into foreign hands for lack of native citizens."[38] Rome remained safe until Constantine moved the seat of the empire east, and the result was that "the emperors thereafter began to view Italy and the western part of the empire almost as the abandoned part, to be neglected and left exposed to the invasions of tyrants and barbarians."[39] The barbarians, who "inundated the land," come in for description, and Bruni discusses the waxing and waning of different alliances of the Romans and Goths. Eventually, he offers a quite detailed discussion of matters such as the events of 410, when "the Goths swept freely over Italy and at last . . . furiously invaded that city which had conquered the world, defiling everything with slaughter and bloodshed—except the sacred places, for which they did show some respect, barbarians though they were."[40] Bruni covers the 452 march westward of Attila and Pope Leo's famous confrontation with the fearsome Hun leader, the attacks of the Vandals, Belisarius' ultimately inefficacious victories, the arrival in Italy of the Lombards, and finally Charlemagne's role in Italian affairs, whence "was born the division of the Roman empire which still exists today."[41]

Bruni then dilates on the fortunes of Roman rule. For him, the real decline was to be seen in the loss of liberty that obtained with the breakup of the Republic. Bruni writes that "the reality and name of empire emerged under the consuls and dictators and military tribunes, the magistrates of a free people. . . . Unconquered by external foes, this people was overwhelmed at last by internal discord and civil war."[42] Bruni and others in his Florentine cohort passionately believed in Florence as an idealized "republic."[43] He and others repeatedly associated the word *libertas* with Florence, and as he goes on his narration, immediately after the just-cited passage, the message is hard to miss: "From that time forth, emperors began to be chosen, and the word *imperator*, which before had meant arms and forts, was brought, as it were, within the city walls as though to signal continuous civil war. The word still referred to a legitimate function, but in reality it signified lordship and domination. Surrounded by armed troops, the citizens were cowed into subservience."[44] Bruni goes on in his overview of the Roman empire during "Late Antiquity," averring that after Odoacer's deposition of Augustulus, "the empire ceased to exist for almost three hundred years."[45] Bruni's *History of the Florentine People*, begun when he was in full vigor and continued until his death, served as a model for a new kind of history writing, one that married a judicious use of sources with a characteristic premodern historiographical aim: the use of examples to instruct a presumed elite. Bruni's usage there of Late Antiquity was perfectly in line with that aim.

Later in life, Bruni struck a more elegiac tone as he undertook his *Italian War against the Goths*. Here a set of events in Late Antiquity serves a different function. He writes in the preface that "it is indeed the business of history to make a literary record of the times whether they are prosperous or adverse, and so, though one prefers better times, one must write about whatever happened."[46] Yet, despite the tone, his preface also reveals another underlying assumption, shared with Biondo and setting him off from a more modern, Gibbon-style view of Late Antiquity as tied to "decline": "As I write these pages, though there are many things that trouble me because of the strong love I feel for my country, I am nevertheless consoled by the following consideration: that even though Italy at that time suffered the most adverse fortune, she was eventually victorious over the foreign invaders, and has remained powerful on land and sea down to our time; her cities, adorned with great wealth, have enjoyed great power in the past and enjoy it today; their glory and jurisdiction extend far and wide."[47] One can observe that there was never any doubt in his mind, or indeed in Biondo's, that something calamitous happened with the traditional "end" of the Roman empire: a great civilization, in Bruni's eyes tied to a great republican tradition of which it had long lost sight, had over time ossified, succumbed to its increasingly lazy citizens' worst impulses, and lost its power.

If for Gibbon the end of the empire meant the "triumph of barbarism and religion" and was to be lamented as such, for Bruni and Biondo the scheme was not so pessimistic. While neither of them seems captive to a providential plan, along the lines of Augustine, nevertheless, the Christian centuries, for Biondo, and the medieval flourishing of the Italian city-states, for Bruni, balanced the loss of ancient Roman culture. Decline there had been: all their requisite sources testified to this notion, deeply embedded as it was in the narratives their culture prized. Both believed there were lessons to be learned from that decline, Bruni especially, even if both changed the focus in their narratives of the medieval centuries to zero in ultimately on exemplary events, those involving individuals and those involving polities, that testified to a kind of reflourishing.

Intellectual history contains within it the story of various cultural moments in which canons become solidified, augmented, or the cause of conscious reflection. Another way to understand the presence of the late antique in the Renaissance is to use canons as a backdrop, something that brings into relief two distinct Italian Renaissance moments, both connected to the late antique: first, what we might term a "Gellian" moment and, second, another cultural moment (also the result of a radical expansion of the canon), which can be described as Platonizing.

The first, Gellian moment, recalls Aulus Gellius, the second-century C.E. author whose *Attic Nights* preserved notes from conversations he had during long winter nights in Attica, so he tells readers in the preface.[48] Divided into twenty books (of which book eight is lacking except for its index), this text recorded notable short questions and answers on topics relating to literature, history, philosophy, geography, and a host of other subjects. Gellius might be considered early in terms of the traditional dating of Late Antiquity, but even if we can see him at the outer edges of the usual chronologies, there is something striking about his method of composition that points to the late antique as a cultural phenomenon: *Attic Nights* is a miscellany, with no apparent order to its contents, and yet there are moments of intellectual virtuosity within it, sometimes all the more powerful for their lack of intellectual arrangement. This type of learned genre of writing can have different functions across a number of diverse cultural environments. One of the most prominent is the manner in which this genre allows its practitioners to reflect on a sense of "classicism" already achieved, even as they use this apparently artless form to define their own intellectual identities, shaped as those are by the classics that loomed before them, as giants on whose shoulders they could only hope to stand.[49]

Gellius had been known to Augustine, to twelfth-century scholars, and to Petrarch.[50] Yet in the fifteenth century, Gellius' preface was rediscovered, and it was a fortuitous time: the 1420s and 1430s, when making excerpt notebooks came to be seen as an important vehicle by which scholars could control and have at their disposal a quantity of information that was increasing exponentially.[51]

Gellius' preface, in which he described his method, told thinkers of the early fifteenth century something they were ready to hear:

> But in the arrangement of my material I have adopted the same haphazard order that I had previously followed in collecting it. For whenever I had taken in hand any Greek or Latin book, or had heard anything worth remembering, I used to jot down whatever took my fancy, of any and every kind, without any definite plan or order; and such notes I would lay away as an aid to my memory, like a kind of literary storehouse, so that when the need arose of a word or a subject which I chanced for the moment to have forgotten, and the books from which I had taken it were not at hand, I could readily find and produce it.[52]

Gellius suggests that a man of good literary taste ought to be conversant with a number of different branches of learning, presenting in *Attic Nights* a "kind of foretaste of the liberal arts; and never to have heard of these, or come in contact with them, is at least unbecoming, if not positively harmful, for a man with even an ordinary education."[53] This short preface can be seen as a manifesto for a style of life that humanists were at once celebrating and creating: one where the reading of venerated ancient material never ends, questions about that material arise, and resolution of those questions in the context of civil conversation became an ideal often aimed at, if, perhaps, less often achieved.

On one hand, the Gellian model was reflected in a number of dialogues of the fifteenth century. None is more appropriate than a little-studied Latin dialogue, set dramatically at the Ferrarese court of Leonello D'Este in the 1440s and written piecemeal in the 1450s and 1460s, titled *On Literary Polish*.[54] Its author, Angelo Decembrio (a humanist writer who worked as a scribe and bibliographer in Spain, Milan, Ferrara, and elsewhere), sets forth in this work a vision of cultural competency that foreshadows some of the sixteenth century's later conduct manuals, even as it also encompasses fifteenth-century ideas. At the outset, Decembrio explicitly refers to Gellius as a model. In the preface, he writes to his dedicatee, Pope Pius II: "So that you might understand, briefly, the order of the book: it has been modeled on Aulus Gellius' *Attic Nights*, or rather on Quintilian's *Institutions*, and the very same advantage that comes from dividing it up into parts and books has been preserved. Indeed, here the book treats no less of oratorical and poetic skill."[55] The reference to Quintilian adds extra authority, suggesting that for Decembrio there is a pedagogical aim; indeed, his work is more ordered than Gellius. But Gellius seems the presiding *numen*, even when it comes to the interlocutors who inhabit the dialogue. A bit later, Decembrio writes:

> To Aulus Gellius, whose example, as well as that of Quintilian, I have promised in this book to imitate, it seemed like a good idea to choose Favorinus and a few others, as if they represented his more frequent teachers. As to me, I have decided in this "Polish" to pick Prince Leonello, Guarino da Verona, and those few but rather famous men who used to carry on disputations with them.[56]

Guarino, one of the fifteenth century's best-known humanist educators, is the voice of scholarly reasonableness in the dialogue. Added force accrues to his character, since it was he who seems primarily responsible for creating the "vulgate" text of Gellius; reconstructing its proper sequence, including the all-important preface; and coming up with a text that served as a basis for the countless manuscripts and printed editions known to the Renaissance.[57]

As the dialogue proceeds, the interlocutors' exemplary functions loom large, even as the overall purpose of the work hints at larger cultural factors beyond its immediate environment. Decembrio's dialogue is less random-seeming than Gellius' text, especially at the outset, as his interlocutors discuss the ideal humanist library: how it should appear, with what books it should be stocked, how one can discern forgeries, and so on. There is a concern for ordering knowledge in the face of a vast, and increasingly growing, classical heritage, and as the dialogue proceeds, there is also the kind of brief, learned discussion on seemingly unrelated points well known to readers of Gellius. Whether certain lines from Cicero should be excised (2.13), the meaning of certain abbreviations in inscriptions (5.54), the significance of the Vatican obelisk (5.55): these and other matters are discussed. Decembrio's Gellian fascination foregrounds the Renaissance's endless preoccupation with antiquity, its love of dialogue, and the point these phenomena had reached by the middle of the fifteenth century.

On the other hand, the Gellian inspiration could serve to induce deeper, more mature reflections, as they did in the fifteenth century's masterpiece of Gellian inspiration, Angelo Poliziano's *Miscellanea*. Poliziano, the fifteenth century's best philologist, completed one "century," or set of one hundred, of these notes during his lifetime, and he left behind an incomplete second century, which was published only in the twentieth century.[58] Poliziano consciously claims Gellius as an inspiration among the Latins (and Aelian among the Greeks), and in the very first note, Poliziano uses a small-seeming matter in Cicero's *Tusculan Disputations* to open up a much broader discussion.[59] At *Tusc.* 1.10.22, Cicero, defining various positions on the soul, says that for Aristotle the soul could be described using the Greek term *endelecheia*. Poliziano opens the discussion by referring to a revered Byzantine thinker who had taught at the Florentine university and with whom Poliziano himself had studied, John Argyropoulos.[60] Poliziano writes that Argyropoulos used to say that Cicero had got this wrong, not understanding that the Aristotelian term should be *entelecheia*, a word that denotes the traditional Aristotelian position and that Aristotle himself uses to describe the soul as a point of completion, the "form" of the person insofar as the form in this case represents the actualization of the hylomorphic entity that the person represents. Cicero's word, instead, suggests that the soul is, as it was for Plato, a principle of motion. The fact that Argyropoulos had been in the habit of saying (so Poliziano reports) that Cicero had been ignorant, not only of Greek but also of philosophy, impels Poliziano to find a way of buttressing Cicero's reputation.

Poliziano uses this textual difficulty to open up a discussion that is as wide-ranging as it is precisely informative. He begins casually enough—indeed, almost playfully—casting his short text as a "defense of Cicero" and more broadly as a defense of the Latins against the Greeks. Still, he goes further than fifteenth-century cliché. Poliziano adduces a series of ancient authorities who praised Cicero's wide-ranging philosophical knowledge and his abilities in Greek. He even retells an anecdote from Plutarch's *Life of Cicero*, to the effect that a Greek contemporary of Cicero, Apollonius Molon, after hearing Cicero speak in Greek, expressed wonder at Cicero's abilities and lamented that what the Greeks thought of as their own unique purchase on eloquence had now passed to the Romans.[61] Throughout his text, Poliziano goes beyond shoring up Cicero's abilities. As he does elsewhere in his work, Poliziano takes account of the late ancient commentators on Aristotle: Alexander of Aphrodisias, Porphyry (in his commentary on the *Categories*), Themistius (in his paraphrase of the second book of Aristotle's *De anima*), and Simplicius, among others, are all mentioned in his discussion.[62] This is not to say, for Poliziano, that Cicero was wrong in his choice of words.

Poliziano's argument is twofold. One trajectory is a standard one for Renaissance thinkers: manuscript transmission is inherently unreliable. The difference of one letter, a *d* versus a *t*, would be unsurprising. Given that Cicero was closer in time to Aristotle than the late ancient commentators, it is likely that he had it right, even if later readings were different. Cicero may have had access to the now-lost exoteric Aristotelian works, in which the conception of soul as continuous motion, as in Plato's *Phaedrus*, might have been more prominent.[63]

The other strand of Poliziano's argument is more interesting, reflecting as it does a theory that has late ancient roots and that has only recently come back into serious scholarly discussion. This is the notion of a fundamental concord between Plato and Aristotle perceived by many late ancient commentators, which Lloyd Gerson has recently brought into relief.[64] For Poliziano, the difference in terminology reflects the fact that different terms, even different fundamental conceptions, do not have to reflect foundational differences between philosophers. Like his friend Pico della Mirandola, from whom he says here that he draws inspiration, Poliziano, like many late ancient commentators, believed both that Plato and Aristotle were in agreement about certain fundamental issues and that the enterprise of philosophy was so large that a division of labor was necessary. If the soul could be seen as the body's final actuality (*entelecheia*), there was also room to concede that it could be seen as an "animating force" or principle of motion (*endelecheia*). Philosophy was large enough to have room for different though ultimately compatible views on important subjects, even if individuals might not always possess intellects capacious enough to encompass these ideas.

Poliziano's position reveals his contact with what can now be seen as a late ancient trend toward finding concord between Plato and Aristotle. The elements that helped bring this trend into being are worthy of reflection. As to Late Antiquity, at least three can be included: first, the establishment of texts and bodies of work as canonical "classics," such as Plato and Aristotle were by the era of Plotinus; second, a system of slow, repetitive reading coupled with oral and eventually written commentary designed to make these classics make sense, at first in a pedagogical situation and then, when in the realm of graphic culture, as elements themselves part of an evolving tradition; and third, again in Late Antiquity, a tendency shared by pagans and Christians to look at philosophical reflection through the prism of monotheism.

"Monotheism" should be understood here not as the adherence to any one system of religious rituals but rather as the projection into logical space of a unitary absolute, along with the philosophical and ideological consequences of that projection. As recent students of Late Antiquity have argued, a key flashpoint among pagans and Christians in, say, the second and third centuries C.E. lay in the realm of language and naming.[65] Celsus, for example, in his late-second-century *On True Doctrine* (preserved in Origen's *Contra Celsum*), wrote that "it makes no difference whether we call Zeus the Most High or Zeus or Adonai or Sabaoth or Amoun like the Egyptians, or Papaeus like the Scythians."[66] The nature of the god was assumed to be the same, whatever regional differences there might have been in cultic practice (and thus whatever concomitant need for linguistic and cultural translation appertained). Yet the Judeo-Christian God was the God who had said "I am Who am," and Christianity, as it grew to be theorized in the early Christian centuries, was not considered the property of one region: Jesus was Jesus, and all who chose to do so could in theory respect his teachings, worship him, and thus belong to the specifically Christian *oikoumene*. Combined with this numinous power, there arose a particular conception of "energized" language when referring to divinity. A certain type of naming was perceived to carry its own particular divine charge, with a sympathy being assumed between the god and the name. Even a committed anti-Christian, Iamblichus (who tellingly lived more than a century later than Celsus), could write in his *De mysteriis* that the original name of a god should not be translated.[67] Overt divisions between "pagans" and "Christians" there indeed were, but as is often the case in such polemics, they were fighting over some of the same basic questions and carrying similar assumptions into the arguments. Renaissance rediscovery of many of the key texts in which these discussions were carried out brought with it explosive possibilities.

Returning to the Renaissance, it is apparent that the elements listed (the establishment of "classical" authors; a pedagogy designed to study, reinforce, and reinterpret those authors; and monotheism as a basis for reflection) were still in force, in a basic sense. Yet much had changed. First, well into the era of Augustine, it was far from clear that Christianity (however diversely it wound up being practiced on a local level in the Middle Ages) would emerge as the one dominant form of religious cult. In the intervening centuries, Christianity had indeed become the dominant form of religious practice, at least in western

Europe. Second, many of the key texts of Late Antiquity, lost to the West in the Middle Ages, were recovered in the fifteenth century. If Poliziano, in his discussion on the soul, foregrounds his knowledge of many of those recently recovered late ancient texts (there specifically a number of the late ancient commentators on Aristotle come to the fore), his friendly rival in late-fifteenth-century Florence, Marsilio Ficino (1433–1499), presents a different perspective, though with him, again, the late ancient texts are key to his method and worldview.

Though he did not himself articulate it in this fashion, the most important lens through which to view Ficino and his relation to Late Antiquity is that of religious orthodoxy: the question was not whether to be a Christian but, rather, what precisely did being a Christian mean? What were the limits of the practices that could be contained within Christianity's larger compass? What texts and authors could a true Christian allow himself to study and engage creatively as sources of reflection? Ficino lived, on one hand, before both the Protestant Reformation and the Council of Trent. On the other hand, his century saw the recovery of a plethora of late ancient texts, many authored by professed anti-Christians, that nonetheless shared a broad family resemblance to Christianity in their central assumptions, especially when it came to the sacramental power of ritual.[68]

One of the difficulties in the history of later Platonic philosophy is the manner in which it has been sanitized by an idealist-oriented historiography of philosophy, beginning, arguably, in the middle eighteenth century with the foundational *Historia critica philosophiae* of Johann Jakob Brucker.[69] There, in his introduction, Brucker made it clear that what had in prior centuries been termed "philosophy" needed to be restricted, so that the word henceforth should denominate that branch of knowledge that can discern and teach the truths accessible to human beings by means of reason alone (whereas theology was that branch of knowledge intended to discern those truths accessible and understandable through revelation). The term had come to be applied promiscuously, in his view, covering even law, medicine, and literature. The historian of philosophy's job was to find (Brucker says "to dig out") what was "systematically" philosophical when he reached back into the past to reconstruct philosophy.[70] In short, Brucker, and the many who followed in his wake, conceived of philosophy in such a way that an entire set of concerns often very important in its history were left out.[71] Religion, law, and a practice-based ethics with examples often drawn from literature all formed part of a notion near and dear to philosophy before the Cartesian era: philosophy as a way of life.[72] When it comes to later Platonism, the area most important here in its relation to Ficino, omitting the "religious" from one's conception of philosophy presents an incomplete picture of the course of later Platonism, from Plotinus, Porphyry, and Iamblichus on through to the end of the fifth century and Proclus.

As to Plotinus, he bequeathed a series of notions that remained part of western philosophy: a hierarchical ordering of reality, with immaterial divinity at the top, and matter and the everyday world we inhabit at the bottom; a propensity toward monotheism; and the belief that one must turn within oneself to communicate with the divine.[73] Yet a decided turn toward including religious ritual within the purview of the "philosopher" became part of later Platonism with the ascendancy of Porphyry's student and eventual antagonist, Iamblichus (c. 245–c. 325), embarrassed about this ritualistic turn as an idealist historiography has been at times. Plotinus' mentalism had served an important function: it enabled him to define the lifestyle of a "philosopher," that is, a person who by the use of mentalistic spiritual exercise could successfully ascend the universe's ontological hierarchy, eventually to achieve ecstatic union with its supreme principle, the One. Yet, as he was writing, a great change was occurring in the late ancient world, among both pagans and Christians. This change had to do precisely with the power and importance of rituals. Iamblichus openly embraced the notion that all people, philosophers included, could and should engage in rituals to assist them in that process of Neoplatonic ascent. For Iamblichus, these rituals fell under the rubric of the term *theourgia*, or "theurgy." These rituals could include chants, the use of "signed" objects (like certain stones, plants, and herbs), and sun worship. These and other techniques exploited the hidden "sympathies," or links that were believed to exist in the cosmos between the earthly and the celestial. Iamblichus in his *De mysteriis* ("On the Mysteries") defines *theurgy* as the efficacious performance of "ineffable acts beyond all human understanding."[74] The Greek etymology of the word *theurgy* (*theion*, "divine," plus *ergon*, "work") suggests that someone engaging in theurgy is "doing divine work," or even "working the divine," the latter meaning suggesting that the human operator has a certain measure of efficacy. This efficacy could be assured only if the rituals were done correctly, so that outward human action, rather than Plotinian inwardness, became thereafter part of Neoplatonic tradition.

Iamblichus also expanded the canon of texts that were thought appropriate to the mission of Platonism. To give one example, he was the first to endorse the dignity of the *Hermetic Corpus*, a body of writings written primarily in Greek mostly in the second century C.E.[75] Like many of his contemporaries, Iamblichus believed these writings were authored by an ancient Egyptian, pre-Platonic sage, thought roughly contemporary with Moses. Hermes Trismegistus served symbolically as a fountainhead of ancient, mysterious, "Egyptian" wisdom.[76] Iamblichus' appropriation of this and other extra-Platonic material broadened the base of texts that could be used in the process of exegesis necessary to find Plato's "true meaning"; it meant that, from Iamblichus' day on, Neoplatonism as an approach would be intentionally eclectic, its representatives seeking out the one unitary truth believed to be contained in many philosophical and religious systems, and it led to a connection with Christianity that lasted until modern times.

As the texts in which these debates and positions were recorded were lost to western thinkers, a set of assumptions emerged that were widely shared as normative, transmitted as they were through the work of St. Augustine and ps.-Dionysius the Areopagite. These included an immaterial, notionally superior world that superintended our mundane material one and whose majesty could be accessed sacramentally; the conception of the human soul as an immortal, discretely individual entity subject to rewards and punishments after death; and a stance toward ascetic meditation that suggested that through it the human being could even in this life, if rarely, have ecstatic contact with the divine. Ficino, like all late medieval Christians, inherited these positions and assumptions. Yet he also was among the first in the West to take a serious and synoptic look at the course of later Platonism, which for him formed part of the divine revelation that had reached a high point in Christ but that continued to be revealed through later interpreters.

Ficino termed this process of continuous revelation the *prisca theologia*, or "ancient theology," and he conceived of it as something rooted in ancient sources.[77] These sources themselves needed continuous and creative reinterpretation by modern thinkers to have their authentic message shine forth. It was unthinkable to Ficino that the treasure trove of new sources uncovered by fifteenth-century thinkers could have no value, and it took an engaged interpreter to bring that value to the fore. Ficino's first encounters with Platonism took place in the 1450s, when as a young medical student he studied Greek. The early 1460s saw him win the attention of Florence's greatest patron, Cosimo de' Medici, an old lion by that point, who encouraged and sponsored Ficino's growing interest in all aspects of Platonism. Cosimo offered Ficino an important Greek manuscript containing Plato's works, and Ficino had access also to a newly found abundance of late ancient Platonic texts, including almost all of what is now possessed of Plotinus, Porphyry, Iamblichus, and Proclus, as well as all the para-Platonic texts that Iamblichus had made respectable, such as the *Hermetic Corpus* and the so-called *Chaldaean Oracles*.

Much in these texts was unremarkable, having been absorbed into late ancient and then medieval Christianity. Yet there were also uncomfortable facts: some of the authors, Porphyry and Iamblichus especially, were overtly anti-Christian, and within these texts there were practices and ideas difficult to square with late medieval Christian practices. Ficino took it as an integral component of his responsibility not only to translate these various texts from Greek to Latin—the Platonic corpus itself, Plotinus' *Enneads*, the works of Porphyry, Iamblichus, and Proclus—but also to explain them and to integrate them into the broad story of the *prisca theologia*.

All of Ficino's works, from his international correspondence network to his *summa*, the *Platonic Theology: On the Immortality of the Soul*, were suffused with references to many late ancient pagan thinkers.[78] A typical Ficinian technique was to report on a practice or idea while simultaneously averring that, though it might function effectively, he did not endorse it. At times, this sort of report could serve the function of "interpreting" a passage in an authority that seemed controversial. One example, from Ficino's *Three Books on Life*, will suffice to make the point.[79] After Plotinus came back into circulation, one problem that Christian thinkers had to confront was a key set of passages in the *Enneads* in which statue-animation was assumed as a reality. This notion raised the question of idolatry.

The *locus classicus* in Plotinus (at *Enneads* 4.3.11) was powerful, revealing much about relatively standard late ancient attitudes.[80] Plotinus wrote:

> And I think that the wise men of old, who made temples and statues in the wish that the gods should be present to them, looking to the nature of the All, had in mind that the nature of soul is everywhere easy to attract, but that if someone were to construct something sympathetic to it and be able to receive a part of it, it would of all things receive soul most easily. That which is sympathetic to it is what imitates it in some way.

When Plotinus writes "the wise men of old" (*hoi palai sophoi*), he is signaling the belief, especially strong in later Platonism, that he and others believed themselves the cultivators of a long tradition. Here the tradition points to the notion that statue animation belonged to an ancient Egyptian tradition embodied in the writings that constituted the *Hermetic Corpus*, especially to the dialogue *Asclepius*, as the lead interlocutor Hermes enlightens the youthful follower Asclepius:

> Our ancestors once erred gravely on the theory of divinity; they were unbelieving and inattentive to worship and reverence for god. But then they discovered the art of making gods. To their discovery they added a conformable power arising from the nature of matter. Because they could not make souls, they mixed this power in and called up the souls of demons or angels and implanted them in likenesses through holy and divine mysteries, whence the idols could have the power to do good and evil.[81]

For Plotinus, it was assumed that the "nature of soul" (*psyches physis*) was everywhere, able, in theory, to be harnessed for material, earthly ends. One needed to construct the right sorts of attractions to enable this process to take place; one needed, in short, to construct "something sympathetic" (*tis prospathes*). It should be stressed that Plotinus was the least inclined, among major later Platonists, to advocate this sort of use of "sympathies," tending more usually to focus on the need to concentrate one's inner energies on the pursuit of the philosophical life.

For other Platonists, especially Iamblichus, the use of ritualistic means to harness the universe's inner, if hidden, powers, was de rigueur. As Christianity evolved alongside later Platonism, certain of these notions were manifested in the way Christians conceived of sacraments, however vitriolic the disagreements between certain pagans and Christians may have seemed on the surface. For Christians, the outline of how sacraments worked was spelled out in St. Augustine's polemics against the Donatist heretics. Later in the Middle Ages, a name was given to this conception, to the effect that sacraments were thought to function *ex opere operato*, "from the work having been worked," which is to say that a sacrament would channel divine power efficaciously if the right ritual were carried out, no matter the moral status of the priest.[82]

One can see the position, then, in which Ficino found himself. On the one hand, there were clear family resemblances between the later Platonic approach to ritual and Christian sacramentalism: humanly initiated rituals designed to channel divine power, whether Christian transubstantiation or pagan theurgy, were assumed to function, since the existence of sympathies between the celestial and earthly realms were not a matter for debate. The questions were: what was permitted? How could a committed, though for his day liberally minded, Christian accommodate the fact that what to some seemed rival religious traditions possessed rituals that functioned just as effectively as Christian ones?

Ficino's method in confronting these questions reflects both his fears about transcending then-malleable orthodoxy and his propensity to see many religious and philosophical traditions as part of a larger whole. He deals with this passage in Plotinus and its ramifications in his *Three Books on Life*, a work written throughout the 1480s and published in 1489. The issue of statue animation raised its head in the third book of that work devoted to promoting the health of scholars, and Ficino signals his affinity to Plotinus at the outset: "Let no man wonder that Soul can be allured as it were by material forms, since indeed she herself has created baits of this kind suitable to herself, to be allured thereby. . . ."[83] Ficino's reasoning, when it comes to "sympathies," is typical and could have been uttered by any one of a number of premodern thinkers: ". . . if the rays of the stars quickly penetrate the whole earth, it cannot easily be denied that they quickly penetrate metal and precious stone when they are engraved with images, and imprint in them wonderful gifts, or at least gifts of some kind, since indeed they generate supremely precious things in the womb of the earth."[84] Like any number of late ancient thinkers, the fifteenth-century Platonist Ficino assumed that the undeniably present influence of the celestial bodes on earthly matters extended beyond what the naked eye could perceive; this relationship was natural, as natural as musical harmonies: "When one lute sounds, does not another one echo it?"[85]

His goal, he avers, is only to interpret Plotinus, yet he addresses the reader directly to say that he does so "provided I will have warned you here at the outset that you must not think I approve the use of images, only recount it."[86] Faced with what he conceives as undeniable evidence of the possibility of using images for earthly goals, Ficino is as ever on the borderline between orthodoxy and heterodoxy, as he refuses to endorse certain practices even as he admits their existence and power:

> It would be unduly curious and perhaps harmful to recite what images they fashioned and how, for the mutual meeting of minds or their alienation, for bringing felicity or inflicting calamity, either to some individual, or to a household, or to a city. I do not affirm that such things can be done. Astrologers, however, think such things can be done, and they teach the method, but I dare not tell it. Porphyry in the book where he sketches the life of his master Plotinus confirms that such can be done.[87]

Thereafter, Ficino recounts Porphyry's well-known anecdote, to the effect that Plotinus' great-souled nature was strong enough to repel a star-spell cast on him by the Egyptian magician Olympius.[88]

Ficino recognizes the positions on the topic of the power of "figures" of the two great thirteenth-century Dominicans, Albert the Great and his more famous pupil, Thomas Aquinas. Albert goes so far as to describe "images to bring calamity and prosperity to someone, which," Ficino hastens to add, "I deliberately pass over."[89] Albert "detests the prayers and fumigations which certain impious people have offered to daemons when they are making images," and yet he "does not disapprove of figures, letters, and sayings impressed upon images for the precise purpose of receiving some gift from a celestial figure. . . ."[90] Ficino discusses Aquinas, "our leader in theology," who "is more fearful of these practices and attributes less to images," even as "in his book *On Fate* he says the constellations give the order of existence and duration, not only to natural things but also to artificial; and that therefore images are fashioned under certain constellations. But if anything worthy of wonder happens to us through them outside the accustomed effects of nature, he rejects it as the work of daemons out to seduce people."[91] Ficino is ambivalent here regarding the power of graven images, made by human hand but nonetheless channeling the divine. He warns against these approaches, though he cannot resist reporting them, hinting at them, or "passing them over" (and thus precisely by his *praeteritio* drawing more attention to the forbidden).

Finally, these tendencies change, in Ficino's *Three Books on Life*, into a barely noticeable yet no less glimmering adumbration of the centuries to come. Even as Ficino looks back to his ancient, late ancient, and medieval sources, expressing an attitude that is characteristically premodern in its appreciation of occult forces such as sympathies, he also looks forward to the ongoing and increasingly more visible debate about the limits of the order of nature, when he mentions Iamblichus directly following the passages just quoted.

Iamblichus was important to Ficino, one of the first Platonists at which Ficino tried his hand as a fledgling Greek-to-Latin translator.[92] Ficino's discussion here at first possesses the same sense of back-and-forth ambivalence noted before:

> Even the Platonists attribute certain wonderful effects of images to the deceptions of daemons. For Iamblichus too says that those who place their trust in images alone . . . are very often deceived in this matter. . . . Iamblichus does not deny, however, that certain natural goods come to pass from images constructed according to a legitimate astrological plan.[93]

Then Ficino enters into the intellectual territory of an as yet untheorized modernity:

> I think, therefore, that it would be safer to trust oneself to medicines than to images; and that the things we said cause celestial power in images can have

> their efficacy rather in medicines than in figures. For it is probable that, if images have any power, they do not so much as acquire it just at the moment of receiving a figure as possess it through a material naturally so disposed; but if an image eventually acquired something when it was engraved, it obtained it not so much through the figure as through the heating produced by hammering.[94]

Ficino stands at the beginning of a three-century intellectual development in which thinkers wrestled with the problem of the limits of nature.[95] Ficino nowhere asserts definitively that a graven image has no actual power. Yet he questions the source of the power, verging toward the notion that the power derives from the natural process of heating rather than from the "figure" impressed upon the image.

Here and elsewhere, Ficino has no doubt that demons exist and can influence events, and the existence of sympathies and other occult forces is a given. Yet the language of natural explanation, undeveloped as it is here, served as part of the genetics of a long cultural conversation yet to come. The end result would be the severing of natural philosophy from philosophy as a whole, as post-Newtonian thinkers gradually but irrevocably conceived of a natural world in which no ultimately unexplainable sympathies could be thought to exist and demons were banished to the realm of literature and the fringes of intellectual life. Mysteries there might be in the natural world, but they were mysteries presumed to have natural solutions, undiscovered as these might be.

Ficino's world was much closer to the world of the late ancient thinkers, Christian and pagan, he so admired than to that of a post-Newtonian natural philosopher. The same could be said for other Renaissance thinkers, from Bruni and Biondo to Poliziano, whose lives and careers spanned the fifteenth century, a crucial period for the rediscovery, consolidation, and eventual absorption of many of Late Antiquity's key textual monuments.

NOTES

1. See Marcone 2008; James 2008; Ando 2008.

2. For some literature on this problem, see Löfstedt 1959; Wright 1991; 2002; Adams 2003; Clackson and Horrocks 2007, esp. 229–304.

3. Cf. James 2008, 25.

4. For an introduction to the literature on Italian Renaissance humanism, see Celenza 2004b; most recently, Hankins 2007.

5. For Petrarch and his importance, see Witt 2000; Rico 1993; Dotti 1992.

6. Petrarch, *Seniles*, 9.1 in Petrarch, *Opera Omnia*, 933–944, at 937; E. Casamassima, "L'autografo Riccardiano della seconda lettera del Petrarca a Urbino V (Senile IX 1)," which is the entire volume *Quaderni petrarcheschi* 3 (1985–1986), transcribes, at pp. 103–134, the letter from the autograph manuscript in MS Florence, Biblioteca Riccardiana,

972, ff.1–16v; the cited passage is at Casamassima, 116; see Rizzo 2002, 37; English trans. in Petrarch, *Letters of Old Age/Rerum senilium libri*, 1:304–327, at 312.

7. Petrarch, *Le familiari*, 22.2; Eng. trans. in Petrarch, *Letters On Familiar Matters*, 3:212.

8. Petrarch, *Invectives*, 94–95.

9. Cf. Witt 2000, 264–265.

10. On Salutati, see Witt 1983; 2000, 292–337.

11. Coluccio Salutati, *Epistolario*, 2:408–419; see Witt 2000, 324–326, whose analysis I follow here.

12. Salutati, *Epistolario*, 2:438, cit. Witt 2000, 325.

13. Salutati, *Epistolario*, 3:76–91.

14. Ibid., 3:80: "hec non michi credas velim, sed ipsos scriptores ante oculos tibi ponas."

15. Ibid., 3:80–81.

16. Ibid., 3:82: ". . . quorum scriptis percipitur quantum tractu temporis ornatus ille locutionis effloruit quantumque maiestas illa prisci sermonis, que cum Cicerone summum apicem tenuit, imminuta est."

17. Ibid.

18. Ibid., ". . . inciderint enim licet Ivones, Bernardi, Hildeberti, Petri Blesenses, Petri Abailardi, Riccardi de Pophis, Iohannes Saberii et alii plures, qui sibi nimis de eloquentia blanditi sunt." Salutati refers here, as Novati points out in note 2, to a number of medieval writers known for, among other things, epistolography: Ivo, bishop of Chartres (c. 1040–1117); Bernard, abbot of Clairvaux (1090–1153); Hildebert, archbishop of Lavardin (c. 1056–1133/34); Peter of Blois (c. 1135–1204); Peter Abelard (1079–1142); Riccardo de Pofi, an otherwise little-known member of the late-thirteenth-century papal court; and John of Salisbury (1115/20–1180).

19. Ibid., 84: "Emerserunt parumper nostro seculo studia litterarum; et primus eloquentie cultor fuit conterraneus tuus Musattus Patavinus, fuit et Gerius Aretinus, maximus Plinii Secundi oratoris . . . imitator."

20. Ibid.: "emerserunt et ista lumina florentina; ut summum vulgaris eloquentiae decus et nulla scientia vel ingenio comparandum qui nostris temporibus floruit, aut etiam cuipiam antiquorum, Dantem Allігherium, pretermittam; Petrarca scilicet et Bocaccius, quorum opera cuncta, ni fallor, posteritas celebrabit: qui tamen quantum ab illis priscis differant facultate dicendi nullum arbitror qui recte iudicare valeat ignorare."

21. On Bruni, see Hankins 2003–2004, 1:9–271; for cultural ambivalence in his generation, see Quint 1985, 423–445; Fubini 1992, 1065–1103; Witt 2000, 432–442.

22. For Chrysoloras' time in Florence and in general on Hellenic studies in Renaissance Italy, see Cortesi 1995; Ciccolella 2008.

23. A number of Bruni's works can be found in Leonardo Bruni 1996, *Opere letterarie e politiche*; for his *History*, see Leonardo Bruni 2001–2004, *History of the Florentine People*.

24. The key texts in the debate are edited and analyzed in Tavoni 1984; see also Celenza 2009; Mazzocco 1993; Fubini 1961.

25. On Biondo Flavio, see Fubini 1969; Hay 1958; Tavoni 1984.

26. Biondo in Tavoni 1984, 208: "Constet vero primum inter nos necessarium est, sive grandibus, sive abiectis, sive dissipatis, sive coercitis ratione verbis oratum fuerit, verba orationum, dum pronunciarentur, fuisse Latina, qualia nunc dicimus 'litterata'."

27. Ibid., 214–215: "Postea vero quam urbs a Gothis et Vandalis capta inhabitarique coepta est, non unus iam aut duo infuscati, sed omnes sermone barbaro inquinati ac penitus sordidati fuerunt; sensimque factum est, ut pro romana latinitate adulterinam hanc barbarica mixtam loquelam habeamus vulgarem."

28. See Hay 1958.

29. Leon Battista Alberti 1996, 6: "Fu Italia più volte occupata e posseduta da varie nazioni: Gallici, Goti, Vandali, Longobardi, e altre simili barbare e molto asprissime genti." See Patota's n. 18 on p. 6 on the meanings of *nazioni* and *genti* as "peoples."

30. Ibid., 6–7: "Onde per questa mistura di dí in dí insalvatichí e viziossi la nostra prima cultissima ed emendatissima lingua." Alberti does not continue with this argument in the way that Pietro Bembo later did in his *Prose della volgar lingua,* whereby the Italian vernacular was born of the interchange between natives and barbarians; see Bembo 1966, 86: "Del come, non si può errare a dire che, essendo la romana lingua e quelle de' Barbari tra sè lontanissime, essi a poco a poco della nostra ora une ora altre voci, e queste troncamente e imperfettamente pigliando, e noi apprendendo similmente delle loro, se ne formasse in processo di tempo e nascessene una nuova, la quale alcuno odore e dell'una e dell'altra ritenesse, che questa volgare è, che ora usiamo."

31. Guarino in Tavoni 1984, 231: "Quarta deinde mixta quaedam emersit seu potius immersit lingua, quam rectius corruptelam linguae quis dixerit."

32. Ibid., 231: ". . . quorum [*sc.* Gothorum, *etc.*] indeleta vestigia luculentum illum romanae suavitatis splendorem macularunt et instar faecis obscenarunt."

33. For further elaboration, see Celenza 2009.

34. Flavio Biondo 1483: "Sed eiusdem detrimenta occasumque celebritatis maxima involvat tegatque obscuritas. Visum est itaque operaeprecium a me factum iri, si annorum mille et triginta, quot ab capta a Gothis urbe Roma in praesens tempus numerantur, ea involucra et omni posteritati admiranda facinora in lucem perduxero."

35. Leonardo Bruni 2001–2004, 1.11 (pp. 18–19).

36. Ibid., 1.13 (pp. 18–19).

37. Ibid., 1.38 (pp. 52–53).

38. Ibid., 1.40 (pp. 52–53).

39. Ibid., 1.40 (pp. 54–55).

40. Ibid., 1.52 (pp. 66–67).

41. Ibid., 1.52–68 (pp. 66–87), quotation from 1.68 (pp. 86–87).

42. Ibid., 1.69 (pp. 86–87).

43. On Bruni and "civic humanism," see Baron 1966; Hankins 2000; Celenza 2004b, 36–39.

44. Bruni 2001–2004, 1.70 (pp. 86–89).

45. Ibid., 1.71 (pp. 88–89).

46. The preface is in Leonardo Bruni 1969, 147–149; an English translation is in Bruni 1988, 195–196.

47. Bruni 1988, 195–196.

48. On Aulus Gellius, see Holford-Strevens 2003; Holford-Strevens and Vardi 2004; the text and translation used here is Aulus Gellius 1927–1928.

49. See Grafton 2004; on "classicism," see Porter 2006.

50. See Grafton 2004, 320–322; the following section is heavily indebted to Grafton.

51. Grafton 2004, 324.

52. Aulus Gellius 1927–1928, pref.

53. Ibid.

54. For literature on Decembrio, see Celenza 2004b; Grafton 1997, 19–49; on Decembrio and Gellius, see Grafton 2004, 318–319, 328–329; there is an edition of the text in Decembrio 2002.

55. Decembrio 2002, 1.1.5: "Cuius futuram seriem ut brevibus intelligas, seu ad opus A. Gellii *Noctium atticarum* seu potius ad Quintiliani *Institutionem oratoriam* formatus est partium et librorum opportunitate eadem fere servata. Nam et hic non minus de oratorio poeticoque tractatur artificio."

56. Ibid., 1.3.1: "Placuit in primis A. Gellio, cuius imaginem et Quintiliani pariter pollicitus sum his libris imitari, Favorinum et quosdam paucos veluti frequentiores sibi magistros eligere. Mihi quoque in hac 'politia' Leonellum principem Guarinumque Veronensem et qui cum eis clariores pauci disputare consueverant, deligendos institui."

57. See Grafton 2004, 321–322.

58. The first *Centuria* is still best read in Poliziano's unpaginated *Opera Omnia* (1498); for the second century, see Poliziano 1978.

59. The note is *Misc.* 1, in Poliziano 1498, B ii(v)—B v(v). It is treated in Garin 1937; Kraye 1983, 83–84.

60. For Argyropoulos' teaching, see Field 1988, 107–126; Hankins 1990, 1: 350.

61. Poliziano 1498, *Misc.* 1, B iv(r).

62. Ibid.

63. Ibid., B iv(v)—B v(r); Poliziano means the definition of soul expounded in Plato, *Phaedrus* 245c.

64. See Gerson 2005b; 2005a.

65. See Athanassiadi and Frede 1999; Assmann 1996.

66. Origen, *Contra Celsum*, 5.41, as cited in Athanassiadi and Frede 1999, 8.

67. *De myst*, 2.4–5, and Assman 1996, 30–31.

68. See Celenza 2004b, 80–114; 2002.

69. See Brucker 1766–1767; for his influence, see Catana 2005; 2008; for background on Brucker, see Schmidt-Biggeman and Stammen 1998.

70. Brucker 1766–1767, 1:15: "Ut itaque de sententia philosophorum sanum rectumque iudicium ferri queat, **totum ex eorum scriptis systema ita eruendum est**, ut ante omnia principia generalia, quae fundamenti loco toti doctrinarum aedificio subiiciuntur, eruantur, et his demum illae superstruantur conclusiones quae ex istis fontibus sponte sua fluunt." [my emphasis]

71. See Celenza 2005, 495–497; Catana 2008.

72. For this perspective, see Hadot 1995; 2002.

73. Celenza 2002; 2010.

74. Iamblichus 1989, 2.11.96.

75. For background and bibliography, see Copenhaver 1992, "Introduction," xiii–lxxxiii.

76. See Fowden 1986.

77. See Allen 1998.

78. See Ficino 2001–2006.

79. For this text, see Ficino 1989.

80. The text and translation used here is Plotinus 1966–1988.

81. See *Asclepius* in Copenhaver 1992, 67–92, at 90.

82. The Augustinian notion is in Augustine 1963–1965, esp. 2, *De baptismo libri VIII*, ed. G. Bavard, at VI.4–5 (pp. 412–414). The connections between the pagan and Christian views were noted by Shaw 1985; 1995.

83. Ficino 1989, 3.1, 244–245.

84. Ibid., 3.16, 322–323.

85. Ibid., 3.17, 330–331.

86. Ibid., 3.15, 320–321.

87. Ibid., 3.18, 340–341.

88. Ibid. The episode is recounted in Porphyry's *Life of Plotinus*, 10, in Plotinus 1966–1988, 1:32–35.

89. Ficino 1989, 3.18, 340–341.

90. Ibid., referring to Albert the Great 1977, 11 (32.103–109), 16 (47.1–21); cit. Kaske and Clarke, in Ficino 1989, 449.

91. Ficino 1989, 3.18, 340–341, referring to (ps.) Thomas Aquinas, *De fato*, in Aquinas 1874–1879, vol. 27 (*Opuscula*): 4 ad fin.; cit. Kaske and Clarke, in Ficino 1989, 450.

92. On this point, see Gentile 1990; Celenza 2002.

93. Ficino 1989, 3.18, 342–343.

94. Ibid.

95. See Daston and Park 1998; Daston 2000.

WORKS CITED

Adams, James Noel. 2003. *Bilingualism and the Latin Language*. Cambridge: Cambridge University Press.

Albert the Great. 1977. *Speculum astronomiae*. Ed. Stefano Caroti et al. Pisa: Domus Galilaeana.

Alberti, Leon Battista. 1996. *Grammatichetta e altri scritti sul volgare*, ed. G. Patota. Rome: Salerno Editrice.

Allen, Michael J. B. 1998. *Synoptic Art: Marsilio Ficino on the History of Platonic Interpretation*. Florence: Olschki.

Ando, Clifford. 2008. "Decline, Fall, and Transformation," *Journal of Late Antiquity* 1: 31–60.

Aquinas, Thomas. 1874–1889. *Opera Omnia*, 34 vols. Paris: Vivés.

Assmann, Jan. 1996. "Translating Gods: Religion as a Factor of Cultural (Un)Translatability." In *The Translatability of Cultures: Figurations of the Space Between*, ed. Sanford Budick and Wolfgang Iser, 25–37. Stanford, CA: Stanford University Press.

Athanassiadi, Polymnia, and Michael Frede, eds. 1999. *Pagan Monotheism in Late Antiquity*. Oxford: Oxford University Press.

Augustine. *Traités anti-Donatistes*. 1963–1965. Various editors. 5 vols. Paris: Desclée De Brouwer.

Baron, Hans. 1966. *The Crisis of the Early Italian Renaissance*, rev. ed. Princeton, NJ: Princeton University Press.

Bembo, Pietro. 1966. *Prose della volgar lingua*. Ed. C. Dionisotti. Turin: UTET.

Biondo, Flavio. 1483. *Historiarum ab inclinatione romanorum imperii*. Venice: Octavianus Scotus.

Brucker, Johann Jakob. 1766–1767. *Historia critica philosophiae a mundi incunabulis ad nostram usque aetatem deducta*, 6 vols. Leipzig: Weidemann.

Bruni, Leonardo. 1969. *Humanistisch-philosophische Schriften mit einer Chronologie seiner Werke und Briefe*, ed. H. Baron. Leipzig: Teubner, 1928; repr. Wiesbaden: Sändig.

———. 1988. *The Humanism of Leonardo Bruni*, ed. and trans. Gordon Griffiths, James Hankins, and David Thompson. Binghamton, NY: MRTS.

———. 1996. *Opere letterarie e politiche*. Ed. Paolo Viti. Turin: UTET.

———. 2001–2004. *History of the Florentine People*, 3 vols. Ed. and trans. James Hankins. Cambridge, MA: Harvard University Press.

Casamassima, Emanuele. 1985–1986. "L'autografo Riccardiano della seconda lettera del Petrarca a Urbino V (Senile IX 1)." = *Quaderni petrarcheschi 3 (1985–1986)*.

Catana, Leo. 2005. "The Concept 'System of Philosophy': The Case of Jacob Brucker's Historiography of Philosophy," *History and Theory* 44: 72–90.

———. 2008. *The Historiographical Concept 'System of Philosophy': Its Origin, Nature, Influence and Legitimacy*. Leiden: Brill.

Celenza, Christopher S. 2002. "Late Antiquity and Florentine Platonism: The 'Post-Plotinian' Ficino." In *Marsilio Ficino: His Theology, His Philosophy, His Legacy*, ed. Michael J. B. Allen and Valerie R. Rees, 71–97. Leiden: Brill.

———. 2004a. "Creating Canons in Fifteenth-Century Ferrara: Angelo Decembrio's *De politia litteraria*, 1.10," *Renaissance Quarterly* 57: 43–98.

———. 2004b. *The Lost Italian Renaissance: Humanists, Historians, and Latin's Legacy*. Baltimore: Johns Hopkins University Press.

———. 2005. "Lorenzo Valla and the Traditions and Transmissions of Philosophy," *Journal of the History of Ideas* 66: 483–506.

———. 2009. "End Game: Humanist Latin in the Late Fifteenth Century." In *Latinitas Perennis II: Appropriation and Latin Literature*, ed. Yanick Maes, Jan Papy, and Wim Verbaal, 201–242. Leiden: Brill.

———. 2010. "Neoplatonism." In *The Classical Tradition*, ed. A. Grafton, G. Most, and S. Settis, 632–636. Cambridge, MA: Harvard University Press.

Ciccolella, Federica. 2008. *Donati Graeci: Learning Greek in the Renaissance*. Leiden: Brill.

Clackson, James, and Geoffrey Horrocks. 2007. *The Blackwell History of the Latin Language*. Oxford: Blackwell.

Copenhaver, Brian P., ed. 1992. *Hermetica*. Cambridge: Cambridge University Press.

Cortesi, Mariarosa. 1995. "Umanesimo greco." In *Lo spazio letterario del medioevo*, vol. 3, ed. G. Cavallo et al., 457–507. Rome: Salerno.

Daston, Lorraine. 2000. "Preternatural Philosophy." In *Biographies of Scientific Objects*, ed. L. Daston, 15–41. Chicago: University of Chicago Press.

Daston, Lorraine, and Katharine Park. 1998. *Wonders and the Order of Nature: 1150–1750*. New York: Zone.

Decembrio, Angelo Camillo. 2002. *De politia litteraria*, ed. Norbert Witten. Munich: Saur.

Dotti, Ugo. 1992. *Vita di Petrarca*. Rome: Laterza.

Ficino, Marsilio. 1989. *Three Books on Life*. Ed. and trans. Carol V. Kaske and John R. Clarke. Binghamton, NY: MRTS.

———. 2001–2006. *Platonic Theology*, 6 vols. Ed. and trans. Michael J. B. Allen and James Hankins. Cambridge, MA: Harvard University Press.

Field, Arthur. 1988. *The Origins of the Platonic Academy of Florence*. Princeton, NJ: Princeton University Press.

Fowden, Garth. 1986. *The Egyptian Hermes: A Historical Approach to the Late Pagan Mind*. Cambridge: Cambridge University Press.

Fubini, Riccardo. 1961. "La coscienza del latino negli umanisti: 'an latina lingua Romanorum esset peculiare idioma'." *Studi medievali, ser. 3*, 2: 505–550.

———. 1969. "Biondo Flavio," *Dizionario biografico degli italiani* 10: 536–577. Rome: Treccani.

———. 1992. "All'uscita della scolastica medievale: Salutati, Bruni, e i *Dialogi ad Petrum Histrum*," *Archivio storico italiano* 150: 1065–1103.

Garin, Eugenio. 1937. "*Endelecheia* e *Entelecheia* nelle discussioni umanistiche," *Atene e roma* 5: 177–187.

Gellius, Aulus. 1927–1928. *The Attic Nights of Aulus Gellius*, 3 vols. Ed. and trans. John C. Rolfe. Cambridge, MA: Harvard University Press.

Gentile, Sebastiano. 1990. "Sulle prime traduzioni dal greco di Marsilio Ficino," *Rinascimento, ser. 2*, 30: 57–104.

Gerson, Lloyd P. 2005a. *Aristotle and Other Platonists*. Ithaca, NY: Cornell University Press.

———. 2005b. "What Is Platonism?" *Journal of the History of Philosophy* 43: 253–276.

Grafton, Anthony. 1997. *Commerce with the Classics: Ancient Books and Renaissance Readers*. Ann Arbor: University of Michigan Press.

———. 2004. "Conflict and Harmony in the *Collegium Gellianum*." In *The Worlds of Aulus Gellius*, ed. Leofranc Holford-Strevens and Amiel Vardi, 318–342. Oxford: Oxford University Press.

Hadot, Pierre. 1995. *Philosophy as a Way of Life*. Ed. A. I. Davidson, trans. M. Chase. Oxford: Blackwell.

———. 2002. *What Is Ancient Philosophy?* Cambridge, MA: Harvard University Press.

Hankins, James. 1990. *Plato in the Italian Renaissance*, 2 vols. Leiden: Brill.

———. 2000, ed. *Renaissance Civic Humanism: Reappraisals and Reflections*. Cambridge: Cambridge University Press.

———. 2003–2004. *Humanism and Platonism in the Italian Renaissance*, 2 vols. Rome: Edizioni di storia e letteratura.

———. 2007. "Humanism, Scholasticism, and Renaissance Philosophy." In *The Cambridge Companion to Renaissance Philosophy*, ed. James Hankins, 30–48. Cambridge: Cambridge University Press.

Hay, Denys. 1958. "Flavio Biondo and the Middle Ages," *Proceedings of the British Academy* 45: 97–125.

Holford-Strevens, Leofranc. 2003. *Aulus Gellius: An Antonine Scholar and His Achievement*. Oxford: Oxford University Press.

Holford-Strevens, Leofranc, and Amiel Vardi, eds. 2004. *The Worlds of Aulus Gellius*. Oxford: Oxford University Press.

Iamblichus. 1989. *De mysteriis*. Ed. Edouard des Places. Paris: Belles Lettres.

James, Edward. 2008. "The Rise and Function of the Concept 'Late Antiquity'," *Journal of Late Antiquity* 1: 20–30.

Kraye, Jill. 1983. "Cicero, Stoicism, and Textual Criticism: Poliziano on *katorthoma*," *Rinascimento, ser. 2*, 23: 79–110.

Löfstedt, Einar. 1959. *Late Latin*. Oslo: Aschehoug.

Marcone, Arnaldo. 2008. "A Long Late Antiquity? Considerations on a Controversial Periodization," *Journal of Late Antiquity* 1: 4–19.

Mazzocco, Angelo. 1993. *Linguistic Theories in Dante and the Humanists: Studies of Language and Intellectual History in Late Medieval and Early Renaissance Italy.* Leiden: Brill.

Petrarch, Francesco. 1554. *Opera Omnia.* Basel: Henricus Petri.

———. 1992. *Letters of Old Age/Rerum senilium libri,* 2 vols. Trans. Aldo S. Bernardo et al. Baltimore: Johns Hopkins University Press.

———. 1997. *Le familiari,* 4 vols. Ed. V. Rossi. Florence: Le lettere. [Reprint of Sansoni edition of 1968]

———. 2003. *Invectives.* Ed. and trans. D. Marsh. Cambridge, MA: Harvard University Press.

———. 2005. *Letters on Familiar Matters,* 3 vols. Trans. Aldo S. Bernardo. New York: Italica Press. [Repr. of Albany: State University of New York Press, vol. 1, 1975, and Baltimore: Johns Hopkins University Press, vols. 2–3, 1982–1985]

Plotinus. 1966–1988. *Enneads,* 7 vols. Ed. and trans. A. H. Armstrong. Cambridge, MA: Harvard University Press.

Poliziano, Angelo. 1498. *Opera Omnia.* Venice: Aldus Manutius.

———. 1978. *Miscellaneorum centuria secunda.* Ed. Vittore Branca and Manlio Pastore Stocchi. Florence: Olschki.

Porter, James I. 2006. "What Is 'Classical' about Classical Antiquity?" In *The Classical Traditions of Greece and Rome,* ed. James I. Porter, 1–65. Princeton, NJ: Princeton University Press.

Quint, David. 1985. "Humanism and Modernity: A Reconsideration of Bruni's Dialogues," *Renaissance Quarterly* 38: 423–445.

Rico, Francisco. 1993. *El sueño del humanismo: De Petrarca a Erasmo.* Madrid: Alleanza.

Rizzo, Silvia. 2002. *Ricerche sul latino umanistico.* Rome: Edizioni di Storia e letteratura.

Salutati, Coluccio. 1891–1911. *Epistolario,* 4 vols. in 5. Ed. Francesco Novati. Rome: Istituto storico italiano per il medio evo.

Schmidt-Biggeman, Wilhelm, and T. Stammen, eds. 1998. *Jacob Brucker (1696–1770): Philosoph und Historiker der europäischen Aufklärung.* Berlin: Akademie-Verlag.

Shaw, Gregory. 1985. "Theurgy: Rituals of Unification in the Neoplatonism of Iamblichus," *Traditio* 41: 1–28.

———. 1995. *Theurgy and the Soul: The Neoplatonism of Iamblichus.* University Park, PA: Pennsylvania State University Press.

Tavoni, Mirko. 1984. *Latino, grammatica, volgare: Storia di una questione umanistica.* Padua: Antenore.

Witt, Ronald G. 1983. *Hercules at the Crossroads: The Life, Works, and Thought of Coluccio Salutati.* Durham, NC: Duke University Press.

———. 2000. *In the Footsteps of the Ancients: The Origins of Humanism from Lovato to Bruni.* Leiden: Brill.

Wright, Roger, ed. 1991. *Latin and the Romance Languages in the Early Middle Ages.* London: Routledge.

———. 2002. "How Latin Came to Be a Foreign Language for All." In *A Sociophilological Study of Late Latin,* ed. idem, 3–17. Turnhout: Brepols.

Index

To Be Noted

- Church buildings named for a saint are listed under "Saint," so you will find S. Agnese fuori le mura, Rome, alphabetized as "Saint Agnese."
- Arabic names beginning with al- are sorted on their first main element, but Arabic names beginning with Abū are sorted at Abū, and names beginning with Ibn are sorted at Ibn. Thus "al-Manṣūr" will be found in the *Ms*, but "Abū Bakr" in the *As*, and "Ibn Sīnā" in the *Is*.
- Greek and Latin names with alternative spellings are given in square brackets, and double-posted or cross-referenced where appropriate. Roman names have multiple parts, and the person may be most generally known by the second or third part of the name (the *nomen* or *cognomen*). In such cases the full Roman name is provided in parentheses, and double-posted or cross-referenced at the full name as well. Thus the reader will find an entry for "Symmachus" (Quintus Aurelius Symmachus), and a cross reference to it at "Quintus Aurelius Symmachus." A similar case is the entry for "Jacobite or West Syriac Church," which is double-posted under "West Syriac or Jacobite Church."
- Syriac names beginning with the title Mār are sorted at Mār; so Mār Isaac will be found in the *Ms*.
- Page numbers in *italics* indicate illustrations.

'Abbasid caliphate, 1068, 1125
'Abd al-Malik (caliph), 1058, 1088–1089
'Abdallah ibn Mu'awiya, 1064
'Abdīšō' of Arphelouna, 1007
Abgar of Edessa, 175, 176, 178, 180, 181, 182, 189, 565, 972
Abīkarib As'ad (king of Ḥimyar), 266–267
Abraha (ruler of Ḥimyar), 284–288, 291–292, 295, 297, 301
Abraham Ałbatanec'i, 122
Abraham of Kashkar, 1007–1008, 1023
Abraham of Pboou, 236
"Abrəha and Aṣbəha" legend, 292
Abū Bakr (caliph), 1087, 1091
Abū Isḥāq, 1082
Abū Manṣūr al-'Ijlī, 1064
Abū Muslim, 157
Acacius (bishop of Amida), 1003
Acheiropoietos, Thessaloniki, 943
Achilles Tatius, 978
Acta Sancti Lupi, 36
Acts of Chalcedon, 888
Acts of Mār Mārī, 998
Acts of Paul, 232
Acts of Peter, 232, 1085
Acts of the Persian Martyrs, 997
Acts of Thekla, 565
Acts of Thomas, 565
Ad familiares (Cicero), 835
Ad Populum edict (320 C.E.), 673
Adam [Jing-Jing], 1022–1023
Adeodatus (son of Augustine of Hippo), 690
'Adī b. Zayd, 307
Adomnán (Irish monk and abbot of Iona), 566, 985
Adone (Marino, 1623), 384
Adontz, Nicholas, 127–128, 130
adultery, law governing, 802–803
Adversus Haereses (Irenaeus of Lyons), 879
Advice to the Bride and Groom (Plutarch), 681
Aediles, Edict of the, 791
Aegidius (Frankish leader), 39
Aelius Aristides [Aristeides], 437–438, 439, 443, 449, 1153, 1176
Aelius Gallus, 1071
Aemilius Asper, 414
Aeneas of Gaza, 455
Aeneid (Virgil), 9, 336, 344
Aethicus Ister, 576, 577
Aëtius [Aetius], 36, 37, 38, 43–46, 105
Afsaruddin, Asma, 1093
Against Aristotle on the Eternity of the World (John Philoponus), 575
Against the Galileans (Julian), 448, 450–451
"Against the Pagans" (Augustine of Hippo), 866
Against Proclus on the Eternity of the World (John Philoponus), 574–575
Agapetus the Deacon, 1153, 1161
Agapius the Greek, 441
Agat'angełos [Agathangelos] (Armenian), 122, 421–422
Agathias of Myrina, 62, 369–370, 372, 386n8, 425, 454, 478, 683, 1066
Agatho (pope), 927

Agora (film), 1149
Agosti, Gianfranco, xxxvii, 361
agriculture and rural environment, 625–644. *See also* climate; peasantry
  in Arabia, 261
  aristocracy and. *See under* aristocracy
  cultivation practices, 631–632
  dispersed and fragmented landholdings, 632–633
  in Egypt, 198, 199–200, 206, 209–210
  imperial decline of sixth century and, 1115
  labor arrangements, 634, 636–637
  Palladius' framework for considering, 625–626
  patronage systems, 640–643
  real estate market, activity of, 633–634
  reciprocity and collective action, tensions associated with, 638–640
  relationship between town and country, 628–631
  tenancy arrangements, 634–635
  village settlements in East, 610, 630–631
Agrimensores, 563
Ahrweiler, Hélène, 1149
air, fire, and the heavens, 529, 530–533, 537. *See also* cosmology
'Ā'isha, suspected adultery of, 1082, 1083
Aizanas ['Ēzānā] (king of Ethiopia), 255, 258, 261, 275–281
Aksūm. *See* Ethiopia
Alamanni, 35, 42
Alans, 36–37, 41
Alaric (Gothic leader), 36, 41, 42, 339
Alaric II (Visigothic king), 15, 40, 47, 794, 838–839
Albert the Great, 1191
Alberti, Leon Battista, 1178
Alcimus Alethius, 409
Alcimus Avitus, 345
Aldfrith (king of Northumbria), 579
Alethia (Claudius Marius Victorius of Marseilles), 345
Alexander of Aphrodisias, 1184
Alexander the Great, 9, 12, 25n7, 364, 437–438, 440
Alexander Romance [*Romance of Alexander; Legend of Alexander*] (Pseudo-Callisthenes), 364–365, 1150, 1153
Alexandria
  Arianism in, 198, 721, 860
  bishopric of, 882, 888
  library at, 19
  Museon, 19
  religious violence at, 445–446, 459–460n43, 860–861
  Serapeum, destruction of, 850, 888
  university quarter, 471
Alexandrian School, 231
Alfred the Great, 894
Algonquin beads, 984, 989
'Alī ibn Abī Ṭālib, family of, 1064
Allāh, and decline of Arab polytheism, 304–305
Altar of Victory, Rome, removal/restoration of, 347, 776–778, 835, 850
altars in Christian churches, 954–955, *955*
Aluoben (Christian missionary to China), xi, 1022, 1023
Alypius (friend of Augustine of Hippo), 414
Ambrose of Milan
  Balkans and, 99
  as bishop, 876, 882, 883, 884, 886, 888
  economic history and, 599
  history writing in Late Antiquity and, 413
  Italian Renaissance interest in, 1175
  on justice and equality, 776, 778
  letters of, 828, 835, 836, 837
  on marriage and family, 677, 682, 683
  monasticism and, 492
  on physics and metaphysics, 539
Ambrosiaster (biblical commentator), 676
amicitia, 816, 830, 832, 836
Ammianus Marcellinus
  on bishops, 819, 881, 887
  on campaigns of disinformation in North Africa, 798
  on Central Asia, 144
  Hellenism and, 457n12
  as historian, 412–413
  on Julian, 478, 855–856
  mental world of Late Antiquity and, 10–11, 13, 21
  on Olybrii, 773
  on religious violence in Alexandria, 861
  Res Gestae, 413
  on rural estates/villas, 606
  on Thrace, 107, 108, 109
  Western kingdoms and, 34, 35
Ammonas (ascetic), 499, 500, 502
Ammonius Saccas, 454, 455, 471, 476
Amos and Kasiseus, Church of, Chapel of Priest John, Khirbet el-Mukhayyat, Jordan, 949, *950*
Amphilochius of Iconium, 366
Amphipolis, Basilica A, northern Greece, 943
"*amr* (God's command)," Qur'ān's and Muḥammad's concern with arrival of, 1090–1099
'Amr ibn al-'Āṣ, 190, 204, 207, 209
An Lushan, 157–158
Ananias of Shirak [Širak], 11, 132, 133, 136n87, 156, 428
Anaolsus (Gothic general), 43
Anastasis Rotunda, Holy Sepulcher, Jerusalem, 941–942, *942*
Anastasius I (emperor), *ii*, xi, 282, 369, 420, 601, 608, 887, 892
Anaxagoras (philosopher), 475
Ancyra, Council of (314 C.E.), 1003
Ando, Clifford, 974

Andovk (prince of Siwnik'), 128
Andrew of Crete [Andrew the Jerusalemite], 1156
Andronicus of Hermopolis, 364, 366
Anemius (bishop), 99
Anianus (referendary of Alaric II), 47
Anicia Juliana, 373
Anicii family in Rome, 598, 605, 606
Anicius Acilius Glabrio Faustus, 797
animal sacrifice, 850, 854–856
animism in Late Antiquity, 971, 977, 980, 983–984, 988–989
Annales (Nicomachus Flavianus), 412, 417
annona, 198, 209, 734, 894
Anonymous Chronicle, 123
Anthemius (emperor), 47, 341
Anthony [Antony] the Great [the Hermit]. *See* Antony the Great
Antioch
  Persian overthrow of, 115–116
  St. Babylas, church of, 942
  special authority of bishopric of, 882
Antioch, Council of (324 C.E.), 1003
Antiochene school, 231
Antiochus Chuzon, 800
Antiquities of the Jews (Josephus), 426, 429
Antonine Constitution (*Constitutio Antoniniana*), 63, 674, 678, 745–747, 749, 754, 791, 827
Antonine Itinerary, 96, 563–564, 571, 605
Antonine plague (165–180 C.E.), 1117
Antoninus (philosopher), 482n84
Antony [Anthony] the Great [the Hermit], 231, 487–488, 494–495, 499–500, 504, 889–890
Aphrahat, 5, 11, 22, 170–172, 1000–1001, 1006
Apion [Appianus] estate and archive, Egypt, 203, 209, 210, 213, 611, 636
Apocalypse of Elijah, 232
Apocalypse of Pseudo-Methodius, 25n17
apocalypticism
  Byzantium, "little eschatology" in, 1157–1160
  in Islam, 1065–1067, 1090–1099
  in religions of Late Antiquity generally, 1065–1067
apocrypha, 917–918, 1084–1085
Apollinarian forgeries, 917–919, 920–921, 924–925
Apollinarians, 865, 918
Apollinarii (father and son poets), 446, 447, 865
Apollinarius of Laodicea, 367
Apollonius Molon, 1184
Apollonius Rhodius, 372, 385n3
Apollonius of Tyana, 364, 372, 495
Apology (Aristeides), 1153
Apology to Constantius (Athanasius), 258
Apophthegmata patrum, 493, 495–499, 497, 504, 1155
Apotheosis (Prudentius), 355n123
Apuleius (Latin prose writer), 857, 1175
Arab conquest. *See* Islam
Arabs and Arabia, 247–254. *See also* Ḥimyar; Islam; Makka
  agriculture, practice of, 261
  Arab language, 307–308
  archaeological sites, pre-Islamic, 248–253
  Byzantine diplomacy in, 253, 259, 283, 284, 293–295
  Christianity in
    Church of the East in Arabia, 1005–1006, 1017–1018
    height of, 305
    Ḥimyar, Christianization of, 294–295
    Lakhmids of Ḥīra, 1005–1006
    Najrān Christians, 281–284, 289, 290, 1006
  cities of, 251, 252
  collapse of Arabian kingdoms in sixth century, 297–299
  economic and climatic crises prior to *hijra*, 305–306
  Elephant, year/battle of, 286–287
  Ethiopia, links to, 247
  ethnogenesis, 306–308
  external sources regarding, 253–254
  geography and climate, 248, *249*, 305–306
  al-Ḥīra, kingdom of, 296, 297, 1005–1006, 1018
  inscriptions and archival documents, pre-Islamic, 251–253, 285–287, 306–307
  Ishmael in Bible, identification with, 68
  Islamic tradition regarding pre-Islamic Arabia, 308–310
  Jafnids, Naṣrids, and Ghassānids [Ghassānites], 293–294, 298
  Lakhmids, 1005–1006, 1018
  long-distance trade, importance of, 259–261
  map, *249*
  origins of term, 247–248
  "out of Arabia" theory of Islamic origins, 1069–1072
  as part of Late Antique world, 1071–1072
  plague of 541–542 in, 305
  Quraysh, tribe of, 272, 286, 287, 295, 301, 303–304, 309–310
  Sasanian Persia and, 12, 295–298
  sedentary and nomadic populations, 261–262
Arator (Latin poet), 339, 345
Aratus (Greek poet), 576
Arcadius (emperor), 417, 790
Arcadius (son of poet Sidonius), 55n125
Arcadius Charisius, 792
archaeology
  in Arabia, 248–253, 305
  barbarian migrations and, 71–72
  Central Asia, effect of Hunnic invasions on, 146–147
  Church of the East, southern wing of, 1017–1018

archaeology (*continued*)
economic history and, 598
in Egypt, 196–197, 207
Ethiopia, important sites in, 256–257
of hospitals, 733
house-churches, 937–938
at monastic sites, 489, 504
settlement patters, trends in, 630–631
architecture, sacred. *See* sacred space
archives, Late Antique use of, 822
Arculf (Frankish bishop), 566
Ardashir (Sasanian ruler), 145, 998, 1068
Arezzo, Geri d', 1176
Argyropoulos, John, 1183
Arianism
in Alexandria/Egypt, 198, 721, 860
barbarian adherence to, 63
bishops and, 888, 889, 891, 892, 894
citizenship and, 748
historical writing in Late Antiquity and, 411
hospitals, association with, 721, 731, 748, 860
Latin poetry and, 345
Ravenna, Arian baptistery at, 944
in Syria, 184
in Western kingdoms, 37, 47, 891, 892
Ariès, Philippe, 669
Aristarchus sacer (Heinsius, 1627), 383
Aristarchus of Samos, 583n64
Aristides (Aelius Aristides) [Aristeides], 437–438, 439, 443, 449, 1153, 1176
aristocracy
bishops and, 15, 882, 1139n48
changes in, 597–599, 606–607, 611–613
conversion to Christianity, 413–414, 863
decline of Western aristocracy, 598–599, 606–607, 615
development of new Byzantine aristocracy, 611–613
history writing in Late Antiquity and Roman aristocracy, 412–415
judicial privileges of, 769–775
marriage, family, and social mobility, 671, 687–692
monetary system and, 597–598, 600
new governing classes, development of, 597–598, 602
patronage systems in rural environments, 640–643
political system of Roman empire and, 1117–1118
proliferation of provinces and, 602
Roman real estate, aristocratic control of, 602–603
rural estates of
Armenian aristocracy, villages owned by, 610
management of estates in Eastern empire, 611–612, 613
Western aristocracy's investment in, 601–602, 603–607, 615
values derived from, 13–16
Aristophanes, 385n3
Aristotle and Aristotelianism
on animate and inanimate, 988
Arabic, translation of Aristotle into, 1024, 1068
Against Aristotle on the Eternity of the World (John Philoponus), 575
Church of the East and, 1007, 1024
Commentary on Aristotle's De Caelo (Simplicius), 574
cosmology of, 573
educational process and, 470, 478, 480n34
on fifth element, 530
Hellenism and, 455
Italian Renaissance, Platonizing in, 1183–1186
in mental world of Late Antiquity, 13, 19
Organon (Aristotle), 470, 1024
on physics and metaphysics, 516, 522, 525, 528–529, 530, 534, 537, 540
on *pneuma*, 534, 537
Topics (Aristotle), 1024
Armenia, 115–134
animal sacrifice in Christian liturgy of, 856
Arab conquests, impact of, 133–134
aristocrats owning villages in, 610
balanced between Rome and Persia, 117, 119
Christian church in, 117, 119–126
dislocation and diaspora, association with, 118–119
economic history of, 132–133
Gregory of Tours on, 115–118
history writing in, 421–422, 428
hospitals for the poor in, 722, 725, 735
literature translated into Armenian, 118
mental world of Late Antiquity in, 11
military in, 129–132
political and social history of, 127–133
Roman empire and, 117, 119, 130–133
Sasanian Persia and, 115–118, 119, 122, 129–130
sliver hexagrams in, 132
Armstrong, A. H., 522
Armstrong, Karen, 1093
Arnobius, 408
arrhae, 675, 678, 690
Arrian (historian), 563
Arsacius (magister militum), 450
Arsenius of Scetis, 499
art history. *See* icons; object relations in Late Antiquity; sacred space; *specific works of art*
Arvandus (Gallic praetorian prefect), 46–47
Aryan myth, 71
As'ad Tubba', 264, 265, 267
Ascensio Isaiae, 232
asceticism. *See* monasticism and asceticism
Ashinas (Turkish sacred clan), 149–150
Asiatic school, Coptic translations from, 232

Aspar (general), 751
Assyrian Church. *See* Church of the East
astral determinism, 66–67
Ataxerxes (Persian ruler), 1071
Athanasius of Alexandria
Apollinarian forgeries attributed to, 917–918
Apology to Constantius, 258
Arian crisis and *annona*, 198
as bishop, 876, 888, 889–890, 893
in Byzantium, 1154
Coptic literature, place in, 234
Ethiopian history and, 258, 274–275
Greek poetry and, 386n9
Life of Anthony (*Vita Antonii*), 386n9, 487–488, 493, 494–495, 498, 505, 889–890
Life of Athanasius, 236
monasticism and asceticism, 494–495
Athaulf (Gothic leader), 36, 42
Athenian Academy, closure of, 477–478, 850
Athens, as state, 1126
Attic Nights (Aulus Gellius), 1181–1183
Attila the Hun, 15, 36, 37, 62, 101–102, 420, 887, 893, 1179
Augustine of Hippo
"Against the Pagans," 866
agriculture and rural environment, evidence for, 636, 638
on anti-Christian riots in Calama, 801
on attendance at Christian services, 866
Aulus Gellius, knowledge of, 1181
as bishop, 876, 882, 884, 885, 886
on citizenship, 745
City of God, 415, 745, 791
conversion of, 539–541
decline of Roman empire, interpretation of, 21
history writing in Late Antiquity and, 414–416
hospital in episcopal palace of, 730–731
Italian Renaissance and, 1175, 1188
Italica, correspondence with, 769
on justice and equality, 767, 769
Latin poetry of, 350n23
letters of, 826, 828, 834, 886
On the Literal Interpretation of Genesis, 540
Magnitude of the Soul, 541
on marriage and family, 682, 683, 684, 687, 689, 690, 691, 698n132
monasticism and asceticism of, 492, 493, 505, 890
on "pagan survivals" in Christian practice, 858
on physics and metaphysics, 517, 530, 531, 535, 538, 539–542
Psalm against the Donatists, 350n23
in rural estates/villas, 605
on sacraments, 1189
on slavery, 687
Augustus (emperor), 7, 8, 14, 34, 673, 749, 1071
Aulus Gellius, 349n16, 1173, 1181–1183
Aurelian (emperor), 96, 880
Aurelius Victor, 409, 410, 411, 413
Ausonius (Latin poet and rhetorician), 336–337, 340, 346, 349n16, 410, 414, 416, 683, 691, 747, 829, 835
authority as criterion in Late Antiquity, 20, 579
Avars, 102, 106, 110
Averintsev, S., 362, 364, 377
Avesta, 17, 18
Avienus (Latin author and translator), 351n42, 563
Avitus (emperor), 45, 47, 101, 341
Avitus (geographical writer), 577
Avitus of Vienne (bishop), 829, 836, 891–892
Axum. *See* Ethiopia
Azzarello, Giuseppina, 611

Babai the Great, 1014, 1015
Babgēn I Ot'msec'i (Armenian catholicos), 128
Babowai (Church of the East catholicos), 1004
Babrius (Greek poet), 385n6
Bactria. *See* Central Asia and the Silk Road
Bagnall, Roger, 196, 697–698n120
Bahram [Bahrām, Vahrām] Chubin (Sasanian general), 1015, 1020
Bahram [Bahrām, Vahrām] I (Sasanian ruler), 768
Bahram [Bahrām, Vahrām] II (Sasanian ruler), 998
Bahram [Bahrām, Vahrām] V Gor [Ghor] (Sasanian ruler), 144, 296, 995
Balavariani, 1153
Balkans, 92–111
Christian church in, 94, 98–99, 103–106, 110
Dalmatia/Salona, 102–106
defined, 92
maps, 93, 94
Pannonia/Sirmium, 95–102
Roman military in, 94, 96, 101–102, 104–105, 109
Spalatum (Split), Diocletian's palace at, 104, 106
Stridon, Jerome on home town of, 101
Thrace/Odessos, 107–110
Banaji, Jairus, xxxvii, 597
baptism
bishop, role of, 885
in Church of the East, 1011–1012
of Constantine, 883
Justinian, forced baptism of pagans mandated by, 849, 859
schismatics, rebaptism of, 880
baptisteries, 937, 938, 944
Bar Shabbā, 1019–1020

barbarians, xix, 60–78. *See also specific peoples, e.g.* Visigoths
Christianity and
alternative view of barbarians provided by, 62, 67–68, 77
diplomatic conversion missions, 65, 68
geographical and astral determinism, 66–67
heterodoxy, association of barbarians with, 18, 37, 63
citizenship, access to, 746, 749–751
"decline and fall" of Roman empire and, 68, 70, 74, 1177–1180
dichotomy of Romans and, 60–62
diplomatic contacts with, 64–65, 68
economic studies and, 77–78
ethnic citizenship of, 748
ethnogenesis theory, 69, 74–77
"Flavius," use of, 750
geographical and astral determinism regarding, 65–67
in history writing in Late Antiquity, 415–417
Italian Renaissance on, 1177–1180
in literature, 61–62
marriages with Romans, 752
mental world of Late Antiquity and, 9, 10, 11
migrations of, 68–74
in military service, 14, 751–752
in modern history, 68–77
new historical approaches to, 77–78
Roman law and, 62–63, 751–754
Roman perceptions of, 61–68
settlement mechanisms, 53–54n87, 752
Western kingdoms founded by. *See* Western kingdoms
Barberini graecus 336 manuscript, 1156
Barberini Ivory, *ii*, 1163
Bardaisan of Edessa [Bardesanus], 8–9, 11, 67, 170, 184, 998, 999, 1027n24, 1068
Barsanuphius of Gaza, 499, 500
Barsauma of Nisibis, 1007, 1010, 1030n76
Barsauma of Samosata, 178–179, 181
Basil of Caesarea. *See also under* hospitals
as bishop, 876, 882, 886
in Byzantium, 1154
Coptic literature and, 234
on education, 473, 476
Eusebius of Caesarea and, 716
Hellenism and, 444
history writing in Late Antiquity and, 411, 412
Letter to Young Men, 444
letters of, 829, 886
liturgy of, 1156
on marriage and family, 680
monasticism and, 492, 493
Syria and, 185
Basil the Cilician, 420
Basilica Nova [Basilica Maxentii/Constantini], Rome, 939
basilicas and churches, 938–943, *940–943*. *See also* sacred space
Batty, Roger, 77
Bauer, Walter, 170
Baur, F. C., 1086, 1087
Ba'ya of Šahrzūr, 1017
Bayān ibn Sim'ān, 1064
The Beard-Hater (Julian), 449
Becker, C. H., 1067
Bede, 429, 566, 579
Beeston, A. F. L., 286
being and reality in Late Antiquity, 518–520
Belisarius (general), 423, 1179
Bell, Richard, 1090, 1091–1092, 1093, 1095, 1096
Belting, Hans, 974
Bemarchius, 409
Benedict Biscop, 579
Benjamin (Egyptian patriarch), 199
Benjamin, Walter, 929, 930, 933n31
Beorgor (Alan king), 37
Besa (ascetic), 234, 236
Bethlehem, Church of the Nativity at, 940–941, 942, 987
betrothals, law governing, 674–675, 678
Beyşehir Occupation Phase, 1115
Bible
apocrypha and pseudepigrapha, 917–918, 1084–1085
bishops in, 877–878
Coptic literature and, 230–231
Greek poetry adapting, 367, 368, 371–372
Ḥimyar, never quoted in inscriptions of, 295
Latin poetry adapting, 343–348
magi associated with Persia, 21–22, 1023
marriage and family in, 680, 681–682
Peshitta, 170, 171, 173, 182, 185
Philoxenus of Mabbug's Syriac translation of, 185–186
pilgrim travelogues quoting, 564, 565, 566
Qur'ān and
Christian Gospels and other documentation compared to, 1078, 1080, 1084, 1086–1087, 1089, 1096, 1097
critical techniques developed for study of Bible and, 1086–1087
Hebrew Bible criticism and, 1086–1087
influenced by Bible, 1072, 1090
Roman and Jewish law compared, 794
stones and stone objects in, 984–985
Bibliotheca (Photius), 826
bimetalism, disintegration of, 599
Biondo, Flavio, 1177, 1178, 1180–1181, 1192
Bird-David, Nurit, 977
Birkeland, Harris, 1092, 1093
bishop of Rome. *See* papacy

bishops, xix, 876–896
architectural complexes of, 943–945, *945*
in Armenian church, 124–126
charity, duty to provide, 885–886. *See also* hospitals
class origins of, 882
communications of, 819–820, 825, 829, 831–832
Constantine's impact on status and influence of, 880–883, 893
in Eastern empire, 895–896
elites and elite values in Late Antiquity and, 15, 882, 1139n48
hierarchy of, 882–883
as missionaries, 889
monarchical episcopate, development of, 877–880
monasticism and asceticism, 889–890
multiple roles of, 878–879, 884–890
orthodoxy of communities, responsibility for, 888–889
as preacher, 885
in Roman judicial system, 777–779, 801, 881–882, 886–887
sacerdotal functions, 885
sanctuary, social division between laity and clergy indicated by, 952, 957
urban environment, role in, 886–888
in Western kingdoms, 890–894
Blachère, Régis, 1084, 1085, 1095
Blavatsky, Madame, 538
Blemyomachia, 365–366, 367
blood sacrifice, 850, 854–856
Boccaccio, Giovanni, 1174, 1176
Bodmer papyri/codex, 365, 371–372, 375, 376, 380
body and soul. *See* physics and metaphysics
Boethius, 47, 351n43, 575, 764, 769
Boitet de Frauville, Claude, 383
bona materna, 673–674
Book of Chastity (*Liber Castitatis*; Īshō'dnaḥ of Basra), 1008
Book of the Laws of the Countries (Bardaisan of Edessa), 998
Book of Rules (Ulpian), 795
Book of Steps, 1006, 1032n103
Books of Miracles (Gregory of Tours), 116
Bordeaux Pilgrim, 564, 565, 566, 935–936, 957
Boswell, James, 724
Boud'hors, Anne, xxxvii, 224
Bowman, A. K., 633
Brahe, Tycho, 576
Braudel, Fernand, xxi
Bréhier, Louis, 1149
Breton kings, 39
Breviarium (Alaric II), 47, 794, 838–839
Breviarium (Eutropius), 420, 429
Britain
conversion of, 894
history writing in, 426–427, 429–430
post-Roman ethnic identity in, 18
Brock, Sebastian, 170, 173, 184, 305, 996, 999
Brodersen, Kai, 570
Brown, Peter
on agriculture and rural environment, 652n161
on barbarians, 73–74, 76
on Byzantium, 1148, 1150, 1157–1158
historiography of Late Antiquity, importance to, xv–xvi, xxii, 4
on Islam, 1055, 1056, 1059, 1064, 1069
Italian Renaissance and, 1172
Latin poetry and, 343
The Making of Late Antiquity (1978), 4
monasticism and, 506n9
on physics and metaphysics, 610
on religion in Late Antiquity, 863
The Rise of Western Christendom (2003), 77, 1148, 1150
The World of Late Antiquity (1971), xv, 4, 73, 1055, 1148
Brucker, Johann Jakob, 1186
Brundage, James, 669
Bruni, Leonardo, 1176–1177, 1179–1181, 1192
Brutus (Cicero), 1177
bubonic plague. *See* plague, Justinianic
bucolic Latin poetry in Late Antique period, 346, 355n112
Buddhism, 144, 150, 151, 158, 1021, 1153
Buhl, Frants, 1091, 1093
Buildings (Procopius), 116, 424
Al-Bukhārī (collector of *ḥadīth*), 1081, 1089
Bulayïq library, 1021–1022
Burgundian kings, 38, 46, 891–892
Burning Bush, Justinianic complex at site of, Sinai, 945, *946*, 954
Buzandaran Patmut'iwnk' (*Epic Histories*), 119
Byzance après Byzance (Iorga, 1935), 1149
Byzance: Grandeur et décadence (Diehl, 1957), 1149
Byzantine History (Malchus), 420
Byzantium, 1148–1165. *See also* Constantinople
bureaucratic-administrative structures, 1125
Christianity in
church hierarchy, imperial reliance on, 612–613
essentially Christian character of Byzantium, 1149–1150, 1151, 1163–1164
heterodoxy and orthodoxy, concern with, 1154–1155, 1164
monasticism and asceticism, 1151, 1158, 1164
Orthodoxy (Christianity as civil religion), development of, 1160–1164
theology as new philosophy, 1154–1156
classical versus Late Antique heritage, 1151–1152
concept of, 1148–1150
economic history of Eastern empire, 607–614

Byzantium (*continued*)
hagiography in, 1152–1154
history writing in Eastern empire. *See under* history writing in Late Antiquity
"little eschatology" in, 1157–1160
liturgy and liturgical poetry, 1156–1157, 1158–1160
as natural geographical entity, 1121
philosophy in, 1151, 1154–1156
resource distribution in, 1134
silk industry in, 612–613

Caecina Mavortius Basilius Decius, 607
Caesarea in Asia Minor, founding of hospital in. *See under* hospitals
Caesarius of Arles, 476, 493, 682, 683, 829, 891–892
Caesars (Julian), 408
Caesars (Suetonius), 410
Caetani, Leone, 1078–1179
Cahill, Thomas, xi
Calasso, Roberto, 384
Caldwell, Craig H., III, xxxvii, 92
Callimachus, 365, 370, 385n3
Calvet, Yves, 1018
Cambyses (Persian ruler), 1071
Cameron, Alan, 343, 363
Cameron, Averil, 863
Candidus (historian), 420
Canon (Mary of Egypt), 1156
canon law, 804
canonicity, 924–927
Capgras syndrome, 975–976, 977, 988
Capito (historian), 420
Caracalla (emperor), 63, 745–746, 749, 750, 791
Carmen Pashcale (Sedulius), 345
Carmina Arcana (Gregory of Nazianzus), 380
Carmina Minora (Claudius Claudianus), 339
Carolingian dynasty, xvii, 10, 31, 34, 40, 49, 348, 820, 829, 891, 893, 905n185
Carter, Robert, 305
Cartesian dualism, 517–518, 530, 540, 542–543, 977
cartography, 567–572, *568*, *569*, *571*, *572*
Casanova, Paul, 1088, 1091
Cassiodorus
Avitus of Vienne compared, 892
barbarians and, 66, 69
Chronicle, 422
cosmology of Ptolemy and, 575
Gothic History, 424
history writing in Late Antiquity and, 422, 423, 424, 426, 427, 429
Institutes, 427, 575
Italian Renaissance interest in, 1175, 1176
mental world of Late Antiquity and, 15
on Paul of Nisibis, 1007
physics and metaphysics of, 541–542
rural and urban environments, relationship between, 629
On the Soul, 541–542
Variae, 831, 832, 836, 837
Western kingdoms, development of, 47
Castalius (historian), 424
castra, 605–606
Catechetical Lectures (Cyril of Jerusalem), 885
catenae, 20, 933n24
Cathemerinon (Prudentius), 347
Cato the Elder, 699n151
Cave of Treasures, 21
Celenza, Christopher, xxxvii, 1172
celibacy, repeal of Augustan penalties for, 673
Celsus (pagan philosopher), 1185
Cento Nuptialis (Ausonius), 336, 340, 352n52
Central Asia and the Silk Road, 142–158. *See also* Turks in Central Asia
Chinese control of, 144, 151–152, 154, 158
Church of the East, expansion of, 144, 151, 158, 1019–1022
climate and geography, 142–143, *143*, 144
cultural-linguistic groups, 143–144
economy, impact of invasion on, 146–148
end of trade network, 157–158
Hunnic invasion, 144–146
map, *143*
Nestorian Monument, Xi'an, China, xi, *xiii*, *xiv*, xv, 151, 158, 996, 1022–1024
northward shift of trade routes, 148–149
religions in, 144, 150, 151, 158, 1019–1122
Sasanian Persia and, 144–145, 157
Western section of Silk Road, 155–157
Cerati, André, 600
Cervidius Scaevola, 809n54
CG (*Codex Gregorianus*), 794, 795, 796, 830, 831, 832
CH (*Codex Hermogenianus*), 794, 795, 796, 830, 831, 832
Chabbi, Jacqueline, 1085
Chalcidius (Platonic commentator), 576
Chaldean Church. *See* Church of the East
Chaldean Oracles, 17, 516, 1188
Chapel of Priest John, Church of Amos and Kasiseus, Khirbet el-Mukhayyat, Jordan, 949, *950*
Chapters/Mirror of Princes (Deacon Agapetus), 1153, 1161
Chararic (Frankish king), 38
charity. *See also* hospitals
bishop's role in providing, 885–886
as Christian value, 719, 723, 730, 866
Charlemagne, xv, 894
chartae. *See* letters
Chavarría Arnau, Alexandra, 603, 607
Chayanov, A. V., 637
Cherubic hymn, 1156
child donations, 230
child exposure, 686

Childebert II (Merovingian king), 821–822
Childeric (Merovingian king), 38
childlessness, repeal of Augustan penalties for, 673
children. *See also* marriage and family
  guardianship of minors, 675, 802
  hospitals for women giving birth, 734–735
  illegitimate, 683, 689
  inheritance, 672, 673–674, 679
  patria potestas, 670, 672, 684, 685, 802
Chilperic (Merovingian king), 821, 822, 904–905n155
China
  An Lushan, rebellion of, 157–158
  bureaucratic-administrative structures, 1125
  Central Asia, control over, 144, 151–152, 154, 158
  economic development in, 1116–1119
  geography, effects of, 1120–1121
  Islamic use of paper and, 1067
  Nestorian Monument, Xi'an, xi, *xiii*, *xiv*, xv, 151, 158, 996, 1022–1024
  population and demographics compared to Western Eurasia, 1113–1114
  ritual penetration of ideologies in, 1131–1132
  Roman empire and, 8, 10, 11, 22, 1111–1112
  Sasanian contact with, 12
  Silk Road, Chinese section of, 152–155
  Sogdian merchant graves in, 153–154
  Xiongnu invasions, 144, 145–146
Chionites, 145, 146
Chloderic (Frankish king), 38
Chosroes. *See entries at* Khusrō
Christ
  historical Jesus movement, 1078, 1093, 1098–1099
  icons and relics of, 971–973, *972*, 985
Christian History (Philip of Side), 418
Christian Topography (Cosmas Indicopleustes), 21, 148–149, 255, 259, 260, 573, 579–580, 1019
Le christianisme dans l'empire perse sous la dynastie sassanide (Labourt, 1904), 997
Christianismes orientaux (1993), 225
Christianity. *See also* Bible; bishops; Church of the East; conversion to Christianity; forgery of religious documents; heterodoxy; liturgy; monasticism and asceticism; object relations in Late Antiquity; orthodoxy; sacred space
  animal sacrifice in, 856
  apocalypticism of, 1065–1067
  in Arabia. *See under* Arabs and Arabia
  Balkans, Christian church in, 94, 98–99, 103–106, 110
  barbarians and. *See under* barbarians
  in Byzantium. *See under* Byzantium
  canon law, 804
  charity, as value of, 719, 723, 730. *See also* hospitals
  citizenship and, 748
  clergy. *See also* bishops
    of Church of the East, 1001–1002
    sanctuary, social division between laity and clergy indicated by, *952*, 955–957, *956*
  coexistence with paganism, 859–862, 1012–1013
  communication in Late Antiquity and, 819–820
  conflict, coercion, and violent incidents, 859–862, 888
  Edict of Toleration (313 C.E.), 849
  education and, 22, 380, 381, 475–477
  in Egypt. *See* Coptic literature, *and under* Egypt
  fluidity of religious identity and, xviii–xix, 864–865, 888, 1012–1013
  Greek poetry and, 365–368, 371–372, 375, 380–382, 386n10
  Hellenism and religious identity. *See under* Hellenism
  history, Christian understanding of, 405–406, 407–408
  Islam, non-Muslim communities under, 1059–1062, 1129
  justice and equality, interest in, 769, 777–779
  Late Antiquity, Christian character of, 1149–1150
  Latin poetry and, 343–348
  law and legal culture affected by, 801–804
  marriage and family, influence on, 667–668, 671, 677, 679–684, 686, 693–694
  "pagan survivals" in, 857–859, 864–865, 1012–1014
  penitential rites, 683
  periodization of Late Antiquity favoring, 5
  power of church to impose views, 682–684, 865
  pragmatic and popular religion, 856–857
  Qur'ān on, 1058, 1060, 1061, 1090
  rise to dominance, narrative of, 849–851, 1185
  ritual penetration of state ideology and, 1132–1133
  Roman empire, Christian universality as spiritual heir to, 10, 13, 18–19, 20–21, 1160–1163
  in Sasanian Persia. *See under* Sasanian Persia
  social repercussions of, 865–866
  Syriac. *See* Syria, Syriac, and Syrians
  terminological issues, 853, 1025
  travel writing and, 564–567
  universalism of, 1058
Christodorus of Coptos, 363, 369, 372
Christology. *See* Council of Chalcedon (451 C.E.) and Chalcedonian controversy; heterodoxy; Nicaea, First Council of; orthodoxy
Chromatius of Aquileia, 414, 492
Chronica (Nepos), 410
Chronica Minora, 53n78
Chronici Canones (Eusebius of Caesarea), 565

Chronicle (Cassiodorus), 422
Chronicle (Eusebius of Caesarea)
continuations of, 411–412, 416, 426, 428–429
history writing in Late Antiquity revolutionized by, 405–407, 407–408, 421
Chronicle (George Hamartolos), 1150
Chronicle (Hydatius), 416
Chronicle (Jacob of Edessa), 429
Chronicle (John Malalas), 1150
Chronicle (Prosper of Aquitaine), 416, 422
"Chronicle of Arbela," 421
Chronicle of Edessa, 421
Chronicle of Joshua the Stylite, 296
Chronicle of Michael the Syrian, 298
Chronicle of Siirt [*Seert*], 172, 998, 999, 1004, 1006–1007, 1008, 1014, 1016, 1019, 1028n29
Chronicle of Thomas, 429
Chronicon Paschale, 428, 721, 722
Chronographer of 354, 410
Chronographia (Eusebius of Caesarea), 118
Chronographia (John Malalas), 429
Church History [*Ecclesiastical History*] (Eusebius), 175, 236, 274, 408, 414, 416, 421, 426, 880, 996
Church History [*Ecclesiastical History*] (Philostorgius), 255, 418
Church History (Socrates), 418–419, 426, 447
Church History (Sozomen), 419, 426
Church History (Theodoret of Cyrrhus), 419, 426
Church History (Theodore Lector), 424
Church History [*Ecclesiastical History*] (Rufinus of Aquileia), 10, 255, 257, 273–274, 414, 415, 418
Church of the East [Nestorians, East Syriac Christianity, Assyrian Church, Chaldean Church], 994–1026
Arab episcopal sees, *Synodicon orientale* providing information about, 254
Arabian influence, 1005–1006, 1017–1018
in Armenia, 126
in Central Asia, 144, 151, 158, 1019–1022
Christology of, 1009–1011, 1024
"Great Slaughter" (344–379 C.E.), 1000–1002, 1006
in Ḥimyar, 282
historiography of, 995–997
Islam, under, 1015–1018, 1024–1026
Jacobite or West Syriac Church and, 1010–1011, 1016, 1024
Jews, relationship with, 999–1001
lay society and practice, 1011–1014
literacy in, 1007–1008
literature of, 1004, 1006–1009
Manichaeism and, 999, 1010–1011, 1024, 1026
mental world of Late Antiquity and, 18
monasticism and school movement, 1006–1009
Nestorian Monument, Xi'an, China, xi, *xiii*, *xiv*, xv, 151, 158, 996, 1022–1024
origins of, 997–1000
sacred space in, 1011–1012
Sasanian Persia and
acculturation to, 1004–1005
court, ecclesiastical relationship with, 1014–1015
persecution of Christians, 1000–1002, 1004, 1006
Synod of 410 C.E., endorsement of, 994–995, 1002–1003
terminological issues, 995–996
Timothy I's philosophical defense of Christianity before al-Mahdī, 1024–1026
unification of Eastern Christians under single hierarchy, 1002–1006
churches and church architecture, 938–943, *940–943*. *See also* sacred space
Chuvin, Pierre, 852–853
Cicero
Ad familiares, 835
Brutus, 1177
De oratore, 805
De republica, 576
Dream of Scipio (*Somnium Scipionis*), 576
Italian Renaissance interest in, 1172, 1175, 1176, 1177, 1183–1184
on law and legal culture, 768, 769, 791, 795, 805
letters of, 829, 835
Life of Cicero (Plutarch), 1184
in mental world of Late Antiquity, 13
on physics and metaphysics, 531, 532, 533, 576
Tusculan Disputations, 1183
Cimitile/Nola, tomb of St. Felix at, 856, 947
cities and towns. *See* urban environment
citizenship, 744–755. *See also* universal citizenship
access to, 744
in ancient Athens, 1126
Antonine Constitution (*Constitutio Antoniniana*) granting, 63, 745–747, 791
barbarians and Roman law, 62–63, 751–754
Christianity and, 748
coloni, 63, 615, 637, 726, 752, 801
conveyance of, 754–755
dediticii excluded from, 746, 750
ethnic, 748
expansion of concept of, 747–749
gentiles, 63, 67, 752, 753, 754
hospitals, citizens not favored in, 719–720, 732
laeti, 63, 752, 753, 754
law and legal culture, at center of, 791
legal privileges and obligations conveyed by, 744, 746, 748–749
liberti, 744, 746–747, 750
marriage and family affected by, 679, 690, 702n242, 752
municipal and regional, 747
peregrini, 746, 749–751
slaves' access to, 744, 746–747, 750

City of God (Augustine), 415, 745, 791
civil and civic values in Late Antiquity, 13, 15
civilization, concept of, 6, 24n4
Claessen, Henri J.-M., 1121
class and class structure. *See also* aristocracy; peasantry; slavery
  bishops, class origins of, 882
  middle class in Byzantium, 607, 608
  poor and powerlessness in Late Antique West, 599–600
  sanctuary, social division between laity and clergy indicated by, 952, 955–957, *956*
  in villages of Eastern Mediterranean, 610
  wage labor in Byzantium, expansion of, 607–608
Classical Receptions Journal, xxi
Classicianus (legal client of Symmachus), 778
Claudian (Christian epigrammist), 377
Claudian (Claudius Claudianus), 338–339, 340, 363, 377, 378, 384, 751, 825
Claudius I (emperor), 176, 178, 180, 181
Claudius II Gothicus (emperor), 96
Claudius Marius Victorius of Marseilles, 345
Claudius Ptolemy, 8, 11, 19, 22, 66, 253, 568, 573–577, 1068
Clement of Alexandria, 443, 978
Clement of Rome, 897n13, 916
Cleopatra, 8
clergy. *See also* bishops
  of Church of the East, 1001–1002
  sanctuary, social division between laity and clergy indicated by, 952, 955–957, *956*
client kingship, 32–36, 42, 43, 44, 98
Climacus, John. *See* John Climacus
climate, 627–628
  in Arabia, 248, *249*, 305–306
  in Central Asia, 142–143, *143*, 144
  in Ethiopia, *249*, 254
  imperial decline of sixth century and, 1114–1116
Clodius Albinus, 598
Clovis (Merovingian king), 15, 38, 49, 892–893
CMCL (*Corpus dei Manoscritti Copti Letterari*) database (Orlandi, 1970s), 227
Codex Gregorianus (*CG*) [*Gregorian Code*], 794, 795, 796, 830, 831, 832
Codex Hermogenianus (*CH*) [*Hermogenian Code*], 794, 795, 796, 830, 831, 832
Codex Justinianus. *See Corpus Iuris Civilis*
Codex Salmasianus, 342–343
Codex Theodosianus. *See Theodosian Code*
"codex of visions," 365
codifications of law, 794, 795–801, 830. *See also specific codes*
coins and coinage. *See* monetary system; numismatics
Collatio of Mosaic and Roman Law (*Lex Dei*), 794
collected letters, 828–840
  format and metadata of original letter, loss of, 833–834
  functions of, 834–840
  as historical sources, 833
  Late antique surge in, 816
  types of letter collections, 828–832
collective action in rural communities, tensions associated with, 638–639
Colluthus of Lycopolis, 369, 370
Cologne Mani Codex, 999
coloni, 63, 615, 637, 726, 752, 801
Columba (Irish missionary and abbot of Iona), 427
Column of Trajan, Rome, 570
Cometas (Greek poet), 382–383
Commemoratio (Ausonius), 352n52
Commentary on Aristotle's De Caelo (Simplicius), 574
Commentary on the Dream of Scipio (Macrobius), 576
Commentary on Micah (Cyril of Alexandria), 1162
Commentary on the Timaeus (Chalcidius), 576
Commentary on the Timaeus (Porphyry), 576
Commentary on the Timaeus (Proclus Diadochus), 452–453, 574
communication in Late Antiquity, 815–840. *See also* collected letters; letters
  archives, use of, 822
  bishops' use of, 819–820, 825, 829
  as cultural index, 820–823
  embassies and envoys, 816–818
  gifts as, 817, 818
  as historical sources, 823–826, 833
  historiography of, 820
  interdependent and performative nature of, 817–818
companionate marriage, 667, 668, 670, 680
comparative state formation. *See* political systems in Late Antiquity
complexity theory, 1140n69
concubinage, 681, 689–690, 703n248
consanguineous marriage, Sasanian practice of, 1005, 1011
consistory hearings, 790
Consolation of Philosophy (Boethius), 764
Constans I (emperor), 411, 850, 862
Constans II (emperor), 131–132, 133
Constantelos, D. J., 738n50
Constantianus (general), 106
Constantine I the Great (emperor)
  Abgar of Edessa as prototype of, 180, 181, 182
  baptism of, 883
  barbarian settlements of, 752
  bishops, impact on institution of, 880–883, 893
  churches and basilicas founded by, 939–941, 944

Constantine I the Great (emperor) (*continued*)
  conversion to Christianity, 850, 851, 1000, 1057
  Donation of Constantine, xix, 893
  Edict of Toleration (313 C.E.), 849
  Ethiopian conversion to Christianity and, 274–275, 293
  Hellenism and, 448
  historical accounts of reign of, 409
  historical writing, new Christian style of, 408
  hospitals, 723, 738n50
  ideology of Christian Roman empire, 21
  judicial procedure under, 765–767, 777–778
  laws of, 798, 799, 801–802
  Life of Constantine (Eusebius of Caesarea), 801, 1161–1162
  marriage and family law under, 673–675, 678, 802
  monetary system, restructuring of, 597, 598, 599, 1118
  new aristocracy under, development of, 597–598, 602
  Pannonia, conquest of, 98, 99
  periodization of Late Antiquity and, 4–5, 9
  Sasanian Persia, relationship with, 1000, 1002
  Zosimus on, 419
Constantine II (emperor), 862
Constantine III (emperor), 42
Constantine IV (emperor), 922
Constantine V (emperor), 1164
Constantinople. *See also* Byzantium
  apocalypticism and, 1066
  as both political and religious capital, 1163, 1164–1165
  Hagia Sophia, 948–949, 954, 960n57, *986*, 986–987, *987*
  history writing in, 417–420, 423–425, 427–430
  liturgical practices in, 953–955
  Sasanian siege of, 896
  special authority of bishopric of, 882–883
Constantinople, Councils of
  I (381 C.E.), 804, 918
  II (553 C.E.), 895, 921–923
  III (680/1 C.E.), 916, 919, 920, 922, 927, 928, 930–931, 1160
Constantinoplis Christiana (Du Cange), 729
Constantius I (emperor), 96
Constantius II (emperor), 99, 100, 275, 278, 281, 293, 449, 598, 721, 722, 850, 862, 1000
Constantius III (emperor), 35, 41, 42–43
Constitutio Antoniniana (Antonine Constitution), 63, 674, 678, 745–747, 749, 754, 791, 827
Constitutio Tanta, 796
Constitutiones Sirmondiani, 830, 831, 832, 838
Consultatio veteris cuiusdam iurisconsulti, 794
Contra Celsum (Origen), 1185
Contra Symmachum (Prudentius), 347
conversion to Christianity, xviii–xix, 863
  by aristocracy, 413–414, 863
  Armenia, conversion of, 119–120
  of Augustine of Hippo, 539–541
  bishops as missionaries, 889
  of Constantine, 850, 851, 1000, 1057
  diplomatic conversion missions, 65, 68
  education leading to, 475–476
  effects of, 865–866
  Ethiopia, conversion of, 273–276
  Greek poetry and, 380
  "pagan survivals" despite, 857–859, 864–865
  rates of, 853–854, 863
  reasons for, 863
  ritual penetration of state ideology and, 1132
  from Zoroastrianism, 1004, 1005, 1010
Cook, Michael, 1053, 1055, 1081, 1084
Cooper, John, 207
Cooper, Kate, 689
copper coinage (*follis*), 608
Coptic Grammatical Categories (Shisha-Halevy, 1986), 233
Coptic literature, 224–238. *See also* Egypt, *and specific authors and works*
  Arab conquest affecting, 224–225, 230, 238
  Bible, importance of, 230–231
  categorization of, 225–226, 229
  Chalcedonian controversy shaping, 229, 236–237
  Damian (patriarch), period of, 237
  dating of surviving manuscripts, 227
  fragmented nature of, 226–227
  Greek influence on, 224, 228–229
  hagiographies, 234–235, 236, 238
  homilies, 229, 235, 236–237
  layered nature of content, 229
  monastic libraries, survival in, 227–228
  Origenist controversy shaping, 229, 231–232, 237
  original language of texts, questions regarding, 228
  Pachomian material, 228, 231–232
  patristic translations, 234–235
  pseudepigrapha, commonness of, 228
  Shenoute, works of, 228, 230, 233–234, 236, 241n61
Coquin, René-Georges, 225–226
Corcoran, Simon, 798
Corippus (Flavius Cresconius Corippus), 343, 370, 751
Cornelius (pope), 724
Cornelius Nepos, 410
Corpus dei Manoscritti Copti Letterari (CMCL database; Orlandi, 1970s), 227
Corpus hermeticum, 516

Corpus Iuris Civilis (*Code, Digest,* and *Novellae* of Justinian)
in Armenia, 130–131
on citizenship, 747
in law and legal culture of Late Antiquity, 789, 791, 792, 794, 795, 796, 797, 800
as letter collection, 830, 838–839
on marriage and family, 672
mental world of Late Antiquity and, 20
in Western kingdoms, 49
correspondence. *See* communication in Late Antiquity
The Corrupting Sea (Horden and Purcell, 2000), 78
Cosmas and Damian, icons in hagiography of, 971–972, 983–984
Cosmas Indicopleustes [Kosmas Indicopleustēs]
on Arabia and Ethiopia, 255, 259, 260, 277, 290
on Central Asia, 148–149
Christian Topography, 21, 148–149, 255, 259, 260, 573, 579–580, 1019
on Church of the East, 1019
cosmological schema of, 573
Hellenism and, 455
mentality of Late Antiquity and, 10–11, 21
world, Late Antique concepts of, 566, 579–580
Cosmic Description (John of Gaza), 377
cosmology
geocentricity of, 583n64
heterodoxy and, 579–580
instrumentalist interpretation of, 584n70
maps and travel writing, relationship to, 572–578
physics and metaphysics of, 529, 530–533, 537
Councils of the Church. *See also* Council of Chalcedon (451 C.E.) and Chalcedonian controversy; Constantinople, Councils of
Ancyra (314 C.E.), 1003
Antioch (324 C.E.), 1003
Ephesus I (431 C.E.), 420, 800, 804, 920, 922, 927–928. *See also* Church of the East; Church of the East, Christology of; Nestorius and Nestorianism;
Ephesus II (Robber Synod, 449 C.E.), 183, 492
Gangra (340 C.E.), 505, 508n79, 722, 1003
Neocaesarea (314/319 C.E.), 1003
Nicaea I (325 C.E.), 420, 804, 882, 888, 916, 1002, 1003
Nicaea II (787 C.E.), 928, 971
Pisidian Laodicea (347/395 C.E.), 1003
Quinisext Council *in Trullo* (691–692 C.E.), 124–125, 920, 1160–1164
Serdica (343 C.E.), 893
Theodosius II, monks required to stay out of Councils by, 1164
Council of Chalcedon (451 C.E.) and Chalcedonian controversy. *See also* Church of the East; Nestorius and Nestorianism; Syria, Syriac, and Syrians
Acts of Chalcedon, 888
Apollonian forgeries and, 917–919, 920–921, 924–925
canons of Council, 804
Church of the East, Christology of, 1009–1011, 1024
Coptic literature shaped by, 229, 236–237
Egyptian Christianity in doctrinal disagreements with empire regarding, 198, 199
Franks and Vandals converted to Chalcedonian orthodoxy, 63
Fronto, letters of (palimpsestic), 829
Jacobite or West Syriac Church, 1010–1011, 1016, 1024
monastic involvement in, 491, 492, 498
Monophysitism/Miaphysitism, 18, 189–190, 283, 420, 579, 895, 924–925, 1010
neo-Chalcedonians, 918, 921, 924–925
Tome (Pope Leo I), 893
countryside. *See* agriculture and rural environment
Courcelle, Pierre, 539
Cowe, S. Peter, 122
creation *ex nihilo*, 575, 577, 579
Cribiore, Raffaella, 210
criminal law, 802–804
Croke, Brian, xxxvii, 405
Crone, Patricia, 302, 1053, 1055, 1080, 1083, 1088
Crook, J., 805
culture and learning. *See also* education; history writing in Late Antiquity; literacy; literature; philosophy; physics and metaphysics
ascetics' apparent rejection of, 487–488, 493, 494–495
authority as criterion, 20, 579
Hellenism and, 437–438, 441, 447, 448
Islamic tradition regarding pre-Islamic Arabia, 309
mental world of Late Antiquity, role in, 19–21, 341
totalization of learning, 19
traditional culture, continued valuation of, 477–479
Curatio (Theodoret of Cyrrhus), 444–445
currency. *See* monetary system
cursus publicus, 546, 819
Cycle (Agathias of Myrina), 369, 372
Cyprian of Antioch, 368, 376, 382, 383
Cyprian of Carthage, 723–724, 857, 879–880, 881, 882
Cyprian the Gaul, 345
Cyraicus, Coptic martyrdom of, 235
Cyril of Alexandria, 183, 234, 861, 888, 917–922, 924–925, 927–928, 1162

Cyril of Jerusalem, 885, 1156
Cyril of Scythopolis, 490
Cyrus and John, Miracles of (Sophronius of Jerusalem), 440–442
Cyrus of Panopolis, 363, 368

Dadīšō' (Church of the East catholicos), 978–980, 1004, 1005, 1008
Damascius (pagan philosopher), 385n4, 453–454, 470
Damasus (pope), 887, 893
Damian (patriarch), Coptic literature under, 237
Daniel of Khuzistan, 1017
Dante Alighieri, 1176
Daoism, 1023
Daphniaca (Agathias of Myrina), 370
David (bishop of Basra), 1019
Davies, Wendy, 605
Davis, Stephen, 985
De actibus Apostolorum (Arator), 339, 345
De cursu stellarum (*On the Course of the Stars;* Gregory of Tours), 576, 577
De deitate Filii et Spiritus Sancti (Gregory of Nyssa), 235
De excidio (Gildas), 426–427
De gentibus Indiae et Bragmanibus (Palladius), 208
De Guignes, Joseph, 145
de Haas, Frans A. J., 515
de Jong, Albert, 1012
De laudibus Dei (Dracontius), 342
De locis sanctis (*On the Holy Places;* Adomnán), 566, 985
De locis sanctis (*On the Holy Places;* Bede), 566
De mensuris et ponderibus (Epiphanius of Salamis), 132
De mortibus boum (Endelechius), 346
De mysteriis (*On the Mysteries;* Iamblichus), 1185, 1187
De opificio mundi (John Philoponus), 580
De oratore (Cicero), 805
de Prémare, Alfred-Louis, 1088–1089
De raptu Proserpinae (Claudius Claudianus), 339
De rebus bellicis, 597–598, 795
De reditu suo (Rutilius Namatianus), 339–340
De republica (Cicero), 576
de Roover, Raymond, 608
De spiritalis historiae gestis (Alcimus Avitus), 345
De vanitate vitae (George of Pisidia), 363–364
Décadence romaine ou Antiquité tardive? (Marrou, 1977), 1150
Decembrio, Angelo, 1182–1183
Decius (emperor), 96, 828, 879
"decline and fall," historiographical themes of, xiv–xv, xix, 4–5
  Augustine's use of, 21
  barbarians associated with collapse of empire, 68, 70, 74, 1177–1180
  bishops and, 890
  in economic history, 606, 614–616
  Islam and, 1054–1055
  in Italian Renaissance, 1172–1173, 1179–1181
  Latin poetry and, 335
  paganism, narrative of decline of, 849–851, 853–854
  reasons for imperial decline of sixth century, 1113–1116
  religion associated with, 70, 850
  Western aristocracy, decline of, 598–599, 606–607, 615
Decline and Fall of the Roman Empire (Gibbon, 1776–1789), xii–xv, xx, 4
  on barbarians, 61, 69–70
  on Byzantium, 1149–1150
  on Islam, 1054, 1055
  Italian Renaissance and, 1172, 1180
  on justice and equality, 767
  Latin poetry and, 336, 338
  on marriage and family, 679
  monasticism and, 505n2
dedicatory letters, 826–827, 837
dediticii, 746, 750
Deioces, tyrant of Media, 780n7
Deliyannis, Deborah, xxi
Della famiglia (Alberti, Leon Battista), 1178
Delogu, Paolo, 615
Demetrios (patriarch of Antioch), 998
Democritus, 528
demographics. *See* population and demographics
demons
  paganism and, 852, 855
  in physics and metaphysics, 536
Demosthenes, 469
Demougeot, Emilienne, 750
Descartes, René, 517–518, 530, 540, 542–543, 977
Description of Hagia Sophia (Paul the Silentiary), 375, 379
Description of Greece (Pausanias of Magnesia), 563
desert fathers. *See* monasticism and asceticism
Desiderius of Cahors, 837, 841n9
Dexippos, 47–408, 417
Dhamar'alī Yuhabirr (king of Ḥimyar), dynasty of, 263–268
diachronic versus synchronic treatments of Late Antiquity, xxi, 5–6
Diadochus of Photike, 501
Dialogue with Trypho (Justin Martyr), 1165n12
Dialogues (Pope Gregory I), 1157
Diatessaron, 174, 175, 176, 182, 185, 189, 355n123
Didache, 877–878, 897n18, 916
Didaskalia, 897n18
Didius Julianus, 602
Diehl, Charles, 1149
Digest of Justinian. *See Corpus Iuris Civilis*
Dillon, John, 516
Dio Cassius, 745

Diocletian (emperor)
in Balkans, 96, 97, 104, 105, 106
Christians, persecution of (303–313), 236, 880
Greek encomium to, 364
Lactantius on, 601
law and legal culture under, 678, 792, 794, 798
Manichaeism, rescript letter against, 794
Maximum Prices edict (301 C.E.), 798
mental world of Late Antiquity and, 5
provinces under, 205, 602
religion, public expenditures on, 854
Spalatum (Split), Diocletian's palace at, 104, 106
Diodore of Tarsus, 411–412
Dionysiaca (Nonnos of Panopolis), 361, 363, 365, 367, 370–371, 375, 376, 378, 381–384
Dionysius the Areopagite [Pseudo-Dionysius], 541, 916–917, 1154, 1155, 1188
Dionysius Periegetes, 385n1, 563
Dioscorides (medical writer), 253
Dioscorus of Alexandria, 198, 236
Dioskoros of Aphroditō [Dioscorus of Aphrodito] and Dioskoros archive, 203, 211, 370, 376
Diospolis, miraculous column of St. George at, 985
diplomacy in Late Antiquity, 64–65. *See also* political systems in Late Antiquity
divination, 855, 862
Divine Institutes (Lactantius), 344, 791
divorce, 667–668, 673, 676–680, 690, 703n255, 802, 804
Doctrina Addai, 172–177, 180–182, 187, 189, 190
The Doctrine of the Subtle Body in Western Tradition (1919), 538
Dodds, E. R., 538, 544n12
Dome of the Rock, Jerusalem, 1058, 1061
Domnio (bishop and martyr), 105
donatio ante nuptias, 668, 675, 678, 690–691
Donation of Constantine, xix, 893
Donatists, 18, 880, 893, 1189
Donner, Fred, 1059, 1062, 1063, 1084, 1087
Doresse, Jean, 275
Dorotheus of Gaza, 501, 505
Dorotheus the Syrian, 1068
Doubts about Galen (Zakariyyā' al-Rāzī), 1068
Doubts about Ptolemy (Ibn al-Haytham), 1068
dowries, 672, 675, 690, 691, 703n248
Dracontius (Latin poet), 342
Drake, H. A., 869n64
Dream of Scipio (*Somnium Scipionis;* Cicero), 576
Drewes, A. J., 278
Drijvers, H. J. W., 170–171, 180
Du Cange, C. du F., 729
dualism, Cartesian, 517–518, 530, 540, 542–543, 977
Dura-Europos house-church, 937, *938*
Durliat, Jean, 215n26
Duval, R., 170, 172
Dyophysites, 18, 921, 924–925. *See also* Church of the East
Dyotheletes, 922, 931

East Syriac Christianity. *See* Church of the East
Eastern empire. *See* Byzantium
Eastern Goths. *See* Ostrogoths
Eastern Philosophy (Ibn Sīnā; Avicenna), 1068
Ecclesiastical History [*Church History*] (Eusebius), 175, 236, 274, 408, 414, 416, 421, 426, 880, 996
Ecclesiastical History [*Church History*] (Philostorgius), 255, 418
Ecclesiastical History [*Church History*] (Rufinus of Aquileia), 10, 255, 257, 273–274, 414, 415, 418
The Echo Maker (Price, 2006), 975
Eclogues (Virgil), 336, 346
economic history, 597–616. *See also* monetary system
aristocracy, changes in, 597–599, 606–607, 611–613. *See also* aristocracy
of Armenia, 132–133
barbarians, new approaches to, 77–78
in Byzantium, 607–614
church hierarchy, Byzantine reliance on, 612–613
Egypt, importance of, 198–201, 208–210
Ethiopia and Arabia, importance of long-distance trade for, 259–261
Islam's emergence as dominant economic power, 615–616
Makka, as commercial power, 300–302
Middle Ages, transition to, 614–616
middle class in Eastern empire, 607, 608
multiple trajectories of, 597–599
pagan practice and, 854
political systems in Late Antiquity and, 1116–1119
poor and powerlessness in Late Antique West, 599–600
pre-*hijra* economic crisis in Arabia, 305–306
provinces, proliferation of, 601, 602
Roman real estate, aristocratic domination of, 602–603
rural estates/villas, Western aristocratic investment in, 601–602, 603–607, 615
Silk Road. *See* Central Asia and the Silk Road
slaves and *mancipia*, 615
taxation, 600, 601, 632–633, 634, 745, 1059, 1117, 1135
urban commercial vitality in Eastern Mediterranean, 608–609, 612–614, 615–616
village settlements in East, 610
wage labor in Eastern empire, expansion of, 607–608
in Western empire, 599–607

Edessa, foundation history of, 174, 175–177, 180–182, 187
Edict *Ad Populum* (320 C.E.), 673
Edict of the Aediles, 791
Edict of Maximum Prices (301 C.E.), 798, 799
Edict of Toleration (313 C.E.), 849
Edictum Perpetuum (Praetorian Edict), 791–792, 793
education, 467–479. *See also* culture and learning
  Athenian Academy, closure of, 477–478, 850
  Christianity and, 22, 380, 381, 475–477
  Church of the East, school movement in, 1006–009
  as classical value, 13, 468
  Greek poetry and, 363, 370, 373–375, 377, 378–380
  Hellenism and, 437–438, 441, 447, 448
  influence of, 474–477
  levels and stages of, 468–471
  mental world of Late Antiquity, role in, 19–21
  of monks, 501–502, 503–505
  paganism and, 475–477
  places of study, 471–472
  rhetorical rules, 373–375
  social and intellectual community, school as, 472–474
  totalization of learning and, 19
  traditional culture, continued valuation of, 477–479
Egeria (Roman pilgrim), 17, 173, 565–566, 936–937, 957
Egidius of Rheims, 821–823
Egypt, 195–214. *See also* Alexandria; Coptic literature
  agricultural importance of, 198, 199–200, 206, 209–210
  Arab conquest of, 199, 214
  Arianism in, 198, 721, 860
  aristocracy, emergence and evolution of, 611–612
  Christianity in
    adoption of religion by empire and, 197
    consolidation of monasteries, 203
    crises shaping, 229–230
    doctrinal disagreements with empire regarding, 198, 199
    ecclesiastical administration, 205–206
    influence of, 213–214
    papyri sources on, 197
    periodization of Late Antiquity and, 213
  communications routes and ports, 207–209
  economic importance of, 198–201, 208–210
  Greek poetry in, 362–363, 365–366, 370
  hospitals in, 729–730
  imperial administration in, 205
  literacy in, 210–212
  map of Egypt and Levant in Late Antiquity, *xlii*
  monastic life, social setting of, 489–490
  Nile, importance of, 195, 196, 199–200, 206–207
  pagarchy in, 205, 612
  papyri sources for, 196–197
  periodization of Late Antiquity in, 212–213
  Persian occupation of, 198–199
  plague of 541–542 in, 201–202, 215n26
  population of, 200–203, 215n26
  uniqueness of, 195–196
  urban environment in, 203–205
Egypt in Late Antiquity (Bagnall, 1993), 195–196
Eichman, Ricardo, 305
ekphrasis, 374
Elements of Astronomy (Proclus Diadochus), 574
Elephant, year/battle of, 286–287, 301
Elesbaa (Ethiopian ruler), 1154
Elias (provincial governor of Caesarea), 715
Elias (hagiographer), 187
Elias (bishop of Merv), 1020
"Elinskij Letopis," 1150
Ełišē [Elishe] (Armenian historian), 123, 422, 428
Elisha (nephew of Church of the East patriarch), 1014, 1035n159
elites. *See* aristocracy
Ella Aṣbəḥa [Kālēb] (king of Ethiopia), 259, 261, 275, 283–284, 288–292
Emmel, Stephen, 233
empires and states in Late Antiquity. *See* political systems in Late Antiquity
Enchiridion (*Handbook;* Pomponius), 781
endelechia, 1183–1185
Endelechius (Latin poet), 346
engagements, law governing, 674–675, 678
England. *See* Britain
Enneads (Plotinus), 522, 530, 533, 1188, 1189
Ennodius of Pavia, 347–348, 422, 423, 836, 1175
entelechia, 1183–1185
environmental change. *See* agriculture and rural environment; climate
environmental determinism, 65–66
Ephesus, First Council of (431 C.E.), 420, 800, 804, 920, 922, 927–928
Ephesus, Second Council of (449 C.E.) [Robber Synod], 183, 492
Ephorus (geographer), 11
Ephrem the Syrian, 170–173, 182–190, 727–728
Ephthalites [Hephthalites], 144–145, 146
epic Greek poetry, 370–371
Epic Histories (Armenian), 422, 610, 722
Epictetus (Greek philosopher), 478
Epigrammata Bobiensia, 351n42
epigrams, 342, 372–373
Epiphanius (*Historia Tripartita*), 426, 429
Epiphanius (sophist), 447, 476
Epiphanius of Salamis, 132, 411
Epiphanius, monastery of, 237
episcopal leadership. *See* bishops

Epistula Apostolorum, 232
epistulae. *See* collected letters; letters
Epistulae Austrasicae, 832
Epithalamium Fridi (Luxurius), 342
Epitome de Caesaribus, 413
Epitome of law (Hermogenian), 795
equality in Late Antiquity. *See* justice and equality
Eratosthenes (geographer), 8, 572–573
eschatology. *See* apocalypticism
Essarhaddon (Assyrian king), 1071
Ethiopia [Aksum, Axum], 254–259
  Arabia, links to, 247
  archaeological sites, 256–257
  conversion to Christianity, 273–280
  decline of, 299–300
  external sources regarding, 258–259
  ʿĒzānā, reign of, 276–281
  geography and climate, *249*, 254
  Ḥimyar as tributary of. *See under* Ḥimyar
  inscriptions from, 257–258, 288–289
  long-distance trade, importance of, 259–261
  map, *249*
  terminological issues, 254–255
ethnic citizenship, 748
ethnic identities, post-Roman, 18
ethnogenesis theory
  Arab identity, origins of, 306–308
  for barbarians in Europe, 69, 74–77
ethopoea, 374
Etymologiae (Isidore of Seville), 427, 576
Eucharist. *See* liturgy
Euchologion, 1157
Eudocia (daughter of Valentinian III), 37
Eudocia, Aelia (empress), 179, 368, 372, 375, 376, 380, 382, 383, 418
Eudoxia, Licinia (empress), 795, 883
Eudoxius of Antioch, 883
Eudoxus of Cnidus, 573
Eufrasius Basilica and ecclesiastical complex, Poreč, Croatia (ancient Parentium, Istria), 944–945, *945*, 949, 950, *952*, 955–957, *956*
Eugippius (hagiographer), 39
Eunapius of Sardis, 21, 362–363, 417–418, 419, 420, 471
Euphorion (Greek poet), 385n3
Eupraxius (imperial official), 420, 800
Euprepius (Alexandrian intellectual), 476
Eurasia in Late Antiquity, map of, *xli*
Euric the Goth, 34, 46
Eusebia (empress), 449
Eusebius of Caesarea
  on Abgar of Edessa, 175
  Armenian sources for, 118
  Basil of Caesarea and, 716
  on bishops, 880, 883
  Chronicle
    Chronici Canones, 565
    Chronographia, 118
    continuations of, 411–412, 416, 426, 428–429
    history writing in Late Antiquity revolutionized by, 405–407, 407–408, 421
  Coptic translations of, 236
  Ecclesiastical History [*Church History*], 175, 236, 274, 408, 414, 416, 421, 426, 880, 996
  Hellenism and, 443, 444, 445, 447
  as historian, 405–407, 407–408, 411, 414, 418, 421, 426, 428–429
  ideology of Christian Roman empire and, 21, 1161–1162
  laws of Constantine preserved in works of, 799
  Life of Constantine, 801, 1161–1162
  Onomasticon, 564–565
  Praeparatio Evangelica, 444
  Rufinus of Aquileia and, 274
  on water used in sacred spaces, 947
Eusebius of Nicomedia, 882, 883, 889
Eusebius of Vericelli, 492
Eustathius of Epiphaneia, 423
Eustathius of Sebaste, 721–722
Eustathius of Thessalonica, 383, 1152
Eustochius of Caesarea, 411
Eutharic (consul and son-in-law of Theoderic), 422
Eutropius (historian), 409–413, 420, 424, 429
Eutyches [monk and heresiarch], 920–921
Eutychianus (historian), 409
Evagrius Ponticus [Evagrius of Pontus], 240n34, 425, 427, 495, 499, 500, 501–502, 505, 832, 836
Evangeliorum libri IV (Juvencus), 344, 372
Evans Grubbs, Judith, 671, 697n105
Ewald, Heinrich, 1086, 1087
Excerpta Valesiana, 426
Expositio totius mundi et gentium, 95, 102, 103, 107, 108, 566, 577, 578, 609
Exuls (Kavafis, 1914), 384
ʿĒzānā [Aizanas] (king of Ethiopia), 255, 258, 261, 275–281
Ezekiel (Church of the East patriarch), 1011

The Fall of Rome and the End of Civilization (Ward-Perkins, 2005), 1149
The Fall of Troy (Triphiodorus of Panopolis), 364
families. *See* marriage and family
Fariana, 773–774
Fāṭima (daughter of Muḥammad), 1064
Faustus of Byzantium, 422, 722
Favorinus (sophist), 449–450, 1182
Festus (historian), 409, 410, 411, 413
Ficino, Marsilio, 1186, 1188–1192
Fiey, Jean-Maurice, 997
fifth element (Aristotle), 530
fire, air, and the heavens, 529, 530–533, 537. *See also* cosmology

Firmilian of Caesarea, 904n166
Firmus of Caesarea, 718
Flandrin, Jean Louis, 669
Flavian of Antioch, 886
Flavian of Constantinople, 920
Flavius Anastasius, 612
"Flavius," barbarian use of, 750
Flavius Cresconius Corippus, 343, 370, 751
Flavius Josephus, 426, 429, 1150
Flavius Licerius Firminus Lupicinus, 422
Flavius Merobaudes, 339
Flavius Valila [Theodobius], 751
Flavius Wallia (Gothic leader), 36, 37, 42
florilegia, 927–929, 1155
Florus (historian), 424
follis (copper coinage), 608
For the Temples (*Pro templis;* Libanius), 804, 856, 863
forgery of religious documents, xix, 916–933. *See also specific forgeries*
  apocrypha and pseudepigrapha, 917–918
  canonicity and, 924–927
  context, efforts to control, 924–926
  copies, originals, and authenticity, 929–931
  crime, not regarded as, 919–920
  ethical dimensions, failure to explore, 919–924
  florilegia, 927–929
  tension between ideology of continuity and inevitability of change leading to, 918–919, 924
  theodicy as means of document testing, 930–931
  theological argumentation, rhetoric of, 916–919, 920, 927, 931–932
  undermining of written authority by, 926–929
Forma Urbis Romae (map), 570–572, *571*, *572*
Forms, Platonic, 525–527
Forte, Antonio, 1023
fortifications, urban and rural, 630
Forty-Eight Saints and Martyrs, Church of, Armenia, 116–117
Forty Martyrs of Sebasteia, 116–117
Fountain of Knowledge (*Pege gnoseos;* John Damascene), 1155
fountains, used in sacred spaces, 947
428 AD: An Ordinary Year at the End of the Roman Empire (Traina, 2009), xxi
Fowden, Elizabeth Key, 1063
Fowden, Garth, 863, 1057, 1059, 1063
Fragmenta Vaticana, 794
Framing the Early Middle Ages (Wickham), 78, 213
Francovich, Riccardo, 614–615
Frange (bookbinder), 211
Frankfurter, David, 853, 855, 863
Franks
  bishops under, 892–893
  bureaucratic-administrative structures, failure to establish, 1127
  Carolingian dynasty, xvii, 10, 31, 34, 40, 49, 348, 820, 829, 891, 893, 905n185
  Chalcedonian orthodoxy, conversion to, 63
  integration of Gallic aristocracy and Frankish ruling class, 615
  kings of, 38–39
  Merovingian dynasty, 10, 38, 40, 49, 50, 599, 615, 821, 892–893, 895, 1129
  post-Roman ethnic identity of, 18
  Roman world, connection to, 50
Fredegund (Merovingian queen), 821
Frederic (Gothic prince), 36, 44, 45, 46
Freud, Sigmund, 977
Fronto (orator and tutor of Marcus Aurelius), 47, 829
Frontonianus of Salona, 106
Frumentius (bishop of Ethiopia), 274–275, 889
fundi, 606
Funk, Wolf-Peter, 231

Gabriel of Maishān, 1016
Gabriel of Sinjār, 1010
Gadara (king of Ethiopia), 277–278
Gaiseric (Vandal king), 37, 44, 45, 47
Gaius (lawyer), 790, 795, 796
Galen (physician and medical writer), 470, 534, 537, 542, 717
Galerius (emperor), 96, 98
Galla Placidia (regent and empress), 36, 44
Gallic Chronicle of 452 C.E., 416
Gallic Chronicle of 511 C.E., 416–417
Gallic War (Julius Caesar), 422
Gangra, Council of (340 C.E.), 505, 508n79, 722, 1003
Garnett, Richard, 384
Garnsey, Peter, 750, 768
Garsoïan, Nina G., 120
Gascou, Jean, 209, 211, 611, 612
Gaudemet, Jean, 679, 697n105
Gaul
  aristocracy of, 615
  bishops in, 891
  history writing in, 416–417
  Latin poetry in, 338–341, 348
  letters and letter collections, 820–821, 829
  rural estates/villas in, 603–604, 607
Gaza, Hellenism and religious violence at, 445, 446
Geary, Patrick, 75
Gelasius (correspondent of Sidonius), 837
Gelasius (pope), 850
Gelasius of Cyzicus, 420
Geminus, 577
gentiles, 63, 67, 752, 753, 754
Gentilismus, 75–76

geography. *See also* world, Late Antique conception of
 of Arabs and Arabia, 248, *249*, 305–306
 cartography, 567–572, *568*, *569*, *571*, *572*
 of Central Asia and the Silk Road, 142–143, *143*, 144
 determinism, geographical, 65–66
 of Ethiopia, *249*, 254
 Late Antiquity, geographical breadth of, xi–xvi, xx–xxi, 3–4
 political systems and, 1119–1121
Geography (Ananias of Širak), 156
Geography (Ptolemy), 568, 573, 582n48, 583n66
geopolitics of Late Antiquity, centrality of Roman empire to, 6–13
George (scholar employed by Makarios of Antioch), 923
George of Alexandria, 408–409, 860–861, 888
George Boktīšō‘, 1024
George the Grammarian, 385n6
George Hamartolos, 1150
George of Izla, 1010
George of Pisidia, 363–364, 367, 382, 386n6
Georgics (Virgil), 336
Georgios Gemistos Plethon, 1152
Georgios Gennadios Scholarios, 1151
Gepids, 102
Gerasa (Jerash, Jordan), St. Timothy's basilica at, 947
German nationalism and barbarian studies, 71–72, 75
Germania (Tacitus), 62, 69, 70
Germanus (patriarch of Constantinople), 987
Germinius (bishop), 99
Gerson, Lloyd, 522, 525, 1184
Gervasius of Tilbury, 567
Gessius, 470, 475
Getica (Jordanes), 69–70, 424
Ghassānids [Ghassānites], 293–294
Giardina, Andrea, 6, 25n8, 212
Gibbon, Edward. *See Decline and Fall of the Roman Empire*
Gibuldus (Alamannic king), 36
Gigantomachy, Greek (Claudian), 377, 379
Gilakios (Armenian commander), 118–119
Gildas, 426–427
Gildo (Moorish king), 35
Gillett, Andrew, xxxvii, 815
Gilliot, Claude, 1088
Giraldus Cambrensis, 578
Glory of the Martyrs (Gregory of Tours), 116
Glycerius (emperor), 46, 47, 105
Gnosticism, 229, 230, 516, 537, 1154
Goar the Alan, 34, 36–37
"god fearers," pagan-Jewish, 854
Godegisel (Vandal king), 37
Godelier, M., 1130
"God's command (*amr*)," Qur'ān's and Muḥammad's concern with arrival of, 1090–1099
Goehring, James, 232, 498
Goffart, Walter, 73, 76
gold coinage in monetary system, 599–600, 608, 614
Goldhill, Simon, 978
Goldziher, Ignác, 1078, 1081
Goody, Jack, 669, 679
Gordian III (emperor), 7
Gorges, Jean-Gerard, 603
Görke, Andreas, 1082–1083
Gospel of Judas, 229, 238n3
Gospel of the Savior, 229
Gothic History (Cassiodorus), 424
Goths
 Gog in Bible, identification with, 67
 in Illyricum, 101, 105–106, 109
 in Jordanes' *Getica*, 69–70
 as kingdom within imperial territory, 43–44
 kings of, 39–40
 mental world of Late Antiquity and, 9
 movement into imperial territory, 41–43
 post-Roman ethnic identity of, 18
grammar, as stage of classical education, 469
Gratian (emperor), 100, 304, 410, 412, 772, 776, 780n13, 850, 883
Gray, Patrick, 917–920, 924, 925
Great Canon (Andrew of Crete), 1156
"Great Slaughter" (344–379 C.E.) of East Syriac Christians, 1000–1002, 1006
Greece
 Athenian Academy, closure of, 477–478, 850
 Athens, as state, 1126
 early Christian churches in, 942, *943*, 947
Greek language, culture, and thought. *See* Hellenism
Greek poetry, 361–384
 audience for, 378–380
 Christianity and, 365–368, 371–372, 375, 380–382, 386n10
 chronological survey of, 36–370
 critical views of, 361–362
 in Egypt, 362–363, 365–366, 370
 genres, 370–373
 later reception of Late Antique works, 382–384
 metrical rules, 376–377
 performance of, 377–378
 rhetorical rules, influence of, 373–375
 significance in Late Antique world, 362–363
 verse paraphrase, importance of, 373, 375–376
Greenwood, Tim, xxxvii, 115
Gregorian Code [*Codex Gregorianus or CG*], 794, 795, 796, 830, 831, 832
Gregory I the Great (pope), 10, 106, 831, 837, 876, 893, 894, 1154, 1157, 1172
Gregory of Antioch, 425, 832
Gregory (Armenian bishop), 125

Gregory the Illuminator, 119, 122–123, 124
Gregory of Nazianzus [Gregory Nazianzen; Gregory the Theologian]
as bishop, 876, 882, 884
in Byzantium, 1151, 1154, 1155
Carmina Arcana, 380
Coptic literary tradition and, 234
on education and school community, 473, 475, 477
Greek poetry of, 362, 366, 369, 371, 377, 379–380, 382–384, 385n6
Hellenism and, 448–449
On His Life, 380
On His Own Verses, 366
history writing in Late Antiquity and, 410, 411, 412
Homilies, imperial manuscript of, 1151
on hospital of Basil of Caesarea, 716, 717, 718, 725, 733
on Julian, 448–449, 725
letter collections, 828, 829
Gregory of Nyssa, 185, 234, 235, 411, 412, 492, 532, 716, 882, 1154
Gregory Palamas, 1155
Gregory of Tours
Armenian visitor and, 115–118, 121, 132
as bishop, 892–893, 895
Books of Miracles, 116
communication in Late Antiquity and, 821–823
On the Course of the Stars (*De cursu stellarum*), 576, 577
Egypt and, 207
as historian, 426
History of the Franks, 115–118, 892–893
Latin poetry and, 348
mental world of Late Antiquity and, 15
on regenerative potential of material objects, 980, 982
on Trinitarian doctrine, 904n159
Western kingdoms, role in, 38, 52n43, 892–893, 895
Grey, Cam, xxxvii, 625
Griffith, Sidney, 175, 183
Grumbates (king of the Chionites), 144, 146
guardianship of minors, 675, 802
Guarino of Verona, 1178, 1183
Gubo Barrayo, 190
Guidobaldi, Federico, 602
Gunderic (Vandal king), 37
Gundioc (Burgundian king), 38, 46
Gundobad (Burgundian king), 38, 46, 49, 892
Gundomadus (Alamannic king), 35
Guran, Petre, xxxvii, 1148
Guria (Syrian martyr), 182, 187
Gwynn, David M., xxxvii, 876
Gyselen, Rika, 130

Ḥabīb (Syriac saint), 182, 188
ḥadīth, 1078, 1081, 1082, 1085
Hadrian (emperor), 674, 791, 792, 793
Hagarism (Crone and Cook, 1977), 1055
Hagia Sophia, Constantinople, 948–949, 954, 960n57, *986*, 986–987, *987*
hagiography
in Byzantium, 1152–1154
in Coptic literature, 234–235, 236, 238
Egeria's travelogue and, 565
icons in hagiography of Cosmas and Damian, 971–972, 983
letter collections, use of, 837
as monastic literature, 494–495
sīra traditions of life of Muḥammad, 1079–1083
Syrian normalizing process in, 170–190
al-Ḥajjāj (governor of Iraq), 1088
Haldon, John, xxxvii, 1111
Hallowell, Alfred, 984
Halsall, Guy, 74
Hamartigenia (Prudentius), 355n123
Handbook (Epictetus), 478
Handy Tables (Ptolemy), 575
Hanno the Carthaginian, 562
Harper, Kyle, xxxvii, 667
Harries, Jill, xxxvii, 341, 789
Hārūn al-Rashīd (caliph), 1024
Ḥasan al-Baṣrī, 1065
Ḥaśšān Yuha'min, 267–268
Hauser, Stefan, 1018
Hausleiter, Arnulf, 305
Hawran (Syrian volcanic plateau), 609–610
Hawting, Gerald, 1070, 1088
Heath, Malcolm, 805
Heather, Peter, 73, 750
heavenly bodies. *See* cosmology
Hecataeus of Miletus, 563
Heinsius, Daniel, 383
Helena, discovery of True Cross by, 176, 178, 179
Helikonios (historian), 417
Helladius of Antinoe, 366
Hellenism, 437–456
Alexander the Great and, 437–438
heterodoxy, associated with, 447
as historiographical concept, 437–440
Islam and, 1067–1069
in Julian's reign, 445–451
in Latin world, 457n12
paideia and, 437–438, 441, 447, 448
philosophy and, 451–456
religious identity and, 440–445
in Julian's reign, 445–451
philosophy and, 453–455
Henoticon (Zeno), 1009
Hephaistion, 576
Hephthalites. *See* Ephthalites
Heptateuch (Latin poem), 345
Heraclius (emperor), xvii, 5, 24, 106, 131–132, 198, 199, 297, 896, 1153

heresy. *See* heterodoxy
Herlihy, David, 669, 688
Hermeias, 460n46
Hermeric (Suevian king), 37
Hermes the Babylonian, 1068
Hermetica and Hermes Trismegistus, 530–531, 1187, 1188, 1189
Hermias of Hermopolis, 363, 366
Hermogenian Code [*Codex Hermogenianus or CH*], 794, 795, 796, 830, 831, 832
Hermogenian[us] (jurist), 794, 795, 830, 832
Hero and Leander (Musaeus the grammarian), 369
Herodian dynasty of Judaea, 34
Herodotus
  on barbarians, 62
  on Deioces, tyrant of Media, 780n7
  on Egypt, 195
  on Ethiopia, 254
  history writing in Late Antiquity and, 407, 410, 411, 412, 413, 414, 421, 429
  travel writing and, 563
Heroikai Theogamiai (Peisander of Laranda), 362, 364
Hesiod, 385n3, 442
Hesychast movement, 1155
Hesychius (bishop of Dalmatia), 105
Hesychius (lawyer and historian), 424
heterodoxy. *See also specific heterodox belief systems*
  accusations under the law, establishment of procedures for, 765–767
  as analytical category, 68
  Armenian exposure to, 120–124, 126
  barbarians associated with, 18, 37, 63
  bishops' responsibility for orthodoxy of communities, 888–889
  Byzantine concern with, 1154–1155, 1164
  Church of the East, Christology of, 1009–1011
  citizenship rights and, 748
  cosmology and, 579–580
  Ephrem the Syrian, heresiology of, 184
  Hellenism associated with, 447
  in Islam, 1061
  Latin poetry addressing, 345
  orthodoxy, Late Antique concern with, xix, 18
  Roman law regarding, 803
  Syrians and, 172–173, 184
Heussi, Karl, 488
Hexaemeron commentary tradition, 577, 580
Hexapla (Origen), 565
Hierakiōn of Oxyrhynchos, 206
Hierios, 613
Hierocles, 408
hijra, 1082–1083
Hilarion of Thavatha, 495, 858
Ḥimyar, 262–273
  Arabia Deserta, conquest of, 272–273
  coinage of, 260
  Dhamar'alī Yuhabirr, dynasty of, 263–268
  Ethiopia, as tributary of, 281–297
    Abraha (Christian Aksūmite), reign of, 284–288, 291–292, 295, 297, 300
    "Abrəha and Aṣbəha" legend, 292
    Christianization of Ḥimyar, 294–295
    Jews, persecution of, 284, 289, 290
    Kālēb (king of Ethiopia) and, 283–284, 288–292
    Najrān massacre and defeat of prince Joseph, 281–284, 289, 290, 1057
    overthrow of Aksūmite rule, 297
  external sources regarding, 253
  'Ēzānā (king of Ethiopia) and, 277–278
  rejection of polytheism and favoring of Judaism in, 265, 266, 269, 270–272, 279–280, 302, 1057
  Sasanian Persia and, 296
  Shuriḥbi'īl Yakkuf, dynasty of, 269
Hindus, under Islam, 1060
Hipparchus (Greek astrologer, astronomer, and geographer), 573, 584n70
Hippocrates (Greek physician), 79n34
Hippodameia (Triphiodorus of Panopolis), 364
Hippolytus of Rome, 893
al-Ḥīra, Arab kingdom of, 296, 297, 1005–1006, 1018
Hishām ibn al-Kalbī, 286, 308
Historia Augusta, 10, 413, 791, 917
Historia critica philosophiae (Brucker), 1186
Historia Lausiaca (*Lausiac History*; Palladius), 495, 819
Historia Monachorum in Aegypto, 495
Historia Religiosa [*Historia Philotheos*] (Theodoret of Cyrrhus), 183, 188, 495
Historia Tripartita (Theodore Lector), 426, 429
historical Jesus movement, 1078, 1093, 1098–1099
A Historical Narrative of the Distress which occurred in Edessa, Amida, and All Mesopotamia (Ps.-Joshua), 421
historiography of Late Antiquity, xi–xvi, xix, xxi–xxii, 3–6. *See also* "decline and fall," historiographical themes of
  barbarians in modern history, 68–77
  Byzantium, concept of, 1148–1150
  Church of the East, 995–997
  on codification process, 800
  communication, study of, 820
  communications as historical sources, 823–826, 833
  Greek poetry, critical views of, 361–362
  Hellenism and, 437–440
  Islam, xv, xvi
    as Late Antique religion, 1053–1056, 1069–1072
    sources for earliest history, problem of, 1056–1057, 1078–1079

historiography of Late Antiquity (*continued*)
in Italian Renaissance. *See* Italian Renaissance and Late Antiquity
Latin poetry, classicizing bias regarding, 335–337
of marriage and family, 669–671
Marxist historiography, 1122, 1148–1149
religion and religious diversity, 851
of Syriac and Syrians, 170–172
History (al-Ṭabarī), 1079
History (Łazar P'arpec'i), 129, 130
History against the Pagans (Orosius), 415
History of Albania (Moses Daskhurantsi), 428
History of the Church of Alexandria, 236
History of the Decline and Fall of the Roman Empire (Gibbon, 1776–1789). *See Decline and Fall of the Roman Empire*
History of Florence (Bruni), 1176
History of the Florentine People (Bruni), 1179–1180
History of the Franks (Gregory of Tours), 115–118, 892–893
History of Joseph the Carpenter, 229
A History of Private Life (Paul Veyne), xviii, 669
history writing in Late Antiquity, 405–430. *See also specific texts and authors*
Arab conquests affecting, 428, 429
in Armenia, 421–422, 428
barbarian invasions, accounting for, 415–417
Christian understanding of history, Eusebius' adaptation of, 405–406, 407–408
classical tradition and, 407
in Eastern empire
395–500 C.E., 417–420
500–600 C.E., 422–425
600–700 C.E., 427–430
influence of new Christian forms in fourth century, 408–412
law and legal culture, historical place of, 791–792
mentality of Late Antiquity, role of history in, 20–22
methodological approaches, 406–407
Roman aristocracy and, 412–415
in Sasanian Persia, 425
in Syriac, 421, 428–429
as unified divine time span, 407–408
in Western kingdoms, 422–423, 426–427
Hodges, Richard, 614–615
Hodgson, Marshall, 1079
Holy Apostles, Church of the, Constantinople, 942
"Holy Land," concept of, 935–937, 978, 979
Holy Sepulcher, Jerusalem, 940–942, *942*, 980, 987
Homer, 364, 368, 371, 373, 375, 442, 443, 503, 504
Homeric Centos, 368, 372, 375, 380
Homilies (John Chrysostom), 1153
Homilies (Gregory of Nazianzus), imperial manuscript of, 1151
homilies in Coptic literature, 229, 235, 236–237
Homily on Easter (Melito of Sardis), 232
Homily on Ephrem (Jacob of Serugh), 187
Homily on Shmouna and Guria (Jacob of Serugh), 187
Homily on the Siege of Constantinople of 626 C.E. (Theodore Synkellos), 1153, 1162
Honorius (emperor), 43, 105, 338, 417, 629, 801, 835
Honorius Augustodunensis, 567
Horace, 828
Horapollo [Horapollon] (Greek poet), 363, 366
Horden, Peregrine, xxxvii, 78, 715
Hormizd IV (Sasanian ruler), 1014
Horologion, 1157
Horsfall, Nicholas, 583n58
Horsiesi (monk), 231, 232
Hosius [Ossius] of Cordoba, 677, 883
hospitals, 715–736
Basil of Caesarea, foundation of
beneficiaries of, 717–720
official concerns regarding, 715–716, 732
purpose of, 716–717, 719
charity, as Christian value, 719, 723, 730
Christian precursors to, 720–724
citizens not specially favored by, 719–720, 732
effects of, 733–736
in Islamic world, 736
Jewish parallels, 726–727
pagan parallels, 725–726
reasons for founding hospitals, 730–733
size and numbers, 728, 729, 734
for slaves, 725–726, 736
space, Christian production of, 732–733
successors of, 727–733
terminological issues, 717, 718
for women giving birth, 734–735
Zoroastrian parallels, 725
"the Hour," Qur'ān's and Muḥammad's concern with arrival of, 1090–1099
house-churches, 937–938, *938*
Hoyland, Robert, xxxviii, 1016, 1053
Hrip'simē (Armenian saint), 119, 122
humanist concerns and Late Antiquity, 1173–175. *See also* Italian Renaissance and Late Antiquity
Humfress, Caroline, 794, 805
Hunger, Herbert, 1149, 1150
Hunneric (Vandal king), 37, 903n150
Huns
Central Asia, Hunnic invasion of, 144–146
in Illyricum, 101–102
mentality of Late Antiquity and, 15
Western kingdoms, establishment of, 36, 37, 45
Huntington, Samuel, 1055
Hurgronje, Snouck, 1090–1091

Hydatius (chronicler), 21, 37, 416
Hyginus (Roman writer), 726
Hymn to Helios the King (Julian), 450
Hymns (Proclus), 368
Hymns against Heresies (Ephrem), 184
Hypatia, 575, 861, 888, 1149
hypostases (One, Intellect, and Soul), 524–527

Iambi ad Seleucum (Amphilochius of Iconium), 366
Iamblichus, 532, 535, 1185–1189, 1191
Iaudas (Berber chief), 606
Ibas of Edessa, 921–922, 925, 927
Ibn 'Abd al-Ḥakam, 207, 209–210
Ibn Abī l-Ḥuqayq, 1082, 1083
Ibn Ḥawqal, 1021
Ibn al-Haytham, 1068
Ibn Hishām, 1079, 1080
Ibn Isḥāq, 1079, 1080
Ibn Khaldūn, 1124
Ibn Sa'd, 300
Ibn Sīnā (Avicenna), 1068
icons. *See also* object relations in Late Antiquity
  animism and, 983–984, 988–989
  of Christ, 971–973, *972*
  Cosmas and Damian, icons in hagiography of, 971–972, 983–984
  flatness and two-dimensionality of, *973*, 973–974
  healing power in paint of, 971–972
  iconoclastic controversy, 974–976
  of Peter, *973*, 973–974
  Pygmalion story and, 983
  regenerative potential of material world and, 983–984
  relics and images, equivalency of, 971–973, *972*, *973*
  of Sergius and Bacchus, 971, *972*, *973*
L'idéologie politique de l'Empire byzantin (Ahrweiler, 1975), 1149
idolatry and object relations. *See* object relations in Late Antiquity
Ignatius of Antioch, 878, 916, 1154
Iliad (Homer), 364, 368, 371, 375, 384, 437
illegitimate children, 683, 689
Illyricum. *See* Balkans
Imago Mundi (Honorius Augustodunensis), 567
imitatio in Latin poetry, 336–338, 344
immaterial and material things. *See* physics and metaphysics
"Imperial History," 410
Imru' al-Qays, 248
incense, use of, 984
incestuous marriage, Sasanian practice of, 1005, 1011
India
  Church of the East, expansion of, 1019
  Egypt, trade with, 208–209
  Hindus, under Islam, 1060
  knowledge of Rome in, 11
  legitimating processes and ideologies of states in, 1127, 1129–1131
  Sasanian contact with, 12
  use of term in Greek and Roman texts, 255
indissolubility, marital doctrine of, 668, 677, 680, 693
inequality, Late Antique concerns about. *See* justice and equality
Inglebert, Hervé, xxxviii, 3
Ingold, Tim, 977
inheritance, 672, 673–674, 679
injustice, Late Antique concerns about. *See* justice and equality
Innocent III (pope), 919
Institutes (Cassiodorus), 427, 575
Institutes (Gaius), 796
Institutes (Justinian), 789–790, 796, 838
Institutiones (Quintilian), 1182
Institutiones grammaticae (*Elements of Latin Grammar;* Priscian), xi–xii, *xii*, xv
Intellect, One, and Soul (three hypostases), 524–527
Introduction to Astronomy (Geminus), 577
Invectives against a Physician (Petrarch), 1174
Iorga, N., 1149
Iran. *See* Sasanian Persia
Ireland
  history writing in, 427
  Priscian's *Institutiones*, Old Irish glosses on, xi–xii, *xii*, xv
Irenaeus (Illyrian saint), 98–99
Irenaeus of Lyons, 879, 1154
Irish Chronicle (Columba), 427
irrigation infrastructure in Egypt, 206
Isaiah of Gaza, 501, 504
Isaurika (Pamprepius), 420
Isidore (envoy of Theophilus of Alexandria), 816–819, 828
Isidore of Pelusium, 499, 500
Isidore of Seville, 66, 427, 576, 577, 631, 693, 1172
Isis, cult of, 854
Islam, 1053–073. *See also* Muḥammad; Qur'ān
  apocalypticism in, 1065–1067
  Armenia, effect of Arab conquests on, 133–134
  bureaucratic-administrative structures, 1125
  Central Asian long-distance trade, end of, 157
  Church of the East under, 1024–1026
  Coptic literature affected by, 224–225, 230, 238
  as economic power, 615–616
  Egypt, Arab conquest of, 199, 214
  Hellenism and, 1067–1069
  in historiography of Late Antiquity, xv, xvi
    as Late Antique religion, 1053–1056, 1069–1072
    sources for earliest history, problem of, 1056–1057, 1078–1079

Islam (*continued*)
  history writing in Late Antique empire and, 428, 429
  holy persons in, 1063–1065
  hospitals, 736
  inscriptions, devotional, 1062–1063
  Khārijīs, 1061, 1064
  as Late Antique religion, 1053–1056, 1069–1072
  legitimating processes and ideologies, 1129
  literature of, 1061–1062
  mental world of Late Antiquity and expansion of, 23–24
  monetary system, continuation of, 615
  non-Muslim communities under, 1059–1062, 1129
  orthodoxy and heterodoxy in, 1061
  "out of Arabia" theory of, 1069–1072
  periodization of Late Antiquity favoring, 5
  political power, association with, 1057–1058
  polytheism in Arabia, decline of, 302–305
  pre-Islamic Arabia, traditions regarding, 308–310
  ritual penetration of state ideology in, 1132
  Sasanian Persia
    Arab conquest of, 297, 1015–1018
    influence of, 1068
  Shī'īs, 1061
  sources for earliest history, problem of, 1056–1057, 1078–1079
  Sunnīs, 1061, 1083
  Syrian Christianity and, 190
  Syrian educational culture, influence of, 478
  Timothy I's philosophical defense of Christianity before al-Mahdī, 1024–1026
  universalism of, 1058–1059
isnād criticism, 1080–1083, 1088
Īšō'dad of Qaṭar, 1017
Īšō'yabh I (Church of the East patriarch), 1014, 1018, 1034n146
Īšō'yabh II (Church of the East patriarch), 1016
Īšō'yabh III (Church of the East patriarch), 1016, 1017, 1025
Italian Renaissance and Late Antiquity, 1172–1196
  Aulus Gellius, influence of, 1181–1183
  barbarian invasions, beliefs about effects of, 1177–1180
  concepts of Late Antiquity and, 1172–1173
  "decline and fall," historiographical themes of, 1172–1173, 1179–1181
  formal versus common speech, debate over, 1177
  humanist concerns and, 1173–1175
  Latin literature and language, interest in, 1174–1177
  philosophy
    Aristotle and Plato, efforts to resolve, 1183–1186
    Christianity and, 1185–11892
    monotheism, viewed through prism of, 1185
    Neoplatonism, 1187
    Platonism and Platonizing, 1183–1192
Italian War against the Goths (Bruni), 1180
Italica (legal client of Symmachus), 769–770, 771, 774–775
Italy in Late Antiquity. *See also* Goths; Lombards; Ostrogoths; Rome
  crisis of sixth and seventh centuries in, 614–615
  decline of aristocracy in, 606–607, 615
  Justinian's reconquest of, 894
  rural estates/villas in, 603–604
itinerarium genre, 563–564, 565, 570, 578
ius civile and *ius gentium*, 791
ius honorarium, 791
ius liberorum, 674, 675
ius publicum, 791

Jabal al-Tayrin, Egypt, impression of Christ's hand at, 985
Jacob Baradeus, 895
Jacob, Christian, 562
Jacob of Edessa, 429
Jacob of Nisibis [James of Nisibis], 11, 119, 185, 189
Jacob of Serug, 186–187, 189
Jacobite or West Syriac Church, 1010–1011, 1016, 1024; *See also* Syria, Syriac, and Syrians; Monophysitism/Miaphysitism
Jafnids, 293–294, 298
Jalons pour une histoire de l'eglise en Iraq (Fiey, 1970), 997
James of Nisibis [Jacob of Nisibis], 11, 119, 185, 189
Jamharat al-nasab (Hishām ibn al-Kalbī), 308
Janin, R., 729
Jenkins, Philip, 996
Jerome
  Aethicus Ister attributed to, 577
  Chronici Canones and *Onomasticon* (Eusebius of Caesarea), translations of, 565
  history writing in Late Antiquity and, 410–416, 423, 427
  on home town of Stridon in Illyricum, 101
  Italian Renaissance interest in, 1175
  mental conception of Late Antiquity, 10
  monasticism and, 490, 491, 492
  on "pagan survivals" in Christian practice, 858
  on resurrection of the body, 528
  on Virgil, 349n16
  women, relationships with, 692, 802, 978
Jerusalem
  Armenia, influence of Jerusalem church in, 120–121
  Dome of the Rock, 1058, 1061
  Holy Sepulcher, 940–942, *942*, 980, 987
  special authority of bishopric, 882–883

Jesus
historical Jesus movement, 1078, 1093, 1098–1099
icons and relics of, 971–973, 972, 985
Jewish War (Josephus), 426, 429
Jews and Judaism
apocalypticism of, 1065
Arabia, decline of polytheism in, 303
Aramaic, rabbinic use of, 25n16
Basil of Caesarea's hospital and, 716, 718
bishops and community relations with, 888
Bordeaux Pilgrim, Jewish sites in, 564
Christian imperial display, use of language of, 174–175
Christian sacrifices patterned on ancient Jewish practices, 856
Church of the East and, 999–1001
citizenship rights, 748
Ḥimyar
Ethiopian conquest, persecution of Jews following, 284, 289, 290
rejection of polytheism and favoring of Judaism in, 265, 266, 269, 270–272, 279–280, 302, 1057
hospitals, Jewish, 726–727
Islam, non-Muslim communities under, 1059–1062
mental world of Late Antiquity and, 18
monastic letters and, 500
pagan-Jewish "god fearers," 854
Qur'ān on, 1058, 1060, 1061, 1090
Roman and Jewish law compared, 794
Syriac world and. *See* Syria, Syriac, and Syrians
Talmudic tradition, authority as criterion in, 20
Jing-Jing [Adam], 1022–1023
Johannis (Corippus), 343
John I (pope), 892
John the Almsgiver, 734
John of Antioch, 428
John of Biclaro, 425, 427
John Cassian, 493, 495, 501, 502, 553n176, 577, 889, 1155–1156
John Chrysostom
as bishop, 876, 883, 884, 885
in Byzantium, 1153, 1154
Coptic literature and, 234–235
On David and Saul III, 235
economic history and, 607, 610
Ekloga of the *Homilies*, 1153
on hospitals, 727, 732, 734
Italica, correspondence with, 769
letter collections, 828, 829
liturgy of, 1156
on marriage, 667–668, 671, 682, 683, 688, 690–691, 692, 693
monasticism and, 491, 492, 502
on "pagan survivals" in Christian practice, 858
John Climacus [John Klimakos; John Klimax; John Climax; John of Sinai], 498, 501, 502, 1154
John of Damascus [John Damascene], 929, 1154, 1155, 1157
John the Deacon, 837
John Diacrinomenos, 420
John of Ephesus, 187–188, 189–190, 201–202, 425, 609, 864, 1010
John of Epiphaneia, 425
John of Fars, 1017
John of Gaza, 369, 374, 377, 385n6
John Geometres, 383
John Hephaestu, 189, 190
John the Lydian, 424, 608, 792
John Lydus, 454
John Malalas, 117, 130, 275, 283, 284, 288, 423, 425, 429, 454, 1150
John Moschos, 441
John the Nazarite, 188
John of Nikiu, 253
John of Phenek [John bar Penkāyē], 1016, 1060
John Philoponus
Against Aristotle on the Eternity of the World, 575
De opificio mundi, 580
On the Eternity of the World against Philoponus (Simplicius), 575
Hellenism and, 455
physics and metaphysics of, 532, 535–536, 542, 548n97, 552n155
Against Proclus on the Eternity of the World, 574–575
world, Late Antique conception of, 530, 574–575, 579–580
John of Sinai [John Climacus; John Climax; John Klimax], 498, 501, 502, 1154
John of Tella, 187, 190
John Troglita, 343
John Tzetzes, 1152
Johnson, Aaron P., xxviii, 437
Johnson, Samuel, 724, 730
Johnson, Scott Fitzgerald, xi, xxviii, 562
Johnston, David, 792
Jones, A. H. M., xv, xxii, 602, 614, 863, 1055
Jordanes, 69–70, 424
Joseph (Ḥimyarite prince), 282–284, 289
Joseph (Church of the East patriarch), 1014
Joseph the Hymnographer [Joseph of Thessalonica; Joseph the Studite], 1157
Josephus (Flavius Josephus), 426, 429, 1150
Joshua the Stylite, Ps.-(Syriac historian), 421
Jovian (emperor), 409
Jovinus (imperial usurper), 37, 38
Judaism. *See* Jews and Judaism

Julian (emperor)
  Armenia and, 121
  The Beard-Hater, 449
  Caesars, 408
  divorce under, 676, 802
  education and, 476–478, 798
  Eusebius of Nicomedia as guardian of, 882
  Against the Galileans, 448, 450–451
  Hellenism and, 445–451, 453
  history writing in Late Antiquity and, 408–409, 411, 413, 418
  hospital of Basil of Caesarea and, 719, 725
  Hymn to Helios the King, 450
  letter collections, 828
  mental world of Late Antiquity and, 21
  paganism, efforts to revive, 849, 855–856, 865, 881, 888
  Syria and, 187
  Western kingdoms and, 35
Julian of Neapolis, 174
Julian Romance, 187
Julian Saba, 183, 185
Julianist doctrine, 295
Julianus (jurist), 809n54
Julianus (sophist), 471
Julius Caesar, 422
Julius Julianus, 882
Julius Nepos, 105
justice and equality, 764–779. *See also* law and legal culture
  accusations, establishment of procedures for, 765–767
  aristocracy, judicial privileges of, 769–775
  Christianity and, 769, 777–779
  imperial influence and, 771–773, 775–778
  importance of philosophical ideas about, 764–765
  tension between, 767–770
Justin I (emperor), 283, 290, 423
Justin II (emperor), 102, 117, 132, 343, 370, 608, 677
Justin Martyr, 1154, 1165n12
Justina (empress), 99
Justinian I (emperor). *See also Corpus Iuris Civilis*
  African and Western re-conquests by, 9, 15, 50, 894
  Apollonian forgeries and, 918
  Arabia and Ethiopia, diplomats sent to, 253, 259, 283, 284, 293
  aristocracy and church hierarchy, reliance on, 612, 613
  Armenia and, 130–131
  Athenian Academy, closure of, 477–478, 850
  Barberini Ivory possibly depicting, *ii*
  bishops under, 894, 895
  churches and basilicas founded by, 945, *946*, 948–949
  divorce laws under, 677, 679
  Egypt under, 198
  expansionist aims of, 1058
  forced baptism of pagans mandated by, 849, 859
  Greek poetry under, 369–370
  history writing under, 423–424
  hospitals and, 729
  in Illyricum, 102, 106, 109–110
  Institutes, 789–790, 796, 838
  letter collections, 828
  monetary system, changes to, 608, 613–614
  pagarchy, edict relating to, 612
  periodization of Late Antiquity and, 5
  religious policy of, 1154
  Republican framework for concept of lawgiving and, 789
  tension between rule-based law and imperial discretion acknowledged by, 790
Justinian II (emperor), 1160–1163
Justinianic Code. See Corpus Iuris Civilis
Justinianic plague (541–542 C.E.). *See* plague, Justinianic
Juvencus, 344–345, 372
Juynboll, G. H. A., 1082

Ka'ba, 286, 295, 302, 304, 309, 1070
Kaiserkritik, 179–181, 190
Kālēb [Ella Aṣbəḥa] (king of Ethiopia), 259, 261, 275, 283–284, 288–292
Kalends of January, celebration of, 858
Kavafis, Konstantinos [Cavafy], 384
Kawād [Kavad, Khavadh] I (Sasanian ruler), 116, 144, 1014
Kellia, monastery at, 489, 504
Kelly, Christopher, 790
Kennet, Derek, 305
Kepler, Johannes, 576
Keydell, Rudolf, 361
Khālid ibn al-Walīd, 297
Khālid ibn Ma'dan, 1065
Khārijīs, 1061, 1064
Khorezmians, 143, 157
Khotanese, 143
Khusrō [Khusro, Khusraw, Khusrau, Chosroes] I Anōshervān [Anūshirwān] (Sasanian ruler), 116–117, 129, 145, 296, 307, 425, 609, 1014, 1015, 1058, 1068
Khusrō [Khusro, Khusraw, Khusrau, Chosroes] II Aparvez (Sasanian ruler), 12, 13, 24, 122, 131, 297, 1010, 1015, 1018
Khuzistan Chronicle, 1020
Kidarites, 145, 146
Kirdīr (Zoroastrian chief priest), 998
Kister, Meir J., 286, 301, 1006, 1098
Kitzinger, Ernst, 975, 988
Kom el-Dikka, Alexandria, 471
Konon (pope), 1160
Koran. *See* Qur'ān
Korotayev, Andrey, 306

Kosmas Indicopleustēs. *See* Cosmas Indicopleustes
Kosmas of Maïouma, 1157
Kossinna, Gustaf, 72, 76
Krader, Lawrence, 1121
Kulikowski, Michael, xxxviii, 31
Kyros (Egyptian official), 199

la Vaissière, Étienne de, xxxviii, 142
labor arrangements for agricultural lands, 634, 636–637
Labourt, Jerome, 997
Lactantius, 344, 409, 601, 769, 791
Ladder of Heavenly Ascent (John Climacus), 498, 502
laeti, 63, 752, 753, 754
Lakhmids, 1005–1006, 1018
Lammens, Henri, 302, 1078–1079
land and land ownership. *See also* agriculture and rural environment
  Armenia, aristocrats owning villages in, 610
  Roman real estate, aristocratic domination of, 602
The Last Byzantine Renaissance (Runciman, 1970), 1152–1153
Late Antiquity, xi–xxiv, 3–24
  agriculture and rural environment in, 625–644. *See also* agriculture and rural environment
  barbarians in, xix, 60–78. *See also* barbarians
  Byzantium and, 1148–165. *See also* Byzantium
  Christian character of, 1149–1150
  citizenship in, 744–755. *See also* citizenship
  collected volumes on, xix–xx, xxi–xxiv
  communication in, 815–840. *See also* communication in Late Antiquity
  cultural reach and legacy of, focus on, xv–xviii, 4
  culture and learning in. *See* culture and learning; education; history writing in Late Antiquity; literature; philosophy
  "decline and fall" in, xiv–xv, xix, 4–5. *See also* "decline and fall," historiographical themes of
  economic history of, 597–616. *See also* economic history
  geographical breadth of, xi–xvi, xx–xxi, 3–4. *See also specific regions and countries*
  Hellenism in, 437–456. *See also* Hellenism
  historiography of, xi–xvi, xix, xxi–xxii, 3–6. *See also* historiography of Late Antiquity
  hospitals, 715–736. *See also* hospitals
  importance of studying, xxii
  Italian Renaissance and, 1172–196. *See also* Italian Renaissance and Late Antiquity
  justice and equality in, 764–779. *See also* justice and equality
  law and legal culture in, 789–807. *See also* law and legal culture
  marriage and family in, 667–694. *See also* marriage and family
  Mediterranean and, xv, xxi, *xl*, 4
  mental world of, 3–24. *See also* mental world of Late Antiquity
  narrative surveys of, xxiii
  periodization of, xx, 4–5, 212–213
  physics and metaphysics of, 513–543. *See also* physics and metaphysics
  political systems in, 111–137. *See also* political systems in Late Antiquity
  religion in, 849–867. *See also* religion in Late Antiquity, *and specific belief systems*
  synchronic versus diachronic treatments of, xxi, 5–6
  unique and definitive aspects of, xviii–xx
  world, conception of, 562–580. *See also* world, Late Antique conception of
The Later Roman Empire (Jones, 1964), xv, 1055
Lateran basilica, Rome, 938–940, *940*, 943, 944, 959n19
Laterculus Malalianus (Theodore of Tarsus), 429
Laterculus Veronensis, 35
Latin literature of Late Antiquity, Renaissance interest in, 1174–1177
Latin poetry, 335–348. *See also specific poets and poetry*
  abundance of, 338
  Christian themes in, 343–348
  classicizing bias, importance of rejecting, 335–337
  in Gaul, 338–341, 348
  imitatio in, 336–338, 344
  in North Africa, 341–343
  Rome and, 339–340, 347
Lausiac History (*Historia Lausiaca;* Palladius), 495, 819
law and legal culture, 789–807. *See also* justice and equality
  accusations, establishment of procedures for, 765–767
  advocates and advocacy in, 805–806
  aristocracy, judicial privileges of, 769–775
  barbarians and Roman law, 62–63, 751–754
  bishops, role of, 777–779, 801, 881–882, 886–887
  canon law, 804
  Christianity and, 801–804
  citizenship at center of, 791
  citizenship, privileges and obligations conveyed by, 744, 746, 748–749
  codifications, 794, 795–801, 830. *See also specific codes*
  consistory hearings, 790
  criminal law, 802–804
  criticisms of, 806
  emperor and imperial administration, role of, 789–790, 792, 805–806

law and legal culture (*continued*)
forms in which law was promulgated, 789–790
history and precedent in, 791–792
ius civile and *ius gentium*, 791
ius honorarium, 791
ius liberorum, 674, 675
ius publicum, 791
judges, role of, 804, 806
Latin and Greek languages, use of, 792–793
letters with dispositive force, 789–790, 821–823, 830–832, 837–840
marriage and family law, 672–679, 802–803
private anthologies and epitomes, 794–795
quaestors, historiographic interest in, 800
religion, efforts to regulate, 849, 850, 859, 862
Republican terms, framed in, 789, 791–792
rescripts, 793–794
rhetorical language of, 805–806
social change affecting, 801–804
tension between rule-based law and imperial discretion, 790
torture, use of, 764, 765, 780n13, 804
Western kingdoms assuming imperial administrative and legal authority, 41, 47–50
Law of Citations, 795
Łazar of P'arpec'i, 129, 130, 422, 428
lead and silver mining in Illyricum, 97–98
learning. *See* culture and learning; education
Legend of Alexander [*Romance of Alexander; Alexander Romance*] (Pseudo-Callisthenes), 364–365, 1150, 1153
Lemerle, Paul, 1152
Leo I the Great (pope), 10, 416, 765–768, 779, 832, 858, 887, 893, 1179
Leo I (emperor), 419, 703n248, 1111
Leo IV (emperor), 1025
Leo VI the Wise (emperor), 1157
Leo of Narbonne, 47
Leontius of Antioch, 721
Leontius of Jerusalem, 918–919
Leovigild (Visigothic king), 38, 40
Leporius, 730–731
Lérins, monastery of, 492–493
Letter to the Armenians (Macarius), 120, 124
Letter to the Monks of Senoun (Philoxenus), 185
Letter to Young Men (Basil of Caesarea), 444
letters, 826–827. *See also* collected letters
ambassadorial, 816–818
amicitia, expression of, 816, 830, 832, 836
dedicatory, 826–827, 837
with dispositive or legal force, 789–790, 821–823, 830–832, 837–840
as historical sources, 824
increase in, 816
literature using epistolary format, 826
physical materials used for, 841n8
as physical objects, 818
survival of, 827–832
Leudast (*comes* of Tours), 821
Lex Dei (*Collatio of Mosaic and Roman Law*), 794
Libanius [Libanios]
on education, 467, 469, 471, 472–473, 474, 478
flexibility of religious convictions, 865
on Hellenism, 449
history writing and, 409, 411, 412, 413
on Julian's sacrifices, 856
letters of, 826, 828, 829, 886
magic, associated with, 857
on marriage and family, 691
Maternus Cynegius, on temple attacks of, 804
mental world of Late Antiquity and, 21
on patronage, 642
Peri ton protostasion, 642
Pro templis (*For the Temples*), 804, 856, 863
Syrian governor criticized by, 806
on villages of Eastern empire, 610
Liberius (bureaucrat working with barbarian rulers), 47–48
liberti, 744, 746–747, 750
libri. *See* collected letters
Libri Theodosiani, 833, 838–840. *See also* *Theodosian Code*
Licinius (emperor), 98, 798, 881, 882, 1161
Life of Abba Aphou of Pemdje, 505
Life of Anthony (*Vita Antonii;* Athanasius of Alexandria), 386n9, 487–488, 493, 494–495, 498, 505, 889–890
Life of Aphou, 232
Life of Apollonius of Tyana (Philostratus), 577
Life of Athanasius, 236
Life of Barlaam and Josaphat, 1153–1154
Life of Barsauma of Samosata, 178–179, 181
Life of Cicero (Plutarch), 1184
Life of St. Columba (Adomnán), 566
Life of Constantine (Eusebius of Caesarea), 801, 1161–1162
Life of St. Cyprian of Antioch (Eudocia), 368, 376, 382, 383
Life of Ephrem, 184–185, 190
Life of Isidore/Philosophical History (Damascius), 385n4 454
Life of Jesus (Renan, 1863), 1078
Life of John of Tella (Elias), 187
Life of St. Mary of Egypt (Sophronios), 1152, 1153–1154, 1156, 1158–1160
Life of Melania the Younger, 685
Life of Pachomius, 504, 505, 720
Life of Plotinus (Porphyry), 513–517, 527
Life of Proclus (Marinus), 372
Life of Pythagoras, 494, 505
Life of Saint Andrew the Fool, 1153

Life of Severinus (*Vita Severini;* Eugippius), 36, 39
Life of Severus (Zacharias Scholasticus), 379, 475
Life of Shenoute (Besa), 236
Life of Sinuthius (*Vita Sinuthii*), 233
Life of Symeon the Stylite, 179
Life of Theodosius, 236
literacy
  in Church of the East, 1007–008
  in Egypt, 210–212
  in Gaul, 820
  in Late Antique world generally, 468–469, 479n11, 503
literature. *See also* Bible; Coptic literature; Greek poetry; hagiography; Latin poetry; *titles of specific works*
  Arabic, translation of Greek texts into, 1067–1069
  in Armenian, 118
  barbarians in, 61–62
  of Church of the East, 1004, 1006–009
  dedicatory letters, 826–827, 837
  epistulary format, using, 826
  of Islam, 1061–1062
  Italian Renaissance interest in Latin literature, 1174–1177
  liturgical poetry in Byzantium, 1156–1157
  monastic and ascetic. *See under* monasticism and asceticism
  pilgrimage texts, 564–566, 570, 578–579, 935–937, 985
  travel accounts, 562–567
Litorius the Hun, 45
liturgy
  Armenia, animal sacrifice in Christian liturgy of, 856
  bishops, sacerdotal functions of, 885
  in Byzantium, 1156–1157, 1158–1160
  in Church of the East, 1012
  sacred space, liturgical function of, 953–955, *955*
Lives of Famous Men (Suetonius), 412
Livy, 410, 412, 413, 414, 415, 791, 1174, 1175
Llandaff charters, 604–605
Lo Cascio, Elio, 599
Lombard, Maurice, 600
Lombards
  aristocracy, effects of Lombard settlement on, 607
  in Illyricum, 102
  Justinian's re-conquest of Italy and, 894
  mentality of Late Antiquity and, 9
  Roman world, connection to, 50
Lucan (Latin poet), 348, 492
Lucchesi, Enzo, 228
Lucian of Samosata, 469
Lucilius (satirist), 365
Lupercalia, condemnation of, 850
Luxurius (Latin poet), 342–343
Maas, Michael, xxxviii, 60
Macarius the Great (Egyptian monk), 499, 500, 502–503
Macarius of Jerusalem (bishop), 120, 124
Macedonius (bishop of Constantinople), 420, 721, 887
Macedonius (Milanese court official), 772–773, 776
Macfarlane, Alan, 669
MacMullen, Ramsay, 863, 865–866
Macrina the Younger, 492
Macrobius, 576, 791, 1175
Macrobius of Seleuceia, 923
magi in Bible associated with Persia, 21–22, 1023
magic, 857, 858–859, 1013–1014
Magnitude of the Soul (Augustine), 541
Magnus Maximus, 768
al-Mahdī (caliph), 1022, 1024, 1025, 1068
Mahomet et Charlemagne (Pirenne, 1937), xiv–xv, 78, 1053, 1054
Majorian [Majorianus] (emperor), 45, 46, 341, 839
Makarios of Antioch, 923
Makarios of Tkoou, 236, 239n19
Makarius the Great, 1154
The Making of Late Antiquity (Brown, 1978), 4
Makka [Mecca]
  Abraha (Christian Aksūmite ruler of Ḥimyar), campaigns of, 285–287, 297, 300
  as commercial power, 300–302
  Islamic tradition regarding pre-Islamic state of, 309, 310
  Ka'ba in, 286, 295, 302, 304, 309, 1070
  Muḥammad's community at, 300
  origins of Islam and, 1070–1071
  polytheism in Arabia, decline of, 302
Malchus (historian), 420
Mālik ibn Dīnār al-Sāmī, 1065
Malkīkarib Yuha'min (king of Ḥimyar), 265–266
Mamre, complex at, 982–983
Ma'nā, metropolitan bishop of Fars, 1004
Manandyan, Hakob A., 132, 136n86
mancipia, 615
Mandeville, Sir John, 566–567
Mandylion (icon of Christ), 971
Mango, Cyril, 983
Mani
  Central Asian depiction of, 151
  Church of the East and, 996, 999, 1019, 1023
  Hellenizing aspects of writing of, 447
  in India, 1019
  Islam and, 1068
  legal treatment of heterodoxy and, 768, 803
  life and career of, 999
  mental world of Late Antiquity and, 5, 12, 17
  Sasanian Persian court and, 768, 1057
  sentenced to death, 768

Manichaeism
in Central Asia, 151, 158, 1022
Christianity, relationship to, 999
in Coptic literature, 229, 230
Diocletian's rescript letter against, 794
distinctive script of, 174
Doctrina Addai and, 175
Hellenism and, 447
Islam, under, 1068
languages used by, 25n16
mental world of Late Antiquity and, 5, 12–13, 18
political support sought by, 1057
in Sasanian Persia, 999, 1010–1011, 1024, 1026
sexual abuse accusations against, 765–768
Manilius (poet and astrologer), 576
Mann, M., 1121, 1131
al-Manṣūr (caliph), 1024, 1068
Manuel Chrysoloras, 1152, 1176
Manuel Moschopoulos, 1152
maps, 567–572, *568*, *569*, *571*, *572*
Mār Abā the Great, 1005, 1008–1009, 1014, 1015, 1019, 1020
Mār 'Abdā, 1006–007
Mār Awgen (ascetic), 184–185
Mār Isaac (bishop of Seleucia-Ctesiphon), 994
Mār Mārī, 998, 1002
Mār Poṣi, 998
Mar Saba Monastery, Kidron Valley, Palestine, 490, *491*
Marathoniaca (Triphiodorus of Panopolis), 364
Marathonius, 721
Marc Antony, 8
Marcella (monastic patron), 492
Marcellina (sister of Ambrose of Milan), 492
Marcellinus (general), 105
Marcellinus (historian), 423, 424, 426, 427
Marcellus, Comte de, 384
Marcian (emperor), 198, 419
Marcian of Heraclea Pontica, 563
Marciana (legal client of Symmachus), 772, 774
Marcianopolis, 108–109
Marcion and Marcionites, 184, 999, 1010–1011, 1023, 1026, 1068
Marcus Aurelius (emperor), 8, 47, 96, 250, 674, 749, 1071
Marino, Giovanni Battista [Giambattista], 384
Marinus (Greek poet and biographer of Proclus), 372, 382, 471
Marius (bishop of Avenches), 426
Marius Victorinus, 410, 539
"Maronite Chronicle," 429
marriage and family, 667–694
adultery, law governing, 802–803
age at marriage, 670, 681, 686, 701n196
arrhae, 675, 678, 690
barbarian-Roman marriages, 752
betrothals, law governing, 674–675, 678
bona materna, 673–674
Christianity, influence of, 667–668, 671, 677, 679–684, 686, 693–694
companionate marriage, 667, 668, 670, 680
concubinage, 681, 689–690, 703n248
consanguineous marriage, Sasanian practice of, 1005, 1011
defining family, 669
diversity and similarity in, 694n8
divorce, 667–668, 673, 676–680, 690, 703n255, 802, 804
donatio ante nuptias, 668, 675, 678, 690–691
dowries, 672, 675, 690, 691, 703n248
Greco-Roman structures, continuity of, 668, 671, 680, 685, 693
in high-mortality, high-fertility society, 668, 669, 670, 685–686
historiography of, 669–671
indissolubility, doctrine of, 668, 677, 680, 693
inheritance, 672, 673–674, 679
material context of, 685–692
minors, guardianship of, 675, 802
monogamy, 670, 673, 680
nuclear versus agnatic or extended structure, 637, 668–670, 672–674, 676, 679, 693
patria potestas, 670, 672, 684, 685, 802
peasant household composition and economy, 637–638
population and demographics affecting, 685–686
provincial custom, influence of, 677–678
remarriage, 667, 668, 673, 674, 680, 686, 701n205, 804
ritual of marriage, development of, 673, 684
Roman family law in Late Antiquity, 672–679, 802–803
sexual exclusivity, 667, 668, 680–682
slavery and, 681, 683, 686, 687
social mobility and, 671, 687–692
tensions within, 684
universal citizenship and, 679, 690, 702n242
urban environment and, 686–687
women, legal status of, 672–674, 675–676
The Marriage of Cadmus and Harmony (Calasso, 1988), 384
Marriage of Philology and Mercury (Martianus Capella), 576–577
Marrou, Henri-Irénée, xxii, 3–4, 24n4, 1148, 1150, 1172
Marthad'īlān Yun'im (king of Ḥimyar), 269
Martial, 342
Martianus Capella, 576–577, 1175
Martin of Braga, 858
Martin of Tours, 348, 492, 858, 860, 890, 892
Martyrdom of Arethas, 283, 288, 290–292, 1154
Martyrdom of Azqir, 254
martyria, church buildings serving as, 942

Marusinac, shrine at, 105
Marutha of Maiferqaṭ, 1002–003
Marxist historiography, 1122, 1148–1149
Mary (mother of Jesus). *See* Virgin Mary
Mary of Egypt, *Life* and *Canon* of, 1152, 1153–1154, 1156, 1158–1160
Masai, François, 539
Masona of Merida, 903n151
Maspero, Gaston, 227
massae, 606
Masties (Moorish leader), 49
Masuna (Moorish leader), 50
material and immaterial things. *See* physics and metaphysics
Maternus Cynegius, 804
Mathisen, Ralph W., xxxviii, 63, 341, 744
Mauri [Moors], 35, 49–50, 343
Maurice (emperor), 5, 12, 62, 122, 131, 198, 425, 1009
Maxentius (emperor), 880, 939
Maximian (bishop of Ravenna), 426
Maximian (emperor), 96
Maximian (poet), 339
Maximim Daia, 798
Maximos Planoudes [Maximus Planudes], 383, 583n66, 1151, 1152
Maximum Prices edict (301 C.E.), 798, 799
Maximus (emperor), 803
Maximus the Confessor, 929, 1154, 1164
Maximus of Ephesus, 365
Maximus of Turin, 858
Maximus Planudes [Maximos Planoudes], 383, 583n66, 1151, 1152
Maxwell, Jaclyn, xxxviii, 849
Mazdakism, 1058
Mazzarino, Santo, 597–598, 599
McCormick, Michael, 78
McGill, Scott, xxxviii, 335
Mecca. *See* Makka
Medici, Cosimo de', 1188
Meditations (Descartes), 530
Mediterranean and Late Antiquity, xv, xxi, 4
Melania the Elder, 490, 492, 701n196
Melania the Younger, 492
Melito of Sardis, 232
Melkite Chronicle, 429
Memmius Vitrasius Orfitus, 776
Memre against Ḥabīb (Philoxenus), 185
Menander the Guardsman (historian), 155, 156, 425, 428
Menander Rhetor, 373, 503, 504
Menas of Constantinople, 922–923
mental world of Late Antiquity, 3–24
  culture and learning, role of, 19–21, 341
  elites and elite values, 13–16
  historical understanding in, 20–22
  historiographical concepts versus, 3–6
  Islam, effects of expansion of, 23–24
  methodological issues, 7
  religious values, 16–19
  Roman empire, geopolitics of, 6–13
  transformation and adaptation in, 22–23
  unity of mentalities across diverse world, problem of, 6, 22
Meropius Pontius Paulinus. *See* Paulinus of Nola
Merovingians, 10, 38, 40, 49, 50, 599, 615, 821, 892–893, 895, 1129
Meršapuh (Armenian bishop), 125
Merv, Central Asia, 144, 151, 157, 1019–1020
Messalians, 1023
Metaphrase of the Psalms, 362, 367–368, 369, 375, 380, 382
metaphysics. *See* physics and metaphysics
Metcalf, Michael, 600, 614
Miaphysitism/Monophysitism, 18, 189–190, 283, 420, 579, 895, 924–925, 1010
Michael Acominatos, 1152
Michael Psellos, 1151
Mickwitz, Gunnar, 598
Migne, J.-P., 366
migrations of barbarian peoples, 68–74
military
  in Armenia, 129–132
  Balkans, Roman military in, 94, 96, 101–102, 104–105, 109
  barbarians in, 14, 751–752
  elite classes and values in mentality of Late Antiquity, 13–16
  hospitals (*valetudinaria*), 726, 727, 736
Millar, Fergus, 830
Miltiades of Rome, 893
Milvian Bridge, Battle of (312 C.E.), 880, 939
mining
  in Egypt, 200
  Illyricum, lead and silver mining in, 97–98
minors, guardianship of, 675, 802
mints. *see also* monetary system; numismatics
  in Alexandria, 861
  in Illyria, 96, 98, 100, 108
  sliver hexagrams in Armenia, 132
  in Thessalonica, 600
Miracles of Cyrus and John (Sophronius of Jerusalem), 440–442
Miracles of Symeon the Younger, 971
Mirkovic, Alexander, 180–181
Mirror of Princes/Chapters (Deacon Agapetus), 1153, 1161
Miscellanea (Poliziano), 1183–1185
Mocsy, A., 750
Modestinus (jurist), 795, 809n54
Modestus (prefect), 731
Modzelewski, Karol, 607
Momigliano, Arnaldo, xxii
Mommsen, Theodor, 93–94
monarchical episcopate, development of, 877–880

monasticism and asceticism, 487–505. *See also under* philosophy
ascetic tradition, Syrian reinvention of, 182–183, 188
bishops and, 889–890
in Byzantium, 1151, 1158, 1164
in Church of the East, 1006–009
Coptic literature surviving in monastic libraries, 227–228
culture and learning, apparent rejection of, 487–488, 493, 494–495
dogmatic conflicts, involvement of monks in, 491, 492, 498
education of monks, 501–502, 503–505
Egypt, consolidation of monasteries in, 203
hospitals run by, 719–722, 729
Islam, holy persons in, 1063–1065
literature of, 493–503
Apophthegmata patrum, 493, 495–499, *497*, 504
in Byzantium, 1155–1156
hagiography, 494–495
letters, 499–501, 504
philosophical writings, 501–503
origins of, 487–489
as philosophical life, 493, 503–505
social setting of, 489–493, *491*
Syrian reinvention of, 182–183, 188
wandering monks and house philosophers, connection between, 492
Monastirine, basilicia at, 105
Monenergism, 923, 928
monetary system. *See also* mints; numismatics
bimetalism, disintegration of, 599
Constantinian restructuring of, 597, 598, 599, 1118
follis (copper coinage), efforts to revalue, 608
gold coinage in, 599–600, 608, 614
Islam, continuity with, 615
Justinian I's changes to, 608, 613–614
restructurings of, 599–601, 608, 613–614
silver-based systems, 132
Western efforts to restructure, 597–601
Mongols, 142, 151, 158, 996, 1122
monogamy in Greco-Roman marriage, 670, 673, 680
Monophysitism/Miaphysitism, 18, 189–190, 283, 420, 579, 895, 924–925, 1010
monotheism, philosophy through prism of, 1185
monotheistic Arabian prophets contemporary with Muḥammad, 303
monotheistic paganism, 854
Monothelete controversy, 123, 198, 922–923, 930–931
Moors [Mauri], 35, 49–50, 343
Moravcsik, Julius, 519
Moselle (Ausonius), 340, 352n52
Moses of Abydos, 236
Moses Daskhurantsi, 428
mosque of 'Amr, 204
Motzki, Harald, 1082, 1083, 1088
Mount Izla, monastery of, 1008
Mousa (Christian astrologer at Sasanian court), 1014
movement of the heavens and the soul, 533–534
Mshabbak, Basilica of, Syria, 942–943, *943*, 948
Mu'āwiya (caliph), 129, 134, 199, 211
al-Mughira ibn Sa'id, 1064
Muḥammad (the prophet), 1078–1099
apocalypticism of, 1066, 1090–1094
Ethiopian sovereigns and, 300
Heraclius as contemporary of, 24
hijra of, 1082–1083
"holy man" qualities of, 1064
monotheistic Arabian prophets contemporary with, 303
origins of Islam and, 1053
as political figure, 1058
Qur'ān and historical Muḥammad, 1084–1087
"satanic verses" and Islamic tradition regarding pre-Islamic Arabia, 310
sīra traditions of life of, 1079–1083, 1085
social/ethical message and purpose of, 1090–1094
sources for life of, problems associated with, 1056–1057, 1078–1079
Muḥammad ibn al-Ḥanafiyya, 1064
Muḥammad ibn al-Qāsim, 1060
municipal citizenship, 747
Murray, Robert, 170
Musa (legal client), 770–771
Musaeus, 369, 370, 382, 383
Musaylima (prophet of the Ḥanīfa), 303, 304, 310
Museon, Alexandria, 19
Musonius Rufus, 680–681, 683
Mussato, Albertino da, 1176
Muziris contract, 609
mythological Greek poetry, 371

Nabateans, 250, 1071
Nabonidus (Babylonian ruler), 250, 1071
Nag Hammadi texts, 227, 490
Najrān Christians and massacre, 281–284, 290, 1006, 1057
al-Namāra inscription, 248
Naqlun, monastic settlements at, 489, 504
Narratio (Sophronius of Jerusalem), 440–442
Narrationes (Pseudo-Nilus of Ancyra), 1153
Narseh II (Sasanian ruler), 295
Naṣr ibn Sayyār, 157
Naṣrids, 293–294, 298
Nativity, Church of the, Bethlehem, 940–941, 942, 987
Natural History (Pliny the Elder), 260, 573

natural world. *See* agriculture and rural environment; object relations in Late Antiquity; world, Late Antique conception of
Naucellius (historian), 412
Nazis and barbarian studies, 72, 75
Nea Anchialos, Basilica A, Greece, 947
Nearchus the Cretan, 563
Nectarius of Constantinople, 882
Nehmé, Laïla, 250
Nemesius of Emesa, 529
Neo-Chalcedonians, 918, 921, 924–925
Neo-Pythagoreans, 505
Neocaesarea, Council of (314/319 C.E.), 1003
Neon (archbishop of Ravenna), orthodox baptistery of, *944*
Neoplatonism
  being and reality in, 519–520
  in Byzantium, 1155
  conversion of Augustine and, 539
  cosmology of, 574–575, 576, 579
  education in Late Antiquity and, 470, 471, 478
  Greek poetry and, 369, 371, 375
  Hellenism and, 451–453, 459–460n43
  on immateriality, 530
  Italian Renaissance and, 1187
  mental world of Late Antiquity and, 17
  monasticism and, 501, 505
  monotheism of, 854
  physics and metaphysics, concern with, 514, 515–516
  on pneumatic vehicle of the soul, 533–536, 538
  on prior simplicity, 522
  of Pseudo-Dionysius, 541
  theurgy in, 1187
  on three hypostases (One, Intellect, and Soul), 525–527
Nepos (Cornelius Nepos), 410
Nepos (Julius Nepos), 105
Nero (emperor), 749, 1179
Nersēs I (Armenian catholicos), 722, 725, 735
Nersēs III (Armenian catholicos), 128
Nestorian Monument, Xi'an, China, xi, *xiii*, *xiv*, xv, 151, 158, 996, 1022–1024
"Nestorians". *See* Church of the East
Nestorius and Nestorianism, 183, 282, 418, 492, 917, 920, 922, 928, 995, 1009, 1025
Neuwirth, Angelika, 1086, 1089
New History (Zosimus), 419
Nicaea, First Council of (325 C.E.), 420, 804, 882, 888, 916, 1002, 1003
Nicaea, Second Council of (787 C.E.), 928, 971
Nicholas (bishop of Myra), 856
Nicomachus Flavianus, 412, 413, 417
Nikephoros Blemmydes, 1151
Nikephoros Gregoras, 1151
Nikulás Bergsson, 578–579
Nilus of Ancyra, 492, 501, 727
Nisibis, school of, 20, 426, 478, 1007–009
nobility and noble values. *See* aristocracy
Nola/Cimitile, tomb of St. Felix at, 856, 947
Nöldeke, Theodor, 1086, 1087, 1092
Nonnos of Panopolis and Nonnian style, 211, 361–369, 372, 374–384. *See also* Greek poetry
Nonnosos (Byzantine ambassador), 253, 259, 291
North Africa. *See also* Vandals
  diversity of settlement patterns in, 631
  Justinianic reconquests in, 9, 15, 50
  olive oil, trade in, 601–602
Notitia Dignitatum, 567, *569*
Novellae, 796, 839. *See also Corpus Iuris Civilis* for *Novellae* of Justinian
Nubel (Moorish king), 35
nuclear family structure, 637, 668–670, 672–674, 676, 679, 693
Numii in Carthage, 601–602
numismatics. *See also* mints; monetary system
  in Arabia and Ethiopia, 258, 260–261, 279, 281, 299
  in Armenia, 132–133
  in Central Asia, 145, 146, 153, 156, 157
  copper coinage (*follis*), 608
  from Illyricum, 98, 99, 100, 108, 109
  loose coins, transactions in, 613–614
  sliver hexagrams in Armenia, 132
Nummius Aemilianus Dexter, 413

object relations in Late Antiquity, 970–990. *See also* icons
  animism, 971, 977, 980, 983–984, 988–989
  Capgras syndrome and, 975–976, 977, 988
  God's immanence, suffusion of physical world with, 971–976
  healing power in icon paint, 971–972
  iconoclastic controversy, 974–976
  idolatry, techniques for avoiding, 971, 974, 976
  metal and mineral objects, reflective qualities of, *981*
  paradise, use of water, light, and decorative elements to suggest, *943*, 947–950, *948*, *950–952*
  Platonic metaphysics of representation and, 974
  regenerative potential of material world, 980–984, *981*
  relics and images, equivalency of, 971–973, *972*, *973*
  stones and stone objects, 984–987, *986*, *987*
  vision, Late Antique conceptions of, 976–980, *979*
Obolensky, Dimitri, 1150
Octoechos, 1157
Odessos (Varna), 107–110
Odoacer (king of Italy), 39, 40, 47, 1180
Odyssey (Homer), 364, 368, 371, 562

Oikonomidès, Nicolas, 613
oikoumene. See world, Late Antique conception of
Ojibwa stones, 984, 985, 988, 989
olive oil trade, 601–602, 608
Olybrius (emperor), 46, 47
Olybrius (Quintus Clodius Hermogenianus Olybrius), 773–777
Olympias (monastic patron), 492
Olympiodorus of Alexandria, 454, 455, 477
Olympiodorus [Olympiodoros] of Thebes, 365, 418, 419, 420, 602
O'Meara, Dominic, 518, 521
On the Course of the Stars (*De cursu stellarum;* Gregory of Tours), 576, 577
On David and Saul III (John Chrysostom), 235
On the Eternity of the World against Philoponus (Simplicius), 575
On Fate (Ficino), 1191
On His Life (Gregory of Nazianzus), 380
On His Own Verses (Gregory of Nazianzus), 366
On the Holy Places (*De locis sanctis;* Adomnán), 566, 985
On the Holy Places (*De locis sanctis;* Bede), 566
On Human Life (George of Pisidia), 382
On the Lapsed (Cyprian of Carthage), 879–880
On the Laws of the Countries (Bardaisan), 170
On the Literal Interpretation of Genesis (Augustine), 540
On Literary Polish (Decembrio), 1182–1183
On the Right Belief, 386n10
On the Sacred Disease, 537
On the Soul (Cassiodorus), 541–542
On Stones (*Orphei Lithica*), 365, 383
On True Doctrine (Celsus), 1185
On the Unity of the Catholic Church (Cyprian of Carthage), 879–880
One, Intellect, and Soul (three hypostases), 524–527
Onomasticon (Eusebius of Caesarea), 564–565
Opinions (*Sententiae;* Paulus), 792, 795
Oppian of Apamea, 385n1
Oppian of Cilicia, 385n1
Optatian (Latin poet), 336–337
Optatus of Milevus, 636–637
Opus Agriculturae (Palladius), 625–626
Ora Maritima (Avienus), 563
Orestes (prefect of Egypt), 861
Orestis tragoedia (Dracontius), 342
Organon (Aristotle), 470, 1024
Origen and Origenist controversy
  in Byzantium, 1154
  Contra Celsum, 1185
  Coptic literature and, 229, 231–232, 237
  Hellenism and, 443
  Hexapla, 565
  monasticism and, 492, 498, 500, 501, 502
  physics and metaphysics, 528, 532, 537
The Origin of Islam in its Christian Environment (Bell, 1925), 1091
The Origins of the European Economy (McCormick, 2001), 78
Orkhon inscriptions, 150
Orlandi, Tito, 225, 227, 229, 231, 232
Orosius (historian and theologian), 10, 21, 415–416, 424, 426, 429, 577
Orphei Lithica (*On Stones*), 365, 383
Orphic Argonautica, 368, 372, 383
orthodoxy
  bishops' responsibility for, 888–889
  Byzantine concern with, 1154–1155, 1164
  canonicity and, 924–927
  Church of the East, Christology of, 1009–1011
  in Islam, 1061
  Late Antique concern with, xix, 18
  Syriac emphasis on, 183–186, 189–190
Orthodoxy (Christianity as civil religion in Byzantium), development of, 1160–1164
Ossius [Hosius] of Cordoba, 677, 883
Ostrogorsky, George, 614
Ostrogoths [Eastern Goths]
  Arian identity of, 63, 893
  destruction of kingdom of, 50
  kings of, 39–40, 48
  local aristocracy, collaboration with, 607
  mental world of Late Antiquity and, 18
Otia Imperialia (Gervasius of Tilbury), 567
Ovid, 336, 340, 348, 351n47

Pachomius [Pachomios] of Tabennesi, 228, 231–232, 490, 493, 499, 500, 504, 720, 723
Pact of 'Umar, 1060–1061
paganism. *See also* conversion to Christianity; religion in Late Antiquity
  Arabia, decline of polytheism in, 302–305
  Christianity, "pagan survivals" in, 857–859, 864–865, 1012–1014
  citizenship rights and, 748
  coexistence with Christianity, 859–862, 1012–1013
  conflict, coercion, and violent incidents, 859–862, 888
  decline throughout Late Antiquity, narrative of, 849–851, 853–854
  demons associated with, 852, 855
  economics affecting, 854
  education and, 475–477
  fluidity of religious identity and, xviii–xix, 864–865, 888, 1012–1013
  Hellenism and religious identity, 440–445
    in Julian's reign, 445–451
    philosophy and, 453–455
  Ḥimyar, rejection of polytheism and favoring of Judaism in, 265, 266, 269, 270–272, 279–280
  hospitals, pagan, 725–726
  Maternus Cynegius, temple attacks of, 804

monotheistic, 854
pragmatic and popular religion, 856–857
proscription of, 679
sacrifice, 850, 854–856
terminological issues, 457–458n13, 852–853
pagarchy in Egypt, 205, 612
Pahlavi Psalter, 1004
paideia. See culture and learning; education
Palestine. *See also* Jerusalem; Syria, Syriac, and Syrians
Bethlehem, Church of the Nativity at, 940–941, 942, 987
"Holy Land," concept of, 935–937, 978, 979
Mar Saba Monastery, Kidron Valley, 490, 491
Palladas (grammarian and epigrammist), 365, 382
Palladius [Palladios] of Galatia (*Historia Lausiaca; De gentibus Indiae et Bragmanibus*), 208, 495, 727, 819
Palladius (Rutilius Taurus Aemilianus Palladius; *Opus Agriculturae*)
on climate, 627
on cultivation practices, 632
as framework for studying Late Antique agricultural and rural environment, 625–626
on labor arrangements, 636
mental world of Late Antiquity and, 10
Opus Agriculturae, 625–626
on peasant household composition and economy, 637
on relationship between town and country, 628–629
Pamprepius of Panopolis, 363, 368–369, 420
Pandectae, 796, 809n54
Panegyric of Florence (Bruni), 1176
Panegyric on Gregory Thaumaturgus (Gregory of Nyssa), 235
Panegyrici latini, 10
Pannonia, 95–102
Pantocrator monastery, hospital run by, 729
Pap (Armenian ruler), 735
Pāpā bar Aggai, 1002
Papaconstantinou, Arietta, xxxviii, 195, 226
papacy [bishops of Rome], 893–894. *See also* specific popes
emperor, as spiritual successor of, 10
letter collections, 828, 831–832
special authority of bishop of Rome, 882–883, 893; *see also Donation of Constantine*
Papas archive, 211, 216n60
paper, Islamic adaptation of, 1067
Papias, 1100n11
Papinian, 795
Paralius, 474, 475
Paraphrase of St. John's Gospel (Nonnos of Panopolis), 367, 369, 372, 374–376, 379–384
Parentalia (Ausonius), 352n52
Paret, Rudi, 1092–1093
Parthians, 8–9, 12, 34, 997–998
Patlagean, Evelyne, 1149
patria (Greek genre), 363, 366
patria potestas, 670, 672, 684, 685, 802
Patricius (poet), 368
patristic writings
in Byzantium, 1154–1156
Coptic translations, 234–235
"traditions of the fathers," 927
patronage systems in rural environments, 640–643
pattern poems, 336, 349n9
Paul (bishop of Constantinople), 887
Paul (monk), 495
Paul of Nisibis, 1007
Paul of Samosata, 880
Paul the Silentiary [Paul Silentiarius], 370, 374, 375, 378, 379, 382, 954, 960n57, 987
Paul of Tamma, 232
Paula (monastic patron and pilgrim), 492, 978
Paulinus of Nola (Pontius Meropius Anicius Paulinus)
animal sacrifices in honor of St. Felix by, 856
as bishop, 888
history writing in Late Antiquity and, 413–414, 416
Latin poetry of, 346–347, 352n52
letters, 835, 837
on marriage and family, 684
on regenerative potential of material objects, 980, 982
on water used in sacred spaces, 947
Paulinus of Pella, 633, 683
Paulus (Severan jurist), 792, 795
Pausanias of Magnesia, 563
P'austus Buzand, 722
Peacock, Thomas Love, 384
peasantry. *See also* agriculture and rural environment
congruence and comparability over time and space, 626
household composition and economy, 637–638
labor arrangements for agricultural lands, 634, 636–637
in Palladius' scheme, 626
patronage systems, 640–643
reciprocity and collective action, tensions associated with, 638–640
slavery, evolution of, 615, 634
terminological issues, 610
in villages of Eastern empire, 610
Peers, Glenn, xxxviii, 970
Pegasius, bishop of Troy, 888
Pege gnoseos (*Fountain of Knowledge;* John Damascene), 1155
Peisander of Laranda, 362, 364

Pelagianism, 345
Pelliot, Paul, 997
penitential rites in Christianity, 683
peregrini, 746, 749–751
Peri ton protostasion (Libanius), 642
Periegesis (Dionysius Periegetes), 563
periodization of Late Antiquity, xx, 4–5, 212–213
Periplous (Hanno the Carthaginian), 562
Periplous of the Black Sea (Arrian), 563
Periplous of the "Outer" Sea (Marcian), 563
Periplous of the Red Sea, 253, 256, 260, 273, 563
Peristephanon (Prudentius), 347
Pērōz (Sasanian ruler), 129, 130, 144, 1004
Pērōzduxt (amulet owner), 1013
Persarmenians, 117
Persian empire. *See* Sasanian Persia
Persis (healing tree in Egypt), 982
Pervigilium Veneris, 343
Peshitta, 170, 171, 173, 182, 185, 1021
Peter Barsymes, 612, 613
Peter, St., icon of, *973*, 973–974
Peter the Patrician, 424
Peters, F. E., 1084, 1086, 1093, 1099n2
Petrarch (Francesco Petrarca), 1174–1175, 1176, 1181
Petronius Maximus, 801
Petronius Probus, 100, 612
Peutinger, Konrad, 567
Peutinger Table, 10, 567–568, *568*, 570–572, 574, 575, 578, 580
Phaedo (Plato), 537
Phaedrus (Plato), 1184
Phaedrus the Greek, 1068
Phaenomena (Aratus), 576
Philip of Macedon, 109, 437
Philip of Side, 418
Philippi, Greece, octagonal church at, 942
Philippic Histories (Pompey Trogus), 25n7
Philo of Alexandria, 544n12, 548n95
Philo of Byblos, 439–440
Philokalia, 1155
philosophy. *See also* justice and equality; physics and metaphysics; *specific philosophers and philosophical schools*
  Athenian Academy, closure of, 477–478, 850
  in Byzantium, 1151, 1154–1156
  Hellenism and, 451–456
  in Italian Renaissance. *See under* Italian Renaissance and Late Antiquity
  monasticism and
    Apophthegmata patrum, 499
    in Byzantium, 1151
    in hagiography, 494–495
    letters of desert fathers, 499–501
    philosophical life, monasticism as, 493, 503–505
    philosophical writings by monks, 501–503
    wandering monks and house philosophers, connection between, 492
  monotheism, through prism of, 1185
  as stage in classical education, 470
Philosophy from Oracles (Porphyry of Tyre), 442
Philostorgius, 254, 255, 265, 418, 420
Philostratus, 449, 577
Philoxenus of Mabbug, 173, 185–186, 187, 188
Phocas (emperor), 5, 198
Photinus of Sirmium, 99
Photius (patriarch of Constantinople), 366, 382, 429, 826
physics and metaphysics, 513–543
  air, fire, and the heavens, 529, 530–533
  Augustine and, 517, 530, 531, 535, 538, 539–542
  being and reality, 518–520
  Cartesian dualism and, 517–518, 530, 540, 542–543, 977
  Cassiodorus and, 541–542
  demons, 536
  immaterial existence, concept of, 528–530
  immoderate living, soul weighed down by, 532
  intelligible versus sensible reality, 518
  material bodies, 527–530
  movement of the heavens and the soul, 533–534
  Neoplatonism's concern with, 514, 515–516
  Plotinus and, 513–517. *See also* Plotinus
  pneuma or spirit, 533–538
  prior simplicity, principle of, 520–524
  representation, Platonic metaphysics of, 974
  three hypostases (One, Intellect, and Soul), 524–527
  unity in, 521–524
  world soul, 526, 527, 533
Piacenza Pilgrim, 566, 985
Pico della Mirandola, Giovanni, 1184
piety, Qur'ān's concern with, 1062–1063
pilgrimage texts, 564–566, 570, 578–579, 935–937, 985
pilgrims' tokens, 971, *972*, 978, *979*
Pindar, 385n3
Pirenne, Henri, xiv–xv, 78, 1053, 1054
Pisenthios (monk), 237
Pisidian Laodicea, Council of (347/395), 1003
Pius II (pope), 1182
plague, Antonine (165–180 C.E.), 1117
plague, Justinianic (541–542 C.E.)
  in Arabia, 305
  divorce laws and, 677
  in Egypt, 201–202, 215n26
  follis, revaluation of, 608
  nature and impact of, 1114
plague of Thucydides (430 B.C.E.), 1114
Planispherium (Ptolemy), 582n48

Plato and Platonism. *See also* Neoplatonism
being and reality in, 519
in Byzantium, 1151, 1155
Cartesian dualism and, 518
Commentary on the Timaeus (Chalcidius), 576
Commentary on the Timaeus (Porphyry), 576
Commentary on the Timaeus (Proclus Diadochus), 452–453, 574
cosmology of Ptolemy and, 573
education in Late Antiquity and, 469, 470
Forms, 525–527
Greek poetry and, 375
Hellenism and, 442, 445, 452, 453
immoderate living, soul weighed down by, 532
Italian Renaissance, Platonizing in, 1183–1192
mental world of Late Antiquity and, 13, 17
monasticism and, 500, 501
Phaedo (Plato), 537
Phaedrus (Plato), 1184
physics and metaphysics, Late Antique concern with, 516
on prior simplicity, 522–523
representation, metaphysics of, 974
Republic (Plato), 525
Timaeus (Plato), 452–453, 535, 576
on vehicle of the soul, 534
Platonic Theology (Proclus of Lycia), 451–452
Platonic Theology: On the Immortality of the Soul (Ficino), 1188
plerophoria, 236, 237
Pliny the Elder, 253, 260, 573
Pliny the Younger, 828, 836, 837, 1175, 1176
Plotinus
on air, fire, and the heavens, 529, 531–532, 537
barbarians and, 66
being and reality in, 519–520
Cartesian dualism and, 517, 518, 540
conversion of Augustine and, 539–540
Enneads, 522, 530, 533, 1188, 1189
Italian Renaissance and, 1186–1191
Life of Plotinus (Porphyry), 513–517, 527
on material bodies, 527, 529–530
mental world of Late Antiquity and, 17
on movement of the heavens and the soul, 533–538, 574
on prior simplicity, 521–524
on three hypostases (One, Intellect, and Soul), 524–527
Plutarch, 449, 532, 533, 681, 683, 1184
pneuma or spirit, 533–538
The Poet of Panopolis (Garnett, 1888), 384
poetry. *See* Greek poetry; Latin poetry
Pohl, Walter, 76
Poimen, Abba, 499
Politian, 383
political systems in Late Antiquity, 1111–1137
Armenia, political and social history of, 127–133
bureaucratic-administrative structures, 1124–1128
complexity theory and, 1140n69
definition and use of "state," 1121–1124
economic development, 1116–1119
geography and, 1119–1121
geopolitics of, 6–13
legitimating processes and ideologies, 1124–1133
nature, constitution, and dynamics of empires, 1112–1116
Orthodoxy (Christianity as civil religion in Byzantium), development of, 1160–1164
power in, 1122–1124, 1134–1137
protostates, 1122–1123
religious institutions and, 1057–1058, 1160–1163
resource distribution in, 1134–1137
ritual penetration of ideologies and, 1128–1133
segmentary states, 1113, 1123, 1134
Syria, Christian political context for, 173–175
typology of, 1122–1123
Poliziano, Angelo, 1183–1186, 1192
Polybius, 413, 419
Polychronios, 930–931
polytheism. *See* paganism
Pompey, conquests of, 440
Pompey Trogus, 25n7
Pomponius (jurist), 791
Pomponius (Latin poet), 346
Pontifex Maximus, as imperial title, 850
popular religion, 856–857
population and demographics
Arabia, sedentary and nomadic populations of, 261–262
in Egypt, 200–203, 215n26
high-mortality, high-fertility society, marriage and family in, 668, 669, 670, 685–686
hospitals, founding of, 731
marriage and family affected by, 685–686
in urban East, 615–616, 619n135
in Western Eurasia versus China, 1113–1114
Poreč, Croatia (ancient Parentium, Istria), Eufrasius Basilica and ecclesiastical complex, 944–945, *945*, 949, 950, *952*, 955–957, *956*
Porphyry of Tyre
Commentary on the Timaeus, 576
Hellenism and, 441–444, 455
history writing in Late Antiquity and, 408
immoderate living, soul weighed down by, 532
Italian Renaissance and, 1186–1188
Life of Plotinus, 513–517, 527
Philosophy from Oracles, 442
on vehicle of the soul, 535, 537
Posidonius (Greek philosopher), 531, 549n102
Posthomerica (Triphiodorus of Panopolis), 378
postliminium, 753
Postumianus (historian), 412
Poussin, Nicholas, 384

poverty
  charity towards the poor, as Christian value, 719, 723, 730, 866
  hospitals serving the poor. *See* hospitals
  power and powerlessness in Late Antique West, 599–600
power in Late Antiquity
  ideological systems and, 1128, 1132–1133
  in political systems, 1122–1124, 1134–1137
  poverty and powerlessness, 599–600
  resource distribution and, 1134–1137
Praeparatio Evangelica (Eusebius of Caesarea), 444
Praetextatus (Vettius Agorius Praetextatus), 776–777, 893
Praetorian Edict (*Edictum Perpetuum*), 791–792, 793
pragmatic religious practice, 856–857
Praktikos (Evagrius), 495, 498
Praxagoras (historian), 409
preachers, bishops as, 885
Premier humanisme byzantin (Lemerle, 1971), 1152
Prester John, 996
Price, Richard, 975
Priestley, Joseph, 536
Primus (bishop), 105
prior simplicity, principle of, 520–524
prisca theologia, 1188
Priscian (Priscianus Caesariensis), xi–xii, xv, 370, 563
Priscillian and Priscillianists, 184, 767, 768, 772, 803
Priscus of Panium, 15, 62, 419–420, 425
Pro templis (*For the Temples;* Libanius), 804, 856, 863
proasteia, 605
Proba (Latin poet), 344–345
Probus (emperor), 96, 97
Proclus Diadochus [Proclus of Lycia]
  Commentary on the Timaeus, 452–453, 574
  cosmology of, 532, 574
  education in Late Antiquity and, 470, 471
  Elements of Astronomy, 574
  on Greek poetry, 368, 369, 372
  Hellenism and, 451–454
  Hymns, 368
  Italian Renaissance and, 1186, 1188
  Life of Proclus (Marinus), 372
  on physics and metaphysics, 532, 535, 551n142
  Platonic Theology, 451–452
  Against Proclus on the Eternity of the World (John Philoponus), 574–575
Procopius [Prokopios] of Caesarea
  on Armenia, 116, 117, 118–119
  on barbarians, 66
  Buildings, 116, 424
  on Flavius Apion I, 611
  Gessius, letter to, 475
  Hellenism and, 454
  on Ḥimyar and Ethiopia, 290–291
  as historian, 423–424, 425
  on Illyricum, 102, 109
  on money supply, 601
  on Peter Barsymes, 612
  on plague of 541–542, 202
  on rural estates/villas, 605
  Secret History, 424
  on Western kingdoms, 53n83
progymnasmata, 469
Prohaeresius, 362
Prolegomena to Platonic Philosophy, 470
Prosper of Aquitaine, 10, 21, 45, 416, 422, 426, 427
prostitution, 681, 683
Protadius, 412
Protoevangelium Jacobi (*Protoevangelium of James*), 229, 1084
Protonike Legend, 176, 177–179, 180–181
protostates, 1122–1123
provinces, proliferation of, 601
Prudentius (Latin poet), 347, 350n22, 752
Psalm against the Donatists (Augustine), 350n23
pseudepigrapha, 917–918, 1084–1085
Pseudo-Callisthenes, 364–365, 1153
Pseudo-Clementine literature, 79n48
Pseudo-Dionysius [Dionysius the Areopagite], 541, 916–917, 1154, 1155, 1188
Pseudo-Macarius, 1157
Pseudo-Methodius, 1163
Pseudo-Nilus of Ancyra, 1153
Pseudo-Scylax, 563
Psychomachia (Prudentius), 347, 350n22
ptochotropheia, 718, 722, 728. *See also* hospitals
Ptolemy (Claudius Ptolemy), 8, 11, 19, 22, 66, 253, 568, 573–577, 1068
Publicola, 636
Purcell, Nicholas, 78
Pygmalion story, 983
Pythagoras and Pythagoreans, 475, 494, 495, 505, 516
Pytheas of Marseille, 563

Q collection, 1089
Qal'at Sim'ān, northern Syria, 945
Qaryat al-Faw wall painting, *1054*
Qenneshre, 20, 190, 478
quaestors, 800
Quinisext Council *in Trullo* (691–692 C.E.), 124–125, 920, 1160–1164
Quintilian, 1182
Quintus Aurelius Symmachus. *See* Symmachus
Quintus of Smyrna [Quintus Smyrnaeus], 362, 364, 367, 383
Quodvultdeus, 21

Qur'ān, 1078–1099
apocalypticism in, 1066, 1090–1099
in Arabia and Ethiopia, 250, 286–287, 307–308, 310
Bible and. *See under* Bible
collection of, 1087–1089, 1099–1100n7
historical Muḥammad and, 1084–1087
on Jews and Christians, 1058, 1060, 1061, 1090
as Late Antique text, 1062–1063
Late Antique world, as witness to Arab participation in, 1071–1072
piety, concern with, 1062–1063
social/ethical message and purpose of, 1090–1094
Quraysh, tribe of, 272, 286, 287, 295, 301, 303–304, 309–310
Qurra ibn Sharīk, 204
Quṣayr 'Amrā, Umayyad frescoes at, xvii, 11, 300

Rabban Hormizd, 1035n156
Rabbula (bishop), 175, 177, 182–183, 185–187, 189, 190, 732, 733
race theory in early 20th century and barbarian migrations, 71–72
Radagaisus (barbarian war leader), 36, 41
Radcliffe-Brown, Alfred Reginald, 1122
Radegunda (abbess and widow of Clotaire I), 348
Rag-i Bibi, Afghanistan, bas-relief from, 12
Rape of Helen (Colluthus of Lycopolis), 369
Rathbone, Dominic, 612
Ravenna
baptisteries at, *944*
S. Vitale, 949, 950–951, *951*
Ravenna Cosmography, 576, 577–578
Ravenna in Late Antiquity (Deliyannis, 2010), xxi
reality in Late Antiquity. *See* physics and metaphysics
Rebillard, Éric, 1167n63
Rechila, Rechiar, and Rechimund (Suevian kings), 37–38, 45, 55–56n115
reciprocity ideology in rural communities, tensions associated with, 638–639
Recognitions (Pseudo-Clementine), 79n48
regional citizenship, 747
Registrum (Pope Gregory I), 831, 837
Regula pasturalis (*Pastoral Rule;* Pope Gregory I), 894
Das Reich der neuen Mitte (Hunger, 1965), 1149, 1150
Relationes (Symmachus), 777, 836
relics
images and, equivalency of, 971–973, *972*, *973*
regenerative potential of material world and, 980–983, *981*
religion in Late Antiquity, 849–867. *See also specific belief systems*
animism, 971, 977, 980, 983–984, 988–989
apocalypticism of, 1065–1067
in Central Asia, 144, 150, 151, 158
conflict, coercion, and violent incidents, 859–862, 888
culture and learning, role of, 19–20
fluidity of religious identity, xviii–xix, 864–865, 888, 1012–1013
generalization of model of religious communities, 17
Gibbon's theory of decline of empire and, 70
Hellenism and. *See under* Hellenism
in Ḥimyar
Christianization of, 294–295
Najrān Christians and massacre, 281–284, 290, 1006
persecution of Jews following Ethiopian conquest, 284, 289, 290
rejection of polytheism and favoring of Judaism in, 265, 266, 269, 270–272, 279–280, 302
historiography of, 851
legal efforts to regulate, 849, 850, 859, 862
magic, 857, 858–859, 1013–1014
mental world, importance to, 16–19
periodization favoring Islam and Christianity, 5
political power, association with, 1057–1058
political systems, ritual penetration of ideologies of, 1128–1133
pragmatic and popular religion, 856–857
rise of Christianity to dominance and decline of paganism, narrative of, 849–851, 853–854, 1185
sacrifice, 850, 854–856
sources for, 851–852
terminological issues, 852–853
universalism of, 1058–1059
remarriage, 667, 668, 673, 674, 680, 686, 701n205, 804
Remigius [Remy] of Rheims, 15, 633, 637
Rémondon, Roger, 612
Renaissance. *See* Italian Renaissance and Late Antiquity
Renan, Ernest, 1078–1079
Renatus Profuturus Frigeridus, 416
Renehan, Robert, 528
renting agricultural lands, 634–635
Republic (Plato), 525
Res Gestae (Ammianus Marcellinus), 413
rescripts, 793–794
Respendial (Alan king), 36
resurrection of the body, 528
rhetoric
Greek poetry influenced by rules of, 373–375
in law and legal culture, 805–806
as stage of classical education, 469–470
theological argumentation as rhetorical process, 916–919, 920, 927, 931–932
Ricimer, 37, 46, 55n117
Riegl, Alois, 3
Riot of the Statues (387 C.E.), 886

Rippin, Andrew, 1069, 1087
The Rise of Western Christendom (Brown, 2003), 77, 1148, 1150
Robber Synod [Second Council of Ephesus] (449 C.E.), 183, 492
Roberts, Michael, 335, 336, 344, 362
Robin, Christian Julien, xxxviii, 247
Robinson, Chase F., 1089
Roman army. *See* military
Roman empire. *See also* Byzantium; "decline and fall," historiographical themes of; political systems in Late Antiquity; Western kingdoms
  Armenia and, 117, 119, 130–133
  bureaucratic-administrative structures, 1125
  China and, 8, 10, 11, 22, 1111–1112
  Christian universality as spiritual heir to, 10, 13, 18–19, 20–21, 1160–1163
  end of, 1112
  geographical openness of, 1121
  legitimating processes and ideologies, 1128
  in mental world of Late Antiquity, 6–13
  ritual penetration of state ideology in, 1132–1133
  Sasanian Persia, relationship with, 1000, 1002
Roman History (Eutropius), 409–410
Roman History (Symmachus), 423
Roman law. *See* law and legal culture
Romana (Jordanes), 424
Romance of Alexander [*Alexander Romance; Legend of Alexander*] (Pseudo-Callisthenes), 364–365, 1150, 1153
Romanos the Melode, 1156
Rome
  Altar of Victory, removal/restoration of, 347, 776–778, 835, 850
  bishops of. *See* papacy
  Christian charity in, 724
  Christianity, conversion of Roman aristocracy to, 413–414
  Column of Trajan, 570
  Constantinople equated with, 1163
  Forma Urbis Romae (map), 570–572, *571*, *572*
  history writing in, 412–415
  Lateran basilica, 938–940, *940*, 943, 944, 959n19
  Latin poetry and, 339–340, 347
  as monastic center, 492
  real estate, aristocratic domination of, 602
  sacks of, 339, 351n49, 415, 893
  S. Agnese fuori le mura, 940, *941*
  SS. Cosmas and Damian, 950
  SS. Giovanni e Paolo, house-church beneath, 938
  S. Lorenzo fuori le mura, 940
  SS. Peter and Marcellinus, 940
  St. Peter's basilica [Vatican], 938, 939–940, 943, 947
  S. Pudenziana, 344, 949–950, *952*
  S. Sebastiano fuori le mura, 940
Rome and the Nomads (Batty, 2007), 77
Romulea (Dracontius), 342
Romulus (symposiarch), 532
Rostovtzeff, Michael, 597
Rothamus (Breton king), 39
Rouche, Michel, 607
Rubenson, Samuel, xxxviii, 487
Rufinus of Aquileia
  on Arabia and Ethiopia, 255, 259, 273–274
  Ecclesiastical History [*Church History*], 10, 255, 257, 273–274, 414, 415, 418
  as historian, 414–415, 426, 429
  mental world of Late Antiquity and, 10
  monasticism and, 492
Rufus of Shotep, 237, 240n39
Rugian kings, 39
Runciman, Steven, 1152–1153
rural environment. *See* agriculture and rural environment
Ruricius of Limoges, 829, 841n9
Rutilius Namatianus, 10, 21, 339–340
Rutilius Taurus Aemilianus Palladius. *See* Palladius
Ryckmans, Jacques, 285–286, 1070

Saba and Sabaeans, 256, 262–263, 270, 277–278, 306
Sabrīšō' (Church of the East patriarch), 1009, 1015, 1018
Sacerdos (director of Basil of Caesarea's hospital), 717
Sacred History or *Chronicle* (Sulpicius Severus), 414
sacred space, 935–962. *See also specific sites*
  altars, 954–955, *955*
  baptisteries, 937, *938*, *944*
  in Church of the East, 1011–1012
  churches and basilicas, 938–943, *940–943*
  funerary functions of churches and basilicas, 940
  "Holy Land," concept of, 635–637
  holy sites, church space identified with, 987
  hospitals, as Christian production of space, 732–733
  house-churches, 937–938, *938*
  iconographic programs, theophanic vision supported by, 950–953, *951*, *952*
  liturgical function of, 953–955, *955*
  martyria, church buildings serving as, 942
  paradise, use of water, light, and decorative elements to suggest, *943*, 947–950, *948*, *950–952*
  sanctuary, organization and separation of, 855–958, *952*, *956*
  screens demarcating, 940, 954–955
  structures associated with churches and basilicas, 943–947, *945–947*
sacrifice, 850, 854–856

Saewulf (pilgrim), 578
Sahak I (Armenian catholicos), 121
Sahak III (Armenian catholicos), 123
Sahak son of Hamazasp, 126
S. Agnese fuori le mura, Rome, 940, *941*
St. Babylas, Antioch, 942
St. Catherine, monastery of, Mount Sinai, *948*
SS. Cosmas and Damian, Rome, 950
St. Felix, tomb of, Nola/Cimitile, 856, 947
St. George at Diospolis, miraculous column at, 985
SS. Giovanni e Paolo, Rome, house-church beneath, 938
S. Lorenzo fuori le mura, Rome, 940
SS. Peter and Marcellinus, Rome, 940
St. Peter's basilica [Vatican], Rome, 938, 939–940, 943, 947
S. Pudenziana, Rome, 344, 949–950, *952*
S. Sebastiano fuori le mura, Rome, 940
St. Timothy's basilica, Gerasa (Jerash, Jordan), 947
S. Vitale, Ravenna, 949, 950–951, *951*
saints, veneration of, 938
Ṣaliḥ ibn Musarriḥ, 1064
Saller, Richard, 670, 698n134
Sallust, 413, 414, 415
Salona (Solin), 102–106
saltus, 605
Salutati, Coluccio, 1175–1176, 1177
Salvian of Marseilles, 21, 62, 681
Salvius Julianus, 791
Salzman, Michele, 859, 863
Samaritans, 174–175, 179
Sambida (Alan leader), 37
San, Santa. *See entries at* Saint
sanctuary space, organization and separation of, 855–958, *952*, *956*
Sandwell, Isabella, 865
Sangibanus (Alan leader), 37
Šahpur. *See entries at* Shapur
Saracens, 201
Sarmatians, 98, 100
Sarris, Peter, 202, 215n26
Sartre, Maurice, 609
Sarus (Roman officer), 42
Sasanian Persia [Sāsānid, Sasanid]
  Arabian kingdoms, relationship with, 12, 295–298
  Armenia and, 115–118, 119, 122, 129–130
  biblical magi, association with, 21–22, 1023
  bureaucratic-administrative structures, 1126–1127
  Central Asia and, 144–145, 157
  Christianity in. *See also* Church of the East
    deportation of Roman Syrians and spread of, 998
    persecution of, 1000–1002, 1004, 1006, 1010
    relationship between Church hierarchy and Sasanian court, 1014–1015
    repeal of persecution and endorsement of Synod of 410 C.E., 994–995, 1002–003
  client kingdoms of eastern border and, 34
  consanguineous marriage, practice of, 1005, 1011
  Constantinople, siege of, 896
  Egypt, occupation of, 198–199
  elites and elite values of, 13–16
  Heraclius, wars with, xvii, 297, 1153
  history writing by, 425
  Islam
    Arab conquest of Persia, 297, 1015–1018
    influence of Persia on, 1068
  legitimating processes and ideologies, 1124, 1126
  Manichaeism under, 999, 1010–1011, 1024, 1026
  mental world of Late Antiquity and, 9, 11–13, 21–22
  Roman empire, relationships with, 1000, 1002
  silver-based monetary system, 132
  torture, use of, 1015, 1029n58
  True Cross, capture of, 1015
  Zoroastrian influence at, 994, 998, 1057
"satanic verses," 310
Satisfactio (Dracontius), 342
Saturnalia (Macrobius), 791
Savchenko, Alexei, 1020–1021
Schacht, Joseph, 1081
Schoeler, Gregor, 1082–1083
Schwartz, Seth, 175
Schweitzer, Albert, 1098–1099
Scirtius [legal client], 773–776
Scourfield, David, 343
screens, in churches, 940, 954–955
Scythians, 62, 1020, 1185
Scythopolis, 613
Sebēos (historian), 428
Secret History (Procopius), 424
Sedulius (Latin poet), 345
seeing, Late Antique conceptions of, 976–980, *979*
segmentary states, 1113, 1123, 1134
Seleucus (historian), 409
Seneca, 1175
Sentences (Menander), 503, 504
Septimius Severus (emperor), 8, 570, 598
Serapeum, Alexandria, destruction of, 850, 888
Serdica, Council of (343), 893
Sergius (bishop of Constantinople), 896
Sergius and Bacchus, icon of, 971, *972*, 973
Sergius the Nazarite, 188
Serjeant, R. B., 1070
Seronatus (Roman official), 55n119, 750
servi, 615, 750
Severus (fifth-century emperor), 47
Severus of Antioch, 189, 236, 366, 476

Severus of Minorca, 888
Sextus Petronius Probus, 410, 777, 959n26
sexual abuse accusations against Manichaeans, 765–768
sexual exclusivity as marital ideal, 667, 668, 680–682
Shahîd, Irfan, xvi
Shapur (Shāpūr, Šahpur) I (Sasanian ruler), 12–13, 881, 998, 999, 1068
Shapur (Shāpūr, Šahpur) II (Sasanian ruler), 5, 144, 295, 994, 998, 1000, 1001, 1006, 1058
Shapur (Shāpūr, Šahpur) III (Sasanian ruler), 121
Shaw, Brent, 670, 686
Shenoute of Atripe, 228, 230, 233–234, 236, 241n61, 490, 828, 858
Shepherd of Hermas, 724, 893
Shi'ite Islam, 1061
Shisha-Halevy, Ariel, 233
Shmouna (Syrian martyr), 182, 187
Shoemaker, Stephen J., xxxviii, 1078
Shuriḥbi'īl Ya'fur (king of Ḥimyar), 268
Shuriḥbi'īl Yakkuf (king of Ḥimyar), dynasty of, 269
Sibylline Oracles, 371
Sidonius Apollinaris
  as bishop, 891–892, 896
  Italian Renaissance interest in, 1175
  as Latin poet, 339, 340–341
  letters of, 828, 829, 836, 837
  mental world of Late Antiquity and, 10, 15
  on military campaigns in Illyricum, 101
  on *peregrini*, 750
  Western kingdoms, development of, 36, 38, 46–47, 49, 55n117
Sigeric of Canterbury, 578
Sigibert (Frankish king), 38
Sigismund (Burgundian king), 892
Silas (Church of the East patriarch), 1014
silk industry in Byzantium, 612–613
Silk Road. *See* Central Asia and the Silk Road
silver and lead mining in Illyricum, 97–98
silver-based monetary systems, 132
Simeon of Bēt Arsham, 253, 1010
Simeon the Mountaineer, 641, 643, 864
Simeon the New Theologian, 1155
Simeon bar Ṣabbā'ē, 1000, 1002
Simeon the Stylite, the elder [Symeon the Stylite, Symeon Stylites], 179, *496*, 889, 945, *972*
Simeon the Stylite, the younger [Symeon the Stylite, Symeon Stylites], 971
Simon (Armenian bishop), 115–117
Simplicianus (archbishop of Milan), 539
Simplicius (philosopher), 454, 455, 478, 574, 575, 1066, 1184
Sinai
  Burning Bush, Justinianic complex at site of, 945, *946*, 954
  St. Catherine, monastery of, *948*
Sion, miraculous column at, 985
Sion Treasure, silver altar revetment from, *955*
sīra traditions of life of Muḥammad, 1079–1083, 1085
Sirmium (Sremska Mitrovica), 95–102
Siwnik', 128–129
Sixtus III (pope), 944
Skalnik, Peter, 1121
slavery
  child exposure and, 686
  citizenship, access to, 744, 746–747, 750
  Constantine on, 777
  evolution of, 615, 634, 687
  hospitals for slaves, 725–726, 736
  rural and urban environments, relationship between, 629
  sexual economy of, 681, 683
Slavs, 9, 106, 110
Smith, Gregory, xxxviii, 513
snorting, religious meaning of, 441–442
social class. *See* aristocracy; class and class structure; peasantry; slavery
Socrates (historian), 418–419, 420, 426, 445–448, 860, 861, 865
Sogdian Ancient Letters, 152
Sogdians. *See* Central Asia and the Silk Road
Somnium Scipionis (*Dream of Scipio*; Cicero), 576
Sophronius [Sophronios] of Jerusalem, 440–442, 456, 1158
Sorabji, Richard, 538
Soter (pope), 724
Soterichus of Oasis, 364, 372
soul and body. *See* physics and metaphysics
Soul, Intellect, and One (three hypostases), 524–527
Sozomen, 174, 419, 420, 426, 445–447, 450, 721, 725, 860, 982, 998
space, sacred. *See* sacred space
Spain. *See also* Visigoths
  decline of aristocracy in, 607
  olive oil, trade in, 601–602
  Priscillianists in, 184, 767, 768
  rural estates/villas in, 603–604, 606
Spalatum (Split), Diocletian's palace at, 104, 106
Speculum Maius (Vincent of Beauvais), 567
spirit or *pneuma*, 533–538
St. *See entries at* Saint
Stadiasmus Magni Maris, 563
Staphylius, 410
states and empires in Late Antiquity. *See* political systems in Late Antiquity
Stephen I (pope), 880, 893
Stephen the Younger, 1164
Stilicho (general), 35, 41, 42, 338, 350n28, 351n47, 751, 825
Stobaeus, Johannes, 531

Stoics and Stoicism
  Antiochene school influenced by, 231
  cosmology of, 531
  Ephrem of Syria and, 184
  in mentality of Late Antiquity, 17
  monasticism and, 500, 501
  Neoplatonism and, 516
  on *pneuma*, 537
  on unity, 521
  on vehicle of the soul, 535
Stone, Lawrence, 669
Strabo, 8, 66, 253
A Study of History (Toynbee, 1961), 1149
substance dualism, 517–518
Suetonius, 410, 412, 1175
Suevi, 37–38, 41, 42, 44
Sulpicius Alexander, 413, 416
Sulpicius Severus, 414, 416, 423, 426
Sunni Islam, 1061, 1083
Suryāyē, 172–173, 175, 190. *See also* Syria, Syriac, and Syrians
Syagrius (king), 39
Symeon Metaphrastes, 1152
Symeon the Stylite, the elder [Simeon the Stylite, Simeon Stylites], 179, 496, 889, 945, 972
Symeon the Stylite, the younger [Simeon the Stylite, Simeon Stylites], 971
Symmachus (Quintus Aurelius Symmachus)
  on agriculture and rural environment, 633, 640, 641
  history writing and, 410, 412, 413, 423
  Italian Renaissance interest in, 1175
  letters of, 828, 835, 836, 886
  on marriage and family, 691–692
  Relationes, 777, 836
  Roman History, 423
  as urban prefect, 769–779, 783n84, 790
Symphosius (Latin poet), 343
synchronic versus diachronic treatments of Late Antiquity, xxi, 5–6
Synerotas (Illyrian saint), 99
Synesius [Synesios] of Cyrene, 366, 379, 385n6, 449, 474, 751, 828
Synodicon orientale, 254, 995, 997
Syria, Syriac, and Syrians, 170–190. *See also* Church of the East
  anti-Jewish polemic and Christian identity, 175, 176, 177–181
  Arab conquest and, 190
  Armenia, influence in, 119–120
  ascetic tradition, reinvention of, 182–183, 188
  Christian political context for, 173–175
  cultural distinctiveness of, 172–173
  distinctive religious tradition, continuation of, 186–188
  early Christian churches in, 942–943, *943*, 948
  Edessa, foundation history of, 174, 175–177, 180–182, 187
  education in, 478
  hagiographic writing, normalizing process in, 170–190
  heterodoxy and, 172–173, 184
  historiography of, 170–172
  history, understanding of, 21
  history writing in, 421, 428–429
  Jacobite or West Syriac Church, 1010–1011, 1016, 1024
  Jewish context of, 171
  Kaiserkritik, anti-Jewish polemic as, 179–181
  mental world of Late Antiquity in, 11
  monasticism, 491–492, 495, *496*
  orthodoxy, emphasis on, 183–186, 189–190
Syrianus (philosopher), 551n142

al-Ṭabarī (biographer of Muḥammad), 1079
Tacitus, 62, 69, 70, 71, 413, 1172, 1175
Talbert, Richard, 570–571, 572, 575
Tarasios (brother of Patriarch Photius), 826
Tardieu, Michel, 1023
Tarpeius (lawyer), 774–775
Tatian, 174, 182
taxation, 600, 601, 632–633, 634, 745, 1059, 1117, 1135
Tebessa, church and martyrium of, North Africa, 945–946
Tell Khwāris mosaic, Nineveh, 1037n192
tenancy of agricultural lands, 634–635
T'ēodoros of Karin, 122, 125
T'ēodoros Rštuni, 129, 133
Terebinth, Mamre, 982–983
Terian, Abraham, 120
Tertullian, 487, 552n155, 723, 978
testamentary powers, 672
Testaments of the Patriarchs, 229
Tha'rān Yuhan'im (king of Ḥimyar), 264–265
Themistius (rhetorician and philosopher), 449, 457n10, 1184
Theocritus (Greek poet), 385n3
Theoderic I the Great [Theodoric] (king of the Ostrogoths in Italy), 36, 37, 39–40, 42, 43, 45–47, 49, 105–106, 422, 892
Theoderic II (Gothic king), 45, 54–55n115
Theoderic Strabo, 751
theodicy as means of testing document authenticity, 930–931
Theodobius [Flavius Valila], 751
Theodore Daphnopates, 1153
Theodore Graptos, 1157
Theodora (empress), 202
Theodore (patriarch of Constantinople), 923
Theodore the Greek, 441
Theodore Lector, 420, 424, 426, 429
Theodore Metochites, 1151, 1152
Theodore of Mopsuestia, 1009
Theodore Prodromos [Theodorus Prodromus], 383

Theodore the Studite, 1154, 1157
Theodore of Sykeon, 858
Theodore Synkellos, 1153, 1162
Theodore of Tarsus (archbishop of Canterbury), 429–430, 579
Theodoret of Cyrrhus
  as bishop, 886
  Church History, 419, 426
  Curatio, 444–445
  Hellenism and, 443–445, 447
  Historia Religiosa [*Historia Philotheos*], 183, 188, 495
  as historian, 419, 420, 426
  letters of, 828, 886
  on monasticism, 491, 495
  Syria and, 172, 182–183, 185, 186, 188
  on violent religious conflict, 860
Theodosian Code (*Codex Theodosianus*)
  in Arabia and Ethiopia, 280–281
  justice and equality, concern with, 765
  in law and legal culture of Late Antiquity, 790, 794–798, 800, 805, 807n9
  as letter collection, 830, 831, 832, 833, 838–840
  Libri Theodosiani, known as, 833, 838–840
  on marriage and family, 672
  mentality of Late Antiquity and, 20
  purpose of, 790
  religious edicts in, 850, 862
  in Syria, 180
  in Western kingdoms, 49
Theodosius (son of Galla Placidia), 36
Theodosius I (emperor)
  Balkans and, 100, 121
  bishops and, 881, 883, 886, 888
  in economic history, 600
  history writing and, 412, 417, 418, 419
  law and legal culture, 751, 766, 804
  on marriage and family, 679
  mentality of Late Antiquity and, 21
  religious practice and, 850, 862
  Western kingdoms and, 41
Theodosius II (emperor)
  Balkans and, 104–105
  bishops and, 881
  Eutyches' defense before, 921
  Greek poetry and, 368
  history writing in Late Antiquity and, 418, 419
  on law and legal culture, 790, 795, 796, 839. *See also Theodosian Code*
  letter collections, 828
  on marriage and family, 676–677
  monks required to stay out of Councils by, 1164
  Novellae, 839
  Syria and, 179, 181
  Theophilus of Alexandria's embassy to, 816–817, 823, 824, 828
  Western kingdoms and, 49
Theodosius of Alexandria, 236
Theodotos (founder of hospital), 726, 727
theology. *See also* Trinitarian doctrine
  Byzantium, theology as new philosophy in, 1154–1156
  Christology. *See* Council of Chalcedon (451 C.E.) and Chalcedonian controversy; heterodoxy; Nicaea, First Council of; orthodoxy
  rhetoric, theological argumentation, and forgery, 916–919, 920, 927, 931–932
Theon of Alexandria, 575
Theophanes (sixth-century historian), 425
Theophanes the Confessor, 253, 738n50
Theophanes Graptos, 1157
Theophanes of Hermopolis, 828
Theophanes of Sicily, 1157
Theophilus [Theophilos] of Alexandria, 231, 232, 236, 445–446, 816–819, 823, 824, 827, 828, 888
Theophilus the Indian, 254, 265, 290
Theophrastus (philosopher), 253
Theophylact of Ochrid, 835
Theophylact Simocatta, 12, 62, 428
Theotokos doctrine, 241n66, 917
theurgy, 1187
Thomas Aquinas, 1191
Thomas Magistros, 1151, 1152
Thrace, 107–110
Three Books on Life (Ficino), 1188, 1190–1191
three hypostases (One, Intellect, and Soul), 524–527
Thucydides, 407, 409, 410, 412–414, 420, 421, 429, 442, 1114
Thunø, Erik, 989
Thuringian kings, 39, 49
Tiberius (emperor), 176, 178, 180, 181, 749
Tibeto-Birman languages, 143–144
Timaeus (Plato), 452–453, 535, 576. *See also entries at Commentary on the Timaeus*
Timotheus (*comes*), 47
Timothy I the Great (Church of the East patriarch), 1022, 1023, 1024–1026
Timothy II Aeluros, 236, 239n19
Tiridates III (Armenian ruler), 421–422
Tisamenos (governor of Syria), 806
To the Righteous, 365
Tokharians, 143, 149
Toleration, Edict of (313 C.E.), 849
Tome (Pope Leo I), 893
Topics (Aristotle), 1024
Torelli, Mario, 598
Torg (Armenian bishop), 120, 125
torture
  Christians, persecution of, 446, 860, 1015
  citizens not to be questioned under, 744, 769
  dediticii, 746
  as Roman legal procedure, 764, 765, 780n13, 804
  Sasanian use of, 1015, 1029n58

totalization of learning, 19
towns and cities. *See* urban environment
Toynbee, Arnold, 1149
traditional religion. *See* paganism
"traditions of the fathers," 927
Traditionskern, 75, 76
Traina, Giusto, xxi
Trajan (emperor), 8, 749, 837
Trajan, Column of, Rome, 570
Trajan's canal, 207
translation movement, 1067–1069
travel genre, 562–567, 570, 578–579
Trdat (Armenian king), 119, 122
Treatise on Solitude and Prayer (Dadīšō'), 979
Trexler, Richard, 974
Tribonian (quaestor), 795, 796, 800
Trimble, Jennifer, 570, 572
Trinitarian doctrine
  Gregory of Tours on, 904n159
  Muslim objections to, 1061
  Syriac amulets with Trinitarian invocations, 1013
  Timothy I's defense of, 1025
Triodion, Palestinian, 1156, 1157
Triodion Synaxaries (Nikephoros Kallistos Xanthopoulos), 1156, 1157
Triphiodorus of Panopolis, 364, 370, 374, 378, 383, 386n8
Trombley, Frank, 173–174
True Cross, 176, 178, 179, 896, 980, 1015
Trullo, Quinisext Council *in* (691–692 C.E.), 124–125, 920, 1160–1164
Tübingen Theosophy, 386n10
Turibius (bishop of Astorga), 767, 768
Turks in Central Asia
  in Arab invasions, 157
  Byzantine relationship with, 1111
  China and, 1111
  control of territory by, 149–152
  nomadic peoples, "Turkicization" of, 143
  Sky and Earth cult of, 144
Tusculan Disputations (Cicero), 1183
Twelve Tablets, Law of, 838
Tylor, Edward Burnett, 977

Uhalde, Kevin, xxxviii, 764, 799
Ulpian (jurist), 745, 793, 795, 806, 811n139
'Umār I (caliph), 209, 1060, 1098
Ummayyad caliphate, 1054, 1064, 1125
unity in physics and metaphysics, 521–524
universal citizenship. *See also* citizenship
  Antonine Constitution (*Constitutio Antoniniana*) granting, 63, 745–747, 791
  conveyance of, 754–755
  marriage and family affected by, 679, 690, 702n242
universalism
  of religions in Late Antiquity, 1058–1059
  Roman empire, Christian universality as spiritual heir to, 10, 13, 18–19, 20–21, 1160–1163
urban environment. *See also specific cities and towns*
  in Arabia, 251
  bishops in, 886–888
  citizenship, municipal, 747
  commercial vitality of Eastern Mediterranean cities, 608–609, 612–614, 615–616
  in Egypt, 203–205
  Forma Urbis Romae (map), 570–572, *571*, *572*
  fortifications, 630
  marriage and family in, 686–687
  mental world of Late Antiquity and, 13, 15
  monasteries and, 492
  population of urban East, 615–616, 619n135
  relationship between town and country, 628–631
Ursinus (papal candidate), 887
'Uthmān (caliph), 1054, 1088, 1089, 1091

Vadomarius (Alamannic king), 35, 42
Vahan (prince of Siwnik'), 129
Vahan Mamikonean [Mamikonian], 122, 129, 130, 422
Vahrām. *See entries at* Bahram
Valens (emperor), 97, 99, 409–410, 411, 716, 722, 723, 752
Valentinian I (emperor), 43, 45, 97, 99–100, 340, 600, 612, 686, 752, 800
Valentinian II (emperor), 772, 775, 776, 779, 883
Valentinian III (emperor), 46, 105, 418, 677, 766, 779, 783n84, 795, 798, 839
Valentinus (gnostic master), 516
Valerian (emperor), 13
Valerian of Cimiez, 768
Valerianus (senator), 772, 773
Valerius Maximus, 1175
valetudinaria, 726, 727, 736. *See also* hospitals
Van Rompay, Lucas, 185
Vance, Eugene, 977
Vandals
  bishops, persecution of, 892
  destruction of kingdom of, 50
  Gallaecia, attack on, 45
  invasion of imperial territory by, 41, 42
  kings of, 37
  Latin poetry and, 341–343
  mental world of Late Antiquity and, 9, 10, 18
Vardan Mamikonean [Mamikonian], 123, 156
Vardik (prince of Mokk'), 133
Variae (Cassiodorus), 831, 832, 836, 837
Varro, 531, 532
Vasak (prince of Siwnik'), 128
Vatican [St. Peter's basilica], Rome, 938, 939–940, 943, 947
vehicle of the soul, 533–538

Venantius Fortunatus, 348, 836
Veroli casket, 386n11
Verona Sacramentary, 684
Versus ad Gratiam Domini (Pomponius), 346
Veyne, Paul, *A History of Private Life* (1987), xviii, 669
Vian, F., 381
Victor (pope), 893
Victor of Tunnuna, 424–425, 427
Victor of Vita, 892, 903n150
Victory, Altar of, Rome, removal/restoration of, 347, 776–778, 835, 850
Vie et mort de Byzance (Bréhier, 1947), 1149
Vigilius (pope), 894, 905n179, 922–923, 925, 927
villages
  Armenia, aristocrats owning villages in, 610
  in Eastern empire, 610, 630–631
  patronage of, 641–643
villas
  fortification and reuse of, 630
  Western aristocratic investment in rural estates, 601–602, 603–607, 615
Villeneuve, François, 250, 610
Vincent of Beauvais, 567
Virchow, Rudolph, 71
Virgil, 8, 9, 349n16, 364, 791
Virgilian centos, 336–337, 343, 346
Virgin Mary
  biography, attempt to reconstruct, 1084–1085
  in Coptic literature, 236–237, 241n66
  Theotokos doctrine, 241n66, 917
Visigoths
  bishops, persecution of, 892
  Chalcedonian orthodoxy, conversion to, 63
  collapse and re-creation of kingdom, 50
  kings of, 40
  mental world of Late Antiquity and, 9, 10, 18
Visio Theophili (Theophilus of Alexandria), 231, 232, 236
vision, Late Antique conceptions of, 976–980, 979
Vision of Dorotheus, 365
visual arts. *See* icons; object relations in Late Antiquity; sacred space; *specific works of art*
Vitae. See entries at Life
Vitalian (general), 109
Vithicabius (Alamannic king), 35
Vitruvius, 65–66
Vrtʻanēs (Armenian bishop), 120

wage labor in Eastern empire, expansion of, 607–608
Walker, Joel, xxxviii, 994
Wallia (Flavius Wallia; Gothic leader), 36, 37, 42
wandering monks, 492
"wandering poets," 338, 363, 381
Wansbrough, John, 1061, 1085, 1086, 1088, 1099–1100n7
Ward-Perkins, Bryan, 73, 1149
water, used in sacred spaces, 947
Watt, Montgomery, 1079, 1083, 1085, 1091–1092, 1093, 1095, 1096
Watts, Edward, xxxviii, 467
Weber, Max, 597, 897n16, 1122
Welch, Alfred, 1088, 1092, 1093
Wellhausen, Julius, 1087
Wen-Ti (Chinese emperor), 1111
Wenskus, Reinhard, 75, 76
Wessel, Susan, xxxix, 916
West Syriac or Jacobite Church, 1010–1011, 1016, 1024. *See also* Syria, Syriac, and Syrians; Monophysitism/Miaphysitism
Western kingdoms, 31–50. *See also specific kingdoms*
  bishops in, 890–894
  client kingship, 32–36, 42, 43, 44
  de facto cession of control to, 41, 44–47
  developmental paradigms for, 31–34
  existence of kingdoms within empire, 35–40, 41, 43–44
  fragility of, 50
  historical process of creation of, 40–41
  history writing in, 422–423, 426–427
  imperial administrative and legal authority, assuming, 41, 47–50
  mental concept of Late Antiquity in, 10
  monasticism in, 492–493
  movement of *reges* and *reguli* from frontier to interior, 40–43
  territorial frontiers, development of, 49–50
  territory, association of king with, 40
Whitaker, C. R., 77
White Monastery, library of, 227, 232–235, 237, 240n39, 490
Wickham, Chris, 78, 212–213, 598, 607, 614, 615, 1118
widows
  Christian social niche for, 684, 686
  minors, guardianship of, 675, 802
Wifstrand, Alfred, 367, 376
Willibald of Eichstätt, 578
wills and testamentary powers, 672
Wipszycka, Ewa, 210
Wisnovsky, Robert, 1067, 1068
Wittgenstein, Ludwig, 457n10
Wolfram, Herwig, 75–76
women. *See also* marriage and family; widows
  agriculture and, 650n126
  as arbiters and symbols of social prestige, 692
  Ephrem the Syrian and, 183, 184, 185
  as guardians of minors, 675, 802
  hospitals for women giving birth, 734–735
  monasticism and, 492
  status in Roman family law, 672–674, 675–676, 802
Wood, Philip, xxxix, 170

world, Late Antique conception of, 562–580
  in cartography, 567–572, *568*, *569*, *571*, *572*
  continuity of, 578–580
  cosmological concepts and, 572–578
  "Holy Land," concept of, 935–937
  itinerarium genre, 563–564, 565, 570, 578
  pilgrimage texts, 564–566, 570, 578–579
  in travel accounts, 562–567
The World of Late Antiquity (Brown, 1971), xv, 4, 73, 1055, 1148
world soul, 526, 527, 533
Wright, W., 170, 171, 172

Xabib (Armenian bishop), 125
Xanthopoulos, Nikephoros Kallistos, 1156, 1157
xenodocheia, 721, 725, 727–728, 729, 731. *See also* hospitals
Xi'an stele [Nestorian Monument], China, xi, *xiii*, *xiv*, xv, 151, 158, 996, 1022–1024
Xiongnu (people), 144, 145–146
Xuanzang (Chinese pilgrim), 150
Xvarr-veh-zād (amulet owner), 1013

Yabhalāhā (Church of the East catholicos), 1003, 1007
Yasin, Ann Marie, xxxix, 935
Yazdāndukt (devout Church of the East woman), 1001
Yazdbozid (on Nestorian Monument), 1022, 1024
Yazdgard [Yazdajird, Yazdegerd, Yazkert] I (Sasanian ruler), 296, 994–995, 1002–1003, 1004, 1014
Yazdgard [Yazdajird, Yazdegerd, Yazkert] II (Sasanian ruler), 123, 296, 995
Yazdgard [Yazdajird, Yazdegerd, Yazkert] III (Sasanian ruler), 157, 297, 1016
Yazdin of Kirkuk, 1015
Yersinia pestis. *See* plague, Justinianic
Yovhannēs Bagaranc'i (Armenian catholicos), 122, 123
Yovhannēs I Mandakuni (Armenian catholicos), 128
Yovhannēs Mayragomec'i (Armenian catholicos), 122
Yovhannēs Ōjunec'i (Armenian catholicos), 123, 124
Yovsēp' (Armenian priest), 121

Zachariah of Mitylene [Zachariah of Gaza; Zacharias of Mitylene; Zacharias Scholasticus], 129, 379, 420, 455, 470, 475
Zacharias of Jerusalem, 896
Zakariyyā' al-Rāzī, 1069
Zamasp (Sasanian ruler), 1005
Zayd ibn Ḥammād, 307
Zeno (emperor), 368–369, 420, 1004, 1009
Zeus Hypsistos, cult of, 854
Zoroastrianism
  apocalypticism of, 1065, 1066–1067
  in Armenia, 422
  in Central Asia, 144, 151, 158, 1021
  converts to Christianity from, 1004, 1005, 1010
  East Syriac Christians, association with persecution of, 994, 998, 1001, 1004
  hospitals of Patriarch Nerses and, 725
  influence at Sasanian court, 994, 998, 1057
  Islam, under, 1060
  mental world of Late Antiquity and, 5, 15, 18
  universalism in, 1058
Zosima (desert father), 1158–1160
Zosimus (historian), 21, 425, 753
al-Zubayr, 'Urwa ibn, 1080, 1082
Zuckerman, Constantin, 202
al-Zuhrī, Ibn Shihāb, 1080, 1082, 1088
Zu'ra (Syriac saint), 187, 188